Honoring America

For Americans, the flag has always had a special meaning. It is a symbol of our nation's freedom and democracy.

Flag Etiquette

Over the years, Americans have developed rules and customs concerning the use and display of the flag. One of the most important things every American should remember is to treat the flag with respect.

- The flag should be raised and lowered by hand and displayed only from sunrise to sunset. On special occasions, the flag may be displayed at night, but it should be illuminated.
- The flag may be displayed on all days, weather permitting, particularly on national and state holidays and on historic and special occasions.
- No flag may be flown above the American flag or to the right of it at the same height.
- The flag should never touch the ground or floor beneath it.
- The flag may be flown at half-staff by order of the president, usually to mourn the death of a public official.
- The flag may be flown upside down only to signal distress.
- The flag should never be carried flat or horizontally, but always carried aloft and free.
- When the flag becomes old and tattered, it should be destroyed by burning. According to an approved custom, the Union (stars on blue field) is first cut from the flag; then the two pieces, which no longer form a flag, are burned.

The American's Creed

I believe in the United States of America as a Government of the people, by the people, for the people, whose just powers are derived from the consent of the governed; a democracy in a republic; a sovereign Nation of many sovereign States; a perfect union, one and inseparable; established upon those principles of freedom, equality, justice, and humanity for which American patriots sacrificed their lives and fortunes.

I therefore believe it is my duty to my Country to love it; to support its Constitution; to obey its laws; to respect its flag, and to defend it against all enemies.

The Pledge of Allegiance

I pledge allegiance to the Flag of the United States of America and to the Republic for which it stands, one Nation under God, indivisible, with liberty and justice for all.

The Star-Spangled Banner

O! say, can you see, by the dawn's early light,
What so proudly we hail'd at the twilight's last gleaming?
Whose broad stripes and bright stars, thro' the perilous fight,
O'er the ramparts we watched were so gallantly streaming?
And the rockets' red glare, the bombs bursting in air,
Gave proof thro' the night, that our flag was still there.
O! say, does that Star-Spangled Banner yet wave
O'er the land of the free and the home of the brave?

On the shore, dimly seen thro' the mist of the deep,
Where the foe's haughty host in dread silence reposes,
What is that which the breeze, o'er the towering steep,
As it fitfully blows, half conceals, half discloses?
Now it catches the gleam of the morning's first beam,
In full glory reflected now shines on the stream.
'Tis the Star-Spangled Banner. O long may it wave
O'er the land of the free and the home of the brave.

And where is that band who so vauntingly swore,
That the havoc of war and the battle's confusion
A home and a country should leave us no more?
Their blood has wash'd out their foul footstep's pollution.
No refuge could save the hireling and slave
From the terror of flight or the gloom of the grave,
And the Star-Spangled Banner in triumph doth wave
O'er the land of the free and the home of the brave.

O thus be it e'er when free men shall stand
Between their lov'd home and war's desolation,
Blest with vict'ry and peace, may the Heav'n-rescued land
Praise the pow'r that hath made and preserv'd us a nation.
Then conquer we must, when our cause it is just,
And this be our motto, "In God is our Trust."
And the Star-Spangled Banner in triumph shall wave
O'er the land of the free and the home of the brave.

Teacher Wraparound Edition

OUR WORLD TODAY

People, Places, and Issues

Senior Author
Richard G. Boehm, Ph.D.

David G. Armstrong, Ph.D.
Francis P. Hunkins, Ph.D.
Dennis Reinhartz, Ph.D.
Merry Lobrecht

Glencoe
McGraw-Hill

New York, New York   Columbus, Ohio   Chicago, Illinois   Peoria, Illinois   Woodland Hills, California

ABOUT THE AUTHORS

NATIONAL GEOGRAPHIC

The National Geographic Society, founded in 1888 for the increase and diffusion of geographic knowledge, is the world's largest nonprofit scientific and educational organization. The Society uses sophisticated communication technologies to convey geographic knowledge to a worldwide membership. The School Publishing Division supports the Society's mission by developing innovative educational programs—ranging from traditional print materials to multimedia programs including CD-ROMS, videos, and software.

Senior Author
Richard G. Boehm

Richard G. Boehm, Ph.D., was one of seven authors of *Geography for Life,* national standards in geography, prepared under Goals 2000: Educate America Act. In 1991 he received the George J. Miller award from the National Council for Geographic Education (NCGE) for distinguished service to geographic education. He has twice won the *Journal of Geography* award for best article. He presently holds the Jesse H. Jones Distinguished Chair in Geographic Education at Southwest Texas State University in San Marcos, Texas.

David G. Armstrong

David G. Armstrong, Ph.D., is Dean of the School of Education at the University of North Carolina at Greensboro. A social studies education specialist with additional advanced training in geography, Dr. Armstrong was educated at Stanford University, University of Montana, and University of Washington. He taught at the secondary level in the state of Washington before beginning a career in higher education. Dr. Armstrong has written books for students and teachers.

Merry Lobrecht

Merry Lobrecht is the Social Studies Curriculum Coordinator for the Humble ISD. She was the recipient of both the 2001 National Council for Geographic Education Distinguished Teacher Achievement Award and the Texas Council of Social Studies Texas Alliance for Geographic Distinguished Teacher Award for 2001.

Francis P. Hunkins

Francis P. Hunkins, Ph.D., is Professor of Education at the University of Washington. He began his career as a teacher in Massachusetts. He received his masters degree in education from Boston University and his doctorate from Kent State University with a major in general curriculum and a minor in geography. Dr. Hunkins has written numerous books and articles.

Dennis Reinhartz

Dennis Reinhartz, Ph.D., is Professor of History and Russian at the University of Texas at Arlington. A specialist in Russian and East European history, as well as in the history of cartography and historical geography, Dr. Reinhartz has written numerous books in these fields. He is a consultant to the U.S. State and Justice Departments and to the U.S. Holocaust Memorial Museum in Washington, D.C.

Glencoe/McGraw-Hill

A Division of The ***McGraw-Hill*** *Companies*

Printed in the United States of America.
Send all inquiries to:
Glencoe/McGraw-Hill
8787 Orion Place
Columbus, Ohio 43240-4027

ISBN 0-07-827382-X (Student Edition) ISBN 0-07-827383-8 (Teacher Wraparound Edition)
1 2 3 4 5 6 7 8 9 027/043 05 04 03 02

CONSULTANTS

Karl Barbir, Ph.D.
Professor of History
Sienna College
Loudonville, New York

Brock Brown, Ph.D.
Associate Professor of Geography and Planning
Southwest Texas State University
San Marcos, Texas

Thomas H. Buckley, Ph.D.
Professor of History
University of Tulsa
Tulsa, Oklahoma

Ramesh Dhussa, Ph.D.
Assistant Professor of Geography
Drake University
Des Moines, Iowa

Charles A. Endress, Ph.D.
Professor of History
Angelo State University
San Angelo, Texas

Dana A. Farnham, Ph.D.
Professor of Anthropology
Lincoln College at Normal
Normal, Illinois

Anne Hardgrove, Ph.D.
Assistant Professor of History
University of Texas at San Antonio
San Antonio, Texas

Ken Hendrickson, Ph.D.
Professor of History
Sam Houston State University
Huntsville, Texas

Terry G. Jordan, Ph.D.
Professor of Geography
University of Texas at Austin
Austin, Texas

Shabbir Mansuri
Director
Susan L. Douglass
Affiliated Scholar
Council on Islamic Education
Fountain Valley, California

Monica Najar, Ph.D.
Assistant Professor of History
Lehigh University
Bethlehem, Pennsylvania

Reverend Marvin O'Dell
Faith Baptist Church
Thousand Oaks, California

Rex C Peebles
Dean of Social and Behavioral Sciences
Austin Community College
Austin, Texas

Bernard Reich, Ph.D.
Professor of Political Science and International Affairs
George Washington University
Washington, D.C.

TEACHER REVIEWERS

Al Boudny
T.H. McDonald Junior High School
Katy, Texas

Diana Bradford
Scobee Middle School
San Antonio, Texas

Kenneth E. Bridges
Huffines Middle School
Lewisville, Texas

Rosemary Conroy
St. Luke School
Shoreline, Washington

Nancy Eudy
Bammel Middle School
Houston, Texas

Carolyn Grogan
Mesa Elementary School
Somis, California

Joan Hinze
Brenham Middle School
Brenham, Texas

Toni Holocek
West Middle School
West, Texas

Rachel Kline
Oak Crest Intermediate School
San Antonio, Texas

Pamela Kniffin
Navasota Intermediate School
Navasota, Texas

Sarah L. Matt
Irma Marsh Middle School
Fort Worth, Texas

Melissa Mitchell
Creekwood Middle School
Kingwood, Texas

Karen Muir
George Fox Middle School
Pasadena, Maryland

Tara Musslewhite
Atascocita Middle School
Humble, Texas

David Nienkamp
Sandy Creek Junior/Senior High School
Fairfield, Nebraska

Megan Phelps
Moorpark Community College
Moorpark, California

Julie Scott
East Valley Middle School
Spokane, Washington

Barbara Vana
Memorial Middle School
Houston, Texas

Michael Yell
Hudson Middle School
Hudson, Wisconsin

Contents

Features

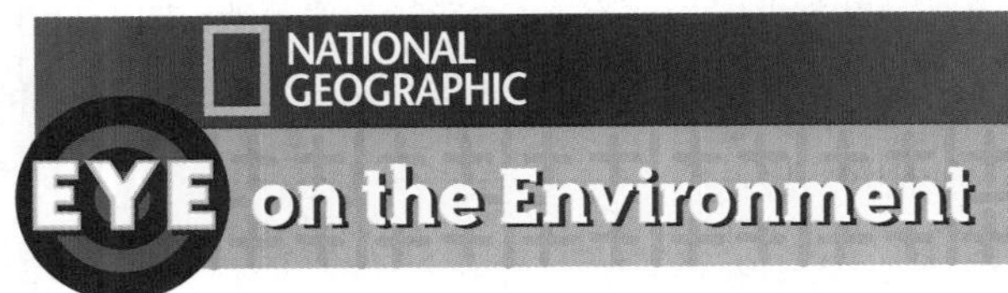

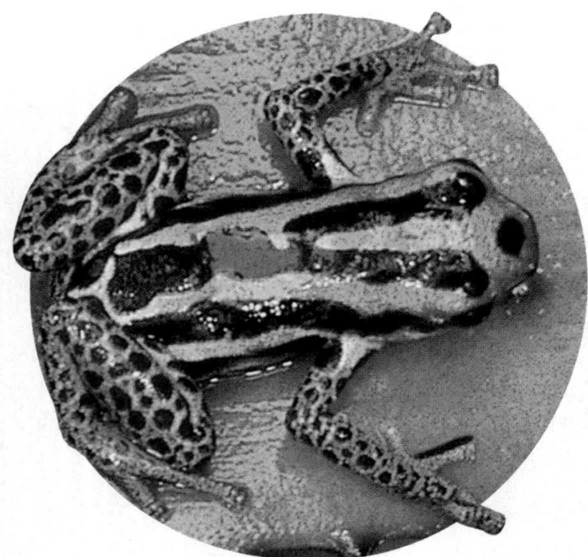

▲ Poison arrow frog

Skills

Social Studies Skills

Critical Thinking Skills

Technology Skills

Study and Writing Skills

Making Connections

Inuits greet with a nose rub

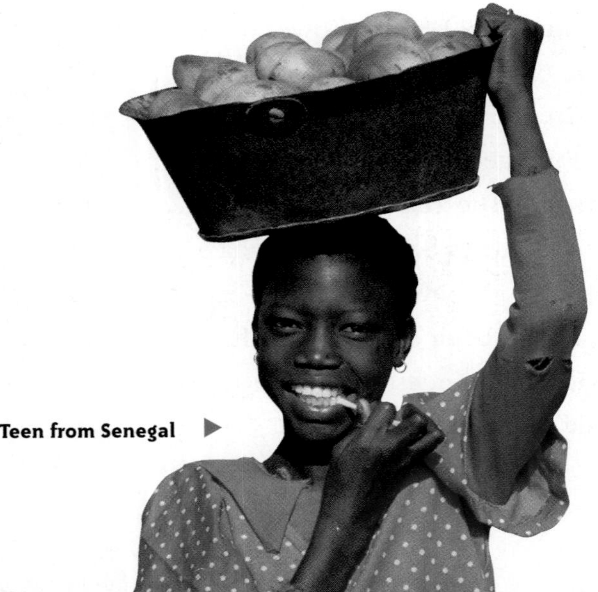

Teen from Senegal ▶

Believe It or Not!

Primary Source

Literature

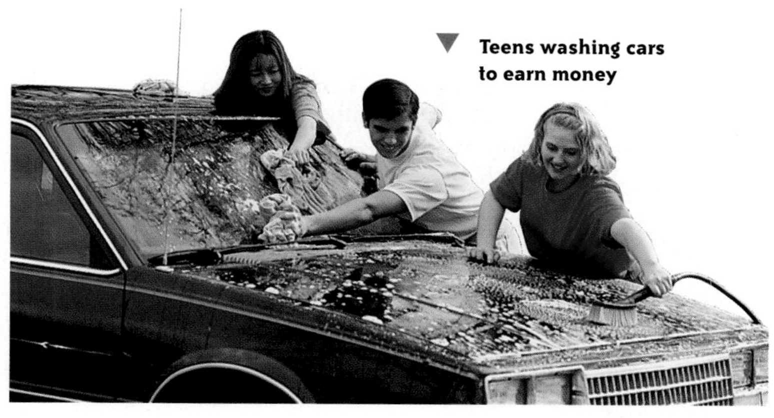

Teens washing cars to earn money

Exploring Economics

Heroes at work

Maps

NATIONAL GEOGRAPHIC Reference Atlas

NATIONAL GEOGRAPHIC Geography Handbook

Unit 1 Learning About Our World

Unit 2 North Africa and Southwest Asia

Unit 3 Asia

Unit 4 Europe

Unit 5 Russia and the Eurasian Republics

Unit 6 Africa South of the Sahara

Unit 7 North America and Middle America

Unit 8 South America

Unit 9 Australia, Oceania, and Antarctica

Charts and Graphs

NATIONAL GEOGRAPHIC Geography Handbook

Unit 1 Learning About Our World

Unit 2 North Africa and Southwest Asia

Unit 3 Asia

Unit 4 Europe

Unit 5 Russia and the Eurasian Republics

Unit 6 Africa South of the Sahara

Unit 7 North America and Middle America

Unit 8 South America

Unit 9 Australia, Oceania, and Antarctica

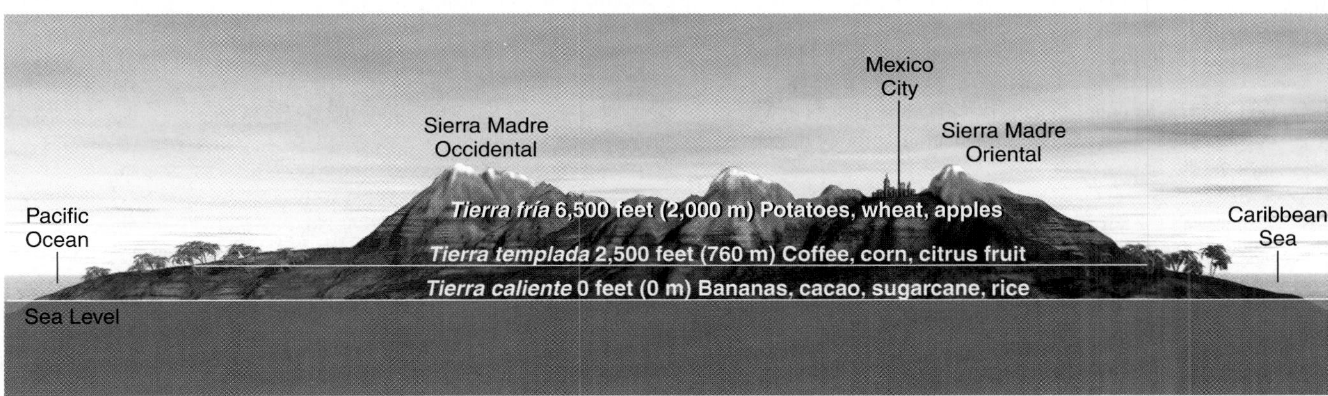

Correlation of

Our World Today To the NCSS Thematic Strands

In *Curriculum for Social Studies: Expectations of Excellence,* the National Council for the Social Studies (NCSS) identified 10 themes that serve as organizing strands for the social studies curriculum at every school level. These themes are interrelated and draw from all of the social science disciplines. Each theme provides student performance expectations in the areas of knowledge, processes, and attitudes. The 10 NCSS themes were the basis for the themes used in *Our World Today.*

Theme and Performance Expectation	Student Pages
I. *Culture* **The study of culture helps students understand similarities and differences within groups of people. By studying a culture's beliefs, values, and traditions, students begin to gain a perspective that helps them relate to different groups. In the middle grades, students begin to examine aspects of culture and how culture influences human behavior.**	
A. Compare similarities and differences in the ways groups, societies, and cultures meet human needs and concerns.	28–29, 31–33, 82–86, 88–93, 170–171, 181, 196–198, 210–214, 236–238, 283–286, 288–291, 296–300, 306–310, 313–314, 317–320, 346–348, 353–354, 357–358, 366–371, 373–376, 410–414, 422–427, 440–445, 450, 459–462, 487–489, 507–508, 537–538, 547–548, 559–561, 585–587, 593–594, 605–606, 617–618, 623–624, 639–641, 645–646, 661–664
B. Explain how information and experiences may be interpreted by people from diverse cultural perspectives and frames of reference.	28–29, 88–93, 195–196, 210–214, 216–219, 240, 247, 280–281, 292–295, 297, 306–310, 313–314, 318–320, 343, 350–351, 357–360, 366–369, 373–376, 404–408, 412–414, 424–425, 436–438, 441, 444–445, 455–457, 460–461, 464–468, 491–493, 508–510, 543–544, 559–561, 564–567, 590–594, 606–607, 617–618, 640–641, 661–664
C. Explain and give examples of how language, literature, the arts, architecture, other artifacts, traditions, beliefs, values, and behaviors contribute to the development and transmission of culture.	28–31, 82–83, 87–93, 149, 171–172, 183, 196–199, 213, 220, 241–242, 245–247, 250, 282, 297, 299, 309, 316, 319, 351–353, 355, 358, 370, 405, 425, 439, 444–446, 456, 461, 524–526, 541–543, 545, 547, 564–565, 585, 596, 639
D. Explain why individuals and groups respond differently to their physical and social environments and/or changes to them on the basis of shared assumptions, values, and beliefs.	28–29, 31–33, 88–93, 114, 125, 181, 196–198, 201, 210–214, 236–238, 242–243, 246–247, 288–291, 297, 306–310, 317–320, 350–351, 353, 357–360, 366–369, 374–376, 405–406, 414, 424–425, 436–438, 441, 443, 455–457, 460–461, 467–468, 493–494, 520–522, 541–543, 564–567, 583–587, 591–592, 617–618, 622–624, 639, 645–646, 661–664
E. Articulate the implications of cultural diversity, as well as cohesion, within and across groups.	24–25, 29, 36, 88–93, 168, 173–179, 200–203, 210–214, 216–219, 238–239, 247–249, 280–281, 297–298, 308, 313–315, 317–320, 350–351, 356–357, 366–371, 372, 375, 400, 443, 450, 455–457, 464–465, 493–494, 496, 522–524, 539, 543–544, 562, 590–591, 594–595, 617–618, 661–662, 668–669
II. *Time, Continuity, and Change* **Understanding time, continuity, and change involves being knowledgeable about what things were like in the past and how things change and develop over time. Knowing how to read and reconstruct the past helps students gain a historical perspective. In the middle grades, students will continue to increase their knowledge of the past and of historical concepts. Students will also begin to learn how individual experiences, social values, and cultural traditions influence interpretations of the past.**	
A. Demonstrate an understanding that different scholars may describe the same event or situation in different ways but must provide reasons or evidence for their views.	53–54, 61, 66, 87, 184, 282, 542
B. Identify and use key concepts such as chronology, causality, change, conflict, and complexity to explain, analyze, and show connections among patterns of historical change and continuity.	30–31, 36, 37, 66, 82–84, 140, 146–147, 156, 165–166, 170–171, 195–198, 214, 235, 236–239, 247–249, 313–315, 366–371, 376, 384, 441, 521, 541–543, 586
C. Identify and describe selected historical periods and patterns of change within and across cultures, such as the rise of civilizations, the development of transportation systems, the growth and breakdown of colonial systems, and others.	22–23, 30–31, 34–35, 37, 82–84, 88–93, 146–147, 168–169, 236–239, 241–244, 245–249, 369–371, 409, 437–438, 441, 443, 455–457, 492, 519–522, 543–544, 559–560, 590, 617, 645–646

Theme and Performance Expectation	Student Pages
D. Identify and use processes important to reconstructing and reinterpreting the past, such as using a variety of sources, providing, validating, and weighing evidence for claims, checking credibility of sources, and searching for causality.	38, 86, 91, 97, 125, 155, 167, 184, 187, 207, 235, 239, 244, 249, 282, 287, 291, 349, 363, 371, 384, 387, 403, 409, 439, 449, 463, 493, 550, 553, 588, 595, 627, 641
E. Develop critical sensitivities such as empathy and skepticism regarding attitudes, values, and behaviors of people in different historical contexts.	25, 26, 32–33, 35, 37, 53–54, 91, 125, 140, 159, 172, 194, 213, 233, 248, 253, 314, 339, 353, 358, 376, 400, 405, 456, 462, 471, 496, 521, 526, 596, 639
F. Use knowledge of facts and concepts drawn from history, along with methods of historical inquiry, to inform decision-making about and action-taking on public issues.	70–71, 140, 372, 525, 579, 600–601
III. *People, Places, & Environments* The study of people, places, and environments will help students as they create their spatial views and geographic perspective of the world. Students begin to make informed and critical decisions about the relationship between humans and their environment. In the middle school years, students can relate their personal experiences to happenings in other environments. These experiences will help students increase their abstract thought when analyzing human behavior in relation to physical and cultural environments.	
A. Elaborate mental maps of locales, regions, and the world that demonstrate understanding of relative location, direction, size, and shape.	49, 97, 129, 187, 223, 303, 363, 371, 471, 518, 553, 571, 599, 627, 657, 673
B. Create, interpret, use, and distinguish various representations of the earth such as maps, globes, and photographs.	30, 53, 58, 62, 76, 92, 97, 134, 155, 215, 237, 280, 331, 336, 344, 359, 386, 394, 411, 426, 439, 463, 471, 487, 504, 528, 540, 542, 557, 562, 591, 607, 622, 644, 661, 667
C. Use appropriate resources, data sources, and geographic tools such as aerial photographs, satellite images, geographic information systems (GIS), map projections, and cartography to generate, manipulate, and interpret information such as atlases, databases, grid systems, charts, graphs, and maps.	46, 54, 56, 77, 103, 113, 152, 156, 164, 204, 214, 303, 337, 395, 409, 423, 427, 449, 450–451, 485, 490, 495, 508, 529, 537, 553, 568, 571, 584, 599, 608, 627, 657, 669, 673
D. Estimate distance, calculate scale, and distinguish other geographic relationships such as population density and spatial distribution patterns.	36, 62, 77, 103, 148, 159, 193, 210–214, 291, 295, 347, 424, 431, 435–436, 444, 471, 503, 518, 540, 553, 568, 571, 583, 595, 623, 644, 657, 673
E. Locate and describe varying landforms and geographic features, such as mountains, plateaus, islands, rain forests, deserts, and oceans, and explain their relationship within the ecosystem.	53–54, 57–60, 64–65, 70–71, 83, 144, 162–164, 182, 192–193, 218, 285, 311–312, 343–345, 363, 404–405, 410–411, 427, 434, 442, 460–462, 486–487, 502–505, 528, 556–559, 582–583, 592–593, 599, 616–617, 621–622, 638–639, 643–644, 660–661, 667–668, 670, 673
F. Describe physical system changes such as seasons, climate and weather, and the water cycle and identify geographic patterns associated with them.	60–61, 69, 136, 144–145, 167, 201–202, 216–217, 295, 336, 342–343, 388, 440–441, 487, 506, 536–537, 607, 619, 624, 662, 667
G. Describe how people create places that reflect cultural values and ideals as they build neighborhoods, parks, shopping centers, and the like.	28–29, 82, 87, 93, 149–151, 171–172, 183, 196–198, 213, 220, 223, 278, 282, 293, 299, 343, 358, 364, 406, 408, 426, 434, 466, 494–495, 541–543, 546, 586–587, 619, 657, 668–669
H. Examine, interpret, and analyze physical and cultural patterns and their interactions, such as land use, settlement patterns, cultural transmission of customs and ideas, and ecosystem changes.	22–23, 26, 28–30, 33–35, 53–55, 60–61, 63–66, 70–71, 77, 82–83, 86, 92, 97, 104, 113, 129, 146, 155, 159, 168–169, 182–183, 192–193, 217, 223, 236–239, 245–249, 308, 331, 342–343, 346–348, 357–358, 360, 374, 376, 388, 413–414, 431, 437–438, 445, 454–457, 467, 471, 488–489, 530–531, 536–539, 542, 550, 553, 558–559, 600–601, 616–617, 621–624, 627, 638–639, 641, 646, 657, 662–663, 668–669, 673
I. Describe ways that historical events have been influenced by, and have influenced, physical and human geographic factors in local, regional, national, and global settings.	30–31, 33, 36, 49, 86, 102–104, 129, 146–148, 168–169, 172, 187, 195–196, 200–201, 203, 207, 213–214, 236–239, 241–244, 245–249, 253, 313–315
J. Observe and speculate about social and economic effects of environmental changes and crises resulting from phenomena such as floods, storms, and drought.	58, 83, 86, 136, 151, 164, 167, 387, 412, 428, 435, 440–441, 471, 556–557, 559
K. Propose, compare, and evaluate alternative uses of land and resources in communities, nations, and the world.	64–66, 70–71, 104, 113, 129, 167, 195, 285, 295, 374, 387, 431, 488, 508–510, 530–531, 584–585, 599–601, 645, 668–670, 673

Theme and Performance Expectation	Student Pages
IV. *Individual Development & Identity* **People and culture influence a person's identity. Examining the different forms of human behavior improve one's understanding of social relationships and the development of personal identity. The study of human behavior helps students become aware of how social processes influence a person's identity. In the middle years, issues of personal identity become important as students begin to view themselves in relation to others.**	
A. Relate personal changes to social, cultural, and historical contexts.	24–25, 28–31, 49, 141, 181, 183, 194, 233, 236–237, 239, 243–244, 245–247, 250, 253, 303, 311, 314, 339, 348, 371, 373–374, 405, 456, 526
B. Describe personal connections to place—as associated with community, nation, and world.	24–25, 27–31, 33, 36–38, 53–54, 79, 114, 129, 146–148, 151, 159, 171–172, 181, 194, 199, 207, 315, 355, 358, 436–437, 449, 496, 522–526, 547, 596, 669
C. Describe the ways family, gender, ethnicity, nationality, and institutional affiliations contribute to personal identity.	24–25, 28–30, 49, 88–93, 108, 125, 140, 146–148, 196–197, 246–247, 253, 280–281, 313–315, 350–355, 373–374, 405, 414, 436–437, 455–457, 471, 493–494, 496–497, 521–525, 526, 529, 547–548, 553, 585–586, 639, 645–646
D. Relate such factors as physical endowment and capabilities, learning, motivation, personality, perception, and behavior to individual development.	22–23, 27–31, 36–37, 70–71, 89, 92–93, 146–147, 149, 169, 194, 197–198, 236, 245–247, 253, 295, 339, 366–369, 373–374, 449, 456, 471, 493, 496, 507–510, 524, 596, 627, 639
E. Identify and describe ways regional, ethnic, and national cultures influence individuals' daily lives.	28–29, 31–33, 88–93, 114, 125, 181, 196–198, 201, 210–214, 236–238, 242–243, 246–247, 288–291, 297, 306–310, 317–320, 350–351, 353, 357–360, 366–369, 374–376, 405–406, 414, 424–425, 436–438, 441, 443, 455–457, 460–461, 467–468, 493–494, 520–521, 541–543, 564–567, 583–587, 591–592, 617–618, 622–624, 639, 645–646, 661–664
F. Identify and describe the influence of perception, attitudes, values, and beliefs on personal identity.	22–23, 27–31, 36–37, 70–71, 89, 92–93, 146–147, 149, 169, 194, 197–198, 236, 245–247, 253, 295, 339, 366–369, 373–374, 449, 456, 471, 493, 496, 507–510, 524, 596, 627, 639
G. Identify and interpret examples of stereotyping, conformity, and altruism.	24–25, 29, 37, 88–93, 140, 146–148, 165, 170, 194, 233, 248, 313, 315, 353, 360, 400, 414, 456–457, 523, 530–531
H. Work independently and cooperatively to accomplish goals.	33, 46, 56, 71, 87, 99, 140, 156, 188, 204, 209, 233, 240, 303, 355, 384, 409, 449, 485, 463, 531, 568, 588, 639, 659
V. *Individuals, Groups, & Institutions* **Institutions, such as schools, governments, and churches, influence people and often reflect a society's values. Because of the vital role that institutions play in people's lives, it is important that students know how institutions develop, what controls and influences them, and how humans react to them. Middle school students will gain experience by studying how institutions change over time. They should also be able to use their understanding to suggest ways how institutions can work for the common good.**	
A. Demonstrate an understanding of concepts such as role, status, and social class in describing the interactions of individuals and social groups.	24–25, 53, 83–84, 114, 140, 146–148, 195–196, 238–239, 242–244, 308, 313–314, 366–370, 400, 414, 438, 443, 455–457, 492–493, 520–521, 544, 549, 553, 645–646
B. Analyze group and institutional influences on people, events, and elements of culture.	31–32, 88–93, 102, 153, 203, 219, 241–242, 253, 346, 363, 437–438, 509–510, 539, 553, 627, 635
C. Describe the various forms institutions take and the interactions of people with institutions.	31–32, 36–37, 79, 88–93, 108, 159, 165, 195–196, 243–244, 279–280, 283, 290–291, 353, 366, 408, 443, 520, 587, 606–607, 635, 668–669
D. Identify and analyze examples of tensions between expressions of individuality and group or institutional efforts to promote social conformity.	106, 170–171, 183, 203, 250, 253, 297, 300, 353, 369–371, 456–457, 493–494, 496
E. Identify and describe examples of tensions between belief systems and government polices and laws.	89, 91, 106, 124, 125, 169, 183, 249, 280–281, 313–315, 353–354, 369–371, 456–457, 499, 520–522, 566, 641
F. Describe the role of institutions in furthering both continuity and change.	31–32, 36–37, 79, 88–93, 102, 108, 153, 165, 195–196, 203, 219, 241–242, 253, 279–280, 346, 363, 408, 437–438, 509–510, 520, 539, 553, 587, 606–607, 627, 635, 668–669

Theme and Performance Expectation	Student Pages
G. Apply knowledge of how groups and institutions work to meet individual needs and promote the common good.	26, 33, 36–38, 49, 71, 91, 233, 246–247, 369, 372, 428, 456, 525, 531, 539, 549, 601, 669
VI. *Power, Authority, & Governance* Studying structures of power, authority, and governance and their functions in the United States and around the world is important for developing a notion of civic responsibility. Students will identify the purpose and characteristics of various types of government and how people try to resolve conflicts. Students will also examine the relationship between individual rights and responsibilities. During the middle school years, students apply what they have learned about rights and responsibilities in more complex contexts.	
A. Examine persistent issues involving the rights, roles, and status of the individual in relation to the general welfare.	24–25, 28–29, 31, 36–38, 88–93, 125, 140, 146–148, 170–171, 233, 236–237, 242–244, 248, 313–314, 353, 373–374, 400, 443, 456, 493, 508–510, 520–521, 523–524, 566, 635, 669
B. Describe the purpose of government and how its powers are acquired, used, and justified.	31–33, 36–37, 83, 102, 106–107, 125, 145–146, 151, 170–171, 201–203, 233, 236–239, 247–249, 279–280, 360, 366–371, 408, 437–438, 509–510, 520–521, 567, 587, 617
C. Analyze and explain ideas and governmental mechanisms to meet needs and wants of citizens, regulate territory, manage conflict, and establish order and security.	26, 31–32, 36–37, 106, 108, 125, 159, 166, 181, 196, 214, 238–239, 281, 314, 369–371, 384, 413, 437–438, 450, 456–457, 494, 499, 509–510, 520–522, 539, 553, 579, 601, 646, 669
D. Describe the ways nations and organizations respond to forces of unity and diversity affecting order and security.	31, 88–93, 102, 111–112, 123–125, 146–148, 170–171, 181, 187, 196, 201, 214, 238–239, 246–249, 280–281, 313–314, 350–351, 353, 369–371, 411, 431, 443, 455–457, 493–496, 520–522, 543–544, 559–560, 606–607
E. Identify and describe the basic features of the political system in the United States and identify representative leaders from various levels and branches of government.	520–521
F. Explain conditions, actions, and motivations that contribute to conflict and cooperations within and among nations.	22–25, 31, 36–37, 49, 102, 108, 111–112, 123–125, 146–148, 170–171, 181, 187, 196, 201, 214, 238–239, 246–249, 280–281, 313–314, 350–351, 353, 369–371, 411, 431, 443, 455–457, 493–496, 520–522, 539, 543–544, 559–560, 606–607, 668–669
G. Describe and analyze the role of technology in communications, transportation, information processing, weapons development, or other areas as it contributes to or helps resolve conflicts.	22–24, 33, 38, 65–66, 102, 113–114, 123, 151, 166–167, 180–181, 194–196, 203, 246–247, 289, 346–348, 370–371, 372, 374, 376, 450, 508–510, 521–522, 543, 579, 669
H. Explain and apply concepts such as power, role, status, justice, and influence to the examination of persistent issues and social problems.	24–25, 28–29, 31, 36–37, 88–93, 108, 125, 140, 146–148, 170–171, 233, 236–237, 242–244, 248, 313–314, 353, 373–374, 400, 443, 456, 493, 508–510, 520–521, 523–524, 566, 635, 669
I. Give examples and explain how governments attempt to achieve their stated ideals at home and abroad.	33, 36–38, 49, 102, 108, 111, 123, 125, 151, 165, 181, 196, 214, 219, 237–239, 247, 280–281, 370, 406, 411, 438, 455–456, 521–522, 525, 564–565, 566–567
VII. *Production, Distribution, & Consumption* Societies try to meet people's needs and wants by trying to answer the basic economic questions: What is to be produced? How should goods be produced? How should goods and services be distributed? How should land, labor, capital, and management be allocated? By studying how needs and wants are met, students learn how trade and government economic policies develop. In the middle grades, students increase their knowledge of economic concepts, principles, and reasoning.	
A. Give and explain examples of ways that economic systems structure choices about how goods and services are to be produced and distributed.	32–33, 107–108, 113–114, 129, 137, 145, 165–166, 180–181, 184, 194–196, 203, 213–214, 284, 289, 292–293, 311–312, 339, 346–348, 373–374, 387, 405–406, 412–413, 460–461, 466, 487–488, 507–510, 538–539, 590, 605–606, 617, 645
B. Describe the role that supply and demand, prices, incentives, and profits play in determining what is produced and distributed in a competitive market system.	32, 113–114, 165–166, 180–181, 195, 211, 217, 280, 286, 293, 295, 312, 331, 346, 373–374, 384, 387, 423, 427, 442, 435, 438, 507–508, 510, 558, 564, 567, 584, 606–607

Theme and Performance Expectation	Student Pages
C. Explain the difference between private and public goods and services.	34, 36, 103, 279, 309, 312, 487–488, 509
D. Describe a range of examples of the various institutions that make up economic systems such as households, business firms, banks, government agencies, labor unions, and corporations.	23, 32–33, 108, 112, 114, 145, 165, 180–181, 277, 286, 290, 298, 346–348, 508, 539, 549–550, 558, 566, 584
E. Describe the role of specialization and exchange in economic process.	23, 32, 37, 108, 113, 123, 165–166, 180–181, 188–189, 195, 217, 244, 247, 285, 277, 295, 370, 423, 435–436, 441, 443, 488, 510, 539, 559, 564, 566, 593, 606, 617, 663
F. Explain and illustrate how values and beliefs influence different economic decisions.	31, 38, 66, 114, 123, 145, 167, 196, 243–244, 293, 346, 370–372, 443, 487–488, 494, 496, 508–509, 559, 579, 585, 646, 668–669
G. Differentiate among various forms of exchange and money.	32, 84, 169, 188–189, 217, 242–243, 247, 411, 424–425, 438, 450, 462, 510, 543, 564, 566, 606, 617, 663
H. Compare basic economic systems according to who determines what is produced, distributed, and consumed.	32–33, 107–108, 113–114, 129, 137, 145, 165–166, 180–181, 184, 194–196, 203, 213, 284, 289, 292–293, 311–312, 339, 346–348, 405–406, 412–413, 460–461, 466, 487–488, 507–510, 538–539, 566, 590, 605–606, 617, 645
I. Use economic concepts to help explain historical and current developments and issues in local, national, or global contexts.	36–38, 113–114, 129, 145, 168–172, 244, 247, 339, 348, 370–371, 373–374, 387, 450–451, 508–510, 521–522, 538–539, 543–544
J. Use economic reasoning to compare different proposals for dealing with a contemporary social issue such as unemployment, acid rain, or high quality education.	64–66, 169, 195, 328, 345, 376, 387, 508–510, 530–531, 579, 584–585
VIII. *Science, Technology, & Society* The study of science, technology, and society is ever changing. It raises questions about who will benefit from it and how fundamental values and beliefs can be preserved in a technology-driven society. By the middle grades, students research the complex relationships among technology, human values, and behavior. Students will learn how technology and science have brought about change and how they have often challenged accepted societal beliefs.	
A. Examine and describe the influence of culture on scientific and technological choices and advancement, such as in transportation, medicine, and warfare.	22–25, 28–31, 37–38, 82–84, 87, 112, 113–114, 148, 169, 196, 198, 212, 245–247, 250, 285–286, 372, 428, 437–438, 450, 494, 496, 508–510, 521–523, 541–543, 662
B. Show through specific examples how science and technology have changed people's perceptions of the social and natural world, such as in their relationship to the land, animal life, family life, and economic wants, needs, and security.	22–25, 33, 37–38, 56, 165–166, 167, 195–196, 244–247, 249–250, 372, 405, 466, 471, 494, 496, 508–510, 521, 585–586, 617, 641, 668–670
C. Describe examples in which values, beliefs, and attitudes have been influenced by new scientific and technological knowledge, such as the invention of the printing press, conceptions of the universe, applications of atomic energy, and genetic discoveries.	22–25, 37–38, 167, 181, 194, 245–247, 249–250
D. Explain the need for laws and policies to govern scientific and technological applications, such as the safety and well-being of workers and consumers and the regulation of utilities, radio, and television.	31–32, 293, 345, 372, 374, 376, 387, 488, 509–510
E. Seek reasonable and ethical solutions to problems that arise when scientific advancements and social norms or values come into conflict.	66, 146, 374, 670
IX. *Global Connections* As countries grow more interdependent, understanding global connections among world societies becomes important. Students will analyze emerging global issues in many different fields. They will also investigate relationships among the different cultures of the world. In the middle years, students analyze the interactions among states and countries and respond to global events and changes.	
A. Describe instances in which language, art, music, belief systems, and other cultural elements can facilitate global understanding or cause misunderstanding.	28–29, 86, 88, 147, 148, 171–172, 183, 198, 220, 237, 245–247, 250, 286, 306, 312, 355, 405, 435, 446, 461, 493, 523, 565, 596, 639

Theme and Performance Expectation	Student Pages
B. Analyze examples of conflict, cooperation, and interdependence among groups, societies, and nations.	25, 36, 88–93, 122–125, 166, 200–203, 247, 278–281, 313–315, 350–351, 400, 413–414, 450–451, 455–457, 493–494, 520, 522–524, 539, 564–567, 606–607, 646, 668, 670
C. Describe and analyze the effects of changing technologies on the global community.	22–25, 28–31, 33, 37–38, 56, 82–84, 87, 112, 113–114, 148, 165–167, 169, 181, 195–196, 198, 212, 244–247, 249–250, 285–286, 372, 405, 428, 437–438, 450, 466, 471, 494, 496, 508–510, 521–523, 541–543, 585–586, 617, 641, 662, 668–670
D. Explore the causes, consequences, and possible solutions to persistent, contemporary, and emerging global issues, such as health, security, resource allocation, economic development, and environmental quality.	33, 35–38, 49, 63–66, 107–108, 122–125, 130–131, 166, 170–172, 373–376, 428, 457, 508–510, 579, 600–601
E. Describe and explain the relationships and tensions between national sovereignty and global interests, in such matters as territory, natural resources, trade, use of technology, and welfare of people.	113–114, 124–125, 170–171, 313–315, 455–457, 539, 579, 600–601
F. Demonstrate understanding of concerns, standards, issues, and conflicts related to universal human rights.	122–125, 170–171, 313–315, 400, 413–414, 455–457, 520–522
G. Identify and describe the roles of international and multinational organizations.	113, 539, 579, 668
X. *Civic Ideals & Practices* **Understanding civic ideals and practices is crucial to complete participation in society and is the main purpose of social studies. Students will learn about civic participation and the role of the citizen within his or her community, country, and world. By the middle grades, students will broaden their understanding to analyze and evaluate relationships between civic ideals and practices.**	
A. Examine the origins and continuing influence of key ideals of the democratic republican form of government, such as individual human dignity, liberty, justice, equality, and the rule of law.	31, 33, 36, 38, 145–146, 170–171, 233, 236–239, 284, 289, 373–376, 406, 520–525, 548, 635
B. Identify and interpret sources and examples of the rights and responsibilities of citizens.	31, 36–37, 38, 140, 170–171, 233, 375–376, 520, 523–525
C. Locate, access, analyze, organize, and apply information about selected public issues—recognizing and explaining multiple points of view.	35, 37, 49, 66, 70–71, 79, 125, 140, 155, 172, 184, 187, 207, 223, 233, 281, 315, 331, 339, 353, 363, 376, 400, 431, 438, 472, 489, 496, 530–531, 553, 579, 600–601, 627, 635
D. Practice forms of civic discussion and participation consistent with the ideals of citizens in a democratic republic.	79, 233, 253, 499, 531, 579, 601, 635
E. Explain and analyze various forms of citizen action that influence public policy decisions.	31, 36–38, 70–71, 170, 371, 400, 456, 493, 496, 499, 520–521, 530–531, 553, 579, 600–601
F. Identify and explain the roles of formal and informal political actors in influencing and shaping public policy and decision-making.	37, 146, 151, 169–170, 233, 353, 371, 375, 400, 456, 496
G. Analyze the influence of diverse forms of public opinion on the development of public policy and decision-making.	31, 36–38, 70–71, 170, 371, 400, 456, 493, 496, 499, 520–521, 530–531, 553, 579, 600–601
H. Analyze the effectiveness of selected public policies and citizen behaviors in realizing the stated ideals of a democratic republican form of government.	31, 33, 36, 38, 145–146, 170–171, 233, 236–239, 284, 289, 373–376, 406, 520–525, 548, 635
I. Explain the relationship between policy statements and action plans used to address issues of public concern.	33, 36–38, 49, 71, 130–131, 145, 159, 167, 281, 313–314, 376, 387, 400, 455–457, 493–494, 510, 525, 549–550, 553, 579, 606, 668
J. Examine strategies designed to strengthen the "common good," which consider a range of options for citizen action.	70–71, 130–131, 233, 400, 428, 530–531, 579, 600–601, 635

From Geography Themes

In the past decade, instruction in geography has been organized around the five themes of geography: location, place, human/environment interaction, movement, and regions. The popularity of these content organizers set the stage for the development of two additional, more comprehensive instructional frameworks: the "Six Essential Elements" and the "Eighteen Geography Standards" within the elements. These two interlocking frameworks provide the structure of the publication *Geography for Life: National Geography Standards 1994.*

6 Essential Elements and

1 The World in Spatial Terms

Geography studies the relationships between people, places, and environments by mapping information about them into a spatial context.

The geographically informed person knows and understands:

1. How to use maps and other geographic representations, tools, and technologies to acquire, process, and report information from a spatial perspective
2. How to use mental maps to organize information about people, places, and environments in a spatial context
3. How to analyze the spatial organization of people, places, and environments on Earth's surface

2 Places and Regions

The identities and lives of individuals and peoples are rooted in particular places and in those human constructs called regions.

The geographically informed person knows and understands:

4. The physical and human characteristics of places
5. That people create regions to interpret Earth's complexity
6. How culture and experience influence people's perception of places and regions

3 Physical Systems

Physical processes shape Earth's surface and interact with plant and animal life to create, sustain, and modify ecosystems.

The geographically informed person knows and understands:

7. The physical processes that shape the patterns of Earth's surface
8. The characteristics and spatial distribution of ecosystems on Earth's surface

to Geography Standards

How the Themes and Standards Compare It is important to keep in mind that the five themes and the standards look at the same geographic universe. The themes represent an instructional approach; they allow a particular focus to be given to the lesson of the moment. The standards comprise the geographic subject matter, skills, and perspectives of geography. The 5 themes flow through all the 18 geography standards and can be used in the instruction of all of them, at any grade level.

The chart below explains the 6 essential elements and lists the standards within each. The chart on pages T24–T29 provides:

- An explanation of the 18 standards
- Which of the five themes relate most closely to each standard
- Page numbers in the student edition of *Our World Today* that utilize each standard

18 Geography Standards

4 Human Systems

People are central to geography in that human activities help shape Earth's surface, human settlements and structures are part of Earth's surface, and humans compete for control of Earth's surface.

The geographically informed person knows and understands:

9. The characteristics, distribution, and migration of human populations on Earth's surface
10. The characteristics, distribution, and complexity of Earth's cultural mosaics
11. The patterns and networks of economic interdependence on Earth's surface
12. The processes, patterns, and functions of human settlement
13. How the forces of cooperation and conflict among people influence the division and control of Earth's surface

5 Environment and Society

The physical environment is modified by human activities, largely as a consequence of the ways in which human societies value and use Earth's natural resources, and human activities are also influenced by Earth's physical features and processes.

The geographically informed person knows and understands:

14. How human actions modify the physical environment
15. How physical systems affect human systems
16. The changes that occur in the meaning, use, distribution, and importance of resources

6 The Uses of Geography

Knowledge of geography enables people to develop an understanding of the relationships between people, places, and environments over time—that is, of Earth as it was, is, and might be.

The geographically informed person knows and understands:

17. How to apply geography to interpret the past
18. How to apply geography to interpret the present and plan for the future

Correlation of *Our World Today* to the National Geography Standards

National Geography Standards & Related Themes	Student Edition Pages
STANDARD 1 **How to use maps and other geographic representations, tools, and technologies to acquire, process, and report information from a spatial perspective** Maps are the most commonly used representations of detailed geographic information on features or places. Along with other tools such as globes, aerial photographs, satellite images, and statistical databases, they bring the whole world into focus. Maps range from simple sketch maps to complex Geographic Information Systems (GIS) analysis. **Related Themes: Location, Place**	46, 48, 52, 54, 56, 58, 59, 62, 68, 69, 72–76, 83, 89, 92, 96, 103, 134–136, 154, 158, 160, 161, 163, 170, 186, 189, 190, 191, 193, 197, 204, 206, 211, 215, 222, 226–228, 237, 243, 252, 254, 255, 262, 264, 266, 272, 273, 304, 305, 307, 330, 331, 334–336, 346, 347, 351, 359, 362, 368, 386, 389–394, 402–403, 407, 411, 424, 430, 431, 435, 436, 444, 448, 451–455, 459, 470, 484–487, 490, 497, 498, 500–504, 518, 522, 528, 530, 533–535, 542, 549, 552, 557, 558, 570, 572–576, 583, 586, 591, 598, 605, 606, 608, 621–623, 626, 628–632, 644, 656, 658, 659, 661, 667, 672, 675
STANDARD 2 **How to use mental maps to organize information about people, places, and environments in a spatial context** A mental map exists only in the mind's eye. It represents each individual's knowledge of the location of geographic features such as countries, cities, seas, mountain ranges, and rivers. A mental map is also made up of approximate size dimensions and cultural characteristics. In scale, it may include our route to a local store or theater, or it may serve as the framework for the location of the Khyber Pass, Brasília, or the Yangtze Gorges. This map grows in complexity as experience, study, and the media bring us new geographic information. **Related Themes: Location, Place, Regions**	27, 46, 49, 52, 53, 54, 56, 68, 69, 84, 89, 97, 99, 104, 113, 125, 144, 150, 159, 168, 180, 182, 187, 200, 201, 203, 207, 212, 223, 253, 273, 278, 283, 285, 290, 296, 298, 306, 317, 319, 332, 342, 363, 387, 431, 445, 449, 466, 471, 486, 494, 499, 502, 518, 529, 553, 571, 582, 599, 618, 620, 621, 623, 627, 638, 657, 666, 667, 673
STANDARD 3 **How to analyze the spatial organization of people, places, and environments on Earth's surface** Human structures organize space. Pattern, regularity, and reason are inherent in the locations of cities, factories, malls, cemeteries, and other human landscape creations. To understand the spatial patterns and processes that organize Earth's surface, it is essential to know concepts such as distance, direction, location, connections, and association. Understanding these concepts enables one to say what factors influence a locational decision for a hospital, a county seat, a sanitary landfill, or a regional shopping center. **Related Themes: Place, Human/Environment Interaction**	36, 46, 52, 53, 54, 56, 62, 104, 113, 125, 144, 150, 151, 152, 154, 162, 168, 180, 193, 200, 210, 215, 218, 278, 290, 342, 357, 404, 405, 407, 410, 412, 422, 434, 459, 464, 488, 494, 502, 534, 535, 540, 568, 589, 604, 623, 629, 638, 643, 660, 666

National Geography Standards & Related Themes	Student Edition Pages
STANDARD 4 **The physical and human characteristics of places** Places may be distinguished by their physical and human characteristics. Physical characteristics include landforms, climate, soils, hydrology, vegetation, and animal life. Human characteristics include language, religion, political and economic systems, population, and quality of life. Places change over time as new technologies, resources, knowledge, and ideologies are introduced and become part of a place's geography. Such change leads to the rise and fall of empires, may derive from shifts in climate or other physical systems, or may be generated by population expansion. **Related Themes: Place, Human/Environment Interaction**	22, 24, 29, 30, 31, 36, 37, 38, 52, 53, 60, 63, 64, 65, 70, 77, 78, 79, 82–86, 88, 90, 102, 103, 104, 137–140, 144–148, 150–155, 162–166, 168–172, 180–183, 188, 191–198, 200–203, 210–214, 216–219, 225, 229–233, 238, 239, 241, 242, 244, 246–249, 257, 278–281, 283–286, 289–300, 306–315, 317–320, 337–339, 342–345, 347, 348, 350, 352, 353, 357–360, 366, 369, 370, 371, 373–376, 391, 395–400, 403, 404, 406, 407, 408, 410–414, 422, 423, 425, 426, 427, 434–438, 441, 442, 444, 445, 446, 454–457, 459–462, 464–468, 486, 487, 489, 491–496, 502–509, 519, 520, 522–525, 535–538, 546, 548, 549, 550, 556–561, 563–567, 573, 578, 579, 581–595, 603–607, 616–624, 629, 634–641, 643, 645, 646, 659–664, 666–669, 674
STANDARD 5 **That people create regions to interpret Earth's complexity** Regions are defined as having one or more common characteristics that give them a measure of unity and make them distinct from surrounding areas. As worlds within worlds, regions simplify geographic analysis by organizing a specific area into a unit of explicit physical and human elements. The criteria in the definition of a region can be as precise as coastline or political boundaries, or as arbitrary as the general location of people loyal to a specific athletic team. Regions are human constructs, created to facilitate the understanding of a large, varied, complex, and changing world. **Related Themes: Regions, Human/Environment Interaction**	24, 25, 27, 30, 33, 54, 73, 82, 113, 114, 144, 151, 152, 163, 180, 188, 201, 210, 212, 213, 216, 238, 285, 286, 290, 291, 292, 293, 294, 295, 296, 297, 299, 306, 308, 309, 310, 311, 313, 314, 315, 317, 342, 347, 348, 356, 357, 358, 366, 391, 395, 404, 410, 412, 413, 422, 425, 426, 427, 437, 438, 440, 443, 445, 459, 464, 467, 488, 489, 502, 503, 504, 536, 537, 538, 556, 559, 565, 566, 567, 573, 582, 589, 591, 592, 594, 604, 616, 622, 623, 639, 641, 644, 660, 663, 667
STANDARD 6 **How culture and experience influence people's perceptions of places and regions** Perception of all places and regions depends upon personal experience, culture, age, gender, and other factors. It is sometimes said that there is no reality, only perception. In geography there is always a mixture of both. For example, a wilderness can be attractive to a camper, a source of anxiety for a child, and a nuisance to a pioneering farmer. **Related Themes: Regions, Place, Movement**	24, 25, 28, 29, 31, 34, 37, 56, 78, 79, 84, 103, 138–140, 161, 166, 167, 169, 171, 188, 195, 196, 197, 209, 217, 225, 230–233, 235, 243, 337, 338–339, 341, 353, 367, 369, 370, 373, 375, 395, 396–400, 413, 425, 437, 453, 460, 485, 486, 501, 507, 509, 510, 520, 523, 533, 547, 578, 579, 634, 635, 637, 659, 666

National Geography Standards & Related Themes	Student Edition Pages
STANDARD 7 **The physical processes that shape the patterns of Earth's surface** Physical processes create natural landscapes and environments arrayed across Earth's surface in spatial patterns. Understanding these forces is indispensable in daily decision-making, such as evaluating home-building sites in earthquake zones or floodplains, or building a highway along the ocean coastline. There is a systematic order in this continual remaking of Earth's surface. The geographically informed person understands the interplay of systems, forces, boundaries, thresholds, and equilibrium as they influence patterns on Earth's surface. **Related Themes: Place, Regions**	52, 53, 57, 58, 59, 60, 61, 63, 64, 145, 151, 153, 163, 164, 165, 196, 216, 295, 374, 405, 412, 487, 504, 505, 534, 535, 536, 537, 556, 563, 643, 662, 666, 668
STANDARD 8 **The characteristics and spatial distribution of ecosystems on Earth's surface** Ecosystems are communities of living things—plants and animals—interacting with each other and with the physical environment. Ecosystems are dynamic and ever changing. They are self-regulating, open systems that maintain flows of energy and matter that naturally move toward maturity, stability, and balance. By understanding how these systems and processes work in shaping the physical environment, students will be better able to comprehend the basic principles that guide environmental management. Such knowledge will enable them to anticipate the consequences of ongoing human effort to transform Earth's landscapes. **Related Themes: Location, Place, Regions**	54, 55, 56, 60, 61, 63, 64, 65, 70, 146, 162, 270, 289, 308, 342, 345, 374, 404, 408, 413, 423, 428, 440, 441, 464, 508, 509, 530, 531, 532, 581, 584, 585, 600, 601, 620, 660, 670
STANDARD 9 **The characteristics, distribution, and migration of human populations on Earth's surface** The characteristics and distribution of human populations are never static. Factors such as natural increase, war, famine, disease, and rate of urbanization play decisive roles in where people live. At any one time, some populations are bound to be migrating—leaving one place, striking out for a second, or possibly settling in a third. The factors that give definition to a nation's population profile, patterns of growth or decline, and inclinations toward migration combine to be significant geographic information. **Related Themes: Human/Environment Interaction, Movement, Regions**	26, 28, 29, 34, 35, 36, 52, 55, 70, 77, 102, 104, 108, 114, 137, 145, 148, 151, 155, 163, 164, 171, 180, 181, 182, 188, 196, 197, 202, 211, 212, 214, 217, 218, 229, 239, 245, 256, 266, 280, 281, 284, 285, 286, 291, 292, 294, 297, 306, 318, 319, 320, 337, 367, 403, 410, 411, 412, 424, 427, 435, 436, 437, 441, 442, 455, 460, 461, 466, 468, 488, 494, 510, 522, 523, 536, 538, 548, 560, 566, 567, 573, 590, 592, 604, 618, 619, 623, 624, 640, 641, 663, 669

National Geography Standards & Related Themes	Student Edition Pages
STANDARD 10 **The characteristics, distribution, and complexity of Earth's cultural mosaics** Culture defines each group's unique view of itself and others, and includes the material goods, skills, and social behavior transmitted to successive generations. It is expressed through art, language, beliefs and institutions, the built environment, and numerous other features. Cultural patterns are never static. They change in response to human migration, diffusion, and the steady introduction of new and competing cultural traits. **Related Themes: Location, Regions, Place**	22, 24, 25, 27, 28, 29, 30, 31, 32, 33, 34, 37, 38, 66, 77, 78, 79, 84, 85, 86, 88, 89, 90, 91, 92, 93, 102, 103, 104, 108, 114, 125, 138–140, 143, 147, 148, 149, 151, 153, 154, 155, 169, 172, 182, 194, 196, 197, 198, 199, 202, 203, 213, 219, 220, 230–233, 236, 237, 238, 242, 244, 245, 246, 247, 248, 250, 269, 283, 284, 286, 291, 293, 294, 295, 296, 297, 298, 309, 310, 311, 312, 314, 315, 316, 338–339, 344, 350, 351, 352, 352, 353, 354, 358, 366, 368, 370, 396–400, 403, 404, 405, 406, 413, 422, 437, 438, 441, 446, 456, 457, 460, 461, 462, 465, 467, 468, 491–496, 519, 521, 522, 523, 525, 526, 542, 543, 544, 546, 547, 560, 561, 564, 565, 578, 579, 584–587, 589–592, 594, 595, 596, 607, 618, 619, 623, 624, 634, 635, 639, 640, 641, 645, 646, 659, 661, 662, 663, 664, 669
STANDARD 11 **The patterns and networks of economic interdependence on Earth's surface** The goods that we need daily to make life work have sources all over the world. Economic networks at all scales, from local to global, have been developed to promote the efficient interchange of goods. Linkages of transportation, communication, language, currency, and custom have been fashioned out of the human desire to have more than what is available locally. For United States citizens, learning about the nature and significance of global interdependence is an essential aspect of being geographically well-informed. **Related Themes: Movement, Regions, Human/Environment Interaction, Location**	24, 32, 33, 35, 37, 38, 78, 79, 86, 102, 108, 138–140, 165, 180, 181, 188, 204, 212, 213, 218, 230–233, 247, 262, 263, 289, 297, 305, 338–339, 358, 372, 373, 396–400, 450, 461, 465, 488, 507, 508, 509, 510, 533, 538, 539, 549, 564, 578, 579, 592, 606, 617, 619, 622, 634, 635, 637, 641, 645, 660, 661, 663, 664
STANDARD 12 **The processes, patterns, and functions of human settlement** Settlement is one of the most basic human responses to the environment. As social animals, humans achieve proximity, shared environments, and the opportunity to engage in effective economic and social interaction through settlement. Nearly half the human population has opted for city residence. However, there is a vast variety of cultural landscapes in urban settings, just as there is in village and town settings for most of the rest of the population. In all varieties of settlements, cultural landscapes reflect local resources and human preferences. **Related Themes: Place, Regions, Movement**	28, 31–38, 55, 77, 83, 85, 86, 102, 108, 113, 137, 145, 151, 152, 165, 166, 167, 171, 183, 194, 195, 202, 203, 211–214, 219, 229, 243, 256, 262, 263, 265, 266, 269, 279, 280, 281, 283, 284, 286, 294, 295, 298, 300, 305, 308, 312–315, 319, 320, 337, 339, 344, 347, 348, 352, 358, 359, 366, 368, 375, 388, 391, 403, 405, 406, 412, 423, 424, 426, 427, 434, 435, 436, 438, 441, 442, 443, 454, 455, 457, 460, 462, 464, 466, 467, 468, 488, 489, 495, 501, 503, 507, 538, 548, 549, 550, 557, 559, 561, 564, 565, 567, 583, 586, 590, 592, 593, 594, 617, 618, 619, 621, 624, 638, 640, 641, 645, 646, 662

National Geography Standards & Related Themes	Student Edition Pages
STANDARD 13 **How the forces of cooperation and conflict among people influence the division and control of Earth's surface** The tendency to divide space into segments that provide identity and a sense of security is universal. This human drive covers all scales, from individual homesteads through neighborhood and city limits to state and national boundaries. We have long declared borders, built walls, demarcated rivers and mountain ridges, and had arbitrary lines mapped across deserts. This trait relates to a wish to enclose that which we desire or perhaps exclude that which is feared. Multinational alliances as well as community interest groups are all motivated by the human capacity for expression of cooperation and conflict in the control of Earth's surface. **Related Themes: Regions, Movement, Human/Environment Interaction**	26, 30, 31, 34, 35, 36, 38, 84, 86, 102, 103, 108, 125, 147, 148, 150, 151, 155, 169, 170, 181, 201, 237, 238, 242, 244–247, 249, 255, 258, 259, 261, 262, 263, 264, 265, 267, 268, 269, 280, 281, 290, 299, 313, 343, 351, 356, 357, 366, 367, 369, 370, 371, 372, 375, 376, 388, 405, 410, 411, 412, 414, 423, 424, 428, 438, 443, 444, 446, 456, 457, 461, 465, 467, 468, 486, 491, 492, 494, 496, 521, 522, 523, 544, 555, 566, 590, 593, 606, 617, 663, 669
STANDARD 14 **How human actions modify the physical environment** When humans first occupied the environment, levels of technology were low enough that modifications of the physical setting were generally simple, although significant over time. However, as we have developed more powerful technology to assist us in such modifications, we have made hot areas cool, cold areas warm, dry areas garden-like, and wet areas habitable. Changing the landscape has become a signature of human use of Earth, and will be a significant theme as we see just what we have gained (and lost) in such transformations. **Related Themes: Human/Environment Interaction, Place, Regions**	38, 52, 54, 60, 61, 63, 64, 65, 66, 70, 71, 83, 85, 145, 146, 152, 166, 167, 195, 209, 218, 270, 289, 308, 312, 357, 360, 374, 376, 391, 445, 466, 509, 536, 550, 558
STANDARD 15 **How physical systems affect human systems** Expanding settlement of floodplains, coastal margins, and seismic zones has brought us face-to-face with striking evidence of ways in which physical systems have profound effects on human systems. Less dramatic—but ultimately more significant—aspects of the effect of physical systems on human systems are such issues as freshwater use, ozone depletion, global warming, and soil loss. Knowledge of Earth's physical systems will be critical to the human use of Earth in the years to come and is central to *Geography for Life.* **Related Themes: Place, Regions, Human/Environment Interaction**	52, 53, 54, 60, 61, 65, 83, 102, 153, 154, 155, 164, 192, 216, 299, 348, 359, 408, 412, 435, 440, 442, 467, 562, 620, 662

National Geography Standards & Related Themes	Student Edition Pages
STANDARD 16 **The changes that occur in the meaning, use, distribution, and importance of resources** We extract, process, market, and consume those things we value in the environment. The activity related to putting values on resources, and the subsequent demands on the environment, establish patterns of economic, political, and cultural interaction. Some natural resources we require: air, water, vegetation—and space. Others commonly used, such as oil, tin, diamonds, bananas, and coffee, have gained their value by human decisions that generally relate to levels of technology and economic development. A geographer must understand what makes an item a resource, and what the subsequent geographic implications of such an appraisal might be. **Related Themes: Human/Environment Interaction, Place, Regions**	53, 55, 61, 63, 64, 65, 66, 70, 71, 83, 84, 85, 86, 99, 103, 113, 145, 151, 152, 153, 155, 164, 167, 171, 181, 195, 202, 203, 210, 211, 217, 284, 290, 291, 293, 307, 309, 310, 311, 312, 315, 319, 320, 345, 346, 347, 348, 357, 358, 360, 405, 407, 410, 412, 414, 423, 425, 426, 427, 435, 436, 437, 442, 443, 444, 445, 450, 454, 455, 456, 458, 460, 462, 465, 466, 467, 468, 487, 488, 489, 503, 504, 505, 519, 521, 556, 558, 559, 564, 579, 582, 584, 586, 591, 592, 603–606, 616–619, 622, 624, 639, 640, 642–645, 660, 661, 663, 664, 666, 668
STANDARD 17 **How to apply geography to interpret the past** An understanding of spatial and environmental perspectives leads to a fuller appreciation of the human use of Earth in the past. By determining how people have assessed their own settings, and gaining understanding of why they used their settings as they did—or changed them the way they did—we can see the role that geography has played in our histories. **Related Themes: Human/Environment Interaction, Movement, Regions**	23, 26, 27, 30, 31, 35, 55, 58, 61, 66, 81–93, 102, 104, 108, 114, 125, 145, 146, 147, 149, 153, 155, 165, 167–172, 181, 182, 183, 188, 194, 195, 196, 200, 201, 203, 211, 213, 214, 217, 218, 219, 233, 235–250, 256–265, 267, 268, 279, 281, 282, 285, 286, 289, 290, 298, 299, 313, 314, 317, 318, 319, 341, 351, 352, 357, 359, 360, 366–373, 388, 400, 406, 408, 410, 411, 413, 414, 422, 424–427, 433, 435, 437, 438, 443, 444, 446, 450, 455, 456, 457, 459–462, 465, 466, 467, 486, 488, 491, 492, 494, 495, 510, 519, 520, 521, 523, 538, 541–545, 550, 555, 559, 560, 562, 564, 566, 567, 584, 585, 586, 590, 591–595, 606, 607, 616, 617, 618, 620, 621, 640, 641, 645, 646, 663, 664, 668, 670, 674
STANDARD 18 **How to apply geography to interpret the present and plan for the future** Geography leads people to think about spatial patterns, connections between places, integration of local to global scales, diversity, and systems. With such a scope, it is easy to see how completely geography influences the present, and how it can be significant in achieving effective planning for the future. Issues that range from resources to population to paths of movement all relate to the essence of geography. Being able to put this breadth of impact to work in planning for the future is one of the benefits of being geographically well-informed. **Related Themes: Regions, Human/Environment Interaction, Place**	22, 23, 55, 61, 66, 153, 161, 183, 214, 260, 268, 270, 283, 341, 346, 360, 376, 403, 414, 424, 453, 460, 508, 539, 644, 670, 674

Scope and Sequence

Themes and Concepts

Each section of *Our World Today* focuses on one central theme, although related themes also appear in each section. The section numbers highlighted here in **red** indicate the central theme that is key to that section. Related themes are listed in black.

Chapter	1	2
Culture and Traditions	Section 1, 2	
Continuity and Change		
Geography and History		Section 1, 2, 3
Individual Action		
Groups and Institutions		
Government and Democracy	Section 2	
Economic Factors		
Science and Technology	Section 1	Section 1, 3
Global Connections		Section 2
Civic Rights and Responsibilities		Section 3

Skills

These are the skills taught in the Chapter *SKILLS LESSON.* Each skill is reinforced in the ***Chapter Skills Activities*** in the Unit Resource books in the TCR and **Glencoe's Skillbuilder Interactive Workbook CD-ROM.**

Chapter	1	2
Skill Category	*Social Studies Skill*	*Social Studies Skill*
Specific Skill	Using Latitude and Longitude	Using a Map Key

3	4	5	6	7
Section 1, 2	Section 2, 3, 4		Section 2, 3	Section 1
Section 1	Section 2		Section 2, 3	Section 2
	Section 1, 2	Section 1, 2	Section 1, 2	Section 1
				Section 1
Section 2	Section 1, 2	Section 1, 2		
		Section 1	Section 3	
	Section 1, 2, 3, 4	Section 1	Section 1, 3	Section 1
Section 1			Section 1	
Social Studies Skill	*Technology Skill*	*Social Studies Skill*	*Critical Thinking Skill*	*Critical Thinking Skill*
Using Latitude and Longitude	Using the Internet	Reading a Circle Graph	Distinguishing Fact from Opinion	Making Comparisons

Chapter	8	9	10	11
Themes and Concepts				
Culture and Traditions	Section 2	Section 1, 2, 3		Section 1, 4
Continuity and Change		Section 1, 2, 3	Section 1, 2, 3	Section 1, 5
Geography and History	Section 1, 2			
Individual Action		Section 1, 2, 3		
Groups and Institutions				Section 5
Government and Democracy		Section 1, 2, 3	Section 2	Section 1, 3, 5
Economic Factors	Section 1, 2		Section 1, 2, 3	Section 1, 2, 3, 4, 5
Science and Technology			Section 1, 2	Section 1
Global Connections		Section 1	Section 2, 3	Section 1, 2, 3, 4
Civic Rights and Responsibilities		Section 1		
Skills				
Skill Category	*Social Studies Skill*	*Social Studies Skill*	*Social Studies Skill*	*Study and Writing Skill*
Specific Skill	Reading a Contour Map	Using B.C. and A.D.	Reading a Population Map	Using Library Resources

12	13	14	15	16
Section 2, 3	Section 2			
Section 1, 2, 3		Section 1, 2		
	Section 1		Section 1, 3	Section 1, 2
Section 2, 3	Section 2	Section 1		
Section 2	Section 3		Section 1, 2	Section 1, 2
		Section 2	Section 3	Section 1
Section 1, 2, 3	Section 3	Section 2	Section 1, 2, 3	Section 1, 2
Section 3	Section 5	Section 1		
		Section 1	Section 3	Section 2
		Section 1		
Study and Writing Skill	*Technology Skill*	*Critical Thinking Skill*	*Critical Thinking Skill*	*Critical Thinking Skill*
Taking Notes	Evaluating a Web Site	Understanding Cause and Effect	Making Predictions	Drawing Inferences and Conclusions

Chapter	17	18	19	20
Themes and Concepts				
Culture and Traditions			Section 3	Section 2
Continuity and Change	Section 1	Section 2	Section 3	
Geography and History	Section 2	Section 1	Section 1	Section 1
Individual Action	Section 1	Section 2	Section 3	Section 2
Groups and Institutions			Section 3	
Government and Democracy	Section 1	Section 2	Section 3	Section 3
Economic Factors	Section 1, 2, 3	Section 1	Section 2	
Science and Technology	Section 1, 2		Section 2	Section 3
Global Connections			Section 2	Section 3
Civic Rights and Responsibilities		Section 2	Section 3	
Skills				
Skill Category	*Technology Skill*	*Social Studies Skill*	*Critical Thinking Skill*	*Social Studies Skill*
Specific Skill	Developing Multimedia Presentations	Reading a Time Zones Map	Mental Mapping	Reading a Physical Map

21	22	23	24	25
	Section 1	Section 1, 2, 3	Section 1, 2	Section 1
	Section 2			
Section 1, 2	Section 1	Section 1, 2, 3	Section 1, 2	Section 1, 2
Section 2	Section 2	Section 1		
Section 1		Section 1, 2	Section 1	
	Section 1, 2	Section 3	Section 1, 2	
Section 1, 2	Section 1, 2	Section 1, 2, 3	Section 1, 2	
Section 1	Section 2		Section 2	
		Section 2		Section 2
		Section 2		
Social Studies Skill	*Critical Thinking Skill*	*Technology Skill*	*Study and Writing Skill*	*Study and Writing Skill*
Interpreting an Elevation Profile	Sequencing and Categorizing Information	Using a Data Base	Outlining	Writing a Report

Classroom Solutions

Reading Strategies

How Can I Help My Students Read and Understand the Textbook?

Social studies teachers do not have to be reading teachers to help students read and understand their textbooks. Often poor readers lack interest in the topic, have trouble concentrating, cannot understand a word or sentence, or are confused as to how the information fits together. These problems can frustrate the student and the teacher, but there are strategies that can be used to improve comprehension and retention of information. Using these reading strategies not only helps poor readers, but also strengthens the reading skills of strong readers.

Activate Prior Knowledge

Activating prior knowledge provides opportunities for students to discover and articulate what they already know about key concepts and ideas. It stimulates student interest and prepares students to incorporate new information into a larger picture. In addition, it helps the teacher to determine a starting place for instruction.

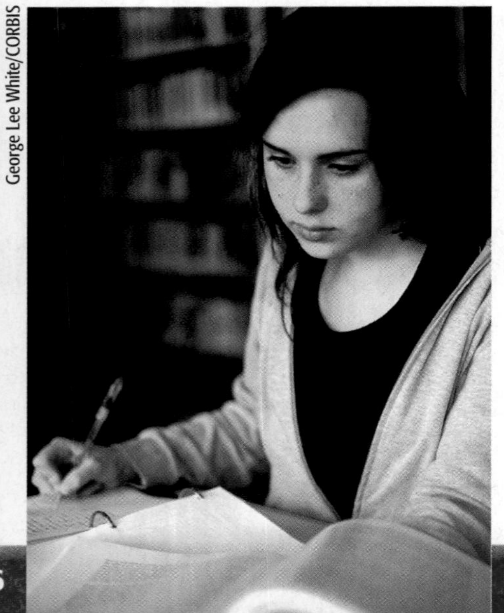
George Lee White/CORBIS

- ✔ Write the topic on the board and have students brainstorm what they know about it. Record their responses on the board.
- ✔ Ask general or specific questions about the topic and see how students respond to them.
- ✔ Present an anticipation guide. An anticipation guide provides a series of statements about an idea or topic. Students read each statement and tell whether they agree or disagree, based on their prior understandings and experiences.
- ✔ Use a K-W-L-H or K-W-L chart to activate prior knowledge and set reading purposes. Students identify what they already **know** (or think they know) and what they **want** to find out about the topic. After reading, students complete the chart.

K	W	L	H
What I **Know**	What I **Want** to Find Out	What I **Learned**	**How** I Can Learn More

Set Reading Purposes

Reading is a purposeful activity. We read to find answers to specific questions, to satisfy curiosity, and to be entertained.

- ✔ Have students preview the reading selection. Tell students to read the title, headings, and subheadings. Draw students' attention to diagrams, tables, and other visuals and their captions. Discuss how these will help comprehension.
- ✔ Prompt students to predict what they might learn in the selection, based on their preview. Invite them to list additional questions they hope to answer through the reading. Have them identify possible problems, such as unfamiliar words or ideas, to watch for as they read.
- ✔ Discuss the need to "shift gears" in reading speed and attention when reading. Support students as they plan how best to read a selection—slowly to watch for new vocabulary and ideas or quickly to review previously learned ideas. They can also discuss new information with a buddy as they read.

Vocabulary Development

Vocabulary knowledge and reading comprehension are closely related.

- ✔ Before students read, preteach vocabulary that is crucial for understanding key topics and concepts.
- ✔ Relate new vocabulary to known words and ideas. After introducing a word and its definition, have students name synonyms or related words they know.
- ✔ If a student encounters an unfamiliar word while reading, have him or her try to pronounce it aloud. Sometimes saying the word will trigger one's memory of its meaning.
- ✔ As students read, help them use prefixes (word parts added to the beginning of base words), suffixes (word parts added to the end of base words), and roots (word elements from which other words are formed) as clues to decipher the meaning of words.
- ✔ Encourage students to use the context of surrounding words and sentences to determine a word's meaning.
- ✔ If context clues and structural analysis fail to help a student understand an important word as

Common Prefixes	Meanings	Examples
un-, dis-, non-, im- and il-	"not" or "the opposite of"	unwrapped, dishonest, nonprofit, immortal, illogical
re-	"again" or "back"	reheat
post-	"after"	postwar
uni-	"one"	unicycle
Common Suffixes	**Meanings**	**Examples**
-ship, -hood	"state of" or "condition of"	friendship, neighborhood
-ment	"act of" or "state of"	management
-ish	"like"	childish
-ous	"full of" or "like"	joyous

they read, have students find the definition in a glossary or dictionary. If the word is not critical for understanding, have students note the word and read on. Later, have students reread the word in context. If the meaning is still unclear, have students consult the dictionary.

Taking Notes

Taking notes challenges readers to determine what is most important and to organize information in a way that makes sense. Note-taking can also help students stay focused as they read. Reviewing notes can build students' retention of important information.

- ✔ Have students take notes after they have read long paragraphs in the section rather than the entire chapter. This helps them focus on important ideas and details and prevents them from losing track of the flow of information.
- ✔ Remind students that as they take notes on the section, they should not take a long time to do it. Students should read, think, write, and move on.
- ✔ Have students take notes using note cards. Notes should be recorded in the students' own words and labeled with the page number where the entire text appears.
- ✔ To use notes to review a passage, have students read through the notes, highlighting the most important information. As they review, encourage students to annotate their notes, making connections between related ideas and clarifying difficult concepts.

Summarizing

Summarizing demands that students identify the most important ideas and details to create a streamlined version of the text.

- ✔ After reading the section, have students recall as much of the information as possible. If the main idea and its supporting details are presented in a certain order, make sure students can recall that organization.
- ✔ As they summarize, students should try to answer as many of the following questions as possible: *who, what, where, when, why,* and *how*.
- ✔ If the section does not have a main idea that is clearly stated, have students create one that is concise but comprehensive. Have students state the main idea in a topic sentence at the beginning of their summaries.
- ✔ Sometimes summaries seem disconnected when details are left out. Students should use connector words such as "and" or "because," along with introductory or closing statements, to make ideas more connected.✦

Reading Comprehension: Be Aware, Reread, and Connect (BARC)

Advice from Dr. Elizabeth Pryor, Ph.D.
Research Center for Educational Technology
Kent State University, Kent, Ohio

Many students think silent reading means just looking at words and saying them in their heads. They do not make the connection that reading is supposed to make sense! Have you ever read a paragraph or a page and then said to yourself, "What was that?" As a good reader, you were aware of your lack of understanding. Poor readers, on the other hand, just keep on reading the words, unaware that they do not understand them.

What strategies do good readers use when this happens? Most reread the text they did not understand. Before rereading I study key words I might have missed. When I reread, sometimes I "whisper read" so I can hear the text as well as read it. As I reread, I try to connect what I am reading with something I already know. If I reread and still don't understand, I read it a third (or fourth) time. Each rereading increases comprehension.

In summary, **Be aware** of understanding as you read, **reread,** and **connect** the reading to what you already know. **BARC!**

Classroom Solutions

Test-Taking Strategies

How Can I Help My Students Succeed on Tests?

It's not enough for students to learn social studies facts and concepts—they must be able to show what they know in a variety of test-taking situations.

How Can I Help My Students Do Well On Objective Tests?

Objective tests may include multiple choice, true/false, and matching questions. Applying the following strategies can help students do their best on objective tests.

Multiple Choice Questions

- ✔ Students should read the directions carefully to learn what answer the test requires—the best answer or the right answer. This is especially important when answer choices include "all of the above" or "none of the above."
- ✔ Advise students to watch for negative words in the questions, such as *not, except, unless, never,* and so forth. If the question contains a negative, the correct answer choice is the one that does not fit.
- ✔ Students should try to mentally answer the question before reading the answer choices.
- ✔ Students should read all the answer choices and cross out those that are obviously wrong. Then they should choose an answer from those that remain.

True/False Questions

- ✔ It is important that students read the entire question before answering. For an answer to be true, the entire statement must be true. If one part of a statement is false, the answer should be marked *False*.
- ✔ Remind students to watch for words like *all, never, every,* and *always*. Statements containing these words are often false.

Matching Questions

- ✔ Students should read through both lists before they mark any answers.
- ✔ Unless an answer can be used more than once, students should cross out each choice as they use it.
- ✔ Using what they know about grammar can help students find the right answer. For instance, when matching a word with its definition, the definition is often the same part of speech (noun, verb, adjective, and so forth) as the word.

How Can I Help My Students Do Well On Essay Tests?

Essay tests require students to provide thorough and well-organized written responses, in addition to telling what they know. Help students use the following strategies on essay tests.

Analyze:	*To **analyze** means to systematically and critically examine all parts of an issue or event.*
Classify or Categorize:	*To **classify** or **categorize** means to put people, things, or ideas into groups, based on a common set of characteristics.*
Compare and Contrast:	*To **compare** is to show how things are similar, or alike. To **contrast** is to show how things are different.*
Describe:	*To **describe** means to present a sketch or impression. Rich details, especially details that appeal to the senses, flesh out a description.*
Discuss:	*To **discuss** means to systematically write about all sides of an issue or event.*
Evaluate:	*To **evaluate** means to make a judgment and support it with evidence.*
Explain:	*To **explain** means to clarify or make plain.*
Illustrate:	*To **illustrate** means to provide examples or to show with a picture or other graphic.*
Infer:	*To **infer** means to read between the lines or to use knowledge and experience to draw conclusions, make a generalization, or form a prediction.*
Justify:	*To **justify** means to prove or to support a position with specific facts and reasons.*
Predict:	*To **predict** means to tell what will happen in the future, based on an understanding of prior events and behaviors.*
State:	*To **state** means to briefly and concisely present information.*
Summarize:	*To **summarize** means to give a brief overview of the main points of an issue or event.*
Trace:	*To **trace** means to present the steps or stages in a process or event in sequential or chronological order.*

Read the Question

The key to writing successful essay responses lies in reading and interpreting questions correctly. Teach students to identify and underline key words in the questions, and to use these words to guide them in understanding what the question asks. Help students understand the meaning of some of the most common key words, listed in the chart on page T38.

Plan and Write the Essay

After students understand the question, they should follow the writing process to develop their answer. Encourage students to follow the steps below to plan and write their essays.

1. Map out an answer. Make lists, webs, or an outline to plan the response.

2. Decide on an order in which to present the main points.

3. Write an opening statement that directly responds to the essay question.

4. Write the essay. Expand on the opening statement. Support key points with specific facts, details, and reasons.

5. Write a closing statement that brings the main points together.

6. Proofread to check for spelling, grammar, and punctuation.

How Can I Help My Students Prepare for Standardized Tests?

Students can follow the steps below to prepare for a test.

Bill Aron/PhotoEdit

- ✔ ***Read About the Test*** Students can familiarize themselves with the format of the test, the types of questions that will be asked, and the amount of time they will have to complete the test.
- ✔ ***Review the Content*** Consistent study throughout the school year will help students build social studies knowledge and understanding. If there are specific objectives or standards that are tested on the exam, help students review these facts or skills to be sure they are proficient.
- ✔ ***Practice*** Provide practice, ideally with real released tests, to build students' familiarity with the content, format, and timing of the real exam. Students should practice all the types of questions they will encounter on the test—multiple choice, short answer, and extended response.
- ✔ ***Analyze Practice Results*** Help students improve test-taking performance by analyzing their test-taking strengths and weaknesses. Spend time discussing students' completed practice tests, explaining why particular answers are right or wrong. Help students identify what kinds of questions they had the most difficulty with. Look for patterns in errors and then tailor instruction to review the appropriate test-taking skills or social studies content.✦

Help Students Learn by Reviewing Graded Tests

Advice from Tara Musslewhite
Humble Independent School District
Humble, Texas

Frequently reviewing graded tests is a great way for students to assess their test-taking skills. It also gives teachers the opportunity to teach test-taking strategies and review content. As the class rereads each test question, guide students to think logically about their answer choices. Show students how to:

1. Read each question carefully to determine its meaning.
2. Look for key words in the question to support their answers.
3. Recognize synonyms in the answer choices that may match phrases in the question.
4. Narrow down answer choices by eliminating ones that don't make sense.
5. Anticipate the answer before looking at the answer choices.
6. Circle questions of which they are unsure and go back to them later. Sometimes a clue will be found in another question on the test.

Classroom Solutions

Alternative Assessment Strategies

How Can I Go Beyond Tests to Assess Students' Understanding of Social Studies Facts and Concepts?

In response to the growing demand for accountability in the classroom, educators must use multiple assessment measures to accurately gauge student performance. In addition to quizzes, tests, essay exams, and standardized tests, assessment today incorporates a variety of performance-based measures and portfolio opportunities.

What Are Some Typical Performance-Based Assessments?

There are many kinds of performance-based assessments. They all share one common characteristic—they challenge students to create products that demonstrate what they know. One good way to present a performance assessment is in the form of an open-ended question.

Writing

Performance-based writing assessments challenge students to apply their knowledge of social studies concepts and information in a variety of written ways. Writing activities are most often completed by one student, rather than by a group.

- ✔ ***Journals*** Students write from the perspective of a historical character or a citizen of a particular historical era.
- ✔ ***Letters*** Students write a letter from one historical figure to another or from a historical figure to a family member or other audience.
- ✔ ***Position Paper or Editorial*** Students explain a controversial issue and present their own opinion and recommendations, supported with strong evidence and convincing reasons.
- ✔ ***Newspaper*** Students write a variety of stories from the perspective of a reporter living in a particular historical time period.
- ✔ ***Biographies and Autobiographies*** Students write about historical figures either from the third person point of view (biography) or from the first person (autobiography).
- ✔ ***Creative Stories*** Students integrate historical events into a piece of fiction, incorporating the customs, language, and geography of the period.
- ✔ ***Poems and Songs*** Students follow the conventions of a particular type of song or poem as they tell about a historical event or person.
- ✔ ***Research Reports*** Students synthesize information from a variety of sources into a well-developed research report.

Oral Presentations

Oral presentations allow students to demonstrate their social studies literacy before an audience. Oral presentations are often group efforts, although this need not be the case.

- ✔ ***Simulations*** Students hold simulations, or reenactments, of actual events, such as trials, acts of civil disobedience, battles, speeches, and so forth.
- ✔ ***Debates*** Students debate two or more sides to a historical policy or issue. Students can debate from a contemporary perspective or in a role play in which they assume a viewpoint held by a historical character.
- ✔ ***Interview*** Students conduct a mock interview of an historical character or bystander.
- ✔ ***Oral Reports*** Students present the results of research efforts in a lively oral report.
- ✔ ***Skits and Plays*** Students use historical events as the basis for a play or skit. Details should accurately reflect customs, language, and the setting of the period.

Visual Presentations

Visual presentations allow students to demonstrate their social studies understandings in a variety of visual formats. Visual presentations can be either group or individual projects.

- ✔ ***Model*** Students make a model to demonstrate or represent a process, place, event, battle, artifact, or custom.
- ✔ ***Museum Exhibit*** Students create a rich display of materials around a topic. Typical displays might include models, illustrations, photographs, videos, writings, and audiotaped explanations.
- ✔ ***Graph or Chart*** Students analyze and represent historical data in a line graph, bar graph, table, or other chart format.
- ✔ ***Drawing*** Students represent or interpret a historical event or period through illustration, including political cartoons.
- ✔ ***Posters and Murals*** Posters and murals may include maps, time lines, diagrams, illustrations, photographs, and written explanations that reflect students' understandings of historical information.

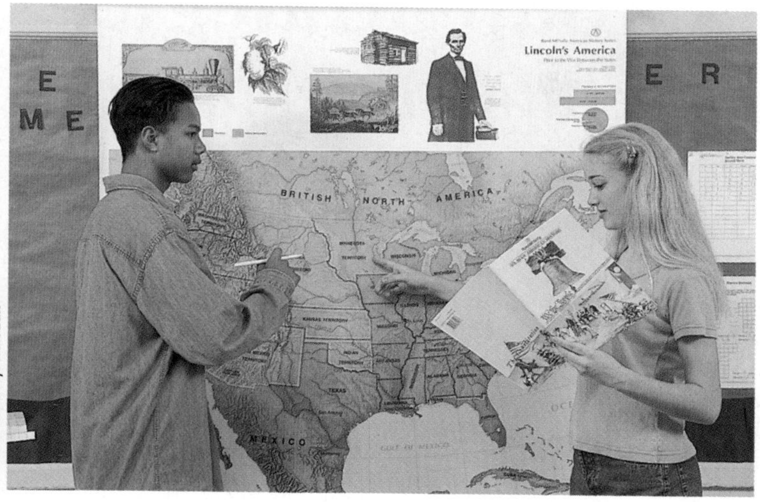

Jonathan Nourok/PhotoEdit

- ✔ ***Quilt*** Students sew or draw a design for a patchwork quilt that shows a variety of perspectives, events, or issues related to a key topic.
- ✔ ***Videotapes*** Students film a video to show historical fiction or to preserve a simulation of a historical event.
- ✔ ***Multimedia Presentation or Slide Show*** Students create a computer-generated multimedia presentation containing historical information and analysis.

How Are Performance Assessments Scored?

There are a variety of means used to evaluate performance tasks. Some or all of the following methods may be used.

- ✔ ***Scoring Rubrics*** A scoring rubric is a set of guidelines for assessing the quality of a process and/or product. It sets out criteria used to distinguish acceptable responses from unacceptable ones, generally along a scale from excellent to poor.
- ✔ ***Models of Excellent Work*** Teacher-selected models of excellent work concretely illustrate expectations and help students set goals for their own projects.
- ✔ ***Student Self-Assessment*** Common methods of self-assessment include ranking work in relation to the model, using a scoring rubric, and writing their own goals and then evaluating how well they have met the goals they set for themselves. Regardless of which method or methods students use, they should be encouraged to evaluate their behaviors and processes, as well as the finished product.
- ✔ ***Peer or Audience Assessment*** Many of the performance tasks target an audience other than the classroom teacher. If possible, the audience of peers should give the student feedback. Have the class create rubrics for specific projects together.
- ✔ ***Observation*** As students carry out their performance tasks, you may want to formally observe students at work. Start by developing a checklist, identifying all the specific behaviors and understandings you expect students to demonstrate. Then observe students as they carry out performance tasks and check off the behaviors as you observe them.
- ✔ ***Interviews*** As a form of ongoing assessment, you may want to conduct interviews with students, asking them to analyze, explain, and assess their participation in performance tasks. When projects take place over an extended period of time, you can hold periodic interviews as well as exit interviews. In this way the interview process allows you to gauge the status of the project and to guide students' efforts along the way.✦

Targeting Multiple Intelligences

Advice from John Cartaina
Consultant, New Jersey Council of Social Studies

Authentic performance assessment provides students with different learning styles opportunities to demonstrate their successful learning. The table below list types of learning styles.

Learning Style	*Characteristics of Students*
Linguistic	*Read regularly, write clearly, and easily understand the written word*
Logical-Mathematical	*Use numbers, logic, and critical thinking skills*
Visual-Spatial	*Think in terms of pictures and images*
Auditory-Musical	*Remember spoken words and produce rhythms and melodies*
Kinesthetic	*Learn from touch, movement, and manipulating objects*
Interpersonal	*Understand and work well with other people*
Intrapersonal	*Have a realistic understanding of their strengths and weaknesses*
Naturalist	*Can distinguish among, classify, and use features of the environment*

You may want to assign activities to students that accommodate their strongest learning styles, but frequently ask them to use their weakest learning styles.

Classroom Solutions

Cooperative Group Strategies

How Can I Use Cooperative Learning to Teach Social Studies?

Today's social and economic climate requires flexibility. Workers must be able to function independently, work well with groups, and engage in fair-minded competition. For this reason, most educators recommend a healthy balance of instructional strategies to foster cooperative, competitive, and individualistic styles of problem solving and learning. Cooperative learning requires students to work together—each with a specific task—to pursue a common goal. Because part of each student's evaluation is determined by the overall quality of the group's work, students help one another accomplish the group goal.

How Do I Form Cooperative Groups?

- ✔ ***Composition*** Most experts recommend that cooperative groups be heterogeneous, reflecting a range of student abilities, backgrounds, and learning styles. However, this does not necessarily mean that students should be assigned to groups on a random basis.
- ✔ ***Group Size*** The size of cooperative groups can change, depending upon the task. Some cooperative tasks are best accomplished in pairs. For most projects, groups of three to five students are ideal.
- ✔ ***Abilities*** Consider the tasks and projects the groups will undertake as you make group assignments. You may want to make sure each group has a strong manager, a strong writer, a strong artist, a good listener, and so forth.
- ✔ ***Balance*** Some teachers use a "family-of-five" approach to grouping. A strong leader heads each group. Two pairs of students with opposing styles or strengths complete the "family." Paired students might exhibit traits such as outgoing and shy, creative and conventional, spontaneous and methodical, and so on. Each group continues to work together throughout the semester or year, with the goal that students develop greater flexibility in their own problem-solving abilities and greater respect for the contributions of others.
- ✔ ***Roles*** In most instances, you will want to assign a specific role for each student to play in a group, such as designer, moderator, recorder, researcher, presenter, graphic artist, actor, and so forth. Roles should be interdependent, requiring students to rely upon one another in order to successfully carry out their individual responsibilities. As students gain experience in working in cooperative groups, turn over more of the responsibility for establishing individual roles and responsibilities to the group.

How Do I Help Groups Run Smoothly?

- ✔ ***Seating Arrangements*** Explain how and where groups should sit. Pairs can sit with desks or chairs face-to-face. Larger groups do well with desks or chairs gathered in a circle or with students seated around a table.
- ✔ ***Warm-Ups*** Provide an introductory activity for new groups. Even when students know one another, they can benefit by making formal introductions and sharing their thoughts on a sentence starter, such as "If I could go anywhere in the world, I would go to . . ." or "If I could have lived at any period in history, I would choose. . ."
- ✔ ***Rules*** Set clear expectations and rules for groups. Typical rules include addressing group members by name, making eye contact, listening politely, expressing disagreement with respect, welcoming others' questions, valuing others' contributions, providing positive feedback, and assisting others when asked.

How Do I Use Cooperative Groups in My Classroom?

- ✔ ***Share and Tell*** Have students form groups of four. Assign each group member a number between one and four. Ask a factual recall question. Have group members discuss the question and come up with an answer. Call out a number between one and four. The student with that number who is first to raise his or her hand answers the question. The group earns a point for a correct answer.
- ✔ ***Circle Partners*** Have the class separate into two equal groups and form two circles, with one circle inside the other. Each student faces a partner in the opposing circle. Ask a question and

Photo

LWA-Dann Tardif/CORBIS STOCK MARKET

have partners discuss the answer. If partners do not know the answer they can ask another pair for help. Then, call on students in the inside circle, the outside circle, or all students to say the answer aloud together.

- ✔ ***In the Know*** Provide students with a set of end-of-chapter questions or other questions covering content you want students to master. Tell students to circulate around the room to find someone who can answer a question on the worksheet. After listening to the answer, the student paraphrases it, writes the answer on the worksheet, and asks the "expert" to read and sign off on the answer if it is correct. Students move on to find a student to answer the next question. The process continues until students have completed their worksheets.
- ✔ ***Open-Ended Projects*** The best long-term projects for cooperative groups are those that are open-ended and multidimensional. That is, the task or question should have many possible answers and should lend itself to many different presentation possibilities.

Multiple intelligences Appropriate projects should challenge students and allow students of various abilities and backgrounds to contribute significantly to solving the problem and executing the project. One way to assess the validity of a potential project is to see whether it requires the use of many different strengths or "intelligences."

Assigning roles Because of the complexity of long-term projects, it is essential that students have clearly assigned roles and responsibilities. Once cooperative groups are established and successful in your classroom, be sure to vary the assignments given to each student from project to project.

Deadlines Define interim and final deadlines to encourage students to pace their efforts appropriately.

How Do I Assess Group and Individual Efforts?

- ✔ ***Expectations*** As with any assignment, set clear guidelines and high expectations for projects. Show models of excellent past projects, if possible, and define what criteria projects must meet to earn the highest grade.
- ✔ ***Group and Individual Grades*** Before students begin, define what percentage of the grade will be based on group work and how much will be based on individual effort. Many teachers give two equally weighted grades: a group grade—the same for each team member—and an individual grade.
- ✔ ***Self-Assessment*** Provide a checklist or rating scale for each group member. Have students evaluate their own contribution to the group, as well as the contributions of other group members. In addition to assessing the quality of the finished product, have students evaluate the processes they used within the group, such as showing respect for others' ideas. Provide space on the evaluation sheet for students to explain why they rated themselves and group members as they did.✦

Troubleshooting

Advice from Carey Boswell, M.Ed.
Humble Independent School District
Humble, Texas

Modern research overwhelmingly suggests that student learning is enhanced when cooperative groups are used in the classroom. Like many other teachers, I was uncertain of how much learning was taking place when I set up cooperative groups. I struggled with noise and control issues and off-task behavior by some students. I found a solution, though.

A cooperative group activity occurs whenever a student works with another student. Cooperative groups do not have to be large groups. Smaller groups ensure that all students are engaged and contribute to the group effort. Smaller groups also guarantee that members perform multiple tasks so that real learning occurs. I often combine two or more small groups into a larger group for short comparative tasks. After making this small adjustment, I am able to assign cooperative group tasks to students at least once a week and student performance, comprehension, and learning has increased in my classroom.

Classroom Solutions

Web Strategies

How Can I Use the Internet to Teach Social Studies?

Aaron Haupt

From the Internet to round-the-clock live newscasts, teachers and students have never before had so much information at their fingertips. Yet never before has it been so confusing to determine where to turn for reliable content and what to do with it once you have found it. In today's world, social studies teachers must not only use the Internet as a source of up-to-the-minute information for students; they must teach students how to find and evaluate sources on their own.

What's Available On the Internet?

- ✔ ***Teacher-Focused Web Sites*** These Web sites provide teaching tips, detailed lesson plans, and links to other sites of interest to teachers and students.
- ✔ ***Historical Documents*** Thousands of primary source documents have now been cataloged and placed on the Web. Some sites provide text-only versions. Others provide photographs of actual documents and artifacts as well as insightful commentary and analysis.
- ✔ ***Geographical Information*** The Web holds a variety of geographical resources, from historical, physical, and political maps; to interactive mapping programs; to information about people and places around the world.
- ✔ ***Statistics*** Government Web sites are rich depositories for statistics of all kinds, including census data and information about climate, education, the economy, and political processes and patterns.
- ✔ ***Reference Sources*** Students can access full-text versions of encyclopedias, dictionaries, atlases, and other reference books, as well as databases containing millions of journal and newspaper articles.
- ✔ ***News*** Traditional media sources, including television, radio, newspapers, and newsmagazines, sponsor Internet sites that provide almost instantaneous news updates, as well as in-depth news coverage and analysis. Extensive archives facilitate research on past news stories.
- ✔ ***Topical Information*** Among the most numerous Web sites are those organized around a particular topic or issue, such as the Civil War or the stock market. These Internet pages may contain essays, analyses, and other commentaries, as well as primary source documents, maps, photographs, video and audio clips, bibliographies, and links to related online resources.
- ✔ ***Organizations*** Many organizations such as museums post Web pages that provide online exhibits, archives, and other information.

Glencoe Online

Glencoe provides an integrated Web curriculum for your textbook. The **Chapter Overview** Web link provides previews and reviews to help students better understand each chapter's organization and content. Engaging **Student Web Activities** challenge students to apply what they've learned. **Self-Check Quizzes** at the end of each chapter let you and your students assess their knowledge. You can also access additional resources, including links relevant to your state.

Finding Things on the Internet

The greatest asset of the Internet—its vast array of materials—is also its greatest deterrent. Many excellent social studies-specific sites provide links to relevant content. Using Internet search engines can also help you find what you need.

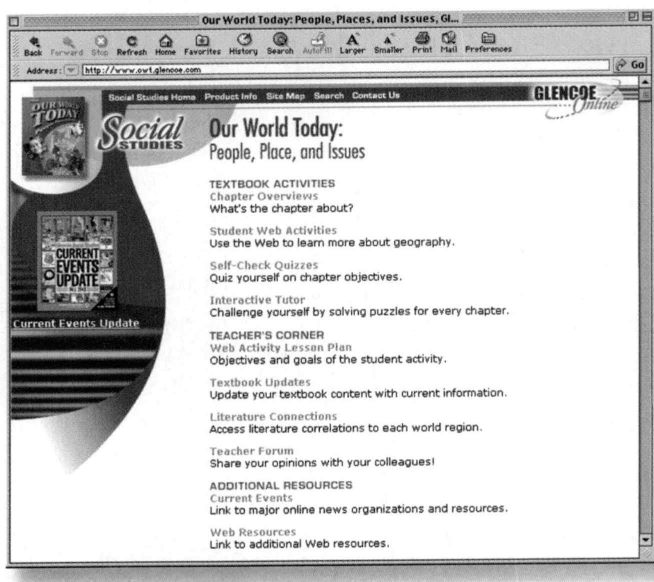

- ✔ A search engine is an Internet search tool. You type in a keyword, name, or phrase, and the search engine lists the URLs for Web sites that match your search. However, a search engine may find things that are not at all related or may miss sites that you would consider of interest. The key is to find ways to define your search.
- ✔ Not all search engines are the same. Each seeks out information a little bit differently. Different search engines use different criteria to determine what constitutes a "match" for your search topic. The Internet holds numerous articles that compare search engines and offer guidelines for choosing those that best meet your needs.
- ✔ An advanced search allows you to refine the search by using a phrase or a combination of words. The way to conduct an advanced search varies from search engine to engine; check the search engine's Help feature for information. Encourage students to review this information regularly for each of the search engines they use.

How Do I Teach Students to Evaluate Web Sites?

Anyone can put up a Web site. Web content is easy to change, too, so Webmasters constantly update their Web sites by adding, modifying, and removing content. These characteristics make evaluating Web sites both more challenging and more important than traditional print resources. Teach students to critically evaluate Web resources, using the questions and criteria below.

1 ***Purpose:*** *What is the purpose of the Web site or Web page? Is it an informational Web page, a news site, a business site, an advocacy site, or a personal Web page? Many sites serve more than one purpose. For instance, a news site may provide current events accompanied by banner ads that market the products advertisers think readers might want.*

2 ***URL:*** *What is the URL, or Web address? Where does the site originate? That can sometimes tell you about the group or business behind the Web page. For example, URLs with .edu and .gov domain names indicate that the site is connected to an educational institution or a government agency, respectively. A .com suffix usually means that a commercial or business interest hosts the Web site, but may also indicate a personal Web page. A nonprofit organization's Web address may end with .org.*

3 ***Authority:*** *Who wrote the material or created the Web site? What qualifications does this person or group have? Who has ultimate responsibility for the site? If the site is sponsored by an organization, are the organization's goals clearly stated?*

4 ***Accuracy:*** *How reliable is the information? Are sources listed so that they can be verified? Is the Web page free from surface errors in spelling and grammar? How does it compare with other sources you've found on the Web and in print?*

5 ***Objectivity:*** *If the site presents itself as an informational site, is the material free from bias? If there is advertising, is it easy to tell the difference between the ads and other features? If the site mixes factual information with opinion, can you spot the difference between the two? If the site advocates an opinion or viewpoint, is the opinion clearly stated and logically defended?*

6 ***Currency:*** *When was the information first placed on the Web? Is the site updated on a regular basis? When was the last revision? If the information is time-sensitive, are the updates frequent enough?*

7 ***Coverage:*** *What topics are covered on the Web site? What is the depth of coverage? Are all sides of an issue presented? How does the coverage compare with other Web and print sources?* ✦

See the *Glencoe Social Studies Guide to Using the Internet* for additional information and teaching strategies.

Make a Classroom Web Page

Advice from Mary Trichel
Atascocita Middle School
Humble Independent School District
Humble, Texas

Set up a classroom Web page with student-friendly access to useful links for class lessons. The Web page can be used by students at school or from their own homes. An easy teacher Web site source can be found at www.quia.com

To preview my Web page, visit the following link: www.quia.com/pages/trichel.html

In addition to quia.com, there are many other teacher-friendly Web page makers available on the Internet free of charge for teacher use. Use a search engine to access these pages and actively involve students in the design, layout, and construction of a class Web page.

Classroom Solutions

Primary Source Strategies

How Do I Use Primary Sources in My Classroom?

PhotoDisc

A primary source is direct evidence of an event, idea, period, or development. It is an oral or written account obtained from actual participants in an event. Examples of primary sources include the following:

- ✔ official documents (records, statistics)
- ✔ political declarations, laws, and rules for governance
- ✔ speeches and interviews
- ✔ diaries, memoirs, and oral histories
- ✔ autobiographies
- ✔ recipes and cookbooks
- ✔ advertisements and posters
- ✔ letters

Physical objects, such as tools and dishes, can be primary sources; so can visual evidence in the form of fine art, photographs, maps, films, and videotapes. Primary sources can also include songs and audio recordings.

Why Use Primary Sources in Your Classroom?

Using primary sources to teach transforms the study of social studies from a passive process to an active one. Students become investigators—finding clues, formulating hypotheses and drawing inferences, making judgments, and reaching conclusions. Bringing primary sources into the classroom stimulates students to think critically about events, issues, and concepts rather than just memorizing dates, names, and generalizations reached by others.

Choosing Primary Sources

- ✔ Provide exposure to a variety of source types, including historic photographs, folk or popular music, financial records or household accounts, as well as letters, journals, and historic documents.
- ✔ When choosing print sources, consider the interests and reading levels of your students. Many texts contain challenging vocabulary and unfamiliar sentence structure. You may need to create a reader's guide that defines key vocabulary and paraphrases the main points of the reading.
- ✔ Some documents may be too long. Decide whether using an excerpt will provide enough information for students to draw conclusions.
- ✔ Depending upon the topic and your instructional objectives, you may need to provide several different primary sources to expose students to a variety of perspectives.
- ✔ Decide how students will access the primary sources: through the Internet, the library, a museum, or other print resources. Consider the possibility of an Internet virtual field trip for students. Moving from URL to URL, students can visit museum sites and other Web pages to view artifacts; interpret economic or census data; and read journals, letters, and official documents.

Anthony Redpath/CORBIS STOCK MARKET

How Do I Introduce Students to Primary Sources?

Carefully explain the nature of primary sources when you introduce them to students. Although primary sources contain valuable clues, be sure to alert students that primary sources contain biases and prejudices, and must be approached with caution. Every primary source reflects the creator's point of view to some degree.

Using Primary Sources in the Classroom

Primary sources provide a rich source of inspiration for a variety of instructional strategies. They can be used to spark interest in a new topic, foster deeper exploration into a historical era, or assess students' understanding of social studies concepts and facts.

- ✔ ***Pre-Reading Activities*** Present a primary source for students to study at the beginning of a new chapter or topic. Have students analyze the source, using the questions and guidelines presented on the next page. Then have students

Aaron Haupt

Interpreting a Primary Source

Before students interpret a primary source, they need to know the context into which the source fits. Then they can use questions and guidelines, such as those below, to help them analyze and interpret the primary source.

Print Sources

- *Who created the source, and what was the purpose for doing so?*
- *Did the writer personally experience or witness the event(s)?*
- *At what point did the writer record the information—as it happened or afterward? How long after?*
- *Who was the intended audience?*
- *Was the writer trying to record facts, express an opinion, or persuade others to take action?*
- *What is the author's main message?*
- *What values does the document convey?*
- *What bias does it reflect?*
- *What information about the topic can you gather from this document?*
- *Compare this document with what you know about the topic. Does it confirm those ideas or introduce a new perspective?*
- *How might other accounts about this topic support or modify the message this source delivers?*

Visual Sources

- *Who created the source, and what was the purpose for doing so?*
- *What does the image show?*
- *What mood does the image convey?*
- *Who or what dominates the image or catches your eye?*
- *How does the view impact the message?*
- *What details can you learn from the image?*
- *What is excluded from view?*
- *What bias does the visual reflect?*
- *What information about the topic can you gather from this visual?*
- *How might other visuals about this topic support or modify the message this one delivers?*

Audio Sources

- *Who created the source? What was the purpose for creating this source?*
- *What is the main idea of the audio?*
- *What mood does the recorder's voice convey?*
- *What bias does the audio text reflect?*
- *What information about the topic can you gather from this audio source?*
- *Compare the information in this source with what you already know about the topic. Does it confirm those ideas or introduce a new perspective?*
- *How might other sources about this topic support or modify the message that this one delivers?*

predict what they might learn in the upcoming lessons.

✔ ***Exploring Information*** Provide a variety of primary sources related to a topic or time period. Have students compare and contrast the items, analyzing the information, making inferences, and drawing conclusions about the period.

✔ ***Evaluation Activities*** Have students evaluate a primary source and tell how it supports or refutes what they learned in the textbook or have students read a primary source document that provides one perspective on a topic, and have students write their own account, presenting another perspective or opinion.✦

Classroom Activity: Reading and Understanding Primary Sources

Advice from Leslie Espinosa
Humble Independent School District
Humble, Texas

1. Before class make a list of student reading partners. Make sure one of the two is a good reader.
2. Have students read a primary source document (or part of a primary source document), taking turns as they go. They should "mark" any words that they do not understand.
3. After each paragraph, the student pair should stop and paraphrase what it says in their own words.
4. Students look up unfamiliar words they've marked and create an illustrated dictionary entry for each term (over the course of the year or semester).
5. Student pairs present their paraphrased primary source to the rest of the class.

Classroom Solutions

Using Maps, Graphs, and Charts

How Can I Use Visuals to Improve Students' Reading Comprehension?

Maps, graphs, and charts are visual tools. By using images rather than words, these tools present complex information in an easy-to-understand format. Teach students the following generalized viewing strategies, and encourage them to apply these strategies as they study each chapter.

- ✔ ***Asking Questions*** Students should start by looking over the graphic and asking themselves questions, such as "What is my purpose for looking at this image?" Then students can identify questions they hope to answer, such as "What is being compared?" or "What are the most important features?"
- ✔ ***Finding Answers*** Next, students should use the graphic's structural features, such as the title, labels, colors, and symbols, to help them find the answers to their questions. If the source of the graphic is available, students should also determine its reliability.
- ✔ ***Drawing Conclusions*** After studying the visual, students should summarize its main points and draw conclusions.
- ✔ ***Connecting*** Before moving on, students should relate what they learned from the visual with what they gained from reading the text selection. Students can examine how the visual supports or extends the meaning of the text.

Maps

Maps show the relative size and location of specific geographic areas. There are as many different kinds of maps as there are uses for them. Two of the most common general purpose maps are political maps and physical maps. Political maps show human-made boundaries, such as state and country borders. Physical maps show physical features, such as mountains and lakes. Special purpose maps might show historical change, cultural features, population, land use, or climate.

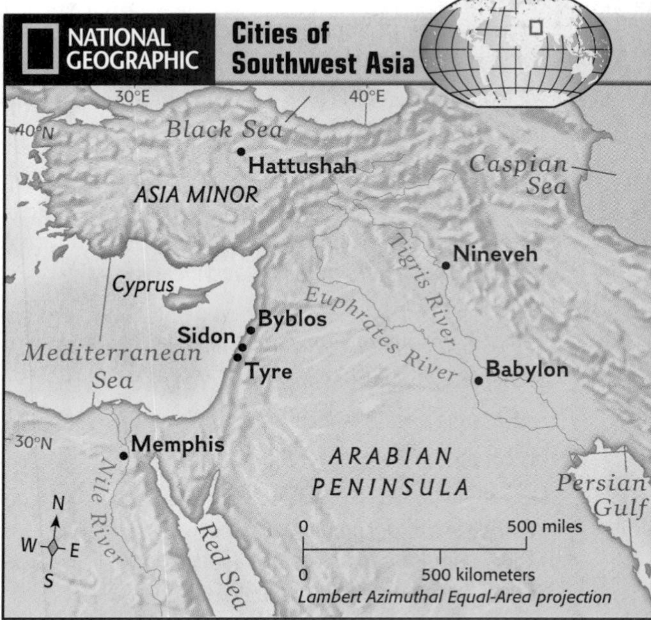

Parts of Maps

All maps contain parts that assist in interpreting the information. Help students learn to identify the following map parts.

- ✔ ***Title*** The map title identifies the area shown on the visual. The title can also identify a map's special focus.
- ✔ ***Map Key*** The map key, or legend, explains the symbols presented on the map, thus unlocking the map's information.
- ✔ ***Compass Rose*** A compass rose is a direction marker. It is a symbol that points out where the cardinal directions—north, south, east, and west—are positioned.
- ✔ ***Scale*** A measuring line, often called a scale bar, indicates the relationship between the distances on the map and the actual distances on Earth. Distance on a map can be determined by measuring the distance between points, then multiplying that measure by the number of miles or kilometers specified in the map scale ratio.
- ✔ ***Latitude and Longitude*** Mapmakers use lines of latitude and longitude to pinpoint exact locations on maps and globes. The imaginary horizontal lines that circle the globe from east to west are lines of latitude, also called parallels. The imaginary vertical lines are lines of longitude, also called meridians. Both parallels and meridians are measured in degrees.

Graphs

Graphs are a way of showing numbers or statistics in a clear, easy-to-read way. Because graphs summarize and present information visually, readers have an easier time understanding the data and drawing conclusions. The most common types of graphs are bar graphs, line graphs, circle graphs, and pictographs.

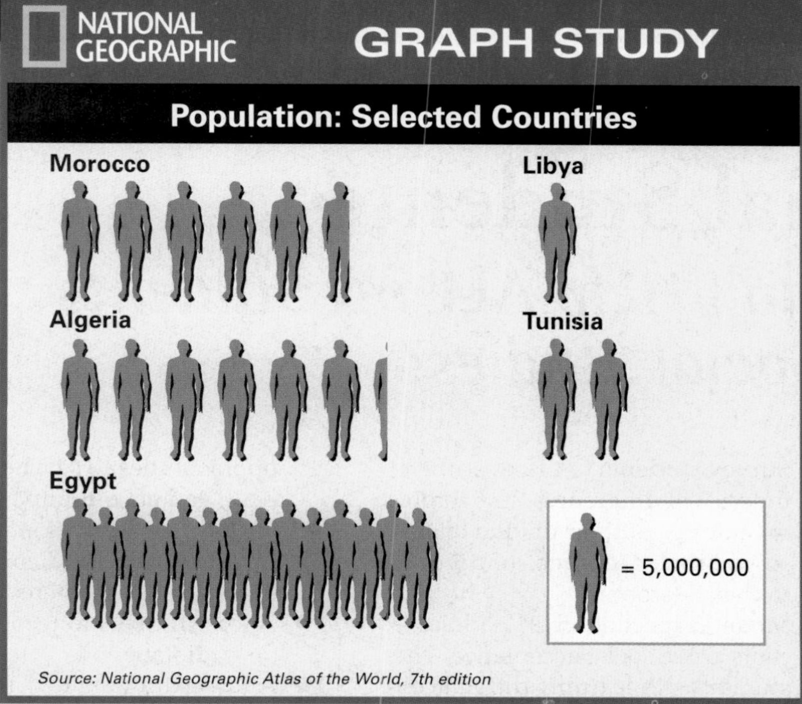

✔ ***Bar Graphs*** A bar graph shows how two or more subjects or statistics compare. It provides information along two sides or axes. The horizontal axis is the line across the bottom of the graph. The vertical axis is the line along the side. The bars may be either vertical or horizontal. In most cases the labels on one axis show quantity, while the labels on the opposite axis show the categories of data being compared.

✔ ***Line Graphs*** A line graph shows change over time. Like a bar graph, it organizes information along the horizontal and vertical axes. The horizontal axis usually shows passing time, such as months, years, or decades. The vertical axis usually shows quantity or amount. Sometimes more than one set of data is shown in a line graph. A double-line graph, for instance, plots data for two related quantities, which may be represented in different colors or patterns.

✔ ***Circle Graphs*** A circle graph, also called a pie graph, shows how each part or percentage relates to the whole. A circle graph enables a viewer to make comparisons between parts and to analyze the relationship of each part to the whole.

✔ ***Pictograph*** A pictograph uses rows of small symbols or pictures, each representing a particular amount. Like a bar graph, a pictograph is useful for making comparisons.

Charts

While all charts present information or data in a visual way, the type of chart is often dictated by the nature of the information and by the chart-maker's purposes.

✔ ***Tables*** Tables show information, including numerical data, in columns and rows. This organized arrangement facilitates comparisons between categories of information. Labels are usually located at the top of each column and on the left-hand side of the table.

✔ ***Diagrams*** Diagrams are specialized drawings. They can show steps in a process; point out parts of an object, organization, or idea; or explain how something works. Arrows or lines may join parts of a figure and can show relationships between parts or the flow of steps.✦

Don't Let Students Overlook Maps, Graphs, and Charts

Advice from Barbara Neff
R.C. Fisher Campus
Athens, Texas

Students often overlook what they see as the "extras" on textbook pages. Remind them that maps, graphs, and charts are excellent tools to study people, places, and events in our world—both past and present. Maps, graphs, and charts are visual aids that will enable students to understand the textbook narrative (and perform better on tests).

Explain to students that they may have to interpret maps, graphs, or charts in their daily lives. Bring some real-life examples to class or have students bring some examples to class. (Examples include travel maps, newspaper maps or graphics, sports data, a map that details the location of a current event, class performance graphs or charts, and so on.)

Maps, graphs, and charts are also an exciting way to study the five themes of geography and the 18 geography standards!

Classroom Solutions

Addressing the Needs of Special Students

How Can I Help ALL my Students Learn Social Studies?

Today's classroom contains students from a variety of backgrounds and with a variety of learning styles, strengths, and challenges. With careful planning, you can address the needs of all students in the social studies classroom. The following tips for instruction can assist your efforts to help all students reach their maximum potential.

Richard Hutchings/PhotoEdit

- ✔ Survey students to discover their individual differences. Use interest inventories of their unique talents so you can encourage contributions in the classroom.
- ✔ Model respect of others. Adolescents crave social acceptance. The student with learning differences is especially sensitive to correction and criticism—particularly when it comes from a teacher. Your behavior will set the tone for how students treat one another.
- ✔ Expand opportunities for success. Provide a variety of instructional activities that reinforce skills and concepts.
- ✔ Establish measurable objectives and decide how you can best help students meet them.
- ✔ Celebrate successes and praise "work in progress."
- ✔ Keep it simple. Point out problem areas—if doing so can help a student affect change. Avoid overwhelming students with too many goals at one time.
- ✔ Assign cooperative group projects that challenge all students to contribute to solving a problem or creating a product.

How Do I Reach Students with Learning Disabilities?

- ✔ Provide support and structure. Clearly specify rules, assignments, and responsibilities.
- ✔ Practice skills frequently. Use games and drills to help maintain student interest.
- ✔ Incorporate many modalities into the learning process. Provide opportunities to say, hear, write, read, and act out important concepts and information.
- ✔ Link new skills and concepts to those already mastered.
- ✔ Allow students to record answers on audiotape.
- ✔ Allow extra time to complete tests and assignments.
- ✔ Let students demonstrate proficiency with alternative presentations, including oral reports, role plays, art projects, and with music.
- ✔ Provide outlines, notes, or tape recordings of lecture material.
- ✔ Pair students with peer helpers, and provide class time for pair interaction.

How Do I Reach Students with Behavioral Disorders?

- ✔ Provide a structured environment with clear-cut schedules, rules, seat assignments, and safety procedures.
- ✔ Reinforce appropriate behavior and model it for students.
- ✔ Cue distracted students back to the task through verbal signals and teacher proximity.
- ✔ Set very small goals that can be achieved in the short term. Work for long-term improvement in the big areas.

How Do I Reach Students with Physical Challenges?

- ✔ Openly discuss with the student any uncertainties you have about when to offer aid.

Mug Shots/CORBIS STOCK MARKET

- ✔ Ask parents or therapists and students what special devices or procedures are needed, and whether any special safety precautions need to be taken.
- ✔ Welcome students with physical challenges into all activities, including field trips, special events, and projects.
- ✔ Provide information to help able-bodied students and adults understand other students' physical challenges.

How Do I Reach Students with Visual Impairments?

- ✔ Facilitate independence. Modify assignments as needed.
- ✔ Teach classmates how and when to serve as guides.
- ✔ Limit unnecessary noise in the classroom, if it distracts the student with visual impairments.
- ✔ Provide tactile models whenever possible.
- ✔ Foster a spirit of inclusion. Describe people and events as they occur in the classroom. Remind classmates that the student with visual impairments cannot interpret gestures and other forms of nonverbal communication.
- ✔ Provide taped lectures and reading assignments.
- ✔ Team the student with a sighted peer for written work.

How Do I Reach Students with Hearing Impairments?

- ✔ Seat students where they can see your lip movements easily and where they can avoid visual distractions.
- ✔ Avoid standing with your back to the window or light source.
- ✔ Use an overhead projector to maintain eye contact while writing.
- ✔ Seat students where they can see speakers.
- ✔ Write all assignments on the board, or hand out written instructions.
- ✔ If the student has a manual interpreter, allow both student and interpreter to select the most favorable seating arrangements.
- ✔ Teach students to look directly at each other when they speak.

How Do I Reach English Language Learners?

- ✔ Remember, students' ability to speak English does not reflect their academic abilities.
- ✔ Try to incorporate the students' cultural experience into your instruction. The help of a bilingual aide may be effective.
- ✔ Avoid cultural stereotypes.
- ✔ Pre-teach important vocabulary and concepts.
- ✔ Encourage students to preview text before they begin reading, noting headings, graphic organizers, photographs, and maps.

How Do I Reach Gifted Students?

- ✔ Make arrangements for students to take selected subjects early and to work on independent projects.
- ✔ Ask "what if" questions to develop high-level thinking skills. Establish an environment safe for risk taking.
- ✔ Emphasize concepts, theories, ideas, relationships, and generalizations.
- ✔ Promote interest in the past by inviting students to make connections to the present.
- ✔ Let students express themselves in alternate ways, such as creative writing, acting, debate, simulations, drawing, or music.
- ✔ Provide students with a catalog of helpful resources, listing such things as agencies that provide free and inexpensive materials, appropriate community services and programs, and community experts.
- ✔ Assign extension projects that allow students to solve real-life problems related to their communities.✦

Customize Your Classroom!

Advice from Marilyn Gerken
Pickerington Local Schools
Pickerington, Ohio

Provide individualized activities and assignments for a variety of student ability levels. Develop learning packets for chapters and units of study with varying formats, levels, and types of assignments. Assign points and contract students based on their selection of activities to be completed. The activities in the Student Edition can be used for many of the learning activities and assignments.

Reference Atlas

NATIONAL GEOGRAPHIC

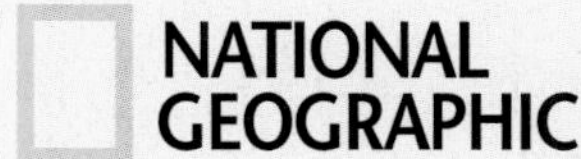

ATLAS KEY

Tundra
Evergreen forest
Mixed forest
Mountains
Grassland
Ice cap
Oceans
Seas
Desert

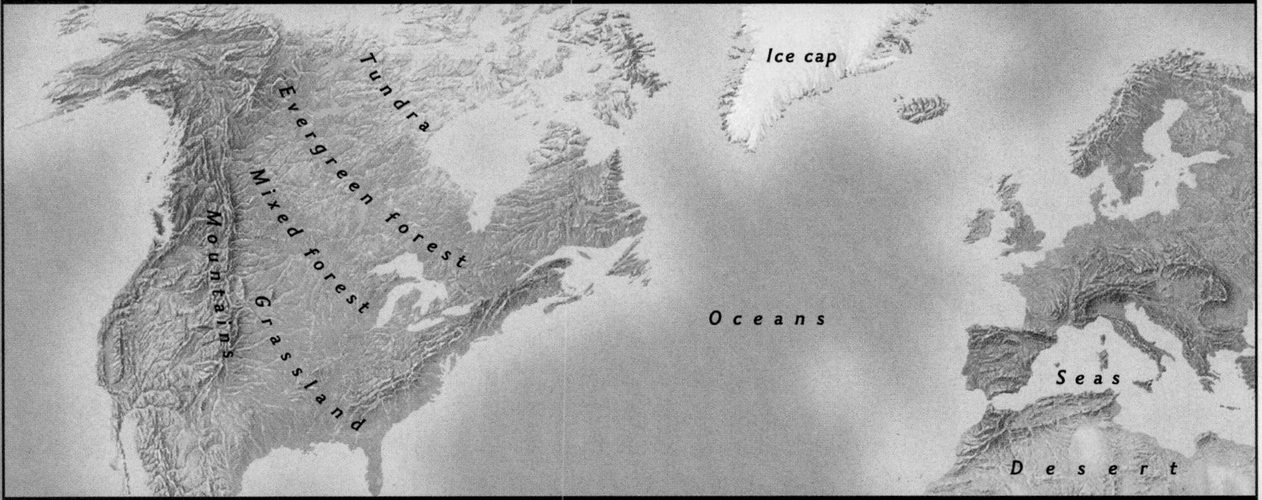

SYMBOL KEY

- Canal
- Claimed boundary
- International boundary
- Depression
- Elevation
- National capital
- Towns
- Below sea level
- Dry salt lake
- Lake
- Rivers
- Lava
- Sand
- Swamp

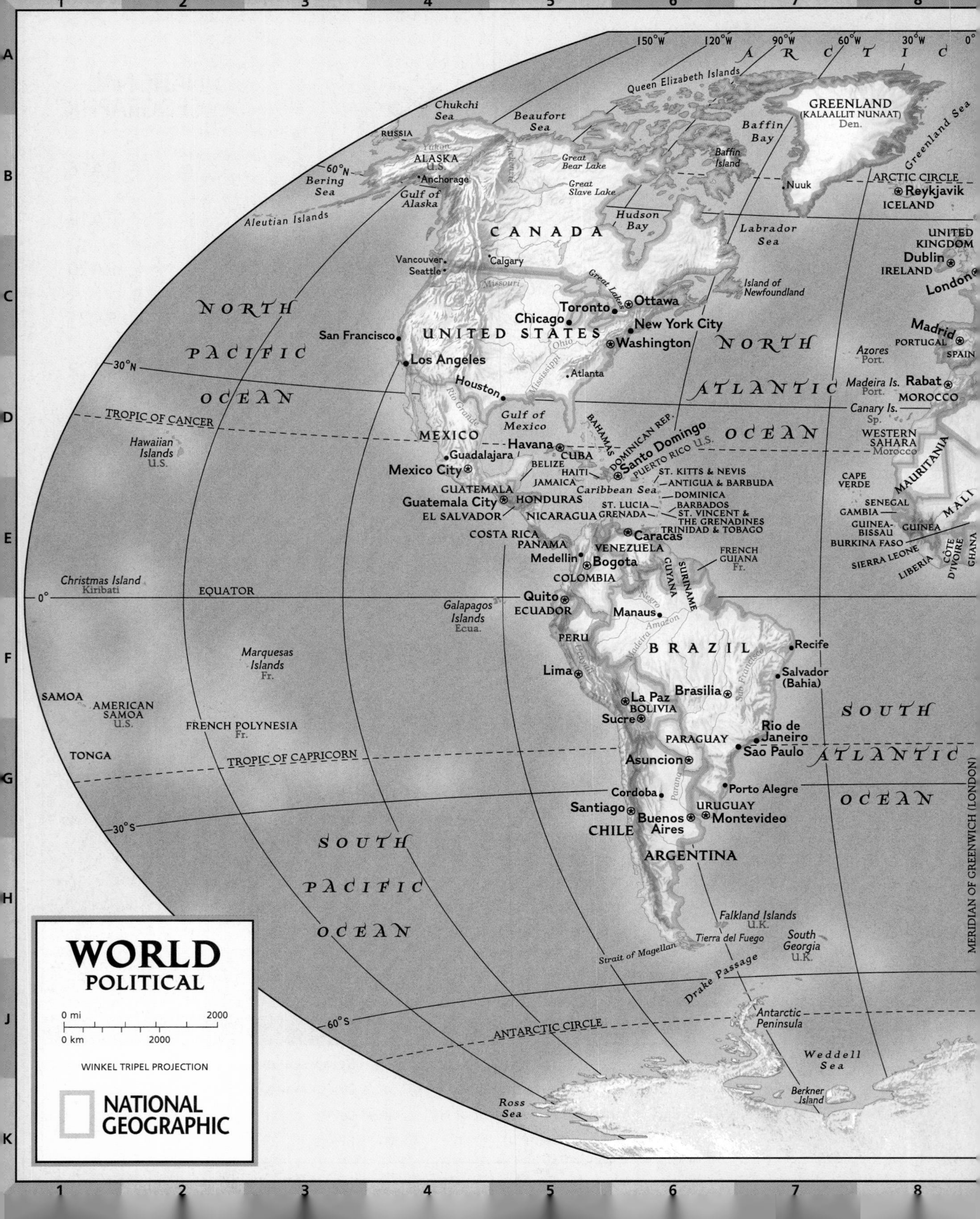

WORLD
POLITICAL
0 mi 2000
0 km 2000
WINKEL TRIPEL PROJECTION
NATIONAL GEOGRAPHIC
ARCTIC
GREENLAND (KALAALLIT NUNAAT) Den.
Queen Elizabeth Islands
Baffin Bay
Baffin Island
Greenland Sea
Chukchi Sea
Beaufort Sea
RUSSIA
ALASKA U.S.
Anchorage
Bering Sea
Gulf of Alaska
Aleutian Islands
Great Bear Lake
Great Slave Lake
Hudson Bay
Nuuk
ARCTIC CIRCLE
Reykjavik
ICELAND
CANADA
Labrador Sea
UNITED KINGDOM
Dublin
IRELAND
London
Vancouver
Seattle
Calgary
Island of Newfoundland
Great Lakes
Ottawa
Toronto
Chicago
New York City
Washington
San Francisco
UNITED STATES
NORTH PACIFIC OCEAN
NORTH ATLANTIC OCEAN
Los Angeles
Atlanta
Houston
Madrid
PORTUGAL
SPAIN
Azores Port.
Madeira Is. Port.
Rabat
MOROCCO
Canary Is. Sp.
TROPIC OF CANCER
Gulf of Mexico
MEXICO
Havana
CUBA
BAHAMAS
DOMINICAN REP.
Santo Domingo
PUERTO RICO U.S.
Hawaiian Islands U.S.
Guadalajara
Mexico City
BELIZE
HAITI
JAMAICA
Caribbean Sea
ST. KITTS & NEVIS
ANTIGUA & BARBUDA
DOMINICA
BARBADOS
ST. LUCIA
GRENADA
ST. VINCENT & THE GRENADINES
TRINIDAD & TOBAGO
GUATEMALA
Guatemala City
HONDURAS
EL SALVADOR
NICARAGUA
COSTA RICA
PANAMA
Caracas
VENEZUELA
WESTERN SAHARA Morocco
MAURITANIA
CAPE VERDE
SENEGAL
GAMBIA
GUINEA-BISSAU
GUINEA
MALI
BURKINA FASO
SIERRA LEONE
LIBERIA
CÔTE D'IVOIRE
GHANA
FRENCH GUIANA Fr.
Medellin
Bogota
COLOMBIA
GUYANA
SURINAME
Christmas Island Kiribati
EQUATOR
Quito
ECUADOR
Galapagos Islands Ecua.
Manaus
Amazon
Negro
Madeira
PERU
BRAZIL
Recife
Marquesas Islands Fr.
Lima
Salvador (Bahia)
Brasilia
La Paz
BOLIVIA
Sucre
SAMOA
AMERICAN SAMOA U.S.
FRENCH POLYNESIA Fr.
TONGA
TROPIC OF CAPRICORN
PARAGUAY
Rio de Janeiro
Sao Paulo
Asuncion
SOUTH ATLANTIC OCEAN
Porto Alegre
Cordoba
Santiago
URUGUAY
Buenos Aires
Montevideo
CHILE
ARGENTINA
SOUTH PACIFIC OCEAN
Falkland Islands U.K.
Tierra del Fuego
South Georgia U.K.
Strait of Magellan
Drake Passage
Antarctic Peninsula
ANTARCTIC CIRCLE
Weddell Sea
Berkner Island
Ross Sea
MERIDIAN OF GREENWICH (LONDON)
150°W
120°W
90°W
60°W
30°W
0°
60°N
30°N
0°
30°S
60°S

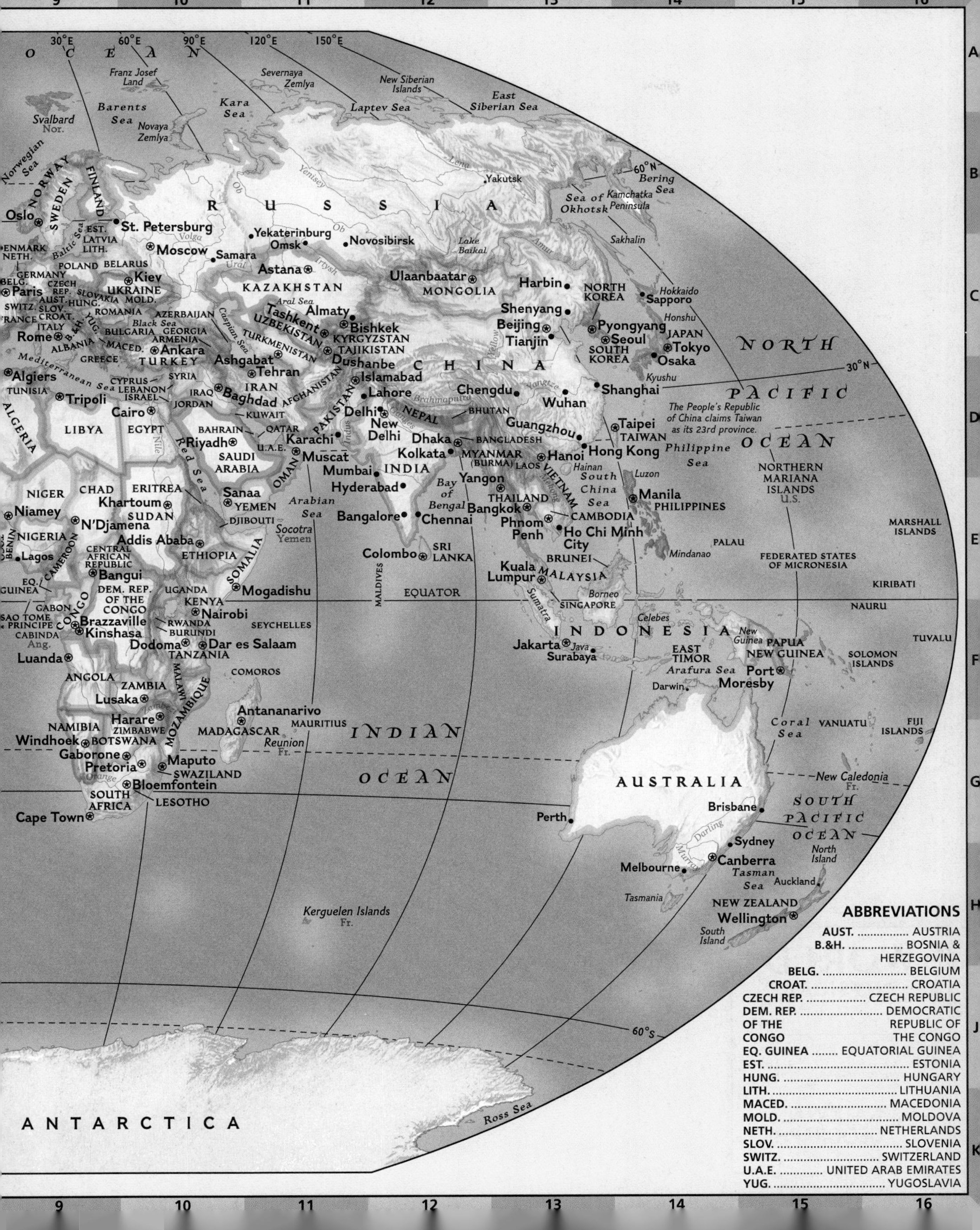

9 10 11 12 13 14 15 16
A B C D E F G H J K
30°E 60°E 90°E 120°E 150°E
O C E A N
Franz Josef Land
Severnaya Zemlya
New Siberian Islands
East Siberian Sea
Laptev Sea
Kara Sea
Barents Sea
Novaya Zemlya
Svalbard Nor.
Norwegian Sea
NORWAY
SWEDEN
FINLAND
Oslo
EST.
LATVIA
LITH.
Baltic Sea
St. Petersburg
Moscow
Volga
DENMARK
NETH.
POLAND
BELARUS
GERMANY
BELG.
Paris
CZECH REP.
SLOVAKIA
UKRAINE
Kiev
MOLD.
AUST.
HUNG.
SWITZ.
SLOV.
FRANCE
CROAT.
ROMANIA
ITALY
B.&H.
YUG.
Rome
BULGARIA
ALBANIA
MACED.
GREECE
Black Sea
Ankara
TURKEY
AZERBAIJAN
GEORGIA
ARMENIA
Caspian Sea
Mediterranean Sea
Algiers
TUNISIA
Tripoli
ALGERIA
CYPRUS
LEBANON
ISRAEL
SYRIA
JORDAN
IRAQ
Baghdad
Cairo
LIBYA
EGYPT
Nile
KUWAIT
BAHRAIN
QATAR
U.A.E.
Riyadh
SAUDI ARABIA
Red Sea
OMAN
Muscat
Sanaa
YEMEN
ERITREA
NIGER
CHAD
Khartoum
SUDAN
Niamey
N'Djamena
DJIBOUTI
Socotra Yemen
NIGERIA
BENIN
Lagos
CAMEROON
Addis Ababa
ETHIOPIA
SOMALIA
CENTRAL AFRICAN REPUBLIC
Bangui
EQ. GUINEA
GABON
SAO TOME & PRINCIPE
CONGO
Brazzaville
Kinshasa
DEM. REP. OF THE CONGO
CABINDA Ang.
UGANDA
KENYA
Nairobi
Mogadishu
RWANDA
BURUNDI
Dodoma
Dar es Salaam
TANZANIA
SEYCHELLES
Luanda
ANGOLA
ZAMBIA
MALAWI
Lusaka
COMOROS
MOZAMBIQUE
Harare
ZIMBABWE
NAMIBIA
Windhoek
BOTSWANA
Gaborone
Pretoria
Orange
Maputo
SWAZILAND
Bloemfontein
SOUTH AFRICA
LESOTHO
Cape Town
Antananarivo
MADAGASCAR
MAURITIUS
Reunion Fr.
R U S S I A
Ob
Yenisey
Lena
Yakutsk
Yekaterinburg
Omsk
Novosibirsk
Samara
Ural
Irtysh
Astana
KAZAKHSTAN
Aral Sea
Almaty
Tashkent
Bishkek
UZBEKISTAN
KYRGYZSTAN
TAJIKISTAN
TURKMENISTAN
Ashgabat
Dushanbe
Tehran
IRAN
AFGHANISTAN
Islamabad
Lahore
PAKISTAN
Indus
Karachi
Delhi
New Delhi
NEPAL
BHUTAN
Brahmaputra
Ganges
Dhaka
BANGLADESH
Kolkata
INDIA
Mumbai
Hyderabad
Bangalore
Chennai
Arabian Sea
Bay of Bengal
Colombo
SRI LANKA
MALDIVES
EQUATOR
Lake Baikal
Ulaanbaatar
MONGOLIA
C H I N A
Yellow
Yangtze
Chengdu
Wuhan
Beijing
Tianjin
Shenyang
Harbin
Amur
Sea of Okhotsk
Kamchatka Peninsula
Sakhalin
60°N
Bering Sea
NORTH KOREA
Pyongyang
Seoul
SOUTH KOREA
Hokkaido
Sapporo
Honshu
JAPAN
Tokyo
Osaka
Kyushu
Shanghai
NORTH
PACIFIC
OCEAN
30°N
The People's Republic of China claims Taiwan as its 23rd province.
Taipei
TAIWAN
Guangzhou
Hong Kong
Philippine Sea
MYANMAR (BURMA)
LAOS
Hanoi
Hainan
VIETNAM
Mekong
Yangon
THAILAND
Bangkok
South China Sea
CAMBODIA
Phnom Penh
Ho Chi Minh City
Luzon
Manila
PHILIPPINES
Mindanao
PALAU
NORTHERN MARIANA ISLANDS U.S.
MARSHALL ISLANDS
FEDERATED STATES OF MICRONESIA
KIRIBATI
NAURU
BRUNEI
Kuala Lumpur
MALAYSIA
Sumatra
SINGAPORE
Borneo
Celebes
I N D O N E S I A
Jakarta
Java
Surabaya
New Guinea
PAPUA NEW GUINEA
EAST TIMOR
Arafura Sea
Port Moresby
Darwin
SOLOMON ISLANDS
TUVALU
Coral Sea
VANUATU
FIJI ISLANDS
INDIAN
OCEAN
AUSTRALIA
New Caledonia Fr.
Perth
Brisbane
Darling
Murray
Sydney
Canberra
Melbourne
Tasmania
Tasman Sea
SOUTH PACIFIC OCEAN
North Island
Auckland
NEW ZEALAND
Wellington
South Island
Kerguelen Islands Fr.
60°S
Ross Sea
A N T A R C T I C A
ABBREVIATIONS
AUST. .... AUSTRIA
B.&H. .... BOSNIA & HERZEGOVINA
BELG. .... BELGIUM
CROAT. .... CROATIA
CZECH REP. .... CZECH REPUBLIC
DEM. REP. OF THE CONGO .... DEMOCRATIC REPUBLIC OF THE CONGO
EQ. GUINEA .... EQUATORIAL GUINEA
EST. .... ESTONIA
HUNG. .... HUNGARY
LITH. .... LITHUANIA
MACED. .... MACEDONIA
MOLD. .... MOLDOVA
NETH. .... NETHERLANDS
SLOV. .... SLOVENIA
SWITZ. .... SWITZERLAND
U.A.E. .... UNITED ARAB EMIRATES
YUG. .... YUGOSLAVIA

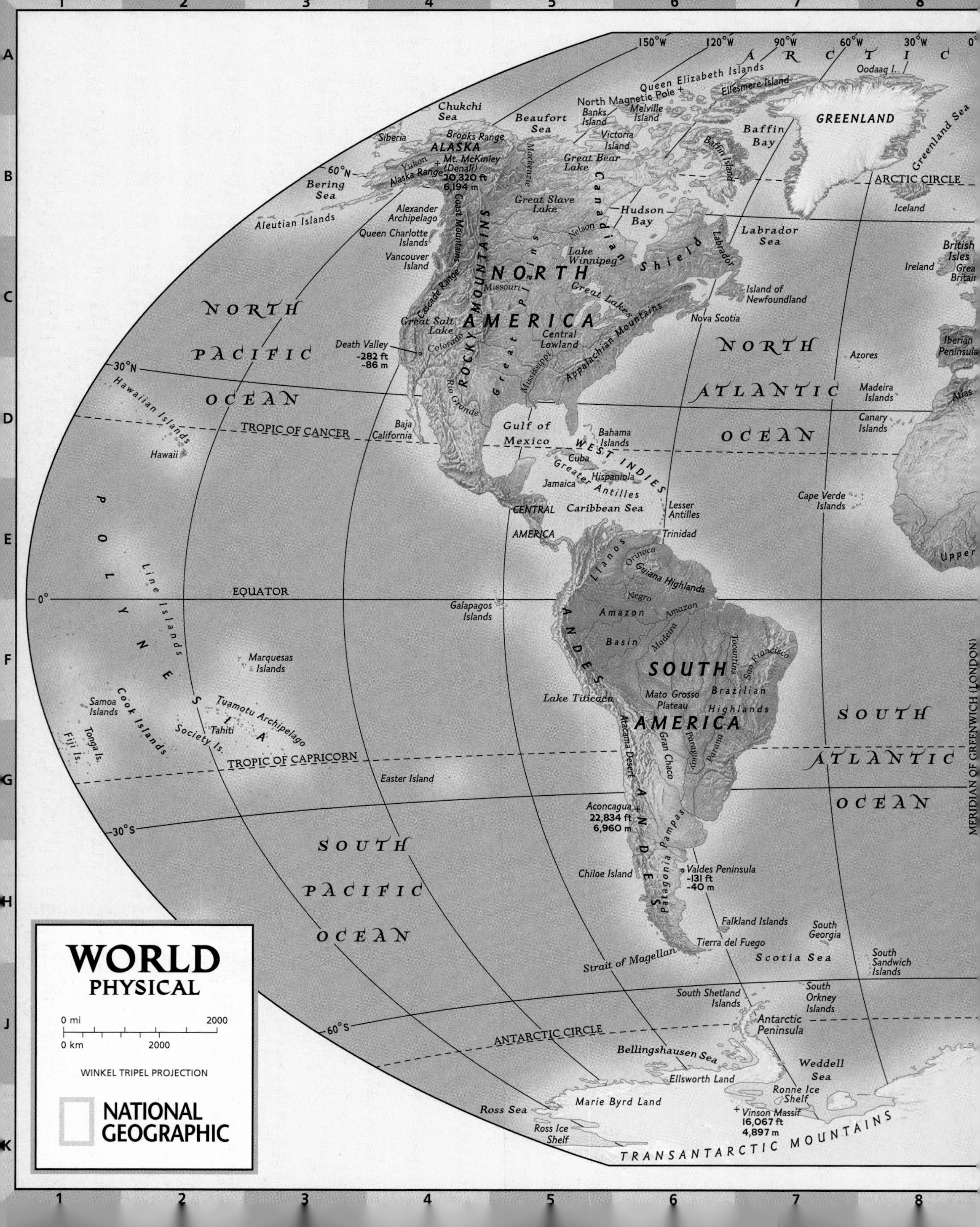

WORLD
PHYSICAL
0 mi 2000
0 km 2000
WINKEL TRIPEL PROJECTION
NATIONAL GEOGRAPHIC
150°W
120°W
90°W
60°W
30°W
ARCTIC
Oodaaq I.
Queen Elizabeth Islands
Ellesmere Island
North Magnetic Pole
Banks Island
Melville Island
Victoria Island
Chukchi Sea
Beaufort Sea
GREENLAND
Greenland Sea
Baffin Bay
Baffin Island
Siberia
Brooks Range
ALASKA
Yukon
Mt. McKinley (Denali)
20,320 ft
6,194 m
Alaska Range
60°N
Bering Sea
Aleutian Islands
Mackenzie
Great Bear Lake
Great Slave Lake
Canadian Shield
Hudson Bay
ARCTIC CIRCLE
Iceland
Alexander Archipelago
Queen Charlotte Islands
Coast Mountains
Vancouver Island
Nelson
Lake Winnipeg
Labrador
Labrador Sea
British Isles
Great Britain
Ireland
ROCKY MOUNTAINS
NORTH AMERICA
Missouri
Cascade Range
Great Lakes
Island of Newfoundland
Nova Scotia
Great Salt Lake
Great Plains
Central Lowland
Appalachian Mountains
Death Valley
-282 ft
-86 m
Colorado
Mississippi
NORTH PACIFIC OCEAN
NORTH ATLANTIC OCEAN
Azores
Iberian Peninsula
Madeira Islands
Atlas
Canary Islands
30°N
Hawaiian Islands
Hawaii
Rio Grande
Baja California
TROPIC OF CANCER
Gulf of Mexico
Bahama Islands
WEST INDIES
Cuba
Greater Antilles
Hispaniola
Jamaica
Caribbean Sea
Lesser Antilles
Cape Verde Islands
CENTRAL AMERICA
Trinidad
Upper
POLYNESIA
Line Islands
Llanos
Orinoco
Guiana Highlands
EQUATOR
0°
Negro
Amazon
Amazon Basin
Madeira
Galapagos Islands
Tocantins
São Francisco
ANDES
Marquesas Islands
SOUTH AMERICA
Mato Grosso Plateau
Brazilian Highlands
Lake Titicaca
Samoa Islands
Cook Islands
Tuamotu Archipelago
Tahiti
Society Is.
Tonga Is.
Fiji Is.
Atacama Desert
Gran Chaco
Paraguay
Paraná
SOUTH ATLANTIC OCEAN
MERIDIAN OF GREENWICH (LONDON)
TROPIC OF CAPRICORN
Easter Island
Aconcagua
22,834 ft
6,960 m
Pampas
30°S
SOUTH PACIFIC OCEAN
Chiloe Island
Valdes Peninsula
-131 ft
-40 m
Patagonia
Falkland Islands
South Georgia
Tierra del Fuego
Scotia Sea
South Sandwich Islands
Strait of Magellan
South Shetland Islands
South Orkney Islands
Antarctic Peninsula
60°S
ANTARCTIC CIRCLE
Bellingshausen Sea
Weddell Sea
Ellsworth Land
Marie Byrd Land
Ronne Ice Shelf
Ross Sea
Vinson Massif
16,067 ft
4,897 m
Ross Ice Shelf
TRANSANTARCTIC MOUNTAINS

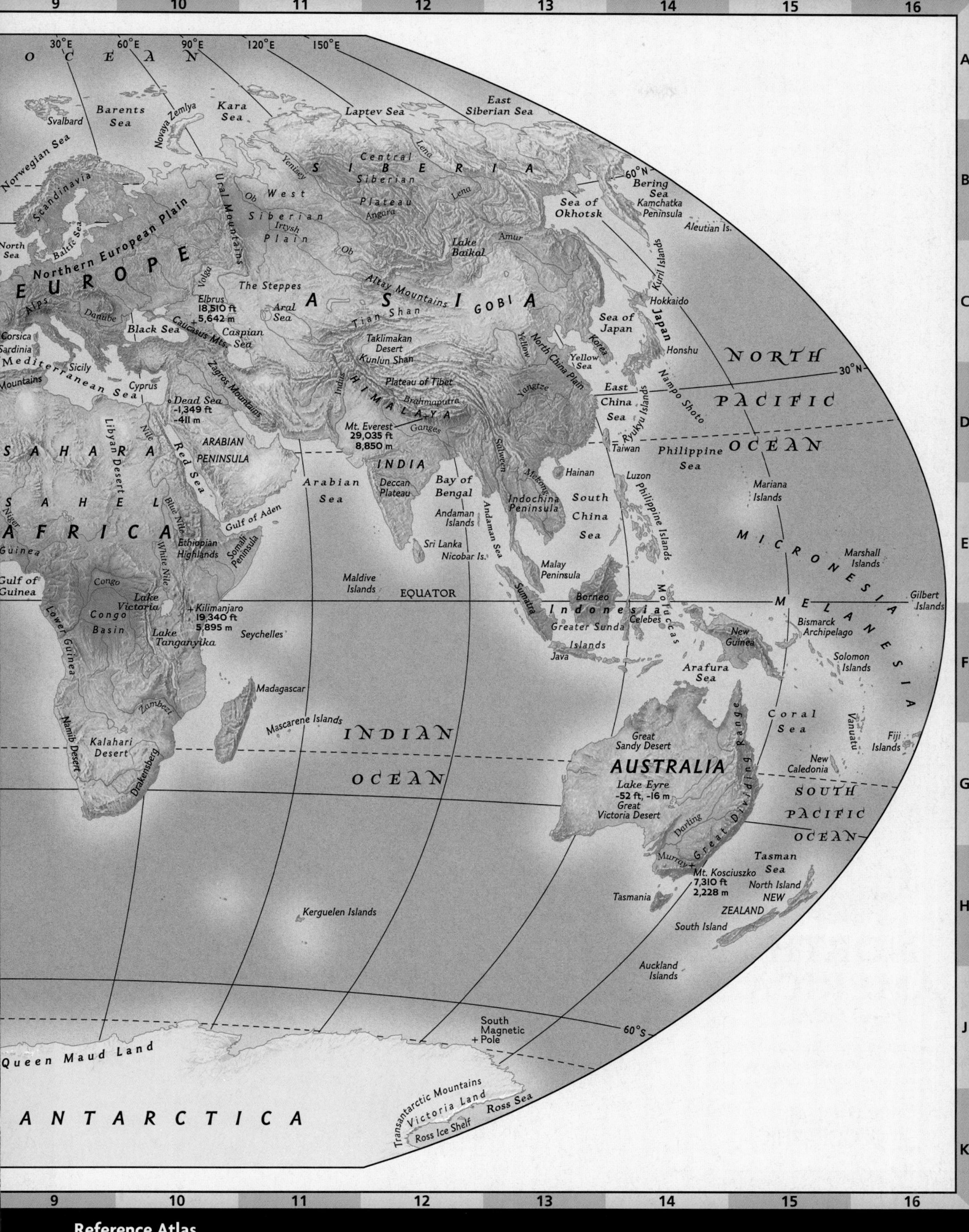

30°E
60°E
90°E
120°E
150°E
OCEAN
Svalbard
Barents Sea
Novaya Zemlya
Kara Sea
Laptev Sea
East Siberian Sea
Norwegian Sea
Scandinavia
Baltic Sea
North Sea
Northern European Plain
EUROPE
Ural Mountains
Ob
West Siberian Plain
Irtysh
Yenisey
SIBERIA
Central Siberian Plateau
Angara
Lena
60°N
Bering Sea
Sea of Okhotsk
Kamchatka Peninsula
Aleutian Is.
Lake Baikal
Amur
Kuril Islands
Volga
Elbrus 18,510 ft 5,642 m
The Steppes
Aral Sea
Altay Mountains
ASIA
GOBI
Hokkaido
Japan
Sea of Japan
Alps
Danube
Black Sea
Caucasus Mts.
Caspian Sea
Tian Shan
Taklimakan Desert
Kunlun Shan
Yellow
North China Plain
Korea
Yellow Sea
Honshu
NORTH
30°N
Corsica
Sardinia
Mediterranean Sea
Sicily
Mountains
Cyprus
Dead Sea -1,349 ft -411 m
Zagros Mountains
Indus
HIMALAYA
Plateau of Tibet
Brahmaputra
Yangtze
East China Sea
Ryukyu Islands
Nampo Shoto
PACIFIC
Mt. Everest 29,035 ft 8,850 m
Ganges
Taiwan
OCEAN
Philippine Sea
SAHARA
Libyan Desert
Nile
Red Sea
ARABIAN PENINSULA
INDIA
Salween
Hainan
Mekong
Luzon
Mariana Islands
SAHEL
Niger
Blue Nile
Arabian Sea
Deccan Plateau
Bay of Bengal
Andaman Islands
Andaman Sea
Indochina Peninsula
South China Sea
Philippine Islands
AFRICA
Gulf of Aden
Ethiopian Highlands
Somali Peninsula
White Nile
Guinea
Sri Lanka
Nicobar Is.
Malay Peninsula
MICRONESIA
Marshall Islands
Gulf of Guinea
Congo
Maldive Islands
EQUATOR
Sumatra
Borneo
Moluccas
Gilbert Islands
Lake Victoria
Congo Basin
Kilimanjaro 19,340 ft 5,895 m
Indonesia
Greater Sunda Islands
Celebes
Java
MELANESIA
Bismarck Archipelago
Lower Guinea
Lake Tanganyika
Seychelles
New Guinea
Solomon Islands
Arafura Sea
Madagascar
Zambezi
Mascarene Islands
INDIAN OCEAN
Great Sandy Desert
Coral Sea
Vanuatu
Fiji Islands
Namib Desert
Kalahari Desert
Drakensberg
AUSTRALIA
Great Dividing Range
New Caledonia
Lake Eyre -52 ft, -16 m
Great Victoria Desert
SOUTH PACIFIC OCEAN
Darling
Murray
Mt. Kosciuszko 7,310 ft 2,228 m
Tasman Sea
North Island
NEW ZEALAND
Tasmania
South Island
Kerguelen Islands
Auckland Islands
South Magnetic Pole
60°S
Queen Maud Land
Transantarctic Mountains
Victoria Land
Ross Sea
Ross Ice Shelf
ANTARCTICA
A B C D E F G H J K

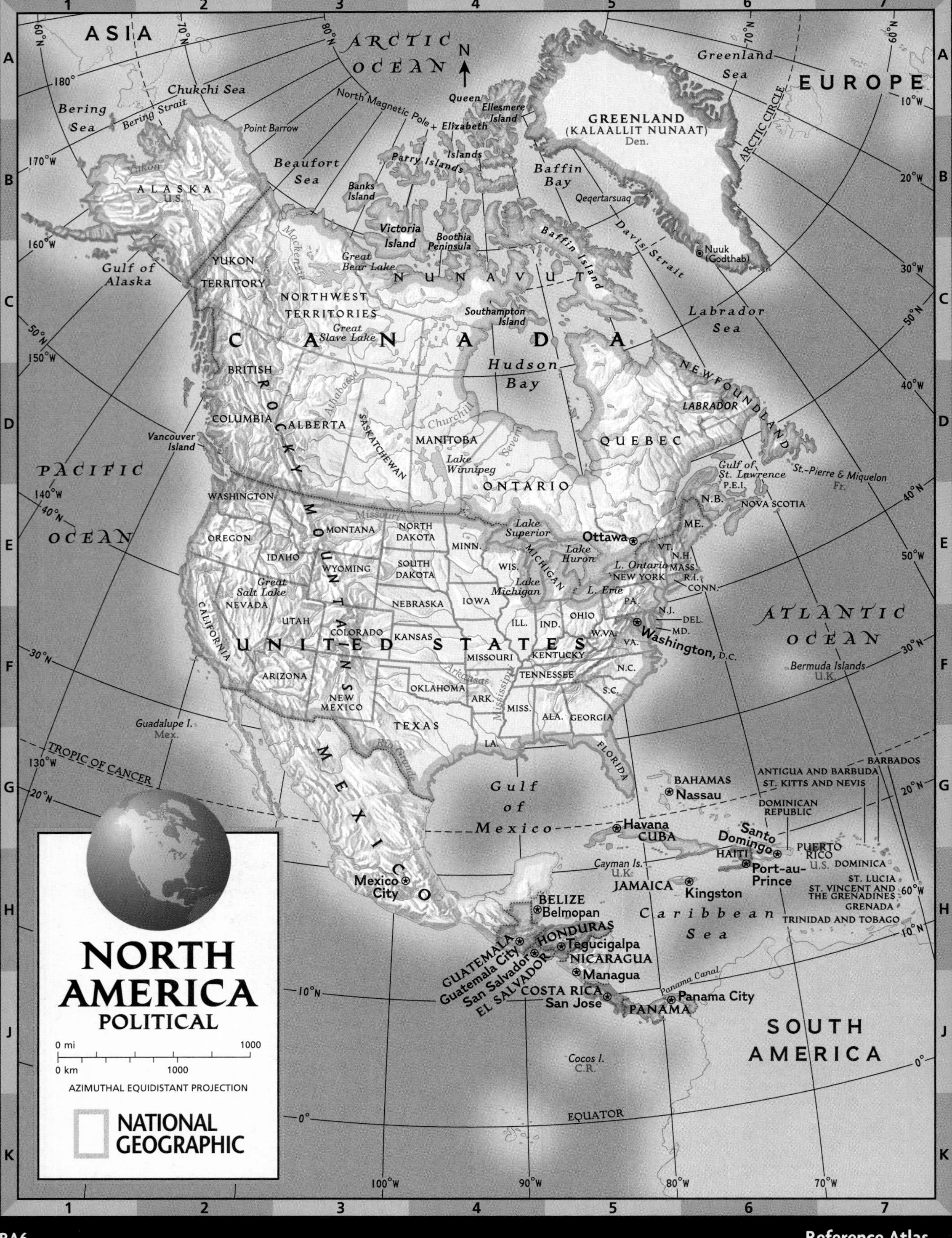
NORTH AMERICA
POLITICAL
0 mi 1000
0 km 1000
AZIMUTHAL EQUIDISTANT PROJECTION
NATIONAL GEOGRAPHIC
ASIA
ARCTIC OCEAN
N
EUROPE
Greenland Sea
GREENLAND
(KALAALLIT NUNAAT)
Den.
ARCTIC CIRCLE
Chukchi Sea
Bering Sea
Bering Strait
Point Barrow
North Magnetic Pole
Queen Elizabeth Islands
Ellesmere Island
Parry Islands
Beaufort Sea
Banks Island
Victoria Island
Boothia Peninsula
Baffin Bay
Qeqertarsuaq
Baffin Island
Davis Strait
Nuuk (Godthab)
ALASKA
U.S.
Yukon
Mackenzie
Gulf of Alaska
YUKON TERRITORY
NORTHWEST TERRITORIES
Great Bear Lake
NUNAVUT
Great Slave Lake
Southampton Island
Labrador Sea
CANADA
Hudson Bay
NEWFOUNDLAND
LABRADOR
BRITISH COLUMBIA
Athabasca
ALBERTA
SASKATCHEWAN
Churchill
MANITOBA
Severn
QUEBEC
Vancouver Island
ROCKY MOUNTAINS
Lake Winnipeg
ONTARIO
Gulf of St. Lawrence
P.E.I.
St.-Pierre & Miquelon
Fr.
PACIFIC OCEAN
WASHINGTON
N.B.
NOVA SCOTIA
Missouri
MONTANA
NORTH DAKOTA
Lake Superior
Ottawa
ME.
OREGON
MINN.
MICHIGAN
Lake Huron
VT.
N.H.
IDAHO
WYOMING
SOUTH DAKOTA
WIS.
L. Ontario
MASS.
NEW YORK
R.I.
Great Salt Lake
Lake Michigan
L. Erie
CONN.
NEVADA
NEBRASKA
IOWA
PA.
N.J.
ATLANTIC OCEAN
CALIFORNIA
UTAH
COLORADO
ILL.
IND.
OHIO
DEL.
MD.
UNITED STATES
KANSAS
W.VA.
VA.
Washington, D.C.
MISSOURI
KENTUCKY
Bermuda Islands
U.K.
ARIZONA
Arkansas
TENNESSEE
N.C.
OKLAHOMA
NEW MEXICO
ARK.
Mississippi
S.C.
MISS.
ALA.
GEORGIA
TEXAS
Guadalupe I.
Mex.
LA.
Rio Grande
FLORIDA
TROPIC OF CANCER
MEXICO
Gulf of Mexico
BAHAMAS
Nassau
BARBADOS
ANTIGUA AND BARBUDA
ST. KITTS AND NEVIS
DOMINICAN REPUBLIC
Havana
CUBA
Santo Domingo
PUERTO RICO
U.S.
HAITI
Port-au-Prince
DOMINICA
Cayman Is.
U.K.
JAMAICA
Kingston
ST. LUCIA
ST. VINCENT AND THE GRENADINES
GRENADA
TRINIDAD AND TOBAGO
Mexico City
BELIZE
Belmopan
Caribbean Sea
HONDURAS
Tegucigalpa
GUATEMALA
Guatemala City
San Salvador
EL SALVADOR
NICARAGUA
Managua
COSTA RICA
San Jose
Panama Canal
Panama City
PANAMA
SOUTH AMERICA
Cocos I.
C.R.
EQUATOR
180°
170°W
160°W
150°W
140°W
130°W
100°W
90°W
80°W
70°W
10°W
20°W
30°W
40°W
50°W
60°W
60°N
70°N
80°N
50°N
40°N
30°N
20°N
10°N
0°
1 2 3 4 5 6 7
A B C D E F G H J K

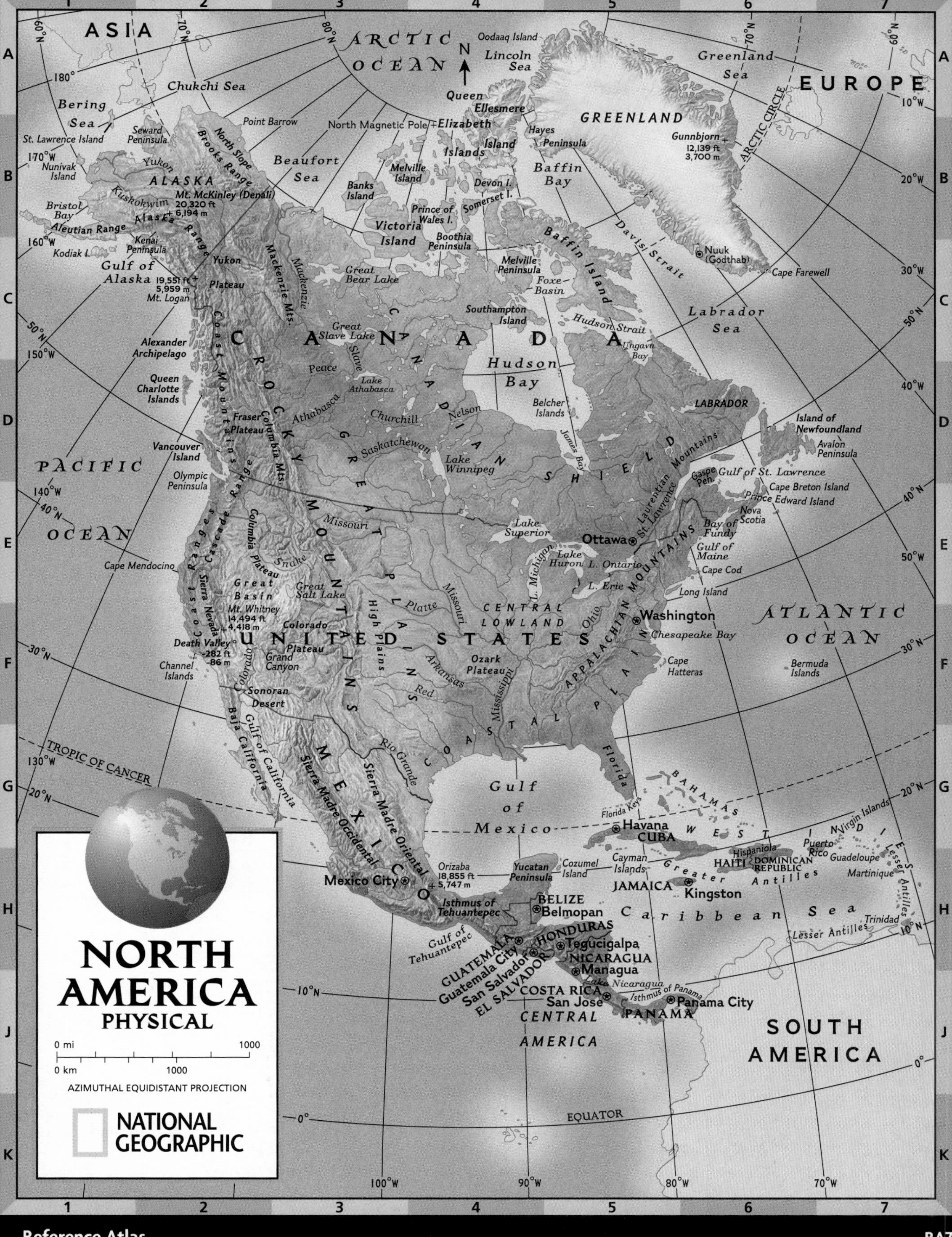
NORTH AMERICA
PHYSICAL
0 mi 1000
0 km 1000
AZIMUTHAL EQUIDISTANT PROJECTION
NATIONAL GEOGRAPHIC
ASIA
ARCTIC OCEAN
EUROPE
GREENLAND
Greenland Sea
Lincoln Sea
Oodaaq Island
Queen Elizabeth Islands
Ellesmere Island
Hayes Peninsula
Gunnbjorn 12,139 ft 3,700 m
ARCTIC CIRCLE
Chukchi Sea
Bering Sea
St. Lawrence Island
Seward Peninsula
Point Barrow
North Magnetic Pole
North Slope
Brooks Range
Beaufort Sea
Nunivak Island
Yukon
ALASKA
Mt. McKinley (Denali) 20,320 ft 6,194 m
Kuskokwim
Bristol Bay
Aleutian Range
Alaska Range
Kenai Peninsula
Kodiak I.
Gulf of Alaska
19,551 ft 5,959 m Mt. Logan
Yukon Plateau
Mackenzie Mts.
Mackenzie
Banks Island
Melville Island
Devon I.
Somerset I.
Baffin Bay
Prince of Wales I.
Victoria Island
Boothia Peninsula
Baffin Island
Davis Strait
Nuuk (Godthab)
Cape Farewell
Great Bear Lake
Melville Peninsula
Foxe Basin
Southampton Island
Hudson Strait
Labrador Sea
Ungava Bay
Great Slave Lake
CANADA
Slave
Peace
Lake Athabasca
Athabasca
Hudson Bay
Belcher Islands
LABRADOR
Island of Newfoundland
Avalon Peninsula
Alexander Archipelago
Queen Charlotte Islands
Coast Mountains
ROCKY MOUNTAINS
Fraser Plateau
Columbia Mts.
Churchill
Nelson
CANADIAN SHIELD
James Bay
Laurentian Mountains
Saskatchewan
Lake Winnipeg
Vancouver Island
PACIFIC OCEAN
Olympic Peninsula
Cascade Range
Coast Ranges
Columbia Plateau
Snake
GREAT PLAINS
Missouri
Lake Superior
Ottawa
St. Lawrence
Gaspe Pen.
Gulf of St. Lawrence
Cape Breton Island
Prince Edward Island
Nova Scotia
Bay of Fundy
Gulf of Maine
Cape Cod
Long Island
L. Michigan
Lake Huron
L. Ontario
L. Erie
APPALACHIAN MOUNTAINS
Cape Mendocino
Sierra Nevada
Great Basin
Great Salt Lake
Mt. Whitney 14,494 ft 4,418 m
Death Valley -282 ft -86 m
Colorado Plateau
Platte
High Plains
CENTRAL LOWLAND
Ohio
Washington
Chesapeake Bay
UNITED STATES
ATLANTIC OCEAN
Channel Islands
Colorado
Grand Canyon
Arkansas
Ozark Plateau
Mississippi
Cape Hatteras
Bermuda Islands
Red
Sonoran Desert
COASTAL PLAIN
Baja California
Gulf of California
Rio Grande
Florida
TROPIC OF CANCER
Sierra Madre Occidental
Sierra Madre Oriental
MEXICO
Gulf of Mexico
BAHAMAS
Florida Keys
Havana
CUBA
WEST INDIES
Virgin Islands
Puerto Rico
Hispaniola
HAITI
DOMINICAN REPUBLIC
Guadeloupe
Martinique
Lesser Antilles
Orizaba 18,855 ft 5,747 m
Mexico City
Yucatan Peninsula
Cozumel Island
Cayman Islands
Greater Antilles
JAMAICA
Kingston
Isthmus of Tehuantepec
BELIZE
Belmopan
Caribbean Sea
Trinidad
Gulf of Tehuantepec
GUATEMALA
Guatemala City
HONDURAS
Tegucigalpa
San Salvador
EL SALVADOR
NICARAGUA
Managua
Lake Nicaragua
Isthmus of Panama
COSTA RICA
San Jose
Panama City
PANAMA
CENTRAL AMERICA
SOUTH AMERICA
EQUATOR

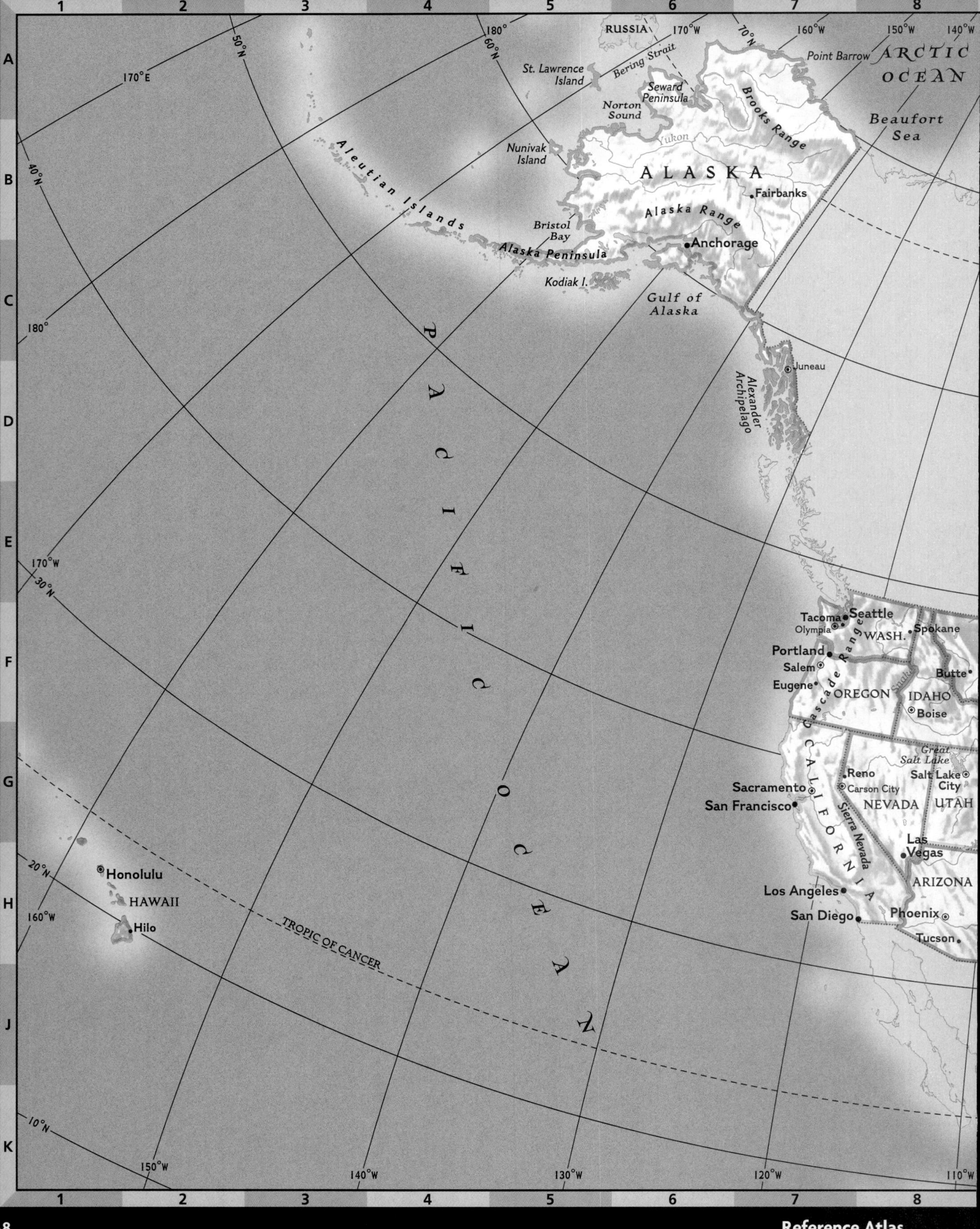

RUSSIA
Bering Strait
St. Lawrence Island
Seward Peninsula
Norton Sound
Point Barrow
ARCTIC OCEAN
Beaufort Sea
Brooks Range
Yukon
Nunivak Island
ALASKA
Fairbanks
Aleutian Islands
Alaska Range
Bristol Bay
Anchorage
Alaska Peninsula
Kodiak I.
Gulf of Alaska
Juneau
Alexander Archipelago
PACIFIC OCEAN
Tacoma
Seattle
Olympia
WASH.
Spokane
Portland
Salem
Eugene
Cascade Range
OREGON
Snake
IDAHO
Boise
Butte
Great Salt Lake
Reno
Carson City
Salt Lake City
Sacramento
San Francisco
CALIFORNIA
Sierra Nevada
NEVADA
UTAH
Las Vegas
ARIZONA
Los Angeles
San Diego
Phoenix
Tucson
Honolulu
HAWAII
Hilo
TROPIC OF CANCER
180°
170°E
170°W
160°W
150°W
140°W
130°W
120°W
110°W
70°N
60°N
50°N
40°N
30°N
20°N
10°N

UNITED STATES
POLITICAL
0 mi
600
0 km
600
OBLIQUE AZIMUTHAL EQUIDISTANT PROJECTION
NATIONAL GEOGRAPHIC
GREENLAND
(KALAALLIT NUNAAT)
Den.
ARCTIC CIRCLE
C A N A D A
MONTANA
Helena
Billings
NORTH DAKOTA
Bismarck
SOUTH DAKOTA
Pierre
MINNESOTA
Minneapolis
St. Paul
WISCONSIN
Milwaukee
Madison
MICHIGAN
Lansing
Detroit
Lake Superior
Lake Huron
L. Michigan
L. Erie
Lake Ontario
WYOMING
Casper
Cheyenne
Sioux City
IOWA
Des Moines
NEBRASKA
Omaha
Lincoln
Chicago
ILLINOIS
IND.
Indianapolis
Springfield
Toledo
Cleveland
OHIO
Columbus
Dayton
Cincinnati
Pittsburgh
PA.
Harrisburg
Buffalo
NEW YORK
Albany
New York City
Montpelier
VT.
N.H.
MAINE
Augusta
Portland
Concord, N.H.
Boston, MASS.
Providence, R.I.
Hartford, CONN.
Trenton, N.J.
Philadelphia
Dover, DEL.
Annapolis, MD.
Baltimore
Washington, D.C.
Richmond
Virginia Beach
VIRGINIA
W. VA.
Charleston
Frankfort
Louisville
KENTUCKY
St. Louis
MISSOURI
Jefferson City
Kansas City
Topeka
KANSAS
Denver
COLORADO
ROCKY MOUNTAINS
Santa Fe
Albuquerque
NEW MEXICO
El Paso
Tulsa
Oklahoma City
OKLAHOMA
ARKANSAS
Little Rock
Memphis
Nashville
TENNESSEE
Raleigh
NORTH CAROLINA
Charlotte
SOUTH CAROLINA
Columbia
Charleston
Atlanta
GEORGIA
Savannah
Birmingham
ALABAMA
Montgomery
MISS.
Jackson
LOUISIANA
Baton Rouge
New Orleans
Tallahassee
Jacksonville
FLORIDA
Tampa
Miami
TEXAS
Fort Worth
Dallas
Austin
San Antonio
Houston
Rio Grande
Arkansas
Mississippi
Missouri
APPALACHIAN MTS.
MEXICO
Gulf of Mexico
Straits of Florida
BAHAMAS
CUBA
HAITI
DOMINICAN REPUBLIC
JAMAICA
PUERTO RICO
U.S.
San Juan
ANTIGUA & BARBUDA
ST. KITTS & NEVIS
DOMINICA
Caribbean Sea
ATLANTIC OCEAN
Bermuda Is.
U.K.

Cape Flattery
Mt. Olympus
7,965 ft
2,428 m
Seattle
CASCADE RANGE
COLUMBIA PLATEAU
ROCKY MOUNTAINS
GREAT PLAINS
CANADA
Columbia
Missouri
Blue Mts.
Clearwater Mts.
Bitterroot Range
Absaroka Range
Bighorn Mts.
Salmon River Mts.
Great Sandy Desert
Snake
Snake River Plain
Shoshone Falls
Wind River Range
Black Hills
Laramie Mts.
N. Platte
Sand Hills
Platte
High Plains
Cape Mendocino
COAST RANGES
SIERRA NEVADA
Great Salt Lake
GREAT BASIN
Wasatch Range
Uinta Mts.
PACIFIC OCEAN
Lake Tahoe
Central Valley
San Francisco
Denver
14,433 ft
4,399 m
Mt. Elbert
Mt. Whitney
14,494 ft
4,418 m
Colorado
Lake Powell
Sangre de Cristo Mts.
San Juan Mts.
Arkansas
Death Valley
-282 ft, -86 m
Lake Mead
Mojave Desert
Grand Canyon
Colorado Plateau
Point Conception
Los Angeles
Channel Islands
Salton Sea
San Diego
Phoenix
Sonoran Desert
Rio Grande
Sacramento Mts.
Llano Estacado
Red
Dallas
Brazos
Edwards Plateau
MEXICO
TROPIC OF CANCER
ARCTIC OCEAN
Point Barrow
Beaufort Sea
Chukchi Sea
North Slope
Brooks Range
RUSSIA
Bering Strait
ARCTIC CIRCLE
Seward Pen.
ALASKA
CANADA
St. Lawrence Island
Yukon
Tanana
Kuskokwim
Alaska Range
Mt. McKinley (Denali)
20,320 ft, 6,194 m
Anchorage
Nunivak Island
Bering Sea
Bristol Bay
Gulf of Alaska
Alexander Archipelago
Alaska Peninsula
Kodiak I.
PACIFIC OCEAN
ALASKA
0 mi 300
0 km 300
130°W
125°W
120°W
115°W
110°W
105°W
100°W
50°N
45°N
40°N
35°N
30°N
25°N
180°
172°W
164°W
156°W
148°W
140°W
132°W
68°N
60°N
52°N

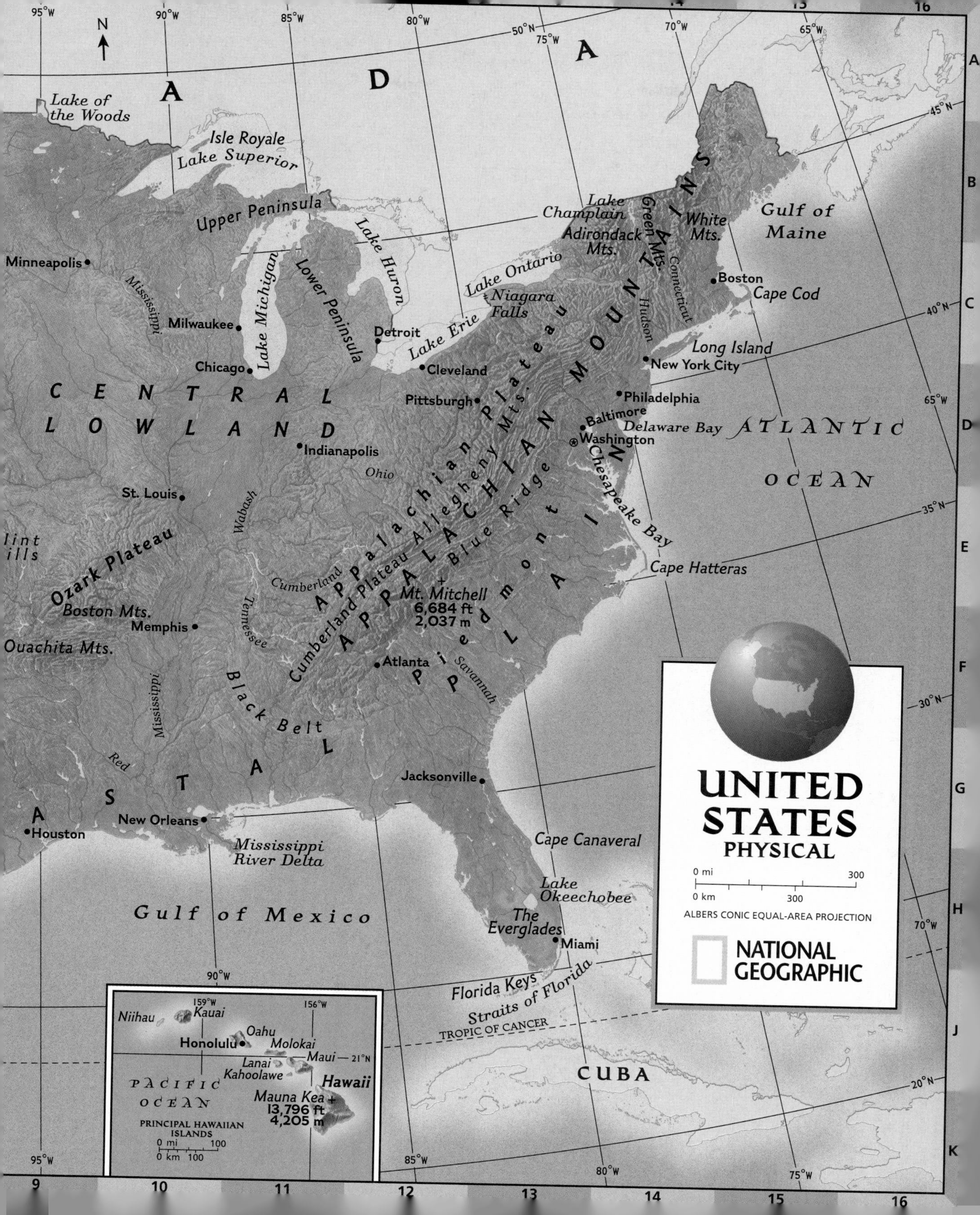

UNITED STATES
PHYSICAL
ALBERS CONIC EQUAL-AREA PROJECTION
NATIONAL GEOGRAPHIC
Lake of the Woods
Isle Royale
Lake Superior
Upper Peninsula
Lake Michigan
Lower Peninsula
Lake Huron
Lake Ontario
Lake Erie
Niagara Falls
Lake Champlain
Adirondack Mts.
Green Mts.
White Mts.
Gulf of Maine
Boston
Cape Cod
Connecticut
Hudson
Long Island
New York City
Philadelphia
Baltimore
Washington
Delaware Bay
Chesapeake Bay
Cape Hatteras
ATLANTIC OCEAN
APPALACHIAN MOUNTAINS
Appalachian Plateau
Allegheny Mts.
Blue Ridge
Piedmont
Cumberland Plateau
Mt. Mitchell
6,684 ft
2,037 m
Minneapolis
Milwaukee
Chicago
Detroit
Cleveland
Pittsburgh
Indianapolis
St. Louis
Memphis
Atlanta
Jacksonville
New Orleans
Houston
Miami
CENTRAL LOWLAND
Mississippi
Ohio
Wabash
Cumberland
Tennessee
Savannah
Red
Ozark Plateau
Boston Mts.
Ouachita Mts.
Black Belt
COASTAL PLAIN
Mississippi River Delta
Gulf of Mexico
Cape Canaveral
Lake Okeechobee
The Everglades
Florida Keys
Straits of Florida
TROPIC OF CANCER
CUBA
Niihau
Kauai
Oahu
Honolulu
Molokai
Maui
Lanai
Kahoolawe
Hawaii
Mauna Kea
13,796 ft
4,205 m
PACIFIC OCEAN
PRINCIPAL HAWAIIAN ISLANDS

RUSSIA
ARCTIC OCEAN
Queen Elizabeth Islands
North Magnetic Pole
Prince Patrick I.
Melville Island
Bathurst Island
Banks Island
Somerset Island
Prince of Wales I.
Victoria Island
Boothia Peninsula
Beaufort Sea
ARCTIC CIRCLE
ALASKA
U.S.
Inuvik
YUKON TERRITORY
Mt. Logan
19,551 ft
5,959 m
Yukon Plateau
Whitehorse
Mackenzie Mts.
Mackenzie
Great Bear Lake
NORTHWEST TERRITORIES
NUNAVUT
CANADIAN
Virginia Falls
Yellowknife
Great Slave Lake
Slave
Peace
Lake Athabasca
Coast Mountains
ROCKY MOUNTAINS
BRITISH COLUMBIA
ALBERTA
Queen Charlotte Islands
Churchill
Fraser Plateau
Prince George
Fraser
Columbia Mts.
Athabasca
GREAT PLAINS
Nelson
PACIFIC OCEAN
Edmonton
SASKATCHEWAN
MANITOBA
Saskatchewan
Vancouver Island
Vancouver
Victoria
Calgary
Saskatoon
Lake Winnipeg
Lake Winnipegosis
Regina
Winnipeg
Lake of the Woods
UNITED STATES
170°W
160°W
150°W
140°W
130°W
120°W
110°W
100°W
80°N
70°N
60°N
50°N
40°N

CANADA
PHYSICAL/POLITICAL
0 mi
400
0 km
400
AZIMUTHAL EQUIDISTANT PROJECTION
NATIONAL GEOGRAPHIC
GREENLAND
(KALAALLIT NUNAAT)
Den.
ICELAND
Ellesmere Island
Devon Island
Baffin Bay
Baffin Island
Davis Strait
Melville Peninsula
Foxe Basin
Southampton Island
Iqaluit
Hudson Strait
Labrador Sea
Ungava Bay
Hudson Bay
Belcher Islands
James Bay
NEWFOUNDLAND
LABRADOR
Cartwright
Happy Valley-Goose Bay
Schefferville
Smallwood Reservoir
Churchill Falls
Island of Newfoundland
St. John's
Avalon Peninsula
QUEBEC
Manicouagan Reservoir
Sept-Iles
Anticosti I.
Gulf of St. Lawrence
St.-Pierre & Miquelon Fr.
Gaspe Pen.
PRINCE EDWARD ISLAND
Charlottetown
Cape Breton I.
NEW BRUNSWICK
NOVA SCOTIA
Fredericton
Saint John
Halifax
Bay of Fundy
ATLANTIC OCEAN
SHIELD
ONTARIO
Chicoutimi
Quebec City
St. Lawrence
Rouyn-Noranda
Lake Nipigon
Thunder Bay
Lake Superior
Sudbury
Montreal
Ottawa
Lake Huron
Lake Michigan
Toronto
L. Ontario
Niagara Falls
London
L. Erie
A V U T
80°N
70°N
60°N
50°N
40°N
40°W
30°W
20°W
10°W
50°W
60°W
70°W
80°W
90°W
A
B
C
D
E
F
G
H
J
K
9
10
11
12
13
14
15
16

UNITED STATES
MEXICO
Tijuana
Mexicali
Sonoran Desert
Baja California
Gulf of California
Ciudad Juarez
Chihuahua
Rio Grande
Sierra Madre Occidental
Sierra Madre Oriental
Nuevo Laredo
Monterrey
Matamoros
Gulf of Mexico
La Paz
False Cape
Mazatlan
Ciudad Madero
Tampico
San Luis Potosi
Leon
Guadalajara
Merida
Cozumel Island
Yucatan Peninsula
Bay of Campeche
Revillagigedo Islands Mex.
Mexico City
Orizaba 18,855 ft 5,747 m
Popocatepetl 17,802 ft 5,426 m
Veracruz
Sierra Madre del Sur
Isthmus of Tehuantepec
Belize City
Belmopan
BELIZE
Gulf of Honduras
Acapulco
Gulf of Tehuantepec
Sierra Madre
GUATEMALA
Guatemala City
Tegucigalpa
EL SALVADOR
San Salvador
Leon
CENTRAL AMERICA
PACIFIC OCEAN
Cocos Island C.R.
MIDDLE AMERICA
PHYSICAL/POLITICAL
0 mi 400
0 km 400
AZIMUTHAL EQUIDISTANT PROJECTION
NATIONAL GEOGRAPHIC

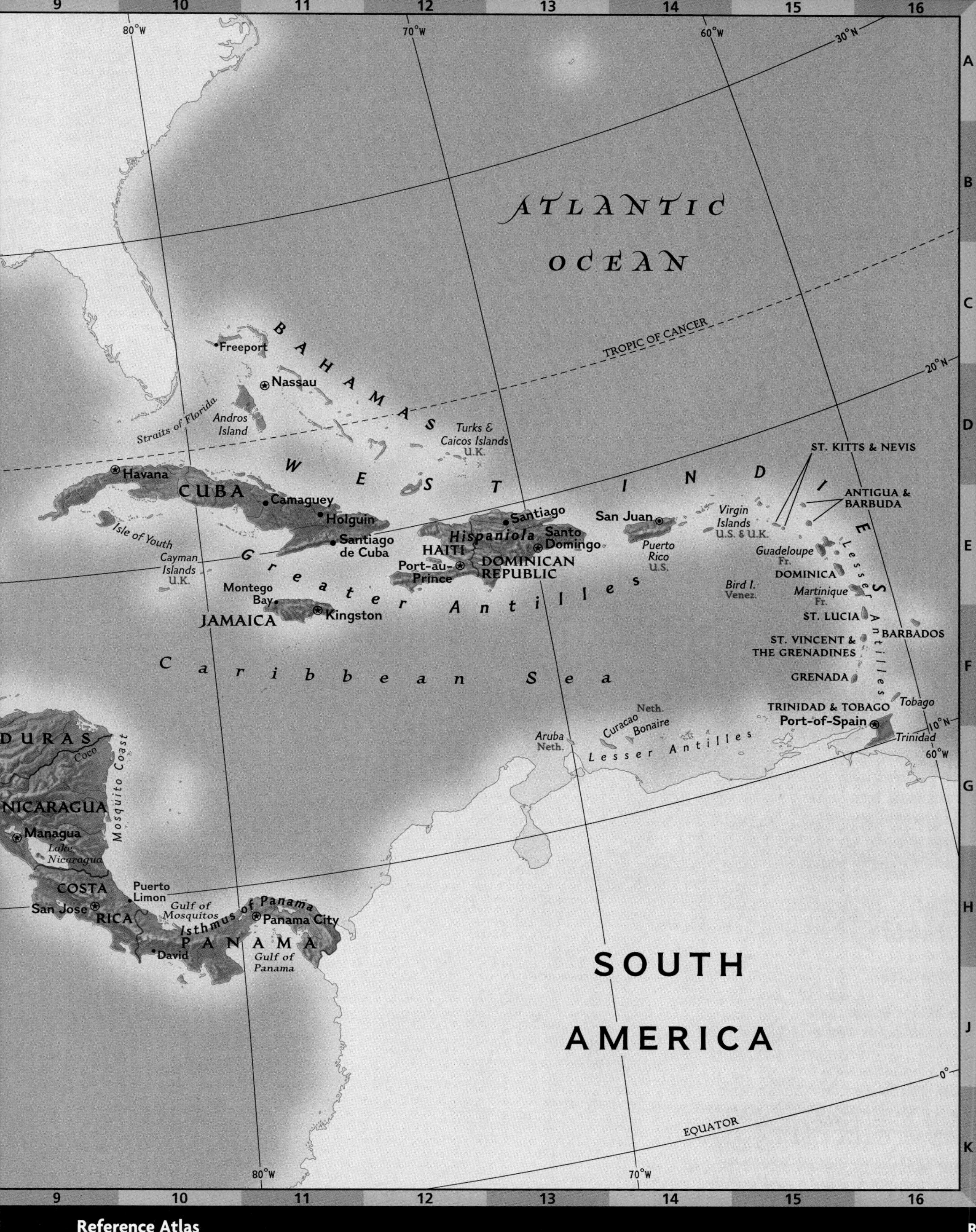
ATLANTIC OCEAN
BAHAMAS
Freeport
Nassau
Andros Island
Straits of Florida
Turks & Caicos Islands U.K.
TROPIC OF CANCER
WEST INDIES
Havana
CUBA
Camaguey
Holguin
Santiago de Cuba
Isle of Youth
Cayman Islands U.K.
Hispaniola
Santiago
Santo Domingo
HAITI
Port-au-Prince
DOMINICAN REPUBLIC
San Juan
Puerto Rico U.S.
Virgin Islands U.S. & U.K.
ST. KITTS & NEVIS
ANTIGUA & BARBUDA
Guadeloupe Fr.
DOMINICA
Martinique Fr.
ST. LUCIA
BARBADOS
ST. VINCENT & THE GRENADINES
GRENADA
TRINIDAD & TOBAGO
Port-of-Spain
Tobago
Trinidad
Lesser Antilles
Bird I. Venez.
Greater Antilles
Montego Bay
Kingston
JAMAICA
Caribbean Sea
Aruba Neth.
Curacao
Bonaire
Neth.
Lesser Antilles
HONDURAS
Coco
Mosquito Coast
NICARAGUA
Managua
Lake Nicaragua
COSTA RICA
San Jose
Puerto Limon
Gulf of Mosquitos
Isthmus of Panama
Panama City
PANAMA
David
Gulf of Panama
SOUTH AMERICA
EQUATOR
80°W
70°W
60°W
30°N
20°N
10°N
0°
9 10 11 12 13 14 15 16
A B C D E F G H J K

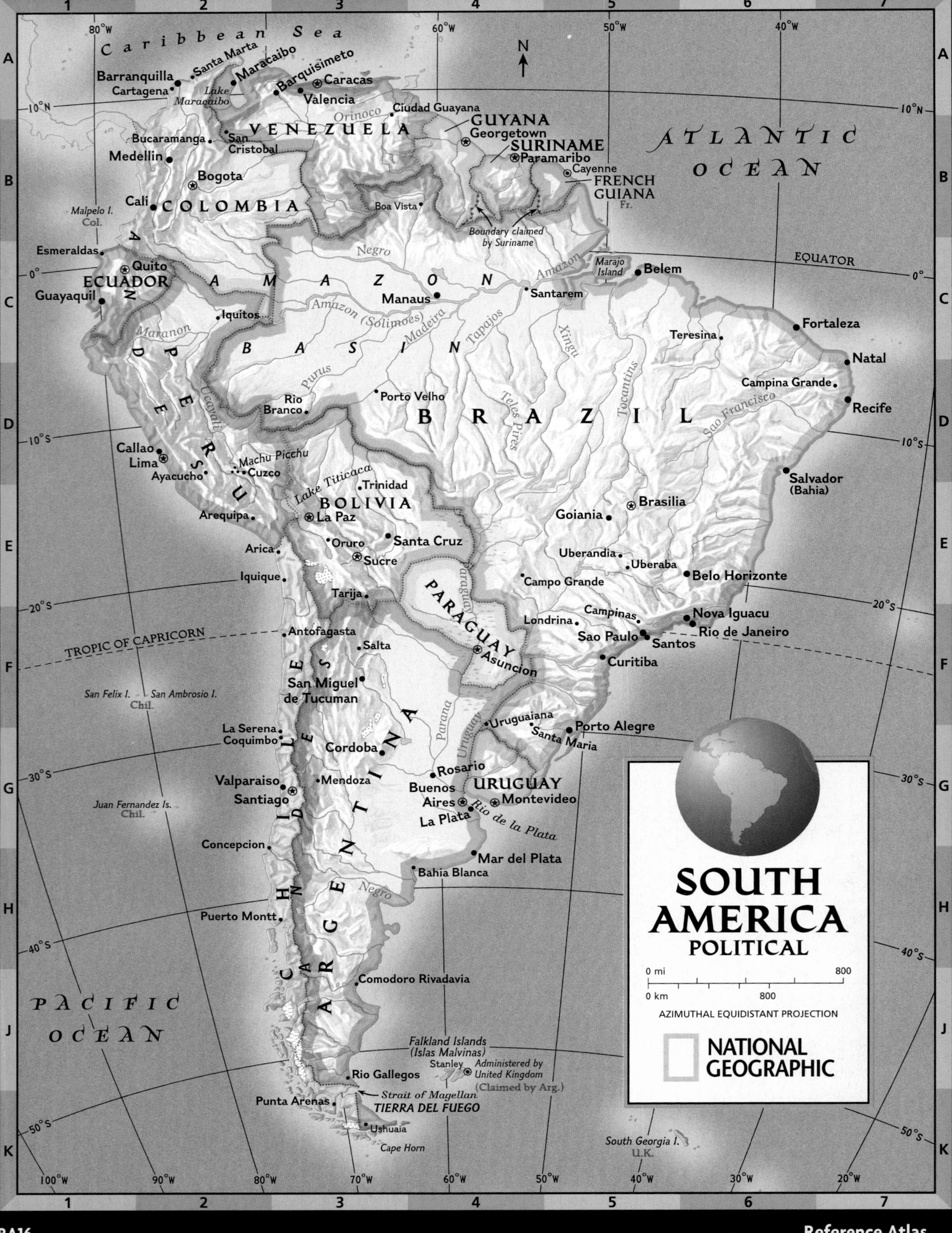
SOUTH AMERICA
POLITICAL
AZIMUTHAL EQUIDISTANT PROJECTION
NATIONAL GEOGRAPHIC
Caribbean Sea
ATLANTIC OCEAN
PACIFIC OCEAN
VENEZUELA
COLOMBIA
ECUADOR
PERU
BRAZIL
BOLIVIA
PARAGUAY
URUGUAY
ARGENTINA
CHILE
GUYANA
SURINAME
FRENCH GUIANA
AMAZON BASIN
ANDES
Barranquilla
Santa Marta
Maracaibo
Barquisimeto
Caracas
Valencia
Cartagena
Ciudad Guayana
Georgetown
Paramaribo
Cayenne
Bucaramanga
San Cristobal
Medellin
Bogota
Cali
Boa Vista
Boundary claimed by Suriname
Esmeraldas
Quito
Guayaquil
Manaus
Santarem
Belem
Iquitos
Fortaleza
Teresina
Natal
Campina Grande
Recife
Porto Velho
Rio Branco
Salvador (Bahia)
Callao
Lima
Machu Picchu
Cuzco
Ayacucho
Trinidad
La Paz
Brasilia
Goiania
Arequipa
Oruro
Santa Cruz
Sucre
Arica
Iquique
Uberandia
Uberaba
Campo Grande
Belo Horizonte
Tarija
Campinas
Nova Iguacu
Londrina
Sao Paulo
Santos
Rio de Janeiro
Antofagasta
Salta
Asuncion
Curitiba
San Miguel de Tucuman
Uruguaiana
Porto Alegre
Santa Maria
La Serena
Coquimbo
Cordoba
Rosario
Valparaiso
Santiago
Mendoza
Buenos Aires
Montevideo
La Plata
Concepcion
Mar del Plata
Bahia Blanca
Puerto Montt
Comodoro Rivadavia
Rio Gallegos
Punta Arenas
Ushuaia
Cape Horn
Strait of Magellan
TIERRA DEL FUEGO
Falkland Islands (Islas Malvinas)
Stanley
Administered by United Kingdom (Claimed by Arg.)
South Georgia I. U.K.
Malpelo I. Col.
San Felix I.
San Ambrosio I. Chil.
Juan Fernandez Is. Chil.
Marajo Island
Lake Maracaibo
Lake Titicaca
Orinoco
Negro
Amazon
Amazon (Solimoes)
Maranon
Madeira
Tapajos
Xingu
Purus
Ucayali
Teles Pires
Tocantins
Sao Francisco
Paraguay
Parana
Uruguay
Rio de la Plata
EQUATOR
TROPIC OF CAPRICORN
0 mi 800
0 km 800

SOUTH AMERICA
PHYSICAL
0 mi 800
0 km 800
AZIMUTHAL EQUIDISTANT PROJECTION
NATIONAL GEOGRAPHIC
Caribbean Sea
ATLANTIC OCEAN
PACIFIC OCEAN
Caracas
Lake Maracaibo
Orinoco
VENEZUELA
GUYANA
Georgetown
SURINAME
Paramaribo
Cayenne
FRENCH GUIANA
Angel Falls
Total drop 3,212 ft 979 m
LLANOS
Bogota
GUIANA HIGHLANDS
Boundary claimed by Suriname
COLOMBIA
Malpelo I.
Quito
ECUADOR
EQUATOR
Negro
Amazon
Marajo Island
AMAZON BASIN
Selvas
Madeira
Tapajos
Xingu
Purus
Ucayali
Teles Pires
Tocantins
Sao Francisco
BRAZIL
ANDES
Lima
Machu Picchu
Lake Titicaca
BOLIVIA
La Paz
MATO GROSSO PLATEAU
BRAZILIAN HIGHLANDS
Brasilia
Altiplano
Sucre
Salar de Uyuni
Paraguay
PARAGUAY
GRAN CHACO
TROPIC OF CAPRICORN
Iguazu Falls
Asuncion
San Felix I.
San Ambrosio I.
Parana
Uruguay
ARGENTINA
PAMPAS
Aconcagua 22,834 ft 6,960 m
Santiago
Buenos Aires
URUGUAY
Montevideo
Rio de la Plata
Juan Fernandez Is.
CHILE
Negro
Chiloe Island
-131 ft -40 m
Valdes Peninsula
PATAGONIA
Gulf of San Jorge
Taitao Peninsula
Wellington I.
Falkland Islands (Islas Malvinas)
Stanley
Strait of Magellan
Tierra del Fuego
Cape Horn
South Georgia I.

EUROPE
POLITICAL
0 mi 400
0 km 400
AZIMUTHAL EQUIDISTANT PROJECTION
NATIONAL GEOGRAPHIC
ATLANTIC OCEAN
ICELAND
Reykjavik
Akureyri
ARCTIC CIRCLE
Norwegian Sea
MERIDIAN OF GREENWICH (LONDON)
Faroe Islands
Den.
Torshavn
Shetland Islands
Lerwick
Orkney Islands
Rockall
U.K.
Isle of Lewis
Inverness
Aberdeen
UNITED KINGDOM
SCOTLAND
Glasgow
Edinburgh
NORTHERN IRELAND
Belfast
IRELAND
Dublin
Cork
Irish Sea
Liverpool
Manchester
WALES
Birmingham
ENGLAND
Cardiff
London
Celtic Sea
Land's End
Southampton
English Channel
North Sea
NORWAY
Trondheim
Alesund
Bergen
Oslo
Stavanger
Tromso
Are
SWEDEN
Sundsvall
Uppsala
Stockholm
Goteborg
Gotland
Gulf of
Skagerrak
DENMARK
Arhus
Copenhagen
Malmo
Baltic
Kiel
Hamburg
NETH.
The Hague
Amsterdam
Brussels
BELGIUM
LUX.
Bonn
Rhine
Frankfurt
GERMANY
Berlin
Gdansk
Bydgoszcz
POLAND
Lodz
Wroclaw
Oder
Prague
CZECH REP.
Bratislava
SLOVAKIA
Vienna
AUSTRIA
Budapest
HUNGARY
Munich
LIECH.
Zurich
Bern
SWITZERLAND
Geneva
ALPS
SLOVENIA
Ljubljana
Zagreb
CROATIA
BOSNIA & HERZEGOVINA
Sarajevo
MONTENEGRO
Tirana
ALBANIA
Le Havre
Brest
Rennes
Paris
Strasbourg
Nantes
FRANCE
La Rochelle
Bay of Biscay
Limoges
Bordeaux
Lyon
Toulouse
MONACO
Nice
Marseille
Donostia-San Sebastian
Pyrenees
ANDORRA
A Coruna
Vigo
Porto
Coimbra
PORTUGAL
Lisbon
Bilbao
Valladolid
Zaragoza
Barcelona
Madrid
SPAIN
Valencia
Cordoba
Seville
Murcia
Cartagena
Cadiz
Malaga
GIBRALTAR
U.K.
Strait of Gibraltar
Cape St. Vincent
Palma
Balearic Islands
Sp.
Mediterranean
Corsica
Fr.
Sardinia
It.
Cagliari
Tyrrhenian Sea
Milan
Turin
Venice
Genoa
SAN MARINO
ITALY
Adriatic Sea
VATICAN CITY
Rome
Naples
Ionian Sea
Palermo
Sicily
Messina
Catania
Valletta
MALTA
AFRICA

A commonly accepted division between Asia and Europe—here marked by a gray line—is formed by the Ural Mountains, Ural River, Caspian Sea, Caucasus Mountains, and the Black Sea with its outlets, the Bosporus and the Dardanelles.
Europe-Asia boundary
RUSSIA
ASIA
KAZAKHSTAN
URAL MOUNTAINS
Barents Sea
White Sea
Kola Peninsula
LAPLAND
FINLAND
ESTONIA
LATVIA
LITHUANIA
BELARUS
UKRAINE
MOLDOVA
ROMANIA
BULGARIA
YUGOSLAVIA
SERBIA
KOSOVO
MACED.
VOJVODINA
TURKEY
GREECE
GEORGIA
AZERBAIJAN
CYPRUS
Black Sea
Sea of Azov
Caspian Sea
Aegean Sea
Caucasus Mountains
Carpathian Mts.
Balkan Mts.
Lake Onega
Lake Ladoga
Murmansk
Kirovsk
Umba
Kem
Archangel
Severodvinsk
Pechora
Tobseda
Syktyvkar
Perm
Kirov
Ufa
Kazan
St. Petersburg
Velikiy Novgorod
Yaroslavl
Nizhniy Novgorod
Tver
Moscow
Samara
Orenburg
Ryazan
Penza
Smolensk
Vitsyebsk
Daugavpils
Vilnius
Kaunas
Minsk
Bryansk
Saratov
Oral
Homyel
Kursk
Chernihiv
Sumy
Kharkiv
Kiev
Poltava
Volgograd
Lviv
Vinnytsya
Donetsk
Rostov
Astrakhan
Dnipropetrovsk
Chisinau
Odesa
Kerch
Crimea
Simferopol
Yalta
Sevastopol
Stavropol
Groznyy
Baku
Tallinn
Riga
Helsinki
Turku
Pori
Tampere
Vaasa
Kuopio
Oulu
Kemi
Lulea
Kiruna
Ivalo
Umea
Bothnia
Warsaw
Krakow
Belgrade
Bucharest
Constanta
Varna
Sofia
Skopje
Istanbul
Thessaloniki
Athens
Peloponnesus
Crete
Iraklio
Rhodes
Nicosia
Bosporus
Dardanelles
Danube
Dniester
Volga
Ural
30°E
40°E
50°E
70°E
60°E
30°N
40°N
50°N
60°N
70°N
80°E
A
B
C
D
E
F
G
H
J
K
9
10
11
12
13
14
15
16

EUROPE
PHYSICAL
0 mi 400
0 km 400
AZIMUTHAL EQUIDISTANT PROJECTION
NATIONAL GEOGRAPHIC
1 2 3 4 5 6 7 8
A B C D E F G H J K
60°N
50°N
40°N
30°N
40°W
30°W
20°W
10°W
0°
10°E
70°N
ARCTIC CIRCLE
MERIDIAN OF GREENWICH (LONDON)
Reykjavik
ICELAND
Faroe Islands
Shetland Islands
Orkney Islands
Outer Hebrides
Highlands
British Isles
Edinburgh
Belfast
UNITED KINGDOM
IRELAND
Dublin
Irish Sea
Great Britain
Cardiff
London
North Sea
Norwegian Sea
N
NORWAY
SWEDEN
SCANDINAVIA
Gulf of
Oslo
Stockholm
Jutland
DENMARK
Copenhagen
Zealand
Baltic
Amsterdam
NETH.
Berlin
NORTH
POLAND
BELGIUM
Brussels
LUX.
GERMANY
Rhine
Oder
Elbe
Prague
CZECH REP.
English Channel
Seine
Paris
Brittany
Loire
FRANCE
Danube
Bratislava
SLOVAKIA
Vienna
LIECH.
Bern
SWITZ.
AUSTRIA
Budapest
HUNGARY
Mont Blanc
15,771 ft
4,807 m
ALPS
SLOVENIA
Ljubljana
Drava
Zagreb
CROATIA
Sava
Danube
ATLANTIC OCEAN
Bay of Biscay
Massif Central
Rhone
Po
MONACO
Riviera
SAN MARINO
BOSNIA &
Sarajevo
HERZEGOVINA
Adriatic Sea
Apennines
Cantabrian Mountains
Pyrenees
Douro
IBERIAN PENINSULA
PORTUGAL
Lisbon
Tagus
Madrid
SPAIN
Ebro
ANDORRA
Corsica
ITALY
VATICAN CITY
Rome
Tirana
ALBANIA
Sardinia
Tyrrhenian Sea
Balearic Islands
Baetic Mountains
GIBRALTAR
Strait of Gibraltar
Mediterranean Sea
Ionian Sea
Sicily
Etna
10,902 ft
3,323 m
Valletta
MALTA
AFRICA

Barents Sea
North Cape
Kola Peninsula
White Sea
Pechora
URAL MOUNTAINS
FINLAND
Bothnia
Lake Region
Lake Onega
Lake Ladoga
Northern Dvina
RUSSIA
NORTH EUROPEAN PLAIN
Europe-Asia boundary
ASIA
Helsinki
Gulf of Finland
Tallinn
ESTONIA
Kama
Volga
Ural
Riga
LATVIA
Moscow
LITHUANIA
Vilnius
RUSSIA
Oka
CENTRAL RUSSIAN UPLAND
Minsk
Dnieper
BELARUS
Don
Warsaw
KAZAKHSTAN
Caspian Depression
Vistula
Kiev
UKRAINE
Carpathian Mountains
Dniester
MOLDOVA
Chisinau
Sea of Azov
Crimea
Elbrus 18,510 ft 5,642 m
Caucasus Mountains
Caspian Sea
ROMANIA
Tisza
Belgrade
Bucharest
Danube
AZERBAIJAN
GEORGIA
Baku
BALKAN PENINSULA
Black Sea
YUGOSLAVIA
BULGARIA
Balkan Mountains
Sofia
Skopje
MACED.
Bosporus
TURKEY
GREECE
Dardanelles
Aegean Sea
Athens
Peloponnesus
Rhodes
Nicosia
CYPRUS
Crete
Sea
30°E
40°E
50°E
60°E
70°E
80°E
30°N
40°N
50°N
60°N
70°N
9 10 11 12 13 14 15 16
A B C D E F G H J K

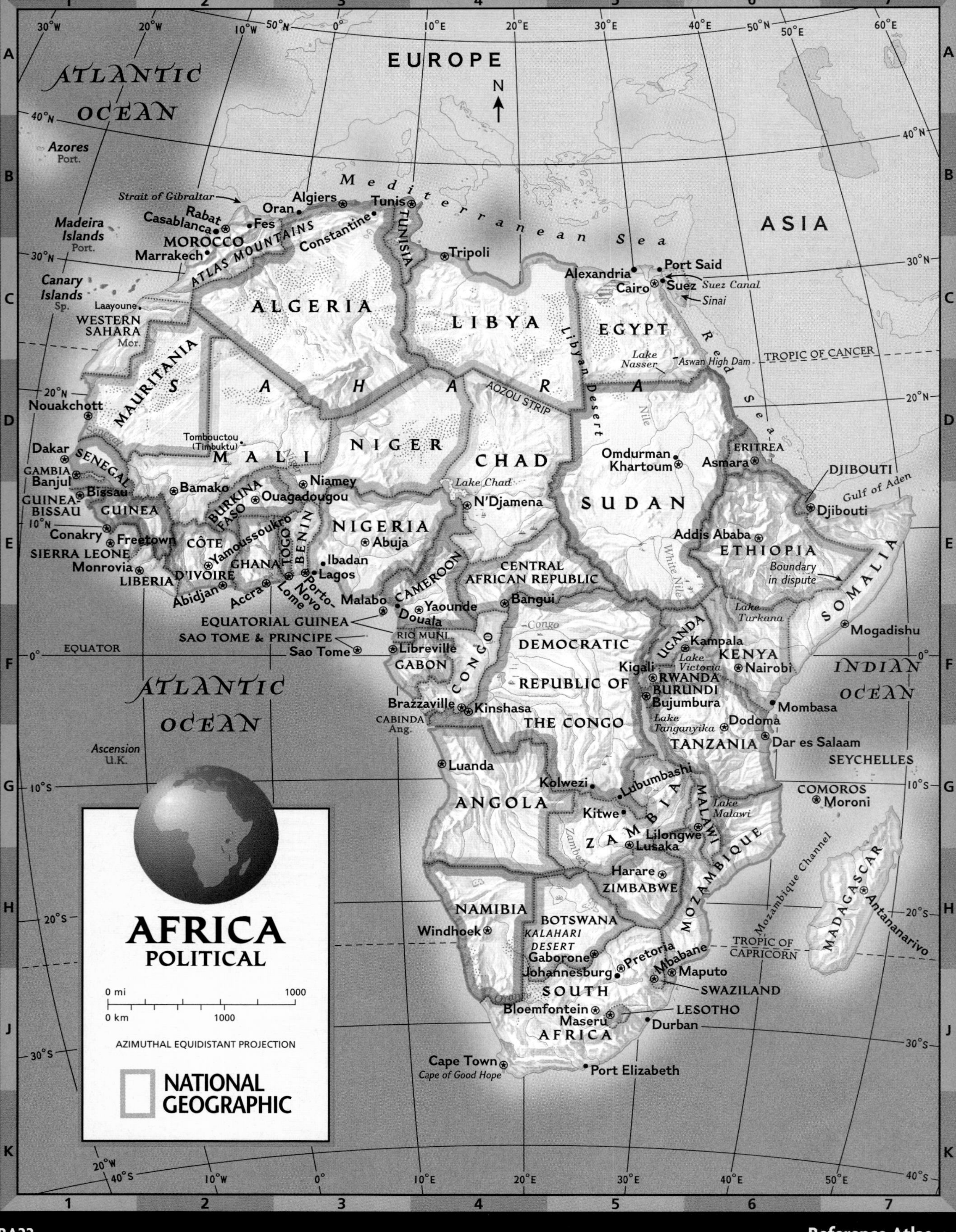
AFRICA
POLITICAL
EUROPE
ASIA
ATLANTIC OCEAN
INDIAN OCEAN
Mediterranean Sea
Red Sea
Gulf of Aden
Mozambique Channel
TROPIC OF CANCER
TROPIC OF CAPRICORN
EQUATOR
SAHARA
ATLAS MOUNTAINS
Libyan Desert
KALAHARI DESERT
AOZOU STRIP
Strait of Gibraltar
Suez Canal
Sinai
Lake Nasser
Aswan High Dam
Lake Chad
Lake Turkana
Lake Victoria
Lake Tanganyika
Lake Malawi
Boundary in dispute
Nile
White Nile
Niger
Senegal
Congo
Zambezi
Orange
Azores Port.
Madeira Islands Port.
Canary Islands Sp.
Ascension U.K.
MOROCCO
Rabat
Casablanca
Fes
Marrakech
ALGERIA
Algiers
Oran
Constantine
TUNISIA
Tunis
LIBYA
Tripoli
EGYPT
Alexandria
Cairo
Port Said
Suez
WESTERN SAHARA Mor.
Laayoune
MAURITANIA
Nouakchott
MALI
Tombouctou (Timbuktu)
Bamako
NIGER
Niamey
CHAD
N'Djamena
SUDAN
Omdurman
Khartoum
ERITREA
Asmara
DJIBOUTI
Djibouti
ETHIOPIA
Addis Ababa
SOMALIA
Mogadishu
SENEGAL
Dakar
GAMBIA
Banjul
GUINEA-BISSAU
Bissau
GUINEA
Conakry
SIERRA LEONE
Freetown
LIBERIA
Monrovia
CÔTE D'IVOIRE
Yamoussoukro
Abidjan
BURKINA FASO
Ouagadougou
GHANA
Accra
TOGO
Lome
BENIN
Porto-Novo
NIGERIA
Abuja
Ibadan
Lagos
CAMEROON
Yaounde
Douala
EQUATORIAL GUINEA
Malabo
RIO MUNI
SAO TOME & PRINCIPE
Sao Tome
GABON
Libreville
CONGO
Brazzaville
CENTRAL AFRICAN REPUBLIC
Bangui
DEMOCRATIC REPUBLIC OF THE CONGO
Kinshasa
Kolwezi
Lubumbashi
CABINDA Ang.
UGANDA
Kampala
KENYA
Nairobi
Mombasa
RWANDA
Kigali
BURUNDI
Bujumbura
TANZANIA
Dodoma
Dar es Salaam
SEYCHELLES
COMOROS
Moroni
ANGOLA
Luanda
ZAMBIA
Lusaka
Kitwe
MALAWI
Lilongwe
MOZAMBIQUE
Maputo
ZIMBABWE
Harare
MADAGASCAR
Antananarivo
NAMIBIA
Windhoek
BOTSWANA
Gaborone
SOUTH AFRICA
Pretoria
Johannesburg
Bloemfontein
Durban
Cape Town
Port Elizabeth
Cape of Good Hope
SWAZILAND
Mbabane
LESOTHO
Maseru
0 mi 1000
0 km 1000
AZIMUTHAL EQUIDISTANT PROJECTION
NATIONAL GEOGRAPHIC

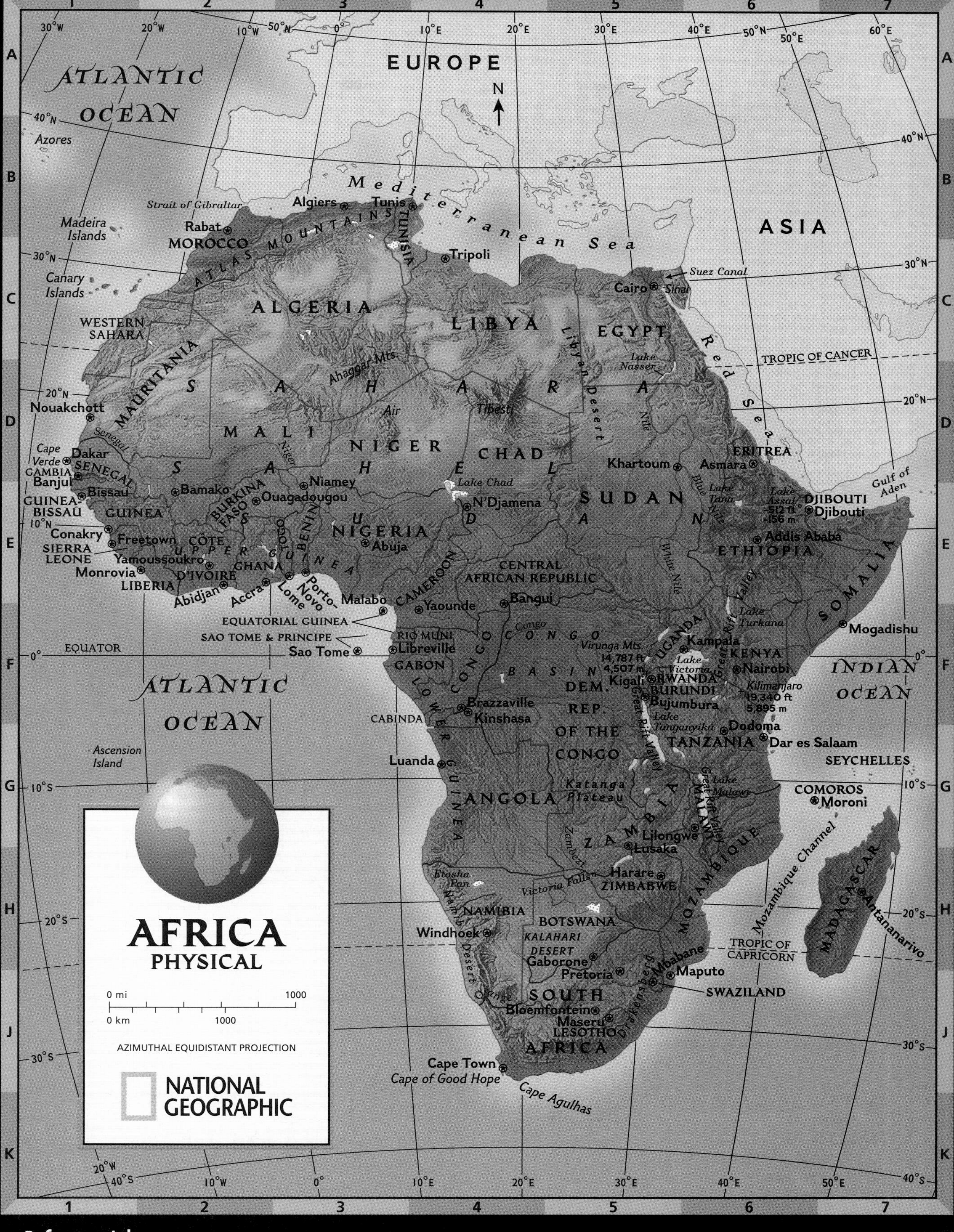

AFRICA
PHYSICAL
0 mi 1000
0 km 1000
AZIMUTHAL EQUIDISTANT PROJECTION
NATIONAL GEOGRAPHIC
EUROPE
ASIA
ATLANTIC OCEAN
INDIAN OCEAN
Mediterranean Sea
Red Sea
Gulf of Aden
Mozambique Channel
TROPIC OF CANCER
EQUATOR
TROPIC OF CAPRICORN
Azores
Madeira Islands
Canary Islands
Cape Verde
Ascension Island
Strait of Gibraltar
ATLAS MOUNTAINS
SAHARA
SAHEL
SUDAN
Ahaggar Mts.
Air
Tibesti
Libyan Desert
Suez Canal
Sinai
Lake Nasser
Nile
Blue Nile
White Nile
Lake Tana
Lake Assal -512 ft -156 m
Lake Chad
Niger
Senegal
UPPER GUINEA
LOWER GUINEA
CONGO BASIN
Congo
Virunga Mts. 14,787 ft 4,507 m
Lake Victoria
Lake Turkana
Great Rift Valley
Kilimanjaro 19,340 ft 5,895 m
Lake Tanganyika
Lake Malawi
Katanga Plateau
Zambezi
Victoria Falls
Etosha Pan
Namib Desert
KALAHARI DESERT
Orange
Drakensberg
Cape of Good Hope
Cape Agulhas
MOROCCO
Rabat
Algiers
Tunis
TUNISIA
Tripoli
ALGERIA
LIBYA
EGYPT
Cairo
WESTERN SAHARA
MAURITANIA
Nouakchott
MALI
NIGER
CHAD
SUDAN
Khartoum
ERITREA
Asmara
DJIBOUTI
Djibouti
ETHIOPIA
Addis Ababa
SOMALIA
Mogadishu
Dakar
SENEGAL
GAMBIA
Banjul
GUINEA-BISSAU
Bissau
GUINEA
Conakry
SIERRA LEONE
Freetown
LIBERIA
Monrovia
CÔTE D'IVOIRE
Yamoussoukro
Abidjan
Bamako
BURKINA FASO
Ouagadougou
GHANA
Accra
TOGO
Lome
BENIN
Porto-Novo
Niamey
NIGERIA
Abuja
N'Djamena
CAMEROON
Yaounde
Malabo
EQUATORIAL GUINEA
SAO TOME & PRINCIPE
Sao Tome
RIO MUNI
Libreville
GABON
CENTRAL AFRICAN REPUBLIC
Bangui
CONGO
Brazzaville
Kinshasa
CABINDA
DEM. REP. OF THE CONGO
UGANDA
Kampala
KENYA
Nairobi
RWANDA
Kigali
BURUNDI
Bujumbura
TANZANIA
Dodoma
Dar es Salaam
SEYCHELLES
COMOROS
Moroni
Luanda
ANGOLA
ZAMBIA
Lusaka
MALAWI
Lilongwe
MOZAMBIQUE
Maputo
ZIMBABWE
Harare
MADAGASCAR
Antananarivo
NAMIBIA
Windhoek
BOTSWANA
Gaborone
Pretoria
Mbabane
SWAZILAND
SOUTH AFRICA
Bloemfontein
Maseru
LESOTHO
Cape Town

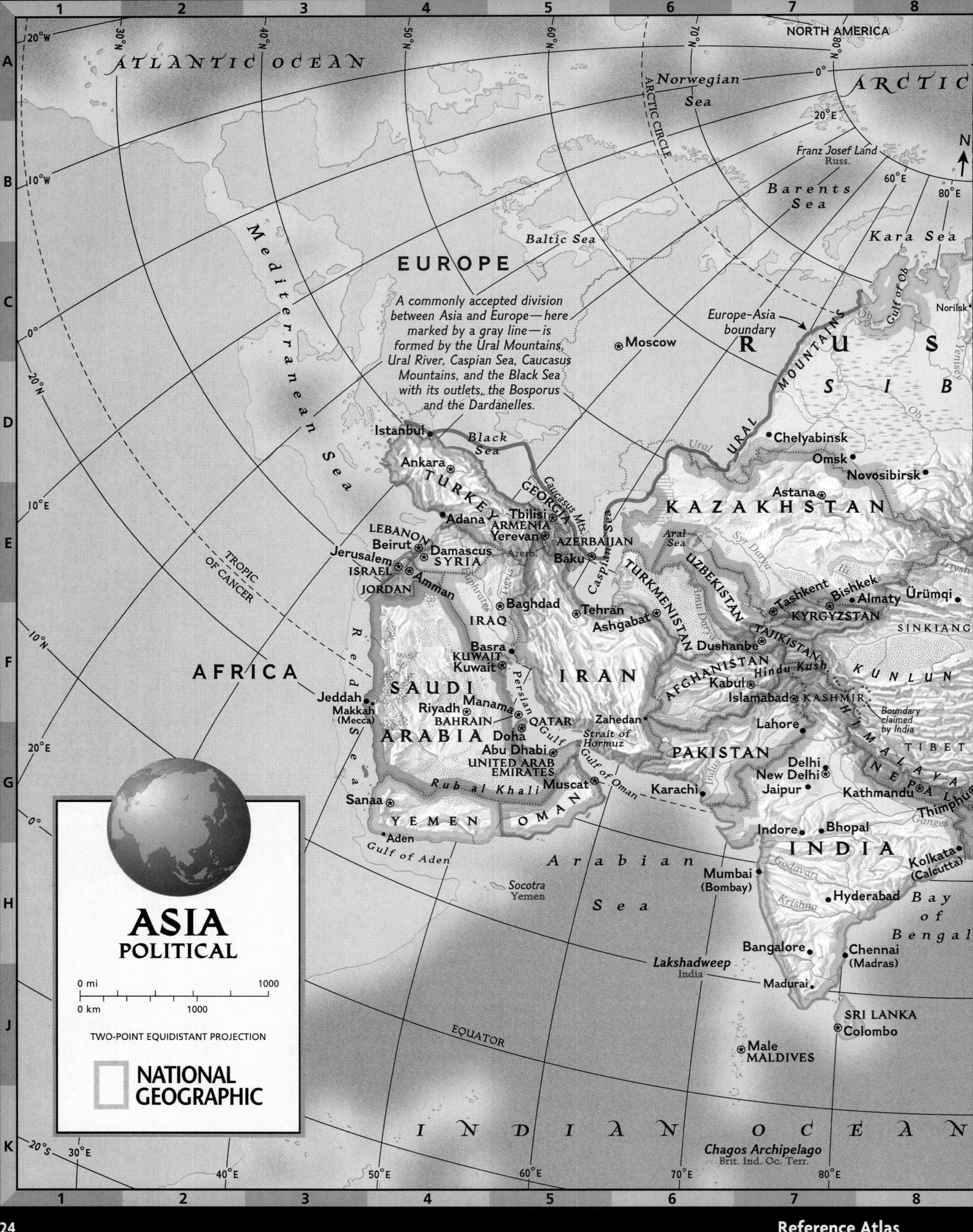

ASIA
POLITICAL
0 mi
1000
0 km
1000
TWO-POINT EQUIDISTANT PROJECTION
NATIONAL GEOGRAPHIC
ATLANTIC OCEAN
NORTH AMERICA
ARCTIC
Norwegian Sea
ARCTIC CIRCLE
Franz Josef Land
Russ.
Barents Sea
Kara Sea
Baltic Sea
EUROPE
Mediterranean Sea
A commonly accepted division between Asia and Europe—here marked by a gray line—is formed by the Ural Mountains, Ural River, Caspian Sea, Caucasus Mountains, and the Black Sea with its outlets, the Bosporus and the Dardanelles.
Europe-Asia boundary
Moscow
URAL MOUNTAINS
Gulf of Ob
Norilsk
Chelyabinsk
Omsk
Novosibirsk
Astana
KAZAKHSTAN
Istanbul
Black Sea
Ankara
TURKEY
GEORGIA
Caucasus Mts.
Tbilisi
ARMENIA
Yerevan
AZERBAIJAN
Baku
Caspian Sea
Aral Sea
Syr Darya
UZBEKISTAN
TURKMENISTAN
Amu Darya
Tashkent
Bishkek
Almaty
Ürümqi
KYRGYZSTAN
SINKIANG
TAJIKISTAN
Dushanbe
Adana
LEBANON
Beirut
Damascus
SYRIA
Jerusalem
ISRAEL
Amman
JORDAN
Euphrates
Tigris
Baghdad
IRAQ
Tehran
Ashgabat
TROPIC OF CANCER
Basra
KUWAIT
Kuwait
Red Sea
AFRICA
IRAN
AFGHANISTAN
Kabul
Hindu Kush
KUNLUN
Islamabad
KASHMIR
Boundary claimed by India
Jeddah
Makkah (Mecca)
SAUDI ARABIA
Riyadh
Manama
BAHRAIN
QATAR
Doha
Persian Gulf
Zahedan
Strait of Hormuz
Lahore
TIBET
Abu Dhabi
UNITED ARAB EMIRATES
Gulf of Oman
PAKISTAN
Indus
Delhi
New Delhi
Jaipur
HIMALAYA
NEPAL
Kathmandu
Thimphu
Ganges
Rub al Khali
Muscat
Karachi
Sanaa
YEMEN
OMAN
Aden
Gulf of Aden
Indore
Bhopal
INDIA
Arabian Sea
Mumbai (Bombay)
Godavari
Kolkata (Calcutta)
Socotra
Yemen
Krishna
Hyderabad
Bay of Bengal
Bangalore
Chennai (Madras)
Lakshadweep
India
Madurai
SRI LANKA
Colombo
EQUATOR
Male
MALDIVES
INDIAN OCEAN
Chagos Archipelago
Brit. Ind. Oc. Terr.

NORTH AMERICA
Bering Strait
Chukchi Sea
North Pole
OCEAN
Wrangel I.
Gulf of Anadyr
Anadyr
Bering Sea
East Siberian Sea
New Siberian Islands
North Land
Laptev Sea
Kolyma Range
Cherskiy Range
Verkhoyansk Range
Commander Is.
Kamchatka Peninsula
Magadan
Sea of Okhotsk
Yakutsk
Lena
Aldan
Sakhalin
Kuril Islands
Amur
Lake Baikal
Irkutsk
Yenisey
MANCHURIA
Hokkaido
Sapporo
Sea of Japan
Vladivostok
Ulaanbaatar
Herlen
MONGOLIA
ALTAY MTS.
GOBI
Changchun
Shenyang
JAPAN
Tokyo
Honshu
Kyoto
Osaka
Hiroshima
Kyushu
NORTH KOREA
Pyongyang
Seoul
SOUTH KOREA
Beijing
Qingdao
Shijiazhuang
Yellow Sea
Yellow
Xuzhou
Lanzhou
Xi'an
Nanjing
Shanghai
East China Sea
Ryukyu Islands
Okinawa
CHINA
Yangtze
Nanchang
Fuzhou
Chengdu
Changsha
Taipei
TAIWAN
Boundary claimed by China
BHUTAN
BANGLADESH
Dhaka
Guiyang
Kunming
Guangzhou
Hong Kong
Macau
The People's Republic of China claims Taiwan as its 23rd province.
Marcus I. Jap.
TROPIC OF CANCER
Bonin Is. Jap.
Volcano Is. Jap.
Parece Vela Jap.
PACIFIC OCEAN
Philippine Sea
Irrawaddy
MYANMAR (BURMA)
Hanoi
Haiphong
LAOS
Vientiane
South China Sea
Hainan
Luzon
Quezon City
Manila
Samar
PHILIPPINES
Leyte
Yangon (Rangoon)
Da Nang
Mindoro
Panay
Negros
THAILAND
Mekong
Bangkok
VIETNAM
CAMBODIA
Phnom Penh
Ho Chi Minh City
Palawan
Mindanao
Andaman Islands India
Gulf of Thailand
Andaman Sea
Bandar Seri Begawan
BRUNEI
SABAH
SARAWAK
MALAYSIA
Nicobar Islands India
Kuala Lumpur
Medan
SINGAPORE
Borneo
Celebes
Halmahera
Morotai
Moluccas
Biak
Jayapura
New Guinea
Kepi
Merauke
Aru Is.
Dolak
Ceram
Buru
INDONESIA
Sumatra
Jambi
GREATER SUNDA ISLANDS
Tanimbar Is.
Mentawai Islands
Java Sea
Dili
EAST TIMOR
Timor Sea
Jakarta
Java
Kupang
AUSTRALIA
EQUATOR
80°N
70°N
60°N
50°N
40°N
30°N
20°N
10°N
0°
10°S
20°S
180°
160°E
120°E
100°E
170°E
160°W
170°W
100°E
110°E
120°E
130°E
140°E
150°E
9
10
11
12
13
14
15
16
A
B
C
D
E
F
G
H
J
K

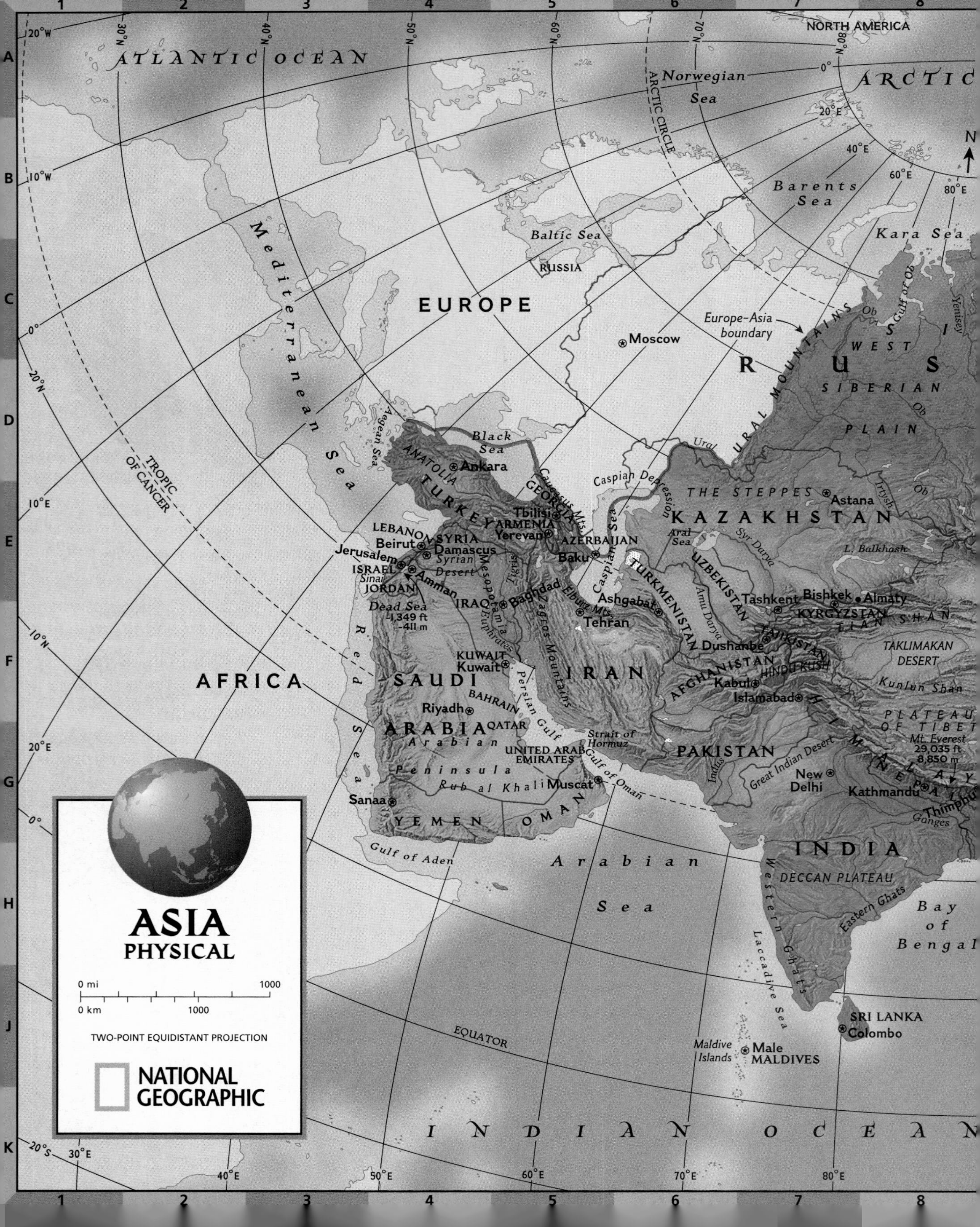
ASIA
PHYSICAL
0 mi
1000
0 km
1000
TWO-POINT EQUIDISTANT PROJECTION
NATIONAL GEOGRAPHIC
ATLANTIC OCEAN
ARCTIC
NORTH AMERICA
Norwegian Sea
ARCTIC CIRCLE
Barents Sea
Kara Sea
Baltic Sea
RUSSIA
EUROPE
Mediterranean Sea
Moscow
Europe-Asia boundary
URAL MOUNTAINS
WEST SIBERIAN PLAIN
Black Sea
Ankara
ANATOLIA
TURKEY
GEORGIA
Tbilisi
ARMENIA
Yerevan
AZERBAIJAN
Baku
Caspian Sea
Caspian Depression
THE STEPPES
Astana
KAZAKHSTAN
Aral Sea
L. Balkhash
UZBEKISTAN
TURKMENISTAN
Ashgabat
Tashkent
Bishkek
Almaty
KYRGYZSTAN
TAJIKISTAN
Dushanbe
TAKLIMAKAN DESERT
LEBANON
SYRIA
Beirut
Damascus
Jerusalem
ISRAEL
JORDAN
Amman
Syrian Desert
Dead Sea -1,349 ft -411 m
IRAQ
Baghdad
Tehran
Elburz Mts.
Zagros Mountains
IRAN
KUWAIT
Kuwait
SAUDI ARABIA
Riyadh
BAHRAIN
QATAR
Persian Gulf
Strait of Hormuz
UNITED ARAB EMIRATES
Gulf of Oman
Muscat
OMAN
YEMEN
Sanaa
Arabian Peninsula
Rub al Khali
Gulf of Aden
AFRICA
Red Sea
TROPIC OF CANCER
AFGHANISTAN
Kabul
Islamabad
HINDU KUSH
PAKISTAN
Indus
Great Indian Desert
New Delhi
Kathmandu
Thimphu
NEPAL
Mt. Everest 29,035 ft 8,850 m
PLATEAU OF TIBET
Kunlun Shan
INDIA
Ganges
DECCAN PLATEAU
Western Ghats
Eastern Ghats
Bay of Bengal
Arabian Sea
Laccadive Sea
Maldive Islands
Male
MALDIVES
SRI LANKA
Colombo
EQUATOR
INDIAN OCEAN

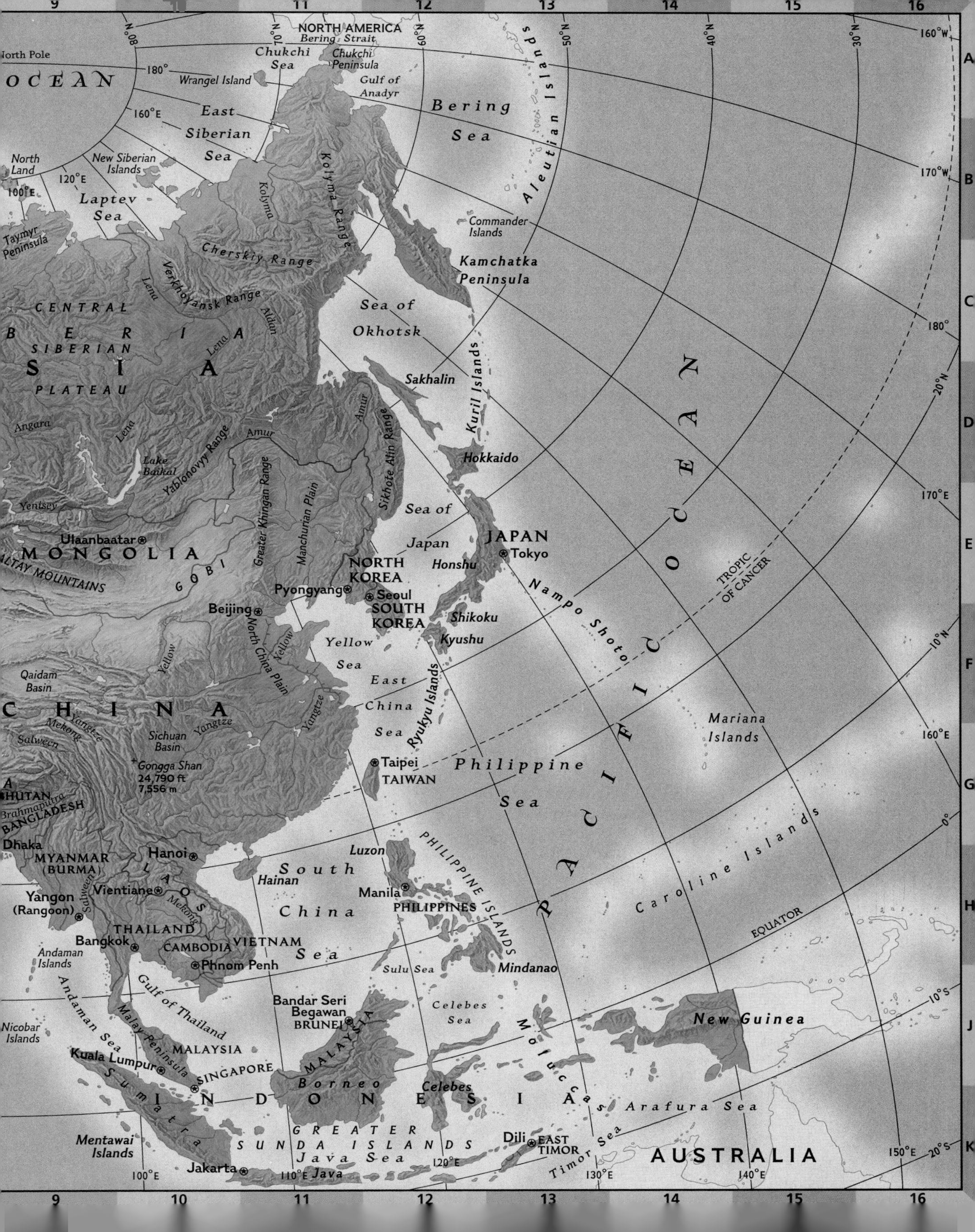

NORTH AMERICA
Bering Strait
Chukchi Sea
Chukchi Peninsula
North Pole
OCEAN
Wrangel Island
Gulf of Anadyr
East Siberian Sea
Bering Sea
Aleutian Islands
North Land
New Siberian Islands
Laptev Sea
Taymyr Peninsula
Kolyma
Kolyma Range
Commander Islands
Cherskiy Range
Kamchatka Peninsula
Verkhoyansk Range
Lena
Aldan
CENTRAL SIBERIAN PLATEAU
SIBERIA
ASIA
Sea of Okhotsk
Sakhalin
Kuril Islands
Amur
Sikhote Alin Range
Angara
Lake Baikal
Yablonovyy Range
Greater Khingan Range
Manchurian Plain
Hokkaido
Yenisey
Sea of Japan
JAPAN
Tokyo
Honshu
Ulaanbaatar
MONGOLIA
ALTAY MOUNTAINS
GOBI
NORTH KOREA
Pyongyang
Seoul
SOUTH KOREA
Beijing
Shikoku
Kyushu
Nampo Shoto
PACIFIC OCEAN
TROPIC OF CANCER
Yellow
North China Plain
Yellow Sea
Qaidam Basin
East China Sea
Ryukyu Islands
CHINA
Yangtze
Mekong
Salween
Sichuan Basin
Gongga Shan 24,790 ft 7,556 m
Taipei
TAIWAN
Philippine Sea
Mariana Islands
BHUTAN
Brahmaputra
BANGLADESH
Dhaka
MYANMAR (BURMA)
Hanoi
LAOS
Luzon
PHILIPPINE ISLANDS
South China Sea
Hainan
Manila
PHILIPPINES
Caroline Islands
Yangon (Rangoon)
Vientiane
THAILAND
Bangkok
CAMBODIA
VIETNAM
Phnom Penh
Andaman Islands
EQUATOR
Sulu Sea
Mindanao
Gulf of Thailand
Andaman Sea
Malay Peninsula
Bandar Seri Begawan
BRUNEI
Celebes Sea
Moluccas
New Guinea
Nicobar Islands
MALAYSIA
Kuala Lumpur
SINGAPORE
Borneo
Celebes
INDONESIA
Sumatra
Arafura Sea
Mentawai Islands
GREATER SUNDA ISLANDS
Java Sea
Dili
EAST TIMOR
Timor Sea
AUSTRALIA
Jakarta
Java
80°N
70°N
60°N
50°N
40°N
30°N
20°N
10°N
0°
10°S
20°S
180°
160°E
120°E
100°E
110°E
130°E
140°E
150°E
160°E
170°E
170°W
160°W
9
10
11
12
13
14
15
16
A
B
C
D
E
F
G
H
J
K

RUSSIA
MONGOLIA
CHINA
NORTH KOREA
SOUTH KOREA
JAPAN
NORTH PACIFIC
INDIAN OCEAN
AUSTRALIA
INDONESIA
MALAYSIA
PHILIPPINES
NEW ZEALAND
PAPUA NEW GUINEA
FEDERATED STATES OF MICRONESIA
MARSHALL ISLANDS
KIRIBATI
SOLOMON ISLANDS
TUVALU
VANUATU
FIJI ISLANDS
TONGA
SAMOA
PALAU
NAURU
EAST TIMOR
BRUNEI
SINGAPORE
THAILAND
CAMBODIA
LAOS
VIETNAM
MYANMAR (BURMA)
INDIA
TAIWAN
Beijing
Ulan Bator
Pyongyang
Seoul
Tokyo
Taipei
Hanoi
Vientiane
Yangon (Rangoon)
Bangkok
Phnom Penh
Manila
Bandar Seri Begawan
Kuala Lumpur
Jakarta
Dili
Koror
Palikir
Majuro
Tarawa
Yaren
Honiara
Funafuti
Port Moresby
Port-Vila
Suva
Apia
Nuku'alofa
Canberra
Wellington
Bering Sea
Sea of Okhotsk
Sea of Japan
Yellow Sea
East China Sea
South China Sea
Philippine Sea
Sulu Sea
Celebes Sea
Java Sea
Arafura Sea
Andaman Sea
Coral Sea
Tasman Sea
Great Australian Bight
KAMCHATKA PENINSULA
ALEUTIAN ISLANDS
KURIL ISLANDS
Sakhalin
Hokkaido
Honshu
Shikoku
Kyushu
NAMPO SHOTO
RYUKYU ISLANDS
Hainan
Luzon
Mindanao
PHILIPPINE ISLANDS
Borneo
Sumatra
Java
Celebes
MOLUCCAS
NEW GUINEA
GREATER SUNDA ISLANDS
LESSER SUNDA ISLANDS
MARIANA ISLANDS
NORTHERN MARIANA ISLANDS U.S.
GUAM U.S.
CAROLINE ISLANDS
MICRONESIA
MELANESIA
POLYNESIA
Ralik Chain
Ratak Chain
Gilbert Islands
Phoenix Is.
Solomon Is.
Santa Cruz Islands
Tokelau N.Z.
AMERICAN SAMOA U.S.
WALLIS AND FUTUNA IS. Fr.
Niue N.Z.
NEW CALEDONIA Fr.
CORAL SEA ISLANDS TERRITORY Austral.
Norfolk Island Austral.
Lord Howe Island Austral.
Kermadec Islands N.Z.
Chatham Island N.Z.
Tasmania
Hawaiian
Lake Baikal
Yablonovyy Range
ALTAY MOUNTAINS
GOBI
Greater Khingan Range
Manchurian Plain
Sikhote Alin Range
Amur
Yellow
Yangtze
Mekong
Darling
TROPIC OF CAPRICORN
105°E
120°E
135°E
150°E
165°E
180°
1 2 3 4 5 6 7 8
A B C D E F G H J K

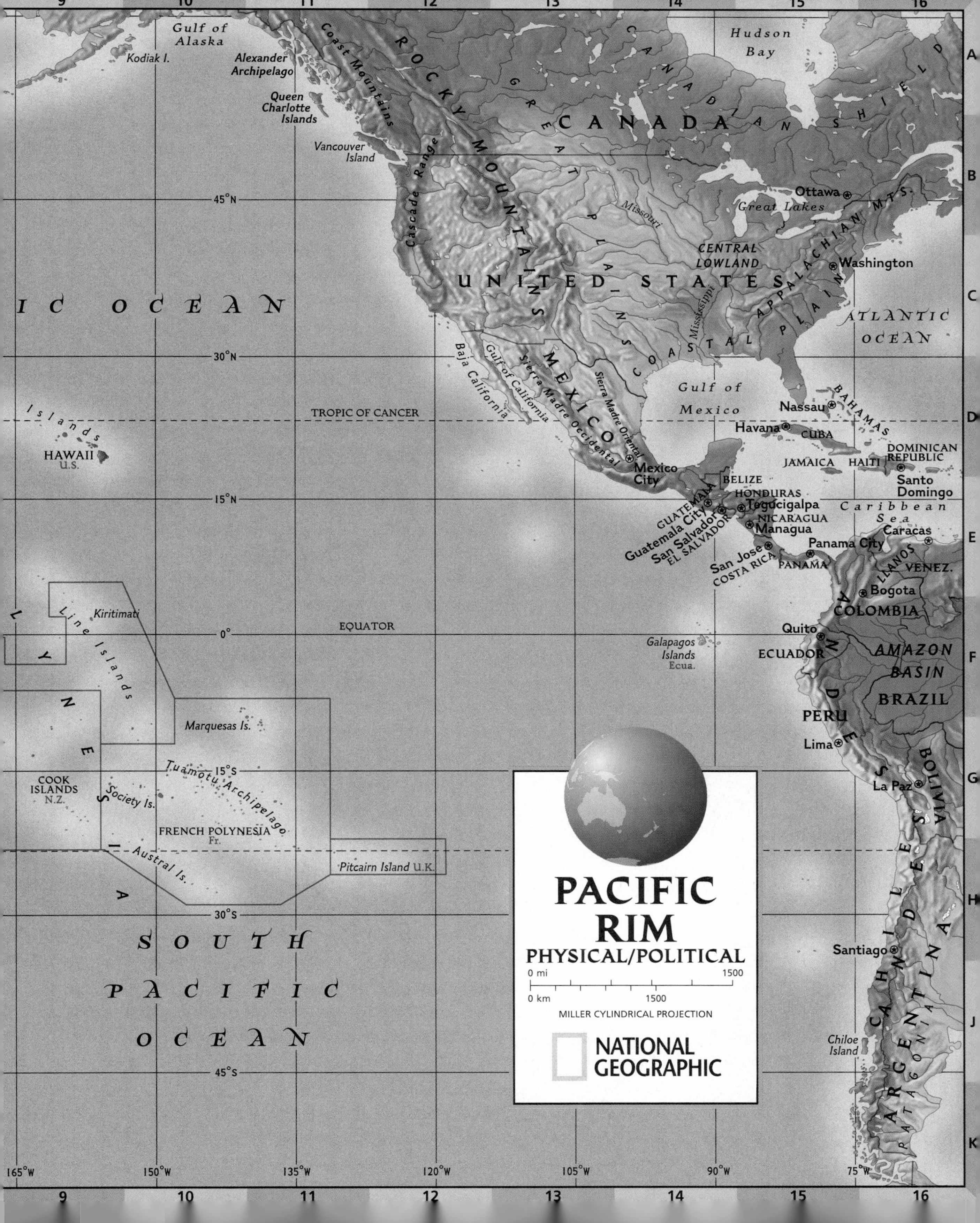

PACIFIC RIM
PHYSICAL/POLITICAL
0 mi 1500
0 km 1500
MILLER CYLINDRICAL PROJECTION
NATIONAL GEOGRAPHIC
Gulf of Alaska
Kodiak I.
Alexander Archipelago
Queen Charlotte Islands
Vancouver Island
Coast Mountains
Cascade Range
ROCKY MOUNTAINS
GREAT PLAINS
CANADIAN SHIELD
CANADA
Hudson Bay
Ottawa
Great Lakes
Missouri
CENTRAL LOWLAND
APPALACHIAN MTS.
Washington
UNITED STATES
Mississippi
COASTAL PLAIN
ATLANTIC OCEAN
PACIFIC OCEAN
Hawaiian Islands
HAWAII U.S.
TROPIC OF CANCER
Baja California
Gulf of California
Sierra Madre Occidental
Sierra Madre Oriental
MEXICO
Gulf of Mexico
Mexico City
Nassau
BAHAMAS
Havana
CUBA
JAMAICA
HAITI
DOMINICAN REPUBLIC
Santo Domingo
BELIZE
HONDURAS
Tegucigalpa
GUATEMALA
Guatemala City
San Salvador
EL SALVADOR
NICARAGUA
Managua
Caribbean Sea
Caracas
Panama City
San Jose
COSTA RICA
PANAMA
LLANOS
VENEZ.
Bogota
COLOMBIA
Kiritimati
Line Islands
POLYNESIA
EQUATOR
Galapagos Islands Ecua.
Quito
ECUADOR
ANDES
AMAZON BASIN
BRAZIL
Marquesas Is.
PERU
Lima
COOK ISLANDS N.Z.
Society Is.
Tuamotu Archipelago
FRENCH POLYNESIA Fr.
Austral Is.
Pitcairn Island U.K.
La Paz
BOLIVIA
SOUTH PACIFIC OCEAN
Santiago
CHILE
ARGENTINA
PATAGONIA
Chiloe Island
45°N
30°N
15°N
0°
15°S
30°S
45°S
165°W
150°W
135°W
120°W
105°W
90°W
75°W

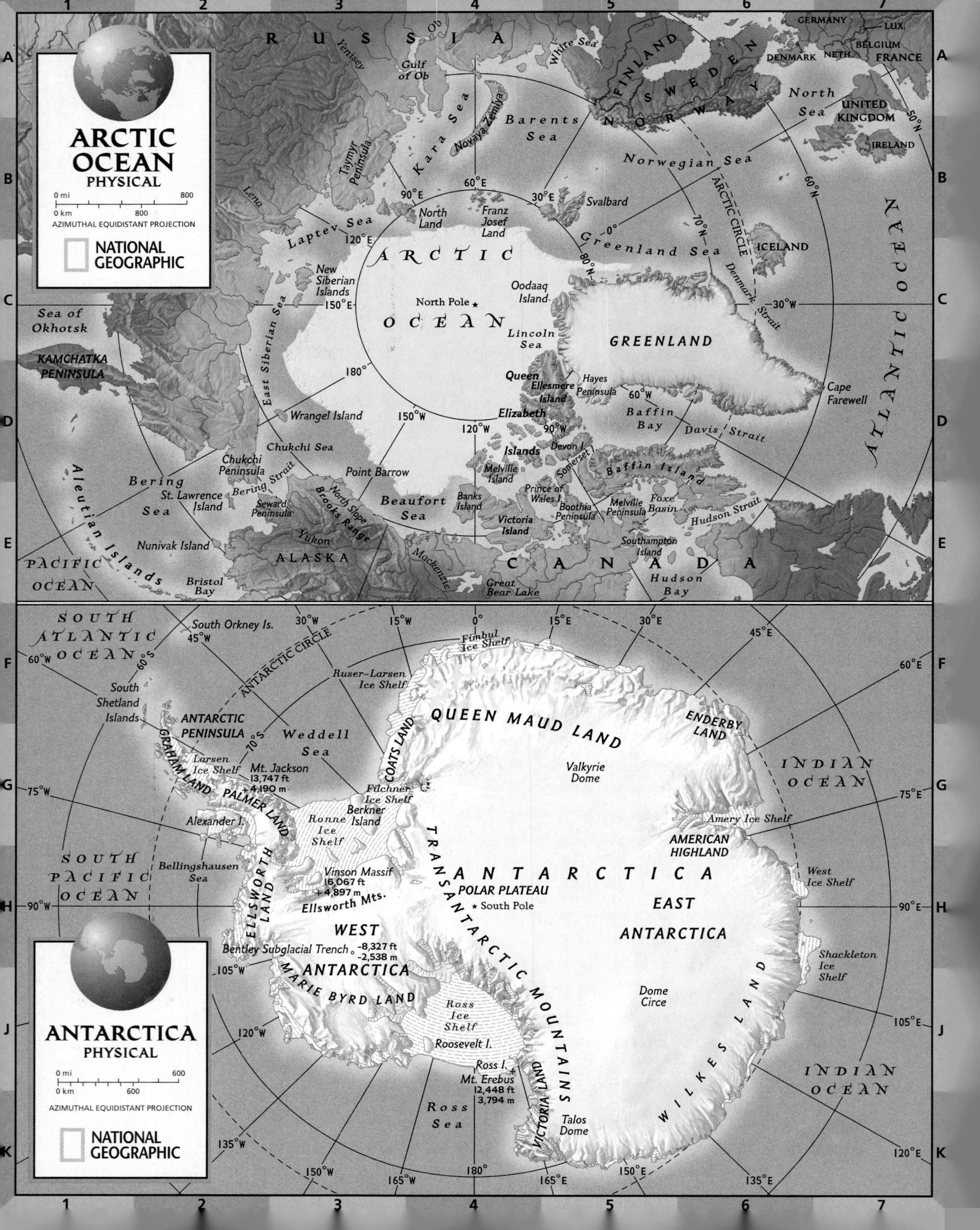
ARCTIC OCEAN
PHYSICAL
AZIMUTHAL EQUIDISTANT PROJECTION
NATIONAL GEOGRAPHIC
RUSSIA
ARCTIC OCEAN
North Pole
GREENLAND
CANADA
ALASKA
ICELAND
FINLAND
SWEDEN
NORWAY
DENMARK
GERMANY
NETH.
BELGIUM
LUX.
FRANCE
UNITED KINGDOM
IRELAND
Barents Sea
Kara Sea
Laptev Sea
East Siberian Sea
Chukchi Sea
Beaufort Sea
Greenland Sea
Norwegian Sea
North Sea
White Sea
Baffin Bay
Hudson Bay
Bering Sea
Sea of Okhotsk
ATLANTIC OCEAN
PACIFIC OCEAN
Arctic Circle
ANTARCTICA
PHYSICAL
AZIMUTHAL EQUIDISTANT PROJECTION
NATIONAL GEOGRAPHIC
ANTARCTICA
WEST ANTARCTICA
EAST ANTARCTICA
South Pole
POLAR PLATEAU
TRANSANTARCTIC MOUNTAINS
QUEEN MAUD LAND
ENDERBY LAND
WILKES LAND
MARIE BYRD LAND
ELLSWORTH LAND
PALMER LAND
GRAHAM LAND
ANTARCTIC PENINSULA
VICTORIA LAND
COATS LAND
AMERICAN HIGHLAND
Weddell Sea
Ross Sea
Bellingshausen Sea
Ronne Ice Shelf
Ross Ice Shelf
Amery Ice Shelf
Vinson Massif 16,067 ft 4,897 m
Mt. Erebus 12,448 ft 3,794 m
Mt. Jackson 13,747 ft 4,190 m
Bentley Subglacial Trench -8,327 ft -2,538 m
SOUTH ATLANTIC OCEAN
SOUTH PACIFIC OCEAN
INDIAN OCEAN
Antarctic Circle

GEOGRAPHY HANDBOOK

A geographer is a person who studies the earth and its people. Have you ever wondered if you could be a geographer? One way to learn how is to use this **Geography Handbook**. It will show you that geography is more than studying facts and figures. It also means doing some of your own exploring of the earth. By learning how to use geographic tools, such as globes, maps, and graphs, you will get to know and appreciate the wonders of our planet.

Geologists studying a volcano ▲

Table of Contents

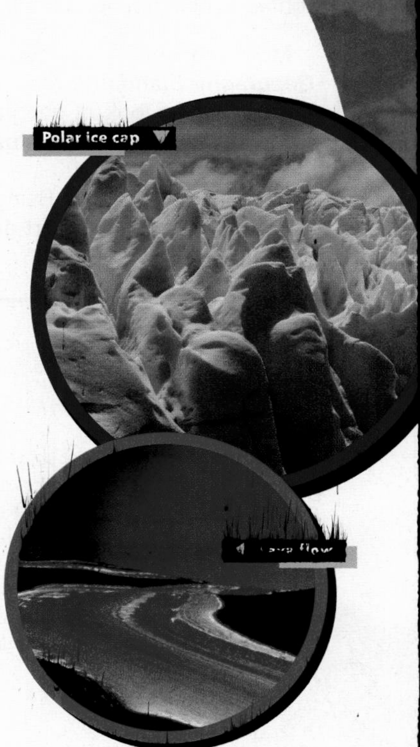

Polar ice cap ▼

Introducing the **GEOGRAPHY HANDBOOK**

LESSON PLAN

Handbook Objectives

1. Understand the purpose and uses of globes and maps.
2. Describe the parts of a map and the different types of maps that geographers use.
3. Demonstrate how to read graphs, charts, and diagrams.

Cultural Kaleidoscope

The Arctic The early Inuit labeled distances on their maps with the time it took to travel rather than with miles. A map would show the distance between what is now Nome and Point Barrow as 10 days rather than as 525 miles (845 km).

Geography Handbook Activity

Using Maps Copy and distribute the political map of the United States in the *Outline Map Resource Book*. Have students color-code the state in which they live. Then have them color-code the states they have visited or passed through. Provide students with an adhesive label to put in the corner of their maps. Ask them to draw a key on the label that explains the meanings of the colors used on their maps. **L1 ELL**

EE1 The World in Spatial Terms: Standard 1

Meeting National Standards

Geography for Life

Turn to pages T22–T29 for more information about the National Standards in Geography and how they are integrated with the five themes as a basis for teaching geography skills and content.

Building Skills

Interpreting Information

Give students practice in identifying characteristics that define *place*. First have them draw a large outline map of the state on poster board. Then have them research the state's plants, animals, and major economic products, and list these items on the back of the poster. Distribute magazines (gardening, wildlife, and local magazines would be most useful) and tell students to find and cut out photos of the items listed on the backs of their posters. Finally, direct the students to paste the photos in the appropriate locations on the outline map, creating a montage of distinctive characteristics of their state.

How Do I Study

Everything you see, touch, use, and even hear is related to geography—the study of the world's people, places, and environments. How can you possibly study such a huge amount of information in your geography class? Where do you start?

Geographers—people who study geography—ask themselves this question, too. To understand how our world is connected, some geographers have broken down the study of geography into five themes. The **Five Themes of Geography** are (1) location, (2) place, (3) human/environment interaction, (4) movement, and (5) regions. These themes are highlighted in blue throughout this textbook.

Most recently, as suggested in the ***Geography Standards for Life,*** geographers have begun to look at geography a different way. They break down the study of geography into **Six Essential Elements,** which are explained for you below. Being aware of these elements will help you sort out what you are learning about geography.

ELEMENT 1 The World in Spatial Terms

Geographers first take a look at where a place is located. **Location** serves as a starting point by asking "Where is it?" Knowing the location of places helps you to orient yourself in space and to develop an awareness of the world around you.

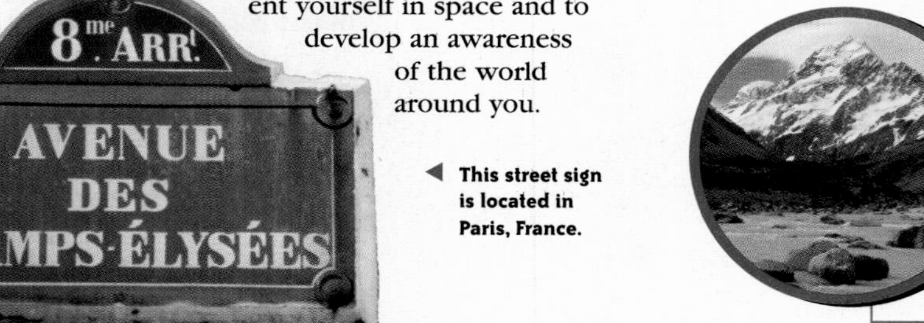

◀ This street sign is located in Paris, France.

ELEMENT 2 Places and Regions

Geographers also look at places and regions. **Place** includes those features and characteristics that give an area its own identity or personality. These can be physical characteristics—such as landforms, climate, plants, and animals—or human characteristics—such as language, religion, architecture, music, politics, and way of life.

To make sense of all the complex things in the world, geographers often group places or areas into regions. **Regions** are united by one or more common characteristics.

Des Moines, Iowa, is a place ▲ characterized by farms. It is also part of a region known as the Corn Belt.

ELEMENT 3 Physical Systems

Why do some places have mountains and other places have flat deserts? When studying places and regions, geographers analyze how physical systems—such as volcanoes, glaciers, and hurricanes—interact and shape the earth's surface. They also look at ecosystems, or communities of plants and animals that are dependent upon one another and their particular surroundings for survival.

◀ A glacier carved this deep valley in New Zealand.

Content Background

Regions Geographers organize regions into three parts: formal regions, functional regions, and perceptual regions. Formal regions are characterized by the presence of a common human property (for example, language, religions, nationality, and political identity) or common physical property (for example, climate, landforms, and vegetation cover). Functional regions are organized around a node or focal point with surrounding areas linked to that node through transportation or communication systems or economic associations. Perceptual regions reflect human feelings or attitudes and are defined by subjective images of the area (for example, New England, southern California, and Corn Belt).

Geography?

Element 4 Human Systems

Geographers also examine human systems, or how people have shaped our world. They look at how boundary lines are determined and analyze why people settle in certain places and not in others. An ongoing theme in geography is the continual **movement** of people, ideas, and goods.

People, vehicles, and goods move quickly through Asmara, the capital of Eritrea.

Element 5 Environment and Society

The study of geography includes looking at **human/environment interaction,** or how and why people change their surroundings. Throughout history, people have cut forests and dammed rivers to build farms and cities. Some activities have led to air and water pollution. The physical environment affects human activities as well. The type of soil and amount of water in a place determines if crops can be grown. Earthquakes and floods also affect human life.

Romanian farmers work in a field near a nuclear power plant.

Element 6 The Uses of Geography

Understanding geography, and knowing how to use the tools and technology available to study it, prepares you for life in our modern society. Individuals, businesses, and governments use geography and maps of all kinds on a daily basis. Computer programs, such as geographic information systems (GIS), allow us to make informed decisions about how to make the best use of our place and region.

A cartographer uses GIS to make a map.

3

Current Events Journal

Ask students to create a flowchart showing how people in a community are interdependent. Explain that this flowchart falls under Essential Element 4, Human Systems.

Interdisciplinary Connections

History Point out to students that each state has a nickname or popular name. Have students make a list of these names and determine which ones are related to physical geography, which are related to human geography, which are related to economic activities, and which are related to an "other" category. Have students turn their lists into a chart using these categories as headings.

Content Background

Careers in Geography Geographers work for the federal government in the Defense Mapping Agency, United States Geologic Survey, Central Intelligence Agency, Army Corps of Engineers, National Science Foundation, Smithsonian Institution, and Office of the Geographer in the Department of State. State environmental and transportation agencies hire geographers as analysts, planners, and cartographers. Some states even have an Office of the State Geographer. In the private sector, geographers work as professors, researchers, and cartographers for GIS companies. Businesses as varied as fast-food chains and ski resorts consult geographers about issues such as the optimal locations for new restaurants and the effects of pollution on the slopes.

FOCUS

Section Objectives

1. Explain how to find an exact location.
2. Understand how maps are made.
3. Explain how to recognize the special parts of a map.
4. Describe how to identify different kinds of maps.

Guide to Reading

Accessing Prior Knowledge
Ask students what they use a key for. Then tell them that a map key "unlocks" the meaning of a map.

Vocabulary Precheck
Have a student read aloud all the dictionary definitions of the word *relief*. Then ask the class to hypothesize which meaning of *relief* will be used in this lesson.

Use the Vocabulary PuzzleMaker to create crossword and word search puzzles.

Section 1 Learning Map Basics

Guide To Reading

Main Idea
Globes and maps provide different ways of showing features of the earth.

Terms to Know
- hemisphere
- latitude
- longitude
- scale bar
- scale
- relief
- elevation
- contour line

What Is a Globe?

A globe is a model of the earth that shows the earth's shape, lands, distances, and directions as they truly relate to one another. A world globe can help you find your way around the earth. By using one, you can locate places and determine distances.

Hemispheres

To locate places on the earth, geographers use a system of imaginary lines that crisscross the globe. One of these lines, the Equator, circles the middle of the earth like a belt. It

NATIONAL GEOGRAPHIC **Hemispheres**

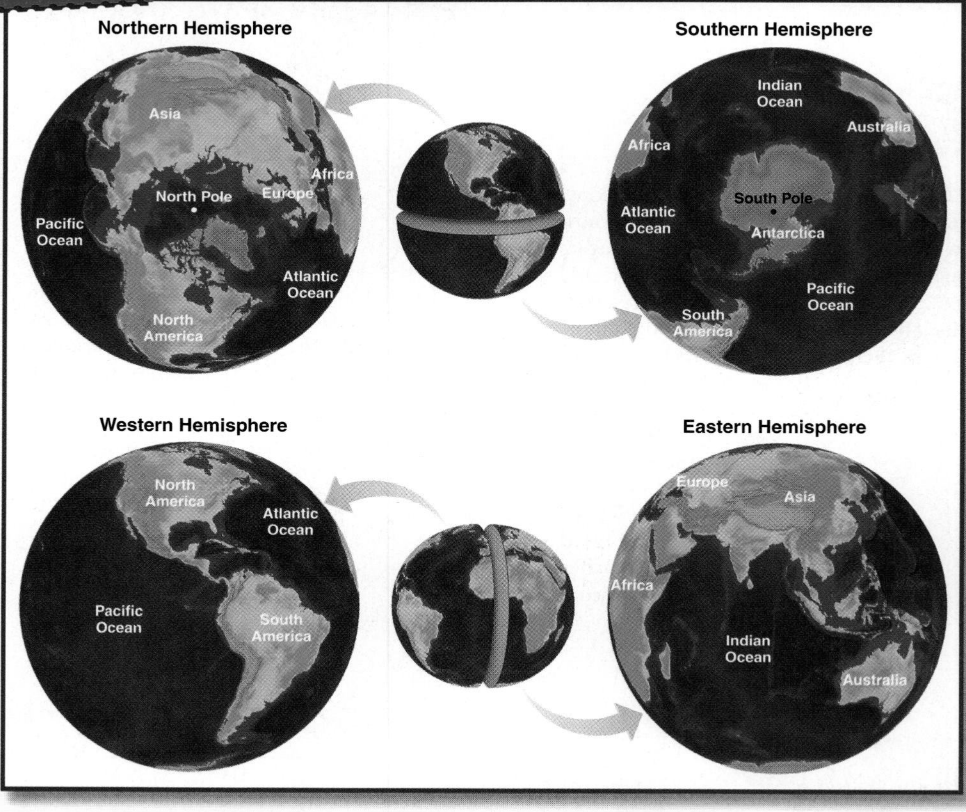

4

Section Resources

Reproducible Masters
- Geography Handbook Strategies and Activities 1
- Geography Handbook Strategies and Activities 2
- Geography Handbook Strategies and Activities 3
- Geography Handbook Strategies and Activities 4
- Geography Handbook Strategies and Activities 6
- Geography Handbook Strategies and Activities 7
- Geography Handbook Strategies and Activities 8
- Outline Map Resource Book

Multimedia
Vocabulary PuzzleMaker Software

Transparencies
- Geography Handbook Transparency 1
- Geography Handbook Transparency 2
- Geography Handbook Transparency 3
- Geography Handbook Transparency 4
- Geography Handbook Transparency 5

divides the earth into "half spheres," or **hemispheres.** Everything north of the Equator is in the Northern Hemisphere. Everything south of the Equator is in the Southern Hemisphere.

Another imaginary line runs from north to south. It helps divide the earth into half spheres in the other direction. Find this line—called the Prime Meridian or the Meridian of Greenwich—on a globe. Everything east of the Prime Meridian for 180 degrees is in the Eastern Hemisphere. Everything west of the Prime Meridian for 180 degrees is in the Western Hemisphere. In which hemispheres is North America located? It is found in both the Northern Hemisphere and the Western Hemisphere.

Latitude and Longitude

The Equator and the Prime Meridian are the starting points for two sets of lines used to find any location. *Parallels* circle the earth like stacked rings and show **latitude,** or distance measured in degrees north and south of the Equator. The letter *N* or *S* following the degree symbol tells you if the location is north or south of the Equator. The North Pole, for example, is at 90°N (North) latitude, and the South Pole is at 90°S (South) latitude.

Two important parallels in between the poles are the Tropic of Cancer at 23½°N latitude and the Tropic of Capricorn at 23½°S latitude. You can also find the Arctic Circle at

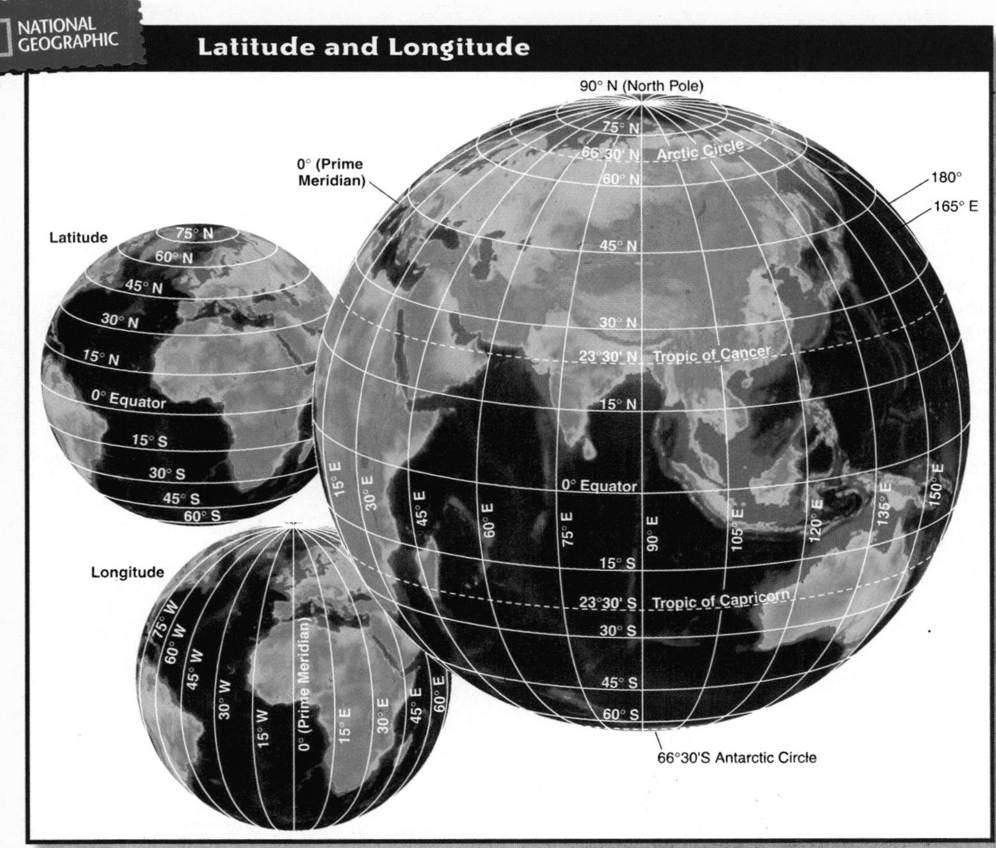

2 Teach

Synthesizing Information

Emphasize the difficulty in portraying the curved surface of the earth on a flat map by giving each student an orange. Using permanent markers, have students draw the outlines of the continents on their oranges. Then ask students to peel the oranges and try to place the peel flat on their desks. Point out that they have to tear the peel to get it to lay flat. **L1**

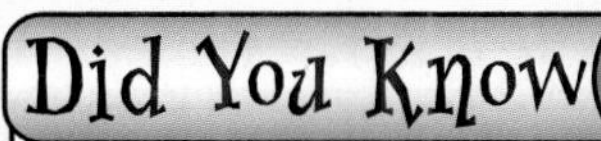

Did You Know

There is a place with no latitude and no longitude. The absolute location where the Prime Meridian and the Equator intersect is 0°N–S, 0°E–W.

Each Geography Handbook Transparency is accompanied by a Student Activity and Teaching Strategy.

Geography Handbook Transparency 1

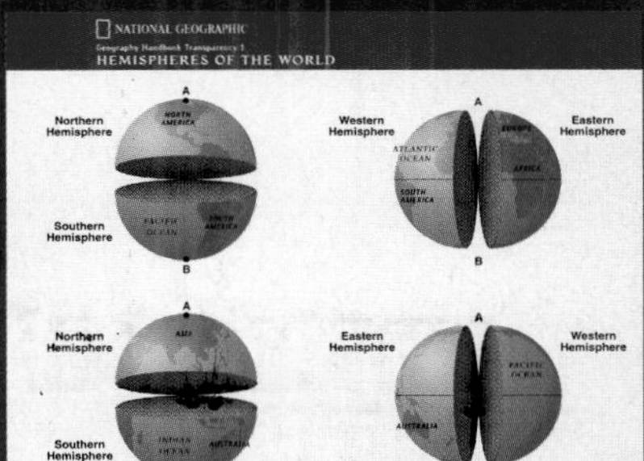

Meeting Special Needs

Study Strategy The grid system is a prerequisite to understanding other aspects of geography, so ensure that all students grasp it at this point. To help students that are having difficulty understanding the grid system, make a simplified grid of three horizontal lines labeled A, B, and C, and three vertical lines labeled 1, 2, and 3. Have students practice naming locations with this simple grid system. When they are comfortable with the basic concept, make a more complex grid of 10 horizontal and 3 vertical lines labeled with degrees. Finally, have students practice on a globe. **L2**

Refer to *Inclusion for the Middle School Social Studies Classroom Strategies and Activities* in the TCR.

Building Skills

Memorizing To help students remember the relationships among latitude, longitude, parallels, and meridians you could tell students that "Lat. Are Flat," meaning that latitude lines are the horizontal, "flat" lines on a map. Write "Parallels show latitude" and "Meridians show longitude" and ask students to come up with mnemonic devices to remember these facts.

Cultural Kaleidoscope

"Grid Language" Citizens of all countries speak the same language of latitude and longitude.

Each Geography Handbook Transparency is accompanied by a Student Activity and Teaching Strategy.

Geography Handbook Transparency 2

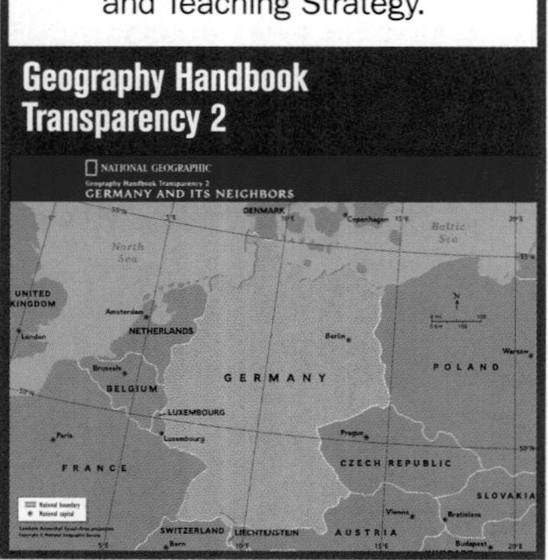

66½°N latitude and the Antarctic Circle at 66½°S latitude.

Meridians run from pole to pole and crisscross parallels. Meridians signify **longitude,** or distance measured in degrees east *(E)* or west *(W)* of the Prime Meridian. The Prime Meridian, or 0° longitude, runs through Greenwich, England. On the opposite side of the earth is the 180° meridian, also called the International Date Line.

Lines of latitude and longitude cross each other in the form of a grid system. You can find a place's absolute location by naming the latitude and longitude lines that cross exactly at that place. For example, the city of Tokyo, Japan, is located at 36°N latitude and 140°E longitude.

How Maps Are Made

For more than 4,000 years, people have made maps to organize their knowledge of the world. The reason for producing maps has not changed over the centuries, but the tools of mapmaking have. Today satellites located thousands of miles in space gather data about the earth below. The data are then sent back to the earth, where computers change the data into images of the earth's surface. Mapmakers analyze and use these images to produce maps.

For modern mapmakers, computers have replaced pen and paper. Most mapmakers use computers with software programs called *geographic information systems (GIS).* With GIS, each kind of information on a map is kept as a separate electronic "layer" in the map's computer files. Because of this modern technology, mapmakers are able to make maps—and change them—more quickly and easily than before.

How to Read a Map

Maps can direct you down the street, across the country, or around the world. An ordinary map holds all kinds of information. Learn the map's code, and you can read it like a book.

Map Key The map key explains the lines, symbols, and colors used on a map. Look at the map of Spain below. Its key shows that dots mark major cities. A circled star indicates the national capital—in Spain's case, the city of Madrid. Some keys tell which lines stand for national boundaries, roads, or railroads. Other map symbols may represent human-made or natural features, such as canals, forests, or natural gas deposits.

Compass Rose An important step in reading any map is to find the direction marker. A map has a symbol that tells you where the *cardinal directions*—north, south, east, and west—are positioned. Sometimes all of these directions are shown with a compass rose. An *intermediate direction,* such as southeast, may also be on the compass rose. Intermediate directions fall between the cardinal directions.

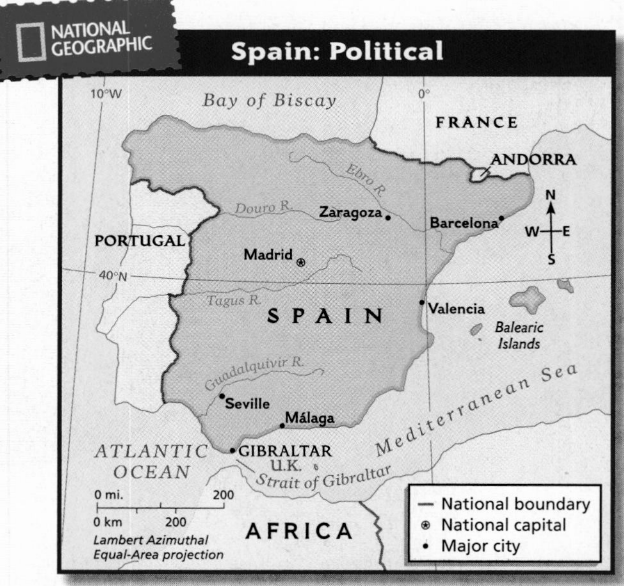

Cooperative Learning Activity

Class Challenge Organize the class into teams. Have each team record the absolute location (in degrees of latitude and longitude) of 20 named places on the globe (cities, natural features, and so on). Then pit teams against each other in a round-robin Absolute Location Tournament. In each round, one team will state the latitude and longitude of five places and time the other team as they locate the places on a globe. The teams will then switch roles. The team with the better time wins the round. **L3**

EE1 The World in Spatial Terms: Standards 1, 3

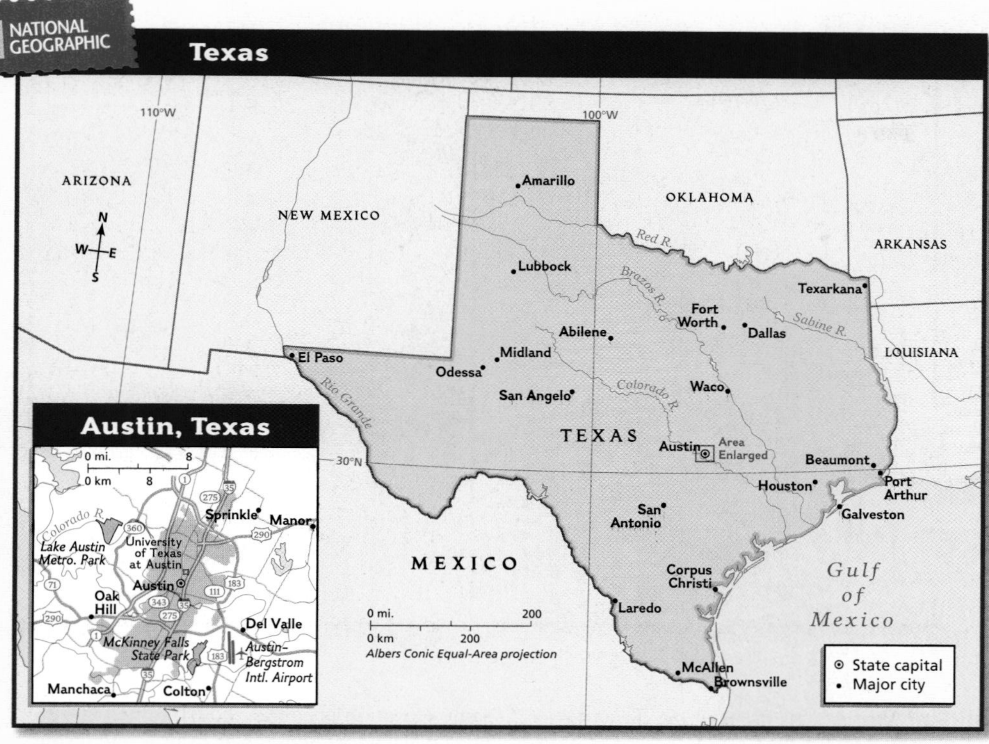

Latitude and Longitude Lines

Like globes, maps have lines of latitude and longitude that form a grid. Every place on the earth has a unique position or "address" on this grid. Knowing this address makes it easier for you to locate cities and other places on a map. For example, what is the grid address of Madrid, Spain? The map on page 6 shows you that the address is 41°N latitude, 4°W longitude.

Scale A measuring line, often called a **scale bar,** helps you determine distance on a map. The map's **scale** tells you what distance on the earth is represented by the measurement on the scale bar. For example, 200 miles on the earth may be represented by 1 inch on the map. Knowing the scale allows you to see how large an area is. Map scale is usually given in both miles and kilometers.

Each map has its own scale. What scale a mapmaker uses depends on the size of the area shown on the map. If you were drawing a map of your backyard, you might use a scale of 1 inch equals 5 feet. In contrast, the scale bar on the inset map above of Austin, Texas, shows that about ¾ inch represents 8 miles. Scale is important when you are trying to compare the size of one area to another.

General Purpose Maps

Maps are amazingly useful tools. You can use them to preserve information, to display data, and to make connections between seemingly unrelated things. Geographers use many different types of maps. Maps that show a wide range of general information about an area are called *general purpose maps.* Two of the most common general purpose maps are political and physical maps.

Each Geography Handbook Transparency is accompanied by a Student Activity and Teaching Strategy.

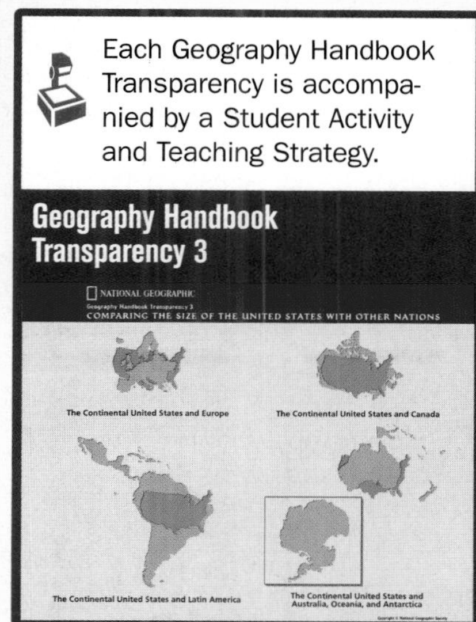

Demonstrating Ideas Write the words "Distance" and "Direction" on the board. Tell students that they could give directions around the world using only these two measures. Ask students how maps show distance *(scale)* and direction *(compass rose)*. Then give students practice in determining distance by showing them how to mark a map scale on the edge of a piece of paper. Have students practice measuring the distance between cities on the map on this page. Next, give students practice in determining direction by having volunteers identify the direction from one city to another. **L2**

Cooperative Learning Activity

Making Maps Organize students into several groups to work as cartographers. Assign each group a particular map—a map of the classroom, the school grounds, or another small area, for example. Different group members should be responsible for the following tasks: measuring and making a scale, using a compass to determine direction and make a compass rose, creating a map key, and creating the map itself. Group members should cooperate to coordinate their work and to display their maps. **L2 ELL**

EE1 The World in Spatial Terms: Standard 1

Each Geography Handbook Transparency is accompanied by a Student Activity and Teaching Strategy.

Geography Handbook Transparency 4

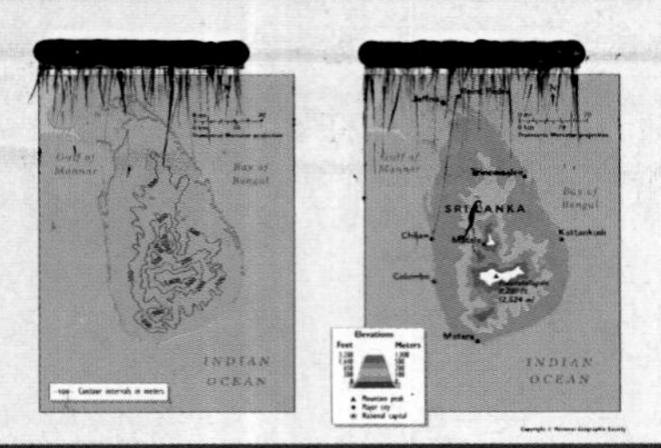

Did You Know

National boundaries run to the center of the earth and to the top of the atmosphere. Airplanes need a country's permission to fly into its air space.

Interdisciplinary Connections

History Until the 1700s, sailors seldom knew exactly where they were because they had only lines of latitude to guide them. John Harrison, an English instrument maker, invented a clock that could keep accurate time at sea. A navigator can determine longitude by figuring the difference between Greenwich Mean Time and the time at the ship's location.

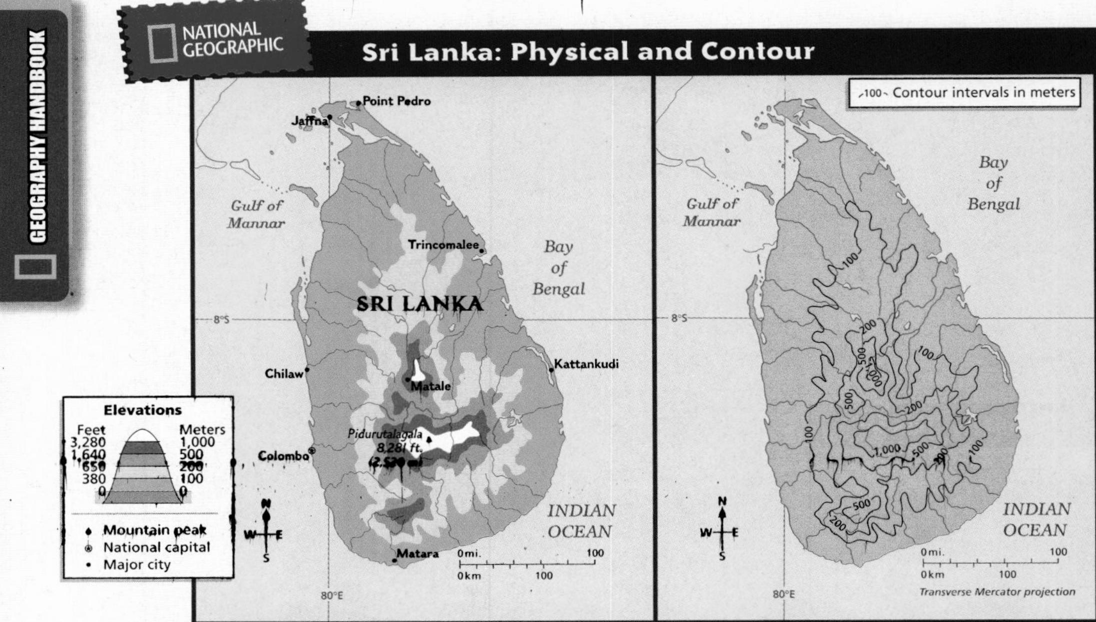

Political Maps *Political maps* show the names and boundaries of countries and identify only major physical features. The political map of Spain on page 6, for example, shows the boundaries between Spain and other countries. It also shows cities and rivers within Spain and bodies of water surrounding Spain.

Physical Maps *Physical maps* call out landforms and water features. The physical map of Sri Lanka above shows rivers and mountains. The colors used on physical maps include brown or green for land, and blue for water. These colors and shadings may show **relief**—or how flat or rugged the land surface is. In addition, physical maps may use colors to show **elevation**—the height of an area above sea level. A key explains what each color and symbol stands for.

Contour Maps One kind of physical map, called a *contour map,* also shows elevation. A contour map has **contour lines**—one line for each major level of elevation. All the land at the same elevation is connected by a line. These lines usually form circles or ovals—one inside the other. If contour lines come very close together, the surface is steep. If the lines are spread apart, the land is flat or rises very gradually. Compare the contour map of Sri Lanka above to its physical map.

Special Purpose Maps

Some maps are made to present specific kinds of information. These are called *thematic* or *special purpose maps.* They usually show themes or patterns, often emphasizing one subject or theme. Special purpose maps may present climate, natural resources, and population density. They may also display historical information, such as battles or territorial changes. The map's title tells what kind of special information it shows. Colors and symbols in the map key are especially important on these types of maps.

One type of special purpose map uses colors to show population density, or the

Meeting Special Needs

Study Strategy To help students remember the several different categories and examples of maps discussed in this section, guide them in creating a graphic organizer entitled "Types of Maps." Branching from this main cell should be two smaller cells labeled "General Purpose Maps" and "Special Purpose Maps." Have students complete the organizer by adding cells labeled with the various maps and connecting them to the correct category. **L1**

Refer to *Inclusion for the Middle School Social Studies Classroom Strategies and Activities* in the TCR.

average number of people living in a square mile or square kilometer. As with other maps, it is important to first read the title and the key. The population density map of Egypt to the right gives a striking picture of differences in population density. The Nile River valley and delta are very densely populated. In contrast, the desert areas east and west of the river are home to few people.

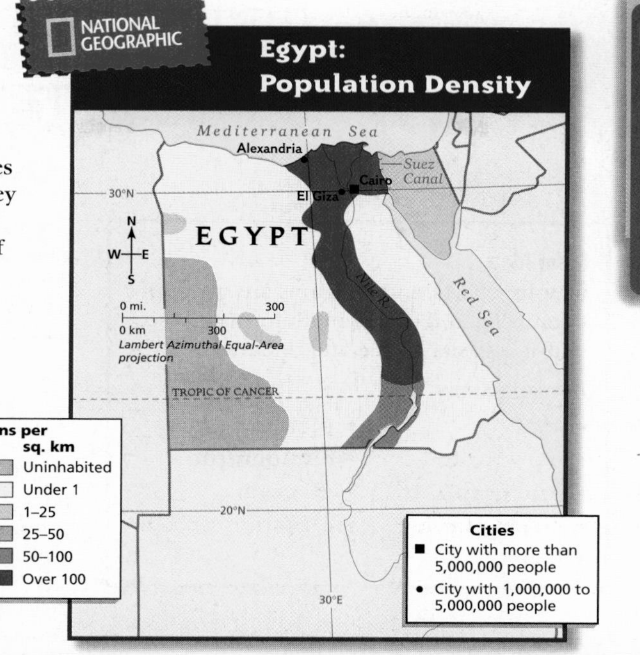

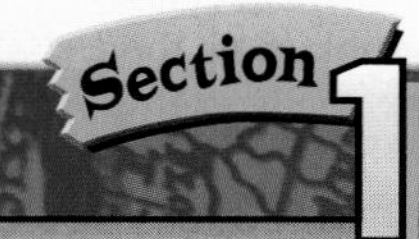

Assessment

Defining Terms

1. **Define** hemisphere, latitude, longitude, scale bar, scale, relief, elevation, contour line.

Recalling Facts

2. Why do people make maps?
3. What are the four cardinal directions?
4. What are two of the most common types of general purpose maps?

Critical Thinking

5. **Drawing Conclusions** Would you use a large scale or a small scale to draw a map showing your route to school? Why?
6. **Synthesizing Information** What imaginary line divides the earth into the Eastern and Western Hemispheres?

Graphic Organizer

7. **Organizing Information** Create a diagram like the one below. In each of the outer ovals, write an example of a feature that you would find on a typical physical map.

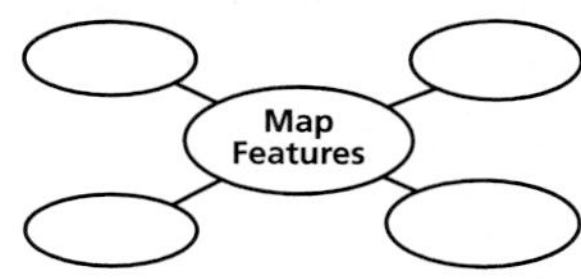

Applying Social Studies Skills

8. **Analyzing Maps** Look at the map of Egypt above. At what latitude and longitude is Alexandria located? Use the key to describe the population density of Alexandria and its surrounding area.

Section 1 Assessment

1. The terms are defined in the Glossary.
2. to organize their knowledge of the world
3. north, south, east, and west
4. physical maps and political maps
5. a small scale; because the map shows a relatively small area
6. the Prime Meridian
7. Answers should include title, key, scale, lines of latitude and longitude, elevation, names of landforms and bodies of water, relief, and map projection.
8. about 32°N, 30°E; the population density is over 250 people per square mile

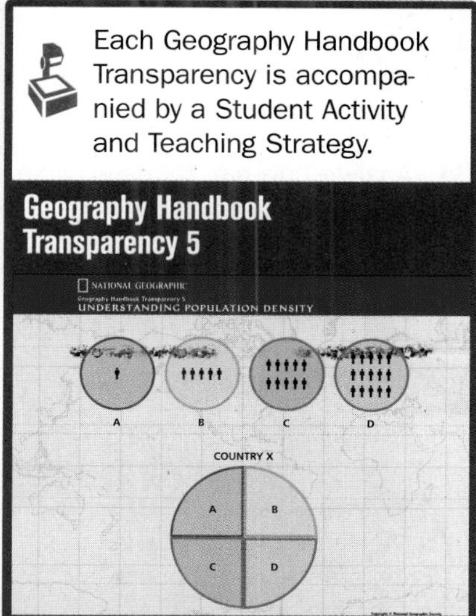
Each Geography Handbook Transparency is accompanied by a Student Activity and Teaching Strategy.

Geography Handbook Transparency 5

3 Assess

Assign the Section 1 Assessment as homework or as an in-class activity.

Enrich

Ask volunteers to bring to class special purpose maps. Special purpose subjects include the path of killer bees, ocean currents, and pizza delivery routes. Even the treasure map that opens Robert Louis Stevenson's classic adventure story, *Treasure Island,* is a special purpose map.

4 Close

Have students scan the textbook and classify the maps according to type: physical, political, or special purpose.

Focus

Section Objectives

1. Analyze how bar, line, and circle graphs present information.
2. Explain how charts and diagrams make data easier to understand.
3. Demonstrate how to read a pictograph and climograph.

Guide to Reading

■ **Accessing Prior Knowledge** Bring several newspapers to class, and have students look through them for charts, graphs, and diagrams. Ask students to summarize the information that several of these visuals portray.

Each Geography Handbook Transparency is accompanied by a Student Activity and Teaching Strategy.

Geography Handbook Transparency 6

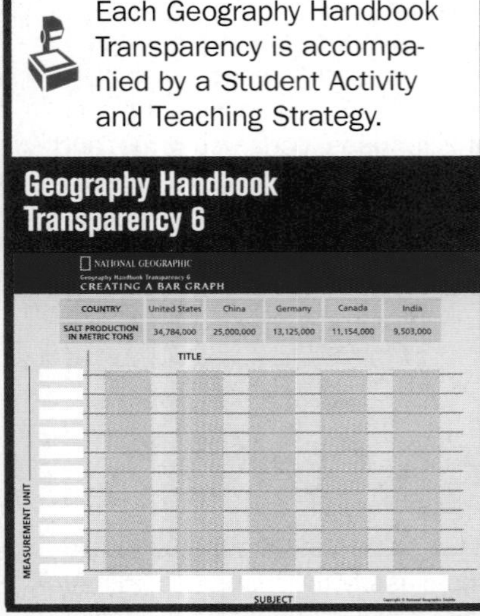

Section 2 Using Graphs, Charts, and Diagrams

Guide To Reading

Main Idea

Graphs, charts, and diagrams are ways of organizing and displaying information so that it is easier to see and understand.

Terms to Know

- axis
- bar graph
- line graph
- circle graph
- chart
- pictograph
- climograph
- diagram
- elevation profile

What Is a Graph?

A graph is a way of summarizing and presenting information visually. Each part of a graph gives useful information. First read the graph's title to find out its subject. Then read the labels along the graph's **axes**—the vertical line along the left side of the graph and the horizontal line along the bottom of the graph. One axis will tell you what is being measured. The other axis tells what units of measurement are being used.

Bar, Line, and Circle Graphs

Bar Graphs Graphs that use bars or wide lines to compare data visually are called **bar graphs.** Look carefully at the bar graph below, which compares world languages. The vertical axis lists the languages. The horizontal axis gives speakers of the language in millions. By comparing the lengths of the bars, you can quickly tell which language is spoken by the most people. Bar graphs are especially useful for comparing quantities, and they may show the bars rising up from the bottom of the graph or extending out from the vertical axis.

NATIONAL GEOGRAPHIC

Comparing World Languages

Languages	Number of Speakers (in millions)
Chinese (Mandarin)	885
English	322
Spanish	266
Bengali	189
Hindi	182
Portuguese	170
Russian	170
Japanese	125
German	98
Chinese (Wu)	77

Source: *National Geographic Atlas of the World,* 1997.

Line Graphs A **line graph** is a useful tool for showing changes over a period of time. The amounts being measured are plotted on the grid above each year, and then are connected by a line. Line graphs sometimes have two or more lines plotted on them. The line graph on page 11 shows that the number of farms in the United States has decreased since 1940. The vertical axis lists the number of farms in millions. The horizontal axis shows the passage of time in ten-year periods from 1940 to 1998.

Section Resources

Reproducible Masters

- Geography Handbook Strategies and Activities 10
- Geography Handbook Strategies and Activities 11
- Geography Handbook Strategies and Activities 12
- Geography Handbook Strategies and Activities 13
- Geography Handbook Strategies and Activities 14
- Geography Handbook Strategies and Activities 16
- Outline Map Resource Book

Multimedia

Vocabulary PuzzleMaker Software

Transparencies

- Geography Handbook Transparency 6
- Geography Handbook Transparency 7
- Geography Handbook Transparency 8
- Geography Handbook Transparency 9

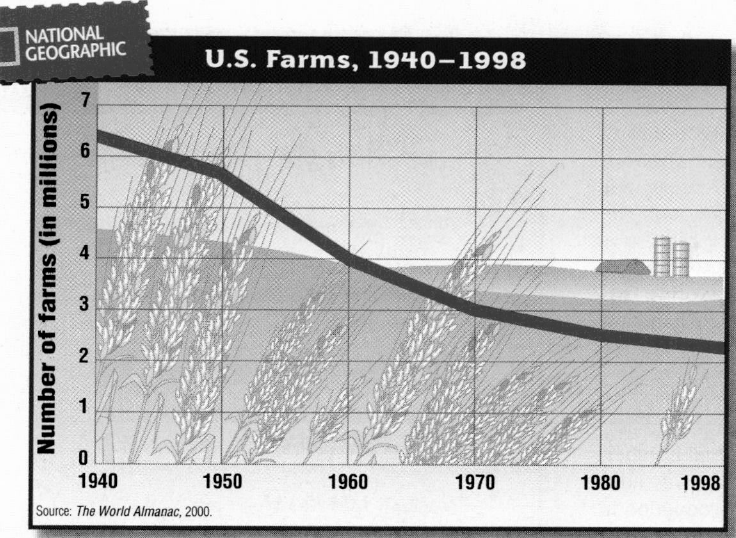

Circle Graphs You can use **circle graphs** when you want to show how the *whole* of something is divided into its *parts*. Because of their shape, circle graphs are often called pie graphs. Each "slice" represents a part or percentage of the whole "pie." On the circle graph below, the whole circle (100 percent) represents the world's population in 2000. The slices show how this population is divided among the world's five largest continents.

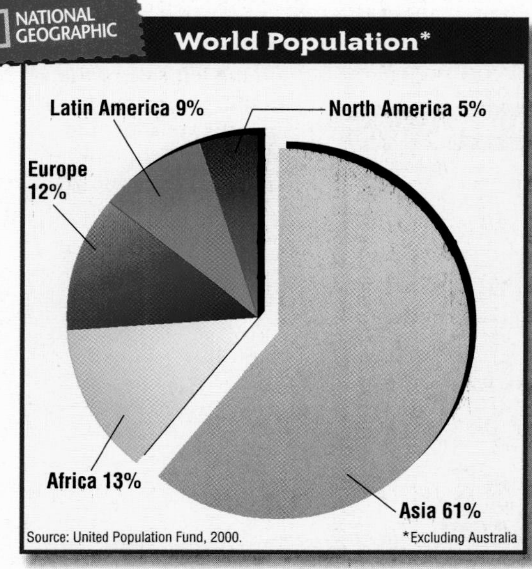

Charts

Charts present related facts and numbers in an organized way. They arrange data, especially numbers, in rows and columns for easy reference. Look at the chart on page 36. To interpret the chart, first read the title. It tells you what information the chart contains. Next, read the labels at the top of each column and on the left side of the chart. They explain what the numbers or data on the chart are measuring. One kind of chart, a *flowchart,* joins certain elements of a chart and a diagram. It can show the order of how things happen or how they are related to each other. The flowchart on page 520 presents the branches of the United States government. Notice how the chart shows the relationship among the tasks and the offices or bodies of each branch.

2 TEACH

Interpreting Graphs Have students study the line graph on this page. **Ask:** **During which 10-year period did the number of U.S. farms decrease the most?** *(1950–1960)* Now have students look at the circle graph on this page. **Ask:** **If Asia's population was expressed as a fraction of the entire world's population, would it be closest to 1/3, 2/3, or 3/4?** *(2/3)* **L1**

Each Geography Handbook Transparency is accompanied by a Student Activity and Teaching Strategy.

Geography Handbook Transparency 7

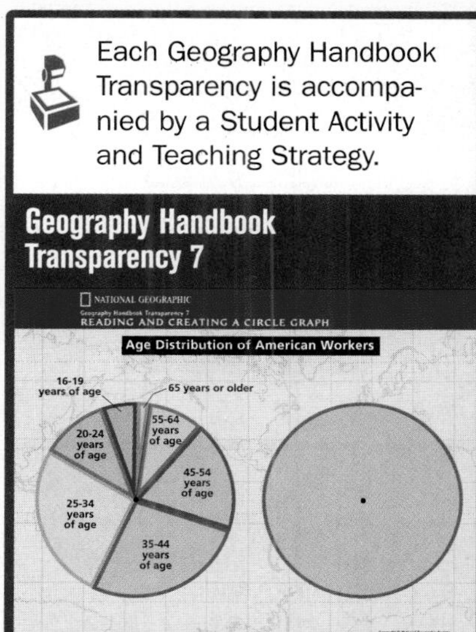

Meeting Special Needs

Kinesthetic Students who do well with the kinesthetic mode of learning can benefit by translating some two-dimensional charts and graphs into three-dimensional models. For example, students can make a line graph using tacks and string, make a bar graph out of blocks, or create a circle graph using play-doh in a pie tin. **L1 ELL** 

Refer to *Inclusion for the Middle School Social Studies Classroom Strategies and Activities* in the TCR.

Each Geography Handbook Transparency is accompanied by a Student Activity and Teaching Strategy.

Analyzing Graphs Have students look at the pictograph on this page. **Ask:** **About how many passenger cars did the United States produce in 2000?** *(5½ million)* **Japan?** *(8 million)* Have students study the climograph on this page. **Ask:** **What are the two coldest months in Moscow?** *(January and February)* **L1**

GEOGRAPHY HANDBOOK

Pictographs

Like bar and circle graphs, pictographs are good for making comparisons. **Pictographs** use rows of small pictures or symbols, with each picture or symbol representing an amount. The pictograph on the right shows the number of automobiles produced in the world's five major automobile-producing countries. The key tells you that one car symbol stands for 1 million automobiles. Pictographs are read like a bar graph. The total number of car symbols in a row adds up to the auto production in each selected country.

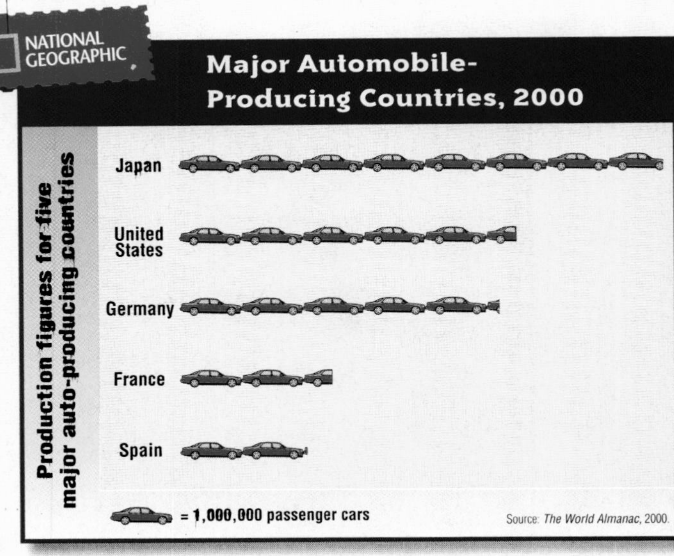

Climographs

A **climograph,** or climate graph, combines a line graph and a bar graph. It gives an overall picture of the climate—the long-term weather patterns—in a specific place. Because climographs include several kinds of information, you need to read them carefully. Note that the vertical bars on the climograph below represent average amounts of precipitation (rain, snow, or sleet) in each month of the year. These bars are measured against the axis on the right side of the graph. The line plotted above the bars represents changes in the average monthly temperature. You measure this line against the axis on the left side of the graph. The names of the months are shown in shortened form on the bottom axis of the graph.

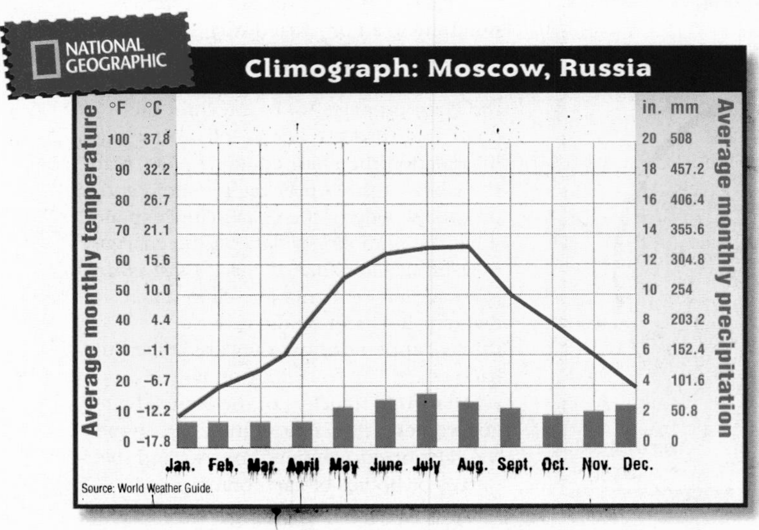

Critical Thinking Activity

Recognizing Bias Point out the source lines at the bottoms of the graphs and charts in this section. Make sure students understand what source lines signify. Then ask students what qualities make an organization a good source of information. Ask them what qualities make a bad source of information. Tell them that some organizations bias their information or delete information in order to support their point of view. Ask them what biases the following sources might have: an industry trade group, a foreign government, and an environmental group. **L3**

EE1 The World in Spatial Terms: Standard 1

NATIONAL GEOGRAPHIC

Africa: Elevation Profile

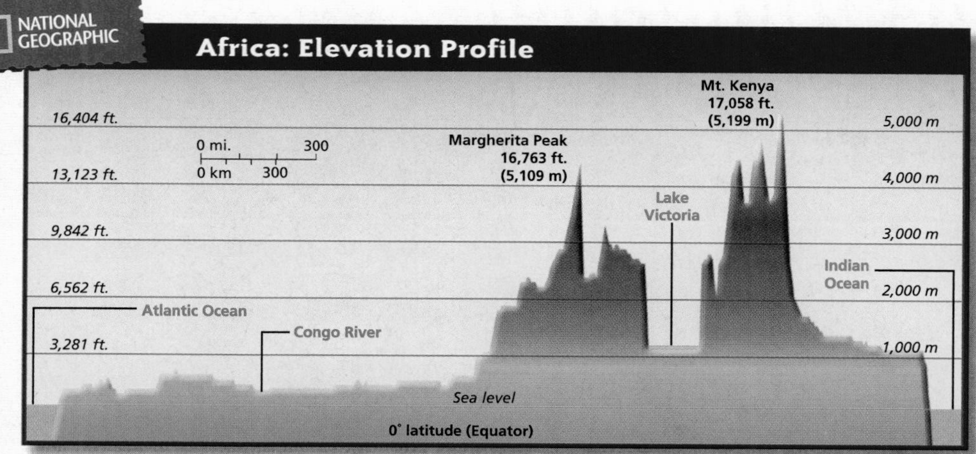

GEOGRAPHY HANDBOOK

Diagrams

Diagrams are drawings that show steps in a process, point out the parts of an object, or explain how something works. You can use a diagram to assemble a stereo. The diagram on page 562 shows how locks enable ships to move through a canal. An **elevation profile** is a type of diagram that can be helpful when comparing the elevations of an area. It shows an exaggerated profile, or side view, of the land as if it were sliced and you were viewing it from the side. The elevation profile of Africa above clearly shows low areas and mountains. The line of latitude at the bottom tells you where this profile was "sliced."

Section 2 Assessment

Defining Terms

1. **Define** axis, bar graph, line graph, circle graph, chart, pictograph, climograph, diagram, elevation profile.

Recalling Facts

2. How does a bar graph differ from a line graph?
3. What percentage does the whole circle in a circle graph always represent?
4. What two features does a climograph show?

Critical Thinking

5. **Synthesizing Information** Draw and label a flowchart showing the steps in some simple process—for example, making a sandwich or doing laundry.

Graphic Organizer

6. **Organizing Information** Create a chart like the one below. In the left column, list the types of graphs that are discussed in this section. In the right column, list what each type of graph is most useful for showing.

Types of Graphs	Useful for showing . . .

Applying Social Studies Skills

7. **Analyzing Graphs** Look at the bar graph on page 10. Which language is the most widely spoken? About how many people speak it?

Section 2 Assessment

1. The terms are defined in the Glossary.
2. A bar graph shows data for a given time. A line graph shows data and how it changes over time.
3. 100 percent
4. average monthly precipitation, temperature
5. Select a student's flowchart for making a sandwich and, if possible, try to follow it exactly. This often demonstrates how difficult it is to create a flowchart without making assumptions.
6. *bar graphs:* compare quantities; *line graphs:* show how quantities change over time; *circle graphs:* show how the whole of something is divided into its parts; *pictograph:* make comparisons; *climograph:* gives annual picture of precipitation and temperature
7. Mandarin Chinese; 885 million people

Assess

Assign the Section 2 Assessment as homework or as an in-class activity.

Reteach

Have students use a decision-making process to identify the best way to graphically display the following information: (1) the total number of students in the class and the number of boys and girls *(circle graph)*; (2) a record of the number of students who attend class each day for a month *(line graph)*; (3) a comparison of the number of students who are of certain heights *(bar graph)*; the number of books read by each student during the summer *(pictograph or bar graph).*

Enrich

Have students construct a chart of their grades in social studies class for one semester.

Close

Point out that statistical information can often be shown in more than one way. Ask students to convert the circle graph on page 11 into a bar graph.

GEOGRAPHIC DICTIONARY

Current Events Journal

Have students identify at least 10 ways to describe the school's relative location. Have them list these ways in their journals. Then have them use a map of the state or a city map that identifies latitude and longitude to find the school's absolute location.

Cultural Kaleidoscope

The Geographer's Language
The terms that geographers use to describe the earth come from many different languages. The term *tsunami* is a Japanese word meaning "overflowing wave." *Mesa* is a Spanish word meaning "table." *Fjord* is a Norwegian word meaning "long, narrow bay."

NATIONAL GEOGRAPHIC

GEOGRAPHIC DICTIONARY

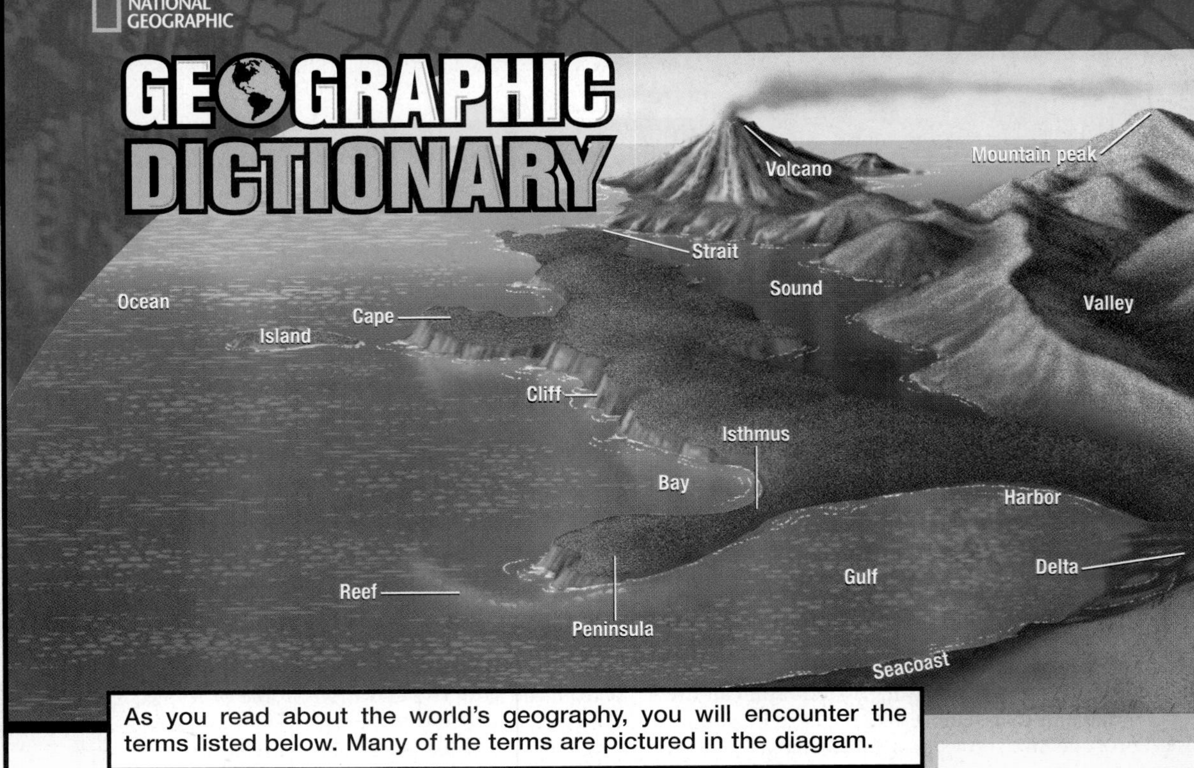

As you read about the world's geography, you will encounter the terms listed below. Many of the terms are pictured in the diagram.

absolute location exact location of a place on the earth described by global coordinates

basin area of land drained by a given river and its branches; area of land surrounded by lands of higher elevations

bay part of a large body of water that extends into a shoreline, generally smaller than a gulf

canyon deep and narrow valley with steep walls

cape point of land that extends into a river, lake, or ocean

channel wide strait or waterway between two landmasses that lie close to each other; deep part of a river or other waterway

cliff steep, high wall of rock, earth, or ice

continent one of the seven large landmasses on the earth

delta flat, low-lying land built up from soil carried downstream by a river and deposited at its mouth

divide stretch of high land that separates river systems

downstream direction in which a river or stream flows from its source to its mouth

elevation height of land above sea level

Equator imaginary line that runs around the earth halfway between the North and South Poles; used as the starting point to measure degrees of north and south latitude

glacier large, thick body of slowly moving ice

gulf part of a large body of water that extends into a shoreline, generally larger and more deeply indented than a bay

harbor a sheltered place along a shoreline where ships can anchor safely

highland elevated land area such as a hill, mountain, or plateau

hill elevated land with sloping sides and rounded summit; generally smaller than a mountain

island land area, smaller than a continent, completely surrounded by water

isthmus narrow stretch of land connecting two larger land areas

lake a sizable inland body of water

latitude distance north or south of the Equator, measured in degrees

longitude distance east or west of the Prime Meridian, measured in degrees

lowland land, usually level, at a low elevation

map drawing of the earth shown on a flat surface

meridian one of many lines on the global grid running from the North Pole to the South Pole; used to measure degrees of longitude

Cooperative Learning Activity

Map Quiz Organize the class into two teams. Provide one team with a map of their county and the other team with a map of their state. Assign each team the following task: Locate every major body of water in your assigned area. Record your findings, including (1) the name of each major body of water; (2) what type of water body it is—lake, river, bay, and so on; and (3) its relative and/or absolute location. When each team has completed its task, have them create a map quiz based on their work. The teams should then trade maps and challenge each other with their quizzes. **L2**

EE1 The World in Spatial Terms: Standard 3

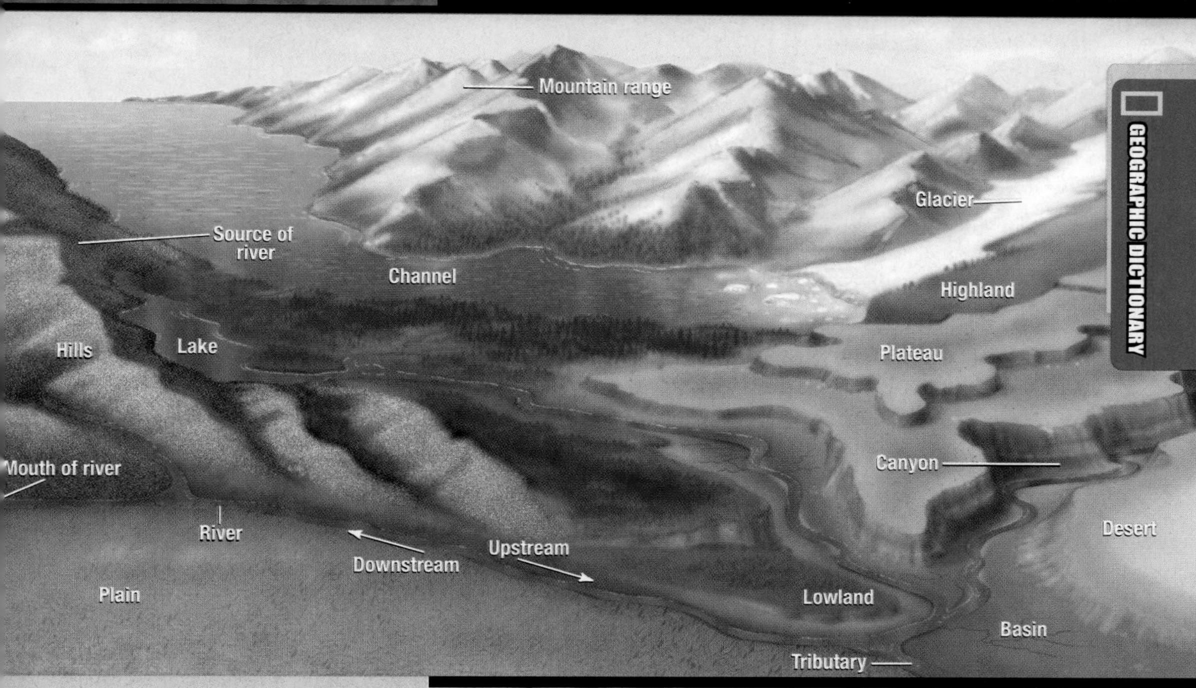

GEOGRAPHIC DICTIONARY

mesa broad, flat-topped landform with steep sides; smaller than a plateau

mountain land with steep sides that rises sharply (1,000 feet or more) from surrounding land; generally larger and more rugged than a hill

mountain peak pointed top of a mountain

mountain range a series of connected mountains

mouth (of a river) place where a stream or river flows into a larger body of water

ocean one of the four major bodies of salt water that surround the continents

ocean current stream of either cold or warm water that moves in a definite direction through an ocean

parallel one of many lines on the global grid that circles the earth north or south of the Equator; used to measure degrees of latitude

peninsula body of land jutting into a lake or ocean, surrounded on three sides by water

physical feature characteristic of a place occurring naturally, such as a landform, body of water, climate pattern, or resource

plain area of level land, usually at low elevation and often covered with grasses

plateau area of flat or rolling land at a high elevation, about 300–3,000 feet high

Prime Meridian line of the global grid running from the North Pole to the South Pole through Greenwich, England; starting point for measuring degrees of east and west longitude

relief changes in elevation over a given area of land

river large natural stream of water that runs through the land

sea large body of water completely or partly surrounded by land

seacoast land lying next to a sea or an ocean

sound broad inland body of water, often between a coastline and one or more islands off the coast

source (of a river) place where a river or stream begins, often in highlands

strait narrow stretch of water joining two larger bodies of water

tributary small river or stream that flows into a large river or stream; a branch of the river

upstream direction opposite the flow of a river; toward the source of a river or stream

valley area of low land between hills or mountains

volcano mountain created as liquid rock and ash erupt from inside the earth

Building Skills

Analyzing Maps Have students use the Reference Atlas on pages RA1–RA30 to find specific examples of all or most of the labels used on the diagram on pages 14–15.

Interdisciplinary Connections

Art Have students use clay to mold a model landscape with all or many of the features mentioned on pages 14–15. Suggest that students paint the model after the clay dries to make it look more realistic. **SS:** 6.3A

Critical Thinking Activity

Synthesizing Information Have students use atlases and other resources to plan a cross-country trip through the United States. Direct them to choose a definite starting point and destination and plot the route between the two points. Have them calculate the approximate distance of the journey, how long the journey might take, and to list points of interest along the way. Allow time for students to share their itineraries. **L2**
SS: 6.21A, 6.21F, 6.22D; **ELA:** 6.5B; **MATH:** 6.8A, 6.11A
EE1 The World in Spatial Terms: Standard 3

Reading Strategies

Helping students become active readers is only the first step in training students for success. The second step is helping students retain and use the knowledge they have gained through reading.

How Can You Help Students Retain What They Read? The better students understand what they read, the more they will remember—so teaching students to use the reading strategies on these pages aids retention. In addition, you can help students use formal study systems such as working with graphic organizers.

Graphic Organizers That Help Students Read and Comprehend Graphic organizers provide a visual format that requires students to restructure information as they analyze and interpret it. In addition, presenting information graphically helps students remember facts and concepts more easily, since they can "picture" it in their mind's eye. Students can productively use graphic organizers prior to reading to activate prior knowledge, during reading to process and analyze information, and after instruction to summarize and draw conclusions. Encourage students to use graphic organizers in the following ways (see *Teacher page 17*).

Be an Active Reader!

How Should I Read My Textbook? Reading your social studies book is different than other reading you might do. Your textbook has a great amount of information in it. It is an example of nonfiction writing—it describes real-life events, people, ideas, and places.

Here are some reading strategies that will help you become an active textbook reader. Choose the strategies that work best for you. If you have trouble as you read your textbook, look back at these strategies for help.

✓ Before You Read

Set a Purpose

- Why are you reading the textbook?
- How might you be able to use what you learn in your own life?

Preview

- Read the chapter title to find out what the topic will be.
- Read the subtitles to see what you will learn about the topic.
- Skim the photos, charts, graphs, or maps.
- Look for vocabulary words that are boldfaced. How are they defined?

Draw From Your Own Background

- What do you already know about the topic?
- How is the new information different from what you already know?

If You Don't Know What A Word Means...

- think about the setting, or *context,* in which the word is used.
- check if prefixes such as *un, non,* or *pre* can help you break down the word.
- look up the word's definition in a dictionary or glossary.

Good Study Habits for Successful Students

As you work with students on reading strategies, keep in mind and share the following tips for helping students retain what they read and prepare for all types of tests.

- **Keep Up:** Frequent review will help students build long-term memory and understanding.
- **Visualize and Recite Information:** Visual images are powerful ones. Students should try to associate a name, event, or idea with a picture. They can visualize the steps in a process or a sequence of events. Students should repeat important information aloud, whenever possible.

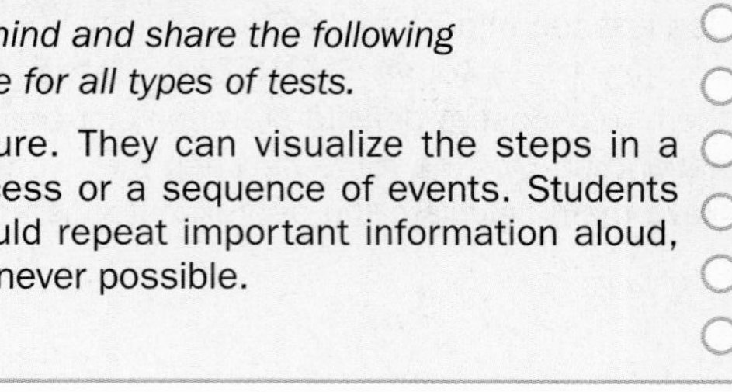

As You Read

Question
- What is the main idea?
- How well do the details support the main idea?
- How do the photos, charts, graphs, and maps support the main idea?

Connect
- Think about people, places, and events in your own life. Are there any similarities with those in your textbook?

Predict
- Predict events or outcomes by using clues and information that you already know.
- Change your predictions as you read and gather new information.

Visualize
- Use your imagination to picture the settings, actions, and people that are described.
- Create graphic organizers to help you see relationships found in the information.

Reading Do's

Do . . .
- ✔ establish a purpose for reading.
- ✔ think about how your own experiences relate to the topic.
- ✔ try different reading strategies.

Reading Don'ts

Don't . . .
- ⃠ ignore how the textbook is organized.
- ⃠ allow yourself to be easily distracted.
- ⃠ hurry to finish the material.

After You Read

Summarize
- Describe the main idea and how the details support it.
- Use your own words to explain what you have read.

Assess
- What was the main idea?
- Did the text clearly support the main idea?
- Did you learn anything new from the material?
- Can you use this new information in other school subjects or at home?

17

Good Study Habits for Successful Students

- **Use the Body:** Incorporate movement into study routines, if possible. Students can march in place or pace while reciting a sequence of events or saying a list of items.
- **Study Groups:** Encourage students to work with others to review for a test. They can discuss important topics and take turns asking and answering questions.
- **The Big Picture:** Essay tests often ask "big picture" questions. To help students get the big picture, have them identify main ideas in reading selections; develop summaries of important topics; and create webs, maps, or other graphic organizers to draw conclusions and analyze relationships.

Reading Strategies

- Use a web to show connections between related ideas, to describe the characteristics of a place or group, or to list examples.
- Use a tree to show a hierarchy of ideas or the structure of an organization or group.
- Use a flowchart to explain steps in a process. Use a time line or chain-of-events diagram to show a chronology or the order of events.
- Analyze causal relationships with a cause-and-effect chart or a problem-and-solution diagram.
- Use a Venn diagram to compare and contrast attributes or characteristics.

Use Writing to Help Students Understand What They Read

Writing provides a way for students to demonstrate what they have learned. More significantly, writing can facilitate greater understanding and richer learning by encouraging writers to transform knowledge into something new. Appropriate writing assignments can help students build social studies concepts in the following ways.

- Writing challenges students to analyze, evaluate, and interpret events.
- Writing invites students to synthesize information from a variety of sources, including students' own prior knowledge and experiences.
- Writing requires students to make connections, draw conclusions, and support their judgments with facts and details.
- The writing process promotes a systematic approach to content analysis by teaching students to focus their thoughts, expand and refine their ideas, and express their viewpoints precisely.

Unit 1 Planning Guide

SUGGESTED PACING CHART

Unit 1 (1 day)	Chapter 1 (5 days)	Chapter 2 (5 days)	Unit 1 (2 days)
Day 1 Introduction	**Day 1** Chapter 1 Intro, Section 1	**Day 1** Chapter 2 Intro, Section 1	**Day 1** Wrap-Up/Projects
	Day 2 Section 2	**Day 2** Section 2	**Day 2** Unit 1 Assessment
	Day 3 Section 3	**Day 3** Section 3	
	Day 4 Chapter 1 Review	**Day 4** Chapter 2 Review	
	Day 5 Chapter 1 Assessment	**Day 5** Chapter 2 Assessment	

For a complete course pacing guide and Teacher Classroom Resources, see:

Interactive Lesson Planner

Use the following tools to easily assess student learning in a variety of ways:

- **Performance Assessment Activities and Rubrics**
- **Section Quizzes**
- **Chapter Tests and Unit Pretests and Posttests**
- **Interactive Tutor Self-Assessment CD-ROM**
- **ExamView® Pro 3.0 Testmaker CD-ROM**
- **MindJogger Videoquiz**
- owt.glencoe.com
- **Standardized Test Practice Workbook**

Note: The following materials may be used when teaching Unit 1.
Chapter level support materials can be found on the chapter resource pages.

TEACHING TRANSPARENCIES

Political Map Transparency 1

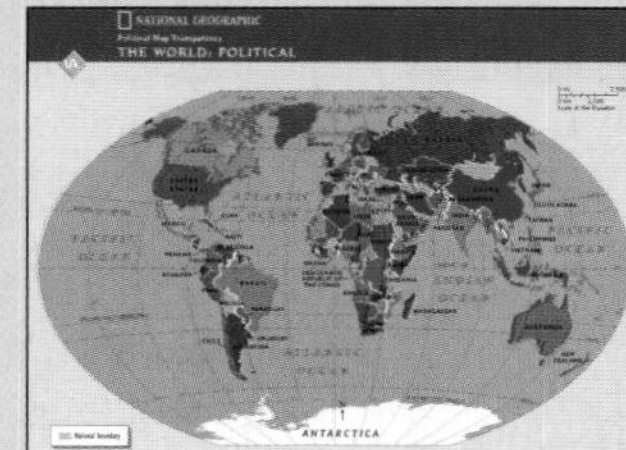

Unit 1 Map Overlay Transparencies

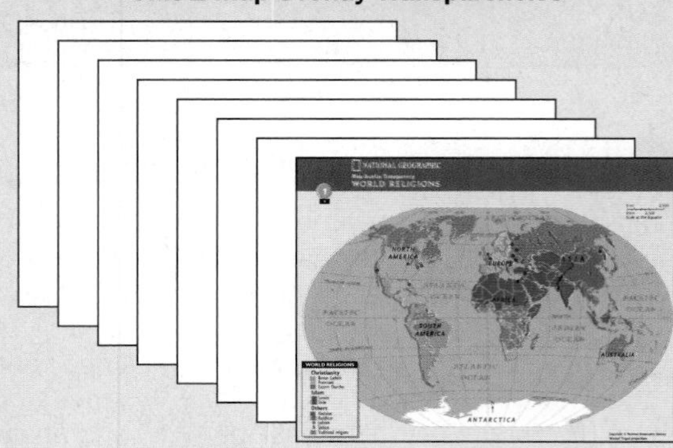

Unit 1 Resources

INTERDISCIPLINARY CONNECTIONS

World Literature Reading 1

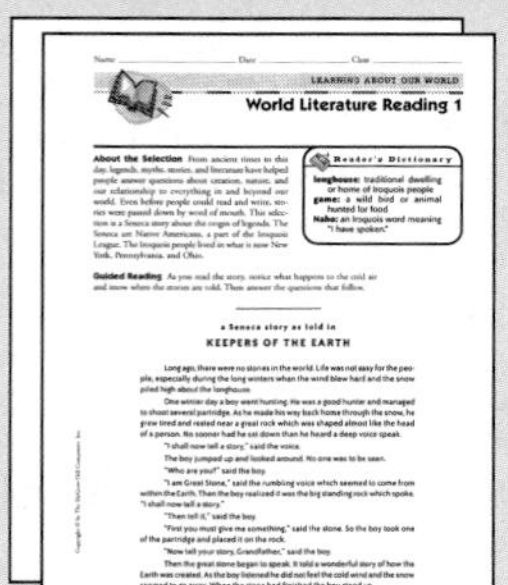

Economics and Geography Activity 1

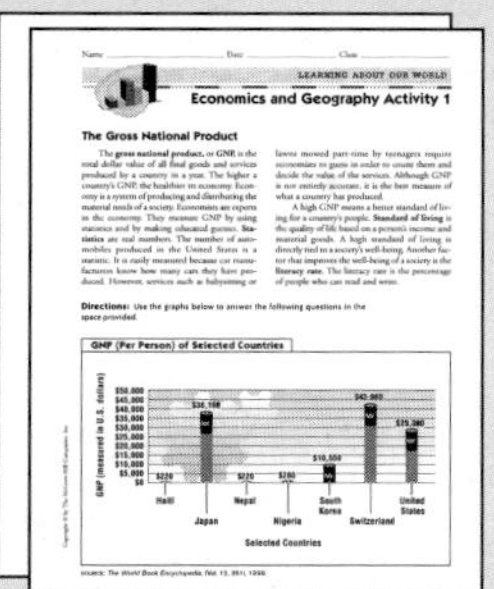

History and Geography Activity 1

MAP AND GEOGRAPHY SKILLS

Building Geography Skills for Life

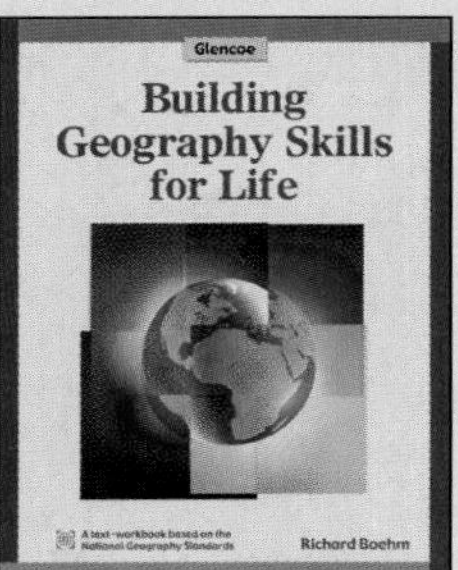

NGS Focus on Geography Literacy

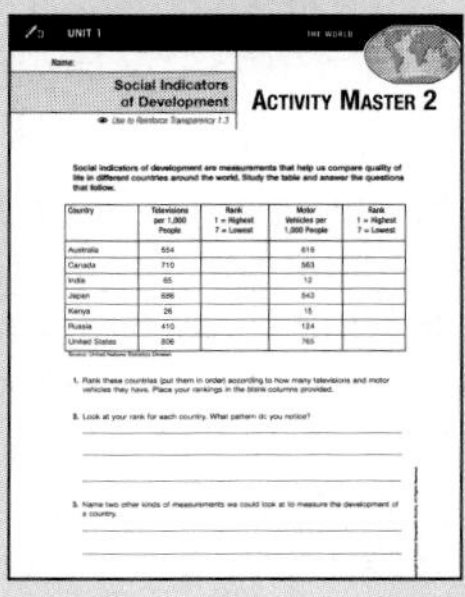

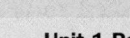

NATIONAL GEOGRAPHIC MapMachine

Find the latest coverage of geography in the news, atlas updates, cartographic activities with interactive maps, an online map store, and links at www.nationalgeographic.com/maps

APPLICATION AND HANDS-ON

Citizenship Activity 1

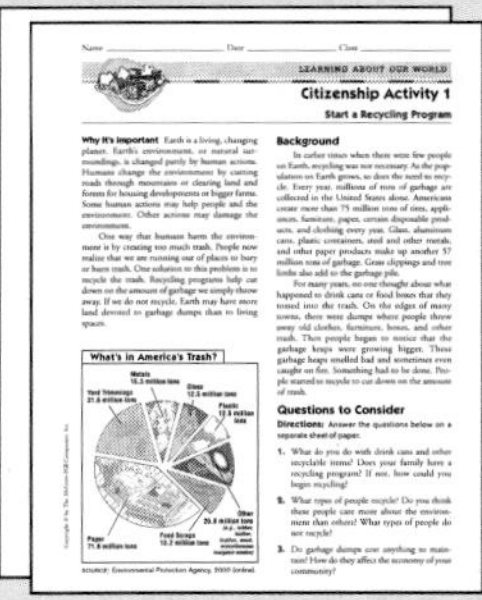

Foods Around the World 1

ENRICHMENT AND EXTENSION

Environmental Case Study 1

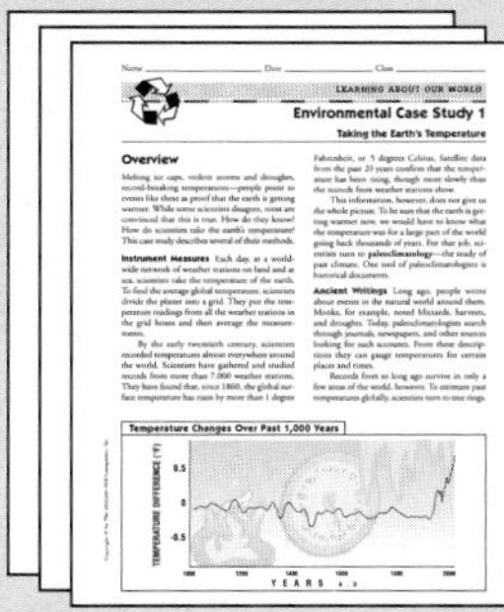

World Music: A Cultural Legacy

ASSESSMENT AND EVALUATION

Unit 1 Pretests

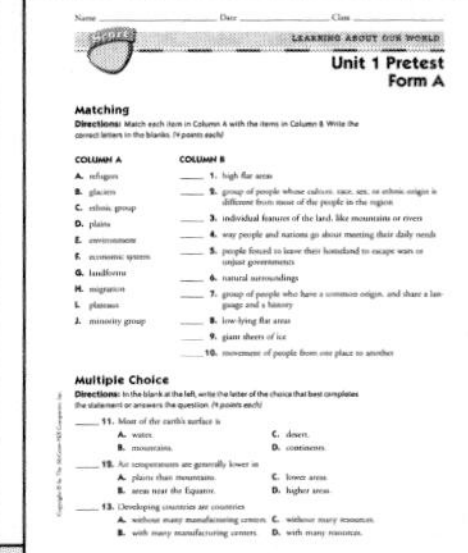

Unit 1 Posttests

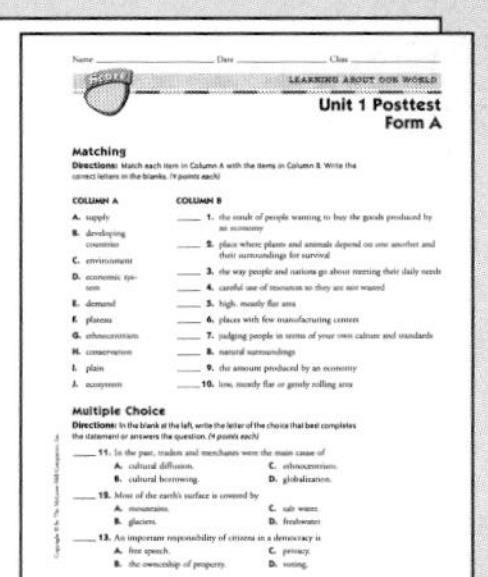

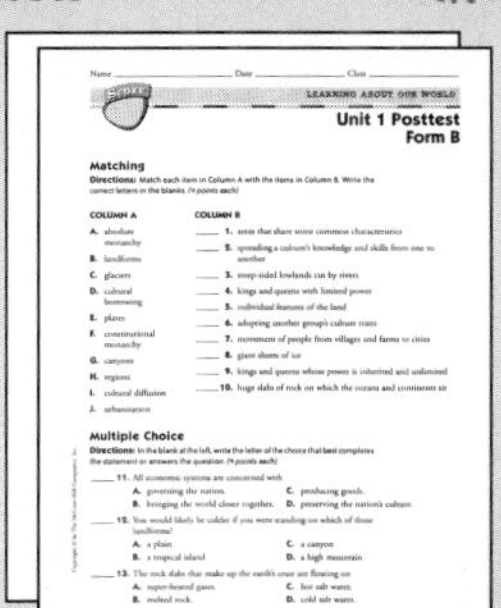

Additional Unit 1 Resources

- owt.glencoe.com
  Our World Today: People, Places, and Issues
  Visit the Glencoe *Our World Today: People, Places, and Issues* Web site for overviews, activities, assessments, and updated charts and graphs.
- socialstudies.glencoe.com
  Glencoe Social Studies
  Visit the Glencoe Web site for social studies activities, updates, and links to other sites.
- www.teachingtoday.glencoe.com
  Glencoe Teaching Today
  This Web site features daily teaching tips, free PDF downloads, annotated Web resources, educational news, and more.
- www.nationalgeographic.com
  NGS ONLINE Visit the National Geographic Society Web site for the latest coverage of geography in the news, atlas updates, activities, links, interactive features, and archives.
- **Glencoe's Guide to Using the Internet**
  Provides an introduction to many of the current technologies on the Internet. Professional resources and teaching strategies included.

Our Web sites provide additional resources. All essential content is covered in the Student Edition.

Bibliography

Literature for the Student

- **Glencoe Middle School World Literature Library**
  Bridge to Terabithia, by Katherine Paterson. Terabithia captures the enchantment of expanding one's intellect.
  A Wrinkle in Time, by Madeleine L'Engle. Two teens travel through the cosmos, one planet at a time, to find their physicist father, and themselves.
- ***Scholastic Kid's Almanac for the 21st Century.*** New York: Scholastic, 1999.
- ***World Holidays,*** by Heather Moehn. NY: Franklin Watts, 2000.

Readings for the Teacher

- ***Encyclopedia of Biomes,*** 3 vols., by Marlene Weigel, ed. Farmington Hills, Mich.: U*X*L, 1999.
- ***The Encyclopedia of World Religions,*** by Robert S. Ellwood and Gregory D. Alles, eds. New York: Facts On File, 1998.

Multimedia Links

- **Glencoe Social Studies Primary Source Document Library**
  The Iceman by David Roberts
  The Poor and Suffering by Mother Teresa
  Universal Declaration of Human Rights by the United Nations
- ***Mapmakers Toolkit.*** Watertown, Mass.: Tom Snyder Productions. Mac/Windows CD-ROM.
- ***Odyssey of Discovery: Earth Systems.*** Portland, Ore.: Pierian Spring. Mac/Windows CD-ROM.

Refer to owt.glencoe.com for additional literature titles and study guides related to this region.

Additional Glencoe Teacher Support

- **Teaching Strategies for the Geography Classroom**
- **Reproducible Lesson Plans**
- **Outline Map Resource Book**
- **Reading in the Content Area**

Service Learning Project

Keeping the Earth Clean

In many communities across the country, local governments participate in "adopt a highway" programs, in which organizations take responsibility for keeping one stretch of a local roadway clean of litter. Have the class investigate what such a program entails and how to arrange to participate in it. If possible, have the class adopt a part of a local roadway. If that is not possible, have the students work in the community to convince others to do so.

Content Background Notes

Use this additional information as lecture notes or discussion prompts throughout the study of Unit 1.

Chapter 1 Our Social World (pp. 20–49)

Global Culture The signs of the globalization of world culture are all around us. Many Chinese now earn extra money by selling products through home party retailing—and they sell the same American makeup, cleaning, and plastic storage products that made product demonstrations a staple of suburban American life. Meanwhile, an American has launched an Internet version of the ancient Chinese game of mah-jongg, which he plays online with fellow enthusiasts in Germany and Wales. In India, diners in one restaurant enjoy Lebanese food while listening to Filipino music and looking at posters of the Grand Ole Opry.

Some critics decry the role that American-based corporations play in this globalization. They say that countries around the world are losing their uniqueness. But multinationals cannot impose American culture everywhere. One makeup company changed the colors it sold in India to adapt to the skin of Indian women, and a major fast-food chain in that country dropped beef from its burgers and served mutton instead.

Languages Anthropologists estimate that about 10,000 languages have been spoken by humans throughout history. Of that number, 6,000 are still in use today. Many are about to die out, because parents in some traditional cultures no longer teach their language to children. As many as 3,000 languages may disappear in the next hundred years.

Chapter 2 Earth Patterns (pp. 50–69)

Biodiversity Scientists argue over exactly how many species of plants and animals actually live on the earth. One suggested as many as 30 million different species. Others believe that this figure is far too high. Whatever the actual total, it is clear that to date we have identified only a fraction of them all—only about 1.75 million.

One reason for such concern over the destruction of the rain forest is that this biological region is rich in living things. Studies show that a hectare (about 2.5 acres) of Panama's rain forest yields as many as 60,000 insect species alone. Yet rain forests—and other environments—yield valuable resources for humans:

- A plant from Madagascar contains a chemical used to treat cancer.
- A microorganism in the hot springs of Yellowstone National Park furnishes a chemical used in easily creating DNA in the laboratory.
- African clawed frogs secrete a powerful chemical that kills bacteria, a chemical that may become an important medicine as antibiotics lose their effectiveness.
- A chemical in the liver of the dogfish shark contains a potential cancer-fighting compound.

Protecting the Environment One obstacle to efforts to save the rain forest is the need of indigenous populations to feed their growing populations. A World Wildlife Fund effort in Madagascar is hoping to overcome this problem. The first step is to revive local people's traditions in viewing the land as sacred. Then the planners hope to develop the area for ecotourism so that local peoples can earn a living while still maintaining the land in its wild state.

The Great Rift Valley Africa's Great Rift Valley is a 3,500-mile (5,633-km) long gash in the earth stretching from Mozambique to the Red Sea. The valley helps demonstrate the theory of plate tectonics. This gash is formed by the separation of the Somali and African Plates. As the plates move apart, hot magma rises to the surface, creating a thin new layer of the earth. The magma sometimes breaks to the surface in volcanoes such as the Virunga Mountains of Uganda. The upwelling of land also builds the highlands of Kenya and Ethiopia.

The Great Rift Valley shows evidence of climate change. Scientists have found the 5,000- to-10,000-year-old shells of freshwater snails in a dry region of Djibouti. Their presence establishes that the climate of East Africa was much wetter then than it is now.

00:00 Out of Time?

If time does not permit teaching each chapter in this unit, you may use the **Reading Essentials and Study Guide** for each chapter.

Unit Overview

The two chapters of this unit introduce students to a basic understanding of how people and physical forces shape our world. The topics include:

- the role of technology in today's world
- the factors that make up the world's cultures
- the growth and movement of the world's populations
- the basic government and economic systems
- the physical geography of the earth
- how people use resources and affect the environment

As an introduction to this region, you may want to engage students by studying an important contemporary issue in this region of the world. The **TIME REPORTS: FOCUS ON WORLD ISSUES** for this region is found on pages 39–45. The feature examines how globalization is bringing different cultures together.

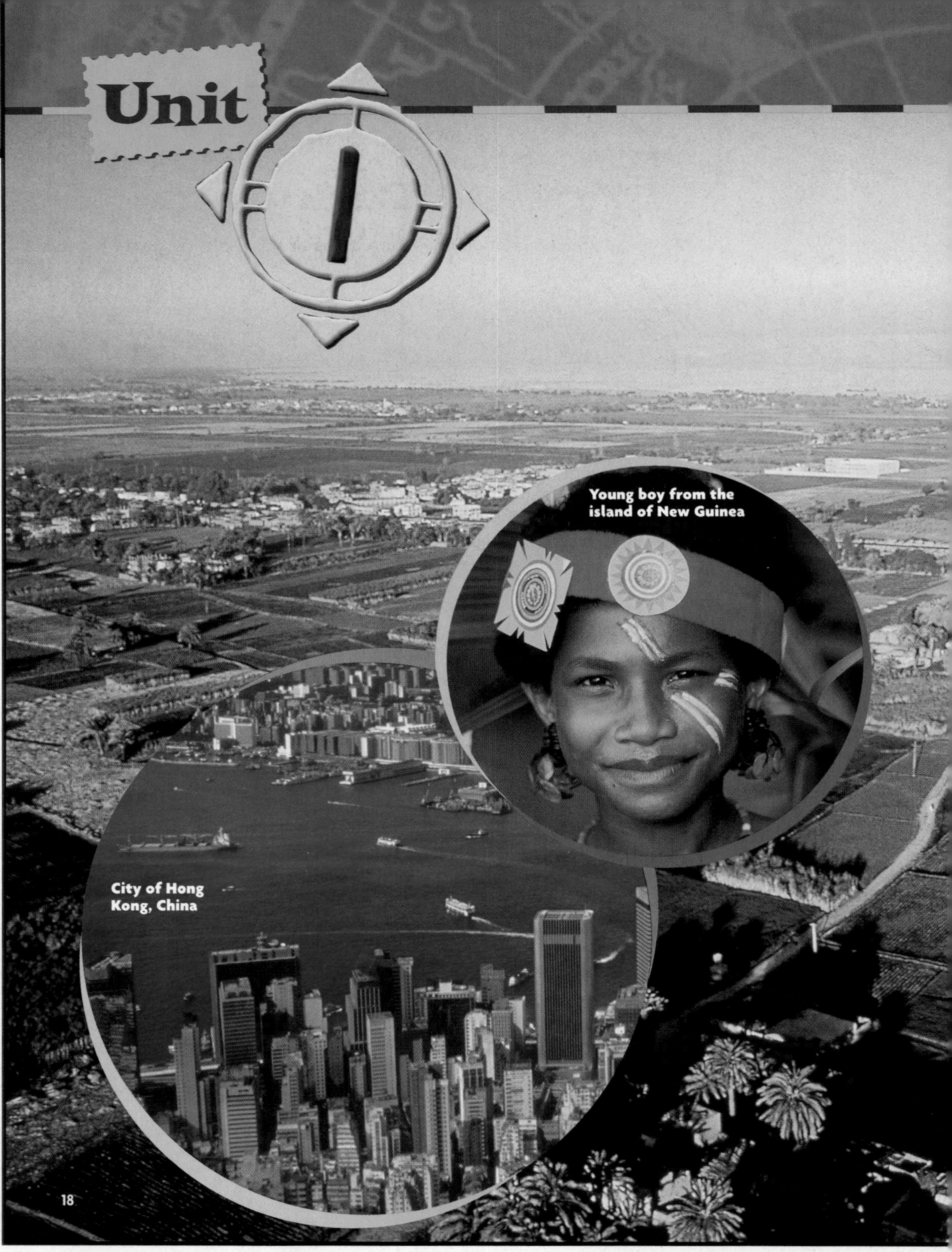

Unit 1

Young boy from the island of New Guinea

City of Hong Kong, China

18

Using the Illustration

Although modern technology and transportation have caused cultures to blend together, there is still a lot of diversity in the world. Hong Kong has one of the highest populations in the world: over 6 million people in an area of 415 square miles (1,076 sq. km). It's an important center of commerce, trade, and shipping. About 2,000 miles away is New Guinea, with a population of about 5 million people in an area of about 320,000 square miles (828,800 sq. km). There is very little industry, and the people there generally produce enough only for their own needs, with few products for export. Ask students to research these two places and write a summary describing and measuring the level of economic development of each place, using such indicators as individual purchasing power, life expectancy, and literacy. **L2**

NATIONAL GEOGRAPHIC

Learning About Our World

You are about to journey to dense rain forests, bleak deserts, bustling cities and marketplaces, and remote villages. You are entering the many worlds of culture. In your study of the earth you will learn about different places and different peoples. Imagine that you could visit any place in the world. Where would you want to go? What would you want to see?

▲ Hot air balloon floating over cultivated fields, Egypt

NGS ONLINE
www.nationalgeographic.com/education

19

These materials are available from Glencoe.

Software

ZipZapMap! World

Transparencies

PicturePack Transparencies

CD-ROM

Picture Atlas of the World, Second Edition

Current Events Journal

Tell students to list in their journals all the different landforms, climates, and types of vegetation they can name. Then have them write a paragraph explaining what meaning all this diversity has for them.

NGS ONLINE

www.nationalgeographic.com/education

This online resource provides lesson plans, atlas updates, cartographic activities with interactive maps, an online map store, and geography links.

Unit Launch Activity

Why Study Other Cultures? Point out that people around the world have many different ways of life—different foods, different kinds of clothing, different housing. Have students offer examples of some of these differences, such as the igloos that the Inuit use for shelter in the cold Arctic or the thatch-built houses on stilts that some Pacific Islanders use. **Ask:** **Why do you think people follow different ways of life around the world?** Have students write the question in their notebooks and refer to it as they study the unit. After completing the unit, ask for volunteers to suggest answers to the question and then discuss each suggestion.

EE4 Human Systems: Standard 10

Chapter 1 Resources

Note: The following materials may be used when teaching Chapter 1.
Section level support materials are shown at point of use in the margins of the Teacher Wraparound Edition.

Timesaving Tools

TeacherWorks™ All-In-One Planner and Resource Center

- **Interactive Teacher Edition** See the **Interactive Teacher Edition** CD-ROM to electronically integrate your Teacher Wraparound Edition and blackline masters.
- **Interactive Lesson Planner** Organize your week, month, semester, or year with all the lesson helps you need. The **Interactive Lesson Planner** CD-ROM contains all Chapter 1 resources.

Use Glencoe's **Presentation Plus!** multimedia teacher tool to easily present dynamic lessons that visually excite your students. Using Microsoft PowerPoint® you can customize the presentations to create your own personalized lessons.

TEACHING TRANSPARENCIES

Graphic Organizer Transparency and Student Activity 1

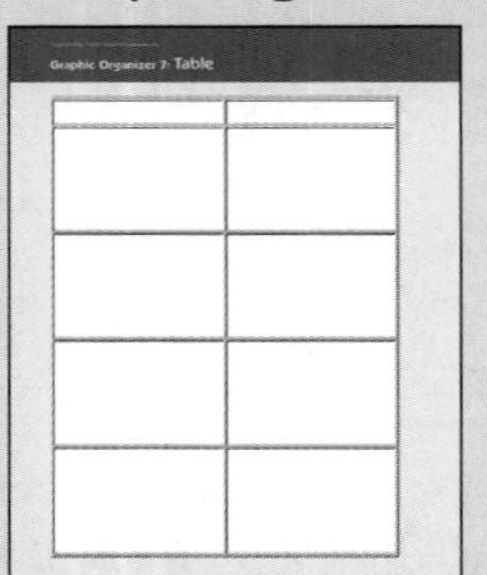

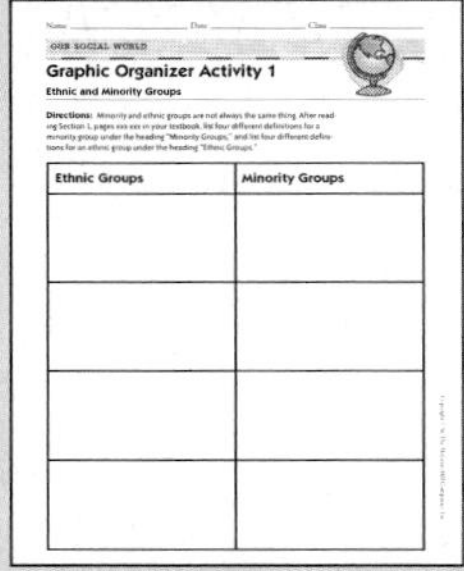

FOLDABLES™ Study Organizer

Foldables are three-dimensional, interactive graphic organizers that help students practice basic writing skills, review key vocabulary terms, and identify main ideas. Every chapter contains a Foldable activity, with additional chapter activities found in the ***Reading and Study Skills Foldables*** booklet.

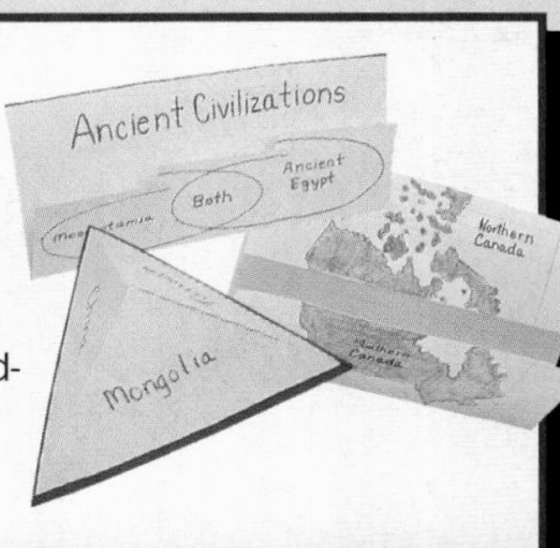

ENRICHMENT AND EXTENSION

Enrichment Activity 1

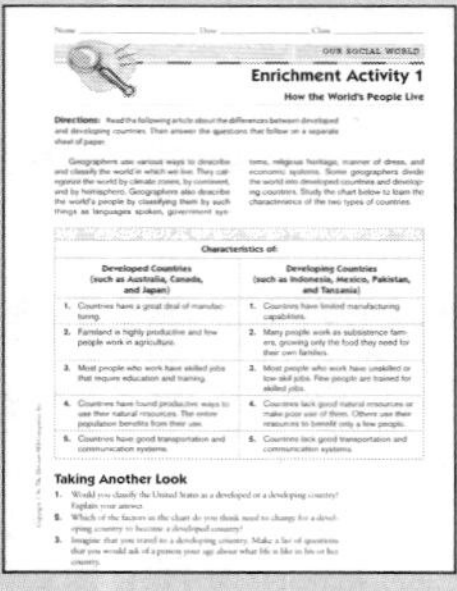

Cooperative Learning Activity 1

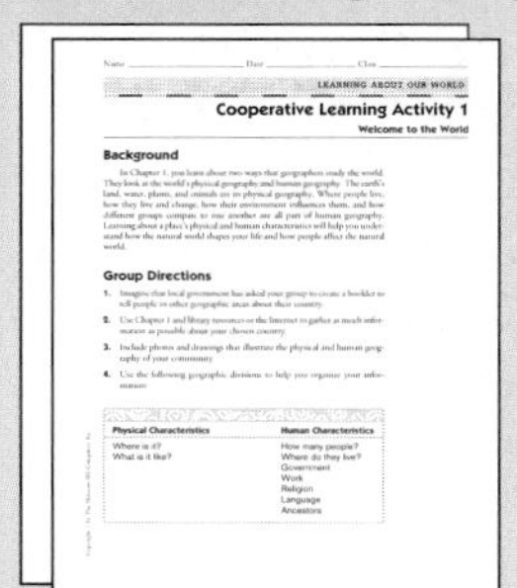

MAP AND GEOGRAPHY SKILLS

Chapter Map Activity 1

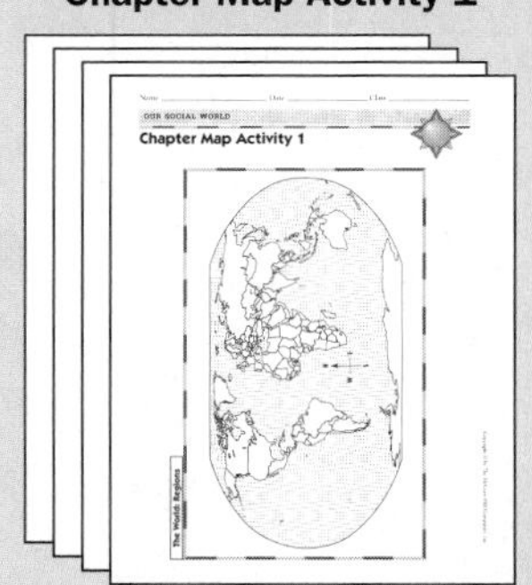

GeoLab Activity 1

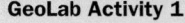

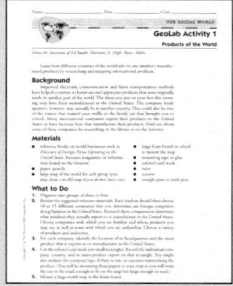

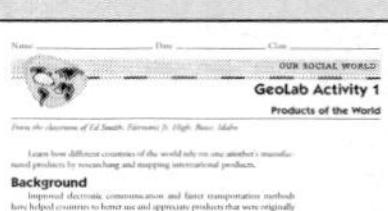

STANDARDIZED ASSESSMENT SKILLS

GLENCOE'S ASSESSMENT ADVANTAGE

Critical Thinking Skills Activity 1

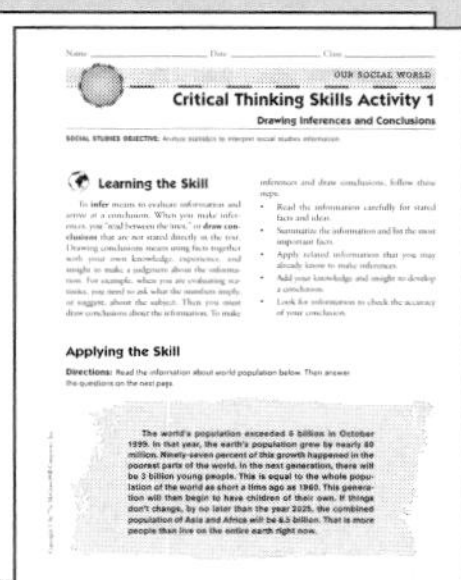

Map and Graph Skills Activity 1

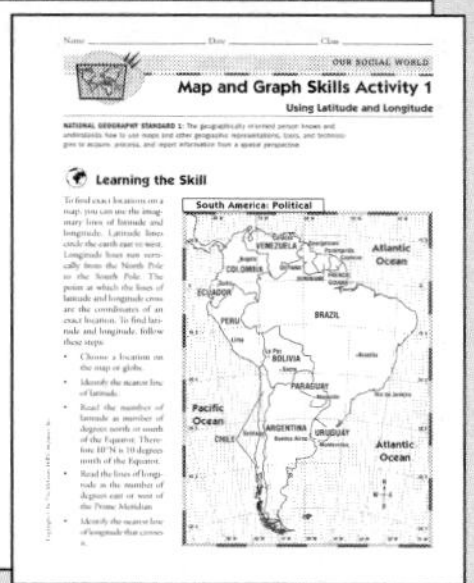

Reading and Writing Skills Activity 1

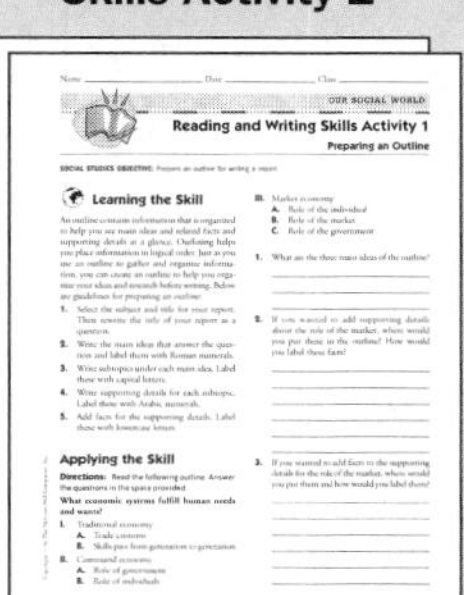

Standardized Test Practice Workbook Activity 1

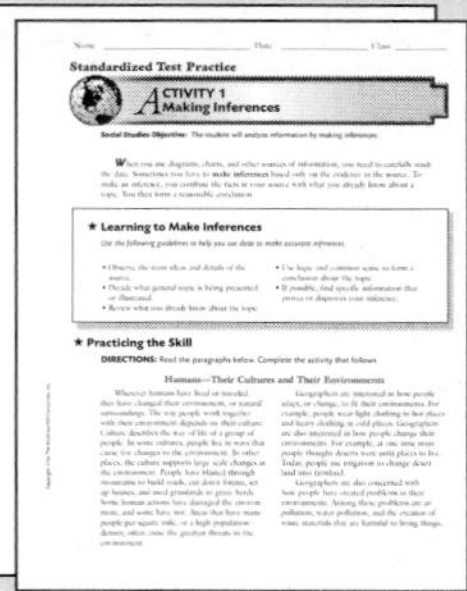

REVIEW AND REINFORCEMENT

Chapter Skills Activity 1

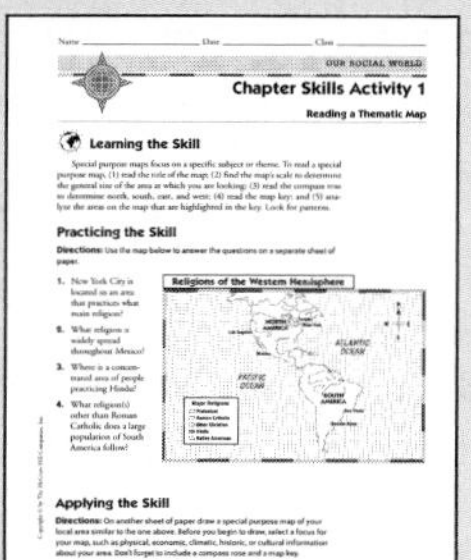

Take-Home Review Activity 1

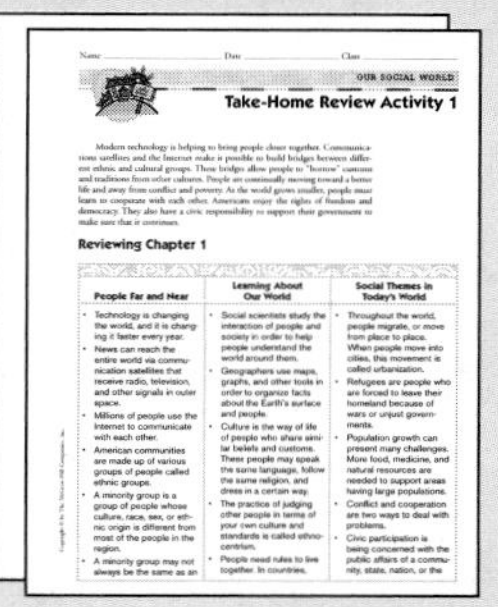

Reteaching Activity 1

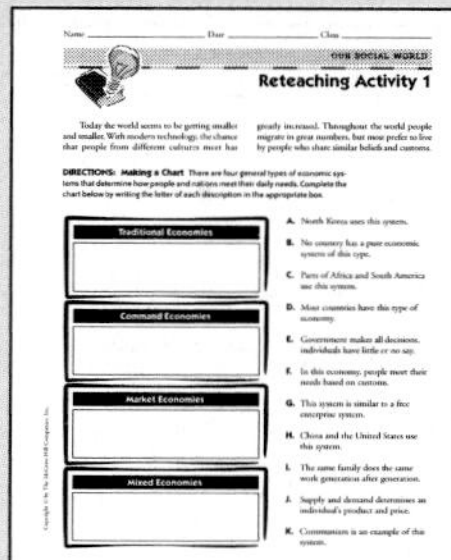

Vocabulary Activity 1

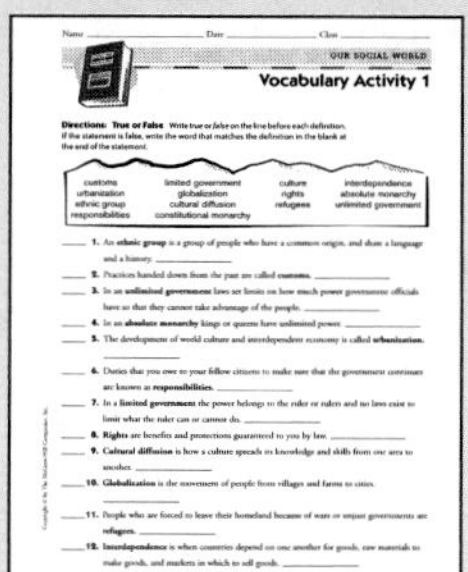

Workbook Activity 1

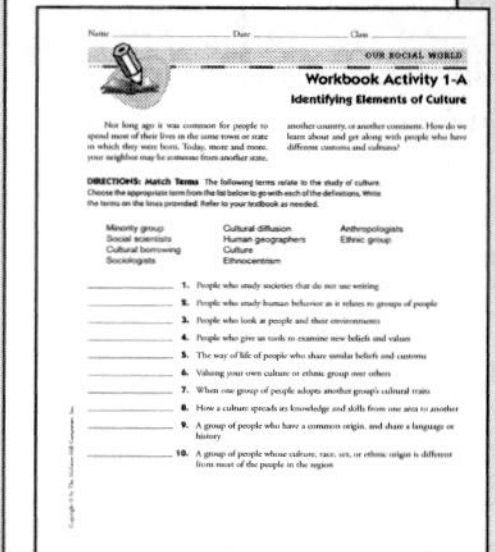

ASSESSMENT

Glencoe's Assessment Advantage

Chapter 1 Test, Form A

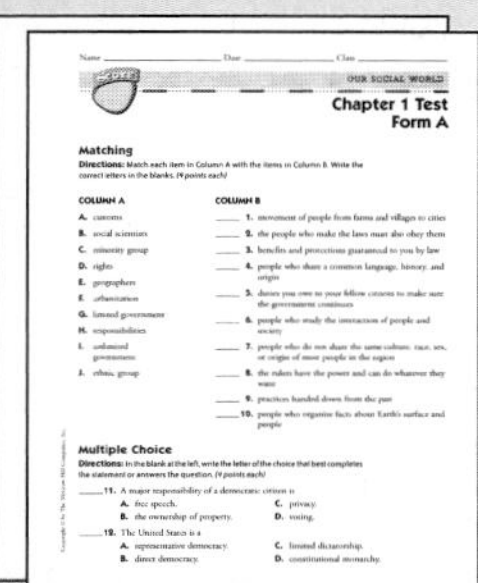

Chapter 1 Test, Form B

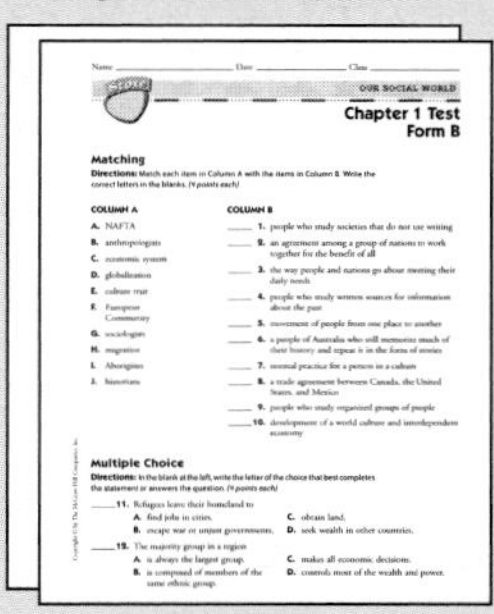

Performance Assessment Activity 1

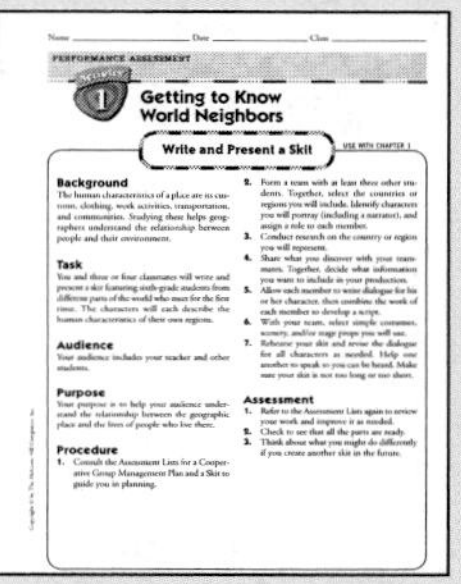

ExamView® Pro 3.0 Testmaker CD-ROM

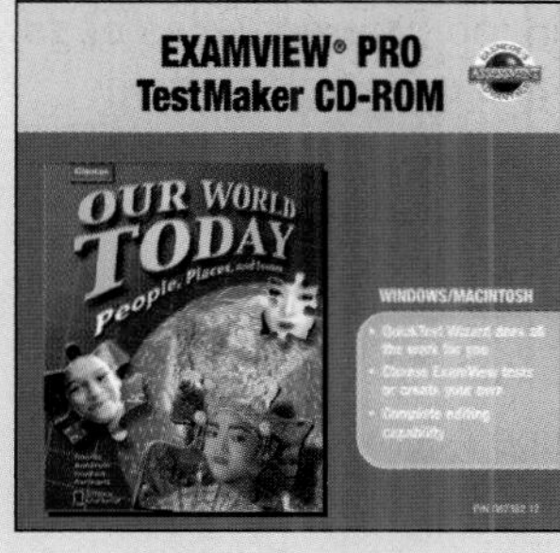

MULTIMEDIA

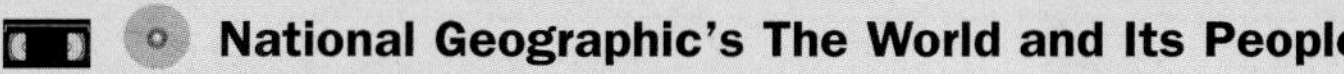

- National Geographic's The World and Its People

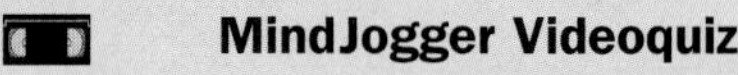

- MindJogger Videoquiz
- Vocabulary PuzzleMaker Software
- Interactive Tutor Self-Assessment CD-ROM
- ExamView® Pro 3.0 Testmaker CD-ROM
- Interactive Lesson Planner CD-ROM
- Interactive Teacher Edition CD-ROM
- Skillbuilder Interactive Workbook CD-ROM, Level 1
- Presentation Plus! CD-ROM
- Audio Program

SPANISH RESOURCES

The following Spanish language materials are available in the Spanish Resources binder:

- **Spanish Chapter Summaries**
- **Spanish Vocabulary Activities**
- **Spanish Guided Reading Activities**
- **Spanish Quizzes and Tests**
- **Spanish Take-Home Review Activities**
- **Spanish Reteaching Activities**

Meeting National Standards

Geography for Life

All of the 18 standards are demonstrated in Unit 1. The following ones are highlighted in Chapter 1:

Section 1 EE1 The World in Spatial Terms: Standard 3

EE4 Human Systems: Standards 9, 10, 11, 12

Section 2 EE5 Environment and Society: Standards 14, 16

EE6 The Uses of Geography: Standards 17, 18

Section 3 EE1 The World in Spatial Terms: Standards 1, 2, 3

EE3 Physical Systems: Standards 7, 8

EE4 Human Systems: Standard 13

For a complete listing of National Geography Standards and entire text correlation, see pages T22–T29.

Chapter 1 Planning Guide

SECTION RESOURCES

Daily Objectives	Reproducible Resources	Multimedia Resources
Section 1 **People Far and Near** **Suggested Pacing = 1 day** **1.** Describe how technology has changed the world. **2.** Distinguish between ethnic groups, majority and minority groups.	Reproducible Lesson Plan 1-1 Daily Lecture and Discussion Notes 1-1 Guided Reading Activity 1-1 Reading Essentials and Study Guide 1-1 Section Quiz 1-1*	Daily Focus Skills Transparency 1-1 Vocabulary PuzzleMaker Software Interactive Tutor Self-Assessment CD-ROM ExamView® Pro 3.0 Testmaker CD-ROM Presentation Plus! CD-ROM
Section 2 **Understanding Culture** **Suggested Pacing = 1 day** **1.** Define what *culture* means. **2.** Describe how and why cultures change. **3.** Explain the different types of government and economic systems.	Reproducible Lesson Plan 1-2 Daily Lecture and Discussion Notes 1-2 Guided Reading Activity 1-2 Reading Essentials and Study Guide 1-2 Section Quiz 1-2*	Daily Focus Skills Transparency 1-2 Vocabulary PuzzleMaker Software Interactive Tutor Self-Assessment CD-ROM ExamView® Pro 3.0 Testmaker CD-ROM Presentation Plus! CD-ROM
Section 3 **Patterns in Today's World** **Suggested Pacing = 1 day** **1.** Describe migration patterns. **2.** Explain the effects of population growth. **3.** Discuss globalization.	Reproducible Lesson Plan 1-3 Daily Lecture and Discussion Notes 1-3 Guided Reading Activity 1-3 Reading Essentials and Study Guide 1-3 Section Quiz 1-3*	Daily Focus Skills Transparency 1-3 Vocabulary PuzzleMaker Software Interactive Tutor Self-Assessment CD-ROM ExamView® Pro 3.0 Testmaker CD-ROM Presentation Plus! CD-ROM

00:00 **Out of Time?** Assign the **Reading Essentials and Study Guide** for this chapter.

*Also available in Spanish

KEY TO ABILITY LEVELS

Teaching strategies have been coded for varying learning styles and abilities.

- L1 **BASIC** activities for all students
- L2 **AVERAGE** activities for average to above-average students
- L3 **CHALLENGING** activities for above-average students
- ELL **ENGLISH LANGUAGE LEARNER** activities

Blackline Master
Software
CD-ROM
Audiocassette
Transparency
Videocassette
Block Scheduling
DVD

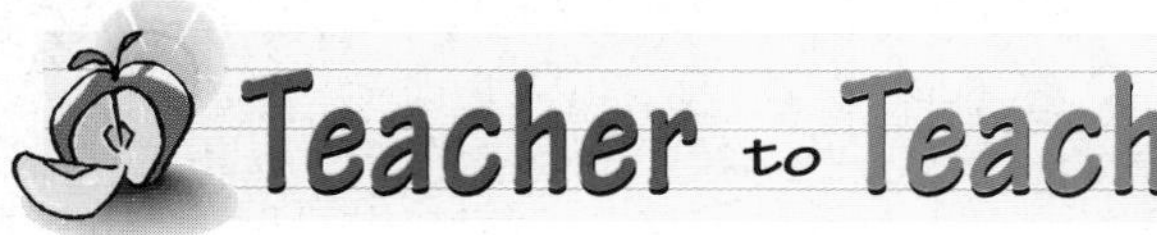

Learning Latitude and Longitude

Beverly A. Blamer
Fremont Middle School
Fremont, Michigan

This activity can be used to help students learn about latitude and longitude and how the grid system shows exact locations. Before class, make large signs for every tenth parallel north and south of the Equator and every fifteenth meridian east and west of the Prime Meridian. Also make signs for the Equator, Arctic and Antarctic Circles, Tropics of Cancer and Capricorn, Prime Meridian, and International Date Line. Take your students and signs to the gymnasium. Have students help you arrange and tape the signs around the room to set up a grid system. Then call out commands such as "Everybody stand on 40°N. Raise your hand if you are also standing at 50°E. You are standing on [name of city]." Repeat with new coordinates until students understand the grid system.

OUR WORLD TODAY Online

Use our Web site for additional resources. All essential content is covered in the Student Edition.

You and your students can visit owt.glencoe.com, the Web site companion to *Our World Today*. This innovative integration of electronic and print media offers your students a wealth of opportunities. The student text directs students to the Web site for the following options:

- Chapter Overviews
- Student Web Activities
- Self-Check Quizzes
- Textbook Updates

Answers are provided for you in the Web Activity Lesson Plan. Additional Web resources and Interactive Tutor puzzles are also available.

TEACHER'S CORNER

Index to National Geographic Magazine:

The following articles may be used for research relating to this chapter:

- "John Glenn: Man With a Mission," by William R. Newcott, June 1999.
- *Physical World,* a National Geographic Special Edition, May 1998.
- "Landsat's Views of a Changing Earth," by Boris Weintraub, November 1997.

National Geographic Society Products Available From Glencoe:

To order the following products for use with this chapter, contact your local Glencoe sales representative or call Glencoe at 1-800-334-7344:

- *STV: World Geography* (Videodisc)
- *STV: Solar System* (Videodisc)
- *PictureShow: Earth's Endangered Environments* (CD-ROM)
- *PictureShow: Dynamic Earth* (CD-ROM)
- *PictureShow: Geology* (CD-ROM)
- *PicturePack: Physical Geography of the World* (Transparencies)

Additional National Geographic Society Products:

To order the following products for use with this chapter, call National Geographic Society at 1-800-368-2728:

- *Atmosphere: On the Air* (Video)
- *Physical Geography of North America Series* (6 Videos)
- *Tool Kit for Teaching Geography* (Geography Lesson Kit)
- *Voices: Poetry and Art From Around the World* (Book)
- *Complete National Geographic: 111 years of National Geographic Magazine* (CD-ROM)
- *MapPack: Continents Series* (Transparencies)
- *MapPack: U.S.A. Regions Series* (Transparencies)
- *PicturePack: Geology* (Transparencies)
- *Latitude and Longitude* (Video)
- *Physical Geography of the Continents Series* (6 Videos)

NGS ONLINE

Access National Geographic's Web site for current events, activities, links, interactive features, and archives.
www.nationalgeographic.com

Introducing
Chapter 1

Our World Today online

Introduce students to chapter content and key terms by having them access Chapter Overview 1 at owt.glencoe.com

Chapter Objectives

1. Describe the impact of technology on world affairs.
2. Explain what makes up a people's culture.
3. Identify the different types of governments and economies.
4. Discuss issues related to human population.

GLENCOE TECHNOLOGY

NATIONAL GEOGRAPHIC

The World and Its People Video Program

Chapter 3 The World's People

The following segments enhance the study of this chapter:

- **The Human Race**
- **Turkana Basin**

Available in DVD and VHS.

MindJogger Videoquiz

Use MindJogger to preview the Chapter 1 content.

Available in VHS.

Chapter 1

Our Social World

The World and Its People NATIONAL GEOGRAPHIC

To learn more about the world's culture regions, view ***The World and Its People*** **Chapter 3** video.

Our World Today online

Chapter Overview Visit the ***Our World Today: People, Places, and Issues*** Web site at owt.glencoe.com and click on **Chapter 1—Chapter Overviews** to preview information about the world's people.

20

Two-Minute Lesson Launcher

Ask students if they have ever visited another country or another part of their country. **Ask:** **How did this other place compare to your home? Were houses and clothing different? Did people speak a different language or eat different foods? How would you compare this other place—and the people who lived in it—to your community? What aspects of culture do you think link different cultures or societies? What aspects separate them?** Try to lead students to see that culture includes many areas of life and that it defines the differences between one community and another.

Categorizing Information Study Foldable Make this foldable to help you organize what you learn about our world, its people, and their cultures.

Step 1 Fold a sheet of paper into thirds from top to bottom.

This forms three sections.

Step 2 Open the paper and refold it into fourths from side to side.

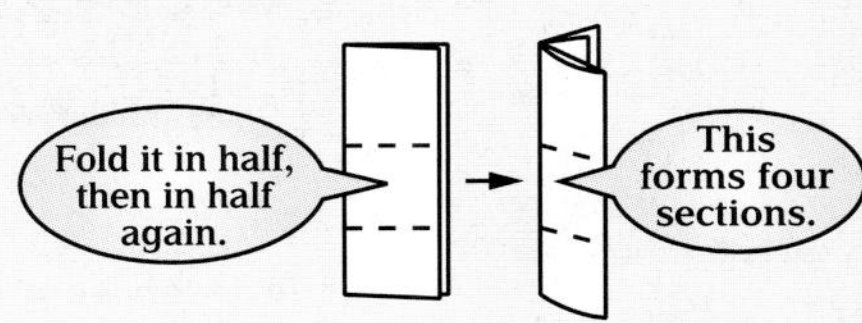

Fold it in half, then in half again.
This forms four sections.

Step 3 Unfold the paper and draw lines along the folds.

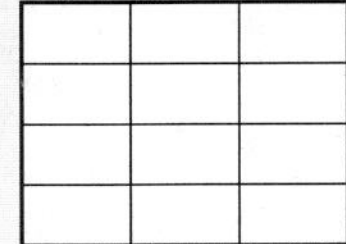

Step 4 Label your table foldable as shown.

	Near	Far
World		
People		
Cultures		

Reading and Writing As you read the chapter, write key words and phrases in your table foldable to help you remember main ideas.

Why It Matters

Discovering Other Cultures

A while ago it was common for people to spend most of their lives in the same town or place in which they were born. Today, your neighbor may be someone from another state, another country, or another continent. How do people in the rest of the world live? How do we get along with them? This book will help you learn about other people and places and what issues are important to them.

◄ **Painted elephants are part of the Dussehra festival in India.**

About the Photos

Dussehra is one of the most important Hindu festivals celebrated in India. It commemorates the victory of Rama, a Hindu deity and hero, over the demon king Ravana, and the triumph of good over evil. It also marks the end of the hot summer and the beginning of the winter season. In Mysore, India, the day is celebrated with a magnificent pro cession. Richly decorated elephants carry actors dressed as deities. Different regions celebrate in their own particular ways, but it is always a joyous occasion, offering lively performances, food, firecrackers, and colorful effigies. Ask students to use this photo to explain the relationship among religious ideas, philosophical ideas, and cultures.

FOLDABLES™ Study Organizer

Purpose This activity requires students to create a table and organize information from the chapter on it. Students group information from the chapter into categories, in effect comparing the world, people, and cultures of their local community ("near") to those of the world at large ("far").

Have students complete ***Reading and Study Skills Foldables*** Activity 1.

Why It Matters

Have students examine why cultural factors spread from one area to another. Create a chart with the headings "Trade," "Technology," and "Movement of People." Ask students to identify examples of each factor of cultural diffusion and borrowing. One example might be the popularity of certain foods, like pizza or tacos. Other examples could be music, fashions, language, and religion. Write students' suggestions under the appropriate columns and discuss them. Can they think of other ways cultures might spread? **Ask:** **How does cultural borrowing affect world cultures?**

FOCUS

Section Objectives

1. Describe how technology has changed the world.
2. Distinguish between ethnic groups, majority and minority groups.

BELLRINGER Skillbuilder Activity

Project transparency and have students answer questions.

This activity is also available as a blackline master.

Daily Focus Skills Transparency 1-1

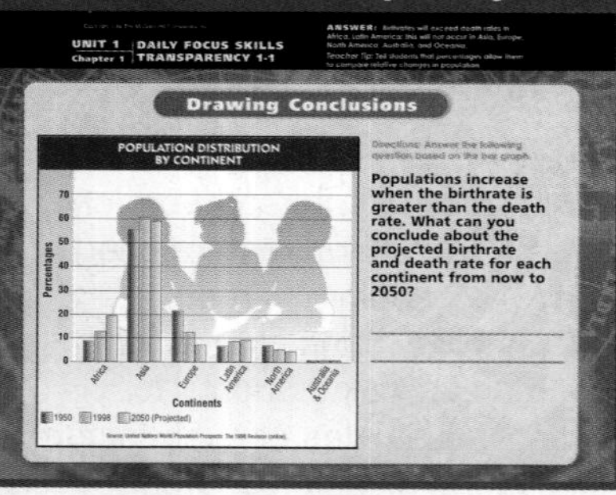

Guide to Reading

■ Vocabulary Precheck
Call on a volunteer to look up the term *minority* in a dictionary and read aloud all of its definitions. Ask students to select the definition that is appropriate for this section.

Use the Vocabulary PuzzleMaker to create crossword and word search puzzles.

Section 1 People Far and Near

Guide to Reading

Main Idea

Modern technology has helped to bring the world's diverse peoples closer together.

Terms to Know

- ethnic group
- custom
- minority group
- majority group

Reading Strategy

Create a diagram like this one. On the spokes list reasons the world may be getting smaller.

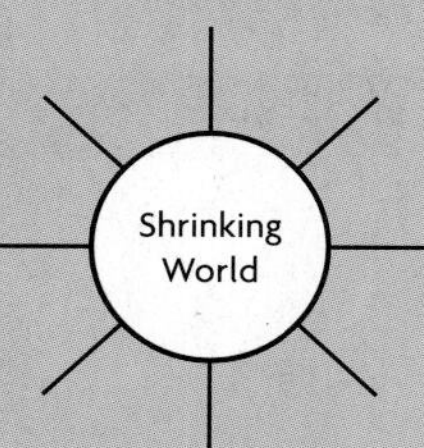

Early in 2001, Ann Bancroft and Liv Arnesen were trying to move into the history books as the first women to cross Antarctica. U.S. residents watched the live newscast on television.

As the women struggled against 100-mile-per-hour winds and temperatures so cold their hair froze, students around the world used the Internet to follow their progress.

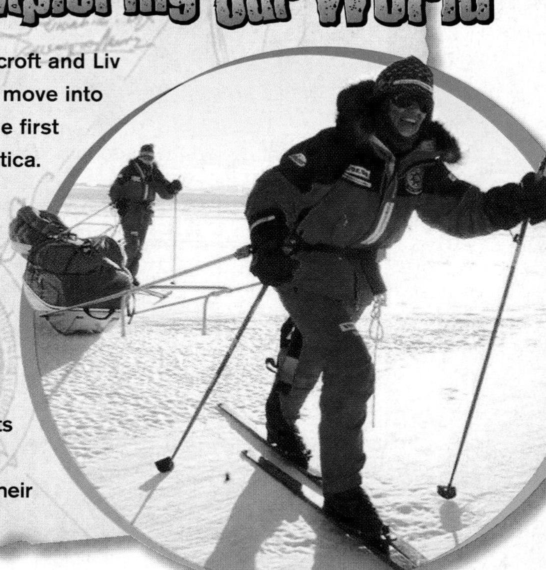

Today, people can talk across an ocean as easily as across a backyard fence. This is what is meant when you hear people say that the world today is shrinking. *Our World Today: People, Places, and Issues* is a book about our shrinking world. It is about the world's peoples, who they are, where they live, and how past experiences helped shape the world they live in today.

Technology Shrinks the World

With modern technology, the world's people have been brought closer together. Because the world is getting smaller, the chance that you will meet people from other cultures is increasing. By studying other people and countries, you will become able to see connections between the United States and the world around us. Learning to understand and respect what makes each culture unique, and recognizing common experiences that link all people will help you

Section Resources

Reproducible Masters
- Reproducible Lesson Plan 1-1
- Daily Lecture and Discussion Notes 1-1
- Guided Reading Activity 1-1
- Reading Essentials and Study Guide 1-1
- Section Quiz 1-1

Transparencies
- Daily Focus Skills Transparency 1-1

Multimedia
- Vocabulary PuzzleMaker Software
- Interactive Tutor Self-Assessment CD-ROM
- Presentation Plus! CD-ROM
- ExamView® Pro 3.0 Testmaker CD-ROM

become an informed member of the global village.

Inventions Change the World When the first telephone cable was laid along the bottom of the Atlantic Ocean in 1956, it could carry only 89 calls between Europe and North America at one time. Forty years later, glass cables as fine as hairs were carrying 3 million long-distance calls at once. Inventions are changing the world and it is changing faster every year.

Jet planes can cross oceans in brief hours, carrying people from one continent to another. Bullet trains speed workers from city to city while subways shuttle them across towns.

Communication satellites receive radio, television, and other signals in outer space. News can be broadcast live to the entire world so that more people than ever can watch. The result is a smaller world.

Internet Technology Millions of people today can use the **Internet** because of improved telephone cables and satellites. But other inventions made the Internet possible in the first place. The most important of these inventions is the computer. Today's hand-held personal computers have more processing power than the computers of the 1960s that helped put an American on the moon! Today, millions of people use the Internet to exchange mail, shop, do research, exchange photographs, play games with friends in other countries, and much more. Again, the world seems to have grown a little smaller.

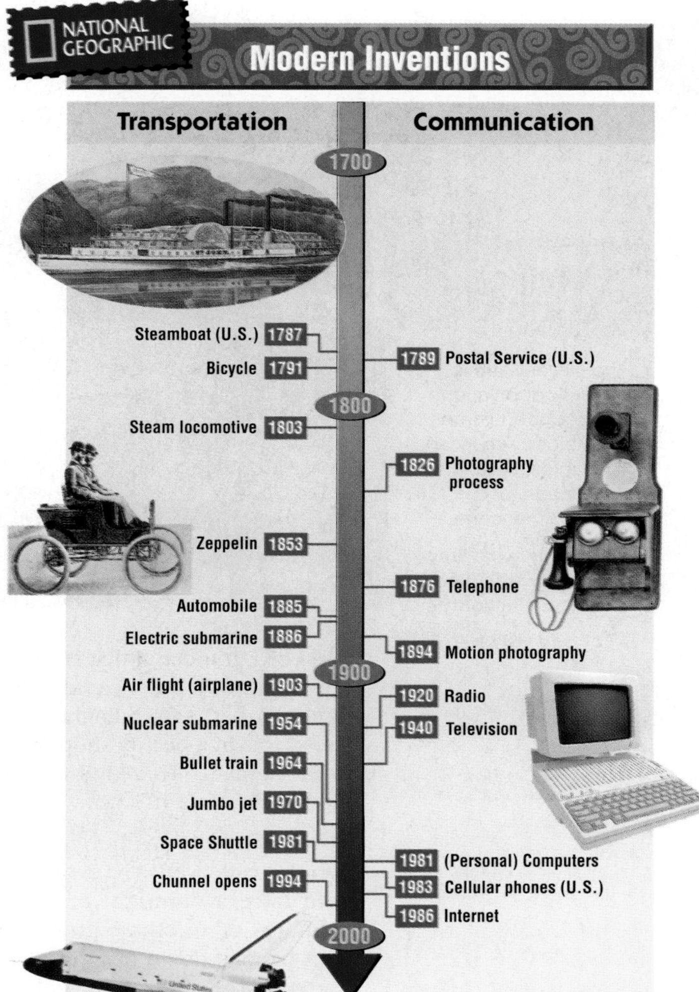

Analyzing the Time Line

In the last century, communication and transportation technologies have evolved at an amazing rate.

Technology **Which 19th century inventions are still used today?**

Reading Check **Name two ways in which technology makes the world seem smaller.**

The World Next Door

Sometimes the world really has become "smaller." A woman in a Houston suburb describes her neighborhood this way: "I was born in Chicago, Illinois, and have lived in the Houston area for 10 years. Inge, the woman next door, is from Denmark. Shiv, her husband,

Cooperative Learning Activity

Then and Now Arrange your class into four groups. Groups 1 and 2 will represent 18th century American and French governments respectively. Groups 3 and 4 will be modern American and Russian governments. Present your class with the following problems: 18th century America will have to go to war with France if France does not remove its war ships from American territory. Modern America will have to go to war with Russia, if Russia does not stop flying military planes over neutral territory. Have the groups research how they would communicate in their particular time period in order to stop the war. They should think about the time it would take, how messages would be carried, and who would be in communication.

EE6 The Uses of Geography: Standard 18

Teach

Making Predictions Ask students for examples of technology that has transcended the boundaries of societies and helped shape the world. Then ask students to envision a future scientific discovery or technological innovation. Have them make predictions about the social, economic, and environmental consequences that might result from such progress. **L2**

Daily Lecture Notes 1-1

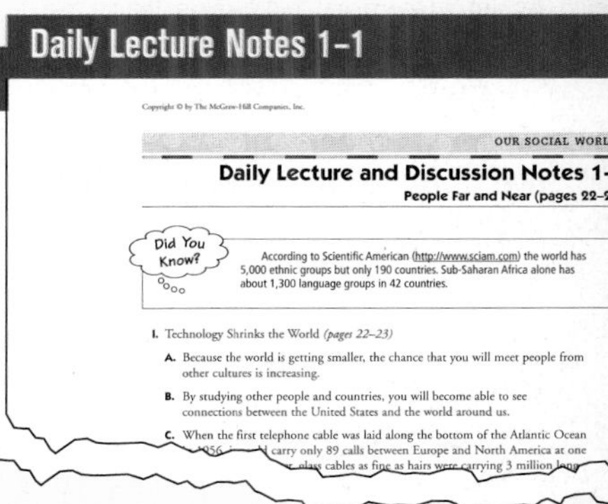
OUR SOCIAL WORLD

Daily Lecture and Discussion Notes 1-1

People Far and Near (pages 22–25)

Did You Know? According to Scientific American (http://www.sciam.com) the world has 5,000 ethnic groups but only 190 countries. Sub-Saharan Africa alone has about 1,300 language groups in 42 countries.

I. Technology Shrinks the World (pages 22–23)

A. Because the world is getting smaller, the chance that you will meet people from other cultures is increasing.

B. By studying other people and countries, you will become able to see connections between the United States and the world around us.

C. When the first telephone cable was laid along the bottom of the Atlantic Ocean ... carry only 89 calls between Europe and North America at one ... glass cables as fine as hairs were carrying 3 million long

Reading Check Answer

Communication technology links people around the world. Faster transportation makes it easy to travel long distances.

Analyzing the Time Line

Answer
automobile, telephone, motion photography

Skills Practice
Trace air travel's evolution *(zeppelin, airplane, jumbo jet, space shuttle)*

Guided Reading Activity 1-1

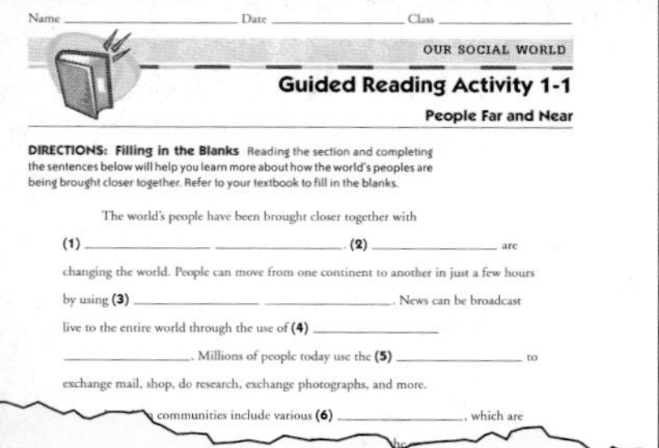

Name ______________ Date ______________ Class ______________

OUR SOCIAL WORLD

Guided Reading Activity 1-1

People Far and Near

DIRECTIONS: Filling in the Blanks Reading the section and completing the sentences below will help you learn more about how the world's peoples are being brought closer together. Refer to your textbook to fill in the blanks.

The world's people have been brought closer together with **(1)** ______________ ______________. **(2)** ______________ are changing the world. People can move from one continent to another in just a few hours by using **(3)** ______________ ______________. News can be broadcast live to the entire world through the use of **(4)** ______________ ______________. Millions of people today use the **(5)** ______________ to exchange mail, shop, do research, exchange photographs, and more.

communities include various **(6)** ______________, which are

Assess

Assign Section 1 Assessment as homework or an in-class activity.

Have students use the Interactive Tutor Self-Assessment CD-ROM to review section 1-1.

More About the Photos

Cities Large cities such as New York and Los Angeles have a lot of diversity in their populations, including many American-born minorities, as well as ethnic groups from around the world. **Ask:** **How does human migration affect the character of a place?**

Caption Answer Many people wrongly consider disabled people as "different" and unable to be productive, so people with disabilities often have difficulty achieving positions of influence in business and politics.

Minority Groups

The largest ethnic minority populations in the United States are African Americans, Hispanics, Asian Americans, and Native Americans.

Issues **In what way are people with disabilities also a minority?**

was born in India, and Seeta and Rajiv, their kids, are Canadian citizens. My daughter's best friend, Ellen, was born in South Africa, and her mother, Janet, is from England. My best friend, Irma, came from Mexico. She works in a beauty shop owned by Van and her husband—a couple from Vietnam." This kind of neighborhood is rapidly becoming common in the United States.

Ethnic Groups American communities include various groups of peoples called **ethnic groups.** An ethnic group is a group of people who have a common origin and share a language and a history. Members of an ethnic group often follow the same **customs**—practices handed down from the past. How many ethnic groups are represented in the Houston neighborhood described above?

Minority Groups Often ethnic groups are also minorities. A **minority group** is a group of people whose culture, race, or ethnic origin is different from that of most of the people in the region. Sometimes the minority group is treated differently from the **majority group.** Majority is normally defined as a number greater than half of a total. When studying societies however, the majority is the group in society that controls most of the wealth and power. However, the majority group is not always the largest group in numbers. For example, South Africa at one time had a government that favored its white citizens and passed laws that restricted the black African population. The blacks were considered a minority even though they made up a much larger percentage of the population. In many cases women are thought of as a minority group because they have less influence than men have in business and politics.

Critical Thinking Activity

Analyzing Information Have students determine the different ethnic groups in their class. Remember that some minorities like Asian Americans have many different ethnic groups, and whites can be Scottish, Italian, and so on. Include a category for mixed ethnicity. Tally the results and have the class make a bar graph showing the proportions of the class's different groups. Now have them identify the different minorities in the class. Besides race, they should look at gender, and can make up new minority categories based on the definition in the text. Make a bar graph with these results and compare it to the first graph.

EE4 Human Systems: Standard 10

It is important to remember that a minority group is not always the same as an ethnic group. For example, Asian Americans are a minority group in the United States, but "Asian" is not an ethnic term. All Asian Americans do not share the same origin, language, or history. Asian Americans may be Vietnamese, Chinese, Japanese, or Cambodian for example. Still others may come from many other places in Asia.

Building Bridges Schools are the place where most young people first meet people from other ethnic groups. Public schools reflect the values in their neighborhoods. As one student says: "Making friends just depends on what you like to do, and who likes to do those things." Curiously, about the time students enter middle school and high school, things begin to change. **Sociologists,** the scientists who study organized groups of people, have found that student friendships start forming along racial lines. Skin color is not the only reason for division between ethnic groups, however. Sometimes groups divide over religious beliefs and values. Building bridges between the "different worlds" in your community and school is possible. You can start by learning about the beliefs and values of other people in the world.

Reading Check Why is Asian not an ethnic term?

Section 1 Assessment

Defining Terms

1. **Define** ethnic group, custom, minority group, majority group.

Recalling Facts

2. **Culture** Explain the difference between a minority group and an ethnic group.
3. **Place** In what country was the group that controlled the wealth and power not the largest ethnic group?
4. **Technology** In what way is technology shrinking the world? Give examples.

Critical Thinking

5. **Understanding Cause and Effect** Why do you think minority groups are sometimes treated differently from the majority?
6. **Making Comparisons** What do you think it means that some groups are divided by religious beliefs and values?

Graphic Organizer

7. **Organizing Information** Create a diagram like this one that describes features of your culture. On the lines write the types of food, clothing, language, music, and so on found in your culture.

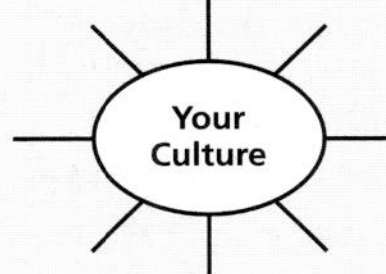

Applying Social Studies Skills

8. **Interpreting Time Lines** Look at the time line on page 23. During which century were most modern communication and modern transportation invented?

Section 1 Assessment

1. The terms are defined in the Glossary.
2. ethnic group: shares an origin, language, or history; minority group: is different from those who hold most of the power
3. South Africa
4. Answers will vary, but should include the communication and transportation technologies that make it faster and easier to reach people and places anywhere in the world.
5. *Possible answer:* because they look or sound different
6. Some people think their beliefs or values are superior and are unaccepting of the beliefs of others.
7. Diagrams will vary.
8. the 20th century

Chapter 1

Section 1, pages 22–25

Section Quiz 1-1

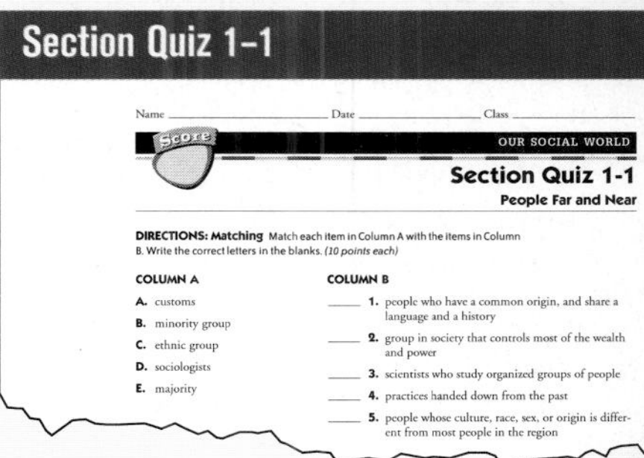

Name ________ Date ________ Class ________

OUR SOCIAL WORLD

Section Quiz 1-1

People Far and Near

DIRECTIONS: Matching Match each item in Column A with the items in Column B. Write the correct letters in the blanks. (20 points each)

COLUMN A	COLUMN B
A. customs	___ 1. people who have a common origin, and share a language and a history
B. minority group	___ 2. group in society that controls most of the wealth and power
C. ethnic group	___ 3. scientists who study organized groups of people
D. sociologists	___ 4. practices handed down from the past
E. majority	___ 5. people whose culture, race, sex, or origin is different from most people in the region

Reteach

Have students write a paragraph about whether they think they are in a minority or majority group and describing how they feel about it.

Reading Check Answer

because all Asians do not share the same origin, language, or history

Reading Essentials and Study Guide 1-1

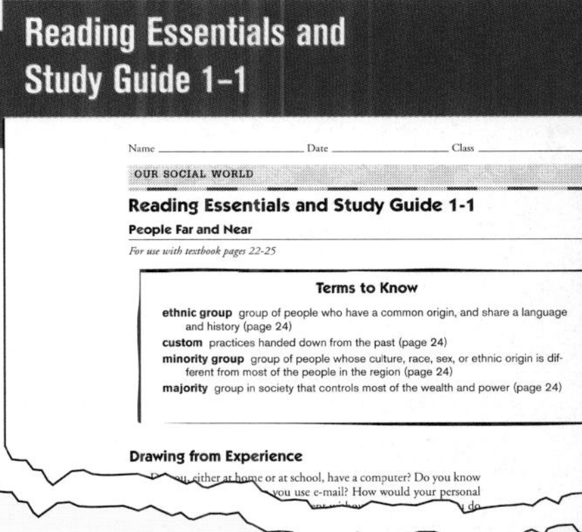

Name ________ Date ________ Class ________

OUR SOCIAL WORLD

Reading Essentials and Study Guide 1-1

People Far and Near

For use with textbook pages 22-25

Terms to Know

ethnic group group of people who have a common origin, and share a language and history (page 24)
custom practices handed down from the past (page 24)
minority group group of people whose culture, race, sex, or ethnic origin is different from most of the people in the region (page 24)
majority group in society that controls most of the wealth and power (page 24)

Drawing from Experience

Close

Have the class pose 10 questions they can ask others about their ethnicity. Have students then interview someone from an ethnic group different from their own.

TEACH

Before students read the feature, tell them to take the role of government officials. Inform them that their task is to make a count of every person in the country. Have them discuss how they would go about getting the information. L2

More About the Census

Two sets of national census records are not available to historians to study. During the War of 1812, when the British burned Washington, D.C., the fires destroyed some parts of the 1790 census, the nation's first count. Decades later, the census from 1890 was completely destroyed in another fire.

Interdisciplinary Connections

Technology The 2000 census became completely automated, using optical scanners to scan the questionnaires filled out by respondents—even scanning written words. The information was then stored immediately on computers. The process was 20 times faster than manually inputting the information.

Making Connections

CULTURE GOVERNMENT PEOPLE TECHNOLOGY

Counting Heads

How do we know there are more than 280 million people in the United States? Who counts the people? Every 10 years since 1790, the United States Census Bureau has counted heads in this country. Why and how do they do this?

The First Census

After the American colonies fought the Revolutionary War and won their independence, the new government required a census. By knowing how many people were in each state, the government could divide the war expenses fairly. The census would also determine the number of people that each state could send to Congress.

The census began in August 1790, about a year after George Washington became president. The census law defined who would be counted, and it required that every household be visited by census takers. These workers walked or rode on horseback to gather their data. By the time it was completed, the census counted 3.9 million people.

The first census asked for little more than one's name and address. Over time, the census added questions to gather more than just population data. By 1820, there were questions about a person's job. Soon after, questions about crime, education, and wages appeared. In 1950 the census used its first computer to process data. Census takers go door-to-door to gather information from those who do not return their census forms in the mail. Now census data are released over the Internet.

▲ The Electric Tabulating Machine processed the 1890 census in 2 1/2 years, a job that would have taken nearly 10 years to complete by hand.

The Census and Race

Sometimes the census itself can cause debate. Many people are uncomfortable with answering questions they believe are their own business. Others worry about how the information might be used or misused. The 2000 census gave rise to concerns about how people are counted and classified into races.

Before 2000, the census form directed individuals to mark only one box from a list of different races. This meant people of mixed races were forced to claim membership in one race. Tiger Woods, for example, might have had to choose between identifying himself as African American or Asian American.

Now, for the first time, the census had allowed people to mark one or more categories for race. Figures show that nearly 7 million people have taken advantage of this new way to be counted.

Making the Connection

1. In what two ways were population data from the first census used?
2. How has technology changed the way census data are collected and processed?
3. **Drawing Conclusions** Why do you think the national and state governments want information about people's education and jobs?

Making the Connection

1. to divide war expenses and to determine representation in Congress
2. Data is collected mostly through the mail rather than relying exclusively on door-to-door surveys. Instead of processing data by hand, it is now done by computers and results are posted on the Internet.
3. *Possible answer:* to help them make better plans about economic growth

Section 2

Understanding Culture

Guide to Reading

Main Idea

People all over the world usually live close to others who follow similar beliefs and like the same foods, music, and clothing.

Terms to Know

- social scientist
- culture
- ethnocentrism
- cultural borrowing
- cultural diffusion
- limited government
- democracy
- unlimited government
- dictatorship
- absolute monarchy
- constitutional monarchy

Reading Strategy

Create a chart like this one. Fill in the spaces with specific examples of cultural borrowing and cultural diffusion.

Cultural Borrowing	Cultural Diffusion

NATIONAL GEOGRAPHIC **Exploring Our World**

Three thousand years ago, the Olmec people lived in Mexico. They sometimes wore skins of jaguars, cats that were sacred to them. This young boy lives in an area where the jaguar is still honored. He is preparing for a jaguar dance. An object from modern culture—a soft drink bottle—is used to make the "jaguar" spots of ash on the boy's clay-covered skin.

Thanks to technology, many of us have the power to "tune in" to the world. By simply pushing a button or clicking a mouse, you can find out why polite Egyptians do not cross their legs in public, who introduced rabbits to Australia, who has made the most points in an NBA basketball game, when Russians celebrate Women's Day, and where people dress in *kangas.* But just knowing facts is not enough. It is far better to learn how to organize information so that it is meaningful and so that it helps you better understand the world.

The Social Sciences

Organizing information to help people understand the world around them is the role of **social scientists.** Social scientists study the interaction of people and society. There are many important disciplines, or fields of study, in the social sciences. Four types of social scientists deal directly with society. **Anthropologists** study people and

27

1 Focus

Section Objectives

1. Define what *culture* means.
2. Describe how and why cultures change.
3. Explain the different types of government and economic systems.

BELLRINGER
Skillbuilder Activity

Project transparency and have students answer questions.

This activity is also available as a blackline master.

Daily Focus Skills Transparency 1-2

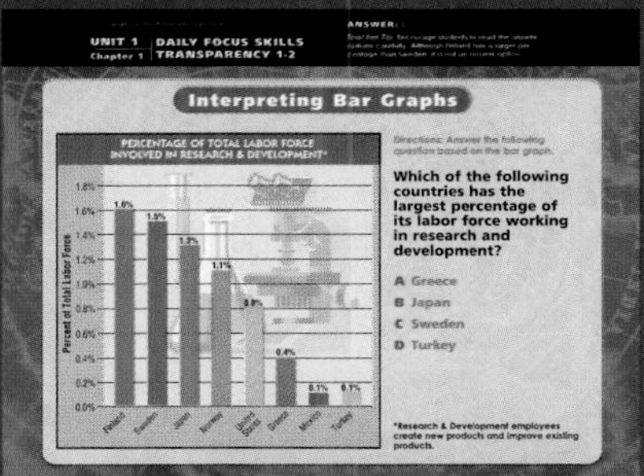

Guide to Reading

Accessing Prior Knowledge
Have volunteers describe the ethnic foods they have eaten. Point out that food is one way cultures differ from one another.

Section Resources

Reproducible Masters

- Reproducible Lesson Plan 1-2
- Daily Lecture and Discussion Notes 1-2
- Guided Reading Activity 1-2
- Reading Essentials and Study Guide 1-2
- Section Quiz 1-2

Transparencies

- Daily Focus Skills Transparency 1-2

Multimedia

- Vocabulary PuzzleMaker Software
- Interactive Tutor Self-Assessment CD-ROM
- Presentation Plus! CD-ROM
- ExamView® Pro 3.0 Testmaker CD-ROM

Chapter 1

Section 2, pages 27–33

Interdisciplinary Connections

Math Give students the following numbers from the *National Geographic Atlas of the World:* Mandarin—885 million; English—322 million; Spanish—266 million; Bengali—189 million; and Hindi—182 million. Tell them that these represent the number of *native* speakers of the five most widely used languages in the world. Give them a world population figure of 6 billion and ask them to calculate the percentage of the world's people that speaks each of these languages. *(Mandarin—14.7%; English—5.4%; Spanish—4.4%; Bengali—3.1%; Hindi—3.0%)* **L1**

Reading Check Answer

They study the interaction of people and society.

More About the Photos

Cultural Universals Human cultures are remarkable for their diversity. Despite this diversity, all cultures have certain features in common. These *cultural universals* include rules about marriage and kinship, ways of obtaining food and providing shelter, artworks, stories or folktales, and ways of settling disputes. **Ask: What other cultural universals can you think of?**

Caption Answer food and housing

NATIONAL GEOGRAPHIC **On Location**

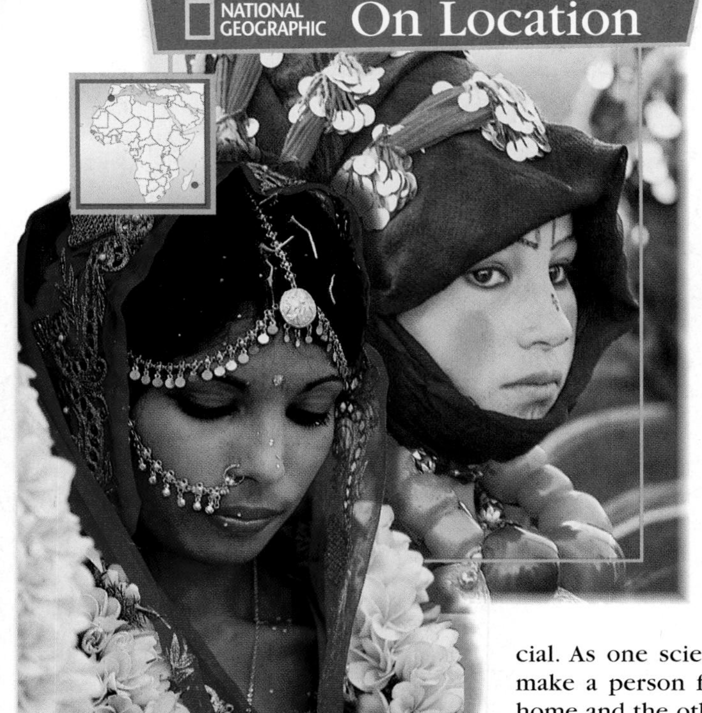

Celebrations

In most cultures, people often bring out their most beautiful clothes for events like weddings. This wedding guest is from Morocco (upper right), and this bride is from Mauritius (above).

Place **What aspects of daily life besides clothing reflect culture?**

societies. **Sociologists** study human behavior as it relates to groups of people. **Historians** study how societies came to be what they are today. **Human geographers** look at people and their environments.

Geographers organize facts about Earth's surface and people. They do this with maps, graphs, and other tools. These tools help geographers to find patterns in the earth's organization. For example, geographers examine why people live where they do and how different industries change the environment. In fact, the work geographers do is so important that you will read more about it in the next chapter.

Social scientists also give us tools to examine new beliefs and values. They look at what makes different people and places special. As one scientist warns: "There are two ways to make a person feel homeless—one is to destroy his home and the other is to make his home look and feel like everybody else's home." In this quotation, the home being talked about is *culture.*

Reading Check **What is the role of social scientists?**

What Is Culture?

Waking up to rock music, putting on denim jeans, and celebrating the Fourth of July are part of the culture of the United States. **Culture** is the way of life of people who share similar beliefs and customs. These people may speak the same language, follow the same religion, and dress in a certain way. The culture of a people also includes their government, food, music, literature, and the ways they make a living. In the United States, people of many cultures live together. But people who live in the United States and who call themselves Americans believe in certain political values, such as freedom of speech, free public education, and the right to practice a religion of their choosing. Americans believe that hard work should be rewarded. Americans pride themselves on getting things done quickly and in a practical way. These beliefs, among others, are part of what defines us as Americans. What other beliefs can you name that define American culture?

Meeting Special Needs

Visual/Spatial Students who do well with this mode of learning can benefit by studying a variety of photographs of people, activities, buildings, and artifacts of different cultures. Bring to class books showing photographs of various nations. Have students find photographs reflecting institutions basic to all societies, including government, economic, educational, and religious institutions. This will help students understand that certain institutions are basic to all societies, but characteristics of these institutions may vary from one society to another. **L2**

Refer to *Inclusion for the Middle School Social Studies Classroom Strategies and Activities* in the TCR.

Once people learn their own culture, it is sometimes hard for them to imagine any other way of life. They may want to judge people in terms of their own culture and their own standards. This practice is called **ethnocentrism.** (Remember the term *ethnic group* from Section 1?) Ethnocentrism means your values are "centered" or based on those of your own particular ethnic group. It is very common for people to prefer their own cultures. In fact, it is very hard not to. Many positive qualities, such as patriotism and taking pride in your nation's history, are ethnocentric feelings. Not all ethnocentric expressions are positive, however. Jokes about certain races or religions are really just ethnocentric statements about a different group of people. By making fun of the ways people are different, we are really saying that our way is better.

Cultural Borrowing Although all people have a culture, a large percentage is "borrowed" from other cultures. **Cultural borrowing** is the adoption by one group of people of another group's culture traits. A culture trait is a normal practice for a person in a culture. The **Maori** of New Zealand traditionally rub noses when they meet. When the Maori shake hands instead, they are using a borrowed culture trait. Today, baseball is a very popular sport in Japan. The Japanese borrowed this game from the United States. Possibly, Americans first borrowed the idea of baseball from a similar game played in Britain called rounder.

Cultural Diffusion **Cultural diffusion** is how a culture spreads its knowledge and skills from one area to another. Merchants and traders used to be the major agents, or causes, of cultural diffusion. They spread cultures when they bought and sold goods.

Today, cultural diffusion occurs through radio, television, telephones, computers, and the Internet. For instance, more than one-fifth of the world's people understand at least some English because of

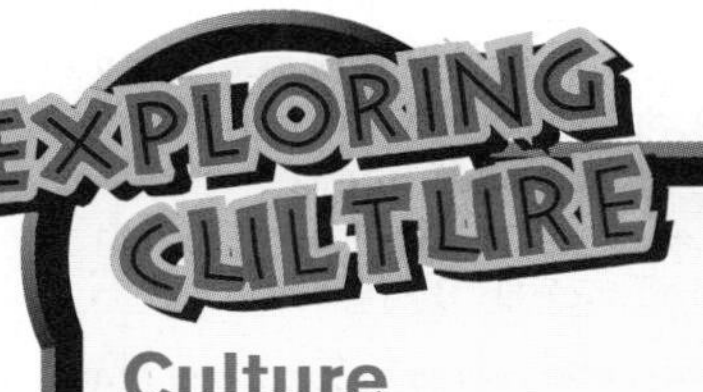

Culture

Cultural differences can be interesting but they can also cause misunderstandings. These can be avoided if we learn how cultures differ from our own. In the photos, Inuit greet with a nose rub, Japanese businessmen bow in meeting (top right), and the French women kiss each other on the cheek (bottom right).

Looking Closer **How do members of your community greet one another?**

Chapter 1

Section 2, pages 27–33

TEACH

Making Comparisons Make the concept of "culture" concrete for students by discussing it in the context of their own culture. For each cultural characteristic (social groups, language, institutions, and so on), have them identify examples from their culture. Write the examples on the board. Then work with students to provide comparative examples from other cultures. **L1**

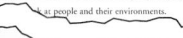

Daily Lecture Notes 1-2

OUR SOCIAL WORLD

Daily Lecture and Discussion Notes 1-2

Understanding Culture (pages 27–33)

Did You Know? Culture is what makes you a stranger when you are away from home. For example, you might not know that Ukrainians enjoy chocolate-coated pork fat at Christmastime and that the Chinese have a special holiday, called Ching Ming, when they spend the day honoring deceased family members.

I. The Social Sciences (pages 27–28)

A. Organizing information to help people understand the world around them is the role of **social scientists.**

B. **Anthropologists** study societies that do not use writing.

C. Sociologists study human behavior as it relates to groups of people.

Answer Answers will vary according to students' ethnic or personal customs.

Ask students: **How many different types of greetings do you use? What are they? With whom do you use each type?** Discuss their responses, and point out differing greetings based on their relationship with each person they greet.

Team-Teaching Activity

Foreign Language Invite the foreign language teacher to class. Have him or her read passages from a work of literature in another language. Then have the teacher or students read a translation of each passage. Discuss the difficulties that arise from translating, such as the problem of translating idioms or the difficulty in recapturing rhythm or rhyme patterns. Ask students for examples of English words or phrases that might be difficult to translate into another language. Discuss why these words might be problematic. Ask students to explain how language can be an aspect of culture that separates cultures or societies. **L3**

EE4 Human Systems: Standard 10

Chapter 1

Section 2, pages 27–33

Applying Map Skills

Answers

1. Africa south of the Sahara
2. North Africa, Southwest Asia, and Central Asia

Skills Practice

Which continents have only one culture region? *(South America, Antarctica, and Australia)*

Guided Reading Activity 1-2

Name ______ Date ______ Class ______

OUR SOCIAL WORLD

Guided Reading Activity 1-2

Understanding Culture

DIRECTIONS: Outlining Reading the section and completing the outline below will help you learn more about how to understand cultures. Refer to your textbook to fill in the blanks.

I. The Social Sciences
  A. The role of ______ ______ is to organize information to help people understand the world around them.
  B. Three types of social scientists deal directly with ______. They include
    1. ______,
    2. ______, and
    3. ______ ______.

II. ______ is the way of life of people who share similar beliefs and customs.
  A. When people judge people in terms of their own culture they are practicing

Reading Check Answer

Answers will vary.

Cultural Kaleidoscope

Dialects are a local form of a language that differs from the main language. Americans might get confused in England, where sweaters are called "jumpers" and trucks are "lorries."

NATIONAL GEOGRAPHIC

World Culture Regions

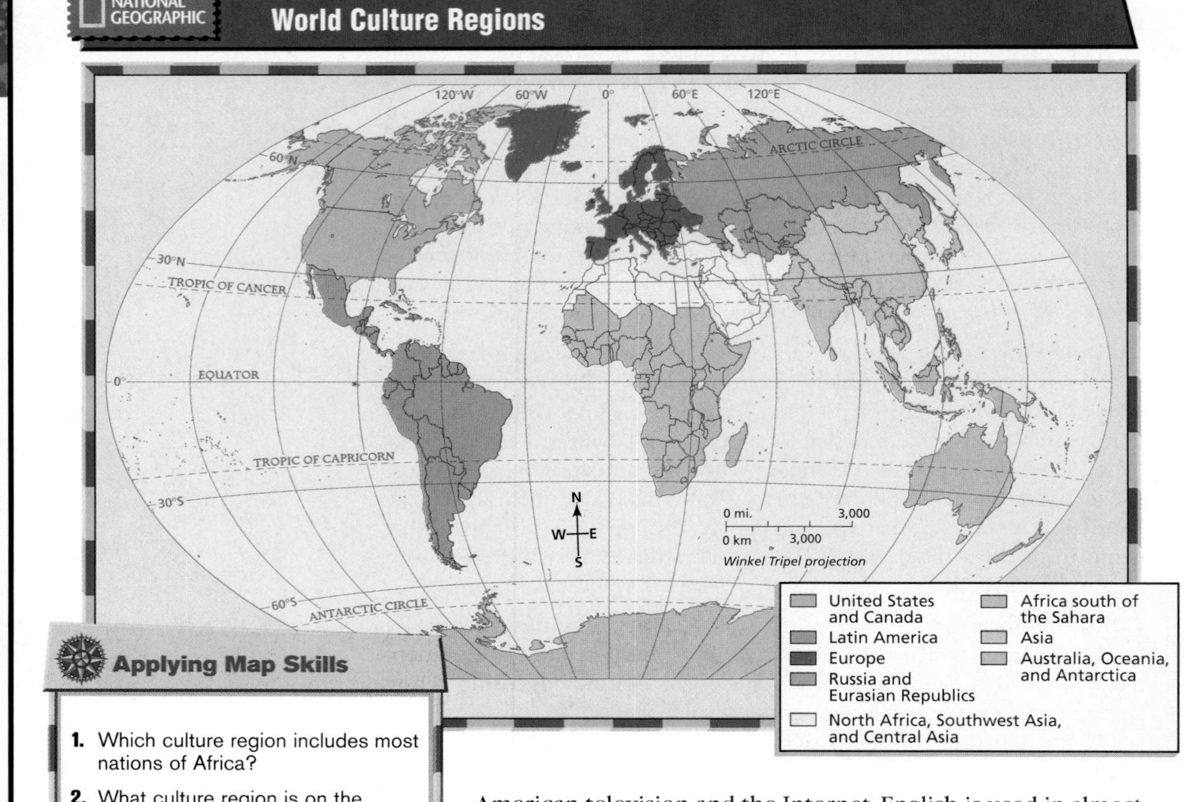

Applying Map Skills

1. Which culture region includes most nations of Africa?
2. What culture region is on the continents of both Africa and Asia?

Find NGS online map resources @ www.nationalgeographic.com/maps

American television and the Internet. English is used in almost 80 percent of Web sites worldwide. Airline pilots use English to communicate when they fly across national borders. Many experts predict that businesspeople worldwide will have to learn English—the language of most computer software—to keep up with world trade. Because of technology, English is the most widely used second language in the world.

Reading Check **Name two ethnocentric values or practices that are common in your community.**

Important Lessons in History

History is the story of the past. For thousands of years, history was passed on by word of mouth. This oral history was how cultures passed on the record of people and events that made them special. Famous epics like *The Iliad,* the story of a 10-year war between the Greeks and the Trojans, began as long poems memorized by professional storytellers. These storytellers were respected and important members of their cultures. Today, **Aborigines** of Australia still memorize much of their history and repeat it in the form of stories to the young people in their clan groups.

Cooperative Learning Activity

World Regions Graph Organize students into eight groups. Inform groups that their task is to create a database and graph showing aspects of world culture regions. Assign each group one of the world culture regions. Have them research information about their region such as population, language, religion, government, and economic activity. Then have each group share its data with the class to create one database with all of the information. Have students then create a graph comparing the populations of the eight world regions. **L3 ELL**

EE4 Human Systems: Standard 10

Eventually, writing became the most important way to keep records of the past. Historians today search through legal documents, diaries, newspapers, and many other written sources for information about the past. They also use artifacts, such as tools and household goods, to try to recreate what happened long ago.

History also tells how past conflicts influence the present. For example, why are millions of people in **Sudan** starving when this African country has large areas of rich farmland? A historian will know that the conflicts of today have their roots in religious wars dating back hundreds of years. Acres of farmland are left unplanted because soldiers burn the land and kill the farmers who try to grow crops in disputed areas.

Studying history can also teach us important lessons and can guide our behavior in the present. A well-known saying is "Those who cannot remember the past are condemned to repeat it." This means that if we do not study our own history, we may end up making the same mistakes of earlier generations.

▲ An African griot, or storyteller, shares cultural stories through song.

✓Reading Check **How was the history of a culture first passed on?**

Government Is Necessary

Most families have rules that guide how the family members behave. These rules might be about mealtimes, chores, homework, or allowances. Without rules, family members would not know how to behave or what to expect from one another. People need rules in order to live together without conflict. In countries, rules are created by governments. In a **limited government** even the people who make the laws must obey them. Constitutions, statements of rights, or other laws set limits on how much power government officials have so that they cannot take advantage of the people.

Democracy is a form of limited government. In a direct democracy, the people govern themselves by voting individually on issues. Direct democracy is still practiced in some small New England towns and in parts of Switzerland. In a representative democracy, people elect representatives. Then the representatives make and enforce laws. The United States is a representative democracy.

In an **unlimited government** power belongs to the ruler or rulers. No rules or laws exist to limit what the ruler can or cannot do. Unlimited governments include dictatorships and absolute monarchies. An example of a **dictatorship** is **Saddam Hussein's** rule in Iraq. In an **absolute monarchy** kings or queens are born into ruling families. Their power is inherited and unlimited. King Fahd ibn Abdul Aziz of Saudi Arabia is an absolute monarch.

Not all monarchies are examples of unlimited government. **Queen Elizabeth II** of England is a monarch, but not an absolute ruler. Britain has a parliament and laws that limit the power of the British kings and queens. Great Britain is a **constitutional monarchy** and is a type of limited government.

✓Reading Check **What is the main difference between limited and unlimited government?**

Categorizing Information

Have students identify examples of limited and unlimited governments. Then ask students to identify the different ways of organizing governments, such as rule by many, by few, or by one. Have students determine the type of organization of each example given. L1

Note-taking tip

Point out to students that the types of government and economic systems are important concepts they will refer to frequently in the course. Suggest that they put the definitions on a note card or some other material that they can keep handy and refer to often.

✓ Reading Check Answer

by word of mouth

3 ASSESS

Assign Section 2 Assessment as homework or an in-class activity.

Have students use the Interactive Tutor Self-Assessment CD-ROM to review Section 1–2.

✓ Reading Check Answer

In limited government, laws exist that set limits on the power of government officials. In unlimited government, absolute power belongs to the ruler.

Critical Thinking Activity

Comparing Governments Saudi Arabia is a country governed by an absolute monarch. The government is heavily influenced by Islamic religious leaders. In addition to a regular police force, Saudi Arabia also has a religious police force that patrols to make sure religious laws are being followed. These include laws that forbid alcohol and drugs and do not permit women to drive. People in Saudi Arabia are divided over whether their country's laws should be strictly based on the Quran, the holy book of the Islamic religion. In the United States, too, there is debate about whether religion should be a part of our government and public institutions. Have your class debate the pros and cons of combining government and religion based on the example in Saudi Arabia.

EE4 Human Systems: Standard 10

Analyzing the Chart

Answer
Answers will vary.

Skills Practice
Define and give examples of primary, secondary, tertiary, and quaternary industries in your community. *(answers will vary)*

Did You Know

Cultures have developed some unusual forms of money. On the island of Yap, in the western Pacific, people use round slabs of stone that are up to 12 feet (3.7 m) across. Why are the stones accepted as money? To get them, someone must travel about 320 miles (515 km) to the island of Palau. The long trip makes the stones very valuable.

Evaluating Information

Have students create a chart of the different economic systems found throughout the world. Their charts should summarize the characteristics of the different systems as well as identify individual societies as examples. **Ask:** **What are the main differences among these systems? What are the benefits of each?**

NATIONAL GEOGRAPHIC

Types of Industries

Classification	Description	Example Product
Primary	Takes natural resources from the earth – mining, forestry, fishing, and agriculture are included here.	Fishing
Secondary	Makes products using the natural resources – construction, factories, and processing plants are in this classification.	Canning plant processes the fish
Tertiary	Provides a service – such as restaurants, supermarkets, hospitals, education, and emergency services.	Supermarket sells the fish
Quaternary	Gathers information– industries in this classification research, gather, and provide information.	Bar codes tell the market when to reorder the fish

Analyzing the Chart

Service industries embrace a wide range of areas, including banking and finance, education, health care, communication, and many others.

Economics **What classification would describe most industry where you live?**

Balancing Our Wants and Needs

The different ways people and nations go about meeting their daily needs are known as *economic systems.* All economic systems are concerned with producing goods.

Traditional Economies In a traditional economy, people meet their needs on the basis of their customs. These have been handed down over many years. In some parts of Africa and South America, for example, children learn their trades from their parents who learned from their parents. In this way the same family does the same work generation after generation.

Command Economies Under a command economy, government makes all the decisions. Individuals have little or no say about basic economic questions such as what and how much to produce and what to charge. North Korea is a country with a command economy. Communism is an example of a command economy.

Market Economies In a market economy, individuals determine for themselves what to produce, who will want it **(demand),** how much to produce **(supply),** and how much to charge **(price).** No country has a pure market economy because governments regulate, or control, some parts of businesses. This system is sometimes called a "free enterprise system."

Mixed Economies Most nations have a mixed economy. The Chinese, for example, have mostly a command economy but are working toward a market system by allowing some private businesses. The United States prides itself on its market economy. However, the government may regulate prices or set rules as in the airline industry and companies that provide gas and electricity.

Cooperative Learning Activity

Developing Nations Divide the class into three groups, with 80 percent in Group A, 15 percent in Group B, and 5 percent in Group C. Group A represents the world's poorest, developing nations. Group B represents mostly industrialized nations. Group C represents fully industrialized nations. Show the class a large candy bar and divide it among the three groups as follows: 80 percent to Group C, 15 percent to Group B, and 5 percent to Group A. Explain to students that this is how the world's wealth is divided. Ask students to explain why this is so, then have groups work together for solutions that would provide a more equitable distribution of wealth.

EE4 Human Systems: Standard 11

Differences in Development

Countries differ in how much manufacturing and industry they have. **Industrialized countries** hold 97 percent of all patents ownership (rights to inventions). Many countries in Europe and North America, as well as Australia, Japan, and South Korea, among others, are industrialized countries. Other countries have only a few manufacturing centers. Many people in these countries grow only enough food for their own families. Countries that are working toward industrialization are called **developing countries.** Most developing countries are found in Africa, Asia, and Latin America.

Many corporations from industrialized countries are now building plants in developing countries. They have found a valuable "resource" in these places—people. The spread of industry has created growing economies in places like Mexico, Taiwan, and China.

Issues faced by developing and industrialized nations can be very different. Increasing population, not enough jobs, poor schools, and lack of social and health services are problems in many developing countries. In more industrialized countries, leaders are looking at ways to clean up pollution, fight crime and drugs, and protect their economies. However, no country is unaffected by the problems of its neighbors.

✓ Reading Check **What are two issues facing most developing countries?**

Assessment

Defining Terms

1. **Define** social scientist, culture, ethnocentrism, cultural borrowing, cultural diffusion, limited government, democracy, unlimited government, dictatorship, absolute monarchy, constitutional monarchy.

Recalling Facts

2. **Culture** What four groups of scientists study society?

3. **Government** People in the United States who call themselves Americans believe in certain political values. What are they?

4. **Culture** What are the main agents of cultural diffusion today?

Critical Thinking

5. **Understanding Cause and Effect** How does history shape a culture?

6. **Making Comparisons** Analyze two kinds of economic systems.

Graphic Organizer

7. **Organizing Information** Create a diagram like this one. In the outer ovals list practices that are characteristic of your government.

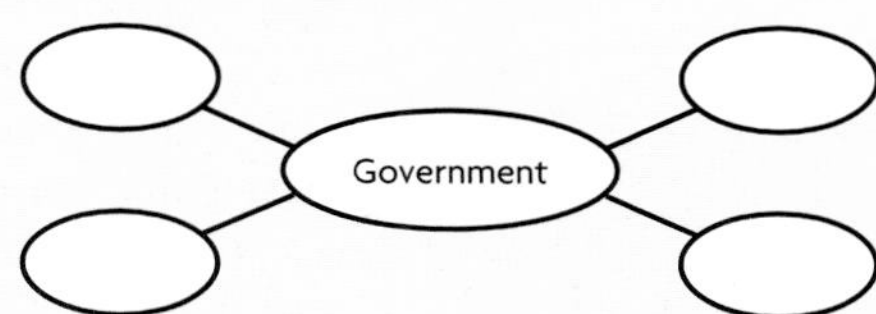

Applying Social Studies Skills

8. **Analyzing Charts** Look at the Types of Industries chart on page 32. Choose your own example product and show how it would go through the different processes.

Section 2 Assessment

1. The terms are defined in the Glossary.
2. anthropologists, sociologists, human geographers, historians
3. freedom of speech, free public education, the right to practice a religion of their choosing
4. radio, television, telephones, computers, the Internet
5. History records a culture's past, thereby explaining present circumstances and guiding present behavior
6. Answers will vary. The systems are defined on page 32 of the text.
7. Students answers could include: limited government, democratic elections, bill of rights, checks and balances
8. Answers will vary.

Chapter 1

Section 2, pages 27–33

Section Quiz 1-2

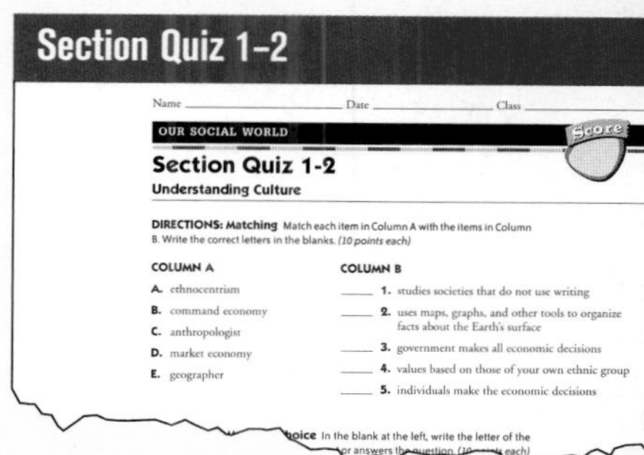

Name ________ Date ________ Class ________

OUR SOCIAL WORLD

Section Quiz 1-2

Understanding Culture

DIRECTIONS: Matching Match each item in Column A with the items in Column B. Write the correct letters in the blanks. *(10 points each)*

COLUMN A	COLUMN B
A. ethnocentrism	____ **1.** studies societies that do not use writing
B. command economy	____ **2.** uses maps, graphs, and other tools to organize facts about the Earth's surface
C. anthropologist	____ **3.** government makes all economic decisions
D. market economy	____ **4.** values based on those of your own ethnic group
E. geographer	____ **5.** individuals make the economic decisions

...hoice In the blank at the left, write the letter of the ... or answers the question. (10 ... each)

✓ Reading Check Answer

Answers may include rising population, too few jobs, poor schools, lack of social and health services.

Reading Essentials and Study Guide 1-2

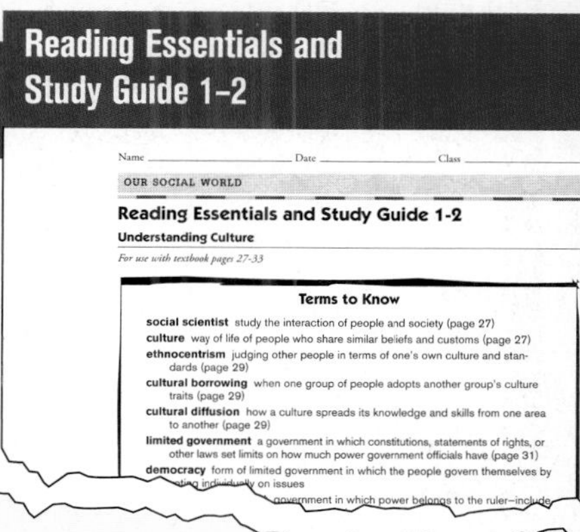

Name ________ Date ________ Class ________

OUR SOCIAL WORLD

Reading Essentials and Study Guide 1-2

Understanding Culture

For use with textbook pages 27-33

Terms to Know

social scientist study the interaction of people and society (page 27)
culture way of life of people who share similar beliefs and customs (page 27)
ethnocentrism judging other people in terms of one's own culture and standards (page 29)
cultural borrowing when one group of people adopts another group's culture traits (page 29)
cultural diffusion how a culture spreads its knowledge and skills from one area to another (page 29)
limited government a government in which constitutions, statements of rights, or other laws set limits on how much power government officials have (page 31)
democracy form of limited government in which the people govern themselves by ... individually on issues
... government in which power belongs to the ruler—include...

Enrich

Have students research and prepare a presentation of the visual arts, music, or literature of another culture. Ask them to explain the relationship between the culture and the art form.

4 Close

Have students write a brief essay explaining each of the eight elements of culture.

Chapter 1

Section 3, pages 34–38

Focus

Section Objectives

1. Describe migration patterns.
2. Explain the effects of population growth.
3. Discuss globalization.

BELLRINGER
Skillbuilder Activity

Project transparency and have students answer questions.

This activity is also available as a blackline master.

Daily Focus Skills Transparency 1-3

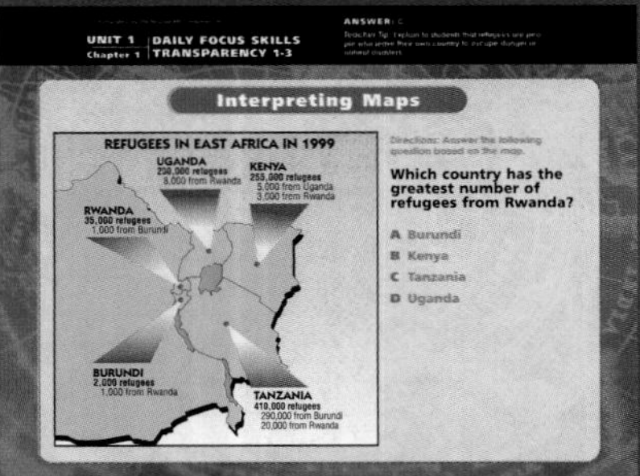

Guide to Reading

■ Accessing Prior Knowledge
Ask students whether they believe their community is crowded. Have them explain their answer.

Use the Vocabulary PuzzleMaker to create crossword and word search puzzles.

Section 3

Patterns in Today's World

Guide to Reading

Main Idea

All over the world people are moving from one place to another looking for freedom, jobs, and a better life.

Terms to Know

- migrate
- urbanization
- refugee
- rights
- responsibilities
- interdependence
- globalization

Reading Strategy

Create a chart like this one. List two regions under each that are experiencing conflict or cooperation at this time.

Conflict	Cooperation

Imagine that you and your friends are in Berlin, Germany. Can you hear the music? Every summer, hundreds of thousands of young people gather here for a music festival. Although most of these young people are here only to visit, many thousands of others come to find jobs and new lives. Germany faces challenges in finding room for its newcomers.

People have been moving from place to place since the dawn of time. Some places "pull" people with opportunities for freedom and a better life. Other places, where poverty is widespread or where governments are unstable, tend to "push" people away. The push and pull of migration is just one of the social forces that shape today's world.

Human Migration

Throughout the world, people **migrate**, or move, in great numbers. More and more people leave villages and farms and move to cities. This movement is called **urbanization**. Nearly half the world's people live in cities—a far higher percentage than ever before.

People move to cities for many reasons. The most common reason is to find jobs. This movement is putting a tremendous strain on the ability of cities to provide basic services such as clean water, sewage removal, housing, and health care.

Section Resources

Reproducible Masters
- Reproducible Lesson Plan 1-3
- Daily Lecture and Discussion Notes 1-3
- Guided Reading Activity 1-3
- Reading Essentials and Study Guide 1-3
- Section Quiz 1-3

Transparencies
- Daily Focus Skills Transparency 1-3

Multimedia
- Vocabulary PuzzleMaker Software
- Interactive Tutor Self-Assessment CD-ROM
- Presentation Plus! CD-ROM
- ExamView® Pro 3.0 Testmaker CD-ROM

When movement is from country to country, problems can increase dramatically. **Refugees** are people who are forced to leave their homeland because of wars or unjust governments. Refugees often do not speak the language or know the customs of the people in their adopted countries. They usually must work at the lowest-paying jobs and often without benefits earned by other workers.

Reading Check What is the most common reason people move to cities from rural areas?

Population Growth

How fast has the earth's population grown? The chart on page 36 shows the rapid increase in world population in recent years. Rapid population growth presents many challenges. An increase in the number of people means that more food is needed. Fortunately, since 1950 world food production has increased faster than population on all continents except Africa. Because so many people there need food, bad weather or war can ruin crops and bring disaster. Millions may suffer from a lack of food.

Also, populations that grow rapidly may use resources more quickly than populations that do not grow as fast. Some countries face shortages of water and housing.

Reading Check Why is rapid population growth a problem for many countries?

Our World Today Online

Web Activity Visit the ***Our World Today: People, Places, and Issues*** Web site at owt.glencoe.com and click on **Chapter 1–Student Web Activities** to learn more about the world population "clock."

NATIONAL GEOGRAPHIC On Location

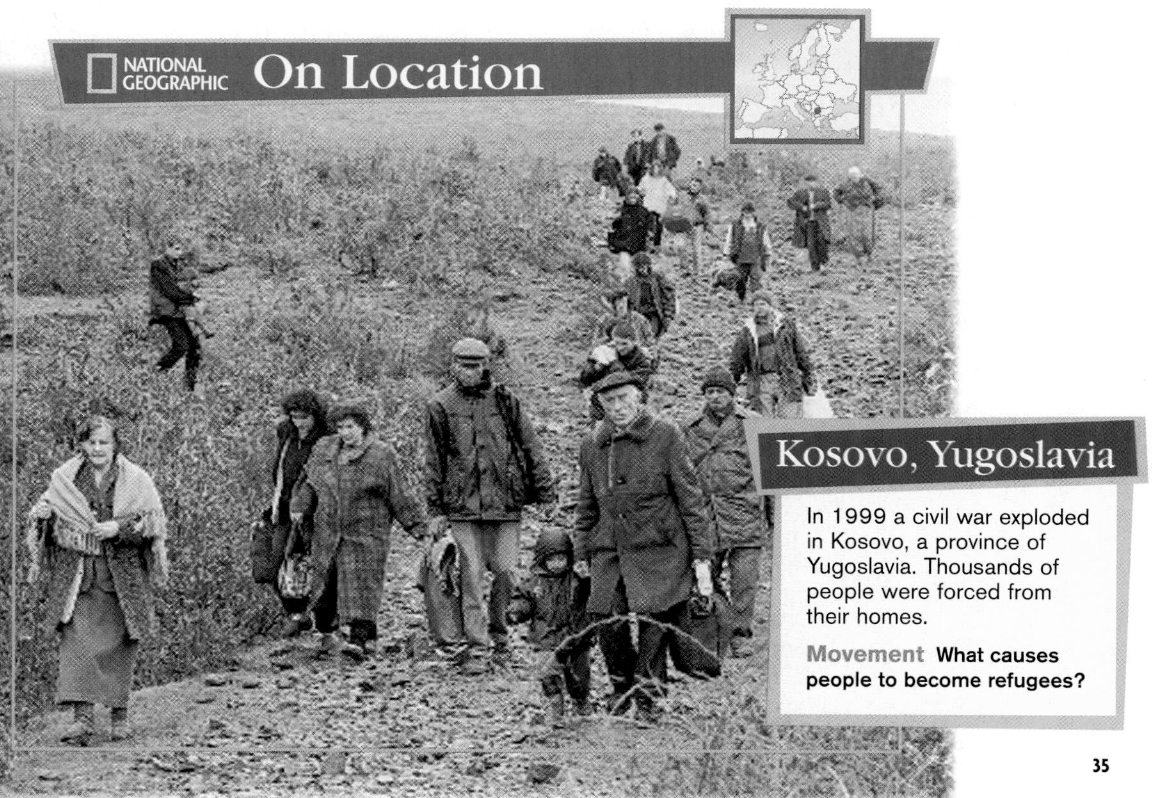

Kosovo, Yugoslavia

In 1999 a civil war exploded in Kosovo, a province of Yugoslavia. Thousands of people were forced from their homes.

Movement **What causes people to become refugees?**

35

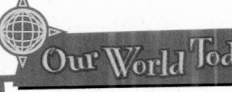

Our World Today Online

Objectives, goals, and answers to the Student Web Activity can be found in the Web Activity Lesson Plan at **owt.glencoe.com**

Reading Check Answer

to find jobs

More About the Photo

Kosovo About 1.5 million Kosovars were driven from their homes during the civil war. Slightly more than half were forced to leave the country until NATO bombing forced Serbia to accept their return.

Caption Answer persecution or disaster

Reading Check Answer

It could lead to shortages in food, resources, water, and housing.

Meeting Special Needs

Interpersonal Have students consider the effects of different levels of population density. They should think about how life would be changed if there were more or fewer people in their community. Then have them create a chart that contains the characteristics of life in low-density and high-density areas. **L2**

Refer to *Inclusion for the Middle School Social Studies Classroom Strategies and Activities* in the TCR.

Analyzing the Graph and Chart

Answer
India

Skills Practice
How would you describe world population growth from A.D. 1 to about 1800? *(much slower than today and remaining fairly steady)*

TEACH

Determining Cause and Effect Create a two-column chart titled "The Population Explosion." Write the words "Causes" and "Effects" as the column headings. Guide students in identifying the causes *(reduced death rates, high birthrates)* and effects *(need for more food and resources, economic strains)*. **L1**

Daily Lecture Notes 1-3

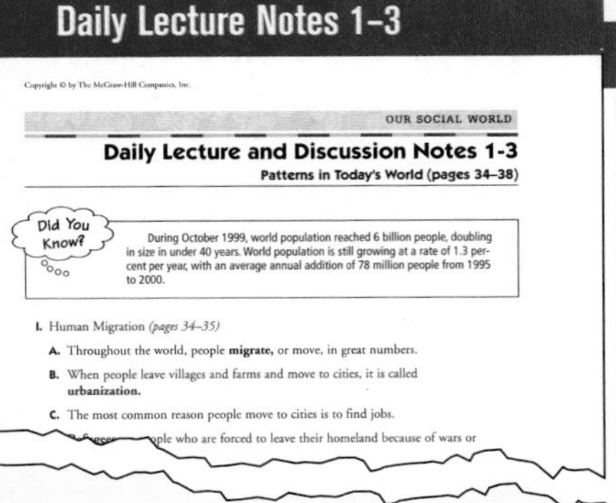

Copyright © by The McGraw-Hill Companies, Inc.

OUR SOCIAL WORLD

Daily Lecture and Discussion Notes 1-3
Patterns in Today's World (pages 34–38)

Did You Know? During October 1999, world population reached 6 billion people, doubling in size in under 40 years. World population is still growing at a rate of 1.3 percent per year, with an average annual addition of 78 million people from 1995 to 2000.

I. Human Migration *(pages 34–35)*

A. Throughout the world, people **migrate,** or move, in great numbers.

B. When people leave villages and farms and move to cities, it is called **urbanization.**

C. The most common reason people move to cities is to find jobs.

✓ Reading Check Answer

Europe and North America

NATIONAL GEOGRAPHIC

World Population

Analyzing the Graph and Chart

The world's population is expected to reach about 9 billion by 2050.

Place Which country has the second-largest number of people?

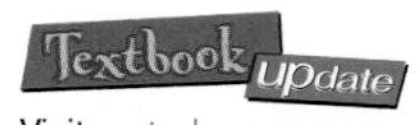

Visit owt.glencoe.com and click on **Chapter 1–Textbook Updates.**

POPULATION GROWTH

Population (in billions): 0, 1, 2, 3, 4, 5, 6

Year: A.D. 1, 500, 1000, 1500, 2000

Source: *The World Almanac,* 2000.

MOST POPULOUS COUNTRIES

Country	Millions of People
China	1,273.3
India	1,033.0
United States	284.5
Indonesia	206.1
Brazil	171.8
Pakistan	145.0
Russia	144.4

Sources: *National Geographic Atlas of the World; The World Almanac,* 2000.

Conflict and Cooperation

Very few, if any, countries have been free of conflict in their history. As technology brings us closer together, however, nations are beginning to understand the importance of cooperation. Disagreement over land is a common reason for conflict between groups and nations. This is especially true when one culture has been displaced, or moved, by another culture. The **Israelis** and **Palestinians,** for example, have been fighting over land for more than 50 years. In eastern Europe, wars have broken out over who should control the land in countries once ruled by the former Soviet Union. These conflicts are also about religion, race, and politics. When groups and nations cooperate, they work together to find peaceful solutions to problems. Or, in the case of the **European Community,** they work together to prevent problems and to benefit from their combined strength. An example of economic cooperation can be found close to home. The **North American Free Trade Agreement (NAFTA)** is an agreement among Canada, the United States, and Mexico to improve trade relations among these countries.

✓ Reading Check **What regions of the world have seen economic cooperation among nations?**

Civic Participation

Civic participation is being concerned with the public affairs of a community, state, nation, or the world. It is being an involved citizen. Some forms of government demand more involvement from their citizens than other types. In a democracy, for example, citizens need to be aware of their rights and responsibilities. **Rights** are benefits and

Cooperative Learning Activity

Mathematics Organize students into six groups and assign each group one of the following continents: Africa, Asia, Australia, Europe, North America, and South America. Direct groups to research the following information on their assigned continent: total population, population density, 10 largest cities, projected population for the year 2010 or 2025. Have each group list its findings on an outline map of the continent. Groups should mark their maps to show population distribution and the locations of the 10 cities. Arrange the maps to form a world map of population on the bulletin board. **L1**

EE4 The World in Spatial Terms: Standard 3

protections guaranteed to you by law. In the United States, for example, you have the right to own property. **Responsibilities** are duties that you owe to your fellow citizens to make sure that the government continues. A major responsibility of democratic citizenship is voting. You also have a responsibility to respect the property and privacy of others. In totalitarian governments, the people have no rights. Their responsibilities are to obey the laws of the land.

✓ Reading Check **How are rights different from responsibilities?**

Globalization

Think of the many ways you use products from other countries. The fruit you put on your breakfast cereal might have come from Mexico or South America. Your running shoes were likely made in China or Taiwan. Your book bag might have been made in India. **Interdependence** exists when countries depend on one another for goods, raw materials to make goods, and markets in which to sell goods. You might hear the world referred to as a "global village." In a village, people depend upon one another to provide what they need to live.

Many people are working to preserve the cultures of peoples such as the Masai in Kenya, Africa. They point out that **globalization**—the

Primary Source

GLOBALIZATION

Kofi Annan, secretary-general of the United Nations, spoke to the General Assembly about globalization.

"If one word [describes] the changes we are living through, it is 'globalization.' . . . What are [the] global issues? I have grouped them under three headings, each of which I relate to a fundamental human freedom . . . First, freedom from want. How can we call human beings free and equal in dignity when over a billion of them are struggling to survive on less than one dollar a day? . . . The second . . . is freedom from fear. . . . We must do more to prevent conflicts from happening at all. . . . The third [is] the freedom of future generations to sustain their lives on this planet. . . . We need to remember the old African wisdom which I learned as a child—that the earth is not ours. It is a treasure we hold in trust for our descendents."

Millennium Report, April 3, 2000.

Analyzing Primary Sources

Do you think these are the only global issues? Do these issues affect you in your daily life? If they do, how? If they don't, do you think you should have to worry about them?

Content Background

In September 2000, the United Nations held a three-day summit meeting with more than 150 world leaders. Organizers wanted to discuss the ways that globalization could improve conditions for people around the world. Globalization is often seen as a way to increase economic trade between countries. Equally important, however, is the exchange of cultures and philosophies, as well as international cooperation in fighting pollution, poverty, disease, and oppression. Leaders who attended the summit resolved that by the year 2015, they would cut in half the number of people who live on less than $1 a day and do not have access to clean water, provide education to all children, and reverse the spread of AIDS and other diseases.

Chapter 1

Section 3, pages 34–38

Guided Reading Activity 1-3

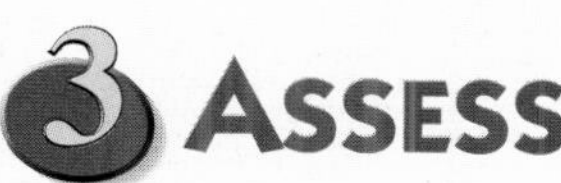
Name ______ Date ______ Class ______

OUR SOCIAL WORLD

Guided Reading Activity 1-3

Patterns in Today's World

DIRECTIONS: Summarizing Reading the section and completing the summary paragraphs below will help you learn more about why people throughout the world move from one place to another. Refer to your textbook to fill in the blanks.

The movement of people from villages and farms to cities is called **(1)** ______. The most common reason for people moving to cities is to **(2)** ______ ______. People who are forced to leave their homelands are known as **(3)** ______.

An increase in population often means that more **(4)** ______ is needed. A population increase can also mean that **(5)** ______ are used more quickly.

A common cause of conflict between nations is disagreement over ______. The Israelis and the **(7)** ______ have been

3 ASSESS

Assign Section 3 Assessment as homework or an in-class activity.

Have students use the Interactive Tutor Self-Assessment CD-ROM to review Section 1–3.

✓ Reading Check Answer

Rights are protections guaranteed to you. Responsibilities are duties you owe your government fellow citizens.

Primary Source

Answer Answers will vary.

Activity Have your students use the Internet to find examples that illustrate Kofi Annan's three global issues. Have students present their findings to the class, using both pictures and facts. They should also describe the Web sites that they use as a source: what organization is behind it, how reliable is it, how up-to-date is the information?

Reading Check Answer

Like in a village, people around the world depend on one another to provide what they need to live.

Section Quiz 1-3

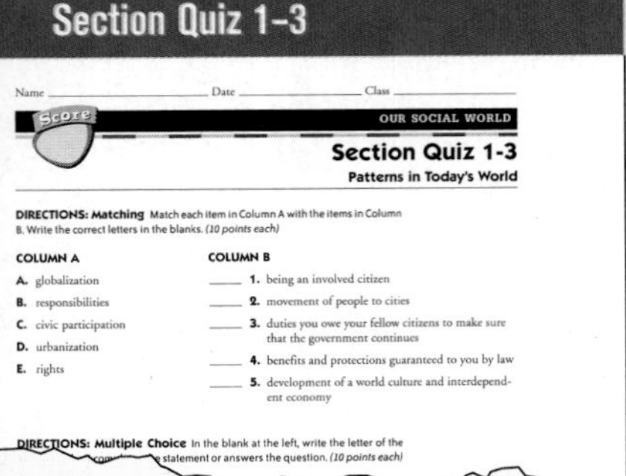
Name ______ Date ______ Class ______

Score

OUR SOCIAL WORLD

Section Quiz 1-3

Patterns in Today's World

DIRECTIONS: Matching Match each item in Column A with the items in Column B. Write the correct letters in the blanks. *(10 points each)*

COLUMN A	COLUMN B
A. globalization	____ **1.** being an involved citizen
B. responsibilities	____ **2.** movement of people to cities
C. civic participation	____ **3.** duties you owe your fellow citizens to make sure that the government continues
D. urbanization	____ **4.** benefits and protections guaranteed to you by law
E. rights	____ **5.** development of a world culture and interdependent economy

DIRECTIONS: Multiple Choice In the blank at the left, write the letter of the ... statement or answers the question. *(10 points each)*

Reading Check Answer

It makes it easier to stay informed, organize, and communicate. Examples will vary.

Reading Essentials and Study Guide 1-3

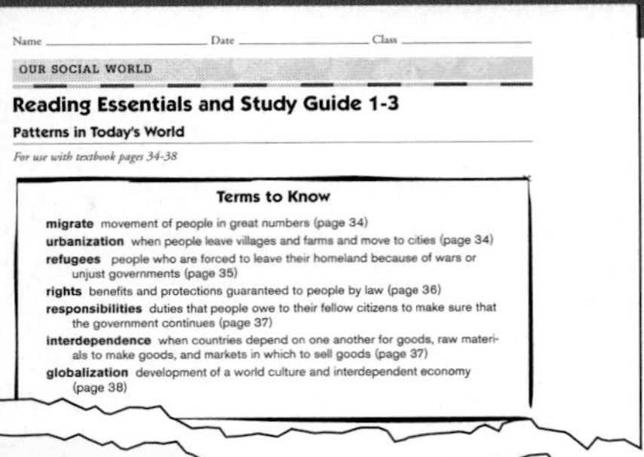
Name ______ Date ______ Class ______

OUR SOCIAL WORLD

Reading Essentials and Study Guide 1-3

Patterns in Today's World

For use with textbook pages 34-38

Terms to Know

migrate movement of people in great numbers (page 34)
urbanization when people leave villages and farms and move to cities (page 34)
refugees people who are forced to leave their homeland because of wars or unjust governments (page 35)
rights benefits and protections guaranteed to people by law (page 36)
responsibilities duties that people owe to their fellow citizens to make sure that the government continues (page 37)
interdependence when countries depend on one another for goods, raw materials to make goods, and markets in which to sell goods (page 37)
globalization development of a world culture and interdependent economy (page 38)

Close

Have students write a summary that highlights the most important points of the section.

development of a world culture and interdependent economy—might erase traditions and customs of smaller groups. An important issue in the world today is how small countries can use products and services of developing nations and still preserve local cultures and values. A saying that has become popular in recent years is that we should "think globally and act locally." What does that expression mean to you?

Reading Check **What is meant by the words "the world is becoming a global village"?**

Technology and World Issues

Technology is a tool. Like any tool, it can be used both wisely and foolishly. The Internet, if used wisely, can help develop better citizens. Citizens can stay better informed. They can organize more easily. They can also communicate with leaders and representatives quickly and directly by e-mail.

Beyond the problem of how technology is used, is the problem of how technology can be shared. Developing countries complain that they do not have access to the information that technology provides. What responsibility, if any, do industrialized countries have to share technology? Because progress, in many ways, is determined by technology, this may be the most important issue of all.

Reading Check **In what way is technology a tool? Give two examples.**

Assessment

Defining Terms

1. **Define** migrate, urbanization, refugee, rights, responsibilities, interdependence, globalization.

Recalling Facts

2. **Place** About how much of the world's population lives in cities?
3. **Movement** What is the most common reason people move to cities?
4. **Government** What responsibilities do people in democracies have?

Critical Thinking

5. **Synthesizing Information** What products found in your classroom were made in other countries?
6. **Understanding Cause and Effect** How can conflict affect human migration?

Graphic Organizer

7. **Organizing Information** Create a diagram like this one and list three results of human migration.

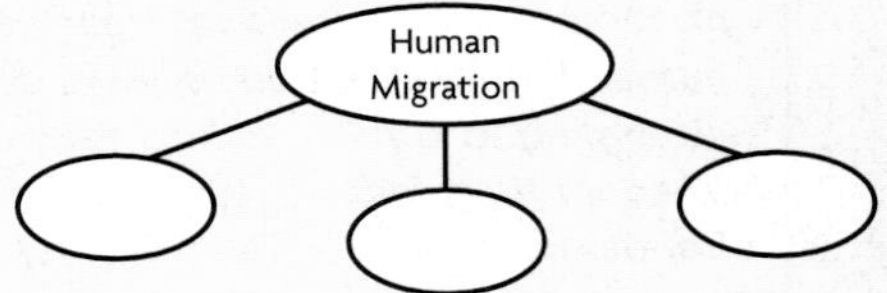

Applying Social Studies Skills

8. **Understanding Citizenship** Describe the civic participation expected of citizens of the United States.

Section 3 Assessment

1. The terms are defined in the Glossary.
2. nearly half the world's people
3. to find jobs
4. voting, respecting the property and privacy of others
5. Answers will vary.
6. Wars or unjust governments can cause people to leave their homeland and migrate to other countries.
7. Answers will vary but can include: strain on resources of host countries or cities, low paying jobs, mixing of cultures, conflict between groups
8. They should be aware of their rights and responsibilities.

TIME REPORTS

FOCUS ON WORLD ISSUES

Our Shrinking World

Indians in Peru use the Internet to line up buyers for their farm goods.

The Global Economy and Your Future

THOMAS MULLER

TIME REPORTS

Focus on World Issues

Teacher Background

Few topics are more controversial than globalization, which is changing the way virtually everyone works. Advocates state that globalization opens up new markets, provides consumers with the goods they want, and creates jobs for those who might otherwise be unable to support their families. Detractors state that globalization takes authority away from local governments and discourages the development of democracy; in addition, foreign corporations often have little concern for worker welfare.

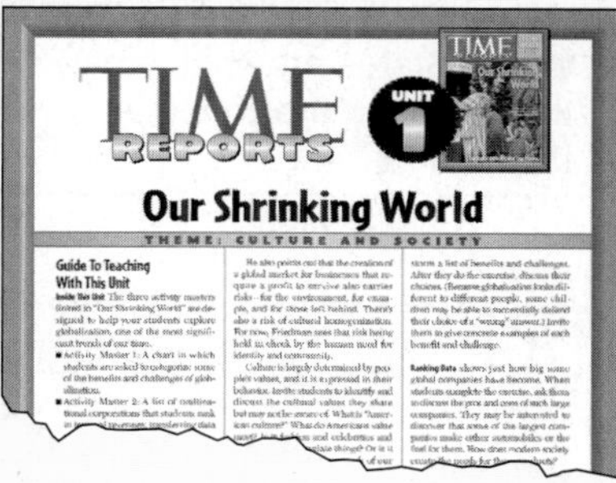

TIME REPORTS UNIT 1

Our Shrinking World

THEME: CULTURE AND SOCIETY

Guide To Teaching With This Unit

Preparing the Student

The term *globalization* came into common usage in the 1980s when countries became increasingly dependent on one another because of growing international trade and the freer flow of money around the world. However, globalization is nothing new—what is new is how fast and efficient international trading has become.

Making Connections

Globalization Ask students: **What did you have for dinner last night?** List the foods on the board. The foods probably will have a variety of ethnic origins. Just a few generations ago, food such as chow mien and lasagna were considered exotic. Today, enchiladas and sushi are available practically everywhere in the United States. Ask students what they think this trend indicates. Encourage them to think of other ways in which their lives are influenced by the widespread interaction among world cultures. For example, how are our clothes, music, and sports influenced by other countries? Then ask students to come up with a definition of the term *globalization*. Emphasize the role that free trade plays in globalization. **L1**

1 Focus

Bring in pictures from magazines, newspapers, and so on that show how average people around the world (in particular teenagers) have been affected by globalization and the mass media. For example, you might choose pictures of students in Africa accessing the Internet and a rural South American child wearing a sweatshirt saying "University of Michigan." Have students discuss the pictures in relationship to globalization.

A Sweatshirt's Global Journey

ANSWER
The cost would probably be higher because workers in the United States are paid more than those in the countries shown here.

Did You Know?

The term *e-commerce* refers to not only doing business over the Internet, but also to using the Internet to enhance business, for example, by supplying product information. In 2001, it was estimated that $8–10 billion worth of business was conducted over the Internet.

TIME REPORTS

FOCUS ON WORLD ISSUES

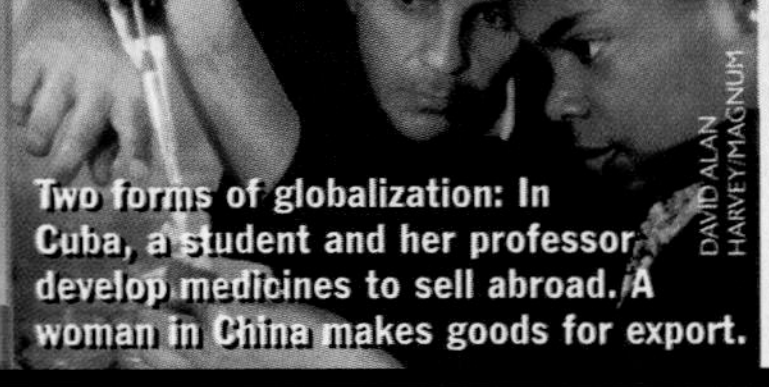

Two forms of globalization: In Cuba, a student and her professor develop medicines to sell abroad. A woman in China makes goods for export.

DAVID ALAN HARVEY/MAGNUM

How Trade Changes Lives

For Nora Lydia Urias Perez, life has never been easy. A single mother, she lived with her five-year-old daughter in the Mexican state of Veracruz. The only work she could find there was on a farm, earning $5 a day. That just wasn't enough.

In 2000 she moved to Nogales, a city just south of the New Mexico border. She got a job in a stapler factory that had moved to Nogales from New York City. Ms. Urias's job paid her $10 a day. To her, it was a fortune.

Thanks to the North American Free Trade Agreement (NAFTA), hundreds of thousands of Mexicans work in factories like Ms. Urias's. Companies in the United States, Japan and Europe own their factories. Their workers assemble products with parts that come from the United States. They send the finished goods—everything from dresses to TVs—back to the United States and Canada.

Global Relationships

This relationship is an example of **globalization**, the linking together of the world's nations through trade. What's driving globalization today is the search for cheap labor. Cheap labor helps manufacturers keep costs low. Low costs can mean lower prices for many things you buy.

A Sweatshirt's Global Journey

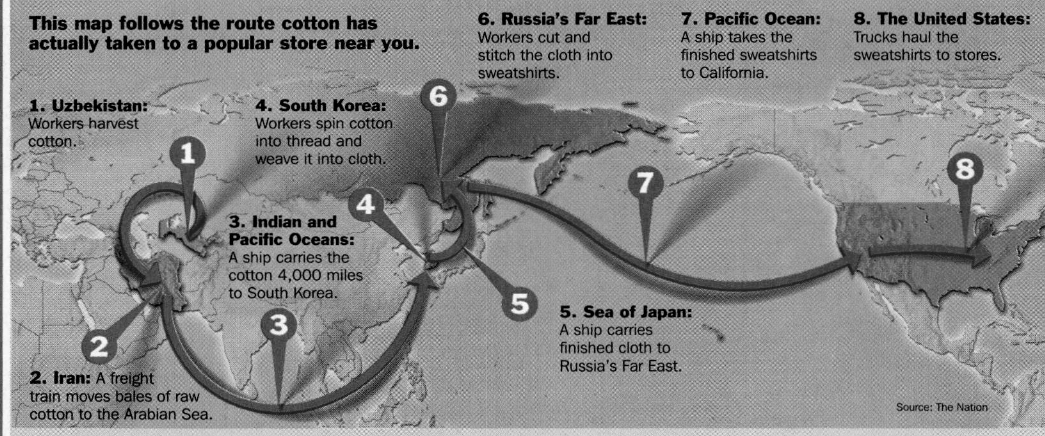

This map follows the route cotton has actually taken to a popular store near you.
1. Uzbekistan: Workers harvest cotton.
2. Iran: A freight train moves bales of raw cotton to the Arabian Sea.
3. Indian and Pacific Oceans: A ship carries the cotton 4,000 miles to South Korea.
4. South Korea: Workers spin cotton into thread and weave it into cloth.
5. Sea of Japan: A ship carries finished cloth to Russia's Far East.
6. Russia's Far East: Workers cut and stitch the cloth into sweatshirts.
7. Pacific Ocean: A ship takes the finished sweatshirts to California.
8. The United States: Trucks haul the sweatshirts to stores.
Source: The Nation

INTERPRETING MAPS

Making Inferences How do you think the price of the sweatshirt might be affected if the sweatshirt were made entirely in the United States?

40

Critical Thinking Activity

Formulating an Opinion Consumer advocate Ralph Nader has stated, "Globalization means control of world economies by giant corporations that don't have an allegiance to a community or don't have any allegiance to a particular country—even the one they're domiciled in—as long as they can make more profit elsewhere." Read this quote to the students. Then have students divide into small groups to discuss whether they agree or disagree with this statement. When they are done, ask each group to share their discussion with the class.

EE4 Human Systems: Standard 11

Some fear global companies may neglect the environment.

Police block a march by globalization's foes in 1999.

A U.S. resident made this Taiwanese movie in China.

Globalization is changing far more than prices. More people, money, and goods are crossing national borders than ever before.

Pop Goes Global

Popular entertainment is no exception. A movie popular in the United States is likely to be a favorite elsewhere. Asians love basketball as much as Americans do. Kids everywhere listen to Latin pop music and wear jeans and sneakers to school.

That doesn't mean all kids think and act the same way. "It is important to see individual differences from one country to the next," advises a woman who has studied teens in 44 nations.

Culture Clash

Companies that forget that advice can get into trouble. A U.S. company opened a theme park outside Paris, France. But the French stayed away. They hated the fast food the park sold. They didn't even like the park's name. It contained the word "Euro," short for "European." The French see themselves as French first, Europeans second.

When the park's owners figured all this out, they made the park more French. They offered food and drinks that suited French tastes, for example. They even put the word "Paris" in the park's name. Today that theme park is one of the most popular in the world.

Good for Everyone?

As the park's owners learned, globalization isn't **"Americanizing"** the world. Local cultures are too strong for that.

But globalization hasn't been good for everyone. The poorest countries have seen little or no increase in trade. Many Americans' jobs have moved to countries where wages are low. And so far the lives of people like Ms. Urias haven't improved much. It costs more to live in Nogales than in Veracruz. So Ms. Urias is still poor.

Gaining Skills

Experts say these problems are only temporary. In recent years trade has created millions of jobs. It has enabled people in poorer countries like Mexico to pick up new skills. The more skilled workers are, the more they get paid.

Ms. Urias looks forward to better times. "I am not saying it will be easy to start life [in Nogales]," she told a reporter. "But at last there is a chance that things for me will get better. There was no chance of that in Veracruz. I had no hope." ■

EXPLORING THE ISSUE

1. **Cause and Effect** How might the health of the U.S. economy shape Ms. Urias's life?
2. **Making Inferences** Why do you think that the poorest countries have seen few gains from globalization?

41

2 TEACH

Identifying Main Ideas

Have students read the subsection titled "Global Relationships." Ask them to write a one-sentence summary of this subsection. Ask volunteers to read their summaries to the class.

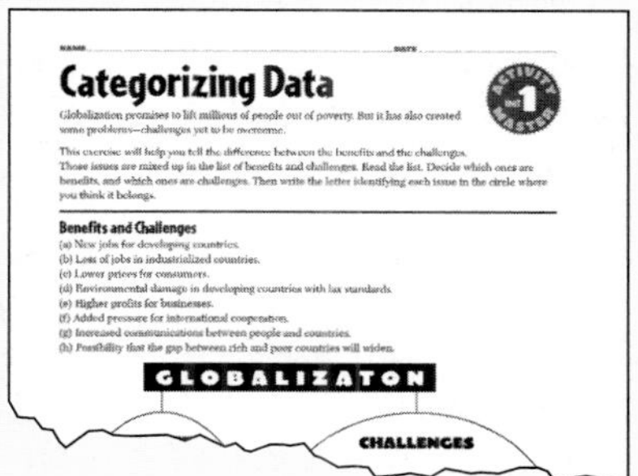

NAME ________ DATE ________

Categorizing Data

Globalization promises to lift millions of people out of poverty. But it has also created some problems—challenges yet to be overcome.

This exercise will help you tell the difference between the benefits and the challenges. Those issues are mixed up in the list of benefits and challenges. Read the list. Decide which ones are benefits, and which ones are challenges. Then write the letter identifying each issue in the circle where you think it belongs.

Benefits and Challenges

(a) New jobs for developing countries.
(b) Loss of jobs in industrialized countries.
(c) Lower prices for consumers.
(d) Environmental damage in developing countries with lax standards.
(e) Higher profits for businesses.
(f) Added pressure for international cooperation.
(g) Increased communications between people and countries.
(h) Possibility that the gap between rich and poor countries will widen.

GLOBALIZATON

CHALLENGES

EXPLORING THE ISSUE

ANSWERS

1. *Possible answer:* Americans must make enough money to purchase the consumer goods she makes or she will not have work.
2. *Possible answer:* The jobs have gone to these countries because the people will work for very low wages. The workers generally have few skills, are not organized, and do not have the ability to fight for higher pay.

Meeting Special Needs

Kinesthetic Dramatizing business activities can increase students sensitivity to the difficulties in interacting with those from another culture. Have students divide into pairs. Each pair should pick a foreign country and then research the business customs and conventions of that country. They should then use their knowledge of these customs to develop a short skit in which one person is an American visiting the country on business. The second person should be a native of the host country. The pair should then present their skit to the class. **L2**

Refer to *Inclusion for the Middle Schcol Social Studies Classroom Strategies and Activities* in the TCR.

TIME REPORTS

Recommended Internet Sites

www.wto.org
The official site of the World Trade Organization (WTO). The WTO deals with rules of trade among nations and attempts to aid in resolving trade disputes.

www.pbs.org/globalization/home.html
This Web site discusses the effects of globalization on human rights.

www.globaled.org/curriculum3.html
Contains a number of lessons on global issues, human rights, and developing nations.

www.maryknoll.org/EDUCA/CORNER/studyguides/edup_la.htm
Contains a set of four lessons on the affect of globalization on Latin America. One of the lessons ("Story Telling—the Human Face of Globalization") contains 16 case studies showing how globalization affects poor people.

EXPLORING THE ISSUE

ANSWERS

1. Trade increases communication among cultures and creates greater understanding of one another's customs and philosophies. People learn how other cultures are similar as well as different.
2. *Possible answers:* vast amounts of information are available immediately; communication around the world is instantaneous; consumers can order items online in just a few minutes rather than going to a store.

TIME REPORTS

Globalization's New Face

The Phoenicians were great sailors. They lived in Southwest Asia, on the coast of Lebanon. They set up **trade routes** all around the Mediterranean Sea. Some experts think they may have sailed to England to bring back tin. They did all this as far back as 700 B.C.

GARWOOD & AINSLIE PLANET PROJECT

▲ **A Yagua tribesman (right) takes part in an Internet poll in the rain forests of Peru.**

As the Phoenicians showed, globalization is not new. People have traded in faraway lands, moved around, and mixed cultures for thousands of years.

What is new is the speed at which these exchanges take place. Technology is shrinking the world. Telephones zip our voices around the world. Jet planes carry us great distances in a few hours. High-speed cargo ships crisscross the oceans, carrying goods from nation to nation.

The Internet

The Internet has changed the way we swap goods, too. Twenty-five years ago, an American importer might have used "snail mail" to order a shipment of French bikes. Today she can check out the manufacturer's stock on his Web page. Then, in seconds, she can e-mail her order halfway around the world.

The deals she makes aren't much different from those the Phoenicians made. They traded timber for horses. She trades money for bicycles.

What's different is that she makes her trades in a flash, and without leaving her seat. She can do more business in the same time, and she can do business anywhere. The Phoenicians could do business only where they could sail.

EXPLORING THE ISSUE

1. **Making Inferences** How might trade help people from different cultures understand one another?
2. **Analyzing Information** How does the Internet make growing up different for you than it was for your parents?

Team-Teaching Activity

Economics Have a teacher with a background in economics discuss the growth of e-commerce (electronic commerce) as it relates to globalization. He or she should talk about how e-commerce is used not only by consumers, but also by companies, particularly within manufacturing industries. Ask the teacher to discuss how treaties such as GATT and NAFTA and regional organizations such as the European Union have affected globalization. **L2**

EE4 Human Systems: Standard 11

Sharing Globalization's Gains

A little more than 6 billion people live on Earth. About half of them get by on less than $2 a day. What does globalization mean to them? So far, not much.

Overall the impact of increased trade has been amazing. The ability of people to make and spend money has grown almost everywhere.

Yet the fruits of globalization haven't been spread evenly. **Industrialized countries** have more to trade than **developing countries**. Foreign companies prefer to build more factories in rich countries than in poor ones.

The result is that countries like Kenya tend to create new jobs slowly. Places like Canada tend to create them more quickly. Some countries in Asia and Africa are barely able to create any new jobs at all.

A Wider Gap

Those differences worry a lot of people. If the trend continues, experts say that the gap between rich and poor countries can only get wider.

What can be done to narrow that gap? There are no easy answers. International businesses are certainly part of it. During the 1990s, private companies spent more than $1 trillion to build factories in developing countries.

Rich nations are also part of the answer. They are already helping poorer countries pay for new roads, phone lines, seaports, and airports. And they are encouraging poor nations to produce things that people elsewhere want to buy.

▲ **Nowhere is the gap between rich and poor clearer than in Pakistan. Here a child laborer makes soccer balls for sale around the world.**

China figured out how to do that years ago. Thanks to trade, the ability of the Chinese to earn and spend money now doubles every 10 years. Finding ways to help about 200 other nations equal that success is one of today's biggest challenges.

EXPLORING THE ISSUE

1. **Making Inferences** Why do you think experts worry about the widening gap between rich and poor countries?
2. **Problem Solving** What would you do to help spread the fruits of globalization more evenly around the globe?

43

Synthesizing Information

Have students research the topic of child labor in developing countries. UNICEF is a good source for information. Have students then research child labor in the United States during the Industrial Revolution. **Ask: Compare the reasons for child labor during the Industrial Revolution to those for child labor in developing countries today. How was child labor stopped in the United States? Do you think these same methods would work in developing countries?** L1

NAME ____ DATE ____

Ranking Data

ACTIVITY UNIT 1 MASTER

In baseball, teams keep score by adding up runs. In business, companies keep score by adding up the year's revenues. Revenues are the money companies collect for what they sell.

This worksheet isn't about baseball. (Sorry.) It's about 10 companies that sell their products all over the world. In the year 2000, these 10 companies led the pack in revenues. Every other company in the world took in less money than they did.

That's a very big deal. To see how big, rank the companies according to the size of their revenues. Then group the companies by the products they make or sell.

Top 10 Global Companies (in alphabetical order)

(a) BP, a British oil and gas company, $148 billion
(b) DaimlerChrysler, a German automaker, $150 billion
(c) Exxon Mobil, a U.S. oil and gas company, $210 billion
(d) Ford Motor, a U.S. automaker, $181 billion
(e) General Electric, a U.S. manufacturer and finance company, $130 billion
(f) General Motors, a U.S. automaker, $185 billion
(g) Mitsubishi, a Japanese trading company, $127 billion
(h) Royal Dutch/Shell Group, a Netherlands oil and gas company, $149 billion
(i) Toyota, a Japanese automaker, $121 billion
(j) WalMart Stores, a U.S. retailer, $194 billion

Source: *Fortune Magazine*

Top 10 Global Companies: Who Makes More?

GROUPED BY PRODUCT

EXPLORING THE ISSUE

ANSWERS

1. Poor people are less able to learn skills to improve their lives. They may be unable to afford food, medical care, or education for their children. They generally do not have the ability to fight for or participate in democratic governments. They may be more willing to engage in warfare because they have little to lose.
2. Answers will vary.

Interdisciplinary Activity

Literature Many students may have already read Sinclair Lewis's novel *The Jungle*. If not, they may want to read it. Have students who have read the book briefly summarize it for those who have not. You will want to make certain that the working conditions of the time are clearly presented. Ask students: **How do you think working conditions in developing countries today are similar to those described in *The Jungle*? How are they different?** *(One way is that because of mass media and telecommunications, it is easier for today's workers to learn about conditions in other parts of the world.)* L2

TIME REPORTS

Preparing for a Smaller World: What Can One Person Do?

Every day in 2000, half a million airline passengers, 1.4 billion e-mail messages, and $1.5 trillion crossed national borders. All that shifting about of people, ideas, and money would have been unthinkable 10 years earlier. The Internet was a toddler. The World Wide Web had just been born.

DAVID STRICK/CORBIS OUTLINE

▲ Which of Pepperdine University's nine teammates was born in the U.S.? It's Anh Nguyen, fourth from left.

What will the world look like 10 years from now? No one can say. But two things are sure. Inventions that create faster ways to communicate will make the world seem a lot smaller than it is today. And more and more Americans will have jobs that require them to deal with people from other nations.

Learning About Other Cultures

You will be able to do that well if you have taken the time to learn about other countries. To really get to know people from other cultures, you need to understand what makes them tick. You can do that best by speaking to them in their own language.

You won't have to leave the United States to need that knowledge. Globalization has enabled more and more people to cross borders to find work. Employers will want to hire people who can work well with people born in other countries.

They will also want to know if you are committed to a **lifetime of learning**. As technology changes, your job will, too. Your need to learn new things won't stop when you leave high school or college.

Globalization is shaping tomorrow's job market. Only you can prepare yourself to thrive in it. And there's no time like today to start. ■

EXPLORING THE ISSUE

1. **Determining Cause and Effect** How does the Internet make the world seem smaller?
2. **Analyzing Information** Modern companies require employees at every level to solve problems they face on the job. Why are lifetime learners better equipped than others to solve problems?

Current Events Journal

Have students read a summary of a recent meeting of an organization such as the World Trade Organization (www.wto.org). Ask students to make a list of the major topics of discussion at the meeting.

Drawing Conclusions Tell students that within recent years, many media companies have merged, resulting in a relatively few remaining organizations. A prime example occurred when America Online (AOL) and Time Warner merged, forming the world's largest media company. **Ask:** What, if any, dangers can you see in an increasingly small number of companies controlling telecommunications and media businesses? L2

EXPLORING THE ISSUE

ANSWERS

1. We can interact with people around the world quickly and cheaply.
2. Learning enhances people's skills and helps them think creatively.

Your Government and You

The Office of the United States Trade Representative is responsible for supporting U.S. trade throughout the world. It enforces U.S. trade regulations and aids in resolving international trade disputes. One important international dispute involves "intellectual property." Some countries, such as China, violate international copyright law by allowing companies to freely copy intellectual property such as books, videotapes, and software without paying royalties to authors. The USTR is active in trying to pressure worldwide enforcement of copyright law. Have students research more about what the USTR is doing on this issue and others by visiting its Web site (www.ustr.gov). Ask them to summarize their findings in a paragraph. L1

TIME REPORTS

REVIEW AND ASSESS

UNDERSTANDING THE ISSUE

1. **Defining Key Terms** Write definitions for the following terms: *globalization, communication, trade route, Americanizing, culture, developing country, lifetime learner.*
2. **Writing to Inform** Write a short article about how globalization shapes the way people live and what they do. Use as many words as you can from the above list.
3. **Writing to Persuade** Overall, is globalization good or bad for the world? Defend your answer in a letter to an imaginary friend who lives in a developing country in Africa.

INTERNET RESEARCH ACTIVITY

4. Navigate to **epals.com**. With your teacher's help, contact two classrooms—one in an industrialized country and one in a developing country. Exchange lists on what imported goods kids in your country and theirs own or use. Compare the lists, and discuss what they say about the importance of trade.
5. Navigate to **www.pbs.org/internet/timeline**. Browse through the time line of Internet history. Write an essay telling how the Internet sped up communication, noting the key milestones described on the time line.

BEYOND THE CLASSROOM

6. **Look through your local newspaper for a week.** Find articles on topics related to globalization. For example, look for stories about the Internet, imports and exports, immigration, and even crimes like drug-smuggling. In an oral report, tell how the articles suggest that globalization is making the world smaller.

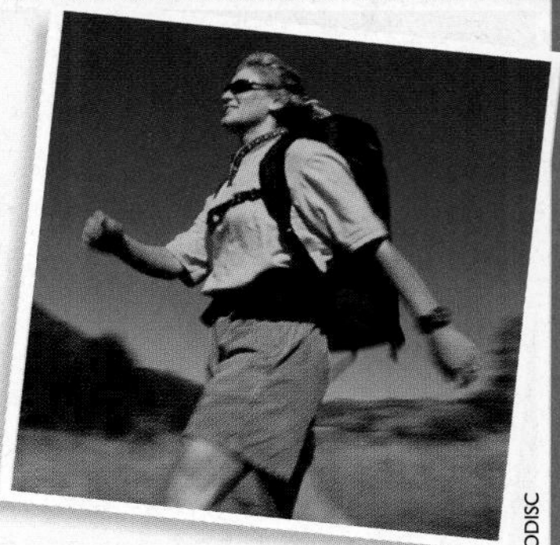

PHOTODISC

▲ More and more Americans are crossing the borders for fun.

7. **Take an inventory of your room at home.** Write down the name of each item made in another country. Count the items imported from the same country. Then make a bar graph to show how many imported items you own. Have each bar stand for one category—clothing, CDs, or sports equipment, for example. Write a caption explaining what the graph says about how important trade is to you.

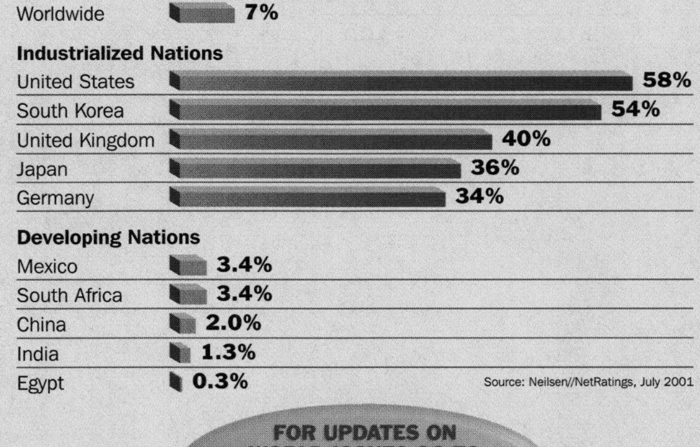

Where in the world are people wired to the Internet at home? Almost everywhere. But industrialized nations have a big lead. People with home access make up a big chunk of the populations of these richer nations. It's just the opposite with developing nations. People with home access make up a tiny part of the populations of these poorer nations. Experts call this gap the "digital divide," and it worries them. The Internet is a tool. Nations must use it to participate fully in world trade.

BUILDING GRAPH READING SKILLS

1. **Drawing Conclusions** Compare the amount of Internet use in industrialized and developing nations.
2. **Determining Cause and Effect** What does a nation need besides Internet access to succeed in world trade?

FOR UPDATES ON WORLD ISSUES GO TO www.timeclassroom.com/glencoe

45

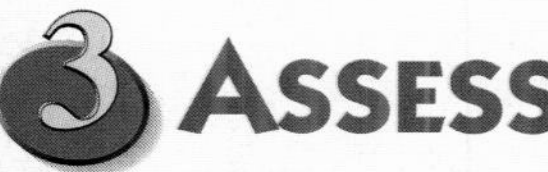

Assess

Have students take the Time Reports Quiz provided in the Teacher's Classroom Resources.

Alternative Assessment
Assign students the alternative assessment project for this unit feature, found in the Teacher's Classroom Resources.

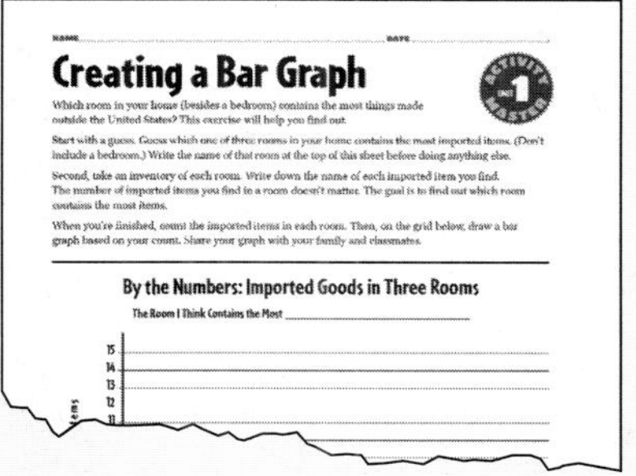

NAME .... DATE ....

Creating a Bar Graph

ACTIVITY 1 MASTER

Which room in your home (besides a bedroom) contains the most things made outside the United States? This exercise will help you find out.

Start with a guess. Guess which one of three rooms in your home contains the most imported items. (Don't include a bedroom.) Write the name of that room at the top of this sheet before doing anything else.

Second, take an inventory of each room. Write down the name of each imported item you find. The number of imported items you find in a room doesn't matter. The goal is to find out which room contains the most items.

When you're finished, count the imported items in each room. Then, on the grid below, draw a bar graph based on your count. Share your graph with your family and classmates.

By the Numbers: Imported Goods in Three Rooms

The Room I Think Contains the Most ____________

15
14
13
12
11

BUILDING GRAPH AND READING SKILLS

ANSWERS

1. It is higher in industrialized countries.
2. *Possible answers:* a hard-working, skilled workforce; a good transportation system; a stable government

Close

Ask students to write a paragraph starting with this topic sentence: *Some of the ways that globalization has changed the way companies conduct business are . . .*

Culminating Activity

To close this lesson, have students complete the Review and Assess section questions and activities above. Students should use classroom discussion, contextual clues, and their student dictionaries to write definitions for terms. Before assigning the Internet activities, it is recommended that you review your school district policy on student Internet use.

Focus on Debate
For further student understanding of the issue, have students debate the pro and con position of the following topic: **Industrialized countries have a responsibility to make certain that workers in developing countries are earning wages that allow them to meet their basic needs, including adequate food, clothing, and medical care. L2**

TEACH

Ask students if they have ever seen or used a road map to get from one place to another. Point out that road maps are special purpose maps. **Ask:** **What special information do these maps contain?** *(road locations; road types; government authority that has responsibility for the roads; relative size of cities and towns; and in some cases, location of service stations, tolls, points of interest)* **L1**

Additional Skills Practice

1. **What areas are shown on the map?** *(parts of Africa, Asia, and Europe)*
2. **What time period does the map cover? How long ago was that?** *(from 3500 B.C. to 1700 B.C.; from 5,500 to 3,700 years ago)*
3. **Which of these ancient civilizations covered the smallest area?** *(Ancient Egypt)*

Additional Skills Resources

 Chapter Skills Activity 1

 Building Geography Skills for Life

GLENCOE TECHNOLOGY

 **Skillbuilder Interactive Workbook CD-ROM, Level 1**

This interactive CD-ROM reinforces student mastery of essential social studies skills.

Social Studies Skill

Reading Thematic Maps

Thematic (special purpose) maps focus on a single theme. This theme may be to show the battles of a particular war or locations of endangered species, for example.

Learning the Skill

To read a special purpose map, follow these steps:

- Read the map title. It tells what kind of special information the map shows.
- Find the map's scale to determine the general size of the area.
- Read the key. Colors and symbols in the map key are especially important on this type of map.
- Analyze the areas on the map that are highlighted in the key. Look for patterns.

Practicing the Skill

Look at the map below to answer the following questions.

1. What is the title of the map?
2. Read the key. What four civilizations are shown on this map?
3. Which civilization was farthest west? East?
4. What do the locations of each of these civilizations have in common?

Applying the Skill

Find a special purpose map in a newspaper or magazine. Pose three questions about the map's purpose, then have a classmate answer the questions.

GO TO Practice key skills with **Glencoe Skillbuilder Interactive Workbook, Level 1.**

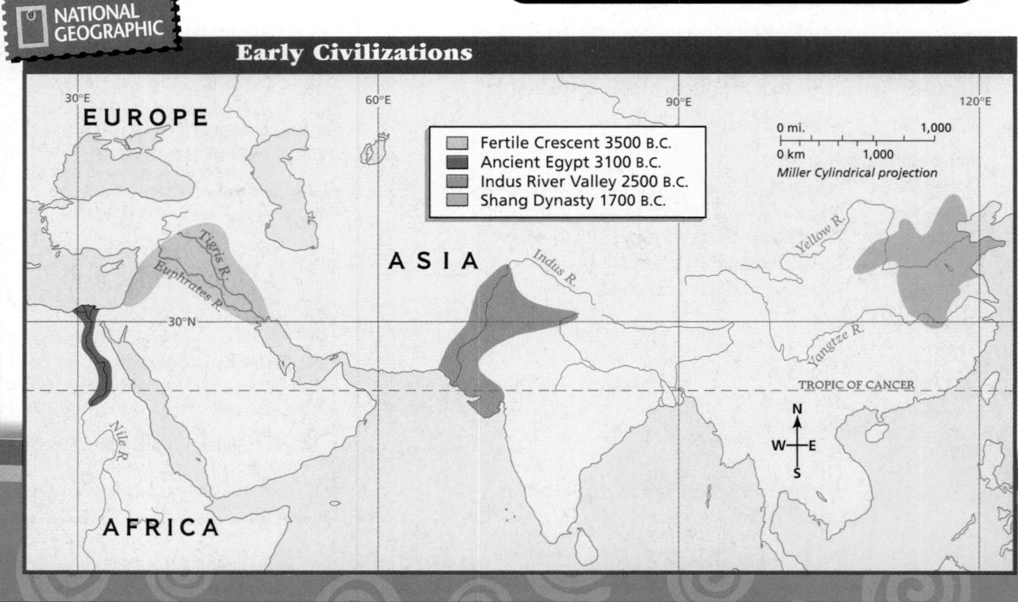

46

Practicing the Skill Answers

1. Early Civilizations
2. Fertile Crescent, Ancient Egypt, Indus River Valley, and Shang Dynasty
3. Ancient Egypt; Shang Dynasty
4. They all developed around rivers.

Applying the Skill
Students should include the map with the three questions.

Reading Review

Section 1 People Far and Near

Terms to Know
ethnic group
custom
minority group
majority group

Main Idea

Modern technology has helped to bring the world's diverse peoples closer together.

✓ Culture Our shrinking world makes it more likely that the people around us will represent other ethnic groups.

✓ Culture It is important to understand what makes people similar and different so that we can get along in a world that is changing.

✓ Place Schools are good places to build bridges between different peoples living in the same region.

Section 2 Understanding Culture

Terms to Know
social scientist
culture
ethnocentrism
cultural borrowing
cultural diffusion
limited government
democracy
unlimited government
dictatorship
absolute monarchy
constitutional monarchy

Main Idea

People all over the world usually live close to others who follow similar beliefs and like the same foods, music, and clothing.

✓ Culture Anthropologists, sociologists, historians, and human geographers are all social scientists who study the interaction of people.

✓ Culture Culture is the way of life of people who share similar beliefs and customs.

✓ Culture Most people have pride in their ethnic group and prefer their own culture.

✓ Culture Culture is continually spreading around the world. It spreads in two main ways, through cultural diffusion and cultural borrowing.

✓ History The story of a people's past helps us to understand its present and possibly its future.

✓ Government People need rules in order to live together.

✓ Economics People all over the world use natural resources to fill their wants and needs.

Section 3 Patterns in Today's World

Terms to Know
migrate
urbanization
refugee
rights
responsibilities
interdependence
globalization

Main Idea

All over the world people are moving from one place to another looking for freedom, jobs, and a better life.

✓ History Throughout the world people are continually moving toward a better life and away from conflict and poverty.

✓ History As the world is getting smaller, people are living closer together and more conflicts are arising. People must learn to cooperate with each other.

✓ Region Americans living in the United States enjoy freedom and democracy. They have a civic responsibility to their government to make sure it continues.

✓ Interdependence The movement of goods and services is helping to bring our world closer together.

Reading Review

Use the Chapter 1 Reading Review to preview, review, condense, or reteach the chapter.

Preview/Review

Use the Terms to Know lists to help students review and study.

Activity Organize the class into teams and quiz them on the Terms to Know. Offer a definition and ask each team to identify the correct term. If they do so correctly, they win a point; if they do not, the other team has an opportunity to do so.

Vocabulary PuzzleMaker Software reinforces the vocabulary terms used in Chapter 1.

The Interactive Tutor Self-Assessment CD-ROM allows students to review Chapter 1 content.

Condense

Have students read the Chapter 1 summary statements.

Chapter 1 Guided Reading Activities

Chapter 1 Audio Program

Reteach

Reteaching Activity 1

Chapter 1 Reading Essentials and Study Guide

Chapter Culminating Activity

Ask students: **What do you think is unique about your town's or state's culture?** Then have students work in groups to survey other students, faculty members, and family members. Have them ask the same question. Groups should collate the responses they receive and present their results to the class in a brief written report. Compile all the results and have the class discuss them. *NOTE: This activity may be completed separately or you may wish students to incorporate it into their Current Events Journals.*

EE2 Places and Regions: Standard 6

Assessment and Activities

GLENCOE TECHNOLOGY

MindJogger Videoquiz
Use MindJogger to review the Chapter 1 content.

 Available in VHS.

Using Key Terms

1. g
2. h
3. i
4. f
5. e
6. d
7. j
8. c
9. b
10. a

Reviewing the Main Idea

11. Technology is making it faster and easier to communicate with or travel to any place in the world.
12. They are where most young people first meet people from other ethnic groups.
13. origin, language, and history
14. social scientist
15. Examples will vary, but borrowing reflects how people adopt practices of another culture and diffusion is when one culture spreads its culture to another.
16. Governments create rules that make it possible for people to live together without conflict.
17. Industrialized countries do most of the world's manufacturing. Developing countries do little manufacturing of their own but are currently working towards greater industrialization.
18. to find jobs
19. Answers will vary, but can include Israel, Rwanda, and some countries of eastern Europe.
20. Answers will vary, but one might be the right to own property

Chapter 1 Assessment and Activities

Using Key Terms

Match the terms in Part A with their definitions in Part B.

A.

1. ethnic group
2. minority group
3. majority group
4. culture
5. ethnocentrism
6. cultural diffusion
7. rights
8. responsibilities
9. urbanization
10. interdependence

B.

a. countries depending on one another
b. people moving from the country to the cities
c. duties that you owe to your government
d. how a country spreads its knowledge and skills
e. people believe their way of life is best
f. way of life of people who share similar beliefs and customs
g. people who have a common origin
h. group of people whose culture, race, or ethnic origin is different from most of the people in the region
i. group in society that controls most of the wealth and power
j. benefits and protections guaranteed by law

Reviewing the Main Idea

Section 1 People Far and Near

11. **Culture** In what way is the world shrinking?
12. **Culture** Why are schools good places to "build bridges" between ethnic groups?
13. **Culture** List three traits that would be common to an ethnic group.

Section 2 Understanding Culture

14. **Culture** If you wanted to study people, what type of scientist might you want to be?
15. **Culture** Give one example of cultural borrowing and one example of cultural diffusion.
16. **Government** Why do countries need governments?
17. **Economics** What is the difference between an industrialized country and a developing country?

Section 3 Patterns in Today's World

18. **Place** Why are so many people moving to cities?
19. **Region** Name two places where there is conflict going on in the world today.
20. **Government** Name one of the rights we have as citizens of the United States.

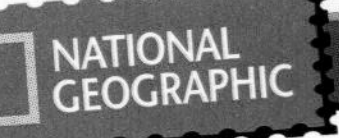

World Culture Regions

Place Location Activity

On a separate sheet of paper, using chapter or unit maps, match the letters on the map with the numbered places listed below.

1. Latin America
2. North Africa, Southwest Asia, and Central Asia
3. Europe
4. Russia
5. East Asia
6. United States and Canada
7. Australia, Oceania, and Antarctica
8. Africa south of the Sahara

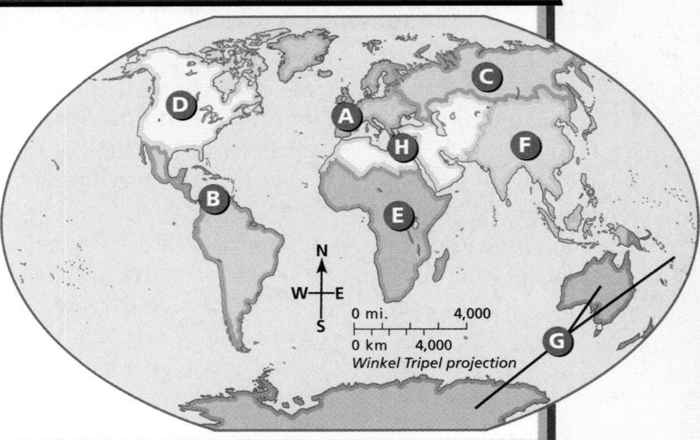

NATIONAL GEOGRAPHIC Place Location Activity

1. B
2. H
3. A
4. C
5. F
6. D
7. G
8. E

Critical Thinking

21. *Possible answers: Help*—provide jobs; raise standard of living; *Harm*—disrupt traditional relationships or ways of living
22. Answers will vary.
23. Outlines will vary, but the three main headings should be: People Far and Near, Understanding Culture, Patterns in Today's World. Facts should be supported by examples from this text.

Self-Check Quiz Visit the ***Our World Today: People, Places, and Issues*** Web site at owt.glencoe.com and click on **Chapter 1–Self-Check Quizzes** to prepare for the Chapter Test.

Critical Thinking

21. **Making Predictions** In what ways do you think a company investing in a developing country could help the people there? How could that same company harm the culture?
22. **Analyzing Information** Imagine that you are a sociologist visiting your school. What characteristics of the local culture would you observe? What conclusions might you develop about your campus culture?
23. **Organizing Information** Create an outline that includes information from each section in this chapter. On your outline, list the title of each section and then list at least three important facts under each title.

Current Events Journal

24. **Analyzing Quotations** Read the following quote and analyze it using information you learned in this chapter. "Own only what you can always carry with you. Know languages, know countries, know people. Let your memory be your travel bag."

Mental Mapping Activity

25. **Focusing on the Region** Create a simple outline map of North America and South America. On the map label the following culture regions.
    - United States and Canada
    - Latin America

Technology Skills Activity

26. **Developing Multimedia Presentations** You are on assignment for your school newspaper. Walk around the halls, attend sports events and fine arts productions, and take photos of many faces around your campus. Scan the photos into presentation software on your computer. Develop a presentation that represents the many cultures that make up your school climate.

The Princeton Review

Standardized Test Practice

Directions: Study the graph, and then answer the following question.

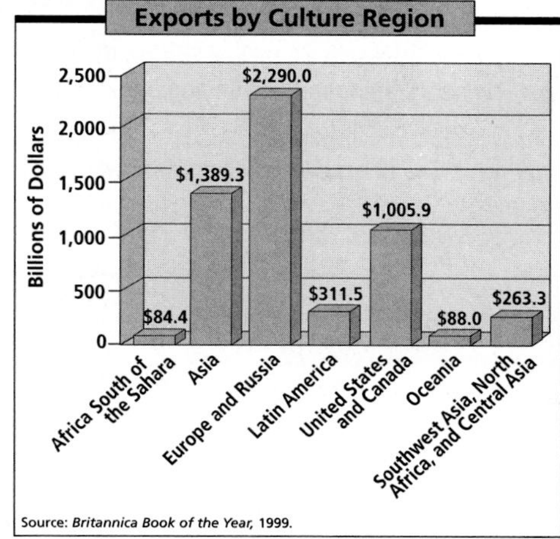

Source: *Britannica Book of the Year,* 1999.

1. According to the graph, what is the combined value of the goods exported by the United States and Canada?

A $1,005,900,000,000
B $1,005,900,000
C $1,005,900
D $1,005

Test-Taking Tip: In order to understand any type of graph, look carefully around the graph for keys that show how it is organized. On this bar graph, the numbers along the left side represent billions of dollars. Therefore, you need to multiply the number on the graph by 1,000,000,000 to get your answer.

Assessment and Activities

Standardized Test Practice

1. A

Tested Objectives:
Analyzing information, reading graphs

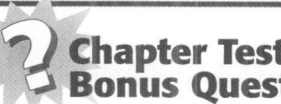

Chapter Test Bonus Question

This question may be used for extra credit on the chapter test.

In the past few decades, the number of people in the world has grown rapidly. Now more and more people live in cities. What are densely populated areas called? *(urban areas)*

Our World Today online

Have students visit the Web site at owt.glencoe.com to review Chapter 1 and take the Self-Check Quiz.

Current Events Journal

24. Students' paragraphs will vary but should address the issues raised in the textbook.

Mental Mapping Activity

25. This exercise helps students visualize the countries and features they have been studying and understand the relationship among various points. All attempts at freehand mapping should be accepted.

Technology Skills Activity

26. Students should talk to the people they photograph to get accurate facts about their subjects' ethnicities and cultures, which students can then use in their presentations.

Chapter 2 Resources

Note: The following materials may be used when teaching Chapter 2.
Section level support materials are shown at point of use in the margins of the Teacher Wraparound Edition.

Timesaving Tools

TeacherWorks™ All-In-One Planner and Resource Center

- **Interactive Teacher Edition** See the **Interactive Teacher Edition** CD-ROM to electronically integrate your Teacher Wraparound Edition and blackline masters.
- **Interactive Lesson Planner** Organize your week, month, semester, or year with all the lesson helps you need. The **Interactive Lesson Planner** CD-ROM contains all Chapter 2 resources.

Use Glencoe's **Presentation Plus!** multimedia teacher tool to easily present dynamic lessons that visually excite your students. Using Microsoft PowerPoint® you can customize the presentations to create your own personalized lessons.

TEACHING TRANSPARENCIES

Graphic Organizer Transparency and Student Activity 2

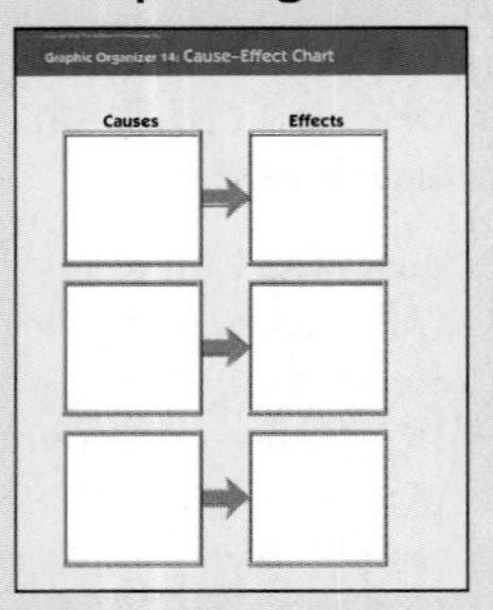

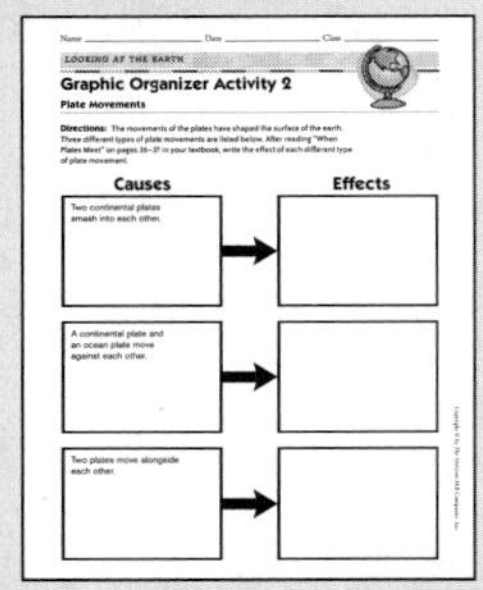

FOLDABLES™ Study Organizer

Foldables are three-dimensional, interactive graphic organizers that help students practice basic writing skills, review key vocabulary terms, and identify main ideas. Every chapter contains a Foldable activity, with additional chapter activities found in the ***Reading and Study Skills Foldables*** booklet.

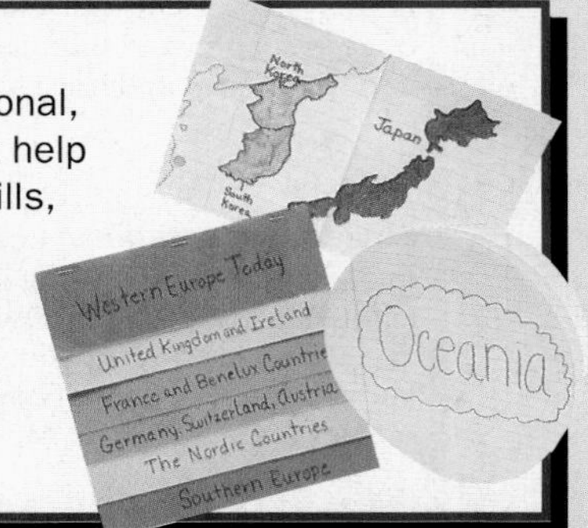

ENRICHMENT AND EXTENSION

Enrichment Activity 2

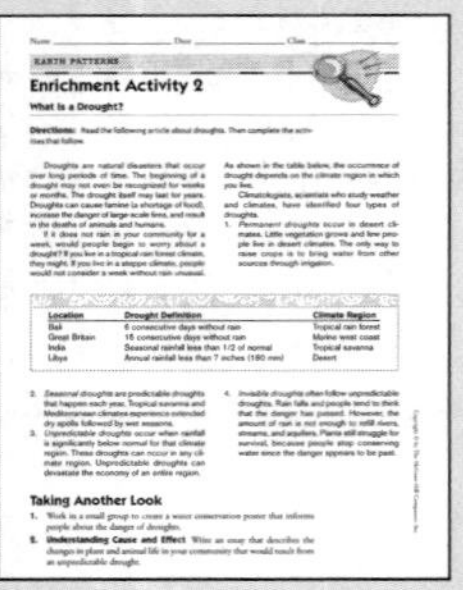

Cooperative Learning Activity 2

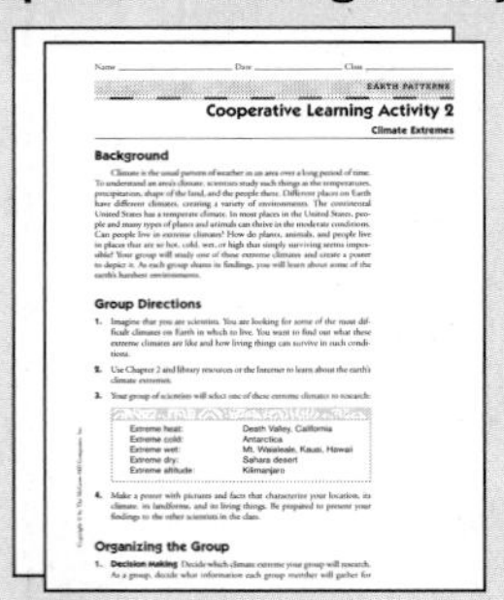

MAP AND GEOGRAPHY SKILLS

Chapter Map Activity 2

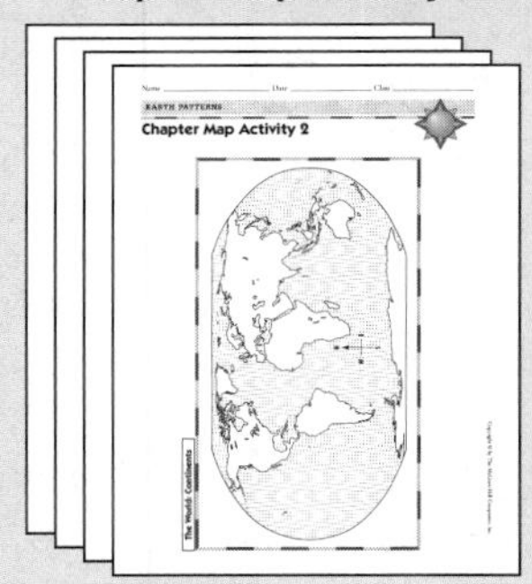

GeoLab Activity 2

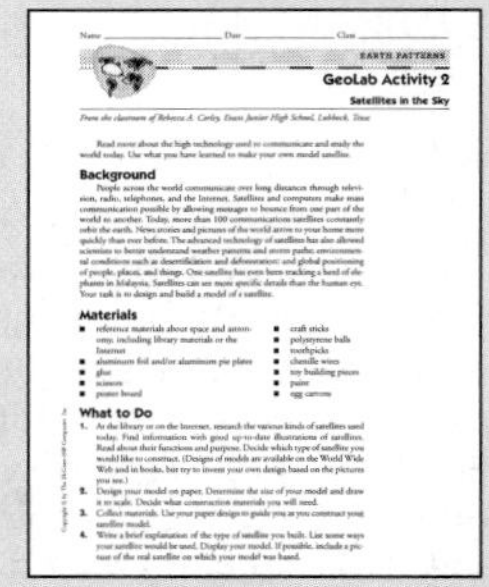

STANDARDIZED ASSESSMENT SKILLS

Critical Thinking Skills Activity 2

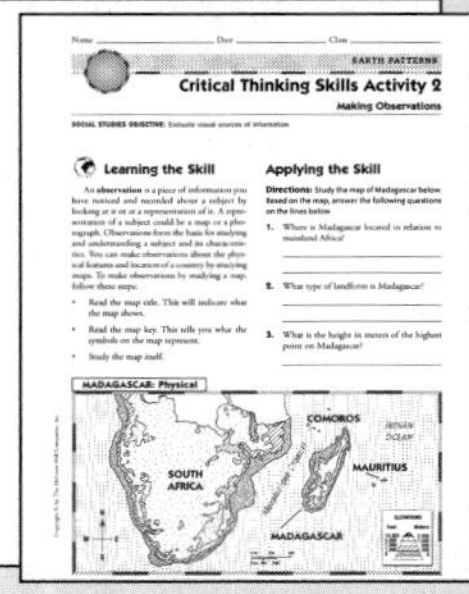

Map and Graph Skills Activity 2

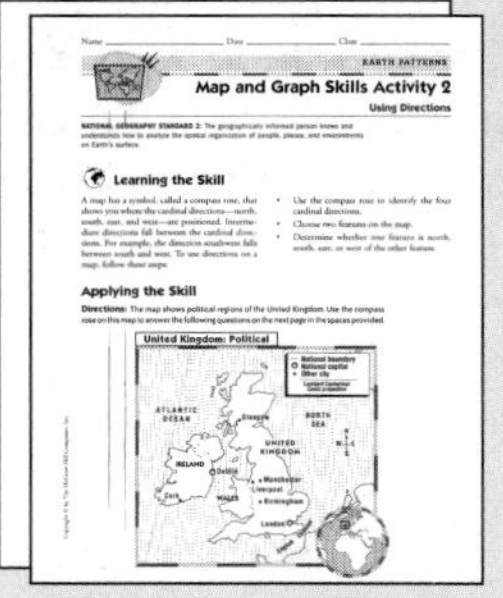

Reading and Writing Skills Activity 2

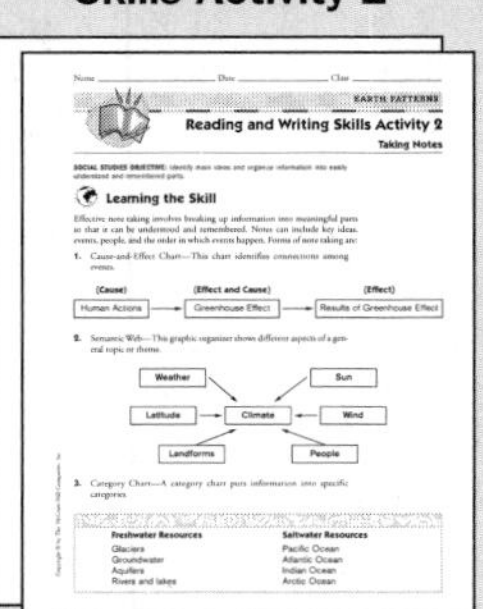

Standardized Test Practice Workbook Activity 2

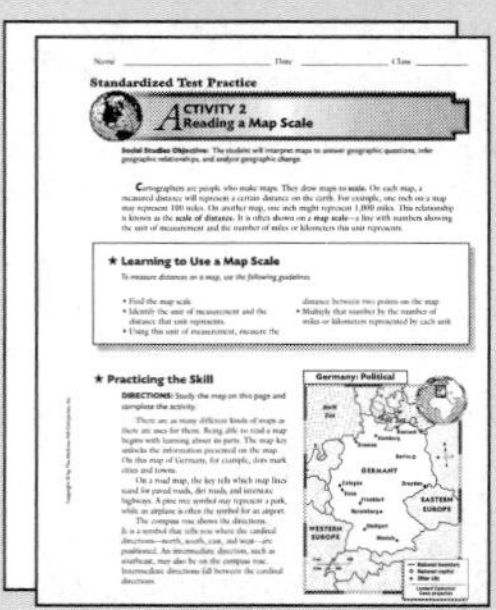

REVIEW AND REINFORCEMENT

Chapter Skills Activity 2

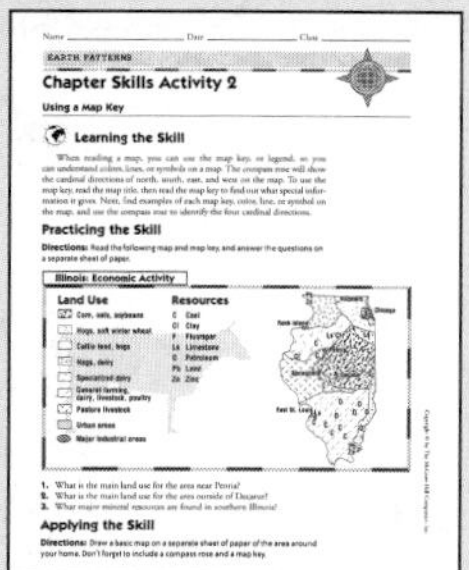

Take-Home Review Activity 2

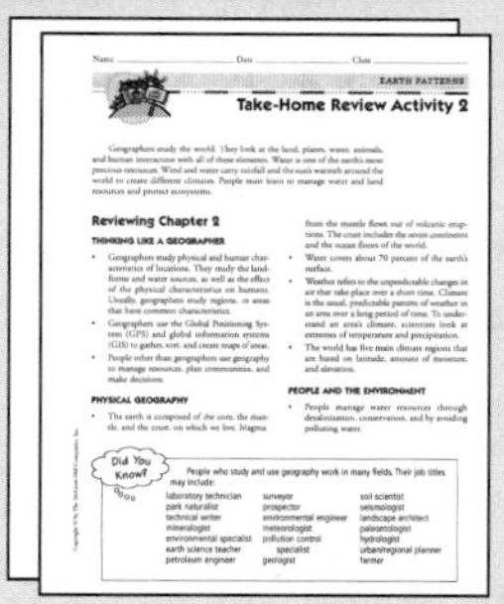

Reteaching Activity 2

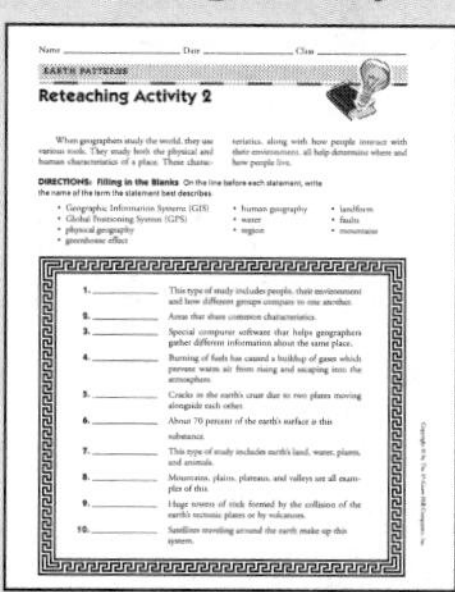

Vocabulary Activity 2

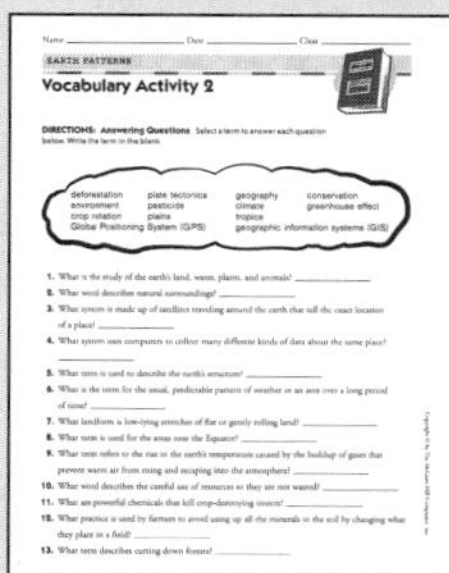

Workbook Activity 2

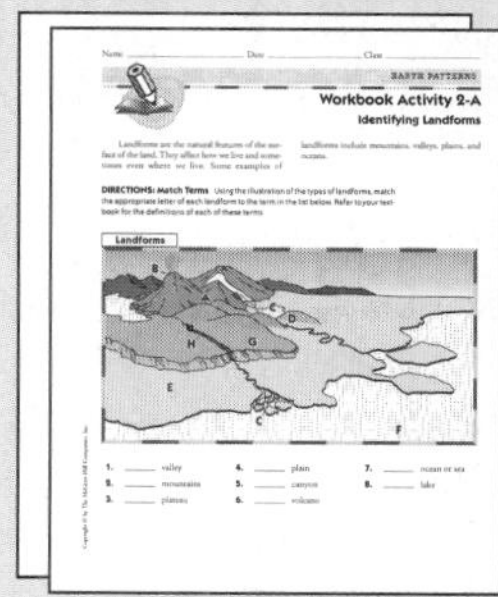

ASSESSMENT

GLENCOE'S ASSESSMENT ADVANTAGE

Chapter 2 Test, Form A

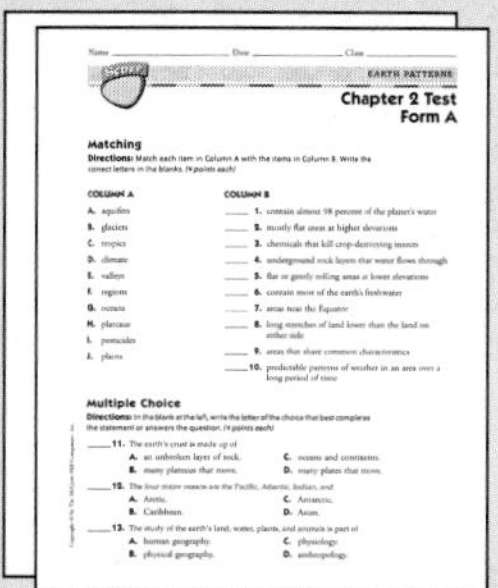

Chapter 2 Test, Form B

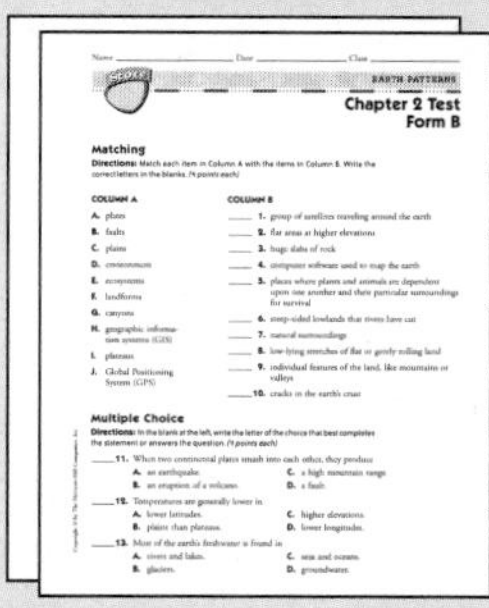

Performance Assessment Activity 2

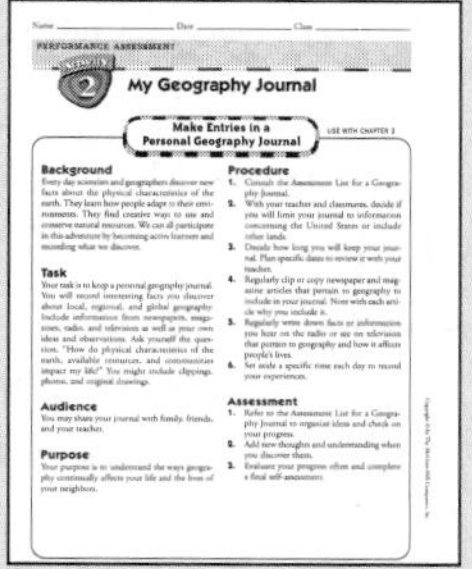

ExamView® Pro 3.0 Testmaker CD-ROM

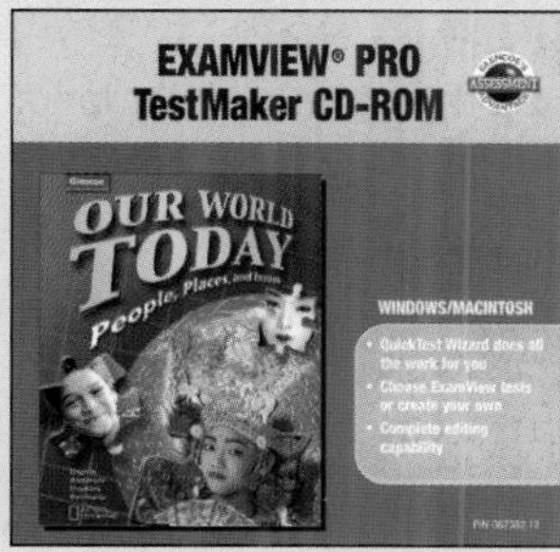

MULTIMEDIA

- **National Geographic's The World and Its People**
- **MindJogger Videoquiz**
- **Vocabulary PuzzleMaker Software**
- **Interactive Tutor Self-Assessment CD-ROM**
- **ExamView® Pro 3.0 Testmaker CD-ROM**
- **Interactive Lesson Planner CD-ROM**
- **Interactive Teacher Edition CD-ROM**
- **Skillbuilder Interactive Workbook CD-ROM, Level 1**
- **Presentation Plus! CD-ROM**
- **Audio Program**

SPANISH RESOURCES

The following Spanish language materials are available in the Spanish Resources binder:

- **Spanish Chapter Summaries**
- **Spanish Vocabulary Activities**
- **Spanish Guided Reading Activities**
- **Spanish Quizzes and Tests**
- **Spanish Take-Home Review Activities**
- **Spanish Reteaching Activities**

Meeting National Standards

Geography for Life

All of the 18 standards are demonstrated in Unit 1. The following ones are highlighted in Chapter 2:

Section 1 **EE1 The World in Spatial Terms: Standards 1, 2, 3**

EE5 Environment and Society: Standards 14, 15, 16

Section 2 **EE3 Physical Systems: Standards 7, 8**

Section 3 **EE2 Places and Regions: Standards 4, 5, 6**

EE5 Environment and Society: Standards 14, 15, 16

For a complete listing of National Geography Standards and entire text correlation, see pages T22–T29.

Local Objectives

Chapter 2 Planning Guide

SECTION RESOURCES

Daily Objectives	Reproducible Resources	Multimedia Resources
Section 1 **Thinking Like a Geographer** **Suggested Pacing = 1 day** **1.** Describe how geographers look at the world. **2.** Discuss what tools geographers use. **3.** Explain how geographers use their knowledge of the earth.	Reproducible Lesson Plan 2-1 Daily Lecture and Discussion Notes 2-1 Guided Reading Activity 2-1 Reading Essentials and Study Guide 2-1 Section Quiz 2-1*	Daily Focus Skills Transparency 2-1 GeoQuiz Transparency 2-1 Vocabulary PuzzleMaker Software Interactive Tutor Self-Assessment CD-ROM ExamView® Pro 3.0 Testmaker CD-ROM Presentation Plus! CD-ROM
Section 2 **Physical Geography** **Suggested Pacing = 1 day** **1.** Discuss the forces that change the earth's surface. **2.** Describe the earth's major landforms. **3.** Explain climate and how it is affected by people.	Reproducible Lesson Plan 2-2 Daily Lecture and Discussion Notes 2-2 Guided Reading Activity 2-2 Reading Essentials and Study Guide 2-2 Section Quiz 2-2*	Daily Focus Skills Transparency 2-2 GeoQuiz Transparency 2-2 Vocabulary PuzzleMaker Software Interactive Tutor Self-Assessment CD-ROM ExamView® Pro 3.0 Testmaker CD-ROM Presentation Plus! CD-ROM
Section 3 **People and the Environment** **Suggested Pacing = 1 day** **1.** Explain why people have to manage water. **2.** Describe how the soil can be damaged by people. **3.** Explain the effects of air pollution.	Reproducible Lesson Plan 2-3 Daily Lecture and Discussion Notes 2-3 Guided Reading Activity 2-3 Reading Essentials and Study Guide 2-3 Section Quiz 2-3*	Daily Focus Skills Transparency 2-3 GeoQuiz Transparency 2-3 Vocabulary PuzzleMaker Software Interactive Tutor Self-Assessment CD-ROM ExamView® Pro 3.0 Testmaker CD-ROM Presentation Plus! CD-ROM

00:00 **Out of Time?** Assign the **Reading Essentials and Study Guide** for this chapter.

*Also available in Spanish

KEY TO ABILITY LEVELS

Teaching strategies have been coded for varying learning styles and abilities.

L1 **BASIC** activities for all students
L2 **AVERAGE** activities for average to above-average students
L3 **CHALLENGING** activities for above-average students
ELL **ENGLISH LANGUAGE LEARNER** activities

Blackline Master
Software
CD-ROM
Audiocassette

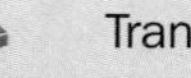

Transparency
Videocassette

Block Scheduling
DVD

Teacher to Teacher

Hurricane Season

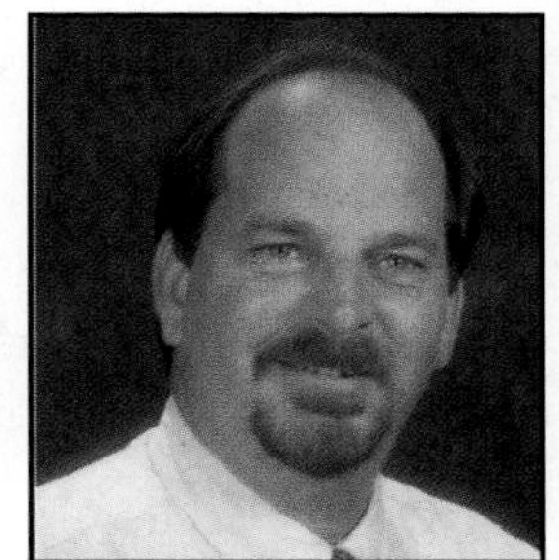

Kim Cavanaugh
Congress Middle School
Boynton Beach, Florida

Provide students with some basic background information about hurricanes. Explain that cyclones are intense storms. Cyclones that form over land are called tornadoes. Tropical cyclones with winds of 74 miles (119 km) per hour that form over the North Atlantic or eastern North Pacific are called hurricanes. They are called typhoons in the western Pacific. Then have students plot the year's current hurricanes. A hurricane tracking chart can be found at **lumahai.soest.hawaii.edu/Tropical_Weather/atlantic_track.gif**

OUR WORLD TODAY Online

Use our Web site for additional resources. All essential content is covered in the Student Edition.

You and your students can visit owt.glencoe.com, the Web site companion to *Our World Today*. This innovative integration of electronic and print media offers your students a wealth of opportunities. The student text directs students to the Web site for the following options:

- Chapter Overviews
- Student Web Activities
- Self-Check Quizzes
- Textbook Updates

Answers are provided for you in the Web Activity Lesson Plan. Additional Web resources and Interactive Tutor puzzles are also available.

TEACHER'S CORNER

Index to National Geographic Magazine:

The following articles may be used for research relating to this chapter:

- "Arctic Submarine," by Glenn Hodges, March 2000.
- "El Niño/La Niña," by Curt Suplee, March 1999.
- *Physical World,* a National Geographic Special Edition, May 1998.
- "Unlocking the Climate Puzzle," by Curt Suplee, May 1998.

National Geographic Society Products Available From Glencoe:

To order the following products for use with this chapter, contact your local Glencoe sales representative or call Glencoe at 1-800-334-7344:

- *PictureShow: Earth's Climate* (CD-ROM)
- *PicturePack: Earth's Climate* (Transparencies)
- *PicturePack: World Geography Library* (Transparencies)
- *GTV: Planetary Manager* (Videodisc)
- *STV: World Geography* (Videodisc)
- *STV: Restless Earth* (Videodisc)
- *STV: Water* (Videodisc)
- *PicturePack: Physical Geography of the World* (Transparencies)
- *PictureShow: Ocean* (CD-ROM)
- *PictureShow: Geology* (CD-ROM)
- *PictureShow: Earth's Endangered Environments* (CD-ROM)

Additional National Geographic Society Products:

To order the following products for use with this chapter, call National Geographic Society at 1-800-368-2728:

- *MapPack: U.S.A. Regions Series* (Transparencies)
- *MapPack: Continents Series* (Transparencies)
- *Physical Geography of the Continents Series* (6 Videos)
- *Physical Earth* (Map)
- *National Geographic Desk Reference* (Book)
- *National Geographic Atlas of the World, Seventh Edition* (Book)
- *The Living Earth* (Video)
- *Water: A Precious Resource* (Video)
- *The Living Ocean* (Video)
- *Ancient Forests* (Video)
- *A Swamp Ecosystem* (Video)

NGS ONLINE

Access National Geographic's Web site for current events, activities, links, interactive features, and archives.
www.nationalgeographic.com

Introducing Chapter 2

Our World Today online

Introduce students to chapter content and key terms by having them access Chapter Overview 2 at owt.glencoe.com

Chapter Objectives

1. Discuss how geographers look at the world and what tools they use.
2. Describe the structure of the earth's interior and landforms.
3. Explain how humans affect the climate and environment.

GLENCOE TECHNOLOGY

NATIONAL GEOGRAPHIC

The World and Its People Video Program

Chapters 1 and 2
Looking at the Earth
The following segments enhance the study of this chapter:

- **Global Sunrise**
- **Kilauea Volcano**
- **Exploring the Ocean**

Available in DVD and VHS.

MindJogger Videoquiz

Use MindJogger to preview the Chapter 2 content.

Available in VHS.

Chapter 2 Earth Patterns

The World and Its People NATIONAL GEOGRAPHIC

To learn more about Earth's structure and landforms, view ***The World and Its People*** **Chapters 1** and **2** videos.

Our World Today online

Chapter Overview Visit the ***Our World Today: People, Places, and Issues*** Web site at owt.glencoe.com and click on **Chapter 2–Chapter Overviews** to preview information about Earth.

50

Two-Minute Lesson Launcher

Before students read the chapter, have them think about the way the earth looks in your area. Ask them how they would describe the land around you—is it flat or hilly or mountainous? Is it dry or wet? Are there large bodies of water nearby? After students have offered some thoughts, ask them if they have any ideas why their part of the earth looks the way it does—that is, how did it get that way? Tell students that in this chapter they will read about the powerful forces that shape the earth—and the way the earth looks as a result.

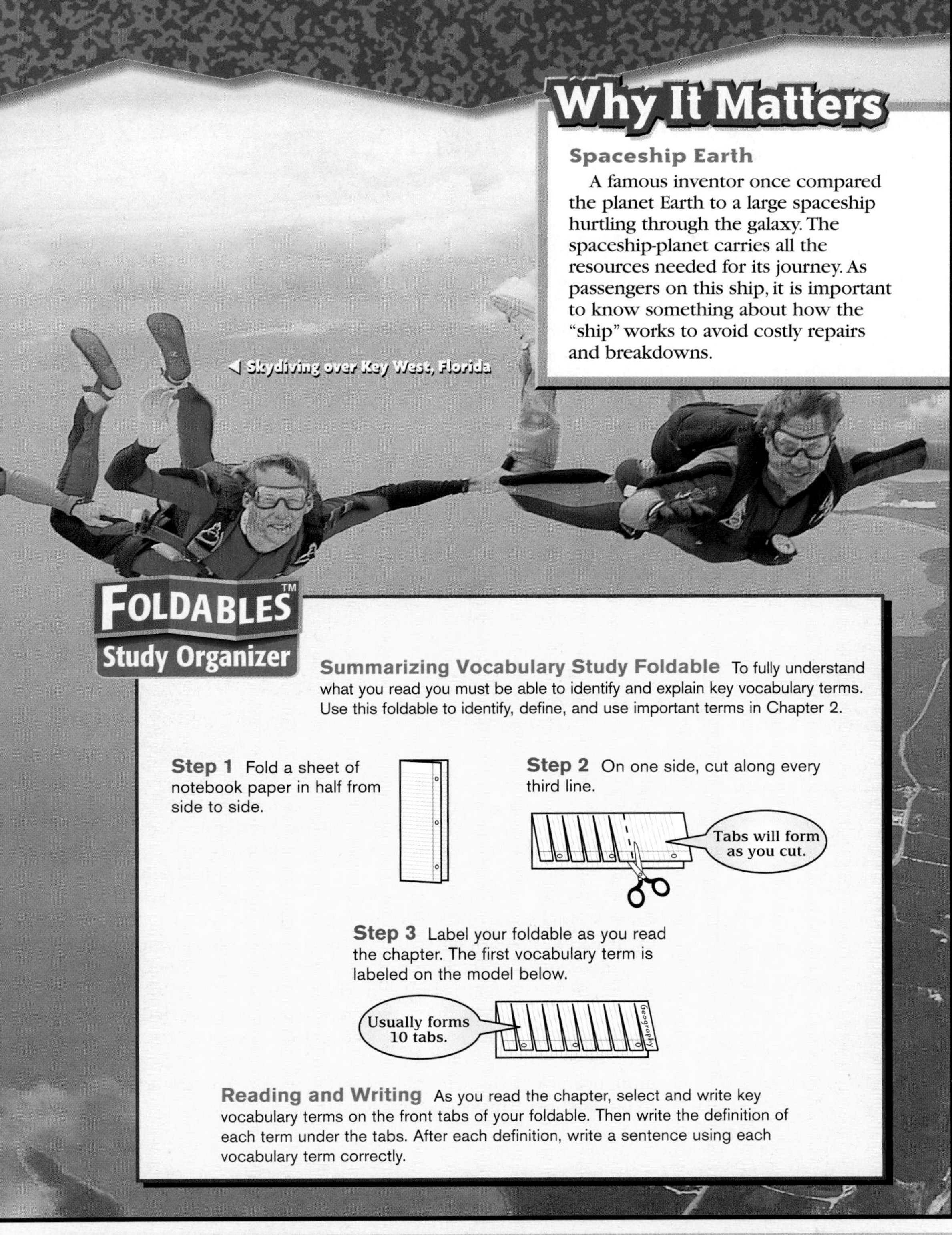

◀ Skydiving over Key West, Florida

Why It Matters

Spaceship Earth

A famous inventor once compared the planet Earth to a large spaceship hurtling through the galaxy. The spaceship-planet carries all the resources needed for its journey. As passengers on this ship, it is important to know something about how the "ship" works to avoid costly repairs and breakdowns.

FOLDABLES™ Study Organizer

Summarizing Vocabulary Study Foldable To fully understand what you read you must be able to identify and explain key vocabulary terms. Use this foldable to identify, define, and use important terms in Chapter 2.

Step 1 Fold a sheet of notebook paper in half from side to side.

Step 2 On one side, cut along every third line.

Tabs will form as you cut.

Step 3 Label your foldable as you read the chapter. The first vocabulary term is labeled on the model below.

Usually forms 10 tabs.
Geography

Reading and Writing As you read the chapter, select and write key vocabulary terms on the front tabs of your foldable. Then write the definition of each term under the tabs. After each definition, write a sentence using each vocabulary term correctly.

About the Photo

These skydivers have a birds' eye view of the Florida Keys' beautiful blue waters. What they can't see is the destruction that is taking place within these once-clear waters. The coral reefs—home to sea turtles, spiny lobsters, sea urchins, fish, and many other types of marine life—are disappearing rapidly. The living corals are being killed by disease and smothered by algae that thrives on pollutants from treated sewage and storm water run-off. The Environmental Protection Agency (EPA) is monitoring Florida's coastal waters to determine changes in the coral reef due to increased human population. They will implement a Water Quality Protection Program based on their findings.

FOLDABLES™ Study Organizer

Purpose Students will make and use a foldable to identify and explain key vocabulary terms in the chapter. As students read the chapter, they will select and write key vocabulary terms on the front of a tab. They should also write the definition and a sentence using each vocabulary term under the appropriate tab.

Have students complete ***Reading and Study Skills Foldables*** Activity 2.

Why It Matters

About 77 percent of all pollution in the oceans originates on land. Plastic and other trash in ocean waters kill fish, sea birds, turtles, seals, and whales. People can help the oceans by recycling. Have your students find out what local arrangements have been made for recycling at your school and in the community. Then have them create posters urging others to recycle and providing information about how to recycle.

They can also learn more about deepwater habitats by exploring the Sustainable Seas Expeditions Web site at **http://sustainableseas.noaa.gov/**. This research project is studying organisms and habitats in the United States's National Marine Sanctuaries.

Chapter 2

Section 1, pages 52–55

Section Objectives

1. Describe how geographers look at the world.
2. Discuss what tools geographers use.
3. Explain how geographers use their knowledge of the earth.

BELLRINGER Skillbuilder Activity

Project transparency and have students answer questions.

This activity is also available as a blackline master.

Daily Focus Skills Transparency 2-1

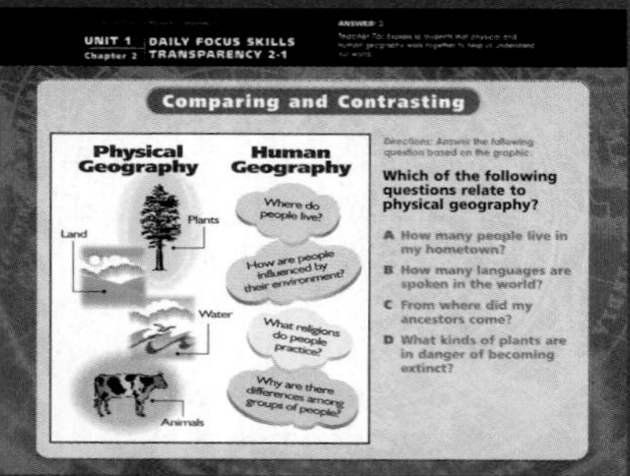

Comparing and Contrasting
Physical Geography
Human Geography
Land
Plants
Water
Animals
Where do people live?
How are people influenced by their environment?
What religions do people practice?
Why are there differences among groups of people?
Which of the following questions relate to physical geography?
A How many people live in my hometown?
B How many languages are spoken in the world?
C From where did my ancestors come?
D What kinds of plants are in danger of becoming extinct?

Guide to Reading

■ **Accessing Prior Knowledge**

Ask: Have you ever given directions to someone? Lead students to see that maps—whether sketches or printed color maps—are ways of representing spatial reality.

Section 1 Thinking Like a Geographer

Guide to Reading

Main Idea

Geographers use various tools to understand the world.

Terms to Know

- geography
- landform
- environment
- region
- Global Positioning System (GPS)
- geographic information systems (GIS)

Reading Strategy

Create a chart like this one and write three details or examples for each heading.

How Geographers View the World
1.
2.
3.
Tools of Geography
1.
2.
3.
Uses of Geography
1.
2.
3.

NATIONAL GEOGRAPHIC Exploring Our World

How would *you* go about making an accurate map of the world? Scientists decided the best way to map the earth was to see it from space. In February 2000, the space shuttle *Endeavour* used a special camera called a radar camera to take pictures of the land below. By using radar, the camera was not hampered by clouds or darkness.

Why do geographers want to know exactly what the earth looks like? Think about the following: In China, the spring flooding of the **Yangtze** (YANG•SEE) **River** threatens people and crops every year. In 1998 the floods killed more than 4,000 people. Using information gathered from land and climate studies, the Chinese government built dams to hold some of the floodwaters back.

This is just one example of how people around the world use geographic knowledge collected from various sources. When you study **geography**, you learn about the earth's land, water, plants, and animals. You learn about how the continents were formed and what causes erosion. This is physical geography. Geographers also study people—where they live, how they live, how they change and are influenced by their environment, and how different groups compare to one another. This is human geography.

Section Resources

Reproducible Masters

- Reproducible Lesson Plan 2-1
- Daily Lecture and Discussion Notes 2-1
- Guided Reading Activity 2-1
- Reading Essentials and Study Guide 2-1
- Section Quiz 2-1

Transparencies

- Daily Focus Skills Transparency 2-1
- GeoQuiz Transparency 2-1

Multimedia

- Vocabulary PuzzleMaker Software
- Interactive Tutor Self-Assessment CD-ROM
- Presentation Plus! CD-ROM
- ExamView® Pro 3.0 Testmaker CD-ROM

A Geographer's View of Place

Geographers look at major issues—like the flooding of the Yangtze—that affect millions of people. They also look at local issues—such as where is the best place for a company to build a new store in town. Whether an issue is major or local, geographers try to understand both its physical characteristics and human systems.

Physical Characteristics Geographers study places. They look at *where* something is located on the earth. They also try to understand what the place is *like*. They ask: What features make a place similar to or different from other places?

To answer this question, geographers identify the landforms of a place. **Landforms** are individual features of the land, such as mountains and valleys. Geographers also look at water. Is the place near an ocean or on a river? Does it have plentiful or very little freshwater? They consider whether the soil will produce crops. They see how much rain the place usually receives and how hot or cold the area is. They find out whether the place has minerals, trees, or other resources.

Human Systems Geographers also observe the social characteristics of the people living in the place. Do many or only a few people live there? Do they live close together or far apart? Why? What kind of government do they have? What religions do they follow? What kinds of work do they do? What languages do they speak?

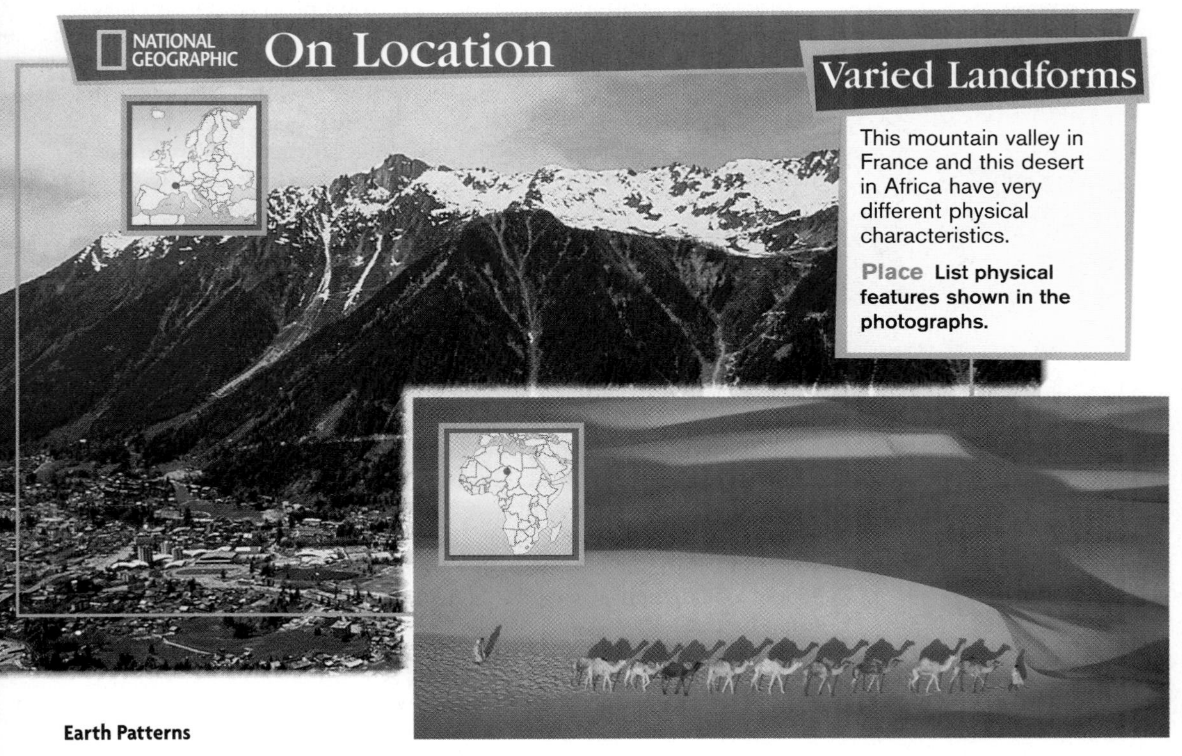

NATIONAL GEOGRAPHIC On Location

Varied Landforms

This mountain valley in France and this desert in Africa have very different physical characteristics.

Place **List physical features shown in the photographs.**

Chapter 2

Section 1, pages 52–55

Making Inferences In the Two-Minute Lesson Launcher on page 50, you asked students to describe the physical characteristics of your area. Have them think again about your area in terms of human systems. How would they describe your area in terms of the human impact on the environment? **L1**

Daily Lecture Notes 2-1

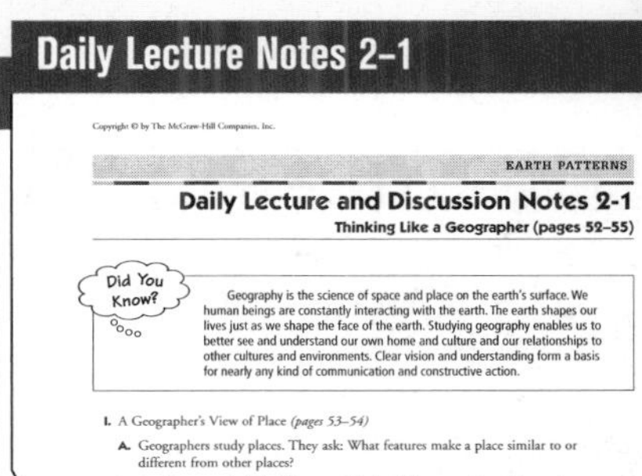

EARTH PATTERNS

Daily Lecture and Discussion Notes 2-1

Thinking Like a Geographer (pages 52–55)

Did You Know?

Geography is the science of space and place on the earth's surface. We human beings are constantly interacting with the earth. The earth shapes our lives just as we shape the face of the earth. Studying geography enables us to better see and understand our own home and culture and our relationships to other cultures and environments. Clear vision and understanding form a basis for nearly any kind of communication and constructive action.

I. A Geographer's View of Place *(pages 53–54)*

A. Geographers study places. They ask: What features make a place similar to or different from other places?

B. **Landforms** are individual features of the land, like mountains, valleys, and

characteristics of the people living in the

More About the Photos

Mont Blanc and the Sahara Mont Blanc rises on the border of France and Italy. Its name—which means "white mountain"—comes from the glacier that covers about 40 square miles (104 sq. km) of its surface. The Sahara, the world's largest hot desert, covers about 3.5 million square miles (9 million sq. km).

Caption Answer *Possible answers:* for Mont Blanc—mountain, valley, forests; for Sahara—desert, shifting dunes, rocky and sandy soil

Team-Teaching Activity

History Invite a teacher with a background in world history to class to discuss the Age of Exploration. Then have students research early maps and people who explored previously unknown areas. They may choose to research Balboa, Alexander Mackenzie, Zebulon Pike, or others. Ask students to prepare a brief report describing the physical and social characteristics that explorers learned about the places they "discovered." **L2** 

EE1 The World in Spatial Terms: Standard 1

Chapter 2

Section 1, pages 52–55

Measure student knowledge of physical features and political entities.

GeoQuiz Transparency 2–1

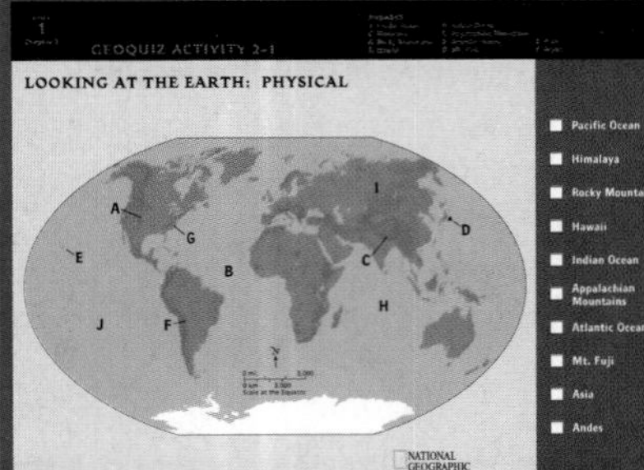

✓ Reading Check Answer

Possible answers: settlement patterns, occupations, government, religion, language

Guided Reading Activity 2–1

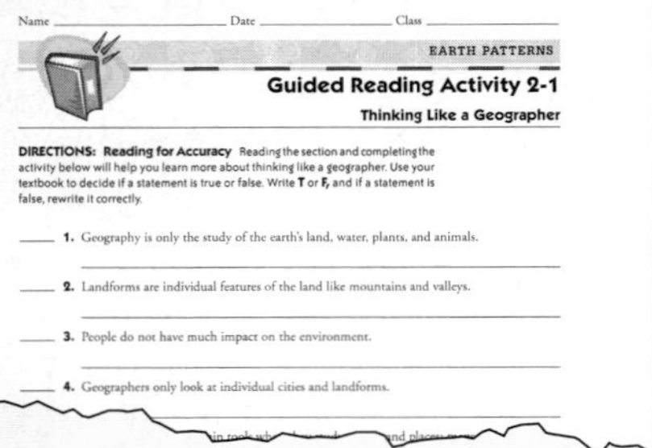
Name ______ Date ______ Class ______

EARTH PATTERNS

Guided Reading Activity 2-1

Thinking Like a Geographer

DIRECTIONS: Reading for Accuracy Reading the section and completing the activity below will help you learn more about thinking like a geographer. Use your textbook to decide if a statement is true or false. Write **T** or **F**, and if a statement is false, rewrite it correctly.

____ **1.** Geography is only the study of the earth's land, water, plants, and animals.

____ **2.** Landforms are individual features of the land like mountains and valleys.

____ **3.** People do not have much impact on the environment.

____ **4.** Geographers only look at individual cities and landforms.

Assign Section 1 Assessment as homework or an in-class activity.

✓ Reading Check Answer

GPS: satellites identify locations; GIS: computer software analyzes data and creates maps

GIS Day

Teens, like Jenna, are putting away their computer video games and booting up GIS software. Jenna joined one of thousands of events taking place on the first International Geographic Information Systems Day in Washington, D.C. Here, the easy-to-use software was demonstrated by the National Geographic Society. GIS is software that helps users visualize geographic situations and problems by mapping and analyzing large amounts of geographic data.

People and Places Geographers are especially interested in how people interact with their **environment,** or natural surroundings. People can have a major impact on the environment. Remember how the Chinese built dams along the Yangtze? When they did so, they changed the way the river behaved in flood season.

Regions Geographers also look at the big picture, or how individual places relate to other places. In other words, geographers look at **regions,** or areas that share common characteristics. Regions can be relatively small—like your state or town. They can also be huge—like all of the western United States. Some regions may even include several countries.

✓ Reading Check What do geographers study to determine the social characteristics of a place?

The Tools of Geography

Geographers need tools to study people and places. Maps and globes are two tools they use to organize information about places.

Collecting Data for Mapping Earth How do geographers gather information so that they can make accurate maps? One way is to take photographs from high above the earth. Some of these are called LANDSAT images and show details such as the shape of the land, what plants cover an area, and how land is being used. Special cameras can even reveal information hidden by ice and snow.

How do geographers accurately label the exact locations of places on a map? Believe it or not, the best way to find a location is from outer space. Satellites traveling around the earth make up the **Global Positioning System (GPS).** A GPS receiver is a special device that receives signals from these satellites. When the receiver is put at a location, the GPS satellite can tell the exact latitude and longitude of that place. As a result, a mapmaker can know where exactly on the earth the particular area is located. GPS devices are even installed in vehicles to help drivers find their way.

Geographic Information Systems Today geographers use another powerful tool in their work—computers. Special computer software called **geographic information systems (GIS)** helps geographers gather many different kinds of information about the same place. After typing in all the data they collect, geographers use the software to combine and overlap the information on special maps.

In the 1990s, a logging company in California wanted to cut down parts of a forest. Environmental groups said that doing so would destroy the nesting areas of some rare birds. Geographers using GIS software created one map that showed the forest and another map that showed the nesting sites—and then overlapped these two maps. People could then see which areas had to be protected and which could be cut.

✓ Reading Check What is the difference between GPS and GIS?

Meeting Special Needs

Visual/Spatial To help students understand the idea that a place can belong to many different regions, use a globe or another model of the earth. Focus on a single city and make a circle around it. Make another circle around a physical region that includes the city and surrounding areas—for example, the river valley to which the city belongs. Make another circle around the state or administrative division in which the city sits, one more around the country as a whole, and finally one around the cultural region. Point out that many of the circles overlap, but all show how the place is linked to other regions in certain ways. Have students write five questions and answers about the geographic characteristics and patterns of the regions they were shown on the globe. **L1**

Uses of Geography

Geographic information is used in planning. Government leaders use geographic information to plan new services in their communities. They might plan how to handle disasters or how much new housing to allow in an area. Companies can see where people are moving in a region in order to make plans for expanding.

Some businesses offer geographic information to their customers. Suppose you were looking for an apartment to rent. Some real estate agents have computer programs that can identify all the apartments of a certain size and price in an area. They can create a map so that you can see exactly where each apartment is located.

Finally, geographic information helps people manage resources. Many natural resources, such as oil or coal, are available only in limited supply and must be managed carefully so that they do not run out. Geographic information can help locate more natural resources.

Reading Check Why do people have to manage resources carefully?

Our World Today
online
Web Activity Visit the ***Our World Today: People, Places, and Issues*** Web site at owt.glencoe.com and click on **Chapter 2–Student Web Activities** to learn more about geographic information systems.

Section 1 Assessment

Defining Terms

1. **Define** geography, landform, environment, region, Global Positioning System (GPS), geographic information systems (GIS).

Recalling Facts

2. **Place** What two kinds of characteristics of a place do geographers study?
3. **Technology** What are the main tools of geography?
4. **Human/Environment Interaction** What are three uses for geography?

Critical Thinking

5. **Understanding Cause and Effect** Identify three physical characteristics of your region. How have these characteristics affected the way people live there?
6. **Categorizing Information** Give five examples of regions. Begin with an area near you that shares common characteristics, then look for larger and larger regions.

Graphic Organizer

7. **Organizing Information** Create a diagram like this one. In the center, write the name of a place you would like to visit. In the outer ovals, identify the types of geographic information you would like to learn about this place.

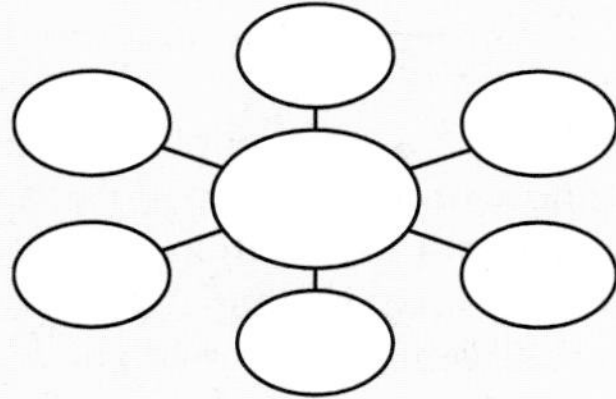

Applying Social Studies Skills

8. **Analyzing Maps** Find Egypt on the map on page RA21 of the **Reference Atlas.** Along what physical feature do you think most Egyptians live? Why? Turn to the population map of Egypt on page 9 of the **Geography Handbook** to see if you are correct.

Chapter 2

Section 1, pages 52–55

Objectives, goals, and answers to the Student Web Activity can be found in the Web Activity Lesson Plan at **owt.glencoe.com**

Section Quiz 2-1

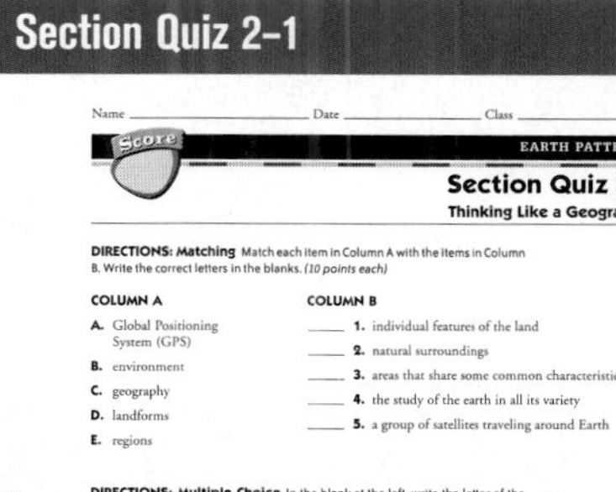
Name ______ Date ______ Class ______

EARTH PATTERNS

Section Quiz 2-1

Thinking Like a Geographer

DIRECTIONS: Matching Match each item in Column A with the items in Column B. Write the correct letters in the blanks. *(10 points each)*

COLUMN A	COLUMN B
A. Global Positioning System (GPS)	___ 1. individual features of the land
B. environment	___ 2. natural surroundings
C. geography	___ 3. areas that share some common characteristics
D. landforms	___ 4. the study of the earth in all its variety
E. regions	___ 5. a group of satellites traveling around Earth

DIRECTIONS: Multiple Choice In the blank at the left, write the letter of the choice that best completes the statement or answers the question. *(10 points each)*

Reading Check Answer

so they are not all used up

Reading Essentials and Study Guide 2-1

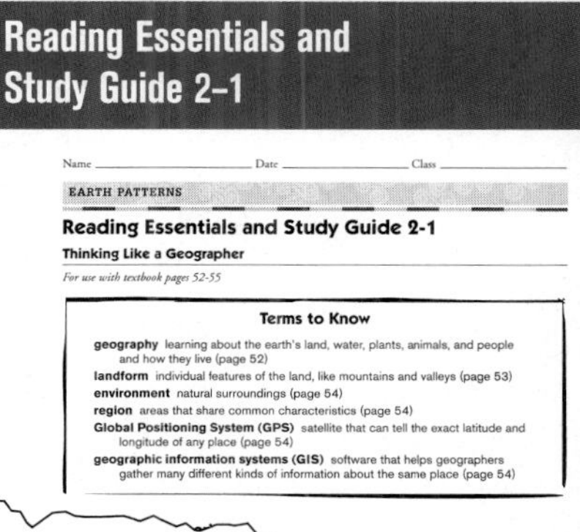
Name ______ Date ______ Class ______

EARTH PATTERNS

Reading Essentials and Study Guide 2-1

Thinking Like a Geographer

For use with textbook pages 52–55

Terms to Know

geography learning about the earth's land, water, plants, animals, and people and how they live (page 52)
landform individual features of the land, like mountains and valleys (page 53)
environment natural surroundings (page 54)
region areas that share common characteristics (page 54)
Global Positioning System (GPS) satellite that can tell the exact latitude and longitude of any place (page 54)
geographic information systems (GIS) software that helps geographers gather many different kinds of information about the same place (page 54)

4 CLOSE

Have students create a concept web for the word *geography.*

Section 1 Assessment

1. The terms are defined in the Glossary.
2. physical, human/social
3. maps, globes
4. to find a location, planning, using resources wisely
5. Answers will vary. Students may mention landforms, climate, resources, and location near water as affecting people.
6. Answers will vary depending on location. Students may mention their suburb, city, county, state, country, and continent.
7. Students may mention location, natural resources, landforms, climate, population density, government, and history.
8. Nile River; because desert covers the rest of the country and water is an important resource

TEACH

Create a map on a transparency showing your school building and the main streets around it. Form students into five groups and give each group a copy of the map. Have each group fill in the map with different information, including places to eat, parking areas, houses, traffic lights, gas stations, or other important features. Display the different maps on an overhead projector. **Ask:** **How are these maps like GIS?** *(They display different information about the same area.)* **L1**

More About GIS

One key to GIS is that a computer can create exact copies of the same base map so that the different layers of information can all be stored on the same scale. Two or more sets of data can be displayed together reliably.

Interdisciplinary Connections

Technology Salt Lake City sits on a fault in the earth's crust, creating the danger of earthquakes. Emergency planners used GIS to simulate damage to roads so they could plot the response time of rescue crews.

Making Connections

CULTURE | GOVERNMENT | PEOPLE | **TECHNOLOGY**

Geographic Information Systems

What if a farmer could save money by applying fertilizer only to the crops that needed it? Today, thanks to computer technology called geographic information systems (GIS), farmers can do just that.

The Technology

Geographic information systems (GIS) use computer software to combine and display a wide range of information about an area. It starts with a map showing a specific location on the earth. This map is then linked with other information about that same place, such as satellite photos, amounts of rainfall, or housing locations.

Think of geographic information systems as a stack of transparencies. Each transparency shows the same general background but highlights different information. The first transparency may show a base map of an area. Only the borders may appear. The second transparency may show only rivers and highways. The third may highlight mountains and other physical features, buildings, or cities.

In a similar way, GIS technology places layers of information onto a base map. It can then switch each layer of information on or off, allowing data to be viewed in many different ways. In the case of the farmer mentioned above, GIS software combines information about soil type, plant needs, and last year's crop to pinpoint exact areas that need fertilizer.

How It Is Used

GIS technology allows users to quickly pull together data from many different sources and construct maps tailored to specific needs. This helps people analyze past events, predict future scenarios, and make sound decisions.

A person who is deciding where to build a new store can use GIS technology to help select the best location. The process might begin with a list of possible sites. The store owner gathers information about the areas surrounding each place. This could include shoppers' ages, incomes, and educations; where shoppers live; traffic patterns; and information about other stores in the area. The GIS software then builds a computerized map composed of these layers of information. The store owner can use the information to decide on a new store location.

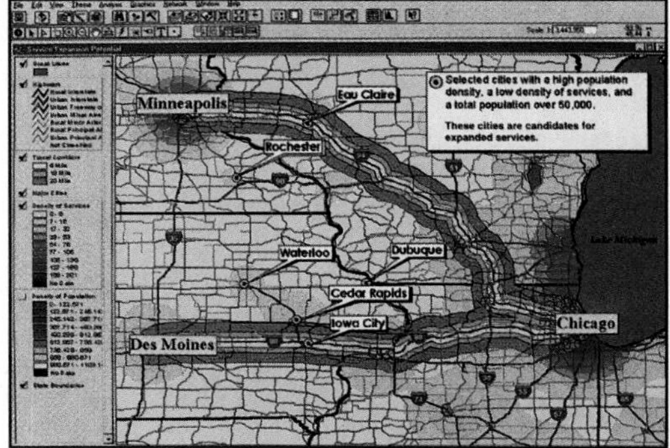

Graphic image created using ArcView® GIS software, and provided courtesy of Environmental Systems Research Institute, Inc.

Making the Connection

1. What is GIS technology?
2. How does GIS software analyze data in a variety of ways?
3. **Drawing Conclusions** Create a list of questions that you would want answered to locate the best place to add a new school to your district.

Making the Connection

1. computer software that can combine and display a variety of information about the same area
2. *Possible answer:* GIS layer different types of information on a base map. The user can choose to display different sets of data at the same time, allowing comparisons.
3. *Possible answers:* What are the settlement patterns, population growth patterns, traffic patterns, and land use information for the community?

Section 2

Physical Geography

Guide to Reading

Main Idea

Landforms in all their variety affect how people live.

Terms to Know

- plate tectonics
- fault
- plain
- plateau
- canyon
- aquifer
- climate
- tropics
- greenhouse effect

Reading Strategy

Create a diagram like this one. In each of the surrounding circles, write the name of a landform and a fact about it.

NATIONAL GEOGRAPHIC **Exploring Our World**

Forces beneath the earth's surface shape the land and the lives of the people who live on it. Here in the Azores Islands, a volcano makes cooking easy. People wrap meat and vegetables in a cloth and bury the bundle in a hole where heat from deep inside the earth rises to the surface. The temperature reaches 200°F (93°C), which is hot enough to steam the food.

It is amazing to think that the earth thousands of miles beneath your feet is so hot that it has turned metal into liquid. Although you may not feel these forces, what lies inside the earth affects what lies on top. Mountains, deserts, and other landscapes were formed over millions of years by forces acting below the earth's surface—and they are still changing today. Some forces work slowly and show no results for thousands of years. Others appear suddenly and have dramatic, and sometimes very destructive, effects.

Forces Beneath the Earth's Crust

You have probably watched science shows about earthquakes and volcanoes. You have probably also seen news on television discussing the destruction caused by earthquakes. These disasters result from forces at work inside the earth.

Plate Movements Scientists have developed a theory about the earth's structure called **plate tectonics.** This theory states that the crust is not an unbroken shell but consists of plates, or huge slabs of rock, that

57

Focus

Section Objectives

1. Discuss the forces that change the earth's surface.
2. Describe the earth's major landforms.
3. Explain climate and how it is affected by people.

BELLRINGER
Skillbuilder Activity

Project transparency and have students answer questions.

This activity is also available as a blackline master.

Daily Focus Skills Transparency 2-2

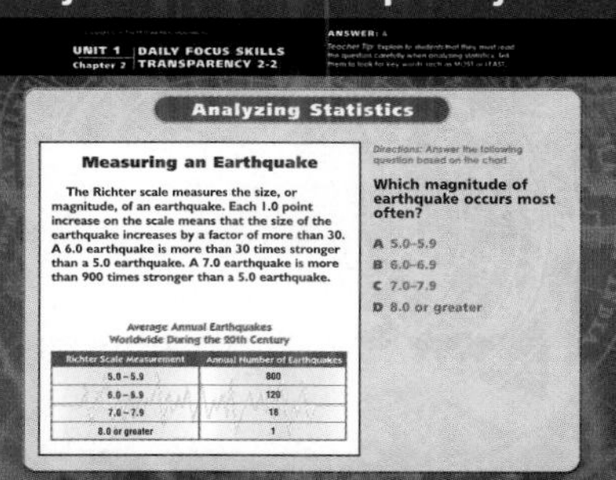

ANSWER: A

UNIT 1 Chapter 2 | DAILY FOCUS SKILLS TRANSPARENCY 2-2

Analyzing Statistics

Measuring an Earthquake

The Richter scale measures the size, or magnitude, of an earthquake. Each 1.0 point increase on the scale means that the size of the earthquake increases by a factor of more than 30. A 6.0 earthquake is more than 30 times stronger than a 5.0 earthquake. A 7.0 earthquake is more than 900 times stronger than a 5.0 earthquake.

Average Annual Earthquakes Worldwide During the 20th Century

Richter Scale Measurement	Annual Number of Earthquakes
5.0–5.9	800
6.0–6.9	120
7.0–7.9	18
8.0 or greater	1

Directions: Answer the following question based on the chart.

Which magnitude of earthquake occurs most often?

A 5.0–5.9
B 6.0–6.9
C 7.0–7.9
D 8.0 or greater

Guide to Reading

■ **Accessing Prior Knowledge** Bring a baseball to class. Hold the ball up and explain to students that the earth is like a baseball. It has an outer shell, like the stitched covering of the ball, and two inner sections that support it.

Use the Vocabulary PuzzleMaker to create crossword and word search puzzles.

Section Resources

Reproducible Masters

- Reproducible Lesson Plan 2-2
- Daily Lecture and Discussion Notes 2-2
- Guided Reading Activity 2-2
- Reading Essentials and Study Guide 2-2
- Section Quiz 2-2

Transparencies

- Daily Focus Skills Transparency 2-2
- GeoQuiz Transparency 2-2

Multimedia

- Vocabulary PuzzleMaker Software
- Interactive Tutor Self-Assessment CD-ROM
- Presentation Plus! CD-ROM
- ExamView® Pro 3.0 Testmaker CD-ROM

Building Skills

Drawing Conclusions Have students read "When Plates Meet" with these questions in mind: **What areas are more likely to experience earthquakes?** *(areas where plates meet)* **What areas are more likely to experience tsunamis?** *(coastal areas)*

Analyzing the Diagram

Answer
Most earthquakes and volcanoes occur along plate boundaries.

Skills Practice
What is the name of an area where two plates are pulling apart? *(fault)*

Reading Check Answer
They produce high mountain ranges.

Tectonic Plate Boundaries

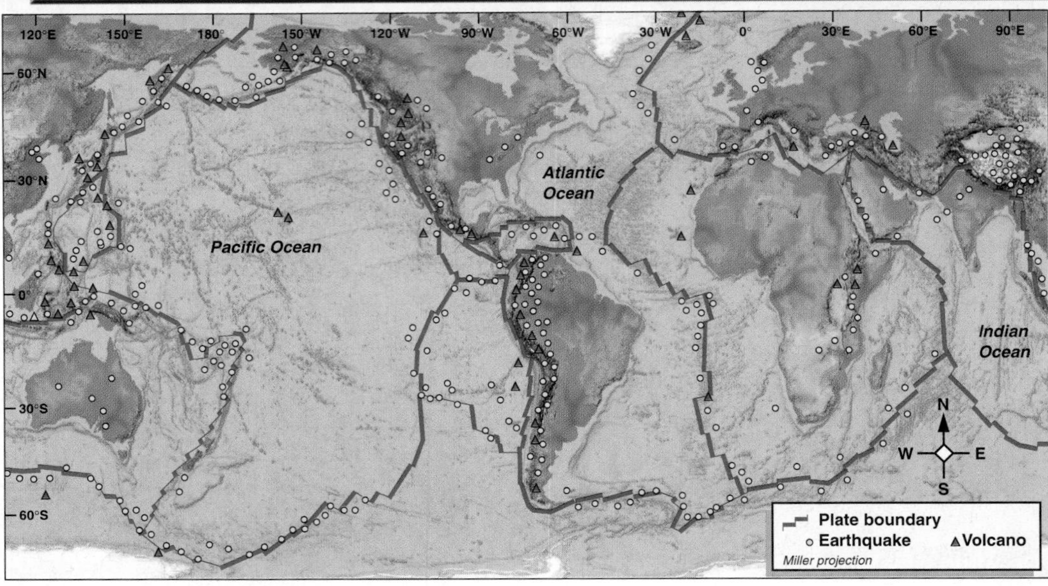

Analyzing the Diagram

Most of North America sits on one plate.

Region **What pattern do you see among plate boundaries, earthquakes, and volcanoes?**

move. The plates float on top of liquid rock just below the earth's crust. They move—but often in different directions. Oceans and continents sit on these gigantic plates, as the diagram above shows.

When Plates Meet Sometimes, these plates push against each other. When this happens, one of three events occurs, depending on what kinds of plates are involved.

If two continental plates smash into each other, the collision produces high mountain ranges. This kind of collision produced the **Himalaya** mountain range in South Asia.

If a continental plate and an ocean plate move against each other, the thicker continental plate slides over the thinner ocean plate. The downward force of the lower plate causes molten rock to build up and perhaps erupt in a volcano or an earthquake.

Sometimes two plates do not meet head-on but move alongside each other. To picture this, put your two hands together and then move them in opposite directions. When this action occurs in the earth, the two plates move apart. This movement creates **faults,** or cracks in the earth's crust. Violent earthquakes can happen near these faults. One of the most famous faults in the United States is the **San Andreas Fault** in California. The earth's movement along this fault caused a severe earthquake in San Francisco in 1906 and another, less serious quake there in 1989.

Reading Check **What happens when two continental plates collide?**

Cooperative Learning Activity

Geology Organize the class into six groups numbered 1 through 6. Have each group split up into three subgroups called A, B, and C. Students in the three subgroups should work together. That is, groups 1A through 6A work together, as do groups 1B through 6B and 1C through 6C. Assign each subgroup one of the following topics: Earth's structure, forces beneath the crust, and forces shaping landforms. Have each subgroup develop ways of teaching their topic. Then send students back to the original groups. Have the subgroups take turns teaching other group members about their topic. **L2**

EE3 Physical Systems: Standard 7

Types of Landforms

Look at the illustration on pages 14 and 15 of the **Geography Handbook.** Notice the many different forms that the land may take. Which ones are familiar to you? Which ones are new to you?

On Land Mountains are huge towers of rock formed by the collision of the earth's tectonic plates or by volcanoes. Some mountains may be a few thousand feet high. Others can soar higher than 20,000 feet (6,096 m). The world's tallest mountain is Mount Everest, located in South Asia's Himalaya mountain ranges. It towers at 29,035 feet (8,850 m)—nearly 5.5 miles (8.9 km) high.

In contrast, **plains** and **plateaus** are mostly flat. What makes them different from each other is their elevation, or height above sea level. Plains are low-lying stretches of flat or gently rolling land. Plateaus are also flat but have higher elevations.

Between mountains or hills lie valleys. A valley is a long stretch of land lower than the land on either side. You often find rivers at the bottom of valleys. **Canyons** are steep-sided lowlands that rivers have cut through plateaus. One of the most famous canyons is the **Grand Canyon** in Arizona. For millions of years, the **Colorado River** flowed over a plateau and carved through rock to form the Grand Canyon.

✓Reading Check **How are plains and plateaus different?**

Bodies of Water

About 70 percent of the earth's surface is water. Most of that water is salt water, which people and animals cannot drink. Only a small percentage is freshwater, which is drinkable. People and most animals need freshwater to live. Many other creatures, however, make their homes in the earth's saltwater oceans and seas.

Valleys vs. Canyons

The Great Rift Valley in Africa is surrounded by mountains (left). Canyons, like the Grand Canyon in Arizona (below), are carved from plateaus.

Place **How are valleys and canyons similar?**

NATIONAL GEOGRAPHIC On Location

59

Chapter 2

Section 2, pages 57–61

Classifying Information

Have students scan the photographs in the text to find examples of the different landforms. **L1**

Daily Lecture Notes 2-2

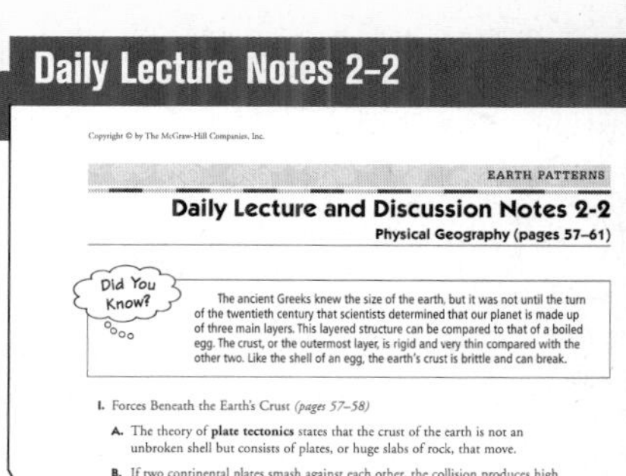
Copyright © by The McGraw-Hill Companies, Inc.

EARTH PATTERNS

Daily Lecture and Discussion Notes 2-2

Physical Geography (pages 57–61)

Did You Know?

The ancient Greeks knew the size of the earth, but it was not until the turn of the twentieth century that scientists determined that our planet is made up of three main layers. This layered structure can be compared to that of a boiled egg. The crust, or the outermost layer, is rigid and very thin compared with the other two. Like the shell of an egg, the earth's crust is brittle and can break.

I. Forces Beneath the Earth's Crust *(pages 57–58)*

A. The theory of **plate tectonics** states that the crust of the earth is not an unbroken shell but consists of plates, or huge slabs of rock, that move.

B. If two continental plates smash against each other, the collision produces high mountain ranges.

✓ Reading Check Answer

Both are generally flat, but plateaus have a higher elevation than plains.

More About the Photos

The Great Rift Valley and the Grand Canyon The Grand Canyon, about a mile deep, was formed fairly recently—about 6 million years ago. The Great Rift Valley of Africa is less steep—about 2,000 to 3,000 feet (610 to 914 m). It is much older—about 30 million years old.

Caption Answer Both valleys and canyons are lowlands, but canyons are more steep-sided and are the result of erosion caused by rivers that cut through plateaus.

Meeting Special Needs

Naturalist Organize the class into teams. Give each team an example of a landform or body of water, such as mountain, valley, ocean, or river. Have teams brainstorm to identify the influence that this geographical feature might have on the lives of people. Remind students that the influence can be both positive and negative (for example, a river can supply freshwater but also flood its banks, endangering the lives of people living near it). Have the groups present their lists to the rest of the class and discuss their findings. **L2**

Refer to *Inclusion for the Middle School Social Studies Classroom Strategies and Activities* in the TCR.

Chapter 2

Section 2, pages 57–61

Guided Reading Activity 2–2

Name ______ Date ______ Class ______

EARTH PATTERNS

Guided Reading Activity 2-2

Physical Geography

DIRECTIONS: Reading for Accuracy Reading the section and completing the activity below will help you learn more about the earth's landforms and climate. Refer to your textbook to decide if a statement is true or false. Write **T** or **F**, and if a statement is false, rewrite it correctly.

____ 1. A theory about the earth's structure is called plate tectonics.

____ 2. If two continental plates smash into each other, the collision produces an earthquake.

____ 3. Plains are low-lying stretches of flat rolling land; plateaus are flat but have higher elevations.

____ 4. Valleys lie between mountains and hills.

3 ASSESS

Assign Section 2 Assessment as homework or an in-class activity.

Have students use the Interactive Tutor Self-Assessment CD-ROM to review Section 2–2.

✓ Reading Check Answer

salt water

Drawing Conclusions The Gulf Stream is a warm current that flows from the Gulf of Mexico along the east coast of North America, then across the Atlantic towards Europe, where it is called the North Atlantic Current. Winds blowing from west to east blow over these warm waters and bring warm air to Europe. **Ask: Which is warmer, Nova Scotia (Canada) or Ireland? Why?** *(Ireland; because Canada lies west of the Gulf Stream and doesn't get the benefits of the wind blowing over the water)*

Believe It or Not!

Mt. Pinatubo

Mt. Pinatubo (PEE•nah•TOO•boh) is a volcanic mountain in the Philippine Islands. Its eruption in the early 1990s impacted the world's climate. The powerful explosion shot ash and sulfur dioxide into the earth's atmosphere, which blocked some of the sun's rays from reaching the earth. The world's climate was cooler for two years after the volcano's blast.

Salt Water All the oceans on the earth are part of a huge, continuous body of salt water—almost 98 percent of the planet's water. The four major oceans are the Pacific Ocean, the Atlantic Ocean, the Indian Ocean, and the Arctic Ocean.

Freshwater Only about 2 percent of the water on the earth is freshwater. Eighty percent of that freshwater is frozen in glaciers, or giant sheets of ice. Only a tiny fraction of the world's freshwater—not even four-hundredths of a percent—is found in lakes and rivers.

When you think of freshwater, you probably think of mighty rivers and huge lakes. People can get freshwater from another source, though. Groundwater is water that fills tiny cracks and holes in the rock layers below the surface of the earth. This is a vital source of water because there is 10 times more groundwater than there is water in rivers and lakes. Groundwater can be tapped by wells. Some areas have **aquifers**, or underground rock layers that water flows through. In regions with little rainfall, both farmers and city dwellers sometimes have to depend on aquifers and other groundwater for most of their water supply.

✓ Reading Check **Which is more plentiful, salt water or freshwater?**

Climate

Climate is the usual, predictable pattern of weather in an area over a long period of time. It is one reason people decide to live in a particular place. One important influence on climate is the angle at which the sun's rays hit the earth. In general, temperatures are higher in places where the rays strike the earth's surface more directly than in places where they strike the surface at an angle. This means that places in low latitudes—regions near the Equator—usually have warmer climates than places at higher latitudes. Generally, warmer climates are found in the **tropics**—areas near the Equator that lie between the **Tropic of Cancer** (23½°N latitude) and the **Tropic of Capricorn** (23½°S latitude).

The combined effects of water, wind, and land also influence the climate at a given place. In general, water warms and cools more slowly than land. In land areas where strong winds blow in from over the ocean, temperatures tend to be less varied than in places at the same latitude that do not benefit from these winds.

Finally, altitude, or elevation, of a place affects its climate. As altitude increases, air temperatures decrease. This means that places at high elevations that are quite close to the Equator can have cool climates.

The Impact of People on Climate You may have noticed that temperatures in large cities are generally higher than those in nearby rural areas. Why is that? City streets and buildings absorb more of the sun's rays than do the plants and trees of rural areas.

Cities are warmer even in winter. People burn fuels to warm houses, power industry, and move cars and buses along the streets. This burning raises the temperature in the city. The burning also releases a cloud of chemicals into the air. These chemicals blanket the city and hold in more of the sun's heat, creating a so-called heat island. The

Team-Teaching Activity

Government Point out that Florida faces high probabilities for both hurricanes and tornadoes. Nevertheless, the population there more than doubled from 1970 to the late 1990s. **Ask: What problems would this population growth cause in the event of a severe storm?** *(need to evacuate, rescue, or provide aid to larger numbers of people if a disaster occurs)* **What can governments do to try to address these problems?** *(plan evacuation routes, have emergency teams ready)* Invite a teacher with knowledge about government to class to discuss recent examples of disasters and how the government responded. **L1**

EE4 Human Systems: Standard 9

burning of fuels is creating a worldwide problem. In the past 200 years, people have burned coal, oil, and natural gas as sources of energy. Burning these fuels releases certain gases into the air.

Many scientists believe that the buildup of these gases presents dangers. It creates a **greenhouse effect**—like a greenhouse, the gases prevent the warm air from rising and escaping into the atmosphere. As a result, the overall temperature of the earth will increase.

In some countries, people are clearing large areas of rain forests. They want to sell the lumber from the trees. They also want to use the land to grow crops or as pasture for cattle. People often clear the forests by burning down trees in an area. This burning releases gases into the air, just like burning oil or natural gas does.

Another danger of clearing the rain forests is related to rainfall. Water on the earth's surface evaporates and then falls as rain. In the rain forests, much of this water evaporates from the leaves of trees. If the trees are cut, less water will evaporate. As a result, less rain will fall. Scientists worry that, over time, the area that now holds rain forests will actually become dry and unable to grow anything.

Not all scientists agree about the greenhouse effect. Some argue that the world is not warming. Others say that even if it is, predictions of disaster are extreme. Many scientists are studying world temperature trends closely. They hope to be able to discover whether the greenhouse effect is a real threat.

✓Reading Check **What is the greenhouse effect?**

Assessment

Define Terms

1. **Define** plate tectonics, fault, plain, plateau, canyon, aquifer, climate, tropics, greenhouse effect.

Recalling Facts

2. **Region** Name three types of landforms.
3. **Movement** What is one reason people decide to settle in a particular area?
4. **Place** What are the world's four oceans?
5. **Region** Why do the areas near the Equator have warmer climates than other areas?

Critical Thinking

6. **Drawing Conclusions** Why do you think it is important to keep groundwater free of dangerous chemicals?
7. **Summarizing** How does clearing of the rain forests affect climate?

Graphic Organizer

8. **Organizing Information** Create a diagram like this one. List at least four sources of freshwater and salt water on the lines under each heading.

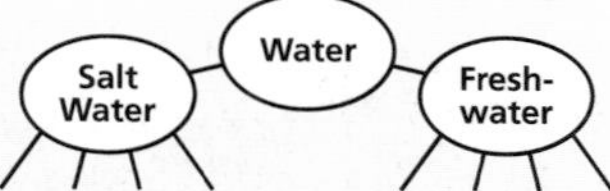

Applying Social Studies Skills

9. **Analyzing Diagrams** Look at the diagram of tectonic plate boundaries on page 58. Why might it be a problem that most of the world's population lives along the western edge of the Pacific Ocean?

Section 2 Assessment

1. The terms are defined in the Glossary.
2. *Possible answers:* mountains, plains, plateaus, valleys, canyons
3. *Possible answer:* climate
4. Pacific, Atlantic, Indian, Arctic
5. Near the Equator, the sun's rays strike the earth's surface more directly.
6. It is a vital source of freshwater for drinking and farming.
7. Burning trees releases gases into the air, creating more heat. Also, when trees are cut, less water evaporates into the air, resulting in less rain.
8. *Possible answers:* freshwater: lakes, rivers, ground water, aquifers; salt water: Atlantic, Pacific, Indian, and Arctic Oceans
9. Many earthquakes and volcanoes occur there.

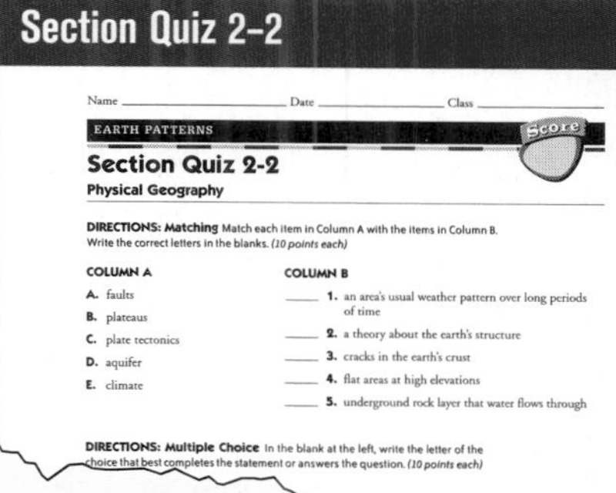

Section Quiz 2-2

Name ________ Date ________ Class ________

EARTH PATTERNS

Score

Section Quiz 2-2

Physical Geography

DIRECTIONS: Matching Match each item in Column A with the items in Column B. Write the correct letters in the blanks. *(10 points each)*

COLUMN A	COLUMN B
A. faults	____ 1. an area's usual weather pattern over long periods of time
B. plateaus	____ 2. a theory about the earth's structure
C. plate tectonics	____ 3. cracks in the earth's crust
D. aquifer	____ 4. flat areas at high elevations
E. climate	____ 5. underground rock layer that water flows through

DIRECTIONS: Multiple Choice In the blank at the left, write the letter of the choice that best completes the statement or answers the question. *(10 points each)*

✓ Reading Check Answer

the effect created by the burning of fossil fuels, which creates a blanket around Earth that traps more of the sun's warmth near the planet

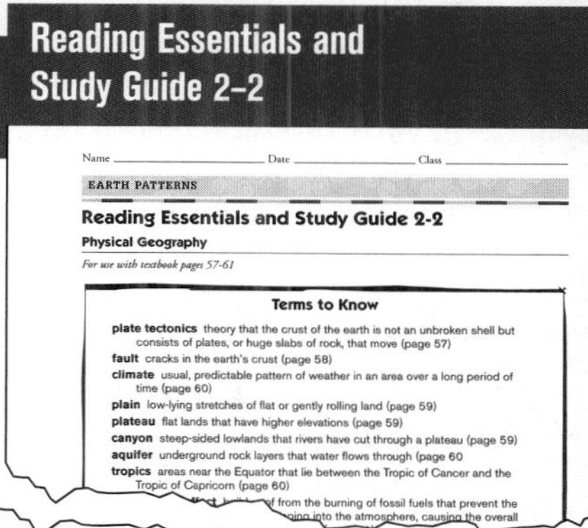

Reading Essentials and Study Guide 2-2

Name ________ Date ________ Class ________

EARTH PATTERNS

Reading Essentials and Study Guide 2-2

Physical Geography

For use with textbook pages 57-61

Terms to Know

plate tectonics theory that the crust of the earth is not an unbroken shell but consists of plates, or huge slabs of rock, that move (page 57)

fault cracks in the earth's crust (page 58)

climate usual, predictable pattern of weather in an area over a long period of time (page 60)

plain low-lying stretches of flat or gently rolling land (page 59)

plateau flat lands that have higher elevations (page 59)

canyon steep-sided lowlands that rivers have cut through a plateau (page 59)

aquifer underground rock layers that water flows through (page 60

tropics areas near the Equator that lie between the Tropic of Cancer and the Tropic of Capricorn (page 60)

CLOSE

Have students investigate one aspect of the earth's structure, or one type of landform or climate zone. Then have them create a poster that explains the characteristics of their subject and shows some examples. **Ask:** **Do people live there? Why or why not?**

TEACH

Create a map of the classroom. Make the perimeter of the room, and then add windows, doors, desks, bookcases, and other features. Before adding each feature, ask students to suggest how it might be represented on the map. *(with different colors or symbols)* Record the suggestions on a key next to the map. Be sure to include a compass rose. Working from the map, have students answer such questions as: **How many windows does the room have? How many desks? L1**

Additional Skills Practice

1. **How are monuments and memorials shown on the map?** *(by yellow squares)*
2. **What direction is the top of the map?** *(north)*
3. **On what street is the Hirshhorn Museum located?** *(Independence Avenue)*

Additional Skills Resources

 Chapter Skills Activity 2

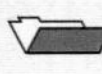 Building Geography Skills for Life

GLENCOE TECHNOLOGY

Skillbuilder Interactive Workbook CD-ROM, Level 1

This interactive CD-ROM reinforces student mastery of essential social studies skills.

Social Studies Skill

Using a Map Key

To understand what a map is showing, you must read the **map key,** or legend. The map key explains the meaning of special colors, symbols, and lines on the map.

Learning the Skill

Colors in the map key may represent different elevations or heights of land, climate areas, or languages. Lines may stand for rivers, streets, or boundaries.

Maps also have a compass rose showing directions. The cardinal directions are north, south, east, and west. North and south are the directions of the North and South Poles. If you stand facing north, east is the direction to your right. West is the direction to your left. The compass rose might also show intermediate directions, or those that fall between the cardinal directions. For example, the intermediate direction northeast falls between north and east. To use a map key, follow these steps:

- Read the map title.
- Read the map key to find out what special information it gives.
- Find examples of each map key color, line, or symbol on the map.
- Use the compass rose to identify the four cardinal directions.

Practicing the Skill

Look at the map of Washington, D.C., below, to answer the following questions.

1. What does a red square represent?
2. What does a blue square represent?
3. Does the Washington Monument lie east or west of the Lincoln Memorial?
4. From the White House, in what direction would you go to get to the Capitol?

Applying the Skill

Find a map in a newspaper or magazine. Use the map key to explain three things the map is showing.

GO TO Practice key skills with Glencoe **Skillbuilder Interactive Workbook, Level 1.**

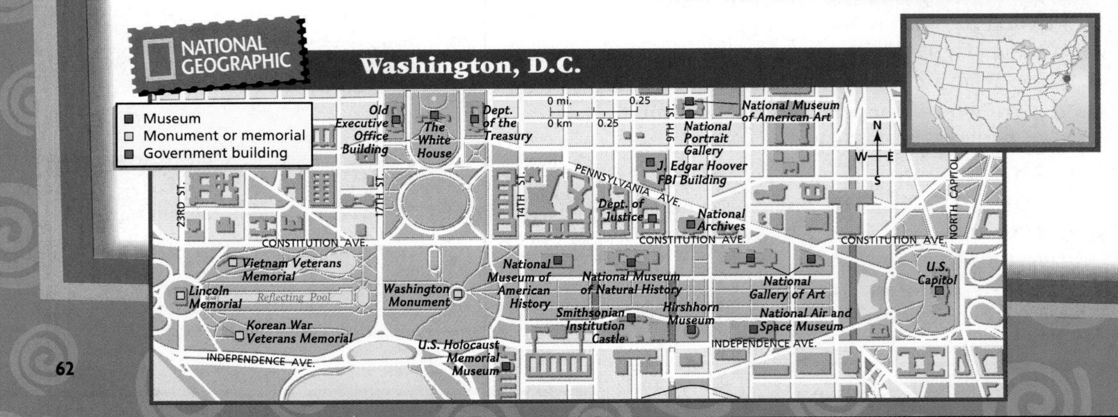

62

Practicing the Skill Answers

1. government buildings
2. museum
3. east
4. southeast

Applying the Skill

Students' responses should demonstrate correct interpretations of the map key in question.

Section 3

People and the Environment

Guide to Reading

Main Idea

The actions people take can have serious effects on the environment.

Terms to Know

- conservation
- pesticide
- ecosystem
- crop rotation
- erosion
- deforestation
- acid rain

Reading Strategy

Create a diagram like this one. On the lines, write at least two problems that are caused by human use of water, land, and air.

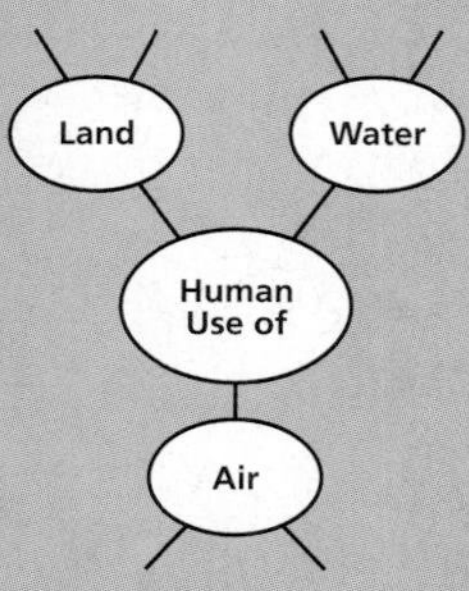

NATIONAL GEOGRAPHIC Exploring Our World

What happens when we harm the environment? It is possible that some plants and animals might be gone forever. This scientist hopes to prevent that. She works at a seed bank. Behind her, stored at −4°F (−20°C), are jars of plant seeds from around the world. Should any of these 4,000 types of plants become extinct, these seeds can start growing them again.

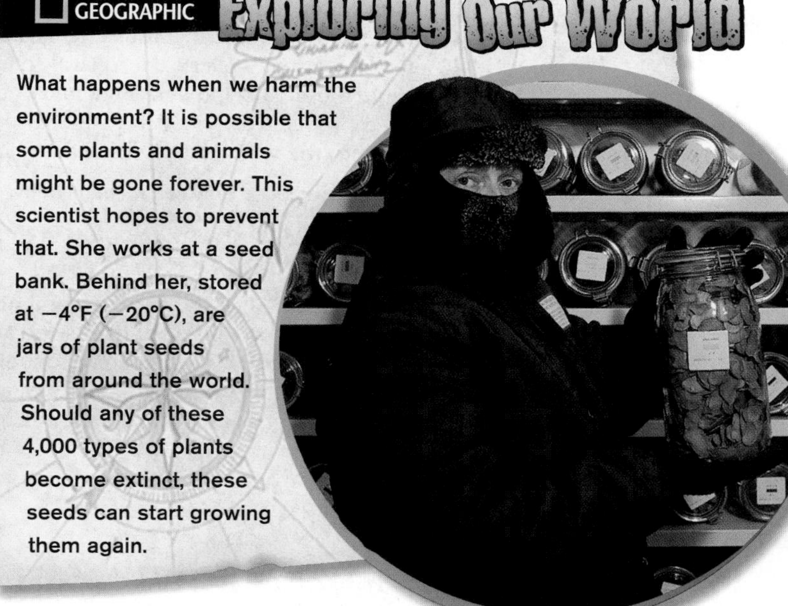

The rapidly growing number of people threatens the delicate balance of life in the world. More and more people use more water. They need more land to live on and to grow more food. Spreading industry fouls the air. Humans must act carefully to be sure not to destroy the earth that gives us life.

Water Use

People, plants, and animals need freshwater to live. People need clean water to drink. They also need water for their crops and their animals. In fact, as much as 70 percent of the water used is for farming. You read earlier that 70 percent of the earth's surface is water. However, only a small fraction of the world's water is freshwater. Because the earth's supply of freshwater is limited, people must manage this precious resource carefully.

63

Section Resources

Reproducible Masters

- Reproducible Lesson Plan 2-3
- Daily Lecture and Discussion Notes 2-3
- Guided Reading Activity 2-3
- Reading Essentials and Study Guide 2-3
- Section Quiz 2-3

Transparencies

- Daily Focus Skills Transparency 2-3
- GeoQuiz Transparency 2-3

Multimedia

- Vocabulary PuzzleMaker Software
- Interactive Tutor Self-Assessment CD-ROM
- Presentation Plus! CD-ROM
- ExamView® Pro 3.0 Testmaker CD-ROM

1 Focus

Section Objectives

1. Explain why people have to manage water.
2. Describe how the soil can be damaged by people.
3. Explain the effects of air pollution.

BELLRINGER Skillbuilder Activity

Project transparency and have students answer questions.

This activity is also available as a blackline master.

Daily Focus Skills Transparency 2-3

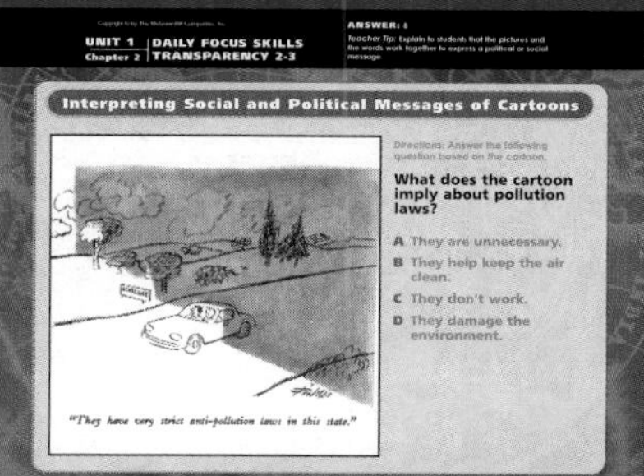

Guide to Reading

■ **Accessing Prior Knowledge**
Have students discuss ideas about the impact of humans on the environment.

■ **Vocabulary Precheck**
Explain to students that the suffix *-tion* means "process" or "action." Have them use this information to determine the meanings of the terms ending with this suffix.

TEACH

Identifying Main Ideas

Ask: **What are the most basic things that people need to live?** *(food, water, and air)* **What happens if those things are not available, or if they are not clean?** *(People will become ill and perhaps die.)* Explain that students will learn about dangers that human actions pose to these resources. **L1**

Reading Check Answer

dangerous chemicals, dirt, or pesticides can seep into the water supply

Daily Lecture Notes 2-3

EARTH PATTERNS

Daily Lecture and Discussion Notes 2-3

People and the Enrivonment (pages 63–66)

Did You Know? Forest areas in developed countries continue to increase slightly each year. Developing countries, however, reduce their forest area each year when they clear land for agriculture, development, and logging. They lose forest area at a rate of at least 140,000 square kilometers every year.

I. Water Use *(pages 63–64)*

A. As much as 70 percent of our water use is for farming.

B. Because the earth's supply of freshwater is limited, people must manage it carefully.

C. Regions that receive heavy rainfall in some months and little or none in other months can manage their water supply by building storage areas to hold the ...ter use.

More About the Photo

Soil Erosion Terracing allows farming on hilly areas that otherwise would not be able to grow crops. Terrace farming is used throughout the world.

Caption Answer Soil is less likely to wash down the hillside.

Water Management Some regions receive heavy rainfall in some months of the year and little, or none, in other months. They can manage their water supply by building storage areas to hold the heavy rains for later use.

Managing water supplies involves two main steps. The first step is **conservation,** or the careful use of resources so that they are not wasted. Did you know that 6 or 7 gallons (23 to 27 liters) of water go down the drain every minute that you shower? Taking short showers instead of baths is an easy way to prevent wasting water.

The second approach to managing the water supply is to avoid polluting water. Some manufacturing processes use water. Sometimes those processes result in dangerous chemicals or dirt entering the water supply. Many farmers overuse fertilizers to help their crops grow. Many also use **pesticides,** or powerful chemicals that kill crop-destroying insects. These products are needed to increase food production, but they can seep into the water supply and cause harm.

Reading Check How can manufacturing and farming harm the water supply?

Land Use

As humans expand their communities, they invade **ecosystems.** These are places where the plants and animals are dependent upon one another—and their particular surroundings—for survival. For example, some people may want to drain a wet, marshy area to get rid of disease-carrying mosquitoes and make the soil useful for farming. When the area

NATIONAL GEOGRAPHIC **On Location**

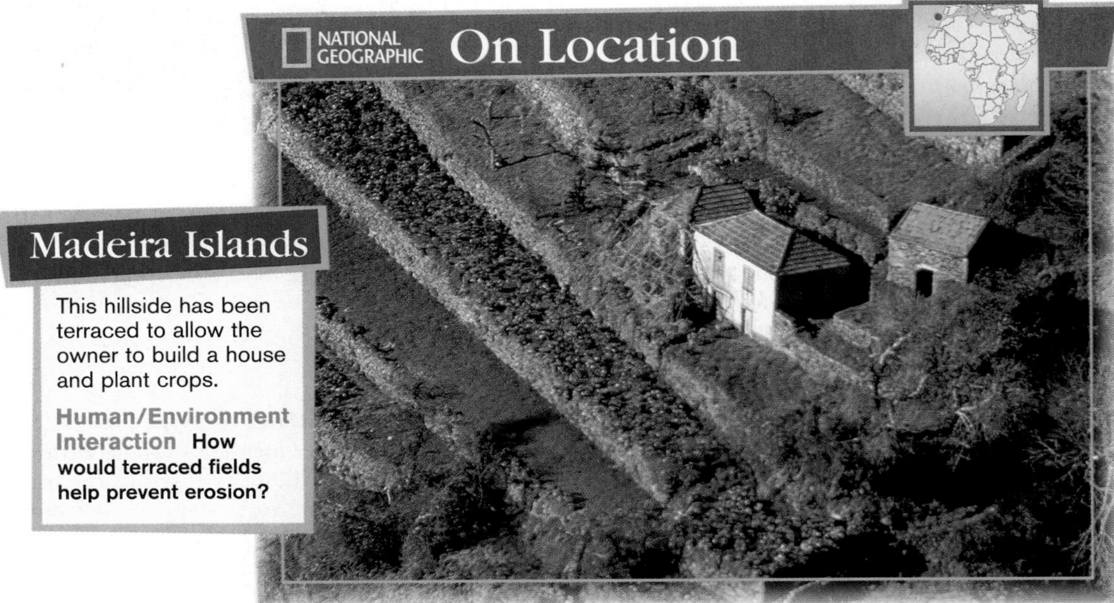

Madeira Islands

This hillside has been terraced to allow the owner to build a house and plant crops.

Human/Environment Interaction How would terraced fields help prevent erosion?

Cooperative Learning Activity

Environmental Posters Organize students into three groups. Assign each group one of the following topics: air pollution, land pollution, water pollution. Have groups investigate their topics as they pertain to their community. Groups should identify the major local threats to the environment and suggest solutions to each threat. Each group should create an illustrated poster presenting its findings. Have groups display their posters on the bulletin board. **L2**

EE5 Environment and Society: Standard 5

is drained, however, the ecosystem is destroyed. In managing land, humans must recognize that some soils are not suited for growing certain crops. Benefits must be weighed against losses.

Soil To grow food, soil needs to have certain minerals. Farmers add fertilizers to the soil to supply some of these minerals. Some also practice **crop rotation,** or changing what they plant in a field to avoid using up all the minerals in the soil. Some crops—like beans—actually restore valuable minerals to the soil. Many farmers now plant bean crops every three years to build the soil back up.

If people do not carefully manage the soil, it can erode away. In **erosion,** wind or water carries soil away, leaving the land less fertile than before. Have you ever seen a group of trees alongside a farmer's field? The farmer may have planted those trees to block the wind and prevent erosion. In the tropics, erosion presents a problem—especially if farmers plant their crops on sloping land. When heavy rains come, the soil may simply wash down the hillside.

Forests Some areas of the world have thick forests of tall trees. Growing populations in these countries often turn to these lush forests as a source of land to grow food. Yet **deforestation,** or cutting down forests, is a problem—especially in the tropics. Rains in these areas are extremely heavy. When the tree roots are no longer there to hold the soil, the water can wash it away. Then farmers have to move to a new area and cut the trees in that section of forest. As a result, more and more of the forest is lost over time.

✓Reading Check **What problem can result from erosion?**

Air Pollution

Industries and vehicles that burn fossil fuels are the main sources of air pollution. Throughout the world, fumes from cars and other vehicles pollute the air. The chemicals in air pollution can seriously damage people's health. These chemicals also combine with precipitation. They then fall as **acid rain,** or rain containing high amounts of chemical pollutants. Acid rain kills fish, damages forests, and eats away at the surfaces of buildings.

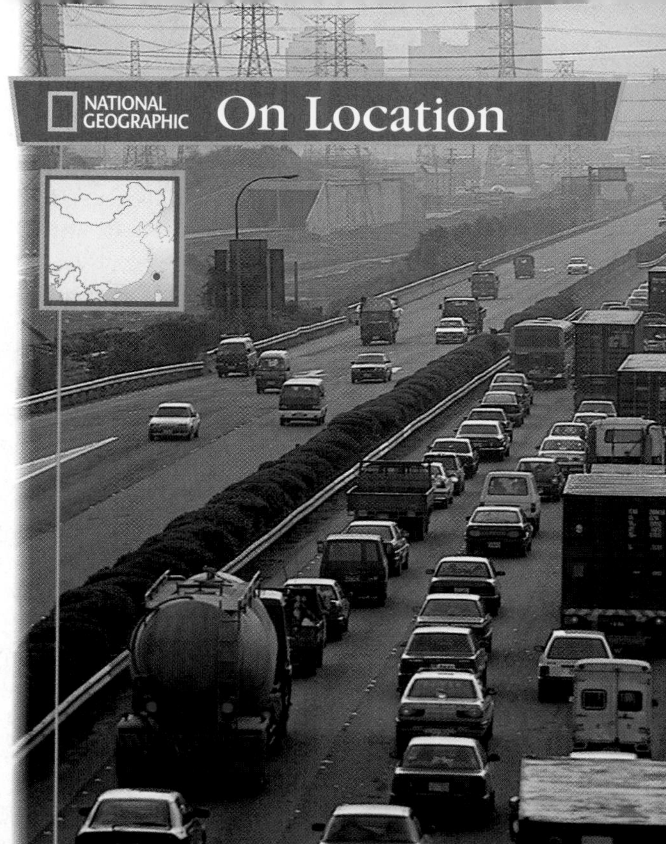

Taiwan

Burning fossil fuels adds harmful chemicals to the air.

Human/Environment Interaction **What are some effects of air pollution?**

More About the Photos

Air Pollution The earth's wind systems can carry pollutants very far. Scientists have found evidence of pesticides in Antarctica, where no such substances have ever been used.

Caption Answer damage to people's health, acid rain, and greenhouse effect

✓ Reading Check Answer

The land is less fertile.

Guided Reading Activity 2-3

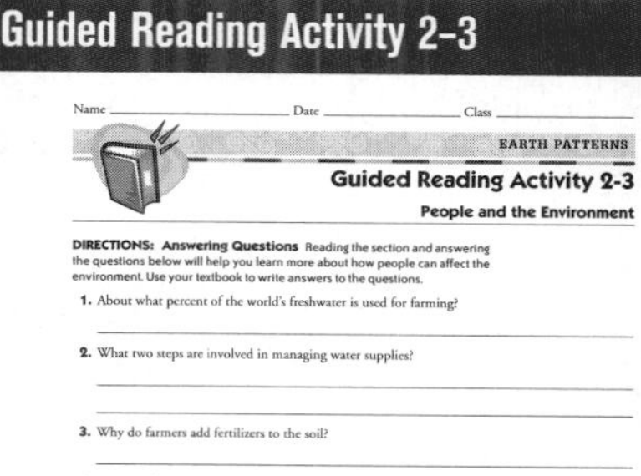
Name ______ Date ______ Class ______

EARTH PATTERNS

Guided Reading Activity 2-3

People and the Environment

DIRECTIONS: Answering Questions Reading the section and answering the questions below will help you learn more about how people can affect the environment. Use your textbook to write answers to the questions.

1. About what percent of the world's freshwater is used for farming?
2. What two steps are involved in managing water supplies?
3. Why do farmers add fertilizers to the soil?
4. How can the pesticides that farmers use to help increase food production also be harmful?

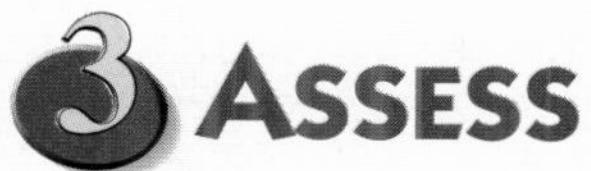

Assign Section 3 Assessment as homework or an in-class activity.

Enrich

Have students find out the physical processes that produce oil. Discuss their results. Ask them why oil is a non-renewable resource and what will happen when we run out of it.

Meeting Special Needs

Auditory/Musical Students who benefit from auditory instruction can retain the lesson better if they participate in partner reading. Pair students and have partners take turns reading paragraphs or sections of the text aloud. The partner not reading should follow the text as it is being read. At the end of each paragraph or section, students should quiz each other on the content. **L1 ELL**

Refer to *Inclusion for the Middle School Social Studies Classroom Strategies and Activities* in the TCR.

✓ Reading Check Answer

the combining of the chemicals in car fumes with precipitation

Section Quiz 2-3

Name ____________ Date ____________ Class ____________

EARTH PATTERNS

Section Quiz 2-3

People and the Environment

DIRECTIONS: Matching Match each item in Column A with the items in Column B. Write the correct letters in the blanks. *(10 points each)*

COLUMN A

A. erosion
B. ecosystem
C. conservation
D. pesticides
E. acid rain

COLUMN B

____ **1.** rain containing high amounts of chemical pollutants
____ **2.** chemicals that kill crop-destroying insects
____ **3.** place where plants and animals are dependent on one another and their surroundings for survival
____ **4.** wind or water carrying soil away
____ **5.** careful use of resources so they are not wasted

DIRECTIONS: Multiple Choice In the blank at the left, write the letter of the ... that best completes the statement or answers the question. *(10 points each)*

✓ Reading Check Answer

Farmers use the rain forests to provide food and income for their families.

Reading Essentials and Study Guide 2-3

Name ____________ Date ____________ Class ____________

EARTH PATTERNS

Reading Essentials and Study Guide 2-3

People and the Environment

For use with textbook pages 63-66

Terms to Know

conservation careful use of resources so they are not wasted (page 64)
pesticide powerful chemicals entering the water supply (page 64)
ecosystem places where the plants and animals are dependent upon one another (page 64)
crop rotation when farmers change what they plant in a field to avoid using up all the minerals in the soil (page 65)
erosion when wind or water carries soil away, leaving the land less fertile than before (page 65)
deforestation cutting down forests (page 65)
acid rain rain containing high amounts of chemical pollutants (page 65)

Close

Have students write a paragraph about the potential damage that humans can do to the environment and what can be done to prevent this.

Some scientists believe that increasing amounts of pollutants in the atmosphere will cause the earth to warm. While not all experts agree, some scientists say that the increase in temperature can have disastrous effects. Glaciers and ice caps may melt, raising the level of the world's seas. Higher seas could flood coastal cities. Warmer temperatures can also affect the land, making it no longer able to produce food.

✓ **Reading Check** What causes highly acidic rain?

Balancing People and Resources

Water, land, and air are among people's most precious resources. We need water and air to live. We need land to grow food. Only by caring for these resources can we be sure that we will still have them to use in the future.

Sometimes, though, protecting the environment for the future seems to clash with feeding people in the present. For example, farmers destroy the rain forests not because they want to but because they need to feed their families. They dislike being told by people in other countries that they should save the rain forests. Before they stop cutting down the rain forests, these farmers will need to find new ways to meet their needs.

✓ **Reading Check** How does saving the rain forests clash with current human needs?

Section 3 Assessment

Defining Terms

1. Define conservation, pesticide, ecosystem, crop rotation, erosion, deforestation, acid rain.

Recalling Facts

2. Human/Environment Interaction How do human activities affect ecosystems?

3. Human/Environment Interaction What are two ways of managing water?

4. Economics Why do farmers practice crop rotation?

Critical Thinking

5. Making Comparisons Which resource—water, soil, or air—do you think is most precious to people? Why?

6. Analyzing Information What ecosystems were affected by the growth of your community?

Graphic Organizer

7. Organizing Information Create a diagram like this one and list three potential results of global warming.

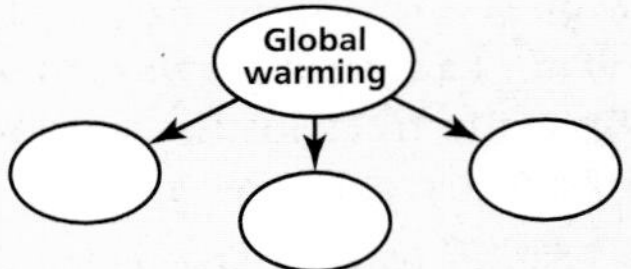

Applying Social Studies Skills

8. Analyzing Photographs Look at the On Location photo of Taiwan on page 65. List ways the environment has been changed and ways it is still being changed.

Section 3 Assessment

1. The terms are defined in the Glossary.
2. They use resources and sometimes pollute land, air, or water.
3. *Possible answers:* collecting rainfall, conservation, and avoiding pollution
4. to restore minerals and keep the soil productive
5. Answers should be well supported.
6. Answers will vary. Students should demonstrate knowledge of *ecosystem.*
7. Glaciers could melt, seas could rise and flood cities, and warmer temperatures could make land less productive than it is now.
8. fossil fuels being burned pollutes the air and causes acid rain; increased pollution in the atmosphere increases global warming

Chapter 2 Reading Review

Section 1 Thinking Like a Geographer

Terms to Know
- geography
- landform
- environment
- region
- Global Positioning System (GPS)
- geographic information systems (GIS)

Main Idea

Geographers use various tools to understand the world.

✓ **Place** Geographers study the physical and social characteristics of places.

✓ **Human/Environment Interaction** Geographers are especially interested in how people interact with their environment.

✓ **Technology** To study the earth, geographers use maps, globes, photographs, the Global Positioning System, and geographic information systems.

✓ **Economics** People can use information from geography to plan, make decisions, and manage resources.

Section 2 Physical Geography

Terms to Know
- plate tectonics
- fault
- plain
- plateau
- canyon
- aquifer
- climate
- tropics
- greenhouse effect

Main Idea

Landforms in all their variety affect how people live.

✓ **Movement** Earthquakes and volcanoes can reshape the land.

✓ **Location** Mountains, plateaus, valleys, and other landforms are found on the earth.

✓ **Science** Humans and most animals need freshwater to live. Only a small fraction of the world's freshwater is found in rivers and lakes.

✓ **Region** The tropics, near the Equator, receive more of the sun's direct rays than other regions.

✓ **Culture** Human actions such as building cities, burning fuels, and clearing the rain forests can affect climate.

Section 3 People and the Environment

Terms to Know
- conservation
- pesticide
- ecosystem
- crop rotation
- erosion
- deforestation
- acid rain

Main Idea

The actions people take can have serious effects on the environment.

✓ **Human/Environment Interaction** People need to manage water resources because the earth's freshwater supply is limited.

✓ **Human/Environment Interaction** Air pollution has damaging effects on the land and on people's health.

This pool formed by an underground spring is an unusual sight in Mexico's Chihuahua Desert. ▶

Reading Review

Use the Chapter 2 Reading Review to preview, review, condense, or reteach the chapter.

Preview/Review

Use the Terms to Know lists to help students review and study.

Activity Play a game in which you challenge teams of students to be the first to identify the correct term from a definition.

Vocabulary PuzzleMaker Software reinforces the vocabulary terms used in Chapter 2.

The Interactive Tutor Self-Assessment CD-ROM allows students to review Chapter 2 content.

Condense

Have students read the Chapter 2 summary statements.

Chapter 2 Guided Reading Activities

Chapter 2 Audio Program

Reteach

Reteaching Activity 2

Chapter 2 Reading Essentials and Study Guide

Chapter Culminating Activity

Ask students: Why does the earth look the way it looks? Have students review Chapter 2 to help answer the question. Students can answer the question by creating a drawing or model of the forces that shape the face of the earth. They could represent physical forces (both those inside the earth and on the surface), or explore the various impacts of humans. *NOTE: This activity may be completed separately or you may wish students to incorporate it into their Current Events Journals.*

EE3 Physical Systems: Standard 7

GLENCOE TECHNOLOGY

MindJogger Videoquiz
Use MindJogger to review the Chapter 2 content.

 Available in VHS.

Using Key Terms

1. f
2. j
3. a
4. c
5. d
6. e
7. b
8. i
9. h
10. g

Reviewing the Main Idea

11. *Any three:* landforms such as mountains, valleys, plains; bodies of water; typical rainfall and temperature; soil; resources
12. *Possible answer:* A place is a specific location; a region is a group of places that have some characteristic in common.
13. *Possible answers:* planning new communities, expanding city services, identifying locations for building
14. They collide head-on or move alongside each other in opposite directions.
15. plateaus
16. Streets and buildings absorb more of the sun's rays than plants and trees. Also more people burn fuels for warming, power, and transportation, which raises temperatures.
17. Chemicals are released into the air, and they hold in more of the sun's heat.
18. conservation and avoiding polluting the water
19. by adding fertilizer or practicing crop rotation
20. *Possible answers:* damaging people's health, acid rain, and global warming

Chapter 2 Assessment and Activities

Using Key Terms

Match the terms in Part A with their definitions in Part B.

A.

1. environment
2. landform
3. region
4. plate tectonics
5. ecosystem
6. geographic information systems
7. erosion
8. canyon
9. fault
10. tropics

B.

a. area that shares common characteristics
b. wearing away of the earth's surface
c. theory that the earth's crust consists of huge slabs of rock that move
d. system of plant, animal, and human interdependence
e. special software that helps geographers gather and use information
f. natural surroundings
g. areas near the Equator
h. crack in the earth's crust
i. steep-sided lowland that a river has cut through a plateau
j. particular feature of the land

Reviewing the Main Ideas

Section 1 Thinking Like a Geographer

11. **Place** Give three examples of the physical characteristics of a place.
12. **Region** How is a region different from a place?
13. **Human/Environment Interaction** Give an example of how people use geographic knowledge.

Section 2 Physical Geography

14. **Movement** In what ways do the plates in the earth's crust move?
15. **Place** Which have a higher elevation—plains or plateaus?
16. **Human/Environment Interaction** Why are cities warmer than nearby rural areas?
17. **Human/Environment Interaction** What problem has been caused by the burning of fuels?

Section 3 People and the Environment

18. **Human/Environment Interaction** What two steps are involved in water management?
19. **Human/Environment Interaction** How can farmers restore the minerals in soil?
20. **Human/Environment Interaction** What two problems can result from air pollution?

The World

Place Location Activity

On a separate sheet of paper, match the letters on the map with the numbered places listed below.

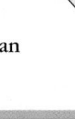

1. North America
2. Pacific Ocean
3. Africa
4. South America
5. Antarctica
6. Australia
7. Atlantic Ocean
8. Asia

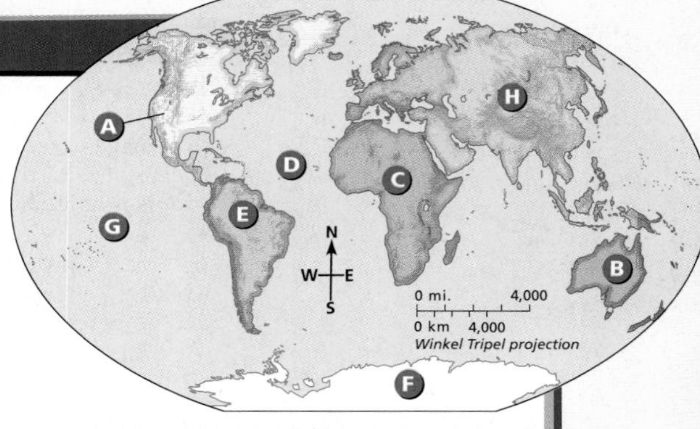

68 CHAPTER 2

Place Location Activity

1. A
2. G
3. C
4. E
5. F
6. B
7. D
8. H

Critical Thinking

21. Answers will vary. Students can call the local water company to find out.
22. Answers will vary. In the first column, students should list their daily activities, such as waking to an alarm clock, listening to the radio, and cooking food in the microwave. In the second column, they should list alternative ways to do these activities.

Self-Check Quiz Visit the ***Our World Today: People, Places, and Issues*** Web site at owt.glencoe.com and click on **Chapter 2–Self-Check Quizzes** to prepare for the Chapter Test.

Critical Thinking

21. **Analyzing Information** From where does the freshwater in your community come? How can you find out?
22. **Sequencing Information** Make a chart like the one below, and list the ways you use electricity from the moment you wake up until you go to sleep. In the second column, write how you would perform the same activity if you had no electricity to rely on.

Activities With Electricity	Without Electricity

Current Events Journal

23. **Writing a Paragraph** Global Positioning System units are now available for people to use for such activities as driving, hiking, and boating. Write a paragraph describing how the use of these units could save lives.

Mental Mapping Activity

24. **Focusing on the Region** Create a map of the world's oceans and continents. Label the following items:
    - Equator
    - Pacific Ocean
    - North America
    - Africa
    - high latitude climate regions
    - tropical climate regions

Technology Skills Activity

25. **Developing Multimedia Presentations** Research how your state's climate influences its culture, including tourist attractions, types of clothing, and the economy. Use your research to develop a television or radio commercial promoting your state.

The Princeton Review

Standardized Test Practice

Directions: Study the maps below, and then answer the question that follows.

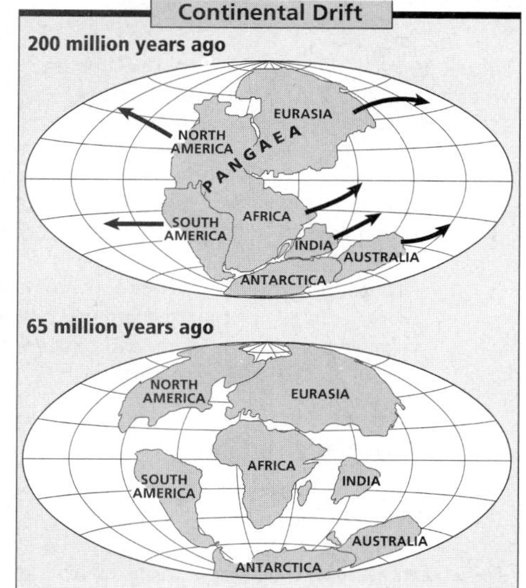

1. **What "supercontinent" do many scientists believe existed 200 million years ago?**
   A Eurasia
   B Pangaea
   C Gondwana
   D Antarctica

Test-Taking Tip: Use information on the maps to answer this question. Read the title above the maps and then the two subtitles. If you reread the question, you see it is asking about a certain time period. Make sure you use the correct map above to answer the question.

69

Assessment and Activities

Standardized Test Practice

1. B

Tested Objectives:
Analyzing Information, reading a map

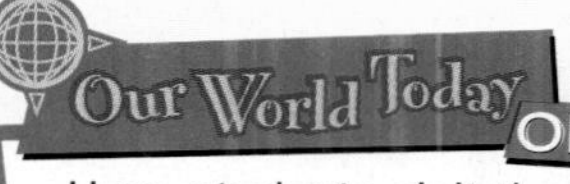

Chapter Test Bonus Question

This question may be used for extra credit on the chapter test.

You are a rugged and steep natural landmark. You rank as a major attraction in almost every country in which you are found. Some people put on all types of clothing and special equipment to see your highest point. What are you? *(a mountain)*

Have students visit the Web site at owt.glencoe.com to review Chapter 2 and take the Self-Check Quiz.

Current Events Journal

23. Student paragraphs will vary.

Mental Mapping Activity

24. This exercise helps students visualize the structure of the earth and understand the relationship of various points. All attempts at freehand mapping should be accepted.

Technology Activity

25. Students should research and summarize their state's climate before writing the commercial. They should focus on their state's unique benefits, using examples of its climate, culture, tourist attractions, clothing worn/needed, and economy.

Write the word *extinction* and ask students what it means. If they have difficulty defining it, break the word into its root (*extinct,* "having ceased to exist"). Point out that plants and animals become extinct as their environments change. The pace of extinction today is much faster than in previous times.

Researching Wildlife Have students research an African animal. Aim for a variety of animals, including not only primates and well-known grazers and hunters, but also birds, fish, reptiles, and insects. Ask students to determine if their animal is threatened with extinction, why that is the case, and what steps are being taken to save the species. One source of information is the African Wildlife Foundation, which carries out programs to protect African species. **L1**

Meeting National Standards

Geography for Life

The following standards are met in the Student Edition feature:

EE1 The World in Spatial Terms: Standard 3

EE5 Environment and Society: Standard 14

EE6 The Uses of Geography: Standard 18

EYE on the Environment

Endangered Spaces

Shrinking Habitats When you think of Africa, what images come to mind? Roaring lions? Sprinting cheetahs? Lumbering elephants? Unless conditions change, some wild African animals may soon be only memories. Many are endangered, primarily because their habitats—their grassland and forest homes—are being destroyed in many ways.

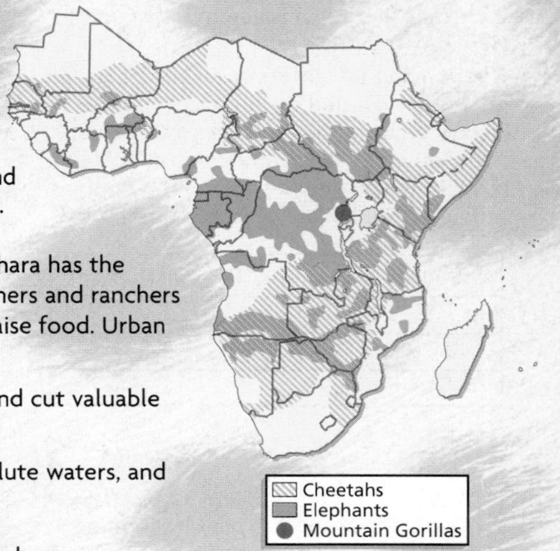

- Population growth — Africa south of the Sahara has the world's highest population growth rate. Farmers and ranchers turn wild lands into fields and pastures to raise food. Urban sprawl also takes over habitats.
- Logging — Logging companies build roads and cut valuable trees, destroying forest habitats.
- Mining — Open pit mines scar the land, pollute waters, and destroy trees.

Cheetahs
Elephants
Mountain Gorillas

As habitats shrink, so do populations of African animals.

- Cheetahs live in Africa's grasslands. As people move into the cheetahs' home, the big cats struggle to survive. Only about 12,000 cheetahs are left in the wild.
- Mountain gorillas live in the misty mountain forests of Central and East Africa. Logging and mining are destroying these forests. Only about 650 mountain gorillas remain.

These and other endangered African animals will survive only if their habitats are saved.

Loggers destroy a forest in the Democratic Republic of the Congo.

Cheetahs are running out of room in Africa.

70 UNIT 1

More About the Issues

Extinction Some biologists suggest that as many as 50 percent of plants and animals around the world are on the path to extinction. There have been five mass extinctions in the history of life on the earth, the most famous one being the extinction of the dinosaurs 65 million years ago. Scientists call the most recent spate the "Sixth Extinction" and say humans are the cause. Even in a protected place like Everglades National Park—1.5 million acres in size—one species of sparrow has dropped in numbers from 6,400 in 1992 to 2,600 just three years later.

Making a Difference

The Cheetah Conservation Fund Cheetahs in Africa are getting a helping hand from the Cheetah Conservation Fund (CCF). This organization is based in Namibia, which is home to about 2,000 cheetahs. Namibian ranchers often trap and shoot cheetahs to protect their livestock. The CCF has donated nearly 70 special herding dogs to ranchers. The dogs protect the livestock and keep cheetahs out of harm's way at the same time. The CCF also teaches villagers and schoolchildren about cheetahs and about why it is important to save these big cats and their habitats.

Namibian children learn about cheetahs.

Protecting Gorillas For nearly 18 years, Dian Fossey studied mountain gorillas in Rwanda. Through her book, *Gorillas in the Mist*, which was made into a movie, Fossey told others about mountain gorillas and how their survival was threatened by habitat destruction and poaching. Fossey established the Karisoke Research Center and an international fund to support gorilla conservation.

Dian Fossey fought fiercely to end gorilla poaching. Although Fossey was murdered at Karisoke in 1985, the Dian Fossey Gorilla Fund International continues its work protecting mountain gorillas and their habitat.

A mountain gorilla

What Can You Do?

Adopt a Cheetah
You and your classmates can help save cheetahs in the wild by adopting one. To learn more, contact the Cheetah Conservation Fund at www.cheetah.org

Find Out More
What animal habitats are endangered where you live? Work with a partner to investigate endangered spaces in your area. Summarize your findings in a report to the class.

Use the Internet
How can people help save vanishing habitats? Check The Nature Conservancy's Web site at www.tnc.org to learn how this group works to preserve habitats worldwide.

71

Habitat Loss The problem of habitat loss affects places the world over. Tropical rain forests are being destroyed at the rate of about 11 square miles (28.5 sq. km) a day, with an estimated three species an hour becoming extinct. Deserts are expanding not only in Africa, but also in Asia, where both the Gobi and the Thar Desert are expanding. In the United States, about 3 million acres (1.2 ha) of open space are lost each year.

3 Assess

Have students work individually or in groups to complete the What Can You Do? activities on page 71.

4 Close

Discuss with students the What Can You Do? activities. You might want to have them write a paragraph explaining why they think endangered animal species should be protected.

For an additional regional case study, use the following:

Environmental Case Study 2

What Can You Do? Teacher Tips

Adopt a Cheetah: The Cheetah Conservation Fund's "Dog Page" on its Web site explains how using dogs to guard flocks actually helps cheetahs. The Web site has many other useful and informative pages.

Find Out More: The World Conservation Management Centre maintains the Red Book, which lists threatened species around the world. The U.S. Fish and Wildlife Service runs the Endangered Species Program, which includes a list, by state, of all endangered plants and animals in the United States.

Unit 2 Planning Guide

SUGGESTED PACING CHART

Unit 2 (1 day)	Chapter 3 (4 days)	Chapter 4 (6 days)	Unit 2 (2 days)
Day 1 Introduction	**Day 1** Chapter 3 Intro, Section 1	**Day 1** Chapter 4 Intro, Section 1	**Day 1** Wrap-Up/Projects
	Day 2 Section 2	**Day 2** Section 2	**Day 2** Unit 2 Assessment
	Day 3 Chapter 3 Review	**Day 3** Section 3	
	Day 4 Chapter 3 Assessment	**Day 4** Section 4	
		Day 5 Chapter 4 Review	
		Day 6 Chapter 4 Assessment	

For a complete course pacing guide and Teacher Classroom Resources, see:

Interactive Lesson Planner

Use the following tools to easily assess student learning in a variety of ways:

- **Performance Assessment Activities and Rubrics**
- **Section Quizzes**
- **Chapter Tests and Unit Pretests and Posttests**
- **Interactive Tutor Self-Assessment CD-ROM**
- **ExamView® Pro 3.0 Testmaker CD-ROM**
- **MindJogger Videoquiz**
- owt.glencoe.com
- **Standardized Test Practice Workbook**

Note: The following materials may be used when teaching Unit 2.
Chapter level support materials can be found on the chapter resource pages.

TEACHING TRANSPARENCIES

Political Map Transparency 2

Unit 2 Map Overlay Transparencies

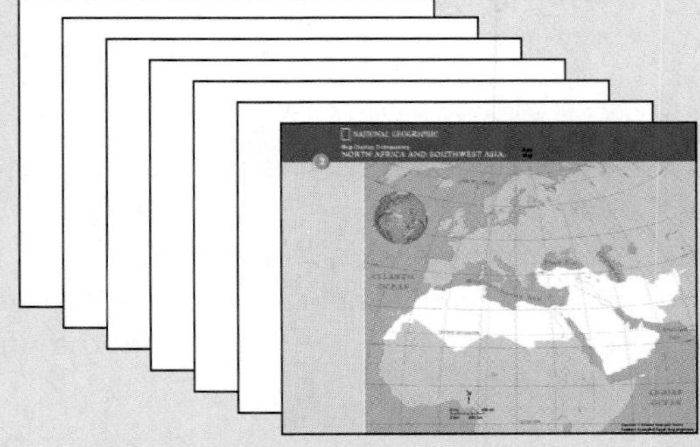

World Cultures Transparencies 1 and 2

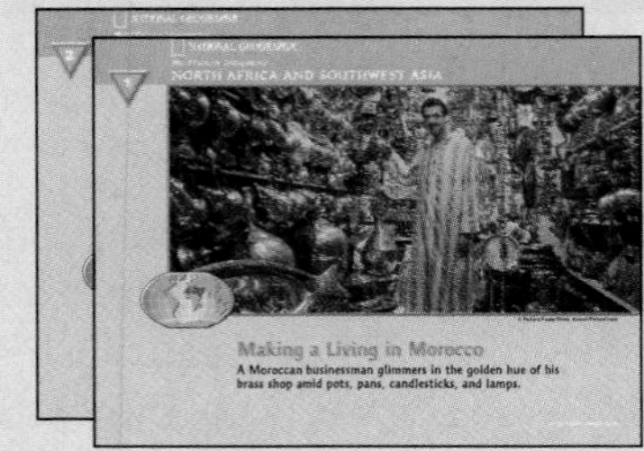

Unit 2 Resources

INTERDISCIPLINARY CONNECTIONS

World Literature Reading 2

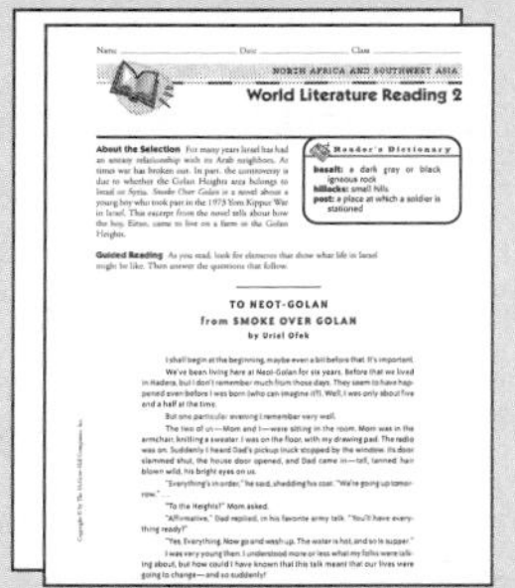

Economics and Geography Activity 2

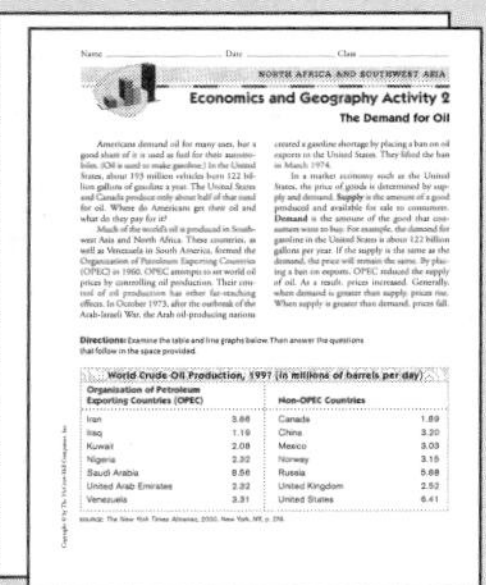

History and Geography Activity 2

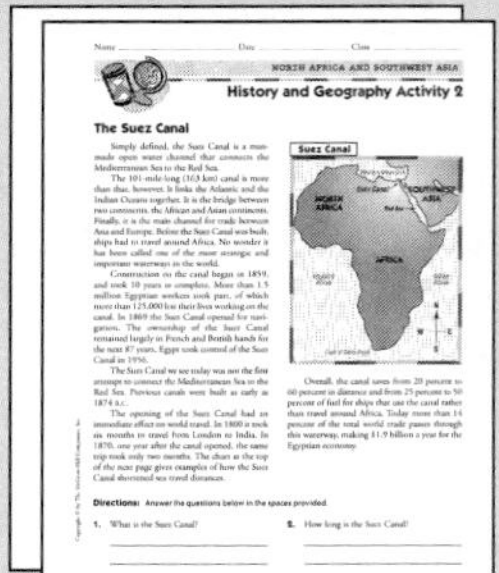

MAP AND GEOGRAPHY SKILLS

Building Geography Skills for Life

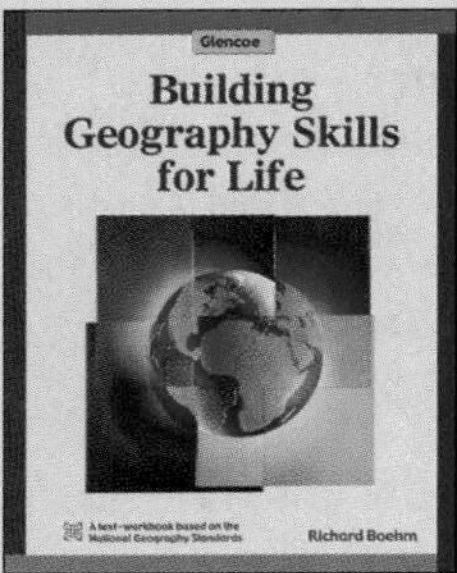

NGS Focus on Geography Literacy

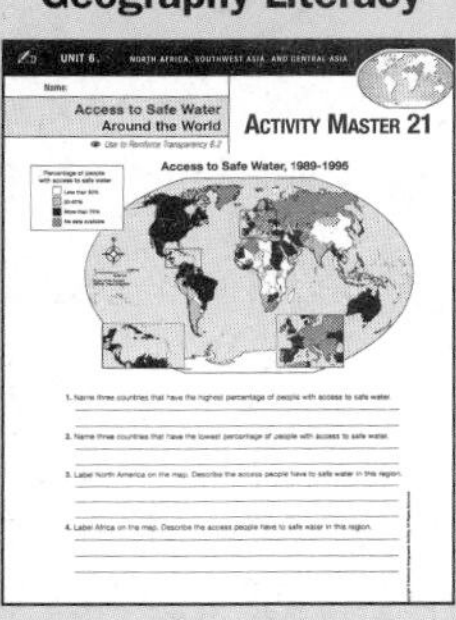

Regional Atlas Activity 2

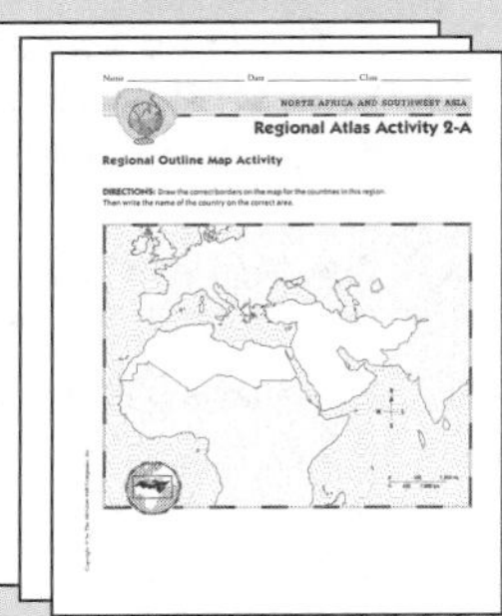

NATIONAL GEOGRAPHIC MapMachine

Find the latest coverage of geography in the news, atlas updates, cartographic activities with interactive maps, an online map store, and links at www.nationalgeographic.com/maps

APPLICATION AND HANDS-ON

Citizenship Activity 2

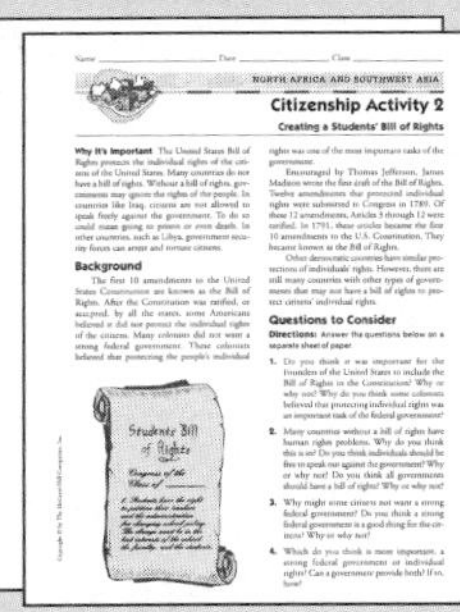

Foods Around the World 6

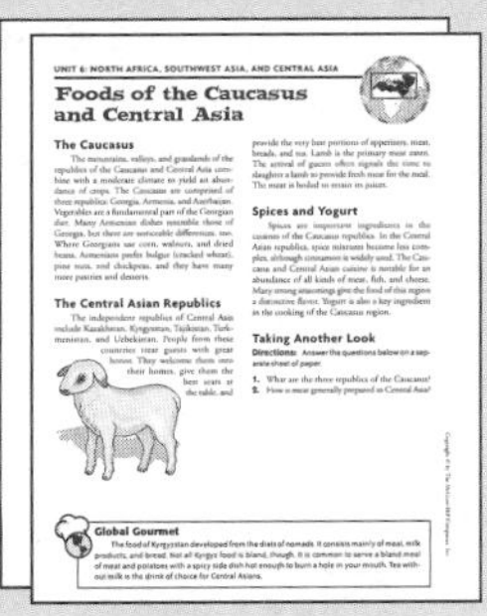

ENRICHMENT AND EXTENSION

Environmental Case Study 2

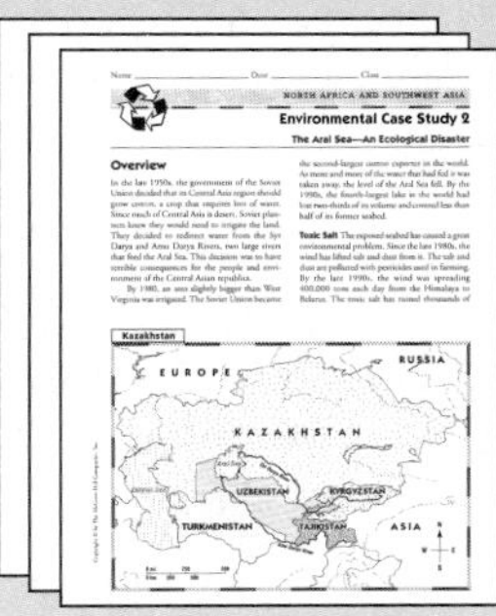

World Music: A Cultural Legacy

ASSESSMENT AND EVALUATION

GLENCOE'S ASSESSMENT ADVANTAGE

Unit 2 Pretests

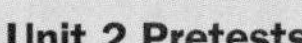

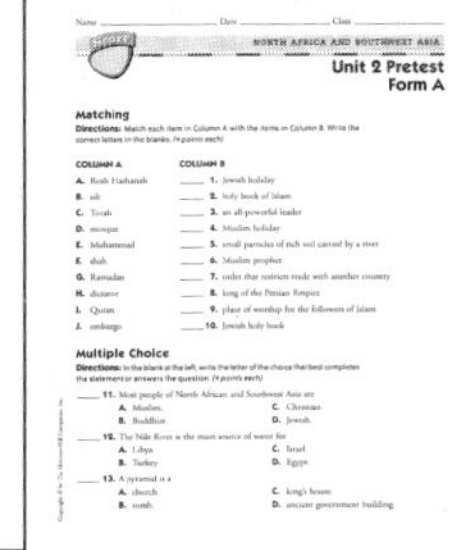

Unit 2 Posttests

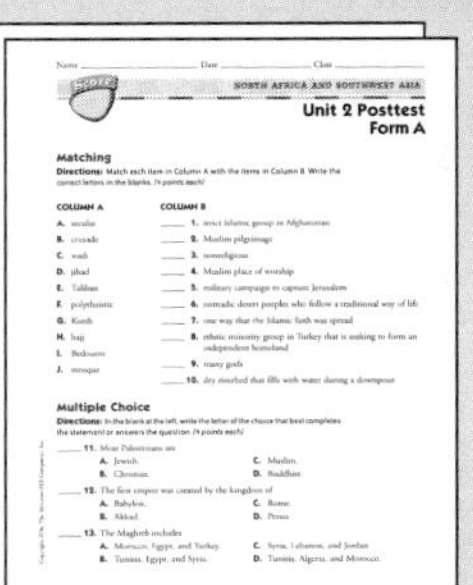

Additional Unit 2 Resources

- **owt.glencoe.com**
  Our World Today: People, Places, and Issues
  Visit the Glencoe *Our World Today: People, Places, and Issues* Web site for overviews, activities, assessments, and updated charts and graphs.
- **socialstudies.glencoe.com**
  Glencoe Social Studies
  Visit the Glencoe Web site for social studies activities, updates, and links to other sites.
- **www.teachingtoday.glencoe.com**
  Glencoe Teaching Today
  This Web site features daily teaching tips, free PDF downloads, annotated Web resources, educational news, and more.
- **www.nationalgeographic.com**
  NGS ONLINE Visit the National Geographic Society Web site for the latest coverage of geography in the news, atlas updates, activities, links, interactive features, and archives.
- **Glencoe's Guide to Using the Internet**
  Provides an introduction to many of the current technologies on the Internet. Professional resources and teaching strategies included.

Our Web sites provide additional resources. All essential content is covered in the Student Edition.

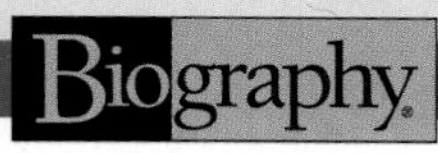

The following videotape programs are available from Glencoe:

- **Great Pyramids of Giza and Other Pyramids** 0-7670-0207-5
- **Mummies and the Wonders of Ancient Egypt** 1-56501-773-0
- **King Tut: The Face of Tutankhaman** 1-56501-159-7
- **Seven Wonders of the Ancient World** 0-7670-0401-9
- **Cleopatra: Destiny's Queen** 1-56501-454-5
- **Tomb of the Gods: The Great Pyramid** 0-7670-0081-1
- **The Great Pharaohs of Egypt** 0-7670-0273-3

To order, call Glencoe at 1-800-334-7344. To find classroom resources to accompany many of these, check:

A&E Television: www.aetv.com

The History Channel: www.historychannel.com

Bibliography

Readings for the Student

- ***Women in the Middle East: Transition and Change,*** by Ramsay M. Harik and Elsa Marston. New York: Franklin Watts, 1996.
- ***Through Middle Eastern Eyes,*** by Robert P. Pearson and Leon F. Clark. NY: Center for International Training and Education, 1993.

Readings for the Teacher

- ***The Islamic World: Beliefs and Civilizations, 600–1600,*** by Peter Mantin and Ruth Mantin. Cambridge: Cambridge University Press, 1993.
- ***The Middle East Today: An Atlas of Reproducible Pages.*** Wellesley, MA.: World Eagle, 1993.

Multimedia Links

- **Glencoe Social Studies Primary Source Document Library**
  Addressing the Nation of Jordan by King Hussein
  Constantinople Under the Turks by Benedetto Ramberti
  Egyptian President Anwar el-Sadat Speaks in Israel by Anwar el-Sadat
  The Fall of Constantinople by Kritovoulos
  The Quran Islamic tradition
- ***Everyday Life in Ancient Egypt.*** Chicago, IL.: Clearvue. CD-ROM, Windows, Macintosh.
- ***Shifting Sands: A History of the Middle East.*** Chatsworth, CA: Aims Multimedia. CD-ROM, Windows, Macintosh.

Refer to owt.glencoe.com for additional literature titles and study guides related to this region.

Additional Glencoe Teacher Support

- **Teaching Strategies for the Geography Classroom**
- **Reproducible Lesson Plans**
- **Outline Map Resource Book**
- **Reading in the Content Area**

Service Learning Project

Connecting Classroom With Community

One of the Five Pillars of Islam is that believers have a responsibility to give a portion of their wealth to the needy. Students can show a similar concern for others in their community by making an effort to help the homeless. They might, for example, collect such useful items as blankets and towels or volunteer to work in a soup kitchen that offers meals to homeless people. Hold a class discussion asking students to identify and explain the importance of voluntary civic participation in our society.

Content Background Notes

Use this additional information as lecture notes or discussion prompts throughout the study of Unit 2.

Chapter 3 North Africa and Southwest Asia—Early Cultures (pp. 80–97)

The Great Flood Dr. Robert Ballard has led a series of National Geographic expeditions to investigate the theory that the Black Sea may be the site of a great flood discussed in sources such as the *Gilgamesh* epic. According to the theory, the Black Sea was once a much smaller and lower freshwater lake. Then the waters of the Mediterranean rose so high that they spilled through the Bosporus and flooded a huge region. These waters destroyed cities on the lake's shores and expanded the body of water to its current size. The catastrophe so scarred people that they remembered it in their legends.

In 1999 Ballard and his team made two important finds. Underwater scans revealed what looked like the contours of an ancient shoreline for the lake—which was found nearly 23 miles (37 km) into the Black Sea. Another key piece of evidence came from a sample of soil from the seabed. The sample included the preserved shells of mussels that were thousands of years old—some of which were freshwater species.

People Great pyramids, built as tombs for Egyptian rulers, rise above desert sands. They are a reminder that some of the world's oldest civilizations developed in this region. Roughly 5,000 years ago, the ancient Egyptians built a kingdom along the life-giving Nile River. The Sumerian civilization, an even older society, flourished in the fertile valley between the Tigris and Euphrates Rivers.

Water still dictates where people settle in this region. Most cities lie along seacoasts or rivers, or near desert oases. Among the largest cities are Cairo, Egypt; Istanbul, Turkey; and Tehran, Iran.

In North Africa and Southwest Asia, most of the people are Arabs. Many other ethnic groups also live in the region. Despite the ethnic diversity, many who live here are united by religion. Most people practice Islam, which developed in this region centuries ago. Two other major religions, Judaism and Christianity, also began here. The country of Israel, the Jewish national homeland, is in this region.

Chapter 4 North Africa and Southwest Asia Today (pp. 98–129)

The Nile Delta The delta of the Nile River—for thousands of years one of the most productive agricultural regions on the earth—is suffering for many reasons. The Aswan Dam, which controls flooding on the Nile, also blocks sediment from flowing downstream. As a result, the delta no longer receives a rich supply of nutrients, as it used to during the annual floods. Farmers must now add fertilizer to the soil, and the salinity of the land is increasing. Delta cities are growing, and concrete is covering larger and larger chunks of land. Finally, the Mediterranean Sea is reaching farther inland, covering parts of the low-lying delta.

At least one positive step has been taken. In the past, delta dwellers cut blocks of soil from the rich earth and then baked them to make bricks for building, reducing valuable farmland. Today laws in Egypt prevent this use of vital farmland for building.

Economy Like water, natural resources are distributed unevenly across the region. This helps to create great differences in living standards. The region includes some of the world's wealthiest nations—and some of its poorest. Enormous reserves of oil and natural gas lie in certain areas, including lands in central North Africa, along the Persian Gulf, and around the Caspian Sea. Countries such as Saudi Arabia and Kuwait, which export petroleum products to fuel-hungry societies, generally enjoy high standards of living.

On the other hand, those countries with economies based on agriculture have much lower standards of living. Only a small percentage of the region's land is suitable for growing crops. In river valleys and along the coasts, where there is water and fertile soil, farmers raise citrus fruits, grapes, dates, grains, and cotton. Nomadic herding is common across the large expanses of this region that are too dry for crops.

The Kurds The Kurds are a people without a country. This distinct ethnic group occupies a region called Kurdistan that extends from eastern Turkey through northern Iraq to western Iran. The Kurds remain a divided population, split under the control of these three governments.

The exact number of Kurds is unknown, although some estimates put them as high as 15 million. The Kurds have long struggled to achieve their own independent state—a right that was recognized in a treaty signed after World War I, but which was later replaced by another treaty omitting reference of Kurdish rights. A powerful nationalist movement has arisen in Turkey, where some Kurds have fought and used terrorism to try to win independence. Along with the appeal of nationalism, these Kurds gain support by pointing to their people's poverty. In the wake of Iraqi attacks on Kurds after the Persian Gulf War of 1991, the United Nations offered protection to the Kurds living in that country. Kurds consider it unlikely that they will be granted independence, however, because Turkey is unwilling to give similar treatment to the Kurds living within its boundaries.

Introducing Unit 2

00:00 Out of Time?

If time does not permit teaching each chapter in this unit, you may use the **Reading Essentials and Study Guide** for each chapter.

Unit Overview

The two chapters of this unit introduce students to two distinct but related cultural regions that stretch from the Atlantic coast of Africa through the eastern shores of the Mediterranean to the vast spaces of Southwest Asia. The countries in this area share the following features:

- rugged landscape that creates many difficulties for human life
- a harsh, dry climate that makes farming difficult
- important deposits of valuable resources
- rich cultures with long histories
- animosity between some religious and ethnic groups

Business district at dusk, Dubai, United Arab Emirates

Man gazing out across the vast expanses of the Sahara

Using the Illustration

There are many contrasts in North Africa and Southwest Asia, where modern innovations often clash with ancient traditions. One of the reasons for these huge differences is the discovery of oil in the region. Oil production has made a great difference in the economies of many countries in Southwest Asia and North Africa. Using the map on page 76 of this text, have students determine which countries produce and export oil. Then have them do research to find out how this affects these countries' economies and standards of living as well as their foreign policies.

NATIONAL GEOGRAPHIC

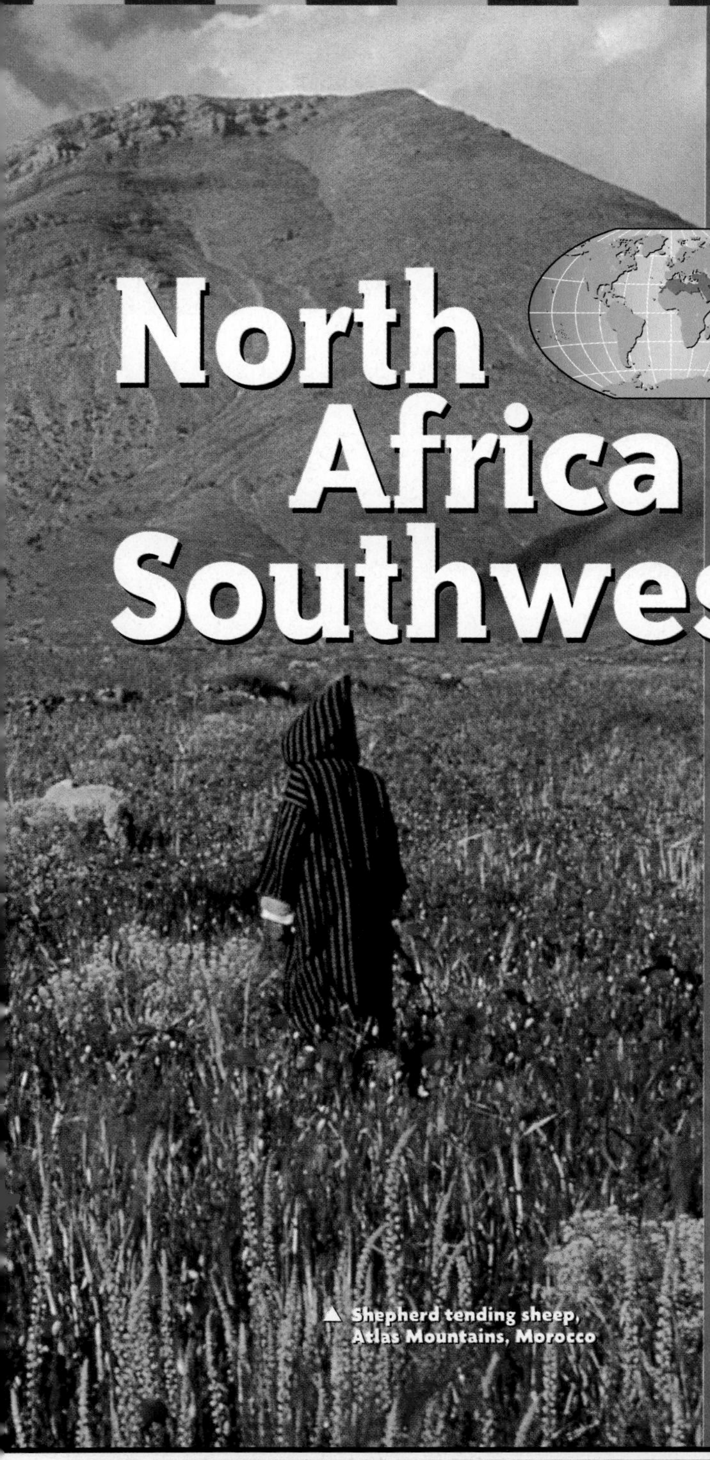

North Africa and Southwest Asia

Ancient Egyptian pyramids overlook industrial smokestacks. Three-thousand-year-old stone temples tower over sparkling new oil derricks. Remote mountain villages and endless desert seas of sand and gravel contrast with modern beaches overrun by tourists. All of these extremes can be found within the culture region of North Africa and Southwest Asia.

▲ Shepherd tending sheep, Atlas Mountains, Morocco

NGS ONLINE
www.nationalgeographic.com/education

73

These materials are available from Glencoe.

Software
ZipZapMap! World

Transparencies
PicturePack Transparencies

CD-ROM
Picture Atlas of the World, Second Edition

Current Events Journal

Have students find the countries covered in this unit on the political map of the world on pages RA2–RA3. Have them notice the great distance from the western to eastern edges of this region. **Ask:** **On what continents are these countries located?** *(Africa, Asia)* **What characteristics could these countries have in common that would tend to unite them? What characteristics would cause conflicts?** Have students write their answers in their notebooks. They can refer to these first thoughts later, as they study the unit.

Unit Launch Activity

Why Is There Conflict in This Region?
Many of the countries in North Africa and Southwest Asia are plagued by conflict. Some have bitter relations with neighbors. Others are torn by divisions within their own societies. Have students study these conflicts to try to determine the causes. *(Possibilities include religion, ethnic differences, and the struggle to control vital resources.)* Then have them discuss which kind of conflict they think is easiest to resolve and which they think would be the most difficult.

EE4 Human Systems: Standard 13

NGS ONLINE
www.nationalgeographic.com/education

This online resource provides lesson plans, atlas updates, cartographic activities with interactive maps, an online map store, and geography links.

LESSON PLAN

Using the Regional Atlas
These features and activities may be used as an introduction to the unit or as teaching tools throughout the course of the unit.

FOCUS

Objectives

1. Locate the major landforms of North Africa and Southwest Asia.
2. Identify the countries and capitals of this region.
3. Compare the populations of the countries in this region.
4. Discuss the chief economic products of this region.

5-Minute Precheck

Have students look at the physical map on this page. Have them identify the names and locations of all the deserts shown on the map. *(Sahara in North Africa, Empty Quarter in Saudi Arabia, Syrian Desert in Syria.)*

More About the Profile

In order to show a variety of physical features, this cross section begins in Morocco and ends at the Afghanistan/Pakistan border along 30°N latitude.

North Africa and Southwest Asia

Physical

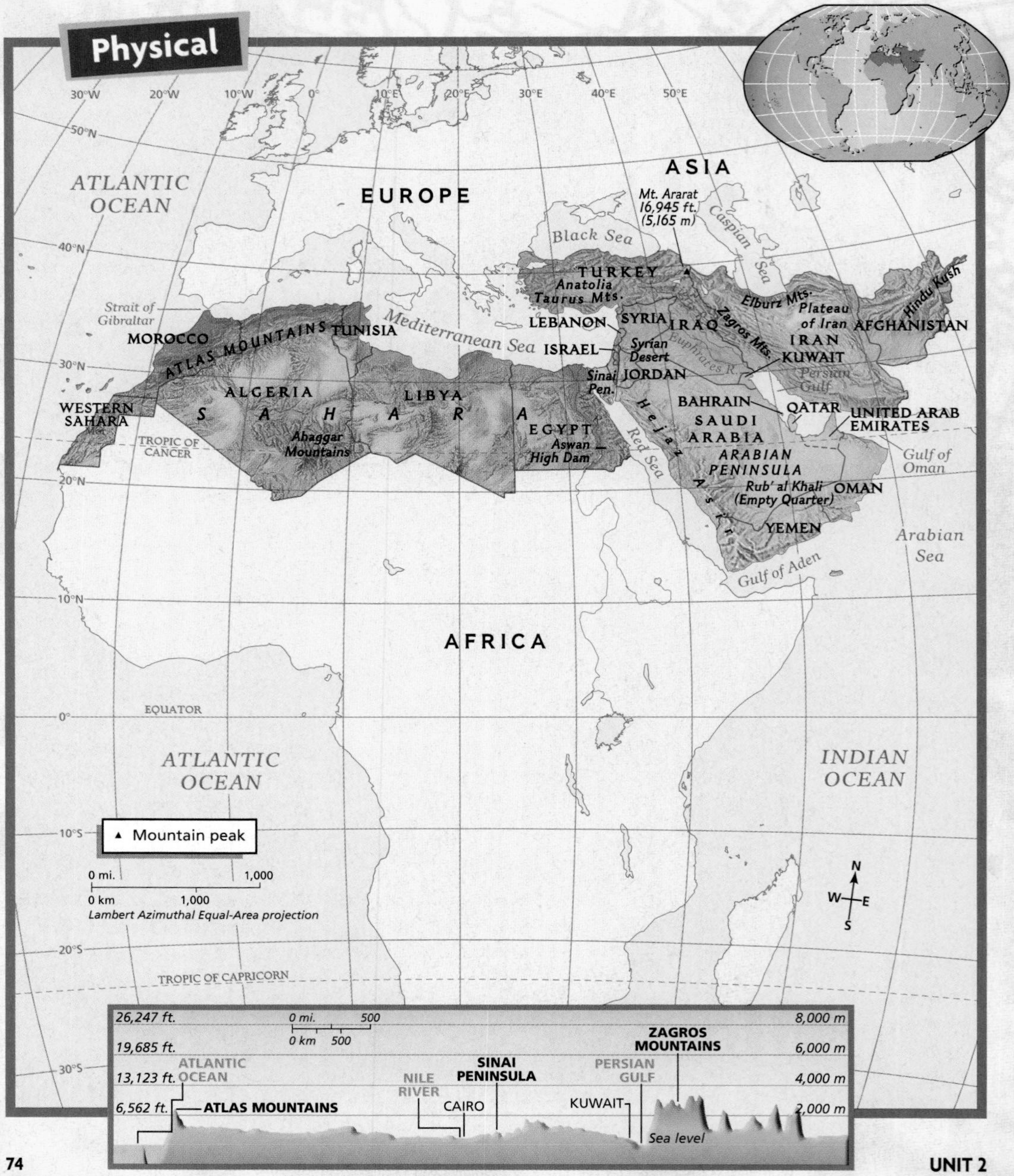

ATLANTIC OCEAN
EUROPE
ASIA
Mt. Ararat 16,945 ft. (5,165 m)
Black Sea
Caspian Sea
TURKEY
Anatolia
Taurus Mts.
Elburz Mts.
Plateau of Iran
Hindu Kush
AFGHANISTAN
Strait of Gibraltar
MOROCCO
ATLAS MOUNTAINS
TUNISIA
Mediterranean Sea
LEBANON
SYRIA
IRAQ
Zagros Mts.
IRAN
ISRAEL
Syrian Desert
Euphrates R.
KUWAIT
Persian Gulf
Sinai Pen.
JORDAN
WESTERN SAHARA
ALGERIA
LIBYA
SAHARA
Ahaggar Mountains
EGYPT
Aswan High Dam
Red Sea
Hejaz
BAHRAIN
QATAR
UNITED ARAB EMIRATES
SAUDI ARABIA
ARABIAN PENINSULA
Rub' al Khali (Empty Quarter)
OMAN
Gulf of Oman
YEMEN
Arabian Sea
Gulf of Aden
TROPIC OF CANCER
AFRICA
EQUATOR
ATLANTIC OCEAN
INDIAN OCEAN
Mountain peak
0 mi. 1,000
0 km 1,000
Lambert Azimuthal Equal-Area projection
TROPIC OF CAPRICORN

26,247 ft. 8,000 m
19,685 ft. 6,000 m
13,123 ft. 4,000 m
6,562 ft. 2,000 m
Sea level
ATLANTIC OCEAN
ATLAS MOUNTAINS
NILE RIVER
CAIRO
SINAI PENINSULA
PERSIAN GULF
KUWAIT
ZAGROS MOUNTAINS

Regional Atlas Activity

Researching Location The greatest population densities in this region tend to be found near bodies of water. The Nile River valley, for example, is one of the world's most heavily populated areas, and the Tigris and Euphrates Rivers are still—as they were millennia ago—home to many cities. Major cities in North Africa and the eastern Mediterranean are located along the Atlantic or Mediterranean coasts. Istanbul sits astride a major waterway. Have students choose one of the cities of the region and research its past. Have them prepare a report explaining why it is located where it is. Suggest that they consider economic and cultural factors as well as geographic factors. **L2**

EE4 Human Systems: Standards 9, 12

UNIT 2

Unit 2

Political

ATLANTIC OCEAN
EUROPE
ASIA
AFRICA
INDIAN OCEAN
Black Sea
Caspian Sea
Mediterranean Sea
Red Sea
Nile R.
Persian Gulf
Gulf of Oman
Arabian Sea
Gulf of Aden
Socotra Yemen
Madeira Is. Port.
Canary Is. Sp.
WESTERN SAHARA Mor.
MOROCCO Rabat
ALGERIA Algiers
TUNISIA Tunis
LIBYA Tripoli
EGYPT Cairo
TURKEY Ankara
LEBANON Beirut
SYRIA Damascus
ISRAEL Jerusalem
JORDAN Amman
IRAQ Baghdad
IRAN Tehran
AFGHANISTAN Kabul
KUWAIT Kuwait
BAHRAIN Manama
QATAR Doha
SAUDI ARABIA Riyadh
UNITED ARAB EMIRATES Abu Dhabi
OMAN Muscat
YEMEN Sanaa
TROPIC OF CANCER
EQUATOR
TROPIC OF CAPRICORN

⊛ National capital

0 mi. 1,000
0 km 1,000
Lambert Azimuthal Equal-Area projection

MAP STUDY

1. What physical feature covers much of North Africa?
2. What is the capital of Saudi Arabia?

2 TEACH

Making Predictions Have students study the physical features of this region and then predict which parts of the region might be used for farming. Then ask students to write generalizations about the relationship between physical geography and land use. **L1**

TRAVEL GUIDE

Syria Many of the marketplaces in Damascus—the capital of Syria—are in the old section of the city on narrow, winding streets. Merchants sell food and objects made of leather, brass, silver, and gold. People go to the marketplaces not only to shop, but also to discuss business and to socialize. Here, as in other markets throughout the region, shoppers haggle or bargain with sellers over the price of goods.

MAP STUDY

Answers
1. Sahara
2. Riyadh

Skills Practice
What country divides the Persian Gulf from the Gulf of Oman? *(United Arab Emirates)*
What is the capital of Turkey? *(Ankara)*

Regional Atlas Activity

Researching Irrigation The earliest cities that archaeologists have uncovered so far lie in the valley of the Tigris and Euphrates Rivers in Southwest Asia and date to about 3500 B.C. Civilizations arose here because the land and rivers provided rich soil for farming. Along these two rivers and the Nile, annual flooding brought nutrients to the soil, allowing farmers to grow crops. Since the floods came at certain times of the year, they were predictable, making farming more reliable. Still, farmers had to retain the water to use later in the year, when there was no rain. Have students research the irrigation methods used in ancient times and report on their findings. **L2**

EE4 Human Systems: Standard 12

REGIONAL ATLAS

North Africa and Southwest Asia

Building Skills

Formulating Questions
Challenge students to generate a list of questions and answers based on the map on this page. They might focus on such issues as the economic benefit of the oil and gas reserves shown on the map, the environmental costs of obtaining these resources, relations between countries with and without these resources, or the reasons for the creation of the different transportation routes. After they have written their questions, ask volunteers to read some aloud. Then have the class discuss them.

MAP STUDY

Answers

1. Europe, North America, Russia, Southern Africa, and Asia
2. Southwest Asia and Caspian Sea

Skills Practice
Which region produces and distributes more oil and natural gas? *(Southwest Asia)*

Oil and Gas Production and Distribution

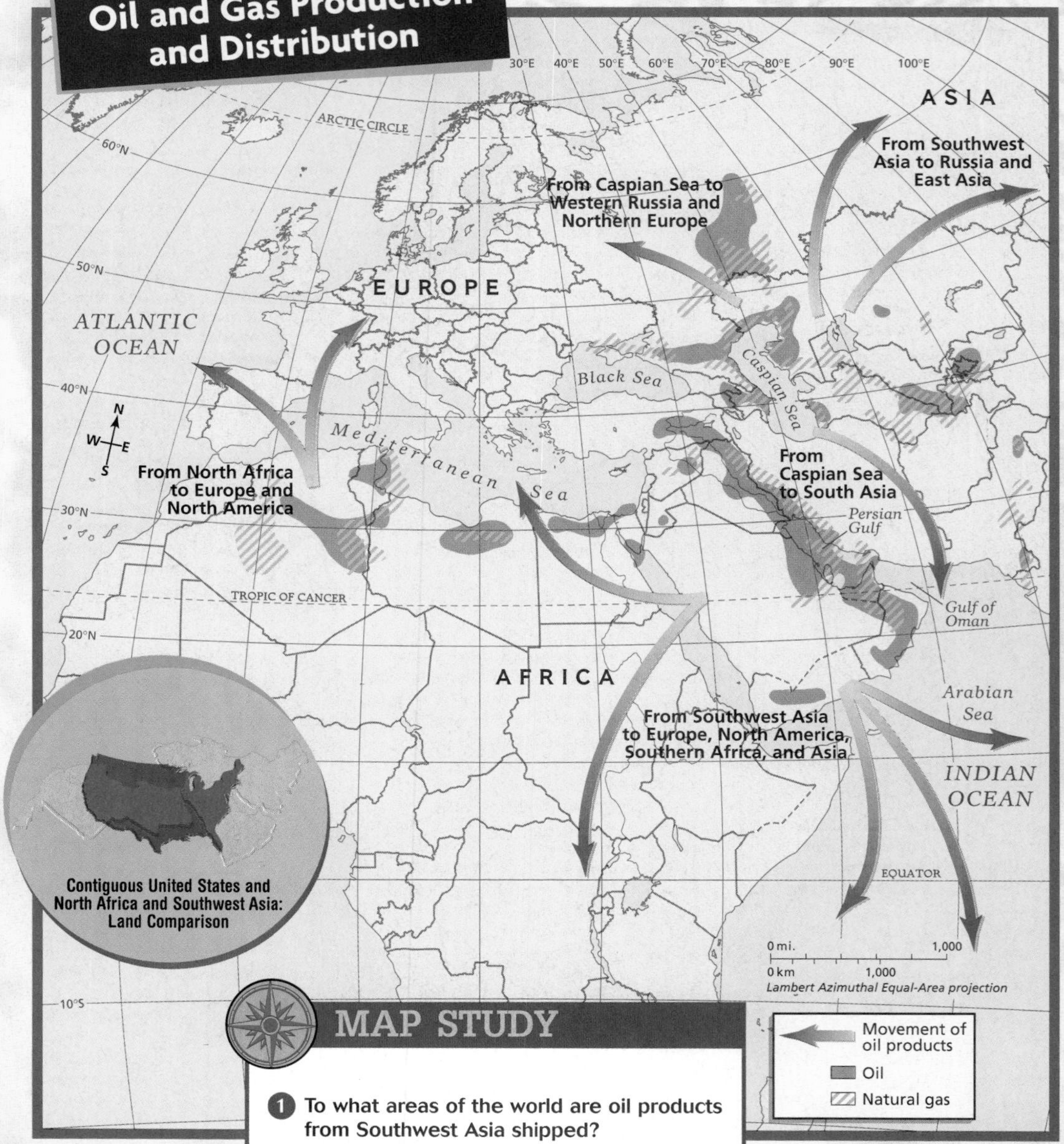

MAP STUDY

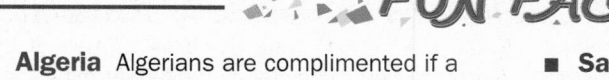

1. To what areas of the world are oil products from Southwest Asia shipped?
2. What oil regions supply oil products to Russia?

76 UNIT 2

FUN FACTS

- **Algeria** Algerians are complimented if a guest leaves some food on the plate at the end of a meal. This indicates that the host has provided more than enough to eat.
- **Oman** This country is one of the hottest in the world. Temperatures here often reach 130°F (54°C).
- **Saudi Arabia** Frankincense and myrrh are fragrant materials that come from trees that grow in this country. Since ancient times, people have burned these materials as incense or used them in perfumes.

Fast Facts

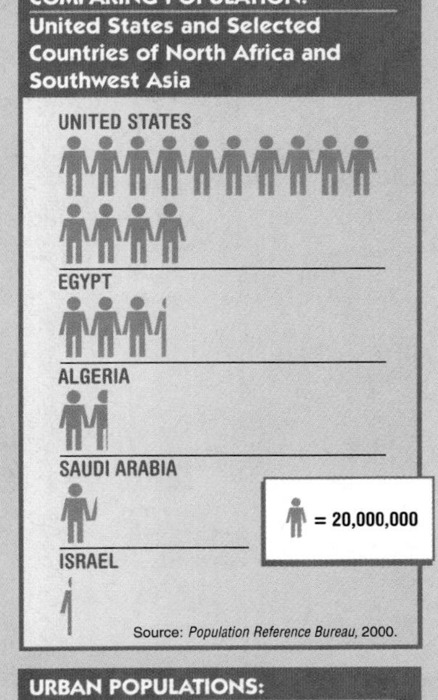

URBAN POPULATIONS: Selected Cities of North Africa, Southwest Asia

CAIRO, EGYPT

TEHRAN, IRAN

ALEXANDRIA, EGYPT

ANKARA, TURKEY

ISTANBUL, TURKEY

= 500,000

Source: *National Geographic Atlas of the World*, 7th Edition, 1999.

Data Bits

Country	Automobiles per 1,000 people	Telephones per 1,000 people
Kuwait	317	227
Lebanon	299	179
Libya	159	68
Morocco	38	50
Yemen	15	13

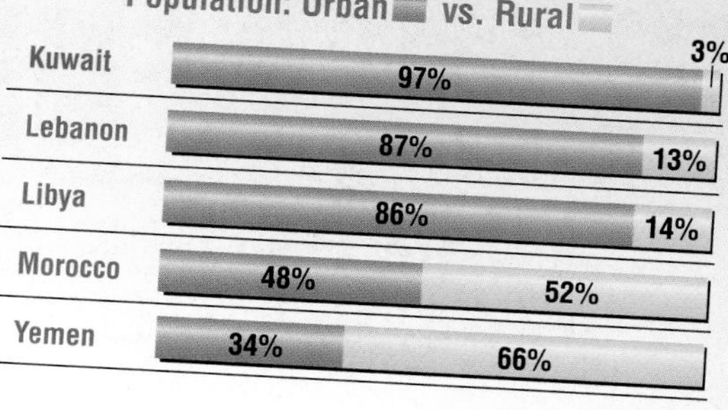

Source: *World Desk Reference*, 2000.

GRAPHIC STUDY

1. What generalization can you make about the rural and urban population split and the number of telephones and automobiles for each country?
2. How does the population of Cairo compare to that of Tehran? How does the population of Ankara compare to that of Cairo?

As an introduction to this region, you may want to engage students by studying an important contemporary issue in this region of the world. The **TIME REPORTS: FOCUS ON WORLD ISSUES** for this region is found on pages 115–121. The feature examines the conflict in the Middle East.

Travel Guide

Southwest Asia The pomegranate is a popular food in Southwest Asia. A picture of the fruit appeared on the pillars of Solomon's temple in Jerusalem. People in the region use the fruit's crimson-colored pulp to make drinks.

GRAPHIC STUDY

Answers

1. Countries with higher urban populations also have more telephones and automobiles.
2. Cairo and Tehran have roughly the same population. The population of Ankara is a little less than half that of Cairo.

Skills Practice

What is the most populous country in the region? *(Egypt)*

Regional Atlas Activity

Passages Khyber Pass through the Hindu Kush of Afghanistan has been a major route for movement between Southwest Asia and South Asia. Centuries ago, invading armies took the pass to reach India. Merchants leading camel caravans used it to carry goods between Asia and the Mediterranean world. Other key passages—such as the Turkish Straits near Istanbul, the Strait of Gibraltar north of Morocco, the Suez Canal in Egypt, and the Strait of Hormuz along the Persian Gulf—are found in this region as well. Organize students into groups and have each group research one of these famous passageways and explain its influence on the region. Have each group present its findings to the class. **L2**

EE1 The World in Spatial Terms: Standard 3

ASSESS

Organize students into groups. Have groups use the maps and graphs from the Unit 2 Regional Atlas to pose questions to quiz one another on North Africa and Southwest Asia.

Current Events Journal

Have students prepare a chart that groups the countries profiled here into two areas: North Africa and Southwest Asia. Their chart might include the name of the country, the capital, the population, and the chief products. Then have them compare the main economic activities in the different areas.

THE HUMANITIES CONNECTION

World Music: A Cultural Legacy

World Art and Architecture Transparencies

Country Profiles

ALGERIA
POPULATION: 31,000,000; 34 per sq. mi.; 13 per sq. km
LANGUAGES: Arabic, French, Berber
MAJOR EXPORT: Petroleum
MAJOR IMPORT: Machinery
CAPITAL: Algiers
LANDMASS: 919,595 sq. mi.; 2,381,741 sq. km

BAHRAIN
POPULATION: 700,000; 2,621 per sq. mi.; 1,013 per sq. km
LANGUAGE: Arabic
MAJOR EXPORT: Petroleum
MAJOR IMPORT: Machinery
CAPITAL: Manama
LANDMASS: 267 sq. mi.; 691 sq. km

EGYPT
POPULATION: 69,800,000; 180 per sq. mi.; 69 per sq. km
LANGUAGE: Arabic
MAJOR EXPORT: Crude Oil
MAJOR IMPORT: Machinery
CAPITAL: Cairo
LANDMASS: 386,662 sq. mi.; 1,001,449 sq. km

IRAN
POPULATION: 66,208,000; 104 per sq. mi.; 40 per sq. km
LANGUAGES: Persian, Kurdish
MAJOR EXPORT: Petroleum
MAJOR IMPORT: Machinery
CAPITAL: Tehran
LANDMASS: 636,296 sq. mi.; 1,647,999 sq. km

IRAQ
POPULATION: 23,600,000; 139 per sq. mi.; 54 per sq. km
LANGUAGES: Arabic, Kurdish
MAJOR EXPORT: Crude Oil
MAJOR IMPORT: Machinery
CAPITAL: Baghdad
LANDMASS: 169,235 sq. mi.; 438,317 sq. km

ISRAEL
POPULATION: 6,400,000; 798 per sq. mi.; 308 per sq. km
LANGUAGES: Hebrew, Arabic
MAJOR EXPORT: Polished Diamonds
MAJOR IMPORT: Chemicals
CAPITAL: Jerusalem*
LANDMASS: 8,019 sq. mi.; 20,770 sq. km

JORDAN
POPULATION: 5,200,000; 146 per sq. mi.; 56 per sq. km
LANGUAGE: Arabic
MAJOR EXPORT: Phosphates
MAJOR IMPORT: Crude Oil
CAPITAL: Amman
LANDMASS: 35,467 sq. mi.; 91,860 sq. km

KUWAIT
POPULATION: 2,300,000; 334 per sq. mi.; 129 per sq. km
LANGUAGE: Arabic
MAJOR EXPORT: Petroleum
MAJOR IMPORT: Foods
CAPITAL: Kuwait
LANDMASS: 6,880 sq. mi.; 17,818 sq. km

* Israel has proclaimed Jerusalem as its capital, but many countries' embassies are located in Tel Aviv.

LEBANON
POPULATION: 4,300,000; 1,071 per sq. mi.; 413 per sq. km
LANGUAGES: Arabic, French
MAJOR EXPORT: Paper
MAJOR IMPORT: Machinery
CAPITAL: Beirut
LANDMASS: 4,015 sq. mi.; 10,399 sq. km

LIBYA
POPULATION: 5,200,000; 7 per sq. mi.; 3 per sq. km
LANGUAGE: Arabic
MAJOR EXPORT: Crude Oil
MAJOR IMPORT: Machinery
CAPITAL: Tripoli
LANDMASS: 679,362 sq. mi.; 1,759,540 sq. km

MOROCCO*
POPULATION: 29,200,000; 106 per sq. mi.; 41 per sq. km
LANGUAGES: Arabic, French, Berber
MAJOR EXPORT: Foods
MAJOR IMPORT: Manufactured Goods
CAPITAL: Rabat
LANDMASS: 275,117 sq. mi.; 712,550 sq. km

OMAN
POPULATION: 2,460,000; 30 per sq. mi.; 12 per sq. km
LANGUAGE: Arabic
MAJOR EXPORT: Petroleum
MAJOR IMPORT: Machinery
CAPITAL: Muscat
LANDMASS: 82,030 sq. mi.; 212,457 sq. km

* Morocco claims the Western Sahara area, but other countries do not accept this claim.

Countries and flags not drawn to scale

78 UNIT 2

- **Egypt** Ancient Egyptian women dyed their hair, wore red lip powder, and painted their fingernails. They used gray, black, or green paint to outline their eyes and color their eyebrows. Men often wore as much makeup as women.
- **Egypt** Ancient Egyptians buried their kings in a secret chamber inside or beneath a pyramid. They filled the chamber with gold and other treasures as well as practical, everyday items. Egyptians believed that the king would need these things in the afterlife.
- **Egypt** A team of archaeologists re-created the bread of ancient Egypt. For the flour, they used emmer wheat—the kind grown in ancient times—and ground it. They created a sourdough starter so the bread would rise.

Unit 2
Regional Atlas

For more information on countries in this region, refer to the Nations of the World Data Bank on pages 690–699.

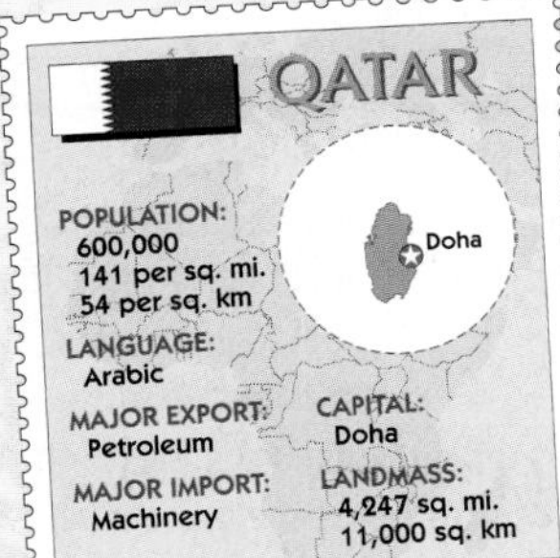

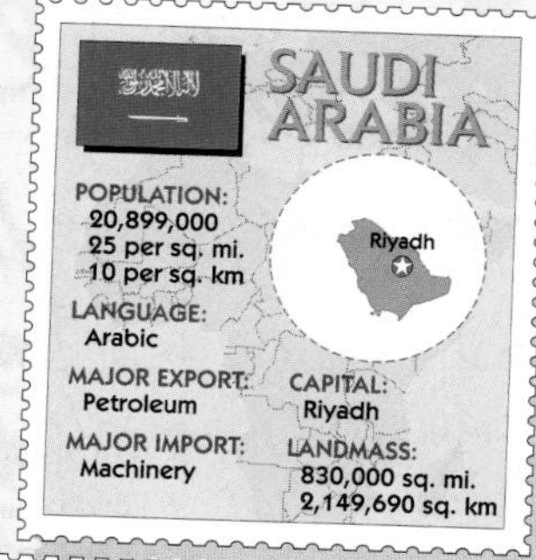

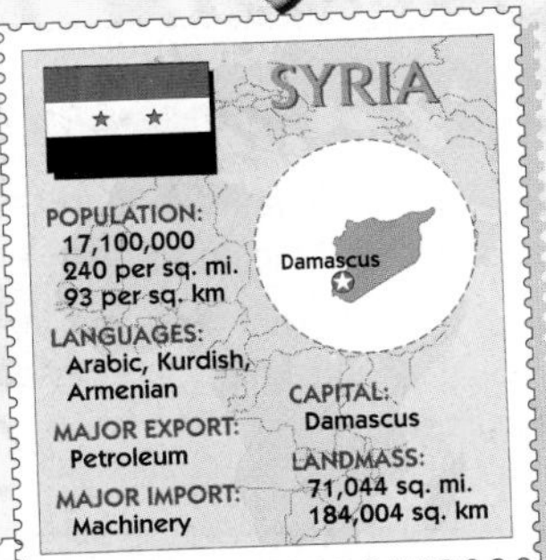

TUNISIA
POPULATION:
9,700,000
153 per sq. mi.
60 per sq. km
LANGUAGES:
Arabic, French
MAJOR EXPORT:
Petroleum
Products
MAJOR IMPORT:
Machinery
CAPITAL:
Tunis
LANDMASS:
63,170 sq. mi.
163,610 sq. km
Tunis

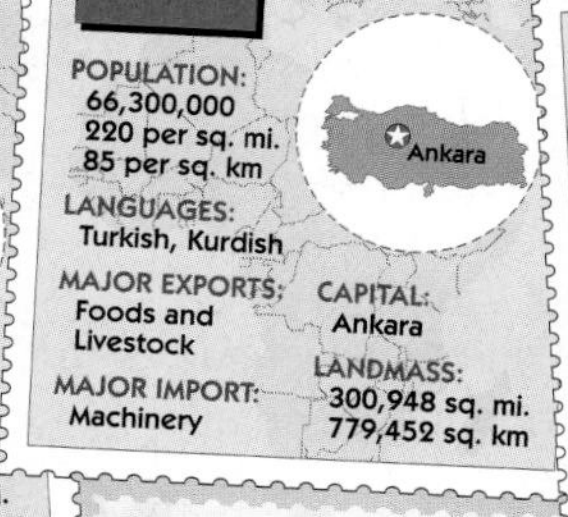

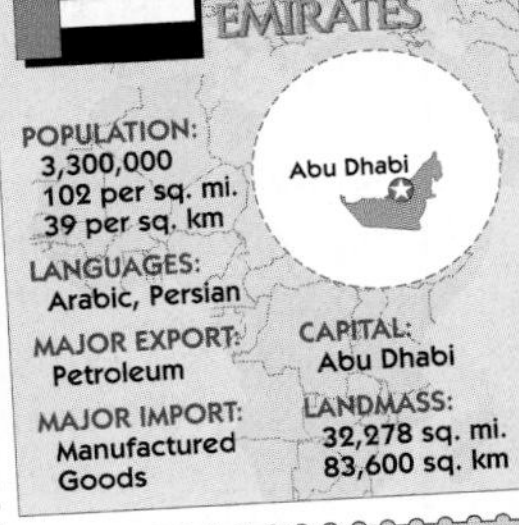

UNITED ARAB EMIRATES
POPULATION:
3,300,000
102 per sq. mi.
39 per sq. km
LANGUAGES:
Arabic, Persian
MAJOR EXPORT:
Petroleum
MAJOR IMPORT:
Manufactured
Goods
CAPITAL:
Abu Dhabi
LANDMASS:
32,278 sq. mi.
83,600 sq. km
Abu Dhabi

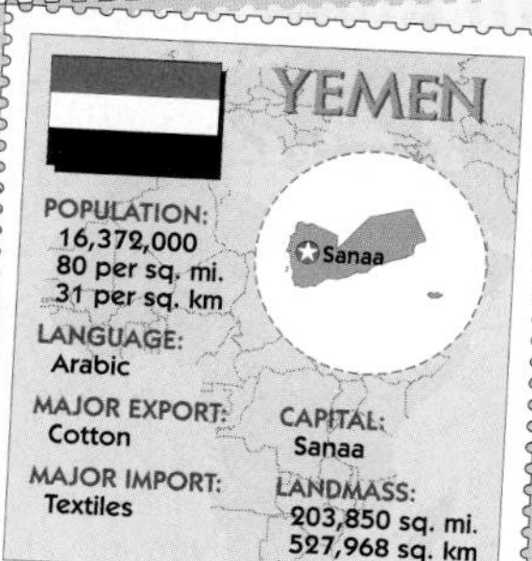

BUILDING CITIZENSHIP

Religious Tolerance In Southwest Asia there are holy places of many religions, including temples, shrines, tombs, and mosques. Because Muslims are forbidden to worship statues or images, in some Islamic countries officials have destroyed ancient shrines and statues revered by Hindus or Buddhists.

1. **Who owns religious properties in the United States?**
2. **Do you think government officials have a responsibility to protect valuable and sacred objects of all religions?**

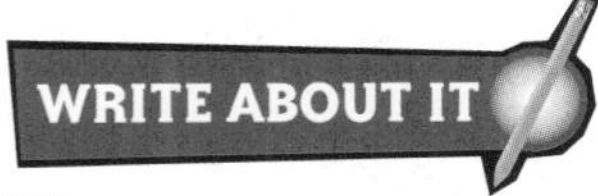

Write a short script that could be read by a television news broadcaster. The script should report on the destruction of a holy site by members of another religion. Present both points of view.

▲ **Destroyed Buddhist statue**

BUILDING CITIZENSHIP

The U.S. Constitution separates church and state but guarantees the right of everyone to worship in their own way. In some other countries, government and religion are combined, and followers of other religions and their holy sites may not be given the same rights and protection.

Answers

1. the religious organizations
2. Answers will vary but should include that the U.S. Constitution prohibits the government from favoring one religion over another.

Write About it! Students' scripts should reflect the fact that the people destroying the statues believe they are following the commands of their own religion. They should also point out what happens when there is no protection for minority religions.

CLOSE

Have students write a paragraph explaining what physical, economic, and cultural features the countries of this region share.

Country Profiles Activity

Economics Assign a country to each student or pair of students. Direct students to use the Country Profiles and library resources to discover their assigned country's major imports, exports, and trading partners. Create a wall chart by pinning a sheet of butcher paper to the bulletin board. Have students enter their findings on the chart. Then call on volunteers to use information on the wall chart to make generalizations about the region's economic activities. **L2**

EE4 Human Systems: Standard 11

Chapter 3 Resources

Note: The following materials may be used when teaching Chapter 3.
Section level support materials are shown at point of use in the margins of the Teacher Wraparound Edition.

Timesaving Tools

TeacherWorks™ All-In-One Planner and Resource Center

- **Interactive Teacher Edition** See the **Interactive Teacher Edition** CD-ROM to electronically integrate your Teacher Wraparound Edition and blackline masters.
- **Interactive Lesson Planner** Organize your week, month, semester, or year with all the lesson helps you need. The **Interactive Lesson Planner** CD-ROM contains all Chapter 3 resources.

Use Glencoe's **Presentation Plus!** multimedia teacher tool to easily present dynamic lessons that visually excite your students. Using Microsoft PowerPoint® you can customize the presentations to create your own personalized lessons.

TEACHING TRANSPARENCIES

Graphic Organizer Transparency and Student Activity 3

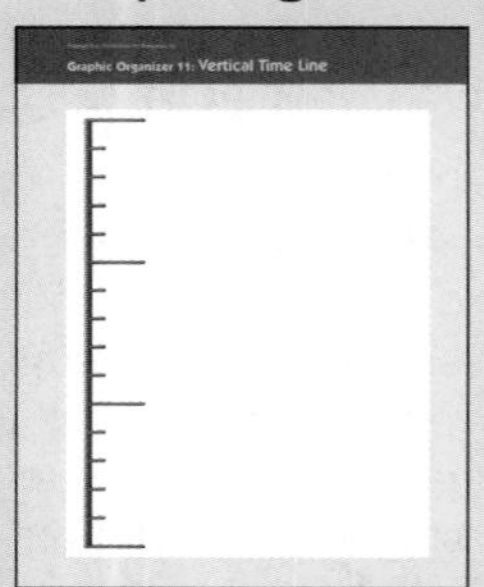

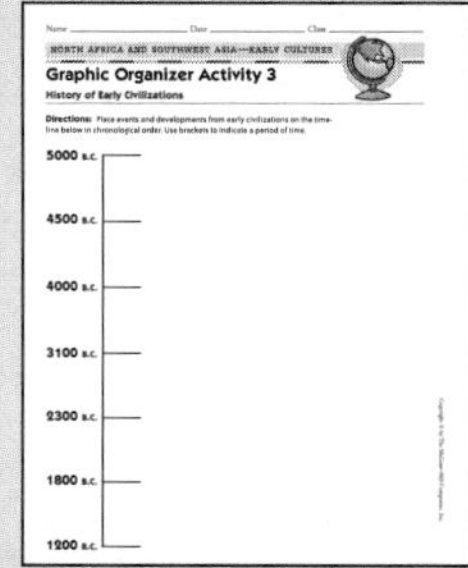

FOLDABLES™ Study Organizer

Foldables are three-dimensional, interactive graphic organizers that help students practice basic writing skills, review key vocabulary terms, and identify main ideas. Every chapter contains a Foldable activity, with additional chapter activities found in the ***Reading and Study Skills Foldables*** booklet.

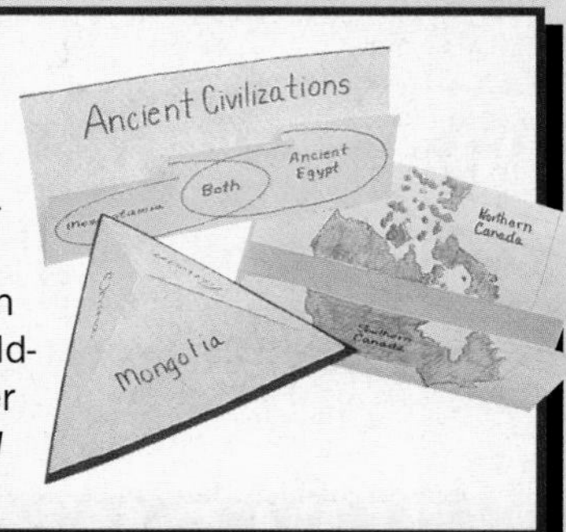

ENRICHMENT AND EXTENSION

Enrichment Activity 3

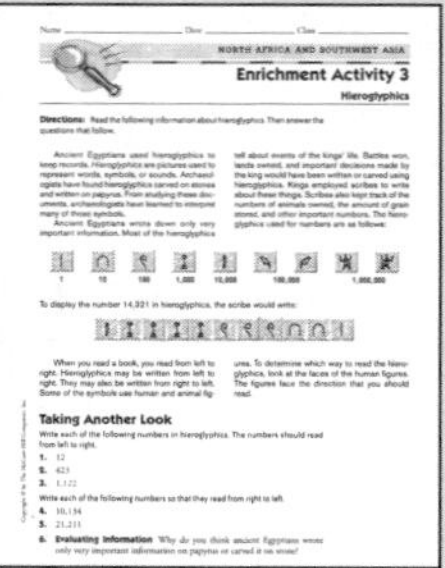

Cooperative Learning Activity 3

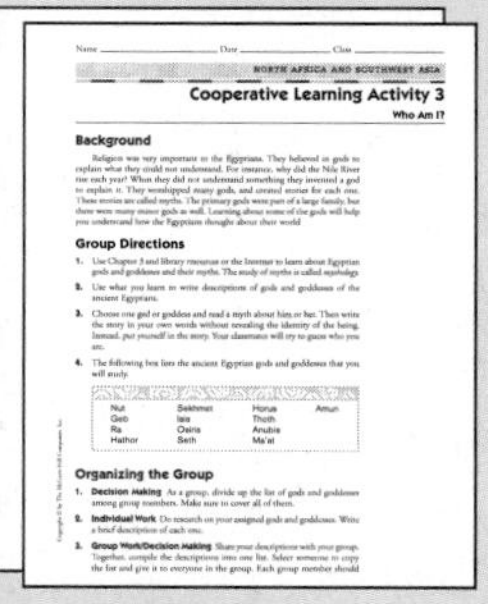

MAP AND GEOGRAPHY SKILLS

Chapter Map Activity 3

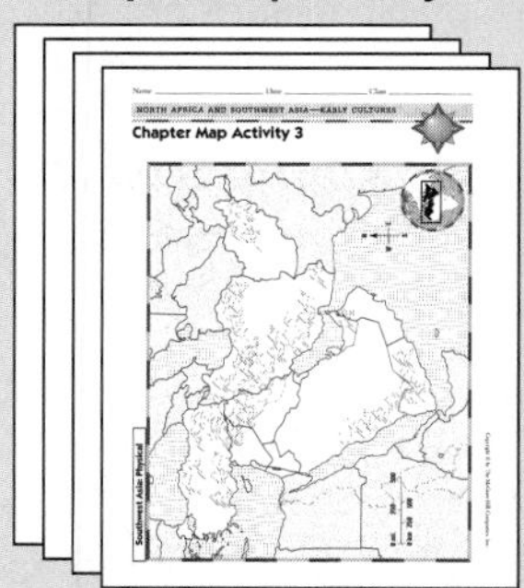

GeoLab Activity 3

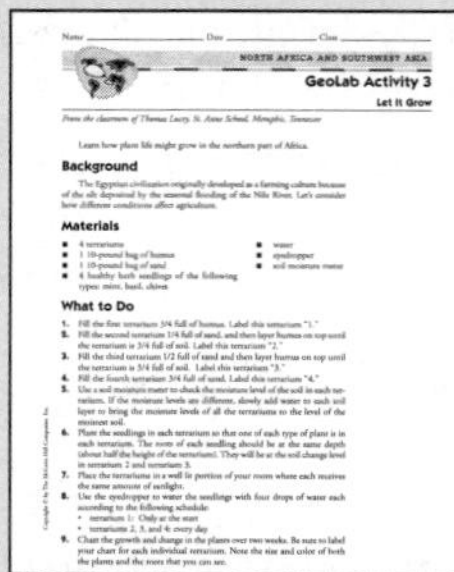

STANDARDIZED ASSESSMENT SKILLS

Critical Thinking Skills Activity 3

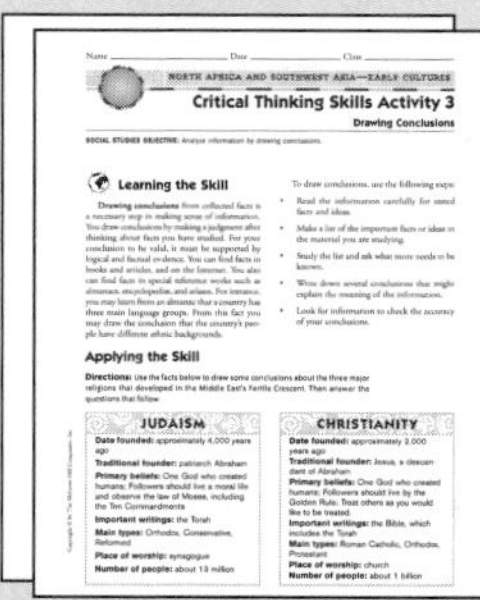

Map and Graph Skills Activity 3

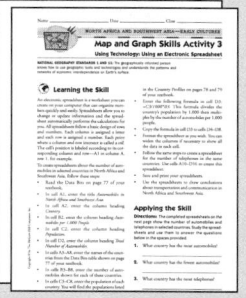

Reading and Writing Skills Activity 3

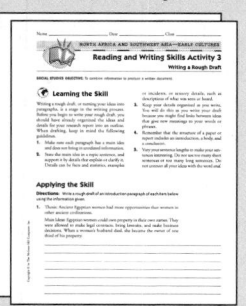

Standardized Test Practice Workbook Activity 3

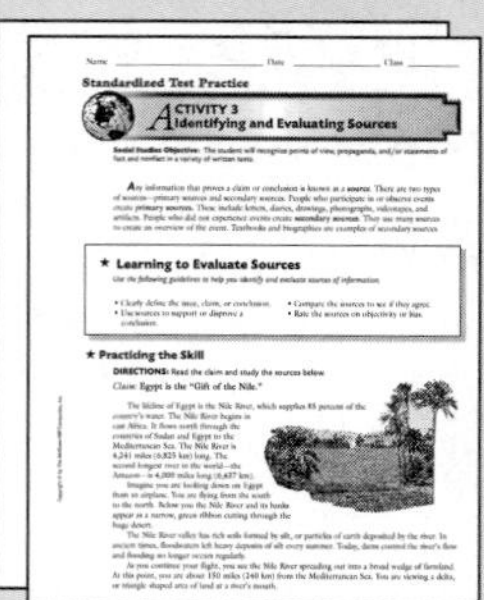

REVIEW AND REINFORCEMENT

Chapter Skills Activity 3

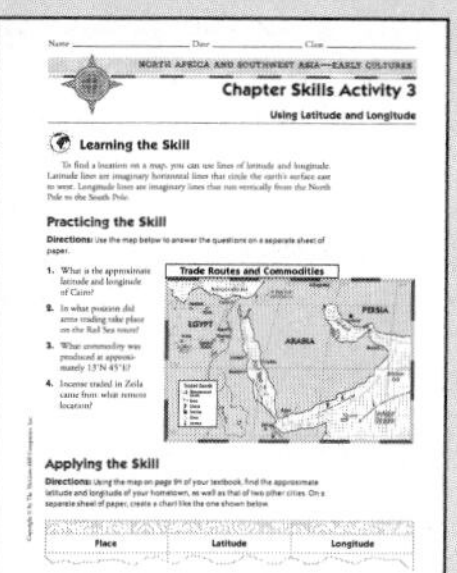

Take-Home Review Activity 3

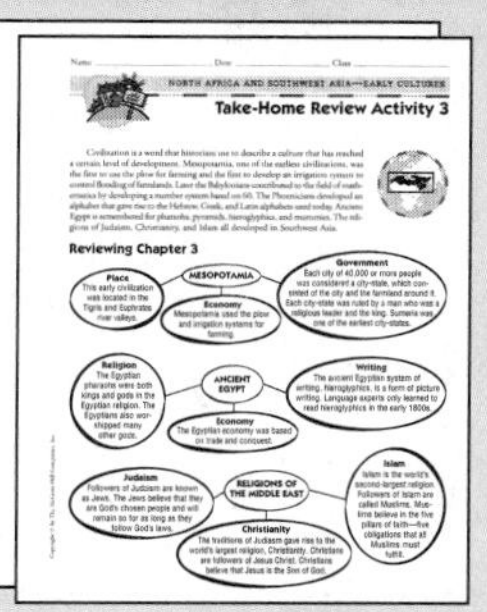

Reteaching Activity 3

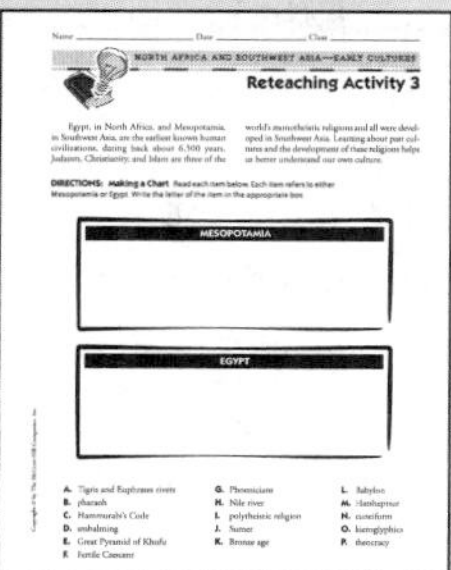

Vocabulary Activity 3

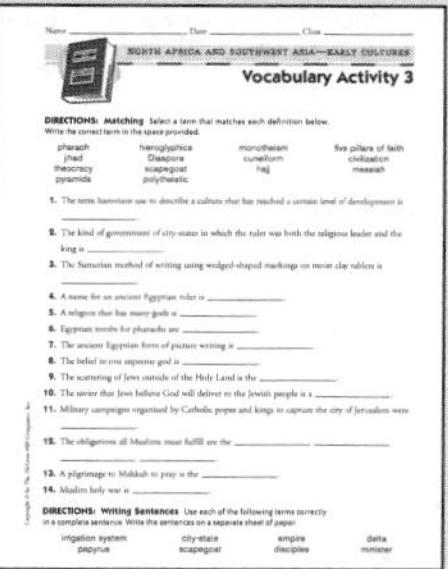

Workbook Activity 3

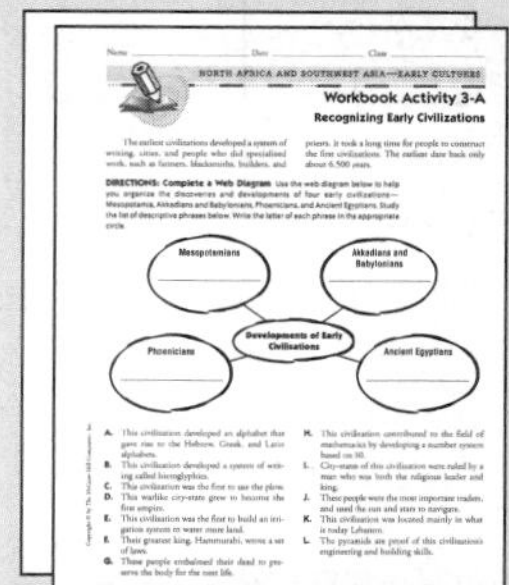

ASSESSMENT

GLENCOE'S ASSESSMENT ADVANTAGE

Chapter 3 Test, Form A

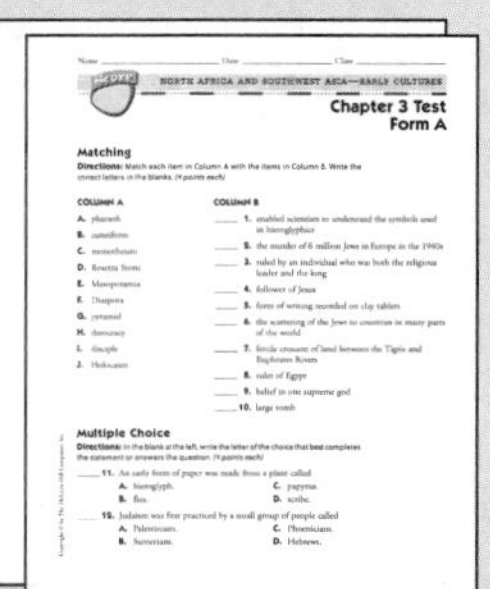

Chapter 3 Test, Form B

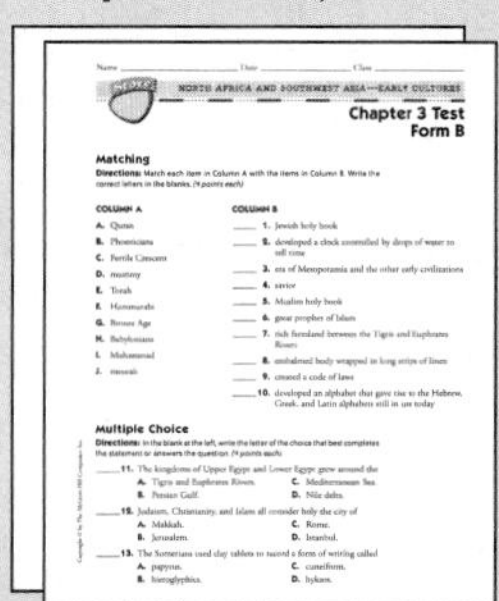

Performance Assessment Activity 3

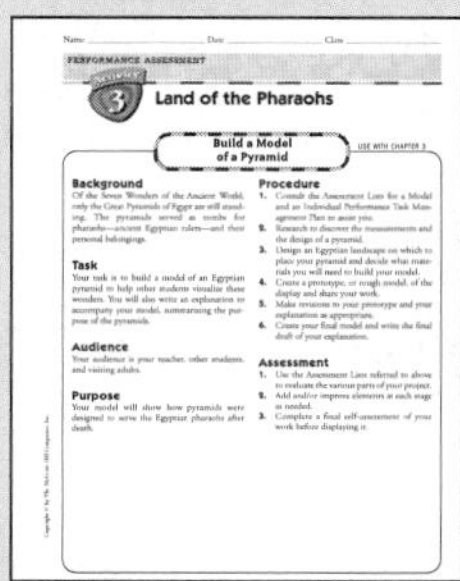

ExamView® Pro 3.0 Testmaker CD-ROM

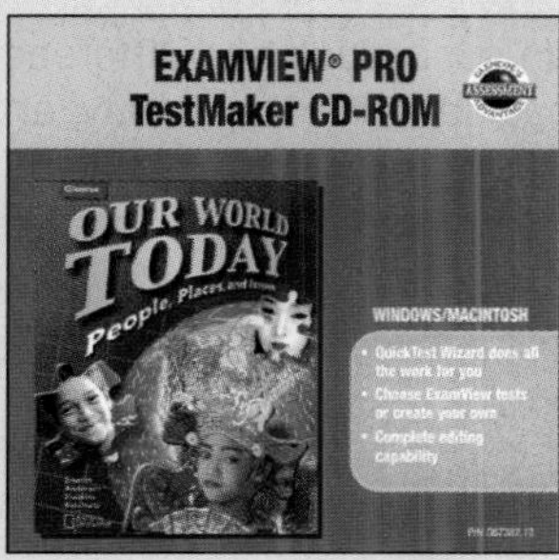

MULTIMEDIA

- **National Geographic's The World and Its People**
- **MindJogger Videoquiz**
- **Vocabulary PuzzleMaker Software**
- **Interactive Tutor Self-Assessment CD-ROM**
- **ExamView® Pro 3.0 Testmaker CD-ROM**
- **Interactive Lesson Planner CD-ROM**
- **Interactive Teacher Edition CD-ROM**
- **Skillbuilder Interactive Workbook CD-ROM, Level 1**
- **Presentation Plus! CD-ROM**
- **Audio Program**

SPANISH RESOURCES

The following Spanish language materials are available in the Spanish Resources binder:

- **Spanish Chapter Summaries**
- **Spanish Vocabulary Activities**
- **Spanish Guided Reading Activities**
- **Spanish Quizzes and Tests**
- **Spanish Take-Home Review Activities**
- **Spanish Reteaching Activities**

Meeting National Standards

Geography for Life

All of the 18 standards are demonstrated in Unit 2. The following ones are highlighted in Chapter 3:

Section 1 **EE2 Places and Regions: Standards 4, 5, 6**

EE4 Human Systems: Standards 9, 10, 11, 12, 13

Section 2 **EE2 Places and Regions: Standards 4, 5, 6**

EE4 Human Systems: Standards 9, 10, 11, 12, 13

For a complete listing of National Geography Standards and entire text correlation, see pages T22–T29.

Local Objectives

Chapter 3 Planning Guide

SECTION RESOURCES

Daily Objectives	Reproducible Resources	Multimedia Resources
Section 1 **Mespotamia and Ancient Egypt** **Suggested Pacing = 1 day** **1.** Explain the early advancements in Mesopotamia. **2.** Discuss the ancient Egyptians' achievements.	Reproducible Lesson Plan 3-1 Daily Lecture and Discussion Notes 3-1 Guided Reading Activity 3-1 Reading Essentials and Study Guide 3-1 Section Quiz 3-1*	Daily Focus Skills Transparency 3-1 Vocabulary PuzzleMaker Software Interactive Tutor Self-Assessment CD-ROM ExamView® Pro 3.0 Testmaker CD-ROM Presentation Plus! CD-ROM
Section 2 **Religions of the Middle East** **Suggested Pacing = 1 day** **1.** Describe the world's three largest monotheistic religions. **2.** Explain similarities and differences among Judaism, Christianity, and Islam.	Reproducible Lesson Plan 3-2 Daily Lecture and Discussion Notes 3-2 Guided Reading Activity 3-2 Reading Essentials and Study Guide 3-2 Section Quiz 3-2*	Daily Focus Skills Transparency 3-2 Vocabulary PuzzleMaker Software Interactive Tutor Self-Assessment CD-ROM ExamView® Pro 3.0 Testmaker CD-ROM Presentation Plus! CD-ROM

00:00 **Out of Time?** Assign the **Reading Essentials and Study Guide** for this chapter.

*Also available in Spanish

KEY TO ABILITY LEVELS

Teaching strategies have been coded for varying learning styles and abilities.

L1 **BASIC** activities for all students
L2 **AVERAGE** activities for average to above-average students
L3 **CHALLENGING** activities for above-average students
ELL **ENGLISH LANGUAGE LEARNER** activities

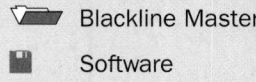

Blackline Master
Software
CD-ROM
Audiocassette
Transparency
Videocassette
Block Scheduling

DVD

Building a Pyramid of Facts

Paula Gordon
Nettleton Intermediate Center
Jonesboro, Arkansas

During the study of this chapter, have students record important facts about Egypt onto individual construction paper triangles. Use one piece of paper per triangle, and make all triangles the same size, preferably isosceles. After students use a large marker to record their facts, have them arrange and tape the triangles into a large pyramid on the wall. (NOTE: About half of the fact statements must be written on upside-down triangles so that readability is not an issue when the triangles are taped on the wall.) Students are usually eager to finish the pyramid, and they often do research on their own to find more facts.

OUR WORLD TODAY *Online*

Use our Web site for additional resources. All essential content is covered in the Student Edition.

You and your students can visit owt.glencoe.com, the Web site companion to *Our World Today*. This innovative integration of electronic and print media offers your students a wealth of opportunities. The student text directs students to the Web site for the following options:

- Chapter Overviews
- Student Web Activities
- Self-Check Quizzes
- Textbook Updates

Answers are provided for you in the Web Activity Lesson Plan. Additional Web resources and Interactive Tutor puzzles are also available.

TEACHER'S CORNER

Index to National Geographic Magazine:

The following articles may be used for research relating to this chapter:

- "Libya: An End to Isolation?," by Andrew Cockburn, November 2000.
- "Valley of the Mummies," by Donovan Webster, October 1999.
- "Abusir Tombs," by Zahi Hawass, November 1998.
- "Valley of the Kings," by Kent R. Weeks, September 1998.

National Geographic Society Products Available From Glencoe:

To order the following products for use with this chapter, contact your local Glencoe sales representative or call Glencoe at 1-800-334-7344:

- *STV: World Geography* (Videodisc)
- *PictureShow: Ancient Civilizations: Egypt and the Fertile Crescent* (CD-ROM)
- *PicturePack: Ancient Civilizations: Ancient Egypt* (Transparencies)

Additional National Geographic Society Products:

To order the following products for use with this chapter, call National Geographic Society at 1-800-368-2728:

- *Pharaoh's Voyage for Eternity* (Video)
- *Who Built the Pyramids?* (Video)
- *Complete National Geographic: 111 Years of National Geographic Magazine* (CD-ROM)
- *Africa* (Video)
- *National Geographic Atlas of the World, Seventh Edition* (Book)
- *Voices: Poetry and Art From Around the World* (Book)
- *PicturePack: The Fertile Crescent* (Transparencies)
- *PicturePack: Ancient Egypt* (Transparencies)
- *PictureShow: Ancient Civilizations: Africa* (CD-ROM)
- *PictureShow: Ancient Civilizations: Egypt & Fertile Crescent* (CD-ROM)
- *Ancient Civilizations: The Fertile Crescent* (Posters)

NGS ONLINE

Access National Geographic's Web site for current events, activities, links, interactive features, and archives.
www.nationalgeographic.com

Introducing Chapter 3

Introduce students to chapter content and key terms by having them access Chapter Overview 3 at owt.glencoe.com

Chapter Objectives

1. Explain how farming, writing, and government developed in Mesopotamia.
2. Examine the artifacts of ancient Egypt.
3. Explain the basic beliefs of Judaism, Christianity, and Islam.
4. Discuss how past civilizations have contributed to our own culture.

GLENCOE TECHNOLOGY

NATIONAL GEOGRAPHIC

The World and Its People Video Program

Chapters 16 and 17 North Africa and Southwest Asia

The following segments enhance the study of this chapter:

- **Mummy of Abusir**
- **The Longest River**
- **Pyramids of Giza**

Available in DVD and VHS.

MindJogger Videoquiz

Use MindJogger to preview the Chapter 3 content.

Available in VHS.

Chapter 3 North Africa and Southwest Asia—Early Cultures

The World and Its People NATIONAL GEOGRAPHIC

To learn more about the people and places of North Africa and Southwest Asia, view ***The World and Its People*** **Chapters 16** and **17** videos.

Our World Today Online

Chapter Overview Visit the ***Our World Today: People, Places, and Issues*** Web site at owt.glencoe.com and click on **Chapter 3—Chapter Overviews** to preview information about North Africa and Southwest Asia.

80

Two-Minute Lesson Launcher

Have students write down everything they know or think they know about Egypt. Have students share their information with a partner. Students may add or delete information. Close the discussion by pointing out that Egypt has a long and rich history and that the country continues to play important political, economic, and cultural roles today. Explain that, in this chapter, they will learn about these aspects of Egypt.

FOLDABLES™
Study Organizer

Compare-Contrast Study Foldable Make and use this foldable to help you determine how Mesopotamia and ancient Egypt were similar and different.

Step 1 Fold a sheet of paper from side to side, leaving a 2-inch tab uncovered along the side.

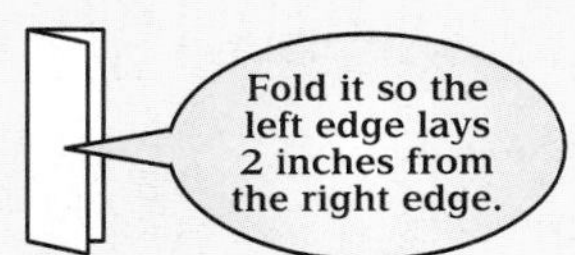
Fold it so the left edge lays 2 inches from the right edge.

Step 2 Turn the paper and fold it into thirds.

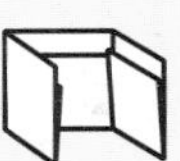

Step 3 Unfold and cut along the two inside fold lines.

Cut along the two folds on the front flap to make 3 tabs.

Step 4 Label your foldable as shown.

Ancient Civilizations
Mesopotamia
Both
Ancient Egypt

Reading and Writing As you read the chapter, write what you learn about these ancient civilizations under the tabs. Be sure to list similarities and differences under the appropriate tabs.

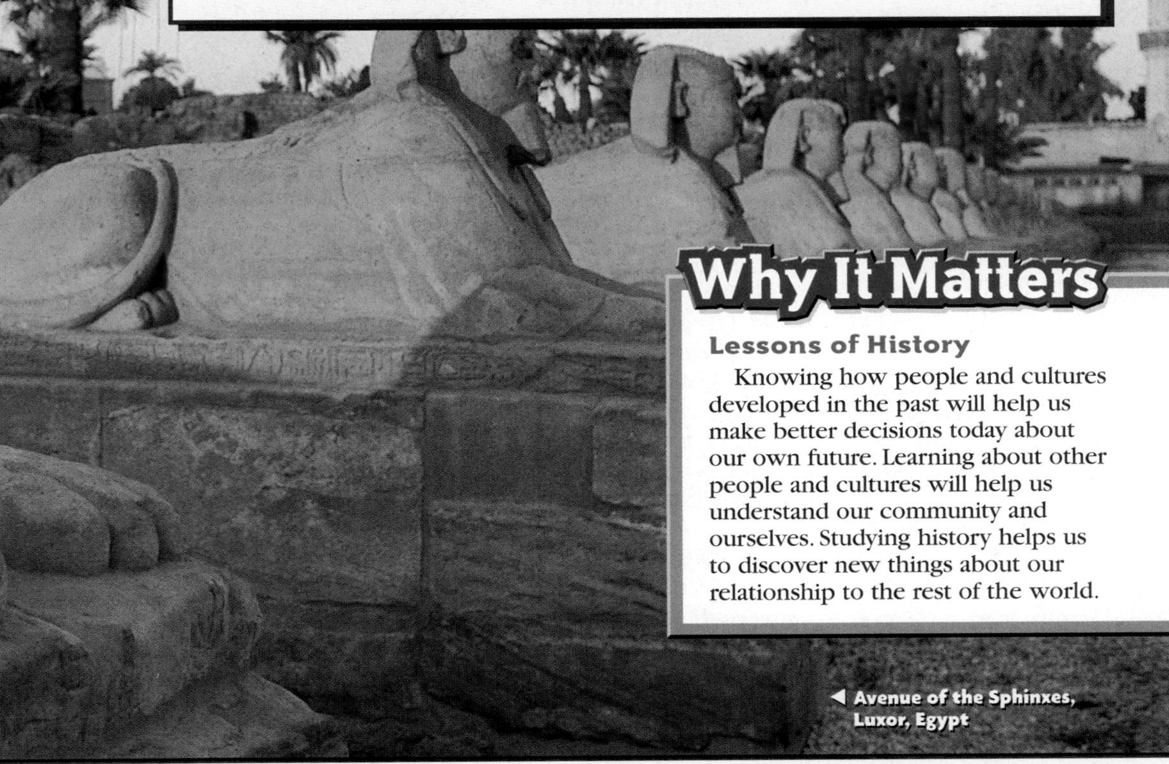

Why It Matters

Lessons of History

Knowing how people and cultures developed in the past will help us make better decisions today about our own future. Learning about other people and cultures will help us understand our community and ourselves. Studying history helps us to discover new things about our relationship to the rest of the world.

◀ Avenue of the Sphinxes, Luxor, Egypt

About the Photo

A sphinx is a being with the head of a human and the body of a lion. In ancient Egypt, the head might assume the face of the reigning pharaoh who, along with the sphinx, was the earthly representation of the sky-god, Horus. In addition, the lion symbolizes kingship and courage. Most people first associate "sphinx" to the Great Sphinx of Egypt, which was 'rediscovered' by the western world when Napoleon's soldiers came across it in 1798. However, there are other sphinxes in Egypt as well. This Avenue of Sphinxes leads to Luxor Temple. They were the guardians of the temple gates and the underworld.

Introducing
Chapter 3

FOLDABLES™ Study Organizer

Purpose Students will make and use a compare-contrast foldable to collect and organize information to compare 1) Mesopotamia and ancient Egypt, and 2) Judaism and Islam. Students will write what they learn about these ancient civilizations and religions, and then will list similarities and differences that they find.

Have students complete ***Reading and Study Skills Foldables*** Activity 3.

Why It Matters

Egypt's dry climate helped preserve the achievements of this ancient land. The lack of humidity not only meant that mud-brick structures remained standing, but also allowed softer materials like wood, textiles, and papyrus scrolls to remain recoverable after thousands of years.

Ask students to write a paragraph in which they agree or disagree with the following sentence: "The Nile gave life to the civilization of ancient Egypt, but the dry climate preserved that civilization." Then have students discuss their answers. **L1**

Section 1 Mesopotamia and Ancient Egypt

1 Focus

1. Explain the early advancements in Mesopotamia.
2. Discuss the ancient Egyptians' achievements.

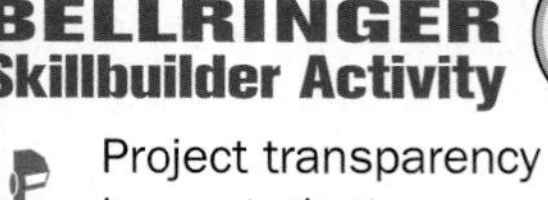

BELLRINGER
Skillbuilder Activity

Project transparency and have students answer questions.

This activity is also available as a blackline master.

Daily Focus Skills Transparency 3-1

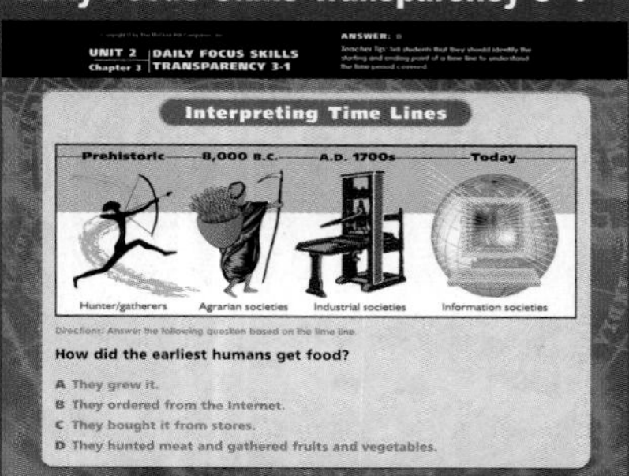
UNIT 2 DAILY FOCUS SKILLS
Chapter 3 TRANSPARENCY 3-1

Interpreting Time Lines

Prehistoric	8,000 B.C.	A.D. 1700s	Today
Hunter/gatherers	Agrarian societies	Industrial societies	Information societies

How did the earliest humans get food?

A They grew it.
B They ordered from the Internet.
C They bought it from stores.
D They hunted meat and gathered fruits and vegetables.

Guide to Reading

■ **Accessing Prior Knowledge**
Ask: Have you ever heard of the pyramids? Where are they? *(Egypt)* What are they? *(tombs for the great rulers of Egypt)*

■ **Vocabulary Precheck**
Inform students that the word *pharaoh* means *great house.*

Guide to Reading

Main Idea

Learning about how past cultures lived helps us better understand our own cultures.

Terms to Know

- civilization
- irrigation system
- city-state
- theocracy
- cuneiform
- empire
- delta
- pharaoh
- polytheistic
- embalm
- pyramid
- hieroglyphics
- papyrus
- scribe

Reading Strategy

Create a chart like the one below. Write facts about Mesopotamia in the M column. Write facts about Egypt in the E column.

	M	E
Religion		
Writing		
Economy		

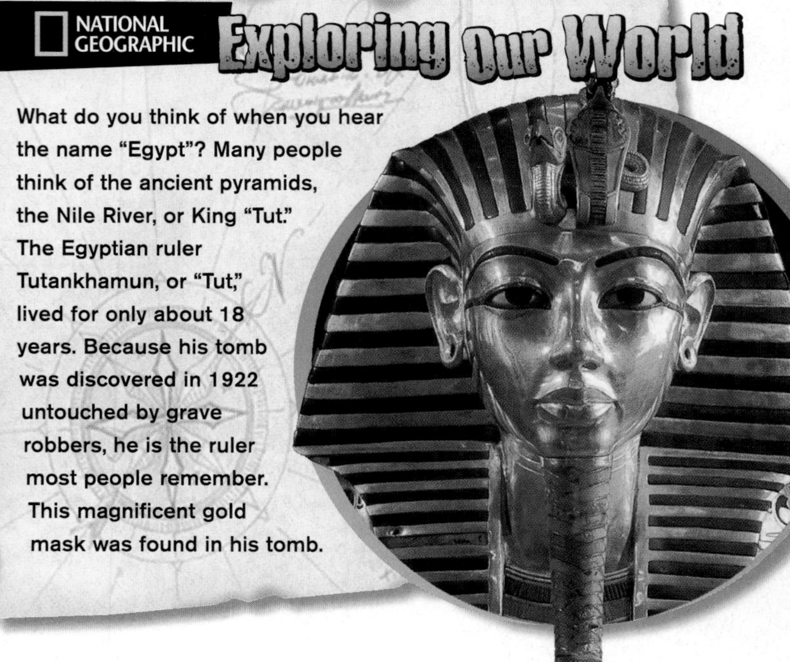

What do you think of when you hear the name "Egypt"? Many people think of the ancient pyramids, the Nile River, or King "Tut." The Egyptian ruler Tutankhamun, or "Tut," lived for only about 18 years. Because his tomb was discovered in 1922 untouched by grave robbers, he is the ruler most people remember. This magnificent gold mask was found in his tomb.

Thanks to television and films, Egypt is probably the most familiar of the ancient civilizations. Movies like *The Mummy* have helped spread knowledge of Egyptian culture, however inaccurate, through the world. **Egypt,** in North Africa, and **Mesopotamia,** in Southwest Asia, were the earliest known human civilizations.

Civilization is a term historians use to describe a culture that has reached a certain level of development. This development includes a system of writing, building cities, and specialized workers, such as farmers, blacksmiths, builders, and priests. The earliest civilizations date back only about 6,500 years.

Mesopotamia

One of the first civilizations grew in the fertile crescent of land between the **Tigris** and **Euphrates Rivers.** The map on page 83 shows you this area. The region then was called Mesopotamia, which means

Section Resources

Reproducible Masters
- Reproducible Lesson Plan 3-1
- Daily Lecture and Discussion Notes 3-1
- Guided Reading Activity 3-1
- Reading Essentials and Study Guide 3-1
- Section Quiz 3-1

Transparencies
- Daily Focus Skills Transparency 3-1

Multimedia
- Vocabulary PuzzleMaker Software
- Interactive Tutor Self-Assessment CD-ROM
- Presentation Plus! CD-ROM
- ExamView® Pro 3.0 Testmaker CD-ROM

"between the rivers." This area of rich farmland—in what is today Syria and Iraq—was the site of the first permanent human settlements. The term *Fertile Crescent* has been used to describe this region. The era of Mesopotamia and the other early civilizations is known as the **Bronze Age** because these cultures often made wide use of the metal bronze, which is a mixture of copper and tin.

Farming Around 4500 B.C. wandering peoples who hunted animals and gathered plants for food settled in large numbers along the banks of the Tigris and Euphrates Rivers. They saw the rich, fertile soil left by the waters from yearly floods and knew it would be a productive area to farm. Over the next 500 years these people dug ditches and built an **irrigation system** to control the flooding and to better water more land. A 12-month calendar, based on the phases of the moon, was developed to better predict the coming of the flood waters. Here, crops like the grain barley and possibly wheat were grown for the first time. The plow was used here for the first time, as well.

Government Some of the villages and towns grew into cities with populations of up to 40,000 people. Each city was considered a small state, or nation. The **city-state** of this time was made up of the city and farmland around it. The city-state was a **theocracy**—it was ruled by an individual who was both the religious leader and the king. These priest-kings had almost absolute power.

Sumer The earliest of these city-states rose in an area called **Sumer,** located near the **Persian Gulf,** where the rivers flow closest to each other. The Sumerians created a form of writing known as **cuneiform.** It was written with wooden triangular-shaped sticks in the form of hundreds of different wedge-shaped markings on moist clay tablets. Cuneiform records became permanent when the clay tablets were allowed to harden in the sun.

Akkad and Babylon Eventually, around 2300 B.C. the warlike kingdom of **Akkad** conquered Sumer and several other city-states to create the first **empire,** or group of states under one ruler. The Akkadian Empire gradually lost control of its empire and gave way to **Babylon** in about 1800 B.C. Babylon's greatest king was **Hammurabi,** who pushed the boundaries of his empire to the Mediterranean Sea. To better rule, Hammurabi wrote a set, or code, of laws. Some of his laws seem cruel by today's standards. However, at that time laws changed often and not all people had to follow the laws. The punishment for the same offense could be a fine or could

NATIONAL GEOGRAPHIC

Mesopotamia and the Fertile Crescent

EUROPE
Black Sea
ASIA MINOR
Mediterranean Sea
PHOENICIA
Tyre
Syrian Desert
Nineveh
Euphrates R.
Tigris R.
AKKAD
Babylon
SUMER
Ur
Eridu
PERSIA
Sinai Pen.
EGYPT
Nile R.
Red Sea
Arabian Desert
Persian Gulf
30°E
40°E
40°N
30°N
20°N
0 mi. 500
0 km 500
Lambert Azimuthal Equal-Area projection
Mesopotamia
Fertile Crescent

Applying Map Skills

1. What feature were most early cities located near?
2. Compare this map to the map on page 75. In what modern-day countries would these cities be located?

Find NGS online map resources@ www.nationalgeographic.com/maps

Chapter 3

Section 1, pages 82–86

Synthesizing Information
Help students create a diagram that shows each stage of the development of Mesopotamia from hunter-gatherers to the first empire. Have students list advancements associated with each of the stages. Discuss how the advancements contributed to the next stage of development.

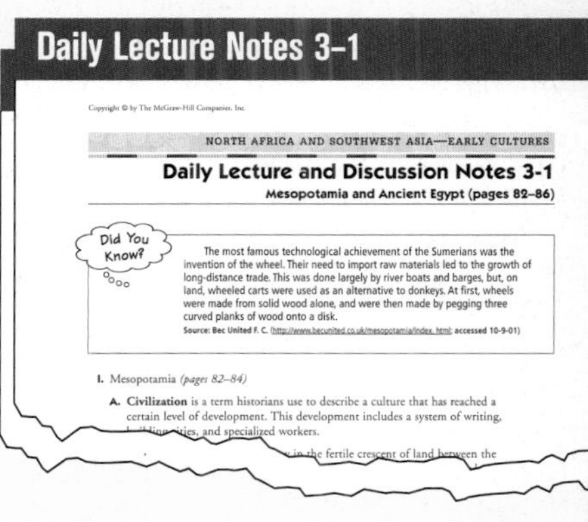
Daily Lecture Notes 3–1

NORTH AFRICA AND SOUTHWEST ASIA—EARLY CULTURES

Daily Lecture and Discussion Notes 3-1

Mesopotamia and Ancient Egypt (pages 82–86)

Did You Know?

The most famous technological achievement of the Sumerians was the invention of the wheel. Their need to import raw materials led to the growth of long-distance trade. This was done largely by river boats and barges, but, on land, wheeled carts were used as an alternative to donkeys. At first, wheels were made from solid wood alone, and were then made by pegging three curved planks of wood onto a disk.

Source: Bec United F. C. (http://www.becunited.co.uk/mesopotamia/index.html; accessed 10-9-01)

I. Mesopotamia *(pages 82–84)*

A. **Civilization** is a term historians use to describe a culture that has reached a certain level of development. This development includes a system of writing, [illegible]ities, and specialized workers.

[illegible] in the fertile crescent of land between the

Applying Map Skills

Answers
1. rivers
2. Iraq, Lebanon

Skills Practice
What city was located on the Tigris River? *(Nineveh)*

Meeting Special Needs

Visual/Spatial The hieroglyphics of ancient Egypt used three types of symbols—*logograms,* in which a symbol stood for a word; *phonograms,* in which symbols representing consonant sounds were combined to sound out a word (there were no symbols for vowel sounds); and *determinatives,* which were symbols used with phonograms to signal exactly which word was meant. The names of pharaohs were spelled out as phonograms inside an oval called a *cartouche.* Several books and activity kits offer hieroglyphic "alphabets"—listings of ancient Egyptian symbols keyed to different consonants. Have students use such a resource to create their own *cartouches.* The Virtual Egypt Web site www.virtual-egypt.com may also be helpful. **L1**

EE4 Human Systems: Standard 10

Chapter 3

Section 1, pages 82–86

Guided Reading Activity 3–1

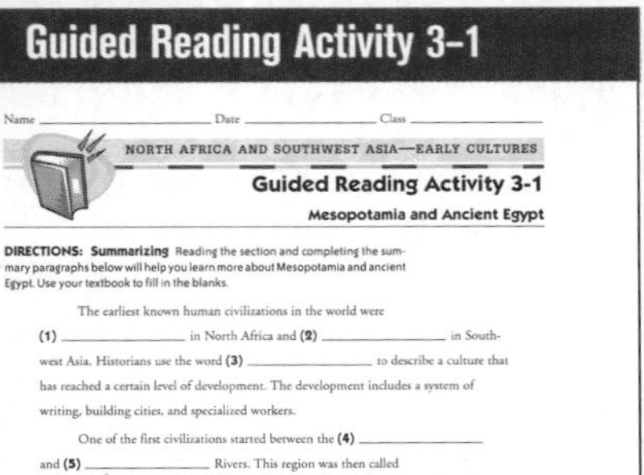
Name ____________ Date ____________ Class ____________

NORTH AFRICA AND SOUTHWEST ASIA—EARLY CULTURES

Guided Reading Activity 3-1

Mesopotamia and Ancient Egypt

DIRECTIONS: Summarizing Reading the section and completing the summary paragraphs below will help you learn more about Mesopotamia and ancient Egypt. Use your textbook to fill in the blanks.

The earliest known human civilizations in the world were **(1)** ____________ in North Africa and **(2)** ____________ in Southwest Asia. Historians use the word **(3)** ____________ to describe a culture that has reached a certain level of development. The development includes a system of writing, building cities, and specialized workers.

One of the first civilizations started between the **(4)** ____________ and **(5)** ____________ Rivers. This region was then called **(6)** ____________. It was an area of rich farmland, so it has been described as **(7)** ____________ ____________. People settled in the region

✓ Reading Check Answer

Sumer, Akkad, and Babylon

Cultural Kaleidoscope

When the Aswan High Dam was built on the Nile River, it created a reservoir 300 miles (483 km) long. The waters would have covered four colossal statues of Ramses II built into a cliff temple, but engineers and scientists moved them. The 66-foot (20-m) tall statues were taken apart and then rebuilt on higher ground.

be death. **Hammurabi's Code** was an attempt to bring some justice and fairness to the idea of law. Hammurabi borrowed cuneiform writing from Sumer and many of their laws as well to create his code.

The Babylonians contributed to the field of mathematics by developing a number system based on 60. From them, we have borrowed the 60-minute hour, 60-second minute, and 360-degree circle. They also used a clock controlled by drops of water to tell time.

The Phoenicians As the peoples of the area warred with neighboring states such as Egypt, they also traded, spreading ideas and cultures. Among the most important traders were the **Phoenicians,** who were located mainly in what is today **Lebanon.** By about 1200 B.C. the Phoenicians had sailed as far as southern Europe and around the southern tip of Africa. They used the sun and the stars to navigate. The Phoenicians also developed an alphabet that gave rise to the Hebrew, Greek, and Latin alphabets still in use today.

✓ Reading Check **What were three important city-states of the Fertile Crescent?**

Ancient Egypt

Like Mesopotamia, Egypt also grew out of a river valley—the **Nile.** The Nile is the longest river in the world. It runs north from its source for 4,241 miles (6,825 km). It passes through the mountains of East Africa, called the Mountains of the Moon by later Greek and Roman geographers, to the **Mediterranean Sea.** At the Mediterranean it forms a great **delta,** a fan-shaped or triangular piece of richly fertile land.

Pharaohs and Gods Hunter-gatherers first began to farm in the Nile Valley at its delta in about 5000 B.C. Eventually, two kingdoms formed, **Upper Egypt** to the south and **Lower Egypt** around the delta. The two kingdoms were united in 3100 B.C. under a great ruler called a **pharaoh.** Pharaoh means "great house," which probably refers to his lavish palace.

The pharaohs were both kings and gods in the Egyptian **polytheistic** religion. Polytheistic means "many gods," which describes most religions of ancient times. The pharaoh ruled as a god, so Egypt's government was a theocracy like those in Mesopotamia. The most important Egyptian gods were Horus, the god of light, Hapi, the river god, and Re, the sun god. Another important god was Osiris, the god of the harvest and eternal life. The Nile brought the Egyptians water and fertile soil, while the sun helped grow their crops.

The Egyptians believed in a form of life after death. To preserve the body for the next life, it was **embalmed,** or preserved immediately after death. Embalming was necessary, for Egyptians believed that the soul could not exist without the body. The embalmed body, or mummy, was wrapped in long strips of linen, a cloth made from the flax plant, which grew along the Nile.

The mummies of poor people were often buried in caves or the desert sand, but rich people's mummies were placed in coffins in often

Exploring Economics

Centers of Trade

Why did some cities develop into rich centers of trade? To succeed at trade, there must be a demand for products and a way to move goods. The peoples of Mesopotamia produced extra food, but they lacked trees for construction and mineral resources to make metals. They were able to trade extra food for other raw materials. Since water is the easiest way to transport goods, cities located nearest rivers and seas became important trading centers.

Content Background

Ancient Mathematics The ancient civilizations of this region developed sophisticated mathematics—some of which still influence our number systems today. Ancient Egyptian mathematicians used a decimal system, or a method of counting in groups of 10. They also had formulas for finding the area and volume of geometric figures, which they used when building the pyramids. The mathematicians of ancient Mesopotamia—the land between the Tigris and Euphrates Rivers—had a number system with a base of 60. Their method of counting is still found today in the way we count time—60 seconds in a minute and 60 minutes in an hour—and in measuring circles—360 degrees makes a complete circle.

NATIONAL GEOGRAPHIC On Location

Ancient Egypt

This mummy (right) was uncovered in the Valley of the Kings, Egypt. The coffin, or sarcophagus (left), made to hold a mummy, was created around 1000 B.C. The hieroglyphics (top) are from the Kom Ombo Temple in Egypt.

History **What were the biggest tombs called?**

very elaborate tombs. Many of these tombs contained fabulous treasures. The biggest tombs belonged to the pharaohs and were called **pyramids.** The largest of these is the **Great Pyramid of Khufu** (Cheops) at El Giza on the west bank of the Nile. It is over 4,500 years old and stands over 40 stories high on 13 acres. That it still stands is proof of ancient Egyptian engineering and building skills. Egyptian sculpture, especially the statues of great pharaohs such as Ramses II, were often monuments, built to glorify the rulers. It is in large part because of these tombs and statues that we know as much as we do about the ancient Egyptian civilization.

Egyptian Writing The ancient Egyptian system of writing is called **hieroglyphics.** Hieroglyphics is a form of picture writing with about 800 signs. The signs were cut into stone or painted on walls and **papyrus** (peh•PIE•rus). Papyrus, like flax, is a plant that grows along the Nile. It was used to make a form of paper, and gives us our root word for paper. Pharaohs kept hundreds of royal officers known as **scribes** to record the government's business.

Language experts only learned to read hieroglyphics in the early 1800s. During Napoleon Bonaparte's invasion of Egypt, a French soldier found what seemed to be a very old stone tablet near the town of Rosetta by the Nile. This stone tablet provided the key that cracked the code for hieroglyphics. The **Rosetta Stone** had the same message

More About the Photos

Mummification was the process of slowly drying a dead body to prevent it from rotting. The process consisted of removing certain internal organs, including the brain, then covering the corpse with a natural salt to absorb the body's water. The body was then filled with spices and wrapped with layers of linen soaked in resin.

Caption Answer pyramids

Assess

Assign Section 1 Assessment as homework or an in-class activity.

Have students use the Interactive Tutor Self-Assessment CD-ROM to review Section 3–1

Section Quiz 3-1

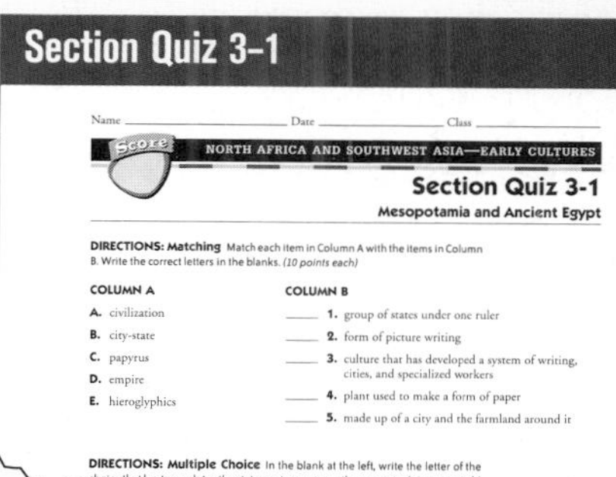

Name ______ Date ______ Class ______

NORTH AFRICA AND SOUTHWEST ASIA—EARLY CULTURES

Section Quiz 3-1

Mesopotamia and Ancient Egypt

DIRECTIONS: Matching Match each item in Column A with the items in Column B. Write the correct letters in the blanks. *(10 points each)*

COLUMN A	COLUMN B
A. civilization	____ **1.** group of states under one ruler
B. city-state	____ **2.** form of picture writing
C. papyrus	____ **3.** culture that has developed a system of writing, cities, and specialized workers
D. empire	____ **4.** plant used to make a form of paper
E. hieroglyphics	____ **5.** made up of a city and the farmland around it

DIRECTIONS: Multiple Choice In the blank at the left, write the letter of the choice that best completes the statement or answers the question. *(10 points each)*

Meeting Special Needs

Interpersonal Many ancient sites in Southwest Asia contain artifacts from simple pottery and carved stone to elaborate and beautiful works of wrought gold or silver. The governments of Southwest Asia work to preserve these remains of their heritage. Encourage students to help preserve the heritage of their own community and to discuss the importance of voluntary civic participation in doing so. By volunteering at a local museum, library, or historical society, they can work to keep the past alive. Their work could range from preparing informational materials to cataloging materials or acting as a tour guide. **L1**

Refer to *Inclusion for the Middle School Social Studies Classroom Strategies and Activities* in the TCR.

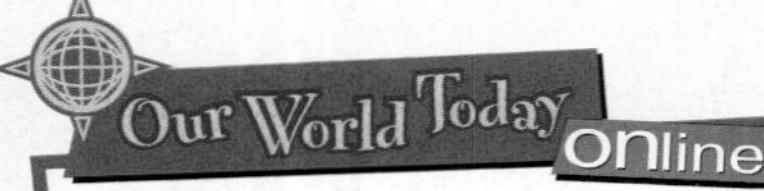

Objectives, goals, and answers to the Student Web Activity can be found in the Web Activity Lesson Plan at **owt.glencoe.com**

Reading Check Answer

to get materials and products they needed

Reading Essentials and Study Guide 3–1

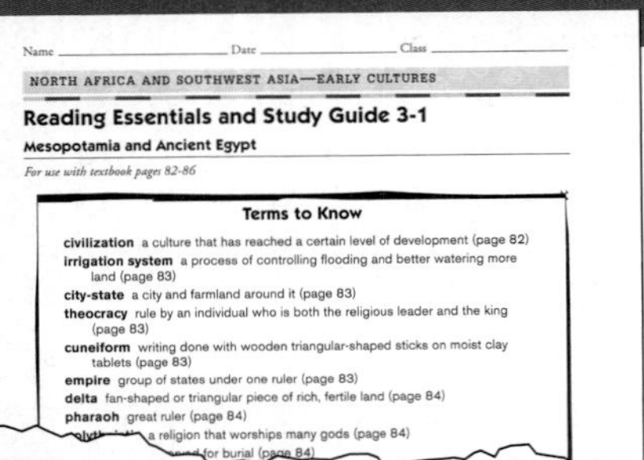
Name ____ Date ____ Class ____

NORTH AFRICA AND SOUTHWEST ASIA—EARLY CULTURES

Reading Essentials and Study Guide 3-1

Mesopotamia and Ancient Egypt

For use with textbook pages 82-86

Terms to Know

civilization a culture that has reached a certain level of development (page 82)
irrigation system a process of controlling flooding and better watering more land (page 83)
city-state a city and farmland around it (page 83)
theocracy rule by an individual who is both the religious leader and the king (page 83)
cuneiform writing done with wooden triangular-shaped sticks on moist clay tablets (page 83)
empire group of states under one ruler (page 83)
delta fan-shaped or triangular piece of rich, fertile land (page 84)
pharaoh great ruler (page 84)
a religion that worships many gods (page 84)
for burial (page 84)

CLOSE

Have students create a bulletin board display about ancient Egypt with images and captions that highlight important features of the country and its people.

Web Activity Visit the ***Our World Today: People, Places, and Issues*** Web site at owt.glencoe.com and click on **Chapter 3–Student Web Activities** to learn more about the Phoenicians.

written three times—in hieroglyphics, a more modern Egyptian language called Demotic, and Greek. Since both the Demotic and Greek could be read, scientists in 1820 were finally able to put meanings to the symbols used in hieroglyphics.

Trade and Conquest Egypt conquered many lands during its long history. It expanded as far as Mesopotamia in the north and southward to the present-day **Sudan.** Egypt also suffered defeats. In 1750 B.C. invaders from Asia, the **Hyksos** or "shepherd kings," conquered Egypt. They ruled for about 150 years until they were overthrown. They left behind various technologies, including horse-drawn chariots. Even then, people and nations that could use technology were able to dominate, or control, other cultures.

Egypt's trade routes stretched far and wide. Egypt sought more gold and gems in the African kingdom of Kush, also near present-day Sudan. The first woman pharaoh, **Hatsheptsut,** sent a trading expedition even farther south to Punt (in present-day **Uganda**) to trade for hard woods, incense, ivory, and other products. To the north, Egypt traded across the eastern Mediterranean with the Phoenicians and the Greeks. Along with trade goods, the Egyptians spread ideas and accomplishments. Egypt, like all great empires of the past, grew weak and was eventually conquered by even greater empires—the Greeks and the Romans.

Reading Check **Why was trade important to the ancient Egyptians?**

Section 1 Assessment

Defining Terms

1. **Define** civilization, irrigation system, city-state, theocracy, cuneiform, empire, delta, pharaoh, polytheistic, embalm, pyramid, hieroglyphics, papyrus, scribe.

Recalling Facts

2. **History** Where was the first civilization, and what was the region called then and now?
3. **History** What were the two early forms of writing, and where did they develop?
4. **Economics** Why were the Phoenicians so important to trade and spreading culture?

Critical Thinking

5. **Understanding Cause and Effect** How did the advancements in early farming methods in the Fertile Crescent lead to increased population growth?

Graphic Organizer

6. **Organizing Information** On a separate sheet of paper, create a diagram like this one. In the outer ovals write the three languages or writing systems that are found on the Rosetta Stone. Next, write what you know about each.

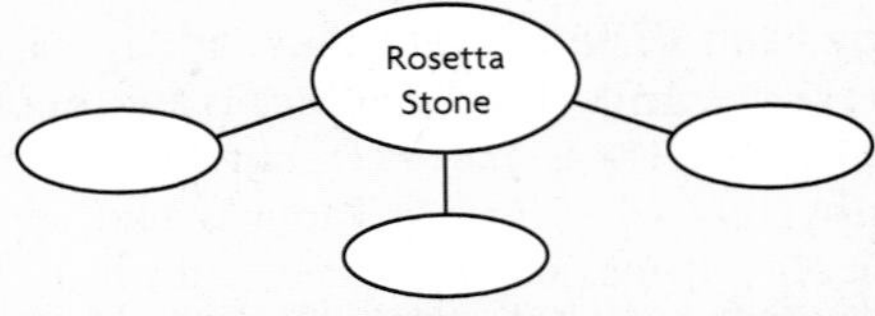

Applying Social Studies Skills

7. **Analyzing Maps** Look at the map on page 83. What do the locations of the towns have in common?

Section 1 Assessment

1. The terms are defined in the Glossary.
2. between the Tigris and Euphrates Rivers; Mesopotamia, Syria
3. cuneiform and hieroglyphics; in Sumer and Egypt, respectively
4. They sailed as far as southern Europe and around the southern tip of Africa and developed an alphabet that gave rise to the Hebrew, Greek, and Latin alphabets that are still used today.
5. *Possible answer:* Improved farming produced new and more reliable crops that could support more people.
6. hieroglyphics of ancient Egypt, Demotic from a later period of Egypt, and Greek
7. They are located along bodies of water.

Making Connections

CULTURE | GOVERNMENT | PEOPLE | TECHNOLOGY

The Egyptian Pyramids

The ancient Egyptians viewed the pharaoh, or king, as the most important person on the earth. They believed he was a god who would continue to guide them after his death. A pyramid served as a tomb for the pharaoh and provided a place where the body would safely pass into the afterlife. Rooms inside the pyramid held food, clothing, weapons, furniture, jewels, and everything else the pharaoh might need in the afterlife.

The Great Pyramid at El Giza

The largest of Egypt's pyramids is the Great Pyramid of Khufu, built nearly 4,500 years ago. When the pyramid was new, it stood 481 feet (147 m) high—as tall as a 50-story building. The square base of the pyramid covers 13 acres (5 ha). More than 2 million limestone and granite blocks were used in building it. These are no ordinary-sized blocks, however. The huge stones weigh an average of 2.5 tons (2.3 t) each.

Construction

For thousands of years, people have wondered how the Egyptians built the pyramids without modern tools or machinery. In 500 B.C., a Greek historian thought it took 100,000 people to build the Great Pyramid. Today archaeologists believe a workforce of about 20,000 did the job in about 20 years. Barges carried supplies and building materials for the pyramid down the Nile River. Nearby quarries supplied most of the stone. Skilled stonecutters carved the stones into the precise size and shape so that no mortar, or cementing material, was needed to hold the stones together.

Engineers think that workers built ramps and used papyrus twine to drag the huge stones to the pyramid. They formed ramps up all four sides of the pyramid and made the ramps higher and longer as the pyramid rose. They then dragged the stones up the ramps. Once finished, the ramps were cleared away. Then stonemasons smoothed and polished the stone, and the finished pyramid towered over the surrounding desert.

Making the Connection

1. Why did the Egyptians build the pyramids?
2. How many workers did both ancient historians and modern archaeologists think it took to build the Great Pyramid?
3. **Sequencing Information** Describe the process experts think Egyptians used to build the pyramids.

◀ The Great Pyramid at El Giza, Egypt

Making the Connection

1. to provide a tomb for the pharaoh and a safe place for the pharaoh to pass into the afterlife
2. In 500 B.C., Greeks thought it took 100,000 people to build the Great Pyramid. Now experts think it took about 20,000.
3. Workers cut stones from nearby quarries, carved them into shape, and pulled them up ramps to the pyramid site. Builders extended the ramps up the sides of the pyramid to carry rocks to the top. After they reached the top, the ramps were cleared away. Stonemasons smoothed and polished the stones.

Making Connections

TEACH

Have students suggest modern ways that important people are honored. *(by building structures like the Washington Monument; by naming structures for a person; by making a statue)* Explain that pyramids were built to honor the pharaohs, or rulers of ancient Egypt. **L1**

More About the Great Pyramid

To underscore the immense size of the Great Pyramid, give students the following height comparisons:

305 feet (93 m) Statue of Liberty

320 ft (98 m) Big Ben

555 ft (169 m) Washington Monument

Interdisciplinary Connections

Mathematics The pyramids show the mathematical skill of the ancient Egyptians. The four sides of the Great Pyramid measure, in feet, 755.43, 756.08, 755.88, and 755.77. Have students calculate the amount of deviation in the four sides. *(756.08 – 755.43, or 0.65 feet—less than 8 inches)* **L1**

Chapter 3

Section 2, pages 88–93

1 Focus

Section Objectives

1. Describe the world's three largest monotheistic religions.
2. Explain similarities and differences among Judaism, Christianity, and Islam.

BELLRINGER Skillbuilder Activity

Project transparency and have students answer questions.

This activity is also available as a blackline master.

Daily Focus Skills Transparency 3-2

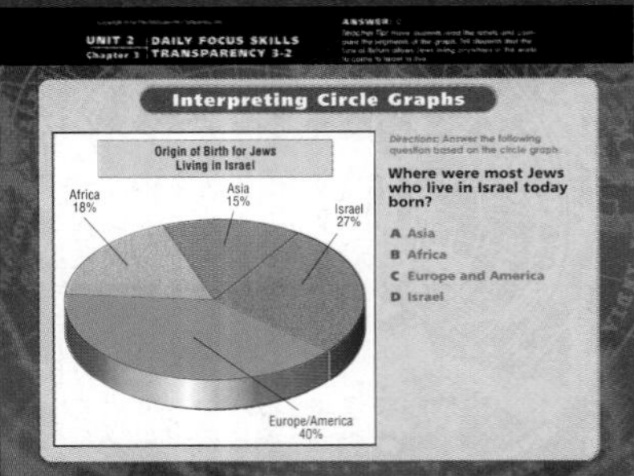

Guide to Reading

■ **Accessing Prior Knowledge**
Ask: Have you ever heard the phrase "Holy Land"? To what place does it refer? *(Israel, which is holy to Jews, Christians, and Muslims)* Point out that in this section students will learn more about the main religions of the Holy Land.

■ **Vocabulary Precheck**
Inform students that *mono* is Greek for *one* and *theism* is from *theos* which is the Greek word for *god.*

Section 2: Religions of the Middle East

Guide to Reading

Main Idea

Three of the world's monotheistic religions—Judaism, Christianity, and Islam—all developed in Southwest Asia.

Terms to Know

- monotheism
- Diaspora
- scapegoat
- messiah
- disciple
- minister
- Crusades
- five pillars of faith
- hajj

Reading Strategy

Create and complete a chart like this one. List important beliefs of each religion.

Religion	Beliefs
Judaism	
Christianity	
Islam	

NATIONAL GEOGRAPHIC Exploring Our World

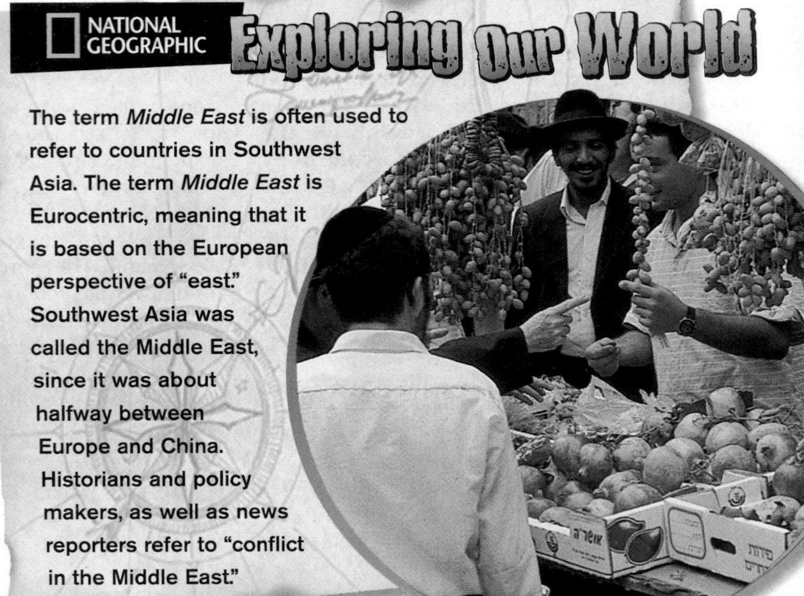

The term *Middle East* is often used to refer to countries in Southwest Asia. The term *Middle East* is Eurocentric, meaning that it is based on the European perspective of "east." Southwest Asia was called the Middle East, since it was about halfway between Europe and China. Historians and policy makers, as well as news reporters refer to "conflict in the Middle East."

Today, Judaism, Christianity, and Islam have become major world faiths. All three religions are examples of **monotheism,** or the belief in one supreme god. All three look to the ancient city of **Jerusalem** as a holy site.

Judaism

Judaism is the oldest of these three world religions. It was first practiced by a small group of people from Mesopotamia called the Hebrews. The followers of Judaism today are known as Jews. We know about the early history of the Jewish people and their religion from their holy book—the **Torah.**

According to Jewish belief, the Hebrew people are descended from Abraham and Sarah, who first worshipped the one God, or Yahweh. The Jews believe that they are God's chosen people and will remain so for as long as they follow God's laws. The most well-known of these laws

Section Resources

Reproducible Masters

- Reproducible Lesson Plan 3-2
- Daily Lecture and Discussion Notes 3-2
- Guided Reading Activity 3-2
- Reading Essentials and Study Guide 3-2
- Section Quiz 3-2

Transparencies

- Daily Focus Skills Transparency 3-2

Multimedia

- Vocabulary PuzzleMaker Software
- Interactive Tutor Self-Assessment CD-ROM
- Presentation Plus! CD-ROM
- ExamView® Pro 3.0 Testmaker CD-ROM

were revealed by the prophet **Moses** and are known as the **Ten Commandments.** The five books of Moses, along with the books of laws and teachings, make up the complete Torah.

Israel became an important and prosperous state under its first three kings—Saul, David, and Solomon. David made the city of Jerusalem Israel's capital in about 1000 B.C. After Solomon's death, the kingdom split in two. Thereafter, the Jews would be conquered and exiled many times.

Eventually, the Jewish people spread to countries in many parts of the world. This scattering of the Jews outside of the Holy Land was called the **Diaspora.** For many hundreds of years, Jews have lived and worked as citizens of different countries. Jewish scholars, writers, artists, and scientists have greatly increased the world's knowledge.

Because they have followed their own religion and customs, however, Jews have sometimes been viewed with suspicion and hatred. Some governments have used Jewish communities as a **scapegoat,** or someone to blame for their troubles. Property belonging to Jewish people has been seized and their lives threatened. More than 6 million Jews were murdered in Europe during the **Holocaust** in the 1940s.

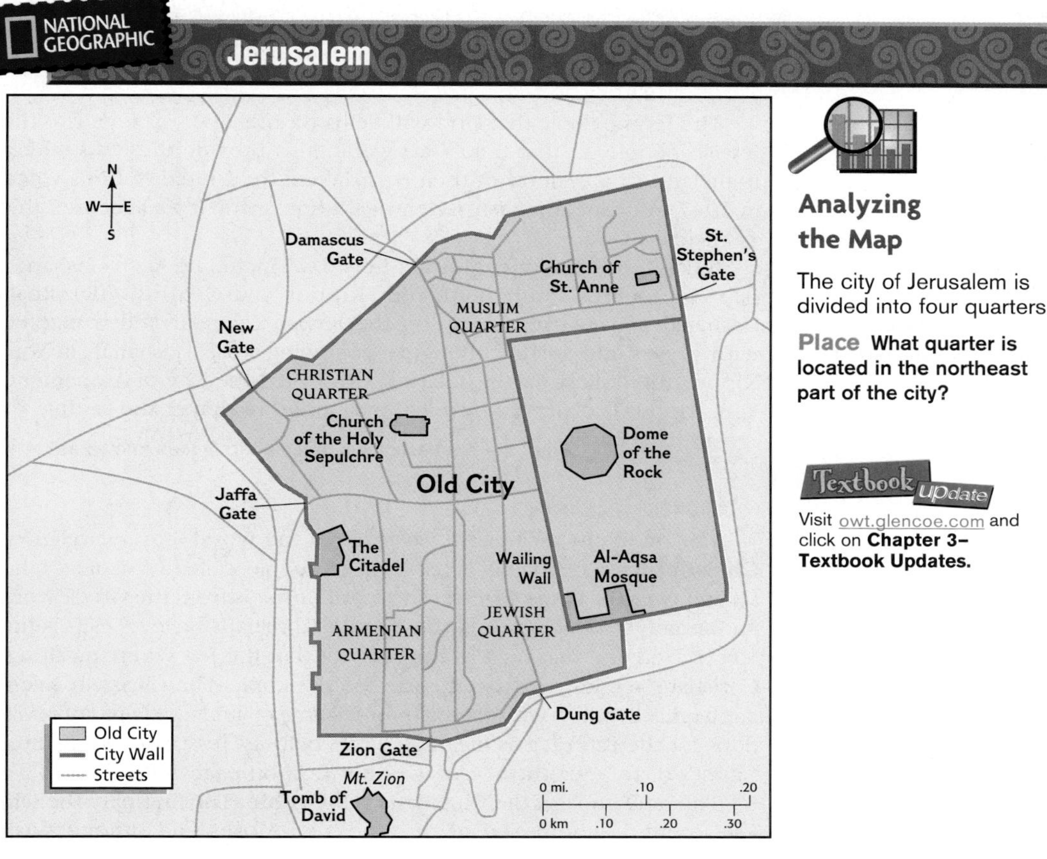

Analyzing the Map

The city of Jerusalem is divided into four quarters.

Place **What quarter is located in the northeast part of the city?**

Textbook update

Visit owt.glencoe.com and click on **Chapter 3–Textbook Updates.**

Chapter 3

Section 2, pages 88–93

TEACH

Categorizing Information

Have students create a four-column chart with the names of the three religions in this section across columns 2, 3, and 4. In the first column, have them list the row's labels: "prophet," "holy book," and "holy days." Then have them fill in the information as they read the section.

Daily Lecture Notes 3-2

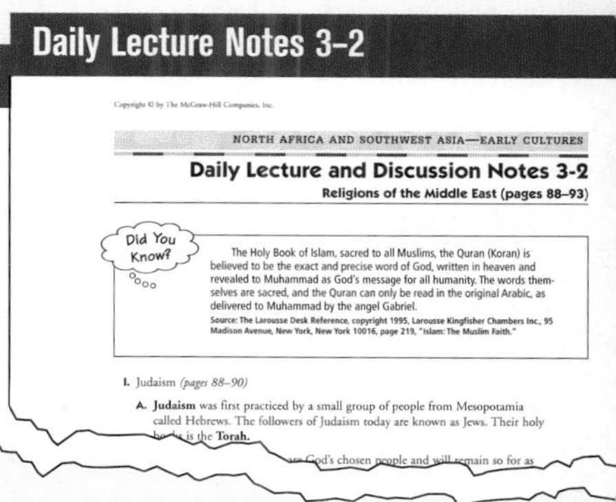

NORTH AFRICA AND SOUTHWEST ASIA—EARLY CULTURES

Daily Lecture and Discussion Notes 3-2

Religions of the Middle East (pages 88–93)

Did You Know?

The Holy Book of Islam, sacred to all Muslims, the Quran (Koran) is believed to be the exact and precise word of God, written in heaven and revealed to Muhammad as God's message for all humanity. The words themselves are sacred, and the Quran can only be read in the original Arabic, as delivered to Muhammad by the angel Gabriel.

I. Judaism (pages 88–90)

A. Judaism was first practiced by a small group of people from Mesopotamia called Hebrews. The followers of Judaism today are known as Jews. Their holy book is the Torah.

Analyzing the Map

Answer
Muslim

Skills Practice
What important religious site is outside of the Old City? *(Tomb of David)*

Team-Teaching Activity

History The site of the city of Jerusalem has been occupied for more than 4,000 years. During that time it has had many rulers, has been destroyed and rebuilt several times, and has become an important center for three major religions. Invite a teacher to class who can describe some of the major events in the history of Jerusalem. Then have students create a time line of key events that led to the importance of the city for the three religions.

EE2 Places and Regions: Standard 4

More About the Photos

Prayer and worship are important practices in the three major monotheistic religions. But they also include laws and moral values for our everyday lives. These practices encourage study of the sacred texts and performing service to others. Ask students to discuss the relationship among religious ideas, philosophical ideas, and cultures.

Caption Answer All are monotheistic and all regard Jerusalem as a holy site.

Reading Check Answer

the Ten Commandments

Did You Know?

Noah's Ark supposedly settled on Mount Ararat, which was once within the borders of Armenia, although it now lies in Turkey. According to legend, Armenians were among the first people in the world to appear after the Great Flood.

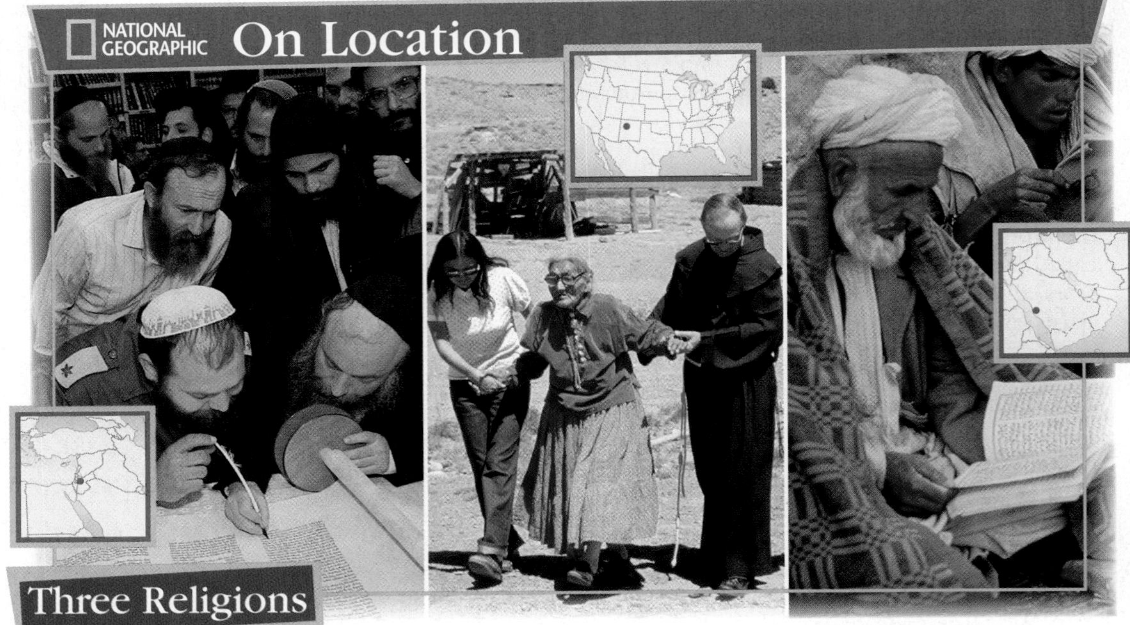

Three Religions

Jewish scholars examine Torah scrolls (left). A Christian missionary priest ministers to a Native American family (center). Muslims study the Quran (right).

Religion **What do all three religions have in common?**

The Jews believe that God will deliver a **messiah,** or savior, to the Jewish people. At that time, God would also provide the Jews with a homeland, or a country of their own. When the United Nations voted in 1947 to create a Jewish state in Palestine, many Jews accepted this as an act of God.

Judaism has several important holy days, including Rosh Hashanah (RAHSH huh•SHAH•nuh) and Yom Kippur (YAHM kih•POOR). Rosh Hashanah is New Year's Day on the Jewish calendar and is marked with prayer and solemn thoughts. Following Rosh Hashanah is Yom Kippur, the holiest day in Judaism. Also called the Day of Atonement, Yom Kippur is observed by a 24-hour period of prayer and fasting.

Reading Check **What are the basic laws revealed to Moses known as?**

Christianity

The traditions of Judaism gave rise to the world's largest religion, **Christianity.** Christianity is made up of people, called Christians, who are followers of **Jesus Christ.** The word *Christ* is from the Greek word for "anointed," which means chosen one. Christians believe Jesus is the Son of God and that he was the Messiah that the Jews were awaiting. Christians see Jesus as the Messiah for all people. The Christian calendar begins in A.D. 1 with the birth of Jesus. "B.C." and "A.D." are abbreviations for the Latin terms meaning "years before Christ" and "years after Christ's birth." (See the **Social Studies Skill** on page 240.)

The holy book of the Christians is the **Bible.** The first part, the Old Testament, is composed of the books of Moses and other Jewish

Meeting Special Needs

Interpersonal Point out that the problems between Israel and the Palestinian Arabs stretch back over many years. Mention that several presidents and other top-ranking officials of the United States have tried to mediate between the two sides to reach a solution. Some schools have peer mediation programs. If that is the case in your school, invite a peer counselor to class to describe what mediation is and how it works. If not, describe the process yourself. After the presentation, have students write a paragraph summarizing how mediation might be applied to the Israeli-Palestinian conflict. **L2**

Refer to *Inclusion for the Middle School Social Studies Classroom Strategies and Activities* in the TCR.

writers. It contains the history and traditions of Judaism that led up to the birth of Jesus. The second part, the New Testament, deals with the birth, the life, and the teachings of Jesus as recorded by his followers, called **disciples.** Christians believe that after Jesus was killed, he rose from the dead, thereby proving the existence of an afterlife with God for all who truly believe.

The disciples spread Jesus' teachings across the Roman world and beyond. However, until about A.D. 300, Christians were persecuted in the Roman Empire. Then the emperor **Constantine the Great** ordered that Christianity become the religion of the state. At this point, Christians were no longer persecuted.

The spread of Christianity was achieved primarily through the work of individuals and missions. The teachings of Jesus were carried to far parts of the globe by missionaries who built churches, schools, and hospitals to **minister** to, or take care of, new Christians. Europe—especially Rome and Constantinople—became the center of Christianity. For hundreds of years, the Christian church shared power with the rulers of many of the nations of Europe. The most famous universities of Europe

Primary Source

COMPARING SCRIPTURE

Although there are many differences between the world's major religions, there are also many similarities. These quotes from Judaism, Christianity, and Islam illustrate the belief in good deeds.

When the holy one loves a man, He sends him a present in the shape of a poor man, so that he should perform some good deed to him, through the merit of which he may draw a cord of grace. **The Torah; Genesis 104a**

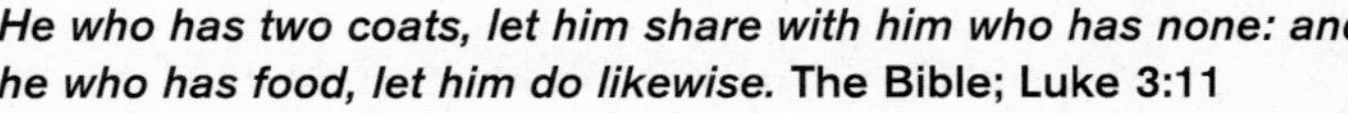

He who has two coats, let him share with him who has none: and he who has food, let him do likewise. **The Bible; Luke 3:11**

Every person's every joint must perform a charity every day the sun comes up: to act justly between two people is a charity. . . . a good word is a charity; every step you take in prayers is a charity; and removing a harmful thing from the road is a charity. **Saying of the Prophet Muhammad**

Analyzing Primary Sources

All three religions share the message of helping others. Why do you suppose there has been such conflict among them?

Critical Thinking Activity

Identifying Main Ideas Have students copy the subheads in this section onto a piece of paper. Tell them to leave ample space beneath each heading to write in additional information. After their outline is copied down, have them read the section and write the main idea under the appropriate heading. After students have completed their exercise, ask for volunteers to read their main ideas aloud. As a class, discuss the different suggestions. **L1**

EE1 The World in Spatial Terms: Standard 1

Chapter 3

Section 2, pages 88–93

Guided Reading Activity 3-2

Name ______ Date ______ Class ______

NORTH AFRICA AND SOUTHWEST ASIA—EARLY CULTURES

Guided Reading Activity 3-2

Religions of the Middle East

DIRECTIONS: Answering Questions Reading the section and answering the questions below will help you learn more about the religions of the Middle East. Use your textbook to write answers to the questions.

1. What do the religions of Judaism, Christianity, and Islam have in common?
2. What items make up the complete Torah, the holy book of the Jews?
3. What are some beliefs of Judaism?

Primary Source

Answer This question should prompt some lively discussion about why religion is seen as a source of conflict.

Activity The Golden Rule of the ethic of reciprocity is found in the scriptures of nearly every religion. It is often regarded as the most concise and general principle of ethics. Basically it states that each person should treat others as they would themselves like to be treated. Ask students to discuss which principles they live by regarding their treatment of others.

3 ASSESS

Assign Section 2 Assessment as homework or an in-class activity.

Have students use the Interactive Tutor Self-Assessment CD-ROM to review Section 3–2.

Chapter 3

Section 2, pages 88–93

Applying Map Skills

Answers

1. 632–661

2. No

Skills Practice

Where did Islam begin?

(in Arabia)

Section Quiz 3-2

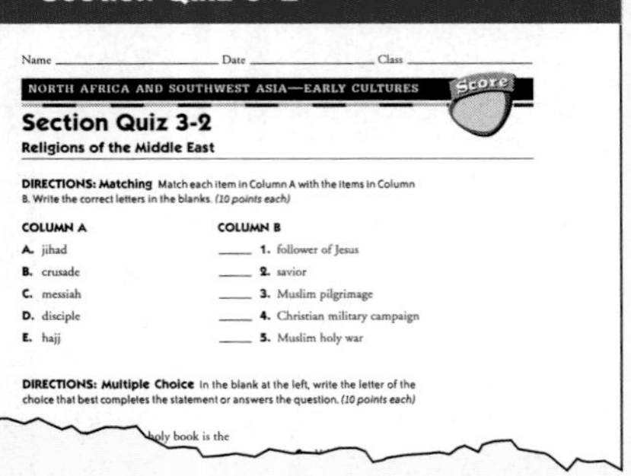

Name ______________ Date ______________ Class ______________

NORTH AFRICA AND SOUTHWEST ASIA—EARLY CULTURES

Section Quiz 3-2

Religions of the Middle East

DIRECTIONS: Matching Match each item in Column A with the items in Column B. Write the correct letters in the blanks. *(10 points each)*

COLUMN A	COLUMN B
A. jihad	____ 1. follower of Jesus
B. crusade	____ 2. savior
C. messiah	____ 3. Muslim pilgrimage
D. disciple	____ 4. Christian military campaign
E. hajj	____ 5. Muslim holy war

DIRECTIONS: Multiple Choice In the blank at the left, write the letter of the choice that best completes the statement or answers the question. *(10 points each)*

...holy book is the

Reading Check Answer

He made Christianity the official religion of Rome.

More About the Quran

For Christians, the Bible is Holy Scripture no matter what language it is written in. For Muslims, the divine Word assumed a specific, Arabic form, and that form is as essential as the meaning that the words convey. Hence only the Arabic Quran is the Quran, and translations are simply interpretations.

NATIONAL GEOGRAPHIC

Spread of Islam

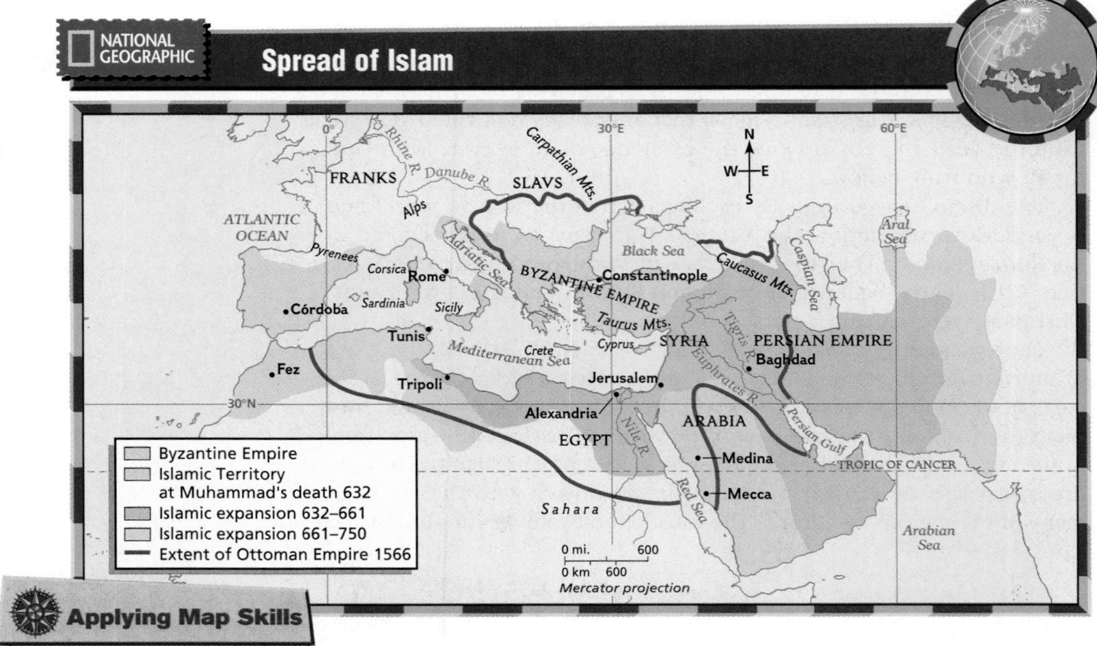

Applying Map Skills

1. Which Islamic expansion included Egypt?
2. Did Islamic territory completely encircle the Mediterranean Sea?

Find NGS online resources @ www.nationalgeographic.com/maps

were begun by Christian scholars. Catholic popes and kings organized military campaigns, called the **Crusades,** to capture the city of Jerusalem. Today, Christians of many denominations look to Jerusalem as a holy city where important churches and shrines are located.

Christians around the world mark important events in the life of Jesus. Christmas celebrates Jesus' birth. Most Christians celebrate Palm Sunday, the occasion when Jesus entered Jerusalem in triumph, and Good Friday, the day of Jesus' crucifixion, or death on a cross. Easter, believed to be the day that God raised Jesus from the dead, is the most important day of the Christian calendar.

Reading Check **Why was Constantine important to spreading Christianity?**

Islam

Jewish and Christian traditions are important to the world's second-largest religion, **Islam.** In the Arabic language, the word *Islam* means "to submit" to the will of God, or Allah. The followers of Islam are called Muslims, or Moslems.

Muslims believe that **Muhammad** is the last and greatest prophet of Allah. The Muslim holy book, the **Quran** (Koran), contains his teachings. Muhammad stressed that it was also important to respect the Torah and the Bible. Jerusalem is important to the Muslims because they believe Muhammad ascended to Allah from there in A.D. 632.

The Quran describes the **five pillars of faith,** or the five obligations all Muslims must fulfill. The first duty is to state your belief in the faith: "There is no god but God, and Muhammad is his messenger." Second, Muslims must pray five times a day, facing the holy city of

Critical Thinking Activity

Religion and Conflict Religion has been a source of conflict in the Middle East for centuries. In the United States, however, many different religions coexist without conflict. Ask students what is different between the Middle East and the United States that allows religions in the United States to exist without conflict. The discussion will vary but students should realize that a major difference is the separation of church and state. In the United States, the government has no control over its citizens' beliefs or type of worship.

Makkah (Mecca). The third obligation is to give to charity. The fourth is to fast, which means not eating or drinking anything from dawn to sunset, during the lunar holy month of Ramadan. Only the young, sick people, pregnant women, and travelers do not have to fast. The last pillar of faith is a pilgrimage, called the **hajj.** Once in each Muslim's life, he or she must, if able, journey to Makkah to pray. The reward for fulfilling all these religious duties is paradise.

The Muslim calendar begins in A.D. 622, the year of the *Hijrah,* when Muhammad was forced to flee for safety from Makkah to Madinah. Muslim dates are written with an "A.H." to signify the years after the *Hijrah.*

Since the time of Muhammad, the Islamic faith has spread widely. In the A.D. 700s, victorious Muslim armies expanded the Muslim empire. Soldiers believed that to die for the faith is to go to Heaven, but Islam restricted just warfare, called *jihad*. Muslims learned from those they conquered. Muslim knowledge in art and architecture, mathematics, medicine, astronomy, geography, history, and other fields was greatly increased.

As mentioned before, Ramadan is a very important holiday on the Muslim calendar. This is the month, according to Muslim beliefs, in which God began to reveal the Quran to Muhammad. Muslims observe Ramadan by fasting from dawn to sunset and refraining from any acts that take their attention away from God.

✓ Reading Check **What is the Islamic pilgrimage known as?**

Section 2 Assessment

Defining Terms

1. **Define** monotheism, Diaspora, scapegoat, messiah, disciple, minister, Crusades, five pillars of faith, hajj.

Recalling Facts

2. **Religion** What are the world's three largest monotheistic religions?
3. **History** Why do historians refer to this area as the Middle East instead of Southwest Asia?
4. **History** Which city in Israel do the three religions look to as a holy site?

Critical Thinking

5. **Making Inferences** Look at the map on page 92. What might be one explanation for Islam not spreading from Spain to France?

Graphic Organizer

6. **Organizing Information** Create a chart like the one below and write key terms to summarize the quotes in the **Primary Source** on page 91.

Key Terms

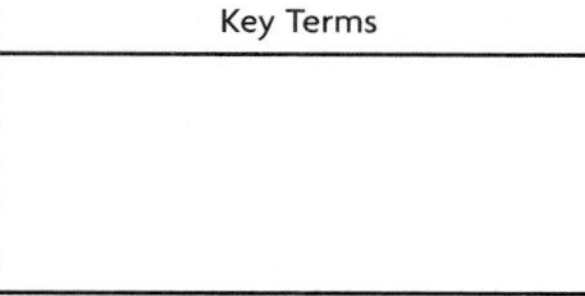

Applying Social Studies Skills

7. **Analyzing Diagrams** Examine the diagram of Jerusalem on page 89. Explain how the city has been divided.

Chapter 3

Section 2, pages 88–93

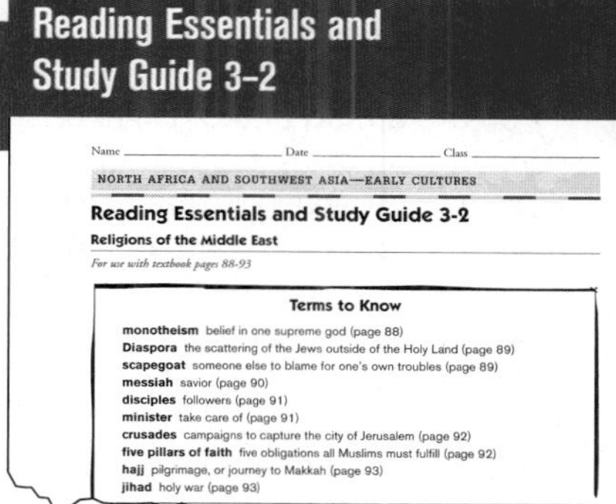
Reading Essentials and Study Guide 3-2

Name ______ Date ______ Class ______

NORTH AFRICA AND SOUTHWEST ASIA—EARLY CULTURES

Reading Essentials and Study Guide 3-2

Religions of the Middle East

For use with textbook pages 88-93

Terms to Know

monotheism belief in one supreme god (page 88)
Diaspora the scattering of the Jews outside of the Holy Land (page 89)
scapegoat someone else to blame for one's own troubles (page 89)
messiah savior (page 90)
disciples followers (page 91)
minister take care of (page 91)
crusades campaigns to capture the city of Jerusalem (page 92)
five pillars of faith five obligations all Muslims must fulfill (page 92)
hajj pilgrimage, or journey to Makkah (page 93)
jihad holy war (page 93)

✓ Reading Check Answer

the hajj

Reteach

Ask students to write one paragraph for each of the religions, summarizing the basic beliefs.

4 Close

Have students create a bulletin board display about the major religious holidays and observances for the different world religions. Ask them to use images and captions to explain the significance of these celebrations in selected contemporary societies. At a minimum, they should mention the major holidays of the three monotheistic religions discussed in this chapter.

Section 2 Assessment

1. The terms are defined in the Glossary.
2. Judaism, Christianity, and Islam
3. From a European perspective it is about halfway between Europe and China
4. Jerusalem
5. the Pyrenees mountains
6. Key terms may include *love, share, charity,* or *prayer.*
7. It has been divided according to religion.

TEACH

Create a map of the neighborhood around the school. Mark street names and include a number of local landmarks, such as the school, a park, and the library. Ask students to describe the locations of the various landmarks by using street names. Suggest that students use the street intersection nearest each landmark. Ask students to share their answers with the class. Point out that identifying locations by using lines of latitude and longitude follows the same principle. Have students read the skill and complete the questions. **L1**

Additional Skills Practice

1. **What is the other name that is used for lines of longitude?** *(meridians)* **For lines of latitude?** *(parallels)*
2. **What city on the map lies almost on the Equator?** *(Singapore)* **On the Prime Meridian (Meridian of Greenwich)?** *(London)*

Additional Skills Resources

 Chapter Skills Activity 3

 Building Geography Skills for Life

GLENCOE TECHNOLOGY

 **Skillbuilder Interactive Workbook CD-ROM, Level 1**

This interactive CD-ROM reinforces student mastery of essential social studies skills.

Social Studies Skill

Using Latitude and Longitude

Learning the Skill

To find an exact location, geographers use a set of imaginary lines. One set of lines—latitude lines—circles the earth's surface east to west. The starting point for numbering latitude lines is the Equator, which is 0° latitude. Every other line of latitude is numbered from 1° to 90° and is followed by an N or S to show whether it is north or south of the Equator. Latitude lines are also called parallels.

A second set of lines—longitude lines—runs vertically from the North Pole to the South Pole. Each of these lines is also called a meridian. The starting point—0° longitude—is called the Prime Meridian (or Meridian of Greenwich). Longitude lines are numbered from 1° to 180° followed by an E or W—to show whether they are east or west of the Prime Meridian.

To find latitude and longitude, choose a place on a map. Identify the nearest parallel, or line of latitude. Is it located north or south of the Equator? Now identify the nearest meridian, or line of longitude. Is it located east or west of the Prime Meridian?

Practicing the Skill

1. On the map below, what is the exact location of Washington, D.C.?
2. What cities on the map lie south of 0° latitude?
3. What city is located near 30°N, 30°E?

Applying the Skill

Turn to page RA2 of the **Reference Atlas.** Determine the latitude and longitude for one city. Ask a classmate to use the information to find and name the city.

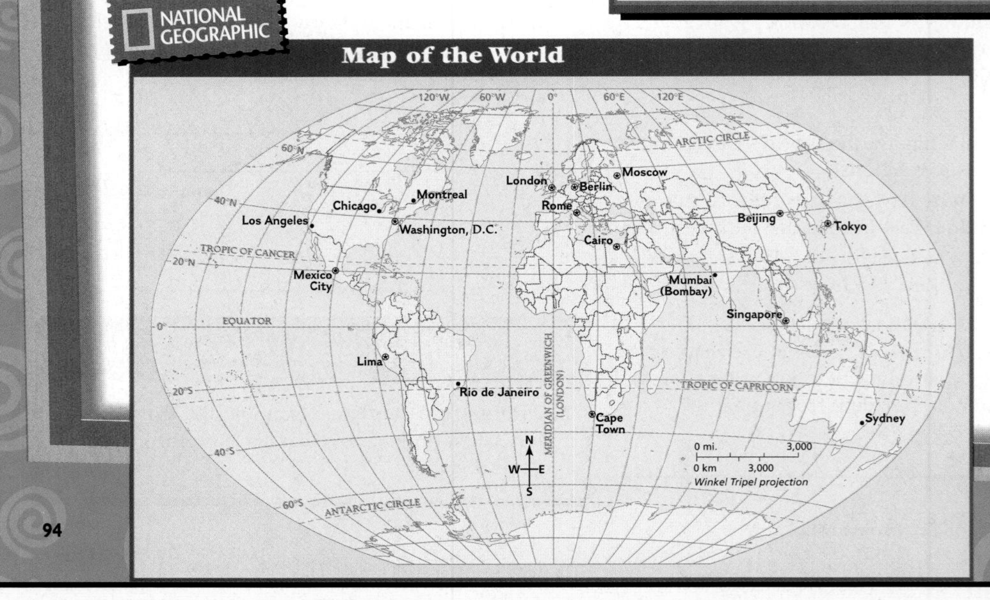

Practicing the Skill Answers

1. about 40°N, 80°W
2. Lima, Rio de Janeiro, Cape Town, Sydney
3. Cairo

Applying the Skill
Monitor students as they carry out the activity.

Chapter 3 Reading Review

Section 1 Mesopotamia and Ancient Egypt

Terms to Know

civilization, irrigation system, city-state, theocracy, cuneiform, empire, delta, pharaoh, polytheistic, embalm, pyramid, hieroglyphics, papyrus, scribe

Main Idea

Learning about how past cultures lived helps us better understand our own cultures.

✓History One of the first civilizations developed in the Fertile Crescent.

✓History Early advancements in Mesopotamia, Sumer, and Phoenicia were in farming, writing, and government.

✓History Ancient Egypt is known for pharaohs, pyramids, hieroglyphics, and mummies.

Section 2 Religions of the Middle East

Terms to Know

monotheism, Diaspora, scapegoat, messiah, disciple, minister, Crusades, five pillars of faith, hajj

Main Idea

Three of the world's monotheistic religions—Judaism, Christianity, and Islam—all developed in Southwest Asia.

✓History Judaism is the world's oldest monotheistic religion. The Jews believe they are God's chosen people.

✓Religion Christians believe Jesus is the Messiah and the Son of God.

✓Religion The Muslims are followers of Islam. Muslims believe Allah is the one God and Muhammad is the messenger.

◄ Desert areas begin where the fertile Nile River Valley ends.

Reading Review

Use the Chapter 3 Reading Review to preview, review, condense, or reteach the chapter.

Preview/Review
Use the Terms to Know lists to help students review and study.

Activity Organize the class into teams and quiz them on the Terms to Know. Offer a definition and ask each team to identify the correct term. If they do so correctly, they win a point; if they do not, the other team has an opportunity to do so.

Vocabulary PuzzleMaker Software reinforces the vocabulary terms used in Chapter 3.

The Interactive Tutor Self-Assessment CD-ROM allows students to review Chapter 3 content.

Condense
Have students read the Chapter 3 summary statements.

Chapter 3 Guided Reading Activities

Chapter 3 Audio Program

Reteach

Reteaching Activity 3

Chapter 3 Reading Essentials and Study Guide

Chapter Culminating Activity

Past and Present Have students create a display that shows achievements and advances that occurred in this region long ago that are still influencing us today. Explain that students can present their results in different ways—as a poster, written report, oral presentation, or multimedia presentation. Whatever means they choose, they should include both technical achievements, such as irrigation, writing systems, and a calendar, and cultural achievements, such as systems of laws and religious beliefs. L2

EE6 The Uses of Geography: Standards 17 and 18

Assessment and Activities

GLENCOE TECHNOLOGY

MindJogger Videoquiz

Use MindJogger to review the Chapter 3 content.

 Available in VHS.

Using Key Terms

1.	c	6.	j
2.	g	7.	f
3.	h	8.	a
4.	d	9.	b
5.	e	10.	i

Reviewing the Main Ideas

11. *Any one:* irrigation, 12-month calendar, growing crops, the plow, cuneiform writing, a number system, clocks.
12. the Fertile Crescent
13. from southern Europe to the southern tip of Africa; by ship; used the sun and stars
14. the Hyksos
15. to preserve the body for the next life
16. they are different names for God
17. a savior
18. different holy books; different holy days; different prophets
19. Judaism: Rosh Hashanah, Yom Kippur; Christianity: Christmas, Palm Sunday, Good Friday, Easter; Islam: Ramadan

Chapter 3 Assessment and Activities

Using Key Terms

Match the terms in Part A with their definitions in Part B.

A.

1. civilization
2. theocracy
3. cuneiform
4. pharaoh
5. polytheistic
6. Diaspora
7. monotheism
8. hajj
9. disciple
10. city-state

B.

a. holy journey in Islam
b. early believer in Jesus Christ
c. culture that has reached level of development where people can specialize their skills
d. god-king of ancient Egypt
e. believing in many gods
f. belief in one God
g. ruled by religious leader who is also a king
h. ancient form of writing in Sumer
i. city and its surrounding countryside
j. scattering of the Jewish people

Reviewing Main Ideas

Section 1 Mesopotamia and Ancient Egypt

11. **History** What was one of the early advancements in ancient Mesopotamia?
12. **History** Where did the earliest city-states arise?
13. **Economics** The Phoenicians were the most important early traders of the region. How did they navigate? Where and how did they travel?
14. **History** Who were the Asians that invaded ancient Egypt?
15. **History** Why did the Egyptians embalm their dead?

Section 2 Religions of the Middle East

16. **Religion** What are the similarities between Yahweh and Allah?
17. **Religion** What is the role of the Messiah in Jewish and Christian religious belief?
18. **Religion** Judaism, Christianity, and Islam are similar in their belief of one supreme god and in viewing Jerusalem in Israel as a holy site. List some of the differences among the three religions.
19. **Religion** What are some of the important holidays in Judaism, Christianity, and Islam?

Southwest Asia

Place Location Activity

On a separate sheet of paper use unit or chapter maps to match the letters on the map with the numbered places listed below.

1. Persian Gulf
2. Zagros Mountains
3. Euphrates River
4. Turkey
5. Iran
6. Israel
7. Iraq
8. Saudi Arabia
9. Makkah
10. Jerusalem

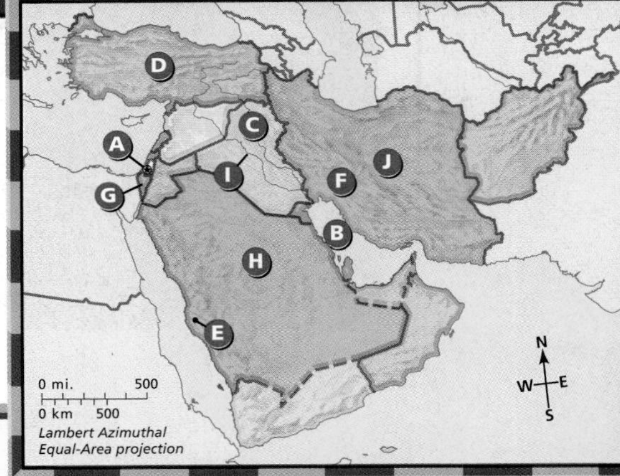

NATIONAL GEOGRAPHIC Place Location Activity

1.	B	6.	G
2.	F	7.	C
3.	I	8.	H
4.	D	9.	E
5.	J	10.	A

Critical Thinking

20. laws define a society's rules of conduct and allow a king to enforce those rules
21. Judaism: Torah
Christianity: Bible
Islam: Quran

Self-Check Quiz Visit the ***Our World Today: People, Places, and Issues*** Web site at owt.glencoe.com and click on **Chapter 3–Self-Check Quizzes** to prepare for the Chapter Test.

Critical Thinking

20. **Analyzing Information** Hammurabi wrote a code of laws to help him rule better. How would laws help a king rule?
21. **Categorizing Information** Create a chart like the one below. Complete the name of the holy book for each of the religions listed.

Religion	Holy Book
Judaism	
Christianity	
Islam	

Currents Events Journal

22. **Summarizing Information** Look through one of the weekly newsmagazines in your library or at home for information on the Middle East. Summarize the article for your journal.

Mental Mapping Activity

23. **Focusing on the Region** Create a simple outline map of Egypt and the Middle East. Draw in the Nile, Tigris, and Euphrates Rivers. Shade the areas where the early civilizations of ancient Egypt and Mesopotamia were located. Locate the cities of Tyre, Nineveh, Babylon, and Ur on your map.

Technology Skills Activity

24. **Using the Internet** Search the Internet and find several newspapers that publish online. Use at least three different sources to research recent discoveries about any ancient cultures in this region. Use the computer to create a report on this topic. You may want to include visual materials for display.

Standardized Test Practice

Directions: Study the map below, and then answer the question that follows.

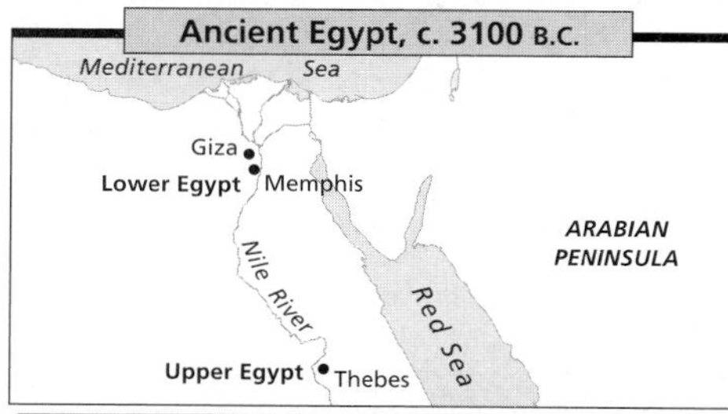

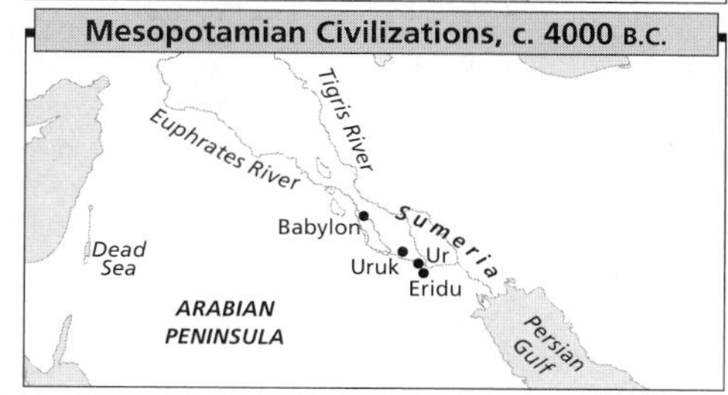

1. **What characteristic did the first Egyptian and Mesopotamian civilizations share?**
   - **A** They were established in the same year.
   - **B** Both civilizations began in North Africa.
   - **C** They both developed on the banks of rivers.
   - **D** People in both civilizations relied on hunting to obtain food.

Test-Taking Tip: When you answer a map question, do *not* rely on your memory of the map. Instead, check each answer choice against the information on the map and get rid of answer choices that are incorrect. Eliminating even one wrong choice will help you locate the correct answer.

Assessment and Activities

Standardized Test Practice

1. C

Tested Objectives:
Analyzing a map, drawing conclusions

Chapter Test Bonus Question

This question may be used for extra credit on the chapter test.

Who developed the numbering system from which we borrowed the 60-minute hour and 60-second minute? *(the Babylonians)*

Our World Today online

Have students visit the Web site at **owt.glencoe.com** to review Chapter 3 and take the Self-Check Quiz.

Current Events Journal

22. Student reports should summarize significant events or characteristics of the region.

Mental Mapping Activity

23. This exercise helps students visualize the location and relationship between the events they have been studying. All attempts at free-hand mapping should be accepted.

Technology Skills Activity

24. Students should list the three sources from the Internet that they used for their report. Their reports may include text, diagrams, timelines, and other illustrations to relate information on a recent discovery.

Chapter 4 Resources

Note: The following materials may be used when teaching Chapter 4.
Section level support materials are shown at point of use in the margins of the Teacher Wraparound Edition.

Timesaving Tools

TeacherWorks™ All-In-One Planner and Resource Center

- **Interactive Teacher Edition** See the **Interactive Teacher Edition** CD-ROM to electronically integrate your Teacher Wraparound Edition and blackline masters.
- **Interactive Lesson Planner** Organize your week, month, semester, or year with all the lesson helps you need. The **Interactive Lesson Planner** CD-ROM contains all Chapter 4 resources.

Use Glencoe's **Presentation Plus!** multimedia teacher tool to easily present dynamic lessons that visually excite your students. Using Microsoft PowerPoint® you can customize the presentations to create your own personalized lessons.

TEACHING TRANSPARENCIES

Graphic Organizer Transparency and Student Activity 4

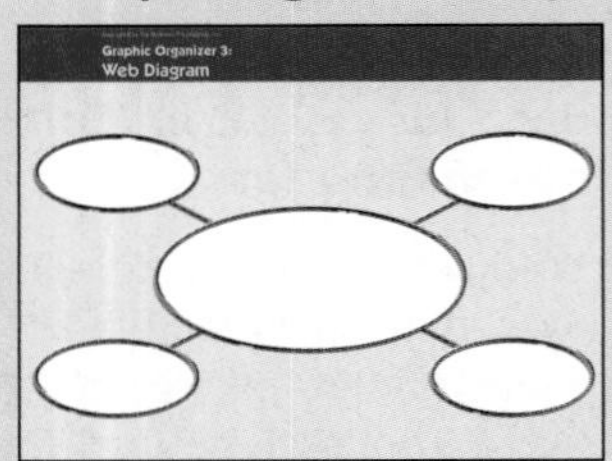

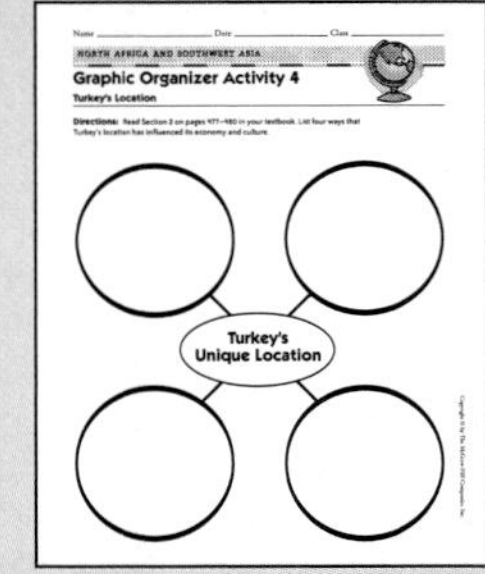

FOLDABLES™ Study Organizer

Foldables are three-dimensional, interactive graphic organizers that help students practice basic writing skills, review key vocabulary terms, and identify main ideas. Every chapter contains a Foldable activity, with additional chapter activities found in the ***Reading and Study Skills Foldables*** booklet.

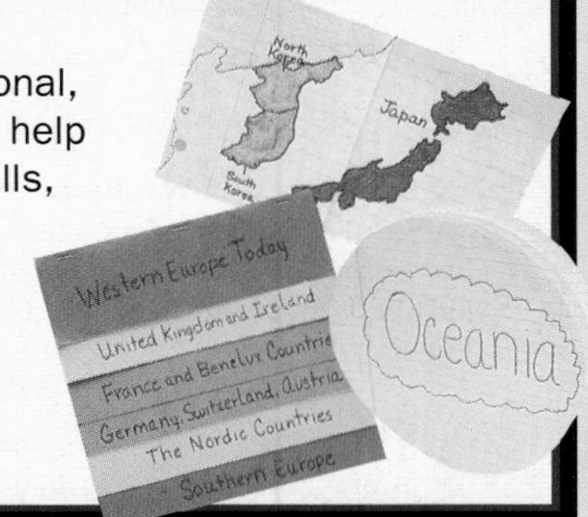

ENRICHMENT AND EXTENSION

Enrichment Activity 4

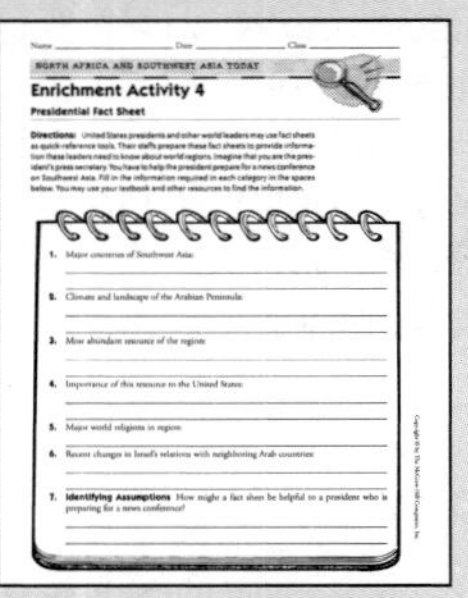

Cooperative Learning Activity 4

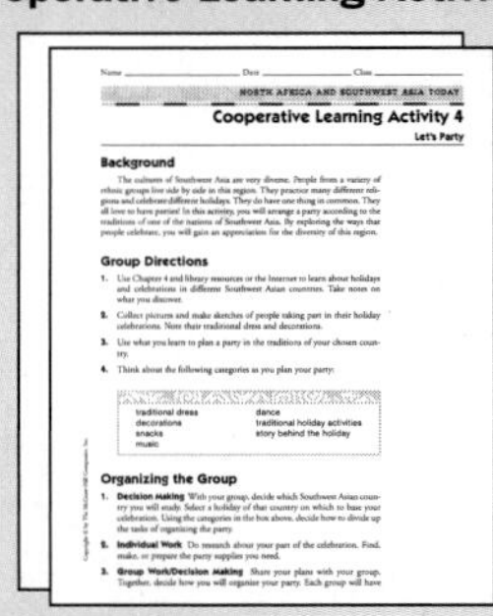

MAP AND GEOGRAPHY SKILLS

Chapter Map Activity 4

GeoLab Activity 4

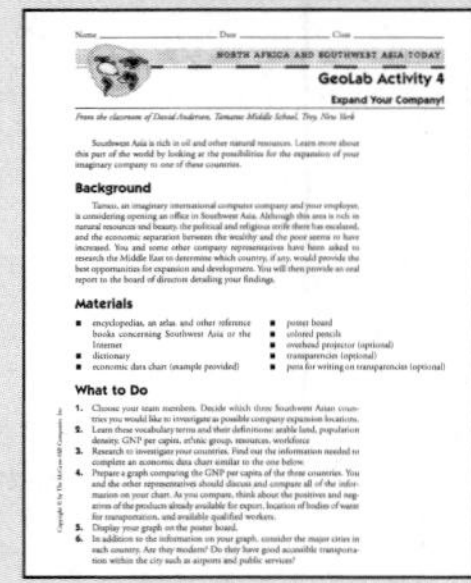

STANDARDIZED ASSESSMENT SKILLS

Glencoe's Assessment Advantage

Critical Thinking Skills Activity 4

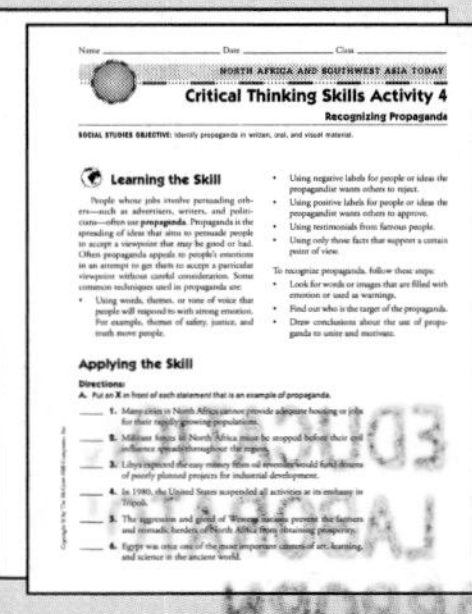

Map and Graph Skills Activity 4

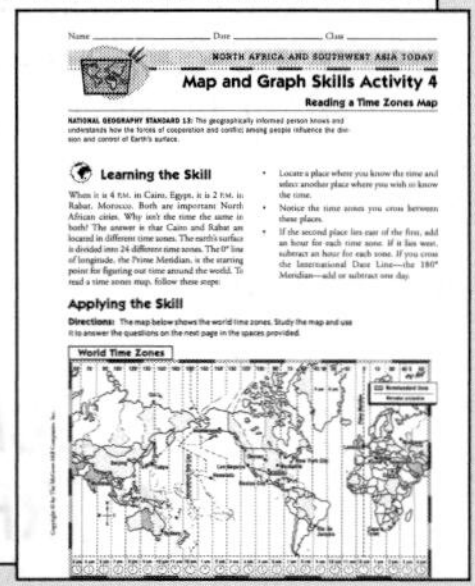

Reading and Writing Skills Activity 4

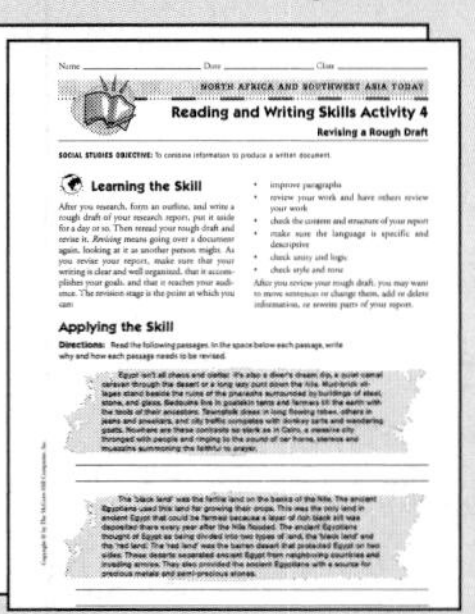

Standardized Test Practice Workbook Activity 4

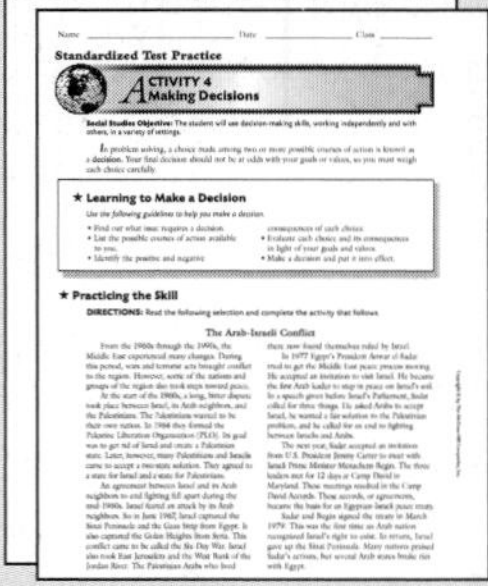

REVIEW AND REINFORCEMENT

Chapter Skills Activity 4

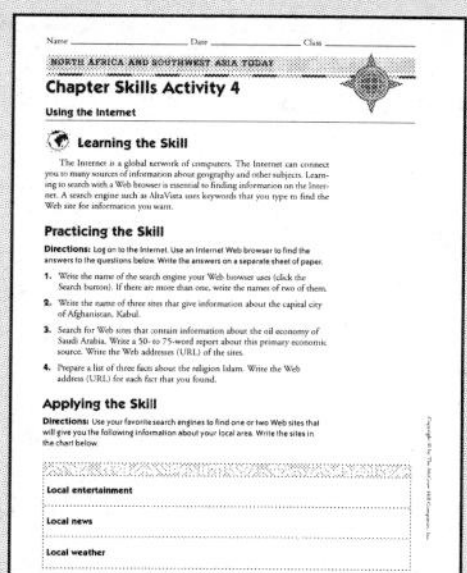

Take-Home Review Activity 4

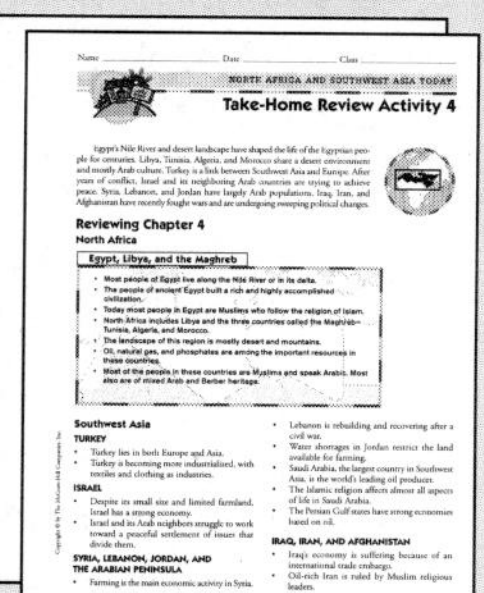

Reteaching Activity 4

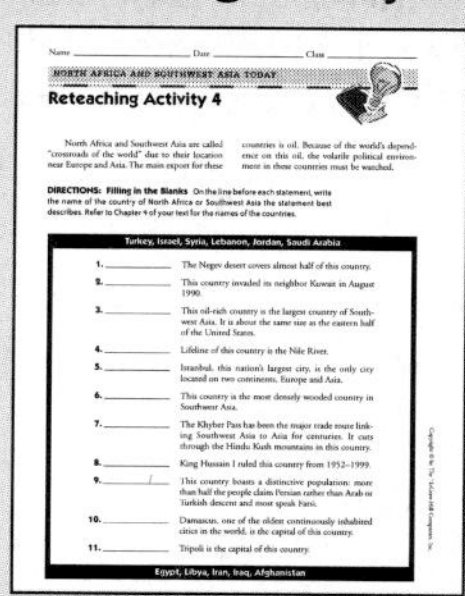

Vocabulary Activity 4

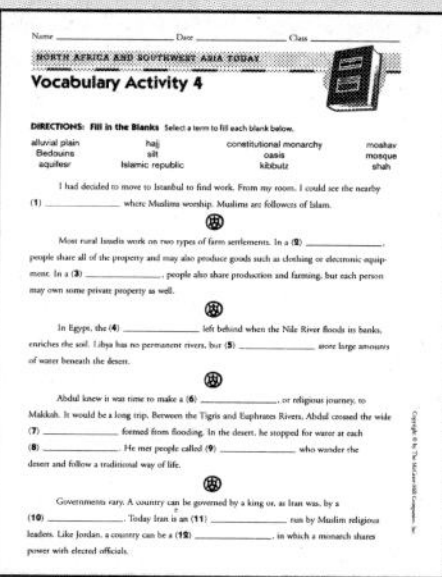

Workbook Activity 4

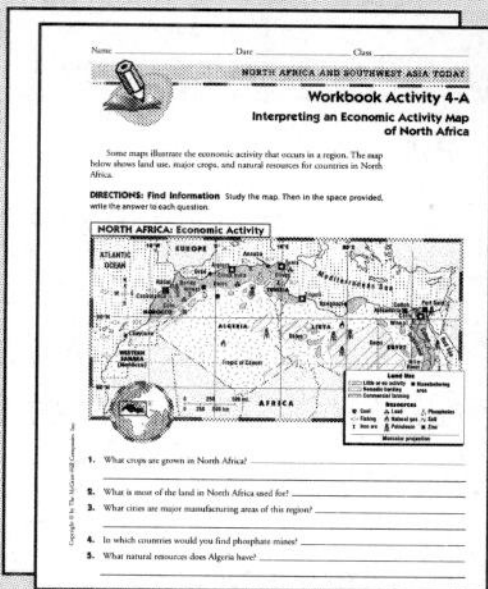

ASSESSMENT

GLENCOE'S ASSESSMENT ADVANTAGE

Chapter 4 Test, Form A

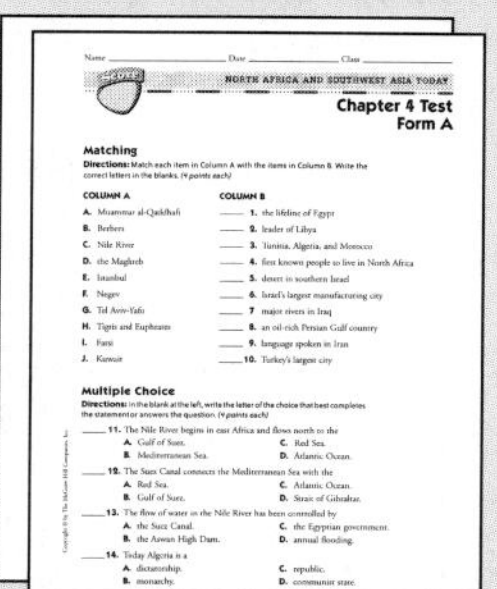

Chapter 4 Test, Form B

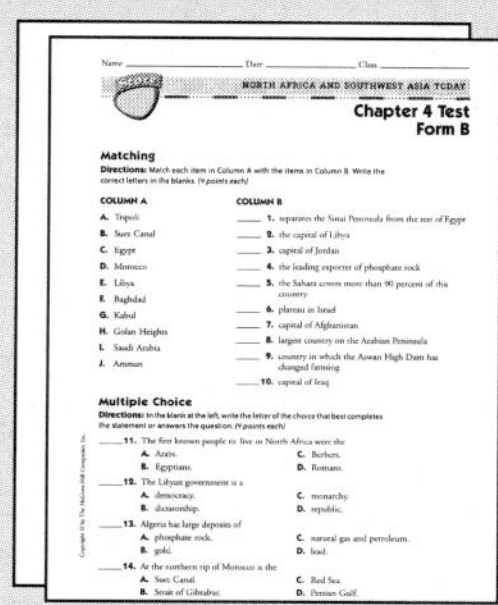

Performance Assessment Activity 4

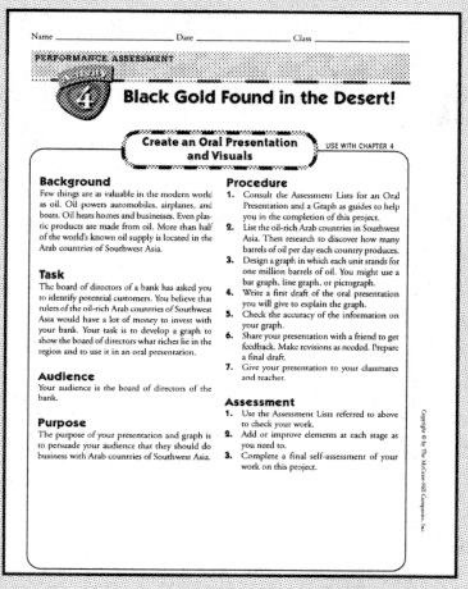

ExamView® Pro 3.0 Testmaker CD-ROM

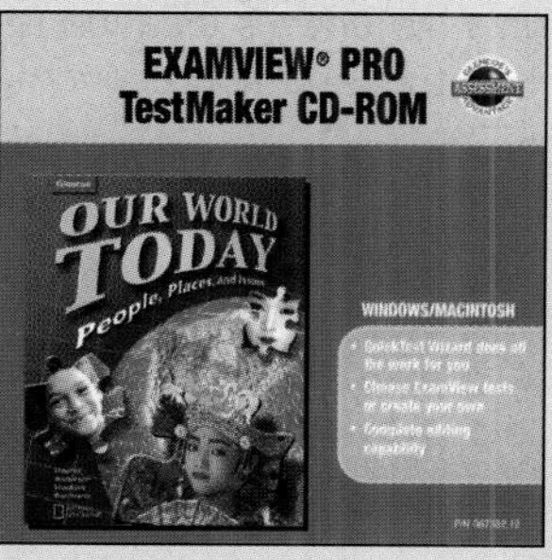

MULTIMEDIA

- **National Geographic's The World and Its People**
- **MindJogger Videoquiz**
- **Vocabulary PuzzleMaker Software**
- **Interactive Tutor Self-Assessment CD-ROM**
- **ExamView® Pro 3.0 Testmaker CD-ROM**
- **Interactive Lesson Planner CD-ROM**
- **Interactive Teacher Edition CD-ROM**
- **Skillbuilder Interactive Workbook CD-ROM, Level 1**
- **Presentation Plus! CD-ROM**
- **Audio Program**

SPANISH RESOURCES

The following Spanish language materials are available in the Spanish Resources binder:

- **Spanish Chapter Summaries**
- **Spanish Vocabulary Activities**
- **Spanish Guided Reading Activities**
- **Spanish Quizzes and Tests**
- **Spanish Take-Home Review Activities**
- **Spanish Reteaching Activities**

Meeting National Standards

Geography for Life

All of the 18 standards are demonstrated in Unit 2. The following ones are highlighted in Chapter 4:

Section 1 **EE4 Human Systems: Standards 9, 10, 11, 12, 13**
EE6 The Uses of Geography: Standard 17

Section 2 **EE4 Human Systems: Standards 9, 10, 11, 12**
EE5 Environment and Society: Standards 14, 15

Section 3 **EE2 Places and Regions: Standards 4, 5, 6**
EE3 Physical Systems: Standards 7, 8

Section 4 **EE1 The World in Spatial Terms: Standards 1, 2, 3**

For a complete listing of National Geography Standards and entire text correlation, see pages T22–T29.

Chapter 4 Planning Guide

SECTION RESOURCES

Daily Objectives	Reproducible Resources	Multimedia Resources
Section 1 **North Africa** **Suggested Pacing = 1 day** **1.** Explain how history and the environment have shaped life in North Africa. **2.** Discuss the economic conditions of North Africa. **3.** Compare the kinds of government the countries of North Africa have.	Reproducible Lesson Plan 4-1 Daily Lecture and Discussion Notes 4-1 Guided Reading Activity 4-1 Reading Essentials and Study Guide 4-1 Section Quiz 4-1*	Daily Focus Skills Transparency 4-1 GeoQuiz Transparency 4-1 Vocabulary PuzzleMaker Software Interactive Tutor Self-Assessment CD-ROM ExamView® Pro 3.0 Testmaker CD-ROM Presentation Plus! CD-ROM
Section 2 **Southwest Asia: Turkey and Israel** **Suggested Pacing = 1 day** **1.** Explain why Turkey's location is unique. **2.** Describe the land and economy of Israel.	Reproducible Lesson Plan 4-2 Daily Lecture and Discussion Notes 4-2 Guided Reading Activity 4-2 Reading Essentials and Study Guide 4-2 Section Quiz 4-2*	Daily Focus Skills Transparency 4-2 GeoQuiz Transparency 4-2 Vocabulary PuzzleMaker Software Interactive Tutor Self-Assessment CD-ROM ExamView® Pro 3.0 Testmaker CD-ROM Presentation Plus! CD-ROM
Section 3 **Syria, Lebanon, Jordan, and Arabia** **Suggested Pacing = 1 day** **1.** Discuss the varied geography of this region. **2.** Describe how oil affects the lives of the people who live here. **3.** Compare the politics of these countries.	Reproducible Lesson Plan 4-3 Daily Lecture and Discussion Notes 4-3 Guided Reading Activity 4-3 Reading Essentials and Study Guide 4-3 Section Quiz 4-3*	Daily Focus Skills Transparency 4-3 GeoQuiz Transparency 4-2 Vocabulary PuzzleMaker Software Interactive Tutor Self-Assessment CD-ROM ExamView® Pro 3.0 Testmaker CD-ROM Presentation Plus! CD-ROM
Section 4 **Iraq, Iran, and Afghanistan** **Suggested Pacing = 1 day** **1.** Explain Iraq's role in regional conflicts. **2.** Discuss how a religious government came to power in Iran. **3.** Describe the religious and political conflicts in Afghanistan.	Reproducible Lesson Plan 4-4 Daily Lecture and Discussion Notes 4-4 Guided Reading Activity 4-4 Reading Essentials and Study Guide 4-4 Section Quiz 4-4*	Daily Focus Skills Transparency 4-4 GeoQuiz Transparency 4-2 Vocabulary PuzzleMaker Software Interactive Tutor Self-Assessment CD-ROM ExamView® Pro 3.0 Testmaker CD-ROM Presentation Plus! CD-ROM

00:00 **Out of Time?** Assign the **Reading Essentials and Study Guide** for this chapter.

*Also available in Spanish

KEY TO ABILITY LEVELS

Teaching strategies have been coded for varying learning styles and abilities.

- **L1** **BASIC** activities for all students
- **L2** **AVERAGE** activities for average to above-average students
- **L3** **CHALLENGING** activities for above-average students
- **ELL** **ENGLISH LANGUAGE LEARNER** activities

Blackline Master
Software
CD-ROM
Audiocassette
Transparency
Videocassette
Block Scheduling
DVD

Teacher to Teacher

Culture Reinforcement

Rick Lyndsey
Roosevelt Full Service
West Palm Beach, Florida

Have students use papier-mâché and Popsicle™ sticks to create the homes and towns of other cultures. For example, they could construct a model of Petra, shown on page 112. Another option is to build a mosque, like the one shown on page 105. After building the structure, students should use various mediums to add color and texture. Finally, have students explain the relationship that exists between the society or culture they have chosen and their architecture.

OUR WORLD TODAY *Online*

Use our Web site for additional resources. All essential content is covered in the Student Edition.

You and your students can visit owt.glencoe.com, the Web site companion to *Our World Today*. This innovative integration of electronic and print media offers your students a wealth of opportunities. The student text directs students to the Web site for the following options:

- Chapter Overviews
- Student Web Activities
- Self-Check Quizzes
- Textbook Updates

Answers are provided for you in the Web Activity Lesson Plan. Additional Web resources and Interactive Tutor puzzles are also available.

TEACHER'S CORNER

Index to National Geographic Magazine:

The following articles may be used for research relating to this chapter:

- "Wrath of the Gods" and "Earthquake in Turkey," by Rick Gore, July 2000.
- "In Focus: Golan Heights," June 2000.
- "Yemen United," by Andrew Cockburn, April 2000.
- "Eyewitness Iraq," by Mike W. Edwards, November 1999.
- "Petra: Ancient City of Stone," by Don Belt, December 1998.

National Geographic Society Products Available From Glencoe:

To order the following products for use with this chapter, contact your local Glencoe sales representative or call Glencoe at 1-800-334-7344:

- *PicturePack: Geography of Asia* (Transparencies)
- *MapPack: Africa* (Transparencies)
- *MapPack: Asia* (Transparencies)
- *Images of the World* (Posters)
- *Eye on the Environment* (Posters)

Additional National Geographic Society Products:

To order the following products for use with this chapter, call National Geographic Society at 1-800-368-2728:

- *Complete National Geographic: 111 Years of National Geographic Magazine* (CD-ROM)
- *Asia* (Video)
- *Israel* (Video)
- *Pollution: World at Risk* (Video)
- *Healing the Earth* (Video)
- *Physical Earth* (Map)
- *Asia Political* (Map)
- *Population* (Map)
- *National Geographic Desk Reference* (Book)
- *National Geographic Atlas of the World, Seventh Edition* (Book)
- *Voices: Poetry and Art From Around the World* (Book)

NGS ONLINE

Access National Geographic's Web site for current events, activities, links, interactive features, and archives.
www.nationalgeographic.com

Introducing Chapter 4

Introduce students to chapter content and key terms by having them access Chapter Overview 4 at owt.glencoe.com

Chapter Objectives

1. Explain the importance of the Nile River to Egypt's people.
2. Describe how religion has affected the development of Southwest Asia.
3. Evaluate the influence of oil on the lives of people on the Arabian Peninsula.
4. Compare the economies and cultures of the countries in this region.

GLENCOE TECHNOLOGY

NATIONAL GEOGRAPHIC

The World and Its People Video Program

Chapters 16 and 17 North Africa and Southwest Asia

The following segments enhance the study of this chapter:

- **Holy City**
- **The Empty Quarter**
- **Hidden Treasure**

Available in DVD and VHS.

MindJogger Videoquiz

Use MindJogger to preview the Chapter 4 content.

Available in VHS.

Chapter 4 North Africa and Southwest Asia Today

The World and Its People NATIONAL GEOGRAPHIC

To learn more about the people and places of North Africa and Southwest Asia, view ***The World and Its People*** **Chapters 16** and **17** videos.

Our World Today online

Chapter Overview Visit the ***Our World Today: People, Places, and Issues*** Web site at owt.glencoe.com and click on **Chapter 4—Chapter Overviews** to preview information about North Africa and Southwest Asia.

98

Two-Minute Lesson Launcher

Point out to students that in this chapter they will learn about countries that are rich in oil, an important resource for the industrial world. Before they read the chapter, ask them: **What role does oil play in your lives and society? What happens when oil prices go up or down? What is the effect of increases and decreases in the supply of oil?** Have students think about the questions and write responses in their notebooks. Have them share responses in groups of four and then in a class discussion. Write the main responses. Students can check and add to these notes as they read the chapter. **L2**

Categorizing Information Study Foldable Asking yourself questions while reading material helps you to focus on what you are reading. Make this foldable to help you ask and answer questions about the people and places in North Africa and Southwest Asia.

Step 1 Fold a sheet of paper in half from side to side, leaving a ½ inch tab along the side.

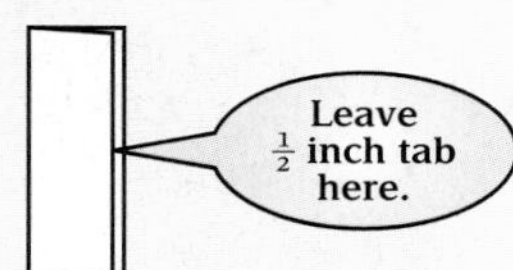

Step 2 Turn the paper and fold it into fourths.

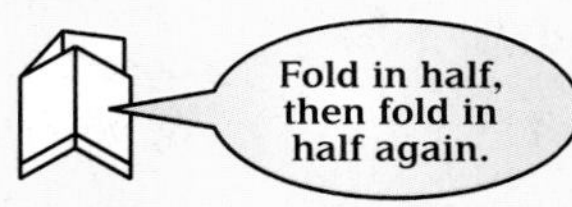

Fold in half, then fold in half again.

Step 3 Unfold and cut up along the three fold lines.

Step 4 Label as shown.

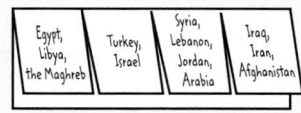

Egypt, Libya, the Maghreb | Turkey, Israel | Syria, Lebanon, Jordan, Arabia | Iraq, Iran, Afghanistan

Reading and Writing As you read, ask yourself questions about these countries. Write your questions and answers under each appropriate tab.

▲ Kin Fahad Stadium in Riyadh, Saudi Arabia

Why It Matters

Crossroads

Because of their location near Europe and Asia, North Africa and Southwest Asia remain even today at the "crossroads of the world." The world depends upon the oil and gas resources found here. Because of this situation, many nations have more reasons than usual for watching closely the events in these oil-rich countries. Achieving peace in this region is of global importance.

About the Photo

The discovery of oil in the 1930s has allowed rapid development of the Arabian Peninsula. Governments have tried to preserve their cultural heritage while promoting improvements. One outcome of development has been the rapid growth of urban centers and the resulting need for increased facilities. The photo illustrates how tradition has been preserved in modern structures. It shows the King Fahad Stadium, which can hold up to 70,000 spectators and has been the site of international competitions. The design of the structure is intended to represent the tents of Bedouin travelers. **Ask:** **How does this photo show the relationship between the Arab culture and its modern architecture?**

FOLDABLES™ Study Organizer

Purpose When making this foldable, students are required to ask themselves questions about the countries and regions of North Africa and Southwest Asia. This reading strategy requires students to ask questions of the chapter material as they read it, thereby helping them focus on main ideas and better understand the material.

Have students complete ***Reading and Study Skills Foldables*** Activity 4.

Why It Matters

Organize students into groups of five. Inform the groups that their task is to create an illustrated wall chart showing an important feature of the region and its significance to the people living there and to the world. Examples might be the Nile, oil, the Suez Canal, and the Turkish Straits. Have the groups display and discuss their completed charts.

Section 1, pages 100–104

1 Focus

Section Objectives

1. Explain how history and the environment have shaped life in North Africa.
2. Discuss the economic conditions of North Africa.
3. Compare the kinds of government the countries of North Africa have.

BELLRINGER
Skillbuilder Activity

Project transparency and have students answer questions.

This activity is also available as a blackline master.

Daily Focus Skills Transparency 4-1

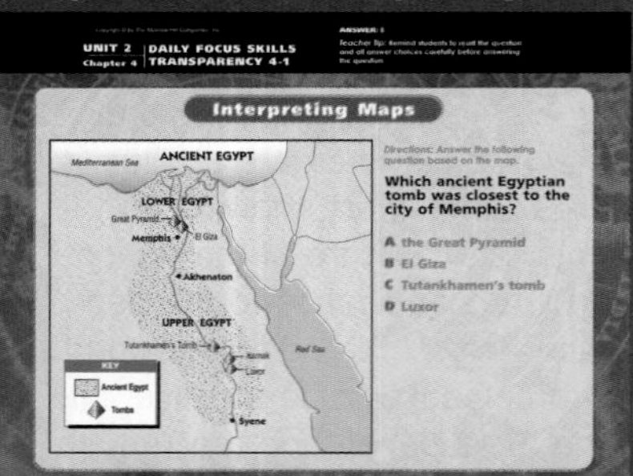

Guide to Reading

■ Vocabulary Precheck
Inform students that the word *delta* derives from the Greek alphabet letter delta, which is shaped like a triangle.

Use the Vocabulary PuzzleMaker to create crossword and word search puzzles.

Section 1 North Africa

Guide to Reading

Main Idea

North Africa's desert landscape has shaped the people and culture for many centuries, as has the Islamic religion.

Terms to Know

- delta
- silt
- oasis
- aquifer
- dictator
- terrorism
- secular
- constitutional monarchy

Reading Strategy

Create a diagram like this one. In the outer ovals, list facts about five of the countries in this section. In the center oval, write three facts that all five countries have in common.

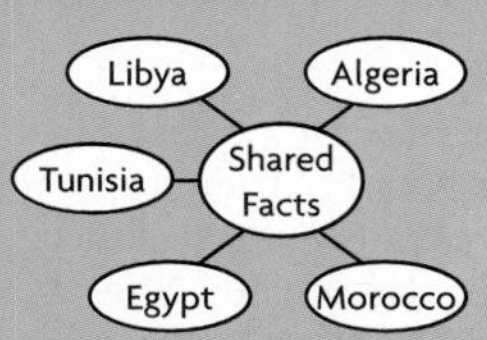

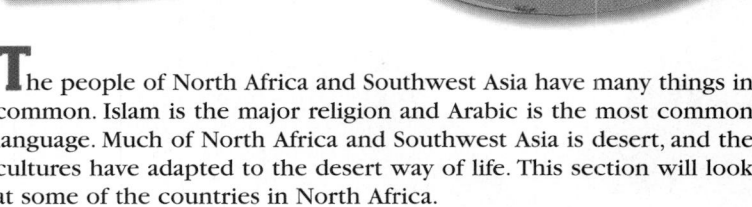

NATIONAL GEOGRAPHIC **Exploring Our World**

The Sahara is the world's largest hot desert. Thousands of years ago, however, it was not a desert at all. Grass and trees covered the region. Evidence of this can be seen in 7,000-year-old rock carvings of giraffes found in the Sahara. Giraffes eat leaves on tall, healthy trees that need water to grow.

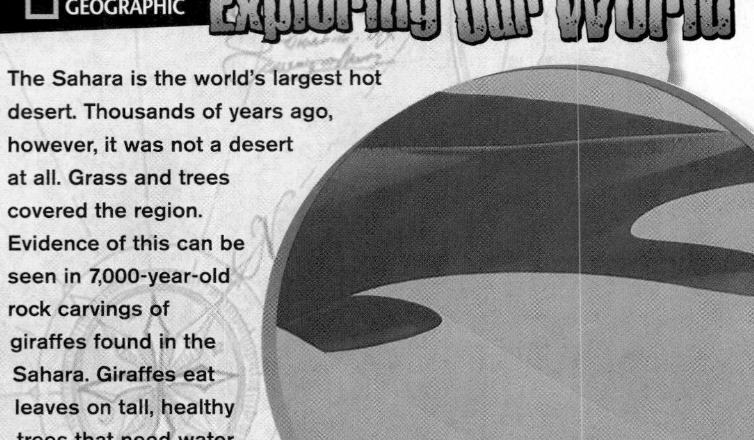

The people of North Africa and Southwest Asia have many things in common. Islam is the major religion and Arabic is the most common language. Much of North Africa and Southwest Asia is desert, and the cultures have adapted to the desert way of life. This section will look at some of the countries in North Africa.

Egypt

Egypt is a large country about the same size as Texas and New Mexico together. Yet most of it is desert. Therefore, Egypt's people crowd into less than 5 percent of the land, or an area a little larger than the size of Maryland. The lifeline of Egypt is the Nile River, which supplies 85 percent of the country's water. From its sources in eastern Africa, the Nile flows 4,241 miles (6,825 km) north to the Mediterranean Sea, making it the world's longest river. Where the river empties into the Mediterranean Sea, you find the Nile's delta. A **delta** is the area formed from soil deposited by a river at its mouth.

For centuries, the Nile's waters would rise in the spring. The swollen river carried **silt**, or small particles of rich soil. When it reached

Section Resources

Reproducible Masters
- Reproducible Lesson Plan 4-1
- Daily Lecture and Discussion Notes 4-1
- Guided Reading Activity 4-1
- Reading Essentials and Study Guide 4-1
- Section Quiz 4-1

Transparencies
- Daily Focus Skills Transparency 4-1
- GeoQuiz Transparency 4-1

Multimedia
- Vocabulary PuzzleMaker Software
- Interactive Tutor Self-Assessment CD-ROM
- Presentation Plus! CD-ROM
- ExamView® Pro 3.0 Testmaker CD-ROM

Egypt, the Nile flooded its banks. As the floodwaters dried, the silt was left behind, enriching the soil and making the land especially good for farming. Dams and channels control the river's flow and its use for farming and generating electric power.

The triangle-shaped **Sinai** (SY•ny) **Peninsula** lies southeast of the Nile delta. This area is a major crossroads between Africa and Southwest Asia. The **Suez Canal** separates the Sinai Peninsula from the rest of Egypt. Egyptians and Europeans built the canal in the mid-1860s. Today the Suez Canal is still one of the world's most important waterways. Ships use the canal to pass from the Mediterranean Sea to the Red Sea. In making this journey, they avoid traveling all the way around Africa.

Egypt's Economy About 40 percent of Egypt's people work in agriculture, though only about 4 percent of Egypt's land is used for farming. Important crops include sugarcane, grains, vegetables, fruits, and cotton. Look at the physical map on page 74. Where do you think the best farmland in Egypt is located?

Farmers rely on dams to control the water needed for their fields. Egypt's largest dam and a major source of electric power is the **Aswan High Dam.** The dams give people control over the Nile's floodwaters. They can store the water for months behind the dams, then release it several times during the year, rather than having just the spring floods. This control allows farmers to harvest two or three crops a year.

The dams bring challenges as well as benefits. They block the flow of silt, making the farmland less fertile. Farmers now rely more heavily on chemical fertilizers to grow crops. In addition, the dams prevent less freshwater from reaching the delta. So, salt water from the Mediterranean Sea flows deeper into the delta, making the land less fertile.

Egyptian factories make food products, textiles, and consumer goods. Egypt's main energy resource, however, is oil, found in and around the Red Sea. Petroleum products make up almost half the value of Egypt's exports. Another important industry is tourism. Visitors come to see the magnificent ruins of ancient Egypt.

✓ Reading Check **Why is the Aswan High Dam important?**

Libya

Except for the coastal lowlands, **Libya** is a desert with only a few oases. An oasis is a green area in a desert fed by underground water. In fact, the Sahara covers more than 90 percent of Libya. During the spring and fall, fierce dust-heavy winds blow from the desert, creating temperatures in coastal areas as high as 110°F (43°C).

Libya has no permanent rivers, but aquifers lie beneath the vast desert. Aquifers are underground rock layers that store large amounts of water. Aquifers are also found in the United States, in drier regions such as northern and western Texas. In the 1990s, the Libyan government built pipelines to carry underground water from the desert to coastal areas.

Politics in Egypt

Egypt is a republic, a government headed by a president. A legislature makes the laws, but the Egyptian president has broad powers in running the country. In recent years, some extremist political and religious groups have opposed the government. These groups have used violence to reach their political goals. The government has tried to stop these attacks, but sometimes innocent tourists are hurt.

2 Teach

Writing Descriptions Ask students to suggest words that might be used to describe a desert. Write their responses on the board or overhead projector. Then have students use the listed words to write a paragraph describing North Africa's desert lands. L1

Daily Lecture Notes 4-1

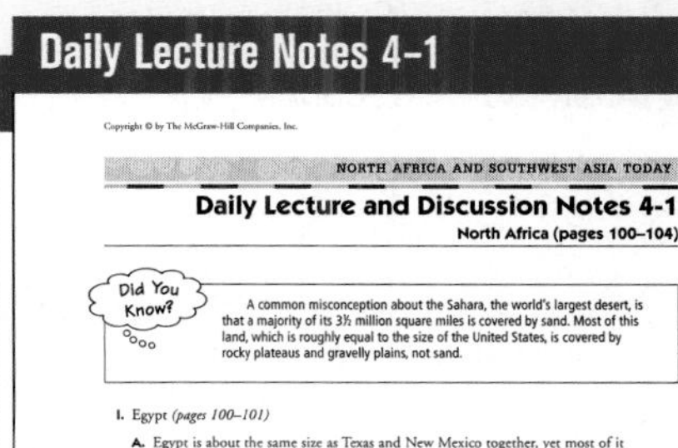

NORTH AFRICA AND SOUTHWEST ASIA TODAY

Daily Lecture and Discussion Notes 4-1

North Africa (pages 100–104)

Did You Know? A common misconception about the Sahara, the world's largest desert, is that a majority of its 3½ million square miles is covered by sand. Most of this land, which is roughly equal to the size of the United States, is covered by rocky plateaus and gravelly plains, not sand.

I. Egypt (pages 100–101)

A. Egypt is about the same size as Texas and New Mexico together, yet most of it is desert.

B. The Nile River supplies 85 percent of the country's water.

C. Dams and channels control the river's flow and its use for farming and

✓ Reading Check Answer

It gives people control over the Nile's floodwaters.

Interdisciplinary Connections

Economics The Aswan High Dam took 10 years to build and cost about $1 billion. Irrigation provided by the dam turned about 900,000 acres (364,217 ha) into arable land. In addition, the hydroelectricity generated at the dam provides about 25 percent of Egypt's power needs.

Critical Thinking Activity

Drawing Conclusions Have students make a chart comparing the positive and negative effects of the Aswan High Dam on life in Egypt. Then ask them to draw conclusions on whether the dam has done more harm or more good. Call on volunteers to state their conclusions and the reasons for them. After a few students have discussed their thoughts, have the class consider the question again to see if any students have changed their minds. Then have them write a paragraph explaining their position. L1

EE5 Environment and Society: Standard 14

Chapter 4

Section 1, pages 100–104

Guided Reading Activity 4-1

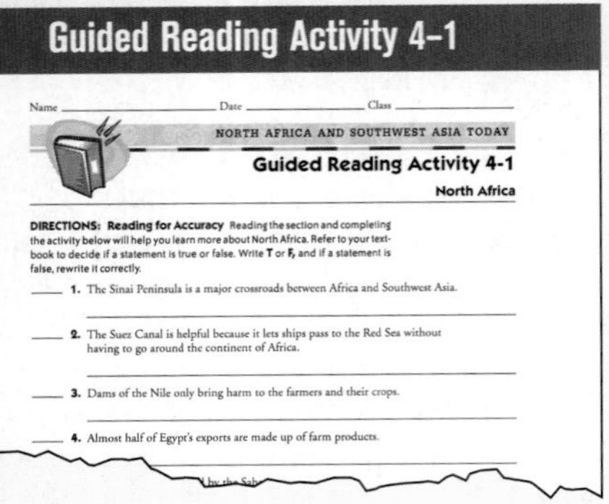

Reading Check Answer

Muammar al-Qaddhafi

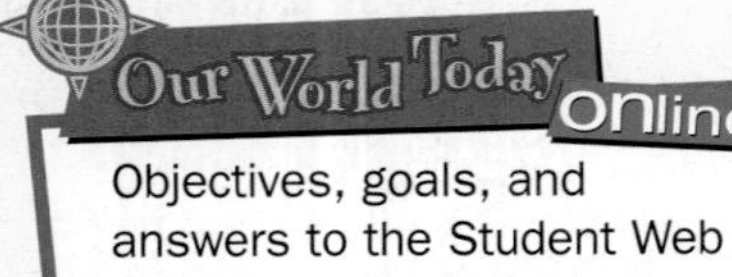

Objectives, goals, and answers to the Student Web Activity can be found in the Web Activity Lesson Plan at owt.glencoe.com

Measure student knowledge of physical features and political entities.

GeoQuiz Transparency 4-1

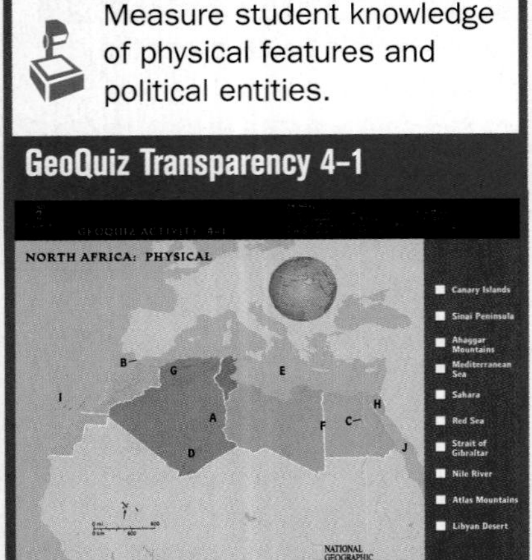

Web Activity Visit the ***Our World Today: People, Places, and Issues*** Web site at owt.glencoe.com and click on **Chapter 4–Student Web Activities** to learn more about Egypt's history.

Poor soil and a hot climate mean that Libya has to import about three-fourths of its food. The discovery of oil in Libya in 1959 brought the country great wealth. Libya's government uses oil money to buy food, build schools and hospitals, and maintain a strong military.

Libya's People Almost all of Libya's 5.2 million people have mixed Arab and Berber heritage. The **Berbers** were the first people known to live in North Africa. During the A.D. 600s, the Arabs brought Islam and the Arabic language to North Africa. Since then, Libya has been a Muslim country, and most of its people speak Arabic. About 86 percent of Libyans live along the Mediterranean coast. Most live in two modern cities—**Tripoli,** the capital, and **Benghazi** (behn•GAH•zee).

Libya's Government In 1969 a military officer named **Muammar al-Qaddhafi** (kuh•DAH•fee) gained power and overthrew the king. Qaddhafi is a **dictator,** or an all-powerful leader. For many years, the United States and other democratic nations have accused Qaddhafi of encouraging **terrorism** against the United States and its citizens. Terrorism is the use of violent acts against civilians to achieve certain goals. The U.S. government worked many years through international courts to prove Libya's involvement in the 1988 terrorist bombing of Pan Am Flight 103 over Lockerbie, Scotland. One Libyan was eventually found guilty in an international court.

Reading Check **Who has governed Libya since 1969?**

The Maghreb

Tunisia, Algeria, and **Morocco** form a region known as the **Maghreb.** *Maghreb* means "the land farthest west" in Arabic. These three countries make up the westernmost part of the Arabic-speaking Muslim world.

Tunisia Tunisia is North Africa's smallest country. Along the fertile eastern coast, farmers grow wheat, olives, fruits, and vegetables. Fishing is also an important industry. Tunisian factories produce food products, textiles, and oil products. In addition, tourism is a growing industry.

In ancient times, Phoenician sailors founded the city of **Carthage** in what is now the northern part of Tunisia. Carthage became a powerful trading center and challenged Rome for control of the Mediterranean. Carthage was defeated by Rome, the city completely destroyed, and its citizens sold into slavery. Tunisia's largest city today is **Tunis,** the capital city of more than 1.3 million people.

Algeria About one and a half times the size of Alaska, Algeria is the largest country in North Africa. Like neighboring Libya, Algeria must import much of its food, which it pays for by selling oil and natural gas. These sales have helped Algeria's industrial growth, but widespread poverty still exists. Many Algerians have moved to France and other European countries to find work.

Critical Thinking Activity

Making Inferences Discuss the rock art of the ancient Sahara. The rock carvings of animals such as rhinos, elephants, and other grazing animals reveal that long ago, the Sahara was covered by grassy savannas rather than the desert sands that prevail today. Even as recently as 7,000 years ago, the land was used for grazing herds of domesticated cattle. A climate shift meant greatly reduced rainfall, which began to produce the arid conditions known today. Have students discuss how people might have responded to that climate shift. *(move their herds to other better-watered areas)* **L1**

EE3 Physical Systems: Standards 7, 8

Over 31 million people live in Algeria and are—as in Libya and Tunisia—of mixed Arab and Berber heritage. If you visited Algeria, you would discover centuries-old Muslim traditions blending with those of France. Why? Algeria became a French possession in 1834. Many people in Algeria's cities speak French as well as Arabic. Also, French dishes are popular, along with local foods.

In 1954, Algerian Arabs rose up against the French and eventually gained their freedom in 1962. Today Algeria is a republic, with a strong president and a legislature. In the early 1990s, members of Muslim political parties opposed many of the government's **secular,** or nonreligious, policies. The Muslims gained enough support to win a national election. The government, however, rejected the election results and imprisoned many Muslim opponents, and a civil war began that has taken many lives.

Morocco Morocco has an economy based on agriculture and industry. Farmers grow sugar beets, grains, fruits, and vegetables for sale to Europe during the winter. Morocco leads the world in the export of phosphate rock and is a leading producer of phosphates, used in fertilizers. An important service industry in Morocco is tourism.

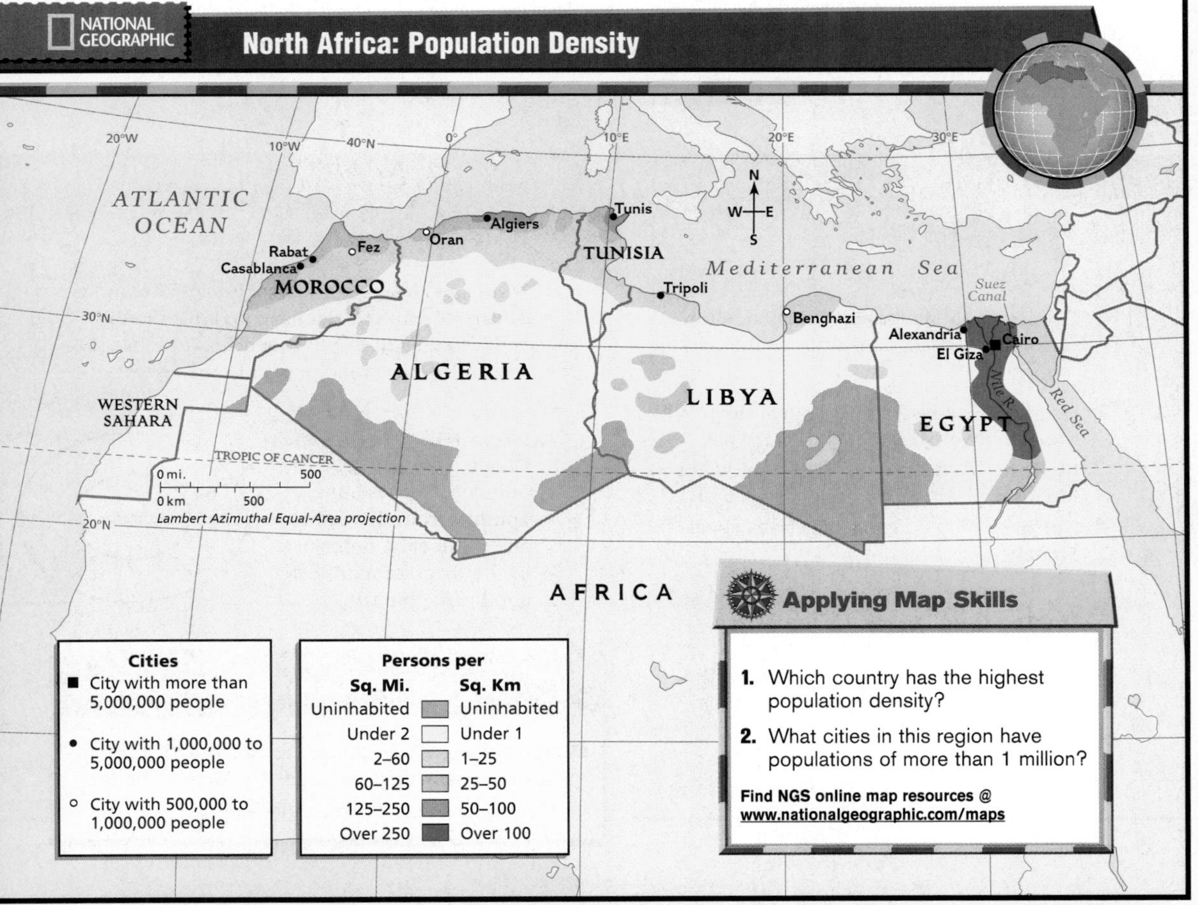

Applying Map Skills

1. Which country has the highest population density?
2. What cities in this region have populations of more than 1 million?

Find NGS online map resources @ www.nationalgeographic.com/maps

Critical Thinking Activity

Analyzing Information Discuss the growth of tourism in North Africa. Have students find information in the text about the countries that have become popular tourist destinations. Then ask students to identify possible reasons that these countries have become attractive to visitors while other countries have not. Call on volunteers to share their ideas with the class. **L2**

EE2 Places and Regions: Standard 6

Chapter 4

Section 1, pages 100–104

Cultural Kaleidoscope

Islam According to Islamic teachings, Muslims must pray five times a day facing the holy city of Makkah. Before those prayer sessions begin, you will hear the crier, or *muezzin,* call to notify people that it is time to pray. The *muezzin* stands in a minaret, which each mosque has. Minarets have distinctive styles in Muslim countries across the world, reflecting the building materials and architectural styles of the local areas.

Assign Section 1 Assessment as homework or an in-class activity.

Have students use the Interactive Tutor Self-Assessment CD-ROM to review Section 4–1.

Applying Map Skills

Answers

1. Egypt
2. Casablanca, Rabat, Algiers, Tunis, Tripoli, Alexandria, El Giza, and Cairo

Skills Practice

Why is the population density around Algiers and Tunis higher than in other areas, except along the Nile River? *(The climate is better there than in the interior, and they are important trading centers.)*

Chapter 4

Section 1, pages 100–104

Section Quiz 4-1

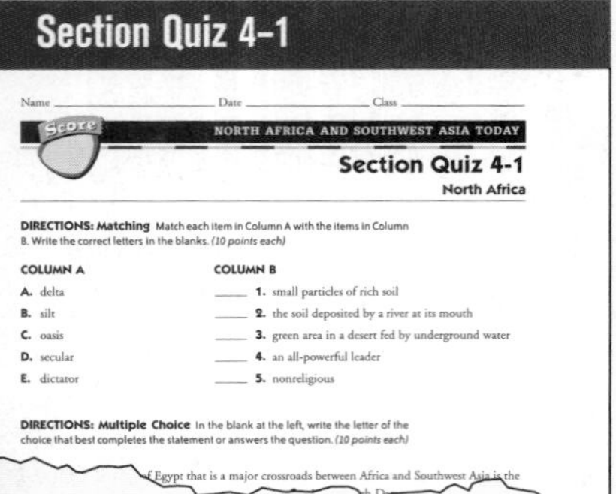
Name ______ Date ______ Class ______

NORTH AFRICA AND SOUTHWEST ASIA TODAY

Section Quiz 4-1

North Africa

DIRECTIONS: Matching Match each item in Column A with the items in Column B. Write the correct letters in the blanks. (10 points each)

COLUMN A	COLUMN B
A. delta	____ 1. small particles of rich soil
B. silt	____ 2. the soil deposited by a river at its mouth
C. oasis	____ 3. green area in a desert fed by underground water
D. secular	____ 4. an all-powerful leader
E. dictator	____ 5. nonreligious

DIRECTIONS: Multiple Choice In the blank at the left, write the letter of the choice that best completes the statement or answers the question. (10 points each)

Egypt that is a major crossroads between Africa and Southwest Asia is the

Reading Check Answer

descendants of Arabs and Berbers in Morocco who conquered much of Spain in the A.D. 700s

Reading Essentials and Study Guide 4-1

Name ______ Date ______ Class ______

NORTH AFRICA AND SOUTHWEST ASIA TODAY

Reading Essentials and Study Guide 4-1

North Africa

For use with textbook pages 100–104

Terms to Know

delta area formed from soil deposited by a river at its mouth (page 100)
silt small particles of rich soil (page 100)
oasis green area in a desert fed by underground water (page 101)
aquifer underground rock layers that store large amounts of water (page 101)
dictator an all-powerful leader (page 102)
terrorism use of violent acts against civilians to achieve certain goals (page 102)
secular non-religious policies (page 103)
constitutional monarchy form of government in which a king or queen is head of state but elected officials run the government (page 104)

Enrich

Have students research the food of one of the countries of North Africa and prepare a menu composed of traditional dishes from that country.

CLOSE

Have students write a 10-question quiz about the most important characteristics of these countries.

The map on page 75 shows you that Morocco's northern tip almost touches Europe. Here you will find the **Strait of Gibraltar.** It separates Africa and Europe—or Morocco and Spain—by only 9 miles (14 km). Like Libya, Morocco was first settled by the Berbers thousands of years ago. During the A.D. 600s, Arab invaders swept into Morocco. A century later, the Arabs and Berbers together crossed the Strait of Gibraltar and conquered Spain. Their descendants, called **Moors,** ruled parts of Spain and developed an advanced civilization until Christian Spanish rulers drove them out in the late 1400s.

Morocco's traditional culture is based on Arab, Berber, and African traditions. Moroccan music today blends the rhythms of these groups, sometimes with a dash of European pop and rock. Morocco also is known for its skilled artisans who make a variety of goods, such as carpets, pottery, jewelry, brassware, and woodwork.

Today Morocco's government is a **constitutional monarchy.** In this form of government, a king or queen is head of state, but elected officials run the government. In Morocco, the monarch still holds many powers, however. Beginning in the 1970s, the Moroccan king claimed the desert region of **Western Sahara,** formerly under Spanish control. The discovery of minerals there sparked a costly war between Morocco and a rebel group wanting Western Sahara to be independent. The United Nations wants to hold a vote that would allow the people of Western Sahara to decide their own future.

Reading Check **Who were the Moors?**

Section 1 Assessment

Defining Terms

1. **Define** delta, silt, oasis, aquifer, dictator, terrorism, secular, constitutional monarchy.

Recalling Facts

2. **Human/Environment Interaction** Why is the Nile River so important to Egypt?
3. **Region** What is a main source of water in Libya?
4. **Culture** Why do many Algerians speak French?

Critical Thinking

5. **Making Predictions** Centuries ago, Moroccan invaders crossed the Strait of Gibraltar into Spain. What effects of this invasion might you expect to see today?
6. **Making Generalizations** Human alterations of earth's features can have positive benefits and also negative consequences. How has the Aswan High Dam helped and hurt Egypt?

Graphic Organizer

7. **Organizing Information** Create a diagram like the one here. Choose one country from this section and fill in each outer part of the diagram with a fact about the country.

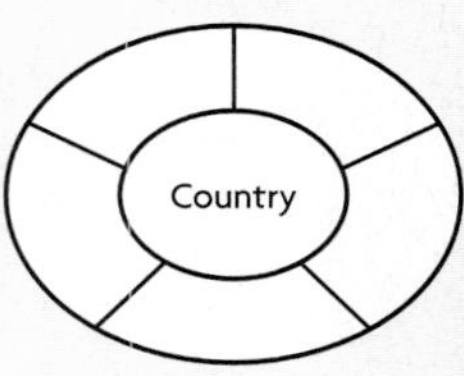

Applying Social Studies Skills

8. **Analyzing Maps** Study the North Africa population density map on page 103. Why is the interior of Algeria so lightly populated?

Section 1 Assessment

1. The terms are defined in the Glossary.
2. It supplies 85 percent of Egypt's water and the rest of the country is desert.
3. aquifers
4. France once held Algeria as a colony.
5. Answers will vary but might include cultural effects such as music, festivals, traditions, language, or architecture.
6. It has helped by controlling flooding, increasing agriculture, and producing electricity. It has hurt by eliminating silt and increasing the need for fertilizers.
7. Answers will vary depending on the country chosen.
8. It is covered by the Sahara.

Section 2

Southwest Asia: Turkey and Israel

Guide to Reading

Main Idea

Turkey and Israel both have strong ties to Europe and the United States.

Terms to Know

- mosque
- kibbutz
- moshav

Reading Strategy

Create a chart like this one, filling in at least two key facts about Turkey and Israel in each category.

Turkey	Fact #1	Fact #2
Land		
Economy		
People		
Israel		
Land		
Economy		
People		

NATIONAL GEOGRAPHIC **Exploring Our World**

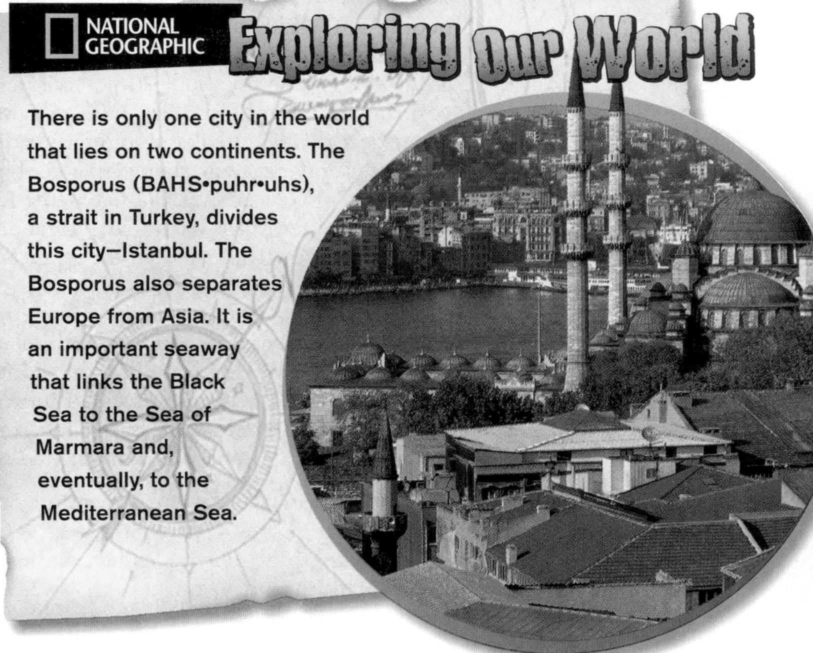

There is only one city in the world that lies on two continents. The Bosporus (BAHS•puhr•uhs), a strait in Turkey, divides this city—Istanbul. The Bosporus also separates Europe from Asia. It is an important seaway that links the Black Sea to the Sea of Marmara and, eventually, to the Mediterranean Sea.

Both **Turkey** and **Israel** have strong cultural ties to Europe. Turkey has a unique location—it bridges the continents of Asia and Europe. The large Asian part of Turkey occupies the peninsula once known as **Asia Minor.** The much smaller European part lies on Europe's Balkan Peninsula. Israel is completely in Southwest Asia, but it was founded by immigrants who came in large part from Europe, Central Asia, and the United States.

Turkey

Three important waterways—the **Bosporus,** the **Sea of Marmara** (MAHR•muh•ruh), and the **Dardanelles** (DAHRD•uhn•EHLZ) separate the Asian and European parts of Turkey. Together, these waterways are called the Turkish Straits. Find these bodies of water on page RA19 of the **Reference Atlas.**

1 Focus

Section Objectives

1. Explain why Turkey's location is unique.
2. Describe the land and economy of Israel.

BELLRINGER Skillbuilder Activity

Project transparency and have students answer questions.

This activity is also available as a blackline master.

Daily Focus Skills Transparency 4-2

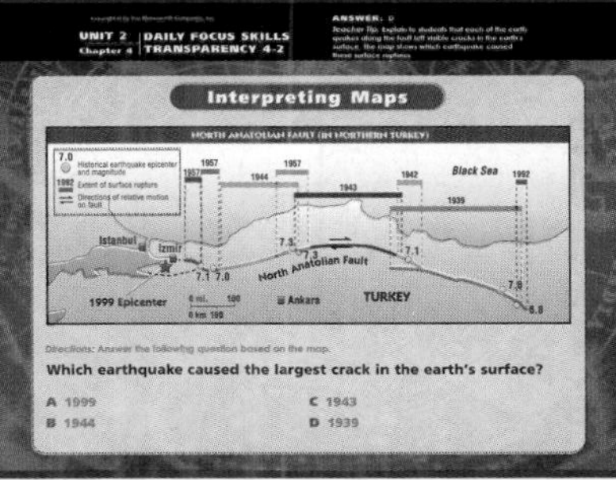

Guide to Reading

■ **Accessing Prior Knowledge**

Ask: In what kinds of locations do cities often rise and thrive? *(along transportation routes such as waterways; amid areas rich in farmland or resources)* Explain that in this chapter, students will learn about an important city that arose along a major waterway.

Section Resources

Reproducible Masters

- Reproducible Lesson Plan 4-2
- Daily Lecture and Discussion Notes 4-2
- Guided Reading Activity 4-2
- Reading Essentials and Study Guide 4-2
- Section Quiz 4-2

Transparencies

- Daily Focus Skills Transparency 4-2
- GeoQuiz Transparency 4-2

Multimedia

- Vocabulary PuzzleMaker Software
- Interactive Tutor Self-Assessment CD-ROM
- Presentation Plus! CD-ROM
- ExamView® Pro 3.0 Testmaker CD-ROM

TEACH

Making Comparisons Write "Modern Israel" and "Ancient Palestine." Have students examine the text and photographs in this section to find items that might be classified under each heading. Describe characteristics of modern Israel that reflect its ancient heritage. **L1**

Measure student knowledge of physical features and political entities.

GeoQuiz Transparency 4-2

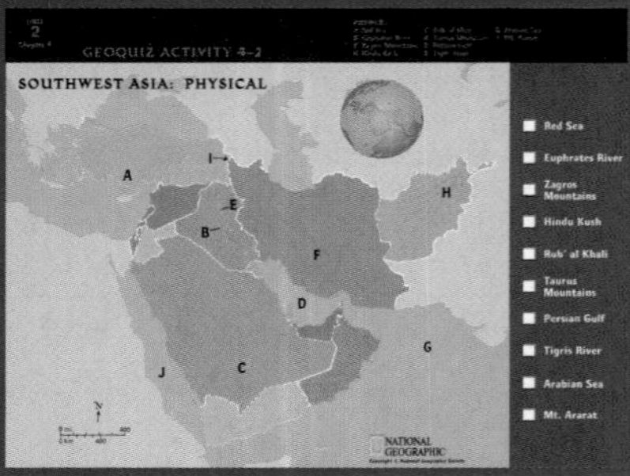

Reading Check Answer

It is the only city in the world that is located on two continents.

Daily Lecture Notes 4-2

NORTH AFRICA AND SOUTHWEST ASIA TODAY

Daily Lecture and Discussion Notes 4-2

Southwest Asia: Turkey and Israel (pages 105–108)

Did You Know? Turkey is home to some of the oldest permanent human settlements. In Çatal Hüyük, Turkey, archaeologists have unearthed some of the oldest known examples of pottery, textiles, and plastered walls. Some of these artifacts date back to 7,000 B.C.

I. Turkey (pages 105–106)

A. The Turkish Straits are made up of three important waterways—the **Bosporus**, the **Sea of Marmara**, and the **Dardanelles**.

B. Turkey's climate varies throughout the country, from hot, dry summers and cold, snowy winters, to hot, dry summers and mild, rainy winters.

Festival Time

Kudret Özal lives in Söğüt, Turkey. Every year, she and her family attend a festival that honors a warrior ancestor. She says, "At night everyone gathers to sing, dance, and tell jokes and stories." According to custom, Kudret wears clothing that covers her head, arms, shoulders, and legs.

Turkey's climate varies throughout the country. If you lived on the large, central plateau, called **Anatolia,** you would experience hot, dry summers and cold, snowy winters. People living in the coastal areas enjoy hot, dry summers and mild, rainy winters. Many of Turkey's people are farmers, growing cotton and fruits on the coast and raising livestock. Wheat is grown in the inland areas. Turkey also has many mineral resources such as coal, copper, and iron. Tourism is a growing industry, thanks to the country's beautiful beaches and historic sites.

Turkey's People About 98 percent of Turkey's more than 66 million people are Muslims. Turkish is the official language, but Arabic and Kurdish are also spoken. Kurdish is the language of the **Kurds,** an ethnic group who make up about 20 percent of Turkey's people. The Turkish government has tried to turn the Kurds away from Kurdish culture and language. Unwilling to abandon their identity, the Kurds have demanded their own independent state. Tensions between the two groups have resulted in violent clashes. Ultimately, the Kurds of Turkey are seeking to unite with other Kurds from Iraq, Iran, and Syria to form an independent homeland called "Kurdistan" in the heart of Southwest Asia. None of the countries involved is willing to see this happen.

Almost 70 percent of Turkey's people live in cities or towns. **Istanbul** is Turkey's largest city with nearly 8 million people. It is the only city in the world located on two continents. Istanbul is known for its beautiful palaces, museums, and mosques. **Mosques** are places of worship for followers of Islam. Thanks to its location at the entrance to the Black Sea, Istanbul is a major trading center.

History and Government Istanbul began as a Greek port called **Byzantium** more than 2,500 years ago. Later it was renamed **Constantinople** after the Roman emperor Constantine the Great. For almost a thousand years, the city was the glittering capital of the Byzantine Empire.

Many of Turkey's people today are descendants of an Asian people called Turks. These people migrated to Anatolia during the A.D. 900s. One group of Turks—the **Ottomans**—conquered Constantinople in the 1400s. They, too, renamed the city, calling it Istanbul. The city served as the brilliant capital of a powerful Muslim empire called the **Ottoman Empire.** At its height, this empire ruled much of southeastern Europe, North Africa, and Southwest Asia.

World War I led to the breakup of the Ottoman Empire. During most of the 1920s and 1930s, **Kemal Atatürk,** a military hero, served as Turkey's first president. Atatürk introduced many political and social changes to modernize the country. Turkey soon began to consider itself European as well as Asian. Most Turkish people, however, continued to practice the Muslim faith. During the 1990s, secular, or nonreligious, political groups struggled for control of Turkey's government. Turkey has been a member of the North Atlantic Treaty Organization (NATO) since 1952 and is seeking to join the European Union. (See Chapter 10.)

Reading Check What is unusual about Turkey's largest city?

Critical Thinking Activity

Evaluating Information About 50,000 tankers and cargo ships travel the Turkish Straits each year. Storms and treacherous currents lead to shipwrecks, and heavy seafaring traffic sometimes produces collisions. Some of these ships carry oil; others haul dangerous cargo like explosives. Discuss the possible harmful effects to the people living near the straits and to the environment. Have students debate what steps the government of Turkey could take to limit or prevent this damage. **L2**

EE5 Environment and Society: Standard 16

Israel

Israel is slightly smaller than the state of New Jersey. The mountains of Galilee lie in Israel's north. East of these mountains is a plateau called the **Golan Heights.** South of the Golan Heights, between Israel and Jordan, is the **Dead Sea.** At 1,349 feet (411 m) below sea level, the shores of the Dead Sea are the lowest place on the earth's surface. The Dead Sea is also the earth's saltiest body of water—about nine times saltier than ocean water. It is an important source of potash, a type of mineral salt.

In southern Israel, a desert called the **Negev** (NEH•gehv) covers almost half the country. A fertile plain no more than 20 miles (32 km) wide lies along the country's Mediterranean coast. To the east, the **Jordan River** cuts through the floor of a long, narrow valley before flowing into the Dead Sea.

Israel's Economy Israel's best farmland stretches along the Mediterranean coastal plain. For centuries, farmers here have grown citrus fruits, such as oranges, grapefruits, and lemons. Citrus fruits are still Israel's major agricultural export. Farther inland, you find that the desert actually blooms. This is possible because farmers add fertilizers to the soil and carefully use scarce water resources.

In very dry areas, crops are grown with drip irrigation. This method uses computers to release specific amounts of water from underground tubes to the roots of plants. Israeli farmers plant fruits and vegetables that do not absorb salts, such as the Negev tomatoes. As a result of technology, Israel's farmers are able to export some food to other countries.

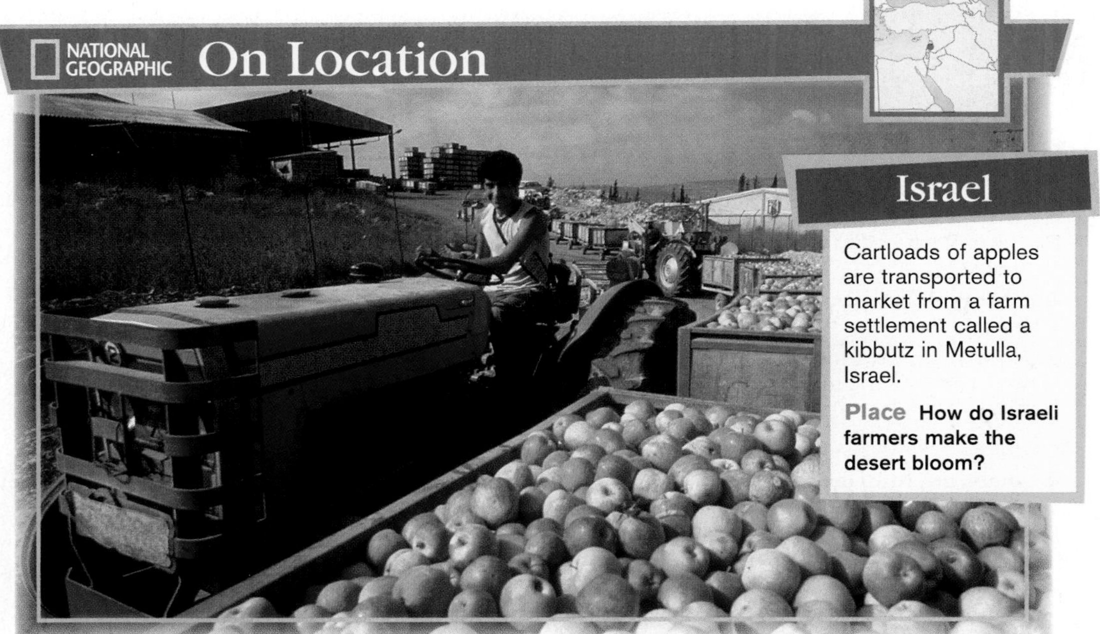

Israel

Cartloads of apples are transported to market from a farm settlement called a kibbutz in Metulla, Israel.

Place **How do Israeli farmers make the desert bloom?**

Chapter 4

Section 2, pages 105–108

Guided Reading Activity 4-2

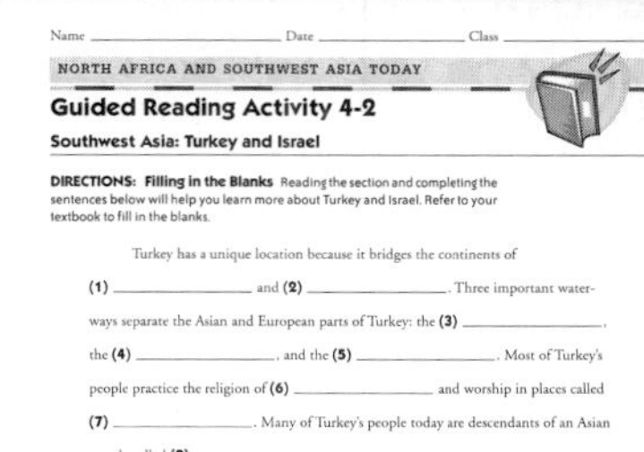
Name ______ Date ______ Class ______

NORTH AFRICA AND SOUTHWEST ASIA TODAY

Guided Reading Activity 4-2

Southwest Asia: Turkey and Israel

DIRECTIONS: Filling in the Blanks Reading the section and completing the sentences below will help you learn more about Turkey and Israel. Refer to your textbook to fill in the blanks.

Turkey has a unique location because it bridges the continents of **(1)** ______ and **(2)** ______. Three important waterways separate the Asian and European parts of Turkey: the **(3)** ______, the **(4)** ______, and the **(5)** ______. Most of Turkey's people practice the religion of **(6)** ______ and worship in places called **(7)** ______. Many of Turkey's people today are descendants of an Asian people called **(8)** ______.

...rael and the **(9)** ______

More About the Photos

Israel A kibbutz differs from a moshav in that under the moshav system, each farm family owns its own land but sells its produce through the moshav. Members of a kibbutz, on the other hand, own and work the land in common. Sometimes a kibbutz also produces manufactured goods.

Caption Answer by using fertilizer and carefully using scarce water resources

Assign Section 2 Assessment as homework or an in-class activity.

Have students use the Interactive Tutor Self-Assessment CD-ROM to review Section 4–2.

Team-Teaching Activity

Government Israel's government is often in the news because the political strength or weakness of the current prime minister has an effect on peace negotiations with its neighbors. Invite a government teacher to class to explain the parliamentary system used in Israel, including such issues as the role of the prime minister and the cabinet, the large number of political parties, coalition governments, votes of no confidence, and the part played by Arab Israeli members of the Knesset. **Ask: What are the similarities and differences to the United States government? L2**

EE4 Human Systems: Standard 9

Section Quiz 4-2

Name ______ Date ______ Class ______

SOUTHWEST ASIA

Section Quiz 4-2
Southwest Asia: Turkey and Israel

DIRECTIONS: Matching Match each item in Column A with the items in Column B. Write the correct letters in the blanks. (10 points each)

COLUMN A	COLUMN B
A. Anatolia	____ 1. places of worship for followers of Islam
B. Istanbul	____ 2. Turkey's large central plateau
C. mosques	____ 3. Turkey's largest city
D. kibbutz	____ 4. a settlement where people share but own private property too
E. moshav	____ 5. farm settlement where property is shared

DIRECTIONS: Multiple Choice In the blank at the left, write the letter of the choice that best completes the statement or answers the question. (10 points each)

Reteach

Have students write five cause-and-effect statements on section content. Have volunteers read either the "cause" or "effect" part of their statements aloud. As each is read, call on other students to complete the statement.

Reading Check Answer

Tel Aviv-Yafo

Reading Essentials and Study Guide 4-2

Name ______ Date ______ Class ______

NORTH AFRICA AND SOUTHWEST ASIA TODAY

Reading Essentials and Study Guide 4-2
Southwest Asia: Turkey and Israel

For use with textbook pages 105–108

Terms to Know

mosque place of worship for followers of Islam (page 106)
kibbutz settlement where property is shared (page 108)
moshav settlement where people share in farming, production, and selling, but each person may own private property as well (page 108)

Drawing from Experience

Do you feel at home in your country? How would you feel if you had no country to call your own? The Jews had no homeland until 1948. The ...

CLOSE

Ask students to imagine that they are visiting Israel. Have them write a postcard to a friend describing what they see.

About 9 percent of Israelis live and work on farm settlements. Some Israelis live in a settlement called a **kibbutz** (kih•BUTS), where property is shared. Another kind of settlement is called a **moshav** (moh•SHAHV). People in a moshav share in farming, production, and selling, but each person may own private property as well.

Israel is the most industrialized country in Southwest Asia. It has been helped by large amounts of aid from Europe and the United States. Israel's skilled workforce produces electronic products, clothing, chemicals, food products, and machinery. Diamond cutting and polishing is also a major industry. **Tel Aviv-Yafo** is the largest manufacturing center. Jerusalem was made the capital of Israel in 1950.

The Israeli People The area that today is Israel has been home to different groups of people over the centuries. The ancient traditions of these groups have led to conflict among their descendants today. About 80 percent of Israel's more than 6 million people are Jews. They have moved to Israel from many countries. The other 20 percent belong to an Arab people called **Palestinians.** Most Palestinians are Muslims, but some are Christians. **Time Reports: Focus on World Issues** (see pages 115–121) looks at the history of the people in this region and explains some of the reasons for the ongoing conflicts between the Israelis and the Arab world and how they are working toward a peaceful settlement of these conflicts.

Reading Check What city is the largest manufacturing center in Israel?

Assessment

Defining Terms

1. **Define** mosque, kibbutz, moshav.

Recalling Facts

2. **Place** What bodies of water form the Turkish Straits?
3. **History** What other names has the city of Istanbul had?
4. **Human/Environment Interaction** What did Israeli farmers use to help them make the desert "bloom"?

Critical Thinking

5. **Analyzing Information** How has Istanbul's location made it a trading center?
6. **Understanding Cause and Effect** Why have violent clashes occurred between the Kurds and the Turkish government?

Graphic Organizer

7. **Organizing Information** On a diagram like this one, label an example of Turkey's culture at the end of each line.

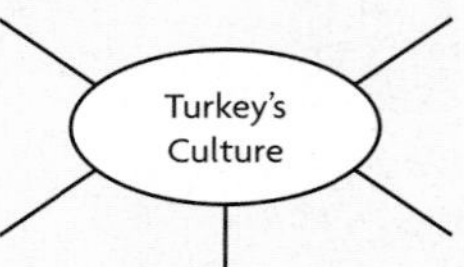

Applying Social Studies Skills

8. **Analyzing Maps** Study the political map on page 75. What country borders Israel to the north? To the northeast? To the east?

Section 2 Assessment

1. The terms are defined in the Glossary.
2. Bosporous, Sea of Marmara, Dardanelles
3. Byzantium, Constantinople
4. fertilizer and water
5. Istanbul occupies a strategic and important position on a strait that connects the Black Sea and the Mediterranean. All trade that goes between these bodies of water must pass near this city. The city is also a gateway for trade between Europe and Asia.
6. The government has tried to move Kurds away from their own culture, while Kurds have tried to achieve an independent state for themselves.
7. Answers will vary.
8. Lebanon; Syria; Jordan

Making Connections

CULTURE | GOVERNMENT | PEOPLE | TECHNOLOGY

Carpet Weaving

For thousands of years, people have been making the hand-knotted floor coverings sometimes called Persian or Turkish rugs. Valued for their rich color and intricate design, these handmade rugs are unique works of art.

▲ Turkish carpet weavers

History

Most experts think that the nomadic peoples of Asia were among the first to make hand-knotted carpets. They used their carpets as wall coverings, curtains, and saddlebags, as well as covering for the bare ground in their tents. The soft, thick rugs blocked out the cold and could also be used as a bed or blanket.

As the nomads moved from place to place, they spread the art of carpet making to new lands and peoples. Throughout the years, the greatest carpet-producing areas have included Turkey, the republics of the Caucasus, Persia (Iran), and Turkmenistan. People in other countries, including Afghanistan, Pakistan, Nepal, India, and China, also became skilled carpet weavers.

Weaving and Knotting

Early nomads wove their carpets from sheep's wool on simple wooden looms that could be rolled up for traveling. Each carpet was woven with two sets of threads. The *warp* threads run from top to bottom, and the *weft* threads are woven from side to side. Hand-tied knots form the carpet's colorful pattern. A skillful weaver can tie about 15 knots a minute. The best carpets, however, can have more than 500 knots per square inch!

Color and Design

The beauty of woven carpets comes from the endless combination of colors and designs. Over the years, various regions developed their own carpet patterns. These were passed down from generation to generation. Often the images hold special meanings. For instance, the palm and coconut often symbolize happiness and blessings.

The very first rugs were colored gray, white, brown, or black—the natural color of the wool. Then people learned to make dyes from plants and animals. The root of the madder plant, as well as certain insects, provided red and pink dye. Turmeric root and saffron supplied shades of yellow, while the indigo plant provided blue.

Making the Connection

1. How did the art of carpet weaving spread from one place to another?
2. What creates the pattern in a Turkish carpet?
3. **Drawing Conclusions** In what way do hand-knotted carpets combine art with usefulness?

Making the Connection

1. As nomads moved from place to place, they brought the craft with them.
2. the color and arrangement of knots
3. *Possible answer:* Each is handmade and a unique work of beauty, but each also serves a useful purpose, such as covering the floor or acting as curtains.

Making Connections

TEACH

Explain to students that rugs are made by tying knots of yarn or thread onto a stiff backing. **Ask: What is the most efficient and quickest way to do this?** *(by machine)* Explain that although most rugs are made by machines today, for most of human history—and still today in some places of the world—another process is used. Then have them read the feature. **L1**

More About Carpets

The oldest known woven carpet—dating from the 200s B.C.—was used by the Huns, a Turkish people, and includes the figures of cavalry riders, deer, flowers, and an abstract checkerboard pattern.

Interdisciplinary Connections

Art Carpet designs vary around the world, although natural patterns like flowers and abstract designs with geometric shapes are common. One typical characteristic of woven carpets is to use a repeated pattern. Give students a piece of graph paper and have them design their own pattern for a woven carpet.

Focus

Section Objectives

1. Discuss the varied geography of this region.
2. Describe how oil affects the lives of the people who live here.
3. Compare the politics of these countries.

BELLRINGER
Skillbuilder Activity

Project transparency and have students answer questions.

This activity is also available as a blackline master.

Daily Focus Skills Transparency 4-3

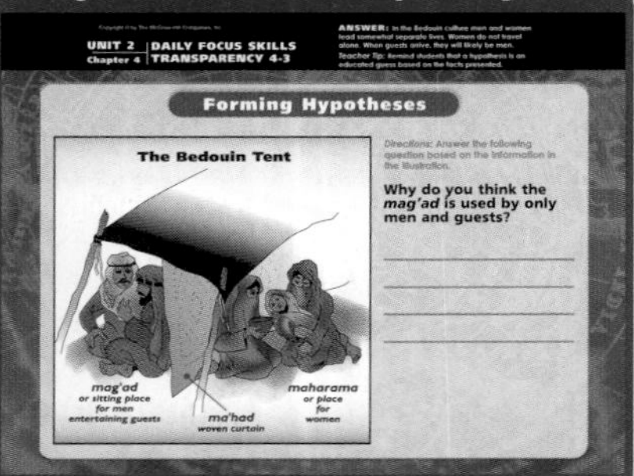

Guide to Reading

■ **Accessing Prior Knowledge**
Ask: **What do you know about the Arab nations of Southwest Asia?** Students might respond that these countries are rich due to oil exports. Tell them that in this chapter they will read about Arab countries that do not have oil wealth.

Section 3

Syria, Lebanon, Jordan, and Arabia

Guide to Reading

Main Idea

Syria, Lebanon, Jordan, and Saudi Arabia have Arab populations but different economies and forms of government.

Terms to Know

- Bedouin
- wadi
- desalinization
- hajj

Reading Strategy

Create a chart like this one, listing three key economic activities for each country.

Country	Economic Activities
Syria	
Lebanon	
Jordan	
Saudi Arabia	

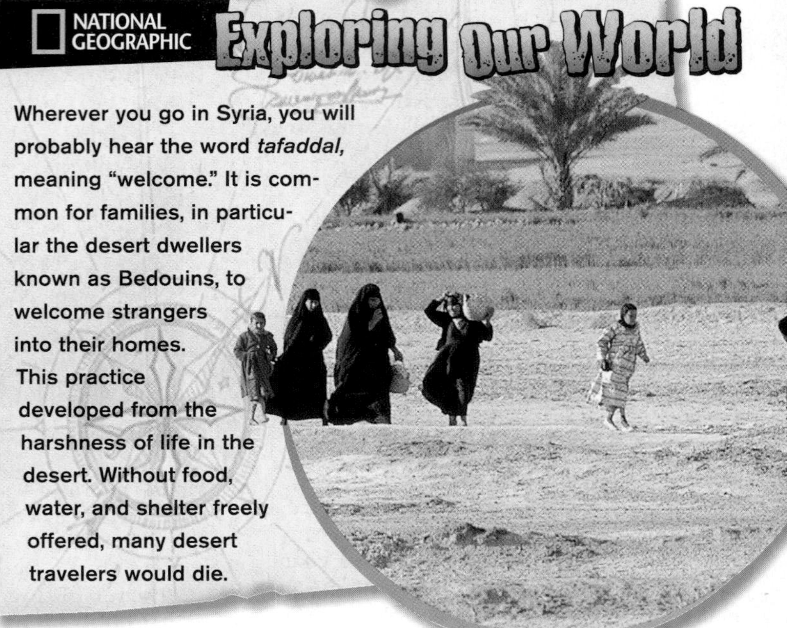

Wherever you go in Syria, you will probably hear the word *tafaddal,* meaning "welcome." It is common for families, in particular the desert dwellers known as Bedouins, to welcome strangers into their homes. This practice developed from the harshness of life in the desert. Without food, water, and shelter freely offered, many desert travelers would die.

People in desert countries greatly value hospitality. Large parts of the countries you will read about in this section are made up of desert. Saudi Arabia makes up about 80 percent of the quite large Arabian Peninsula. Yemen, Oman, and the Persian Gulf States—Kuwait, Bahrain, and the United Arab Emirates—make up the rest.

Syria

Syria's land includes fertile coastal plains and valleys along the Mediterranean Sea. The vast Syrian Desert covers the eastern region. Agriculture is Syria's main economic activity. Farmers raise mostly cotton, wheat, and fruits. The Syrian government has built dams on the **Euphrates River,** which provide water for irrigation as well as hydroelectric power for cities and industries. Future conflict with both Turkey and Iraq over Euphrates water is a possibility.

Section Resources

Reproducible Masters
- Reproducible Lesson Plan 4-3
- Daily Lecture and Discussion Notes 4-3
- Guided Reading Activity 4-3
- Reading Essentials and Study Guide 4-3
- Section Quiz 4-3

Transparencies
- Daily Focus Skills Transparency 4-3
- GeoQuiz Transparency 4-2

Multimedia
- Vocabulary PuzzleMaker Software
- Interactive Tutor Self-Assessment CD-ROM
- Presentation Plus! CD-ROM
- ExamView® Pro 3.0 Testmaker CD-ROM

Syria's People Almost half of Syria's 17.1 million people live in rural areas. A few are **Bedouins**—nomadic desert peoples who follow a traditional way of life. Most other Syrians live in cities. **Damascus,** the capital, is one of the oldest continuously inhabited cities in the world. It was founded as a trading center more than 5,000 years ago.

Islam has deeply influenced Syria's traditional arts and buildings. In many Syrian cities, you can see spectacular mosques and palaces. As in other Arab countries, hospitality is a major part of life in Syria. Group meals are a popular way of strengthening family ties and friendships. The most favorite foods are lamb, flat bread, and bean dishes flavored with garlic and lemon.

Syria's Government In 1946 Syria became an independent country. Since the 1960s, one political party has controlled Syria's government. It does not allow many political freedoms. As of May 2000, Syria was one of seven nations named by the U.S. government as being "state sponsors" of terrorism. This means that the United States believes that these countries help organize terrorist attacks by providing money or a base of operations. Other countries suspected of supporting terrorists include Libya, Iran, Iraq, Sudan, North Korea, Cuba, and Afghanistan.

✓Reading Check **On what river has Syria built dams?**

Lebanon

Lebanon is about half the size of New Jersey. Because the country is so small, you can swim in the warm Mediterranean Sea, then play in the snow in the mountains, both on the same day.

Music

The most common stringed instrument of Southwest Asia is the oud. Often pear-shaped, its neck bends sharply backward. Music from this region uses semitones that are not heard in Western music. Semitones are the "invisible" notes that lie between the black and white keys of a piano. Legend says that the oud owes its special tones to the birdsongs absorbed by the wood from which the oud was made.

Looking Closer **What instrument in our culture do you think came from the oud?**

GO TO **World Music: A Cultural Legacy**
Hear music of this region on Disc 1, Track 25.

Chapter 4

Section 3, pages 110–114

TEACH

Making a Chart Create a chart with "Syria," "Lebanon," "Jordan," and "Arabian Peninsula" as column headings. Down the left side of the chart, list the headings "Physical features," "Economy," "People," "Cities," "Government," and "Religion." Have students copy these headings into their notebooks and fill in the relevant details as they read the section. **L1**

✓ Reading Check Answer

Euphrates River

Answer guitar, mandolin, or lute

Activity Have students look up "oud" on the Internet, noting its many different forms and tracing its travels from the Islamic world into Europe.

World Music: A Cultural Legacy

Use the accompanying Teacher Guide for background information, discussion questions, and worksheets about the music of this region.

Cooperative Learning Activity

Solving a Puzzle Point out that people have been living in cities in Southwest Asia for thousands of years. Records dating to the 1400s B.C. refer to Damascus. Describe how archaeologists piece together clues to ancient civilizations. If possible, supplement your presentation with photographs showing the partial evidence from which archaeologists work. Then organize students into groups and give them photographs of two ancient objects that you have cut into pieces of random sizes. Have the groups try to reassemble their "artifacts," and then try to interpret what they were used for. Have the groups share their findings with the class. **L1 ELL**

EE6 The Uses of Geography: Standard 17

Daily Lecture Notes 4–3

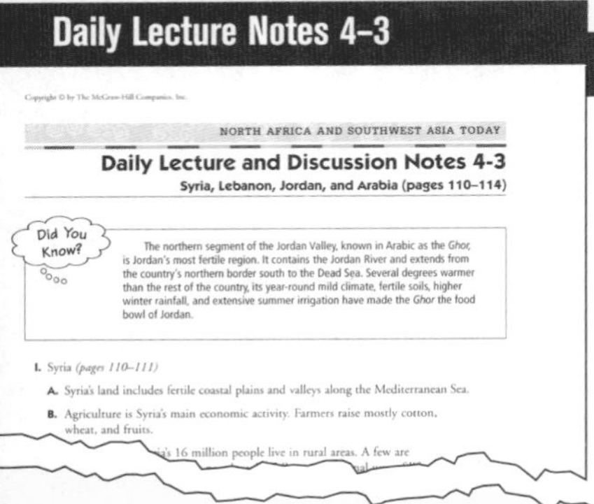

NORTH AFRICA AND SOUTHWEST ASIA TODAY

Daily Lecture and Discussion Notes 4-3

Syria, Lebanon, Jordan, and Arabia (pages 110–114)

Did You Know? The northern segment of the Jordan Valley, known in Arabic as the *Ghor*, is Jordan's most fertile region. It contains the Jordan River and extends from the country's northern border south to the Dead Sea. Several degrees warmer than the rest of the country, its year-round mild climate, fertile soils, higher winter rainfall, and extensive summer irrigation have made the *Ghor* the food bowl of Jordan.

I. Syria *(pages 110–111)*

A. Syria's land includes fertile coastal plains and valleys along the Mediterranean Sea.

B. Agriculture is Syria's main economic activity. Farmers raise mostly cotton, wheat, and fruits.

...ia's 16 million people live in rural areas. A few are

✓ Reading Check Answer

It was badly damaged in a civil war that lasted from 1975 to 1991.

Guided Reading Activity 4–3

Name ______ Date ______ Class ______

NORTH AFRICA AND SOUTHWEST ASIA TODAY

Guided Reading Activity 4-3

Syria, Lebanon, Jordan, and Arabia

DIRECTIONS: Answering Questions Reading the section and answering the questions below will help you learn more about Syria, Lebanon, Jordan, and Arabia. Use your textbook to write answers to the questions.

1. What kind of land does Syria include?
2. What is the main economic activity of Syria?
3. Where do more than half of Syria's people live?
4. What is the capital and largest city of Lebanon?
5. What languages are spoken in Lebanon?

✓ Reading Check Answer

phosphates, potash, pottery, chemicals, and processed foods

Assign Section 3 Assessment as homework or an in-class activity.

Have students use the Interactive Tutor Self-Assessment CD-ROM to review Section 4–3.

Cedar trees once covered Lebanon. King Solomon used them to build the Jewish Temple. Cedars were used in the Bible as symbols of beauty, strength, endurance, and pride. Now only a few groves survive. Still, Lebanon is the most densely wooded of all the Southwest Asian countries.

The Lebanese People More than 80 percent of Lebanon's nearly 4.3 million people live in coastal urban areas. **Beirut** (bay•ROOT), the capital and largest city, was once a major banking and business center. European tourists called Beirut "the Paris of the East" because of its elegant shops and sidewalk cafés. Today, however, Beirut is still rebuilding after a civil war that lasted from 1975 to 1991.

Lebanon's civil war arose between groups of Muslims and Christians. About 70 percent of the Lebanese are Arab Muslims and most of the rest are Arab Christians. Many lives were lost in the war, many people fled as refugees, and Lebanon's economy was almost destroyed. Israel invaded Lebanon during the civil war.

Arabic is the most widely spoken language in Lebanon. French is also an official language. Why? France ruled Lebanon before the country became independent in the 1940s. Local foods reflect a blend of Arab, Turkish, and French influences.

✓ Reading Check **Why is Beirut in the process of rebuilding?**

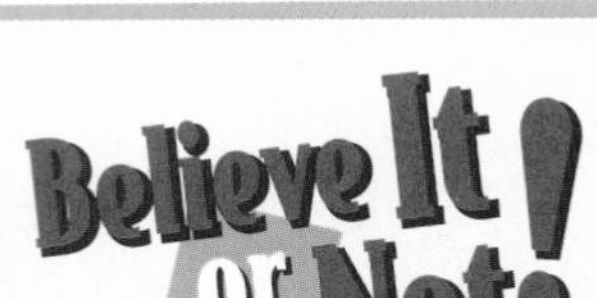

Petra

Petra was built during the 300s B.C. The city's temples and monuments were carved out of cliffs in the Valley of Moses in Jordan. It was a major center of the spice trade that reached as far as China, Egypt, Greece, and India. Archaeologists have found dams, rock-carved channels, and ceramic pipes that brought water to the 30,000 people who once lived here.

Jordan

A land of contrasts, Jordan stretches from the fertile Jordan River valley in the west to dry, rugged country in the east. Jordan lacks water resources. However, small amounts of irrigated farmland lie in the Jordan River valley. Here farmers grow wheat, fruits, and vegetables. Jordan's desert is home to tent-dwelling Bedouins, who raise livestock.

Jordan also lacks energy resources. The majority of its people work in service and manufacturing industries. The leading manufactured goods are phosphate, potash, pottery, chemicals, and processed foods.

People and Government Most of Jordan's 5.2 million people are Arab Muslims. They include more than 1 million Palestinian refugees. **Amman** is the capital and largest city. At least 5,000 years old, Amman is sprinkled with Roman ruins.

During the early 1900s, the Ottoman Empire ruled this area. After the Ottoman defeat in World War I, the British set up a territory that became known as Jordan, which became an independent country in 1946.

Jordan has a constitutional monarchy. Elected leaders govern, but a king or queen is the official head of state. From 1952 to 1999, **King Hussein I** (hoo•SAYN) ruled Jordan. He worked to blend the country's traditions with modern ways of life. In 1994, Hussein signed a peace treaty with neighboring Israel. He was helped in his work by his American-born wife, **Queen Noor.** Since 1978, Queen Noor has played a major role in promoting Arab-Western relations. The present ruler of Jordan is Hussein's son, **King Abdullah II** (uhb•dul•LAH).

✓ Reading Check **What are Jordan's leading manufactured goods?**

Meeting Special Needs

Interpersonal Organize students into three groups and assign each group one of the countries discussed in Section 3. Instruct the groups to create a study guide for their assigned country. Make sure each group member makes a copy of the completed study guide. Then have the class separate into new groups of three, with each new group including one member from each of the original three groups. Students can use their study guides to teach the other group members about their country. **L1**

Refer to *Inclusion for the Middle School Social Studies Classroom Strategies and Activities* in the TCR.

World Oil Reserves

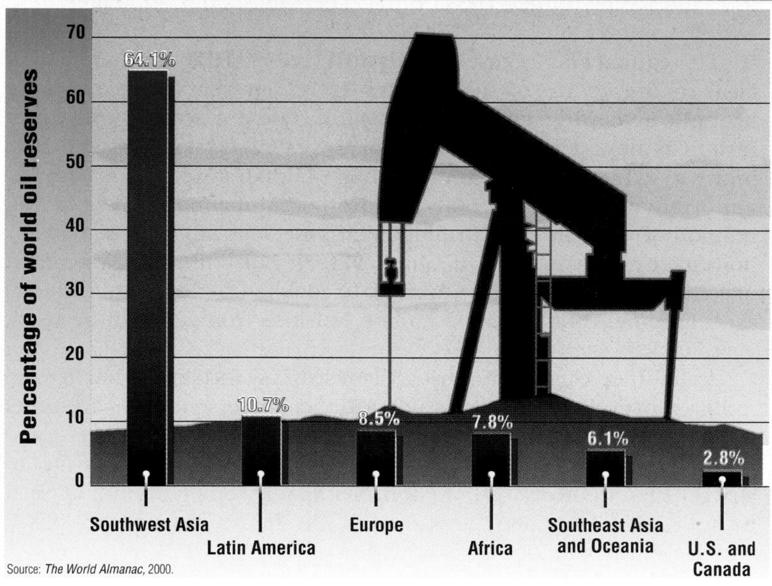

Source: *The World Almanac*, 2000.

Analyzing the Graph

Southwest Asia has more oil than all other regions of the world combined.

Region **What percentage of the world's oil reserves does Southwest Asia hold?**

Visit owt.glencoe.com and click on **Chapter 4–Textbook Updates.**

Saudi Arabia

Saudi Arabia, the largest country in Southwest Asia, is about the size of the eastern half of the United States. Vast deserts cover this region. The largest and harshest desert is the Rub' al-Khali, or Empty Quarter, in the southeast.

Saudi Arabia has no rivers or permanent bodies of water. Water for farming sometimes comes from seasonal **wadis,** or dry riverbeds filled by rainwater from rare downpours. The desert also holds oases.

An Oil-Based Economy Saudi Arabia holds about 25 percent of the world's oil. This entire region of North Africa and Southwest Asia is by far the world's leading producer of oil. The graph above compares the amount of oil reserves in Southwest Asia with those of other regions. Saudi Arabia belongs to the **Organization of Petroleum Exporting Countries (OPEC).** Today the 11 OPEC countries supply more than 40 percent of the world's oil. By increasing or reducing supply, they are able to influence world oil prices.

Oil has helped Saudi Arabia boost its standard of living. Money earned by selling oil has built schools, hospitals, roads, and airports. Aware that someday its oil will run out, Saudi Arabia's government has been trying to broaden its economy. In recent years, it has given more emphasis to industry and agriculture. To get more water and grow more food, the government of Saudi Arabia has spent much money on irrigation and another process called **desalinization,** which takes salt out of seawater.

Posing Questions Ask students to pose and answer five questions using the World Oil Reserves graph on this page. Guide students to use all available information on the graph, and to test a variety of skills such as math, making comparisons, generalizing, categorizing, and so on. **L2**

Analyzing the Graph

Answer
64.1 percent

Skills Practice
What region has the next largest share of oil reserves? How large are those reserves? *(Latin America; 10.7 percent of the world's total)*

Did You Know?

Petroleum is used to produce detergents, synthetic rubber, and products used to make drugs, nylon, plastics, polyester fabrics, food additives, explosives, dyes, and many other goods.

Team-Teaching Activity

Mathematics Point out that petroleum, or crude oil, is used to produce a great variety of products, including gasoline, kerosene, and other products. Tell students that each barrel, containing 42 gallons of crude oil, produces 21 gallons of gasoline, 3 gallons of jet fuel, 9 gallons of gas oil and distillates, less than 4 gallons of lubricants, and 3 gallons of heavier residues. Have them use these figures to create a circle graph showing the percentage of each product that comes from a barrel of crude oil. Invite a math teacher to class to review calculating percentages. **L3**

EE5 Environment and Society: Standard 16

Chapter 4

Section 3, pages 110–114

Section Quiz 4-3

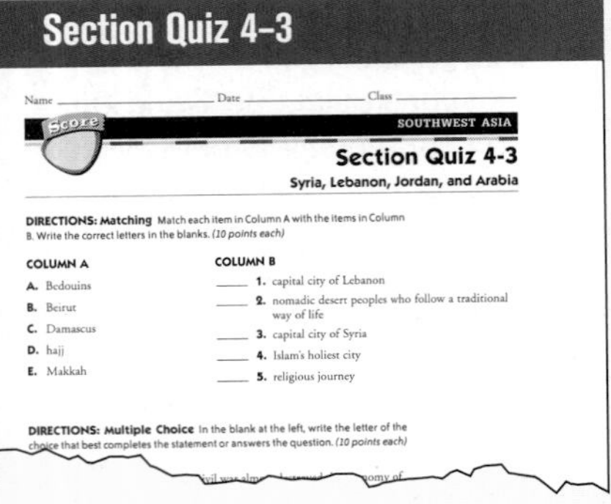

Name ______ Date ______ Class ______

SOUTHWEST ASIA

Section Quiz 4-3

Syria, Lebanon, Jordan, and Arabia

DIRECTIONS: Matching Match each item in Column A with the items in Column B. Write the correct letters in the blanks. (10 points each)

COLUMN A	COLUMN B
A. Bedouins	____ 1. capital city of Lebanon
B. Beirut	____ 2. nomadic desert peoples who follow a traditional way of life
C. Damascus	____ 3. capital city of Syria
D. hajj	____ 4. Islam's holiest city
E. Makkah	____ 5. religious journey

DIRECTIONS: Multiple Choice In the blank at the left, write the letter of the choice that best completes the statement or answers the question. (10 points each)

Reading Check Answer

Islamic religion

Reading Essentials and Study Guide 4-3

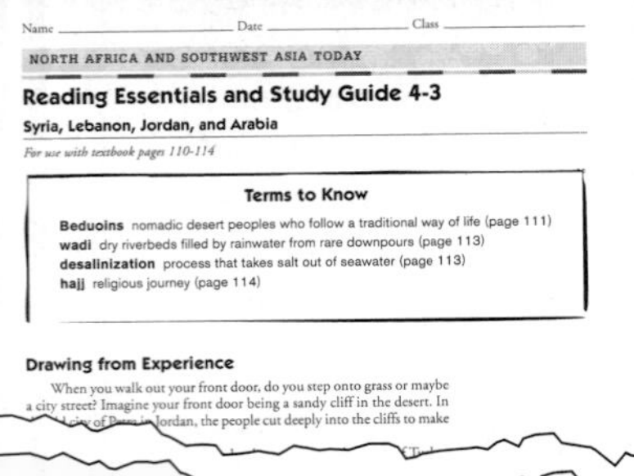

Name ______ Date ______ Class ______

NORTH AFRICA AND SOUTHWEST ASIA TODAY

Reading Essentials and Study Guide 4-3

Syria, Lebanon, Jordan, and Arabia

For use with textbook pages 110–114

Terms to Know

Bedouins nomadic desert peoples who follow a traditional way of life (page 111)
wadi dry riverbeds filled by rainwater from rare downpours (page 113)
desalinization process that takes salt out of seawater (page 113)
hajj religious journey (page 114)

Drawing from Experience

When you walk out your front door, do you step onto grass or maybe a city street? Imagine your front door being a sandy cliff in the desert. In ... Jordan, the people cut deeply into the cliffs to make

Enrich

Have students research the Five Pillars of Islam and prepare a display that explains them.

4 CLOSE

Have students write a paragraph describing how oil and Islam affect life in the countries of the Arabian Peninsula.

History and People The people of Saudi Arabia were once divided into many different family groups. In 1932 a monarchy led by the Saud family unified the country. The Saud family still rules Saudi Arabia.

The capital and largest city, **Riyadh** (ree•YAHD), sits amid a large oasis in the center of the country. In recent years, oil wealth has brought sweeping changes to Riyadh. Once a small rural town, Riyadh is now a modern city with towering skyscrapers and busy highways. In western Saudi Arabia, Makkah (Mecca) is another important city. In the A.D. 600s, the prophet Muhammad preached the religion of Islam in Makkah. Since that time, Makkah has been Islam's holiest city. As you read in Chapter 3, all Muslims are expected to make a **hajj**, or religious journey, to Makkah at least once during their lifetime. Today, about 2 million Muslims from around the world visit Makkah each year.

As in other Muslim countries, Islam strongly influences life in Saudi Arabia. Government, business, school, and home schedules are timed to Islam's five daily prayers and two major yearly celebrations. Saudi customs concerning the roles of men and women in public life are stricter than in most Muslim countries. Saudi women are not allowed to drive cars. They may work outside the home, but only in jobs in which they avoid close contact with men.

Reading Check What influences almost every part of Saudi Arabian culture?

Assessment

Defining Terms

1. **Define** Bedouin, wadi, desalinization, hajj.

Recalling Facts

2. **Government** Why are many people in the United States suspicious of the Syrian government?
3. **Culture** Why was Beirut called "the Paris of the East"?
4. **Culture** What is the importance of the city of Makkah?

Critical Thinking

5. **Understanding Cause and Effect** How could a dam on the Euphrates River cause conflict between Turkey, Syria, and Iraq?
6. **Drawing Conclusions** How could the nations belonging to OPEC affect your life?

Graphic Organizer

7. **Organizing Information** Create a diagram like this one. Inside the large oval, list characteristics that Syria, Lebanon, and Jordan share.

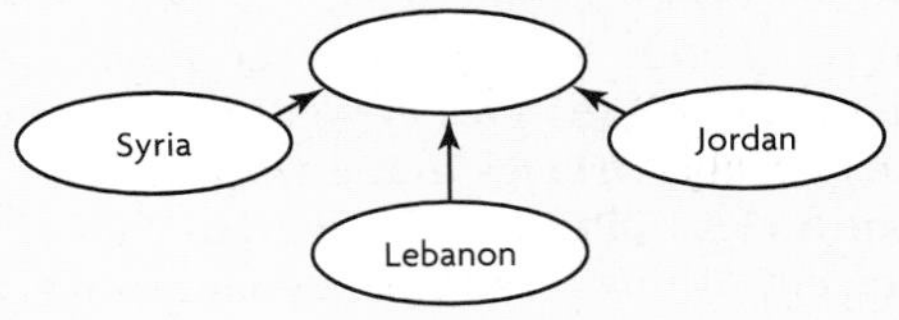

Applying Social Studies Skills

8. **Analyzing Graphs** Examine the World Oil Reserves graph on page 113. Which region of the world has the third largest reserves of oil?

Section 3 Assessment

1. The terms are defined in the Glossary.
2. because of connections with terrorist activities
3. because of its elegant shops and sidewalk cafes
4. It is Islam's holiest city, and all Muslims are expected to make a journey to it at least once in their lives, if they are able.
5. because dams built by one country upstream reduce the water available to other countries downstream
6. They control the production and price of oil, which affects the availability and prices of gasoline and other petroleum-based products in our country.
7. *Possible answers:* Muslim majority, Arabic is spoken, varied land.
8. Europe

TIME REPORTS

FOCUS ON WORLD ISSUES

The Arab-Israeli Conflict

Will words replace violence in the Holy Land's quarrel?

AMIT SHABI—REUTERS

Focus on World Issues

Teacher Background

The Arab-Israeli conflict has been a thorn in the side of world governments since the end of World War II. To understand why this is such a heated issue, it is important to remember that this area has strong religious and cultural significance for many people.

TIME REPORTS UNIT 2

The Arab-Israeli Conflict

THEME: CONFLICT AND COOPERATION

Guide To Teaching With This Unit

Preparing the Student

Have students locate Israel on a map. Note the strategic location of this region between Europe, Asia, and Africa. Point out Jerusalem, the West Bank, the Gaza Strip, and the Golan Heights.

Tell students that after the founding of Israel in 1948, many of the Arabs who lived in this area (the Palestinians) were forced to move to other locations such as Lebanon, the West Bank, and the Gaza Strip. Some of today's Palestinians are fourth-generation refugees. According to the United Nations High Commissioner for Refugees, Palestinians have been uprooted longer than any other current group.

Making Connections

Conflict **Ask students:** **Have you ever felt you were treated unfairly by an adult such as a parent or teacher? Have you ever been forced to give up something that you felt was yours? How did this make you feel?** Both the Palestinians and the Israelis have similar feelings. The Palestinians feel they have been unfairly forced to give up their homeland. The Israelis feel the Arabs have treated them with disrespect in not accepting their right to live in Israel. Such feelings are deep-seated and affect us all. International law cannot be upheld when local governments are in turmoil. In addition, trading is difficult when governments are unstable.

TIME REPORTS

1 Focus

Ask students: **What have you heard about the Arab-Israeli conflict? What do you know about the differences between the two groups? How are their religions and customs different? What do you think each side wants?**

Encourage the students to be nonjudgmental in their views of those customs and religions that may differ from their own.

Write the major points made by students on the board. Ask the other students whether they agree or disagree with each statement.

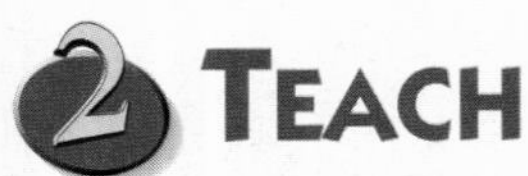

2 Teach

Identifying Main Ideas

After students have read the "United in Grief" section, have them write a paragraph describing the main idea they learned from their reading. L1

More About the Photo

Historic Moment At the time this photograph was taken, it was in magazines and on news broadcasts around the world. **Ask:** **What is the significance of shaking hands in our culture? Do you think shaking hands would have the same meaning to Prime Minister Rabin and PLO leader Arafat?**

TIME REPORTS

FOCUS ON WORLD ISSUES

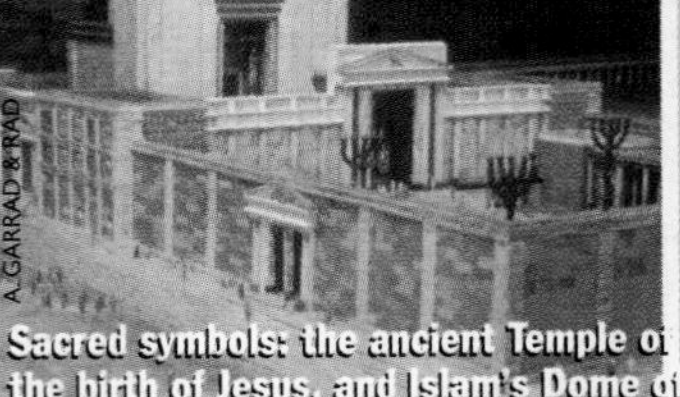

A.GARRAD & RAD

Sacred symbols: the ancient Temple of the Jews, the birth of Jesus, and Islam's Dome of the Rock.

United in Grief

In April 2001 two couples shook hands in Amman, the capital of Jordan. One couple, Ayelet and Tzvika Shahak, were Israeli. They are citizens of Israel, a nation that Jews consider their **homeland**.

The other couple, Amal and Jamal al-Durra, were **Palestinian**. Most Palestinian Arabs are Muslims, and about 1 million of them are Israeli citizens. But like the al-Durras, most have no country to call their own. They believe that the land Israel occupies is their homeland.

CYNTHIA JOHNSON

Historic moment: Israeli Prime Minister Yitzhak Rabin and Palestinian leade[r] Yasser Arafat shake hands at the White House in 199[3]

Since Israel's founding in 1948, the conflict between the Israelis and the Palestinians has taken thousands of lives. Those of the Shahaks' daughter and the al-Durras' son were among them.

A Borderless Battleground

A peace group brought the Shahaks and the al-Durras together in Amman. Their common grief united them. Yet in all other ways they stood miles apart. The al-Durras want the 3.7 million Palestinians now outside Israel to be able to live on Israeli soil. The Shahaks, like most Israelis, oppose that idea. They fear that Palestinians would soon take over their nation.

The meeting gave Mr. Shahak some hope for the future, however. "Just the fact of Jamal's willingness to look for a solution means to me that perhaps eventually there will be someone to talk to," he said. "But it seems to me that there's still a long way to go."

Most Israelis and Palestinians would agree. Israelis and Arabs have fought four major wars since 1948. The violence has never completely stopped. And it has boiled over into the nations of North Africa and Southwest Asia.

One Small Nation

Israel is a tiny country, a bit smaller than New Jersey. Its population of nearly 6 million, mostly made up of Jews, is smaller than New York City's.

Outside of Israel, about 395 million people live in 19 North African and Southwest Asian nations. Almost all of them are Muslims, followers of the Islamic faith. Together, those 19 nations

116

Meeting Special Needs

Visual/Spatial Give students a blank map of Israel and the area surrounding it, including parts of Lebanon, Syria, Jordan, and Egypt. Have them label the following countries/areas: Israel, Egypt, Lebanon, Syria, Jordan, Gaza Strip, West Bank, and Golan Heights. They should also label Jerusalem. Have students color each area/country a different color. Seeing how close these areas are to one another and how small Israel is in comparison to the Arab countries can help students grasp the difficulties in resolving this conflict. L1

Refer to *Inclusion for the Middle School Social Studies Classroom Strategies and Activities* in the TCR.

CYNTHIA JOHNSON

ART RESOURCE—PHOTO RESEARCHERS, SUPERSTOCK

Palestinian militant: student leader Qais Adwan

ALFRED YAGOBZADEH—SIPA FOR TIME

ALBERT FACELLY—SIPA FOR TIME

Israeli military officer: Colonel Noam Tibon

TIME REPORTS

cover more land than the United States and Mexico combined.

Outsized Impact

Despite its small size, Israel has had a major impact on its neighbors. This is especially true of Muslim nations populated by Arabs, or people who speak Arabic. (People in Turkey, Iran, and Afghanistan speak other languages.)

In the early part of the 20th century, most Arabs lived in small villages. They felt a strong loyalty to their **clan**, or group of related families. Those Arabs who moved to cities began to see themselves as citizens of a nation. Few Arabs, however, thought of themselves as members of a community of nations with a common purpose.

Israel's birth in 1948 changed all that, creating the region's only true democracy. Despite support for Israel from the United Nations, Arabs questioned Israel's right to the land. Suddenly the Muslim world shared a goal—driving the Israelis out.

Israel survived war with its Arab neighbors in 1948, 1956, 1967, and 1973. In 1979 Israel signed a peace treaty with Egypt. Israel also signed a treaty with Jordan in 1994.

Yet some Muslim nations still consider themselves at war with Israel. Among them are a few oil-rich nations, such as Iran, Iraq, Libya, and Syria. Those nations send money—and sometimes weapons—to the Palestinian Liberation Organization (PLO), headed by Yasser Arafat. The PLO's main goal is to set up an independent Palestinian nation. People like the Shahaks and the al-Durras know that. And they hope their leaders find a fair way to get both sides what they want.

EXPLORING THE ISSUE

1. **Analyzing Information** What might make people who share a language and a religion feel loyal to one another, wherever they live?
2. **Making Inferences** In the year 2000, 600,000 Palestinians still lived in 59 refugee camps set up by the United Nations. How might growing up in a camp make young people angry?
3. **Cause and Effect** Why might Israel's democracy and economic success make the region's kings and self-appointed leaders uneasy?

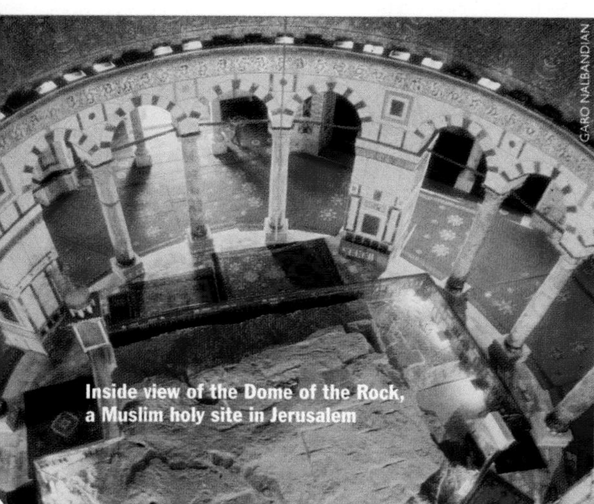

GARO NALBANDIAN

Inside view of the Dome of the Rock, a Muslim holy site in Jerusalem

117

Summarizing Information

Ask students: What does the section titled "Outsized Impact" say about how the founding of Israel affected Arabs? What were some of the ways that the Arabs responded?

You may find it helpful to have students refer to the time line in the "Years of Tears Chronology" subsection at the end of this chapter.

EXPLORING THE ISSUE

ANSWERS

1. People who share a common language can communicate easily with one another and there is less chance for misunderstanding. Sharing a common religion means sharing beliefs, customs, and values, which are fundamental ways in which human beings are tied to one another.
2. *Possible answers:* These young people have no sense of having a home. They may hear stories from their elders about how they were pushed out of their homes when Israel was founded.
3. *Possible answers:* Their citizens might wonder why they are not as affluent as the Israelis. They might then want to overthrow their leaders and become a democracy, too.

Team-Teaching Activity

History Have a teacher who is knowledgeable about current events update the class on what has been happening with the Arab-Israeli conflict since this report was written. Request that the teacher discuss specific recent incidents and ask students to explain how the incidents might be perceived by both Jews and Arabs. **L1**

EE4 Human Systems: Standard 13

TIME REPORTS

Did You Know?

Israel is defined as a religious state. The government does not prohibit discrimination and it does not promise that everyone will be treated equally. Religious minorities can be discriminated against in terms of housing and jobs.

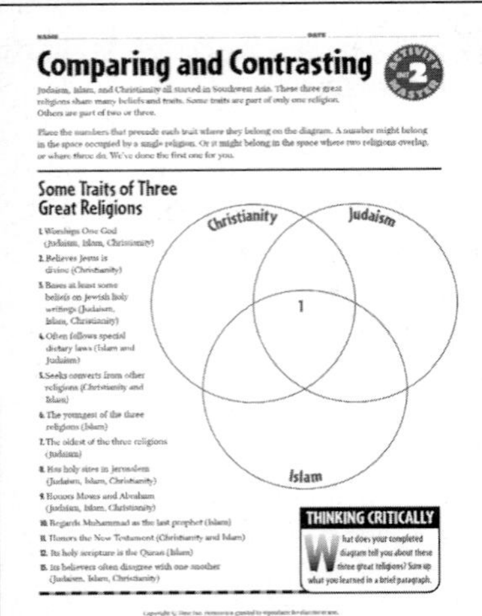
Comparing and Contrasting

Some Traits of Three Great Religions

Christianity

Judaism

Islam

1

THINKING CRITICALLY

EXPLORING THE ISSUE

ANSWERS

1. They realized this site had religious significance for Jews and might have thought Israeli voters would agree that Muslims should not have complete control over it.
2. Answers will vary. Many people felt the Israeli officials acted aggressively in entering the site; Palestinians responded violently, as did Israeli soldiers.

TIME REPORTS

Conflict on Holy Ground

A 35-acre plot of land sits atop a hill in the heart of Jerusalem, Israel's capital city. The hilltop is a beautiful place, filled with fountains, gardens, buildings, and domes. Many key events in the early history of Christianity took place here. The hill also has a special hold on Jews and Muslims.

Muslims call the hilltop Haram al-Sharif, or the Noble Sanctuary. A house of worship called the al-Aqsa Mosque sits there, as does a glittering, gilded dome. The dome covers a sacred rock. Muslims believe that Muhammad, the last and greatest prophet of Islam, rose to heaven from that rock.

Jews call the hill the Temple Mount. It is the most sacred site of Judaism, the Jewish religion. Two great Jewish temples once stood there. On the western side of the hill is a wall that held back the earth below the second of the temples. Jews come from all over the world to pray at the Western Wall.

From Insult to Injury

Generally only Muslims are allowed to enter the Noble Sanctuary. In September 2000, some heavily guarded Israeli politicians entered the site to challenge that rule. Rioting broke out. It spread to the Gaza Strip and to an area called the **West Bank**, where 900,000 Arabs live.

Palestinians named the daily, bloody rioting that followed the **al-Aqsa Intifadeh** (uprising). Fighting stopped for a while in June 2001. But the mutual trust that had been growing since 1993, when serious peace talks began, was dead.

▲ **Temple Mount/Haram al-Sharif was originally the site of King Solomon's Temple, built around 960 B.C.**

EXPLORING THE ISSUE

1. **Making Inferences** Why might the Israeli politicians have thought their tour of the mount would help them win the support of Israeli voters?
2. **Drawing Conclusions** Do you think the al-Aqsa Intifadeh created sympathy for the Palestinians? Why or why not?

Interdisciplinary Activity

Science When the Israelis developed their homeland, people said they "made the desert bloom." Ask a science teacher to explain how crops are generally grown in the United States. Afterwards, have students research ways the Israelis accomplish this task. Students should learn about types of crops grown, farming methods used, and the ecological consequences of this type of farming. Have them report their findings to the class. Then have the class compare Israeli agriculture to American. **L2**

EE5 Environment and Society: Standards 14, 15

The Search for Peace

Kiyan Khaled al-Sayfi is a Palestinian teenager. She lives in a refugee camp in Bethlehem. Bethlehem is a city in the West Bank, an area between Israel and Jordan. "I expect to die at any moment by a stray bullet from an Israeli soldier," she said one month after the al-Aqsa Intifadeh began. "It is a terrible feeling."

About 15 miles away, near the town of Hebron, Colonel Noam Tibon, 38, was in charge of 2,000 Israeli soldiers. "My 70-year-old parents," he said, "are very worried about the situation in Israel. They went through all the wars here. But they don't stop dreaming of peace for my children, their grandchildren."

ALBERT FACELLY—SIPA FOR TIME

Teenager Kiyan Khaled al-Sayfi in Bethlehem

Missing Deadlines

Will that dream ever come true? The answer depends on what Israelis and Palestinians are willing to give up. Mainly, the Palestinians want land they can call their own. The Israelis want to be able to live in peace in their own country. In 1993, both groups agreed on a plan to reach those goals. If all went well, by 2000 the Palestinians would have their own nation in the West Bank and the Gaza Strip.

Yet all didn't go well. By the summer of 2000, several problems still had to be solved. For one thing, Israel wanted all of Jerusalem to be its capital. The Palestinians wanted to make the eastern half of Jerusalem their capital.

Control of the Temple Mount was another sticking point. Another obstacle was Israel's firm refusal to give Palestinians everywhere the right to move to Israel. Still another was the nearly 300 Jewish settlements in the West Bank, the Gaza Strip, and East Jerusalem. The Palestinians wanted them destroyed.

The truce that halted the al-Aqsa Intifadeh in June 2001 wasn't a real peace. But when one comes, teens like Kiyan won't have to fear for their lives. And Colonel Tibon's children—or their children—will see his parents' dreams come true.

EXPLORING THE ISSUE

1. **Comparing** What hopes and fears might Kiyan and Colonel Tibon have in common?
2. **Explaining** Why would Israel not want to give all Palestinians the right to move to Israel?

Current Events Journal

Instruct students to pick articles from two different publications covering the same current event about the Arab-Israeli conflict. Tell students to read both articles carefully and write their responses to the following: **Do you think the articles present both the Arab and the Israeli sides of the issue? What differences in approach can you see in the articles?**

Did You Know

In the summer of 2001, Palestinian authorities estimated that about one-third of the people in the Gaza Strip and West Bank were living in poverty on less than $1.50 a day. Some of these people had jobs in Israel, but with the start of the al-Aqsa Intifada, most of them lost their jobs.

EXPLORING THE ISSUE

ANSWERS

1. Both fear for their personal safety and that of their relatives. They both hope the area will see peace someday.
2. being outnumbered by Palestinians; fear for Israelis' safety and religious freedom; costs of resettlement

Critical Thinking Activity

Interpreting Points of View Have students split into two groups. Have each student in the first group write an essay in which he or she pretends to be a young Jew who moves to Israel from Europe shortly after World War II. Instruct each student in the second group to write an essay about how it would feel to be a young Palestinian who was forced to move to a refugee camp as a result of Israel being established. Students should discuss how they felt about moving and the hardships they faced. **L2**

EE4 Human Systems: Standard 13

Recommended Internet Sites

www.unhcr.ch
The United Nations High Commissioner for Refugees (UNHCR) Web site provides information on refugees. Click on "The World." When the world map appears, click on the Middle East. Select a country to learn about its refugees.

fyi.cnn.com
Search for news on a particular subject such as Israel or Palestine. Teacher resources include lesson plans and activity ideas.

www.nara.gov/education/teaching/ishome.html
Provides a lesson plan on the U.S. recognition of Israel.

EXPLORING THE ISSUE

ANSWERS

1. The organization hopes to build understanding among individual young people, hoping they will spread this understanding to others.
2. Answers will vary.

NAME ________ DATE ________

Interpreting Tables

ACTIVITY MASTER 2

The United States tries to cooperate with other nations in a number of ways. The chart on this page will help you explore two of them.

- The first way is military aid. Military aid helps other nations equip and train their armed forces.
- The second way is economic aid. Among other things, economic aid helps poorer nations build roads, schools, hospitals, as well as train and hire teachers.
- Sometimes the United States sends nations items—weapons, for example, or food. Sometimes it loans money to nations. Other times it gives countries grants—money they don't have to pay back.
- The tables show where the nations are that get the most U.S. aid. It also shows the support the United States gives two Southwest Asian nations. To learn more, decide whether the statements below the charts are true or false.

Two Ways the United States Helps Other Nations
(in thousands of dollars—add 000)

Top Donations of U.S. Military Aid		Top Donations of U.S. Economic Aid	
Israel	$1,800,000	Africa South of the Sahara	$1,555,944
Egypt	$1,301,000	Israel	$1,200,000
Africa South of the Sahara	$16,343	Egypt	$810,743
Latin American Nations	$11,052	Latin American Nations	$740,895
European Nations*	$376,055	Asian Nations**	$599,872
Asian Nations**	$6,751	Newly Independent States***	$559,142
Newly Independent States***	$3,904	European Nations*	$507,946

Label the following statements True (T) or False (F).

____ 1. The information about military and economic aid is presented in two tables.
____ 2. The information comes from the U.S. State Department.
____ 3. One table shows that the United States gave Israel $1,800,000,000 in military aid in 1997.

Promoting Peace: What Can One Person Do?

What can an individual do to help reduce tensions in Southwest Asia? Israelis Ayelet and Tzvika Shahak asked themselves that question after a Palestinian's bomb killed their daughter. They decided to promote understanding. Their group brought them together with Palestinians Amal and Jamal al-Durra.

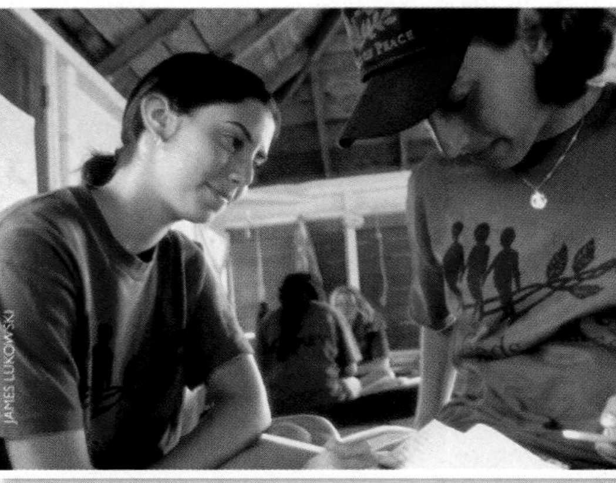

▲ **The camp broke down barriers for Israeli Dana Gadalyahu and Palestinian Ayah el-Rozi, both 15.**

John Wallach, an American, set up another group, Seeds of Peace. Every summer Seeds of Peace brings about 150 Muslim and Jewish teenagers to a camp in Maine. "The whole point," Wallach says, "is to let young people see that the differences are wide, that they are deep, but that it's up to them to find a way to resolve them."

John Wallach (left) with camp counselor Jared Fishman

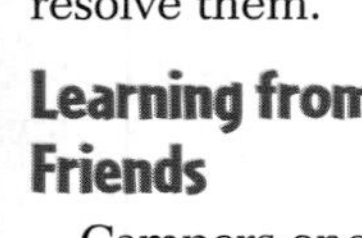

Learning from Friends

Campers one recent summer came from the nations of Israel, Egypt, Jordan, Tunisia, Morocco, and Qatar. Palestinian Sara Jabari, 15, came from the West Bank. She and Dana Naor, 13, an Israeli from a Tel Aviv suburb, became fast friends. Their friendship helped them understand each other's point of view. "She is so nice," Sara said of Dana. "I really got a new idea of the Israelis from Dana."

Do students in your school understand the Arab and Israeli points of view? If not, you could help your fellow students see how complex the issue is. Set up a discussion panel. Bring together people on each side and have them discuss their views. The Seeds of Peace website (**www.seedsofpeace.org**) can suggest other ideas. ■

EXPLORING THE ISSUE

1. **Analyzing Information** Why is Seeds of Peace an appropriate name for John Wallach's group?
2. **Making Inferences** Do you think it was harder for the Shahaks and al-Durras to meet than it was for the campers?

120

Your Government and You

The United States government has long been involved in the quest for peace in the Middle East. The United States embassy in Israel maintains a Web site (**www.usembassyisrael.org.il/publish/peace/peace1.htm**) that contains discussions of U.S. peace-making efforts along with related documents and photographs. Have students pick a specific topic or event (such as the 1978 Camp David Accords) and use this Web site to research it and write a report. **L2**

EE4 Human Systems: Standard 13

TIME REPORTS

REVIEW AND ASSESS

UNDERSTANDING THE ISSUE

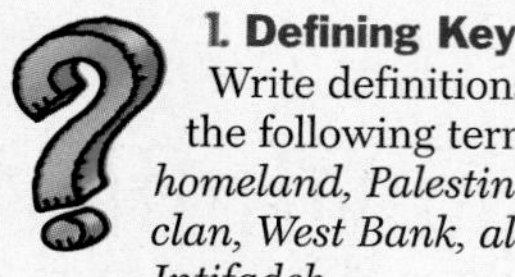

1. **Defining Key Terms** Write definitions for the following terms: *homeland, Palestinian, clan, West Bank, al-Aqsa Intifadeh.*
2. **Writing to Inform** In a 300-word article, describe the roadblocks that kept Israel and the Palestinians from ending their conflict in 2000. Use the terms listed above.
3. **Writing to Persuade** Israel once proposed letting Palestinians control the top of the Temple Mount, or Haram al-Sharif. Israelis would control the bottom portion, where they believe the remains of their ancient temples are buried. Write a short essay on why this plan might be a good idea, a bad one, or a little of each.

INTERNET RESEARCH ACTIVITIES

4. Navigate to the United Nations websites of both Palestine **www.palestine-un.org/index.html** and Israel **www.israel-un.org**. What does each side stress about its history? What does each side leave out? Report your findings to your class.
5. Christians trace their religion's roots to the Holy Land. To learn how one Christian group views the conflict, go to the website of Churches for a Middle East Peace **www.cmep.org**. Browse the site to find out what goals CMEP shares with Palestinian Muslims and Israeli Jews. Discuss those goals.

BEYOND THE CLASSROOM

6. **Research another ethnic or religious conflict**—the 1994 war in Rwanda, for example, or the 1999 conflict in Kosovo. How is the conflict you chose like the Arab-Israeli conflict? How is it different? Summarize your conclusions.
7. With your teacher's help, **make e-pals** with students in Israel and in Arab countries. A group called e-PALS (**www.epals.com**) can help you. Ask your e-pals to tell you how the dispute between Arabs and Israelis affects them.

JAMES LUKOWSKI

▲ **Trust-building exercise at Seeds of Peace.**

Years of Tears

Timeline of Major Arab-Israeli Conflicts, 1948-2001

1948-49 First Arab-Israeli War. Israel wins control of Western Jerusalem and most of the former Palestine.

1956 Second Arab-Israeli War. The UN ends it; no side gains.

1967 Third Arab-Israeli War. Israel wins control of the Gaza Strip and the Sinai Peninsula from Egypt; the Golan Heights from Syria; and the West Bank, including East Jerusalem, from Jordan.

1973-74 Fourth Arab-Israeli War. Israel defeats Arab invaders.

1987-1993 First Palestinian Intifadeh (uprising). Ends when both sides agree to a timetable for creating a Palestinian state.

2000-2001 Second Palestinian Intifadeh takes about 600 lives.

1940 1950 1960 1970 1980 1990 2000

BUILDING SKILLS FOR READING TIMELINES

1. **Analyzing the Data** Timelines help you understand the sequence of events. What was the longest period of time between wars?
2. **Making Inferences** Make a list of the land Israel won after each war. What does that list suggest about the role wars play in setting boundaries between nations?

FOR UPDATES ON WORLD ISSUES GO TO www.timeclassroom.com/glencoe

121

ASSESS

Have students take the Time Reports Quiz or do the Alternative Assessment Project provided in the Teacher's Classroom Resources.

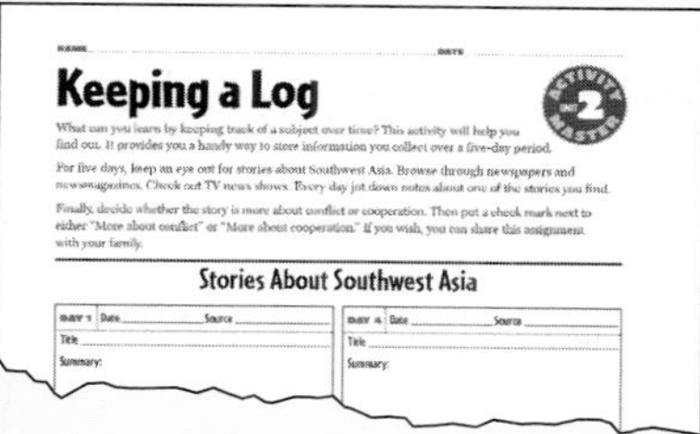

NAME .... DATE ....

Keeping a Log

ACTIVITY MASTER 2

What can you learn by keeping track of a subject over time? This activity will help you find out. It provides you a handy way to store information you collect over a five-day period.

For five days, keep an eye out for stories about Southwest Asia. Browse through newspapers and newsmagazines. Check out TV news shows. Every day jot down notes about one of the stories you find.

Finally, decide whether the story is more about conflict or cooperation. Then put a check mark next to either "More about conflict" or "More about cooperation." If you wish, you can share this assignment with your family.

Stories About Southwest Asia

DAY 1 Date ______ Source ______
Title ______
Summary:

DAY 4 Date ______ Source ______
Title ______
Summary:

BUILDING SKILLS FOR READING CHRONOLOGIES

ANSWERS

1. 13 years: between the Fourth Arab-Israeli War and the First Palestinian Intifada.
2. First Arab-Israeli War: Western Jerusalem, most of former Palestine; Second Arab-Israeli War: nothing; Third Arab-Israeli War: Gaza Strip, Sinai Peninsula, Golan Heights, West Bank; Fourth Arab-Israeli War: nothing; First Palestinian Intifada: time-table for Palestinian state; Second Palestinian Intifada: nothing.

CLOSE

Ask students to write a paragraph starting with this topic sentence: *Working for a just and peaceful solution to the Arab-Israeli conflict is important to the entire world because . . .*

Culminating Activity

To close this lesson, have students complete the Review and Assess section questions and activities above. Students should use classroom discussion, contextual clues, and their student dictionaries to write definitions for terms. Before assigning the Internet activities, it is recommended that you review your school district policy on student Internet use.

Focus on Debate

As a final activity for further student understanding of the issue, have students debate the pro and con position of the following topic: **Jerusalem, which is seen by many religions as a holy city, should be governed by the United Nations, thereby allowing access to all religious groups.**

Section 4, pages 122–125

1 Focus

1. Explain Iraq's role in regional conflicts.
2. Discuss how a religious government came to power in Iran.
3. Describe the religious and political conflicts in Afghanistan.

BELLRINGER
Skillbuilder Activity

Project transparency and have students answer questions.

This activity is also available as a blackline master.

Daily Focus Skills Transparency 4-4

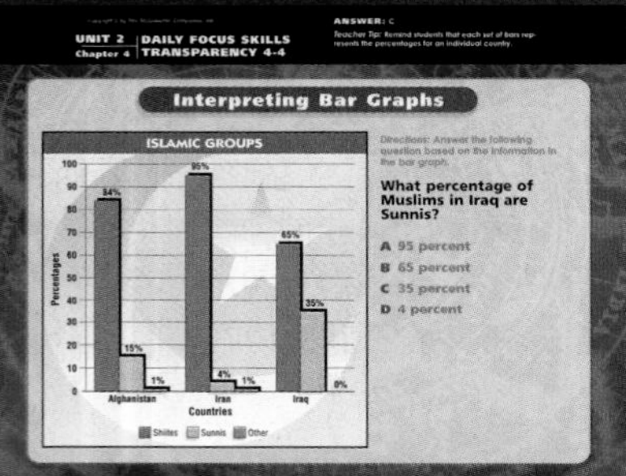

Guide to Reading

Vocabulary Precheck
Have students guess at the meaning of the term *Islamic republic* based on what they know about the two words making up this compound.

Use the Vocabulary PuzzleMaker to create crossword and word search puzzles.

Iraq, Iran, and Afghanistan

Guide to Reading

Main Idea

Iraq, Iran, and Afghanistan have recently fought wars and undergone sweeping political changes.

Terms to Know

- alluvial plain
- embargo
- shah
- Islamic republic

Reading Strategy

Create a chart like this one and list one fact about the people in each country.

Country	People
Iraq	
Iran	
Afghanistan	

Muslims approach this colorful Islamic mosque in Baghdad, Iraq, for dawn prayers. The Islamic religion strongly influences life in Iran, Iraq, and Afghanistan. Government and religious leaders seek to influence people's behavior through laws and policies. Although Iran's leaders have reduced such policies over the years, Afghanistan is ruled by a small, strict Islamic group.

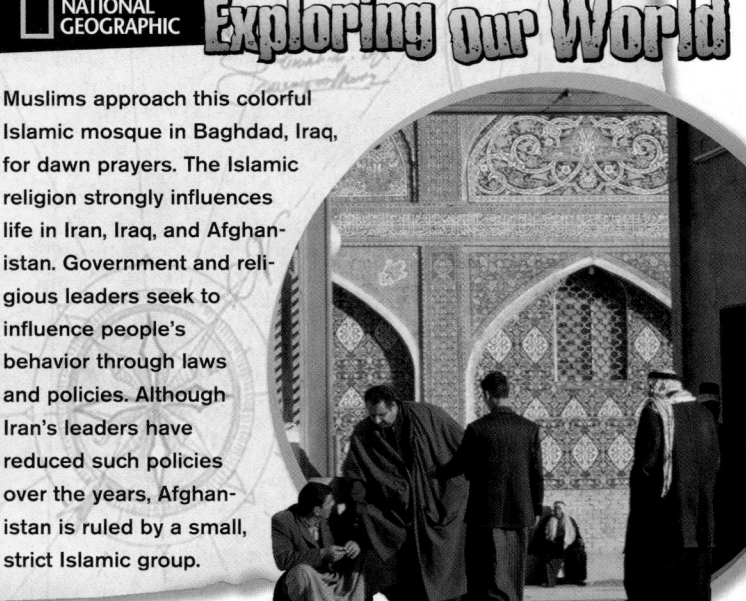

Iraq, Iran, and Afghanistan are located in a region where some of the world's oldest civilizations developed. This region has experienced turmoil throughout history and even today.

Iraq

As you read in Chapter 3, the world's first known cities arose between the Tigris and Euphrates Rivers. These rivers are the major geographic features of **Iraq.** Between the two rivers is an **alluvial plain**—an area that is built up by rich fertile soil left by river floods. Most farming takes place here—growing wheat, barley, dates, cotton, and rice.

Oil is the country's major export. Iraq's factories process foods and make textiles, chemicals, and construction materials.

People and Government About 70 percent of Iraq's 23.6 million people live in urban areas. **Baghdad,** the capital, is the largest city.

Section Resources

Reproducible Masters
- Reproducible Lesson Plan 4-4
- Daily Lecture and Discussion Notes 4-4
- Guided Reading Activity 4-4
- Reading Essentials and Study Guide 4-4
- Section Quiz 4-4

Transparencies
- Daily Focus Skills Transparency 4-4
- GeoQuiz Transparency 4-2

Multimedia
- Vocabulary PuzzleMaker Software
- Interactive Tutor Self-Assessment CD-ROM
- Presentation Plus! CD-ROM
- ExamView® Pro 3.0 Testmaker CD-ROM

From the A.D. 700s to 1200s, Baghdad was the center of a large Muslim empire that made many advances in the arts and sciences. Muslim Arabs make up the largest group in Iraq's population. The second-largest group consists of another Muslim people, the Kurds, who want to form their own country.

Modern Iraq gained its independence as a kingdom in 1932. In 1958 the last king was overthrown in a revolt. Since then, military leaders have governed Iraq as a dictatorship. The current leader, **Saddam Hussein** (sah•DAHM hoo•SAYN), rules with an iron hand.

In the 1980s, Iraq, with aid from Western and Arab countries, fought a bloody war with its neighbor Iran. The fighting cost thousands of lives and billions of dollars in damage to cities and oil-shipping ports in the Persian Gulf. In 1990, partly because of a dispute over oil, Iraq invaded neighboring **Kuwait.** By April of 1991, at the end of the **Persian Gulf War,** a United Nations force led by the United States pushed Iraqi troops out of Kuwait. This operation was known as "Desert Storm."

After the Persian Gulf War, Saddam Hussein refused to cooperate with the demands of the United Nations. In response, the United States and other nations put an **embargo** on trade with Iraq. An embargo is an order that restricts trade with another country. Since then, Iraq has not exported as much oil as before and cannot import certain goods. This has severely damaged Iraq's economy.

✓Reading Check **What two rivers have influenced the history of Iraq?**

NATIONAL GEOGRAPHIC **On Location**

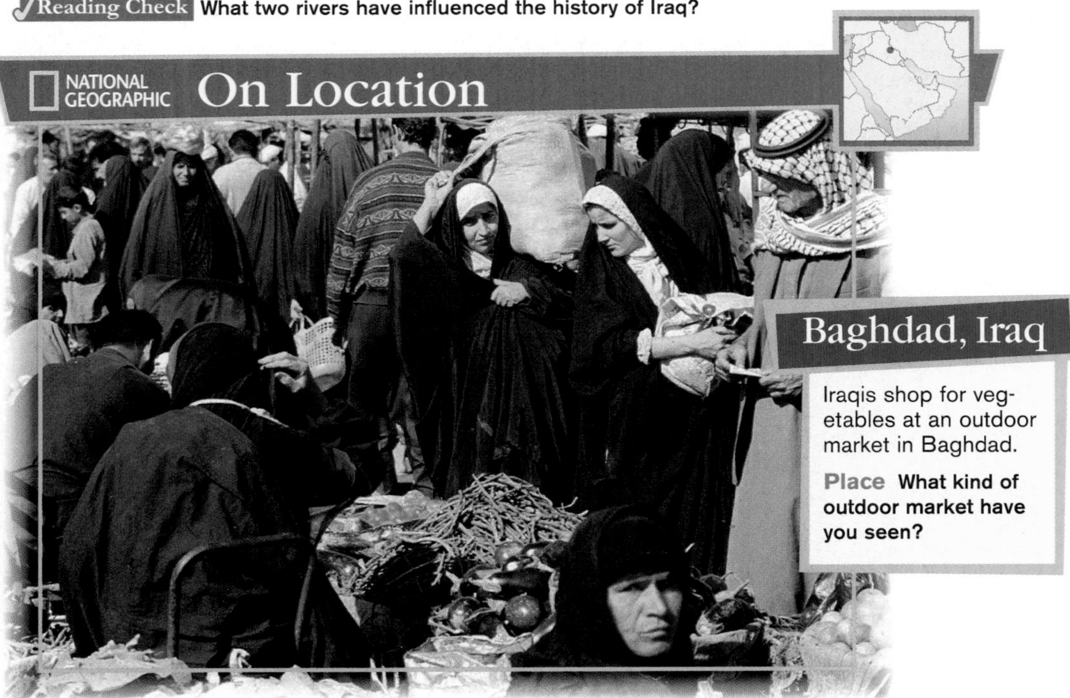

Baghdad, Iraq

Iraqis shop for vegetables at an outdoor market in Baghdad.

Place What kind of outdoor market have you seen?

Chapter 4

Section 4, pages 122–125

2 TEACH

Determining Cause and Effect Challenge students to determine the impact that climate and landscape have on economic activities, housing, clothing, and recreation in Iraq, Iran, and Afghanistan. Ask students to use these examples to write a paragraph explaining the cause-and-effect relationship between physical geography and life in these countries. **L1**

✓ Reading Check Answer

Tigris and Euphrates Rivers

Daily Lecture Notes 4-4

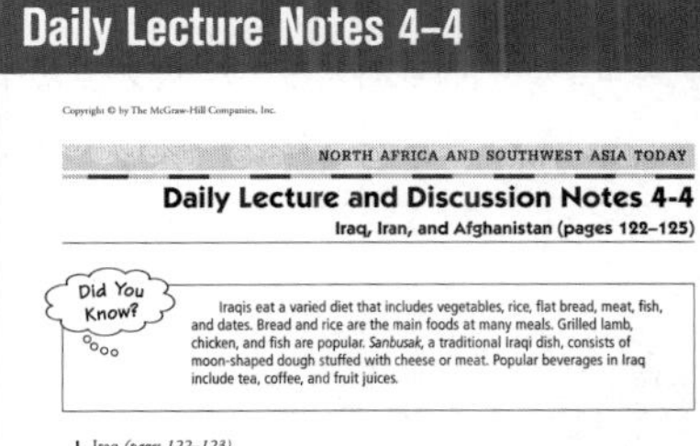

NORTH AFRICA AND SOUTHWEST ASIA TODAY

Daily Lecture and Discussion Notes 4-4

Iraq, Iran, and Afghanistan (pages 122–125)

Did You Know? Iraqis eat a varied diet that includes vegetables, rice, flat bread, meat, fish, and dates. Bread and rice are the main foods at many meals. Grilled lamb, chicken, and fish are popular. *Sanbusak*, a traditional Iraqi dish, consists of moon-shaped dough stuffed with cheese or meat. Popular beverages in Iraq include tea, coffee, and fruit juices.

I. Iraq *(pages 122–123)*

A. The Tigris and Euphrates Rivers are the major geographic features of Iraq.

B. Between the two rivers is an **alluvial plain**—an area that is built up by rich fertile soil left by river floods.

More About the Photo

Baghdad In addition to the outdoor markets and colorful bazaars, central Baghdad has modern banks, department stores, and hotels. Industrial and residential districts extend in all directions from the city's center.

Caption Answer Answers will vary.

Critical Thinking Activity

History The body of water created where the Tigris and Euphrates Rivers join, near the head of the Persian Gulf, is called the Shatt-al-Arab. Iraq and Iran have long struggled over control of this waterway. This issue was the chief cause of the bloody war fought by the two countries in the 1980s. Have students form three groups to research the causes and results of the Iran-Iraq war. Then designate one group to present Iran's view of the issues, one to present Iraq's view, and one to give the U.S. perspective. **L2**

EE4 Human Systems: Standard 13

More About the Photos

Women in Afghanistan When women do appear in public in Afghanistan, they wear a long gown called a *burka* that covers them from head to foot.

Caption Answer an Islamic republic; a group called the Taliban

Guided Reading Activity 4-4

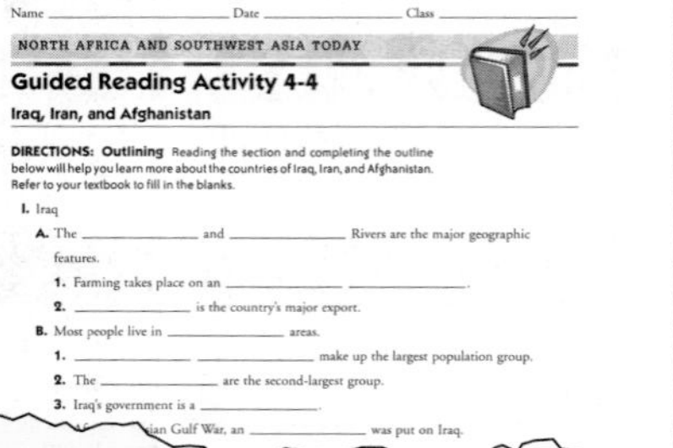
Name ________ Date ________ Class ________

NORTH AFRICA AND SOUTHWEST ASIA TODAY

Guided Reading Activity 4-4

Iraq, Iran, and Afghanistan

DIRECTIONS: Outlining Reading the section and completing the outline below will help you learn more about the countries of Iraq, Iran, and Afghanistan. Refer to your textbook to fill in the blanks.

I. Iraq
  A. The ________ and ________ Rivers are the major geographic features.
    1. Farming takes place on an ________ ________.
    2. ________ is the country's major export.
  B. Most people live in ________ areas.
    1. ________ ________ make up the largest population group.
    2. The ________ are the second-largest group.
    3. Iraq's government is a ________.
    ...ian Gulf War, an ________ was put on Iraq.

Assess

Assign Section 4 Assessment as homework or an in-class activity.

Have students use the Interactive Tutor Self-Assessment CD-ROM to review Section 4–4.

Reading Check Answer

More than half are Persians, not Arabs or Turks, as found in other Southwest Asian countries. They speak Farsi.

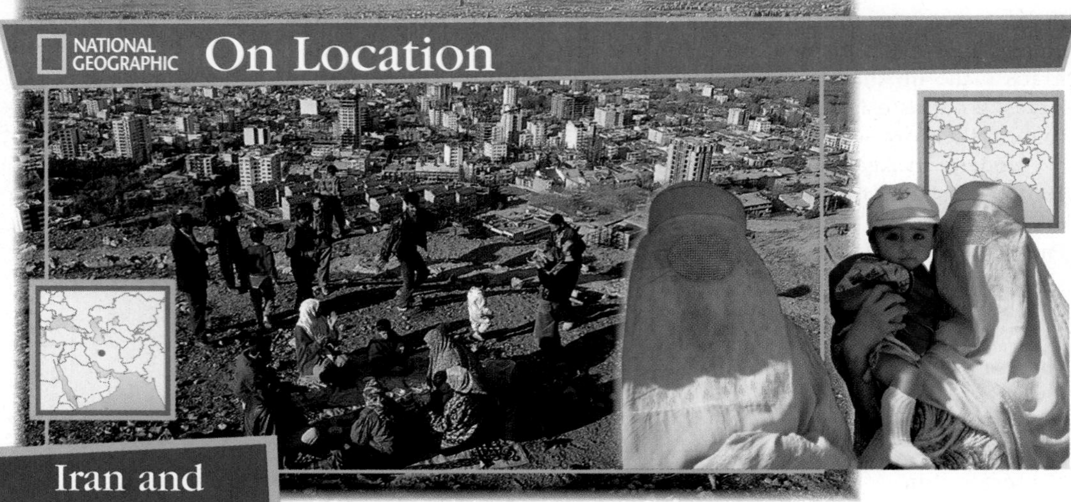

Iran and Afghanistan

An Iranian family picnics in the hills above Tehran (left). In Afghanistan, women are rarely allowed in public (right).

Government What form of government does Iran have? What group leads Afghanistan?

Iran

Once known as Persia, **Iran** is about the size of Alaska. Iran is an oil-rich nation and is where the first oil wells in Southwest Asia were drilled in 1908. Like Saudi Arabia, Iran is trying to promote other industries in order to become less dependent on oil earnings. With limited supplies of water, less than 12 percent of Iran's land can be farmed. Some farmers use ancient underground channels to bring water to their fields. They grow wheat, rice, sugar beets, and cotton. Iran is also the world's largest producer of pistachio nuts.

The Iranian People Iran's 66.1 million people differ from those of other Southwest Asian countries. More than one-half are Persians, not Arabs or Turks. The Persians' ancestors migrated from Central Asia centuries ago. They speak **Farsi,** or Persian, the official language of Iran. Other languages include Kurdish, Arabic, and Turkish. About 60 percent of Iranians live in urban areas. **Tehran,** located in northern Iran, is the largest city and the capital. Iran is also home to about 2 million people from Iraq and Afghanistan who have fled recent wars. Nearly 98 percent of Iran's people practice some form of Islam.

Iran's Government About 2,000 years ago, Iran was the center of the powerful Persian Empire ruled by kings known as **shahs.** In 1979 Muslim religious leaders overthrew the last monarchy. Iran now has an **Islamic republic,** a government run by Muslim religious leaders. The government has introduced laws based on its understanding of the Quran. Followers of religions other than Islam have been persecuted. Many Western customs seen as a threat to Islam are now forbidden. Like Syria, Iran has been accused by many Western governments of supporting terrorists.

Reading Check How do Iranians differ in ethnic background from most other Southwest Asians?

Meeting Special Needs

Verbal/Linguistic Suggest that students who learn better verbally re-create the information in the map and photos in Chapter 4 in verbal form. Have them review each to identify what information they can learn about the three countries in Section 4. Guide students' observations by asking questions such as: **What physical features influence the climate of these countries? Where do most people live in each country? What resources influence economic activities in these countries?** Then have them write their findings in sentences and use these as study aids. **L1**

Refer to *Inclusion for the Middle School Social Studies Classroom Strategies and Activities* in the TCR

Afghanistan

A landlocked nation, **Afghanistan** (af•GA•nuh•STAN) is mostly covered with the rugged peaks of the **Hindu Kush** mountain range. The Khyber (KY•buhr) Pass cuts through the mountains and for centuries has been a major trade route linking Southwest Asia with other parts of Asia. The capital city, **Kabul** (KAH•buhl), lies in a valley. The country's 26 million people are divided into about 20 different ethnic groups.

A Country at War During the 1980s, the Afghan people fought against Soviet troops who had invaded their country. When the Soviets pulled out in 1989, the Afghan people faced poverty, food shortages, and rising crime. The country collapsed into civil war. Many people turned to the **Taliban,** a group of fighters educated at strict Islamic schools in Pakistan. By 1996, the Taliban had taken control of the capital, Kabul, and about 80 percent of the country. They set up very strict laws based on their view of the religion of Islam. For example, men had to wear beards, and women had to cover themselves in public and could not hold jobs or go to school. In the north, a group known as the **Northern Alliance** continued to battle with the Taliban but with little success. In October 2001, the United States accused the Taliban of supporting terrorists and began bombing Taliban forces. The United States also sent aid to the Northern Alliance. By mid-November, the Taliban government had collapsed and the Northern Alliance had captured Kabul. The United Nations then began working with local leaders to create a new government for Afghanistan.

✓Reading Check **What trade route cuts through the Hindu Kush?**

Assessment

Defining Terms

1. **Define** alluvial plain, embargo, shah, Islamic republic.

Recalling Facts

2. **Economics** What is Iraq's major export?
3. **Culture** What group had gained control of most of Afghanistan by 1996?
4. **Government** What type of government does Iran have? Why do so many Western nations consider it a threat?

Critical Thinking

5. **Understanding Cause and Effect** Why have Iraq and the United States continued to treat each other with hostility?
6. **Drawing Conclusions** Why have so few governments recognized the Taliban government in Afghanistan?

Graphic Organizer

7. **Organizing Information** Create a chart like this one for each of the following countries: Iraq, Iran, and Afghanistan. Then write one fact about the country under each heading.

Country		
Capital	Landforms	Agriculture
People	Religion	Government

Applying Social Studies Skills

8. **Analyzing Maps** Study the physical map on page 74. Between what two bodies of water is Iran located?

Section 4 Assessment

1. The terms are defined in the Glossary.
2. oil
3. the Taliban
4. an Islamic republic; it has been accused of supporting terrorists
5. Because of Iraq's refusal to cooperate with UN demands, the U.S. led other countries in putting an embargo on Iraq.
6. They are concerned with events that they have heard of in areas controlled by the Taliban.
7. Students should complete the table with information from the section.
8. Persian Gulf, Caspian Sea

Chapter 4

Section 4, pages 122–125

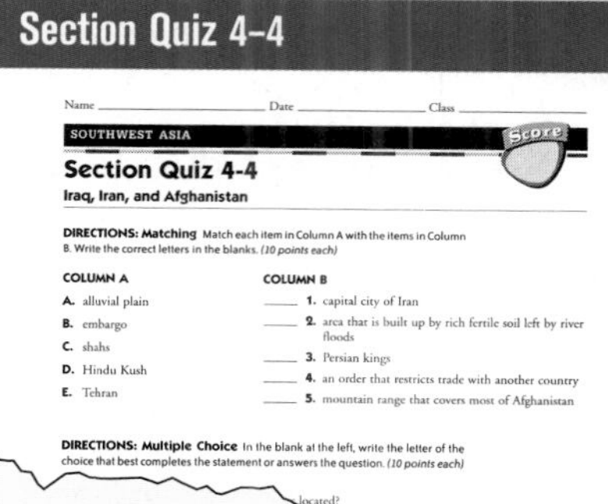

Section Quiz 4-4

Name ______ Date ______ Class ______

SOUTHWEST ASIA

Score

Section Quiz 4-4

Iraq, Iran, and Afghanistan

DIRECTIONS: Matching Match each item in Column A with the items in Column B. Write the correct letters in the blanks. *(10 points each)*

COLUMN A	COLUMN B
A. alluvial plain	____ 1. capital city of Iran
B. embargo	____ 2. area that is built up by rich fertile soil left by river floods
C. shahs	____ 3. Persian kings
D. Hindu Kush	____ 4. an order that restricts trade with another country
E. Tehran	____ 5. mountain range that covers most of Afghanistan

DIRECTIONS: Multiple Choice In the blank at the left, write the letter of the choice that best completes the statement or answers the question. *(10 points each)*

Reteach

Write a country and a category on a flash card, such as "Iran—climate" or "Iraq—people." Show the flash cards to the class and ask volunteers to supply information about the country that fits the category.

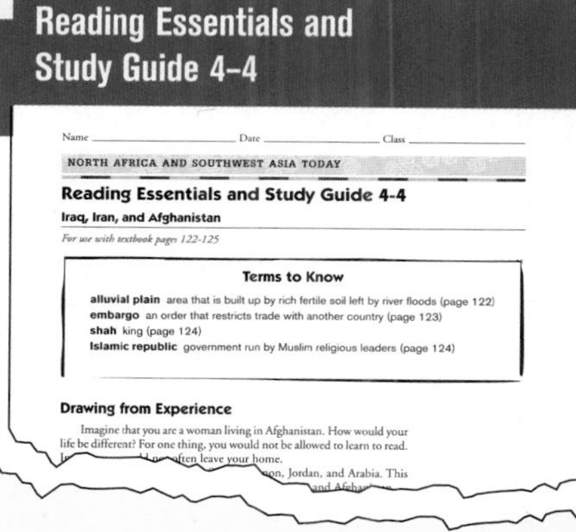

Reading Essentials and Study Guide 4-4

Name ______ Date ______ Class ______

NORTH AFRICA AND SOUTHWEST ASIA TODAY

Reading Essentials and Study Guide 4-4

Iraq, Iran, and Afghanistan

For use with textbook pages 122-125

Terms to Know

alluvial plain area that is built up by rich fertile soil left by river floods (page 122)
embargo an order that restricts trade with another country (page 123)
shah king (page 124)
Islamic republic government run by Muslim religious leaders (page 124)

Drawing from Experience

Imagine that you are a woman living in Afghanistan. How would your life be different? For one thing, you would not be allowed to learn to read.

✓ Reading Check Answer

One

CLOSE

Have students write three paragraphs comparing these three countries, with one paragraph each on their economies, government, and people.

TEACH

Point out to students that search engines often have tips on tailoring a search to produce desirable results. In "Yahoo!," for example, using a plus sign (such as "mosques + Iran") brings up only those sites that contain both words. Using a minus sign (such as "mosques – Spain") eliminates sites that have the undesirable word.

Additional Skills Practice

1. **What three things are needed to log onto the Internet?** *(computer, modem, and account with an Internet service provider)*
2. **How would you search for information on climate in Iran?** *(access a search engine or online encyclopedia and type in "Iran + climate" in the search box)*
3. **How would you search for information on recent earthquakes in Iran?** *(access a search engine or online news service and type in "Iran + earthquake" in the search box)*

Additional Skills Resources

 Chapter Skills Activity 4

 Building Geography Skills for Life

Technology Skill

Using the Internet

To learn more about almost any topic imaginable, use the **Internet**—a global network of computers. Many features, such as e-mail, interactive educational classes, and shopping services are offered on the Net.

▲ The National Geographic Society's Web site

Learning the Skill

To get on the Internet, you need three things: (a) a personal computer, (b) a device that connects your computer to the Internet, and (c) an account with an Internet service provider (ISP). An ISP is a company that enables you to log on to the Internet, usually for a fee.

After you are connected, the easiest way to access Internet sites is to use a "Web browser," a program that lets you view and explore information on the World Wide Web. The Web consists of many documents called "Web sites," each of which has its own address, or Uniform Resource Locator (URL). Many URLs start with the keystrokes *http://*

If you do not know the exact URL of a site, commercial "search engines" such as Google or Yahoo! can help you find information. Type a subject or name into the "search" box, and then press Enter. The search engine lists available sites that may have the information you are looking for.

Practicing the Skill

Follow these steps to learn how the Internet can help you find information about Iran.

1. Log on to the Internet and access a search engine.
2. Search by typing "Iran" in the search box.
3. Scroll the list of Web sites that appears when the search is complete. Select a site to bring up and read or print.
4. If you get "lost" on the Internet, click on the back arrow key at the top of the screen until you find a familiar site.
5. Continue selecting sites until you have enough information to write a short report on natural resources found in Iran.

Applying the Skill

Follow the above steps to locate information about *oil and natural gas in Iraq.* Use the information you gather to create a chart or graph showing the amount of oil and natural gas Iraq has exported in the past five years.

126

Practicing the Skill Answers

Monitor students' searches to see that they are seeking the correct information. Warn them that some of the sources might be in a foreign language. Students should organize the information they collect into a report.

Applying the Skill
Advise students that they can put more than one word in a search box. Show them how to search for **Iraq** AND **oil.** Students should organize the information they find into a report or graph or chart.

Reading Review

Section 1 North Africa

Terms to Know
delta
silt
oasis
aquifer
dictator
terrorism
secular
constitutional monarchy

Main Idea
North Africa's desert landscape has shaped the people and culture for many centuries, as has the Islamic religion.
✓ **Location** Most people of Egypt live along the Nile River or in its delta.
✓ **Economics** Forty percent of Egypt's workers live by farming, but industry has grown in recent years.
✓ **Region** North Africa includes Egypt, Libya and the three countries called the Maghreb—Tunisia, Algeria, and Morocco.
✓ **Economics** Oil, natural gas, and phosphates are among the important resources in these countries.
✓ **Culture** Most of the people in these countries are Muslims and speak Arabic.

Section 2 Southwest Asia: Turkey and Israel

Terms to Know
mosque
kibbutz
moshav

Main Idea
Turkey and Israel both have strong ties to Europe and the United States.
✓ **Location** Turkey lies in both Europe and Asia.
✓ **Economics** Tourism is a growing industry in Turkey, thanks to beautiful beaches and historic sites.
✓ **Culture** About 80 percent of Israel's population are Jews. They have moved to Israel from many countries.
✓ **History** Israel and its Arab neighbors continue to work toward a peaceful settlement of issues that divide them.

Section 3 Syria, Lebanon, Jordan, and Arabia

Terms to Know
Bedouin
wadi
desalinization
hajj

Main Idea
Syria, Lebanon, Jordan, and Saudi Arabia have Arab populations but different economies and forms of government.
✓ **Economics** Farming is the main economic activity in Syria.
✓ **History** Lebanon is rebuilding and recovering after a civil war.
✓ **Economics** Saudi Arabia is the world's leading oil producer.

Section 4 Iraq, Iran, and Afghanistan

Terms to Know
alluvial plain
embargo
shah
Islamic republic

Main Idea
Iraq, Iran, and Afghanistan have recently fought wars and undergone sweeping political changes.
✓ **Economics** Iraq is suffering because of an international trade embargo.
✓ **Culture** Oil-rich Iran is ruled by Muslim religious leaders.
✓ **Economics** Afghanistan is mountainous and relatively undeveloped.

Reading Review

Use the Chapter 4 Reading Review to preview, review, condense, or reteach the chapter.

Preview/Review

Use the Terms to Know lists to help students review and study.

Activity Have students identify the country for which each term is relevant. Read the terms aloud, one at a time, and ask for volunteers to categorize each. Note that some terms may apply to more than one country.

Vocabulary PuzzleMaker Software reinforces the vocabulary terms used in Chapter 4.

The Interactive Tutor Self-Assessment CD-ROM allows students to review Chapter 4 content.

Condense

Have students read the Chapter 4 summary statements.

Chapter 4 Guided Reading Activities

Chapter 4 Audio Program

Reteach

Reteaching Activity 4

Chapter 4 Reading Essentials and Study Guide

Chapter Culminating Activity

Creating Maps Have students create illustrated maps of North Africa and Southwest Asia. Their maps could highlight the region's geographical features, with illustrations showing the different types of climates, vegetation, or landscapes. Students might show the region's resources and economic activities. The maps could also display the important historical and cultural sites found throughout the region. Encourage students to illustrate their maps with photographs and other images that demonstrate the variety of this region. *NOTE: This activity may be completed separately or you may wish students to incorporate it into their Current Events Journals.*

EE1 The World in Spatial Terms: Standards 1, 3

GLENCOE TECHNOLOGY

MindJogger Videoquiz
Use MindJogger to review the Chapter 4 content.

 Available in VHS.

Using Key Terms

1. f
2. g
3. e
4. c
5. d
6. a
7. h
8. i
9. b
10. j

Reviewing the Main Ideas

11. Mediterranean Sea and Red Sea
12. constitutional monarchy
13. most of Libya is a desert
14. the land farthest west
15. oil or petroleum
16. Istanbul
17. 1950
18. It is the capital of Syria and one of the oldest continuously inhabited cities in the world.
19. Organization of Petroleum Exporting Countries
20. More than half are Persian, not Arabs or Turks as in other Southwest Asian countries, and they speak Farsi.

Critical Thinking

21. because the rest of the region is covered by desert
22. Oil is important because of its value throughout the world for fuels and petroleum-based products. Its abundance in any particular country gives that country power. Water is obviously vital to life as well as to farming, the economy, and trade. Its scarcity in any particular country makes that country vulnerable to neighbors who have a larger supply of water.

Chapter 4 Assessment and Activities

Using Key Terms

Match the terms in Part A with their definitions in Part B.

A.

1. oasis
2. secular
3. delta
4. shah
5. hajj
6. kibbutz
7. silt
8. terrorism
9. aquifer
10. embargo

B.

a. Israeli community
b. underground rock layer that stores water
c. Iran's monarch
d. religious pilgrimage
e. area formed by soil at a river's mouth
f. water and vegetation surrounded by desert
g. nonreligious
h. small particles of rich soil
i. violence against civilians
j. restricts trade with another country

Reviewing the Main Ideas

Section 1 North Africa

11. **Movement** What two bodies of water does the Suez Canal connect?
12. **Government** What type of government does Morocco have today?
13. **Human/Environment Interaction** Why must Libya depend on aquifers for water?
14. **Region** What does *Maghreb* mean?
15. **Economics** What energy resource is important to almost all of North Africa's countries?

Section 2 Southwest Asia: Turkey and Israel

16. **Place** What is Turkey's largest city?
17. **History** In what year was Jerusalem made the capital of Israel?

Section 3 Syria, Lebanon, Jordan, and Arabia

18. **History** What makes Damascus an important city?
19. **Economics** What is OPEC?

Section 4 Iraq, Iran, and Afghanistan

20. **Culture** How do the people of Iran differ from other Southwest Asian peoples?

North Africa

Place Location Activity

On a separate sheet of paper, match the letters on the map with the numbered places listed below.

1. Red Sea
2. Morocco
3. Libya
4. Algeria
5. Atlas Mountains
6. Nile River
7. Cairo
8. Tunisia
9. Tripoli
10. Sinai Peninsula

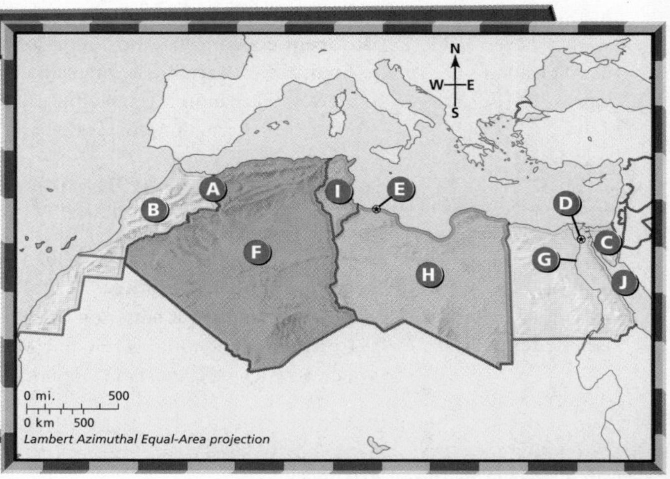

A B C D E F G H I J
N W E S
0 mi. 500
0 km 500
Lambert Azimuthal Equal-Area projection

NATIONAL GEOGRAPHIC Place Location Activity

1. J
2. B
3. H
4. F
5. A
6. G
7. D
8. I
9. E
10. C

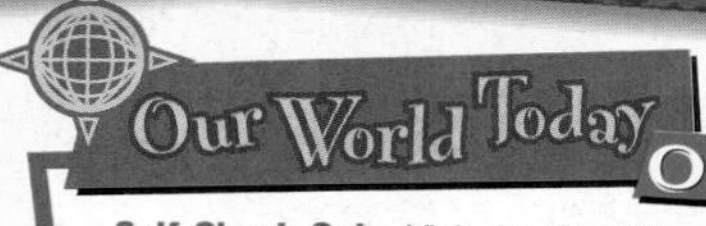

Self-Check Quiz Visit the ***Our World Today: People, Places, and Issues*** Web site at owt.glencoe.com and click on **Chapter 4–Self-Check Quizzes** to prepare for the Chapter Test.

Critical Thinking

21. **Understanding Cause and Effect** Why are the most densely populated areas of North Africa along the Mediterranean Sea and the Nile River?
22. **Analyzing Information** On a chart like this, list a reason for the importance of oil and water to Southwest Asia and one result of their abundance or scarcity.

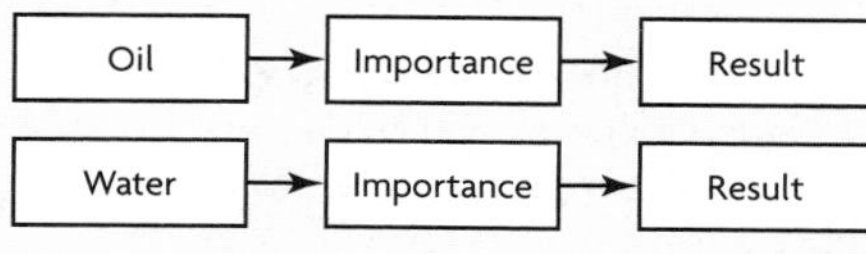

Current Events Journal

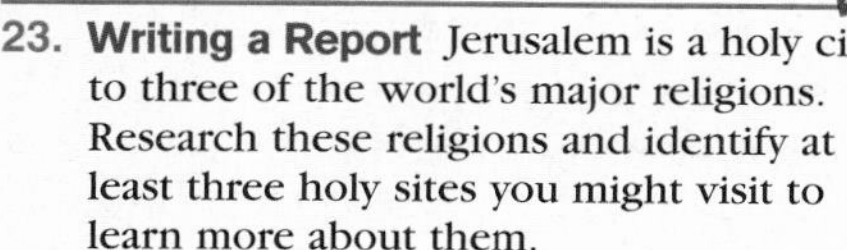

23. **Writing a Report** Jerusalem is a holy city to three of the world's major religions. Research these religions and identify at least three holy sites you might visit to learn more about them.

Mental Mapping Activity

24. **Focusing on the Region** Draw a simple outline map of North Africa, and then label the following:

- Mediterranean Sea
- Egypt
- Red Sea
- Libya
- Atlantic Ocean
- Morocco
- Nile River
- Tunisia
- Atlas Mountains
- Algeria

Technology Skills Activity

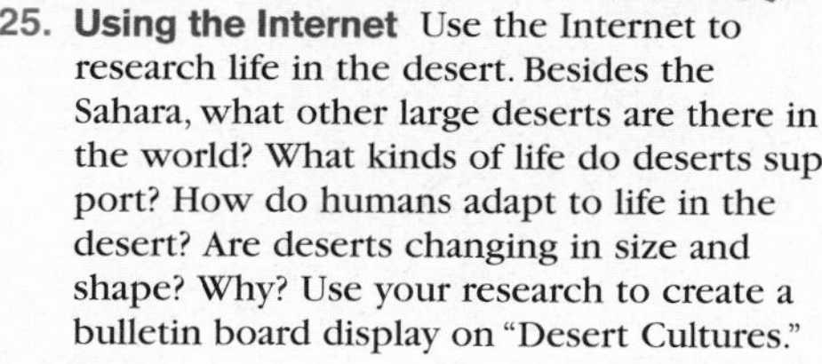

25. **Using the Internet** Use the Internet to research life in the desert. Besides the Sahara, what other large deserts are there in the world? What kinds of life do deserts support? How do humans adapt to life in the desert? Are deserts changing in size and shape? Why? Use your research to create a bulletin board display on "Desert Cultures."

The Princeton Review

Standardized Test Practice

Directions: Study the graph, and then answer the question that follows.

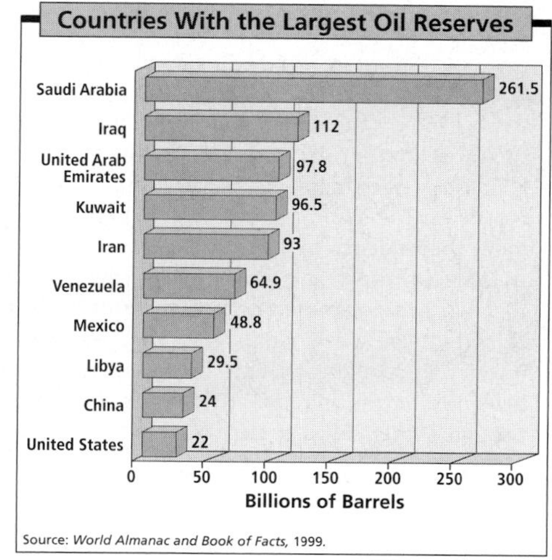

1. **How many of the 10 countries with the largest oil reserves are located in Southwest Asia?**

   A one
   B three
   C five
   D seven

Test-Taking Tip: You need to rely on your memory as well as analyze the graph to answer this question. Look at each country, and then think back to the countries you studied in Chapter 4. Which of those listed on the graph did you just learn about?

Assessment and Activities

Standardized Test Practice

1. C

Tested Objectives: Analyzing a graph, synthesizing information

Chapter Test Bonus Question

This question may be used for extra credit on the chapter test.

What group of people have partial control of the West Bank and Gaza Strip? *(Palestinian Arabs)*

Our World Today online

Have students visit the Web site at **owt.glencoe.com** to review Chapter 4 and take the Self-Check Quiz.

Current Events Journal

23. Students' reports should identify the religion related to each holy site and explain the site's significance.

Mental Mapping Activity

24. This exercise helps students visualize the countries and geographic features they have been studying and understand the relationship among various points. All attempts at freehand mapping should be accepted.

Technology Skills Activity

25. Students should search the Internet for information on deserts. Their posters might include maps, text, and illustrations, all aimed at demonstrating the unique conditions and cultures of the world's deserts.

Write the following heading on the board: "Water, water everywhere." Ask students to identify various sources of water. Guide them by offering such examples as oceans, lakes, rivers, glaciers, and so on. List their responses under the heading. Then point out that water covers about 70 percent of the earth's surface.

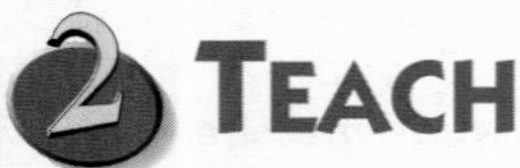

Analyzing Information Ask students to speculate how the earth could have a shortage of water when the amount of water never changes. Explain that less than 1 percent of the world's water is fresh and readily accessible. Then point out that this water is distributed very unevenly across the earth, and remind students that North Africa and Southwest Asia are among the world's driest regions.

Meeting National Standards

Geography for Life

The following standards are met in the Student Edition feature:

EE5 Environment and Society: Standards 14, 15, 16

EE6 The Uses of Geography: Standard 18

EYE on the Environment

A Water Crisis

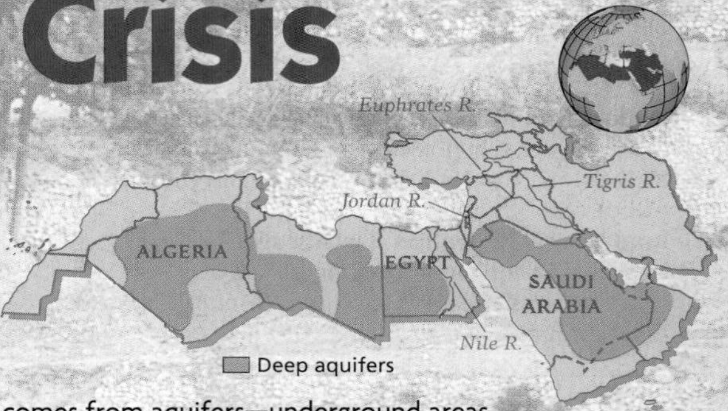

Draining the Rivers The ball game is over. You are hot, sweaty, and thirsty. You press the button on the drinking fountain, but no water comes out. A crisis? Consider this: Many people in Southwest Asia and North Africa never have enough water to meet their needs.

Most of the usable water in this region comes from aquifers—underground areas that store large amounts of water—and from the Jordan, Tigris, Euphrates, and Nile Rivers. Despite these great rivers, water is scarce. The rivers flow through several countries. As each country takes its share of water, less remains for those downstream. A few countries have desalinization plants that turn seawater into freshwater. Desalinization is expensive, though. Water resources are further strained by many factors.

- Population growth — By 2020, about 541 million people will inhabit the region. That is too many people for the existing water supplies.
- Irrigation — About 70 percent of water supplies in Southwest Asia are used to irrigate crops.
- Pollution — River water in many places is polluted by salt, sewage, and chemicals.

Finding Solutions Faced with growing demand and decreasing supplies, countries in this region are looking for creative solutions to the water crisis.

- Some countries are recycling wastewater to use on crops.
- Advances in technology are making desalinization more affordable.
- Countries are building dams to regulate water. They also are constructing pipelines to carry water to where it is most needed.

Camels crossing Egypt's desert drink water piped from the Nile River, 300 miles (483 km) away.

More About the Issues

Irrigation The earliest recorded use of irrigation occurred in Mesopotamia in Southwest Asia. Today irrigation remains a major use of freshwater in the region. Problems related to traditional methods of irrigation continue to plague the region's farmers, however. Because the climate is so hot and dry, surface irrigation systems lose a high percentage of water to evaporation. High rates of evaporation lead to the accumulation of certain minerals in the soil—and these minerals can make the soil unproductive for farming. To address such problems, many governments in the region have encouraged the use of newer technologies, such as drip irrigation.

NATIONAL GEOGRAPHIC

Making a Difference

Wise Water Ways Scientist Sandra Postel is trying to educate others on ways to use water more wisely. In her book, *Last Oasis: Facing Water Scarcity*, Postel argues that we can no longer meet rising demands for water by building larger dams and drilling deeper wells. Instead of reaching out for more water, Postel argues, everyone needs to do more with less water. People need to conserve and recycle water and to use it more efficiently. Through her research, Postel has found that farmers, industries, and cities could cut their water use by as much as 50 percent. Water could be saved by practicing water conservation methods such as drip irrigation and water recycling. Postel hopes that governments around the world will work together to protect one of the earth's most precious resources.

Author Sandra Postel

Meeting Demand A group in Southwest Asia and North Africa is studying ways to ease water shortages in the region. The Water Demand Management Research Network (WDMRN) is made up of scientists and government representatives who are studying ways to meet the growing needs for water. The WDMRN shares information with other water researchers and holds meetings to encourage cooperation between all countries in the region.

Worker takes a drink of water at a desalinization plant, Kuwait.

What Can You Do?

Conserve Water
Saving water is as easy as turning off a faucet. Practice water conservation by taking shorter showers and by turning off the water while brushing your teeth. What other ways can you conserve water at home or at school?

Find Out More
Investigate the pathway drinking water takes in your community. Collaborate with classmates to create a bulletin board display showing how water gets from its source to a drinking fountain in your school.

Use the Internet
The United States has water disputes, too. The Colorado River has been called the "river of contention." Research the Colorado River controversy. A good place to start: the Colorado River Water Users Association at http://crwua.mwd.dst.ca.us. Share what you find with your classmates.

131

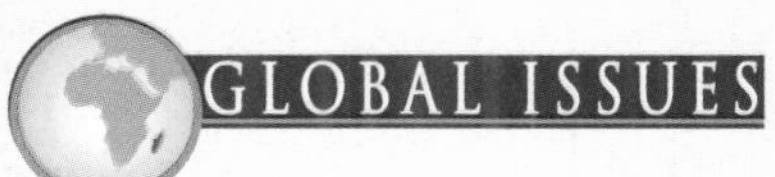

Interdependence Establishing a fair system of access to freshwater is a worldwide problem. Even within the United States, some western states are engaged in legal battles with each other over water rights.

Have students work individually or in groups to complete the What Can You Do? activities on page 131.

Discuss with students the What Can You Do? activities. Consider inviting a representative of the local water utility to the class to give a presentation on water-related issues and to answer students' questions.

For an additional regional case study, use the following:

Environmental Case Study 2

What Can You Do? Teacher Tips

Conserve Water Many publications list simple ways that people can reduce their use of water. Encourage students to find and report these steps to the class.

Find Out More Suggest that students look for answers to such questions as: What is the source of the community's drinking water? How is this water treated and transported to homes? What problems confront the community's water supply?

Use the Internet After completing their research on the Internet, students might create a chart that shows the differing views of the various sides in the Colorado River water dispute.

Unit 3 Planning Guide

SUGGESTED PACING CHART

Unit 3 (1 day)	Chapter 5 (4 days)	Chapter 6 (5 days)	Chapter 7 (4 days)	Chapter 8 (4 days)	Unit 3 (2 days)
Day 1 Introduction	**Day 1** Chapter 5 Intro, Section 1	**Day 1** Chapter 6 Intro, Section 1	**Day 1** Chapter 7 Intro, Section 1	**Day 1** Chapter 8 Intro, Section 1	**Day 1** Wrap-Up/Projects
	Day 2 Section 2	**Day 2** Section 2	**Day 2** Section 2	**Day 2** Section 2	**Day 2** Unit 3 Assessment
	Day 3 Chapter 5 Review	**Day 3** Section 3	**Day 3** Chapter 7 Review	**Day 3** Chapter 8 Review	
	Day 4 Chapter 5 Assessment	**Day 4** Chapter 6 Review	**Day 4** Chapter 7 Assessment	**Day 4** Chapter 8 Assessment	
		Day 5 Chapter 6 Assessment			

For a complete course pacing guide and Teacher Classroom Resources, see:

Interactive Lesson Planner

Use the following tools to easily assess student learning in a variety of ways:

- **Performance Assessment Activities and Rubrics**
- **Section Quizzes**
- **Chapter Tests and Unit Pretests and Posttests**
- **Interactive Tutor Self-Assessment CD-ROM**
- **ExamView® Pro 3.0 Testmaker CD-ROM**
- **MindJogger Videoquiz**
- **owt.glencoe.com**
- **Standardized Test Practice Workbook**

Note: The following materials may be used when teaching Unit 3.
Chapter level support materials can be found on the chapter resource pages.

TEACHING TRANSPARENCIES

Political Map Transparency 3

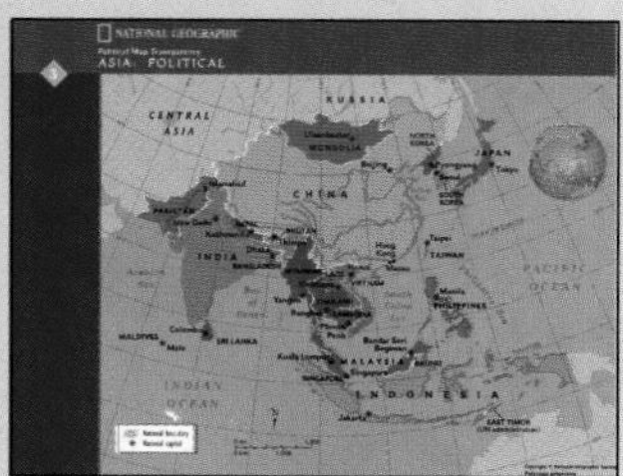

Unit 3 Map Overlay Transparencies

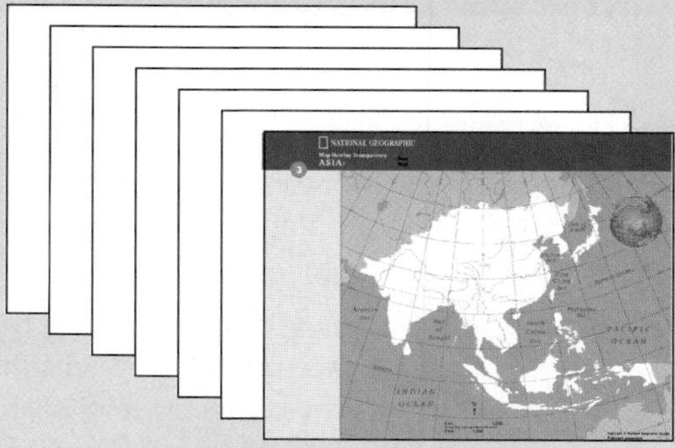

World Cultures Transparencies 3 and 4

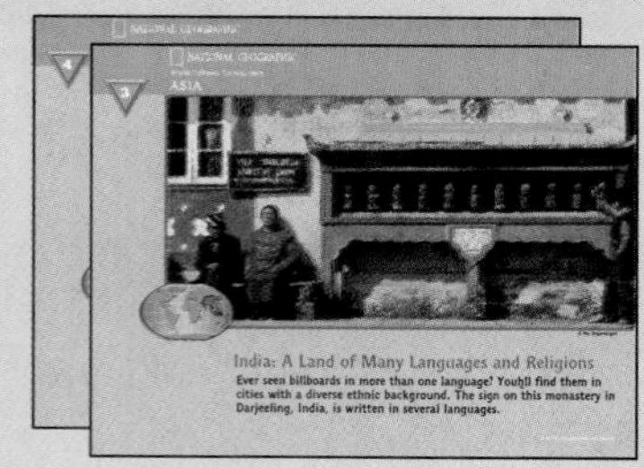

Unit 3 Resources

INTERDISCIPLINARY CONNECTIONS

World Literature Reading 3

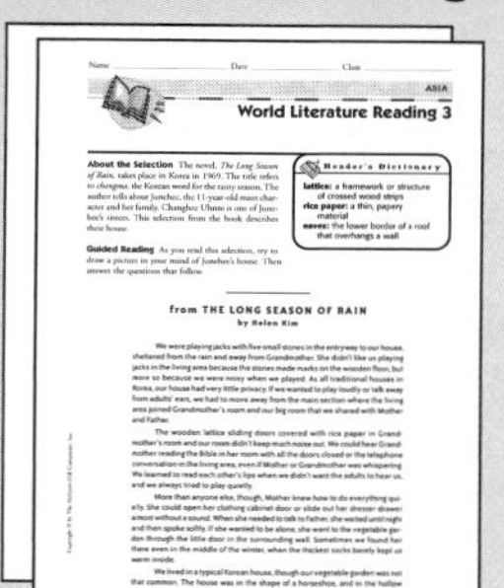

Economics and Geography Activity 3

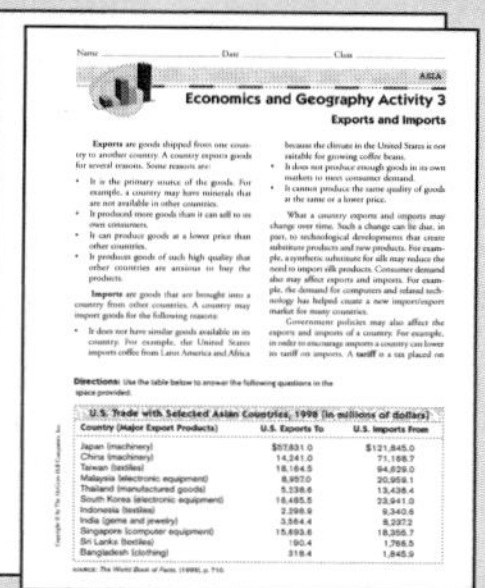

History and Geography Activity 3

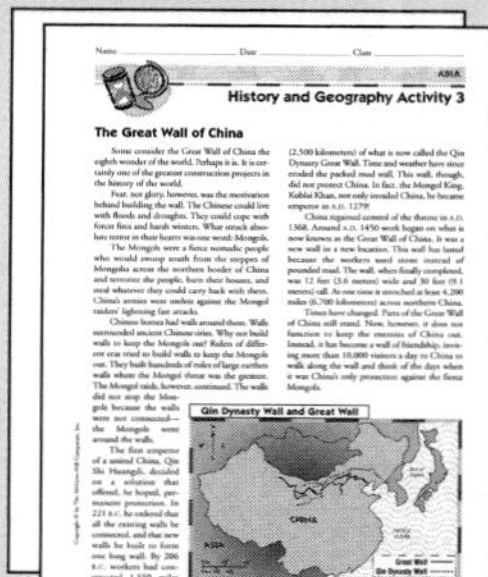

MAP AND GEOGRAPHY SKILLS

Building Geography Skills for Life

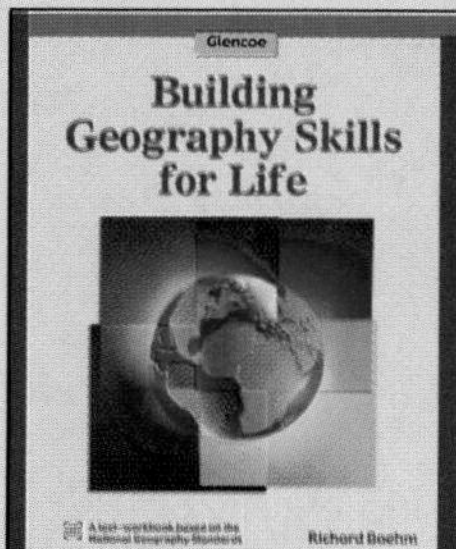

NGS Focus on Geography Literacy

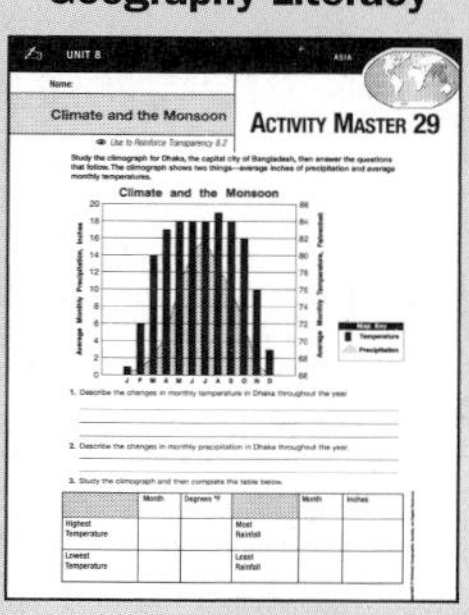

Regional Atlas Activity 3

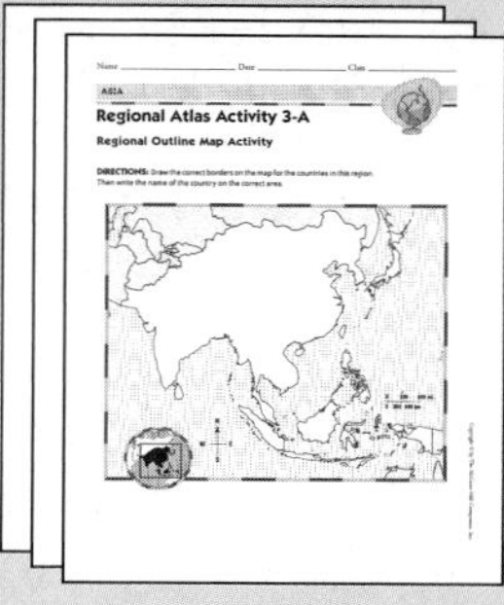

NATIONAL GEOGRAPHIC MapMachine

Find the latest coverage of geography in the news, atlas updates, cartographic activities with interactive maps, an online map store, and links at www.nationalgeographic.com/maps

APPLICATION AND HANDS-ON

Citizenship Activity 3

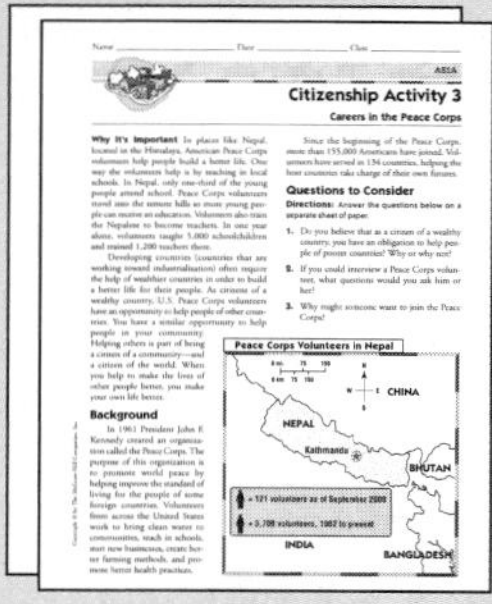

Foods Around the World 8

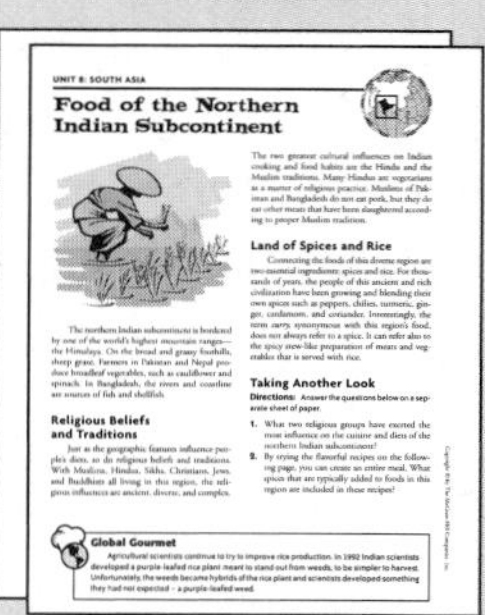

ENRICHMENT AND EXTENSION

Environmental Case Study 3

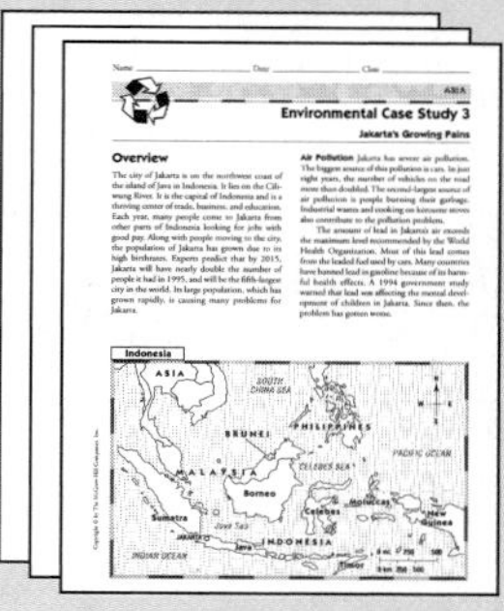

World Music: A Cultural Legacy

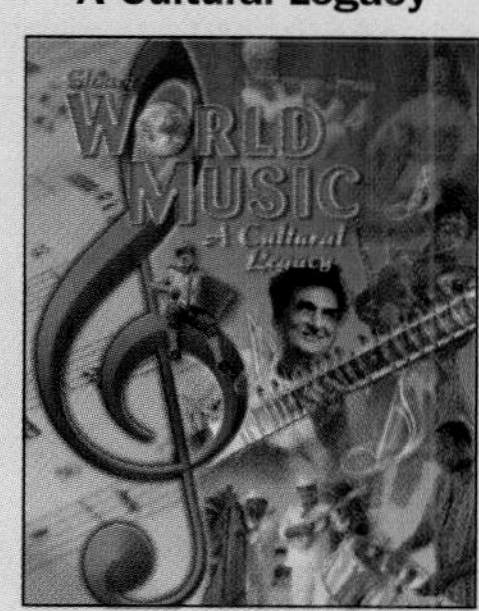

ASSESSMENT AND EVALUATION

GLENCOE'S ASSESSMENT ADVANTAGE

Unit 3 Pretests

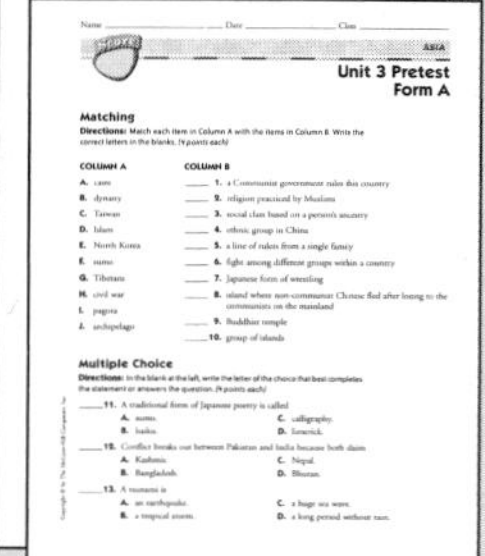

Unit 3 Posttests

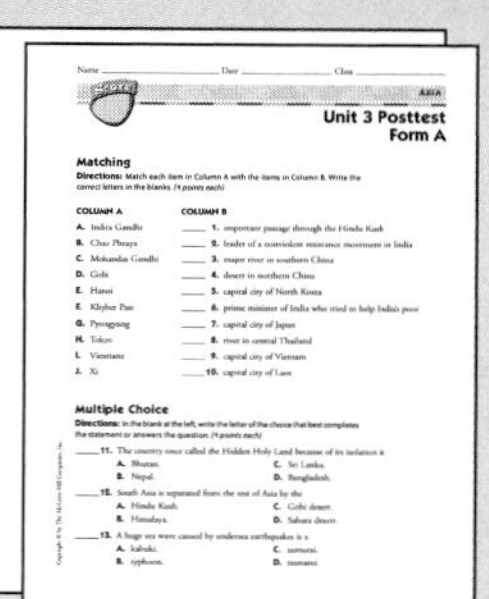

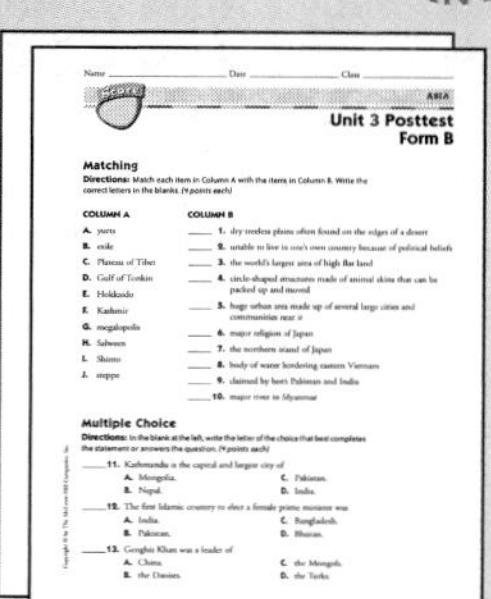

Additional Unit 3 Resources

- owt.glencoe.com
  Our World Today: People, Places, and Issues
  Visit the Glencoe *Our World Today: People, Places, and Issues* Web site for overviews, activities, assessments, and updated charts and graphs.
- socialstudies.glencoe.com
  Glencoe Social Studies
  Visit the Glencoe Web site for social studies activities, updates, and links to other sites.
- www.teachingtoday.glencoe.com
  Glencoe Teaching Today
  This Web site features daily teaching tips, free PDF downloads, annotated Web resources, educational news, and more.
- www.nationalgeographic.com
  NGS ONLINE Visit the National Geographic Society Web site for the latest coverage of geography in the news, atlas updates, activities, links, interactive features, and archives.
- **Glencoe's Guide to Using the Internet**
  Provides an introduction to many of the current technologies on the Internet. Professional resources and teaching strategies included.

Our Web sites provide additional resources. All essential content is covered in the Student Edition.

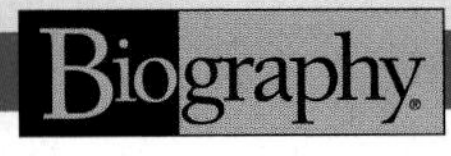

The following videotape programs are available from Glencoe:

- **The Great Wall of China** 0-7670-0361-6
- **Hirohito** 1-56501-461-8
- **Korea: The Forgotten War** 1-56501-540-1
- **Mahatma Gandhi: Pilgrim of Peace** 0-7670-0668-2
- **Democracy Crushed: Tiananmen Square** 0-7670-1459-6
- **Vietnam: A Soldier's Diary** 0-7670-0772-7
- **China's Boxer Rebellion** 0-7670-0617-8
- **China's Forbidden City** 0-7670-0649-6
- **Confucius: Words of Wisdom** 0-7670-0407-8

To order, call Glencoe at 1-800-334-7344. To find classroom resources to accompany many of these, check:

A&E Television: www.aetv.com

The History Channel: www.historychannel.com

Bibliography

Literature for the Student

- **Glencoe Middle School World Literature Library**
  Shabanu: Daughter of the Wind, by Suzanne Fisher Staples. Women in the nomadic culture of the Pakistan desert dwellers.
  So Far From the Bamboo Grove, by Yoko Kawashima Watkins, Jean Fritz. True story of a young girl forced to flee her home in Korea for Japan at the end of World War II.

Readings for the Teacher

- ***Vietnam,*** by Ole Steen Hansen. Austin, TX: Raintree Steck Vaughn, 1997.
- ***Imperial China,*** by Hazel Mary Martell. Austin, TX: Raintree Steck Vaughn, 1999.

Multimedia Links

- **Glencoe Social Studies Primary Source Document Library**
  The *Analects* by Confucius
  Buddha's Sermons, Oral tradition
  China's Cultural Revolution by Yan Jiaqi and Gao Gao
  Dinner With Attila the Hun by Priscus
  The Hindi *Upanishads*, Author unknown
- ***Assignment: Southeast Asia.*** Boston: Christian Science Monitor Video, 1993. 60 minutes.
- ***History and Culture of China.*** Fairfield, Conn.: Queue. CD-ROM, Win/Mac.

Refer to owt.glencoe.com for additional literature titles and study guides related to this region.

Additional Glencoe Teacher Support

- **Teaching Strategies for the Geography Classroom**
- **Reproducible Lesson Plans**
- **Outline Map Resource Book**
- **Reading in the Content Area**

Service Learning Project

Connecting Classroom With Community

China has a long tradition of honoring parents and ancestors. As a result, the elderly in this culture are accorded great respect. Suggest that students show similar respect in their own community by visiting a community center that serves senior citizens. They might assist clients with meals, record their memories to create a community memory bank, or simply provide company. Have students complete a project summary report that includes such information as: How did this project help my community? What did I learn while completing this project?

Content Background Notes

Use this additional information as lecture notes or discussion prompts throughout the study of Unit 3.

Chapter 5 South Asia (pp. 142–159)

Devastating Earthquake In January 2001, a powerful earthquake struck the northern Indian state of Gujarat. Tragically, the quake came on Republic Day, a national holiday that celebrates the country's independence. Early estimates suggested the death toll would reach 30,000, making the quake the worst in India's history and the worst in the world since a 1990 quake shook Iran. Other estimates put the damage caused by the quake at more than $5 billion. Some of the damage came to historical and cultural sites that attract millions of visitors. India had no nationwide disaster relief system. In the aftermath of the earthquake, the country's leaders began planning to create one.

The Sundarbans One of the treasures of Bangladesh is the Sundarbans, the swampy region formed by the deltas of the Ganges, Brahmaputra, and Meghna Rivers. This biologically rich area is home to one of the largest mangrove forests in the world. Bangladesh has created three wildlife sanctuaries in the region that total some 2,228 square miles (5,771 sq. km). The region is home to a large population of Bengal tigers and to more than 300 different kinds of birds. Other notable animals include the estuarine crocodile, Indian python, and king cobra. The region is still largely wild and virtually uninhabited, although some people live on its outskirts and enter the Sundarbans in the late spring to harvest honey.

Chapter 6 China and Its Neighbors (pp. 160–187)

Falun Gong One-time Chinese government employee Li Hongzhi hoped to help other Chinese build greater spiritual peace. In 1992 he founded a movement called Falun Gong, which means "Law of the Wheel-Breathing Exercise." Followers use meditation and exercise to achieve calm and good health.

The Chinese government is hardly calm about Falun Gong, however. In April 1999, the movement shocked China's rulers by sending 10,000 members to demonstrate outside Communist Party headquarters in Beijing. The crowd stood silently in place, with the goal of winning the government's recognition of their movement. They got just the reverse—in July 1999, the government declared Falun Gong illegal. Since then, it has charged the movement with threatening the government, disrupting social stability, and endangering the health of followers. Estimates of Falun Gong members range as high as 70 million. According to some, this number is greater than the number of people who belong to the country's Communist Party. Other countries, including the United States, have urged the Chinese government to refrain from persecuting members of the movement. China has shown no signs of softening its stand.

Chapter 7 Japan and the Koreas (pp. 190–207)

Oldest Monarchy Japan has the world's oldest monarchy—a continuous line of emperors and empresses that reaches back about 2,000 years. Current Emperor Akihito is the 125th emperor in that line. Nestled in the middle of bustling, modern Tokyo sits nearly 300 acres of parkland and private buildings that make up the Imperial Palace complex, home to Japan's emperors since 1869. The Palace complex is surrounded by moats and, in some areas, by walls and towers. Inside, Japan's imperial family and the workers who support them follow a life of tradition and privacy. Imperial guards and court officials protect the emperor and his family from the public, erecting what has been called the "chrysanthemum curtain," named for the flower that serves as the emperor's symbol.

Reconciliation in Korea In 2000 North Korea and South Korea moved closer than ever before toward improved relations. In June South Korean president Kim Dae-Jung met with North Korean leader Kim Jong Il, launching a series of steps toward decreasing tensions in the peninsula. These included agreements to set up permanent liaison offices; to hold regular, high-level talks; and to allow family members separated by the border for nearly 50 years to visit with one another. Later in 2000, the American secretary of state met with North Korea's leader as well, another indication of an improved situation in Korea. For his efforts to promote peace, South Korea's leader won the 2000 Nobel Peace Prize.

Chapter 8 Southeast Asia (pp. 208–223)

Muslim Pop One of the world's top singing groups is a quintet from Malaysia called Raihan. The group—whose name means "a sense of paradise"—sings traditional Islamic songs called *nasyids.* They perform the songs with the sound of contemporary pop music, however, giving the Islamic faith a modern feel. Audiences have responded to the group's music. Their first album not only became Malaysia's top seller but also broke previous records for sales of one album. Record companies in Malaysia quickly tried to sign up other religious singers to capture a share of the market. Even a group of female singers has appeared. These women—all married and mothers—had to ask their husbands' permission to perform.

00:00 Out of Time?

If time does not permit teaching each chapter in this unit, you may use the **Reading Essentials and Study Guide** for each chapter.

Unit Overview

The four chapters of this unit introduce students to a culture region in which a large percentage of the world's people live. The countries in this region share the following features:

- high population densities
- deadly natural hazards—typhoons, floods, volcanoes, earthquakes
- expanding economies
- rich natural resources
- ancient religions and cultures

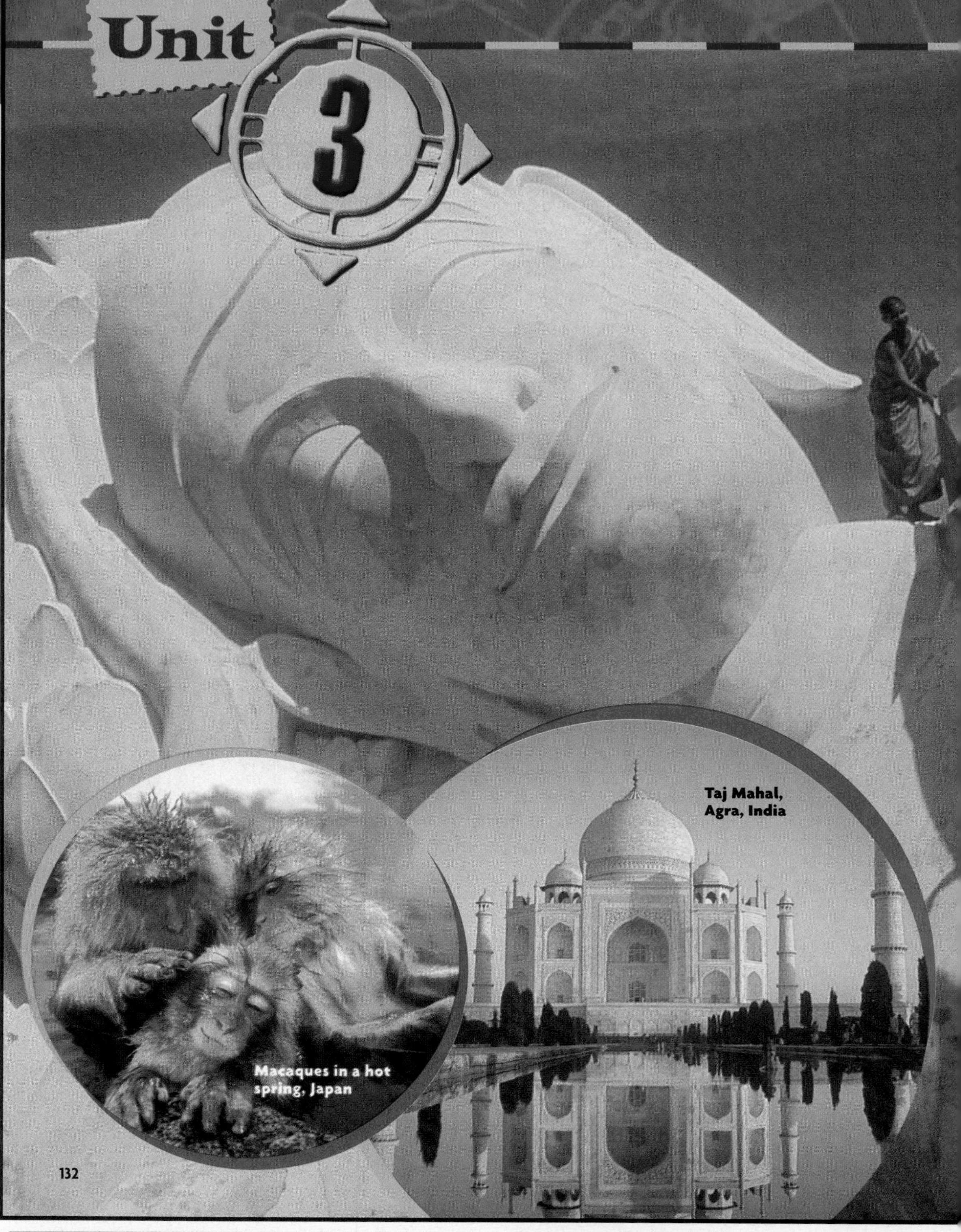

Taj Mahal, Agra, India

Macaques in a hot spring, Japan

Using the Illustration

Visual Instruction Buddha is typically shown in only a few poses. The reclining Buddha shown above represents the moment when he enters final nirvana. Thai artists tried to achieve the essence of an ancient sculpture believed to have been made in the Buddha's lifetime. Images of the Buddha are common throughout the region because kings hoped to gain credit for placing as many as possible in their realms. **Ask:** **What Asian countries besides Thailand are likely to display images of the Buddha?** Students can read the text to find which countries have large Buddhist populations. *(Bhutan, Cambodia, China, Japan, the Koreas, Laos, Mongolia, Myanmar, Nepal, Singapore, Sri Lanka, Vietnam)*

Introducing Unit 3

NATIONAL GEOGRAPHIC

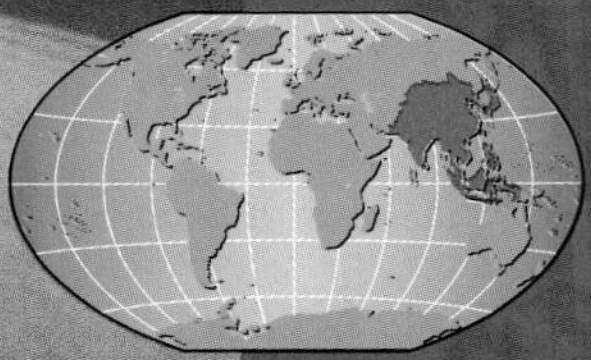

Asia

For many people in the Western Hemisphere, the region of Asia—in the Eastern Hemisphere—brings to mind exotic images. Ancient temples stand in dense rain forests. Farmers work in flooded rice fields. Pandas nibble bamboo shoots. Yet bustling cities, gleaming skyscrapers, and high-technology industries also can be found here. Turn the page to learn more about this region and its 3 billion people.

▲ Monks wrapping statue of Buddha in yellow cloth, Thailand

NGS ONLINE
www.nationalgeographic.com/education

NATIONAL GEOGRAPHIC

These materials are available from Glencoe.

 Software

ZipZapMap! World

Transparencies

PicturePack Transparencies

CD-ROM

Picture Atlas of the World, Second Edition

Current Events Journal

Point out that India's rate of population growth—about 2 percent a year—is half of what it was 50 years ago. Inform students that the country has about 1 billion people. **Ask: With a growth rate of 2 percent, how many people are added to the country each year?** *(about 20 million)* **What effects would this population growth have on the country?** *(Answers might include overcrowding, a lack of food and water, and strains on the economy and government.)* **L1**

Unit Launch Activity

The Influence of China and India Asia has two of the oldest civilizations on the earth. China and India began to develop their civilizations thousands of years ago. Through trade, conquest, and religious conversion, these two civilizations strongly influenced many of their neighbors. Although other countries in Asia have their own distinctive cultures, China and India clearly have left their stamp on the ways of thinking and living in other countries. Before students begin studying Unit 3, inform them of the importance of these two cultures to the other countries of Asia. As they read, have them keep track of examples of this influence. When they have completed studying the unit, ask for volunteers to share their examples with the class.

EE4 Human Systems: Standard 9

NGS ONLINE
www.nationalgeographic.com/education

This online resource provides lesson plans, atlas updates, cartographic activities with interactive maps, an online map store, and geography links.

NATIONAL GEOGRAPHIC **REGIONAL ATLAS**

Lesson Plan

Using the Regional Atlas
These features and activities may be used as an introduction to the unit or as teaching tools throughout the course of the unit.

Focus

Objectives

1. Locate Asia and describe its major landforms.
2. Identify the countries and capitals of Asia.
3. Compare the populations of the countries in Asia.

5-Minute Precheck

Have students look at the physical map on this page. **Ask:** **Would you say that most of the land in Asia was lowland or highland?** *(highland)* **What effect is that fact likely to have on agriculture?** *(The region has limited amounts of arable land as a result.)*

More About the Profile

In order to show a variety of physical features, this cross section begins at the India-Pakistan border and ends at Mount Fuji, Japan.

Asia

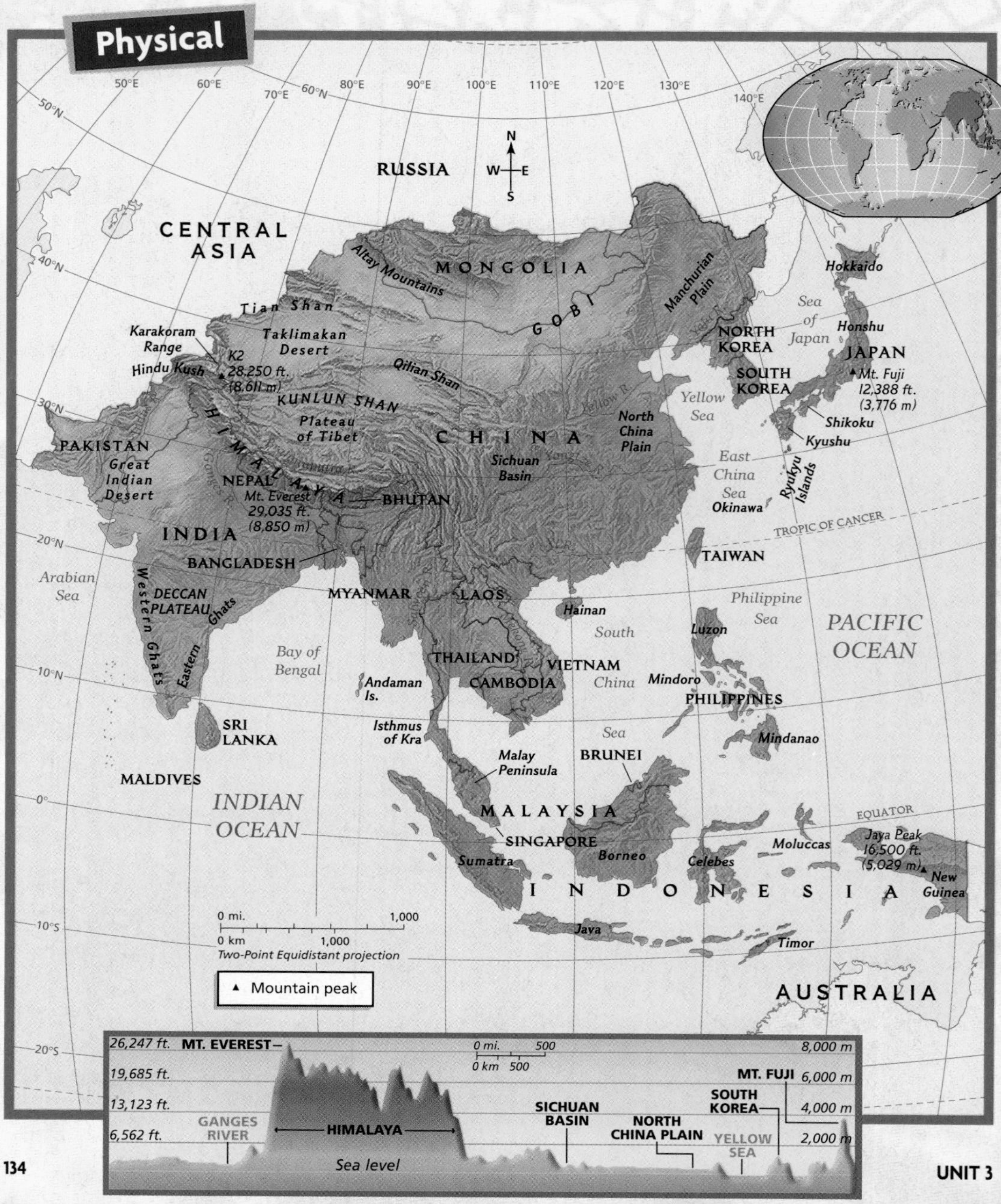

Physical

Two-Point Equidistant projection

▲ Mountain peak

Regional Atlas Activity

Making Comparisons Assign each student a city in Asia on the map on pages RA22–RA23. Then have the students find a city in the Western Hemisphere along the same line of latitude as the Asian city they have been assigned. Tell students to use the maps in the Unit 3 Regional Atlas and the text to compare one aspect of the two cities, such as the landforms or population density. Instruct them to present their comparisons in the form of a chart. **L2**

EE1 The World in Spatial Terms: Standard 1

UNIT 3

Political

RUSSIA
CENTRAL ASIA
MONGOLIA
Ulaanbaatar
CHINA
Beijing
NORTH KOREA
Pyongyang
SOUTH KOREA
Seoul
JAPAN
Tokyo
Sea of Japan
Yellow Sea
East China Sea
Amur R.
Yellow R.
Yangtze R.
Salween R.
Xi R.
KASHMIR
Islamabad
PAKISTAN
Indus R.
New Delhi
NEPAL
Kathmandu
Brahmaputra R.
Thimphu
BHUTAN
Ganges R.
BANGLADESH
Dhaka
INDIA
Irrawaddy R.
Arabian Sea
Bay of Bengal
MYANMAR
Yangon (Rangoon)
LAOS
Vientiane
Hanoi
Mekong R.
THAILAND
Bangkok
VIETNAM
CAMBODIA
Phnom Penh
Macau
Hong Kong
Taipei
TAIWAN
The People's Republic of China claims Taiwan as its 23rd province.
TROPIC OF CANCER
South China Sea
Philippine Sea
PACIFIC OCEAN
Manila
PHILIPPINES
SRI LANKA
Colombo
Male
MALDIVES
BRUNEI
Bandar Seri Begawan
Kuala Lumpur
MALAYSIA
SINGAPORE
EQUATOR
INDIAN OCEAN
INDONESIA
Jakarta
Dili
EAST TIMOR (UN administration)
AUSTRALIA
60°E 80°E 100°E 120°E 140°E
60°N 40°N 20°N 0° 20°S

- National capital
- Territorial capital
- Major city

0 mi. 1,000
0 km 1,000
Two-Point Equidistant projection

N W E S

MAP STUDY

1. What river runs through China's Sichuan Basin?
2. What is the capital of Thailand?

Unit 3

TEACH

Making Comparisons Give students a pair of countries in Asia. Have them use the maps on these two pages to compare the two countries in terms of size, location, and physical features. Then have them write a paragraph about their comparisons. Ask for volunteers to read their paragraphs to the class. **L1**

MAP STUDY

Answers

1. Yangtze River
2. Bangkok

Skills Practice

What is the largest country in Asia? *(China)* **What seven rivers have their sources in the Plateau of Tibet?** *(Indus, Ganges, Brahmaputra, Irawaddy, Mekong, Yangtze, Salween)*

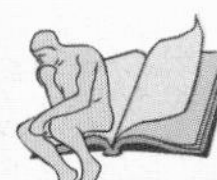

THE HUMANITIES CONNECTION

World Music: A Cultural Legacy

World Art and Architecture Transparencies

Regional Atlas Activity

Hindu Festivals Organize students into groups, and then assign each group one of the following Hindu festivals: Diwali, Durga Puja or Dassehra, Holi, Janannath, Makara-Sankranti, Pongal, Ramlila, and Vaisakhi. Ask groups to find out what their festival commemorates and how Hindus celebrate it. Have groups share their findings with the class in an oral report, a visual display, or a skit. **L1**

EE4 Human Systems: Standard 10

Building Skills

Making Generalizations
Have students study the map on this page and then develop a generalization based on its information. *(Example: Monsoon winds affect regions near the coast more than those in the interior.)* Ask for volunteers to read their generalizations to the class.

Interdisciplinary Connections

Science The wet monsoons bring about 60 inches (152 cm) of rain to most of Southeast Asia each year, although some areas can receive several times that amount.

MAP STUDY

Answers

1. more than 60 inches
2. northeast

Skills Practice

How many inches of rain do northwest China and Mongolia receive each year? *(less than 20 inches)*

Asia

Monsoons

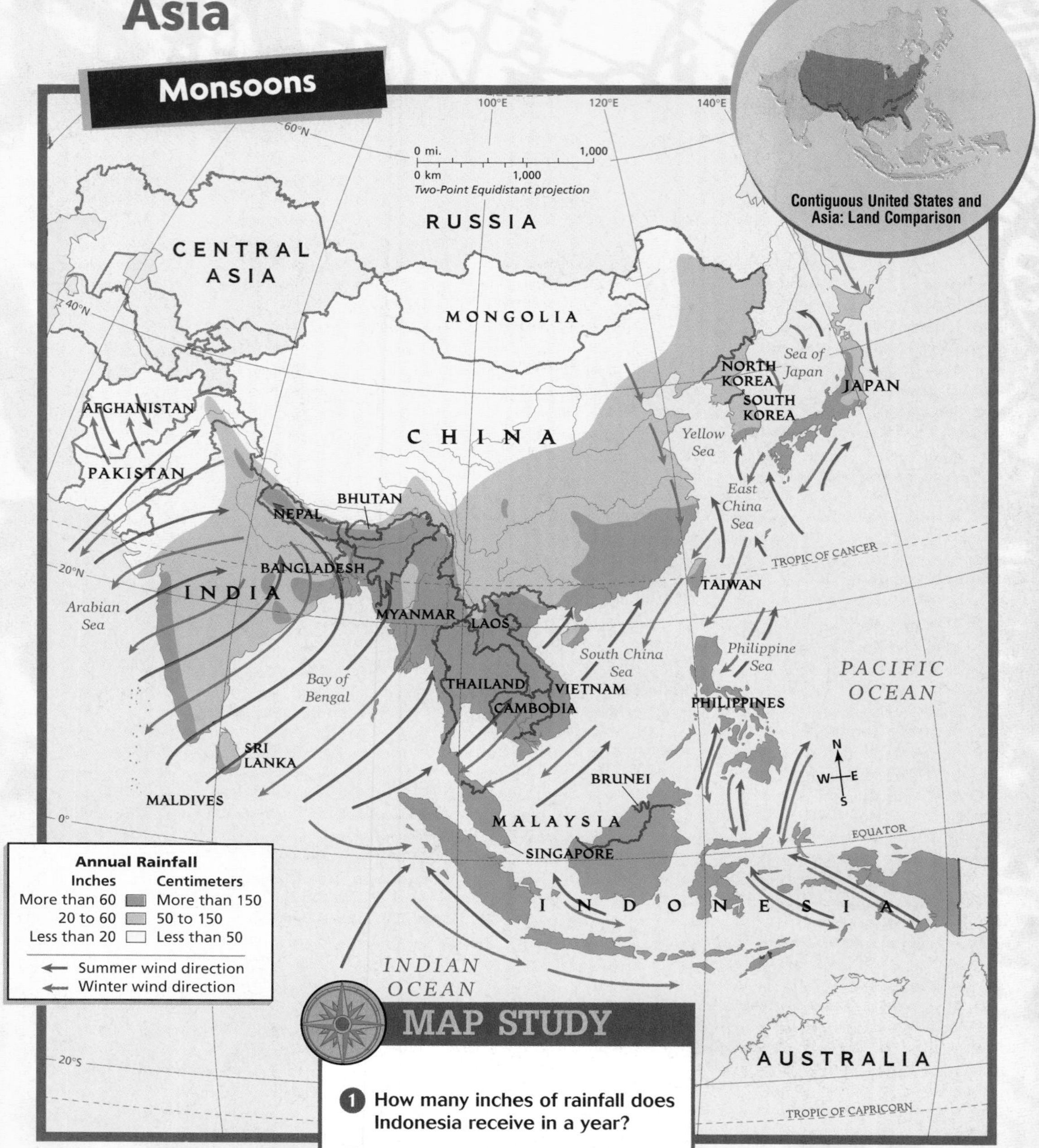

0 mi. 1,000
0 km 1,000
Two-Point Equidistant projection

Contiguous United States and Asia: Land Comparison

Annual Rainfall

Inches		Centimeters
More than 60	▇	More than 150
20 to 60	▒	50 to 150
Less than 20	☐	Less than 50

← Summer wind direction
← Winter wind direction

MAP STUDY

1. How many inches of rainfall does Indonesia receive in a year?
2. In what general direction do most of the summer monsoons blow?

136 UNIT 3

Content Background

The Spratly Islands China, Taiwan, Vietnam, Malaysia, and the Philippines all claim the Spratly Islands in the South China Sea. These countries are not interested in what is on these mostly uninhabited islands but in what might be *beneath* them—deposits of oil and other valuable resources. How are such disputes settled? One criterion for assigning possession is based on claims dating back to ancient times, but none of the countries has had lasting possession. Maintaining control for 50 consecutive years makes a strong claim, but, again, none of the five qualifies. The United Nations Law of the Sea allows countries to claim islands within 200 miles of their shores, but this does not apply to any of the five countries either.

Unit 3

Fast Facts

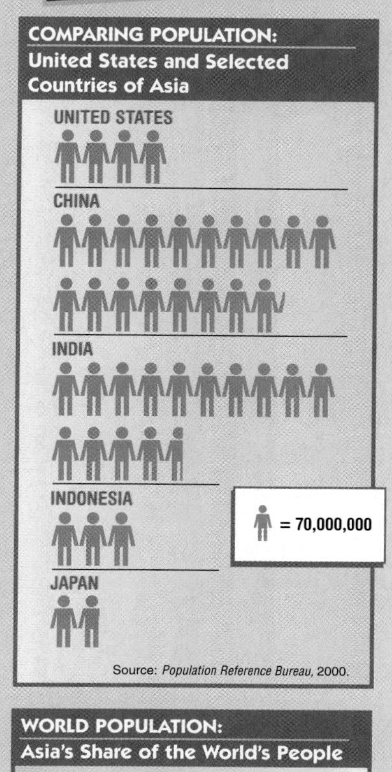

WORLD POPULATION: Asia's Share of the World's People

Rest of World 39.3%
China 20.7%
India 16.8%
Indonesia 3.4%
Pakistan 2.4%
Japan 2.1%
Bangladesh 2.2%
Rest of Asia 13.1%

Source: *Population Reference Bureau,* 2000.

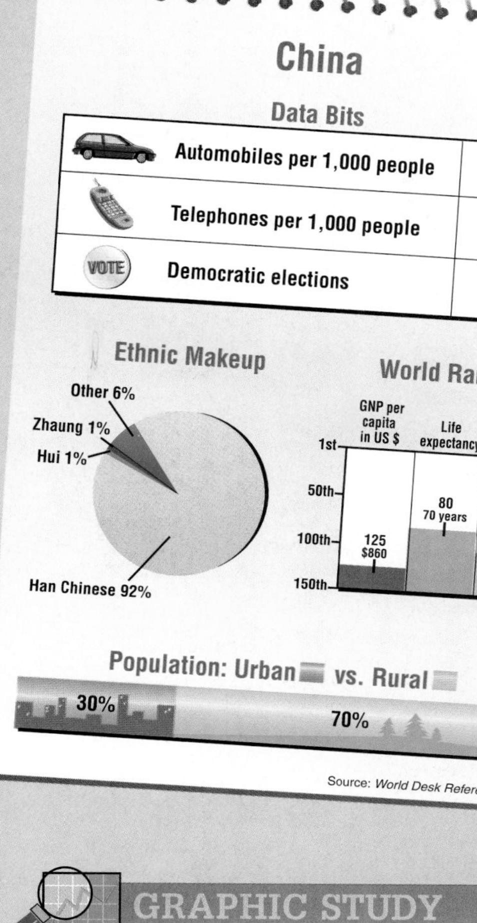

GRAPHIC STUDY

1. Which Asian country's population is nearest the United States?
2. What percentage of the world's population lives in Asia?

Asia 137

TIME REPORTS FOCUS ON WORLD ISSUES

As an introduction to this region, you may want to engage students by studying an important contemporary issue in this region of the world. The **TIME REPORTS: FOCUS ON WORLD ISSUES** for this region is found on pages 173–179. This feature examines what is happening to China's political structure as the government begins instituting some free enterprise practices.

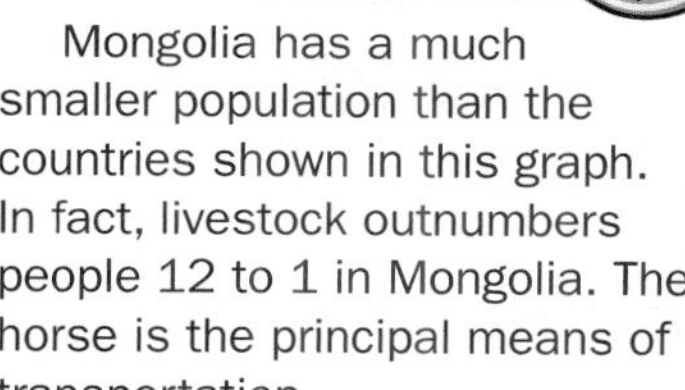

Mongolia has a much smaller population than the countries shown in this graph. In fact, livestock outnumbers people 12 to 1 in Mongolia. The horse is the principal means of transportation.

GRAPHIC STUDY

Answers

1. Indonesia
2. 60.7 percent

Skills Practice

How does China compare in population to the United States? *(about 4 1/2 times larger)* **How does India's population compare to the United States?** *(about 3 1/2 times larger)*

FUN FACTS

- **Bhutan** This Himalayan country is called Land of the Thunder Dragon because of its violent storms.
- **China/Mongolia** *Gobi* is Mongolian for "place without water."
- **India** In the ancient Indian language of Sanskrit, *Himalaya* means "abode of snow."
- **Indonesia** More Muslims live in Indonesia than in any other country in the world.
- **Singapore** The name *Singapore* is derived from the Sanskrit *Singa Pur,* which means "city of the lion." This name was probably given to the area by Sumatrans who settled there in the 1200s.

Current Events Journal

Have students use the Country Profiles to write down which Asian countries speak European languages. *(French: Cambodia, Laos; English: Brunei, India, Malaysia, Maldives, Pakistan, Philippines, Singapore, Sri Lanka).* **Ask: Why do you think English and French are spoken in these countries?** *(They once were colonies of England or France, except for the Philippines, which was an American colony.)*

Cultural Kaleidoscope

Bangladesh When someone does a favor for someone else in Bangladesh, the custom is not to say thanks but to return the favor.

Brunei The sultan of Brunei, with a net worth of more than $30 billion, is one of the richest people in the world.

Did You Know

A mandarin was a public official in Imperial China. Over time, the term came to be used to describe the food eaten by "mandarins," as foreigners called members of China's upper class.

REGIONAL ATLAS

Country Profiles

BANGLADESH
POPULATION: 133,500,000 2,383 per sq. mi. 933 per sq. km
LANGUAGE: Bengali
MAJOR EXPORT: Clothing
MAJOR IMPORT: Machinery
CAPITAL: Dhaka
LANDMASS: 55,598 sq. mi. 143,998 sq. km
Dhaka
BHUTAN
POPULATION: 900,000 50 per sq. mi. 19 per sq. km
LANGUAGES: Dzonkha, Local Languages
MAJOR EXPORT: Cardamom
MAJOR IMPORT: Fuels
CAPITAL: Thimphu
LANDMASS: 18,147 sq. mi. 47,001 sq. km
Thimphu
BRUNEI
POPULATION: 323,000 145 per sq. mi. 56 per sq. km
LANGUAGES: Malay, English, Chinese
MAJOR EXPORT: Crude Oil
MAJOR IMPORT: Machinery
CAPITAL: Bandar Seri Begawan
LANDMASS: 2,226 sq. mi. 5,765 sq. km
Bandar Seri Begawan
CAMBODIA
POPULATION: 13,100,000 187 per sq. mi. 72 per sq. km
LANGUAGES: Khmer, French
MAJOR EXPORT: Timber
MAJOR IMPORT: Construction Materials
CAPITAL: Phnom Penh
LANDMASS: 69,898 sq. mi. 181,035 sq. km
Phnom Penh
CHINA
POPULATION: 1,273,300,000 343 per sq. mi. 132 per sq. km
LANGUAGE: Mandarin Chinese
MAJOR EXPORT: Machinery
MAJOR IMPORT: Machinery
CAPITAL: Beijing
LANDMASS: 3,705,820 sq. mi. 9,598,032 sq. km
Beijing
INDIA
POPULATION: 1,033,000,000 814 per sq. mi. 314 per sq. km
LANGUAGES: Hindi, English, Local Languages
MAJOR EXPORTS: Gems and Jewelry
MAJOR IMPORT: Crude Oil
CAPITAL: New Delhi
LANDMASS: 1,269,346 sq. mi. 3,287,591 sq. km
New Delhi
INDONESIA
POPULATION: 206,100,000 278 per sq. mi. 107 per sq. km
LANGUAGES: Bahasa Indonesia, Local Languages
MAJOR EXPORT: Textiles
MAJOR IMPORT: Manufactured Goods
CAPITAL: Jakarta
LAND MASS: 741,101 sq. mi. 1,919,443 sq. km
Jakarta
JAPAN
POPULATION: 127,100,000 871 per sq. mi. 336 per sq. km
LANGUAGE: Japanese
MAJOR EXPORT: Machinery
MAJOR IMPORT: Manufactured Goods
CAPITAL: Tokyo
LANDMASS: 145,875 sq. mi. 377,815 sq. km
Tokyo
LAOS
POPULATION: 5,400,000 59 per sq. mi. 23 per sq. km
LANGUAGES: Lao, French
MAJOR EXPORT: Wood Products
MAJOR IMPORT: Machinery
CAPITAL: Vientiane
LANDMASS: 91,429 sq. mi. 236,800 sq. km
Vientiane

Countries and flags not drawn to scale

138 UNIT 3

Regional Atlas Activity

Acrostic Poems Assign each student a country or physical feature in Asia. Give students time to research their subject and then have them develop an acrostic poem describing the place. An acrostic poem is one in which each word begins with a letter of the subject's name. *(For example, the words for China could be Communist government; Home to Hong Kong; Industrializing; Near North Korea; Ancient culture.)* **L2**

EE4 Places and Regions: Standard 4

UNIT 3

For more information on countries in this region, refer to the Nations of the World Data Bank on pages 690–699.

Interdisciplinary Connections

Art People in Japan have made an art—called *origami*—out of folding paper. They create decorative objects such as animals, fish, or flowers. There are about 100 traditional origami patterns, but each year new designs are developed.

History Sikhism, which combines elements of Hinduism and Islam, was founded by Guru Nanak, who lived between 1469 and 1539. Sikhs differ from Hindus in that they reject the caste system, the priesthood, pilgrimages, begging, and bathing in sacred streams. Sikhs accept the equality of men and women and believe in one God. Their holiest place is the Golden Temple at Amritsar in the state of Punjab.

5-Minute Precheck

Write "6 billion" and inform students that this number represents the population of the world. Then write "3.3 billion." **Ask: What does this number represent?** *(the population of Asia)* In view of this fact, have them consider Asia's importance to the world. Ask for volunteers to express their thoughts.

Country Profiles Activity

Using Maps Play a geographical riddle game with students in which you give them a set of directions and they have to identify both the starting point *and* the endpoint. For example, you could say, "From this city, you move by ship south into the Indian Ocean, turn to the east, and then head northeast to reach a city in Myanmar." *(starting point: Colombo, Sri Lanka; ending point: Yangon)* Organize students into teams and allow each team a few seconds to provide the answer. If they cannot, give another team a chance to do so. Award points for correct answers and create a fictional award such as "Champion Puzzle Solvers" for the team with the most points. **L2**

EE1 The World in Spatial Terms: Standard 1

Regional Atlas

Country Profiles

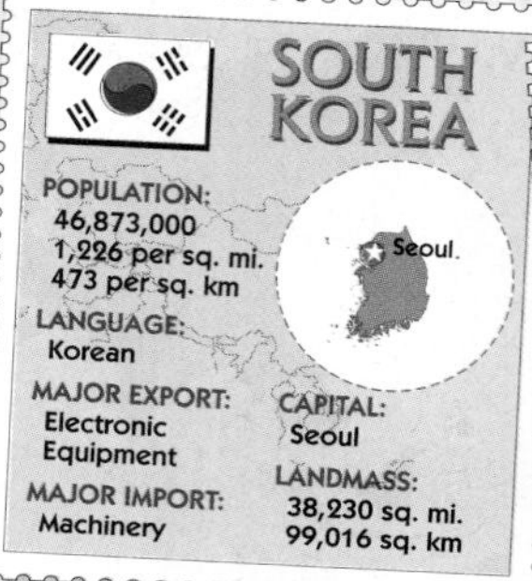

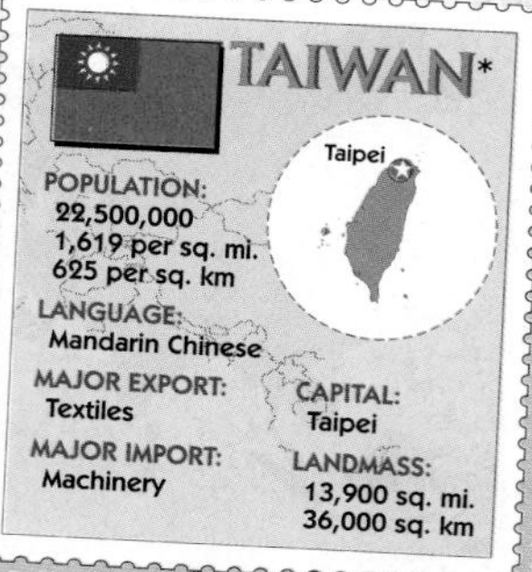

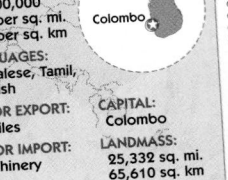

* The People's Republic of China claims Taiwan as its 23rd province.

THAILAND
POPULATION:
62,400,000
314 per sq. mi.
121 per sq. km
LANGUAGES:
Thai, Local Languages
MAJOR EXPORT:
Manufactured Goods
MAJOR IMPORT:
Machinery
CAPITAL:
Bangkok
LANDMASS:
198,457 sq. mi.
514,001 sq. km
Bangkok

VIETNAM
POPULATION:
78,700,000
611 per sq. mi.
239 per sq. km
LANGUAGES:
Vietnamese, Chinese
MAJOR EXPORT:
Crude Oil
MAJOR IMPORT:
Machinery
CAPITAL:
Hanoi
LANDMASS:
127,242 sq. mi.
329,556 sq. km
Hanoi

Countries and flags not drawn to scale

Building Citizenship

Women's Rights Not all countries have the same laws for men and women. In some countries, women are not allowed to own property, vote, go to school, or work. Part of the reason for this is that women's contributions to society in the area of raising children and running a household are not valued as much as men's contributions.

Why is it important in the United States that men and women have equal rights and that those rights are protected by the law?

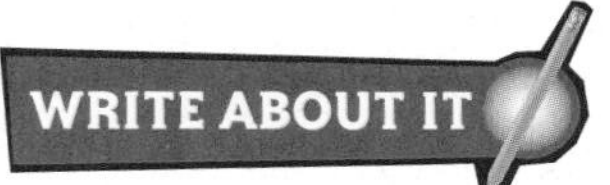

Imagine that you are a sixth grade exchange student from an Asian country. Write a letter to your sister at home describing some activities that girls in your American school take part in on an equal basis with boys.

Vietnamese mother and baby ▶

Fun Facts

- **Taiwan** Leaving rice in one's bowl is considered impolite in Taiwan. The Taiwanese teach their children to finish all of their food out of respect for their parents and for the farmers who grew it.
- **India** In India, wealthy people honor special guests by decorating rice dishes with thin sheets of silver or gold leaf.
- **Thailand** Thais always honor their king and his image. When the king's picture is on a stamp, Thais wet the stamp with a damp sponge rather than licking it, which would show disrespect.
- **The Koreas** Cooks in the Koreas try to serve meals that include all the traditional colors: red, green, yellow, white, and black.

Cultural Kaleidoscope

Malaysia Malaysians think that the durian is the best of all fruits. It has a green, spiny rind and a flavored, soft pulp. However, it gives off a rather strong odor that some people think is unpleasant.

Did You Know?

The Philippines is one of the world's major sources of movies. Only three countries in the world make more films.

Building Citizenship

Answer
The United States is founded on the concepts of equality and equal rights. Women contribute to all aspects of U.S. society.

Write About it! Responses should include boys and girls together in school, girls and women involved in sports, more women in politics and business, and freedom to do anything that boys and men can do. Students should also realize that with these freedoms come risks and responsibilities. In sports, for example, girls risk being injured, which many cultures consider unacceptable.

UNIT 3

Three generations of a Chinese family

Unit 3
Regional Atlas

More About the Photo

Family Since Kongfuzi (Confucius) began teaching in the 500s B.C., family has been a central feature of life in China. The philosopher urged that children should show deep respect to their parents, who gave the gift of life. Such an attitude, he said, was the most fundamental way of acting morally.

Assess

Organize students into groups. Have the groups use the Unit 3 Regional Atlas to quiz one another on the physical and cultural characteristics of the countries of Asia.

Enrich

Have students choose one country from Asia and create an annotated map that uses images and captions to show the natural, cultural, and historical sites that a tourist might visit.

Close

Have students write a one-sentence summary of the Regional Atlas introduction.

Fun Facts

- **Indonesia** About 1 out of every 15 cups of coffee consumed around the world and about 1 in every 20 cups of tea come from crops grown on plantations in Indonesia.
- **China/Nepal** Mount Everest—the tallest mountain in the world—is named for Sir George Everest, a British colonial official who surveyed the Himalaya in the 1860s. Tibetans call the mountain *Chomolungma*, which means "Goddess Mother of the World."
- **Pakistan** K2 is another lofty mountain near Everest. It was so named because it was the second mountain measured in a survey of the Karakoram Range carried out in the 1850s.

Chapter 5 Resources

Note: The following materials may be used when teaching Chapter 5. Section level support materials are shown at point of use in the margins of the Teacher Wraparound Edition.

Timesaving Tools

TeacherWorks™ All-In-One Planner and Resource Center

- **Interactive Teacher Edition** See the **Interactive Teacher Edition** CD-ROM to electronically integrate your Teacher Wraparound Edition and blackline masters.
- **Interactive Lesson Planner** Organize your week, month, semester, or year with all the lesson helps you need. The **Interactive Lesson Planner** CD-ROM contains all Chapter 5 resources.

Use Glencoe's **Presentation Plus!** multimedia teacher tool to easily present dynamic lessons that visually excite your students. Using Microsoft PowerPoint® you can customize the presentations to create your own personalized lessons.

TEACHING TRANSPARENCIES

Graphic Organizer Transparency and Student Activity 5

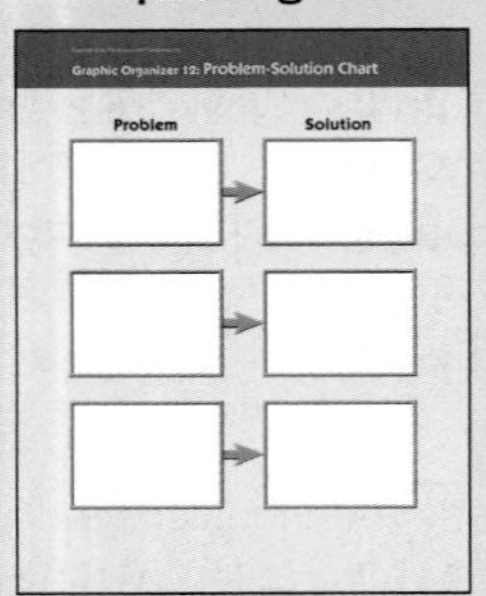

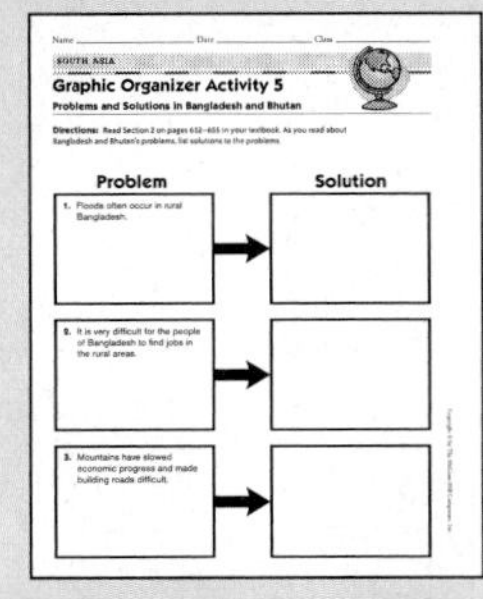

FOLDABLES™ Study Organizer

Foldables are three-dimensional, interactive graphic organizers that help students practice basic writing skills, review key vocabulary terms, and identify main ideas. Every chapter contains a Foldable activity, with additional chapter activities found in the ***Reading and Study Skills Foldables*** booklet.

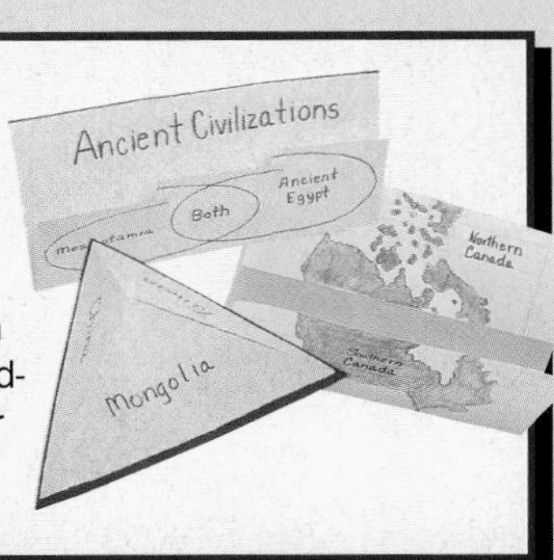

ENRICHMENT AND EXTENSION

Enrichment Activity 5

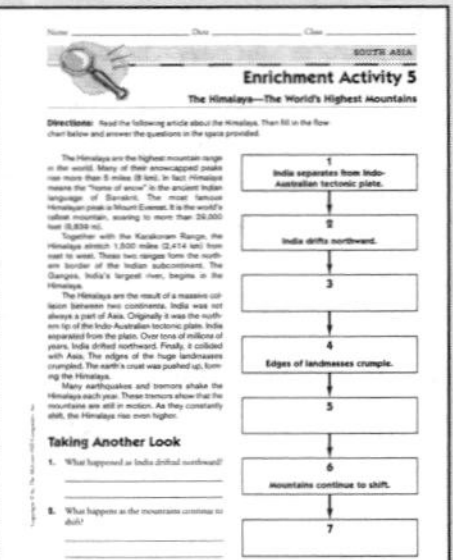

Cooperative Learning Activity 5

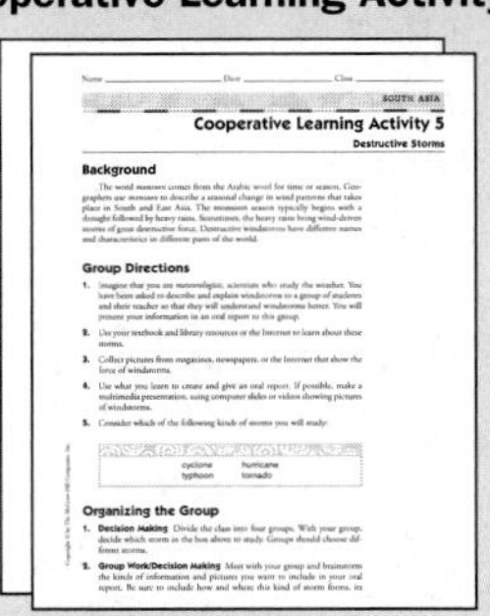

MAP AND GEOGRAPHY SKILLS

Chapter Map Activity 5

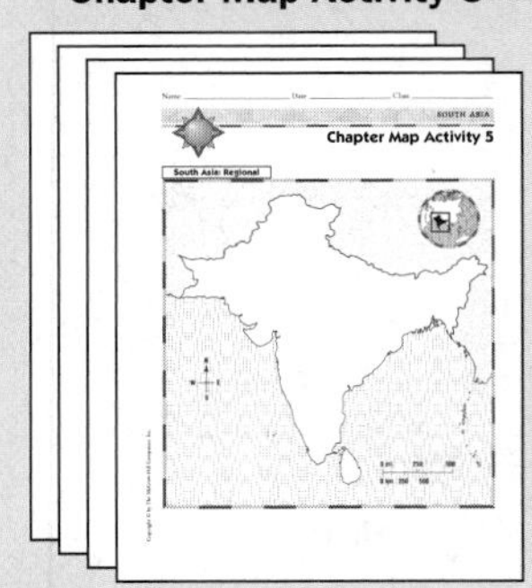

GeoLab Activity 5

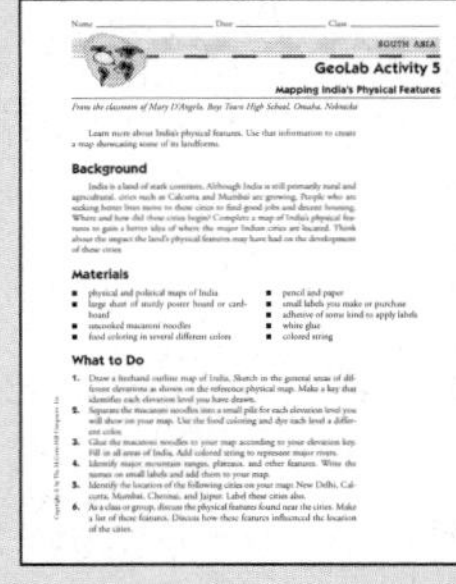

STANDARDIZED ASSESSMENT SKILLS

GLENCOE'S ASSESSMENT ADVANTAGE

Critical Thinking Skills Activity 5

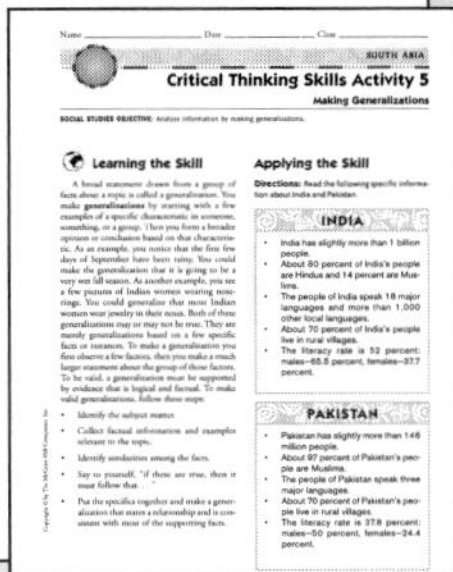

Map and Graph Skills Activity 5

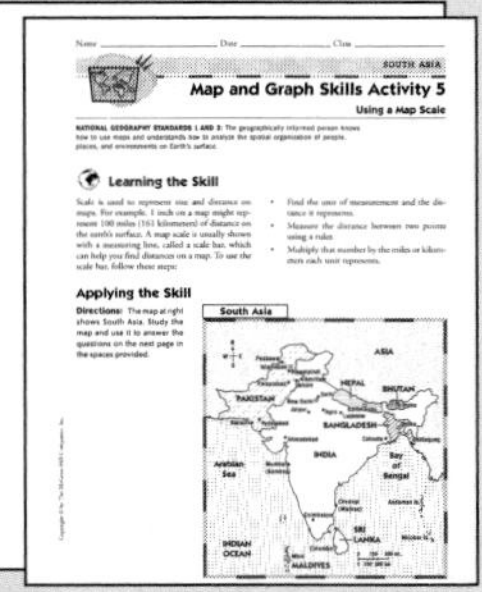

Reading and Writing Skills Activity 5

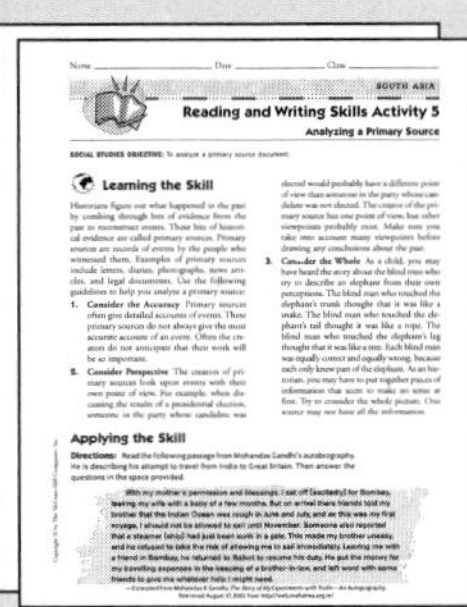

Standardized Test Practice Workbook Activity 5

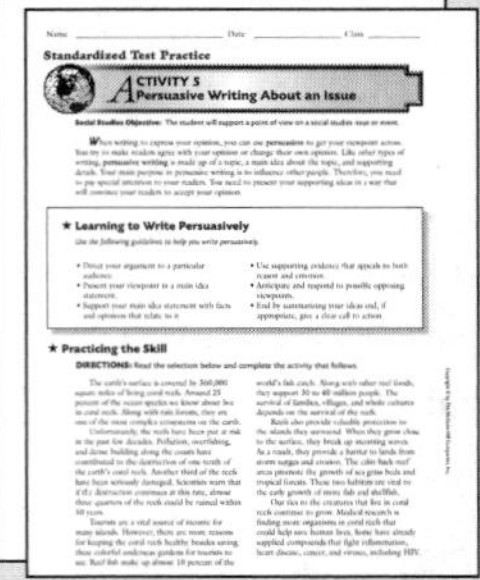

REVIEW AND REINFORCEMENT

Chapter Skills Activity 5

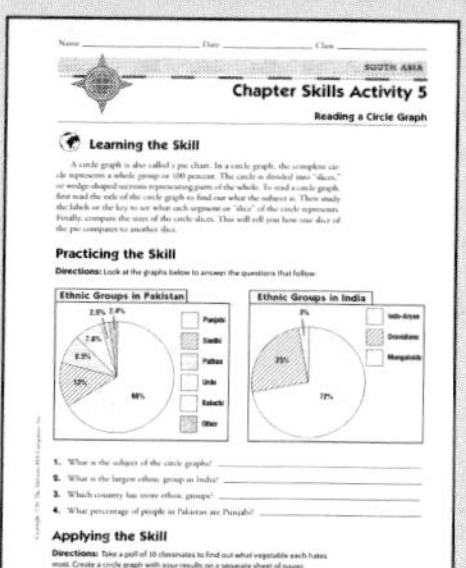

Take-Home Review Activity 5

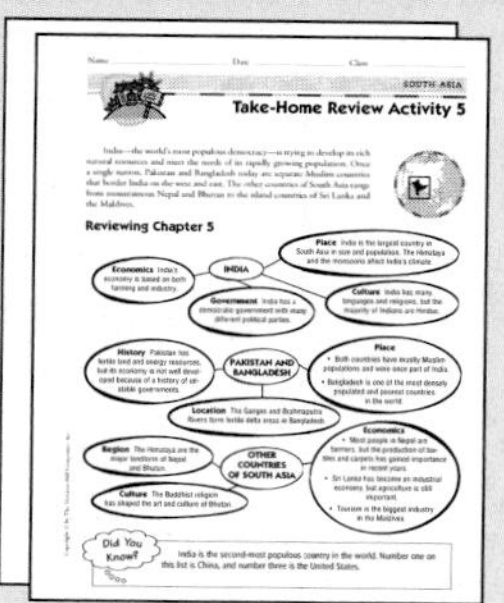

Reteaching Activity 5

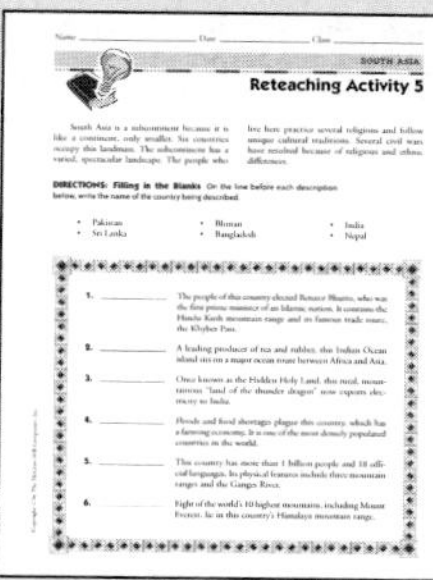

Vocabulary Activity 5

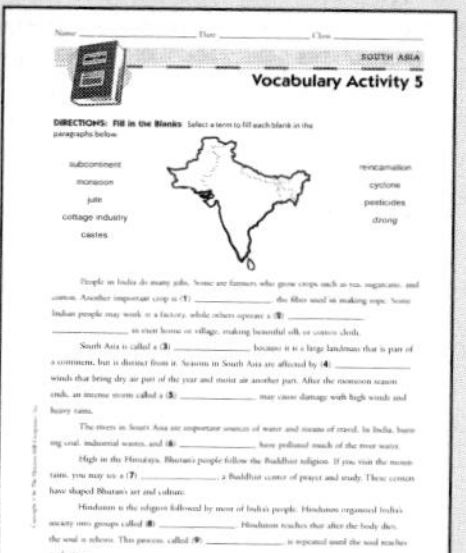

Workbook Activity 5

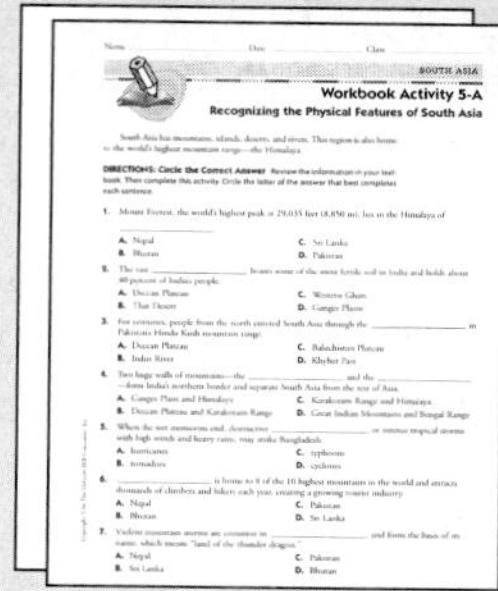

ASSESSMENT

GLENCOE'S ASSESSMENT ADVANTAGE

Chapter 5 Test, Form A

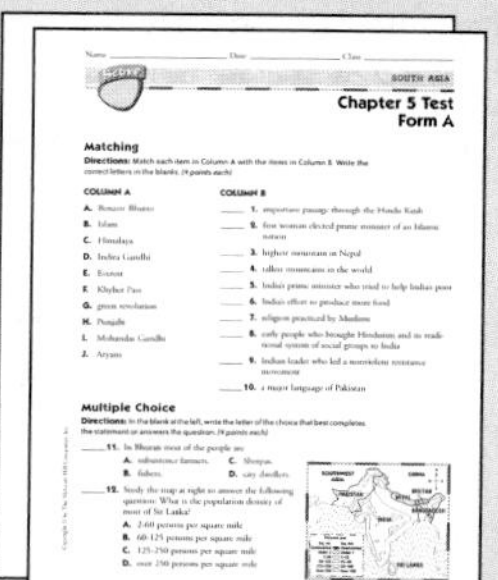

Chapter 5 Test, Form B

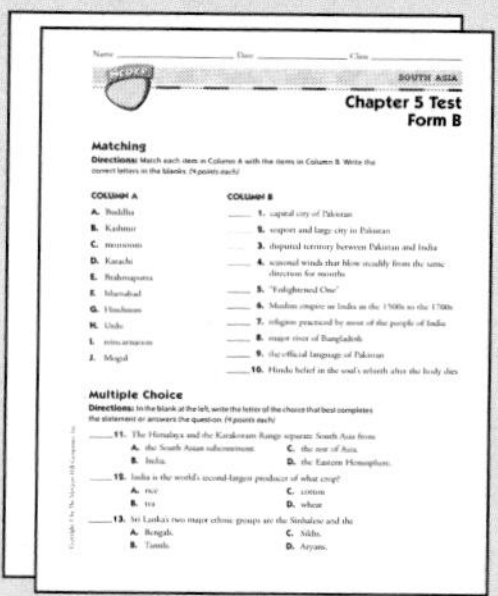

Performance Assessment Activity 5

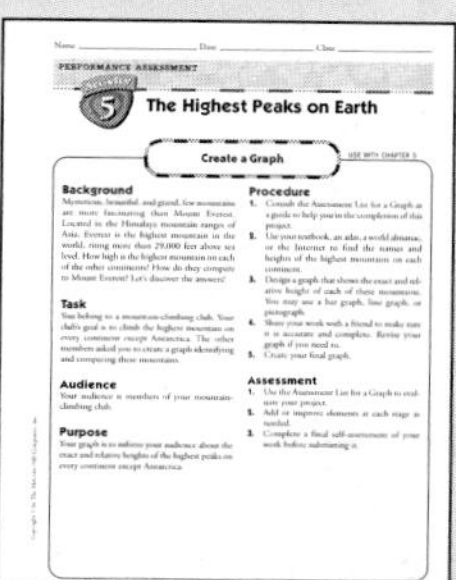

ExamView® Pro 3.0 Testmaker CD-ROM

MULTIMEDIA

- **National Geographic's The World and Its People**
- **MindJogger Videoquiz**
- **Vocabulary PuzzleMaker Software**
- **Interactive Tutor Self-Assessment CD-ROM**
- **ExamView® Pro 3.0 Testmaker CD-ROM**
- **Interactive Lesson Planner CD-ROM**
- **Interactive Teacher Edition CD-ROM**
- **Skillbuilder Interactive Workbook CD-ROM, Level 1**
- **Presentation Plus! CD-ROM**
- **Audio Program**

SPANISH RESOURCES

The following Spanish language materials are available in the Spanish Resources binder:

- **Spanish Chapter Summaries**
- **Spanish Vocabulary Activities**
- **Spanish Guided Reading Activities**
- **Spanish Quizzes and Tests**
- **Spanish Take-Home Review Activities**
- **Spanish Reteaching Activities**

Meeting National Standards

Geography for Life

All of the 18 standards are demonstrated in Unit 3. The following ones are highlighted in Chapter 5:

Section 1 **EE3 Human Systems: Standards 7, 8**
EE4 Human Systems: Standards 9, 10, 11, 12, 13
EE5 Environment and Society: Standards 14, 15, 16

Section 2 **EE4 Human Systems: Standards 9, 10, 11, 12, 13**
EE5 Environment and Society: Standards 14, 15, 16

For a complete listing of National Geography Standards and entire text correlation, see pages T22–T29.

Local Objectives

____

____

Chapter 5 Planning Guide

SECTION RESOURCES

Daily Objectives	Reproducible Resources	Multimedia Resources
Section 1 **India** **Suggested Pacing = 1 day** **1.** Explain how India's agriculture and industry have evolved. **2.** Describe India's political and environmental challenges. **3.** Discuss India's history and culture.	Reproducible Lesson Plan 5-1 Daily Lecture and Discussion Notes 5-1 Guided Reading Activity 5-1 Reading Essentials and Study Guide 5-1 Section Quiz 5-1*	Daily Focus Skills Transparency 5-1 GeoQuiz Transparency 5-1 Vocabulary PuzzleMaker Software Interactive Tutor Self-Assessment CD-ROM ExamView® Pro 3.0 Testmaker CD-ROM Presentation Plus! CD-ROM
Section 2 **Other Countries of South Asia** **Suggested Pacing = 1 day** **1.** Compare the main physical and cultural features of the countries in the region. **2.** Describe the economies of the countries in this region.	Reproducible Lesson Plan 5-2 Daily Lecture and Discussion Notes 5-2 Guided Reading Activity 5-2 Reading Essentials and Study Guide 5-2 Section Quiz 5-2*	Daily Focus Skills Transparency 5-2 GeoQuiz Transparency 5-1 Vocabulary PuzzleMaker Software Interactive Tutor Self-Assessment CD-ROM ExamView® Pro 3.0 Testmaker CD-ROM Presentation Plus! CD-ROM

00:00 **Out of Time?** Assign the **Reading Essentials and Study Guide** for this chapter.

*Also available in Spanish

KEY TO ABILITY LEVELS

Teaching strategies have been coded for varying learning styles and abilities.

L1 **BASIC** activities for all students
L2 **AVERAGE** activities for average to above-average students
L3 **CHALLENGING** activities for above-average students
ELL **ENGLISH LANGUAGE LEARNER** activities

Blackline Master
Software
CD-ROM
Audiocassette
Transparency
Videocassette
Block Scheduling
DVD

Religions of the World

Destin L. Haas
Benton Central
Junior/Senior High
Oxford, Indiana

Have students work in pairs and choose one of the following religions to research: Buddhism, Confucianism, Islam, Judaism, Hinduism, or Christianity. For the religion that pairs choose, they should find out the following information: (1) Where and when was it founded? (2) Who was the founder? (3) What is the holy book used? (4) What are some of the beliefs and practices of that religion? (5) What are some of the main holy days and what is their significance? (6) Where is the religion practiced in the world?

Pairs should present this information in three ways: (1) as a poster or another visual; (2) as an oral presentation; and (3) as a written report. They should include a bibliography.

OUR WORLD TODAY Online

Use our Web site for additional resources. All essential content is covered in the Student Edition.

You and your students can visit owt.glencoe.com, the Web site companion to *Our World Today*. This innovative integration of electronic and print media offers your students a wealth of opportunities. The student text directs students to the Web site for the following options:

- Chapter Overviews
- Student Web Activities
- Self-Check Quizzes
- Textbook Updates

Answers are provided for you in the Web Activity Lesson Plan. Additional Web resources and Interactive Tutor puzzles are also available.

NATIONAL GEOGRAPHIC TEACHER'S CORNER

Index to National Geographic Magazine:

The following articles may be used for research relating to this chapter:

- "Nepal," by T.D. Allman, November 2000.
- "Rana Tharu Women," by Debra Kellner, September 2000.
- "In Search of the Clouded Leopard," by Jesse Oak Taylor-Ide, September 2000.
- "The Temples of Angkor," by Douglas Preston, August 2000.

National Geographic Society Products Available From Glencoe:

To order the following products for use with this chapter, contact your local Glencoe sales representative or call Glencoe at 1-800-334-7344:

- *STV: World Geography* (Videodisc)
- *Picture Atlas of the World* (CD-ROM)
- *PictureShow: Ancient Civilizations: India and China* (CD-ROM)
- *PicturePack: Ancient Civilizations: Ancient India* (Transparencies)
- *MapPack: Asia* (Transparencies)

Additional National Geographic Society Products:

To order the following products for use with this chapter, call National Geographic Society at 1-800-368-2728:

- *Complete National Geographic: 111 Years of National Geographic Magazine* (CD-ROM)
- *Voices: Poetry and Art From Around the World* (Book)
- *National Geographic Desk Reference* (Book)
- *National Geographic Atlas of the World, Seventh Edition* (Book)
- *Asia* (Video)
- *Asia Political* (Map)
- *Population* (Map)

NGS ONLINE

Access National Geographic's Web site for current events, activities, links, interactive features, and archives.
www.nationalgeographic.com

Introducing
Chapter 5

Introduce students to chapter content and key terms by having them access Chapter Overview 5 at owt.glencoe.com

Chapter Objectives

1. Describe the land, economy, and people of India.
2. Compare the land, economies and cultures of India's neighboring countries.

GLENCOE TECHNOLOGY

NATIONAL GEOGRAPHIC

The World and Its People Video Program

Chapter 23 South Asia
The following segments enhance the study of this chapter:

- **Indian Railways**
- **Mount Everest**

Available in DVD and VHS.

MindJogger Videoquiz
Use MindJogger to preview the Chapter 5 content.

Available in VHS.

Chapter 5
South Asia

The World and Its People NATIONAL GEOGRAPHIC

To learn more about the people and places of South Asia, view ***The World and Its People*** **Chapter 23** video.

Our World Today online

Chapter Overview Visit the ***Our World Today: People, Places, and Issues*** Web site at owt.glencoe.com and click on **Chapter 5—Chapter Overviews** to preview information about South Asia.

142

Two-Minute Lesson Launcher

Explain to students that in this chapter they will read about countries in which religion is a major part of people's lives. Before reading the chapter, have them suggest different ways that religion can affect people's lives. Ask volunteers to offer their ideas, and write their responses. Have students copy these ideas into their notebooks. Suggest that as they read the chapter, they look to see if there are any suggestions they can add to the list.

FOLDABLES™ Study Organizer

Categorizing Information Study Foldable Make this foldable to organize information from the chapter to help you learn more about the land, economy, government, history, and religions of six South Asian countries.

Step 1 Collect four sheets of paper and place them about ½ inch apart.

Keep the edges straight.

Step 2 Fold up the bottom edges of the paper to form 8 tabs.

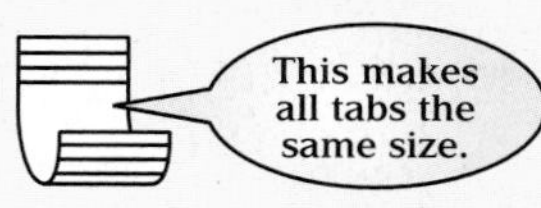

This makes all tabs the same size.

Step 3 When all the tabs are the same size, crease the paper to hold the tabs in place and staple the sheets together. Turn the paper and label each tab as shown.

SOUTH ASIA
General Information
Bangladesh
Sri Lanka
Bhutan
Nepal
Pakistan
India

Staple together along the fold.

Reading and Writing As you read, use your foldable to write down the main ideas about each South Asian country. Record the main ideas under each appropriate tab of your foldable.

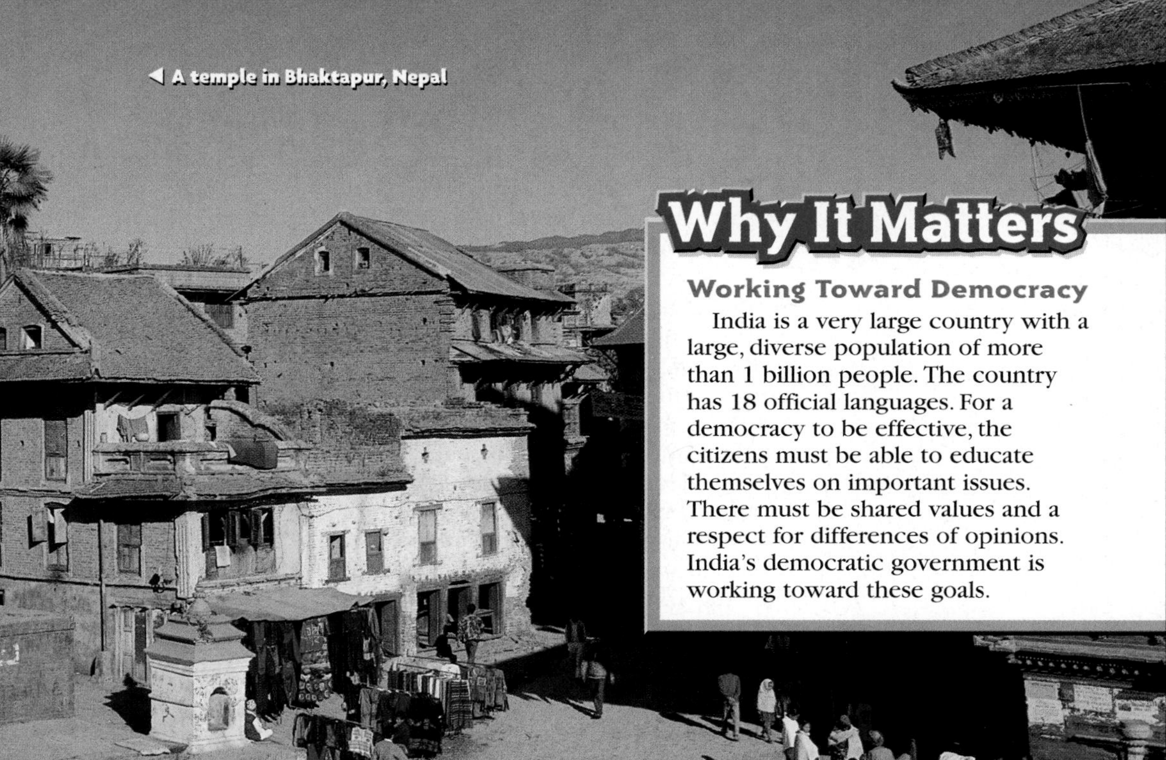

◀ A temple in Bhaktapur, Nepal

Why It Matters

Working Toward Democracy

India is a very large country with a large, diverse population of more than 1 billion people. The country has 18 official languages. For a democracy to be effective, the citizens must be able to educate themselves on important issues. There must be shared values and a respect for differences of opinions. India's democratic government is working toward these goals.

About the Photo

Bhaktapur is one of three major towns of the Kathmandu Valley in Nepal. This small valley is crowded with more than 2,500 large temples and monuments. It is known as the city of temples and shrines. Temples here are dedicated to a plethora of gods and goddesses from both Hinduism and Buddhism. The pagoda style building, as seen in this temple's multi-roofed structure and numerous spires, is one of several styles of architecture in the Kathmandu Valley. These buildings and monuments are still used by the many local people who worship as part of their everyday lives.

Introducing
Chapter 5

FOLDABLES™ Study Organizer

Purpose This activity requires students to create a table and organize information from the chapter on it. Students group information about each country in the chapter—as well as general information about South Asia—under the appropriate heading, in effect comparing the land, economy, government, history, and religion of the countries of South Asia.

Have students complete ***Reading and Study Skills Foldables*** Activity 5.

Why It Matters

To give students some idea of the difficulty India faces in achieving democratic government, break students into groups of five each. To simulate the many languages spoken in India, tell the students that they can only communicate with the person sitting directly next to them (right or left). If they want to communicate across the circle, they must use an interpreter. They cannot correct the interpreter's translation of their thoughts since they (supposedly) cannot understand. You may even direct them to cover their ears when not talking to the person on their right or left. Ask them to discuss an issue of highly emotional content, such as how far parental authority should extend, or how much authority school officials should have in students' personal or private lives. They should soon become frustrated with the inability to communicate freely.

Focus

Section Objectives

1. Explain how India's agriculture and industry have evolved.
2. Describe India's political and environmental challenges.
3. Discuss India's history and culture.

BELLRINGER Skillbuilder Activity

Project transparency and have students answer questions.

This activity is also available as a blackline master.

Daily Focus Skills Transparency 5-1

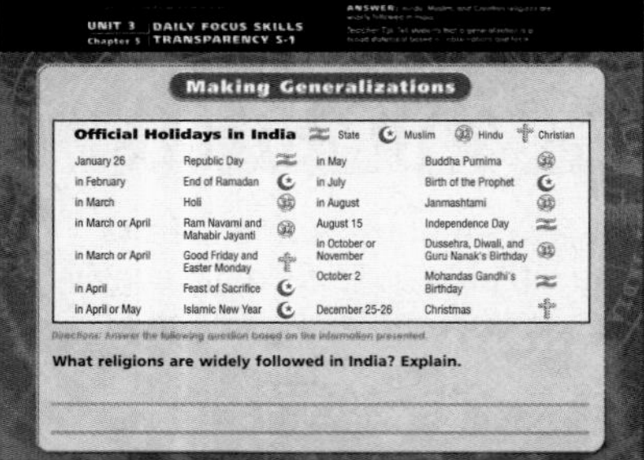

UNIT 3 Chapter 5 | DAILY FOCUS SKILLS TRANSPARENCY 5-1

Making Generalizations

Official Holidays in India (State, Muslim, Hindu, Christian)

Date	Holiday	Type	Date	Holiday	Type
January 26	Republic Day	State	in May	Buddha Purnima	Hindu
in February	End of Ramadan	Muslim	in July	Birth of the Prophet	Muslim
in March	Holi	Hindu	in August	Janmashtami	Hindu
in March or April	Ram Navami and Mahabir Jayanti	Hindu	August 15	Independence Day	State
in March or April	Good Friday and Easter Monday	Christian	in October or November	Dussehra, Diwali, and Guru Nanak's Birthday	Hindu
in April	Feast of Sacrifice	Muslim	October 2	Mohandas Gandhi's Birthday	State
in April or May	Islamic New Year	Muslim	December 25-26	Christmas	Christian

What religions are widely followed in India? Explain.

Guide to Reading

■ **Accessing Prior Knowledge**

Ask: What country is the world's largest democracy? After students give answers, point out that this distinction belongs to India. As they read this section, ask students to discuss the similarities and differences between the democratic governments of India and the United States.

India

Guide to Reading

Main Idea

India is trying to develop its resources and meet the needs of its rapidly growing population.

Terms to Know

- subcontinent
- monsoon
- green revolution
- jute
- cottage industry
- prime minister
- pesticide
- caste
- reincarnation

Reading Strategy

Create a chart like this one. Then fill in at least two key facts about India under each category.

India	
Land	Economy
History	Religion

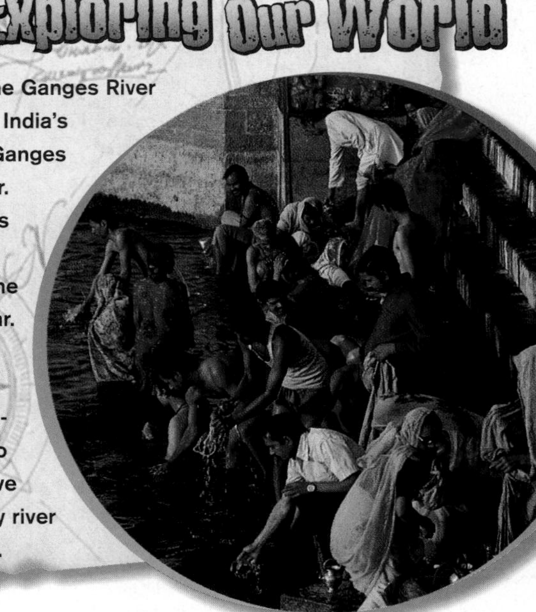

Stone steps lead to the Ganges River at this village in India. India's Hindus consider the Ganges River to be a holy river. About 1 million Hindus from all areas of India come to pray and bathe in its waters every year. People also use the river to do their laundry. In addition, industries dump waste into it. Today there is grave concern that the holy river is seriously polluted.

India and several other countries—Pakistan, Bangladesh (BAHNG•gluh•DEHSH), Nepal, Bhutan, Sri Lanka, and the Maldives—make up the South Asian subcontinent. A **subcontinent** is a large landmass that is part of another continent but distinct from it.

India's Land and Economy

Two huge walls of mountains—the **Karakoram** (KAH•rah•KOHR•ahm) **Range** and the **Himalaya** (HIH•muh•LAY•uh)—form India's northern border and separate South Asia from the rest of Asia. (See the map of Asia on page 134.) The tallest mountains in the world, the Himalaya's snowcapped peaks average more than 5 miles (8 km) in height. Mountain ranges also line India's southern coasts.

Most of India is warm or hot all year. The Himalaya block cold northern air from sweeping south into the country. **Monsoons**, or seasonal winds that blow steadily from the same direction for months, also influence the climate. During the rainy season (May through October), southern monsoon winds bring moist air from the Indian Ocean. The map on page 136 shows monsoon patterns for summer and winter.

Section Resources

Reproducible Masters

- Reproducible Lesson Plan 5-1
- Daily Lecture and Discussion Notes 5-1
- Guided Reading Activity 5-1
- Reading Essentials and Study Guide 5-1
- Section Quiz 5-1

Transparencies

- Daily Focus Skills Transparency 5-1
- GeoQuiz Transparency 5-1

Multimedia

- Vocabulary PuzzleMaker Software
- Interactive Tutor Self-Assessment CD-ROM
- Presentation Plus! CD-ROM
- ExamView® Pro 3.0 Testmaker CD-ROM

The Green Revolution Today, India raises most of the food it needs. In the past it was very different. The world's worst recorded food disaster, known as the **Bengal Famine,** happened in 1943 when the United Kingdom ruled India. An estimated 4 million people died of starvation that year alone. When India won its independence in 1947, government officials turned their attention to improving India's farm output. The **green revolution** was an effort to use modern techniques and science to increase production of food.

To produce more food, farmers planted more than one crop per year. If the farmers relied only on the monsoon rains to water their crops, they could only plant once per year. The government built dams to collect the water. The dams stored the water and spread it out through irrigation ditches during the dry season. Farmers could then plant twice a year.

The second part of the green revolution was to use improved seeds. New, stronger strains of wheat, rice, and corn were developed that could withstand diseases and droughts and produce more grains. Between 1947 and 1980, farm production improved by more than 30 percent.

Today, India's farmers raise a variety of crops, including rice, wheat, cotton, tea, sugarcane, and jute. **Jute** is a plant fiber used for making rope, burlap bags, and carpet backing. India is the world's second-largest rice producer, after China.

Industry Huge factories in India's cities turn out cotton textiles and produce iron and steel. Oil and sugar refineries loom over many urban skylines. Recently, American computer companies have opened offices in India, making it an important source of computer software. Mining is another major industry. India has rich deposits of coal, iron ore, manganese, and bauxite. Its major exports are gems and jewelry.

Many Indian products are manufactured in cottage industries. A **cottage industry** is a home- or village-based industry in which family members, including children, supply their own equipment to make goods. Items produced in cottage industries include cotton cloth, silk cloth, rugs, leather products, and metalware.

NATIONAL GEOGRAPHIC **On Location**

Two Views of India

The growing middle class live comfortable lives in India's suburbs (above), but the poor in India's cities must struggle to survive (left).

Human/Environment Interaction

How would the green revolution benefit India's people?

The World's Largest Democracy

Like the United States, India is a democracy. The Indian parliament, or congress, has two houses. One house is made up of representatives of the states and is called the Council of States. The other house—called the House of the People—is like our House of Representatives.

More About the Photos

Bangalore These middle-class homes sit in a suburb of Bangalore, once the capital of a princely state and now the center of India's computer industry, earning it the name "India's Silicon Valley." Despite the country's increasing prosperity, more than one-third of the people live in poverty.

Caption Answer More food would be available and would be more affordable.

TEACH

Making Comparisons Point out to students that India's monsoon winds cause distinct wet and dry seasons in that country. **Ask: What seasonal patterns affect climate in your community? What factors cause these patterns to occur? L1**

Daily Lecture Notes 5-1

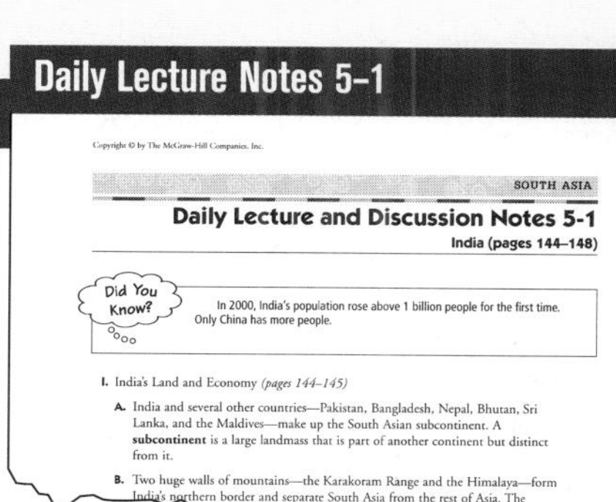

SOUTH ASIA

Daily Lecture and Discussion Notes 5-1

India (pages 144–148)

Did You Know? In 2000, India's population rose above 1 billion people for the first time. Only China has more people.

I. India's Land and Economy *(pages 144–145)*

A. India and several other countries—Pakistan, Bangladesh, Nepal, Bhutan, Sri Lanka, and the Maldives—make up the South Asian subcontinent. A **subcontinent** is a large landmass that is part of another continent but distinct from it.

B. Two huge walls of mountains—the Karakoram Range and the Himalaya—form India's northern border and separate South Asia from the rest of Asia. The ... ld, the Himalaya's snowcapped peaks average more

Meeting Special Needs

Kinesthetic Bring a small fan to class. Have several students stand shoulder to shoulder at the front of the class. Take the fan and position yourself behind the standing students. Point the fan toward the students and turn it on. Ask students seated in the main part of the classroom whether they feel the breeze from the fan. *(The standing students should effectively block the air; if they do not, aim the fan lower.)* Point out that the Himalaya act in the same way to block the cold winds from the north. **L1**

Refer to *Inclusion for the Middle School Social Studies Classroom Strategies and Activities in the TCR.*

More About the Photos

Leaders of India A beloved leader in the Indian National Congress, Mohandas K. Gandhi was called Mahatma, the "Great Soul," by millions of followers. Jawaharlal Nehru, also a nationalist, was the first prime minister of independent India. Indira Gandhi, the daughter of Jawaharlal Nehru, was prime minister of India from 1966–77 and 1980–84.

Caption Answer The United Kingdom

Reading Check Answer

democracy

Guided Reading Activity 5-1

Name ______ Date ______ Class ______

SOUTH ASIA

Guided Reading Activity 5-1

India

DIRECTIONS: Answering Questions Reading the section and answering the questions below will help you learn more about the country of India. Use your textbook to fill in the blanks.

1. What is a subcontinent?
2. What forms India's northern border?
3. Describe the climate of India.
4. What is important to India's economy?

Assess

Assign Section 1 Assessment as homework or an in-class activity.

Have students use the Interactive Tutor Self-Assessment CD-ROM to review Section 5–1.

The most important difference between the two systems is that most of the power to run the government of India is held not by the president, but by the **prime minister,** who is appointed by the ruling party. The first prime minister of India was Jawaharlal Nehru, who was elected in 1947. While in office, Mr. Nehru pursued peace between India and all other countries. His daughter, Indira Gandhi, was also elected prime minister. Except for a short period, she led India from 1966 until her assassination in 1984. Mrs. Gandhi tried to help India's poor by providing low-cost housing and giving land to those who owned none. She also helped to extend voting rights.

Environmental Challenges India's economic growth has brought challenges to its environment. Thousands of acres of forests have been cleared for farming. Both water and land have been polluted from burning coal, industrial wastes, and **pesticides,** or chemicals used to kill insects that destroy crops. The Ganges is considered by many experts to be one of the world's most polluted rivers.

All of these developments have played a part in destroying animal habitats. India's elephants, lions, tigers, leopards, monkeys, and panthers have been greatly reduced in number. The government has set up more than 350 national parks and preserves to save these animals.

Reading Check What form of government does India have?

India's History and People

About 4,000 years ago, the first Indian civilization built well-planned cities along the **Indus River** valley, in present-day Pakistan. In the 1500s B.C., warriors known as **Aryans** (AR•ee•uhns) entered the subcontinent from Central Asia. They set up kingdoms in northern India. Aryan beliefs gradually blended with the practices of the local people to form the religion of **Hinduism.**

NATIONAL GEOGRAPHIC **On Location**

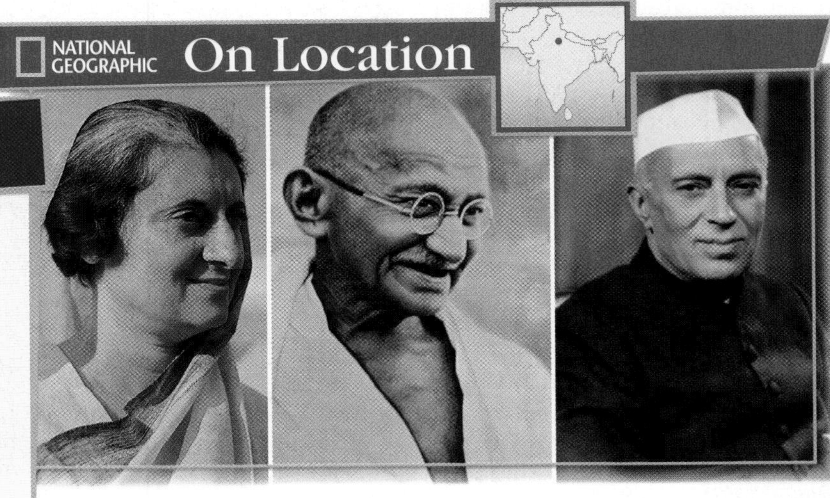

Leaders of India

Indira Gandhi (left) Mohandas Gandhi (center), and Jawaharlal Nehru (right) were instrumental in bringing democracy to India.

History **Which country ruled India before it won its independence?**

Critical Thinking Activity

Making Generalizations Display facts comparing India as a whole with the state of Kerala. Include the following statistics:

Per capita Gross National Product (GNP) in U.S. dollars (1996): India—380; Kerala—350

Infant mortality per 1,000 live births (1998): India—72; Kerala—17

Women's life expectancy in years (1998): India—59; Kerala—74

Literacy rate among women (1996): India—38; Kerala—87

Have students use this information to write a generalization about life in Kerala compared to that in India as a whole. Ask volunteers to share their generalizations with the class. **L1**

EE4 Human Systems: Standard 9

Music

The tabla is a pair of connected drums from India. The drums are made of wood in the shape of a cylinder. Wooden pegs and leather straps hold the skin tightly onto the right-hand drum. The skin on the left-hand drum is kept slightly loose so that players can push down into it. This creates lower and higher pitches. Although the tabla emerged in India 500 years ago, it is now heard in modern pop and jazz music all over the world.

Looking Closer **Which drum do you think has more variation in sound? Why?**

GO TO **World Music: A Cultural Legacy**
Hear music of this region on Disc 2, Track 13.

Over time, Hinduism organized India's society into groups called castes. A **caste** was a social class based on a person's ancestry. A person was born into a particular caste. People married within their caste, and certain occupations belonged to the specific castes. People could not move from one caste to another. The caste system still influences Indian life, although laws now forbid unfair treatment of one group by another.

Buddhism started in India about 500 B.C., but was largely driven out by 300 B.C. You will read more about Buddhism later in this unit. The religion of Islam also influenced India's history. In the A.D. 700s, Muslims from Southwest Asia brought Islam to India. In the 1500s, they founded the **Mogul** (MOH•guhl) **Empire** and ruled India for 200 years.

The British were the last of India's conquerors, ruling from the 1700s to the mid-1900s. They built roads, railroads, and seaports. They also made large profits from the plantations, mines, and factories they set up. An Indian leader named **Mohandas Gandhi** (moh•HAHN•duhs GAHN•dee) led a nonviolent resistance movement to free India from Britain's rule. When India won its independence from the United Kingdom in 1947, many Muslims were afraid that their voices would not be heard by the Hindu majority. East and West Pakistan were created, one on each side of India, as Muslim homelands. In 1971, East Pakistan became the nation of **Bangladesh.**

Religion About 80 percent of India's people are Hindus, or followers of Hinduism. Hindus worship a supreme being that can take many different god-like and animal-like forms. Hinduism teaches that after the body dies, the soul is reborn, often in an animal or human form.

Answer the left-hand drum because the tension of the drum head can change

The Language of the Drum Before learning to play drums in India, you must first learn how to speak the sounds of the drum. Depending on hand position, number of fingers used, and the part of the drum that is struck, a great variety of sounds are attainable, and each one of these "hits" has a name.

World Music: A Cultural Legacy

Use the accompanying Teacher Guide for background information, discussion questions, and worksheets about the music of this region.

Measure student knowledge of physical features and political entities.

GeoQuiz Transparency 5-1

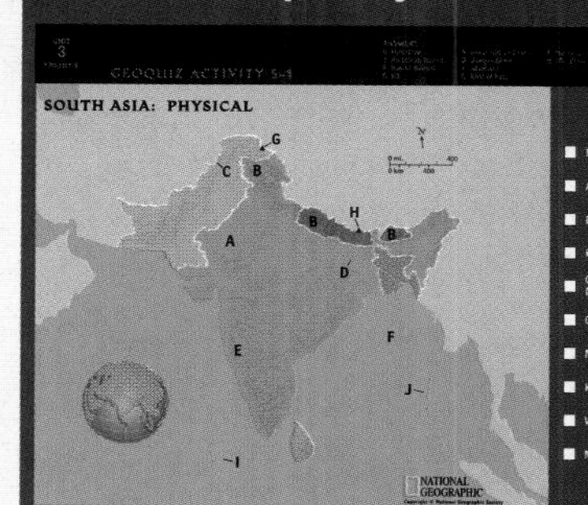

Content Background

Caste System India's caste system dates from about 1000 B.C., when the Aryans invaded the area. The Aryans had recognized four main groups, which gradually evolved into the four *varna: Brahman,* the priests; *Kshatriya,* warriors and officials; *Vaishya,* or merchants, craftspeople, and landed farmers; and *Shudra,* the peasants and workers. Giving this last group—the most numerous by far—the lowest status allowed the Aryans to maintain control over the majority population. A fifth group, the outcastes, included those who did not fit in the first four. Over time, these groups developed into nearly 3,000 smaller groups called *jati.* The lowest caste and the outcastes suffered discrimination. Mohandas Gandhi urged his country to abandon the system, and great strides have been made. In 1997 a member of the lowest caste was named India's president.

Section Quiz 5-1

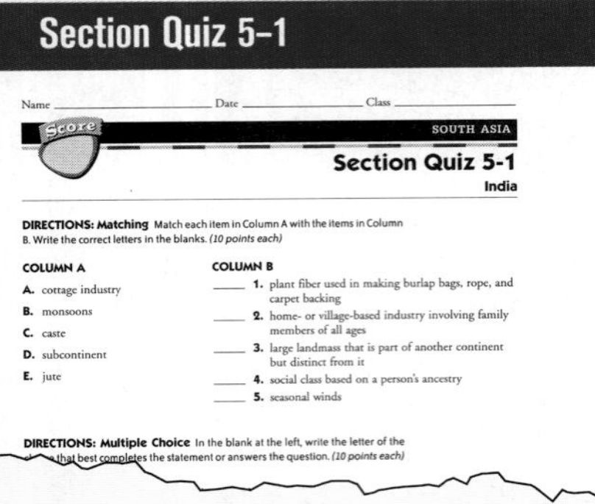
Name ______ Date ______ Class ______

SOUTH ASIA

Score

Section Quiz 5-1
India

DIRECTIONS: Matching Match each item in Column A with the items in Column B. Write the correct letters in the blanks. *(10 points each)*

COLUMN A	COLUMN B
A. cottage industry	____ **1.** plant fiber used in making burlap bags, rope, and carpet backing
B. monsoons	____ **2.** home- or village-based industry involving family members of all ages
C. caste	____ **3.** large landmass that is part of another continent but distinct from it
D. subcontinent	____ **4.** social class based on a person's ancestry
E. jute	____ **5.** seasonal winds

DIRECTIONS: Multiple Choice In the blank at the left, write the letter of the ... that best completes the statement or answers the question. *(10 points each)*

Reading Check Answer

about 70 percent

Reading Essentials and Study Guide 5-1

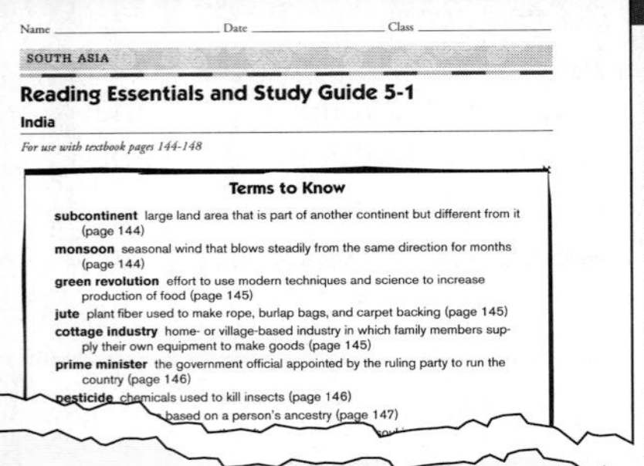
Name ______ Date ______ Class ______

SOUTH ASIA

Reading Essentials and Study Guide 5-1
India

For use with textbook pages 144-148

Terms to Know

subcontinent large land area that is part of another continent but different from it (page 144)
monsoon seasonal wind that blows steadily from the same direction for months (page 144)
green revolution effort to use modern techniques and science to increase production of food (page 145)
jute plant fiber used to make rope, burlap bags, and carpet backing (page 145)
cottage industry home- or village-based industry in which family members supply their own equipment to make goods (page 145)
prime minister the government official appointed by the ruling party to run the country (page 146)
pesticide chemicals used to kill insects (page 146)
... based on a person's ancestry (page 147)

4 Close

Ask students to write a paragraph stating how their lives would be different if they lived in India.

▲ This statue represents Shiva, one of Hinduism's many dieties.

This process, called **reincarnation**, is repeated until the soul reaches perfection. For this reason, many Hindus believe it is wrong to kill any living creature. Cows are believed to be sacred and are allowed to roam freely.

One of the most popular holidays is **Diwali** (dee•VAH•lee), the Festival of Lights. It is a Hindu celebration marking the coming of winter and the victory of good over evil. Indians also like watching movies. India's movie industry turns out more films than Hollywood.

Islam has over 140 million followers in India. Other religions include Christianity, Sikhism (SEE•KIH•zuhm), Buddhism, and Jainism (JY•NIH•zuhm). Conflict sometimes occurs between Hindus and followers of the other religions. The **Sikhs,** who practice Sikhism, believe in one God as Christians and Muslims do, yet Sikhs also have other beliefs similar to Hindus. Today, many Sikhs would like to form their own independent state.

Daily Life More than 1 billion people call India their home. The country has 18 official languages, of which Hindi is the most widely used. English is often spoken in business and government, however. About 70 percent of the people live in farming villages. The government has been working to provide villagers with electricity, drinking water, better schools, and paved roads. Still, many villagers stream to cities to find jobs and a better standard of living.

✓Reading Check **What percentage of India's people live in rural villages?**

Section 1 Assessment

Defining Terms

1. **Define** subcontinent, monsoon, green revolution, jute, cottage industry, prime minister, pesticide, caste, reincarnation.

Recalling Facts

2. **Location** What two mountain ranges form India's northern border?
3. **Culture** What is the most widely followed religion in India?
4. **History** What Indian leader led a movement that brought India its independence in 1947?

Critical Thinking

5. **Understanding Cause and Effect** How do monsoon winds affect India's climate?
6. **Drawing Conclusions** What challenges do you think the caste system might have caused in India?

Graphic Organizer

7. **Organizing Information** India is becoming a more modern country but still has many traditional ways. Create a chart like this one. Then list both modern and traditional aspects of India.

Modern Aspects	Traditional Aspects

Applying Social Studies Skills

8. **Analyzing Maps** Look at the population density map on page 154. What are the most densely populated areas of India?

148

Section 1 Assessment

1. The terms are defined in the Glossary.
2. Karakoram and Himalaya
3. Hinduism
4. Mohandas Gandhi
5. In the cool and hot seasons, monsoon winds from the north bring dry air. In the wet seasons, monsoon winds from the Indian Ocean bring moist air and rain.
6. difficulty in building trust between groups and in providing equal healthcare, education, and opportunities to all citizens.
7. *Modern:* high-rise buildings, movie industry, high-technology industries; *Traditional:* high percentage of farming villages, caste system, cottage industries
8. the north, in the Ganges River Plain, and on the southwest and southeast coastal plains

Making Connections

CULTURE | GOVERNMENT | PEOPLE | TECHNOLOGY

Shah Jahan of India

Considered one of the world's most beautiful buildings, the Taj Mahal was built by the Muslim emperor Shah Jahan of India. He had it built to house the grave of his beloved wife, Mumtaz Mahal. She died in 1631 shortly after giving birth to their fourteenth child.

The Taj Mahal, Agra, India ▲

Background

While they were married, Mumtaz Mahal and Shah Jahan were constant companions. The empress went everywhere with her husband, even on military expeditions. She encouraged her husband to perform great acts of charity toward the poor. This earned her the love and admiration of the Indian people.

After his wife's death, Shah Jahan ordered the construction of the finest monument ever built. A team of architects, sculptors, calligraphers, and master builders participated in the design. More than 20,000 laborers and skilled craft workers from India, Persia, the Ottoman Empire, and Europe worked together to build the monument. For 22 years they worked to complete the Taj Mahal, which holds a tomb, mosque, rest house, elaborate garden, and arched gateway.

The Mausoleum

The central part of the Taj Mahal is the domed marble mausoleum, or tomb, built on a square marble platform. The central dome is 213 feet (65 m) tall, and four smaller domed chambers surround it. A high minaret, or tower, marks each corner of the platform.

Inside the central chamber, delicately carved marble screens enclose the caskets of Mumtaz Mahal and Shah Jahan. He was buried next to his wife after his death in 1666. Following Islamic tradition, the caskets face east toward Makkah, the religious capital of Islam.

The white marble from which the mausoleum is built seems to change color throughout the day as it reflects light from the sun and moon. Detailed flower patterns are carved into the marble walls and inlaid with colorful gemstones. Verses from Islamic religious writings are etched in calligraphy into the stone archways.

Making the Connection

1. Who is buried in the Taj Mahal?
2. Who built the Taj Mahal and how long did it take?
3. **Understanding Cause and Effect** How did Shah Jahan's feelings for his wife affect the grave site he built for her?

Making the Connection

1. Mumtaz Mahal and Shah Jahan
2. Shah Jahan ordered it built, requiring the work of more than 20,000 laborers and skilled craft workers. It took them 22 years to complete it.
3. *Possible answer:* His love for his wife led him to build for her tomb one of the finest monuments in the world.

TEACH

Write the names of the following buildings: Washington Monument, Jefferson Memorial, Lincoln Memorial. **Ask: What do these structures have in common?** *(They are memorials to people who have died.)* Tell students that they are going to read about another famous memorial. **L1**

More About the Taj Mahal

The Taj Mahal embodies the principles of symmetry and balance. The four smaller domes balance the large central dome. Their pattern is repeated in the four graceful minarets. The four sides of the building each have a large central arch flanked by smaller arches on angled walls that create the Taj Mahal's octagonal shape. The desire for symmetry is very clear in two side buildings. On one side is a mosque, which faces east. On the opposite side is an identical structure called a *jawab,* or "answer," the purpose of which is to mirror the mosque and complete the sense of balance.

Interdisciplinary Connections

Art Have students create a work—through art, the written word, or song—that pays tribute to someone they respect or admire.

Chapter 5

Section 2, pages 150–155

Focus

Section Objectives

1. Compare the main physical and cultural features of the countries in the region.
2. Describe the economies of the countries in this region.

BELLRINGER
Skillbuilder Activity

Project transparency and have students answer questions.

This activity is also available as a blackline master.

Daily Focus Skills Transparency 5-2

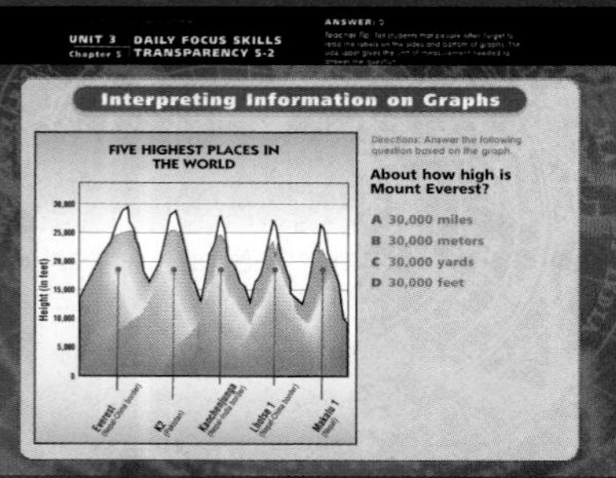

Guide to Reading

■ **Accessing Prior Knowledge**
Ask: **Which is a bigger problem for a farmer, too much rain or too little?** *(Both are major problems.)* Inform students that in this chapter, they will read about Bangladesh, which suffers from these two opposite problems.

Guide to Reading

Main Idea

The other countries of South Asia include once-united Pakistan and Bangladesh, mountainous Nepal and Bhutan, and the island country of Sri Lanka.

Terms to Know

- cyclone
- dzong

Reading Strategy

Create and fill in a chart like this one, listing the main economic activities in these countries of South Asia.

Country	Economic Activity
Pakistan	
Bangladesh	
Nepal	
Bhutan	
Sri Lanka	

Section 2 Other Countries of South Asia

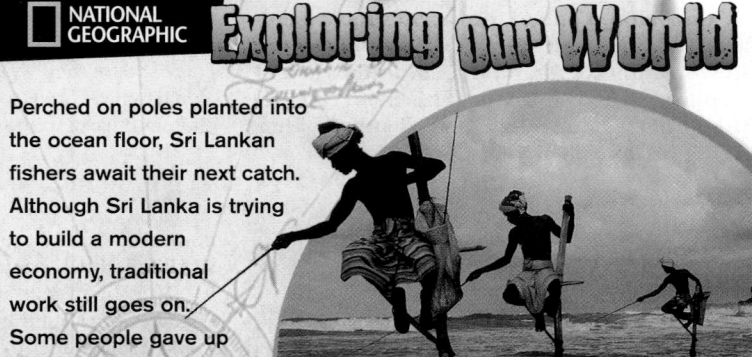

Perched on poles planted into the ocean floor, Sri Lankan fishers await their next catch. Although Sri Lanka is trying to build a modern economy, traditional work still goes on. Some people gave up fishing when Sri Lanka seemed ready to become a major tourist destination. However, years of ethnic warfare have kept tourists away and slowed the economy.

Two countries in South Asia—**Pakistan** and **Bangladesh**—are largely Muslim. They share the same religion, but have very different cultures and languages. Two other countries—**Nepal** and **Bhutan**—are landlocked kingdoms. **Sri Lanka** and the **Maldives** are island republics.

Pakistan

Pakistan is about twice the size of California. Towering mountains occupy most of northern and western Pakistan. The world's second-highest peak, K2, rises 28,250 feet (8,611 m) in the Karakoram Range. Another mountain range, the **Hindu Kush,** lies in the far north. Several passes cut through its rugged peaks. The best known is the **Khyber Pass.** For centuries, it has been used by people traveling through South Asia from the north.

Pakistan and India both claim **Kashmir,** a mostly Muslim territory on the border between the two countries. Both countries want to

Section Resources

Reproducible Masters
- Reproducible Lesson Plan 5-2
- Daily Lecture and Discussion Notes 5-2
- Guided Reading Activity 5-2
- Reading Essentials and Study Guide 5-2
- Section Quiz 5-2

Transparencies
- Daily Focus Skills Transparency 5-2
- GeoQuiz Transparency 5-1

Multimedia
- Vocabulary PuzzleMaker Software
- Interactive Tutor Self-Assessment CD-ROM
- Presentation Plus! CD-ROM
- ExamView® Pro 3.0 Testmaker CD-ROM

control the entire region, mainly for its vast water resources. This dispute over Kashmir has sparked three wars between Pakistan and India. In fact, it threatens not only the countries of South Asia, but also the rest of the world because both Pakistan and India have nuclear weapons.

Pakistan's People Since independence, Pakistan has had many changes of government. Some of these governments were elected, including a female prime minister, **Benazir Bhutto.** Bhutto was the first woman elected prime minister of an Islamic nation. In other cases, the army seized power from an elected government. The most recent army takeover occurred in 1999, and military leaders still control the country.

About 97 percent of Pakistanis are Muslims. The influence of Islam is seen in large, domed mosques and people bowed in prayer at certain times of the day. Among the major languages are **Punjabi** and **Sindhi.** The official language, **Urdu,** is the first language of only 9 percent of the people. English is widely spoken in government.

Almost 70 percent of Pakistan's people live in rural villages. Most follow traditional customs and live in small homes of clay or sun-dried mud. Pakistanis live in large cities as well. **Karachi,** a seaport on the Arabian Sea, is a sprawling urban area. It has traditional outdoor markets, modern shops, and hotels. In the far north lies **Islamabad,** the capital. The government built this well-planned, modern city to draw people inland from crowded coastal areas.

✓ Reading Check **Why do India and Pakistan both claim Kashmir?**

Bangladesh

Bangladesh, about the size of Wisconsin, is nearly surrounded by India. Although Bangladesh is a Muslim country like Pakistan, it shares many cultural features with eastern India.

Seeing Bangladesh for the first time, you might describe the country with one word—water. Two major rivers—the **Brahmaputra** (BRAHM•uh•POO•truh) **River** and the **Ganges River**—flow through the lush, low plains that cover most of Bangladesh.

As in India, the monsoons affect Bangladesh. When the monsoons end, cyclones may strike Bangladesh. A **cyclone** is an intense tropical storm system with high winds and heavy rains. Cyclones, in turn, may be followed by deadly tidal waves that surge up from the **Bay of Bengal.** As deadly as the cyclones and tidal waves may be, it is worse if the rains come too late. When this happens, crops often fail and there is widespread hunger.

A Farming Economy Most people of Bangladesh earn their living by farming. Rice is the most important crop. The fertile soil and plentiful water make it possible for rice to be grown and harvested three times a year. Other crops include sugarcane, jute, and wheat. Cash crops of tea grow in hilly regions in the east. Despite good growing conditions, Bangladesh cannot grow enough food for its people. Its farmers have few modern tools and use outdated farming methods. In addition, the disastrous floods can drown crops and cause food shortages.

teen Scene

School's Out!

Adil Husain is on his way home from middle school. In Pakistan, schooling only goes to grade 10. After grade 10, Adil must decide whether to go to intermediate college (grades 11 and 12) and then the university. Like most Pakistanis, Adil is Muslim. He prays when he hears the call from the mosque. Afterward, he wants to start a game of cricket with his friends. "It's a lot like baseball where teams of 11 players bat in innings and try to score runs. Our rules and equipment are different, though. You should try it!"

Chapter 5

Section 2, pages 150–155

Note-taking tip

Suggest that students write notes about the same topic—such as physical characteristics, people, politics, economics—for each country to facilitate comparisons.

✓ Reading Check Answer

for its vast water resources

Making Comparisons Have students create two line or bar graphs comparing the countries in this section. In the first graph, they should show the size in area of the countries. In the second, have them show the populations. Remind students that they can get the needed data from the Country Profiles in the Unit 3 Regional Atlas. After they have prepared their graphs, have them explain why they chose the particular type of graph. L2

Meeting Special Needs

Naturalistic To clarify why deforested slopes cause problems in heavy rains, ask students to compare what happens when rain falls on paved streets versus when it falls on planted areas. Students should recognize that in planted areas, the rain is more likely to soak into the earth. In paved areas, however, the water pools on the surface. Explain that mountains without trees act similarly to pavement—the water simply runs down the mountainsides. When the slopes are covered by trees, however, the roots of the plants can hold the water before it runs off. L1 ELL

Refer to *Inclusion for the Middle School Social Studies Classroom Strategies and Activities* in the TCR.

TEACH

Applying Information
Explain that the temperature drops 4°F for every 1,000 feet of increased elevation. Then ask students to calculate the temperature at the top of Mount Everest if the temperature at sea level is 80°F *(-36°F).* **L3**

Analyzing the Graph

Answer
Mount McKinley

Skills Practice
How much higher than Mount McKinley is Mount Everest? *(more than 7,500 feet, or about 2,300 m)*

Reading Check Answer
floods, tidal waves, drought

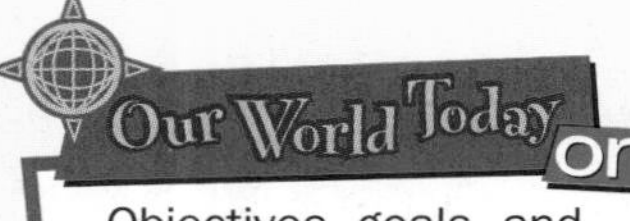

Our World Today Online

Objectives, goals, and answers to the Student Web Activity can be found in the Web Activity Lesson Plan at **owt.glencoe.com**

Highest Mountain on Each Continent

Analyzing the Graph

Mount Everest is the tallest mountain on the earth.

Place **What is the tallest mountain in North America?**

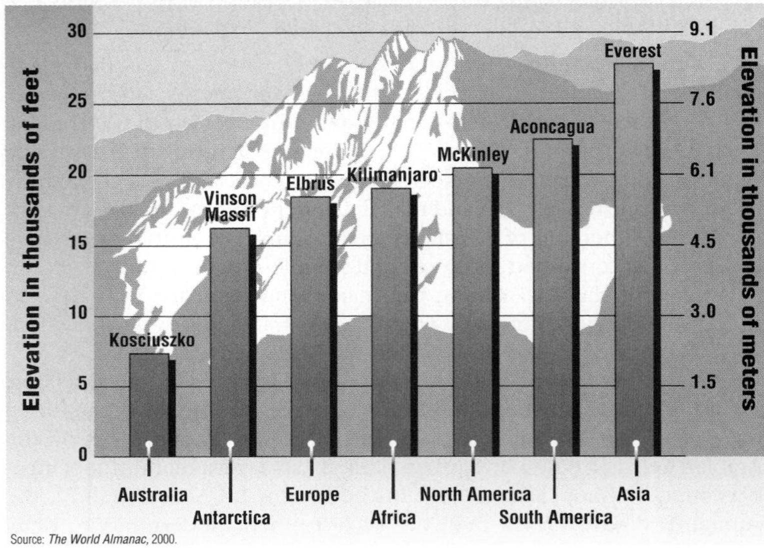

Source: *The World Almanac,* 2000.

The People With about 133.5 million people, Bangladesh is one of the most densely populated countries in the world. It is also one of the poorest countries. More than 80 percent of the people live in rural areas. Because of floods, people in rural Bangladesh have to build their houses on platforms. Many people have moved to crowded urban areas to find work in factories. The largest city is **Dhaka** (DA•kuh), Bangladesh's capital and major port. Most of Bangladesh's people speak **Bengali.**

Reading Check **What are three ways the climate may cause disasters in Bangladesh?**

Nepal

Nepal—about the size of Arkansas—forms a steep stairway to the world's highest mountain range. The Himalaya, dominating about 80 percent of Nepal's land area, are actually three mountain ranges running side by side. Nepal is home to 8 of the 10 highest mountains in the world. **Mount Everest,** the highest, soars 29,035 feet (8,850 m). Nepal's rugged mountains attract thousands of climbers and hikers each year, creating a growing tourist industry.

Nepal's economy depends almost entirely on farming. Farmers grow rice, sugarcane, wheat, corn, and potatoes to feed their families. Most fields are located on the southern plains or on the lower mountain slopes. As the population has increased, Nepalese farmers have moved higher up the slopes. There they clear the forests for new fields and use the cut trees for fuel. Stripped of trees, however, the

Our World Today Online

Web Activity Visit the ***Our World Today: People, Places, and Issues*** Web site at owt.glencoe.com and click on **Chapter 5–Student Web Activities** to learn more about Nepal.

Team-Teaching Activity

Science Mount Everest—the highest peak in the world—attracts thousands of mountain climbers annually. Invite the science teacher to class to discuss the history of attempts to climb the mountain—from George Mallory's ill-fated 1924 foray to the first success by Sir Edmund Hillary and Tenzing Norgay in 1953 to the multiple ascents today. Have the teacher explain the dangers posed by the high altitudes and freezing temperatures and the benefits offered by modern equipment such as bottled oxygen, stronger synthetic rope, and better clothing. Then have students take the role of an Everest climber and write a diary entry explaining their fascination with this mighty mountain. **L1** 

EE1 The World in Spatial Terms: Standard 2

slopes erode very easily. During the rainy season, valleys often are flooded, fields destroyed, and rivers filled with mud.

Nepal's People Nepal has 23.5 million people. Most are related to peoples in northern India and Tibet. One group—the **Sherpa**—is known for its skill in guiding mountain climbers. About 85 percent of Nepal's people live in rural villages. A growing number live in **Kathmandu,** Nepal's capital and largest city. Nepal is a parliamentary democracy ruled by a prime minister, who is appointed by Nepal's king.

The founder of Buddhism, **Siddartha Gautama** (sihd•DAHR•tuh GOW•tuh•muh), was born in the Kathmandu region about 563 B.C. Raised as a prince, Gautama gave up his wealth and became a holy man in India. Known as the **Buddha,** or "Enlightened One," he taught that people could find peace from life's troubles by living simply, doing good deeds, and praying. Buddhism later spread to other parts of Asia.

Today Hinduism is the official religion in Nepal, but Buddhism is practiced as well. If you visit Nepal, you will find temples and monuments of both religions scattered throughout the country.

✓Reading Check **What are the two main religions in Nepal?**

Bhutan

East of Nepal lies an even smaller kingdom—Bhutan. Bhutan is about half the size of Indiana. The map on page 135 shows you that a small part of India separates Bhutan from Nepal.

As in Nepal, the Himalaya are the major landform of Bhutan. Violent mountain storms are common and are the basis of Bhutan's name, which means "land of the thunder dragon." In the foothills of the Himalaya, the climate is mild. Thick forests cover much of this area. To the south—along Bhutan's border with India—lies an area of plains and river valleys.

More than 90 percent of Bhutan's people are subsistence farmers. They live in the fertile mountain valleys and grow oranges, rice, corn, potatoes, and the spice cardamom. People also herd cattle and yaks, which are a type of oxen. Bhutan is trying to develop its economy, but the mountains slow progress. Building roads is difficult, and there are no railroads. Bhutan has built hydroelectric plants to create electricity from rushing mountain waters. It now exports electricity to India. Tourism is a new industry. However, the government limits the number of tourists in order to protect Bhutan's cultural traditions.

NATIONAL GEOGRAPHIC **On Location**

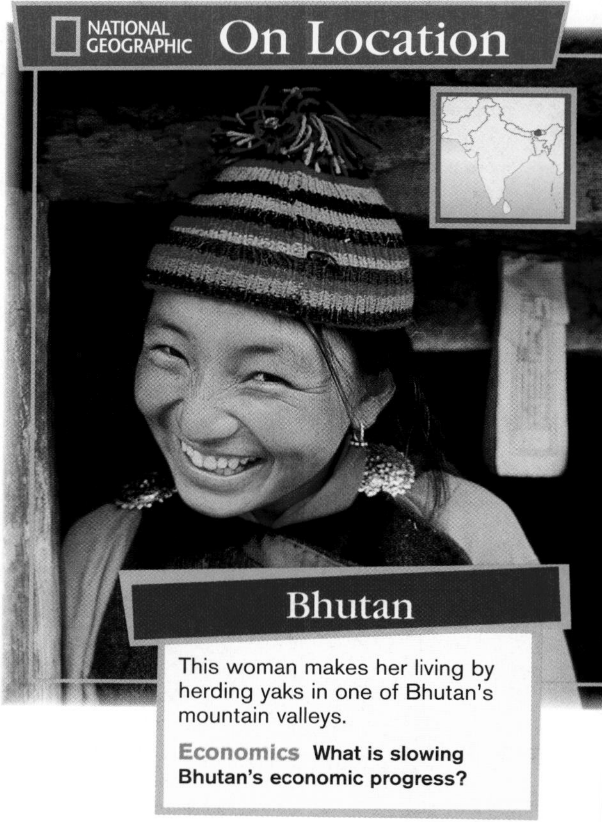

Bhutan

This woman makes her living by herding yaks in one of Bhutan's mountain valleys.

Economics **What is slowing Bhutan's economic progress?**

Content Background

Bhutan Buddhism gives Bhutan's people a deep sense of the sacredness of all life. As a result, no animals are killed. This deep belief, combined with the country's remoteness and lack of modernization, created some unusual situations. The capital of Thimphu has about 30,000 people. In recent years, more dogs than vehicles roamed the streets. There were no traffic lights and only a handful of gas stations in the town. One westerner who visited Thimphu in the early 1990s noted that it was not unusual to find black bears or wild boars in people's yards.

Daily Lecture Notes 5-2

SOUTH ASIA

Daily Lecture and Discussion Notes 5-2

Other Countries of South Asia (pages 150–155)

Did You Know? The events surrounding a Pakistani wedding last for three or four days. Trees, lampposts, and bushes near the bride's house are decorated with small, white lights, similar to the lights some Americans put up at Christmas. Pakistani brides wear red dresses at the wedding ceremony.

I. Pakistan *(pages 150–151)*

A. Pakistan is largely Muslim.

B. Kashmir is a mostly Muslim territory on the northern border of India and Pakistan. Kashmir is currently divided between the two countries. Both nations want to control the entire region, mainly for its vast water resources. This dispute over Kashmir has sparked three wars between Pakistan and India.

most of northern and western Pakistan. The

✓ Reading Check Answer

Hinduism and Buddhism

Did You Know

Have you ever dreamed of climbing Mount Everest? On your trip you would walk through the world's highest garbage dump. Over the past 40 years, mountaineers have left 16 tons (15 t) of discarded oxygen bottles, abandoned tents, leftover food and other junk on Everest's slopes.

More About the Photo

Bhutan Yak herding is still the main occupation in the high mountain valleys of Bhutan. Restricted tourism by the Bhutanese government has preserved traditional ways, and this kingdom reflects a peaceful way of life long gone in other parts of the Himalaya.

Caption Answer The mountains make transportation difficult.

Guided Reading Activity 5-2

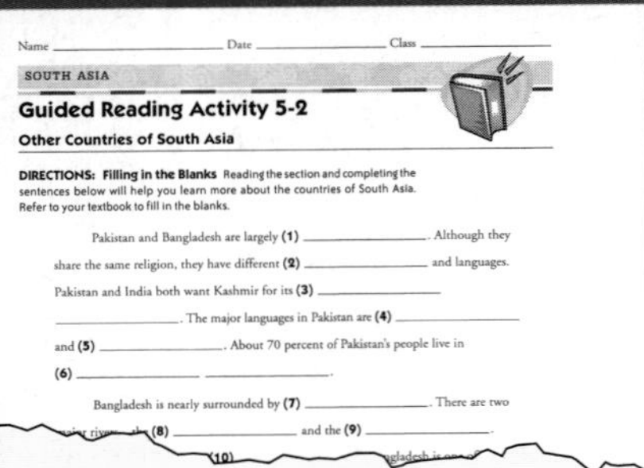
Name ____ Date ____ Class ____

SOUTH ASIA

Guided Reading Activity 5-2

Other Countries of South Asia

DIRECTIONS: Filling in the Blanks Reading the section and completing the sentences below will help you learn more about the countries of South Asia. Refer to your textbook to fill in the blanks.

Pakistan and Bangladesh are largely (1) ____. Although they share the same religion, they have different (2) ____ and languages. Pakistan and India both want Kashmir for its (3) ____. The major languages in Pakistan are (4) ____ and (5) ____. About 70 percent of Pakistan's people live in (6) ____.

Bangladesh is nearly surrounded by (7) ____. There are two major rivers—the (8) ____ and the (9) ____ (10) ____

ASSESS

Assign Section 2 Assessment as homework or an in-class activity.

Have students use the Interactive Tutor Self-Assessment CD-ROM to review Section 5–2.

Applying Map Skills

Answers

1. 125–250 persons per square mile (50–100 per sq. km)
2. Karachi, Mumbai, Delhi, Chennai, Calcutta, Dhaka

Skills Practice

What geographic feature accounts for the pattern of population density in central Pakistan? *(the Indus River)*

Reading Check Answer

Buddhism

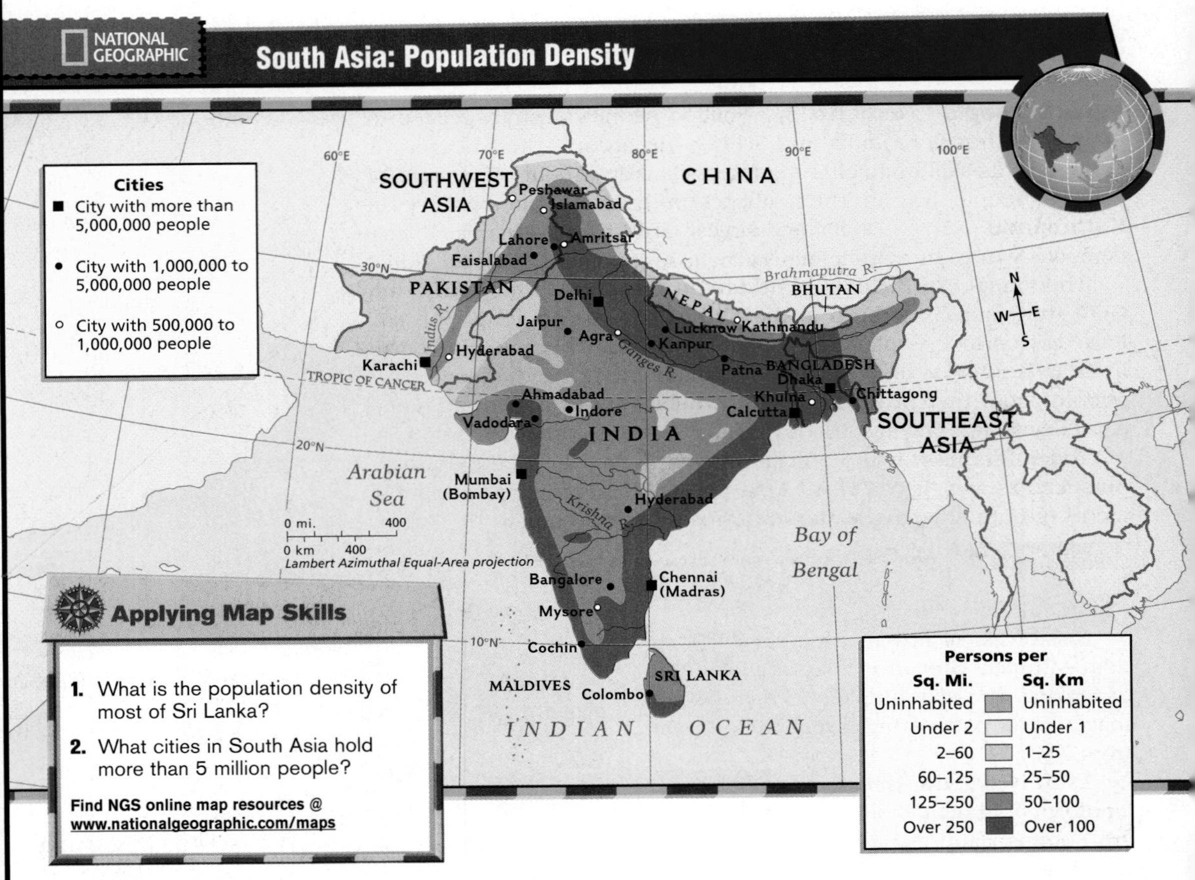

Applying Map Skills

1. What is the population density of most of Sri Lanka?
2. What cities in South Asia hold more than 5 million people?

Find NGS online map resources @ www.nationalgeographic.com/maps

Bhutan's People Bhutan has about 900,000 people. Most speak the Dzonkha dialect and live in rural villages that dot southern valleys and plains. **Thimphu,** the capital, is located in the southern area.

Bhutan was once called the Hidden Holy Land because of its isolation. Most people remain deeply loyal to Buddhism. In Bhutan, Buddhist centers of prayer and study are called **dzongs.** They have shaped the country's art and culture.

For many years, Bhutan was ruled by strong kings. In 1998 the country began to move toward democracy. At that time, the ruling king agreed to share his power with an elected legislature.

Reading Check **What is the main religion in Bhutan?**

Sri Lanka

Pear-shaped Sri Lanka lies about 20 miles (32 km) off the southeastern coast of India. A little larger than West Virginia, Sri Lanka is an island of white beaches, dense forests, and abundant wildlife. Monsoon winds and heavy rains combine with the island's warm temperatures and fertile soil to make Sri Lanka a good place to farm.

Content Background

Altitude Living in the high altitudes of the Himalaya requires physical adjustments to allow survival. The higher the altitude, the thinner the air. The drop in air pressure means that the alveoli, or air sacs, in the lungs cannot transmit as much oxygen to red blood cells. The Sherpas of Nepal have a swelling of blood vessels near the carotid arteries in the neck, some thickening of the walls of blood vessels in the lungs, and slightly increased blood pressure. Those who visit high altitudes for short periods may suffer altitude sickness, which can include shortness of breath, some nausea, and even chest pains. Even experienced climbers speak of the difficulties caused by the lack of oxygen. One climber who has scaled Everest four times describes the sensation as "like running on a treadmill and breathing through a straw."

Farmers grow rice and other food crops in lowland areas. In higher elevations, tea, rubber, and coconuts grow on large plantations. The country is one of the world's leading producers of tea and rubber. Sri Lanka is also famous for its sapphires, rubies, and other gemstones. Forests contain many valuable woods, such as ebony and satinwood, and a variety of birds and animals.

Sri Lanka's People For centuries, Sri Lanka prospered because of its location on an important ocean route between Africa and Asia. Beginning in the A.D. 1500s, Sri Lanka—then known as Ceylon—came under the control of European countries. The British ruled the island from 1802 to 1948, when it became independent. In 1972 Ceylon took the name of Sri Lanka, an ancient term meaning "brilliant land." Today, Sri Lanka is a republic with a president who carries out ceremonial duties. Real power is held by a prime minister, who is the head of government.

Sri Lankans belong to two major ethnic groups: the **Sinhalese** (sihng•guh•LEEZ) and the **Tamils** (TA•muhlz). Forming about 74 percent of the population, the Sinhalese live in the southern and western parts of the island. They speak Sinhalese and are mostly Buddhist. The Tamils make up about 18 percent of the population. They live in the north and east, speak Tamil, and are Hindus.

Since 1983 the Tamils and the Sinhalese have fought a violent civil war. The Tamils claim they have not been treated justly by the majority Sinhalese. They want to set up a separate Tamil nation in northern Sri Lanka. Thousands of Sri Lankans have lost their lives in the fighting.

✓ Reading Check **What are the two main ethnic groups in Sri Lanka?**

Section 2 Assessment

Defining Terms

1. **Define** cyclone, dzong.

Recalling Facts

2. **History** Why has the Khyber Pass been important?
3. **Human/Environment Interaction** What problems are caused by stripping the trees off the slopes in Nepal?
4. **Place** How do Bhutan's people earn a living?

Critical Thinking

5. **Summarizing Information** What were the teachings of the Buddha?
6. **Formulating an Opinion** What could Bangladesh do to increase food production?

Graphic Organizer

7. **Organizing Information** Create a time line like this one. List four events from Sri Lanka's history and their dates.

Applying Social Studies Skills

8. **Analyzing Maps** Look at the population density map on page 154 and the physical map on page 134. What is the population density of the southern part of Nepal? The northern part? Explain the difference.

Section 2 Assessment

1. The terms are defined in the Glossary.
2. It has been a passage through South Asia from the north.
3. slopes erode, valleys flood, fields are destroyed and rivers fill with mud
4. Most are subsistence farmers.
5. that people find peace by living simply, doing good deeds, and praying
6. It could modernize its farming methods and control flooding.
7. *Possible answers:* 1500s: under control of European countries; 1802–1948: Ruled by Britain; 1972: named Sri Lanka; 1983: civil war begins
8. *South*—125–250 persons per square mile; *North*—Under 2 persons per square mile; The least populous part is covered by the Himalaya.

Chapter 5

Section 2, pages 150–155

Section Quiz 5-2

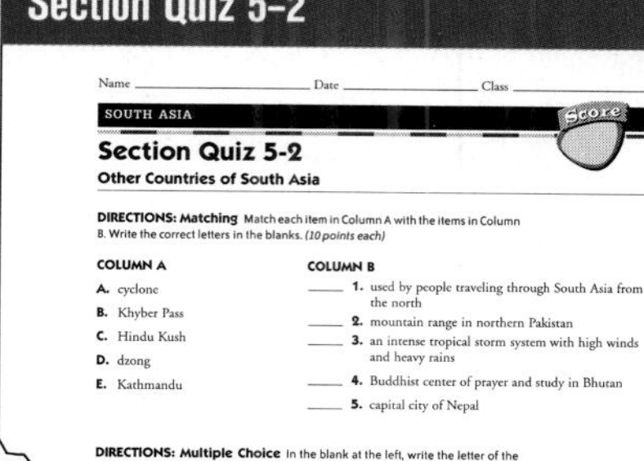

Name ______ Date ______ Class ______

SOUTH ASIA

Score

Section Quiz 5-2

Other Countries of South Asia

DIRECTIONS: Matching Match each item in Column A with the items in Column B. Write the correct letters in the blanks. *(10 points each)*

COLUMN A	COLUMN B
A. cyclone	____ **1.** used by people traveling through South Asia from the north
B. Khyber Pass	____ **2.** mountain range in northern Pakistan
C. Hindu Kush	____ **3.** an intense tropical storm system with high winds and heavy rains
D. dzong	____ **4.** Buddhist center of prayer and study in Bhutan
E. Kathmandu	____ **5.** capital city of Nepal

DIRECTIONS: Multiple Choice In the blank at the left, write the letter of the choice that best completes the statement or answers the question. *(10 points each)*

Reteach

Have students prepare an outline or concept map of the section content, listing the subheadings and writing three or four key facts under each.

✓ Reading Check Answer

Sinhalese and Tamils

Reading Essentials and Study Guide 5-2

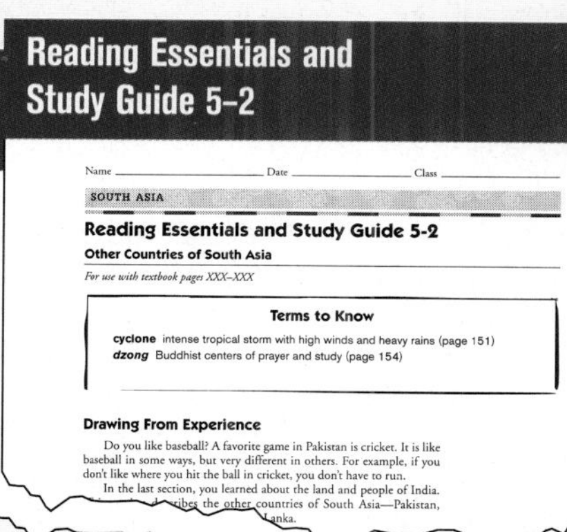

Name ______ Date ______ Class ______

SOUTH ASIA

Reading Essentials and Study Guide 5-2

Other Countries of South Asia

For use with textbook pages XXX–XXX

Terms to Know

cyclone intense tropical storm with high winds and heavy rains (page 151)

dzong Buddhist centers of prayer and study (page 154)

Drawing From Experience

Do you like baseball? A favorite game in Pakistan is cricket. It is like baseball in some ways, but very different in others. For example, if you don't like where you hit the ball in cricket, you don't have to run.

In the last section, you learned about the land and people of India. ... the other countries of South Asia—Pakistan, ... Lanka.

CLOSE

Have students write a paragraph that completes the sentence, "[*Name of country*] is unusual because . . . ." Tell them they can write about any of the countries in the section.

TEACH

Conduct a survey in the class. Ask students how many arrive at school (1) on foot, (2) by bicycle, (3) on a school bus, (4) by public transportation, or (5) by car. Tally the results and then ask students to convert the responses to percentages. Create a circle and explain that it represents the whole class. Make a slice corresponding to the percentage of the first group of students. Then prompt students to make the remaining slices. **L1**

Additional Skills Practice

1. Suppose you had figures showing different areas where the government spent its money in a single year. **Could you use a circle graph to present these figures? Why or why not?** *(yes; because each spending area represents a part of all spending)*
2. Suppose you had figures showing how much the government spent for two different years. **Could you use a single circle graph to show these figures? Why or why not?** *(no; because a circle graph shows parts of a whole, not a comparison of two different totals)*

Additional Skills Resources

 Chapter Skills Activity 5

 Building Geography Skills for Life

Social Studies Skill

Reading a Circle Graph

Have you ever watched someone dish out pieces of pie? When the pie is cut evenly, everybody gets the same size slice. If one slice is cut a little larger, however, someone else gets a smaller piece.

Learning the Skill

A **circle graph** is like a sliced pie. Often it is even called a pie chart. In a circle graph, the complete circle represents a whole group—or 100 percent. The circle is divided into "slices," or wedge-shaped sections representing parts of the whole.

To read a circle graph, follow these steps:

- Read the title of the circle graph to find out what the subject is.
- Study the labels or the key to see what each "slice" represents.
- Compare the sizes of the circle slices.

Practicing the Skill

Look at the graph below to answer the following questions.

1. What is the subject of the circle graph?
2. Which religion in South Asia has the most followers?
3. What percentage practice Islam?
4. What is the combined percentage of Buddhist and Christian followers?

Applying the Skill

Quiz at least 10 friends about the capitals of India, Pakistan, and Bangladesh. Create a circle graph showing what percentage knew (a) all three capitals, (b) two capitals, (c) one capital, or (d) no capitals.

GO TO Practice key skills with **Glencoe Skillbuilder Interactive Workbook, Level 1.**

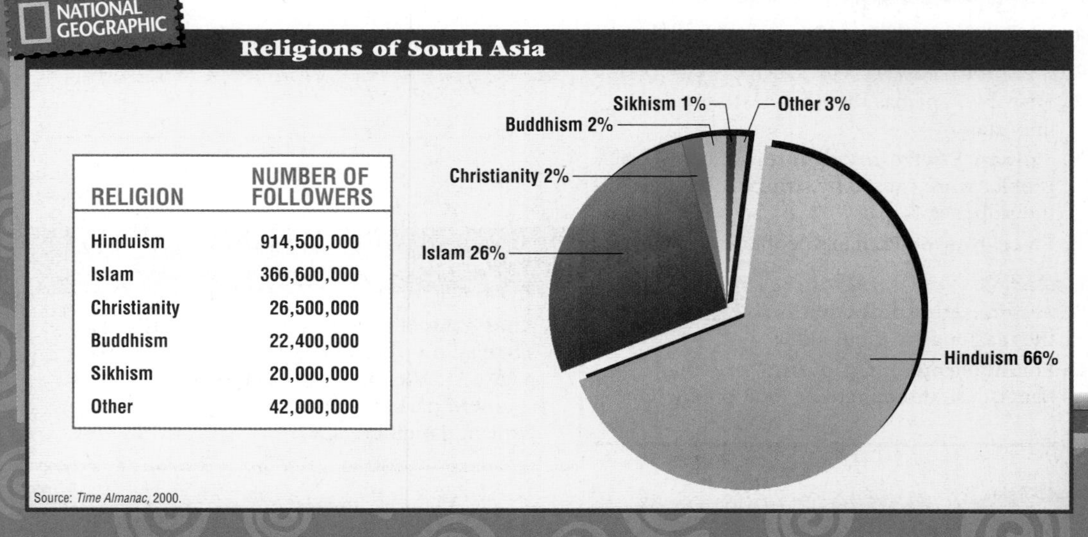

RELIGION	NUMBER OF FOLLOWERS
Hinduism	914,500,000
Islam	366,600,000
Christianity	26,500,000
Buddhism	22,400,000
Sikhism	20,000,000
Other	42,000,000

Practicing the Skill Answers

1. religions practiced in South Asia
2. Hinduism
3. 26 percent
4. 4 percent

Applying the Skill

Students' circle graphs will vary according to the results they obtained for their question, but each circle graph should contain up to four "slices"—knew all three capitals; knew two; knew one; and knew none (unless one of those categories had no respondents). Be sure that students include a key or labels to identify the slices.

Chapter 5 Reading Review

Section 1 India

Terms to Know
subcontinent
monsoon
green revolution
jute
cottage industry
prime minister
pesticide
caste
reincarnation

Main Idea

India is trying to develop its resources and meet the needs of its rapidly growing population.

✓**Place** India is the largest country in South Asia in size and population.
✓**Place** The Himalaya and the monsoons affect India's climate.
✓**Economics** India's economy is based on both farming and industry.
✓**Culture** India has many religions, but the majority of Indians are Hindus.
✓**Human/Environment Interaction** The green revolution has greatly improved India's production of food.

Section 2 Other Countries of South Asia

Terms to Know
cyclone
dzong

Main Idea

The other countries of South Asia include once-united Pakistan and Bangladesh, mountainous Nepal and Bhutan, and the island country of Sri Lanka.

✓**Region** Pakistan and India both claim Kashmir. This has led to wars between the two countries.
✓**History** Since independence, Pakistan has had many changes of government. Some of the changes were through elections and some through military takeovers.
✓**Place** Bangladesh is a densely populated and poor country.
✓**Region** The Himalaya are the major landform of Nepal and Bhutan.
✓**Economics** Sri Lanka is one of the world's leading producers of tea and rubber.

A teacher and his students have classes outdoors on a pleasant day in Bhutan. ▶

Reading Review

Use the Chapter 5 Reading Review to preview, review, condense, or reteach the chapter.

Preview/Review
Use the Terms to Know lists to help students review and study.

Activity Form the class into two teams and give the teams a quiz of the chapter's terms by reading a definition and having them identify the correct word.

Vocabulary PuzzleMaker Software reinforces the vocabulary terms used in Chapter 5.

The Interactive Tutor Self-Assessment CD-ROM allows students to review Chapter 5 content.

Condense
Have students read the Chapter 5 summary statements.

Chapter 5 Guided Reading Activities

Chapter 5 Audio Program

Reteach

Reteaching Activity 5

Chapter 5 Reading Essentials and Study Guide

Chapter Culminating Activity

Designing a Web Page South Asia is home to several important religions, including Hinduism, Buddhism, Islam, Jainism, and Sikhism. Have students research one of these religions and prepare an outline for a Web site about that religion. Students' outlines should show what the topic and main idea will be on each Web page. The outline might also suggest illustrations that could be included on each Web page. If students have time and interest, suggest that they design the opening page for the Web site or show how one of the detailed pages would look. *NOTE: This activity may be completed separately or you may wish students to incorporate it into their Current Events Journals.*

EE4 Human Systems: Standard 10

Assessment and Activities

GLENCOE TECHNOLOGY

MindJogger Videoquiz
Use MindJogger to review the Chapter 5 content.

 Available in VHS.

Using Key Terms

1.	b	6.	i
2.	g	7.	f
3.	h	8.	a
4.	j	9.	e
5.	d	10.	c

Reviewing the Main Ideas

11. the Karakoram and Himalaya ranges
12. They block cold air from the north.
13. cotton cloth, silk cloth, rugs, leather products, metalware
14. Hinduism
15. the Karakoram Range and the Hindu Kush Range
16. crops fail and there is widespread hunger
17. farm
18. The mountains make it difficult to build roads and railroads there.
19. because of its isolation and Buddhist religion
20. The minority Tamils want an independent state.
21. It is on an important ocean route between Africa and Asia.

Chapter 5 Assessment and Activities

 Using Key Terms

Match the terms in Part A with their definitions in Part B.

A.

1. monsoon
2. cyclone
3. green revolution
4. jute
5. subcontinent
6. reincarnation
7. pesticide
8. caste
9. dzong
10. cottage industry

B.

a. social class based on a person's ancestry
b. seasonal wind
c. family members supply their own equipment to make goods
d. large landmass that is part of another continent but distinct from it
e. Buddhist center for prayer and study
f. chemical used to kill insects
g. intense storm system with high winds
h. a government effort to use modern farming methods
i. the belief that after the body dies, the soul is reborn
j. plant fiber used for making rope, burlap bags, and carpet backing

 Reviewing the Main Ideas

Section 1 India

11. **Place** What forms a barrier between South Asia and the rest of Asia?
12. **Place** How do the Himalaya affect India's climate?
13. **Economics** What kinds of goods are produced by India's cottage industries?
14. **Culture** What religion do most Indians practice?

Section 2 Other Countries of South Asia

15. **Place** What mountain ranges occupy much of Pakistan?
16. **Human/Environment Interaction** What often happens when the rains come too late in Bangladesh?
17. **Economics** What do most of the people of Bangladesh do for a living?
18. **Human/Environment Interaction** How do mountains hinder economic development in Bhutan?
19. **History** Why was Bhutan once called the Hidden Holy Land?
20. **History** What is the basis of the civil war in Sri Lanka?
21. **Location** How did Sri Lanka's location allow it to prosper for many centuries?

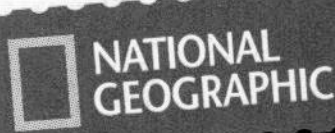

South Asia

Place Location Activity

On a separate sheet of paper, match the letters on the map with the numbered places listed below.

1. Ganges River
2. New Delhi
3. Brahmaputra River
4. Indus River
5. Sri Lanka
6. Himalaya
7. Bangladesh
8. Mumbai
9. Western Ghats
10. Deccan Plateau

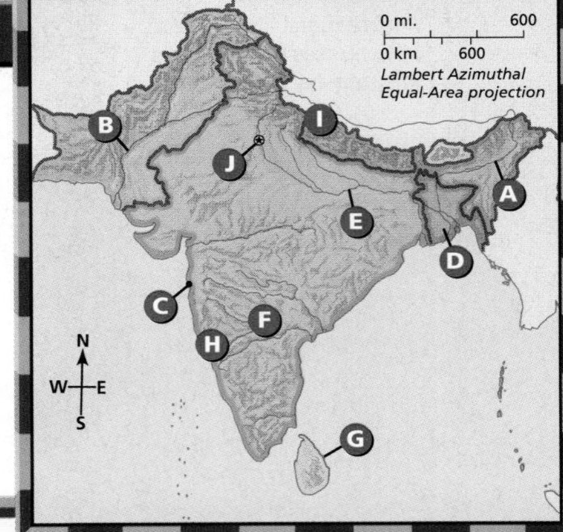

NATIONAL GEOGRAPHIC Place Location Activity

1.	E	6.	I
2.	J	7.	D
3.	A	8.	C
4.	B	9.	H
5.	G	10.	F

Critical Thinking

22. Answers will vary but might include such issues as undernourishment, poor health care, and educational problems. Solutions might include lowering the birthrate, producing more food, and developing industry.
23. Answers will vary, depending on the physical feature selected.

Self-Check Quiz Visit the ***Our World Today: People, Places, and Issues*** Web site at owt.glencoe.com and click on **Chapter 5–Self-Check Quizzes** to prepare for the Chapter Test.

Critical Thinking

22. **Identifying Alternatives** In this chapter you read about South Asia, a region with much poverty. What problems do you think a country faces when it has so many poor people? What are some solutions to this poverty?
23. **Understanding Cause and Effect** Create a chart like this one. List a physical feature of South Asia in the left-hand box. In the right-hand box, explain how that feature affects people's lives.

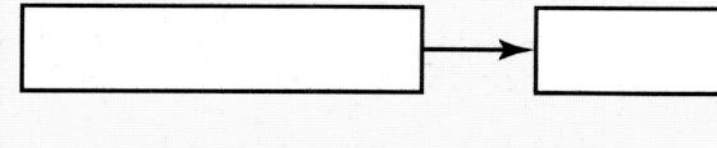

Current Events Journal

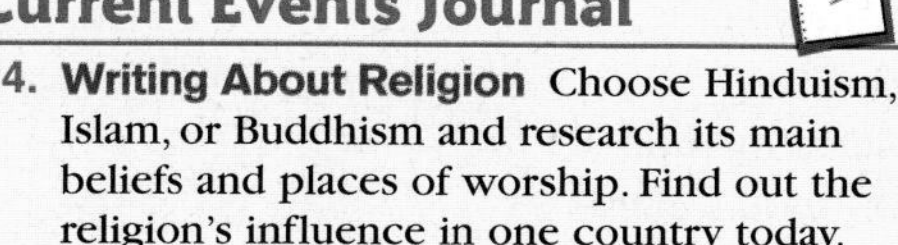

24. **Writing About Religion** Choose Hinduism, Islam, or Buddhism and research its main beliefs and places of worship. Find out the religion's influence in one country today. After your research is complete, create a poster that presents your findings.

Mental Mapping Activity

25. **Focusing on the Region** Create a simple outline map of South Asia, and then label the following:

- Bay of Bengal
- Sri Lanka
- Kashmir
- Pakistan
- Nepal
- Indian Ocean
- Bhutan
- Bangladesh
- Deccan Plateau
- New Delhi

Technology Skills Activity

26. **Using the Internet** Use the Internet to research tourism in one of the following countries: Nepal, India, or Sri Lanka. Create a travel brochure about a trip to the country, featuring information on the equipment and clothing that is needed, the availability of guides, costs, and so on.

The Princeton Review

Standardized Test Practice

Directions: Study the graph below, and then answer the following questions.

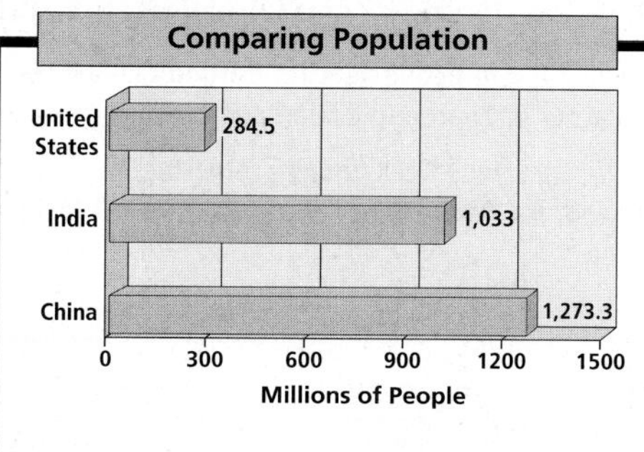

1. **How many people live in India?**
   - **A** 1,033
   - **B** 1,000,033
   - **C** 1,033,000,000
   - **D** 1,033,000,000,000
2. **About how many more people live in India than in the United States?**
   - **F** 2.5 times as many
   - **G** 3.5 times as many
   - **H** 4.5 times as many
   - **J** 5.5 times as many

Test-Taking Tip: You often need to use math skills in order to understand graphs. Look at the information along the sides and bottom of the graph to find out what the bars on the graph mean. Notice that on the graph above, the numbers represent millions of people. Therefore, you need to multiply the number on each bar by 1,000,000 to get the correct answer.

Assessment and Activities

Standardized Test Practice

1. C
2. G

Tested Objectives:
Reading a graph, analyzing information

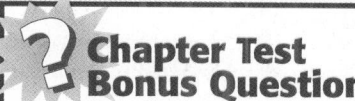

Chapter Test Bonus Question

This question may be used for extra credit on the chapter test.

What religion is practiced by most people in Pakistan? *(Islam)*

Our World Today online

Have students visit the Web site at **owt.glencoe.com** to review Chapter 5 and take the Self-Check Quiz.

Current Events Journal

24. Students' posters should focus on the central tenets of these major religions.

Mental Mapping Activity

25. This exercise helps students visualize the countries and geographic features they have been studying and understand the relationship among various points. Accept all attempts at freehand mapping that show places in the correct relationship to one another.

Technology Skills Activity

26. Students' brochures could be enhanced with photographs from the chosen country.

Chapter 6 Resources

Note: The following materials may be used when teaching Chapter 6.
Section level support materials are shown at point of use in the margins of the Teacher Wraparound Edition.

Timesaving Tools

TeacherWorks™ All-In-One Planner and Resource Center

- **Interactive Teacher Edition** See the **Interactive Teacher Edition** CD-ROM to electronically integrate your Teacher Wraparound Edition and blackline masters.
- **Interactive Lesson Planner** Organize your week, month, semester, or year with all the lesson helps you need. The **Interactive Lesson Planner** CD-ROM contains all Chapter 6 resources.

Use Glencoe's **Presentation Plus!** multimedia teacher tool to easily present dynamic lessons that visually excite your students. Using Microsoft PowerPoint® you can customize the presentations to create your own personalized lessons.

TEACHING TRANSPARENCIES

Graphic Organizer Transparency and Student Activity 6

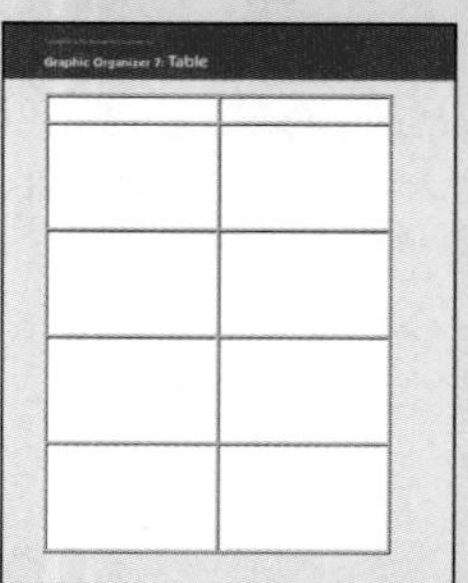

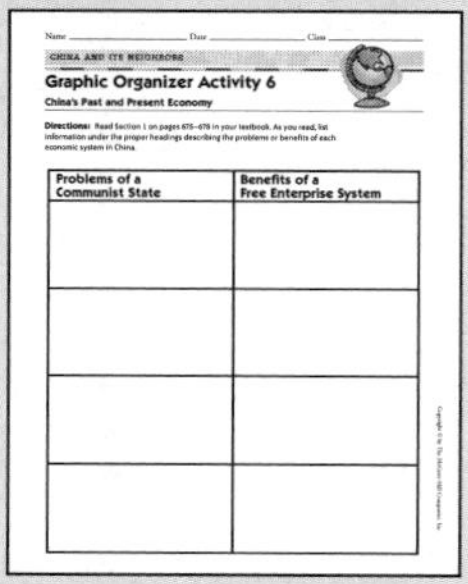

FOLDABLES™ Study Organizer

Foldables are three-dimensional, interactive graphic organizers that help students practice basic writing skills, review key vocabulary terms, and identify main ideas. Every chapter contains a Foldable activity, with additional chapter activities found in the ***Reading and Study Skills Foldables*** booklet.

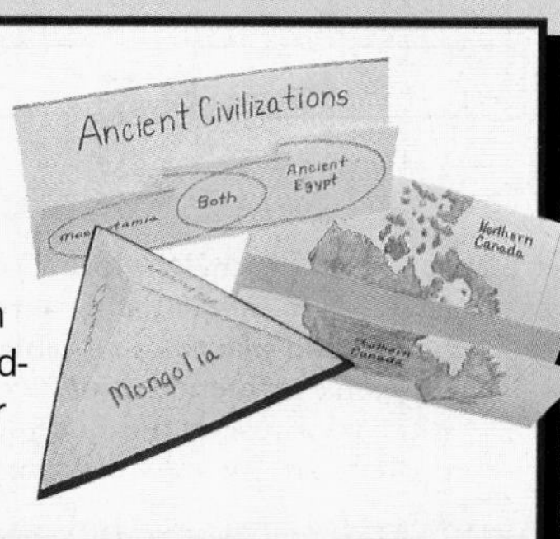

ENRICHMENT AND EXTENSION

Enrichment Activity 6

Cooperative Learning Activity 6

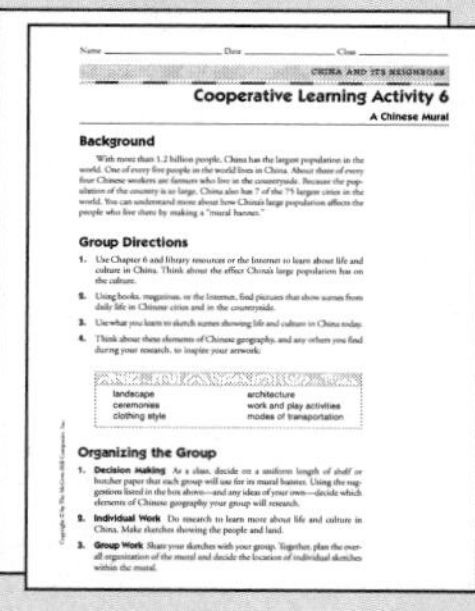

MAP AND GEOGRAPHY SKILLS

Chapter Map Activity 6

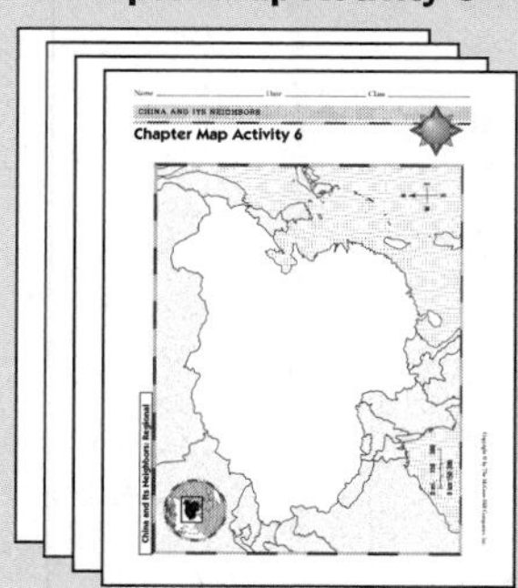

GeoLab Activity 6

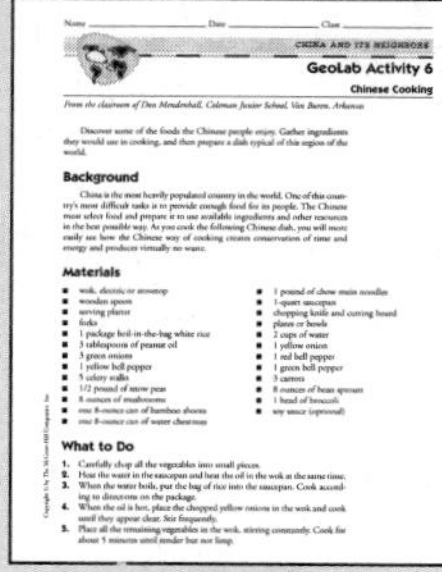

STANDARDIZED ASSESSMENT SKILLS

Critical Thinking Skills Activity 6

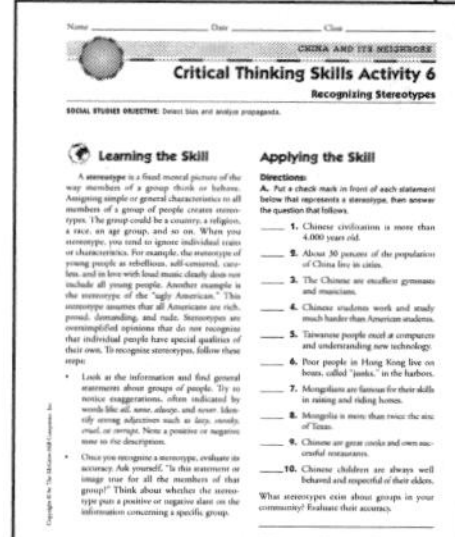

Map and Graph Skills Activity 6

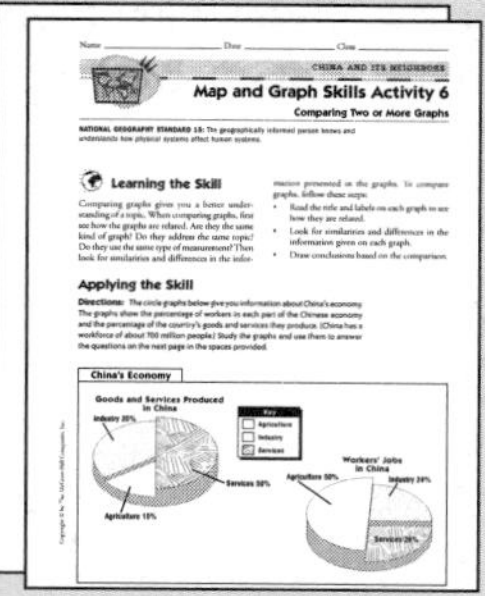

Reading and Writing Skills Activity 6

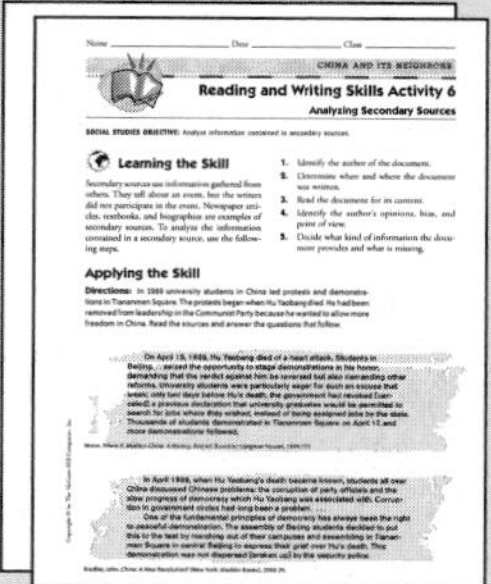

Standardized Test Practice Workbook Activity 6

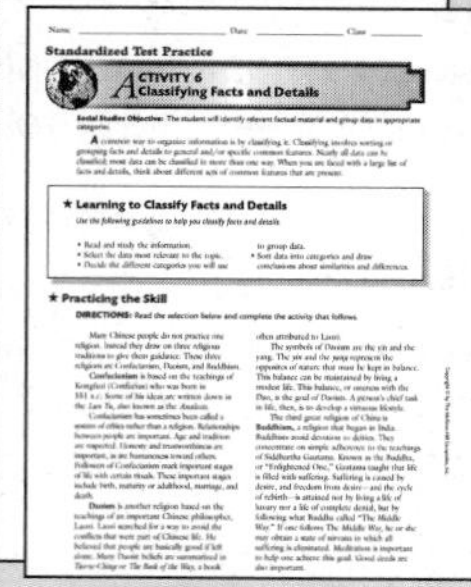

REVIEW AND REINFORCEMENT

Chapter Skills Activity 6

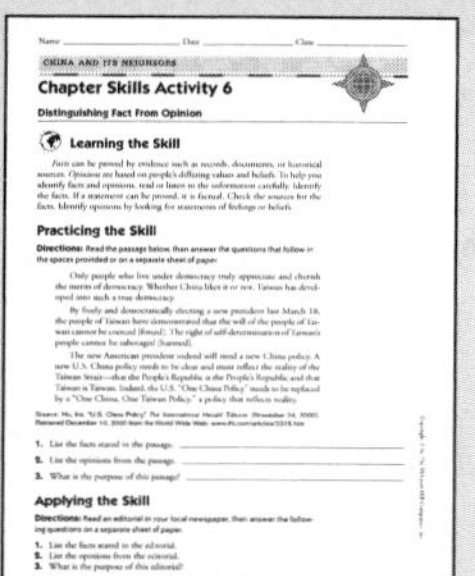

Take-Home Review Activity 6

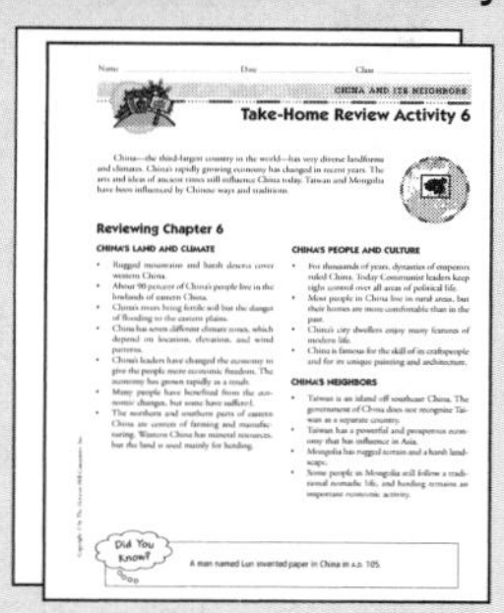

Reteaching Activity 6

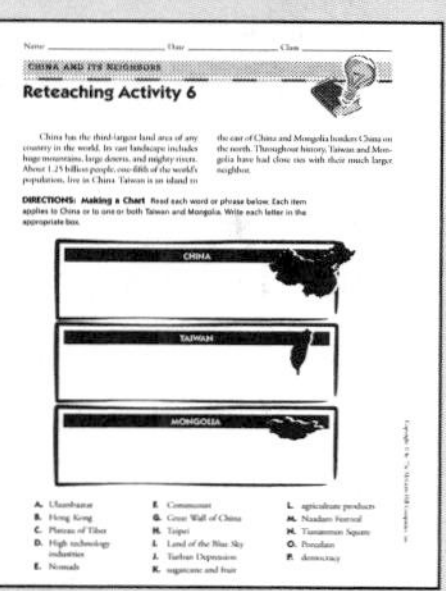

Vocabulary Activity 6

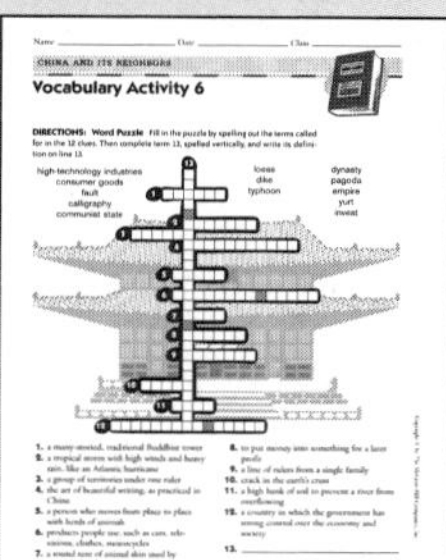

Workbook Activity 6

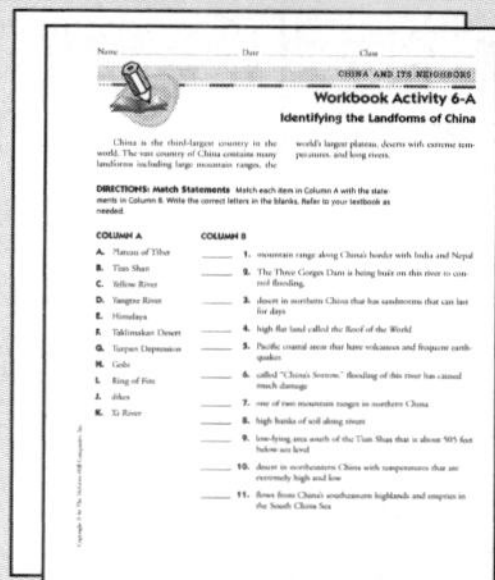

ASSESSMENT

GLENCOE'S ASSESSMENT ADVANTAGE

Chapter 6 Test, Form A

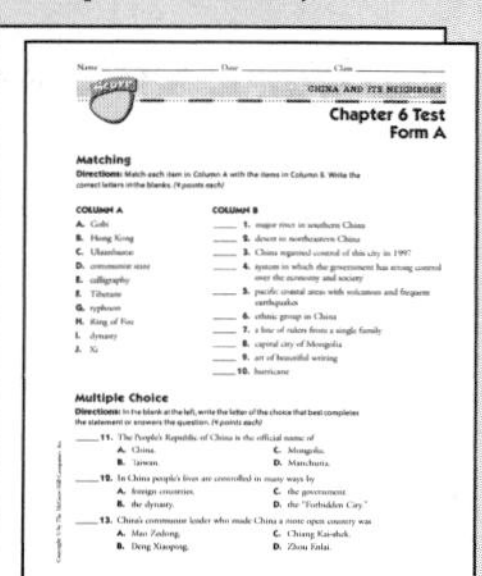

Chapter 6 Test, Form B

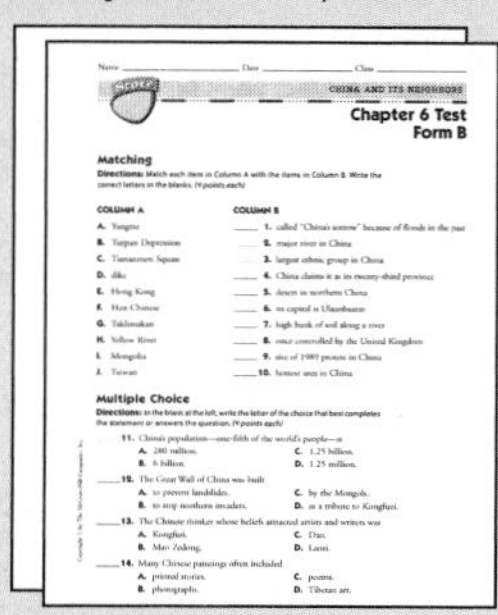

Performance Assessment Activity 6

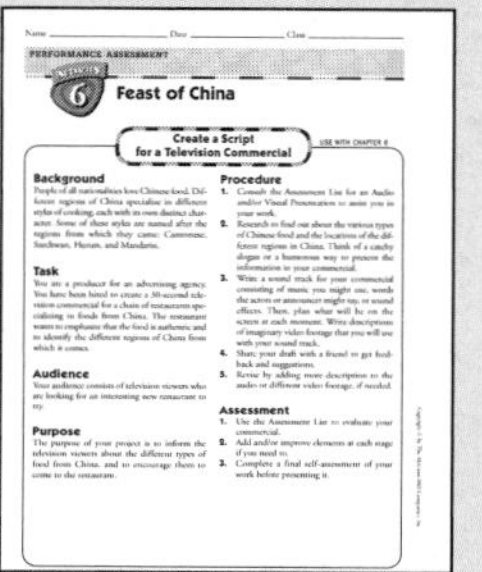

ExamView® Pro 3.0 Testmaker CD-ROM

MULTIMEDIA

- National Geographic's The World and Its People
- MindJogger Videoquiz
- Vocabulary PuzzleMaker Software
- Interactive Tutor Self-Assessment CD-ROM
- ExamView® Pro 3.0 Testmaker CD-ROM
- Interactive Lesson Planner CD-ROM
- Interactive Teacher Edition CD-ROM
- Skillbuilder Interactive Workbook CD-ROM, Level 1
- Presentation Plus! CD-ROM
- Audio Program

SPANISH RESOURCES

The following Spanish language materials are available in the Spanish Resources binder:

- **Spanish Chapter Summaries**
- **Spanish Vocabulary Activities**
- **Spanish Guided Reading Activities**
- **Spanish Quizzes and Tests**
- **Spanish Take-Home Review Activities**
- **Spanish Reteaching Activities**

Meeting National Standards

Geography for Life

All of the 18 standards are demonstrated in Unit 3. The following ones are highlighted in Chapter 6:

Section 1 **EE2 Places and Regions: Standards 4, 5, 6**

EE5 Environment and Society: Standards 14, 15, 16

Section 2 **EE4 Human Systems: Standards 9, 10, 11, 12, 13**

EE6 The Uses of Geography: Standards 17, 18

Section 3 **EE2 Places and Regions: Standards 4, 5, 6**

EE4 Human Systems: Standards 9, 10, 11, 12, 13

For a complete listing of National Geography Standards and entire text correlation, see pages T22–T29.

Local Objectives

____

Chapter 6 Planning Guide

SECTION RESOURCES

Daily Objectives	Reproducible Resources	Multimedia Resources
Section 1 **China's Land and Economy** **Suggested Pacing = 1 day** **1.** Discuss the varied landforms found in China. **2.** Describe how China's economy is changing.	Reproducible Lesson Plan 6-1 Daily Lecture and Discussion Notes 6-1 Guided Reading Activity 6-1 Reading Essentials and Study Guide 6-1 Section Quiz 6-1*	Daily Focus Skills Transparency 6-1 GeoQuiz Transparency 6-1 Vocabulary PuzzleMaker Software Interactive Tutor Self-Assessment CD-ROM ExamView® Pro 3.0 Testmaker CD-ROM Presentation Plus! CD-ROM
Section 2 **China's People and Culture** **Suggested Pacing = 1 day** **1.** Explain how China's history influences life there today. **2.** Contrast urban and rural China. **3.** Summarize what arts China is known for.	Reproducible Lesson Plan 6-2 Daily Lecture and Discussion Notes 6-2 Guided Reading Activity 6-2 Reading Essentials and Study Guide 6-2 Section Quiz 6-2*	Daily Focus Skills Transparency 6-2 Vocabulary PuzzleMaker Software Interactive Tutor Self-Assessment CD-ROM ExamView® Pro 3.0 Testmaker CD-ROM Presentation Plus! CD-ROM
Section 3 **China's Neighbors** **Suggested Pacing = 1 day** **1.** Explain why many people moved to Taiwan. **2.** Describe the people of Mongolia.	Reproducible Lesson Plan 6-3 Daily Lecture and Discussion Notes 6-3 Guided Reading Activity 6-3 Reading Essentials and Study Guide 6-3 Section Quiz 6-3*	Daily Focus Skills Transparency 6-3 Vocabulary PuzzleMaker Software Interactive Tutor Self-Assessment CD-ROM ExamView® Pro 3.0 Testmaker CD-ROM Presentation Plus! CD-ROM

00:00 **Out of Time?** Assign the **Reading Essentials and Study Guide** for this chapter.

*Also available in Spanish

KEY TO ABILITY LEVELS

Teaching strategies have been coded for varying learning styles and abilities.

L1 **BASIC** activities for all students
L2 **AVERAGE** activities for average to above-average students
L3 **CHALLENGING** activities for above-average students
ELL **ENGLISH LANGUAGE LEARNER** activities

Blackline Master
Software
CD-ROM
Audiocassette
Transparency
Videocassette
Block Scheduling
DVD

Charting Population Growth

Janet S. D'Meo-Townley
Park Middle School
Scotch Plains, New Jersey

Have students use Skittles® to represent the population and simulate population growth. Between 2 paper plates, shake 2 Skittles. For every "S" that shows, add another Skittle to the plate. Record the number on a table. Repeat this process for 15 shakes (or "generations"), and graph the data in a table. A variation of this activity is to remove one Skittle for every two Skittles that touch, in addition to adding a Skittle for every "S" that shows. Graph the data and make predictions about future population growth, particularly for Asian countries.

OUR WORLD TODAY Online

Use our Web site for additional resources. All essential content is covered in the Student Edition.

You and your students can visit owt.glencoe.com, the Web site companion to *Our World Today*. This innovative integration of electronic and print media offers your students a wealth of opportunities. The student text directs students to the Web site for the following options:

- Chapter Overviews
- Student Web Activities
- Self-Check Quizzes
- Textbook Updates

Answers are provided for you in the Web Activity Lesson Plan. Additional Web resources and Interactive Tutor puzzles are also available.

NATIONAL GEOGRAPHIC TEACHER'S CORNER

Index to National Geographic Magazine:

The following articles may be used for research relating to this chapter:

- "Beijing: New Face for the Ancient Capital," by Todd Carrel, March 2000.
- "Black Dragon River," by Simon Winchester, February 2000.
- "Tibet Embraces the New Year," by Ian Baker, January 2000.
- "South China Sea: Crossroads of Asia," by Tracy Dahlby, December 1998.

National Geographic Society Products Available From Glencoe:

To order the following products for use with this chapter, contact your local Glencoe sales representative or call Glencoe at 1-800-334-7344:

- *STV: World Geography* (Videodisc)
- *Picture Atlas of the World* (CD-ROM)
- *PictureShow: Ancient Civilizations: China and India* (CD-ROM)
- *PicturePack: Geography of Asia* (Transparencies)
- *MapPack: Asia* (Transparencies)
- *ZipZapMap! World* (Software)

Additional National Geographic Society Products:

To order the following products for use with this chapter, call National Geographic Society at 1-800-368-2728:

- *Complete National Geographic: 111 Years of National Geographic Magazine* (CD-ROM)
- *Voices: Poetry and Art From Around the World* (Book)
- *National Geographic Desk Reference* (Book)
- *National Geographic Atlas of the World, Seventh Edition* (Book)
- *Asia* (Video)
- *Asia Political* (Map)
- *Cultures* (Map)
- *Population* (Map)

NGS ONLINE

Access National Geographic's Web site for current events, activities, links, interactive features, and archives.
www.nationalgeographic.com

Introducing Chapter 6

Our World Today Online

Introduce students to chapter content and key terms by having them access Chapter Overview 6 at owt.glencoe.com

Chapter Objectives

1. Discuss the landforms and climates of China.
2. Contrast the economy of China in the past to the economy today.
3. Explain the influence of China's past on the people today.
4. Describe the geography and people of Taiwan and Mongolia.

GLENCOE TECHNOLOGY

NATIONAL GEOGRAPHIC

The World and Its People Video Program

Chapter 24 China

The following segments enhance the study of this chapter:

- **The Giant Panda**
- **Minority Games**

Available in DVD and VHS.

MindJogger Videoquiz

Use MindJogger to preview the Chapter 6 content.

Available in VHS.

Chapter 6 China and Its Neighbors

The World and Its People NATIONAL GEOGRAPHIC

To learn more about the people and places of China, view ***The World and Its People*** **Chapter 24** video.

Our World Today Online

Chapter Overview Visit the ***Our World Today: People, Places, and Issues*** Web site at owt.glencoe.com and click on **Chapter 6—Chapter Overviews** to preview information about China.

160

Two-Minute Lesson Launcher

More than 4,000 miles (6,437 km) long, the Great Wall of China deserves its reputation as one of humankind's most impressive structures. First begun in the 200s B.C., the wall that stands now largely dates from around A.D. 1500. Thousands of tourists come from around the world every day to a well-maintained section of the wall near Beijing. Inform students of these facts about the Great Wall of China. **Ask:** **What does this information tell you about China?** *(Possible answers: China is an ancient civilization with a long history; China fascinates people all over the world; China once had conflict with its neighbors; China had a powerful government, which organized people to build this structure.)*

Identifying Main Ideas Study Foldable Make this foldable to help you identify key facts about the people and places of China and its neighbors.

Step 1 Fold the paper from the top right corner down so the edges line up. Cut off the leftover piece.

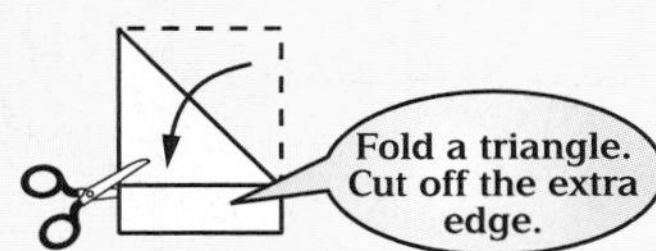
Fold a triangle. Cut off the extra edge.

Step 2 Fold the triangle in half. Unfold.

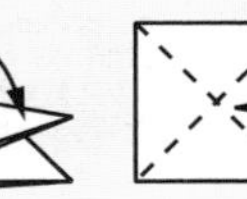

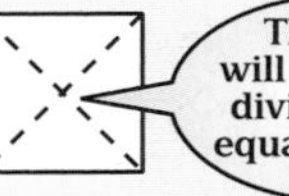
The folds will form an X dividing four equal sections.

Step 3 Cut up one fold line and stop at the middle. This forms two triangular flaps.

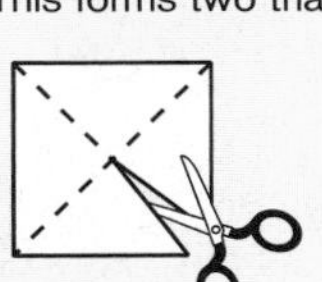

Step 4 Draw an X on one tab and label the other three the following: Flap 1: Mongolia; Flap 2: China; Flap 3: Taiwan.

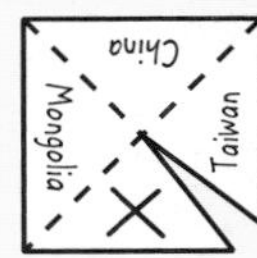
China
Mongolia
Taiwan

Step 5 Fold the X flap under the other flap and glue together.

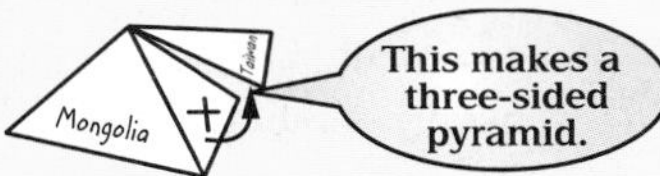
Mongolia
This makes a three-sided pyramid.

Reading and Writing As you read, write main ideas inside the foldable under each appropriate pyramid wall.

Why It Matters

Opening to Trade

Built to keep out foreigners, the Great Wall of China is so large that it can be seen from space. Despite this high visibility, much about China remains a mystery to the rest of the world. For centuries, China has worked to protect its culture from outside influences. Recently, however, the need to develop its economy has motivated China to begin opening its doors to trade with other countries.

◀ Part of the Great Wall of China

About the Photo

In the northern part of China are the cold, windswept plains of Inner Mongolia. These plains provide the only easy land route into the agricultural region of China from western Asia. Ch'in Shih Huang Ti originally started to build the Great Wall along this frontier during the Han period (207 B.C. to A.D. 220), one of the magnificent periods in China's long history. The purpose of the wall was to keep the nomads of Inner Mongolia and other "barbarians" from attacking settled areas in agricultural China.

Introducing Chapter 6

FOLDABLES™ Study Organizer

Purpose This activity will provide students with an opportunity to review what they know and to think about what they would like to know about Mongolia, China, and Taiwan. The resulting foldable can be used as an assessment tool at the end of the chapter to determine what students have learned.

Have students complete ***Reading and Study Skills Foldables*** Activity 6.

Why It Matters

Ask students why the Great Wall is an obsolete concept for isolating a nation today. Students should respond that the Internet has made instant communication a virtual fact of life. Ask students to vote on this question: Which machine (technology) would you rather be without—a computer or a car? Many students will realize that their computer can take them places cars will never go.

Chapter 6

Section 1, pages 162–166

Focus

Section Objectives

1. Discuss the varied landforms found in China.
2. Describe how China's economy is changing.

BELLRINGER Skillbuilder Activity

Project transparency and have students answer questions.

This activity is also available as a blackline master.

Daily Focus Skills Transparency 6-1

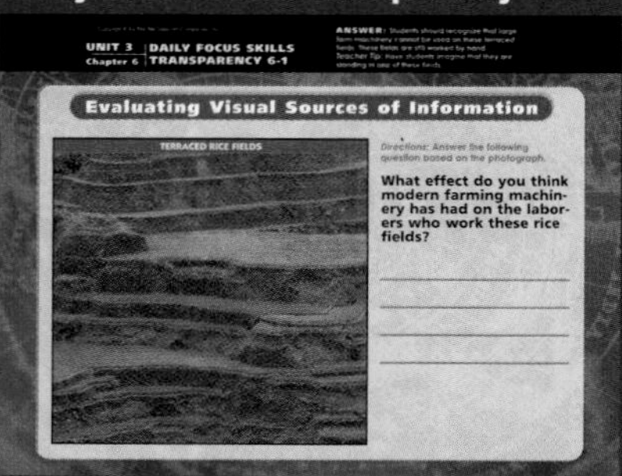

Guide to Reading

■ **Accessing Prior Knowledge**

Ask: Which country is the most populous nation in the world? *(China)* How can the panda—which lives in sparsely populated wild areas—survive in China? *(China is a large and varied country that has some very isolated and untamed areas.)*

Use the Vocabulary PuzzleMaker to create crossword and word search puzzles.

Guide to Reading

Main Idea

China—the third-largest country in the world—has very diverse landforms. China's rapidly growing economy has changed in recent years.

Terms to Know

- dike
- fault
- communist state
- free enterprise system
- invest
- consumer goods
- "one-country, two-systems"

Reading Strategy

Create a diagram like this one. Then list two facts under each heading in the outer ovals.

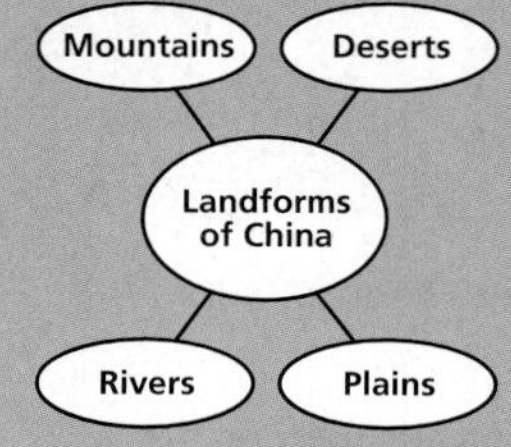

Section 1 China's Land and Economy

Giant pandas look cute and cuddly, but actually they are somewhat hot-tempered. You would be hot-tempered too if your habitat were dwindling in size. Fewer than 1,000 pandas live in the wild, and about 140 live in zoos. The wild pandas make their home on the eastern edge of the Plateau of Tibet. They eat mainly bamboo stems and leaves.

China (officially called the **People's Republic of China**) lies in the central part of eastern Asia. It is the third-largest country in area, after Russia and Canada. China is just slightly larger than the United States.

China's Land and Climate

The physical map on the next page shows the many landforms found within China's vast area. Rugged mountains cover about one-third of the country. Find the Himalaya, Kunlun Shan, Tian Shan, and Altay mountain ranges.

The world's largest plateau is also in China. This high, flat land, commonly called the "Roof of the World," is really the **Plateau of Tibet.** Its height averages about 13,000 feet (3,962 m) above sea level. Scattered shrubs and grasses cover the plateau's harsh landscape. Pandas, golden monkeys, and other rare animals roam the thick forests found at the eastern end of this plateau.

Section Resources

Reproducible Masters

- Reproducible Lesson Plan 6-1
- Daily Lecture and Discussion Notes 6-1
- Guided Reading Activity 6-1
- Reading Essentials and Study Guide 6-1
- Section Quiz 6-1

Transparencies

- Daily Focus Skills Transparency 6-1
- GeoQuiz Transparency 6-1

Multimedia

- Vocabulary PuzzleMaker Software
- Interactive Tutor Self-Assessment CD-ROM
- Presentation Plus! CD-ROM
- ExamView® Pro 3.0 Testmaker CD-ROM

In addition to very high elevations, western China has some extremely low areas. The Turpan Depression, east of the Tian Shan, lies about 505 feet (154 m) *below* sea level. It is partly filled with salt lakes. It also is the hottest area of China. Daytime temperatures can reach as high as 122°F (50°C). Can you find the Turpan Depression on the physical map below? Use the elevation key as a guide.

In the north of China, mountain ranges circle desert areas. One of these areas is the **Taklimakan Desert.** It is an isolated region with very high temperatures. Sandstorms here may last for days and create huge, drifting sand dunes. Farther east lies another desert, the **Gobi.** Instead of sand, the Gobi has rocks and stones. Temperatures here can range from 110°F (43°C) in the day to as low as -30°F (-34°C) on winter nights.

The map below shows you that plains also run along the coasts of the South China and East China Seas. These fertile plains are rich in mineral resources. Almost 90 percent of China's people live here. This region is one of the most scenic areas in China.

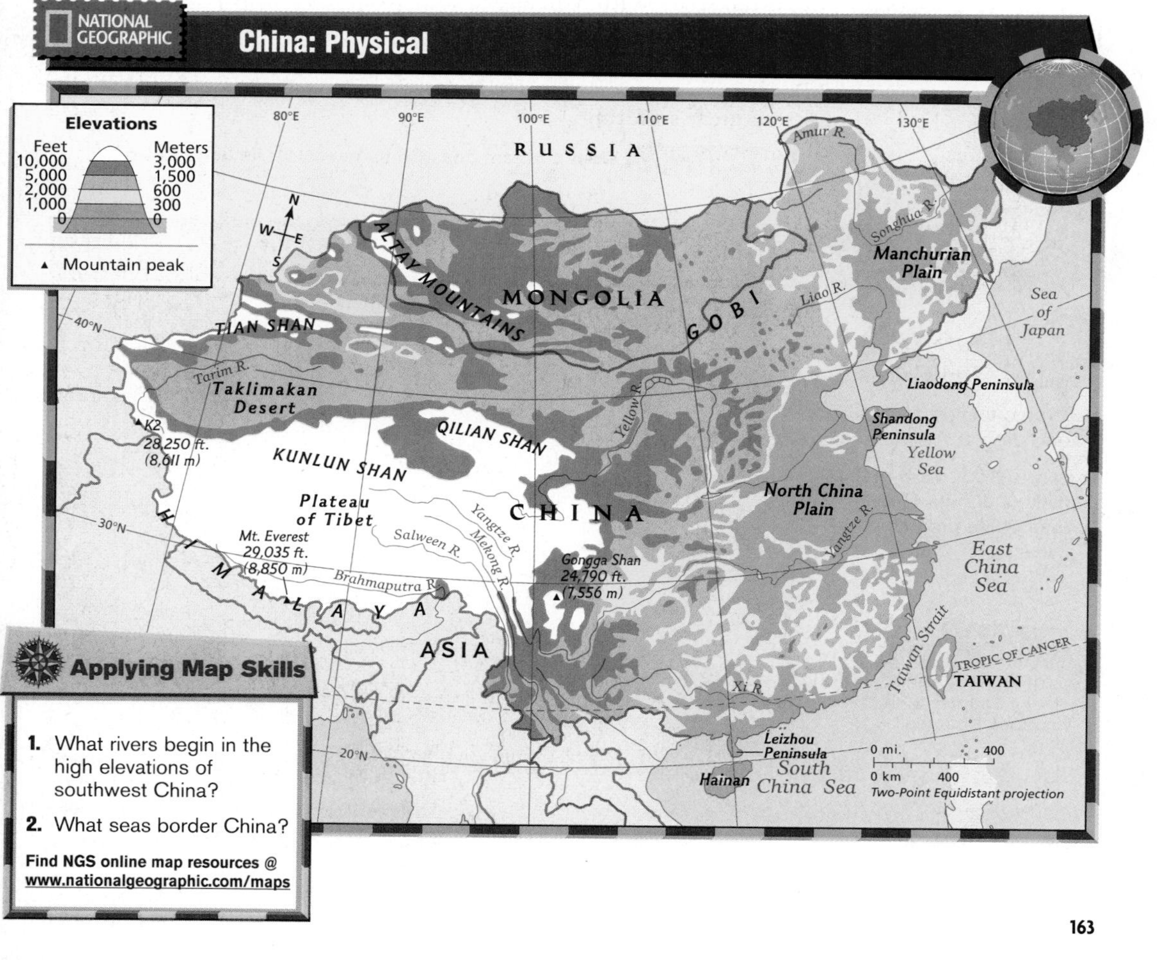

Applying Map Skills

1. What rivers begin in the high elevations of southwest China?
2. What seas border China?

Find NGS online map resources @ www.nationalgeographic.com/maps

163

Chapter 6

Section 1, pages 162–166

2 TEACH

Analyzing Information Tell students to write the headings "Early People's Republic of China" and "China Today" in their notebooks. Tell them that as they read the section, they should record facts about China's economy under the appropriate heading. Then have them write a paragraph comparing and contrasting the economy of China in these two periods. Ask students to summarize how trade has influenced the facts they recorded under "China Today." **L1**

Daily Lecture Notes 6-1

CHINA AND ITS NEIGHBORS

Daily Lecture and Discussion Notes 6-1

China's Land and Economy (pages 162–166)

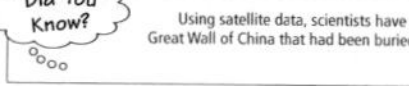

Did You Know? Using satellite data, scientists have discovered more than 600 miles of the Great Wall of China that had been buried beneath sand, dirt, and silt.

I. China's Land and Climate *(pages 162–165)*

A. Many landforms are found within China's vast area, which is slightly larger than the United States. Between the Himalaya and the Kunlun Shan lies the Plateau of Tibet. The world's largest plateau, this high flat land is called the Roof of the World. Its height averages about 13,000 feet above sea level. The Turpan Depression, in contrast, lies about 505 feet below sea level.

B. The Taklimakan Desert is an isolated region with very high temperatures. ... days and create huge, drifting sand dunes. Farther ... of sand, the Gobi has ... and stones.

Applying Map Skills

Answers

1. Yellow, Yangtze, Mekong, Salween, Brahmaputra
2. Yellow Sea, East China Sea, South China Sea

Skills Practice

Describe the elevation of western China. *(highland plateaus and mountains)* **Eastern China?** *(lowland plain)*

Team-Teaching Activity

Language Arts Invite a language arts teacher to class to discuss the main features of descriptive writing. The teacher should touch on such subjects as using vivid words, giving details, comparing, drawing on words that convey the five senses (sight, hearing, smell, taste, and touch), and having a vantage point from which the scene is described. After reviewing these principles, have students write a paragraph describing a walk through one region of China. Then ask volunteers to read their paragraphs aloud, and have the class discuss how the piece reveals elements of descriptive writing and helps form a mental map of the place. **L1**

EE1 The World in Spatial Terms: Standard 2

Chapter 6

Section 1, pages 162–166

Objectives, goals, and answers to the Student Web Activity can be found in the Web Activity Lesson Plan at **owt.glencoe.com**

Analyzing the Graph

Answer
about 205 million tons

Skills Practice
What country ranks second in rice production? *(India)*

✓ Reading Check Answer
flooding causes damage and kills many people

Guided Reading Activity 6-1

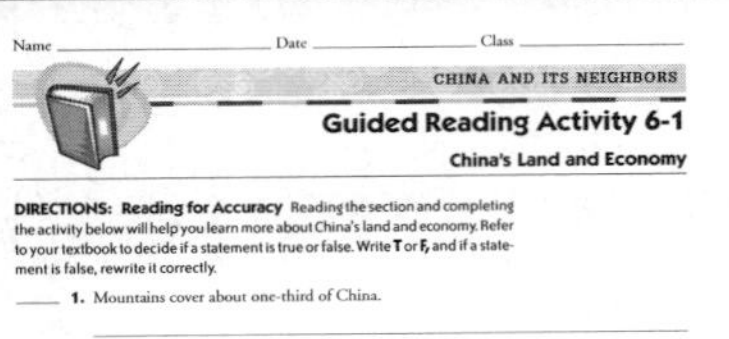

Name ______ Date ______ Class ______

CHINA AND ITS NEIGHBORS

Guided Reading Activity 6-1

China's Land and Economy

DIRECTIONS: Reading for Accuracy Reading the section and completing the activity below will help you learn more about China's land and economy. Refer to your textbook to decide if a statement is true or false. Write T or F, and if a statement is false, rewrite it correctly.

____ 1. Mountains cover about one-third of China.

____ 2. The rest of China is very fertile and full of grasslands.

____ 3. The Yellow River valley is a very important farming area.

____ 4. The Yellow River brought much devastation from flooding until dams and dikes were built.

Our World Today online

Web Activity Visit the ***Our World Today: People, Places, and Issues*** Web site at owt.glencoe.com and click on **Chapter 6–Student Web Activities** to learn more about China's rivers.

Rivers Three of China's major waterways—the **Yangtze** (YANG•SEE), **Yellow,** and **Xi** (SHEE) **Rivers**—flow through the plains and southern highlands. They serve as important transportation routes and also as a source of soil. How? For centuries, these rivers have flooded their banks in the spring. The floodwaters have deposited rich soil to form flat river basins that can be farmed. China's most productive farmland is found in valleys formed by these major rivers.

Despite their benefits, the rivers of China also have brought much suffering. The Chinese call the Yellow River "China's sorrow." In the past, its flooding cost hundreds of thousands of lives and caused much damage. To control floods, the Chinese have built dams and **dikes,** or high banks of soil, along the rivers. Turn to page 167 to learn more about the **Three Gorges Dam,** a project under way on the Yangtze River.

An Unsteady Land In addition to floods, people in eastern China face another danger—earthquakes. Their part of the country stretches along the **Ring of Fire,** a name that describes Pacific coastal areas with volcanoes and frequent earthquakes. Eastern China lies along a **fault,** or crack in the earth's crust. As a result, earthquakes in this region are common—and can be very violent. Because so many people live in eastern China, these earthquakes can bring great suffering.

✓ Reading Check **What problem does China have with its large rivers?**

NATIONAL GEOGRAPHIC

Leading Rice-Producing Countries

Analyzing the Graph

The most important food crop in Asia is rice.

Economics **How many millions of tons of rice does China produce in a year?**

Textbook update

Visit owt.glencoe.com and click on **Chapter 6–Textbook Updates.**

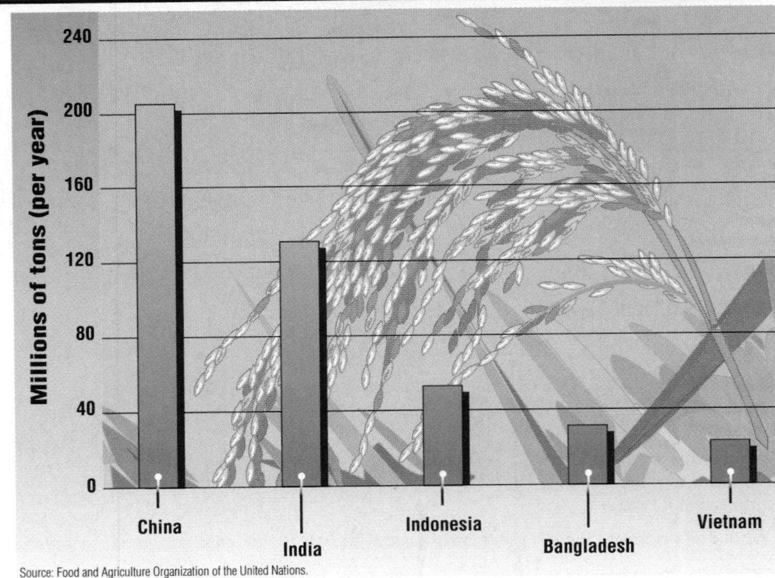

Source: Food and Agriculture Organization of the United Nations.

Cooperative Learning Activity

Making a Diorama Have students work in groups to create a diorama of the regions of China. Students should research to learn more about each region, such as average temperatures and rainfall and the kinds of plants and animals found there. The research will yield images that they can use as the basis for their display. Have the groups work together to assemble the display. When it is complete, have the class compare and contrast the different regions of China. They should also describe how the physical geography affects the lives of the people who live in the region. In their descriptions, students might include such aspects as patterns of population, location of economic activities, and foreign and domestic policies that have been influenced by the region's geography. **L1 ELL**

A New Economy

Since 1949, China has been a **communist state,** in which the government has strong control over the economy and society as a whole. Government officials—not individuals or businesses—decide what crops are grown, what products are made, and what prices are charged. China discovered that the communist system created many problems. China fell behind other countries in technology, and manufactured goods were of poor quality.

In recent years, China's leaders have begun many changes to make the economy stronger. Without completely giving up communism, the government has allowed many features of the **free enterprise system** to take hold. In this system, the government allows individuals to choose what jobs they want and where to start their own businesses. Workers can keep the profits they make. Farmers can grow and sell what they wish.

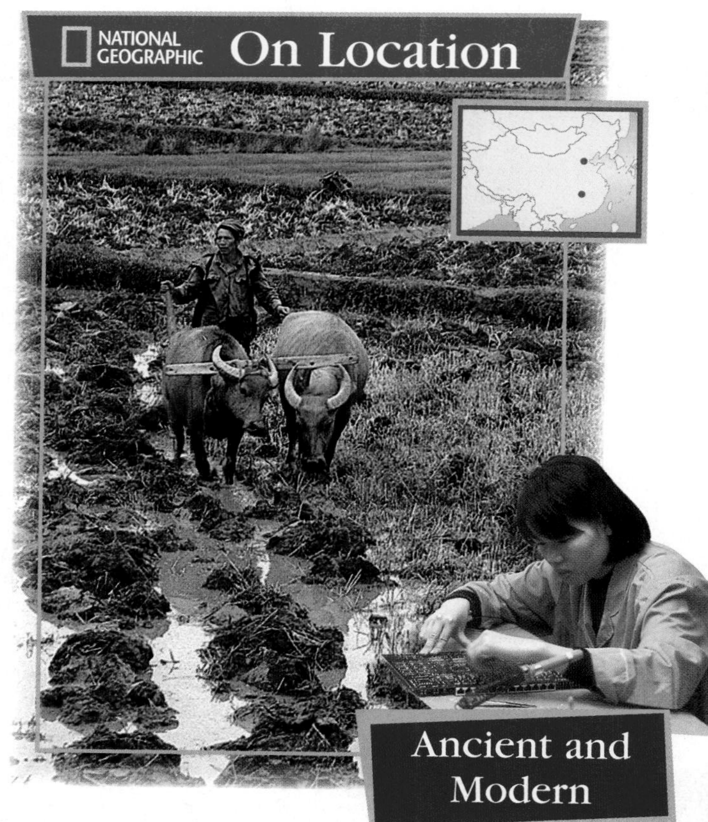

Ancient and Modern

In China's rural areas ancient farming methods are still used (left). However, in the industrialized cities, high technology is being developed (right).

Government How has the government affected how things are done in China?

As a result of these and other changes, China's economy has boomed. The total value of goods and services produced in China increased four times from 1978 to 1999. Farm output also rose rapidly. Because of mountains and deserts, only 10 percent of China's land is farmed. Yet China is now a world leader in producing various agricultural products.

Foreign Trade Eager to learn about new business methods, China has asked other countries to **invest,** or put money into developing Chinese businesses. Many companies in China are now jointly owned by Chinese and foreign businesspeople. Foreign companies expect two benefits from investing in China. First, they can pay Chinese workers less than they pay workers in their own countries. Second, companies in China have hundreds of millions of possible customers for their goods.

Results of Growth Because of economic growth, more of China's people are able to get jobs in manufacturing and service industries. Wages have increased, and more goods are available to buy. Some Chinese now enjoy a good standard of living. They can afford **consumer goods,** or products such as televisions, cars, and motorcycles.

Critical Thinking Activity

Formulating an Opinion Discuss the vote in the United States Congress in 2000 to have permanent normal trade relations (PNTR) with China. Critics of the plan cited China's poor record on human rights and the environment and the possibility that increased trade with China would lead to American manufacturing jobs being transferred to China, where labor costs are lower. Supporters argued that by increasing trade, the United States could contribute to slowly transforming China to behave more desirably in these areas. Have students research the current scope of American trade with China and how the situation is currently viewed. **L1**

EE4 Human Systems: Standard 11

More About the Photos

Ancient and Modern Modernization efforts by China's Communist government in both agriculture and industry have allowed China's economy to boom in recent years. The government's aim is to build a society with strict political control—tightly governing the media and all political activities—but relatively free economic opportunity.

Caption Answer It has moved from a command economy to more of a free enterprise system.

3 ASSESS

Assign Section 1 Assessment as homework or an in-class activity.

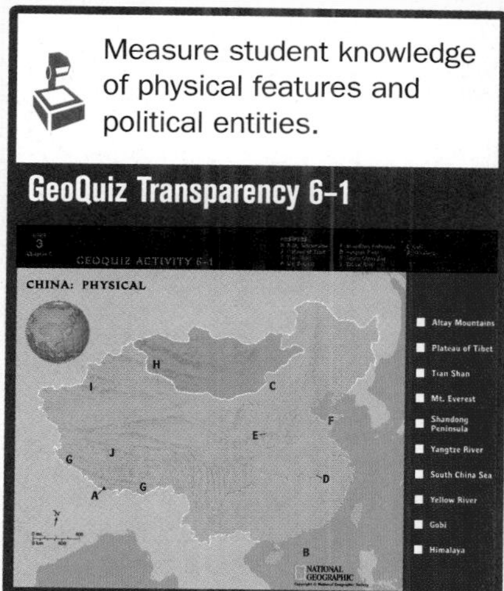

Measure student knowledge of physical features and political entities.

GeoQuiz Transparency 6-1

Section Quiz 6-1

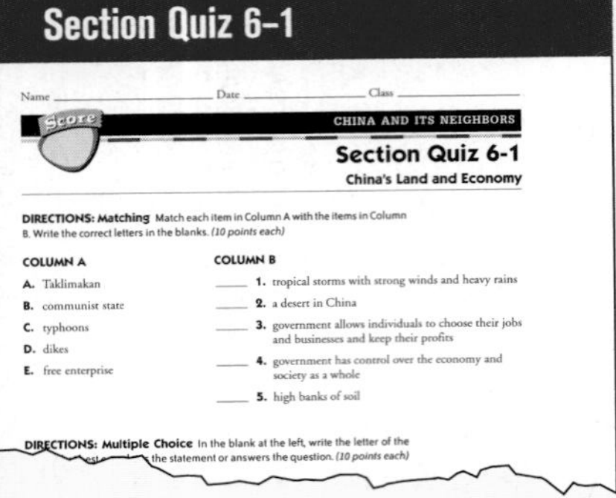
Name ______ Date ______ Class ______

Score — CHINA AND ITS NEIGHBORS

Section Quiz 6-1
China's Land and Economy

DIRECTIONS: Matching Match each item in Column A with the items in Column B. Write the correct letters in the blanks. *(10 points each)*

COLUMN A	COLUMN B
A. Taklimakan	____ 1. tropical storms with strong winds and heavy rains
B. communist state	____ 2. a desert in China
C. typhoons	____ 3. government allows individuals to choose their jobs and businesses and keep their profits
D. dikes	____ 4. government has control over the economy and society as a whole
E. free enterprise	____ 5. high banks of soil

DIRECTIONS: Multiple Choice In the blank at the left, write the letter of the ... the statement or answers the question. *(10 points each)*

✓ Reading Check Answer

China's promise to allow Western freedoms and capitalism to exist side-by-side with communism in Hong Kong and Macau

Reading Essentials and Study Guide 6-1

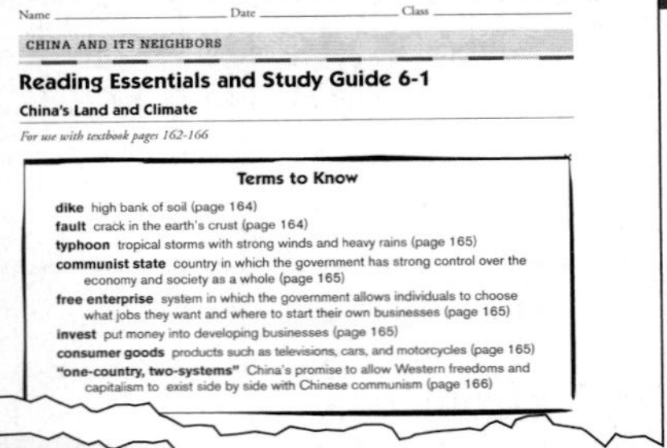
Name ______ Date ______ Class ______

CHINA AND ITS NEIGHBORS

Reading Essentials and Study Guide 6-1
China's Land and Climate

For use with textbook pages 162–166

Terms to Know

dike high bank of soil (page 164)
fault crack in the earth's crust (page 164)
typhoon tropical storms with strong winds and heavy rains (page 165)
communist state country in which the government has strong control over the economy and society as a whole (page 165)
free enterprise system in which the government allows individuals to choose what jobs they want and where to start their own businesses (page 165)
invest put money into developing businesses (page 165)
consumer goods products such as televisions, cars, and motorcycles (page 165)
"one-country, two-systems" China's promise to allow Western freedoms and capitalism to exist side by side with Chinese communism (page 166)

4 CLOSE

Have students summarize a paragraph from the section in a sentence. Collect the sentences, omit key words, and have students supply the missing words.

Not everyone has adjusted well to the new economy. Many Chinese find that prices have risen faster than their incomes. Some Chinese have become very rich, while others remain poor.

China's economic growth has also hurt the environment. Many factories dump poisonous chemicals into rivers. Others burn coal, which gives off smoke that pollutes the air. This pollution leads to lung disease, which causes one-fourth of all deaths in China.

Hong Kong and Macau The cities of **Hong Kong** and **Macau** (muh•KOW) are an important part of the economic changes taking place in China. Both cities were once controlled by a European country—Hong Kong by the United Kingdom, and Macau by Portugal. China regained control of Hong Kong in 1997 and of Macau in 1999. Both cities are centers of manufacturing, trade, and finance. Chinese leaders hope that the successful businesses in these cities will help spur economic growth in the rest of the country.

At the same time, foreign companies that are considering investing in these cities must ask themselves whether China will stand by its **"one-country, two-systems"** pledge. The pledge refers to China's promise to allow Western freedoms and capitalism to exist side by side with Chinese communism. The **Time Reports: Focus on World Issues** on pages 173–179 looks closely at how free enterprise may affect China's lack of freedom.

✓ Reading Check **To what does "one-country, two-systems" refer?**

Section 1 Assessment

Defining Terms

1. **Define** dike, fault, communist state, free enterprise system, invest, consumer goods, "one-country, two-systems."

Recalling Facts

2. **Place** What are China's two large deserts?
3. **Region** What two very important functions do China's rivers perform?
4. **Economics** What has caused China's economy to boom?

Critical Thinking

5. **Analyzing Information** How are China's rivers both a blessing and a disaster?
6. **Making Comparisons** How is a communist economic system different from a free enterprise system?
7. **Analyzing Information** What benefits does China receive from foreign investments?

Graphic Organizer

8. **Organizing Information** Create a diagram like this one. In the proper places on the oval, fill in the physical features you would encounter if you traveled completely around China.

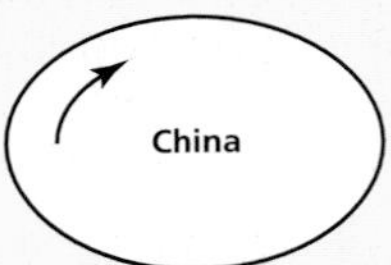

Applying Social Studies Skills

9. **Analyzing Maps** Look at the political map on page 135. What is the capital of China?

166

Section 1 Assessment

1. The terms are defined in the Glossary.
2. Taklimakan, Gobi
3. They carry fertile soil to land and provide transportation.
4. more free enterprise
5. They improve soil and provide transportation but flooding causes extreme damage.
6. communist system: government controls economy; free enterprise system: individuals run businesses.
7. Investment teaches new business methods and encourages growth.
8. NW: Altay Mnts; N: Gobi; NE: Manchurian Plain; E: North China Plain; S: Plateau of Tibet; W: Taklimakan Desert
9. Beijing

Making Connections

The Three Gorges Dam

Since 1919, Chinese officials have dreamed of building a dam across the Yangtze, the third-longest river in the world. Curving through the heart of China, the river provides an important highway for moving people and products from town to town. Yet the Yangtze is unpredictable. For thousands of years, floods have harmed the millions of people who live along its banks. Now construction is under way to build the dam.

The Dam

In 1994 the Chinese government began a 17-year-long project to build a massive dam. It will eventually be 1.5 miles (2.4 km) wide and more than 600 feet (183 m) high. The dam, called the Three Gorges Dam, is being built about halfway between Chongqing and Wuhan (see the map on page 170). The dam will benefit China in several ways. First, it will control water flow and stop floods. Second, its system of locks will allow large ships to travel inland. This will reduce trade and transportation costs for the millions of people who live inland. Third, the dam will create electricity using turbines—water-driven engines.

Controversy

Even with all the proposed benefits, many people within China and elsewhere have questioned the wisdom of building the dam. When completed, the dam will create a deep reservoir nearly 400 miles (644 km) long. This reservoir will flood more than 100 towns and force nearly 2 million people to move. Many of these people must leave the farms that their families have worked for centuries. Historians point out that the reservoir will also wash away more than 1,000 important historical sites, including the homeland of the first people to settle the region about 4,000 years ago.

Environmentalists caution that the dam may create pollution and health risks. Industrial sites, once they lie underwater, may leak hazardous chemicals. Sewage from communities surrounding the dam could flow directly into the reservoir and into the Yangtze River. In the past, this problem was less serious because the fast-moving waters of the Yangtze carried waste quickly out to sea.

Making the Connection

1. How have the unpredictable waters of the Yangtze River affected the Chinese?
2. Create a physical map of China showing the major rivers. Mark where the Three Gorges Dam is being built.
3. **Interpreting Points of View** List three reasons in support of constructing the Three Gorges Dam and three reasons against it.

◀ All but the very top of these towering gorges (left) will be deep underwater when the huge dam is completed (far left).

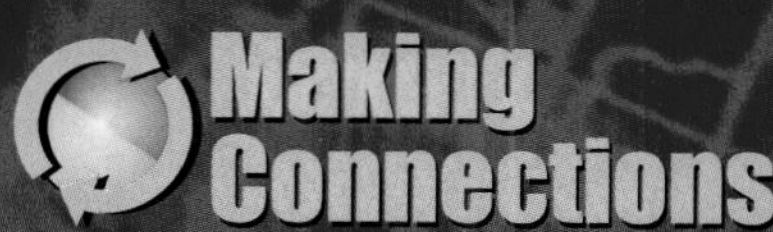

Teach

Inform students that it takes about four hours to drive from New York City to Boston. Explain that the reservoir created by the Three Gorges Dam will be about the same length as the distance between those two cities. L1

More About Three Gorges Dam

Problems such as cost overruns are plaguing the project, which may not meet its 2009 completion goal. Some experts believe that the dam will cost three times the original estimate.

Interdisciplinary Connections

Math Give students the following figures, which show the number of megawatts of electricity generated by the world's four largest dams:

Itaipu (Brazil and Paraguay)—12,600
Grand Coulee (U.S.)—10,100
Guri (Venezuela)—10,100
Tucuruii (Brazil)—7,500

Have students compare these figures to the 18,200 megawatts projected as the output of the Three Gorges Dam. They could express their comparisons as a bar graph.

Making the Connection

1. Flooding has caused massive death and destruction.
2. Students' maps should show the Yellow, Yangtze, and Xi Rivers, among others. Students should locate the Three Gorges Dam about halfway between the cities of Chongqing and Wuhan on the Yangtze River.
3. *For:* eliminate flooding, allow oceangoing vessels to gain access to the interior, and generate electricity; *Against:* displace nearly 2 million people, destroy historical sites, and cause pollution

1 FOCUS

Section Objectives

1. Explain how China's history influences life there today.
2. Contrast urban and rural China.
3. Summarize what arts China is known for.

BELLRINGER
Skillbuilder Activity

Project transparency and have students answer questions.

This activity is also available as a blackline master.

Daily Focus Skills Transparency 6-2

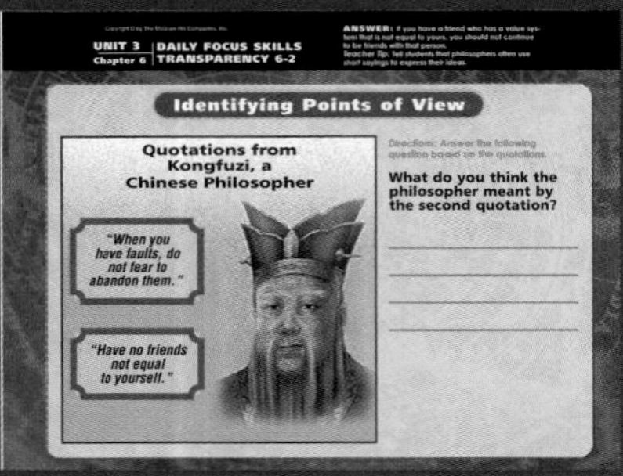

Guide to Reading

■ **Accessing Prior Knowledge**
Ask: **What do you think of when you hear the word *China*?** List responses and have students identify which are examples of Chinese culture.

■ **Vocabulary Precheck**
Ask students what they think *human rights* and *exile* mean. Then have them search the section to confirm their guesses.

Section 2 China's People and Culture

Guide to Reading

Main Idea

The arts and ideas of ancient times still influence China today.

Terms to Know

- dynasty
- human rights
- exile
- calligraphy
- pagoda

Reading Strategy

Create a chart like this one. Then list two key facts in the right column for each item in the left column.

China	
History	
Government	
Urban and Rural Life	
Arts	

NATIONAL GEOGRAPHIC Exploring Our World

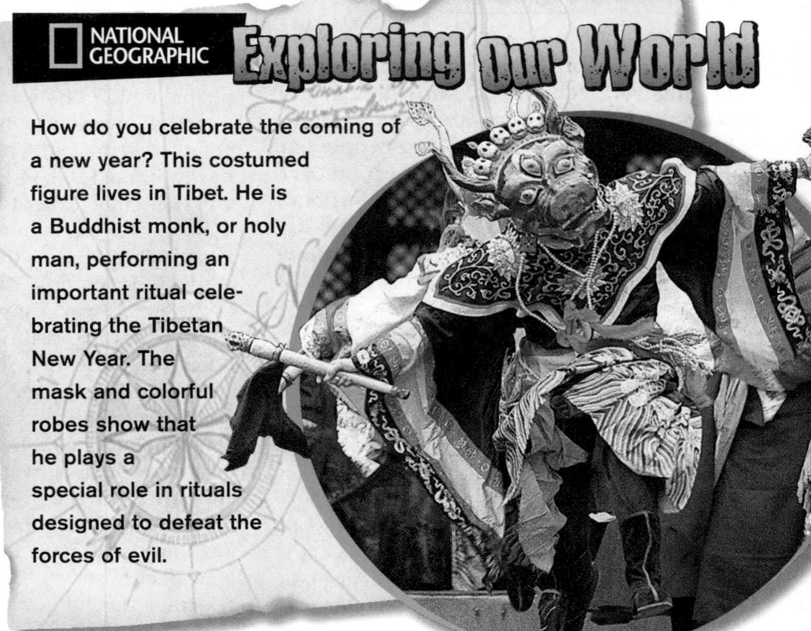

How do you celebrate the coming of a new year? This costumed figure lives in Tibet. He is a Buddhist monk, or holy man, performing an important ritual celebrating the Tibetan New Year. The mask and colorful robes show that he plays a special role in rituals designed to defeat the forces of evil.

China's population of 1.27 billion is about one-fifth of the world's people. About 92 percent of these people belong to the ethnic group called **Han Chinese.** They have a distinctive culture. The remaining 8 percent belong to 55 other ethnic groups. Most of these groups, such as the **Tibetans,** live in the western part of China. They have struggled to protect their traditions from Han Chinese influences.

China's History

China's civilization is more than 4,000 years old. For many centuries until the early 1900s, rulers known as emperors or empresses governed China. Many lived in the Imperial Palace, located in the heart of Beijing. A **dynasty,** or line of rulers from a single family, would hold power until it was overthrown. Then a new leader would start a new dynasty. Under the dynasties, China built a highly developed culture and conquered neighboring lands.

Section Resources

Reproducible Masters

- Reproducible Lesson Plan 6-2
- Daily Lecture and Discussion Notes 6-2
- Guided Reading Activity 6-2
- Reading Essentials and Study Guide 6-2
- Section Quiz 6-2

Transparencies

- Daily Focus Skills Transparency 6-2

Multimedia

- Vocabulary PuzzleMaker Software
- Interactive Tutor Self-Assessment CD-ROM
- Presentation Plus! CD-ROM
- ExamView® Pro 3.0 Testmaker CD-ROM

As their civilization developed, the Chinese tried to keep out foreign invaders. In many ways, this was easy. On most of China's borders, natural barriers such as seas, mountains, and deserts already provided protection. Still, invaders threatened from the north. To defend this area, the Chinese began building the **Great Wall of China** about 2,200 years ago. Over the centuries, the wall was continually rebuilt and lengthened. In time, it snaked more than 4,000 miles (6,437 km) from the Yellow Sea in the east to the deserts of the west. It still stands today.

Culture Chinese thinkers believed that learning was a key to good behavior. About 500 B.C., a thinker named **Kongfuzi** (KOONG•FOO•DZUH), or Confucius, taught that people should be polite, honest, brave, and wise. Children were to obey their parents, and every person was to respect the elderly and obey the country's rulers. Kongfuzi's teachings shaped China's government and society until the early 1900s.

During Kongfuzi's time, another thinker named **Laozi** (LOW•DZUH) arose. His teachings, called **Daoism** (DAHW•ehzm), stated that people should live simply and in harmony with nature. While Kongfuzi's ideas appealed to government leaders, Laozi's beliefs attracted artists and writers.

Buddhism came to China from South Asia about A.D. 100. This religion taught that prayer, right thoughts, and good deeds could help people find relief from life's problems. Over time, the Chinese mixed Buddhism, Daoism, and the ideas of Kongfuzi. This mixed spiritual heritage still influences many Chinese people today.

The early Chinese were inventors as well as thinkers. Did you know that they were using paper and ink before people in other parts of the world? Other Chinese inventions included silk, the clock, the magnetic compass, printed books, gunpowder, and fireworks. For hundreds of years, China was the most advanced civilization in the world.

Communist China Foreign influences increasingly entered China during the 1700s and 1800s. Europeans especially wanted to get such fine Chinese goods as silk, tea, and pottery. The United Kingdom and other countries used military power to force China to trade.

In 1911 a Chinese uprising under the Western-educated **Dr. Sun Yat-sen** overthrew the last emperor. China became a republic, or a country governed by elected leaders. Disorder followed until the Nationalist political party took over. The Communist Party gained power as well. After World War II, the Nationalists and the Communists fought for control of China. **General Chiang Kai-shek** (jee•AHNG KY•SHEHK) led the Nationalists. **Mao Zedong** (MOW DZUH• DOONG) led the Communists.

In 1949 the Communists won and set up the People's Republic of China under Mao Zedong and **Zhou Enlai** (JOH ehn•LY). The Nationalists fled to the offshore island of Taiwan. There they set up a rival government.

✓Reading Check **Why was the Great Wall of China built?**

Labor Costs

There's a good chance your clothes and shoes were manufactured in China. Some American companies can manufacture their products at much lower costs in China because the wages paid to workers there are low by U.S. standards. These companies pay more and offer better working conditions than Chinese employers. Still, human rights activists are concerned about exploiting workers to make higher profits for U.S. companies.

Chapter 6

Section 2, pages 168–172

TEACH

Analyzing Information

Make a circle and shade in one-fourth of the circle's area. **Ask: What fact about China's population does this signify?** *(China has about one-fourth of the world's people.)* Then make a time line with marks for every 500 years up to 4,000. Make one bar stretching 200–250 years and another that stretches the entire 4,000. **Ask: What do these two bars compare?** *(the age of the United States and the age of civilization in China)* L1

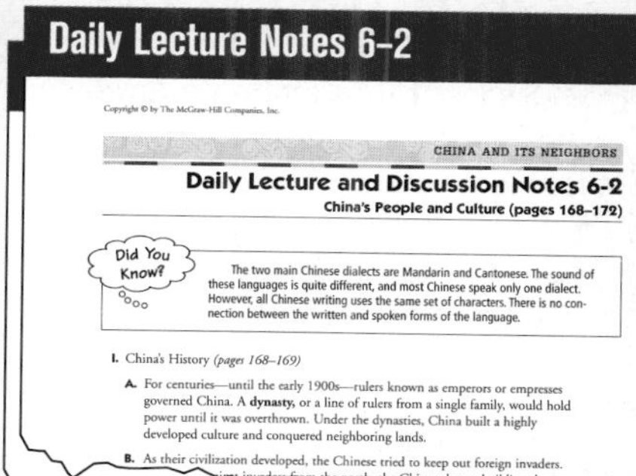

Daily Lecture Notes 6–2

CHINA AND ITS NEIGHBORS

Daily Lecture and Discussion Notes 6-2

China's People and Culture (pages 168–172)

Did You Know? The two main Chinese dialects are Mandarin and Cantonese. The sound of these languages is quite different, and most Chinese speak only one dialect. However, all Chinese writing uses the same set of characters. There is no connection between the written and spoken forms of the language.

I. China's History *(pages 168–169)*

A. For centuries—until the early 1900s—rulers known as emperors or empresses governed China. A **dynasty**, or a line of rulers from a single family, would hold power until it was overthrown. Under the dynasties, China built a highly developed culture and conquered neighboring lands.

B. As their civilization developed, the Chinese tried to keep out foreign invaders. ... from the north, the Chinese began building the ... years ago. It still stands today.

✓ Reading Check Answer

to defend China from invaders coming from the north

Team-Teaching Activity

Literature Invite a literature teacher to class or have students read excerpts from Chinese poems, such as this example from Ma Zhiyuan: "Heaven has made you rich,/ But why do you indulge in luxury!/ Good days and pleasant nights do not last long./ You, slaves of wealth, how your hearts are like iron/ To have vainly squandered the wind-and-moon in an embroidered hall." Have a class discussion about how these poems exemplify the values of Kongfuzi or Laozi. L1

EE4 Human Systems: Standard 10

Chapter 6

Section 2, pages 168–172

Current Events Journal

Show a photo of the Chinese students who protested in Tiananmen Square in 1989 and have students write what freedoms they would have asked for if they had lived in China at that time. Ask students to compare the role of citizens in China with the role of citizens in the United States.

Note-taking tip

Suggest that students divide their notebooks into three columns labeled "Ancient History," "Recent Times," and "China Today." Then have them categorize their notes in the correct period.

Applying Map Skills

Answers

1. Harbin, Shenyang, Beijing, Tianjin, Shanghai, Hangzhou, Hong Kong
2. Over 250 persons per square mile (over 100 per sq. km)

Skills Practice

What is the population density of most of Mongolia? *(under 2 persons per square mile, or under 1 per sq. km)*

China's Government and Society

After 1949 the Communists completely changed the mainland of China. All land and factories were taken over by the government. Farmers were organized onto large government farms, and women joined the industrial workforce. Dams and improved agricultural methods brought some economic benefits. Yet many government plans went wrong, and individual freedoms were lost. Many people were killed because they opposed communism.

After Mao Zedong died in 1976, a new Communist leader, **Deng Xiaoping** (DUHNG SHOW•PIHNG), decided to take a new direction. He wanted to make China a more open country. One way to do this was to give people more economic freedom. The government kept tight control over all political activities, however. It continued to deny individual freedoms and acted harshly against any Chinese who criticized its actions. In 1989 thousands of students gathered in Beijing's **Tiananmen** (TEE•EHN•AHN•MEHN) **Square.** The students called for more democracy in China. The government answered by sending in tanks and troops. These forces killed thousands of protesters and arrested many more.

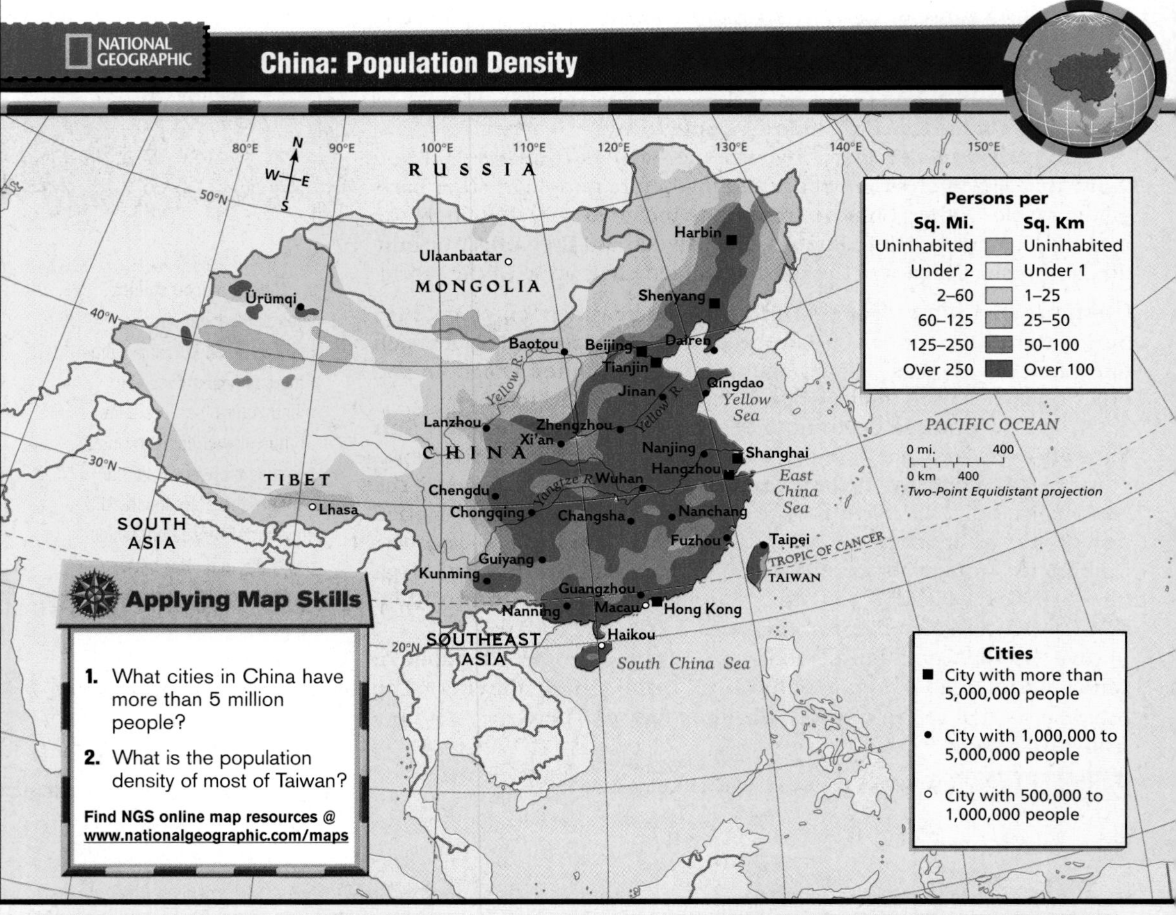

Meeting Special Needs

Visual/Spatial Have students prepare a bulletin board display that presents and explains the individual and group achievements of ancient China. Students can portray such activities as making silk; creating bronzes; inventing gunpowder, paper, ink, printing, and paper money; and so on. Their displays should include illustrations of each achievement and brief captions describing the significance of each. **L1 ELL**

Refer to *Inclusion for the Middle School Social Studies Classroom Strategies and Activities* in the TCR.

Countries around the world have protested the Chinese government's continued harsh treatment of people who criticize it. They say that Chinese leaders have no respect for **human rights**—the basic freedoms and rights, such as freedom of speech, that all people should enjoy. Because of China's actions, some people say that other countries should not trade with China.

China's leaders have also been criticized for their actions in Tibet. Tibet was once a separate Buddhist kingdom. China took control of the area in 1950 and crushed a rebellion there about nine years later. The Tibetan people have demanded independence since then. The **Dalai Lama** (DAH•ly LAH•muh), the Buddhist leader of Tibet, now lives in exile in India and the United States. Someone in **exile** is unable to live in his or her own country because of political beliefs. The Dalai Lama travels around the world trying to win support for his people.

NATIONAL GEOGRAPHIC **On Location**

Urban Life

Hundreds of thousands of people use bicycles—not cars—to get around Beijing and other cities.

Place **About how many people live in China's cities?**

Rural Life About 70 percent of China's people live in rural areas. The map on page 170 shows that most Chinese are crowded into the fertile river valleys of eastern China. Families work hard in their fields. They often use hand tools because mechanical equipment is too expensive.

Village life has improved in recent years. Most rural families now live in three- or four-room houses. They have enough food and some modern appliances. Many villages have community centers. People gather there to watch movies and play table tennis and basketball.

Urban Life More than 360 million Chinese people live in cities. China's cities are growing rapidly as people leave farms in hope of finding better-paying jobs. Living conditions in the cities are crowded, but most homes and apartments have heat, electricity, and running water. Many people now earn enough money to buy extra clothes and televisions. They also have more leisure time to attend concerts or Chinese operas, walk in parks, or visit zoos.

✓ Reading Check **Why have people in other countries criticized China's government?**

China's Culture

China is famous for its traditional arts. Chinese craft workers make bronze bowls, jade jewelry, decorated silk, glazed pottery, and fine porcelain. The Chinese are also known for their painting, sculpture, and architecture.

Chapter 6

Section 2, pages 168–172

More About the Photos

Beijing Beijing has not always been the capital of China, but it has served in that role almost continuously since the 1200s. The northern section contains the Imperial City, the ancient capital. At the heart of this area is the famous Forbidden City, where the imperial family lived.

Caption Answer more than 360 million people

Guided Reading Activity 6-2

Name ___ Date ___ Class ___

CHINA AND ITS NEIGHBORS

Guided Reading Activity 6-2

China's People and Culture

DIRECTIONS: Filling in the Blanks Reading the section and completing the sentences below will help you learn more about China's people and culture. Refer to your textbook to fill in the blanks.

China's population makes up about (1) ___ of all of the people in the world. Most belong to the ethnic group called (2) ___. As China's civilization developed, they wanted to keep out (3) ___. To defend the northern area, they built the (4) ___.

A Chinese thinker named (5) ___ said people should be ___ (7) ___ and wise. Another

3 ASSESS

Assign Section 2 Assessment as homework or an in-class activity.

Have students use the Interactive Tutor Self-Assessment CD-ROM to review Section 6–2.

✓ Reading Check Answer

because of Chinese leaders' harsh treatment of people who criticize them and for their treatment of Tibet

Critical Thinking Activity

Synthesizing Information Give students the following sayings of Kongfuzi: (1) Have no friends not equal to yourself. (2) When you have faults, do not fear to abandon them. (3) Learning without thought is labor lost; thought without learning is perilous. (4) The cautious seldom err. Have students discuss the sayings and, after a specified time, reach a consensus about what the sayings mean. Ask students to present their interpretations of the sayings in poster form. **L1**

EE4 Human Systems: Standard 10

Section Quiz 6-2

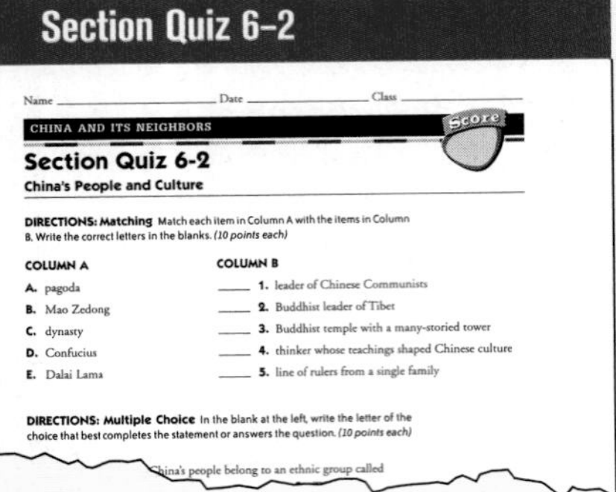
Name ______ Date ______ Class ______

CHINA AND ITS NEIGHBORS

Section Quiz 6-2

China's People and Culture

DIRECTIONS: Matching Match each item in Column A with the items in Column B. Write the correct letters in the blanks. *(10 points each)*

COLUMN A	COLUMN B
A. pagoda	____ 1. leader of Chinese Communists
B. Mao Zedong	____ 2. Buddhist leader of Tibet
C. dynasty	____ 3. Buddhist temple with a many-storied tower
D. Confucius	____ 4. thinker whose teachings shaped Chinese culture
E. Dalai Lama	____ 5. line of rulers from a single family

DIRECTIONS: Multiple Choice In the blank at the left, write the letter of the choice that best completes the statement or answers the question. *(10 points each)*

China's people belong to an ethnic group called

Reteach

List the key people discussed in this section. Then have students identify each and explain their significance in history and their influence today.

Reading Check Answer

because the written language has more than 50,000 characters

Reading Essentials and Study Guide 6–2

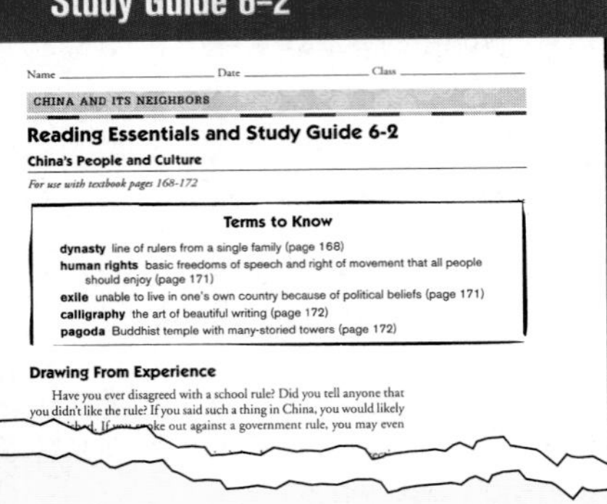
Name ______ Date ______ Class ______

CHINA AND ITS NEIGHBORS

Reading Essentials and Study Guide 6-2

China's People and Culture

For use with textbook pages 168-172

Terms to Know

dynasty line of rulers from a single family (page 168)
human rights basic freedoms of speech and right of movement that all people should enjoy (page 171)
exile unable to live in one's own country because of political beliefs (page 171)
calligraphy the art of beautiful writing (page 172)
pagoda Buddhist temple with many-storied towers (page 172)

Drawing From Experience

Have you ever disagreed with a school rule? Did you tell anyone that you didn't like the rule? If you said such a thing in China, you would likely ... If you spoke out against a government rule, you may even

4 Close

Have students create a travelogue that describes the sights and sounds they would experience in a trip through China.

The Chinese love of nature has influenced painting and poetry. Chinese artists paint on long panels of paper or silk. Artwork often shows scenes of mountains, rivers, and forests. Artists attempt to portray the harmony between people and nature.

Many Chinese paintings include a poem written in **calligraphy,** the art of beautiful writing. Chinese writing is different from the print you are reading right now. It uses characters that represent words or ideas instead of letters that represent sounds. There are more than 50,000 Chinese characters, but the average person recognizes only about 8,000. It takes many years to learn to write Chinese.

The Chinese developed the first porcelain centuries ago. Porcelain is made from coal dust and fine, white clay. Painted porcelain vases from early China are considered priceless today.

Most buildings in China's cities are modern. Yet traditional buildings still stand. Some have large, tiled roofs with edges that curve gracefully upward. Others are Buddhist temples with many-storied towers called **pagodas.** These buildings hold large statues of the Buddha.

Foods Cooking differs greatly from region to region. In coastal areas, people enjoy fish, crab, and shrimp dishes. Central China is famous for its spicy dishes made with hot peppers. Most Chinese eat very simply. A typical Chinese meal includes vegetables with bits of meat or seafood, soup, and rice or noodles. Often the meat and vegetables are cooked quickly in a small amount of oil over very high heat. This method—called stir-frying—allows the vegetables to stay crunchy.

✓ Reading Check **Why does it take many years to learn to read and write Chinese?**

Assessment

Defining Terms

1. Define dynasty, human rights, exile, calligraphy, pagoda.

Recalling Facts

2. History Who are two thinkers who influenced life in China?

3. History Who led the Nationalists after World War II? Who led the Communists after World War II? Who won control of China?

4. Culture What scenes are commonly found in Chinese paintings?

Critical Thinking

5. Making Predictions How might the teachings of Kongfuzi prevent rebellions in China?

6. Summarizing Information Why did Europeans want to force China to trade with them?

Graphic Organizer

7. Organizing Information Create a time line like this one. Then list at least five dates and their events in China's history.

Applying Social Studies Skills

8. Analyzing Maps Look at the population density map on page 170. How does the population density in western China differ from that in eastern China?

Section 2 Assessment

1. The terms are defined in the Glossary.
2. Kongfuzi and Laozi
3. Nationalists: Chiang Kai-shek; Communists: Mao Zedong; the Communists
4. scenes of nature, such as landscapes of mountains, rivers, and forests
5. He taught that people should obey the country's rulers.
6. They wanted fine Chinese goods such as silk, tea, and pottery.
7. Answers will vary.
8. Population density in eastern China is far greater—up to 125 times greater—than in the west.

TIME REPORTS

FOCUS ON WORLD ISSUES

Will Good Times Set China Free?

Shanghai Building Boom

NETWORK

Focus on World Issues

Teacher Background

For many centuries, China was the dominant civilization of East Asia. It influenced many other East Asian countries in culture, education, government, and the arts. The Chinese also invented gunpowder, porcelain, and printing.

While China is slightly smaller than the United States, it has nearly 1.3 billion people, over four times as many people. Population density has been an important factor in China's political history.

TIME REPORTS UNIT 3

Will Good Times Set China Free?

THEME: CAPITALISM AND DEMOCRACY

Guide To Teaching With This Unit

Using the Reproducibles

Preparing the Student

During the first half of the twentieth century, China experienced a great deal of unrest. In 1949, Mao Zedong established a Communist dictatorship. When the Communists took over mainland China, several million Nationalists fled to the island of Taiwan where they established a government.

In 1978, China began making market-economy reforms, and production skyrocketed. Today's government tightly controls the political environment while economic control is comparatively weak.

Making Connections

Totalitarianism **Ask students:** **Have you ever felt your freedom was unfairly restricted by the United States government? Name some of the ways that the U.S. government restricts our freedom.**

Discuss that in China, people's rights are restricted much more severely. There is only one political party and speaking out against it can be risky. While the United States is a nation of laws, China is a nation of totalitarian rulers who can do pretty much as they wish. Ask students to compare and contrast the limits and functions of the Chinese and U.S. governments. They should identify reasons for limiting the power of government.

TIME REPORTS

1 Focus

Have students respond to the following: **What do you think it would be like to live in a country where there was only one political party? What are the advantages and disadvantages?**

Write students' responses. Place the advantages in one column and the disadvantages in a second column.

Did You Know?

Qi Gong is the name of techniques used for spiritual and physical well-being. The Chinese government tolerates groups that emphasize the physical aspects of this tradition. However, some groups place greater emphasis on the spiritual aspects. The largest is Falun Gong. These religious groups are outlawed by the government.

Comparing and Contrasting

ANSWER
$929 billion

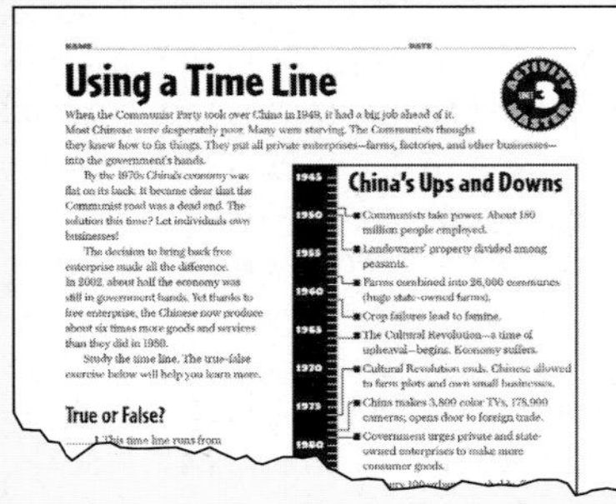

TIME REPORTS

FOCUS ON WORLD ISSUES

One protester stopped the tanks of the world's biggest army outside Tiananmen Square in 1989.

No Easy Choices

Lloyd Zhao was a wanted man in 2001. He lived in Beijing, China's capital, where he spent hours every day on the Internet. His goal: to keep his religion alive.

The religion, Falun Gong, was barely 10 years old. Some call it a **cult**—a phony religion. Whatever it is, China's Communist leaders fear it. Any large group threatens their hold on power, and Falun Gong was very big. It had several million followers in 2000.

The government outlawed Falun Gong in 1999. It put as many as 6,000 of its followers in jail. But the Internet prevented the government from putting Falun Gong completely out of business. Its followers used it to stay in touch with each other and with their leaders.

Their effort to outwit the government is a reminder that China is a **police state**, a country whose leaders often crush their opponents.

Because of the Internet, fresh ideas are circulating in China. The government can't control those ideas. It may even stop trying, now that it is preparing to host the 2008 Olympics. Whatever it does, it can't alter the fact that ideas from around the world are changing China forever.

A Closed Society

As recently as the 1970s, China's Communist government banned almost all communication with other countries. It told the Chinese what they could read. It told them where they could live and work. It decided what factories could make and what farms could produce.

It could do this because the government owned all enterprises—factories, farms, stores, and railroads, among other things. And it had the world's largest army to back it up.

During the late 1970s, it became clear that this arrangement wasn't working. China's farms couldn't feed the nation. Its factories produced goods few people wanted.

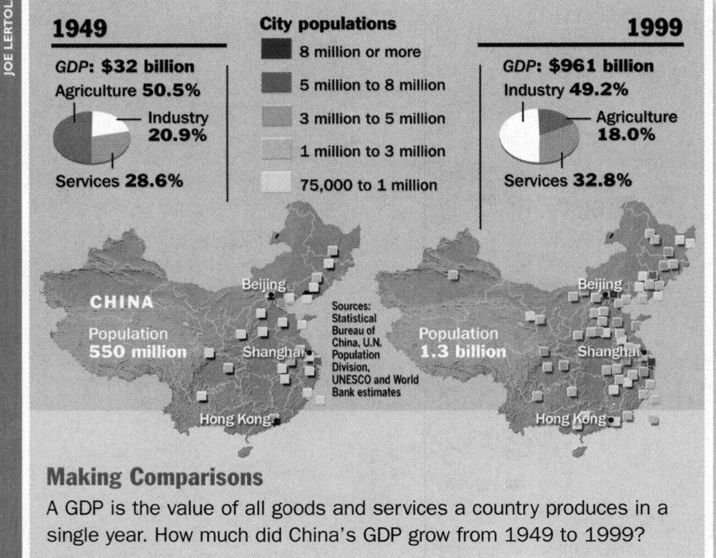

Making Comparisons

A GDP is the value of all goods and services a country produces in a single year. How much did China's GDP grow from 1949 to 1999?

174

Team-Teaching Activity

Communications Ask students why a totalitarian government like China's would want to limit the use of communication technology such as the Internet and satellite television. Have a teacher with knowledge in the subject speak to the class about the reasons totalitarian governments attempt to control access to the Internet and outside broadcasts or publications. The teacher should explain the policies China uses to prevent exposure to these technologies and whether the government has been successful. Ask students if they can think of other countries besides China that might attempt to control the media and why they would want to do so. Discuss the "unwanted" cultural traits that teenagers in these countries might pick up from the Internet or satellite TV. **L2**

 **EE4 Human Systems: Standard 10**

Job-seekers line up in Beijing.

HIROJI KUBOTA—MAGNUM

Farmers vote for village leaders.

JAIME FLORACRUZ/TIMEPIX

Britain gave Hong Kong back to China in 1997.

JEFFREY AARONSON/NETWORK ASPEN

So in 1978 China's government took a big step. It let individuals own their own businesses. It let farmers till their own plots. And it let them keep the money they earned.

Free enterprise worked wonders. China's economy blossomed. Wages went up. Families were able to buy refrigerators, TV sets, computers, and sometimes even automobiles. To bring modern know-how to China, the government let citizens study abroad, hook up to cable TV, and surf the Internet.

New Problems

But with the good news came problems. Better-organized factories and farms needed fewer workers, and millions lost their jobs. Crime increased, and so did shady dealings by government officials. Water and air pollution, already bad, got worse.

The Chinese don't need or want outsiders to help them solve those problems. What they do want is the technology that makes modern economies run. China must buy that machinery from more industrialized nations.

NG HAN GUAN/ASSOCIATED PRESS—AP

In July 2001 the Chinese celebrated when they learned they would host the 2008 Olympics.

China pays for those imports with exports—items that carry a "Made in China" label. That trade has connected China's economy to those of nations everywhere.

Globalization has brought China out of its shell. The Internet and the daring of people like Zhao have linked the Chinese to each other and to new ideas. China "watchers" wonder if these changes will bring democracy to China.

EXPLORING THE ISSUE

1. **Making Inferences** Why might China's leaders see the Internet as a threat to their power?
2. **Cause and Effect** China's government let people own farms and businesses and keep the money they earn. How did this decision help make China's economy grow?

2 TEACH

Identifying Main Ideas

As students finish reading each subsection, ask them for one-sentence summaries of that subsection. Write the suggested sentences.

More About the Photos

Voting Have students look at the photograph of farmers voting. **Ask:** **How do you think these farmers learned about the candidates? Do you think the farmers were well-informed?**

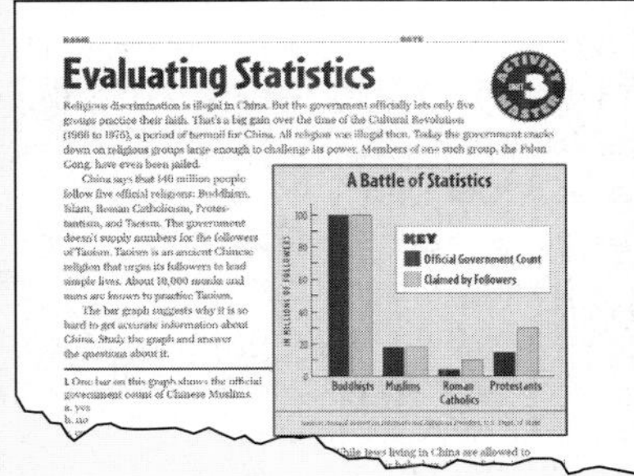

NAME .... DATE ....

Evaluating Statistics

ACTIVITY MASTER 3

Religious discrimination is illegal in China. But the government officially lets only five groups practice their faith. That's a big gain over the time of the Cultural Revolution (1966 to 1976), a period of turmoil for China. All religion was illegal then. Today the government cracks down on religious groups large enough to challenge its power. Members of one such group, the Falun Gong, have even been jailed.

China says that 140 million people follow five official religions: Buddhism, Islam, Roman Catholicism, Protestantism, and Taoism. The government doesn't supply numbers for the followers of Taoism. Taoism is an ancient Chinese religion that urges its followers to lead simple lives. About 10,000 monks and nuns are known to practice Taoism.

The bar graph suggests why it is so hard to get accurate information about China. Study the graph and answer the questions about it.

1. One bar on this graph shows the official government count of Chinese Muslims.
a. yes
b. no

While Jews living in China are allowed to

EXPLORING THE ISSUE

ANSWERS

1. Chinese people can see how people in other countries live; learn about democratic principles and freedom of choice; and discover that people in democracies live more affluent lives.
2. People were able to buy consumer goods and start new businesses.

Meeting Special Needs

Logical/Mathematical Instruct students to go to a store that offers a wide variety of consumer goods. They should take a list of five categories of goods, which might include toys, various electronics, footwear, kitchen items, clothing, and school supplies. Students should look at 6 to 10 items in each category and keep track of the number that are made in China and the number that are made in other countries. They should use the results to create a bar chart and answer the following questions: **What kind of items are made in China, and how does this compare to items made in other countries?**

Refer to *Inclusion for the Middle School Social Studies Classroom Strategies and Activities* in the TCR.

TIME REPORTS

Recommended Internet Sites

www.hrichina.org
Founded by Chinese scholars and scientists to monitor the implementation of human rights in China and report abuses.

fyi.cnn.com/2001/fyi/
Contains a lesson plan built around a CNN discussion of Falun Gong and the Chinese government's crackdown on it.

www.askasia.org/
Contains a number of lesson plans and exercises dealing with Asia in general and China in particular.

www.nytimes.com/learning/teachers/lessons/
In the archives, there are lesson plans about China, including human rights issues.

EXPLORING THE ISSUE

ANSWERS

1. Lei is freer than her parents; however, because of her economic freedom, she may feel she has less security than her parents did.
2. The government does not want any dissent, discussion of opposing ideas, or loss of power.

TIME REPORTS

Limited Freedoms

Young Chinese today enjoy freedoms that their parents could only dream of. They can't criticize government leaders in print, but they can discuss just about anything else. Young people also have the luxury of working, living, and traveling wherever they want.

DAVID J. COULSON—AP

Concerts by rocker Cui Jian were once banned.

Such freedoms please people like Lei Xia. Lei, 22, is a guide on a tourist boat that sails up and down China's longest river, the Yangtze. Not long ago she and a friend decided to quit their jobs. They plan to go to Beijing to look for work. "Compared with my parents' generation," Lei said, "maybe I am lucky. I can choose for myself."

Crushing Dissent

One thing Lei can't choose is China's leaders. The Communist Party officials who run the government will do anything to hold onto power.

They made that clear in 1989. During the spring, students protesting China's lack of democracy camped out on Beijing's main plaza, Tiananmen Square. Ordered to clear them out, soldiers killed at least 300 people. This human rights abuse shocked the world.

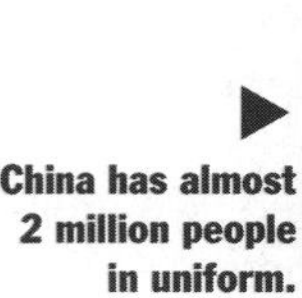

China has almost 2 million people in uniform.

The government continues to crush **dissent**, or opposition. In 1999 it sentenced leaders of a new political party to eight years in jail. Their crime: calling for an end to **one-party rule**. In 2001 the government shut down thousands of cybercafes. **Cybercafes** let people sip tea and surf the Web for as little as 20 cents an hour. Those shut down had let customers tap into anti-government websites.

Baton of Democracy

In June 2001, 20,000 people gathered in a park in Hong Kong, an island city in southeast China. They lighted candles in honor of the people killed in Tiananmen Square. A banner hanging over their heads read, "Pass on the baton of democracy." That's exactly what Chinese leaders don't want their citizens to do.

EXPLORING THE ISSUE

1. **Analyzing** Lei says "Maybe I am lucky" instead of simply "I am lucky." Why might she be unsure?
2. **Explaining** Why do you think China's leaders oppose a two-party system?

176

Critical Thinking Activity

Drawing Conclusions The Chinese people saw the collapse of the Soviet Union and other eastern European countries and the political upheaval and economic hardships that have befallen that entire region. In addition, they have seen extensive fighting in eastern Europe. All of these governments were previously communist. **Ask: Do you think seeing the collapse of the Communist governments of eastern Europe made the Chinese people more or less likely to fight for democracy? Why?** L2

EE4 Human Systems: Standard 13

The Road to Democracy

People who are free to run their own businesses usually want to choose their own governments. That's what happened in Taiwan, China's island province. Since 1949, Taiwan—a haven for anti-Communists—has gone its own way. It is now a free society with free elections.

But one party ruled it with an iron fist for nearly 40 years. Taiwan's 22 million people became better educated during that time. Taiwan became a showcase for free enterprise. Yet it wasn't until 1986, after those gains were made, that Taiwan's government let new political parties form. In 2000, the Taiwanese elected a member of one of the new parties as their president.

China could follow the same path, experts say. If it does, it could become a full democracy in 40 or 50 years.

Grassroots Democracy

Taiwan prepared its people for democracy slowly. The Taiwanese began electing village, county, and city governments in 1950.

China may be building democracy from the ground up, too. About 900 million farmers live in the nation's 928,000 villages. People in most of those villages have elected their leaders since the 1980s. "Now we have better management," says Li Dongju, whose husband heads a village committee in Hebei Province. "That's because our leaders enjoy the approval of the people."

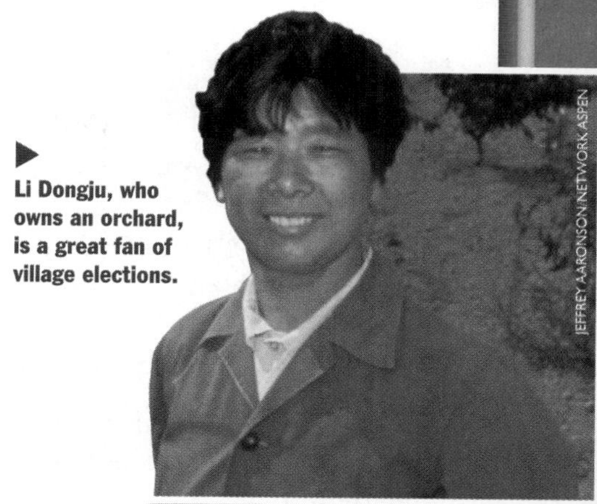

▶ **Li Dongju, who owns an orchard, is a great fan of village elections.**

JEFFREY AARONSON/NETWORK ASPEN

Li and her fellow villagers are learning what it means to be ruled by laws. Laws govern village elections. Laws tell village leaders what they can and can't do. And if the leaders break those laws, another law explains how they can be removed from office.

No laws rule China at the national level, however. Officials in Beijing are free to do just about anything they want. Sometimes visitors to China are arrested as foreign spies or agents. But the Internet and China's new economy are changing everything. "People are thinking rather than blindly following directions," says a Beijing businessman.

Free enterprise has led to democracies in Taiwan, South Korea, and Thailand. It can happen in China too.

EXPLORING THE ISSUE

1. **Evaluating Information** How can you tell that the United States is a nation ruled by law?
2. **Analyzing Information** How might mainland China's size make it hard to create a democracy there?

177

Synthesizing Information

Some people believe that the United States should not have free trade with China as long as the government is committing human rights abuses against its citizens. Instruct students to research and report on the types of human rights abuses commonly committed in China and the ways in which the United States might respond to these abuses. They should include how China's hosting the 2008 Olympics might affect its human rights policies.

EXPLORING THE ISSUE

ANSWERS

1. The U.S. Constitution specifies individual rights and government controls and creates a court system.
2. *Possible answers:* problems controlling outlying rural areas; poor communications and transportation systems make it difficult for people to be well-informed

Making Comparisons

The June 4, 1989, Tiananmen Square massacre was a major turning-point in the relationship between the Chinese government and its citizens. Have students research this event and give a brief report to the class. Discuss. how Tiananmen compares to student demonstrations in the United States.

Interdisciplinary Activity

Language Arts Some people think a major drawback to the spread of democracy in China is the large number of different dialects found in the country. Have students research these dialects and write a paper briefly discussing the most common dialects, along with the percentage of people that speak each one. The paper should also discuss the difficulties multiple dialects cause and the steps that have been taken to overcome these difficulties. **L2**

EE4 Human Systems: Standard 10

Current Events Journal

Have students read two or more recent articles about human rights abuses in China. Based on ideas discussed in the section titled "Promoting Democracy: What Can One Person Do?" have students write about the actions they personally might take in response to these abuses.

EXPLORING THE ISSUE

ANSWERS

1. *Possible answer:* Human rights are of international concern because tyranny in one country can spread to others.
2. It draws the world's attention to the government's behavior. It can force democracies to react, for example, by imposing sanctions.

Have students take the Time Reports Quiz or do the Alternative Assessment project for this unit provided in the Teacher's Classroom Resources.

Promoting Democracy: What Can One Person Do?

About 2.1 billion people throughout the world are unable to choose their own governments. Slightly more than half of them live in China.

What can the United States do to urge China's leaders to pass some of their power to ordinary citizens? Confronting China's leaders directly hasn't worked.

What might work, some experts say, is an indirect approach. For example, the U.S. could encourage Asian governments to raise the issue of human rights on their own. Or it could get China to sit down and discuss common problems—like disease control. Human rights might then be slipped into these discussions. That way, China's leaders might be less likely to feel they were being singled out.

Taking Action

You can help promote respect for human rights in China and other countries. For example, you could find out what your representatives in Congress are doing about the issue. Then you could write them, either supporting or disagreeing with their stands.

Since 1961, a group called Amnesty International (AI) has fought to make governments respect their citizens' rights. Its most successful weapon has been the letter-writing campaign. To learn how such campaigns work, go to AI's Web page **www.amnestyusa.org** and click "Act!" on the top row.

GREG GIRARD—CONTACT

Internet portals like sohu.com bring new ideas to China.

"What you do may seem terribly insignificant," Mohandas Gandhi said, "but it is terribly important that you do it anyway." Gandhi knew what he was talking about. He led the campaign that won India its independence in 1947. ■

EXPLORING THE ISSUE

1. **Evaluating** China's leaders say that no one outside China has the right to comment on the way they treat their citizens. Why do you agree or disagree?
2. **Cause and Effect** How might letter-writing campaigns make governments think twice about jailing opponents?

Your Government and You

Secretary of State Collin Powell has said, "China and the United States have very, very important common interests." He has stated that these include economic and trade interests. However, our government is very concerned about the lack of human rights in China. The U.S. State Department has a site that discusses the relationship between China and the U.S. (**www.usembassy-china.org.cn/english/politicsindex.html**). This site contains useful information on many topics, including economic relationships and human rights issues. Have students choose a speech or report on the site and summarize it. **L3**

REVIEW AND ASSESS

UNDERSTANDING THE ISSUE

1. **Defining Key Terms** Write definitions for the following terms: *cybercafe, cult, police state, free enterprise, globalization, dissent, one-party rule.*
2. **Writing to Inform** In a brief essay, explain how village elections could prepare China's farmers for democracy. Use the terms *free elections, approval by the people,* and *rule of law.*
3. **Writing to Persuade** To get the Chinese to accept free enterprise, one of their leaders once said, "To get rich is glorious." Do you agree with this statement? Write a brief essay to explain your answer.

INTERNET RESEARCH ACTIVITY

4. Explore the website of China's embassy in Washington, D.C.: **www.china-embassy.org/eng**. Browse the site until you find a topic that interests you. Write a brief report explaining what that topic teaches you about modern-day China.
5. Use the Web to research a specific episode in the history of Chinese immigration to the United States. You might start with the story of the "Chinese Ellis Island" at **www.angel-island.com** or by browsing through the site of the Organization of Chinese Americans **www.ocanatl.org**. Give an oral report of your findings to your class.

BEYOND THE CLASSROOM

6. Visit a library to find books about life in China today. Two places to start: *River Town: Two Years on the Yangtze* by Peter Hessler, and *The Chinese* by Jasper Becker. Write a short report about a chapter in one of the books.
7. Interview a person in your community who once lived in China. Why did this person move to America? What does he or she think are the most startling differences between the United States and China? What does this person most miss about China? Write a brief portrait of that person. Include his or her answers to the above questions.

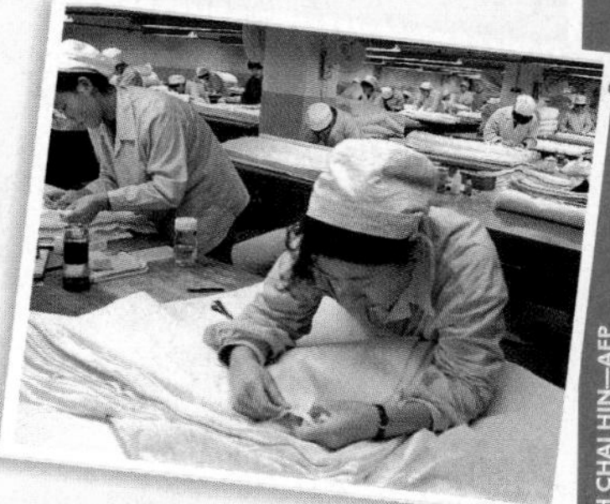

GOH CHAI HIN—AFP

▲ China makes many of the clothes Americans wear.

U.S. Trade With China

Top Five Imports and Exports Between China and the U.S.

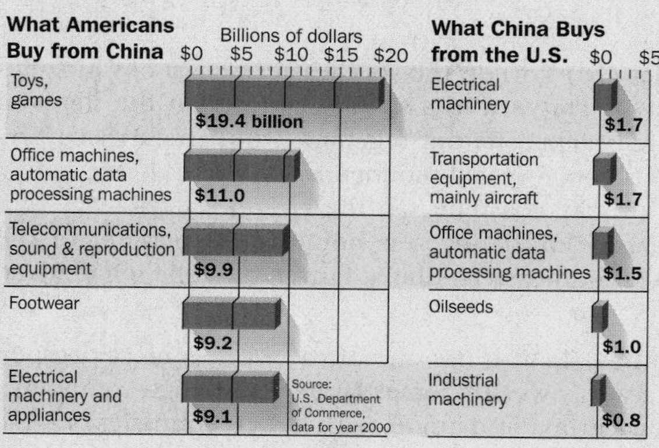

What China Buys from the U.S. ($0–$5)	
Electrical machinery	$1.7
Transportation equipment, mainly aircraft	$1.7
Office machines, automatic data processing machines	$1.5
Oilseeds	$1.0
Industrial machinery	$0.8

BUILDING SKILLS FOR READING TABLES

1. **Analyzing Data** How do the two "shopping lists" at left differ from one another? How do those differences suggest ways each nation can help the other?
2. **Making Inferences** American factories in China typically pay workers about half what they would pay in the U.S. How does this fact help explain why the U.S. buys more from China than China buys from the U.S.?

FOR UPDATES ON WORLD ISSUES GO TO www.timeclassroom.com/glencoe

179

BUILDING SKILLS FOR READING GRAPHS

ANSWERS

1. The United States imports much more from China than China does from us. We buy many inexpensive items, such as toys and footwear, whereas a major item China buys is machinery. By importing Chinese goods, we help China's economy so they can buy machines from us. This then helps them further develop their economy.
2. Americans can save money by buying Chinese goods. U.S. goods are expensive for Chinese.

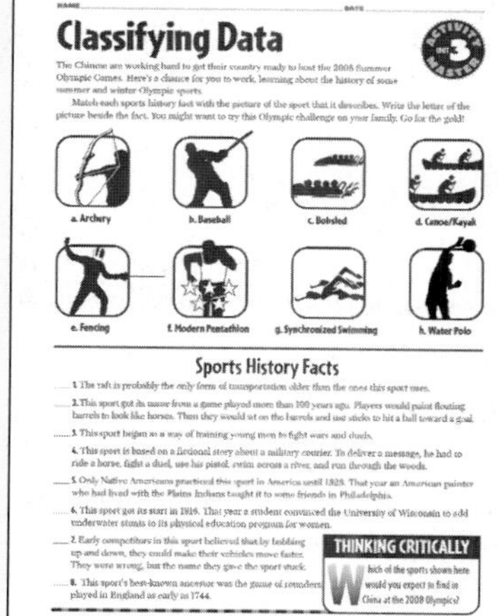

Classifying Data

a. Archery b. Baseball c. Bobsled d. Canoe/Kayak
e. Fencing f. Modern Pentathlon g. Synchronized Swimming h. Water Polo

Sports History Facts

THINKING CRITICALLY

CLOSE

Ask students to write a paragraph starting with this topic sentence: *People throughout the world should be concerned about human rights abuses in China because . . .*

Culminating Activity

To close this lesson, have students complete the Review and Assess section questions and activities above. Students should use classroom discussion, contextual clues, and their student dictionaries to write definitions for terms. Before assigning the Internet activities, it is recommended that you review your school district policy on student Internet use.

Focus on Debate

Have students debate the pro and con position of the following topic: **As long as the Chinese people are doing okay economically and can buy consumer items like televisions and washing machines, they will not care if they do not have political freedom.**

EE6 The Uses of Geography: Standard 18

1 Focus

Section Objectives

1. Explain why many people moved to Taiwan.
2. Describe the people of Mongolia.

BELLRINGER Skillbuilder Activity

Project transparency and have students answer questions.

This activity is also available as a blackline master.

Daily Focus Skills Transparency 6-3

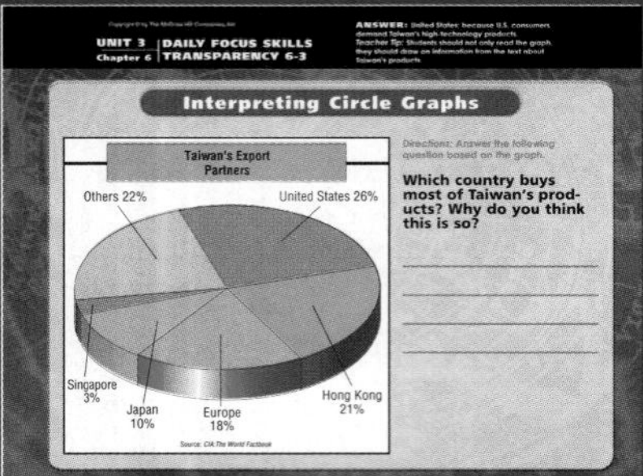

Guide to Reading

■ **Accessing Prior Knowledge** Remind students that the Communists took over China in 1949. **Ask: What happened to those who had fought against the Communists?** Explain that in this section, students will find out.

■ **Vocabulary Precheck** Explain what a *yurt* is. Then ask students what other word in the Terms to Know is related to yurt *(nomad)*. **Why?** *(A portable home would be useful to nomadic people.)*

Section 3 China's Neighbors

Guide to Reading

Main Idea

Taiwan and Mongolia have been influenced by Chinese ways and traditions.

Terms to Know

- high-technology industry
- steppe
- nomad
- empire
- yurt

Reading Strategy

Create a diagram like this one. Then write statements that are true of each country under their headings in the outer ovals. Where the ovals overlap, write statements that are true of both countries.

NATIONAL GEOGRAPHIC Exploring Our World

In the remote, harsh land of western Mongolia, a centuries-old tradition continues. Hunters train eagles to bring their kill back to the human hunter. The people say that female eagles make the best hunters. Because they weigh more than males, they can capture larger prey. Like all eagles, they have superb vision—eight times better than a human's.

Taiwan is an island close to China's mainland, and Mongolia borders China on the north. Throughout history, Taiwan and Mongolia have had close ties to their larger neighbor.

Taiwan

About 100 miles (161 km) off the southeastern coast of China lies the island country of **Taiwan.** It is slightly larger than the states of Connecticut and Massachusetts put together. Through Taiwan's center runs a ridge of steep, forested mountains. On the east, the mountains descend to a rocky coastline. On the west, they fall away to a narrow, fertile plain. This flat area is home to 90 percent of the island's people. Like southeastern China, Taiwan has mild winters and hot, rainy summers.

Taiwan's Economy Taiwan has one of the world's most prosperous economies. Taiwan's wealth comes largely from high-technology industries, manufacturing, and trade with other countries. **High-technology industries** produce computers and other kinds of

Section Resources

Reproducible Masters

- Reproducible Lesson Plan 6-3
- Daily Lecture and Discussion Notes 6-3
- Guided Reading Activity 6-3
- Reading Essentials and Study Guide 6-3
- Section Quiz 6-3

Transparencies

- Daily Focus Skills Transparency 6-3

Multimedia

- Vocabulary PuzzleMaker Software
- Interactive Tutor Self-Assessment CD-ROM
- Presentation Plus! CD-ROM
- ExamView® Pro 3.0 Testmaker CD-ROM

electronic equipment. Workers in Taiwan's factories make many different products, including computers, calculators, radios, televisions, and telephones. You have probably seen goods from Taiwan sold in stores in your community.

Taiwan has a growing economic influence on its Asian neighbors. Many powerful companies based in Taiwan have recently built factories in the People's Republic of China and Thailand. Despite their political differences, Taiwan and mainland China have increased their economic ties since the 1990s.

Agriculture also contributes to Taiwan's booming economy. The island's mountainous landscape limits the amount of land that can be farmed. Still, some farmers have built terraces on mountainsides to grow rice. Other major crops include sugarcane and fruits. In fact, Taiwan's farmers produce enough food not only to feed their own people but also to export.

Taiwan's History and People For centuries, Taiwan was part of China's empire. Then in 1895, Japan took the island after defeating China in war. The Japanese developed the economy of Taiwan but treated the people very harshly. After Japan's loss in World War II, Taiwan returned to China.

In 1949 the Nationalists under Chiang Kai-shek arrived in Taiwan from the Chinese mainland. Along with them came more than 1 million refugees fleeing communist rule. Fearing a communist invasion, the Nationalists kept a large army in the hope of someday retaking the mainland. They also blocked other political groups from sharing in the government.

By the early 1990s, local Taiwanese were allowed more opportunities in government. The one-party system ended, and Taiwan became a democracy. Taiwan still claims to be a Chinese country, but many people would like to declare Taiwan independent. China claims Taiwan as its twenty-third province and believes that it should be under China's control. China has threatened to use force against Taiwan if the island declares its independence.

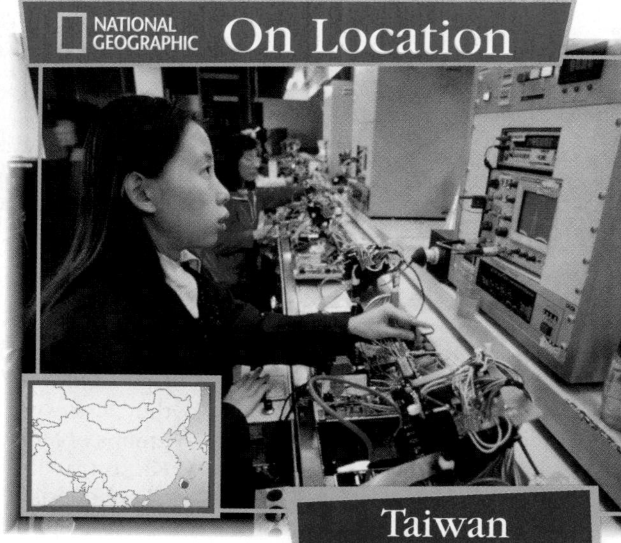

Many electronic industries have headquarters in Taiwan.

Place What kinds of products do high-technology factories in Taiwan produce?

About 75 percent of Taiwan's 22.5 million people live in urban areas. The most populous city—with 2.6 million people—is the capital, **Taipei.** This bustling center of trade and commerce has tall skyscrapers and modern stores. If you stroll through the city, however, you will see Chinese traditions. Buddhist temples, for example, still reflect traditional Chinese architecture.

Reading Check **What is the capital of Taiwan?**

Chapter 6

Section 3, pages 180–183

2 TEACH

Outlining Have students prepare an outline of the section by writing down the subheadings and listing four or five key points under each. **L1**

More About the Photo

Taiwan's Economy The prosperity of Taiwan is evident in this fact: About 80 percent of Taiwan's people own their own homes, the highest rate of home ownership in the world.

Caption Answer computers, calculators, radios, televisions, and telephones

Daily Lecture Notes 6-3

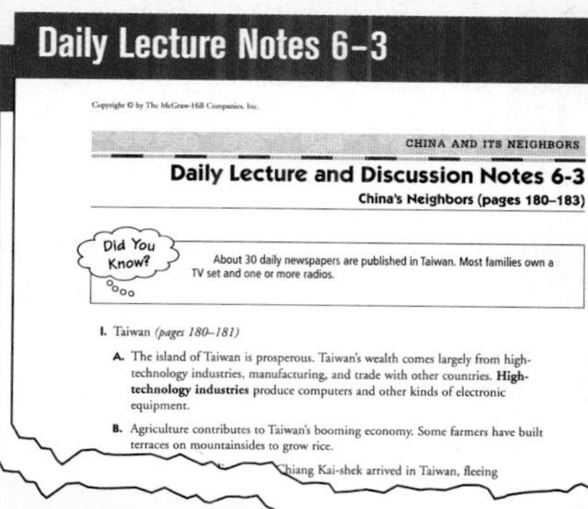

CHINA AND ITS NEIGHBORS

Daily Lecture and Discussion Notes 6-3

China's Neighbors (pages 180–183)

Did You Know? About 30 daily newspapers are published in Taiwan. Most families own a TV set and one or more radios.

I. Taiwan *(pages 180–181)*

A. The island of Taiwan is prosperous. Taiwan's wealth comes largely from high-technology industries, manufacturing, and trade with other countries. **High-technology industries** produce computers and other kinds of electronic equipment.

B. Agriculture contributes to Taiwan's booming economy. Some farmers have built terraces on mountainsides to grow rice.

Chiang Kai-shek arrived in Taiwan, fleeing

Reading Check Answer

Taipei

Team-Teaching Activity

History Invite a teacher to class who can discuss the Chinese civil war and the background of Taiwan's status. The teacher should review the clashes between the Nationalists and Communists, their cooperation during World War II, the resumption of the conflict after 1945, and the U.S. role in this conflict. The teacher should also tell the class about the special relationship the United States has with Taiwan and the diplomacy that must be observed when, for example, leaders of these two nations meet. Then have students look up current news stories about Taiwan and China to find the current status of the relationship between the leaders of the two lands. **L1**

EE4 Human Systems: Standard 13

More About the Photo

Ulaanbaatar Mongolia's capital was originally called *Da Khure,* after the monastery founded there. In 1911 the city became *Niislel Khureheh* ("capital of Mongolia"). The current name, given in 1924, means "Red Hero" and reflects the Communist regime of the time.

Caption Answer because the country has more than 260 days of sunshine per year

Interdisciplinary Connections

Music One folk tradition of Mongolia is called *kumay,* or "throat singing." A singer can produce the equivalent of two or three different voices at the same time.

Guided Reading Activity 6–3

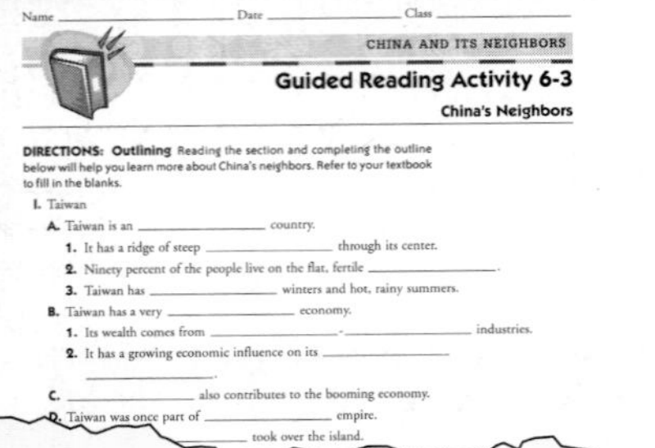
Name ________ Date ________ Class ________

CHINA AND ITS NEIGHBORS

Guided Reading Activity 6-3

China's Neighbors

DIRECTIONS: Outlining Reading the section and completing the outline below will help you learn more about China's neighbors. Refer to your textbook to fill in the blanks.

I. Taiwan
A. Taiwan is an ________ country.
1. It has a ridge of steep ________ through its center.
2. Ninety percent of the people live on the flat, fertile ________.
3. Taiwan has ________ winters and hot, rainy summers.
B. Taiwan has a very ________ economy.
1. Its wealth comes from ________-________ industries.
2. It has a growing economic influence on its ________ ________.
C. ________ also contributes to the booming economy.
D. Taiwan was once part of ________ empire.
________ took over the island.

3 ASSESS

Assign Section 3 Assessment as homework or an in-class activity.

NATIONAL GEOGRAPHIC **On Location**

Ulaanbaatar

Ulaanbaatar in Mongolia began as a Buddhist community in the early 1600s. Today it is a modern cultural and industrial center.

Place **Why is Mongolia known as the Land of the Blue Sky?**

Mongolia

Landlocked **Mongolia** is a large country about the size of Alaska. Rugged mountains and high plateaus rise in the west and central regions. The bleak landscape of the Gobi spreads over the southeast. The rest of the country is covered by **steppes,** the dry treeless plains often found on the edges of a desert.

Known as the Land of the Blue Sky, Mongolia boasts more than 260 days of sunshine per year. Yet its climate has extremes. Rainfall is scarce, and fierce dust storms sometimes sweep across the landscape. Temperatures are very hot in the summer. In the winter, they fall below freezing at night.

For centuries, most of Mongolia's people were **nomads.** Nomads are people who move from place to place with herds of animals. Even today, many Mongolians tend sheep, goats, cattle, or camels on the country's vast steppes. Important industries in Mongolia use products from these animals. Some factories use wool to make textiles and clothing. Others use the hides of cattle to make leather and shoes. Some farmers grow wheat and other grains. Mongolia also has deposits of copper and gold.

Mongolia's History and People Mongolia's people are famous for their skills in raising and riding horses. In the past, they also were known as fierce fighters. In the 1200s, many groups of Mongols joined together under one leader, **Genghis Khan** (JEHNG•guhs KAHN). He led Mongol armies on a series of conquests. The Mongols eventually carved out the largest land empire in history, ruling 80 percent of Eurasia by A.D. 1300. An **empire** is a collection of different territories under one ruler. The **Mongol Empire** stretched from China all the way to eastern Europe.

During the 1300s, the Mongol Empire weakened and fell apart. China ruled the area that is now Mongolia from the 1700s to the early 1900s. In 1924 Mongolia gained independence and created a strict communist government under the guidance of the Soviet Union. The country finally became a democracy in 1990. Since then, the Mongolian economy has moved slowly from government control to a free enterprise system.

Content Background

Taiwan One of the favorite places of the people of Taipei is the Lin Family Garden. Built in the 1800s by the wealthiest family in Taiwan, the garden is now a public park. The garden follows traditional Chinese garden design, with small mountains, small streams of running water, pools that reflect the surroundings, and stones set in patterns. The Taiwanese feel they can gain peace and balance here by contemplating nature.

About 90 percent of Mongolia's 2.4 million people are Mongols. They speak the Mongol language. More than 60 percent of the people live in urban areas. The largest city is the capital, **Ulaanbaatar** (OO•LAHN•BAH•TAWR). Mongolians in the countryside live on farms. A few still follow the nomadic life of their ancestors. These herder-nomads live in **yurts,** large circle-shaped structures made of animal skins that can be packed up and moved from place to place.

Mongolians still enjoy the sports and foods of their nomadic ancestors. The favorite meal is boiled sheep's meat with rice, washed down with tea. The biggest event of the year is the **Naadam Festival,** held all over the country in mid-summer. It consists of a number of sporting events, including wrestling, archery, and horse racing.

Since before the days of the Mongol Empire, most people in Mongolia have been Buddhists. Buddhism has long influenced Mongolian art, music, and literature. Traditional music has a wide range of instruments and singing styles. In one style of Mongolian singing, male performers produce harmonic sounds from deep in the throat, releasing several notes at once.

For centuries, Buddhist temples and other holy places dotted the country. Under communism, religious worship was discouraged. Many of these historic buildings were either destroyed or left to decay. Today, people are once again able to practice their religion. They have restored or rebuilt many of their holy buildings.

✓Reading Check **What religion do most Mongolians practice?**

Assessment

Defining Terms

1. **Define** high-technology industry, steppe, nomad, empire, yurt.

Recalling Facts

2. **Economics** What kinds of products are made in Taiwan?

3. **Government** Why has Taiwan not claimed independence from China?

4. **History** What Mongol warrior conquered much of Eurasia by A.D. 1300?

Critical Thinking

5. **Understanding Cause and Effect** Why did many people flee to Taiwan from China in 1949?

6. **Drawing Conclusions** Why do you think communist leaders discouraged religious worship in Mongolia?

Graphic Organizer

7. **Organizing Information** Create a diagram like this one. Then write either Taiwan or Mongolia in the center oval. Write at least one fact about the country under the headings in each of the outer ovals.

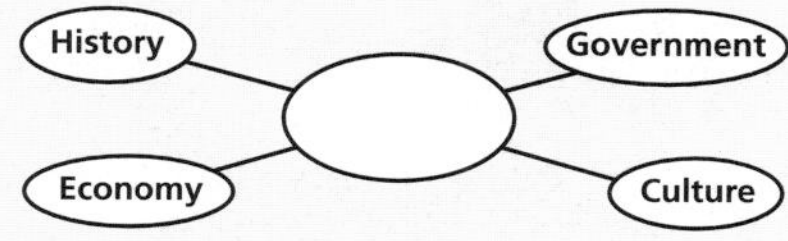

Applying Social Studies Skills

8. **Analyzing Maps** Look at the physical map on page 163. What mountains rise in western Mongolia? What desert is found in southern and southeastern Mongolia?

Section 3 Assessment

1. The terms are defined in the Glossary.
2. electronic goods
3. China has threatened to use force against the island if it does so.
4. Genghis Khan
5. They did not wish to live under Communist rule.
6. *Possible answer:* Communism discourages any religious worship as an attempt to gain the people's undivided allegiance to the state.
7. Diagrams will vary.
8. Altay Mountains; Gobi

Chapter 6

Section 3, pages 180–183

Section Quiz 6-3

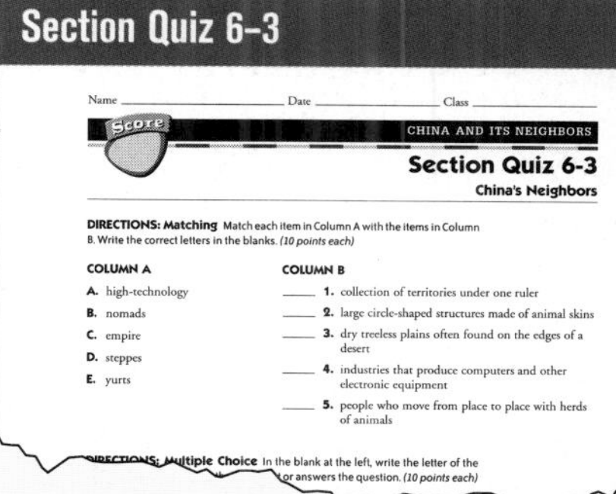

Name ______ Date ______ Class ______

Score

CHINA AND ITS NEIGHBORS

Section Quiz 6-3

China's Neighbors

DIRECTIONS: Matching Match each item in Column A with the items in Column B. Write the correct letters in the blanks. *(10 points each)*

COLUMN A	COLUMN B
A. high-technology	____ **1.** collection of territories under one ruler
B. nomads	____ **2.** large circle-shaped structures made of animal skins
C. empire	____ **3.** dry treeless plains often found on the edges of a desert
D. steppes	____ **4.** industries that produce computers and other electronic equipment
E. yurts	____ **5.** people who move from place to place with herds of animals

DIRECTIONS: Multiple Choice In the blank at the left, write the letter of the ... or answers the question. *(10 points each)*

Reteach

Have students brainstorm words that describe Taiwan or Mongolia. Have other students identify which country is described by each word.

✓ Reading Check Answer

Buddhism

Reading Essentials and Study Guide 6-3

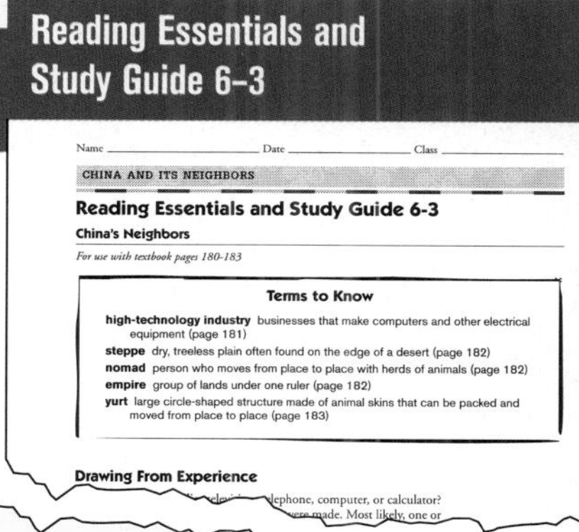

Name ______ Date ______ Class ______

CHINA AND ITS NEIGHBORS

Reading Essentials and Study Guide 6-3

China's Neighbors

For use with textbook pages 180-183

Terms to Know

high-technology industry businesses that make computers and other electrical equipment (page 181)
steppe dry, treeless plain often found on the edge of a desert (page 182)
nomad person who moves from place to place with herds of animals (page 182)
empire group of lands under one ruler (page 182)
yurt large circle-shaped structure made of animal skins that can be packed and moved from place to place (page 183)

Drawing From Experience

...elephone, computer, or calculator? ...were made. Most likely, one or

Close

Have students write one paragraph about Taiwan and Mongolia, explaining how both are influenced by China and different from China.

Critical Thinking Skill

TEACH

Write the following phrases: "The movie grossed $35 million on its opening weekend of business." "The movie was exciting—you should see it!" **Ask: Which sentence states a fact and which states an opinion?** *(The first is a fact, the second an opinion.)* Ask students to explain the difference. **L1**

Additional Skills Practice

1. **Are all opinions of equal value? Does anything make one person's opinion more valid than another person's opinion?** *(Possible answer: Informed, or expert, opinions should carry more validity than uninformed opinions.)*
2. **Some people say, "Statistics never lie." Is that true or not?** *(Possible answer: Statistics can be misleading if they do not try to present a full picture of the situation being analyzed.)*

Additional Skills Resources

 Chapter Skills Activity 6

 Building Geography Skills for Life

GLENCOE TECHNOLOGY

 **Skillbuilder Interactive Workbook CD-ROM, Level 1**

This interactive CD-ROM reinforces student mastery of essential social studies skills.

Critical Thinking Skill

Distinguishing Fact From Opinion

Distinguishing fact from opinion can help you make reasonable judgments about what others say and write. Facts can be proved by evidence such as records, documents, or historical sources. Opinions are based on people's differing values and beliefs.

Learning the Skill

The following steps will help you identify facts and opinions:

- Read or listen to the information carefully. Identify the facts. Ask: Can these statements be proved? Where would I find information to prove them?
- If a statement can be proved, it is factual. Check the sources for the facts. Often statistics sound impressive, but they may come from an unreliable source.
- Identify opinions by looking for statements of feelings or beliefs. The statements may contain words like *should, would, could, best, greatest, all, every,* or *always.*

Practicing the Skill

Read the paragraph below, and then answer the questions that follow.

> Anyone who thinks the Internet is not used in China has been asleep at the mouse. China's government-owned factories and political system may seem old-fashioned. When it comes to cyberspace, however, China is moving at Net speed. Internet use is growing explosively. In 1997 only 640,000 Chinese were using the Internet. By 2000, the number had increased to 12.3 million. The Phillips Group estimates that by 2005, the online population should hit 85 million.

1. Identify facts. Can you prove that Chinese Internet use is increasing?
2. Note opinions. What phrases alert you that these are opinions?
3. What is the purpose of this paragraph?

Applying the Skill

Watch a television commercial. List one fact and one opinion that are stated. Does the fact seem reliable? How can you prove the fact?

GO TO Practice key skills with **Glencoe Skillbuilder Interactive Workbook, Level 1.**

◀ **Chinese students attend an Internet exhibit in Beijing.**

CHAPTER 6

Practicing the Skill Answers

1. In 1997 only 640,000 Chinese were using the Internet. By 2000, the number had increased to 12.3 million." These facts prove Internet use is increasing.
2. The rhetorical writing in the first few sentences, and the estimate of Internet usage in 2005, are opinions. Phrases such as "old-fashioned," "Net speed," and "should" signify opinion.
3. to show that China is becoming modernized and its Internet usage is growing rapidly

Applying the Skill

Ask volunteers to share their examples of facts and opinions from television commercials. Have the class discuss what key words in the sentences suggest that they are fact or opinion.

Reading Review

Section 1 China's Land and Economy

Terms to Know
- dike
- fault
- communist state
- free enterprise system
- invest
- consumer goods
- "one-country, two-systems"

Main Idea

China—the third-largest country in the world—has very diverse landforms. China's rapidly growing economy has changed in recent years.

✓ **Place** Rugged mountains and harsh deserts cover western China.

✓ **Place** About 90 percent of China's people live in the lowlands of eastern China.

✓ **Human/Environment Interaction** China's rivers bring fertile soil along with the danger of flooding to the eastern plains.

✓ **Economics** China's leaders have changed the economy to give the people more economic freedom. The economy has grown rapidly as a result.

✓ **Economics** Many companies in China are now jointly owned by Chinese and foreign businesspeople. Foreign companies can pay workers less than they pay workers in their own countries, and they have a great number of possible customers in the Chinese people.

Section 2 China's People and Culture

Terms to Know
- dynasty
- human rights
- exile
- calligraphy
- pagoda

Main Idea

The arts and ideas of ancient times still influence China today.

✓ **History** The ancient teachings of Kongfuzi, Daoism, and Buddhism still influence the people of China.

✓ **History** For thousands of years, dynasties of emperors ruled China. Today, Communist leaders keep tight control over all areas of political life.

✓ **Culture** China is famous for the skill of its craft workers and for its distinctive painting and architecture.

Section 3 China's Neighbors

Terms to Know
- high-technology industry
- steppe
- nomad
- empire
- yurt

Main Idea

Taiwan and Mongolia have been influenced by Chinese ways and traditions.

✓ **Government** Taiwan is an island off southeast China. The government of China does not recognize Taiwan as a separate country.

✓ **Economics** Taiwan's prosperous economy has influenced other Asian economies.

✓ **Place** Mongolia has rugged terrain and a harsh landscape.

✓ **Culture** Some people in Mongolia still follow a traditional nomadic lifestyle, and herding remains an important economic activity.

Reading Review

Use the Chapter 6 Reading Review to preview, review, condense, or reteach the chapter.

Preview/Review

Use the Terms to Know lists to help students review and study.

Activity Have students group the terms according to category—physical geography or human geography. Read the terms aloud, one at a time, and ask for volunteers to categorize each.

Vocabulary PuzzleMaker Software reinforces the vocabulary terms used in Chapter 6.

The Interactive Tutor Self-Assessment CD-ROM allows students to review Chapter 6 content.

Condense

Have students read the Chapter 6 summary statements.

Chapter 6 Guided Reading Activities

Chapter 6 Audio Program

Reteach

Reteaching Activity 6

Chapter 6 Reading Essentials and Study Guide

Chapter Culminating Activity

China's Economy With its size and resources, China is an economic powerhouse. Have students research China's economic output in agriculture, manufacturing, and mining and prepare an illustrated display that shows the country's products. The display should also reveal how China's economy is changing and where it ranks among world economies. Graphs that chart China's trade with the United States could also be included. *NOTE: This activity may be completed separately or you may wish students to incorporate it into their Current Events Journals.*

EE5 Environment and Society: Standard 16

Assessment and Activities

GLENCOE TECHNOLOGY

MindJogger Videoquiz
Use MindJogger to review the Chapter 6 content.

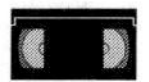
Available in VHS.

Using Key Terms

1.	e	6.	b
2.	i	7.	a
3.	h	8.	f
4.	j	9.	d
5.	c	10.	g

Reviewing the Main Ideas

11. in the eastern part of the country
12. Yangtze, Yellow, Xi
13. Increased industrialization has meant more burning of coal to produce energy, which pollutes the air.
14. *Possible answers:* individuals can choose their jobs, decide where to start businesses, keep profits; foreign companies have invested
15. Kongfuzi believed that people should be polite, honest, brave, and wise; that children should obey parents; and that subjects should obey rulers. Laozi believed that people should live simply and in harmony with nature.
16. a republic
17. because it has one of the world's most prosperous economies and has a growing economic influence on its Asian neighbors
18. The land is very dry, and much of it is covered by mountains or desert.
19. The main industries use wool to make textiles and clothing or cattle hides to make leather and shoes.

Chapter 6 Assessment and Activities

Using Key Terms

Match the terms in Part A with their definitions in Part B.

A.

1. invest
2. dynasty
3. exile
4. high-technology industry
5. dike
6. communist state
7. "one-country, two-systems"
8. calligraphy
9. human rights
10. yurt

B.

a. promise to allow capitalism and communism to exist side-by-side
b. country whose government has strong control over the economy and society
c. high bank of soil along a river to prevent flooding
d. basic freedoms of speech and movement
e. to put money into
f. the art of beautiful writing
g. nomadic tent made of animal skins
h. state of being unable to live in one's own country because of political beliefs
i. line of rulers from the same family
j. business that produces electronic equipment

Reviewing the Main Ideas

Section 1 China's Land and Economy

11. **Place** Where do most of China's people live?
12. **Place** What three major rivers flow through the plains and southern highlands of China?
13. **Human/Environment Interaction** How has the new economy contributed to air pollution in China?
14. **Economics** Give three reasons why China's economy has boomed.

Section 2 China's People and Culture

15. **Culture** What are the ideas of Kongfuzi? Of Laozi?
16. **Government** What kind of government did China have between 1911 and 1949?

Section 3 China's Neighbors

17. **Economics** Why is Taiwan's economy important in Asia?
18. **Place** How does Mongolia's landscape prevent much farming?
19. **Economics** How are Mongolia's main industries related to herding?

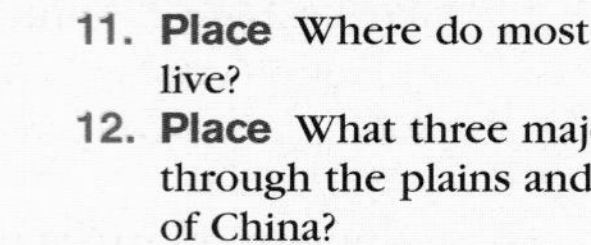

China

Place Location Activity

On a separate sheet of paper, match the letters on the map with the numbered places listed below.

1. Plateau of Tibet
2. Yellow River
3. Yangtze River
4. Hong Kong
5. Gobi
6. Beijing
7. Mongolia
8. Shanghai
9. Taklimakan Desert
10. Himalaya

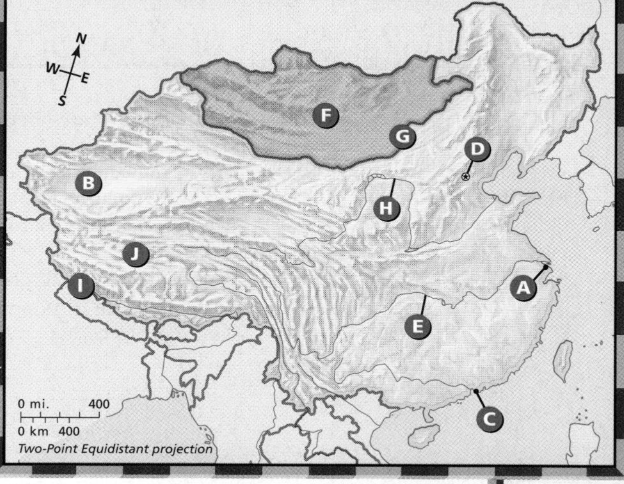

NATIONAL GEOGRAPHIC Place Location Activity

1.	J	6.	D
2.	H	7.	F
3.	E	8.	A
4.	C	9.	B
5.	G	10.	I

Critical Thinking

20. *Possible answer:* Chinese rulers did not want Europeans to influence the Chinese people. They were mainly interested in internal development and protecting their borders from invaders.
21. Students' charts will vary.

Current Events Journal

22. Suggest that students use Internet resources to find images they can copy and paste into their time lines.

Self-Check Quiz Visit the ***Our World Today: People, Places, and Issues*** Web site at owt.glencoe.com and click on **Chapter 6–Self-Check Quizzes** to prepare for the Chapter Test.

Critical Thinking

20. **Drawing Conclusions** Why do you think China wanted to be isolated from European countries in the 1700s and 1800s?
21. **Organizing Information** Create a chart like the one below. Under each heading, write at least two facts about China.

Land	Economy	History	Government	People

Current Events Journal

22. **Creating a Time Line** Learn more about an event that is happening in China, Mongolia, or Taiwan today. Find out what important events led up to this one and what effect they have had on what is happening now. Create a time line showing your findings. Include illustrations and photos.

Mental Mapping Activity

23. **Focusing on the Region** Create a simple outline map of China and its neighbors, and then label the following:
    - Himalaya
    - Yellow River
    - Taiwan
    - Beijing
    - Gobi
    - Ulaanbaatar
    - Yangtze River
    - Hong Kong

Technology Skills Activity

24. **Developing a Multimedia Presentation** Using the Internet, research one of the arts of China. You might choose painting, architecture, literature, music, or a craft such as casting bronze or making silk. Create a museum exhibit that presents your findings. Include photographs showing examples of works from different periods in Chinese history.

The Princeton Review

Standardized Test Practice

Directions: Study the map below, and then answer the questions that follow.

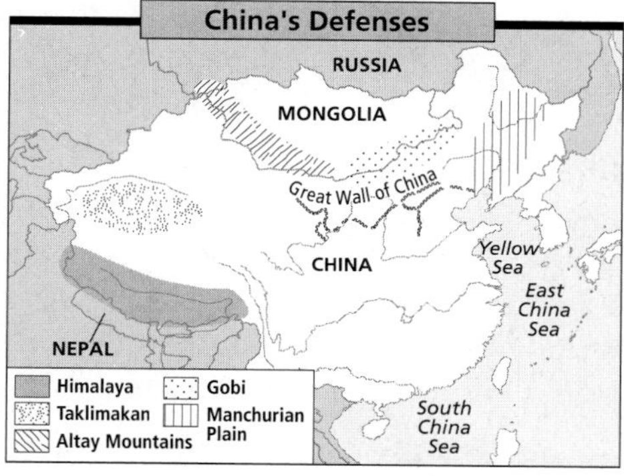

1. **Where is the Gobi?**
   - **A** Near China's Russian border
   - **B** In the southwestern part of China
   - **C** In the Himalaya
   - **D** Along China's border with Mongolia
2. **Which of the following is NOT one of China's natural defenses?**
   - **F** The Great Wall of China
   - **G** The Gobi
   - **H** The South China Sea
   - **J** The Himalaya

Test-Taking Tip: Pay attention to key words such as *not* or *except* in a test question. In this case, all of the answer choices are natural defenses of China except for the correct answer. Look at the map closely, using its title, legend, and information shown on it to find the correct answer choice.

Assessment and Activities

Standardized Test Practice

1. D
2. F

Tested Objectives: Reading a map, analyzing information

Chapter Test Bonus Question

This question may be used for extra credit on the chapter test.

What city was recently returned to China by the United Kingdom? *(Hong Kong)*

Our World Today online

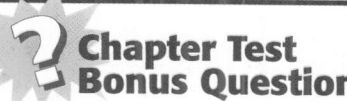

Have students visit the Web site at **owt.glencoe.com** to review Chapter 6 and take the Self-Check Quiz.

Mental Mapping Activity

23. This exercise helps students visualize the countries and geographic features they have been studying and understand the relationship among various points. Accept all attempts at freehand mapping that show places in the correct relationship to one another.

Technology Skills Activity

24. Remind students that museum exhibits identify the object and when and where it was made. They also list the materials used and briefly describe the features that show how the object expresses—and departs from—a particular artistic style or period.

1 Focus

Ask students to name highways or industrial complexes in their area that are named for a product or an industry. List their contributions. Then point out that one of the world's oldest and most famous trade routes was named for a product—the Silk Road.

2 Teach

Classifying Information
Have students suggest ways that people exchange ideas today. Have them classify their suggestions into the categories "direct contact" (such as travel to other countries) and "long-distance communication" (such as using radio, television, telephones, or the Internet).

Meeting National Standards

Geography for Life
The following standards are met in the Student Edition feature:

- **EE1 The World in Spatial Terms: Standards 1, 3**
- **EE2 Places and Regions: Standards 4, 6**
- **EE4 Human Systems: Standard 11**
- **EE5 Environment and Society: Standards 15, 16**

Soft and sleek, silk is a valuable textile.

The Silk Road

Was there really a road made of silk? Well, not exactly. Silk, however, was one of the main products carried along the Silk Road—a system of trade routes that linked ancient China and the empires of the West. When Chinese silk became fashionable in Rome, the precious cloth traveled the Silk Road.

A Risky Route

The road itself was anything but soft and smooth. Traveling from China, camels laden with silk and other cargo trudged through deserts, including the Taklimakan, a name meaning "go in and you won't come out." Sandstorms and intense heat made passage difficult. Farther along the route, the Pamir mountain range thrust an ice- and snow-covered barrier in the way. The road was dangerous as well. Bandits attacked often, stealing valuable goods.

Few traveled the entire 4,000-mile (6,437-km) series of routes. Instead, merchants bought goods in trading posts and oases along the way and sold them at other markets farther along, much as relay runners pass a baton.

Chinese Secret Agent

Zhang Qian, an agent on a secret mission for Chinese Emperor Wudi, may have started the silk trade. In 139 B.C. invaders swept into China, despite China's Great Wall. Zhang Qian was sent far into Central Asia to find allies to help fight the invaders. He found no allies. Instead, he brought back strong horses for the military, which he had bought with bolts of silk.

Soon the Chinese were trading silk with the Parthian Empire, now present-day Iran. It is said that Rome wanted silk after its soldiers spotted silk banners fluttering above Parthian troops. By the A.D. 100s, China and Rome were trading a variety of goods. From the East came such exotic items as silk, spices, and fruits. Rome paid in glass, wool, and ivory, but mostly in gold.

Ideas also traveled the Silk Road. From India, the religion of Buddhism reached China. Christianity and Islam spread eastward as well. Chinese techniques for making paper and explosives traveled west. Western methods of cloth manufacturing and better gun design went to China. The process for making silk, however, traveled nowhere until much later. The Chinese successfully guarded their secret—that silk was made from the strands of a silkworm's cocoon.

For centuries, goods and ideas traveled between East and West. In the 1300s, however, the Silk Road began to decline as sea routes proved safer than land routes. Nevertheless, even today, parts of the Silk Road are busy with trade—and tourism. In addition to camels, tour buses now travel the caravan routes.

QUESTIONS

1. How is the Silk Road "made of silk"?
2. What were some obstacles along the Silk Road?

A man and his camel travel the Silk Road in China. ▶

Answers to the Questions

1. because silk was the chief good that was traded along the road
2. the harsh Taklimakan Desert; the high, cold Pamir Mountains; bandit attacks

NATIONAL GEOGRAPHIC

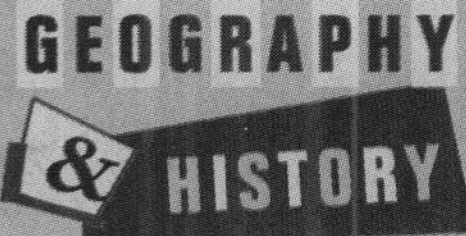

Time Line

- **139 B.C.:** Zhang Qian travels west into Central Asia
- **130 B.C.–A.D. 900:** First period in which Silk Road flourishes
- **c. 100 B.C.:** Hybrid camels are bred to carry goods
- **c. 100 B.C.–A.D. 600:** Independent principalities arise in Central Asia along Silk Road
- **c. A.D. 100:** Kushan people of Afghanistan first use the stirrup, which spreads along the Silk Road
- **c. A.D. 100:** Buddhism begins to spread along Silk Road
- **A.D. 1200–1600:** Second period in which Silk Road flourishes

3 Assess

Have students answer the questions on page 188.

4 Close

Have students make a list of the kinds of goods that are traded around the world today. Which do they think are as valuable and desirable as silk was in more ancient times?

Geography and History Activity

Using Maps Have students compare the map of the Silk Road to the map of Asia in the Reference Atlas on pages RA24–RA25. Have them make a list of the countries through which the Silk Road passed.

EE4 Human Systems: Standard 11

Chapter 7 Resources

Note: The following materials may be used when teaching Chapter 7.
Section level support materials are shown at point of use in the margins of the Teacher Wraparound Edition.

Timesaving Tools

TeacherWorks™ All-In-One Planner and Resource Center

- **Interactive Teacher Edition** See the **Interactive Teacher Edition** CD-ROM to electronically integrate your Teacher Wraparound Edition and blackline masters.
- **Interactive Lesson Planner** Organize your week, month, semester, or year with all the lesson helps you need. The **Interactive Lesson Planner** CD-ROM contains all Chapter 7 resources.

Use Glencoe's **Presentation Plus!** multimedia teacher tool to easily present dynamic lessons that visually excite your students. Using Microsoft PowerPoint® you can customize the presentations to create your own personalized lessons.

TEACHING TRANSPARENCIES

Graphic Organizer Transparency and Student Activity 7

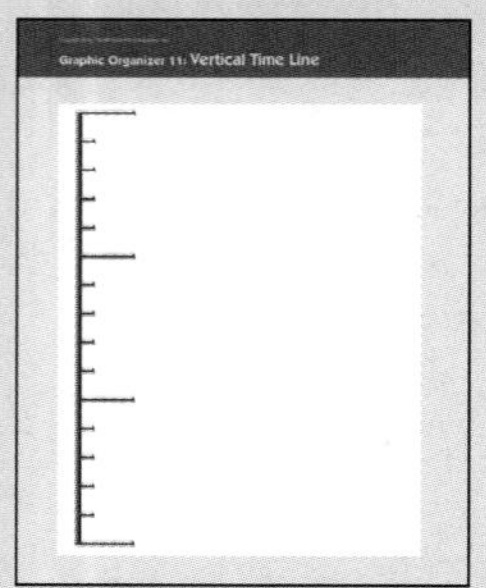

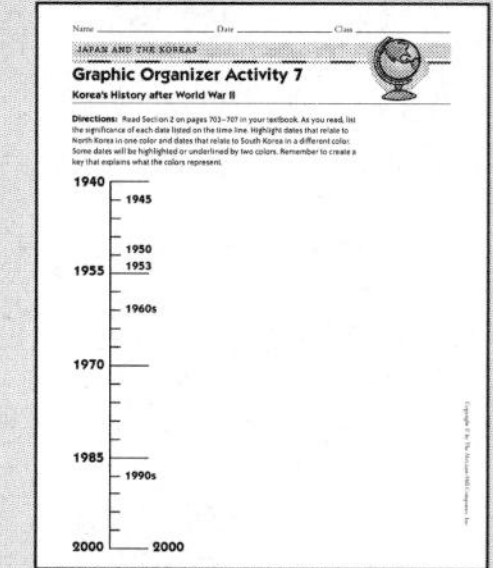

FOLDABLES™ Study Organizer

Foldables are three-dimensional, interactive graphic organizers that help students practice basic writing skills, review key vocabulary terms, and identify main ideas. Every chapter contains a Foldable activity, with additional chapter activities found in the ***Reading and Study Skills Foldables*** booklet.

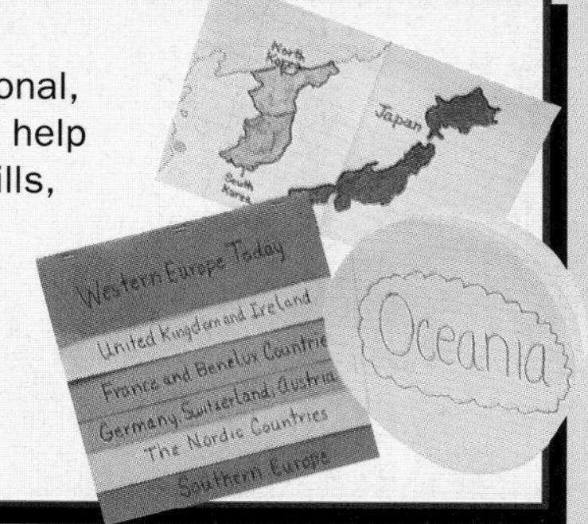

ENRICHMENT AND EXTENSION

Enrichment Activity 7

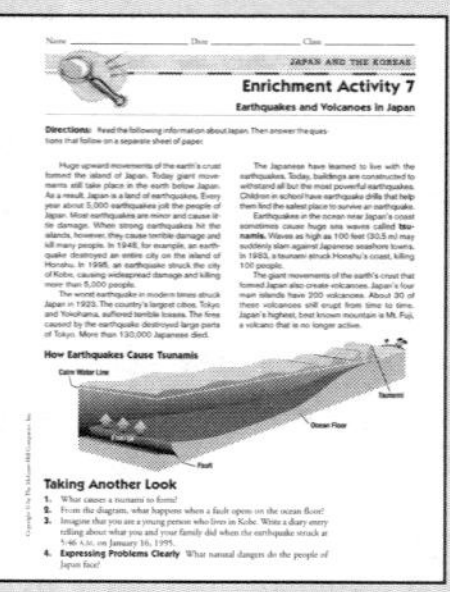

Cooperative Learning Activity 7

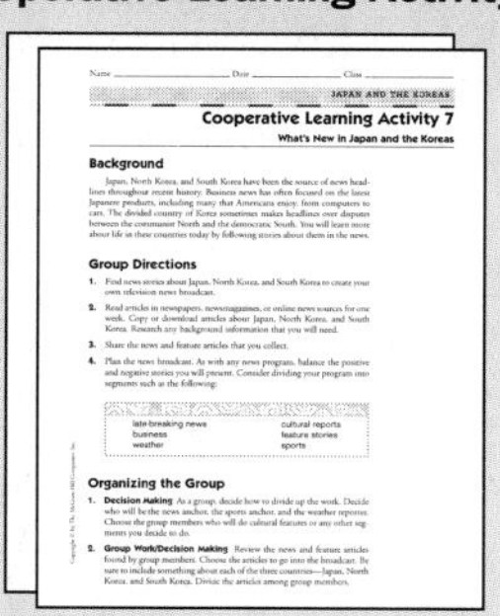

MAP AND GEOGRAPHY SKILLS

Chapter Map Activity 7

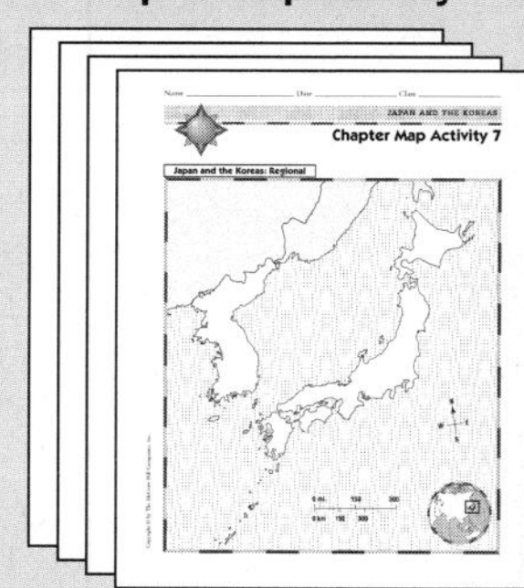

GeoLab Activity 7

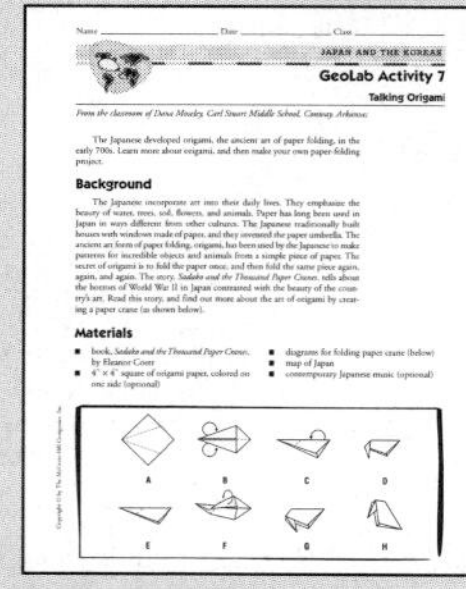

STANDARDIZED ASSESSMENT SKILLS

GLENCOE'S ASSESSMENT ADVANTAGE

Critical Thinking Skills Activity 7

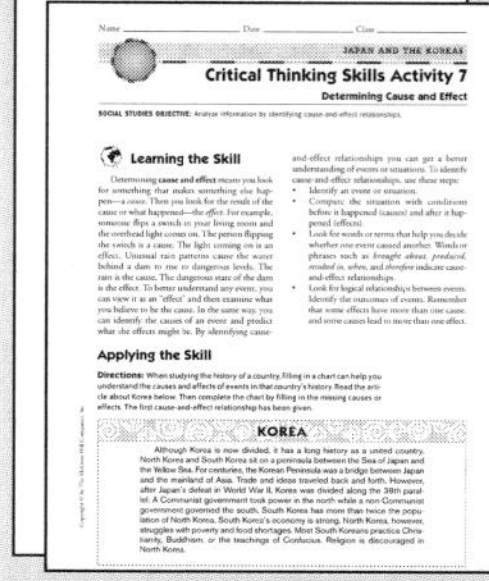

Map and Graph Skills Activity 7

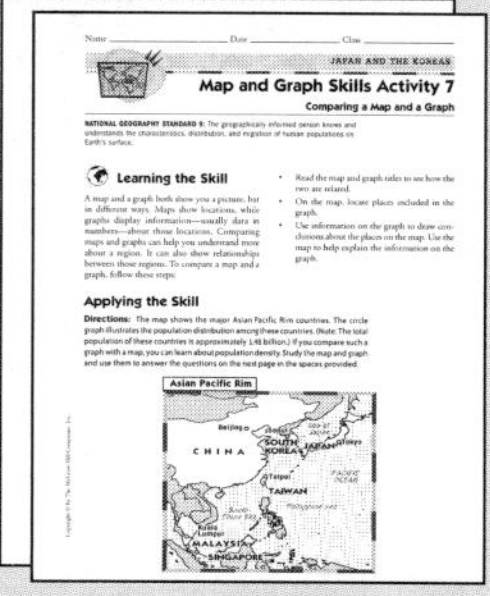

Reading and Writing Skills Activity 7

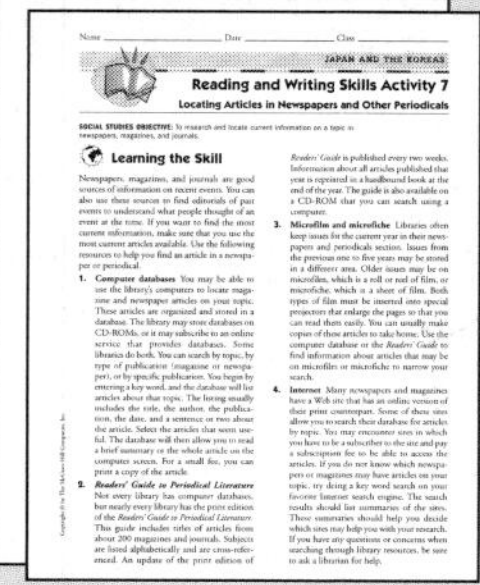

Standardized Test Practice Workbook Activity 7

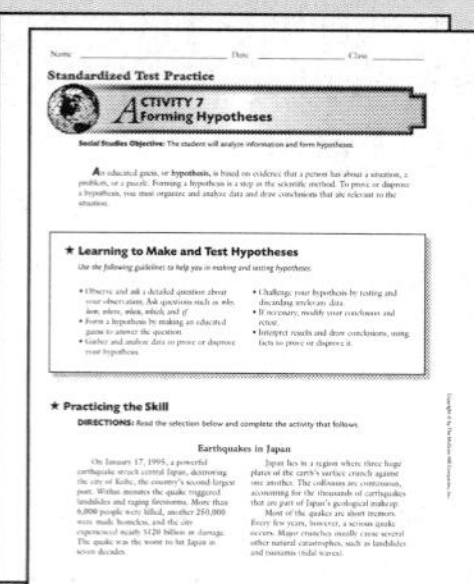

REVIEW AND REINFORCEMENT

Chapter Skills Activity 7

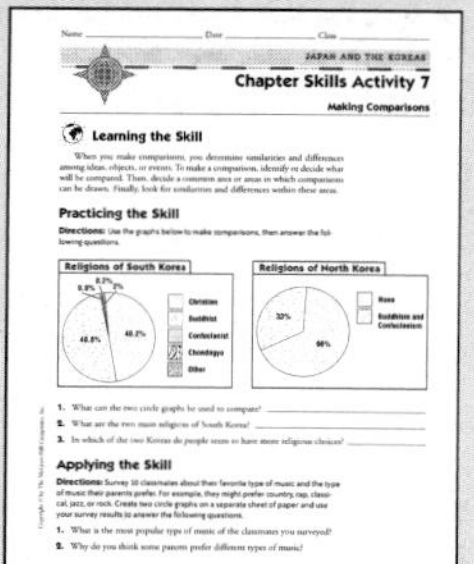

Take-Home Review Activity 7

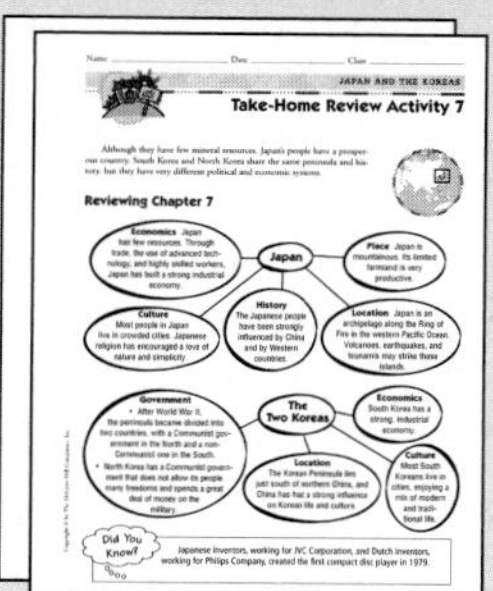

Reteaching Activity 7

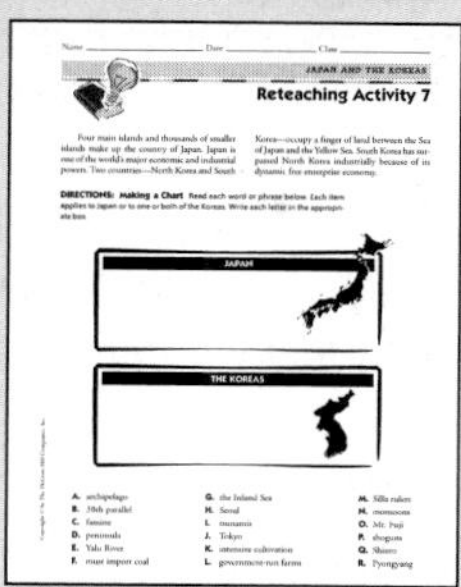

Vocabulary Activity 7

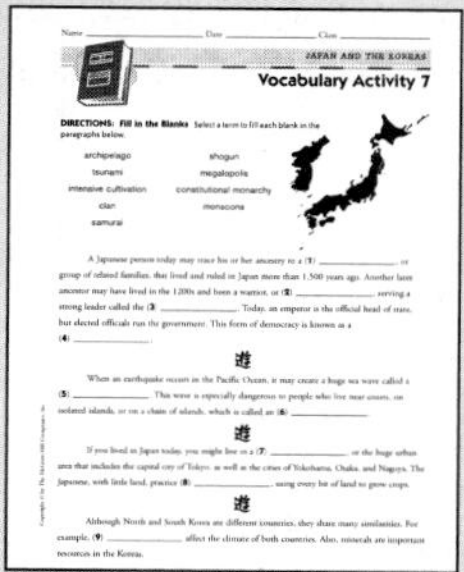

Workbook Activity 7

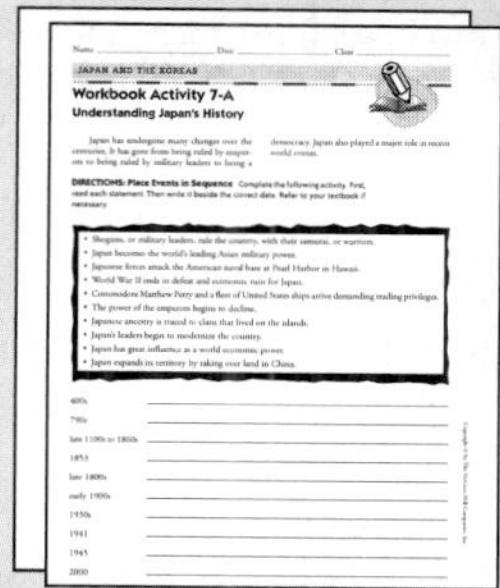

ASSESSMENT

GLENCOE'S ASSESSMENT ADVANTAGE

Chapter 7 Test, Form A

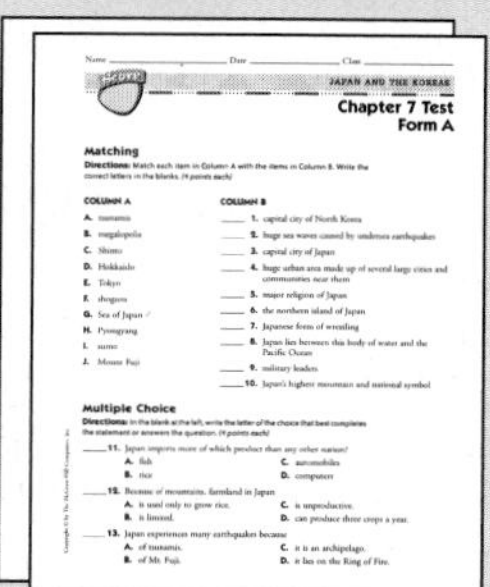

Chapter 7 Test, Form B

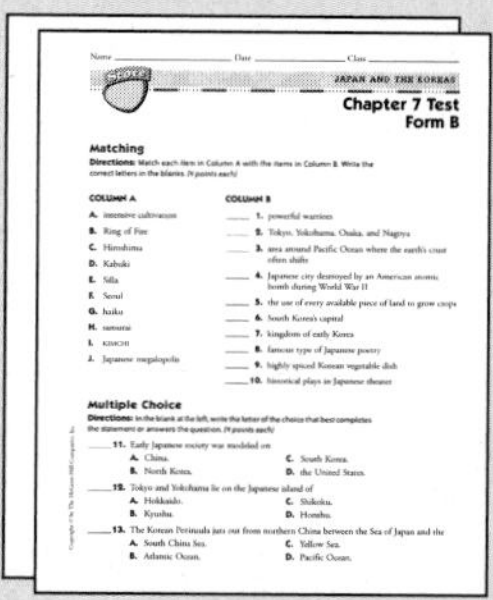

Performance Assessment Activity 7

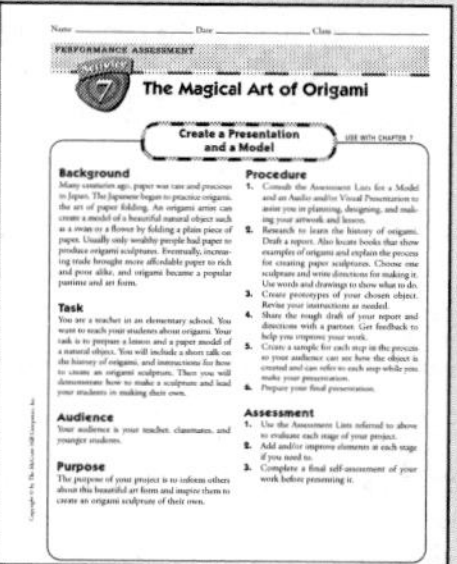

ExamView® Pro 3.0 Testmaker CD-ROM

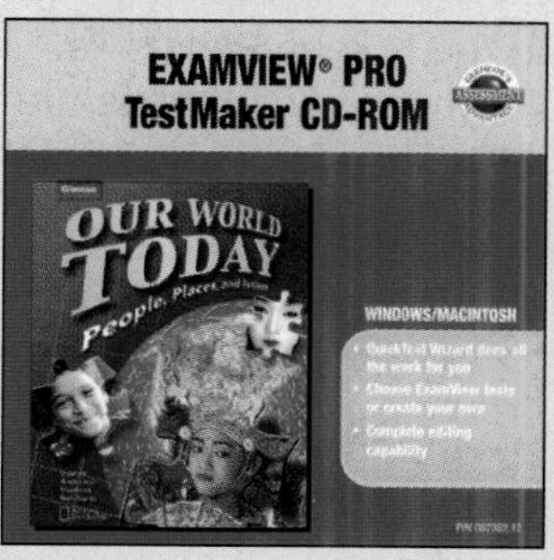

MULTIMEDIA

- National Geographic's The World and Its People
- MindJogger Videoquiz
- Vocabulary PuzzleMaker Software
- Interactive Tutor Self-Assessment CD-ROM
- ExamView® Pro 3.0 Testmaker CD-ROM
- Interactive Lesson Planner CD-ROM
- Interactive Teacher Edition CD-ROM
- Skillbuilder Interactive Workbook CD-ROM, Level 1
- Presentation Plus! CD-ROM
- Audio Program

SPANISH RESOURCES

The following Spanish language materials are available in the Spanish Resources binder:

- Spanish Chapter Summaries
- Spanish Vocabulary Activities
- Spanish Guided Reading Activities
- Spanish Quizzes and Tests
- Spanish Take-Home Review Activities
- Spanish Reteaching Activities

Meeting National Standards

Geography for Life

All of the 18 standards are demonstrated in Unit 3. The following ones are highlighted in Chapter 7:

Section 1
EE4 Human Systems: Standards 9, 10, 11, 12, 13
EE5 Environment and Society: Standards 14, 15, 16

Section 2
EE4 Human Systems: Standards 9, 10, 11, 12, 13
EE5 Environment and Society: Standards 14, 15, 16
EE6 The Uses of Geography: Standard 17

For a complete listing of National Geography Standards and entire text correlation, see pages T22–T29.

Local Objectives

____

____

Chapter 7 Planning Guide

SECTION RESOURCES

Daily Objectives	Reproducible Resources	Multimedia Resources
Section 1 **Japan** **Suggested Pacing = 1 day** **1.** Explain what economic activities are important in Japan. **2.** Describe how the past has influenced Japan. **3.** Summarize how religion has shaped culture in Japan.	Reproducible Lesson Plan 7-1 Daily Lecture and Discussion Notes 7-1 Guided Reading Activity 7-1 Reading Essentials and Study Guide 7-1 Section Quiz 7-1*	Daily Focus Skills Transparency 7-1 GeoQuiz Transparency 7-1 Vocabulary PuzzleMaker Software Interactive Tutor Self-Assessment CD-ROM ExamView® Pro 3.0 Testmaker CD-ROM Presentation Plus! CD-ROM
Section 2 **The Two Koreas** **Suggested Pacing = 1 day** **1.** Locate the Korean Peninsula. **2.** Explain why the two Koreas are divided. **3.** Compare life in North and South Korea.	Reproducible Lesson Plan 7-2 Daily Lecture and Discussion Notes 7-2 Guided Reading Activity 7-2 Reading Essentials and Study Guide 7-2 Section Quiz 7-2*	Daily Focus Skills Transparency 7-2 GeoQuiz Transparency 7-1 Vocabulary PuzzleMaker Software Interactive Tutor Self-Assessment CD-ROM ExamView® Pro 3.0 Testmaker CD-ROM Presentation Plus! CD-ROM

00:00 **Out of Time?** Assign the **Reading Essentials and Study Guide** for this chapter.

*Also available in Spanish

KEY TO ABILITY LEVELS

Teaching strategies have been coded for varying learning styles and abilities.

L1 **BASIC** activities for all students
L2 **AVERAGE** activities for average to above-average students
L3 **CHALLENGING** activities for above-average students
ELL **ENGLISH LANGUAGE LEARNER** activities

Blackline Master
Software
CD-ROM
Audiocassette
Transparency
Videocassette
Block Scheduling
DVD

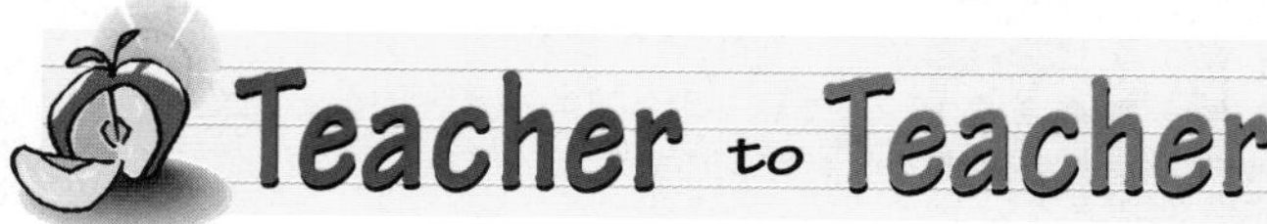

Making a Human Graph

Kim Cavanaugh
Congress Middle School
Boynton Beach, Florida

Ask students to define the terms *culture* and *culture region.* Ask them to describe the traits that define culture *(language, religions, customs, food, clothing styles, and so on).* As students give ideas, write the topics on the board, across the top. Ask students to choose the one thing that they think most defines them culturally, and then have them stand in a straight row in front of that topic on the board. Record the number of students in each row. Then have the students transfer that information to a bar graph or pictograph.

OUR WORLD TODAY *Online*

Use our Web site for additional resources. All essential content is covered in the Student Edition.

You and your students can visit **owt.glencoe.com**, the Web site companion to *Our World Today*. This innovative integration of electronic and print media offers your students a wealth of opportunities. The student text directs students to the Web site for the following options:

- Chapter Overviews
- Student Web Activities
- Self-Check Quizzes
- Textbook Updates

Answers are provided for you in the Web Activity Lesson Plan. Additional Web resources and Interactive Tutor puzzles are also available.

TEACHER'S CORNER

Index to National Geographic Magazine:

The following articles may be used for research relating to this chapter:

- "Japan's Imperial Palace," by Robert M. Poole, January 2001.
- "Sumo," by T.R. Reid, July 1997.
- "Okinawa: Claiming Its Birthright," by Arthur Rich, June 1997.
- "Kuril Islands," by Charles E. Cobb, Jr., October 1996.
- "The Great Tokyo Fish Market," by T.R. Reid, November 1995.
- "Geisha," by Jodi Cobb, October 1995.

National Geographic Society Products Available From Glencoe:

To order the following products for use with this chapter, contact your local Glencoe sales representative or call Glencoe at 1-800-334-7344:

- *STV: World Geography* (Videodisc)
- *Picture Atlas of the World* (CD-ROM)
- *MapPack: Asia* (Transparencies)
- *PicturePack: Geography of Asia* (Transparencies)
- *ZipZapMap! World* (Software)
- *GeoBee* (CD-ROM)
- *Images of the World* (Posters)
- *Eye on the Environment* (Posters)

Additional National Geographic Society Products:

To order the following products for use with this chapter, call National Geographic Society at 1-800-368-2728:

- *Complete National Geographic: 111 Years of National Geographic Magazine* (CD-ROM)
- *Voices: Poetry and Art From Around the World* (Book)
- *National Geographic Desk Reference* (Book)
- *National Geographic Atlas of the World, Seventh Edition* (Book)
- *Asia* (Video)
- *Japan* (Video)
- *Physical Earth* (Map)
- *Asia Political* (Map)
- *Population* (Map)
- *Democratic Government Series* (Video)

NGS ONLINE

Access National Geographic's Web site for current events, activities, links, interactive features, and archives.
www.nationalgeographic.com

Introducing Chapter 7

Introduce students to chapter content and key terms by having them access Chapter Overview 7 at owt.glencoe.com

Chapter Objectives

1. Explain the significance of the location of Japan and the two Koreas.
2. Describe the economy and culture of Japan.
3. Compare the economies and governments of North and South Korea.

GLENCOE TECHNOLOGY

NATIONAL GEOGRAPHIC

The World and Its People Video Program

Chapter 25 Japan and the Koreas

The following segments enhance the study of this chapter:

- **Tokyo Fish Market**
- **The Haenyo of Cheju**

Available in DVD and VHS.

MindJogger Videoquiz

Use MindJogger to preview the Chapter 7 content.

Available in VHS.

Chapter 7 Japan and the Koreas

The World and Its People NATIONAL GEOGRAPHIC

To learn more about the people and places of Japan and the Koreas, view ***The World and Its People*** **Chapter 25** video.

Our World Today Online

Chapter Overview Visit the ***Our World Today: People, Places, and Issues*** Web site at owt.glencoe.com and click on **Chapter 7—Chapter Overviews** to preview information about Japan and the Koreas.

Two-Minute Lesson Launcher

Ask students to identify companies or products that they associate with Japan or South Korea. They are likely to be able to name several. Then ask them what companies or products they associate with North Korea. There will be few correct responses. Explain that for many decades, North Korea has been isolated from the world while South Korea and Japan have actively engaged in world trade. In this chapter they will learn the impacts of these decisions.

FOLDABLES™ Study Organizer

Compare-Contrast Study Foldable Make this foldable to help you compare and contrast the people and places of Japan and the Koreas.

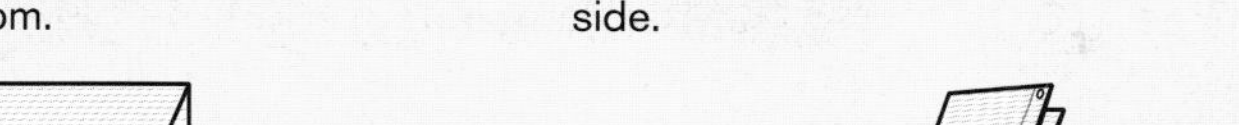

Step 1 Fold one sheet of paper in half from top to bottom.

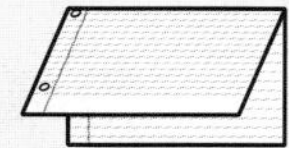

Step 2 Fold it in half again, from side to side.

Step 3 Unfold the paper once. Sketch an outline of the Koreas and Japan across both tabs and label them as shown.

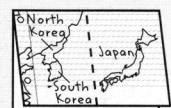

Step 4 Cut up the fold of the top flap only.

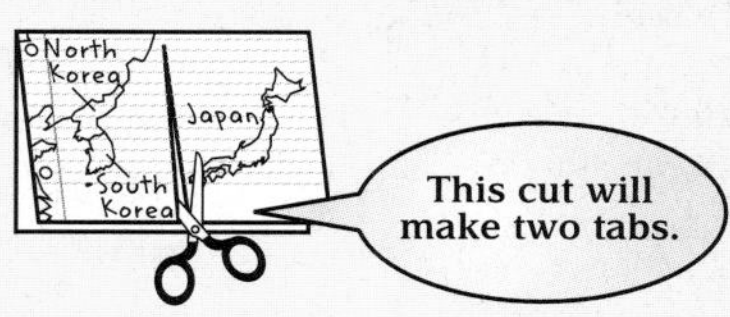

Reading and Writing As you read the chapter, write what you learn about these countries under the appropriate tab. Use your notes to determine how these countries are alike and different.

Why It Matters

Rebuilding

Only about 50 years ago, Japan and Korea were areas destroyed by war. Japan and South Korea recovered to become important centers of technology with prosperous economies. North Korea, under a communist system of government, has not enjoyed economic growth. Today, challenges arise as these nations learn to relate to one another.

◀ Mount Fuji is the national symbol of Japan.

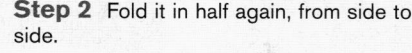

About the Photo

Mount Fuji, a dormant volcano, is one of Japan's most famous tourist attractions and one of the country's great natural wonders. In this photo ancient meets modern with Mount Fuji overlooking one of Japan's modern marvels—the Bullet Train. Japan is where regular, high-speed railways were born. The country's Shinkansen ("Bullet Train") network has been developed over more than 35 years, and today carries more than 100 million passengers per year at speeds up to 170 miles per hour. The city of Tokyo takes a central position in the Shinkansen network with most lines starting there and carrying passengers to the west and north of the densely populated nation. The Bullet Trains have a reputation for being safe, fast, comfortable, and quiet.

Introducing
Chapter 7

FOLDABLES™ Study Organizer

Purpose Students make and use a compare-contrast foldable to help them organize the similarities and differences between Japan and the Koreas. As students read the chapter and fill in information on their foldable, they analyze the similarities and differences of the people and places of Japan and the Koreas.

Have students complete ***Reading and Study Skills Foldables*** Activity 7.

Why It Matters

Tell students that Japan's industrial output rose spectacularly from the 1950s to the 1990s when a sharp recession settled in. Meanwhile, four of Japan's neighbors earned the nickname "little dragons." They were Hong Kong, Singapore, South Korea, and Taiwan. Ask students why that nickname might have been given to them *(because of the fierce economic growth).* Ask students what country they think grew the fastest during the late 1990s? *(China)*

Chapter 7

Section 1, pages 192–198

Focus

Section Objectives

1. Explain what economic activities are important in Japan.
2. Describe how the past has influenced Japan.
3. Summarize how religion has shaped culture in Japan.

BELLRINGER
Skillbuilder Activity

Project transparency and have students answer questions.

This activity is also available as a blackline master.

Daily Focus Skills Transparency 7-1

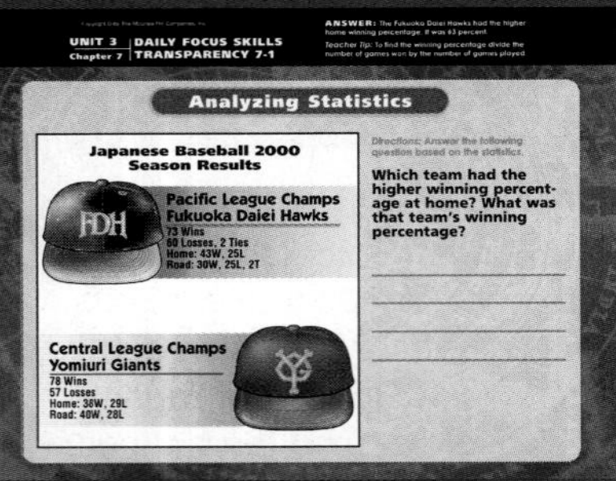

Guide to Reading

■ **Accessing Prior Knowledge**
Ask: What symbolizes the United States? *(bald eagle, flag, Statue of Liberty)* Then ask students to give ideas about items that symbolize Japan. Ask students to analyze the similarities and differences between these two nations as they learn about Japan.

Japan

Guide to Reading

Main Idea

Although Japan's people have few mineral resources, they have built a prosperous country.

Terms to Know

- tsunami
- archipelago
- intensive cultivation
- clan
- shogun
- samurai
- constitutional monarchy
- megalopolis

Reading Strategy

Create a chart like this one. In the right column, write a fact about Japan for each topic in the left column.

Japan	Fact
Land	
Economy	
History	
People	

NATIONAL GEOGRAPHIC Exploring Our World

Early one morning in 1995, the ground in the Japanese port city of Kobe (KOH•bay) began to shake. The earthquake passed in less than a minute—but the destruction was immense. Buildings and bridges like this one collapsed. Gas lines broke, and the leaking gas caught fire. Thousands of people died, and the damage exceeded $100 billion.

The city of Kobe suffered an earthquake because Japan lies on the **Ring of Fire.** This name refers to an area surrounding the Pacific Ocean where the earth's crust often shifts. Japan experiences thousands of earthquakes a year. People in Japan also have to deal with tsunamis (tsu•NAH•mees). These huge sea waves caused by undersea earthquakes are very destructive along Japan's Pacific coast.

Japan's Land

Japan is an archipelago, or a group of islands, off the coast of eastern Asia between the Sea of Japan and the Pacific Ocean. Four main islands and thousands of smaller ones make up Japan's land area. The four largest islands are **Hokkaido** (hoh•KY•doh), **Honshu, Shikoku** (shee•KOH•koo), and **Kyushu** (KYOO•SHOO).

These islands are actually the peaks of mountains that rise from the floor of the Pacific Ocean. The mountains are volcanic, but many are no longer active. The most famous peak is **Mount Fuji,** Japan's highest mountain and national symbol. Rugged mountains and steep, forested hills dominate most of Japan. Narrowly squeezed between the

Section Resources

Reproducible Masters

- Reproducible Lesson Plan 7-1
- Daily Lecture and Discussion Notes 7-1
- Guided Reading Activity 7-1
- Reading Essentials and Study Guide 7-1
- Section Quiz 7-1

Transparencies

- Daily Focus Skills Transparency 7-1
- GeoQuiz Transparency 7-1

Multimedia

- Vocabulary PuzzleMaker Software
- Interactive Tutor Self-Assessment CD-ROM
- Presentation Plus! CD-ROM
- ExamView® Pro 3.0 Testmaker CD-ROM

seacoast and the mountains are plains. The **Kanto Plain** in eastern Honshu is Japan's largest plain. It holds **Tokyo,** the capital, and **Yokohama,** one of Asia's major port cities. You will find most of Japan's cities, farms, and industries on the coastal plains.

No part of Japan is more than 70 miles (113 km) from the sea. In bay areas along the jagged coasts lie many fine harbors and ports. The northern islands catch cold arctic winds and ocean currents. The Pacific Ocean, on the other hand, sends warm ocean currents to the southern part of Japan.

✓Reading Check **What are the two major landforms in Japan?**

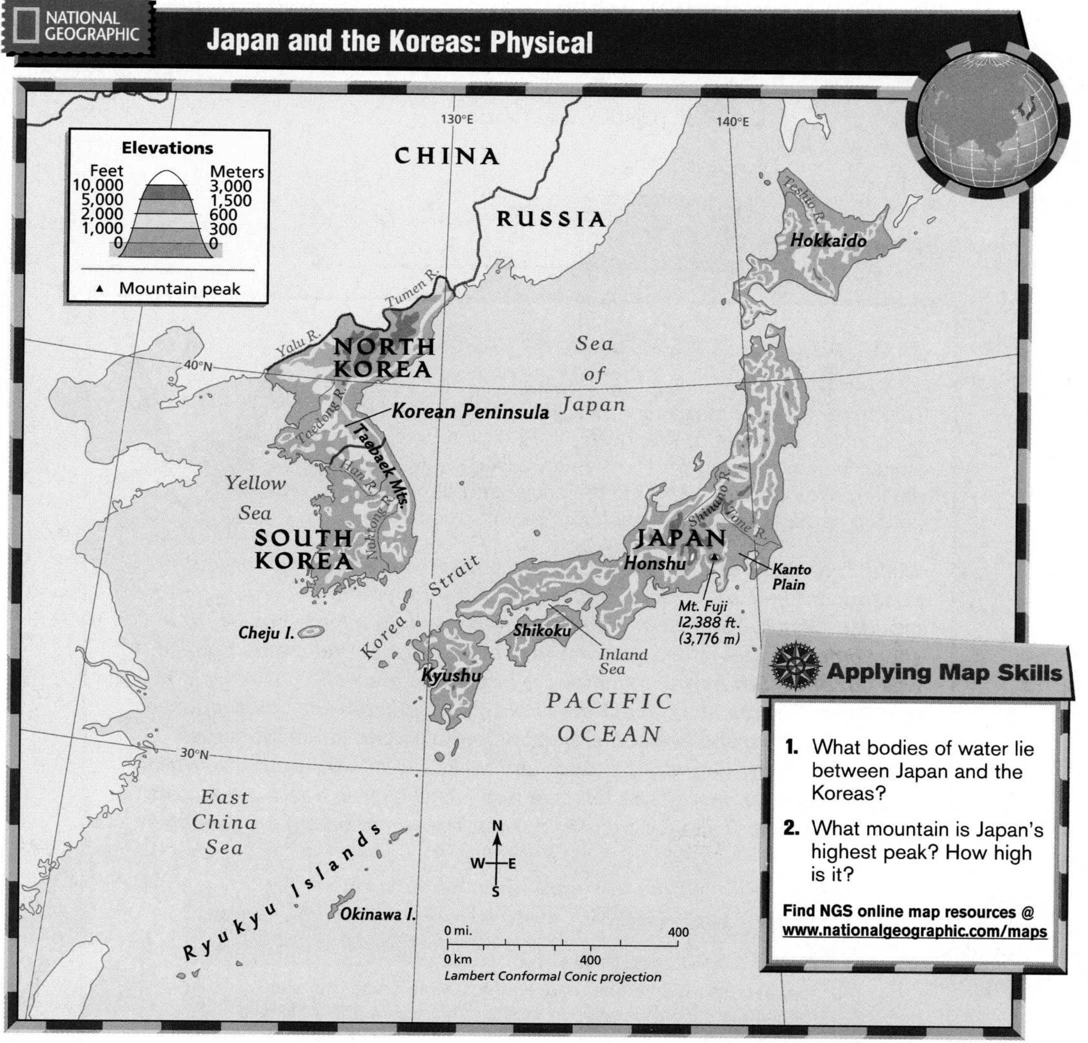

2 TEACH

Understanding Cause and Effect Give students a fact about Japan, such as "lies on the Ring of Fire." Then have them predict effects that might result from this fact. *(danger of earthquakes; need to have organized civil defense measures; need to design buildings to withstand earthquakes)* Other facts you might offer: The country is made up of many islands; sits near China; has few mineral resources; has many people. **L1**

✓ Reading Check Answer

mountains and plains

Creating a Display Ask students to create collages titled "Life in the Ring of Fire," showing earthquakes and volcanoes in Japan. Students might include maps that show where these events occurred, time lines highlighting the worst incidences, photographs showing the extent of the damage, and first-person accounts of what it was like to live through these disasters. **L1**

Applying Map Skills

Answers

1. Sea of Japan, Korea Strait
2. Mt. Fuji; 12,388 ft. (3,776 m)

Skills Practice

Why is the "Inland Sea" so named? *(because the island of Shikoku mostly protects it from the open ocean)*

Team-Teaching Activity

Science Invite a science teacher to class to discuss the different engineering methods that can be used to prevent extensive earthquake damage. For example, earthquakes make soft soil dangerous, causing buildings erected on such soil to collapse—unless they have pilings that are sunk very deep into the earth. Japanese cities may suffer extensive damage because—since wood is scarce and expensive—house walls tend not to have much wood, making the walls more likely to move and, as a result, roofs to collapse. After the presentation, have students work in groups to prepare posters listing "Do's and Don'ts of Engineering in Earthquake Zones." **L1**

EE5 Environment and Society: Standard 15

Chapter 7

Section 1, pages 192–198

Lecture Notes 7-1

JAPAN AND THE KOREAS

Daily Lecture and Discussion Notes 7-1

Japan (pages 192–198)

The Japanese call their country *Nippon* or *Nihon*, which means "source of the sun." The name *Japan* may have come from *Zipangu*, the Italian name given to the country by Marco Polo, a Venetian traveler of the late 1200s. Polo had heard of the Japanese islands while traveling through China.

I. Japan's Land *(pages 192–193)*

A. Japan experiences thousands of earthquakes a year. People in Japan also have to deal with **tsunamis.** These huge sea waves, caused by undersea earthquakes, are very destructive along Japan's Pacific coast.

B. Japan is an **archipelago,** or a group of islands, off the coast of eastern Asia between the Sea of Japan and the Pacific Ocean. Four main islands and ... aller ones make up Japan's land area. The four largest islands ... Shikoku, and Kyushu.

Literature

Answer Sadako was suffering from an illness caused by a military action. In some sense she was a soldier in the war. She was a symbol of what had happened to the nation as a whole. People wanted her to recover just as Japan was to recover.

Current Events Journal

Suggest that students use graphic organizers to link related information about Japan. For example, they can divide their notes about physical geography under the headings "Landforms" and "Bodies of Water." They could split information on the economy under "Industry" and "Agriculture."

Japan's Economy

Japan's industries have benefited from having highly skilled workers. The people of Japan value hard work, cooperation, and education. After high school graduation, many Japanese students go on to a local university.

Industry Japan has few mineral resources, so it must import raw materials, such as iron ore, coal, and oil. However, Japan is an industrial giant known around the world for the variety and quality of its manufactured goods. Japan's modern factories use new technology and robots to make their products quickly and carefully. These products include automobiles and other vehicles. The graph on page 12 in the **Geography Handbook** shows you that Japan leads the world in automobile production. Japan's factories also produce consumer goods such as electronic equipment, watches, small appliances, and calculators. Other factories produce industrial goods such as steel, cement, fertilizer, plastics, and fabrics.

Literature

SADAKO AND THE THOUSAND PAPER CRANES

by Eleanor Coerr

This book tells the true story of a young Japanese girl living in the aftermath of World War II. Radiation from the atomic bomb dropped on Hiroshima caused Sadako to get leukemia. Sadako turned to the ancient art of origami (folding paper to make objects) for strength and courage.

While Sadako closed her eyes, Chizuko put some pieces of paper and scissors on the bed . . . "I've figured out a way for you to get well," she said proudly. "Watch!" She cut a piece of gold paper into a large square. In a short time she had folded it over and over into a beautiful crane. Sadako was puzzled. "But how can that paper bird make me well?" "Don't you remember that old story about the crane?" Chizuko asked. "It's supposed to live for a thousand years. If a sick person folds one thousand paper cranes, the gods will grant her wish and make her healthy again." . . . With the golden crane nearby she felt safe and lucky. Why, in a few weeks she would be able to finish the thousand. Then she would be strong enough to go home.

Source: Sadako and the Thousand Paper Cranes by Eleanor Coerr. Copyright 1977. The Putnam Publishing Group.

Analyzing Literature

Sadako died before she reached the 1000th crane, but she became a national heroine in Japan. What was it about Sadako that made other Japanese people feel connected to her and proud of her?

Cooperative Learning Activity

Team Effort A popular Japanese proverb says "the nail that sticks out gets hammered down." Individualism is not valued in Japan. From an early age, Japanese children are taught that cooperation and loyalty to the group are the most important qualities. The ideas of teamwork, mutual help, and belonging are cultivated at work. Have students work in groups to draw up lists of those behaviors or qualities that contribute to the success of a team effort and those that can create challenges to group success. After the groups state their findings to the class, have the class as a whole discuss which set of values is promoted in their own culture. **L1** 

EE4 Human Systems: Standard 10

Agriculture Farmland is very limited. Yet Japan's farmers use fertilizers and modern machinery to produce high crop yields. They also practice **intensive cultivation**—they grow crops on every available piece of land. You can see crops growing on terraces cut in hillsides and even between buildings and highways. In warmer areas, farmers harvest two or three crops a year. The chief crop is rice, a basic part of the Japanese diet. Other important crops include sugar beets, potatoes, fruits, and tea. Seafood forms an important part of the people's diet. Although Japan's fishing fleet is large, the country imports more fish than any other nation.

Past and Present

Past and present come together in Japan. Here, a priest of the ancient Shinto religion blesses a family's shiny new car.

Place **Where was this car probably made? Why?**

Economic Challenges Japan is one of the world's leading exporters. Because of trade restrictions, the country imports few finished goods from other countries, however. This has led to disagreements with trading partners who want to export more goods to Japan.

Another challenge facing Japan is preserving the environment. Air pollution from power plants has produced acid rain. Because of overfishing, supplies of seafood have dropped. The government has passed laws to limit the amount of fish that can be caught each year.

✓Reading Check **What are some products made by Japanese manufacturers?**

Japan's History and Government

Japan's history reaches back many centuries. The Japanese trace their ancestry to various **clans**, or groups of related families, that originally came from the mainland of Asia and lived on the islands as early as the late A.D. 400s.

The Japanese developed close ties with China on the Asian mainland. Ruled by emperors, Japan modeled its society on the Chinese way of life. The Japanese also borrowed the Chinese system of writing and accepted the Buddhist religion brought by Chinese missionaries. Today most Japanese practice Buddhism along with **Shinto,** Japan's own traditional nature religion.

In the 790s, the power of Japanese emperors began to decline. From the late 1100s to the 1860s, Japan was ruled by **shoguns**, or military leaders, and powerful land-owning warriors known as the

More About the Photo

Shinto Although the religion had been followed for centuries, Shinto did not have a name in Japan until the A.D. 500s. Then, as Buddhism made gains, traditional beliefs were given the name Shinto, which means "the way of *kami*" (the spiritual or divine).

Caption Answer Japan; it is the world's leading car manufacturer

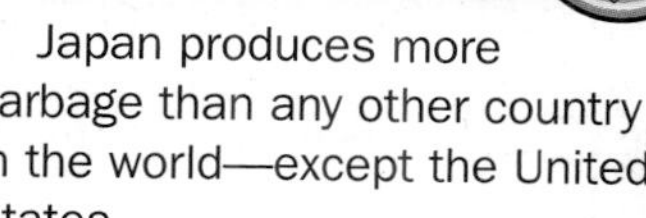

Japan produces more garbage than any other country in the world—except the United States.

✓ Reading Check Answer

automobiles and other motor vehicles, consumer goods (electronic equipment, watches, small appliances, and calculators), steel, cement, fertilizer, plastics, fabrics

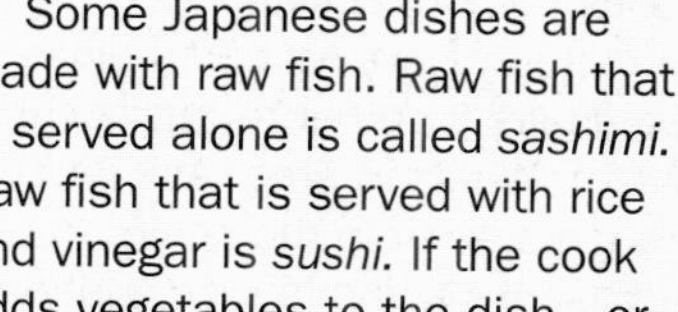

Some Japanese dishes are made with raw fish. Raw fish that is served alone is called *sashimi*. Raw fish that is served with rice and vinegar is *sushi*. If the cook adds vegetables to the dish—or substitutes vegetables for the fish—the dish is called *norimaki*.

Critical Thinking Activity

Analyzing Information Write the following Japanese proverb: "Failure is the source of success." Then ask students to analyze the information under Japan's Economy and Japan's History and Government for examples that confirm the proverb. For each example, direct students to find passages that describe a failure and the success that came from that failure. Encourage students to share and compare their examples and passages. **L2**

EE2 Places and Regions: Standard 4

Cultural Kaleidoscope

Japan Tea came to Japan from China around A.D. 800. It quickly became a beverage of the rich, although the poor occasionally used it as a medicine. In the 1400s, the practice of drinking tea became very popular throughout Japan. This was due, in part, to the Japanese court's adoption of the Buddhist tea ceremony.

Guided Reading Activity 7-1

Name ________ Date ________ Class ________

JAPAN AND THE KOREAS

Guided Reading Activity 7-1

Japan

DIRECTIONS: Answering Questions Reading the section and answering the questions below will help you learn more about the country of Japan. Use your textbook to write answers to the questions.

1. Why does Japan experience so many earthquakes and tsunamis?
2. What makes up Japan's land area?
3. What is Japan known for in industry?
4. What do Japanese farmers practice?

Reading Check Answer

constitutional monarchy

Creating a Model Ask students to create a model to illustrate population density and its effect on culture. Have students place five chairs together to represent California's land area. Ask four students to sit in the chairs to represent California's population density. Then separate the five chairs to represent Japan's land area in islands. Have four students sit on only two chairs to show how only half of Japan is habitable (the rest of Japan is too mountainous for habitation).

Hard Hats to School?

Okajima Yukiko and Sataka Aya walk along ash-covered sidewalks to Kurokami Junior High School. Why are they wearing hard hats? Their city is near Japan's Mount Oyama Volcano, which has just erupted. Yukiko and Aya have grown up facing the dangers of volcanic eruptions, earthquakes, and tsunamis. At school their first class starts at 8:30 A.M., and their last class ends at 3:40 P.M. Yukiko and Aya must go to school every second Saturday of the month, too.

samurai. Like China, Japan did not want to trade with foreign countries. In 1853 the United States government sent a fleet headed by Commodore Matthew Perry to Japan to demand trading privileges. In response to this action and other outside pressures, the Japanese started trading with other countries.

In the late 1800s, Japanese leaders began to use Western ideas to modernize the country, improve education, and set up industries. By the early 1900s, Japan was the leading military power in Asia.

In the 1930s, Japan needed more resources for its growing population. It took land in China and spread its influence to Southeast Asia. In 1941 Japanese forces attacked the American naval base at **Pearl Harbor** in Hawaii. This attack caused the United States to enter World War II. After four years of fighting, Japan surrendered when the United States dropped atomic bombs on the cities of **Hiroshima** and **Nagasaki.** By that time, many of Japan's cities lay in ruins and the economy had collapsed. With help from the United States, Japan became a democracy and quickly rebuilt its ruined economy.

Government Japan's democracy is in the form of a **constitutional monarchy.** The emperor is the official head of state, but elected officials run the government. Voters elect representatives to the national legislature. The political party with the most members chooses a prime minister to lead the government.

Japan has great influence as a world economic power. In addition, it gives large amounts of money to poorer countries. Japan is not a military power, though. Because of the suffering that World War II caused, the Japanese have chosen to keep Japan's military small.

The government of Japan has improved health care and education for its people. Japan has the lowest infant death rate in the world and its literacy rate is almost 100 percent. The crime rate in Japan is very low.

Reading Check What kind of government does Japan have?

Japan's People and Culture

Although about the size of California, Japan has 127.1 million people—nearly one-half the population of the United States. Most of Japan's people belong to the same Japanese ethnic background. Look at the map on page 197 to see where most of Japan's people live. About three-fourths are crowded into urban areas on the coastal plains. The four large cities of Tokyo, Yokohama, Nagoya, and Osaka form a **megalopolis,** or a huge urban area made up of several large cities and communities near them.

Japan's cities have tall office buildings, busy streets, and speedy highways. Homes and apartments are small and close to one another. Many city workers crowd into subway trains to get to work. Men work long hours and arrive home very late. Women often quit their jobs to raise children and return to work when the children are grown.

You still see signs of traditional life, even in the cities. Parks and gardens give people a chance to take a break from the busy day. It is

Team-Teaching Activity

Government Invite a teacher with a background in government to discuss the parliamentary system of government in Japan. The discussion should address such issues as elections, the selection of the prime minister and the cabinet, coalition governments, and votes of no confidence. Then have students make a chart comparing government in Japan to that in the United States, placing the similarities in one column and the differences in another. **L1** 

EE4 Human Systems: Standard 12

common to see a person dressed in a traditional garment called a kimono walking with another person wearing a T-shirt and jeans.

Only 22 percent of Japan's people live in rural areas. In both rural and urban Japan, the family traditionally has been the center of one's life. Each family member had to obey certain rules. Grandparents, parents, and children all lived in one house. Family ties still remain strong, but each family member is now allowed more freedom. Many family groups today consist only of parents and children.

Religion Many Japanese practice two religions—Shinto and Buddhism. Shinto began in Japan many centuries ago. It teaches respect for nature, love of simple things, and concern for cleanliness and good manners. Shinto is different from other religions for several reasons. First, there is no person who founded or started the religion. Shinto did not spread to other areas of the world, but stayed mostly in Japan. Also, there is no collection of writings that make up scripture, such as the Bible or the Quran. Buddhism also teaches respect for nature and the need to achieve inner peace.

Traditional Arts Japan's religions have influenced the country's arts. Many paintings portray the beauty of nature, often with a few simple brush strokes. Some even include verses of poetry. Haiku (HY•koo) is a well-known type of Japanese poetry that is written according to a very specific formula. Turn to page 199 to learn more about haiku.

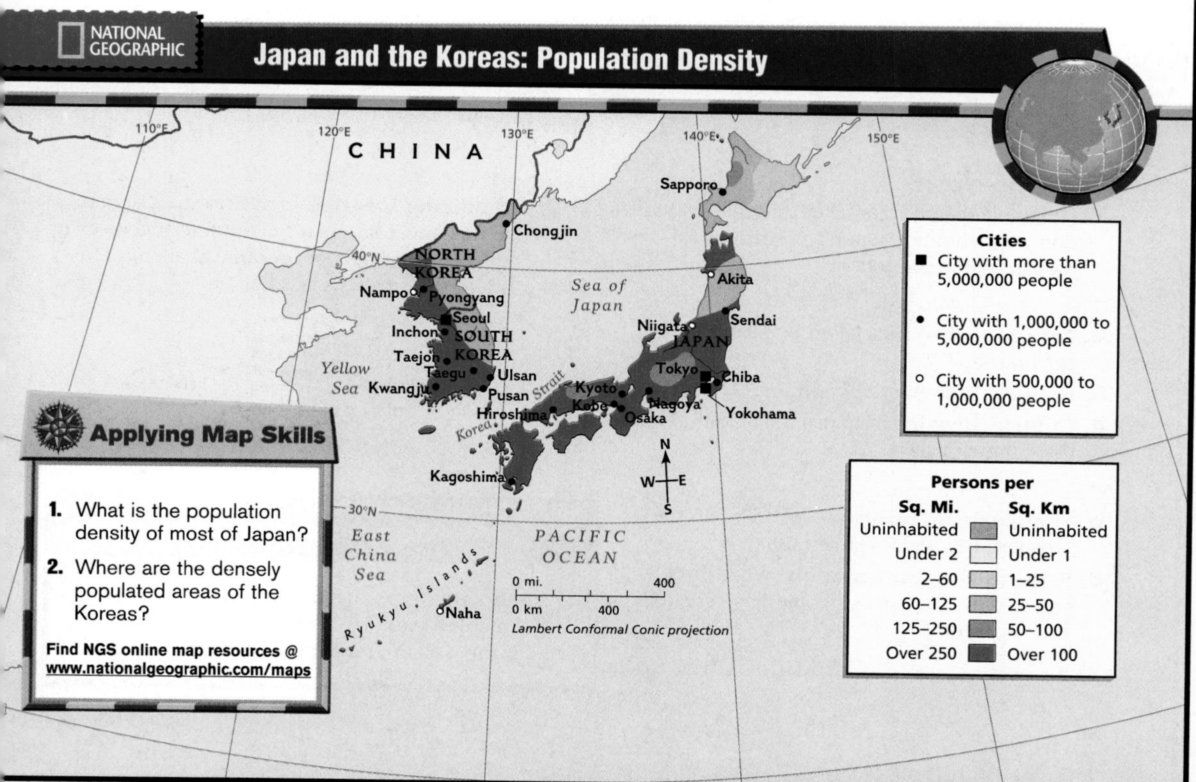

Content Background

Shinto All Japanese belong to the State Shinto—Japan's official religion. Shinto has no founder or sacred book. Its followers worship numerous gods, emperors, heroes, and ancestors. State Shinto demands loyalty to the emperor, who is believed to be descended from the Sun Goddess. Another division of Shinto, Shrine Shinto, centers its rites around state-supported shrines. At these locales, priests pray for peace, good harvests, and prosperity for all. Festivals held at these shrines incorporate many Buddhist practices.

3 Assess

Assign Section 1 Assessment as homework or an in-class activity.

Have students use the Interactive Tutor Self-Assessment CD-ROM to review Section 7–1.

Applying Map Skills

Answers

1. over 250 people per square mile (over 100 per sq. km)
2. along the west coast of the Korean Peninsula

Skills Practice

What Japanese cities have more than 5 million people? *(Tokyo and Yokohama)*

Section Quiz 7-1

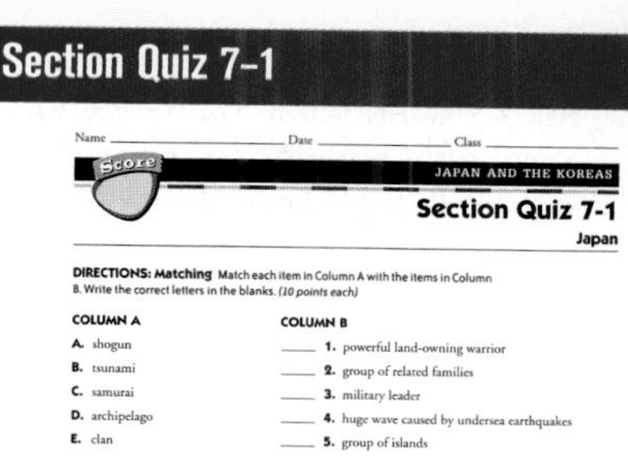
Name ____ Date ____ Class ____

JAPAN AND THE KOREAS

Section Quiz 7-1

Japan

DIRECTIONS: Matching Match each item in Column A with the items in Column B. Write the correct letters in the blanks. (10 points each)

COLUMN A	COLUMN B
A. shogun	___ 1. powerful land-owning warrior
B. tsunami	___ 2. group of related families
C. samurai	___ 3. military leader
D. archipelago	___ 4. huge wave caused by undersea earthquakes
E. clan	___ 5. group of islands

DIRECTIONS: Multiple Choice In the blank at the left, write the letter of the choice that best completes the statement or answers the question. (10 points each)

Chapter 7

Section 1, pages 192–198

Reteach

Have students write a paragraph explaining how a lack of land resources in Japan has affected the use of technology there.

✓ Reading Check Answer

Shinto, Buddhism

Reading Essentials and Study Guide 7-1

Name ______ Date ______ Class ______

JAPAN AND THE KOREAS

Reading Essentials and Study Guide 7-1

Japan

For use with textbook pages 192–198

Terms to Know

tsunamis huge sea waves caused by undersea earthquakes (page 192)
archipelago group of islands (page 192)
intensive cultivation growing crops on every available piece of land (page 194)
clan group of related families (page 195)
shogun military leader in Japan (page 195)
samurai Japanese warrior (page 195)
constitutional monarchy government headed by a king or queen, but run by elected officials (page 196)
megalopolis huge urban area made up of several large cities and communities near them (page 196)

Enrich

Have students use primary and secondary sources to research the culture of the samurai and prepare a display summarizing their findings.

CLOSE

Have students write a paragraph analyzing what is unique about Japan and how Japan is like other countries.

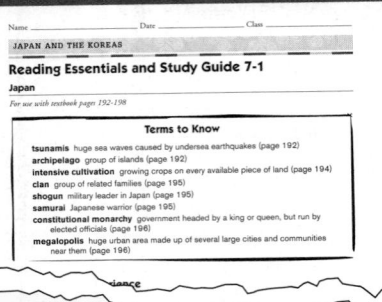

The Japanese also have a rich heritage of literature and drama. Many scholars believe that the world's first novel came from Japan. The novel is called *The Tale of Genji* and was written by a noblewoman about A.D. 1000. Since the 1600s, Japanese theatergoers have attended the historical plays of the Kabuki theater. In Kabuki plays, actors wearing brilliantly colored costumes perform on colorful stages.

Many of Japan's sports have their origins in the past. A popular sport is sumo, an ancient Japanese form of wrestling. In sumo wrestling, two players try to force their opponent to touch the ground with any part of their body other than the feet. The players may not punch, kick, or pull hair during the competition. To participate in sumo wrestling, a person should weigh about 300 pounds (136 km). Two ancient martial arts—judo and karate—also developed in this area. Today, martial arts are practiced both for self-defense and for exercise.

Modern Pastimes Along with these traditional arts, the people of Japan enjoy modern pastimes. Many Japanese are enthusiastic about baseball, and the professional leagues in Japan field several teams. Several Japanese players have become stars in the major leagues of the United States. Despite Japan's strong emphasis on education, life is not all work for Japanese young people. They enjoy rock music, modern fashions, television, and movies. Japanese cartoon shows are popular around the world.

✓ Reading Check What two religions are found in Japan?

Assessment

Defining Terms

1. **Define** tsunami, archipelago, intensive cultivation, clan, shogun, samurai, constitutional monarchy, megalopolis.

Recalling Facts

2. **Location** Why does Japan experience earthquakes?
3. **History** Who were the samurai?
4. **Culture** How have Japan's religions influenced the country's arts?

Critical Thinking

5. **Summarizing Information** Why do the Japanese not want a large military?
6. **Synthesizing Information** What three values of the Japanese people have created good workers?

Graphic Organizer

7. **Organizing Information** Create a diagram like this one. List Japan's economic successes in the large oval and its economic challenges in each of the smaller ovals.

Applying Social Studies Skills

8. **Analyzing Maps** Look at the population density map on page 197. Which Japanese cities have more than 5 million people?

Section 1 Assessment

1. The terms are defined in the Glossary.
2. It sits on the Ring of Fire, an area where the earth's crust often shifts.
3. powerful land-owning warriors who ruled Japan from the late 1100s to the 1860s
4. Shinto and Buddhism teach respect for nature, and many paintings and poems express the beauty of nature.
5. because of the suffering caused by World War II
6. education, hard work, cooperation
7. *Successes:* industrial giant; intensive cultivation of land; productive fishing fleet; *Challenges:* disagreements with trading partners; pollution; overfishing
8. Tokyo and Yokohama

Making Connections

CULTURE | GOVERNMENT | PEOPLE | TECHNOLOGY

Haiku

Haiku is a type of poetry that first became popular in Japan during the 1600s. A haiku is a three-line poem, usually about nature and human emotions. The traditional haiku requires 17 syllables—5 in the first line, 7 in the second line, and 5 in the third line. All of the haiku below, written by famous Japanese poets, concern the subject of New Year's Day.*

For this New Year's Day,
The sight we gaze upon shall be
Mount Fuji.
Sôkan

That is good, this too is good,—
New Year's Day
In my old age.
Rôyto

New Year's Day;
Whosoever's face we see,
It is care-free.
Shigyoku

New Year's Day:
My hovel,
The same as ever.
Issa

New Year's Day:
What luck! What luck!
A pale blue sky!
Issa

The dawn of New Year's Day;
Yesterday,
How far off!
Ichiku

▲ This Japanese wood-block print shows two girls playing a New Year's game.

The first dream of the year;
I kept it a secret,
And smiled to myself.
Shô-u

*The translations may have affected the number of syllables.
Excerpts from *Haiku, Volume II.* Copyright © 1952 by R.H. Blyth. Reprinted by permission of Hokuseido Press.

Making the Connection

1. How does the poet Shigyoku think most people react to New Year's Day?
2. From his poem, how can you tell that Ichiku sees the New Year as a new beginning?
3. **Making Comparisons** Compare the two poems by Issa. How does his mood change from one to the other?

Teach

Ask students to name some poems they have read and to describe their reactions to these poems. Then remind students that reading poetry is different from reading prose. Poetry demands more of the reader than prose does. In a short story or novel, the reader can often get the gist of the plot without necessarily understanding every word. A poem, however, should be read slowly and carefully several times. Each word in a poem is important, and the sound of a poem is also extremely important.

More About Haiku

Perhaps the foremost master of haiku was Matsuo Basho, who lived in the 1600s. At first a samurai, Basho became a noted poet and critic. The haiku form had existed before him, but it had become trivial and silly. Basho's gemlike verses elevated the haiku to a new art form that used compressed language to suggest eternal truths.

Interdisciplinary Connections

Literature Originally, haiku were meant to describe something in nature while evoking an emotional response. Have students attempt writing a haiku about nature. Remind them that the best haiku use very concrete details.

Making the Connection

1. It makes them feel lighthearted and carefree.
2. He conveys the idea that yesterday is gone and forgotten.
3. In the first poem, Issa indicates that his life will continue being miserable. In the second, he feels blessed by the beauty of the world around him.

Chapter 7

Section 2, pages 200–203

1 Focus

Section Objectives

1. Locate the Korean Peninsula.
2. Explain why the two Koreas are divided.
3. Compare life in North and South Korea.

BELLRINGER Skillbuilder Activity

Project transparency and have students answer questions.

This activity is also available as a blackline master.

Daily Focus Skills Transparency 7-2

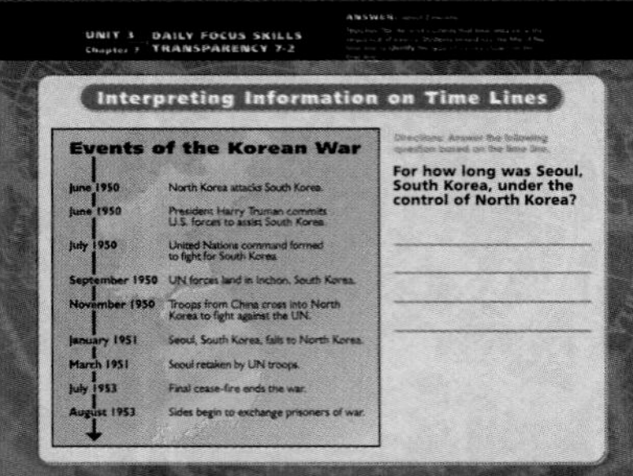

UNIT 3 Chapter 7 DAILY FOCUS SKILLS TRANSPARENCY 7-2

Interpreting Information on Time Lines

Events of the Korean War

June 1950	North Korea attacks South Korea.
June 1950	President Harry Truman commits U.S. forces to assist South Korea.
July 1950	United Nations command formed to fight for South Korea.
September 1950	UN forces land in Inchon, South Korea.
November 1950	Troops from China cross into North Korea to fight against the UN.
January 1951	Seoul, South Korea, falls to North Korea.
March 1951	Seoul retaken by UN troops.
July 1953	Final cease-fire ends the war.
August 1953	Sides begin to exchange prisoners of war.

Directions: Answer the following question based on the time line.

For how long was Seoul, South Korea, under the control of North Korea?

Guide to Reading

■ **Accessing Prior Knowledge** Ask students why they think these two countries share the same name but are separated. After students have suggested reasons, have them read the section.

Use the Vocabulary PuzzleMaker to create crossword and word search puzzles.

Section 2 The Two Koreas

Guide to Reading

Main Idea

South Korea and North Korea share the same peninsula and history, but they have very different political and economic systems.

Terms to Know

- dynasty
- monsoon
- famine

Reading Strategy

Create a time line like this one to record four important dates and their events in Korean history.

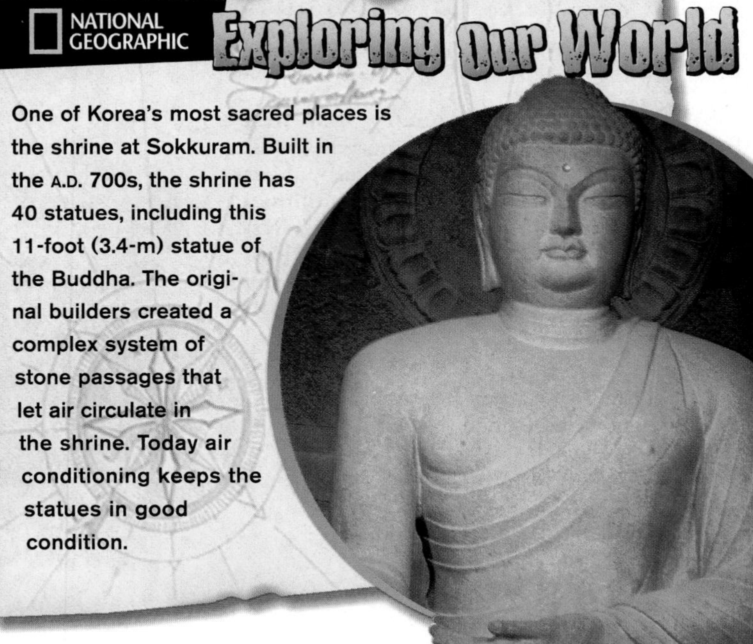

NATIONAL GEOGRAPHIC **Exploring Our World**

One of Korea's most sacred places is the shrine at Sokkuram. Built in the A.D. 700s, the shrine has 40 statues, including this 11-foot (3.4-m) statue of the Buddha. The original builders created a complex system of stone passages that let air circulate in the shrine. Today air conditioning keeps the statues in good condition.

The **Korean Peninsula** juts out from northern China, between the Sea of Japan and the Yellow Sea. For centuries, this piece of land held a unified country. Today the peninsula is divided into two nations—Communist **North Korea** and non-Communist **South Korea.** For nearly 50 years after World War II, the two governments were bitter enemies. Since the 1990s, they have been drawing closer together.

A Divided Country

The Koreans trace their ancestry to people who settled on the peninsula thousands of years ago. From the 100s B.C. until the early A.D. 300s, neighboring China ruled Korea. When Chinese control ended, separate Korean kingdoms arose throughout the peninsula.

From A.D. 668 to 935, a single kingdom called **Silla** (SHIH•luh) united much of the peninsula. During this time, Korea made many cultural and scientific advances. For example, Silla rulers built one of the world's earliest astronomical observatories in the A.D. 600s.

Other **dynasties,** or ruling families, followed the Silla. In the 1400s, scholars invented a new way of writing the Korean language. This new

Section Resources

Reproducible Masters

- Reproducible Lesson Plan 7-2
- Daily Lecture and Discussion Notes 7-2
- Guided Reading Activity 7-2
- Reading Essentials and Study Guide 7-2
- Section Quiz 7-2

Transparencies

- Daily Focus Skills Transparency 7-2
- GeoQuiz Transparency 7-1

Multimedia

- Vocabulary PuzzleMaker Software
- Interactive Tutor Self-Assessment CD-ROM
- Presentation Plus! CD-ROM
- ExamView® Pro 3.0 Testmaker CD-ROM

system—called *hangul* (HAHN•GOOL)—used only 28 symbols to write words. This is far fewer than the thousands of characters needed to write Chinese, making the Korean system much easier to learn.

The Korean Peninsula was a stepping stone between Japan and mainland Asia. Trade and ideas went back and forth. In 1910 the Japanese conquered Korea and made it part of their empire. They governed the peninsula until the end of World War II in 1945.

Division and War After World War II, troops from the Communist Soviet Union took over the northern half of Korea. American troops occupied the southern half. Korea eventually divided along the 38th parallel. A communist state arose in what came to be called North Korea. A noncommunist government controlled South Korea.

In 1950 the armies of North Korea attacked South Korea. They hoped to unite all of Korea under communist rule. United Nations countries, led by the United States, rushed to support South Korea. The **Korean War** finally ended in 1953—without a peace treaty or a victory for either side. By the 1960s, two separate countries had developed on the Korean Peninsula.

After years of bitterness, the two Koreas in the 1990s developed closer relations. In the year 2000, led by a "unification flag," athletes of North and South Korea marched together in the opening ceremony of the Sydney, Australia, Olympics. That same year the leaders of North Korea and South Korea held a meeting for the first time since the division.

✓ Reading Check **Why is the Korean Peninsula divided?**

South Korea

South Korea, much of which is covered by mountains, lies at the southern end of the Korean Peninsula. Most South Koreans live in coastal areas where they are affected by monsoons. A **monsoon** is the

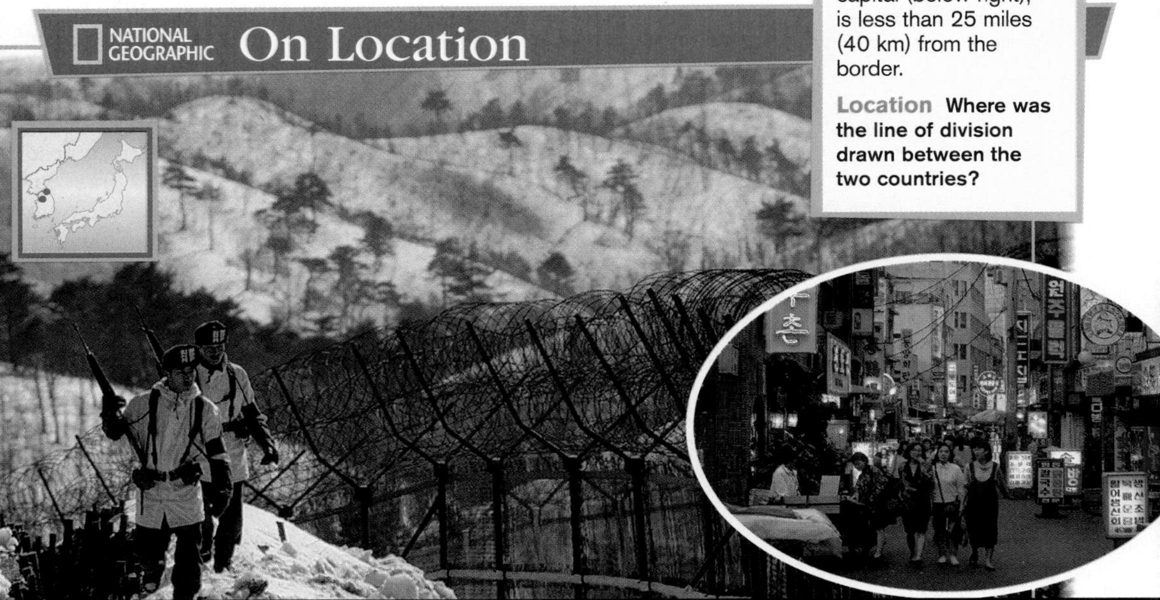

Korean Border

Nearly 50 years after the fighting stopped in Korea, troops still patrol the border between North and South Korea (below left). Seoul, South Korea's modern capital (below right), is less than 25 miles (40 km) from the border.

Location **Where was the line of division drawn between the two countries?**

Chapter 7

Section 2, pages 200–203

TEACH

Categorizing Information

Organize students into two teams. Read them a series of statements, and require teams to say whether the statement applies to North Korea, South Korea, or both. **L1**

✓ Reading Check Answer

because the Communists held one half and an American-backed government held the other half

More About the Photos

The Border The border between North and South Korea is a demilitarized zone (DMZ), where only small weapons are allowed. Inside this region is the village of Panmunjom, where the two sides carried out the truce negotiations that ended the fighting in 1953.

Caption Answer along the 38th parallel

Daily Lecture Notes 7-2

JAPAN AND THE KOREAS

Daily Lecture and Discussion Notes 7-2

The Two Koreas (pages 200–203)

Did You Know? Until the early 1900s, Korea's economy was based entirely on agriculture, and almost all Koreans worked as farmers. After the early 1900s, the country underwent vast changes. Today industry is far more important than agriculture in both North Korea and South Korea.

I. A Divided Country *(pages 200–201)*

A. The Korean Peninsula juts out from northern China, between the Sea of Japan and the Yellow Sea. Today the peninsula is divided into two nations—Communist North Korea and non-Communist South Korea.

B. China ruled Korea until the A.D. 300s. From A.D. 668 to 935, a single kingdom called Silla united much of the peninsula. Other **dynasties**, or ruling families,

Team-Teaching Activity

History Invite a teacher with a background in world history to discuss the circumstances around the Korean War. Suggest that the teacher discuss such issues as the early Cold War years in Europe, the Communist takeover in China in 1949, and the North Korean invasion that launched the Korean War. Have the teacher also discuss the successful American-South Korean counterattack and the entry of China into the war. Have students discuss how these events might have affected the views of people in the two Koreas. **L1**

EE4 Human Systems: Standard 13

More About the Photo

Sonun-sa Temple Although the majority of South Koreans are Buddhist, many Koreans became Christian after the first missionaries were allowed into the country in 1882.

Caption Answer China

Guided Reading Activity 7-2

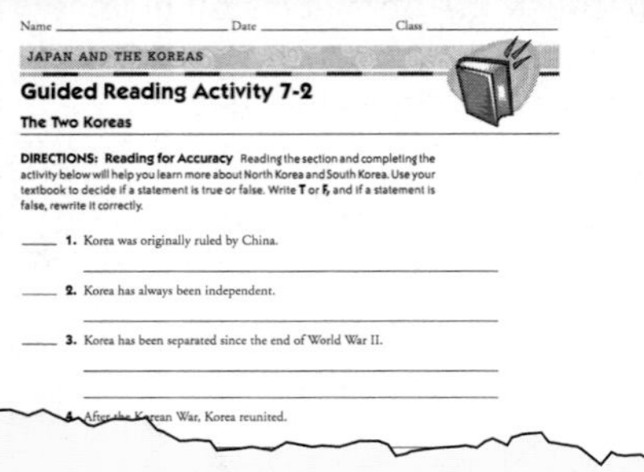
Name ______ Date ______ Class ______

JAPAN AND THE KOREAS

Guided Reading Activity 7-2

The Two Koreas

DIRECTIONS: Reading for Accuracy Reading the section and completing the activity below will help you learn more about North Korea and South Korea. Use your textbook to decide if a statement is true or false. Write **T** or **F**, and if a statement is false, rewrite it correctly.

____ 1. Korea was originally ruled by China.

____ 2. Korea has always been independent.

____ 3. Korea has been separated since the end of World War II.

____ 4. After the Korean War, Korea reunited.

Reading Check Answer

Christianity, Buddhism, and Confucianism

ASSESS

Assign Section 2 Assessment as homework or an in-class activity.

Have students use the Interactive Tutor Self-Assessment CD-ROM to review Section 7–2.

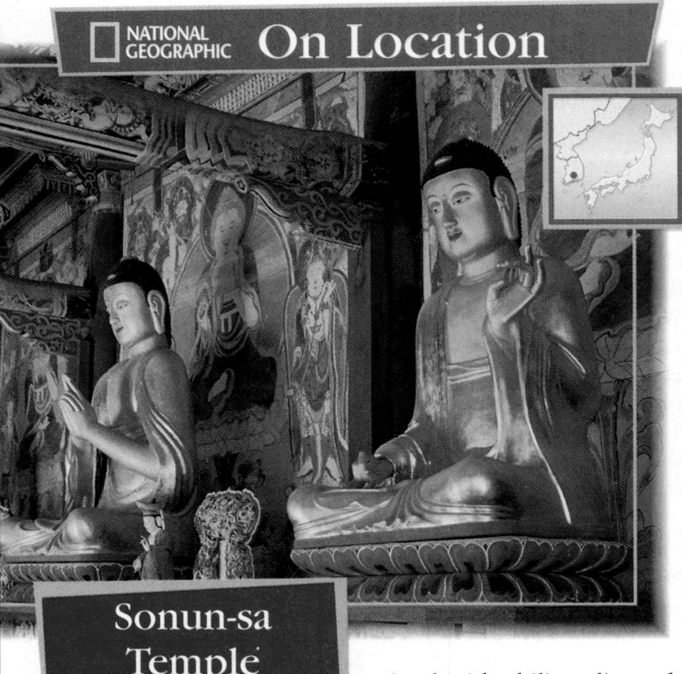

Sonun-sa Temple

Gilded Buddhas such as these at Sonun-sa Temple adorn many Buddhist temples throughout South Korea.

History **Which country influenced the religion of South Korea?**

seasonal wind that blows over Asia for months at a time. During the summer, a monsoon from the south brings hot, humid weather. In the winter, a monsoon blows in from the north, bringing cold, dry weather.

Manufacturing and trade dominate South Korea's economy. High-technology and service industries have grown tremendously. The country is a leading exporter of ships, cars, textiles, computers, and electronic appliances. In the 1990s, South Korea faced economic difficulties, but it remains one of the economic powers of Asia.

South Korean farmers own their land, although most of their farms are very small. The major crops are rice, barley, onions, potatoes, cabbage, apples, and tangerines. Rice is the country's basic food item. One of the most popular Korean dishes is *kimchi,* a highly spiced blend of vegetables mixed with chili, garlic, and ginger. Many farmers also raise livestock, especially chickens. Some add to their income by fishing.

South Korea's People The people of the two Koreas belong to the same Korean ethnic group. South Korea has nearly 49 million people. More than 80 percent live in cities and towns in the coastal plains. South Korea's capital, **Seoul,** is the largest city.

Most city dwellers live in tall apartment buildings. Many own cars, but they also use buses, subways, and trains to travel to and from work. In rural areas, people live in small, one-story homes made of brick or concrete blocks. A large number of South Koreans have emigrated to the United States since the end of the Korean War.

Buddhism, Confucianism, and Christianity are South Korea's major religions. The Koreans have developed their own culture, but Chinese religion and culture influenced the traditional arts of Korea. In Seoul you will discover ancient palaces modeled after the Imperial Palace in Beijing, China. Historic Buddhist temples—like Sokkuram—dot the hills and valleys of the countryside. Within these temples are beautifully carved figures of the Buddha in stone, iron, and gold. One of the great achievements of early Koreans was pottery. Korean potters still make bowls and dishes that are admired around the world.

Like Japan, Korea has a tradition of martial arts. Have you heard of tae kwon do? This martial art originated in Korea. Those who study it learn mental discipline as well as self-defense.

Reading Check **What are the major religions in South Korea?**

Meeting Special Needs

Naturalistic Korean cooks balance their meals by following the rule of Five Flavors—including tastes that are salt, sweet, sour, bitter, and hot. Soy sauce and bean paste supply the salty flavor; honey, sugar, and sweet potatoes add sweetness; vinegar provides sourness; ginger contributes bitterness; and mustard and chili peppers add heat. Garlic, green onions, sesame seeds, cinnamon, and eggs are some of the other ingredients found in many Korean dishes. Have interested students bring some of these seasonings to class or prepare a Korean dish and bring it to class. **L1**

Refer to *Inclusion for the Middle School Social Studies Classroom Strategies and Activities* in the TCR.

North Korea

Separated from China by the **Yalu River,** Communist North Korea is slightly larger than South Korea. Like South Korea, monsoons affect the climate, but the central mountains block some of the winter monsoon. The eastern coast generally has warmer winters than the rest of the country.

The North Korean government owns and runs factories and farms. It spends much money on the military. Unlike prosperous South Korea, North Korea is economically poor. Coal and iron ore are plentiful, but industries suffer from old equipment and power shortages.

About 75 percent of North Korea's rugged landscape is forested. This leaves little land to farm, yet more than 40 percent of North Korea's people are farmers who work on large, government-run farms. These farms do not grow enough food to feed the country. A lack of fertilizer recently produced **famines,** or severe food shortages.

North Korea's People North Korea has about 22 million people. Nearly 60 percent live in urban areas along the coasts and river valleys. **Pyongyang** is the capital and largest city. Largely rebuilt since the Korean War, Pyongyang has many modern buildings and monuments to Communist leaders. Most of these monuments honor Kim Il Sung, who became North Korea's first ruler in the late 1940s. After Kim's death in 1994, his son Kim Jong Il became the ruler.

The Communist government discourages the practice of religion, although many people still hold to their traditional beliefs. The government also places the needs of the communist system over the needs of individuals and families.

Reading Check **Who controls the economy of North Korea?**

Web Activity Visit the ***Our World Today: People, Places, and Issues*** Web site at owt.glencoe.com and click on **Chapter 7–Student Web Activities** to learn more about South Korea.

Section 2 Assessment

Defining Terms

1. **Define** dynasty, monsoon, famine.

Recalling Facts

2. **Location** Where is the Korean Peninsula?
3. **History** Why did Korea become divided?
4. **Economics** What products are made in South Korea?

Critical Thinking

5. **Making Comparisons** How does the standard of living in South Korea differ from that in North Korea?
6. **Summarizing Information** What country has had the greatest influence on the culture and arts of South Korea? Explain.

Graphic Organizer

7. **Organizing Information** Create a diagram like this one. Write facts about each country's economics, government, and natural resources in the outer ovals. Where the ovals overlap, write facts that are common to both countries.

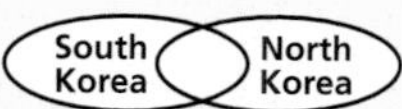

Applying Social Studies Skills

8. **Analyzing Maps** Turn to the population density map on page 197. What is the most populous city on the Korean Peninsula? In which country is it located?

Section 2 Assessment

1. The terms are defined in the Glossary.
2. It juts out from northern China between the Sea of Japan and the Yellow Sea.
3. because the Communists controlled the north and an American-based non-communist government ruled the south
4. ships, cars, textiles, computers, and electronic appliances
5. The standard of living in South Korea is quite high, but most people living in North Korea are very poor.
6. China; South Korea modeled its capital after the Chinese capital, and Buddhism influenced the country as well
7. Answers will vary.
8. Seoul; South Korea

Section Quiz 7-2

Name ______ Date ______ Class ______

JAPAN AND THE KOREAS

Section Quiz 7-2

The Two Koreas

DIRECTIONS: Matching Match each item in Column A with the items in Column B. Write the correct letters in the blanks. (10 points each)

COLUMN A	COLUMN B
A. Korean Peninsula	___ 1. severe food shortage
B. famine	___ 2. capital city of North Korea
C. Seoul	___ 3. juts out from northern China between the Sea of Japan and Yellow Sea
D. Pyongyang	___ 4. capital city of South Korea
E. *hangul*	___ 5. system for writing the Korean language

Our World Today Online

Objectives, goals, and answers to the Student Web Activity can be found in the Web Activity Lesson Plan at **owt.glencoe.com**

Reading Check Answer

the government

Reading Essentials and Study Guide 7-2

Name ______ Date ______ Class ______

JAPAN AND THE KOREAS

Reading Essentials and Study Guide 7-2

The Two Koreas

For use with textbook pages 200–203

Terms to Know

dynasty ruling family (page 200)
monsoon wind that blows for months at a time in certain seasons over Asia (page 201)
famine severe lack of food (page 203)

Drawing From Experience

Have you ever seen someone perform martial arts in movies or video games? Perhaps you know of classes in your area that teach these skills. Korea invented one popular martial art—tae kwon do.

Close

Have students prepare a bulletin board display comparing and contrasting the Koreas.

TEACH

Give students the following situation: Suppose you want to buy a portable CD player, and you must choose among three models. Ask students what criteria they would use to make the purchase. *(Students may respond that they would compare such characteristics of the three models as price, sound quality, and size.)* L1

Additional Skills Practice

1. **In comparing two countries' economic performance, what factors might you compare?** *(products made, gross national product, or relative wealth of people)*
2. **In terms of physical geography, what factors can you use to compare two countries?** *(landforms, climate, location in relation to Equator, location in relation to other countries, size)*

Additional Skills Resources

 Chapter Skills Activity 7

 Building Geography Skills for Life

GLENCOE TECHNOLOGY

 **Skillbuilder Interactive Workbook CD-ROM, Level 1**

This interactive CD-ROM reinforces student mastery of essential social studies skills.

Critical Thinking Skill

Making Comparisons

When you make comparisons, you determine similarities and differences among ideas, objects, or events. By comparing maps and graphs, you can learn more about a region.

Learning the Skill

Follow these steps to make comparisons:

- Identify or decide what will be compared.
- Determine a common area or areas in which comparisons can be drawn.
- Look for similarities and differences within these areas.

Practicing the Skill

Use the map and graph below to make comparisons and answer these questions:

1. What is the title of the map? The graph?
2. How are the map and graph related?
3. Which country has the most exports and imports?
4. Does a country's size have any effect on the amount it exports? Explain.
5. What generalizations can you make about this map and graph?

Applying the Skill

Survey your classmates about an issue in the news. Summarize the opinions and write a paragraph comparing the different opinions.

GO TO Practice key skills with **Glencoe Skillbuilder Interactive Workbook, Level 1.**

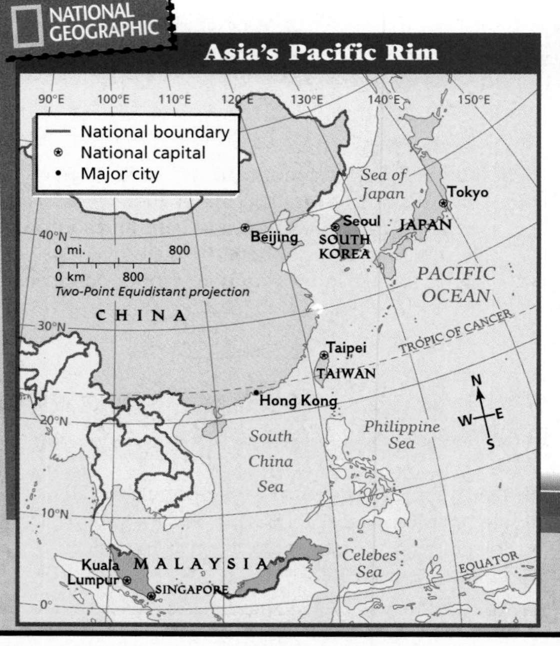

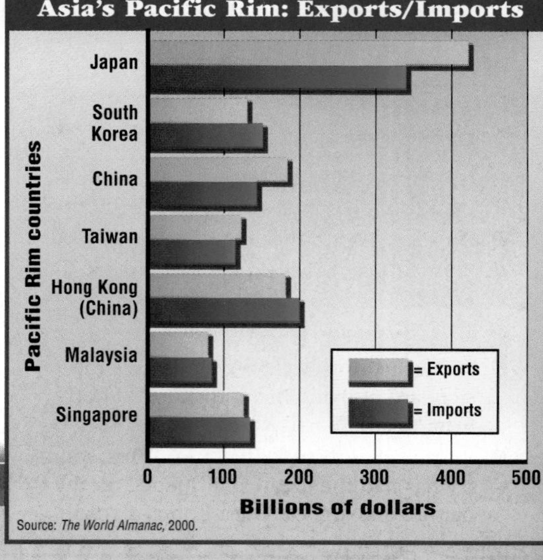

Practicing the Skill Answers

1. Asia's Pacific Rim; Asia's Pacific Rim: Exports/Imports
2. The graph includes places labeled on the map.
3. Japan
4. No; Japan is much smaller in size than China, yet it exports and imports more than twice as much as China.
5. Many countries and places along Asia's Pacific Rim are highly industrialized, and they spend billions of dollars in exports and earn billions of dollars in imports.

Applying the Skill

Students' answers will vary depending on the issue chosen and the opinions heard. Have them present their results in a graph.

Reading Review

Section 1 Japan

Terms to Know
tsunami
archipelago
intensive cultivation
clan
shogun
samurai
constitutional monarchy
megalopolis

Main Idea
Although Japan's people have few mineral resources, they have built a prosperous country.

✓ **Location** Japan is an archipelago along the Ring of Fire in the western Pacific Ocean. Volcanoes, earthquakes, and tsunamis may strike these islands.

✓ **Economics** Japan is mountainous, but with intensive cultivation its limited farmland is very productive.

✓ **Economics** Japan has few resources. Through trade, the use of advanced technology, and highly skilled workers, Japan has built a strong industrial economy.

✓ **History** The Japanese people have been strongly influenced by China and by Western countries.

✓ **Culture** Most people in Japan live in crowded cities.

✓ **Culture** Japanese religion has encouraged a love of nature and simplicity.

Section 2 The Two Koreas

Terms to Know
dynasty
monsoon
famine

Main Idea
South Korea and North Korea share the same peninsula and history, but they have very different political and economic systems.

✓ **Culture** The Korean Peninsula lies just south of northern China, and China has had a strong influence on Korean life and culture.

✓ **Government** After World War II, the peninsula became divided into two countries, with a communist government in North Korea and a noncommunist one in South Korea.

✓ **Economics** South Korea has a strong industrial economy.

✓ **Culture** Most South Koreans live in cities, enjoying a mix of modern and traditional life.

✓ **Government** North Korea has a communist government that does not allow its people many freedoms and spends a great deal of money on the military. It is economically poor.

Because of its beautiful forest-covered mountains, Korea was once known as Land of the Morning Calm. ▶

Reading Review

Use the Chapter 7 Reading Review to preview, review, condense, or reteach the chapter.

Preview/Review

Use the Terms to Know lists to help students review and study.

Activity Have students choose 10 of the words, including some from each section, and create an illustrated glossary.

Vocabulary PuzzleMaker Software reinforces the vocabulary terms used in Chapter 7.

The Interactive Tutor Self-Assessment CD-ROM allows students to review Chapter 7 content.

Condense

Have students read the Chapter 7 summary statements.

Chapter 7 Guided Reading Activities

Chapter 7 Audio Program

Reteach

Reteaching Activity 7

Chapter 7 Reading Essentials and Study Guide

Cultural Kaleidoscope

Korea In A.D. 935, a kingdom called *Koryo* took control of much of the Korean Peninsula. The modern name *Korea* is derived from the name of that ancient kingdom.

Chapter Culminating Activity

Preparing a Database Have students collect information from both primary and secondary sources about the three countries in this section. Ask them to use computer software; interviews; biographies; oral, print, and visual material; and artifacts as sources of information. Have them organize their findings into a database comparing the countries in terms of size, population, major products and crops, main exports and imports, literacy rate, life expectancy, form of government, and other factors. Students should include the source of their information and differentiate between the primary and secondary sources. *NOTE: This activity may be completed separately or you may wish students to incorporate it into their Current Events Journals.*

EE2 Places and Regions: Standard 4

Assessment and Activities

GLENCOE TECHNOLOGY

MindJogger Videoquiz
Use MindJogger to review the Chapter 7 content.

 Available in VHS.

Using Key Terms

1.	e	6.	i
2.	f	7.	d
3.	j	8.	a
4.	b	9.	g
5.	c	10.	h

Reviewing the Main Ideas

11. through intensive cultivation, or growing crops on every available piece of land
12. *Consumer goods:* electronic equipment, watches, small appliances, calculators, automobiles, and other vehicles; *Industrial goods:* steel, cement, fertilizer, plastics, and fabrics
13. It modernized, with improved education and newly started industries.
14. Tokyo, Yokohama, Nagoya, and Osaka
15. painting, poetry, literature, and drama (Kabuki)
16. China
17. After Soviet and American troops occupied the two halves of the country, two different governments—one Communist and one not—took power in the two halves.
18. The summer monsoon from the south brings hot, humid weather. The winter monsoon from the north brings cold, dry weather.
19. manufacturing and trade
20. Limited farm land produced even less food because there wasn't enough fertilizer.

Chapter 7 Assessment and Activities

Using Key Terms

Match the terms in Part A with their definitions in Part B.

A.

1. monsoon
2. tsunami
3. intensive cultivation
4. shogun
5. archipelago
6. dynasty
7. constitutional monarchy
8. clan
9. famine
10. megalopolis

B.

a. group of related families
b. Japanese military leader
c. chain of islands
d. emperor is the official head of state, but elected officials run the government
e. seasonal wind that blows over a continent for months at a time
f. huge wave caused by an undersea earthquake
g. severe food shortage
h. huge supercity
i. ruling family
j. growing crops on every available piece of land

Reviewing the Main Ideas

Section 1 Japan

11. **Human/Environment Interaction** How do Japan's farmers achieve high crop yields?
12. **Economics** What consumer goods and industrial goods are made in Japan?
13. **History** How did Japan change in the late 1800s?
14. **Location** What four cities make up Japan's megalopolis?
15. **Culture** What are three of Japan's traditional arts?

Section 2 The Two Koreas

16. **Location** What large Asian nation lies north of the Korean Peninsula?
17. **History** Why did Korea become divided in 1945?
18. **Location** How do summer and winter monsoons differ in Korea?
19. **Economics** What are the main economic activities in South Korea?
20. **Human/Environment Interaction** Why has North Korea suffered from famine in recent years?

Japan and the Koreas

Place Location Activity

On a separate sheet of paper, match the letters on the map with the numbered places listed below.

1. Mount Fuji
2. Sea of Japan
3. North Korea
4. South Korea
5. Tokyo
6. Honshu
7. Yalu River
8. Seoul
9. Pyongyang
10. Hokkaido

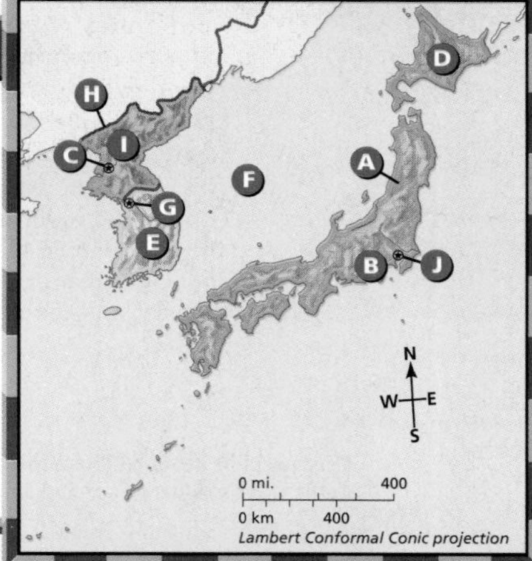

Place Location Activity

1.	B	6.	A
2.	F	7.	H
3.	I	8.	G
4.	E	9.	C
5.	J	10.	D

Critical Thinking

21. Answers will vary but might include the fact that all communist countries experience some difficulties in changing to a free market economy and that China, which has a communist system, is on the border and may pressure North Korea to act in certain ways.
22. Answers will vary.

Self-Check Quiz Visit the ***Our World Today: People, Places, and Issues*** Web site at owt.glencoe.com and click on **Chapter 7–Self-Check Quizzes** to prepare for the Chapter Test.

Critical Thinking

21. **Drawing Conclusions** Why might North Korea find it difficult to change from a communist system to a noncommunist system? Keep in mind the country's location.
22. **Organizing Information** Create a chart like this one. In each column, write two main ideas about Japan, South Korea, and North Korea as they relate to the topics in the first column.

Topic	Japan	South Korea	North Korea
Land			
Economy			
History			
People			

Current Events Journal

23. **Writing a Poem** As you recall, a haiku is a traditional Japanese poem that requires 17 syllables—5 in the first line, 7 in the second line, and 5 in the third line. Write a haiku in which you describe a scene from life in Japan or the Koreas today.

Mental Mapping Activity

24. **Focusing on the Region** Create a map of Japan and the Koreas, and add these labels:
    - Honshu
    - North Korea
    - Korean Peninsula
    - Pacific Ocean
    - Tokyo
    - Sea of Japan

Technology Skills Activity

25. **Using the Internet** Use the Internet to research traditional Japanese culture. You might look at Japanese gardens, Buddhism, literature, or painting. Create a bulletin board display with pictures and write captions that explain what the images show.

The Princeton Review

Standardized Test Practice

Directions: Read the paragraph below, and then answer the following questions.

In A.D. 1185 Japan's emperor gave political and military power to a shogun, or general. The shogun system proved to be quite strong. Even though the Mongol warrior Kublai Khan tried twice to invade Japan, he did not succeed. On the first invasion in 1274, Japanese warriors and the threat of a storm forced the Mongols to leave. On the second invasion in 1281, 150,000 Mongol warriors came by ship, but a typhoon arose and destroyed the fleet. The Japanese thought of the storm as the kamikaze, or "divine wind." They believed that their islands were indeed sacred.

1. **In what century did shoguns gain political power in Japan?**
   - **A** tenth century
   - **B** eleventh century
   - **C** twelfth century
   - **D** thirteenth century
2. **In what century did the Mongol warrior Kublai Khan try to invade Japan?**
   - **F** tenth century
   - **G** eleventh century
   - **H** twelfth century
   - **J** thirteenth century

Test-Taking Tip: Century names are a common source of error. Remember, in Western societies, a baby's first year begins at birth and ends at age one. Therefore, if you are now 14 years old, you are in your fifteenth year. Using the same type of thinking, what century began in 1201?

207

Assessment and Activities

Standardized Test Practice

1. C
2. J

Tested Objectives: Analyzing information, synthesizing information

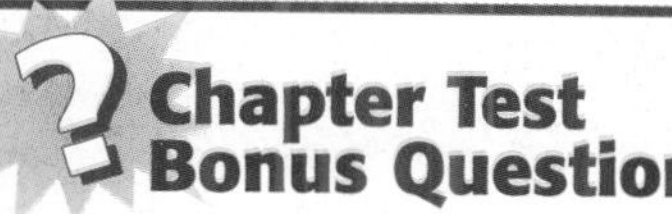

Chapter Test Bonus Question

This question may be used for extra credit on the chapter test.

How do ocean currents affect Japan's economy? *(A warm current from the Pacific Ocean flows north, warming southern Japan. Warm water is better for fishing.)*

Have students visit the Web site at **owt.glencoe.com** to review Chapter 7 and take the Self-Check Quiz.

Current Events Journal

23. Students' poems should follow the syllabic pattern of haiku, include concrete details, and convey an emotion about the scene described.

Mental Mapping Activity

24. This exercise helps students visualize the countries and geographic features they have been studying and understand the relationship among various points. Accept all attempts at freehand mapping that show places in the correct relationship to one another.

Technology Skills Activity

25. Display students' bulletin boards in the classroom and have students discuss the different art forms that were presented.

Chapter 8 Resources

Note: The following materials may be used when teaching Chapter 8.
Section level support materials are shown at point of use in the margins of the Teacher Wraparound Edition.

Timesaving Tools

TeacherWorks™ All-In-One Planner and Resource Center

- **Interactive Teacher Edition** See the **Interactive Teacher Edition** CD-ROM to electronically integrate your Teacher Wraparound Edition and blackline masters.
- **Interactive Lesson Planner** Organize your week, month, semester, or year with all the lesson helps you need. The **Interactive Lesson Planner** CD-ROM contains all Chapter 8 resources.

Use Glencoe's **Presentation Plus!** multimedia teacher tool to easily present dynamic lessons that visually excite your students. Using Microsoft PowerPoint® you can customize the presentations to create your own personalized lessons.

TEACHING TRANSPARENCIES

Graphic Organizer Transparency and Student Activity 8

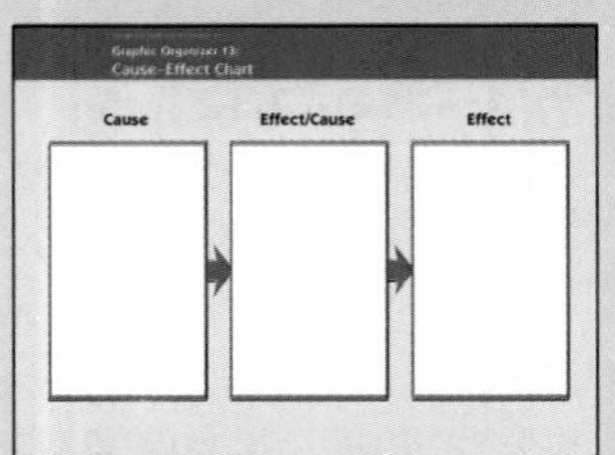

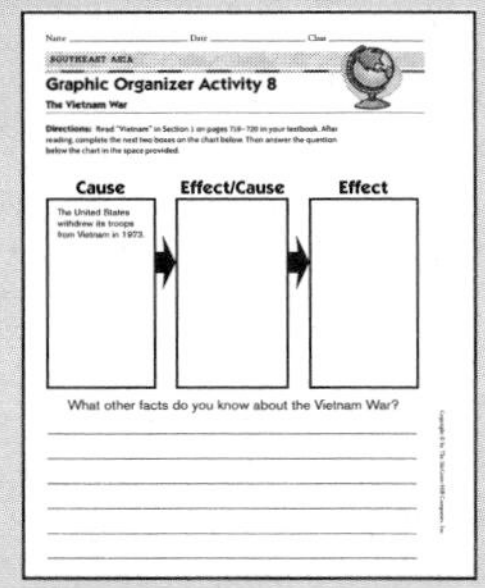

FOLDABLES™ Study Organizer

Foldables are three-dimensional, interactive graphic organizers that help students practice basic writing skills, review key vocabulary terms, and identify main ideas. Every chapter contains a Foldable activity, with additional chapter activities found in the ***Reading and Study Skills Foldables*** booklet.

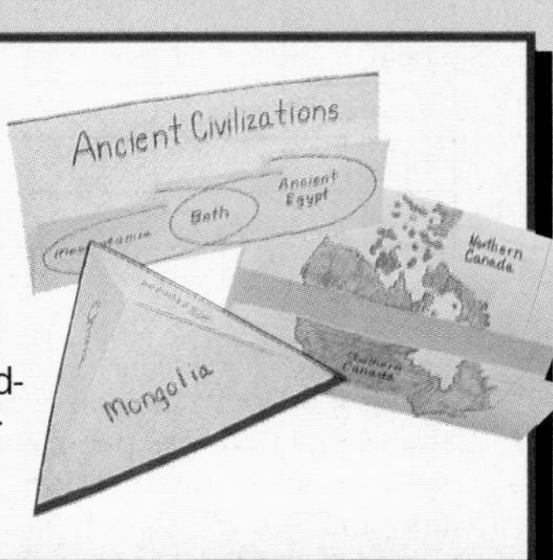

ENRICHMENT AND EXTENSION

Enrichment Activity 8

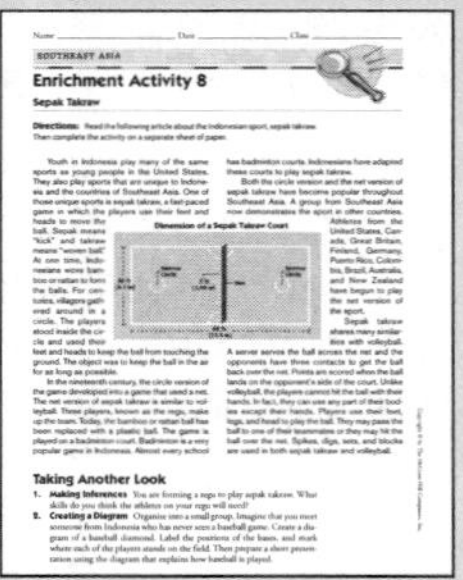

Cooperative Learning Activity 8

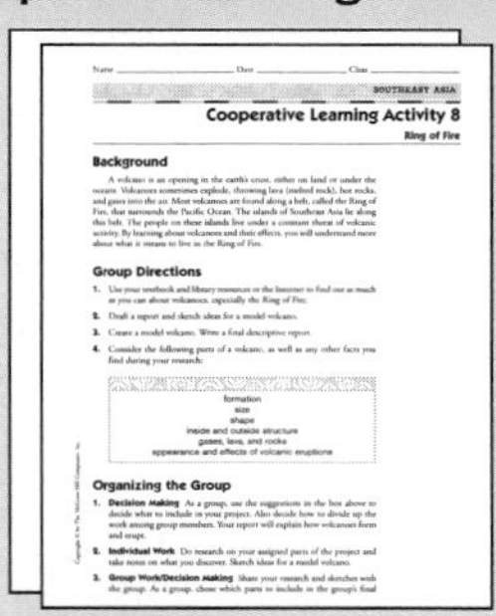

MAP AND GEOGRAPHY SKILLS

Chapter Map Activity 8

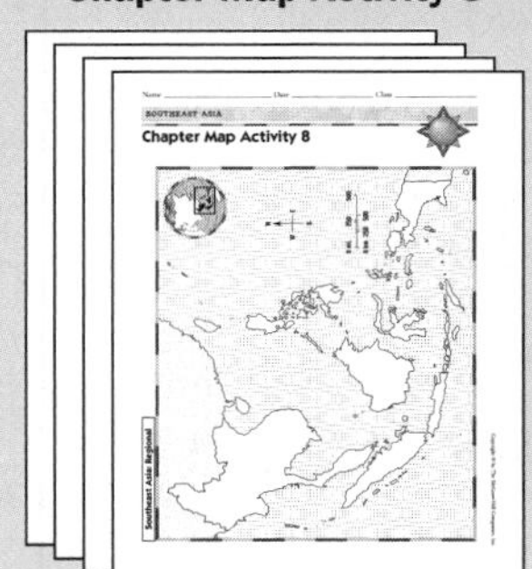

GeoLab Activity 8

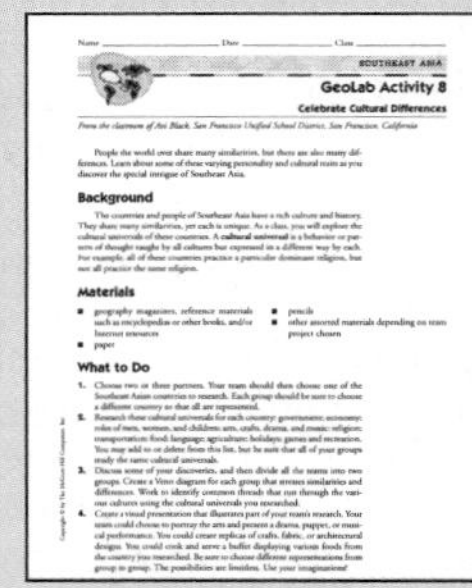

STANDARDIZED ASSESSMENT SKILLS

GLENCOE'S ASSESSMENT ADVANTAGE

Critical Thinking Skills Activity 8

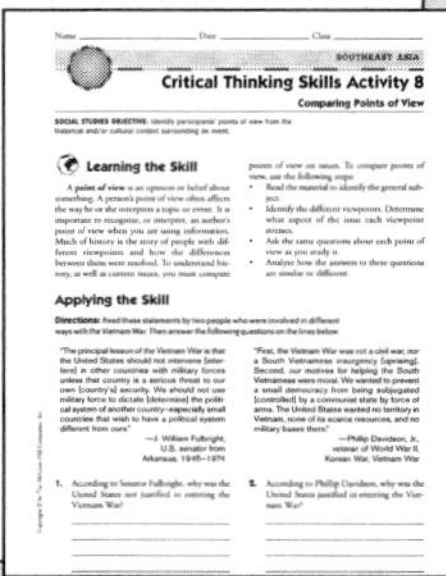

Map and Graph Skills Activity 8

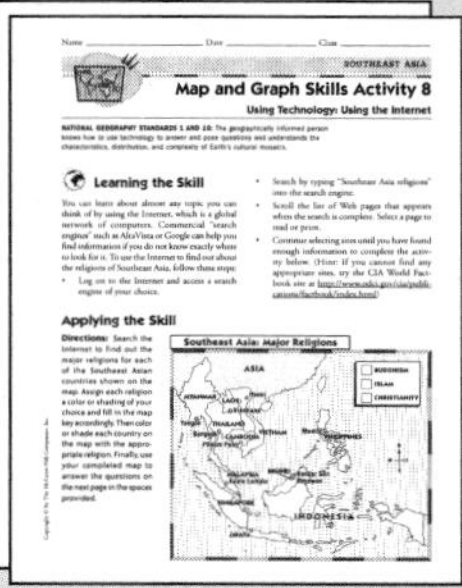

Reading and Writing Skills Activity 8

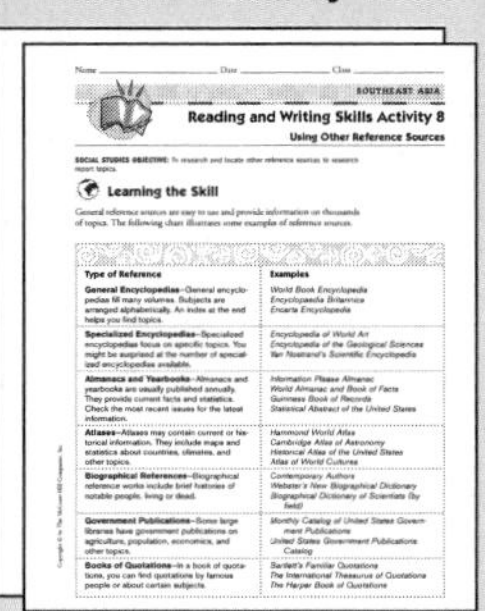

Standardized Test Practice Workbook Activity 8

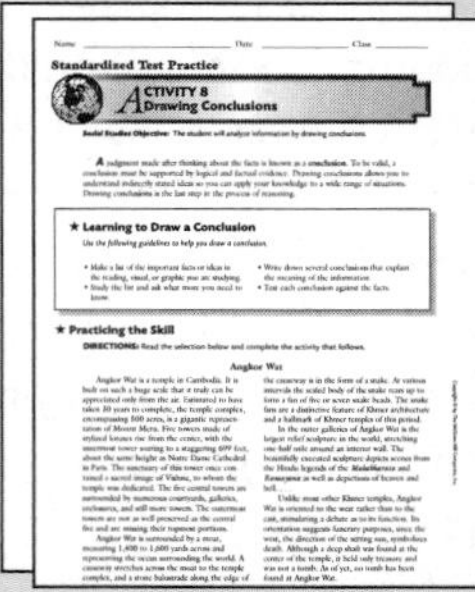

REVIEW AND REINFORCEMENT

Chapter Skills Activity 8

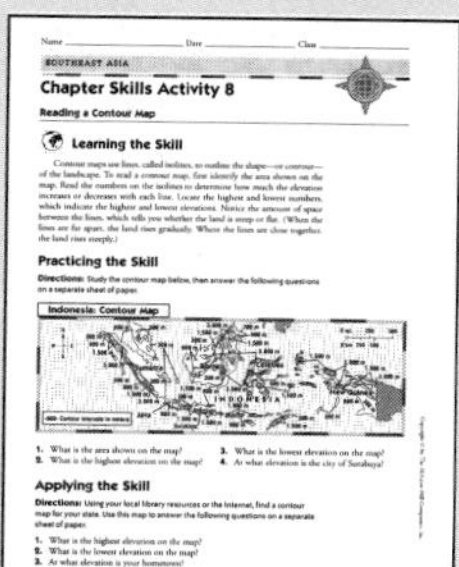

Take-Home Review Activity 8

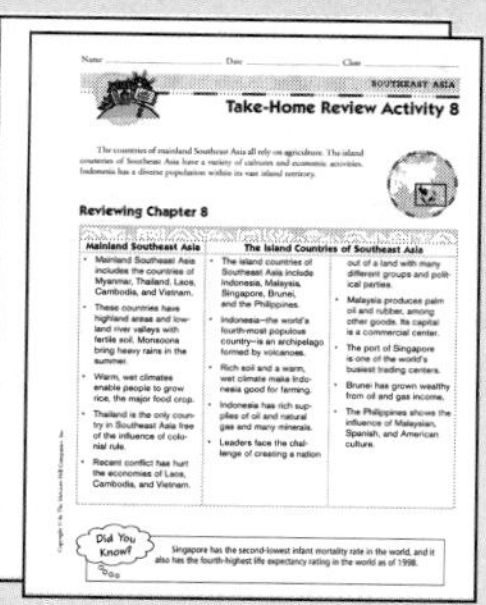

Reteaching Activity 8

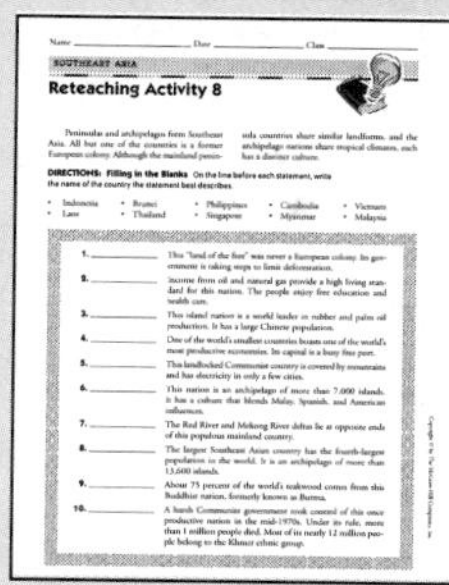

Vocabulary Activity 8

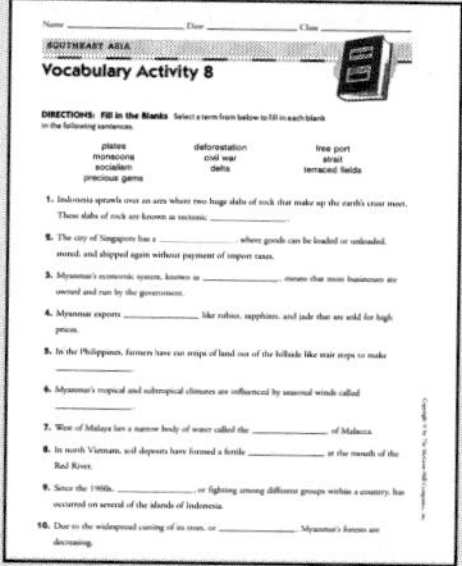

Workbook Activity 8

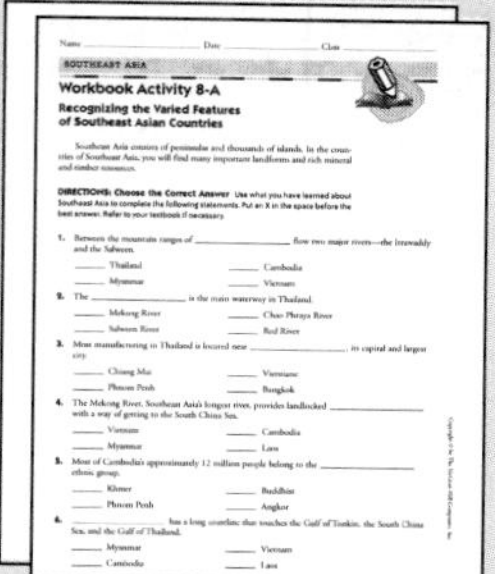

ASSESSMENT

GLENCOE'S ASSESSMENT ADVANTAGE

Chapter 8 Test, Form A

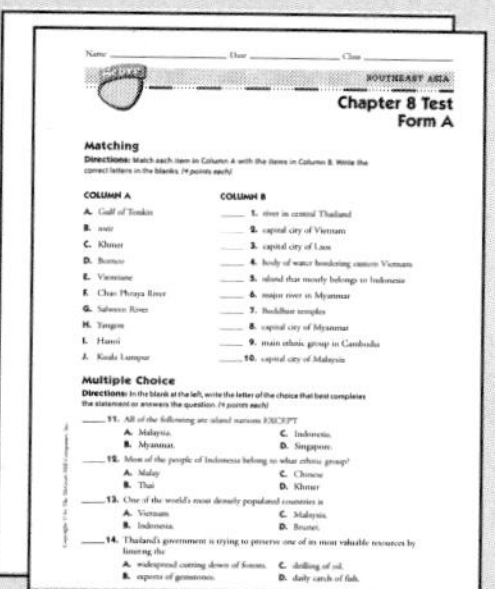

Chapter 8 Test, Form B

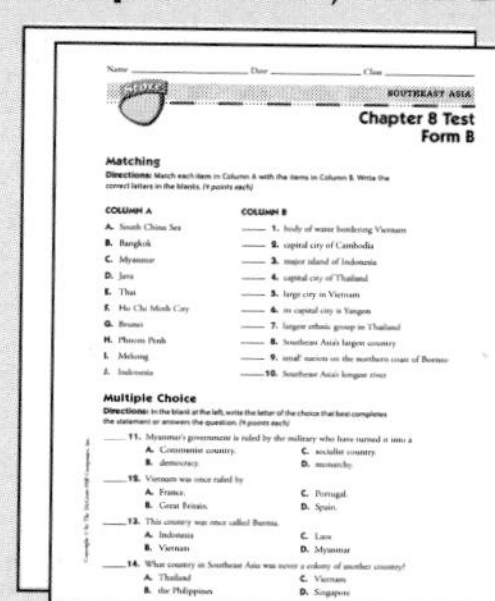

Performance Assessment Activity 8

ExamView® Pro 3.0 Testmaker CD-ROM

MULTIMEDIA

- National Geographic's The World and Its People
- MindJogger Videoquiz
- Vocabulary PuzzleMaker Software
- Interactive Tutor Self-Assessment CD-ROM
- ExamView® Pro 3.0 Testmaker CD-ROM
- Interactive Lesson Planner CD-ROM
- Interactive Teacher Edition CD-ROM
- Skillbuilder Interactive Workbook CD-ROM, Level 1
- Presentation Plus! CD-ROM
- Audio Program

SPANISH RESOURCES

The following Spanish language materials are available in the Spanish Resources binder:

- Spanish Chapter Summaries
- Spanish Vocabulary Activities
- Spanish Guided Reading Activities
- Spanish Quizzes and Tests
- Spanish Take-Home Review Activities
- Spanish Reteaching Activities

Meeting National Standards

Geography for Life

All of the 18 standards are demonstrated in Unit 3. The following ones are highlighted in Chapter 8:

Section 1 **EE1 The World in Spatial Terms: Standards 1, 2, 3**

EE2 Places and Regions: Standards 4, 5, 6

Section 2 **EE2 Places and Regions: Standards 4, 5, 6**

EE3 Physical Systems: Standards 7, 8

EE4 Human Systems: Standards 9, 10, 11, 12, 13

For a complete listing of National Geography Standards and entire text correlation, see pages T22–T29.

Local Objectives

Chapter 8 Planning Guide

SECTION RESOURCES

Daily Objectives	Reproducible Resources	Multimedia Resources
Section 1 **Mainland Southeast Asia** **Suggested Pacing = 1 day** **1.** Describe the people and geography of Myanmar and Thailand. **2.** Explain how war has affected Laos and Cambodia. **3.** Discuss Vietnam and its history.	Reproducible Lesson Plan 8-1 Daily Lecture and Discussion Notes 8-1 Guided Reading Activity 8-1 Reading Essentials and Study Guide 8-1 Section Quiz 8-1*	Daily Focus Skills Transparency 8-1 GeoQuiz Transparency 8-1 Vocabulary PuzzleMaker Software Interactive Tutor Self-Assessment CD-ROM ExamView® Pro 3.0 Testmaker CD-ROM Presentation Plus! CD-ROM
Section 2 **Island Southeast Asia** **Suggested Pacing = 1 day** **1.** Compare the people and economic activities of the island countries of Southeast Asia. **2.** Name the groups that have influenced these countries.	Reproducible Lesson Plan 8-2 Daily Lecture and Discussion Notes 8-2 Guided Reading Activity 8-2 Reading Essentials and Study Guide 8-2 Section Quiz 8-2*	Daily Focus Skills Transparency 8-2 GeoQuiz Transparency 8-1 Vocabulary PuzzleMaker Software Interactive Tutor Self-Assessment CD-ROM ExamView® Pro 3.0 Testmaker CD-ROM Presentation Plus! CD-ROM

00:00 **Out of Time?** Assign the **Reading Essentials and Study Guide** for this chapter.

*Also available in Spanish

KEY TO ABILITY LEVELS

Teaching strategies have been coded for varying learning styles and abilities.

L1 **BASIC** activities for all students
L2 **AVERAGE** activities for average to above-average students
L3 **CHALLENGING** activities for above-average students
ELL **ENGLISH LANGUAGE LEARNER** activities

Blackline Master
Software
CD-ROM
Audiocassette
Transparency
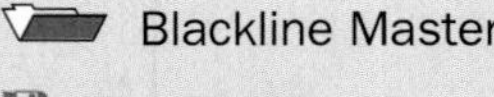
Videocassette
Block Scheduling
DVD

Teacher to Teacher

"Made in ???"

Daniel Hanczar
West Allegheny Middle School
Imperial, Pennsylvania

With parental permission, have students detach and bring to class clothing labels; tags from purses, book bags, tennis shoes, and towels; labels from canned goods or other food products; and so on. Then have students draw small pictures of the products, color them, and attach the "Made in . . ." or "Product of . . ." labels to the appropriate item. Post all pictures and labels on a large map of the world in their countries of origin. Have students pose and answer questions about the origins of their products, paying particular attention to any patterns they see among countries and world regions. Students enjoy seeing and learning where common items they buy originated.

OUR WORLD TODAY Online

Use our Web site for additional resources. All essential content is covered in the Student Edition.

You and your students can visit owt.glencoe.com, the Web site companion to *Our World Today*. This innovative integration of electronic and print media offers your students a wealth of opportunities. The student text directs students to the Web site for the following options:

- Chapter Overviews
- Student Web Activities
- Self-Check Quizzes
- Textbook Updates

Answers are provided for you in the Web Activity Lesson Plan. Additional Web resources and Interactive Tutor puzzles are also available.

NATIONAL GEOGRAPHIC TEACHER'S CORNER

Index to National Geographic Magazine:

The following articles may be used for research relating to this chapter:

- "Wild Gliders: The Creatures of Borneo's Rain Forest," by Tim Laman, October 2000.
- "The Temples of Angkor," by Douglas Preston, August 2000.
- "Tam Dao: Vietnam's Sanctuary Under Siege," by Michael J. McRae, June 1999.

National Geographic Society Products Available From Glencoe:

To order the following products for use with this chapter, contact your local Glencoe sales representative or call Glencoe at 1-800-334-7344:

- *STV: World Geography* (Videodisc)
- *Picture Atlas of the World* (CD-ROM)
- *MapPack: Asia* (Transparencies)
- *PicturePack: Geography of Asia* (Transparencies)
- *ZipZapMap! World* (Software)
- *GeoBee* (CD-ROM)
- *Images of the World* (Posters)
- *Eye on the Environment* (Posters)

Additional National Geographic Society Products:

To order the following products for use with this chapter, call National Geographic Society at 1-800-368-2728:

- *Complete National Geographic: 111 Years of National Geographic Magazine* (CD-ROM)
- *Voices: Poetry and Art From Around the World* (Book)
- *National Geographic Desk Reference* (Book)
- *National Geographic Atlas of the World, Seventh Edition* (Book)
- *Asia* (Video)
- *Asia Political* (Map)
- *Population* (Map)
- *Communism* (Video)

NGS ONLINE

Access National Geographic's Web site for current events, activities, links, interactive features, and archives.
www.nationalgeographic.com

Introducing Chapter 8

Our World Today online

Introduce students to chapter content and key terms by having them access Chapter Overview 8 at owt.glencoe.com

Chapter Objectives

1. Describe the land, resources, economies, and cultures of the mainland countries of Southeast Asia.
2. Compare the landforms, people, and economies of the island countries of Southeast Asia.

GLENCOE TECHNOLOGY

NATIONAL GEOGRAPHIC

The World and Its People Video Program

Chapter 26 Southeast Asia
The following segments enhance the study of this chapter:

- **Vietnamese New Year**
- **Philippine Hot Spot**
- **Bali**

Available in DVD and VHS.

MindJogger Videoquiz

Use MindJogger to preview the Chapter 8 content.

Available in VHS.

Chapter 8 Southeast Asia

The World and Its People NATIONAL GEOGRAPHIC

To learn more about the people and places of Southeast Asia, view ***The World and Its People* Chapter 26** video.

Our World Today online

Chapter Overview Visit the ***Our World Today: People, Places, and Issues*** Web site at owt.glencoe.com and click on **Chapter 8—Chapter Overviews** to preview information about Southeast Asia.

208

Two-Minute Lesson Launcher

Write the names of the countries in Southeast Asia. Have students write everything they know or think they know about these nations in their notebooks. Ask students to pair up. Then have students compare lists. They may add or delete information. Have each pair share one fact with the class. Make a master list on an overhead projector of all shared information. *(Students are likely to have heard of Vietnam due to the long war there; they may also know of other countries as a result of recent news stories.)* After students have read the chapter, review this list with the class to see which facts were confirmed, which were contradicted, and which were not covered. Those not covered can be topics for further research.

Study Organizer

Identifying Main Ideas Study Foldable Make this foldable to help you identify key facts about the people and places of Southeast Asia.

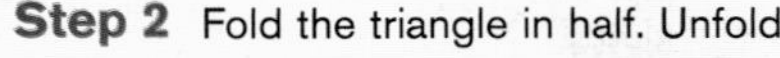

Step 1 Fold the paper from the top right corner down so the edges line up. Cut off the leftover piece.

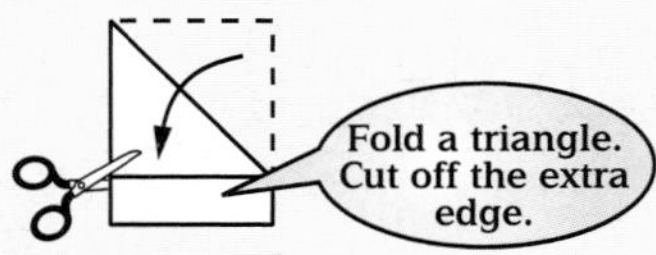

Fold a triangle. Cut off the extra edge.

Step 2 Fold the triangle in half. Unfold.

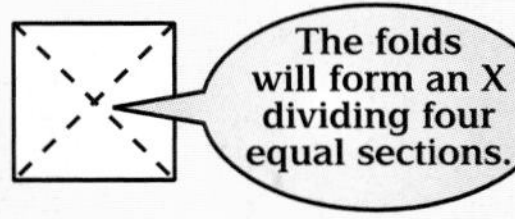

The folds will form an X dividing four equal sections.

Step 3 Cut up one fold line and stop at the middle. This forms two triangular flaps.

Step 4 Draw an X on one tab and label the other three the following: Flap 1: Mainland Countries; Flap 2: Island Countries; Flap 3: The Philippines.

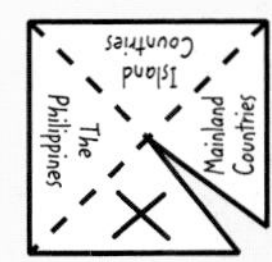

Step 5 Fold the X flap under the other flap and glue together.

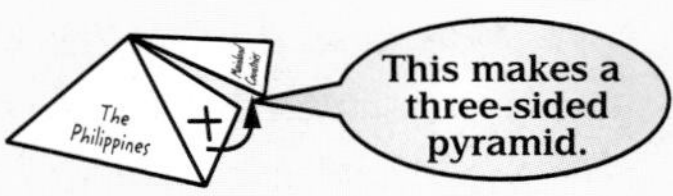

The Philippines
This makes a three-sided pyramid.

Reading and Writing As you read, write main ideas inside the foldable under each appropriate pyramid wall.

Why It Matters

A High Price for Prosperity

Some Southeast Asian countries—such as Indonesia, Malaysia, and Singapore—have become very important economic centers, manufacturing goods and exporting natural resources. One possible price paid for this economic prosperity might be in the destruction of the region's most beautiful landscapes.

▲ Outside restaurants are popular in Singapore.

About the Photo

Singapore, or "The Lion City" as the name *Singa Pur* translates, became a central sea port and exporter of rare and exotic foods in the 19th century. Among the precious cargo sailing from Singapore were sago, tea, sugar, cloves, coriander, cassia, nutmeg, and black pepper. Today the spirit of Singapore is captured best in its colorful open-air restaurants and street stands. Some of Singapore's most famous dishes—satays, laksa lemak, char kway teow (stir-fried rice noodles), chili crab, and otak-otak (spicy char-grilled fish cakes) exemplify the island nation's love of chili and spices.

Introducing Chapter 8

FOLDABLES™ Study Organizer

Purpose Students will make and use a foldable to summarize the main ideas after reading the chapter. This reading strategy requires students to read with the purpose of identifying and describing key facts about the countries of Southeast Asia. As the students read they are required to record what they have learned about the geography, economy, and culture of the countries of Southeast Asia.

Have students complete ***Reading and Study Skills Foldables*** Activity 8.

Why It Matters

Statistics are used to measure the economic growth of areas. Tell students that in order to be accurate you should compare like things. For example, the countries with the most computers are the United States, Japan, and Germany. But the countries with the highest *rate of computers per population* are Singapore, the United States, and Switzerland. Looking at rate "evens the playing field" for countries like those in Southeast Asia with smaller populations.

Chapter 8

Section 1, pages 210–214

Focus

Section Objectives

1. Describe the people and geography of Myanmar and Thailand.
2. Explain how war has affected Laos and Cambodia.
3. Discuss Vietnam and its history.

BELLRINGER
Skillbuilder Activity

Project transparency and have students answer questions.

This activity is also available as a blackline master.

Daily Focus Skills Transparency 8-1

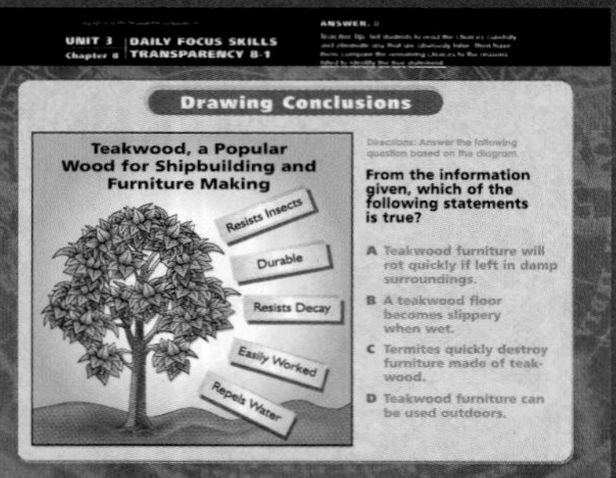

Guide to Reading

Accessing Prior Knowledge Point to Southeast Asia on a map of the world and show the region's proximity to China, India, and Australia. Ask students to collect evidence of these countries' influences on Southeast Asia as they read the section.

Mainland Southeast Asia

Guide to Reading

Main Idea

The countries of mainland Southeast Asia rely on agriculture as a major source of wealth.

Terms to Know

- monsoon
- precious gems
- deforestation
- socialism
- civil war
- delta

Reading Strategy

Create a chart like this one for each of these countries: Myanmar, Thailand, Laos, Cambodia, and Vietnam. Fill in the right column on each chart with facts about the countries.

Country	
Topic	Key Fact
Land	
Economy	
People	

NATIONAL GEOGRAPHIC **Exploring Our World**

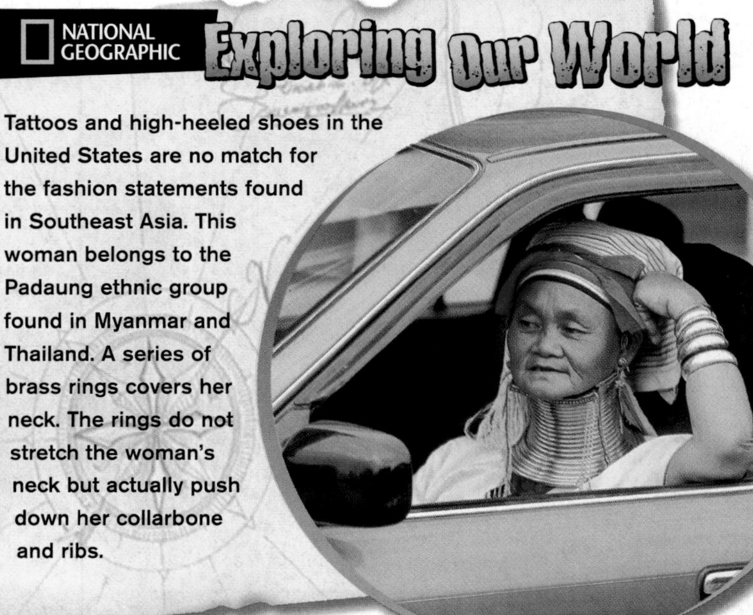

Tattoos and high-heeled shoes in the United States are no match for the fashion statements found in Southeast Asia. This woman belongs to the Padaung ethnic group found in Myanmar and Thailand. A series of brass rings covers her neck. The rings do not stretch the woman's neck but actually push down her collarbone and ribs.

South of China and east of India lies **Southeast Asia.** This region includes thousands of islands and a long arm of land called the **Malay Peninsula.** Several countries lie entirely on the mainland of Southeast Asia. They are Myanmar, Thailand, Laos, Cambodia, and Vietnam.

Myanmar

Myanmar, once called Burma, is about the size of Texas. Rugged, steep mountains sweep through its western and eastern borders. Two wide rivers—the **Irrawaddy** (IHR•ah•WAH•dee) and the **Salween**—flow through vast lowland plains between these mountain ranges.

Monsoons, or seasonal winds that blow over a continent for months at a time, cause the wet summers and dry winters in Myanmar.

About two-thirds of the country's people farm. The main crops are rice, sugarcane, beans, and nuts. Some farmers work their fields with tractors, but most rely on plows drawn by water buffalo.

Section Resources

Reproducible Masters
- Reproducible Lesson Plan 8-1
- Daily Lecture and Discussion Notes 8-1
- Guided Reading Activity 8-1
- Reading Essentials and Study Guide 8-1
- Section Quiz 8-1

Transparencies
- Daily Focus Skills Transparency 8-1
- GeoQuiz Transparency 8-1

Multimedia
- Vocabulary PuzzleMaker Software
- Interactive Tutor Self-Assessment CD-ROM
- Presentation Plus! CD-ROM
- ExamView® Pro 3.0 Testmaker CD-ROM

Factories produce and export such goods as soap, noodles, paper, textiles, and glass bottles. Myanmar also exports precious gems such as rubies, sapphires, and jade. **Precious gems** are valuable and can be sold for high prices. In addition, the country provides about 75 percent of the world's teakwood. Myanmar's valuable forests are decreasing because of **deforestation,** or the widespread cutting of trees.

About 75 percent of Myanmar's 47.8 million people live in rural areas. The most densely populated part of the country is the fertile Irrawaddy River valley. Many rural dwellers build their homes on poles above the ground for protection from floods and wild animals.

The capital and largest city, **Yangon** (formerly called Rangoon), is famous both for its modern university and its gold-covered Buddhist temples. Buddhism is the main religion in Myanmar. Most people are of Burman heritage, and Burmese is the main language.

Myanmar was part of British India for many years. It became an independent republic in 1948. Since then, military leaders have turned Myanmar into a socialist country. **Socialism** is an economic system in which most businesses are owned and run by the government. Some

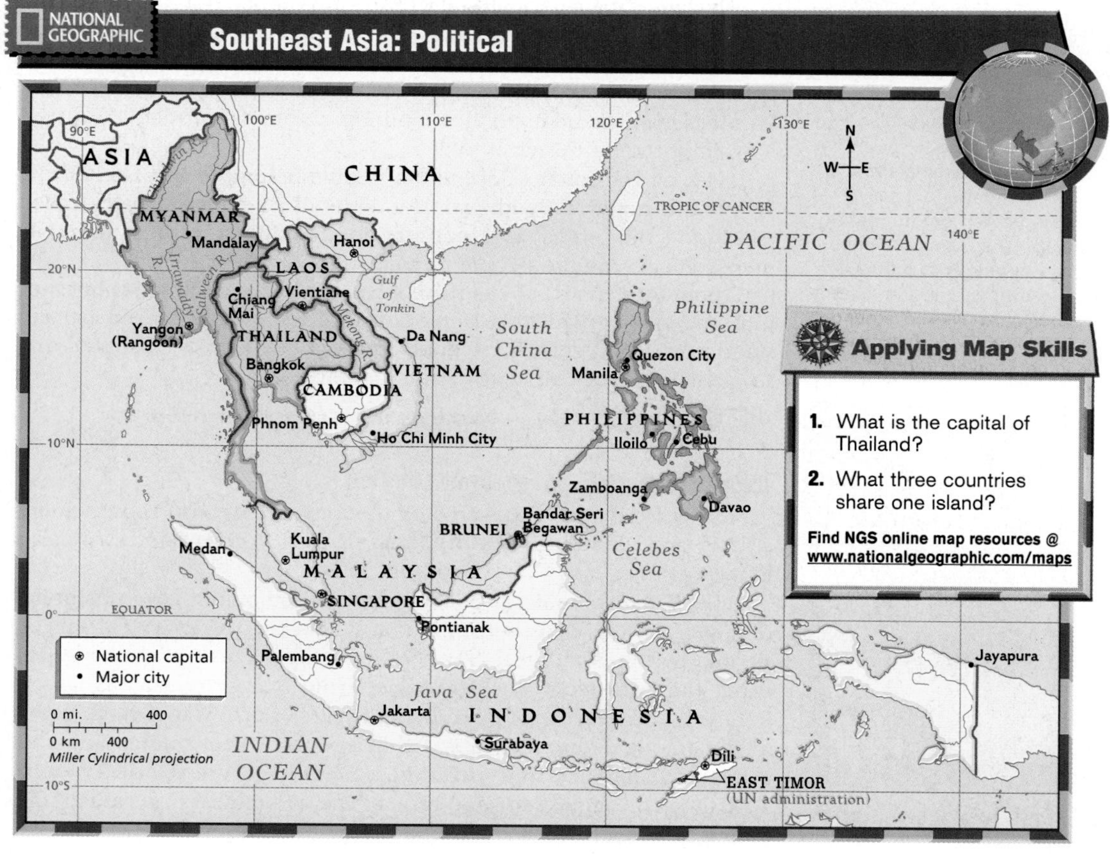

Applying Map Skills

1. What is the capital of Thailand?
2. What three countries share one island?

Find NGS online map resources @ www.nationalgeographic.com/maps

Chapter 8

Section 1, pages 210–214

TEACH

Restating Information

Have students read the first sentence on this page. Demonstrate restating by rewording the sentence: Myanmar produces few modern products such as electronics or cars. Have students practice the skill with other sentences in the section. **L1**

Daily Lecture Notes 8-1

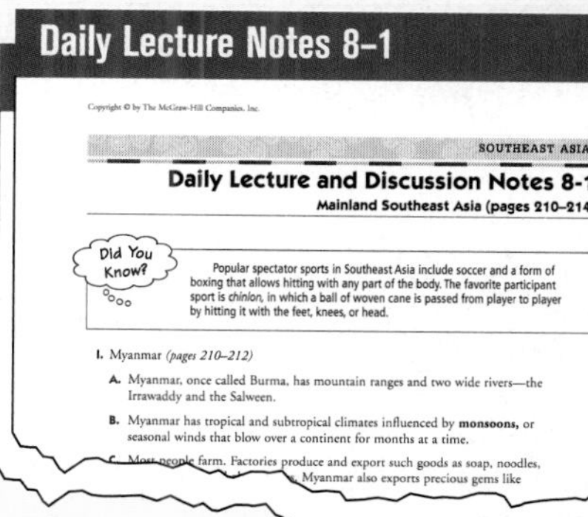
SOUTHEAST ASIA

Daily Lecture and Discussion Notes 8-1

Mainland Southeast Asia (pages 210–214)

Did You Know? Popular spectator sports in Southeast Asia include soccer and a form of boxing that allows hitting with any part of the body. The favorite participant sport is chinlon, in which a ball of woven cane is passed from player to player by hitting it with the feet, knees, or head.

I. Myanmar *(pages 210–212)*

A. Myanmar, once called Burma, has mountain ranges and two wide rivers—the Irrawaddy and the Salween.

B. Myanmar has tropical and subtropical climates influenced by **monsoons,** or seasonal winds that blow over a continent for months at a time.

C. Most people farm. Factories produce and export such goods as soap, noodles, ... Myanmar also exports precious gems like

Applying Map Skills

Answers

1. Bangkok
2. Brunei, Malaysia, and Indonesia share the island of Borneo.

Skills Practice

What is the capital of Myanmar? *(Yangon)*

Team-Teaching Activity

Government Invite a teacher to class who has a background in government. Discuss the government and human rights situation in Myanmar. Ask the teacher to describe the restrictions that the military government places on protests and detail its steps against Aung San Suu Kyi. Have the teacher also mention the role that independent human rights organizations play in focusing attention on governments' actions to punish citizens for trying to exercise their rights. Then have students debate whether such actions are helpful or harmful to the people they are trying to help. **L2**

EE4 Human Systems: Standard 12

Guided Reading Activity 8-1

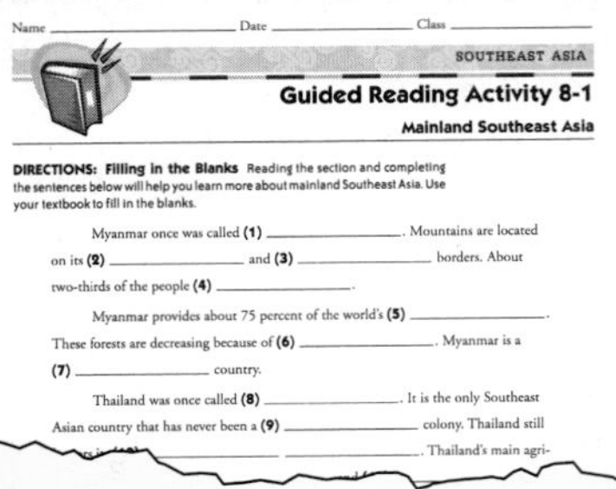
Name ____ Date ____ Class ____

SOUTHEAST ASIA

Guided Reading Activity 8-1

Mainland Southeast Asia

DIRECTIONS: Filling in the Blanks Reading the section and completing the sentences below will help you learn more about mainland Southeast Asia. Use your textbook to fill in the blanks.

Myanmar once was called **(1)** ____. Mountains are located on its **(2)** ____ and **(3)** ____ borders. About two-thirds of the people **(4)** ____.

Myanmar provides about 75 percent of the world's **(5)** ____. These forests are decreasing because of **(6)** ____. Myanmar is a **(7)** ____ country.

Thailand was once called **(8)** ____. It is the only Southeast Asian country that has never been a **(9)** ____ colony. Thailand still ____ ____. Thailand's main agri-

Reading Check Answer

the Irrawaddy River valley

Cultural Kaleidoscope

Thailand If you are in Thailand in April, you might get wet. Thais celebrate the New Year in April. They mark this holiday by pouring buckets of water on people. The tradition began as a gesture symbolizing hope for rain for crops.

Reading Check Answer

rubber, teakwood

3 ASSESS

Assign Section 1 Assessment as homework or an in-class activity.

Have students use the Interactive Tutor Self-Assessment CD-ROM to review Section 8–1.

people have struggled to build a democracy in Myanmar. A woman named **Aung San Suu Kyi** (AWNG SAN SOO CHEE) has become a leader in this struggle. In 1991 she was awarded the Nobel Peace Prize for her efforts to bring political changes without violence.

Reading Check Where is Myanmar's most densely populated area?

Thailand

The map on page 211 shows you that **Thailand** looks like a flower on a stem. The "flower" is the northern part, located on the mainland. The "stem" is a narrow strip on the Malay Peninsula. The country's main waterway—the **Chao Phraya** (chow PRY•uh) River—flows through a central plain. Like Myanmar, Thailand has wet summer monsoons and dry winter monsoons.

Once called Siam, *Thailand* means "land of the free." It is the only Southeast Asian country that has never been a European colony. The Thai people trace their independence as a kingdom back to the A.D. 1200s. Thailand still has a king or queen and honors its royal family.

Thailand's main agricultural exports are rubber and teakwood. The government has taken steps to limit deforestation to protect these industries. Thailand is one of the world's leading exporters of tin and gemstones. Most manufacturing is located near **Bangkok,** the capital. Workers make cement, textiles, clothing, and metal products. Tourism is an important industry as well.

Most of Thailand's 62.4 million people belong to the Thai ethnic group and practice Buddhism. Hundreds of Buddhist temples called *wats* dot the cities and countryside. Buddhist monks, or holy men, walk among the people to receive food offerings.

About 80 percent of Thais live in rural villages, although thousands look for jobs in Bangkok. Here, beautiful temples and royal palaces stand next to modern skyscrapers and crowded streets. Bangkok has so many cars that daily traffic jams last for hours.

Reading Check What are Thailand's major agricultural exports?

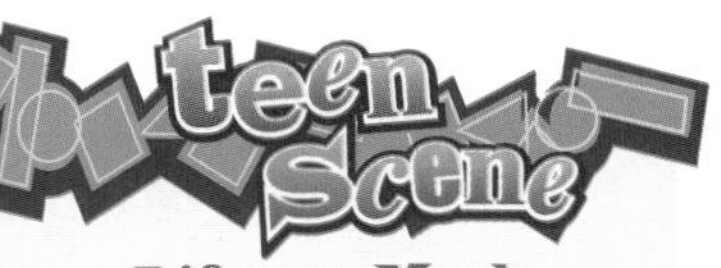

Life as a Monk

After his grandfather died, Nattawud Daoruang became a novice Buddhist monk. "You see," he says, "Thai Buddhists believe they can get to paradise by holding on to a monk's robe. So I became a monk for a month to help my grandfather get to paradise. The novice monks had to get up at 5:00 A.M. and meditate. In the afternoons, we walked around the village with the monks to get food and drink."

Laos and Cambodia

Landlocked **Laos** is covered by mountains. Southern Laos includes a fertile area along the **Mekong** (MAY•KAWNG) River, Southeast Asia's longest river.

Laos is an economically poor country. Its communist government has only recently allowed tourism. About 80 percent of Laos's 5.4 million people live in rural areas. Farmers grow rice, sweet potatoes, sugarcane, and corn along the Mekong's fertile banks. Industry is largely undeveloped because of isolation and years of civil war. A **civil war** is a fight among different groups within a country. The country lacks railroads and has electricity in only a few cities. **Vientiane** (vyehn•TYAHN) is the largest city and capital. The communist government discourages religion, but most Laotians remain Buddhists.

Meeting Special Needs

Auditory/Musical Students who benefit from auditory instruction can retain the lesson better if they participate in partner reading. Pair students and have partners take turns reading paragraphs or sections of the text aloud. The partner not reading should follow the text as it is being read. At the end of each paragraph or section, students should quiz each other on the content. **L1 ELL**

Refer to *Inclusion for the Middle School Social Studies Classroom Strategies and Activities* in the TCR.

Architecture

The temple of Angkor Wat in northwestern Cambodia was built during the 1100s. Dedicated to the Hindu god Vishnu, much of the temple is covered with elaborately carved characters from Hindu legends. The Khmer people designed Angkor Wat to represent the Hindu view of the universe. The moat surrounding the temple stood for the oceans. The tall central tower symbolized Mount Meru, center of the universe and home of the various forms of the Hindu supreme being.

Looking Closer **How does the design of Angkor Wat reflect beliefs of the builders?**

Cambodia For many years Cambodia was a rich farming country that exported rice and rubber. By the 1980s, its economy was in ruins because of years of civil war and harsh communist rule. Cambodia's few factories produce food items, chemicals, and textiles.

Most of Cambodia's 13.1 million people belong to the **Khmer** (kuh•MEHR) ethnic group. About 80 percent live in rural villages. The rest live in cities such as the capital, **Phnom Penh** (puh•NAWM PEHN). Buddhism is Cambodia's main religion.

In modern times, Cambodia was under French rule, finally becoming independent in 1953. Since the 1960s, it has experienced almost constant warfare among rival political groups. A communist government led by the dictator Pol Pot took control in the mid-1970s, and the people suffered great hardships. Many people from the cities were forced to move to rural areas and work as farmers. Between 1.6 and 2 million Cambodians died. Some fled to other countries. In 1993 Cambodia brought back its king, but rivalry among political groups continues.

✓Reading Check **Why is Cambodia's economy in ruins?**

Vietnam

Vietnam's long eastern coastline borders the Gulf of Tonkin, the South China Sea, and the Gulf of Thailand. In the north lies the fertile delta of the Red River. A **delta** is an area of land formed by soil deposits at the mouth of a river. In the south you find the wide, swampy delta of the Mekong River. Monsoons bring wet and dry seasons.

Farmers grow large amounts of rice, sugarcane, cassava, sweet potatoes, corn, bananas, and coffee in river deltas. Vietnam's mountain forests provide wood, and the South China Sea yields large catches of fish.

Chapter 8

Section 1, pages 210–214

Answer The carvings are characters from Hindu legends, and the overall design represents the Hindu view of the universe.

More About Khmer Temples Angkor Wat is the largest of more than 100 temples in the Angkor area. There are about 1,000 Khmer temples across Southeast Asia.

World Art and Architecture Transparencies

Use these transparencies with accompanying strategies and activities to introduce students to other types of architecture of the region.

✓ Reading Check Answer

The country has suffered almost constant warfare since the 1960s.

Measure student knowledge of physical features and political entities.

GeoQuiz Transparency 8-1

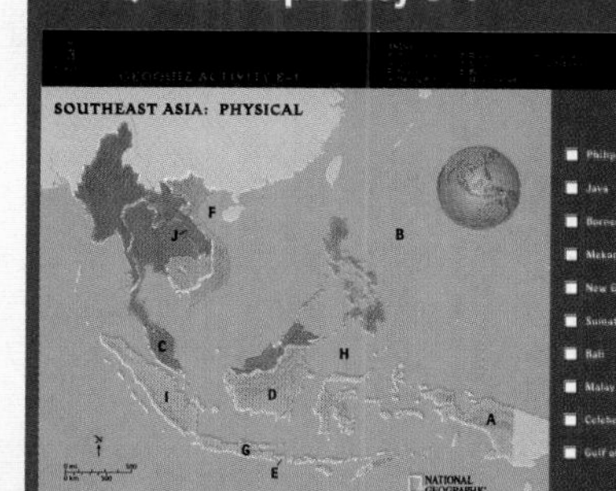

Content Background

Angkor Explain how impressive the Angkor area is in terms not only of its art but also its technology. The entire complex was designed as a method of controlling the floodwaters of the river flowing through the area. By creating canals, artificial lakes, and irrigation channels, the Khmer rulers were able to keep the area as a vast, functioning rice paddy. The achievement helped support their rule—the kings, by controlling the water that ensured people's survival, demonstrated their power. **Ask:** **How might a king abuse this power, and how might that be prevented?**

Chapter 8

Section 1, pages 210–214

Section Quiz 8-1

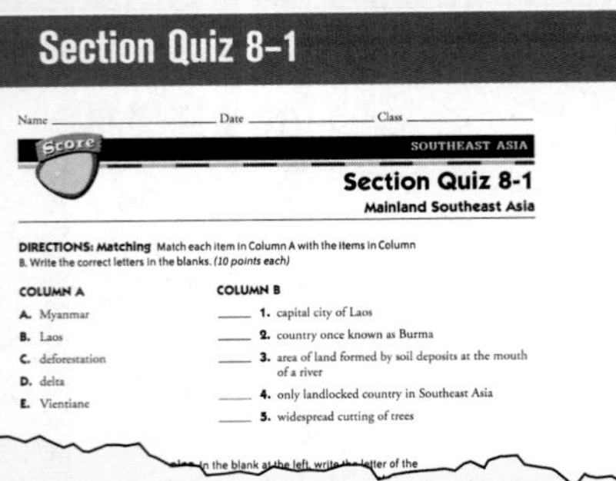

Name ____________ Date ____________ Class ____________

SOUTHEAST ASIA

Score

Section Quiz 8-1

Mainland Southeast Asia

DIRECTIONS: Matching Match each item in Column A with the items in Column B. Write the correct letters in the blanks. *(10 points each)*

COLUMN A	COLUMN B
A. Myanmar	____ 1. capital city of Laos
B. Laos	____ 2. country once known as Burma
C. deforestation	____ 3. area of land formed by soil deposits at the mouth of a river
D. delta	____ 4. only landlocked country in Southeast Asia
E. Vientiane	____ 5. widespread cutting of trees

…in the blank at the left, write the letter of the…

Review

Have students each make a list of four facts and a fib about mainland Southeast Asia. Then put students in groups to compare lists. Students try to guess which are fibs.

✓ Reading Check Answer

Ho Chi Minh City

Reading Essentials and Study Guide 8–1

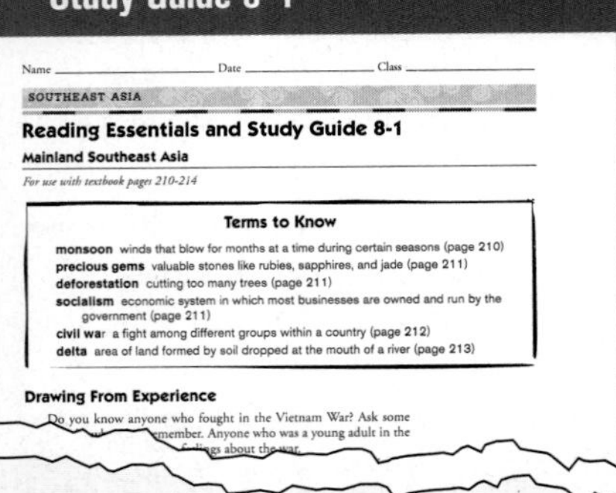

Name ____________ Date ____________ Class ____________

SOUTHEAST ASIA

Reading Essentials and Study Guide 8-1

Mainland Southeast Asia

For use with textbook pages 210-214

Terms to Know

monsoon winds that blow for months at a time during certain seasons (page 210)
precious gems valuable stones like rubies, sapphires, and jade (page 211)
deforestation cutting too many trees (page 211)
socialism economic system in which most businesses are owned and run by the government (page 211)
civil war a fight among different groups within a country (page 212)
delta area of land formed by soil dropped at the mouth of a river (page 213)

Drawing From Experience

Do you know anyone who fought in the Vietnam War? Ask some … remember. Anyone who was a young adult in the … feelings about the war.

4 Close

Have students prepare a bulletin board display that uses images and captions to describe life in mainland Southeast Asia.

With almost 80 million people, Vietnam has the largest population in mainland Southeast Asia. About 80 percent live in the countryside. The largest urban area is **Ho Chi Minh** (HOH CHEE MIHN) **City,** named for the country's first Communist leader. It used to be called **Saigon** (sy•GAHN). Vietnam's capital, **Hanoi,** is located in the north. Most people are Buddhists and belong to the Vietnamese ethnic group. The rest are Chinese, Cambodians, and other Asian ethnic groups. Vietnamese is the major language, but Chinese, English, and French are also spoken.

The ancestors of Vietnam's people came from China more than 2,000 years ago. From the late 1800s to the mid-1950s, Vietnam was under French rule. Vietnamese Communists drove out the French in 1954. The Communist government controlled northern Vietnam, while an American-supported government ruled the south. In the 1960s, fighting between these two groups led to the **Vietnam War.** During this 10-year conflict, more than 3 million Americans helped fight against the Communists. The United States eventually withdrew its forces in 1973. Within two years, the Communists had captured the south.

In recent years, Vietnam's Communist leaders have opened the country to Western ideas, businesses, and tourists. They also have loosened government controls on the economy. In these two ways, the Communist leaders hope to raise Vietnam's standard of living.

✓ Reading Check **What is the largest urban area in Vietnam?**

Section 1 Assessment

Defining Terms

1. **Define** monsoon, precious gems, deforestation, socialism, civil war, delta.

Recalling Facts

2. **Economics** What does Myanmar export?
3. **History** What led to the Vietnam war?
4. **Economics** What has slowed the economies of Laos and Cambodia?

Graphic Organizer

5. **Organizing Information** Create a time line like this one. Then list four events and their dates in Vietnam's history.

Critical Thinking

6. **Summarizing Information** What makes Thailand unique among the countries of Southeast Asia?
7. **Making Predictions** In recent years, the Communist leaders in Vietnam have tried to improve the country's standard of living. How do they hope to do this? Do you think these actions will help? Why or why not?

Applying Social Studies Skills

8. **Analyzing Maps** Look at the political map on page 211. What city is located at 21°N 106°E?

Section 1 Assessment

1. The terms are defined in the Glossary.
2. soap, noodles, paper, textiles, bottles, rubies, sapphires, jade, teakwood
3. fighting between the Communists in the north and the American-supported government in the south
4. civil wars
5. c. a.d. 1: Ancestors of today's people come from China; late 1800s–1950s: France rules area; 1954: Vietnamese Communists drive French out; 1960s: Vietnam War; 1975: Country united
6. It is the only Southeast Asian country never to have been a colony.
7. by welcoming Western ideas, businesses, and tourists and by loosening government controls on the economy; answers will vary
8. Hanoi, Vietnam

Reading a Contour Map

A trail map would show the paths you could follow if you went hiking in the mountains. How would you know if the trail follows an easy, flat route, though, or if it cuts steeply up a mountain? To find out, you need a **contour map.**

Learning the Skill

Contour maps use lines to outline the shape—or contour—of the landscape. Each contour line connects all points that are at the same elevation. This means that if you walked along one contour line, you would always be at the same height above sea level.

Where the contour lines are far apart, the land rises gradually. Where the lines are close together, the land rises steeply. For example, one contour line may be labeled 1,000 meters (3,281 ft.). Another contour line very close to the first one may be labeled 2,000 meters (6,562 ft.). This means that the land rises 1,000 meters (3,281 ft.) in just a short distance.

To read a contour map, follow these steps:

- Identify the area shown on the map.
- Read the numbers on the contour lines to determine how much the elevation increases or decreases with each line.
- Locate the highest and lowest numbers, which indicate the highest and lowest elevations.
- Notice the amount of space between the lines, which tells you whether the land is steep or flat.

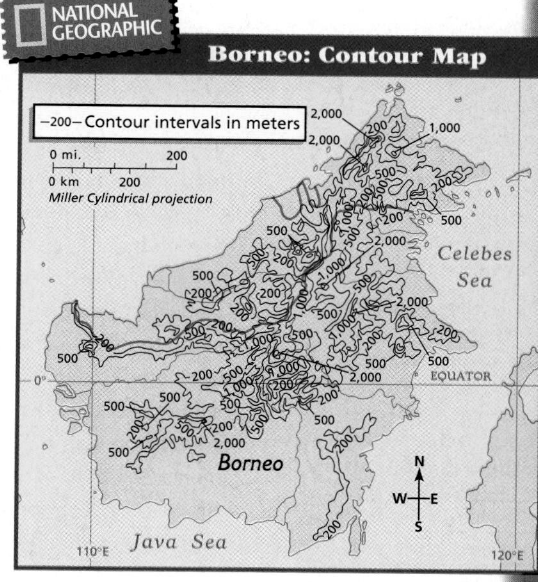

Practicing the Skill

Study the contour map above, then answer the following questions.

1. What area is shown on the map?
2. What is the lowest elevation on the map?
3. What is the highest elevation on the map?
4. Where is the landscape flattest? How can you tell?
5. How would you describe the physical geography of this island?

Applying the Skill

Turn to page 8 in the **Geography Handbook.** Use the contour map there to answer the five questions above.

Social Studies Skill

TEACH

Create a simple trail map with two routes leading from a town to a lake. One route should be short and direct, and the other should be long and circuitous. **Ask: Which route would you walk?** Most will select the shorter route. Then make contour lines to show that the shorter route goes over a mountain while the longer one covers flat land. Ask students again which route they would choose. **L1**

Additional Skills Practice

1. **What do contour lines show?** *(They show the points that have the same elevation.)*
2. **What kind of slope would you expect to see if contour lines are far apart?** *(gradual)*
3. **What kind of slope would you expect to see if contour lines are close together?** *(steep)*

Additional Skills Resources

 Chapter Skills Activity 8

 Building Geography Skills for Life

GLENCOE TECHNOLOGY

 **Skillbuilder Interactive Workbook CD-ROM, Level 1**

This interactive CD-ROM reinforces student mastery of essential social studies skills.

Practicing the Skill Answers

1. the island of Borneo
2. 200 meters and lower
3. 2,000 meters
4. along the coast and the southern part of the island; there is a wide area before the first contour line occurs
5. The island is rugged, with high elevations in the center.

Applying the Skill

1. Sri Lanka
2. 100 meters and lower
3. 1,000 meters
4. along the coast and the northern part of the island; there is a wide area here before the first contour line occurs
5. The island is mostly lowland, with a hilly center.

Section Objectives

1. Compare the people and economic activities of the island countries of Southeast Asia.
2. Name the groups that have influenced these countries.

BELLRINGER Skillbuilder Activity

Project transparency and have students answer questions.

This activity is also available as a blackline master.

Daily Focus Skills Transparency 8-2

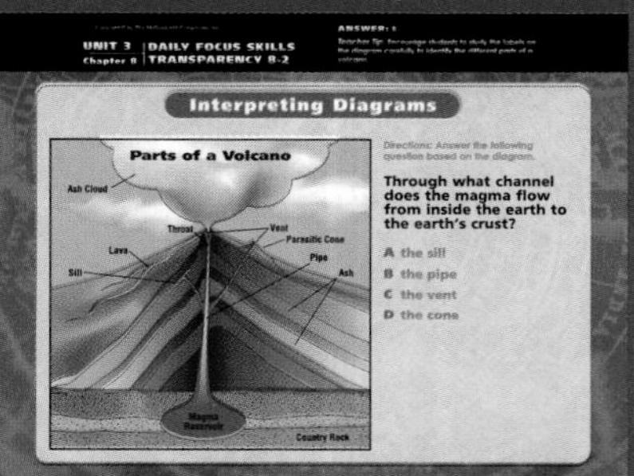

Guide to Reading

■ **Accessing Prior Knowledge**

Ask: What problems would you expect to find in governing a country of many islands? How would those problems change if the people were from many ethnic groups? Explain that in this section, students will read about a very populous country that faces these problems.

Section 2

Island Southeast Asia

Guide to Reading

Main Idea

The island countries of Southeast Asia have a variety of cultures and economic activities.

Terms to Know

- plate
- strait
- free port
- terraced field

Reading Strategy

Create a chart like this one. As you read, list two facts about each country in the right column.

Country	Facts
Indonesia	
Malaysia	
Singapore	
Brunei	
Philippines	

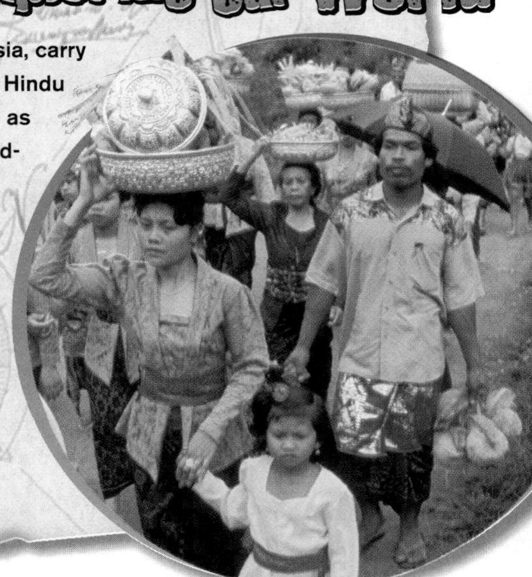

Villagers in Bali, Indonesia, carry food and gifts to a local Hindu temple. In Bali, it seems as though there is an unending chain of religious festivals. More than 60 festivals a year are dedicated to such events and items as percussion instruments, the birth of a Hindu goddess, woodcarving, and learning.

The island countries of Southeast Asia are Indonesia, Malaysia, Singapore, Brunei (bru•NY), and the Philippines. Indonesia sprawls over an area where two of the earth's tectonic plates meet. Tectonic **plates** are the huge slabs of rock that make up the earth's crust. Indonesia's location on top of these plates causes it to experience earthquakes.

Indonesia

Indonesia is Southeast Asia's largest country. It is an archipelago of more than 13,600 islands. The physical map on page 134 shows you the major islands of Indonesia—**Sumatra, Java,** and **Celebes** (SEH•luh•BEEZ). Indonesia also shares two large islands with other countries. Most of the island of **Borneo** belongs to Indonesia. In addition, Indonesia controls the western half of **New Guinea.** Another country—**Papua New Guinea**—lies on the eastern half.

Section Resources

Reproducible Masters

- Reproducible Lesson Plan 8-2
- Daily Lecture and Discussion Notes 8-2
- Guided Reading Activity 8-2
- Reading Essentials and Study Guide 8-2
- Section Quiz 8-2

Transparencies

- Daily Focus Skills Transparency 8-2
- GeoQuiz Transparency 8-1

Multimedia

- Vocabulary PuzzleMaker Software
- Interactive Tutor Self-Assessment CD-ROM
- Presentation Plus! CD-ROM
- ExamView® Pro 3.0 Testmaker CD-ROM

The volcanoes that formed Indonesia have left a rich covering of ash that makes the soil good for farming. Because Indonesia lies on the Equator, its climate is tropical. Monsoons bring a wet season and a dry season. The tropical climate, combined with fertile soil, has allowed dense rain forests to spread.

Indonesia's Economy Foreign companies build factories on the island of Java because labor is inexpensive. In addition, the island's location makes it easy to ship goods. Agriculture provides work for nearly half of the people of Indonesia. Farmers grow rice, coffee, cassava, tea, coconuts, and rubber trees. Cattle and sheep are also raised.

Indonesia has large reserves of oil and natural gas. Its mines yield tin, silver, nickel, copper, bauxite, and gold. Dense rain forests provide teak and other valuable woods. Some companies that own large tracts of land are cutting down the trees very quickly. The environment suffers from this deforestation. Tree roots help keep the soil in place during heavy rains. When the trees are cut down, the rich soil runs off into the sea.

Indonesia's People Indonesia has about 206 million people—the fourth-largest population in the world. It is also one of the world's most densely populated countries. On Java you will find **Jakarta** (juh•KAHR•tuh), Indonesia's capital and largest city.

Most of Indonesia's people belong to the Malay ethnic group. They are divided into about 300 smaller groups with their own languages. The official language, Bahasa Indonesia, is taught in schools.

Indonesia has more followers of Islam than any other country. Other religions, such as Christianity and Buddhism, are also practiced. On the beautiful island of Bali, Hindu beliefs are held by most of the people.

Thousands of years ago, Malays from mainland Southeast Asia settled the islands that are today Indonesia. Their descendants set up Buddhist and Hindu kingdoms. These kingdoms grew wealthy by controlling the trade that passed through the waterways between the Indian and Pacific Oceans. In the A.D. 1100s, traders from Southwest Asia brought Islam to the region. Four hundred years later, Europeans arrived to acquire the valuable spices grown here. They brought Christianity to the islands. The Dutch eventually controlled most of the islands as a colony. Independence finally came to Indonesia in 1949.

Since the 1960s, unrest and civil war have occurred on several islands. Most recently, the people of East Timor, who are largely Roman Catholic and were once ruled by Portugal, voted for independence. While Indonesia accepted the results of this election, some people in East Timor have not. With so many different ethnic groups, many small political parties arise. As a result, Indonesia's democratic leaders find it difficult to form a government that is strong enough to deal with the challenges facing the country.

✓Reading Check **When did Indonesia win its independence?**

Exchange of Knowledge

In early times merchants and traders were responsible for the exchange of knowledge as well as goods. Malacca, in Malay, was the richest seaport in the world in the 1500s. Merchants from India, China, and Japan, met Portuguese, British, and Dutch traders. Today, thanks to its geographical location, Singapore has replaced Malacca as the chief center of trade.

Content Background

Deforestation Deforestation not only causes environmental damage but might also have severe health consequences. Dangerous forest fires raged across Indonesia in 1997. Caused by the application of slash-and-burn techniques on an industrial scale—to clear huge amounts of land for the creation of plantations—the fires burned out of control in a time of drought. As a result, an area about the size of New Jersey went up in smoke—and that smoke had devastating consequences. It was so thick that ships in the Straits of Malacca collided, a plane crash in Sumatra killed 234 people, and about 20 million people suffered respiratory diseases. Although Indonesia's government banned clearing large tracts of land in this way, companies continued to do so, producing another air pollution hazard in 1999.

Categorizing Information

Develop a database of Indonesia's characteristics, such as reserves of oil, location along shipping lines, and a large population. Read these items one at a time and have students identify whether it describes Indonesia's physical geography, economy, or culture. Some features can be placed in more than one category. **L1**

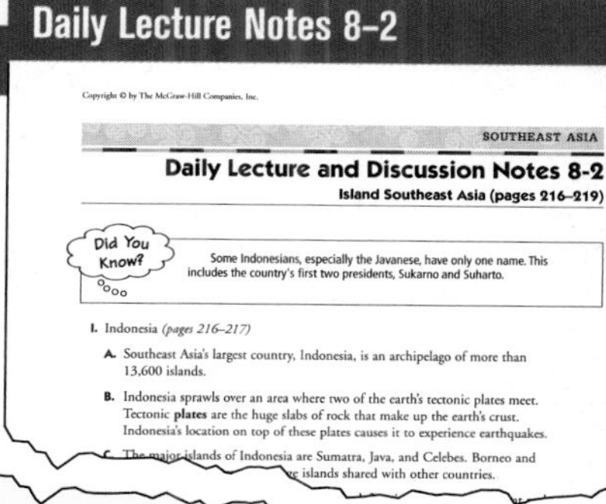
Daily Lecture Notes 8-2

SOUTHEAST ASIA

Daily Lecture and Discussion Notes 8-2

Island Southeast Asia (pages 216–219)

Did You Know? Some Indonesians, especially the Javanese, have only one name. This includes the country's first two presidents, Sukarno and Suharto.

I. Indonesia (pages 216–217)

A. Southeast Asia's largest country, Indonesia, is an archipelago of more than 13,600 islands.

B. Indonesia sprawls over an area where two of the earth's tectonic plates meet. Tectonic **plates** are the huge slabs of rock that make up the earth's crust. Indonesia's location on top of these plates causes it to experience earthquakes.

C. The major islands of Indonesia are Sumatra, Java, and Celebes. Borneo and ... islands shared with other countries.

✓ Reading Check Answer

1949

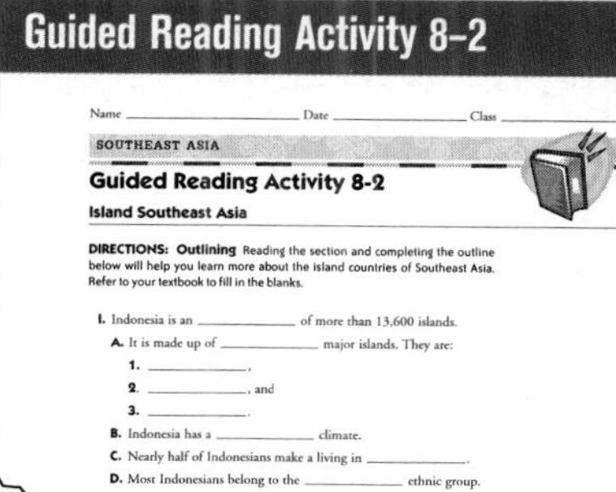
Guided Reading Activity 8-2

Name ________ Date ________ Class ________

SOUTHEAST ASIA

Guided Reading Activity 8-2

Island Southeast Asia

DIRECTIONS: Outlining Reading the section and completing the outline below will help you learn more about the island countries of Southeast Asia. Refer to your textbook to fill in the blanks.

I. Indonesia is an ________ of more than 13,600 islands.

A. It is made up of ________ major islands. They are:

1. ________,

2. ________, and

3. ________.

B. Indonesia has a ________ climate.

C. Nearly half of Indonesians make a living in ________.

D. Most Indonesians belong to the ________ ethnic group.

E. Indonesia's main religions are ________, ________, ________.

More About the Photos

Rubber British scientist Joseph Priestly gave rubber its name when he learned it could be used to rub out pencil marks.

Caption Answer palm oil, wood

Reading Check Answer

in Kuala Lumpur, Malaysia

ASSESS

Assign Section 2 Assessment as homework or an in-class activity.

Section Quiz 4-3

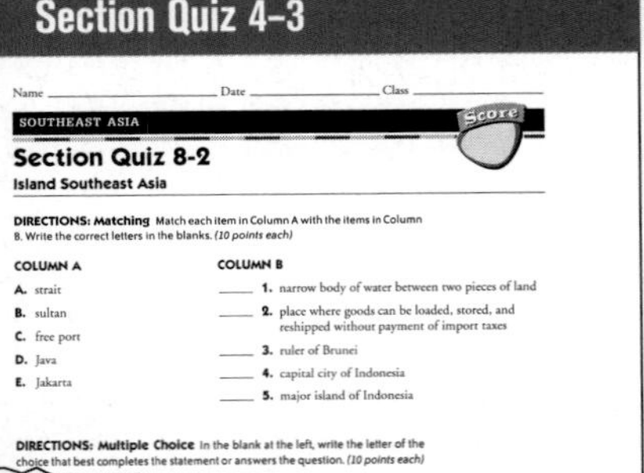

Name ______ Date ______ Class ______

SOUTHEAST ASIA — Score

Section Quiz 8-2

Island Southeast Asia

DIRECTIONS: Matching Match each item in Column A with the items in Column B. Write the correct letters in the blanks. *(10 points each)*

COLUMN A	COLUMN B
A. strait	____ 1. narrow body of water between two pieces of land
B. sultan	____ 2. place where goods can be loaded, stored, and reshipped without payment of import taxes
C. free port	____ 3. ruler of Brunei
D. Java	____ 4. capital city of Indonesia
E. Jakarta	____ 5. major island of Indonesia

DIRECTIONS: Multiple Choice In the blank at the left, write the letter of the choice that best completes the statement or answers the question. *(10 points each)*

Did You Know?

More farmers die from snake bites in Malaysia than anywhere else in the world.

NATIONAL GEOGRAPHIC **On Location**

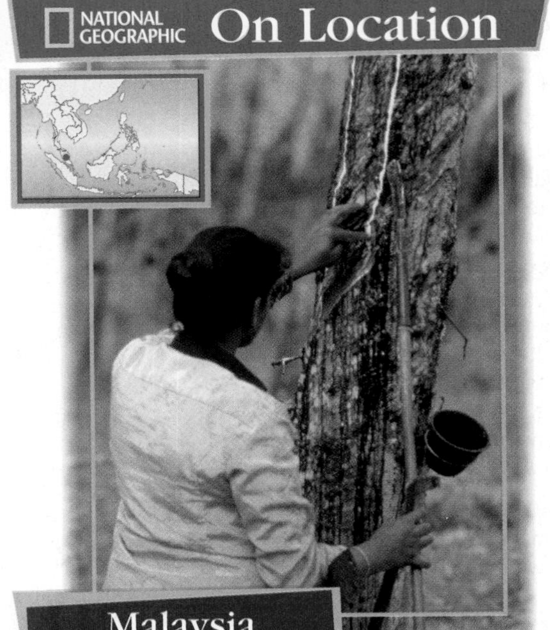

Malaysia

A Malaysian worker taps a rubber tree to get the milky liquid called latex.

Human/Environment Interaction What other Malaysian products are grown for export?

Malaysia

Dense rain forests and rugged mountains make up the landscape of **Malaysia.** The **Strait of Malacca** lies to the west of one part of Malaysia—the Malay Peninsula. A **strait** is a narrow body of water between two pieces of land. The Strait of Malacca is an important waterway for trade between the Indian Ocean and the Java Sea.

Malaysia is one of the world's leaders in exporting rubber and palm oil. Large amounts of wood are also exported. Malaysia is rich in minerals such as tin, iron ore, copper, and bauxite, as well as in oil and natural gas. Factory workers make high-technology and consumer goods. Malaysia's ports are important centers of trade. **Kuala Lumpur** (KWAH•luh LUM•PUR) is the capital and largest city. The Petronas Towers—the tallest buildings in the world—soar above this city. In contrast, many rural villagers live in thatched-roof homes built on posts a few feet off the ground.

Most of Malaysia's 22.7 million people belong to the Malay ethnic group. Their ancestors came from southern China about 4,000 years ago. In the 1800s, the British—who then ruled Malaysia—brought in Chinese and South Asian workers to mine tin and to work on rubber plantations. As a result, in marketplaces today you can hear Malay, Chinese, Tamil, and English spoken. Most Malaysians are Muslims, but there are large numbers of Hindus, Buddhists, and Christians.

Reading Check Where are the world's tallest buildings located?

Singapore, Brunei, and the Philippines

Singapore lies off the southern tip of the Malay Peninsula. It is made up of Singapore Island and 58 smaller islands. Singapore is one of the world's smallest countries, yet it has one of the world's most productive economies.

The city of Singapore is the capital and takes up much of Singapore Island. Once covered by rain forests, Singapore Island now has highways, factories, office buildings, and docks.

The city of Singapore has one of the world's busiest harbors. It is a **free port,** a place where goods can be loaded or unloaded, stored, and shipped again without payment of import taxes. Huge amounts of goods pass through this port. Singapore's many factories make high-tech goods, machinery, chemicals, and paper products. Because of their productive trade economy, the people of Singapore enjoy a high standard of living.

Meeting Special Needs

Visual/Spatial Malaysia and Indonesia are known for an art form called *batik,* a Javanese word meaning "drop." To create a *batik* pattern, wax is first dripped onto a fabric. When the fabric is dyed, the dye enters only the areas that are not covered by wax. After the dye has dried, the fabric is boiled to remove the wax. A beautiful pattern remains on the fabric. Show students some examples of Malaysian art and ask them to explain the relationship between Malaysia and the art they see. Then give them a blank sheet of paper and have them create a *batik* design that evokes the spirit of that art. **L1**

Refer to *Inclusion for the Middle School Social Studies Classroom Strategies and Activities* in the TCR.

Founded by the British in the early 1800s, Singapore became an independent republic in 1965. Most of the country's 4 million people are Chinese, but Malaysians and Indians make up about 25 percent of the population. These people practice Buddhism, Islam, Christianity, Hinduism, and traditional Chinese religions.

Brunei On the northern coast of Borneo lies another small nation—**Brunei.** Oil and natural gas exports provide about half of the country's income. Brunei's citizens receive free education and medical care, and low-cost housing, fuel, and food. Today the government is investing in new industries to avoid too much reliance on revenues from fuels. All political and economic decisions are made by Brunei's ruler, or sultan, who governs with a firm hand.

The Philippines The Philippines is an archipelago of more than 7,000 islands of volcanic mountains and forests. Lava from volcanoes provides fertile soil for agriculture. Farmers have built terraces on the steep slopes of the mountains. **Terraced fields** are strips of land cut out of a hillside like stair steps. The land can then hold water and be used for farming.

Named after King Philip II of Spain, the Philippines spent more than 300 years as a Spanish colony. As a result of the **Spanish-American War,** the United States controlled the islands from 1898 until World War II. In 1946 the Philippines became an independent democratic republic.

The Philippines is the only Christian country in Southeast Asia. About 90 percent of Filipinos follow the Roman Catholic religion, brought to the islands by Spanish missionaries. The culture today blends Malay, Spanish, and American influences.

✓ **Reading Check** For whom was the Philippines named and why?

Our World Today Online
Web Activity Visit the ***Our World Today: People, Places, and Issues*** Web site at owt.glencoe.com and click on **Chapter 8–Student Web Activities** to learn more about the Philippines.

Section 2 Assessment

Defining Terms

1. **Define** plate, strait, free port, terraced field.

Recalling Facts

2. **Location** What five islands are the largest in Indonesia?
3. **Economics** Why do the people of Singapore enjoy a high standard of living?
4. **Culture** What religion do most Filipinos practice?

Critical Thinking

5. **Summarizing Information** How does Brunei's government use its fuel income?
6. **Understanding Culture** Why is it difficult for government officials to rule Indonesia?

Graphic Organizer

7. **Organizing Information** Create a diagram like this one. In the center, list similarities of the countries listed. In the outer ovals, write two ways that the country differs from the others.

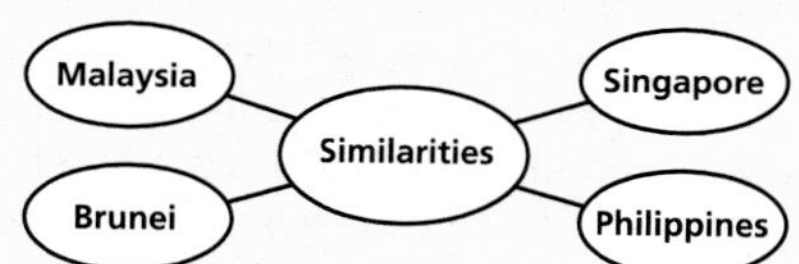

Applying Social Studies Skills

8. **Analyzing Maps** Look at the physical map on page 134. What is the highest point of land in Indonesia?

Section 2 Assessment

1. The terms are defined in the Glossary.
2. Sumatra, Java, Celebes, Bornea, and New Guinea
3. because Singapore has a very productive trade economy
4. Roman Catholicism
5. Fuel income pays for free education and medical care and low-cost housing, food, and fuel for all the country's people.
6. There are many different ethnic groups and many small political parties.
7. Students' diagrams will vary.
8. Jaya Peak on New Guinea

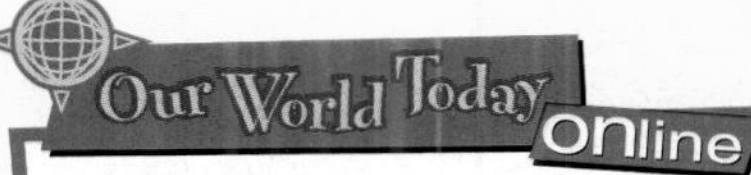

Objectives, goals, and answers to the Student Web Activity can be found in the Web Activity Lesson Plan at **owt.glencoe.com**

✓ Reading Check Answer

King Philip II of Spain; the Philippines were a Spanish colony

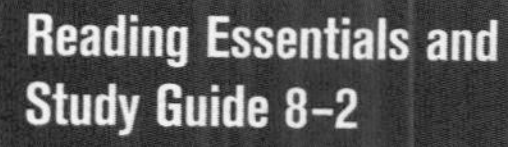

Reading Essentials and Study Guide 8–2

SOUTHEAST ASIA

Reading Essentials and Study Guide 8-2
Island Southeast Asia

For use with textbook pages 216–219

Terms to Know
plates huge slabs of rock that make up the earth's crust (page 216)
strait narrow body of water between two pieces of land (page 218)
free port place where goods can be loaded or unloaded, stored, and shipped again without payment of import taxes (page 218)
terraced field strips of land cut out of a hillside like stair steps (page 219)

Drawing From Experience
What do the soles of your shoes and tires on a car have in common? They both may be made of rubber. What is rubber and where does it come from? ...rubber comes from the sap of a rubber tree. Many

Enrich

Have students research and report on the history of Spanish or American involvement in the Philippines.

Close

Have students write a pen pal letter to a teenager in one of the island countries of Southeast Asia. Have them compare that country with the United States.

TEACH

Ask: Have you ever seen a puppet show? *(Students might mention puppet shows they saw as children on TV or in movies.)* Explain that in Indonesia, puppet shows are a very special part of the culture of all people, including adults. L1

More About Shadow Puppets

Despite the heavy demands placed on the *dalang* in shadow puppetry, there are many thousands of these performers entertaining people across Indonesia. Shadow puppets are found throughout Southeast Asia and in China. Only in Indonesia, however, are the shows performed by a single puppeteer.

Interdisciplinary Connections

Drama Have students work in groups to write a script for a short play. They might base it on a folktale. Then have them perform their play. If time allows, have students design puppets.

Making Connections

CULTURE | GOVERNMENT | PEOPLE | TECHNOLOGY

Shadow Puppets

Late at night, long after dark has fallen on a small stage in Java, a shadow puppet show is about to begin. The glow of a lamp shines behind a wide linen screen. Puppets stand hidden from direct view. The "good" characters are on the right. The "bad" ones are placed on the left. The audience waits anxiously on the other side of the screen. Once the story begins, the performance will continue until dawn.

The Performance

Wayang kulit, the ancient Indonesian shadow puppet theater, dates back at least 1,000 years. Today there are several thousand puppeteers. This makes shadow puppets the strongest theater tradition in Southeast Asia.

Shadow puppets are flat leather puppets, many with movable limbs and mouths, that are operated by sticks. During the show, the puppets cast their shadows onto the screen. The *dalang,* or puppeteer, sits behind the screen and manipulates the figures. He brings each to life in one of the more than 200 traditional puppet stories.

The Stories

Although Islam is now the major religion of Indonesia, much of the traditional shadow puppet theater is based on stories from two ancient Hindu epics from India. At one time the principal purpose of shadow puppetry was to provide moral and religious instruction in Hinduism. Now the stories combine Hindu themes with elements of Buddhism and Islam, as well as Indonesian history and folklore. Often the performance is given in celebration of public or religious holidays or to honor a wedding or birth.

▼ The *dalang* and his orchestra

The Puppeteer

The skill of the *dalang* is critical to the show's success. The *dalang* operates all the puppets, narrates the story, provides sound effects, and directs the gong, drum, and flute orchestra that accompanies the puppet show. The puppeteer changes his voice to create an individual sound for each character. The *dalang* performs without a script or notes, adding jokes and making small changes to suit the crowd and the occasion. Because a shadow puppet show can last as long as nine hours, the *dalang* must have both a tremendous memory and great endurance.

Many *dalang*s carve their own puppets, having learned this art from earlier generations. Each figure must appear in a specific size, body build, and costume. Even the shape of the eyes tells about the figure's character and mood.

Making the Connection

1. How do shadow puppets move?
2. What kinds of stories do shadow puppet shows present?
3. **Drawing Conclusions** In what way is the *dalang* a master of many different art forms?

Making the Connection

1. They are operated by sticks.
2. traditional stories with religious themes and Indonesian history and folklore
3. The *dalang* must operate all the puppets, tell the story, use different voices for the puppets, and direct the music that accompanies the performance.

Reading Review

Section 1 Mainland Southeast Asia

Terms to Know
monsoon
precious gems
deforestation
socialism
civil war
delta

Main Idea
The countries of mainland Southeast Asia rely on agriculture as a major source of income.

✓ **Region** Mainland Southeast Asia includes the countries of Myanmar, Thailand, Laos, Cambodia, and Vietnam.
✓ **Place** These countries have highland areas and lowland river valleys with fertile soil. Monsoons bring heavy rains in the summer.
✓ **History** Thailand is the only country in Southeast Asia free of the influence of colonial rule.
✓ **Economics** Conflict has hurt the economies of Laos, Cambodia, and Vietnam.

Section 2 Island Southeast Asia

Terms to Know
plate
strait
free port
terraced field

Main Idea
The island countries of Southeast Asia have a variety of cultures and economic activities.

✓ **Region** The island countries of Southeast Asia include Indonesia, Malaysia, Singapore, Brunei, and the Philippines.
✓ **Place** Indonesia—the world's fourth most-populous country—is an archipelago formed by volcanoes.
✓ **Economics** Indonesia has rich supplies of oil, natural gas, and minerals.
✓ **Government** Indonesia's leaders face the challenge of creating a nation out of a land with many different groups and political parties.
✓ **Economics** Malaysia produces palm oil and rubber, among other goods. Its capital, Kuala Lumpur, is a commercial center.
✓ **Economics** The port of Singapore is one of the world's busiest trading centers.
✓ **Culture** The Philippines shows the influence of Malaysian, Spanish, and American culture.

People in Bangkok, Thailand, face traffic snarls and pollution that are among the worst in the world. ▶

Reading Review

Use the Chapter 8 Reading Review to preview, review, condense, or reteach the chapter.

Preview/Review

Use the Terms to Know lists to help students review and study.

Activity Have students draw up a matching quiz of the 10 terms from the chapter and their definitions. Then have them exchange quizzes with another student and take the quiz their partners prepared.

Vocabulary PuzzleMaker Software reinforces the vocabulary terms used in Chapter 8.

The Interactive Tutor Self-Assessment CD-ROM allows students to review Chapter 8 content.

Condense

Have students read the Chapter 8 summary statements.

Chapter 8 Guided Reading Activities

Chapter 8 Audio Program

Reteach

Reteaching Activity 8

Chapter 8 Reading Essentials and Study Guide

Chapter Culminating Activity

Country Photo Album Have students choose one of the countries studied in this chapter and imagine that they have visited there. Ask them to create a photo album that shows what they saw in the country. They should look for photographs that show the landscape, cities, places of interest, and people of their chosen country. With each photograph, have them write a brief caption that identifies the subject of the photo and gives additional information about it. *NOTE: This activity may be completed separately or you may wish students to incorporate it into their Current Events Journals.*

EE2 Places and Regions: Standard 4

GLENCOE TECHNOLOGY

MindJogger Videoquiz
Use MindJogger to review the Chapter 8 content.

 Available in VHS.

Using Key Terms

1. f
2. a
3. g
4. j
5. i
6. c
7. b
8. d
9. e
10. h

Reviewing the Main Ideas

11. tin, gemstones
12. Laos, Cambodia, and Vietnam
13. by opening the country to Western ideas, businesses, and tourists and by loosening government control of the economy
14. farming
15. Because Indonesia sits in the midst of several seas and near the Pacific and Indian Oceans, it is a convenient point from which to ship goods.
16. because of all the ethnic groups on the islands
17. It is a transportation corridor between the Indian Ocean and the Java Sea.
18. manufacturing
19. oil and natural gas
20. Most of the people are Roman Catholic, as in Spain.

Chapter 8 Assessment and Activities

Using Key Terms

Match the terms in Part A with their definitions in Part B.

A.

1. free port
2. delta
3. plates
4. strait
5. deforestation
6. terraced field
7. civil war
8. socialism
9. precious gems
10. monsoon

B.

a. land made from soil deposited at the mouth of a river
b. war fought between groups within a country
c. strip of land cut out of a hillside
d. economic system in which the government owns many businesses
e. stones such as rubies, sapphires, and jade
f. place where shipped goods are not taxed
g. slabs of rock that make up the earth's crust
h. seasonal wind that blows over a continent for months at a time
i. the widespread cutting of trees
j. narrow body of water that runs between two land areas

Reviewing the Main Ideas

Section 1 Mainland Southeast Asia

11. **Economics** Thailand is one of the world's leading exporters of what two items?
12. **History** What countries have poor economies because of recent conflict?
13. **Economics** How is Vietnam trying to improve its economy?

Section 2 Island Southeast Asia

14. **Economics** How do nearly half of the people of Indonesia make a living?
15. **Location** How does location make Indonesia a center of trade?
16. **Government** Why does Indonesia have many political parties?
17. **Place** Why is the strait of Malacca important?
18. **Economics** What economic activity is important in Singapore besides its shipping industry?
19. **Economics** What resources have made Brunei wealthy?
20. **Culture** How does religion show Spanish influence in the Philippines?

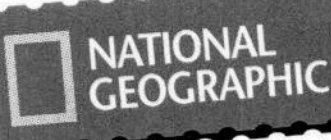

Southeast Asia

Place Location Activity

On a separate sheet of paper, match the letters on the map with the numbered places listed below.

1. Mekong River
2. South China Sea
3. Gulf of Tonkin
4. Hanoi
5. Indonesia
6. Singapore
7. Thailand
8. Vietnam
9. Indian Ocean
10. Philippines

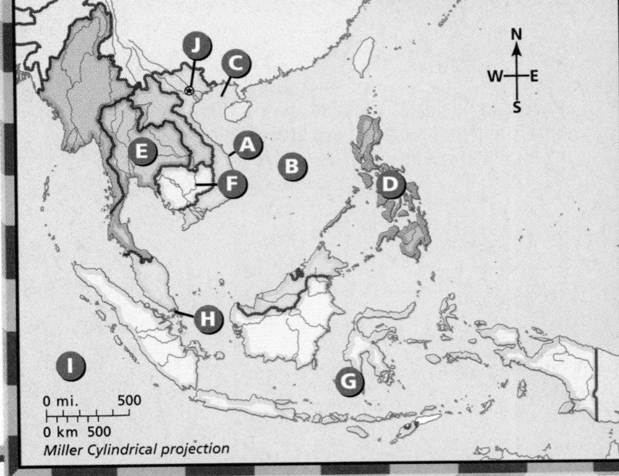

NATIONAL GEOGRAPHIC **Place Location Activity**

1. F
2. B
3. C
4. J
5. G
6. H
7. E
8. A
9. I
10. D

Critical Thinking

21. *Possible answer:* Unless they diversify, the country's economy will suffer and the standard of living will drop significantly due to the loss of oil revenues.
22. Students' charts will vary.

Current Events Journal

23. Students who choose a musical topic might wish to include audio samples of the music they discuss.

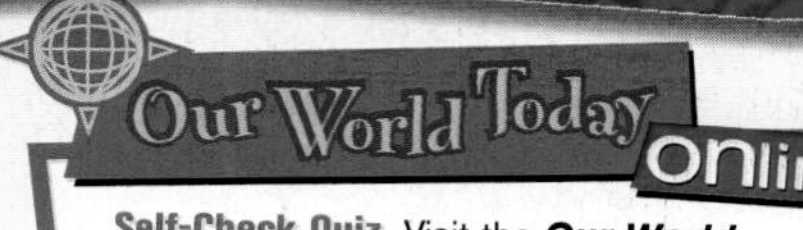

Self-Check Quiz Visit the ***Our World Today: People, Places, and Issues*** Web site at owt.glencoe.com and click on **Chapter 8–Self-Check Quizzes** to prepare for the Chapter Test.

Critical Thinking

21. **Predicting Outcomes** Experts believe that Brunei has enough oil reserves to last until 2018. What might happen to the country's economy and standard of living at that time?
22. **Organizing Information** Create a chart like this one. Under each column, write two facts about a country in Southeast Asia. Write about three countries—one from mainland Southeast Asia, Indonesia, and another from island Southeast Asia.

Country	Land	Economy	People

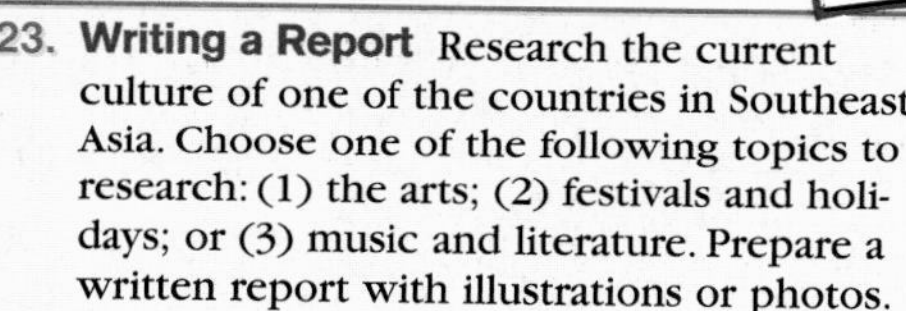

Current Events Journal

23. **Writing a Report** Research the current culture of one of the countries in Southeast Asia. Choose one of the following topics to research: (1) the arts; (2) festivals and holidays; or (3) music and literature. Prepare a written report with illustrations or photos.

Mental Mapping Activity

24. **Focusing on the Region** Draw a map of Southeast Asia, then label the following:

- Borneo
- Irrawaddy River
- Java
- Malay Peninsula
- Philippines
- South China Sea
- Strait of Malacca
- Thailand

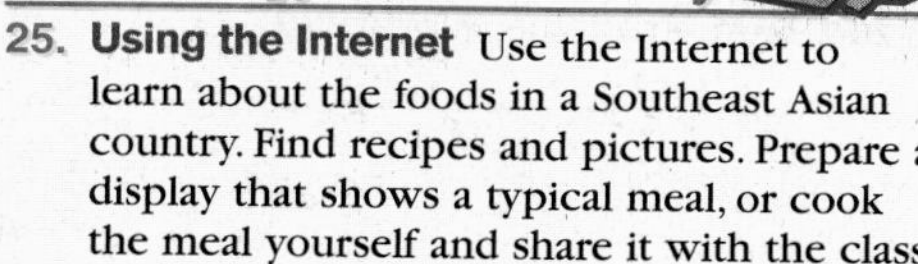

Technology Skills Activity

25. **Using the Internet** Use the Internet to learn about the foods in a Southeast Asian country. Find recipes and pictures. Prepare a display that shows a typical meal, or cook the meal yourself and share it with the class.

Standardized Test Practice

Directions: Study the graph below, and then answer the questions that follow.

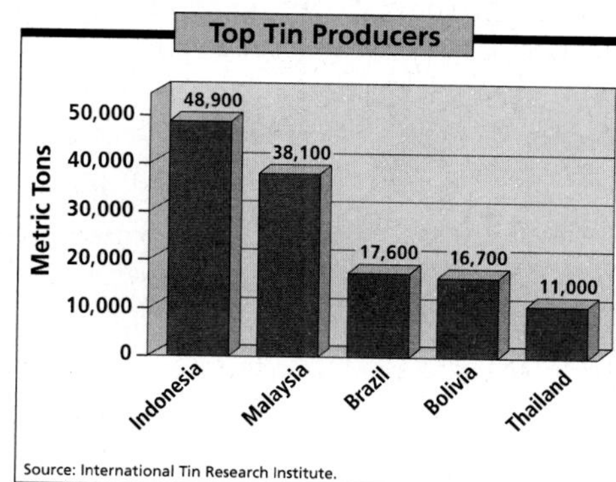

1. **About how much tin does Indonesia produce each year?**
   A 48,900 metric tons
   B 48,000,900 metric tons
   C 48.9 million metric tons
   D 48.9 billion metric tons
2. **About how much tin does Brazil produce each year?**
   F 17,600 metric tons
   G 17,600,000 metric tons
   H 17.6 million metric tons
   J 17.6 billion metric tons

Test-Taking Tip: In order to understand any type of graph, look carefully around the graph for keys that show how it is organized. On this bar graph, the numbers along the left side represent the exact number shown. You do not have to multiply by millions or billions to find the number of metric tons.

Assessment and Activities

Standardized Test Practice

1. A
2. F

Tested Objectives: Reading a graph, analyzing information

Chapter Test Bonus Question

This question may be used for extra credit on the chapter test.

Which country in this region is named for a king of Spain? *(the Philippines)*

Our World Today Online

Have students visit the Web site at **owt.glencoe.com** to review Chapter 8 and take the Self-Check Quiz.

Mental Mapping Activity

24. This exercise helps students visualize the countries and geographic features they have been studying and understand the relationship among various points. Accept all attempts at freehand mapping that show places in the correct relationship to one another.

Technology Skills Activity

25. Several Internet sources offer international recipes. Large food stores often carry ingredients for international foods. As an alternative, students could contact an ethnic restaurant in the area that serves food from the region and obtain a menu of foods in that way.

Unit 4 Planning Guide

SUGGESTED PACING CHART

Unit 4 (1 day)	Chapter 9 (5 days)	Chapter 10 (5 days)	Chapter 11 (7 days)	Chapter 12 (5 days)	Unit 4 (2 days)
Day 1 Introduction	**Day 1** Chapter 9 Intro, Section 1	**Day 1** Chapter 10 Intro, Section 1	**Day 1** Chapter 11 Intro, Section 1	**Day 1** Chapter 12 Intro, Section 1	**Day 1** Wrap-Up/Projects
	Day 2 Section 2	**Day 2** Section 2	**Day 2** Section 2	**Day 2** Section 2	**Day 2** Unit 4 Assessment
	Day 3 Section 3	**Day 3** Section 3	**Day 3** Section 3	**Day 3** Section 3	
	Day 4 Chapter 9 Review	**Day 4** Chapter 10 Review	**Day 4** Section 4	**Day 4** Chapter 12 Review	
	Day 5 Chapter 9 Assessment	**Day 5** Chapter 10 Assessment	**Day 5** Section 5	**Day 5** Chapter 12 Assessment	
			Day 6 Chapter 11 Review		
			Day 7 Chapter 11 Assessment		

For a complete course pacing guide and Teacher Classroom Resources, see:

Interactive Lesson Planner

Use the following tools to easily assess student learning in a variety of ways:

- **Performance Assessment Activities and Rubrics**
- **Section Quizzes**
- **Chapter Tests and Unit Pretests and Posttests**
- **Interactive Tutor Self-Assessment CD-ROM**
- **ExamView® Pro 3.0 Testmaker CD-ROM**
- **MindJogger Videoquiz**
- **owt.glencoe.com**
- **Standardized Test Practice Workbook**

Note: The following materials may be used when teaching Unit 4.
Chapter level support materials can be found on the chapter resource pages.

TEACHING TRANSPARENCIES

Political Map Transparency 4

Unit 4 Map Overlay Transparencies

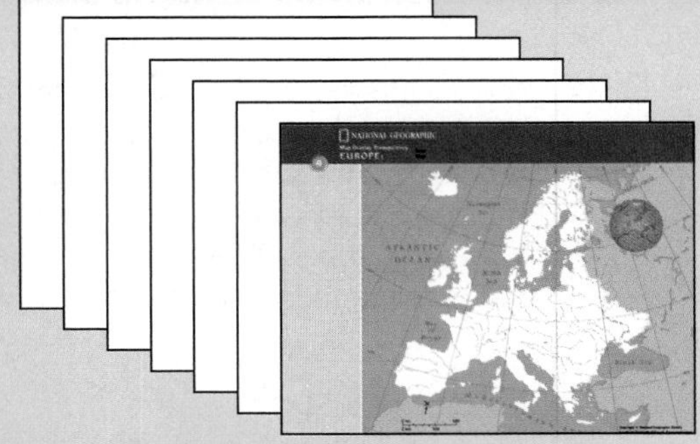

World Cultures Transparencies 5 and 6

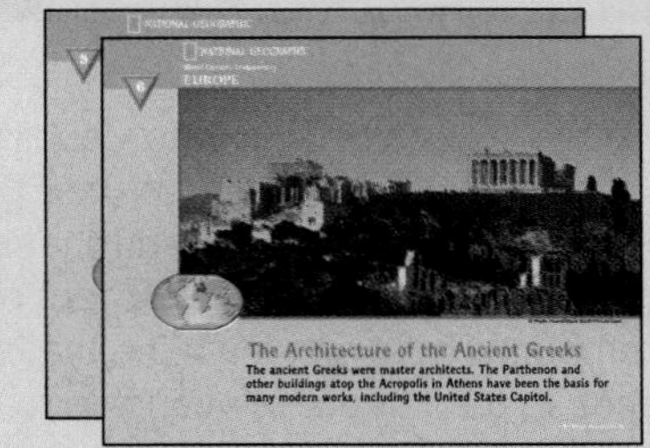

Unit 4 Resources

INTERDISCIPLINARY CONNECTIONS

World Literature Reading 4

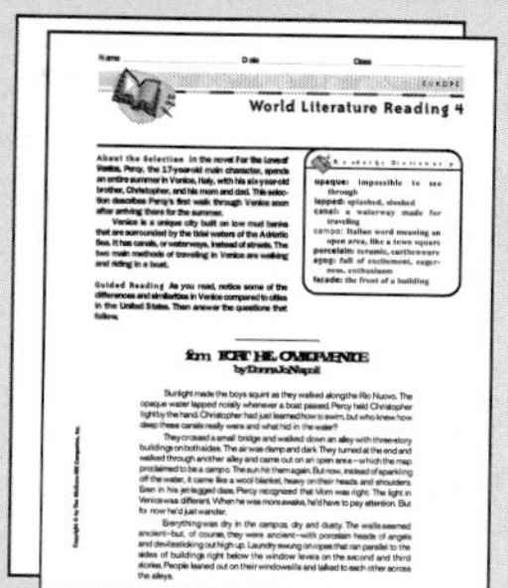

Economics and Geography Activity 4

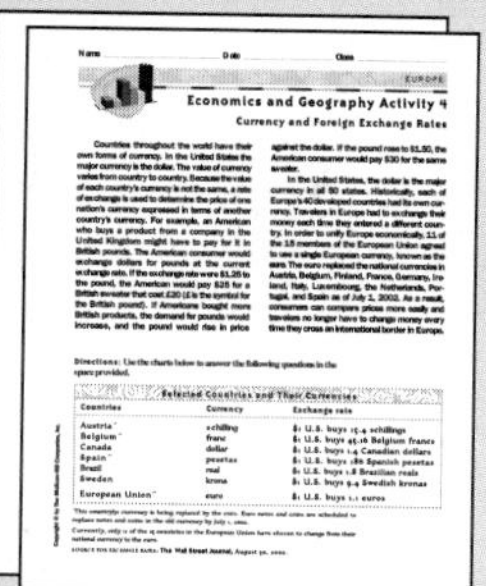

History and Geography Activity 4

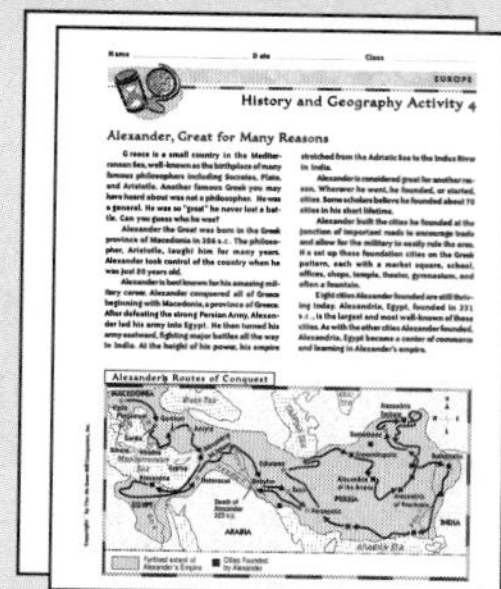

MAP AND GEOGRAPHY SKILLS

Building Geography Skills for Life

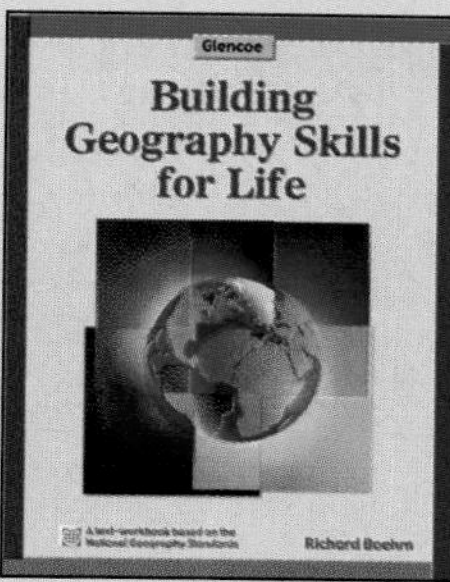

NGS Focus on Geography Literacy

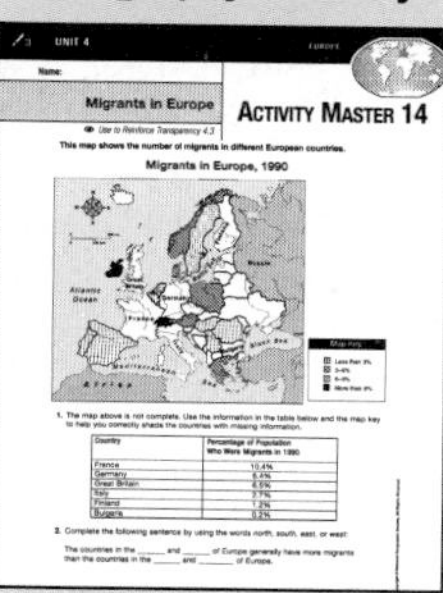

Regional Atlas Activity 4

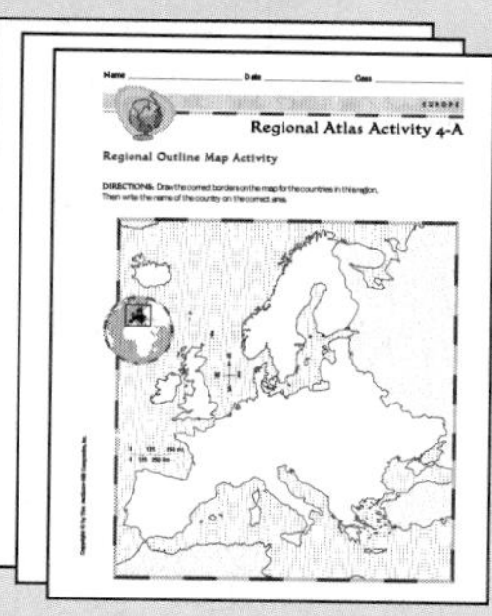

NATIONAL GEOGRAPHIC MapMachine

Find the latest coverage of geography in the news, atlas updates, cartographic activities with interactive maps, an online map store, and links at www.nationalgeographic.com/maps

APPLICATION AND HANDS-ON

Citizenship Activity 4

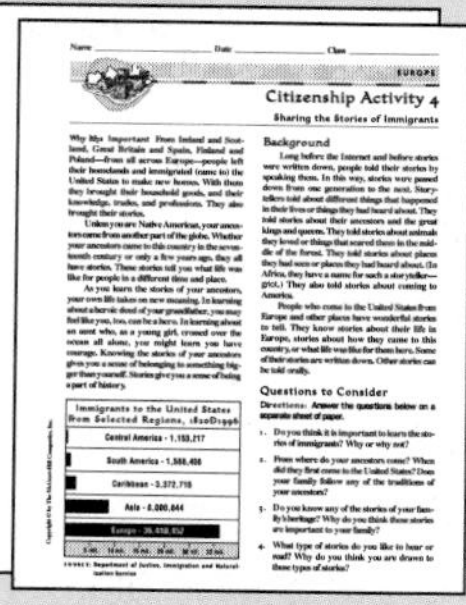

Foods Around the World 4

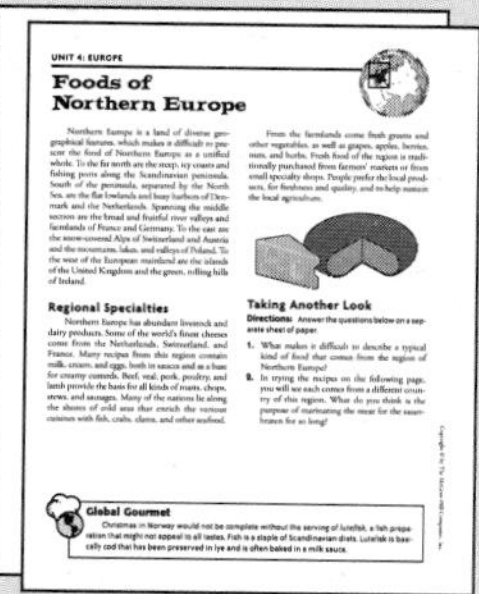

ENRICHMENT AND EXTENSION

Environmental Case Study 4

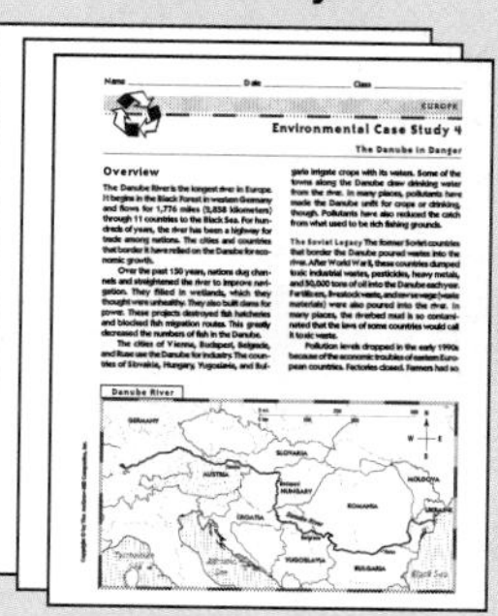

World Music: A Cultural Legacy

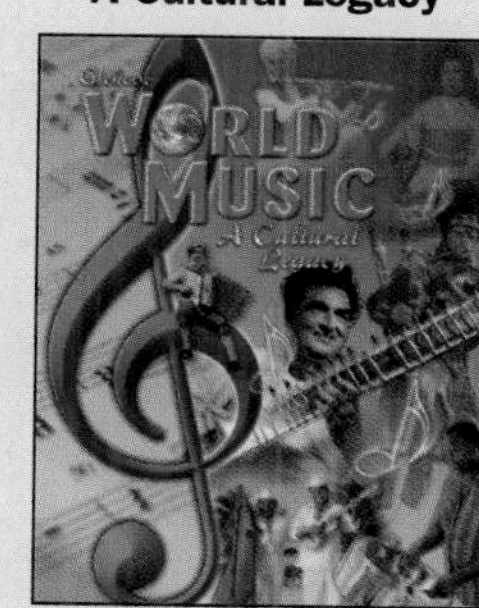

ASSESSMENT AND EVALUATION

GLENCOE'S ASSESSMENT ADVANTAGE

Unit 4 Pretests

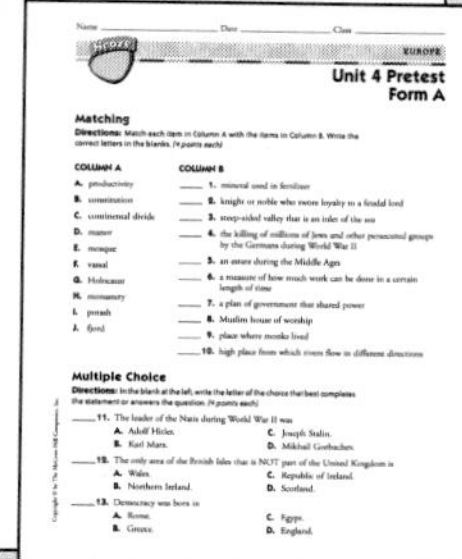

Unit 4 Posttests

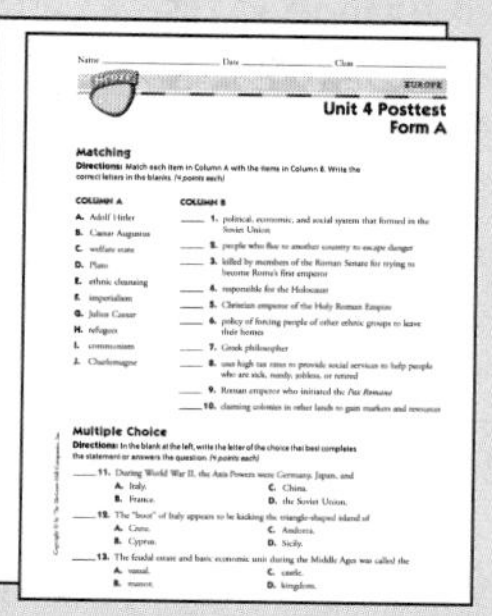

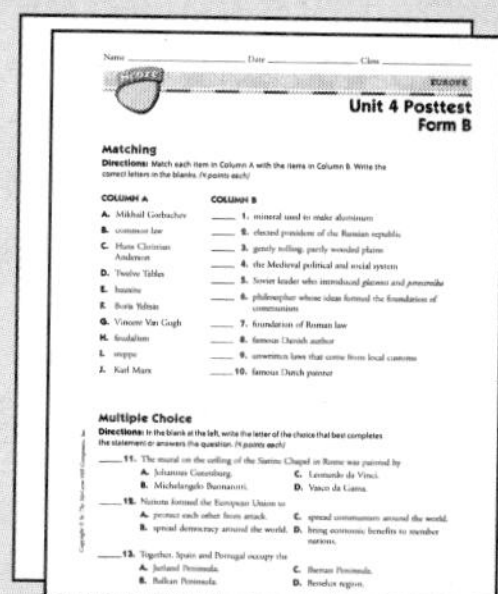

Additional Unit 4 Resources

- owt.glencoe.com
  Our World Today: People, Places, and Issues
  Visit the Glencoe *Our World Today: People, Places, and Issues* Web site for overviews, activities, assessments, and updated charts and graphs.
- socialstudies.glencoe.com
  Glencoe Social Studies
  Visit the Glencoe Web site for social studies activities, updates, and links to other sites.
- www.teachingtoday.glencoe.com
  Glencoe Teaching Today
  This Web site features daily teaching tips, free PDF downloads, annotated Web resources, educational news, and more.
- www.nationalgeographic.com
  NGS ONLINE Visit the National Geographic Society Web site for the latest coverage of geography in the news, atlas updates, activities, links, interactive features, and archives.
- **Glencoe's Guide to Using the Internet**
  Provides an introduction to many of the current technologies on the Internet. Professional resources and teaching strategies included.

Our Web sites provide additional resources. All essential content is covered in the Student Edition.

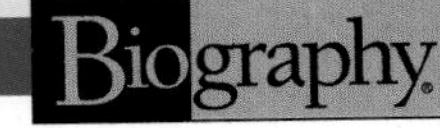

The following videotape programs are available from Glencoe:

- **Ancient Rome** 0-7670-1263-1
- **Mystical Monuments of Ancient Greece** 1-7670-0012-9
- **Constantine: The Christian Emperor** 0-7670-0577-5
- **Michelangelo** 1-56501-425-1
- **Napolean Bonaparte: The Glory of France** 0-7670-1211-9
- **The War in Europe** 1-56501-993-8
- **Anne Frank** 0-7670-1409-X
- **Eiffel Tower** 1-56501-465-0

To order, call Glencoe at 1-800-334-7344. To find classroom resources to accompany many of these, check:

A&E Television: www.aetv.com

The History Channel: www.historychannel.com

Bibliography

Literature for the Student

- **Glencoe Middle School World Literature Library**
  Number the Stars by Lois Lowry. Recounts the heroic 1943 evacuation of nearly 7,000 endangered Jews from Denmark to safety in Sweden during the period of Nazi occupation.
  I, Juan de Pareja by Eliabeth Trevino. Historical fiction set against the backdrop of 17th century Seville, Spain, and the lives of painters Diego Velaquez and Juan de Paraja.
- ***The Diary of Anne Frank***

Readings for the Teacher

- ***Europe On File***™. New York: Facts On File, 1997.
- ***Europe Today: An Atlas of Reproducible Pages,*** revised edition. Wellesley, Mass.: World Eagle, 1996.

Multimedia Links

- **Glencoe Social Studies Primary Source Document Library**
  The Black Plague, from *The Decameron* by Giovanni Boccaccio
  The Chernobyl Disaster by Yevgeny Velikov
  Churchill Rallies the British by Winston Churchill
  Da Vinci on Painting by Leonardo da Vinci
- ***Let's Visit France.*** Fairfield, Conn.: Queue. Mac/Windows CD-ROM.
- ***Making of the German Nation.*** Chicago, Ill.: Clearvue. Mac/Windows CD-ROM.

Refer to owt.glencoe.com for additional literature titles and study guides related to this region.

Additional Glencoe Teacher Support

- **Teaching Strategies for the Geography Classroom**
- **Reproducible Lesson Plans**
- **Outline Map Resource Book**
- **Reading in the Content Area**

Service Learning Project

Connecting Classroom With Community

The opposing sides of the conflict in Northern Ireland overcame their differences with the aid of a mediator. Many schools have established peer mediation programs. The steps include creating ground rules for the mediation, having the parties express their views without interruption, encouraging the parties to identify and discuss possible resolutions, and leading the parties to settle on a solution. Have students set up a peer mediation program in their school.

Content Background Notes

Use this additional information as lecture notes or discussion prompts throughout the study of Unit 4.

Chapter 9 Europe—Early History (pp. 234–253)

Olive Oil Olives were first grown in the eastern Mediterranean region about 6,000 years ago. Phoenician sailors brought them to Greece and Spain. Greeks planted olives in their colonies in Italy. Today Spain, Italy, and Greece produce about 74 percent of the world's olive oil output—nearly 500 million gallons a year. In a friendly rivalry, producers in the three countries vigorously debate which nation has the best quality oil.

Olive oil has gained in popularity in the past few decades not only because of its flavor but for health reasons. A 1970 study linked olive oil in the diet of southern Europeans to the fact that these people had the lowest rate of heart disease of all western nations. Later studies connected olive oil to other health benefits, including a reduced risk of breast cancer among women. These studies and other trends have helped contribute to a fivefold increase in U.S. imports of olive oil from the early 1980s to the late 1990s. Among Mediterranean peoples, this sudden popularity is probably not surprising. An ancient Greek myth says that the goddess Athena won a contest in which she and other gods gave gifts to humankind. Her gift—the olive tree—won the contest because it was deemed the most useful gift.

Chapter 10 Europe—Modern History (pp. 254–273)

The Euro By 2001, fifteen European countries belonged to the economic and political organization called the European Union (EU). All of the westernmost countries of Europe except Switzerland are members, as are seven countries in southern and northern Europe. Most members of the EU use a common currency, the euro. The euro was launched in 1999, although at first only for record-keeping and trading. By 2002, actual EU currency was to become available as the official currency in participating countries. After a brief transition period, member countries are to drop their national currencies in favor of the euro. Thus, the French franc, the German deutschmark, the Italian lira, and other well-known European currencies will cease to function as a means of exchange.

The United Kingdom, Sweden, and Denmark decided to not join with other member countries in adopting the common currency. Danish participation was denied in 2000, when, in a national referendum, the Danish people voted against using the euro.

Chapter 11 Western Europe Today (pp. 276–303)

Iceland: The Gene Laboratory Iceland's status as an isolated land with a homogeneous population has made the country a focus of modern genetics research. The country's 300,000 people are largely descended from the Nordic immigrants who arrived on the island in the 800s and 900s. As a result, the variations in Iceland's gene pool are fairly narrow. At the same time, the country's tradition of accurately recording genealogies makes it possible to trace the ancestry of today's islanders. These combined factors have led to an ambitious study of human genetics.

A native Icelander started a company that is studying the DNA of Icelanders who suffer from the same diseases. Scientists hope to identify genetic causes for these diseases—a task made more simple because of the population's small degree of genetic variation. In 1998 the company signed an agreement with a major drug manufacturer. The deal gives the drugmaker the right to the genetic information as a basis for developing new medicines. Icelanders, in turn, will be given those new medicines for free.

Also in 1998, Iceland's parliament approved the creation of a vast national database containing genetic information on the country's people. The move has stirred some controversy. Critics fear that information in the database could be abused, but supporters hope that Iceland's unique status could be useful in helping science cure some serious diseases.

Chapter 12 Eastern Europe Today (pp. 304–331)

Chernobyl's Legacy The 1986 nuclear disaster at the Chernobyl power plant continues to haunt Ukraine. The rate of thyroid cancers among people in the nearby area has skyrocketed. The plant itself needs attention. The concrete shell surrounding the reactor that exploded is cracked and leaking. Rebuilding the shell and disposing of nuclear waste will cost hundreds of millions of dollars—money Ukraine does not have.

Some problems lurk in the future. Environmental scientists say that radiation in the Dneiper River, near Chernobyl, will peak 60 to 90 years from now, causing problems then.

In 2000, Ukraine—under pressure from other countries—finally decided to shut down the last reactors at Chernobyl. That may not be the end of the story, however. Many scientists are worried about the possibility of a similar disaster elsewhere. Fourteen other nuclear plants have the same flawed design as the Chernobyl works. They are located in Lithuania and Russia. In addition, 25 other Soviet-built plants in eastern Europe and Russia have designs that are considered less safe than those employed in western countries.

00:00 Out of Time?

If time does not permit teaching each chapter in this unit, you may use the **Reading Essentials and Study Guide** for each chapter.

Unit Overview

The four chapters in this unit introduce students to the history, geography, and peoples of Europe. The chapters describe the physical and human features of these countries and explore their contributions to world culture. Before beginning to study the unit, point out to students that the countries of Europe share the following features:

- several related language families account for most of the languages spoken
- most people share a form of the Christian religion
- most countries are democratic
- most countries follow free market economies, and most people enjoy relatively high standards of living

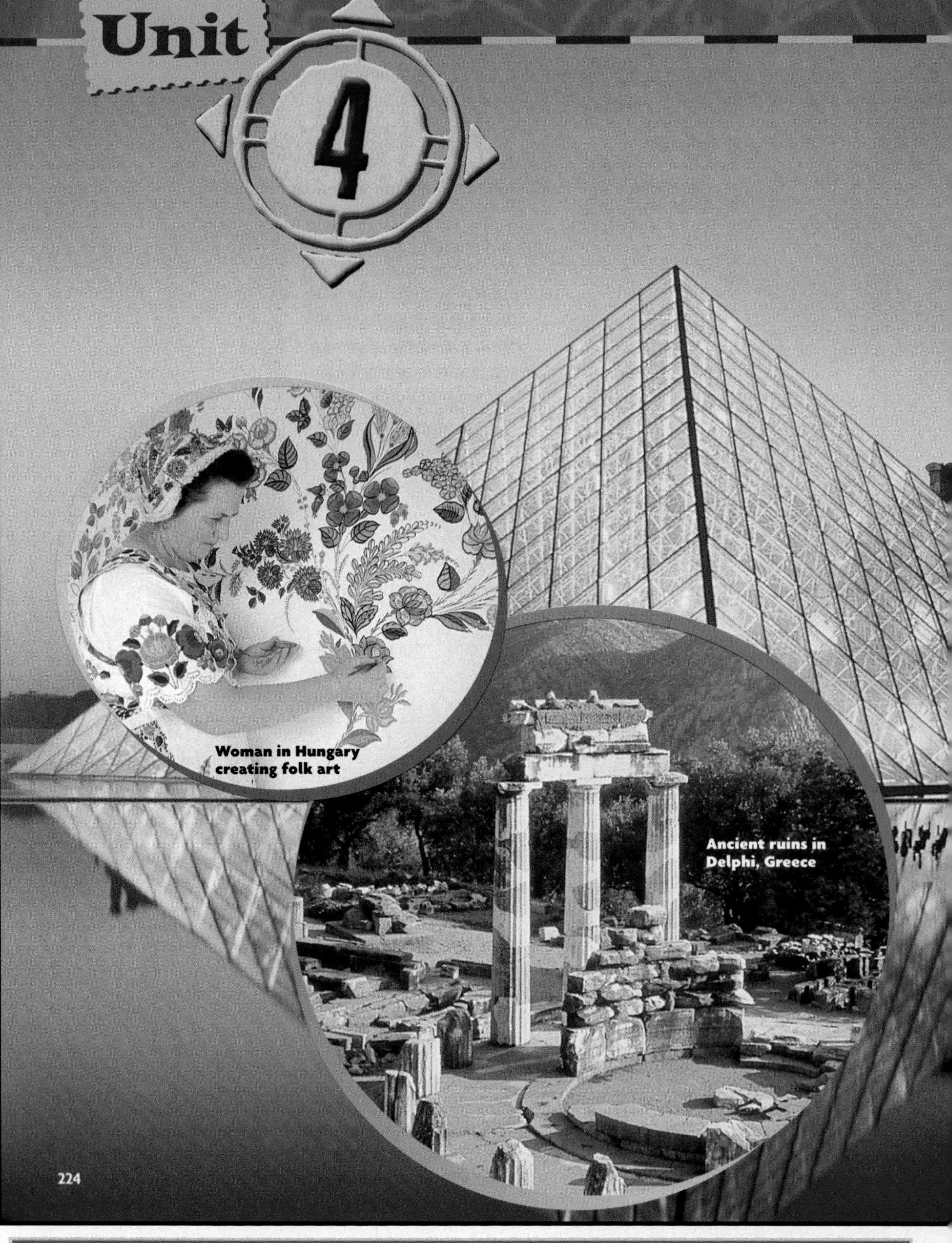

Woman in Hungary creating folk art

Ancient ruins in Delphi, Greece

Using the Illustration

The Louvre is on the original site of a royal castle built by King Philip II of France in the late 1100s. In the 1540s, King Francis I tore down the castle and began the first phase of construction on the structure now known as the Louvre. It first became an art museum in 1793, after the French Revolution. In the 1980s and 1990s, the museum was updated and renovated. The glass pyramid—designed by renowned architect I.M. Pei—was part of this. **Ask: What can you tell about Europe from the photos on these pages?** *(Europe has ancient cultures, evident from the Greek ruins; cities with impressive modern structures; and a lively tradition of folk art.)*

NATIONAL GEOGRAPHIC

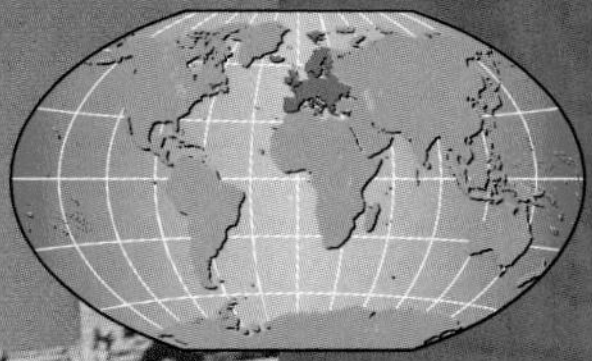

Europe

Relatively small as continents go, Europe is rich in history and culture. Like the United States, most nations in Europe are industrialized and have high standards of living. Unlike the United States, however, the people of Europe do not share a common language or government.

▲ The Louvre museum, Paris, France

NGS ONLINE
www.nationalgeographic.com/education

225

NATIONAL GEOGRAPHIC

These materials are available from Glencoe.

Software
ZipZapMap! World

Transparencies
PicturePack Transparencies

CD-ROM
Picture Atlas of the World, Second Edition

Current Events Journal

Have students look at a map of Europe and ask them what they notice. They should see that Europe is a small area with many countries. Have students list in their journals the effects that might result from this fact. *(conflicts over land, need to share resources)* Suggest that as they study the unit they look for details that show these effects.

NGS ONLINE
www.nationalgeographic.com/education

This online resource provides lesson plans, atlas updates, cartographic activities with interactive maps, an online map store, and geography links.

Unit Launch Activity

Why Study Europe? Point out that people have been living in Europe for many thousands of years and that they have significantly altered the environment. **Ask: How do countries in general use the environment?** Suggest that they think about resources, waterways, and recreational uses. **How do human actions harm the environment?** Suggest to students that they look for evidence of human use of the environment as they study this unit. Then have the class discuss the questions: **How do Europeans use the environment? What impact do those uses have? L2**

EE5 Environment and Society: Standard 14

NATIONAL GEOGRAPHIC

REGIONAL ATLAS

LESSON PLAN

Using the Regional Atlas
These features and activities may be used as an introduction to the unit or as teaching tools throughout the course of the unit.

Focus

Objectives

1. Describe the relative size and location of Europe.
2. Name the major physical features of Europe.
3. Identify the countries that make up Europe.
4. Describe the population density of Europe.

5-Minute Precheck

Have students look at the physical map of Europe on this page. Have them describe, in general terms, the landscape of Europe. *(mountains throughout the south; a vast lowland plain in the middle; some countries are islands and peninsulas)*

More About the Profile

In order to show a variety of physical features, this cross section begins at Lisbon, Portugal, and ends at Warsaw, Poland.

Europe

Physical

▲ Mountain peak
0 mi. 500
0 km 500
Lambert Azimuthal Equal-Area projection

20°W 10°W 0° 10°E 20°E 30°E
ARCTIC CIRCLE
MERIDIAN OF GREENWICH (LONDON)
60°N 50°N 40°N

ICELAND
Faroe Is.
Shetland Is.
Orkney Is.
ATLANTIC OCEAN
Norwegian Sea
North Sea
Baltic Sea
NORWAY
SWEDEN
SCANDINAVIA
FINLAND
ESTONIA
LATVIA
LITHUANIA
RUSSIA
RUSSIA
BELARUS
UKRAINE
MOLDOVA
Crimean Peninsula
Black Sea
Jutland
DENMARK
IRELAND
UNITED KINGDOM
British Isles
Thames R.
NETH.
GERMANY
Elbe R.
NORTH EUROPEAN PLAIN
POLAND
Oder R.
Vistula R.
Dnieper R.
BELG.
LUX.
Rhine R.
Seine R.
Loire R.
FRANCE
Bay of Biscay
CZECH REP.
SLOVAKIA
Carpathian Mountains
AUSTRIA
LIECH.
SWITZ.
ALPS
Mt. Blanc 15,771 ft. (4,807 m)
Matterhorn 14,690 ft. (4,478 m)
Hungarian Plain
HUNGARY
ROMANIA
SLOV.
CROATIA
BOSN. & HERZG.
YUG.
Danube R.
Balkan Peninsula
BULGARIA
MACED.
ALBANIA
GREECE
Aegean Sea
Adriatic Sea
Apennines
SAN MARINO
MONACO
Corsica
Sardinia
ITALY
Sicily
MALTA
Crete
CYPRUS
ANDORRA
Pyrenees
PORTUGAL
SPAIN
Ebro R.
Douro R.
Tagus R.
IBERIAN PENINSULA
Strait of Gibraltar
Mediterranean Sea

26,247 ft. 8,000 m
19,685 ft. 6,000 m
13,123 ft. 4,000 m
6,562 ft. 2,000 m
0 mi. 500
0 km 500
ALPS
PYRENEES
— LISBON Sea level WARSAW —

Regional Atlas Activity

Analyzing Maps On the board, copy the puzzle shown at right, omitting the letters above the lines. Have students complete the acrostic with names of physical features from the map above. Provide hints, such as "Body of water east of Greece" or "River in northern Germany." L2

EE2 Places and Regions: Standard 4

AE**G**EAN SEA
ELBE RIVER
P**O** RIVER
HUN**G**ARIAN PLAIN
CA**R**PATHIAN MOUNTAINS
ALPS
A**P**ENNINES
R**H**INE RIVER
P**Y**RENEES

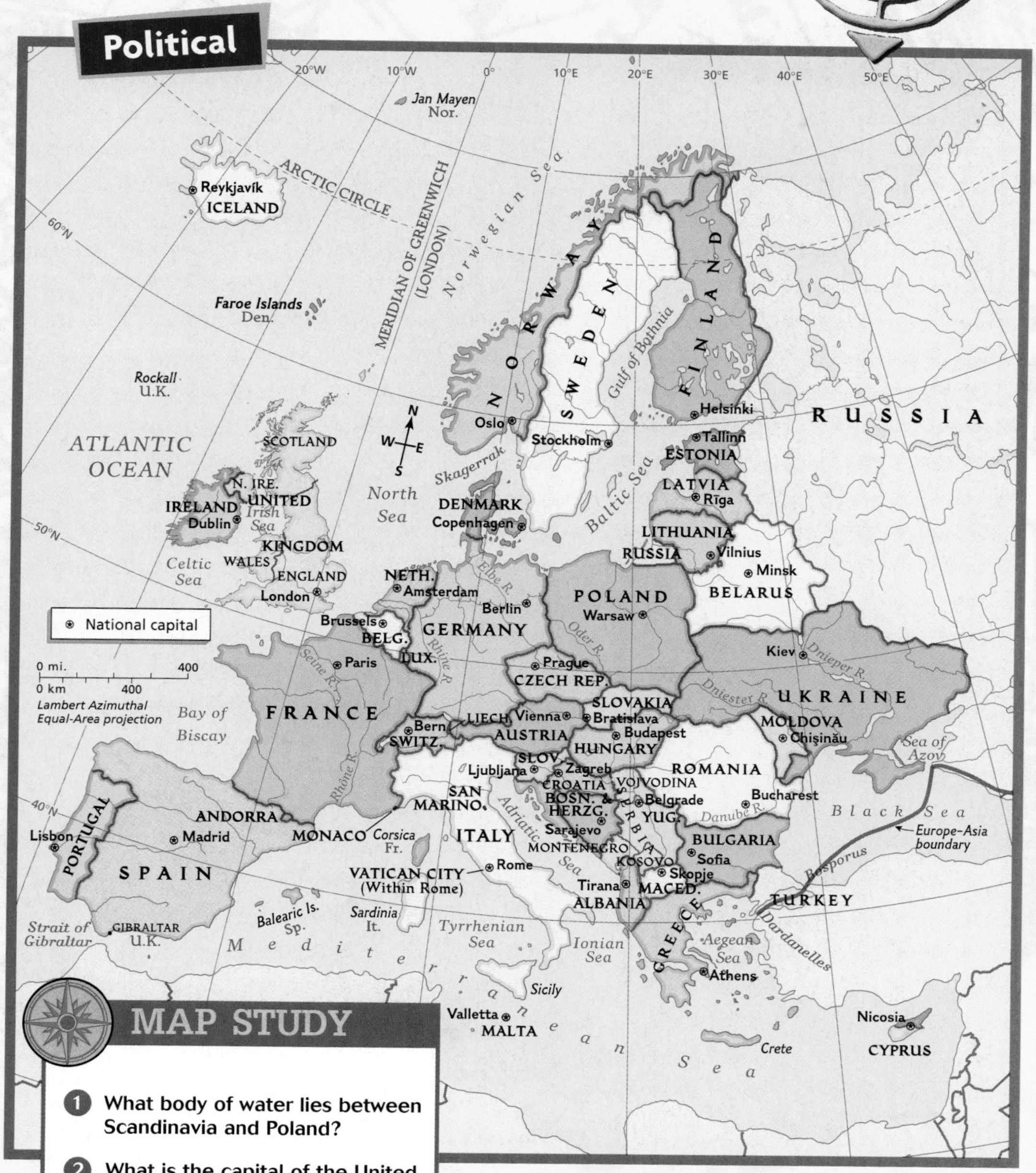

UNIT 4

Political

ATLANTIC OCEAN
Jan Mayen Nor.
Reykjavík
ICELAND
ARCTIC CIRCLE
MERIDIAN OF GREENWICH (LONDON)
Norwegian Sea
Faroe Islands Den.
Rockall U.K.
NORWAY
SWEDEN
FINLAND
Gulf of Bothnia
Oslo
Stockholm
Helsinki
RUSSIA
Tallinn
ESTONIA
LATVIA
Riga
LITHUANIA
RUSSIA
Vilnius
Minsk
BELARUS
SCOTLAND
N. IRE.
UNITED KINGDOM
IRELAND
Dublin
Irish Sea
WALES
ENGLAND
London
Celtic Sea
North Sea
Skagerrak
DENMARK
Copenhagen
Baltic Sea
NETH.
Amsterdam
Berlin
POLAND
Warsaw
Brussels
BELG.
LUX.
GERMANY
Prague
CZECH REP.
Kiev
UKRAINE
Paris
FRANCE
Bay of Biscay
Bern
SWITZ.
LIECH.
Vienna
Bratislava
SLOVAKIA
AUSTRIA
Budapest
HUNGARY
MOLDOVA
Chişinău
Sea of Azov
SLOV.
Ljubljana
Zagreb
CROATIA
VOJVODINA
ROMANIA
Bucharest
SAN MARINO
BOSN. & HERZG.
Belgrade
YUG.
SERBIA
Sarajevo
MONTENEGRO
KOSOVO
Skopje
MACED.
Tirana
ALBANIA
BULGARIA
Sofia
Black Sea
Europe-Asia boundary
Bosporus
TURKEY
Dardanelles
GREECE
Aegean Sea
Athens
Crete
Nicosia
CYPRUS
ANDORRA
Madrid
Lisbon
PORTUGAL
SPAIN
MONACO
Corsica Fr.
ITALY
Rome
VATICAN CITY (Within Rome)
Adriatic Sea
Balearic Is. Sp.
Sardinia It.
Tyrrhenian Sea
Ionian Sea
Sicily
Valletta
MALTA
Mediterranean Sea
Strait of Gibraltar
GIBRALTAR U.K.
20°W
10°W
0°
10°E
20°E
30°E
40°E
50°E
60°N
50°N
40°N

National capital

0 mi. 400
0 km 400
Lambert Azimuthal Equal-Area projection

MAP STUDY

1. What body of water lies between Scandinavia and Poland?
2. What is the capital of the United Kingdom?

227

2 TEACH

Making Comparisons Have students use the Nations of the World Databank on pages 690–699 to identify the countries that rank in the top 10 for Gross National Product (GNP). **Ask: What world regions are represented in this list? What regions are not represented?** Then have students pose and answer five questions comparing Europe to other world regions using information in the databank.

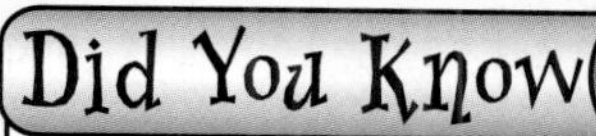

Europe is the only continent without a major desert.

MAP STUDY

Answers
1. Baltic Sea
2. London

Skills Practice
What body of water separates the Mediterranean Sea from the Atlantic Ocean? *(Strait of Gibraltar)*

Regional Atlas Activity

Analyzing Maps Have students study the physical maps of Europe, Asia, and North Africa in the Reference Atlas. Point out that Asia and Africa often have had a great deal of influence on European culture and history—and vice versa. **Ask: What features of physical geography would contribute to this fact?** *(Europe and Asia are connected; there are no major geographical barriers preventing people from moving to Europe from Asia, or in the opposite direction—in fact, the presence of lowland steppes make such movement easy; Europe lies near Africa and—through the Mediterranean Sea—has easy access to Africa.)* **L2**

EE1 The World in Spatial Terms: Standard 3

Creating a Graph Have students write down the population of Germany, shown on page 231. Then have them look at the Country Profiles in three other Regional Atlases in this textbook to find the largest population in three other culture regions. Have them copy that information on the same sheet. Finally, have them create a bar graph that compares the information on the four countries. **L1**

Cultural Kaleidoscope

Denmark Trolls originated in Danish legend. Folklore explains that trolls spend their nights burying treasure and their days guarding their loot.

TRAVEL GUIDE

Hungarians usually greet each other by shaking hands. If their hands are dirty, they offer elbows.

MAP STUDY

Answers

1. Germanic
2. Spanish, Portuguese, Galician, Catalan, French, Italian, Sardinian, Romanian, and Moldavian

Skills Practice

From what language family do most eastern European languages come? *(Slavic)*

NATIONAL GEOGRAPHIC

REGIONAL ATLAS

Europe

Languages

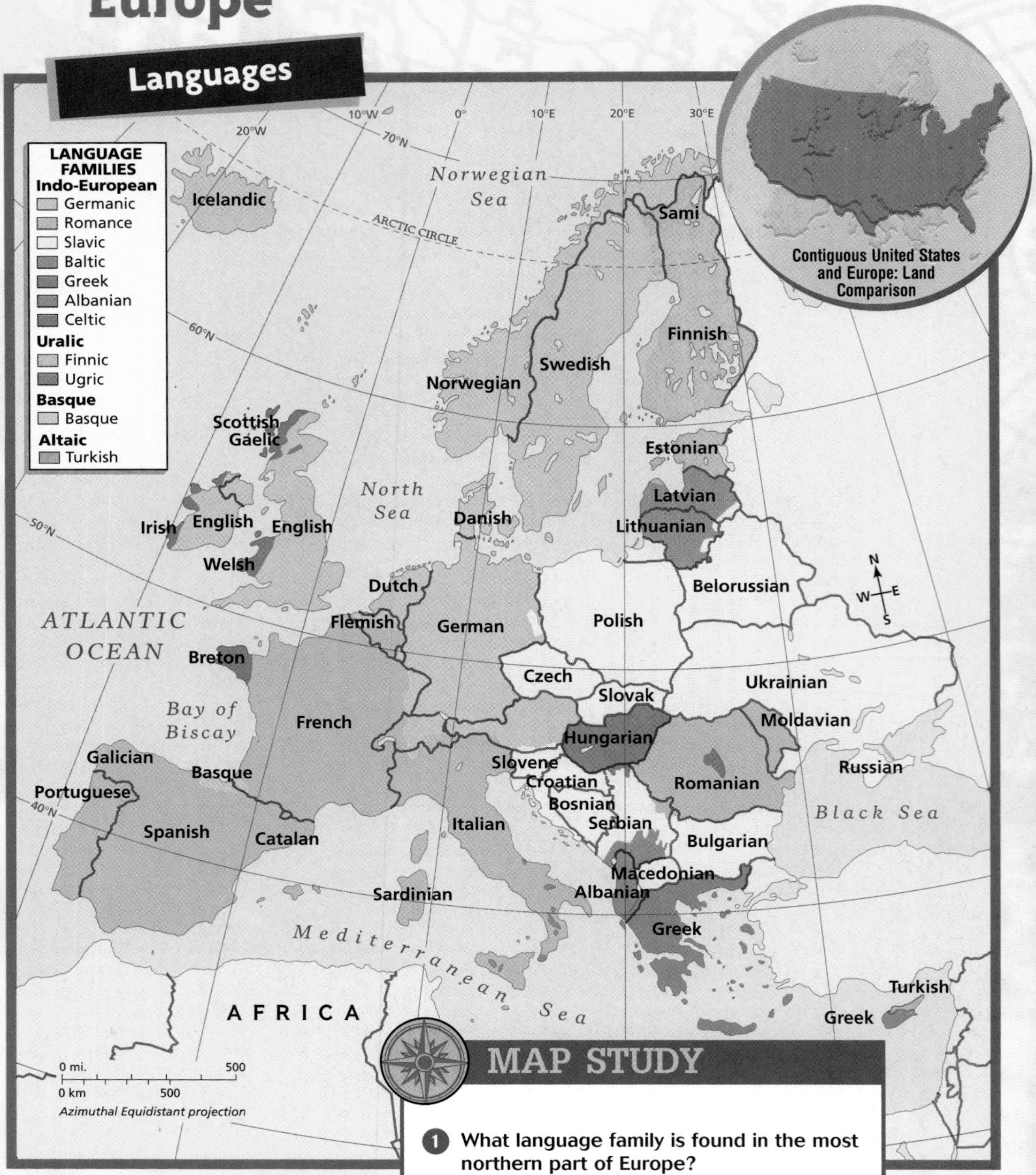

LANGUAGE FAMILIES

Indo-European
- Germanic
- Romance
- Slavic
- Baltic
- Greek
- Albanian
- Celtic

Uralic
- Finnic
- Ugric

Basque
- Basque

Altaic
- Turkish

Icelandic, Sami, Finnish, Swedish, Norwegian, Scottish Gaelic, Estonian, Latvian, Lithuanian, Irish, English, Welsh, Danish, Dutch, Flemish, German, Polish, Belorussian, Breton, Czech, Slovak, Ukrainian, Moldavian, French, Hungarian, Galician, Basque, Slovene, Croatian, Russian, Portuguese, Romanian, Bosnian, Serbian, Spanish, Catalan, Italian, Bulgarian, Macedonian, Albanian, Sardinian, Greek, Turkish

Norwegian Sea, ARCTIC CIRCLE, North Sea, ATLANTIC OCEAN, Bay of Biscay, Black Sea, Mediterranean Sea, AFRICA

20°W, 10°W, 0°, 10°E, 20°E, 30°E, 70°N, 60°N, 50°N, 40°N

0 mi. 500
0 km 500
Azimuthal Equidistant projection

Contiguous United States and Europe: Land Comparison

MAP STUDY

1. What language family is found in the most northern part of Europe?
2. What are three Romance languages?

228 UNIT 4

Regional Atlas Activity

Categorizing Regions Inform students that Europe is often divided into regions, in which several countries are grouped together according to common characteristics. Tell them that, for example, the countries of Spain, Italy, and Greece are often called the Mediterranean countries. **Ask: What characteristics do these countries share?** *(southern location, Mediterranean coastlines, generally high elevations, peninsular)* Ask them what the map of European languages above shows about how countries could be grouped together according to language or how languages cut across national boundaries. **L1**

EE2 Places and Regions: Standard 5

Fast Facts

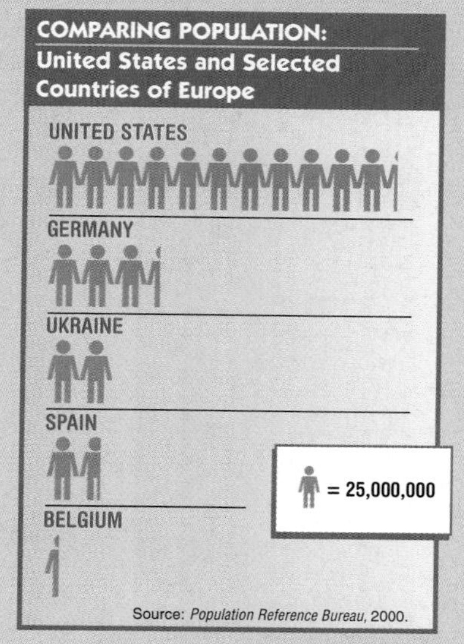

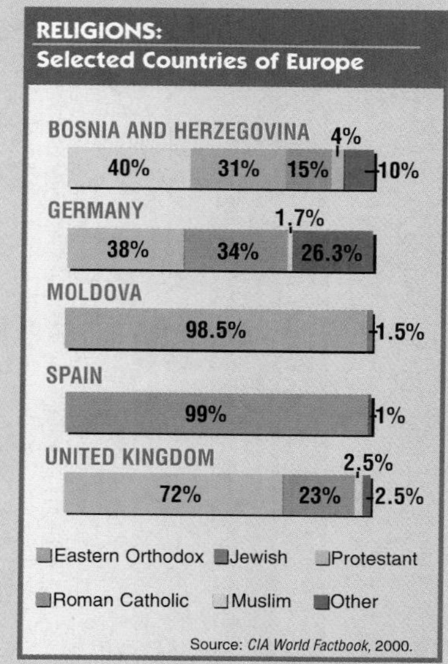

Data Bits

Country	Automobiles per 1,000 people	Telephones per 1,000 people
Austria	469	492
Finland	379	556
France	442	575
Greece	223	516
Ireland	272	411

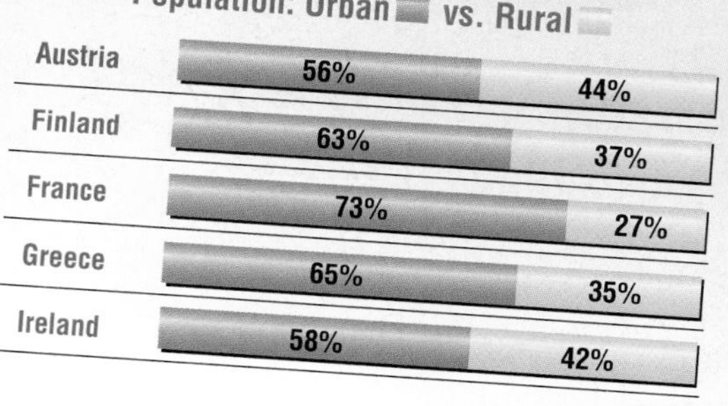

Source: *World Desk Reference*, 2000.

GRAPHIC STUDY

1. Which two countries have the fewest automobiles per 1,000 people?
2. Roughly, what is the population of Germany? What percentage of the population is Protestant?

Unit 4

Regional Atlas

As an introduction to this region, you may want to engage students by studying an important contemporary issue in this region of the world. The **TIME REPORTS: FOCUS ON WORLD ISSUES** for this region is found on pages 321–327. The feature examines how increased cooperation between nations is changing Europe.

Making Comparisons Have students look at the countries in the Comparing Population chart. Then have them use the Country Profiles listings to see if the countries on the chart include Europe's *most* populous country and the *least* populous country. If not, have them list the names of those countries and their populations. Then have them draw a pictogram comparing the populations of the listed countries to that of the United States. **L1**

GRAPHIC STUDY

Answers

1. Greece and Ireland
2. About 85 to 90 million people; about 38 percent

Skills Practice

Which country in the lower chart has the greatest percentage of Roman Catholic followers in the population? *(Spain)*

FUN FACTS

- **Bulgaria** Bulgarians shake their head from side to side to denote "yes" and nod up and down to denote "no."
- **Greece** The people of Greece are well known for their hospitality. The tradition of hospitality may stem from the ancient belief that one needed to treat strangers kindly in case they were gods in disguise. Indeed, ancient Greek myths include stories in which some mortals are rewarded for kindness to strangers, and others are punished for treating strangers inhospitably.
- **Czech Republic** Czechs give each other marzipan candies shaped like pigs for good luck in the New Year.

REGIONAL ATLAS

Country Profiles

THE HUMANITIES CONNECTION

World Music: A Cultural Legacy

World Art and Architecture Transparencies

Building Skills

Using Decimals If students are taking notes on the areas or populations of Europe's countries, suggest that they use shorthand by converting the numbers into decimals. Thus, Austria's population of 8,087,000 becomes 8.1 million; Iceland's 300,000 is written as .3 million.

Cultural Kaleidoscope

Austria Dinner guests in Austria bring their host an odd number of flowers. To bring an even number would be considered unlucky. They also avoid bringing roses, which symbolize romantic love.

Determining Cause and Effect The tiny state of Andorra has two heads of state: the French president and a Spanish bishop. Have students locate Andorra on the political map on page 227 to explain why. **L1**

ALBANIA
POPULATION: 3,460,000; 312 per sq. mi.; 120 per sq. km
LANGUAGE: Albanian
MAJOR EXPORT: Asphalt
MAJOR IMPORT: Machinery
CAPITAL: Tirana
LANDMASS: 11,100 sq. mi.; 28,748 sq. km

ANDORRA
POPULATION: 100,000; 571 per sq. mi.; 220 per sq. km
LANGUAGES: Catalan, French, Spanish
MAJOR EXPORT: Electricity
MAJOR IMPORT: Manufactured Goods
CAPITAL: Andorra la Vella
LANDMASS: 175 sq. mi.; 453 sq. km

AUSTRIA
POPULATION: 8,087,000; 250 per sq. mi.; 96 per sq. km
LANGUAGE: German
MAJOR EXPORT: Machinery
MAJOR IMPORT: Petroleum
CAPITAL: Vienna
LANDMASS: 32,377 sq. mi.; 83,856 sq. km

BELARUS
POPULATION: 10,167,000; 127 per sq. mi.; 49 per sq. km
LANGUAGES: Belarussian, Russian
MAJOR EXPORT: Machinery
MAJOR IMPORT: Fuels
CAPITAL: Minsk
LANDMASS: 80,154 sq. mi.; 207,598 sq. km

BELGIUM
POPULATION: 10,300,000; 874 per sq. mi.; 337 per sq. km
LANGUAGES: Flemish, French
MAJOR EXPORTS: Iron and Steel
MAJOR IMPORT: Fuels
CAPITAL: Brussels
LANDMASS: 11,783 sq. mi.; 30,518 sq. km

BOSNIA and HERZEGOVINA
POPULATION: 3,400,000; 172 per sq. mi.; 66.5 per sq. km
LANGUAGE: Serbo-Croatian
MAJOR EXPORT: N/A
MAJOR IMPORT: N/A
CAPITAL: Sarajevo
LANDMASS: 19,741 sq. mi.; 51,129 sq. km

BULGARIA
POPULATION: 8,188,000; 191 per sq. mi.; 74 per sq. km
LANGUAGE: Bulgarian
MAJOR EXPORT: Machinery
MAJOR IMPORT: Fuels
CAPITAL: Sofia
LANDMASS: 42,823 sq. mi.; 110,912 sq. km

CROATIA
POPULATION: 4,700,000; 216 per sq. mi.; 83 per sq. km
LANGUAGE: Serbo-Croatian
MAJOR EXPORT: Transport Equipment
MAJOR IMPORT: Machinery
CAPITAL: Zagreb
LANDMASS: 21,829 sq. mi.; 56,538 sq. km

CYPRUS
POPULATION: 900,000; 395 per sq. mi.; 152 per sq. km
LANGUAGES: Greek, Turkish
MAJOR EXPORT: Citrus Fruits
MAJOR IMPORT: Manufactured Goods
CAPITAL: Nicosia
LANDMASS: 2,277 sq. mi.; 5,897 sq. km

CZECH REPUBLIC
POPULATION: 10,284,000; 338 per sq. mi.; 130 per sq. km
LANGUAGES: Czech, Slovak
MAJOR EXPORT: Machinery
MAJOR IMPORT: Crude Oil
CAPITAL: Prague
LANDMASS: 30,450 sq. mi.; 78,864 sq. km

DENMARK
POPULATION: 5,325,000; 320 per sq. mi.; 124 per sq. km
LANGUAGE: Danish
MAJOR EXPORT: Machinery
MAJOR IMPORT: Machinery
CAPITAL: Copenhagen
LANDMASS: 16,638 sq. mi.; 43,092 sq. km

ESTONIA
POPULATION: 1,441,000; 83 per sq. mi.; 32 per sq. km
LANGUAGE: Estonian
MAJOR EXPORT: Textiles
MAJOR IMPORT: Machinery
CAPITAL: Tallinn
LANDMASS: 17,413 sq. mi.; 45,099 sq. km

Countries and flags not drawn to scale

Regional Atlas Activity

Drawing Conclusions Tell students that the Channel Tunnel (Chunnel) links the United Kingdom and France. Denmark's Storebaelt ("Great Belt") Bridge is the second-longest suspension bridge in the world. It connects the island on which Copenhagen is located to the mainland. This 1-mile (1.6-km) bridge is part of a much longer transportation system called the Oresund Fixed Link. The Fixed Link stretches 9.3 miles (14.9 km) across the North Sea from Copenhagen to Malmö, Sweden. It includes a bridge, a roadway built on an artificial island, and a tunnel. **Ask: Why would people in Europe invest in these elaborate structures?** *(to allow easier access from one place to another; to increase trade and communication between countries)* **L1**

EE4 Human Systems: Standard 11

UNIT 4

For more information on countries in this region, refer to the Nations of the World Data Bank on pages 690–699.

FINLAND
POPULATION: 5,170,000; 40 per sq. mi.; 15 per sq. km
LANGUAGES: Finnish, Swedish
MAJOR EXPORT: Paper
MAJOR IMPORT: Foods
CAPITAL: Helsinki
LANDMASS: 130,558 sq. mi.; 338,145 sq. km

FRANCE
POPULATION: 59,067,000; 281 per sq. mi.; 109 per sq. km
LANGUAGE: French
MAJOR EXPORT: Machinery
MAJOR IMPORT: Crude Oil
CAPITAL: Paris
LANDMASS: 210,026 sq. mi.; 543,965 sq. km

GERMANY
POPULATION: 82,200,000; 596 per sq. mi.; 230 per sq. km
LANGUAGE: German
MAJOR EXPORT: Machinery
MAJOR IMPORT: Machinery
CAPITAL: Berlin
LANDMASS: 137,857 sq. mi.; 357,046 sq. km

GREECE
POPULATION: 10,900,000; 213 per sq. mi.; 83 per sq. km
LANGUAGE: Greek
MAJOR EXPORT: Foods
MAJOR IMPORT: Machinery
CAPITAL: Athens
LANDMASS: 50,962 sq. mi.; 131,990 sq. km

HUNGARY
POPULATION: 10,076,000; 281 per sq. mi.; 108 per sq. km
LANGUAGE: Hungarian
MAJOR EXPORT: Machinery
MAJOR IMPORT: Crude Oil
CAPITAL: Budapest
LANDMASS: 35,919 sq. mi.; 93,030 sq. km

ICELAND
POPULATION: 300,000; 8 per sq. mi.; 3 per sq. km
LANGUAGE: Icelandic
MAJOR EXPORT: Fish
MAJOR IMPORT: Machinery
CAPITAL: Reykjavík
LANDMASS: 39,769 sq. mi.; 103,001 sq. km

IRELAND
POPULATION: 3,800,000; 140 per sq. mi.; 54 per sq. km
LANGUAGES: English, Irish Gaelic
MAJOR EXPORT: Chemical Products
MAJOR IMPORT: Foods
CAPITAL: Dublin
LANDMASS: 27,137 sq. mi.; 70,284 sq. km

ITALY
POPULATION: 57,717,000; 496 per sq. mi.; 192 per sq. km
LANGUAGE: Italian
MAJOR EXPORT: Metals
MAJOR IMPORT: Machinery
CAPITAL: Rome
LANDMASS: 116,324 sq. mi.; 301,277 sq. km

LATVIA
POPULATION: 2,430,000; 97 per sq. mi.; 38 per sq. km
LANGUAGES: Latvian, Russian
MAJOR EXPORT: Wood
MAJOR IMPORT: Fuels
CAPITAL: Rīga
LANDMASS: 24,942 sq. mi.; 64,599 sq. km

LIECHTENSTEIN
POPULATION: 32,000; 516 per sq. mi.; 200 per sq. km
LANGUAGE: German
MAJOR EXPORT: Machinery
MAJOR IMPORT: Machinery
CAPITAL: Vaduz
LANDMASS: 62 sq. mi.; 160 sq. km

LITHUANIA
POPULATION: 3,700,000; 147 per sq. mi.; 57 per sq. km
LANGUAGES: Lithuanian, Polish, Russian
MAJOR EXPORTS: Foods and Livestock
MAJOR IMPORT: Minerals
CAPITAL: Vilnius
LANDMASS: 25,174 sq. mi.; 65,200 sq. km

LUXEMBOURG
POPULATION: 432,000; 433 per sq. mi.; 167 per sq. km
LANGUAGES: Luxembourgian, German, French
MAJOR EXPORT: Steel Products
MAJOR IMPORT: Minerals
CAPITAL: Luxembourg
LANDMASS: 998 sq. mi.; 2,586 sq. km

Europe 231

Unit 4 Regional Atlas

Making Predictions About 30,000 years ago, bison and rhinoceroses wandered the land that is now France. Scientists know this because they have identified these animals in cave paintings found in France and dating from this period. **Ask: What probably happened to these animals?** *(They were probably overhunted or driven elsewhere.)* **L1**

Cultural Kaleidoscope

Rome, Italy Rome was the first area of Europe that had professional barbers. They first set up shop in 303 B.C. Early Romans prized dark hair as much as a good cut, and they used dyes made by boiling walnut shells and leeks to darken their hair. The dyes were so harsh, however, that they often made the Romans' hair fall out.

Making Inferences San Marino is the world's smallest republic and Europe's oldest existing country, with about 1,600 years of independent existence. Its inhabitants, however, do not have their own national language. Have students locate San Marino on the map on page 227. **Ask: What language do its people probably speak?** *(Italian)* Then have them check their answer on the Country Profile "stamp" on page 232. **L1**

Regional Atlas Activity

Mapping an Empire The achievements of ancient Rome can still be seen throughout Europe. In Rome itself are the Colosseum, Pantheon, and the Forum. Italy has the buried cities of Pompeii and Herculaneum and parts of the Roman road called the Appian Way. Southern France has the aqueduct called the Pont du Gard, and another impressive aqueduct is found in Segovia, Spain. Remains of Hadrian's Wall can be found in the United Kingdom. Give students an outline map of Europe and a list of Roman sites. Have them place the sites on the map so they can see the extent of the Roman Empire. **L2**

EE4 Human Systems: Standard 10

Regional Atlas

Country Profiles

MACEDONIA, Former Yugoslav Republic of
POPULATION: 2,019,000; 203 per sq. mi.; 79 per sq. km
LANGUAGES: Macedonian, Albanian
MAJOR EXPORT: Manufactured Goods
MAJOR IMPORT: Fuels
CAPITAL: Skopje
LANDMASS: 9,928 sq. mi.; 25,713 sq. km

MALTA
POPULATION: 400,000; 3,279 per sq. mi.; 1,265 per sq. km
LANGUAGES: Maltese, English
MAJOR EXPORT: Machinery
MAJOR IMPORT: Foods
CAPITAL: Valletta
LANDMASS: 122 sq. mi.; 316 sq. km

MOLDOVA
POPULATION: 4,284,000; 324 per sq. mi.; 126 per sq. km
LANGUAGES: Moldovan, Russian
MAJOR EXPORT: Foods
MAJOR IMPORT: Petroleum
CAPITAL: Chişinău
LANDMASS: 13,217 sq. mi.; 33,999 sq. km

MONACO
POPULATION: 33,000; 55,000 per sq. mi.; 17,368 per sq. km
LANGUAGE: French
MAJOR EXPORT: N/A
MAJOR IMPORT: N/A
CAPITAL: Monaco
LANDMASS: 0.6 sq. mi.; 1.9 sq. km

NETHERLANDS
POPULATION: 16,000,000; 999 per sq. mi.; 385 per sq. km
LANGUAGE: Dutch
MAJOR EXPORT: Manufactured Goods
MAJOR IMPORT: Raw Materials
CAPITAL: Amsterdam
LANDMASS: 16,023 sq. mi.; 41,499 sq. km

NORWAY
POPULATION: 4,462,000; 36 per sq. mi.; 14 per sq. km
LANGUAGE: Norwegian
MAJOR EXPORT: Petroleum
MAJOR IMPORT: Machinery
CAPITAL: Oslo
LANDMASS: 125,182 sq. mi.; 324,220 sq. km

POLAND
POPULATION: 38,674,000; 320 per sq. mi.; 124 per sq. km
LANGUAGE: Polish
MAJOR EXPORT: Manufactured Goods
MAJOR IMPORT: Machinery
CAPITAL: Warsaw
LANDMASS: 120,725 sq. mi.; 312,677 sq. km

PORTUGAL
POPULATION: 9,992,000; 280 per sq. mi.; 108 per sq. km
LANGUAGE: Portuguese
MAJOR EXPORT: Clothing
MAJOR IMPORT: Machinery
CAPITAL: Lisbon
LANDMASS: 35,672 sq. mi.; 92,389 sq. km

ROMANIA
POPULATION: 22,460,000; 245 per sq. mi.; 95 per sq. km
LANGUAGES: Romanian, Hungarian, German
MAJOR EXPORT: Textiles
MAJOR IMPORT: Fuels
CAPITAL: Bucharest
LANDMASS: 91,699 sq. mi.; 237,499 sq. km

SAN MARINO
POPULATION: 26,000; 1,083 per sq. mi.; 426 per sq. km
LANGUAGE: Italian
MAJOR EXPORT: Building Stone
MAJOR IMPORT: Manufactured Goods
CAPITAL: San Marino
LANDMASS: 24 sq. mi.; 61 sq. km

SLOVAKIA
POPULATION: 5,401,000; 285 per sq. mi.; 110 per sq. km
LANGUAGES: Slovak, Hungarian
MAJOR EXPORT: Transport Equipment
MAJOR IMPORT: Machinery
CAPITAL: Bratislava
LANDMASS: 18,921 sq. mi.; 49,006 sq. km

SLOVENIA
POPULATION: 1,978,000; 253 per sq. mi.; 98 per sq. km
LANGUAGES: Slovene, Serbo-Croatian
MAJOR EXPORT: Transport Equipment
MAJOR IMPORT: Machinery
CAPITAL: Ljubljana
LANDMASS: 7,819 sq. mi.; 20,251 sq. km

Countries and flags not drawn to scale

Travel Guide

Favorite foods of the Dutch are chocolate spread on bread for breakfast and smoked eel for the main meal.

Current Events Journal

Suggest that students compare the countries of Europe in terms of size and population. Have them create a two-column chart in their notebooks with the column headings "Area" and "Population." Then have them find the five largest and five most populous countries and write the names under the appropriate heading.

Cultural Kaleidoscope

Portugal Bakers in Sintra, Portugal, make delicious, bite-sized cheese tarts. Local legend says that a thirteenth-century king loved the tarts so much that he allowed his subjects to use them to pay their taxes.

Assess

Organize students into groups. Have groups use the maps and graphs from the Unit 4 Regional Atlas to quiz one another on the geography of Europe.

Regional Atlas Activity

Identifying Locations Have students locate the following cities on the map of Europe on pages RA16–RA17: London and Edinburgh, (United Kingdom); Paris, Nantes, Bordeaux, and Marseilles (France); Barcelona and Madrid (Spain); Rome and Venice (Italy); Berlin and Hamburg, (Germany); Vienna (Austria); Warsaw (Poland); Stockholm (Sweden); and Oslo (Norway). **Ask:** **What do almost all of these cities have in common?** *(All but Madrid are located near water.)* **What does this fact of location tell you about these cities?** *(They probably arose as ports or along transportation routes.)* **L2**

EE6 The Uses of Geography: Standard 17

For more information on countries in this region, refer to the Nations of the World Data Bank on pages 690–699.

SPAIN
POPULATION:
39,800,000
204 per sq. mi.
79 per sq. km
LANGUAGES:
Spanish, Catalan, Galician, Basque
MAJOR EXPORTS:
Cars and Trucks
MAJOR IMPORT:
Machinery
CAPITAL:
Madrid
LANDMASS:
194,897 sq. mi.
504,782 sq. km
Madrid
SWEDEN
POPULATION:
8,856,000
51 per sq. mi.
20 per sq. km
LANGUAGE:
Swedish
MAJOR EXPORT:
Paper Products
MAJOR IMPORT:
Crude Oil
CAPITAL:
Stockholm
LANDMASS:
173,732 sq. mi.
449,964 sq. km
Stockholm
SWITZERLAND
POPULATION:
7,200,000
451 per sq. mi.
174 per sq. km
LANGUAGES:
German, French, Italian, Romansch
MAJOR EXPORT:
Precision Instruments
MAJOR IMPORT:
Machinery
CAPITAL:
Bern
LANDMASS:
15,941 sq. mi.
41,288 sq. km
Bern
UKRAINE
POPULATION:
49,100,000
210 per sq. mi.
81 per sq. km
LANGUAGES:
Ukrainian, Russian
MAJOR EXPORT:
Metals
MAJOR IMPORT:
Machinery
CAPITAL:
Kiev
LANDMASS:
233,206 sq. mi.
604,001 sq. km
Kiev
UNITED KINGDOM
POPULATION:
60,000,000
637 per sq. mi.
246 per sq. km
LANGUAGES:
English, Welsh, Scottish Gaelic
MAJOR EXPORT:
Manufactured Goods
MAJOR IMPORT:
Foods
CAPITAL:
London
LANDMASS:
94,248 sq. mi.
244,101 sq. km
London
VATICAN CITY
POPULATION:
1,000
LANGUAGES:
Italian, Latin
MAJOR EXPORT:
N/A
MAJOR IMPORT:
N/A
CAPITAL:
N/A
LANDMASS:
0.2 sq. mi.
0.4 sq. km
YUGOSLAVIA
(Serbia and Montenegro)
POPULATION:
10,646,000
270 per sq. mi.
104 per sq. km
LANGUAGES:
Serbo-Croatian, Albanian, Hungarian
MAJOR EXPORT:
Manufactured Goods
MAJOR IMPORT:
Machinery
CAPITAL:
Belgrade
LANDMASS:
39,450 sq. mi.
102,173 sq. km
Belgrade

BUILDING CITIZENSHIP

Participation All citizens are expected to obey the laws of their country. Sometimes, however, the right thing to do is not clear. During World War II, many people in Germany broke the law by helping Jews escape Nazi persecution. During Communist rule, many citizens in Eastern Europe bought and sold goods on the black market.

What do you think would have happened to people helping the Jews if they had been caught?

In the U.S. we work to change laws we believe are unfair. Trying to influence the decisions of our elected leaders is an important part of being an active citizen. Write a letter to your school board explaining why you think students should or should not wear uniforms.

Should students have to wear uniforms? ▼

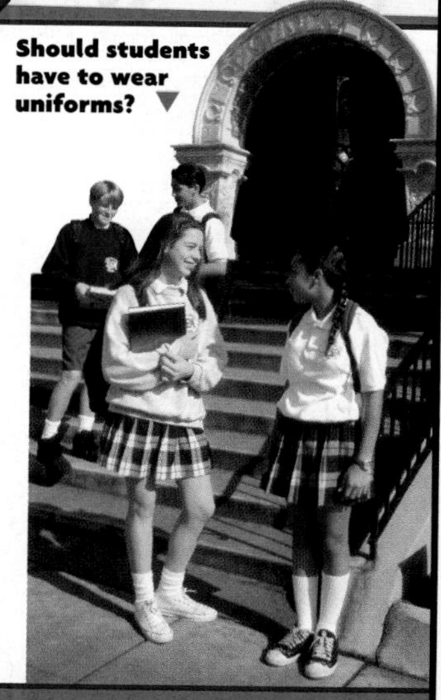

BUILDING CITIZENSHIP

Answer Even if a law appears to be wrong, people who break the law must accept the consequences. The people helping the Jews believed so strongly that what they were doing was right that they were willing to risk jail or death.

Write About It! Students should recognize the authority of the school board to make rules for student dress and conduct. Their letters should argue why uniforms will or will not improve the school. They may be asked to consider the trade-off between community and individual rights.

Enrich

Have students choose one of the countries profiled on these pages and prepare a display on the country's national symbols. The display should identify the meaning behind the symbols and colors on its flag.

CLOSE

Tell students that Europe is sometimes called "a peninsula of peninsulas." Have them write a paragraph explaining how that statement is true.

Country Profiles Activity

Charting Major Exports Have students make a chart with three columns. The column headings should read "Food Products," "Manufactured Goods," and "Natural Resources." Have students look at the Major Exports entry in each Country Profile. Tell them to write each country name in the appropriate column based on what kind of export the country has. Have them compare the entries in each column to see whether the economies of Europe are primarily based on agriculture, industry, or natural resources. **L1**

Chapter 9 Resources

Note: The following materials may be used when teaching Chapter 9.
Section level support materials are shown at point of use in the margins of the Teacher Wraparound Edition.

Timesaving Tools

TeacherWorks™ All-In-One Planner and Resource Center

- **Interactive Teacher Edition** See the **Interactive Teacher Edition** CD-ROM to electronically integrate your Teacher Wraparound Edition and blackline masters.
- **Interactive Lesson Planner** Organize your week, month, semester, or year with all the lesson helps you need. The **Interactive Lesson Planner** CD-ROM contains all Chapter 9 resources.

Use Glencoe's **Presentation Plus!** multimedia teacher tool to easily present dynamic lessons that visually excite your students. Using Microsoft PowerPoint® you can customize the presentations to create your own personalized lessons.

TEACHING TRANSPARENCIES

Graphic Organizer Transparency and Student Activity 9

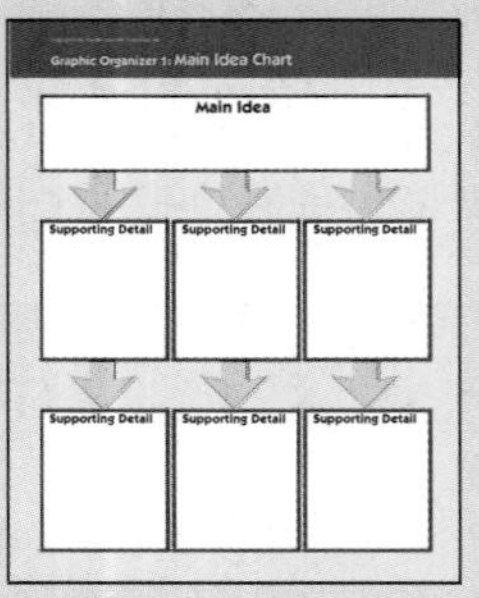

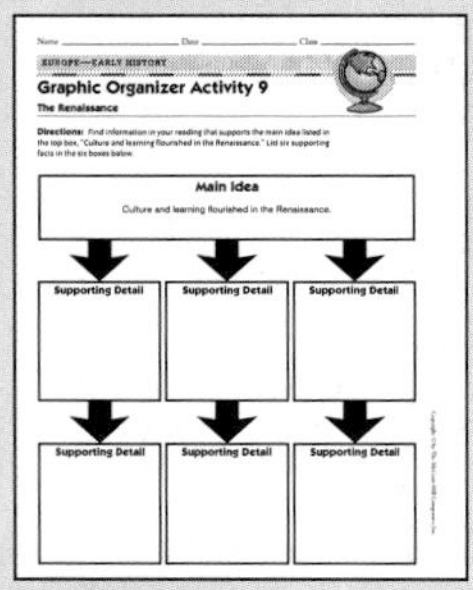

FOLDABLES™ Study Organizer

Foldables are three-dimensional, interactive graphic organizers that help students practice basic writing skills, review key vocabulary terms, and identify main ideas. Every chapter contains a Foldable activity, with additional chapter activities found in the ***Reading and Study Skills Foldables*** booklet.

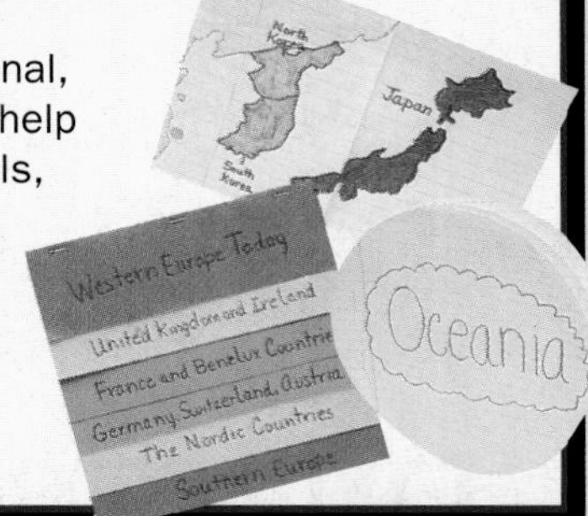

ENRICHMENT AND EXTENSION

Enrichment Activity 9

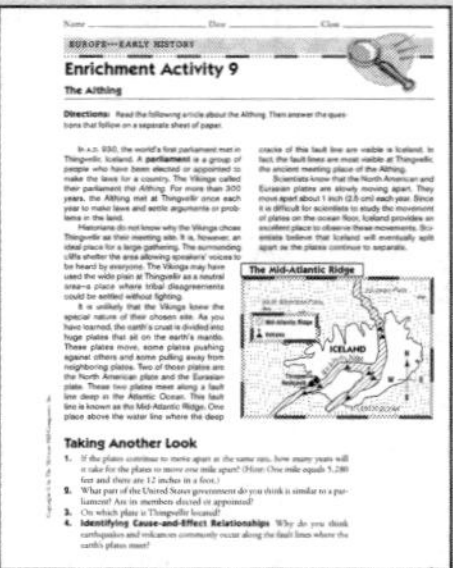

Cooperative Learning Activity 9

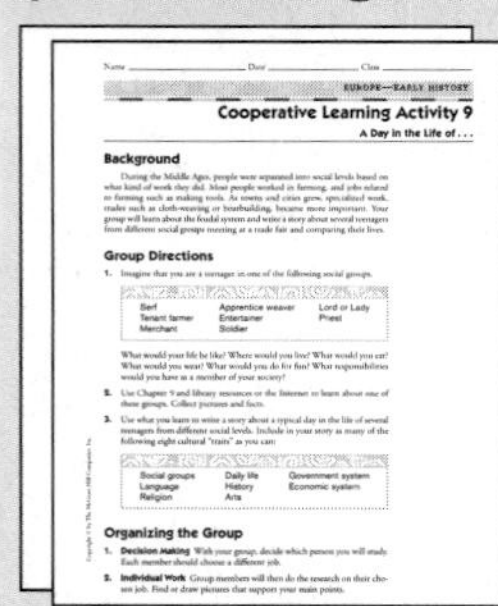

MAP AND GEOGRAPHY SKILLS

Chapter Map Activity 9

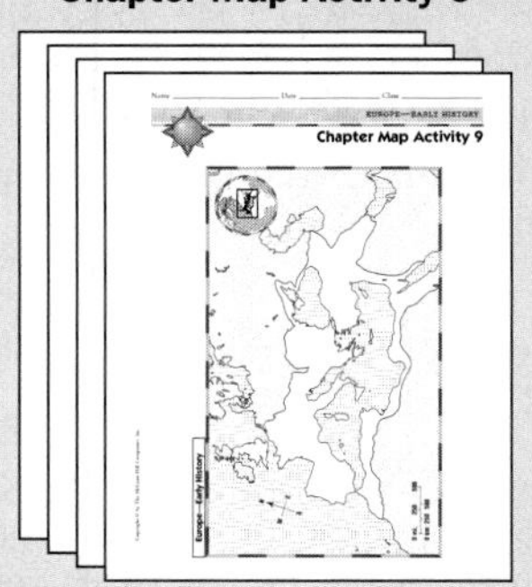

GeoLab Activity 9

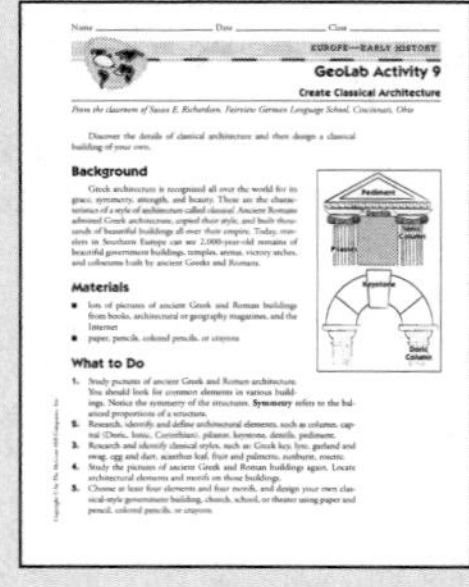

STANDARDIZED ASSESSMENT SKILLS

GLENCOE'S ASSESSMENT ADVANTAGE

Critical Thinking Skills Activity 9

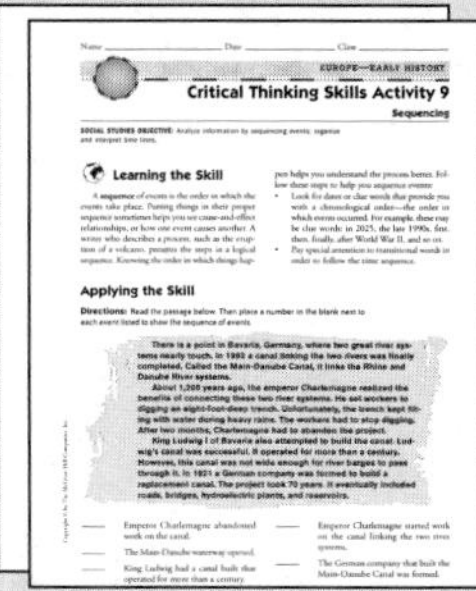

Map and Graph Skills Activity 9

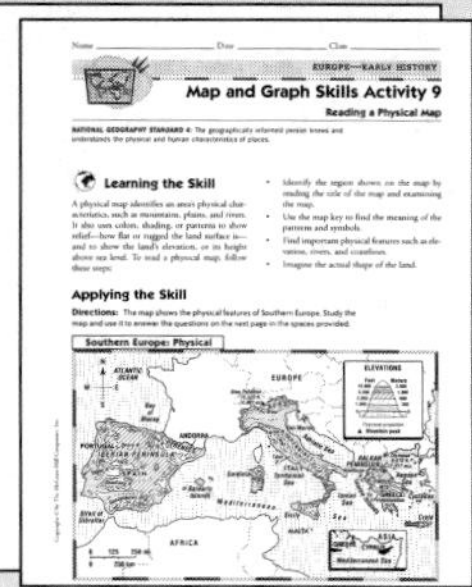

Reading and Writing Skills Activity 9

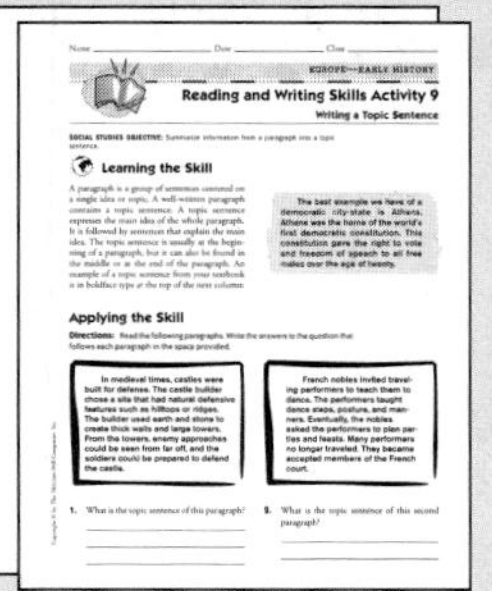

Standardized Test Practice Workbook Activity 9

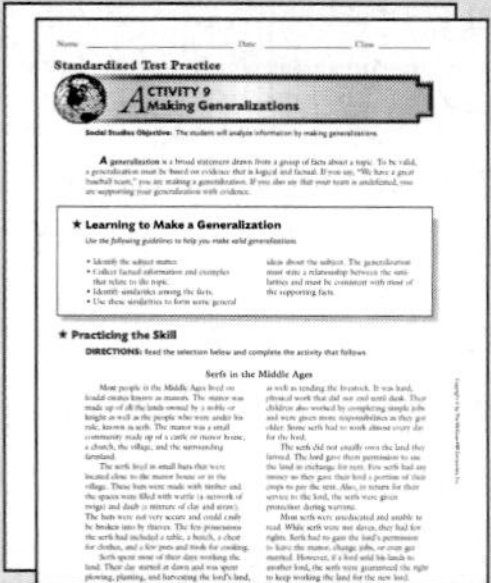

REVIEW AND REINFORCEMENT

Chapter Skills Activity 9

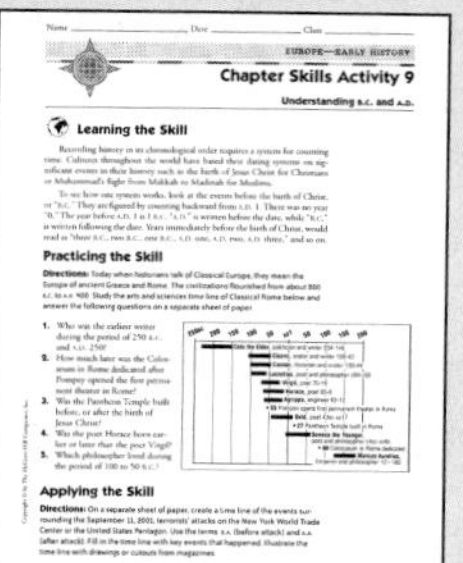

Take-Home Review Activity 9

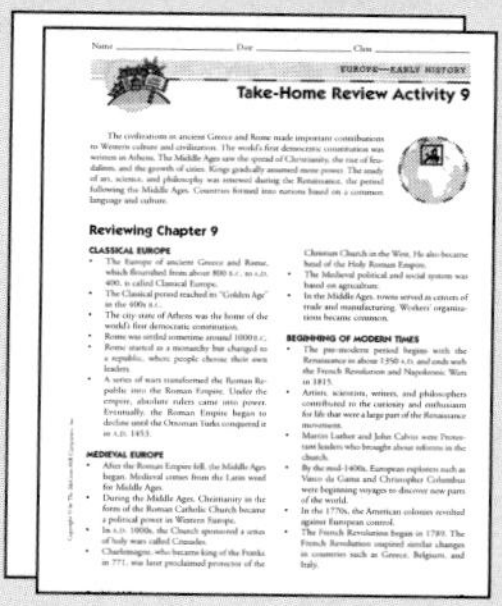

Reteaching Activity 9

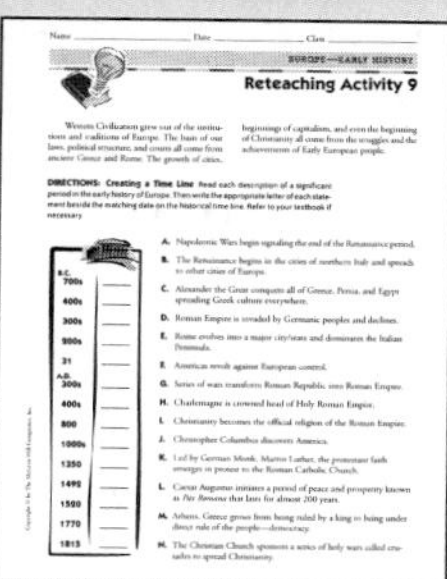

Vocabulary Activity 9

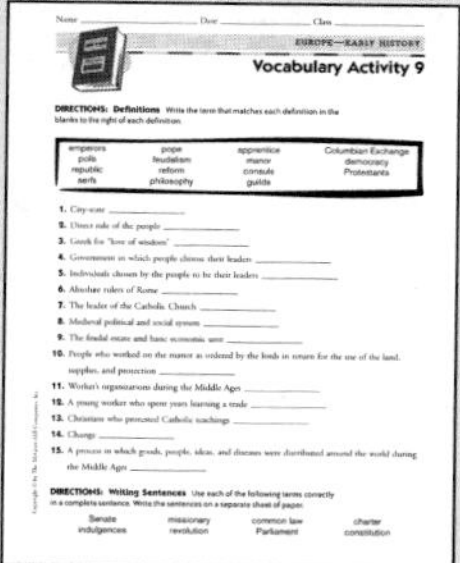

Workbook Activity 9

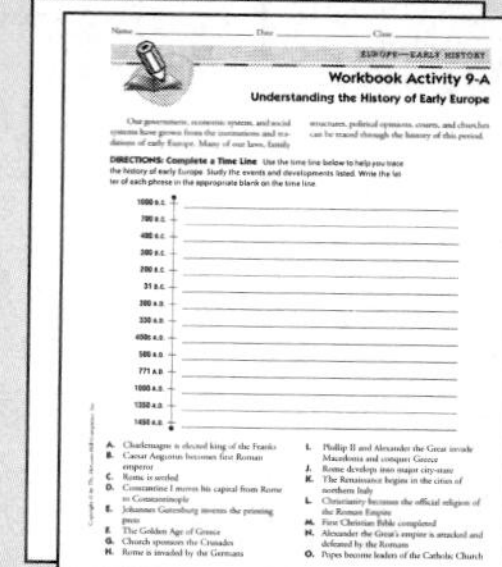

ASSESSMENT

Chapter 9 Test, Form A

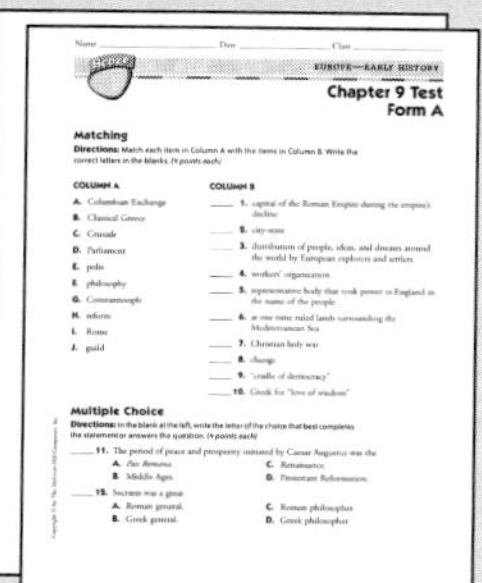

Chapter 9 Test, Form B

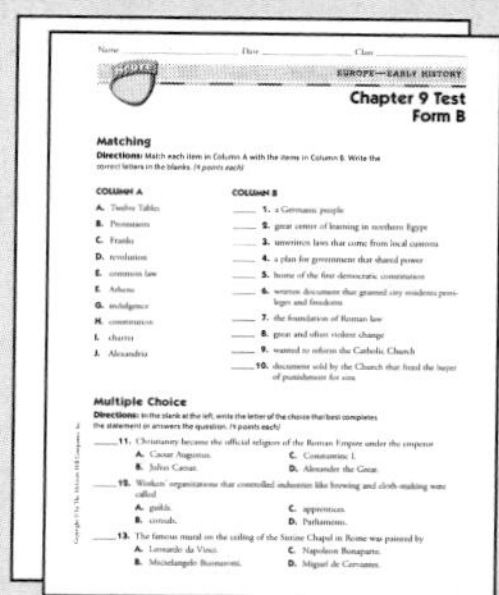

Performance Assessment Activity 9

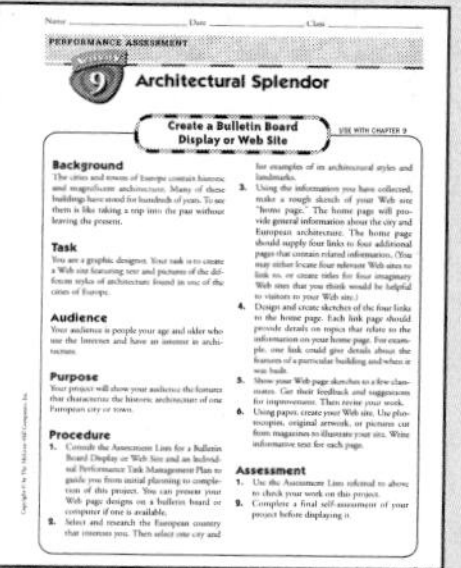

ExamView® Pro 3.0 Testmaker CD-ROM

MULTIMEDIA

- National Geographic's The World and Its People
- MindJogger Videoquiz
- Vocabulary PuzzleMaker Software
- Interactive Tutor Self-Assessment CD-ROM
- ExamView® Pro 3.0 Testmaker CD-ROM
- Interactive Lesson Planner CD-ROM
- Interactive Teacher Edition CD-ROM
- Skillbuilder Interactive Workbook CD-ROM, Level 1
- Presentation Plus! CD-ROM
- Audio Program

SPANISH RESOURCES

The following Spanish language materials are available in the Spanish Resources binder:

- **Spanish Chapter Summaries**
- **Spanish Vocabulary Activities**
- **Spanish Guided Reading Activities**
- **Spanish Quizzes and Tests**
- **Spanish Take-Home Review Activities**
- **Spanish Reteaching Activities**

Meeting National Standards

Geography for Life

All of the 18 standards are demonstrated in Unit 4. The following ones are highlighted in Chapter 9:

Section 1 **EE4 Human Systems: Standards 9, 10, 11, 12, 13**
EE5 The Uses of Geography: Standard 17

Section 2 **EE4 Human Systems: Standards 9, 10, 11, 12, 13**
EE5 Environment and Society: Standards 14, 15, 16

Section 3 **EE4 Human Systems: Standards 9, 10, 11, 12, 13**
EE5 Environment and Society: Standards 14, 15, 16
EE6 The Uses of Geography: Standards 17, 18

For a complete listing of National Geography Standards and entire text correlation, see pages T22–T29.

Chapter 9 Planning Guide

SECTION RESOURCES

Daily Objectives	Reproducible Resources	Multimedia Resources
Section 1 **Classical Europe** **Suggested Pacing = 1 day** **1.** Identify significant accomplishments of Greek culture. **2.** Explain how Alexander spread Greek culture. **3.** Describe the Roman system of government and law.	Reproducible Lesson Plan 9-1 Daily Lecture and Discussion Notes 9-1 Guided Reading Activity 9-1 Reading Essentials and Study Guide 9-1 Section Quiz 9-1*	Daily Focus Skills Transparency 9-1 Vocabulary PuzzleMaker Software Interactive Tutor Self-Assessment CD-ROM ExamView® Pro 3.0 Testmaker CD-ROM Presentation Plus! CD-ROM
Section 2 **Medieval Europe** **Suggested Pacing = 1 day** **1.** Explain the importance of Christianity as a political influence in Medieval Europe. **2.** Describe the medieval social and political systems.	Reproducible Lesson Plan 9-2 Daily Lecture and Discussion Notes 9-2 Guided Reading Activity 9-2 Reading Essentials and Study Guide 9-2 Section Quiz 9-2*	Daily Focus Skills Transparency 9-2 Vocabulary PuzzleMaker Software Interactive Tutor Self-Assessment CD-ROM ExamView® Pro 3.0 Testmaker CD-ROM Presentation Plus! CD-ROM
Section 3 **The Beginning of Modern Times** **Suggested Pacing = 1 day** **1.** Explain advances in arts, science, and nationhood achieved during the Renaissance. **2.** Identify the causes of the Reformation. **3.** Compare the causes and results of revolutions in the Americas and Europe.	Reproducible Lesson Plan 9-3 Daily Lecture and Discussion Notes 9-3 Guided Reading Activity 9-3 Reading Essentials and Study Guide 9-3 Section Quiz 9-3*	Daily Focus Skills Transparency 9-3 Vocabulary PuzzleMaker Software Interactive Tutor Self-Assessment CD-ROM ExamView® Pro 3.0 Testmaker CD-ROM Presentation Plus! CD-ROM

00:00 **Out of Time?** Assign the **Reading Essentials and Study Guide** for this chapter.

*Also available in Spanish

KEY TO ABILITY LEVELS

Teaching strategies have been coded for varying learning styles and abilities.

L1 **BASIC** activities for all students
L2 **AVERAGE** activities for average to above-average students
L3 **CHALLENGING** activities for above-average students
ELL **ENGLISH LANGUAGE LEARNER** activities

Blackline Master
Software
CD-ROM
Audiocassette
Transparency
Videocassette
Block Scheduling
DVD

Teacher to Teacher

European Art—Phases and Schools

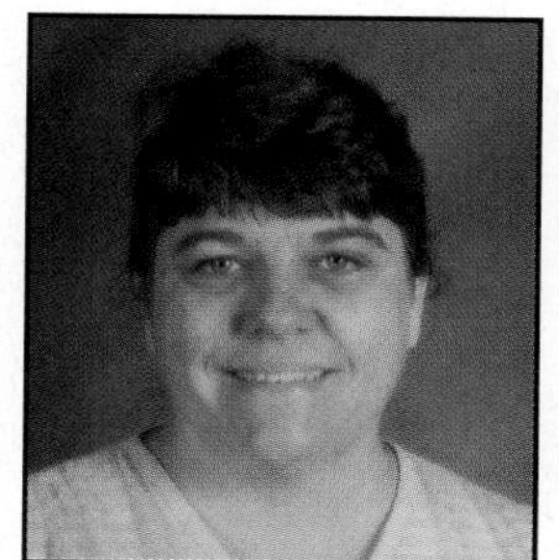

Camille King-Thompson
Williston Middle School
Williston, Florida

With the aid of the art teacher, have a class discussion about the progression that European art has made and its impact on art throughout the world. Have students look at examples of styles of European art from different periods, such as realism, pointilism, impressionism, cubism, and abstract expressionism. Then ask students to choose the style or piece of art they like the best and explain why they like it. Finally, ask students to do research and write a short report on their piece of art, explaining the relationship between the piece or style of art and the particular society it came from. Students should describe ways in which societal issues influenced the piece or style of art.

OUR WORLD TODAY Online

Use our Web site for additional resources. All essential content is covered in the Student Edition.

You and your students can visit owt.glencoe.com, the Web site companion to *Our World Today*. This innovative integration of electronic and print media offers your students a wealth of opportunities. The student text directs students to the Web site for the following options:

- Chapter Overviews
- Student Web Activities
- Self-Check Quizzes
- Textbook Updates

Answers are provided for you in the Web Activity Lesson Plan. Additional Web resources and Interactive Tutor puzzles are also available.

TEACHER'S CORNER

Index to National Geographic Magazine:

The following articles may be used for research relating to this chapter:

- "Ancient Greece, Parts I, II, and III," by Caroline Alexander, December 1999, February and March 2000.
- "Italy's Endangered Art," by Erla Zwingle, August 1999.
- "Monaco," by Richard Conniff, May 1996.

National Geographic Society Products Available From Glencoe:

To order the following products for use with this chapter, contact your local Glencoe sales representative or call Glencoe at 1-800-334-7344:

- *GeoBee* (CD-ROM)
- *PicturePack: Geography of Europe* (Transparencies)
- *MapPack: Europe* (Transparencies)
- *STV: World Geography* (Videodisc)
- *Picture Atlas of the World* (CD-ROM)

Additional National Geographic Society Products:

To order the following products for use with this chapter, call National Geographic Society at 1-800-368-2728:

- *Complete National Geographic: 111 Years of National Geographic Magazine* (CD-ROM)
- *Europe* (Video)
- *Cultures* (Map)
- *PicturePack: Ancient Greece* (Transparencies)
- *PicturePack: Ancient Rome* (Transparencies)
- *PicturePack: The Middle Ages* (Transparencies)
- *PicturePack: The Renaissance* (Transparencies)
- *PictureShow: Ancient Civilizations: Greece & Rome* (CD-ROM)
- *PictureShow: The Middle Ages* (CD-ROM)
- *PictureShow: The Renaissance* (CD-ROM)
- *Ancient Civilizations: Ancient Greece* (Posters)
- *Ancient Civilizations: Ancient Rome* (Posters)

NGS ONLINE

Access National Geographic's Web site for current events, activities, links, interactive features, and archives.
www.nationalgeographic.com

Introducing

Chapter 9

Introduce students to chapter content and key terms by having them access Chapter Overview 9 at owt.glencoe.com

Chapter Objectives

1. Describe the governments and culture of ancient Greece and Rome.
2. Explain the importance of religion in European history.
3. Outline events that defined the beginnings of the Modern Age.

GLENCOE TECHNOLOGY

NATIONAL GEOGRAPHIC

The World and Its People Video Program

Chapters 10–13 Europe

The following segments enhance the study of this chapter:

- **Gondolas of Venice**
- **Dracula's Castle**
- **The New Forest**

 Available in DVD and VHS.

MindJogger Videoquiz

Use MindJogger to preview the Chapter 9 content.

 Available in VHS.

Chapter 9 Europe—Early History

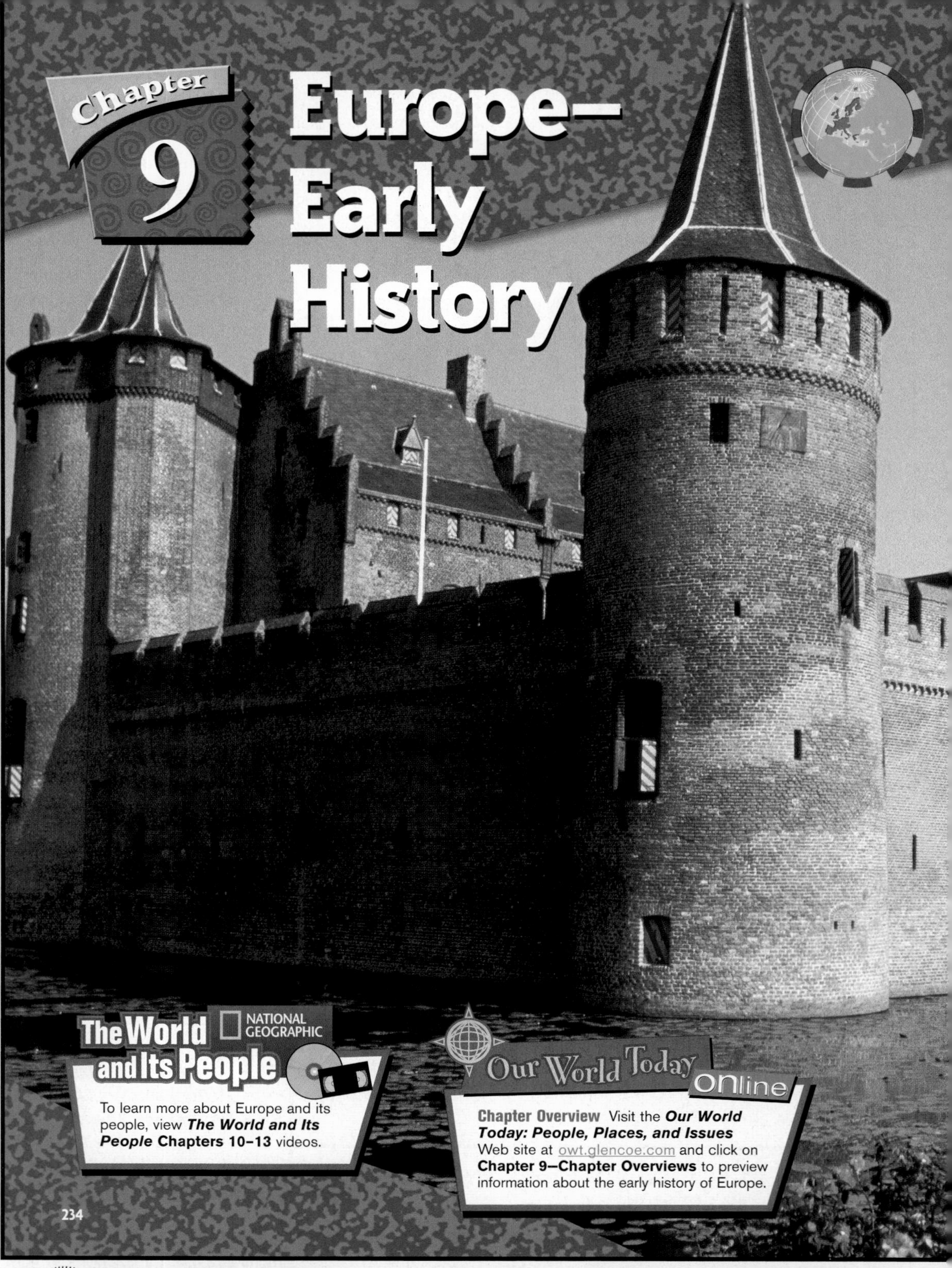

The World and Its People NATIONAL GEOGRAPHIC

To learn more about Europe and its people, view ***The World and Its People*** **Chapters 10–13** videos.

Our World Today online

Chapter Overview Visit the ***Our World Today: People, Places, and Issues*** Web site at owt.glencoe.com and click on **Chapter 9—Chapter Overviews** to preview information about the early history of Europe.

234

Two-Minute Lesson Launcher

Tell students that this chapter discusses cultures that created the foundations for the government and culture of the United States. **Ask: What do you know about ancient Greece and Rome?** *(Most will have seen movies about gladiators or Christian persecution.)* As the students read the chapter, have them write down things they learn about Greece and Rome that were important achievements and why.

Sequencing Events Study Foldable Make this foldable to help you organize information and sequence events into a flowchart about the early history of Europe.

Step 1 Fold a sheet of paper in half from side to side.

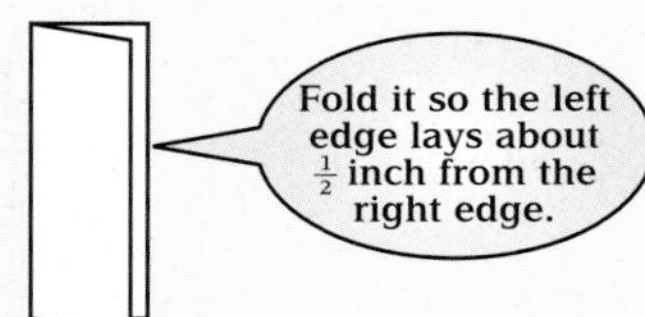

Fold it so the left edge lays about ½ inch from the right edge.

Step 2 Turn the paper and fold it into thirds.

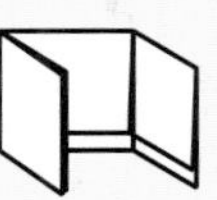

Step 3 Unfold and cut the top layer only along both folds.

This will make three tabs.

Step 4 Turn the paper and label it as shown.

Reading and Writing As you read the chapter, list events that occurred during these three periods in European history under the appropriate tab of your foldable.

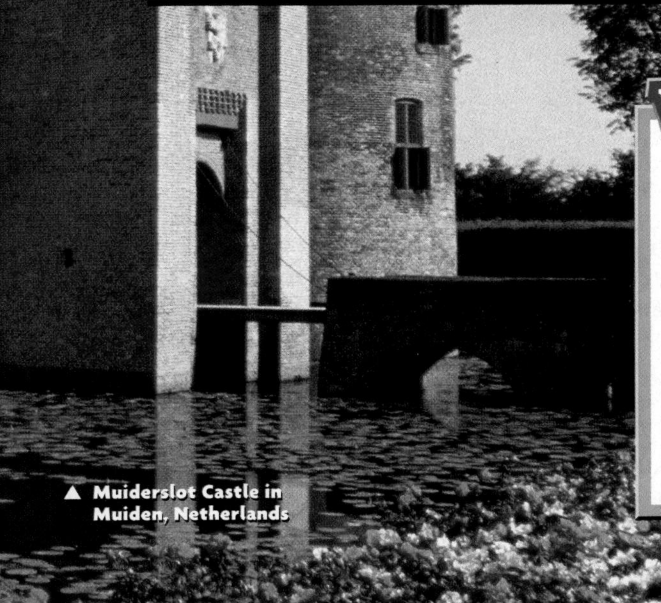

▲ Muiderslot Castle in Muiden, Netherlands

Why It Matters

Roots of Western Culture

Our government, economic system, and social systems have grown from the institutions and traditions of Europe. Our laws, family structure, political opinions, and courts have roots in ancient Greek and Roman customs. Medieval Europe saw the growth of cities and the beginning of capitalism. Finally, new Christian churches were founded in Germany, Scotland, and Switzerland.

About the Photo

American industrialists of the late 19th and early 20th century have been compared to the nobles of medieval Europe. These industrialists built magnificent homes, many of which have been turned into museums or historical parks. Ask your students how these "American Castles" differed from the castles of medieval Europe. What purpose did these homes serve? As part of the lesson, you may want to show a segment from the "American Castles" series broadcast on PBS and A&E network.

Introducing Chapter 9

FOLDABLES Study Organizer

Purpose Students will make and use a foldable to organize events from the early history of Europe. As students read the chapter, they are required to sequence and describe important events. When students have completed the activity, they should have a flowchart that outlines the events of classical, medieval, and premodern Europe.

Have students complete ***Reading and Study Skills Foldables*** Activity 9.

Why It Matters

Have students create a chart with two columns. Label one column "European" and the other "American." In each column, have students list important characteristics of the modern United States that originated in each of the regions. Examples might include government, language, religion, cars, sports, computers, etc. Ask for volunteers to present and discuss their charts.

More About the Photo

Castles in medieval Europe were primarily defensive structures intended to extend control over adjacent territories. The walls and turrets were designed to withstand attacks and siege. Whenever possible, castles were built on hills or islands that provided natural defenses. When that wasn't possible, moats were dug to provide additional defense.

Focus

Section Objectives

1. Identify significant accomplishments of Greek culture.
2. Explain how Alexander spread Greek culture.
3. Describe the Roman system of government and law.

BELLRINGER
Skillbuilder Activity

Project transparency and have students answer questions.

This activity is also available as a blackline master.

Daily Focus Skills Transparency 9-1

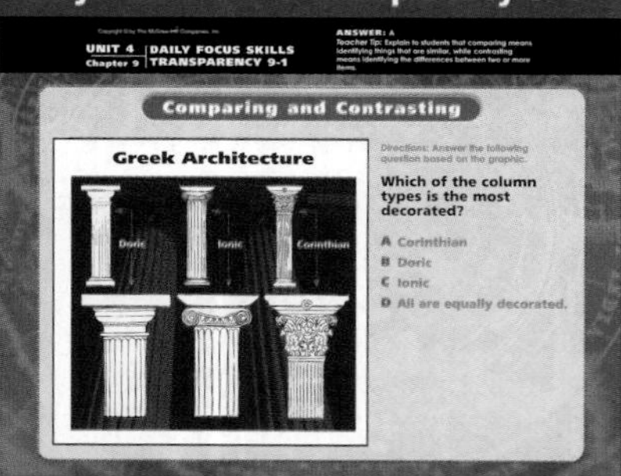

Guide to Reading

■ Accessing Prior Knowledge
Have the class discuss and give examples of different forms of government.

■ Vocabulary Precheck
Have students find the meanings of *monarchy* and *republic.* Then have them identify synonyms, or words with the same meanings. *(monarchy—kingdom; republic—democracy)*

Section 1 Classical Europe

Guide to Reading

Main Idea

Ancient Greece and Rome made important contributions to Western culture and civilization.

Terms to Know

- classical
- polis
- democracy
- philosophy
- republic
- consul
- Senate
- emperor

Reading Strategy

Create a chart like the one below. Write one fact that you already know about each category in the "Know" column. After reading the section, write one fact that you have learned about each category in the "Learn" column.

Category	Know	Learn
Greece		
Rome		
Roman law		
Christianity		

NATIONAL GEOGRAPHIC Exploring Our World

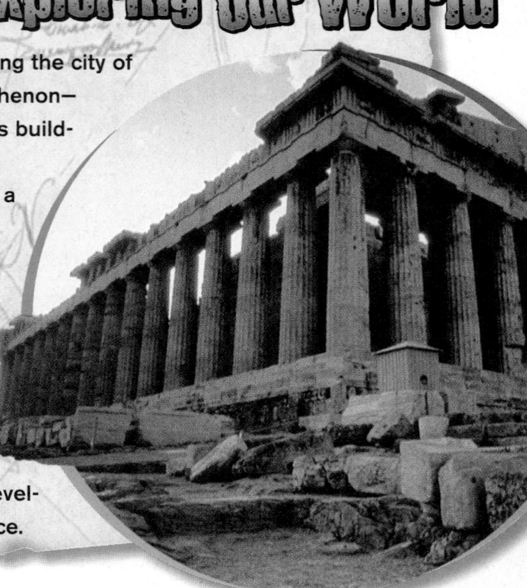

High on a hill overlooking the city of Athens stands the Parthenon—one of the most famous buildings in the world. The Parthenon was built as a temple to Athena, the ancient Greek goddess of wisdom. Started in 447 B.C., the building took 15 years to complete. It is just one of many buildings that show us the civilization that developed in ancient Greece.

When historians talk of **classical** Europe they mean the Europe of ancient Greece and Rome. These civilizations flourished from about 800 B.C. to A.D. 400.

The Golden Age of Greece

Much of European, or Western, civilization grew out of the achievements of **Classical Greece.** This Classical period reached its "Golden Age" in the 400s B.C. By that time, the city-state, or **polis,** had grown from being ruled by a king to the almost direct rule of the people, or **democracy.** Classical Greece has been called the "cradle of democracy" because we trace the beginnings of our political system to this time.

Athens **Athens** is the best example we have of a democratic city-state. It was the home of the world's first democratic constitution. All free males over the age of 20 had the right to vote and speak freely.

Athenian artists produced famous and influential works of philosophy, literature, and drama. **Philosophy** is Greek for the "love of wisdom." Two great philosophers, **Socrates** and his student **Plato,** sought

Section Resources

Reproducible Masters

- Reproducible Lesson Plan 9-1
- Daily Lecture and Discussion Notes 9-1
- Guided Reading Activity 9-1
- Reading Essentials and Study Guide 9-1
- Section Quiz 9-1

Transparencies

- Daily Focus Skills Transparency 9-1

Multimedia

- Vocabulary PuzzleMaker Software
- Interactive Tutor Self-Assessment CD-ROM
- Presentation Plus! CD-ROM
- ExamView® Pro 3.0 Testmaker CD-ROM

to understand and explain human nature. **Aristotle,** a student of Plato's, wrote about the natural environment in which people lived. Greek writers and dramatists dealt with these timeless themes in their poems and plays.

Conflict Between the City-States During this period, city-states such as Athens and **Sparta** wanted to expand their empires. These two rivals often fought against each other. They united temporarily, during the Persian War, when they prevented the Persians from invading Greece. However, from 431–404 B.C. they were again fighting each other. Sparta finally defeated Athens in the Peloponnesian War, which further divided and weakened all of Greece.

Greek Culture Spread In the 300s B.C., Phillip II of Macedonia and his son, **Alexander the Great** invaded the northern border of Greece. They easily conquered all of Greece. Alexander went on to conquer an empire that included Persia and Egypt and stretched eastward into India. Although his empire barely survived his death, Alexander spread Greek culture everywhere he invaded. Over time Greek customs mixed with Persian and Egyptian culture. The empire's important center was at **Alexandria** in northern Egypt. There a great center of learning, a museum-library, was founded. The empire lasted until it came under attack from the Romans in about 200 B.C.

▲ Greek theater comedy mask

✓Reading Check **Why has Greece been called the "cradle of democracy"?**

The Rise of Rome

According to legend, the city of **Rome** was founded by twin brothers, Romulus and Remus, who had, as infants, been left to die on the banks of the Tiber River. Instead of drowning, they were rescued by a she-wolf,

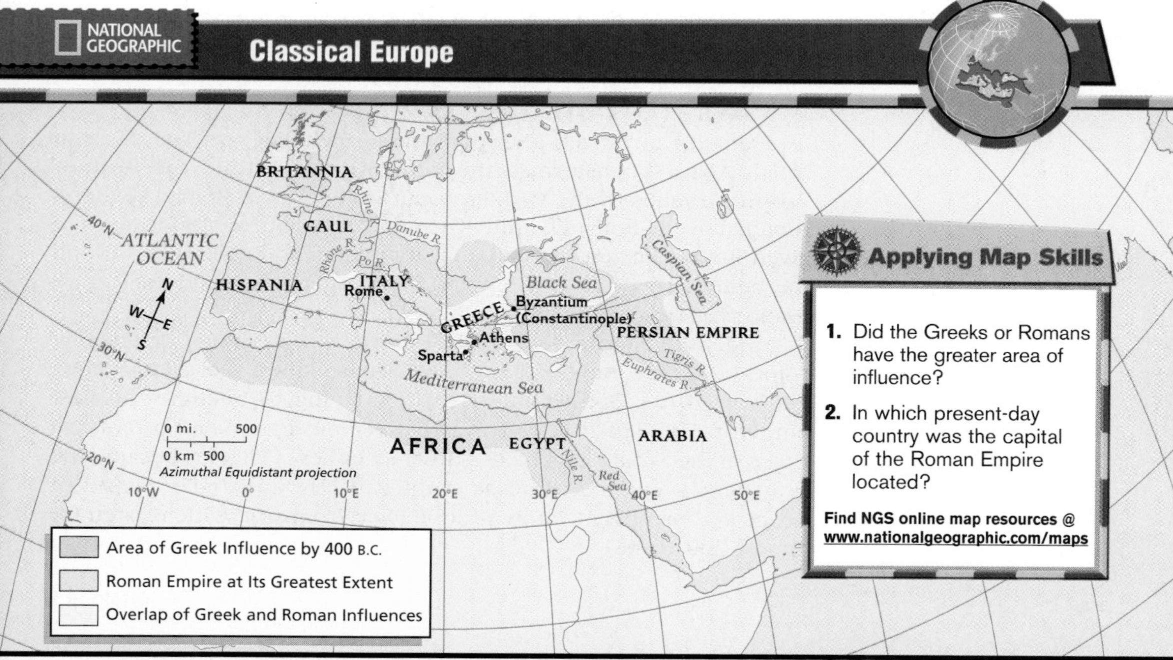

Applying Map Skills

1. Did the Greeks or Romans have the greater area of influence?
2. In which present-day country was the capital of the Roman Empire located?

Find NGS online map resources @ www.nationalgeographic.com/maps

Team-Teaching Activity

Literature The Trojan Wars, a legendary conflict between the Greeks and the people of Troy, stirred the imagination of the ancient Greeks more than any other event and inspired Roman literature as well. The story of the Trojan Wars is told in the *Iliad* and the *Odyssey* of Homer. Invite an English teacher to class to tell students the story of Odysseus's journey home from the Trojan Wars as related in the *Odyssey*. **Ask: Why is the story of the *Odyssey* such an enduring legend?** Have the students discuss how the *Odyssey* represents a great hero overcoming many obstacles to reach his goal. **What are other examples of literature with universal themes that have transcended their own cultures or societies?**

EE4 Human Systems: Standard 13

TEACH

Sequencing Information
Have students create a time line covering the period 800 B.C. to A.D. 400. Have them show the approximate time of significant events in ancient Greece and Rome as well as the span of the Golden Age and the *Pax Romana.* **L2**

✓ Reading Check Answer

because we trace the beginnings of our political system to this time

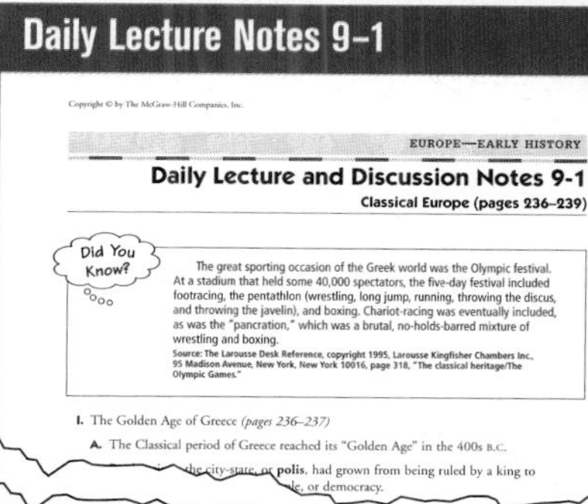

Daily Lecture Notes 9-1

EUROPE—EARLY HISTORY

Daily Lecture and Discussion Notes 9-1

Classical Europe (pages 236–239)

Did You Know?

The great sporting occasion of the Greek world was the Olympic festival. At a stadium that held some 40,000 spectators, the five-day festival included footracing, the pentathlon (wrestling, long jump, running, throwing the discus, and throwing the javelin), and boxing. Chariot-racing was eventually included, as was the "pancration," which was a brutal, no-holds-barred mixture of wrestling and boxing.

Source: The Larousse Desk Reference, copyright 1995, Larousse Kingfisher Chambers Inc., 95 Madison Avenue, New York, New York 10016, page 318, "The classical heritage/The Olympic Games."

I. The Golden Age of Greece *(pages 236–237)*

A. The Classical period of Greece reached its "Golden Age" in the 400s B.C.

... the city-state, or **polis**, had grown from being ruled by a king to ... le, or democracy.

Applying Map Skills

Answers

1. Romans
2. Italy

Skills Practice

Over how many continents did the Roman Empire extend? *(three—Europe, Asia, and Africa)*

Chapter 9

Section 1, pages 236–239

Guided Reading Activity 9-1

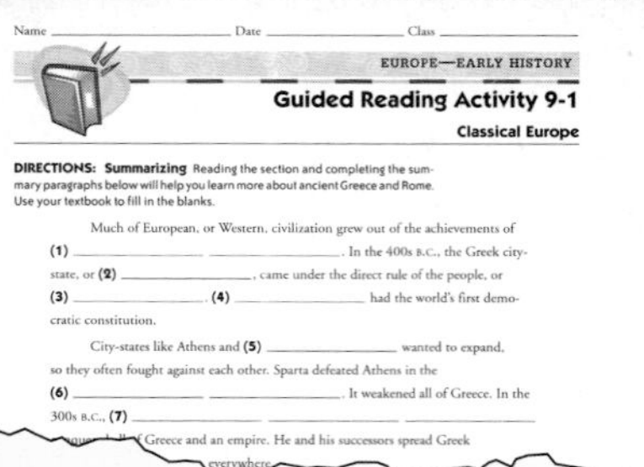
Name ______ Date ______ Class ______

EUROPE—EARLY HISTORY

Guided Reading Activity 9-1

Classical Europe

DIRECTIONS: Summarizing Reading the section and completing the summary paragraphs below will help you learn more about ancient Greece and Rome. Use your textbook to fill in the blanks.

Much of European, or Western, civilization grew out of the achievements of **(1)** ______ ______. In the 400s B.C., the Greek city-state, or **(2)** ______, came under the direct rule of the people, or **(3)** ______. **(4)** ______ had the world's first democratic constitution.

City-states like Athens and **(5)** ______ wanted to expand, so they often fought against each other. Sparta defeated Athens in the **(6)** ______ ______. It weakened all of Greece. In the 300s B.C., **(7)** ______ ______ ______

... Greece and an empire. He and his successors spread Greek ... everywhere

More About the Photo

The dedication ceremonies for the Colosseum in A.D. 80 included 100 days of games and competition. The Colosseum measures 620 by 530 feet (190 by 155 meters) and could seat 50,000 spectators.

Caption Answer Answers will vary but should include sports stadiums, convention centers, and concert auditoriums.

✓ Reading Check Answer

Greek democracy, republican government, and Roman law

ASSESS

Assign Section 1 Assessment as homework or an in-class activity.

Have students use the Interactive Tutor Self-Assessment CD-ROM to review Section 9–1.

NATIONAL GEOGRAPHIC **On Location**

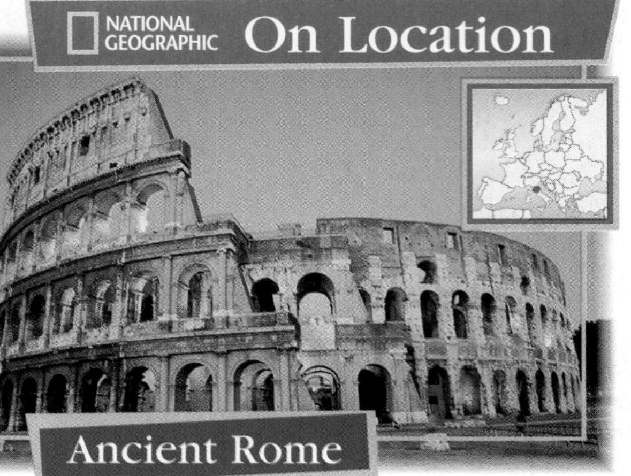

Ancient Rome

The Colosseum was built as an arena for gladiator fights.

Place **Name some arenas we have for public events today.**

who then raised them as her cubs. When grown, the twins built the city on seven hills in central Italy. They fought over who should be king, and Romulus emerged the victor.

Historical Rome What we know for fact is that Rome was settled sometime around 1000 B.C. By about 700 B.C. it had evolved into a major city-state that began to dominate much of the **Italian Peninsula.** Rome lacked natural resources and had only a few good harbors, but it had much more fertile land than Greece. The Romans were therefore a mostly agricultural society and were less likely to live in cities. Italy was more easily invaded than mountainous Greece, so the Romans developed a strong army. Roman art, religion, mythology, and the Latin alphabet were borrowed from the Greeks.

The Roman Republic Rome started as a monarchy but changed to a republic. In a **republic,** people choose their leaders. Rome was led by two **consuls,** individuals elected by the people of Rome to represent them. They reported to the **Senate.** Members of the Senate were landowners who served for life. All of this and more was guaranteed by the system of **Roman law.** The foundation of Roman law was the **Twelve Tables.** The "tables" were actually bronze tablets on which laws regarding wills, courts, and property were recorded. The laws applied to all citizens of Rome, both common and noble. Along with Greek democracy, republican government and Roman law were important contributions to Western civilization and the Modern Age.

✓ Reading Check **What three important developments from Greece and Rome influenced Western civilization?**

From Republic to Empire

From 264 to 146 B.C. a series of wars—including the Punic Wars in North Africa—transformed the Roman Republic into the **Roman Empire.** Eventually the Mediterranean Sea became a "Roman lake" surrounded by the Roman Empire. The peoples conquered by Rome were given Roman citizenship and equality under the Roman law. Beyond the boundaries of its vast empire, Rome opened up trade with civilizations as far away as India and China.

Under the empire, Senators lost power to **emperors,** or absolute rulers, of Rome. Supporters of the Senate killed the great Roman general **Julius Caesar** in 44 B.C. for trying to become the first emperor. This led to a civil war between Caesar's supporters and those of the Senate. In 31 B.C., Caesar's nephew Octavius became the first Roman emperor, **Caesar Augustus.** He initiated a period of peace and prosperity known as the ***Pax Romana,*** which lasted for almost 200 years.

Cooperative Learning Activity

Organize students into four groups. Have each of the groups research the functions of the Roman Senate. Have them consider such items as who the senators were, who they represented, the issues they debated, and the rules of debate. Have each group prepare a presentation of their findings. Then conduct a mock Senate debate. Combine the groups into two teams. Have the teams debate a current event issue following the rules from the Roman Senate and representing the interests of Roman Senators.

EE6 The Uses of Geography: Standard 17

Christianity and Rome **Jesus Christ** was born a citizen of Rome in Palestine under Caesar Augustus and carried out his teaching during the early *Pax Romana.* Two disciples, **Peter** and **Paul,** established the new Christian Church in Rome. Even though the early Christians were cruelly persecuted, Christianity spread over the Roman world. In the A.D. 300s, under the emperors **Constantine I** and **Theodosius I,** Christianity became the official religion of the Roman Empire.

The Decline of the Empire After the period of the *Pax Romana* the Roman Empire began to decline. In A.D. 330, Constantine I moved the capital from Rome in Italy eastward to the newly built city of **Constantinople,** near the Black Sea. Constantine tried to save the empire by reforming the government, but it was too late. Plagues that came in from Asia over trade routes killed numerous people. People fled the cities and escaped to villas, or country estates.

Finally, in the A.D. 400s, the northern frontier defenses crumbled. Rome was left open to invasion by various groups of Germanic peoples. (One group, the Huns, introduced a new technology unknown to the Roman cavalry—the stirrup. The stirrup allowed the Huns to use their weapons while riding horses.) The Germans came to rule over Rome and much of Italy and Europe. The **Eastern Roman Empire,** or Byzantine Empire, did not fall to the Germans but continued on for another 1,000 years until its conquest by the Ottoman Turks in A.D. 1453.

▲ Roman soldier's breast plate

Reading Check **How did technology play a role in the decline of the Roman Empire?**

Section 1 Assessment

Defining Terms

1. Define classical, polis, democracy, philosophy, republic, consul, Senate, emperor.

Recalling Facts

2. Government In its democratic constitution, what two rights did Athens give all free males over the age of 20?

3. Culture Name four influences that Greece had on Roman culture.

Critical Thinking

4. Analyzing Information Why do you suppose some of Rome's citizens wanted absolute rulers instead of elected senators?

5. Making Connections What is one freedom that American democracy has today that was clearly not recognized in the Roman Empire?

Graphic Organizer

6. Creating Time Lines Create a time line like this. Place the letter of the event next to its date.

A. Greek empire is attacked by Rome
B. Julius Caesar is killed
C. Germans invade Rome
D. Rome is settled
E. Octavius becomes the first Roman emperor

1000 B.C. — 200 B.C. — 44 B.C. — 31 B.C. — A.D. 400

Applying Social Studies Skills

7. Making Inferences Why do you think the story of Romulus and Remus was created?

Section 1 Assessment

1. The terms are defined in the Glossary.
2. the right to vote and to speak freely
3. art, religion, mythology, and the Latin alphabet
4. *Possible answer:* an absolute ruler can make decisions without having to discuss, debate, or compromise.
5. *Possible answer:* They might have curried favor with the ruler and expected to receive favorable treatment.
6. **A.** 200 B.C. **B.** 44 B.C. **C.** A.D. 400 **D.** 1000 B.C. **E.** 31 B.C.
7. This exercise helps students understand the importance of mythology in preserving and relating history and the connection between myth and history. All reasonable attempts at answers should be accepted.

Chapter 9

Section 1, pages 236–239

Section Quiz 9-1

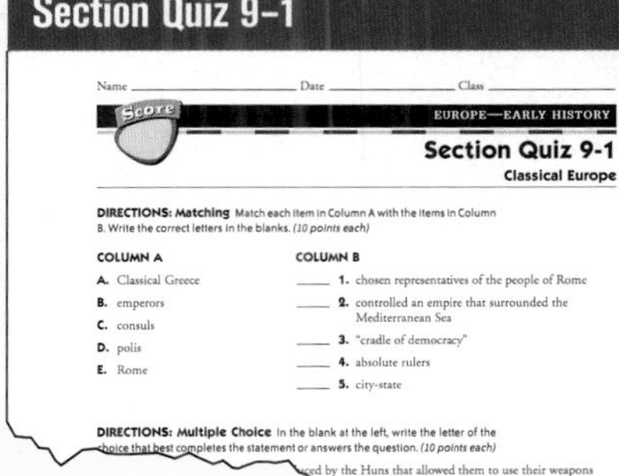

Name ______ Date ______ Class ______

Score — EUROPE—EARLY HISTORY

Section Quiz 9-1
Classical Europe

DIRECTIONS: Matching Match each item in Column A with the items in Column B. Write the correct letters in the blanks. *(10 points each)*

COLUMN A	COLUMN B
A. Classical Greece	____ **1.** chosen representatives of the people of Rome
B. emperors	____ **2.** controlled an empire that surrounded the Mediterranean Sea
C. consuls	____ **3.** "cradle of democracy"
D. polis	____ **4.** absolute rulers
E. Rome	____ **5.** city-state

DIRECTIONS: Multiple Choice In the blank at the left, write the letter of the choice that best completes the statement or answers the question. *(10 points each)*

ced by the Huns that allowed them to use their weapons

Reading Check Answer

the stirrup allowed the Huns to use weapons while riding horses, which led to the Romans' defeat

Reading Essentials and Study Guide 9-1

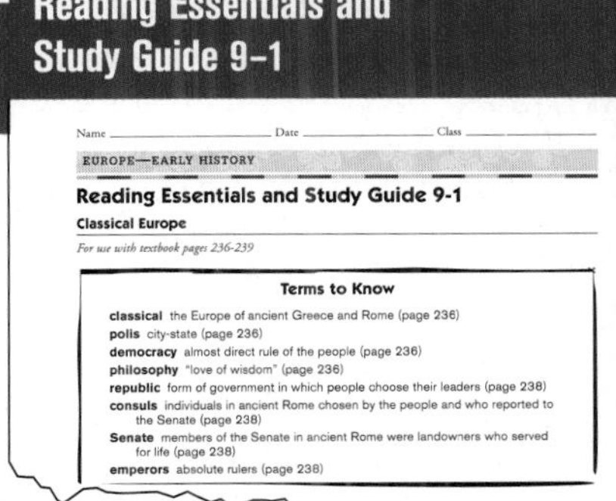

Name ______ Date ______ Class ______

EUROPE—EARLY HISTORY

Reading Essentials and Study Guide 9-1
Classical Europe

For use with textbook pages 236-239

Terms to Know

classical the Europe of ancient Greece and Rome (page 236)
polis city-state (page 236)
democracy almost direct rule of the people (page 236)
philosophy "love of wisdom" (page 236)
republic form of government in which people choose their leaders (page 238)
consuls individuals in ancient Rome chosen by the people and who reported to the Senate (page 238)
Senate members of the Senate in ancient Rome were landowners who served for life (page 238)
emperors absolute rulers (page 238)

4 CLOSE

Have students research the art of Greece and Rome. Have them write a paragraph that describes how social issues influenced art there.

Social Studies Skill

TEACH

Compare the Western calendar with alternative dating methods, such as those found in the Hebrew, Chinese, and Muslim calendars. The conversion to the Western calendar's year 2000 is as follows:

	Beginning Date	Year 2000
Hebrew	3760 B.C.	5760
Chinese	2637 B.C.	4637
Muslim	A.D. 622	1378

Additional Skills Practice

1. **How is the number of years between two B.C. dates calculated?** *(the later date is subtracted from the earlier date)*
2. **How is the number of years between two A.D. dates calculated?** *(the earlier date is subtracted from the later date)*
3. **How is the number of years between a B.C. date and an A.D. date calculated?** *(the two dates are added together)*

GLENCOE TECHNOLOGY

Skillbuilder Interactive Workbook CD-ROM, Level 1

This interactive CD-ROM reinforces student mastery of essential social studies skills.

Social Studies Skill

Using B.C. and A.D.

Cultures throughout the world have based their dating systems on significant events in their history. For example, Islamic countries use a dating system that begins with Muhammad's flight from Makkah to Madinah. For Western cultures, the most important event was the birth of Jesus Christ.

Learning the Skill

About 515, a Christian monk developed a system that begins dating from *anno Domini,* Latin for "the year of the Lord." Although some historians believe that the monk made a small mistake in his figuring of the exact year of Christ's birth, his system of dating has lasted. Events before the birth of Christ, or "B.C.," are figured by counting backward from A.D. 1. There was no year "0." The year before A.D. 1 is 1 B.C. Notice that "A.D." is written before the date, while "B.C." is written following the date.

Practicing the Skill

Study the time line of Classical Europe to answer the following questions.

1. How old was Plato when he became a student of Socrates?
2. For how long did Alexander the Great rule?
3. How old was Julius Caesar when he was assassinated?
4. Who was emperor nearly 500 years after the rule of Alexander the Great?

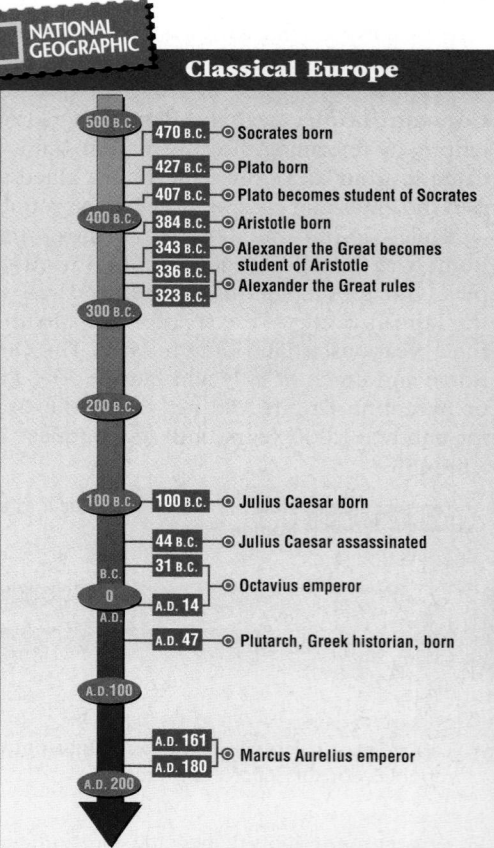

NATIONAL GEOGRAPHIC

Classical Europe

500 B.C.
470 B.C. Socrates born
427 B.C. Plato born
407 B.C. Plato becomes student of Socrates
400 B.C.
384 B.C. Aristotle born
343 B.C. Alexander the Great becomes student of Aristotle
336 B.C.–323 B.C. Alexander the Great rules
300 B.C.
200 B.C.
100 B.C.
100 B.C. Julius Caesar born
44 B.C. Julius Caesar assassinated
31 B.C.–A.D. 14 Octavius emperor
B.C. 0 A.D.
A.D. 47 Plutarch, Greek historian, born
A.D. 100
A.D. 161–A.D. 180 Marcus Aurelius emperor
A.D. 200

Applying the Skill

Create a time line using the terms B.M.B. (before my birth) and A.M.B. (after my birth). Fill in the time line with key events that happened before and after you were born. Illustrate the time line with drawings or cutouts from magazines.

GO TO Practice key skills with **Glencoe Skillbuilder Interactive Workbook, Level 1.**

240

Practicing the Skill Answers

1. 20 years old
2. for 13 years
3. 56 years old
4. Marcus Aurelius

Applying the Skill
Students' time lines will vary.

Section 2

Medieval Europe

Guide to Reading

Main Idea

The Middle Ages saw the spread of Christianity, the growth of cities, and the growing powers of kings.

Key Terms

- bishop
- pope
- missionary
- monastery
- convent
- common law
- feudalism
- vassal
- manor
- tenant
- serf
- guild
- apprentice
- charter

Reading Strategy

Create a chart like the one below. Fill in the chief duty or role of each of these members of society.

Lord	
Vassal	
Guild member	
Apprentice	
Serf	

NATIONAL GEOGRAPHIC **Exploring Our World**

Majestic cathedrals like this one at Reims, France, draw tourists from all over the world. The cathedral was begun in 1211 and took 80 years to complete, although the decorations continued for centuries. It is almost 500 feet (152 m) long, making it one and a half times the length of a football field. Twenty-five kings of France received their crowns here.

With the disappearance of the Roman Empire, a new age, which we call the **Middle Ages,** began. ***Medieval*** is derived from a Latin word for "Middle Ages." It is a fitting name for the 1,000-year period that lies between Classical and Modern times. Medieval Europe combined characteristics of the Roman Empire with the newer ways of Christianity and the peoples of Europe.

The Rise of Christianity

It was during the Middle Ages that Christianity, in the form of the Roman Catholic Church, became a political power in western Europe. A leader called a **bishop** headed each major Christian community. By the A.D. 500s, the bishops of Rome, now known as **popes,** became the leaders of the Catholic Church. The influence of the Church was so strong at this time that the popes also became important political figures.

In eastern Europe, the Byzantine Empire, started by Constantine I, continued. There, Christianity was known as **Eastern Orthodoxy.** It was not under the leadership of the popes in Rome, but rather the emperors in Constantinople.

1 Focus

Section Objectives

1. Explain the importance of Christianity as a political influence in Medieval Europe.
2. Describe the medieval social and political systems.

BELLRINGER
Skillbuilder Activity

Project transparency and have students answer questions.

This activity is also available as a blackline master.

Daily Focus Skills Transparency 9-2

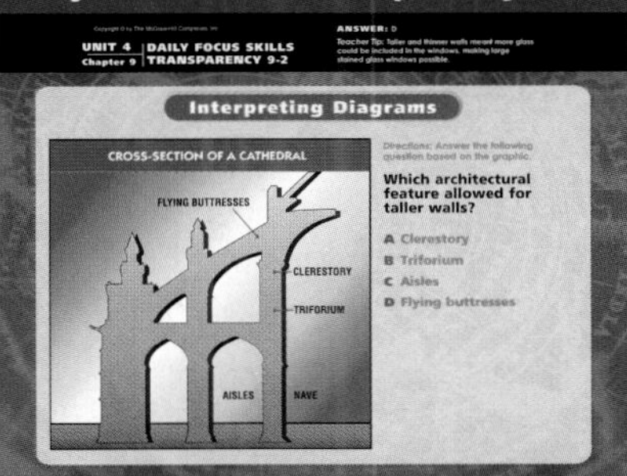

Guide to Reading

■ **Vocabulary Precheck**
Ask students to offer definitions of *vassal, tenant,* and *serf.* Write the definitions on the board. As they study the section, have students change the definition as they learn about the terms.

Use the Vocabulary PuzzleMaker to create crossword and word search puzzles.

Section Resources

Reproducible Masters
- Reproducible Lesson Plan 9-2
- Daily Lecture and Discussion Notes 9-2
- Guided Reading Activity 9-2
- Reading Essentials and Study Guide 9-2
- Section Quiz 9-2

Transparencies
- Daily Focus Skills Transparency 9-2

Multimedia
- Vocabulary PuzzleMaker Software
- Interactive Tutor Self-Assessment CD-ROM
- Presentation Plus! CD-ROM
- ExamView® Pro 3.0 Testmaker CD-ROM

Chapter 9

Section 2, pages 241–244

Teach

Analyzing Information Ask students to find a picture of a castle or cathedral from Medieval Europe. Have them write a paragraph telling about the building and attach it to the picture. The pictures and reports can then be used to create a collage on a bulletin board.

Reading Check Answer

They were sent to every part of Europe.

Daily Lecture Notes 9-2

Copyright © by The McGraw-Hill Companies, Inc.

EUROPE—EARLY HISTORY

Daily Lecture and Discussion Notes 9-2

Medieval Europe (pages 241–244)

Did You Know? In medieval times, Christians from all over Europe were willing to travel for months and even years to visit the places in Palestine associated with Jesus Christ. To journey to these sites, European pilgrims were willing to put up with almost any degree of hardship and danger.

Source: The Larousse Desk Reference, copyright 1995, Larousse Kingfisher Chambers Inc., 95 Madison Avenue, New York, New York 10016, page 327. "The medieval Christian Church/Pilgrims."

I. The Rise of Christianity (pages 241–242)

A. It was during the Middle Ages that Christianity in the form of the Roman Catholic Church became a political power in western Europe. By the A.D. 500s, ... leaders of the Church

Reading Check Answer

He was protector of the Christian Church of the West and head of the Holy Roman Empire.

Guided Reading Activity 9-2

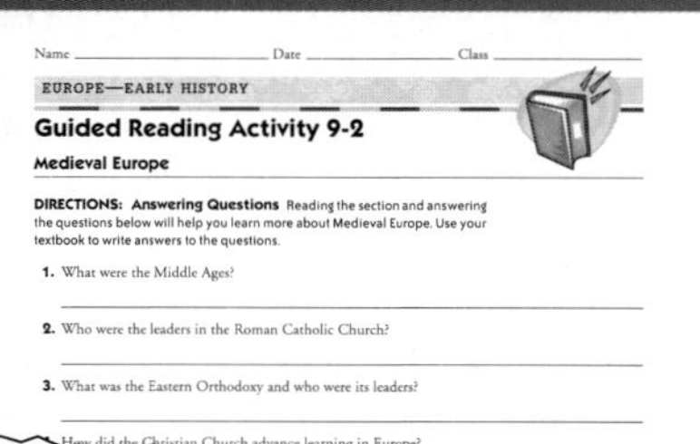

Name ______ Date ______ Class ______

EUROPE—EARLY HISTORY

Guided Reading Activity 9-2

Medieval Europe

DIRECTIONS: Answering Questions Reading the section and answering the questions below will help you learn more about Medieval Europe. Use your textbook to write answers to the questions.

1. What were the Middle Ages?
2. Who were the leaders in the Roman Catholic Church?
3. What was the Eastern Orthodoxy and who were its leaders?
4. How did the Christian Church advance learning in Europe?

▲ Jeweled cross and Bible

Spreading the Faith By A.D. 500, the first Christian Bible was completed. The early popes sent **missionaries,** teachers of Christianity, to every part of Europe. Many of the missionaries were monks and nuns. Monks were men who devoted their lives to prayer, study, and good works and lived in **monasteries.** Women who did similarly were nuns and lived in **convents.** Monks and nuns not only helped the poor and needy, but they were teachers as well. Through its schools, the Christian Church greatly advanced learning in Europe. In the 1100s, the Church also founded the first universities, institutions of higher learning, at Bologna in Italy and Oxford in England.

Beginning in the A.D. 1000s, the Church sponsored a series of holy wars called **Crusades.** It sent armies to capture Jerusalem in Palestine from the Islamic caliphs, or rulers. The Church also crusaded in northern and eastern Europe for about 400 years to spread Christianity.

Reading Check How did missionaries help spread Christianity?

The Holy Roman Empire

The Germans combined their **common law,** the unwritten laws that come from local customs, with Roman law and founded kingdoms all over Europe—from Spain to England to Germany and Italy. Many of these kingdoms soon became Christian. The early kings, like the German tribal chiefs before them, were elected by all nobles and knights. Over time, however, the kings became more independent and powerful. The crown was passed down to the next generation, usually the king's first-born son.

Charlemagne One of the most important German kingdoms was that of the **Franks.** By the A.D. 700s it controlled much of what would become France and Germany. In fact, the name "France" comes from the word *Franks.* In 771 **Charlemagne** was elected king of the Franks. Through war he added more of Germany and parts of Spain and Italy, including Rome, to the kingdom of the Franks.

On Christmas Day in the year 800, Charlemagne knelt before the pope in the Church of St. Peter in Rome and was proclaimed the protector of the Christian Church in the West. He also was crowned the head of the Roman Empire in the West. That empire came to be known as the **Holy Roman Empire.**

After Charlemagne's death in 814, his empire was inherited by his son and grandsons and broke up into several kingdoms. These kingdoms were the foundations for modern Germany, Italy, France, and Spain. At about the same time, several Germanic groups like the Angles, Saxons, Jutes, and Danes helped to found the first English kingdom. "England" gets its name from "Angle land."

Reading Check What was Charlemagne's role in the spread of Christianity?

Medieval Society

Most people during the Middle Ages were not kings, warriors, traders, or explorers—they were farmers. The medieval political and social system—called **feudalism**—was based on agriculture. Under

Content Background

Maps Although the Greeks envisioned a spherical Earth and had proposed a system of longitude and latitude, the maps of medieval Europe were much more simple. Ask students to find examples of the more than 600 maps that survived from the period. They are sometimes called "T-O" maps because they were round, or O-shaped, depicting the earth as a flat circular dish, and they were divided into three parts, or a "T", by bodies of water. Asia was above the T, Europe was at the lower left, and Africa was at the lower right. The vertical part of the T, separating Europe from Africa, was the Mediterranean Sea. The horizontal part was the Danube and the Nile Rivers, flowing in a line on opposite sides of the Mediterranean. The entire known world was surrounded by the great Ocean Sea.

feudalism, lords would give land to a noble or knight to work, govern, and defend. In return, those who received the land swore loyalty to the lords and became their **vassals.** Those knights who did not receive land usually served in the armies of the lords, often hoping to be rewarded with land for their service.

The Manor The feudal estate and basic economic unit was called the **manor.** At its heart was usually a manor house or a castle. Most of the population of the manor was made up of common people who farmed and performed other tasks as well. There were two types of farmers. Those who paid rent for their land and then worked the land freely as they pleased were known as **tenants.** The other much larger group was the **serfs.**

Serfs were not as free and were usually poorer than tenant farmers. In return for the use of land, seed, tools, and protection, serfs had to work as ordered by the lords of the manors, whether in the fields or elsewhere. Often the serfs worked on roads, walls, fortifications, and at other hard jobs. Some might become millers making flour out of grain, coopers making barrels and buckets, or blacksmiths making tools, weapons, or horseshoes out of iron and other metals. In times of trouble, male serfs also became foot soldiers who served under the direction of the cavalry of knights.

These were often quite violent times, and the common people rarely strayed too far from the safety of the manor. On occasion the manors might be visited by wanderers with special skills. For example, tinkers made a living by moving from estate to estate, patching pots or fixing other metal objects. Minstrels and other troubadours entertained by playing music, juggling, or acting as comedians or fools.

✓ Reading Check **What did a vassal receive for his service to a lord?**

Web Activity Visit the ***Our World Today: People, Places, and Issues*** Web site at owt.glencoe.com and click on **Chapter 9—Student Web Activities** to learn more about the Crusades.

NATIONAL GEOGRAPHIC

Medieval Europe c. 1200 A.D.

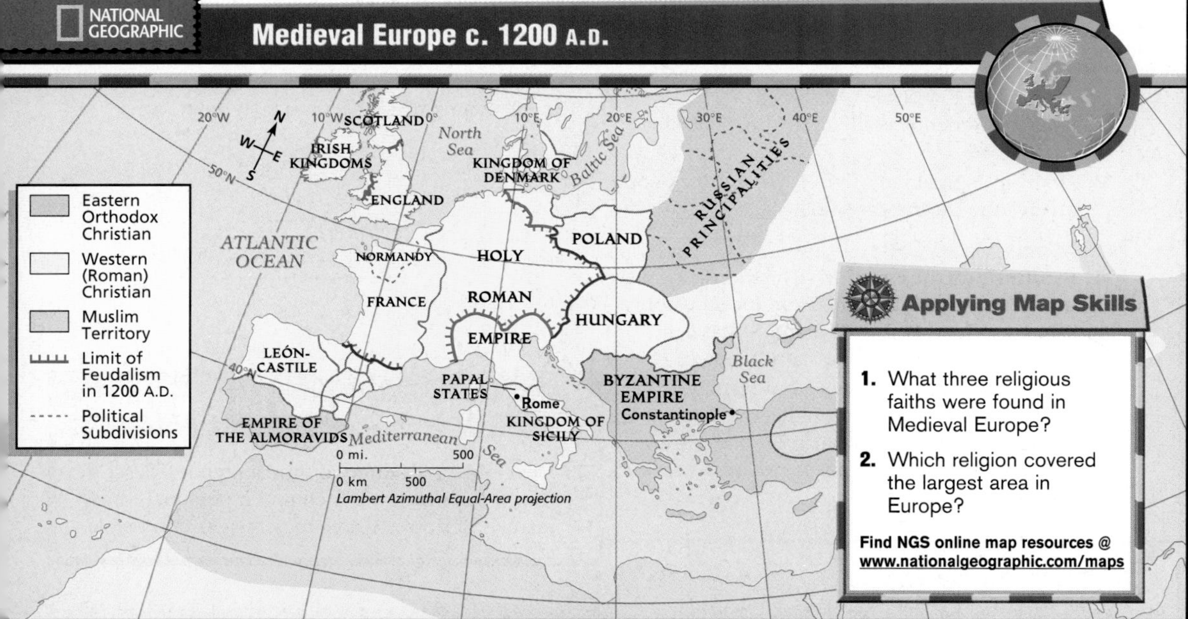

Applying Map Skills

1. What three religious faiths were found in Medieval Europe?
2. Which religion covered the largest area in Europe?

Find NGS online map resources @ www.nationalgeographic.com/maps

Critical Thinking Activity

Drawing Conclusions There was little privacy in the manor house. The cramped living quarters and the lack of heating did much to foster togetherness. It was not uncommon for nobles to have huge beds (12 feet wide) that allowed a noble, his wife, their children, some servants, and key members of the lord's "fellowship" (his knights) to sleep together in the dead of winter. Fortunately, Medieval people liked being clean. During the warm weather, on one of the many religious holidays, you would easily find freshly bathed, cleanly dressed peasants. **Ask: How do you think Medieval people heated their homes? Why might it be difficult for them to take baths? What would they do to stay clean in cold weather? Where do you think the term "spring cleaning" came from?**

Our World Today online

Objectives, goals, and answers to the Student Web Activity can be found in the Web Activity Lesson Plan at **owt.glencoe.com**

ASSESS

Assign Section 2 Assessment as homework or an in-class activity.

Have students use the Interactive Tutor Self-Assessment CD-ROM to review Section 9–2.

✓ Reading Check Answer

land

Applying Map Skills

Answers

1. Eastern Orthodox Christianity, Western (Roman) Christianity, and Islam
2. Western Christianity

Skills Practice

Were the Irish Kingdoms within the limits of feudalism? *(No)*

Chapter 9

Section 2, pages 241–244

Section Quiz 9-2

Did You Know

According to a Medieval saying "City air makes one free." Legally, if a serf lived in a city for a year and a day he was free.

Reading Check Answer

for protection against powerful nobles

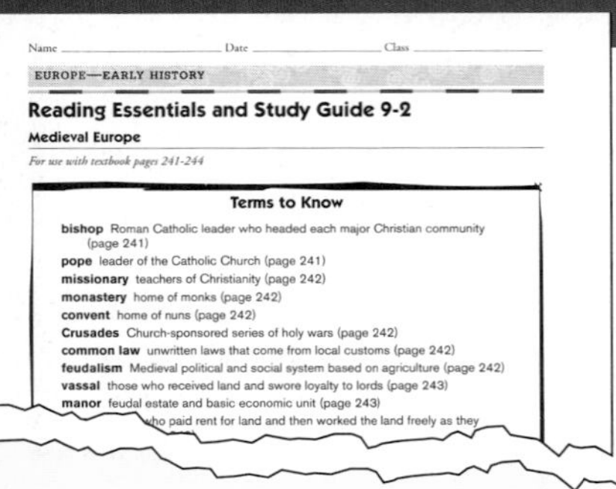

Reading Essentials and Study Guide 9-2

4 CLOSE

Have students create a display of a manor and its lands.

▲ Stained glass showing a craftsman at work

The Growth of Cities

Towns in the Middle Ages were fairly independent and free of the feudal lords' control. Towns served as centers of trade and manufacturing. Their importance increased during the Crusades because the Christian armies needed supplies. By the twelfth century, towns hosted great trade fairs, where merchants from far and wide came together to do business.

Manufacturing came under the control of workers' organizations known as **guilds.** Different guilds controlled industries such as brewing, cloth making, boat building, and many others. Young workers, called **apprentices,** spent years learning a trade so that they could join a guild. With experience, the apprentices became journeymen and eventually master craftsmen.

Over time, some towns grew into cities and became political and religious centers as well. The new, more powerful kings and churchmen understood the importance of cities. They built great cathedrals and granted the residents privileges and freedoms in written documents called **charters.** By doing this, the kings won the support of the townspeople. This support was useful in times of war and for protection against powerful nobles. The kings also raised money by collecting taxes from the towns in return for granting charters.

Reading Check **Why did kings want the support of large cities?**

Section 2 Assessment

Defining Terms

1. **Define** bishop, pope, missionary, monastery, convent, common law, feudalism, vassal, manor, tenant, serf, guild, apprentice, charter.

Recalling Facts

2. **History** When was the first Christian Bible completed?
3. **History** What kind of work were most people involved in during the Middle Ages?

Critical Thinking

4. **Evaluating Information** Common laws were unwritten laws that came from local customs. What are the possible difficulties that can arise from having such unwritten laws?
5. **Analyzing Information** Rome has been known as the Roman Republic, the Roman Empire, and the Holy Roman Empire. How do these labels signify major political changes?

Graphic Organizer

6. **Organizing Information** Create a triangle like the one below. On the lines, list serfs, vassals, and tenants in the order they would be ranked under a lord in the feudal system. Consider how much a person owned when you rank them.

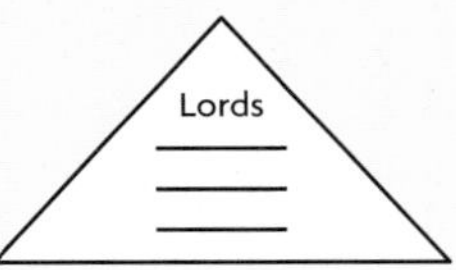

Applying Social Studies Skills

7. **Describing** In three to four sentences, describe life on the manor for a common person. Use as many descriptive words (adjectives) as possible.

Section 2 Assessment

1. The terms are defined in the Glossary.
2. before A.D. 500
3. farming
4. *Possible answers:* laws are open to interpretation and may not be uniformly applied; different customs may conflict; as conditions change common law may no longer apply.
5. Political power changed from the citizens, to an absolute ruler, to a ruler of both the church and the state.
6. lord, vassal, tenant, serf
7. This exercise helps students to visualize and articulate conditions during Medieval times. All reasonable attempts at realistic descriptions should be accepted.

The Beginning of Modern Times

Guide to Reading

Main Idea

The study of science, art, and education was renewed in the period following the Middle Ages.

Key Terms

- indulgences
- Protestant
- reform
- Columbian Exchange
- revolution
- divine right of kings
- Parliament
- constitution

Reading Strategy

Create a time line like the one below. As you read, add the following terms to the line in the correct order.

Protestant Reformation
Age of Exploration
American Revolution
Renaissance
French Revolution

NATIONAL GEOGRAPHIC **Exploring Our World**

From the 1300s to the 1600s, important cultural achievements in the arts and learning spread throughout Europe. Merchant families used their wealth to help artists and scholars explore new ways of thinking. The result was the Renaissance—a French word meaning "rebirth." Michelangelo's statue of David is one of the many masterpieces from this period.

The growth of cities and trade and the gradual breakup of feudalism led to the end of the Middle Ages. Because of the important developments that shaped life as we know it today in the West, historians trace the beginnings of the "Modern Age" from these times. This pre-modern period begins with the **Renaissance** in about A.D. 1350 and ends with the **French Revolution** and Napoleonic Wars in 1815.

The Renaissance

Around 1350 interest in education, art, and science peaked in several parts of Europe, especially in the cities and towns. To many people, this was the beginning of a new golden age like that of ancient Greece and Rome. The Renaissance began in the cities of northern Italy and spread to other cities of Europe.

Section Resources

Reproducible Masters
- Reproducible Lesson Plan 9-3
- Daily Lecture and Discussion Notes 9-3
- Guided Reading Activity 9-3
- Reading Essentials and Study Guide 9-3
- Section Quiz 9-3

Transparencies
- Daily Focus Skills Transparency 9-3

Multimedia
- Vocabulary PuzzleMaker Software
- Interactive Tutor Self-Assessment CD-ROM
- Presentation Plus! CD-ROM
- ExamView® Pro 3.0 Testmaker CD-ROM

1 Focus

Section Objectives

1. Explain advances in arts, science, and nationhood achieved during the Renaissance.
2. Identify the causes of the Reformation.
3. Compare the causes and results of revolutions in the Americas and Europe.

BELLRINGER Skillbuilder Activity

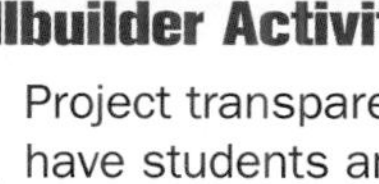

Project transparency and have students answer questions.

This activity is also available as a blackline master.

Daily Focus Skills Transparency 9-3

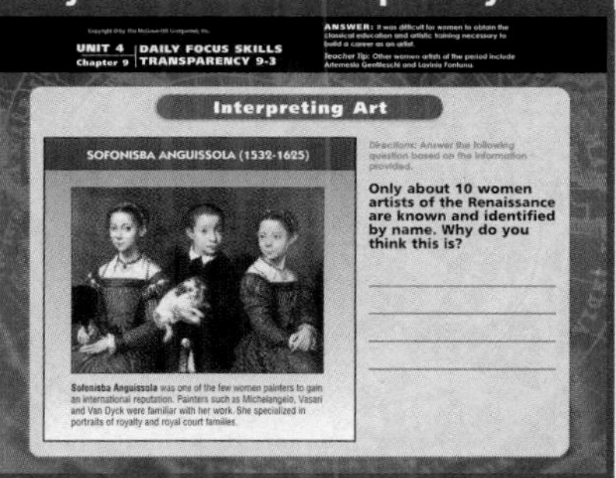

Guide to Reading

■ **Accessing Prior Knowledge**
Ask students to identify any revolutions they know of. Ask who fights in a revolution and why.

■ **Vocabulary Precheck**
Have students look up the words *reformation* and *revolution* and explain the differences and similarities.

TEACH

Making Inferences On a world map, locate Europe and India. Point out that the Americas were unknown to Europeans at that time. Ask students why the Portuguese explorers may have tried to reach India by sailing around Africa. *(They could stay near land.)* Why didn't explorers want to try to reach India by sailing west across the Ocean? *(They would have to navigate unknown oceans without landmarks.)*

Daily Lecture Notes 9-3

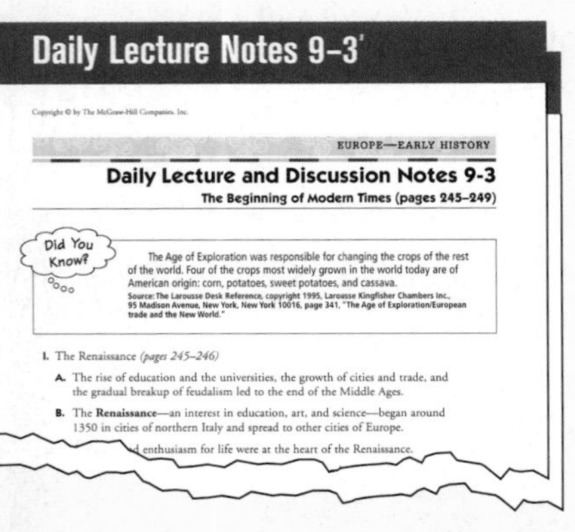

EUROPE—EARLY HISTORY

Daily Lecture and Discussion Notes 9-3

The Beginning of Modern Times (pages 245–249)

Did You Know?

The Age of Exploration was responsible for changing the crops of the rest of the world. Four of the crops most widely grown in the world today are of American origin: corn, potatoes, sweet potatoes, and cassava.

Source: The Larousse Desk Reference, copyright 1995, Larousse Kingfisher Chambers Inc., 95 Madison Avenue, New York, New York 10016, page 341, "The Age of Exploration/European trade and the New World."

I. The Renaissance *(pages 245–246)*

A. The rise of education and the universities, the growth of cities and trade, and the gradual breakup of feudalism led to the end of the Middle Ages.

B. The **Renaissance**—an interest in education, art, and science—began around 1350 in cities of northern Italy and spread to other cities of Europe.

...d enthusiasm for life were at the heart of the Renaissance.

✓ Reading Check Answer

It made books more numerous and less expensive.

Guided Reading Activity 9-3

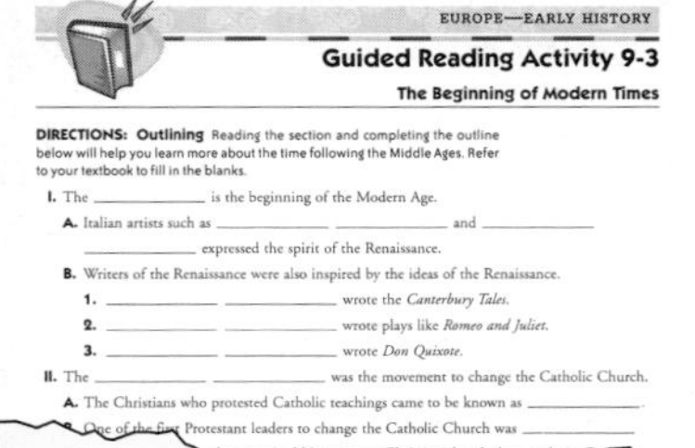

Name ______ Date ______ Class ______

EUROPE—EARLY HISTORY

Guided Reading Activity 9-3

The Beginning of Modern Times

DIRECTIONS: Outlining Reading the section and completing the outline below will help you learn more about the time following the Middle Ages. Refer to your textbook to fill in the blanks.

I. The ______ is the beginning of the Modern Age.

A. Italian artists such as ______ ______ and ______ ______ expressed the spirit of the Renaissance.

B. Writers of the Renaissance were also inspired by the ideas of the Renaissance.

1. ______ ______ wrote the *Canterbury Tales.*
2. ______ ______ wrote plays like *Romeo and Juliet.*
3. ______ ______ wrote *Don Quixote.*

II. The ______ ______ was the movement to change the Catholic Church.

A. The Christians who protested Catholic teachings came to be known as ______.

B. One of the first Protestant leaders to change the Catholic Church was ______ ... who organized his own new Christian church that taught in G...

▲ The Sistine Chapel

Renaissance Artists The artists, scientists, and philosophers of Greece and Rome had taken pride in their ability to think and to appreciate the beauty in human beings and nature. Curiosity and enthusiasm for life were at the heart of the Renaissance. No one better expressed this revived spirit than two Italians, **Leonardo da Vinci** and **Michelangelo Buonarotti.** (See page 250 for some of the achievements of Leonardo da Vinci.)

The painter and sculptor Michelangelo expressed human emotions such as anger, sorrow, and strength in his paintings and sculptures. His most famous work is the mural on the ceiling of the Sistine Chapel in the Vatican Palace in Rome. It covers over 6,000 square feet (1,828 sq. m) and is made up of 145 separate paintings. It took nearly five years to complete.

The Printing Press Writers were also inspired by the ideas of the Renaissance. Until this time, most literature was written in Medieval Latin. To reach a wider audience, writers began to use the language they spoke every day instead of Latin or French, the language of the educated. So, **Geoffrey Chaucer** wrote *The Canterbury Tales* and **William Shakespeare** wrote plays such as *Hamlet* and *Romeo and Juliet* in English. **Miguel de Cervantes** wrote his novel *Don Quixote* in Spanish.

These works were reproduced in many copies for the first time by the printing press, which was invented by **Johannes Gutenberg** around 1450. While the Chinese had developed a printing process, Gutenberg introduced the idea of movable type. He has been called the "father of printing in the Western world." The printing press made books more numerous and less expensive, thereby encouraging more people to learn to read and write.

Nationhood During the Renaissance, western European rulers became more powerful. They used their power to unite their countries, creating nations based on a common language and culture. England was strengthened by the first Tudor king, Henry VII and his famous granddaughter Elizabeth I. King Ferdinand and Queen Isabella united Spain by driving out the last of the Muslims and Jews. By the 1450s, the kings of France finally liberated their country from the English.

✓ Reading Check **How did the printing press make it easier for people to learn to read and write?**

The Protestant Reformation

Many of the new ideas given birth in the Renaissance led to questions about religion. Some people believed that Church leaders were more interested in wealth than religion. Others disagreed with corrupt practices of the Church. One of these practices was selling of documents called **indulgences,** which freed their owners of punishment for sins they had committed. Because these Christians "protested" Catholic teachings, they came to be called **Protestants.** The movement to **reform,** or change, the Catholic Church was called the **Protestant Reformation.**

Team-Teaching Activity

Graphic Arts Until the invention of photocopying, the process of printing was largely unchanged from the days of Gutenberg. Although it has been mechanized, printing still involves transferring ink from raised letters or an image onto paper. Ask a graphic arts teacher to come to class to discuss and demonstrate how books, brochures, pictures, and posters are produced. Ask the teacher to discuss what natural resources the process uses. Ask students to think of the different ways they use printed materials.

EE5 Environment and Society: Standard 14

One of first Protestant leaders to challenge the Catholic Church was **Martin Luther,** a German monk and scholar. In 1520, the pope banished Luther from the Catholic Church for his criticism. Luther organized his own new Christian church, which taught in German, not Latin, from a Bible that Luther himself had translated into German. This split between the Catholics and Protestants led to many long years of religious wars in Europe.

Another early Protestant leader was **John Calvin.** His followers in France were called Huguenots, and in England they were called Puritans. Many came to the Protestant cause seeking not only greater religious freedom, but also political, economic, and intellectual freedom. The Puritans eventually sought freedom in the Americas to practice their own religion.

✓Reading Check **What was the Protestant Reformation?**

The Age of Exploration

By the mid-1400s, Europe began to reach out beyond its boundaries in a great age of discovery and exploration. The Portuguese began to sail southward in the Atlantic, down the West African coast, seeking a way to the profitable spice trade in Asia. In 1488, **Bartholomeu Dias** reached the Cape of Good Hope at the southern tip of Africa. Ten years later, **Vasco da Gama** sailed around it to India.

While the Portuguese were searching for a way around Africa, King Ferdinand and Queen Isabella of Spain were trying to find another way to Asia. In 1492, they sent an Italian navigator, **Christopher Columbus,** with three small ships—the *Niña,* the *Pinta,* and the *Santa María*—westward across the Atlantic. Although he never realized it himself, Columbus had landed in a part of the world unknown to Europeans at that time. He called its people "Indians" because he believed he had sailed to the East Indies in Asia.

▲ **The Pope acts as money changer while selling indulgences.**

The Dutch, English, and French soon joined the Spanish and Portuguese in exploring and settling and trading with the Americas, Asia, and Africa. Eventually—in addition to trade goods—people, diseases, and ideas were distributed around the world in a process called the **Columbian Exchange.** Europeans unknowingly brought to the Americas diseases such as measles and small pox, which infected and killed millions of Native Americans. These natives had been used as laborers on plantations and in mines. In their place, traders eventually transported more than 20 million Africans to the Americas as enslaved persons, until the slave trade was outlawed in the early 1800s.

✓Reading Check **Which European nation first began exploration around the coast of Africa?**

Revolution

A **revolution** is a great and often violent change. In the Americas, the colonies won freedom from their European mother countries. In Europe, the people fought for freedom from their kings, queens, and nobles.

Chapter 9

Section 3, pages 245–249

✓ Reading Check Answer

The movement to reform, or change, the Catholic Church.

Interdisciplinary Connections

Religion Martin Luther dealt the symbolic blow that began the Reformation when he nailed his Ninety-Five Theses to the door of the Wittenberg Church. That document contained an attack on papal abuses and the sale of indulgences by church officials. Luther defended his position before the Emperor at the Diet of Worms and when asked to recant his views was said to have replied "Here I stand. I cannot do otherwise."

✓ Reading Check Answer

Portugal

ASSESS

Assign Section 3 Assessment as homework or an in-class activity.

Have students use the Interactive Tutor Self-Assessment CD-ROM to review Section 9–3.

Content Background

Christopher Columbus Few people thought the world was flat when Columbus set out on his voyage for India. What was in doubt was the exact circumference of the earth and, therefore, the westward distance from Europe to India. Columbus relied on thousand-year-old maps made by Ptolemy that both underestimated the earth's diameter and overestimated the eastward extent of Asia. This had the effect of making the westward distance from Europe to Asia seem much smaller than it actually is and made Columbus believe, erroneously, that India could be reached by sailing west. This has to be one of the most monumental "errors" in history. Have students use a globe to trace Columbus's voyage from Spain to the Americas. Then have them analyze the path he would have needed to take in order to reach Asia.

Literature

The Scarlet Pimpernel was written in 1905, more than 100 years after the events it describes. It tells of a brave band of Englishmen who risk their lives to rescue the intended victims of the guillotine. Their leader is an enigmatic hero known only by his calling card: the red, star-shaped wildflower known as the Scarlet Pimpernel.

Answer These questions can be used to start a class discussion on the roles and motives of people during revolutions. Not everyone is involved in the conflict, and not everyone involved is motivated by revolutionary zeal.

Section Quiz 9-3

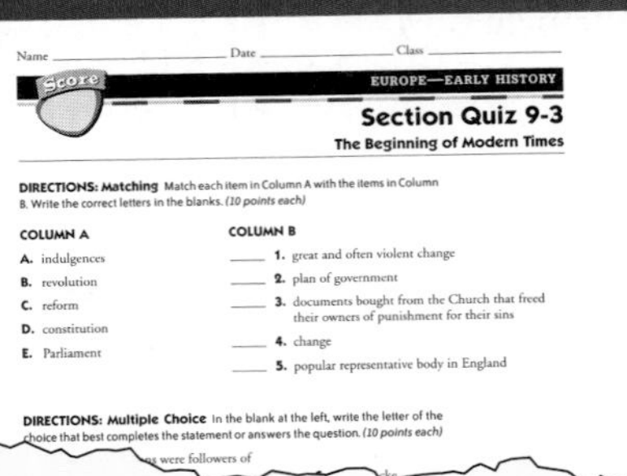

Name ____________ Date ____________ Class ____________

Score

EUROPE—EARLY HISTORY

Section Quiz 9-3

The Beginning of Modern Times

DIRECTIONS: Matching Match each item in Column A with the items in Column B. Write the correct letters in the blanks. *(10 points each)*

COLUMN A	COLUMN B
A. indulgences	____ **1.** great and often violent change
B. revolution	____ **2.** plan of government
C. reform	____ **3.** documents bought from the Church that freed their owners of punishment for their sins
D. constitution	____ **4.** change
E. Parliament	____ **5.** popular representative body in England

DIRECTIONS: Multiple Choice In the blank at the left, write the letter of the choice that best completes the statement or answers the question. *(10 points each)*

The Rule of the People The eighteenth century ended with great changes to Europe and many of its American colonies. The belief in the **divine right of kings**—that European kings and queens ruled by the will of God—was fading. In learning about the examples from ancient Greece and Rome, people came to feel that they should play a greater, more direct role in government. Philosophers such as **John Locke** and **Jean Jacques Rousseau** looked at the nature of man and government. They believed that government should serve them and protect them and their freedom. However, this also meant that they had to take more responsibility for themselves and their own actions.

British Democracy In some cases, revolutionary changes came more peacefully than in others. Over many centuries, Britain had slowly developed a system of shared power and responsibility. The king ruled with the **Parliament,** a popular representative body that gradually took power in the name of the people. Eventually, British kings and queens were forced to accept a **constitution,** a plan for government that shared power but gave most of it to the Parliament.

Literature

THE SCARLET PIMPERNEL

by Baroness Orczy

During and after the French Revolution, many nobles were executed by the lower classes that had rebelled against them. The number of these executions shocked the people of Europe. *The Scarlet Pimpernel* is a novel about an English nobleman who helps aristocrats escape from France. The hero—as true heroes will—minimizes his heroic actions.

"It had all occurred in such a miraculous way. She and her husband had understood that they had been placed on the list of 'suspected persons,' which meant that their trial and death was but a matter of days—of hours, perhaps. Then came the hope of salvation: the mysterious [letter], signed with the scarlet device; . . . the flight with her two children; the covered cart; . . . Every moment under that cart she expected recognition, arrest. [These young Englishmen] . . . had risked their lives to save them all, as they had already saved scores of other innocent people. And all only for sport? Impossible! . . . she thought that he . . . rescued his fellow-men from terrible and unmerited death, through a higher and nobler motive than his friend would have her believe."

Source: Baroness Orczy. *The Scarlet Pimpernel.* Doubleday and Company, Inc., 1961.

Analyzing Literature

Do you think that the Scarlet Pimpernel's actions were really just for sport? Why or why not? Do you think they were right to try to save the French nobility? Would you?

Meeting Special Needs

Visual/Spatial To reinforce the verbal descriptions in this chapter, have students collect pictures and photographs that illustrate the cultures and events described. They can clip pictures from travel brochures or magazines, can make copies from books, or can download images from the Internet. Organize the students into groups and give each group a selection of pictures. Have the groups discuss each picture and determine what it depicts and what time period it illustrates.

Democracy in the Americas In the 1770s, the American colonies, beginning with the thirteen British colonies in North America, revolted against British control. The new United States, its **Declaration of Independence, Constitution,** and representative Congress, became a model for many of these revolutions. By the 1830s, most of the Spanish, Portuguese, and British colonies in the Americas south of Canada had also gained their independence.

The French Revolution In the 1780s, revolution erupted in Europe as well, starting with France. The **French Revolution** began in 1789 and went through several stages. When King Louis XVI and Queen Marie Antoinette opposed the new French constitution that limited their powers, they were executed. By 1799, **Napoleon Bonaparte**—a military hero of the French Revolution—became the dictator, the absolute leader, of France. He declared himself emperor of a new French Empire in 1803. Eventually, people almost everywhere in Europe reacted against Napoleon and went to war against France. Napoleon was finally defeated in 1815.

The revolution in France stimulated Latin Americans and other European peoples to demand more personal and political control over their lives. Countries such as Greece, Belgium, Italy, and Germany also experienced revolutions.

✓Reading Check **How was the growth of democracy in Britain different from that in France?**

Assessment

Defining Terms

1. **Define** indulgences, Protestant, reform, Columbian Exchange, revolution, divine right of kings, Parliament, constitution.

Recalling Facts

2. **History** What was the movement to reform the Catholic Church called?
3. **People** Who is known as the "father of printing in the Western world"?

Critical Thinking

4. **Examining Results** Describe the effects of the process called the Columbian Exchange.
5. **Making Connections** How might a revolution in one country encourage political changes around the world?

Graphic Organizer

6. **Identifying People** Create a table like the one below. In the right column, write what each individual is historically recognized for.

Person	Historical Recognition
Michelangelo	
Johannes Gutenberg	
Martin Luther	
Christopher Columbus	
Napoleon Bonaparte	

Applying Social Studies Skills

7. **Identifying** Why do you suppose the period known as the Renaissance was considered a "rebirth"?

Section 3 Assessment

1. The terms are defined in the Glossary.
2. the Reformation
3. Johannes Gutenberg
4. Native Americans were killed and to replace their labor, Africans were brought to America as slaves.
5. The success of revolutionaries in one country may encourage revolutionary changes elsewhere.
6. *Michelangelo:* Renaissance Art; *Johannes Gutenberg:* Printing Press; *Martin Luther:* Protestant Reformation; *Christopher Columbus:* sailing to the Americas; *Napoleon Bonaparte:* French Empire
7. Interest in arts, science, and culture were "reborn" after being in decline during the Middle Ages.

Cultural Kaleidoscope

Great Britain does not celebrate an Independence Day like the Fourth of July. However, Guy Fawkes Day, November 5, is celebrated in England with fireworks and bonfires. It marks the anniversary of an unsuccessful plot to blow up the British parliament.

Reading Essentials and Study Guide 9-3

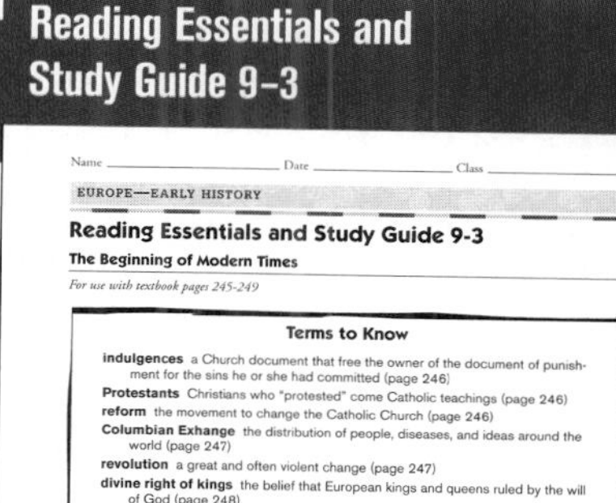
Name ______ Date ______ Class ______

EUROPE—EARLY HISTORY

Reading Essentials and Study Guide 9-3

The Beginning of Modern Times

For use with textbook pages 245-249

Terms to Know

indulgences a Church document that free the owner of the document of punishment for the sins he or she had committed (page 246)
Protestants Christians who "protested" come Catholic teachings (page 246)
reform the movement to change the Catholic Church (page 246)
Columbian Exhange the distribution of people, diseases, and ideas around the world (page 247)
revolution a great and often violent change (page 247)
divine right of kings the belief that European kings and queens ruled by the will of God (page 248)
Parliament a popular representative body that gradually took power in the name of the people (page 248)
ent that shared power, but gave most o it to the

✓ Reading Check Answer

In Great Britain the change occurred more peacefully and over a long period of time.

Close

Have students create a three-column chart with the headings "Renaissance," "Reform," and "Revolution." Have them fill in the chart with important events and people from this section.

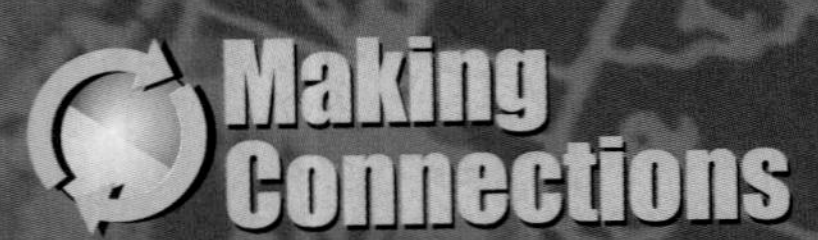

Making Connections

CULTURE | GOVERNMENT | PEOPLE | TECHNOLOGY

Leonardo da Vinci

The Italian Leonardo da Vinci is considered one of the greatest artists of the Renaissance. He painted the *Mona Lisa* and the *Last Supper*, two of the world's best-known paintings. He was also a talented architect, engineer, and inventor.

The Artist

Leonardo da Vinci was born in 1452 in a small town near Florence, Italy. As the son of a wealthy man, he received the best education that Florence could offer. Leonardo became known for his ability to create sculptures and paintings that looked almost lifelike. Much of his success in this area came from his keen interest in nature. He also studied human anatomy and used this knowledge to make his figures realistic.

The Inventor

As a child, Leonardo was fascinated with machines and began to draw his own inventions. The first successful parachute jump was made from the top of a French tower in 1783—but Leonardo had sketched a parachute in 1485. He designed flying machines, armored tanks, and aircraft landing gear. He even drew a diver's suit that used tubes and air chambers to allow a swimmer to remain underwater for long periods of time.

Leonardo's Notebooks

Much of what we know about Leonardo comes from the thousands of pages of notes and sketches he kept in his notebooks. He used mirror, or reverse, writing, starting at the right side of the page and moving across to the left. No one is sure why Leonardo wrote this way. Some think he was trying to keep people from reading and stealing his ideas. He may also have been trying to hide his thoughts from the Roman Catholic Church, whose teachings sometimes conflicted with his ideas. From a practical standpoint, writing in reverse probably helped him avoid smearing wet ink, since he was left-handed.

▲ Leonardo da Vinci

▲ The *Mona Lisa*

Making the Connection

1. What are two of Leonardo's best-known works?
2. Why might Leonardo have written his notebooks in mirror writing?
3. **Understanding Cause and Effect** In what way did Leonardo's interest in the world around him influence his work?

Teach

Ask students if they have ever heard the phrase "Renaissance person." Explain that the words refer to someone who has talents and interests in many different areas. **Ask: Can you think of anyone to whom this term could be applied? Why? L1**

More About Leonardo

One of Leonardo's works was completed 500 years late. In 1482 Leonardo designed an equestrian statue for his patron, the duke of Milan. Soon after, the French invaded the city, and Leonardo had to abandon the work. In the 1970s, an American art collector decided to create the statue as a tribute to him. The final piece, a bronze horse that stands 24 feet (7 m) high and was based on Leonardo's designs, was completed in September 1999 in Milan.

Interdisciplinary Connections

Art One of the hallmarks of Renaissance painting is the use of linear perspective to create the illusion of three dimensions. Architect Filippo Brunelleschi developed the first principles of perspective in the early 1400s. Show some examples of medieval and Renaissance art so that students can see the contrast.

Making the Connection

1. the *Mona Lisa* and the *Last Supper*
2. perhaps to keep others from stealing his ideas, to hide them from the Church, or to keep the pages neat and unsoiled by smeared ink
3. He used knowledge gained from his study of nature to make his paintings more realistic.

Reading Review

Section 1 Classical Europe

Terms to Know
classical
polis
democracy
philosophy
republic
consuls
Senate
emperor

Main Idea

Ancient Greece and Rome made important contributions to Western culture and civilization.

✓ Government The world's first democratic constitution was written in Athens.
✓ History Alexander the Great conquered all of Greece.
✓ History Rome grew from Republic to Empire.
✓ Religion Christianity spread over the Roman world.
✓ History The Roman Empire was invaded by Germanic peoples and declined.

Section 2 Medieval Europe

Terms to Know
bishop
pope
missionary
monastery
convent
common law
feudalism
vassal
manor
tenant
serf
guild
apprentice
charter

Main Idea

The Middle Ages saw the spread of Christianity, the growth of cities, and the growing powers of kings.

✓ Religion The Roman Catholic Church became a political power in western Europe.
✓ History The first Christian Bible was completed by A.D. 500.
✓ History Charlemagne was crowned head of the Roman Empire in the West and proclaimed Protector of the Christian Church in the West.
✓ Government Feudalism was the medieval political and social system.

Section 3 The Beginning of Modern Times

Terms to Know
indulgences
Protestant
reform
Columbian Exchange
revolution
divine right of kings
Parliament
constitution

Main Idea

The study of science, art, and education was renewed in the period following the Middle Ages.

✓ Culture Important cultural achievements in the arts and learning spread throughout Europe in the period known as the Renaissance.
✓ History Johannes Gutenberg invented the printing press.
✓ Government Countries formed into nations based on a common language and culture.
✓ Religion The Protestant faith emerged in protest to the Roman Catholic Church.
✓ History Christopher Columbus set sail across the Atlantic.
✓ Government Revolution erupted in the Americas and Europe.

Reading Review

Use the Chapter 9 Reading Review to preview, review, condense, or reteach the chapter.

Preview/Review

Use the Terms to Know lists to help students review and study.

Activity Have students identify the time period for which each term is relevant. Read the terms aloud, one at a time, and ask for volunteers to categorize each. Note that some terms may apply to more than one country.

Vocabulary PuzzleMaker Software reinforces the vocabulary terms used in Chapter 9.

The Interactive Tutor Self-Assessment CD-ROM allows students to review Chapter 9 content.

Condense

Have students read the Chapter 9 summary statements.

Chapter 9 Guided Reading Activities

Chapter 9 Audio Program

Reteach

Reteaching Activity 9

Chapter 9 Reading Essentials and Study Guide

Chapter Culminating Activity

Travel Brochure Tell students to imagine they work for the 'U-R-There' time-travel agency. Have them create a four-page travel brochure that highlights the attractions for one of the periods in this chapter. Explain that the travel brochure should include both physical and cultural features that visitors would want to see. Advise students that an effective brochure includes appealing visuals as well as brief, engaging text. *NOTE: This activity may be completed separately or you may wish students to incorporate it into their Current Events Journals.*

EE2 Places and Regions: Standard 6

Assessment and Activities

GLENCOE TECHNOLOGY

MindJogger Videoquiz
Use MindJogger to review the Chapter 9 content.

Available in VHS.

Using Key Terms

1.	e	6.	b
2.	a	7.	j
3.	d	8.	h
4.	f	9.	g
5.	c	10.	i

Reviewing the Main Ideas

11. Greece
12. Philip II and his son, Alexander the Great
13. Christianity
14. various groups of German peoples
15. Roman Catholic Church
16. Vassals were knights or nobles who received land and swore loyalty to a lord; serfs were poor farmers who in return for use of land, seeds, tools, and protection had to work as ordered by the lords of the manor.
17. feudalism
18. a printing press with movable type
19. Protestants
20. being the first to "discover" America
21. in the Americas and in Europe

Critical Thinking

22. Answers may include: the beginnings of our political system can be traced to Greece, the Greeks developed the first democratic constitution, republican government and codified law developed in Rome, and Greece and Rome developed art, philosophy, and an alphabet.
23. The power of the state and the church were combined in one person so there were no checks on abuse.

Chapter 9 Assessment and Activities

Using Key Terms

Match the terms in Part A with their definitions in Part B.

A.

1. emperor
2. common law
3. feudalism
4. apprentice
5. indulgences
6. Protestants
7. polis
8. philosophy
9. missionary
10. guild

B.

a. unwritten laws from customs
b. "protested" Catholic teachings
c. freed owners from punishment for sins
d. medieval political and social system
e. absolute ruler
f. young worker learning a trade
g. teacher of Christianity
h. "love of wisdom"
i. workers' organization
j. city-state

Reviewing the Main Ideas

Section 1 Classical Europe

11. **Government** Where was the first democratic constitution written?
12. **History** Who conquered all of Greece?
13. **Religion** Which religion spread all over the Roman world?
14. **History** Who invaded the Roman Empire?

Section 2 Medieval Europe

15. **Religion** Which religious group became a political power in western Europe?
16. **Economics** Explain the difference between vassals and serfs.
17. **Government** Name the political and social system in medieval Europe.

Section 3 The Beginning of Modern Times

18. **History** What did Johannes Gutenberg invent?
19. **Religion** Which faith emerged out of protest to the Catholic Church?
20. **History** What is Christopher Columbus historically known for?
21. **Government** Where were revolutions taking place?

Classical Europe

Place Location Activity

On a separate sheet of paper, match the letters on the map with the numbered places listed below.

1. Alexandria
2. Macedonia
3. Mediterranean Sea
4. Constantinople
5. Black Sea
6. Greece
7. Athens
8. Rome
9. Tiber River
10. Sparta

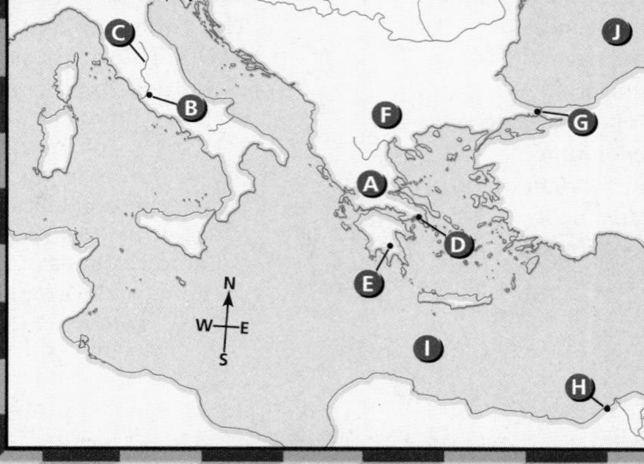

NATIONAL GEOGRAPHIC Place Location Activity

1.	H	6.	A
2.	F	7.	D
3.	I	8.	B
4.	G	9.	C
5.	J	10.	E

Self-Check Quiz Visit the ***Our World Today: People, Places, and Issues*** Web site at owt.glencoe.com and click on **Chapter 9–Self-Check Quizzes** to prepare for the Chapter Test.

Critical Thinking

22. **Making Connections** In what ways have our political and social lives today been influenced by ancient Greek and Roman customs?
23. **Drawing Conclusions** Eastern Orthodoxy was ruled by emperors rather than by popes. This made the emperors very powerful. What kinds of problems might have occurred because of this?

Current Events Journal

24. **Writing a Paragraph** Imagine that you are the writer of a tourism book for France. Write a short paragraph describing the cathedral on page 241. Use the information provided in the beginning of Section 2 of this chapter.

Mental Mapping Activity

25. **Identifying People and Places** Create a simple outline map of Europe that includes Germany, Italy, France, Rome, and Greece. Place the letter of the individual's name next to the place from which he originated.

- a. Michelangelo Buonarotti
- b. Alexander the Great
- c. Julius Caesar
- d. Socrates
- e. Charlemagne
- f. Leonardo da Vinci
- g. Christopher Columbus
- h. Napoleon Bonaparte
- i. Martin Luther
- j. Plato

Technology Skills Activity

26. **Using the Internet** Search the Internet for information on the Twelve Tables of Roman law. After reading about the laws, note the ones that you strongly agree or disagree with and tell why. For example, tablet 4 states that "a dreadfully deformed child shall be quickly killed." In our society, this is obviously illegal and inhumane.

The Princeton Review

Standardized Test Practice

Directions: Read the paragraphs below, and then answer the question that follows.

The ancient Greeks held the Olympic Games in Olympia every four years. The games were a religious festival in honor of Zeus, the Greeks' chief god. Trading and wars stopped while the games took place. The first Greek calendar began with the supposed date of the first Olympic Games in 776 B.C.

Athletes came from all over the Greek-speaking world to compete. Only male athletes, however, were allowed to take part, and women were not permitted even as spectators. Olympic events at first consisted only of a footrace. Later the broad jump, the discus throw, boxing, and wrestling were added. The Greeks crowned Olympic winners with wreaths of olive leaves and held parades in their honor.

1. **From the paragraphs, which of the following statements about Greek culture is NOT correct?**
   - **F** The Greeks valued individual achievements.
   - **G** The Greeks believed in many gods.
   - **H** The Greeks believed in being healthy.
   - **J** The Greeks discouraged individual glory.

Test-Taking Tip: Read all the choices carefully before choosing the one that does NOT describe Greek culture. Eliminate answers that you know are incorrect. For example, all the Olympic events were performed by individuals, not by teams. Therefore, answer F does describe Greek culture. The question, however, is asking for the statement that does NOT describe Greek culture.

253

Assessment and Activities

Standardized Test Practice

1. J

Tested Objectives:
Analyzing information, synthesizing information

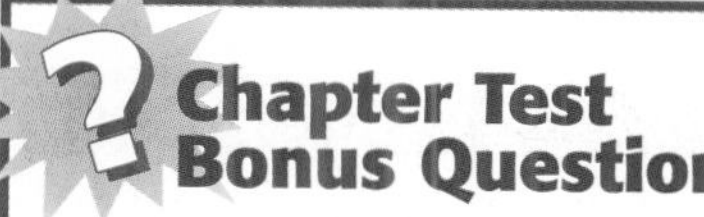

This question may be used for extra credit on the chapter test.

The revolution in this country began in 1789 and stimulated revolutionary change in Latin America and Europe.

What country is it? *(France)*

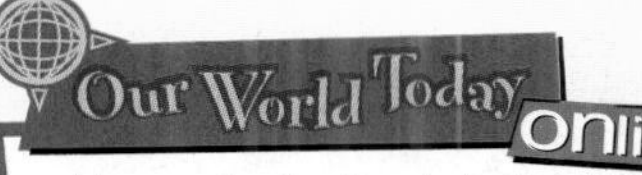

Have students visit the Web site at **owt.glencoe.com** to review Chapter 9 and take the Self-Check Quiz.

Current Events Journal

24. Ask volunteers to share their paragraphs. Have students discuss what they thought was important to include for a tourism book and why.

Mental Mapping Activity

25. This exercise helps students visualize the areas they have been studying and how cultures interacted to spread new ideas and achievements. Accept all reasonable attempts at freehand mapping that show locations and relations.

Technology Skills Activity

26. Students' answers will vary. They should compare Roman law to the laws or accepted norms of today.

Chapter 10 Resources

Note: The following materials may be used when teaching Chapter 10.
Section level support materials are shown at point of use in the margins of the Teacher Wraparound Edition.

Timesaving Tools

TeacherWorks™ All-In-One Planner and Resource Center

- **Interactive Teacher Edition** See the **Interactive Teacher Edition** CD-ROM to electronically integrate your Teacher Wraparound Edition and blackline masters.
- **Interactive Lesson Planner** Organize your week, month, semester, or year with all the lesson helps you need. The **Interactive Lesson Planner** CD-ROM contains all Chapter 10 resources.

Use Glencoe's **Presentation Plus!** multimedia teacher tool to easily present dynamic lessons that visually excite your students. Using Microsoft PowerPoint® you can customize the presentations to create your own personalized lessons.

TEACHING TRANSPARENCIES

Graphic Organizer Transparency and Student Activity 10

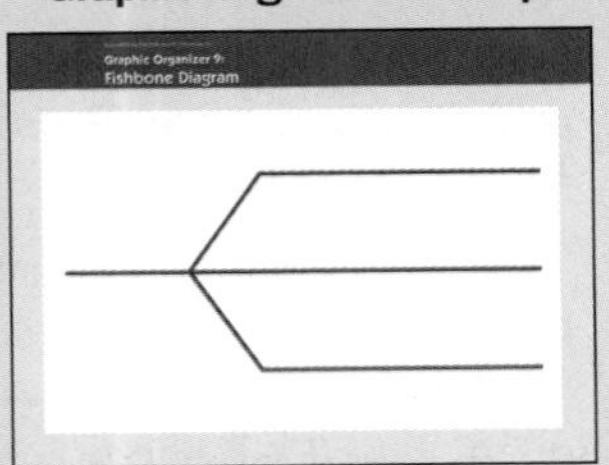

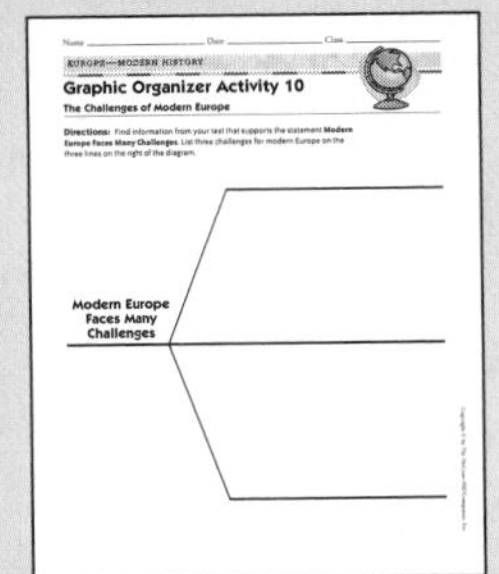

FOLDABLES™ Study Organizer

Foldables are three-dimensional, interactive graphic organizers that help students practice basic writing skills, review key vocabulary terms, and identify main ideas. Every chapter contains a Foldable activity, with additional chapter activities found in the ***Reading and Study Skills Foldables*** booklet.

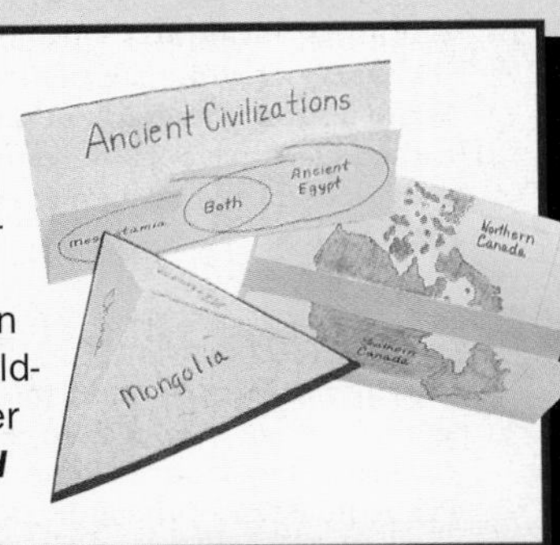

ENRICHMENT AND EXTENSION

Enrichment Activity 10

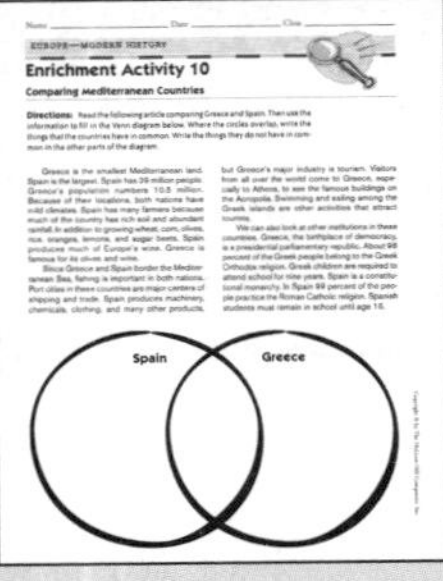

Cooperative Learning Activity 10

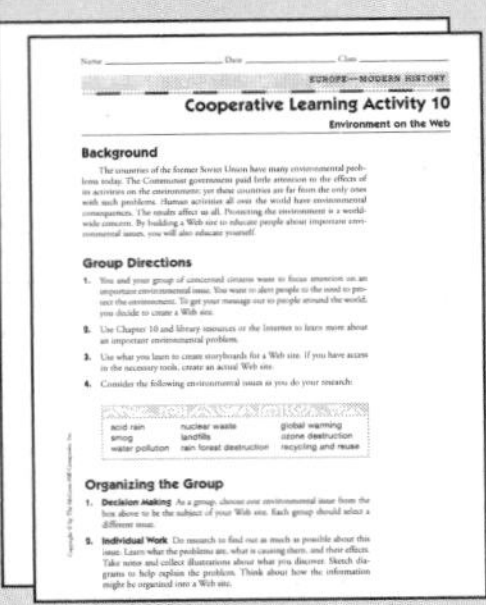

MAP AND GEOGRAPHY SKILLS

Chapter Map Activity 10

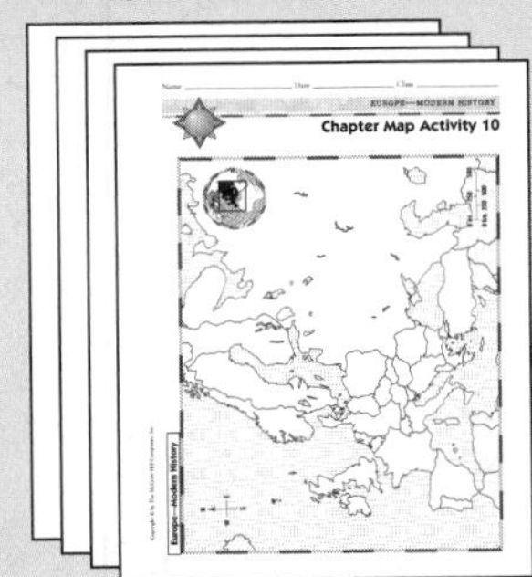

GeoLab Activity 10

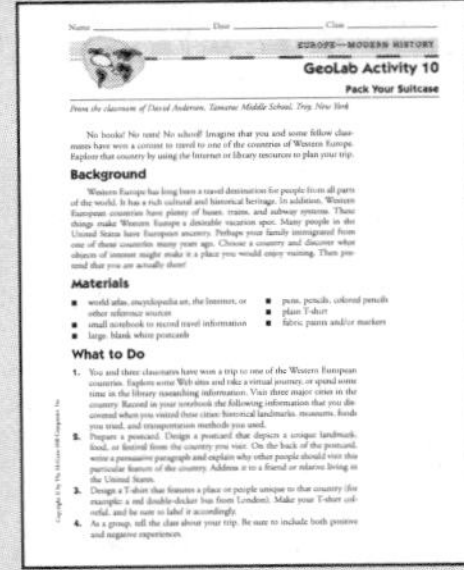

STANDARDIZED ASSESSMENT SKILLS

GLENCOE'S ASSESSMENT ADVANTAGE

Critical Thinking Skills Activity 10

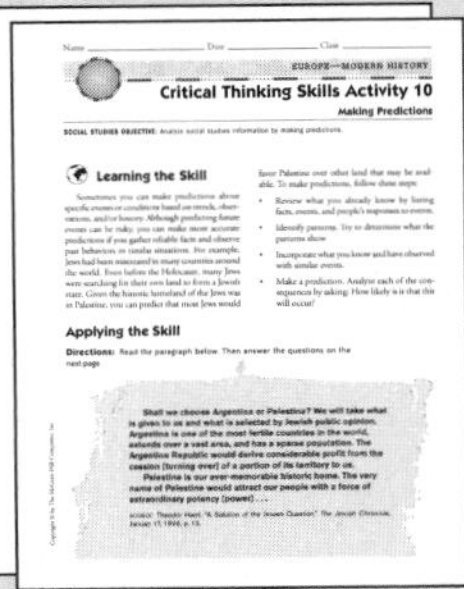

Map and Graph Skills Activity 10

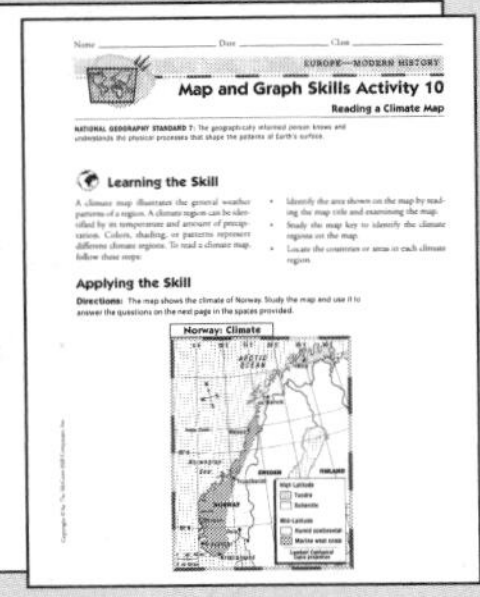

Reading and Writing Skills Activity 10

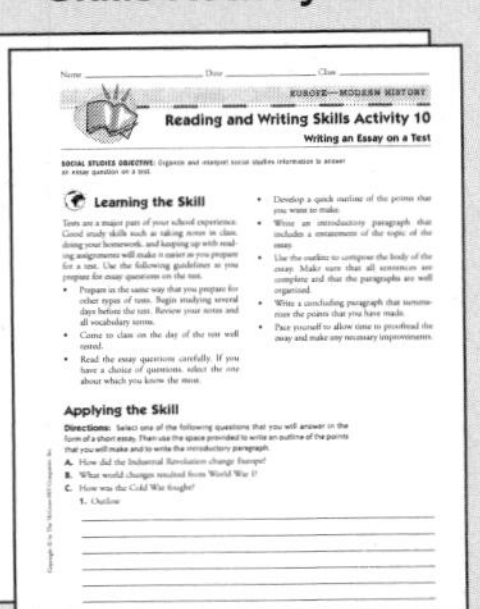

Standardized Test Practice Workbook Activity 10

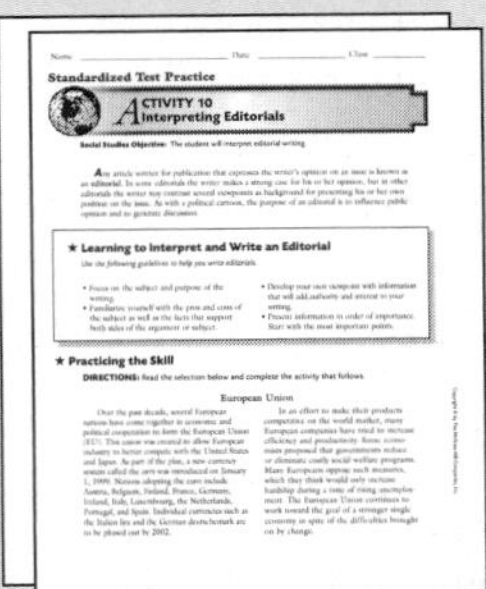

REVIEW AND REINFORCEMENT

Chapter Skills Activity 10

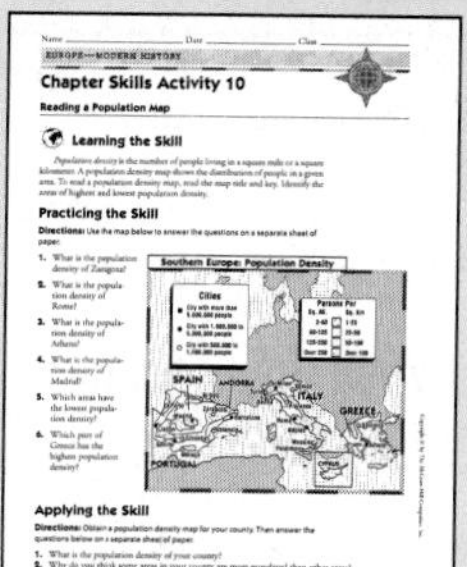

Take-Home Review Activity 10

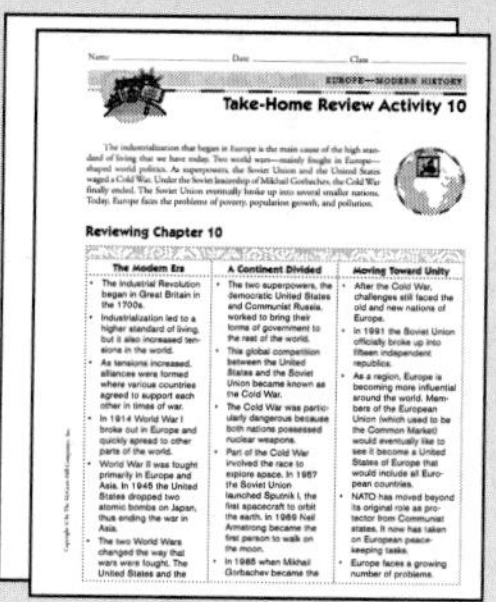

Reteaching Activity 10

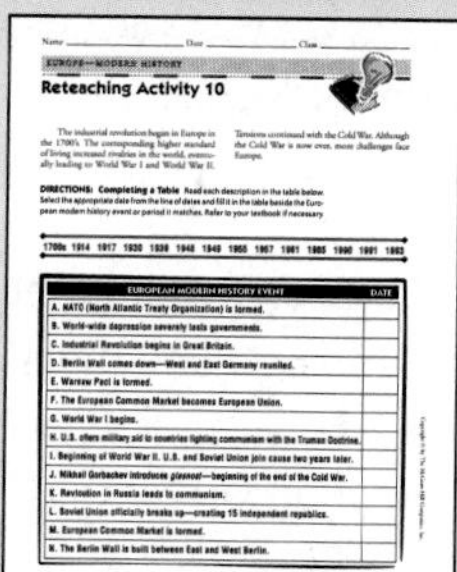

Vocabulary Activity 10

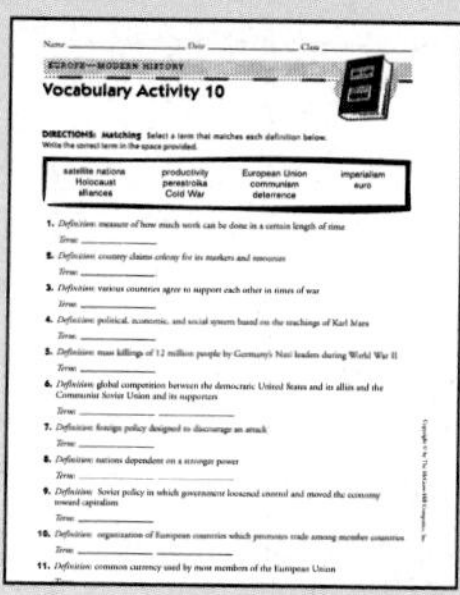

Workbook Activity 10

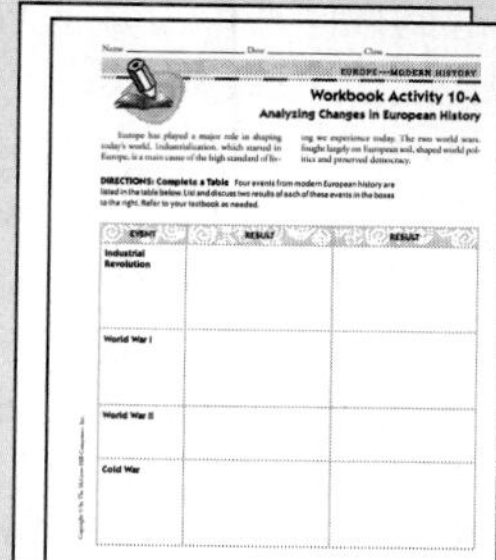

ASSESSMENT

Chapter 10 Test, Form A

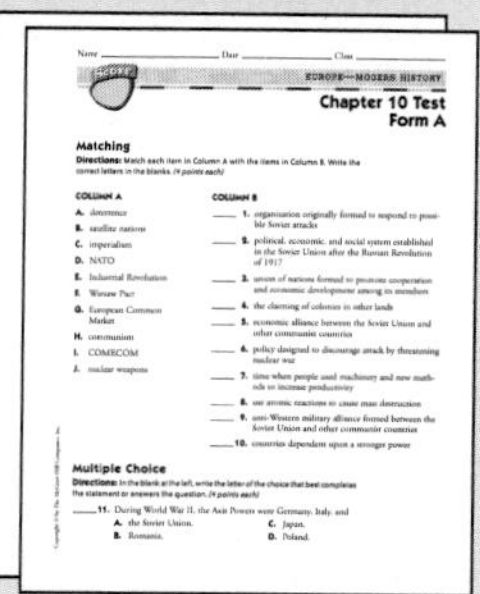

Chapter 10 Test, Form B

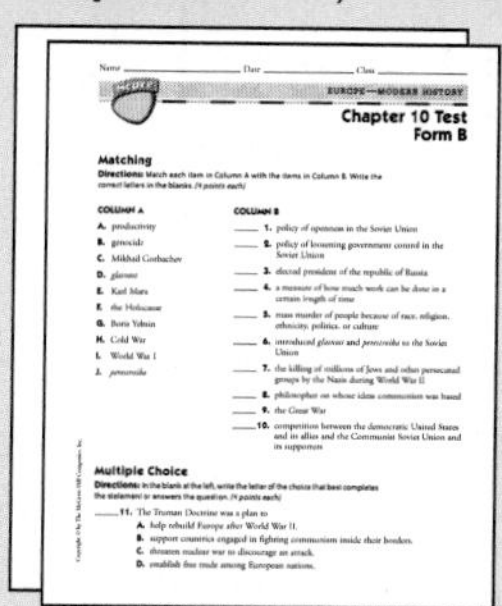

Performance Assessment Activity 10

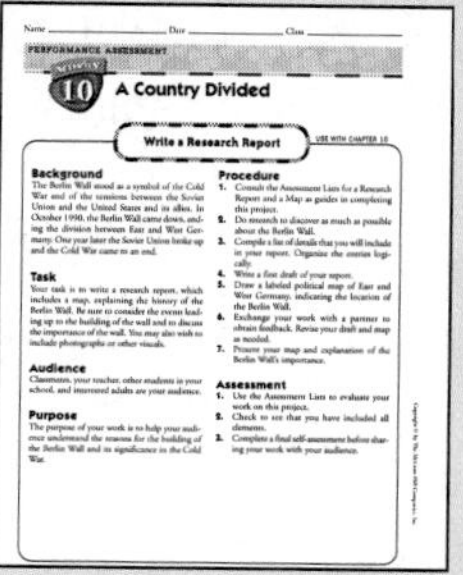

ExamView® Pro 3.0 Testmaker CD-ROM

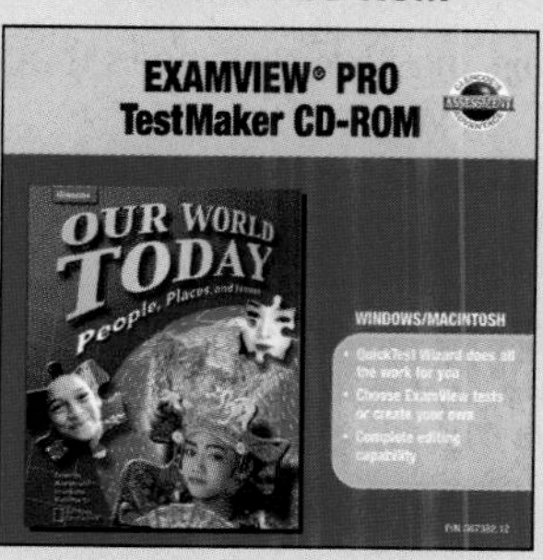

MULTIMEDIA

- National Geographic's The World and Its People
- MindJogger Videoquiz
- Vocabulary PuzzleMaker Software
- Interactive Tutor Self-Assessment CD-ROM
- ExamView® Pro 3.0 Testmaker CD-ROM
- Interactive Lesson Planner CD-ROM
- Interactive Teacher Edition CD-ROM
- Skillbuilder Interactive Workbook CD-ROM, Level 1
- Presentation Plus! CD-ROM
- Audio Program

SPANISH RESOURCES

The following Spanish language materials are available in the Spanish Resources binder:

- Spanish Chapter Summaries
- Spanish Vocabulary Activities
- Spanish Guided Reading Activities
- Spanish Quizzes and Tests
- Spanish Take-Home Review Activities
- Spanish Reteaching Activities

Meeting National Standards

Geography for Life

All of the 18 standards are demonstrated in Unit 4. The following ones are highlighted in Chapter 10:

Section 1 EE4 Human Systems: Standards 12, 13
EE5 Environment and Society: Standard 14, 15, 16

Section 2 EE2 Places and Regions: Standards 4, 5, 6
EE6 The Uses of Geography: Standards 17, 18

Section 3 EE1 The World in Spatial Terms: Standards 1, 2, 3
EE3 Physical Systems: Standards 7, 8
EE6 The Uses of Geography: Standards 17, 18

For a complete listing of National Geography Standards and entire text correlation, see pages T22–T29.

Chapter 10 Planning Guide

SECTION RESOURCES

Daily Objectives	Reproducible Resources	Multimedia Resources
Section 1 **The Modern Era** **Suggested Pacing = 1 day** **1.** Discuss the Industrial Revolution and the social changes it created. **2.** Explain how industrialization created new rivalries between European countries. **3.** Explain how the two World Wars changed the balance of power in the world.	Reproducible Lesson Plan 10-1 Daily Lecture and Discussion Notes 10-1 Guided Reading Activity 10-1 Reading Essentials and Study Guide 10-1 Section Quiz 10-1*	Daily Focus Skills Transparency 10-1 Vocabulary PuzzleMaker Software Interactive Tutor Self-Assessment CD-ROM ExamView® Pro 3.0 Testmaker CD-ROM Presentation Plus! CD-ROM
Section 2 **A Continent Divided** **Suggested Pacing = 1 day** **1.** Explain the circumstances that created the Cold War. **2.** Discuss the events that led to the end of the Cold War.	Reproducible Lesson Plan 10-2 Daily Lecture and Discussion Notes 10-2 Guided Reading Activity 10-2 Reading Essentials and Study Guide 10-2 Section Quiz 10-2*	Daily Focus Skills Transparency 10-2 Vocabulary PuzzleMaker Software Interactive Tutor Self-Assessment CD-ROM ExamView® Pro 3.0 Testmaker CD-ROM Presentation Plus! CD-ROM
Section 3 **Moving Toward Unity** **Suggested Pacing = 1 day** **1.** Discuss the outcome of the breakup of the Soviet Union. **2.** Explain how Europe has become more united. **3.** Explain the problems facing Europe today.	Reproducible Lesson Plan 10-3 Daily Lecture and Discussion Notes 10-3 Guided Reading Activity 10-3 Reading Essentials and Study Guide 10-3 Section Quiz 10-3*	Daily Focus Skills Transparency 10-3 Vocabulary PuzzleMaker Software Interactive Tutor Self-Assessment CD-ROM ExamView® Pro 3.0 Testmaker CD-ROM Presentation Plus! CD-ROM

00:00 **Out of Time?** Assign the **Reading Essentials and Study Guide** for this chapter.

*Also available in Spanish

KEY TO ABILITY LEVELS

Teaching strategies have been coded for varying learning styles and abilities.

L1 **BASIC** activities for all students
L2 **AVERAGE** activities for average to above-average students
L3 **CHALLENGING** activities for above-average students
ELL **ENGLISH LANGUAGE LEARNER** activities

Blackline Master
Software
CD-ROM
Audiocassette
Transparency
Videocassette
Block Scheduling
DVD

Passport Portfolios

Kristine Louise Edwards
Dodge Intermediate School
Twinsburg, Ohio

Create a contract for students to work independently on preparing a "portfolio" of a selected country. Assign points for each of the following activities they complete: (A) Utilize five resources for research=10 points. (B) Make a landforms map of your selected country=15 points. (C) Design a portfolio cover with the selected country's flag=5 points. (D) Create a Venn diagram comparing the culture of the selected country with that of the United States=15 points. (E) Orally present an art project, music, or recipe from your selected country=25 points. (F) Complete a written report on your selected country=30 points. Then have students share their portfolios with one another.

OUR WORLD TODAY Online

Use our Web site for additional resources. All essential content is covered in the Student Edition.

You and your students can visit owt.glencoe.com, the Web site companion to *Our World Today*. This innovative integration of electronic and print media offers your students a wealth of opportunities. The student text directs students to the Web site for the following options:

- Chapter Overviews
- Student Web Activities
- Self-Check Quizzes
- Textbook Updates

Answers are provided for you in the Web Activity Lesson Plan. Additional Web resources and Interactive Tutor puzzles are also available.

NATIONAL GEOGRAPHIC TEACHER'S CORNER

Index to National Geographic Magazine:

The following articles may be used for research relating to this chapter:

- "In Search of Vikings," by Priit J. Vesilind, May 2000.
- "Mystery Ships From a Danish Bog," by Michael Klesius, May 2000.
- "Civilized Denmark," by Garrison Keillor, July 1998.
- "Iceland's Trial by Fire," by Glenn Oeland, May 1997.

National Geographic Society Products Available From Glencoe:

To order the following products for use with this chapter, contact your local Glencoe sales representative or call Glencoe at 1-800-334-7344:

- *GeoBee* (CD-ROM)
- *PictureShow: World War I Era* (CD-ROM)
- *PictureShow: World War II Era* (CD-ROM)
- *STV: World Geography* (Videodisc)
- *Picture Atlas of the World* (CD-ROM)
- *PicturePack: Geography of Europe* (Transparencies)
- *MapPack: Europe* (Transparencies)

Additional National Geographic Society Products:

To order the following products for use with this chapter, call National Geographic Society at 1-800-368-2728:

- *Complete National Geographic: 111 Years of National Geographic Magazine* (CD-ROM)
- *Europe* (Video)
- *Europe: The Road to Unity (Video)*
- *Europe Political* (Map)
- *Cultures (Map)*
- *Population (Map)*
- *Voices: Poetry and Art From Around the World (Book)*
- *National Geographic Desk Reference (Book)*
- *PicturePack: World War I Era* (Transparencies)
- *PicturePack: World War II Era* (Transparencies)

NGS ONLINE

Access National Geographic's Web site for current events, activities, links, interactive features, and archives.
www.nationalgeographic.com

Introducing
Chapter 10

Introduce students to chapter content and key terms by having them access Chapter Overview 10 at owt.glencoe.com

Chapter Objectives

1. Discuss the Industrial Revolution and the social changes it created.
2. Explain how industrialization led to greater rivalry between nations.
3. Discuss the events that contributed to the Cold War.
4. Explain the breakup of the Soviet Union and its aftereffects on Europe.

GLENCOE TECHNOLOGY

NATIONAL GEOGRAPHIC

The World and Its People Video Program

Chapters 10–13 Europe
The following segments enhance the study of this chapter:

- **Avalanche!**
- **Shipwreck**
- **Fire and Ice**

Available in DVD and VHS.

MindJogger Videoquiz
Use MindJogger to preview the Chapter 10 content.

Available in VHS.

Chapter 10 Europe—Modern History

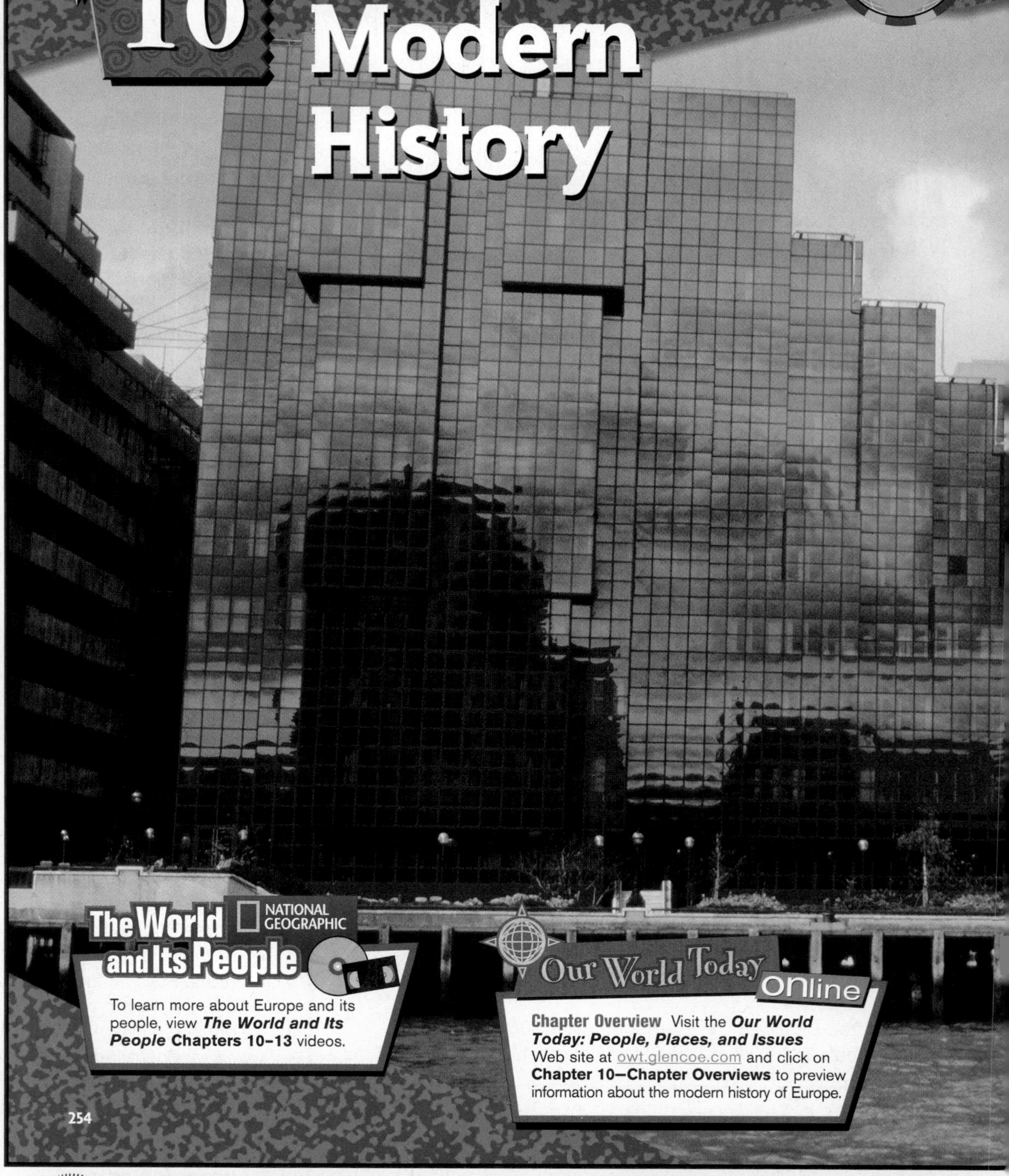

The World and Its People — NATIONAL GEOGRAPHIC

To learn more about Europe and its people, view ***The World and Its People*** **Chapters 10–13** videos.

Our World Today online

Chapter Overview Visit the ***Our World Today: People, Places, and Issues*** Web site at owt.glencoe.com and click on **Chapter 10—Chapter Overviews** to preview information about the modern history of Europe.

254

Two-Minute Lesson Launcher

Have your students look at the labels in their clothing and on electronic goods (like personal stereos or calculators) to see where they were made. Make a list of the different countries. Most will probably be developing countries. **Ask:** **Why do American companies have factories in these countries?** *(Labor is cheaper because people need work. Since it costs less to manufacture goods, the companies can sell their product for less.)* **Why do these countries want American factories?** *(It provides employment and raises the standard of living.)* After students read the chapter, see if they can find parallels between the rise of industry in 18th-century England with today's global manufacturing practices.

FOLDABLES™ Study Organizer

Summarizing Information Study Foldable Make the following foldable to help you organize and summarize information about historic events and modern events in Europe, and how they are related.

Step 1 Fold a sheet of paper from side to side, leaving a 2-inch tab uncovered along the side.

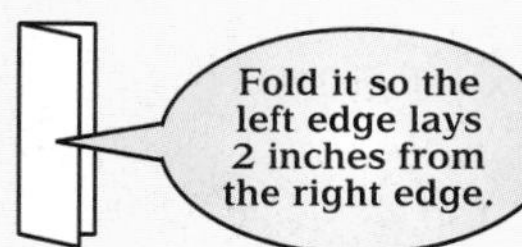
Fold it so the left edge lays 2 inches from the right edge.

Step 2 Turn the paper and fold it into thirds.

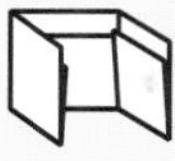

Step 3 Unfold and cut along the two inside fold lines.

Cut along the two folds on the front flap to make 3 tabs.

Step 4 Label the foldable as shown.

EUROPE: MODERN HISTORY
The Modern Era
Continent Divided
Move Toward Unity

Reading and Writing As you read about the modern history of Europe, write important facts under each appropriate tab of your foldable.

◀ A modern office building stands next to Billingsgate Fish Market in London, England.

Why It Matters

The Modern Era

Europe has played a major role in shaping today's world. Industrialization, which started in Europe, is one of the reasons for the high standard of living we experience today. Two world wars, fought largely on European soil, shaped world politics and preserved democracy.

About the Photo

For much of the 18th century, Great Britain was known as the workshop of the world. By the 19th century, industry began to spread to other countries in Europe, as well as the United States. When these countries began to industrialize, they could use Great Britain as a model. Often, they would change existing British techniques to suit the needs of their own country. As more and more countries industrialized around the world, there were new Industrial Revolutions that varied according to the time and place they occurred.

Introducing

Chapter 10

FOLDABLES™ Study Organizer

Purpose Students will make and use a foldable to organize and evaluate information about historic events and modern events in Europe. Students are required to group information from the chapter into categories, and then evaluate how the facts are related.

Have students complete ***Reading and Study Skills Foldables*** Activity 10.

Why It Matters

Use this activity to demonstrate how industrial practices can lead to rivalry and even war between nations. Place your students into four groups. Propose the following scenario to each group.

1. They all manufacture woolen hats.
2. They all buy wool from the same place: the Island of Sheep.
3. They have all become rich from making hats and can afford armies and navies
4. The Island of Sheep has such a demand for its wool that it can charge more, and it favors the groups that will pay more.
5. There are so many woolen hats that customers want to pay less.
6. There's too much competition among groups for the same wool and the same hat customers.

Have the groups come up with proposals that ensure their supply of wool and their position as the only hat supplier in the world. Make sure each group explains the possible consequences of their proposals.

FOCUS

Section Objectives

1. Discuss the Industrial Revolution and the social changes it created.
2. Explain how industrialization created new rivalries between European countries.
3. Explain how the two World Wars changed the balance of power in the world.

BELLRINGER
Skillbuilder Activity

Project transparency and have students answer questions.

This activity is also available as a blackline master.

Daily Focus Skills Transparency 10-1

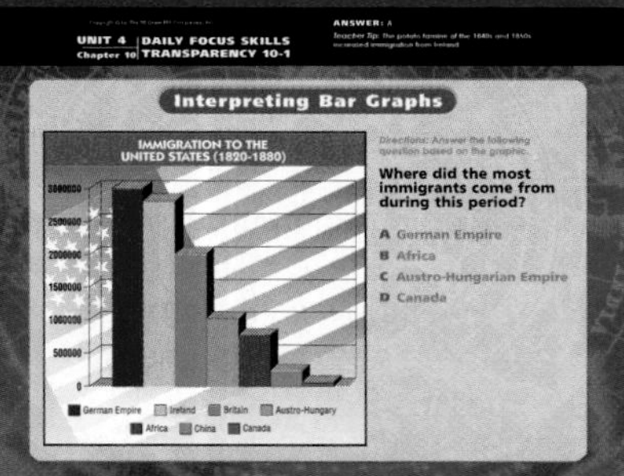

Guide to Reading

Accessing Prior Knowledge Ask students to think about how their clothing is made. How do they think it was made before automated factories were created? *(Individuals spun the wool or cotton thread, wove it by hand on a loom, then cut and stitched the clothes by hand.)*

Section 1 The Modern Era

Guide to Reading

Main Idea

Industrialization led not only to a higher standard of living for some, but also to increased tensions in the world. Two world wars changed the balance of power in the world.

Terms to Know

- productivity
- human resources
- textiles
- cottage industry
- union
- strike
- imperialism
- alliance
- communism
- Holocaust
- genocide

Reading Strategy

Create a chart like the one below. Write three statements of fact under the Fact column. In the Opinion column, write three statements that show how you feel about the fact statement.

Fact	Opinion

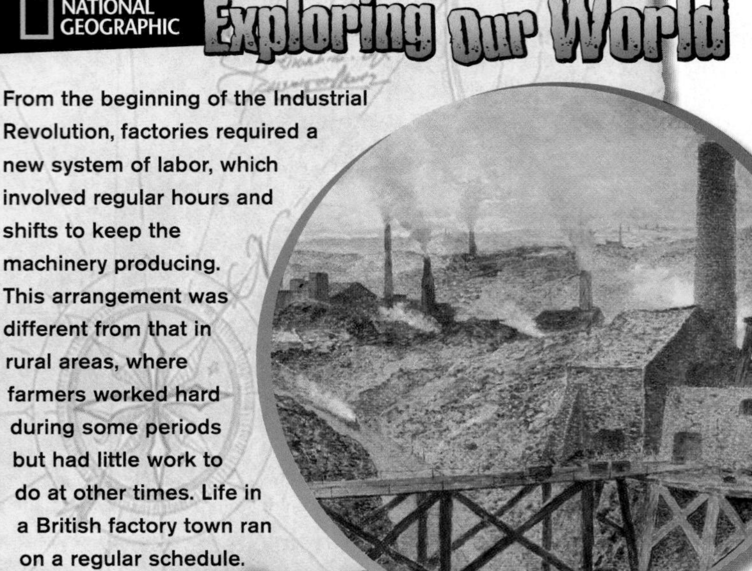

NATIONAL GEOGRAPHIC **Exploring Our World**

From the beginning of the Industrial Revolution, factories required a new system of labor, which involved regular hours and shifts to keep the machinery producing. This arrangement was different from that in rural areas, where farmers worked hard during some periods but had little work to do at other times. Life in a British factory town ran on a regular schedule.

The **Industrial Revolution** began in Great Britain in the 1700s. It was a time when people used machinery and new methods to increase **productivity.** Productivity is a measure of how much work can be done in a certain length of time. The changes these machines brought were so great that they led to a revolution in the ways work was done and people lived. Today, machines touch every part of our lives.

A Rapidly Changing World

The Industrial Revolution started in Britain for several reasons. Britain had a ready supply of natural resources such as coal and iron, which were needed to make and run machinery. There was also a plentiful supply of raw materials such as wool and imported cotton, used to make cloth. There was also a source of people—**human resources**—who could be hired to work the machines. As farmers relied more on machines to plant and harvest crops, fewer people were needed to grow crops. Many people who used to work on the farms went to the cities to find work in factories and shops.

Section Resources

Reproducible Masters

- Reproducible Lesson Plan 10-1
- Daily Lecture and Discussion Notes 10-1
- Guided Reading Activity 10-1
- Reading Essentials and Study Guide 10-1
- Section Quiz 10-1

Transparencies

- Daily Focus Skills Transparency 10-1

Multimedia

- Vocabulary PuzzleMaker Software
- Interactive Tutor Self-Assessment CD-ROM
- Presentation Plus! CD-ROM
- ExamView® Pro 3.0 Testmaker CD-ROM

Major Industries **Textiles,** or woven cloth, was the first industry to be moved to factories. Before that, spinning and cloth weaving had been a **cottage industry** carried out by family members working in their own homes. With industrialization, huge quantities of cloth could be produced in factories that employed many workers. Textile mills became even more productive when steam replaced waterpower for running the machinery.

The steam engine was invented by John Newcomen in the early 1700s and was used to pump water out of coal mines. In 1769, James Watt invented a more efficient steam engine, which was used for textile mills, riverboats, and locomotives. Inventions like the railroad stimulated even more industries and growth. By the early 1800s, the Industrial Revolution spread from Britain to much of western Europe and North America.

✓**Reading Check** How did machinery affect the textile industry?

Changing Lifestyles

Towns and cities grew, as people's lives changed dramatically. At first, industrial workers, including women and children, had to work hard for long hours often under dangerous conditions. Eventually, the workers formed groups called unions. A **union** spoke for all the workers in a factory or industry and bargained for better working conditions, higher pay, and a shorter working day. If a factory owner refused these demands, union members often went on **strike.** That is, they refused to work until their demands were met.

Overall, the Industrial Revolution made life more difficult for people in the short term, but easier in the long run. For example, because manufactured cotton clothing was better and cheaper, people could afford more. They then could afford to change clothes and wash them more often. This new cleanliness helped to reduce sickness and disease, so people generally lived healthier and longer.

The Industrial Revolution also resulted in strong economies in western Europe. It was because of this economic strength that Europe was able to dominate the world in the 1800s and early 1900s.

✓**Reading Check** How did the Industrial Revolution improve people's lives?

NATIONAL GEOGRAPHIC **On Location**

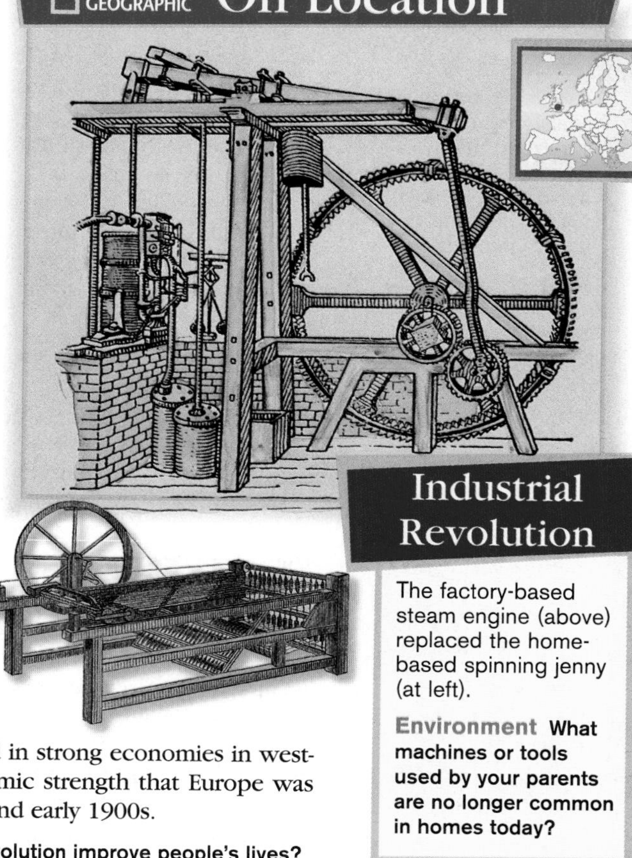

Industrial Revolution

The factory-based steam engine (above) replaced the home-based spinning jenny (at left).

Environment **What machines or tools used by your parents are no longer common in homes today?**

2 TEACH

Brainstorming Ask students to look around the room and think of how it would be different if there were no factories or mass manufacturing. *(Possible answers: limited supplies of books, paper, pencils, etc.; fewer windows; wearing the same clothes every day)*

✓ Reading Check Answer

Huge quantities of cloth could be produced.

Daily Lecture Notes 10-1

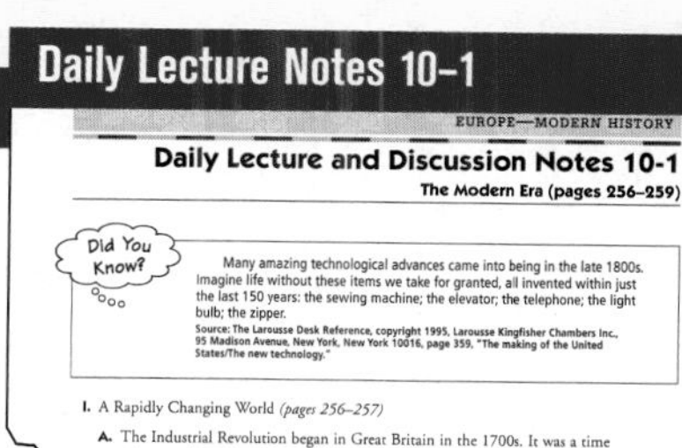

EUROPE—MODERN HISTORY

Daily Lecture and Discussion Notes 10-1

The Modern Era (pages 256–259)

Did You Know?

Many amazing technological advances came into being in the late 1800s. Imagine life without these items we take for granted, all invented within just the last 150 years: the sewing machine; the elevator; the telephone; the light bulb; the zipper.

Source: The Larousse Desk Reference, copyright 1995, Larousse Kingfisher Chambers Inc., 95 Madison Avenue, New York, New York 10016, page 359, "The making of the United States/The new technology."

I. A Rapidly Changing World *(pages 256–257)*

A. The Industrial Revolution began in Great Britain in the 1700s. It was a time when people used machinery and new methods to increase productivity.

...olution in Britain were that Britain had a

More About the Photos

Technology Although seldom used today, the steam engine made it possible to develop other sources of power, such as the gasoline engine.

Caption Answer *Possible answers:* typewriter, record turntable, slide rule, clothespin, carbon paper

✓ Reading Check Answer

Clothing was cheaper, making it easier for people to stay clean. This reduced disease.

Cooperative Learning Activity

Making Posters England went through great changes because of the Industrial Revolution, particularly in the following areas: pollution, health, working conditions, social classes, and transportation. Divide your class into groups. Have each research one of those topics as it pertains to 19th-century England. Have each group make a poster that illustrates important points or examples and use it as part of a presentation. Have the class discuss how their various topics might have connections to one another.

EE5 Environment and Society: Standard 14

EE4 Human Systems: Standard 12

More About the Photos

World War II World War II was fought in Europe, the Pacific, and North Africa. The only military action on American soil was the bombing of Pearl Harbor in Hawaii.

Caption Answer *Possible answers:* London, England; Berlin, Germany; Hiroshima, Japan

Guided Reading Activity 10-1

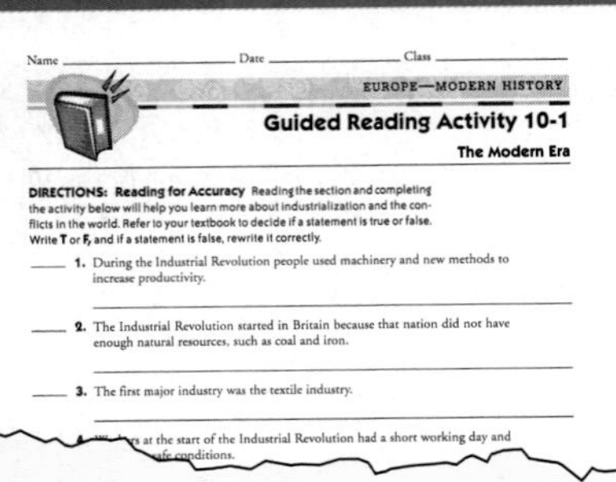
Name ______ Date ______ Class ______

EUROPE—MODERN HISTORY

Guided Reading Activity 10-1

The Modern Era

DIRECTIONS: Reading for Accuracy Reading the section and completing the activity below will help you learn more about industrialization and the conflicts in the world. Refer to your textbook to decide if a statement is true or false. Write **T** or **F**, and if a statement is false, rewrite it correctly.

____ **1.** During the Industrial Revolution people used machinery and new methods to increase productivity.

____ **2.** The Industrial Revolution started in Britain because that nation did not have enough natural resources, such as coal and iron.

____ **3.** The first major industry was the textile industry.

at the start of the Industrial Revolution had a short working day and conditions.

Assess

Assign Section 1 Assessment as homework or an in-class activity.

Have students use the Interactive Tutor Assessment CD-ROM to review Section 10-1.

Building Skills

Sequencing Using the information on pages 258–259 of this text, have students list the sequence of circumstances leading to World War II.

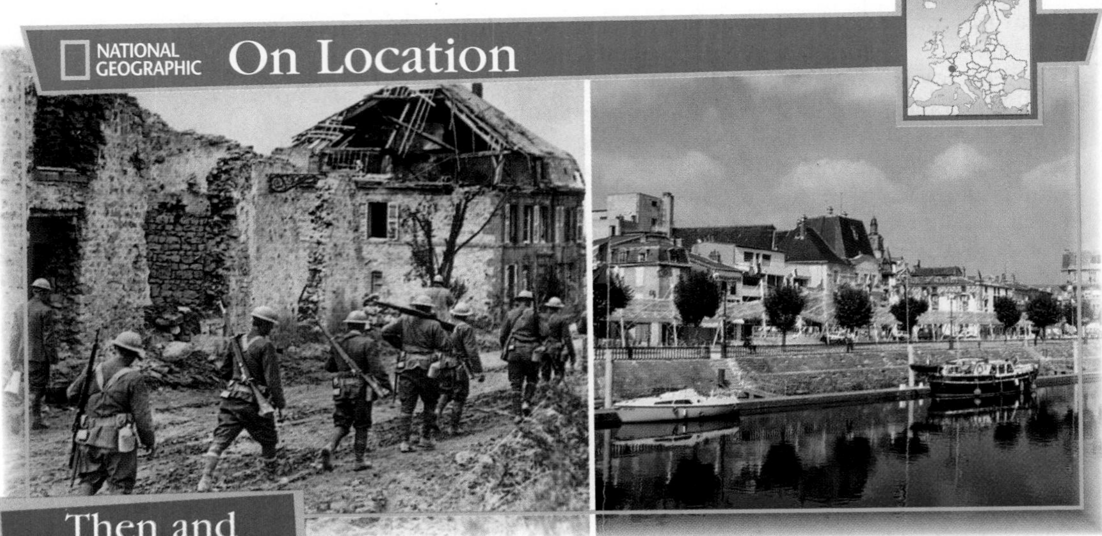

Then and Now

Verdun, France was nearly destroyed during World War II (above). Today it is a thriving commercial center and tourist attraction (right).

Place **Name another city that has been rebuilt since WWII.**

Rivalry Between Nations

Industrialization created new rivalries among the countries of Europe. Britain, France, Germany, and other European countries competed around the world for markets and resources for their factories. Under a system called **imperialism,** European countries claimed colonies in Africa and Asia in the late 1800s. European nations built up armies and navies to protect themselves and their empires. Different **alliances** were formed, whereby various countries agreed to support one another in times of war.

World War I In 1914, a war broke out in Europe that quickly spread to the European colonies and other areas of the world. It was known as the **Great War,** and later called **World War I.** This war was not like any earlier wars. With the techniques learned in the Industrial Revolution, machines designed for war were mass-produced. Tanks, heavy artillery, machine guns, and airplanes helped to make the war more violent than any before it. In the four years of the war, millions of people were killed or wounded, and many European cities and villages were destroyed.

New Problems Arise As a result of the war, many once-strong countries became weak. Germany was blamed for starting the war and was asked to pay for much of it. The United States and Japan became great powers. A revolution in Russia in 1917 led to a new political, economic, and social system called **communism.** Communism was based on the teachings of a German philosopher named Karl Marx. Marx believed that industrialization had created two classes of people—those who owned the means of producing goods and those who worked to produce the goods. He wrote that this system was unfair and needed to be overthrown.

Critical Thinking Activity

Making Inferences Have students research the European languages spoken by the countries in Africa. They can use an almanac or find the information on the Internet. *(They should find that the main European languages are French, English, and Portuguese.)* Using their findings, have students group the African countries according to the European language they speak, then have them locate the countries on a map. Ask them why these African countries speak European languages. *(Answer: They were once colonies of France, Belgium, England, or Portugal.)*

EE4 Human Systems: Standard 10

World War II In the 1930s, worldwide depression severely tested the ability of many governments to provide for their citizens. The problems that were not solved after World War I eventually led to new alliances in Europe. Germany became a dictatorship under Adolf Hitler and his National Socialist German Worker's party. Its members, called **Nazis,** believed in German superiority. By 1939, Germany, Italy, and Japan (the **Axis Powers**) were at war with Britain, France, and China (the **Allies**). In 1941, the United States and Soviet Union joined the Allies in the war that became known as World War II.

During the war, Hitler began the **Holocaust,** which killed over 12 million people. Over 6 million of the victims were Jews. Other persecuted groups included the Romany people (called Gypsies), Serbians, individuals with disabilities, and many other groups that were classified as "undesirable" by the Nazi leaders. The Holocaust is an example of the war crime of **genocide,** or the mass murder of a people because of race, religion, ethnicity, politics, or culture.

World War II was fought primarily in Europe and Asia. Italy and Germany were finally defeated in May 1945. In August, the United States—in an effort to end the war in Asia—dropped two atomic bombs on the Japanese cities of Hiroshima and Nagasaki. From this global conflict, the United States and the Soviet Union emerged as superpowers.

Reading Check What was the Holocaust?

▲ Hitler at a Nazi rally, Dortmund, Germany

Section 1 Assessment

Defining Terms
1. **Define** productivity, human resources, textiles, cottage industry, union, strike, imperialism, alliance, communism, Holocaust, genocide.

Recalling Facts
2. **History** Where did the Industrial Revolution begin?
3. **Government** Name the new political, economic, and social system that was envisioned by Karl Marx.

Critical Thinking
4. **Comparing and Contrasting** How did people's living habits change after the introduction of factories? Do you think people were generally better off?
5. **Evaluating Information** Why did the new military equipment introduced in World War I change the way wars were fought?

Graphic Organizer
6. **Organizing Information** Create a diagram like the one below and fill in the names of the countries that made up the two powers fighting each other in World War II.

Axis Powers	Allies

Applying Social Studies Skills
7. **Analyzing Maps** Refer to the **Reference Atlas** map of the world on pages RA2 and RA3. Which of the Allies was nearest to Japan?

Section 1 Assessment

1. The terms are defined in the Glossary.
2. England
3. communism
4. They moved to cities to be closer to factories; they worked long hours under dangerous conditions until unions were formed; clothing was more affordable; they could stay cleaner and live healthier lives. Student opinion will likely vary.
5. They made the war more violent than any before it.
6. Axis: Germany, Italy, Japan; Allies: Britain, France, China, United States, Russia
7. China

Chapter 10
Section 1, pages 256–259

Section Quiz 10-1

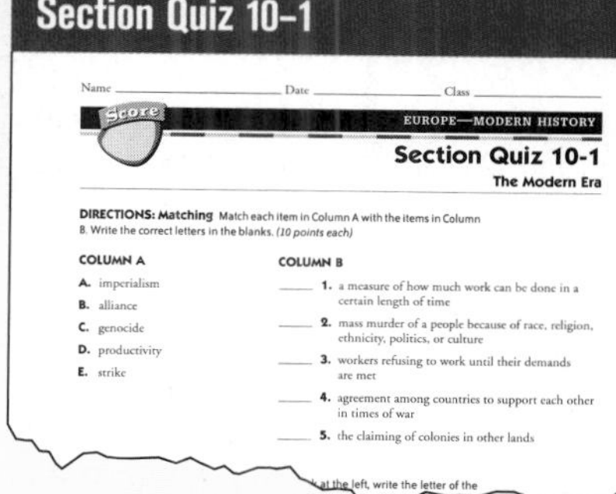
Section Quiz 10-1
The Modern Era

Reading Check Answer
the Nazi genocide of over 12 million people during World War II

Reading Essentials and Study Guide 10-1

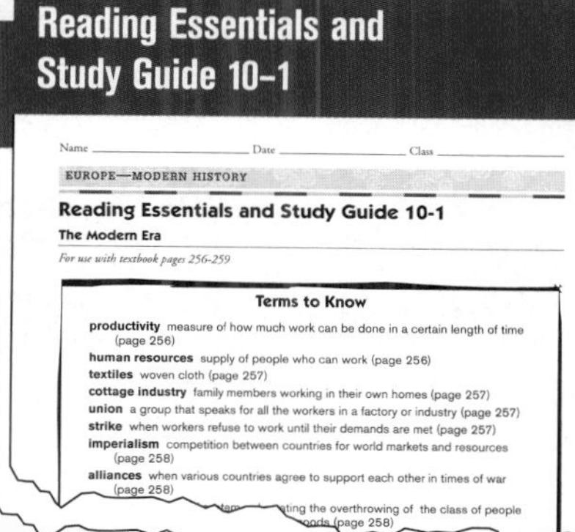
Reading Essentials and Study Guide 10-1
The Modern Era

4 CLOSE

Have students research daily life in the 18th century, and write an essay about what life was like before the Industrial Revolution. They might include information about clothes, transportation, health, sanitary conditions, recreation, education, and occupations.

Teach

Explain to students that often prejudice and intolerance come from ignorance and fear. Ask the class to name groups (religious, ethnic, social, political) that they think might often be the victims of prejudice. Have each student write a question, asking for specific information about one of the groups they know little about. Collect their questions and give them out to other students to answer. Answers might have to be researched, but they should be unbiased and supported with examples. Share responses with the class and discuss how recent current events have led to some prejudice.

More About the Holocaust

Unfortunately, events like the Holocaust were not limited to World War II. In the early 20th century, over half the Armenian population of Turkey was massacred. African Americans were often the targets of violent prejudice in the United States. Mass murder is still happening around the world today. In eastern Europe and Africa, ethnic conflicts have led to the slaughter of many innocent people.

Making Connections

CULTURE | GOVERNMENT | PEOPLE | TECHNOLOGY

The Holocaust

The Holocaust is one of the most horrifying events in human history. *Holocaust* is a word that means complete and total destruction. Learning about the Holocaust is important so that crimes against humanity such as this will never occur again.

The Final Solution

Adolf Hitler, chancellor of Germany, believed that the Germanic peoples of the world, called Aryans, were a superior race. His goal was to populate Europe with one "master" race of people. During the years before and during World War II, Hitler's government persecuted many racial, religious, and ethnic groups that he considered "undesirable." These included Gypsies, Jehovah's Witnesses, people with disabilities, and political dissidents of all backgrounds.

The chief target of Hitler's plan—which he called his "Final Solution"—was the Jews. Jewish communities throughout Germany and German-controlled territory suffered terribly. Jews, forced to wear identification badges, were blamed for all Germany's economic and social problems.

Between 1939 and 1945, Hitler's Nazi forces attempted to exterminate the Jews in every country Germany invaded, as well as in those countries that were Nazi allies. Jews from Germany, Poland, the Soviet Union, France, Belgium, the Netherlands, Greece, and Hungary were among those killed during the Holocaust.

▲ Auschwitz Nazi concentration camp in Oswiecim, Poland

Mass Murder

In the early years of the war, Jewish people in Eastern Europe were rounded up, gathered together, machine-gunned, and buried in mass graves. Later, millions of Jews were uprooted and forced into concentration camps. Few people survived these. Those too young, sick, or elderly for heavy labor were executed in gas chambers. In all, more than 6 million Jews and 1 million Gypsies were murdered during the Holocaust.

Making the Connection

1. What was the Holocaust?
2. Why did Hitler want to rid Europe of its Jewish people?
3. **Understanding Cause and Effect** How can studying about the Holocaust today help prevent another atrocity from happening in the future?

Making the Connection

1. The organized murder of Jews and other ethnic, religious, or political groups by the Germans during World War II.
2. He wanted to eliminate any group that he considered undesirable and he particularly targeted Jews.
3. Answers will vary. One possible response is that showing the horrors forced upon a peoples simply because of race and beliefs will help people see the inhuman results of hatred and intolerance.

Section 2

A Continent Divided

Guide to Reading

Main Idea

Two powers, the democratic United States and the Communist Soviet Union, worked to bring their forms of government to the war-torn nations of Europe.

Terms to Know

- Cold War
- nuclear weapon
- deterrence
- satellite nation
- blockade
- airlift
- glasnost
- perestroika
- capitalism

Reading Strategy

As you read, fill in a time line like the one below with an event that occurred during that year.

1948 ______
1955 ______
1957 ______
1985 ______
1989 ______

NATIONAL GEOGRAPHIC **Exploring Our World**

For nearly 30 years, armed guards patrolled a 103-mile (166-km) wall that divided the German city of Berlin into eastern and western halves. During that time, the citizens of East Berlin were not allowed to travel freely to West Berlin. In late 1989, the wall finally came down. Germans from both parts of the city came together and celebrated.

After World War II, much of Europe was in ruins. The total defeat of Germany, Italy, and Japan left a power gap that would be filled by the rival United States and Soviet Union.

The Cold War

The global competition between the democratic United States and its allies and the Communist Soviet Union and its supporters came to be called the **Cold War.** It was a dangerous time because by 1948 both sides had **nuclear weapons.** Nuclear weapons use atomic reactions to release enormous power and cause mass destruction. It was a "cold" war because countries never mobilized armies in an official war.

The Cold War began in Europe. In 1948, the United States started a loan program called the **Marshall Plan** to help rebuild Europe and try to stop the spread of communism. Under the Marshall Plan, factories were rebuilt, mines were reopened, and roads were repaired and

1 Focus

Section Objectives

1. Explain the circumstances that created the Cold War.
2. Discuss the events that led to the end of the Cold War.

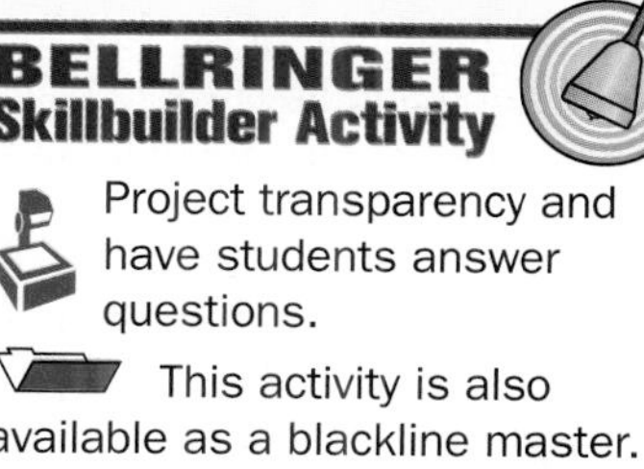

BELLRINGER Skillbuilder Activity

Project transparency and have students answer questions.

This activity is also available as a blackline master.

Daily Focus Skills Transparency 10-2

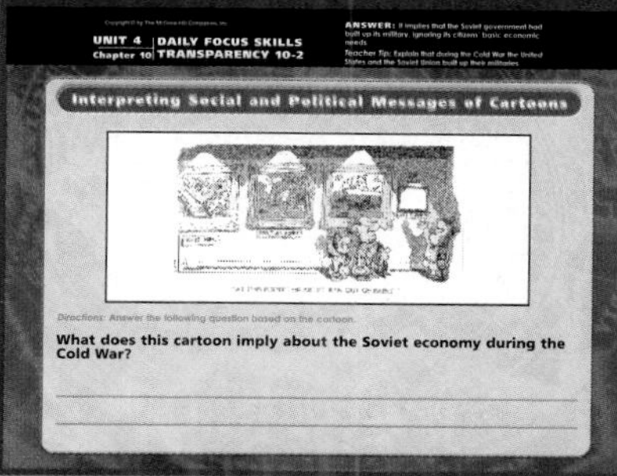

UNIT 4 Chapter 10 DAILY FOCUS SKILLS TRANSPARENCY 10-2
Interpreting Social and Political Messages of Cartoons
What does this cartoon imply about the Soviet economy during the Cold War?

Guide to Reading

■ **Vocabulary Precheck**
Ask students why the term *cold war* was used to describe the conflict between the United States and the Soviet Union.

Use the Vocabulary Puzzle-Maker to create crossword and word search puzzles.

Section Resources

Reproducible Masters
- Reproducible Lesson Plan 10-2
- Daily Lecture and Discussion Notes 10-2
- Guided Reading Activity 10-2
- Reading Essentials and Study Guide 10-2
- Section Quiz 10-2

Transparencies
- Daily Focus Skills Transparency 10-2

Multimedia
- Vocabulary PuzzleMaker Software
- Interactive Tutor Self-Assessment CD-ROM
- Presentation Plus! CD-ROM
- ExamView® Pro 3.0 Testmaker CD-ROM

a global competition between the United States and the Soviet Union

2 TEACH

Sequencing Events Write the following events on the board, overhead projector, or powerpoint presentation and have your class date them and place them in the correct order: NATO is formed, World War II ends in Europe, Mikhail Gorbachev becomes the leader of the Soviet Union, the Berlin Wall is built, the Marshall Plan is started. *(1945: WWII ends; 1948: Marshall Plan; 1949: NATO; 1961: Berlin Wall; 1985: Gorbachev)*

Applying Map Skills

Answers

1. Western
2. Soviet Union, German Democratic Republic, Czechoslovakia, Hungary, Romania, Bulgaria

Skills Practice

Which Eastern European countries are landlocked? *(Czechoslovakia, Hungary)*

replaced. The economies of Western Europe—those countries liberated and occupied by the United States and Great Britain during World War II—began to grow.

Reading Check What was the Cold War?

West European Nations Cooperate

In 1948 under the **Truman Doctrine,** named after U.S. President Harry S Truman, the United States offered military aid to countries such as Greece and Turkey that were engaged in fighting communism inside their borders. In 1949, the North Atlantic Treaty Organization (NATO) was formed to respond to possible attacks by the Soviet Union. In forming NATO, each member country agreed to treat an attack on any other member as an attack on itself. The NATO countries believed that the Soviet Union would not attack Western Europe if Soviet leaders thought such an attack would trigger nuclear war with the United States. This policy is known as **deterrence** because it is designed to deter, or discourage, an attack.

Eventually, to help themselves, Western European countries began to cooperate with one another. First the small countries Belgium, the Netherlands, and Luxembourg joined together in 1948 to form the **Benelux** trade union, an arrangement for the free movement of money, goods, and people among these nations. Then West Germany,

Applying Map Skills

1. Were there more countries in Western Europe or Eastern Europe?
2. Which Eastern European countries were on the border with Western Europe?

Find NGS online map resources@ www.nationalgeographic.com/maps

Critical Thinking Activity

Comparing and Contrasting Have your students research the North Atlantic Treaty Organization (NATO) to find out when and why it was started, who the members are, and what its current role in the world is. Divide the class into groups, each representing one of the members of NATO. Have each group come up with three reasons why it is important that their country belongs to NATO. Afterwards, have groups share their reasons and see if there are any similarities or differences between countries.

EE4 Human Systems: Standard 13

France, and Italy came together with the Benelux countries to form the European Coal and Steel Community. In 1957, this became the **European Common Market.** The members agreed to tax-free trade among themselves. Workers from one member country could take jobs in any of the other countries. Between 1957 and 1986 Denmark, Great Britain, Ireland, Spain, Portugal, and Greece also joined the Common Market (known today as the **European Union**), which moved toward greater cooperation and economic development.

✓Reading Check **Why did the countries of Western Europe join NATO?**

The Soviet Community

In Eastern Europe, the Soviet Union made **satellite nations** of those countries surrounding it. Satellite nations are dependent upon a stronger power. They were strictly controlled by the Soviet Union. Bulgaria, Romania, Czechoslovakia, Hungary, Poland, and East Germany became communist. With these countries, the Soviet Union created the Communist Economic Community, or COMECON, primarily for its own economic benefit.

In 1955, the Soviet Union formed its satellites into an anti-Western military alliance known as the **Warsaw Pact.** It was named after the Polish capital city of Warsaw, where the treaty of alliance was signed.

Yugoslavia and Albania also became communist but refused to be put under Soviet control. During the Cold War, Yugoslavia, India, Egypt, and Indonesia formed the Non-Aligned Community. Its members tried to stay neutral—to not support either side—during the Cold War.

✓Reading Check **In what way was the Warsaw Pact like NATO?**

A Clash Between Superpowers

During the Cold War, there were many "hot spots," or areas of tension and conflict. Some of them were China, Korea, Cuba, and Vietnam. The earliest, however, and one of the most important was Berlin.

Divided Berlin At the end of World War II, the Allies (the United States, the Soviet Union, Great Britain, and France) occupied Germany and its capital city of Berlin. In 1948, to promote peace and German recovery, the United States, Great Britain, and France decided to unite their occupation zones. The Soviet Union was against any plan that would strengthen Germany, its historical enemy. Berlin was located deep in the Soviet zone, but jointly occupied by the four powers. In June 1948, the Soviets **blockaded,** or closed off, all land and water traffic into Berlin. They hoped this would force the other three powers to leave the city.

In response, the United States and Great Britain began an **airlift,** or a system of carrying supplies into Berlin by airplane. Day and night the planes flew tons of food, fuel, and raw materials into the city. This heroic effort caused the Soviets to finally end the 11-month blockade of Berlin. That same year, two separate governments were set up—a democratic one for West Germany with Bonn as its new

Exploring Economics

Restructuring

Imagine a family-owned business in which the head of the family makes all the decisions. These include which businesses to begin, who will do which jobs, what products to produce, and how much to pay employees. Then, suddenly the head of the family disappears. Family members now must make all the decisions though they have had no experience. Like this example, for most Soviet citizens, taking control of the local economy was a difficult change.

✓ Reading Check Answer

to form an alliance in order to respond to possible attacks by the Soviet Union

Daily Lecture Notes 10-2

EUROPE—MODERN HISTORY

Daily Lecture and Discussion Notes 10-2

A Continent Divided (pages 261–265)

Did You Know? In addition to airlifting food, fuel, and raw materials to the people blockaded by the Soviets in Berlin, one American pilot, Lieutenant Gale S. Halverson, regularly dropped candy, attached to parachutes made from handkerchiefs, for the children.

I. The Cold War *(pages 261–262)*
   A. The global competition between the democratic United States and its allies and the Communist Soviet Union and its supporters came to be called the Cold War.
   B. The Cold War was a dangerous time because both sides had nuclear weapons.
   C. Under the Marshall Plan, the United States lent money to help rebuild Europe and ... the spread of communism.

✓ Reading Check Answer

It was also a military alliance, but against the West.

Guided Reading Activity 10-2

Name ______ Date ______ Class ______

EUROPE—MODERN HISTORY

Guided Reading Activity 10-2

A Continent Divided

DIRECTIONS: Answering Questions Reading the section and answering the questions below will help you learn more about the conflict between the United States and the Soviet Union. Use your textbook to write answers to the questions.

1. What was the Cold War?
2. Why did the United States set up the Marshall Plan?
3. Why did the NATO countries follow a policy known as deterrence?
4. How did Western European countries begin to cooperate with each other after World War II?

Team-Teaching Activity

Economics Invite a teacher with a background in economics to class to discuss how business was run under communism and how it runs in a capitalist system. Then make a chart on the board, with a heading for the Soviet Union and one for the United States. Have students answer the following questions for each column: *Who determines what new businesses should begin? How do people get jobs? How are salaries determined? Who controls the prices of consumer goods? Who gets the business profits?* Afterwards, discuss the advantages and disadvantages of each system.

EE4 Human Systems: Standard 12

3 ASSESS

Assign Section 2 Assessment as homework or an in-class activity.

More About the Photo

Berlin After the airlift ended in 1949, Berlin remained divided into East and West. It wasn't until 1990 that the city reunited and again became Germany's capital.

Caption Answer Even though the Soviets closed off land and water routes into Berlin, the West was able to maintain its hold there by bringing in supplies by airplane.

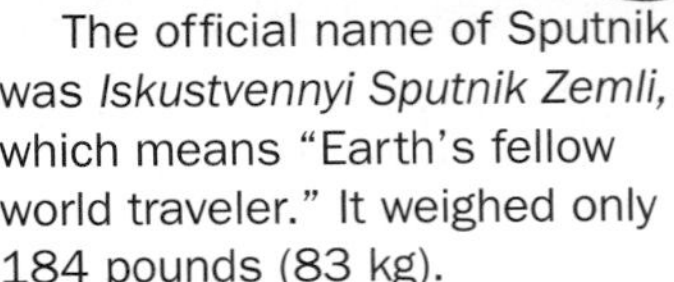

Did You Know

The official name of Sputnik was *Iskustvennyi Sputnik Zemli,* which means "Earth's fellow world traveler." It weighed only 184 pounds (83 kg).

✓ Reading Check Answer

with a wall

Section Quiz 10-2

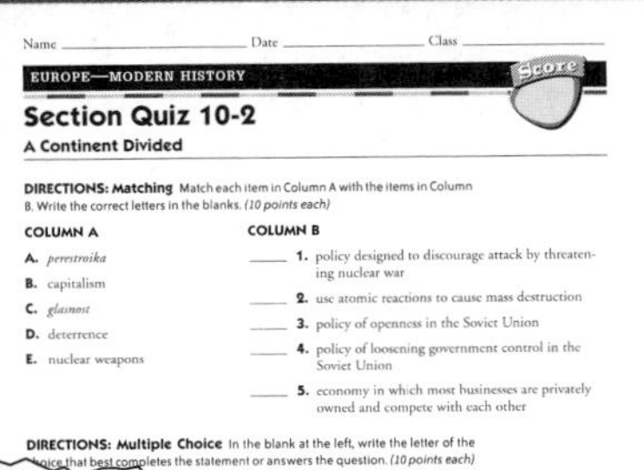

Name ______ Date ______ Class ______

EUROPE—MODERN HISTORY

Score

Section Quiz 10-2

A Continent Divided

DIRECTIONS: Matching Match each item in Column A with the items in Column B. Write the correct letters in the blanks. *(10 points each)*

COLUMN A	COLUMN B
A. *perestroika*	____ **1.** policy designed to discourage attack by threatening nuclear war
B. capitalism	____ **2.** use atomic reactions to cause mass destruction
C. *glasnost*	____ **3.** policy of openness in the Soviet Union
D. deterrence	____ **4.** policy of loosening government control in the Soviet Union
E. nuclear weapons	____ **5.** economy in which most businesses are privately owned and compete with each other

DIRECTIONS: Multiple Choice In the blank at the left, write the letter of the choice that best completes the statement or answers the question. *(10 points each)*

Germany, and Romania were members of

Berlin Airlift

Residents of Berlin (right) wave to an American airlift plane. A line of planes (left) wait to be unloaded at a Berlin airfield.

Technology **How did airplane technology affect Soviet military strategy in Germany?**

capital and a communist one for East Germany with East Berlin, in the Soviet zone, as its capital. West Berlin remained a democratic stronghold surrounded by communism.

The Berlin Wall Many people in East Germany were unhappy under communist rule. About 3 million people fled to West Berlin in search of political freedom and better living conditions. The East German government wanted to stop these escapes, and in August 1961 the government built a wall between East and West Berlin. The wall, with Soviet soldiers guarding it, became a symbol of the split between Eastern and Western Europe. Many East Germans continued to risk their lives trying to escape over or under the wall.

The Race to Space Part of the Cold War between the United States and the Soviet Union involved the race to explore space. The Soviets first took the lead. In 1957, they launched *Sputnik I,* the first spacecraft to orbit the earth. Four years later Soviet astronaut Yuri Gagarin became the first human being to circle the earth.

Then the United States became the leader. In 1969, Neil Armstrong became the first person to walk on the moon. During the 1970s, the first landings on Venus and Mars were made by U.S. crewless spacecraft. Later, space vehicles explored Jupiter, Saturn, and beyond. The space race brought fame and glory to both powers. Today the United States and Russia are cooperating partners in the international space station project.

✓ Reading Check **How did the Soviet Union separate the people of East and West Berlin?**

Cooperative Learning Activity

Creating Walls Draw a line down the middle of the room with a piece of chalk or masking tape. Half of your students should be on the side with the door. The other half should have limited or no access to "the outside world." Tell your students that they should imagine a wall where the line is. From now on, they can't communicate with their friends on the other side of the line. Those on the side with the door will have free access to the rest of the school. Those on the other side of the line will have to get permission to leave and are stuck with the supplies they have on hand. Have the class discuss the consequences of dividing the classroom.

EE4 Human Systems: Standard 13

The End of the Cold War

During the cold war, the Soviet Union spent large sums of money on military and space ventures. In spite of plans to improve consumer housing and agriculture, the economies of the Soviet Union and its satellites kept falling further and further behind the United States and its Western European allies.

In 1985, Mikhail Gorbachev became the leader of the Soviet Union. He introduced reforms to try to get the Soviet economy moving again. Under **glasnost,** or openness, the Soviet people could criticize the system without fear of being punished. Free elections were held in which many noncommunists gained office. Under the policy of **perestroika,** or restructuring, Gorbachev loosened government control and moved the economy toward **capitalism.** Under capitalism, most businesses are privately owned, and there is competition to try to create better products at lower prices.

In the late 1980s, as the Soviet Union moved slowly toward democracy and capitalism, tensions within the country and its satellites increased. Some people thought that Gorbachev was moving too quickly with his reforms. Others thought he was not moving fast enough. At the same time, many ethnic groups in the Soviet Union were demanding independence. All of the satellite nations also moved toward freedom from Soviet domination. The Cold War was coming to an end.

Reading Check **Which Russian leader moved the Soviet Union toward democracy?**

Our World Today online

Web Activity Visit the ***Our World Today: People, Places, and Issues*** Web site at owt.glencoe.com and click on **Chapter 10–Student Web Activities** to learn more about the Cold War.

Section 2 Assessment

Defining Terms

1. **Define** Cold War, nuclear weapon, deterrence, satellite nation, blockade, airlift, glasnost, perestroika, capitalism.

Recalling Facts

2. **History** What was the purpose of the Marshall Plan?
3. **Place** Which countries were considered satellites of the Soviet Union?

Critical Thinking

4. **Comparing and Contrasting** What are the similarities and differences between a "cold" war and a "hot" war?
5. **Analyzing Information** How did the space race reflect tensions between the United States and the Soviet Union?

Graphic Organizer

6. **Organizing Information** Create a chart like this. Explain how each of the following events intensified the Cold War.

Marshall Plan	
Truman Doctrine	
NATO	
Warsaw Pact	

Applying Social Studies Skills

7. **Analyzing Maps** Look at the map of Western and Eastern Europe on page 262. Name the Western European countries that shared a border with countries in Eastern Europe.

Chapter 10

Section 2, pages 261–265

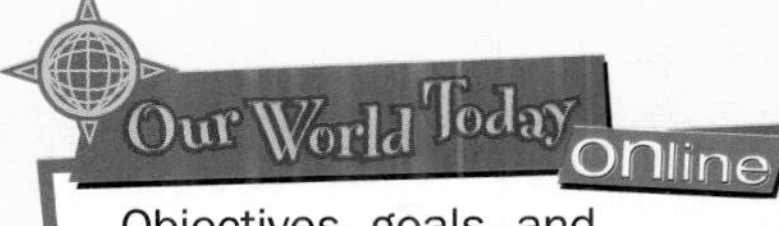

Objectives, goals, and answers to the Student Web Activity can be found in the Web Activity Lesson Plan at **owt.glencoe.com**

Reading Check Answer

Mikhail Gorbachev

Reading Essentials and Study Guide 10–2

Name ______ Date ______ Class ______

EUROPE—MODERN HISTORY

Reading Essentials and Study Guide 10-2

A Continent Divided

For use with textbook pages 261-265

Terms to Know

Cold War global competition between the democratic United States and its allies and the Communist Soviet Union (page 261)

nuclear weapons weapons that use atomic reactions to release enormous power and cause mass destruction (page 261)

deterrence policy designed to deter, or discourage, an attack (page 262)

satellite nations nations that are dependent upon a stronger power (page 263)

blockade closing off of land and water traffic into Berlin by the Soviet Union (page 263)

airlift system of carrying supplies into Berlin by airplane

glasnost openness (page 265)

perestroika loosening of government control and moving the Soviet economy

4 Close

Have students look up the Russian term *perestroika* to find out its English translation. (*"restructuring"*) Ask students why they think that term was used to describe Gorbachev's policies. *(He restructured Russia's economy.)*

Section 2 Assessment

1. The terms are defined in the Glossary.
2. to help rebuild Europe after WWII
3. Bulgaria, Romania, Czechoslovakia, Hungary, Poland, East Germany
4. In a cold war there's no official declaration of war or direct military confrontation.
5. They were competing to see who could be first and claim the glory.
6. *Marshall Plan:* improved economies of Western Europe to stop spread of communism; *Truman Doctrine:* military aid to countries fighting communism; *NATO:* military alliance of Western nations against Soviets; *Warsaw Pact:* anti-Western military alliance between the Soviet Union and its satellites
7. Finland, Federal Republic of Germany, Austria, Yugoslavia, Greece, Turkey

TEACH

Display a map of your city or county. Have students draw a freehand copy of the map. Ask them to mark on the map those areas where they think many people live and those where they think few people live. Point out that geographers express these differences as population density. Ask students what impact the population density of their city or county has on their lives. L1

Additional Skills Practice

1. **How is population density expressed?** *(as the number of people living in every square mile or square kilometer of an area)*
2. **How is population density shown on maps?** *(Distinct colors represent different ranges of population density.)*
3. **How is the population size of different cities shown on maps?** *(Different symbols represent different levels of population.)*

Additional Skills Resources

 Chapter Skills Activity 10

 Building Geography Skills for Life

GLENCOE TECHNOLOGY

 **Skillbuilder Interactive Workbook CD-ROM, Level 1**

This interactive CD-ROM reinforces student mastery of essential social studies skills.

Social Studies Skill

Reading a Population Map

Population density is the number of people living in a square mile or square kilometer. A **population density map** shows you where people live in a given region. Mapmakers use different colors to represent different population densities. The darker the color, the more dense, or crowded, the population is in that particular area. Cities that are shown by dots or squares also represent different population sizes.

Learning the Skill

To read a population density map, follow these steps:

- Read the title of the map.
- Study the map key to determine what the colors mean.
- On the map, find the areas that have the lowest and highest population density.
- Identify what symbols are used to show how heavily populated the cities are.

Practicing the Skill

Look at the map below to answer the following questions.

1. What color stands for 125–250 people per square mile (50–100 per sq. km)?
2. Which cities have more than 1 million people?
3. Which areas have the lowest population density? Why?

Applying the Skill

Obtain a population density map of your state. What is the population density of your area? What is the nearest city with 1 million people?

GO TO Practice key skills with **Glencoe Skillbuilder Interactive Workbook, Level 1.**

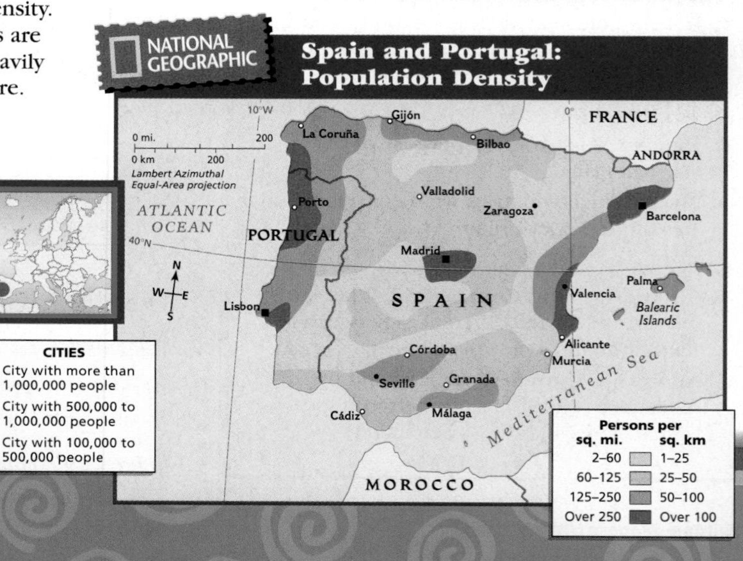

266

Practicing the Skill Answers

1. red
2. Barcelona, Lisbon, Madrid
3. north central Spain, the interior of eastern Spain, and the interior of southern and south western Spain; these tend to be highland areas and may be too dry to support much farming

Applying the Skill
Verify students' answers for accuracy.

Moving Toward Unity

Guide to Reading

Main Idea

Although the Cold War is over, many challenges still face the old and new nations of Europe.

Terms to Know

- European Union
- Euro

Reading Strategy

Create a chart like the one below and write one key fact about each topic.

Soviet Union	
Yugoslavia	
European Union	
NATO	
Greenhouse effect	

NATIONAL GEOGRAPHIC **Exploring Our World**

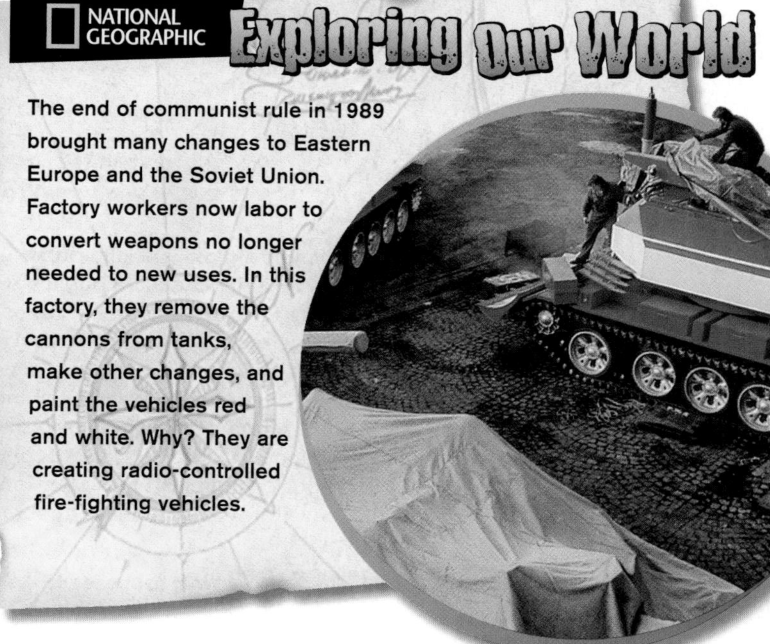

The end of communist rule in 1989 brought many changes to Eastern Europe and the Soviet Union. Factory workers now labor to convert weapons no longer needed to new uses. In this factory, they remove the cannons from tanks, make other changes, and paint the vehicles red and white. Why? They are creating radio-controlled fire-fighting vehicles.

In 1989, massive protests occurred in East Germany and the communist government resigned. In Poland, for the first time, a communist government had lost power as a result of a democratic election. The Berlin Wall came down, and West and East Germany reunited in October 1990. By 1991, all of the Soviet satellite nations—even Mongolia in distant Central Asia—had thrown off communist rule in favor of democracy.

The End of the Soviet Union

The movement toward democracy spread to the Soviet Union. In May 1990, **Boris Yeltsin,** a reformer and former Communist, was elected president of Russia, the largest of the 15 Soviet republics. Meanwhile, people in the other 14 republics began to shake off Soviet rule. Freed from daily Russian control, fierce ethnic fighting broke out among various groups in many of these republics.

267

1 Focus

Section Objectives

1. Discuss the outcome of the breakup of the Soviet Union.
2. Explain how Europe has become more united.
3. Explain the problems facing Europe today.

BELLRINGER Skillbuilder Activity

Project transparency and have students answer questions.

This activity is also available as a blackline master.

Daily Focus Skills Transparency 10-3

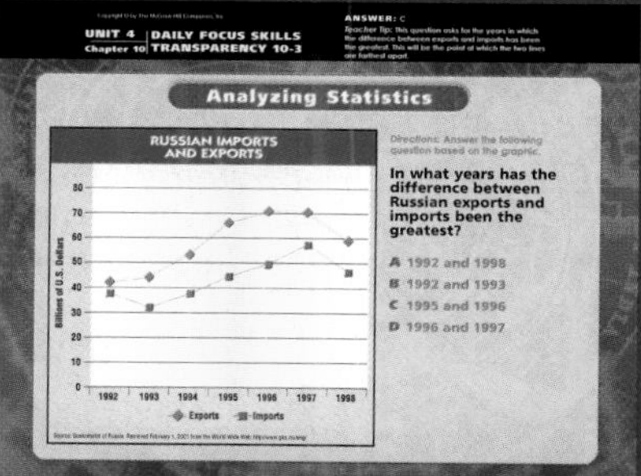

Guide to Reading

■ **Accessing Prior Knowledge**
Ask students if they can name any European currencies (*Possible answers:* English pound, French franc, German mark, Italian lira)

■ **Vocabulary Precheck**
Ask students why "greenhouse" is used to describe the build-up of carbon dioxide in the atmosphere.

Section Resources

Reproducible Masters
- Reproducible Lesson Plan 10-3
- Daily Lecture and Discussion Notes 10-3
- Guided Reading Activity 10-3
- Reading Essentials and Study Guide 10-3
- Section Quiz 10-3

Transparencies
- Daily Focus Skills Transparency 10-3

Multimedia
- Vocabulary PuzzleMaker Software
- Interactive Tutor Self-Assessment CD-ROM
- Presentation Plus! CD-ROM
- ExamView® Pro 3.0 Testmaker CD-ROM

Chapter 10

Section 3, pages 267–270

More About the Photo

Standing for Democracy In August 1991, leaders from the government and military tried to seize power and return control to the Communist Party. Yeltsin and thousands of Russians bravely resisted the rebels.

Caption Answer The reforms in government led to tensions within the Soviet Union and its satellites, and would change the way Russians lived. Also, those who had been in power didn't want to lose their status.

TEACH

Identifying Main Ideas Have students write down the headings in this section. Under each heading, have them write three facts that they learned from their reading.

✓ Reading Check Answer

They became independent from Soviet rule.

Daily Lecture Notes 10-3

EUROPE—MODERN HISTORY

Daily Lecture and Discussion Notes 10-3

Moving Toward Unity (pages 267–270)

Did You Know?

The new currency of the European Union, the euro, comes in several denominations. Notes (paper, or bills) are in amounts of 500, 200, 100, 50, 20, 10, and 5 euro. Coins are in amounts of 2 euro, 1 euro, 50 euro cent, 20 euro cent, 10 euro cent, 5 euro cent, 2 euro cent, and 1 euro cent. Vending machines have been adapted to accept euro notes and coins: There are more than 3.5 million vending machines in the European Union Member States!

Source: Europa—The European Union On-Line (http://europa.eu.int, accessed 10-9-01)

I. The End of the Soviet Union *(pages 267–268)*

A. The Berlin Wall came down, and West and East Germany reunited in October 1989.

B. By 1991, all of the Soviet satellite nations had thrown off communist rule in ... emocracy.

NATIONAL GEOGRAPHIC On Location

Standing for Democracy

Russia's president, Boris Yeltsin, stood on a tank in defiance of a communist group that wanted to stop Russia's move to democracy.

Government Why do you think some people did not want Russia to move to democracy?

The Soviet Union officially broke up on Christmas Day 1991. In its place are 15 independent republics stretching across Europe and Asia and moving toward democracy. **Yugoslavia,** a communist country, and democratic **Czechoslovakia** also broke up. After much fighting and civil wars, Yugoslavia became the independent republics Slovenia, Croatia, Bosnia and Herzegovina, Macedonia, and a smaller Yugoslavia made up of Serbia and Montenegro. Czechoslovakia peacefully became the Czech Republic and Slovakia. All of these countries today have major problems due to poor economies, ethnic tensions, and a lack of understanding of democracy. You will read more about these eastern European countries in Chapter 12.

✓ **Reading Check** What happened to the republics of the Soviet Union?

The New Europe

Since the fall of communism and the Soviet Union, there is no longer a political division between western and eastern Europe—although cultural and economic differences remain. As a result of cooperation, Europe is becoming more of an economic power in the world. The Common Market became the **European Union** (EU) in 1993. At that time, the twelve members included the United Kingdom, Ireland, France, Luxembourg, Spain, Portugal, Denmark, the Netherlands, Belgium, Germany, Italy, and Greece. Austria, Finland, and Sweden joined in 1995. Fourteen other nations, including many from eastern Europe, have applied for membership.

The European Union is moving toward greater unity. Some Europeans would eventually like to see it become a United States of Europe that would include all European countries. In January 2002 most of its members began using a common currency, the **Euro** to replace their national currencies. This means that citizens of countries in the EU are using the same type of money to buy goods and services.

Meeting Special Needs

Visual/Spatial To help students understand the recent changes in Europe, it can be helpful for them to look at a map. Find an old map of the Soviet Union. Have students compare it to a recent map of eastern Europe. **Ask:** **How many independent republics were formed when the Soviet Union broke up in 1991? What are the names of these new countries?**

EE1 The World in Spatial Terms: Standard 3

The countries of Europe have cooperated in the areas of science and technology, as well as politics and economics. Europe had one of the first treaties on nuclear energy. The European Atomic Energy Community (EURATOM) has wide powers, including the right to conclude contracts, obtain raw materials, and establish standards to protect workers and the general population against the dangers of radiation.

✓ Reading Check **What is the name of the new European Union currency?**

Facing the Region's Problems

There is a growing number of problems in Europe—and the world—that Europeans are actively trying to solve. The income gap between the rich and poor nations of Europe needs to be lessened. Population growth must be controlled, and the increasing food and health needs of existing populations must be met.

NATO as Peacekeeper Some eastern European countries have joined NATO, and others are on the waiting list. Poland, Hungary, and the Czech Republic are NATO members. Countries that have applied for NATO membership include Estonia, Romania, Bulgaria, and Slovenia. However, the expansion of NATO to Russia's western border is also creating tensions among Russia, the United States, and Europe. NATO is moving beyond its original role as a protector from communist states. It has also taken on European peacekeeping tasks. Since 1990, through NATO, the United States and Europe have supported United Nations efforts in areas such as Iraq and Kuwait and in the former Yugoslav republics of Bosnia and Herzegovina, Serbia and Montenegro, and Macedonia. Sometimes there is not complete agreement among all the members on how NATO forces should be employed.

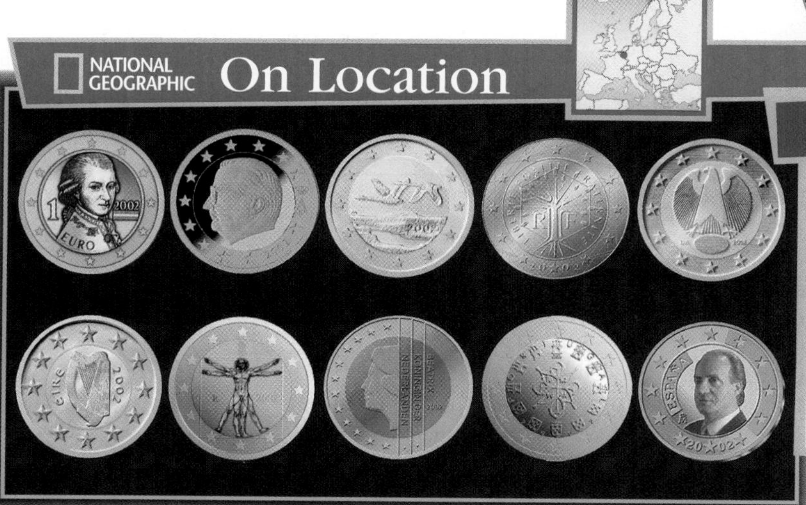

The Euro

Ten different national sides of the one Euro coin are shown, along with the front image that does not change.

Place **How many coins can you identify by the images chosen to represent the country?**

Chapter 10

Section 3, pages 267–270

Guided Reading Activity 10-3

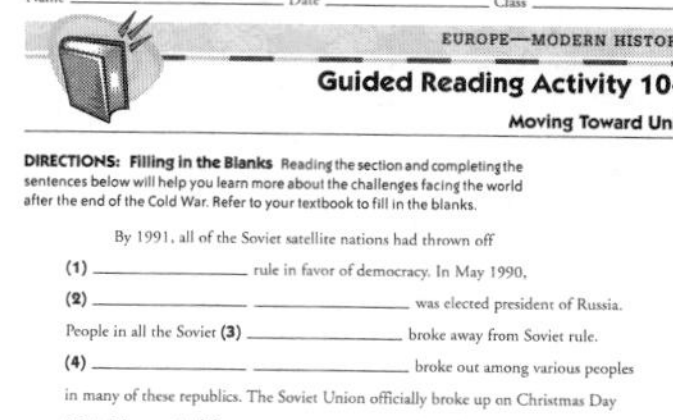
Name ______ Date ______ Class ______

EUROPE—MODERN HISTORY

Guided Reading Activity 10-3

Moving Toward Unity

DIRECTIONS: Filling in the Blanks Reading the section and completing the sentences below will help you learn more about the challenges facing the world after the end of the Cold War. Refer to your textbook to fill in the blanks.

By 1991, all of the Soviet satellite nations had thrown off **(1)** ______ rule in favor of democracy. In May 1990, **(2)** ______ ______ was elected president of Russia. People in all the Soviet **(3)** ______ broke away from Soviet rule. **(4)** ______ ______ broke out among various peoples in many of these republics. The Soviet Union officially broke up on Christmas Day 1991. It became 15 **(5)** ______ republics. **(6)** ______ became the independent republics of Slovenia, Croatia, Bosnia-Herzegovina, Macedo- ... choslovakia became the Czech Republic and

Assign Section 3 Assessment as homework or an in-class activity.

Have students use the Interactive Tutor Self-Assessment CD-ROM to review Section 10–3.

✓ Reading Check Answer

the Euro

More About the Photo

In January 2002, Euro notes and coins began replacing the currencies of the 11 members of the European Monetary Union (EMU).

Caption Answer *Top row:* Austria (Mozart), Belgium (King Albert), Finland (two swans over a lake), France (Tree of Life), German (Federal Eagle); *bottom row:* Ireland (Irish harp), Italy (Leonardo da Vinci drawing), Netherlands (Queen Beatrix), Portugal (seal with castles and coats of arms), Spain (King Juan Carlos). Luxembourg, the 11th member of the EMU is not represented yet.

Team-Teaching Activity

Math Invite a math teacher to class to discuss how to convert the Euro to dollar amounts and vice versa. Look in the newspaper or on the Internet to find the exchange rate of the Euro compared to the dollar. **Ask:** **How many Euros to a dollar? How many dollars to a Euro? If a CD cost $10, how many Euros would it cost? If a jacket costs 100 Euros, how many dollars would it cost?** Compare the dollar exchange rates of other currencies.

EE4 Human Systems: Standard 11

Chapter 10

Section 3, pages 267–270

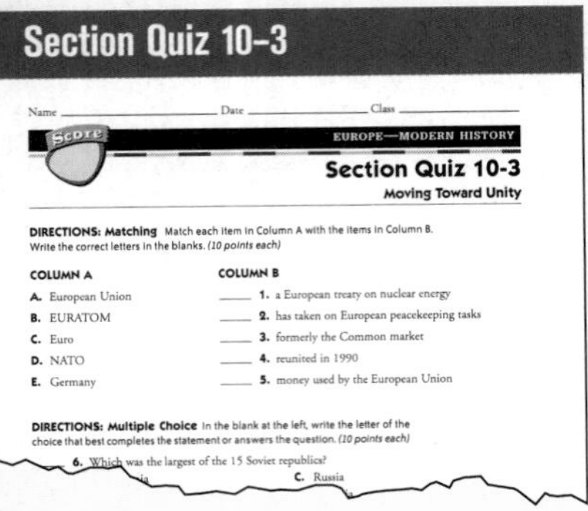

Section Quiz 10-3

Name ______ Date ______ Class ______

EUROPE—MODERN HISTORY

Section Quiz 10-3

Moving Toward Unity

DIRECTIONS: Matching Match each item in Column A with the items in Column B. Write the correct letters in the blanks. *(10 points each)*

COLUMN A	COLUMN B
A. European Union	____ **1.** a European treaty on nuclear energy
B. EURATOM	____ **2.** has taken on European peacekeeping tasks
C. Euro	____ **3.** formerly the Common market
D. NATO	____ **4.** reunited in 1990
E. Germany	____ **5.** money used by the European Union

DIRECTIONS: Multiple Choice In the blank at the left, write the letter of the choice that best completes the statement or answers the question. *(10 points each)*

____ **6.** Which was the largest of the 15 Soviet republics?

C. Russia

✓ Reading Check Answer

Possible answers: ethnic conflicts, gap between rich and poor, population growth, rising health and food needs, disagreements about NATO's role, pollution

Reading Essentials and Study Guide 10-3

Name ______ Date ______ Class ______

EUROPE—MODERN HISTORY

Reading Essentials and Study Guide 10-3

Moving Toward Unity

For use with textbook pages 267-270

Terms to Know

European Union the new name for the old European Common Market (page 268)

Euro common currency for the European Union (page 268)

Drawing from Experience

Have you ever tried to work on a problem alone or when others were working against you? Have you ever worked on a problem with other people who were as interested as you were in solving it? Which way allowed you to solve the problem in the easiest way? Cooperation among coun- ... foundations of the European Union.

... discussed the lack of progress during the Cold War.

CLOSE

Have students read a recent newspaper or look at a news Web site. Have them find an article about Europe and write a paragraph that summarizes the key points of the article.

Environmental Issues Yet another important challenge for Europe comes from environmental problems. In France, rivers like the Seine and the Loire are polluted as are the major canals. In the Netherlands, water is not drunk or used on gardens without being filtered first. Nowhere is the problem more acute than in the Rhine River. As the river flows north, it passes through a continuous band of cities and industrial regions. By the time it reaches the Netherlands it is carrying a staggering 25 million tons of industrial water per year. This is all dumped into the North Sea. In its rush to develop and compete, the Soviet Union did damage to the natural environment across Europe and Asia. The resulting air, water, and land pollution from these environmental disasters needs to be cleaned up and reversed.

One pressing issue is the growing greenhouse effect. Heavy use of coal and oil fuels results in a build-up of carbon dioxide gas in the atmosphere. Scientists believe that this may cause the earth's average temperature to rise. Even a slight rise could result in polar ice cap melting and flooding in some coastal regions of the world.

Europeans are realizing that international cooperation and increased contact among peoples hold the key to overcoming the regions—and the world's—most pressing challenges and crises. Because of their history, Europeans have learned the importance of working together to deal with major problems.

✓ Reading Check **What are two important issues facing Europeans today?**

Section 3 Assessment

Defining Terms

1. **Define** European Union, Euro.

Recalling Facts

2. **History** What smaller independent republics were formed after the breakup of Yugoslavia?

3. **Economics** What is the European Union trying to achieve?

Critical Thinking

4. **Making Inferences** Why did freedom from Soviet rule lead to ethnic fighting in many former Soviet satellites?

5. **Drawing Conclusions** Do you think Russia will join the European Union? Why or why not?

Graphic Organizer

6. **Organizing Information** Create a list showing some of the problems still facing Europe.

1. ______
2. ______
3. ______
4. ______

Applying Social Studies Skills

7. **Summarizing** Write a paragraph that summarizes the end of the Soviet Union. In your summary be sure to include important events that led to the break up, any key people who created change, and the final outcome of the break up.

Section 3 Assessment

1. The terms are defined in the Glossary.
2. Slovenia, Croatia, Bosnia, Herzegovina, Macedonia, Yugoslavia
3. greater economic unity between European countries
4. Without strong Soviet control, there was freedom to express old resentment and conflicts.
5. *Possible answers:* It will join for more economic power and easier trade. It won't join to maintain its independence from other European countries.
6. *Possible answers:* ethnic conflicts, gap between rich and poor, population growth, rising health and food needs, disagreements about NATO's role, pollution
7. Answers will vary.

Chapter 10 Reading Review

Section 1 The Modern Era

Terms to Know
- productivity
- human resources
- textiles
- cottage industry
- union
- strike
- imperialism
- alliance
- communism
- Holocaust
- genocide

Main Idea

Industrialization led not only to a higher standard of living for some, but also to increased tensions in the world. Two world wars changed the balance of power in the world.

✓Economics Machinery made it possible to increase productivity, leading to the Industrial Revolution.

✓Culture Industry changed the way people worked and lived.

✓Economics Competition for markets and resources led to imperialism and friction among European countries.

✓History The two World Wars changed the way wars were fought and created new political power for the United States and the Soviet Union.

Section 2 A Continent Divided

Terms to Know
- Cold War
- nuclear weapon
- deterrence
- satellite nation
- blockade
- airlift
- glasnost
- perestroika
- capitalism

Main Idea

Two powers, the democratic United States and the Communist Soviet Union, worked to bring their forms of government to the war-torn nations of Europe.

✓History Competition between the United States and the Soviet Union started a cold war.

✓Economics Western European countries joined together to form the European Common Market, which moved toward greater cooperation and economic development.

✓Government The Soviet Union made satellites of its surrounding nations.

✓History Berlin became a "hot spot" for conflict between the superpowers, symbolized by the Berlin Wall.

✓Government As its satellites began to rebel, the Soviet Union under Mikhail Gorbachev moved towards a more open system that allowed privately owned businesses.

Section 3 Moving Toward Unity

Terms to Know
- European Union
- Euro

Main Idea

Although the Cold War is over, many challenges still face the old and new nations of Europe.

✓History In 1991, the Soviet Union officially broke up into 15 independent republics.

✓Economics The fall of the Soviet Union increased Europe's global influence and strengthened the movement towards greater political and economic unity.

✓Human/Environment Interaction Problems still remain in Europe, including poverty, population growth, and pollution.

Reading Review

Use the Chapter 10 Reading Review to preview, review, condense, or reteach the chapter.

Preview/Review

Use the Terms to Know lists to help students review and study.

Activity Have students group the terms according to one of the following categories: industry, war, economics, politics. Some words may go under more than one category. Read a term out loud and ask for volunteers to categorize it and explain why they chose that category.

Vocabulary PuzzleMaker Software reinforces the vocabulary terms used in Chapter 10.

The Interactive Tutor Self-Assessment CD-ROM allows students to review Chapter 10 content.

Condense

Have students read the Chapter 10 summary statements.

Chapter 10 Guided Reading Activities

Chapter 10 Audio Program

Reteach

Reteaching Activity 10

Chapter 10 Reading Essentials and Study Guide

Chapter Culminating Activity

Personal Perspectives Have students do more research about Mikhail Gorbachev's policies of **glasnost** and **perestroika.** Discuss with the class how these policies might have changed life for Russians. Then, have your students write two letters as if they were a Russian citizen writing to a friend in the United States. The first letter should describe the writer's life before these policies were implemented (around 1985). The second should be dated a year later and describe how life has changed.

EE4 Human Systems: Standard 12

Assessment and Activities

GLENCOE TECHNOLOGY

MindJogger Videoquiz
Use MindJogger to review the Chapter 10 content.

 Available in VHS.

Using Key Terms

1.	g	6.	h
2.	a	7.	j
3.	f	8.	b
4.	i	9.	e
5.	c	10.	d

Reviewing the Main Ideas

11. People had to work on a regular schedule. Living conditions improved because manufactured goods were less expensive.
12. so they could have markets and resources for their factories
13. *Possible answers:* a world-wide depression; new alliances after WWI; Hitler became dictator of Germany
14. a loan program started by the United States to help rebuild Europe after WWII; it restored the economies of Western Europe
15. They were started to fight communism and attacks by the Soviets.
16. an alliance of countries that wished to remain neutral during the Cold War; Yugoslavia, India, Egypt, Indonesia
17. to prevent people from fleeing to West Berlin from East Berlin
18. glasnost, perestroika
19. poor economies, ethnic tensions, lack of understanding democracy
20. a common currency used by most EU members
21. They created environmental disasters in Europe and Asia.

Chapter 10 Assessment and Activities

 Using Key Terms

Match the terms in Part A with their definitions in Part B.

A.

1. productivity
2. union
3. imperialism
4. communism
5. genocide
6. Cold War
7. deterrence
8. glasnost
9. capitalism
10. Euro

B.

a. group that bargains for better working conditions
b. openness
c. mass murder of a people because of race, religion, ethnicity, politics, or culture
d. European Union common currency
e. economic system where businesses are privately held
f. countries claim colonies for their resources and markets
g. how much work can be done in a certain length of time
h. conflict between the United States and the Soviet Union
i. political system that called for the overthrow of the industrialized system
j. designed to discourage a first attack

 Reviewing the Main Ideas

Section 1 The Modern Era

11. **History** How did the Industrial Revolution change working and living conditions?
12. **Economics** Why did European countries find it necessary to have colonies?
13. **History** What were some of the problems that led to World War II?

Section 2 A Continent Divided

14. **History** What was the Marshall Plan, and why was it important?
15. **History** How did the Truman Doctrine and NATO intensify the Cold War?
16. **Government** What was the Non-Aligned Community, and which nations belonged to it?
17. **History** Why did the Soviet Union build the Berlin Wall?
18. **Government** What were some of the policies that Mikhail Gorbachev introduced?

Section 3 Moving Toward Unity

19. **Government** What are some of the problems facing the new republics formed after the breakup of the Soviet Union?
20. **Economics** What is the Euro?
21. **Human/Environment Interaction** How has Soviet economic development and competition affected the environment?

The Allies and Axis Powers

Place Location Activity

On a separate sheet of paper, match the letters on the map with the numbered places listed below.

1. Germany
2. Italy
3. United Kingdom
4. France
5. China
6. Soviet Union
7. Japan
8. United States

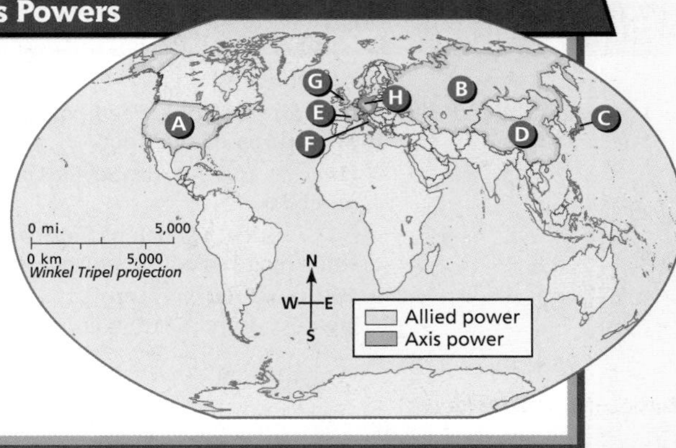

NATIONAL GEOGRAPHIC Place Location Activity

1.	H	5.	D
2.	F	6.	B
3.	G	7.	C
4.	E	8.	A

Critical Thinking

22. *Possible answers:* Western Europe could become stronger economically, Russia and/or its former satellites could become part of a European trade agreement
23. *Possible answers:* Marshall Plan; Truman Doctrine; formation of NATO, Benelux, and European Union; Warsaw Pact; Berlin Wall; space race

Self-Check Quiz Visit the ***Our World Today: People, Places, and Issues*** Web site at owt.glencoe.com and click on **Chapter 10–Self-Check Quizzes** to prepare for the Chapter Test.

Critical Thinking

22. **Predicting Consequences** What changes will occur in Europe as a result of the European Union and the collapse of the Soviet Union?
23. **Sequencing Events** List five events that made the Cold War "colder."

1. ______
2. ______
3. ______
4. ______
5. ______

Current Events Journal

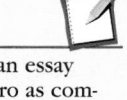

24. **Writing and Evaluating** Write an essay explaining why adopting the Euro as common European currency is a good or bad idea. Find out why the European Union thinks a common currency is important and how Europeans are adapting to it. Use the Technology Skills Activity to provide more information to support your arguments.

Mental Mapping

25. **Focusing on the Region** Draw a simple outline map of Europe and label the following:

- the United Kingdom
- Germany
- Italy
- France
- Russia
- Spain
- Greece

Technology Skills Activity

26. **Using the Internet** Research the national currencies that are being used in at least five European countries until the Euro is adopted. Note what each country's currency is called and when the country plans to phase it out. Use this information to support your ideas in the Current Events Journal above.

The Princeton Review

Standardized Test Practice

Directions: Study the map, then answer the question that follows.

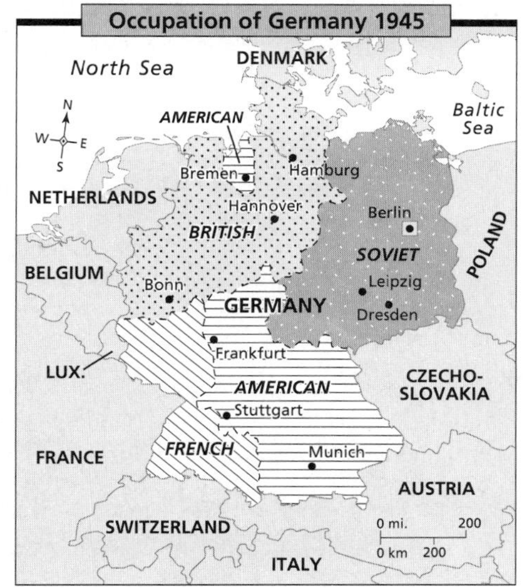

1. In 1945, what country controlled the land surrounding Berlin, Germany's capital?

F the United Kingdom
G the Soviet Union
H the United States
J France

Test-Taking Tip: This question asks you to synthesize information on the map with prior knowledge. Notice that the map does not specifically state that the United Kingdom, for example, controlled a portion of Germany. Instead, it refers to this area as "British."

273

Assessment and Activities

Standardized Test Practice

1. G

Tested Objectives:
Reading a map, analyzing information

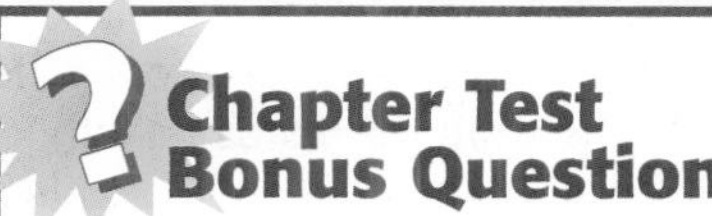

Chapter Test Bonus Question

This question may be used for extra credit on the chapter test.

What was it called when European nations claimed colonies in Africa and Asia? *(Imperialism)*

Have students visit the Web site at **owt.glencoe.com** to review Chapter 10 and take the Self-Check Quiz.

Current Events Journal

24. Student essays will vary, but they should include an explanation of the Euro and why it was adopted. Their opinions should be supported by examples.

Mental Mapping Activity

25. This exercise helps students visualize the countries they've been studying and understand the relationships of various points. Accept all attempts at freehand mapping that show places in correct relation to one another.

Technology Skills Activity

26. Students' reports should include brief text descriptions of each site as well as illustrations.

EYE on the Environment

1 Focus

Ask: **What images, feelings, or phrases come to mind when you think of rain?** *(Students are likely to respond with such ideas as wetness, gloominess, and so on.)* As they answer, lead them to think of the contribution that rain makes to life by offering such words as "growth," "spring," "flowers blooming," and so on. As students see the vital role that rain plays in promoting life on Earth, write the words "death" and "disease" on the board. Explain that in this feature, students will see how these words are also connected with rain.

2 Teach

Problem Solving Explain to students that several issues make solving acid rain difficult. One is the expense of converting polluting facilities to nonpolluting technology or of installing scrubbers and other pollution-control devices. Another is the huge number of automobiles in the world, because their exhaust contributes to acid rain as well. A third problem is the international dimension—the source of the pollution is often not the same country where the effects are felt. Ask students if they can identify any other issues that might slow remedies to acid rain. Have them suggest ways of overcoming each problem. **L2**

EYE on the Environment

RAIN, RAIN Go Away

Acid Rain Have you ever sucked on a lemon slice? Yow! Lemons make you pucker up because they are high in acid. Rainwater can be acidic, too. Any form of precipitation that contains high amounts of acid is known as acid rain. In some parts of the world, rain or snow falls that is as acidic as lemon juice.

Why does this happen? When cars and trucks burn gasoline, or when factories and power plants burn coal, sulfur and nitrogen compounds are produced. High in the atmosphere, these gases mix with moisture to form sulfuric acid and nitric acid. These acids make rainwater much more acidic than normal. Acid rain is a problem because it

- harms fish and other animals in lakes and streams;
- damages trees and crops;
- washes nutrients out of soils.

Taking Action Europeans are very concerned about acid rain and its effects. Half of the trees in Germany's Black Forest are sick or dying. Forests in Norway, Austria, Poland, France, and the Czech Republic have also been damaged. In Sweden, 20 percent of the lakes contain few or no fish. The same is true of most lakes in southern Norway.

Many European countries are trying to reduce acid rain by

- installing filters on factory smokestacks;
- putting special exhaust systems on motor vehicles;
- building new factories that do not burn coal.

A German factory spews chemicals that cause acid rain.

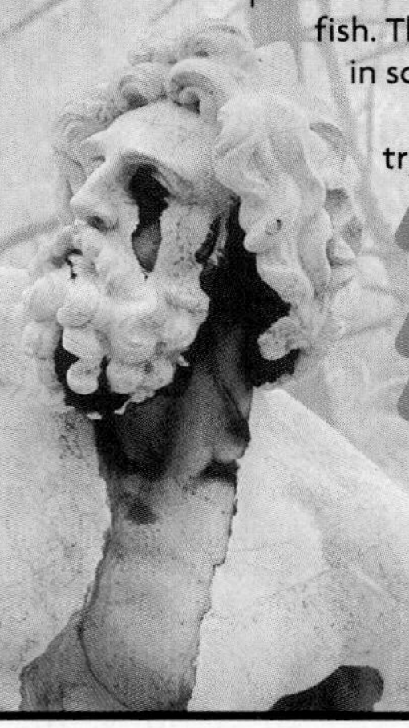

Acid rain eats away at a statue in Rome.

More About the Issues

Students in a middle school near Schenectady, New York, are taking a novel approach to cutting acid rain. Under American law, power plants are given so many "allowances" per year to give off sulphur dioxide, a component of acid rain. Plants that do not pollute are permitted to sell their allowances to plants that do pollute. The hope is that through this system, plants will move to non-polluting methods of producing energy so that they do not have to buy allowances. The students learned that anyone, not just power plants, can buy these allowances. They have raised $24,000 in the past few years, buying allowances that cover 313 tons of sulphur dioxide emission. As a result, overall pollution has been reduced.

Making a Difference

Acid Rain 2000 A project called Acid Rain 2000 is giving students across Europe a chance to study acid rain and its effects. From 2000 to 2005, participating students will be collecting four kinds of environmental data at study sites in Europe.

- **WEATHER** — Each day, students record the wind direction and the acidity of precipitation.
- **PLANTS** — Once a month, students check the condition of trees and other plants at their sites.
- **SOIL** — Once a month, students test the soil at their sites for acid and plant nutrient levels.
- **LICHENS** — Twice a year, students record the condition of plants called lichens. Since lichens die if the air is too polluted, they are good indicators of a site's air quality.

Acid Rain 2000 participants e-mail the data they collect to Northamptonshire Grammar School, near Northampton, England. There, students and staff process the data and publish the project's findings on the Internet. Acid Rain 2000 hopes to show which areas in Europe are most sensitive to acid rain.

Student collects weather data

Lichens

What Can You Do?

Collect Data
Although Acid Rain 2000 is a European project, you can collect similar kinds of data at a study site in your community. For more information about how to set up a site and collect data, contact Acid Rain 2000 at *www.brixworth.demon.co.uk/acidrain2000*

Investigate
Does acid rain affect your community? If so, what impact has acid rain had on the environment? What are local industries doing to combat the problem? Motor vehicle exhaust contributes to acid rain. What can you do to limit vehicle use on a daily basis?

Use the Internet
Learn more about the international problem of acid rain. Good sites include *www.brixworth.demon.co.uk/acidrain2000/sites.htm* and the acid rain home page of the U.S. Environmental Protection Agency at *www.epa.gov/docs/airmarkets/acidrain*

275

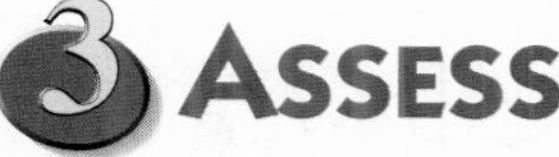

ASSESS

Have students work individually or in groups to complete the What Can You Do? activities on page 275.

CLOSE

Discuss with students the What Can You Do? activities. You may emphasize the international nature of the problem of acid rain by having students write paragraphs that explain how wind patterns can cause pollution in one country to produce acid rain in another.

For an additional regional case study, use the following:

Environmental Case Study 4

Meeting National Standards

Geography for Life

The following standards are met in the Student Edition feature:

EE5 Environment and Society: Standards 14, 15

EE6 The Uses of Geography: Standards 17, 18

What Can You Do? Teacher Tips

Collect Data You may wish to visit the site first so that you can guide students as to which pages to visit.

Investigate The local health department or state environmental agency might have information about pollution issues in your community.

Use the Internet The EPA Web site has specific information aimed at students and teachers as well as more technical industry information.

Chapter 11 Resources

Note: The following materials may be used when teaching Chapter 11.
Section level support materials are shown at point of use in the margins of the Teacher Wraparound Edition.

Timesaving Tools

TeacherWorks™ All-In-One Planner and Resource Center

- **Interactive Teacher Edition** See the **Interactive Teacher Edition** CD-ROM to electronically integrate your Teacher Wraparound Edition and blackline masters.
- **Interactive Lesson Planner** Organize your week, month, semester, or year with all the lesson helps you need. The **Interactive Lesson Planner** CD-ROM contains all Chapter 11 resources.

Use Glencoe's **Presentation Plus!** multimedia teacher tool to easily present dynamic lessons that visually excite your students. Using Microsoft PowerPoint® you can customize the presentations to create your own personalized lessons.

TEACHING TRANSPARENCIES

Graphic Organizer Transparency and Student Activity 11

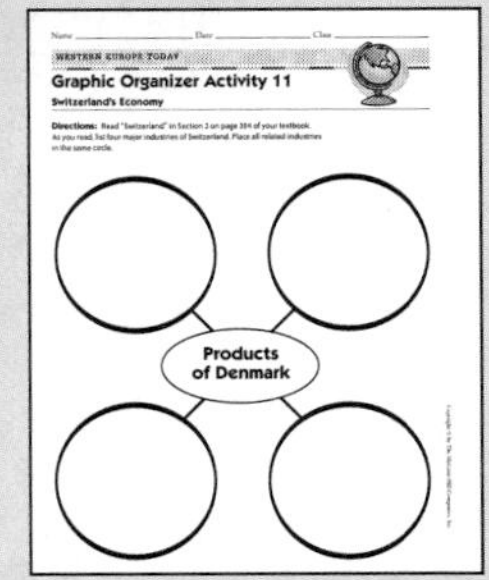

FOLDABLES™ Study Organizer

Foldables are three-dimensional, interactive graphic organizers that help students practice basic writing skills, review key vocabulary terms, and identify main ideas. Every chapter contains a Foldable activity, with additional chapter activities found in the ***Reading and Study Skills Foldables*** booklet.

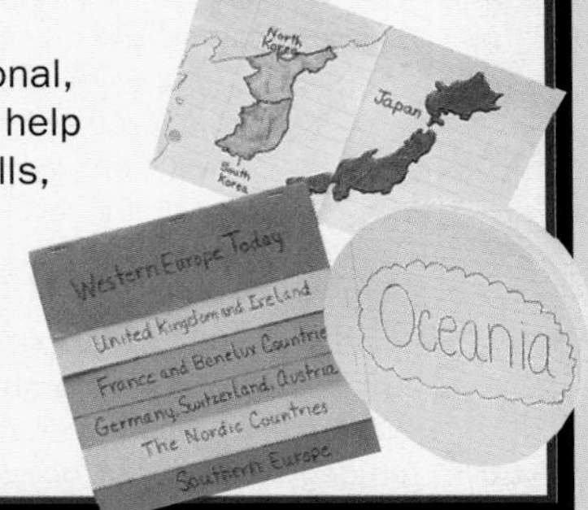

ENRICHMENT AND EXTENSION

Enrichment Activity 11

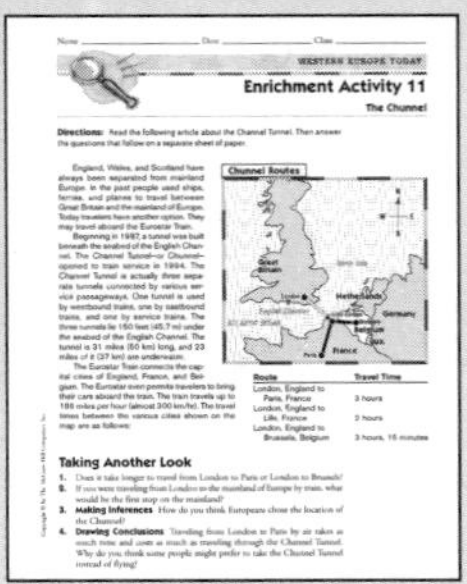

Cooperative Learning Activity 11

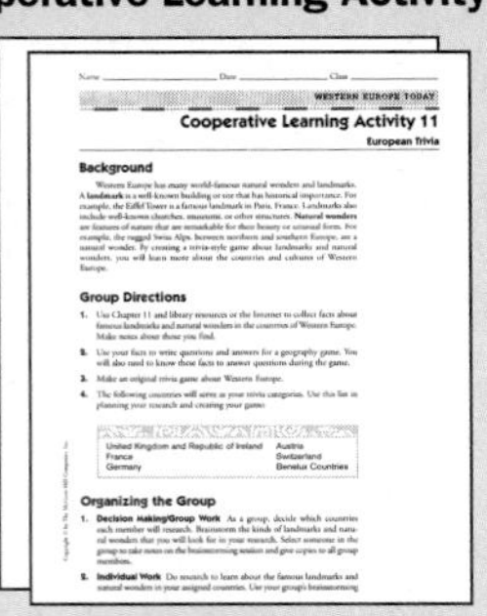

MAP AND GEOGRAPHY SKILLS

Chapter Map Activity 11

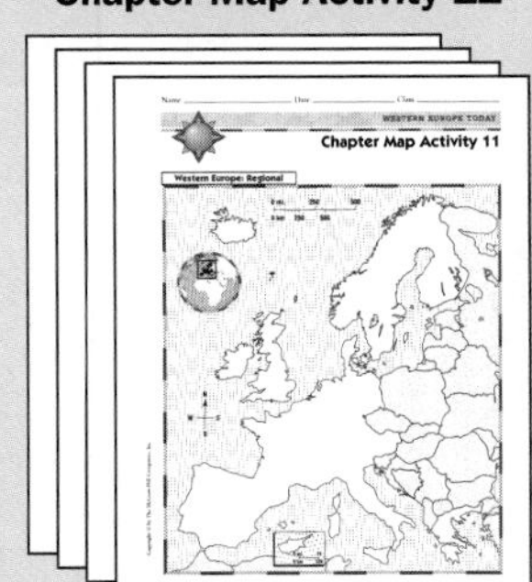

GeoLab Activity 11

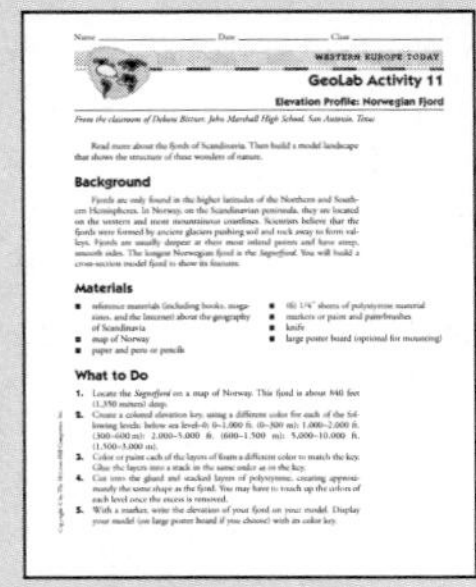

STANDARDIZED ASSESSMENT SKILLS

GLENCOE'S ASSESSMENT ADVANTAGE

Critical Thinking Skills Activity 11

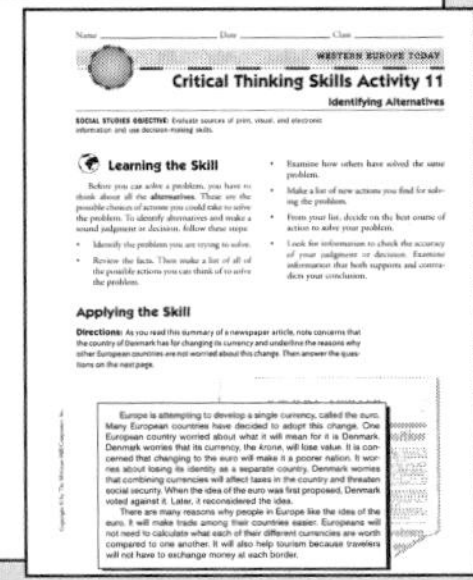

Map and Graph Skills Activity 11

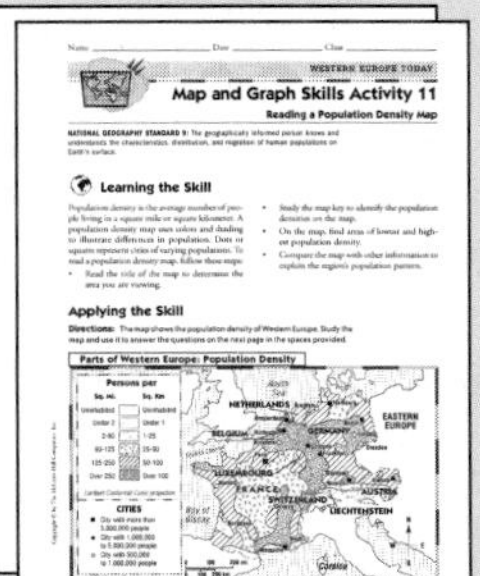

Reading and Writing Skills Activity 11

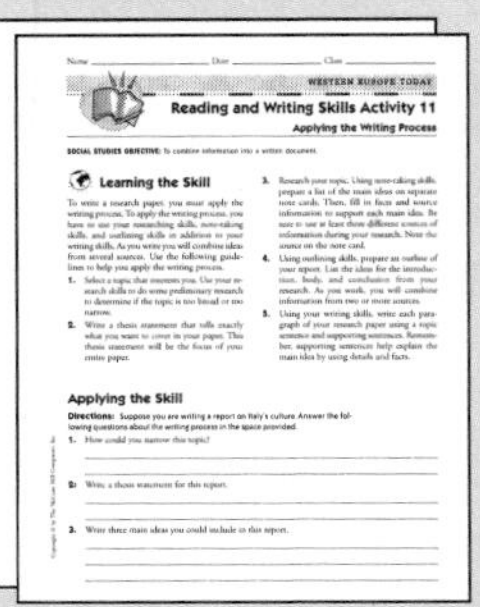

Standardized Test Practice Workbook Activity 11

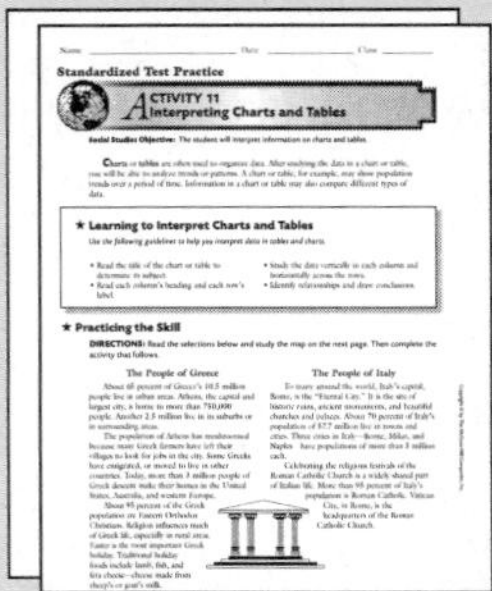

REVIEW AND REINFORCEMENT

Chapter Skills Activity 11

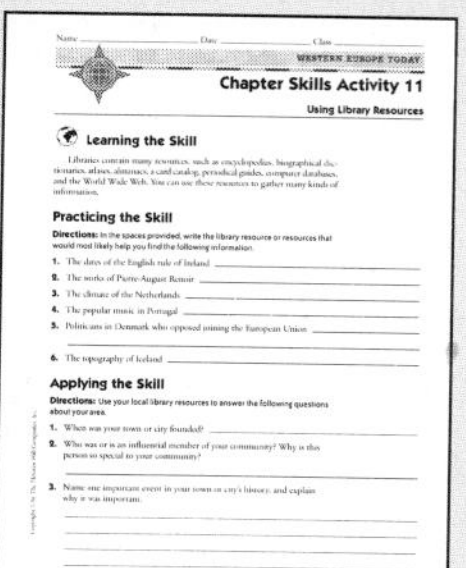

Take-Home Review Activity 11

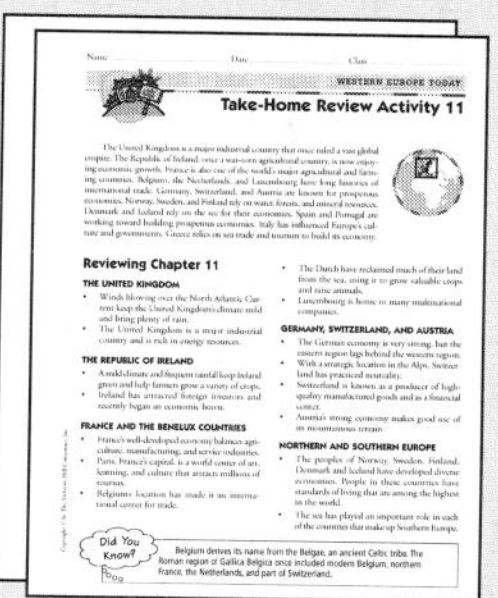

Reteaching Activity 11

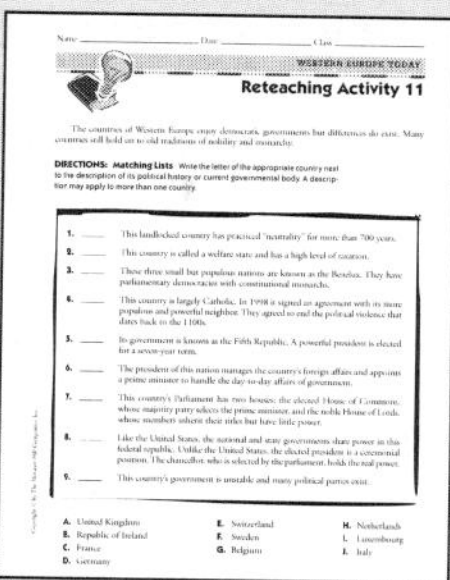

Vocabulary Activity 11

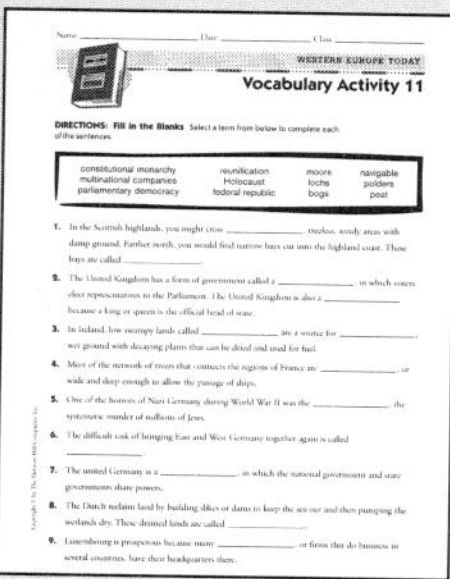

Workbook Activity 11

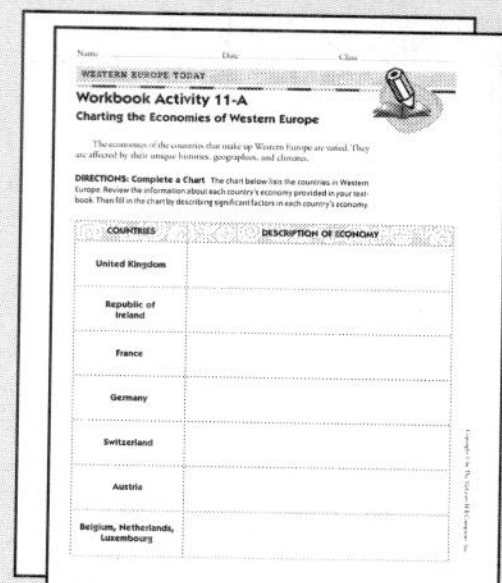

ASSESSMENT

GLENCOE'S ASSESSMENT ADVANTAGE

Chapter 11 Test, Form A

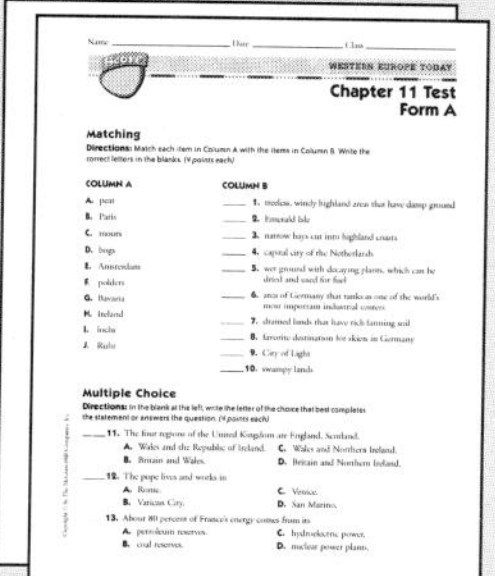

Chapter 11 Test, Form B

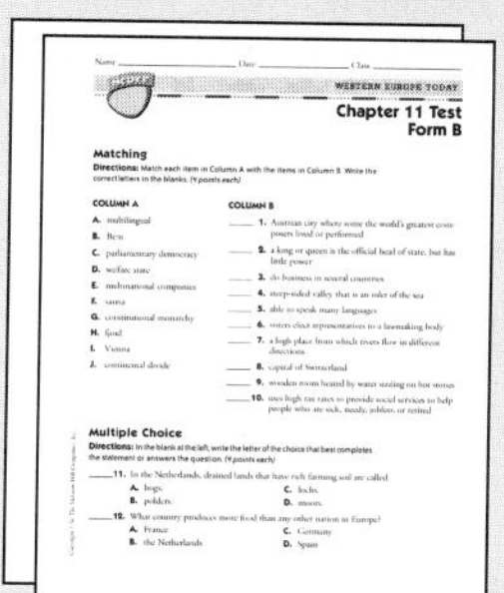

Performance Assessment Activity 11

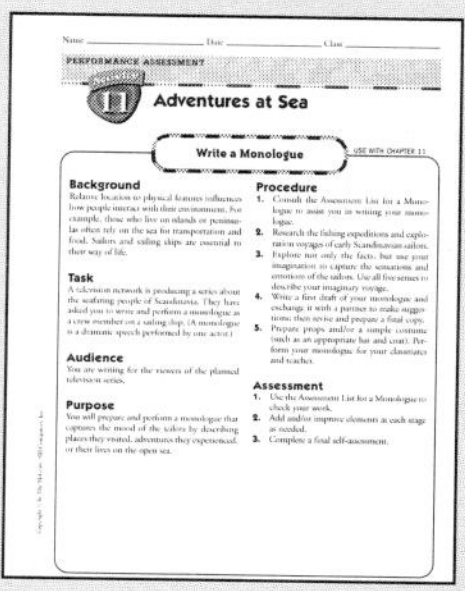

ExamView® Pro 3.0 Testmaker CD-ROM

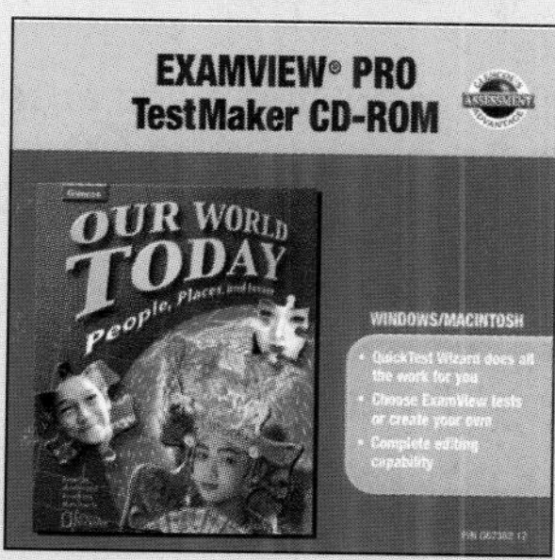

MULTIMEDIA

- National Geographic's The World and Its People
- MindJogger Videoquiz
- Vocabulary PuzzleMaker Software
- Interactive Tutor Self-Assessment CD-ROM
- ExamView® Pro 3.0 Testmaker CD-ROM
- Interactive Lesson Planner CD-ROM
- Interactive Teacher Edition CD-ROM
- Skillbuilder Interactive Workbook CD-ROM, Level 1
- Presentation Plus! CD-ROM
- Audio Program

SPANISH RESOURCES

The following Spanish language materials are available in the Spanish Resources binder:

- Spanish Chapter Summaries
- Spanish Vocabulary Activities
- Spanish Guided Reading Activities
- Spanish Quizzes and Tests
- Spanish Take-Home Review Activities
- Spanish Reteaching Activities

Meeting National Standards

Geography for Life

All of the 18 standards are demonstrated in Unit 4. The following ones are highlighted in Chapter 11:

Section 1 EE1 The World in Spatial Terms: Standards 1, 2, 3
EE6 The Uses of Geography: Standard 17

Section 2 EE4 Human Systems: Standards 9, 10, 11, 12, 13

Section 3 EE2 Places and Regions: Standards 4, 5, 6

Section 4 EE4 Human Systems: Standards 9, 11, 12, 13

Section 5 EE1 The World in Spatial Terms: Standards 1, 2, 3
EE2 Places and Regions: Standard 4

For a complete listing of National Geography Standards and entire text correlation, see pages T22–T29.

Chapter 11 Planning Guide

SECTION RESOURCES

Daily Objectives	Reproducible Resources	Multimedia Resources
Section 1 **The United Kingdom and Ireland** **Suggested Pacing = 1 day** **1.** Discuss the economies and governments of the United Kingdom and Ireland. **2.** Explain the history and culture of the United Kingdom and Ireland.	Reproducible Lesson Plan 11-1 Daily Lecture and Discussion Notes 11-1 Guided Reading Activity 11-1 Reading Essentials and Study Guide 11-1 Section Quiz 11-1*	Daily Focus Skills Transparency 11-1 GeoQuiz Transparency 11-1 Vocabulary PuzzleMaker Software Interactive Tutor Self-Assessment CD-ROM ExamView® Pro 3.0 Testmaker CD-ROM Presentation Plus! CD-ROM
Section 2 **France and the Benelux Countries** **Suggested Pacing = 1 day** **1.** Discuss the economy and people of France. **2.** Compare the cultures and economies of the Benelux countries.	Reproducible Lesson Plan 11-2 Daily Lecture and Discussion Notes 11-2 Guided Reading Activity 11-2 Reading Essentials and Study Guide 11-2 Section Quiz 11-2*	Daily Focus Skills Transparency 11-2 GeoQuiz Transparency 11-1 Vocabulary PuzzleMaker Software Interactive Tutor Self-Assessment CD-ROM ExamView® Pro 3.0 Testmaker CD-ROM Presentation Plus! CD-ROM
Section 3 **Germany, Switzerland, and Austria** **Suggested Pacing = 1 day** **1.** Discuss the economy and government of Germany. **2.** Compare the geography and economies of Switzerland and Austria.	Reproducible Lesson Plan 11-3 Daily Lecture and Discussion Notes 11-3 Guided Reading Activity 11-3 Reading Essentials and Study Guide 11-3 Section Quiz 11-3*	Daily Focus Skills Transparency 11-3 GeoQuiz Transparency 11-1 Vocabulary PuzzleMaker Software Interactive Tutor Self-Assessment CD-ROM ExamView® Pro 3.0 Testmaker CD-ROM Presentation Plus! CD-ROM
Section 4 **The Nordic Countries** **Suggested Pacing = 1 day** **1.** Describe the landscapes and climates of the Nordic countries. **2.** Compare the economies and people of this region.	Reproducible Lesson Plan 11-4 Daily Lecture and Discussion Notes 11-4 Guided Reading Activity 11-4 Reading Essentials and Study Guide 11-4 Section Quiz 11-4*	Daily Focus Skills Transparency 11-4 GeoQuiz Transparency 11-4 Vocabulary PuzzleMaker Software Interactive Tutor Self-Assessment CD-ROM ExamView® Pro 3.0 Testmaker CD-ROM Presentation Plus! CD-ROM
Section 5 **Southern Europe** **Suggested Pacing = 1 day** **1.** Compare the geography and people of Spain and Portugal. **2.** Summarize the history and cultural contributions of Italy. **3.** Explain how physical geography has shaped life and history in Greece.	Reproducible Lesson Plan 11-5 Daily Lecture and Discussion Notes 11-5 Guided Reading Activity 11-5 Reading Essentials and Study Guide 11-5 Section Quiz 11-5*	Daily Focus Skills Transparency 11-5 GeoQuiz Transparency 11-5 Vocabulary PuzzleMaker Software Interactive Tutor Self-Assessment CD-ROM ExamView® Pro 3.0 Testmaker CD-ROM Presentation Plus! CD-ROM

00:00 **Out of Time?** Assign the **Reading Essentials and Study Guide** for this chapter.

*Also available in Spanish

Teacher to Teacher

Europe in a Box

Phillip G. Hays
Conrad Weiser Middle School
Robesonia, Pennsylvania

Students create a cereal box showing the culture of their chosen country. Each student brings in an empty cereal box and chooses one country from Europe. Students use drawings, photos from magazines, and other visual aids to design their boxes. On the front panel of the box, students should show a map of the country and visuals of the land. The back panel should show photos of the people. On the side panels, students should create charts and graphs to illustrate the economy. The box top lists statistics about the country. The name of the cereal should reflect the country's name or a part of its culture—Ukraine Krispies, Londonberry Loops. Three items representing the land, the people, and the economy are placed inside the box (e.g., a wool scarf to represent sheep raising). Students then incorporate main and supporting ideas to create a 30-second commercial to advertise their "cereal."

OUR WORLD TODAY Online

Use our Web site for additional resources. All essential content is covered in the Student Edition.

You and your students can visit owt.glencoe.com, the Web site companion to *Our World Today*. This innovative integration of electronic and print media offers your students a wealth of opportunities. The student text directs students to the Web site for the following options:

- Chapter Overviews
- Student Web Activities
- Self-Check Quizzes
- Textbook Updates

Answers are provided for you in the Web Activity Lesson Plan. Additional Web resources and Interactive Tutor puzzles are also available.

NATIONAL GEOGRAPHIC TEACHER'S CORNER

Index to National Geographic Magazine:

The following articles may be used for research relating to this chapter:

- "London," by Simon Worrall, June 2000.
- "Tale of Three Cities," by Joel L. Swedlow, August 1999.
- *Biodiversity,* a National Geographic Special Edition, February 1999.
- "Naples Unabashed," by Erla Zwingle, March 1998.

National Geographic Society Products Available From Glencoe:

To order the following products for use with this chapter, contact your local Glencoe sales representative or call Glencoe at 1-800-334-7344:

- *PicturePack: Geography of Europe* (Transparencies)
- *Picture Atlas of the World* (CD-ROM)
- *Physical Geography of the World* (Transparencies)
- *MapPack: Europe* (Transparencies)

Additional National Geographic Society Products:

To order the following products for use with this chapter, call National Geographic Society at 1-800-368-2728:

- *Complete National Geographic: 111 Years of National Geographic Magazine* (CD-ROM)
- *GeoKit: Pollution* (Kit)
- *Europe* (Video)
- *Weather: Come Rain, Come Shine* (Video)
- *Democratic Government Series* (5 Videos)
- *Europe: The Road to Unity* (Video)
- *Capitalism, Communism, Socialism Series* (3 Videos)
- *National Geographic Atlas of the World, Seventh Edition* (Book)

NGS ONLINE

Access National Geographic's Web site for current events, activities, links, interactive features, and archives.
www.nationalgeographic.com

Introducing Chapter 11

Introduce students to chapter content and key terms by having them access Chapter Overview 11 at owt.glencoe.com

Chapter Objectives

1. Describe the government and economy of the United Kingdom and its relationship with Ireland.
2. Compare the economies and cultures of France and the Benelux countries.
3. Discuss the economies of Germany, Switzerland, and Austria.
4. Explain how physical geography affects life in the Nordic countries.
5. Describe the cultural contributions of southern Europe.

GLENCOE TECHNOLOGY

NATIONAL GEOGRAPHIC

The World and Its People Video Program

Chapters 10–12 Western Europe

The following segments enhance the study of this chapter:

- **Crazy for Tulips**
- **Bears of Svalbard**
- **Gran Paradiso**

Available in DVD and VHS.

MindJogger Videoquiz

Use MindJogger to preview the Chapter 11 content.

Available in VHS.

Chapter 11 Western Europe Today

The World and Its People NATIONAL GEOGRAPHIC

To learn more about the people and places of western Europe, view ***The World and Its People* Chapters 10–12** videos.

Our World Today online

Chapter Overview Visit the ***Our World Today: People, Places, and Issues*** Web site at owt.glencoe.com and click on **Chapter 11—Chapter Overviews** to preview information about western Europe.

Two-Minute Lesson Launcher

Tell students that this chapter discusses countries that had a profound effect on the history and culture of the United States. **Ask: What examples can you give of the influence that the United Kingdom, Ireland, France, and Germany had on American history?** *(British people settled the 13 Atlantic colonies; many American places carry British and French names; Irish and German immigrants poured into the country in the 1800s; United Kingdom, France, and the United States were allies fighting against Germany in the two World Wars of the twentieth century.)* As they read the chapter, have students look for other ways in which the history of these countries has affected their own economies and cultures.

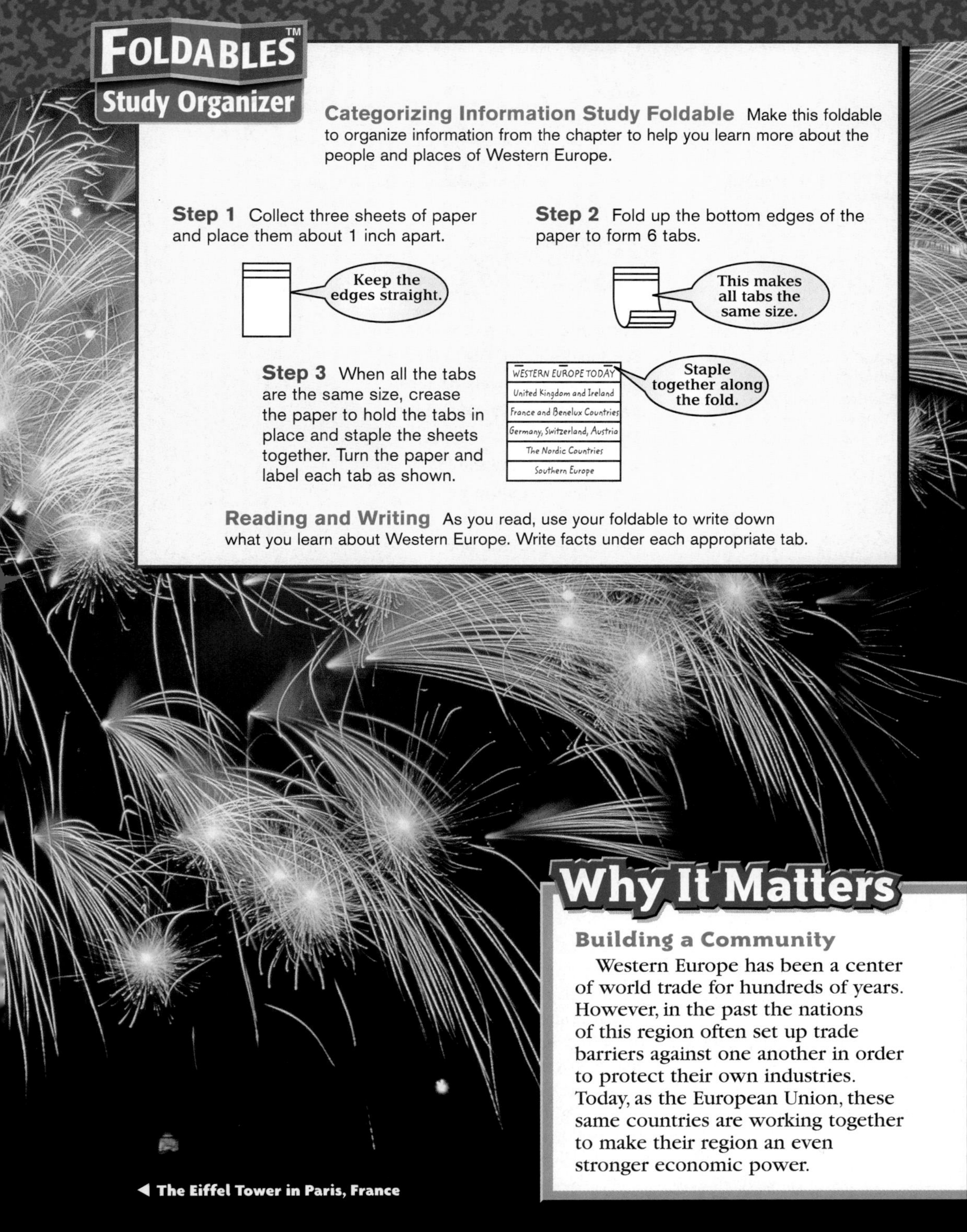

FOLDABLES™ Study Organizer

Categorizing Information Study Foldable Make this foldable to organize information from the chapter to help you learn more about the people and places of Western Europe.

Step 1 Collect three sheets of paper and place them about 1 inch apart.

Step 2 Fold up the bottom edges of the paper to form 6 tabs.

Step 3 When all the tabs are the same size, crease the paper to hold the tabs in place and staple the sheets together. Turn the paper and label each tab as shown.

Reading and Writing As you read, use your foldable to write down what you learn about Western Europe. Write facts under each appropriate tab.

Why It Matters

Building a Community

Western Europe has been a center of world trade for hundreds of years. However, in the past the nations of this region often set up trade barriers against one another in order to protect their own industries. Today, as the European Union, these same countries are working together to make their region an even stronger economic power.

◀ The Eiffel Tower in Paris, France

About the Photo

Bastille Day, July 14, is a national holiday in France celebrated with parades, speeches, and fireworks. It commemorates the 1789 "storming of the Bastille," an infamous Paris prison, in the opening days of the French Revolution. Ask students to compare Bastille Day with the Fourth of July. Why are these holidays important to the people of France and the United States?

Introducing

Chapter 11

FOLDABLES™ Study Organizer

Purpose This activity requires students to create a table and organize information from the chapter on it. Students group information from the chapter into categories, in effect comparing the people and places of the countries of western Europe.

Have students complete ***Reading and Study Skills Foldables*** Activity 11.

Why It Matters

The European Union's mission is to organize relations between the Member States and between their peoples in a coherent manner and on the basis of solidarity. However, there are many difficulties trying to unite different countries and cultures. Organize students into five groups and assign one of the following topics to each: *money, language, laws, defense, social programs.* Have students prepare a brief presentation on how their topic presents barriers to unification and what they think could be done to overcome the barriers.

Chapter 11

Section 1, pages 278–281

FOCUS

Section Objectives

1. Discuss the economies and governments of the United Kingdom and Ireland.
2. Explain the history and culture of the United Kingdom and Ireland.

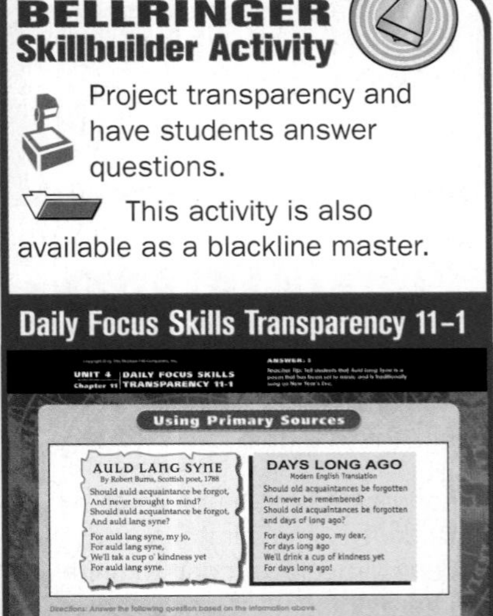

BELLRINGER
Skillbuilder Activity

Project transparency and have students answer questions.

This activity is also available as a blackline master.

Daily Focus Skills Transparency 11-1

UNIT 4 DAILY FOCUS SKILLS TRANSPARENCY 11-1
Using Primary Sources
AULD LANG SYNE
DAYS LONG AGO
What does Auld Lang Syne mean?
A old, long signs
B days long ago
C old acquaintances
D forget the past

Guide to Reading

■ **Accessing Prior Knowledge** Remind students that American law and government are based on practices followed in one of the countries of western Europe. Ask them to identify that country. *(United Kingdom; some may answer England or Great Britain)*

Section 1

The United Kingdom and Ireland

Guide to Reading

Main Idea

The United Kingdom and Ireland are small in size, but their people have had a great impact on the rest of the world.

Terms to Know

- parliamentary democracy
- constitutional monarchy
- peat
- bog

Reading Strategy

Create a diagram like this one. Fill in the names of the four regions that make up the United Kingdom and one fact about each. Create a second diagram for Ireland and include one fact about it.

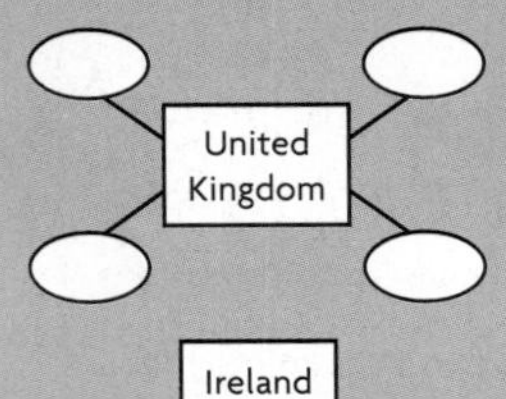

Every year millions of tourists visit London, England. They come to see the crown jewels or dungeons in the Tower of London. They also visit the Houses of Parliament and the tall clock known as Big Ben. You cannot be afraid of heights if you ride one of London's newest attractions. Known as the London Eye, it is the tallest Ferris wheel in the world.

Also known as the **British Isles,** the countries of the **United Kingdom** and the **Republic of Ireland** lie in the North Atlantic Ocean, west of the European continent. While sharing similar physical characteristics, these two countries differ culturally.

The United Kingdom

About the size of Oregon, the United Kingdom is made up of four regions. **England** dominates the United Kingdom, in population and economic strength. However, **Scotland** and **Wales** are important parts of the United Kingdom. Both were conquered by England centuries ago. Today, movements for independence have grown in both countries, as seen by the popularity of the movie *Braveheart,* a film about the Scottish freedom-fighter William Wallace. In Wales, great effort has been made to keep the little-used Welsh language alive by teaching it in school. (Language is one of the most important ways to keep a people's culture

Section Resources

Reproducible Masters

- Reproducible Lesson Plan 11-1
- Daily Lecture and Discussion Notes 11-1
- Guided Reading Activity 11-1
- Reading Essentials and Study Guide 11-1
- Section Quiz 11-1

Transparencies

- Daily Focus Skills Transparency 11-1
- GeoQuiz Transparency 11-1

Multimedia

- Vocabulary PuzzleMaker Software
- Interactive Tutor Self-Assessment CD-ROM
- Presentation Plus! CD-ROM
- ExamView® Pro 3.0 Testmaker CD-ROM

The United Kingdom's fourth region—**Northern Ireland**—shares the island of Ireland with the Republic of Ireland.

The Economy Over 250 years ago, inventors and scientists here sparked the **Industrial Revolution.** Today, the United Kingdom is still a major industrial and trading country. Manufactured goods and machinery are the leading exports, though new computer and electronic industries are gradually replacing older industries. Service industries such as banking, insurance, communications, and health care employ most of the country's people.

Farming is very efficient here. Still, the United Kingdom must import about one-third of its food. Why? A lack of farmland and a limited growing season make it impossible to feed the large population.

The Government The United Kingdom is a **parliamentary democracy,** a form of government in which voters elect representatives to a lawmaking body called Parliament. It has two houses—the House of Commons and the House of Lords. The political party that has the largest number of members in the House of Commons chooses the government's leader, the prime minister. The House of Lords has little power. Most members of the Lords are nobles who have inherited their titles or who have been given titles by the Queen.

NATIONAL GEOGRAPHIC **Western Europe: Political**

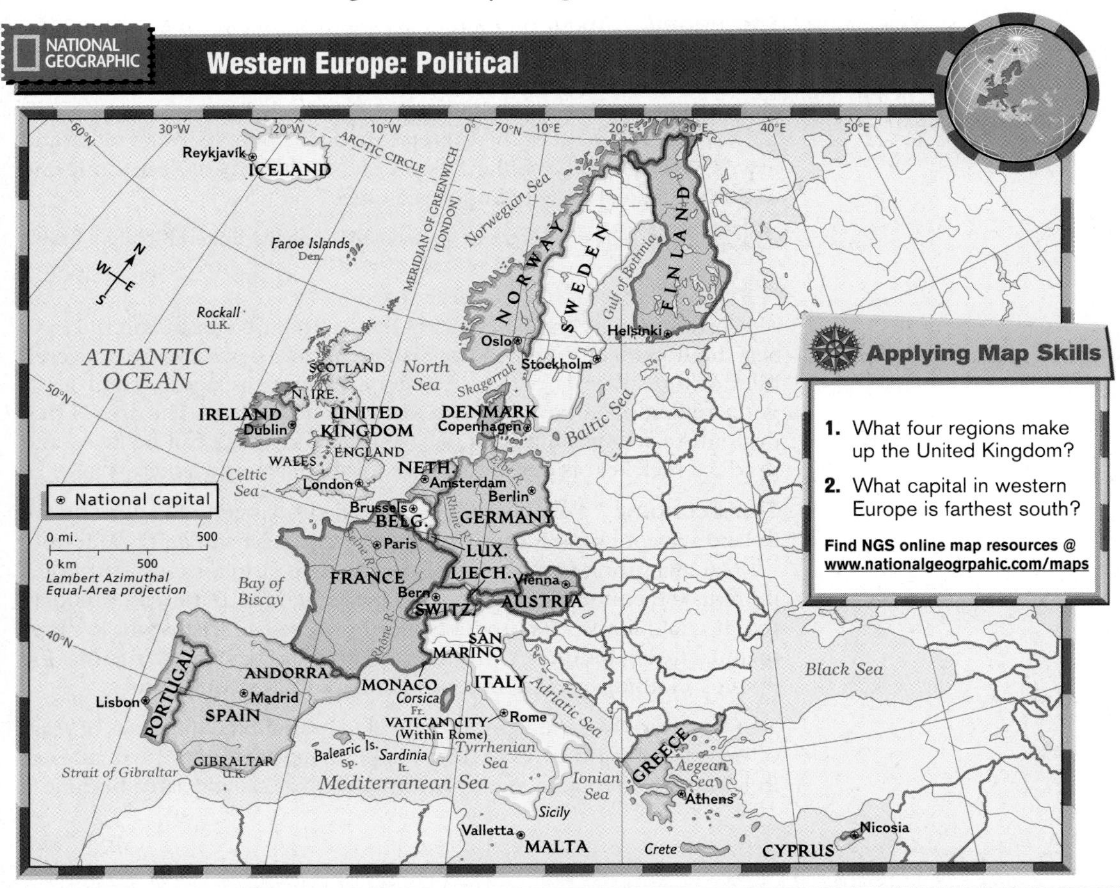

Applying Map Skills

1. What four regions make up the United Kingdom?
2. What capital in western Europe is farthest south?

Find NGS online map resources @ www.nationalgeogrpahic.com/maps

Chapter 11
Section 1, pages 278–281

2 TEACH

Analyzing Information Give students a map of Ireland. Ask why it's divided between two countries. Write down answers and ask again after students have read the chapter. **L1** 

Daily Lecture Notes 11-1

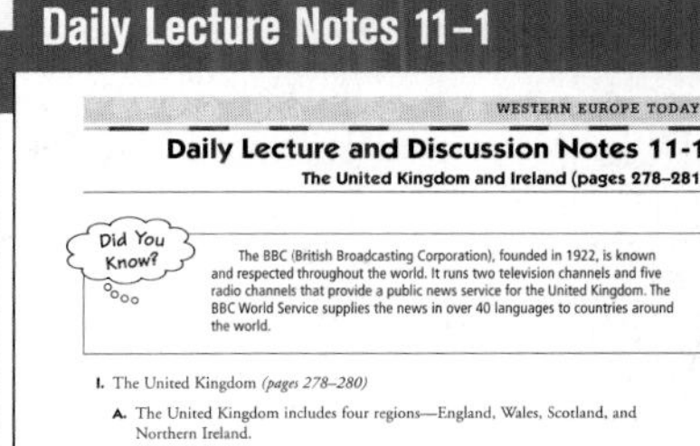
WESTERN EUROPE TODAY

Daily Lecture and Discussion Notes 11-1
The United Kingdom and Ireland (pages 278–281)

Did You Know? The BBC (British Broadcasting Corporation), founded in 1922, is known and respected throughout the world. It runs two television channels and five radio channels that provide a public news service for the United Kingdom. The BBC World Service supplies the news in over 40 languages to countries around the world.

I. The United Kingdom (pages 278–280)
A. The United Kingdom includes four regions—England, Wales, Scotland, and Northern Ireland.
B. In northern England, Wales, and Scotland, cross **moors**—treeless, windy highland areas that have damp ground.
...ays, or **lochs,** cut into the highland coasts.

Applying Map Skills

Answers
1. England, Scotland, Wales, and Northern Ireland
2. Bern, Switzerland

Skills Practice
Which western European countries are islands? *(United Kingdom, Ireland)*

Guided Reading Activity 11-1

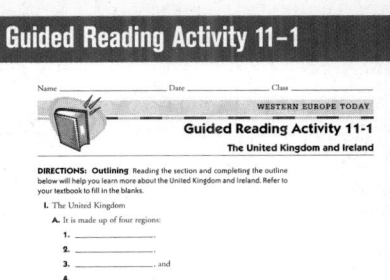

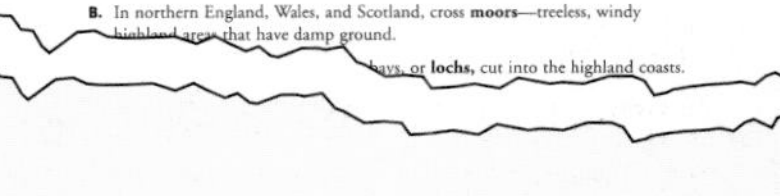
Name ________ Date ________ Class ________

WESTERN EUROPE TODAY

Guided Reading Activity 11-1
The United Kingdom and Ireland

DIRECTIONS: Outlining Reading the section and completing the outline below will help you learn more about the United Kingdom and Ireland. Refer to your textbook to fill in the blanks.

I. The United Kingdom
A. It is made up of four regions:
1. ________.
2. ________.
3. ________, and
4. ________.
...United Kingdom is a major ________ and ________

Team-Teaching Activity

Literature English authors are renowned for their love of nature and skill at evoking the landscape of the United Kingdom. The lyrics of William Wordsworth, the naturalistic prose of Thomas Hardy, and the stirring descriptions written by the Brontë sisters convey the beauty—and at times harshness—of the lake country, western England, and the northern moors, respectively. Invite an English teacher to class to read some descriptive passages penned by British authors. Using the passages, make a list of words describing England's physical geography. Then use a physical map of England to try to identify the areas in the literature. **L2**

EE4 Human Systems: Standard 10

More About the Photos

The Republic of Ireland gained independence from British rule after centuries of rebellion. Today, the two countries share many economic and political ties.

Caption Answer Northern Ireland

Reading Check Answer

parliamentary democracy

3 Assess

Assign Section 1 Assessment as homework or an in-class activity.

Have students use the Interactive Tutor Self-Assessment CD-ROM to review Section 11–1.

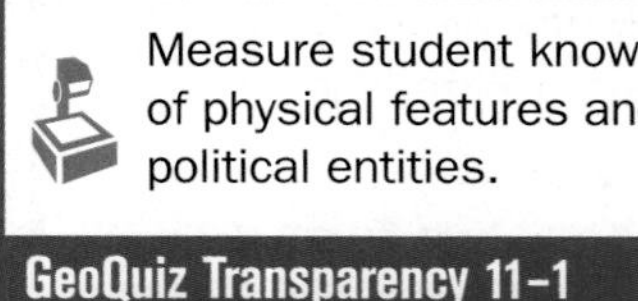

Measure student knowledge of physical features and political entities.

GeoQuiz Transparency 11–1

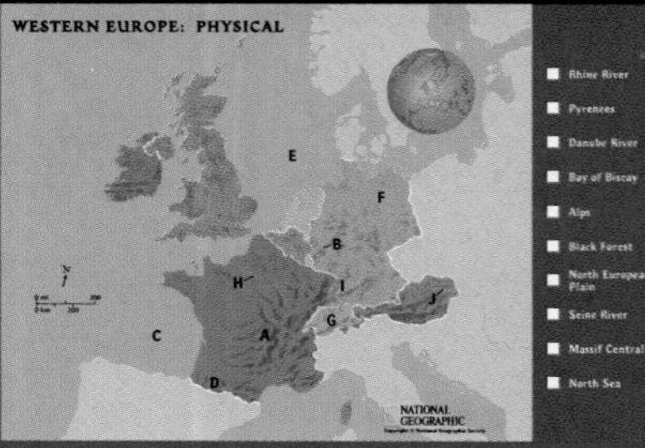

NATIONAL GEOGRAPHIC **On Location**

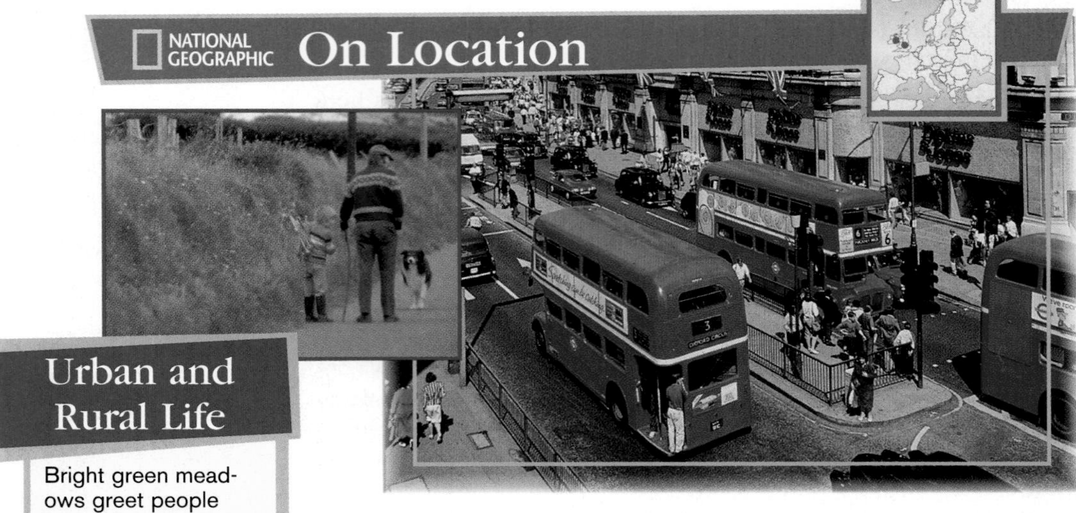

Urban and Rural Life

Bright green meadows greet people who venture into Ireland's countryside (above). In London, doubledecker buses show their bright colors (right).

Government **Which Ireland is part of the United Kingdom?**

The United Kingdom's government is also a **constitutional monarchy,** in which a queen or king is the official head of state. The monarch represents the country at public events but has little power.

The People About 60 million people live in the United Kingdom. The British people speak English, although Welsh and Scottish Gaelic are spoken in some areas. Most people are Protestant Christians, although immigrants practice Islam and other religions.

About 90 percent of the United Kingdom's people live in cities and towns. With about 12 million people, the capital city of **London** is one of Europe's most heavily populated cities.

Reading Check **What form of government does the United Kingdom have?**

The Republic of Ireland

Surrounded by the blue waters of the Atlantic Ocean and the Irish Sea, the Republic of Ireland has lush green meadows and tree-covered hills. As a result, it is called the Emerald Isle. At Ireland's center lies a wide, rolling plain covered with forests and farmland. The area is rich in **peat,** or wet ground with decaying plants, which can be dried and used for fuel. Peat is dug from **bogs,** or low swampy lands.

The Economy Potatoes, barley, wheat, sugar beets, and turnips are Ireland's major crops. Farmers raise sheep and beef and dairy cattle, too.

Manufacturing employs more people than farming and contributes more to the country's economy. Ireland joined the European Union so that it could market its products more widely. The Irish work in many manufacturing industries, processing foods and beverages, and making textiles, clothing, pharmaceuticals, and computer equipment.

The Northern Ireland Conflict Ireland has suffered hundreds of years of unrest under British rule. The southern, mostly Catholic, counties of Ireland won independence from Britain in 1922, and later became a

Meeting Special Needs

Interpersonal Organize the class into six groups numbered 1 through 6. Have each group split up into four subgroups called A, B, C, and D. Have all students in the four subgroups meet together. (That is, groups 1A through 6A get together, as do groups 1B through 6B, and so on.) Assign each subgroup one of the following topics: land and climate; economy; history; and culture. Have the students in each subgroup develop ways of teaching information about their topic in relation to the United Kingdom. Then send students back to the original groups. Have the subgroups take turns teaching other group members about their topic. **L1**

Refer to *Inclusion for the Middle School Social Studies Classroom Strategies and Activities* in the TCR.

republic. The northern counties, where many British Protestants had settled, remained part of the United Kingdom. Peace still did not come to the island. The **Nationalists,** who are typically Catholic, want the six counties of Northern Ireland to be reunited with the Republic. The **Loyalists,** who are typically Protestant, prefer that Northern Ireland remain under British rule. The fighting between these two groups, which the Irish refer to as "the troubles," has led to many deaths.

In 1998 officials of the United Kingdom and the Republic of Ireland met with leaders of the different sides in Northern Ireland. They all signed an agreement to end the political violence. The agreement gave Northern Ireland its own elected assembly, made up of Catholic and Protestant members, to govern Northern Ireland. Although disagreements continue to occur, many hope that the peace will last.

The People The Irish trace their ancestry to the **Celts** who settled Ireland around 500 B.C. Gaelic, a Celtic language, and English are Ireland's two official languages.

Today, Ireland is an urban nation. About 58 percent of the country's people live in cities or towns. Nearly one-third live in or around **Dublin,** the capital. Life often centers on the neighborhood church.

Irish music and folk dancing, are performed around the world. Of all the arts, however, the Irish have had the greatest influence on literature. Playwright **George Bernard Shaw,** poet William Butler Yeats, and novelist James Joyce are some of the country's best-known writers.

✓Reading Check **How are Northern Ireland and the Republic of Ireland different?**

Assessment

Defining Terms

1. **Define** moor, loch, parliamentary democracy, constitutional monarchy, peat, bog.

Recalling Facts

2. **Region** What are the four regions of the United Kingdom?
3. **Economics** What are the two leading exports of the United Kingdom?
4. **Economics** Why did Ireland join the European Union?

Critical Thinking

5. **Analyzing Information** Why does the House of Lords have little power in the United Kingdom's Parliament?
6. **Understanding Cause and Effect** What disagreement has led to fighting in Northern Ireland?

Graphic Organizer

7. **Organizing Information** Create two diagrams like this one, one for the United Kingdom and one for the Republic of Ireland. Under each heading, list as many facts as you can for both countries.

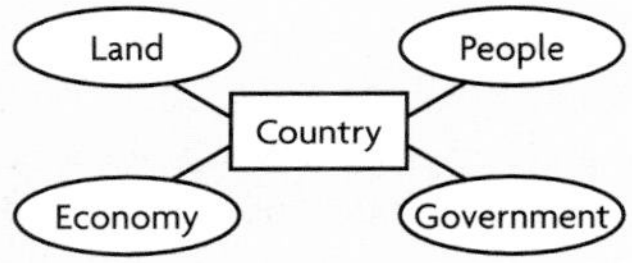

Applying Social Studies Skills

8. **Analyzing Maps** Look at the political map on page 279. What is the capital of the United Kingdom? Of the Republic of Ireland?

Chapter 11

Section 1, pages 278–281

Section Quiz 11-1

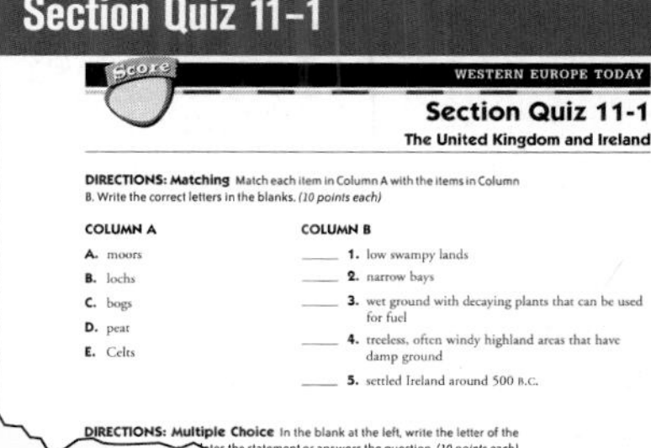
WESTERN EUROPE TODAY

Section Quiz 11-1

The United Kingdom and Ireland

DIRECTIONS: Matching Match each item in Column A with the items in Column B. Write the correct letters in the blanks. *(10 points each)*

COLUMN A	COLUMN B
A. moors	____ 1. low swampy lands
B. lochs	____ 2. narrow bays
C. bogs	____ 3. wet ground with decaying plants that can be used for fuel
D. peat	____ 4. treeless, often windy highland areas that have damp ground
E. Celts	____ 5. settled Ireland around 500 B.C.

DIRECTIONS: Multiple Choice In the blank at the left, write the letter of the ... the statement or answers the question. *(10 points each)*

✓ Reading Check Answer

The Republic of Ireland is an independent country. Northern Ireland is still part of the United Kingdom.

Reading Essentials and Study Guide 11-1

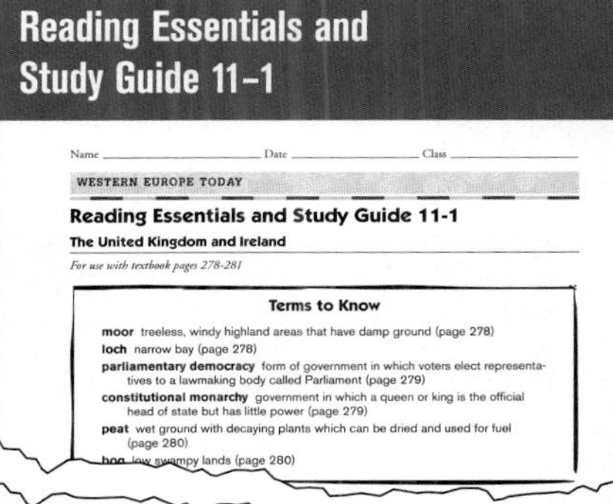
Name ______ Date ______ Class ______

WESTERN EUROPE TODAY

Reading Essentials and Study Guide 11-1

The United Kingdom and Ireland

For use with textbook pages 278–281

Terms to Know

moor treeless, windy highland areas that have damp ground (page 278)
loch narrow bay (page 278)
parliamentary democracy form of government in which voters elect representatives to a lawmaking body called Parliament (page 279)
constitutional monarchy government in which a queen or king is the official head of state but has little power (page 279)
peat wet ground with decaying plants which can be dried and used for fuel (page 280)
bog low swampy lands (page 280)

Have students research the history of Northern Ireland and prepare an oral presentation describing characteristics of the society today that resulted from historical factors such as invasion and colonization.

Section 1 Assessment

1. The terms are defined in the Glossary.
2. England, Scotland, Wales, and Northern Ireland
3. manufactured goods and machinery
4. to market its products more widely
5. Members inherit their titles and may have little interest in politics; they have not been elected and so do not have the support of a political constituency.
6. The mainly Protestant Northern Ireland wishes to remain part of the United Kingdom while the Catholic Republic of Ireland wants a united Ireland.
7. Students should list facts from the text under the appropriate category.
8. London; Dublin

TEACH

Although many different societies and cultures exist in the world, they often build structures that serve the same purposes—for shelter, as meeting places for government or religious purposes, for transportation, and even as tombs and monuments. Ask students for examples of each. *(Any home; the Capitol building; churches and temples; bridges, roads, and tunnels; the pyramids and Washington Monument)* Have students consider the relationships that exist between societies and their architecture as they read about Stonehenge. **L1**

More About Mysterious Monuments

Nature has recently revealed a structure similar to Stonehenge. For centuries, a layer of peat covered a circle made of logs along Great Britain's North Sea coast. Recently the sea washed the peat away, exposing the wooden posts in a circle 22 feet (6.7 m) wide. Archaeologists have dated the structure reminiscent of Stonehenge as about 4,000 years old. Ask students how this society's belief system affected their building technology.

Making Connections

CULTURE | GOVERNMENT | PEOPLE | TECHNOLOGY

Stonehenge

Stonehenge, one of the world's best-known and most puzzling ancient monuments, stands in southern England.

History of Stonehenge

The most noticeable part of Stonehenge is its huge stones set up in four circular patterns. A circular ditch and mound form a border around the site. Shallow dirt holes also circle the stones.

Stonehenge was built over a period of more than 2,000 years. The earliest construction, that of the circular ditch and mound, probably began about 3100 B.C. The outer ring of large pillars, topped with horizontal rocks, was built about 2000 B.C. An inner ring of stone pillars also supports horizontal stones.

There was no local source of stone, so workers carried it from an area that was about 20 miles (32 km) north. The stones are huge—up to 30 feet (9 m) long and 50 tons (45 t) in weight. Before setting the stones in place, workers smoothed and shaped them. They carved joints into the stones so that they would fit together perfectly. Then the builders probably used levers and wooden supports to raise the stones into position.

About 500 years later, builders added the third and fourth rings of stones. This time they used bluestone, which an earlier group of people had transported 240 miles (386 km) from the Preseli Mountains of Wales.

What Does It Mean?

Although much is known about when people built Stonehenge, experts do not agree on who built it. Early theories suggested that an ancient group known as Druids or the Romans built the monument. Now archaeologists believe that the monument was completed long before either of these groups came to the area.

▲ Stonehenge

An even greater mystery is *why* Stonehenge was built. Most experts agree that Stonehenge was probably used as a place of worship. Some believe that the series of holes, stones, and archways were used as a calendar. By lining up particular holes and stones, people could note the summer and winter solstices. They could also keep track of the months. Some scientists think that early people used the site to predict solar and lunar eclipses.

Making the Connection

1. About how old is Stonehenge?
2. From where did the stones used at Stonehenge come?
3. **Sequencing Information** Describe the order in which Stonehenge was built.

Making the Connection

1. about 5,100 years old
2. Some came from 20 miles (32 km) away; others came from 240 miles (386 km) away.
3. The circular ditch and mound were built about 3100 B.C.; the outer ring of pillars was built about 2000 B.C., as was an inner ring; two more rings were added about 1500 B.C.

Section 2

France and the Benelux Countries

Guide to Reading

Main Idea

France and the Benelux countries are important cultural, agricultural, and manufacturing centers of Europe.

Terms to Know

- navigable
- republic
- polder
- multinational company
- multilingual

Reading Strategy

Create a diagram like this one. Then list two countries that have major products in these categories. List two products for each country.

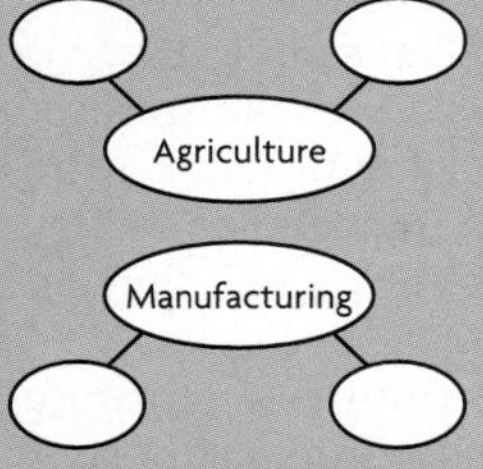

NATIONAL GEOGRAPHIC **Exploring Our World**

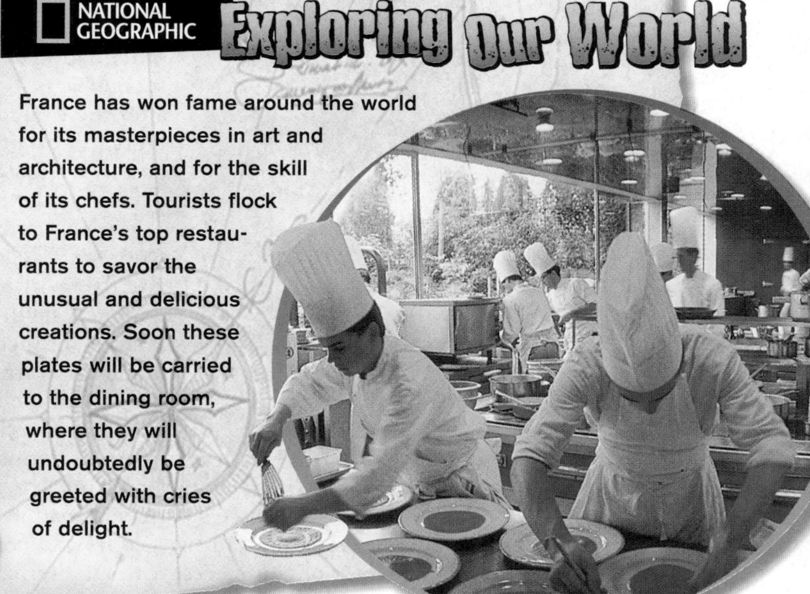

France has won fame around the world for its masterpieces in art and architecture, and for the skill of its chefs. Tourists flock to France's top restaurants to savor the unusual and delicious creations. Soon these plates will be carried to the dining room, where they will undoubtedly be greeted with cries of delight.

France and its neighbors in the west of Europe rank as major economic and cultural centers of the world. Today, joined in economic partnership in the European Union, they look forward to a peaceful and prosperous twenty-first century.

France

The largest country in western Europe, **France** is still smaller than the state of Texas. France's landscape is made up of high mountain ranges that separate it from Spain, Italy, and Switzerland, a large flat plain, and several rivers. Most of these rivers are **navigable,** or wide and deep enough to allow the passage of ships.

Most of France has a climate that is ideal for agriculture. The rich soil in France's flat lowland area makes France an important food producer. In many French towns, you can find open-air markets displaying an abundance of fresh farm produce.

1 Focus

Section Objectives

1. Discuss the economy and people of France.
2. Compare the cultures and economies of the Benelux countries.

BELLRINGER
Skillbuilder Activity

Project transparency and have students answer questions.

This activity is also available as a blackline master.

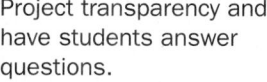

Daily Focus Skills Transparency 11-2

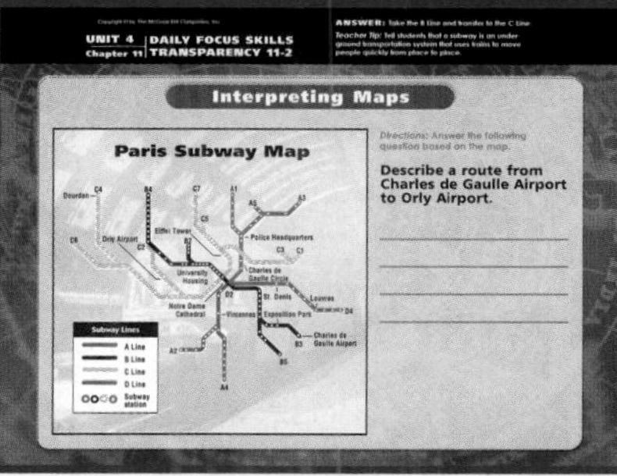

Guide to Reading

■ **Vocabulary Precheck**

Explain that the suffix *-or* means "one who," *-ation* means "act of," and *-able* means "can be." Point out that a *navigator* is "one who sails," and *navigation* is "the act of sailing." Ask students to explain what *navigable* means. (*can be sailed*)

Section Resources

Reproducible Masters
- Reproducible Lesson Plan 11-2
- Daily Lecture and Discussion Notes 11-2
- Guided Reading Activity 11-2
- Reading Essentials and Study Guide 11-2
- Section Quiz 11-2

Transparencies
- Daily Focus Skills Transparency 11-2
- GeoQuiz Transparency 11-1

Multimedia
- Vocabulary PuzzleMaker Software
- Interactive Tutor Self-Assessment CD-ROM
- Presentation Plus! CD-ROM
- ExamView® Pro 3.0 Testmaker CD-ROM

TEACH

Graphing Data Write these numbers on the board: China—$4.42; France—$1.32; Germany—$1.81; India—$1.69; Italy—$1.18; Japan—$2.9; United Kingdom—$1.25; United States—$8.51. These statistics represent the total output, in billions of dollars, of the world's leading economies in a recent year. Have students create a graph depicting the economic ranks of these countries. Ask them to compare the western European countries to countries from other regions. *(Germany—fourth; France—sixth; United Kingdom—seventh)* **L2**

Daily Lecture Notes 11–2

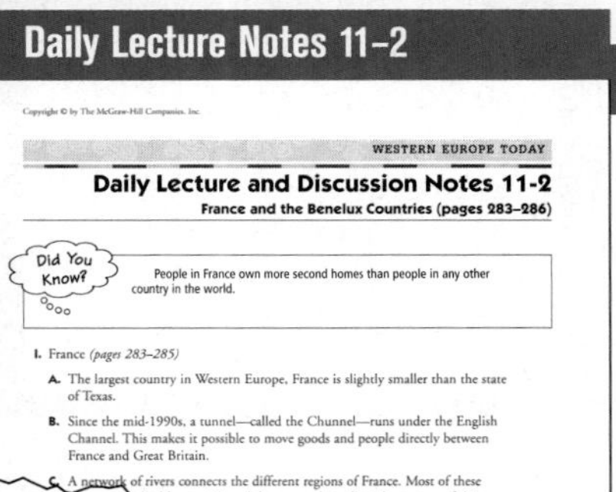

WESTERN EUROPE TODAY

Daily Lecture and Discussion Notes 11-2

France and the Benelux Countries (pages 283–286)

Did You Know? People in France own more second homes than people in any other country in the world.

I. France *(pages 283–285)*

A. The largest country in Western Europe, France is slightly smaller than the state of Texas.

B. Since the mid-1990s, a tunnel—called the Chunnel—runs under the English Channel. This makes it possible to move goods and people directly between France and Great Britain.

C. A network of rivers connects the different regions of France. Most of these ... **igable,** or wide and deep enough to allow the passage of ships

More About the Photos

In 1789 the French people overthrew their king in the bloody French Revolution. The 1862 novel *Les Miserables* deals with the tragic circumstances of the poor in France after the revolution.

Caption Answer The Pledge of Allegiance

NATIONAL GEOGRAPHIC **On Location**

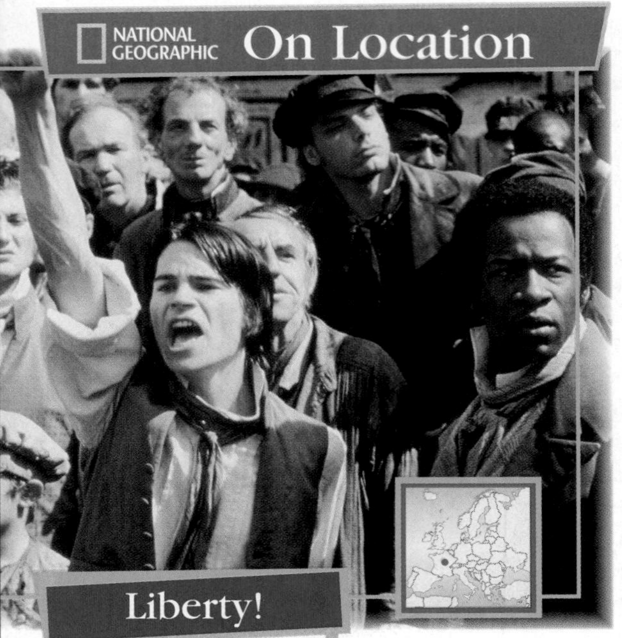

Liberty!

Les Miserables was a popular novel by Victor Hugo before it became a Broadway play. The story portrays the struggle of the French people for "liberty, equality, and fraternity."

History **What important pledge used by Americans also contains the word *liberty*?**

France's Economy France's well-developed economy relies on agriculture and manufacturing. Most people, however, work in service industries such as banking, commerce, communications, and tourism. Tourists from all over the world flock to visit France's historic and cultural sites, such as palaces and museums. They also come to enjoy the blue skies, rocky cliffs, and lovely beaches of France's Mediterranean coast.

France produces more food than any other nation in Europe. In fact, it ranks as the second-largest food exporter in the world, after the United States. Yet only 5 percent of French workers labor on farms. Their success is a tribute to France's fertile soil, mild climate, and modern farming methods.

French farmers grow grains, sugar beets, fruits, and vegetables. They also raise beef and dairy cattle. In addition, vineyards are a common sight. The grapes are used to make famous French wines. Olives are grown along the warm, dry Mediterranean coast.

France's natural resources include bauxite, iron ore, and coal. France has small petroleum reserves and little hydroelectric power. How does the nation power its industries? About 80 percent of France's electricity comes from nuclear power plants.

Workers produce a variety of manufactured goods, including steel, chemicals, textiles, airplanes, cars, and computers. France is also a leading center of commerce, with an international reputation in fashion.

The French People "Liberté . . . Egalité . . . Fraternité" (Liberty, Equality, Fraternity)—France's national motto—describes the spirit of the French people. Although they have regional differences, the French share a strong national loyalty. Most French trace their ancestry to the Celts, Romans, and Franks of early Europe. They speak French, and about 90 percent of them are Roman Catholic.

France's government is known as the **Fifth Republic.** A **republic** is a strong national government headed by elected leaders. A powerful president, elected for a seven-year term, leads the nation. The French president manages the country's foreign affairs. He or she appoints a prime minister to run the day-to-day affairs of government.

About three-fourths of France's 59.2 million people live in cities and towns. **Paris,** the capital and largest city, with its suburbs has a population of more than 10 million people. The city is home to many universities, museums, and other cultural sites. Outstanding cultural figures who lived in Paris include the writer Victor Hugo and the painters Claude Monet and Pierre-Auguste Renoir. Each year, millions

Team-Teaching Activity

Government Invite a teacher with a background in government to class to discuss the government of France, comparing it to the United States government. Ask the teacher to focus on such issues as the different relative powers of the national and regional governments, the relative powers of the presidents, and the role of the prime minister in France. Have students form groups and create Venn diagrams that place characteristics of American government in one circle, traits of French government in the other circle, and characteristics of both in the area where the circles overlap. **L2**

EE4 Human Systems: Standard 12

of tourists flock to the City of Light, as Paris is called. They visit such sites as the Eiffel Tower, the cathedral of Notre Dame, and the Louvre (LOOV), one of the world's most famous art museums.

✓Reading Check **What is the main religion in France?**

The Benelux Countries

The name *Benelux* comes from combining the first letters of three countries' names: Belgium, the Netherlands, and Luxembourg. These three countries cooperated to form a trade partnership in 1948. These small countries have much in common. Their lands are low, flat, and densely populated. Most people live in cities, work in businesses or factories, and enjoy a high standard of living. All three nations are members of the European Union. They are also parliamentary democracies with constitutional monarchies.

Belgium About the size of Maryland, **Belgium** touches France, Luxembourg, Germany, and the Netherlands. Lying near major industrial regions, Belgium has long been a trade and manufacturing center. Belgian lace, Belgian chocolate, and Belgian diamond-cutting all enjoy a worldwide reputation for excellence. With few natural resources of their own, the Belgian people import metals, fuels, and raw materials. They use these materials to make vehicles, chemicals, and textiles, which are then exported.

Most of the people are Roman Catholic. The country has two main cultural and language groups. The Flemings in the north speak Flemish, a language based on Dutch. The south is home to the French-speaking Walloons. Tensions sometimes arise between the two groups, especially because there is more wealth and industry in the north than in the south. Most Belgians live in crowded urban areas. **Brussels,** the capital and largest city, is an international center for trade.

The Netherlands The **Netherlands**—about half the size of Maine—is one of the most densely populated countries in the world. Sometimes called Holland, its people are known as the Dutch.

Netherlands means "lowlands." True to its name, nearly half of this small, flat country lies below sea level. Without defenses against the sea, high tides would flood much of the country twice a day. To protect and reclaim their land from the sea, the Dutch have developed a simple method of building dikes to keep the sea out, then draining and pumping the wetlands dry. Once run by windmills, pumps are now driven by steam or electricity. These drained lands, called **polders,** have rich farming soil. The Dutch also build factories, airports, and even towns on them. The Delta Plan Project, completed in 1986, consists of huge barriers that keep the North Sea from overflowing the countryside during storms.

High technology makes small farms so productive that the Dutch can export cheese, vegetables, and flowers. In fact, the Netherlands ranks third in the world—after the United States and France—in the value of its agricultural exports. However, because machines make farming more productive, most people work in service industries, manufacturing, and trade.

Web Activity Visit the ***Our World Today: People, Places, and Issues*** Web site at owt.glencoe.com and click on **Chapter 11—Student Web Activities** to learn more about the Delta Plan Project.

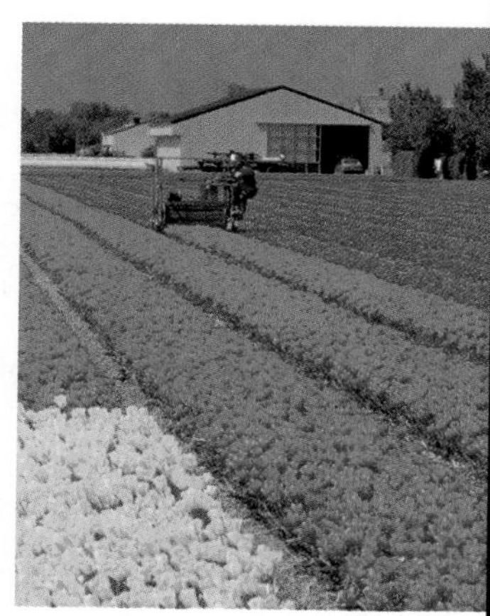

▲ **A tulip field in the Netherlands**

✓ Reading Check Answer

Roman Catholic

Guided Reading Activity 11–2

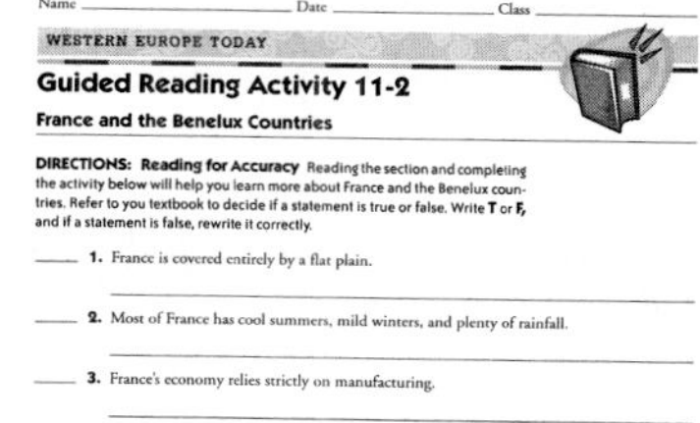

Name ________ Date ________ Class ________

WESTERN EUROPE TODAY

Guided Reading Activity 11-2

France and the Benelux Countries

DIRECTIONS: Reading for Accuracy Reading the section and completeing the activity below will help you learn more about France and the Benelux countries. Refer to you textbook to decide if a statement is true or false. Write **T** or **F**, and if a statement is false, rewrite it correctly.

____ 1. France is covered entirely by a flat plain.

____ 2. Most of France has cool summers, mild winters, and plenty of rainfall.

____ 3. France's economy relies strictly on manufacturing.

____ 4. France produces more food than any other nation in Europe.

... Fifth Republic.

Our World Today Online

Objectives, goals, and answers to the Student Web Activity can be found in the Web Activity Lesson Plan at owt.glencoe.com

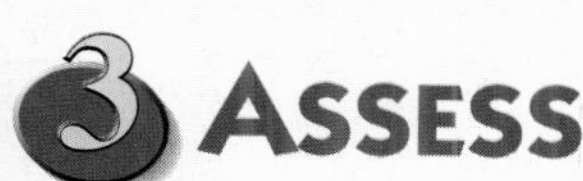

Assign Section 2 Assessment as homework or an in-class activity.

Section Quiz 11–2

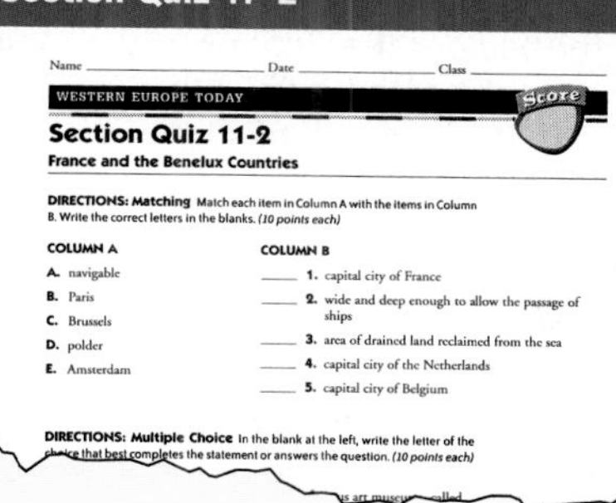

Name ________ Date ________ Class ________

WESTERN EUROPE TODAY

Section Quiz 11-2

France and the Benelux Countries

DIRECTIONS: Matching Match each item in Column A with the items in Column B. Write the correct letters in the blanks. *(10 points each)*

COLUMN A	COLUMN B
A. navigable	____ 1. capital city of France
B. Paris	____ 2. wide and deep enough to allow the passage of ships
C. Brussels	____ 3. area of drained land reclaimed from the sea
D. polder	____ 4. capital city of the Netherlands
E. Amsterdam	____ 5. capital city of Belgium

DIRECTIONS: Multiple Choice In the blank at the left, write the letter of the choice that best completes the statement or answers the question. *(10 points each)*

... art museum called ...

Critical Thinking Activity

Making Comparisons Economists measure a country's economic performance by looking at gross domestic product (GDP)—the total value of all goods and services produced in a country in a given year. Economists use *per capita* GDP to compare the relative wealth of people in different countries. Write the following numbers: Luxembourg: $33,119; United States: $29,326; Norway: $26,771; Switzerland: $25,902; Denmark: $25,514; Iceland: $24,836; Japan: $24,574; Canada: $23,761; Belgium: $23,242; Austria: $23,077. These figures represent the top ten countries in terms of per capita GDP in a recent year. **Ask: How would you describe the levels of economic development of the smaller countries of western Europe?** *(Luxembourg, Switzerland, and Austria all have highly productive economies.)* **L2**

Chapter 11

Section 2, pages 283–286

Reteach

Have students identify the two main cultural groups of Belgium. Have them summarize the differences that cause conflict between these cultures. Then have students list reasons that these cultures might cooperate with each other.

✓ Reading Check Answer

steel and banking

Reading Essentials and Study Guide 11-2

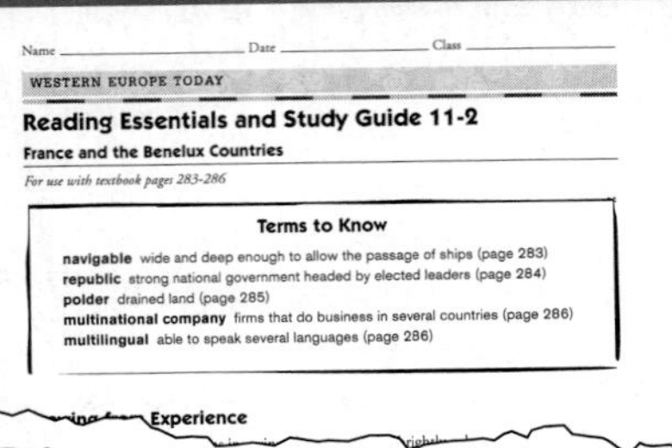
Name ______ Date ______ Class ______

WESTERN EUROPE TODAY

Reading Essentials and Study Guide 11-2

France and the Benelux Countries

For use with textbook pages 283–286

Terms to Know

navigable wide and deep enough to allow the passage of ships (page 283)
republic strong national government headed by elected leaders (page 284)
polder drained land (page 285)
multinational company firms that do business in several countries (page 286)
multilingual able to speak several languages (page 286)

...Experience

Enrich

Have students use a variety of primary and secondary sources to identify and explain the following issues: ethnic conflict and cooperation in Belgium, reclaiming land from the sea in the Netherlands, or the factors that influence the economy of Luxembourg.

Close

Have students imagine that they live in one of the Benelux countries and draw a picture of the view from their house.

About 90 percent of the Dutch live in cities and towns. Amsterdam is the capital and largest city. Living in a densely populated country, the Dutch make good use of their space. Houses are narrow but tall, and apartments are often built on canals and over highways. Some of Amsterdam's most famous people are the painters Rembrant, van Ryn, and Vincent van Gogh. You may already have read *The Diary of Anne Frank.* This Dutch teenager's autobiography tells how she and her family tried to hide from the German Nazis during World War II.

About two-thirds of the Dutch people are Protestant. Others are Roman Catholic, and a small number of immigrants are Muslims. The people of the Netherlands speak Dutch, but most also speak English.

Luxembourg Southeast of Belgium lies **Luxembourg,** one of Europe's smallest countries. The entire country is only about 55 miles (89 km) long and about 35 miles (56 km) wide.

Despite its size, Luxembourg is prosperous. Many **multinational companies,** firms that do business in several countries, have their headquarters here. It is home to the second-largest steel-producing company in Europe and is a major banking center as well.

Why is Luxembourg so attractive to foreign companies? First, the country is centrally located. Second, most people in this tiny land are **multilingual,** or able to speak several languages. They speak Luxembourgian, a blend of old German and French; French, the official language of the law; and German, used in most newspapers.

✓ **Reading Check** **What industries are important in Luxembourg?**

Assessment

Defining Terms

1. **Define** navigable, republic, polder, multinational company, multilingual.

Recalling Facts

2. **Economics** Name five of France's agricultural products.
3. **Culture** What are the two major cultures and languages of Belgium?
4. **Human/Environment Interaction** How do the Dutch protect their land from the sea?

Critical Thinking

5. **Drawing Conclusions** France is the second-largest food exporter in the world. Why is that remarkable?
6. **Analyzing Information** Why do foreign companies come to Luxembourg?

Graphic Organizer

7. **Organizing Information** Create a diagram like this one. In the center circle list three characteristics that are shared by these countries.

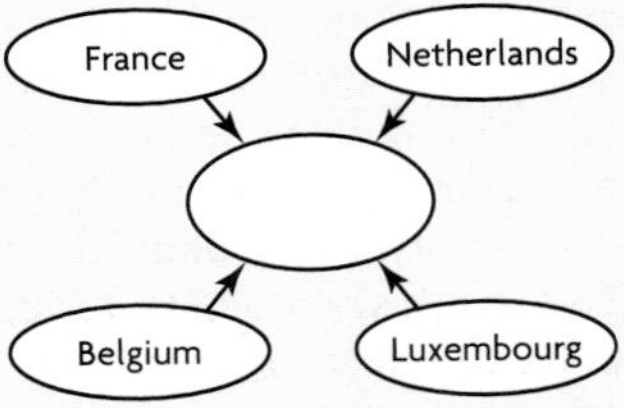

Applying Social Studies Skills

8. **Analyzing Maps** Turn to the political map on page 279. What country borders France, Belgium, the Netherlands, and Luxembourg?

Section 2 Assessment

1. The terms are defined in the Glossary.
2. *Any five:* grains, sugar beets, fruits, vegetables, beef, dairy cattle, grapes, olives, cheese
3. Flemings speak Flemish; Walloons speak French
4. by building dikes and pumping the water out
5. because only 5 percent of French workers are involved in agriculture
6. It is centrally located and most people are multilingual.
7. *Any three:* European; border Germany; at least some people speak French; industrialized; prosperous; Protestant and/or Catholic
8. Germany

Study and Writing Skill

Using Library Resources

Your teacher has assigned a major research report, so you go to the library. As you wander the aisles surrounded by books, you wonder: Where do I start my research? Which reference tools should I use?

Learning the Skill

Libraries contain many resources. Here are brief descriptions of important ones:

- **Encyclopedia:** set of books containing short articles on many subjects arranged alphabetically
- **Biographical Dictionary:** brief biographies listed alphabetically by last names
- **Atlas:** collection of maps and charts
- **Almanac:** reference updated yearly that provides current statistics and historical information on a wide range of subjects
- **Card Catalog:** listing of every book in the library, either on cards or computerized; search for books by author, subject, or title
- **Periodical Guide:** set of books listing topics covered in magazines and newspaper articles
- **Computer Database:** collections of information organized for rapid search and retrieval
- **World Wide Web:** collection of information on the Internet accessed with a Web browser *(Caution: Some information may not be reliable.)*

Practicing the Skill

Suppose you are assigned a research report dealing with Denmark. Read the questions below, and then decide which of the resources on the left you would use to answer each question and why.

1. During which years did Queen Margarethe rule Denmark?
2. What is the current population of Denmark?
3. Besides "The Little Mermaid," what stories did Danish author Hans Christian Andersen write?

Applying the Skill

Using library resources, research the origins and main stories of Icelandic sagas. Find out if the sagas say anything about the land or environment of Iceland. Present the information you find to the class.

◄ The Little Mermaid statue in Copenhagen

TEACH

Ask: **How do you find an unknown phone number?** *(check the directory or call directory assistance)* **How do you find out what programs are showing on television on any given day?** *(check an on-screen or print television guide)* Point out that a library card catalog serves the same function—it indicates the location of resources in a library like a phone directory and summarizes those resources like a television guide. Tell students that in this feature they will learn about other library research guides. **L1**

Additional Skills Practice

1. **How is a dictionary organized?** *(alphabetically)* **How are encyclopedias and biographical dictionaries organized?** *(alphabetically)*
2. **Where would you find the location of cities in Norway?** *(atlas)*
3. **Where would you find a listing of recent articles written about Iceland?** *(periodical guide)*

Additional Skills Resources

- Chapter Skills Activity 11
- Building Geography Skills for Life

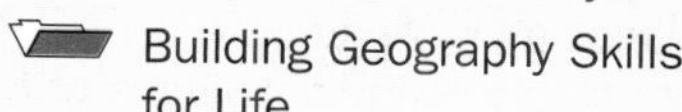

Practicing the Skill Answers

1. encyclopedia, biographical dictionary
2. almanac, World Wide Web
3. encyclopedia, biographical dictionary, card catalog

Applying the Skill

You might wish to inform the school librarian before assigning this activity so that he or she can research the available materials and thus be prepared for students' research.

Chapter 11

Section 3, pages 288–291

Focus

Section Objectives

1. Discuss the economy and government of Germany.
2. Compare the geography and economies of Switzerland and Austria.

BELLRINGER
Skillbuilder Activity

Project transparency and have students answer questions.

This activity is also available as a blackline master.

Daily Focus Skills Transparency 11–3

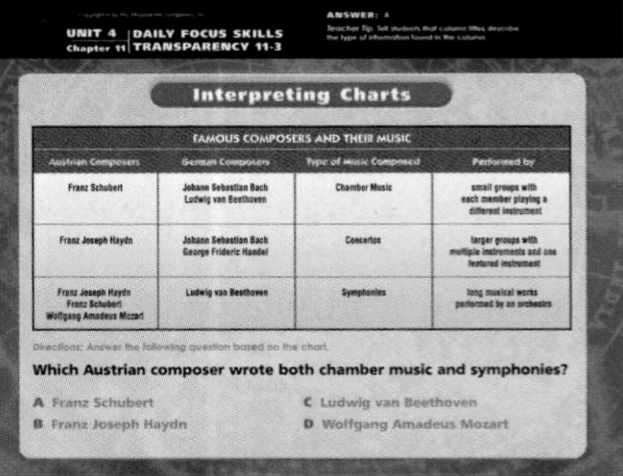

UNIT 4 Chapter 11 | DAILY FOCUS SKILLS TRANSPARENCY 11-3

ANSWER: A

Teacher Tip: Tell students that column titles describe the type of information found in the column.

Interpreting Charts

FAMOUS COMPOSERS AND THEIR MUSIC			
Austrian Composers	German Composers	Type of Music Composed	Performed by
Franz Schubert	Johann Sebastian Bach Ludwig van Beethoven	Chamber Music	small groups with each member playing a different instrument
Franz Joseph Haydn	Johann Sebastian Bach George Frideric Handel	Concertos	larger groups with multiple instruments and one featured instrument
Franz Joseph Haydn Franz Schubert Wolfgang Amadeus Mozart	Ludwig van Beethoven	Symphonies	long musical works performed by an orchestra

Directions: Answer the following question based on the chart.

Which Austrian composer wrote both chamber music and symphonies?

A Franz Schubert
B Franz Joseph Haydn
C Ludwig van Beethoven
D Wolfgang Amadeus Mozart

Guide to Reading

■ **Vocabulary Precheck**
Write the following definitions on the board: "not joining either side in a fight"; and "to rejoin separated parts." Have students identify the correct terms. *(neutrality, reunification)*

Section 3

Germany, Switzerland, and Austria

Guide to Reading

Main Idea

Germany, Switzerland, and Austria are known for their mountain scenery and prosperous economies.

Terms to Know

- autobahn
- federal republic
- reunification
- neutrality
- continental divide

Reading Strategy

Create a diagram like this one. Under the headings fill each oval with facts about each country. Put statements that are true of all three countries where the ovals overlap.

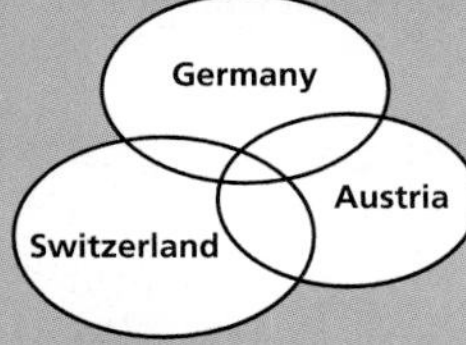

NATIONAL GEOGRAPHIC Exploring Our World

Bavaria, the beauty spot of Germany, was the home of King Ludwig II, who became king of Bavaria at the age of 18. Disillusioned after a lost war with the Prussians, Ludwig lost all interest in politics and became increasingly eccentric. Ludwig built three "fairy tale castles" at stupendous expense before dying a mysterious—and some say not accidental—death.

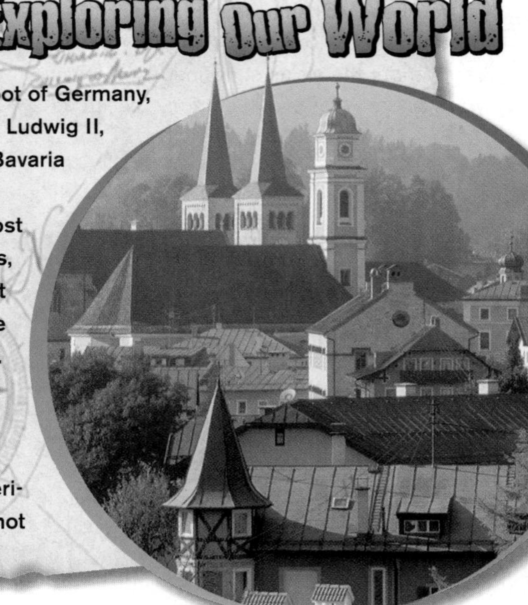

Today **Germany, Switzerland,** and **Austria** are adjusting to the changes sweeping Europe since the fall of communism. Germany, in particular, is facing challenges of reuniting its eastern and western sectors.

Germany

About the size of Montana, Germany lies in the heart of Europe. Mountains in the south and plains in the north form the physical landscape of Germany. The Alps rise in the southern German state of **Bavaria.** The lower slopes of these mountains—a favorite destination for skiers—are covered with forests.

One of Europe's most important waterways flows through Germany. The **Danube River** winds eastward across southern Germany. Rivers are also important in northern Germany, where they are used to transport raw materials and manufactured goods. The **Rhine River,** in the west, forms part of the border with France.

Section Resources

Reproducible Masters

- Reproducible Lesson Plan 11-3
- Daily Lecture and Discussion Notes 11-3
- Guided Reading Activity 11-3
- Reading Essentials and Study Guide 11-3
- Section Quiz 11-3

Transparencies

- Daily Focus Skills Transparency 11-3
- GeoQuiz Transparency 11-1

Multimedia

- Vocabulary PuzzleMaker Software
- Interactive Tutor Self-Assessment CD-ROM
- Presentation Plus! CD-ROM
- ExamView® Pro 3.0 Testmaker CD-ROM

Because of the rivers and productive land, Germany's northern plain has many cities and towns. **Berlin,** the capital, is the major center of the northeast. To the west lies **Hamburg,** Germany's largest port city, located on the Elbe River.

An Economic and Industrial Power Germany is a global economic power and a leader in the European Union. In fact, an area in western Germany called the **Ruhr** ranks as one of the world's most important industrial centers. The Ruhr developed around rich deposits of coal and iron ore. Battles have been fought among Europe's leaders for control of this productive area. Factories here produce high-quality steel, ships, cars, machinery, chemicals, and electrical equipment.

The growth of factories, service industries, and high technology in the last decade has used up the supply of workers. Thus, a growing number of immigrants, or guest workers, have come from Turkey, Italy, Greece, and the former Yugoslav republics. Sometimes they are the targets of racist attacks. When the economy takes a downturn and jobs are scarce, native-born people sometimes resent foreign laborers.

Lying just north of the Alps, Germany's **Black Forest** is famous for its beautiful scenery and for its wood products. Is the forest really black? No, but in places the trees grow so close together that the forest appears to be black. The Black Forest has suffered severe damage. Smoke containing sulfur and other chemicals from factories and automobiles makes the rain more acidic. The Germans have not yet found a solution to the acid rain problem because much of the pollution is formed in other countries.

Germany imports about one-third of its food, although it is a leading producer of beer, wine, and cheese. Farmers raise livestock and grow grains, vegetables, and fruits. Superhighways called **autobahns,** along with railroads, rivers, and canals, link Germany's cities.

Germany's Government Like the United States, Germany is a **federal republic** in which a national government and state governments share powers. An elected president serves as Germany's head of state, but he or she carries out only ceremonial duties. The chancellor, chosen by one of the two houses of parliament, is the real head of the government.

One of the challenges of the current government has been **reunification**—bringing the two parts together under one government. (Remember that Germany was divided into East and West after World War II.) This process has been difficult. Workers in East Germany had less experience and training in modern technology than workers in West Germany. After reunification, many old and inefficient factories in the east could not compete with the more advanced industries in the west and were forced to close. Unlike western Germany, the number of people without jobs has risen in the eastern part.

▲ A cuckoo clock from the Black Forest region of Germany

People Most of Germany's 82.2 million people trace their ancestry to groups who settled in Europe from about the A.D. 100s to 400s. The people speak German, a language that is related to English. Roman

2 TEACH

Making Comparisons Have students compare the governments of East and West Germany before reunification. Have them discuss which government was adopted after reunification and why. **L2**

Daily Lecture Notes 11-3

WESTERN EUROPE TODAY

Daily Lecture and Discussion Notes 11-3

Germany, Switzerland, and Austria (pages 288–291)

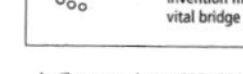

The ancient German city of Mainz was the home of Johannes Gutenberg. Gutenberg developed a new printing process using movable type in 1436. His invention made the written word available to more people and served as a vital bridge from the Middle Ages to the Renaissance.

I. Germany *(pages 288–290)*

A. About the size of Montana, Germany lies in the heart of Europe.

B. The Danube River, one of Europe's most important waterways, flows through Germany.

C. An area in western Germany called the Ruhr ranks as one of the world's most ...rial centers. The Ruhr developed around rich deposits of coal ...ht among Europe's leaders for control of

Interdisciplinary Connections

Science Switzerland's Alpine forests have been under stress in recent years, just as Germany's Black Forest has suffered. Growing levels of acid rain and higher levels of ozone are damaging the needles of these evergreens. Weakened trees become susceptible to bark beetles and other pests, which eventually kill the trees and then spread to others.

Team-Teaching Activity

Health Organize students into four groups. Assign two of the groups to research what health care was like in the two countries of West Germany and East Germany during the years of the Cold War. Have the other two groups investigate health care in the western and eastern parts of Germany today. After the groups have conducted their research, have them present their findings to the class and contrast health care in the two regions. Then have them try to identify factors in the past that shaped those current developments. Ask the health teacher to help students identify factors that could influence health in these regions. **L1**

EE5 Environment and Society: Standard 15

Guided Reading Activity 11-3

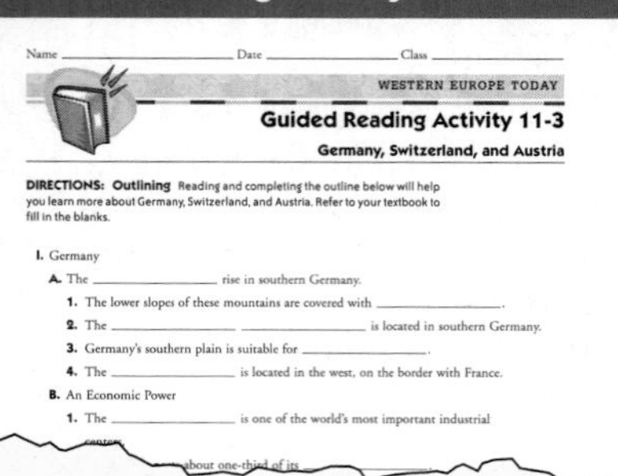

Name ______ Date ______ Class ______

WESTERN EUROPE TODAY

Guided Reading Activity 11-3

Germany, Switzerland, and Austria

DIRECTIONS: Outlining Reading and completing the outline below will help you learn more about Germany, Switzerland, and Austria. Refer to your textbook to fill in the blanks.

I. Germany
   A. The ______ rise in southern Germany.
      1. The lower slopes of these mountains are covered with ______.
      2. The ______ ______ is located in southern Germany.
      3. Germany's southern plain is suitable for ______.
      4. The ______ is located in the west, on the border with France.
   B. An Economic Power
      1. The ______ is one of the world's most important industrial centers.

Reading Check Answer

one-third

More About the Photos

Swiss Economy Just three companies account for about 90 percent of foreign sales funneling into Switzerland. One of these companies is a chocolate manufacturer. The others make metals and pharmaceuticals.

Caption Answer machinery, pharmaceuticals, high-tech electronic equipment, clocks and watches, chemicals, cheese

3 ASSESS

Assign Section 3 Assessment as homework or an in-class activity.

Have students use the Interactive Tutor Self-Assessment CD-ROM to review Section 11–3.

NATIONAL GEOGRAPHIC **On Location**

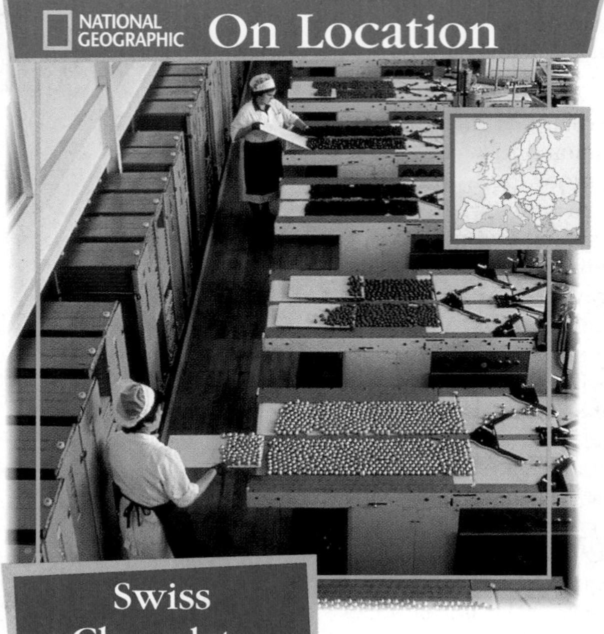

Swiss Chocolate

Switzerland's factories produce some of the best chocolate in the world.

Economics What other products are made in Switzerland?

Catholics and Protestants make up most of the population and are fairly evenly represented. **Munich** (MYOO•nikh), the largest city in southern Germany, is known for its theaters, museums, and concert halls. Berlin has also emerged as a cultural center.

Reading Check **How much of its food does Germany import?**

Switzerland and Austria

The **Alps** form most of the landscape in Switzerland, Austria, and **Liechtenstein.** That is why they are called the Alpine countries. Liechtenstein is a tiny country—only 60 square miles (155 sq. km)—sandwiched between Switzerland and Austria. The rugged Swiss Alps prevent easy travel between northern and southern Europe. For centuries, landlocked Switzerland guarded the few routes that cut through this barrier.

Switzerland The Swiss have enjoyed a stable democratic government for more than 700 years. Because of its location in the Alps, Switzerland has practiced **neutrality**—refusing to take sides in disagreements and wars between countries. As a result of this peaceful history, the Swiss city of **Geneva** is today the center of many international organizations.

The Alps make Switzerland the continental divide of central Europe. A **continental divide** is a high place from which rivers flow in different directions. Several rivers, including the Rhine and the Rhône, begin in the Swiss Alps. Dams built on Switzerland's rivers produce great amounts of hydroelectric power. Most of Switzerland's industries and its richest farmlands are found on a high plateau between two mountain ranges. **Bern,** Switzerland's capital, and **Zurich,** its largest city, are also located on this plateau.

Although it has few natural resources, Switzerland is a thriving industrial nation. Using imported materials, Swiss workers make high-quality goods such as electronic equipment, clocks, and watches. They also produce chemicals and gourmet foods such as chocolate and cheese. Tourism is an important industry, as are banking and insurance.

Zurich and Geneva are important centers of international finance. Recently, Swiss and Austrian banks have been criticized for keeping gold and deposits belonging to Jews sent to concentration camps during the Holocaust. International pressure has resulted in some of these deposits being returned to the heirs.

As you might expect given its location, Switzerland has many different ethnic groups and religions. Did you know that the country has four

Content Background

Switzerland The local divisions in Switzerland, called cantons, are like American states but retain more control over local affairs. The national legislature has two houses. Like the U.S. Congress, one has a set number of members from each canton, and the other is based on proportional representation. The Swiss people retain significant power, however. Laws passed by the legislature can be reviewed by the people in a national referendum and either approved or rejected. The people, not the executive, have this veto power. The national executive is a seven-member council, where each member heads one of the executive departments. **Ask: How do Switzerland's citizens influence the political process? Compare this and Switzerland's government to America's.**

national languages? They are German, French, Italian, and Romansch. Most Swiss speak German, and many speak more than one language.

Austria Austria is a landlocked country lying in the heart of Europe. The Alps cover three-fourths of Austria. In fact, Austria is one of the most mountainous countries in the world. Have you ever seen the movie *The Sound of Music*? It took place in Austria's spectacular mountains. Austria's climate is similar to Switzerland's. In winter, lowland areas receive rain, and mountainous regions have snow. Summers are cooler in Austria than they are in Switzerland.

Austria's economy is strong and varied. The mountains provide valuable timber and hydroelectric power. They also attract millions of tourists who enjoy hiking and skiing. Factories produce machinery, chemicals, metals, and vehicles. Farmers raise dairy cattle and other livestock, sugar beets, grains, potatoes, and fruits.

Most of Austria's 8.1 million people live in cities and towns and work in manufacturing or service jobs. The majority of people speak German. About 90 percent of the people are Roman Catholic.

Vienna, on the Danube River, is the capital and largest city. It has a rich history as a center of culture and learning. Some of the world's greatest composers, including Mozart, Schubert, and Haydn, lived or performed in Vienna. The city's concert halls, historic palaces and churches, and grand architecture continue to draw musicians today.

Reading Check What economic benefits do Austria's mountains provide?

▲ Young people dance in one of Vienna's many ballrooms.

Assessment

Defining Terms

1. **Define** autobahn, federal republic, reunification, neutrality, continental divide.

Recalling Facts

2. **Human/Environment Interaction** What has damaged the Black Forest?
3. **Culture** What are Switzerland's four languages?
4. **Economics** What types of jobs do most Austrians have?

Critical Thinking

5. **Understanding Cause and Effect** What problems have emerged as a result of German reunification?
6. **Analyzing Information** How have the Alps helped Switzerland maintain its neutrality?

Graphic Organizer

7. **Organizing Information** Create a diagram like the one below. On the lines list two facts about Austria's physical features, two facts about Austria's people, and four facts about Austria's economy.

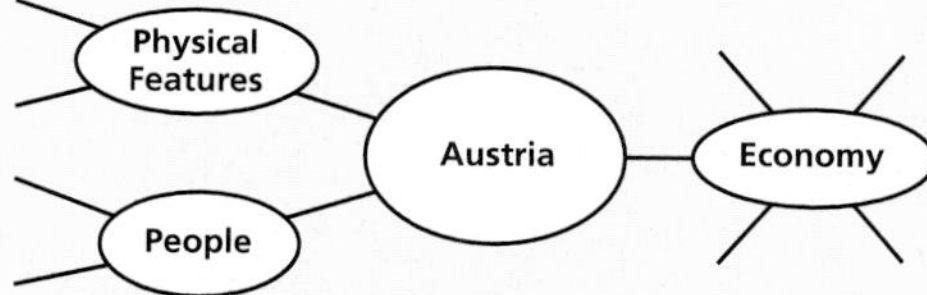

Applying Social Studies Skills

8. **Analyzing Maps** Look at the political map on page 279. The city of Frankfurt, Germany is located at what degree of latitude?

Section 3 Assessment

1. The terms are defined in the Glossary.
2. acid rain
3. German, Italian, French, Romansch
4. manufacturing or service
5. East German workers were not as well-trained in modern technology, and factories there were old and inefficient. The German government has tried to close the economic gap between the two parts of the country.
6. The Alps are a natural barrier that have kept foreign armies from invading Switzerland or using it as an invasion route to reach other countries.
7. Students' diagrams will vary.
8. about 50°N

Chapter 11

Section 3, pages 288–291

Section Quiz 11-3

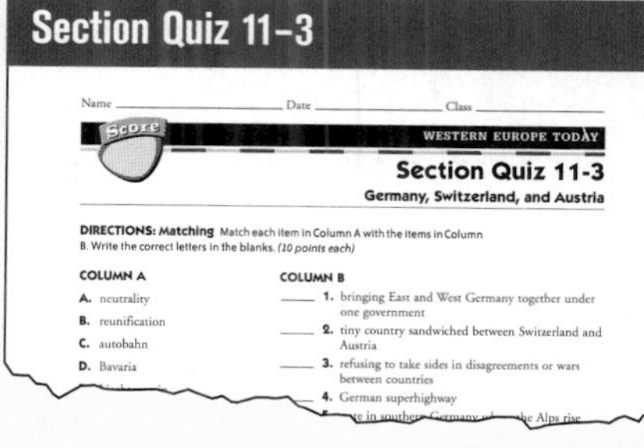

Name ____ Date ____ Class ____

WESTERN EUROPE TODAY

Section Quiz 11-3

Germany, Switzerland, and Austria

DIRECTIONS: Matching Match each item in Column A with the items in Column B. Write the correct letters in the blanks. (10 points each)

COLUMN A	COLUMN B
A. neutrality	___ 1. bringing East and West Germany together under one government
B. reunification	___ 2. tiny country sandwiched between Switzerland and Austria
C. autobahn	___ 3. refusing to take sides in disagreements or wars between countries
D. Bavaria	___ 4. German superhighway

Reading Check Answer

timber, hydroelectric power, iron ore, coal, and attraction to tourists

Reteach

Have students write four questions and their answers about the geographic distributions and patterns of each country in this section. They can use the maps, charts, graphs, and databank in this textbook as sources. Then have pairs of students take turns trying to answer their partner's questions.

Reading Essentials and Study Guide 11-3

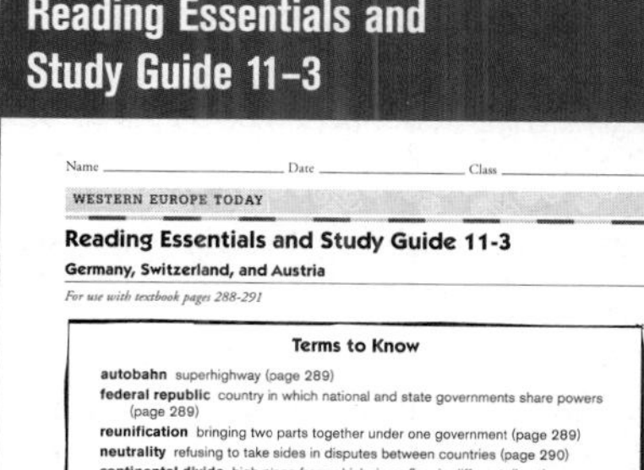

Name ____ Date ____ Class ____

WESTERN EUROPE TODAY

Reading Essentials and Study Guide 11-3

Germany, Switzerland, and Austria

For use with textbook pages 288–291

Terms to Know

autobahn superhighway (page 289)
federal republic country in which national and state governments share powers (page 289)
reunification bringing two parts together under one government (page 289)
neutrality refusing to take sides in disputes between countries (page 290)
continental divide high place from which rivers flow in different directions (page 290)

4 CLOSE

Have students write a paragraph contrasting the economies of these three countries.

Chapter 11

Section 4, pages 292–295

1 Focus

Section Objectives

1. Describe the landscapes and climates of the Nordic countries.
2. Compare the economies and people of this region.

BELLRINGER Skillbuilder Activity

Project transparency and have students answer questions.

This activity is also available as a blackline master.

Daily Focus Skills Transparency 11–4

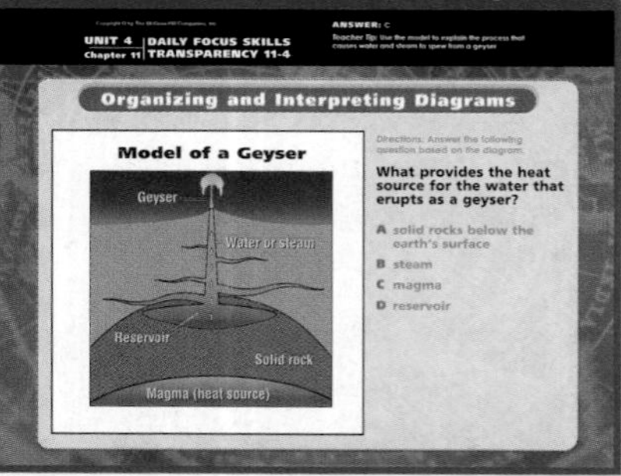

Guide to Reading

■ Accessing Prior Knowledge
Ask students if they are familiar with stories of the Vikings. Have them recount the stories. In this section they will read about people descended from the Vikings.

■ Vocabulary Precheck
Inform students that two of the Terms to Know are Nordic words. *(fjord, sauna)* Ask them to find their definitions.

Section 4

The Nordic Countries

Guide to Reading

Main Idea

The Nordic countries have developed diverse economies, and their people enjoy a high standard of living.

Terms to Know

- fjord
- welfare state
- heavy industry
- sauna
- geyser
- geothermal energy

Reading Strategy

Create a chart like this one for each of the following countries: Norway, Sweden, Finland, Denmark, and Iceland. Fill in at least two key facts for (1) the land, (2) the economy, and (3) the people of each country.

Country	(1)
	(2)
	(3)

NATIONAL GEOGRAPHIC Exploring Our World

An ocean of snow covers northern Sweden in winter, when the sun is above the horizon for only a few hours a day and summer seems light-years away. Here, near Sweden's border with Norway, a footbridge used in summer to cross a ravine is almost buried in snow. Instead of using the footbridge, a hardy Swede zips by on his snowmobile.

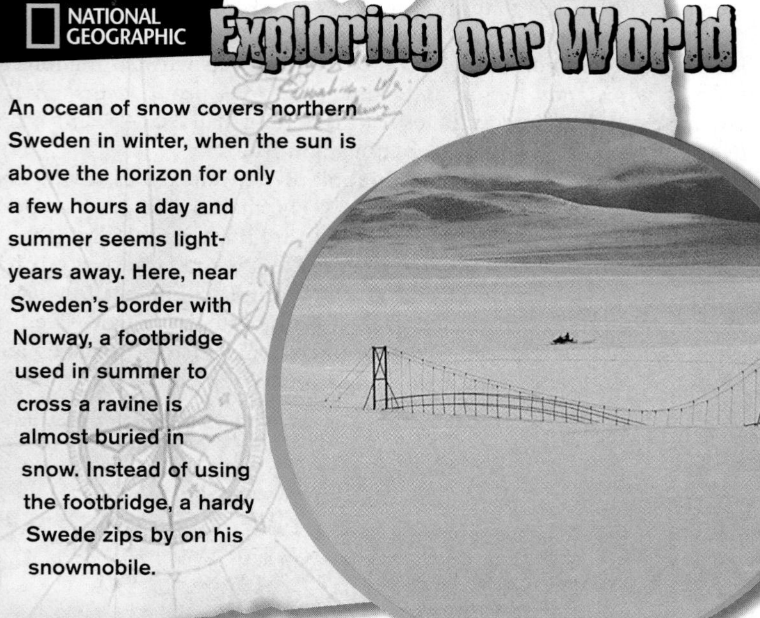

The northernmost part of Europe is made up of five countries: **Norway, Sweden, Finland, Denmark,** and **Iceland.** People in these countries have standards of living that are among the highest in the world.

Norway

Norway's long, jagged coastline on the Atlantic Ocean includes many **fjords** (fee•AWRDS), or steep-sided, glacial-cut valleys that are inlets of the sea. The fjords provide Norway with sheltered harbors and beautiful scenery that is popular with tourists.

Norway's far northern location results in a mostly cold climate. However, a mild climate is found along Norway's southern and western coasts due to warm winds from the **North Atlantic Current.** As you might expect, most of Norway's 4.5 million people live in the south within 10 miles (16 km) of the coast.

Section Resources

Reproducible Masters

- Reproducible Lesson Plan 11-4
- Daily Lecture and Discussion Notes 11-4
- Guided Reading Activity 11-4
- Reading Essentials and Study Guide 11-4
- Section Quiz 11-4

Transparencies

- Daily Focus Skills Transparency 11-4
- GeoQuiz Transparency 11-4

Multimedia

- Vocabulary PuzzleMaker Software
- Interactive Tutor Self-Assessment CD-ROM
- Presentation Plus! CD-ROM
- ExamView® Pro 3.0 Testmaker CD-ROM

Norway is a wealthy country, partly because of oil and natural gas pumped from beneath the North Sea. Today it is one of the world's largest oil exporters. The seas themselves provide an important export—fish. Warm ocean currents keep most of Norway's harbors ice-free all year.

Norway is a parliamentary democracy. It has a monarchy but is governed by an elected prime minister. In 1994, Norway voted not to join the European Union so that it could keep control of its own economy. EU membership is still hotly debated, however.

The people of Norway greatly value their cultural traditions. Elaborate folk dress is often seen at weddings and village festivals. Norwegians are a very modern people, though. Three-fourths of the population live in urban centers like the capital, **Oslo.** More than one-third own computers. When they are not typing on keyboards, they may be skiing or riding snowmobiles.

✓ Reading Check **What type of government does Norway have?**

Sweden

Like Norway, Sweden is a wealthy, industrial country. Its prosperity comes from abundant natural resources, including iron ore deposits and extensive pine forests. Exports include machinery, motor vehicles, paper products, wood, and electronic products. Only about 8 percent of Sweden's land can be used for farming. Swedish farmers have developed efficient ways to grow crops, and their farms supply most of the nation's food.

Sweden's economic wealth enabled it to become a **welfare state** —a country that uses high rates of taxation to provide services to people who are sick, needy, jobless, or retired. Sweden is a parliamentary democracy and joined the European Union.

NATIONAL GEOGRAPHIC **On Location**

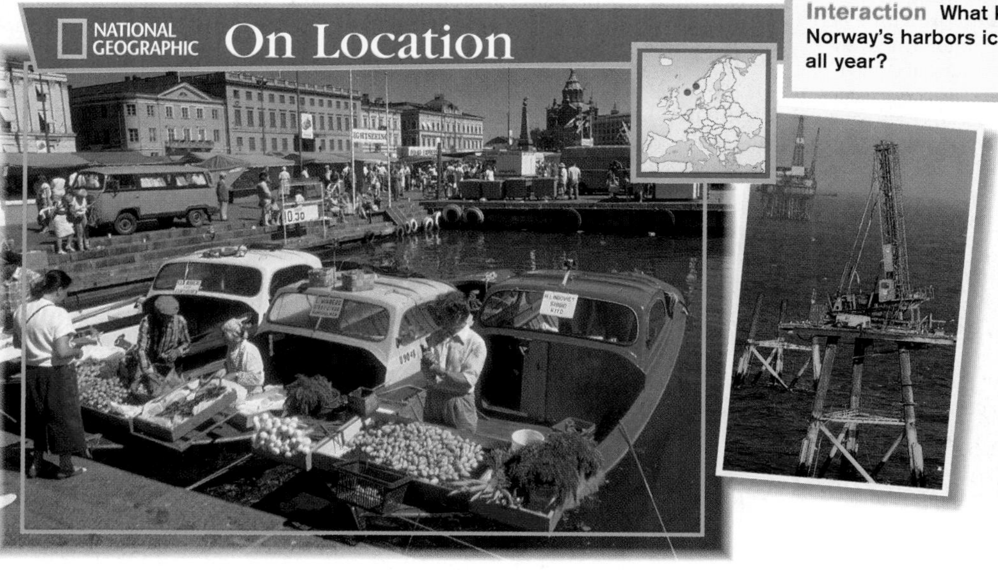

Norway's Economy

A shopper goes from boat to boat looking for bargains in Bergen, Norway's water market (below left). Europe's richest oil and natural gas fields are found in the North Sea (below right).

Human/Environment Interaction **What keeps Norway's harbors ice-free all year?**

Chapter 11

Section 4, pages 292–295

2 TEACH

Outlining Have students create a concept web with one of the Nordic countries in the center. They should have five secondary areas—"Land," "Climate," "Economy," "History," and "People." Then have them put details connecting to each of these areas. **L1**

✓ Reading Check Answer

parliamentary democracy

Daily Lecture Notes 11–4

WESTERN EUROPE TODAY

Daily Lecture and Discussion Notes 11-4

Scandinavian Countries (pages 292–295)

Did You Know? About 150,000 offshore islands serve as a barrier that helps to protect Norway's coast from Atlantic storms.

I. Norway *(pages 292–293)*

A. The countries of Norway, Sweden, Finland, Denmark, and Iceland make up the countries of Scandinavia.

B. The long, jagged Atlantic Ocean coastline of Norway includes many **fjords,** or steep-sided valleys that are inlets of the sea.

C. Norway is a wealthy country. It is the world's second-largest oil exporter, after ... is another major export.

More About the Photos

The North Sea Pollution has become a problem in the North Sea, not only as a result of oil and gas drilling but from the heavy shipping activity in its waters. Countries bordering this sea have reached several agreements aimed at cutting this pollution, but enforcement has been spotty.

Caption Answer the North Atlantic Current

Team-Teaching Activity

Science Invite the science teacher to the class to explain about the Northern Lights, or *Aurora Borealis.* This spectacular sky display is caused by solar winds. Electrically charged particles in these winds reach the earth's upper atmosphere and react with charged particles near the magnetic North Pole to create light effects. If possible, have the teacher show photographs of the lights so students can identify the arcing patterns and shifting colors. Point out that the Norwegian town of Tromso is one of the most active spots on the earth for seeing the *Aurora Borealis.* **Ask: How do you think early cultures in this area interpreted this phenomenon? L1**

EE3 Physical Systems: Standard 7

Reading Check Answer

iron ore and pine forests

Guided Reading Activity 11-4

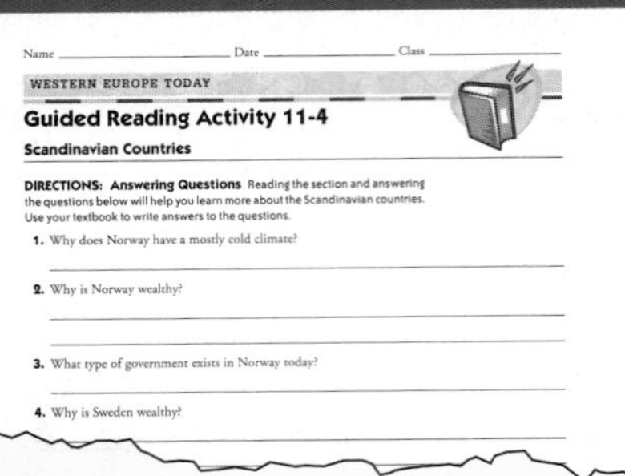
Name ______ Date ______ Class ______

WESTERN EUROPE TODAY

Guided Reading Activity 11-4

Scandinavian Countries

DIRECTIONS: Answering Questions Reading the section and answering the questions below will help you learn more about the Scandinavian countries. Use your textbook to write answers to the questions.

1. Why does Norway have a mostly cold climate?
2. Why is Norway wealthy?
3. What type of government exists in Norway today?
4. Why is Sweden wealthy?

ASSESS

Assign Section 4 Assessment as homework or an in-class activity.

Have students use the Interactive Tutor Self-Assessment CD-ROM to review Section 11–4.

Reading Check Answer

Siberia

Section Quiz 11-4

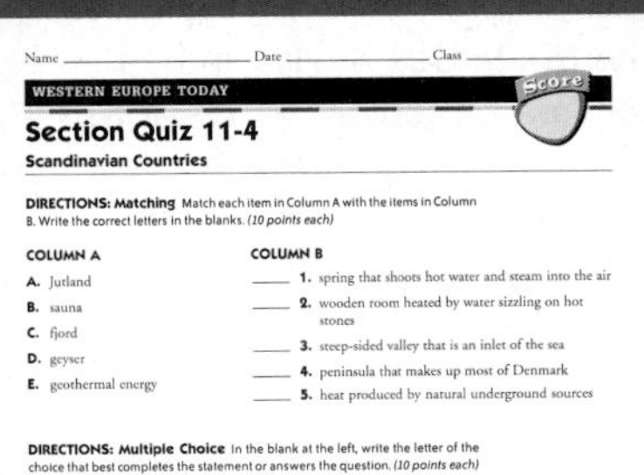
Name ______ Date ______ Class ______

WESTERN EUROPE TODAY

Section Quiz 11-4

Scandinavian Countries

DIRECTIONS: Matching Match each item in Column A with the items in Column B. Write the correct letters in the blanks. (10 points each)

COLUMN A	COLUMN B
A. Jutland	____ 1. spring that shoots hot water and steam into the air
B. sauna	____ 2. wooden room heated by water sizzling on hot stones
C. fjord	____ 3. steep-sided valley that is an inlet of the sea
D. geyser	____ 4. peninsula that makes up most of Denmark
E. geothermal energy	____ 5. heat produced by natural underground sources

DIRECTIONS: Multiple Choice In the blank at the left, write the letter of the choice that best completes the statement or answers the question. (10 points each)

Most of Sweden's almost 9 million people live in cities in the southern lowlands. Stockholm is the country's capital and largest city. Sweden's high standard of living has attracted more than 1 million immigrants from nearby Norway and Denmark and distant Turkey and Vietnam.

Reading Check What two natural resources have helped make Sweden wealthy?

Finland

Finland holds some of the largest unspoiled wilderness in Europe. Most of Finland's wealth comes from its huge forests of spruce, pine, and birch. Paper and wood products are important exports. In recent years, **heavy industry**—or manufactured goods such as machinery—has driven Finland's economy. The Finns are also leaders in the electronic communications industry. In fact, Finns as young as 10 carry mobile phones to school. In 1995 Finland joined the European Union.

The ancestors of the Finns settled in the region thousands of years ago, probably coming from what is now Siberia in Russia. As a result, Finnish language and culture differ from those of other Nordic countries.

Most of Finland's more than 5 million people live in towns and cities on the southern coast. **Helsinki,** the capital, has over 1 million people, but the city has still kept a small-town atmosphere. For example, there are no high-rise buildings. With snow on the ground for about half of the year, Finns enjoy cross-country skiing. After outdoor activities, many Finns enjoy relaxing in **saunas,** or wooden rooms heated by water sizzling on hot stones.

Reading Check Where did the ancestors of the Finns come from?

teen Scene

Cozy Ballet?

Helle Oelkers (far right) is a member of one of Europe's finest ballet companies—the Royal Danish Ballet. Helle likes to think that her performance encourages audience members to feel *hygge*. *Hygge* means feeling cozy and snug. She explains, "The greatest compliment a Dane can give is to thank someone for a cozy evening."

Denmark and Iceland

Both Denmark and Iceland are countries whose histories are closely tied to the sea. For centuries, Iceland was ruled by Denmark. For this reason Danish is still widely spoken and understood in Iceland.

Most of Denmark is made up of a peninsula known as Jutland. Denmark also includes nearly 500 islands, only 100 of which have people living on them. Denmark also rules the large island of Greenland. Throughout history, Denmark's location has made it a link for people and goods between the Nordic countries and the rest of Europe. Ferries and bridges connect Jutland and the islands. A bridge and tunnel now join Denmark's Zealand Island to Sweden.

Denmark has some of the richest farmland in northern Europe. Danish farm products include butter, cheese, bacon, and ham. Royal Copenhagen porcelain, a famous Danish export, is among the finest in the world. The Danes also invented and export the world-famous Lego toy building blocks. In 1993 Denmark joined the European Union.

The more than 5 million Danes enjoy a high standard of living. About 85 percent of them live in cities or towns. **Copenhagen,** Denmark's capital, is the largest city in northern Europe. In Copenhagen's harbor is

Content Background

Vikings in the New World In the 960s, Erik Thorvaldsson, or Erik the Red, left Norway with his father for Iceland. A few years later, Erik was banished for killing too many people. He found another island that—despite its barren landscape—he called "Greenland" to entice settlers. A few years later, a trading expedition led by Bjarni Herjolfsson was blown west, where it sighted a shoreline covered by woods. He did not stop, but Erik's son, Leif the Lucky, later retraced the route, which took him to the Americas. Around 1004, Thorfinn Karlsefni planted the first European colony of more than 100 Vikings in the Americas. The next year, his wife Gudrid gave birth to a son, Snorri, the first European child born in the Americas. Conflict with Native Americans led the Vikings to abandon the colony around 1007.

a famous attraction: a statue of the Little Mermaid. (See the photo on page 287.) She is a character from a story by the Danish author Hans Christian Andersen. Andersen, who lived and wrote during the 1800s, is one of Denmark's most famous writers.

Iceland Iceland, an island in the North Atlantic, is a land of hot springs and **geysers**—springs that shoot hot water and steam into the air. The people of Iceland make the most of this unusual environment. They use **geothermal energy**, or heat produced by natural underground sources, to heat most of their homes, buildings, and swimming pools.

What makes such natural wonders possible? Sitting on top of a fault line, Iceland is at the mercy of constant volcanic activity. Every few years, one of the country's 200 volcanoes erupts. The volcanoes heat the springs that appear across the length of Iceland.

Iceland's economy depends heavily on fishing. Fish exports provide the money to buy food and consumer goods from other countries. Iceland is concerned that overfishing will reduce the amount of fish available. To reduce its dependence on the fishing industry, Iceland has introduced new manufacturing and service industries.

About 99 percent of the 380,000 Icelanders live in urban areas. More than half the people live in the capital city of **Reykjavík** (RAY•kyah•veek). The people have a passion for books, magazines, and newspapers. In fact, the literacy rate in Iceland is 100 percent.

✓Reading Check **How do the people of Iceland take advantage of the country's geysers?**

Assessment

Defining Terms

1. **Define** fjord, welfare state, heavy industry, sauna, geyser, geothermal energy.

Recalling Facts

2. **Location** Name the five Nordic countries.
3. **Economics** What resource produces most of Norway's wealth?
4. **History** Why do some Icelanders speak Danish?

Critical Thinking

5. **Analyzing Information** How has Denmark's location affected its relationship with the rest of Europe?
6. **Understanding Cause and Effect** Why is Finnish culture different from the rest of the Nordic countries?

Graphic Organizer

7. **Organizing Information** Create a diagram like the one below that models three effects on Iceland that result because of its location on a fault line.

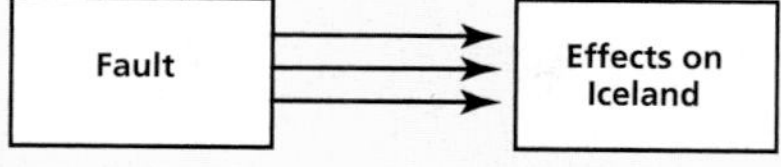

Applying Social Studies Skills

8. **Analyzing Maps** Study the political map on page 279. Which Nordic capital lies the farthest north? Which Nordic capital lies the farthest south?

Section 4 Assessment

1. The terms are defined in the Glossary.
2. Norway, Sweden, Finland, Denmark, Iceland
3. oil
4. Denmark ruled Iceland for centuries
5. It has been a link between mainland Europe and the Nordic countries.
6. Finland was probably originally settled by people from Siberia in eastern Russia.
7. presence of geysers and hot springs; geothermal energy; volcanic activity
8. Reykjavik; Copenhagen

Chapter 11

Section 4, pages 292–295

Reteach

Write the name of a country and a category of information on a flash card, such as "Denmark—climate" or "Iceland—people." Show the flash cards to the class and ask for volunteers to supply a piece of information about the country that fits in that category.

✓ Reading Check Answer

They use them to generate geothermal power.

Reading Essentials and Study Guide 11-4

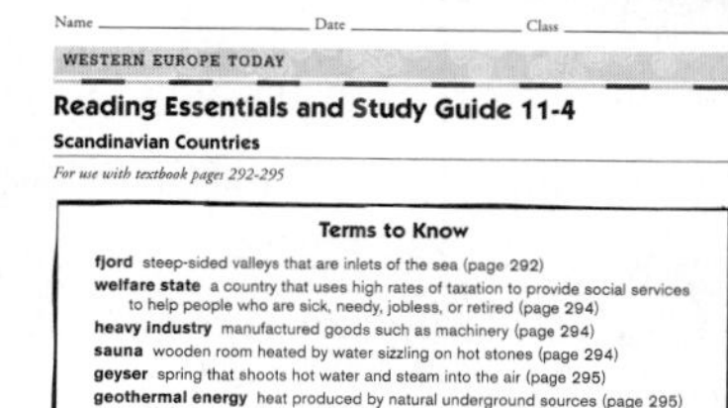
Name ______ Date ______ Class ______

WESTERN EUROPE TODAY

Reading Essentials and Study Guide 11-4

Scandinavian Countries

For use with textbook pages 292-295

Terms to Know

fjord steep-sided valleys that are inlets of the sea (page 292)
welfare state a country that uses high rates of taxation to provide social services to help people who are sick, needy, jobless, or retired (page 294)
heavy industry manufactured goods such as machinery (page 294)
sauna wooden room heated by water sizzling on hot stones (page 294)
geyser spring that shoots hot water and steam into the air (page 295)
geothermal energy heat produced by natural underground sources (page 295)

Drawing from Experience

Close

Have students create a bulletin board display about one of the countries in this section with images and captions that highlight important features of the country.

Chapter 11

Section 5, pages 296–300

1 Focus

Section Objectives

1. Compare the geography and people of Spain and Portugal.
2. Summarize the history and cultural contributions of Italy.
3. Explain how physical geography has shaped life and history in Greece.

BELLRINGER Skillbuilder Activity

Project transparency and have students answer questions.

This activity is also available as a blackline master.

Daily Focus Skills Transparency 11-5

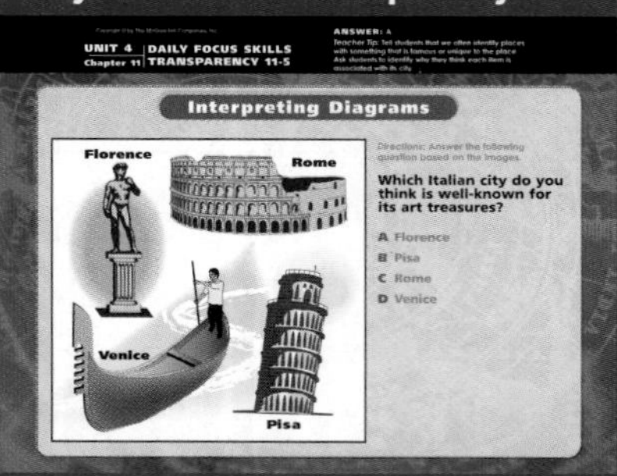

Guide to Reading

■ **Accessing Prior Knowledge**
Remind students that most of the countries of Latin America were once colonies of Spain and Portugal. **Ask:** What does this suggest about the past of these two countries? *(They once led powerful empires.)*

Section 5 Southern Europe

Guide to Reading

Main Idea

The sea has played an important role in each of the countries of southern Europe.

Terms to Know

- dry farming
- parliamentary republic
- sirocco
- coalition government

Reading Strategy

Create a chart like this one for each of the following countries: Spain, Portugal, Italy, and Greece. Fill in at least one key fact about each country for each category listed.

Country	
Land	
Economy	
Government	
People	

NATIONAL GEOGRAPHIC **Exploring Our World**

The "running of the bulls" is an annual and controversial event in Pamplona, a city in northern Spain. Although animal rights groups object to it, each morning during the weeklong Festival of San Fermín, a half dozen bulls are released to run along the city's narrow streets. People risk their lives running ahead of the bulls. Their goal is to stay in the race as long as possible.

Spain, Portugal, Italy, and **Greece**—and several tiny countries make up southern Europe. A long cultural heritage has produced many of the world's greatest writers, artists, and musicians. As you read in Chapter 9, it was the people of ancient Greece and Rome who played an especially important role in the development of Western civilization.

The Iberian Peninsula

Spain—about twice the size of Oregon—and Portugal—slightly smaller than Indiana—share the **Iberian Peninsula.** Tiny **Andorra,** with only 175 square miles (453 sq. km), perches high in the Pyrenees mountain range near Spain's border with France.

Portugal and most of Spain have mild winters and hot summers. Much of the interior of the peninsula is a dry plateau. In many areas the reddish-yellow soil is poor, and the land is dry-farmed to grow crops such as wheat and vegetables. In **dry farming** irrigation is not used. Instead the land is left unplanted every few years so that it can store moisture. Some farmers also herd sheep, goats, and cattle.

Section Resources

Reproducible Masters
- Reproducible Lesson Plan 11-5
- Daily Lecture and Discussion Notes 11-5
- Guided Reading Activity 11-5
- Reading Essentials and Study Guide 11-5
- Section Quiz 11-5

Transparencies
- Daily Focus Skills Transparency 11-5
- GeoQuiz Transparency 11-5

Multimedia
- Vocabulary PuzzleMaker Software
- Interactive Tutor Self-Assessment CD-ROM
- Presentation Plus! CD-ROM
- ExamView® Pro 3.0 Testmaker CD-ROM

Growing Economies Spain and Portugal both belong to the European Union. Once slow in developing manufacturing, the two countries in recent years have worked hard to catch up economically with other European Union nations.

Spain is one of the world's leading producers of olive oil. Portuguese farmers grow potatoes, grains, fruits, olives, and grapes. In addition, Portugal is the world's leading exporter of cork. The cork comes from the bark of certain oak trees, which grow well in central Portugal.

Millions of people travel to the Iberian Peninsula to enjoy the sunny climate, beautiful beaches, and ancient castles and cathedrals. Andorra draws millions of tourists each year who flock to its duty-free shops. Spain and Portugal also depend on the tourist industry. Manufacturing industries benefit both countries' economies as well. Spanish workers mine rich deposits of iron ore and make processed foods, clothing, footwear, steel, and automobiles.

The Government Both Spain and Portugal are modern democracies. Spain is a constitutional monarchy, in which a king or queen is head of state, but elected officials run the government. Portugal is a **parliamentary republic**, with a president as head of state. A prime minister, chosen by the legislature, is the head of government. Andorra is a semi-independent principality—it is governed by both Spain and France.

The People Most people in Spain and Portugal are Roman Catholic. Despite similar histories, the people of Spain and Portugal have their cultural differences. Portugal developed a unified culture based on the Portuguese language, while Spain remained a "country of different countries." The Spanish people do not all speak the same language or even have a single culture.

The **Basque** people in the Pyrenees see themselves as completely separate from Spain. They speak Basque, a language unlike any other in the world. Having lived in Spain longer than any other group, many Basques want independence in order to preserve their way of life. Some Basque groups have even used violence against the Spanish government.

Lisbon is Portugal's busy capital, but Portugal is mostly rural. On the other hand, more than three-fourths of Spain's people live in cities and towns. **Madrid,** Spain's capital, has nearly 5 million people and ranks as one of Europe's leading cultural centers. Madrid faces the usual urban challenges of heavy traffic and air pollution. Fast-paced **Barcelona** is Spain's leading seaport and industrial center.

You find some centuries-old traditions even in the modern cities. For example, most Spanish families usually do not eat dinner until 9 or 10 o'clock at night. On special occasions, Spaniards enjoy paella, a traditional dish of shrimp, lobster, chicken, ham, and vegetables mixed with seasoned rice.

Rock and jazz music are popular with young Spaniards and Portuguese, but the people of each region have their own traditional songs and dances as well. Spanish musicians often accompany

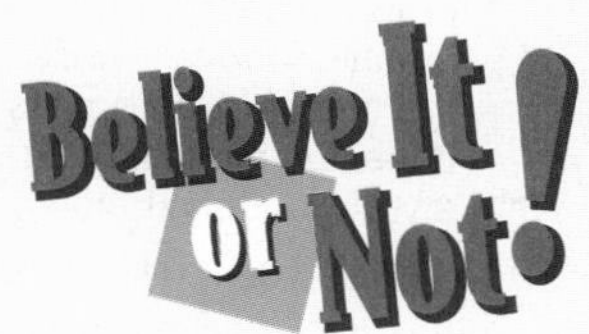

Islamic Art

The Muslims brought scientific knowledge to Spain. They introduced methods of irrigation, and new crops. They also brought literature, music, and art.

Islam forbids art that includes human forms. As a result, Muslim artists created complex patterns and elaborate designs. The tile below is an example of the beautiful mosaics seen today the world over.

Chapter 11

Section 5, pages 296–300

Making Comparisons Make a table with three columns. List the characteristics of people living in the Iberian Peninsula, Italy, and Greece. Have students analyze the similarities and differences of the people in these countries.

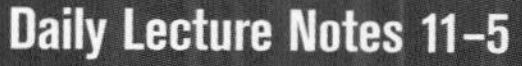

WESTERN EUROPE TODAY

Daily Lecture and Discussion Notes 11-5

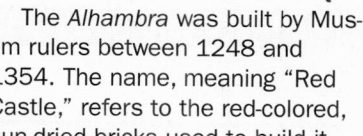

Southern Europe (pages 296–300)

Did You Know? More than 45 million tourists visit Spain each year, making it one of the three most visited countries in the world.

I. The Iberian Peninsula (pages 296–298)

A. Spain and Portugal share the **Iberian Peninsula.** Tiny **Andorra** perches high in the Pyrenees mountain range near Spain's border with France.

B. Portugal and most of Spain have mild winters and hot summers.

C. **Dry farming** is a method in which the land is left unplanted every few years so that it can store moisture.

...producers of olive oil.

TRAVEL GUIDE

The *Alhambra* was built by Muslim rulers between 1248 and 1354. The name, meaning "Red Castle," refers to the red-colored, sun-dried bricks used to build it.

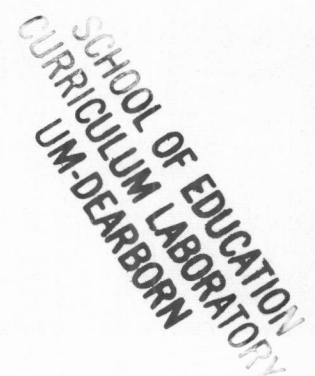

Meeting Special Needs

Visual/Spatial Organize students into five or six groups and supply each group with 10 large index cards. Inform groups that their task is to create a set of 10 information cards on the Iberian Peninsula. First, have group members spend time discussing what they think are the 10 most important features of the region. Then direct groups to create their cards. Some group members could design visuals to illustrate the features on the fronts of the cards. Others could research the features and write brief descriptions of them for the backs of the cards. Call on the groups to present their cards to the class. Have them explain why they selected the features they chose. **L1**

Refer to *Inclusion for the Middle School Social Studies Classroom Strategies and Activities* in the TCR.

More About the Photos

Gondolas Gondolas are to Venice what taxis are to New York. Each boat carries up to six passengers, costs about $30,000, and lasts over 20 years. Because of their unique design, gondolas are easily maneuvered through crowded canals, even when fully loaded.

Caption Answer from agriculture to a leading industrial economy

Guided Reading Activity 11-5

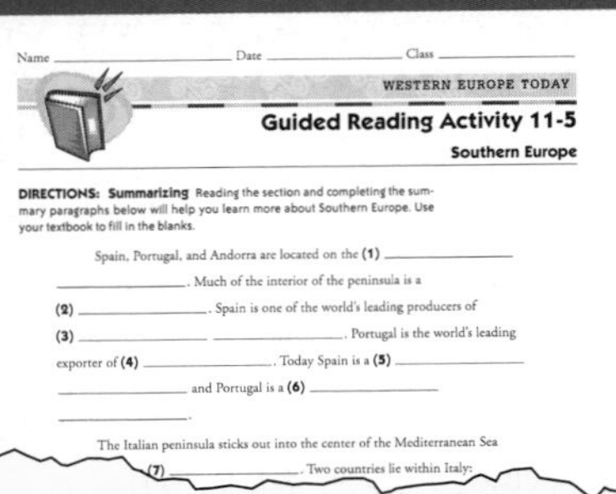

Reading Check Answer

cork

Measure student knowledge of physical features and political entities.

GeoQuiz Transparency 11-5

NATIONAL GEOGRAPHIC On Location

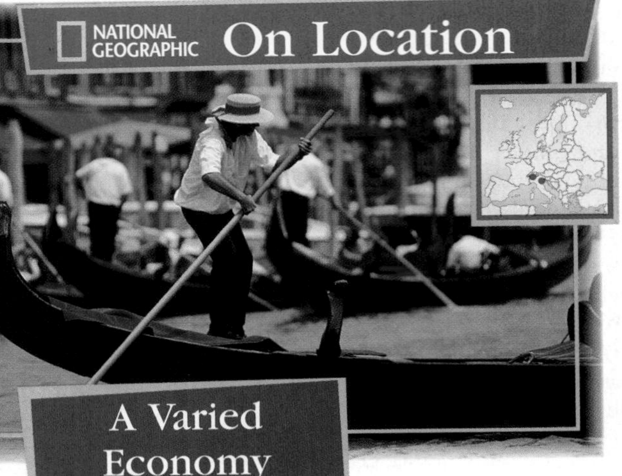

A Varied Economy

The canals of Venice draw thousands of tourists (above)—while the city of Milan boasts a fashion industry with stylish models (below).

Economics How has Italy's economy changed in the past 50 years?

singers and dancers on guitars, castanets, and tambourines. Spanish dances, such as the bolero and flamenco, and soulful Portuguese music known as fado have spread throughout the world.

Reading Check In what export does Portugal lead the world?

Italy

The Italian peninsula sticks out from Europe into the center of the Mediterranean Sea. The peninsula looks like a boot about to kick a triangle-shaped football. The "football" is **Sicily,** an island that belongs to Italy. Two tiny countries—**San Marino** and **Vatican City**—lie within the Italian "boot."

The Alps tower over northern Italy, while the rumbling of volcanic mountains echoes through the southern part of the peninsula and the island of Sicily. Throughout history, the southern part of Italy has experienced volcanic eruptions and earthquakes.

Most of Italy has a mild climate of sunny summers and rainy winters. In spring and summer, hot dry winds called **siroccos** blow across Italy from North Africa.

Italy's Economy In the past 50 years, Italy has changed from a mainly agricultural country into one of the world's leading industrial economies. Many of those goods are produced by small, family-owned businesses rather than by large corporations. Italian businesses are known for creating new designs and methods for making products. Italy is a member of the European Union.

Northern Italy is the center of manufacturing. Tourism is also important in northern and central Italy. Resorts in the Alps attract skiers. **Venice,** to the northeast, is built on 117 islands. You find no cars in this city, which is crisscrossed by canals and relies on boats for transportation. In central Italy lies **Rome,** the seat of the ancient Roman Empire. It is from the Vatican City, surrounded by Rome, that the pope guides the Catholic Church. In Rome, you can see ancient ruins and magnificent churches and palaces.

Southern Italy is poorer and less industrialized than northern and central Italy. Unemployment and poverty are common. Many southern Italians have moved to northern Italy or to other parts of Europe.

Italy's Government After World War II, Italy became a democratic republic. Yet democracy did not bring a stable government. Rivalry between the wealthy north and the poorer south has caused political tensions. In addition, many political parties exist, and no single party has been strong enough to gain control. Instead, Italy has seen many **coalition governments,** where two or more political parties work together to run a country.

Critical Thinking Activity

Figuring Percentages Write the following figures on the chalkboard: "Total: 581.8 million;" "Eastern Europe: 193.6 million;" "Northern Europe: 24.2 million;" "Southern Europe: 118.1 million;" "Western Europe: 245.9 million." Inform students that these figures represent the populations of the different regions of Europe and the continent as a whole. *(Note: Russia is not included in these figures.)* Have them calculate the percentages to determine what share of the continent's population lives in southern Europe. *(Eastern: 33.3%; Northern: 4.2%; Southern: 20.3%; Western: 42.3%)* Have them create a circle graph showing the data. **L2**

EE1 The World in Spatial Terms: Standard 1

Italy's People About 70 percent of Italy's nearly 58 million people live in towns and cities, and more than 90 percent of Italians work in manufacturing and service industries. Most Italians—more than 95 percent—are Roman Catholic. Celebrating the church's religious festivals is a widely shared part of Italian life. Vatican City in Rome is the headquarters of the Roman Catholic Church. The pope, who is the head of the church, lives and works here. Vatican City has many art treasures as well as the world's largest church, St. Peter's Basilica.

The people of Italy speak Italian, which developed from Latin, the language of ancient Rome. Italian is closely related to French and Spanish. Pasta, made from flour and water, is the basic dish in Italy. Some pasta dishes are spaghetti, lasagna, and ravioli.

✓Reading Check **Why have coalition governments been necessary in Italy?**

Greece

The Greek mainland sits on the southern tip of the Balkan Peninsula, which juts out from Europe into the Mediterranean Sea. Greece also includes 2,000 islands around the mainland. Like other Mediterranean areas, Greece is often shaken by earthquakes. Mountain ranges divide Greece into many separate regions. Historically, this has kept people in one region isolated from people in other regions.

Of the 2,000 Greek islands, only about 170 have people living on them. The largest Greek island, covering more than 3,000 square miles (7,770 sq. km), is **Crete.** Farther east in the Mediterranean is the island country of **Cyprus.** Once under Turkish and then British rule, Cyprus became independent in 1960. For centuries Greeks and Turks have lived on Cyprus, but fighting between the two groups has resulted in a divided country.

Architecture

For 800 years the Leaning Tower of Pisa has stood as a monument to construction mistakes. Begun in 1173, the tower began to tilt even before it was finished. Over time the tower moved even more, until by 1990, it leaned 12 feet (3.7 m) to the south. Fearing the tower would fall over, experts closed it. They added 800 tons (726 t) of lead weights to its base. They also removed 30 tons (27 t) of subsoil from underneath the north side of the tower in hopes that it would sink the opposite way. Visitors have once more returned to the tower.

Looking Closer **Why do you think experts fixed the tower's problem but still left it leaning?**

Cooperative Learning Activity

Celebrating Ethnic Diversity The people of southern Europe have many festivals and holidays. Some might be celebrated in your community if immigrants from these lands settled there. Other groups living in your community have their own special occasions. Have students investigate which ethnic groups are in your community, learn what special days these groups observe, and find out how they celebrate these days. Then have students create posters or brochures that celebrate the ethnic diversity in the community by illustrating one of the festivals.

EE4 Human Systems: Standards 9, 10

Assign Section 5 Assessment as homework or an in-class activity.

Have students use the Interactive Tutor Self-Assessment CD-ROM to review Section 11–5.

✓ Reading Check Answer

There are many political parties and no single party has been strong enough to gain control.

Did You Know?

The name *Greece* comes from the Latin word *Graeci,* the name that the Romans gave to the people who lived in what is today northern Greece.

Answer to continue to attract tourists to the famed tower

Ask students: **Do you think people should act to preserve and protect old buildings? Why or why not?**

World Art and Architecture Transparencies

Use these transparencies with accompanying strategies and activities to introduce students to other types of architecture of the region.

Chapter 11

Section 5, pages 296–300

Section Quiz 11-5

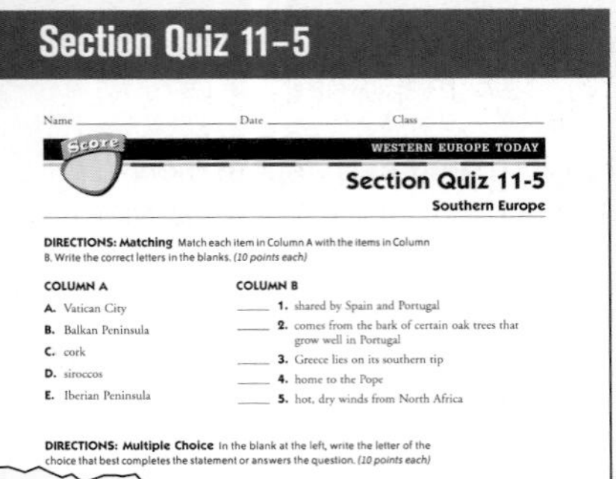

Name ____ Date ____ Class ____

WESTERN EUROPE TODAY

Section Quiz 11-5

Southern Europe

DIRECTIONS: Matching Match each item in Column A with the items in Column B. Write the correct letters in the blanks. (10 points each)

COLUMN A	COLUMN B
A. Vatican City	____ 1. shared by Spain and Portugal
B. Balkan Peninsula	____ 2. comes from the bark of certain oak trees that grow well in Portugal
C. cork	____ 3. Greece lies on its southern tip
D. siroccos	____ 4. home to the Pope
E. Iberian Peninsula	____ 5. hot, dry winds from North Africa

DIRECTIONS: Multiple Choice In the blank at the left, write the letter of the choice that best completes the statement or answers the question. (10 points each)

Reading Check Answer

shipping and tourism

Reading Essentials and Study Guide 11-5

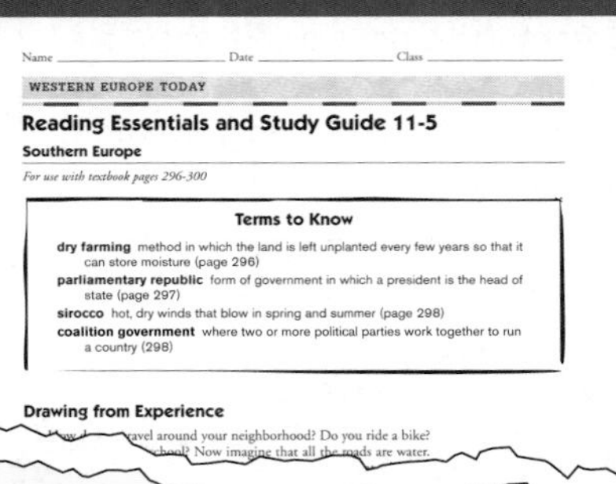

Name ____ Date ____ Class ____

WESTERN EUROPE TODAY

Reading Essentials and Study Guide 11-5

Southern Europe

For use with textbook pages 296–300

Terms to Know

dry farming method in which the land is left unplanted every few years so that it can store moisture (page 296)

parliamentary republic form of government in which a president is the head of state (page 297)

sirocco hot, dry winds that blow in spring and summer (page 298)

coalition government where two or more political parties work together to run a country (298)

Drawing from Experience

4 CLOSE

Tell students to imagine they are on a vacation in southern Europe. Have them write a letter home describing the things that they have seen, using standard grammar, spelling, sentence structure, and punctuation.

▲ Greek folk dancers in traditional costumes

Greece's Economy Greece belongs to the European Union but has one of the least industrialized economies in Europe. Because of the poor, stony soil, most people living in the highlands must graze sheep and goats. Greece must import food, fuels, and many manufactured goods. Farmers cultivate sugar beets, grains, citrus fruits, and tobacco. Greece has important crops of olives, used for olive oil, and grapes, used for wine.

No part of Greece is more than 85 miles (137 km) from the sea. Greece still has one of the largest shipping fleets in the world, including oil tankers, cargo ships, fishing boats, and passenger vessels. Shipping is vital to the economy.

Tourism is another key industry. Each year millions of visitors come to Greece to visit historic sites, such as the Parthenon in the capital city of **Athens** and the temple of Apollo at Delphi. Others come to relax on beaches and to enjoy the beautiful island scenery.

Greece's Government and People Today, Greece is a parliamentary republic. About 65 percent of Greece's 10.9 million people live in urban areas. The Greeks of today have much in common with their ancestors. They debate political issues with great enthusiasm, and they value the art of storytelling.

More than 95 percent of Greeks are Greek Orthodox Christians. Religion influences much of Greek life, especially in rural areas. Easter is the most important Greek holiday. Traditional holiday foods include lamb, fish, and feta cheese—made from sheep's or goat's milk.

Reading Check What are two key industries in Greece?

Section 5 Assessment

Defining Terms

1. **Define** dry farming, parliamentary republic, sirocco, coalition government.

Recalling Facts

2. **Location** What three countries are located on the Iberian Peninsula?
3. **Economics** Which is the more prosperous region in Italy—north or south?
4. **Culture** List four things tourists see in Italy.

Critical Thinking

5. **Analyzing Information** Why is it expected that Greece's economy would be dependent upon the sea?
6. **Understanding Cause and Effect** Why do the Basque people feel separate from the rest of Spain?

Graphic Organizer

7. **Organizing Information** In a chart like this one, list facts about Spain, Portugal, and Greece for each category.

	Spain	Portugal	Greece
Land			
Economy			
Cities			
People			

Applying Social Studies Skills

8. **Analyzing Maps** Turn to the political map on page 279. What body of water touches most of the southern countries of Europe?

300

Section 5 Assessment

1. The terms are defined in the Glossary.
2. Spain, Portugal, and Andorra
3. North
4. *Possible answers:* the Alps, Venice, Rome, Vatican City
5. No part of Greece is more than 85 miles from the sea.
6. The Basques live in an isolated region of northern Spain, where they have developed a totally separate language, and unique culture.
7. Students' charts will vary.
8. the Mediterranean Sea

Reading Review

Section 1 The United Kingdom and Ireland

Terms to Know
- peat
- bog
- parliamentary democracy
- constitutional monarchy

Main Idea

The United Kingdom and Ireland are small in size, but their people have had a great impact on the rest of the world.

✓Economics The United Kingdom is a major industrial and trading country.

✓Economics Manufacturing is important to Ireland's economy.

✓History After years of conflict, a peace plan was adopted in Northern Ireland.

Section 2 France and the Benelux Countries

Terms to Know
- navigable
- polder
- republic
- multinational company
- multilingual

Main Idea

France and the Benelux countries are important cultural, agricultural, and manufacturing centers of Europe.

✓Culture Paris is a world center of art, learning, and culture.

✓Location Belgium's location has made it an international center for trade.

✓Economics Luxembourg is home to many multinational companies.

Section 3 Germany, Switzerland, and Austria

Terms to Know
- autobahn
- federal republic
- reunification
- neutrality
- continental divide

Main Idea

Germany, Switzerland, and Austria are known for their mountain scenery and prosperous economies.

✓Economics The German economy is very strong.

✓Economics Switzerland produces high-quality manufactured goods.

✓Economics Austria's economy makes use of its mountainous terrain.

Section 4 The Nordic Countries

Terms to Know
- fjord
- sauna
- geyser
- welfare state
- heavy industry
- geothermal energy

Main Idea

The Nordic countries have developed diverse economies, and their people enjoy a high standard of living.

✓Region The Nordic countries include Norway, Sweden, Finland, Denmark, and Iceland.

✓Culture Finnish culture differs from other Nordic countries.

✓Economics Sweden's prosperity comes from forests and iron ore.

Section 5 Southern Europe

Terms to Know
- dry farming
- sirocco
- parliamentary republic
- coalition government

Main Idea

The sea has played an important role in each of the countries of southern Europe.

✓Location Spain and Portugal occupy the Iberian Peninsula.

✓Economics Italy is one of the world's leading industrial economies.

✓Place Greece consists of a mountainous mainland and 2,000 islands.

Reading Review

Use the Chapter 11 Reading Review to preview, review, condense, or reteach the chapter.

Preview/Review
Use the Terms to Know lists to help students review and study.

Activity Give students a quiz of the chapter's terms by reading a definition and having them identify the correct word.

Vocabulary PuzzleMaker Software reinforces the vocabulary terms used in Chapter 11.

The Interactive Tutor Self-Assessment CD-ROM allows students to review Chapter 11 content.

Condense
Have students read the Chapter 11 summary statements.

Chapter 11 Guided Reading Activities

Chapter 11 Audio Program

Reteach

Reteaching Activity 11

Chapter 11 Reading Essentials and Study Guide

Chapter Culminating Activity

Illustrated Time Line Have students choose one of the countries profiled in this chapter and create an illustrated time line of that country's history. Advise them to include events from ancient as well as modern times and to address the country's cultural contributions as well as political events. They can prepare their time lines as bulletin board displays or as multimedia presentations. *NOTE: This activity may be completed separately or you may wish students to incorporate it into their Current Events Journals.*

EE4 Human Systems: Standards 9, 10, 12

Assessment and Activities

GLENCOE TECHNOLOGY

MindJogger Videoquiz
Use MindJogger to review the Chapter 11 content.

 Available in VHS.

Using Key Terms

1.	h	6.	d
2.	j	7.	a
3.	i	8.	g
4.	c	9.	f
5.	b	10.	e

Reviewing the Main Ideas

11. England, Scotland, Wales, and Northern Ireland
12. Gaelic and English languages, Catholic religion
13. the name of the current government in France
14. They have such high population density that they need more land.
15. Eastern Germany has old and inefficient factories that cannot compete with the more advanced industries in the west.
16. because of Switzerland's heritage of neutrality, which is a result of its location in the Alps
17. because of oil and natural gas and fish exports
18. 100 percent
19. The Basque people see their culture as separate from Spain's and want to preserve their way of life.
20. The soil is too poor and rocky for farming. Shipping and sea-related activities are more dominant economic activities.

Chapter 11 Assessment and Activities

Using Key Terms

Match the terms in Part A with their definitions in Part B.

A.

1. multilingual
2. heavy industry
3. coalition government
4. neutrality
5. dry farming
6. welfare state
7. polder
8. autobahn
9. constitutional monarchy
10. multinational company

B.

a. land reclaimed from the sea
b. leaving land unplanted to store moisture
c. refusing to take sides
d. country that uses tax money to help people in need
e. company that has offices in several countries
f. government that has a king or queen but is run by elected officials
g. superhighway
h. able to speak several languages
i. two or more political parties working together to run a country
j. production of industrial goods

Reviewing the Main Ideas

Section 1 The United Kingdom and Ireland

11. **Region** What regions make up the United Kingdom?
12. **Culture** Name the major language(s) and religion of the Republic of Ireland.

Section 2 France and the Benelux Countries

13. **Government** What is the Fifth Republic?
14. **Economics** Why do the Dutch reclaim land from the sea?

Section 3 Germany, Switzerland, and Austria

15. **Government** What challenges does the reunification of Germany bring?
16. **Location** Why is Geneva the center of many international organizations?

Section 4 The Nordic Coutries

17. **Economics** Why is Norway wealthy?
18. **Culture** What is Iceland's literacy rate?

Section 5 Southern Europe

19. **Culture** Why do the Basque people want independence from Spain?
20. **Economics** How does the rocky landscape influence Greece's economy?

NATIONAL GEOGRAPHIC **Western Europe**

Place Location Activity

On a separate sheet of paper, match the letters on the map with the numbered places listed below.

1. Ireland
2. North Sea
3. Belgium
4. Austria
5. Switzerland
6. Spain
7. Norway
8. Portugal
9. Sweden
10. Iceland

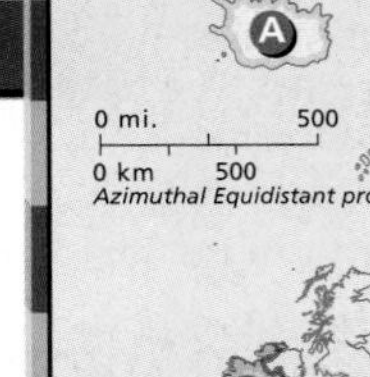

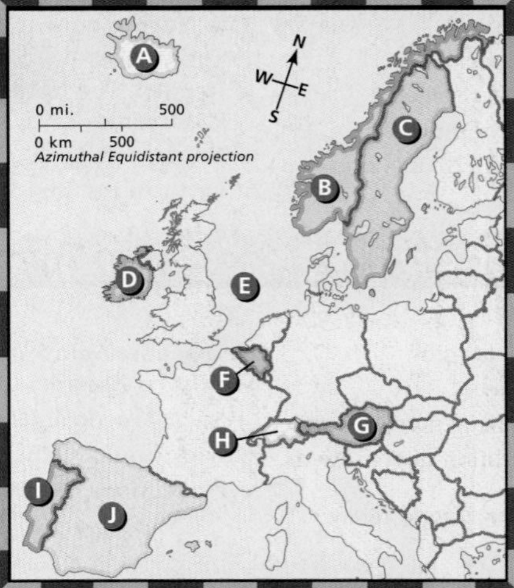

NATIONAL GEOGRAPHIC **Place Location Activity**

1.	D	6.	J
2.	E	7.	B
3.	F	8.	I
4.	G	9.	C
5.	H	10.	A

Critical Thinking

21. "Fire" is appropriate because the island experiences geysers and volcanoes due to its location along a fault line. "Ice" is appropriate because many areas are covered by ice due to its northern latitude.
22. Students' outlines will vary.

Self-Check Quiz Visit the ***Our World Today: People, Places, and Issues*** Web site at owt.glencoe.com and click on **Chapter 11–Self-Check Quizzes** to prepare for the Chapter Test.

Critical Thinking

21. **Analyzing Information** Why is the name Land of Fire and Ice appropriate for Iceland?
22. **Organizing Information** Create an outline of each country in Section 5. Use the following guide as your base outline.
    - I. Name of Country
        - A. Land
        - B. Economy
        - C. People

Current Events Journal

23. **Writing a News Broadcast** Research an important event that recently took place in one of the countries studied in this chapter. Write and present a news broadcast about the event. Make a prediction about how the event might affect life in the future.

Mental Mapping Activity

24. **Focusing on the Region** Create a simple outline map of western Europe, and then label the following:
    - United Kingdom
    - France
    - Germany
    - Sweden
    - Italy
    - Spain
    - Switzerland
    - Iceland

Technology Skills Activity

25. **Using a Spreadsheet** List the names of the western European countries in a spreadsheet, beginning with cell A2 and continuing down the column. Find each country's population and record the figures in column B. In column C list each country's area in square miles. Title column D "Population Density" then divide column B by column C to find the population density. Print and share your spreadsheet with the class.

The Princeton Review

Standardized Test Practice

Directions: Study the graph below, and then answer the question that follows.

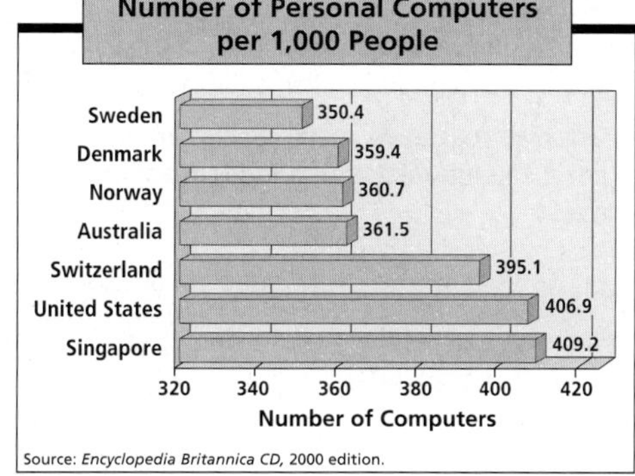

Source: *Encyclopedia Britannica CD*, 2000 edition.

1. **Which Nordic country has the highest number of personal computers per 1,000 people?**
   - **A** Singapore
   - **B** Switzerland
   - **C** Denmark
   - **D** Norway

Test-Taking Tip: Use the information on the graph to help you answer this question. Look carefully at the information on the bottom and the side of a bar graph to understand what the bars represent. The important word in the question is *Nordic*. Other countries may have more personal computers, but which Nordic country listed on the graph has the most personal computers per 1,000 people?

Assessment and Activities

Standardized Test Practice

1. D

Tested Objectives:
Analyzing information, catagorizing information

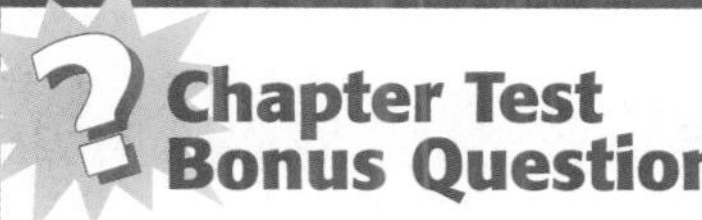

Chapter Test Bonus Question

This question may be used for extra credit on the chapter test.

The country in which you plan to vacation:

(1) has coastal areas on the Mediterranean and the Atlantic; (2) is famous for its wine and cheese; (3) is a world center of art and learning.

Where will you be taking your vacation? *(France)*

Our World Today online

Have students visit the Web site at **owt.glencoe.com** to review Chapter 11 and take the Self-Check Quiz.

Current Events Journal

23. Students should incorporate main and supporting ideas in their written and oral presentations. Afterwards, discuss in class whether the reports cover the Five W's and One H of journalism: *Who, What, Where, When, Why,* and *How.*

Mental Mapping Activity

24. This exercise helps students visualize the countries and geographic features they have been studying and understand the relationship among various points. Accept all attempts at freehand mapping.

Technology Skills Activity

25. Students' spreadsheets or databases should have clearly defined fields and accurate records with no typographical or other errors. Encourage students to include bar graphs or other means of showing comparative information.

Chapter 12 Resources

Note: The following materials may be used when teaching Chapter 12. Section level support materials are shown at point of use in the margins of the Teacher Wraparound Edition.

Timesaving Tools

TeacherWorks™ All-In-One Planner and Resource Center

- **Interactive Teacher Edition** See the **Interactive Teacher Edition** CD-ROM to electronically integrate your Teacher Wraparound Edition and blackline masters.
- **Interactive Lesson Planner** Organize your week, month, semester, or year with all the lesson helps you need. The **Interactive Lesson Planner** CD-ROM contains all Chapter 12 resources.

Use Glencoe's **Presentation Plus!** multimedia teacher tool to easily present dynamic lessons that visually excite your students. Using Microsoft PowerPoint® you can customize the presentations to create your own personalized lessons.

TEACHING TRANSPARENCIES

Graphic Organizer Transparency and Student Activity 12

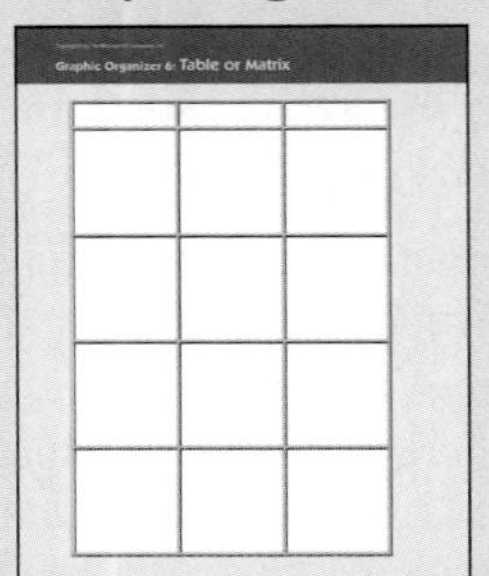

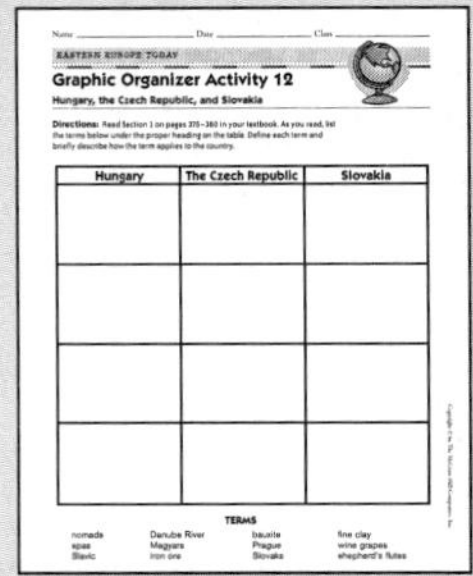

FOLDABLES™ Study Organizer

Foldables are three-dimensional, interactive graphic organizers that help students practice basic writing skills, review key vocabulary terms, and identify main ideas. Every chapter contains a Foldable activity, with additional chapter activities found in the ***Reading and Study Skills Foldables*** booklet.

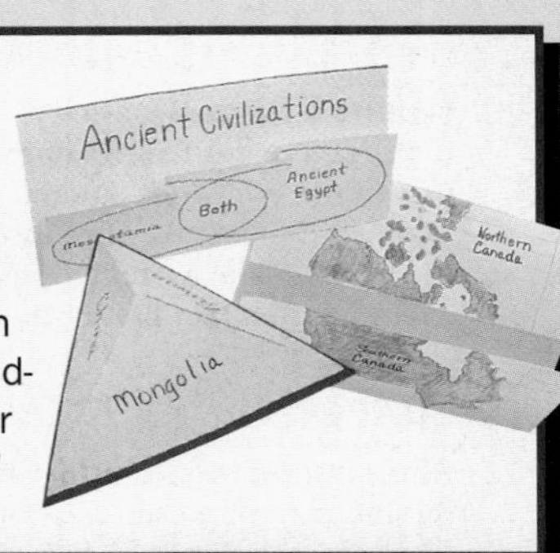

ENRICHMENT AND EXTENSION

Enrichment Activity 12

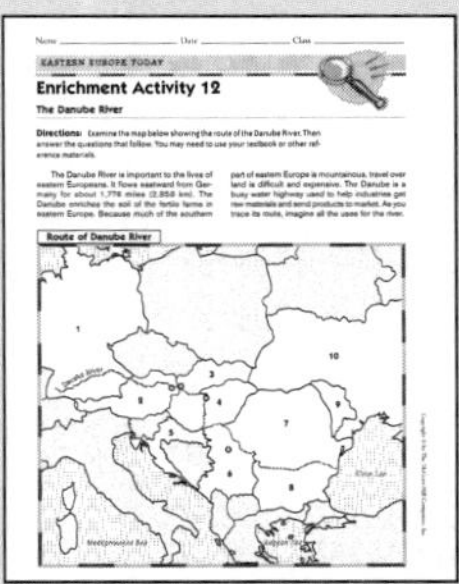

Cooperative Learning Activity 12

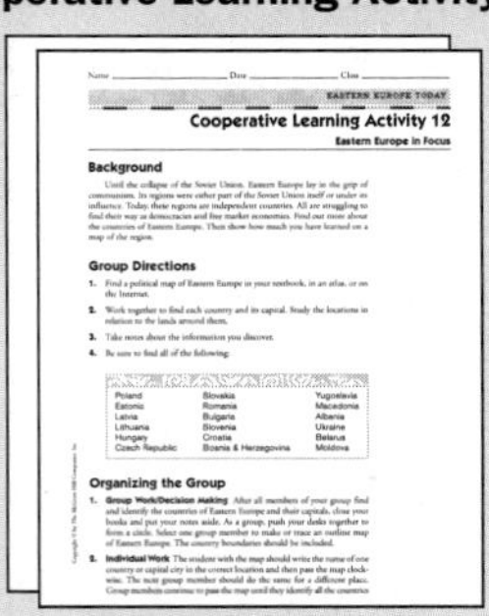

MAP AND GEOGRAPHY SKILLS

Chapter Map Activity 12

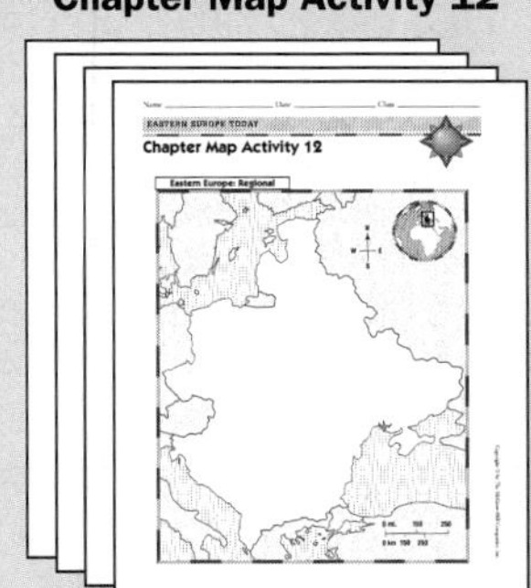

GeoLab Activity 12

STANDARDIZED ASSESSMENT SKILLS

Glencoe's Assessment Advantage

Critical Thinking Skills Activity 12

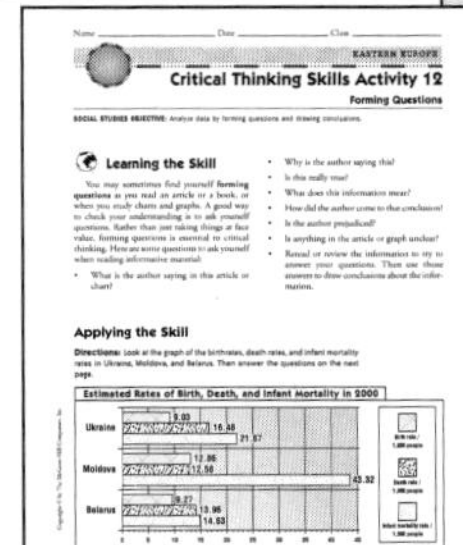

Map and Graph Skills Activity 12

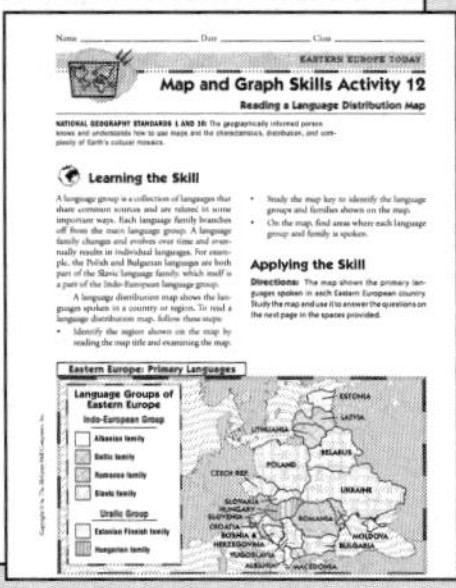

Reading and Writing Skills Activity 12

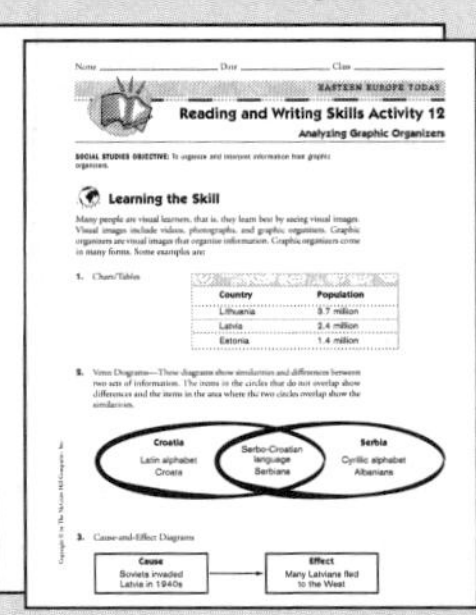

Standardized Test Practice Workbook Activity 12

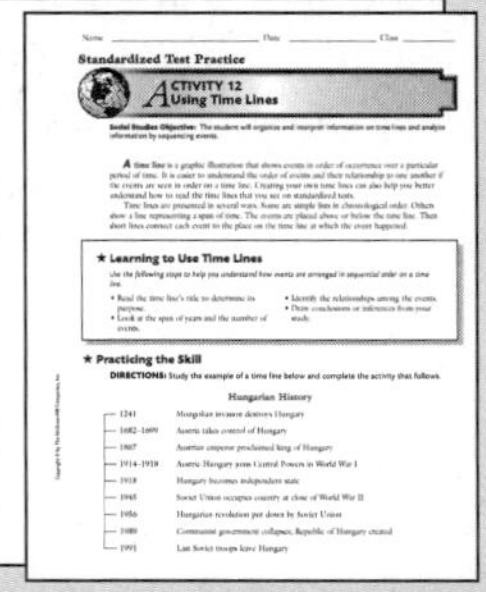

REVIEW AND REINFORCEMENT

Chapter Skills Activity 12

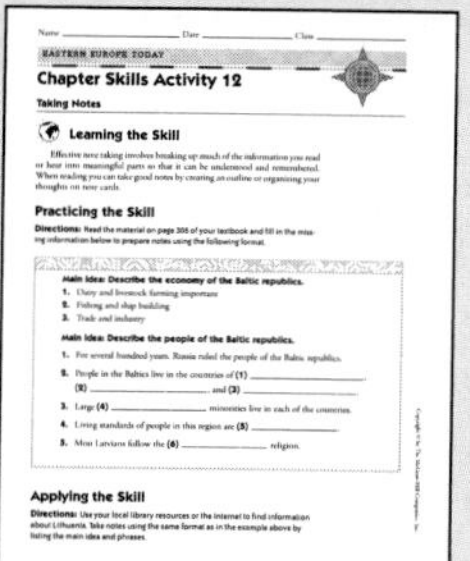

Take-Home Review Activity 12

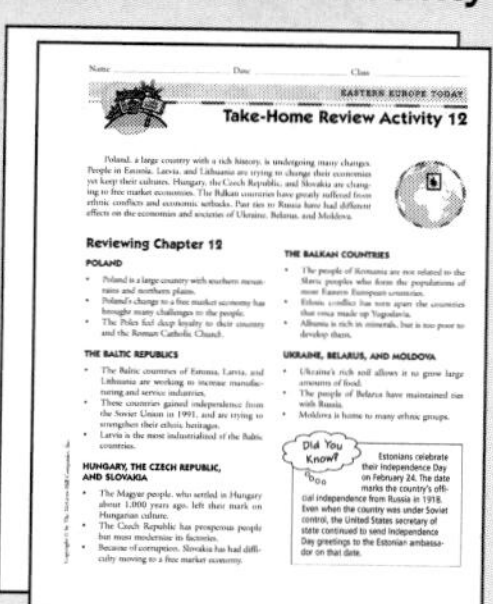

Reteaching Activity 12

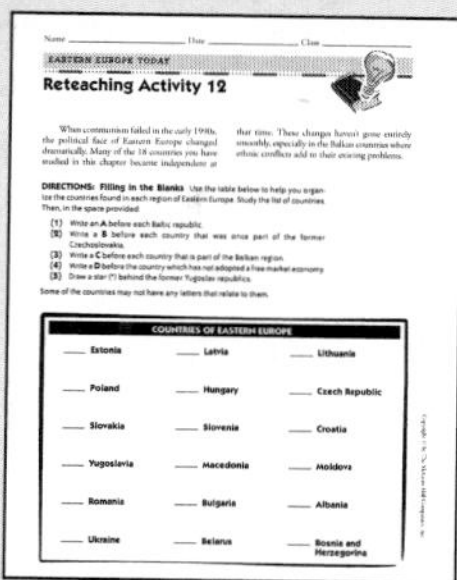

Vocabulary Activity 12

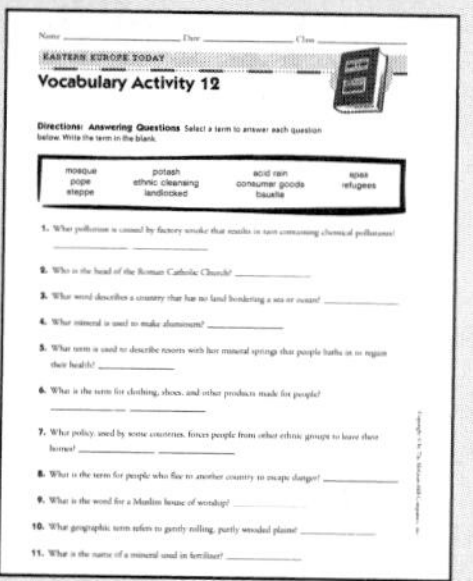

Workbook Activity 12

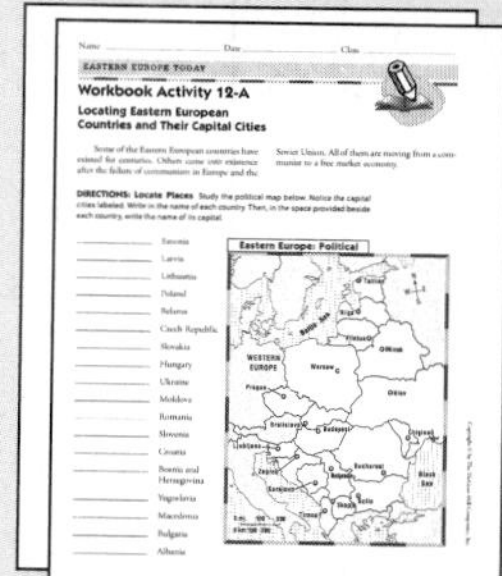

ASSESSMENT

GLENCOE'S ASSESSMENT ADVANTAGE

Chapter 12 Test, Form A

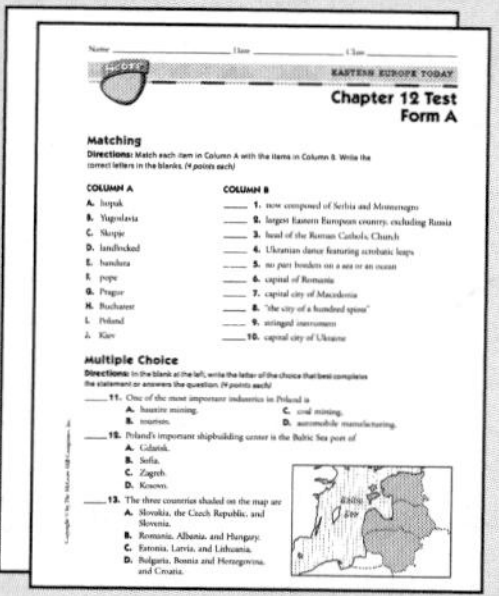

Chapter 12 Test, Form B

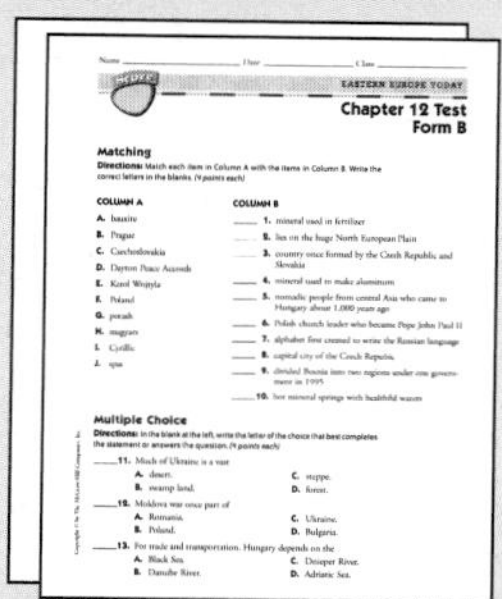

Performance Assessment Activity 12

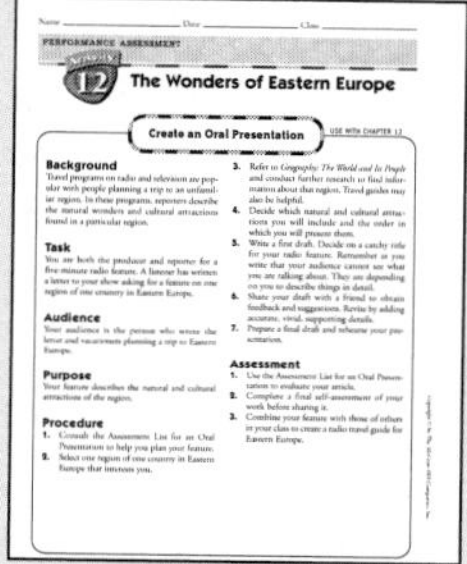

ExamView® Pro 3.0 Testmaker CD-ROM

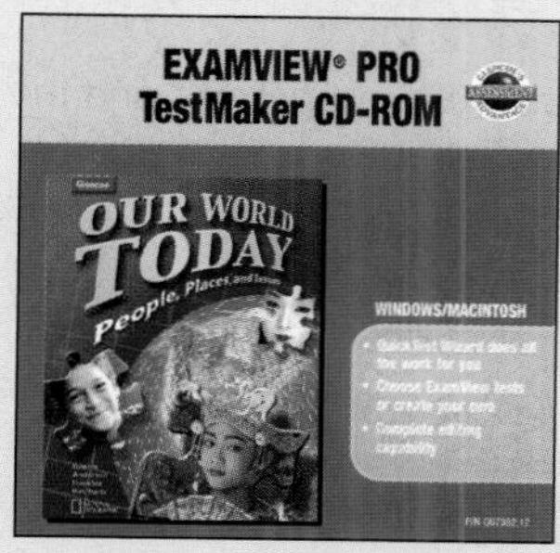

MULTIMEDIA

- **National Geographic's The World and Its People**
- **MindJogger Videoquiz**
- **Vocabulary PuzzleMaker Software**
- **Interactive Tutor Self-Assessment CD-ROM**
- **ExamView® Pro 3.0 Testmaker CD-ROM**
- **Interactive Lesson Planner CD-ROM**
- **Interactive Teacher Edition CD-ROM**
- **Skillbuilder Interactive Workbook CD-ROM, Level 1**
- **Presentation Plus! CD-ROM**
- **Audio Program**

SPANISH RESOURCES

The following Spanish language materials are available in the Spanish Resources binder:

- **Spanish Chapter Summaries**
- **Spanish Vocabulary Activities**
- **Spanish Guided Reading Activities**
- **Spanish Quizzes and Tests**
- **Spanish Take-Home Review Activities**
- **Spanish Reteaching Activities**

Meeting National Standards

Geography for Life

All of the 18 standards are demonstrated in Unit 4. The following ones are highlighted in Chapter 12:

Section 1
EE3 Physical Systems: Standards 7, 8
EE4 Human Systems: Standards 10, 11, 12
EE5 Environment and Society: Standards 14, 15, 16

Section 2
EE4 Human Systems: Standards 9, 10, 13

Section 3
EE4 Human Systems: Standards 9, 10, 11, 12, 13
EE5 Environment and Society: Standards 14, 15, 16

For a complete listing of National Geography Standards and entire text correlation, see pages T22–T29.

Local Objectives

Chapter 12 Planning Guide

SECTION RESOURCES

Daily Objectives	Reproducible Resources	Multimedia Resources
Section 1 **East Central Europe** **Suggested Pacing = 1 day** **1.** Describe the customs and beliefs of the Polish people. **2.** Explain how the economies of the Baltic republics have changed in recent years. **3.** Compare the people and economic activities of Hungary, the Czech Republic, and Slovakia.	Reproducible Lesson Plan 12-1 Daily Lecture and Discussion Notes 12-1 Guided Reading Activity 12-1 Reading Essentials and Study Guide 12-1 Section Quiz 12-1*	Daily Focus Skills Transparency 12-1 GeoQuiz Transparency 12-1 Vocabulary PuzzleMaker Software Interactive Tutor Self-Assessment CD-ROM ExamView® Pro 3.0 Testmaker CD-ROM Presentation Plus! CD-ROM
Section 2 **The Balkan Countries** **Suggested Pacing = 1 day** **1.** Compare the economies and the peoples of the Balkan countries. **2.** Explain why Yugoslavia broke up into separate countries.	Reproducible Lesson Plan 12-2 Daily Lecture and Discussion Notes 12-2 Guided Reading Activity 12-2 Reading Essentials and Study Guide 12-2 Section Quiz 12-2*	Daily Focus Skills Transparency 12-2 GeoQuiz Transparency 12-1 Vocabulary PuzzleMaker Software Interactive Tutor Self-Assessment CD-ROM ExamView® Pro 3.0 Testmaker CD-ROM Presentation Plus! CD-ROM
Section 3 **Ukraine, Belarus, and Moldova** **Suggested Pacing = 1 day** **1.** Describe the landforms of Ukraine, Belarus, and Moldova. **2.** Compare the economies, history, and culture of Ukraine, Belarus, and Moldova.	Reproducible Lesson Plan 12-3 Daily Lecture and Discussion Notes 12-3 Guided Reading Activity 12-3 Reading Essentials and Study Guide 12-3 Section Quiz 12-3*	Daily Focus Skills Transparency 12-3 GeoQuiz Transparency 12-1 Vocabulary PuzzleMaker Software Interactive Tutor Self-Assessment CD-ROM ExamView® Pro 3.0 Testmaker CD-ROM Presentation Plus! CD-ROM

00:00 **Out of Time?** Assign the **Reading Essentials and Study Guide** for this chapter.

*Also available in Spanish

KEY TO ABILITY LEVELS

Teaching strategies have been coded for varying learning styles and abilities.

- **L1** **BASIC** activities for all students
- **L2** **AVERAGE** activities for average to above-average students
- **L3** **CHALLENGING** activities for above-average students
- **ELL** **ENGLISH LANGUAGE LEARNER** activities

Blackline Master
Software
CD-ROM
Audiocassette
Transparency
Videocassette
Block Scheduling
DVD

Teacher to Teacher

Ten Clues

Give each student a 4" × 6" note card and a specific country of Europe. Then have each student draw an outline of the country he or she has been assigned. On the back of their cards, students should write 10 clues to help with the identification of their country. Then have students exchange cards and work in pairs to quiz each other on the countries' identifications.

Sue Brinkley
Hampshire Unit School
Hampshire, Tennessee

OUR WORLD TODAY Online

Use our Web site for additional resources. All essential content is covered in the Student Edition.

You and your students can visit **owt.glencoe.com**, the Web site companion to *Our World Today*. This innovative integration of electronic and print media offers your students a wealth of opportunities. The student text directs students to the Web site for the following options:

- Chapter Overviews
- Student Web Activities
- Self-Check Quizzes
- Textbook Updates

Answers are provided for you in the Web Activity Lesson Plan. Additional Web resources and Interactive Tutor puzzles are also available.

TEACHER'S CORNER

Index to National Geographic Magazine:

The following articles may be used for research relating to this chapter:

- "Albanians: A People Undone," by Priit J. Vesilind, February 2000.
- "Eyewitness Kosovo," by Alexandra Boulat, February 2000.
- "Romania's New Day," by Ed Vuilliamy, September 1998.
- "In Focus: Bosnia," (no author), June 1996.
- "Macedonia," by Priit J. Vesilind, March 1996.

National Geographic Society Products Available From Glencoe:

To order the following products for use with this chapter, contact your local Glencoe sales representative or call Glencoe at 1-800-334-7344:

- *GeoBee* (CD-ROM)
- *PictureShow: Earth's Climate* (CD-ROM)
- *PictureShow: Earth's Endangered Environments* (CD-ROM)
- *PicturePack: Geography of Europe* (Transparencies)
- *MapPack: Europe* (Transparencies)

Additional National Geographic Society Products:

To order the following products for use with this chapter, call National Geographic Society at 1-800-368-2728:

- *Complete National Geographic: 111 Years of National Geographic Magazine* (CD-ROM)
- *GeoKit: Pollution* (Kit)
- *Europe* (Video)
- *Weather: Come Rain, Come Shine* (Video)
- *Europe: The Road to Unity* (Video)
- *Communism* (Video)
- *Pollution: World at Risk* (Video)
- *Technology's Price* (Video)
- *Population* (Map)
- *Europe Political* (Map)
- *Voices: Poetry and Art From Around the World* (Book)
- *National Geographic Desk Reference* (Book)
- *National Geographic Atlas of the World, Seventh Edition* (Book)

NGS ONLINE

Access National Geographic's Web site for current events, activities, links, interactive features, and archives.
www.nationalgeographic.com

Introduce students to chapter content and key terms by having them access Chapter Overview 12 at owt.glencoe.com

Chapter Objectives

1. Discuss the land, economy, and culture of Poland.
2. Compare the economies and cultures of the Baltic republics.
3. Identify similarities and differences among the Balkan countries.
4. Describe the economies and people of Ukraine, Belarus, and Moldova.

GLENCOE TECHNOLOGY

NATIONAL GEOGRAPHIC

The World and Its People Video Program

Chapter 13 Eastern Europe
The following segments enhance the study of this chapter:

- **Down the Dunajec**
- **Poland's Storks**
- **Dracula's Castle**

Available in DVD and VHS.

MindJogger Videoquiz
Use MindJogger to preview the Chapter 12 content.

Available in VHS.

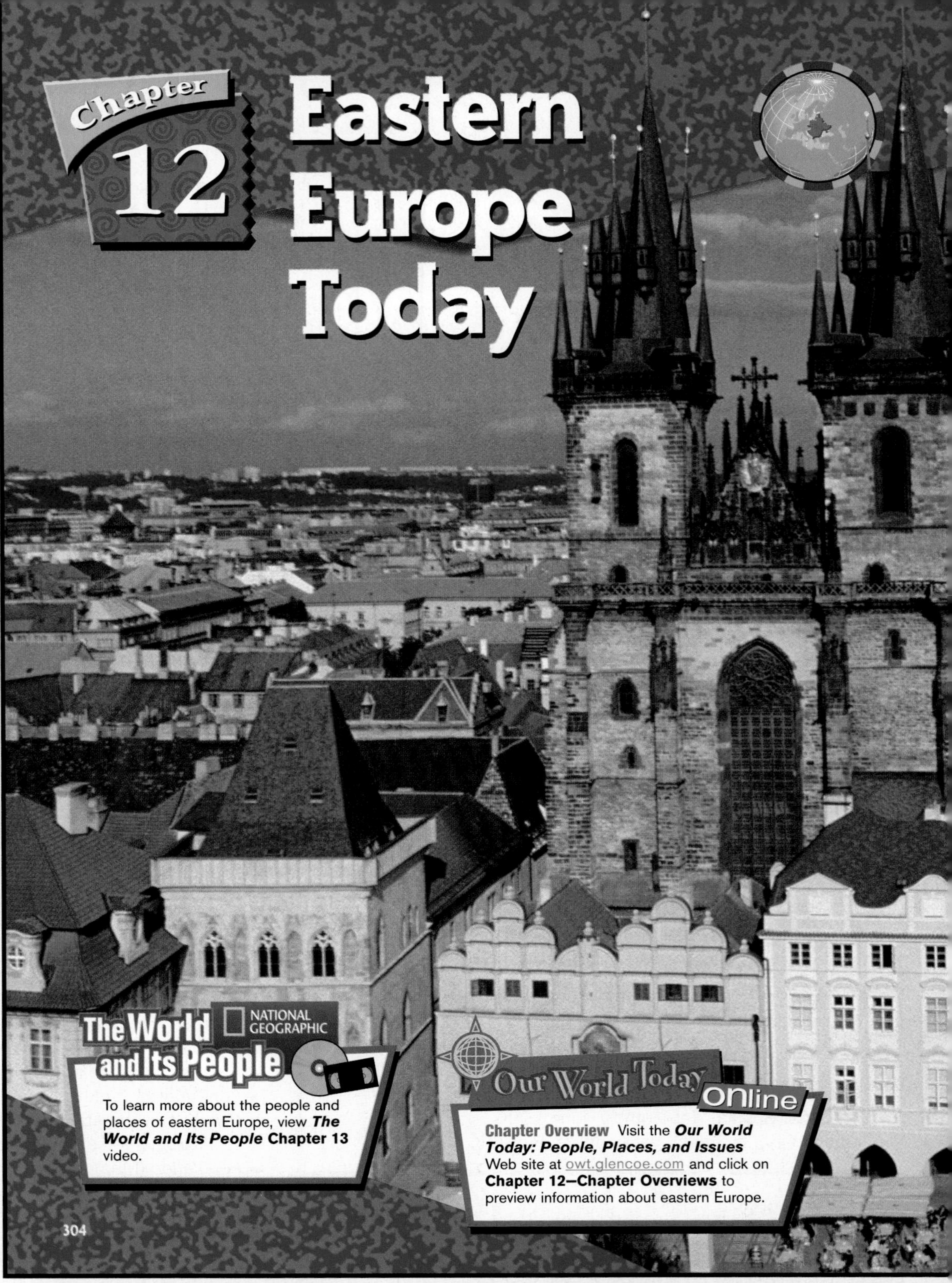

Chapter 12 Eastern Europe Today

The World and Its People — NATIONAL GEOGRAPHIC

To learn more about the people and places of eastern Europe, view ***The World and Its People*** **Chapter 13** video.

Our World Today online

Chapter Overview Visit the ***Our World Today: People, Places, and Issues*** Web site at owt.glencoe.com and click on **Chapter 12—Chapter Overviews** to preview information about eastern Europe.

304

Two-Minute Lesson Launcher

Before reading Chapter 12, have students scan the photographs throughout the chapter. **Ask:** **How would you describe the people and places that you see? What evidence can you see that these countries and cultures are very old? What evidence of more modern developments can you see?** Have students write their conclusions in their notebooks. When the class is done studying the chapter, have them review their impressions and see if they have any additional—or different—comments.

Compare-Contrast Study Foldable Make the following foldable to help you compare and contrast what you learn about Western Europe and Eastern Europe.

Step 1 Fold a sheet of paper in half from side to side.

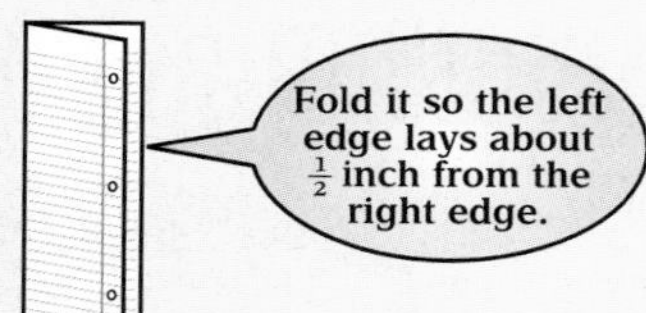

Fold it so the left edge lays about ½ inch from the right edge.

Step 2 Turn the paper and fold it into thirds.

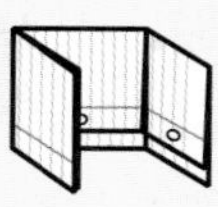

Step 3 Unfold and cut the top layer only along both folds.

This will make three tabs.

Step 4 Label as shown.

Reading and Writing Before you read Chapter 12, record what you learned about Western Europe in Chapter 11 under the Western Europe tab of your foldable. As you read Chapter 12, write what you learn about Eastern Europe under the correct tab. Then list ways these two regions are similar under the middle tab.

Why It Matters

From Communism to Democracy

Since the fall of communism, the countries of eastern Europe have continued to change. The formation of new democratic governments has led to closer ties with other free nations in Europe. The economic influence of eastern Europe grows as the region becomes a new market for western goods. The changes are not occurring smoothly, however, and many challenges have to be met.

◄ Starometske Namesti and Tyn Church in Prague, Czech Republic

About the Photo

Cherished as one of the most beautiful cities in the world, Prague lies in the center of Europe. Som times called the "City of One Hundred Spires," Prague is alive with towers and other beautiful buildings that reflect a rich and unique architectural heritage. The city is also known for being one of the cultural centers of eastern Europe. Museums and galleries are plentiful as are concerts and theater performances. Musical events in Prague today offer a variety of styles including classical, Dixieland jazz, folk and world music, and pop. **Ask:** **What does the variety of architecture, museums, and music tell you about Prague's society?**

Introducing

Chapter 12

FOLDABLES™ Study Organizer

Purpose Students make and use a compare-contrast foldable to collect and organize information about western Europe and eastern Europe. Students will compare and contrast characteristics of the two regions by using a Venn diagram.

Have students complete ***Reading and Study Skill Foldables*** Activity 12.

Why It Matters

Compare free market and command economic systems. Help students understand the difficulty of changing from a communist to free market system for the countries in this chapter. Tell them to recall a time in their lives when they moved from a familiar, comfortable way of life to something different. Point out that even if the change was for the better, they still may have had difficulty adjusting. Have them write a paragraph describing difficulties they felt in this transition. **Ask:** **How much more difficult would it be if an entire society were undergoing such change?**

Focus

Section Objectives

1. Describe the customs and beliefs of the Polish people.
2. Explain how the economies of the Baltic republics have changed in recent years.
3. Compare the people and economic activities of Hungary, the Czech Republic, and Slovakia.

BELLRINGER
Skillbuilder Activity

Project transparency and have students answer questions.

This activity is also available as a blackline master.

Daily Focus Skills Transparency 12-1

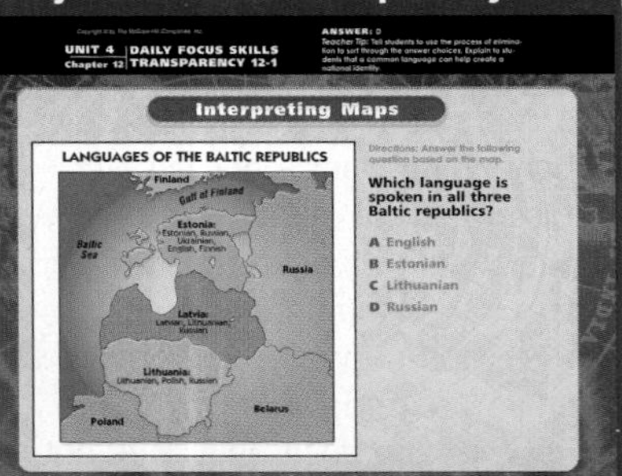

Guide to Reading

■ **Accessing Prior Knowledge**
Poland sits between strong neighbors, Russia and Germany, and has had serious problems as a result. Ask students to explain how location and resources can influence a country's foreign policy and its ability to control territory. Ask for examples of places that have suffered at the hands of more powerful neighbors.

Guide to Reading

Main Idea

The countries of East Central Europe are undergoing many changes to their political and economic systems.

Terms to Know

- acid rain
- pope
- landlocked
- bauxite
- spa

Reading Strategy

Create a chart like this one, and write one fact about the people of each country in East Central Europe.

Country	People
Poland	
Estonia	
Latvia	
Lithuania	
Hungary	
Czech Republic	
Slovakia	

Section 1

East Central Europe

NATIONAL GEOGRAPHIC Exploring Our World

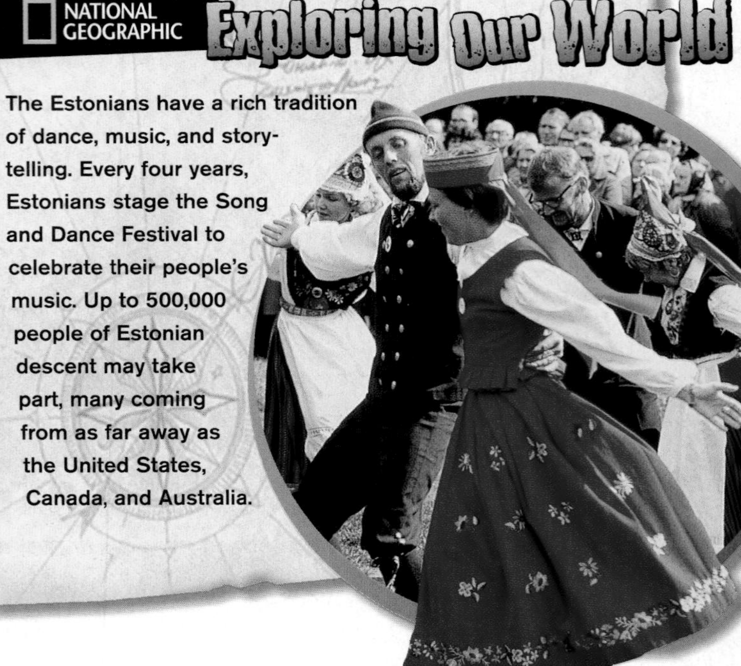

The Estonians have a rich tradition of dance, music, and storytelling. Every four years, Estonians stage the Song and Dance Festival to celebrate their people's music. Up to 500,000 people of Estonian descent may take part, many coming from as far away as the United States, Canada, and Australia.

East Central Europe is a region sandwiched between western Europe, the Baltic Sea, the Balkan Peninsula, and the countries of Ukraine and Belarus to the east. **Poland, Estonia, Latvia, Lithuania, Hungary,** the **Czech Republic,** and **Slovakia** make up this region. Though close together in distance, these countries have distinct histories and customs. This region of the world has undergone great changes in recent years.

Poland

Poland is one of the largest countries in eastern Europe. About the size of New Mexico, Poland lies on the huge North European Plain, which stretches from France to Russia. Many Polish people live in this fertile central region. Warm winds blowing across Europe from the Atlantic Ocean bring mild weather year-round.

Section Resources

Reproducible Masters

- Reproducible Lesson Plan 12-1
- Daily Lecture and Discussion Notes 12-1
- Guided Reading Activity 12-1
- Reading Essentials and Study Guide 12-1
- Section Quiz 12-1

Transparencies

- Daily Focus Skills Transparency 12-1
- GeoQuiz Transparency 12-1

Multimedia

- Vocabulary PuzzleMaker Software
- Interactive Tutor Self-Assessment CD-ROM
- Presentation Plus! CD-ROM
- ExamView® Pro 3.0 Testmaker CD-ROM

Poland is dotted with almost 2 million small farms, on which about 28 percent of Poles work. Farmers here grow more potatoes and rye than any other country in Europe. Other crops include wheat, sugar beets, fruits, and vegetables. Some farmers raise cattle, pigs, and chickens.

Most mining and manufacturing take place in Poland's central and southern regions. The mountains hold copper, zinc, and lead. Poland also has petroleum and natural gas, and produces hydroelectric power. Coal mining is one of the most important industries. Factories process foods and make machines, transportation equipment, and chemicals. Warsaw is Poland's capital and the city of **Gdańsk** (guh•DAHNSK), a Baltic Sea port, is an important shipbuilding center.

NATIONAL GEOGRAPHIC

Eastern Europe: Political

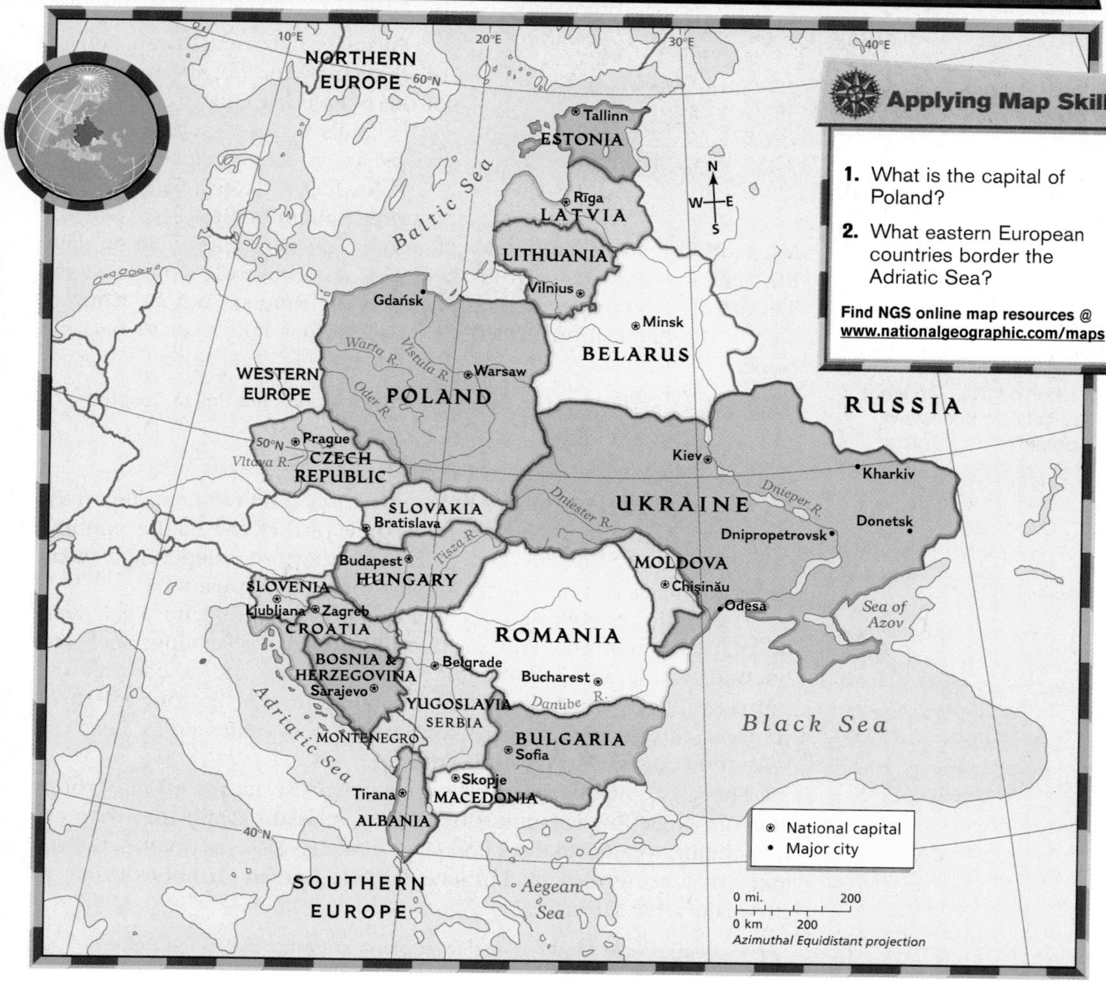

NORTHERN EUROPE, WESTERN EUROPE, SOUTHERN EUROPE, ESTONIA, Tallinn, LATVIA, Rīga, LITHUANIA, Vilnius, BELARUS, Minsk, POLAND, Gdańsk, Warsaw, CZECH REPUBLIC, Prague, SLOVAKIA, Bratislava, HUNGARY, Budapest, UKRAINE, Kiev, Kharkiv, Donetsk, Dnipropetrovsk, Odesa, MOLDOVA, Chişinău, RUSSIA, ROMANIA, Bucharest, SLOVENIA, Ljubljana, CROATIA, Zagreb, BOSNIA & HERZEGOVINA, Sarajevo, YUGOSLAVIA, SERBIA, MONTENEGRO, Belgrade, BULGARIA, Sofia, MACEDONIA, Skopje, ALBANIA, Tirana, Baltic Sea, Black Sea, Sea of Azov, Adriatic Sea, Aegean Sea, Warta R., Vistula R., Oder R., Vltava R., Tisza R., Dniester R., Dnieper R., Danube R.

⊛ National capital
• Major city

0 mi. 200 / 0 km 200 — Azimuthal Equidistant projection

Applying Map Skills

1. What is the capital of Poland?
2. What eastern European countries border the Adriatic Sea?

Find NGS online map resources @ www.nationalgeographic.com/maps

Chapter 12

Section 1, pages 306–310

2 TEACH

Graphing Data Give students this information: Ethnic Groups in Poland: Polish—97.6 percent, Other—2.4 percent; Religion in Poland: Roman Catholic—95 percent, Other—5 percent. Have students graph the data into two circle graphs. **Ask: Is Poland diverse or homogeneous? L1**

Applying Map Skills

Answers

1. Warsaw
2. Slovenia, Croatia, Bosnia and Herzegovina, Albania, Yugoslavia (Montenegro)

Skills Practice

Why are Lithuania, Latvia, and Estonia called the Baltic republics? *(They border the Baltic Sea.)*

Daily Lecture Notes 12-1

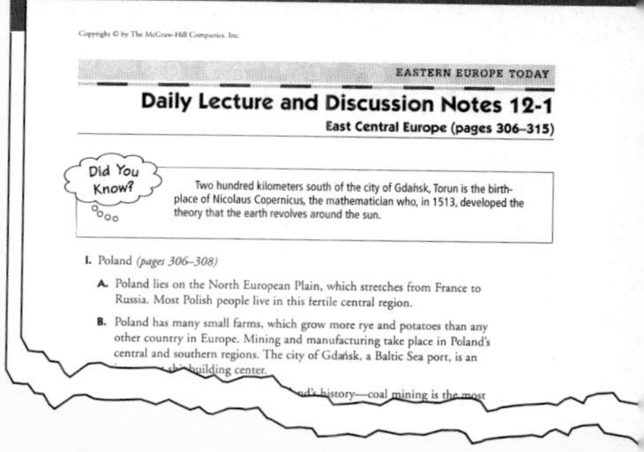

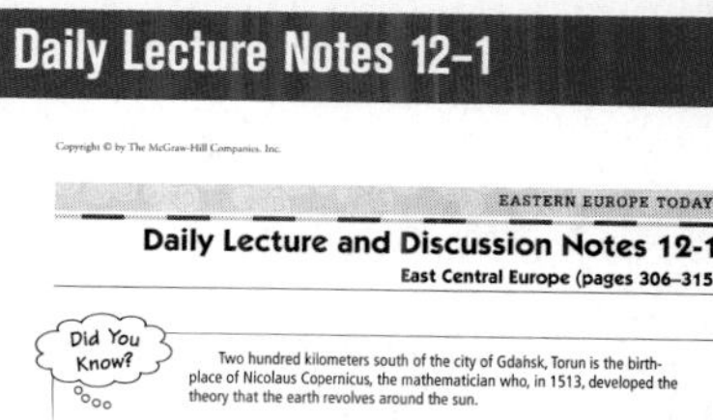

EASTERN EUROPE TODAY

Daily Lecture and Discussion Notes 12-1

East Central Europe (pages 306–315)

Did You Know? Two hundred kilometers south of the city of Gdańsk, Torun is the birthplace of Nicolaus Copernicus, the mathematician who, in 1513, developed the theory that the earth revolves around the sun.

I. Poland (pages 306–308)

A. Poland lies on the North European Plain, which stretches from France to Russia. Most Polish people live in this fertile central region.

B. Poland has many small farms, which grow more rye and potatoes than any other country in Europe. Mining and manufacturing take place in Poland's central and southern regions. The city of Gdańsk, a Baltic Sea port, is an ... building center.

Critical Thinking Activity

Problem Solving Inform students that coal is Poland's chief source of energy and the principal cause of its air and water pollution. Discuss the health problems associated with burning fossil fuels, particularly coal. Then have students work in small groups to research the connection between using coal as fuel and respiratory ailments. Ask groups to report their findings to the class. Then have the class discuss options the Poles might follow to improve their environment. They should use the problem-solving process to identify the problem, gather information, list and consider options, consider advantages and disadvantages, and choose a solution. **L2**

EE5 Environment and Society: Standard 14

More About the Photo

Rīga Rīga has always been an important port despite the fact that the waters of the Baltic Sea freeze in winter and early spring. Icebreaking ships are often used to clear a channel.

Caption Answer dairy farming, beef production, fishing, and shipbuilding

Guided Reading Activity 12-1

Name ______ Date ______ Class ______

EASTERN EUROPE TODAY

Guided Reading Activity 12-1

East Central Europe

DIRECTIONS: Reading for Accuracy Reading the section and completing the activity below will help you learn more about East Central Europe. Refer to your textbook to decide if a statement is true or false. Write **T** or **F**, and if a statement is false, rewrite it correctly.

____ 1. Poland's climate is mostly cold year-round.

____ 2. About 28 percent of Poland's people work on the nation's farms.

____ 3. One of the most important industries in Poland is lead mining.

____ 4. Polish factories have caused some of the worst water and air pollution in Europe.

... republics are located on fertile farmland.

✓ Reading Check Answer

religion and loyalty to their country

3 ASSESS

Assign Section 1 Assessment as homework or an in-class activity.

Have students use the Interactive Tutor Self-Assessment CD-ROM to review Section 12–1.

✓ Reading Check Answer

Protestant Lutheran and Roman Catholic

NATIONAL GEOGRAPHIC **On Location**

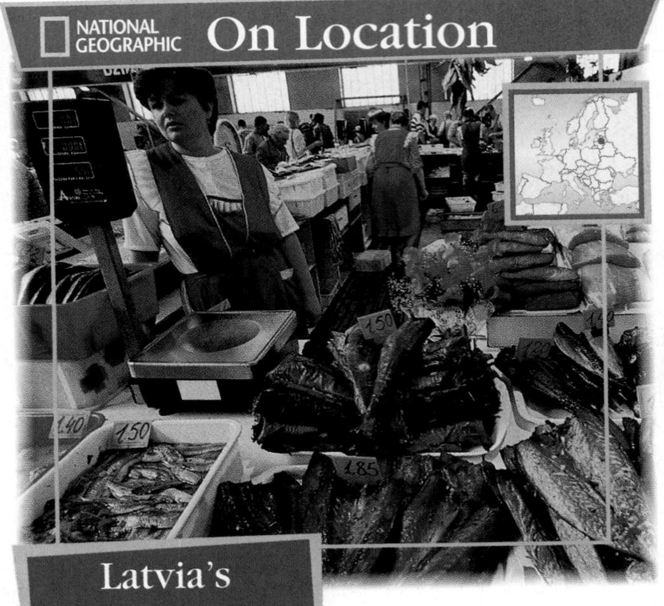

Latvia's Economy

Fish caught in the nearby Baltic Sea are sold in Rīga's Central Market.

Economics On what is Latvia's economy based?

Environmental Challenges Under Communist rule, Polish factories caused some of the worst water and air pollution in Europe. Since 1989 the government has moved to clean up the environment. Still, problems continue because Polish factories rely on burning coal. Factory smoke causes **acid rain,** or rain containing chemical pollutants.

Daily Life About 38.6 million people live in Poland. Almost all of them are ethnic Poles. Poles belong to the large ethnic group called Slavs and speak Polish, a Slavic language.

Poland is more rural than nations in other parts of Europe. About one-third of the people live in the countryside. As Poland's economy changes, more people are moving to cities.

Poles feel a deep loyalty to their country. Religion unites Poles as well. Most are Roman Catholic, and religion has a strong influence on daily life. Poles were very proud in 1978 when Karol Wojtyla (voy•TEE•wah) was named **pope,** or head of the Roman Catholic Church. Taking the name John Paul II, he was the first Pole ever to become pope.

✓ **Reading Check** What two beliefs or attitudes unite the Polish people?

The Baltic Republics

The small Baltic republics of Estonia, Latvia, and Lithuania lie on the shores of the Baltic Sea. For most of their history, the Baltic republics have been under Russian control. Though they are independent today, these countries still have large Russian minority populations.

The Baltic republics are located on poor, swampy land. Their well-developed economies are based mainly on dairy farming, beef production, fishing, and shipbuilding. In recent years, increased trade and industry have raised standards of living in this region. All three republics are moving toward free-market economies and closer ties with the countries in western Europe.

There is considerable tension between the native ethnic groups and the large Russian minorities. Many Russians claim that they are now being treated like second-class citizens. Most people in Estonia and Latvia are Protestant Lutherans, while Roman Catholics make up the majority in Lithuania.

✓ **Reading Check** What two major religions are practiced in the Baltic republics?

Meeting Special Needs

Visual/Spatial Help visual learners keep track of the characteristics of the Baltic republics by providing an outline map of the region. Using the unit and chapter maps, have them write in the names and capitals of each country. Then suggest that they annotate the map with information on the physical geography, economy, and people, color-coding their annotations by using a different color for each class of information (such as red for landforms, blue for economic features, and so on). Students can use their completed maps as a study aid. **ELL L1**

Refer to *Inclusion for the Middle School Social Studies Classroom Strategies and Activities* in the TCR.

Hungary, the Czech Republic, and Slovakia

In the center of eastern Europe, you find Hungary, the Czech (CHEHK) Republic, and Slovakia (sloh•VAH•kee•uh). The Czech Republic and Slovakia once were partners in a larger country known as Czechoslovakia.

Hungary Hungary, almost the size of Indiana, is **landlocked,** meaning that its land does not border a sea or an ocean. Hungary depends on the Danube River for trade and transportation. It's capital, Budapest, is divided in two by this river. Hungary's farmers grow corn, sugar beets, wheat, and potatoes in the country's rich soil. Grapes, grown to make wine, are also an important crop. Hungary has important natural resources such as coal, petroleum, and natural gas. Workers also mine **bauxite,** a mineral used to make aluminum. Service industries, such as financial services and tourism, now thrive.

About 90 percent of Hungary's 10 million people are descended from the **Magyars,** a nomadic people from Central Asia who came to Hungary about 1,000 years ago. Almost all speak the Hungarian language. About two-thirds are Roman Catholic, while another one-fourth is Protestant. Two-thirds of Hungarians live in towns and cities.

The Czech Republic The Czech Republic is also a landlocked country. Many areas are known for their natural beauty. In the mountains to the north and south, you can visit **spas,** or resorts with hot mineral springs that people bathe in to improve their health.

The Czechs enjoy a high standard of living compared to other eastern European countries. Large fertile areas make the Czech Republic a major agricultural producer. Farmers grow grains, sugar beets, potatoes,

Music

Early European shepherds were probably the first to play bagpipes. The bag is made from an animal's hide or stomach. To inflate the bag, air is blown through a tube or pumped with a bellows—a small air pump—under one arm. This air escapes through hollow sticks or bones in a controlled way to make different notes. The "drone" pipes produce a steady note, while the "chanter" pipes produce the melody.

Looking Closer Do you think drone or chanter pipes would be more difficult to control? Why?

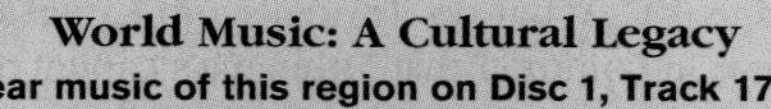

World Music: A Cultural Legacy
Hear music of this region on Disc 1, Track 17.

309

Chapter 12

Section 1, pages 306–310

Section Quiz 12-1

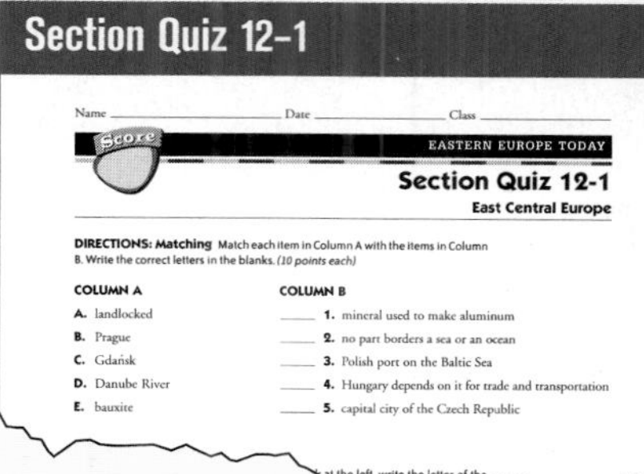

Name ______ Date ______ Class ______

EASTERN EUROPE TODAY

Section Quiz 12-1

East Central Europe

DIRECTIONS: Matching Match each item in Column A with the items in Column B. Write the correct letters in the blanks. *(10 points each)*

COLUMN A	COLUMN B
A. landlocked	____ **1.** mineral used to make aluminum
B. Prague	____ **2.** no part borders a sea or an ocean
C. Gdańsk	____ **3.** Polish port on the Baltic Sea
D. Danube River	____ **4.** Hungary depends on it for trade and transportation
E. bauxite	____ **5.** capital city of the Czech Republic

Reteach

Have students work in small groups to write 10 questions and answers about the section content, including maps. Then have groups use their questions to quiz other groups.

Answer the chanter pipes; because they play the melody, whereas the drone only plays one note

Musical Melting Pot Europeans played almost exclusively wind instruments such as bagpipes, horns, and flutes until Turks and Arabs invaded the Balkan, Iberian, and Italian Peninsulas. The Turks and Arabs brought string and percussion instruments, which are now considered part of the *European* classical tradition.

World Music: A Cultural Legacy

Use the accompanying Teacher Guide for background information, discussion questions, and worksheets about the music of this region.

Cooperative Learning Activity

Creating Comic Books Organize students into groups, and assign each group one of the following topics: Hungary as part of the Roman Empire; Magyar rule in Hungary; Hungary during the Renaissance; Hungary under the Hapsburgs; Hungary before and during World War I; Hungary during World War II; the Hungarian uprising of 1956; political changes in Hungary between 1988 and 1990. Encourage groups to research their topics using both primary sources, such as interviews and autobiographies, and secondary sources, such as encyclopedias and films. Then have them create comic books based on their research. They can use software to help with the illustrations. Distribute comics about history that the groups can use as models. **L1**

EE6 The Uses of Geography: Standard 17

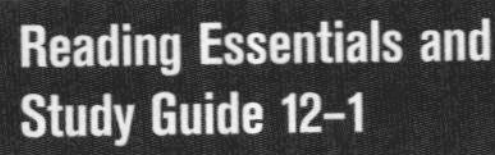

Reading Essentials and Study Guide 12-1

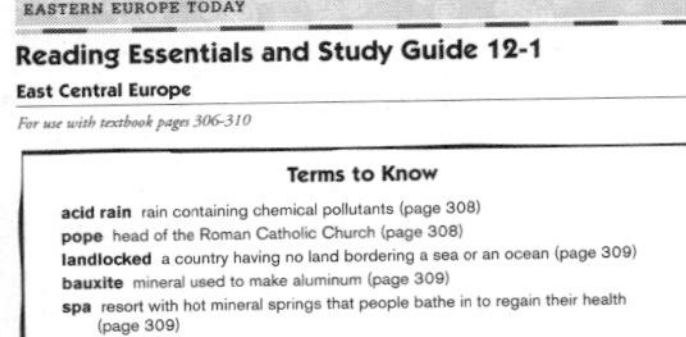

Name ______ Date ______ Class ______

EASTERN EUROPE TODAY

Reading Essentials and Study Guide 12-1

East Central Europe

For use with textbook pages 306–310

Terms to Know

acid rain rain containing chemical pollutants (page 308)
pope head of the Roman Catholic Church (page 308)
landlocked a country having no land bordering a sea or an ocean (page 309)
bauxite mineral used to make aluminum (page 309)
spa resort with hot mineral springs that people bathe in to regain their health (page 309)

Drawing from Experience

The pope, the head the of the Catholic Church, lives inside of Rome, Italy. Do you think all popes are Italian? Where do you think Pope John ... he is Polish!

Reading Check Answer

potatoes and sugarbeets

Measure student knowledge of physical features and political entities.

GeoQuiz Transparency 12-1

CLOSE

Ask students to prepare a written travelogue on one country of East Central Europe for tourists. They should use standard grammar, spelling, punctuation, and sentence structure.

and other foods. The country has some petroleum and natural gas. Minerals include limestone, coal, and kaolin, a fine clay used for pottery.

Prague (PRAHG), the capital, is a center of service industries, tourism, and high-technology manufacturing. Although manufacturing provides many consumer products, many factories are old, inefficient, and harmful to the environment. The Czechs are trying to modernize them to continue their prosperity.

Today the Czech Republic is a parliamentary democracy, with a powerful president assisted by a prime minister. Two-thirds of the Czech Republic's 10.3 million people live in cities. Prague is often called "the city of a hundred spires" because of its many church steeples. More recently, the Czech Republic has been a leading European center of jazz.

Slovakia Farmers in the lowlands of Slovakia grow barley, corn, potatoes, sugar beets, and wine grapes. The mountains are rich in iron ore, lead, zinc, and copper. Factories produce iron and steel products, cement, plastics, textiles, and processed foods.

Slovaks make up most of the population. They have a language and culture different from the Czechs'. Most Slovaks are Roman Catholic. Nearly 60 percent of Slovakia's 5.4 million people live in modern towns and cities. Tourists visit villages to see people dress in traditional clothes for festivals. You might even see musicians playing folk music on shepherds' flutes and bagpipes.

Reading Check **What crops are common to Hungary, the Czech Republic, and Slovakia?**

Section 1 Assessment

Defining Terms

1. **Define** acid rain, pope, landlocked, bauxite, spa.

Recalling Facts

2. **Culture** What is Poland's language and major religion?
3. **Culture** What is the difference between the religion of Lithuania and that of the other Baltic republics?
4. **Economics** What are three of the Czech Republic's natural resources?

Critical Thinking

5. **Analyzing Information** What has been the cause of considerable tension in the Baltic republics?
6. **Analyzing Information** Why do the Czechs have a high standard of living?

Graphic Organizer

7. **Organizing Information** Create a diagram like the one below. Choose one country of East Central Europe and write its name in the center oval. Then add at least two facts under the heading in each outer oval.

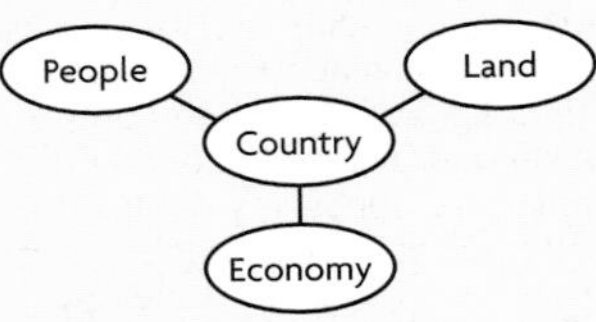

Applying Social Studies Skills

8. **Analyzing Maps** Refer to the political map on page 307. What do Estonia's and Latvia's capitals have in common that Lithuania's capital does not?

310

Section 1 Assessment

1. The terms are defined in the Glossary.
2. Polish; Roman Catholic
3. Lithuania's religion is Roman Catholic, Latvia's and Estonia's is Protestant Lutheran.
4. petroleum, natural gas, limestone, coal, and kaolin
5. conflict between native ethnic groups and the large Russian populations living there
6. Fertile areas make the Czech Republic a food producer, factories produce manufactured goods, the country attracts tourists, and the country has important resources.
7. Students' diagrams will vary.
8. They are ports on the Baltic Sea.

Section 2

The Balkan Countries

Guide to Reading

Main Idea

The Balkan countries have greatly suffered from ethnic conflicts and economic setbacks.

Terms to Know

- consumer goods
- ethnic cleansing
- refugee
- mosque

Reading Strategy

Create a chart like this one. For each Balkan country, write a fact or cause in the left box. Then write an effect that results from that fact in the right box.

Cause → Effect

NATIONAL GEOGRAPHIC **Exploring Our World**

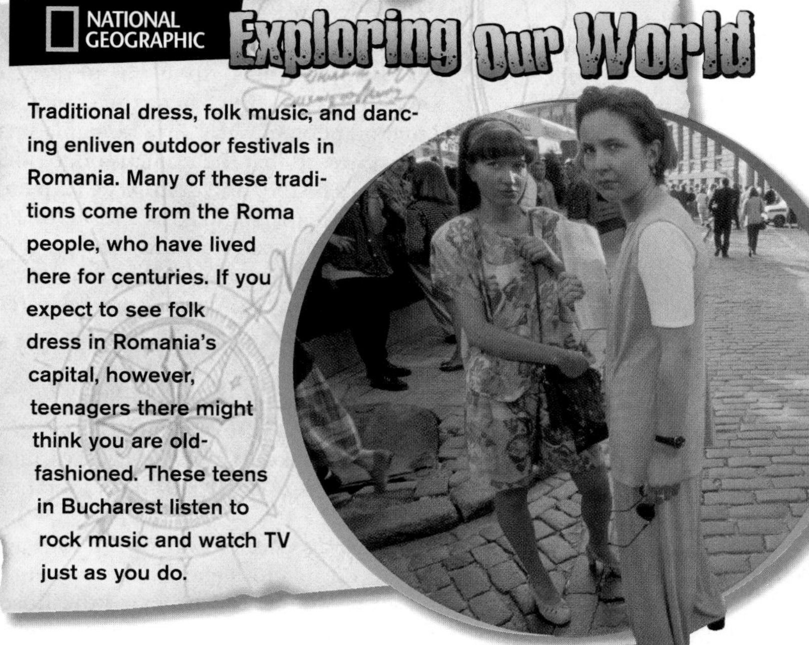

Traditional dress, folk music, and dancing enliven outdoor festivals in Romania. Many of these traditions come from the Roma people, who have lived here for centuries. If you expect to see folk dress in Romania's capital, however, teenagers there might think you are old-fashioned. These teens in Bucharest listen to rock music and watch TV just as you do.

Europe's **Balkan Peninsula** lies between the Adriatic Sea and the Black Sea. The political map on page 307 shows you that several countries make up this Balkan region. They are **Romania, Bulgaria,** the former **Yugoslav** republics, and **Albania.**

Romania

Romania sits on the northeastern edge of the Balkan Peninsula. The **Carpathian Mountains** take up about one-third of the country's land area. A vast plateau covers central Romania. A coastal region along the Black Sea includes the mouth of the Danube River. Winters can be very cold and foggy, with much snow. Summers are hot and sunny, but rainfall is abundant.

Romania's economic activities include farming, manufacturing, and mining. The forested mountains and central plateau contain deposits of coal, petroleum, and natural gas. Oil derricks rise in the

1 Focus

Section Objectives

1. Compare the economies and the peoples of the Balkan countries.
2. Explain why Yugoslavia broke up into separate countries.

BELLRINGER Skillbuilder Activity

Project transparency and have students answer questions.

This activity is also available as a blackline master.

Daily Focus Skills Transparency 12-2

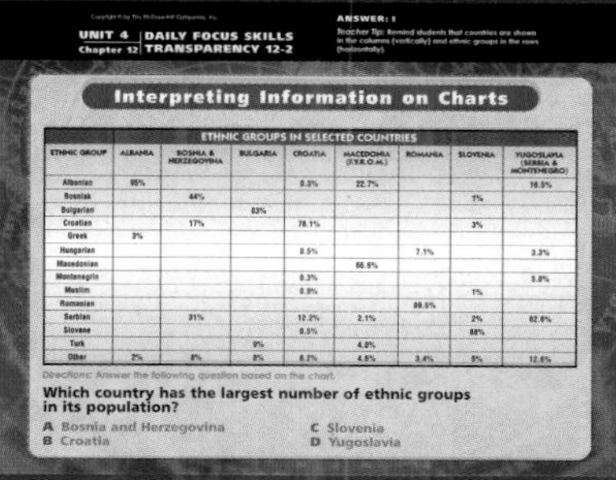

UNIT 4 Chapter 12 | DAILY FOCUS SKILLS TRANSPARENCY 12-2

ANSWER:

Teacher Tip: Remind students that countries are shown in the columns (vertically) and ethnic groups in the rows (horizontally).

Interpreting Information on Charts

ETHNIC GROUPS IN SELECTED COUNTRIES

ETHNIC GROUP	ALBANIA	BOSNIA & HERZEGOVINA	BULGARIA	CROATIA	MACEDONIA (F.Y.R.O.M.)	ROMANIA	SLOVENIA	YUGOSLAVIA (SERBIA & MONTENEGRO)
Albanian	95%			0.3%	22.7%			16.5%
Bosniak		44%					1%	
Bulgarian			83%					
Croatian		17%		78.1%			3%	
Greek	3%							
Hungarian				0.5%		7.1%		3.3%
Macedonian					66.6%			
Montenegrin				0.3%				5.0%
Muslim				0.9%			1%	
Romanian						89.5%		
Serbian		31%		12.2%	2.1%		2%	62.6%
Slovene				0.5%			88%	
Turk			9%		4.0%			
Other	2%	8%	8%	8.2%	4.8%	3.4%	5%	12.6%

Directions: Answer the following question based on the chart.

Which country has the largest number of ethnic groups in its population?

A Bosnia and Herzegovina
B Croatia
C Slovenia
D Yugoslavia

Guide to Reading

■ **Accessing Prior Knowledge**
Ask students to describe the ethnic and religious makeup of their community. Have them discuss how people there cooperate and work together despite diversity. Explain that in this section, they will read about an area where diversity has produced conflict.

Section Resources

Reproducible Masters

- Reproducible Lesson Plan 12-2
- Daily Lecture and Discussion Notes 12-2
- Guided Reading Activity 12-2
- Reading Essentials and Study Guide 12-2
- Section Quiz 12-2

Transparencies

- Daily Focus Skills Transparency 12-2
- GeoQuiz Transparency 12-1

Multimedia

- Vocabulary PuzzleMaker Software
- Interactive Tutor Self-Assessment CD-ROM
- Presentation Plus! CD-ROM
- ExamView® Pro 3.0 Testmaker CD-ROM

TEACH

Graphing Data Have students use the Country Profiles section of the Unit 4 Regional Atlas to identify the population of each country in the Balkans. Have them plot their data on a graph. **Ask: Which country is most populous?** *(Romania)* **Which is the least populous?** *(Macedonia)* **How many times more populous is the larger country than the smaller?** *(about 11 times)* **L2**

Reading Check Answer

French, Italian, Spanish

Daily Lecture Notes 12–2

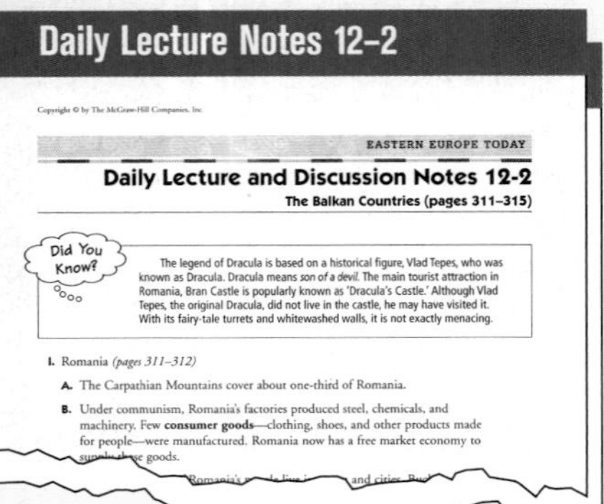

EASTERN EUROPE TODAY

Daily Lecture and Discussion Notes 12-2

The Balkan Countries (pages 311–315)

Did You Know? The legend of Dracula is based on a historical figure, Vlad Tepes, who was known as Dracula. Dracula means *son of a devil.* The main tourist attraction in Romania, Bran Castle is popularly known as 'Dracula's Castle.' Although Vlad Tepes, the original Dracula, did not live in the castle, he may have visited it. With its fairy-tale turrets and whitewashed walls, it is not exactly menacing.

I. Romania *(pages 311–312)*

A. The Carpathian Mountains cover about one-third of Romania.

B. Under communism, Romania's factories produced steel, chemicals, and machinery. Few **consumer goods**—clothing, shoes, and other products made for people—were manufactured. Romania now has a free market economy to supply these goods.

Note-taking tip

Remind students that scanning a passage before reading can help them develop a sense of its main ideas. Have students scan the text under "The Bulgarians" for main ideas. *(Ancestry, language, religion)*

Reading Check Answer

the Cyrillic alphabet

south. Orchards and vineyards stretch along Romania's western, eastern, and southern borders. Farmers also grow grains, vegetables, and herbs here.

Despite abundant resources, Romania's economy has been held back by the communist policies of the past. Under communism, Romania's factories produced steel, chemicals, and machinery. Few **consumer goods**—clothing, shoes, and other products made for people—were manufactured. Romania now has a free-market economy to supply these goods, but aging factories must be updated for Romania's economy to grow. In addition, the country needs to heal an environment widely damaged by air and water pollution.

The Romanians About 56 percent of Romania's people live in towns and cities. Bucharest, the capital and largest city, has more than 2 million people. What does Romania's name tell you about its history? If you guessed that the Romans once ruled this region, you are correct. Romania's history and culture were greatly influenced by the Romans. The Romanian language is closer to French, Italian, and Spanish—which are all based on Latin—than it is to other eastern European languages. In other ways, the Romanians are more like their Slavic neighbors. Many Romanians are Eastern Orthodox Christians.

Reading Check **To what other languages is Romanian related?**

Believe It or Not!

Transylvania

The region of central Romania known as Transylvania was the setting for English author Bram Stoker's vampire novel *Dracula*. Recently, a doctor noticed that many myths about vampires matched the symptoms of rabies, including pain from bright lights. He found that rabies had spread through the region at the same time that the vampire tales began.

Bulgaria

Mountainous Bulgaria lies south of Romania. Fertile valleys and plains are tucked among Bulgaria's mountains. The coast along the Black Sea has warmer year-round temperatures than the mountainous inland areas.

Bulgaria's economy rests on both agriculture and manufacturing. Wheat, corn, and sugar beets grow in the fertile valleys. Roses are grown in the central Valley of the Roses. Their sweet-smelling oil is used in perfumes. Manufacturing depends on the country's deposits of zinc and coal. Factories produce machinery, metals, textiles, and processed foods. Tourism is growing as visitors flock to Bulgaria's resorts on the Black Sea.

The Bulgarians Most of Bulgaria's 8.1 million people trace their ancestry to the Slavs, Turks, and other groups from Central Asia. Most Slavic people use the **Cyrillic** (suh•RIH•lihk) alphabet, which was first created to write the Slavic language. The Bulgarian language is also written in this Cyrillic alphabet. Most Bulgarians practice the **Eastern Orthodox Christian** religion. About 9 percent of the people are Muslim Turks.

Sofia, with over 1 million people, is the capital and largest city. During the summer, Bulgarians join vacationers from other countries at resorts on the Black Sea coast. Here, modern hotels line wide, sandy beaches.

Reading Check **What alphabet is used in many Slavic languages?**

Team-Teaching Activity

Language Arts Invite a foreign language teacher to class to discuss the different language families in Europe. Have the teacher point out the language chart on page 319. (The teacher might mention that the chart shows only national languages and does not include those spoken by smaller groups, such as Basque and Catalan in Spain or Sami in the Nordic countries.) Suggest that the teacher offer students examples of common words from the Germanic, Romance, or Slavic languages that show the similarities among languages in that family. Then have students identify which language groups are represented in eastern Europe. **L1**

EE4 Human Systems: Standard 10

Former Yugoslav Republics

The former Yugoslav republics used to be one country called **Yugoslavia.** In the early 1990s, long-simmering disputes among ethnic groups boiled to the surface and tore the country apart. Five countries emerged: **Slovenia, Croatia, Bosnia and Herzegovina** (HEHRT•seh•GAW•vee•nah), Yugoslavia (made up of **Serbia** and **Montenegro),** and **Macedonia,** also known as the Former Yugoslav Republic of Macedonia (or F.Y.R.O.M.).

After the breakup, Serbia, the strongest country, kept the name of Yugoslavia. It wished to regain control of parts of the other former Yugoslav republics. Serbia also wanted to make sure that Serbs living in the other republics would not lose their rights. As a result, wars erupted throughout the 1990s. Some countries forced people from other ethnic groups to leave their homes, a policy called **ethnic cleansing.** Hundreds of thousands of people died or were murdered. About the same number became **refugees,** or people who flee to another country to escape danger. These wars left the region badly scarred, without promise of long-term peace.

Slovenia Slovenia, in the northwest of the Balkans region, has rugged mountains and fertile, densely populated valleys. Of all the countries of the old Yugoslavia, Slovenia is the most peaceful and prosperous. With many factories and service industries, it also has the region's highest standard of living. About 52 percent of the 2 million Slovenians live in towns and cities. Most are Roman Catholic.

Croatia Croatia spreads along the island-studded coast of the Adriatic Sea. Then it suddenly swings inland, encompassing rugged mountains and a fertile plain. **Zagreb,** the capital and largest city, lies in this inland area. An industrialized republic, Croatia supports agriculture as well. Tourists once flocked to Croatia's beautiful Adriatic beaches, but war has damaged many places.

The Croats, a Slavic group, make up 78 percent of Croatia's 4.7 million people. Another 12 percent are Serbs. Both Croats and Serbs speak the same Serbo-Croatian language, but they use different alphabets. The Croats use the Latin alphabet, the same one that you use for English. The Serbs write with the Cyrillic alphabet. Religion also divides Croats and Serbs. Croats are mainly Roman Catholic, while Serbs are Eastern Orthodox Christians.

NATIONAL GEOGRAPHIC **On Location**

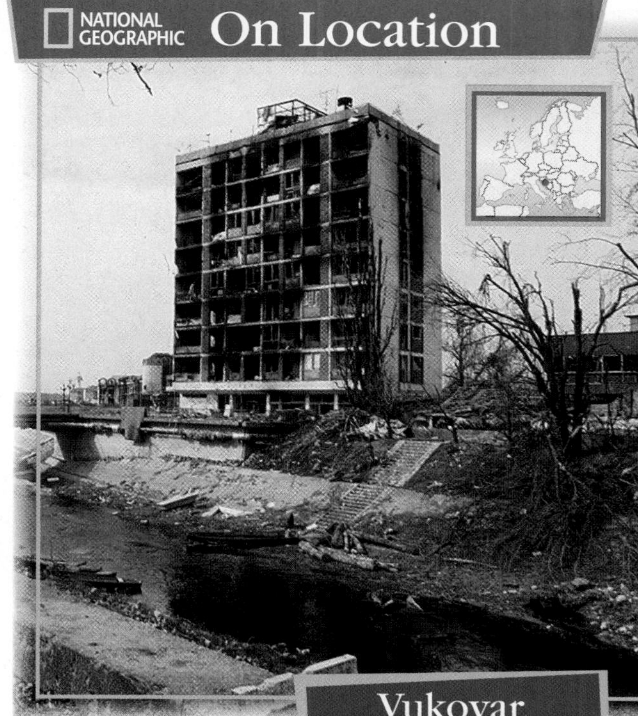

Vukovar, Croatia

In 1991 Serbs attacked Vukovar in a revolt against Croatian independence. The revolt became a war, which lasted many years and took many lives.

Place **What are some ways the war affected Croatia?**

Drawing Conclusions On the board, write the following headings: "Country," "Ethnic Groups," and "Religions." Call on volunteers to list details about each country in the Balkans under the appropriate headings. Then have students use the information in the chart to determine which countries have similar ethnic groups, which have similar religions, and which are different from their neighbors. **L1**

More About the Photos

Croatia The war in the former Yugoslav republics lasted from 1991–1995. During these four years, nearly 1 million refugees from Bosnia and Herzegovina flooded into Croatia, prompting Croatia's government to ask for international humanitarian and financial aid. **Ask:** **How do characteristics of Bosnia today reflect this history of war?**

Caption Answer buildings were destroyed, many lives were lost, tourism suffered

Guided Reading Activity 12-2

Name ____ Date ____ Class ____

EASTERN EUROPE TODAY

Guided Reading Activity 12-2

The Balkan Countries

DIRECTIONS: Outlining Reading the section and completing the outline below will help you learn more about the Balkan countries. Use your textbook to fill in the blanks.

I. Romania
   A. The ____ ____ take up one-third of the land.
   B. Economic activities include:
      1. ____
      2. ____, and
      3. ____
   C. The forested mountains and central plateau contain ____ of ____ and natural gas.
   ____ and towns.

Meeting Special Needs

Interpersonal Organize students into several groups. Have each group create a board game that people in the Balkan countries could use to learn about the free market economy. Suggest that groups use Monopoly as a model but that they name the squares after streets in a Balkan city. They can check maps of cities in travel guides for street names. Help groups create cards that reflect situations in a free market economy, such as "You priced your product too high for the market. Lose 1 turn." or "Your investment paid off. Win $500." Give groups a chance to explain their games to the other students. **L3**

Refer to *Inclusion for the Middle School Social Studies Classroom Strategies and Activities* in the TCR.

Chapter 12

Section 2, pages 311–315

Primary Source

Answer Answers will vary.

Activity Have students research the refugees from the former Yugoslav republics. Ask them to imagine that they are among those refugees. Have the students write a diary entry about the day they were forced to leave home. Ask them to use their senses of sight, smell, and hearing to describe in detail the events that are taking place around them. Ask them to describe their feelings.

3 ASSESS

Assign Section 2 Assessment as homework or an in-class activity.

Section Quiz 12-2

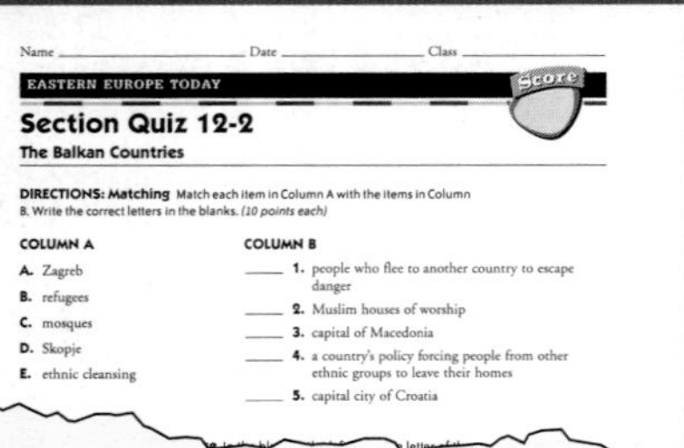

Name ______ Date ______ Class ______

EASTERN EUROPE TODAY

Score

Section Quiz 12-2

The Balkan Countries

DIRECTIONS: Matching Match each item in Column A with the items in Column B. Write the correct letters in the blanks. (10 points each)

COLUMN A	COLUMN B
A. Zagreb	___ 1. people who flee to another country to escape danger
B. refugees	___ 2. Muslim houses of worship
C. mosques	___ 3. capital of Macedonia
D. Skopje	___ 4. a country's policy forcing people from other ethnic groups to leave their homes
E. ethnic cleansing	___ 5. capital city of Croatia

✓ Reading Check Answer

Slovenia, Croatia, Bosnia and Herzegovina, Yugoslavia (Serbia and Montenegro), and the Former Yugoslav Republic of Macedonia

Primary Source

ZLATA'S DIARY

by Zlata Filipović

Young Zlata Filipović kept a diary about her experiences in Sarajevo.

"BOREDOM!!! SHOOTING!!! SHELLING!!! PEOPLE BEING KILLED!!! DESPAIR!!! HUNGER!!! MISERY!!! FEAR!!! That's my life! The life of an innocent eleven-year-old schoolgirl!!!! A schoolgirl without a school. A child without games, without friends, without the sun, without birds, without nature, without fruit, without chocolate or sweets, with just a little powdered milk. In short, a child without a childhood. A wartime child. . . . I once heard that childhood is the most wonderful time of your life. And it is. I loved it, and now an ugly war is taking it all away from me. Why? I feel sad. I feel like crying. I am crying."

Taken from *Zlata's Diary: A Child's Life in Sarajevo,* © 1994 by Viking Penguin. Translation copyright Fixotet editions Robert Laffont, 1994.

Analyzing Primary Sources

Making Inferences What little things do you think you would miss the most if war or another tragedy took them from you?

Bosnia and Herzegovina Mountainous and poor, Bosnia and Herzegovina has an economy based mainly on crops and livestock. **Sarajevo** (SAR•uh•YAY•voh), the capital, has the look of an Asian city, with its marketplaces and **mosques,** or Muslim houses of worship. Many of the Bosnian people are Muslims, followers of the religion of Islam. Others are Eastern Orthodox Serbs or Roman Catholic Croats. Serbs began a bitter war after Bosnia's independence in 1992. The **Dayton Peace Accords** divided Bosnia into two regions under one government in 1995. American and other troops came as peacekeepers.

Yugoslavia (Serbia and Montenegro) All that is left of Yugoslavia is Serbia and its reluctant partner, Montenegro. Inland plains and mountains cover the area. The economies of these two republics are based on agriculture and industry. The region's largest city is **Belgrade.** The 10.7 million Serbs and Montenegrins practice the Eastern Orthodox faith.

Serbia has faced growing unrest in some of its local provinces. Muslim Albanians living in the province of **Kosovo** want independence from Serbia. Also living in Kosovo is a smaller group of Eastern Orthodox Serbs. For centuries, Albanians and Serbs here have felt a deep anger toward each other. In 1999 Serb forces tried to push the Albanians out of Kosovo. The United States and other nations bombed Serbia to force it to withdraw its troops. Even with the help of United Nations peacekeeping troops, peace in Kosovo remains shaky.

Macedonia (F.Y.R.O.M.) Macedonia's 2 million people, mostly farmers, are a mix of different ethnic groups from the Balkans. In **Skopje** (SKAW•pyeh), Macedonia's capital, there is an amazing mix of ancient Christian churches, timeworn Turkish markets, and modern shopping centers. Close to Kosovo, Macedonia handled a huge wave of ethnic Albanian refugees from Kosovo who fled Serb forces in 1999.

✓ **Reading Check** **What nations were formed from the former Yugoslavia?**

Critical Thinking Activity

Categorizing Information Have students work in pairs to organize Section 2's information in a chart. Have each student prepare a chart with the column headings "Landforms," "Economy," "People," and "History." Then have both students in each pair draw up a list of two or three facts about each country in the section. Have students take turns reading their facts to each other. The partner then has the task of placing each one in the correct category by writing it under the appropriate column heading. **L1**

EE2 Places and Regions: Standard 4

Albania

Bordering the Adriatic Sea, Albania is slightly larger than the state of Maryland. Mountains cover most of the country, contributing to Albania's isolation from neighboring countries. A small coastal plain runs along the Adriatic Sea.

Albania is a very poor country. Although the country has valuable mineral resources, it lacks the money to mine them. Most Albanians farm—growing corn, grapes, olives, potatoes, sugar beets, and wheat—in mountain valleys.

The Albanians Almost two-thirds of Albanians live in the countryside. The capital and largest city, **Tirana,** and its suburbs have a population of more than 500,000. Although 3.4 million people live in Albania, another 3.2 million Albanians live in nearby countries. These refugees fled Albania to escape the violence that swept the country after communism's fall in the early 1990s.

About 70 percent of Albanians are Muslim. The rest are Christian—either Eastern Orthodox or Roman Catholic. While the Communists opposed religion, Albania's democratic government has allowed people to practice their faith. As a result, many mosques and churches have opened across the country. The most famous Albanian in recent times was the Catholic nun **Mother Teresa,** who served the poor in Calcutta, India.

✓ Reading Check **What is the main religion in Albania?**

Section 2 Assessment

Defining Terms

1. **Define** consumer goods, ethnic cleansing, refugee, mosque.

Recalling Facts

2. **Place** What is the capital of Romania?
3. **Economics** How are roses used in Bulgaria?
4. **History** Which of the former Yugoslav republics is most prosperous?

Critical Thinking

5. **Drawing Conclusions** How do you think people in the Balkans feel about the recent changes in their countries?
6. **Understanding Cause and Effect** What effect did the policy of ethnic cleansing have on the people of Serbia?

Graphic Organizer

7. **Organizing Information** Create a chart like the one below and complete it by filling in two facts under each country name.

Romania	Bulgaria	Slovenia	Croatia
Bosnia and Herzegovina	Yugoslavia	Macedonia	Albania

Applying Social Studies Skills

8. **Analyzing Maps** Study the political map on page 307. What countries are found on the east coast of the Adriatic Sea?

Chapter 12

Section 2, pages 311–315

Reteach

Have students write two key facts about each country in the Balkan region.

Reading Essentials and Study Guide 12–2

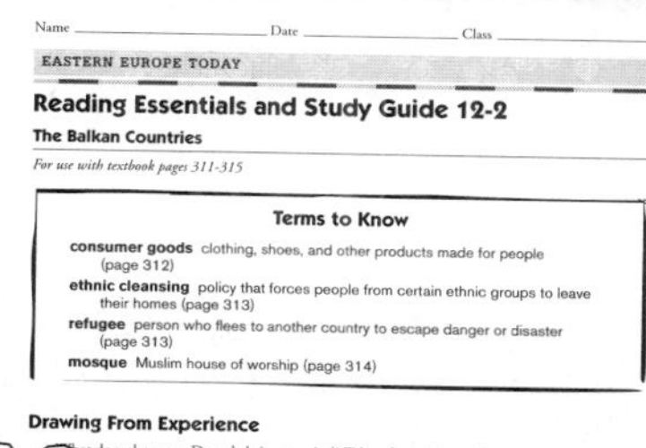
Name ______ Date ______ Class ______

EASTERN EUROPE TODAY

Reading Essentials and Study Guide 12-2

The Balkan Countries

For use with textbook pages 311-315

Terms to Know

consumer goods clothing, shoes, and other products made for people (page 312)

ethnic cleansing policy that forces people from certain ethnic groups to leave their homes (page 313)

refugee person who flees to another country to escape danger or disaster (page 313)

mosque Muslim house of worship (page 314)

Drawing From Experience

Dracula bring to mind? Tales of vampires stalk-

sylvania? Where is Transylva-

✓ Reading Check Answer

Islam

Enrich

Have students research the traditional culture of one of the countries in the region, such as Hungarian dances or folk costume in Slovenia. Have them report their findings to the class.

4 CLOSE

Give students an outline map of the Balkans and have them fill in the names of the countries and capitals.

Section 2 Assessment

1. The terms are defined in the Glossary.
2. Bucharest
3. Roses are grown so that their sweet-smelling oils can be used in perfume.
4. Slovenia
5. Students' answers will vary but should suggest that people's feelings will depend on the situation in each particular country. Some countries have fared well since the fall of communism, and others have not.
6. Many people lost their lives and many became refugees.
7. Students' charts will vary.
8. Slovenia, Croatia, Yugoslavia (Montenegro), Albania, Bosnia and Herzegovina

Making Connections

CULTURE | GOVERNMENT | PEOPLE | TECHNOLOGY

TEACH

Name or show some examples of folk art—such as quilts, pottery, wood carvings, or dolls. **Ask:** **What functions do folk arts serve for their societies?** *(as decoration; as an expression of cultural values; as a celebration of a group's identity)* **What aspect of Ukrainian culture influences their folk art?** *(early myths and Christianity)* **L2**

More About Ukranian Legends

Pysanky also play a role in maintaining the world, according to Ukrainian legend. Stories say that a serpentlike monster lives in a cave, chained to the walls. Each year, he sends out agents to see if *pysanky* are still being made. If not, the chains are loosened and he is released to do mischief and evil. If they are, the monster remains in chains.

Interdisciplinary Connections

Art The most famous decorated Easter eggs are the handiwork of the Russian jeweler Peter Carl Fabergé. He created gold-and-jewel-encrusted objects that were the artistic height of decorated eggs. The eggs, produced for the family of Russia's ruling czars, were made for special occasions. Each egg opened to reveal a surprise inside. Forty of the original 50 imperial eggs still exist.

Ukrainian Easter Eggs

Ukrainians have a rich folk art tradition that dates back thousands of years. It includes pottery, textiles, and woodworking. The best-known Ukrainian art form, however, is that of *pysanky,* or decorated eggs.

History

Ukrainian Easter eggs are known worldwide for their beauty and skillful designs. Many of the designs date back to a time when people in the region worshiped a sun god. According to legend, the sun god preferred birds over all other creatures. Birds' eggs became a symbol of birth and new life, and people believed the eggs could ward off evil and bring good luck. Eggs were decorated with sun symbols and used in ceremonies that marked the beginning of spring.

When Christianity took hold in Ukraine in A.D. 988, the tradition of decorative eggs continued. The egg came to represent religious rebirth and new life. People decorated eggs in the days before Easter, then gave them as gifts on Easter morning.

Technique

The word *pysanky* comes from Ukrainian words meaning "things that are written upon." This phrase helps explain the wax process used to decorate the eggs. An artist uses a pin or a tool called a *kistka* to "write" a design in hot wax onto the egg. The egg is then dipped into yellow dye, leaving the wax-covered portion of the eggshell white. After removing the egg from the dye, the artist writes with hot wax over another section of the egg. This portion stays yellow as the egg is dipped into a second dye color. The process continues, with the artist adding wax and dipping the egg into a darker and darker color. At the end, the artist removes the wax layers to reveal the multicolored design.

Making the Connection

1. What is *pysanky* and when did it originate?
2. What role does placing wax onto the eggshell play in creating a decorative egg?
3. **Drawing Conclusions** What purposes, other than entertainment, might folk art accomplish?

◀ Ukrainian Easter eggs

316 CHAPTER 12

Making the Connection

1. *Pysanky* is the art of decorating eggs. The first eggs were made thousands of years ago when people from the region worshipped a sun god.
2. Areas covered by wax retain the color underneath when the egg is plunged into dye.
3. *Possible answers:* to build a sense of pride and identity; to embody legends and traditions

Section 3

Ukraine, Belarus, and Moldova

Guide to Reading

Main Idea

Past ties to Russia have had different effects on the economies and societies of Ukraine, Belarus, and Moldova.

Terms to Know

- steppe
- potash

Reading Strategy

Create a diagram like this one. Under the country name, list at least one fact that shows the Soviet Union's effect on these countries.

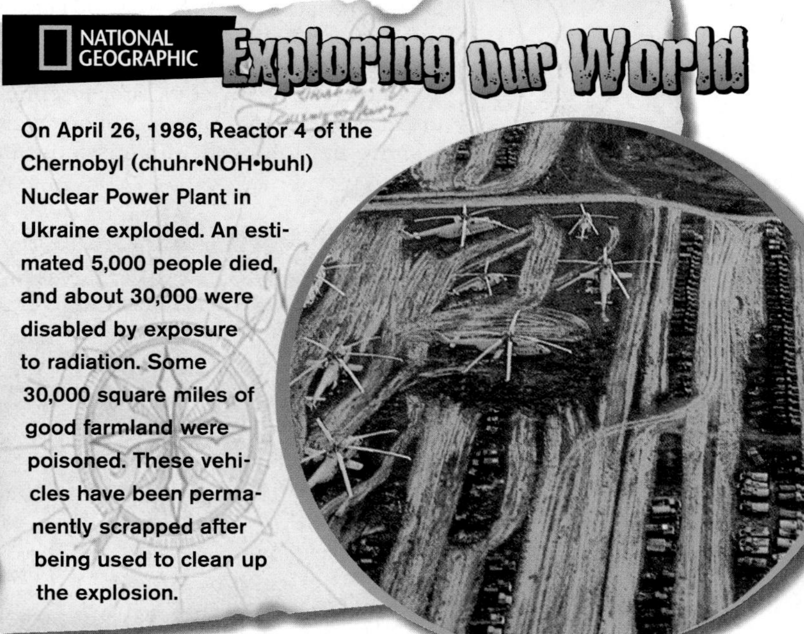

On April 26, 1986, Reactor 4 of the Chernobyl (chuhr•NOH•buhl) Nuclear Power Plant in Ukraine exploded. An estimated 5,000 people died, and about 30,000 were disabled by exposure to radiation. Some 30,000 square miles of good farmland were poisoned. These vehicles have been permanently scrapped after being used to clean up the explosion.

Ukraine, Belarus (BEE•luh•ROOS), and **Moldova** (mawl•DAW•vuh) once belonged to the Soviet Union. When the Soviet Union broke apart in late 1991, Ukraine, Belarus, and Moldova became independent. Since then, they have struggled to build new economies.

Ukraine

Slightly smaller than Texas, Ukraine is by far the largest eastern European country (excluding Russia). The Carpathian Mountains rise along its southwestern border. Farther east, a vast steppe, or gently rolling, partly wooded plain, makes up the country. Nearly 23,000 rivers twist across the steppe, most of which are too shallow for ships. The most important waterway, the **Dnieper** (NEE•puhr) **River,** has been made navigable so that ships can carry goods to distant markets. The **Crimean Peninsula** juts into the Black Sea. Most of Ukraine has cold winters and warm summers.

317

1 Focus

Section Objectives

1. Describe the landforms of Ukraine, Belarus, and Moldova.
2. Compare the economies, history, and culture of Ukraine, Belarus, and Moldova.

BELLRINGER Skillbuilder Activity

Project transparency and have students answer questions.

This activity is also available as a blackline master.

Daily Focus Skills Transparency 12-3

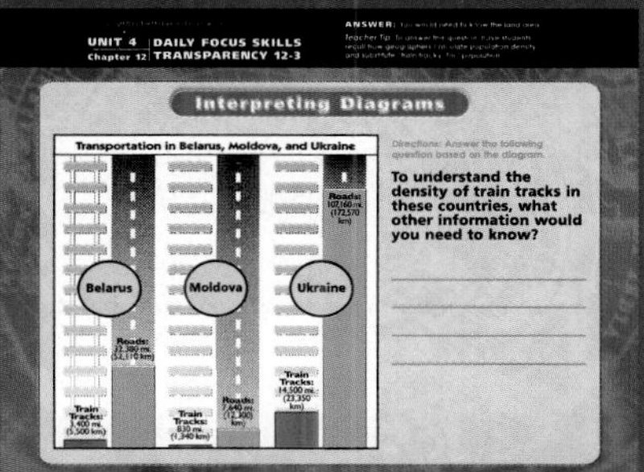

Guide to Reading

■ **Accessing Prior Knowledge**

Ask: What do you think of when you hear a region called a "breadbasket"? *(that it produces large quantities of grain)* Inform students that in this section, they will read about such a region.

■ **Vocabulary Precheck**

Have students look up the definitions of *steppe* and *potash* and use each word in a sentence.

Section Resources

Reproducible Masters

- Reproducible Lesson Plan 12-3
- Daily Lecture and Discussion Notes 12-3
- Guided Reading Activity 12-3
- Reading Essentials and Study Guide 12-3
- Section Quiz 12-3

Transparencies

- Daily Focus Skills Transparency 12-3
- GeoQuiz Transparency 12-1

Multimedia

- Vocabulary PuzzleMaker Software
- Interactive Tutor Self-Assessment CD-ROM
- Presentation Plus! CD-ROM
- ExamView® Pro 3.0 Testmaker CD-ROM

TEACH

Making Comparisons Have students scan the section for names of crops and manufactured goods produced in Ukraine, Belarus, and Moldova. Then have them copy the information and add it to a chart with the headings "Country," "Crops," and "Manufactured Goods." Remind them to use their charts as study aids. **L1**

Applying Map Skills

Answers

1. Kiev
2. 60–125 people per sq. mi.

Skills Practice

What cities of over 1 million people are found in Ukraine? *(Kiev, Kharkiv, Dnipropetrovsk, Donetsk, Lviv, and Odesa)*

Daily Lecture Notes 12-3

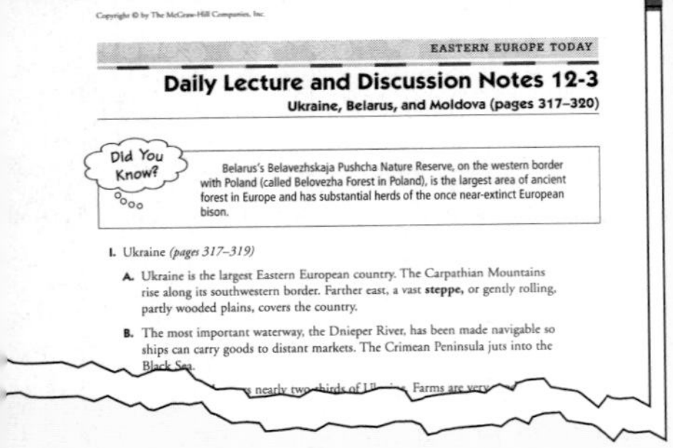

Copyright © by The McGraw-Hill Companies, Inc.

EASTERN EUROPE TODAY

Daily Lecture and Discussion Notes 12-3

Ukraine, Belarus, and Moldova (pages 317–320)

Did You Know? Belarus's Belavezhskaja Pushcha Nature Reserve, on the western border with Poland (called Belovezha Forest in Poland), is the largest area of ancient forest in Europe and has substantial herds of the once near-extinct European bison.

I. Ukraine (pages 317–319)

A. Ukraine is the largest Eastern European country. The Carpathian Mountains rise along its southwestern border. Farther east, a vast **steppe**, or gently rolling, partly wooded plains, covers the country.

B. The most important waterway, the Dnieper River, has been made navigable so ships can carry goods to distant markets. The Crimean Peninsula juts into the Black Sea.

Rich dark soil covers nearly two-thirds of Ukraine. Farms are very productive, earning the country the name "breadbasket of Europe." Farmers grow sugar beets, potatoes, and grains and raise cattle and sheep. Factories make machinery, processed foods, and chemicals.

The Ukrainians Early Slavic groups settled and traded along the rivers of the region. During the A.D. 800s, warriors from Nordic countries united these groups into a large state centered on the city of Kiev (KEE•ihf). A century later, the people of Kiev accepted the Eastern Orthodox faith and built one of Europe's most prosperous civilizations. After 300 years of freedom, the people of Kiev were conquered by Mongols, then Lithuanians and Poles, and finally the Russians.

In the 1930s, Soviet dictator Joseph Stalin brought Ukraine's farms under government control. Millions were murdered or starved in the famine that followed. Millions more died when Germans invaded

NATIONAL GEOGRAPHIC

Eastern Europe: Population Density

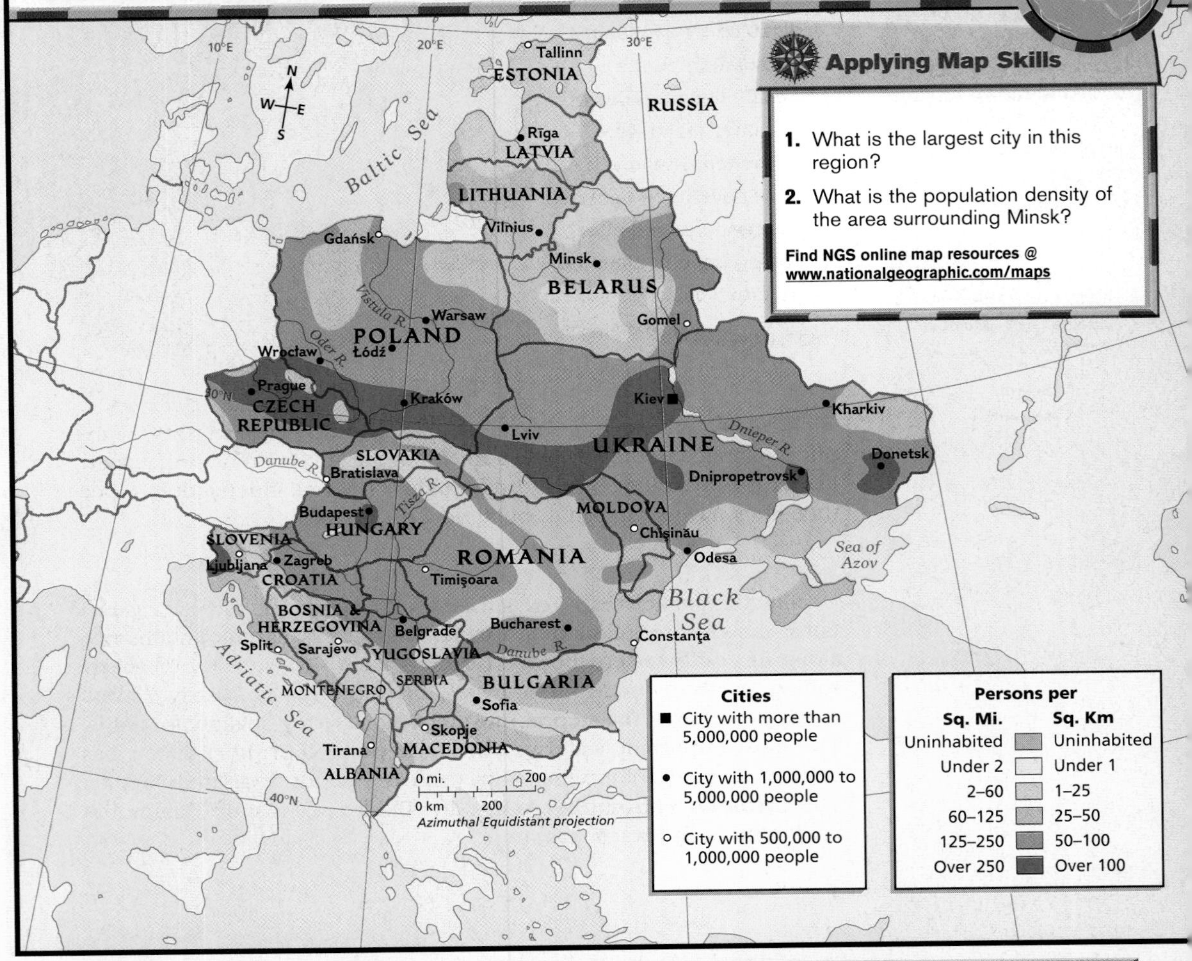

ESTONIA, Tallinn, LATVIA, Rīga, LITHUANIA, Vilnius, RUSSIA, BELARUS, Minsk, Gomel, POLAND, Gdańsk, Warsaw, Łódź, Wrocław, Kraków, CZECH REPUBLIC, Prague, SLOVAKIA, Bratislava, HUNGARY, Budapest, UKRAINE, Kiev, Kharkiv, Lviv, Dnipropetrovsk, Donetsk, MOLDOVA, Chişinău, Odesa, ROMANIA, Timişoara, Bucharest, Constanţa, SLOVENIA, Ljubljana, CROATIA, Zagreb, Split, BOSNIA & HERZEGOVINA, Sarajevo, YUGOSLAVIA, SERBIA, MONTENEGRO, Belgrade, BULGARIA, Sofia, MACEDONIA, Skopje, ALBANIA, Tirana, Baltic Sea, Black Sea, Sea of Azov, Adriatic Sea, Danube R., Dnieper R., Vistula R., Oder R., Tisza R.

0 mi. 200 / 0 km 200 — Azimuthal Equidistant projection

Applying Map Skills

1. What is the largest city in this region?
2. What is the population density of the area surrounding Minsk?

Find NGS online map resources @ www.nationalgeographic.com/maps

Cities

- ■ City with more than 5,000,000 people
- • City with 1,000,000 to 5,000,000 people
- ○ City with 500,000 to 1,000,000 people

Persons per Sq. Mi.	Persons per Sq. Km
Uninhabited	Uninhabited
Under 2	Under 1
2–60	1–25
60–125	25–50
125–250	50–100
Over 250	Over 100

Team-Teaching Activity

Science Have the science teacher visit the class and explain the issues related to nuclear energy and the accident at Chernobyl. The presentation should include a discussion of how nuclear reactors work, why radiation is dangerous, what safety measures are required to limit the danger, and what went wrong at Chernobyl. When the presentation is finished, have students work in groups to research the matter further and then debate whether they believe nuclear energy is promising or too dangerous to use. They should consider future environmental consequences that could result from innovations in nuclear energy. **L2**

EE5 Environment and Society: Standard 14

Language Families of Europe

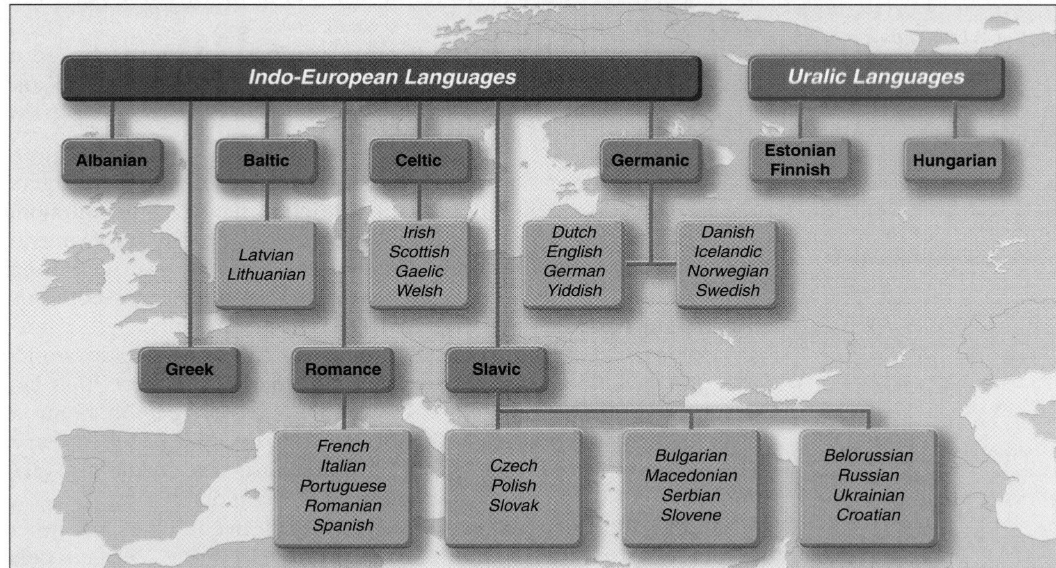

Ukraine during World War II. Finally in 1991, with the decline of Soviet power, Ukraine once again became a free nation.

Ukraine has over 49 million people. Nearly 75 percent are ethnic Ukrainians. About 22 percent are Russians, who live mainly in eastern areas. The people follow the Eastern Orthodox religion and speak Ukrainian, a Slavic language closely related to Russian.

More than 70 percent of the people live in cities. Kiev, the capital, has over 3 million people. Modern Ukrainians, even teenagers, enjoy listening to folk music played on a stringed instrument called a bandura and watching the acrobatic leaps of the *hopak* dance.

Reading Check **Why is Ukraine called the "breadbasket of Europe"?**

Analyzing the Chart

Seven main language families stem from Indo-European origins.

History **From what language family did Ukrainian develop?**

Belarus and Moldova

Belarus, slightly smaller than Kansas, is largely lowlands. Visiting Belarus, you would see wide stretches of birch tree groves, vast forested marshlands, and wooden villages surrounded by fields. Summers are cool and wet, and winters are cold.

Farmers grow potatoes, grains, vegetables, sugar beets, and fruits. Factory workers make equipment, chemicals, and construction materials. Food processing is another important industry. In addition to having petroleum and natural gas, Belarus has **potash**, a mineral used in fertilizer.

Slavic groups first settled the area that is today Belarus in the A.D. 600s. Surrounded by larger countries, Belarus was under foreign rule

Chapter 12

Section 3, pages 317–320

Analyzing the Chart

Answer
Slavic

Skills Practice
What type of language is Hungarian? *(Uralic)*

Guided Reading Activity 12-3

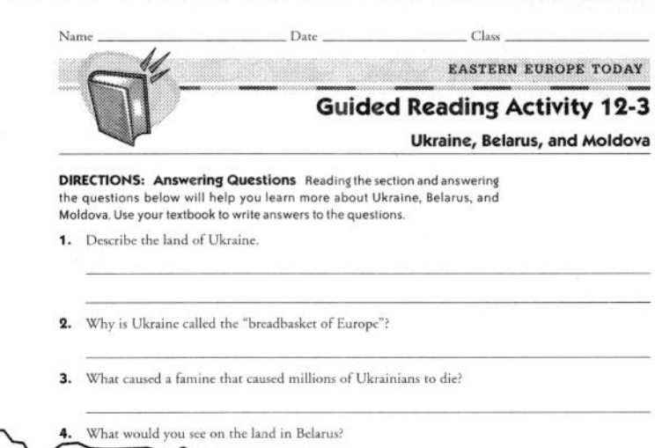

Name ______ Date ______ Class ______

EASTERN EUROPE TODAY

Guided Reading Activity 12-3

Ukraine, Belarus, and Moldova

DIRECTIONS: Answering Questions Reading the section and answering the questions below will help you learn more about Ukraine, Belarus, and Moldova. Use your textbook to write answers to the questions.

1. Describe the land of Ukraine.
2. Why is Ukraine called the "breadbasket of Europe"?
3. What caused a famine that caused millions of Ukrainians to die?
4. What would you see on the land in Belarus?

Reading Check Answer

its farms are very productive

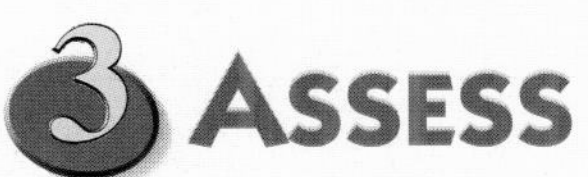

Assign Section 3 Assessment as homework or an in-class activity.

Section Quiz 12-3

Name ______ Date ______ Class ______

EASTERN EUROPE TODAY

Section Quiz 12-3

Ukraine, Belarus, and Moldova

DIRECTIONS: Matching Match each item in Column A with the items in Column B. Write the correct letters in the blanks. *(10 points each)*

COLUMN A	COLUMN B
A. Ukraine	____ 1. capital city of Belarus
B. bandura	____ 2. stringed instrument
C. steppe	____ 3. the "breadbasket of Europe"
D. Romania	____ 4. Moldova was a part of this country
E. Minsk	____ 5. gently rolling, partly wooded plain

DIRECTIONS: Multiple Choice In the blank at the left, write the letter of the choice that best completes the statement or answers the question. *(10 points each)*

Critical Thinking Activity

Categorizing Information After students have read the section, organize them into teams. Explain that team members must try to identify Ukraine, Belarus, Moldova, or all three from short clues. For each correct answer, a team earns one point. After all the students have had turns, total the points to see which team wins. Use clues such as "breadbasket of Europe" *(Ukraine)*; "previously a Communist country" *(all three)*; and "Chisinau is the main city" *(Moldova)*. **L1**

EE2 Places and Regions: Standard 4

Chapter 12

Section 3, pages 317–320

Objectives, goals, and answers to the Student Web Activity can be found in the Web Activity Lesson Plan at owt.glencoe.com

Reteach

Have students prepare a chart comparing the physical and cultural characteristics of Belarus and Moldova.

✓ Reading Check Answer

Russia

Reading Essentials and Study Guide 12-3

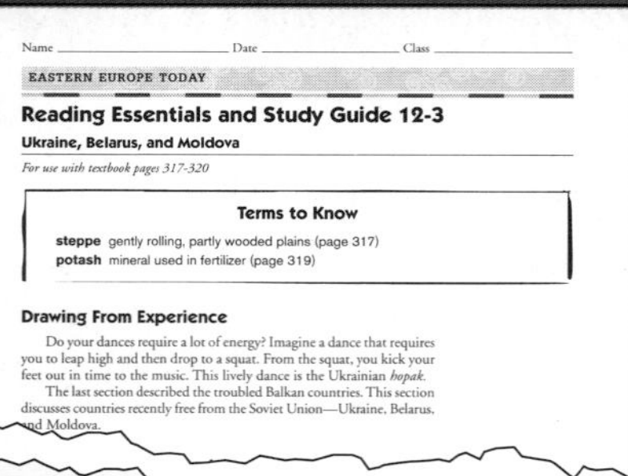

Name ________ Date ________ Class ________

EASTERN EUROPE TODAY

Reading Essentials and Study Guide 12-3

Ukraine, Belarus, and Moldova

For use with textbook pages 317-320

Terms to Know

steppe gently rolling, partly wooded plains (page 317)
potash mineral used in fertilizer (page 319)

Drawing From Experience

Do your dances require a lot of energy? Imagine a dance that requires you to leap high and then drop to a squat. From the squat, you kick your feet out in time to the music. This lively dance is the Ukrainian *hopak*.

The last section described the troubled Balkan countries. This section discusses countries recently free from the Soviet Union—Ukraine, Belarus, and Moldova.

CLOSE

Have students imagine they are visiting these three countries. Ask them to write three postcards to a friend back home. Each postcard should describe what they see in one of these countries.

Our World Today Online

Web Activity Visit the ***Our World Today: People, Places, and Issues*** Web site at owt.glencoe.com and click on **Chapter 12–Student Web Activities** to learn more about the effects of Chernobyl's nuclear disaster.

for most of its history. Communist Party leaders control Belarus's government and have maintained close ties with Russia. Foreign companies have been unwilling to do business here. In addition, Belarus is still linked to neighboring Russia's weak economy.

The 10 million people of Belarus are mostly Eastern Orthodox Slavs. Their Belorussian language is closely related to Russian and Ukrainian and is written in Cyrillic. Two-thirds of Belarus's people live in cities. **Minsk,** the largest city, is the capital.

Moldova Moldova is mostly a rolling hilly plain sliced by rivers. These waterways form valleys that hold rich fertile soil. This soil, along with mild winters and warm summers, provides productive farmland. Farmers grow sugar beets, grains, potatoes, apples, and tobacco. Some grow grapes used to make wine. Factories turn out processed foods, machinery, metals, construction materials, and textiles.

Moldova's flag looks similar to Romania's flag. Why? Moldova once was part of Romania. About two-thirds of the people trace their language and culture to that country. Moldova's eastern region, home to many Russians, Ukrainians, and Turks, recently declared independence. This is an important issue to Moldova because that region also produces about 80 percent of the country's electricity.

Moldova has 4.3 million people. About half live in cities, but much of Moldova's culture is still based on a rural way of life. Villagers celebrate special occasions with lamb, cornmeal pudding, and goat's milk cheese. The main city is the capital, **Chişinău** (KEE•shee•NOW).

✓ Reading Check **With what nation does Belarus have close ties?**

Section 3 Assessment

Defining Terms

1. **Define** steppe, potash.

Recalling Facts

2. **Location** Where is the Crimean Peninsula located?
3. **Government** What type of government does Belarus have?
4. **Economics** Name three of Moldova's agricultural products.

Critical Thinking

5. **Categorizing Information** List four agricultural products and three manufactured products of Ukraine.
6. **Understanding Cause and Effect** Why is the culture of Moldova similar to that of Romania?

Graphic Organizer

7. **Organizing Information** Create a time line like this one. Then label five important periods or events in Ukraine's history.

|—————|—————|—————|—————|

Applying Social Studies Skills

8. **Analyzing Maps** Compare the political and population maps on pages 307 and 318. What is the population density around Ukraine's Dniester River?

Section 3 Assessment

1. The terms are defined in the Glossary.
2. in southern Ukraine extending into the Black Sea
3. Communist
4. *Any three:* sugar beets, grains, potatoes, apples, tobacco, grapes
5. *Agriculture*—sugar beets, potatoes, grains, cattle, sheep; *Products*—machinery, processed foods, chemicals
6. because Moldova was once part of Romania
7. *800s*—Nordic warriors create a state in Kiev; *900s*—Kievans take Orthodox faith; *1200s*—Mongol conquest; *1930s*—farms brought under Soviet control; *1991*—Ukraine becomes independent
8. over 250 people per sq. mi.

TIME REPORTS

FOCUS ON WORLD ISSUES

The European Union: Good for Everyone?

A Common Currency for a Common Market

AVANTIS/ZUMO PRESS/NEWSCOM

Making Connections

Free Trade Divide students into groups. Tell each group to imagine what the United States would be like if we did not have free trade among the states. Students should assume that each state prints its own currency, controls who can enter that state, and charges tariffs (taxes) on items coming from other states. Have the groups discuss the disadvantages of this system. Can they think of any advantages? Have groups discuss this topic and then present their advantages and disadvantages to the class as a whole. After students have completed their presentations, explain that these are the kinds of problems that Europe is working to solve.

TIME REPORTS

Focus on World Issues

Teacher Background

With increasing globalization, it has become more difficult for individual European countries to compete in the world marketplace. In addition, since the breakup of the Soviet Union, the nations of eastern Europe have needed support in implementing democratic governments and marketplace economies. The European Union has played an increasingly important role in tackling these problems.

The concept of a unified Europe gained strength after World War II. The 1951 establishment of the European Coal and Steel Community (ECSC) and the 1957 establishment of the European Economic Community (EEC) were both major milestones along the way. In 1992, the Treaty on European Union was signed in the Netherlands.

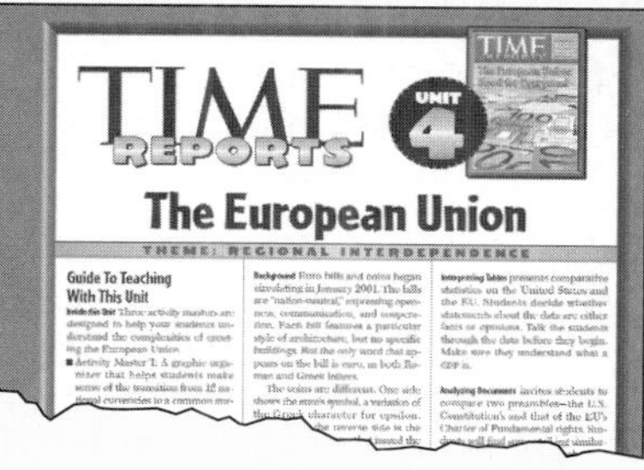
TIME REPORTS UNIT 4

The European Union

THEME: REGIONAL INTERDEPENDENCE

Guide To Teaching With This Unit

Preparing the Student

Remind students that both western and eastern Europe have traditionally been composed of small, autonomous countries, each with its own currency, tariffs, and security forces. Over the centuries, numerous major wars have been fought, resulting in loss of life, regional and ethnic hostilities, and shifting national boundaries.

TIME REPORTS

TIME REPORTS

FOCUS ON WORLD ISSUES

Europeans began using new currency in January 2002. The impact was gigantic—like this mocked-up coin.

1 Focus

Ask students the following question: **What services do you think a democratic government should provide for its people?** Encourage students to think about this in the very broadest sense. Some items might include free trade, a common currency, free elections, individual rights, an army, and free public education. Then tell students that if a country is small and must interact with many other countries, providing economic and political security can be difficult. The European Union is designed to simplify these activities.

Have students examine the "Europe in 2002" map. Be sure to discuss any changes that have taken place in EU membership since this map was created.

Europe in 2002

ANSWERS

1. Current EU members are in western Europe. Nations that want to join are in eastern Europe.
2. *Possible answers:* The nations of eastern Europe do not have as long a history of democratic government as those in western Europe. In addition, they tend to be less stable and not as well off economically. These differences could cause disagreement on economic and political issues.

Building a United Europe

Damien Barry had a problem. He wanted to work in Paris, France. The trouble was, the French were fussy. French people could work in France. And so could people from 14 other loosely united European nations. All 15 nations belonged to the **European Union**, or the EU. Barry wasn't from an EU nation. He was from Brooklyn, New York.

But that didn't stop him. Ireland is an EU nation. It grants citizenship to anyone with an Irish parent or grandparent. Barry had Irish grandparents. He applied for an Irish passport and got one. Soon after that he had a job in a French bank.

A Big Story for Americans

Barry would never give up his U.S. citizenship. Yet he's not letting go of his Irish passport, either. "It's worth a million dollars to me," he said.

Barry's story suggests how much the EU matters to Americans. The 15 EU nations form the world's largest trading group. That gives them awesome power to control jobs and the price of many things you buy.

That's not all. By 2020, the EU plans to expand to 30 nations. Right now, the U.S. deals one-on-one with countries like Poland and Estonia. In the future, it will have to deal with them through the EU.

What's more, the EU is piecing together a small army. That army will change the U.S. military's role in Europe. "In the next 10 years," TIME magazine said in 2001, "there may be no bigger story than the EU."

Europe in 2002

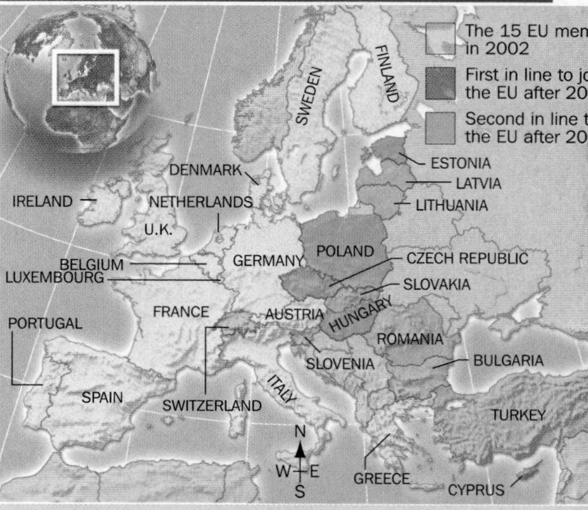

INTERPRETING MAPS

1. **Categorizing** In what part of Europe—east or west—are most current EU members? In which part are nations that want to join?
2. **Making Inferences** Why might it be hard for all these nations to agree on important issues?

322

Team-Teaching Activity

Economics Ask a teacher with a background in economics to discuss the significance of the EU's having a single currency, the euro. Have the teacher emphasize the role of a common currency in the establishment of free trade. Ask the teacher to lead a class discussion about why some countries might not want to adopt the common currency. Some reasons might be that some countries (especially those in eastern Europe) have weaker economies than others. Other countries associate their currency with their national identity. **L2**

EE4 Human Systems: Standard 11

The new euro exchanged for bread.

Farm animals' health is a big EU concern.

This Dutchman is one of hundreds of pro soccer players in the EU.

CENTRAL AUDIOVISUAL LIBRARY, EUROPEAN COMMISSION

Common Problems

What is the EU? Simply put, it is a group of nations that have joined forces to solve common problems. Finding a safe way to recycle used batteries is one problem. Convincing Europeans to stop smoking is another. Making sure goods flow freely within Europe is still another. The EU is a **free trade zone**. That means EU nations don't tax goods they import from each other.

The EU hopes to help its members prosper. But it has another goal—bringing peace to a continent with a long history of conflict.

A Heap of Trouble

To get the euro to shoppers by January 2002, the EU sent 56 billion coins to banks in 12 nations. The coins weighed 168,000 tons—24 times more than the Eiffel Tower in Paris, France!

Weak Government

Some people compare the EU with the United States around 1785. The U.S. government had little muscle then. It had no president, no army, no power to raise money. The states had all the money and almost all the power.

In many ways, the EU is like that. Officials at EU offices in Brussels, Belgium, make a lot of decisions, but they have no **authority** to force member nations to give up their armies. They can't even make them stop printing money.

In 1789, America's original 13 states agreed to give up powers like those. They did it by approving the U.S. Constitution.

The EU doesn't have a constitution. Its members are joined by treaties, or written agreements. Without a constitution to guide them, it's hard to get all 15 nations to agree on anything.

New Money

One thing most EU members have agreed on is a common currency, the **euro**. In January 2002, most EU nations replaced their own money with the euro. Three nations—Britain, Denmark and Sweden—chose not to make the switch immediately.

In 2001, Damien Barry got paid in French francs. Now he gets paid in euros. When he goes to Italy and Holland, he no longer carries Italian lira and Dutch guilders. Like his Irish passport, the euro has made his life easier. And it's done the same for the more than 300 million Europeans who use the euro every day.

CENTRAL AUDIOVISUAL LIBRARY, EUROPEAN COMMISSION

EXPLORING THE ISSUE

1. **Making Generalizations** Three EU nations refused to replace their currencies with the euro. Why might a nation want to keep its own currency?
2. **Cause and Effect** How might the EU affect your life—today, and in the future?

323

2 TEACH

Identifying Main Ideas
Have students read the subsection titled "Common Problems." Ask them to state the main idea presented in this section. Write their answers. Then have them find examples in the text that support this idea. **L1**

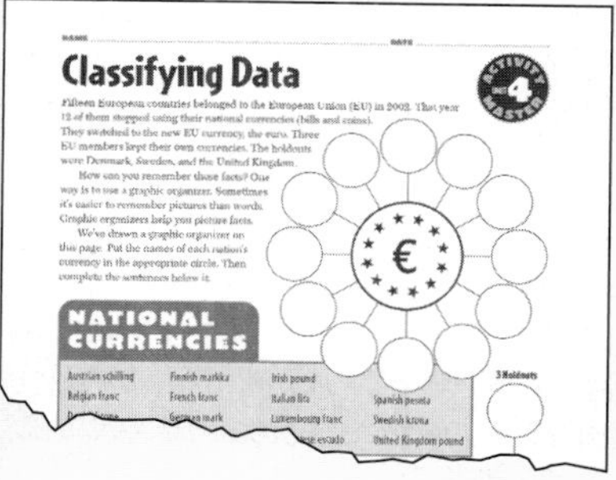

EXPLORING THE ISSUE

ANSWERS

1. *Possible answers:* Some countries feel that having their own currency is vital to their identity, and that being able to control interest rates and exchange rates is vital for a stable economy.
2. *Possible answers:* It simplifies travel within Europe. It may make it more difficult for a U.S. citizen to get a job in Europe. Increased trade between European countries could reduce Europe's trade with the United States.

Meeting Special Needs

Auditory/Musical Have students listen to the anthem of the European Union. (It can be obtained at a number of Web sites, including **europa.eu.int/abc/symbols/anthem/index_en.htm**). Then have students respond to the following questions: **Can you identify the music?** *(the last movement of Beethoven's Ninth Symphony)* **How does the anthem make you feel? How do you think these feelings match the goals of the European Union? Why are symbols such as anthems important to the EU? L1**

Refer to *Inclusion for the Middle School Social Studies Classroom Strategies and Activities* in the TCR.

TIME REPORTS

Making Comparisons Canada, the United States, and Mexico have joined together under NAFTA, the North American Free Trade Agreement. Have students research NAFTA and write a paragraph about how it is similar to the EU, and how it differs.

More About the Photo

Jean Monnet Ask: Why would reducing an individual country's supply of coal and steel decrease the chance of war?

EXPLORING THE ISSUE

ANSWERS

1. International control of steel and energy production makes it more difficult for individual countries to wage war. Free trade, a common currency, open borders, and a European security force make people feel more united.
2. Businesses no longer have to worry about paying tariffs when exporting goods to another EU country. Time and money is saved in not having to perform currency exchanges.

TIME REPORTS

From Peace to Prosperity

World War II ended in 1945. It was the third time in 75 years that Germany and France had fought each other.

Could another war be prevented? A Frenchman named Jean Monnet thought so. He proposed taking coal and steel production out of the hands of individual countries. Without fuel and steel, he said, nations couldn't wage war.

UPI/CORBIS-BETTMANN

U.S. President John F. Kennedy shares a smile with Jean Monnet.

In 1951, six nations accepted Monnet's proposal. They were Belgium, West Germany, Italy, Luxembourg, the Netherlands, and France. They set up an organization that told each nation how much coal and steel it could produce.

A Free Trade Zone

That was a big step. But there were bigger ones to come. In 1957, all six agreed to stop taxing goods they imported from each other. Those taxes acted like walls, stopping goods from moving between nations. By removing those walls, the six nations created a **common market**.

Common markets were nothing new. The United States had had one for more than 150 years. California never taxed beef "imported" from Texas, for instance. Free trade was new for Europe, however. And it helped businesses there grow.

How the EU Grew

1951: France, Germany, Italy, the Netherlands, Belgium and Luxembourg agree to pool their coal, iron ore, and steel industries.

1973: Denmark, Ireland, and the United Kingdom join.

1981: Greece joins.

1986: Spain and Portugal join.

1995: Austria, Finland, and Sweden join.

Growing Pains

Nine nations eventually joined the original six. Looking ahead, the EU expects to let about 15 other nations join by 2020.

Getting 30 nations to work together won't be easy. But no one doubts that the EU's impact on the world is going to grow. Somewhere Jean Monnet, who died in 1979, must be smiling.

EXPLORING THE ISSUE

1. **Explaining** In what ways might the simple fact of the EU's existence promote peace?
2. **Cause and Effect** How might a common market help businesses grow?

324

Critical Thinking Activity

Drawing Conclusions Briefly remind students about the importance of Sir Winston Churchill who led Britain through World War II. Then tell the students that Churchill made the statement, "But we have our own dream and our own task. We are with Europe, but not of it. We are linked but not combined. We are interested and associated but not absorbed." **Ask students:** Do you think Winston Churchill would be in favor of or against the European Union? Why? Have students do some research to find out about the United Kingdom's role in the EU and why people there might feel separate from the rest of Europe. **L2**

EE4 Human Systems: Standard 13

A Model for Change

Hungary had a bumpy 50 years after World War II. This East European nation suffered under Communist rule from 1948 to 1990. Now Hungarians have a democratic government. Individuals there can own their own businesses again. Those changes put Hungary on track to joining the EU.

Qualifying for entry wasn't easy. Hungary's government had to budget its spending. It had to sell factories and land it owned to private citizens. Thousands of workers lost their jobs.

Creating Jobs

Hungarians were willing to make the sacrifices, because they wanted to join the EU. Once in, they would be able to sell what they made to other EU members. Those sales would create jobs at home and make lives easier for Hungarians.

Would Hungary have changed if the EU didn't exist? Certainly. But chances are it wouldn't have changed so fast—and so completely. The EU has served as a model for Hungary and other former Communist nations to follow.

The EU has been especially good for the United States. Every day the U.S. and the EU nations sell each other goods worth $2 billion. In 1999, EU citizens bought $32 billion worth of goods from Texas and California alone. That money paid the salaries of at least 327,000 Texans and Californians.

Ads for Democracy

The U.S. and the EU compete with each other. They often disagree on major issues. But they are firm friends, and both are good advertisements for democracy and free trade. The prospect of joining their "club" has spurred Hungary and other nations to change—and to change quickly.

The Top Two **Output of goods and services in 1999, in trillions of dollars**

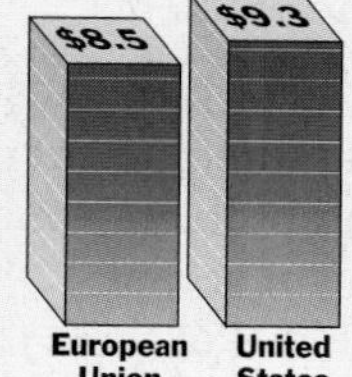

Analyzing information One of every 10 people in the world live in the U.S. or in EU nations. But every year U.S. and EU workers together create more than half the world's goods and services. Why do you think this is so?

▲ **U.S. President George W. Bush confers with a high EU official.**

EXPLORING THE ISSUE

1. **Comparing** How are the U.S. and the EU alike?
2. **Making Inferences** Why might a Hungarian worker be both for and against change?

Recommended Internet Sites

www.eurunion.org

The official Web site of the European Commission's ambassador to the U.S. contains a wealth of information on the EU. Within this site is the "A-Z Index of European Union Web sites" (**www.eurunion.org/infores/euindex.htm**).

The Top Two

ANSWER

The United States and Europe are more technologically advanced, and their citizens use more consumer goods than most countries.

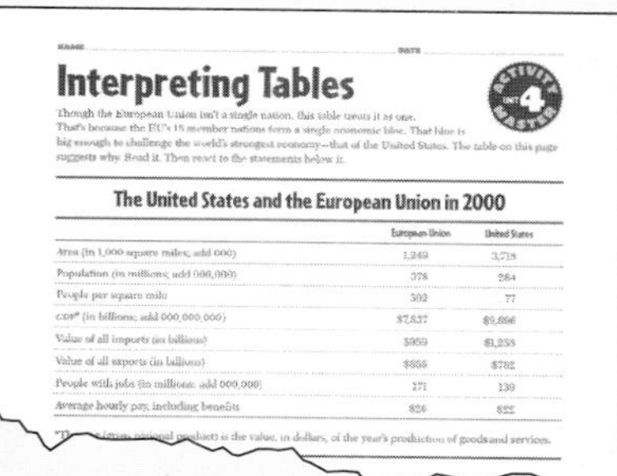

NAME ______ DATE ______

Interpreting Tables

Though the European Union isn't a single nation, this table treats it as one. That's because the EU's 15 member nations form a single economic bloc. That bloc is big enough to challenge the world's strongest economy—that of the United States. The table on this page suggests why. Read it. Then react to the statements below it.

The United States and the European Union in 2000

	European Union	United States
Area (in 1,000 square miles; add 000)	1,249	3,718
Population (in millions; add 000,000)	378	284
People per square mile	302	77
GDP* (in billions; add 000,000,000)	$7,837	$9,896
Value of all imports (in billions)	$969	$1,258
Value of all exports (in billions)	$888	$782
People with jobs (in millions; add 000,000)	171	139
Average hourly pay, including benefits	$26	$22

*Th[illegible] (gross national product) is the value, in dollars, of the year's production of goods and services.

EXPLORING THE ISSUE

ANSWERS

1. *Possible answers:* Like the countries of the EU, U.S. states have a common currency, no tariffs, and open borders between them.
2. *For:* They will be able to freely sell to other EU countries, hopefully increasing the number of available jobs. *Against:* Some workers lost jobs when the government sold industries that it owned.

Interdisciplinary Activity

Language Arts Have students write lyrics for the European Union anthem. The lyrics should be written in English and should emphasize the EU's goals, such as strength through solidarity, peace, and democracy. Have students work individually or in small groups. When they are done, have them share their results. Discuss the problem with having the anthem lyrics in a single language, such as English. **L1**

EE4 Human Systems: Standard 10

TIME REPORTS

Current Events Journal

Have students create a chart that lists all the members of the European Union in the order in which they joined. After each country's name, they should write the year it joined. Compare this list to the map on page 322. **Ask:** **What nations have joined since this map was created?**

Did You Know

Another important difference between the EU and the U.S. centers around the death penalty. The EU is strongly opposed to it in all cases, while 37 U.S. states have death penalty statutes.

EXPLORING THE ISSUE

ANSWERS

1. In all four disputes, at least one side believes that the other is trying to unfairly control it.
2. They all involve controversial subjects that at least one side believes are of global importance. For example, global warming and food safety could affect everyone.

TIME REPORTS

Resolving Differences: What Can One Person Do?

The EU and the United States are good friends. But friends have their differences. Here are four:

1. The U.S. doesn't trade with Libya, Iran, and Cuba. It tried to get EU nations to do the same, but the EU refused. Companies in EU nations want to be free to sell goods to anyone.

2. The EU put limits on some U.S. companies that do business in Europe. Some Americans don't think the EU should be able to tell U.S. companies how to run their businesses.

3. Another dispute involved food. U.S. food companies wanted to grow **genetically altered crops** that resisted disease. So their scientists invented new types of crops. Many Europeans are afraid that those crops might pose health risks. Some EU countries won't even allow those products inside their borders.

4. Global warming is another sticking point. Scientists fear that gases from factories and automobiles keep the earth's heat from escaping into space.

SCIENCE SOURCE/PHOTO RESEARCHERS

▲ Genetically altered foods are creating an EU controversy.

EU nations and the U.S. can't agree on the best way to solve the problem.

Choose one of the four problems. Research each side's argument. Then create a solution to the problem—one you think both sides might accept.

Make your views public. Put them in a letter. Send the letter to your representatives in Congress. You might even want to send a copy to the European Union's ambassador to the United States. Address: Ambassador, Delegation of the European Commission to the United States, 2300 M Street, NW, Washington, D.C., 20037.

EXPLORING THE ISSUE

1. **Analyzing Information** What might all four disputes have to do with each side's view of its "rights?"
2. **Making Predictions** How might these disputes affect parts of the world outside the U.S. and the EU?

326

Your Government and You

While the United States and Europe have long been friends, there are many ongoing differences between the two countries. Twice a year, an EU-U.S. summit is held. Areas of concern are discussed along with proposed solutions. Students can read about some of these issues at the Web site **www.eurunion.org/partner/summit.htm**. Have students explain one difference they've read about to the rest of the class. Then ask students their opinion about who they agree with on the issue, and why. **L2**

EE4 Human Systems: Standard 13

REVIEW AND ASSESS

UNDERSTANDING THE ISSUE

1. **Defining Key Terms** Write definitions for the following terms: *European Union, import tax, free trade zone, common market, authority, genetically-altered crops,* and *euro.*

2. **Writing to Inform** Write a short article about the European Union, explaining how it could affect the lives of your fellow students. Use as many words as you can from the above list.

3. **Writing to Persuade** Write a letter to an imaginary friend in Denmark. Convince your friend that all European countries should use the euro.

INTERNET RESEARCH ACTIVITY

4. Navigate to **http://europa.eu.int.** Click on the English words, then ABC and Institutions. Read about the EU's three main governing bodies. Choose one and write a brief description of it in your own words. Then decide, with your classmates, how those bodies work together and which ones have the most power.

5. Navigate to **http://europa.eu.int/abc/symbols/index_en.htm.** Research the symbols of the European union: the flag, the anthem, and Europe Day. How is the EU's flag like—and different from—the first U.S. flag? Download the EU anthem. Why do you think the EU chose it? How is Europe Day like Independence Day in the U.S.? Put your answers in a 250-word essay.

BEYOND THE CLASSROOM

6. **Research the history of the U.S. dollar.** How hard was it to get Americans to accept U.S. currency in 1792? ask your parents about the U.S. $2.00 bill. How did they react to its introduction? How is the dollar like the euro? Explain your answers in an article appropriate for a school newspaper.

7. **Divide the class into three teams.** Debate this resolution: "It is unfair for the EU to let only European citizens work in EU countries." A panel of student judges will decide which team has the most convincing arguments.

CENTRAL AUDIOVISUAL LIBRARY, EUROPEAN COMMISSION

The EU flag: golden stars in a blue sky represent the nations

It's All About Jobs!

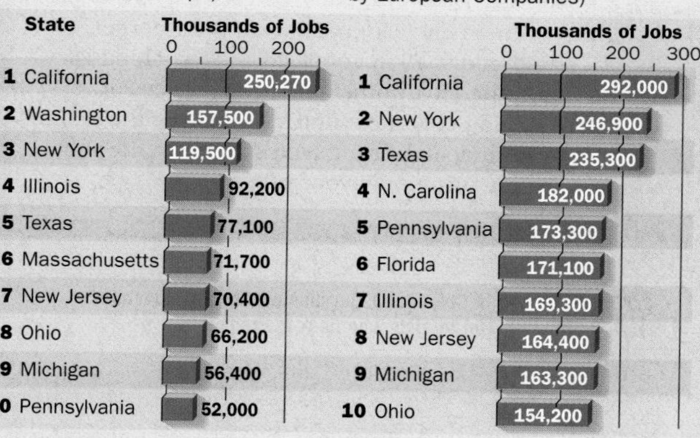

Where U.S. Exports Create Jobs
(Top 10 States with Jobs Created by Exports to Europe)

State	Thousands of Jobs
1 California	250,270
2 Washington	157,500
3 New York	119,500
4 Illinois	92,200
5 Texas	77,100
6 Massachusetts	71,700
7 New Jersey	70,400
8 Ohio	66,200
9 Michigan	56,400
10 Pennsylvania	52,000

Where Europe's Money Creates Jobs
(Top 10 States with Jobs Created by European Companies)

State	Thousands of Jobs
1 California	292,000
2 New York	246,900
3 Texas	235,300
4 N. Carolina	182,000
5 Pennsylvania	173,300
6 Florida	171,100
7 Illinois	169,300
8 New Jersey	164,400
9 Michigan	163,300
10 Ohio	154,200

Source: European-American Business Council. Note: "Europe" refers to the 15 EU members plus four members of a related group, the European Free Trade Association (Iceland, Liechtenstein, Norway, and Switzerland).

BUILDING SKILLS FOR READING TABLES

1. **Analyzing Data** Using an almanac, find the 10 states with the largest populations. How many of those states are listed among the top 10 on each graph? What relationships do you see between state populations and jobs supported by exports? How might state populations influence the number of jobs European companies create in the U.S.? Put your answers in a short report.

2. **Making Inferences** European companies create more jobs in Florida and North Carolina than exports do. How might you explain this?

FOR UPDATES ON WORLD ISSUES GO TO www.timeclassroom.com/glencoe

327

3 ASSESS

Have students take the Time Reports Quiz or do the Alternative Assessment project for this unit provided in the Teacher's Classroom Resources.

Analyzing Documents

Document A: Preamble to the U.S. Constitution

Document B: Preamble to the EU Charter

BUILDING SKILLS FOR READING CHARTS

ANSWERS

1. Eight of the largest ten states are listed in "U.S. Exports Create Jobs" and nine are listed in "Europe's Money Creates Jobs."
2. *Possible answer:* Florida and North Carolina don't have their own high-tech industries, but they have a desirable location and work force that attracts European companies with a U.S. market.

4 CLOSE

Ask students to write a paragraph starting with this topic sentence: *The European Union has had a positive effect on the world because . . .*

Culminating Activity

To close this lesson, have students complete the Review and Assess section questions and activities above. Students should use classroom discussion, contextual clues, and their student dictionaries to write definitions for terms. Before assigning the Internet activities, it is recommended that you review your school district policy on student Internet use.

Focus on Debate

As a final activity for further student understanding of the issue, have students debate the pro and con position of the following topic: **The United States should seek to create a union with Canada and Mexico similar to the European Union. L2**

 **EE4 Human Systems: Standard 11**

TEACH

Have students read and take notes on the material under the heading Poland in Section 1. Remind them that notes should be written as phrases. When students are done, have volunteers exchange notes with another student. Then have the second student try to re-create the key facts in the section by reading the notes. Have the class compare what the student says to what is written in the textbook. Whether or not the two versions match, you should be able to explain that effective note-taking is a skill that students can use to re-create a lesson or their reading. **L1**

Additional Skills Practice

1. **What questions would you ask to find the main ideas on the subject of Poland's environmental challenges?** *(What types of pollution are found in Poland?)*
2. **Why is it necessary to record information about the source on note cards for a research paper?** *(so that the source can be cited when writing the research paper, and the source can be rechecked if necessary)*

Additional Skills Resources

 Chapter Skills Activity 12

 Building Geography Skills for Life

Study and Writing Skill

Taking Notes

Effective note taking involves more than just writing facts in short phrases. It involves breaking up information into meaningful parts so that it can be remembered.

Learning the Skill

To take good notes, follow these steps:

- Write key points and important facts and figures quickly and neatly. Use abbreviations and phrases.
- Copy words, statements, or diagrams from the board or your research.
- Ask the teacher to repeat important points you do not understand.
- When studying textbook material, organize your notes into an outline (see page 654) or concept map that links important information.
- For a research report, take notes on cards. Note cards should include the title, author, and page number of sources.

Practicing the Skill

Suppose you are writing a research report on eastern Europe. First, identify main idea questions about this topic, such as "Who has ruled Poland?" or "What economic activities are found in the Czech Republic?" Then research each question.

Using this textbook as a source, read the material on pages 307 and 309–310 and prepare notes like this:

Main Idea: What economic activities are found in Poland?
1. Agriculture:
2. Mining:
3. Manufacturing:
Main Idea: What economic activities are found in the Czech Republic?
1.
2.
3.

Applying the Skill

In an encyclopedia or on the Internet, find information about Poland's coal industry and the environmental consequences of burning coal. Take notes by writing the main idea and supporting facts. Then rewrite the article using only your notes.

◀ A Czech teenager displays Soviet souvenirs for tourists who flock to Prague.

Practicing the Skill Answers

1. Agriculture: grains, sugar beets, potatoes, and other foods
2. Mining: petroleum, natural gas, and kaolin
3. Other: service industries, tourism, and high-technology manufacturing.

Applying the Skill

Have students print out the pages of the Web sites they visit for information on Poland's coal industry and environmental consequences. Check their notes against the original information to be sure that they identified the key points correctly.

Chapter 12 Reading Review

Section 1 East Central Europe

Terms to Know
acid rain
pope
landlocked
bauxite
spa

Main Idea
The countries of East Central Europe are undergoing many changes to their political and economic systems.

✓ **Culture** The Poles feel deep loyalty to their country and the Catholic Church.
✓ **Economics** The Baltic countries of Estonia, Latvia, and Lithuania are moving toward free-market economies and closer ties with western Europe.
✓ **Economics** The Czech Republic is prosperous but must modernize its factories.

Section 2 The Balkan Countries

Terms to Know
consumer goods
ethnic cleansing
refugee
mosque

Main Idea
The Balkan countries have greatly suffered from ethnic conflicts and economic setbacks.

✓ **Culture** Romanian history and culture were greatly influenced by the Romans. The Romanian language is not like other Eastern European languages, however in other ways, Romanians are like their Slavic neighbors.
✓ **History** Ethnic conflicts have torn apart the former Yugoslav republics.
✓ **Economics** Albania is rich in minerals but is too poor to mine them.

Section 3 Ukraine, Belarus, and Moldova

Terms to Know
steppe
potash

Main Idea
Past ties to Russia have had different effects on the economies and societies of Ukraine, Belarus, and Moldova.

✓ **Geography** Ukraine's rich soil allows it to grow large amounts of food.
✓ **Culture** The government of Belarus has maintained ties with Russia.
✓ **Culture** Moldova's eastern region, home to many Russians, Ukranians, and Turks, has declared its independence.

Sculptures and chandeliers made of salt decorate this room in a Polish salt mine. ▶

Reading Review

Use the Chapter 12 Reading Review to preview, review, condense, or reteach the chapter.

Preview/Review
Use the Terms to Know lists to help students review and study.

Activity Have students draw up a matching quiz of ten terms and their definitions from the chapter. Then have them exchange quizzes with another student and take the quiz their partner prepared.

Vocabulary PuzzleMaker Software reinforces the vocabulary terms used in Chapter 12.

The Interactive Tutor Self-Assessment CD-ROM allows students to review Chapter 12 content.

Condense
Have students read the Chapter 12 summary statements.

Chapter 12 Guided Reading Activities

Chapter 12 Audio Program

Reteach

Reteaching Activity 12

Chapter 12 Reading Essentials and Study Guide

Chapter Culminating Activity

Making a Presentation Remind students that the countries of eastern Europe face many challenges in their transition from their past political and economic systems to democracy and free market economies. Have students choose two of the countries studied in this chapter and research how those two countries have managed this transition. Ask them to create a presentation that compares the two countries' performances. Their presentation can take the form of a bulletin board, a report, or a multimedia display. *NOTE: This activity may be completed separately or you may wish students to incorporate it into their Current Events Journals.*

EE4 Human Systems: Standard 11

Assessment and Activities

GLENCOE TECHNOLOGY

MindJogger Videoquiz
Use MindJogger to review the Chapter 12 content.

 Available in VHS.

Using Key Terms

1. b
2. h
3. g
4. a
5. j
6. d
7. f
8. e
9. i
10. c

Reviewing the Main Ideas

11. coal mining
12. increased trade and industry
13. Prague
14. inexperience with manufacturing consumer goods, inefficient factories, and environmental damage
15. Eastern Orthodox Christianity
16. disputes among ethnic groups
17. When communism fell in the early 1990s, violence broke out among various ethnic groups. These Albanians fled the country as refugees to avoid the violence.
18. Kiev
19. Russian and Ukrainian
20. Moldova once was part of Romania.

Critical Thinking

21. Muslim Albanians living in Kosovo want independence from Serbia. Serb forces tried to push the Albanians out of Kosovo.
22. Students' charts will vary. The facts provided should relate directly to the reason given for the categorization of the country.

Chapter 12 Assessment and Activities

Using Key Terms

Match the terms in Part A with their definitions in Part B.

A.

1. spa
2. ethnic cleansing
3. acid rain
4. pope
5. steppe
6. landlocked
7. mosque
8. consumer goods
9. refugee
10. bauxite

B.

a. head of the Roman Catholic Church
b. resort with hot mineral springs
c. a mineral that is mined and used to make aluminum
d. having no access to the sea
e. products made for people
f. Muslim house of worship
g. rain containing chemical pollutants
h. forcing people from other ethnic groups to leave their homes
i. person who must flee to another country to escape danger or disaster
j. gently rolling, partly wooded plain

Reviewing the Main Ideas

Section 1 East Central Europe

11. **Economics** What is one of Poland's most important industries?
12. **History** What has raised standards of living in the Baltic republics?
13. **Place** What is the capital of the Czech Republic?

Section 2 The Balkan Countries

14. **Economics** What factors are holding back Romania's economy?
15. **Culture** What is the main religion of Bulgaria?
16. **History** What caused Yugoslavia to fall apart?
17. **History** Over 3 million Albanians live outside of Albania in nearby countries. Explain why.

Section 3 Ukraine, Belarus, and Moldova

18. **Place** What is the capital of Ukraine?
19. **Culture** To what languages is Belorussian similar?
20. **History** Why does Moldova's flag look similar to Romania's flag?

Eastern Europe

Place Location Activity

On a separate sheet of paper, match the letters on the map with the numbered places listed below.

1. Danube River
2. Black Sea
3. Croatia
4. Albania
5. Latvia
6. Hungary
7. Warsaw
8. Carpathian Mountains
9. Baltic Sea
10. Ukraine

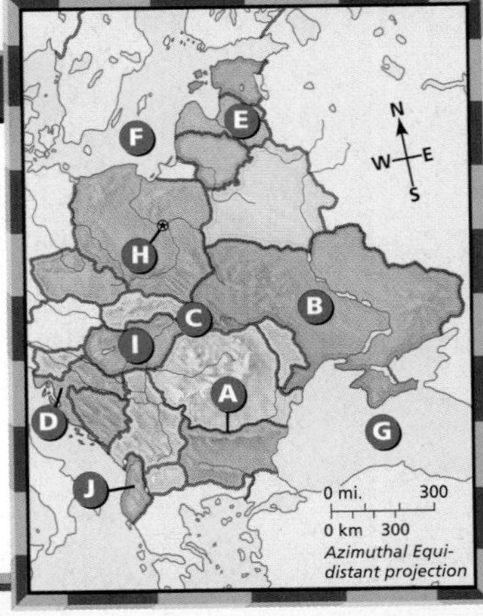

NATIONAL GEOGRAPHIC Place Location Activity

1. A
2. G
3. D
4. J
5. E
6. I
7. H
8. C
9. F
10. B

Current Events Journal

23. You might offer students the following cinquain as an example:

"Ukraine
rich breadbasket
struggling, suffering, rebelling
finally a free nation
Frontier."

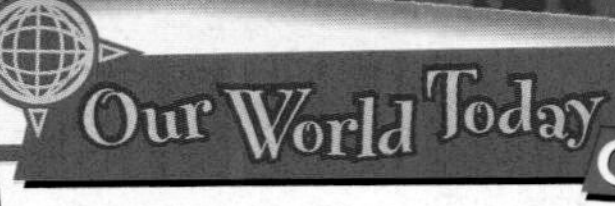

Self-Check Quiz Visit the ***Our World Today: People, Places, and Issues*** Web site at owt.glencoe.com and click on **Chapter 12–Self-Check Quizzes** to prepare for the Chapter Test.

Critical Thinking

21. **Understanding Cause and Effect** What has led to the unrest in the part of Yugoslavia known as Serbia?
22. **Categorizing Information** In a chart like the one below, identify eastern European countries that are succeeding and ones that continue to struggle economically. Include one fact that explains each situation.

Countries That Are Succeeding	Countries That Are Struggling

Current Events Journal

23. **Writing a Poem** A cinquain is a poem with five lines. The first line is a one-word title. Line two has two words that describe the title. Line three has three action words that describe the title. Line four is a four-word phrase that expresses a feeling about the subject. Line five is one word that is a synonym or restatement of the title. Write a cinquain about a current issue in one eastern European country.

Mental Mapping Activity

24. **Focusing on the Region** Create a map of eastern Europe, then label the following:

- Poland
- Albania
- Czech Republic
- Serbia
- Hungary
- Lithuania
- Black Sea
- Danube River
- Ukraine
- Adriatic Sea

Technology Skills Activity

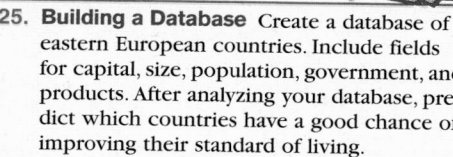

25. **Building a Database** Create a database of eastern European countries. Include fields for capital, size, population, government, and products. After analyzing your database, predict which countries have a good chance of improving their standard of living.

Standardized Test Practice

Directions: Study the map below, and then answer the question that follows.

1. **Which of these eastern European countries has NOT applied for membership in the European Union?**
   A Ukraine
   B Poland
   C Estonia
   D Czech Republic

Test-Taking Tip: This is a tricky question because all the choices are eastern European countries. You need to study the map to see which answer choice is not listed on the map. Use the process of elimination to narrow your answer choices.

331

Assessment and Activities

Standardized Test Practice

1. A

Tested Objectives:
Analyzing information, reading a map

Chapter Test Bonus Question

This question may be used for extra credit on the chapter test.

This country is well-known for its rich folk art tradition of creating elaborate and beautiful Easter eggs. What is this country? *(Ukraine)*

Our World Today online

Have students visit the Web site at **owt.glencoe.com** to review Chapter 12 and take the Self-Check Quiz.

Mental Mapping Activity

24. This exercise helps students visualize the countries and geographic features they have been studying and to understand the relationship among various points. Accept all attempts at freehand mapping that show places in a correct relationship to one another.

Technology Skills Activity

25. After completing this activity, students should discuss all the different factors that help a country succeed in taking care of its people and meeting its goals.

Unit 5 Planning Guide

SUGGESTED PACING CHART

Unit 5 (1 day)	Chapter 13 (5 days)	Chapter 14 (4 days)	Unit 5 (2 days)
Day 1 Introduction	**Day 1** Chapter 13 Intro, Section 1	**Day 1** Chapter 14 Intro, Section 1	**Day 1** Wrap-Up/Projects
	Day 2 Section 2	**Day 2** Section 2	**Day 2** Unit 5 Assessment
	Day 3 Section 3	**Day 3** Chapter 14 Review	
	Day 4 Chapter 13 Review	**Day 4** Chapter 14 Assessment	
	Day 5 Chapter 13 Assessment		

For a complete course pacing guide and Teacher Classroom Resources, see:

Interactive Lesson Planner

Use the following tools to easily assess student learning in a variety of ways:

- **Performance Assessment Activities and Rubrics**
- **Section Quizzes**
- **Chapter Tests and Unit Pretests and Posttests**
- **Interactive Tutor Self-Assessment CD-ROM**
- **ExamView® Pro 3.0 Testmaker CD-ROM**
- **MindJogger Videoquiz**
- **owt.glencoe.com**
- **Standardized Test Practice Workbook**

Note: The following materials may be used when teaching Unit 5.
Chapter level support materials can be found on the chapter resource pages.

TEACHING TRANSPARENCIES

Political Map Transparency 5

Unit 5 Map Overlay Transparencies

World Cultures Transparencies 7 and 8

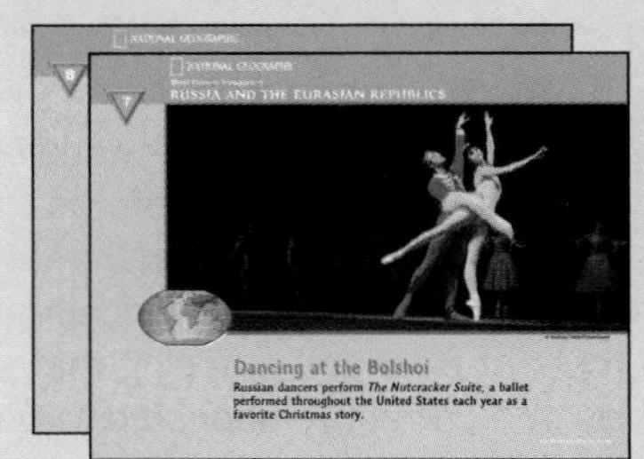

Unit 5 Resources

INTERDISCIPLINARY CONNECTIONS

World Literature Reading 5

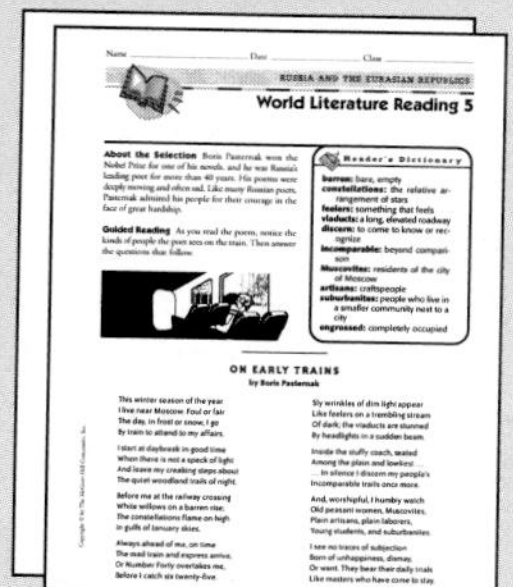

Economics and Geography Activity 5

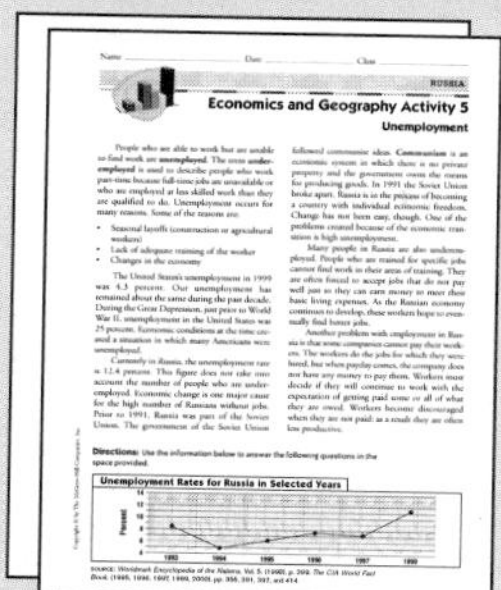

History and Geography Activity 5

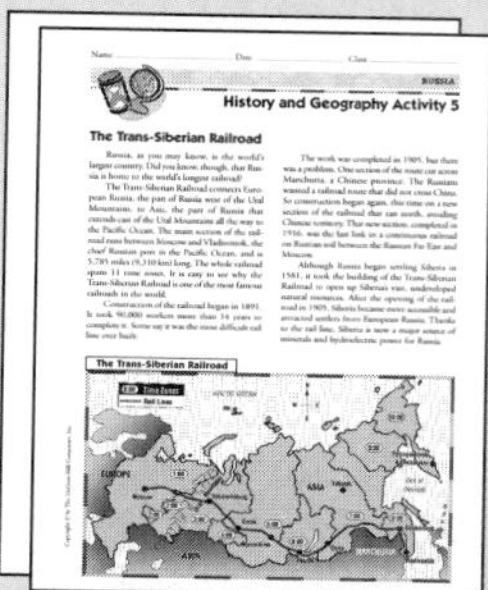

MAP AND GEOGRAPHY SKILLS

Building Geography Skills for Life

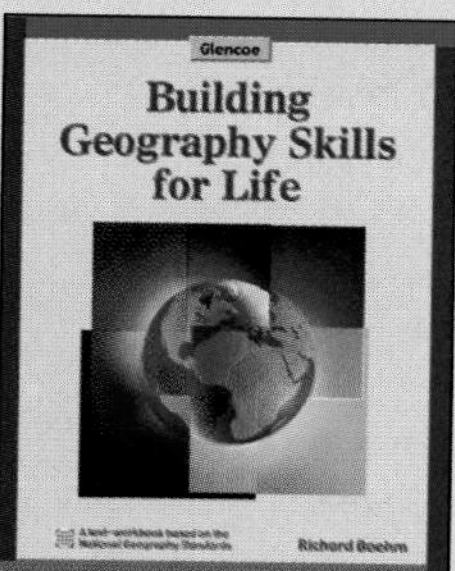

NGS Focus on Geography Literacy

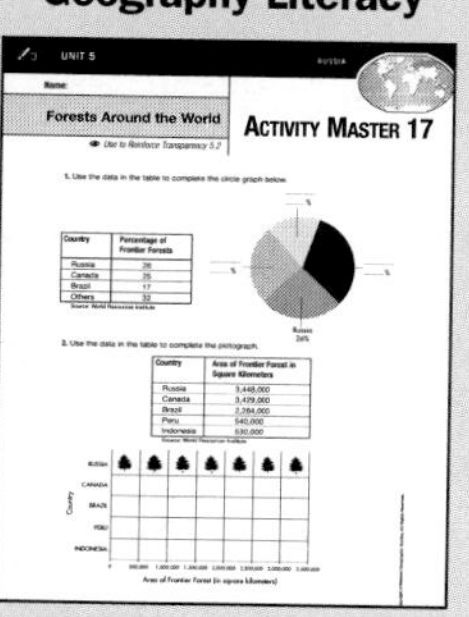

Regional Atlas Activity 5

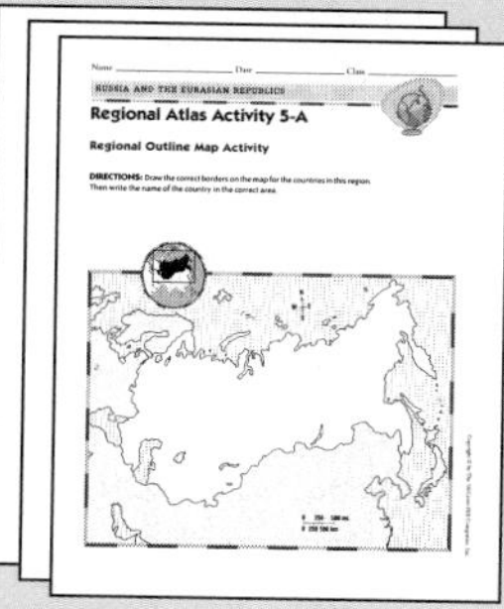

NATIONAL GEOGRAPHIC MapMachine

Find the latest coverage of geography in the news, atlas updates, cartographic activities with interactive maps, an online map store, and links at www.nationalgeographic.com/maps

APPLICATION AND HANDS-ON

Citizenship Activity 5

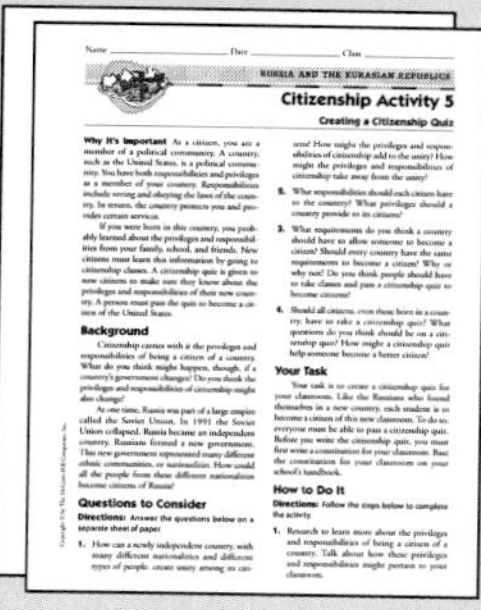

Foods Around the World 5

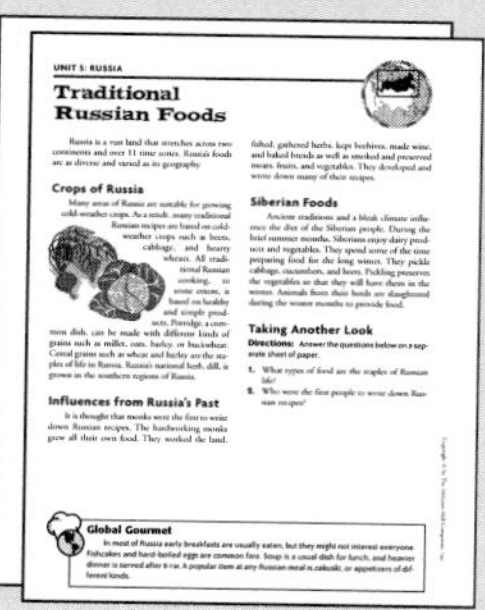

ENRICHMENT AND EXTENSION

Environmental Case Study 5

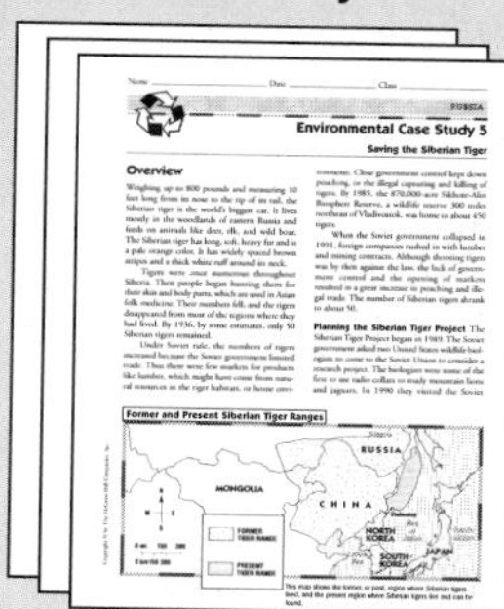

World Music: A Cultural Legacy

ASSESSMENT AND EVALUATION

GLENCOE'S ASSESSMENT ADVANTAGE

Unit 5 Pretests

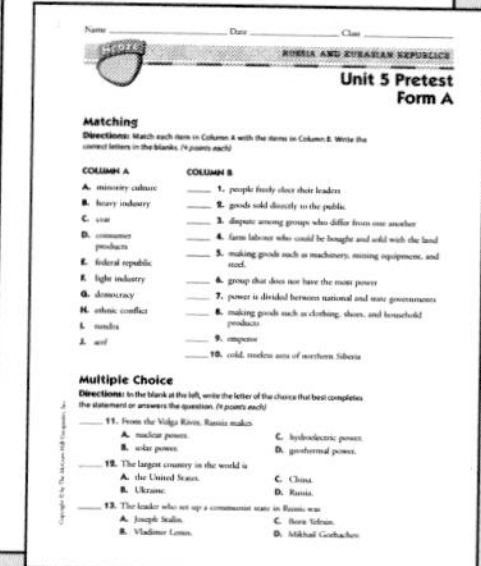

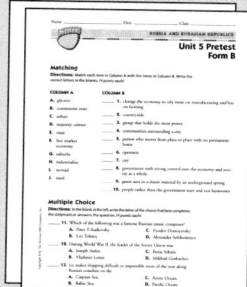

Unit 5 Posttests

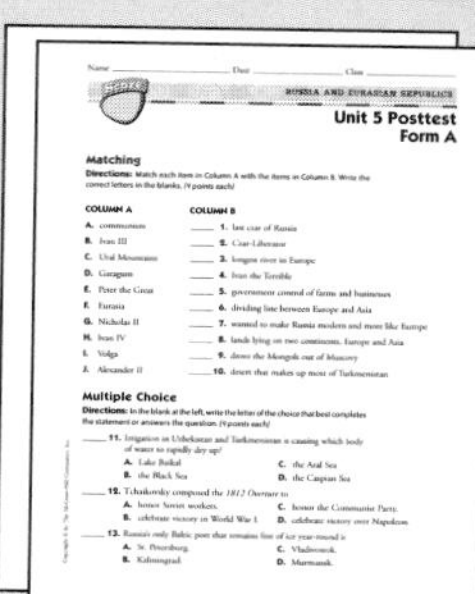

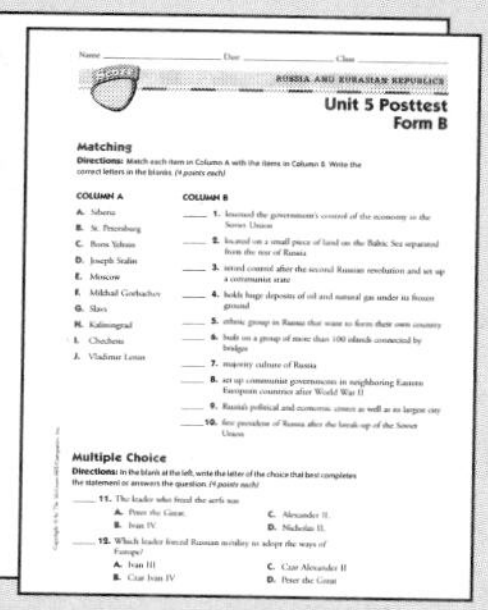

Additional Unit 5 Resources

interNET RESOURCES

- owt.glencoe.com
  Our World Today: People, Places, and Issues
  Visit the Glencoe *Our World Today: People, Places, and Issues* Web site for overviews, activities, assessments, and updated charts and graphs.
- socialstudies.glencoe.com
  Glencoe Social Studies
  Visit the Glencoe Web site for social studies activities, updates, and links to other sites.
- www.teachingtoday.glencoe.com
  Glencoe Teaching Today
  This Web site features daily teaching tips, free PDF downloads, annotated Web resources, educational news, and more.
- www.nationalgeographic.com
  NGS ONLINE Visit the National Geographic Society Web site for the latest coverage of geography in the news, atlas updates, activities, links, interactive features, and archives.
- **Glencoe's Guide to Using the Internet**
  Provides an introduction to many of the current technologies on the Internet. Professional resources and teaching strategies included.

Our Web sites provide additional resources. All essential content is covered in the Student Edition.

THE HISTORY CHANNEL. A&E Biography.

The following videotape programs are available from Glencoe:

- **Faberge: Imperial Jeweler** 1-56501-878-8
- **Ivan the Terrible** 0-7670-0517-1
- **Joseph Stalin** 1-56501-820-6

To order, call Glencoe at 1-800-334-7344. To find classroom resources to accompany many of these, check:

A&E Television: www.aetv.com

The History Channel: www.historychannel.com

Bibliography

Literature for the Student

- **Glencoe Middle School World Literature Library**
  Letters From Rifka, by Karen Hesse. A family flees from Russia to America, but Rifka is left behind in Poland.
- ***Russia and the Independent States,*** rev. ed. By Daniel C. Diller. Washington, D.C.: Congressional Quarterly, 1993.
- ***Russia: Then and Now.*** Minneapolis: Lerner, 1993.

Readings for the Teacher

- ***CIS and Eastern Europe On File.*** New York: Facts On File, 1993.
- ***Teaching About the Former Soviet Union: History, Language, Culture, Art,*** rev. ed. By Patricia Winpenny, et al. Denver: Center for Teaching International Relations, 1994.

Multimedia Links

- **Glencoe Social Studies Primary Source Document Library**
  Bolsheviks Seize Power in Russia, by Vladimir Ilyich Lenin
  The Communist Manifesto, by Karl Marx
  Emancipation of Russian Serfs, by Czar Alexander II
  Napoleon at Moscow, by Baron Claude François de Méneval
  Stalin's Bloody Purge Begins, by Edvard Radzinsky
- ***The Rise and Fall of the Soviet Union.*** Tapeworm, 1992. 2 videocassettes, 124 minutes.

Refer to owt.glencoe.com for additional literature titles and study guides related to this region.

Additional Glencoe Teacher Support

- **Teaching Strategies for the Geography Classroom**
- **Reproducible Lesson Plans**
- **Outline Map Resource Book**
- **Reading in the Content Area**

Service Learning Project

Connecting Classroom With Community

Pollution is a very serious problem in Russia. Have students investigate a pollution-related issue that interests them, such as waste disposal, conservation, water pollution, global warming, or ozone depletion. Then have them identify ways that they can do something to try to alleviate this problem. They could participate in fund-raising or letter-writing campaigns, join an environmental group that works toward a goal that they share, or begin their own local clean-up effort.

Content Background Notes

Use this additional information as lecture notes or discussion prompts throughout the study of Unit 5.

Chapter 13 Russia and Its Neighbors (pp. 340–363)

The Sky Is Falling One June morning in 1908, the stillness in remote central Siberia was shattered by a massive explosion in the air. Scientists estimate the blast was as strong as 10 to 15 megatons of dynamite—as powerful as many atomic bombs. The power of the blast was enough to flatten about 2,000 square miles (5,180 sq. km) of trees in the forest—an area more than half the size of Rhode Island. It was strong enough that the resulting shaking of the earth registered on seismographs in western Europe. Yet this massive explosion left no crater on the ground. What caused the "Tunguska Event," named for the river near where the explosion occurred?

Various explanations have been offered for this event, from the appearance of a black hole to the explosion of a power plant in a spaceship piloted by extraterrestrials. Today most scientists believe that the blast was the result of either an asteroid or a comet tumbling to Earth and burning up in the atmosphere. Comets—made of ice and dust—are more likely than rocky asteroids to burn up in the atmosphere, explaining why no crater has been found. However, some metallic fragments have been found in tree resin in the area, suggesting that the object was an asteroid. Whether asteroid or comet, the fragment must have been huge; scientists suggest a weight anywhere from 100,000 to 1 million tons (90,719 to 907,185 metric tons). Research at Tunguska continues, as scientists hope to learn more about Earth's explosive visitor.

A Mammoth Project Siberia is home to another fascinating research project—one attempting to reach not out in space but back in time. About 20,000 years ago, wooly mammoths lumbered across Siberia. These massive creatures—which measured up to 8.5 feet (2.6 m) across at the shoulders and weighed about 14,000 pounds (6,350 kg)—thrived in the cold Ice Age climate. One mammoth—47 years old—died and was later frozen in ice. Scientists used jackhammers to chisel a huge block of ice holding its remains. Then they used a helicopter to carry that block of ice to a nearby cave, where they are defrosting the animal so they can study it. Because they want to be sure not to destroy any evidence, the scientists have to defrost their sample very carefully—using hand-held hair dryers. By studying the mammoth and remains of other plants and animals trapped in the ice, scientists believe they can learn a wealth of information about the biology of the Ice Age world.

Chapter 14 Russia—Past and Present (pp. 364–387)

The Kremlin One of the most familiar sites from Russia is Moscow's famous Kremlin, the fortress that was the center of the old city. The name *Kremlin* means "fortified town" in Russian, and this collection of buildings standing behind stout walls is precisely that—a walled city within a city. Full of palaces, churches, and military facilities, the Kremlin speaks of Russia's imperial past.

Construction of the Kremlin first began in 1147, when Moscow was founded, and the original citadel walls were finished 10 years later. By the 1300s, Moscow had become the center of the Russian Orthodox faith, and from then on, the Kremlin became home to some of Russia's most magnificent churches. Today five cathedrals rise within the walls of this enclave. The oldest is the Cathedral of the Assumption, built in the 1400s. The Cathedral of the Archangel Michael holds the burial tombs of all of Russia's czars over a period of hundreds of years.

The Kremlin also has armories, palaces from the days of the czars, the massive 40-ton (36–metric ton) Tsar Cannon (built in the 1580s and unworkable), and the 200-ton (181–metric ton) Tsar Bell (also unworkable). The complex is still in use. The ornate Senate building, built during the reign of Catherine the Great, today serves as the official residence of Russia's president.

Icons One of the hallmarks of the Russian Orthodox Church is the veneration of icons. Icons are painted images of Jesus and Mary, the archangels and apostles, church fathers, and important figures from the Old Testament. The style of icon painting is distinctive, drawing from ancient Greek, Roman, and Egyptian practices. Icon art looks different from western painting because it does not attempt to portray physical features in a realistic manner. Figures are less three-dimensional, and the relative sizes of figures are determined not by the actual size of the people represented or their placement nearer or farther from the viewer (as in western art), but according to their spiritual importance. The more significant the figure, the larger the size. The colors used by icon painters are distinctive as well and, again, aim to convey spiritual meaning, not physical reality. Icon painting originated in the Eastern Orthodox Church of the Byzantine Empire. Russian icon painters adapted the art but developed a distinctly Russian style that included darker colors and a more forgiving portrayal of Jesus than was often found in Byzantine art.

OUT OF TIME?

If time does not permit teaching each chapter in this unit, you may use the **Reading Essentials and Study Guide** for each chapter.

Unit Overview

The two chapters in this unit introduce students to the geography, culture, and history of Russia and its neighbors. Before beginning to study the unit, point out to students the following characteristics of this region:

- physical features that have a historical and economic impact
- recent changes that have dramatically altered political and economic life
- distinctive, rich cultural traditions
- environmental problems due to development

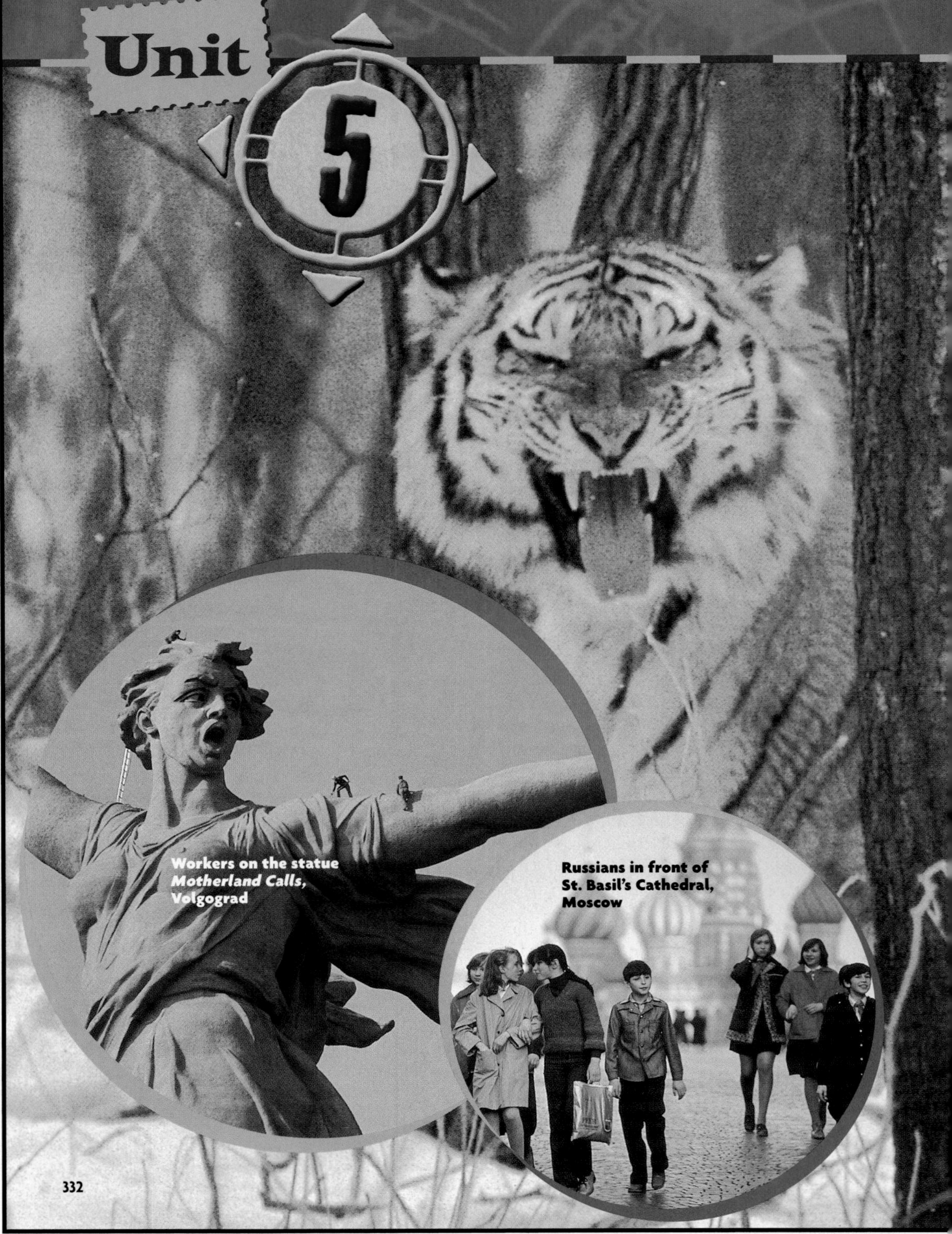

Workers on the statue *Motherland Calls*, Volgograd

Russians in front of St. Basil's Cathedral, Moscow

332

Using the Illustration

Siberian tigers are in great danger of extinction. They once roamed a huge territory that included not only Siberia but China and the Korean Peninsula. The disorder that followed the collapse of the Soviet Union resulted in funding cuts for conservation activity and left the borders more porous, opening the way for a surge in illegal hunting. A single Siberian tiger is worth $15,000—far beyond the typical income of people in the region. As a result of this surge in hunting, today there are fewer than 500 of these animals in the wild. Have students research more about Siberia. They can do individual or group presentations on one of the following aspects of Siberia: physical features and climate, resources, ecology, history, economics, people.

NATIONAL GEOGRAPHIC

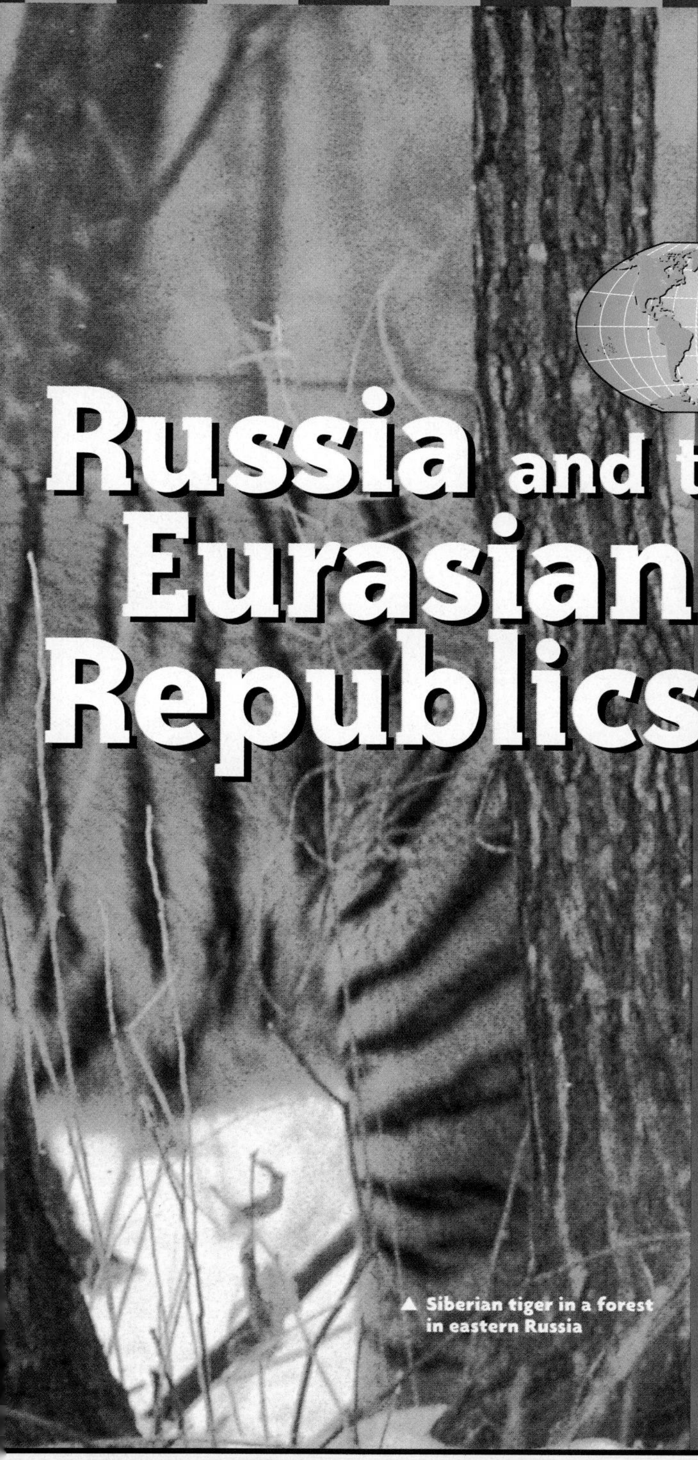

Russia and the Eurasian Republics

If you had to describe Russia in one word, that word would be BIG! Russia is the largest country in the world in area. Its almost 6.6 million square miles (17 million sq. km) are spread across two continents—Europe and Asia. As you can imagine, such a large country faces equally large challenges. In 1991, Russia emerged from the Soviet empire as an independent country. Since then it has been struggling to unite its many ethnic groups, set up a democratic government, and build a stable economy.

▲ Siberian tiger in a forest in eastern Russia

NGS ONLINE
www.nationalgeographic.com/education

These materials are available from Glencoe.

Software

ZipZapMap! World

Transparencies

PicturePack Transparencies

CD-ROM

Picture Atlas of the World, Second Edition

Current Events Journal

Have students find Russia on the map on pages RA2–RA3. **Ask:** **How would you describe Russia's size compared to other countries?** *(very large)* Have students consider what impact this great size has on life in Russia. Ask them to write about such issues as transportation, communication, and government control over all regions.

NGS ONLINE
www.nationalgeographic.com/education

This online resource provides lesson plans, atlas updates, cartographic activities with interactive maps, an online map store, and geography links.

Unit Launch Activity

What Challenges Do Russians Face?
In recent years, Russia has undergone many major changes: the end of Communist rule and the adoption of democratic government, the shrinking of the Russian Empire and the rise of ethnic conflict, and the transformation from a command to a market economy. Organize students into groups, and have each research one of the challenges facing the Russian people. Then have each group use problem-solving techniques to identify which challenge they think is the most important and design a three-part presentation: an explanation of what that challenge is, reasons that it is so difficult, and how to implement a solution to overcome those difficulties. Have each group present its findings to the class, who should be prepared to debate the effectiveness of the solution.

Lesson Plan

Using the Regional Atlas
These features and activities may be used as an introduction to the unit or as teaching tools throughout the course of the unit.

Focus

Objectives

1. Locate Russia and describe its landforms and climates.
2. Compare Russia to its neighbors.

5-Minute Precheck

Have students look at the map on pages RA2–RA3. **Ask:** **Is Russia in Europe or in Asia?** *(both; the Ural Mountains, which divide Europe and Asia, are inside Russia)* Ask if there are any other countries that sit on more than one continent. *(Turkey, which has a very small European section)*

More About the Profile

In order to show a variety of physical features, this cross section begins at the Belarus-Russia border and ends at the Kamchatka Peninsula along 55°N latitude.

NATIONAL GEOGRAPHIC **REGIONAL ATLAS**

Russia and the Eurasian Republics

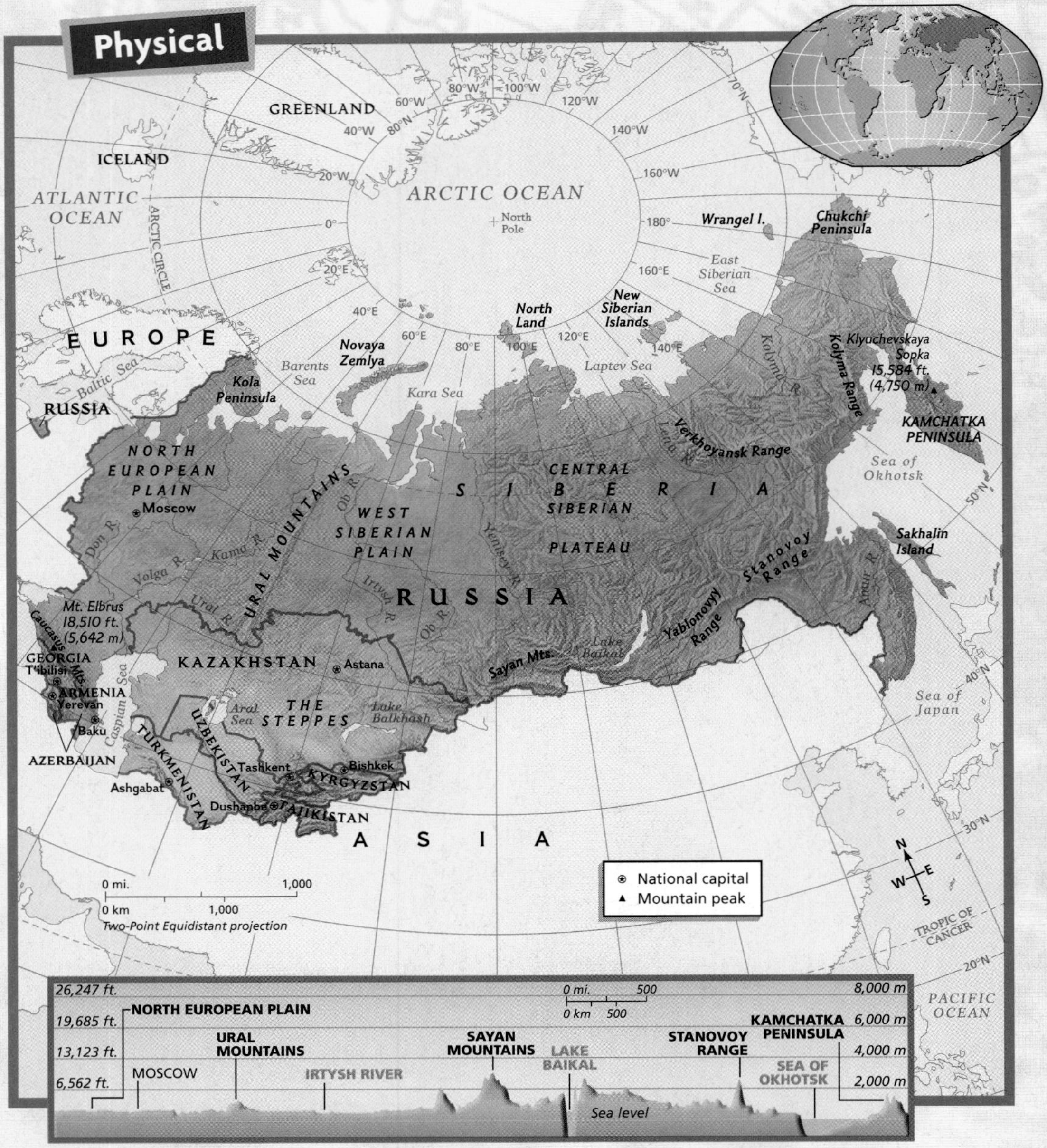

Physical

334 UNIT 5

Regional Atlas Activity

Analyzing Population Write the following information on the board:

	Russia	World Average
Birthrate per 1,000 people	9.3	25.0
Death rate per 1,000 people	15.0	9.3
Rate of natural increase per 1,000 people	–5.7	15.7

Ask: **What can you conclude about the population of Russia from these statistics? Why?** *(It is declining because there are fewer births per 1,000 people than deaths.)* **How does this compare to the world in general?** *(The Russian population is declining, but the population of the world in general is increasing—birthrate far exceeds death rate.)* **L2**

EE4 Human Systems: Standard 9

Unit 5

UNIT 5

Political

MAP STUDY

1. Where are most Russian cities located? Why are they located here?
2. What is the capital of Russia?

2 TEACH

Making Comparisons Have students look at the political map of Russia on page 335 and the map of Russian winters on page 336. Have them compare the Russian winter in four different Russian cities. Then have them speculate on the impact that these differences will have on life in the different cities. **L1**

Interdisciplinary Connections

History The name *Russia* comes from *Rus*—the name that people gave to the Vikings who started invading the area in the A.D. 800s. *Rus* is probably a mispronunciation of what the Vikings called themselves—*rothsmen,* or "rowers."

MAP STUDY

Answers

1. the south of Russia; the climate is warmer
2. Moscow

Skills Practice

On what body of water is Russia's largest coastline? *(Arctic Ocean)*

Regional Atlas Activity

Researching Features Organize students into groups and assign each group one of the landforms or bodies of water in Russia. For example, one group could be assigned the Ural Mountains, another the Volga River, and so on. Have each group conduct research about their physical feature with the goal of explaining how that feature affects the lives of Russians. They can look at the economic and cultural benefits of the feature or the obstacles to development that the feature offers. Have the groups also find information about how the people of Russia affect that geographical feature through their actions. After concluding their research, have each group prepare a bulletin board display about their feature. **L2**

EE5 Environment and Society: Standards 14

NATIONAL GEOGRAPHIC

REGIONAL ATLAS

Cultural Kaleidoscope

Russia The potato is a staple of the Russian diet. It was not always so popular, however. When the government ordered peasants to plant potatoes on common ground in 1840, "anti-potato" riots broke out in 10 Russian provinces.

Travel Guide

Guests in Russia often bring gifts of flowers to their hosts. They always give an odd number of flowers, however, since an even number of flowers is used for funerals.

Did You Know

Lake Baikal is so deep that it would take an entire year for the volume of water from all the rivers on the earth to fill it.

MAP STUDY

Answers

1. 120 to 160 days
2. Vladivostok

Skills Practice

How many hours of sunshine does Moscow have in January? *(1 hour)*

Russia

The Russian Winter

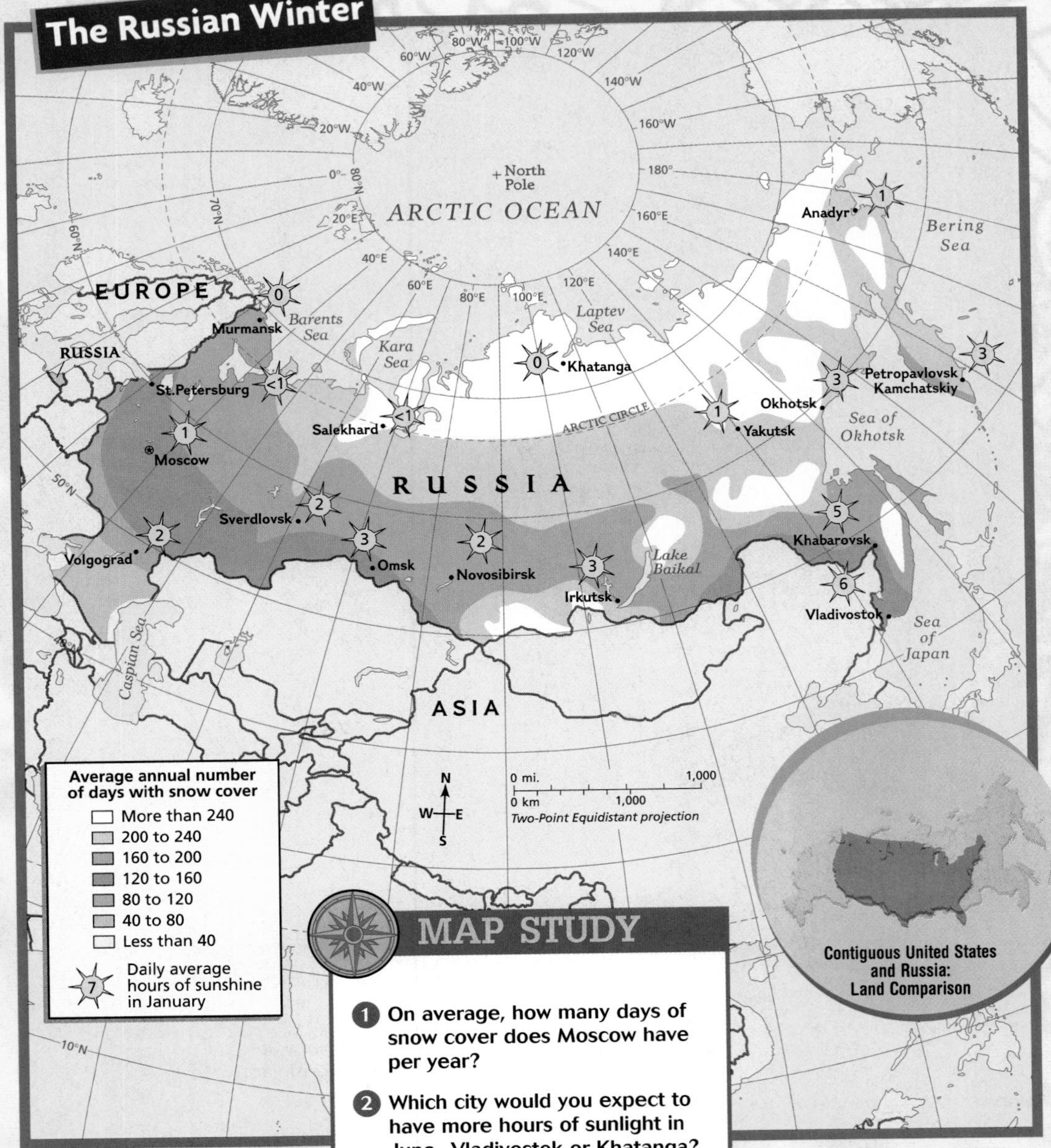

ARCTIC OCEAN · North Pole · EUROPE · RUSSIA · ASIA · Barents Sea · Kara Sea · Laptev Sea · Bering Sea · Sea of Okhotsk · Sea of Japan · Caspian Sea · Lake Baikal · ARCTIC CIRCLE

Murmansk · St. Petersburg · Moscow · Volgograd · Salekhard · Sverdlovsk · Omsk · Novosibirsk · Irkutsk · Khatanga · Yakutsk · Okhotsk · Anadyr · Petropavlovsk Kamchatskiy · Khabarovsk · Vladivostok

Average annual number of days with snow cover

- More than 240
- 200 to 240
- 160 to 200
- 120 to 160
- 80 to 120
- 40 to 80
- Less than 40
- Daily average hours of sunshine in January

0 mi. 1,000
0 km 1,000
Two-Point Equidistant projection

Contiguous United States and Russia: Land Comparison

MAP STUDY

1. On average, how many days of snow cover does Moscow have per year?
2. Which city would you expect to have more hours of sunlight in June—Vladivostok or Khatanga?

336 UNIT 5

Regional Atlas Activity

Making Comparisons Have your students identify the Russian cities located above latitude 60°N on this map. Then have them look at other maps in the Reference Atlas to find at least five other cities around the world located above 60°N. Afterwards, students should use the Internet to find out what today's temperature is in each city. Have your students organize their information into a chart that lists the cities (and their countries), their latitude and longitude, and their temperatures. **Ask:** **Which city has the lowest and which has the highest temperature? How does it compare to the temperature in your own location? What factors might cause the differences in temperatures? L2**

EE1 The World in Spatial Terms: Standard 3

Fast Facts

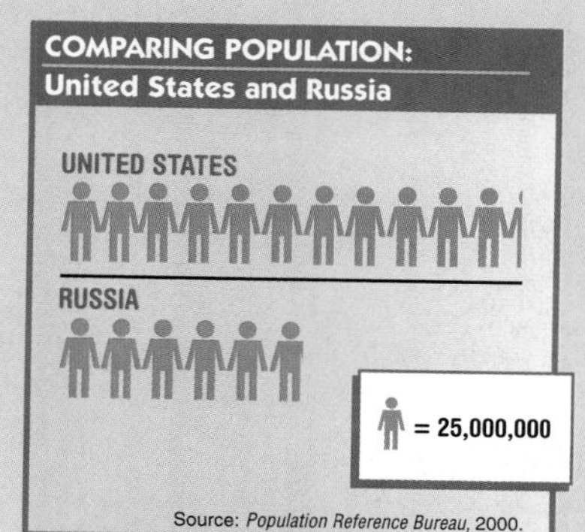

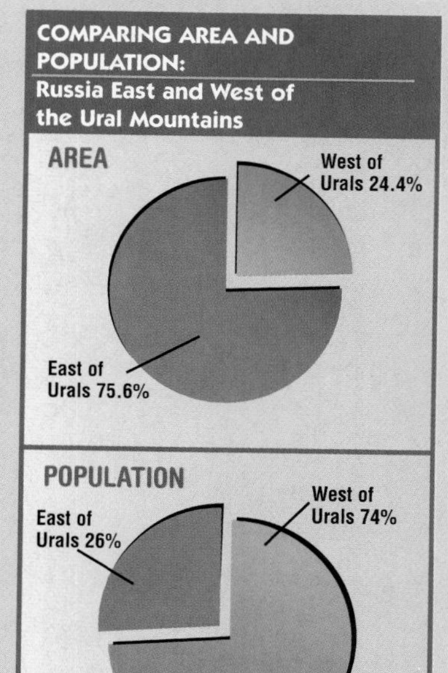

Russia

Data Bits

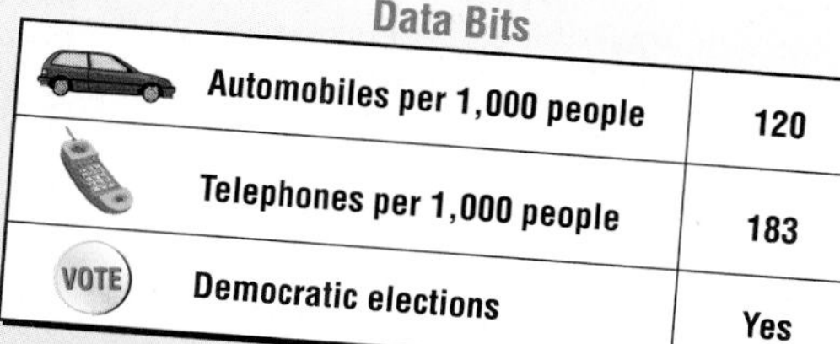

Automobiles per 1,000 people	120
Telephones per 1,000 people	183
Democratic elections	Yes

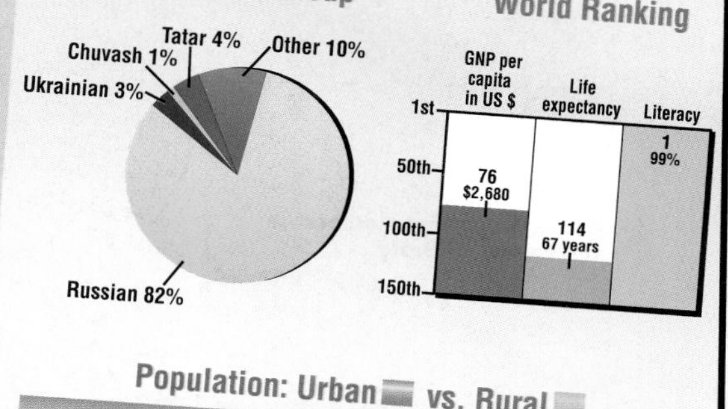

Population: Urban vs. Rural

76%

24%

Source: World Desk Reference, 2000.

GRAPHIC STUDY

1. Which country, Russia or the U.S., has a **higher** population?
2. What percentage of Russia's people live west of the Ural Mountains?

Unit 5
Regional Atlas

As an introduction to this region, you may want to engage students by studying an important contemporary issue in this region of the world. The **TIME REPORTS: FOCUS ON WORLD ISSUES** for this region is found on pages 377–383. The feature examines Russia's transition from communist state to emerging democracy.

GRAPHIC STUDY

Answers

1. United States
2. 74 percent

Skills Practice

Where do most people in Russia live—cities or the country? *(Cities, 76% live in urban areas.)*

Interdisciplinary Connections

Science The average life expectancy in Georgia—about 72 years—is among the highest in the region. Many Georgians live well beyond this average. In the early 1990s, for example, there were more than 20,000 Georgians aged 90 or older. Georgians attribute their longevity to their country's healthful climate.

Regional Atlas Activity

Ethnic Distribution Write the following information: Belarus—31.9 percent; Estonia—29 percent; Kazakhstan—47.4 percent; Kyrgyzstan—16.2 percent; Latvia—32.6 percent; Lithuania—8.2 percent; Moldova—23.1 percent; Ukraine—32.8 percent. Explain that these are the percentages of ethnic Russians living in each of these countries. Have students rank the countries according to these percentages, from highest to lowest. *(Kazakhstan, Ukraine, Latvia, Belarus, Estonia, Moldova, Kyrgyzstan, Lithuania)* **Ask:** **What problems might be caused by having a high proportion of Russians in a country?** *(possible tension with other ethnic groups within the country)* **L1**

EE4 Human Systems: Standard 9

Did You Know?

Georgia has been controlled by many different peoples. The Byzantine Empire and Persia fought over this land, and in A.D. 645 it was conquered by the Arabs. Later, Georgia was part of the Mongol and Ottoman Empires and the Soviet Union.

Interdisciplinary Connections

Literature The folklore of Kyrgyzstan is preserved in the *Manas*, the longest oral chronicle of its kind in the world. It tells the adventures of the hero Manas the Strong.

Cultural Kaleidoscope

Kazakhstan The Kazakhs preserve many ancient traditions. Families sit on carpets and eat from low tables. Almost everyone can play the domras—a two-stringed musical instrument.

3 Assess

Have students answer the Map Study and Graphic Study questions on pages 335–337.

NATIONAL GEOGRAPHIC

Regional Atlas

Country Profiles

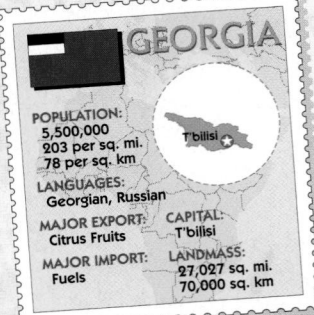

▼ **Reindeer pulling sled across the tundra, Siberia**

Countries and flags not drawn to scale

Fun Facts

- **Russia** Russian names often end in "ov" or "vich." *Ov* simply means "son of." The name *Ivanov* means "son of Ivan." The suffix "vich" also refers to the father's name, but it was originally restricted only to those in the upper class. So someone with the last name of *Ivanovich* might have an ancestor who was a dignitary named Ivan.
- **Georgia** After a wedding ceremony in Georgia, the bride and groom traditionally return to the groom's house. When the couple crosses the threshold, they stomp on a ceramic plate. The one who breaks the plate first will be the "boss" in the marriage. The number of broken pieces represents the amount of problems the couple may later face together.

For more information on countries in this region, refer to the Nations of the World Data Bank on pages 690–699.

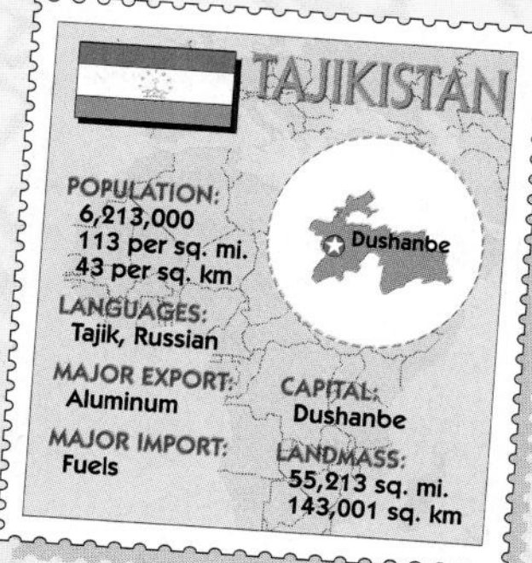

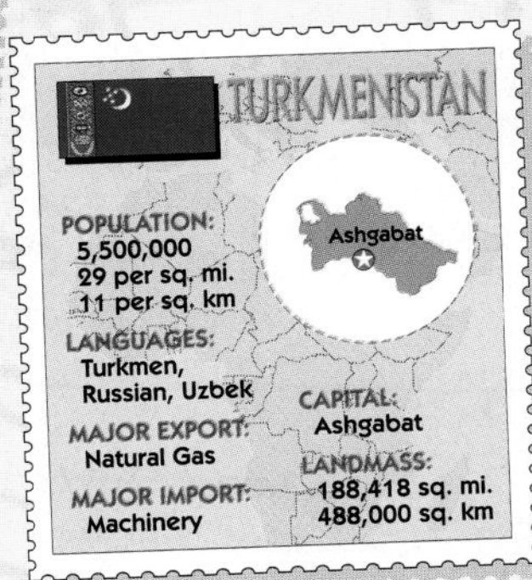

TURKMENISTAN
POPULATION:
5,500,000
29 per sq. mi.
11 per sq. km
LANGUAGES:
Turkmen,
Russian, Uzbek
MAJOR EXPORT:
Natural Gas
MAJOR IMPORT:
Machinery
CAPITAL:
Ashgabat
LANDMASS:
188,418 sq. mi.
488,000 sq. km
Ashgabat

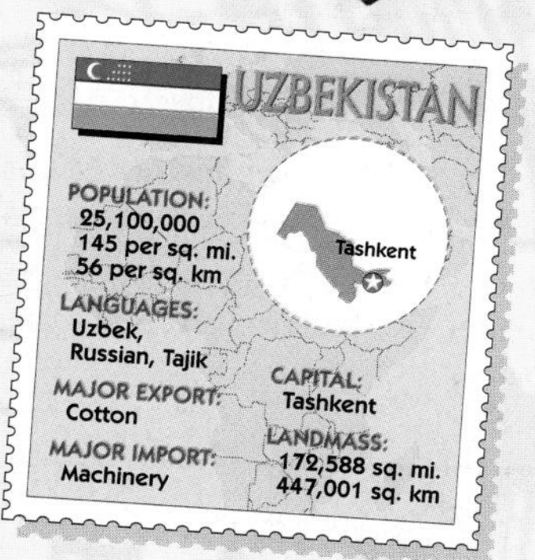

BUILDING CITIZENSHIP

Initiative Under communism, the government is the main employer. Many people no longer had a steady income when the Soviet Union broke apart. The government could no longer take care of them. People had to figure out on their own how to solve the problem of making enough money to feed their families. In other words, they had to show initiative.

Describe a time when you showed initiative to solve a problem you faced.

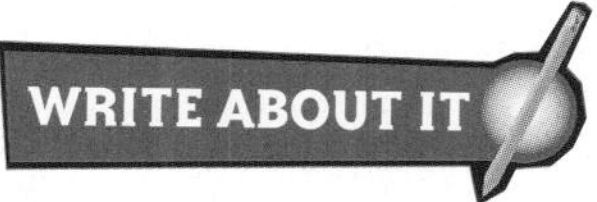

You can develop initiative with practice. Use the problem-solving process to identify a business you could start alone or with some friends. Gather information, list and consider your options, consider the advantages and disadvantages, and make a decision.

Teens washing cars to earn money ▼

Regional Atlas Activity

Drawing Conclusions Uzbekistan, Turkmenistan, and Tajikistan were countries that few people knew about until they suddenly became critical players in the worldwide crisis caused by terrorist actions in New York and Washington, D.C., on September 11, 2001. The three countries all share a border with Afghanistan, a key target in the fight against the terrorists. Until they were thrust into the spotlight, these Muslim countries were trying to overcome their own problems. Like other former Soviet republics, their economies have suffered since independence, and they are also troubled by ethnic and religious conflicts. **Ask:** **What geographic factors of these three countries have recently caused changes in their foreign relations? What elements have changed Americans' perceptions of Uzbekistan, Turkmenistan, and Tajikistan? L2**

BUILDING CITIZENSHIP

Answer Student answers will vary. You can explain that in order to have initiative, it helps to have a stable environment in which to start. When the Soviet Union collapsed and switched to a free market economy, there were no laws or government administration in place to help people who wanted to take advantage of the new economic climate. Without that support, it has been difficult for Russians to solve their financial problems.

Write About It! Students can work in groups to decide on a business. They should research what finances they would need to start it, if they would need to contact government or private agencies, who their competition would be, where they would locate, and to whom they would market.

CLOSE

Have students make a two-column chart in their notebooks. Have them write the headings "European Russia" and "Asian Russia" at the top of each column. Then have them study the text, maps, and graphs in the Regional Atlas and fill in information about each part of Russia under the appropriate heading. They might include such details as climate and landforms, cities, cultural information, populations, economics, and so on.

Chapter 13 Resources

Note: The following materials may be used when teaching Chapter 13.
Section level support materials are shown at point of use in the margins of the Teacher Wraparound Edition.

Timesaving Tools

TeacherWorks™ All-In-One Planner and Resource Center

- **Interactive Teacher Edition** See the **Interactive Teacher Edition** CD-ROM to electronically integrate your Teacher Wraparound Edition and blackline masters.
- **Interactive Lesson Planner** Organize your week, month, semester, or year with all the lesson helps you need. The **Interactive Lesson Planner** CD-ROM contains all Chapter 13 resources.

Use Glencoe's **Presentation Plus!** multimedia teacher tool to easily present dynamic lessons that visually excite your students. Using Microsoft PowerPoint® you can customize the presentations to create your own personalized lessons.

TEACHING TRANSPARENCIES

Graphic Organizer Transparency and Student Activity 13

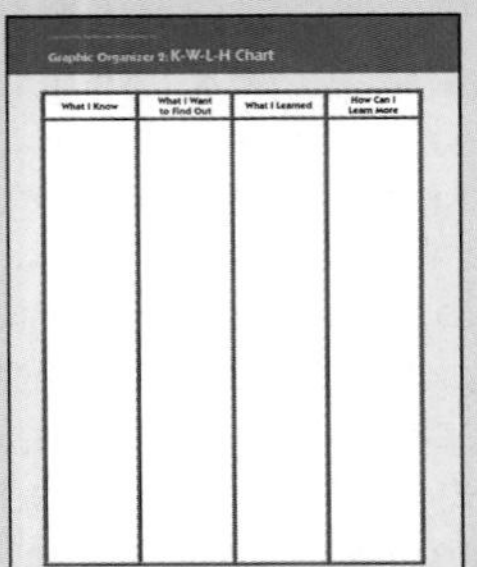

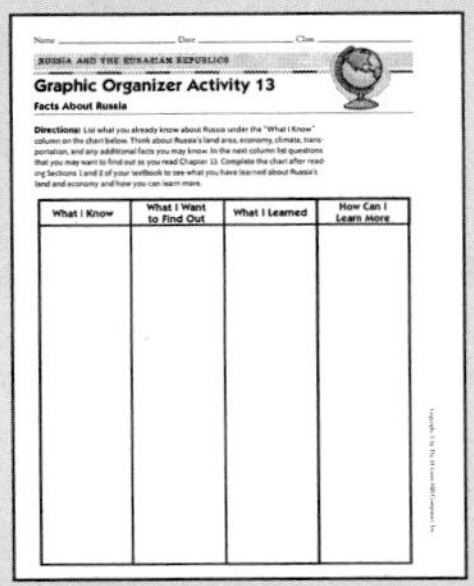

FOLDABLES™ Study Organizer

Foldables are three-dimensional, interactive graphic organizers that help students practice basic writing skills, review key vocabulary terms, and identify main ideas. Every chapter contains a Foldable activity, with additional chapter activities found in the ***Reading and Study Skills Foldables*** booklet.

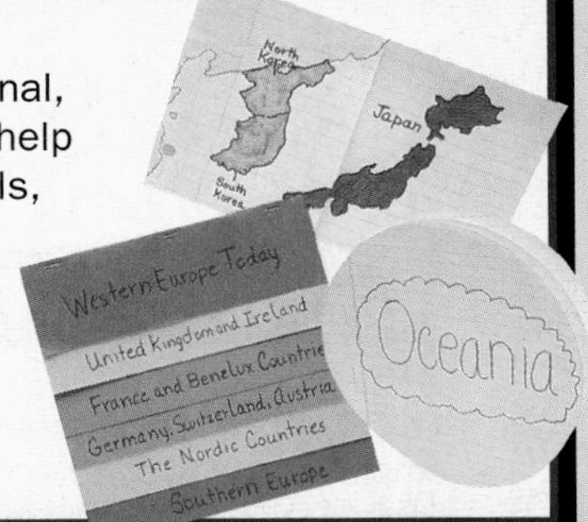

ENRICHMENT AND EXTENSION

Enrichment Activity 13

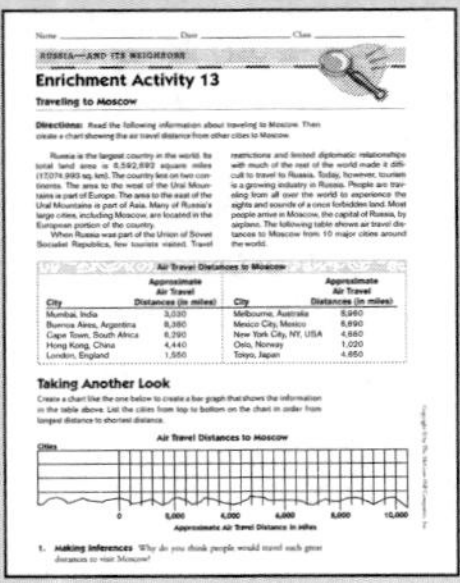

Cooperative Learning Activity 13

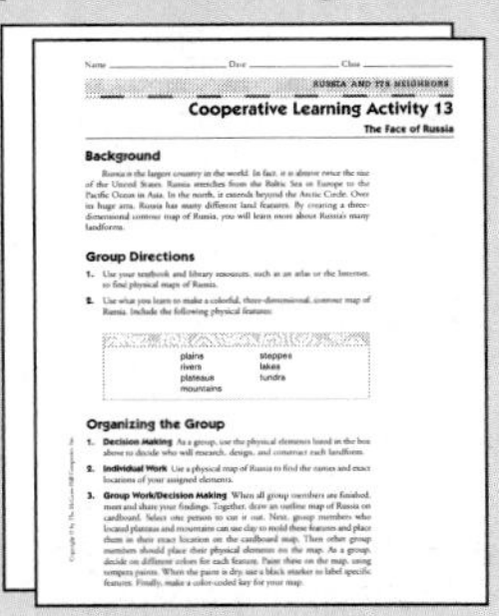

MAP AND GEOGRAPHY SKILLS

Chapter Map Activity 13

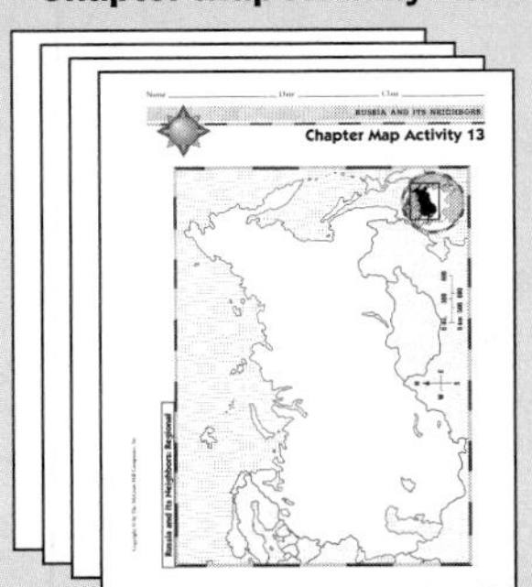

GeoLab Activity 13

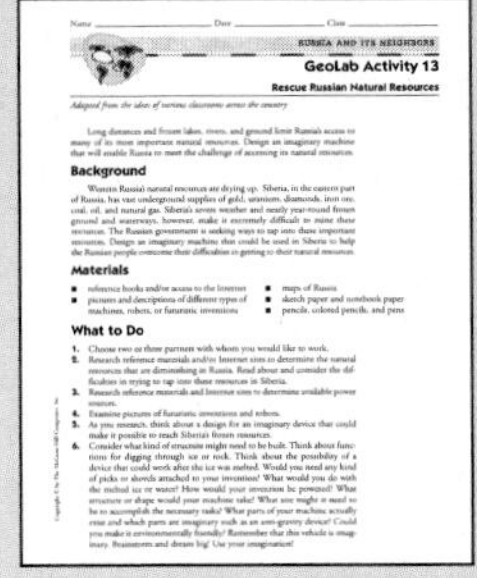

STANDARDIZED ASSESSMENT SKILLS

GLENCOE'S ASSESSMENT ADVANTAGE

Critical Thinking Skills Activity 13

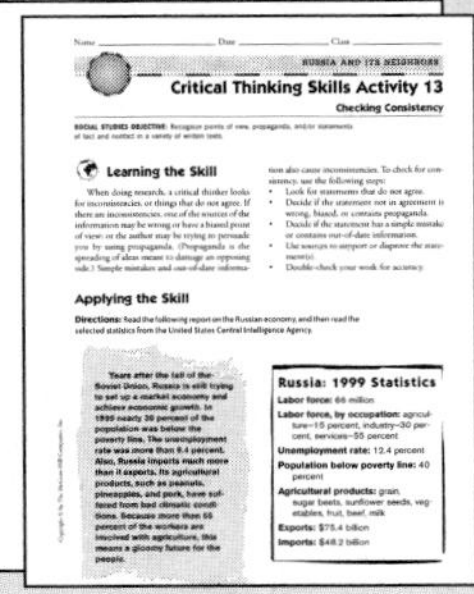

Map and Graph Skills Activity 13

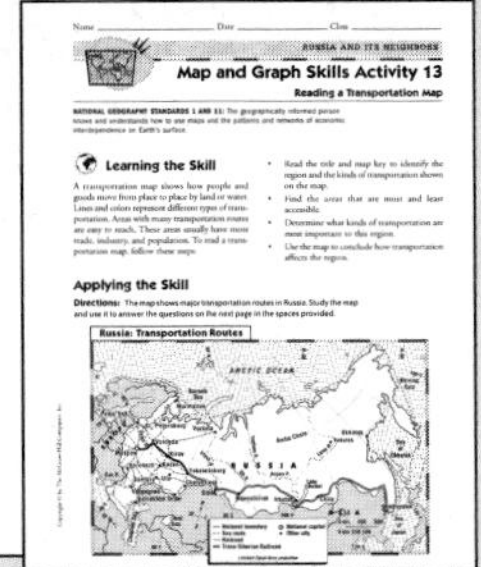

Reading and Writing Skills Activity 13

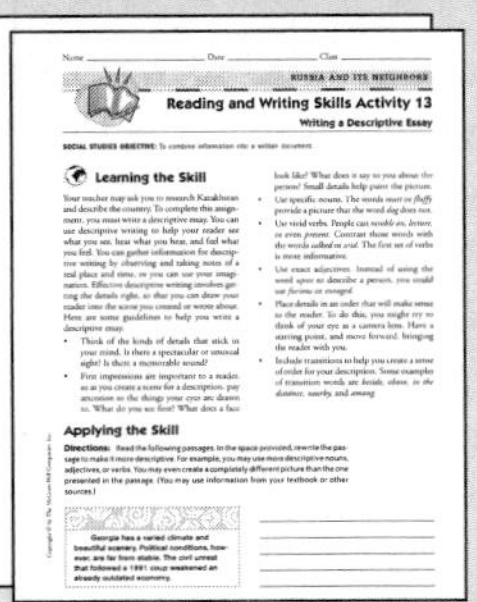

Standardized Test Practice Workbook Activity 13

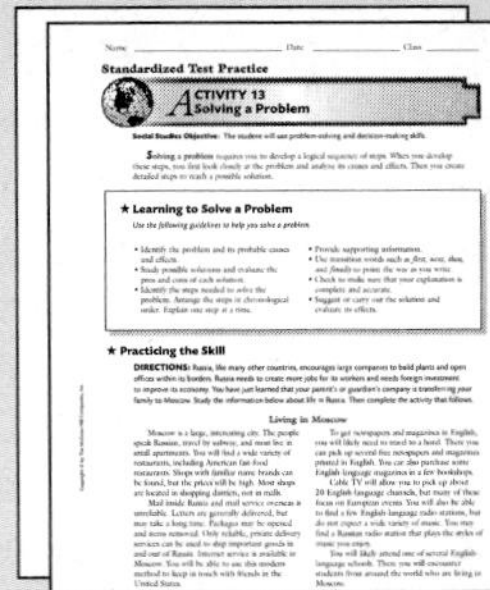

REVIEW AND REINFORCEMENT

Chapter Skills Activity 13

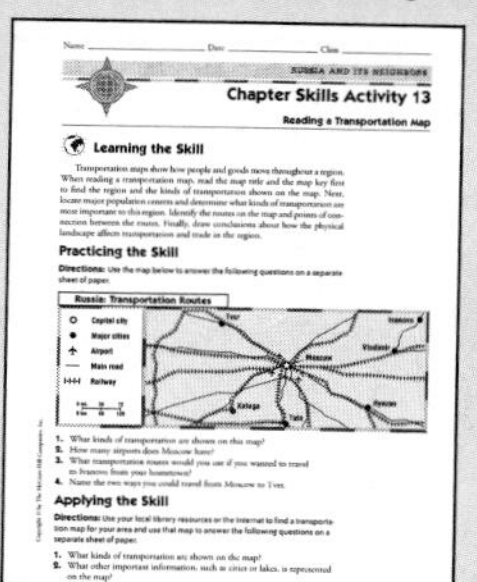

Take-Home Review Activity 13

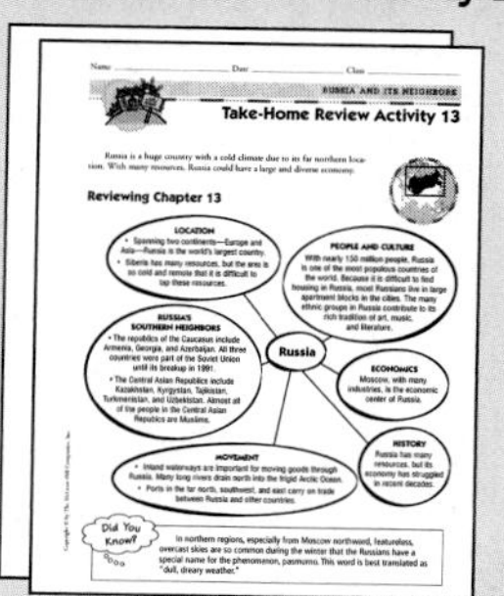

Reteaching Activity 13

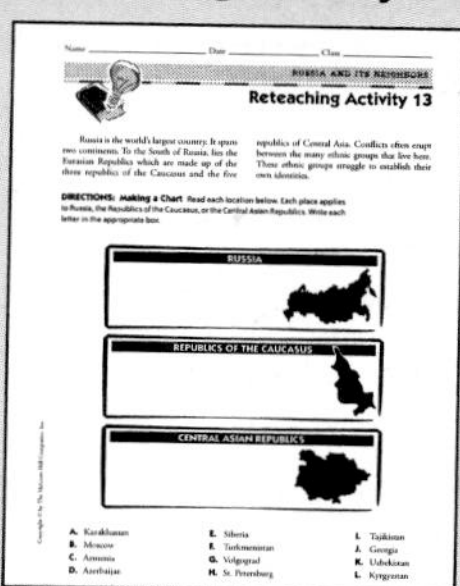

Vocabulary Activity 13

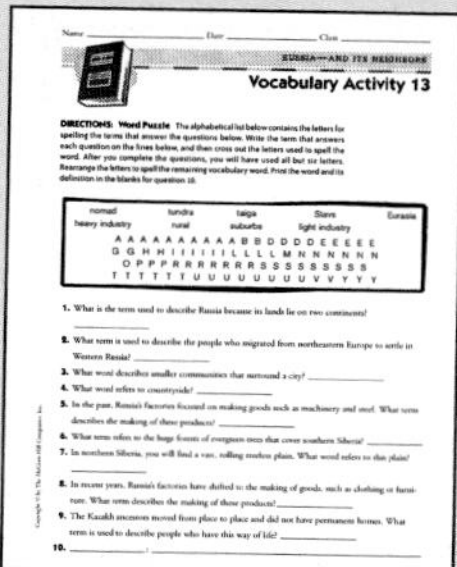

Workbook Activity 13

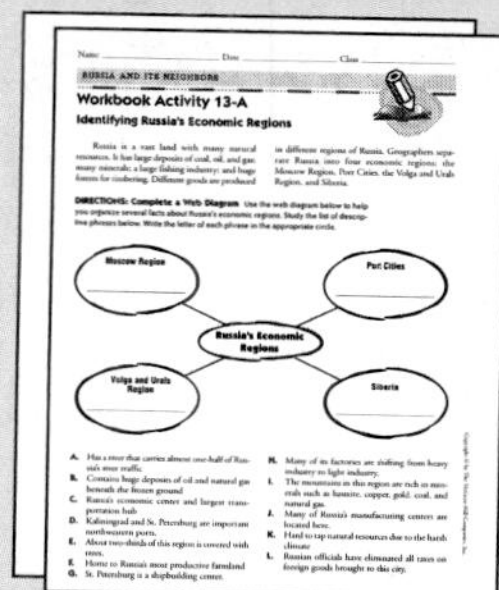

ASSESSMENT

GLENCOE'S ASSESSMENT ADVANTAGE

Chapter 13 Test, Form A

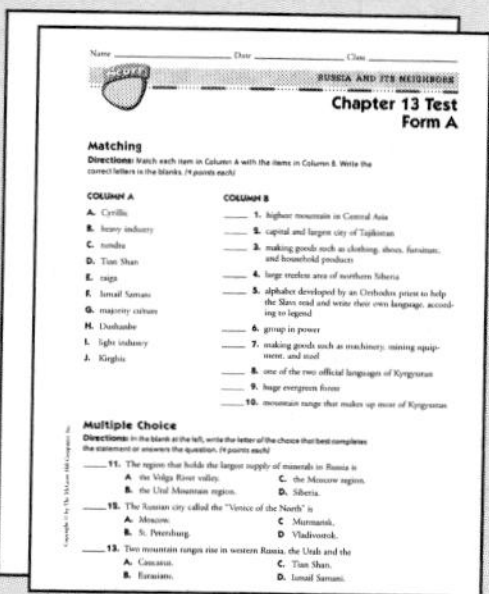

Chapter 13 Test, Form B

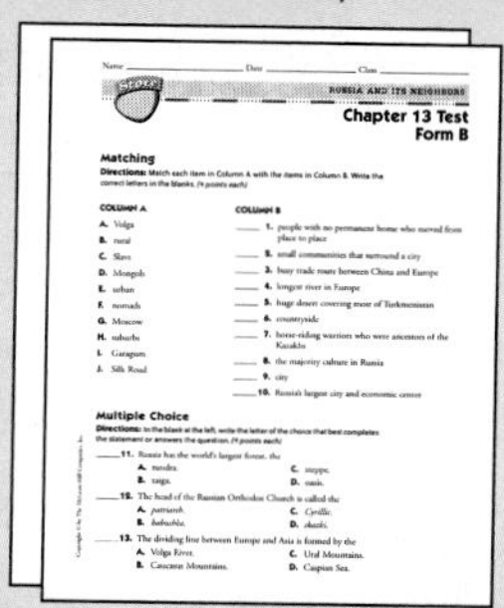

Performance Assessment Activity 13

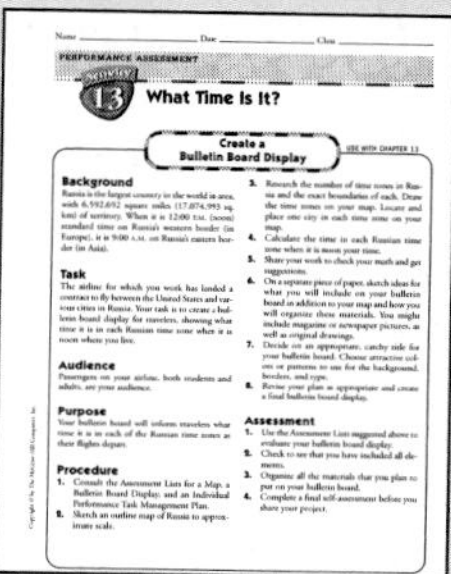

ExamView® Pro 3.0 Testmaker CD-ROM

MULTIMEDIA

- **National Geographic's The World and Its People**
- **MindJogger Videoquiz**
- **Vocabulary PuzzleMaker Software**
- **Interactive Tutor Self-Assessment CD-ROM**
- **ExamView® Pro 3.0 Testmaker CD-ROM**
- **Interactive Lesson Planner CD-ROM**
- **Interactive Teacher Edition CD-ROM**
- **Skillbuilder Interactive Workbook CD-ROM, Level 1**
- **Presentation Plus! CD-ROM**
- **Audio Program**

SPANISH RESOURCES

The following Spanish language materials are available in the Spanish Resources binder:

- **Spanish Chapter Summaries**
- **Spanish Vocabulary Activities**
- **Spanish Guided Reading Activities**
- **Spanish Quizzes and Tests**
- **Spanish Take-Home Review Activities**
- **Spanish Reteaching Activities**

Meeting National Standards

Geography for Life

All of the 18 standards are demonstrated in Unit 5. The following ones are highlighted in Chapter 13:

Section 1 **EE1 The World in Spatial Terms:** Standards 1, 2, 3

EE2 Places and Regions: Standards 4, 5, 6

EE5 Environment and Society: Standards 15, 16

Section 2 **EE4 Human Systems:** Standards 9, 10, 12

Section 3 **EE3 Physical Systems:** Standards 7, 8

EE4 Human Systems: Standards 10, 13

EE6 The Uses of Geography: Standards 17, 18

For a complete listing of National Geography Standards and entire text correlation, see pages T22–T29.

Chapter 13 Planning Guide

SECTION RESOURCES

Daily Objectives	Reproducible Resources	Multimedia Resources
Section 1 **The Russian Land** **Suggested Pacing = 1 day** **1.** Describe the landforms and climates found in Russia. **2.** Compare Russia's economic regions.	Reproducible Lesson Plan 13-1 Daily Lecture and Discussion Notes 13-1 Guided Reading Activity 13-1 Reading Essentials and Study Guide 13-1 Section Quiz 13-1*	Daily Focus Skills Transparency 13-1 GeoQuiz Transparency 13-1 Vocabulary PuzzleMaker Software Interactive Tutor Self-Assessment CD-ROM ExamView® Pro 3.0 Testmaker CD-ROM Presentation Plus! CD-ROM
Section 2 **The People of Russia** **Suggested Pacing = 1 day** **1.** Discuss the different ethnic groups in Russia. **2.** Explain the main features of Russian culture.	Reproducible Lesson Plan 13-2 Daily Lecture and Discussion Notes 13-2 Guided Reading Activity 13-2 Reading Essentials and Study Guide 13-2 Section Quiz 13-2*	Daily Focus Skills Transparency 13-2 Vocabulary PuzzleMaker Software Interactive Tutor Self-Assessment CD-ROM ExamView® Pro 3.0 Testmaker CD-ROM Presentation Plus! CD-ROM
Section 3 **Russia's Southern Neighbors** **Suggested Pacing = 1 day** **1.** Discuss how the people of these countries earn a living. **2.** Explain how independence from the Soviet Union has effected these countries.	Reproducible Lesson Plan 13-3 Daily Lecture and Discussion Notes 13-3 Guided Reading Activity 13-3 Reading Essentials and Study Guide 13-3 Section Quiz 13-3*	Daily Focus Skills Transparency 13-3 GeoQuiz Transparency 13-3 Vocabulary PuzzleMaker Software Interactive Tutor Self-Assessment CD-ROM ExamView® Pro 3.0 Testmaker CD-ROM Presentation Plus! CD-ROM

00:00 **Out of Time?** Assign the **Reading Essentials and Study Guide** for this chapter.

*Also available in Spanish

KEY TO ABILITY LEVELS

Teaching strategies have been coded for varying learning styles and abilities.

L1 **BASIC** activities for all students
L2 **AVERAGE** activities for average to above-average students
L3 **CHALLENGING** activities for above-average students
ELL **ENGLISH LANGUAGE LEARNER** activities

Blackline Master
Software
CD-ROM
Audiocassette
Transparency
Videocassette
Block Scheduling
DVD

ABC's of Russia

Wanda J. Petersen
Landrum Middle School
Ponte Vedra, Florida

With a partner, have students create an ABC book on Russia. Students should match the letters of the alphabet to a particular aspect of Russia. For example, *K* could stand for *Kremlin,* followed by a sentence or two describing the Kremlin. Each item should be accompanied by an illustration, whether a photograph or drawing. Students should use standard grammar, spelling, sentence structure, and punctuation in the written portions of their booklet. Students can compile the booklet on a computer, including a title page and front and back covers. The booklets can be bound and the title pages laminated and then donated to an elementary school library.

OUR WORLD TODAY Online

Use our Web site for additional resources. All essential content is covered in the Student Edition.

You and your students can visit owt.glencoe.com, the Web site companion to *Our World Today*. This innovative integration of electronic and print media offers your students a wealth of opportunities. The student text directs students to the Web site for the following options:

- Chapter Overviews
- Student Web Activities
- Self-Check Quizzes
- Textbook Updates

Answers are provided for you in the Web Activity Lesson Plan. Additional Web resources and Interactive Tutor puzzles are also available.

NATIONAL GEOGRAPHIC TEACHER'S CORNER

Index to National Geographic Magazine:

The following articles may be used for research relating to this chapter:

- "Remote Russia: Expedition to the Putorana Plateau," by Fen Montaigne, November 2000.
- "The Caspian Sea," by Robert Cullen, May 1999.
- "Russia's Iron Road," by Fen Montaigne, June 1998.
- "Nenets: Surviving on the Siberian Tundra," by Fen Montaigne, March 1998.
- "Lethal Legacy: Pollution in the Former U.S.S.R.," by Mike Edwards, August 1994.

National Geographic Society Products Available From Glencoe:

To order the following products for use with this chapter, contact your local Glencoe sales representative or call Glencoe at 1-800-334-7344:

- *STV: World Geography* (Videodisc)
- *Picture Atlas of the World* (CD-ROM)
- *ZipZapMap! World* (Software)
- *GeoBee* (CD-ROM)
- *MapPack: Asia* (Transparencies)
- *MapPack: Europe* (Transparencies)

Additional National Geographic Society Products:

To order the following products for use with this chapter, call National Geographic Society at 1-800-368-2728:

- *Complete National Geographic: 111 Years of National Geographic Magazine* (CD-ROM)
- *Rise and Fall of the Soviet Union* (Video)
- *Russia: After the U.S.S.R.* (Video)
- *1917: Revolution in Russia* (Video)
- *Asia* (Video)
- *Europe* (Video)
- *National Geographic Atlas of the World, Seventh Edition* (Book)
- *GeoKit: Weather* (Kit)
- *Physical Earth* (Map)
- *Asia: Political* (Map)
- *Europe: Political* (Map)
- *National Geographic Desk Reference* (Book)

NGS ONLINE

Access National Geographic's Web site for current events, activities, links, interactive features, and archives.
www.nationalgeographic.com

Introducing Chapter 13

Introduce students to chapter content and key terms by having them access Chapter Overview 13 at owt.glencoe.com

Chapter Objectives

1. Identify the location and the landforms of Russia.
2. Describe the economy of Russia.
3. Discuss the cultural aspects of Russia.
4. Explain how Russia's newly independent neighbors have recently changed.

GLENCOE TECHNOLOGY

NATIONAL GEOGRAPHIC

The World and Its People Video Program

Chapters 14 and 18 Russia and Its Neighbors
The following segments enhance the study of this chapter:

- **The Biggest Cat**
- **Lake Baikal**
- **Oil Boom**

Available in DVD and VHS.

MindJogger Videoquiz
Use MindJogger to preview the Chapter 13 content.

Available in VHS.

Chapter 13 Russia and Its Neighbors

The World and Its People NATIONAL GEOGRAPHIC

To learn more about Russia and its neighboring countries, view ***The World and Its People*** **Chapters 14** and **18** videos.

Our World Today online

Chapter Overview Visit the ***Our World Today: People, Places, and Issues*** Web site at owt.glencoe.com and click on **Chapter 13—Chapter Overviews** to preview information about Russia.

340

Two-Minute Lesson Launcher

Ask: What is meant by calling Russia a "Eurasian" country? *(It is found in both Europe and Asia.)* If students cannot answer, have them look at the map of the world on pages RA2–RA3. Ask for volunteers to answer the question based on Russia's location. **Then ask:** How might being in both Europe and Asia affect Russia? *(Its culture reflects both European and Asian influences.)* How might its size and location affect its ability to control its territory and influence its domestic policies? *(There's a great variety of cultural differences.)* **L2**

Introducing Chapter 13

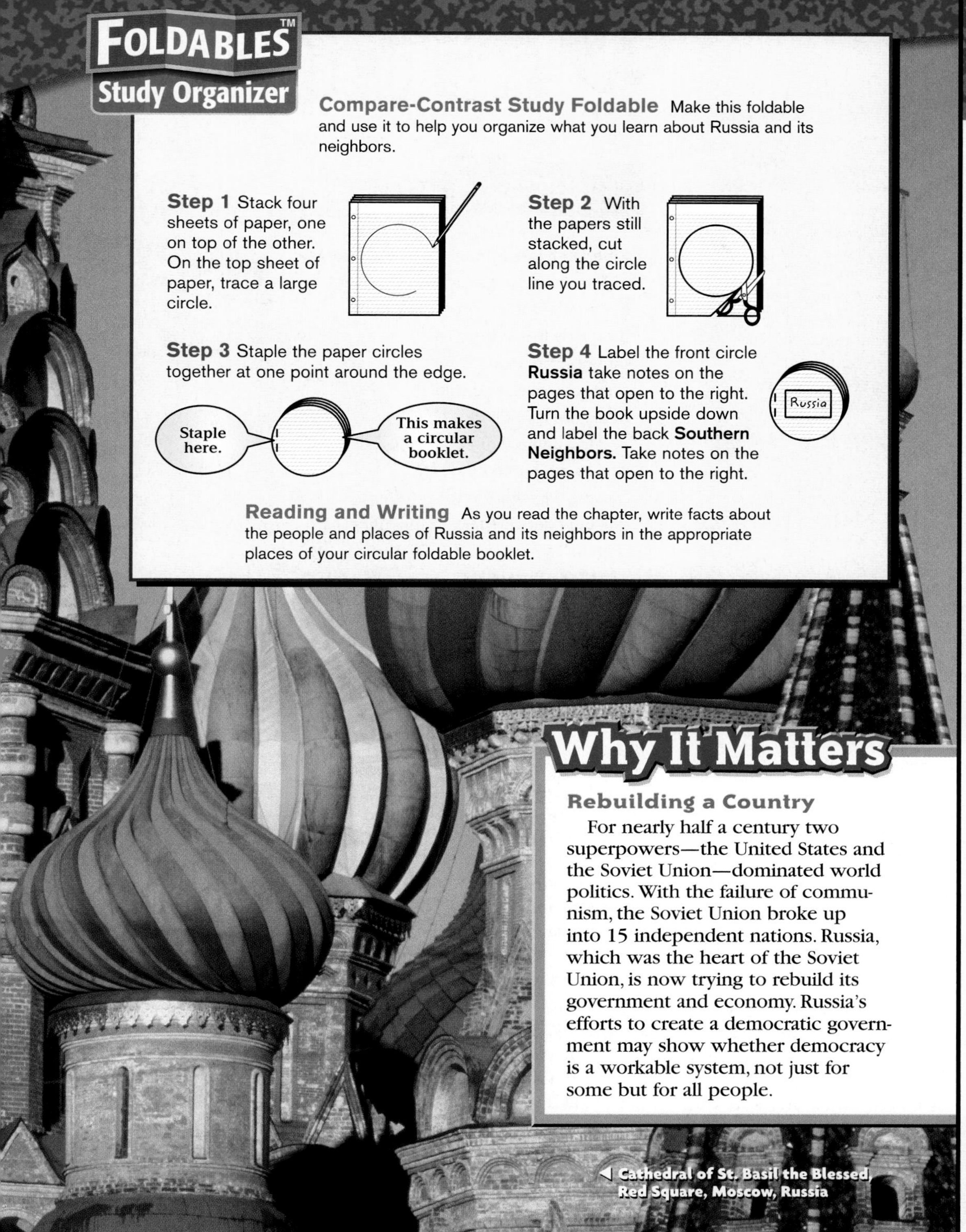

FOLDABLES™ Study Organizer

Compare-Contrast Study Foldable Make this foldable and use it to help you organize what you learn about Russia and its neighbors.

Step 1 Stack four sheets of paper, one on top of the other. On the top sheet of paper, trace a large circle.

Step 2 With the papers still stacked, cut along the circle line you traced.

Step 3 Staple the paper circles together at one point around the edge.

Staple here.
This makes a circular booklet.

Step 4 Label the front circle **Russia** take notes on the pages that open to the right. Turn the book upside down and label the back **Southern Neighbors.** Take notes on the pages that open to the right.

Russia

Reading and Writing As you read the chapter, write facts about the people and places of Russia and its neighbors in the appropriate places of your circular foldable booklet.

Why It Matters

Rebuilding a Country

For nearly half a century two superpowers—the United States and the Soviet Union—dominated world politics. With the failure of communism, the Soviet Union broke up into 15 independent nations. Russia, which was the heart of the Soviet Union, is now trying to rebuild its government and economy. Russia's efforts to create a democratic government may show whether democracy is a workable system, not just for some but for all people.

◀ Cathedral of St. Basil the Blessed, Red Square, Moscow, Russia

FOLDABLES™ Study Organizer

Purpose Students make and use a compare-contrast foldable to help them organize the similarities and differences between Russia and the Eurasian republics—Russia's southern neighbors. As students read the chapter and fill in information on their foldable, they analyze the similarities and the differences of the people, places, and economies of Russia and its southern neighbors.

Have students complete ***Reading and Study Skills Foldables*** Activity 13.

Why It Matters

On the board write: Armenia, Georgia, Azerbaijan, Kazakhstan, Kyrgyzstan, Tajikistan, Uzbekistan, and Turkmenistan. Ask students what they know about these countries. There will probably be little response. Divide students into groups for each country. Have each group locate its country on a map and find out information about the country's economy, government, and social issues since becoming independent from the Soviet Union.

About the Photo

Ask your students if anyone can identify the building in the photo, what it might be used for, and what's special about its features. The cathedral was built by Ivan the Terrible in the 16th century to commemorate a Russian victory. It is actually eight churches built around a ninth, all on the same foundation. A tenth church was added later over the grave of Basil the Blessed, and that's how the cathedral got its present name. The cathedral is located in Red Square, a vast open space that has been the site of military parades and celebrations, as well as demonstrations. **Ask: What makes this cathedral unique to Russia? What are the similarities and differences between it and the National Cathedral in Washington, D.C.?**

Focus

Section Objectives

1. Describe the landforms and climates found in Russia.
2. Compare Russia's economic regions.

BELLRINGER Skillbuilder Activity

Project transparency and have students answer questions.

This activity is also available as a blackline master.

Daily Focus Skills Transparency 13-1

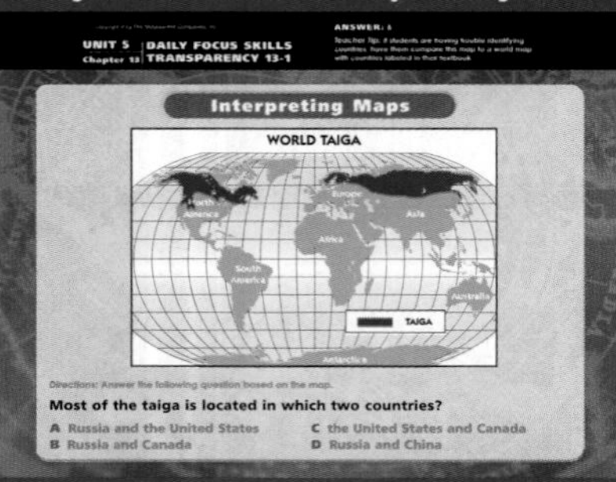

Guide to Reading

■ **Accessing Prior Knowledge**
Before students look at this chapter, ask them what animals they think live in Russia. Then have them read the Exploring Our World feature. **Ask: Are you surprised that tigers live in Russia?** Have them write other facts about Russia that surprise them.

■ **Vocabulary Precheck**
Have students speculate on the meaning of *tundra*. Then ask them to find the term in the text to check the definition.

Guide to Reading

Main Idea

Most people in Russia live west of the Urals, where the climate is mild. The people of Russia have met the challenges created by the country's gigantic size and harsh climates.

Terms to Know

- Eurasia
- urban
- suburb
- consumer goods
- rural
- tundra
- taiga
- steppe
- communism
- heavy industry
- light industry

Reading Strategy

Create a chart like this one. Give a specific name of each type of physical feature listed.

Russia	
Lakes	
Mountains	
Plateaus	
Rivers	

NATIONAL GEOGRAPHIC Exploring Our World

Siberian tigers hunt in the eastern forests of Russia—sometimes even climbing trees to find food. Only a few hundred now live in the wild, though. The animals they hunt—elk, deer, and wild boar—are dwindling, and the tigers themselves are hunted by people. Poachers who kill the tigers illegally can sell a skin for $15,000. Russia is trying to enforce laws to save these animals.

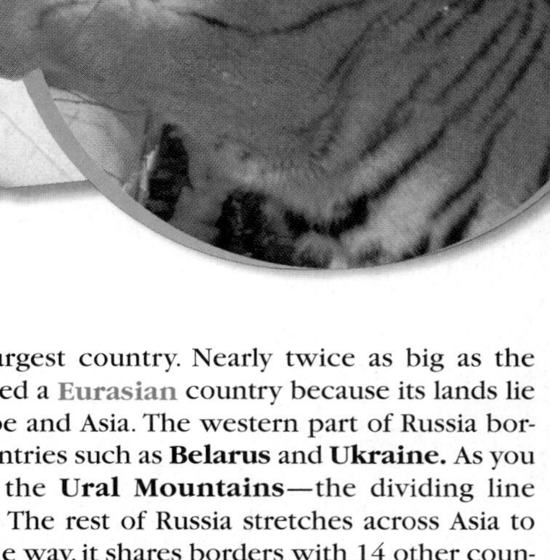

Russia is the world's largest country. Nearly twice as big as the United States, Russia is called a **Eurasian** country because its lands lie on two continents—Europe and Asia. The western part of Russia borders eastern European countries such as **Belarus** and **Ukraine.** As you move east, you run into the **Ural Mountains**—the dividing line between Europe and Asia. The rest of Russia stretches across Asia to the Pacific Ocean. Along the way, it shares borders with 14 other countries. Russia is so wide that it includes 11 time zones from east to west. When it is 12:00 P.M. (noon) in eastern Russia and people are eating lunch, people in western Russia are still sound asleep at 1:00 A.M.

Russia's Climate

As you can see from the map on page 334, Russia's southern border is in the middle latitudes while the north reaches past the **Arctic Circle.** Russia has a long coastline along the **Arctic Ocean.** Ice makes shipping difficult or impossible most of the year. Even many of Russia's ports on the Baltic Sea and Pacific Ocean are closed by ice part of the year.

Section Resources

Reproducible Masters
- Reproducible Lesson Plan 13-1
- Daily Lecture and Discussion Notes 13-1
- Guided Reading Activity 13-1
- Reading Essentials and Study Guide 13-1
- Section Quiz 13-1

Transparencies
- Daily Focus Skills Transparency 13-1
- GeoQuiz Transparency 13-1

Multimedia
- Vocabulary PuzzleMaker Software
- Interactive Tutor Self-Assessment CD-ROM
- Presentation Plus! CD-ROM
- ExamView® Pro 3.0 Testmaker CD-ROM

Russia's gigantic size and harsh climates make transportation difficult within the country as well. If you visited Russia, you would discover that, unlike in the United States, railroads, rivers, and canals still are important means of getting around. With about 100,000 miles (160,000 km) of track, railroads are the leading movers of people and goods in Russia.

European Russia Two mountain ranges rise in western Russia—the Urals and the Caucasus (KAW•kuh•suhs). The Ural Mountains, very old and worn down, do not reach very high. Their length is extensive, though, running from the Arctic Ocean to Russia's southern boundary. The Ural Mountains form the geographical boundary between the continents of Europe and Asia.

In general, the part of Russia that lies in Europe is warmer than Asian Russia. Large plains cover European Russia, which lies west of the Ural Mountains. The plains have a mild climate, and about 75 percent of the population lives in European Russia. This region holds the national capital, **Moscow,** and other important cities such as **St. Petersburg** and **Volgograd.**

Russia's **urban,** or city, areas are large and modern with stone or concrete buildings and wide streets. Tall buildings hold apartments for

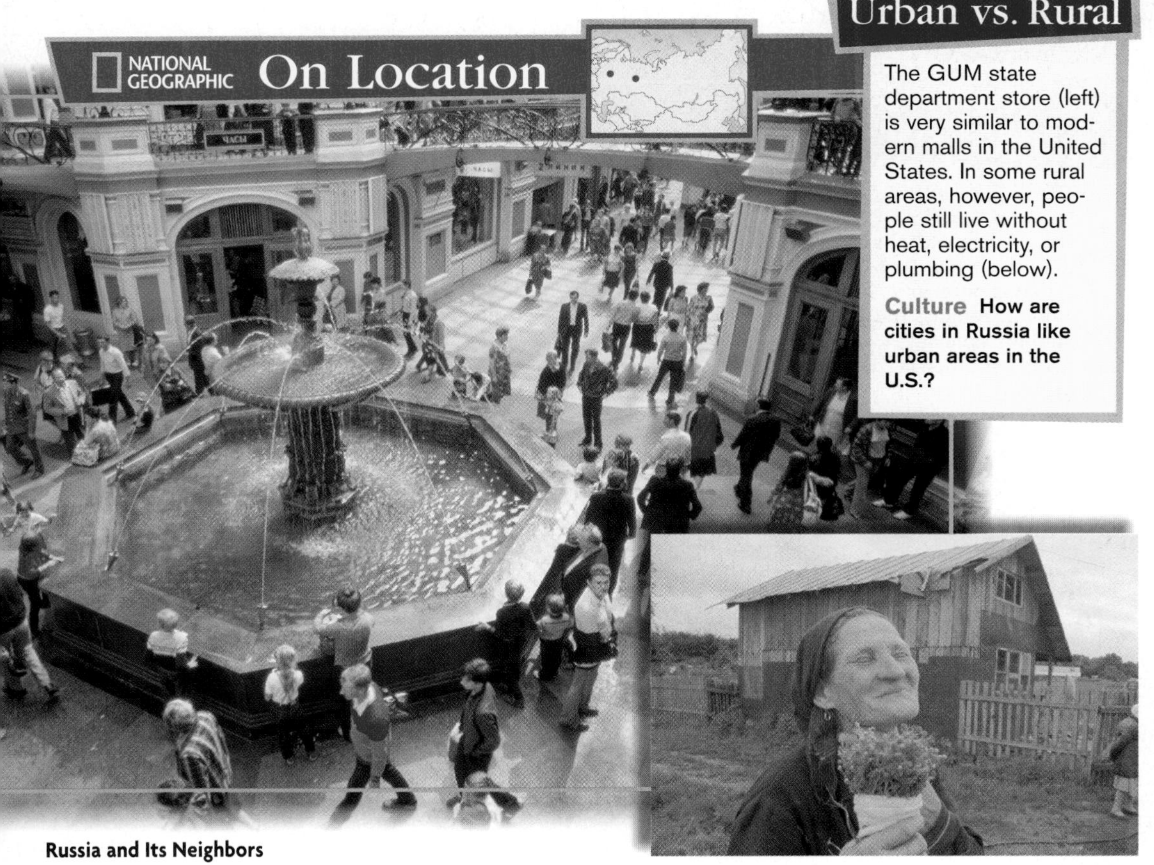

Urban vs. Rural

The GUM state department store (left) is very similar to modern malls in the United States. In some rural areas, however, people still live without heat, electricity, or plumbing (below).

Culture How are cities in Russia like urban areas in the U.S.?

Chapter 13

Section 1, pages 342–348

TEACH

Making Predictions Ask students to analyze how Russia's harsh climates might affect ways of life there. Call on volunteers to offer their suggestions to the class and give the reasons for their ideas. **L1**

Daily Lecture Notes 13-1

RUSSIA AND ITS NEIGHBORS

Daily Lecture and Discussion Notes 13-1

The Russian Land (pages 342–348)

Did You Know?

Russia's most identifiable architectural feature is its onion-domed churches, which evolved when the wooden churches of the north were translated into brick and colorful tilework. In the world of art, religious icons, futurism, and revolutionary graphic art are instantly recognizable Russian forms.

I. Russia's Climate *(pages 342–346)*

A. Russia's southern border is in the middle latitudes while the north reaches past the **Arctic Circle.** Russia has a long coastline along the **Arctic Ocean.**

B. Many of Russia's ports on the Baltic Sea and Pacific Ocean are closed by ice part of the year.

C. Russia's gigantic size and harsh climates make transportation difficult within the

More About the Photos

The GUM The largest department store in Moscow is referred to by its acronym *GUM,* taken from the three Russian words that mean "state department store." The store sells everything from coats to caviar.

Caption Answer They're large and modern, with tall buildings, wide streets, and many people.

Cooperative Learning Activity

Writing a Petition Have students form small groups, each representing a different region of Russia. Ask them to imagine that they are Russian citizens and they must draw up a petition to make one change in the region. Students should use a problem-solving process to create their petitions, including identifying the problem they want to change, gathering information, considering options, advantages, or disadvantages, and deciding on a solution. Possible topics include landforms, climates, economics, environment, cultures, and history. Their petitions should incorporate the main and supporting ideas they need to make their point. Afterwards, the groups should orally present their petitions to the rest of the class. **L2**

EE The Uses of Geography: Standard 18

More About the Photos

The Steppes The soil on the steppes has a 3-foot (91-cm) thick top layer of humus, which is why it is so fertile.

Caption Answer evergreen trees

Making Comparisons Write the headings "City Life" and "Country Life." Ask students to offer information on urban and rural life in Russia and the factors responsible for people choosing either city or country life. Note their responses under the appropriate heading. Then have students use the information to write a script for a brief television news feature on life in Russia. Call on volunteers to present their features to the rest of the class. **L2**

Guided Reading Activity 13-1

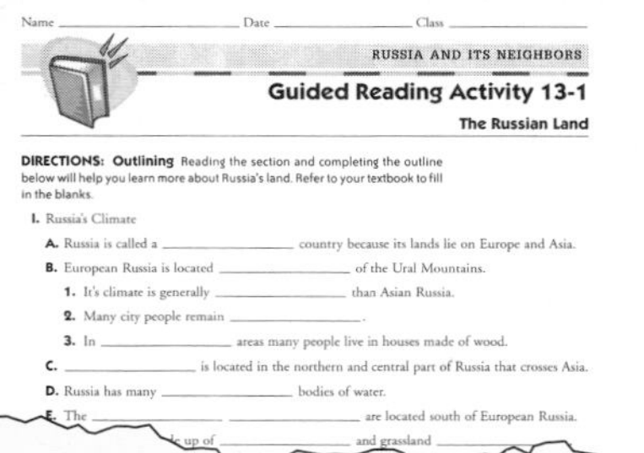
Name ______ Date ______ Class ______

RUSSIA AND ITS NEIGHBORS

Guided Reading Activity 13-1

The Russian Land

DIRECTIONS: Outlining Reading the section and completing the outline below will help you learn more about Russia's land. Refer to your textbook to fill in the blanks.

I. Russia's Climate

A. Russia is called a ______ country because its lands lie on Europe and Asia.

B. European Russia is located ______ of the Ural Mountains.

1. It's climate is generally ______ than Asian Russia.

2. Many city people remain ______.

3. In ______ areas many people live in houses made of wood.

C. ______ is located in the northern and central part of Russia that crosses Asia.

D. Russia has many ______ bodies of water.

E. The ______ ______ are located south of European Russia.

...up of ______ and grassland ______.

NATIONAL GEOGRAPHIC On Location

Vegetation in Russia

The tundra (left) is found in northern Russia. South of the tundra is the huge expanse of taiga woods (center). The steppes dominate southwest Russia (right).

Place **What type of vegetation grows on the taiga?**

hundreds of small families. Many of these apartments are small and cramped, however. When people in cities relax, they spend time with their families and friends, take walks through parks, or attend concerts, movies, and the circus.

Russian cities have changed in recent years. New cars speed down Moscow's streets. More people are building large houses outside the city limits, where few people lived before. As a result, Russia is developing its first **suburbs,** or smaller communities that surround a city.

Large numbers of Russia's city dwellers remain poor. These people lack the money to buy the **consumer goods** that are now more and more available. Consumer goods are items sold directly to the public, such as clothes, radios, and automobiles. The poor must stand in long lines to get the food they need to survive. Some of them resent the success of the newly wealthy people.

In Russia's **rural** areas, or countryside, most people live in houses built of wood. As in the United States, the quality of health care and education is often lower in rural areas than in the cities. Over the years, many people have left rural areas to find work in Russia's cities.

Tundra In the northern part of Siberia is a large, treeless region where only the top few inches of the ground thaw during the summer. This is called **tundra.** The few people who live there make their living by fishing, hunting seals and walruses, or herding reindeer. Because there are

Critical Thinking Activity

Interpreting Information Have students research the Trans-Siberian Railroad and create a display about it. Students' projects should address the physical and economic aspects of the railroad. The display should include a map of the route the railroad follows, images revealing the landscape through which the train passes, and text or visual information that describes the economic regions that the railroad traverses. Students should explain why the route goes through particular towns and regions. **L1**

EE1 The World in Spatial Terms: Standard 3

few trees, many of the huts are made of walrus skins. For two months out of the year, while the sun stays visible for most of the night, temperatures may rise to 70°F. (21°C) Because the distances are great and the land is usually covered in ice and snow, people may use helicopters for travel.

South of the tundra is the world's largest forest, the taiga (TY•guh). The forest of evergreen trees stretches 4,000 (6,436 km) miles across the country in a belt 1,000 to 2,000 (1,609 to 3,218 km) miles wide. Like the tundra, few people live in this area. Those who do support themselves by lumbering or hunting. This area is so sparsely populated that forest fires sometimes burn for weeks before anyone notices.

Inland Water Areas Russia touches many inland bodies of water. In the southwest, it borders on the **Black Sea.** Through this sea, Russia can reach the Mediterranean Sea. If you look at the physical map on page 334, you will find another large sea in southwestern Russia—the **Caspian Sea.** About the size of California, the Caspian Sea is actually the largest inland body of water in the world. Like the Great Salt Lake in Utah, the Caspian Sea has salt water, not freshwater. Russia shares this sea with four other countries—Azerbaijan, Iran, Turkmenistan, and Kazakhstan.

High in the Central Siberian Plateau is **Lake Baikal.** This is the world's deepest freshwater lake. In fact, Lake Baikal holds almost 20 percent of the world's supply of unfrozen freshwater. It is also the world's oldest lake, dating back more than 30 million years. Some of the plant and fish species in the lake can be traced to prehistoric times. No other lake in the world has so many unusual and rare species. As a result, Lake Baikal is a huge natural laboratory that attracts scientists from all over the world. Tourists travel by train to see the lake's shimmering blue waters.

Unfortunately, a large paper mill nearby has polluted the Lake Baikal region. The paper mill is a major source of jobs and wealth. An important problem for this region is how to both save the lake and keep the badly needed industry.

Russia has several important rivers. The **Volga**—the longest river in Europe—is an important transportation route. It and other rivers of European Russia are connected by canals. These transport people and goods from one city to another.

The Caucasus and Central Asia To the south of European Russia lay the high, rugged **Caucasus Mountains.** This is a fertile region of valleys where many non-Russian people live. Thirteen different ethnic groups live in the eight countries, or republics, that border Russia in this region. Many, like the Armenians, have cultures far older than that of the Russians.

Central Asia is a land of desert and grassland steppes occupied by Turkish- and Persian-speaking peoples. These people were forced to settle down on the land as farmers by the conquering Russians. Fewer than 10 percent of the people here even speak Russian. You will learn more about the countries in these regions in Section 3.

✓Reading Check **What is an important problem for the Lake Baikal region?**

Fighting Pollution

In the United States, our government passes strong laws to prevent or limit pollution. However, some companies that contribute to the pollution problem fight the laws because making their companies pollution-free is very expensive. Fortunately, our government is strong and able to enforce the anti-pollution laws. In Russia, however, the new government is not strong enough to enforce the anti-pollution laws it has passed and many companies are still polluting areas such as Lake Baikal.

Chapter 13

Section 1, pages 342–348

Making Generalizations

Ask students to brainstorm words that describe Siberia. *(Possibilities include unpopulated, cold, treeless, tundra, and so on.)* Have them write a paragraph about Siberia using those words.

Measure student knowledge of physical features and political entities.

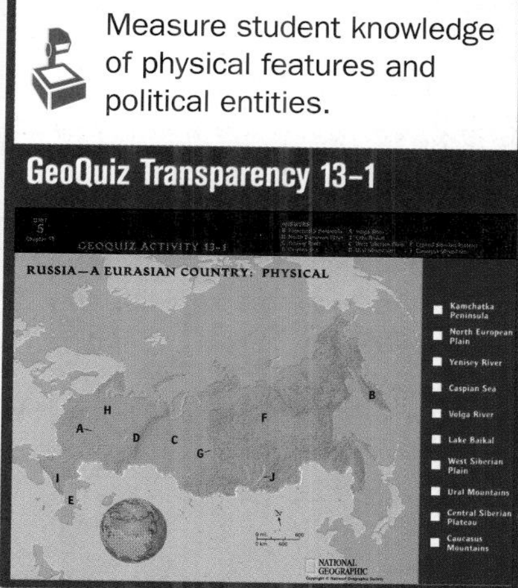

Note-taking tip

Have students look at the Main Idea in the Guide to Reading on page 342. Tell them to identify the two phrases that describe Russia in that sentence *(most people live west of Urals, meet challenge of gigantic size and harsh climates)* and write them on a sheet of paper. As students read the section, have them list facts that support each phrase.

✓ Reading Check Answer

pollution

Content Background

The Volga River Russia's Volga River is the longest river in Europe and the chief river of western Russia. It flows nearly 2,200 miles (3,541 km) from Moscow to the Caspian Sea. The area along the river holds a large part of Russia's population and for centuries has been a vital part of Russian agriculture. The Volga has long been one of the chief means of transporting goods in Russia. Today transport is hampered by dams and reservoirs built along the river to provide cities with water and hydroelectric power. Still, the river and its tributaries carry more than half of the freight moved along Russia's inland waterways. **Ask:** **How do Russians use the Volga?** *(for agriculture and transportation)* **How have they modified it?** *(by building dams and reservoirs)* **Why did the Russians build these structures?** *(to provide water and power)*

Chapter 13

Section 1, pages 342–348

Organizing Information
Have students create a chart with the economic regions as column headings. Have them write these row labels: "Location," "Resources," "Industry," and "Agriculture." As they read, have them fill in the chart with information from the text.

Cultural Kaleidoscope

Russia In the past, Russian and Soviet governments banished criminals and political prisoners to the frigid lands of Siberia. Prisoners were forced to work in factories and mines. Today the Russian government offers high salaries and long vacations to attract workers to the region.

Applying Map Skills

Answers

1. coal, petroleum, natural gas
2. corn, barley, oats, potatoes, and flax

Skills Practice
Where are most of Russia's mineral resources found? *(Siberia)*

Russia's Economic Regions

Russia has large deposits of coal, oil, and natural gas. It also has many minerals, including nickel, iron ore, tin, and gold. The southwestern area can produce rich yields of grains. Russia's fishing industry is among the largest in the world. The vast forests of Siberia provide plenty of timber. Many people who live in Russia have jobs relating to the rich resources found there.

Even with these resources, Russia's economy is not strong. Under **communism,** it was very difficult for individual people to start their own companies or run their own farms. The state wanted people to work for government factories and on large, government-owned farms because the government had strong control over the economy and society as a whole. The Russian people have not had very much experience in creating jobs, starting businesses, and making money. You will learn more about the changing Russian economy in Chapter 14. For now, we will look at what Russia's economy produces.

NATIONAL GEOGRAPHIC

Russia: Economic Activity

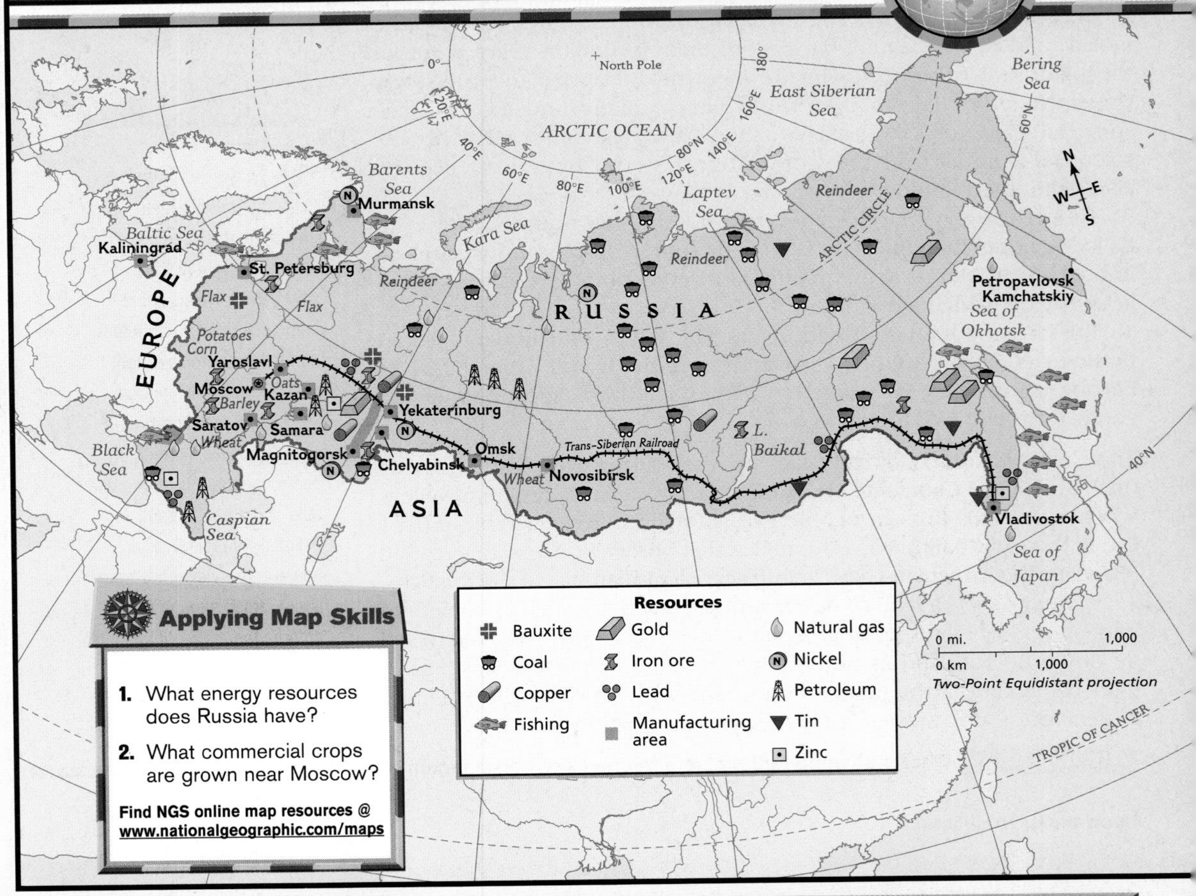

Resources

- Bauxite
- Coal
- Copper
- Fishing
- Gold
- Iron ore
- Lead
- Manufacturing area
- Natural gas
- Nickel
- Petroleum
- Tin
- Zinc

0 mi. 1,000
0 km 1,000
Two-Point Equidistant projection

Applying Map Skills

1. What energy resources does Russia have?
2. What commercial crops are grown near Moscow?

Find NGS online map resources @ www.nationalgeographic.com/maps

Team-Teaching Activity

Government Ask a teacher with a background in government to talk to the class about how governments can attract investment to their regions. Steps include tax breaks, loans for construction, cutting prices for land or facilities, or allowing businesses to keep a greater share of profits. After the discussion, organize students into four groups and assign each group one of Russia's economic regions. Instruct groups to study the economic resources in their region and then—taking the role of government officials from that region—devise a plan to attract foreign investors. Call on groups to present their plans. Then have the class discuss which plan seems most likely to succeed.

EE5 Environment and Society: Standard 16

Russia is divided into four different economic regions: the Moscow Region, Port Cities, the Volga and Urals Region, and Siberia. Today people living in these regions face many challenges.

The Moscow Region About 800 years old, Moscow is the political and cultural center of Russia. The largest city in Russia, Moscow is the country's economic center and largest transportation hub as well. Look at the economic activity map on page 346. Many of Russia's manufacturing centers are located in the western part of Russia. In the past, many of the country's factories focused on **heavy industry**, or making goods such as machinery, mining equipment, and steel. In recent years, more factories have shifted to **light industry**, or the making of such goods as clothing, shoes, furniture, and household products. Today factories make more consumer goods.

Some farming also takes place in the Moscow region. Farmers raise dairy cattle, barley, oats, potatoes, corn, and sugar beets. Other crops include flax, which is used to make textiles. Railroads and canals crisscross Moscow and the area to carry raw materials.

Port Cities Russia has two important northwestern ports—**Kaliningrad** and **St. Petersburg.** Look at the map on page 346. Do you see that Russia owns a small piece of land on the Baltic Sea separated from the rest of the country? The port of Kaliningrad is located on this land. This city is Russia's only Baltic port that remains free of ice year-round. Russian officials, hoping to increase trade here, have eliminated all taxes on foreign goods brought to this city. However, companies that deliver goods to this port must still transport their goods another 200 miles (322 km) through other countries to reach the nearest inland part of Russia. In summer when St. Petersburg's port is not frozen, ships can travel another 500 miles (805 km) north to reach this city.

St. Petersburg, once the capital of Russia, is another important port and a cultural center. The city was built by Czar Peter the Great in the early 1700s on a group of more than 100 islands connected by bridges. Large palaces stand gracefully on public squares. (You will read more about this beautiful city when we look at Russian culture.) Factories in St. Petersburg make light machinery, textiles, and scientific and medical equipment. Located on the **Neva River** near the Gulf of Finland, the city is also a shipbuilding center.

Murmansk, in Russia's far north, and **Vladivostok,** in the east, are other important port cities. Vladivostok is Russia's largest port on the Pacific Ocean. Trade in these port cities brings needed goods to the Russian people.

NATIONAL GEOGRAPHIC

Comparing Latitudes

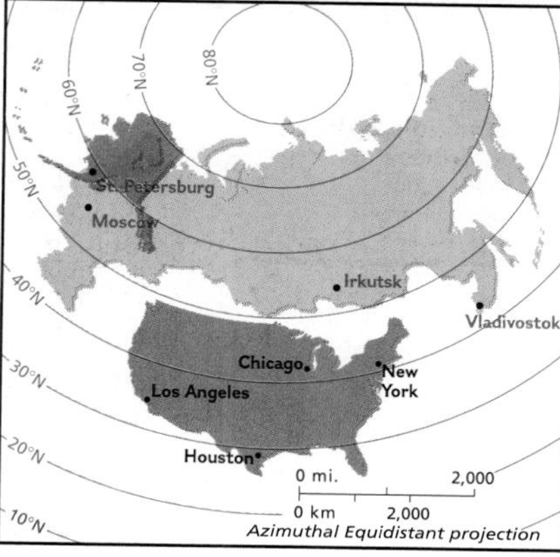

Analyzing the Map

As you can see in this map, ports in the contiguous United States are at much lower latitudes than Russian ports and are not affected by freezing weather.

Location **Look at the political map of the United States on page 475. What body of water is close to the same latitude as St. Petersburg?**

Analyzing the Map

Answer
Bering Sea

Skills Practice
Which Russian port is at the lowest latitude? *(Vladivostok)*

ASSESS

Assign Section 1 Assessment as homework or an in-class activity.

Have students use the Interactive Tutor Self-Assessment CD-ROM to review Section 13–1.

Section Quiz 13-1

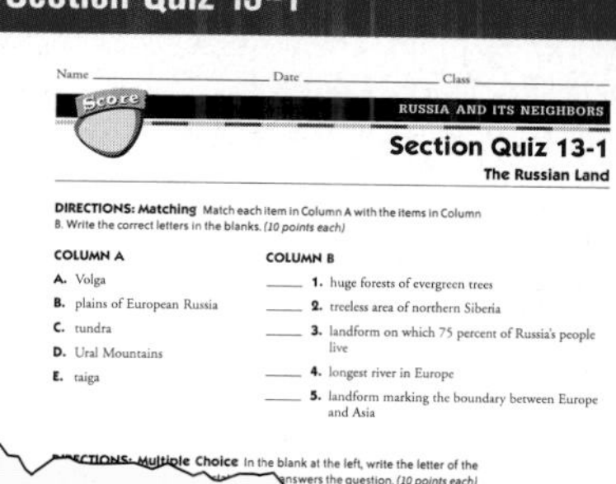
Name ______ Date ______ Class ______
RUSSIA AND ITS NEIGHBORS
Section Quiz 13-1
The Russian Land

DIRECTIONS: Matching Match each item in Column A with the items in Column B. Write the correct letters in the blanks. (10 points each)

COLUMN A	COLUMN B
A. Volga	___ 1. huge forests of evergreen trees
B. plains of European Russia	___ 2. treeless area of northern Siberia
C. tundra	___ 3. landform on which 75 percent of Russia's people live
D. Ural Mountains	___ 4. longest river in Europe
E. taiga	___ 5. landform marking the boundary between Europe and Asia

DIRECTIONS: Multiple Choice In the blank at the left, write the letter of the ... answers the question. (10 points each)

Meeting Special Needs

Interpersonal Organize the class into five groups numbered 1 through 5. Have each group split up into five subgroups called A, B, C, D, and E. Have all students in the five subgroups meet together. (That is, groups 1A through 5A get together, as do groups 1B through 5B, and so on.) Assign each subgroup one of the following topics: the Moscow region; port cities; the Volga region; the Urals region; and Siberia. Have the students in each subgroup develop ways of teaching information about the economy in their assigned region. Then send students back to the original groups. Have the subgroups take turns teaching other group members about their topic. **L1**

Refer to *Inclusion for the Middle School Social Studies Classroom Strategies and Activities* in the TCR.

Chapter 13

Section 1, pages 342–348

Objectives, goals, and answers to the Student Web Activity can be found in the Web Activity Lesson Plan at owt.glencoe.com

Reading Check Answer

because minerals and fuels of western Russia have been used up

Reteach

Write a number of false statements about Russia's economic regions. Ask for volunteers to rephrase the statements so that they are true.

Reading Essentials and Study Guide 13-1

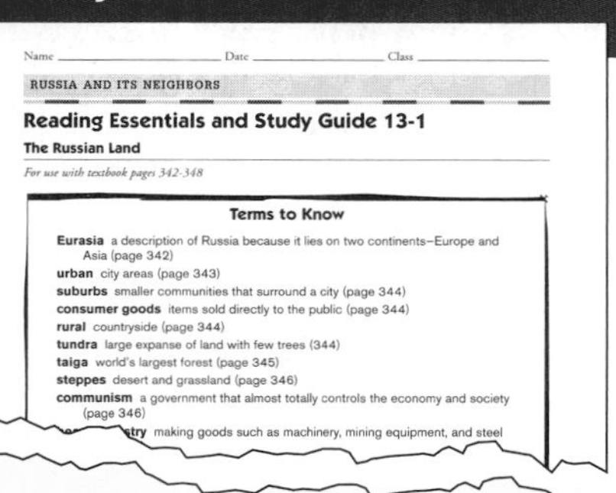

Name ______ Date ______ Class ______

RUSSIA AND ITS NEIGHBORS

Reading Essentials and Study Guide 13-1

The Russian Land

For use with textbook pages 342–348

Terms to Know

Eurasia a description of Russia because it lies on two continents—Europe and Asia (page 342)
urban city areas (page 343)
suburbs smaller communities that surround a city (page 344)
consumer goods items sold directly to the public (page 344)
rural countryside (page 344)
tundra large expanse of land with few trees (344)
taiga world's largest forest (page 345)
steppes desert and grassland (page 346)
communism a government that almost totally controls the economy and society (page 346)
...try making goods such as machinery, mining equipment, and steel

4 Close

Have students create an annotated map that describes the resources and products of Russia's different economic regions.

Web Activity Visit the ***Our World Today: People, Places, and Issues*** Web site at owt.glencoe.com and click on **Chapter 13–Student Web Activities** to learn more about St. Petersburg.

Siberia This region has the largest supply of minerals in Russia, including iron ore, uranium, gold, diamonds, and coal. Huge deposits of oil and natural gas lie beneath the frozen ground of northern Siberia. About two-thirds of Siberia is covered with trees that could support a timber industry. The people here also fish, hunt, and herd reindeer.

Tapping all of these resources is very difficult, however. Siberia is mostly undeveloped because of its harsh, cold climate. Another problem is size—it can take eight or more days to travel across all of Russia by train. Finding a way to develop the remote resources of Siberia is very important for Russia's economic future. Many of the minerals and fuels of western Russia have been used up. The industrial centers there need the resources from Siberia.

The Volga and Urals Region Tucked between the Moscow area and Siberia lies the industrial region of the Volga River and Ural Mountains. The Volga River carries almost one-half of Russia's river traffic. It provides water for irrigation and for hydroelectric power—the power generated by fast-flowing water. The region is also home to Russia's most productive farmlands.

The Ural Mountains are rich in minerals. Workers here mine copper, gold, lead, nickel, and bauxite, a mineral used to make aluminum. The mountains have energy resources of coal, oil, and natural gas.

Reading Check **Why are Siberia's mineral resources important?**

Section 1 Assessment

Defining Terms

1. **Define** Eurasian, urban, suburb, consumer goods, rural, tundra, taiga, steppe, communism, heavy industry, light industry.

Recalling Facts

2. **Culture** What is the political and cultural center of Russia?
3. **Location** What mountain range separates Europe and Asia?

Critical Thinking

4. **Analyzing Information** Why is Kaliningrad such an important port in Russia?
5. **Drawing Conclusions** How have economic changes affected the lives of people since the collapse of the Soviet Union?

Graphic Organizer

6. **Organizing Information** Create a chart like the one below and list the most important method of transportation for the locations listed.

Place	Transportation Method
Volga	
Kaliningrad	
Siberia	
Moscow	

Applying Social Studies Skills

7. **Analyzing Maps** Turn to the economic activity map on page 346. In what part of Russia does most of the manufacturing take place?

Section 1 Assessment

1. The terms are defined in the Glossary.
2. Moscow
3. Ural Mountains
4. It's the only Baltic port that is free of ice year-round.
5. It's more difficult because people are used to working for the government and are not experienced in creating jobs or running companies as individuals.
6. Charts will vary but should contain:
   Volga: boat
   Kalingrad: boat
   Siberia: train
   Moscow: train, canal boat
7. the west

Technology Skill

Evaluating a Web Site

Why Learn This Skill?

The Internet has become a valuable research tool. It is convenient to use, and the information contained on the Internet is plentiful. However, some Web site information is not necessarily accurate or reliable. When using the Internet as a research tool, the user must distinguish between quality information and inaccurate or incomplete information.

▲ The Peace Corps Web site is government sponsored.

Learning the Skill

There are a number of things to consider when evaluating a Web site. Most important is to check the accuracy of the source and content. The author and publisher or sponsor of the site should be clearly indicated, and the user must also determine the usefulness of the site. The information on the site should be current, and the design and organization of the site should be appealing and easy to navigate.

To evaluate a Web site, ask yourself the following questions:

- Are the facts on the site documented?
- Does the site contain a bibliography?
- Is the author clearly identified?
- Does the site explore the topic in-depth or only scratch the surface?
- Does the site contain links to other useful and up-to-date resources?
- Is the information easy to access? Is it properly labeled?

Practicing the Skill

Visit the Peace Corps Web site listed below and answer the following questions.

1. Who is the author or sponsor of the Web site?
2. What links does the site contain? Are they appropriate to the topic?
3. What sources were used for the information contained on the site?
4. Does the site explore the topic in-depth? Why or why not?
5. Is the design of the site appealing? Why or why not?

Applying the Skill

Locate two other Web sites about Russia. Evaluate them for accuracy and usefulness, and then compare them to the Peace Corps site listed below.
(www.peacecorps.gov/kids/world/europemed/russia.html)

Technology Skill

TEACH

Have students explore the Peace Corps Web site **www.peacecorps.gov/kids/world/europemed/russia.html** to find out about Russian food and holidays and what Russian kids like to do. Divide them into three groups, each exploring one of these subjects in detail. They should use information from this Web site and at least one other Web site. Have them use this information to make a presentation about the topic. After each presentation, ask students how Russian tastes and customs compare to Americans'. **Ask: Why are some activities the same in both cultures? L1**

ADDITIONAL SKILL PRACTICE

1. **How is the Peace Corps involved in Russian education?** *(They provide English teaching and up-to-date textbooks.)*
2. **How do you greet a friend in Russia?** *(Privyet)*

Additional Skills Resources

Chapter Skills Activity 13

GLENCOE TECHNOLOGY

Skillbuilder Interactive Workbook CD-ROM, Level 1

This interactive CD-ROM reinforces student mastery of essential social studies skills.

Practicing the Skill Answers

1. The Peace Corps
2. Links to other parts of the world where there are Peace Corps volunteers. Yes.
3. The U.S. government (specifically FirstGov, a public-private agency that provides government information on the Web)
4. It's not in-depth about Russia because the information is related to Peace Corps activities there.
5. Yes. It's tailored to children and is colorful, clear and easy to use.

Applying the Skill
Suggest that students try a search engine like Yahooligans!, Excite, or Google to find other Web sites about Russia.

Chapter 13

Section 2, pages 350–354

1 Focus

Section Objectives

1. Discuss the different ethnic groups in Russia.
2. Explain the main features of Russian culture.

BELLRINGER Skillbuilder Activity

Project transparency and have students answer questions.

This activity is also available as a blackline master.

Daily Focus Skills Transparency 13-2

UNIT 5 Chapter 13 DAILY FOCUS SKILLS TRANSPARENCY 13-2

Drawing Conclusions

FATHER FROST

Why do you think St. Nicholas became Father Frost under the Communist leadership in Russia?

Guide to Reading

Russia has produced some of the world's best-known music and literature. Ask students if they can identify any famous Russian works or their creators. When they read the section, have them note recognizable names and why they know them.

Use the Vocabulary PuzzleMaker to create crossword and word search puzzles.

Guide to Reading

Main Idea

Russia's people enjoy a culture rich in art, music, literature, and religion.

Terms to Know

- Slav
- majority culture
- minority culture

Reading Strategy

Create a chart like this one. List one or two examples for Russia beside each heading.

Art	
Music	
Literature	
Religion	

Section 2 The People of Russia

NATIONAL GEOGRAPHIC Exploring Our World

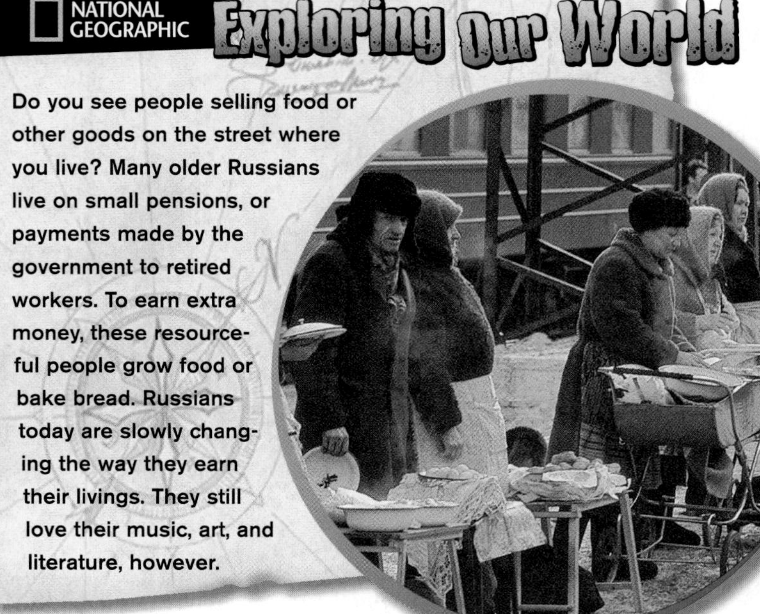

Do you see people selling food or other goods on the street where you live? Many older Russians live on small pensions, or payments made by the government to retired workers. To earn extra money, these resourceful people grow food or bake bread. Russians today are slowly changing the way they earn their livings. They still love their music, art, and literature, however.

Russia is one of the most populous countries in the world, with nearly 145 million people. It is a huge land, with more than 150 different ethnic groups. Most of the people, however, are Russian.

Ethnic Groups

Russians, along with Ukrainians and Belorussians, are part of a larger group of people called **Slavs.** Hundreds of years ago, the Slavs migrated from northeastern Europe to settle in western Russia. In Russia today, 80 percent of the people are Slavs. Slavs are the **majority culture.**

Besides the Slavs, many other ethnic groups live in Russia. Each of these groups has its own distinctive language and culture. Some of the groups have a Christian heritage, while others are Islamic, Buddhist, or Jewish. These cultures are called **minority cultures** because they are not the group that controls most of the wealth and power in the society.

Section Resources

Reproducible Masters

- Reproducible Lesson Plan 13-2
- Daily Lecture and Discussion Notes 13-2
- Guided Reading Activity 13-2
- Reading Essentials and Study Guide 13-2
- Section Quiz 13-2

Transparencies

- Daily Focus Skills Transparency 13-2

Multimedia

- Vocabulary PuzzleMaker Software
- Interactive Tutor Self-Assessment CD-ROM
- Presentation Plus! CD-ROM
- ExamView® Pro 3.0 Testmaker CD-ROM

When the Soviet Union existed, the central government kept tight control over its people. When the Soviet Union fell apart, many old feuds and remembered wrongs came to the surface. Fighting broke out among many of the people who had been enemies in the past and whose differences had never been resolved. Like many other areas of the world, one of the biggest challenges facing people in this region is to learn how to cooperate and how to protect people who belong to minority cultures.

Reading Check What is the largest, most powerful ethnic group in Russia?

Culture in Russia

Russia has a rich tradition of art, music, and literature. Russians view these cultural achievements with pride. Some of their most beloved works of art are based on religious, historical, or folk themes.

NATIONAL GEOGRAPHIC

Russia: Population Density

0 mi. 1,000
0 km 1,000
Two-Point Equidistant projection

Persons per Sq. Mi.	Persons per Sq. Km
Uninhabited	Uninhabited
Under 2	Under 1
2–60	1–25
60–125	25–50
125–250	50–100
Over 250	Over 100

Cities
- ■ City with more than 5,000,000 people
- • City with 1,000,000 to 5,000,000 people
- ○ City with 500,000 to 1,000,000 people

Applying Map Skills

1. What general area of Russia has the highest population density?
2. What is the population density of most of eastern Russia?

Find NGS online map resources @ www.nationalgeographic.com/maps

Chapter 13

Section 2, pages 350–354

Reading Check Answer

Slavs

Interdisciplinary Connections

Architecture The churches of Russia are famous for their "onion domes," bulbous domes that often have deep grooves cut into them. Russian architects developed the onion domes in the 1600s and 1700s. They are not only attractive but practical—Russia's heavy snows slide off these domes.

2 TEACH

Synthesizing Information

Find an example of a Russian folktale, or *skazki* and read it to your class. Have your students pick out familiar elements that they've heard in other fairy tales. Then list the elements that were new to them. How might these relate to what they've learned about Russia? **L1**

Applying Map Skills

Answers

1. western Russia
2. under 2 persons per square mile (1 per sq. km)

Skills Practice

Which cities have more than 5 million people? *(Moscow and St. Petersburg)*

Cooperative Learning Activity

Writing a Skit Organize students into pairs. Have students in each pair take the part of people representing two different groups in Russian society. They might be the members of different ethnic groups, people who live in a city or in the country, people from different professions, or people from western and eastern Russia. Tell the pairs to do some research in order to write a brief skit in which the two Russians they portray describe life in Russia as they know it. Through this discussion, students should be able to reveal their understanding of the differences in Russia today by identifying these different points of view. **L2**

Refer to *Inclusion for the Middle School Social Studies Classroom Strategies and Activities* in the TCR.

More About the Photo

Russian Ballet Russia has many important ballet companies. The Mariinsky Ballet—once known as the Kirov—and the Bolshoi Ballet in Moscow have influenced dancers around the world.

Caption Answer *Possible answers:* Sleeping Beauty, The Nutcracker, Swan Lake, Firebird

Daily Lecture Notes 13-2

RUSSIA AND ITS NEIGHBORS

Daily Lecture and Discussion Notes 13-2

The People of Russia (pages 350–354)

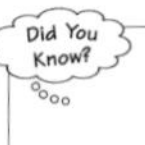

Russians originally believed in a variety of major and minor gods. According to tradition, Christianity was first introduced in Russia in A.D. 988, by Prince Vladimir whose grandmother Olga was converted to the Eastern Orthodox faith in Constantinople. The religion in Constantinople at the time was Eastern Catholicism or Orthodoxy (from Greek *orthos doxos* "true faith"); hence the Russian Church is Orthodox rather than Roman Catholic.

I. Ethnic Groups (*pages 350–351*)

A. Russia is one of the most populous countries in the world, with nearly 150 million people and 150 different ethnic groups.

B. In Russia today, 80 percent of the people are **Slavs**—the majority culture.

If you are visiting Moscow and want a quick bite for lunch, just ask where you can find a *chizburger.* Muscovites will guide you to the city's McDonald's. Be prepared to stand in line, though. About 50,000 people lunch there every day.

NATIONAL GEOGRAPHIC On Location

Russian Ballet

Ballet in Russia dates back to 1738 with the founding of the first dancing school in St. Petersburg for the children of palace servants. Today, the St. Petersburg Mariinsky Ballet, is one of Europe's leading ballet companies.

Culture Name a famous ballet written by a Russian composer.

Art and Music If you wanted to see Russian culture at its best, you would probably go to St. Petersburg. It was founded in 1703 by **Peter the Great.** Peter came to the Russian throne in 1698. Nearly 7 feet tall, he had boundless energy. After becoming czar, he took an 18-month tour of England and visited the Netherlands. Unlike most tourists, Peter stopped at shipyards, factories, and laboratories. He learned carpentry and enough skill in dentistry and surgery to want to practice on others. When he returned home, Peter forced the Russian nobility to adopt the ways of western Europe. In fact, those who refused to study math and geometry were not allowed to get married!

Peter built St. Petersburg to face Europe as a "window on the West." The city has so many beautiful museums and statues that it is also called the "Venice of the North" after the cultural center of Italy. While in St. Petersburg, you might visit Mariinsky (MAH•ree•IHN•skee) Theater. One of Russia's top ballet companies dances here, and Russian ballet dancers are famous around the world. Composer **Peter Tchaikovsky** (chy•KAWF•skee) wrote some of the world's favorite ballets, including *Sleeping Beauty* and *The Nutcracker.* **Nikolay Rimsky-Korsakov** used Russian folktales and tunes in his operas and other works. **Igor Stravinsky's** *Firebird* came from a Russian legend.

If you enjoy painting, you would definitely want to stroll through St. Petersburg's Hermitage Museum. Originally built to hold the art collection of the czars, the museum now displays these works for the public. It has works by Russian and European painters and sculptors.

Russian Literature Russians enjoy all kinds of literature. The Russian storytelling tradition is one of the oldest and richest in the world. The cultural diversity of Russia's peoples, stretching from the Baltic coast to the farthest reaches of Siberia, has resulted in a rich folk heritage. These stories, or *skazki,* were passed down orally from generation to generation, until finally they were recorded in print. Beasts and creatures with magical powers are common in these tales that grew out of a land with dark forests and long, cold winters.

The great novels and plays of Russia also reflect Russian themes. These are mostly political, however. **Leo Tolstoy's** novel *War and Peace* recounts how Russians rallied to defeat the French emperor Napoleon Bonaparte. **Fyodor Dostoyevsky** (FEE•uh•dor DAHS•tuh•YEHF•skee) wrote many novels that explored Russian life during the late 1800s. In the 1970s, **Alexander Solzhenitsyn** (SOHL•zhuh•NEET•suhn) wrote novels that revealed the harsh conditions of Communist society.

Meeting Special Needs

Inefficient Readers Point out to students that the main idea of a paragraph often appears in the first sentence, and that the remainder of the paragraph often supplies supporting details. Have them read the second paragraph on this page to see whether it follows this model. Ask volunteers, using their own words, to express the paragraph's main idea and supporting details. Then have them practice this skill with other paragraphs in this section. **L1**

Refer to *Inclusion for the Middle School Social Studies Classroom Strategies and Activities* in the TCR.

Religion in Russia In spite of Communist laws in the past forbidding the practice of religion, the Russian Orthodox Church is very popular. Russian Orthodox is a Christian faith. It is headed by a figure called the *patriarch*. The word *patriarch* is a Greek term for "father."

Russian Orthodoxy was responsible for a special alphabet called Cyrillic. According to legend, this alphabet was developed by St. Cyril, an Orthodox priest, to help the Slavs read and write their own language. He invented new letters for sounds in the Slavic language that were not present in the Greek or Latin languages.

While more than 70 percent of the Russian population is Russian Orthodox, this is by no means the only religion in Russia. Many Muslims (followers of Islam), Roman Catholics, Protestants, and Buddhists today live within Russia's boundaries. Many of the Jews that at one time lived in Russia have now emigrated to other areas. Today, fewer than 1 million Jews live in Russia.

Family Life in Russia About three-fourths of Russians live in cities, mostly in large apartment blocks. The typical Russian apartment is small, often with just a bedroom, living room, kitchen, and bathroom for a family of four. The living room may also be used as a bedroom.

It is very hard to find housing in the cities in Russia. For this reason, many generations may share the same home. This can be very helpful, however, because many Russian mothers work outside of the

Primary Source

ALEXANDER SOLZHENITSYN

(1918–)

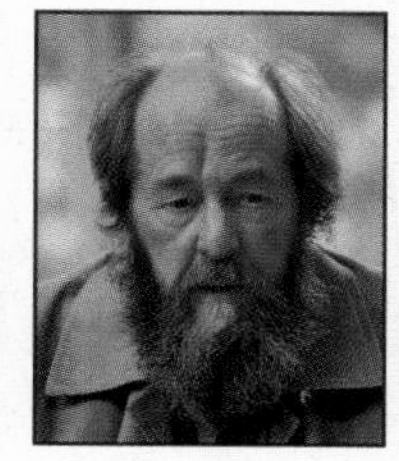

For many years Russian author Alexander Solzhenitsyn was the voice of protest for his people, speaking out through his novels about injustices in the Soviet Union's Communist system. Since the people could not "see" freedom for themselves, he used his great literary talent to bring truth to as many people as possible.

"The sole substitute for an experience which we have not ourselves lived through is art and literature,"* he wrote. *"Wherever else it fails, art always has won its fight against lies, and it always will."

Source: Nobel Lecture, 1972 by Alexander Isayevich Solzhenitsyn

Analyzing Primary Sources

1. What does Solzhenitsyn mean when he says that literature can substitute for an experience we have not had? Do you agree?
2. Describe an event you "experienced" through art. This might include a scary story or a powerful scene from a film.

Team-Teaching Activity

Literature Invite a literature teacher to class to describe Nikolai Gogol's play *The Government Inspector* (often called *The Inspector General*). In this play, written in the 1830s during czarist times, corrupt town officials fear the upcoming arrival of a government inspector who is to enter their midst in disguise. When a stranger enters the town, the officials assume he is the inspector and treat him with overwhelming courtesy, which the clever stranger takes full advantage of. After he leaves, the officials are shocked when the real inspector shows up. Have the teacher explain the use of irony and satire in this and other works of Russian literature. Then have students give examples of Russian life and explain why they would be appropriate for satire. **L2**

EE2 Places and Regions: Standard 6

Chapter 13

Section 2, pages 350–354

Guided Reading Activity 13–2

Name ________ Date ________ Class ________

RUSSIA AND ITS NEIGHBORS

Guided Reading Activity 13-2

The People of Russia

DIRECTIONS: Summarizing Reading the section and completing the summary paragraphs below will help you learn more about the people of Russia. Use your textbook to fill in the blanks.

Most of the people in Russia are **(1)** ________. They are part of a larger group of people called **(2)** ________. They make up 80 percent of Russia's people and are the **(3)** ________ ________. Other ethnic groups also live in Russia. These cultures are called **(4)** ________ ________, because they are not the most powerful group. When the **(5)** ________ ________ fell apart, fighting broke out among many of the people whose differences had never been resolved.

The city of **(6)** ________ ________ is an important ... was founded in 1703 by **(7)** ________

Assign Section 2 Assessment as homework or an in-class activity.

Have students use the Interactive Tutor Self-Assessment CD-ROM to review Section 13–2.

Primary Source

Answers

1. Solzhenitsyn believes that a good writer can describe a physical or emotional experience in a way that allows readers to feel, or at least understand, the experience as if they had lived it themselves. Students would probably prefer reading Solzhenitsyn's experiences rather than living them—he wrote about the terrible times he endured in a Soviet prison.
2. Answers will vary, but students should describe why they felt differently from other times they read a book or watched a movie.

Chapter 13

Section 2, pages 350–354

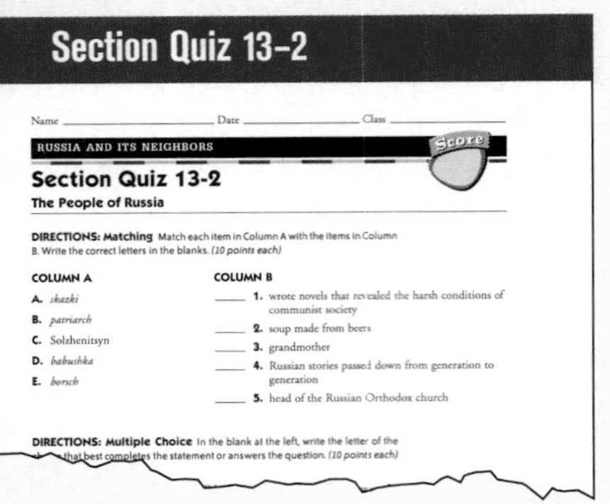

Section Quiz 13-2

Name ______ Date ______ Class ______

RUSSIA AND ITS NEIGHBORS

Score

Section Quiz 13-2

The People of Russia

DIRECTIONS: Matching Match each item in Column A with the items in Column B. Write the correct letters in the blanks. *(10 points each)*

COLUMN A	COLUMN B
A. *skazki*	____ 1. wrote novels that revealed the harsh conditions of communist society
B. *patriarch*	____ 2. soup made from beets
C. Solzhenitsyn	____ 3. grandmother
D. *babushka*	____ 4. Russian stories passed down from generation to generation
E. *borsch*	____ 5. head of the Russian Orthodox church

DIRECTIONS: Multiple Choice In the blank at the left, write the letter of the ... that best completes the statement or answers the question. *(10 points each)*

Reading Check Answer

Families get together to celebrate holidays.

Reading Essentials and Study Guide 13-2

Name ______ Date ______ Class ______

RUSSIA AND ITS NEIGHBORS

Reading Essentials and Study Guide 13-2

The People of Russia

For use with textbook pages 350-354

Terms to Know

Slavs people who, hundreds of years ago, migrated from northeastern Europe to settle in western Russia (page 350)

minority culture not the most powerful group (page 350)

majority culture the most powerful group (page 350)

Drawing from Experience

How many people from different ethnic groups or cultures do you know? Russia has more than 150 different ethnic groups.

In the last section you learned about the Russian land and climates. ... the country's people and culture.

Enrich

Have students research and report on relations between the United States and Russia since the end of the Cold War.

4 Close

Have students create a group of picture postcards showing Russia today. They should have a picture on one side and text about the site on the other.

▲ A babushka selling Russian folk art

home. The grandmother, or *babushka*, may take care of the cooking, cleaning, and caring for the young children. Shopping for food can take a long time because it sometimes means waiting in long lines.

There are many similarities between American and Russian women. As in the United States, women and men have equal rights in Russia. But also like the United States, women are still expected to do most of the household work. Women in Russia earn less than men for the same work. There is an active women's movement in Russia, and many women have begun to demand more help in the home from Russian men.

Celebrations and Food Russians enjoy small family get-togethers as well as national holidays. New Year's Eve is the most festive nonreligious holiday for Russians. Children decorate a fir tree and exchange presents with others in their families. Russians also celebrate the first day of May with parades and speeches. May Day honors Russian workers.

If you have dinner with a Russian family, you might begin with a big bowl of *borscht,* a soup made from beets, or *shchi,* a soup made from cabbage. Next, you might have meat turnovers, called *piroshki.* For the main course, you are likely to eat meat, poultry, or fish with boiled potatoes. On special occasions, Russians like to eat caviar. This delicacy is eggs of the sturgeon, a fish from the Caspian Sea.

Reading Check **What are some ways that Russian and American cultures are similar?**

Section 2 Assessment

Defining Terms

1. Define Slav, majority culture, minority culture.

Recalling Facts

2. Culture What Russian composer wrote the world famous ballets *Sleeping Beauty* and *The Nutcracker*?

3. Government What did the Communist government try to do to religion in Russia?

4. Culture What is the major religion of Russia?

Critical Thinking

5. Synthesizing Information How would your family's living conditions change if you lived in a typical Russian apartment?

6. Making Predictions Art ideas are frequently drawn from life. What themes do you think you will see in future Russian arts?

Graphic Organizer

7. Organizing Information Create a diagram like this one, and list two facts for each topic in the four outer ovals.

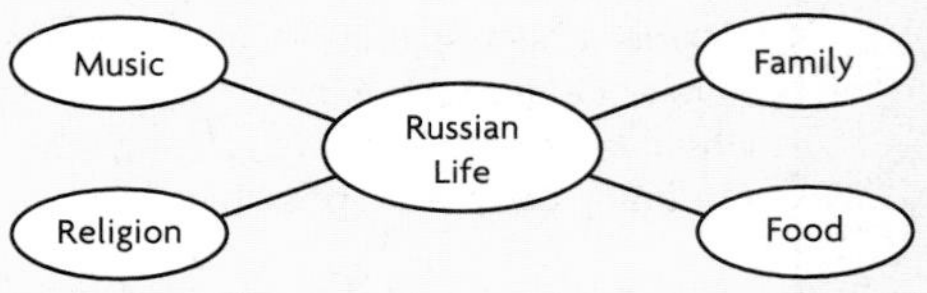

Applying Social Studies Skills

8. Analyzing Maps Look at the population density map on page 351. What city is located at about 55°N latitude and 38°E longitude? What is the estimated population of this city?

354 CHAPTER 13

Section 2 Assessment

1. The terms are defined in the Glossary.
2. Tchaikovsky
3. The Communists passed laws forbidding its practice.
4. Russian Orthodox
5. Student answers will vary but they should talk about cramped conditions and different generations living together.
6. *Possible answer:* Art in the future will probably address the difficulties Russians experience in making the transition to a free market economy and to democracy.
7. Student diagrams should be supported by facts from the section.
8. Moscow, more than 5 million people

Making Connections

CULTURE | GOVERNMENT | PEOPLE | TECHNOLOGY

Count Leo Tolstoy

Count Leo Tolstoy (1828–1910) was a famous Russian novelist. Two of his epic works are *War and Peace* and *Anna Karenina.* What is not generally known is that Tolstoy also wrote for children. He wrote: "[These writings] will be used to teach generations of all Russian children, from the czar's to the peasant's, and from these readers they will receive their first poetic impressions, and having written these books, I can now die in peace."

Russian literature, even stories for children, contains more suffering and tragedy than American children would appreciate. The stories also celebrate qualities such as helpfulness, compassion, mercy, and justice. These are the values needed to survive difficult times. This story is an example of just such literature.

The Grandfather and His Little Grandson

by Count Leo Tolstoy (1828–1910)

The grandfather had become very old. His legs would not carry him, his eyes could not see, his ears could not hear, and he was toothless. And when he ate, he was untidy. His son and the son's wife no longer allowed him to eat with them at the table and had him take his meals near the stove. They gave him his food in a cup. Once he tried to move the cup closer to him and it fell to the floor and broke. The daughter-in-law scolded the old man, saying that he damaged everything around the house and broke their cups, and she warned him that from that day on she would give him his food in a wooden dish. The old man sighed and said nothing.

One day the old man's son and his wife were sitting in their hut, resting. Their little son was playing on the floor. He was putting together something out of small bits of wood. His father asked him: "What are you making, Misha?" And Misha said: "I'm making a wooden bucket. When you and Mommie get old, I'll feed you out of this wooden bucket."

The young peasant and his wife looked at each other and tears appeared in their eyes. They were shamed to have treated the old man so unkindly, and from that day they again ate with him at the table and took better care of him.

Source: "The Grandfather and His Little Grandson" from *A Harvest of Russian Children's Literature,* edited by Miriam Morton. Copyright © 1967. University of California Press (Berkeley and Los Angeles, CA)

▲ Russian grandfather

Making the Connection

1. What reasons did Leo Tolstoy give for writing stories for children?
2. What do you think the young peasant and his wife learned from their son?
3. **Making Comparisons** Compare this story with one you learned as a child. How are they different? How are they the same?

Making the Connection

1. He wanted to teach children and give them their first introduction to literature.
2. that if they treat the old man unkindly their son will learn from their actions and treat them the same way someday
3. Student answers will vary, but you might find some appropriate stories that they can compare to this one.

Making Connections

TEACH

Tolstoy once wrote: "Happy families are all alike. Every unhappy family is unhappy in its own way." Ask your students if they agree or disagree with Tolstoy and why. Do they think this story is a good example of Tolstoy's statement? Why or why not? L2

More About Leo Tolstoy

Tolstoy's family were aristocratic landowners, but even with his privileged background, he was determined to improve conditions for the peasant serfs. Many of his writings address moral and social issues, and they've had a strong influence on many writers and leaders, including Mohandas Gandhi.

Interdisciplinary Connections

Psychology Tolstoy is famous for the psychological realism in his work. Discuss the realistic elements of this story with your students. What emotions and issues does Tolstoy examine? Ask your students (or find a story in a magazine or newspaper) about how old people are treated today. What parallels are there to the story and what differences?

Chapter 13

Section 3, pages 356–360

Focus

Section Objectives

1. Discuss how the people of these countries earn a living.
2. Explain how independence from the Soviet Union has effected these countries.

BELLRINGER Skillbuilder Activity

Project transparency and have students answer questions.

This activity is also available as a blackline master.

Daily Focus Skills Transparency 13–3

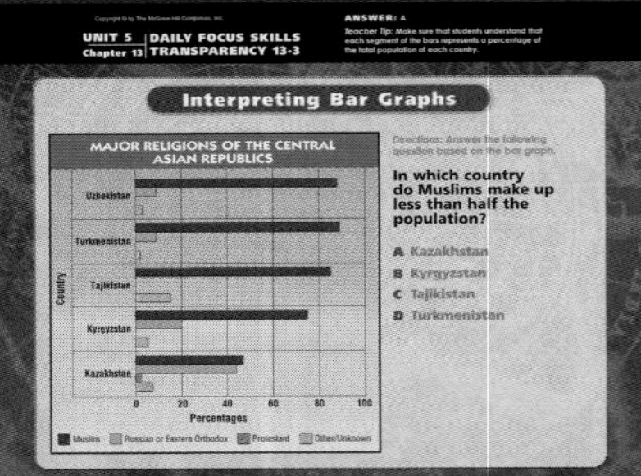

ANSWER: A
UNIT 5 Chapter 13 DAILY FOCUS SKILLS TRANSPARENCY 13-3
Teacher Tip: Make sure that students understand that each segment of the bars represents a percentage of the total population of each country.
Interpreting Bar Graphs
MAJOR RELIGIONS OF THE CENTRAL ASIAN REPUBLICS
Uzbekistan
Turkmenistan
Tajikistan
Kyrgyzstan
Kazakhstan
Country
0 20 40 60 80 100
Percentages
Muslim
Russian or Eastern Orthodox
Protestant
Other/Unknown
Directions: Answer the following question based on the bar graph.
In which country do Muslims make up less than half the population?
A Kazakhstan
B Kyrgyzstan
C Tajikistan
D Turkmenistan

Guide to Reading

■ Accessing Prior Knowledge Have students locate Armenia, Georgia, and Azerbaijan on the map on pages RA2–RA3. **Ask: What effect do you think having larger neighbors might have on these countries?** *(They have probably been threatened over time by their larger neighbors.)*

Guide to Reading

Main Idea

Many different ethnic groups live in the Eurasian Republics.

Terms to Know

- ethnic conflict
- nomad
- oasis
- elevation

Reading Strategy

Create a chart like this one. In the left column, list the Eurasian Republics. In the right column, list the dominant religion in the republic.

Republic	Religion

Section 3

Russia's Southern Neighbors

NATIONAL GEOGRAPHIC Exploring Our World

For centuries, the city of Bukhara was a stop along an ancient trading route called the Silk Road, which stretched from China to Europe. In the past, precious Chinese silk was carried on the backs of camels. Silk is still sold in Bukhara's markets. Today, however, international trade communications occur through a system of fiber-optic cables laid along the ancient tracks of the Silk Road camels.

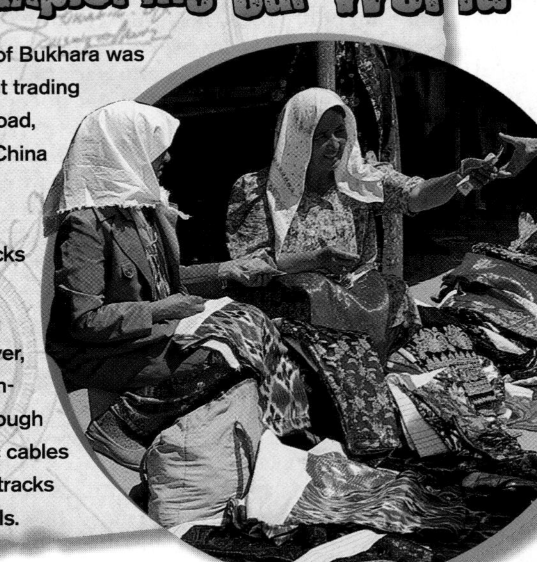

The Eurasian Republics are made up of the three republics of the **Caucasus** and the five republics of **Central Asia.** The peoples of this region have all been ruled at one time or another by Arabs, Turks, Persians, and Russians. Disagreements among these countries and among the ethnic groups within the countries have sparked violent conflicts. Most of the conflicts are disagreements over who owns the land.

The Caucasus

The republics of the Caucasus include **Armenia, Georgia,** and **Azerbaijan.** These republics became independent in 1991 for the first time in centuries. Since then, the region has struggled to develop its own industries and businesses.

Making this effort more difficult is the conflict between ethnic Armenia and neighboring Azerbaijan. Many Christian Armenians live in Azerbaijan, but want to become part of Armenia. This dispute led

Section Resources

Reproducible Masters
- Reproducible Lesson Plan 13-3
- Daily Lecture and Discussion Notes 13-3
- Guided Reading Activity 13-3
- Reading Essentials and Study Guide 13-3
- Section Quiz 13-3

Transparencies
- Daily Focus Skills Transparency 13-3
- GeoQuiz Transparency 13-3

Multimedia
- Vocabulary PuzzleMaker Software
- Interactive Tutor Self-Assessment CD-ROM
- Presentation Plus! CD-ROM
- ExamView® Pro 3.0 Testmaker CD-ROM

Azerbaijan to cut off needed supplies of fuel and other resources to Armenia. The economy of both countries has been seriously hurt by this conflict.

Azerbaijan is split in two by Armenian territory. The Azeris are Muslims who speak their own language called Azeri. The Azeris are excellent weavers and craftspeople and are productive farmers. Their hand-knotted rugs are highly valued for their rich color and intricate designs.

Ethnic conflicts have also erupted in Georgia and hurt its efforts to move toward democracy. **Ethnic conflicts** are disagreements or fights between two or more groups who differ from each other. The majority culture of dominant Georgians is Christian and the people speak Georgian, a distinctive language. They are skilled farmers whose products make up one-third of the country's goods. Georgia also has natural resources such as copper and coal.

✓ Reading Check **What republics are included in the republics of the Caucasus?**

The Central Asian Republics

The Central Asian Republics include **Kazakhstan, Kyrgystan** (KIHR•gih•STAN), **Tajikistan, Turkmenistan,** and **Uzbekistan.** All five Central Asian Republics are Islamic countries. (See the map on page 359.)

Kazakhstan The Kazakh ancestors were horse-riding warriors called the **Mongols.** They were **nomads** who moved from place to place and did not have permanent homes. They were forced to give up their nomadic ways when they became part of the Soviet Union. Many Russians moved to this area in the mid-1900s to enforce Communist laws. The environment has been badly damaged, because many factories were built quickly. Nuclear, chemical, and industrial waste has polluted the land and water of this region.

NATIONAL GEOGRAPHIC On Location

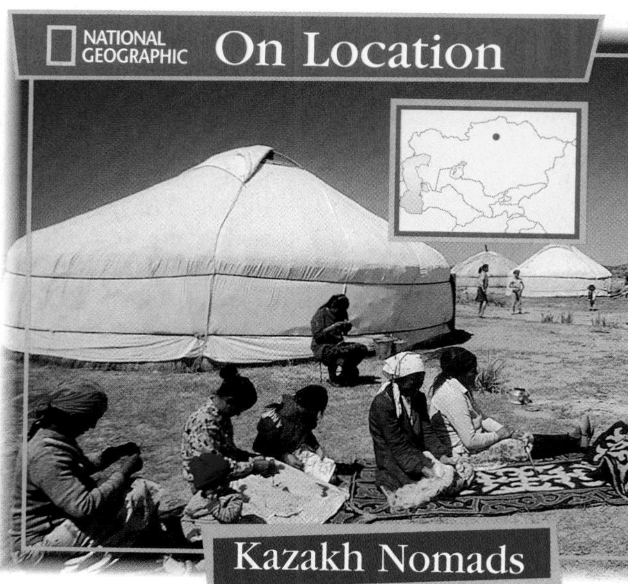

Kazakh Nomads

The traditional home of Kazakhs—called a yurt—can be easily taken apart and moved.

Culture **Why would the Mongols and early Kazakh people need a house that could be moved?**

Uzbekistan Uzbekistan is slightly larger than California in area. Uzbekistan is one of the world's largest cotton producers. This boom in cotton, unfortunately, has had disastrous effects on the environment. Large farms needing irrigation have nearly drained away the rivers flowing into the **Aral Sea.** Receiving less freshwater, the sea has steadily shrunk, and its salt level has increased. Fish and wildlife have died, and salt particles have polluted the air and soil. To create prosperity, Uzbek leaders want to

Team-Teaching Activity

History Invite a teacher with a background in world history to class to discuss the sufferings of Armenians under the Ottomans and the Turks. Severe persecution began in the 1890s when Ottoman soldiers killed hundreds of thousands of Armenians. Attacks continued in the 1910s when as many as a million Armenians might have been killed in what some call "the Armenian Holocaust." When the presentation is completed, have students discuss whether they think international bodies such as the United Nations or independent alliances of nations should intervene in such conflicts. **L2**

EE4 Human Systems: Standard 13

2 TEACH

Using a Map Have students look at the physical map of Asia on pages RA24–RA25. Have them locate the five countries discussed in this section. **Ask: Why are these countries called "Central Asian Republics"?** *(because they are located in the center of Asia)* **L1**

Daily Lecture Notes 13-3

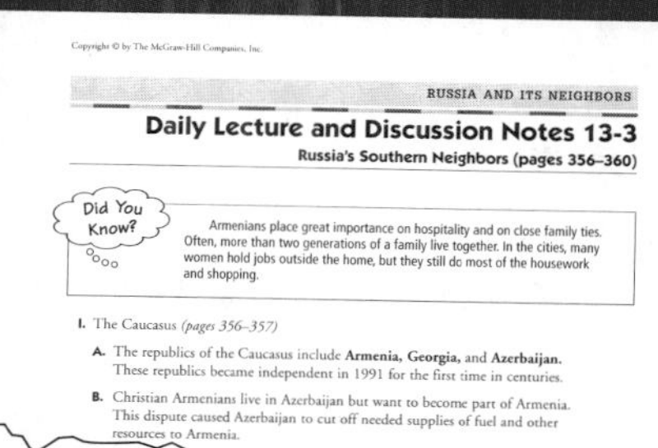

RUSSIA AND ITS NEIGHBORS

Daily Lecture and Discussion Notes 13-3

Russia's Southern Neighbors (pages 356–360)

Did You Know? Armenians place great importance on hospitality and on close family ties. Often, more than two generations of a family live together. In the cities, many women hold jobs outside the home, but they still do most of the housework and shopping.

I. The Caucasus *(pages 356–357)*

A. The republics of the Caucasus include **Armenia, Georgia,** and **Azerbaijan.** These republics became independent in 1991 for the first time in centuries.

B. Christian Armenians live in Azerbaijan but want to become part of Armenia. This dispute caused Azerbaijan to cut off needed supplies of fuel and other resources to Armenia.

...eak their own language called Azeri.

More About the Photo

Yurts A wheel called a *shaneraq* is used to pull together the yurt frame. It is considered a national symbol of Kazakhstan in celebration of the nomadic way of life.

Caption Answer because they are nomads who frequently move

✓ Reading Check Answer

Armenia, Georgia, Azerbaijan

Answer Answers will vary, but might include schools, community centers, parks, coffee shops, shopping malls

Ask students: **What are some popular gathering places in other countries or cultures?** Have students do research, if necessary, in order to compare these places to those they know. **What types of people gather there? How do people socialize? Where are these places usually located?**

Guided Reading Activity 13–3

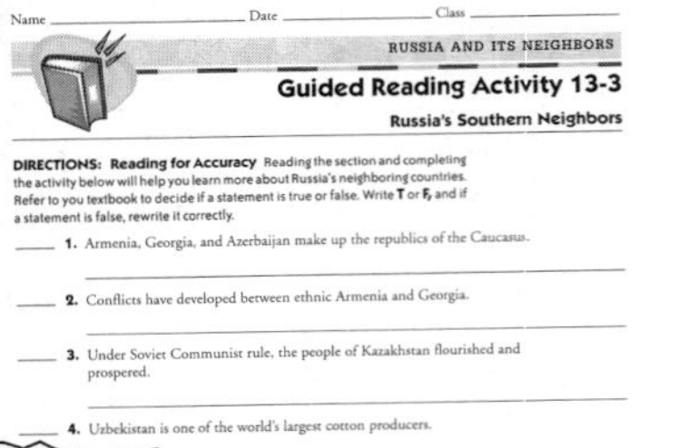
Name ______ Date ______ Class ______

RUSSIA AND ITS NEIGHBORS

Guided Reading Activity 13-3

Russia's Southern Neighbors

DIRECTIONS: Reading for Accuracy Reading the section and completing the activity below will help you learn more about Russia's neighboring countries. Refer to you textbook to decide if a statement is true or false. Write **T** or **F**, and if a statement is false, rewrite it correctly.

____ **1.** Armenia, Georgia, and Azerbaijan make up the republics of the Caucasus.

____ **2.** Conflicts have developed between ethnic Armenia and Georgia.

____ **3.** Under Soviet Communist rule, the people of Kazakhstan flourished and prospered.

____ **4.** Uzbekistan is one of the world's largest cotton producers.

Did You Know?

Estimates suggest that irrigation would have to be halted for 30 years to bring the Aral Sea back to its 1960 water level.

Architecture

In 1983, two towns from opposite sides of the world—Boulder, Colorado, and Dushanbe, Tajikistan—became "sister cities." From Dushanbe came the largest gift ever from any former Soviet nation to the United States. The gift was a beautiful *chaikhona,* or teahouse. In Tajikistan, a *chaikhona* serves as a community center where men gather to drink beverages, tell stories, hear news, and socialize. It often becomes the very heart of a city. In Boulder, men and women of all ages come here to appreciate this part of Tajik culture.

Looking Closer **What are some gathering places in your community?**

use newly discovered deposits of oil, gas, and gold. This would create more pollution in the region.

Most of Uzbekistan's 25.1 million people are Uzbeks who generally live in fertile valleys and oases. An **oasis** is a green area in a desert watered by an underground spring. **Tashkent,** the capital, is the largest city and industrial center in Central Asia. About 2,000 years ago, the oases of Tashkent, Bukhara, and Samarqand were part of the busy trade route—the **Silk Road**—that linked China and Europe.

Kyrgyzstan The lofty **Tian Shan** (tee•AHN SHAHN) mountain range makes up most of Kyrgyzstan. The climate depends on an area's height above sea level, or **elevation.** Lower valleys and plains have warm, dry summers and chilly winters. Higher areas have cool summers and bitterly cold winters. The harsh climate and lack of fertile soil hinder farmers, but they manage to grow cotton, vegetables, and fruits. Many also raise sheep or cattle. Kyrgyzstan has few industries, but it does have valuable deposits of mercury and gold.

More than half of the people belong to the Kyrgyz ethnic group. Differences among clans, or family groups, often separate one part of the country from another. Kyrgyzstan is a bilingual country—one that has two official languages. These are Kirghiz, related to Turkish, and Russian. About 40 percent of the people live in cities, such as the capital, **Bishkek.**

Tajikistan **Tajikistan** is also very mountainous. Ismail Samani Peak, once called Communist Peak, is the highest mountain in Central Asia and is located here.

Agriculture is the most important activity in Tajikistan. Farmers grow cotton, rice, and fruits in fertile river valleys. Mountain streams provide water for irrigation as well as for hydroelectric power.

Meeting Special Needs

Visual/Spatial Students who are visual learners might need visual cues to help them grasp the information explained in the section. Suggest that they refer to the different maps as they read the subsections on each country. For example, it will be more meaningful for these learners to see the high elevations of the Tian Shan mountains on the physical map than just to read the text description. Have them look at the photographs in the chapter and see if they can relate them to locations on the physical map. **L1**

Refer to *Inclusion for the Middle School Social Studies Classroom Strategies and Activities* in the TCR.

The largest city is **Dushanbe** (doo•SHAM•buh), the capital. Most of Tajikistan's people are Tajiks, who are related to the Persians. Another 25 percent are Uzbeks, a group related to the Turks. In 1992 a bitter civil war broke out between rival clans. Many people were killed, and the economy was severely damaged. Despite a peace agreement in 1997, tensions still remain high.

Turkmenistan **Turkmenistan** is larger than neighboring Uzbekistan, but it has far fewer people. Why? Most of this vast land—about 85 percent of it—is part of a huge desert called the **Garagum** (GAHR•uh•GOOM). Making up the northern and central region, *Garagum* means "black sand."

Despite the harshness of the land and climate, agriculture is the leading economic activity. Raising livestock is another important activity. However, not enough produce is available to feed everyone in the country, and much food has to be imported.

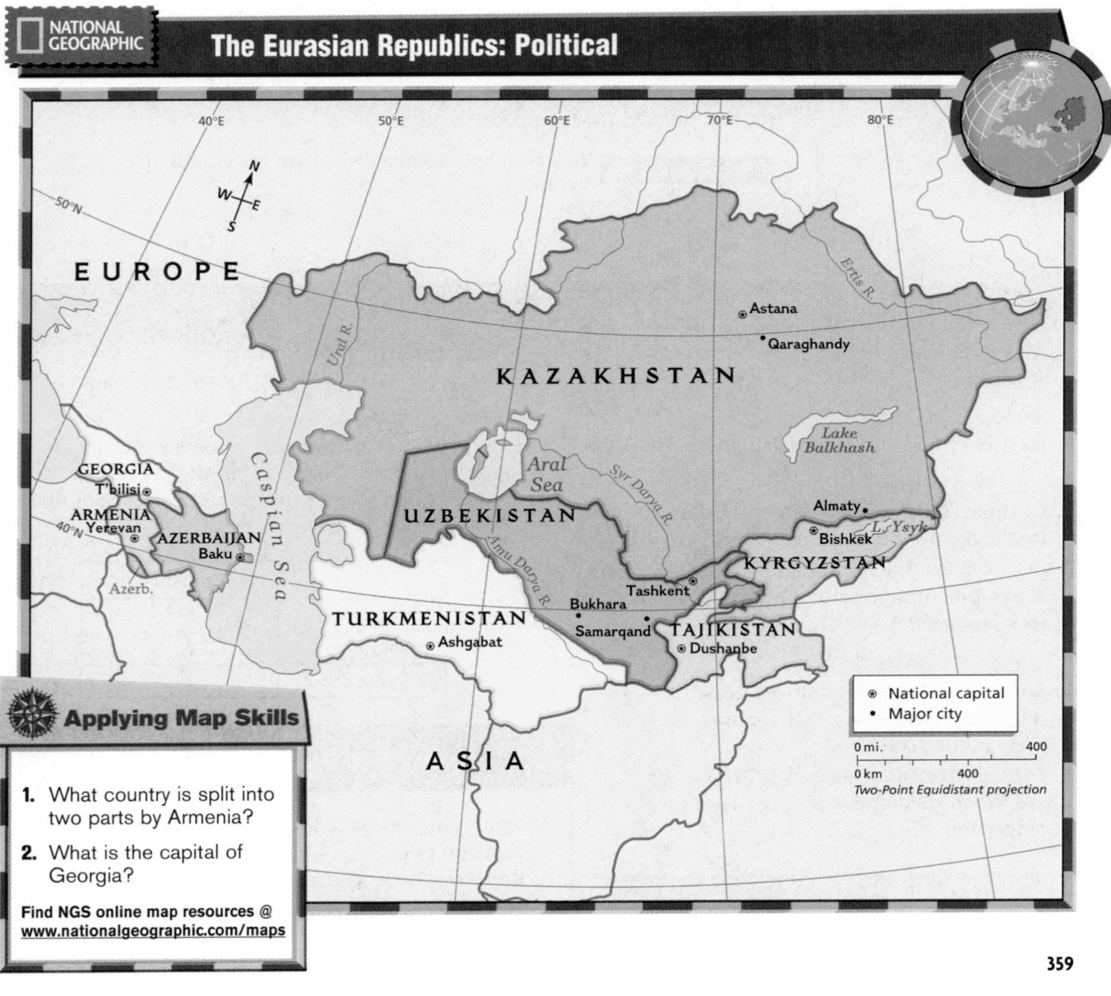

Applying Map Skills

1. What country is split into two parts by Armenia?
2. What is the capital of Georgia?

Find NGS online map resources @ www.nationalgeographic.com/maps

Chapter 13

Section 3, pages 356–360

Assign Section 3 Assessment as homework or an in-class activity.

Have students use the Interactive Tutor Self-Assessment CD-ROM to review Section 13–3.

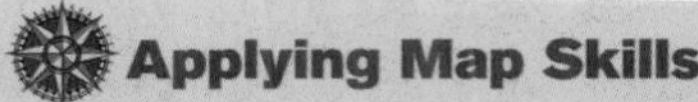

Applying Map Skills

Answers

1. Azerbaijan
2. T'bilisi

Skills Practice

Which of the Caucasus republics is landlocked? *(Armenia)*

Measure student knowledge of physical features and political entities.

GeoQuiz Transparency 13-3

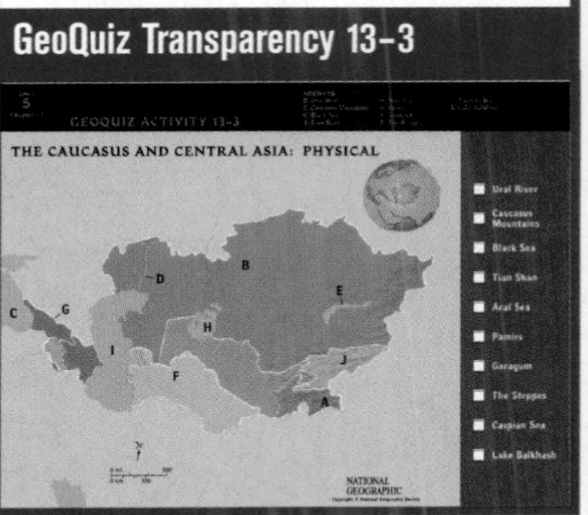

Critical Thinking Activity

Making Comparisons Have students create a chart that compares these countries in terms of resources, economic activities, population, ethnic mix, and most important challenges. When they have finished their work, have them write a brief essay describing the factors necessary for a free market economy, identifying which country they think is most likely to succeed in achieving one, and explaining why they believe this. Organize the class into groups based on the country chosen, and have the class debate the selections based on the reasons provided by students. **L2**

EE4 Human Systems: Standard 11

Section Quiz 13-3

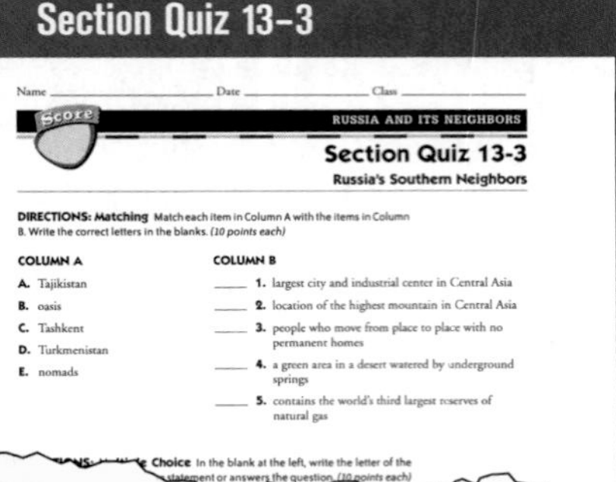
Name ______ Date ______ Class ______

RUSSIA AND ITS NEIGHBORS

Section Quiz 13-3
Russia's Southern Neighbors

DIRECTIONS: Matching Match each item in Column A with the items in Column B. Write the correct letters in the blanks. *(10 points each)*

COLUMN A	COLUMN B
A. Tajikistan	____ 1. largest city and industrial center in Central Asia
B. oasis	____ 2. location of the highest mountain in Central Asia
C. Tashkent	____ 3. people who move from place to place with no permanent homes
D. Turkmenistan	____ 4. a green area in a desert watered by underground springs
E. nomads	____ 5. contains the world's third largest reserves of natural gas

Choice In the blank at the left, write the letter of the statement or answers the question. *(10 points each)*

Reteach

Have students create a concept web for three of the Central Asian Republics covering such aspects as physical geography, economy, and people.

✓ Reading Check Answer

because that region has oases formed by mountain streams

Reading Essentials and Study Guide 13-3

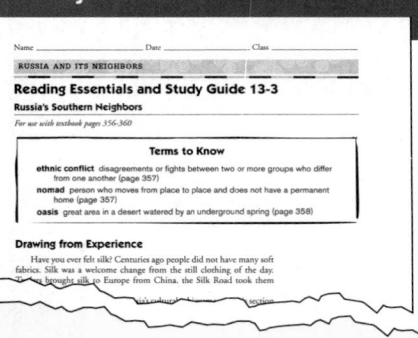

Name ______ Date ______ Class ______

RUSSIA AND ITS NEIGHBORS

Reading Essentials and Study Guide 13-3
Russia's Southern Neighbors

For use with textbook pages 356-360

Terms to Know

ethnic conflict disagreements or fights between two or more groups who differ from one another (page 357)
nomad person who moves from place to place and does not have a permanent home (page 357)
oasis great area in a desert watered by an underground spring (page 358)

Drawing from Experience

Have you ever felt silk? Centuries ago people did not have many soft fabrics. Silk was a welcome change from the still clothing of the day. Traders brought silk to Europe from China. the Silk Road took them

CLOSE

Give students an outline map of the Central Asian Republics. Have them create an annotated map that describes the resources and products of the different regions.

Turkmenistan is important to world energy markets because it contains the world's third-largest reserves of natural gas. Estimates of the total gas resource range as high as 535 trillion cubic feet. Turkmenistan is hoping that its oil and natural gas resources will give it a brighter future.

Turkmenistan is a one-party state dominated by its president and his closest advisers. In spite of having a democratic constitution, the current president retains absolute control over the country. In 1999, the Democratic Party was renamed the Communist Party.

More than 75 percent of Turkmenistan's 5.5 million people belong to the Turkmen ethnic group. **Ashgabat,** the capital, is the country's largest city and leading economic and cultural center. More than one-half of Turkmenistan's people live in rural areas, though. Turkmen villages usually are located near oases formed by mountain streams.

The Turkmen people were nomads who raised camels and other livestock in the desert. Under Soviet rule, the nomads were forced to settle on farms. In the 1950s, Soviet engineers built a large irrigation and shipping canal. This technological feat greatly increased the land area used for growing cotton. However, as in Uzbekistan, cotton growing has helped to dry up the Aral Sea.

✓ Reading Check **Why do most Turkmen live along the southern border?**

Section 3 Assessment

Defining Terms

1. Define ethnic conflict, nomad, oasis, elevation.

Recalling Facts

2. Culture What are the different ethnic groups that make up the Central Asian Republics?

3. Economics What conflict is making economic development more difficult for the republics of the Caucasus?

Critical Thinking

4. Summarizing Information How has religion played a part in the ethnic conflicts in the Caucasus?

5. Understanding Cause and Effect What are the results of diverting the rivers that empty into the Aral Sea?

Graphic Organizer

6. Organizing Information Create a chart like the one shown below. Fill in the chart with information about Georgia and Uzbekistan that you learned in this section.

	Georgia	Uzbekistan
Ethnic group		
Natural resources		
Economic activity		

Applying Social Studies Skills

7. Analyzing Maps Look at the political map chart on page 335. Which of the Eurasian Republics do not share a border with Russia?

Section 3 Assessment

1. The terms are defined in the Glossary.
2. Mongols, Uzbeks, Kyrgyz, Tajiks, Ashgabat
3. ethnic conflict
4. Armenian Christians and Muslim Azeris are fighting over territory.
5. The Aral Sea receives less freshwater, it has shrunk, the salt level has increased, wildlife have died, salt particles from the dry seabed are polluting the land.
6. Student diagrams should be supported by facts from the section.
7. Armenia, Turkmenistan, Uzbekistan, Kyrgyzstan, Tajikistan

Chapter 13 Reading Review

Section 1 The Russian Land

Terms to Know
Eurasia
urban
suburb
consumer goods
rural
tundra
taiga
steppe
communism
heavy industry
light industry

Main Idea
Most people in Russia live west of the Urals, where the climate is mild. The people of Russia have met the challenges created by the country's gigantic size and harsh climates.

- ✓ **Location** Spanning two continents—Europe and Asia—Russia is the world's largest country.
- ✓ **Region** 75 percent of the people live in the western half of Russia, which is mostly a lowland plain.
- ✓ **Economics** The people of Siberia support themselves by fishing, hunting, herding reindeer, and lumbering.
- ✓ **Movement** Inland waterways, such as rivers and canals as well as railroads are important for moving goods through Russia.

Section 2 The People of Russia

Terms to Know
Slav
majority culture
minority culture

Main Idea
Russia's people enjoy a culture rich in art, music, literature, and religion.

- ✓ **Culture** Russia is a huge, populous country with more than 150 different ethnic groups.
- ✓ **Culture** The city of St. Petersburg in Russia has many beautiful museums and statues.
- ✓ **Religion** The Russian Orthodox Church has provided the people of Russia with religious beliefs, beautiful churches, and the Cyrillic alphabet.

Section 3 Russia's Southern Neighbors

Terms to Know
ethnic conflict
nomad
oasis
elevation

Main idea
Many different ethnic groups live in the Eurasian Republics.

- ✓ **Economics** The Caucasus Republics have struggled to develop their own industries and businesses, but are facing many ethnic conflicts.
- ✓ **Environment** The Central Asian Republics have a great deal of pollution in their land, air, and water.
- ✓ **Environment** The Aral Sea is drying up because farms are draining away the rivers that feed it to irrigate their crops.

Camels walk where fish once swam in the Aral Sea. ▶

Reading Review

Use the Chapter 13 Reading Review to preview, review, condense, or reteach the chapter.

Preview/Review

Use the Terms to Know lists to help students review and study.

Activity Assign students a selection of terms from each section and have them write sentences using the assigned words. Have volunteers read their sentences aloud.

Vocabulary PuzzleMaker Software reinforces the vocabulary terms used in Chapter 13.

The Interactive Tutor Self-Assessment CD-ROM allows students to review Chapter 13 content.

Condense

Have students read the Chapter 13 summary statements.

Chapter 13 Guided Reading Activities

Chapter 13 Audio Program

Reteach

Reteaching Activity 13

Chapter 13 Reading Essentials and Study Guide

Chapter Culminating Activity

Illustrated Charts Have students consider how geography, climate, and history have shaped the lives of people in these countries. Have them create a chart with three headings—"Effects of Geography," "Effects of Climate," and "Effects of History." Have them write examples of these effects under the appropriate heading. Suggest that they can illustrate their charts with photographs, maps, or diagrams. Display students' finished charts in the classroom. *NOTE: This activity may be completed separately or you may wish students to incorporate it into their Current Events Journals.* **L2**

EE4 Places and Regions: Standard 4

Assessment and Activities

GLENCOE TECHNOLOGY

MindJogger Videoquiz
Use MindJogger to review the Chapter 13 content.

 Available in VHS.

Using Key Terms

1. d
2. f
3. i
4. c
5. j
6. a
7. g
8. e
9. h
10. b

Reviewing the Main Ideas

11. Moscow
12. It's the only port that remains ice-free year round.
13. The Volga
14. Siberia
15. Slavs
16. St. Petersburg
17. the Communists created laws forbidding its practice
18. Ethnic conflict
19. Different ethnic groups disagree over who owns the land

Chapter 13 Assessment and Activities

 Using Key Terms

Match the terms in Part A with their definitions in Part B.

A.

1. majority culture
2. light industry
3. rural
4. steppe
5. consumer goods
6. taiga
7. hydroelectric power
8. ethnic conflict
9. heavy industry
10. urban

B.

a. huge, subarctic evergreen forest
b. relating to cities
c. dry, treeless grassland
d. the most powerful culture group
e. a disagreement or fight between two or more groups who differ from one another
f. production of consumer goods
g. electricity generated by water
h. production of industrial goods
i. relating to the countryside
j. products for personal use, such as clothing

Reviewing the Main Ideas

Section 1 The Russian Land

11. **Culture** What is the political and cultural center of Russia?
12. **Economics** Why is Kaliningrad so important to Russia?
13. **Movement** What river carries almost half of Russia's river traffic?
14. **Location** What part of Russia has the most minerals?

Section 2 The People of Russia

15. **Culture** What is the majority culture in Russia?
16. **Culture** In which city would you find the Hermitage Museum and many of Russia's museums, theaters, and ballets?
17. **History** What happened to religion during the Communist rule of Russia?

Section 3 Russia's Southern Neighbors

18. **Economics** What has seriously hurt the the economies of Armenia and Azerbaijan?
19. **Culture** Why have the republics been in conflict?

Russia—A Eurasian Country

Place Location Activity

On a separate sheet of paper, match the letters on the map with the numbered places listed below.

1. Ural Mountains
2. Kamchatka Peninsula
3. Lake Baikal
4. Volga River
5. Moscow
6. Lena River
7. West Siberian Plain
8. Caspian Sea
9. Caucasus Mountains
10. Sakhalin Island

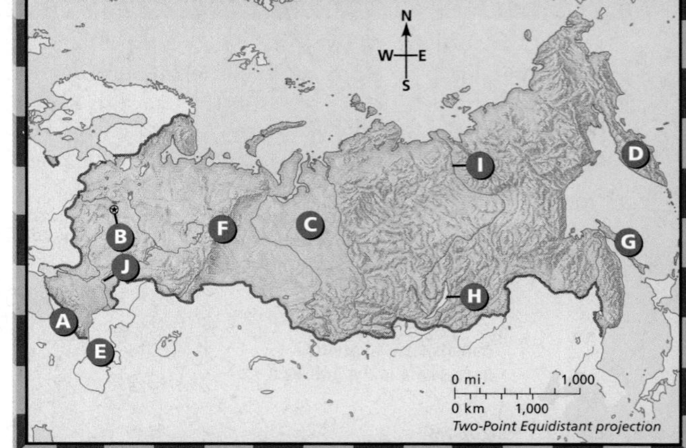

NATIONAL GEOGRAPHIC Place Location Activity

1. F
2. D
3. H
4. J
5. B
6. I
7. C
8. E
9. A
10. G

Critical Thinking

20. It's made it weaker because the government no longer has a strong control and Russian people don't have much experience creating jobs, starting businesses, or making money.
21. Students' charts will vary.

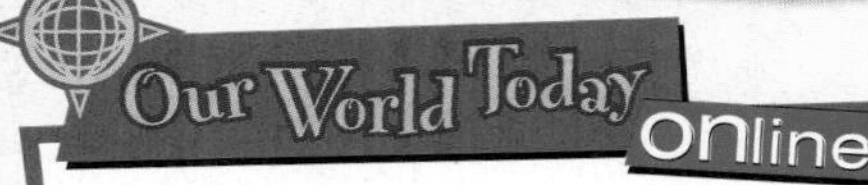

Self-Check Quiz Visit the ***Our World Today: People, Places, and Issues*** Web site at owt.glencoe.com and click on **Chapter 13–Self-Check Quizzes** to prepare for the Chapter Test.

Critical Thinking

20. **Making Generalizations** How have recent changes in Russia affected its economy?
21. **Organizing Information** Create a chart like this one. Then list the similarities and differences between the economies of two Central Asian Republics.

Country	Similarities	Differences

Current Events Journal

22. **Writing a Paragraph** Read a newspaper or magazine article about Russia or one of its neighbors and imagine yourself in the scene. Write a description using vivid words to portray the sights, sounds, and people you would encounter. What is the location? What can you hear? What can you see? Describe what is happening.

Mental Mapping Activity

23. **Focus on the Region** Create a simple outline map of Russia and label the following:
    - Black Sea
    - Caspian Sea
    - Aral Sea
    - Volga River
    - Ural Mountains
    - St. Petersburg
    - Moscow
    - Lake Baikal

Technology Skills Activity

24. **Using the Internet** Search the Internet for information on the problems facing the Aral Sea. Find out what distinctive creatures live in the Aral Sea that cannot be found anywhere else in the world. Find a map that shows what countries border the Aral Sea.

The Princeton Review

Standardized Test Practice

Directions: Read the paragraph below, and then answer the following question.

For 70 years, the Communist government of the Soviet Union stopped at nothing to industrialize the country. Soviet leaders gave little thought to the health of the people or to the land they were ruining. From St. Petersburg to Vladivostok, across more than 8 million square miles, the Russian environment shows decay. Today Russia's great rivers are sewers of chemicals and human waste. Air in more than 200 cities is at least five times more polluted than standards allow, putting millions at risk of lung diseases. Tons of nuclear waste lie under Arctic waters, and the use of toxic fertilizers has poisoned the soil.

Adapted from "The U.S.S.R.'s Lethal Legacy" by Mike Edwards, *National Geographic,* August 1994.

1. **Which of the following best explains why the Russian environment is so polluted today?**
   F Soviet leaders did not care about the health of the people.
   G Soviet leaders wanted to industrialize the country at all costs.
   H Farmers were careless about the chemicals they spread on their fields.
   J Eastern Russia is not as polluted as western Russia.

Test-Taking Tip: Notice that the question asks for the *best* explanation. Read all the choices carefully before choosing the best one. Although all of the answer statements might be true, you need to find the best answer to the question.

Assessment and Activities

Standardized Test Practice

1. G

Tested Objectives:
Finding the main idea, analyzing information

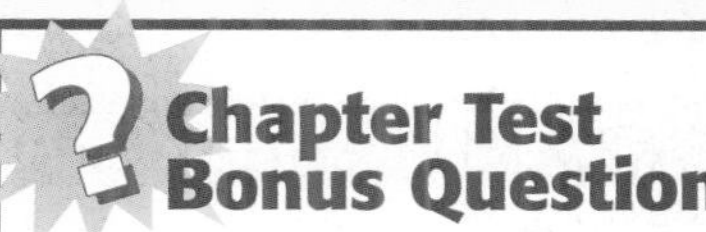

This question may be used for extra credit on the chapter test.

What cultural feature of Georgia and Armenia is different from all the other countries covered in the Eurasian Republics? *(Religion—they are Orthodox Christian, and all the other countries are Muslim.)*

Have students visit the Web site at owt.glencoe.com to review Chapter 13 and take the Self-Check Quiz.

Current Events Journal

22. Make a list of words that could describe Russian sights, sounds, smells, sensations. Students might want to do additional research about the photos.

Mental Mapping Activity

23. This exercise helps students visualize the countries and geographic features they have been studying and understand the relationship among various points. All attempts at freehand mapping should be accepted.

Technology Skills Activity

24. Students' presentations should cover all of the subjects described in the assignment.

Chapter 14 Resources

Note: The following materials may be used when teaching Chapter 14.
Section level support materials are shown at point of use in the margins of the Teacher Wraparound Edition.

Timesaving Tools

TeacherWorks™ All-In-One Planner and Resource Center

- **Interactive Teacher Edition** See the **Interactive Teacher Edition** CD-ROM to electronically integrate your Teacher Wraparound Edition and blackline masters.
- **Interactive Lesson Planner** Organize your week, month, semester, or year with all the lesson helps you need. The **Interactive Lesson Planner** CD-ROM contains all Chapter 14 resources.

Use Glencoe's **Presentation Plus!** multimedia teacher tool to easily present dynamic lessons that visually excite your students. Using Microsoft PowerPoint® you can customize the presentations to create your own personalized lessons.

TEACHING TRANSPARENCIES

Graphic Organizer Transparency and Student Activity 14

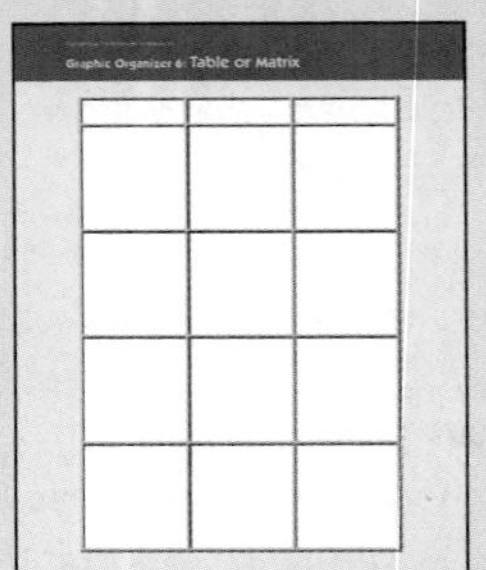

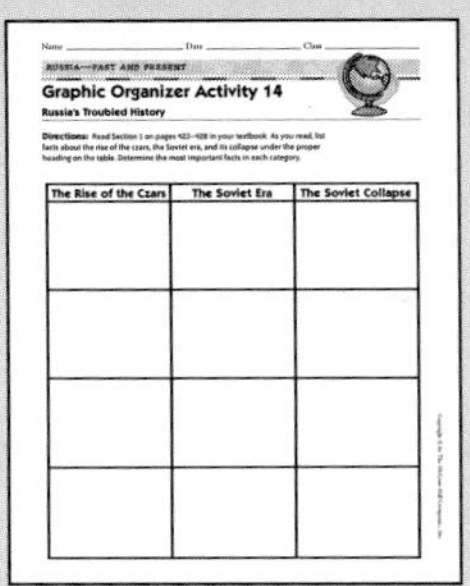

FOLDABLES™ Study Organizer

Foldables are three-dimensional, interactive graphic organizers that help students practice basic writing skills, review key vocabulary terms, and identify main ideas. Every chapter contains a Foldable activity, with additional chapter activities found in the ***Reading and Study Skills Foldables*** booklet.

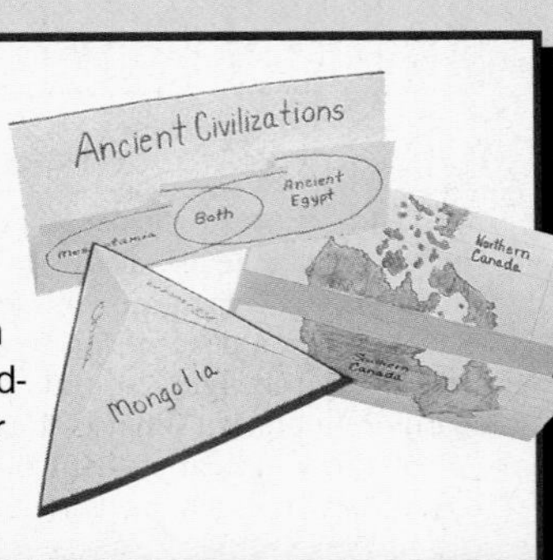

ENRICHMENT AND EXTENSION

Enrichment Activity 14

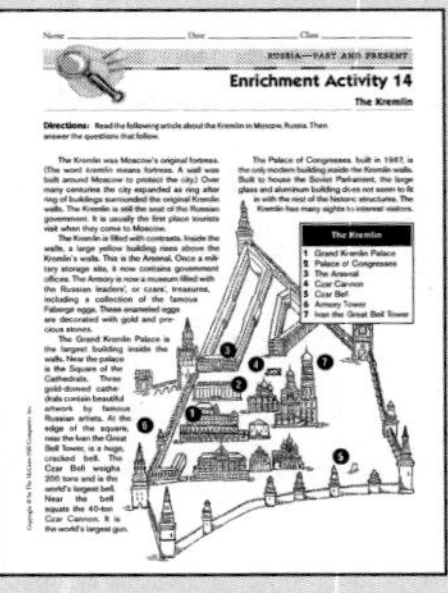

Cooperative Learning Activity 14

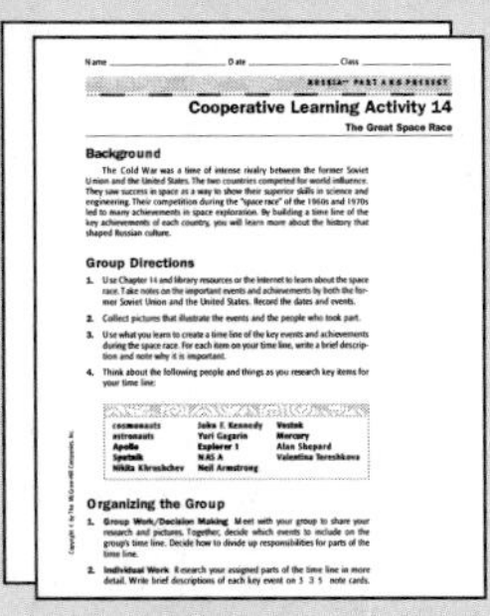

MAP AND GEOGRAPHY SKILLS

Chapter Map Activity 14

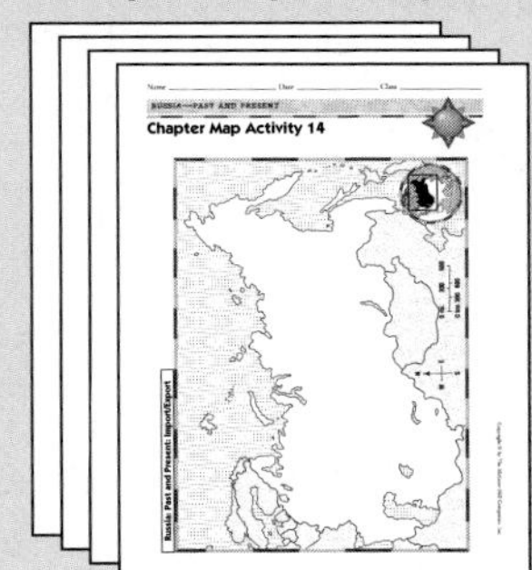

GeoLab Activity 14

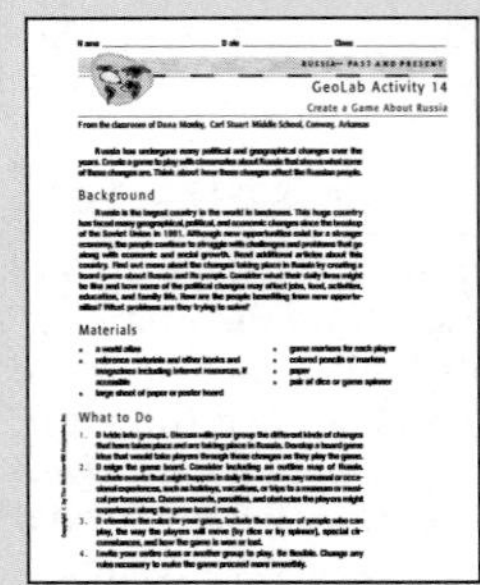

STANDARDIZED ASSESSMENT SKILLS

Glencoe's Assessment Advantage

Critical Thinking Skills Activity 14

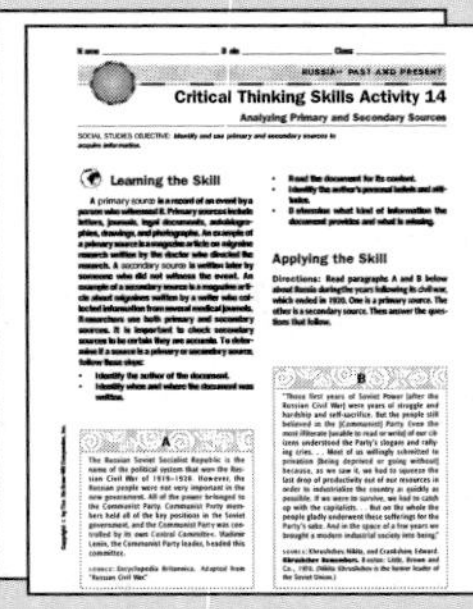

Map and Graph Skills Activity 14

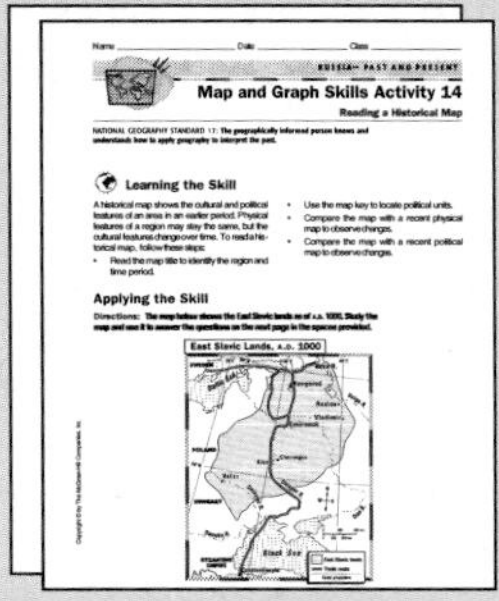

Reading and Writing Skills Activity 14

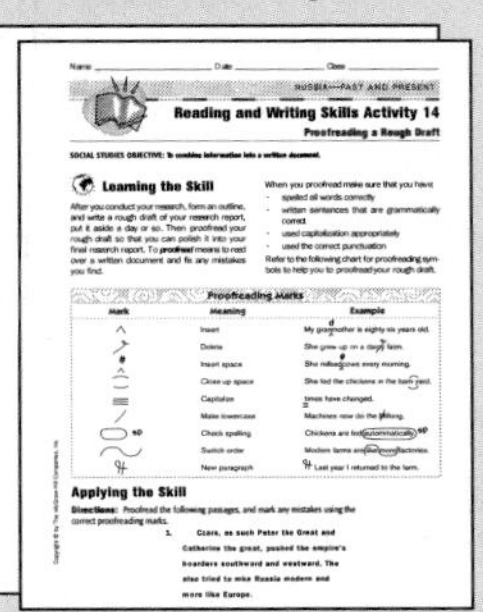

Standardized Test Practice Workbook Activity 14

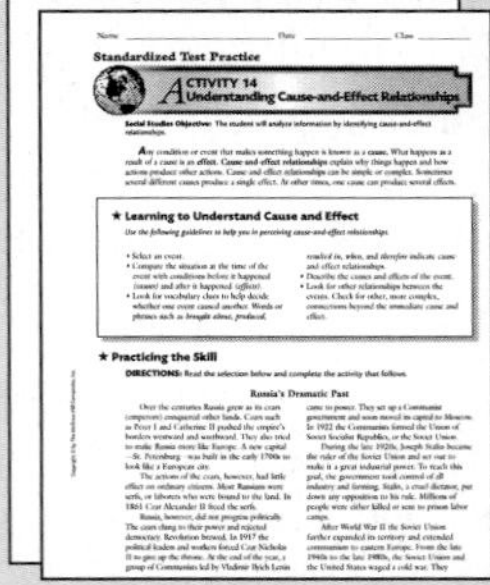

REVIEW AND REINFORCEMENT

Chapter Skills Activity 14

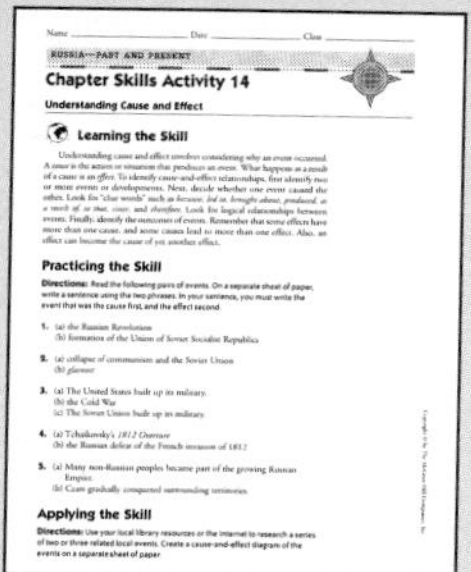

Take-Home Review Activity 14

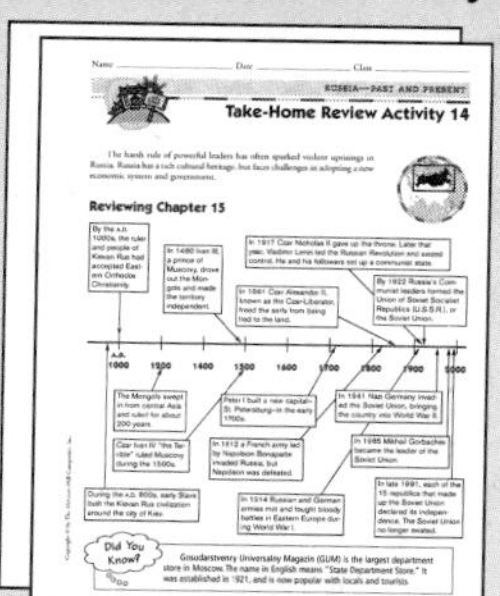

Reteaching Activity 14

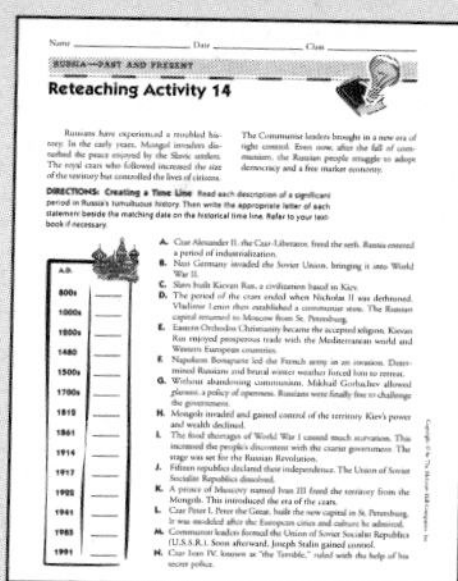

Vocabulary Activity 14

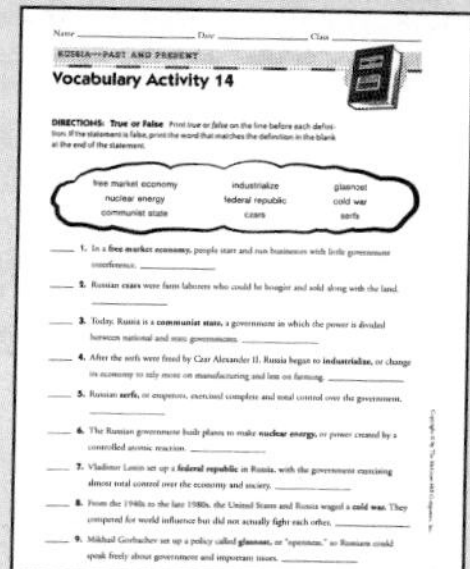

Workbook Activity 14

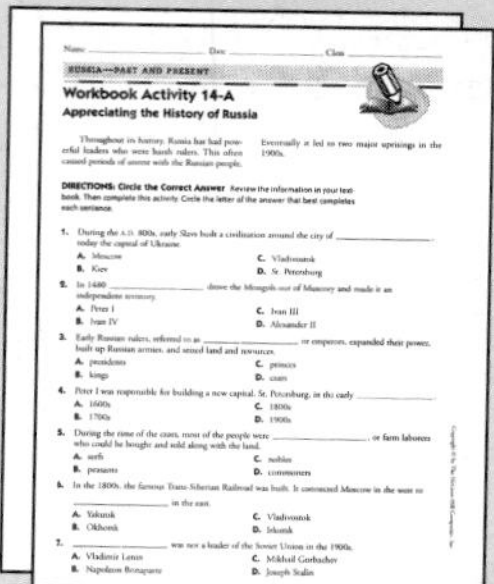

ASSESSMENT

GLENCOE'S ASSESSMENT ADVANTAGE

Chapter 14 Test, Form A

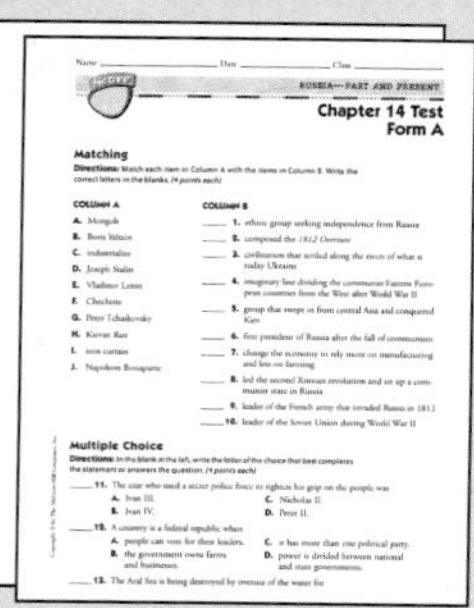

Chapter 14 Test, Form B

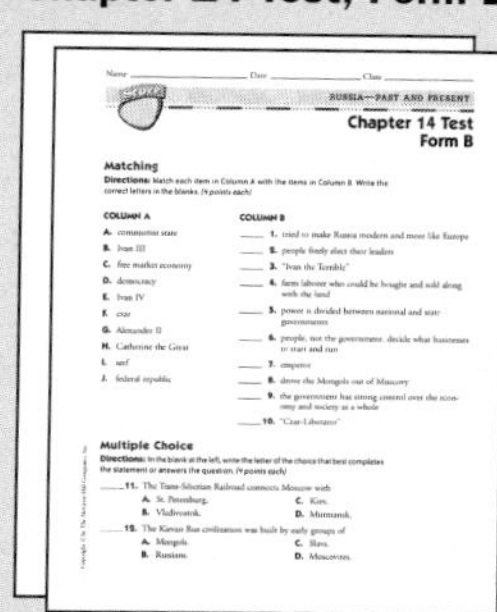

Performance Assessment Activity 14

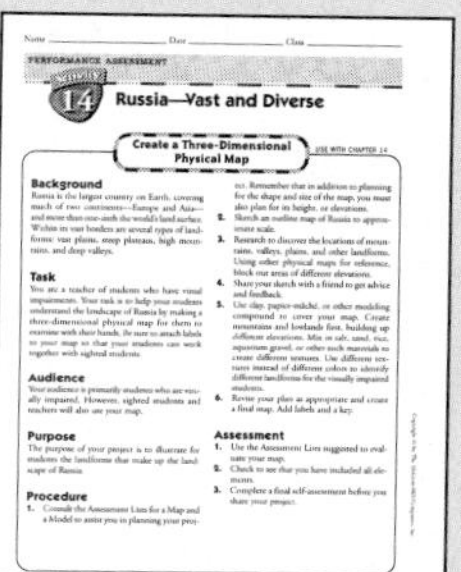

ExamView® Pro 3.0 Testmaker CD-ROM

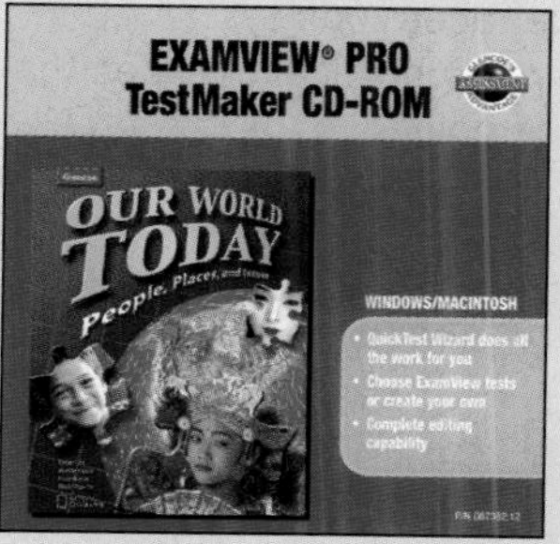

MULTIMEDIA

- **National Geographic's The World and Its People**
- **MindJogger Videoquiz**
- **Vocabulary PuzzleMaker Software**
- **Interactive Tutor Self-Assessment CD-ROM**
- **ExamView® Pro 3.0 Testmaker CD-ROM**
- **Interactive Lesson Planner CD-ROM**
- **Interactive Teacher Edition CD-ROM**
- **Skillbuilder Interactive Workbook CD-ROM, Level 1**
- **Presentation Plus! CD-ROM**
- **Audio Program**

SPANISH RESOURCES

The following Spanish language materials are available in the Spanish Resources binder:

- **Spanish Chapter Summaries**
- **Spanish Vocabulary Activities**
- **Spanish Guided Reading Activities**
- **Spanish Quizzes and Tests**
- **Spanish Take-Home Review Activities**
- **Spanish Reteaching Activities**

Meeting National Standards

Geography for Life

All of the 18 standards are demonstrated in Unit 5. The following ones are highlighted in Chapter 14:

Section 1
EE1 The World in Spatial Terms: Standards 1, 2, 3
EE4 Human Systems: Standards 9, 11, 12, 13
EE6 The Uses of Geography: Standards 17, 18

Section 2
EE2 Places and Regions: Standards 4, 5, 6
EE4 Human Systems: Standards 9, 11, 12, 13
EE5 Environment and Society: Standards 14, 15, 16

For a complete listing of National Geography Standards and entire text correlation, see pages T22–T29.

Local Objectives

Chapter 14 Planning Guide

SECTION RESOURCES

Daily Objectives	Reproducible Resources	Multimedia Resources
Section 1 **A Troubled History** **Suggested Pacing = 1 day** **1.** Describe life in Russia under the czars. **2.** Discuss life in Russia under Communist rule. **3.** Explain why the Soviet Union collapsed.	Reproducible Lesson Plan 14-1 Daily Lecture and Discussion Notes 14-1 Guided Reading Activity 14-1 Reading Essentials and Study Guide 14-1 Section Quiz 14-1*	Daily Focus Skills Transparency 14-1 GeoQuiz Transparency 14-1 Vocabulary PuzzleMaker Software Interactive Tutor Self-Assessment CD-ROM ExamView® Pro 3.0 Testmaker CD-ROM Presentation Plus! CD-ROM
Section 2 **A New Russia** **Suggested Pacing = 1 day** **1.** Discuss the economic challenges that Russia faces today. **2.** Explain the political changes that Russia is undergoing.	Reproducible Lesson Plan 14-2 Daily Lecture and Discussion Notes 14-2 Guided Reading Activity 14-2 Reading Essentials and Study Guide 14-2 Section Quiz 14-2*	Daily Focus Skills Transparency 14-2 Vocabulary PuzzleMaker Software Interactive Tutor Self-Assessment CD-ROM ExamView® Pro 3.0 Testmaker CD-ROM Presentation Plus! CD-ROM

00:00 **Out of Time?** Assign the **Reading Essentials and Study Guide** for this chapter.

*Also available in Spanish

KEY TO ABILITY LEVELS

Teaching strategies have been coded for varying learning styles and abilities.

L1 **BASIC** activities for all students
L2 **AVERAGE** activities for average to above-average students
L3 **CHALLENGING** activities for above-average students
ELL **ENGLISH LANGUAGE LEARNER** activities

Blackline Master
Software
CD-ROM
Audiocassette
Transparency
Videocassette
Block Scheduling
DVD

A Geographic Coat of Arms

April Robinson
Baxter Elementary School
Baxter, Tennessee

Have students interview family members to find out the countries of origin and careers of early family members. After plotting a family tree, students should design a coat of arms on a large piece of poster board. A map of the world should be the background. Draw the routes that family members took to arrive in the United States. Include drawings of ships, planes, and other types of transportation used. Embellish the coats of arms with samples of items that portray the careers of ancestors as they migrated toward your home city or town (slivers of wood to portray lumbering or shipbuilding, seeds to portray farming, and so on). Then have students carefully paint their final product.

OUR WORLD TODAY Online

Use our Web site for additional resources. All essential content is covered in the Student Edition.

You and your students can visit owt.glencoe.com, the Web site companion to *Our World Today*. This innovative integration of electronic and print media offers your students a wealth of opportunities. The student text directs students to the Web site for the following options:

- Chapter Overviews
- Student Web Activities
- Self-Check Quizzes
- Textbook Updates

Answers are provided for you in the Web Activity Lesson Plan. Additional Web resources and Interactive Tutor puzzles are also available.

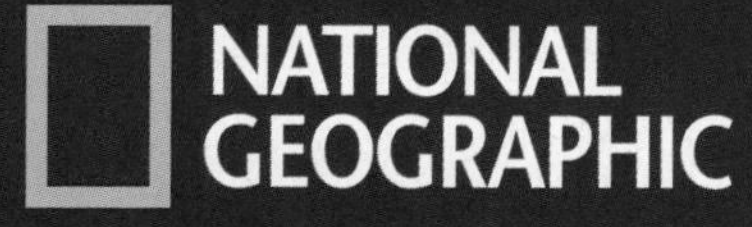

TEACHER'S CORNER

Index to National Geographic Magazine:

The following articles may be used for research relating to this chapter:

- "The Caspian Sea," by Robert Cullen, May 1999.
- "Stellar's Sea-Eagles," by Klaus Nigge, March 1999.
- *Biodiversity,* a National Geographic Special Edition, February 1999.
- "A Comeback for the Cossacks," by Mike Edwards, November 1998.

National Geographic Society Products Available From Glencoe:

To order the following products for use with this chapter, contact your local Glencoe sales representative or call Glencoe at 1-800-334-7344:

- *STV: World Geography* (Videodisc)
- *Picture Atlas of the World* (CD-ROM)
- *ZipZapMap! World* (Software)
- *GeoBee* (CD-ROM)
- *MapPack: Europe* (Transparencies)

Additional National Geographic Society Products:

To order the following products for use with this chapter, call National Geographic Society at 1-800-368-2728:

- *Europe: The Road to Unity* (Video)
- *Russia: Then and Now Series* (Video)
- *Capitalism, Communism, Socialism Series* (3 Videos)
- *Pollution: World at Risk* (Video)
- *Healing the Earth* (Video)
- *Nuclear Energy: The Question Before Us* (Video)
- *Complete National Geographic: 111 Years of National Geographic Magazine* (CD-ROM)
- *Voices: Poetry and Art From Around the World* (Book)
- *National Geographic Desk Reference* (Book)
- *National Geographic Atlas of the World, Seventh Edition* (Book)

NGS ONLINE

Access National Geographic's Web site for current events, activities, links, interactive features, and archives.
www.nationalgeographic.com

Introducing
Chapter 14

Introduce students to chapter content and key terms by having them access Chapter Overview 14 at owt.glencoe.com

Chapter Objectives

1. Compare Russia under the czars and the Communists.
2. Explain why the Soviet Union collapsed.
3. Discuss the economic and political issues in Russia today.
4. Describe life in Russia today.

GLENCOE TECHNOLOGY

NATIONAL GEOGRAPHIC

The World and Its People Video Program

Chapter 15 Russia—Past and Present

The following segments enhance the study of this chapter:

- **Return to Russia**
- **Circus School**

Available in DVD and VHS.

MindJogger Videoquiz

Use MindJogger to preview the Chapter 14 content.

Available in VHS.

Chapter 14 Russia—Past and Present

The World and Its People NATIONAL GEOGRAPHIC

To learn more about Russia's land and economy, view ***The World and Its People*** **Chapter 15** video.

Our World Today Online

Chapter Overview Visit the ***Our World Today: People, Places, and Issues*** Web site at owt.glencoe.com and click on **Chapter 14—Chapter Overviews** to preview information about Russia.

364

Two-Minute Lesson Launcher

Have students look at the photographs in the unit. **Ask:** **Based on these photographs, how does life in Russia look similar to life in your country? What aspects of life look different?** Suggest that students write their responses to these questions in their notebooks. As they read the chapter, they can review their ideas to see if they wish to revise or add to them with information from the text.

FOLDABLES™ Study Organizer

Categorizing Information Study Foldable When you group information into categories, it is easier to make sense of what you are learning. Make this foldable to help you learn about Russia's past and present.

Step 1 Fold one sheet of paper in half from top to bottom.

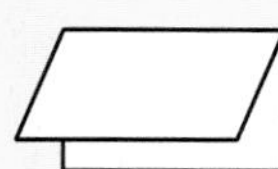

Step 2 Fold it in half again, from side to side.

Step 3 Unfold the paper once. Cut up the inside fold of the top flap only.

Step 4 Turn the paper and sketch a map of the U.S.S.R. and Russia on the front tabs. Label your foldable as shown.

Reading and Writing As you read the chapter, write under the appropriate flaps of your foldable what you learn about the former U.S.S.R. and present-day Russia.

Why It Matters

A New Government

Russia is a land rich in natural resources but with a troubled political history. The various peoples in Russia have had little experience with "hands-on" government. This experience is needed for a stable democracy to work. On the other hand, a strong, central government is needed to create policies to prevent continued air and water pollution and to build up the economy. How will Russia meet both of these aims? The answer is important to us all.

◀ Statue of Vladimir Lenin at the Exhibition of Economic Achievement Moscow, Russia

Introducing

Chapter 14

FOLDABLES™ Study Organizer

Purpose This foldable will help students organize information about Russia's past and present. When grouping information from the chapter into two categories—*Past:* U.S.S.R. and *Present:* Russia—students are required to determine what is relevant factual information and group this data into the appropriate categories.

Have students complete ***Reading and Study Skills Foldables*** Activity 14.

Why It Matters

Organize students into groups to investigate the following environmental issues in Russia: air pollution, water pollution, and land pollution. Have each group conduct research to identify what caused the problem, the extent of the problem, what steps the Russian government is taking to address the problem, what help Russia is receiving from outside organizations and countries, and the prospects for improving the situation. Have each group create a display showing the results of their findings.

About the Photos

Although the Soviet Union collapsed in 1991, statues of Vladimir Lenin—the leader of the Russian Revolution and founder of the communist Soviet state—are still very common in Russia, as are other monuments to communism honoring everything from leaders and war heroes to farmers and their equipment. The Exhibition of Economic Achievement was originally used in 1939 as an agricultural exposition, celebrating the triumphs of Russia under the rule of Joseph Stalin. Have your students think of statues or monuments in your town. Whom do these memorials commemorate and why? What are the similarities and differences in the ways the two societies use monuments?

Focus

Section Objectives

1. Describe life in Russia under the czars.
2. Discuss life in Russia under Communist rule.
3. Explain why the Soviet Union collapsed.

BELLRINGER Skillbuilder Activity

Project transparency and have students answer questions.

This activity is also available as a blackline master.

Daily Focus Skills Transparency 14-1

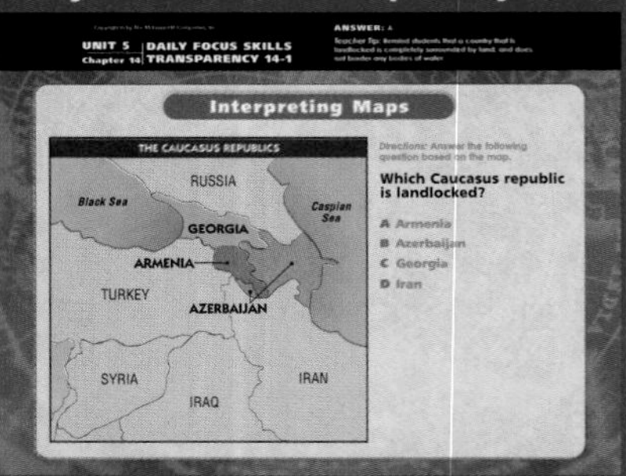

Guide to Reading

Accessing Prior Knowledge
Have the class discuss what a revolution is and how it can transform a society.

Vocabulary Precheck
Have students find the meanings of the words *czar* and *serf.* Then have them identify synonyms, or words that have the same meanings. *(czar—emperor; serf—slave, servant)*

Section 1 A Troubled History

Guide to Reading

Main Idea

The harsh rule of powerful leaders has often sparked violent uprisings in Russia.

Terms to Know

- czar
- serf
- industrialize
- communist state
- Cold War
- glasnost

Reading Strategy

Create a chart like this one. List three main czars and important things to remember about them.

Czar	Importance

NATIONAL GEOGRAPHIC Exploring Our World

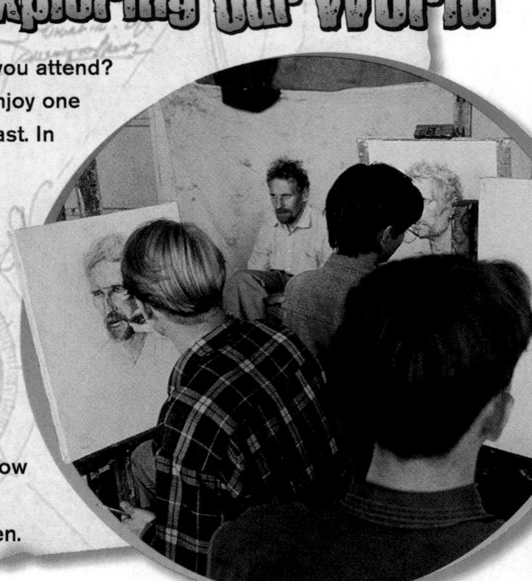

How old is the school you attend? Russian art students enjoy one reminder of Russia's past. In 1764 the empress Catherine the Great enlarged the Russian Academy of Fine Arts to train Russian artists. The empress hoped they would develop the skills shown by artists in western Europe. The school, now known as the Repin Institute, remains open.

As you read in Chapter 13, Russia is the largest country in the world. Early in its history, however, it was a small territory on the edge of Europe. Strong rulers gradually expanded the Russian territory. Their harsh rule led to unrest, eventually resulting in two major upheavals—one in 1917, the other in 1991.

The History of Russia

To understand the challenges facing Russia today, let us go back through Russia's history. Modern Russians descend from early groups of Slavs who settled along the rivers of what is today Ukraine and Russia. During the A.D. 800s, these early Slavs built a civilization around the city of **Kiev,** today the capital of **Ukraine.** This civilization was called **Kievan Rus** (kee•AY•vuhn ROOS). By the 1000s, the ruler and people of Kievan Rus had accepted Eastern Orthodox Christianity. They prospered from trade with the Mediterranean world and western Europe.

In the 1200s, the **Mongols** swept in from Central Asia and conquered Kiev. Under their rule, Kiev lost much of its wealth and power. Meanwhile, Moscow became the center of a new Slavic territory,

Section Resources

Reproducible Masters
- Reproducible Lesson Plan 14-1
- Daily Lecture and Discussion Notes 14-1
- Guided Reading Activity 14-1
- Reading Essentials and Study Guide 14-1
- Section Quiz 14-1

Transparencies
- Daily Focus Skills Transparency 14-1
- GeoQuiz Transparency 14-1

Multimedia
- Vocabulary PuzzleMaker Software
- Interactive Tutor Self-Assessment CD-ROM
- Presentation Plus! CD-ROM
- ExamView® Pro 3.0 Testmaker CD-ROM

called **Muscovy** (muh•SKOH•vee). In 1480 **Ivan III,** a prince of Muscovy, drove out the Mongols and made the territory independent.

Rise of the Czars Muscovy slowly developed into the country we know today as Russia. Russian rulers expanded their power, built up their armies, and seized land and other resources. They called themselves **czars,** or emperors. (Sometimes you will see this word written *tsar.*) They had complete and total control over the government. As a citizen of Muscovy, you would have feared **Czar Ivan IV,** who ruled during the 1500s. Known as "Ivan the Terrible," Ivan IV used a secret police force to tighten his iron grip on the people and control their lives.

The czars gradually conquered nearby territories. As a result, many non-Russian peoples became part of the growing Russian Empire. (Russia today still suffers from ethnic tensions caused by these conquests.) Czars, such as **Peter the Great** and **Catherine the Great,** pushed the empire's borders southward and westward. They also tried to make Russia modern and more like Europe. As explained in Chapter 13, Peter built a new capital—St. Petersburg—in the early 1700s. Built close to Europe near the Baltic coast, St. Petersburg was designed like a European city with its elegant palaces, public squares, and canals. If you had been a Russian noble at this time, you would have spoken French as well as Russian. You also would have put aside traditional Russian dress, worn European clothes, and attended fancy balls and parties.

Early Russia

Ivan III, or "Ivan the Great," (left) ruled Muscovy until 1505. His grandson, Ivan IV, also known as "Ivan the Terrible," (right) used a secret police force to control the people of Muscovy.

History **Who drove the Mongols out of Kiev?**

NATIONAL GEOGRAPHIC On Location

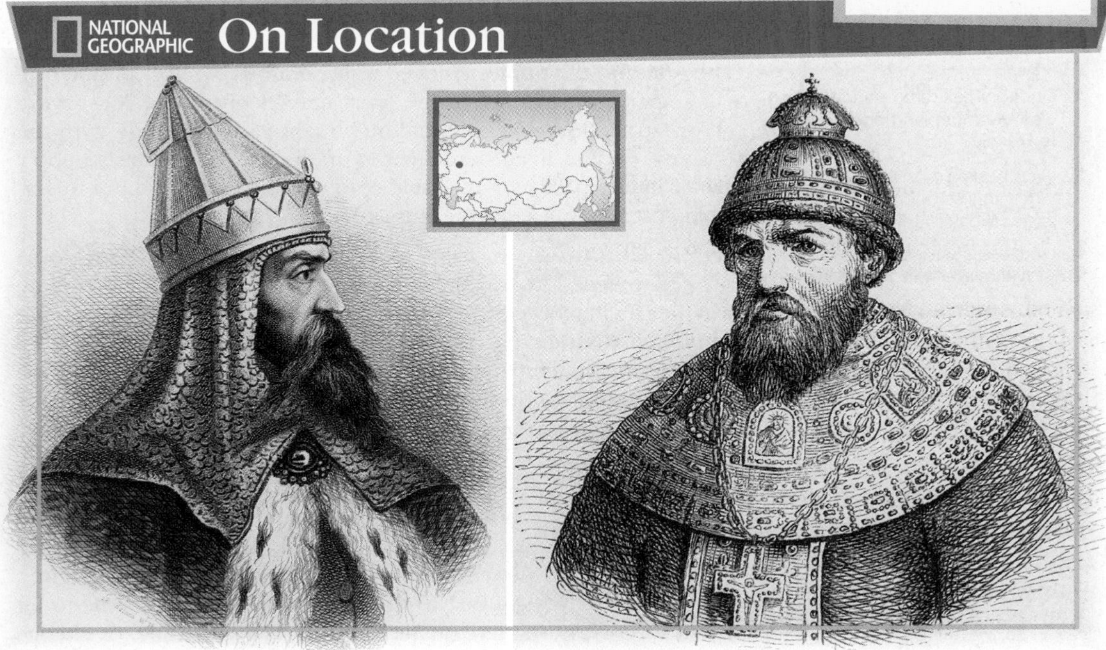

Chapter 14

Section 1, pages 366–371

2 TEACH

Making Generalizations
Have students create a chart of Russian history with four major periods: early Russia, Russia under the czars, Communist Russia, and Russia after 1991. Have them write facts about each period under the appropriate heading. Then ask them to make a generalization about life in Russia in each period. **L1**

Daily Lecture Notes 14-1

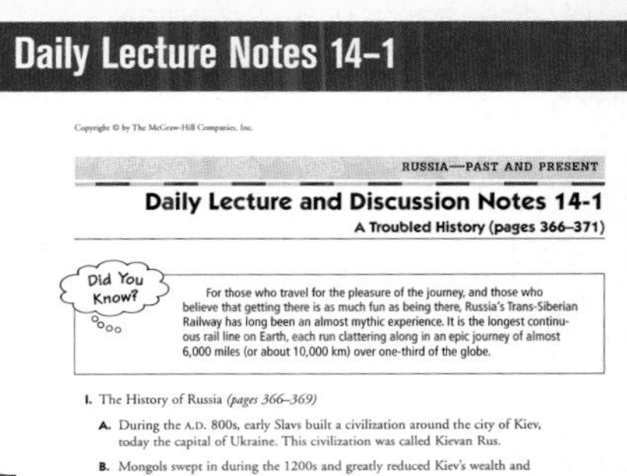

RUSSIA—PAST AND PRESENT

Daily Lecture and Discussion Notes 14-1

A Troubled History (pages 366–371)

Did You Know? For those who travel for the pleasure of the journey, and those who believe that getting there is as much fun as being there, Russia's Trans-Siberian Railway has long been an almost mythic experience. It is the longest continuous rail line on Earth, each run clattering along in an epic journey of almost 6,000 miles (or about 10,000 km) over one-third of the globe.

I. The History of Russia (*pages 366–369*)

A. During the A.D. 800s, early Slavs built a civilization around the city of Kiev, today the capital of Ukraine. This civilization was called Kievan Rus.

B. Mongols swept in during the 1200s and greatly reduced Kiev's wealth and power.

More About the Photo

Early Russia Ivan III was the first czar of Russia, but Ivan IV was its most powerful. Under his rule, Russia expanded its territory and increased contact with western Europe.

Caption Answer Ivan III

Team-Teaching Activity

Government Ask a teacher with a background in government to discuss the Soviet Union's government. Have the discussion focus on these areas: Communist Party control of the government; government control of most areas of life; central government planning; and government censorship and punishment of dissidents. **Ask: What difficulties would these characteristics create for the country as it tried to move to democracy? What skills and attitudes would people have to learn to make democratic government work?** Have the class discuss these issues. **L1**

EE6 The Uses of Geography: Standards 17, 18

Building Skills

Context Clues Help students learn to define words by using context clues. Ask for volunteers to identify a word that is unfamiliar to them. Help them guess at the meaning of the word by understanding the context in which it is used. Suggest that students write these words on a note card and check their guesses against the dictionary. That way they can be sure that they correctly understand new words they encounter in reading.

Applying Map Skills

Answers

1. 1524–1689
2. 1945

Skills Practice

What lines of longitude does present day Russia lie within? *(approx. 30°E and 170°W)*

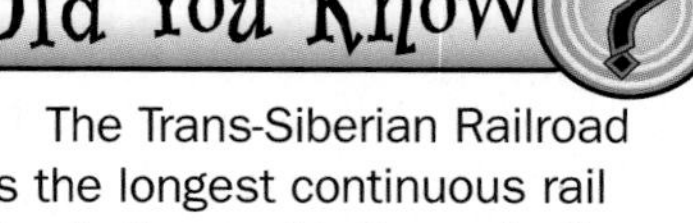

The Trans-Siberian Railroad is the longest continuous rail line in the world. Begun in the 1880s, the 5,750-mile (9,254-km) line was completed in 1916.

NATIONAL GEOGRAPHIC

Expansion of Russia

Applying Map Skills

1. During which time period was the most land added to Russia?
2. Was Russia's land area larger in 1945, or is it larger today?

Find NGS online map resources @ www.nationalgeographic.com/maps

The czar and the nobles enjoyed rich, comfortable lives. At the bottom of society, however, were the great masses of people. Most were **serfs,** or farm laborers, who could be bought and sold along with the land. These people lived hard lives, working on the nobles' country estates or in city palaces. Few could read or write. They did not follow Western customs, but kept the Russian traditions.

Dramatic Changes In 1812, a French army led by **Napoleon Bonaparte** invaded Russia. Brave Russian soldiers and the fierce winter weather finally forced the French to retreat. The year 1812 became a symbol of Russian patriotism. Have you ever heard the *1812 Overture,* with its dramatic ending that includes the ringing of bells and the bursts of cannon fire? Written by the Russian composer **Peter Tchaikovsky,** this musical masterpiece celebrates the Russian victory over Napoleon.

In the late 1800s, Russia entered a period of economic and social change. The Russian Empire expanded southward into the Caucasus Mountains and eastward into Central Asia and toward China and the Pacific Ocean. In 1861 **Czar Alexander II,** known as the Czar-Liberator, freed the serfs from being tied to the land. His new law did little to lift them out of poverty, though. Russia began to **industrialize,** or change its economy to rely more on manufacturing and less on farming.

Meeting Special Needs

Auditory/Musical Obtain a recording of Tchaikovsky's *1812 Overture.* Explain that the work was written to commemorate Russia's victory over Napoleon. (The initial performance was outdoors, one reason that Tchaikovsky was able to include the famous cannons.) Point out that in the central section of the piece, Tchaikovsky uses the French and Russian national anthems ("La Marseillaise" and "God Save the Czar") to clash against each other, representing the clash of the French and Russian armies. Play the ending so students can hear the cannons roar, the triumph of the Russian anthem, and the church bells. After listening, have them discuss how such a piece of music would make Russians feel about their country and why it appeals to societies all over the world. **L1 ELL**

Railroads, including the famous **Trans-Siberian Railroad,** spread across the country. It linked Moscow in the west with Vladivostok on Russia's Pacific coast.

✓Reading Check **What was the name of the civilization that early Slavs built in the area that is today Ukraine?**

The Soviet Era

In 1914, World War I broke out in Europe. Russian and German armies met and fought bloody battles in eastern Europe. Unprepared for war, Russia suffered many defeats and had few victories. As the fighting dragged on, shortages of food in Russian cities caused much starvation. The Russian people blamed the czars for their troubles.

The Russian Revolution In 1917, political leaders, soldiers, and factory workers forced **Czar Nicholas II** to give up the throne. Later that year, a political rebel named **Vladimir Lenin** (VLAH•deh•meehr LEN•in) led a second revolution and seized control. He and his followers set up a **communist state.** A communist state is a country whose government has almost total control over the economy and society as a whole. Fearing invasion, the Communists moved Russia's capital from coastal St. Petersburg to Moscow.

Growth of Soviet Power By 1922, after a brutal civil war, Russia's Communist leaders were securely in power. In that year, they formed the **Union of Soviet Socialist Republics (U.S.S.R.),** or the Soviet Union. This vast territory included Russia and most of the conquered territories of the old Russian Empire. After Lenin died in 1924, Communist Party officials disagreed over who was to lead the country.

Within a few years, **Joseph Stalin** won out over the others and became the Soviet Union's leader. Under Stalin's orders, the government took complete control over the economy. Those who opposed Stalin's actions were killed or sent to remote prison camps deep in the vast forests of icy Siberia. Millions of people were brutally murdered or forced into slave labor under Stalin's rule.

Our World Today online

Web Activity Visit the ***Our World Today: People, Places, and Issues*** Web site at owt.glencoe.com and click on **Chapter 14–Student Web Activities** to learn more about the Russian Revolution.

NATIONAL GEOGRAPHIC On Location

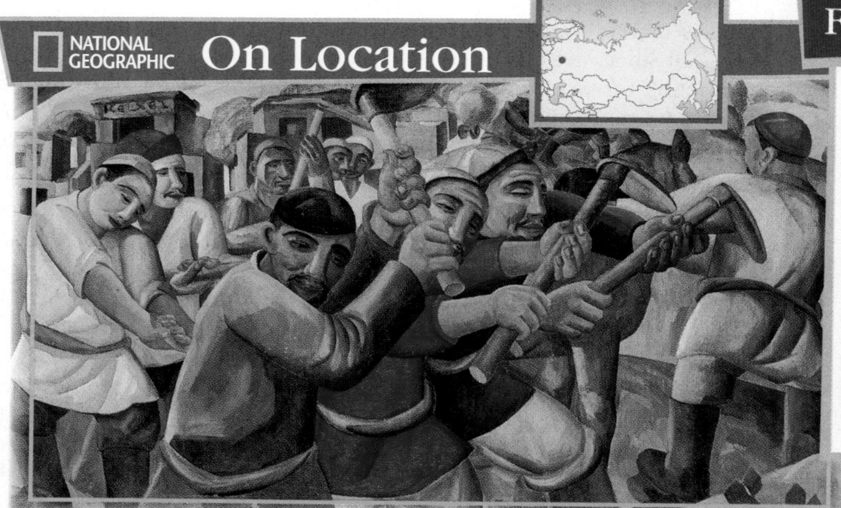

Collective Farm Workers

In an effort to increase food production, Stalin combined small peasant farms into large collectives, shown in this painting by Alexander Volkov. Peasant resistance turned the experiment into a disaster.

Government How do you think Stalin dealt with the farmers who resisted?

Chapter 14

Section 1, pages 366–371

✓ Reading Check Answer

Kievan Rus

Our World Today online

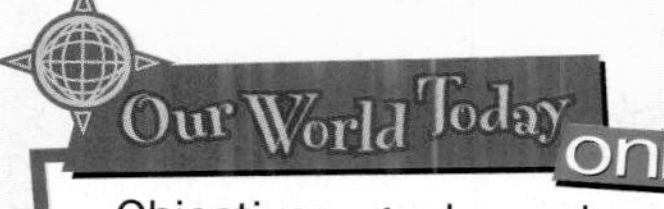

Objectives, goals, and answers to the Student Web Activity can be found in the Web Activity Lesson Plan at owt.glencoe.com

More About the Photos

Collective Farm Workers Under Stalin's collective farming program, peasants were forced to turn over their grain to the government. Millions of peasants lost their land or died as a result of collectivization.

Caption Answer He had them killed or sent to prison camps.

Measure student knowledge of physical features and political entities.

GeoQuiz Transparency 14-1

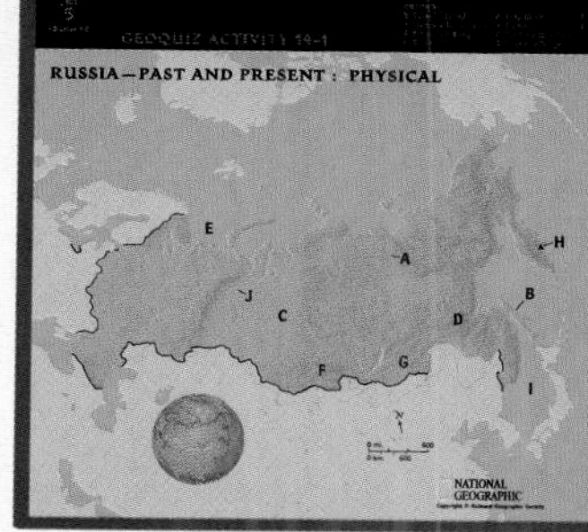

Critical Thinking Activity

Understanding Cause and Effect Write a list of statements on the board, such as "Serfs freed but remain poor," "Opponents killed or sent to prison camps," and "Czars expand Russia's borders." Have students identify the period in Russian history in which it belongs. When the exercise is complete, ask students to evaluate the relationships between past conflicts and current conditions in Russia. What common themes do they see in Russian history? L2

EE4 Human Systems: Standard 12

Answer Russian royalty lived extravagantly. The post-revolutionary government did not tolerate such excesses.

Activity Have students design an egg using sequins or glitter.

World Art and Architecture Transparencies

Use these prints with accompanying strategies and activities to introduce other arts of the region.

Guided Reading Activity 14-1

Name ________ Date ________ Class ________

RUSSIA—PAST AND PRESENT

Guided Reading Activity 14-1
A Troubled History

DIRECTIONS: Answering Questions Reading the section and answering the questions below will help you learn more about Russia's troubled history. Use your textbook to write answers to the questions.

1. Where did the early Slavs build a civilization, and what was it called?
2. Why was Napoleon Bonaparte not successful in conquering Russia?
3. After Nicholas II was forced to give up the throne, what happened?

Assign Section 1 Assessment as homework or an in-class activity.

Have students use the Interactive Tutor Self-Assessment CD-ROM to review Section 14–1.

Art

Peter Carl Fabergé was no ordinary Russian jeweler. His successful workshop designed extravagant jeweled flowers, figures, and animals. He is most famous for crafting priceless gold Easter eggs for the czar of Russia and other royalty in Europe and Asia. Each egg was unique and took nearly a year to create. Lifting the lid of the egg revealed a tiny surprise. One egg Fabergé created (shown here) held an intricate ship inside.

Looking Closer **Why do you think Fabergé's workshop closed after the Russian Revolution of 1917?**

Fabergé egg ▲

In 1941, Nazi Germany invaded the Soviet Union, bringing the country into World War II. During the conflict, the Soviets joined with Great Britain and the United States to defeat the Germans. Millions of Russians—soldiers and civilians—died in what Russians call the Great Patriotic Fatherland War.

A Superpower When World War II ended, Stalin wanted to protect the Soviet Union from any more invasions. He sent troops to set up communist governments in neighboring Eastern European countries. These countries formed what was called an "iron curtain" behind which corruption and brutality were the norm. Stalin and the leaders who followed him spent large amounts of money on the military and weapons. The Soviet Union became one of the two most powerful nations in the world. The other superpower—the United States—opposed Soviet actions. These two nations engaged in the **Cold War**, competing for world influence without breaking out in actual fighting. They even competed in areas outside the world. Both the Soviet Union and the United States launched rockets in a bid to be first in outer space.

The Cold War Years From 1940 to about 1980—the Cold War years—the Soviet economy faced many problems. The government factories and businessess had no competition and no one was allowed to make a profit. Factories became inefficient and produced poor-quality goods. The government cared more about making tanks and airplanes for military purposes than cars and refrigerators. As a result, people had few consumer goods to buy. Food often became scarce, and people often waited in long lines to buy bread, milk, and

Cooperative Learning Activity

Illustrated Time Line Organize students into five groups and assign each group one of the following historical periods: 900s–1400s, 1400s–1800s, 1800s–1917, 1920–1990, and 1991–present. Have each group research its assigned time period and choose events to include on an illustrated time line of Russian history. On the classroom wall, attach a long strip of paper on which the dates are written. Have groups place annotated illustrations of their selected events in appropriate places along the time line. Suggest that they use yarn to connect each illustration with its correct date. **L2**

EE4 Human Systems: Standard 9

other necessary items. As during World War I, the Russian people and those living in Soviet-controlled areas became very unhappy.

The Soviet Union had another challenge. This vast empire included not only Russians but also people from many other ethnic groups. Instead of being scattered throughout the country, people in each of these other groups generally lived together in the same area. They resented the control of the government in Moscow, which they believed favored Slavic Russians. They wanted to leave the Soviet Union and form their own countries.

▲ Mikhail Gorbachev tried to lesson the Russian government's control of the economy and society.

Soviet Collapse In 1985, **Mikhail Gorbachev** (GAWR•buh•CHAWF) became the leader of the Soviet Union. Gorbachev hoped to lessen the government's control of the economy and society. He allowed farmers and factory managers to make many of their own decisions. He allowed people to speak freely about the government and important issues, a policy called **glasnost,** or "openness." Instead of strengthening the country, however, his policies only made people doubt the communist system even more. People's demands for more and more changes eventually led to the collapse of both communism and the Soviet Union.

By late 1991, each of the 15 republics that made up the Soviet Union had declared its independence. The Soviet Union no longer existed. Russia emerged as the largest and most powerful of those republics. Although a rough road lay ahead, many Russians were thrilled by the end of communism and the chance to enjoy freedom.

✓Reading Check **What were three reasons for the breakup of the Soviet Union?**

Section 1 Assessment

Defining Terms

1. **Define** czar, serf, industrialize, communist state, Cold War, glasnost.

Recalling Facts

2. **History** Why did Peter the Great build a new capital of Russia?
3. **History** Who led the 1917 revolution in Russia?
4. **History** What happened to the Soviet Union in 1991?

Critical Thinking

5. **Understanding Cause and Effect** What problems were created when Mikhail Gorbachev allowed the policy of glasnost in Russia?
6. **Analyzing Information** How did glasnost weaken the communist system?

Graphic Organizer

7. **Organizing Information** In a chart like this one, write facts that show the contrast between the nobles and the serfs of Russia.

Nobles	Serfs

Applying Social Studies Skills

8. **Creating Mental Maps** Create your own map of early Russian territory. Label where Kievan Rus was located. Then label where Peter the Great moved the capital.

Section 1 Assessment

1. The terms are defined in the Glossary.
2. He wanted it to be more European and closer to Europe.
3. Vladimir Lenin
4. It became 15 independent republics.
5. People began to doubt the Communist system more than before.
6. People demanded more changes.
7. Nobles: spoke French and Russian, wore European clothes, attended fancy parties, rich, comfortable; Serfs: laborers, could be bought and sold, lived hard lives, couldn't read or write, followed Russian traditions
8. This exercise helps students visualize historic Russia. All attempts at freehand mapping should be accepted.

Chapter 14

Section 1, pages 366–371

Section Quiz 14-1

Name ______ Date ______ Class ______

Score

RUSSIA—PAST AND PRESENT

Section Quiz 14-1

A Troubled History

DIRECTIONS: Matching Match each item in Column A with the items in Column B. Write the correct letters in the blanks. *(10 points each)*

COLUMN A	COLUMN B
A. *glasnost*	____ 1. emperor
B. serf	____ 2. change the economy to rely more on manufacturing and less on farming
C. Cold War	____ 3. competition for world influence between the Soviet Union and the United States
D. czar	____ 4. openness
E. industrialize	____ 5. farm laborer who could be bought and sold with the land

...iple Choice In the blank at the left, write the letter of the ... answers the question. *(10 points each)*

✓ Reading Check Answer

The economy had problems, people of different ethnic groups wanted independence from Russia, glasnost made people doubt the Communist system.

Reteach

Have students create a concept web of Russian history.

Reading Essentials and Study Guide 14-1

Name ______ Date ______ Class ______

RUSSIA—PAST AND PRESENT

Reading Essentials and Study Guide 14-1

A Troubled History

For use with textbook pages 366-371

Terms to Know

czar emperor (page 367)
serf farm laborer who could be bought and sold along with the land (page 368)
industrialize to change an economy to rely more on manufacturing and less on farming (page 368)
communist state country whose government has almost total control over the economy and society (page 369)
cold war competing for world influence without actually fighting (page 370)
glasnot ????

Drawing From Experience

... "duck and cover"? If you had lived ... school, students learned ...

4 CLOSE

Have students create a display that illustrates the Communist period in Russian history.

Teach

Tell students to imagine that they must spend all day every day for two months in a space the size of the classroom with small compartments on the side for sleeping. Tell them that they must live and work in this space with the same two people every day. **Ask: What characteristics must a person have to live in these circumstances?** *(patience, tolerance, discipline)* Point out that this is how cosmonauts who served on *Mir* actually lived. L1

More About *Mir*

The living area of *Mir* was divided into crews' quarters (with a chair, a sleeping bag, and a porthole); bathroom facilities (with a toilet, sink, and shower); and a galley (with a table, cooking areas, and facilities for storing trash). The space station also had a stationary bike to use for exercise.

Interdisciplinary Connections

Science Students can visit the NASA Web site *(spaceflight.nasa.gov)* for information about the International Space Station. Included are a virtual reality tour of the station, a tracking map that shows the location of the station in real time, and a way of identifying when you can see the space station fly overhead.

Making Connections

CULTURE | GOVERNMENT | PEOPLE | TECHNOLOGY

Cooperative Space Ventures

The space age officially began in 1957, when Russia launched *Sputnik I.* It was the first artificial satellite to orbit the earth.

The Space Race

The Russians sent the first man into space in 1961, when cosmonaut Yuri Gagarin orbited the earth. A few weeks later, Alan Shepard made the United States's first space flight. John Glenn was the first astronaut to orbit the earth in 1962. After this, the "space race" between the United States and Russia was of global importance. It was feared that one country could dominate the world if it had the right equipment in space.

Over the years, both Russia and the United States launched many spacecraft. In 1986, the Russian space station *Mir,* which means "peace," began to orbit the earth. This was the first permanently staffed laboratory in space. Astronauts from more than a dozen countries were invited to participate on the space station *Mir.* The astronauts and Russian cosmonauts performed many experiments about the effects of weightlessness.

In 1993 the United States and Russia decided to work jointly to build an International Space Station. On November 2, 2000, the International Space Station had its first permanent human inhabitants. The crew was made up of both Russian cosmonauts and American astronauts. Finally, on March 22, 2001, after 15 years of use, *Mir* was allowed to plummet back to Earth.

Making the Connection

1. What country launched the space age?
2. How have the United States and Russia cooperated on space ventures?
3. **Making Predictions** What space technology do you think we will see in the future? What social consequences might result from this?

NATIONAL GEOGRAPHIC

***Mir* Space Station Core Module**

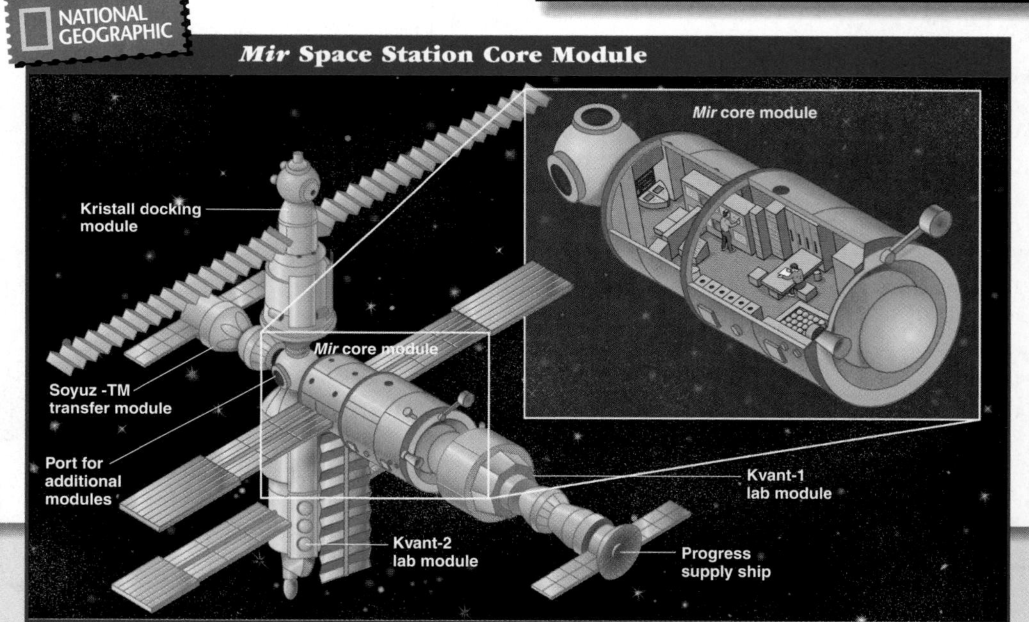

Making the Connection

1. Russia
2. They jointly built the International Space Station and its first crew was American and Russian.
3. Answers will vary. *Possible predictions:* a bigger and better space station, passenger shuttles to the moon, crewed missions to Mars. *Possible consequences:* new settlements outside of Earth, new energy or mineral resources from space, new technologies and discoveries.

Section 2

A New Russia

Guide to Reading

Main Idea

Russia has a rich cultural heritage but faces challenges in adopting a new economic system and government.

Terms to Know

- free market economy
- nuclear energy
- federal republic

Reading Strategy

Create a diagram like this one. Then write four challenges facing Russia.

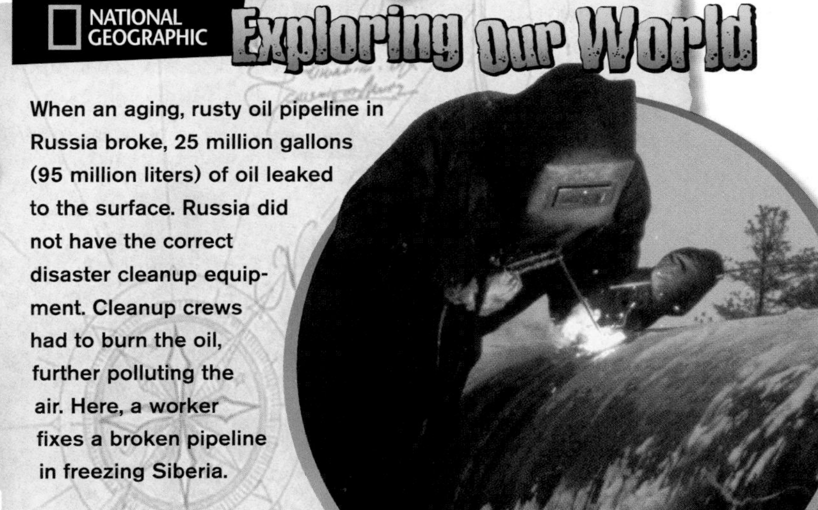

When an aging, rusty oil pipeline in Russia broke, 25 million gallons (95 million liters) of oil leaked to the surface. Russia did not have the correct disaster cleanup equipment. Cleanup crews had to burn the oil, further polluting the air. Here, a worker fixes a broken pipeline in freezing Siberia.

The Russian people have been working to move away from the strict, tightly controlled rules of the czars and Communists. They are moving toward a democratic government and an economy based on competition and private ownership. They have found that these changes do not come easily.

From Communism to Free Enterprise

The fall of communism turned Russia's economy upside down. The new Russian government turned to a free market economy, the system followed in the United States. Under a **free market economy**, the people, not the government, decide what businesses to start and run. Today Russian factory managers can decide what products to make. People can open businesses—such as restaurants, stores, or computer companies—and choose their own careers.

The Russian people gained freedom, but staying free is hard work. People now can make their own decisions, but those decisions do not always lead to success. Businesses can fail. People may become

373

1 Focus

Section Objectives

1. Discuss the economic challenges that Russia faces today.
2. Explain the political changes that Russia is undergoing.

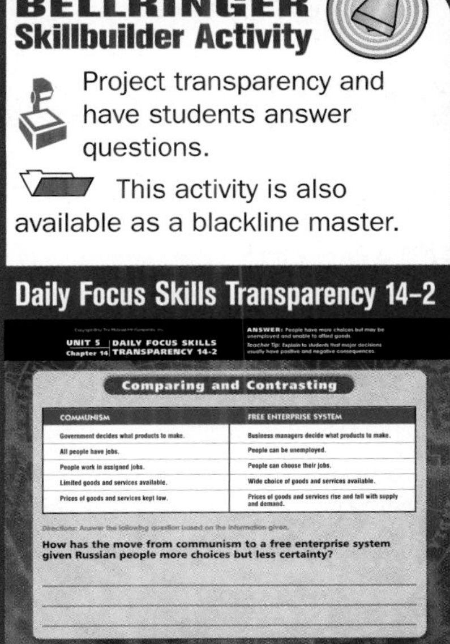

BELLRINGER Skillbuilder Activity

Project transparency and have students answer questions.

This activity is also available as a blackline master.

Daily Focus Skills Transparency 14-2

UNIT 5 Chapter 14 | DAILY FOCUS SKILLS TRANSPARENCY 14-2

ANSWER: People have more choices but may be unemployed and unable to afford goods.
Teacher Tip: Explain to students that major decisions usually have positive and negative consequences.

Comparing and Contrasting

COMMUNISM	FREE ENTERPRISE SYSTEM
Government decides what products to make.	Business managers decide what products to make.
All people have jobs.	People can be unemployed.
People work in assigned jobs.	People can choose their jobs.
Limited goods and services available.	Wide choice of goods and services available.
Prices of goods and services kept low.	Prices of goods and services rise and fall with supply and demand.

Directions: Answer the following question based on the information given.

How has the move from communism to a free enterprise system given Russian people more choices but less certainty?

Guide to Reading

■ **Accessing Prior Knowledge**
Ask: What challenges do you think Russia faces in changing from the old Soviet ways? Write students' suggestions on the board. As they study the section, have them add to or take items away from the list.

Use the Vocabulary PuzzleMaker to create crossword and word search puzzles.

Section Resources

Reproducible Masters
- Reproducible Lesson Plan 14-2
- Daily Lecture and Discussion Notes 14-2
- Guided Reading Activity 14-2
- Reading Essentials and Study Guide 14-2
- Section Quiz 14-2

Transparencies
- Daily Focus Skills Transparency 14-2
- GeoQuiz Transparency 14-1

Multimedia
- Vocabulary PuzzleMaker Software
- Interactive Tutor Self-Assessment CD-ROM
- Presentation Plus! CD-ROM
- ExamView® Pro 3.0 Testmaker CD-ROM

Distinguishing Differences
Have students create a two-column chart comparing life under the Soviet regime to life in Russia today. L1

Reading Check Answer
the people

Daily Lecture Notes 14-2

RUSSIA—PAST AND PRESENT
Daily Lecture and Discussion Notes 14-2
A New Russia (pages 373–376)

Did You Know? Many Russians celebrate the end of winter and the coming of spring with a Pancake Week. The celebration announces the end of winter, and prepares people for Lent. People wear brightly colored masks and costumes, and join in the festivities of eating, drinking, and dancing. Throughout the week people feast on pancakes served with honey, caviar, fresh cream, and butter.

I. From Communism to Free Enterprise (pages 373–374)
A. The fall of communism turned Russia's economy upside down. The new Russian government turned to a market economy, the system followed in the United States. Under a free market economy, the people, not the government, decide what businesses to start and run.
Under communism, everybody had jobs. Workers today can lose their jobs

More About the Photos

Shortages Under Communism In Soviet days, Russian stores were often short of goods. In order to get what they wanted, many people bought goods in the illegal economy. They used this so-called black market for anything from food to medicines to spare parts with which to fix home appliances.

Caption Answer because prices have risen and now some people are unemployed

Reading Check Answer
They leave dangerous by-products in the air.

unemployed. Under communism, everybody had jobs. Workers today can lose their jobs when business is poor.

In addition, the government no longer sets prices for food and other goods. When prices were set low, the Russian people could afford the goods, but they often faced shortages. Without government controls, prices have risen. Higher prices make it harder to buy necessities such as food and clothing. It is hoped that, in the future, factories will start producing more goods. Now that manufacturers and producers know they can receive higher prices and more profits for their goods, supplies should increase.

Reading Check **Who decides what businesses to start and run in a free market economy?**

Environmental Issues

Pollution is a serious problem in Russia today. Forest lands in Russia have been cut without replanting seedlings to hold the soil. This is causing serious soil erosion in some areas. Chemical fertilizers have been heavily used to increase crop production. These chemicals can build up in the soil over time and destroy its ability to grow food.

NATIONAL GEOGRAPHIC On Location

Food Shortages

Under communism, prices were low, but people faced shortages and had to wait in line to buy goods.

Economics **Why can many Russians today not afford goods and services?**

Air Pollution The government built power plants to make **nuclear energy,** or energy from controlled atomic reactions. Nuclear power plants can leave dangerous by-products in the air. Air pollution from heavy industry is also particularly bad. Gases are given off by coal-fired electric plants, vehicles, and other forms of transportation in major cities. It has caused many people to suffer from lung diseases. Rising numbers of people have cancer, and people in Russia are dying sooner.

Water Pollution Chemicals that are used in agriculture and industry often end up in rivers and lakes. Poor sewer systems also pollute water systems in Russia. Yet another source of water pollution is the chemical weapons that were developed by the Soviet Union during the Cold War. Many of these are buried in dumps throughout Russia. Age is causing the weapons to deteriorate and some of the chemicals are finding their way into groundwater or nearby waterways.

Reading Check **What pollution problems do nuclear power plants create?**

Team-Teaching Activity

Health As the text points out, life expectancy in Russia has been falling in recent years. Invite a health teacher to class to discuss the factors that can influence life expectancy, including the spread of communicable diseases; environmental problems; lifestyle problems (poor diet, lack of exercise, and unhealthful habits such as smoking, drinking alcohol, and taking drugs); and problems in the health care system (lack of medicines, reduced use of vaccines, poor quality or insufficient facilities, and so on). Then have students conduct research to discover what factors in the economy have contributed to the decrease in Russian life expectancy. Have them write a report on their findings. L2

EE4 Human Systems: Standard 10

NATIONAL GEOGRAPHIC **On Location**

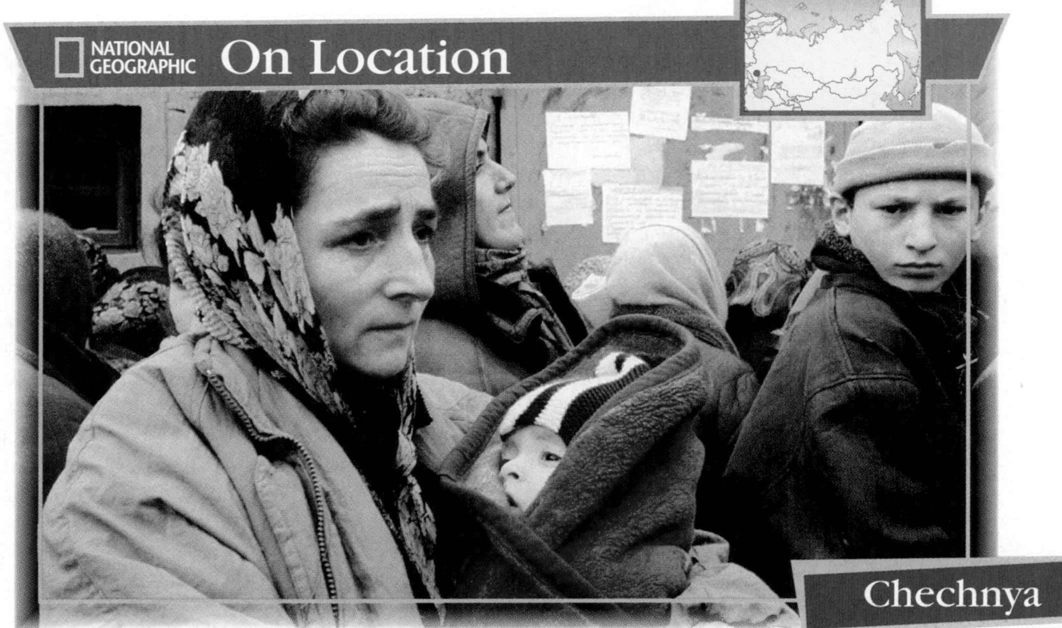

Chechnya

These Chechens are standing in line to receive humanitarian aid after Russian rebels fought in this area.

Culture **Why might Chechens want to be independent from Russia?**

Political Challenges

Today Russia is a democracy, a government in which people freely elect their leaders. Russia, like the United States, is also a **federal republic.** This means that power is divided between national and state governments. A president is elected to lead the nation.

A Russian president has stronger powers than an American president. For example, the Russian president can issue orders that become laws even if they are not passed by the legislature. Russia's first two presidents—**Boris Yeltsin** (BOH•rehs YEHL•tzehn) and **Vladimir Putin** (VLAH•deh•meehr POO•tihn)—used their powers to help develop and strengthen Russia's economy.

In adjusting to a new form of government, Russians face important political challenges. Democracy is built on the idea of the rule of law. In the past, Russian leaders did what they wanted to do. In the new system, they must learn to follow the law. Also, past governments punished people who criticized their decisions. In a democracy, officials have to respect other opinions.

Another challenge results from the fact that Russia is home to many different ethnic groups. Some of these groups want to form their own countries. Among these groups are the **Chechens** (CHEH•chehnz), who live in **Chechnya** (CHEHCH•nee•uh) near the Caspian Sea and Caucasus Mountains in southern Russia. Russian troops have fought Chechen forces to keep Chechnya a part of Russia.

✓Reading Check **Why is being home to different ethnic groups a challenge for Russia?**

More About the Photos

Chechnya Chechnya declared itself independent from the Soviet Union in 1991. The Russian government did not recognize Chechnya's independence and invaded the republic in 1994.

Caption Answer Chechens are a different ethnic group from Russians, and they are Muslims rather than Russian Orthodox.

Guided Reading Activity 14-2

Name ________ Date ________ Class ________

RUSSIA—PAST AND PRESENT

Guided Reading Activity 14-2

A New Russia

DIRECTIONS: Filling in the Blanks Reading the section and completing the sentences below will help you learn more about the new Russia. Refer to your textbook to fill in the blanks.

The government controlled Russia's **(1)** ________ under communism. After communism fell, Russia turned to a **(2)** ________ ________ economy.

Under communism, the environment was not **(3)** ________. The government built plants to make **(4)** ________ energy, which produces **(5)** ________ by-products. People are **(6)** ________ sooner due to the effects of **(7)** ________.

... **(8)** ________, and also a

Assess

Assign Section 2 Assessment as homework or an in-class activity.

Have students use the Interactive Tutor Self-Assessment CD-ROM to review Section 14–2.

✓ Reading Check Answer

Some of these groups want to form their own countries.

Critical Thinking Activity

Predicting Consequences Point out that under communism, Russians were accustomed to obeying the government without question. Ask students to predict how freedom might affect people's attitudes and behavior. Have students consider the following question: **What skills might Russians need to develop to handle their newfound freedom?** *(Answers might include the ability to negotiate, to take risks, and to make economic decisions.)* **What responsibilities will Russian citizens have with their new rights?** *(taking part in government, voting, obeying laws voluntarily)* Have them write a letter to a Russian that identifies and explains the importance of voluntary civic participation in Russia's new, more democratic society. **L2**

EE2 Places and Regions: Standard 6

Chapter 14

Section 2, pages 373–376

Section Quiz 14-2

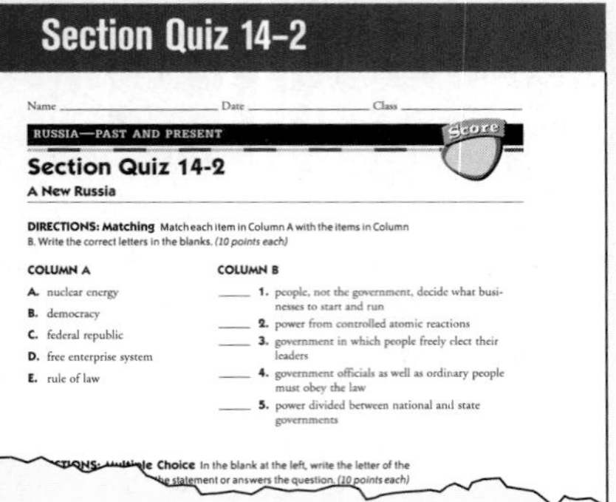
Name ______ Date ______ Class ______

RUSSIA—PAST AND PRESENT

Score

Section Quiz 14-2

A New Russia

DIRECTIONS: Matching Match each item in Column A with the items in Column B. Write the correct letters in the blanks. *(10 points each)*

COLUMN A	COLUMN B
A. nuclear energy	____ 1. people, not the government, decide what businesses to start and run
B. democracy	____ 2. power from controlled atomic reactions
C. federal republic	____ 3. government in which people freely elect their leaders
D. free enterprise system	____ 4. government officials as well as ordinary people must obey the law
E. rule of law	____ 5. power divided between national and state governments

DIRECTIONS: Multiple Choice In the blank at the left, write the letter of the ... statement or answers the question. *(10 points each)*

✓ Reading Check Answer

the change from communist to democratic government, creating a free market economy, trust among different ethnic groups, cleaning the environment

Reading Essentials and Study Guide 14-2

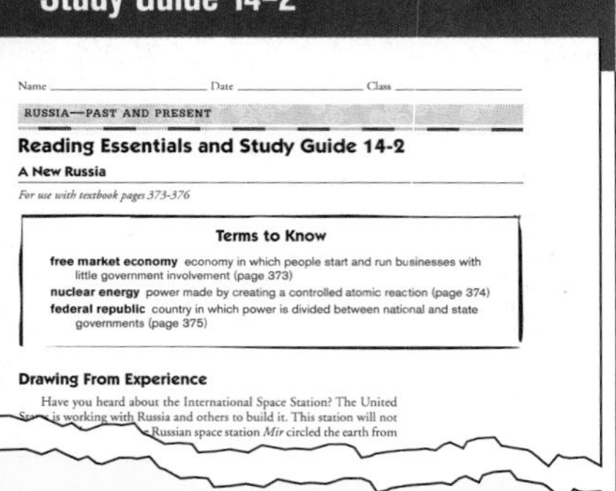
Name ______ Date ______ Class ______

RUSSIA—PAST AND PRESENT

Reading Essentials and Study Guide 14-2

A New Russia

For use with textbook pages 373–376

Terms to Know

free market economy economy in which people start and run businesses with little government involvement (page 373)

nuclear energy power made by creating a controlled atomic reaction (page 374)

federal republic country in which power is divided between national and state governments (page 375)

Drawing From Experience

Have you heard about the International Space Station? The United States is working with Russia and others to build it. This station will not ... Russian space station *Mir* circled the earth from

4 Close

Have students research and prepare a presentation about the latest political developments in Russia or one of the Eurasian Republics.

The Challenge of Change

Russia and the Eurasian Republics are presently facing many challenges. The most important of these have been discussed in the last two chapters. One of these is the change from a communist to a democratic government. Another challenge involves creating a free market economy. People must be given an opportunity to learn, work, and raise families. Third, if the region is to have peace, trust must grow among the different ethnic groups. Finally, the land, air, and waterways must be cleaned up and preserved for future generations.

The free countries of the world have many reasons to want Russia to succeed. If the Russian people cannot live under a democratic government, will they try to turn back to communism? Is an unstable Russia dangerous for Europe? A strong, free Russia may guide neighboring countries toward democracy. Russia has seen two revolutions in the last century, one violent and one peaceful. The problem faced by the world is how to best help this region reach its goals so that there will be no more violent Russian revolutions.

✓ Reading Check **What are some of the challenges facing Russia and the Eurasian Republics?**

Assessment

Defining Terms

1. **Define** free market economy, nuclear energy, federal republic.

Recalling Facts

2. **Environment** How has the government added to the problem of pollution?
3. **Environment** What are three sources of water pollution in Russia?
4. **Government** Why has there been fighting with Chechnya?

Critical Thinking

5. **Synthesizing Information** After years of living under Communist rule, why is it hard for Russians to live under democracy?
6. **Making Predictions** Russia is now a federal republic, and government officials need to learn how to make decisions in a democracy. How do you think that will affect life in Russia in the future?

Graphic Organizer

7. **Organizing Information** Create a diagram like this one, and list two facts about Russia for each topic in the four outer ovals. Facts should reflect the conditions in Russia today.

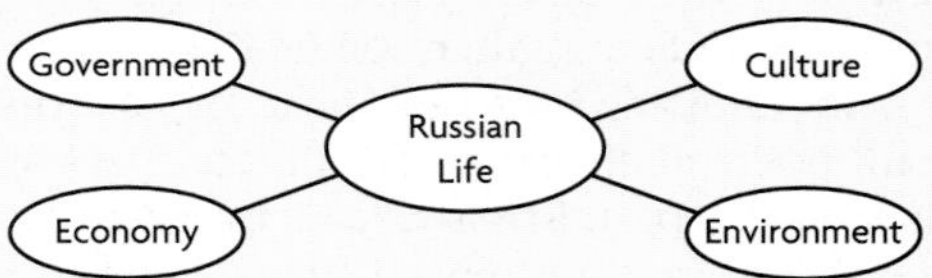

Applying Social Studies Skills

8. **Comparing Governments** Compare Russia's government during communism and since it has changed to a democratic government. List similarities and differences.

Section 2 Assessment

1. The terms are defined in the Glossary.
2. They were concerned with building factories, not protecting the environment.
3. chemicals from agriculture and industry, poor sewer systems, buried chemical weapons
4. Ethnic groups in Chechnya want to form their own country.
5. They are not used to running their own businesses and careers; there was no unemployment under communism; the government set price controls, but now the free market has high prices.
6. Answers will vary.
7. Diagrams will vary.
8. *Similarities:* president has strong powers, can issue orders without legislature; *Differences:* people elect leaders, leaders subject to laws

TIME REPORTS

FOCUS ON WORLD ISSUES

The New Russia

Is Democracy Working?

SOVFOTO/EASTFOTO

Focus on World Issues

Teacher Background

Following the defeat of Russia in World War I, the Communists seized control of the government, eventually taking over the entire territory that became the Soviet Union. Because of the government's repressive policies, the economy performed poorly. From 1985–1991, Mikhail Gorbachev attempted to modernize communism by making the economy less centralized. However, this attempt ultimately failed, leading to the December 1991 breakup of the Soviet Union.

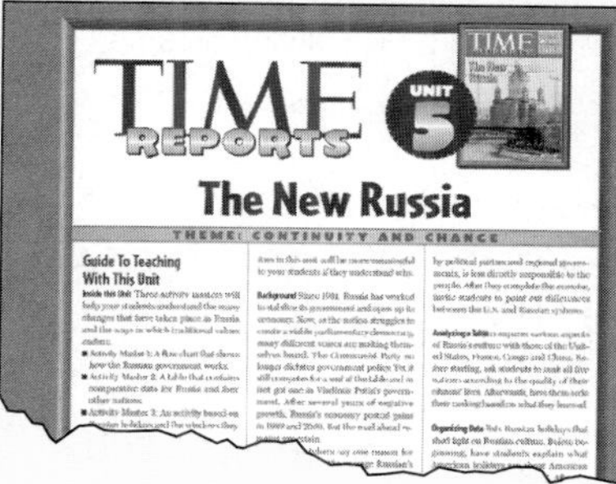
TIME REPORTS UNIT 5

The New Russia

THEME: CONTINUITY AND CHANGE

Guide To Teaching With This Unit

Preparing the Student

Explain to students that the breakup of the Soviet Union resulted in 15 independent nations, with Russia being the largest. Without any preparation, Russia went from being a highly restrictive, totalitarian government to a democracy. This report discusses the problems Russians continue to encounter because of this sudden transition.

Making Connections

Democracy **Ask students:** **How does U.S. society prepare young people to participate in democracy?** List the student's ideas on the board. Ideas might include taking government and civics courses in school, reading and hearing about politics in newspapers and on television, and watching adults vote. **Ask:** **How is this different from what happened in 1991 when the Soviet Union suddenly broke up? Why do you think it has been difficult for the Russian people to get a good start on a stable democratic government?**

TIME REPORTS

FOCUS ON WORLD ISSUES

SOVFOTO/EASTFOTO

CHRISTOPHER MORRIS/BLACK STAR

In Moscow a cathedral destroyed by the Communists has been rebuilt. Older Russians are especially pleased.

1 Focus

Point to Russia on a world map and mention that it is the world's largest country. **Ask: What have you heard about life in Russia today?** Students might mention that Russians can now vote and own businesses. However, most of them are poor and there is a great deal of corruption, even among government officials.

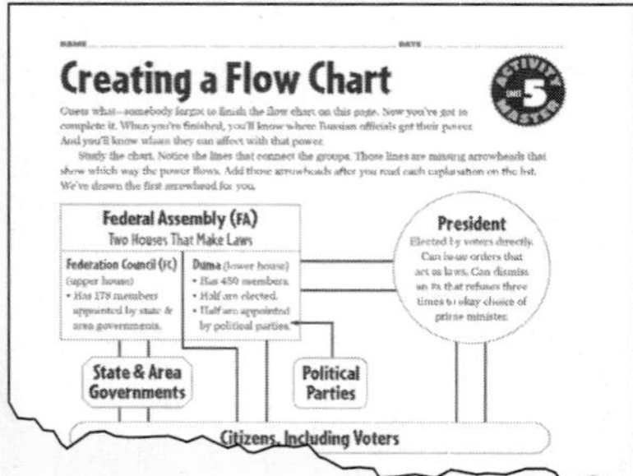

NAME .... DATE ....

Creating a Flow Chart

ACTIVITY MASTER UNIT 5

Guess what—somebody forgot to finish the flow chart on this page. Now you've got to complete it. When you're finished, you'll know where Russian officials get their power. And you'll know whom they can affect with that power.

Study the chart. Notice the lines that connect the groups. Those lines are missing arrowheads that show which way the power flows. Add those arrowheads after you read each explanation on the list. We've drawn the first arrowhead for you.

Federal Assembly (FA)
Two Houses That Make Laws

Federation Council (FC) (upper house)
• Has 178 members appointed by state & area governments.

Duma (lower house)
• Has 450 members.
• Half are elected.
• Half are appointed by political parties.

President
Elected by voters directly. Can issue orders that act as laws. Can dismiss an [illegible] that refuses three times to okay choice of prime minister.

State & Area Governments

Political Parties

Citizens, Including Voters

Did You Know?

The average Russian has a purchasing power of $7,700 a year, compared to $36,200 in the United States. Forty percent of Russians live below the poverty line.

Inventing a Nation

Daniel Strigin lives in Moscow, the capital of Russia. There he shares a tiny, three-room apartment with his mother, his grandmother, his wife—and the parts of a one-seat airplane. Strigan, 30, is what Russians call a **kulibini**—a part-time inventor. By day he works as a computer technician. By night and on weekends, he works on his dream of flying a plane he built himself.

Prefab housing goes up in Provideniya, a port city west of Alaska in Russia's Far East.

WOLFGANG KAEHLER/CORBIS

Strigin is one of tens of thousands of *kulibini* in Russia. "There is something in the Russian man's soul," he says, "that pushes him to invent."

The impulse to invent is something Russia needs badly today. Its Communist government collapsed in 1991. Since then the country of 146 million people has been struggling to remake itself as a democracy.

Remarkable Gains

So far Russia has made impressive strides:

- Russians now elect their leaders, something they had never been allowed to do before.
- Russians now own factories, shops, restaurants, and other **enterprises**, or businesses. Before 1991, the government owned everything.
- Russia has shrunk its borders. Once it had been the Soviet Union's leading power. But that union fell to pieces. The republics that were part of it went their own way. Now all 15 of those former republics, including Russia, are independent nations.

Russia still has a long way to go. Its elected leaders sometimes act illegally to silence their critics. The government still owns all the nation's land. Steel companies and other huge businesses ended up in the hands of a few powerful people. Criminal gangs and dishonest public officials thrive. And in Chechnya, part of the Russian Federation, rebels have been at

378

Team-Teaching Activity

Government Have a teacher with a background in political science talk about the Russian government today. He or she should talk about how government policies affect the average Russian and what the government is doing to try to improve citizens' lives. If possible, the teacher should discuss how the average Russian lives, the types of schools children attend, and the kinds of jobs people have. Efforts by foreign governments and the international community to stabilize the government and economy should also be discussed. Have students discuss how the new Russian government compares to the United States government. **L2**

EE4 Human Systems: Standard 10

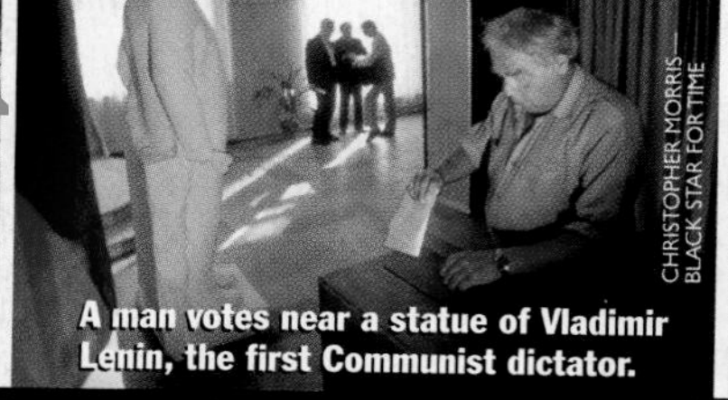
A man votes near a statue of Vladimir Lenin, the first Communist dictator.

A man dressed as a bear advertises a new restaurant in St. Petersburg.

Billboards near St. Basil Cathedral are evidence of the new Russian economy.

war with the government since 1994. The **Russian Federation** is Russia's official name.

Misery For Many

The reforms caused great hardship. In the shift to privately owned enterprises, thousands of farms and factories failed. Millions lost their jobs, and the government had no money with which to help them. In 1999, 55 million people—one out of three Russians—scraped by on less than $6 a month.

Millions landed on their feet, however. "Everyone willing to work hard has a chance nowadays," said a restaurant owner. "Not everyone is prepared to do that. I haven't taken a day off since I opened this place."

Where Russians Work

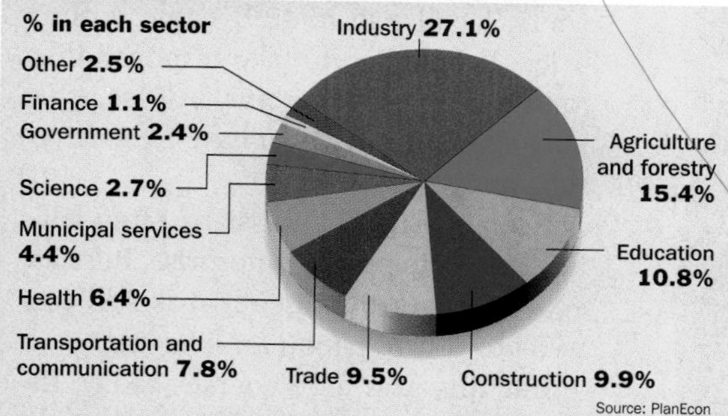

Source: PlanEcon

INTERPRETING GRAPHS

Explaining How does this graph tell you that about one in four Russians makes or sells industrial products?

EXPLORING THE ISSUE

1. **Making Inferences** Why might younger Russians find it easier than older Russians to learn to rely on themselves?
2. **Compare and Contrast** Suppose all the states in the United States became independent nations. How might that situation be like—and unlike—what happened to the Soviet Union?

Misplaced Trust

Russia's Communist government didn't ask Russians to plan their lives. "You did what was expected of you," said one woman. "We didn't think to ask questions or doubt the [Communist] system. Now," she added, "I can't imagine being so trusting."

Today's Russia has many strengths. Despite its stockpile of nuclear weapons, it is no longer a military superpower. But it remains the world's largest country, and its people are well educated. Its natural resources—oil, lumber, and minerals—are plentiful. And many of its privately owned factories have at last figured out how to make first-rate products.

"A Russian is **inventive**," says one of Daniel Strigin's *kulibini* friends, "because he has to find solutions in bad conditions."

Bad conditions haunt today's Russia. Time will tell whether its people have the will—and the inventiveness—to overcome them.

379

2 TEACH

Identifying Main Ideas
As students finish reading each subsection, have them write a one-sentence summary of that subsection. Ask volunteers to share their sentences.

After the students have finished reading the report, ask them to state its main idea. What message does Russia's experience send to all of us? One important point is that citizens must be carefully prepared to take part in a democracy. **L1**

Where Russians Work

ANSWER
It shows that 27.1% work in industry, a little more than one in four.

EXPLORING THE ISSUE

ANSWERS

1. Younger Russians have not lived for as many years (or maybe not at all) under a totalitarian regime that told them where to work, provided housing, and took care of their health care and other needs.
2. *Like:* Each state would have its own government, laws, army, taxes, currency. *Unlike:* American states have a number of things in common, such as a common language and a democratic government.

Meeting Special Needs

Auditory/Musical Have a group of 6 to 8 students research Russian folk music and dance. Books and tapes on folk music and dance are available at the public library. The students may want to see if they can find a local person, such as a person of Russian descent, who would be able to help them learn about Russian music and dance. The students should practice one or more folk dances and then present them to the class. If facilities allow, perhaps they can teach the dance to the entire class. Afterwards, discuss how the music and dances reflect Russian culture. **L1**

Refer to *Inclusion for the Middle School Social Studies Classroom Strategies and Activities* in the TCR.

TIME REPORTS

Recommended Internet Sites

news.bbc.co.uk
Enter "Collapse of USSR" in the Search box to find a time line, maps, photos, and a feature on how life has changed in each of the 15 former Soviet countries.

pbs.org/weta/faceofrussia/
This site has information on Russian culture, and what it was like to live in a communist society. It also has lesson plans.

More About the Photos

Stalin Ask: **What do you think this man liked about his life under Stalin's rule?**

EXPLORING THE ISSUE

ANSWERS

1. While today's Russia has many problems, people no longer live under a totalitarian government that steals their freedom and ultimately their lives.
2. If word gets around that these officials are mistreating people, they will not be re-elected.

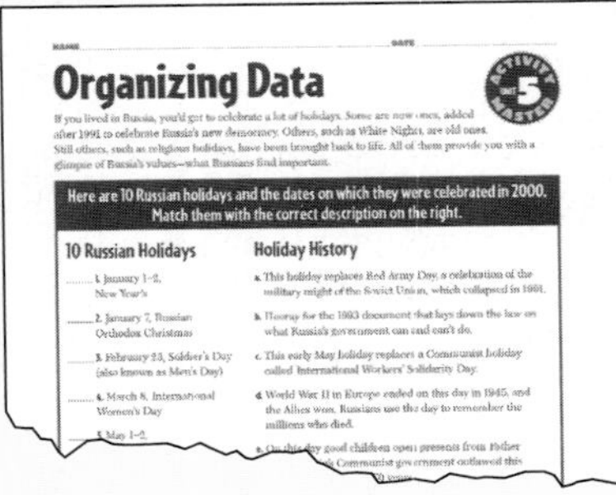

NAME .... DATE ....

Organizing Data

ACTIVITY 5 MASTER

If you lived in Russia, you'd get to celebrate a lot of holidays. Some are new ones, added after 1991 to celebrate Russia's new democracy. Others, such as White Nights, are old ones. Still others, such as religious holidays, have been brought back to life. All of them provide you with a glimpse of Russia's values—what Russians find important.

Here are 10 Russian holidays and the dates on which they were celebrated in 2000. Match them with the correct description on the right.

10 Russian Holidays	Holiday History
____ 1. January 1–2, New Year's	a. This holiday replaces Red Army Day, a celebration of the military might of the Soviet Union, which collapsed in 1991.
____ 2. January 7, Russian Orthodox Christmas	b. Hooray for the 1993 document that lays down the law on what Russia's government can and can't do.
____ 3. February 23, Soldier's Day (also known as Men's Day)	c. This early May holiday replaces a Communist holiday called International Workers' Solidarity Day.
____ 4. March 8, International Women's Day	d. World War II in Europe ended on this day in 1945, and the Allies won. Russians use the day to remember the millions who died.
____ 5. May 1–2	e. On this day good children open presents from Father ... Communist government outlawed this ...

TIME REPORTS

Are Russians Better Off?

Valentina Fedotova cries when she tells her story. In 1946, she was a student nurse in the Ukrainian city of Kiev. One day the secret police arrested her. They never told her why. After a four-minute "trial," she was shipped off to Russia's brutally cold Siberia. There she spent 10 years in a labor camp, working year-round mining gold. After 10 years, she was freed. But her sentence required her to stay in Siberia for 10 more years. By the time those years were up, Fedotova was a broken woman. She never left the far east, where she now lives alone.

CHRISTOPHER MORRIS/BLACK STAR

▼ **Many older Russians long for earlier times. This war veteran's hero is Joseph Stalin, a brutal dictator.**

Millions of people who lived through the Soviet era, from 1917 to 1991, have similar stories. The Communist government headed by Joseph Stalin between 1924 and 1953 imprisoned, executed or starved to death tens of millions of people. Prisoners in labor camps built canals, railroads, hydroelectric stations, mines, and other industries.

The Price of Freedom

The freedom that followed the Soviet Union's collapse in 1991 came with a price. People had to take responsibility for their lives. "In today's Russia," a businessman says, "you have to learn to rely on yourself."

Even self-reliant Russians often suffer. Thanks to private enterprise, Russia's economy is growing. Yet it is still too weak to provide a job for everyone.

But Russia is a democracy today. Its government is no longer free to destroy lives like Valentina Fedotova's. That fact alone, most Russians believe, makes them better off today than ever. ■

EXPLORING THE ISSUE

1. **Finding the Main Idea** How does Fedotova's story illustrate the main point of this article?
2. **Contrasting** Elected leaders are less likely than dictators to arrest and imprison people without cause. Why do you think this is so?

380

Critical Thinking Activity

Indentifying Alternatives A major problem in Russia today is corruption at every level of government. Bribing is common place. Students may have little understanding of how this makes it difficult to conduct even ordinary business. Ask them how they would feel if they had to pay a bribe to get a driver's license or to avoid a speeding ticket. A major problem is that the world's stable governments may be reluctant to help such a government. Other governments may be afraid their aid will only reach corrupt officials. Have students brainstorm about how the United States might attempt to help the Russian people overcome this current situation, reduce corruption, and create a more stable society. **L2**

EE6 The Uses of Geography: Standard 18

TIME REPORTS

The Road to Somewhere

As the Soviet Union was ending in 1991, protesters gathered in Moscow's Red Square. One man held a sign that said, "70 Years to Nowhere." The sign spoke of the past—the years of Communist rule that had led to a dead end.

What about the next 70 years? They should bring fairer courts, for one thing. Russian judges are used to taking the government's side. Soon juries will be deciding many cases, making courts more even-handed.

Jobs and Health

Tomorrow's Russians will be wealthier and healthier than today's. Today hospital patients must supply their own food, sheets, and medicine. Life expectancy for men today is only 59 years—down from 64 in 1989.

But Russia's healthcare system is getting stronger, along with the nation's economy. A stronger economy will mean more jobs and less poverty. Steady jobs should persuade Russian men to stop abusing alcohol. That drug is shortening their lives.

How quickly will those changes come? It all depends on how quickly Russians change the way they think. Russians don't yet have democracy in their hearts. They are not used to voting or taking part in community affairs, either as volunteers or as elected officials. They tend to think it is more important to help themselves than their neighbors.

EAST NEWS/GETTY IMAGES/NEWSCOM

▲ Russian students hope to enjoy freedoms their parents never knew.

Self-Serve Government

Government workers think the same way. Few see themselves as **public servants**. Many of them serve themselves first. People must pay money "under the table" to get driver's licenses, fair treatment by police, and permits to build houses.

Today "70 Years to Somewhere" could be Russia's slogan. It's just far too early to say what that somewhere will be.

EXPLORING THE ISSUE

1. **Explaining** Why might a stronger Russian economy lead to better health?
2. **Problem Solving** What could the United States do to help Russians learn to put "democracy in their hearts"?

381

Interpreting Information

Have students research the lives of average Russian citizens. **Ask: What kinds of jobs do they have? Where do they live? Do they own cars, washing machines, TVs, stereos? What do teenagers do for recreation?** Then have them write a report titled "A Day in the Life of . . ." in which they describe a day in the life of an average teenager in Russia. **L2**

Did You Know

Russian organized crime conducts its business in the same way as transnational corporations. Criminals have learned from the globalization of private industry how to best use telecommunications, the Internet, and other resources.

EXPLORING THE ISSUE

ANSWERS

1. *Possible answers:* Health care will be better because of better training and facilities; people will eat better and therefore be healthier; people who can work and support their families are less likely to abuse alcohol.
2. *Possible answers:* show Russians that citizens' participation in government is good for individuals and the country as a whole; teach them that with rights come responsibilities.

Interdisciplinary Activity

Health Ask students about the type of health care they expect to get in the United States. What do they do when they get sick? How is their care paid for? What kind of treatment would they get if they were ill or in an accident? Tell them that in Russia under the Communist government, Russians had free health care, but it wasn't always the best. Have them research the Russian health care system to see how it has changed in the new free economy. **Ask: How does it compare to the American system as far as providing health care to all citizens and giving the best and most up-to-date treatment?** Have students debate the pros and cons of the two systems. **L3**

EE4 Human Systems: Standard 11

TIME REPORTS

Making Comparisons

It is important to remember that 15 nations were created when the Soviet Union dissolved. Instruct students to research the government and economy of one of the other 14 countries. They should then write a report briefly comparing this nation to Russia. The report should discuss the stability of the government and how well the average citizen is doing. **L2**

Current Events Journal

Have students divide a piece of paper into two columns. They should label one column *Former Soviet Union* and the second column *Russia Today.* In the *Former Soviet Union* column, they should list the advantages of life in the Soviet Union. Below this list, they should list the disadvantages of life in the Soviet Union. This process should be repeated for the *Russia Today* column.

Making Generalizations

As shown in the map on page 383, Russia spans 11 time zones. In fact, it is 1.8 times the size of the United States. **Ask:** **Do you think it is easier to have a democracy in a large country or a small country? Why? L2**

TIME REPORTS

Helping Russia Rebuild: What Can One Person Do?

In July 2000, former hockey star Mike Gartner made boys in two Russian hockey clubs very happy. One club was in Penza, a town outside Moscow. The other club was far to the east in Novokuznetsk, a city in Siberia. Gartner gave each club something it couldn't afford—hockey equipment worth thousands of dollars.

Goals & Dreams

Gartner heads the Goals & Dreams program of the National Hockey League Players' Association (NHLPA). "We're not doing this to try to make future NHL hockey players," Gartner said. "The goal is to try to make kids better people."

That's also the goal of the head of Novokuznetsk's hockey. "We are working toward a healthier lifestyle for our youth," he said.

That's not easy in a nation as hard-pressed as Russia. The Novokuznetsk club gives its members free food and medical care. But it has no money left over to buy equipment.

Encouraging Words

You can help Russians simply by supporting efforts like the NHLPA's. You don't have to send sports equipment. You don't have to send money. Just send those groups a letter, letting them know how much you appreciate their efforts. Groups that provide assistance to others gain strength just from knowing that others care.

▲ **Former pro hockey star Mike Gartner meets members of a Russian hockey club.**

Many groups are helping Russia today. One is the Eurasia Foundation, based in Washington, D.C. (**www.eurasia.org**). The World Wildlife Federation is another (**www.wwf.ru/eng/index.html**).

And don't forget Goals & Dreams (**www.nhlpa.com**). "We have stacks of letters from kids and families thanking us," Mike Gartner said. "This is a great job—kind of like being Santa Claus."

382

Your Government and You

The Center for Strategic and International Studies (CSIS) is a bipartisan effort to provide world leaders with insight into a wide variety of global issues. The CSIS has organized the Global Organized Crime Project. Students can visit its Web site (www.csis.org/goc/) to learn more about its efforts. Its leader, former CIA Director R. James Woolsey, has stated that organized crime is as great a threat to the United States and the world as the Cold War. Just like the Cold War threatened our security, so do international crime networks. **Ask:** **What kinds of business is organized crime involved in? Why would it be considered a threat? L2**

EE4 Human Systems: Standard 13

REVIEW AND ASSESS

UNDERSTANDING THE ISSUE

1. **Defining Key Terms** Write definitions for the following terms: *kulibini, Russian Federation, Commonwealth of Independent States, stockpile, inventive, public servant, economy.*

2. **Writing to Inform** Pretend you are in a Russian middle school. Write a letter to an American friend explaining Russia's problems. Use at least five of the key terms listed above.

3. **Writing to Persuade** "In today's Russia, you have to learn to rely on yourself." Write a letter to an imaginary Russian friend. Explain why self-reliance is a good thing.

INTERNET RESEARCH ACTIVITY

4. Russian army units have "adopted" a few thousand of the 1 million to 2 million Russian kids who have no home. Children as young as 11 live on army bases, wear uniforms, and attend school. They are not sent to war. Elsewhere children do fight wars. To learn about them, explore **www.child-soldiers.org** and **www.uschild-soldiers.org**. List ways that real child soldiers seem like, and are different from, Russian kids in uniform. Compare your list with those of your classmates.

5. Since 1999, the Library of Congress has brought Russian officials to the United States to see democracy at work. Explore the Russian Leadership Program's website at **http://lcweb.loc.gov/rlp**. In a short essay, describe the program and explain how it might benefit both Russians and Americans. Put your answers in a 250-word essay.

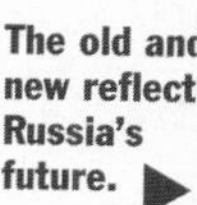

The old and new reflect Russia's future. ▶

SERGEI GUNEYEV/TIMEPIX

BEYOND THE CLASSROOM

6. **Visit your school or local library** to learn about the Soviet Union. Working in groups, find out what it was like to live under a Communist government. What basic freedoms did Russians not have? Discuss your findings with your classmates.

7. **Research another nation** that has exchanged one-party rule for democracy. What might Russians learn from the other nation's experience? Put your findings in a short report.

RUSSIA'S 11 TIME ZONES

The earth is divided into 24 time zones, one for each hour of the day. Russia spans 11 time zones, stretching nearly halfway around the globe. We've labeled Russia's time zones from A to K. There's an hour's difference between each zone. It's always earlier in the East, where the sun rises, than in the West.

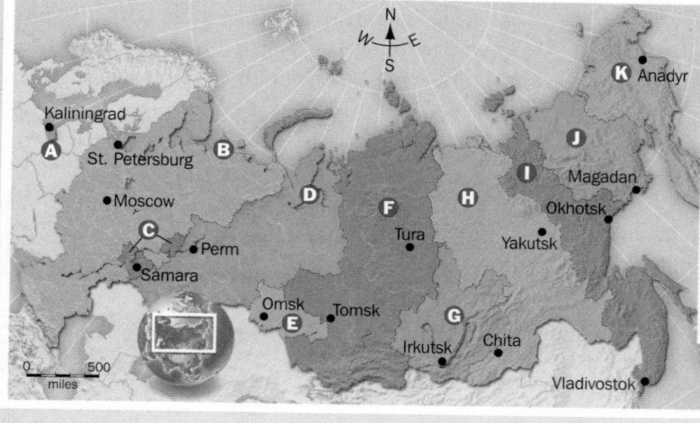

BUILDING MAP READING SKILLS

1. **Interpreting Maps** If it's 9:00 A.M. in Kaliningrad, what time is it in Moscow? What time is it in Tura, Chita, Vladivostok, and Magadan? Suppose it is 2:00 A.M., January 20, in Tomsk. What time and day is it in Samara?

2. **Transferring Data** Across the top of a sheet of paper, write the name of one city in each time zone, from Kaliningrad to Anadyr. Draw a clock beneath each name. Set the sixth clock at midnight. Draw the correct time on the 10 other clocks.

FOR UPDATES ON WORLD ISSUES GO TO www.timeclassroom.com/glencoe

383

ASSESS

Have students take the Time Reports Quiz or do the Alternative Assessment project for this unit provided in the Teacher's Classroom Resources.

NAME .... DATE ....

Analyzing a Table

ACTIVITY 5 MASTER

How can you get a sharper picture of life in Russia? One way is to compare numbers that describe Russia with those that describe other countries. The table on this page does just that. Read it. Then decide whether statements about it are true or false.

How Five Nations Measure Up

	China	D.R. Congo*	France	Russia	US
People in millions	1,273	54	59	146	281
% of population who live in cities	36%	29%	73%	78%	75%
Years a person can expect to live	70	51	78	67	72
% of population with jobs	58%	30%	43%	50%	50%
% of pop. age 15+ who are able to read	82%	77%	99%	98%	97%
Calories eaten by one person per day	2,741	1,879	3,588	2,928	3,603
Corruption ranking**	57	Not avail.	23	79	16
Freedom compared with other nations***	7.6	6.5	1.2	4.3	1.1

Sources: *Encyclopedia Britannica* (2001), *UN Human Development Report* (1999), *World Desk Reference* 2000

BUILDING MAP READING SKILLS

ANSWERS

1. Moscow: 10:00 A.M.; Tura: 2:00 P.M.; Chita: 4:00 P.M.; Vladivostok: 5:00 P.M.; Magadon: 6:00 P.M.; 11:00 P.M., January 19
2. Answers will vary.

CLOSE

Ask students to write a paragraph starting with this topic sentence: *Some of the ways the Russian government could encourage its citizens to participate in democracy are . . .*

Culminating Activity

To close this lesson, have students complete the Review and Assess section questions and activities above. Students should use classroom discussion, contextual clues, and their student dictionaries to write definitions for terms. Before assigning the Internet activities, it is recommended that you review your school district policy on student Internet use.

Focus on Debate

Have students debate the pro and con position of the following topic: **The average Russian citizen was better off under the Communist government of the Soviet Union than he or she is today. L2**

EE6 The Uses of Geography: Standard 18

Critical Thinking Skill

TEACH

Write the following sentences on the board: (A) José ate dinner. (B) José was hungry. (C) José brushed his teeth. Ask students to put the sentences in a logical order. *(B, A, C)* Ask for volunteers to explain why this is a sensible order. *(José's hunger caused him to eat, and eating caused him to need to brush his teeth.)* Explain that these three sentences are a simple example of cause and effect. Then have them read the feature and practice the skill. **L1**

Additional Skills Practice

1. **Which is the cause in this pair of facts? (A) Resources in Siberia have not been well developed. (B) Siberia is a remote region with a harsh environment.** *(Cause—B; Effect—A)*
2. **How can one event be both a cause and an effect?** *(It can result from one event but cause yet another—like José eating dinner in the TEACH activity.)*

Additional Skills Resources

 Chapter Skills Activity 14

 Building Geography Skills for Life

GLENCOE TECHNOLOGY

 **Skillbuilder Interactive Workbook CD-ROM, Level 1**

This interactive CD-ROM reinforces student mastery of essential social studies skills.

Critical Thinking Skill

Understanding Cause and Effect

Understanding cause and effect involves considering *why* an event occurred. A *cause* is the action or situation that produces an event. What happens as a result of a cause is an *effect.*

Learning the Skill

To identify cause-and-effect relationships, follow these steps:

- Identify two or more events or developments.
- Decide whether one event caused the other. Look for "clue words" such as *because, led to, brought about, produced, as a result of, so that, since,* and *therefore*.
- Look for logical relationships between events, such as "She overslept, and then she missed her bus."
- Identify the outcomes of events. Remember that some effects have more than one cause, and some causes lead to more than one effect. Also, an effect can become the cause of yet another effect.

Practicing the Skill

For each number below, identify which statement is the cause and which is the effect.

1. (A) Russia's capital was moved from coastal St. Petersburg to Moscow in the heart of the country.
   (B) The capital of Russia was threatened by an outside invasion.

▲ Revolutionary leaders and philosophers Lenin, Engels, and Marx

2. (A) Revolutionary leaders seized control of the Russian government.
   (B) During World War I, shortages of food in Russian cities caused much starvation.
   (C) Discontent grew among the Russian people.
3. (A) The Soviet government kept prices for goods and services very low.
   (B) Many goods and services were in short supply in the Soviet Union.

Applying the Skill

In your local newspaper, read an article describing a current event. Determine at least one cause and one effect of that event. Show the cause-and-effect relationship in a diagram like the one here:

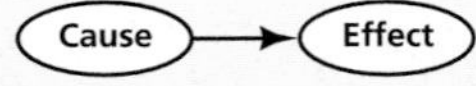

GO TO Practice key skills with **Glencoe Skillbuilder Interactive Workbook, Level 1.**

Practicing the Skill Answers

1. *Cause*—B; *Effect*—A
2. *Cause*—B; *First Effect*—C; *Second Effect*—A
3. *Cause*—A; *Effect*—B

Applying the Skill

Have students submit a copy of the newspaper article along with their chart. Check their responses for correct interpretation of the cause and effect relationship.

Reading Review

Section 1 A Troubled History

Terms to Know
- czar
- serf
- industrialize
- communist state
- Cold War
- glasnost

Main Idea

The harsh rule of powerful leaders has often sparked violent uprisings in Russia.

✓History Emperors called czars ruled the Russian Empire from 1480 to 1917.

✓History The czars expanded Russian territory to reach from Europe to the Pacific.

✓Government Under the Communists, Russia became part of the Soviet Union.

✓History In 1991 the Soviet Union broke apart, and Russia became an independent republic.

Section 2 A New Russia

Terms to Know
- free market economy
- nuclear energy
- federal republic

Main Idea

Russia has a rich cultural heritage but faces challenges in adopting a new economic system and government.

✓Economics The change to a free market economy has been a challenge for Russians as they face rising unemployment and rising prices.

✓Government Russians have had to learn how to live in a democracy.

✓Government Some non-Russian ethnic groups want to create independent nations outside of Russia.

Young people strolling and singing in St. Petersburg ▶

Reading Review

Use the Chapter 14 Reading Review to preview, review, condense, or reteach the chapter.

Preview/Review

Use the Terms to Know lists to help students review and study.

Activity Have students create crossword puzzles for ten of the terms from the chapter, exchange papers with another student, and try to complete their partner's puzzle.

Vocabulary PuzzleMaker Software reinforces the vocabulary terms used in Chapter 14.

The Interactive Tutor Self-Assessment CD-ROM allows students to review Chapter 14 content.

Condense

Have students read the Chapter 14 summary statements.

Chapter 14 Guided Reading Activities

Chapter 14 Audio Program

Reteach

Reteaching Activity 14

Chapter 14 Reading Essentials and Study Guide

Chapter Culminating Activity

Creating a Web Site Have students prepare an outline for their own Web site that summarizes Russian history or culture. Students' outlines should show what the topic and main idea will be on each Web page. The outline might also suggest illustrations that they could include on each Web page. If students have time and interest, suggest that they design the opening page for the Web site or show how one of the detailed pages would look. *NOTE: This activity may be completed separately or you may wish students to incorporate it into their Current Events Journal.*

EE4 Human Systems: Standard 10

Assessment and Activities

Chapter 14 Assessment and Activities

GLENCOE TECHNOLOGY

MindJogger Videoquiz
Use MindJogger to review the Chapter 14 content.

 Available in VHS.

Using Key Terms

1. c
2. f
3. e
4. a
5. b
6. d
7. g

Reviewing the Main Ideas

8. Ivan IV (*or* Ivan the Terrible)
9. 1922
10. because they opposed his actions
11. The Soviet Union collapsed.
12. free enterprise system
13. Boris Yeltsin and Vladimir Putin
14. democratic government, greater freedom, and an economy based on competition and private ownership
15. erosion and chemicals in the land; air pollution from industry and vehicles; water pollution from chemicals, sewers, and drainage
16. If it succeeds, Russia could guide neighbors towards democracy, and if it doesn't, Russia could turn back to communism or be a danger to Europe.

Using Key Terms

Match the terms in Part A with their definitions in Part B.

A.

1. Cold War
2. nuclear energy
3. czar
4. industrialize
5. serf
6. federal republic
7. free market economy

B.

a. to change an economy to manufacturing
b. a farm laborer bound to the land he worked
c. period of tension without actual fighting
d. power is divided between national and state governments with a president who leads the nation
e. former emperor of Russia
f. power from a controlled atomic reaction
g. people decide what businesses to start and run

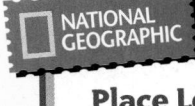

Reviewing the Main Ideas

Section 1 A Troubled History

8. **History** Which czar used a secret police force to maintain strict control over the people?
9. **History** When was the Union of Soviet Socialist Republics formed?
10. **Government** Why did Stalin send people to Siberia?
11. **History** What took place in the Soviet Union in 1991?

Section 2 A New Russia

12. **Economics** What type of economic system has the new Russian government adopted?
13. **History** Who were Russia's first two presidents?
14. **Government** What are some changes Russians face as a result of their changing government?
15. **Human/Environment Interaction** What are some environmental problems facing Russia today?
16. **Government** Why do free countries of the world want Russia's new government to succeed?

NATIONAL GEOGRAPHIC Russia–Past and Present

Place Location Activity

On a separate sheet of paper, match the letters on the map with the numbered places listed below.

1. St. Petersburg
2. Caspian Sea
3. Moscow
4. Baltic Sea
5. Vladivostok
6. Sea of Japan
7. Irkutsk
8. Omsk

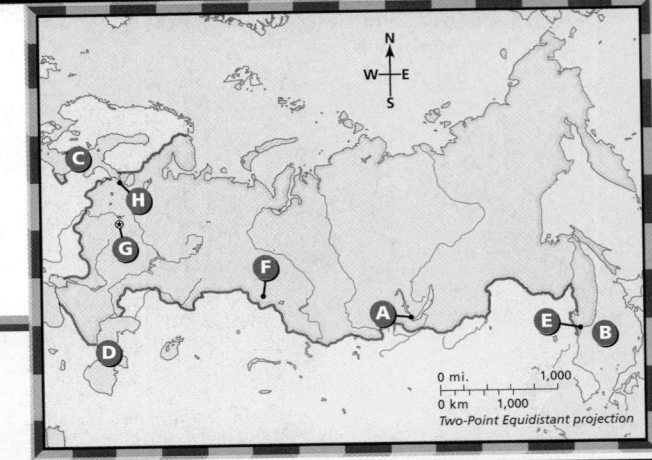

NATIONAL GEOGRAPHIC Place Location Activity

1. H
2. D
3. G
4. C
5. E
6. B
7. A
8. F

Critical Thinking

17. Because Russia was unprepared for war, its people suffered from food shortages and other deprivations. Discontent grew and the people were ready to follow someone who would promise them a better life.
18. Possible answers: factory managers decide what products to make; people can open businesses and choose their own careers; people may become unemployed; prices have risen.

Self-Check Quiz Visit the ***Our World Today: People, Places, and Issues*** Web site at owt.glencoe.com and click on **Chapter 14–Self-Check Quizzes** to prepare for the Chapter Test.

Critical Thinking

17. **Understanding Cause and Effect** How did World War I help lead to the Russian Revolution?
18. **Organizing Information** Create a diagram like this one. Complete it with four characteristics of the free enterprise system in Russia.

Current Events Journal

19. **Writing a News Article** Learn about the nuclear disaster at Chernobyl. Find out what happened and its effects on the local people, animals, and land. Write a news article that might have appeared a few days after the explosion. Then write a follow-up article on how the explosion is still affecting Russia and neighboring countries today.

Mental Mapping Activity

20. **Focusing on the Region** Create a simple outline map of Russia and label the following:
    - Arctic Ocean
    - Pacific Ocean
    - Vladivostok
    - Moscow
    - Bering Sea
    - St. Petersburg
    - Siberia
    - Baltic Sea

Technology Skills Activity

21. **Developing Multimedia Presentations** Choose an environmental or political problem that the Russian people have faced in the last 10 years. Research your choice and create a multimedia presentation on this problem. Include information on when, what, where, and other interesting facts. Use pictures, maps, and time lines to make your presentation more visual.

The Princeton Review

Standardized Test Practice

Directions: Read the paragraph below, and then answer the question that follows.

You may be surprised to know that Kazakhstan was—and still is—important to the exploration of outer space. The Russian space center Baikonur (by•kuh•NOOR) lies in south-central Kazakhstan. During the Soviet period, Baikonur was used for many space launches. Several historic "firsts in space" occurred here. For example, the first satellite was launched in 1957. The first crewed flight took place when cosmonaut Yuri Gagarin orbited the earth in 1961. In addition, the flight of the first woman in space, Valentina Tereshkova, was launched in 1963. After the Soviet collapse, the Russian-owned center remained in independent Kazakh territory.

1. **The Soviet space program at Baikonur holds great importance, mostly because**
   - **F** it is located in south-central Kazakhstan.
   - **G** it provides jobs for the people who live near the launch site.
   - **H** many "first in space" flights were launched from it.
   - **J** Valentina Tereshkova was the first woman in space.

Test-Taking Tip: When a question uses the word *most* or *mostly*, it means that more than one answer may be correct. Your job is to pick the *best* answer. For example, Baikonur's location in Kazakhstan may be important to the people who live near it, which is answer G. Another answer, however, provides a more general reason for Baikonur's importance.

Assessment and Activities

Standardized Test Practice

1. H

Tested Objectives:
Analyzing information, drawing conclusions

Chapter Test Bonus Question

This question may be used for extra credit on the chapter test.

What city was once the capital of Russia under the czars? *(St. Petersburg)*

Our World Today Online

Have students visit the Web site at **owt.glencoe.com** to review Chapter 14 and take the Self-Check Quiz.

Current Events Journal

19. Make sure that students' articles incorporate main and supporting ideas and cover: *Who, What, Where, When, Why,* and *How.*

Mental Mapping Activity

20. This exercise helps students visualize the countries they have been studying and understand the relationships among various points. All attempts at freehand mapping should be accepted.

Technology Skills Activity

21. After students have completed their presentations, ask for volunteers to show them to the class. Then discuss the similarities and differences to similar issues in the United States.

1 Focus

Ask students if they have ever experienced severe winter weather. Have volunteers describe the difficulty people and machines have in functioning under these conditions. Point out that armies can have the same problems, especially large armies of hundreds of thousands of troops (as in the cases of the French and German invasions). Then have students read the feature describing the history-changing effects of Russia's climate.

2 Teach

Synthesizing Information

Tell students that physical features—like weather—can have a major impact on an army's success or failure in battle. Give students a list of physical features—such as forests, swamps, hills, deserts, or islands—and ask how armies could benefit or face difficulties from having to fight or move through that feature. **L1**

Meeting National Standards

Geography for Life

The following standards are met in the Student Edition feature:

EE5 Environment and Society: Standard 15

EE6 The Uses of Geography: Standard 17

Napoleon and troops retreat from Russia.

RUSSIA'S STRATEGY:

Freeze Your Foes

Winter weather can cancel school, bring flu outbreaks, and stop traffic. It can even change history. Such was the case when French ruler Napoleon Bonaparte thought he had conquered the Russian Empire.

In fact, Napoleon did not want to conquer Russia. His real enemy was Great Britain. Napoleon wanted Russia and other countries to stop trading with Great Britain. Yet Russia's czar, Alexander I, refused. By 1812, Napoleon was determined to change Alexander's mind. In June, leading an army of more than half a million soldiers, Napoleon invaded Russia. To reach Moscow and the czar, Napoleon had to fight his way across the Russian countryside.

By the time Napoleon's battle-weary forces reached Moscow, supplies were scarce. All along the route, Russians had burned villages as they retreated, leaving no food or shelter. Reaching Moscow, Napoleon found the city in flames and nearly empty of people. The czar had moved to St. Petersburg. Napoleon took Moscow without a fight, but most of the city was in ashes.

Winter Wins a War

With winter approaching, Napoleon waited in Moscow for Alexander I to offer peace. The czar remained silent, however. With dwindling supplies and many of his troops lacking winter clothes, Napoleon was forced to retreat. He tried to take a new way back, but the Russians made Napoleon use the same ruined route he had used before. Armed bands of Russians attacked at every turn. Starving and desperate to escape the bitter cold, several of Napoleon's soldiers threw themselves into burning buildings. Most of Napoleon's troops never made it out of Russia.

History Repeats

More than a century later, during World War II, Russia's winter was again a mighty foe. On June 22, 1941, Adolf Hitler's German army invaded Russia, then part of the Soviet Union. As the German army fought its way to Moscow, Soviet leader Joseph Stalin issued his own "scorched-earth policy." Soviet citizens burned anything of use to the invaders. By December, German troops were within sight of the Kremlin, Moscow's government center, when winter struck.

Snow buried the invaders. Temperatures fell below freezing. Grease in guns and oil in vehicles froze solid. German soldiers suffered frostbite and died. The Soviets were better clothed and had winterized their tanks and trucks. Stalin's troops pushed back the German army. Once again the Russians triumphed with help from "General Winter."

QUESTIONS

1. **After Napoleon conquered Moscow in 1812, why did he retreat?**
2. **How did Russia's winter affect fighting in World War II?**

388

German prisoners of Russia's winter ▶

Answers to the Questions

1. He was waiting for the czar to offer peace, but the czar never did. Napoleon's army was without food and supplies, so it could not stay any longer in Moscow.
2. Snow stopped the equipment and the soldiers; bitter cold prevented vehicles from working and froze the German soldiers.

NATIONAL GEOGRAPHIC

Time Line

- **June 1812:** Napoleon's army invades Russia
- **Sept 1812:** Napoleon takes Moscow
- **Nov 1812:** Retreat finished
- **June 1941:** German army invades Russia
- **July 1941:** German army reaches 400 miles into Russia
- **Oct 1941:** German army advances on Moscow
- **Dec 1941:** Advance on Moscow slowed by winter
- **Dec 1941:** Soviet counter-attack begins to drive Germans back

Average Winter Temperatures

EUROPE
Moscow
RUSSIA
ASIA
N W E S

Napoleon's Advance, June–October 1812
German Forces Front Line, December 1941

< -40°F
-40° to -31°F
-30° to -21°F
-20° to -11°F
-10° to 0°F
0° to 10°F
11° to 20°F
21° to 30°F
> 30°F

3 Assess

Have students answer the questions on page 388.

4 Close

Have students take the role of a Russian in either 1812 during Napoleon's invasion or in 1941 during Hitler's invasion. Have them write a poem, essay, or song in praise of "General Winter."

Geography and History Activity

Annotated Maps Have students conduct further research about Napoleon's or Hitler's invasions of Russia. Have them prepare an annotated map that highlights key events and places in these two conflicts.

EE1 The World in Spatial Terms: Standards 1, 3

Unit 6 Planning Guide

SUGGESTED PACING CHART

Unit 6 (1 day)	Chapter 15 (5 days)	Chapter 16 (4 days)	Chapter 17 (5 days)	Unit 6 (2 days)
Day 1 Introduction	**Day 1** Chapter 15 Intro, Section 1	**Day 1** Chapter 16 Intro, Section 1	**Day 1** Chapter 17 Intro, Section 1	**Day 1** Wrap-Up/Projects
	Day 2 Section 2	**Day 2** Section 2	**Day 2** Section 2	**Day 2** Unit 6 Assessment
	Day 3 Section 3	**Day 3** Chapter 16 Review	**Day 3** Section 3	
	Day 4 Chapter 15 Review	**Day 4** Chapter 16 Assessment	**Day 4** Chapter 17 Review	
	Day 5 Chapter 15 Assessment		**Day 5** Chapter 17 Assessment	

For a complete course pacing guide and Teacher Classroom Resources, see:

Interactive Lesson Planner

Use the following tools to easily assess student learning in a variety of ways:

- **Performance Assessment Activities and Rubrics**
- **Section Quizzes**
- **Chapter Tests and Unit Pretests and Posttests**
- **Interactive Tutor Self-Assessment CD-ROM**
- **ExamView® Pro 3.0 Testmaker CD-ROM**
- **MindJogger Videoquiz**
- owt.glencoe.com
- **Standardized Test Practice Workbook**

Note: The following materials may be used when teaching Unit 6. Chapter level support materials can be found on the chapter resource pages.

TEACHING TRANSPARENCIES

Political Map Transparency 6

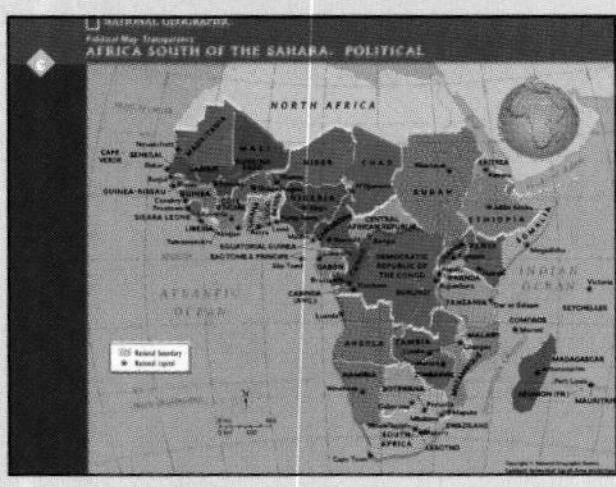

Unit 6 Map Overlay Transparencies

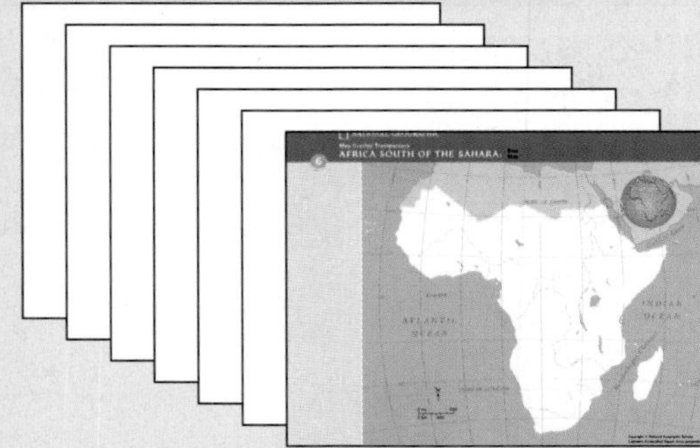

World Cultures Transparencies 9 and 10

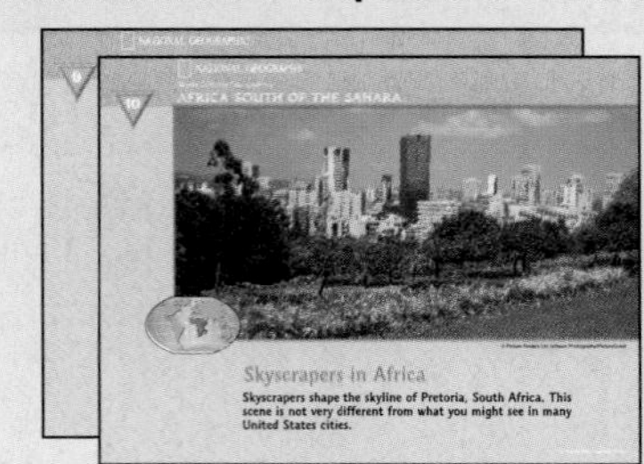

Unit 6 Resources

INTERDISCIPLINARY CONNECTIONS

World Literature Reading 6

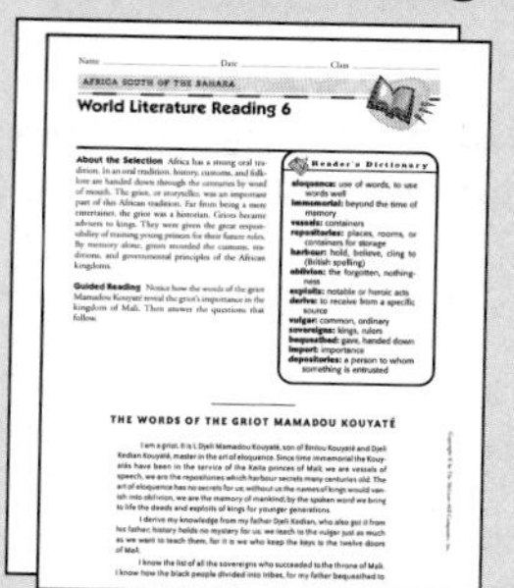

Economics and Geography Activity 6

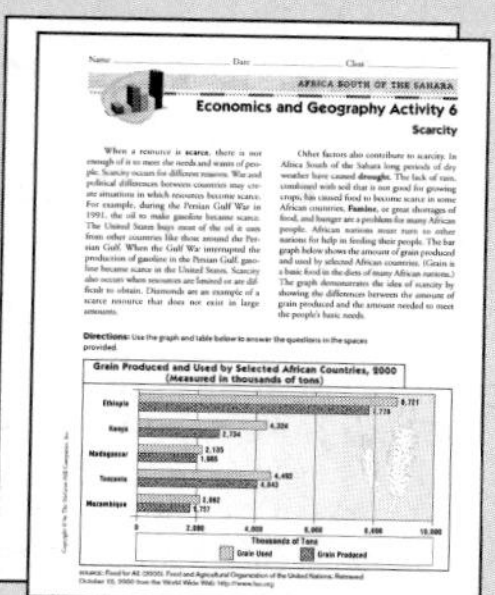

History and Geography Activity 6

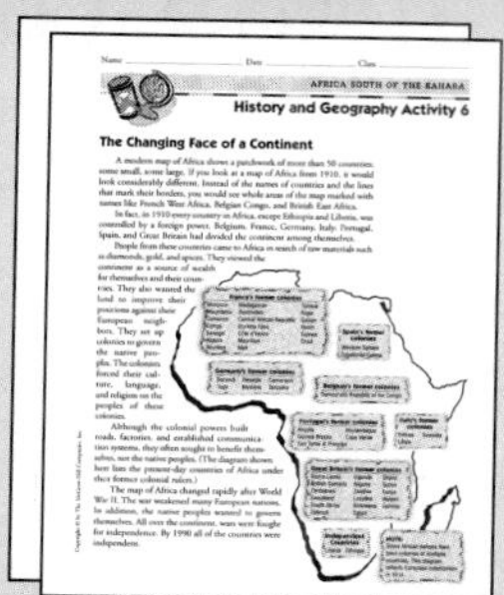

MAP AND GEOGRAPHY SKILLS

Building Geography Skills for Life

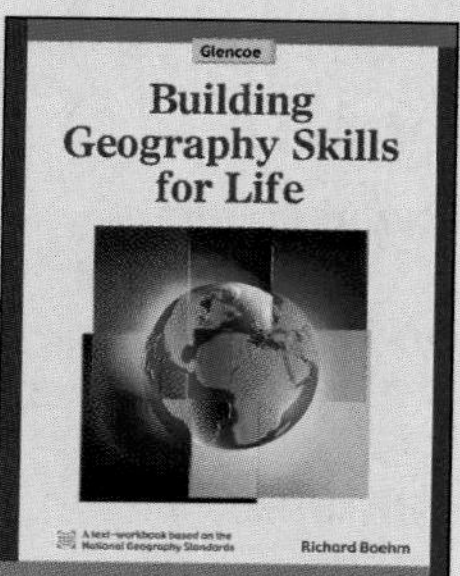

NGS Focus on Geography Literacy

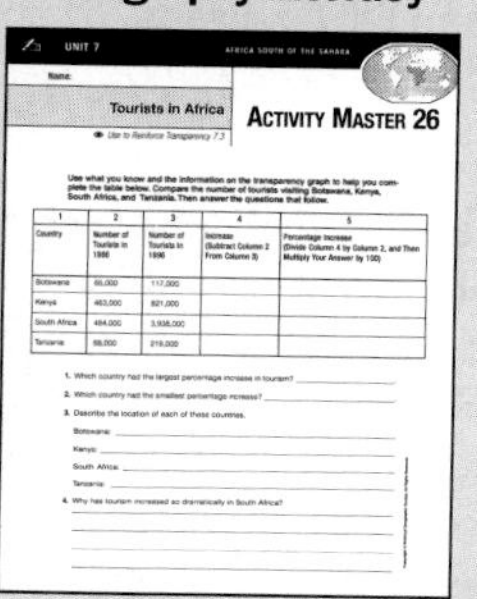

Regional Atlas Activity 6

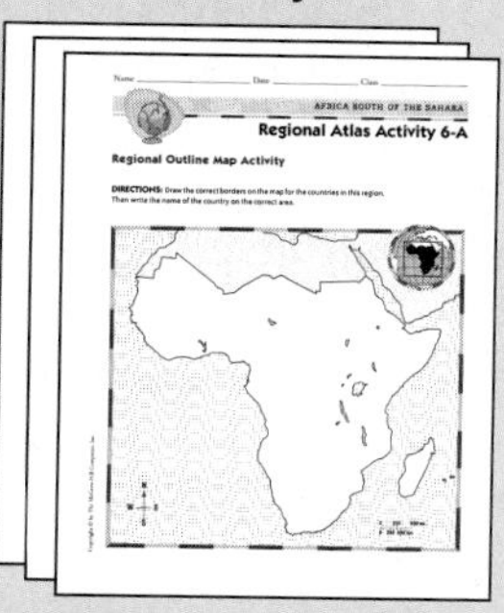

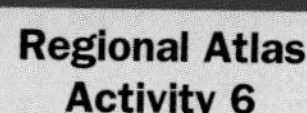

NATIONAL GEOGRAPHIC MapMachine

Find the latest coverage of geography in the news, atlas updates, cartographic activities with interactive maps, an online map store, and links at www.nationalgeographic.com/maps

APPLICATION AND HANDS-ON

Citizenship Activity 6

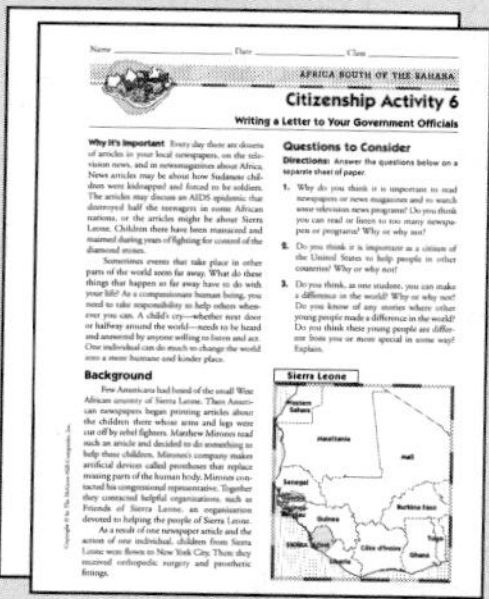

Foods Around the World 7

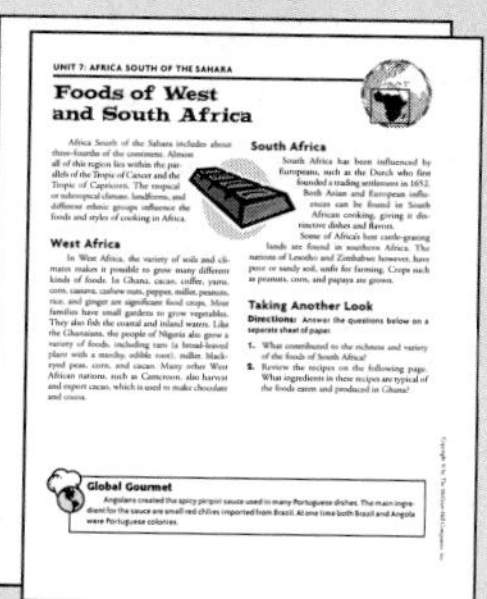

ENRICHMENT AND EXTENSION

Environmental Case Study 6

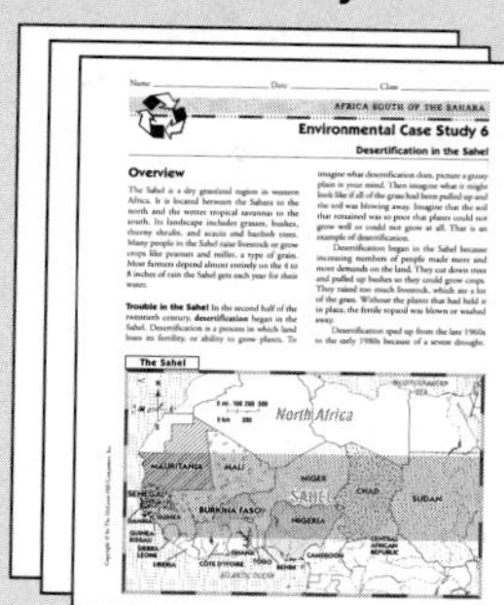

World Music: A Cultural Legacy

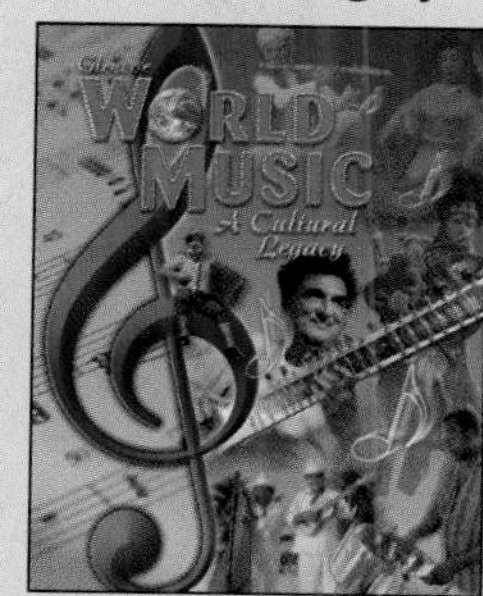

ASSESSMENT AND EVALUATION

Unit 6 Pretests

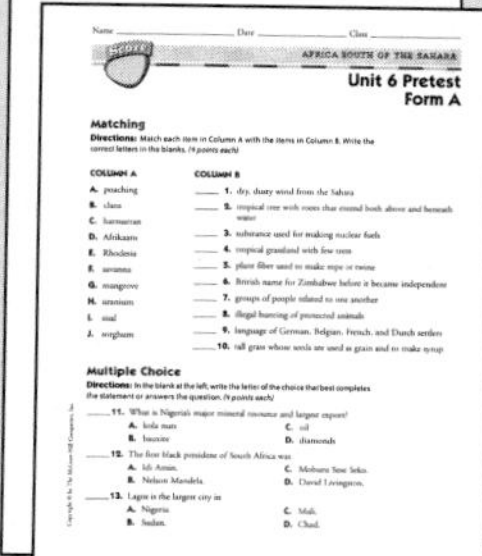

Unit 6 Posttests

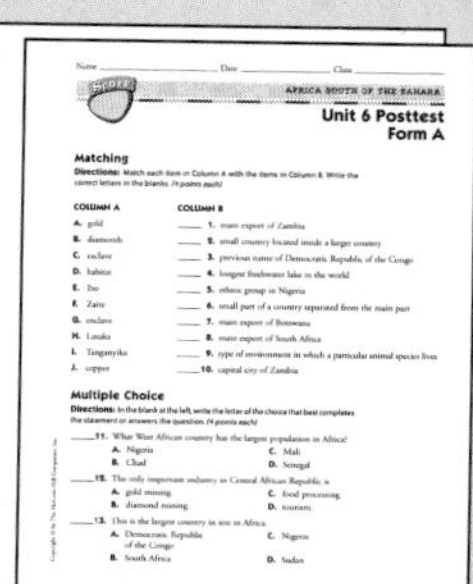

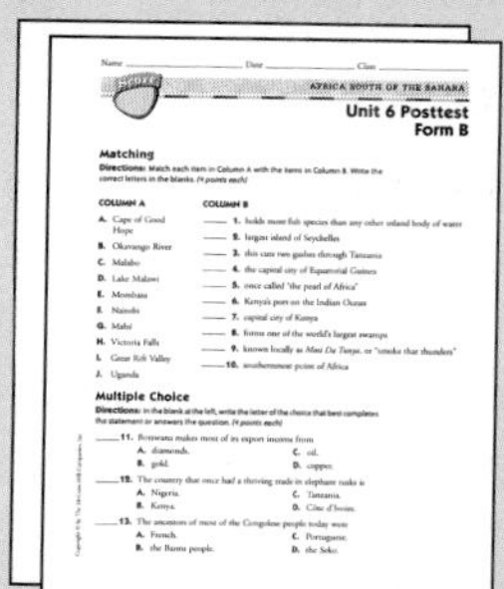

Additional Unit 6 Resources

interNET RESOURCES

- owt.glencoe.com
  Our World Today: People, Places, and Issues
  Visit the Glencoe *Our World Today: People, Places, and Issues* Web site for overviews, activities, assessments, and updated charts and graphs.
- socialstudies.glencoe.com
  Glencoe Social Studies
  Visit the Glencoe Web site for social studies activities, updates, and links to other sites.
- www.teachingtoday.glencoe.com
  Glencoe Teaching Today
  This Web site features daily teaching tips, free PDF downloads, annotated Web resources, educational news, and more.
- www.nationalgeographic.com
  NGS ONLINE Visit the National Geographic Society Web site for the latest coverage of geography in the news, atlas updates, activities, links, interactive features, and archives.
- **Glencoe's Guide to Using the Internet**
  Provides an introduction to many of the current technologies on the Internet. Professional resources and teaching strategies included.

Our Web sites provide additional resources. All essential content is covered in the Student Edition.

The following videotape program is available from Glencoe:

- **Nelson Mandela: Journey to Freedom** 0-7670-0113-3

To order, call Glencoe at 1-800-334-7344. To find classroom resources to accompany many of these, check:

A&E Television: www.aetv.com

The History Channel: www.historychannel.com

Bibliography

Literature for the Student

- **Glencoe Middle School World Literature Library**
  Journey to Jo'berg: A South African Story by Beverley Naidoo. A young girl faces the reality of apartheid.
  The Glory Field by Walter Dean Myers. Saga of an African American family and their lives from Africa to South Carolina.
- ***Great African Kingdoms,*** by Sean Sheehan. Austin, TX: Raintree Steck Vaughn, 1999.
- ***The Day Gogo Went to Vote: South Africa, April 1994,*** by Elinor Batezat Sisulu and Sharon Wilson. Boston: Little, Brown, 1996.

Readings for the Teacher

- ***Africa Today: A Reproducible Atlas.*** Wellesley, MA: World Eagle, 1994.
- ***Introduction to African Civilizations,*** by John G. Jackson. New York: Citadel, 1990.

Multimedia Links

- **Glencoe Social Studies Primary Source Document Library**
  The End of Apartheid by F.W. de Klerk
  Stanley Searches for Livingstone in Africa by Henry M. Stanley
- ***Africa: Continent of Contrasts.*** Huntsville, TX: Educational Video Network, 1994. Videocassette, 34 minutes.
- ***They Come in Peace: A New Democratic South Africa.*** Niles, IL: United Learning, 1994. Videocassette, 27 minutes.

Refer to owt.glencoe.com for additional literature titles and study guides related to this region.

Additional Glencoe Teacher Support

- **Teaching Strategies for the Geography Classroom**
- **Reproducible Lesson Plans**
- **Outline Map Resource Book**
- **Reading in the Content Area**

Service Learning Project

Connecting Classroom With Community

Many people in Africa suffer from poor nutrition. Many people in industrialized societies have problems of poor nutrition as well. Obesity rates are high in the United States. Encourage students to organize a campaign to promote good nutrition. Have them look up the recommendations of the Food Guide Pyramid and the cautions that nutritionists offer regarding eating such substances as fats, sodium, and sugar. Then have them stage a Nutrition Fair in which they teach others how to create balanced diets.

Content Background Notes

Use this additional information as lecture notes or discussion prompts throughout the study of Unit 6.

Chapter 15 East and Central Africa (pp. 402–431)

Human Origins The Great Rift Valley, an ancient rock formation, has proven beneficial to archaeologists seeking evidence of the earliest humans. Many important fossils have been uncovered in East Africa, from Ethiopia to Kenya and Tanzania. Early in the 1900s, scientists believed that humans had originated in Asia. In 1959 Mary Leakey—who worked along with her husband Louis—discovered teeth and a human skull that were about 1.75 million years old. This was twice as old as scientists had thought the human race to be, and the find turned their attention to Africa.

Many digs have taken place along the Great Rift Valley since then, and scientists have made many spectacular finds. Evidence found by the Leakeys, their son Richard, and other archaeologists suggests that several kinds of early humans and near-humans lived side by side in the area a few million years ago. Sometime between 4 million and 2 million years ago, the near-human strains died out. The true humans eventually evolved into *Homo sapiens.* National Geographic magazine has published a series of articles titled "The Dawn of Humans" over the years. These articles summarize the various finds made in Africa and in other parts of the world.

The Megatransect In late 1999, J. Michael Fay began an ambitious walk through the rain forests of Central Africa. Beginning at Bomassa, Congo, a town on the Sangha River (a tributary of the mighty Congo), Fay planned to march about 1,200 miles (1,931 km) through 13 forests that adjoin. His goal was to make an accurate survey of the plant and animal life in these forests—before continued human intervention destroys them. Like Meriwether Lewis, Fay recorded in notebooks everything he saw. His records also included sound recordings and videotapes. Fay also used high-technology methods—a GPS device—to help track his route. Low-tech solutions were useful, too. Each day one of Fay's companions played out a cord from a handheld device that measured the distance walked that day. Since the adventurers were sure that the line would be eaten by insects, they brought plenty of spare cords. Interested students can read field reports from Fay at National Geographic Society's Web site.

Chapter 16 West Africa (pp. 432–449)

The British Liberia It is well known that freed slaves from the United States settled in Liberia, creating a home for African Americans who wished to resettle in Africa. Less well known is Sierra Leone, where British antislavery crusaders created settlements for freed slaves from Jamaica and North America—nearly 40 years before the first American freed slaves settled in Liberia. About 1,200 of these settlers had been enslaved in the American colonies. Promised their freedom—and land—by the British, they escaped from bondage and fought alongside British troops during the American Revolution. When the war ended, they were resettled in Nova Scotia, but the British never fulfilled the promise to give them land. In 1792 these 1,200 people traveled to Sierra Leone, where they founded Freetown—now the country's capital.

After 1808, when the British banned the slave trade, Sierra Leone became an important base for British naval ships that patrolled African waters and seized slave ships. From 1807 to 1864, the British brought more than 50,000 Africans who were liberated from these ships to settle in Sierra Leone.

The Palaces of Abomey The town of Abomey, in modern Benin, was once the flourishing capital of the kingdom of Abomey (formerly called Dahomey). The kingdom was a powerful state in West Africa from the late 1600s to the mid-1800s. Today archaeologists are working at the site of the Royal Palaces. Among the finds are a series of bas-reliefs that were used to decorate an area called the Hall of Jewels. These reliefs celebrated the achievements of the Fon people, who founded Abomey. Rain and insects have damaged the reliefs. As a result, the archaeological work must begin with restoring the bas-reliefs. Then the crew will develop plans for their long-term preservation.

Chapter 17 South Africa and Its Neighbors (pp. 452–471)

Telling the Truth During the apartheid era, many black South Africans suffered at the hands of white officials and police officers. In the mid-1990s, when the majority black government was first formed in South Africa, there was concern that revenge could poison race relations and hamper the new government's efforts to build for the future. One of the key steps in avoiding this problem was the creation of South Africa's Truth and Reconciliation Commission. The Commission was chaired by Desmond Tutu, the black archbishop of the Anglican Church in South Africa, who had won a Nobel Peace Prize for his stand against apartheid.

Tutu led the Commission through hearings that included statements from more than 20,000 people. The purpose was to help South Africans be reconciled to the past by telling the truth about it—and then forgiving those who committed atrocities. As one Commission member said: "If we cannot understand what made people think and do what they did, these conflicts will arise again within our society." As part of its mission to tell the full story of apartheid, the Commission's final report revealed crimes committed not only by government forces but also by those who struggled against apartheid.

Introducing Unit 6

00:00 Out of Time?

If time does not permit teaching each chapter in this unit, you may use the **Reading Essentials and Study Guide** for each chapter.

Unit Overview

The three chapters of this unit introduce students to a cultural region that covers most of the continent of Africa. The countries in this region share the following features:

- a location almost entirely in the tropics
- the world's fastest-growing and youngest population
- challenges to the environment, especially natural resources and wildlife
- a struggle to improve the quality of life
- political and economic difficulties caused in part by a colonial past

Waterfront of Cape Town, South Africa

Woman making butter in Chad

Using the Illustration

Many African countries have set aside land as nature preserves to save the endangered animals of Africa—and to generate income by attracting eco-tourists. Among the most famous parks are Kruger National Park in South Africa, Tsavo in Kenya, and Serengeti in Tanzania. Recently South Africa, Mozambique, and Zimbabwe agreed to combine Kruger with parks in the two other countries, forming a larger entity that can better protect species by giving them ample space to migrate. Have students investigate and report on one of Africa's parks, creating a poster that shows the location of the park, what visitors can see, and what programs are being used to study or protect the animals, and the economic benefits they give to African countries. **ELL L2**

EE3 Physical Systems: Standard 8

Giraffe on a plain in Kenya ▼

NATIONAL GEOGRAPHIC

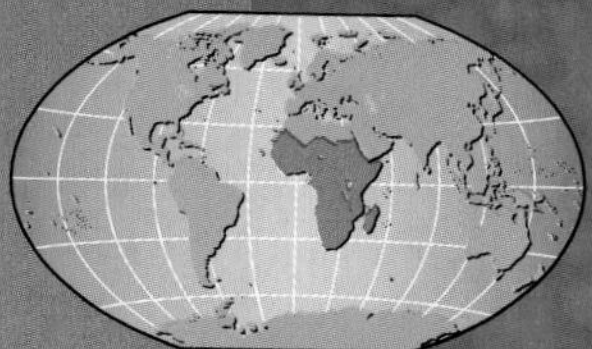

Africa South of the Sahara

The region of Africa south of the Sahara is home to more than 2,000 ethnic groups. Its hot, humid forests and dry grasslands support a variety of wild animals. Both people and animals face tough challenges in this region. The people are struggling to build stable governments and economies. The animals are threatened with extinction as human activities destroy natural habitats.

NGS ONLINE
www.nationalgeographic.com/education

391

NATIONAL GEOGRAPHIC

These materials are available from Glencoe.

Software

ZipZapMap! World

Transparencies

PicturePack Transparencies

CD-ROM

Picture Atlas of the World, Second Edition

Current Events Journal

In their notebooks, have students write words or phrases that they associate with Africa. Tell them to refer back to their lists of "perceptions" as they read the unit. They may need to cross off some words or phrases as they add new ones.

NGS ONLINE
www.nationalgeographic.com/education

This online resource provides lesson plans, atlas updates, cartographic activities with interactive maps, an online map store, and geography links.

Unit Launch Activity

Why Study Africa? Africa faces difficult challenges. Ethnic divisions have disrupted many countries in recent years. AIDS has reached epidemic proportions in some countries. Developing nations struggle to establish order and economic growth as they compete against more industrialized countries. Traditional values and practices are challenged by the modern world. Some countries are threatened by desertification, habitat loss, poaching, and the effects of resource extraction. Inform students of these challenges and have them list ideas for possible solutions. Have them refer back to their lists when they have completed the unit and explain why their ideas would or wouldn't work. **L2**

EE4 Human Systems: Standards 10, 13

NATIONAL GEOGRAPHIC

REGIONAL ATLAS

LESSON PLAN

Using the Regional Atlas

These features and activities may be used as an introduction to the unit or as teaching tools throughout the course of the unit.

FOCUS

Objectives

1. Locate the region and describe its major landforms.
2. Identify the countries and capitals of the region.
3. Compare the populations of the countries in the region.
4. Discuss the chief economic products of the countries.

5-Minute Precheck

Have students look at the political map on page 393. Have them write down the four countries they think are the largest. Then have them check the Country Profiles to see if they were correct. *(Sudan—963,600 sq. mi.; Democratic Republic of the Congo—905,568 sq. mi.; Chad—495,755 sq. mi.; Niger—489,191 sq. mi.)*

More About the Profile

In order to show a variety of physical features, this cross section along the Equator begins at Libreville in Gabon and ends in Somalia.

Africa South of the Sahara

Physical

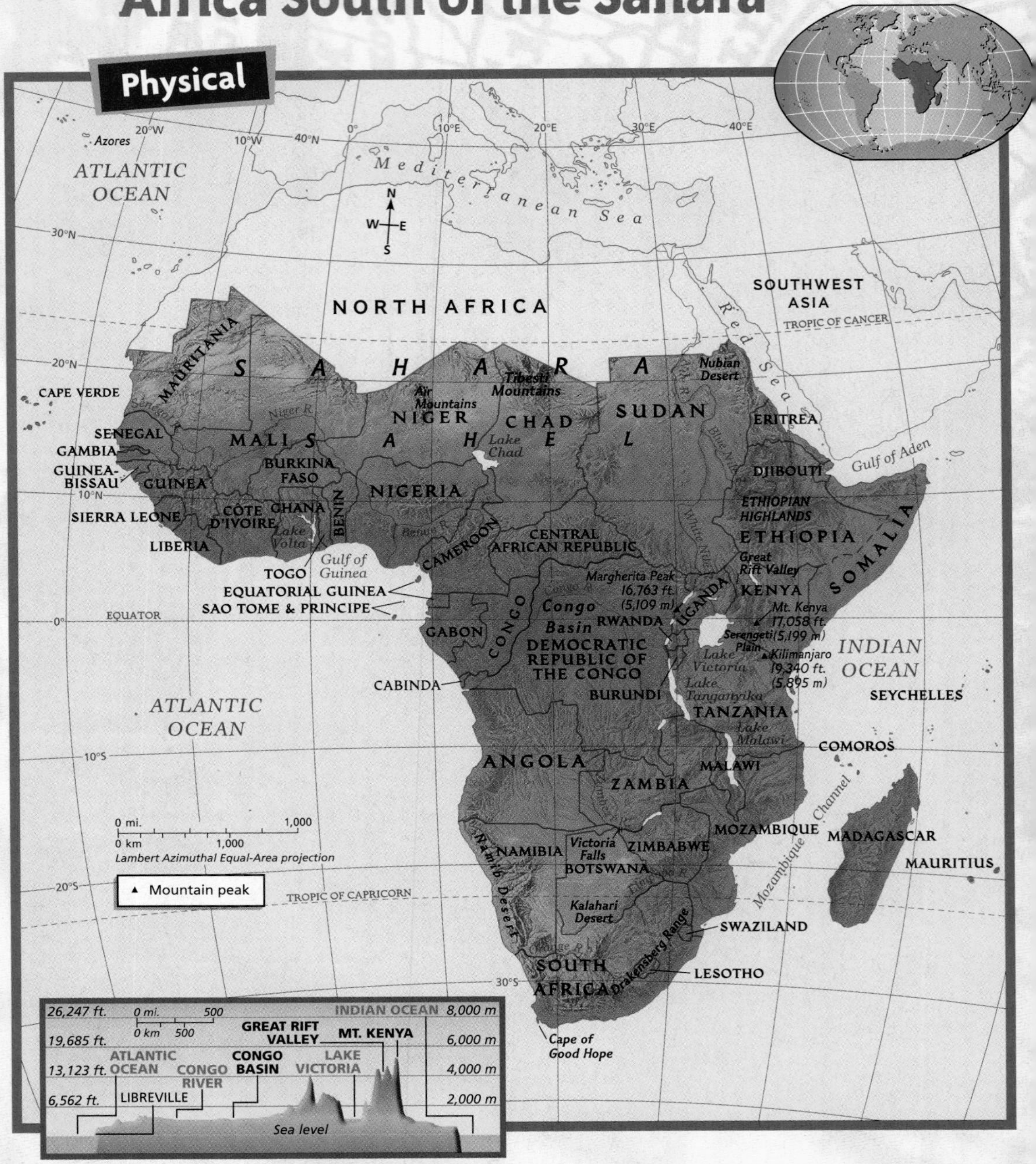

392 UNIT 6

Content Background

Cameroon's Deadly Lake Lake Nyos, in Cameroon, sits on a pool of hot magma. This magma lets out carbon dioxide gas, which is dangerous. The gas builds up in the bottom of the lake. In August 1986, the pressure of this gas became too great, and it escaped into the air in a killing cloud that soon settled over nearby villages. Thousands of animals and 1,700 people died. After a decade passed, people began to return to the lake shore. The gases are building up again, however. Scientists are installing a series of pipes from the gas layer to the surface. They hope to release the gas slowly over time so they can prevent another massive, deadly leak. **Ask: Why would people want to live by Lake Nyos and what effect would it have on their lives? L1**

UNIT 6

Political

Azores Port.
20°W
10°W
40°N
0°
10°E
30°E
40°E
50°E
30°N
20°N
10°N
0°
10°S
20°S
ATLANTIC OCEAN
Mediterranean Sea
NORTH AFRICA
SOUTHWEST ASIA
Red Sea
TROPIC OF CANCER
CAPE VERDE
Praia
Nouakchott
MAURITANIA
Sénégal R.
SENEGAL
Dakar
Banjul
GAMBIA
GUINEA-BISSAU
Bissau
GUINEA
Conakry
Freetown
SIERRA LEONE
Monrovia
LIBERIA
MALI
Bamako
Niger R.
BURKINA FASO
Ouagadougou
Niamey
NIGER
CÔTE D'IVOIRE
Yamoussoukro
Abidjan
GHANA
Accra
TOGO
Lomé
BENIN
Porto-Novo
NIGERIA
Abuja
Benue R.
CHAD
Lake Chad
N'Djamena
SUDAN
Khartoum
Nile R.
Blue Nile R.
White Nile R.
ERITREA
Asmara
DJIBOUTI
Djibouti
Gulf of Aden
Addis Ababa
ETHIOPIA
SOMALIA
Mogadishu
CAMEROON
Yaoundé
Malabo
CENTRAL AFRICAN REPUBLIC
Bangui
EQUATORIAL GUINEA
SAO TOME & PRINCIPE
São Tomé
EQUATOR
Libreville
GABON
CONGO
Congo R.
Brazzaville
Kinshasa
CABINDA Ang.
DEMOCRATIC REPUBLIC OF THE CONGO
RWANDA
Kigali
BURUNDI
Bujumbura
UGANDA
Kampala
KENYA
Lake Victoria
Nairobi
INDIAN OCEAN
Victoria
SEYCHELLES
Lake Tanganyika
TANZANIA
Dar es Salaam
Lake Malawi
COMOROS
Moroni
Luanda
ANGOLA
MALAWI
Lilongwe
ZAMBIA
Lusaka
Zambezi R.
Harare
ZIMBABWE
MOZAMBIQUE
Mozambique Channel
MADAGASCAR
Antananarivo
MAURITIUS
Port Louis
RÉUNION Fr.
NAMIBIA
Windhoek
BOTSWANA
Gaborone
Limpopo R.
Pretoria
Maputo
Mbabane
SWAZILAND
SOUTH AFRICA
Orange R.
Bloemfontein
Maseru
LESOTHO
Cape Town
ATLANTIC OCEAN
N S E W
National capital
TROPIC OF CAPRICORN
0 mi. 1,000
0 km 1,000
Lambert Azimuthal Equal-Area projection

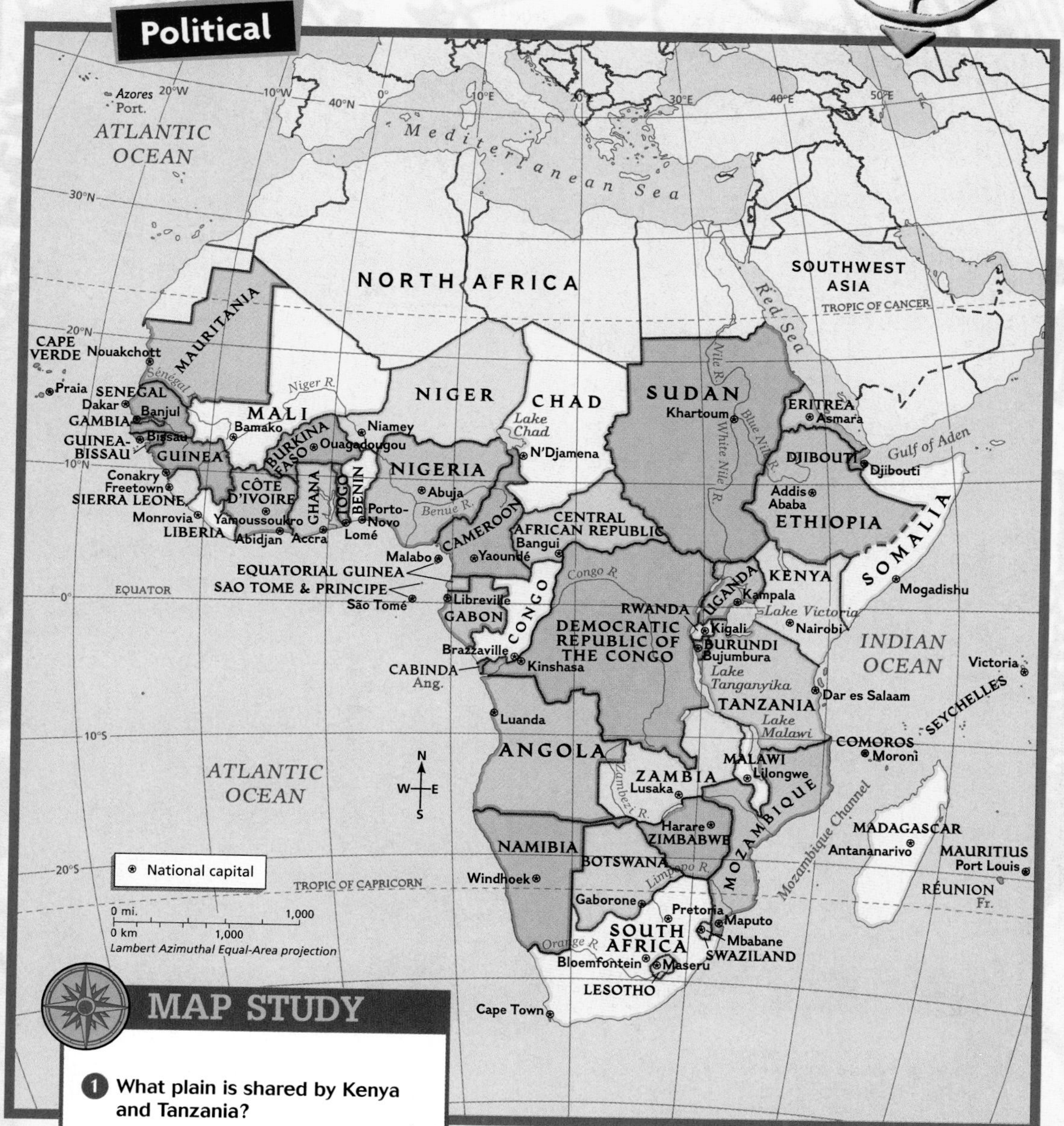

MAP STUDY

1. What plain is shared by Kenya and Tanzania?
2. What is the capital of Nigeria?

393

Unit 6

2 TEACH

Synthesizing Information Have students study the physical features of these regions. Then have them choose a place or geographic feature shown on the map. Have them write at least five adjectives to describe their place or feature. Call on students to share their adjectives. Then have other students try to identify the place or feature. **L1**

Using a Map Have students look at the political map on this page. **Ask: Which country has a coastline on two oceans?** *(South Africa)* **What 16 countries are landlocked?** *(Mali, Burkina Faso, Niger, Chad, Sudan, Ethiopia, Central African Republic, Uganda, Rwanda, Burundi, Malawi, Zambia, Zimbabwe, Botswana, Swaziland, Lesotho)* **What 6 countries are only on islands?** *(Cape Verde Islands, São Tomé and Príncipe, Madagascar, Comoros, Seychelles, Mauritius)*

MAP STUDY

Answers

1. Serengeti Plain
2. Abuja

Skills Practice
What country is completely surrounded by South Africa? *(Lesotho)* **Which is longer, the Atlantic Ocean coast or the Indian Ocean coast?** *(Atlantic)*

Regional Atlas Activity

Mental Mapping Help students develop a mental map of Africa south of the Sahara by playing a location game. Assign one or more countries to each student. Instruct students to write clues about the location of the countries they were assigned. *(Example: This country is east of Gabon. It borders the Central African Republic. It is west and north of the Democratic Republic of the Congo. It has a coastline on the Atlantic Ocean. Answer—Congo.)* Have each student read these clues, one at a time, until a classmate can identify the country. You could also use the clues as part of a team competition. Award points based on the number of clues a team needs to correctly identify the country, with more points received the fewer the clues used. **L2**

EE1 The World in Spatial Terms: Standard 2

Unit 6
Regional Atlas

Making Generalizations Have students study the map on this page and then make a generalization based on its information. *(Example: Most nations with diamond deposits are in western or southern Africa.)* Ask for volunteers to read their generalizations aloud. **L1**

Interdisciplinary Connections

Economics Minerals are not the only valuable resource in Africa. Markets for crocodile leather and leopard fur have resulted in severely reduced numbers of Nile crocodiles and leopards. Rhinoceroses have been hunted to near extinction for their horns. Elephant ivory is also popular, and the number of African elephants has plummeted from about 2 million in the early 1970s to only about 600,000 in 1990.

MAP STUDY

Answers

1. diamonds, rubies, emeralds, and sapphires
2. Atlantic Ocean

Skills Practice

In what countries are emeralds mined? *(Tanzania, Mozambique, Zambia, Zimbabwe, Botswana, South Africa, and Madagascar)*

NATIONAL GEOGRAPHIC

REGIONAL ATLAS

Africa South of the Sahara

Gems and Minerals

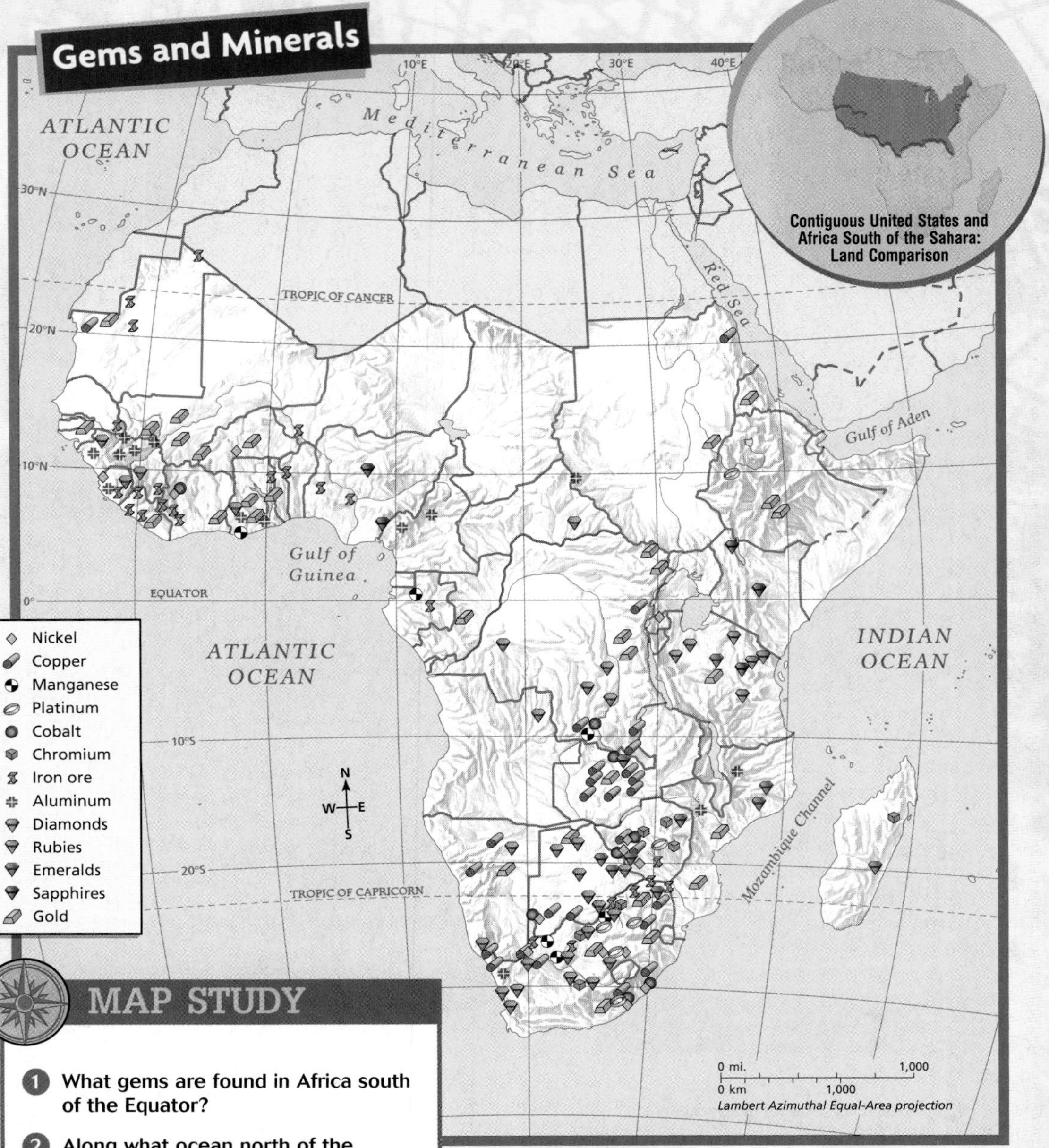

ATLANTIC OCEAN

Mediterranean Sea

Red Sea

Gulf of Aden

TROPIC OF CANCER

Gulf of Guinea

EQUATOR

INDIAN OCEAN

Mozambique Channel

TROPIC OF CAPRICORN

Contiguous United States and Africa South of the Sahara: Land Comparison

- Nickel
- Copper
- Manganese
- Platinum
- Cobalt
- Chromium
- Iron ore
- Aluminum
- Diamonds
- Rubies
- Emeralds
- Sapphires
- Gold

0 mi. 1,000
0 km 1,000
Lambert Azimuthal Equal-Area projection

MAP STUDY

1. What gems are found in Africa south of the Equator?
2. Along what ocean north of the Equator is the most gold found?

Regional Atlas Activity

Locating Places A United Nations report recently predicted that conflict over water is likely to become a significant problem in Africa in the next 25 years. The report says that 11 countries are currently in a situation of water scarcity or water stress, meaning that the country has less than 42 cubic feet (1.2 cu. m) of water per person per year. The report predicts that 14 more countries are likely to join this list in the coming years, accounting for nearly half of Africa's people. The report expects the most severe problems in areas where countries share rivers or lakes. Have students look at the physical map on page 392 and identify areas where this situation applies. **L1**

EE6 The Uses of Geography: Standard 18

Unit 6 Regional Atlas

Fast Facts

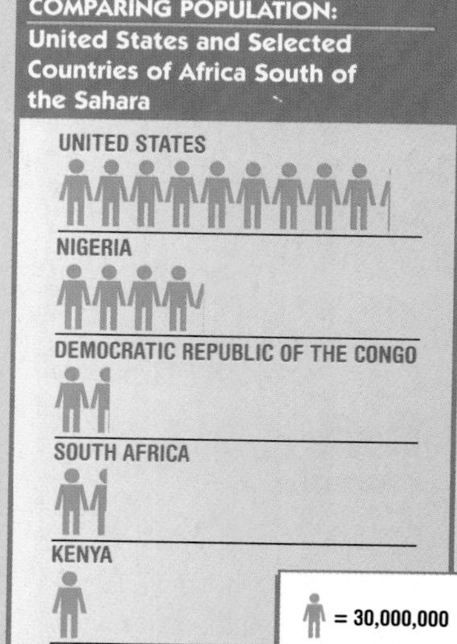

Source: *Population Reference Bureau*, 2000.

SELECTED RURAL AND URBAN POPULATIONS: Africa South of the Sahara

	Rural	Urban
WEST AFRICA		
Niger	83%	17%
Cape Verde	56%	44%
CENTRAL AFRICA		
Angola	68%	32%
Central African Republic	61%	39%
EAST AFRICA		
Rwanda	95%	5%
Djibouti	17%	83%
SOUTHERN AFRICA		
Lesotho	84%	16%
South Africa	55%	45%

Source: *Population Reference Bureau*, 2000.

Data Bits

Country	Automobiles per 1,000 people	Telephones per 1,000 people
Ghana	5	6
Mauritania	8	5
Sudan	10	4
Tanzania	1	3
Zambia	17	9

Religions

Country	Islam	Christian	Traditional Beliefs	Other
Ghana	11%	43%	38%	8%
Mauritania	100%	—	—	—
Sudan	70%	9%	20%	1%
Tanzania	33%	33%	30%	4%
Zambia	0.5%	63%	36%	.5%

Source: *World Desk Reference*, 2000.

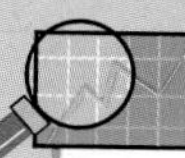

GRAPHIC STUDY

1. Which country has the highest percentage of Christians? Which has the lowest percentage?
2. Of the African countries shown in the chart at lower left, which is least urbanized? Which is most urbanized?

As an introduction to this region, you may want to engage students by studying an important contemporary issue in this region of the world. The **TIME REPORTS: FOCUS ON WORLD ISSUES** for this region is found on pages 415–421. The feature examines the movement of refugees in Africa.

Cultural Kaleidoscope

Lesotho As many as 250,000 men at a time may be gone from this country to work in the mines of South Africa. As a result, women do most of the farming and make many day-to-day family decisions.

GRAPHIC STUDY

Answers

1. Zambia; Mauritania
2. Rwanda; Djibouti

Skills Practice

How many people live in Kenya? *(about 30 million)* **How does Kenya's population compare to Nigeria's?** *(Nigeria's population is about 4 times larger.)*

FUN FACTS

- **Africa** About 90 percent of Africa lies within the tropics—the largest tropical region of any continent.
- **Chad** The Tibesti Mountains cover an area of more than 50,000 square miles (129,500 sq. km) and reach heights of over 11,000 feet (3,353 m). One of the world's most rugged and inaccessible places, the Tibesti Mountains have long served as a refuge for desert bandits.
- **Namibia** About 100,000 people in Namibia and other parts of southwest Africa speak Khoisan languages. These languages are not related to any others spoken in Africa. Many words in Khoisan are expressed with unusual "click" sounds.

Regional Atlas

Country Profiles

ANGOLA
POPULATION: 12,479,000; 26 per sq. mi.; 10 per sq. km
LANGUAGES: Portuguese, Local Languages
MAJOR EXPORT: Crude Oil
MAJOR IMPORT: Machinery
CAPITAL: Luanda
LANDMASS: 481,354 sq. mi.; 1,246,700 sq. km

BENIN
POPULATION: 6,600,000; 152 per sq. mi.; 58 per sq. km
LANGUAGES: French, Fon, Yoruba
MAJOR EXPORT: Cotton
MAJOR IMPORT: Foods
CAPITAL: Porto-Novo
LANDMASS: 43,484 sq. mi.; 112,622 sq. km

BOTSWANA
POPULATION: 1,600,000; 7 per sq. mi.; 2 per sq. km
LANGUAGES: English, Setswana
MAJOR EXPORT: Diamonds
MAJOR IMPORT: Foods
CAPITAL: Gaborone
LANDMASS: 231,805 sq. mi.; 600,372 sq. km

BURKINA FASO
POPULATION: 12,300,000; 116 per sq. mi.; 45 per sq. km
LANGUAGES: French, Local Languages
MAJOR EXPORT: Cotton
MAJOR IMPORT: Machinery
CAPITAL: Ouagadougou
LANDMASS: 105,869 sq. mi.; 274,200 sq. km

BURUNDI
POPULATION: 6,200,000; 577 per sq. mi.; 222 per sq. km
LANGUAGES: Kirundi, French
MAJOR EXPORT: Coffee
MAJOR IMPORT: Machinery
CAPITAL: Bujumbura
LANDMASS: 10,747 sq. mi.; 27,834 sq. km

CAMEROON
POPULATION: 15,456,000; 84 per sq. mi.; 33 per sq. km
LANGUAGES: French, English, Local Languages
MAJOR EXPORT: Crude Oil
MAJOR IMPORT: Machinery
CAPITAL: Yaoundé
LANDMASS: 183,569 sq. mi.; 475,442 sq. km

CAPE VERDE
POPULATION: 400,000; 256 per sq. mi.; 100 per sq. km
LANGUAGES: Portuguese, Crioulo
MAJOR EXPORT: Shoes
MAJOR IMPORT: Foods
CAPITAL: Praia
LANDMASS: 1,557 sq. mi.; 4,033 sq. km

CENTRAL AFRICAN REPUBLIC
POPULATION: 3,600,000; 15 per sq. mi.; 5 per sq. km
LANGUAGES: French, Sango, Arabic, Hunsa
MAJOR EXPORT: Diamonds
MAJOR IMPORT: Foods
CAPITAL: Bangui
LANDMASS: 240,535 sq. mi.; 622,984 sq. km

CHAD
POPULATION: 8,700,000; 17 per sq. mi.; 6 per sq. km
LANGUAGES: French, Arabic, Sara, Sango
MAJOR EXPORT: Cotton
MAJOR IMPORT: Machinery
CAPITAL: N'Djamena
LANDMASS: 495,755 sq. mi.; 1,284,000 sq. km

COMOROS
POPULATION: 600,000; 834 per sq. mi.; 322 per sq. km
LANGUAGES: Arabic, French, Comoran
MAJOR EXPORT: Vanilla
MAJOR IMPORT: Rice
CAPITAL: Moroni
LANDMASS: 719 sq. mi.; 1,862 sq. km

CONGO
POPULATION: 3,100,000; 23 per sq. mi.; 9 per sq. km
LANGUAGES: French, Lingala, Monokutuba
MAJOR EXPORT: Crude Oil
MAJOR IMPORT: Machinery
CAPITAL: Brazzaville
LANDMASS: 132,047 sq. mi.; 342,000 sq. km

Countries and flags not drawn to scale

Current Events Journal

Have students write at least five questions about the physical geography of Africa south of the Sahara. Tell students to include direction, key, scale, or physical map questions such as: **In what direction would you travel from Ethiopia to Somalia?** *(east)*; **How does Senegal compare in elevation to Burundi?** *(Senegal is a lowland coastal plain from 0 to 1,000 feet above sea level; Burundi is a mountainous region from 5,000 to 10,000 feet high.)* Allow time for students to write questions and challenge one another. You may also want to repeat this activity at the end of the unit.

Did You Know

Burkina Faso means "land of the honest people." Burkina Faso's economy is heavily dependent on cattle, goats, and sheep. About 50 percent of the country's export income is derived from the sale of livestock.

Travel Guide

Telephones are rare in Cameroon and mail service is unreliable. People communicate by *radio trattoir,* or "pavement radio." This is a system of passing news by verbal relay.

Content Background

African Families Family is extremely important in many African countries. In Cameroon, a family may house and feed a distant relative who is in need, even when it causes hardship. In Zimbabwe, parents care for their children and expect the children to care for them in their old age. For centuries, families across Africa were typically extended families, with several generations living in the same household. In recent decades, urbanization and the development of a money economy have changed that, and the nuclear family became more common. The stresses caused by war and AIDS have ravaged the family further in some countries. **Ask: What are the similarities and differences in the way Africans and Americans feel about families?**

UNIT 6

For more information on countries in this region, refer to the Nations of the World Data Bank on pages 690–699.

CONGO, Democratic Republic of the
POPULATION: 53,600,000; 59 per sq. mi.; 23 per sq. km
LANGUAGES: French, Lingala, Kingwana
MAJOR EXPORT: Diamonds
MAJOR IMPORT: Manufactured Goods
CAPITAL: Kinshasa
LANDMASS: 905,568 sq. mi.; 2,345,409 sq. km

CÔTE D'IVOIRE
POPULATION: 16,400,000; 131 per sq. mi.; 51 per sq. km
LANGUAGES: French, Dioula
MAJOR EXPORT: Cocoa
MAJOR IMPORT: Foods
CAPITALS: Yamoussoukro, Abidjan
LANDMASS: 124,504 sq. mi.; 322,463 sq. km

DJIBOUTI
POPULATION: 600,000; 67 per sq. mi.; 26 per sq. km
LANGUAGES: French, Arabic
MAJOR EXPORTS: Hides and Skins
MAJOR IMPORT: Foods
CAPITAL: Djibouti
LANDMASS: 8,958 sq. mi.; 23,200 sq. km

EQUATORIAL GUINEA
POPULATION: 500,000; 46 per sq. mi.; 17 per sq. km
LANGUAGES: Spanish, French, Fang, Bubi, Ibo
MAJOR EXPORT: Petroleum
MAJOR IMPORT: Machinery
CAPITAL: Malabo
LANDMASS: 10,831 sq. mi.; 28,051 sq. km

ERITREA
POPULATION: 4,300,000; 92 per sq. mi.; 35 per sq. km
LANGUAGES: Afar, Amharic, Arabic, Tigre
MAJOR EXPORT: Livestock
MAJOR IMPORT: Processed Foods
CAPITAL: Asmara
LANDMASS: 46,842 sq. mi.; 121,320 sq. km

ETHIOPIA
POPULATION: 65,400,000; 154 per sq. mi.; 60 per sq. km
LANGUAGES: Amharic, Tigrinya, Orominga
MAJOR EXPORT: Coffee
MAJOR IMPORTS: Foods and Livestock
CAPITAL: Addis Ababa
LANDMASS: 424,934 sq. mi.; 1,100,574 sq. km

GABON
POPULATION: 1,197,000; 12 per sq. mi.; 4 per sq. km
LANGUAGES: French, Local Languages
MAJOR EXPORT: Crude Oil
MAJOR IMPORT: Machinery
CAPITAL: Libreville
LANDMASS: 103,347 sq. mi.; 267,667 sq. km

GAMBIA
POPULATION: 1,400,000; 321 per sq. mi.; 123 per sq. km
LANGUAGES: English, Mandinka, Fula, Wolof
MAJOR EXPORT: Peanuts
MAJOR IMPORT: Foods
CAPITAL: Banjul
LANDMASS: 4,361 sq. mi.; 11,295 sq. km

GHANA
POPULATION: 19,900,000; 216 per sq. mi.; 83 per sq. km
LANGUAGES: English, Local Languages
MAJOR EXPORT: Gold
MAJOR IMPORT: Machinery
CAPITAL: Accra
LANDMASS: 92,100 sq. mi.; 238,537 sq. km

GUINEA
POPULATION: 7,600,000; 80 per sq. mi.; 31 per sq. km
LANGUAGES: French, Local Languages
MAJOR EXPORT: Bauxite
MAJOR IMPORT: Petroleum Products
CAPITAL: Conakry
LANDMASS: 94,926 sq. mi.; 245,857 sq. km

GUINEA-BISSAU
POPULATION: 1,200,000; 86 per sq. mi.; 33 per sq. km
LANGUAGES: Portuguese, Crioulo, Local Languages
MAJOR EXPORT: Cashews
MAJOR IMPORT: Foods
CAPITAL: Bissau
LANDMASS: 13,948 sq. mi.; 36,125 sq. km

Country Profiles Activity

Have students prepare a chart that lists the countries profiled here by region—West Africa, Central Africa, East Africa, and southern Africa. Their chart might include the name of the country, the capital, the population, and the chief exports. Then have them compare the main economic activities in the different regions. **L1**

EE1 The World in Spatial Terms: Standard 1

Unit 6 Regional Atlas

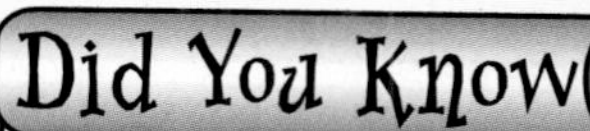

Did You Know

According to tradition, Ethiopians are descendants of the Biblical rulers Solomon and the Queen of Sheba.

TRAVEL GUIDE

When visiting Cape Verde, you may enjoy the *Funáná,* lively dance music with a strong beat. The music was forbidden in Cape Verde during colonial times. After the islands received independence, the music revived.

THE HUMANITIES CONNECTION

World Music: A Cultural Legacy

World Art and Architecture Transparencies

Cultural Kaleidoscope

Niger Students in Niger get their teacher's attention by snapping their fingers rather than raising their hands.

Regional Atlas

Cultural Kaleidoscope

Liberia Liberia was founded as a settlement for African Americans who were freed from slavery. It was founded in 1822, and the first settlement was named Monrovia after American President James Monroe. The American connection is also evident in the country's flag, which has a total of 13 red and white stripes and a single white star in a field of deep blue.

Because of its elevation, Lesotho does not have a tropical climate like that of the surrounding region. For the same reason, Lesotho is free of many of the diseases common in other parts of Africa.

Interdisciplinary Connections

Economics Malawi sits on the shores of Lake Malawi, home to more different species of fish than any other freshwater lake in the world. Malawi uses this resource in an unusual way—divers collect the beautifully colored fish and sell them to companies that market them for aquarium collectors around the world. Some fish can bring hundreds of dollars to the diver who catches them.

Country Profiles

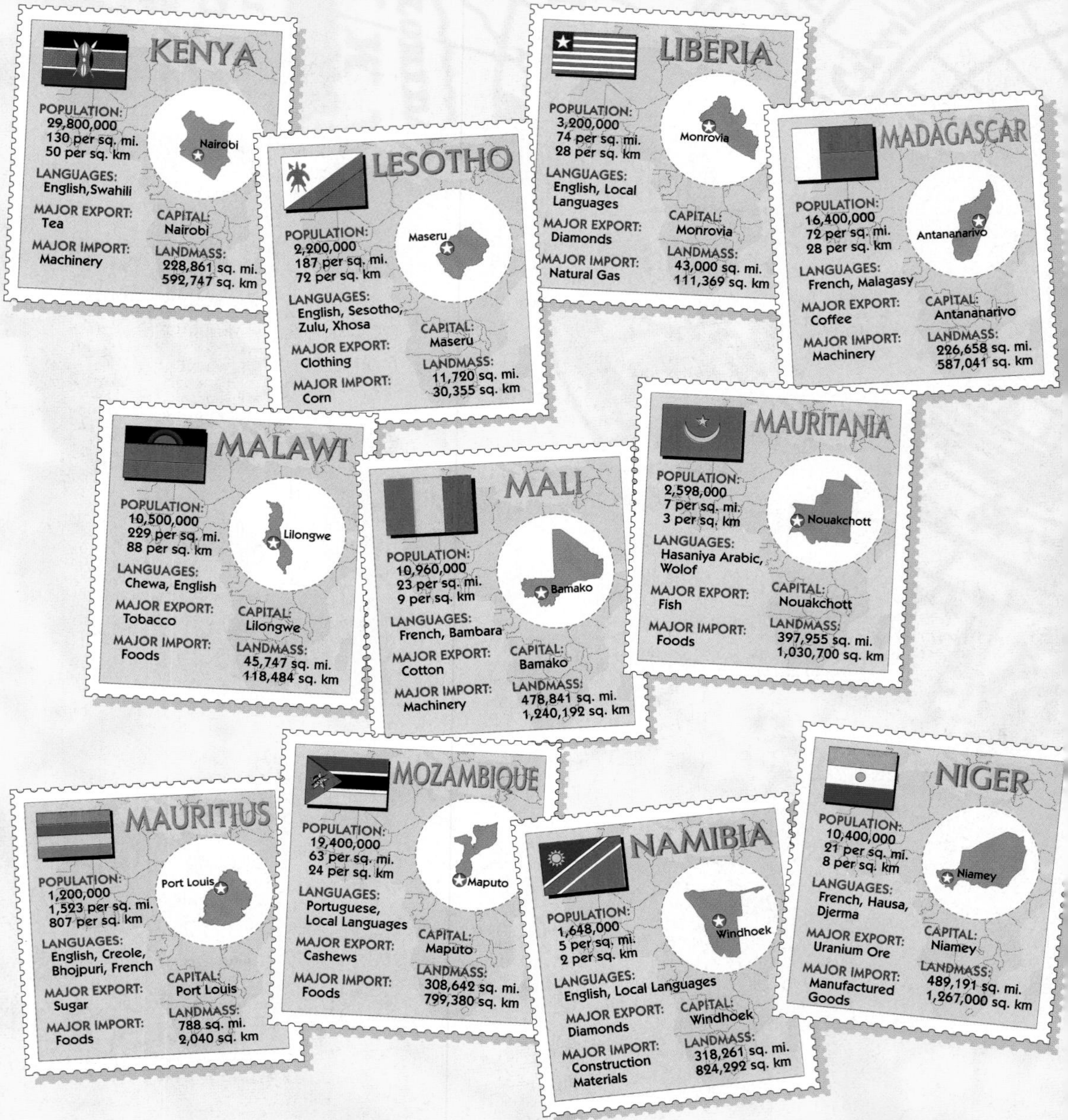

KENYA
POPULATION: 29,800,000; 130 per sq. mi.; 50 per sq. km
LANGUAGES: English, Swahili
MAJOR EXPORT: Tea
MAJOR IMPORT: Machinery
CAPITAL: Nairobi
LANDMASS: 228,861 sq. mi.; 592,747 sq. km

LIBERIA
POPULATION: 3,200,000; 74 per sq. mi.; 28 per sq. km
LANGUAGES: English, Local Languages
MAJOR EXPORT: Diamonds
MAJOR IMPORT: Natural Gas
CAPITAL: Monrovia
LANDMASS: 43,000 sq. mi.; 111,369 sq. km

LESOTHO
POPULATION: 2,200,000; 187 per sq. mi.; 72 per sq. km
LANGUAGES: English, Sesotho, Zulu, Xhosa
MAJOR EXPORT: Clothing
MAJOR IMPORT: Corn
CAPITAL: Maseru
LANDMASS: 11,720 sq. mi.; 30,355 sq. km

MADAGASCAR
POPULATION: 16,400,000; 72 per sq. mi.; 28 per sq. km
LANGUAGES: French, Malagasy
MAJOR EXPORT: Coffee
MAJOR IMPORT: Machinery
CAPITAL: Antananarivo
LANDMASS: 226,658 sq. mi.; 587,041 sq. km

MALAWI
POPULATION: 10,500,000; 229 per sq. mi.; 88 per sq. km
LANGUAGES: Chewa, English
MAJOR EXPORT: Tobacco
MAJOR IMPORT: Foods
CAPITAL: Lilongwe
LANDMASS: 45,747 sq. mi.; 118,484 sq. km

MALI
POPULATION: 10,960,000; 23 per sq. mi.; 9 per sq. km
LANGUAGES: French, Bambara
MAJOR EXPORT: Cotton
MAJOR IMPORT: Machinery
CAPITAL: Bamako
LANDMASS: 478,841 sq. mi.; 1,240,192 sq. km

MAURITANIA
POPULATION: 2,598,000; 7 per sq. mi.; 3 per sq. km
LANGUAGES: Hasaniya Arabic, Wolof
MAJOR EXPORT: Fish
MAJOR IMPORT: Foods
CAPITAL: Nouakchott
LANDMASS: 397,955 sq. mi.; 1,030,700 sq. km

MAURITIUS
POPULATION: 1,200,000; 1,523 per sq. mi.; 807 per sq. km
LANGUAGES: English, Creole, Bhojpuri, French
MAJOR EXPORT: Sugar
MAJOR IMPORT: Foods
CAPITAL: Port Louis
LANDMASS: 788 sq. mi.; 2,040 sq. km

MOZAMBIQUE
POPULATION: 19,400,000; 63 per sq. mi.; 24 per sq. km
LANGUAGES: Portuguese, Local Languages
MAJOR EXPORT: Cashews
MAJOR IMPORT: Foods
CAPITAL: Maputo
LANDMASS: 308,642 sq. mi.; 799,380 sq. km

NAMIBIA
POPULATION: 1,648,000; 5 per sq. mi.; 2 per sq. km
LANGUAGES: English, Local Languages
MAJOR EXPORT: Diamonds
MAJOR IMPORT: Construction Materials
CAPITAL: Windhoek
LANDMASS: 318,261 sq. mi.; 824,292 sq. km

NIGER
POPULATION: 10,400,000; 21 per sq. mi.; 8 per sq. km
LANGUAGES: French, Hausa, Djerma
MAJOR EXPORT: Uranium Ore
MAJOR IMPORT: Manufactured Goods
CAPITAL: Niamey
LANDMASS: 489,191 sq. mi.; 1,267,000 sq. km

Countries and flags not drawn to scale

FUN FACTS

- **Lesotho** This country has no forests and is subject to severe soil erosion. The government sponsors projects to help the environment. Tree Planting Day is an official holiday celebrated on March 21.
- **Namibia** The Namib Desert has some of the largest sand dunes in the world. In the southern part of the desert, dunes reach heights of 660 feet (201 m) and may spread up to 1 mile (1.6 km) wide. Tourists come here to sandboard.
- **Rwanda** Rwanda's oral literary tradition consists of myths, fables, folktales, poetry, and proverbs. Relatively few Rwandans can read and write, so stories are passed from one generation to another by storytellers.

UNIT 6

For more information on countries in this region, refer to the Nations of the World Data Bank on pages 690–699.

NIGERIA
POPULATION: 126,600,000; 354 per sq. mi.; 137 per sq. km
LANGUAGES: English, Hausa, Yoruba, Igbo
MAJOR EXPORT: Petroleum
MAJOR IMPORT: Machinery
CAPITAL: Abuja
LANDMASS: 356,669 sq. mi.; 923,768 sq. km

RWANDA
POPULATION: 7,300,000; 718 per sq. mi.; 277 per sq. km
LANGUAGES: Kinyarwanda, French, English
MAJOR EXPORT: Coffee
MAJOR IMPORT: Foods
CAPITAL: Kigali
LANDMASS: 10,169 sq. mi.; 26,338 sq. km

SAO TOME and PRINCIPE
POPULATION: 200,000; 537 per sq. mi.; 207 per sq. km
LANGUAGES: Portuguese, Crioulo
MAJOR EXPORT: Cocoa
MAJOR IMPORT: Textiles
CAPITAL: São Tomé
LANDMASS: 372 sq. mi.; 964 sq. km

SENEGAL
POPULATION: 9,700,000; 128 per sq. mi.; 49 per sq. km
LANGUAGES: French, Wolof, Pulaar, Diola
MAJOR EXPORT: Fish
MAJOR IMPORT: Foods
CAPITAL: Dakar
LANDMASS: 75,955 sq. mi.; 196,722 sq. km

SEYCHELLES
POPULATION: 100,000; 571 per sq. mi.; 220 per sq. km
LANGUAGES: English, French, Creole
MAJOR EXPORT: Fish
MAJOR IMPORT: Foods
CAPITAL: Victoria
LANDMASS: 175 sq. mi.; 453 sq. km

SIERRA LEONE
POPULATION: 5,400,000; 195 per sq. mi.; 75 per sq. km
LANGUAGES: English, Mende, Temne, Krio
MAJOR EXPORT: Diamonds
MAJOR IMPORT: Foods
CAPITAL: Freetown
LANDMASS: 27,699 sq. mi.; 71,740 sq. km

SOMALIA
POPULATION: 7,500,000; 30 per sq. mi.; 11 per sq. km
LANGUAGES: Somali, Arabic
MAJOR EXPORT: Livestock
MAJOR IMPORT: Textiles
CAPITAL: Mogadishu
LANDMASS: 246,201 sq. mi.; 637,657 sq. km

SOUTH AFRICA
POPULATION: 43,600,000; 92 per sq. mi.; 35 per sq. km
LANGUAGES: Afrikaans, English, Local Languages
MAJOR EXPORT: Gold
MAJOR IMPORT: Transport Equip.
CAPITALS: Pretoria, Cape Town, Bloemfontein
LANDMASS: 471,445 sq. mi.; 1,221,037 sq. km

SUDAN
POPULATION: 31,800,000; 33 per sq. mi.; 13 per sq. km
LANGUAGES: Arabic, Nubian, Ta Bedawie
MAJOR EXPORT: Cotton
MAJOR IMPORT: Petroleum Products
CAPITAL: Khartoum
LANDMASS: 963,600 sq. mi.; 2,495,712 sq. km

SWAZILAND
POPULATION: 1,100,000; 164 per sq. mi.; 63 per sq. km
LANGUAGES: English, Swazi
MAJOR EXPORT: Soft Drink Concentrates
MAJOR IMPORT: Machinery
CAPITAL: Mbabane
LANDMASS: 6,704 sq. mi.; 17,364 sq. km

TANZANIA
POPULATION: 36,200,000; 99 per sq. mi.; 38 per sq. km
LANGUAGES: Swahili, English
MAJOR EXPORT: Coffee
MAJOR IMPORT: Machinery
CAPITAL: Dar es Salaam
LANDMASS: 364,900 sq. mi.; 945,087 sq. km

Unit 6 Regional Atlas

Did You Know

During the 1600s and 1700s, Madagascar was used as a base by pirates. Among them was the notorious Scottish pirate named Captain Kidd.

TRAVEL GUIDE

The people of Mali never use the left hand to accept food or money. When shaking hands, a Malian shows special respect by touching his or her right elbow with the fingers of the left hand.

Interdisciplinary Connections

Science The Welwitschia is a plant that grows in the Namib Desert. Its trunk spreads to a width of more than 5 feet (1.5 m). Two giant green leaves grow out from the trunk and split into ribbonlike shreds. The plants may live as long as 2,000 years.

Regional Atlas Activity

Migration Much of Africa south of the Sahara is inhabited by descendants of the Bantu people who lived in West Africa about 500 B.C. Over hundreds of years, they developed the ability to mine and to work metals. As a result, they had iron tools for farming and iron tips for hunting weapons. With more food, the population grew. About 2,000 years ago, the population had increased so much that some Bantu moved to new areas searching for new land. Over hundreds of years, Bantu-speaking groups spread throughout Central, East, and southern Africa. Today about 60 to 80 million of their descendants live in Africa, speaking the many Bantu-related languages. Ask students to research and explain the factors responsible for Bantu migration. L1

EE2 Places and Regions: Standard 4

REGIONAL ATLAS

Interdisciplinary Connections

History Hundreds of years ago, what is now Zimbabwe was a flourishing stone city named Great Zimbabwe. The country is named for this city. Many carved stone figurines of a bird were found in the ruins of the city. This bird is now a national symbol found on Zimbabwe's flag.

BUILDING CITIZENSHIP

Answer Trying to find and punish all the people who had committed crimes would continue the hatred that had divided South Africa. By pardoning political crimes, Mandela focused the country on a unified future rather than a divided past.

Write About It! Student answers will vary, but should include a description or drawing of the flag. Although not always official, the colors on African flags frequently refer to the people, resources, environment, and other characteristics of the country. A good Web site to research flags is Flags of the World (FOTW) at **fotw.digibel.be/flags**.

Country Profiles

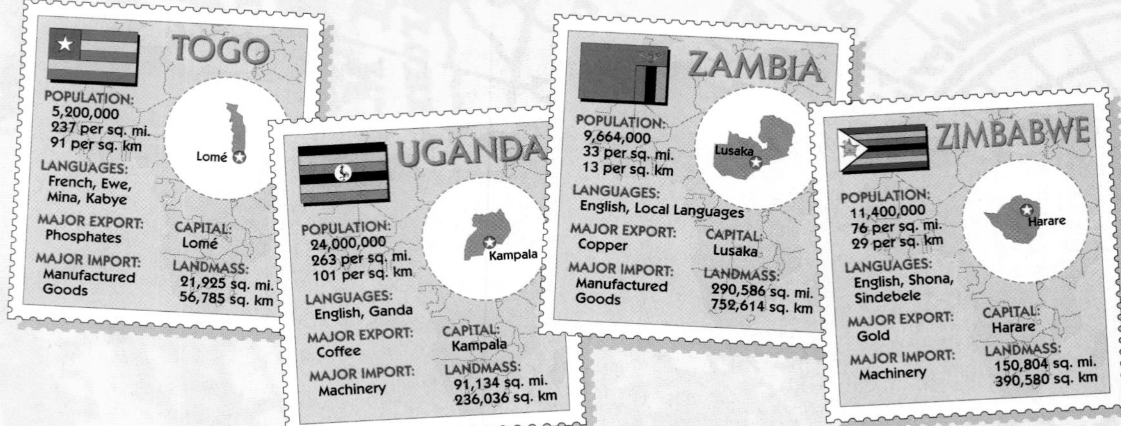

TOGO
POPULATION: 5,200,000
237 per sq. mi.
91 per sq. km
LANGUAGES: French, Ewe, Mina, Kabye
MAJOR EXPORT: Phosphates
MAJOR IMPORT: Manufactured Goods
CAPITAL: Lomé
LANDMASS: 21,925 sq. mi.
56,785 sq. km
Lomé
UGANDA
POPULATION: 24,000,000
263 per sq. mi.
101 per sq. km
LANGUAGES: English, Ganda
MAJOR EXPORT: Coffee
MAJOR IMPORT: Machinery
CAPITAL: Kampala
LANDMASS: 91,134 sq. mi.
236,036 sq. km
Kampala
ZAMBIA
POPULATION: 9,664,000
33 per sq. mi.
13 per sq. km
LANGUAGES: English, Local Languages
MAJOR EXPORT: Copper
MAJOR IMPORT: Manufactured Goods
CAPITAL: Lusaka
LANDMASS: 290,586 sq. mi.
752,614 sq. km
Lusaka
ZIMBABWE
POPULATION: 11,400,000
76 per sq. mi.
29 per sq. km
LANGUAGES: English, Shona, Sindebele
MAJOR EXPORT: Gold
MAJOR IMPORT: Machinery
CAPITAL: Harare
LANDMASS: 150,804 sq. mi.
390,580 sq. km
Harare

Countries and flags not drawn to scale

BUILDING CITIZENSHIP

Closing the Door on Racism By 1994, South Africa's racist policy of apartheid was officially over. Nelson Mandela became the first black person to be elected president of South Africa. Just three years earlier he had been released from jail after spending 27 years there for anti-apartheid activities. When he became president, he created a panel to grant pardons to both blacks and whites who had admitted to committing political crimes in the past. Mandela believed that only by "closing the door" on the past could the country move on to its future.

Why do you think Nelson Mandela was willing to pardon people?

▼ Women at an antiapartheid rally in South Africa

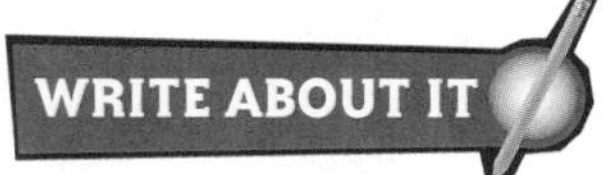

The flags of African countries often represent the history or culture of the country. For example, the "Y" shape in the South African flag symbolizes a divided people going forward in unity. Research the flag of an African country and write a paragraph about the meaning of the flag.

Content Background

Culture and History Between A.D. 1000 and 1500, the Shona people built nearly 300 stone-walled fortresses throughout southern Africa. The largest was called Great Zimbabwe, meaning "house of stone." It was the religious and trading center of the Shona kingdom. Great Zimbabwe included fortress walls, temples, marketplaces, and homes spread out on a fertile, gold-rich plateau south of the Zambezi River. The most impressive part of the city was an area called the Great Enclosure, which had an outer wall 16.5 feet (5 m) thick and 32 feet (9.8 m) high. Inside the wall, a maze of interior walls and hidden passages protected the house of the king, the Great Temple, and other religious buildings.

UNIT 6

View over terraced fields and small settlements, Kabale, Uganda

Africa South of the Sahara 401

FUN FACTS

- **Côte d'Ivoire** French sailors came to this region in the late 1400s in search of ivory. They are responsible for the name, which means "Ivory Coast."
- **Ghana** In Ghana, it is impolite and defiant for a child to look an adult in the eye.
- **Guinea** At family celebrations in Guinea, *griots,* or traditional singers, are hired to sing about individual guests.

Unit 6
Regional Atlas

3 ASSESS

Assign the Building Citizenship as homework or as an in-class activity.

Reteach

Give students an outline map of the region. Have them complete the map by writing in the names of major physical features, including

- Mountains (Aïr Mountains, Tibesti Mountains, Mt. Kenya, Kilimanjaro, Drakensberg Range)
- Plateaus (Ethiopian Highlands)
- Deserts (Sahara, Sahel, Namib Desert, Kalahari Desert)
- Lakes (Lake Victoria, Lake Tanganyika, Lake Malawi)
- Rivers (Niger River, Congo River, Blue Nile River, White Nile River, Zambezi River)
- Other (Great Rift Valley, Serengeti Plain, Victoria Falls)

Enrich

Have students choose a country in Africa south of the Sahara. Have them research that country and prepare a bulletin board display that discusses the main ethnic, religious, and language groups in the country.

4 CLOSE

Have students write a paragraph that summarizes what they think are the main physical, economic, and cultural characteristics shared by the countries of Africa south of the Sahara.

Chapter 15 Resources

Note: The following materials may be used when teaching Chapter 15.
Section level support materials are shown at point of use in the margins of the Teacher Wraparound Edition.

Timesaving Tools

TeacherWorks™ All-In-One Planner and Resource Center

- **Interactive Teacher Edition** See the **Interactive Teacher Edition** CD-ROM to electronically integrate your Teacher Wraparound Edition and blackline masters.
- **Interactive Lesson Planner** Organize your week, month, semester, or year with all the lesson helps you need. The **Interactive Lesson Planner** CD-ROM contains all Chapter 15 resources.

Use Glencoe's **Presentation Plus!** multimedia teacher tool to easily present dynamic lessons that visually excite your students. Using Microsoft PowerPoint® you can customize the presentations to create your own personalized lessons.

TEACHING TRANSPARENCIES

Graphic Organizer Transparency and Student Activity 15

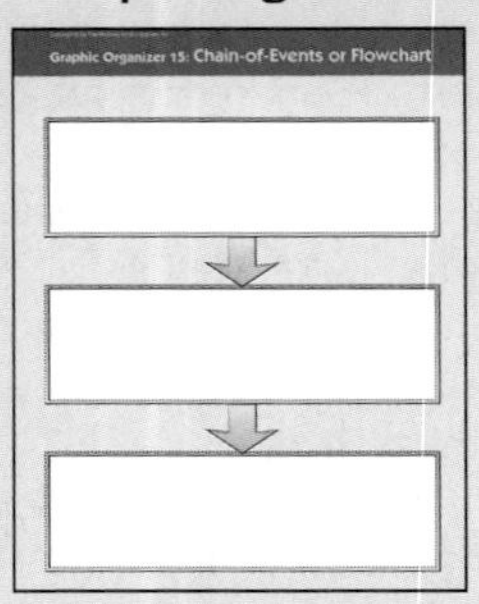
Graphic Organizer 15: Chain-of-Events or Flowchart

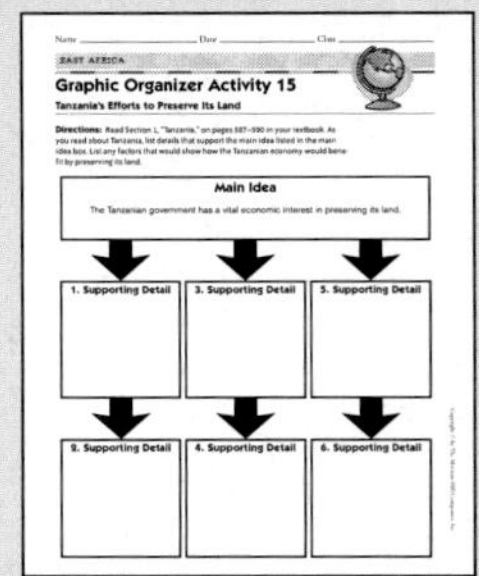
EAST AFRICA
Graphic Organizer Activity 15
Tanzania's Efforts to Preserve Its Land
Main Idea
The Tanzanian government has a vital economic interest in preserving its land.
1. Supporting Detail | 2. Supporting Detail | 3. Supporting Detail
4. Supporting Detail | 5. Supporting Detail | 6. Supporting Detail

FOLDABLES™ Study Organizer

Foldables are three-dimensional, interactive graphic organizers that help students practice basic writing skills, review key vocabulary terms, and identify main ideas. Every chapter contains a Foldable activity, with additional chapter activities found in the ***Reading and Study Skills Foldables*** booklet.

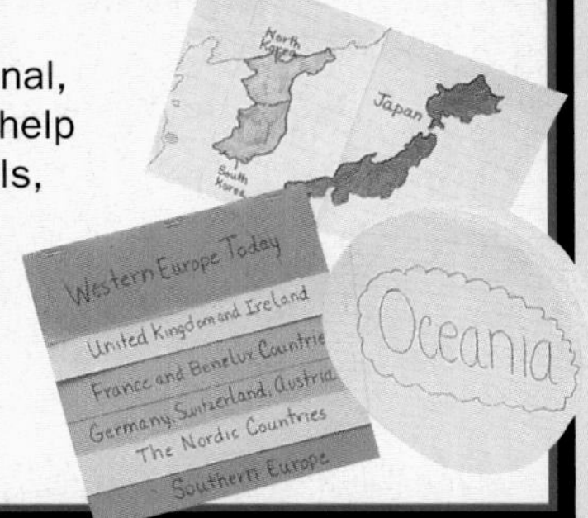

ENRICHMENT AND EXTENSION

Enrichment Activity 15

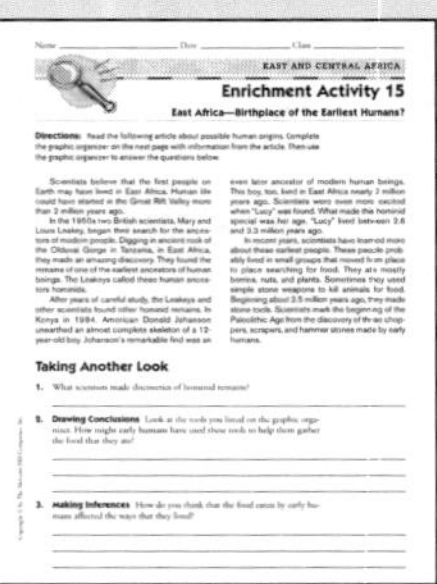
EAST AND CENTRAL AFRICA
Enrichment Activity 15
East Africa—Birthplace of the Earliest Humans?
Taking Another Look

Cooperative Learning Activity 15

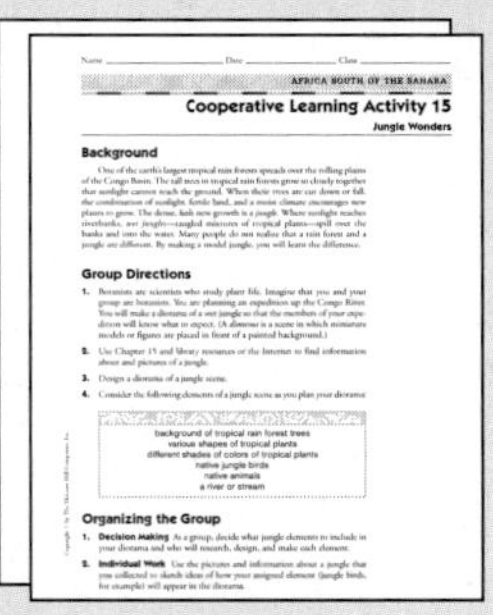
AFRICA SOUTH OF THE SAHARA
Cooperative Learning Activity 15
Jungle Wonders
Background
Group Directions
Organizing the Group

MAP AND GEOGRAPHY SKILLS

Chapter Map Activity 15

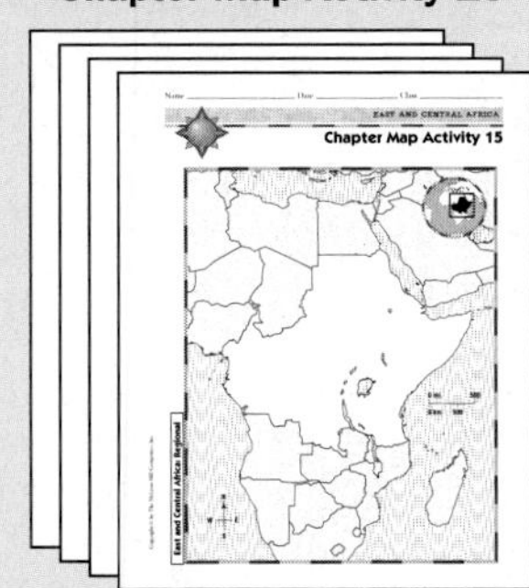
EAST AND CENTRAL AFRICA
Chapter Map Activity 15

GeoLab Activity 15

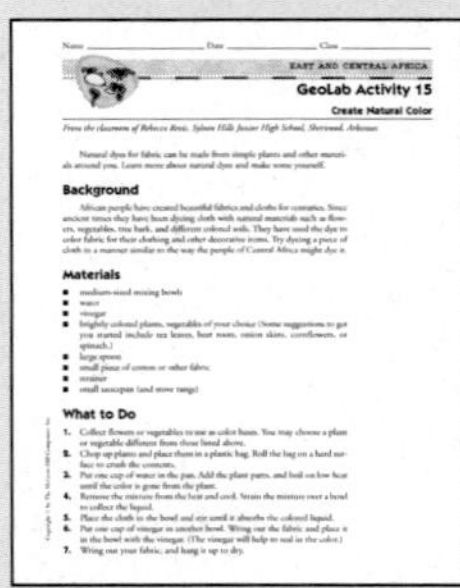
EAST AND CENTRAL AFRICA
GeoLab Activity 15
Create Natural Color
Background
Materials
What to Do

STANDARDIZED ASSESSMENT SKILLS

GLENCOE'S ASSESSMENT ADVANTAGE

Critical Thinking Skills Activity 15

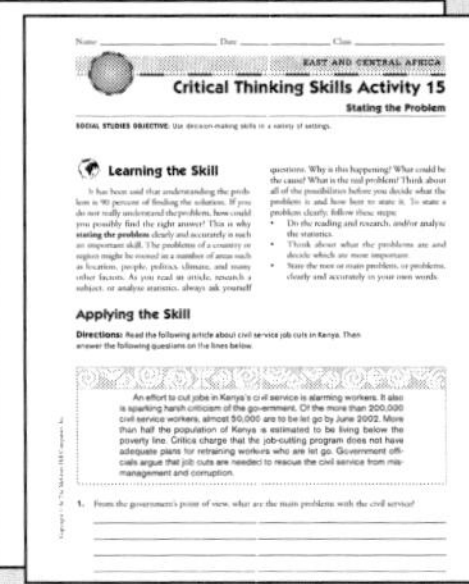
EAST AND CENTRAL AFRICA
Critical Thinking Skills Activity 15
Stating the Problem
Learning the Skill
Applying the Skill

Map and Graph Skills Activity 15

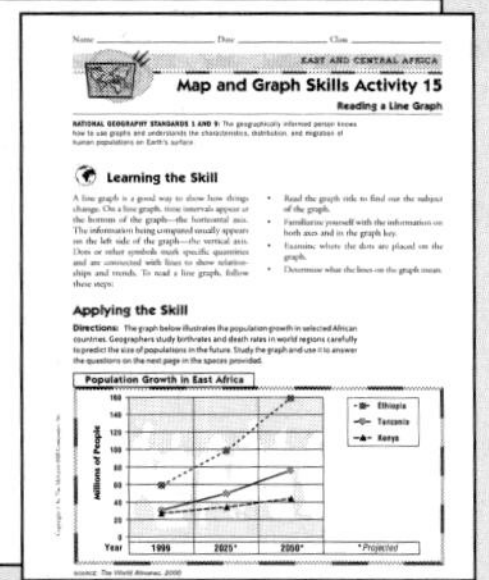
EAST AND CENTRAL AFRICA
Map and Graph Skills Activity 15
Reading a Line Graph
Learning the Skill
Applying the Skill
Population Growth in East Africa

Reading and Writing Skills Activity 15

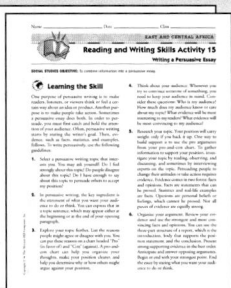

Standardized Test Practice Workbook Activity 15

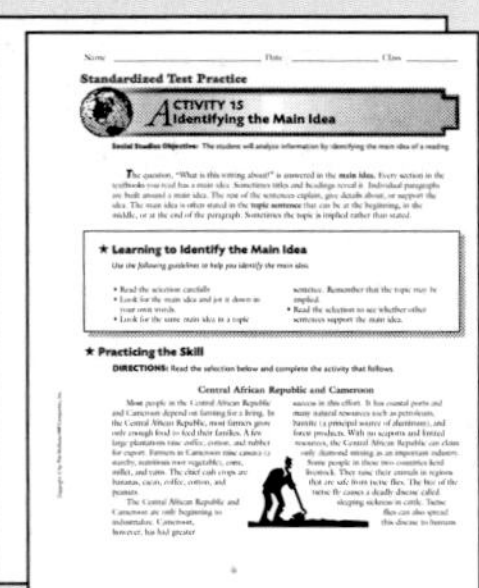
Standardized Test Practice
Activity 15
Identifying the Main Idea
Learning to Identify the Main Idea
Practicing the Skill
Central African Republic and Cameroon

REVIEW AND REINFORCEMENT

Chapter Skills Activity 15

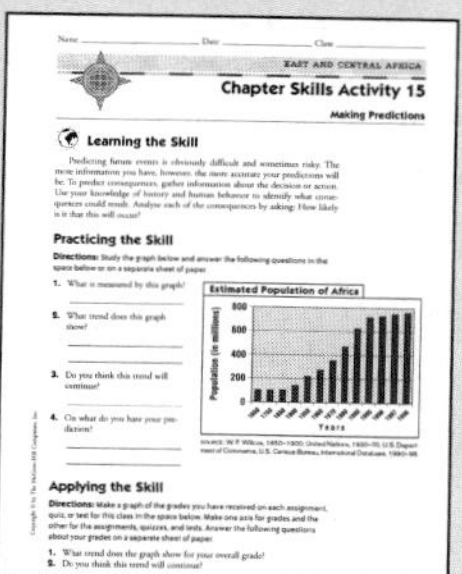

Take-Home Review Activity 15

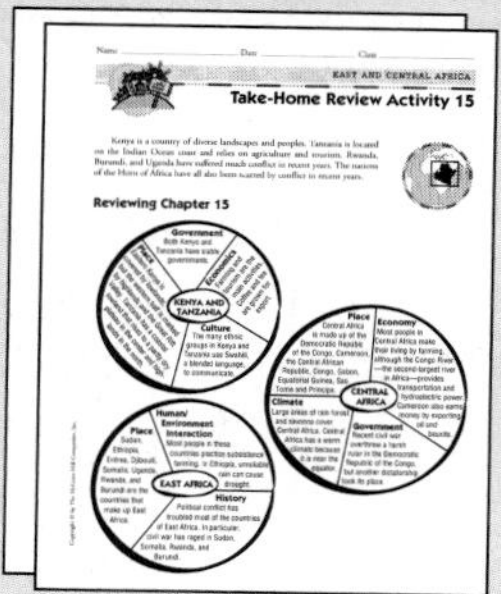

Reteaching Activity 15

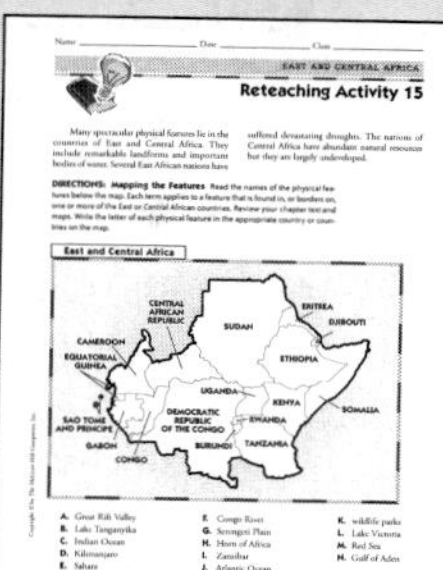

Vocabulary Activity 15

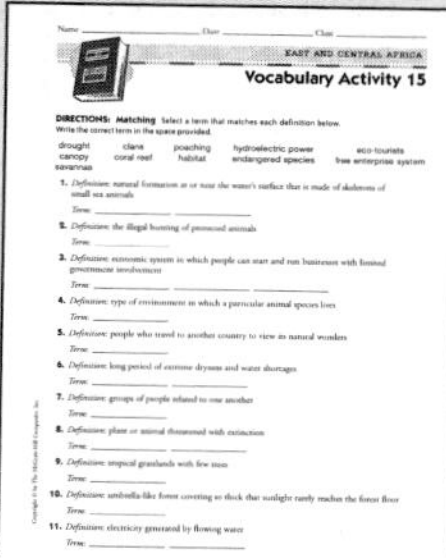

Workbook Activity 15

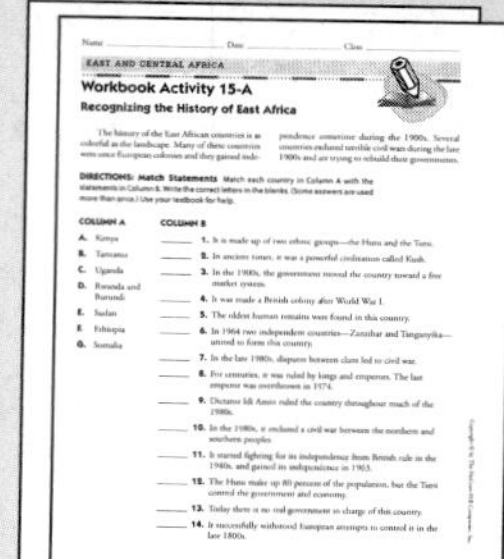

ASSESSMENT

Chapter 15 Test, Form A

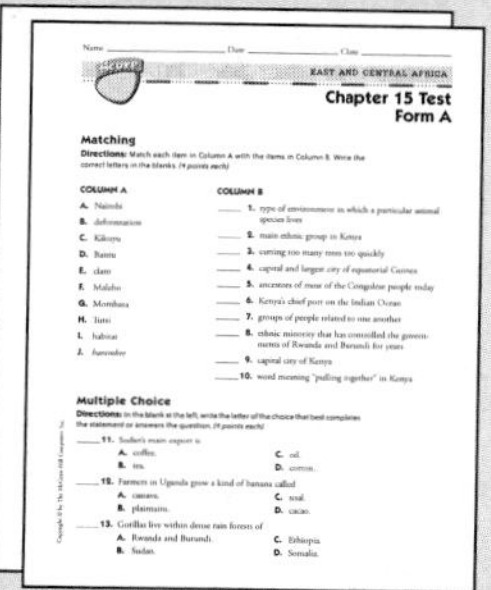

Chapter 15 Test, Form B

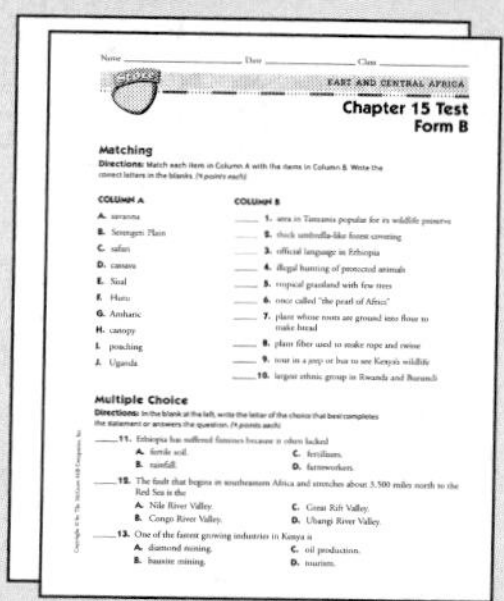

Performance Assessment Activity 15

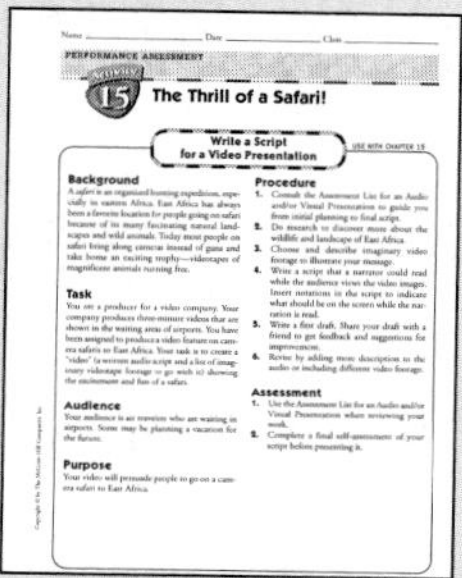

ExamView® Pro 3.0 Testmaker CD-ROM

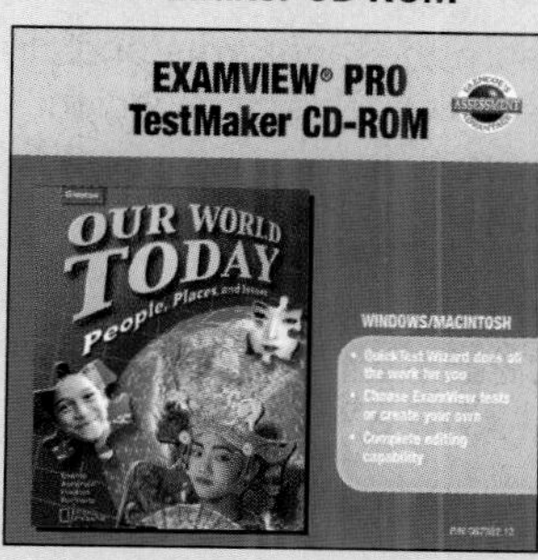

MULTIMEDIA

- National Geographic's The World and Its People
- MindJogger Videoquiz
- Vocabulary PuzzleMaker Software
- Interactive Tutor Self-Assessment CD-ROM
- ExamView® Pro 3.0 Testmaker CD-ROM
- Interactive Lesson Planner CD-ROM
- Interactive Teacher Edition CD-ROM
- Skillbuilder Interactive Workbook CD-ROM, Level 1
- Presentation Plus! CD-ROM
- Audio Program

SPANISH RESOURCES

The following Spanish language materials are available in the Spanish Resources binder:

- Spanish Chapter Summaries
- Spanish Vocabulary Activities
- Spanish Guided Reading Activities
- Spanish Quizzes and Tests
- Spanish Take-Home Review Activities
- Spanish Reteaching Activities

Meeting National Standards

Geography for Life

All of the 18 standards are demonstrated in Unit 6. The following ones are highlighted in Chapter 15:

Section 1 EE4 Human Systems: Standards 9, 10, 12, 13

Section 2 EE4 Human Systems: Standards 9, 10, 11, 13

EE5 Environment and Society: Standards 14, 15, 16

Section 3 EE2 Places and Regions: Standards 4, 6

EE4 Human Systems: Standards 9, 10, 12, 13

EE5 Environment and Society: Standard 14

For a complete listing of National Geography Standards and entire text correlation, see pages T22–T29.

Local Objectives

Chapter 15 Planning Guide

SECTION RESOURCES

Daily Objectives	Reproducible Resources	Multimedia Resources
Section 1 **East Africa: Kenya and Tanzania** **Suggested Pacing = 1 day** **1.** Identify the landforms found in Kenya and Tanzania. **2.** Describe the activities most important to these countries' economies. **3.** Compare the histories and people of Kenya and Tanzania.	Reproducible Lesson Plan 15-1 Daily Lecture and Discussion Notes 15-1 Guided Reading Activity 15-1 Reading Essentials and Study Guide 15-1 Section Quiz 15-1*	Daily Focus Skills Transparency 15-1 GeoQuiz Transparency 15-1 Vocabulary PuzzleMaker Software Interactive Tutor Self-Assessment CD-ROM ExamView® Pro 3.0 Testmaker CD-ROM Presentation Plus! CD-ROM
Section 2 **Other Countries of East Africa** **Suggested Pacing = 1 day** **1.** Compare the landforms and climates of the countries in this region. **2.** Describe the major challenges facing each of these countries.	Reproducible Lesson Plan 15-2 Daily Lecture and Discussion Notes 15-2 Guided Reading Activity 15-2 Reading Essentials and Study Guide 15-2 Section Quiz 15-2*	Daily Focus Skills Transparency 15-2 GeoQuiz Transparency 15-1 Vocabulary PuzzleMaker Software Interactive Tutor Self-Assessment CD-ROM ExamView® Pro 3.0 Testmaker CD-ROM Presentation Plus! CD-ROM
Section 3 **Central Africa** **Suggested Pacing = 1 day** **1.** Describe the landforms found in the countries of Central Africa. **2.** Explain the factors preventing the Democratic Republic of the Congo from reaching its economic potential. **3.** Compare the economies and people of the countries in this region.	Reproducible Lesson Plan 15-3 Daily Lecture and Discussion Notes 15-3 Guided Reading Activity 15-3 Reading Essentials and Study Guide 15-3 Section Quiz 15-3*	Daily Focus Skills Transparency 15-3 GeoQuiz Transparency 15-3 Vocabulary PuzzleMaker Software Interactive Tutor Self-Assessment CD-ROM ExamView® Pro 3.0 Testmaker CD-ROM Presentation Plus! CD-ROM

00:00 **Out of Time?** Assign the **Reading Essentials and Study Guide** for this chapter.

*Also available in Spanish

KEY TO ABILITY LEVELS

Teaching strategies have been coded for varying learning styles and abilities.

L1 **BASIC** activities for all students
L2 **AVERAGE** activities for average to above-average students
L3 **CHALLENGING** activities for above-average students
ELL **ENGLISH LANGUAGE LEARNER** activities

 Blackline Master
 Software
 CD-ROM
 Audiocassette
 Transparency
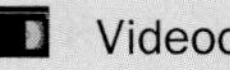 Videocassette
Block Scheduling
 DVD

Teacher to Teacher

Solutions to Poaching

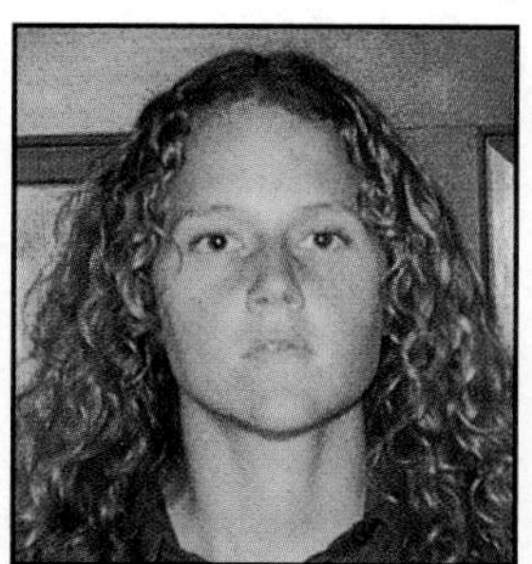

Dawn Forman
Hawthorne Junior/ Senior High
Gainesville, Florida

This is a cooperative learning activity in which students develop solutions to the problem of poaching in African countries such as Kenya, Uganda, and Rwanda. Organize students into groups and have groups use the Internet to research the causes of poaching. Students should find at least five Web sites to use as sources of information. Have students list as many options as they can think of. They should then consider each of their options, weighing the advantages and disadvantages, before concluding to solutions. Have each group prepare a poster highlighting the causes of poaching and at least two solutions to prevent poaching. This activity helps students feel like they can make a difference.

OUR WORLD TODAY Online

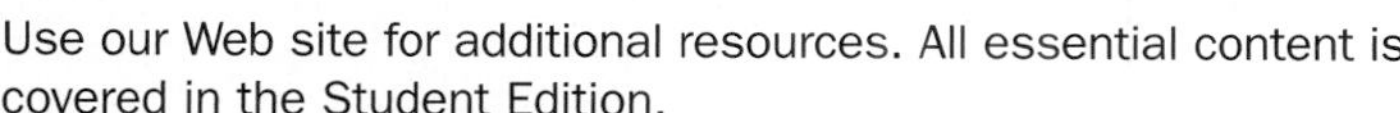

Use our Web site for additional resources. All essential content is covered in the Student Edition.

You and your students can visit owt.glencoe.com, the Web site companion to *Our World Today*. This innovative integration of electronic and print media offers your students a wealth of opportunities. The student text directs students to the Web site for the following options:

- Chapter Overviews
- Student Web Activities
- Self-Check Quizzes
- Textbook Updates

Answers are provided for you in the Web Activity Lesson Plan. Additional Web resources and Interactive Tutor puzzles are also available.

NATIONAL GEOGRAPHIC TEACHER'S CORNER

Index to National Geographic Magazine:

The following articles may be used for research relating to this chapter:

- "Masai Passage to Manhood," by Carol Beckwith, September 1999.
- "Zanzibar's Endangered Red Colobus Monkey," by Tom Struhsaker, November 1998.
- "In Focus: Central Africa's Cycle of Violence," by Mike Edwards, June 1997.

National Geographic Society Products Available From Glencoe:

To order the following products for use with this chapter, contact your local Glencoe sales representative or call Glencoe at 1-800-334-7344:

- *STV: World Geography* (Videodisc)
- *Picture Atlas of the World* (CD-ROM)
- *PictureShow: Earth's Endangered Environments* (CD-ROM)
- *MapPack: Africa* (Transparencies)
- *PicturePack: Geography of Africa* (Transparencies)

Additional National Geographic Society Products:

To order the following products for use with this chapter, call National Geographic Society at 1-800-368-2728:

- *Complete National Geographic: 111 Years of National Geographic Magazine* (CD-ROM)
- *Healing the Earth* (Video)
- *Endangered Animals: Survivors on the Brink* (Video)
- *Africa* (Video)
- *Jane Goodall* (Video)
- *Physical Earth* (Map)
- *Population* (Map)
- *Voices: Poetry and Art From Around the World* (Book)
- *National Geographic Desk Reference* (Book)
- *PicturePack: Ancient Civilizations: Africa* (Transparencies)
- *PictureShow: Ancient Civilizations: Africa* (CD-ROM)

NGS ONLINE

Access National Geographic's Web site for current events, activities, links, interactive features, and archives. www.nationalgeographic.com

Introducing Chapter 15

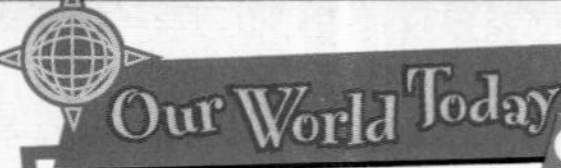

Introduce students to chapter content and key terms by having them access Chapter Overview 15 at owt.glencoe.com

Chapter Objectives

1. Describe the geography and economy of Kenya and Tanzania.
2. Explain the similarities and differences among the countries of East Africa.
3. Describe the geography, history, and people of the Democratic Republic of the Congo.
4. Compare the geography and cultures of the countries of Central Africa.

GLENCOE TECHNOLOGY

NATIONAL GEOGRAPHIC

The World and Its People Video Program

Chapters 20 and 21
East and Central Africa
The following segments enhance the study of this chapter:

- **Korup National Forest**
- **Photographing Ndoki**
- **Great Rift Valley**
- **Gorillas**

Available in DVD and VHS.

MindJogger Videoquiz
Use MindJogger to preview the Chapter 15 content.

Available in VHS.

Chapter 15 East and Central Africa

The World and Its People NATIONAL GEOGRAPHIC

To learn more about the people and places of East and Central Africa, view ***The World and Its People*** **Chapters 20** and **21** videos.

Our World Today online

Chapter Overview Visit the ***Our World Today: People, Places, and Issues*** Web site at owt.glencoe.com and click on **Chapter 15—Chapter Overviews** to preview information about East and Central Africa.

402

Two-Minute Lesson Launcher

In this chapter, students will learn about a part of the world where people have to balance economic development with preserving natural areas. **Ask:** **How might people use undeveloped land for economic purposes? Which do you think is more important—preserving forests and the wildlife that depend on them or using the land to try to develop a nation's economy to improve people's lives? Why? Is there a way to preserve the land and still use it for economic profit? L1**

FOLDABLES™ Study Organizer

Compare-Contrast Study Foldable Make this foldable to compare and contrast traditional and modern cultures in East and Central Africa.

Step 1 Fold one sheet of paper in half from side to side.

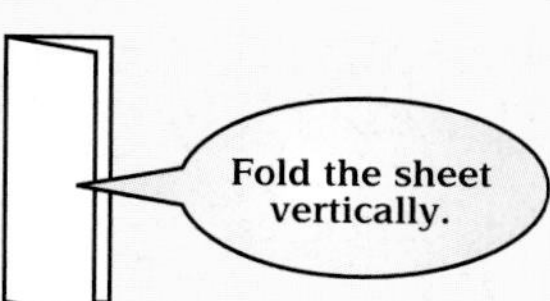
Fold the sheet vertically.

Step 2 Fold again, one inch from the top. (Tip: The middle knuckle of your index finger is about one inch long.)

Step 3 Open and label as shown.

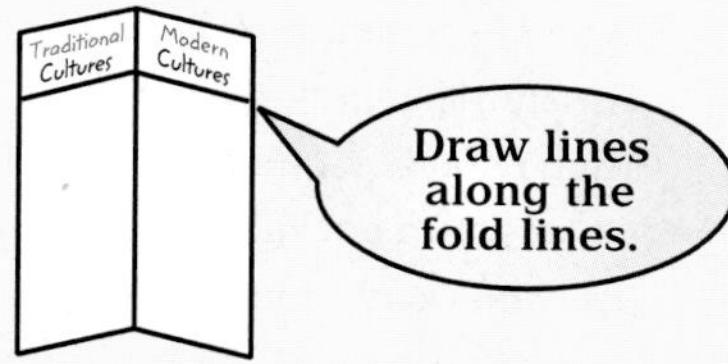
Traditional Cultures
Modern Cultures
Draw lines along the fold lines.

Reading and Writing As you read this chapter, record information in the two columns of your foldable chart. Be sure to write the information you find in the appropriate column of your foldable.

▲ Elephants on the Serengeti Plain in Tanzania

Why It Matters

Rich in Heritage

Some of Africa's most important early civilizations flourished in the location that is now part of East and Central Africa. These societies grew to become large and complex as they developed the skills to master the region's difficult environment. They were successful farmers, herders, metalworkers, artisans, and merchants. Today, the people of this region are facing difficult challenges just to survive.

About the Photo

Tanzania is home to 5 large national parks: Mikumi, Ngurdoto, Arusha, Manyara, and Serengeti. They cover 10,000 square miles. The parks management is based on detailed studies of the ecology in each area. These studies are done by scientists funded by many international organizations. This insures that the animals and plants are protected. Outside of these parks, employees of the Game Department of Tanzania not only have to fight poaching, but they must also protect crops. For example, elephants have often been known to damage banana and maize crops on the north edge of Manyara National Park. Sometimes game wardens have to shoot the same wild animals they are trying to protect.

FOLDABLES™ Study Organizer

Purpose Students will make and use a compare-contrast foldable to collect and organize information about traditional and modern cultures in East and Central Africa. Students will analyze similarities and differences of traditional cultures and modern cultures in East and Central Africa by using the foldable.

Have students complete ***Reading and Study Skills Foldables*** Activity 15.

Why It Matters

Help students understand how the increase in life expectancy and population have caused a conflict between human interests and animal conservation. Ask them if they've ever had people stay at their house for a visit. Ask them how it felt to give up their beds and share living space. Then have them imagine that the guests decided to live with the family. How would they feel about the crowded living conditions? Imagine that these guests made it more difficult to get food. Now think of the "guests" as African people, and themselves as African wildlife. Tell students that, with East African people living longer, and more children surviving infancy, the population has increased dramatically in recent years. As people need more land, the animal habitat is shrinking.

Chapter 15

Section 1, pages 404–408

FOCUS

Section Objectives

1. Identify the landforms found in Kenya and Tanzania.
2. Describe the activities most important to these countries' economies.
3. Compare the histories and people of Kenya and Tanzania.

BELLRINGER
Skillbuilder Activity

Project transparency and have students answer questions.

This activity is also available as a blackline master.

Daily Focus Skills Transparency 15-1

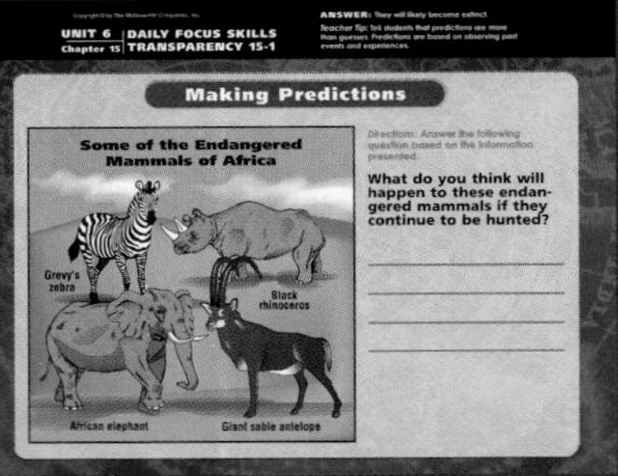

Guide to Reading

■ **Accessing Prior Knowledge**
Ask: What do you think of when you hear the word *Africa?* Most students think of elephants, giraffes, and tribal peoples like the Masai. Tell them that Kenya embodies these traditional views as well as those of modern, industrial Africa.

Section 1

East Africa: Kenya and Tanzania

Guide to Reading

Main Idea

Both Kenya and Tanzania are countries of diverse landscapes and peoples.

Terms to Know

- coral reef
- poaching
- free enterprise system
- cassava
- sisal
- habitat
- eco-tourist

Reading Strategy

Create a chart like this one. Then list facts about the land, economy, and people of Kenya and Tanzania.

Fact	Kenya	Tanzania
Land		
Economy		
People		

NATIONAL GEOGRAPHIC **Exploring Our World**

The Masai (mah•SY) are one of Kenya's many ethnic groups. Rituals have shaped their lives for hundreds of years. Young men take part in an important four-day ceremony. When it ends, they become elders and help make group decisions. In the ceremony, elders tell them, "Drop your weapons and use your head and wisdom instead."

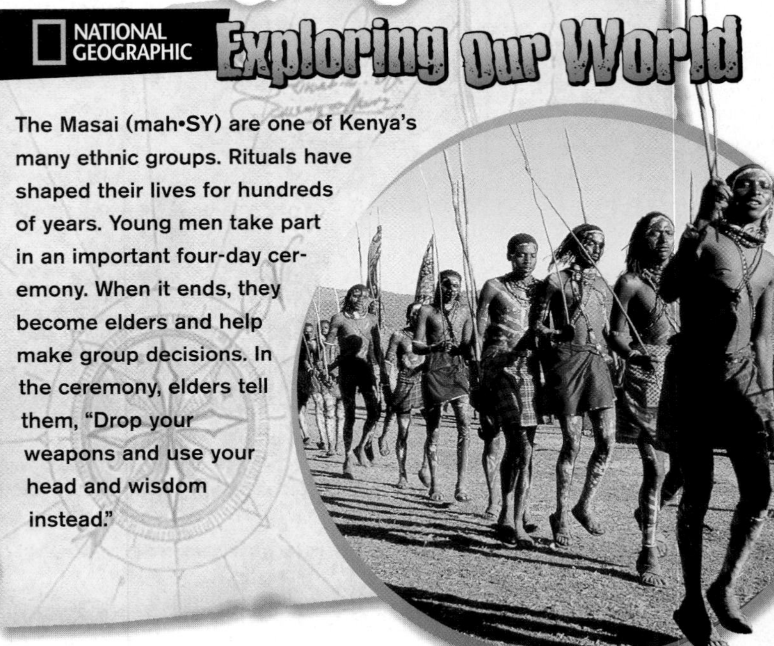

Both traditional and modern cultures meet in **Kenya.** The **Masai** follow ways of life similar to their ancestors, while city dwellers live in apartments and work in offices. **Tanzania** has one of the largest wild animal populations in the world.

Kenya

Kenya is about two times the size of Nevada. The country's Indian Ocean coastline has stretches of white beaches lined with palm trees. Offshore lies a **coral reef,** a natural formation at or near the water's surface that is made of the skeletons of small sea animals. Lions, elephants, rhinoceroses, and other wildlife roam an upland plain. Millions of acres are set aside by the government to protect plants and wildlife. Still, in recent years there has been heavy **poaching,** the illegal hunting of protected animals.

Section Resources

Reproducible Masters
- Reproducible Lesson Plan 15-1
- Daily Lecture and Discussion Notes 15-1
- Guided Reading Activity 15-1
- Reading Essentials and Study Guide 15-1
- Section Quiz 15-1

Transparencies
- Daily Focus Skills Transparency 15-1
- GeoQuiz Transparency 15-1

Multimedia
- Vocabulary PuzzleMaker Software
- Interactive Tutor Self-Assessment CD-ROM
- Presentation Plus! CD-ROM
- ExamView® Pro 3.0 Testmaker CD-ROM

In the western part of the country are highlands and the **Great Rift Valley.** (See photo on page 59.) This valley is really a fault—a crack in the earth's crust. The Great Rift Valley begins in southeastern Africa and stretches about 3,500 miles (5,633 km) north to the Red Sea. Lakes have formed in many places and volcanoes also dot the area. One of them—**Mt. Kenya**—rises 17,058 feet (5,199 m) high. It is in the Great Rift Valley that fossils of the earliest human ancestors, dating back about 4 million years, have been found.

Kenya's Economy Kenya has a developing economy based on a **free enterprise system.** In this economic system, people can start and run businesses with limited government involvement. Kenya's capital, **Nairobi** (ny•ROH•bee), has become a center of business and commerce for all of East Africa. Foreign companies have set up regional headquarters in this city.

Many Kenyans remain poor, however. Farmers raise corn, bananas, cassava, and sweet potatoes. **Cassava** is a plant whose roots are ground to make porridge. Some larger farms raise coffee and tea for export. In recent years, the weather has not been good for crops. Also,

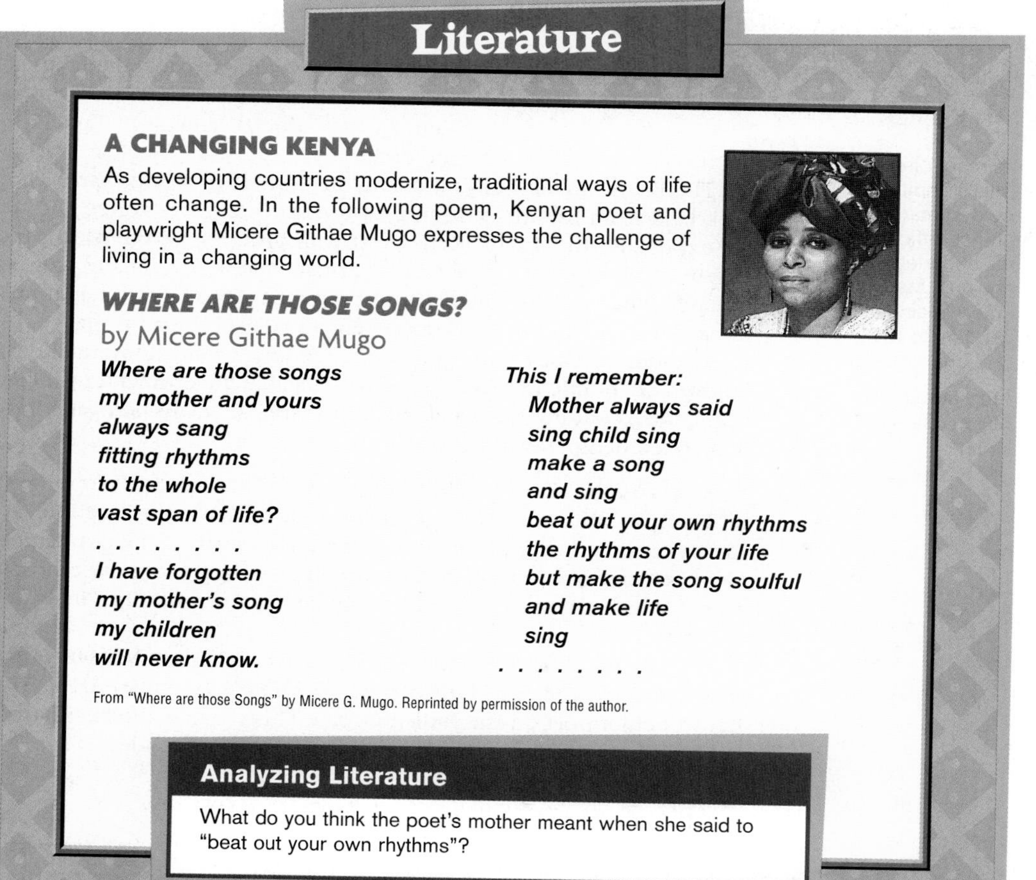

Literature

A CHANGING KENYA

As developing countries modernize, traditional ways of life often change. In the following poem, Kenyan poet and playwright Micere Githae Mugo expresses the challenge of living in a changing world.

WHERE ARE THOSE SONGS?

by Micere Githae Mugo

Where are those songs
my mother and yours
always sang
fitting rhythms
to the whole
vast span of life?
. . . .
I have forgotten
my mother's song
my children
will never know.

This I remember:
Mother always said
sing child sing
make a song
and sing
beat out your own rhythms
the rhythms of your life
but make the song soulful
and make life
sing
. . . .

From "Where are those Songs" by Micere G. Mugo. Reprinted by permission of the author.

Analyzing Literature

What do you think the poet's mother meant when she said to "beat out your own rhythms"?

Chapter 15

Section 1, pages 404–408

TEACH

Classifying Information Have students identify the major economic activities in Kenya. *(agriculture, international businesses, tourism)* Then have them create a graphic organizer that identifies these main activities and shows the subdivisions that make up each. *(For example, agriculture can be split into subsistence farming, with the crops corn, cassava, potatoes, sweet potatoes, bananas; into nomadic herding; and into cash crops, which are coffee and tea.)* **L1**

Daily Lecture Notes 15-1

EAST AND CENTRAL AFRICA

Daily Lecture and Discussion Notes 15-1

East Africa: Kenya and Tanzania (pages 404–408)

Did You Know? Motion pictures are popular throughout Kenya. People living in the cities can attend movie theaters, but people in rural areas wait for mobile motion-picture units to bring films to them. These mobile units operate on a regular schedule.

I. Kenya *(pages 404–406)*

A. Kenya is about two times the size of Nevada. Offshore in the Indian Ocean lies a **coral reef,** a natural formation at or near the water's surface that is made up of the skeletons of small sea animals.

Literature

Micere Githae Mugo taught at Nairobi University in Kenya, where she was a fierce critic of the government. After a 1982 coup failed, the government cracked down on university students and teachers. Mugo left the country before she could be arrested. Since then, she has lived and taught in Zimbabwe and the United States.

Answer The phrase means "Make your own life."

Meeting Special Needs

Math How valuable is tourism in Kenya? Each lion produces $27,000 in income, and a herd of elephants generates $610,000 from tourists. The money is used to maintain the country's parks and to support tribes living in the area. Give students the following information: The average acre of land in Kenya has a value of $0.36 in terms of the crops it produces. That same acre, if used as a game preserve, generates $18 in income from tourists. Have students calculate the increased value of land from tourism over agriculture. *(The increase is $17.64 per acre, or 5,000%.)* Then have students discuss the potential drawbacks of relying on tourism. **L1**

Refer to *Inclusion for the Middle School Social Studies Classroom Strategies and Activities* in the TCR.

More About the Photos

Nairobi Kenya's capital was founded in the 1890s as a rail center when the British built a railroad in East Africa. It became the capital of British East Africa in 1905 and remained Kenya's capital after gaining independence.

Caption Answer 1.5 million people

Guided Reading Activity 15–1

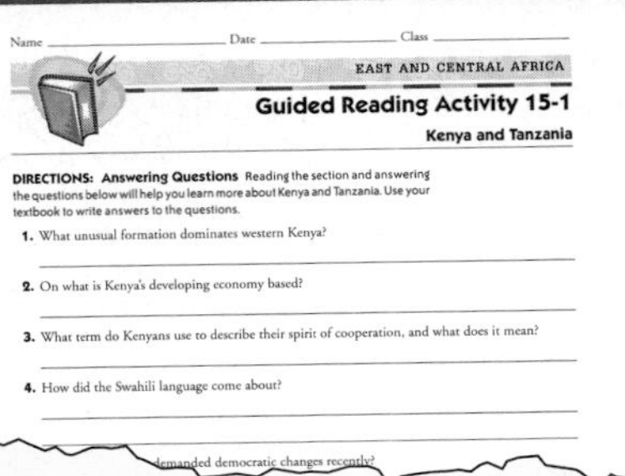
Name ______ Date ______ Class ______

EAST AND CENTRAL AFRICA

Guided Reading Activity 15-1

Kenya and Tanzania

DIRECTIONS: Answering Questions Reading the section and answering the questions below will help you learn more about Kenya and Tanzania. Use your textbook to write answers to the questions.

1. What unusual formation dominates western Kenya?
2. On what is Kenya's developing economy based?
3. What term do Kenyans use to describe their spirit of cooperation, and what does it mean?
4. How did the Swahili language come about?

...demanded democratic changes recently?

Reading Check Answer

Mombasa

3 ASSESS

Assign Section 1 Assessment as homework or an in-class activity.

Have students use the Interactive Tutor Self-Assessment CD-ROM to review Section 15–1.

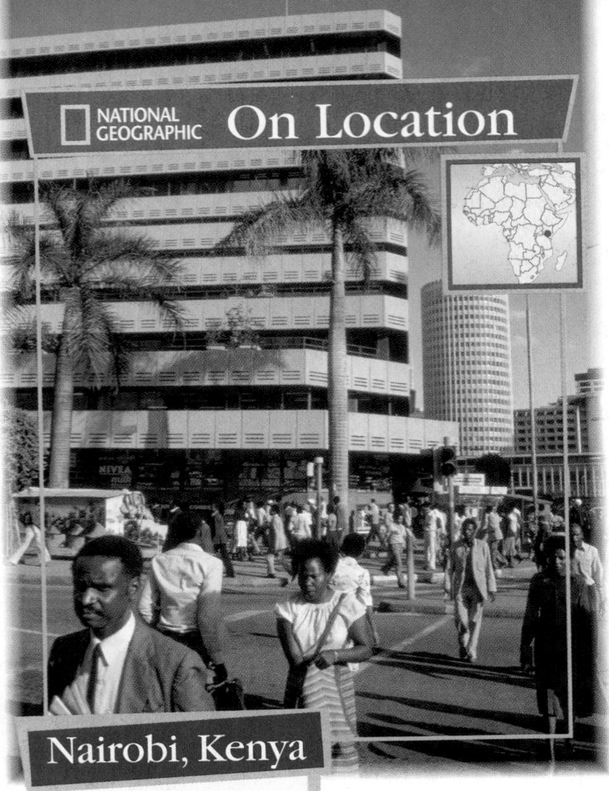

Like most cities, Kenya's capital has crowded markets, high-rise office buildings, and elegant mansions. Many city workers maintain close ties to relatives in the countryside.

Place **About how many people live in Nairobi?**

corrupt practices of government officials have hurt the economy.

One of the fastest-growing industries in Kenya is tourism. Thousands of tourists visit each year. Visitors often take tours called safaris in jeeps and buses to see the country's wildlife in its natural surroundings.

Kenya's People The people of Kenya believe in *harambee,* which means "pulling together." The spirit of *harambee* has led the different ethnic groups to build schools and clinics in their communities. They have raised money to send good students to universities.

History and Government During the A.D. 700s, Arab traders from Southwest Asia settled along the coast where a blending of cultures took place. The **Swahili** language came about from this blending. The name *Swahili* comes from an Arabic word meaning "of the coast." The language includes features of several African languages as well as Arabic. Today Swahili is one of Kenya's two official languages. English is the other.

The British made Kenya a colony in 1918 after World War I. They took land from the Africans and set up farms to grow coffee and tea for export. By the 1940s, Kenya's African groups like the **Mau Mau** fought in violent civil wars to end British rule. Kenya finally won its independence in 1963 and became a republic. The country's first president, **Jomo Kenyatta** (JOH•moh kehn•YAHT•uh), won respect as an early leader in Africa's movement for freedom. Under Kenyatta, Kenya enjoyed economic prosperity and had a stable government. In recent years, the economy has weakened. In response, many Kenyans have demanded democratic changes.

Kenya Today Kenya's 29.8 million people are divided among 40 different ethnic groups. The **Kikuyu** (kee•KOO•yoo) people are Kenya's main group, making up less than one-fourth of the population. Most Kenyans live in rural areas where they struggle to grow crops. In recent years, large numbers of people have moved to cities in search of a better life.

About one-third of Kenya's people live in cities. Nairobi is the largest city, with 1.5 million people. **Mombasa** (mohm•BAH•sah) is Kenya's chief port on the Indian Ocean. This city has the best harbor in East Africa, making it an ideal site for oceangoing trade.

✓ Reading Check **What city is Kenya's chief port?**

Critical Thinking Activity

Determining Cause and Effect Kenya's chief exports are coffee and tea, which earn about half the country's income from foreign trade. **Ask:** **What might happen to Kenya's foreign trade in a year with bad weather?** *(Trade income would drop because the coffee and tea harvests decrease.)* **What happens if other countries begin producing more coffee or tea?** *(Kenya will either sell less or the price will decline, meaning that the value of Kenya's products will go down.)* **What would you suggest that the government of Kenya do to improve the economy in light of these issues?** *(Possible responses: concentrate on developing manufacturing; encourage more tourism)* **L1**

EE4 Human Systems: Standard 11

Tanzania

Tourists flock to Tanzania's **Serengeti** (SEHR•uhn•GEH•tee) **Plain,** famous for its wildlife preserve, huge grasslands, and patches of trees and shrubs. To the north, near the Kenyan border, a snowcapped mountain called **Kilimanjaro** towers over this region. It is the highest point in Africa. The Great Rift Valley cuts two gashes through Tanzania, one in the center of the country and the other along the western border. Unusual fish swim in the deep, dark waters of Lake Tanganyika (TAN•guhn•YEE•kuh). Lake Victoria, also in Tanzania, is Africa's largest lake and one of the sources of the Nile River.

Tanzania's Economy More than 80 percent of all Tanzanians work in farming or herding. Important export crops are coffee and sisal, a plant fiber used to make rope and twine. Do you enjoy eating baked ham? If so, you might have tasted the spice called cloves, often used to flavor ham. The islands of Zanzibar and Pemba, off the coast of Tanzania, produce more cloves than any other place in the world.

NATIONAL GEOGRAPHIC — **East and Central Africa: Political**

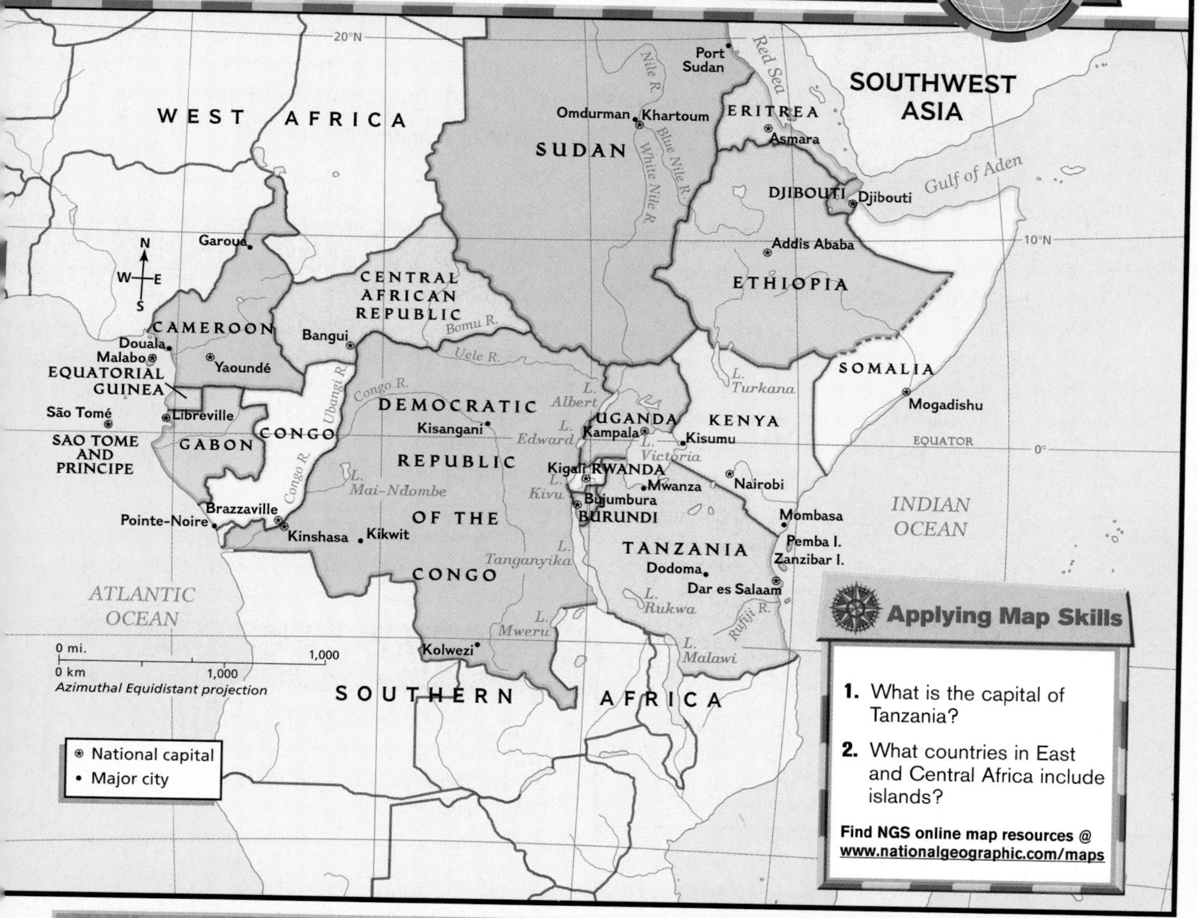

⊛ National capital
• Major city

0 mi. 1,000
0 km 1,000
Azimuthal Equidistant projection

Applying Map Skills

1. What is the capital of Tanzania?
2. What countries in East and Central Africa include islands?

Find NGS online map resources @ www.nationalgeographic.com/maps

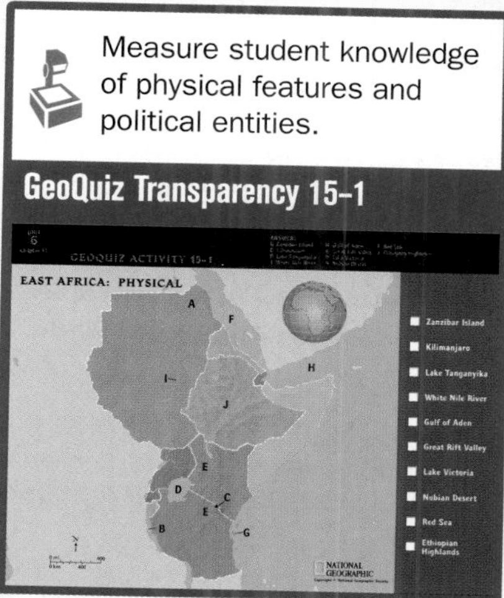

Measure student knowledge of physical features and political entities.

GeoQuiz Transparency 15–1

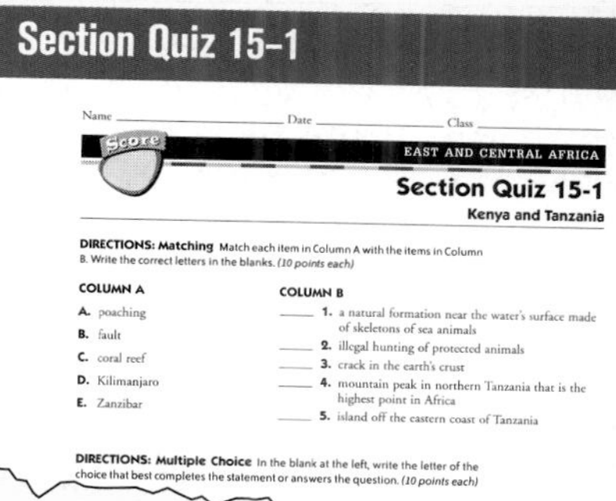

Section Quiz 15–1

Name ______ Date ______ Class ______

EAST AND CENTRAL AFRICA

Section Quiz 15-1
Kenya and Tanzania

DIRECTIONS: Matching Match each item in Column A with the items in Column B. Write the correct letters in the blanks. (10 points each)

COLUMN A	COLUMN B
A. poaching	____ 1. a natural formation near the water's surface made of skeletons of sea animals
B. fault	____ 2. illegal hunting of protected animals
C. coral reef	____ 3. crack in the earth's crust
D. Kilimanjaro	____ 4. mountain peak in northern Tanzania that is the highest point in Africa
E. Zanzibar	____ 5. island off the eastern coast of Tanzania

DIRECTIONS: Multiple Choice In the blank at the left, write the letter of the choice that best completes the statement or answers the question. (10 points each)

Applying Map Skills

Answers

1. Dar es Salaam
2. Tanzania, Equatorial Guinea, São Tomé and Príncipe

Skills Practice

What capital sits on the shores of Lake Victoria?

(Kampala, Uganda)

Team-Teaching Activity

Language Arts Invite a language arts teacher to class to discuss the formation of languages in relation to Swahili, one of the languages spoken in Tanzania as well as in Kenya. Have the teacher explain how Swahili combines Arabic with local African languages from the coast and how the language was spread by coastal traders and caravans that entered the interior of East Africa. Ask students to suggest other examples of languages created by combining elements of two distinct languages and how these languages might have been created. They might mention Haitian Creole, formed of French and African languages, and the "Spanglish" that combines Spanish and English in the United States. **ELL L1**

EE4 Human Systems: Standards 10, 12

Chapter 15

Section 1, pages 404–408

Reteach

Have students write newspaper headlines that summarize the main idea of each subsection.

✓ Reading Check Answer

Sisal is an important export crop.

Reading Essentials and Study Guide 15-1

Name ____________ Date ____________ Class ____________

EAST AND CENTRAL AFRICA

Reading Essentials and Study Guide 15-1

East Africa: Kenya and Tanzania

For use with textbook pages 404–408

Terms to Know

coral reef natural formation near the water's surface that is made of skeletons of small sea animals (page 404)
poaching illegal hunting of protected animals (page 404)
free enterprise system economic system in which people can start and run businesses with little government involvement (page 405)
cassava plant whose roots are ground into flour to make bread (page 405)
sisal plant fiber used to make rope and twine (page 407)
habitat environment in which a certain kind of animal lives (page 408)
eco-tourist person who travels to another country to view its natural wonders (page 408)

Enrich

Have students prepare oral reports about the Serengeti or other national parks or preserves of Tanzania.

CLOSE

Have students explain why Tanzania would be of interest to the following scientists: a geologist, an archaeologist, an anthropologist, and a zoologist.

I Am a Samburu

Nimfa Lekuuk is a member of the Samburu of northern Kenya. The word *Samburu* means "the people with the white goats." Nimfa wears the traditional clothes of Samburu women. She is in standard 7 now. "Standard" is the Kenyans' term for *grade.* She studies language, math, history, geography, science, arts and crafts, and religion.

Tourism is a fast-growing industry in Tanzania. The government has set aside several national parks to protect the habitats of the country's wildlife. A **habitat** is the type of environment in which a particular animal species lives. Serengeti National Park covers about 5,600 square miles (14,504 sq. km). Lions and wild dogs hunt among thousands of zebras, wildebeests, and antelopes. The park attracts many **eco-tourists,** or people who travel to another country to view its natural wonders.

Tanzania's leaders are also taking steps to preserve farmland. In recent years, many trees have been cut down. Without trees, the land cannot hold soil or rainwater in place. As a result, the land dries out, and soil blows away. To prevent the land from becoming desert, the government of Tanzania has announced a new policy. For every tree that is cut down, five new trees should be planted.

History and Government Tanzania's 36.2 million people include more than 120 different ethnic groups. Each group has its own language, but most people also speak Swahili. The two main religions are Christianity and Islam. In 1964 the island country of Zanzibar united with the former German colony of Tanganyika to form Tanzania. Since then, Tanzania has been one of Africa's more politically stable republics. During the 1960s, Tanzania's socialist government controlled the economy. By the 1990s, however, it had moved toward a free market system. In taking this step, Tanzania's leaders hoped to improve the economy and reduce poverty. Meanwhile, the government also moved toward more democratic elections with more than one political party.

✓ Reading Check **Why is sisal important to Tanzania?**

Section 1 Assessment

Defining Terms

1. **Define** coral reef, poaching, free enterprise system, cassava, sisal, habitat, eco-tourist.

Recalling Facts

2. **Place** Describe the Great Rift Valley.
3. **Culture** What are Kenya's official languages?
4. **Culture** What are the two major religions of Tanzania?

Critical Thinking

5. **Evaluating Information** Why might two countries such as Tanganyika and Zanzibar unite?
6. **Analyzing Information** Why would the government of Tanzania put so much effort into preserving its national parks?

Graphic Organizer

7. **Organizing Information** Review the information about the history and government of Kenya. Then, on a time line like the one below, label four important events and their dates in Kenya's history.

Applying Social Studies Skills

8. **Analyzing Maps** Study the political map on page 407. Name the four bodies of water that border Tanzania. On what body of water is Dar es Salaam located?

Section 1 Assessment

1. The terms are defined in the Glossary.
2. a highlands area in southeastern Africa, 3,500 miles long, formed by a fault, with many lakes and volcanoes
3. Swahili and English
4. Christianity and Islam
5. *Possible answer:* to combine economic and political strengths.
6. to attract tourists for economic profit
7. Possible answers: 700s—Arabs settle in coastal areas; 1918—becomes colony of England; 1940s—civil wars against British rule; 1963—Kenya becomes an independent republic
8. Indian Ocean, Lake Malawi, Lake Tanganyika, Lake Victoria; Indian Ocean

Critical Thinking Skill

Making Predictions

Predicting consequences is obviously difficult and sometimes risky. The more information you have, however, the more accurate your predictions will be.

Learning the Skill

Follow these steps to learn how to better predict consequences:

- Gather information about the decision or action you are considering.
- Use your knowledge of history and human behavior to identify what consequences could result.
- Analyze each of the consequences by asking yourself: How likely is it that this will occur?

Practicing the Skill

Study the graph below, and then answer these questions:

1. What is measured on this graph? Over what time period?
2. In what year did the fewest tourists visit Kenya?
3. What trend does the graph show?
4. Do you think this trend is likely to continue?
5. On what do you base this prediction?
6. What are three possible consequences of this trend?

Applying the Skill

Analyze three articles in your local newspaper. Predict three consequences of the actions in each of the articles. On what do you base your predictions?

GO TO Practice key skills with **Glencoe Skillbuilder Interactive Workbook, Level 1.**

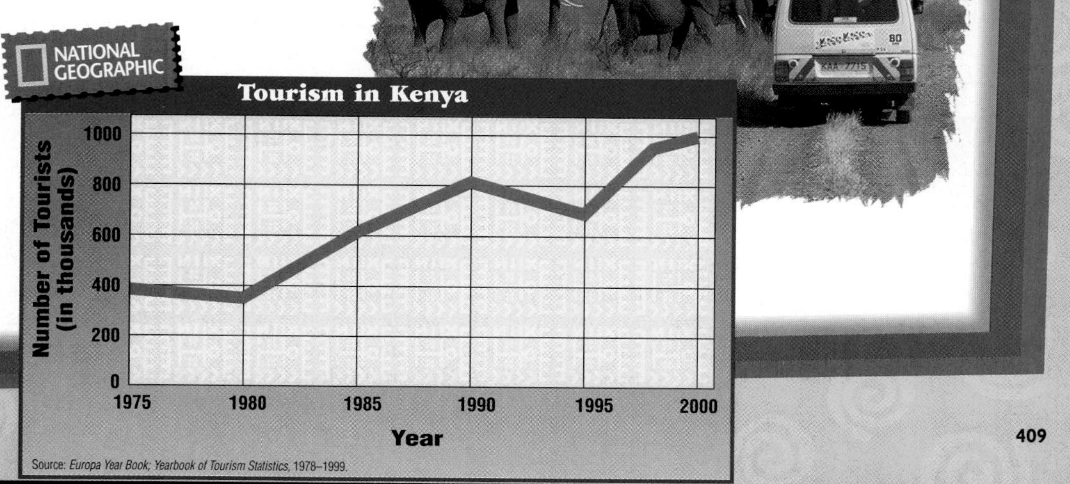

Critical Thinking Skill

TEACH

Ask: **What is the weather going to be like tomorrow? How do you know?** *(Possible responses: heard or read a weather report; guessing based on what the weather is like today)* Point out that in this situation, either the weather reporter or the students themselves were making a prediction. Explain that in this feature, students will learn how to use data to make their predictions more reliable than just guessing. **L1**

Additional Skills Practice

1. **Why should you analyze trends before making predictions?** *(to make the predictions more accurate)*
2. **How can you generate lists of possible consequences of an action?** *(Possible answers: brainstorming; talking to other people)*

Additional Skills Resources

- Chapter Skills Activity 15
- Building Geography Skills for Life

GLENCOE TECHNOLOGY

Skillbuilder Interactive Workbook CD-ROM, Level 1

This interactive CD-ROM reinforces student mastery of essential social studies skills.

Practicing the Skill Answers

1. tourism in Kenya; 1975–2000
2. 1980
3. that the number of tourists visiting Kenya has steadily increased
4. Yes, but at a slower rate
5. The rise in tourists evened out a little from 1997 to 2000.
6. *Possible answers:* Kenya's economy will continue benefiting from tourism, but at a slower rate. The wildlife in Kenya will continue to be protected for tourism purposes. Perhaps more land will be set aside for nature preserves to draw more tourists to the country.

Applying the Skill
Ask students to hand in copies of the articles along with their predictions.

Chapter 15

Section 2, pages 410–414

1 Focus

1. Compare the landforms and climates of the countries in this region.
2. Describe the major challenges facing each of these countries.

BELLRINGER Skillbuilder Activity

Project transparency and have students answer questions.

This activity is also available as a blackline master.

Daily Focus Skills Transparency 15-2

UNIT 6 Chapter 15 | DAILY FOCUS SKILLS TRANSPARENCY 15-2

ANSWER: Khartoum, Sudan, has a desert climate because of the small amount of rainfall it receives. Teacher Tip: Ask students which information (temperature or rainfall) is more important in identifying a desert climate.

Interpreting Information on Tables

Addis Ababa, Ethiopia

Month	Jan.	Feb.	Mar.	Apr.	May	June	July	Aug.	Sept.	Oct.	Nov.	Dec.
Average Temperature*	61°	63°	65°	64°	65°	62°	60°	60°	61°	61°	60°	58°
Rainfall	0.7"	1.5"	2.7"	3.4"	3.4"	5.2"	10.5"	11.1"	7.3"	1.1"	0.4"	0.4"

Khartoum, Sudan

Month	Jan.	Feb.	Mar.	Apr.	May	June	July	Aug.	Sept.	Oct.	Nov.	Dec.
Average Temperature*	73°	75°	82°	88°	93°	93°	89°	87°	89°	89°	82°	75°
Rainfall	0"	0"	0"	0"	0.1"	0.3"	1.9"	2.7"	0.8"	0.2"	0"	0"

*Temperatures in Fahrenheit

Directions: Answer the following question based on the table.

Which city do you think has a desert climate? Why?

Guide to Reading

■ **Accessing Prior Knowledge** Have students look at the political map on page 407. **Ask:** Why is the region from Eritrea to Somalia called "the Horn of Africa"?

Use the Vocabulary PuzzleMaker to create crossword and word search puzzles.

Section 2 Other Countries of East Africa

Guide to Reading

Main Idea

The other countries of East Africa have all been scarred by conflict in recent years.

Terms to Know

- drought
- plate
- clan
- endangered species
- genocide
- refugee

Reading Strategy

Create a chart like this one. Choose three countries of East Africa. Write the cause of conflict in each country next to that country's name. Then write the effects of that conflict.

Country	Cause of conflict	Effects of conflict

In the late 1100s and early 1200s, a king named Lalibela ruled Ethiopia. He had his subjects build Christian churches by carving them out of solid rock. First they cut a huge rectangular trench into the ground. Then they carved the rock inside that trench to form the church. This ancient church is just 1 of 11 ordered built by Lalibela.

The northern part of East Africa is a region called the **Horn of Africa.** This region got its name because it is shaped like a horn that juts out into the Indian Ocean. The countries here are **Sudan, Ethiopia, Eritrea** (EHR•uh•TREE•uh), **Djibouti** (jih•BOO•tee), and **Somalia.** West of Kenya and Tanzania lie **Uganda, Rwanda,** and **Burundi.** All three are landlocked—their land does not touch a sea or an ocean. Instead, they use three large lakes for transportation and trade.

Sudan

Sudan is the largest country in Africa—about one-third the size of the continental United States. Nomads raise camels and goats in the north. Most of Sudan's people live along the Nile River or one of its tributaries. Like the Egyptians, they use water from the Nile to irrigate their fields. Farmers grow sugarcane, grains, nuts, dates, and cotton—the country's leading export. Oil fields in the south offer another possibility of income.

Section Resources

Reproducible Masters

- Reproducible Lesson Plan 15-2
- Daily Lecture and Discussion Notes 15-2
- Guided Reading Activity 15-2
- Reading Essentials and Study Guide 15-2
- Section Quiz 15-2

Transparencies

- Daily Focus Skills Transparency 15-2
- GeoQuiz Transparency 15-1

Multimedia

- Vocabulary PuzzleMaker Software
- Interactive Tutor Self-Assessment CD-ROM
- Presentation Plus! CD-ROM
- ExamView® Pro 3.0 Testmaker CD-ROM

Sudan's People and History In ancient times, Sudan was the center of a powerful civilization called Kush. The people of Kush had close cultural and trade ties with the Egyptians to the north. Kushites traded metal tools for cotton and other goods from India, Arabia, and China. They built a great capital at Meroë (MAR•oh•EE). In Meroë were huge temples, stone palaces, and small pyramids. Kush began to lose power around A.D. 350.

During the A.D. 500s, missionaries from Egypt brought Christianity to the area. About 900 years later, Muslim Arabs entered northern Sudan and converted its people to Islam. From the late 1800s to the 1950s, the British and the Egyptians together ruled the entire country. Sudan became an independent nation in 1956. Since then, military leaders generally have ruled Sudan. In the 1980s, the government began a "reign of terror" against the southern Christian peoples. The fighting has disrupted the economy and caused widespread hunger, especially in the south. A recent **drought**—a long period of extreme dryness and water shortages—made the situation worse. Millions of people have starved to death, and major outbreaks of diseases have swept through the country. To end the war, the government has announced that it might allow the south to become independent. **Time Reports: Focus on World Issues** on pages 415–421 looks at Sudanese refugees.

✓Reading Check What is the main export of Sudan?

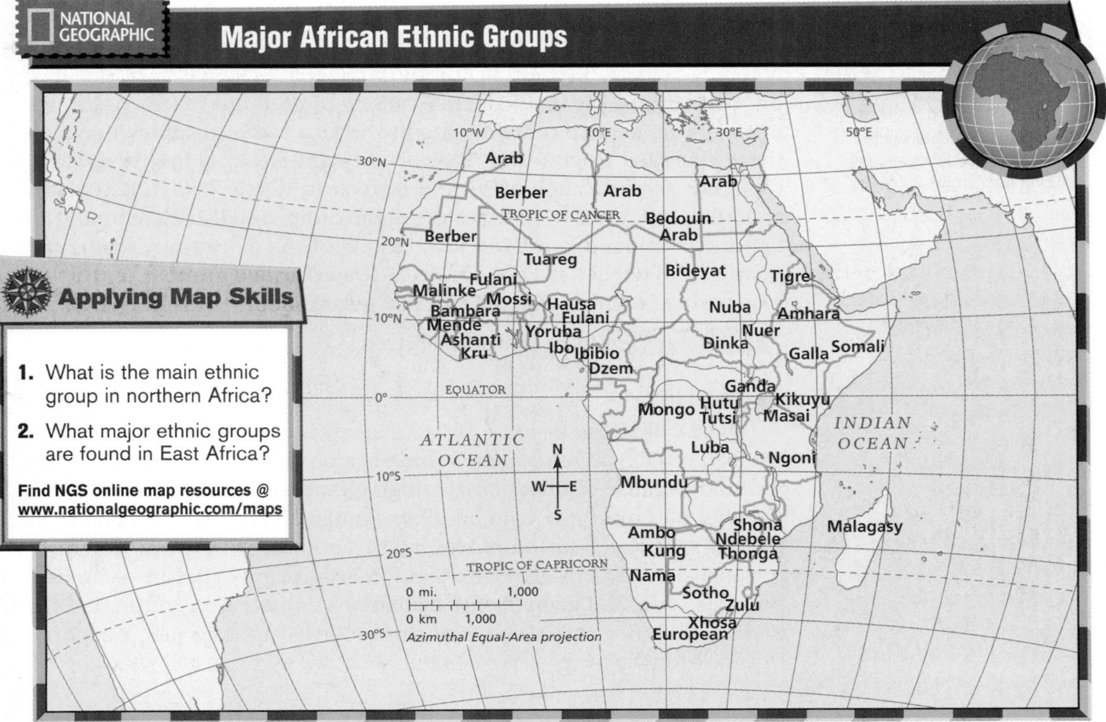

Applying Map Skills

1. What is the main ethnic group in northern Africa?
2. What major ethnic groups are found in East Africa?

Find NGS online map resources @ www.nationalgeographic.com/maps

Chapter 15

Section 2, pages 410–414

TEACH

Making Generalizations

Have students look at Rwanda and Burundi on the maps in this chapter. **Ask:** **Based on what you see on these maps, why are these two countries studied together?** *(Possible answers: similar geography, close proximity to each other, have same ethnic groups)* **L1**

Daily Lecture Notes 15–2

EAST AND CENTRAL AFRICA

Daily Lecture and Discussion Notes 15-2

Other Countries of East Africa (pages 410–414)

The main dish in the Sudanese diet is *ful* (also spelled *fool*). This dish consists of broad beans cooked in oil. Goat, lamb, beef, and chicken are served occasionally, but the majority of the Sudanese people do not eat much meat.

I. Sudan *(pages 410–411)*

A. Sudan is the largest country in Africa—about one-third the size of the continental United States.

B. Farmers along the Nile River grow sugarcane, grains, nuts, dates, and cotton—the country's leading export.

C. In ancient times, Sudan was the center of the powerful Kush Empire. The British ... ruled Sudan together until it gained its independence in 1956.

... een the northern and ... people

Applying Map Skills

Answers

1. Arab
2. Tigre, Amhara, Galla, Somali, Nuba, Nuer, Dinka, Ganda, Hutu, Tutsi, Masai, Kikuyu, and Ngoni

Skills Practice

What group is most prominent in the Sahel? *(Tuareg)*

Team-Teaching Activity

Health AIDS is a devastating problem in Africa south of the Sahara, which has about two-thirds of the world's cases of infection with HIV, the virus that causes AIDS. This region also accounts for about 90 percent of all deaths by AIDS, because poverty and relatively poor health care systems make it difficult for victims to afford the drugs available in industrialized countries. Invite the health teacher to class to discuss the way HIV attacks the body's immune system and the treatments available now. Then have the teacher discuss the obstacles to combating the disease in Africa. Have students research and discuss the impact that the widespread AIDS epidemic has on the people and economies of Africa and what the international community is doing to help. **L2**

EE4 Human Systems: Standard 9

Reading Check Answer

famine

Cultural Kaleidoscope

Sudan The name of the country now called Sudan has varied throughout history. Ancient Egyptians called it *Kush*. The Greeks considered it part of a land they called *Abyssinia*. To the Romans, it was *Nubia*. The Arabs called it *bilad as sudan*, or "land of the blacks."

Ethiopia About 40 percent of Ethiopians belong to the Ethiopian Orthodox Christian Church. This faith is different from both Roman Catholicism and Eastern Orthodox religions, because it includes many customs adapted from Judaism. The Ethiopian Church observes the Sabbath on Saturday, cantors chant the liturgy; and there is an emphasis on clean and unclean foods.

Guided Reading Activity 15-2

Name ______ Date ______ Class ______

EAST AND CENTRAL AFRICA

Guided Reading Activity 15-2

Other Countries of East Africa

DIRECTIONS: Summarizing Reading the section and completing the summary paragraphs below will help you learn more about other countries in East Africa. Use your textbook to fill in the blanks.

The Horn of Africa is located at the (1) ______ part of East Africa. The largest country in Africa, (2) ______, is one-third the size of the United States. Most people live along the (3) ______. In ancient times, a civilization called (4) ______ was a powerful civilization in the area.

Sudan became independent in (5) ______. (6) ______ have generally ruled since then.

Ethiopia is a (7) ______ country, about twice the size of Texas. Since 1974 Ethiopia has been trying to build a (8) ______ government.

Reading Check Answer

disputes between different clans

Ethiopia and Eritrea

Landlocked Ethiopia is almost twice the size of Texas. Famine brought Ethiopia to the world's attention in the 1980s. At that time, a drought turned fields once rich in crops into seas of dust. Despite food aid, more than 1 million Ethiopians died.

Since 1974 Ethiopia has been trying to build a democratic government. This goal is hindered by warfare with neighboring **Eritrea,** a small country that broke away from Ethiopia in 1993. Eritrean women formed about one-third of the army that won the war. After the war ended, the new government passed laws that gave Eritrean women more rights than they had ever had before.

Muslims now form about 45 percent of Ethiopia's 65.4 million people. About 40 percent of Ethiopians are Christians. Others practice traditional African religions. Almost 80 languages are spoken in Ethiopia. Amharic, similar to Hebrew and Arabic, is the official language.

Reading Check **What crisis brought Ethiopia to the world's attention?**

▲ In May 2000, this woman voted in Ethiopia's second-ever democratic election.

Djibouti and Somalia

The tiny country of Djibouti is one of the hottest, driest places on the earth. This country lies at the northern tip of the Great Rift Valley, where three of the earth's plates join. **Plates** are huge slabs of rock that make up the earth's crust. In Djibouti, two of these plates are pulling away from each other. As they separate, fiery hot rock rises to the earth's surface, causing volcanic activity.

Somalia Shaped like the number seven, Somalia is almost as large as Texas. Like Eritrea and Djibouti, much of Somalia is hot, dry country where farming is difficult. Nearly all the people of Somalia are Muslims, but they are deeply divided. They belong to different **clans,** or groups of people related to one another. In the late 1980s, disputes between these clans led to civil war. When a drought struck a few years later, hundreds of thousands of people starved to death. The United States and other countries tried to restore some order and distribute food. The fighting continued, however, and often kept the aid from reaching the people who needed it. Even today, clan-based armed groups control various parts of Somalia. There is no real government that is in charge.

Reading Check **What kind of conflict led to civil war in Somalia?**

Uganda

Once called "the pearl of Africa," Uganda is a fertile, green land about the size of Oregon. Although Uganda lies on the Equator, temperatures are mild because of the country's high elevation. Uganda's rich soil and plentiful rain make the land good for farming. More than 80 percent of Uganda's workers are employed in agriculture. Most work on small, privately owned farms. They grow plantains—a kind of banana—cassava, potatoes, corn, and grains. Some plantations grow coffee, cotton, and tea for export. Coffee makes up nearly three-fourths of the country's exports. Uganda's few factories make cement, soap, sugar, metal, and shoes.

Critical Thinking Activity

Synthesizing Information Organize students into 8 groups. Inform groups that their task is to create a wall poster on one of the 8 countries in this region; assign each group to a country. Then assign each group the following areas of study—land and climate; economy; history and government; and culture. Groups should develop or locate a number of images that illustrate their areas. They then should create their section of the poster. Some group members might do artwork or design, while others might write captions. Have groups combine their finished sections to create the wall poster. **L1**

EE2 Places and Regions: Standard 4

Kampala, Uganda

Public transportation in Kampala includes passenger boats on Lake Victoria.

Culture **How does this compare to public transportation where you live?**

Uganda's People About two-thirds of Ugandans are Christians. The remaining one-third practice Islam or traditional African religions. At one time there were large numbers of Hindus and Sikhs from South Asia living in the country. A dictator, Idi Amin, drove them out in 1972. Recently, the government invited them back, and many have returned.

The people of Uganda belong to more than 40 different ethnic groups. They have a rich cultural heritage of songs, folktales, and poems. In the past, these were passed by word of mouth from one generation to the next. Today this heritage has been preserved in books.

History and Government The dictator Idi Amin's cruel rule hurt Uganda throughout much of the 1980s. Civil wars forced Amin out of power. The role of local chiefs or kings has been reduced since independence to try to lessen tribal fighting.

Ugandans now have one of the fastest-growing economies in Africa. Uganda also enjoys a stable government. It is a republic with an elected president and legislature. Still, the future is clouded. Uganda, along with other African countries, faces a new threat: the disease called AIDS. Hundreds of thousands of Ugandans have died from it, and many more are infected with HIV, the virus that causes AIDS.

✓ Reading Check **What kind of government does Uganda have today?**

Rwanda and Burundi

Rwanda and Burundi are located in inland East Africa. High elevation gives both Rwanda and Burundi a moderate climate even though they lie near the Equator. Gorillas live within rain forests here. Because of illegal hunting, or poaching, gorillas are now an endangered species. An **endangered species** is a plant or an animal threatened with extinction.

More About the Photos

Lake Victoria Lake Victoria is the largest lake in Africa and the third-largest in the world. The Caspian Sea is first, and Lake Superior is second.

Caption Answer Answers will vary.

Travel Guide

Rwanda preserves a greater percentage of its land for national parks than any other country in Africa. Volcanoes National Park was the first wildlife park on the continent. It is the home of mountain gorillas.

✓ Reading Check Answer

a republic with an elected president and legislature

3 Assess

Assign Section 2 Assessment as homework or an in-class activity.

Have students use the Interactive Tutor Self-Assessment CD-ROM to review Section 15–2.

Section Quiz 15-2

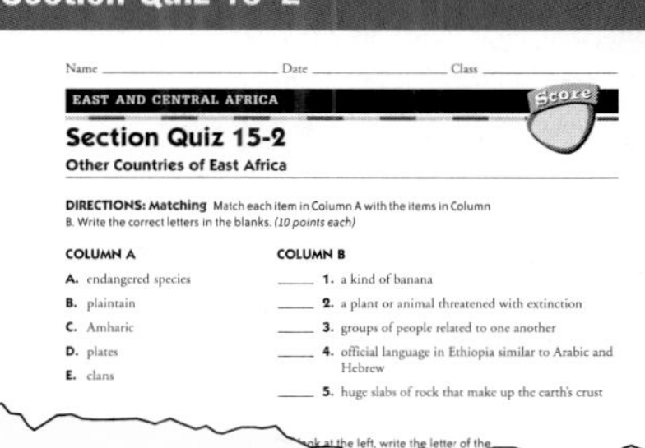

Name ____ Date ____ Class ____

EAST AND CENTRAL AFRICA

Score

Section Quiz 15-2

Other Countries of East Africa

DIRECTIONS: Matching Match each item in Column A with the items in Column B. Write the correct letters in the blanks. *(10 points each)*

COLUMN A	COLUMN B
A. endangered species	____ 1. a kind of banana
B. plaintain	____ 2. a plant or animal threatened with extinction
C. Amharic	____ 3. groups of people related to one another
D. plates	____ 4. official language in Ethiopia similar to Arabic and Hebrew
E. clans	____ 5. huge slabs of rock that make up the earth's crust

Meeting Special Needs

Logical/Mathematical Give students the following figures, which represent the population (in millions) of the countries of East Africa: Burundi—5.7; Djibouti—0.7; Eritrea—4.0; Ethiopia—59.7; Kenya—28.8; Rwanda—8.2; Somalia—7.1; Tanzania—31.3; Uganda—22.8. Have them construct a chart that displays this information. They could select a bar graph, a table, or some other form. For further skills practice, provide your students with the latest statistics on the spread of AIDS in these countries. Have them add this information to their charts. **L2**

Refer to *Inclusion for the Middle School Social Studies Classroom Strategies and Activities* in the TCR.

Chapter 15

Section 2, pages 410–414

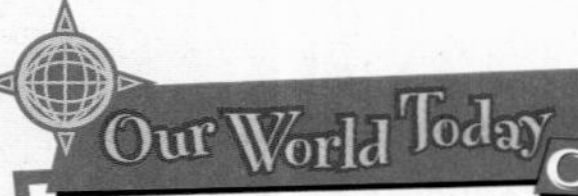

Objectives, goals, and answers to the Student Web Activity can be found in the Web Activity Lesson Plan at owt.glencoe.com

✓ Reading Check Answer

Hutu

Reading Essentials and Study Guide 15-2

Name ________________ Date ________________ Class ________________

EAST AND CENTRAL AFRICA

Reading Essentials and Study Guide 15-2

Other Countries of East Africa

For use with textbook pages 410–414

Terms to Know

drought long period of extreme dryness and water shortages (page 411)
plates huge slabs of rock that make up the earth's crust (page 412)
clan group of people related to one another (page 412)
endangered species plant or animal threatened with extinction (413)
refugee person who flees to another country to escape persecution or disaster (page 414)

Drawing from Experience

Enrich

Have students conduct research to determine the current status of the situation between the Hutus and Tutsis in Rwanda and Burundi. Tell them to look for examples of cooperation as well as conflict.

CLOSE

Have students create a concept web for the countries covered in this section. Have them include facts about the geography, history, and culture of each country.

Web Activity Visit the ***Our World Today: People, Places, and Issues*** Web site at owt.glencoe.com and click on **Chapter 15–Student Web Activities** to learn more about Rwanda's mountain gorillas.

Coffee is the main export crop in Burundi and Rwanda. The people who live along Lake Kivu and Lake Tanganyika also fish. Because both countries are landlocked, they have trouble getting their goods to foreign buyers. Few paved roads and no railroads exist. Most goods must be transported by road to Lake Tanganyika, where boats take them to Tanzania or the Democratic Republic of the Congo.

Ethnic Conflict Rwanda and Burundi are among the most densely populated countries in Africa. Two ethnic groups form most of the population of both countries—the **Hutu** and the **Tutsi.** The Hutu make up 80 percent or more of the population in both Rwanda and Burundi. Over the years, however, the Tutsi have controlled the governments and economies. Since the countries became independent in 1962, the Hutu have tried to gain some of this power.

That effort led to civil war and genocide in the 1990s. **Genocide** is the deliberate destruction of a group of people because of their race or culture. A Hutu-led government in Rwanda killed hundreds of thousands of Tutsi people. Two million more became **refugees,** or people who flee to another country to escape persecution or disaster. The fighting between the Hutu and Tutsi has lessened, but both countries face many challenges as they try to rebuild with the help and cooperation of the international community.

✓ Reading Check **Which ethnic group makes up the majority of the population in Rwanda and Burundi?**

Assessment

Defining Terms

1. **Define** drought, plate, clan, endangered species, genocide, refugee.

Recalling Facts

2. **History** To what nation did Eritrea once belong?
3. **Government** Describe the current political situation in Somalia.
4. **Region** What endangered species lives in the forests of Rwanda and Burundi?

Critical Thinking

5. **Evaluating Information** How could a deadly epidemic, such as AIDS, affect a country's economy?
6. **Analyzing Information** How do ethnic differences create problems for the countries of East Africa?

Graphic Organizer

7. **Organizing Information** Create a diagram like the one below. Then write two facts about Sudan under each of the category headings in the outer ovals.

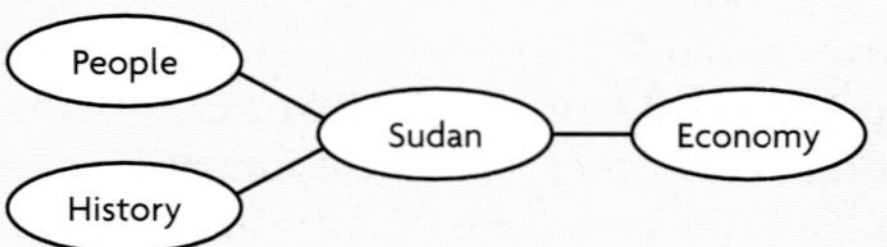

Applying Social Studies Skills

8. **Analyzing Maps** Study the political map on page 407. What are the four landlocked countries of East Africa?

Section 2 Assessment

1. The terms are defined in the Glossary.
2. Ethiopia
3. There is no real government in charge. Armed groups from different clans control various areas.
4. gorillas
5. Answers should include such issues as the cost of health care, loss of workers, and loss of skilled people who could help build the country's future.
6. Ethnic differences have led to conflict, civil war, and massive killings.
7. Students' diagrams will vary.
8. Uganda, Rwanda, Burundi, Ethiopia

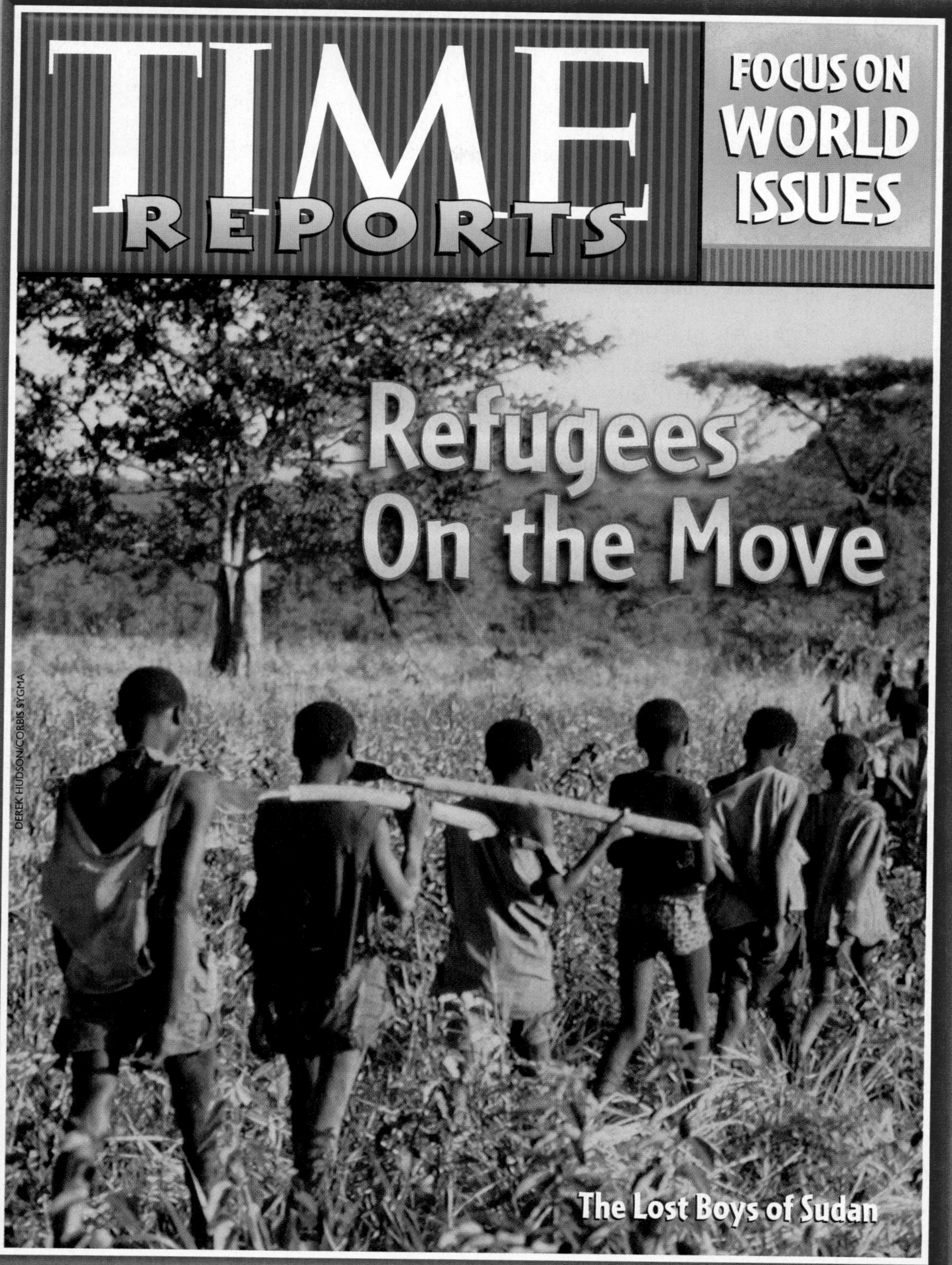

TIME REPORTS

FOCUS ON WORLD ISSUES

Refugees On the Move

The Lost Boys of Sudan

DEREK HUDSON/CORBIS SYGMA

Making Connections

Diversity **Ask students: What do you think the words *diverse* and *inclusive* mean when Americans use them to discuss their society? Do you think America is an inclusive society? Why or why not?** Discuss the fact that many nations are composed of different groups, or tribes, that do not get along. These groups may have very different customs, religions, and views of the world. They do not understand America's concept of "strength through diversity." When one group gains control of the government, it may attempt to destroy other groups, even to the point of killing them or forcing them to flee for their lives. These people become refugees. Many come to the United States. Compare the way these citizens might be treated in their country to their life in the United States.

TIME REPORTS

Focus on World Issues

Teacher Background

The Office of the United Nations High Commissioner on Refugees (UNHCR) was first set up in 1951 and assigned the task of resettling European refugees left homeless after World War II. At that time there were approximately 1.2 million refugees, most of whom were resettled in Europe.

Today, the number of refugees is much greater. This has put an enormous strain on the UNHCR and other organizations and countries wanting to help displaced persons.

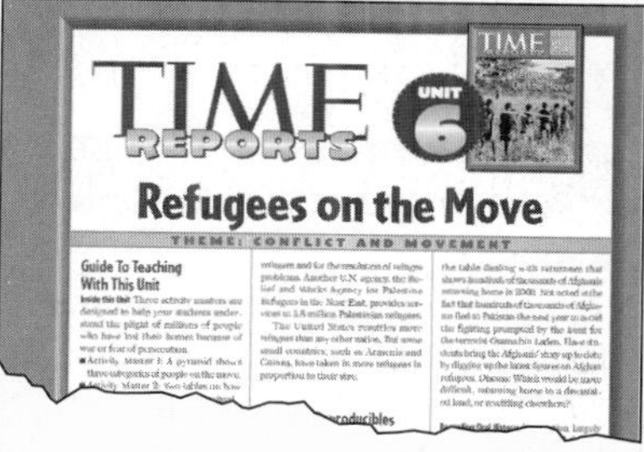
TIME REPORTS UNIT 6

Refugees on the Move

THEME: CONFLICT AND MOVEMENT

Guide To Teaching With This Unit

Preparing the Student

In many parts of Africa, religious and cultural conflicts have led to refugee problems. Many of these conflicts have their roots in colonialism. When Europeans created countries in Africa, they determined boundaries without regard to cultural allegiances. The artificial states that were formed often threw together people of different ethnic groups with different languages and age-old rivalries. Colonial government also worsened political inequalities that had already existed among the different groups.

1 Focus

Ask students to write a paragraph summarizing what they understand about refugees in the world, not just in Africa. Remind them that this is not to place fault or blame, but to explain the circumstances surrounding the problem, including as many causes as they can surmise.

Then put students in small groups to share their paragraphs and to create a list of non-judgmental statements about what they believe are the main causes of the refugee crisis and the main issues needing to be resolved. Finally, bring the groups back together and create a master list. Let the students debate the merits of all the points included on the list.

Africans on the Move

ANSWER
None of these countries have refugees leaving their borders, but they are countries with internal displacements.

Evaluating Information

Pass out a copy of the Universal Declaration of Human Rights that was adopted by the UN in 1948. You can obtain it at **www.un.org/rights**. It has 30 articles. Have students read it and then in groups or individually ask them to choose the five rights that they think are most important. Afterwards have the class share their ratings and explain why they think some rights are more important than others. **L2**

TIME REPORTS

FOCUS ON WORLD ISSUES

At a refugee camp, boys collected sticks and reeds to make huts, then cooked a rare meal of beans.

The Lost Boys of Sudan

In November 1987, William Deng was tending cattle several miles from his village in southern Sudan. Two brothers and some cousins were with him. One afternoon they heard distant gunfire but ignored it. "The next morning," William said, "we saw the smoke. I climbed a tree and saw that my whole village was burned."

They raced to the village. There they learned that government troops had swept through. "Nobody was left standing," William said. "Some were wounded; some were killed. My father was dead. So we just ran away. I was 5."

The boys headed toward Ethiopia. Crossing marshlands and desert, they joined thousands of other Sudanese, mostly boys. They walked for two months. They ate berries, dried leaves, birds, and mice—anything they could find. Thousands died. "You think that maybe later that will be you," said one boy.

Into Ethiopia

The survivors finally reached a refugee camp in Ethiopia. **Refugees** are people forced by fear to find refuge, or shelter, outside their countries.

In 1991 Ethiopia closed its camps. Soldiers forced all of the "Lost Boys of Sudan," as they came to be called, back to their homeland.

After a year in Sudan, 10,000 of the boys fled to a refugee camp in Kenya. And there they stayed—some for as long as 10 years.

All Too Common

Sadly, William's experience is not unique. Throughout Africa south of the Sahara, millions of people have had to flee their homes. Most live in crowded camps set up by groups such as the United Nations. There they wait—until it is safe to go home, or until another country lets them stay.

Africans on the Move

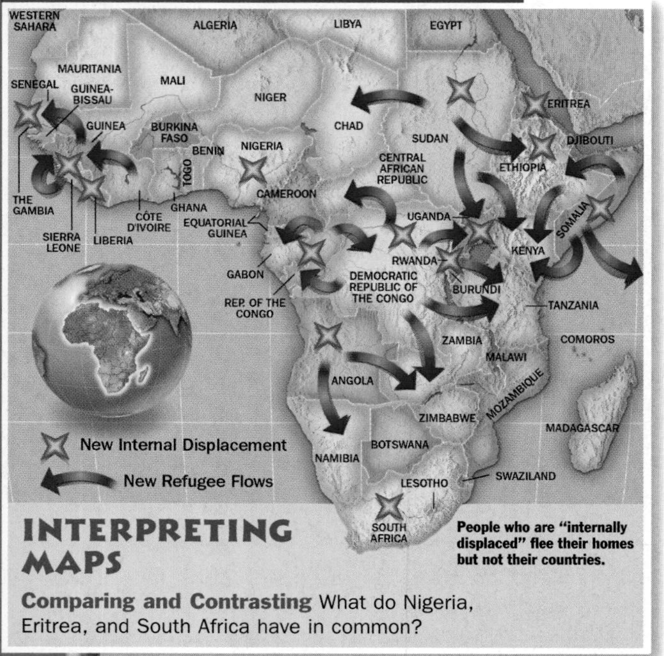

INTERPRETING MAPS

Comparing and Contrasting What do Nigeria, Eritrea, and South Africa have in common?

416

Team-Teaching Activity

Psychology Have a teacher who is knowledgeable about psychology discuss the adjustment problems these children faced when their families were killed and they were forced to leave their homes. The teacher may want to introduce Maslow's Hierarchy of Needs. At first the children struggled to meet their most fundamental physical needs, such as food, shelter, and safety. Those who survived and were sent to other countries to start a new life could try to meet higher-level needs, such as love and esteem. These needs can be met when people are accepted and cared for by those around them and learn skills to support themselves. After students have finished reading this report, have them discuss how the "Lost Boys of Sudan" fit this psychological pattern. **L2**

EE4 Human Systems: Standard 9

Older boys "adopted" younger ones.

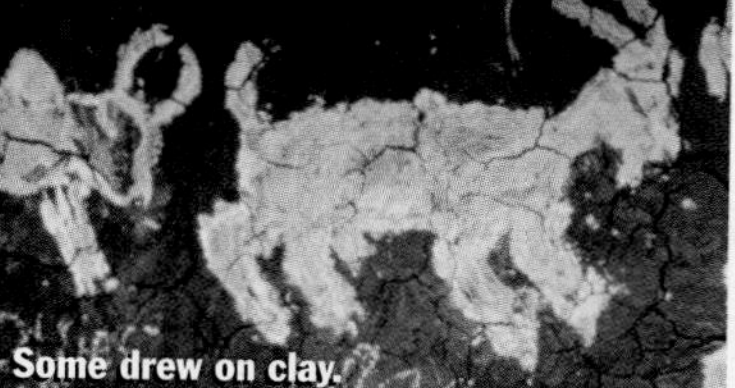

Some drew on clay.

The youngest wore the faces of suffering.

TOP PHOTOS: DEREK HUDSON/CORBIS SYGMA

The Lost Boys are victims of a war that began in 1983. The government has been heartless. U.S. President George W. Bush explained in 2001, "Some 2 million Sudanese have lost their lives; 4 million more have lost their homes." The Sudan, he concluded, is a "disaster area for human rights."

Human rights include the right to safety, to food, and to shelter, among other things. In democracies, they also include the rights of citizens to choose their own leaders.

Defining Refugees' Rights

In 1951, members of the United Nations agreed to guarantee basic human rights to refugees. They signed a **convention**, or special document, that gives refugees a unique legal status, or position. That status gives them the right to **asylum**, or safety, in foreign countries. It also gives them the right to be treated like any other foreign resident of their host country.

The convention defines refugees as people who leave their countries to flee **persecution**. Persecution is unfair treatment based on such characteristics as race, religion, or ethnic background. Recently the United Nations expanded this definition. Today people whose governments can't protect them from the dangers of war are also entitled to refugee status, the UN says.

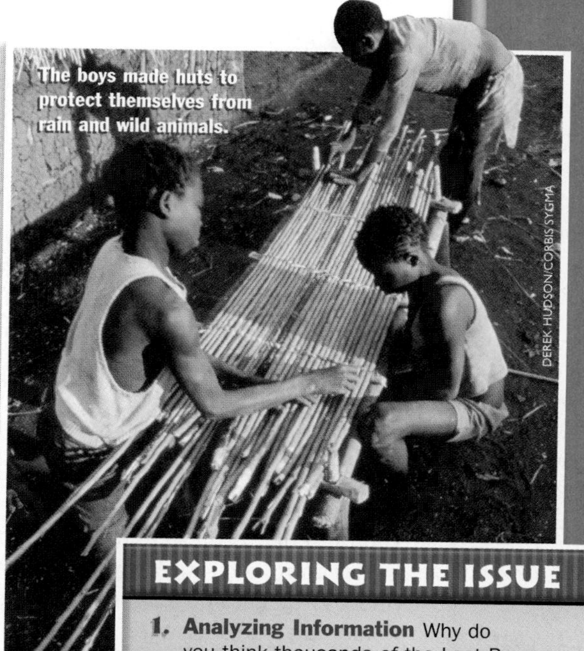

The boys made huts to protect themselves from rain and wild animals.

DEREK HUDSON/CORBIS SYGMA

EXPLORING THE ISSUE

1. **Analyzing Information** Why do you think thousands of the Lost Boys traveled together instead of alone?
2. **Making Predictions** How might your life change if you no longer had the basic human rights listed here?

Environmental Refugees

People who flee natural disasters, such as floods and famines, aren't refugees. They are "displaced persons" or "environmental refugees." Immigrants aren't refugees, either. Immigrants may leave their countries to get an education or find a better job. Refugees like the Lost Boys of Sudan have little choice. They flee their countries to find safety.

2 TEACH

Identifying Main Ideas

As students read each subsection, have them write one sentence that expresses the main idea. Have volunteers offer their sentences and discuss to what extent they do or do not capture the main idea. L1

More About the Photos

Lost Boys Ask: **Where do you think these young people learned the skills they needed to build their own shelters?**

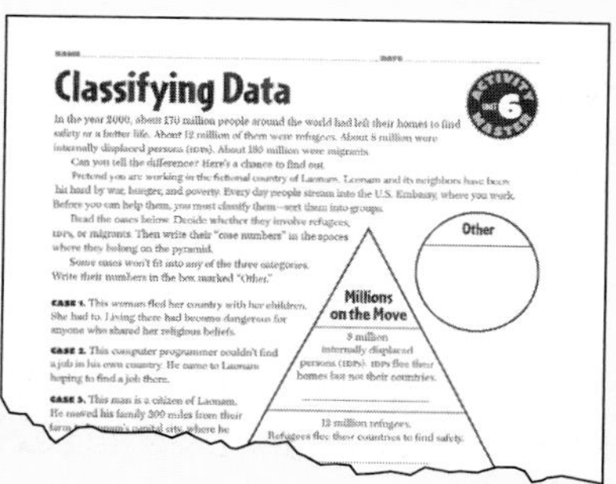

EXPLORING THE ISSUE

ANSWERS

1. *Possible answers:* a group provides more protection and emotional support; they could share their skills; older boys could care for younger ones
2. Answers will vary.

Meeting Special Needs

Intrapersonal Write the following questions: **Do you think you would have the ability to survive on your own as these young people did? What qualities do you have that you think would help you survive? How do you think this experience would change the way you felt about others and how you lived your life in the future?**

Divide students into small groups and have them discuss their responses to these questions. Then have them write a short essay that summarizes their responses. L2

Refer to *Inclusion for the Middle School Social Studies Classroom Strategies and Activities* in the TCR.

TIME REPORTS

Recommended Internet Sites

www.unhcr.ch
The official Web site of the United Nations Commissioner for Refugees contains up-to-date information on refugees, along with statistics. Clicking on Research/Evaluation will take you to Teaching Tools.

www.un.org/CyberSchoolBus/briefing/refugees
Provides a general discussion of what constitutes a refugee, along with reports on current refugee problems.

Synthesizing Information
Have groups pick a country with refugee camps. Each group should research ways that the UN, its member nations, and relief organizations are helping the refugees. Groups should make a presentation that answers the following: **What are conditions like in the camps? Are there schools for the children? How can the organizations find permanent homes and jobs for the refugees? L2**

EXPLORING THE ISSUE

ANSWERS

1. Displaced people disrupt the countries into which they flee and require possibly scarce food, shelter, and medical care. They may spread diseases, such as AIDS.
2. Governments may not have the resources to provide these services. They may not want to encourage refugees to stay or more to enter their country.

TIME REPORTS

Africa's Troubled Past

Refugees have existed in many places, not only countries in Africa. Yet rarely has the flow of refugees been as widespread as it is today. Worldwide, about 35 million people were on the move in the year 2000. Some 21 million of them were **internally displaced persons (IDPs)**—people who flee to safety inside their own countries. About 14 million more were refugees seeking freedom from war and persecution outside their countries. During the year 2000, Africa alone held more than 3 million refugees and at least 11 million IDPs.

▲ War chased thousands of terrified Burundians into the Congo in 1995.

The Impact of Violence

The presence of these uprooted people is reshaping Africa. Away from their villages, refugees no longer grow crops, worsening food shortages. The crush of refugees drains the resources of the already poor countries that host them. And refugees spread AIDS, a disease that by 2001 had killed the parents of 12 million African children.

Many experts trace Africa's refugee problem back to the late 1800s. That's when European nations began to carve the continent into colonies. Africa's 2,000 ethnic groups speak around one thousand languages. But European colonizers failed to respect those differences. They set up boundaries that split individual tribes into many pieces. Other borders forced traditional enemies such as Rwanda's Hutu and Tutsi tribes to share the same space.

How America Is Different

Americans living in Britain's 13 colonies didn't face such problems in 1776. When the U.S. was born, most Americans spoke English and shared similar values. They were ready to rule themselves as a democracy.

Africa's colonies became independent nearly two centuries later. But they contained groups that had little interest in working together. That made it hard for democracy to take root. In many nations, armed groups muscled their way to power. Such struggles for control turned millions of Africans into refugees.

EXPLORING THE ISSUE

1. **Making Inferences** In what ways might Africa's refugee problem hurt all Africans?
2. **Analyzing Information** How might the refugee problem keep governments from building roads and providing services such as education and health care?

418

Critical Thinking Activity

Making Comparisons Remind students about the Unit 2 Time Reports titled "The Arab-Israeli Conflict." Have the class respond to the following questions: **How were the problems encountered by the Jewish refugees after the end of World War II similar to those of the Sudanese refugees? How were they different? How is the plight of today's Palestinian refugees similar to that of the Sudanese? How is it different? L2**

EE4 Human Systems: Standard 9

TIME REPORTS

Struggling to Survive

When refugees enter another country, they may face dangers. In 1997, for example, soldiers rounded up refugees who had lived many years in Tanzania. They forced the refugees into camps. "I never thought the Tanzanian government would do this to us," said a woman who fled Burundi in 1971. "I am now held in a refugee camp, but my children are still outside. They have no money to come here."

Even refugees allowed to stay in private homes face risks. "We are frequently arrested by the police," said an Ethiopian who fled to Kenya. "They require bribes before they will release us."

Refugee Children

For children, refugee life brings special problems. Those separated from their parents must fend for themselves. Some girls and boys are forced to become soldiers. Others must work for little or no pay. Abby, 14, fled the war in Sierra Leone. Now she lives in a refugee camp in Guinea. "In the morning," she said, "I fetch water, sweep, and pray. Then I go find a job for the day. I usually pound rice. I get no food, only [a tiny amount of money]. I will be in the sun until evening. I feel pain all over my body. I don't go to school. I live with my grandmother, and she is very old. I need to take care of her."

Many of the overcrowded camps are dirty and unhealthy. But until their countries become safe again, the refugees have few choices. Either they stay in the camps, or they return home to the horrors they fled.

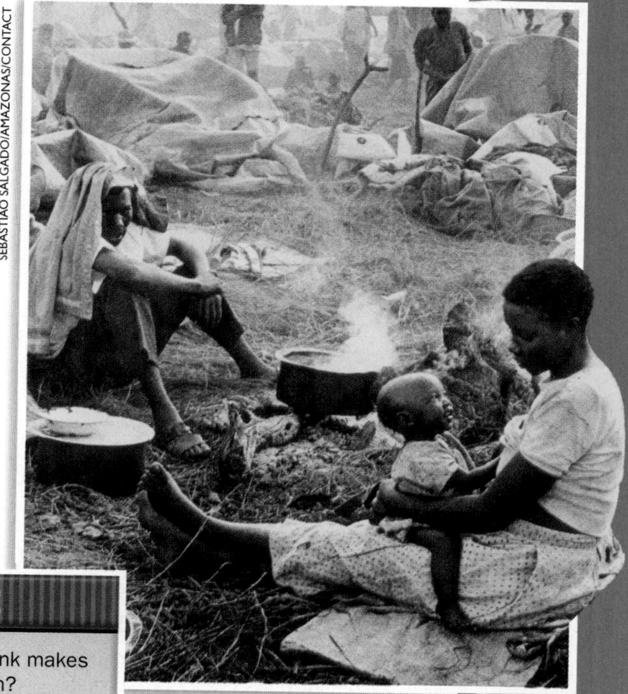

SEBASTIAO SALGADO/AMAZONAS/CONTACT

▲ **A refugee camp at Benako, Tanzania, overflowed with Rwandans in 1994.**

EXPLORING THE ISSUE

1. **Drawing Conclusions** What do you think makes many refugee camps so difficult to live in?
2. **Problem Solving** Gather information from the text to identify problems faced by refugees in camps. Consider changes that might be made to the camps to improve life there.

419

Understanding Cause and Effect

Afghanistan has a long history of people fleeing the country as refugees. After the September 11, 2001, terrorist attack on the United States, even more Afghans fled the country, knowing U.S. retaliation was coming. Have students research and write a report about the history of Afghan refugees, the problems they have faced, and to what countries they have fled. **L2**

Did You Know

In August, 2001, the Kakuma refugee camp in Kenya housed 77,000 people. The corrugated metal buildings stretched for 10 miles.

EXPLORING THE ISSUE

ANSWERS

1. People are separated from their homes and families, so they lack a traditional support system. Camps are often crowded and lack sanitary facilities, causing disease.
2. *Possible answers:* separation of families, overcrowding, unsanitary conditions, harassment by soldiers or governments, child exploitation. The UN, its member countries, and relief agencies can combine resources of money, manpower, and political pressure to improve conditions in camps and help return refugees to their homes.

Interdisciplinary Activity

Literature Considerable literature has been written by and about refugees. Following World War II, many books were written by European Jews who were displaced during the war and by people from eastern Europe who fled Soviet persecution. Have students read a biographical work or a work of fiction about a refugee from an area in which they are interested. When they are done reading, they should write a book report. Instruct them to focus on the feelings of the primary character(s). **Why did the characters become refugees? What difficulties did they have in adjusting to their new homeland? L3**

EE4 Human Systems: Standard 10

TIME REPORTS

Current Events Journal

Instruct students to go to the Web site of the United Nations Commissioner For Refugees (www.unhcr.ch) to find the current listing of the 10 countries with the most refugees fleeing their borders. They should use this information to create a pie chart showing the percentage of refugees coming from each of the 10 countries.

EXPLORING THE ISSUE

ANSWERS

1. *Possible answers:* using everyday appliances, understanding laws and what is expected of you in school; understanding American slang and customs
2. *Possible answers:* helping them with grocery shopping, cooking dinner, doing the laundry, and going to the bank

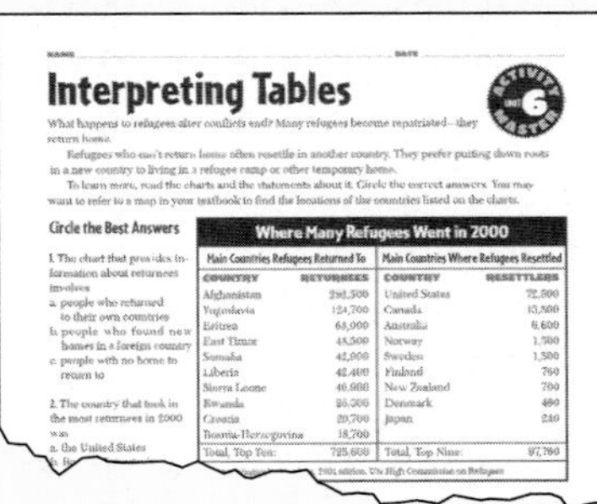

NAME ________ DATE ________

Interpreting Tables

What happens to refugees after conflicts end? Many refugees become repatriated—they return home.

Refugees who can't return home often resettle in another country. They prefer putting down roots in a new country to living in a refugee camp or other temporary home.

To learn more, read the charts and the statements about it. Circle the correct answers. You may want to refer to a map in your textbook to find the locations of the countries listed on the charts.

Circle the Best Answers

1. The chart that provides information about returnees involves
a. people who returned to their own countries
b. people who found new homes in a foreign country
c. people with no home to return to

2. The country that took in the most returnees in 2000 was
a. the United States

Where Many Refugees Went in 2000

Main Countries Refugees Returned To		Main Countries Where Refugees Resettled	
COUNTRY	RETURNEES	COUNTRY	RESETTLERS
Afghanistan	[illegible]	United States	72,500
Yugoslavia	124,700	Canada	13,500
Eritrea	63,000	Australia	6,600
East Timor	48,500	Norway	1,500
Somalia	42,000	Sweden	1,500
Liberia	42,400	Finland	760
Sierra Leone	40,800	New Zealand	700
Rwanda	26,300	Denmark	480
Croatia	20,700	Japan	240
Bosnia-Herzegovina	18,700		
Total, Top Ten:	725,600	Total, Top Nine:	97,780

2001 edition. UN High Commission on Refugees

TIME REPORTS

Helping Refugees: What Can One Person Do?

Countries that offer asylum to refugees are known as **host countries**. Starting life over in a host country can be hard for refugees and their families. William Deng and Joseph Maker are among more than 3,000 Lost Boys of Sudan who have found refuge in the United States. William lives in Grand Rapids, Michigan. Joseph lives in Houston, Texas, as do 170 other Lost Boys. In both places, local people taught them how to take buses, shop, and even use faucets and refrigerators. Many of those helpers were volunteers.

Eventually, many refugees who get such help grow to love their adopted country. They come to love it as much as or even more than people born there.

STEVE LISS

◀ These Michigan second graders are learning English at school.

Strangers in a New Land

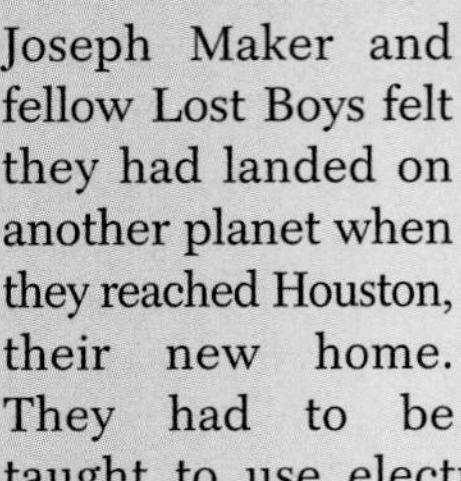

HOUSTON CHRONICLE

▲ Joseph Maker fo[und] a warm welcome [in] Houston, Texas.

Joseph Maker and fellow Lost Boys felt they had landed on another planet when they reached Houston, their new home. They had to be taught to use electricity, running water, air conditioners, flush toilets, stoves, and telephones.

Packaged foods baffled them. At the refugee camp in Kenya, they had eaten the same meal—beans and lentils—every day for nine years. In Houston they discovered junk food—and the fear of getting fat. "I've heard in America, people can become big," said Joseph's friend James Thon Aleer.

The newcomers also had to learn new ways to act. In Sudan, it's disrespectful to look into the eyes of the person you're speaking to. In America, it's impolite to look away. Joseph and his friends adopted the American way, something they think helped all of them get jobs.

One thing they picked up quickly was American humor. The tag on James Thon Aleer's key chain says "Don't Mess with Texas."

EXPLORING THE ISSUE

1. **Categorizing** If you were an African refugee in your community, what things might confuse you the most?
2. **Problem Solving** How might volunteers help refugees adapt to life in your community?

420

Your Government and You

Many countries around the world, including the United States, grant asylum to refugees. Each year, the United States sets quotas for the number of refugees it will accept from different continents. This number has been shrinking, from 142,000 in 1992 to 90,000 in 2000. Have students divide into groups. **Ask:** **How can we encourage our government to become more active in helping refugees? What can we do on an individual basis to help refugees around the world and in our communities?** Have the groups share their responses, and decide which options are best. If possible, implement one of the solutions. **L3**

EE6 The Uses of Geography: Standard 18

REVIEW AND ASSESS

UNDERSTANDING THE ISSUE

1. **Defining Key Terms** Write definitions for the following terms: *refugee, refugee camp, internally displaced person, human rights, asylum, convention,* and *persecution.*
2. **Writing to Inform** Write a 250-word article about the refugee issue that a school newspaper could publish. Use the key terms listed above.
3. **Writing to Persuade** "There is no greater sorrow on Earth than the loss of one's native land." A Greek thinker wrote those words about 2,500 years ago. Is his statement as true today? Write a short essay to explain.

INTERNET RESEARCH ACTIVITIES

4. Navigate to the United States Committee for Refugees website at **www.refugees.org/index.cfm.** Click on the button for News and Resources. Write a brief report on current "refugee hot spots" in Africa south of the Sahara. Be prepared to report on these problems in class.
5. Navigate to the website of the United Nations High Commissioner for Refugees at **www.unhcr.ch**. Click on the World, then click on the map of Africa. Report on what the UN is doing to ease refugee problems in two nations south of the Sahara.

BEYOND THE CLASSROOM

6. **Visit your school or local library** to find books in which young refugees share their experiences. (Enter the key words "refugee children" on the Amazon.com website, and you can find some titles to start with.) Bring those books to class to share with your classmates.

STEVE LISS

▲ This Hmong boy from Laos now lives in Wisconsin.

7. **Research a refugee problem outside Africa.** List ways that it is like—and different from—refugee problems in Africa. Report your findings to your classmates.
8. **Work in groups** to come up with ways young people could make it easier for newcomers to your community. Put your suggestions on a poster. Include phone numbers of groups that provide services for refugees. Display the poster for all students to see.

Where the World's Refugees Come From

(Top 15 Sources of Refugees as of January 1, 2001)

Palestinians	4,000,000
Afghanistan	3,600,000
Sudan	460,000
Iraq	450,000
Burundi	420,000
Angola	400,000
Sierra Leone	400,000
Burma	380,000
Somalia	370,000
Dem. Rep. of Congo	350,000
Eritrea	350,000
Croatia	315,000
Vietnam	300,000
Bosnia and Herzegovina	250,000
El Salvador	230,000
Total:	**12,275,000**

Around the world in 2001, more than 14 million people lived as refugees. This table lists the 15 nations that most of them fled. Besides refugees, at least 21 million others are internally displaced persons (IDPs). IDPs seek safety inside their nation's borders but far from their homes.

Source: U.S. Committee for Refugees

BUILDING SKILLS FOR READING TABLES

1. **Categorizing** Use your text to categorize the 15 nations listed here under one of five regions: Africa, Central America, Eastern Europe, Southeast Asia, and Southwest Asia.
2. **Analyzing Data** Which of the above regions have the greatest and smallest number of refugees?
3. **Transferring Data** Create a bar graph based on the country data in this table.

FOR UPDATES ON WORLD ISSUES GO TO www.timeclassroom.com/glencoe

3 ASSESS

Have students take the Time Reports Quiz or do the Alternative Assessment project for this unit provided in the Teacher's Classroom Resources.

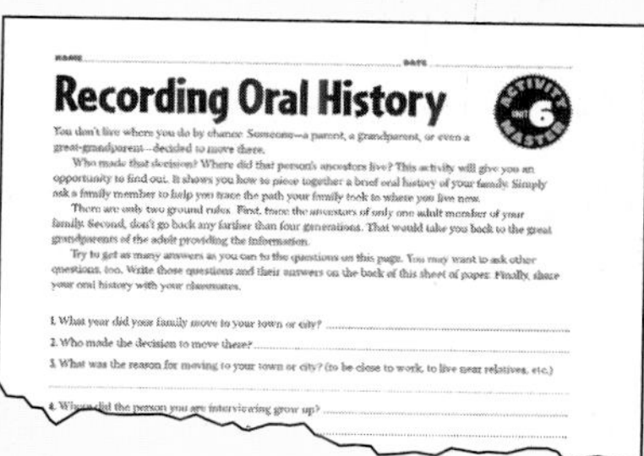

Recording Oral History

BUILDING SKILLS FOR READING TABLES

ANSWERS

1. *Africa:* Sudan, Burundi, Angola, Sierra Leone, Somalia, Dem. Rep. of Congo, Eritrea; *Central America:* El Salvador; *Eastern Europe:* Croatia, Bosnia and Herzegovina; *Southeast Asia:* Burma, Vietnam; *Southwest Asia:* Palestinians, Afghanistan, Iraq.
2. *greatest:* Southwest Asia; *smallest:* Central America
3. The bar graph can illustrate the number of refugees in each country or region.

4 CLOSE

Ask students to write a paragraph starting with this sentence: *The plight of refugees is a global issue because . . .*

Culminating Activity

To close this lesson, have students complete the Review and Assess section questions and activities above. Students should use classroom discussion, contextual clues, and their student dictionaries to write definitions for terms. Before assigning the Internet activities, it is recommended that you review your school district policy on student Internet use.

Focus on Debate

Have students debate the pro and con position of the following: **The United States should take in as many refugees as possible, provide them with what they need to live, and help them to develop skills they need to get jobs and become productive citizens. L2**

EE6 The Uses of Geography: Standard 18

FOCUS

1. Describe the landforms found in the countries of Central Africa.
2. Explain the factors preventing the Democratic Republic of the Congo from reaching its economic potential.
3. Compare the economies and people of the countries in this region.

BELLRINGER Skillbuilder Activity

Project transparency and have students answer questions.

This activity is also available as a blackline master.

Daily Focus Skills Transparency 15-3

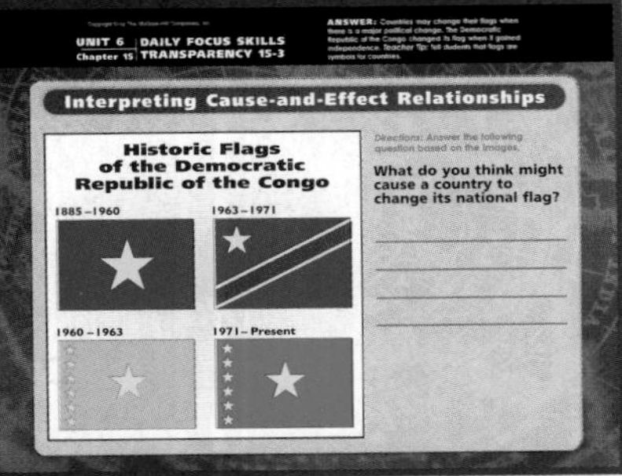

UNIT 6 DAILY FOCUS SKILLS
Chapter 15 TRANSPARENCY 15-3
Interpreting Cause-and-Effect Relationships
Historic Flags of the Democratic Republic of the Congo
1885–1960
1963–1971
1960–1963
1971–Present
What do you think might cause a country to change its national flag?

Guide to Reading

■ **Accessing Prior Knowledge**
Ask students what kind of natural resources are valuable to a country. *(timber, minerals, water power)* Explain that in this section they will read about a country that has all of these resources.

Central Africa

Guide to Reading

Main Idea

Central Africa has rich natural resources that are largely undeveloped because of civil war and poor government decisions.

Terms to Know

- savanna
- canopy
- hydroelectric power
- tsetse fly
- deforestation

Reading Strategy

Create a chart like this one. Choose two countries of Central Africa. Then list two facts about the people of each country.

Country	Fact #1	Fact #2

In the 2000 Olympic Summer Games, the gold medal in men's soccer went to Cameroon's team, the Indomitable Lions. The streets of Cameroon's capital, Yaoundé, and other cities were jammed with wildly excited fans screaming with joy. Cameroon's president even declared the following Monday a national holiday to celebrate the victory.

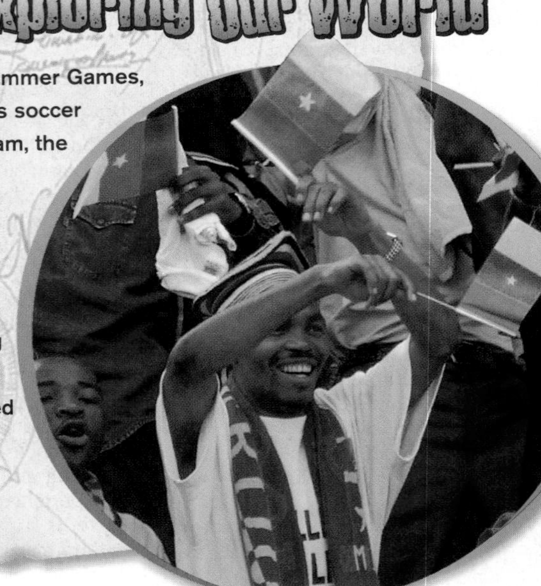

Central Africa includes seven countries. They are the **Democratic Republic of the Congo, Cameroon,** the **Central African Republic, Congo, Gabon** (ga•BOHN), **Equatorial Guinea,** and **São Tomé** (sow too•MAY) **and Príncipe** (PREEN•see•pee). Africa's second-longest river—the **Congo River**—flows through the center of the Democratic Republic of the Congo in the very heart of Africa.

Democratic Republic of the Congo

One-fourth the size of the United States, the Democratic Republic of the Congo has only about 23 miles (37 km) of coastline. Most of its land borders other African countries—nine in all.

High, rugged mountains rise in the eastern part of the country. Here you will find four large lakes—Lake Albert, Lake Edward, Lake Kivu, and Lake Tanganyika. **Lake Tanganyika** is the longest freshwater lake in the world. It is also the second deepest, after Russia's Lake Baikal. Savannas, or tropical grasslands with few trees, cover the highlands in the far north and south of the country. In these areas, lions and leopards stalk antelopes and zebras for food.

Section Resources

Reproducible Masters

- Reproducible Lesson Plan 15-3
- Daily Lecture and Discussion Notes 15-3
- Guided Reading Activity 15-3
- Reading Essentials and Study Guide 15-3
- Section Quiz 15-3

Transparencies

- Daily Focus Skills Transparency 15-3
- GeoQuiz Transparency 15-3

Multimedia

- Vocabulary PuzzleMaker Software
- Interactive Tutor Self-Assessment CD-ROM
- Presentation Plus! CD-ROM
- ExamView® Pro 3.0 Testmaker CD-ROM

One of the world's largest rain forests covers the center of the Democratic Republic of the Congo. The treetops form a **canopy,** or an umbrella-like forest covering so thick that sunlight rarely reaches the forest floor. More than 750 different kinds of trees grow here. The rain forests are being destroyed at a rapid rate, however, as they are cleared for timber and farmland.

The mighty Congo River—about 2,800 miles (4,506 km) long—weaves its way through the country on its journey to the Atlantic Ocean. The river current is so strong that it carries water about 100 miles (161 km) into the ocean. The Congo River and its tributaries, such as the Kasai River, provide **hydroelectric power,** or electricity generated by flowing water. In fact, these rivers produce more than 10 percent of all the world's hydroelectric power. The Congo is also the country's highway for trade and travel.

The Economy The Democratic Republic of the Congo has the opportunity to be a wealthy nation. The country exports gold, petroleum, diamonds, and copper. It is Central Africa's main source of industrial diamonds, as shown on the graph below. These diamonds are used in making strong industrial tools that cut metal. The country's factories make steel, cement, tires, shoes, textiles, processed foods, and beverages.

The Democratic Republic of the Congo has not been able to take full advantage of its rich resources, however. Why? One reason is the difficulty of transportation. Many of the minerals are found deep in the country's interior. Lack of roads and the thick rain forests make it hard to reach these areas. Another reason is political unrest. For many years, power-hungry leaders kept the nation's wealth for themselves. Then a

Leading Diamond-Producing Countries

Analyzing the Graph

Three of the world's top diamond-producing countries are in Africa south of the Sahara.

Economics What two countries produce the most diamonds in Africa?

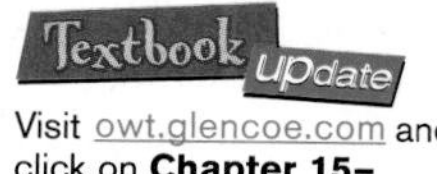

Visit owt.glencoe.com and click on **Chapter 15–Textbook Updates.**

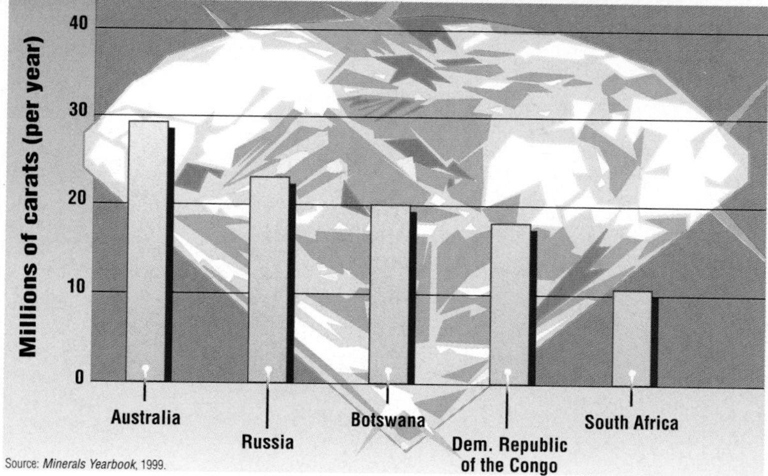

Chapter 15

Section 3, pages 422–427

Analyzing the Graph

Answer
Botswana and the Democratic Republic of the Congo

Skills Practice
About how many diamonds are produced each year in the Democratic Republic of the Congo? *(about 18,000 carats)*

Cultural Kaleidoscope

Democratic Republic of the Congo Among the ethnic groups living in this vast land are the Mbuti—people who grow no higher than about 59 inches (150 cm) of adult height. The Mbuti live a nomadic, hunter-gatherer life.

Measure student knowledge of physical features and political entities.

GeoQuiz Transparency 15-3

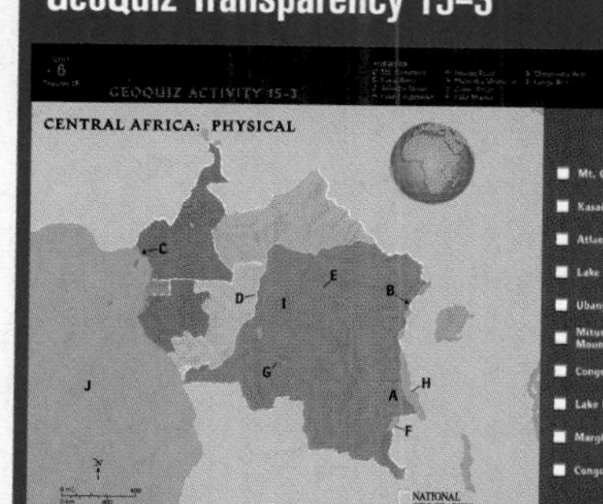

Team-Teaching Activity

History Invite a teacher with a background in world history to class to explain how the legacy of colonialism has caused problems for the countries of Africa. The discussion could include such points as the failure of European countries to train people who could administer government functions, the generally inadequate educational systems, national borders made problematic by ethnic differences, and damaging economic policies. Specifics from the history of the Democratic Republic of the Congo could be used to exemplify these problems. Have students discuss what role the United States might play today to help African nations overcome their challenges. **L1**

EE2 Places and Regions: Standard 6

Chapter 15

Section 3, pages 422–427

TEACH

Analyzing a Map Have students look at the physical map of Africa on page RA21. Have them locate the Democratic Republic of the Congo and note its location in relation to other countries. Have them speculate on how its size, location, and short coastline might affect its history and economic development. Tell them to write their ideas and check them as they study the section. **L1**

Daily Lecture Notes 15-3

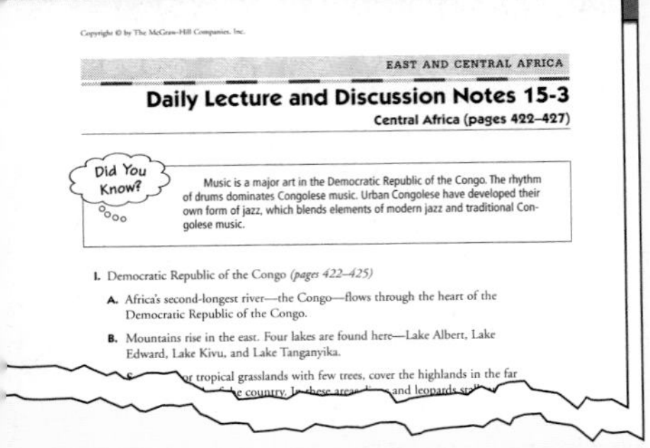

EAST AND CENTRAL AFRICA

Daily Lecture and Discussion Notes 15-3

Central Africa (pages 422–427)

Did You Know? Music is a major art in the Democratic Republic of the Congo. The rhythm of drums dominates Congolese music. Urban Congolese have developed their own form of jazz, which blends elements of modern jazz and traditional Congolese music.

I. Democratic Republic of the Congo (pages 422–425)

A. Africa's second-longest river—the Congo—flows through the heart of the Democratic Republic of the Congo.

B. Mountains rise in the east. Four lakes are found here—Lake Albert, Lake Edward, Lake Kivu, and Lake Tanganyika.

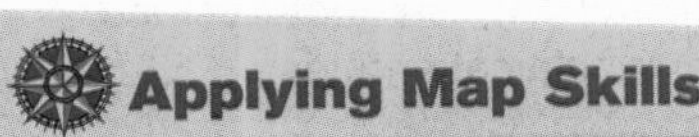

Applying Map Skills

Answers

1. Kenya, Tanzania, Uganda
2. Ethiopia

Skills Practice

How does Central Africa's elevation change as you move from west to east? *(The elevation rises.)*

civil war broke out in the late 1990s. This war has hurt efforts to develop the country's economy.

The People of the D.R.C. The Democratic Republic of the Congo's 53.6 million people consist of as many as 250 different ethnic groups. One of these groups is the Kongo people, after whom the country is named. The country's official language is French, but many people speak local languages, such as Lingala or Kingwana. More than 75 percent of Congolese are Christians. Most of these are Roman Catholic.

Most people in the Democratic Republic of the Congo live in rural areas. Less than one-third are city dwellers. Still, **Kinshasa,** the capital, has about 3 million people. After years of civil war, life in the country is still unsettled. The economy has nearly collapsed, and many people in the cities are without work.

In rural areas people follow traditional ways of life. They plant seeds, tend fields, and harvest crops. Most of the harvest goes to feeding the

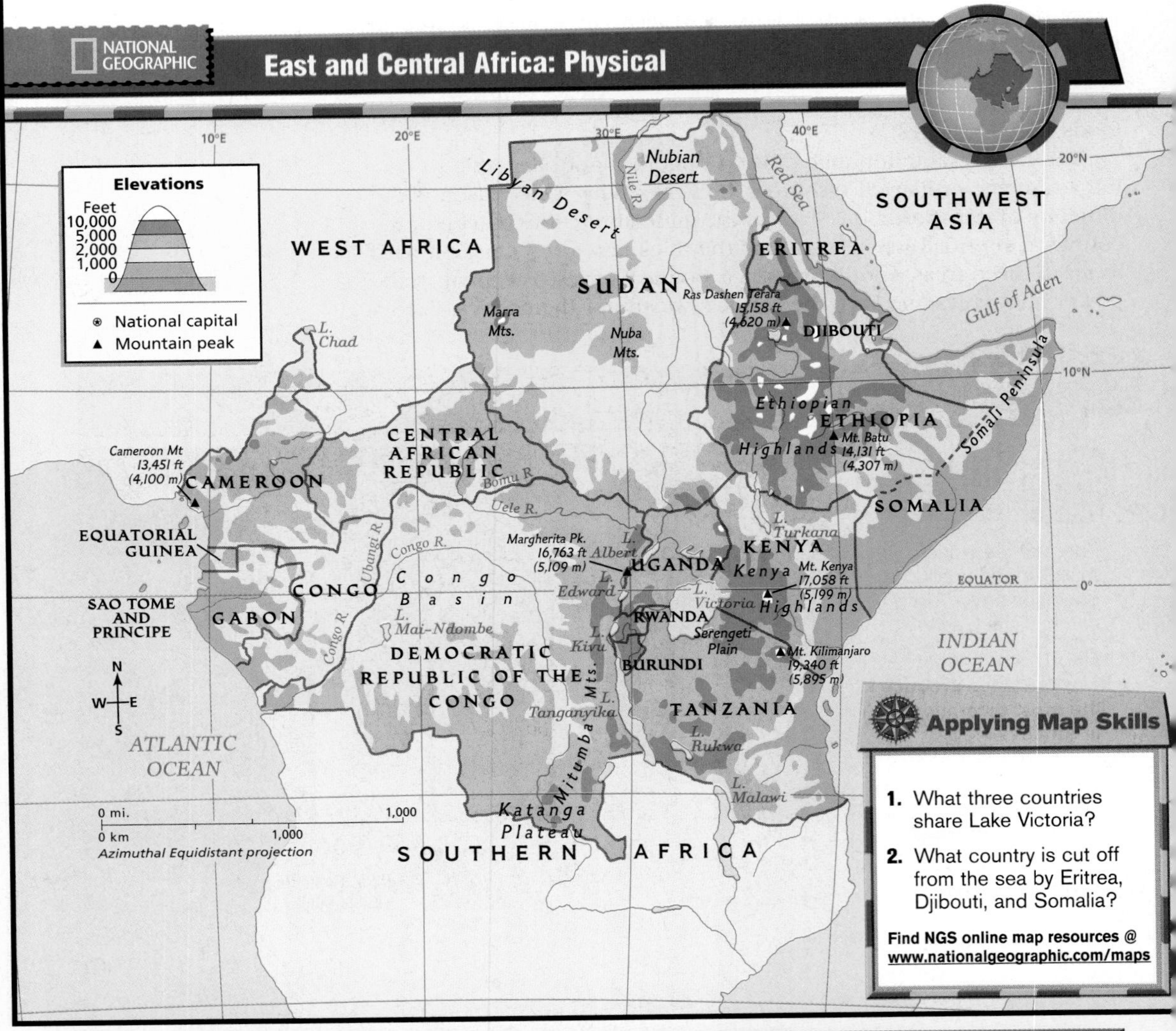

NATIONAL GEOGRAPHIC

East and Central Africa: Physical

Applying Map Skills

1. What three countries share Lake Victoria?
2. What country is cut off from the sea by Eritrea, Djibouti, and Somalia?

Find NGS online map resources @ www.nationalgeographic.com/maps

Critical Thinking Activity

Drawing Conclusions Have students list obstacles to the economic development of the Democratic Republic of the Congo. Next, have them identify and list the country's major resources. Then encourage students to use this information to draw conclusions about the most serious economic challenges facing the people of this country. Finally, have them suggest steps that people could take to try to overcome those challenges including future technological innovations that might help. **L2**

EE5 Environment and Society: Standards 15, 16

family. Any extra goes to the local market—or to the boats moving along the rivers—to sell or trade for goods the people need.

History and Government The Congo region was first settled about 10,000 years ago. The Bantu people—ancestors of most of the Congolese people today—moved here from Nigeria around the A.D. 600s and 700s. Several powerful kingdoms arose in the savannas south of the rain forests. The largest of these kingdoms was the **Kongo.**

In the late 1400s, European traders arrived in Central Africa. During the next 300 years, European and African agents enslaved many people from the Congo region. Most of these Africans were transported to the Americas.

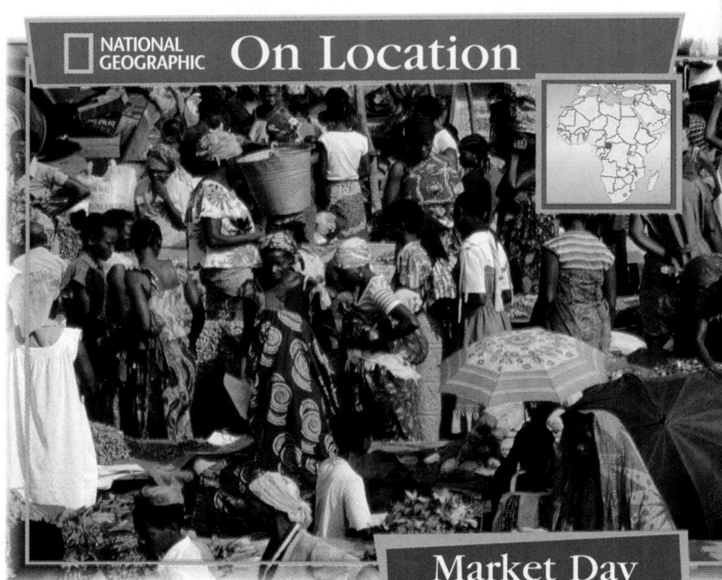

Market Day

This marketplace in Kinshasa, Democratic Republic of the Congo, is bustling with activity.

Culture How is this market different from where your family shops? How is it similar?

Like many other African nations, the Democratic Republic of the Congo was once a European colony. It became independent in 1960, and was renamed **Zaire.** A harsh dictator named Mobutu Sese Seko ruled Zaire until civil wars in neighboring Rwanda and Burundi sparked a civil war in Zaire. In 1997, Mobutu's government was finally overthrown, and again the country was given a new name. Zaire became the Democratic Republic of the Congo and another dictator took power. The country has not yet been able to organize a stable government.

✓Reading Check **What kind of government does the Democratic Republic of the Congo now have?**

Cameroon and the Central African Republic

Find Cameroon and the Central African Republic on the map on page 424. These countries lie just north of the Equator. Most people in the Central African Republic and Cameroon farm for a living. A few large plantations raise cacao, cotton, tobacco, and rubber for export. Some people herd livestock in areas that are safe from tsetse flies. A parasite that is often transmitted by the bite of the **tsetse** (SEET•see) **fly** causes a deadly disease called sleeping sickness. Turn to page 428 to find out more about sleeping sickness.

These two countries are only beginning to industrialize, or base their economies more on manufacturing and less on farming. Cameroon has had greater success in this effort. It has coastal ports and forest products, petroleum, and bauxite. The Central African Republic can claim only diamond mining as an important industry.

Chapter 15

Section 3, pages 422–427

More About the Photo

Market Day Farmers grow cassava, plantains, corn, rice, beans, and peanuts. Surplus harvest goes to market. As this market is in Kinshasa, the DRC's capital, located on the Congo River, there is a wide variety of goods traded here. The Congo links shoppers and merchants to this nation's only ocean port at Matadi.

Caption Answer enclosed supermarkets vs. open air, crowding, packaging, bartering vs. money use; comparable to farmers' markets, people get the goods they need

✓ Reading Check Answer

a dictatorship

Note-taking tip

Have students write the main idea of each subsection and give three supporting details. Then have them take turns reading their supporting details to a partner and having their partner state the main idea.

Guided Reading Activity 15–3

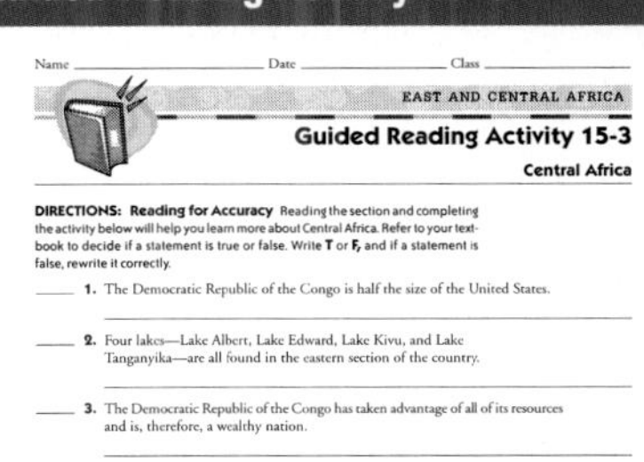
Name ______ Date ______ Class ______

EAST AND CENTRAL AFRICA

Guided Reading Activity 15-3

Central Africa

DIRECTIONS: Reading for Accuracy Reading the section and completing the activity below will help you learn more about Central Africa. Refer to your textbook to decide if a statement is true or false. Write **T** or **F**, and if a statement is false, rewrite it correctly.

____ 1. The Democratic Republic of the Congo is half the size of the United States.

____ 2. Four lakes—Lake Albert, Lake Edward, Lake Kivu, and Lake Tanganyika—are all found in the eastern section of the country.

____ 3. The Democratic Republic of the Congo has taken advantage of all of its resources and is, therefore, a wealthy nation.

____ 4. One of the four major ethnic groups is the Kongo people after whom the ... named.

Meeting Special Needs

Verbal/Linguistic Suggest that students who learn better verbally re-create the information in the maps and charts in Chapter 15 in verbal form. Have them review each map to identify what information they can learn. Guide students' observations by asking questions such as: **What physical features influence the climate of these countries? Which ethnic groups live in each country? What resources influence economic activities in these countries?** Then have them write their findings in sentences and use these as study aids. **L1**

Refer to *Inclusion for the Middle School Social Studies Classroom Strategies and Activities* in the TCR.

More About the Photos

Rural Living In equatorial countries, the weather is hot and rainy. People want houses which will shelter them from the rain, but which will allow air to circulate. In Gabon, lumber is abundant, so wooden roofs are common. The eastern DRC is a grassland, so thatched roofs are used.

Caption Answer Climate and available materials influence house styles.

Reading Check Answer

It has a greater variety of resources and coastal ports that can be used to ship goods.

ASSESS

Assign Section 3 Assessment as homework or an in-class activity.

Have students use the Interactive Tutor Self-Assessment CD-ROM to review Section 15–3.

Reading Check Answer

lumber and petroleum

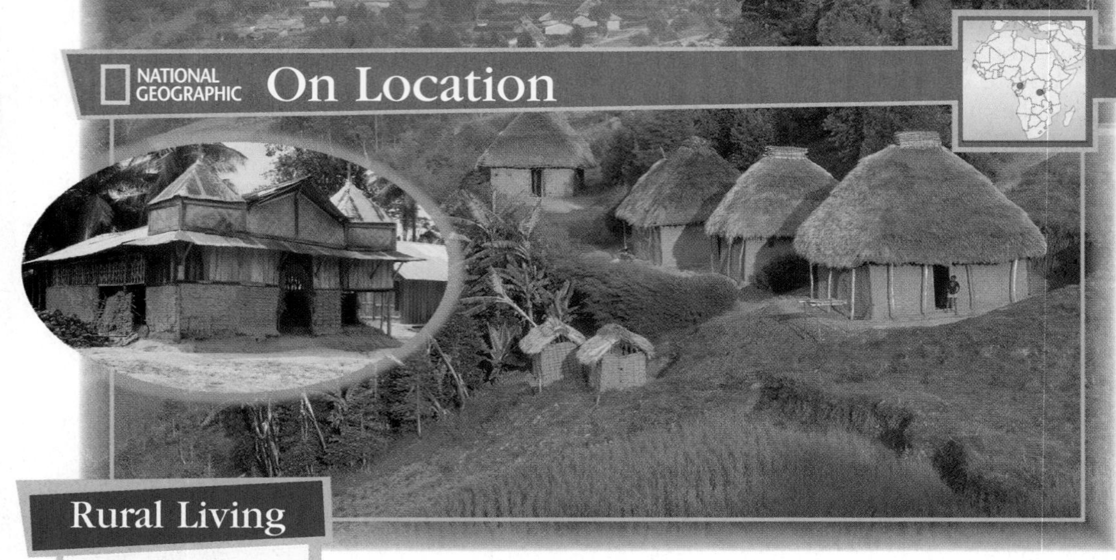

Rural Living

A row of thatch houses stands in a village in rural Democratic Republic of the Congo (right). This village in Gabon (above) boasts a very different type of house.

Culture **Why might house styles differ from country to country?**

Originally a German colony until 1918 and then a colony of France until 1960, the Central African Republic recognizes French as its official language. Yet most of its people speak Sango, the national language of the Central African Republic, to ease communication among the many ethnic groups. Cameroon, divided between the British and the French until 1960, uses both English and French as its official languages.

Reading Check **Why has Cameroon had greater success than the Central African Republic in industrializing?**

Congo and Gabon

Congo and Gabon both won their independence from France in 1960. In Congo, a plain stretches along the Atlantic coast and rises to low mountain ranges and plateaus. Here the Congo River supports most of the country's farmlands and industries. To the north, a large swampy area along the Ubangi River supports dense vine thickets and tropical trees. Both the Ubangi and Congo Rivers provide Congo with hydroelectric power. They also make Congo the door to the Atlantic Ocean for trade and transport.

More than half of Congo's and Gabon's people farm small plots of land. Both countries' economies rely on exports of lumber. They are beginning to depend more on rich offshore oil fields, however, for their main export. Congo also exports diamonds. Gabon suffers from **deforestation**, or the cutting of too many trees too quickly. Gabon also has valuable deposits of manganese and uranium.

Only about 1.2 million people live in Gabon—mainly along rivers or in the coastal capital, **Libreville.** Congo's 3.1 million people generally live along the Atlantic coast or near the capital, **Brazzaville.**

Reading Check **What two exports are most important to Congo and Gabon?**

Cooperative Learning Activity

Travel Brochure Put students into groups to create a four-page travel brochure that highlights the attractions of one of the countries in this chapter. Explain that the travel brochure should include both physical and cultural features that visitors would want to see. Remind students that one part of the brochure should have practical information such as clothing appropriate for climate, language(s) used in the country, and currency. Advise students that an effective brochure includes appealing visuals as well as brief, engaging text. **L2**

EE2 Places and Regions: Standard 4

Island Countries

Once a Spanish colony, Equatorial Guinea won its independence in 1968. Equatorial Guinea includes land on the mainland of Africa and five islands. Today the country is home to about 500,000 people. Most live on the mainland, although the capital and largest city—**Malabo** (mah•LAH•boh)—is on the country's largest island.

Farming, fishing, and harvesting wood are the country's main economic activities. For many years, timber and cacao grown in the islands' rich volcanic soil were the main exports. Oil was recently discovered and now leads all other exports.

The island country of São Tomé and Príncipe gained its independence from Portugal in 1975. The Portuguese had first settled here about 300 years earlier. At that time, no people lived on the islands. Today about 200,000 people live here, with almost all living on the main island of São Tomé.

São Tomé and Príncipe are volcanic islands. As a result, the soil is rich and productive. Farmworkers on the islands grow various crops, including coconuts and bananas for export. The biggest export crop, however, is cacao, which makes cocoa and chocolate.

✓Reading Check **Which of these island countries is also located on the African mainland?**

Assessment

Defining Terms

1. **Define** savanna, canopy, hydroelectric power, tsetse fly, deforestation.

Recalling Facts

2. **Economics** Why has the Democratic Republic of the Congo not taken full advantage of its resources?
3. **Place** How has Cameroon's location helped it prosper?
4. **Economics** What natural resource was recently discovered in Equatorial Guinea?

Critical Thinking

5. **Evaluating Information** Why do you think Europeans wanted to colonize parts of Africa, such as the Congo?
6. **Understanding Cause and Effect** How could furniture buyers in the United States affect lumber exports in Central Africa?

Graphic Organizer

7. **Organizing Information** Complete a chart like this with one fact about each country.

Country	Fact
Democratic Republic of the Congo	
Cameroon	
Central African Republic	
Congo	
Gabon	
Equatorial Guinea	
São Tomé & Príncipe	

Applying Social Studies Skills

8. **Analyzing Maps** Study the political map on page 407. The Ubangi River forms part of the boundaries of which countries?

Section 3 Assessment

1. The terms are defined in the Glossary.
2. because transportation is difficult and there is political unrest
3. Cameroon has coastal ports which stimulate trade and bring both money and goods into the country.
4. oil
5. *Possible answer:* Europeans desired natural resources in the region.
6. Answers should focus on the desire of American buyers for the valuable woods in the region. If deforestation decreases the supply of wood for international trade, the economies of Central Africa will slump.
7. Answers will vary.
8. Central African Republic, Congo, and Democratic Republic of the Congo

Chapter 15

Section 3, pages 422–427

Section Quiz 15-3

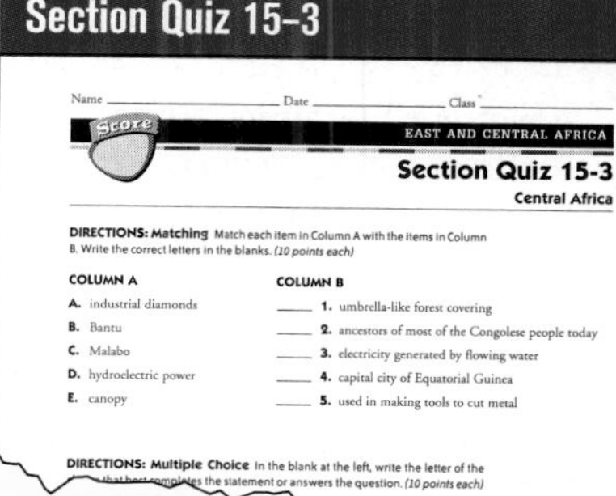

Name ____ Date ____ Class ____

Score — EAST AND CENTRAL AFRICA

Section Quiz 15-3

Central Africa

DIRECTIONS: Matching Match each item in Column A with the items in Column B. Write the correct letters in the blanks. (10 points each)

COLUMN A	COLUMN B
A. industrial diamonds	___ 1. umbrella-like forest covering
B. Bantu	___ 2. ancestors of most of the Congolese people today
C. Malabo	___ 3. electricity generated by flowing water
D. hydroelectric power	___ 4. capital city of Equatorial Guinea
E. canopy	___ 5. used in making tools to cut metal

DIRECTIONS: Multiple Choice In the blank at the left, write the letter of the ... the statement or answers the question. (10 points each)

✓ Reading Check Answer

Equatorial Guinea

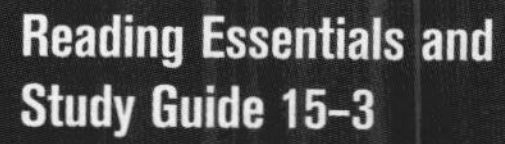

Reading Essentials and Study Guide 15-3

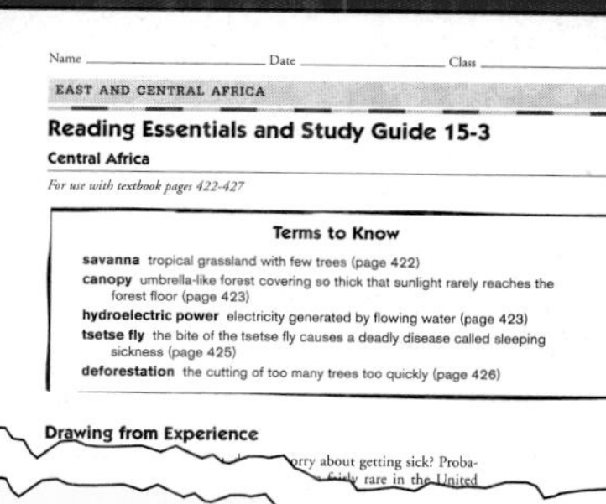

Name ____ Date ____ Class ____

EAST AND CENTRAL AFRICA

Reading Essentials and Study Guide 15-3

Central Africa

For use with textbook pages 422-427

Terms to Know

savanna tropical grassland with few trees (page 422)
canopy umbrella-like forest covering so thick that sunlight rarely reaches the forest floor (page 423)
hydroelectric power electricity generated by flowing water (page 423)
tsetse fly the bite of the tsetse fly causes a deadly disease called sleeping sickness (page 425)
deforestation the cutting of too many trees too quickly (page 426)

Drawing from Experience

Enrich

Have students research the history of one of the countries covered in this section and prepare an illustrated report displaying what they found.

4 CLOSE

Have students take an imaginary trip along the Congo River and describe the landscapes they would see.

TEACH

Point out that there are two kinds of diseases. Noncommunicable diseases are based on inheritance or lifestyle, whereas communicable diseases are spread by contact. Ask students if they have ever had a cold or flu. Point out that these are common diseases spread from one person to another. Explain that some diseases are transmitted by contact with animals. L1

More About Tsetse Flies

The threat of sleeping sickness has had a significant impact on settlement patterns in Africa. People avoid areas with large numbers of these flies, cutting down on the land that can be used for farming and other purposes.

Interdisciplinary Connections

Science Malaria is another dangerous disease that afflicts people in Africa, as well as in other areas of the world. Have students research the disease to find out where it is found, what causes the disease, what health problems it causes, how it is treated, and what steps are being taken to prevent it. Have them present their findings to the class in an illustrated report or oral presentation.

Making Connections

CULTURE | GOVERNMENT | PEOPLE | TECHNOLOGY

Battling Sleeping Sickness

Since the 1300s, people in Africa south of the Sahara have battled a disease now commonly called sleeping sickness. Yet it was not until the early 1900s that scientists began to understand the disease and that it was transmitted through the bite of an infected tsetse fly.

The Tsetse Fly

Found only in parts of Africa, the tsetse fly is the common name for any of about 21 species of flies that can transmit sleeping sickness. The flies are larger than the houseflies common to the United States. Tsetse flies thrive in forests and in areas of thick shrubbery and trees near lakes, ponds, and rivers.

Although the bite of a tsetse fly is painful, the bite itself is not necessarily harmful. What gives the tsetse fly its dreadful reputation is the disease-causing parasite it may carry.

Sleeping Sickness

The World Health Organization (WHO) estimates that more than 60 million people in Africa are at risk of being infected with sleeping sickness. As many as 500,000 people carry the disease. If left untreated, the disease leads to a slow breakdown of bodily functions and, eventually, death. Sleeping sickness need not be fatal. When the disease is treated in its early stages, most people recover. Treatment is expensive, however, and many of those infected lack medical care. Even if they are cured, they may become infected again.

Governments Work Together

To prevent the spread of sleeping sickness requires a united action on the part of the governments of the many African nations affected by the disease. Thirty-seven African countries lie within the African tsetse belt. This belt covers a total of 10 million sq. km in an area stretching from Senegal to South Africa. African leaders have met in conferences and passed a resolution calling for the eradication of the sleeping-sickness-causing tsetse flies from the continent. Perhaps working together to fight a common enemy will encourage the governments to consult on other regional issues, as well.

Making the Connection

1. Where do tsetse flies live?
2. What causes sleeping sickness?
3. **Drawing Conclusions** Why is treatment of infected humans only part of the solution to eliminating sleeping sickness?

◄ Children in Central Africa have learned to report bites of the tsetse fly.

Making the Connection

1. in forests and thick shrubbery near lakes, ponds, and rivers in some areas of Africa south of the Sahara
2. a parasite that some tsetse flies carry
3. Natural areas where the flies live must be cleared to reduce the number of flies, which will limit the danger to people. In addition, animals that have the parasite need to be removed so that the parasite is not spread.

Chapter 15 Reading Review

Section 1 East Africa: Kenya and Tanzania

Terms to Know
- coral reef
- poaching
- free enterprise system
- cassava
- sisal
- habitat
- eco-tourist

Main Idea

Both Kenya and Tanzania are countries of diverse landscapes and peoples.

✓ Place The western part of Kenya is marked by highlands and the wide Great Rift Valley.

✓ Economics Many people in Kenya are farmers. Coffee and tea are grown for export. Tourism is also a major industry in Kenya.

✓ Culture Kenya's people come from many different cultures. They speak Swahili and English.

✓ Economics Farming and tourism are the main economic activities in Tanzania.

✓ Government Tanzania's government has been stable and democratic.

Section 2 Other Countries of East Africa

Terms to Know
- drought
- plate
- clan
- endangered species
- genocide
- refugee

Main Idea

The other countries of East Africa have all been scarred by conflict in recent years.

✓ History Sudan has been torn by a civil war between the northern Muslim Arabs and the southern Christian peoples.

✓ Human/Environment Interaction In the past, drought has caused severe famine in Ethiopia.

✓ History Fighting between rival clans and drought have caused suffering in Somalia.

✓ History Rwanda and Burundi have suffered a brutal civil war between the Hutu and the Tutsi ethnic groups.

Section 3 Central Africa

Terms to Know
- savanna
- canopy
- hydroelectric power
- tsetse fly
- deforestation

Main Idea

Central Africa has rich natural resources that are largely undeveloped because of civil war and poor government decisions.

✓ Movement The Congo River—the second-largest river in Africa—provides transportation and hydroelectric power.

✓ Place The Democratic Republic of the Congo has many resources but has not been able to take full advantage of them.

✓ Government A recent civil war in the Democratic Republic of the Congo overthrew a harsh ruler, but an elected government is not yet in place.

✓ Culture Although English and French are the official languages of the Central African Republic, most of its people speak Sango. Sango is the national language and eases communication among the many ethnic groups.

✓ Economics The economies of Congo and Gabon rely on exports of lumber.

Reading Review

Use the Chapter 15 Reading Review to preview, review, condense, or reteach the chapter.

Preview/Review

Use the Terms to Know lists to help students review and study.

Activity Have students create crossword puzzles for 10 of the terms from the chapter, exchange papers with another student, and try to complete their partner's puzzle.

Vocabulary PuzzleMaker Software reinforces the vocabulary terms used in Chapter 15.

The Interactive Tutor Self-Assessment CD-ROM allows students to review Chapter 15 content.

Condense

Have students read the Chapter 15 summary statements.

Chapter 15 Guided Reading Activities

Chapter 15 Audio Program

Reteach

Reteaching Activity 15

Chapter 15 Reading Essentials and Study Guide

Chapter Culminating Activity

Illustrated Encyclopedias Have students work in small groups to create an illustrated encyclopedia for East and Central Africa. Offer the following as a sample entry: "T is for Tanganyika . . . a lake in southeastern Central Africa on the border between the Democratic Republic of the Congo and Tanzania. Lake Tanganyika is the world's longest freshwater lake and the second-deepest, after Lake Baikal in Russia." Students may consult almanacs and encyclopedias for items beginning with certain letters. Display the finished encyclopedias. *NOTE: This activity may be completed separately or you may wish students to incorporate it into their Current Events Journals.* L1

EE2 Places and Regions: Standard 4

Assessment and Activities

GLENCOE TECHNOLOGY

MindJogger Videoquiz
Use MindJogger to review the Chapter 15 content.

Available in VHS.

Using Key Terms

1. f
2. i
3. e
4. j
5. h
6. c
7. a
8. b
9. d
10. g

Reviewing the Main Ideas

11. "pulling together"
12. on the islands of Zanzibar and Pemba
13. lions, wild dogs, wildebeests, antelope
14. Goods are taken by road to Lake Tanganyika, then sent by boat to Tanzania or the Democratic Republic of the Congo.
15. Hutu and Tutsi
16. Sudan
17. Lack of roads and thick rainforests make it hard to transport mineral resources for trade.
18. Cameroon's coastal ports provide a place to ship and receive materials for its industrial development.
19. French. It was a colony of France prior to gaining independence.
20. the Portuguese

Assessment and Activities

Using Key Terms

Match the terms in Part A with their definitions in Part B.

A.

1. canopy
2. tsetse fly
3. poaching
4. endangered species
5. habitat
6. savanna
7. hydroelectric power
8. drought
9. refugee
10. eco-tourist

B.

a. electricity created by flowing water
b. extended period of extreme dryness
c. tropical grassland with few trees
d. person who flees to another country for safety
e. hunting and killing animals illegally
f. topmost layer of a rain forest
g. people who travel to view natural wonders
h. environment in which an animal species normally lives
i. insect whose bite can cause sleeping sickness
j. plant or animal in danger of dying out

Reviewing the Main Ideas

Section 1 East Africa: Kenya and Tanzania

11. **Culture** What does the term *harambee* mean to Kenyans?
12. **Economics** In which part of Tanzania are cloves produced?
13. **Region** Name some of the animals that live on the Serengeti Plain.

Section 2 Other Countries of East Africa

14. **Economics** How do Burundi and Rwanda get their goods to foreign buyers?
15. **Culture** What two ethnic groups are fighting in Rwanda and Burundi?
16. **Place** What is the largest country in Africa?

Section 3 Central Africa

17. **Economy** How has transportation affected the economy of the Democratic Republic of the Congo?
18. **Human/Environment Interaction** How has being a coastal country helped Cameroon become more industrialized?
19. **Culture** What is the official language of the Central African Republic? Why?
20. **History** Who originally settled São Tomé and Príncipe?

East and Central Africa

Place Location Activity

On a separate sheet of paper, match the letters on the map with the numbered places listed below.

1. Congo River
2. Cameroon
3. Kilimanjaro
4. Central African Republic
5. Sudan
6. Tanzania
7. Democratic Republic of the Congo
8. Somalia
9. Rwanda
10. Gabon

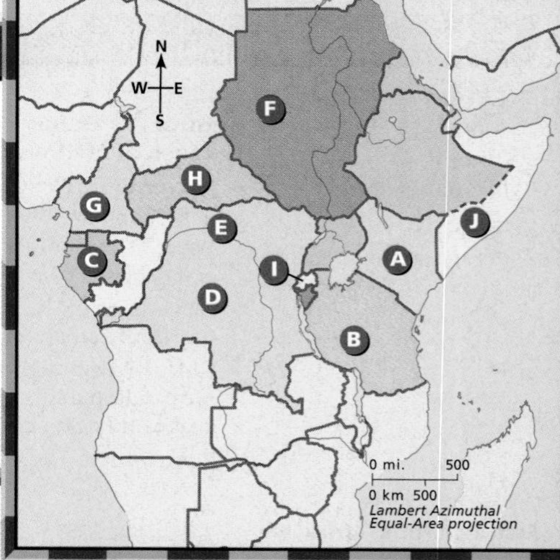

NATIONAL GEOGRAPHIC **Place Location Activity**

1. E
2. G
3. A
4. H
5. F
6. B
7. D
8. J
9. I
10. C

Critical Thinking

21. Good transportation is needed to move goods to markets.
22. Trees are cut down; Land cannot hold soil or rain water in place; Land dries; Soil blows away; Desert.

Current Events Journal

23. Have students illustrate their posters with photos and maps and use them to give a presentation to the class.

Self-Check Quiz Visit the ***Our World Today: People, Places, and Issues*** Web site at owt.glencoe.com and click on **Chapter 15–Self-Check Quizzes** to prepare for the Chapter Test.

Critical Thinking

21. **Analyzing Information** Much of East Africa depends on agriculture as a main economic activity. Why is a good transportation system important to an agricultural society?
22. **Sequencing Information** In a diagram like the one below, describe and put in order the steps that can lead to the creation of a desert.

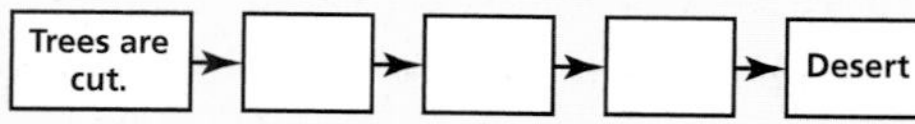

Current Events Journal

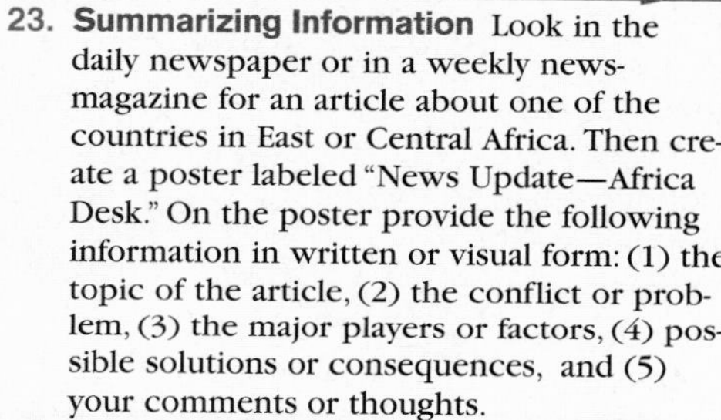

23. **Summarizing Information** Look in the daily newspaper or in a weekly newsmagazine for an article about one of the countries in East or Central Africa. Then create a poster labeled "News Update—Africa Desk." On the poster provide the following information in written or visual form: (1) the topic of the article, (2) the conflict or problem, (3) the major players or factors, (4) possible solutions or consequences, and (5) your comments or thoughts.

Mental Mapping Activity

24. **Focusing on the Region** Create a simple outline map of Africa, then label the following:
    - Sudan
    - Indian Ocean
    - Kenya
    - Tanzania
    - Democratic Republic of the Congo
    - Lake Victoria
    - Uganda
    - Congo
    - Nile River

Technology Skills Activity

25. **Developing a Multimedia Presentation** Choose one of Africa's endangered animals and create a multimedia presentation about it. Include pictures or video clips of the animal, maps of its habitat area, and the steps being taken to protect this animal.

Standardized Test Practice

Directions: Study the map below, and then answer the following question.

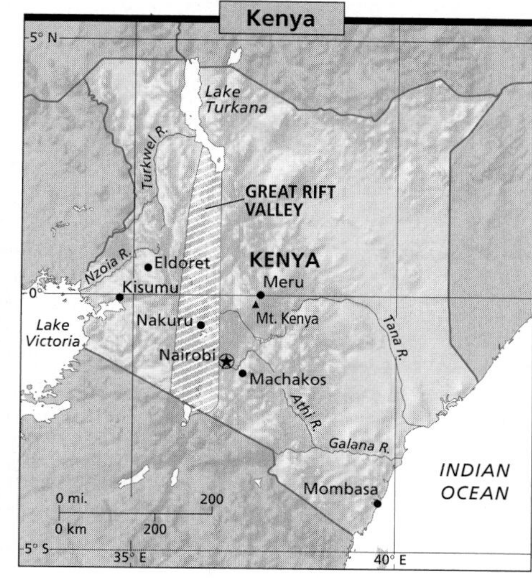

1. **About how many miles is it from Nairobi to Mombasa?**
   F 100 miles
   G 200 miles
   H 300 miles
   J 400 miles

Test-Taking Tip: Look carefully at the map key to understand its *scale,* or distance from one point to another. If you find it hard to judge distances by eye, use a small piece of scrap paper to measure the units described in the key.

431

Assessment and Activities

Standardized Test Practice

1. H

Tested Objectives: Analyzing a map, drawing conclusions

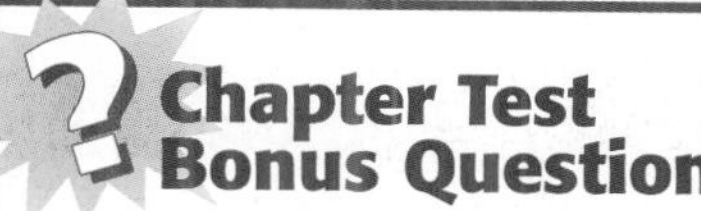

Chapter Test Bonus Question

This question may be used for extra credit on the chapter test.

What type of ecosystem covers a large portion of Central Africa north and south of the Equator? *(tropical rain forest)*

Our World Today online

Have students visit the Web site at **owt.glencoe.com** to review Chapter 15 and take the Self-Check Quiz.

Mental Mapping Activity

24. This exercise helps students visualize the countries and geographic features they have been studying and understand the relationship among various points. Accept all attempts at freehand mapping that show places in the correct relationship to one another.

Technology Skills Activity

25. Students might broaden their study by applying what they have learned to endangered animals in other parts of the world.

Chapter 16 Resources

Note: The following materials may be used when teaching Chapter 16.
Section level support materials are shown at point of use in the margins of the Teacher Wraparound Edition.

Timesaving Tools

TeacherWorks™ All-In-One Planner and Resource Center

- **Interactive Teacher Edition** See the **Interactive Teacher Edition** CD-ROM to electronically integrate your Teacher Wraparound Edition and blackline masters.
- **Interactive Lesson Planner** Organize your week, month, semester, or year with all the lesson helps you need. The **Interactive Lesson Planner** CD-ROM contains all Chapter 16 resources.

Use Glencoe's **Presentation Plus!** multimedia teacher tool to easily present dynamic lessons that visually excite your students. Using Microsoft PowerPoint® you can customize the presentations to create your own personalized lessons.

TEACHING TRANSPARENCIES

Graphic Organizer Transparency and Student Activity 16

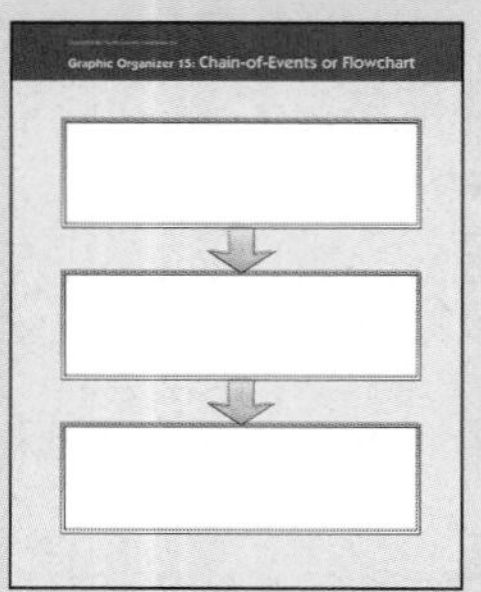

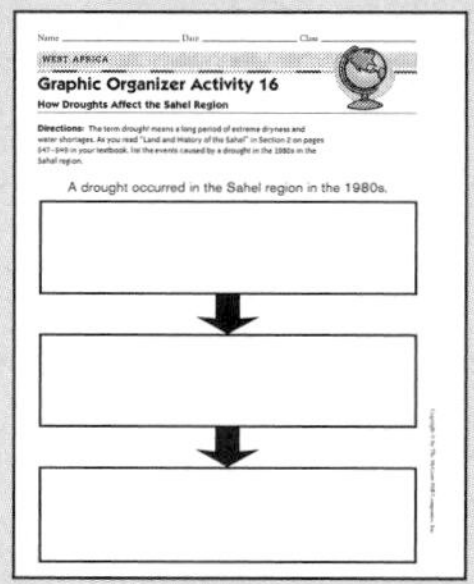

FOLDABLES™ Study Organizer

Foldables are three-dimensional, interactive graphic organizers that help students practice basic writing skills, review key vocabulary terms, and identify main ideas. Every chapter contains a Foldable activity, with additional chapter activities found in the ***Reading and Study Skills Foldables*** booklet.

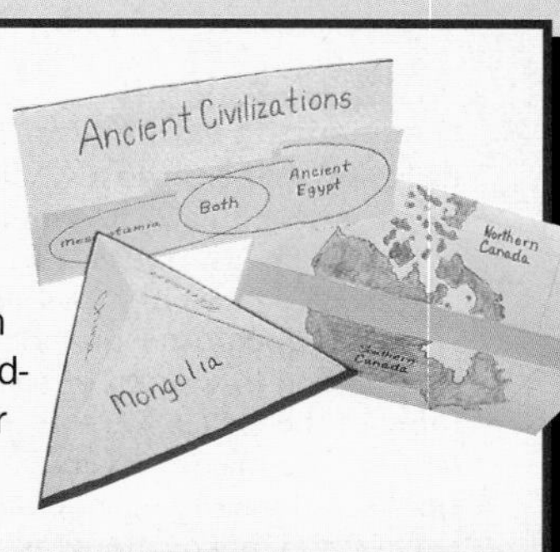

ENRICHMENT AND EXTENSION

Enrichment Activity 16

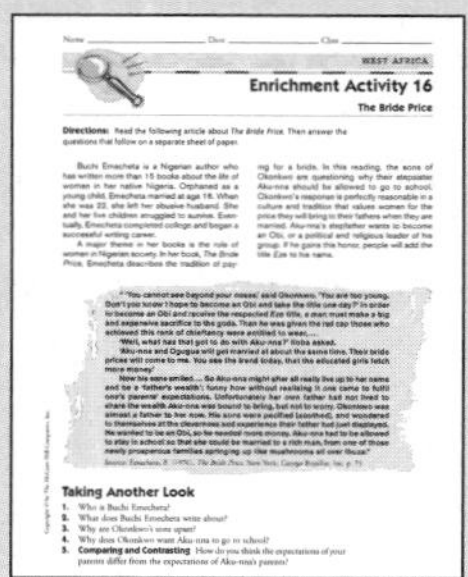

Cooperative Learning Activity 16

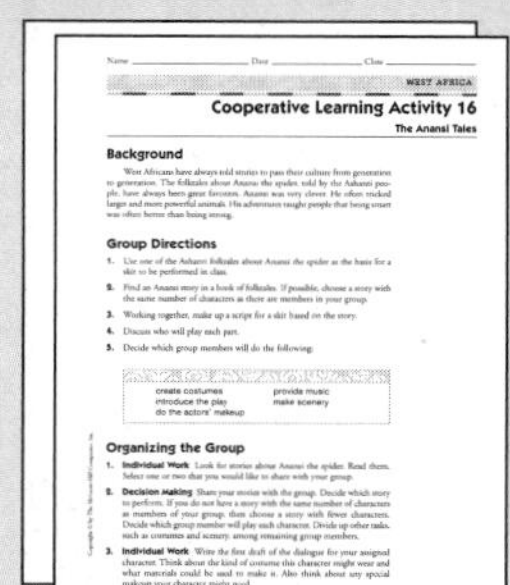

MAP AND GEOGRAPHY SKILLS

Chapter Map Activity 16

GeoLab Activity 16

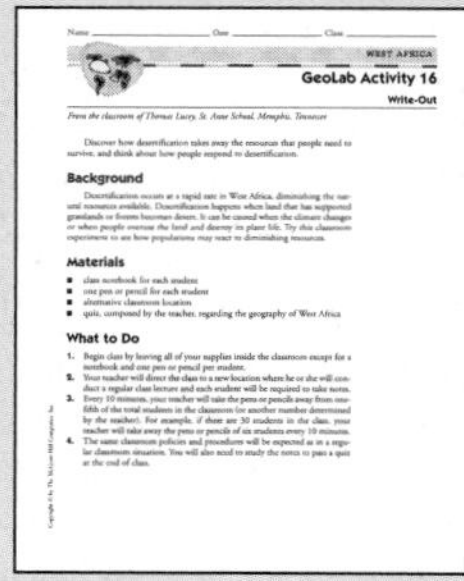

STANDARDIZED ASSESSMENT SKILLS

Critical Thinking Skills Activity 16

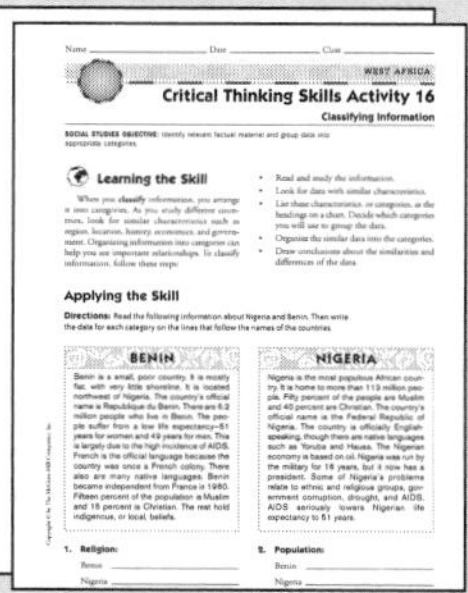

Map and Graph Skills Activity 16

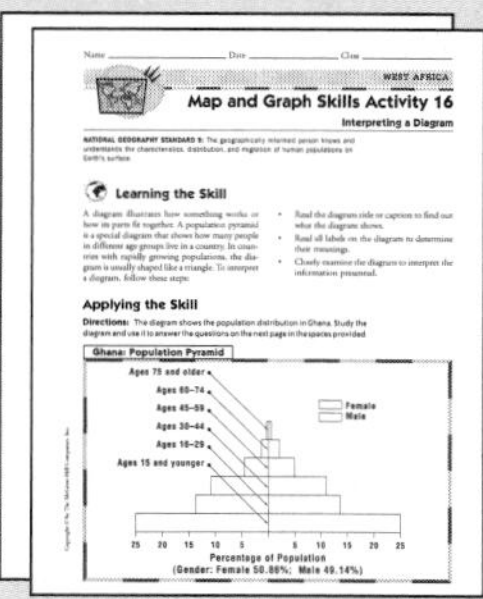

Reading and Writing Skills Activity 16

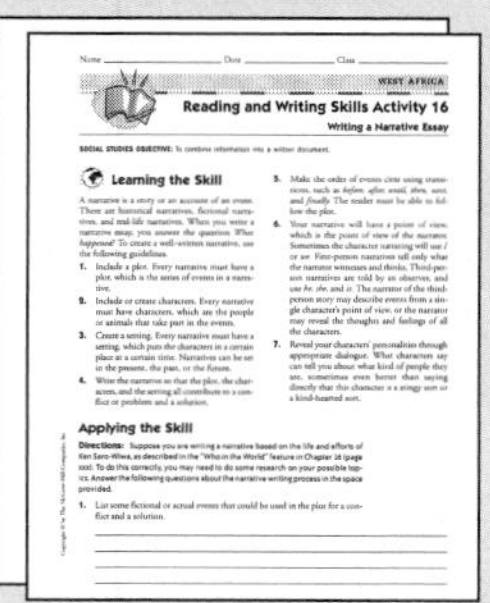

Standardized Test Practice Workbook Activity 16

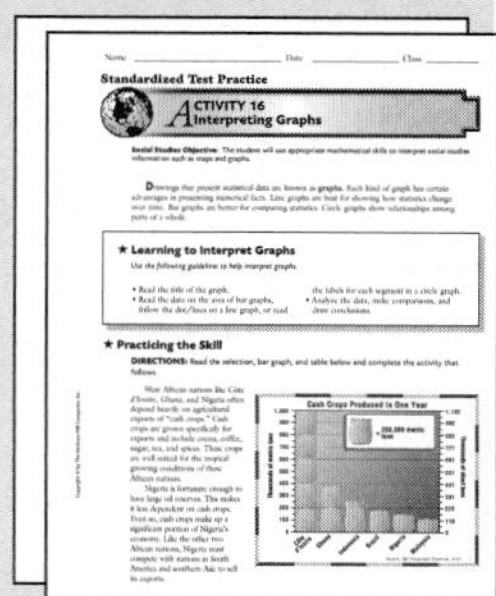

REVIEW AND REINFORCEMENT

Chapter Skills Activity 16

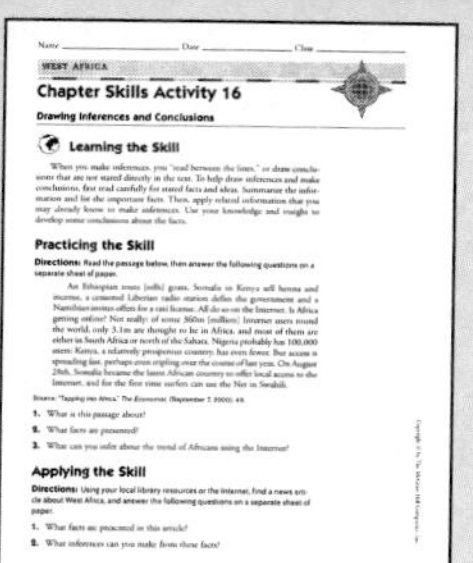

Take-Home Review Activity 16

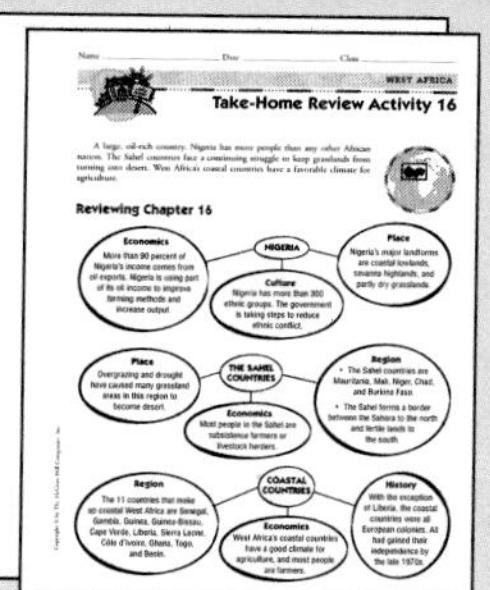

Reteaching Activity 16

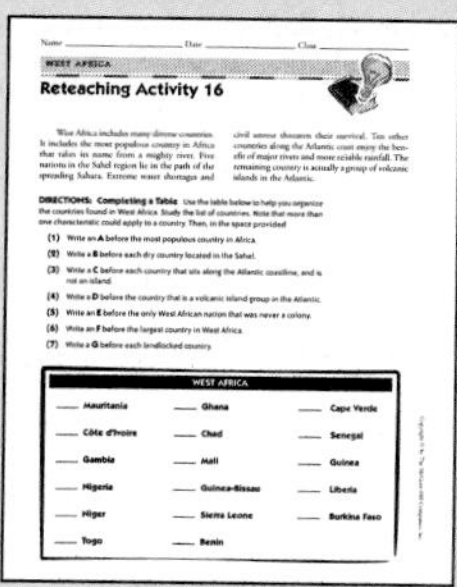

Vocabulary Activity 16

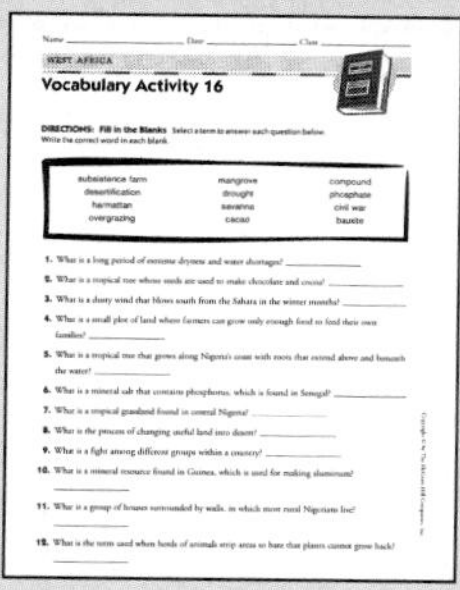

Workbook Activity 16

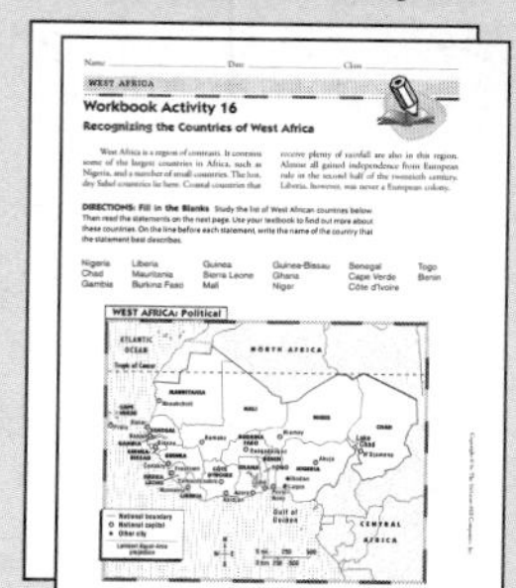

ASSESSMENT

GLENCOE'S ASSESSMENT ADVANTAGE

Chapter 16 Test, Form A

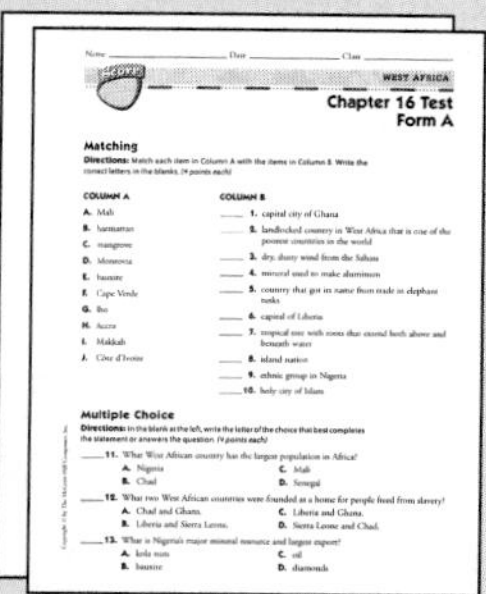

Chapter 16 Test, Form B

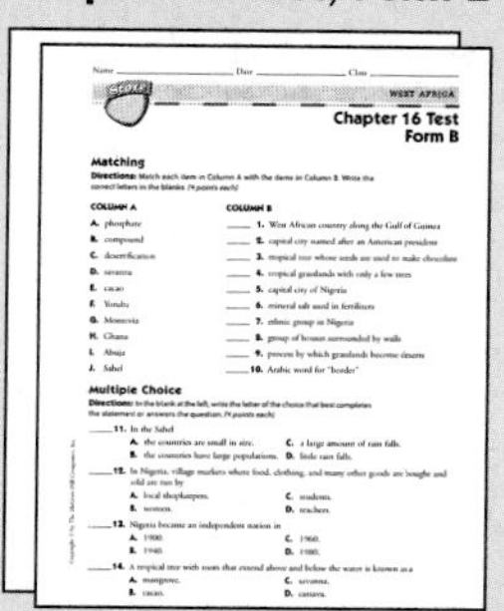

Performance Assessment Activity 16

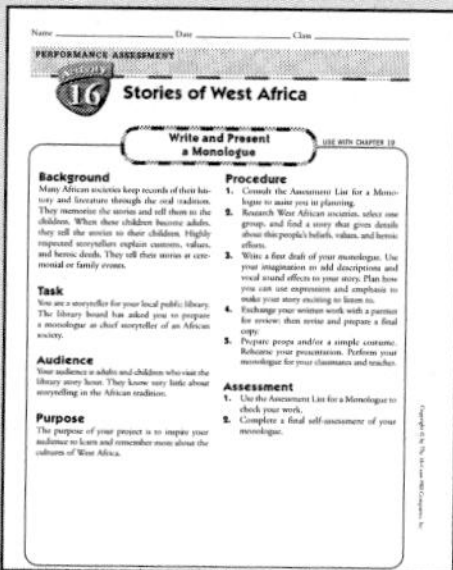

ExamView® Pro 3.0 Testmaker CD-ROM

MULTIMEDIA

- **National Geographic's The World and Its People**
- **MindJogger Videoquiz**
- **Vocabulary PuzzleMaker Software**
- **Interactive Tutor Self-Assessment CD-ROM**
- **ExamView® Pro 3.0 Testmaker CD-ROM**
- **Interactive Lesson Planner CD-ROM**
- **Interactive Teacher Edition CD-ROM**
- **Skillbuilder Interactive Workbook CD-ROM, Level 1**
- **Presentation Plus! CD-ROM**
- **Audio Program**

SPANISH RESOURCES

The following Spanish language materials are available in the Spanish Resources binder:

- **Spanish Chapter Summaries**
- **Spanish Vocabulary Activities**
- **Spanish Guided Reading Activities**
- **Spanish Quizzes and Tests**
- **Spanish Take-Home Review Activities**
- **Spanish Reteaching Activities**

Meeting National Standards

Geography for Life

All of the 18 standards are demonstrated in Unit 6. The following ones are highlighted in Chapter 16:

Section 1 **EE4 The World in Spatial Terms: Standards 1, 2, 3**

EE4 Human Systems: Standards 9, 10

Section 2 **EE2 Places and Regions: Standards 4, 5, 6**

EE3 Physical Systems: Standards 7, 8

EE4 Human Systems: Standards 9, 10, 11, 12, 13

EE5 Environment and Society: Standards 14, 15, 16

For a complete listing of National Geography Standards and entire text correlation, see pages T22–T29.

Local Objectives

___

Chapter 16 Planning Guide

SECTION RESOURCES

Daily Objectives	Reproducible Resources	Multimedia Resources
Section 1 **Nigeria** **Suggested Pacing = 1 day** **1.** Describe the land and climates found in Nigeria. **2.** Explain Nigeria's economy. **3.** Compare Nigeria's ethnic groups.	Reproducible Lesson Plan 16-1 Daily Lecture and Discussion Notes 16-1 Guided Reading Activity 16-1 Reading Essentials and Study Guide 16-1 Section Quiz 16-1*	Daily Focus Skills Transparency 16-1 GeoQuiz Transparency 16-1 Vocabulary PuzzleMaker Software Interactive Tutor Self-Assessment CD-ROM ExamView® Pro 3.0 Testmaker CD-ROM Presentation Plus! CD-ROM
Section 2 **Other Countries of West Africa** **Suggested Pacing = 1 day** **1.** Describe the Sahel's location and its history. **2.** Explain how people in the Sahel countries live. **3.** Compare the coastal countries, their history, and peoples.	Reproducible Lesson Plan 16-2 Daily Lecture and Discussion Notes 16-2 Guided Reading Activity 16-2 Reading Essentials and Study Guide 16-2 Section Quiz 16-2*	Daily Focus Skills Transparency 16-2 GeoQuiz Transparency 16-1 Vocabulary PuzzleMaker Software Interactive Tutor Self-Assessment CD-ROM ExamView® Pro 3.0 Testmaker CD-ROM Presentation Plus! CD-ROM

00:00 **Out of Time?** Assign the **Reading Essentials and Study Guide** for this chapter.

*Also available in Spanish

KEY TO ABILITY LEVELS

Teaching strategies have been coded for varying learning styles and abilities.

L1 **BASIC** activities for all students
L2 **AVERAGE** activities for average to above-average students
L3 **CHALLENGING** activities for above-average students
ELL **ENGLISH LANGUAGE LEARNER** activities

Blackline Master
Software
CD-ROM
Audiocassette
Transparency
Videocassette
Block Scheduling
DVD

World Hunger

Peter John Arroyo
Space Coast Middle School
Port St. John, Florida

Remind students that hunger is often commonplace among people living in developing countries. Many of the people are subsistence farmers who grow only enough to feed their families. Plan a Hunger Awareness Day at school to show students the seriousness of world hunger. To prepare for this event, ask students to (1) find 20 Web sites regarding world hunger; (2) find two hunger events advertised on the Internet with an explanation of how students can get involved; and (3) design and produce a poster regarding world hunger. Display the posters around the school on the designated Hunger Awareness Day. Have each student turn in a one-page report listing the 20 Web sites they found as well as a paragraph summarizing what they learned about world hunger.

OUR WORLD TODAY Online

Use our Web site for additional resources. All essential content is covered in the Student Edition.

You and your students can visit owt.glencoe.com, the Web site companion to *Our World Today*. This innovative integration of electronic and print media offers your students a wealth of opportunities. The student text directs students to the Web site for the following options:

- Chapter Overviews
- Student Web Activities
- Self-Check Quizzes
- Textbook Updates

Answers are provided for you in the Web Activity Lesson Plan. Additional Web resources and Interactive Tutor puzzles are also available.

TEACHER'S CORNER

Index to National Geographic Magazine:

The following articles may be used for research relating to this chapter:

- "People of Heaven," by Peter Godwin, August 2000.
- "African Marriage Rituals," by Carol Beckwith and Angela Fisher, November 1999.
- "African Gold," by Carol Beckwith and Angela Fisher, October 1996.

National Geographic Society Products Available From Glencoe:

To order the following products for use with this chapter, contact your local Glencoe sales representative or call Glencoe at 1-800-334-7344:

- *STV: World Geography* (Videodisc)
- *Picture Atlas of the World* (CD-ROM)
- *PicturePack: Geography of Africa* (Transparencies)
- *MapPack: Africa* (Transparencies)
- *ZipZapMap! World* (Software)

Additional National Geographic Society Products:

To order the following products for use with this chapter, call National Geographic Society at 1-800-368-2728:

- *Complete National Geographic: 111 Years of National Geographic Magazine* (CD-ROM)
- *Africa* (Video)
- *Endangered Animals: Survivors on the Brink* (Video)
- *Healing the Earth* (Video)
- *Physical Earth* (Map)
- *Population* (Map)
- *National Geographic Atlas of the World, Seventh Edition* (Book)
- *PicturePack: Ancient Civilizations: Africa* (Transparencies)
- *PictureShow: Ancient Civilizations: Africa* (CD-ROM)

NGS ONLINE

Access National Geographic's Web site for current events, activities, links, interactive features, and archives.
www.nationalgeographic.com

Introducing
Chapter 16

Introduce students to chapter content and key terms by having them access Chapter Overview 16 at owt.glencoe.com

Chapter Objectives

1. Identify the physical features and climates of the countries of West Africa.
2. Explain how West Africa's economies relate to the natural resources in the region.
3. Compare the different peoples that live in West Africa.
4. Explain the impact of historical influences on West Africa.

GLENCOE TECHNOLOGY

NATIONAL GEOGRAPHIC

The World and Its People Video Program

Chapter 19 West Africa
The following segments enhance the study of this chapter:

- **Dino Dig**
- **Rain Forest Walkway**

Available in DVD and VHS.

MindJogger Videoquiz
Use MindJogger to preview the Chapter 16 content.

Available in VHS.

Chapter 16 West Africa

The World and Its People NATIONAL GEOGRAPHIC

To learn more about the people and places of West Africa, view ***The World and Its People*** **Chapter 19** video.

Our World Today online

Chapter Overview Visit the ***Our World Today: People, Places, and Issues*** Web site at owt.glencoe.com and click on **Chapter 16—Chapter Overviews** to preview information about West Africa.

432

Two-Minute Lesson Launcher

Ask students what kind of environment they think of when they hear the name Africa. *(They are likely to offer such ideas as rain forest and desert.)* Write their suggestions. Then have them look at the physical map on page RA21. Point out that Africa extends from north of the Tropic of Cancer to south of the Tropic of Capricorn. Ask them, based on that information, what answers they might give now. Write these new suggestions and have them copy both sets of responses. Advise them to refer to their notes as they study the chapter to see which gives a more accurate picture of Africa. **L1**

Summarizing Information Study Foldable Make this foldable to determine what you already know, to identify what you want to know, and to summarize what you learn about West Africa.

Step 1 Fold a sheet of paper into thirds from top to bottom.

Step 2 Turn the paper horizontally, unfold, and label the three columns as shown.

Know | Want to Know | Learned

Reading and Writing Before you read the chapter, write what you already know about West Africa under the "Know" tab. Write what you want to know about West Africa under the "Want to Know" tab. Then, as you read the chapter, write what you learn under the "Learned" tab. Be sure to include information you wanted to know (from the second column).

Why It Matters

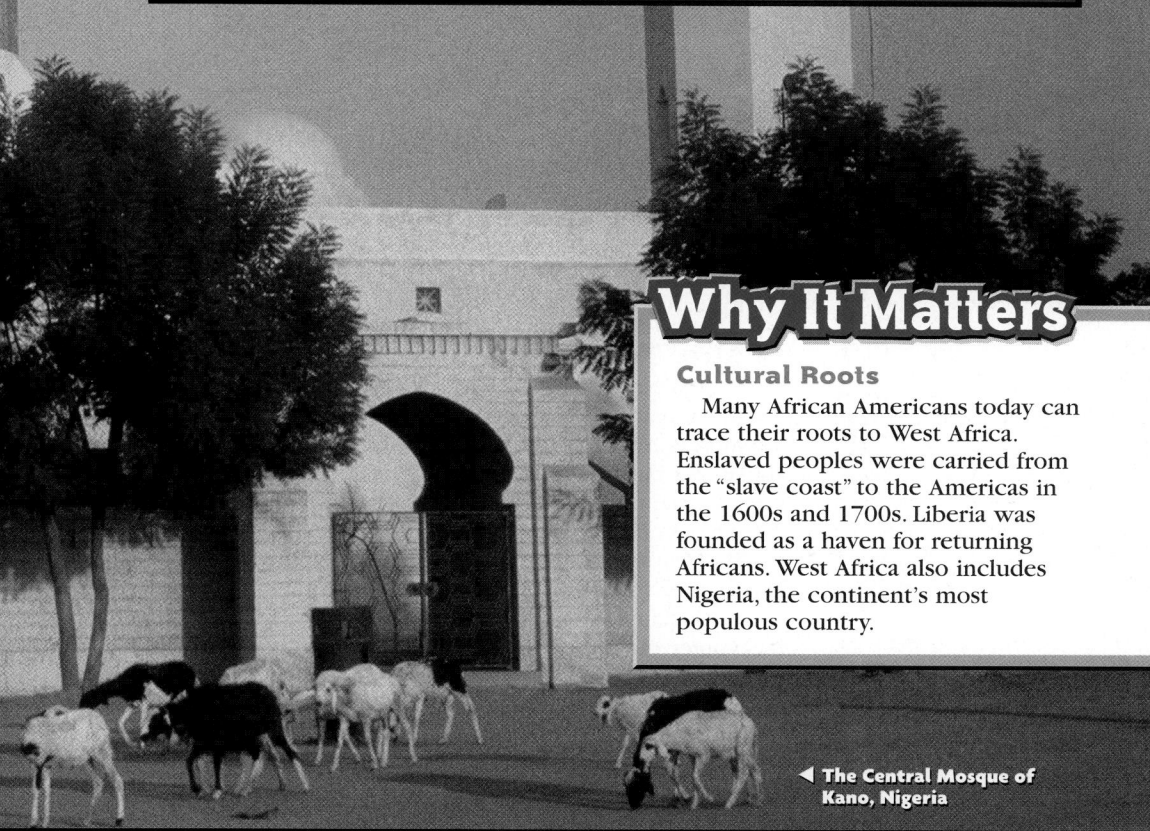

Cultural Roots

Many African Americans today can trace their roots to West Africa. Enslaved peoples were carried from the "slave coast" to the Americas in the 1600s and 1700s. Liberia was founded as a haven for returning Africans. West Africa also includes Nigeria, the continent's most populous country.

◀ The Central Mosque of Kano, Nigeria

About the Photos

Kano is one of the largest cities in Nigeria. It is located in the northern part of the country, which is where much of Nigeria's Islamic population lives. Christianity was established in the southern part of the country by Protestant and Roman Catholic missionaries in the late 19th century. Today, both Christianity and Islam continue to be the major religions in Nigeria, though many people also follow the practices and beliefs of the indigenous African religions. Independent Nigerian churches, such as Cherubim and Seraphim, combine Christian worship with African religious practices like drumming and dancing. **Ask: What are other ways Christianity varies from one society to another?**

Introducing

Chapter 16

FOLDABLES™ Study Organizer

Purpose This activity will provide students with an opportunity to review what they know and think about what they would like to know about West Africa. The resulting foldable can be used as an assessment tool at the end of the chapter to determine what students have learned.

Have students complete ***Reading and Study Skills Foldables*** Activity 16.

Why It Matters

European contact has had a profound influence on Nigeria and the rest of West Africa. Have students use this text and other resources to come up with a list of ways that European contact has affected these nations. *(Possible responses: slave trade, religion, exploitation of resources, language, division of ethnic groups to form countries)* Divide students into groups and have each group research and present one topic on the list, discussing the history of the subject as well as the positive and negative effects on Africa.

Section Objectives

1. Describe the land and climates found in Nigeria.
2. Explain Nigeria's economy.
3. Compare Nigeria's ethnic groups.

BELLRINGER Skillbuilder Activity

Project transparency and have students answer questions.

This activity is also available as a blackline master.

Daily Focus Skills Transparency 16-1

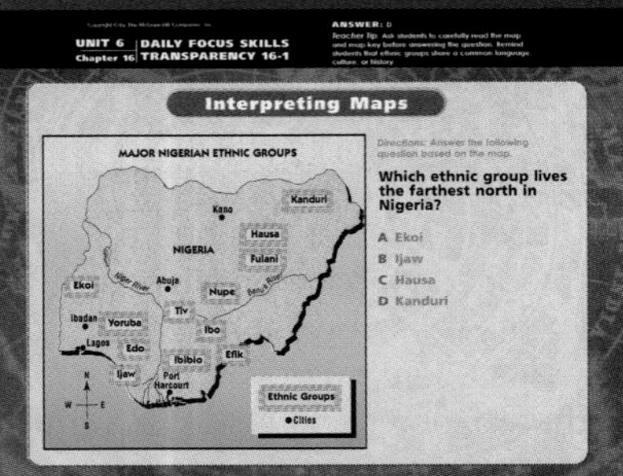

Reading Check Answer

mangrove swamps, rain forests, and savannas

Guide to Reading

■ **Accessing Prior Knowledge**
Ask: What region of the world has the largest share of the world's oil reserves? *(Southwest Asia)* Point out that some countries in other regions have substantial quantities of oil as well.

Nigeria

Guide to Reading

Main Idea

A large, oil-rich country, Nigeria has more people than any other African nation.

Terms to Know

- mangrove
- savanna
- harmattan
- subsistence farm
- cacao
- compound
- civil war

Reading Strategy

Create a chart like the one below. Then list two facts about Nigeria in each category.

Nigeria	Fact #1	Fact #2
Land		
Economy		
People		

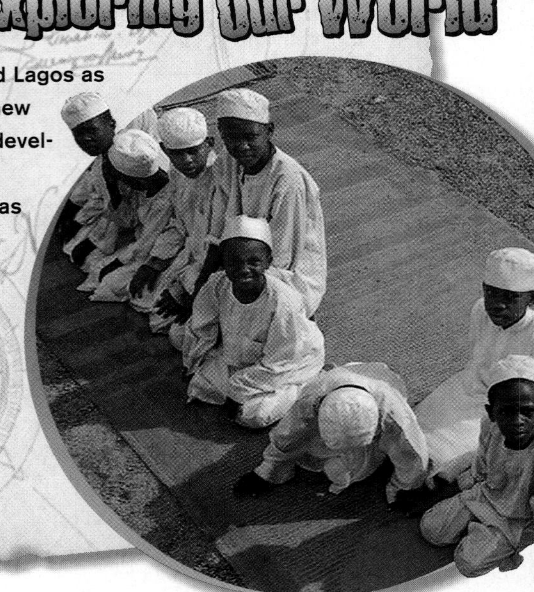

In 1991 Abuja replaced Lagos as Nigeria's capital. The new city was built in an undeveloped region in central Nigeria. Today Abuja has new buildings and a network of roads linking it with other parts of the country. It also has schools. These children prepare to pray at the Islamic Academy in Abuja.

The West African country of **Nigeria** takes its name from the **Niger River,** which flows through western and central Nigeria. One of the largest nations in Africa, Nigeria is more than twice the size of California.

From Tropics to Savannas

Nigeria has a long coastline on the Gulf of Guinea, an arm of the Atlantic Ocean. Along Nigeria's coast, the land is covered with mangrove swamps. A **mangrove** is a tropical tree with roots that extend both above and beneath the water. As you travel inland, the land becomes vast tropical rain forests. Small villages appear in only a few clearings. The forests gradually thin into savannas in central Nigeria. **Savannas** are tropical grasslands with only a few trees. Highlands and plateaus also make up this area. Most of the country has high average temperatures and seasonal rains. The grasslands of the far north have a dry climate. In the winter months, a dusty wind called the **harmattan** blows south from the Sahara.

Reading Check What kinds of vegetation are found in Nigeria?

Section Resources

Reproducible Masters

- Reproducible Lesson Plan 16-1
- Daily Lecture and Discussion Notes 16-1
- Guided Reading Activity 16-1
- Reading Essentials and Study Guide 16-1
- Section Quiz 16-1

Transparencies

- Daily Focus Skills Transparency 16-1
- GeoQuiz Transparency 16-1

Multimedia

- Vocabulary PuzzleMaker Software
- Interactive Tutor Self-Assessment CD-ROM
- Presentation Plus! CD-ROM
- ExamView® Pro 3.0 Testmaker CD-ROM

Economic Challenges

Nigeria is one of the world's major oil-producing countries. More than 90 percent of the country's income comes from oil exports. The government has used money from oil to build highways, schools, skyscrapers, and factories. These factories make food products, textiles, chemicals, machinery, and vehicles. Still, more than one-third of Nigeria's people lack jobs and live in poverty.

Nigeria began to experience economic troubles during the 1980s. As a result of falling world oil prices, Nigeria's income dropped. At the same time, many people left their farms in search of better-paying jobs in the cities. In addition, a few years of low rainfall meant smaller harvests. As a result, food production fell. Nigeria—which had once exported food—had to import food to feed its people.

Despite oil resources, Nigeria's people mainly work as farmers. Most have **subsistence farms,** or small plots that grow just enough

NATIONAL GEOGRAPHIC **West Africa: Political**

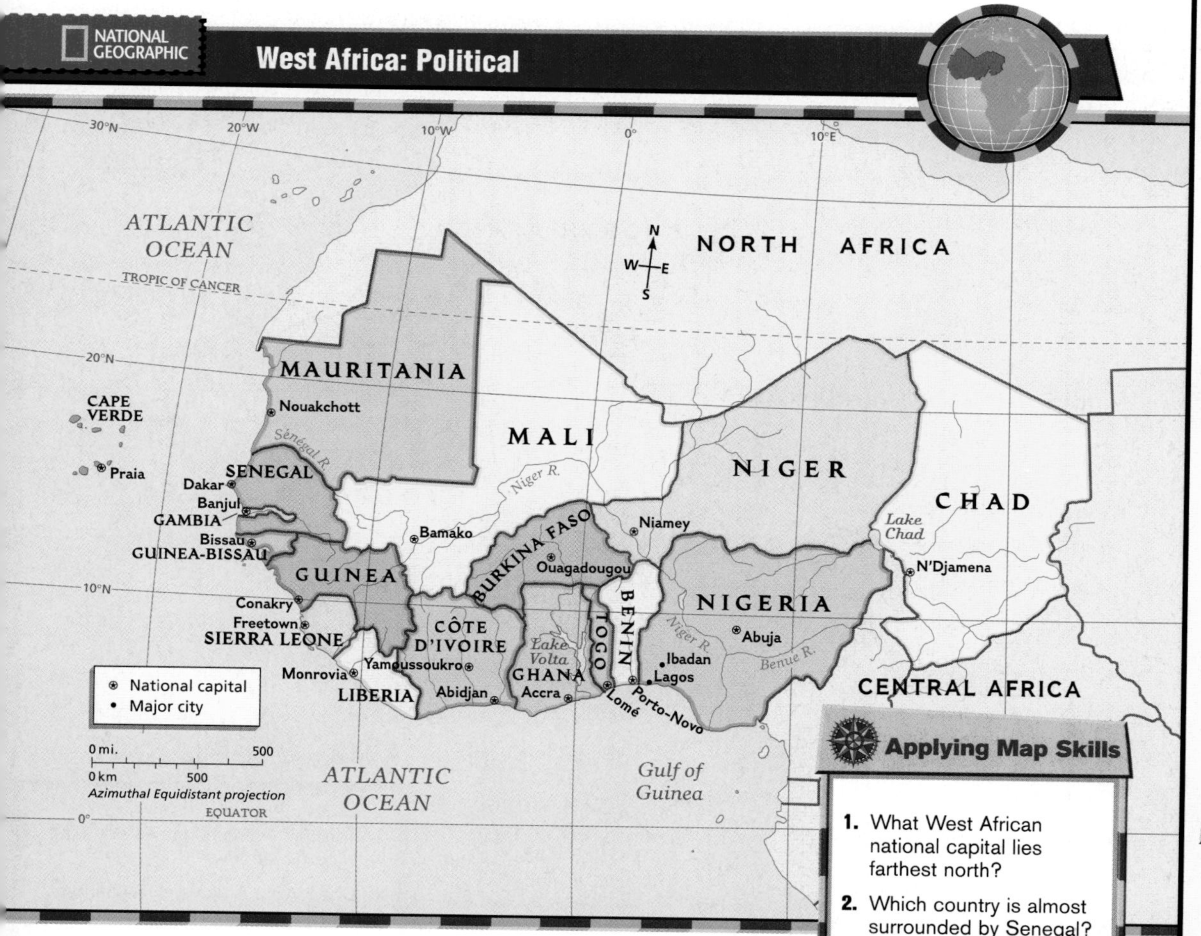

30°N 20°W 10°W 0° 10°E

ATLANTIC OCEAN

TROPIC OF CANCER

N W E S

NORTH AFRICA

20°N

MAURITANIA

Nouakchott

CAPE VERDE

Praia

Sénégal R.

MALI

Niger R.

NIGER

CHAD

SENEGAL

Dakar

Banjul

GAMBIA

Bissau

GUINEA-BISSAU

Bamako

BURKINA FASO

Ouagadougou

Niamey

Lake Chad

N'Djamena

10°N

GUINEA

Conakry

Freetown

SIERRA LEONE

CÔTE D'IVOIRE

Lake Volta

GHANA

TOGO

BENIN

NIGERIA

Niger R.

Abuja

Benue R.

Ibadan

Lagos

Monrovia

Yamoussoukro

LIBERIA

Abidjan

Accra

Lomé

Porto-Novo

CENTRAL AFRICA

⊛ National capital
• Major city

0 mi. 500
0 km 500
Azimuthal Equidistant projection

ATLANTIC OCEAN

Gulf of Guinea

0° EQUATOR

West Africa

Applying Map Skills

1. What West African national capital lies farthest north?
2. Which country is almost surrounded by Senegal?

Find NGS online map resources @ www.nationalgeographic.com/maps

Team-Teaching Activity

History Have students discuss how history has affected ways of life in Nigeria. Suggest that they begin with the arrival of Europeans in the late 1400s and end with the situation today. Ask students to pay close attention to how European influences affected ethnic groups, religions, and languages in Nigeria. You might invite a teacher with a background in world history to talk to the class about the end of colonialism in the 1960s. Then have students work in groups to construct a time line showing what they think are the key historical events in Nigeria. **L1**

EE4 Human Systems: Standard 12

Chapter 16

Section 1, pages 434–438

TEACH

Making Inferences Point out that for some questions, the answers are "right there" whereas others require students to "think and search," or to interpret the information in the text. Give examples of these two types of questions. **Ask: Where is Nigeria's coastline?** *(The answer, along the Gulf of Guinea, is "right there" on page 434.)* **Is the land drier in the north or south of the country?** *(The answer can be inferred from the fact that the south has swamps and rain forests whereas the north has a dry climate.)* Have students pose questions of these two types. **L1**

Daily Lecture Notes 16-1

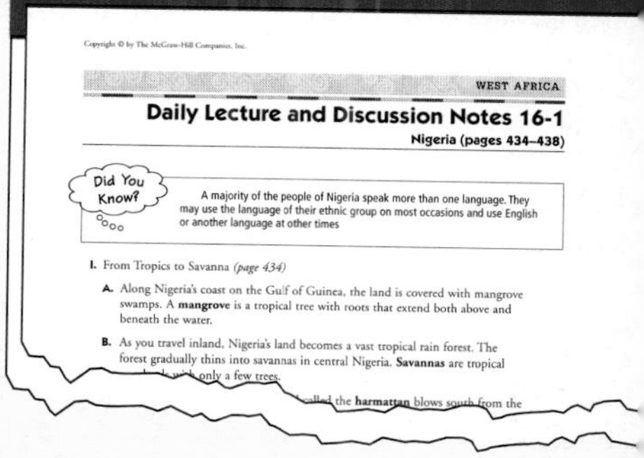

WEST AFRICA

Daily Lecture and Discussion Notes 16-1

Nigeria (pages 434–438)

Did You Know? A majority of the people of Nigeria speak more than one language. They may use the language of their ethnic group on most occasions and use English or another language at other times.

I. From Tropics to Savanna (page 434)

A. Along Nigeria's coast on the Gulf of Guinea, the land is covered with mangrove swamps. A **mangrove** is a tropical tree with roots that extend both above and beneath the water.

B. As you travel inland, Nigeria's land becomes a vast tropical rain forest. The forest gradually thins into savannas in central Nigeria. **Savannas** are tropical ... only a few trees.

... the **harmattan** blows south from the

Applying Map Skills

Answers

1. Nouakchott
2. Gambia

Skills Practice

What city is located on Nigeria's coast? *(Lagos)*

✓ Reading Check Answer

to build highways, schools, skyscrapers, and factories

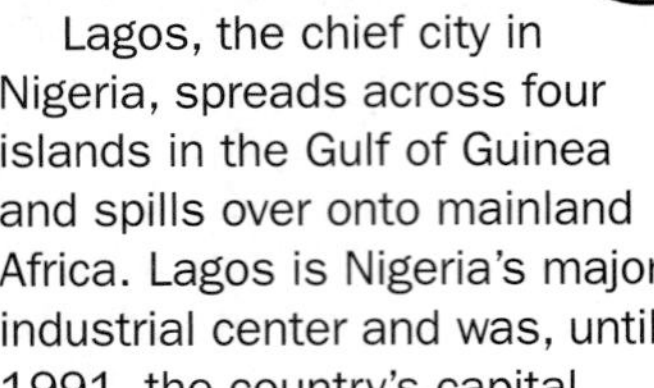

Did You Know?

Lagos, the chief city in Nigeria, spreads across four islands in the Gulf of Guinea and spills over onto mainland Africa. Lagos is Nigeria's major industrial center and was, until 1991, the country's capital.

Guided Reading Activity 16-1

Name ____ Date ____ Class ____

WEST AFRICA

Guided Reading Activity 16-1
Nigeria

DIRECTIONS: Filling in the Blanks Reading the section and completing the sentences below will help you learn more about the country of Nigeria. Use your textbook to fill in the blanks.

Nigeria's land is covered with (1) ____ swamps. The farther inland you travel the land becomes (2) ____ ____. Finally, the land becomes woodlands and
(3) ____. During the winter, a dusty wind, called the
(4) ____, blows from the Sahara.
Most of Nigeria's income comes from (5) ____. More than
(6) ____ of the country's people live in (7) ____

Applying Map Skills

Answers

1. Guinea, Mali, Niger, Benin (border of), and Nigeria
2. The land rises as you move north.

Skills Practice

What river flows from the east to join the Niger River in Nigeria? *(Benue River)*

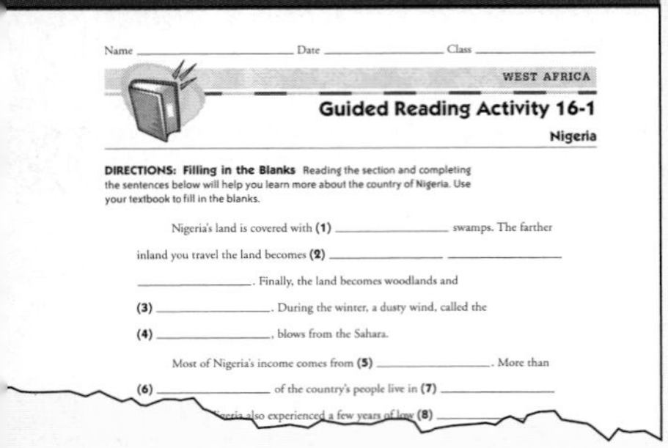

to feed their families. Some work on larger farms that produce such cash crops as rubber, peanuts, palm oil, and cacao. The **cacao** is a tropical tree whose seeds are used to make chocolate and cocoa. Nigeria is a leading producer of cacao beans.

✓ Reading Check How has Nigeria's government used money from oil exports?

Nigeria's People

About 126.6 million people live in Nigeria—more people than in any other country in Africa. The map on page 444 shows that most of the people live along the coast and around the city of **Kano** in the north.

One of the strongest bonds that Africans have is a sense of belonging to a group or family. Nigeria has more than 300 ethnic groups. The four largest are the Hausa (HOW•suh), Fulani (foo•LAH•nee), Yoruba (YAWR•uh•buh), and Ibo (EE•boh). Nigerians speak many different

NATIONAL GEOGRAPHIC

West Africa: Physical

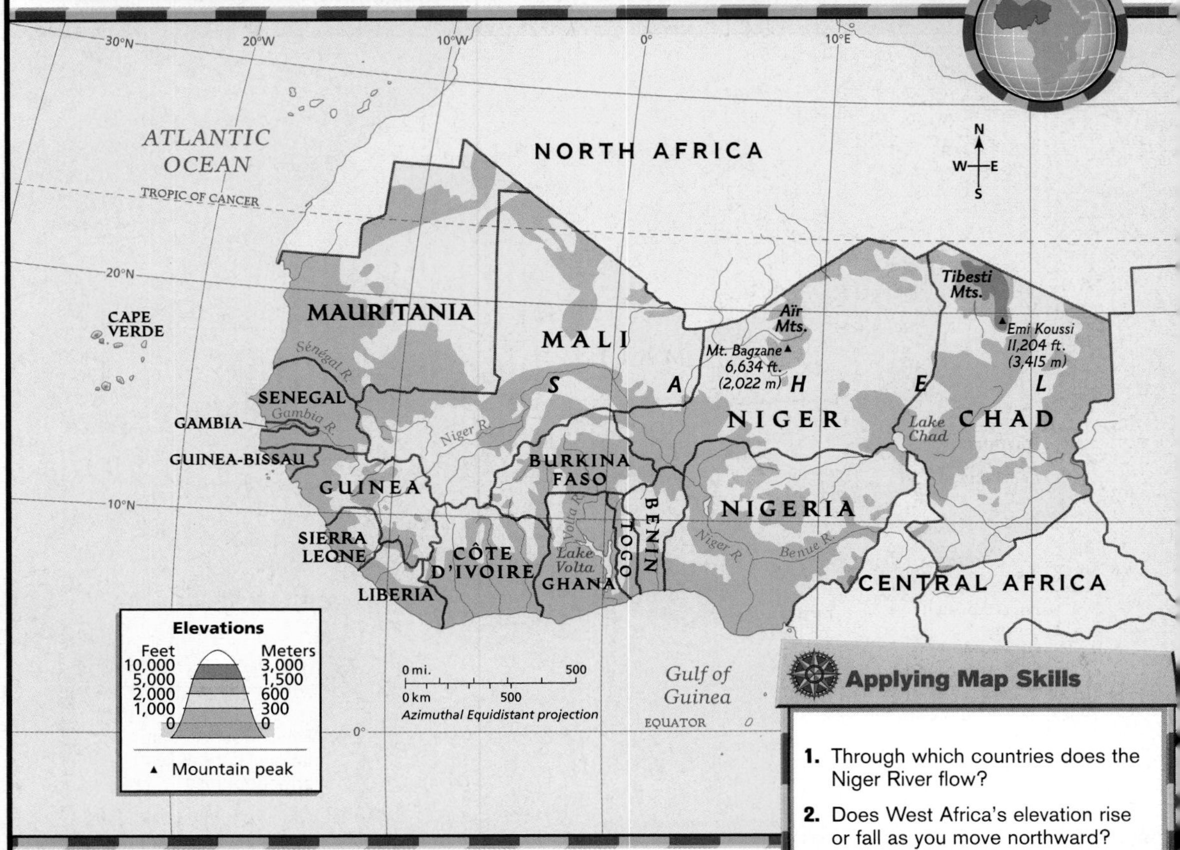

Applying Map Skills

1. Through which countries does the Niger River flow?
2. Does West Africa's elevation rise or fall as you move northward?

Find NGS online map resources @ www.nationalgeographic.com/maps

436

Meeting Special Needs

Visual/Spatial Visual learners can better grasp the different features of Nigeria by locating information on maps as the information is read. Pair visual learners with other students. Have the other students read key passages in the text. As they do so, have the visual learners find the correct map for this information and see how the map shows what the text describes. **L1**

Refer to *Inclusion for the Middle School Social Studies Classroom Strategies and Activities* in the TCR.

Nigeria's Economy

Nigerian women canoe past an oil refinery in the Niger River delta (left). Cacao pods are harvested in Nigeria (above).

Human/Environment Interaction **What are Nigeria's important cash crops?**

African languages. They use English in business and government affairs, though. About one-half of Nigeria's people are Muslim, and another 40 percent are Christian. The remaining 10 percent practice traditional African religions.

About 60 percent of Nigerians live in rural villages. The typical family lives in a **compound,** or a group of houses surrounded by walls. Usually the village has a weekly market run by women. The women sell locally-grown products such as meat, cloth, yams, nuts, and palm oil. The market also provides a chance for friends to meet.

Long-standing rural ways are changing, however. Many young men now move to the cities to find work. The women stay in the villages to raise children and to farm the land. The men, when they are able, return home to see their families and to share the money they have made.

Nigeria's largest city is the port of **Lagos,** the former capital. Major banks, department stores, and restaurants serve the 11 million people who live in Lagos and its surrounding areas. **Ibadan** (EE•bah•DAHN), Kano, and Abuja (ah•BOO•jah) lie inland. **Abuja,** the present capital, is a planned city that was begun during the 1980s.

Nigerians take pride in both old and new features of their culture. Artists make elaborate wooden masks, metal sculptures, and colorful cloth. In the past, Nigerians passed on stories, sayings, and riddles by word of mouth from one generation to the next. In 1986 Nigerian writer **Wole Soyinka** (WAW•lay shaw•YIHNG•ka) became the first African to win the Nobel Prize in literature.

History and Government The earliest known inhabitants of the area were the **Nok** people. They lived between the Niger and Benue Rivers between 300 B.C. and A.D. 200. The Nok were known as skilled metalworkers and traders.

Chapter 16

Section 1, pages 434–438

More About the Photos

Niger River The Niger River is Africa's third-longest river, after the Nile and the Congo. The Malinke people call it the *Joliba,* meaning "great river." Originating in Guinea, the river flows northeast before it turns south.

Caption Answer rubber, peanuts, palm oil, and cacao

Assign Section 1 Assessment as homework or an in-class activity.

Have students use the Interactive Tutor Self-Assessment CD-ROM to review Section 16–1.

Measure student knowledge of physical features and political entities.

GeoQuiz Transparency 16–1

Critical Thinking Activity

Analyzing Information As they read the section on Nigeria, have students identify serious challenges that Nigeria might face in the future. Have them list at least one challenge for each subheading. For example, for the section From Tropics to Savannas, the challenge might be "communicating with isolated villages in the rain forest." Tell students that they also need to explain why they chose that challenge. When they have finished, have volunteers read their suggestions aloud. Have the class discuss possible ways Nigeria could work to meet these challenges. **L2**

EE6 The Uses of Geography: Standard 18

Chapter 16

Section 1, pages 434–438

Section Quiz 16-1

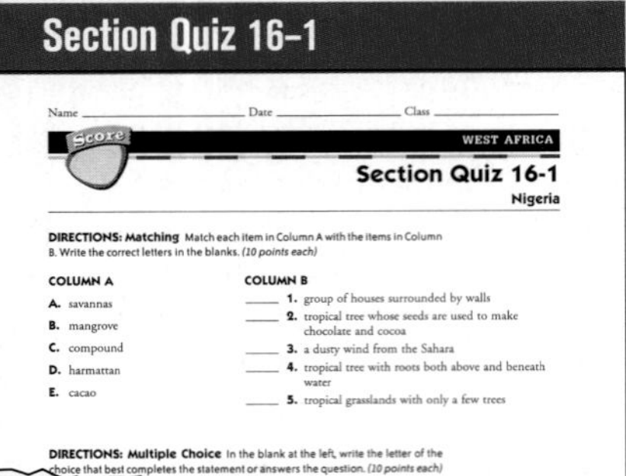
Name ______ Date ______ Class ______

WEST AFRICA

Section Quiz 16-1

Nigeria

DIRECTIONS: Matching Match each item in Column A with the items in Column B. Write the correct letters in the blanks. (10 points each)

COLUMN A	COLUMN B
A. savannas	___ 1. group of houses surrounded by walls
B. mangrove	___ 2. tropical tree whose seeds are used to make chocolate and cocoa
C. compound	___ 3. a dusty wind from the Sahara
D. harmattan	___ 4. tropical tree with roots both above and beneath water
E. cacao	___ 5. tropical grasslands with only a few trees

DIRECTIONS: Multiple Choice In the blank at the left, write the letter of the choice that best completes the statement or answers the question. (10 points each)

Reteach

Have students create a country profile of Nigeria. They should summarize facts under the headings: "Landscapes," "Economy," "People," and "Government."

Reading Check Answer

Hausa, Fulani, Yoruba, and Ibo

Reading Essentials and Study Guide 16-1

Name ______ Date ______ Class ______

WEST AFRICA

Reading Essentials and Study Guide 16-1

Nigeria

For use with textbook pages 434–438

Terms to Know

mangrove tropical tree with roots both above and below the water (page 434)
savanna tropical grassland with only a few trees (page 434)
harmattan dusty wind that blows from the Sahara (page 434)
subsistence farm small plot where farmers can grow only enough to feed their families (page 435)
cacao tropical tree whose seeds are used to make chocolate and cocoa (page 436)
compound group of houses surrounded by walls (page 437)
civil war a fight among different groups within a country (page 438)

Experience

4 CLOSE

Have students write a pen-pal letter to a Nigerian teenager named Elizabeth Tofa. Their letters should reflect what they have learned about Nigeria.

Over the centuries, powerful city-states and kingdoms became centers of trade and the arts. People in the north came in contact with Muslim cultures and adopted the religion of Islam. People in the south developed cultures based on traditional African religions.

During the 1400s, Europeans arrived in Africa looking for gold and Africans to take overseas as enslaved laborers. In 1884 European leaders divided most of Africa into colonies. The borders of these colonies, however, often sliced through ethnic lands. As a result, many ethnic groups found their members living in two or more separate territories. By the early 1900s, the British had taken control of Nigeria.

In 1960 Nigeria finally became an independent country. Ethnic, religious, and political disputes soon tore it apart, however. One ethnic group, the Ibo, tried to set up its own country. A **civil war**—a fight between different groups within a country—resulted. In this bloody war, starvation and conflict led to 2 million deaths. The Ibo were defeated, and their region remained part of Nigeria.

Nigeria has faced the challenge of building a stable government. Military leaders have often ruled the country. In 1999 Nigerians were able to vote for a president in free elections. Nigerians are continung to work towards greater national unity, but face enormous problems.

Reading Check What are the four largest ethnic groups in Nigeria?

Section 1 Assessment

Defining Terms

1. **Define** mangrove, savanna, harmattan, subsistence farm, cacao, compound, civil war.

Recalling Facts

2. **Place** Describe the changes in Nigeria's physical geography as you move from the coast inland.
3. **Place** What is the capital of Nigeria?
4. **Culture** How many ethnic groups are represented by the people of Nigeria?

Critical Thinking

5. **Understanding Cause and Effect** Why did a drop in oil prices cause economic troubles in Nigeria in the 1980s?
6. **Drawing Conclusions** Why do you think an ethnic group, such as the Ibo, would want to set up their own country?

Graphic Organizer

7. **Organizing Information** On a time line like the one below, place the following events and their dates in order: Nigeria becomes independent. Nok people work in metal and trade for goods. Free elections are held. British take control of Nigeria.

Applying Social Studies Skills

8. **Analyzing Maps** Study the physical map on page 436. Into what larger body of water does the Niger River empty?

Section 1 Assessment

1. The terms are defined in the Glossary.
2. coastline with swamps; vast tropical rain forest; highlands and plateaus with savannas; grasslands
3. Abuja
4. over 300
5. Nigeria's income dropped.
6. to control their own lives and ensure their own interests
7. 300 B.C. to A.D. 200: Nok people work in metal and trade; early 1900s: British take control of Nigeria; 1960: Nigeria becomes independent; 1999: free elections are held
8. Gulf of Guinea (or Atlantic Ocean)

Critical Thinking Skill

Drawing Inferences and Conclusions

Suppose your teacher brought to class a colorful wooden mask, and a classmate said, "Wow. That's from Nigeria." You might infer that your classmate has an interest in African art and, therefore, recognizes the mask as coming from Nigeria.

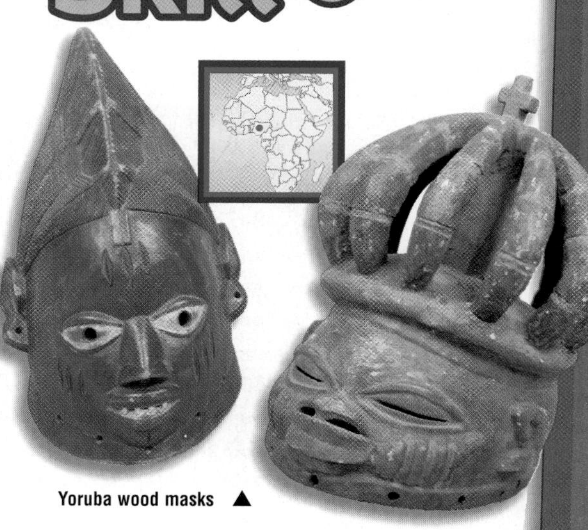
Yoruba wood masks ▲

Learning the Skill

To *infer* means to evaluate information and arrive at a conclusion. When you make inferences, you "read between the lines" or draw conclusions that are not stated directly in the text. You must use the available facts *and* your own knowledge and experience to form a judgment or opinion about the material.

Use the following steps to help draw inferences and make conclusions:

- Read carefully for stated facts and ideas.
- Summarize the information and list the important facts.
- Apply related information that you may already know to make inferences.
- Use your knowledge and insight to develop some conclusions about these facts.

Practicing the Skill

Read the passage below, and then answer the questions that follow.

> Nigerian art forms reflect the people's beliefs in spirits and nature. Yoruba masks are carved out of wood, reflecting the forces of nature and gods. The masks are used in ceremonies to help connect with the spirit of their ancestors. The masks also appear at funerals in order to please the spirits of the dead. Of all the Yoruba masks, the helmet masks of the Epa cult are the most spectacular.

1. What topic is the writer describing?
2. What facts are presented?
3. What can you infer about the role of masks in Nigerian life?
4. What do you already know about religious ceremonies?
5. What conclusion can you make about traditional religions in Nigeria?

Applying the Skill

Study the photos of Nigerians on page 437. What can you infer about life in Nigeria from the photographs? What evidence supports this inference, or conclusion?

GO TO Practice key skills with **Glencoe Skillbuilder Interactive Workbook, Level 1.**

Critical Thinking Skill

TEACH

Give students the following situation: Suppose you walk into your family's living room late at night. The television is on, and a sibling is sleeping on the couch. The floor is covered with popcorn. **Ask: What do you think happened?** *(The sibling fell asleep with the television on and dropped the popcorn.)* Explain that in reaching this conclusion, students made inferences—that is, they reached a conclusion based on the available evidence. **L1**

Additional Skills Practice

1. **What conclusion could you draw about the weather from seeing the wet footprints of a cat on the kitchen floor?** *(that it is raining or snowing)*
2. **What could you infer about the environment from the fact that a group of people used camels to transport goods?** *(The people probably lived in a desert.)*

Additional Skills Resources

  Chapter Skills Activity 16

Building Geography Skills for Life

GLENCOE TECHNOLOGY

 **Skillbuilder Interactive Workbook CD-ROM, Level 1**

This interactive CD-ROM reinforces student mastery of essential social studies skills.

Practicing the Skill Answers

1. the connection between Yoruba art forms and spirits and nature
2. Yoruba masks are made of wood; masks are used in ceremonies, including funerals.
3. They play a role in spiritual life.
4. Answers will vary.
5. They involve beliefs in spirits that interact with living people.

Applying the Skill

Answers will vary but might include such inferences as: Cacao is an important economic crop; Nigeria includes both traditional aspects (as shown by the women in canoes) and modern aspects (shown by the oil factory).

Section Objectives

1. Describe the Sahel's location and its history.
2. Explain how people in the Sahel countries live.
2. Compare the coastal countries, their history, and peoples.

BELLRINGER
Skillbuilder Activity

Project transparency and have students answer questions.

This activity is also available as a blackline master.

Daily Focus Skills Transparency 16-2

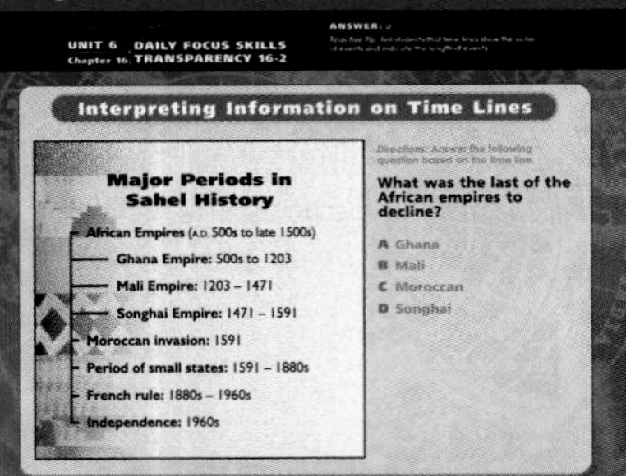
UNIT 6 DAILY FOCUS SKILLS
Chapter 16 TRANSPARENCY 16-2
Interpreting Information on Time Lines
Major Periods in Sahel History
African Empires (A.D. 500s to late 1500s)
Ghana Empire: 500s to 1203
Mali Empire: 1203 – 1471
Songhai Empire: 1471 – 1591
Moroccan invasion: 1591
Period of small states: 1591 – 1880s
French rule: 1880s – 1960s
Independence: 1960s
What was the last of the African empires to decline?
A Ghana
B Mali
C Moroccan
D Songhai

Guide to Reading

■ **Accessing Prior Knowledge**

Ask: Can a desert grow and shrink? After hearing students' responses, explain that in this section they will learn that a desert can indeed grow—and that its growth has important effects on people's lives.

Section 2

Other Countries of West Africa

Guide to Reading

Main Idea

The Sahel countries face a continuing struggle to keep grasslands from turning into desert, but the coastal countries receive plenty of rainfall.

Terms to Know

- overgraze
- drought
- desertification
- bauxite
- phosphate

Reading Strategy

Create five charts like this one, filling in at least one key fact about five West African countries for each category.

Country	
Land	
Economy	
Culture	

NATIONAL GEOGRAPHIC **Exploring Our World**

Slowly but surely, the desert is creeping into grassy inland areas of West Africa north of Nigeria. Over the past 100 years, a stretch of the Sahara about 100 miles (161 km) wide has swallowed parts of countries in West Africa. This growing desert is like an invading army slowly taking over the countries of the vast Sahel.

Five countries—**Mauritania** (MAWR•uh•TAY•nee•uh), **Mali** (MAH•lee), **Burkina Faso** (bur•KEE•nuh FAH•soh), **Niger** (NY•juhr), and **Chad**—are located in an area known as the **Sahel.** The word *Sahel* comes from an Arabic word that means "border." In addition to the Sahel countries, West Africa includes 11 coastal countries. One country—**Cape Verde**—is a group of islands in the Atlantic Ocean. The other countries, including **Togo** and **Benin,** stretch along the Gulf of Guinea and the Atlantic coast.

Land and History of the Sahel

The Sahel receives little rainfall, so only short grasses and small trees can support grazing animals. Most people have traditionally herded livestock. Their flocks, unfortunately, have overgrazed the land in some places. When animals overgraze land, they strip areas so bare that plants cannot grow back. Then bare soil is blown away by winds.

Section Resources

Reproducible Masters
- Reproducible Lesson Plan 16-2
- Daily Lecture and Discussion Notes 16-2
- Guided Reading Activity 16-2
- Reading Essentials and Study Guide 16-2
- Section Quiz 16-2

Transparencies
- Daily Focus Skills Transparency 16-2
- GeoQuiz Transparency 16-1

Multimedia
- Vocabulary PuzzleMaker Software
- Interactive Tutor Self-Assessment CD-ROM
- Presentation Plus! CD-ROM
- ExamView® Pro 3.0 Testmaker CD-ROM

In the Sahel, dry and wet periods usually follow each other. When the seasonal rains do not fall, drought takes hold. A **drought** is a long period of extreme dryness and water shortage. The latest drought occurred in the 1980s. Rivers dried up, crops failed, and millions of animals died. Thousands of people died of starvation. Millions of others fled to more productive southern areas. Overgrazing and drought have led to **desertification** where grasslands have become deserts.

History From the A.D. 500s to 1500s, three great African empires—**Ghana** (GAH•nuh), **Mali,** and **Songhai** (SAWNG•hy)—arose in the Sahel. These empires controlled the trade in gold, salt, and other goods between West Africa and the Arab lands of North Africa and Southwest Asia. To learn more about the salt trade, turn to page 450.

In the early 1300s, Mali's most famous ruler, **Mansa Musa,** made a journey in grand style to Makkah. This is the holy city of Islam located in the Arabian Peninsula. A faithful Muslim, Mansa Musa made his capital, Tombouctou (TOH•book•TOO), a leading center of Islamic learning. People came from all over the Muslim world to study there.

Invaders from North Africa defeated Songhai—the last of the great empires—in the late 1500s. During the 1800s, the Sahel region came under French rule. The French created five colonies in the area. In 1960 these five colonies became the independent nations of Mauritania, Mali, Upper Volta (now Burkina Faso), Niger, and Chad.

✓ Reading Check **What has caused the desertification of the Sahel?**

The People of the Sahel

The Sahel countries are large in size but have small populations. If you look at the population map on page 444, you will see that most people live in the southern areas of the Sahel. Rivers flow here, and the land can be farmed or grazed. Yet even these areas do not have enough water and fertile land to support large numbers of people.

Clothing

To protect themselves from the hot Saharan sun, the Tuareg people wear layers of clothing under their long flowing robes. These loose cotton clothes help slow the evaporation of sweat and conserve body moisture. As a sign of respect for their superiors, Tuareg men cover their mouths and faces with veils. Women usually wear veils only for weddings. The veils are made of blue cloth dyed from crushed indigo. The blue dye easily rubs off onto the skin, earning the men the nickname "the Blue Men of the Desert."

Looking Closer How is the clothing of the Tuareg appropriate for the land in which they live?

Content Background

A Grand Caravan Mansa Musa's pilgrimage to Makkah included 12,000 slaves carrying gold-covered staffs. About 80 camels set out with 300 pounds of gold each, which the emperor generously distributed during the trip. This journey notified the world of the wealth of West Africa. In fact, so much gold was given away on Mansa Musa's journey that the world price of gold fell.

Analyzing Information
Have students research and report on the music of Africa south of the Sahara. Suggest that they include information on how the music spread to the United States and influenced spirituals, jazz, blues, and rock and roll. **L2**

Answer It protects them from the heat and conserves body moisture.

Ask students: How is the clothing that you and your classmates wear suited to the climate in which you live? Discuss their responses, and point out differing clothing needs with the change of seasons.

✓ **Reading Check Answer**
overgrazing and drought

TRAVEL GUIDE 

On special occasions, Ghanaians wear clothing made from kente cloth. This cotton fabric is handwoven in narrow stripes that are then sewn together. Each pattern tells a story or represents an event.

Chapter 16

Section 2, pages 440–445

Daily Lecture Notes 16–2

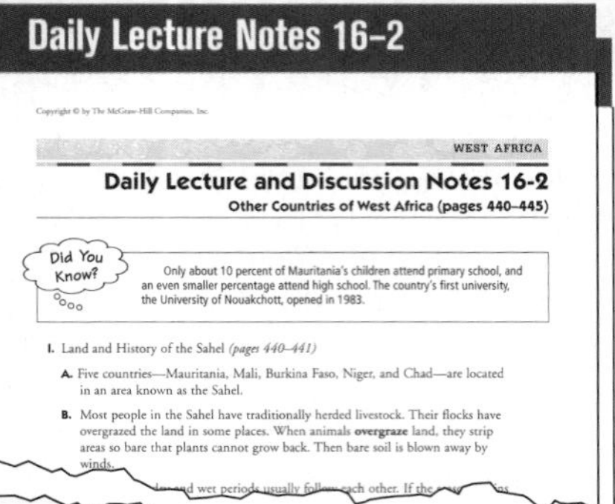

WEST AFRICA

Daily Lecture and Discussion Notes 16-2

Other Countries of West Africa (pages 440–445)

Did You Know? Only about 10 percent of Mauritania's children attend primary school, and an even smaller percentage attend high school. The country's first university, the University of Nouakchott, opened in 1983.

I. Land and History of the Sahel *(pages 440–441)*

A. Five countries—Mauritania, Mali, Burkina Faso, Niger, and Chad—are located in an area known as the Sahel.

B. Most people in the Sahel have traditionally herded livestock. Their flocks have overgrazed the land in some places. When animals **overgraze** land, they strip areas so bare that plants cannot grow back. Then bare soil is blown away by winds.

Today most people in the Sahel live in small towns. They are subsistence farmers who grow grains, such as millet and sorghum (SAWR•guhm). For years, many people were nomads. Groups such as the Tuareg (TWAH•rehg), for example, would cross the desert with herds of camels. The Fulani herded cattle, goats, and sheep. The recent droughts forced many of them to give up their traditional way of life and move to the towns. Here they often live in crowded camps of tents.

Two countries in the Sahel, Mali and Burkina Faso, are among the poorest countries in the world. The landlocked countries of the Sahel have problems getting their products to overseas markets.

The people of the Sahel practice a mix of African, Arab, and European traditions. Most are Muslims and follow the Islamic religion. They speak Arabic as well as a variety of African languages. In many of the larger cities, French is also spoken.

✓ Reading Check **Why have many people in the Sahel given up the nomadic lifestyle?**

✓ **Reading Check Answer**

Droughts forced many to move to towns.

Making Comparisons Have students compare urban and rural ways of life in coastal West Africa. Then ask students to discuss why rural people are more likely to preserve traditional ways of life than urban people. *(Urban people are likely to have more contact with other cultures, weakening traditional ties.)* **L1**

The Coastal Countries

If you look at the map on page 444, you will see the Cape Verde Islands off the Atlantic Coast. Skipping to **Senegal,** follow the countries in order around the coast: **Gambia, Guinea-Bissau, Guinea, Sierra Leone, Liberia, Côte d'Ivoire, Ghana,** Togo, and Benin.

Sandy beaches, thick mangrove swamps, and rain forests cover the shores of West Africa's coastal countries. Highland areas with grasses and trees lie inland. Several major rivers flow from these highlands to the coast. They include the Senegal, Gambia, Volta, and Niger Rivers. Rapids and shallow waters prevent large ships from traveling far inland.

Because they border the ocean, the coastal countries receive plenty of rainfall. Warm currents in the Gulf of Guinea create a moist, tropical rain forest climate in most coastal lowlands year-round. For many years, tropical disease, thick rain forests, and river rapids kept European explorers from entering the interior.

Damage to rain forests is also a problem along the densely settled West African coast, where forests have been cleared to make space for palm, coffee, cacao, and rubber plantations, as well as for many small farms. Population pressure on cultivated land is increasing rapidly. Dense clusters of settlements ring port cities such as **Abidjan** (Côte d'Ivoire), **Accra** (Ghana), and Lagos and **Port Harcourt** (Nigeria). Oil discoveries in eastern Nigeria and Gabon are now attracting even more people to the West African coast.

Despite rich agricultural resources, coastal West African countries import more in industrial goods than they export in natural products. Why? Agricultural products often rise and fall in price suddenly, and their value is not equal to finished goods. To meet their countries' needs, governments have to borrow money from other countries or international organizations.

✓ Reading Check **What is attracting people to the West African coast?**

Monoculture

The economies of some West African countries, such as Côte d'Ivoire, depend upon the production of one or two major crops. This practice is called monoculture. While this has the advantage of being able to produce enough product to export, it also has disadvantages. If worldwide demand for the product drops, the price also drops. A major drought or epidemic could destroy harvests and wipe out the nation's only major source of income.

✓ **Reading Check Answer**

oil discoveries

Meeting Special Needs

Interpersonal Organize students into five groups and assign one of the Sahel countries to each group. Have group members research and prepare a mini-lesson about their assigned country. Each lesson should cover such topics as landscapes, resources, economic activities, and cultures. Then form new groups consisting of one member from each original group. Have each member in the new groups teach the other group members about the country he or she researched. **L1**

Refer to *Inclusion for the Middle School Social Studies Classroom Strategies and Activities* in the TCR.

History of the Coastal Countries

Ancient Ghana, an empire located at the headwaters of the Senegal and Niger Rivers, flourished between A.D. 700 and 1200. The people of Ghana knew how to make iron weapons, which they used to conquer neighboring groups of farmers and herders. Located on trade routes that connected the gold mines in the rain forests of West Africa with the copper and salt mines in the Sahara, Ghana prospered by taxing the goods that moved north and south along these trade routes. Ghana also had major deposits of gold.

The capital city of ancient Ghana covered a square mile and housed 30,000 people. The kingdom had a well-developed bureaucracy, controlled a large population, and could field an army of 200,000 warriors—at a time when major European battles involved only small numbers of soldiers. The wealth of the king's court was legendary. Europeans called Ghana "the land of gold." This empire fell into decay in the 1200s.

In later times, the powerful and wealthy kingdoms of **Ashanti** and **Abomey** ruled West Africa's coastal region. These kingdoms were centers of trade, learning, and the arts. From the late 1400s to the early 1800s, Europeans set up trading posts along the West African coast. From these posts they traded with Africans for gold, ivory, and other goods that people in Europe wanted.

Effects of Slave Trade Many African states had sold people as slaves to Europeans and Asians long before the Portuguese reached Africa. Most of these slaves were prisoners of war captured in local battles. Only after the development of European sailing ships did the trade in human beings become a major source of income for the kings of West African states, however.

The Europeans also enslaved and forced millions of Africans to migrate to the Americas to work on plantations and in mines. This trade in human beings, which also took place among African countries, was a disaster for West Africa. The removal of so many young and skilled people devastated West African families, villages, and economies.

The French, British, and Portuguese eventually divided up the coastal region and set up colonies to obtain the region's rich resources. In 1957 Ghana became the first country in Africa to become independent. By the late 1970s, no West African country was under European rule.

Reading Check What two things allowed ancient Ghana to prosper economically?

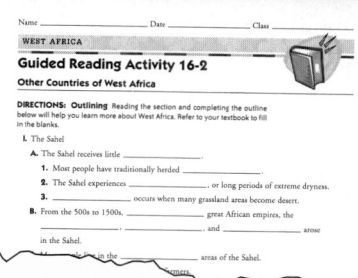

NATIONAL GEOGRAPHIC **On Location**

Niger Highway

Rivers of West Africa provide not only water but transportation. Here, freight boats on the Niger River deliver goods to Benin's people.

Place **What prevents large ships from traveling far inland on West Africa's rivers?**

More About the Photos

West Africa's Rivers The Gambia River is used for transportation, freight deliveries, and mail. The river is also navigated by oceangoing vessels.

Caption Answer rapids and shallow water

Guided Reading Activity 16-2

WEST AFRICA
Guided Reading Activity 16-2
Other Countries of West Africa

DIRECTIONS: Outlining Reading the section and completing the outline below will help you learn more about West Africa. Refer to your textbook to fill in the blanks.

I. The Sahel
A. The Sahel receives little ________.
1. Most people have traditionally herded ________.
2. The Sahel experiences ________, or long periods of extreme dryness.
3. ________ occurs when many grassland areas become desert.
B. From the 500s to 1500s, ________ great African empires, the ________, ________, and ________ arose in the Sahel.

Understanding Cause and Effect West Africa's history has been largely shaped by trade—including the slave trade. Ask students to describe the ways in which West African societies today reflect this history. **L2**

3 ASSESS

Assign Section 2 Assessment as homework or an in-class activity.

Reading Check Answer

taxing goods moved along trade routes; major gold deposits

Team-Teaching Activity

Language Arts The peoples of West Africa have a long tradition of oral literature that has been preserved by special artists named *griots.* Griots are storytellers who relate the achievements of an ethnic group. In relating the achievements of warriors and heroes, they preserve the traditions and values of the group. Invite a language arts teacher to class to outline the typical elements of oral literature in general and of the griots in particular. Then invite students to write a story showing these elements and give an oral performance of it. **ELL L1**

EE4 Human Systems: Standard 10

Chapter 16

Section 2, pages 440–445

Cultural Kaleidoscope

Côte d'Ivoire French missionaries brought Christianity to Côte d'Ivoire in the 1600s. The church of Our Lady of Peace in Yamoussoukro is the largest Christian place of worship in Africa.

Applying Map Skills

Answers

1. Lagos, Ibadan, Ogbomosho, Abuja, and Kano
2. along the Gulf of Guinea

Skills Practice

Why are northern Mali and central Mauritania largely uninhabited? *(These areas are deserts.)*

Section Quiz 16-2

Name ______ Date ______ Class ______

WEST AFRICA

Section Quiz 16-2

Other Countries of West Africa

DIRECTIONS: Matching Match each item in Column A with the items in Column B. Write the correct letters in the blanks. *(10 points each)*

COLUMN A	COLUMN B
A. overgrazing	____ 1. leading center of Islamic learning in ancient times
B. drought	____ 2. long periods of extreme dryness and water shortages
C. Tombouctou	____ 3. grasslands stripped so bare by feeding animals that plants cannot grow back
D. Cape Verde	____ 4. West African country that is a group of islands
E. Liberia	____ 5. only West African nation that was never a colony

DIRECTIONS: Multiple Choice In the blank at the left, write the letter of the choice that best completes the statement or answers the question. *(10 points each)*

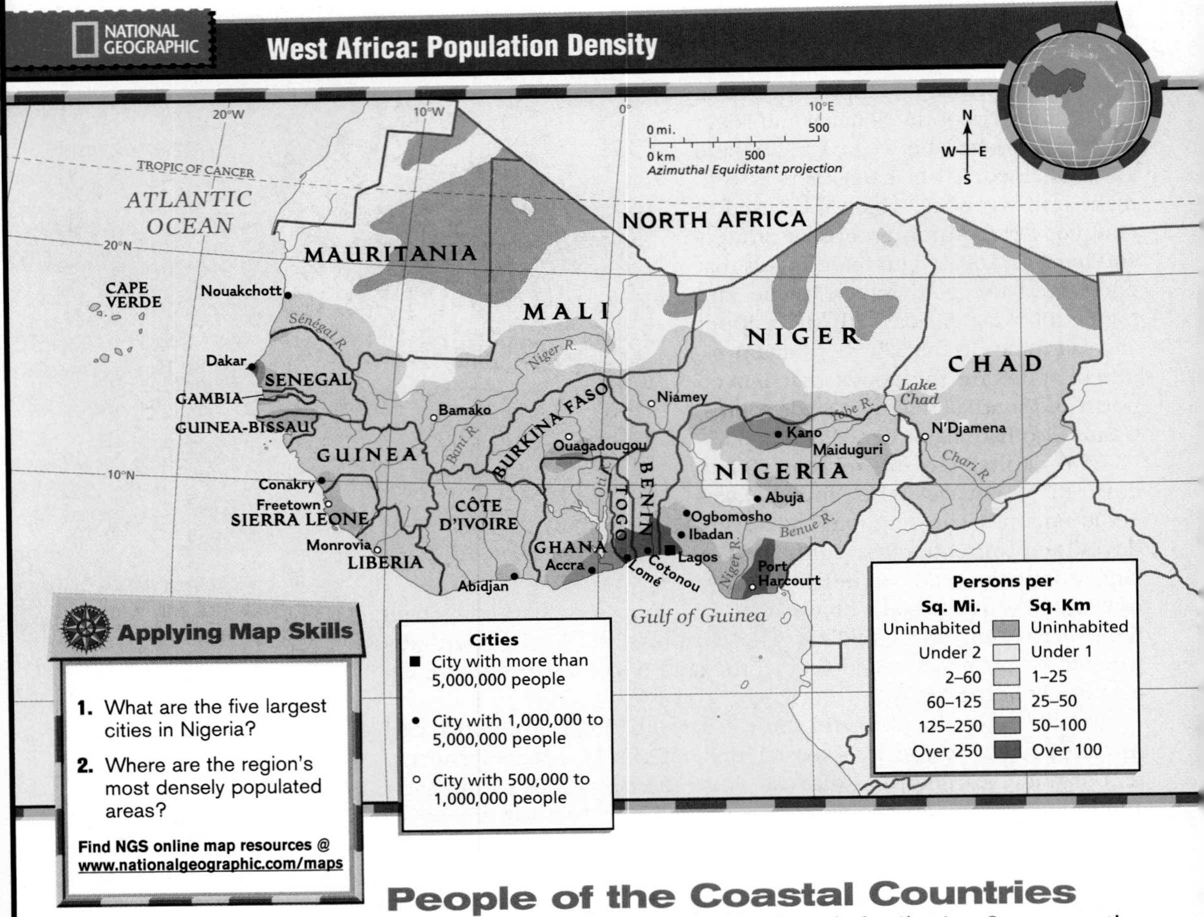

Applying Map Skills

1. What are the five largest cities in Nigeria?
2. Where are the region's most densely populated areas?

Find NGS online map resources @ www.nationalgeographic.com/maps

People of the Coastal Countries

People in coastal West Africa cherish family ties. Some practice traditional African religions, whereas others are Christian or Muslim. Local African languages are spoken in everyday conversation. Reflecting the region's colonial histories, languages such as French, English, and Portuguese are used in business and government. Most of the people in Gambia, Senegal, and Guinea work in agriculture. Guinea is also rich in bauxite and diamonds. **Bauxite** is a mineral used to make aluminum. Guinea has about 25 percent of the world's reserves of bauxite. Senegal is an important source of phosphate. **Phosphate** is mineral salt that has phosphorus, which is used in fertilizers.

Liberia is the only West African nation that was never a colony. African Americans freed from slavery founded Liberia in 1822. **Monrovia,** Liberia's capital, was named for James Monroe—the president of the United States when Liberia was founded. From 1989 to 1996, a civil war cost many lives and destroyed much of the country's economy.

Meeting Special Needs

Naturalistic Organize the class into two teams, and then split each team into smaller groups. Have the groups in one half create dioramas showing the environment of the rain forest in the coastal countries of West Africa. Have the groups in the other half create dioramas showing the environment of the steppe areas in the Sahel countries. Have the different groups write questions about the geographic features shown in the models of the other group. When each team presents its dioramas to the class they should answer the questions and explain the features they highlighted. Afterwards, have students compare the features in the models. In what other world regions can these environments be found? **L1**

Like Liberia, Sierra Leone was founded as a home for people freed from slavery. The British ruled Sierra Leone from 1787 to 1961. Most of the land is used for farming, but the country also has mineral resources, especially diamonds.

Côte d'Ivoire has a French name that means "ivory coast." From the late 1400s to the early 1900s, a trade in elephant ivory tusks in Côte d'Ivoire brought profits to European traders. Today the ivory trade is illegal, and the country protects its few remaining elephants. The port of Abidjan is the largest urban area and economic center. It has towering office buildings and wide avenues. Abidjan is the official seat of government, but **Yamoussoukro** (YAH•moo•SOO•kroh), some 137 miles (220 km) inland, has been named the new capital.

Ghana's people belong to about 100 ethnic groups. The Ashanti and the Fante are the largest. Many groups still keep their local kings, but these rulers have no political power. The people respect these ceremonial rulers and look to them to keep traditions alive. About 35 percent of Ghana's people live in cities. Accra, on the coast, is the capital and largest city. A giant dam on the Volta River provides hydroelectric power to urban areas. The dam also has created **Lake Volta,** the world's largest artificial lake.

✓ Reading Check **What are the capitals of Ghana and Côte d'Ivoire?**

Our World Today Online
Web Activity Visit the ***Our World Today: People, Places, and Issues*** Web site at owt.glencoe.com and click on **Chapter 16–Student Web Activities** to learn more about Liberia.

Section 2 Assessment

Defining Terms

1. **Define** overgraze, drought, desertification, bauxite, phosphate.

Recalling Facts

2. **History** What three great empires ruled in the Sahel from A.D. 500 to 1500?
3. **Economics** What types of goods must West African countries import?
4. **History** Which West African country was never a colony?
5. **Government** How much political power do the local kings in Ghana have?

Critical Thinking

6. **Making Predictions** What problems do you think will arise as people move from the Sahel to more productive areas?
7. **Drawing Conclusions** Why do governments of coastal West African countries have to borrow money?
8. **Analyzing Information** What West African products do you use?

Graphic Organizer

9. **Organizing Information** On a diagram like this one, record at least three different facts about the three ancient African empires of Ghana, Mali, and Songhai.

Ghana	Mali	Songhai

Applying Social Studies Skills

10. **Analyzing Maps** Study the population density map on page 444. Why would you expect the heavy population centers to be located along the coast?

Section 2 Assessment

1. The terms are defined in the Glossary.
2. Ghana, Mali, and Songhai
3. industrial
4. Liberia
5. None. They are ceremonial.
6. Answers will vary.
7. Agricultural exports often don't earn enough to pay for industrial imports, so the countries can't meet their people's needs.
8. Answers will vary but might include palm, coffee, cacao, rubber.
9. All three empires controlled the trade in gold, salt, and other goods; Mali's ruler, Mansa Musa, made his capital, Tombouctou, a leading center of Islamic learning; invaders from North Africa defeated Songhai, the last of the great empires, in the late 1500s.
10. Close to ports and oil discoveries.

Chapter 16

Section 2, pages 440–445

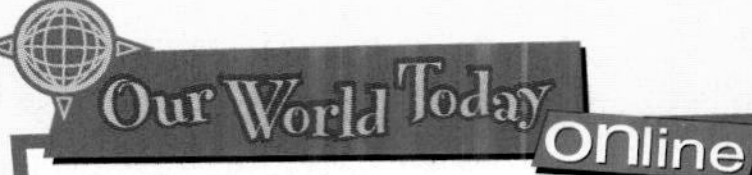

Objectives, goals, and answers to the Student Web Activity can be found in the Web Activity Lesson Plan at **owt.glencoe.com**

Reteach

Have students list three key facts about each country discussed in this section.

✓ Reading Check Answer

Accra; Yamoussoukro

Reading Essentials and Study Guide 16–2

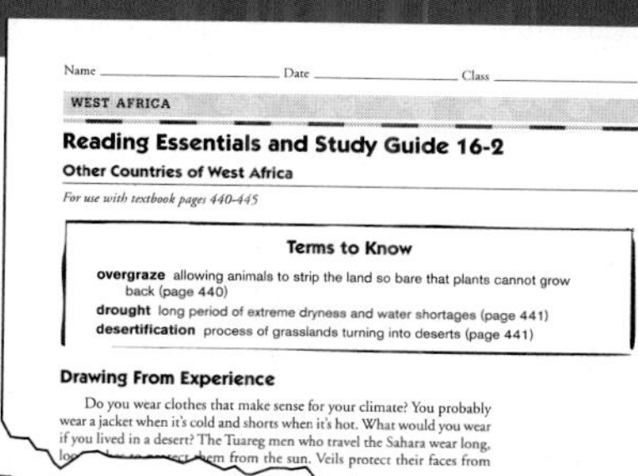
Name ______ Date ______ Class ______

WEST AFRICA

Reading Essentials and Study Guide 16-2

Other Countries of West Africa

For use with textbook pages 440–445

Terms to Know

overgraze allowing animals to strip the land so bare that plants cannot grow back (page 440)
drought long period of extreme dryness and water shortages (page 441)
desertification process of grasslands turning into deserts (page 441)

Drawing From Experience

Do you wear clothes that make sense for your climate? You probably wear a jacket when it's cold and shorts when it's hot. What would you wear if you lived in a desert? The Tuareg men who travel the Sahara wear long, [illegible] from the sun. Veils protect their faces from

CLOSE

Have students use the maps and text in this chapter to write a 10-question quiz that reflects what they think are the most important characteristics of the coastal countries of West Africa.

TEACH

Ask: What kinds of buildings are common to all societies? *(Examples are government buildings, recreational facilities, museums, stadiums or arenas, transportation facilities, and shopping areas.)* Help students understand that religious structures fall in this category. **L1**

More About Great Mosque

A visitor to Djenné described the spring repair of the Great Mosque in this way: "This is a festival at once awesome, messy, meticulous, and fun. For weeks beforehand mud is cured. . . . [When the signal comes,] a hundred voices roar, and the throng sets off on a massive mud-fetch. . . . Crowds of young women, heads erect under the burden of buckets brimming with water, approach. . . . Other teams, bringing mud, charge shouting through the main square and swarm across the mosque's terrace."

Interdisciplinary Connections

Architecture Have students research a famous building in their own community. Have them prepare a poster that shows how the structure reflects the physical environment.

Making Connections

CULTURE | GOVERNMENT | PEOPLE | TECHNOLOGY

Great Mosque of Djenné

In the West African city of Djenné (jeh•NAY), Mali, stands a huge structure built entirely of mud. It is the Great Mosque of Djenné, and it covers an area the size of a city block. Considered one of Africa's greatest architectural wonders, the existing Great Mosque is actually the third mosque to occupy the location.

Djenné

Located between the Sahara and the African savanna, the city of Djenné was an important crossroads on a trade route connecting northern and southern Africa. Caravans and boats carried gold, salt, and other goods through the city.

During the A.D. 1200s, the ruler of Djenné ordered the construction of the first Great Mosque. Having recently converted to Islam, he had his palace torn down to make room for the huge house of worship. The city became an important Islamic religious center. Over the years, political and religious conflicts led to a decline in the city. People abandoned the Great Mosque, and a second, much smaller one replaced it. Then in 1906, builders began to raise a new Great Mosque. Today the Great Mosque is once more an important part of the religious life of the people of Djenné.

The Great Mosque

Built facing east toward Makkah, the holy city of Islam, the Great Mosque of Djenné is constructed from the same sun-dried mud bricks as most of the rest of the city. The mud walls of the mosque vary in thickness between 16 and 24 inches (41 and 61 cm), providing insulation to keep the interior cool. Roof vents can be removed at night to allow cooler air inside.

With its five stories and three towers, or minarets, the mosque rises above the surrounding buildings. Inside the mosque, the main prayer hall is open to the sky. Although the mosque contains loudspeakers used to issue the call to prayer, there are few other modern improvements.

Maintaining the Mosque

Rain, wind, and heat can damage mud structures, and without care the Great Mosque would soon deteriorate. Each spring the people of Djenné plaster the mosque from top to bottom with fresh mud. It is a great festival day, and nearly everyone volunteers. Workers climb up the sides of the mosque on wooden rods permanently mounted to the walls. They dump mud and water onto the walls, then smooth it with their bare hands. The townspeople know that, with such care, the Great Mosque will remain a place of worship for generations to come.

Making the Connection

1. When was the first Great Mosque built?
2. What elements of the Great Mosque help keep the inside cool?
3. **Making Comparisons** In what way is the Great Mosque like the other buildings in Djenné? In what way is it different?

◀ Great Mosque of Djenné

CHAPTER 16

Making the Connection

1. A.D. 1200s
2. The mud walls provide insulation to keep the interior cool; roof vents can be removed at night to allow cooler air inside.
3. It is similar to other buildings in that it is made of sun-dried mud brick. It is different because it faces toward Makkah, because it is taller than other buildings in the city, and because people from all over the city help repair the walls each spring.

Reading Review

Section 1 Nigeria

Terms to Know
- mangrove
- savanna
- harmattan
- subsistence farm
- cacao
- compound
- civil war

Main Idea

A large, oil-rich country, Nigeria has more people than any other African nation.

✓ **Place** Nigeria's major landforms are coastal lowlands, savannas, highlands, plateaus, and partly dry grasslands.

✓ **Economics** More than 90 percent of Nigeria's income comes from oil exports.

✓ **Culture** Nigeria has more than 300 ethnic groups. The four largest ethnic groups are the Hausa, Fulani, Yoruba, and Ibo.

Section 2 Other Countries of West Africa

Terms to Know
- overgraze
- drought
- desertification
- bauxite
- phosphate

Main Idea

The Sahel countries face a continuing struggle to keep grasslands from turning into desert, but the coastal countries receive plenty of rainfall.

✓ **Region** The Sahel countries are Mauritania, Mali, Niger, Chad, and Burkina Faso.

✓ **Region** The Sahel receives little rainfall, so only short grasses and small trees can support grazing animals.

✓ **Human/Environment Interaction** Overgrazing and drought have caused many grassland areas in this region to become desert.

✓ **Region** The 11 countries that make up coastal West Africa are Senegal, Gambia, Guinea, Guinea-Bissau, Cape Verde, Liberia, Sierra Leone, Côte d'Ivoire, Ghana, Togo, and Benin.

✓ **Economics** West Africa's coastal countries import more in industrial goods than they export in natural products.

The port of Abidjan, Côte d'Ivoire ▶

Reading Review

Use the Chapter 16 Reading Review to preview, review, condense, or reteach the chapter.

Preview/Review

Use the Terms to Know lists to help students review and study.

Activity Have students draw up a matching quiz of 10 terms and their definitions from the chapter. Then have them exchange quizzes with another student and take the quiz their partners prepared.

Vocabulary PuzzleMaker Software reinforces the vocabulary terms used in Chapter 16.

The Interactive Tutor Self-Assessment CD-ROM allows students to review Chapter 16 content.

Condense

Have students read the Chapter 16 summary statements.

Chapter 16 Guided Reading Activities

Chapter 16 Audio Program

Reteach

Reteaching Activity 16

Chapter 16 Reading Essentials and Study Guide

Chapter Culminating Activity

Charting Information Have students work in groups to prepare a chart or other display that shows the similarities and differences among at least five countries in West Africa. Tell students that their countries should include Nigeria and two countries from both the Sahel and the coast regions. Suggest that they address such issues as landforms, climate, economies, history, and people. Remind them to include both similarities and differences. Have the groups present their findings to the class. *NOTE: This activity may be completed separately or you may wish students to incorporate it into their Current Events Journals.* **L2**

EE2 Places and Regions: Standard 4

Assessment and Activities

GLENCOE TECHNOLOGY

MindJogger Videoquiz
Use MindJogger to review the Chapter 16 content.

 Available in VHS.

Using Key Terms

1.	i	**6.**	d
2.	c	**7.**	a
3.	h	**8.**	e
4.	j	**9.**	g
5.	b	**10.**	f

Reviewing the Main Ideas

11. oil
12. because different ethnic groups have sought control over the country or tried to set up their own country
13. Wole Soyinka
14. Hausa, Fulani, Yoruba, Ibo
15. border
16. Mali's most famous ruler and a Muslim who made Tombouctou a leading center of Islamic learning
17. Islam
18. overgrazing and drought
19. Rapids and shallow waters prevent it.
20. African states selling people as slaves to Europeans and Asians
21. Ghana
22. Ashanti and Fante

Chapter 16 Assessment and Activities

Using Key Terms

Match the terms in Part A with their definitions in Part B.

A.

1. overgraze	6. phosphate
2. harmattan	7. desertification
3. drought	8. cacao
4. mangrove	9. subsistence farm
5. compound	10. savanna

B.

a. process in which deserts expand
b. a group of houses surrounded by a wall
c. a dusty wind that blows south from the Sahara
d. mineral salt used in fertilizers
e. tropical tree whose seeds are used to make cocoa and chocolate
f. tropical grassland with scattered trees
g. produces enough to support a family's needs
h. extended period of extreme dryness
i. when animals strip the land so bare that plants cannot grow
j. tropical tree with roots above and beneath the water

 Reviewing the Main Idea

Section 1 Nigeria

11. **Economics** What is Nigeria's major export?
12. **History** Why have there been so many conflicts in Nigeria since 1960?
13. **Culture** Who was the first African to win the Nobel Prize in literature?
14. **Culture** What are the four largest ethnic groups in Nigeria?

Section 2 Other Countries of West Africa

15. **Region** What is the meaning of the word *Sahel?*
16. **History** Who was Mansa Musa?
17. **Culture** What religion do most people of the Sahel follow?
18. **History** What has led to desertification in the Sahel?
19. **Movement** Why are ships unable to sail very far inland in coastal West Africa?
20. **History** What was the slave trade?
21. **History** What early kingdom was called "the land of gold"?
22. **Culture** What are the largest ethnic groups in Ghana?

West Africa

Place Location Activity

On a separate sheet of paper, match the letters on the map with the numbered places listed below.

1. Gulf of Guinea	6. Lagos
2. Nigeria	7. Mali
3. Niger River	8. Ghana
4. Liberia	9. Chad
5. Cape Verde	10. Monrovia

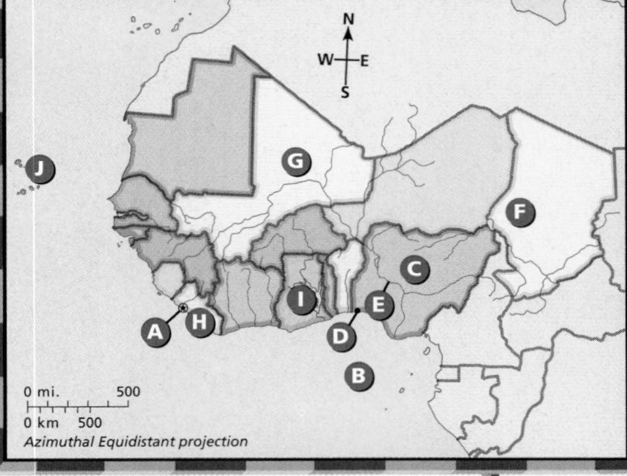

NATIONAL GEOGRAPHIC

Place Location Activity

1.	B	6.	D
2.	C	7.	G
3.	E	8.	I
4.	H	9.	F
5.	J	10.	A

Critical Thinking

23. Answers will vary but might include such challenges as desertification, ethnic conflict, or economic development.
24. Time lines will vary. Have students justify why they chose the five events as the most important.

Assessment and Activities

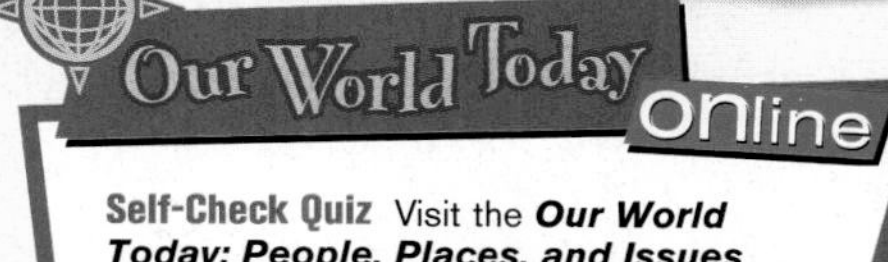

Self-Check Quiz Visit the ***Our World Today: People, Places, and Issues*** Web site at owt.glencoe.com and click on **Chapter 16–Self-Check Quizzes** to prepare for the Chapter Test.

Critical Thinking

23. **Evaluating Information** What do you feel is the major challenge facing the countries of West Africa today? Explain your answer.
24. **Sequencing Information** After reviewing the entire chapter, choose what you feel are five of the most important events in the history of West Africa. Place those events and their dates on a time line like this one.

Current Events Journal

25. **Writing a Poem** Read a newspaper or magazine article about one of the countries of West Africa. Imagine that you are there and write an "I am . . ." poem. Begin each line with the words "I am . . ." and then complete it with a description, action, or emotion that you feel relates to the subject. Share your poem with the rest of the class.

Mental Mapping Activity

26. **Focusing on the Region** Create a simple outline map of West Africa, then label the following:

- Niger River
- Senegal
- Atlantic Ocean
- Côte d'Ivoire
- Gulf of Guinea
- Chad
- Tropic of Cancer
- Mali
- Nigeria
- Mauritania
- Niger
- Liberia

Technology Skills Activity

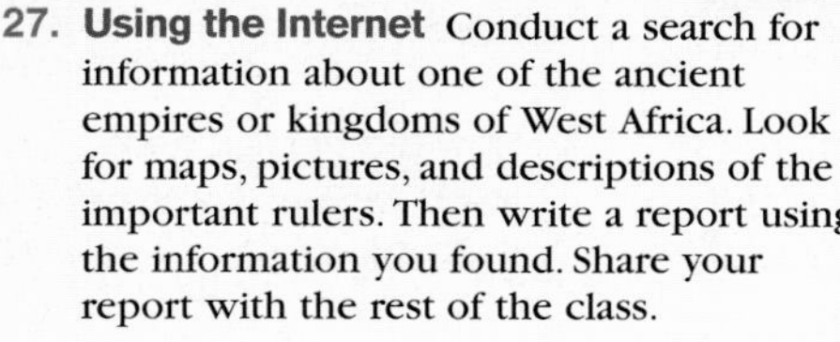

27. **Using the Internet** Conduct a search for information about one of the ancient empires or kingdoms of West Africa. Look for maps, pictures, and descriptions of the important rulers. Then write a report using the information you found. Share your report with the rest of the class.

The Princeton Review

Standardized Test Practice

Directions: Study the graph, and then answer the question that follows.

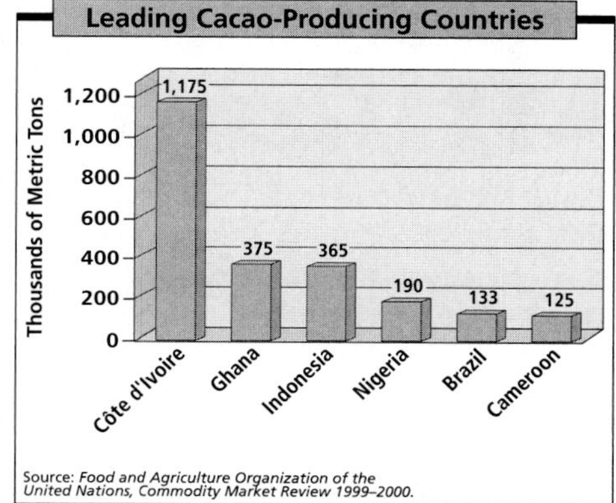

1. **What countries on the graph are leading cacao-producing countries from West Africa?**
   A Ghana, Indonesia, and Nigeria
   B Côte d'Ivoire, Ghana, and Indonesia
   C Côte d'Ivoire, Nigeria, and Cameroon
   D Côte d'Ivoire, Ghana, and Nigeria

Test-Taking Tip: The important words in this question are "from West Africa." You need to use information on the graph as well as information you learned in Chapter 16 to answer this question. As with any graph, read the title bar and information along the side and bottom of the graph first. Then analyze and compare the sizes of the bars to one another.

449

Standardized Test Practice

1. D

Tested Objectives:
Reading a graph, synthesizing information

Chapter Test Bonus Question

This question may be used for extra credit on the chapter test.

This country in West Africa was founded by African Americans who had been freed from slavery in the United States. It was never a colony. What country is it? *(Liberia)*

Our World Today online

Have students visit the Web site at owt.glencoe.com to review Chapter 16 and take the Self-Check Quiz.

Current Events Journal

25. Students' poems should highlight the key features of the country, including its geography, economy, and culture. Remind students to begin each line with "I am." Point out that the poem does not need to rhyme.

Mental Mapping Activity

26. This exercise helps students visualize the countries and geographic features they have been studying and understand the relationship among various points. Accept all attempts at freehand mapping that show places in the correct relationship to one another.

Technology Skills Activity

27. Students' projects should include not only the report, but also the evaluation of Internet sources. You may wish to discuss what criteria to use in evaluating the Web sites before students conduct their assessment.

Focus

Ask: **Have you ever traded items with a friend?** Have volunteers describe the situation and how the two people arrived at an understanding of the value of the two items traded. Then explain that trading has existed between groups of people for thousands of years. Point out that in ancient Africa, people traded for a good that students might consider very common.

Teach

Tracing Trade Routes
Ask: **What is the most important resource in the world today?** *(Possible responses: oil, water, food)* **What makes these goods so valuable?** *(Oil is needed to power industry, cars, and electricity; water and food are needed for survival.)* Have students choose one good that is exported and research where it is found or produced and what routes it follows when sold. **L1**

Meeting National Standards

Geography for Life
The following standards are met in the Student Edition feature:

- **EE1** The World in Spatial Terms: Standard 3
- **EE4** Human Systems: Standard 11
- **EE5** Environment and Society: Standard 16

People trade salt and other goods at a market on the Niger River in ancient Africa.

PLEASE PASS THE SALT:
Africa's Salt Trade

Passing the salt at dinner may not be a big deal, but in parts of Africa, salt built empires. How did such a basic substance come to play such an important role in Africa?

Good as Gold

Salt is essential for life. Every person contains about 8 ounces (227 g) of salt—enough to fill several saltshakers. Salt helps muscles work, and it aids in digesting food. In hot climates, people need extra salt to replace the salt lost when they sweat. In tropical Africa, salt has always been precious.

Salt is plentiful in the Sahara and scarce in the forests south of the Sahara (in present-day countries such as Ghana and Côte d'Ivoire). These conditions gave rise to Africa's salt trade. Beginning in the A.D. 300s, Berbers drove camels carrying European glassware and weapons from Mediterranean ports into the Sahara. At the desert's great salt deposits, such as those near the ancient sites of Terhazza and Taoudenni, they traded European wares for salt.

The salt did not look like the tiny crystals in a saltshaker. It was in the form of large slabs, as hard as stone. The slabs were pried from hardened salt deposits that were left on the land long ago when landlocked seas evaporated. The salt slabs were loaded onto camels, and the animals were herded south. To people in the south, salt was literally worth its weight in gold. The slabs were cut into equal-sized blocks and exchanged for gold and other products such as ivory and kola nuts. Salt was also traded for enslaved people.

Rise and Decline

Before camels arrived in Africa from Asia in A.D. 300, only a trickle of trade, mostly carried by human porters, made it across the blistering desert. In time, caravans of thousands of camels loaded with tons of salt arrived at southern markets.

Local kings along the trade routes put taxes—payable in gold—on all goods crossing their realms. The ancient empires of Mali, Ghana, and Songhai rose to great power from wealth brought by the salt trade.

Trade routes also provided avenues for spreading ideas and inventions. By the A.D. 800s, Arab traders brought to Africa a system of weights and measures, a written language, and the concept of money. They also brought a new religion: Islam.

Today trucks have replaced many of the camels. Salt no longer dominates trade in the region. However, salt is still important, and the salt trade continues in Mali and in the markets of other West African nations.

QUESTIONS

1. What goods were exchanged in the salt trade?
2. How did the salt trade affect regions south of the Sahara?

A present-day salt caravan in Niger ▶

Answers to the Questions

1. European wares, gold, ivory, kola nuts, enslaved people
2. Local kings rose to power by collecting tax on the salt and other trade goods; trade routes helped spread ideas and inventions.

NATIONAL GEOGRAPHIC

Time Line

- A.D. **200:** Camels introduced to the Sahara by this time
- **700–900:** Berbers develop caravan routes linking Mediterranean ports to West Africa
- **900s:** Islam enters West Africa
- **900–1100:** Kingdom of Ghana flourishes
- **1200–1450:** Kingdom of Mali controls West Africa
- **c. 1312–1327:** Reign of Mansa Musa over Mali
- **1450–1590:** Kingdom of Songhai thrives

Salt Trade Routes

Did You Know

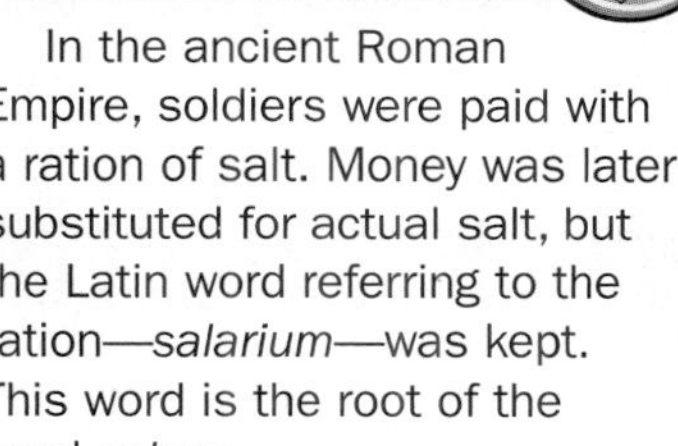

In the ancient Roman Empire, soldiers were paid with a ration of salt. Money was later substituted for actual salt, but the Latin word referring to the ration—*salarium*—was kept. This word is the root of the word *salary.*

3 Assess

Have students answer the questions on page 450.

4 Close

Have students write a paragraph explaining why the salt trade arose in West Africa and what impact this trade had.

Geography and History Activity

Trade Routes Have students research the oceangoing trade routes that connected cities on the east coast of Africa to the Muslim and Indian worlds. Have them create an illustrated map or poster that shows the routes followed, the main trading ports, and the goods that were exchanged. Have them also report on how the exchanges affected society and culture in East Africa. **L2**

EE1 The World in Spatial Terms: Standard 1

Chapter 17 Resources

Note: The following materials may be used when teaching Chapter 17.
Section level support materials are shown at point of use in the margins of the Teacher Wraparound Edition.

Timesaving Tools

TeacherWorks™ All-In-One Planner and Resource Center

- **Interactive Teacher Edition** See the **Interactive Teacher Edition** CD-ROM to electronically integrate your Teacher Wraparound Edition and blackline masters.
- **Interactive Lesson Planner** Organize your week, month, semester, or year with all the lesson helps you need. The **Interactive Lesson Planner** CD-ROM contains all Chapter 17 resources.

Use Glencoe's **Presentation Plus!** multimedia teacher tool to easily present dynamic lessons that visually excite your students. Using Microsoft PowerPoint® you can customize the presentations to create your own personalized lessons.

TEACHING TRANSPARENCIES

Graphic Organizer Transparency and Student Activity 17

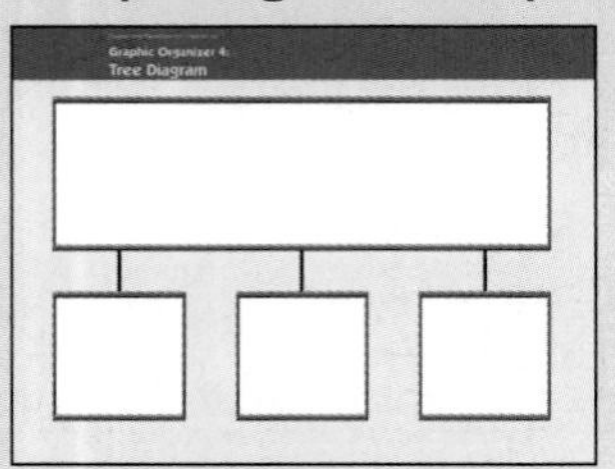

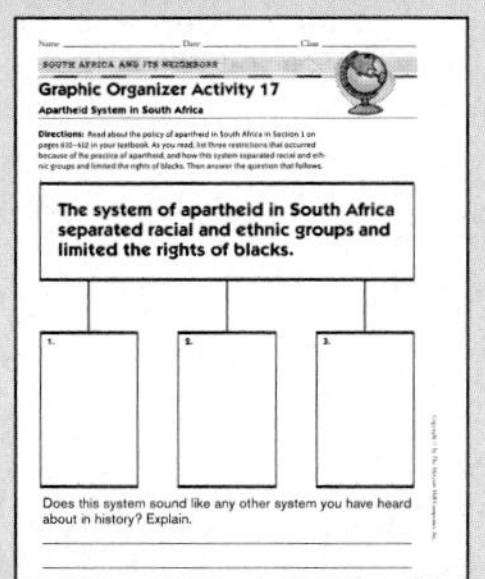

FOLDABLES™ Study Organizer

Foldables are three-dimensional, interactive graphic organizers that help students practice basic writing skills, review key vocabulary terms, and identify main ideas. Every chapter contains a Foldable activity, with additional chapter activities found in the ***Reading and Study Skills Foldables*** booklet.

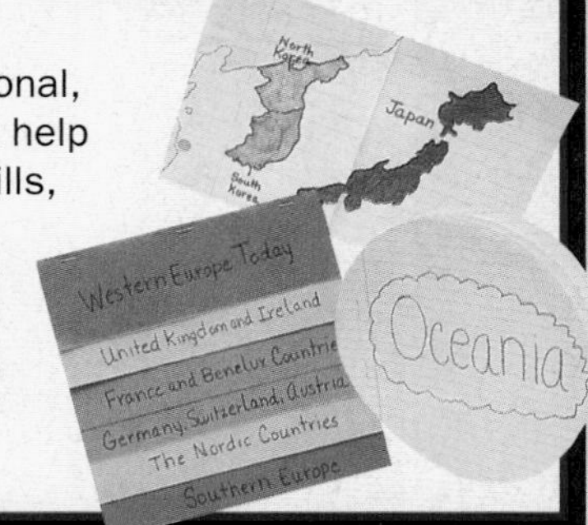

ENRICHMENT AND EXTENSION

Enrichment Activity 17

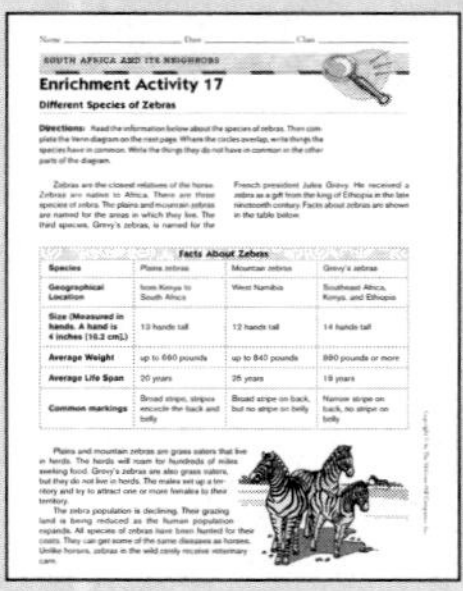

Cooperative Learning Activity 17

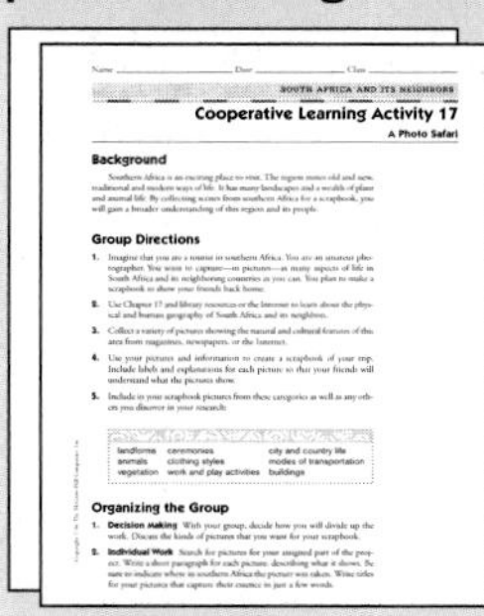

MAP AND GEOGRAPHY SKILLS

Chapter Map Activity 17

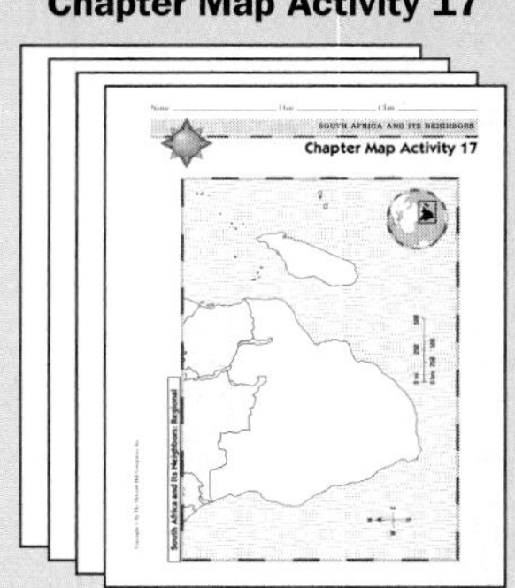

GeoLab Activity 17

STANDARDIZED ASSESSMENT SKILLS

Glencoe's Assessment Advantage

Critical Thinking Skills Activity 17

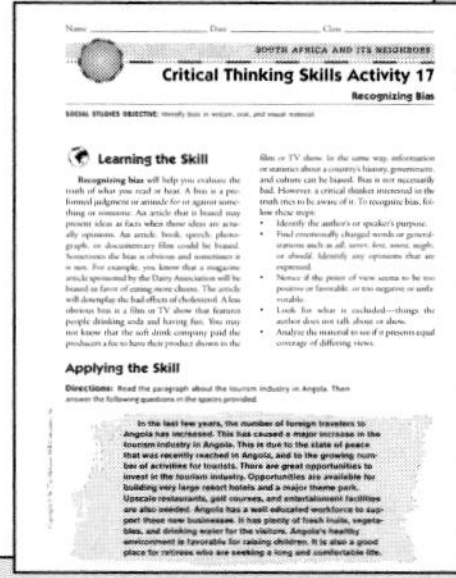

Map and Graph Skills Activity 17

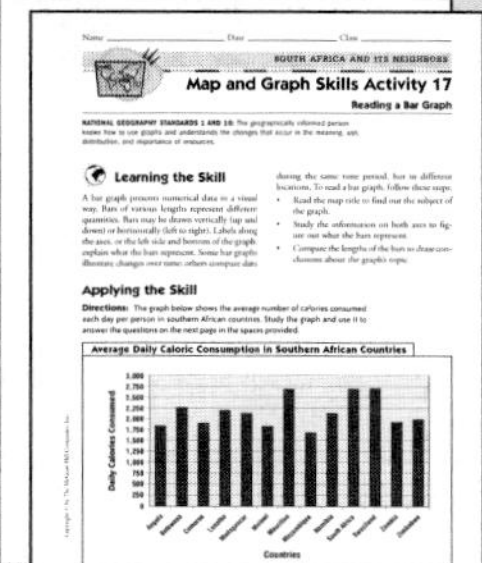

Reading and Writing Skills Activity 17

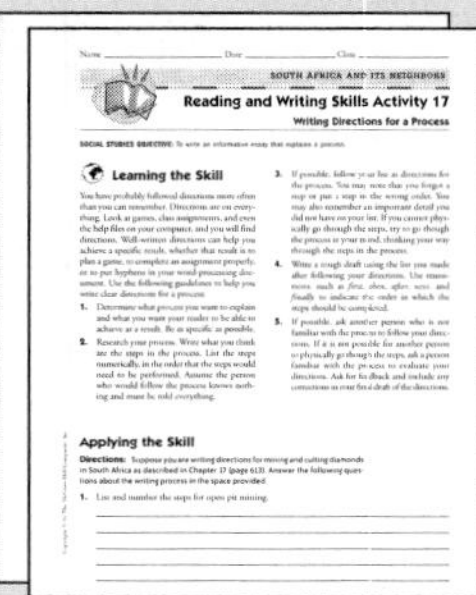

Standardized Test Practice Workbook Activity 17

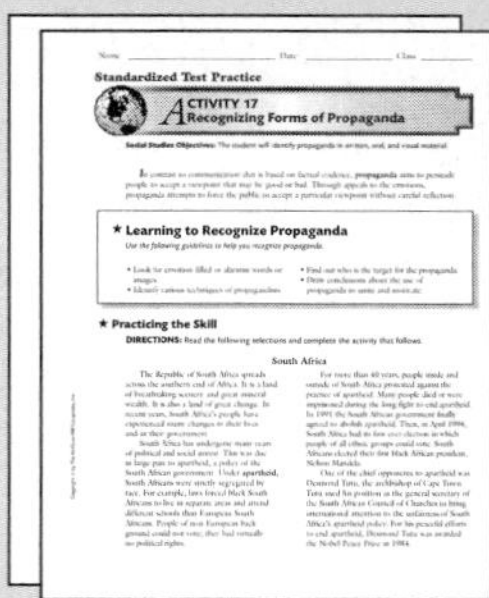

REVIEW AND REINFORCEMENT

Chapter Skills Activity 17

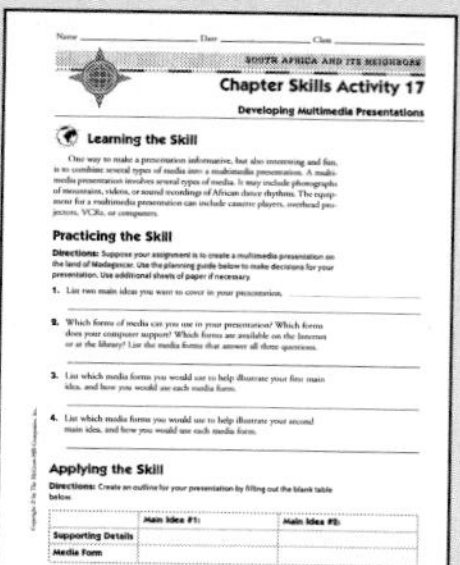

Take-Home Review Activity 17

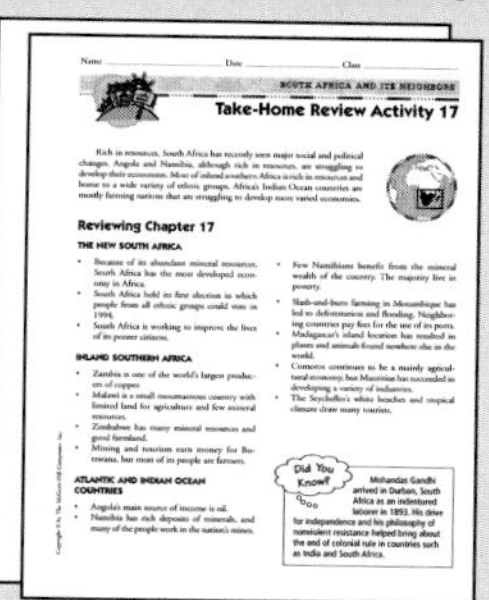

Reteaching Activity 17

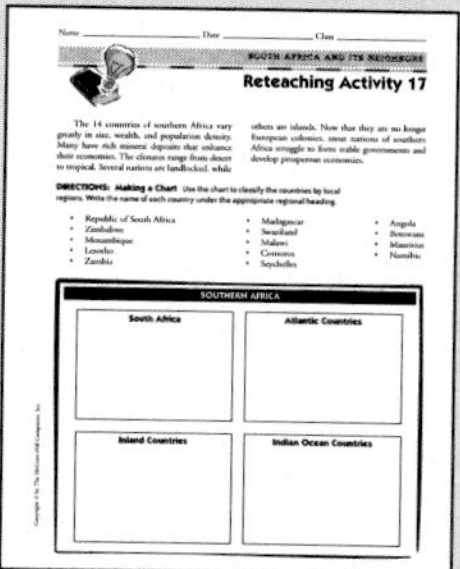

Vocabulary Activity 17

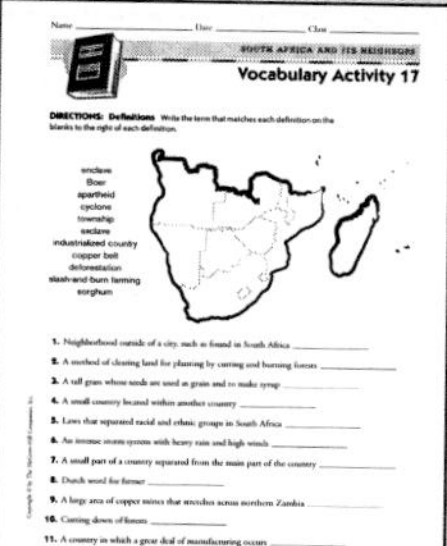

Workbook Activity 17

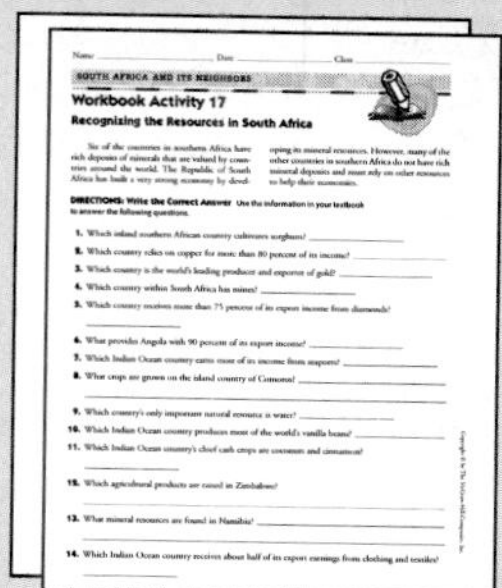

ASSESSMENT

GLENCOE'S ASSESSMENT ADVANTAGE

Chapter 17 Test, Form A

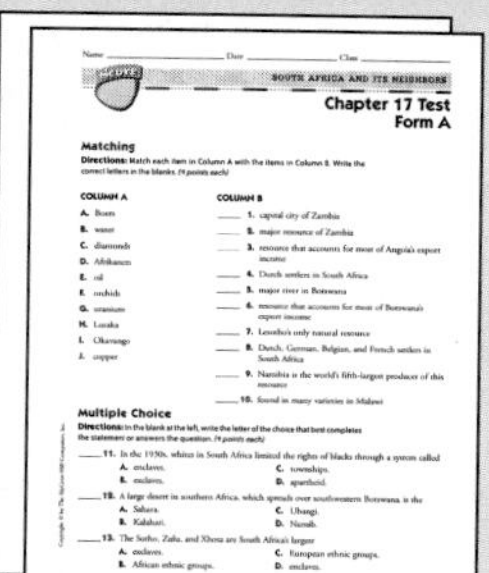

Chapter 17 Test, Form B

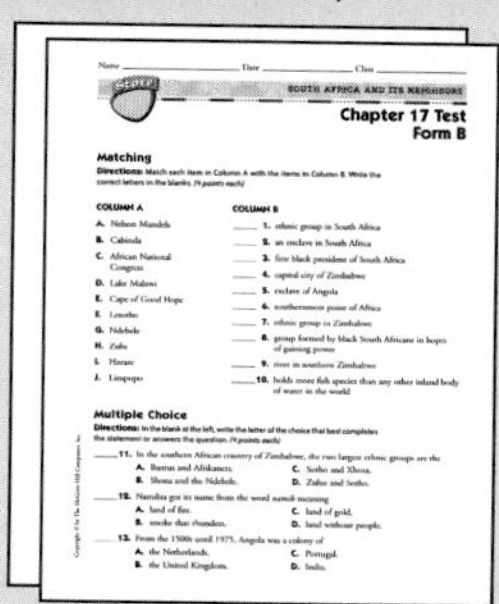

Performance Assessment Activity 17

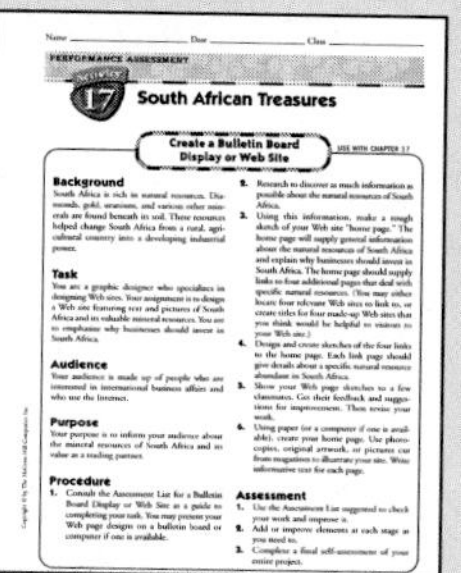

ExamView® Pro 3.0 Testmaker CD-ROM

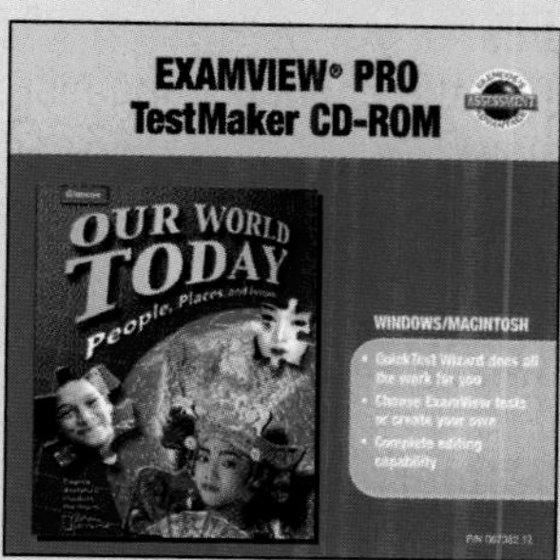

MULTIMEDIA

- National Geographic's The World and Its People
- MindJogger Videoquiz
- Vocabulary PuzzleMaker Software
- Interactive Tutor Self-Assessment CD-ROM
- ExamView® Pro 3.0 Testmaker CD-ROM
- Interactive Lesson Planner CD-ROM
- Interactive Teacher Edition CD-ROM
- Skillbuilder Interactive Workbook CD-ROM, Level 1
- Presentation Plus! CD-ROM
- Audio Program

SPANISH RESOURCES

The following Spanish language materials are available in the Spanish Resources binder:

- Spanish Chapter Summaries
- Spanish Vocabulary Activities
- Spanish Guided Reading Activities
- Spanish Quizzes and Tests
- Spanish Take-Home Review Activities
- Spanish Reteaching Activities

Meeting National Standards

Geography for Life

All of the 18 standards are demonstrated in Unit 6. The following ones are highlighted in Chapter 17:

Section 1 — **EE4 Human Systems: Standards 9, 10, 12**
EE5 Environment and Society: Standard 16

Section 2 — **EE2 Places and Regions: Standard 4**
EE3 Physical Systems: Standards 7, 8
EE5 Environment and Society: Standards 14, 15, 16

Section 3 — **EE2 Places and Regions: Standard 4**
EE5 Environment and Society: Standards 14, 15, 16

For a complete listing of National Geography Standards and entire text correlation, see pages T22–T29.

Chapter 17 Planning Guide

SECTION RESOURCES

Daily Objectives	Reproducible Resources	Multimedia Resources
Section 1 **The New South Africa** **Suggested Pacing = 1 day** **1.** Describe the landforms and resources of the Republic of South Africa. **2.** Discuss the people and recent changes in the Republic of South Africa.	Reproducible Lesson Plan 17-1 Daily Lecture and Discussion Notes 17-1 Guided Reading Activity 17-1 Reading Essentials and Study Guide 17-1 Section Quiz 17-1*	Daily Focus Skills Transparency 17-1 GeoQuiz Transparency 17-1 Vocabulary PuzzleMaker Software Interactive Tutor Self-Assessment CD-ROM ExamView® Pro 3.0 Testmaker CD-ROM Presentation Plus! CD-ROM
Section 2 **Inland Southern Africa** **Suggested Pacing = 1 day** **1.** Identify Zambia's most important resource. **2.** Describe the economy and history of Malawi. **3.** Explain the challenges to Zimbabwe's economy. **4.** Discuss how climate affects Botswana's people.	Reproducible Lesson Plan 17-2 Daily Lecture and Discussion Notes 17-2 Guided Reading Activity 17-2 Reading Essentials and Study Guide 17-2 Section Quiz 17-2*	Daily Focus Skills Transparency 17-2 GeoQuiz Transparency 17-1 Vocabulary PuzzleMaker Software Interactive Tutor Self-Assessment CD-ROM ExamView® Pro 3.0 Testmaker CD-ROM Presentation Plus! CD-ROM
Section 3 **Atlantic and Indian Ocean Countries** **Suggested Pacing = 1 day** **1.** Compare the landforms and economies of Angola and Namibia. **2.** Explain what has caused deforestation in Mozambique and Madagascar. **3.** Discuss why Madagascar has such unusual plants and animals.	Reproducible Lesson Plan 17-3 Daily Lecture and Discussion Notes 17-3 Guided Reading Activity 17-3 Reading Essentials and Study Guide 17-3 Section Quiz 17-3*	Daily Focus Skills Transparency 17-3 GeoQuiz Transparency 17-1 Vocabulary PuzzleMaker Software Interactive Tutor Self-Assessment CD-ROM ExamView® Pro 3.0 Testmaker CD-ROM Presentation Plus! CD-ROM

00:00 **Out of Time?** Assign the **Reading Essentials and Study Guide** for this chapter.

*Also available in Spanish

KEY TO ABILITY LEVELS

Teaching strategies have been coded for varying learning styles and abilities.

L1 BASIC activities for all students
L2 AVERAGE activities for average to above-average students
L3 CHALLENGING activities for above-average students
ELL ENGLISH LANGUAGE LEARNER activities

Blackline Master
Software
CD-ROM
Audiocassette
Transparency
Videocassette
Block Scheduling
DVD

Teacher to Teacher

African Masks

Ida Haskew Smith
South Pittsburg Elementary
South Pittsburg, Tennessee

Explain to students that masks are an important art form in Africa. When Africans put on a mask, they stop being themselves and become the force or spirit they are trying to please. Usually masks were worn by dancers at important ceremonies, such as ceremonies for the dead, initiations into secret societies, preparations for war, or rituals to ward off evil spirits or to appeal to good spirits. Masks also had to affect human onlookers. Their power was increased as the masks swayed and bobbed with the motions of the dancers wearing them. Have students make their own masks out of paper, feathers, and other items, much like the various ethnic groups in Africa. Students' masks, however, must reflect their own communities' resources and/or historical interests.

OUR WORLD TODAY Online

Use our Web site for additional resources. All essential content is covered in the Student Edition.

You and your students can visit owt.glencoe.com, the Web site companion to *Our World Today*. This innovative integration of electronic and print media offers your students a wealth of opportunities. The student text directs students to the Web site for the following options:

- Chapter Overviews
- Student Web Activities
- Self-Check Quizzes
- Textbook Updates

Answers are provided for you in the Web Activity Lesson Plan. Additional Web resources and Interactive Tutor puzzles are also available.

TEACHER'S CORNER

Index to National Geographic Magazine:

The following articles may be used for research relating to this chapter:

- "Zulu: People of Heaven, Heirs to Violence," by Peter Godwin, August 2000.
- "Cheetahs: Ghosts of the Grasslands," by Richard Conniff, December 1999.
- "Restoring Madagascar," by Virginia Morell, February 1999.

National Geographic Society Products Available From Glencoe:

To order the following products for use with this chapter, contact your local Glencoe sales representative or call Glencoe at 1-800-334-7344:

- *STV: World Geography* (Videodisc)
- *Picture Atlas of the World* (CD-ROM)
- *MapPack: Africa* (Transparencies)
- *PicturePack: Geography of Africa* (Transparencies)
- *ZipZapMap! World* (Software)
- *GeoBee* (CD-ROM)

Additional National Geographic Society Products:

To order the following products for use with this chapter, call National Geographic Society at 1-800-368-2728:

- *Complete National Geographic: 111 Years of National Geographic Magazine* (CD-ROM)
- *Africa* (Video)
- *Endangered Animals: Survivors on the Brink* (Video)
- *Healing the Earth* (Video)
- *South Africa: After Apartheid* (Video)
- *Physical Earth* (Map)
- *Population* (Map)
- *Voices: Poetry and Art From Around the World* (Book)
- *National Geographic Desk Reference* (Book)
- *National Geographic Atlas of the World, Seventh Edition* (Book)

NGS ONLINE

Access National Geographic's Web site for current events, activities, links, interactive features, and archives.
www.nationalgeographic.com

Introducing Chapter 17

Introduce students to chapter content and key terms by having them access Chapter Overview 17 at owt.glencoe.com

Chapter Objectives

1. Describe the geography, history, economy, and people of the Republic of South Africa.
2. Summarize the physical features, people, and histories of the inland countries of southern Africa.
3. Compare the geography, economies, and cultures of the countries of southern Africa that border the Atlantic and Indian Oceans.

GLENCOE TECHNOLOGY

NATIONAL GEOGRAPHIC

The World and Its People Video Program

Chapter 22 South Africa and Its Neighbors

The following segments enhance the study of this chapter:

- **Soweto**
- **Leaping Lemurs**
- **Sand and Sea**

Available in DVD and VHS.

MindJogger Videoquiz

Use MindJogger to preview the Chapter 17 content.

Available in VHS.

Chapter 17 South Africa and Its Neighbors

The World and Its People NATIONAL GEOGRAPHIC

To learn more about the people and places of South Africa and its neighbors, view ***The World and Its People* Chapter 22** video.

Our World Today online

Chapter Overview Visit the ***Our World Today: People, Places, and Issues*** Web site at owt.glencoe.com and click on **Chapter 17—Chapter Overviews** to preview information about South Africa and its neighbors.

452

Two-Minute Lesson Launcher

Inform students that southern Africa includes several countries that have large deposits of such minerals as gold, diamonds, copper, and others. **Ask: What impact do you think these resources have on the countries' economies?** *(Students are likely to say that the countries are wealthy from selling these resources.)* Explain that all of the countries in the region have not been able to take advantage of these resources to generate wealth. **What factors might prevent a country from benefiting from these resources?** *(control of the resources by other countries; difficulty in tapping these resources due to geography and lack of money)* **L2**

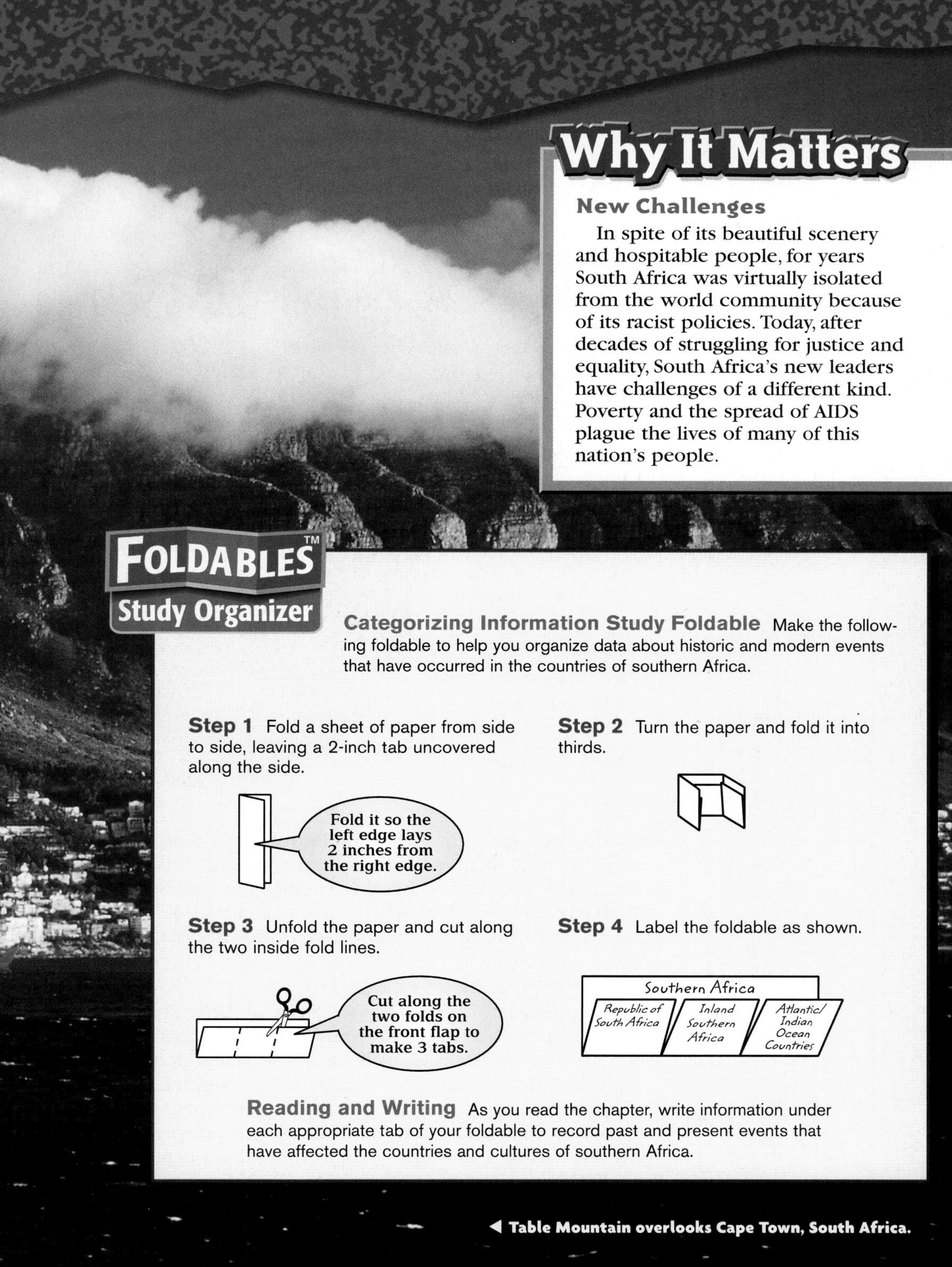

Why It Matters

New Challenges

In spite of its beautiful scenery and hospitable people, for years South Africa was virtually isolated from the world community because of its racist policies. Today, after decades of struggling for justice and equality, South Africa's new leaders have challenges of a different kind. Poverty and the spread of AIDS plague the lives of many of this nation's people.

FOLDABLES™ Study Organizer

Categorizing Information Study Foldable Make the following foldable to help you organize data about historic and modern events that have occurred in the countries of southern Africa.

Step 1 Fold a sheet of paper from side to side, leaving a 2-inch tab uncovered along the side.

Fold it so the left edge lays 2 inches from the right edge.

Step 2 Turn the paper and fold it into thirds.

Step 3 Unfold the paper and cut along the two inside fold lines.

Cut along the two folds on the front flap to make 3 tabs.

Step 4 Label the foldable as shown.

Southern Africa
Republic of South Africa
Inland Southern Africa
Atlantic/ Indian Ocean Countries

Reading and Writing As you read the chapter, write information under each appropriate tab of your foldable to record past and present events that have affected the countries and cultures of southern Africa.

◀ Table Mountain overlooks Cape Town, South Africa.

Introducing Chapter 17

FOLDABLES™ Study Organizer

Purpose This activity requires students to create a foldable and organize information from the chapter on it. Students are required to record historic and modern events that occurred in the Republic of South Africa, inland southern Africa, and the Atlantic and Indian Ocean countries of southern Africa on the appropriate tabs of the foldable.

Have students complete ***Reading and Study Skills Foldables*** Activity 17.

Why It Matters

Help students understand the idea of creating a new, improved government system. Ask them to think of a time when they saw or experienced bullying on the playground. Game rules are designed to make sure all children are treated fairly, and to keep them safe. The citizens of South Africa are emerging from a struggle for justice and equality. Have students imagine they are writing laws for such a new government. Brainstorm the most important rights and freedoms they would guarantee their citizens. Then, have small groups choose five ideas and write them as laws.

About the Photo

On the coasts of nations around the world, towns have grown to provide safe harbors and a place to exchange and distribute goods brought there by ship. Fresh water and food are needed by the crew, and shore leave is prized. When a merchant sells some of his cargo, new cargo can then be purchased and brought back to the home port for sale. Shipping is very important to the economies of many countries. While Cape Town is the most populous port city in South Africa, it follows Durban in shipping volume. Port Elizabeth and East London are also major ports.

Chapter 17

Section 1, pages 454–457

Focus

Section Objectives

1. Describe the landforms and resources of the Republic of South Africa.
2. Discuss the people and recent changes in the Republic of South Africa.

BELLRINGER
Skillbuilder Activity

Project transparency and have students answer questions.

This activity is also available as a blackline master.

Daily Focus Skills Transparency 17-1

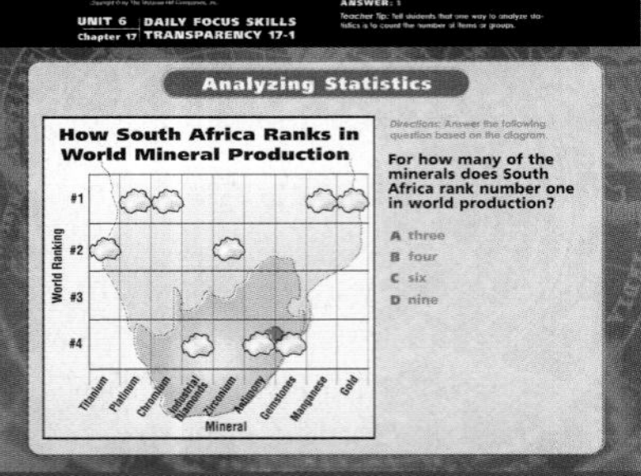

Guide to Reading

■ Accessing Prior Knowledge Tell students that South Africa's distance from the Equator is about the same as that of Texas. Explain that in this section, they will see how South Africa is similar to Texas.

The New South Africa

Guide to Reading

Main Idea

Rich in resources, South Africa has recently seen major social and political changes.

Terms to Know

- industrialized country
- Boer
- apartheid
- township
- enclave

Reading Strategy

Create a time line like this one. Then list five key events and their dates in South Africa's history.

NATIONAL GEOGRAPHIC Exploring Our World

Cape Town's Table Mountain is famous for its flat top. A cable car takes people to the top. If you are physically fit and have four hours to spare, you can also climb the mountain. From the top, you can see Cape Town—South Africa's legislative capital. The country's executive capital is Pretoria, while the judicial capital is Bloemfontein.

South Africa (officially called the **Republic of South Africa**) is a land of beautiful scenery and great mineral wealth. It is also a land of great change. Here you will find the continent's biggest mammal, the African elephant, and smallest mammal, the miniature shrew. To protect these creatures, the government has set aside land as national parks.

A Land Rich in Resources

South Africa borders the Atlantic Ocean on the west and the Indian Ocean on the south and east. The **Namib Desert** reaches into the northwest. The **Cape of Good Hope** is the southernmost point of Africa.

South Africa is the most industrialized country in Africa. An **industrialized country** is one in which a great deal of manufacturing occurs. Not all South Africans benefit from this prosperous economy, however. In rural areas, many people continue to depend on subsistence farming and live in poverty.

Section Resources

Reproducible Masters
- Reproducible Lesson Plan 17-1
- Daily Lecture and Discussion Notes 17-1
- Guided Reading Activity 17-1
- Reading Essentials and Study Guide 17-1
- Section Quiz 17-1

Transparencies
- Daily Focus Skills Transparency 17-1
- GeoQuiz Transparency 17-1

Multimedia
- Vocabulary PuzzleMaker Software
- Interactive Tutor Self-Assessment CD-ROM
- Presentation Plus! CD-ROM
- ExamView® Pro 3.0 Testmaker CD-ROM

South Africa's economy is supported in several ways. In terms of mineral resources, South Africa is one of the richest countries in the world. It is the world's largest producer and exporter of gold. South Africa also has large deposits of diamonds, chromite, platinum, and coal. The country also exports machinery, chemicals, clothing, and processed foods. Among the crops cultivated are corn, wheat, fruits, cotton, sugarcane, and potatoes. Ranchers on the high plains raise sheep, cattle for beef, and dairy cows.

✓Reading Check **How have South Africa's resources helped its economy?**

South Africa's History and People

About 43.6 million people live in South Africa. Black African ethnic groups make up about 78 percent of the population. Most trace their ancestry to Bantu-speaking peoples who settled throughout Africa between A.D. 100 and 1000. The largest groups in South Africa today are the **Sotho** (SOO•too), **Zulu,** and **Xhosa** (KOH•suh).

In the 1600s, the Dutch settled in South Africa. They were known as the **Boers,** a Dutch word for farmers. German, Belgian, and French settlers joined them. Together these groups were known as Afrikaners

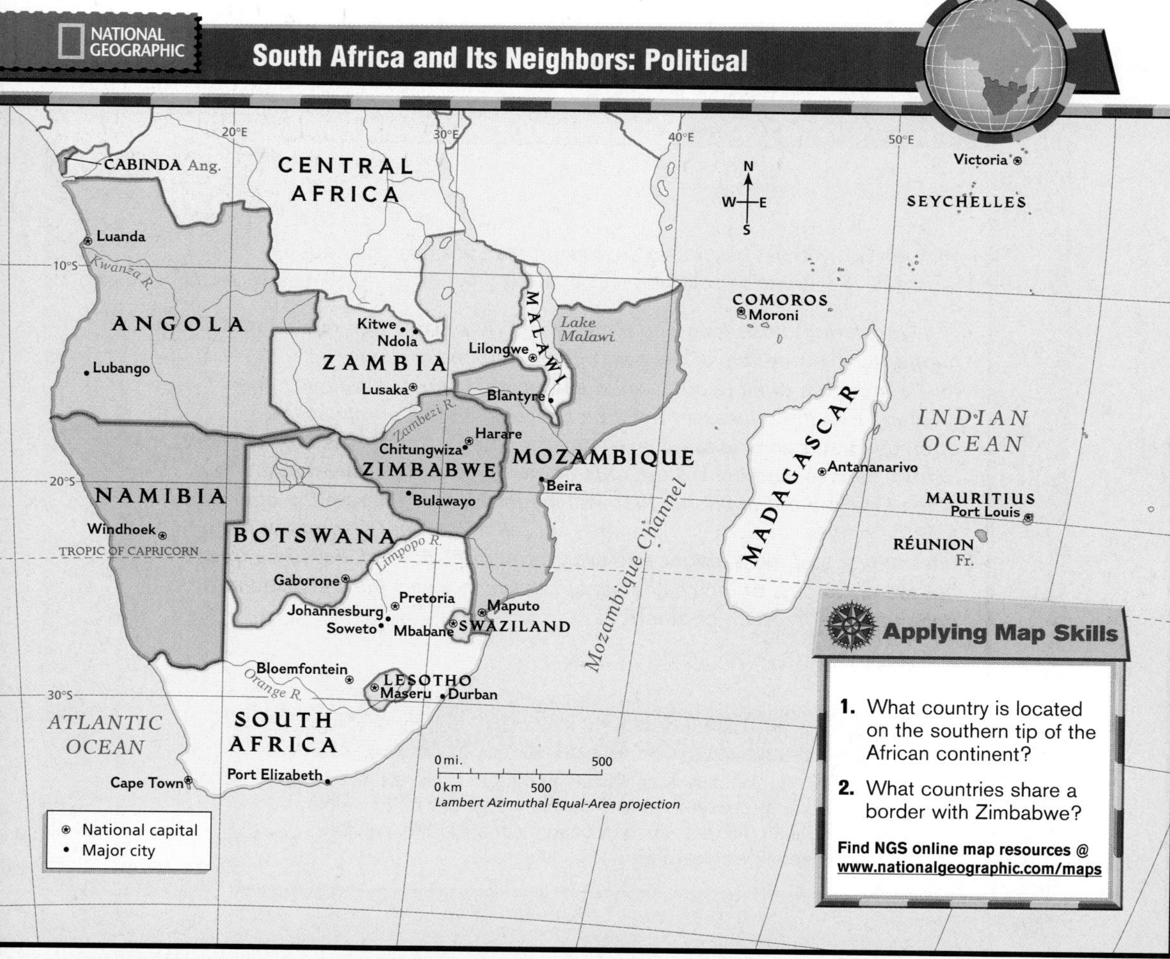

TEACH

Categorizing Information Create a four-column chart, using the following as column headings: "The Land," "The Economy," "The History," and "The People." Then relate a set of facts about the Republic of South Africa. Have students write each fact under the appropriate heading. **L1**

Daily Lecture Notes 17–1

Copyright © by The McGraw-Hill Companies, Inc.

SOUTH AFRICA AND ITS NEIGHBORS

Daily Lecture and Discussion Notes 17-1

The New South Africa (pages 454–457)

Did You Know? The Republic of South Africa has three capitals. Parliament meets in Cape Town, the legislative capital. All government departments have their headquarters in Pretoria, the administrative capital. The highest court meets in Bloemfontein, the country's judicial capital.

I. A Land Rich in Resources (pages 454–455)

A. In South Africa you will find the continent's biggest animal, the African elephant, and smallest mammal, the miniature shrew. To protect these creatures, the government has set aside land as national parks.

B. The Namib Desert lies in northwest South Africa. The Cape of Good Hope is the southernmost point of Africa.

...alized country in Africa.

✓ Reading Check Answer

The economy is supported by several types of resources—minerals, industrial and consumer goods, agriculture, and ranching.

Applying Map Skills

Answers

1. South Africa
2. South Africa, Botswana, Zambia, and Mozambique

Skills Practice

What country is completely surrounded by South Africa? *(Lesotho)*

Team-Teaching Activity

History Invite a teacher with a background in world history to class to talk about the history of South Africa, explaining how the policy of apartheid first developed and how it came to be abandoned. Have the teacher cover such key events as the arrival of the British, the Boers' Great Trek, the Boer War and conflict with the Zulus, independence, and the formation of the white minority government. Then have him or her discuss the extent of apartheid laws, the homelands policy, life in the townships, and the struggle against apartheid—both at home and in the international community. Have students select a topic to research and prepare an annotated time line that uses text and images to explain what happened and why. **L1**

EE4 Human Systems: Standards 12, 13

Chapter 17

Section 1, pages 454–457

Guided Reading Activity 17-1

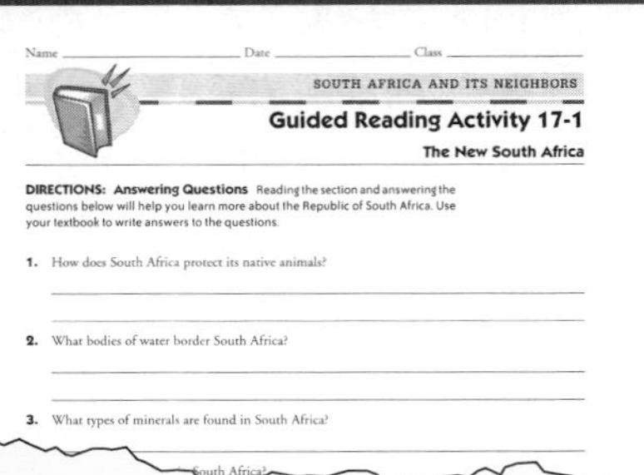
Name ______ Date ______ Class ______

SOUTH AFRICA AND ITS NEIGHBORS

Guided Reading Activity 17-1

The New South Africa

DIRECTIONS: Answering Questions Reading the section and answering the questions below will help you learn more about the Republic of South Africa. Use your textbook to write answers to the questions.

1. How does South Africa protect its native animals?

2. What bodies of water border South Africa?

3. What types of minerals are found in South Africa?

3 ASSESS

Assign Section 1 Assessment as homework or an in-class activity.

Primary Source

Answer Nelson Mandela spent 27 years in prison because of his fight against apartheid. He is comparing his walk out of prison to the long road that blacks in South Africa must "walk" to political freedom. The walk is a symbol of the small steps that must be taken in order to reach the final goal of freedom and respect.

and spoke their own language—Afrikaans (A•frih•KAHNS). They pushed Africans off the best land and set up farms and plantations. They brought many laborers from India to work on sugar plantations.

The British first came to South Africa in the early 1800s. Later, the discovery of diamonds and gold attracted many more British settlers. Tensions between the British and the Afrikaners resulted in the 1902 defeat of the Afrikaners in the Boer War. In 1910 Afrikaner and British territories became the Union of South Africa. It was part of the British Empire and was ruled by whites. Black South Africans founded the **African National Congress** (ANC) in 1912 in hopes of gaining power.

In the 1930s, the whites set up a system of apartheid, or "apartness." **Apartheid** (uh•PAHR•TAYT) made it illegal for different races and ethnic groups to mix, thus limiting the rights of blacks. For example, laws forced black South Africans to live in separate areas, called "homelands." People of non-European background were not even allowed to vote.

For more than 40 years, people inside and outside South Africa protested against the practice of apartheid. Many black Africans were jailed for their actions in the long struggle for justice and equality.

Primary Source

NELSON MANDELA

(1918–)

Through his work and experiences, Nelson Mandela has come to symbolize the struggle for freedom in South Africa.

"It was during those long and lonely years [in prison] that my hunger for the freedom of my own people became a hunger for the freedom of all people, white and black. I knew as well as I knew anything that the oppressor must be liberated just as surely as the oppressed. A man who takes away another man's freedom is a prisoner of hatred, he is locked behind the bars of prejudice and narrow-mindedness. When I walked out of prison, that was my mission, to liberate the oppressed and the oppressor both. . . . We have not taken the final step of our journey, but the first step on a longer and even more difficult road. For to be free is not merely to cast off one's chains, but to live in a way that respects and enhances the freedom of others."

From *The Long Walk to Freedom*, the autobiography of Nelson Mandela.

Analyzing Primary Sources

What do you think Mandela is referring to in his title ***The Long Walk to Freedom***? What is the walk a symbol for? Use the Internet to find a secondary source about Nelson Mandela. Research Mandela's life using the source.

Critical Thinking Activity

Drawing Conclusions Discuss how other countries brought pressure on the government of South Africa to abandon its policy of apartheid. Steps taken included economic sanctions against trade with South Africa and the refusal to allow South Africans to participate in world events such as the Olympics. Describe other instances of sanctions, such as the ban on arms sales to Yugoslavia under the rule of Slobodan Milosevic and the international sanctions against Saddam Hussein in Iraq. Then have students discuss whether sanctions are effective and if so, in what situations. **L1**

EE4 Human Systems: Standard 11

The United Nations declared that apartheid was "a crime against humanity." Many countries cut off trade with South Africa. Finally, in 1991 apartheid ended. South Africa held its first democratic election in April 1994, electing **Nelson Mandela** as the first black president.

The People South Africa has 11 official languages, including Afrikaans, English, Zulu, and Xhosa. About two-thirds of South Africans are Christians while the rest practice traditional African religions.

One of the challenges facing South Africa today is to develop a better standard of living for its poorer people. Most European South Africans live in modern homes and enjoy a high standard of living. Most black African, Asian, and mixed-group South Africans live in rural areas and crowded **townships**, or neighborhoods outside cities. The government has introduced measures to improve education and basic services.

Another challenge facing South Africa is the AIDS epidemic. Millions of people throughout Africa have been infected with the virus that causes AIDS. South Africa is one of the countries hit hardest.

Lesotho and Swaziland Within South Africa lie two other African nations—**Lesotho** (luh•SOO•too) and **Swaziland.** These tiny kingdoms are **enclaves**—small countries located inside a larger country. Both are poor countries that depend heavily on South Africa. Lesotho's only natural resource is water, some of which it sells to South Africa. Many of Lesotho's and Swaziland's people are engaged in subsistence farming. Others work in mines in South Africa.

How do Lesotho and Swaziland earn money from South Africa?

Section 1 Assessment

Defining Terms
1. **Define** industrialized country, Boer, apartheid, township, enclave.

Recalling Facts
2. **Place** Name the largest mammal and the smallest mammal in Africa.
3. **Government** Who is Nelson Mandela?
4. **Culture** What challenges face South Africa?

Critical Thinking
5. **Drawing Conclusions** How did the rest of the world view apartheid?
6. **Analyzing Information** Why do you think workers in Lesotho and Swaziland travel to South Africa to work in mines?

Graphic Organizer
7. **Organizing Information** In a chart like the one below, write the resources and products of South Africa in the two boxes.

South Africa	
Resources	Products

Applying Social Studies Skills
8. **Analyzing Maps** Study the political map on page 455. What are the three national capitals of the Republic of South Africa?

Section 1 Assessment

1. The terms are defined in the Glossary.
2. African elephant; miniature shrew
3. the first black African president of South Africa
4. developing a better standard of living for its poor people; fighting AIDS
5. The United Nations declared that apartheid was "a crime against humanity."
6. because their own countries do not have enough jobs
7. *Resources:* gold, diamonds, chromite, platinum, coal, fertile soil, land for herding; *Products:* machinery, chemicals, clothing, processed foods, corn, wheat, fruits, cotton, sugarcane, potatoes, sheep, cattle for beef, dairy cows
8. Pretoria, Bloemfontein, and Cape Town.

Chapter 17

Section 1, pages 454–457

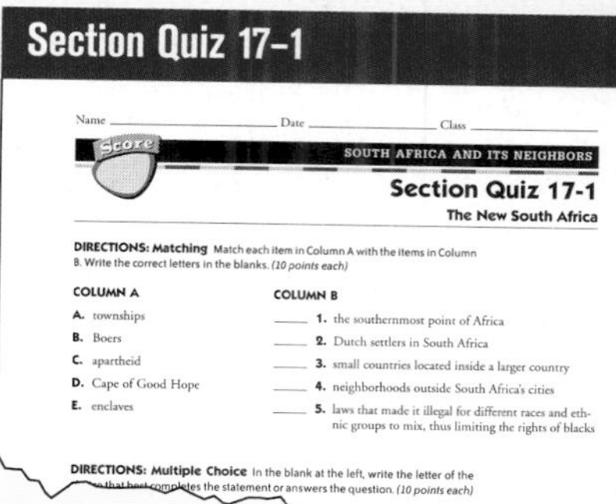
Section Quiz 17–1

Name ______ Date ______ Class ______

SOUTH AFRICA AND ITS NEIGHBORS

Section Quiz 17-1
The New South Africa

DIRECTIONS: Matching Match each item in Column A with the items in Column B. Write the correct letters in the blanks. *(10 points each)*

COLUMN A	COLUMN B
A. townships	____ 1. the southernmost point of Africa
B. Boers	____ 2. Dutch settlers in South Africa
C. apartheid	____ 3. small countries located inside a larger country
D. Cape of Good Hope	____ 4. neighborhoods outside South Africa's cities
E. enclaves	____ 5. laws that made it illegal for different races and ethnic groups to mix, thus limiting the rights of blacks

DIRECTIONS: Multiple Choice In the blank at the left, write the letter of the ... completes the statement or answers the question. *(10 points each)*

Enrich
Have students research Nelson Mandela's contributions to the peaceful ending of apartheid, and describe his influence on South Africa today.

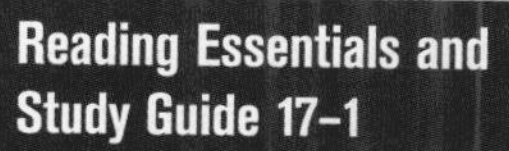

by selling water to South Africa and working in South Africa's mines

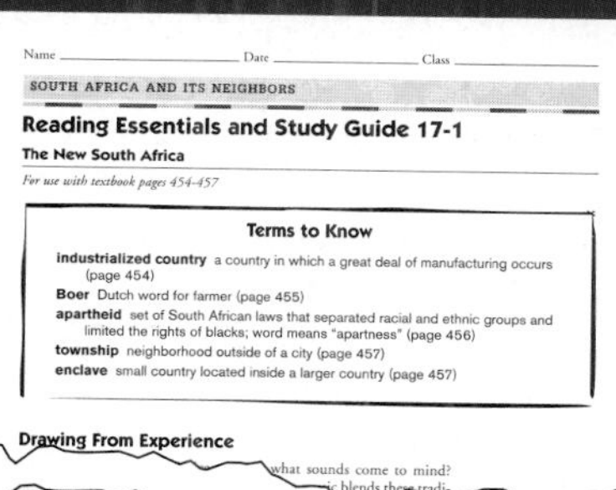
Reading Essentials and Study Guide 17–1

Name ______ Date ______ Class ______

SOUTH AFRICA AND ITS NEIGHBORS

Reading Essentials and Study Guide 17-1
The New South Africa

For use with textbook pages 454–457

Terms to Know

industrialized country a country in which a great deal of manufacturing occurs (page 454)
Boer Dutch word for farmer (page 455)
apartheid set of South African laws that separated racial and ethnic groups and limited the rights of blacks; word means "apartness" (page 456)
township neighborhood outside of a city (page 457)
enclave small country located inside a larger country (page 457)

Drawing From Experience

CLOSE
Have students answer the question: **How did apartheid violate human rights?** *(blacks did not have the same rights as whites, including the right to vote)*

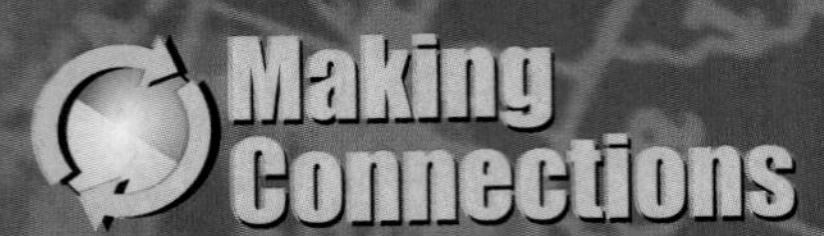

Teach

Ask students if they have heard the expression "a diamond in the rough." **Ask:** **What does the phrase mean?** *(something precious that has not yet been polished to show its brilliance)* Explain that in this feature, they will learn how diamonds are formed, mined, shaped, and polished. **L1**

More About Diamonds

About 80 percent of diamonds are used for industrial cutting and polishing. Diamonds were once used in phonograph needles, which were used to play wax records on turntables.

Interdisciplinary Connections

Science Diamonds, the hardest substance found in nature, are also the most desired because of their brilliance and sparkle. When diamonds are cut well, they reflect more light than other gems. The largest diamond was dug from a mine near Pretoria, in South Africa. It was about the size of a person's fist and weighed 3,106 carats (about 1.4 pounds [.64 kg]). When cut, it made 9 large jewels and more than 100 smaller ones. The largest jewel was called the Star of Africa.

Making Connections

CULTURE | GOVERNMENT | PEOPLE | TECHNOLOGY

Mining and Cutting Diamonds

A diamond is a mineral made entirely of carbon. It is the hardest known substance on the earth and the most popular gemstone. Most diamonds formed billions of years ago deep inside the earth's mantle. There, intense pressure and heat transformed carbon into diamond crystal.

Mining

There are two major techniques used for mining diamonds: open pit and underground mining. In open pit mining, the earth is dug out in layers, creating a series of steps or roads that circle down into a pit. After drills and explosives loosen the rock containing diamonds, shovels and trucks remove it. When the pit becomes too deep to reach easily, underground mining may begin.

Underground mining requires sinking a shaft into the ground and tunneling to the rock. Explosives blast the rock loose, and the resulting rubble is crushed and carried to the surface for further processing.

To remove the diamonds, the crushed rock is mixed with water and placed in a washing pan. Heavier minerals, such as diamonds, settle to the bottom, while lighter wastes rise to the top and overflow. Next, the heavier mixture travels to a grease table. Diamonds cling to the grease while other wetted minerals flow past. Workers continue the sorting and separating by hand.

Cutting

The newly mined diamond resembles a piece of glass, not a sparkling jewel. To enhance their brilliance and sparkle, gem-quality diamonds are precisely cut and polished. The cutter uses high-speed diamond-tipped tools to cut facets, or small flat surfaces, into the stone. One of the most popular diamond cuts is the brilliant cut, which has 58 facets. The job of the cutter requires extreme skill, because the angles of the facets must be exactly right to bring out the diamond's beauty.

Making the Connection

1. Of what are diamonds made?
2. Why are gemstone diamonds cut and polished?
3. **Making Comparisons** How are open pit and underground diamond mining techniques alike? How are they different?

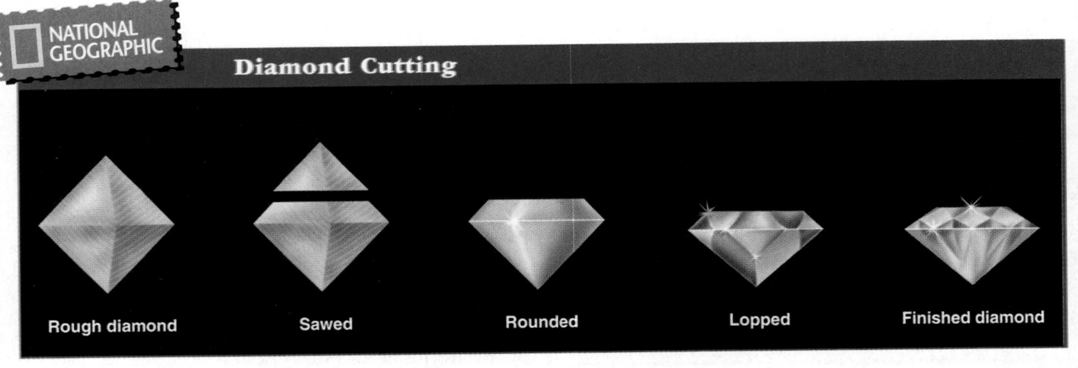

458 CHAPTER 17

Making the Connection

1. carbon
2. to eliminate imperfections and to enhance brilliance and sparkle
3. Both methods involve separating diamonds from the surrounding rock. Open pit mining involves digging out the rock that contains diamonds in layers creating a pit. Underground mining involves tunneling to the rock that contains diamonds.

Section 2

Inland Southern Africa

Guide to Reading

Main Idea

Most of inland southern Africa is rich in resources and home to a wide variety of ethnic groups.

Terms to Know

- copper belt
- sorghum

Reading Strategy

Create a chart like this one. Then list the main economic activities of each country.

Country	Economic Activities
Zambia	
Malawi	
Zimbabwe	
Botswana	

NATIONAL GEOGRAPHIC **Exploring Our World**

Hundreds of years ago, southern Africa had powerful, wealthy kingdoms. They traded gold to cities on the eastern coast. The largest kingdom and city was Great Zimbabwe, a Bantu word meaning "stone houses." The city, part of which is shown here, flourished from about A.D. 1100 to 1450. It covered nearly 100 acres (40 ha) and, along with the surrounding valley,

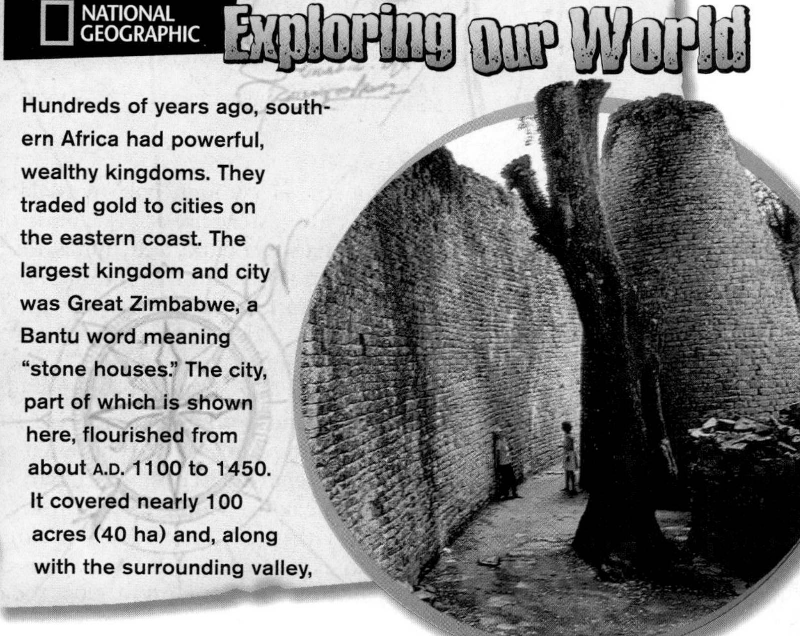

The four countries of inland southern Africa include **Zambia, Malawi** (mah•LAH•wee), **Zimbabwe,** and **Botswana** (baht•SWAH•nah). They have several things in common. First, they all are landlocked. A high plateau dominates much of their landscape and gives them a mild climate. In addition, about 70 percent of the people practice subsistence farming in rural villages. Thousands move to cities each year to look for work.

Zambia

Zambia is slightly larger than Texas. The **Zambezi** (zam•BEE•zee) **River**—one of southern Africa's longest rivers—crosses the country. The Kariba Dam—one of Africa's largest hydroelectric projects—spans the Zambezi River. Also along the Zambezi River are the spectacular Victoria Falls, named in honor of British Queen Victoria, who ruled in the 1800s. The falls are known locally as *Mosi oa Tunya*—or "smoke that thunders."

1 Focus

Section Objectives

1. Identify Zambia's most important resource.
2. Describe the economy and history of Malawi.
3. Explain the challenges to Zimbabwe's economy.
4. Discuss how climate affects Botswana's people.

BELLRINGER Skillbuilder Activity

Project transparency and have students answer questions.

This activity is also available as a blackline master.

Daily Focus Skills Transparency 17-2

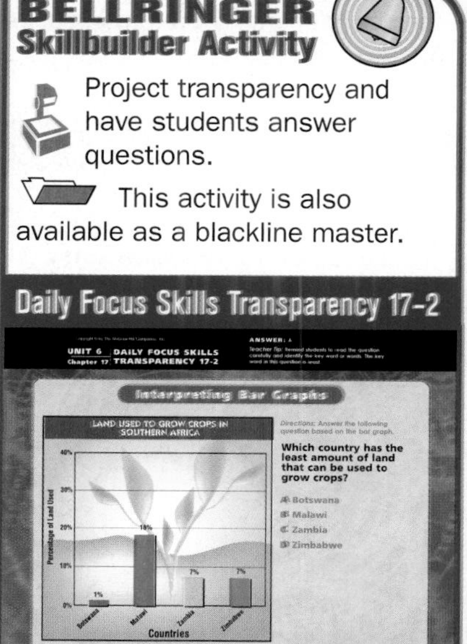

Guide to Reading

■ **Accessing Prior Knowledge** Have students find Zambia, Malawi, Zimbabwe, and Botswana on a map. **Ask:** **How does location make economic development difficult for these countries?** *(being landlocked, transportation of goods is difficult)*

Section Resources

Reproducible Masters

- Reproducible Lesson Plan 17-2
- Daily Lecture and Discussion Notes 17-2
- Guided Reading Activity 17-2
- Reading Essentials and Study Guide 17-2
- Section Quiz 17-2

Transparencies

- Daily Focus Skills Transparency 17-2
- GeoQuiz Transparency 17-1

Multimedia

- Vocabulary PuzzleMaker Software
- Interactive Tutor Self-Assessment CD-ROM
- Presentation Plus! CD-ROM
- ExamView® Pro 3.0 Testmaker CD-ROM

TEACH

Charting Information Have students scan the section for names of crops and resources found in these four countries. Then have them copy the information into a chart with the headings "Country," "Crops," and "Resources." Remind them to use their charts as study aids. **L1**

Reading Check Answer

Zambia's economy suffers because its income goes down.

Daily Lecture Notes 17–2

SOUTH AFRICA AND ITS NEIGHBORS

Daily Lecture and Discussion Notes 17-2

Inland Southern Africa (pages 459–462)

Did You Know? As the spread of the HIV virus continues in Africa, Zambia is wrestling with the idea of requiring its presidential candidates to be tested for the virus before they are allowed to run for office. The country's Permanent Human Rights Commission hopes that debate on the issue can result in a national consensus.

I. Zambia (pages 459–460)

A. The Zambezi River crosses Zambia. The spectacular Victoria Falls lie along the river.

B. A large area of copper mines, known as a **copper belt**, stretches across northern Zambia. One of the world's major producers of copper, Zambia relies on it for ... percent of its income. As a result, when world copper prices go ...

Reading Check Answer

green plains and grasslands

Guided Reading Activity 17–2

Name ______ Date ______ Class ______

SOUTH AFRICA AND ITS NEIGHBORS

Guided Reading Activity 17-2

Inland Southern Africa

DIRECTIONS: Outlining Reading the section and completing the outline below will help you learn more about the countries of Zambia, Malawi, Zimbabwe, and Botswana. Use your textbook to fill in the blanks.

I. Zambia

A. The ______ ______ is one of southern Africa's longest rivers.

1. The ______ ______ is one of Africa's largest hydroelectric projects.

2. The ______ ______ are named in honor of a British queen.

B. A ______ ______ stretches across northern Zambia.

C. Zambia gained its independence from the ______ in ______.

A large area of copper mines, known as a **copper belt,** stretches across northern Zambia. One of the world's major producers of copper, Zambia relies on it for more than 80 percent of its income. As a result, when world copper prices go down, Zambia's income goes down too. As copper reserves dwindle, the government has encouraged city dwellers to return to farming. Zambia must import much of its food.

Once a British colony, Zambia gained its independence in 1964. The country's 9.8 million people belong to more than 70 ethnic groups and speak many languages. English is the official language. Those who live in urban areas such as **Lusaka,** the capital, work in mining and service industries. Villagers grow corn, rice, and other crops to support their families. Their main food is porridge made from corn.

Reading Check What happens to Zambia when copper prices go down?

Malawi

If you travel through narrow Malawi, you see green plains and grasslands in western areas. Vast herds of elephants, zebras, and antelope roam national parks and animal reserves here.

The Great Rift Valley runs through eastern Malawi. In the middle of it lies beautiful **Lake Malawi.** This lake holds about 500 fish species, more than any other inland body of water in the world. Malawi is also famous for its more than 400 orchid species.

Malawi has few mineral resources and little industry. Tobacco, tea, sugar, coffee, and peanuts are exported. Farmers also grow **sorghum,** a tall grass whose seeds are used as grain and to make syrup. Donations, loans, and foreign aid help support Malawi's people.

Bantu-speaking people arrived in the area about 2,000 years ago, bringing with them knowledge of iron working. The most famous European explorer to reach Malawi was the Scottish missionary **David Livingstone** during the mid-1800s. Today most people in Malawi are Protestant Christians as a result of the teachings of missionaries.

In 1964 the British colony became independent. Malawi has recently returned to democratic government after a long period of rule by a dictator. After years of harsh government, the works of many modern writers emphasize themes such as human rights and abuse of power.

Malawi is one of the most densely populated countries in Africa. It has 229 people per square mile (88 people per sq. km). Jobs are scarce, so thousands of men seek work in South Africa and Zambia.

Reading Check What types of landforms cover western Malawi?

Democracy in Action

AIDS is a serious problem for many African countries. The governments of some countries, such as Zimbabwe, do not have the resources to deal with the disease. Other countries, such as Botswana, are working with the international community to combat the spread of HIV, the virus that causes AIDS. Because of Botswana's stable, democratic government, clinics have been established, roads are well maintained, and medical supplies can be quickly distributed. Botswana has a good chance for a successful treatment program.

Zimbabwe

Crossing Zimbabwe, you might think you were in the western United States. The vast plateau is studded with large outcrops of rock. The **Limpopo River** winds through southern lowlands. The Zambezi River crosses the north.

Mining gold, copper, iron ore, and asbestos provides most of the country's income. Some large plantations grow coffee, cotton, and

Critical Thinking Activity

Summarizing Information The black majority government of Zimbabwe inherited a difficult economic situation when it took power. Although whites were a minority, they owned most of the large farms—about 40 percent of the country's land. The government promised to redistribute this land to blacks, but such action did not take place quickly, producing unrest. In the meantime, this prospect discouraged white farmers from developing their land and led some to leave the country, draining the nation of wealth. Have students research the current economic situation in Zimbabwe and summarize what steps the government has taken to improve the economy. **L2**

 **EE4 Human Systems: Standard 11**

Music

The talking drum is a popular instrument in Africa south of the Sahara. Animal skins cover both ends and are held together by strings. While holding the drum under the arm, the musician strikes one skin with a curved wooden mallet. By squeezing down on the strings with the arm, the skins are stretched tighter and the pitch of the drum becomes higher. The loosening and tightening of the strings give the drum its characteristic "talking" sound.

Looking Closer **How is the talking drum different from the traditional drums in the United States?**

GO TO **World Music: A Cultural Legacy**
Hear music of this region on Disk 2, Track 1.

tobacco. Europeans own many of the large plantations, while many Africans work only small plots. Since the 1980s, the government has tried to redistribute land to Africans. Progress has been slow, and with President Mugabe's support, protesters recently took over large and small European-owned farms to force changes.

Another serious challenge to Zimbabwe's economy comes from the spread of AIDS. People who have the disease often cannot work to support their families. Many children have been orphaned by AIDS. The government lacks the means to effectively deal with the AIDS crisis.

Zimbabwe takes its name from an ancient African city and trading center—**Great Zimbabwe.** This remarkable stone fortress was built by an ethnic group called the Shona in the A.D. 1100s to 1400s. The **Shona** and the **Ndebele** (ehn•duh•BEH•leh) ruled large stretches of south-central Africa until the late 1800s. In the 1890s, the British controlled the area and called it Rhodesia. They named it after **Cecil Rhodes,** a British businessman who expanded British rule in Africa.

Europeans ran Rhodesia and owned all the best farmland. In response, the Africans organized into political groups and fought European rule. In 1980 free elections brought an independent African government to power. The country was renamed Zimbabwe.

Today Zimbabwe has about 11.4 million people. Most of them belong to the Shona and Ndebele ethnic groups. About half of the population is Christian. The other half practices traditional African religions. The largest city is **Harare** (hah•RAH•ray), the capital.

✓Reading Check **How has AIDS affected Zimbabwe's economy?**

Web Activity Visit the ***Our World Today: People, Places, and Issues*** Web site at owt.glencoe.com and click on **Chapter 17–Student Web Activities** to learn more about Zimbabwe.

Meeting Special Needs

Inefficient Readers Students who do not read efficiently benefit from having a specific purpose for reading. Point out the Reading Strategy at the beginning of the section. Have students read the instructions and copy the grid into their notebooks. Then have them look for information to fill in the chart as they read. **L1**

Refer to *Inclusion for the Middle School Social Studies Classroom Strategies and Activities* in the TCR.

A master drummer using a talking drum can converse, tell stories, and even crack jokes.

Answer In traditional American drums, there are no strings to tighten the drum head. Each drum is stretched tight when it is made.

World Music: A Cultural Legacy
Use the Teacher Guide for background information, discussion questions, and worksheets about the music of the region.

3 ASSESS

Assign Section 2 Assessment as homework or an in-class activity.

Objectives, goals, and answers to the Student Web Activity can be found in the Web Activity Lesson Plan at owt.glencoe.com

✓ Reading Check Answer

Many workers have been lost; many children have become orphans, which means they need additional help to survive; and health care costs have risen.

Chapter 17

Section 2, pages 459–462

Section Quiz 17-2

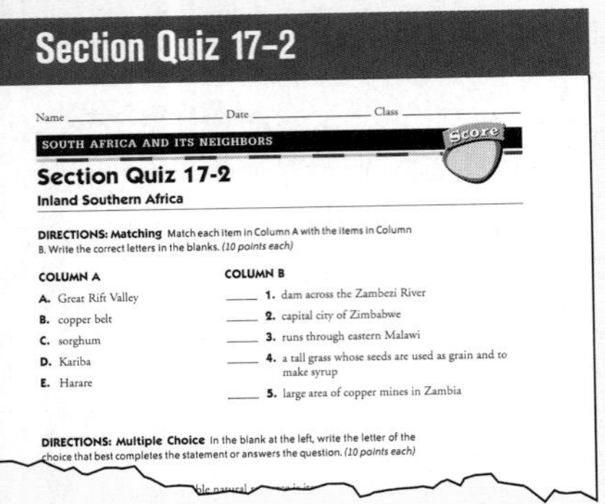
Name ______ Date ______ Class ______

SOUTH AFRICA AND ITS NEIGHBORS

Score

Section Quiz 17-2
Inland Southern Africa

DIRECTIONS: Matching Match each item in Column A with the items in Column B. Write the correct letters in the blanks. *(10 points each)*

COLUMN A	COLUMN B
A. Great Rift Valley	____ 1. dam across the Zambezi River
B. copper belt	____ 2. capital city of Zimbabwe
C. sorghum	____ 3. runs through eastern Malawi
D. Kariba	____ 4. a tall grass whose seeds are used as grain and to make syrup
E. Harare	____ 5. large area of copper mines in Zambia

DIRECTIONS: Multiple Choice In the blank at the left, write the letter of the choice that best completes the statement or answers the question. *(10 points each)*

Reading Check Answer

diamonds

Reading Essentials and Study Guide 17-2

Name ______ Date ______ Class ______

SOUTH AFRICA AND ITS NEIGHBORS

Reading Essentials and Study Guide 17-2
Inland South Africa

For use with textbook pages 459–462

Terms to Know

copper belt large area of copper mines in Zambia (page 460)
sorghum tall grass whose seeds are used as grain and to make syrup (page 460)

Drawing From Experience

Have you ever seen a waterfall? Imagine one that is a mile wide and falls 355 feet. This is the roaring Victoria Falls in Zambia. Earth scientists list it as one of the seven wonders of the world.

The last section described South Africa and the two countries within it—Lesotho and Swaziland. This section discusses four countries without coast: Zambia, Malawi, Zimbabwe, and Botswana.

CLOSE

Give students an outline map of southern Africa. Have them create an annotated map that describes the geography, resources, and products of the inland countries.

Botswana

Botswana lies in the center of southern Africa. The vast **Kalahari Desert** spreads over southwestern Botswana. This hot, dry area has rolling, red sands and low, thorny shrubs. The Okavango River in the northwest forms one of the largest swamp areas in the world. This area of shifting streams has much wildlife.

Botswana's national emblem (as well as its basic monetary unit) is a one-word motto—*Pula*—meaning "rain." In Botswana, there is never much of it. From May to October, the sun bakes the land. Droughts strike often, and many years can pass before the rains fall again.

Botswana is rich in mineral resources. Diamonds account for more than 75 percent of Botswana's export income. Thousands of tourists visit Botswana's game preserves every year. Farming is difficult, and the country grows only about 50 percent of its food needs. It must import the rest. To earn a living, many people work in South Africa for several months a year.

After nearly 80 years of British colonial rule, Botswana became independent in 1966. Today it has one of Africa's strongest democracies. Most of Botswana's people are Christians, although a large number practice traditional African religions. The official language is English, but 90 percent of the population speak an African language called Setswana. **Gaborone** is the capital and largest city.

Reading Check **What is Botswana's biggest source of export income?**

Assessment

Defining Terms

1. **Define** copper belt, sorghum.

Recalling Facts

2. **Economics** What is Zambia's most important export?
3. **Place** What makes Lake Malawi unique?
4. **Culture** Where did Zimbabwe get its name?

Graphic Organizer

5. **Organizing Information** Choose two of the countries in this section. Put the name and three facts about each country in the outer ovals. Where the ovals overlap, put facts that are true of both countries.

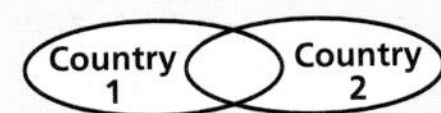

Critical Thinking

6. **Synthesizing Information** Imagine that someone from Great Zimbabwe traveled to that country today. What do you think he or she would describe as the greatest difference between then and now?
7. **Analyzing Information** Why do you think the people of Botswana chose *Pula,* or "rain," as their motto?

Applying Social Studies Skills

8. **Analyzing Maps** Study the political map on page 455. What five African nations does the Tropic of Capricorn cross?

Section 2 Assessment

1. The terms are defined in the Glossary.
2. copper
3. It holds more fish species than any other lake in the world.
4. from Great Zimbabwe, an ancient African city and trading center
5. Answers will vary depending on the countries chosen.
6. Answers might suggest the technology in use today.
7. Answers should include the importance of rain to the people of Botswana.
8. Namibia, Botswana, South Africa, Mozambique, and Madagascar

Technology Skill

Developing Multimedia Presentations

Your geography homework is to make a presentation about Botswana. You want to make your presentation informative but also interesting and fun. How can you do this? One way is to combine several types of media into a **multimedia presentation.**

Learning the Skill

A multimedia presentation involves using several types of media, including photographs, videos, or sound recordings. The equipment can range from simple cassette players to overhead projectors to VCRs to computers and beyond. In your presentation on Botswana, for example, you might show photographs of cheetahs in the Okavango River delta or women fishing. You could also play a recording of local music or find a video of people working in diamond mines. If you have the proper equipment, you can then combine all these items on a computer.

Computer multimedia programs allow you to combine text, video, audio, art or graphics, and animation. The tools you need include computer graphic and drawing programs, animation programs that make certain images move, and systems that tie everything together. Your computer manual will tell you which tools your computer can support.

Practicing the Skill

Use the following questions as a guide when planning your presentation:

1. Which forms of media do I want to include? Video? Sound? Animation? Photographs? Graphics?
2. Which of the media forms does my computer support?
3. Which kinds of media equipment are available at my school or local library?
4. What types of media can I create to enhance my presentation?

Applying the Skill

Plan and create a multimedia presentation on a country discussed in this unit. List three ideas you would like to cover. Use as many multimedia materials as possible and share your presentation with the class.

▼ Various equipment is needed to make multimedia presentations. For example, photographs and videos of cheetahs will make your report on Botswana more interesting.

Technology Skill

TEACH

Ask: **What is easier to remember—something you see and hear or something you read?** The question is likely to generate several different responses. Point out that this is why multimedia presentations are so effective—they appeal to the many different ways that people acquire information. Inform students that the skills they develop in this area might well be useful in their work lives.

Discuss the technologies mentioned and demonstrate some if needed. You might, for example, play African music on a cassette or CD player or show a clip from a documentary on a videocassette player. You could demonstrate several media at once using a CD-ROM encyclopedia on a computer. **L1**

Additional Skills Practice

1. **What type of media is used in the textbook to convey information?** *(print media, including photographs, maps, graphics)*
2. **Why are computers useful multimedia tools?** *(because you can use them to present many different kinds of media)*

Additional Skills Resources

- Chapter Skills Activity 17
- Building Geography Skills for Life

Practicing the Skill Answers

1. Discuss with the class the benefits of each type of media.
2. You might wish to invite a computer teacher to class to discuss the different hardware and software in using media on computers.
3. Have students check with the school media center to find the answer to this question.
4. Have students debate the value of each of these media for a project on Botswana.

Applying the Skill
If time is limited or equipment not available, you could suggest to students that they outline their presentation showing the kinds of content that they would include and the types of media they would use to convey that content.

Focus

Section Objectives

1. Compare the landforms and economies of Angola and Namibia.
2. Explain what has caused deforestation in Mozambique and Madagascar.
3. Discuss why Madagascar has such unusual plants and animals.

BELLRINGER
Skillbuilder Activity

Project transparency and have students answer questions.

This activity is also available as a blackline master.

Daily Focus Skills Transparency 17-3

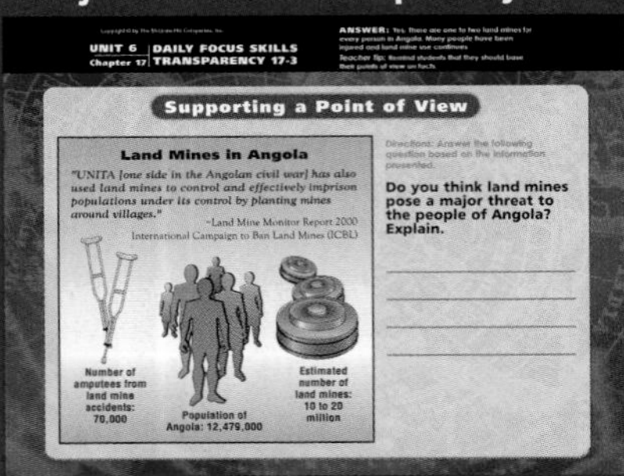

Guide to Reading

■ Vocabulary Precheck
Have students find the meaning of the word *exclave* in the text. Help them locate Cabinda, Swaziland, and Lesotho on the map on page 455. Have them use these examples to compare the definitions of *exclave* and *enclave*.

Section 3

Atlantic and Indian Ocean Countries

Guide to Reading

Main Idea

Africa's Atlantic and Indian Ocean countries are struggling to develop their economies.

Terms to Know

- exclave
- slash-and-burn farming
- deforestation
- cyclone

Reading Strategy

Create a diagram like this one. Choose one Atlantic and one Indian Ocean country. Write facts about each in the outer ovals under its heading. Where the ovals overlap, write statements that are true of both countries.

NATIONAL GEOGRAPHIC **Exploring Our World**

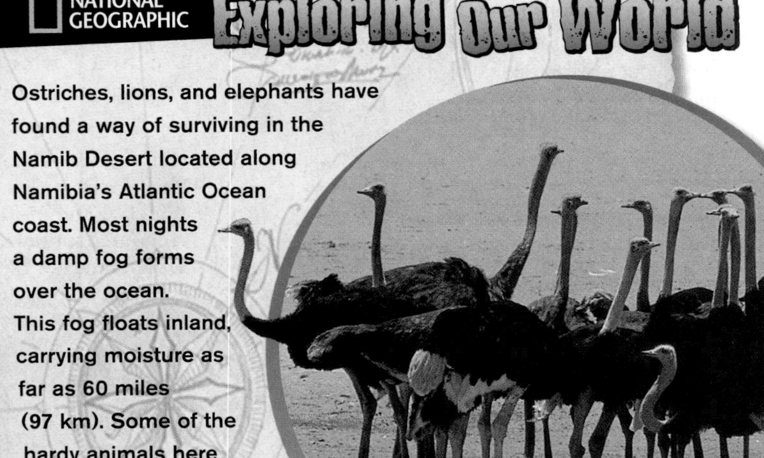

Ostriches, lions, and elephants have found a way of surviving in the Namib Desert located along Namibia's Atlantic Ocean coast. Most nights a damp fog forms over the ocean. This fog floats inland, carrying moisture as far as 60 miles (97 km). Some of the hardy animals here survive by eating moistened tree leaves or finding small water holes.

Angola and **Namibia** have long coastlines on the Atlantic Ocean and are known as southern Africa's Atlantic countries. **Mozambique** and four island countries—**Madagascar** (MA•duh•GAS•kuhr), **Comoros** (KAH•muh•ROHZ), **Seychelles** (say•SHEHL), and **Mauritius** (maw•RIH•shuhs)—form southern Africa's Indian Ocean region.

Angola

Angola is almost twice the size of Texas. Angola also includes a tiny exclave called **Cabinda.** An **exclave** is a small part of a country that is separated from the main part. Hilly grasslands cover northern Angola. The southern part of the country is a rocky desert. In Cabinda, rain forests thrive.

Angola's main economic activity is agriculture. About 85 percent of the people make their living from subsistence farming. Some farmers grow coffee and cotton for export. Angola's main source of income,

Section Resources

Reproducible Masters
- Reproducible Lesson Plan 17-3
- Daily Lecture and Discussion Notes 17-3
- Guided Reading Activity 17-3
- Reading Essentials and Study Guide 17-3
- Section Quiz 17-3

Transparencies
- Daily Focus Skills Transparency 17-3
- GeoQuiz Transparency 17-1

Multimedia
- Vocabulary PuzzleMaker Software
- Interactive Tutor Self-Assessment CD-ROM
- Presentation Plus! CD-ROM
- ExamView® Pro 3.0 Testmaker CD-ROM

however, is oil. Oil deposits off the coast of Cabinda account for 90 percent of Angola's export earnings. Other important industries include diamond mining, fish processing, and textiles. Still, Angola is not a wealthy country. Different groups have struggled for control of the country, which has hurt the economy.

Most of Angola's people trace their ancestry to the Bantu-speaking peoples who spread across much of Africa many centuries ago. In the 1400s, the Kongo kingdom ruled a large part of northern Angola.

From the 1500s until its independence in 1975, Angola was a colony of Portugal. Portugal is still an important trading partner, and Portuguese is the official language. Bantu and other African languages are also widely spoken. Almost 50 percent of Angolans practice the Roman Catholic faith brought to Angola by the Portuguese.

After Angola gained its independence, civil war broke out among different political and ethnic groups. The fighting has lasted more than 25 years and continues to bring great suffering to the people.

✓ Reading Check Why is Angola's economy weak, even though it has rich resources?

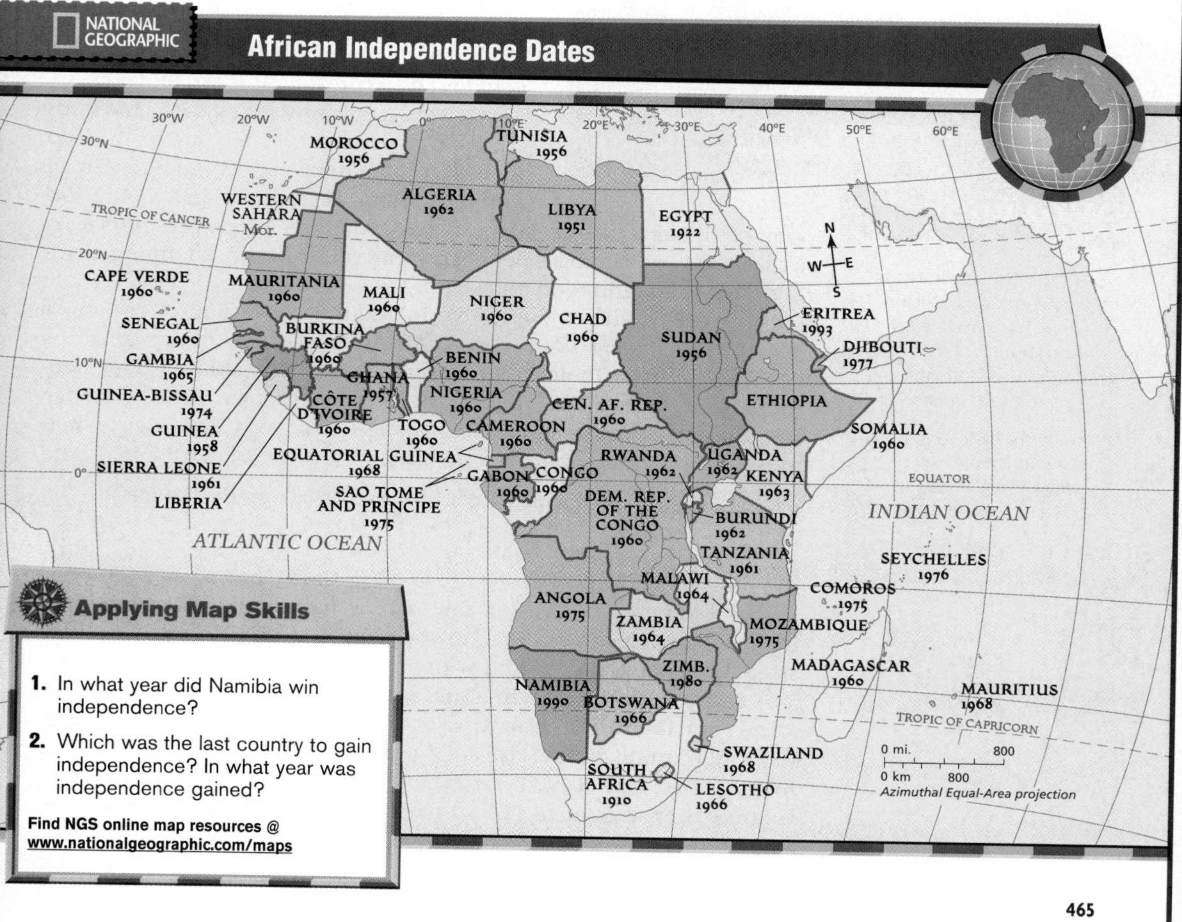

Applying Map Skills

1. In what year did Namibia win independence?
2. Which was the last country to gain independence? In what year was independence gained?

Find NGS online map resources @ www.nationalgeographic.com/maps

465

Chapter 17

Section 3, pages 464–468

Teach

Making Comparisons Have students make a chart comparing Angola and Namibia. Bases of comparison may include landscapes, economic activities, history, and people. Have volunteers share their comparisons with the class. **L1**

✓ Reading Check Answer

Groups struggling for control of the country have hurt the economy.

Applying Map Skills

Answers

1. 1990
2. Eritrea; 1993

Skills Practice

How many years after South Africa's independence did Lesotho and Swaziland gain theirs? *(Lesotho: 56; Swaziland: 58)*

Team-Teaching Activity

Math Invite the math teacher to class to discuss the kinds of data that bar graphs and circle graphs are most useful in showing. Write the following statistics about world deserts: Sahara—3.5 million sq. miles; Gobi—500,000 sq. miles; Patagonia—300,000 sq. miles; Empty Quarter—250,000 sq. miles; Kalahari—225,000 sq. miles; Namib—60,000 sq. miles. Then give students the following statistics about land use in Namibia: Forests—15.2%; Pasture—46.2%; Farmland—0.8%; Other (including desert)—37.8%. Ask them which kind of graph would best compare the sizes of different deserts in the world. *(bar graph)* Then ask which kind of graph would best show the information about land use in Namibia. *(circle graph)* Have them prepare a bar or circle graph showing the data. **L1**

EE1 The World in Spatial Terms: Standard 1

Chapter 17

Section 3, pages 464–468

Daily Lecture Notes 17-3

SOUTH AFRICA AND ITS NEIGHBORS

Daily Lecture and Discussion Notes 17-3

Atlantic and Indian Ocean Countries (pages 464–468)

Did You Know? The Chokwe people live in Angola and Zambia. They do not recognize a single leader, but instead are loyal to local chiefs. The chiefs consult with a group of elders and ritual experts before making decisions.

I. Angola (pages 464–465)

A. Angola includes a tiny exclave called Cabinda. An **exclave** is a small part of a country that is separated from the main part.

B. Although its main economic activity is agriculture, Angola's main source of income is oil. Oil deposits off the coast of Cabinda account for 90 percent of Angola's export earnings.

...ot a wealthy country. Different groups have struggled for control of...

Reading Check Answer

1990

More About the Photo

Maputo Maputo and two other Mozambique ports—Beira and Nacala—have among the finest harbors in all of Africa.

Caption Answer a fierce civil war

Guided Reading Activity 17-3

Name ______ Date ______ Class ______

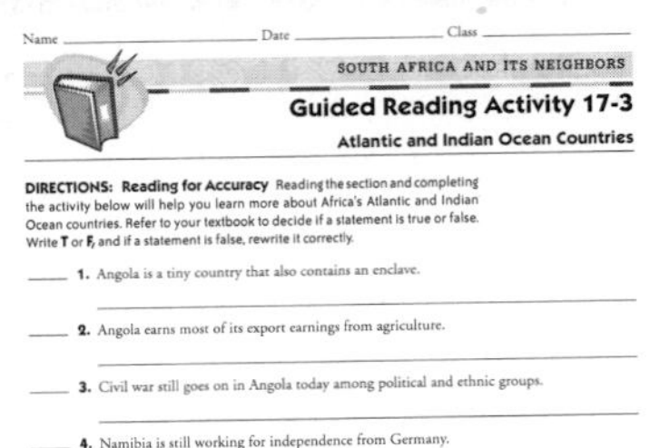

SOUTH AFRICA AND ITS NEIGHBORS

Guided Reading Activity 17-3

Atlantic and Indian Ocean Countries

DIRECTIONS: Reading for Accuracy Reading the section and completing the activity below will help you learn more about Africa's Atlantic and Indian Ocean countries. Refer to your textbook to decide if a statement is true or false. Write **T** or **F**, and if a statement is false, rewrite it correctly.

____ 1. Angola is a tiny country that also contains an enclave.

____ 2. Angola earns most of its export earnings from agriculture.

____ 3. Civil war still goes on in Angola today among political and ethnic groups.

____ 4. Namibia is still working for independence from Germany.

NATIONAL GEOGRAPHIC **On Location**

Maputo, Mozambique

A high-rise building is being constructed in Maputo. Hotels and industrial projects are helping the city's economy to grow.

Economics **What slowed industrial growth in Maputo in the 1980s and 1990s?**

Namibia

Namibia is one of Africa's newest countries. Namibia became independent in 1990 after 75 years of rule by the Republic of South Africa. Before that it was a colony of Germany.

A large plateau runs through the center of the country. This area of patchy grassland is the most populous section of Namibia. The rest is made up of deserts. The **Namib Desert,** located along Namibia's Atlantic coast, is a narrow ribbon of towering dunes and rocks. Tourists come from all over the world to "sand-board" down these dunes. The Kalahari Desert stretches across the southeastern part of the country. As you might guess, most of Namibia has a hot, dry climate.

Namibia has rich deposits of diamonds, copper, gold, zinc, silver, and lead. It is the world's fifth-largest producer of uranium, a substance used for making nuclear fuels. The economy depends on the mining, processing, and exporting of these minerals.

Despite this mineral wealth, most of Namibia's people live in poverty. The income from mineral exports goes to a small group of Namibia's people and to the foreign companies that have invested in Namibia's mineral resources. As a result, half of Namibia's people depend on subsistence farming, herding, and working in food industries.

Only 1.8 million people live in Namibia. It is one of the most sparsely populated countries in Africa. In fact, in the language of Namibia's Nama ethnic group, *namib* means "the land without people." Most Namibians belong to African ethnic groups. A small number are of European ancestry. Namibians speak African languages, while most of the white population speaks Afrikaans and English.

✓Reading Check **When did Namibia become an independent country?**

Mozambique

Sand dunes, swamps, and fine natural harbors line Mozambique's long Indian Ocean coastline. In the center of this Y-shaped country stretches a flat plain covered with grasses and tropical forests.

Most people in Mozambique are farmers. Some practice **slash-and-burn farming**—a method of clearing land for planting by cutting and burning forest. Slash-and-burn farming along with commercial logging has caused **deforestation,** or cutting down of forests. Deforestation can, in turn, lead to flooding during the rainy season. Such floods drove millions of people from their homes in early 2000.

Team-Teaching Activity

Science Invite the science teacher to class to explain the short-term benefits but long-term costs of slash-and-burn agriculture. Ask the teacher to discuss the large expanse of land needed to support slash-and-burn farming over a period of many years and the amount of time required to allow the land to rebound. Have him or her also discuss the pros and cons of the techniques used in settled farming, such as using fertilizers, leaving fields fallow, cycling through crops, planting windbreaks, and so on. After the presentation is complete, have students create charts comparing the two sets of agricultural techniques. **L2**

EE5 Environment and Society: Standard 14

Mozambique also experiences deadly cyclones. A **cyclone** is an intense storm system with heavy rain and high winds.

Mozambique's major crops are cashews, cotton, sugarcane, tea, coconuts, and tropical fruits. The main source of income, however, comes from its seaports. South Africa, Zimbabwe, Swaziland, and Malawi all pay to use the docks at Maputo, the capital, and other ports.

During the 1980s and early 1990s, a fierce civil war slowed industrial growth. In recent years, however, foreign companies have begun to invest in metal production, natural gas, fishing, and transportation services.

Most of Mozambique's 19.4 million people belong to one of 16 major African ethnic groups. A former colony of Portugal, Mozambique's official language is Portuguese, but most people speak African languages. About half of the people practice traditional African religions. Most of the rest are Muslim or Christian.

✓ Reading Check **What is a negative result of slash-and-burn farming?**

Madagascar

The island of Madagascar broke away from the African mainland about 160 million years ago. As a result, it has many plants and animals that are not found elsewhere. It produces most of the world's vanilla beans. The main cash crop is coffee, and rice is also grown. About 80 percent of the island has been slashed and burned by people who must farm and herd to survive. The government has taken steps to save what forests are left.

Only about 22 percent of Madagascar's people are city dwellers. **Antananarivo** (AHN•tah•NAH•nah•REE•voh), the capital, lies in the central plateau. Called "Tana" for short, this city is known for it colorful street markets, where craftspeople sell a variety of products.

Music revolves around dance rhythms that reflect Madagascar's Southeast Asian and African heritage. The people are known for their rhythmic style of singing accompanied only by hand clapping.

✓ Reading Check **Why does Madagascar have wildlife that appears nowhere else on the earth?**

▲ This ring-tailed lemur lives on the island of Madagascar.

Small Island Countries

Far from Africa in the Indian Ocean are three other island republics—Comoros, Seychelles, and Mauritius. The people of these countries have many different backgrounds.

Comoros Volcanoes formed Comoros thousands of years ago. Dense tropical forests cover Comoros today. Most of the 600,000 people are farmers. The main crops are rice, vanilla, cloves, coconuts, and bananas. Even though agriculture employs 80 percent of the workforce, Comoros cannot grow enough food for its growing population. The government is trying to encourage industry, including tourism.

The people of Comoros are a mixture of Arabs, Africans, and people from Madagascar. They speak Arabic, French, and Comoran. Most

✓ Reading Check Answer

deforestation

3 ASSESS

Assign Section 3 Assessment as homework or an in-class activity.

Have students use the Interactive Tutor Self-Assessment CD-ROM to review Section 17–3.

✓ Reading Check Answer

because it separated from the mainland 160 million years ago

Section Quiz 17-3

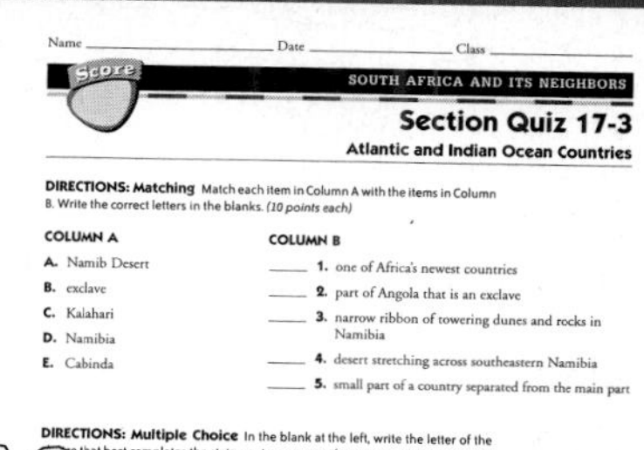

Name ____ Date ____ Class ____

Score

SOUTH AFRICA AND ITS NEIGHBORS

Section Quiz 17-3

Atlantic and Indian Ocean Countries

DIRECTIONS: Matching Match each item in Column A with the items in Column B. Write the correct letters in the blanks. *(10 points each)*

COLUMN A	COLUMN B
A. Namib Desert	____ 1. one of Africa's newest countries
B. exclave	____ 2. part of Angola that is an exclave
C. Kalahari	____ 3. narrow ribbon of towering dunes and rocks in Namibia
D. Namibia	____ 4. desert stretching across southeastern Namibia
E. Cabinda	____ 5. small part of a country separated from the main part

DIRECTIONS: Multiple Choice In the blank at the left, write the letter of the [illegible] that best completes the statement or answers the question. *(10 points each)*

Meeting Special Needs

Visual/Spatial Organize students into five groups and assign one of the five countries covered in this section to each. Instruct students to develop an illustrated poster with three or more images that convey the variety of life in their assigned country. For example, they might choose a coffee plantation, a landscape showing deforestation, or a street market in Antananarivo to portray Madagascar. Suggest that they obtain their images by drawing them or by researching on the Internet. Call on each group to display their images and explain the significance of each. **ELL L1**

Refer to *Inclusion for the Middle School Social Studies Classroom Strategies and Activities* in the TCR.

Chapter 17

Section 3, pages 464–468

Reteach

Have students organize the content of the section into outline form.

Reading Check Answer

volcanoes

Reading Essentials and Study Guide 17-3

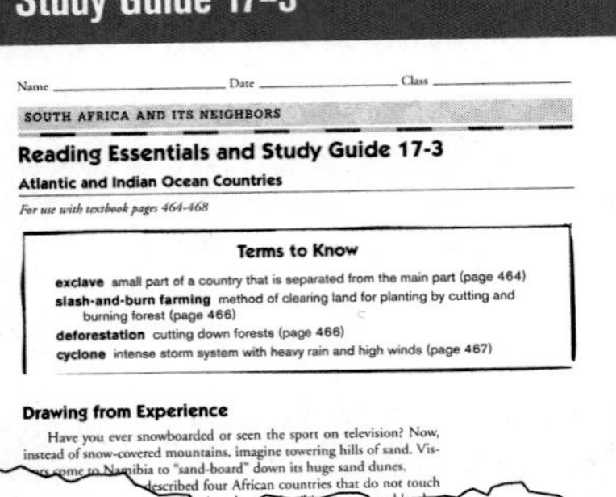
Name ______ Date ______ Class ______

SOUTH AFRICA AND ITS NEIGHBORS

Reading Essentials and Study Guide 17-3

Atlantic and Indian Ocean Countries

For use with textbook pages 464–468

Terms to Know

exclave small part of a country that is separated from the main part (page 464)
slash-and-burn farming method of clearing land for planting by cutting and burning forest (page 466)
deforestation cutting down forests (page 466)
cyclone intense storm system with heavy rain and high winds (page 467)

Drawing from Experience

Have you ever snowboarded or seen the sport on television? Now, instead of snow-covered mountains, imagine towering hills of sand. Visitors come to Namibia to "sand-board" down its huge sand dunes.

Enrich

Have students research one of the animals unique to Madagascar and report on its characteristics.

CLOSE

Ask students to prepare a travelogue on one of the countries in this section that tells visitors about the most important and interesting features of the country.

practice Islam. Once ruled by France, the people of Comoros declared their independence in 1975. Since then, they have suffered from fighting among political groups for control of the government.

Seychelles About 90 islands form the country of Seychelles. About 40 of the islands are granite with high green peaks. The rest are small, flat coral islands with few people. Nearly 90 percent of the country's 100,000 people live on Mahé, the largest island.

Seychelles was not inhabited until the 1700s. Under French and then British rule, it finally became independent in 1976. Most of the country's people are of mixed African, European, and Asian descent. Coconuts and cinnamon are the chief cash crops. Fishing and tourism are important industries as well.

Mauritius Like Comoros, the islands of Mauritius were formed by volcanoes. Sugar is its main agricultural export. Clothing and textiles account for about half of the country's export earnings. Tourism is an important industry, too.

Mauritians come from many different backgrounds. About 70 percent are descendants of settlers from India. The rest are of African, European, or Chinese ancestry. Because of this varied ethnic heritage, the foods of Mauritius have quite a mix of ingredients. You can sample Indian chicken curry, Chinese pork, African-made roast beef, and French-style vegetables.

Reading Check What natural force created the islands of Comoros and Mauritius?

Assessment

Defining Terms

1. **Define** exclave, slash-and-burn farming, deforestation, cyclone.

Recalling Facts

2. **Economics** What is Angola's main source of income?
3. **Place** What two deserts can be found in Namibia?
4. **Location** Where are most of the world's vanilla beans grown?

Critical Thinking

5. **Understanding Cause and Effect** Why is Namibia one of the most sparsely populated countries in Africa?
6. **Evaluating Information** How do the foods of Mauritius show its heritage?

Graphic Organizer

7. **Organizing Information** Create a diagram like the one below. Then write facts about Madagascar that fit the category heading in each of the outer ovals.

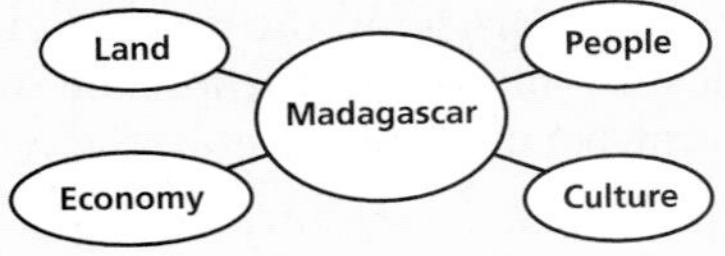

Applying Social Studies Skills

8. **Analyzing Maps** Study the map of African independence dates on page 465. Which southern African country first achieved independence?

Section 3 Assessment

1. The terms are defined in the Glossary.
2. oil
3. the Namib and the Kalahari
4. Madagascar
5. Most of Namibia is uninhabitable desert.
6. People of widely varied ethnicities have brought their homeland's foods with them.
7. Answers will vary.
8. South Africa

Reading Review

Section 1 The New South Africa

Terms to Know
industrialized country
Boer
apartheid
township
enclave

Main Idea
Rich in resources, South Africa has recently seen major social and political changes.

✓ Economics Because of its abundant mineral resources, South Africa has the most industrialized economy in Africa.
✓ Government In 1994 South Africa held its first democratic election in which people from all ethnic groups could vote.
✓ Government South Africa is working to improve the lives of its poorer citizens.

Section 2 Inland Southern Africa

Terms to Know
copper belt
sorghum

Main Idea
Most of inland southern Africa is rich in resources and home to a wide variety of ethnic groups.

✓ Economics Zambia is one of the world's largest producers of copper.
✓ Economics Zimbabwe has many mineral resources and good farmland.
✓ Economics Mining and tourism earn money for Botswana, but many of its people work in South Africa for several months a year.

Section 3 Atlantic and Indian Ocean Countries

Terms to Know
exclave
slash-and-burn farming
deforestation
cyclone

Main Idea
Africa's Atlantic and Indian Ocean countries are struggling to develop their economies.

✓ Economics Angola's main source of income is oil.
✓ Culture Few Namibians benefit from the country's rich mineral wealth. Most live in poverty.
✓ Human/Environment Interaction Slash-and-burn farming in Mozambique has led to deforestation and flooding. Neighboring countries pay fees for the use of Mozambique's ports.
✓ Location Madagascar's island location has resulted in many plants and animals found nowhere else in the world.
✓ Economics Comoros continues to be a mainly agricultural economy, but Mauritius has succeeded in developing a variety of industries.
✓ Economics Seychelles's beaches and tropical climate draw many tourists.

Reading Review

Use the Chapter 17 Reading Review to preview, review, condense, or reteach the chapter.

Preview/Review

Use the Terms to Know lists to help students review and study.

Activity Assign students a selection of related terms from each section and have them write a paragraph using the assigned words. Have volunteers read their sentences aloud.

Vocabulary PuzzleMaker Software reinforces the vocabulary terms used in Chapter 17.

The Interactive Tutor Self-Assessment CD-ROM allows students to review Chapter 17 content.

Condense

Have students read the Chapter 17 summary statements.

Chapter 17 Guided Reading Activities

Chapter 17 Audio Program

Reteach

Reteaching Activity 17

Chapter 17 Reading Essentials and Study Guide

Chapter Culminating Activity

Illustrated Report Have students prepare an illustrated report that demonstrates how physical geography and climate affect the people of one of the countries in southern Africa. Remind them that in discussing physical geography, they should address not only the location of the country and the landforms found in it but also the natural resources, which can have an impact on the economy. Suggest that they include different kinds of maps in their report, and remind them to include keys that explain the different information on each map. *NOTE: This activity may be completed separately or you may wish students to incorporate it into their Current Events Journals.* **L2**

EE1 The World in Spatial Terms: Standards 1, 3

Assessment and Activities

GLENCOE TECHNOLOGY

MindJogger Videoquiz
Use MindJogger to review the Chapter 17 content.

 Available in VHS.

Using Key Terms

1. e
2. b
3. f
4. g
5. i
6. a
7. j
8. c
9. h
10. d

Reviewing the Main Ideas

11. Cape of Good Hope
12. 1994
13. water
14. Zambezi River
15. northern Zambia
16. donations, loans, and foreign aid
17. an ancient African city
18. Great Britain
19. Portugal
20. "the land without people"
21. Portuguese
22. coffee

Chapter 17 Assessment and Activities

Using Key Terms

Match the terms in Part A with their definitions in Part B.

A.

1. copper belt
2. cyclone
3. exclave
4. slash-and-burn farming
5. township
6. apartheid
7. Boer
8. deforestation
9. sorghum
10. enclave

B.

a. separating racial and ethnic groups
b. storm with high circular winds
c. widespread cutting of trees
d. small nation located inside a larger country
e. large area of copper mines
f. small part of a nation separated from the main part of the country
g. areas of forest are cleared by burning
h. tall grass used as grain and to make syrup
i. settlement outside cities in South Africa
j. Dutch farmer in South Africa

Reviewing Main Ideas

Section 1 The New South Africa

11. **Location** What is the southernmost point of Africa?
12. **History** When was South Africa's first election allowing all people to vote?
13. **Economics** What is Lesotho's only important natural resource?

Section 2 Inland Southern Africa

14. **Place** What river crosses Zambia?
15. **Economics** Where is the copper belt?
16. **Economics** How are the people of Malawi supported?
17. **History** What was Great Zimbabwe?
18. **History** Who ruled Botswana for nearly 80 years?

Section 3 Atlantic and Indian Ocean Countries

19. **History** What European country colonized Angola?
20. **Culture** What does *namib* mean?
21. **Culture** What is the official language of Mozambique?
22. **Economics** What is Madagascar's main cash crop?

South Africa and Its Neighbors

Place Location Activity

On a separate sheet of paper, match the letters on the map with the numbered places listed below.

1. Madagascar
2. Lake Malawi
3. Zambezi River
4. Kalahari Desert
5. Angola
6. Zimbabwe
7. Pretoria
8. Mozambique
9. South Africa
10. Namibia

0 mi. 500
0 km 500
Lambert Azimuthal Equal-Area projection

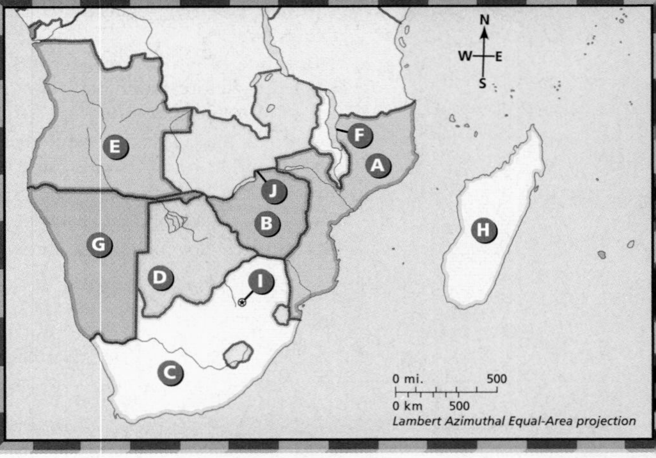

NATIONAL GEOGRAPHIC Place Location Activity

1. H
2. F
3. J
4. D
5. E
6. B
7. I
8. A
9. C
10. G

Critical Thinking

23. *Possible answer:* South Africa has abundant mineral resources; a variety of industries, including manufacturing; productive farms and ranches; and uses high-technology approaches to production.
24. Answers will vary, but positive factors might include an end to reliance on uncertain single-commodity exports and increased income; negatives might include pollution and loss of traditional cultures.

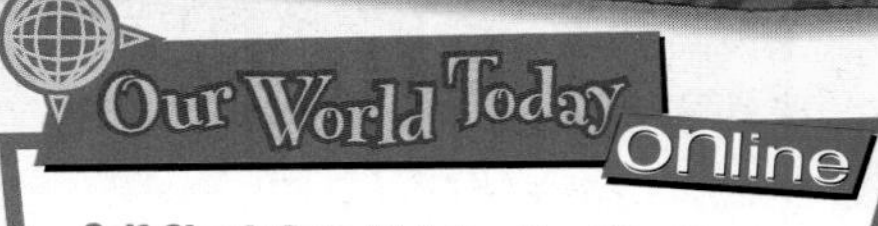

Self-Check Quiz Visit the ***Our World Today: People, Places, and Issues*** Web site at owt.glencoe.com and click on **Chapter 17–Self-Check Quizzes** to prepare for the Chapter Test.

Critical Thinking

23. **Supporting Generalizations** What facts support the statement "South Africa has the most industrialized economy in Africa"?
24. **Evaluating Information** Many countries of southern Africa are hoping to build and improve their industries. On a chart like the one below, list the positive and negative aspects of industrialization under the correct headings.

Industrialization	
Positives	Negatives

Current Events Journal

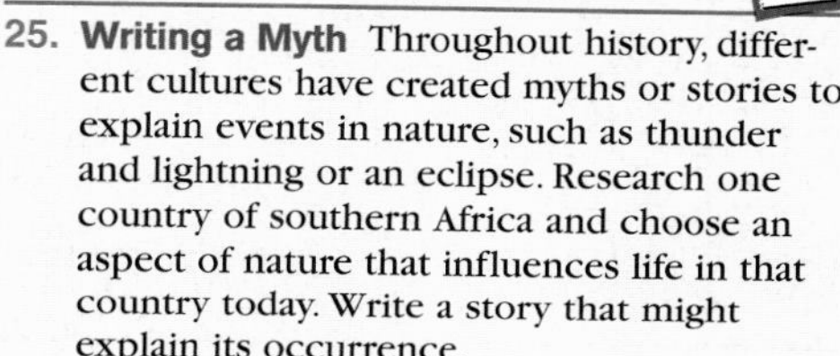

25. **Writing a Myth** Throughout history, different cultures have created myths or stories to explain events in nature, such as thunder and lightning or an eclipse. Research one country of southern Africa and choose an aspect of nature that influences life in that country today. Write a story that might explain its occurrence.

Mental Mapping Activity

26. **Focusing on the Region** Create a simple outline map of Africa, then label the following:

- Atlantic Ocean
- Pretoria
- Madagascar
- Angola
- South Africa
- Cape Town
- Namib Desert
- Mozambique
- Indian Ocean
- Kalahari Desert

Technology Skills Activity

27. **Using the Internet** The Zulu are a well-known ethnic group in Africa. Research this group on the Internet. Write a speech answering these questions: Who are the Zulu? How have they affected the history of southern Africa? Where do they live today?

The Princeton Review

Standardized Test Practice

Directions: Study the map below, and then answer the question that follows.

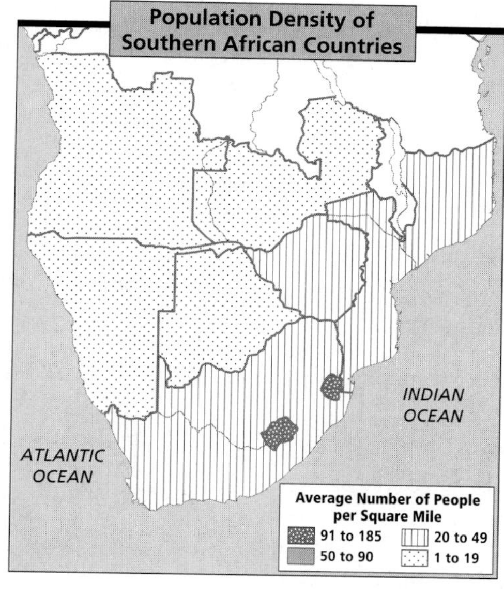

1. **Which country has the fewest people per square mile?**
   - **A** Lesotho
   - **B** Egypt
   - **C** South Africa
   - **D** Namibia

Test-Taking Tip: This question involves both recalling where countries are located as well as using the legend. Start with the answer choices. Think about what you learned about each country. You may be able to get rid of wrong answer choices simply by recalling these facts.

Assessment and Activities

Standardized Test Practice

1. D

Tested Objectives:
Reading a map, analyzing information

Chapter Test Bonus Question

This question may be used for extra credit on the chapter test.

Where does the ring-tailed lemur live? *(Madagascar)*

Our World Today online

Have students visit the Web site at **owt.glencoe.com** to review Chapter 17 and take the Self-Check Quiz.

Current Events Journal

25. Encourage students to share their stories, re-create a setting like that found years ago, when listeners crowded around a fire, and the storyteller used voice and gestures to make a story come alive.

Mental Mapping Activity

26. This exercise helps students visualize the countries and geographic features they have been studying and to understand the relationship among various points. Accept all attempts at freehand mapping that show places in the correct relationship to one another.

Technology Skills Activity

27. For variety, you might assign some students to research other peoples who live in southern Africa.

Unit 7 Planning Guide

SUGGESTED PACING CHART

Unit 7 (1 day)	Chapter 18 (4 days)	Chapter 19 (5 days)	Chapter 20 (5 days)	Chapter 21 (4 days)	Unit 7 (2 days)
Day 1 Introduction	**Day 1** Chapter 18 Intro, Section 1	**Day 1** Chapter 19 Intro, Section 1	**Day 1** Chapter 20 Intro, Section 1	**Day 1** Chapter 21 Intro, Section 1	**Day 1** Wrap-Up/Projects
	Day 2 Section 2	**Day 2** Section 2	**Day 2** Section 2	**Day 2** Section 2	**Day 2** Unit 7 Assessment
	Day 3 Chapter 18 Review	**Day 3** Section 3	**Day 3** Section 3	**Day 3** Chapter 21 Review	
	Day 4 Chapter 18 Assessment	**Day 4** Chapter 19 Review	**Day 4** Chapter 20 Review	**Day 4** Chapter 21 Assessment	
		Day 5 Chapter 19 Assessment	**Day 5** Chapter 20 Assessment		

For a complete course pacing guide and Teacher Classroom Resources, see:

Interactive Lesson Planner

Use the following tools to easily assess student learning in a variety of ways:

- **Performance Assessment Activities and Rubrics**
- **Section Quizzes**
- **Chapter Tests and Unit Pretests and Posttests**
- **Interactive Tutor Self-Assessment CD-ROM**
- **ExamView® Pro 3.0 Testmaker CD-ROM**
- **MindJogger Videoquiz**
- **owt.glencoe.com**
- **Standardized Test Practice Workbook**

Note: The following materials may be used when teaching Unit 7. Chapter level support materials can be found on the chapter resource pages.

TEACHING TRANSPARENCIES

Political Map Transparency 7

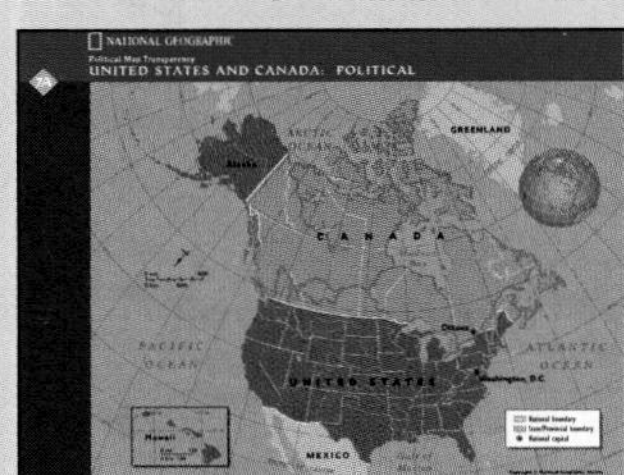

Unit 7 Map Overlay Transparencies

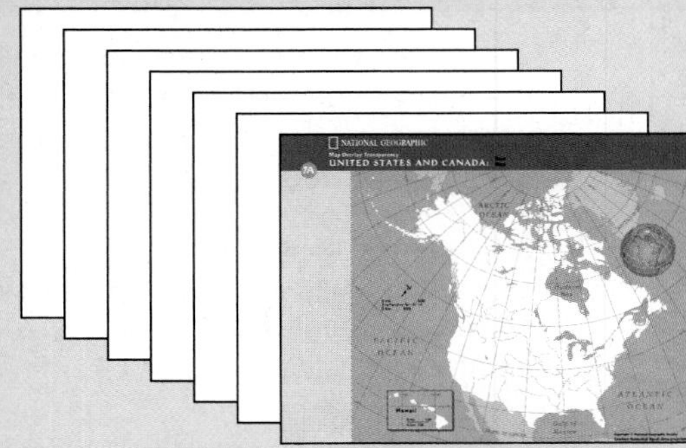

World Cultures Transparencies 11 and 12

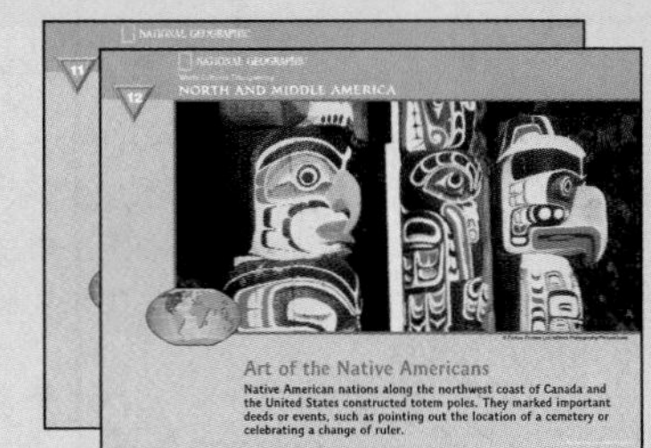

Unit 7 Resources

INTERDISCIPLINARY CONNECTIONS

World Literature Reading 7

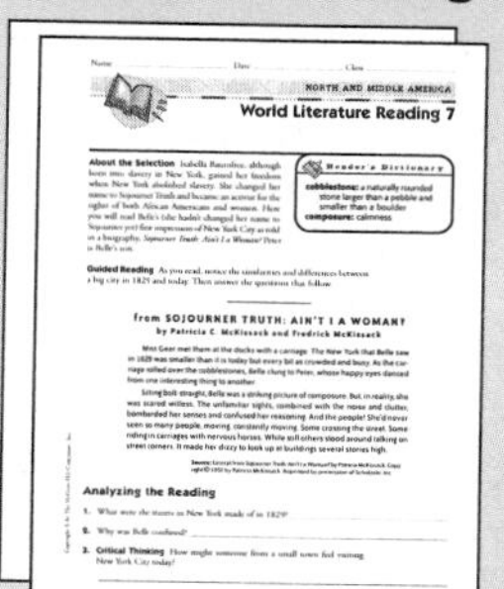

Economics and Geography Activity 7

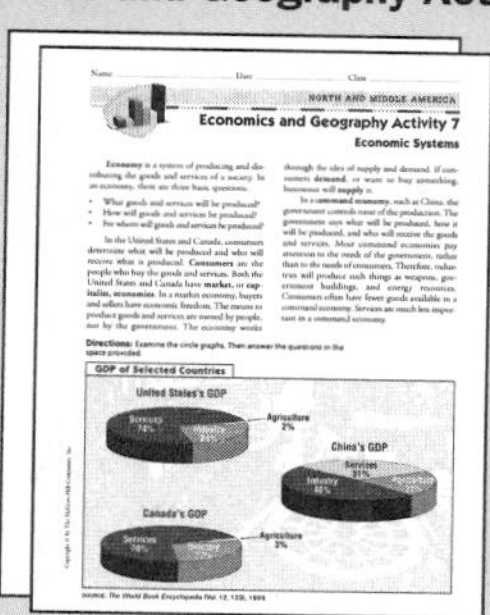

History and Geography Activity 7

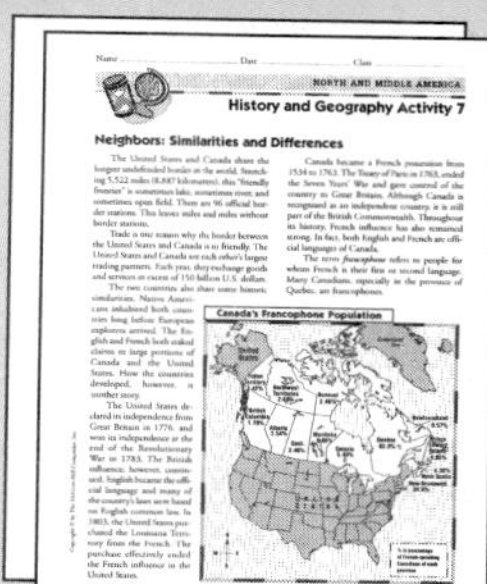

MAP AND GEOGRAPHY SKILLS

Building Geography Skills for Life

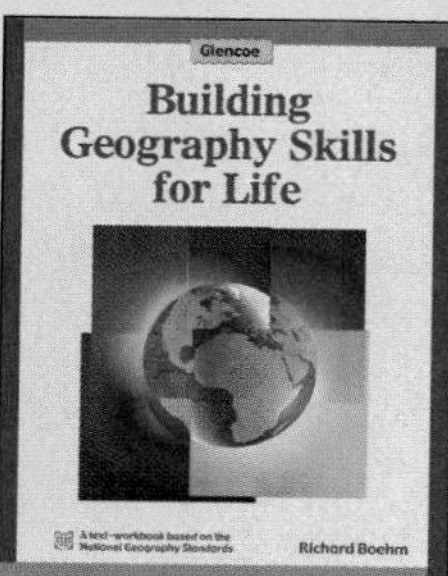

NGS Focus on Geography Literacy

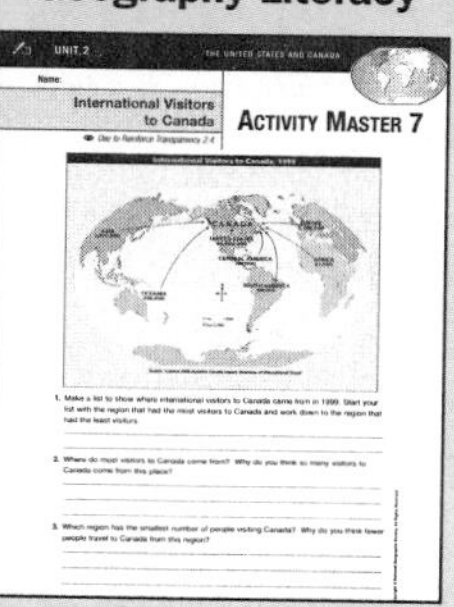

Regional Atlas Activity 7

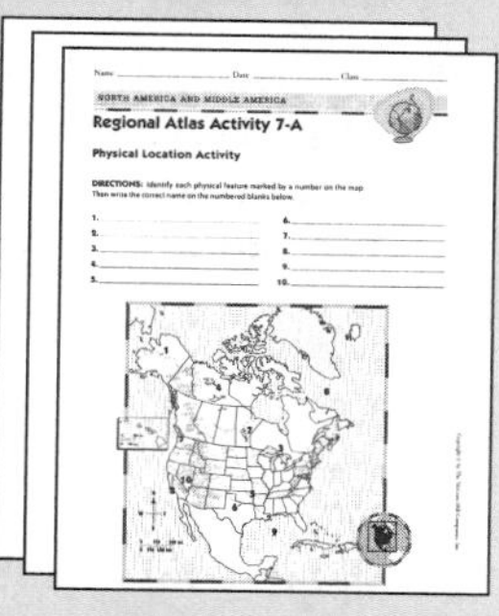

NATIONAL GEOGRAPHIC MapMachine

Find the latest coverage of geography in the news, atlas updates, cartographic activities with interactive maps, an online map store, and links at www.nationalgeographic.com/maps

APPLICATION AND HANDS-ON

Citizenship Activity 7

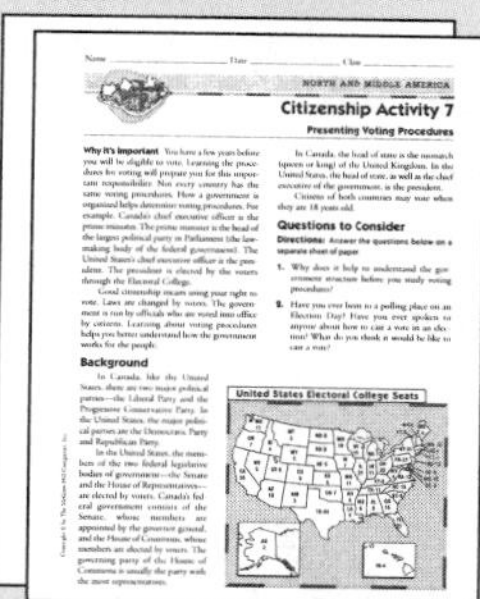

Foods Around the World 2

ENRICHMENT AND EXTENSION

Environmental Case Study 7

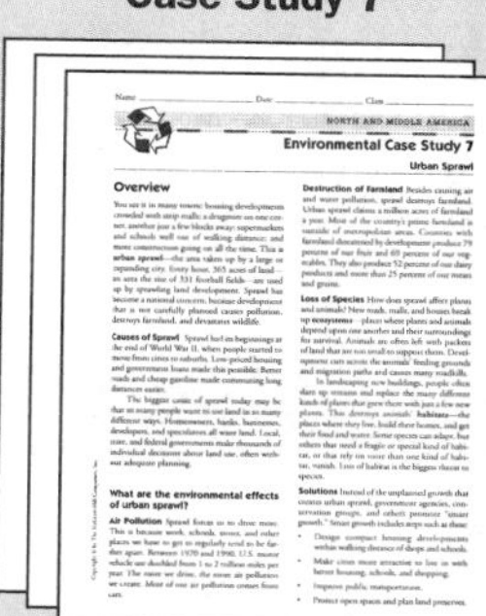

World Music: A Cultural Legacy

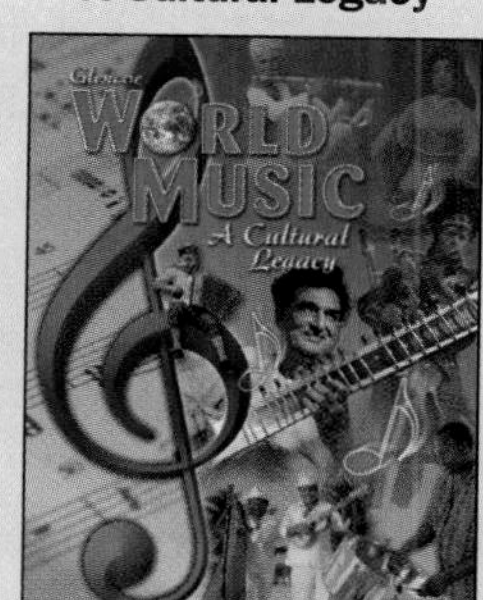

ASSESSMENT AND EVALUATION

GLENCOE'S ASSESSMENT ADVANTAGE

Unit 7 Pretests

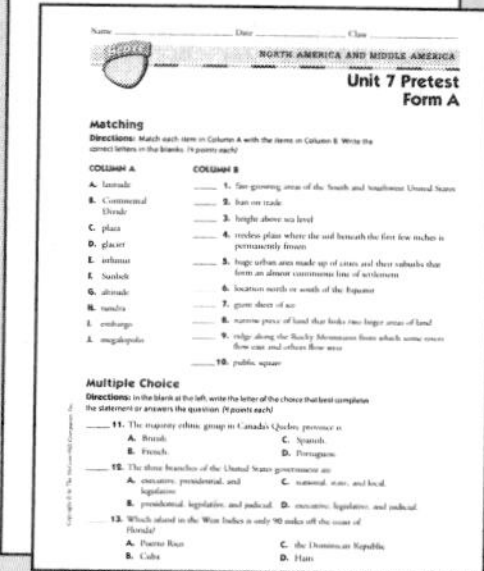

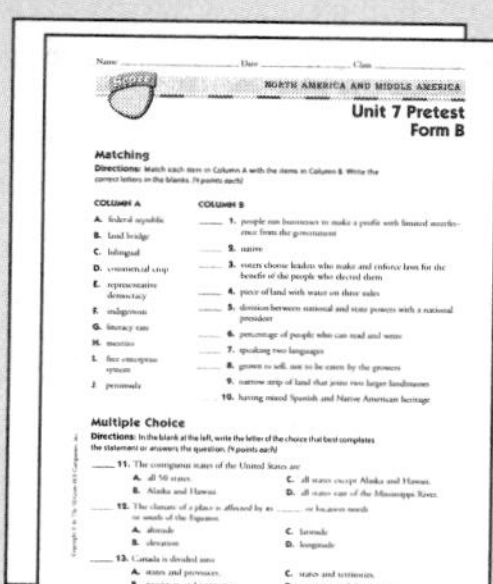

Unit 7 Posttests

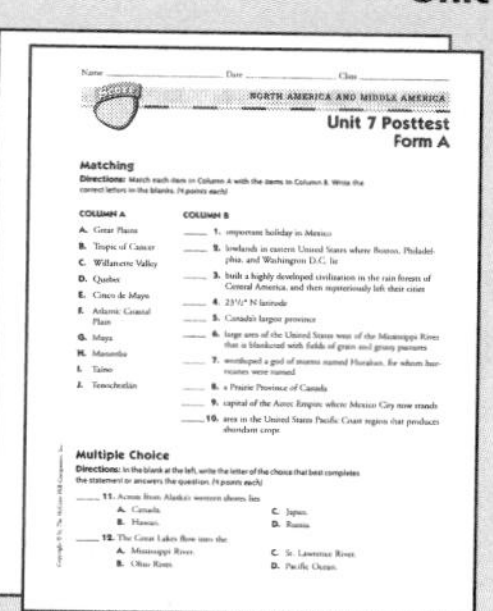

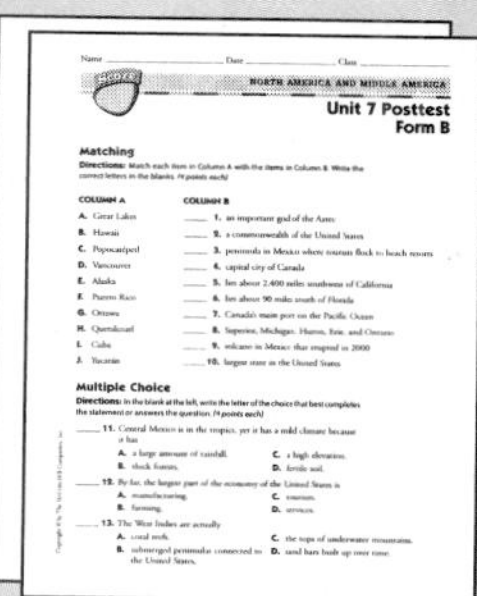

Additional Unit 7 Resources

interNET RESOURCES

- **owt.glencoe.com**
  Our World Today: People, Places, and Issues
  Visit the Glencoe *Our World Today: People, Places, and Issues* Web site for overviews, activities, assessments, and updated charts and graphs.
- **socialstudies.glencoe.com**
  Glencoe Social Studies
  Visit the Glencoe Web site for social studies activities, updates, and links to other sites.
- **www.teachingtoday.glencoe.com**
  Glencoe Teaching Today
  This Web site features daily teaching tips, free PDF downloads, annotated Web resources, educational news, and more.
- **www.nationalgeographic.com**
  NGS ONLINE Visit the National Geographic Society Web site for the latest coverage of geography in the news, atlas updates, activities, links, interactive features, and archives.
- **Glencoe's Guide to Using the Internet**
  Provides an introduction to many of the current technologies on the Internet. Professional resources and teaching strategies included.

Our Web sites provide additional resources. All essential content is covered in the Student Edition.

The following videotape programs are available from Glencoe:

- **The Secret Mounds of Prehistoric America** 1-56501-681-5
- **The Pueblo Cliff Dwellers** 0-7670-0613-5
- **Mexico: A Story of Courage and Conquest** 0-7670-1622-X
- **The Aztec Empire** 0-7670-0542-2
- **Pancho Villa: Outlaw Hero** 0-7670-0315-2
- **The Maya** 0-7670-0697-6
- **Cuba and Castro** 0-7670-1426-X

To order, call Glencoe at 1-800-334-7344. To find classroom resources to accompany many of these, check:

A&E Television: www.aetv.com

The History Channel: www.historychannel.com

Bibliography

Literature for the Student

- **Glencoe Middle School World Literature Library**
  Dragonwings, by Lawrence Yep. In the early twentieth century, Moon Shadow, an 8-year-old boy, leaves China to join his father in San Francisco.
  Julie of the Wolves, by Jean Craig George. The drama of the conflict between modern and traditional Inuit values.
- ***Haiti: Land of Inequality,*** by Mary C. Turck and Eric Black. Minneapolis: Lerner, 1999.

Readings for the Teacher

- ***Gale Encyclopedia of Multicultural America: Primary Documents.*** Farmington Hills, Mich.: Gale Research, 2000.
- ***The Cambridge Encyclopedia of Latin America and the Caribbean.*** New York: Cambridge University Press, 1992.

Multimedia Links

- **Glencoe Social Studies Primary Source Document Library**
  Columbus Reaches the Americas by Christopher Columbus
  The Life of a Maquiladora Worker by Maria Ibarra with David Bacon
  The Persian Gulf War by Colin Powell
- ***Canadian Treasures.*** Burnaby, B.C.: Ingenuity Works. Mac/Windows CD-ROM.
- ***The Regions of the United States.*** Niles, Ill.: United Learning, 1993, 1994, 1995. 5 videocassettes, 18 minutes each.

Refer to ***owt.glencoe.com*** *for additional literature titles and study guides related to this region.*

Additional Glencoe Teacher Support

- **Teaching Strategies for the Geography Classroom**
- **Reproducible Lesson Plans**
- **Outline Map Resource Book**
- **Reading in the Content Area**

Service Learning Project

Developing an Emergency Plan

Different areas of the United States are susceptible to different kinds of extreme weather or other natural hazards. The Southeast, for example, can be hit by hurricanes; the Plains states by tornadoes; the Northeast by heavy blizzards; and the West by wildfires. Have students find out what natural disasters are most likely to hit their area—and what recommendations public safety officials have for people to act responsibly and safely in such emergencies.

Content Background Notes

Use this additional information as lecture notes or discussion prompts throughout the study of Unit 7.

Chapter 18 Canada (pp. 484–499)

Quebec Perhaps the single most pressing political issue in Canada is the ongoing debate over the separation of Quebec. The separatist movement first gained prominence in the 1970s, and the separatist Parti Québécois (PQ) won a substantial majority of seats in the provincial legislature in 1976. In 1979 PQ leader René Lévesque, later prime minister of the province, made French the official language of Quebec. The next year he held a provincial referendum on the question of separation. By a nearly 60-40 margin, voters turned it down. Even a majority of French-speaking Quebecers voted no.

In 1995 the province voted on a new separation referendum. This time, the vote was extremely close, with only 50.6 percent saying yes and 49.4 percent voting no. Interestingly, French speakers now approved separation by a 60-40 margin. Other groups, including English speakers and Native Americans, voted against separation by a 95-5 vote, however.

The current provincial prime minister has vowed to hold another referendum on the issue, but no date has been scheduled. For now, Quebecers are concentrating on rebuilding their economy. One strategy is to increase ties with the United States and Europe. More than 80 percent of the province's exports go to the United States, and these ties have generated nearly 300,000 new jobs.

Chapter 19 The United States (pp. 500–529)

Damage to the Gulf Agricultural runoff from the Mississippi River basin is causing damage in the Gulf of Mexico. About 7 million tons of fertilizer is used on farms located in the vast, productive river basin each year. Some of that nitrogen-rich material washes into the river and, over time, flows out into the Gulf of Mexico. That is when the trouble starts. Algae thrive on the nitrogen, creating vast algae blooms that can spread as much as 7,000 square miles (18,130 sq. km). The algae suck up oxygen, which makes it impossible for other creatures to live. Scientists say that swimmers such as fish and shrimp can simply move elsewhere, but bottom-dwelling creatures such as starfish and clams die off in large numbers.

Chapter 20 Mexico (pp. 532–553)

Desert Spring Water One of Mexico's most enchanting sites is *Quatro Ciénegas* (KWAH • troh see • AY • nay • gahs), or "Four Marshes." Although it is located in the middle of the burning Chihuahuan Desert, *Quatro Ciénegas* brims with life—waterborne life. The area holds several lakes, pools, and canals that are fed by underground springs. This surface water supports scores of plant and animal species, some of which are unique to the area. Local farmers tap the springwater for irrigation, but scientists say there is no evidence yet that the underground aquifers are being depleted. Still, they warn that human intervention does threaten this fragile area. The Mexican government has protected this unusual desert wetland by making it a biological reserve.

Chapter 21 Central America and the West Indies (pp. 554–571)

The Treasures of Copán Among the several important regional sites of the ancient Maya was Copán, in western Honduras. For decades, archaeologists have explored the monumental buildings and temples of the city, which was the center of a kingdom of about 20,000 people. Recent excavations have yielded important new findings. One is an altar built by the last dynastic king of Copán that depicts himself and his 15 predecessors, including the dynasty's founder, Sun-Eyed Green Quetzal Macaw. Archaeologists digging deep under the city's central monument found a royal burial chamber housing a skeleton that they believe might be the remains of the dynastic founder. The storied king apparently had lived a difficult life—the skeleton showed signs of an unhealed broken arm, a dislocated shoulder, missing teeth, and arthritis.

Volcanic Isle Montserrat was once home to recording studios used by world-famous rock stars and to million-dollar vacation homes with spectacular views. In 1995 life on this island in the Lesser Antilles changed dramatically, however. That year, the volcanic Soufriere Hills erupted, launching fire and ash into the sky. Two years later, new explosions triggered massive mudslides that led to the evacuation of more than half of the island's 11,000 people. The mudslides covered two-thirds of the island and completely buried its capital city. Many islanders remained, determined to rebuild their lives. They faced major challenges. Scientists have found that the ash spewed by the volcano contains a dangerous mineral that could cause a serious lung disease. Also, after several months of staying quiet, the volcano began erupting again in late 1999. Montserrat is not yet safe.

Introducing Unit 7

00:00 Out of Time?

If time does not permit teaching each chapter in this unit, you may use the **Reading Essentials and Study Guide** for each chapter.

Unit Overview

The chapters of this unit introduce students to the geography, culture, and peoples of North America and Middle America. The chapters detail the landforms, climate, economy, history, government, and lifestyles found in these countries. Before beginning to study the unit, point out to students that although these countries are all part of the continent of North America, similarities are shared by regions, as follows:

- The large northern countries of Canada and the United States have diverse populations and democratic governments.
- Both countries have varied economies, with a generally high standard of living.
- The southern part of the continent—including Mexico, Central America, and the West Indies—is made up of many smaller countries.
- Mexico, Central America, and many of the islands of the West Indies have a strong Spanish influence on language and culture.

◀ Skier in Idaho's stretch of the Rocky Mountains

▲ Mexican boy carrying decorated cross for religious celebration

Farm on the Manitoba plains

472

Using the Illustration

The Rocky Mountains dominate the western landscapes of both the United States and Canada, and they are geologically related to the Sierra Madre Oriental mountain range in Mexico. All three countries have similar landforms to the west of these mountains. Canada and Mexico both have large plateaus, and the United States has the Great Basin. **Ask:** **How do you think having similar landforms affected the growth of the United States and Canada?** *(The mountains had a similar impact on development. High mountains like the Rockies slowed migration to the west, as well as making communication difficult between the western and eastern parts of both countries.)*

NATIONAL GEOGRAPHIC

North America and Middle America

North America is a large continent that stretches from above the Arctic Circle to a few degrees north of the Equator. Home to many cultures and peoples, it is a land of stark contrasts. The United States and Canada, in the northern part of the continent, share a similar history and a common language. Mexico and Central America also have a common language and history, and—with the islands of the Caribbean—make up a region known as Middle America. Middle America is not technically a separate continent, but it can be defined as a culture region.

NGS ONLINE
www.nationalgeographic.com/education

473

Unit Launch Activity

How Do Canada and the United States Compare? These two close neighbors enjoy many similarities—but they are different as well. **Ask:** **How do the countries differ in land and climate? How are their economies both similar and different? In what ways are the people of the two countries like and unlike each other?** Encourage students to keep a record of stories that they hear about the United States and Canada on television and radio or read in newspapers or magazines. Have them take notes on the content of the unit as well. When they are finished, ask for volunteers to recount their examples. Then have the class discuss the question: **How are Canada and the United States similar and different? L1**

EE2 Places and Regions: Standard 4

These materials are available from Glencoe.

Software

ZipZapMap! World

Transparencies

PicturePack Transparencies

CD-ROM

Picture Atlas of the World, Second Edition

Current Events Journal

After students have completed their study of Unit 7, have them choose one specific aspect of the culture of North or Middle America that interests them. In their journals students should describe that feature in terms of taste, smell, feel, look, and sound. Have students then illustrate their ideas using poster board and markers or paint. They might use cassette recorders to illustrate sounds. Display students' work on class bulletin boards.

NGS ONLINE
www.nationalgeographic.com/education

This online resource provides lesson plans, atlas updates, cartographic activities with interactive maps, an online map store, and geography links.

Lesson Plan

Using the Regional Atlas
These features and activities may be used as an introduction to the unit or as teaching tools throughout the course of the unit.

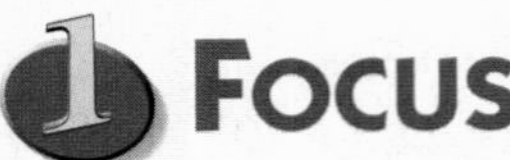

1 Focus

Objectives

1. Describe the relative size and location of North America and Middle America.
2. Name the major physical features of North America and Middle America.
3. Identify the smaller units into which North America and Middle America are divided.
4. Compare the languages of North America and Middle America.

5-Minute Precheck

Have students look at the political map on page 475 and describe the locations of the two national capitals, Washington, D.C., and Ottawa. *(between Maryland and Virginia; in eastern Ontario)*

More About the Profile

In order to show a variety of physical features, this cross section begins at Vancouver Island and ends at Nova Scotia.

NATIONAL GEOGRAPHIC **REGIONAL ATLAS**

The United States and Canada

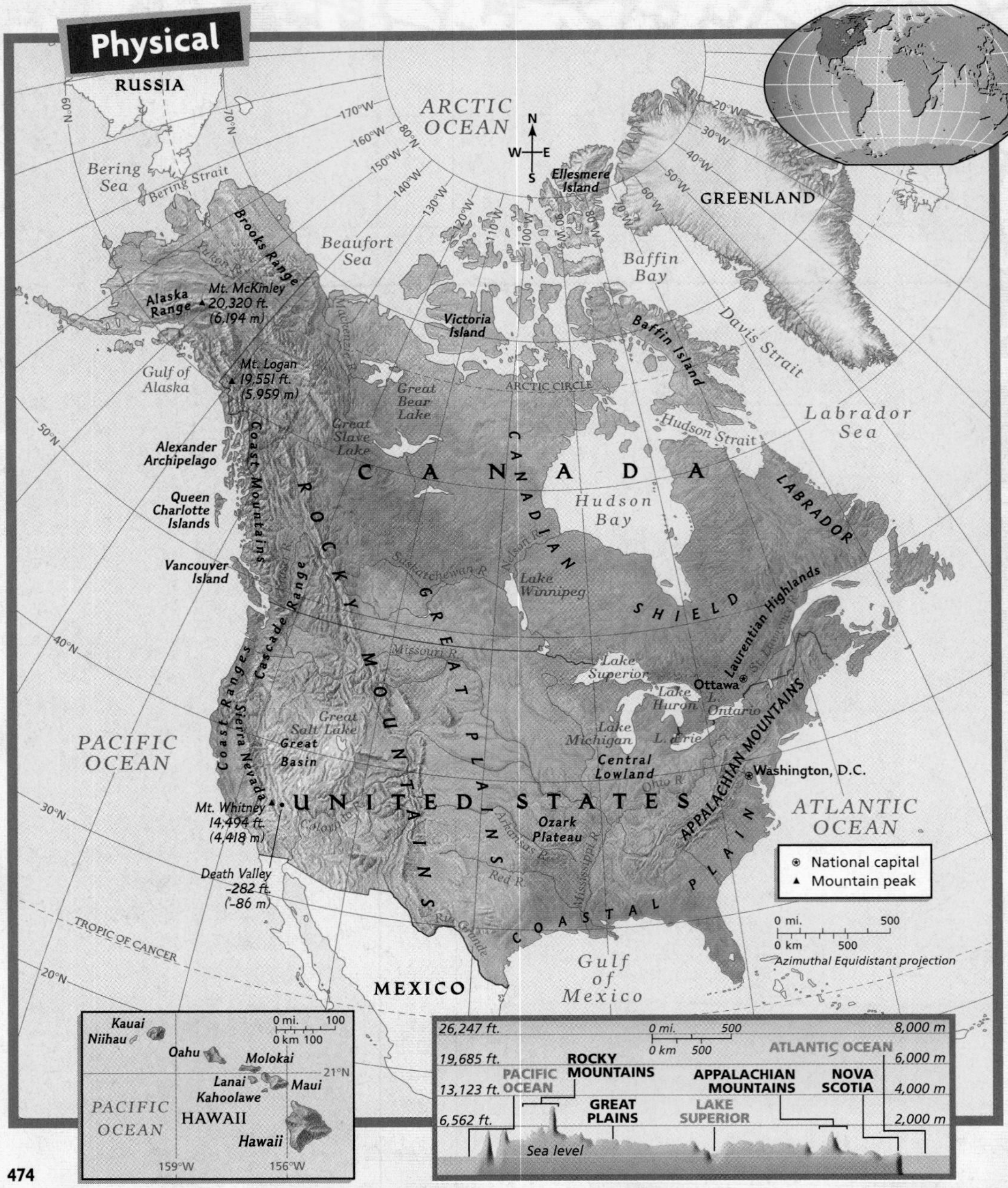

Physical
RUSSIA
ARCTIC OCEAN
Bering Sea
Bering Strait
Beaufort Sea
Ellesmere Island
GREENLAND
Baffin Bay
Baffin Island
Davis Strait
Brooks Range
Alaska Range
Mt. McKinley 20,320 ft. (6,194 m)
Victoria Island
Gulf of Alaska
Mt. Logan 19,551 ft. (5,959 m)
Great Bear Lake
ARCTIC CIRCLE
Hudson Strait
Labrador Sea
Great Slave Lake
Alexander Archipelago
Coast Mountains
C A N A D A
Hudson Bay
LABRADOR
Queen Charlotte Islands
Vancouver Island
ROCKY MOUNTAINS
CANADIAN SHIELD
Saskatchewan R.
Nelson R.
Lake Winnipeg
Laurentian Highlands
Cascade Range
GREAT PLAINS
Missouri R.
Lake Superior
Ottawa
Lake Huron
L. Ontario
Lake Michigan
L. Erie
APPALACHIAN MOUNTAINS
PACIFIC OCEAN
Great Salt Lake
Great Basin
Coast Ranges
Sierra Nevada
Central Lowland
Washington, D.C.
Mt. Whitney 14,494 ft. (4,418 m)
UNITED STATES
Ozark Plateau
ATLANTIC OCEAN
Death Valley -282 ft. (-86 m)
Red R.
Mississippi R.
COASTAL PLAIN
National capital
Mountain peak
TROPIC OF CANCER
Rio Grande
MEXICO
Gulf of Mexico
0 mi. 500
0 km 500
Azimuthal Equidistant projection
Kauai
Niihau
Oahu
Molokai
Lanai
Maui
Kahoolawe
HAWAII
Hawaii
PACIFIC OCEAN
159°W
156°W
21°N
0 mi. 100
0 km 100
26,247 ft.
19,685 ft.
13,123 ft.
6,562 ft.
Sea level
8,000 m
6,000 m
4,000 m
2,000 m
ROCKY MOUNTAINS
PACIFIC OCEAN
GREAT PLAINS
APPALACHIAN MOUNTAINS
LAKE SUPERIOR
NOVA SCOTIA
ATLANTIC OCEAN

474

Regional Atlas Activity

Class Challenge Have students use atlases and other resources to plan a cross-country trip through the United States or Canada. Direct them to choose a definite starting point and destination and to plot the route between the two points. (Alternatively, you could assign starting and ending points to students.) Have them calculate the approximate distance of the journey and list specific points of interest along the way. Allow time for students to share their itineraries and compare their routes and points of interest. **L1 ELL**

EE1 The World in Spatial Terms: Standard 1

UNIT 7

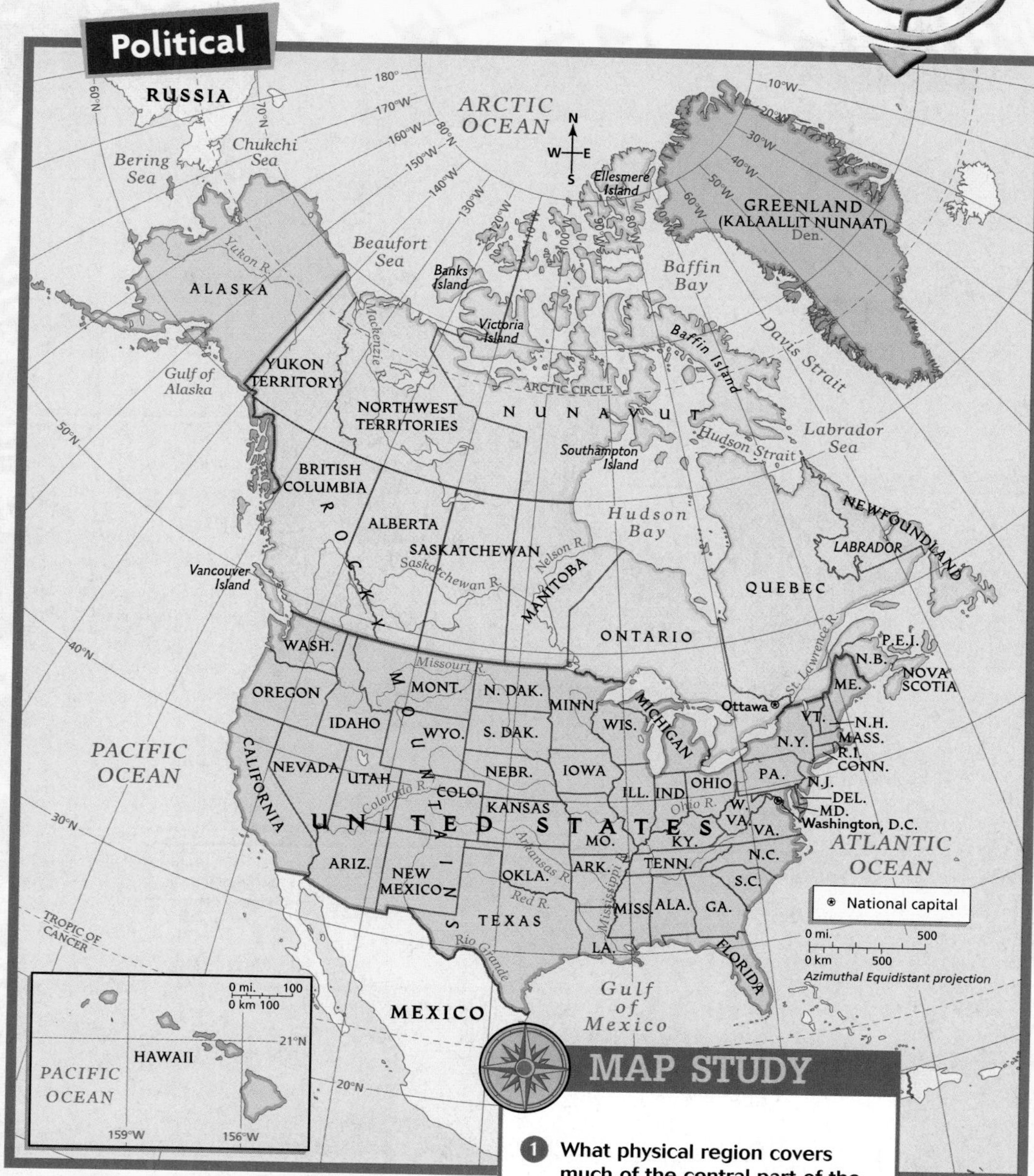

Political

North America and Middle America

MAP STUDY

1. What physical region covers much of the central part of the United States and Canada?
2. What is the capital of Canada?

475

Unit 7
Regional Atlas

TEACH

Making Comparisons
Have the students compare the elevation profiles of North America and Middle America. **Ask: Which is higher, the Rocky Mountains or Pico de Orizaba in Mexico's Sierra Madre Oriental Mountains?** *(Orizaba)* **What river separates the United States and Mexico?** *(the Rio Grande)*

Cultural Kaleidoscope

Canada Canadians call Alberta, Saskatchewan, and Manitoba, which are located on the Great Plains, the *Prairie Provinces. Prairie* is a French word that means "grassy field" or "meadow."

MAP STUDY

Answers
1. the Great Plains
2. Ottawa

Skills Practice
Which state in the United States does not touch either Canada or another state? *(Hawaii)* **What country borders the United States on the south?** *(Mexico)*

Regional Atlas Activity

Interpreting Maps Give students some time to study the physical features of the United States and Canada shown on the map on page 474. Then have them work in small groups to write five location questions based on the physical features. Offer the following question as an example: What mountain range extends through the western region of both the United States and Canada? *(Rocky Mountains)* Have groups compete against each other, posing and answering questions and giving points, as in a quiz show. Encourage groups to challenge one another with their questions. **L2**

EE1 The World in Spatial Terms: Standard 3

REGIONAL ATLAS

THE HUMANITIES CONNECTION

World Music: A Cultural Legacy

World Art and Architecture Transparencies

Interdisciplinary Connections

History In 1804 Haiti became the first country in Latin America to win independence. The most recent was Saint Kitts and Nevis, a nation composed of two islands in the Caribbean, which won independence from the United Kingdom in 1983. Some West Indies islands are still possessions of European countries. Puerto Rico has its own government but is associated with the United States.

5-Minute Precheck

Ask students what facts they know about Middle America. On the board, write "Physical" and "People." Prompt students to suggest which category each fact belongs to.

Middle America

Physical

120°W 110°W 100°W 90°W 80°W 70°W
40°N 30°N 20°N 10°N 0° 10°S

Baja California
SIERRA MADRE OCCIDENTAL
MEXICAN PLATEAU
SIERRA MADRE ORIENTAL
Río Grande
Gulf of Mexico
ATLANTIC OCEAN
Bermuda Is.
BAHAMAS
Nassau
TROPIC OF CANCER
Havana
CUBA
Yucatán Peninsula
Pico de Orizaba 18,855 ft. (5,747 m)
Mexico City
MEXICO
SIERRA MADRE DEL SUR
Greater Antilles
HAITI
DOMINICAN REPUBLIC
Port-au-Prince
Santo Domingo
Puerto Rico
Kingston
JAMAICA
Hispaniola
ANTIGUA AND BARBUDA
ST. KITTS AND NEVIS
Guadeloupe
Lesser Antilles
DOMINICA
Martinique
ST. LUCIA
ST. VINCENT AND THE GRENADINES
BARBADOS
GRENADA
Port of Spain
TRINIDAD AND TOBAGO
BELIZE
Belmopan
HONDURAS
Tegucigalpa
Guatemala City
GUATEMALA
San Salvador
EL SALVADOR
Caribbean Sea
Mosquito Coast
Managua
NICARAGUA
Lake Nicaragua
San José
COSTA RICA
Panama City
Isthmus of Panama
PANAMA
N W E S
EQUATOR
PACIFIC OCEAN
0 mi. 1,000
0 km 1,000
Lambert Azimuthal Equal-Area projection
National capital
Mountain peak

19,685 ft. 13,123 ft. 6,561 ft.
6,000 m 4,000 m 2,000 m
0 mi 100
0 km 100
PACIFIC OCEAN
PUERTO VALLARTA
MEXICO CITY
POPOCATÉPETL
ORIZABA
BAY OF CAMPECHE
VERACRUZ
Sea Level

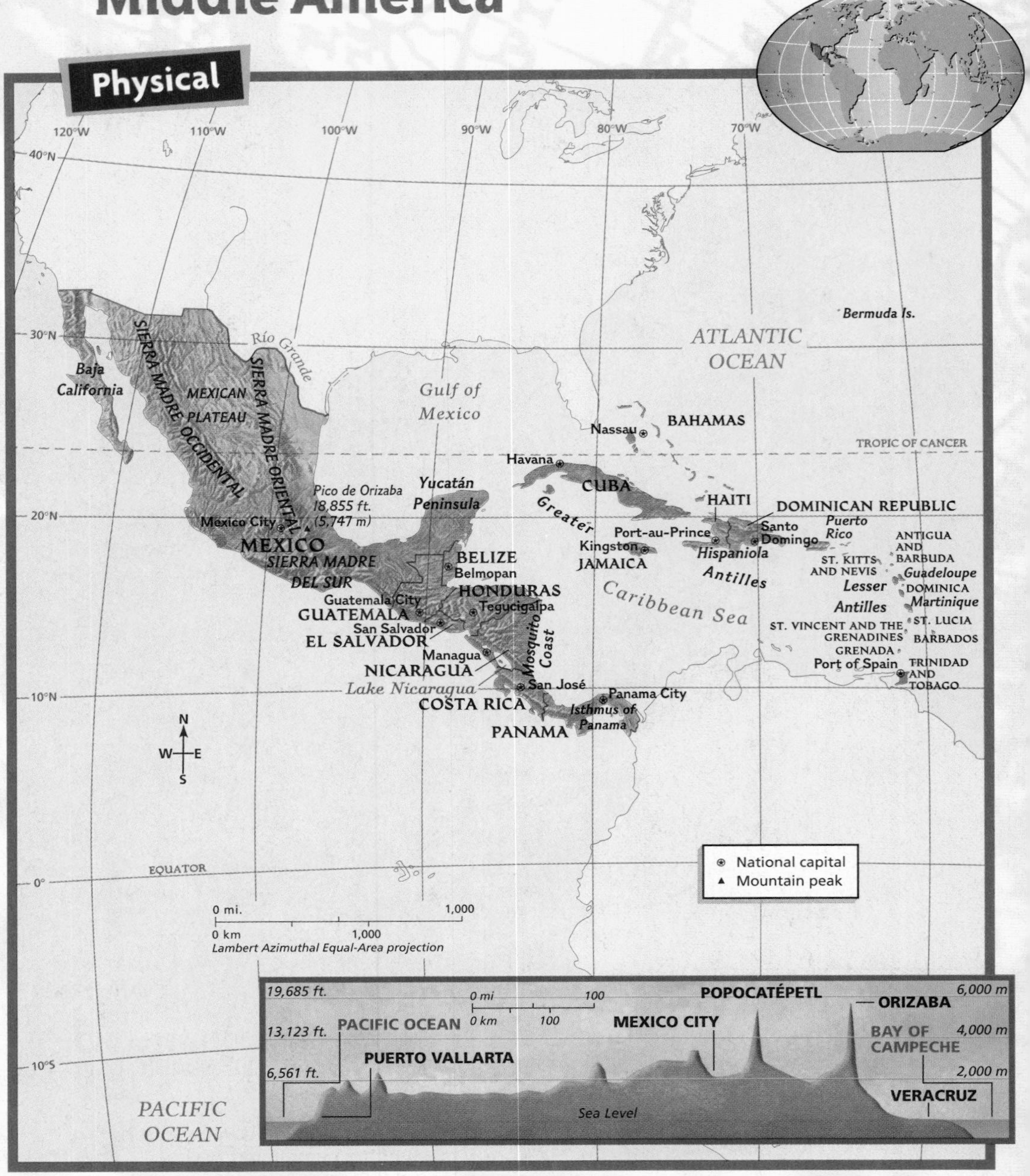

476 UNIT 7

Regional Atlas Activity

Analyzing Information Have students look at the physical map on the page. **Ask: What islands seem to be an extension of continental landforms?** Students should recognize that Cuba seems to extend from the Yucatán Peninsula. Cuba and the other islands of the Greater Antilles are, in fact, the remnants of the same system of fault mountains that formed the Yucatán. Over millions of years, those mountains have eroded, and sea levels have risen, leaving the highest bits of land as isolated islands. Encourage students to research how the islands of the Lesser Antilles were formed. **L1**

EE3 Physical Systems: Standard 7

UNIT 7

Political

120°W 110°W 100°W 90°W 80°W 70°W 60°W
40°N 30°N 20°N 10°N 0° 10°S
Rio Grande
Gulf of Mexico
ATLANTIC OCEAN
PACIFIC OCEAN
Caribbean Sea
TROPIC OF CANCER
EQUATOR
Bermuda U.K.
Monterrey
MEXICO
Guadalajara
Mexico City
Nassau
BAHAMAS
Havana
CUBA
Cayman Is. U.K.
Kingston
JAMAICA
Port-au-Prince
HAITI
DOMINICAN REPUBLIC
Santo Domingo
Puerto Rico U.S.
Virgin Islands U.S. & U.K.
ANTIGUA AND BARBUDA
ST. KITTS AND NEVIS
Guadeloupe Fr.
DOMINICA
Martinique Fr.
ST. LUCIA
ST. VINCENT AND THE GRENADINES
BARBADOS
GRENADA
Port-of-Spain
TRINIDAD AND TOBAGO
BELIZE
Belmopan
GUATEMALA
Guatemala City
HONDURAS
Tegucigalpa
San Salvador
EL SALVADOR
NICARAGUA
Managua
San José
COSTA RICA
Panama City
PANAMA
N S E W
National capital
Major city
0 mi. 1,000
0 km 1,000
Lambert Azimuthal Equal-Area projection

MAP STUDY

1. What physical region covers much of the central part of Mexico?
2. What is the capital of Cuba?

Unit 7 Regional Atlas

Interpreting a Map Have students look at the political map on this page. **Ask: What is different about the way the name Martinique is treated on the map?** *(Martinique is followed by "Fr.")* **What does this difference mean?** *(Martinique is not an independent country but a territory under another government.)* Have them find other similar places on the map. *(Cayman Islands; Virgin Islands; Puerto Rico; Bermuda; Guadeloupe)* **L1**

Cultural Kaleidoscope

Haiti Most of Haiti is mountainous. Its name comes from a Native American word meaning "high ground."

MAP STUDY

Answers

1. The Mexican Plateau
2. Havana

Skills Practice

The Panama Canal cuts across the Isthmus of Panama. **Which two bodies of water does the canal connect?** *(The Caribbean Sea and the Pacific Ocean)* **Why was a canal built there?** *(It is the narrowest part of Central America.)*

Regional Atlas Activity

Research Activity Point out to students that maize (corn)—first grown in modern Mexico—was unknown in Europe, Africa, or Asia until European explorers reached the Americas. Have students do research to find food crops that originated in the Americas and then spread to other areas. Then have them research one of the crops. They should learn what kind of growing conditions—soil, temperature, rainfall—the crop needs, where in Latin America it was originally found, and how and where it's used today. Have them prepare a display that summarizes their findings. **L2**

EE5 Environment and Society: Standard 16

Note-taking tip

Remind students that Spanish is the predominant language in Middle America. Suggest that they can more easily remember the languages of the different countries of Middle America by noting the *exceptions*—those in which Spanish is not the main language.

Cultural Kaleidoscope

Belize's relatively small population is a blend of many peoples and cultures. Mayans descended from the original inhabitants of the area. Creoles are descendents of Europeans and enslaved Africans, while mestizos are a mix of Europeans and Mayans. Mennonites are a strict religious sect who moved to Belize from Canada and Mexico. More recently, immigrants have arrived from Lebanon, China, and India.

MAP STUDY

Answers

1. English, Spanish, French
2. England, Spain, France

Skills Practice

Which country has three language groups? *(Canada)*
What are the languages spoken there? *(English, French, and native languages)*

North America and Middle America

Major Languages

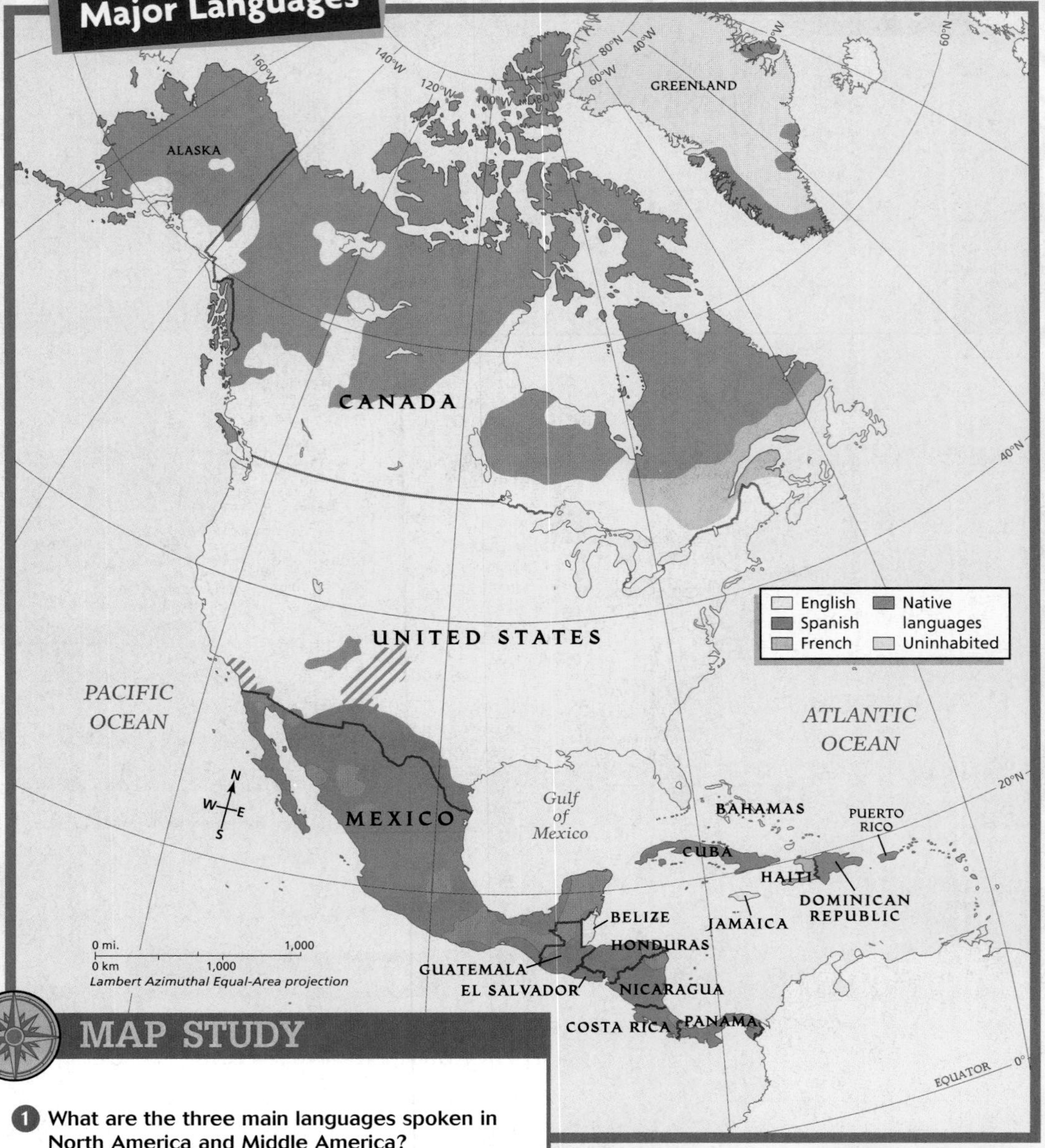

English
Spanish
French
Native languages
Uninhabited

ALASKA
GREENLAND
CANADA
UNITED STATES
MEXICO
PACIFIC OCEAN
ATLANTIC OCEAN
Gulf of Mexico
BAHAMAS
CUBA
HAITI
DOMINICAN REPUBLIC
PUERTO RICO
JAMAICA
BELIZE
HONDURAS
GUATEMALA
EL SALVADOR
NICARAGUA
COSTA RICA
PANAMA
EQUATOR

0 mi. 1,000
0 km 1,000
Lambert Azimuthal Equal-Area projection

MAP STUDY

1. What are the three main languages spoken in North America and Middle America?
2. In what countries did these languages originate?

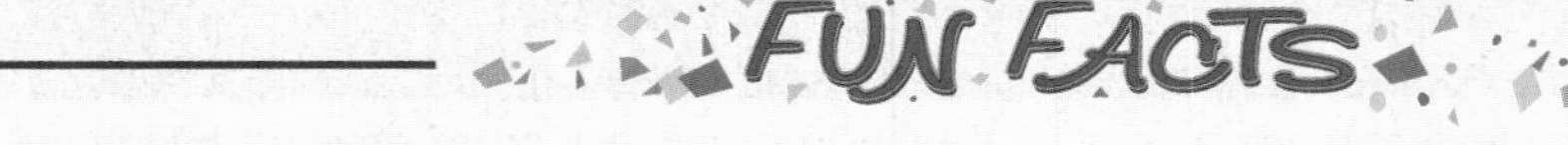

- **Dominican Republic** Dominicans point with puckered lips rather than a finger.
- **Jamaica** A staple of Jamaican cooking is "jerk" meat. No one is sure where the term *jerk* comes from, but the spicy dish was probably first cooked by runaway slaves in the 1600s.
- **Canada** The western Canadian town Medicine Hat is named after a Native American legend where a healer lost his headdress in a stream.
- **Costa Rica** Although Costa Rica's landmass is .03% of the planet, its plants and animals make up 6% of the world's biodiversity.

Unit 7
Regional Atlas

Fast Facts

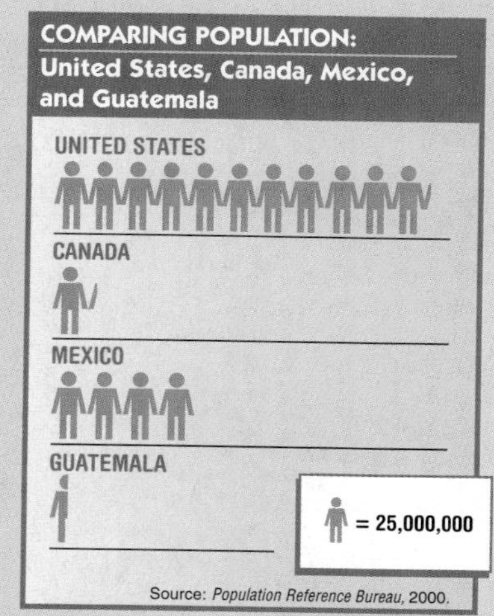

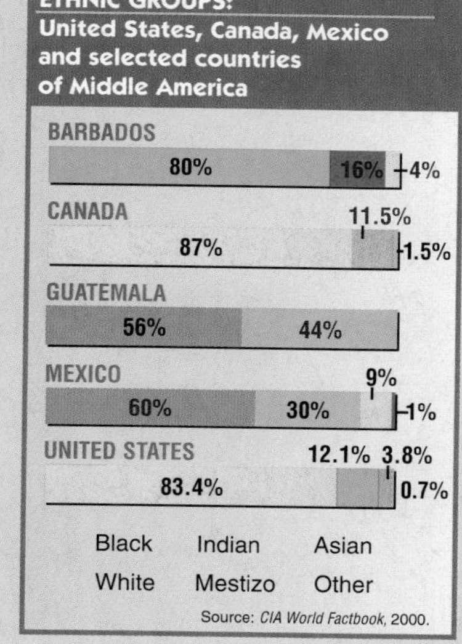

Mexico

Data Bits

Automobiles per 1,000 people	93
Telephones per 1,000 people	96
VOTE Democratic elections	Yes

Religions

Protestant 6%
Other 4%
Roman Catholic 90%

World Ranking

	GNP per capita in US $	Life expectancy	Literacy
Rank	61	62	94
	$3,700	72 years	90%

Axis: 1st, 50th, 100th, 150th

Population: Urban vs. Rural

Urban 75%, Rural 25%

Source: World Desk Reference, 2000.

GRAPHIC STUDY

1. What is life expectancy in Mexico?
2. What countries have a majority of mestizos (people of mixed European and Native American ancestry)?

As an introduction to this region, you may want to engage students by studying an important contemporary issue in this region of the world. The **TIME REPORTS: FOCUS ON WORLD ISSUES** for this region is found on pages 511–517. The feature examines the war on terrorism.

GRAPHIC STUDY

Answers

1. 72 years

2. Guatemala and Mexico

Skills Practice

What percentage of Mexicans lives in cities? *(75%)* **How does Guatemala's population compare to Canada's?** *(Guatemala has less than half of Canada's population.)*

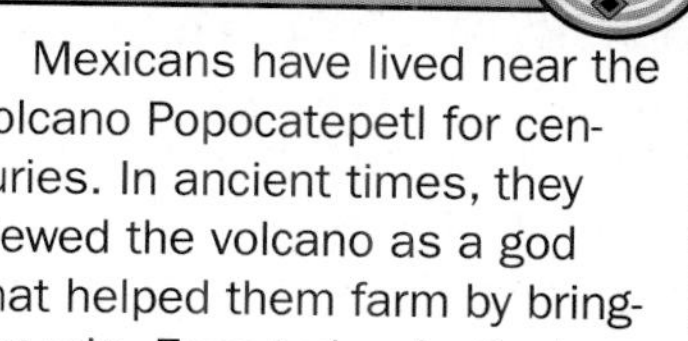

Mexicans have lived near the volcano Popocatepetl for centuries. In ancient times, they viewed the volcano as a god that helped them farm by bringing rain. Even today, festivals timed to the farming cycle honor this mountain.

Regional Atlas Activity

Making Comparisons Have students use the charts on pages 479, 137, and 633 to compare the GNP per capita, life expectancy, and literacy of Mexico, China, and Australia. Have them compare the levels of economic development of these countries based on these three indicators. **L2**

EE4 Human Systems: Standard 11

NATIONAL GEOGRAPHIC

REGIONAL ATLAS

Synthesizing Information Have students choose a country and investigate its flag. They should find out what colors and symbols are used on the flag and why. Have them create a presentation that displays the flag and explains its significance. **L1**

TRAVEL GUIDE 

The Cajun people of Louisiana are the descendants of French Canadians who were driven from their homes in an area called Acadia—now the province of Nova Scotia—by the British after the French and Indian War. *Cajun* is a slurred version of the word *Acadian.* The Cajuns enjoy many spicy dishes. Favorites include jambalaya, a dish that includes rice, ham, sausage, chicken, and seafood; and gumbo, a thick soup of vegetables and meat or seafood.

Did You Know 

British traditions remain strong in Barbados. Although the island achieved independence from the United Kingdom in 1996, it still recognizes Britain's Queen Elizabeth II as its head of state.

Country Profiles

ANTIGUA and BARBUDA
POPULATION: 100,000; 588 per sq. mi.; 227 per sq. km
LANGUAGE: English
MAJOR EXPORT: Petroleum Products
MAJOR IMPORTS: Foods and Livestock
CAPITAL: St. John's
LANDMASS: 170 sq. mi.; 440 sq. km
(Map label: St. Johns)

BAHAMAS
POPULATION: 301,000; 56 per sq. mi.; 22 per sq. km
LANGUAGES: English, Creole
MAJOR EXPORT: Pharmaceuticals
MAJOR IMPORT: Foods
CAPITAL: Nassau
LANDMASS: 5,382 sq. mi.; 13,939 sq. km

BARBADOS
POPULATION: 300,000; 1807 per sq. mi.; 698 per sq. km
LANGUAGE: English
MAJOR EXPORT: Sugar
MAJOR IMPORTS: Manufactured Goods
CAPITAL: Bridgetown
LANDMASS: 166 sq. mi.; 430 sq. km

BELIZE
POPULATION: 300,000; 34 per sq. mi.; 13 per sq. km
LANGUAGE: English
MAJOR EXPORT: Sugar
MAJOR IMPORT: Machinery
CAPITAL: Belmopan
LANDMASS: 8,867 sq. mi.; 22,965 sq. km

CANADA
POPULATION: 31,000,000; 8 per sq. mi.; 3 per sq. km
LANGUAGES: English, French
MAJOR EXPORT: Newsprint
MAJOR IMPORT: Crude Oil
CAPITAL: Ottawa
LANDMASS: 3,849,670 sq. mi.; 9,970,610 sq. km

COSTA RICA
POPULATION: 3,700,000; 187 per sq. mi.; 72 per sq. km
LANGUAGE: Spanish
MAJOR EXPORT: Coffee
MAJOR IMPORT: Raw Materials
CAPITAL: San José
LANDMASS: 19,730 sq. mi.; 51,100 sq. km

CUBA
POPULATION: 11,178,000; 261 per sq. mi.; 101 per sq. km
LANGUAGE: Spanish
MAJOR EXPORT: Sugar
MAJOR IMPORT: Petroleum
CAPITAL: Havana
LANDMASS: 42,804 sq. mi.; 110,861 sq. km

DOMINICA
POPULATION: 100,000; 345 per sq. mi.; 133 per sq. km
LANGUAGES: English, French
MAJOR EXPORT: Bananas
MAJOR IMPORT: Manufactured Goods
CAPITAL: Roseau
LANDMASS: 290 sq. mi.; 751 sq. km

DOMINICAN REPUBLIC
POPULATION: 8,600,000; 457 per sq. mi.; 176 per sq. km
LANGUAGE: Spanish
MAJOR EXPORT: Ferronickel
MAJOR IMPORT: Foods
CAPITAL: Santo Domingo
LANDMASS: 18,816 sq. mi.; 48,734 sq. km

EL SALVADOR
POPULATION: 6,400,000; 788 per sq. mi.; 304 per sq. km
LANGUAGE: Spanish
MAJOR EXPORT: Coffee
MAJOR IMPORT: Raw Materials
CAPITAL: San Salvador
LANDMASS: 8,124 sq. mi.; 21,041 sq. km

GRENADA
POPULATION: 97,000; 729 per sq. mi.; 282 per sq. km
LANGUAGES: English, French
MAJOR EXPORT: Bananas
MAJOR IMPORT: Foods
CAPITAL: St. George's
LANDMASS: 133 sq. mi.; 344 sq. km

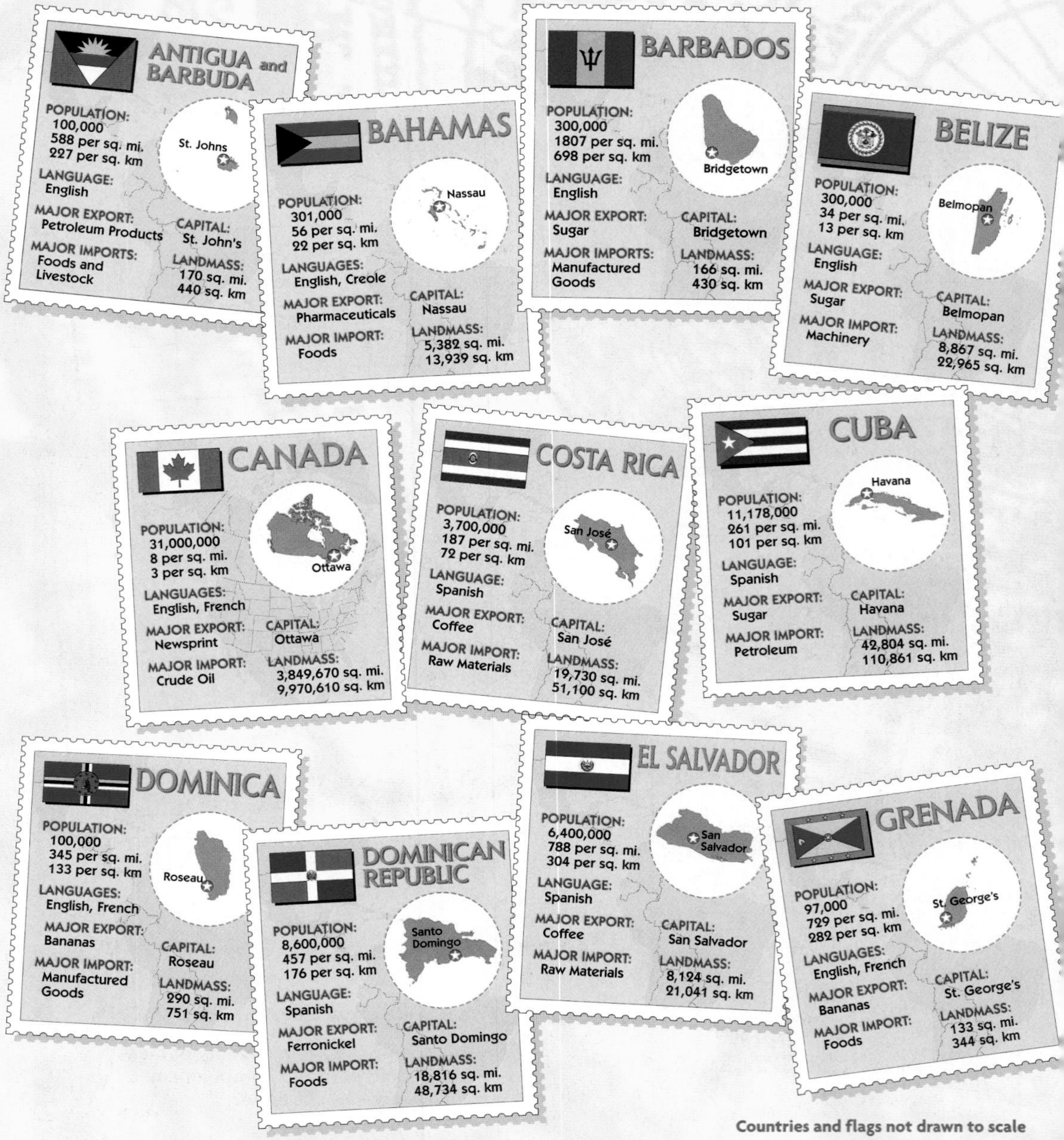

Countries and flags not drawn to scale

Regional Atlas Activity

Making Charts Point out to students that all the nations of North and Middle America were once colonies of European countries. Have students look at the Country Profiles and the map on page 478. **Ask:** **What information suggests which European countries ruled the countries in this region?** *(language)* **Which European countries had colonies in the area?** *(Britain, Spain, France).* Have students create a chart with headings for each European colonial power. Then they should write the names of each North and Middle American country under the appropriate heading. (Some may be under two headings.) **L1**

EE6 The Uses of Geography: Standard 18

UNIT 7

For more information on countries in this region, refer to the Nations of the World Data Bank on pages 690–699.

GUATEMALA

POPULATION:
13,000,000
309 per sq. mi.
119 per sq. km
LANGUAGES:
Spanish, Mayan Languages
MAJOR EXPORT:
Coffee
MAJOR IMPORT:
Petroleum
CAPITAL:
Guatemala City
LANDMASS:
42,042 sq. mi.
108,889 sq. km

Guatemala City

HAITI

POPULATION:
7,751,000
723 per sq. mi.
279 per sq. km
LANGUAGES:
French, Creole
MAJOR EXPORT:
Manufactured Goods
MAJOR IMPORT:
Machinery
CAPITAL:
Port-au-Prince
LANDMASS:
10,714 sq. mi.
27,750 sq. km

Port-au-Prince

HONDURAS

POPULATION:
6,700,000
155 per sq. mi.
60 per sq. km
LANGUAGE:
Spanish
MAJOR EXPORT:
Bananas
MAJOR IMPORT:
Machinery
CAPITAL:
Tegucigalpa
LANDMASS:
43,277 sq. mi.
112,088 sq. km

Tegucigalpa

JAMAICA

POPULATION:
2,621,000
618 per sq. mi.
238 per sq. km
LANGUAGES:
English, Creole
MAJOR EXPORT:
Alumina
MAJOR IMPORT:
Machinery
CAPITAL:
Kingston
LANDMASS:
4,244 sq. mi.
10,991 sq. km

Kingston

MEXICO

POPULATION:
99,734,000
132 per sq. mi.
51 per sq. km
LANGUAGES:
Spanish, Native American Languages
MAJOR EXPORT:
Crude Oil
MAJOR IMPORT:
Machinery
CAPITAL:
Mexico City
LANDMASS:
756,066 sq. mi.
1,958,201 sq. km

Mexico City

NICARAGUA

POPULATION:
5,200,000
104 per sq. mi.
40 per sq. km
LANGUAGE:
Spanish
MAJOR EXPORT:
Coffee
MAJOR IMPORT:
Manufactured Goods
CAPITAL:
Managua
LANDMASS:
50,193 sq. mi.
129,999 sq. km

Managua

PANAMA

POPULATION:
2,900,000
97 per sq. mi.
38 per sq. km
LANGUAGE:
Spanish
MAJOR EXPORT:
Bananas
MAJOR IMPORT:
Machinery
CAPITAL:
Panama City
LANDMASS:
29,762 sq. mi.
77,082 sq. km

Panama City

PUERTO RICO*

POPULATION:
3,887,652
1,132 per sq. mi.
437 per sq. km
LANGUAGES:
Spanish, English
MAJOR EXPORT:
Pharmaceuticals
MAJOR IMPORT:
Chemical Products
CAPITAL:
San Juan
LANDMASS:
3,435 sq. mi.
8,897 sq. km

San Juan

ST. KITTS and NEVIS

POPULATION:
40,000
396 per sq. mi.
153 per sq. km
LANGUAGE:
English
MAJOR EXPORT:
Machinery
MAJOR IMPORT:
Electronic Goods
CAPITAL:
Basseterre
LANDMASS:
101 sq. mi.
261 sq. km

Basseterre

ST. LUCIA

POPULATION:
154,000
647 per sq. mi.
250 per sq. km
LANGUAGES:
English, French
MAJOR EXPORT:
Bananas
MAJOR IMPORT:
Foods
CAPITAL:
Castries
LANDMASS:
238 sq. mi.
617 sq. km

Castries

* U.S. Commonwealth

Unit 7

3 ASSESS

Organize students into groups. Have groups use the maps and graphs from the Unit 7 Regional Atlas to quiz one another on the features of North and Middle America.

Reteach

Have students use the Country Profiles chart to come up with questions about patterns that exist in this world region. Use their questions to quiz the class.

Cultural Kaleidoscope

Guatemala In the Guatemalan town of Santiago, people celebrate All Saints' Day (November 2) by flying giant kites to raise the souls of the dead to Heaven and turn away evil spirits. Families compete to see who can make the best kite.

Did You Know?

On the shores of Canada's Georgian Bay are strange-looking landforms called flowerpots. Wind and water have worn away the bases of these tall rock formations. What remains are wide tops covered with flowers, plants, and shrubs.

Regional Atlas Activity

Research Activity Point out that in earlier times, people in different regions of North and Middle America developed particular styles of cooking that combined the traditions of the people who settled there with the foods available in that region due to its physical geography and climate. Have students choose a region and generate a list of dishes typical of that region. You might ask them to devise a menu. Have them annotate their list or menu to explain whether the different dishes are based on the culture of those who settled there or the local availability of ingredients. **L2**

EE6 The Uses of Geography: Standard 17

Comparing Information

Have students list the seven countries that make up Central America. Then ask them to use the Country Profiles to compare the exports and imports in these countries. **Ask:** **What are the similarities and differences?** *(Many export agricultural goods like bananas or coffee, and import machinery or raw goods.)*

TRAVEL GUIDE 

The islands of Trinidad and Tobago are actually parts of South America that broke away from the mainland. Trinidad is only seven miles from Venezuela.

BUILDING CITIZENSHIP

Answer
If encouraged to think about it, most students will realize that someone in their family is involved with a church, Boy Scouts or Girl Scouts, or community sports. Some may work with clinics, shelters, food kitchens, or other service organizations.

Write About It! Students may make up an organization like an animal shelter or an after-school club, or they may be familiar with a church, Scouts, or other nonprofit organization. Their responses should include a description of the organization, its members, and some of the things they do. Students should present their talks orally.

Country Profiles

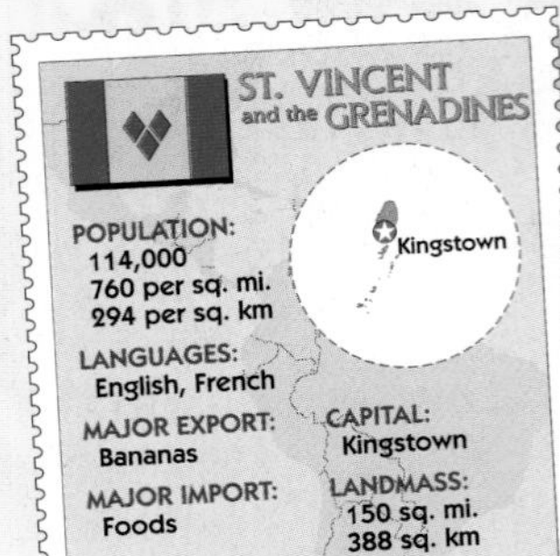

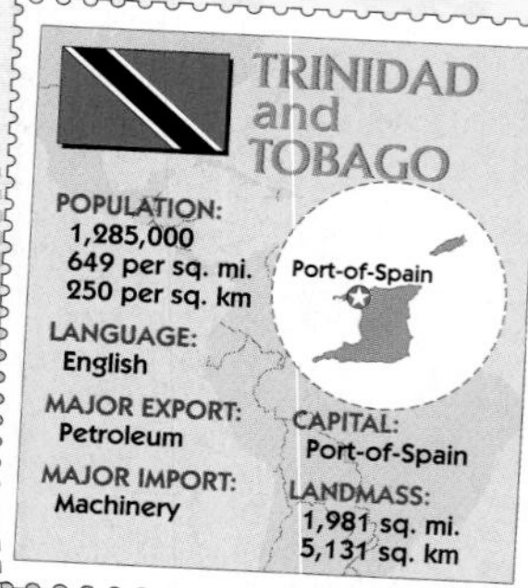

TRINIDAD and TOBAGO
Port-of-Spain
POPULATION:
1,285,000
649 per sq. mi.
250 per sq. km
LANGUAGE:
English
MAJOR EXPORT:
Petroleum
MAJOR IMPORT:
Machinery
CAPITAL:
Port-of-Spain
LANDMASS:
1,981 sq. mi.
5,131 sq. km

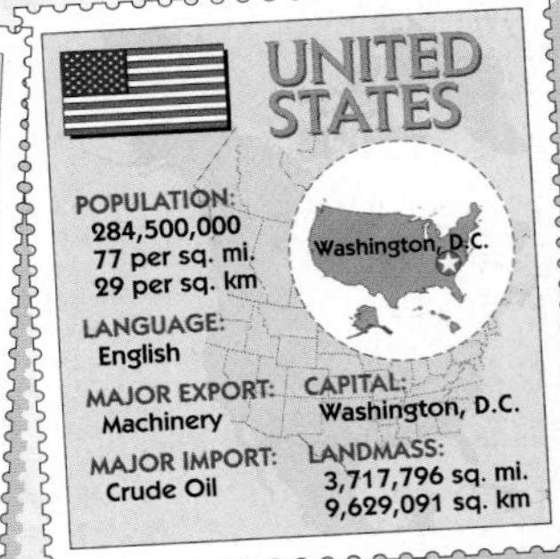

Countries and flags not drawn to scale

BUILDING CITIZENSHIP

Building Better Communities Many people in the United States try to improve their communities or help other people by volunteering in nonprofit and civic organizations. Nonprofit organizations may be churches, boys and girls clubs, sporting and leisure clubs, homeless shelters, or other social agencies. They supply services and assistance that the government or business is unable to provide. More than half of all Americans volunteer at least three hours per week in nonprofit organizations.

Tell about a nonprofit organization supported by you or someone you know.

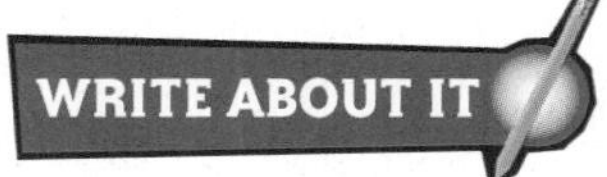

Imagine that you are the head of a nonprofit organization and you have been invited to your school to tell the students about it. Knowing that your efforts may inspire students to participate, write a short talk describing the organization's activities.

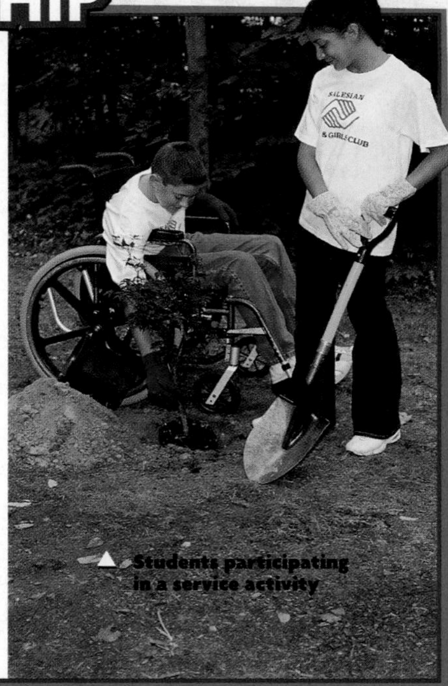

Students participating in a service activity

Content Background

NAFTA El Paso, Texas and Juarez, Mexico are separated by the Rio Grande, the river that separates Mexico and the United States. The cities are connected by a bridge, but even more important is the economic connection created by the North American Free Trade Agreement (NAFTA). Today, there are 400 factories in Juarez and more than 2000 along the U.S.-Mexican border. These factories—mostly owned by U.S., Japanese, and European companies—assemble products from parts shipped to them from the United States. The finished goods are then sent back to the United States. This arrangement provides jobs for Mexicans, inexpensive goods for Americans, and economic growth for American border towns like El Paso.

UNIT 7

Spider monkey and Mayan ruins, Mexico ▲

Content Background

Many Mayan ruins are located in dense forests, where they were covered by foliage and hidden for centuries. Finding these ruins was often frustrating. One enterprising archaeologist realized that he might be able to get information from native *chicleros,* the men who harvested the sap of chicle trees, which was used to make chewing gum. By questioning the men in the chicle camps, the archaeologist was able to locate many ruins, which otherwise might never have been found.

More About the Photo

The Maya The Mayan people lived in southern Mexico, Guatemala, and parts of Belize and Honduras. The peak of their civilization was probably between A.D. 300 to 900, when they built their finest pyramids and made significant advances in astronomy and writing.

Did You Know

The Mosquito Coast stretches about 500 miles along the Caribbean Coast from Honduras to Nicaragua. The remote area has few roads because of its extensive lagoons, swamps, and rivers, which are prone to seasonal flooding and, indeed, are good breeding grounds for mosquitoes.

Enrich

Have students research one of the countries in the Caribbean. Then have them prepare a poster advertising the country's attractions.

4 CLOSE

Have students write a brief paragraph in which they summarize the physical and social characteristics of a country they studied in this section.

Chapter 18 Resources

Note: The following materials may be used when teaching Chapter 18. Section level support materials are shown at point of use in the margins of the Teacher Wraparound Edition.

Timesaving Tools

TeacherWorks™ All-In-One Planner and Resource Center

- **Interactive Teacher Edition** See the **Interactive Teacher Edition** CD-ROM to electronically integrate your Teacher Wraparound Edition and blackline masters.
- **Interactive Lesson Planner** Organize your week, month, semester, or year with all the lesson helps you need. The **Interactive Lesson Planner** CD-ROM contains all Chapter 18 resources.

Use Glencoe's **Presentation Plus!** multimedia teacher tool to easily present dynamic lessons that visually excite your students. Using Microsoft PowerPoint® you can customize the presentations to create your own personalized lessons.

TEACHING TRANSPARENCIES

Graphic Organizer Transparency and Student Activity 18

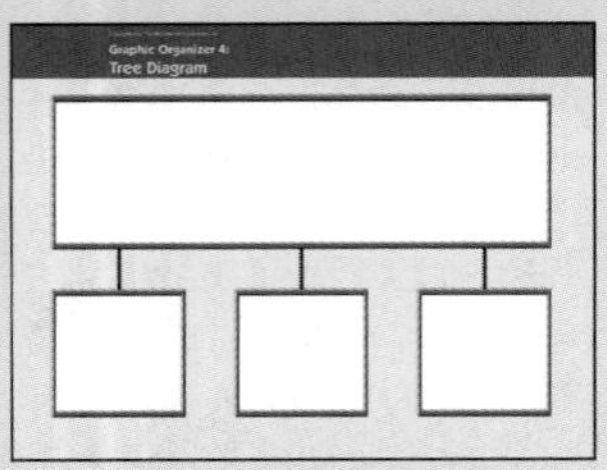

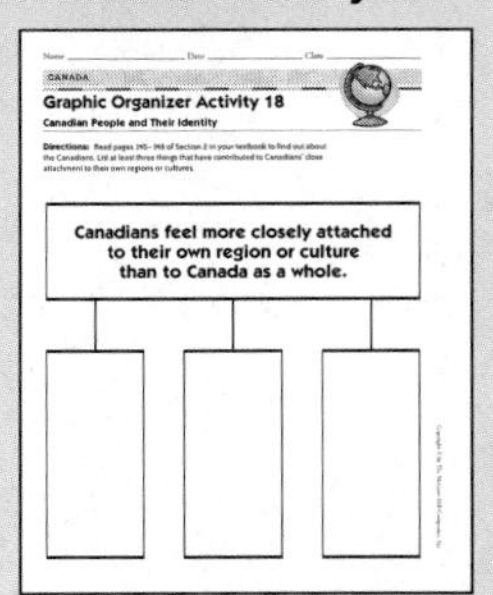

FOLDABLES™ Study Organizer

Foldables are three-dimensional, interactive graphic organizers that help students practice basic writing skills, review key vocabulary terms, and identify main ideas. Every chapter contains a Foldable activity, with additional chapter activities found in the ***Reading and Study Skills Foldables*** booklet.

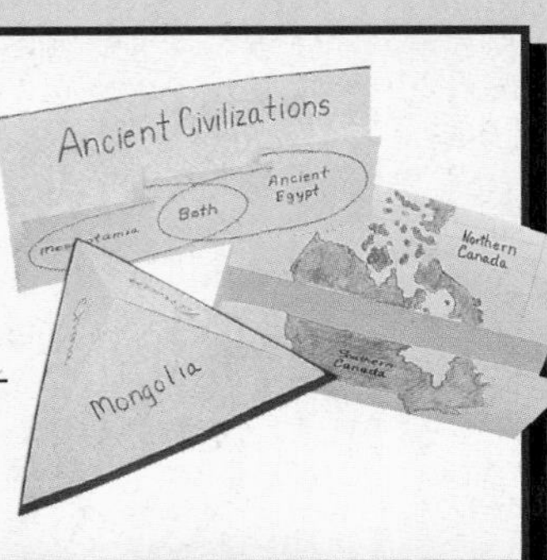

ENRICHMENT AND EXTENSION

Enrichment Activity 18

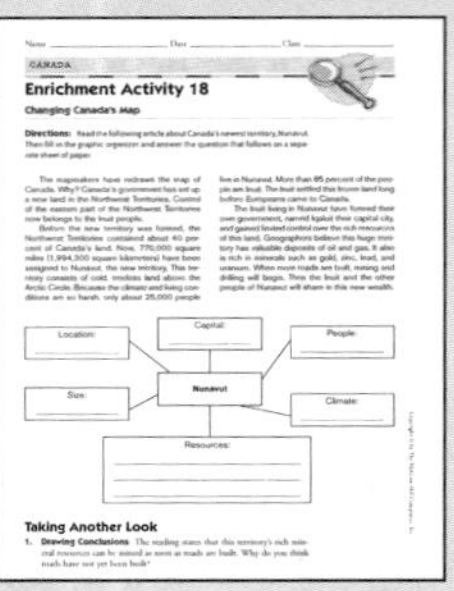

Cooperative Learning Activity 18

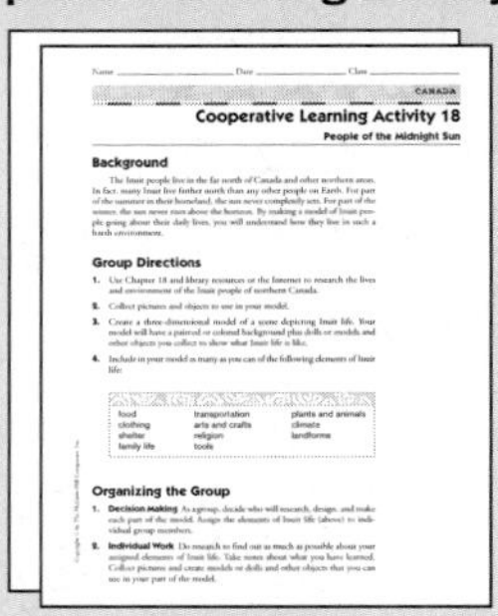

MAP AND GEOGRAPHY SKILLS

Chapter Map Activity 18

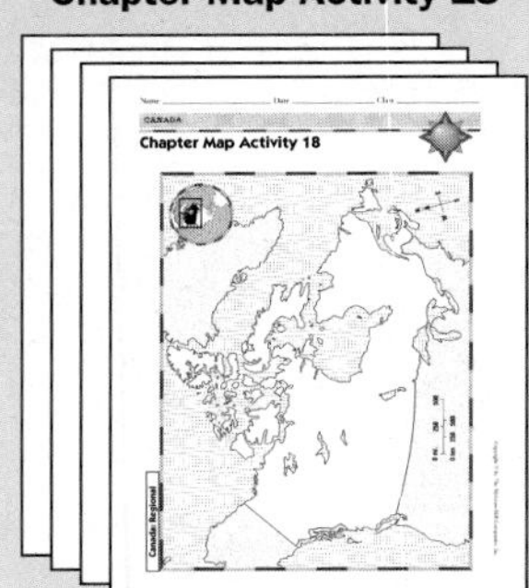

GeoLab Activity 18

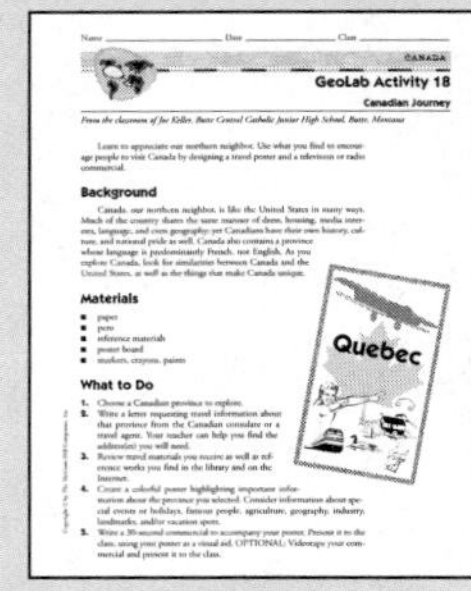

STANDARDIZED ASSESSMENT SKILLS

GLENCOE'S ASSESSMENT ADVANTAGE

Critical Thinking Skills Activity 18

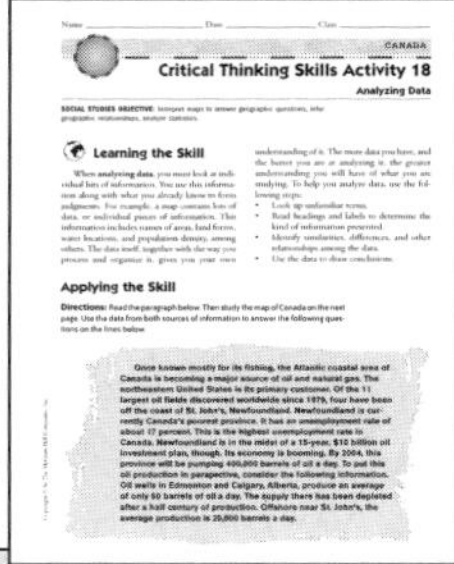

Map and Graph Skills Activity 18

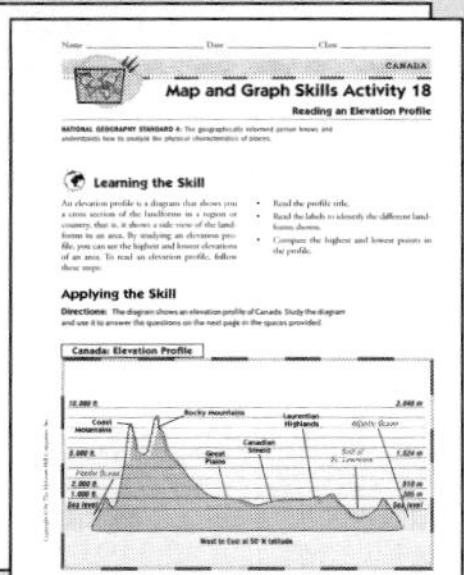

Reading and Writing Skills Activity 18

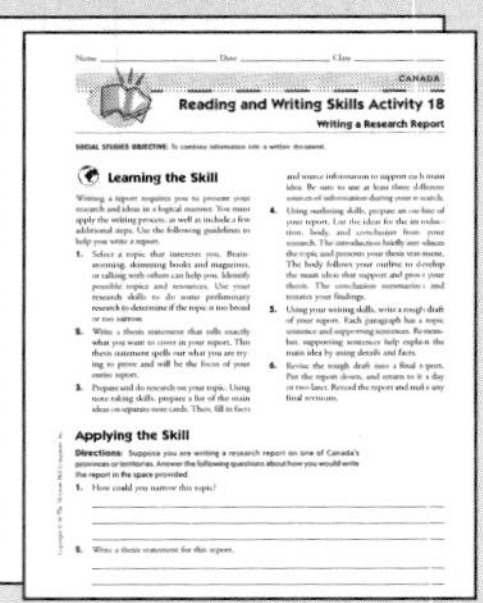

Standardized Test Practice Workbook Activity 18

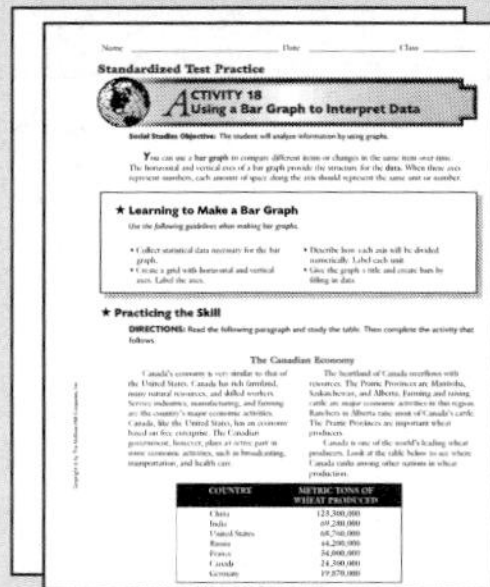

REVIEW AND REINFORCEMENT

Chapter Skills Activity 18

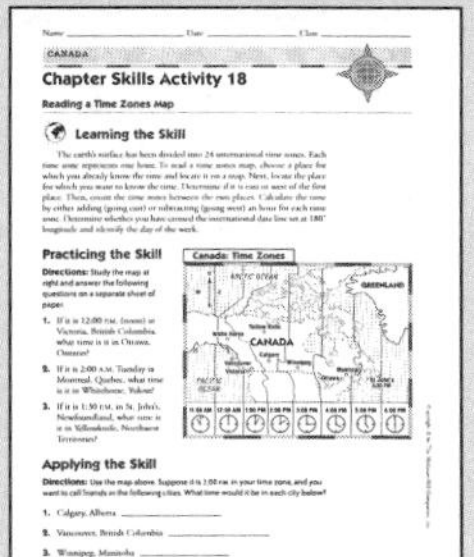

Take-Home Review Activity 18

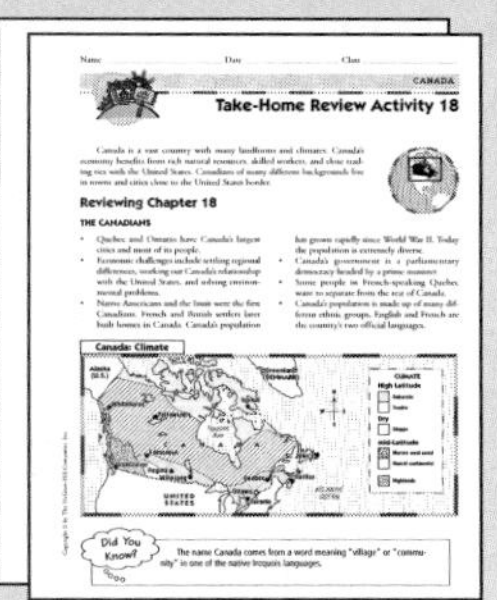

Reteaching Activity 18

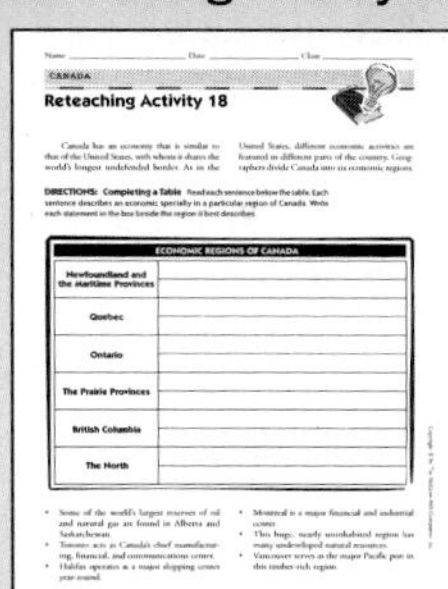

Vocabulary Activity 18

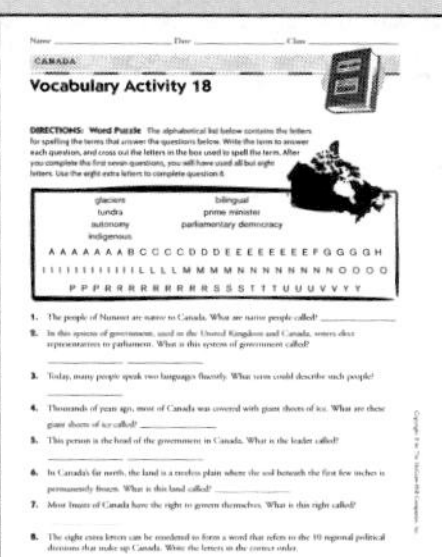

Workbook Activity 18

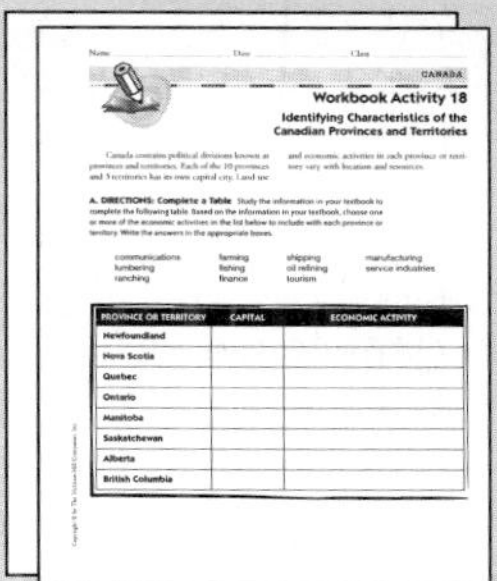

ASSESSMENT

Glencoe's Assessment Advantage

Chapter 18 Test, Form A

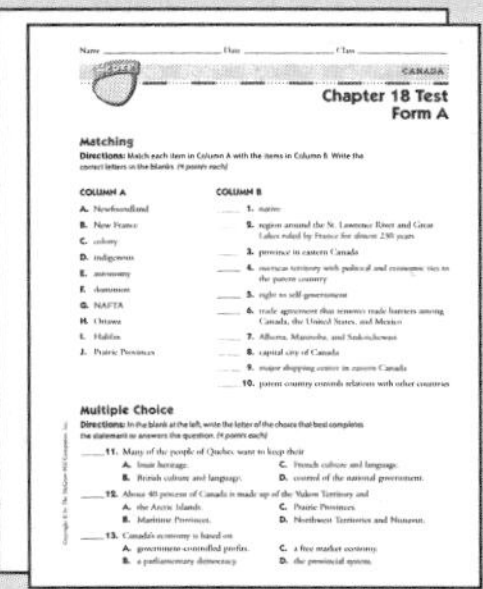

Chapter 18 Test, Form B

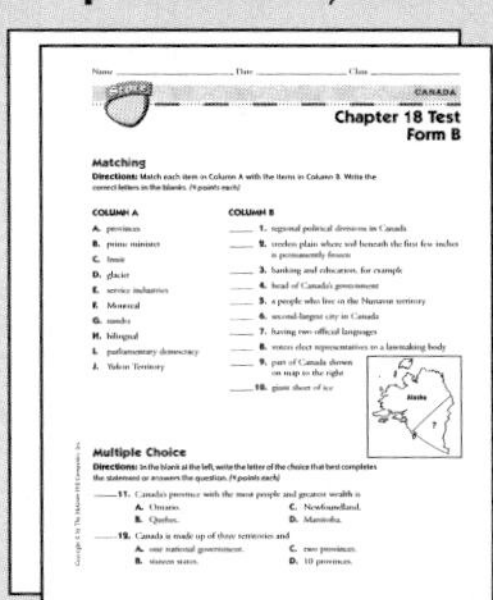

Performance Assessment Activity 18

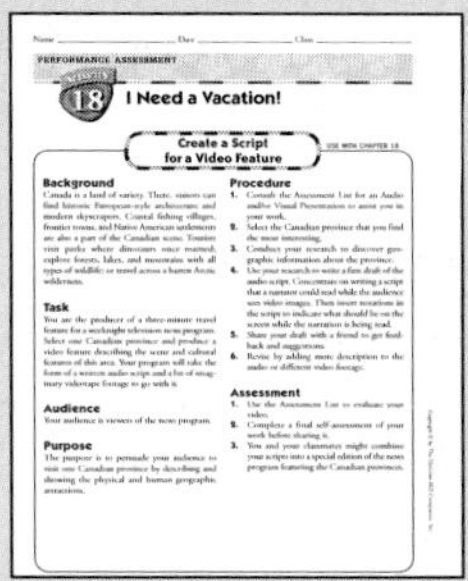

ExamView® Pro 3.0 Testmaker CD-ROM

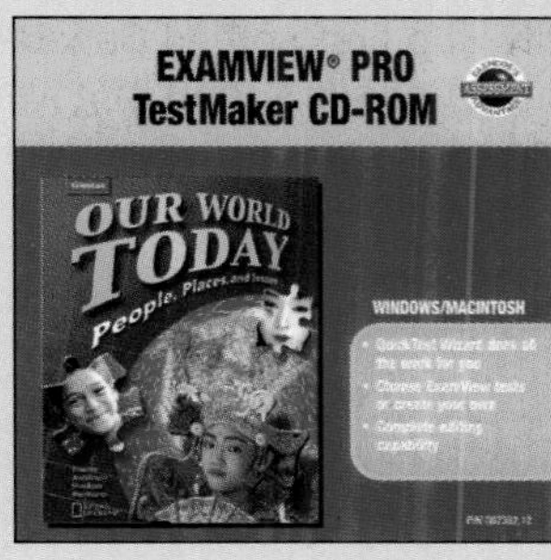

MULTIMEDIA

- National Geographic's The World and Its People
- MindJogger Videoquiz
- Vocabulary PuzzleMaker Software
- Interactive Tutor Self-Assessment CD-ROM
- ExamView® Pro 3.0 Testmaker CD-ROM
- Interactive Lesson Planner CD-ROM
- Interactive Teacher Edition CD-ROM
- Skillbuilder Interactive Workbook CD-ROM, Level 1
- Presentation Plus! CD-ROM
- Audio Program

SPANISH RESOURCES

The following Spanish language materials are available in the Spanish Resources binder:

- Spanish Chapter Summaries
- Spanish Vocabulary Activities
- Spanish Guided Reading Activities
- Spanish Quizzes and Tests
- Spanish Take-Home Review Activities
- Spanish Reteaching Activities

Meeting National Standards

Geography for Life

All of the 18 standards are demonstrated in Unit 7. The following ones are highlighted in Chapter 18:

Section 1 **EE3 Physical Systems: Standards 7, 8**

EE5 Environment and Society: Standards 14, 15, 16

Section 2 **EE4 Human Systems: Standards 9, 10, 11, 12, 13**

EE5 Environment and Society: Standard 14

EE6 The Uses of Geography: Standards 17, 18

For a complete listing of National Geography Standards and entire text correlation, see pages T22–T29.

Local Objectives

Chapter 18 Planning Guide

SECTION RESOURCES

Daily Objectives	Reproducible Resources	Multimedia Resources
Section 1 **Canada's Major Regions** **Suggested Pacing = 1 day** **1.** Explain how Canada's landforms and climate have affected where Canadians live. **2.** Compare Canada's economy to that of the United States. **3.** Compare the different economies of Canada's provinces.	Reproducible Lesson Plan 18-1 Daily Lecture and Discussion Notes 18-1 Guided Reading Activity 18-1 Reading Essentials and Study Guide 18-1 Section Quiz 18-1*	Daily Focus Skills Transparency 18-1 GeoQuiz Transparency 18-1 Vocabulary PuzzleMaker Software Interactive Tutor Self-Assessment CD-ROM ExamView® Pro 3.0 Testmaker CD-ROM Presentation Plus! CD-ROM
Section 2 **The Canadians** **Suggested Pacing = 1 day** **1.** Identify who first settled Canada. **2.** Describe Canada's form of government. **3.** Explain what groups make up the Canadian people.	Reproducible Lesson Plan 18-2 Daily Lecture and Discussion Notes 18-2 Guided Reading Activity 18-2 Reading Essentials and Study Guide 18-2 Section Quiz 18-2*	Daily Focus Skills Transparency 18-2 Vocabulary PuzzleMaker Software Interactive Tutor Self-Assessment CD-ROM ExamView® Pro 3.0 Testmaker CD-ROM Presentation Plus! CD-ROM

00:00 **Out of Time?** Assign the **Reading Essentials and Study Guide** for this chapter.

*Also available in Spanish

KEY TO ABILITY LEVELS

Teaching strategies have been coded for varying learning styles and abilities.

L1 **BASIC** activities for all students
L2 **AVERAGE** activities for average to above-average students
L3 **CHALLENGING** activities for above-average students
ELL **ENGLISH LANGUAGE LEARNER** activities

Blackline Master
Software
CD-ROM
Audiocassette
Transparency
Videocassette
Block Scheduling
DVD

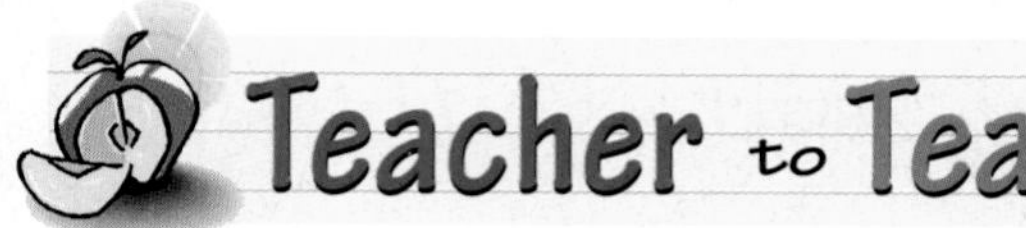

World Tour

William Sim
L.L. Wright Middle School
Ironwood, Michigan

Students travel the world. They select a city with a minimum population of 1 million people in 10 different countries. Then they construct a world map on a large piece of styrofoam. Placing a pushpin into their hometown, they travel to their first city and add a pushpin there. They must research 5 items about the city: famous landmark, famous person from there and his or her significance, general physical landscape, year of founding, and flag of the country in which the city is located. For each city, students must draw or list the 5 items on small pieces of paper, and insert the papers with toothpicks near the city's pushpin. After the 10 cities are visited, the student connects all pushpins with a string in the order in which the cities were visited.

Use our Web site for additional resources. All essential content is covered in the Student Edition.

You and your students can visit owt.glencoe.com, the Web site companion to *Our World Today*. This innovative integration of electronic and print media offers your students a wealth of opportunities. The student text directs students to the Web site for the following options:

- Chapter Overviews
- Student Web Activities
- Self-Check Quizzes
- Textbook Updates

Answers are provided for you in the Web Activity Lesson Plan. Additional Web resources and Interactive Tutor puzzles are also available.

NATIONAL GEOGRAPHIC TEACHER'S CORNER

Index to National Geographic Magazine:

The following articles may be used for research relating to this chapter:

- "The Untamed Yukon River," by Michael Parfit, July 1998.
- "Prince Edward Island: A World Apart No More," by Ian Darragh, May 1998.
- "A Dream Called Nunavut," by Michael Parfit, September 1997.

National Geographic Society Products Available From Glencoe:

To order the following products for use with this chapter, contact your local Glencoe sales representative or call Glencoe at 1-800-334-7344:

- *GeoBee* (CD-ROM)
- *PicturePack: Earth's Climate* (Transparencies)
- *PicturePack: Geography of North America* (Transparencies)
- *PictureShow: Earth's Endangered Environments* (CD-ROM)
- *PicturePack: Looking at Ecosystems* (Transparencies)
- *MapPack: Continents: North America* (Transparencies)
- *GTV: A Geographic Perspective on American History* (Videodisc)

Additional National Geographic Society Products:

To order the following products for use with this chapter, call National Geographic Society at 1-800-368-2728:

- *Complete National Geographic: 111 years of National Geographic Magazine* (CD-ROM)
- *GeoKit: Pollution* (Kit)
- *Physical Geography of North America Series* (6 Videos)
- *The Living Ocean* (Video)
- *Investigating Global Warming* (Video)
- *Technology's Price* (Video)
- *North America Political* (Map)
- *Canada Political* (Map)
- *National Geographic Desk Reference* (Book)
- *National Geographic Atlas of the World, Seventh Edition* (Book)
- *Physical Geography of North America Series* (6 Videos)

NGS ONLINE

Access National Geographic's Web site for current events, activities, links, interactive features, and archives.
www.nationalgeographic.com

Introducing
Chapter 18

Our World Today online

Introduce students to chapter content and key terms by having them access Chapter Overview 18 at owt.glencoe.com

Chapter Objectives

1. Describe the landscapes and climates of Canada.
2. Explain Canada's economic resources, activities, and challenges.
3. Discuss the history and government of Canada.
4. Compare the Canadian peoples and their cultures.

GLENCOE TECHNOLOGY

NATIONAL GEOGRAPHIC

The World and Its People Video Program

Chapter 5 Canada

The following segments enhance the study of this chapter:

- **Newfoundland**
- **Seals in Winter**

Available in DVD and VHS.

MindJogger Videoquiz

Use MindJogger to preview the Chapter 18 content.

Available in VHS.

Chapter 18 Canada

The World and Its People NATIONAL GEOGRAPHIC

To learn more about Canada's people and places, view ***The World and Its People*** **Chapter 5** video.

Our World Today online

Chapter Overview Visit the ***Our World Today: People, Places, and Issues*** Web site at owt.glencoe.com and click on **Chapter 18—Chapter Overviews** to preview information about Canada.

484

Two-Minute Lesson Launcher

Bring in a section from the local newspaper and hold it up before the class. **Ask:** **What connection does this newspaper have to Canada?** If students are unable to answer, tell them that Canada's trees are used to make newsprint, the paper on which newspaper is printed. Point out that the newsprint used for the paper you hold may have come from Canada. The country produces more than one-fourth of all the newsprint manufactured in the world, and nearly 90 percent of its output is exported. Inform students that in this chapter they will read more about Canada and its resources. **L1**

FOLDABLES™ Study Organizer

Compare-Contrast Study Foldable Make this foldable to help you analyze the similarities and differences between the landforms, climate, and cultures of northern and southern Canada.

Step 1 Mark the midpoint of the side edge of a sheet of paper.

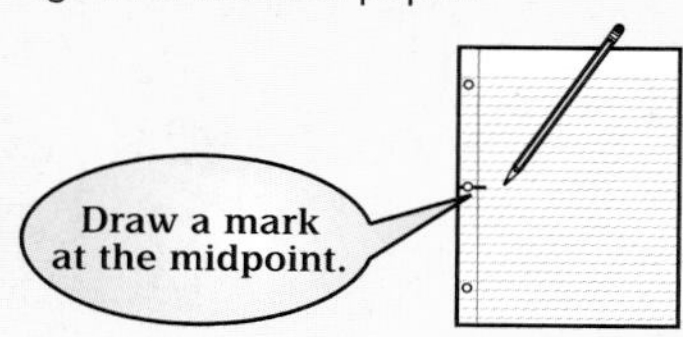

Step 2 Turn the paper and fold the outside edges in to touch at the midpoint.

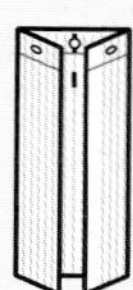

Step 3 Turn and label your foldable as shown.

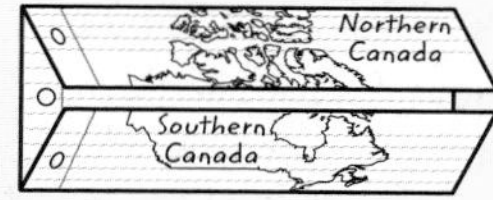

Reading and Writing As you read the chapter, collect and write information under the appropriate tab that will help you compare and contrast northern and southern Canada.

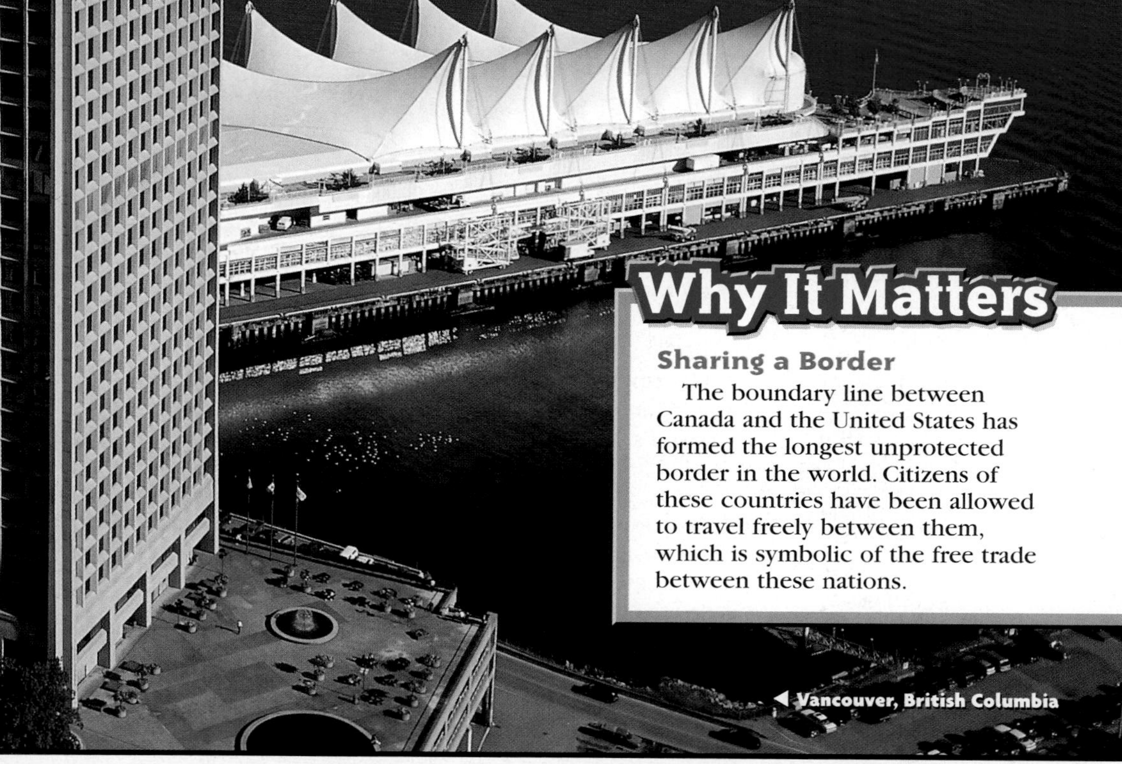

Why It Matters

Sharing a Border

The boundary line between Canada and the United States has formed the longest unprotected border in the world. Citizens of these countries have been allowed to travel freely between them, which is symbolic of the free trade between these nations.

◀ Vancouver, British Columbia

About the Photos

Vancouver is located on the Pacific Coast of Canada and is the country's main seaport and third largest city (after Toronto and Montreal). Although it has the most temperate climate in Canada, it often rains there. Vancouver's dramatic setting makes it a popular tourist destination, and it is known for its parks and many recreational and cultural activities. It's also the location of many Hollywood movies, which are filmed there because production is often less expensive than in the United States.

Introducing

Chapter 18

FOLDABLES™ Study Organizer

Purpose Students will make and use a compare-contrast foldable to help them organize the similarities and differences between northern and southern Canada. As students read the chapter and fill in information on their foldable, they compare and contrast facts that show how the landforms, climate, and cultures differ and are the same in northern and southern Canada.

Have students complete ***Reading and Study Skills Foldables*** Activity 18.

Why It Matters

Ask students to name physical and cultural features that they know the United States and Canada share. If they have difficulty coming up with examples, have them look at the physical map of the region on page 474. They should be able to identify such features as the Rocky Mountains, the Great Lakes, and the Great Plains. Cultural examples include a common language *(English)*, common sports, and popular performers. See if students can come up with professional teams or sports figures from Canada. *(For example, the Toronto Blue Jays are in baseball's American League.)* They may also know Canadian celebrities such as Celine Dion, Alanis Morissette, and Peter Jennings.

Chapter 18

Section 1, pages 486–489

Focus

Section Objectives

1. Explain how Canada's landforms and climate have affected where Canadians live.
2. Compare Canada's economy to that of the United States.
3. Compare the different economies of Canada's provinces.

BELLRINGER
Skillbuilder Activity

Project transparency 18–1 and have students answer questions.

This activity is also available as a blackline master.

Daily Focus Skills Transparency 18-1

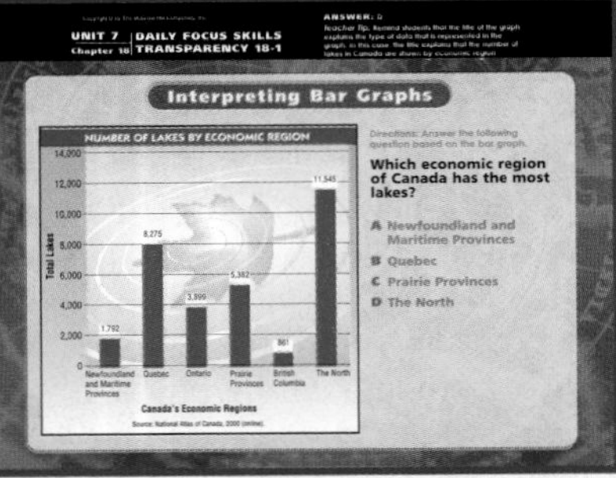

UNIT 7 Chapter 18
DAILY FOCUS SKILLS TRANSPARENCY 18-1
Interpreting Bar Graphs
Which economic region of Canada has the most lakes?
A Newfoundland and Maritime Provinces
B Quebec
C Prairie Provinces
D The North

Guide to Reading

■ Accessing Prior Knowledge

Ask: How large do you think Canada is compared to the United States? Have students write their answers on a piece of paper and check them for accuracy as they read the section.

Canada's Major Regions

Guide to Reading

Main Idea

Canada is a vast country with many landforms, climates, resources, and peoples.

Terms to Know

- province
- Nunavut
- indigenous
- glacier
- tundra
- service industry
- overfishing

Reading Strategy

Create a chart like this one and list Canada's provinces in the left column. In the right column, list the main economic activities in each province.

Province	Economic Activities

NATIONAL GEOGRAPHIC Exploring Our World

Have you ever seen a lumbering, snarling grizzly bear up close and personal? Many tourists come to Banff National Park in western Canada hoping to spot such a creature. Located in the Rocky Mountains, Banff is Canada's oldest, best-loved, and busiest national park. More than 4 million visitors a year are drawn to its spectacular mountain scenery.

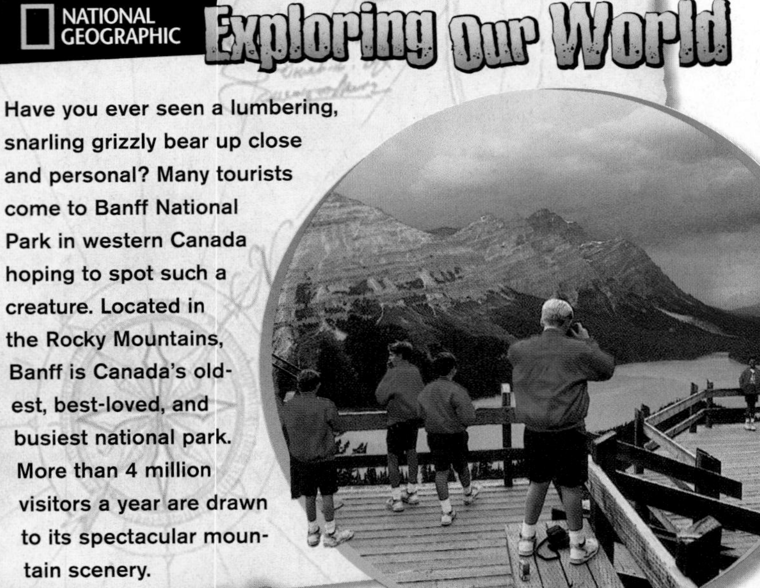

Vikings first landed their ships on its eastern coast around A.D. 1000. Niagara Falls thunders in the southeast. Grizzly bears roam its western regions. What country are we describing? It is Canada.

Landforms and Climate

The map on the next page shows you that Canada is located north of the contiguous United States. Between Canada and the United States lies the world's longest undefended border. The friendship developed between the two countries has allowed thousands of people to cross this border every day. Canada is the world's second-largest country in land area. Only Russia is larger. Instead of being made up of states, Canada has 10 **provinces,** or regional political divisions. It also includes 3 territories. The newest territory, **Nunavut** (NOO•nuh•vuht), in the north of Canada was created in 1999 as a homeland for Canada's **indigenous,** or native, people. You will learn more about Nunavut in the next section.

Section Resources

Reproducible Masters

- Reproducible Lesson Plan 18-1
- Daily Lecture and Discussion Notes 18-1
- Guided Reading Activity 18-1
- Reading Essentials and Study Guide 18-1
- Section Quiz 18-1

Transparencies

- Daily Focus Skills Transparency 18-1
- GeoQuiz Transparency 18-1

Multimedia

- Vocabulary PuzzleMaker Software
- Interactive Tutor Self-Assessment CD-ROM
- Presentation Plus! CD-ROM
- ExamView® Pro 3.0 Testmaker CD-ROM

Thousands of years ago, huge **glaciers,** or giant sheets of ice, covered most of Canada. The weight of these glaciers pushed much of the land down and created a large, low basin. Highlands rose on the western, eastern, and northern edges of this basin. Water filled the land that was pushed very low. As a result, Canada today has many lakes and inland waterways—more than any other country in the world.

The map below shows you that Canada generally has a cool or cold climate. In Canada's far north, people shiver in the cold tundra climate. A **tundra** is a treeless plain where the soil beneath the first few inches is permanently frozen. Farther south, between 70°N and 50°N latitude, Canadians experience cool summers and long, cold winters. Southeastern Canada has a milder climate and, as you would expect, most Canadians live in this area. The warmest temperatures are found along Canada's southwest coastline.

✓Reading Check **Why do you think most of Canada's people live in the southern part of the country?**

The Economy of Canada

Canada's economy is similar to that of the United States. Canada is known for fertile farmland, rich natural resources, and skilled workers. Manufacturing, farming, and service industries are the country's major economic activities. **Service industries** are businesses, such as banking and education, which provide services to people instead of producing goods. Fishing, mining, and lumbering are also important to the Canadian economy.

Canada, like the United States, has a free market economy in which people start and run businesses with limited government involvement. Canada's government, however, plays a more direct role in the

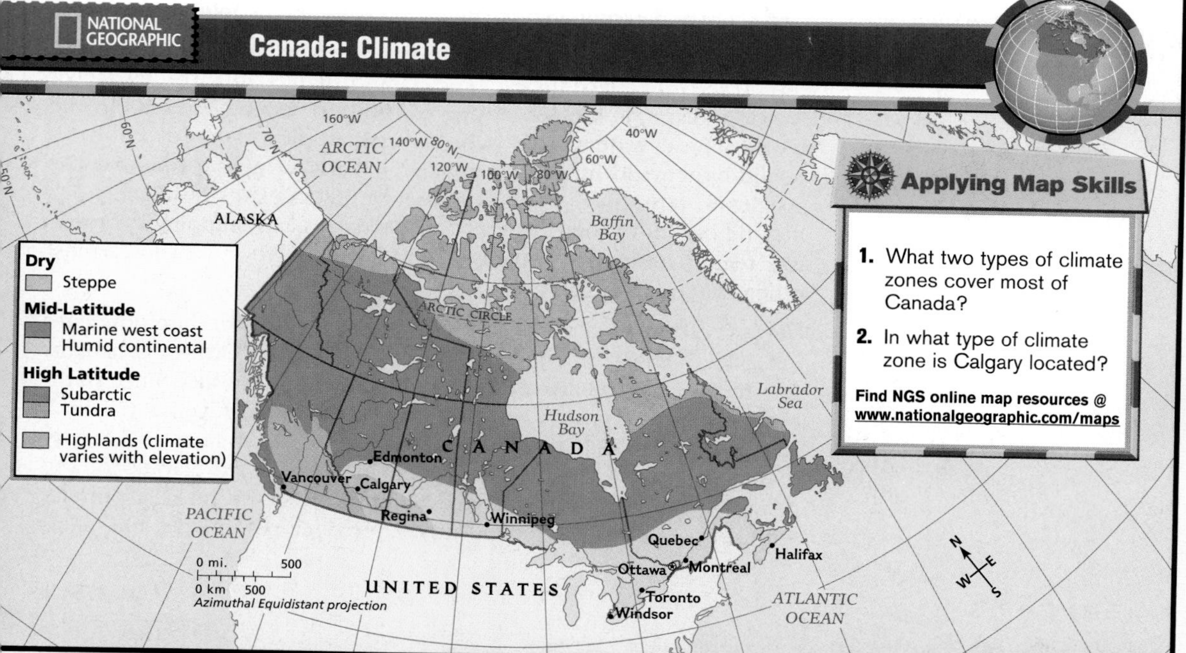

Applying Map Skills

1. What two types of climate zones cover most of Canada?
2. In what type of climate zone is Calgary located?

Find NGS online map resources @ www.nationalgeographic.com/maps

Cooperative Learning Activity

Creating a Map Puzzle Explain to students that you're going to make a giant map of Canada. Organize them into groups and assign each group one of Canada's provinces or territories. Have students draw their province or territory on a large piece of poster board. To make the map pieces somewhat proportional, groups with larger land areas should use two pieces of poster board. Instruct the students to draw pictures, use magazine photos, and make charts on their map pieces to illustrate the following information about their area: major cities; important landforms and climate; ethnic groups, languages, and cultures; economic activities; famous people, products, or sights. Afterwards, arrange the pieces into a huge map of Canada. It won't be exact, but it should convey a sense of the country's shape and make-up. **L2**

EE1 The World in Spatial Terms: Standard 1

Chapter 18

Section 1, pages 486–489

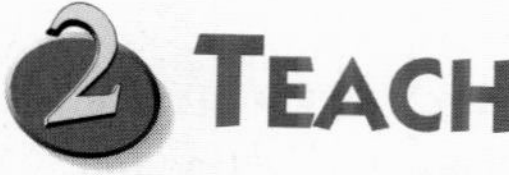

TEACH

Making Comparisons

Canada and the United States both have free market economies, although there are differences between the two. Have students read The Economy of Canada and compare the economic practices of the two countries. **Ask: What are the various ways these countries organize their economic systems? L2**

Daily Lecture Notes 18–1

CANADA

Daily Lecture and Discussion Notes 18-1

Canada's Major Regions (pages 486–489)

Did You Know? The rocks of the Canadian Shield were formed in Precambrian times 500 million years ago. Two tectonic plates converged, causing the surface rock to be forced down into the interior of the earth, where it melted. Over millions of years, that rock slowly rose back to the surface and cooled.

I. Canada's Landforms and Climate *(pages 486–487)*

A. Canada is made up of 10 **provinces,** or regional political divisions. It also has three territories.

B. Between Canada and the United States lies the world's longest undefended border. No military troops prevent the thousands of people from crossing this

covered most of Canada. These glaciers

✓ Reading Check Answer

It has a milder climate.

Applying Map Skills

Answers

1. subarctic and tundra
2. steppe (dry)

Skills Practice

What city has a marine west coast climate? *(Vancouver)*

Chapter 18

Section 1, pages 486–489

More About the Photo

Saskatchewan More than half of Canada's wheat is grown in Saskatchewan. The building of the Canadian Pacific Railway in the late 1800s helped farmers migrate to Saskatchewan and provided a way for them to get their grain to market.

Caption Answer ranching, oil and natural gas

✓ Reading Check Answer

In a free market economy, people start and run businesses with limited government involvement.

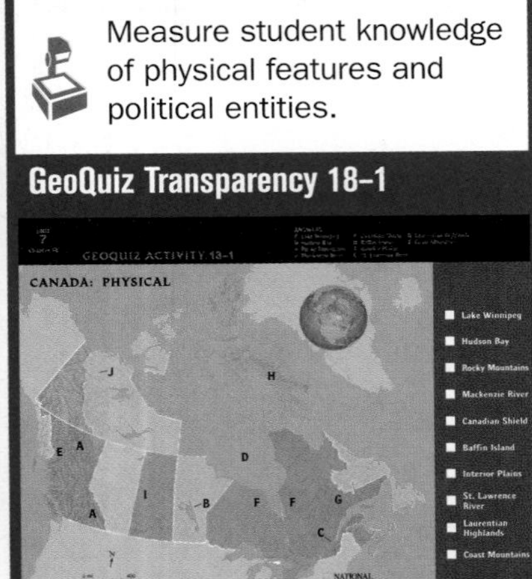

Measure student knowledge of physical features and political entities.

GeoQuiz Transparency 18–1

3 ASSESS

Assign Section 1 Assessment as homework or an in-class activity.

NATIONAL GEOGRAPHIC On Location

Nighttime Harvest

At harvest time in southern Saskatchewan, the work goes on around the clock. The farms in the Prairie Provinces are large and depend on machinery.

Economics **What other economic activities take place in the Prairie Provinces?**

Canadian economy. For example, Canada's national and provincial governments provide health care for citizens. Broadcasting, transportation, and electric power companies are heavily regulated. These public services might not have been available in Canada's remote areas without government assistance.

About $1 billion worth of trade passes between Canada and the United States each day. In 1992 Canada, the United States, and Mexico entered into the North American Free Trade Agreement (NAFTA) to remove trade barriers among the three countries. This agreement took effect in 1994. Some Canadians do not support NAFTA because they fear that their economy is too dependent on the United States. They worry that the American economy is so large that it will dominate the partnership.

✓ Reading Check **What is a free market economy?**

Canada's Economy

Fishing, manufacturing, farming, ranching, and energy production are Canada's important industries. As you would expect, geography plays a major role in where industries are located. Factors such as nearness to the ocean, location along the border with the United States, and oil and coal deposits determine where industries, jobs, and people can be found.

Fishing Fishing has been the major industry in **Newfoundland** and the **Maritime Provinces.** The Grand Banks, off the coast of Newfoundland, is known as one of the best fishing grounds in the world. These waters have been overfished, however. **Overfishing** results when too many fish are taken without giving time for the species to reproduce. The government now regulates how many fish may be caught in these waters. **Halifax** is a major shipping center in this region. Its harbor remains open in winter when ice closes most other eastern Canadian ports.

Manufacturing Manufacturing and service industries are dominant in Canada's largest province, **Quebec.** Almost one-fourth of Canadians live in Quebec, where agriculture and fishing are also important. **Montreal,** an important port on the St. Lawrence River, is Canada's second-largest city and a major financial and industrial center. The city of **Quebec,** founded by the French in 1608, is the capital of the province. Many historic sites and a European charm make it popular with tourists. Canada's second-largest province is **Ontario,** but it has

Content Background

Shared Cities The United States and Canada share a 5,522 mile (8,887-km) border, the largest continuous border in the world. It is also an undefended border. In several spots, cities on both sides of the border share commerce, trade, and tourism. The two cities named Niagara Falls are one example, and the pair of Great Lakes cities named Sault Ste. Marie are another. The largest pairing, though, is Windsor, in Canada's province of Ontario, and Detroit, in the state of Michigan. The two cities sit on the opposite banks of the Detroit River and enjoy a thriving international trade. Each day thousands of people cross the two bridges and tunnels connecting these cities. Some cross to work at their jobs; others visit the sites of the neighboring city or use it as the launching point for travel in the other country.

the most people and greatest wealth. Ontario produces more than half of Canada's manufactured goods. Southern Ontario also has fertile land and a growing season long enough for commercial farming. Farmers here grow grains, fruits, and vegetables and raise beef and dairy cattle.

Toronto, the capital of Ontario, is Canada's largest city. It is also the country's chief manufacturing, financial, and communications center. **Ottawa,** the capital city of Canada, lies in Ontario near the border with Quebec. Many Canadians work in government offices in Ottawa.

Farming, Ranching and Energy Production Farming and ranching are major economic activities in the Prairie Provinces of **Manitoba, Saskatchewan,** and **Alberta.** Canada is one of the world's biggest producers of wheat, most of which is exported to Europe and Asia. Some of the world's largest reserves of oil and natural gas are found in Alberta and Saskatchewan. These resources contribute to Canada's wealth. Huge pipelines carry the oil and gas to other parts of Canada and to the United States. Canada is the fifth-largest producer of energy in the world.

Thick forests blanket much of **British Columbia.** The province helps make Canada the world's leading producer of newsprint, the type of paper used for printing newspapers. Fishing and tourism are also strong economic activities in British Columbia. Fishing fleets sail out into the Pacific Ocean to catch salmon and other kinds of fish. **Vancouver** is a bustling trade center and the nation's main Pacific port.

✓ Reading Check **Which city is Canada's communications center?**

Assessment

Defining Terms

1. **Define** province, Nunavut, indigenous, glacier, tundra, service industry, overfishing.

Recalling Facts

2. **History** What is unusual about the border between Canada and the United States?
3. **Place** Who lives in the north of Canada?
4. **Economics** Which province is the world's leading producer of newsprint?

Critical Thinking

5. **Analyzing Information** What province in Canada has the most people and the most economic activity?
6. **Drawing Conclusions** Explain why some Canadians fear NAFTA.

Graphic Organizer

7. **Organizing Information** Create a chart like this one. Then list each province, the resources found in it, and major cities located there, if any.

Province	Resources	Cities

Applying Social Studies Skills

8. **Analyzing Maps** Look at the political map on page 475. Name the Canadian provinces that border the United States.

Section 1 Assessment

1. The terms are defined in the Glossary.
2. The U.S.-Canadian border is the world's longest undefended border.
3. Canada's indigenous, or native, people.
4. British Columbia
5. Ontario
6. They fear that their economy is too dependent on the United States. They worry that the American economy is so large that it will dominate the partnership.
7. Students' completed charts may vary. Check facts for accuracy.
8. British Columbia, Alberta, Saskatchewan, Manitoba, Ontario and Quebec

Chapter 18

Section 1, pages 486–489

Section Quiz 18-1

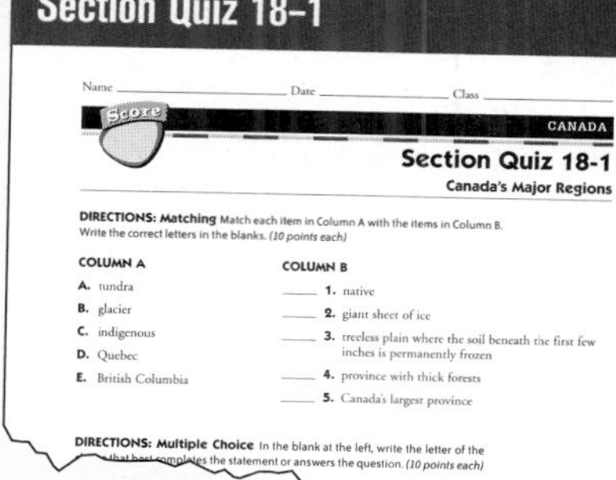
Name ______ Date ______ Class ______

Score

CANADA

Section Quiz 18-1

Canada's Major Regions

DIRECTIONS: Matching Match each item in Column A with the items in Column B. Write the correct letters in the blanks. *(10 points each)*

COLUMN A	COLUMN B
A. tundra	____ **1.** native
B. glacier	____ **2.** giant sheet of ice
C. indigenous	____ **3.** treeless plain where the soil beneath the first few inches is permanently frozen
D. Quebec	____ **4.** province with thick forests
E. British Columbia	____ **5.** Canada's largest province

DIRECTIONS: Multiple Choice In the blank at the left, write the letter of the ... completes the statement or answers the question. *(10 points each)*

✓ Reading Check Answer

Toronto

Reading Essentials and Study Guide 18-1

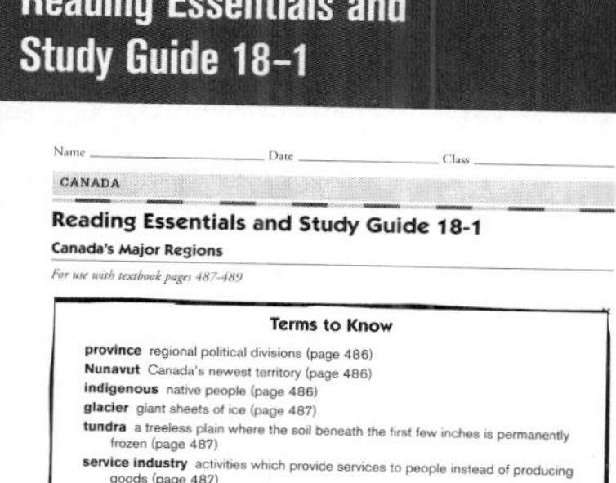
Name ______ Date ______ Class ______

CANADA

Reading Essentials and Study Guide 18-1

Canada's Major Regions

For use with textbook pages 487-489

Terms to Know

province regional political divisions (page 486)
Nunavut Canada's newest territory (page 486)
indigenous native people (page 486)
glacier giant sheets of ice (page 487)
tundra a treeless plain where the soil beneath the first few inches is permanently frozen (page 487)
service industry activities which provide services to people instead of producing goods (page 487)
overfishing when too many fish are taken without giving time for the species to reproduce (page 488)

CLOSE

Have students write want ads for jobs in Canada. Call on volunteers to read their ads and have the rest of the class identify in which regions the various jobs might exist.

TEACH

Ask: **Why do countries not set their clocks to the same time?** Provide this explanation: The earth rotates 360° in 24 hours; therefore, when it is day on one side of the earth, it is night on the other. To clarify time relationships among places, the world has been divided into time zones based on the earth's rotation. Then have students read the skill feature. **L1**

Additional Skills Practice

1. **If you leave Nashville at 8:00 P.M. on an eight-hour flight to Rome, what time will you arrive?** *(11:00 A.M. the next day)*
2. **Suppose you leave Los Angeles on Monday and travel westward to Sydney, Australia. On what day will you arrive in Sydney? Why?** *(Tuesday; since you crossed the International Date Line going westward, you add a day)*

Additional Skills Resources

 Chapter Skills Activity 18

 Building Geography Skills for Life

GLENCOE TECHNOLOGY

 **Skillbuilder Interactive Workbook CD-ROM, Level 1**

This interactive CD-ROM reinforces student mastery of essential social studies skills.

Social Studies Skill

Reading a Time Zones Map

The earth revolves 360° in 24 hours. The earth's surface has been divided into 24 time zones. Each time zone represents 15° longitude, or the distance that the earth rotates in 1 hour.

Learning the Skill

The Prime Meridian, or 0° longitude, is the starting point for figuring out time around the world. Traveling west from 0° longitude, it becomes 1 hour earlier. Traveling east, it becomes 1 hour later. The international date line is set at the 180° line of longitude. Traveling west across this imaginary line, you add a day. Traveling east, you subtract a day. To read a time zones map:

- Choose a place for which you already know the time and locate it on the map.
- Locate another place and determine if it is east or west of the first place.
- Calculate the time by either adding (going east) or subtracting (going west) an hour for each time zone.
- Determine whether you have crossed the International Date Line, and identify the day of the week.

Practicing the Skill

1. On the map below, if it is 4 P.M. in Rio de Janeiro, what time is it in Honolulu?
2. If it is 10:00 A.M. in Tokyo on Tuesday, what day and time is it in Moscow?

Applying the Skill

Imagine you have a friend living in Rome, Italy. What time (your time) would you call if you wanted to talk to your friend after 7:00 P.M.?

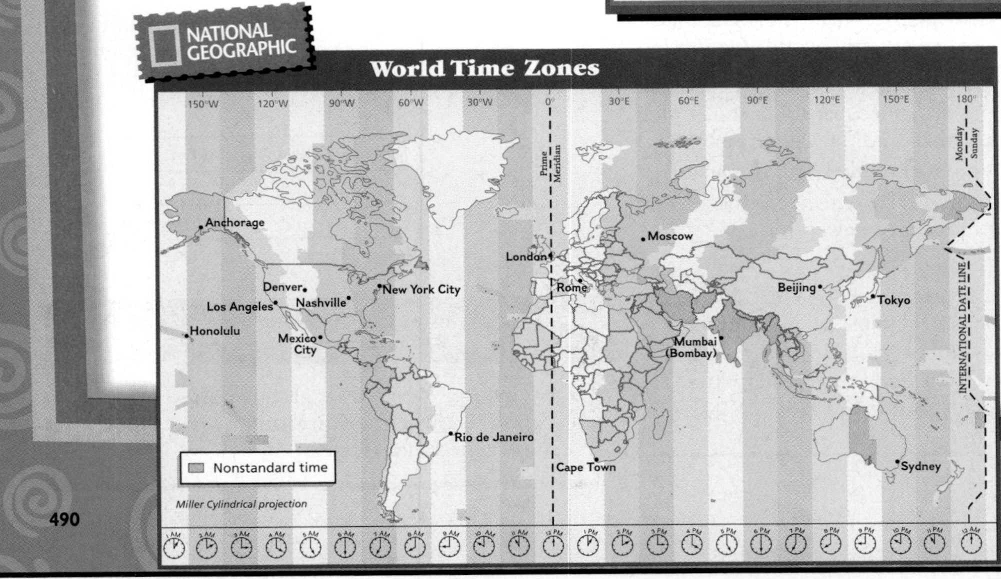

490

Practicing the Skill Answers

1. 9:00 A.M.
2. 3:00 A.M. on Tuesday

Applying the Skill

After 1:00 P.M. in the eastern time zone of North America, 12:00 P.M. in the Central time zone; 11:00 A.M. in the mountain time zone; 10:00 A.M. in the Pacific time zone; and 9:00 A.M. in Alaska

Section 2

The Canadians

Guide to Reading

Main Idea

Canadians of many different backgrounds live in towns and cities close to the United States border.

Terms to Know

- colony
- dominion
- parliamentary democracy
- prime minister
- bilingual
- autonomy

Reading Strategy

Create a chart like this one and give at least two facts about Canada for each topic.

History		
Population		
Culture		

NATIONAL GEOGRAPHIC **Exploring Our World**

Arrêt or Stop? People living in Quebec need to know both words when they cross the street. Canada has two official languages—English and French. All government documents are printed in both languages. In Quebec, even the school system is divided into French and English.

Like the United States, Canada's population is made up of many different cultures. The largest group of Canadians has a European heritage, but the country is home to people from all continents. Yet unlike the United States, Canada has had difficulty achieving a strong sense of being one nation. The country's vast distances and largely separate cultures have made Canadians feel more closely attached to their own region or culture than to Canada as a whole.

Canada's History

Inuit and other Native Americans lived for thousands of years in Canada before European settlers arrived. Some lived in coastal fishing villages. Others were hunters and gatherers constantly on the move. Still others founded permanent settlements. The first Europeans in Canada were Viking explorers who landed in about A.D. 1000. They lived for a while on the Newfoundland coast but eventually left.

In the 1500s, both Britain and France claimed areas of Canada. French explorers, settlers, and missionaries founded several cities. The most important were Quebec and Montreal. For almost 230 years,

1 Focus

Section Objectives

1. Identify who first settled Canada.
2. Describe Canada's form of government.
3. Explain what groups make up the Canadian people.

Project transparency 18–2 and have students answer questions.

This activity is also available as a blackline master.

Daily Focus Skills Transparency 18-2

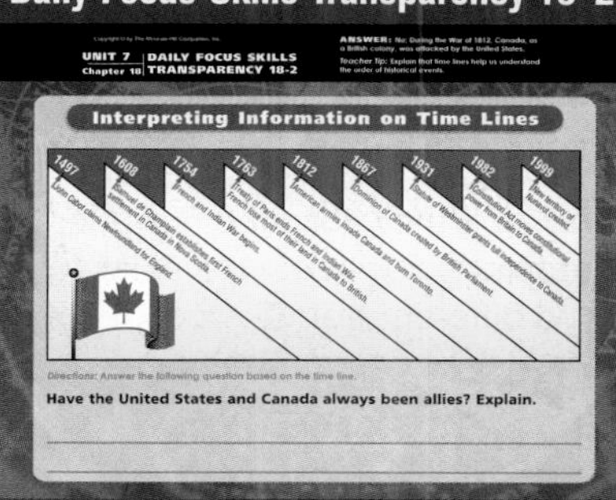

Guide to Reading

■ Vocabulary Precheck

Point out that the prefix *bi* means "two" and that *lingua* means "language." Have students use these clues to define the term *bilingual.*

Use the Vocabulary PuzzleMaker to create crossword and word search puzzles.

Section Resources

Reproducible Masters

- Reproducible Lesson Plan 18-2
- Daily Lecture and Discussion Notes 18-2
- Guided Reading Activity 18-2
- Reading Essentials and Study Guide 18-2
- Section Quiz 18-2

Transparencies

- Daily Focus Skills Transparency 18-2

Multimedia

- Vocabulary PuzzleMaker Software
- Interactive Tutor Self-Assessment CD-ROM
- Presentation Plus! CD-ROM
- ExamView® Pro 3.0 Testmaker CD-ROM

Answer The Inuit wore one layer of clothing with the fur against their skin, trapping warm air close to the body. They wore another layer with the fur outside, and the clothing moved to create a breeze and prevent overheating.

Ask students: **How did the Inuit provide shelter in an environment without stone or wood?** *(by making homes of ice)*

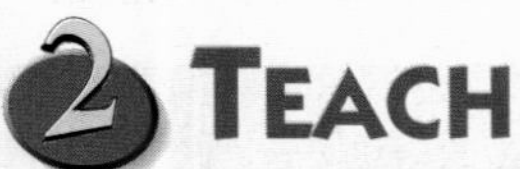

TEACH

Making Comparisons After students have read the section, have them write a short paragraph in which they describe how the people of Canada are similar to and different from the people of the United States. **L1 ELL**

Daily Lecture Notes 18–2

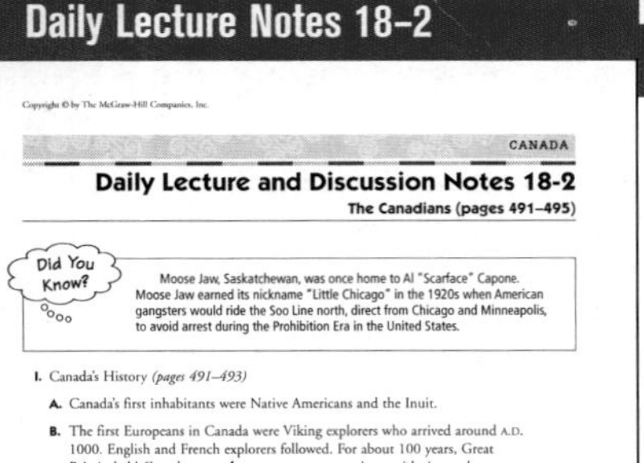

CANADA

Daily Lecture and Discussion Notes 18-2

The Canadians (pages 491–495)

Did You Know? Moose Jaw, Saskatchewan, was once home to Al "Scarface" Capone. Moose Jaw earned its nickname "Little Chicago" in the 1920s when American gangsters would ride the Soo Line north, direct from Chicago and Minneapolis, to avoid arrest during the Prohibition Era in the United States.

I. Canada's History *(pages 491–493)*

A. Canada's first inhabitants were Native Americans and the Inuit.

B. The first Europeans in Canada were Viking explorers who arrived around A.D. 1000. English and French explorers followed. For about 100 years, Great Britain held Canada as a **colony**—an overseas territory with ties to the parent country.

Clothing

The Inuit of the Canadian Arctic designed their clothes for protection from the harsh climate. Traditional clothing was made up of a caribou or sealskin parka, pants, mittens, and boots. In winter the Inuit wore their furs facing toward the skin. This created air pockets that trapped warm air close to the body. On top they wore another layer with the fur facing outward. The clothing flapped as the wearer moved, creating a breeze that kept the person from overheating while running or working.

Looking Closer How does traditional clothing protect the Inuit from the harsh climate?

France ruled the area around the St. Lawrence River and the Great Lakes. This region was called New France.

During the 1600s and 1700s, England and France fought each other for territory around the globe. Eventually, by 1763, the British gained control of all of Canada. Tragically, European warfare and diseases were destroying the Native American cultures during this time.

From Colony to Nation For about 100 years, Great Britain held Canada as a colony. A **colony** is an overseas territory with political and economic ties to the parent country. While Canada was ruled by Great Britain, English and French areas were kept separate. Each region had its own colonial government. In 1867 the different colonies of Canada became one nation known as the Dominion of Canada. As a **dominion,** Canada had its own government to run local affairs. Great Britain, however, still controlled Canada's relations with other countries.

The new Canadian government promised continued protection for the French language and culture in Quebec. Yet many English-speaking Canadians did not always keep this promise. French speakers often claimed that they were treated unfairly because of their heritage. Canada often was torn apart by disputes between the two ethnic groups.

During the 1900s, Canadians fought side by side with the British and Americans in two World Wars. Canada's loyal support in these conflicts gradually led to the nation's full independence. In 1982 Canadians peacefully won the right to change their constitution without British approval. Today, only one major link between Canada and Britain remains. The British king or queen still reigns as king or queen of Canada, but this is a ceremonial position with no real power.

Canada's Government The Canadians have a British-style parliamentary democracy. In a **parliamentary democracy,** voters elect

Cooperative Learning Activity

History Organize students into several groups and assign each group a time period in Canadian history. Determine reasonable time periods—perhaps 50- or 100-year increments starting in 1600. Using several sheets of butcher paper, have groups construct a time line. Direct groups to research their time period and select 10 important events to enter on the time line. Have group representatives write their selections on the time line along with annotations explaining each event. **L2**

EE6 The Uses of Geography: Standard 17

representatives to a lawmaking body called Parliament. These representatives then choose an official called the **prime minister** to head the government. Since the British king or queen visits Canada only once in a while, a Canadian official called the governor-general carries out most of the government's ceremonial duties.

✓ Reading Check What was the result of Great Britain keeping the French and British areas separate?

A Bilingual Country

Canada's history of being colonized by both France and Britain means that today, two European languages and cultures exist side by side. About one-third of the Canadians are descended from French-speaking settlers. (By comparison, in the United States, only 1 person out of 20 originally came from France.) Most of these people live in Quebec. In Quebec, the French, not the British, are the majority ethnic group.

The people of Quebec have long refused to give up their French language and customs. They did not want to "become English." As a result, Canada today is a **bilingual** country, with two official languages.

Primary Source

A DECLARATION OF FIRST NATIONS

"We the Original Peoples of this land know the Creator put us here.
The Creator gave us laws that govern all our relationships to live in harmony with nature and mankind.
The Laws of the Creator defined our rights and responsibilities.
The Creator gave us our spiritual beliefs, our languages, our culture, and a place on Mother Earth, which provided us with all our needs.
We have maintained our Freedom, our Languages, and our Traditions from time immemorial.
We continue to exercise the rights and fulfill the responsibilities and obligations given to us by the Creator for the land upon which we were placed.
The Creator has given us the right to govern ourselves and the right to self-determination.
The rights and responsibilities given to us by the Creator cannot be altered or taken away by any other Nation."

Analyzing Primary Sources

The U.S. Declaration of Independence states that ". . . all men are created equal, that they are endowed by their Creator with certain **unalienable** Rights. . ." Look up the meaning of *unalienable*. Then, identify the line in the Declaration of First Nations that supports this statement.

Critical Thinking Activity

Predicting Consequences Have students form into groups and develop a list of consequences that might result if Quebec were indeed to separate from the rest of Canada. They should consider such issues as the impact on the economy of Quebec and of the other provinces, how transportation and communication across the new national borders would take place, how Canada's government would have to change, and what changes would affect people in their daily lives. Ask for representatives to offer the group's predictions. As a class, discuss which predictions are most likely to come true if Quebec does secede. **L3**

EE6 The Uses of Geography: Standard 18

Chapter 18

Section 2, pages 491–495

Guided Reading Activity 18-2

✓ Reading Check Answer

Each region had its own colonial government.

3 ASSESS

Assign Section 2 Assessment as homework or an in-class activity.

Have students use the Interactive Tutor Self-Assessment CD-ROM to review Section 18–2.

Primary Source

Answer *Unalienable* means incapable of being surrendered. The rights and responsibilities given to us by the Creator cannot be altered or taken away by any other Nation.

Activity Have students organize into groups and stage a debate about whether the Native Americans of Canada should or should not be given more control over land and resources. Give each group time to prepare its arguments and questions for the other side.

Did You Know?

Quebec's Winter Carnival is famous for its beautiful and elaborate snow and ice sculptures. However, Quebec is not the only city that has a tradition of this icy art form. West Ellis, Wisconsin, and Breckenridge, Colorado, also hold annual snow sculpture competitions. Participants in these and the Quebec events come from all over the world.

Reading Check Answer

English and French

Section Quiz 18-2

Name ________ Date ________ Class ________

CANADA

Score

Section Quiz 18-2

The Canadians

DIRECTIONS: Matching Match each item in Column A with the items in Column B. Write the correct letters in the blanks. *(10 points each)*

COLUMN A	COLUMN B
A. bilingual	____ **1.** right to self-government
B. prime minister	____ **2.** voters elect representatives to lawmaking body
C. colony	____ **3.** an official who heads the government
D. autonomy	____ **4.** having two official languages
E. parliamentary democracy	____ **5.** overseas territory with political and economic ties to the parent country

DIRECTIONS: Multiple Choice In the blank at the left, write the letter of the choice that best completes the statement or answers the question. *(10 points each)*

Reading Check Answer

the Inuit

Time to Play

Fifteen-year-old Natalie Menard has been playing ice hockey since she was five years old. Natalie also enjoys visiting her cousin Angela, who lives in Toronto, Ontario. More than 6 miles (10 km) of covered walkways and underground tunnels in downtown Toronto connect subways with shops, offices, hotels, and restaurants. Natalie and Angela walk from place to place without even thinking of the weather.

An official language is one that is recognized by the government as being a legal language for conducting government business. Government documents and publications in Canada are printed in English and French. Traffic signs are also printed in both languages. School students learn to speak both languages. Of course, some areas of the country favor one language over the other. What language do you think is more popular in Quebec?

For many years, many French-speaking people have wanted Quebec to secede, or withdraw, from Canada. They would like Quebec to become an independent country, apart from the rest of the Canadian provinces. They do not believe that French culture can be protected in a largely English-speaking country. So far, they have been defeated in two very important votes on this issue. However, Canada's future as a united country is still uncertain.

✓ Reading Check **What are Canada's two official languages?**

Nunavut, A New Territory

As you have already learned, the first peoples of Canada were Inuit and other Native Americans. In recent years, the Canadian government has given the first peoples more control over their land. In 1999, the new territory of Nunavut was created for the Inuit. *Nunavut* is an Inuit word that means "our land." The Inuit now control the government and mineral rights in this new territory. In this way, most of the Inuit living in Canada have **autonomy**, the right to govern themselves. When issues involve other nations, however, the national government of Canada still makes the decisions.

Nunavut is almost three times the size of the state of Texas. Part of it lies on the North American continent, but more than half of Nunavut is made up of hundreds of islands in the Arctic Ocean. As large as it is, Nunavut does not include all of Canada's Inuit people. Many live in Quebec, Labrador, and the Northwest Territories.

The population of Nunavut is also different from the rest of Canada because of its age. More than 60 percent of the population is under the age of 25. Finding jobs to take care of the young population is difficult because there is not much industry in this region. The government is the largest employer, but there are not enough jobs. People often must hunt and fish to make sure they have enough food and warm clothes to stay alive. Nunavut must develop an economy that will grow along with its population so that its citizens will not have to depend on government welfare.

✓ Reading Check **For whom was Nunavut created?**

A Growing Ethnic Diversity

Like the United States, Canada has opened its doors to a great many immigrants. Canada opened its doors to Ukrainians, who settled in the Prairie Provinces about 100 years ago. Many other settlers came from Italy, Hungary, and other European countries.

Meeting Special Needs

Logical/Mathematical Give students the following figures, which represent the population (in millions) of Canada's 10 provinces: Alberta—2.85; British Columbia—3.95; Manitoba—1.15; New Brunswick—.76; Newfoundland—.56; Nova Scotia—.95; Ontario—11.4; Prince Edward Island—.14; Quebec—7.42; Saskatchewan—1.0. (Note: The populations of the territories are much smaller and cannot be compared on the same graph.) Have them construct a chart or graph that displays this information. They could choose a circle or bar graph, a table, or some other form. Have students explain why they chose the kind of graphic they constructed. **L2**

Refer to *Inclusion for the Middle School Social Studies Classroom Strategies and Activities* in the TCR.

In the 1960s, Canada welcomed refugees and other people who lost their homes due to war or natural disasters. Many of these people came from Asia, especially China, Southeast Asia, and India. Cities such as Vancouver on the west coast have sizeable Asian populations. Many Africans have also migrated to Canada.

Canada also has a long history of religious diversity. Most Canadians are Roman Catholic or Protestant. Still, many also follow Judaism, Buddhism, Hinduism, or Islam.

Our World Today online
Web Activity Visit the Our World Today: People, Places, and Issues Web site at owt.glencoe.com and click on Chapter 18–Student Web Activities to learn more about Quebec's French culture.

Food, Sports, and Recreation Because Canada has such ethnic diversity, people here can enjoy a variety of tasty foods. People from many different groups have settled in cities such as Toronto. You can walk down the street and sample the foods of Ukraine, Greece, Italy, the Caribbean, and Asia all in the same day.

Canadians enjoy a variety of activities, especially outdoor sports. You will find local parks and national parks crowded with people exercising and having fun. Many young Canadians enjoy playing ice hockey. They also take part in other winter sports, including skiing, skating, curling, and snowboarding. During the summer, they might go sailing on Lake Ontario. Professional football and hockey are popular spectator sports. Many Canadian sports fans also flock to see the major league baseball games played in Toronto's and Montreal's large indoor stadiums.

Reading Check What groups make up Canada's diverse population?

Section 2 Assessment

Defining Terms

1. **Define** colony, dominion, parliamentary democracy, prime minister, bilingual, autonomy.

Recalling Facts

2. **History** Who were the first peoples to live in Canada?
3. **Government** What is the new territory that was created in 1999, and what does its name mean?
4. **Culture** Name four activities enjoyed by Canadians.

Critical Thinking

5. **Analyzing Information** What is the link between Canada and Great Britain?
6. **Summarizing Information** What are two reasons for Canada's ethnic diversity?

Graphic Organizer

7. **Organizing Information** Create a diagram like this one. List two examples under each heading in the outer ovals.

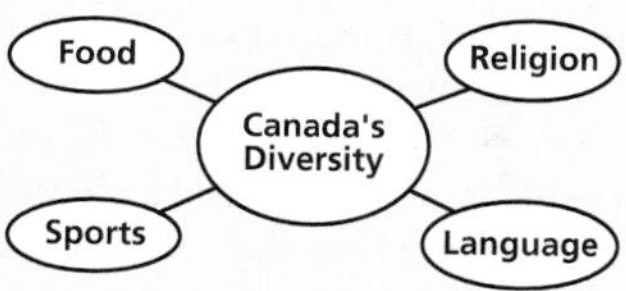

Applying Social Studies Skills

8. **Analyzing Maps** Study the major languages map on page 478. How does the language pattern in Canada differ from that of the United States?

Chapter 18

Our World Today online

Objectives, goals, and answers to the Student Web Activity can be found in the Web Activity Lesson Plan at owt.glencoe.com

Reading Check Answer

people of British and French ancestry, Inuit and other Native Americans; Recent immigrants include people from Ukraine, Italy, other European countries, Southeast Asia, India, and Africa.

Reading Essentials and Study Guide 18–2

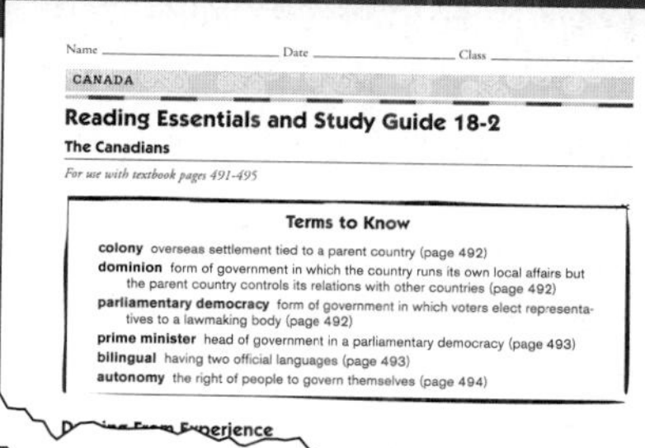
Name ______ Date ______ Class ______

CANADA

Reading Essentials and Study Guide 18-2

The Canadians

For use with textbook pages 491–495

Terms to Know

colony overseas settlement tied to a parent country (page 492)
dominion form of government in which the country runs its own local affairs but the parent country controls its relations with other countries (page 492)
parliamentary democracy form of government in which voters elect representatives to a lawmaking body (page 492)
prime minister head of government in a parliamentary democracy (page 493)
bilingual having two official languages (page 493)
autonomy the right of people to govern themselves (page 494)

Close

Canada celebrates its nationhood on July 1, a holiday called Canada Day. Have students assume the role of a Canadian political leader and write a Canada Day speech he or she might give honoring the country's history and diversity.

Section 2 Assessment

1. The terms are defined in the Glossary.
2. Native Americans and Inuits
3. Nunavut, "our land"
4. Possible answers include ice hockey, skiing, skating, curling, snowboarding, sailing, attending spectator sports including football, hockey and baseball.
5. The king or queen of the United Kingdom is also the king or queen of Canada but has no real power there.
6. early settlers, recent immigrants
7. Students' answers may vary. Check completed diagrams for accuracy.
8. The United States speaks mostly English everywhere. Canada has 3 major language groups: English in the south, French in the east, and Native in the north.

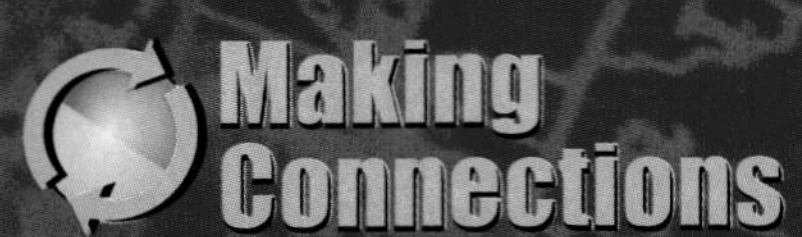

TEACH

Have students do a presentation on one of the indigenous tribes of Canada. Students should research the history of the group, its traditions and culture, and its present political and economic situation, including examples of conflict and cooperation between these groups and the Canadian majority. Reports can be in the form of a poster or a multimedia presentation. **L2**

More About Matthew Coon Come

Matthew Coon Come didn't meet any white people until he was six, when he was taken away to a residential school. He was a 21-year-old law student when he was asked by Cree elders to run for election as the band's deputy chief.

Interdisciplinary Connections

Environment Many native peoples still follow traditional ways of life. One of their major concerns is the disappearance of forestland and, with it, the habitats of wildlife that these people depend on. Ask your students if they can think of examples of environmental issues that affect native peoples. *(Possible answers: destruction of the rain forest in Brazil, oil drilling in Alaska)*

Making Connections

CULTURE | GOVERNMENT | PEOPLE | TECHNOLOGY

Matthew Coon Come: Man With a Mission

The National Chief of the Mistissini First Nation of the Cree, Ne-Ha-Ba-Nus, "the one who wakes up with the sun," is also known as Matthew Coon Come. Matthew's goal is to preserve the right of the native peoples to choose whether they will live in the cities or the wilderness.

A Proud Chief

In 1990 Matthew Coon Come led a fight against a proposed hydroelectric project, which would have flooded Cree lands in Quebec. He helped organize a canoe trip to get publicity for Cree leaders. The trip was from James Bay, through Lake Erie, down the Hudson River, and finally to New York City. The strategy was brilliantly effective. Coon Come gained much-needed worldwide attention and made his plea directly to New Yorkers, who cancelled their plans to buy power from the proposed project.

As Grand Chief of the Crees of northern Quebec, Matthew Coon Come has become a foe of industry and politicians who want to separate Quebec from Canada. He has stated that even if Quebec secedes, the Native Americans living in Quebec choose to stay part of Canada. Coon Come speaks for only 12,000 Cree, Inuit, Nadkapi, and Innu people, but they live on two-thirds of the land area of Quebec.

What if the Native American peoples who control two-thirds of the territory should elect to leave the new Quebec and rejoin Canada? Would this mean a problem for the newly formed Quebec nation? No one is really sure what would happen in that case.

For recognition of his leadership in environmental, human rights, and tribal communities, Matthew Coon Come has received numerous awards.

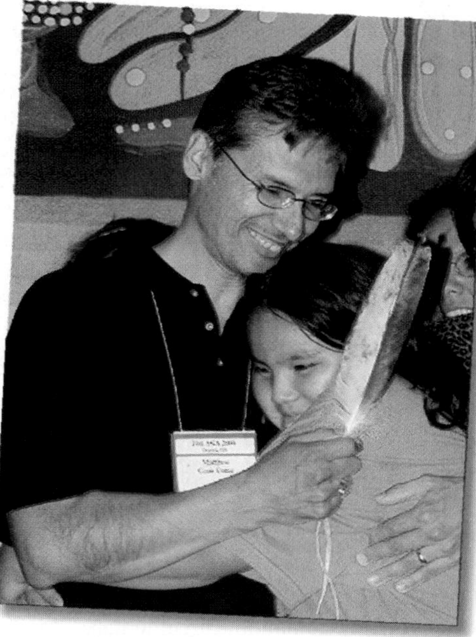

▲ Matthew Coon Come

Making the Connection

1. Why was Matthew Coon Come so opposed to the proposed hydroelectric project?
2. How will the Native Americans be affected if Quebec is successful in seceding from Canada?
3. **Synthesizing Information** Matthew Coon Come has his Christian name and his Cree name. They represent the two worlds he lives in. Develop a new name for yourself and explain what it represents.

Making the Connection

1. It would have flooded Cree lands in Quebec.
2. If native peoples were to stay part of Canada, they would be an unincorporated group within Quebec.
3. Answers will vary.

Reading Review

Section 1 Canada's Major Regions

Terms to Know
- province
- Nunavut
- indigenous
- glacier
- tundra
- service industry
- overfishing

Main Idea

Canada is a vast country with many landforms, climates, resources, and peoples.

✓ **Region** Canada, the second-largest country in the world, is rich in natural resources.

✓ **Economics** Canada's economy is rich in fertile farmland, natural resources, and skilled workers.

✓ **Economics** One of the best fishing grounds in the world is found in the Grand Banks off the coast of Newfoundland.

✓ **Place** Quebec is the largest province.

✓ **Culture** Quebec and Ontario have Canada's largest cities and most of its people.

✓ **Region** Most of Canada has a cool or cold climate. Milder temperatures are found in the southern part of the country.

Section 2 The Canadians

Terms to Know
- colony
- dominion
- parliamentary democracy
- prime minister
- bilingual
- autonomy

Main Idea

Canadians of many different backgrounds live in towns and cities close to the United States border.

✓ **History** Inuit and other Native Americans were the first Canadians. French and British settlers later built homes in Canada. Large numbers of immigrants have recently come from Asia and eastern Europe.

✓ **Government** Canada's government is a parliamentary democracy headed by a prime minister.

✓ **Culture** Some people in French-speaking Quebec want to separate from the rest of Canada.

✓ **Culture** Canada's native peoples have recently been given more autonomy to govern themselves.

Horseshoe Falls, Canada—one of the two waterfalls that makes up Niagara Falls ▶

Reading Review

Use the Chapter 18 Reading Review to preview, review, condense, or reteach the chapter.

Preview/Review

Use the Terms to Know lists to help students review and study.

Activity Have students create crossword puzzles for 10 of the terms from the chapter, exchange papers with another student, and try to complete their partner's puzzle.

Vocabulary PuzzleMaker Software reinforces the vocabulary terms used in Chapter 18.

The Interactive Tutor Self-Assessment CD-ROM allows students to review Chapter 18 content.

Condense

Have students read the Chapter 18 summary statements.

Chapter 18 Guided Reading Activities

Chapter 18 Audio Program

Reteach

Reteaching Activity 18

Chapter 18 Reading Essentials and Study Guide

Chapter Culminating Activity

Ask students: How have climate and history affected the way Canadians live? Have students use the notes they took during their reading of Chapter 18 to help answer the question. Students can answer the question by creating a chart with two headings—"Effects of Climate" and "Effects of History." Have them write a list of effects under each column heading. *NOTE: This activity may be completed separately or you may wish students to incorporate it into their Current Events Journal.* **L1**

EE4 Human Systems: Standard 12

Assessment and Activities

GLENCOE TECHNOLOGY

MindJogger Videoquiz
Use MindJogger to review the Chapter 18 content.

 Available in VHS.

Using Key Terms

1.	h	6.	j
2.	b	7.	c
3.	f	8.	a
4.	i	9.	e
5.	g	10.	d

Reviewing the Main Ideas

11. free market economy
12. the Prairie Provinces of Manitoba, Saskatchewan, and Alberta
13. Ontario
14. The government provides health care and owns broadcasting, transportation, and electric power companies.
15. the Inuit
16. manufacturing, farming, and service industries
17. the waters have been overfished
18. to protect Quebec's French culture in a largely English-speaking North America
19. English and French
20. the Inuit and other Native Americans

Chapter 18 Assessment and Activities

Using Key Terms

Match the terms in Part A with their definitions in Part B.

A.

1. province
2. glacier
3. Nunavut
4. indigenous
5. overfishing
6. dominion
7. service industry
8. bilingual
9. prime minister
10. parliamentary democracy

B.

a. having or speaking two languages
b. giant sheet of ice
c. businesses that provide services to people
d. voters elect representatives to a lawmaking body called Parliament
e. government leader chosen by Parliament
f. Canada's newest territory created in 1999
g. too many fish are taken without giving time for the species to reproduce
h. regional political division
i. native
j. nation that has its own government to run local affairs

Reviewing the Main Ideas

Section 1 Canada's Major Regions

11. **Economics** What kind of economy does Canada have?
12. **Region** Which three provinces are good agricultural areas?
13. **Location** Which province is the most heavily populated?
14. **Government** Describe two ways in which Canada's government plays a role in the nation's economy.
15. **History** Who are the main inhabitants of many of Canada's northern regions?
16. **Economics** What are three economic activities of British Columbia?
17. **Human/Environment Interaction** Explain why Canada's government must regulate how many fish can be caught in the Grand Banks.

Section 2 The Canadians

18. **Culture** Why do some of Quebec's people want independence from Canada?
19. **Culture** What are Canada's two official languages?
20. **History** Who were the first people of Canada?

NATIONAL GEOGRAPHIC Canada

Place Location Activity

On a separate sheet of paper, match the letters on the map with the numbered places listed below.

1. Hudson Bay
2. Nunavut
3. British Columbia
4. Ottawa
5. Quebec (province)
6. St. Lawrence River
7. Rocky Mountains
8. Winnipeg
9. Ontario
10. Nova Scotia

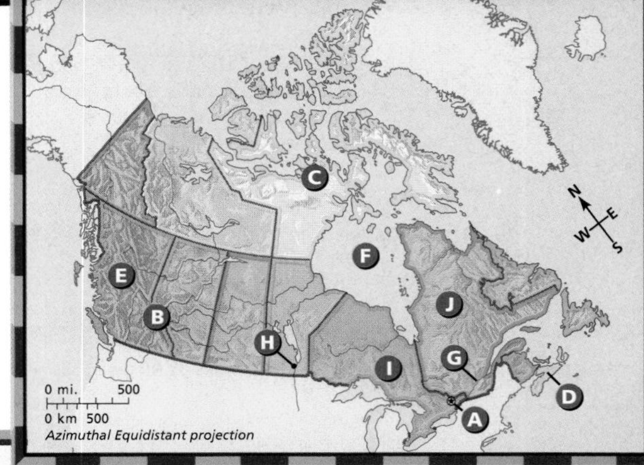

NATIONAL GEOGRAPHIC Place Location Activity

1.	F	6.	G
2.	C	7.	B
3.	E	8.	H
4.	A	9.	I
5.	J	10.	D

Critical Thinking

21. Northeast and northwest Canada have subarctic climates. The southeast is milder and humid. The southwest has the warmest temperatures along the coast, but the temperature varies in the highlands.
22. The climate is mildest along the southern border.
23. Answers will vary depending on the province or territory chosen.

Self-Check Quiz Visit the ***Our World Today: People, Places, and Issues*** Web site at owt.glencoe.com and click on **Chapter 18–Self-Check Quizzes** to prepare for the Chapter Test.

Critical Thinking

21. **Making Comparisons** Compare the climates of western and eastern Canada.
22. **Analyzing Information** Why do most Canadians live in the south of Canada?
23. **Categorizing Information** Choose one of Canada's provinces or territories. Complete a chart like the one below with at least two facts or examples under the headings.

Province or Territory	Landforms	Resources
	Major Cities	Products

Current Events Journal

24. **Writing a Speech** List what you know about Matthew Coon Come. Take the role of either an environmentalist, a Native American, a vice president of the hydroelectric project, a school teacher, or a parent of five children living in Montreal. Write a short speech explaining your views of the hydroelectric project or the secession of Quebec.

Mental Mapping Activity

25. **Focusing on the Region** Create a simple outline map of Canada. Refer to the map on page 475, and then label the following on your map:
   - Arctic Ocean
   - Quebec (province)
   - Pacific Ocean
   - Ontario
   - Atlantic Ocean
   - British Columbia
   - Rocky Mountains
   - Nunavut
   - Hudson Bay
   - Ottawa

Technology Skills Activity

26. **Using the Internet** Access the Internet and search for information on the Inuit and the new territory of Nunavut. Create an illustrated time line that shows the steps leading to the creation of the new territory.

The Princeton Review

Standardized Test Practice

Directions: Study the graph below, and then answer the questions that follow.

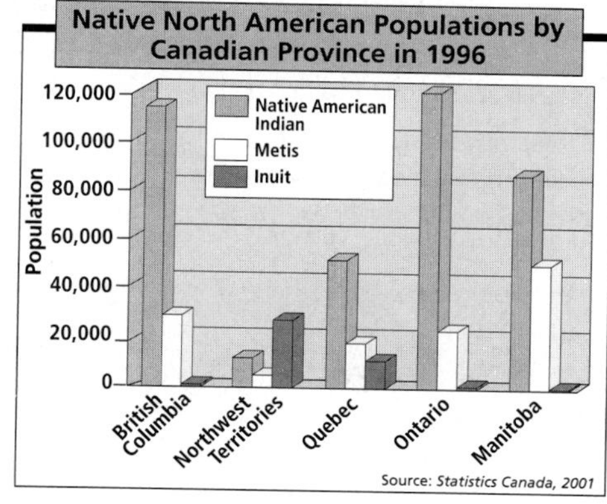

1. **Which of the following provinces has the largest Native American population?**
   - **A** Northwest Territories
   - **B** Manitoba
   - **C** Ontario
   - **D** British Columbia
2. **In what part of Canada does most of the Inuit population live?**
   - **F** The northern part of the country
   - **G** Along the U.S. border
   - **H** Near the Atlantic coast
   - **J** In cities such as Toronto and Ontario

Test-Taking Tip: Sometimes you cannot answer a question directly from the information in a map or a graph. In these cases, you have to make an *inference,* or draw a conclusion, that is supported by information in the map or graph. The clues may also help you get rid of wrong choices.

499

Assessment and Activities

Standardized Test Practice

1. C
2. F

Tested Objectives:
Reading a bar graph, interpreting information

Chapter Test Bonus Question

This question may be used for extra credit on the chapter test.

What is the capital of Nunavut? *(Iqaluit)*

Have students visit the Web site at **owt.glencoe.com** to review Chapter 18 and take the Self-Check Quiz.

Current Events Journal

24. Students' speeches will vary, either supporting or attacking Matthew Coon Come, depending on the "speaker."

Mental Mapping Activity

25. This exercise helps students visualize the countries and geographic features they have been studying and to understand the relationships among various points. All attempts at freehand mapping should be accepted.

Technology Skills Activity

26. Students' projects should show a time line with correct time scale and illustrations—perhaps with captions—that show Inuit culture and the creation of Nunavut.

Chapter 19 Resources

Note: The following materials may be used when teaching Chapter 19.
Section level support materials are shown at point of use in the margins of the Teacher Wraparound Edition.

Timesaving Tools

TeacherWorks™ All-In-One Planner and Resource Center

- **Interactive Teacher Edition** See the **Interactive Teacher Edition** CD-ROM to electronically integrate your Teacher Wraparound Edition and blackline masters.
- **Interactive Lesson Planner** Organize your week, month, semester, or year with all the lesson helps you need. The **Interactive Lesson Planner** CD-ROM contains all Chapter 19 resources.

Use Glencoe's **Presentation Plus!** multimedia teacher tool to easily present dynamic lessons that visually excite your students. Using Microsoft PowerPoint® you can customize the presentations to create your own personalized lessons.

TEACHING TRANSPARENCIES

Graphic Organizer Transparency and Student Activity 19

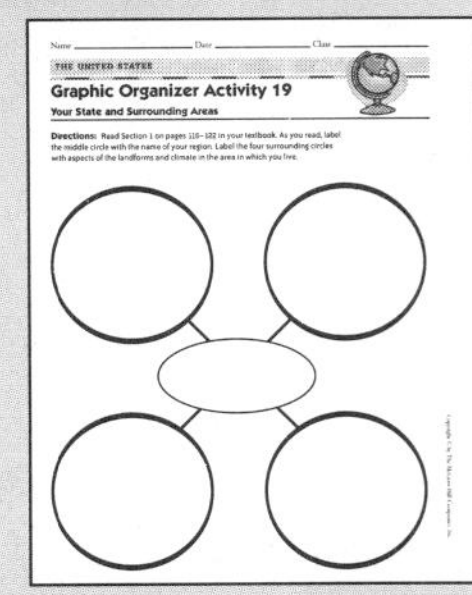

FOLDABLES™ Study Organizer

Foldables are three-dimensional, interactive graphic organizers that help students practice basic writing skills, review key vocabulary terms, and identify main ideas. Every chapter contains a Foldable activity, with additional chapter activities found in the ***Reading and Study Skills Foldables*** booklet.

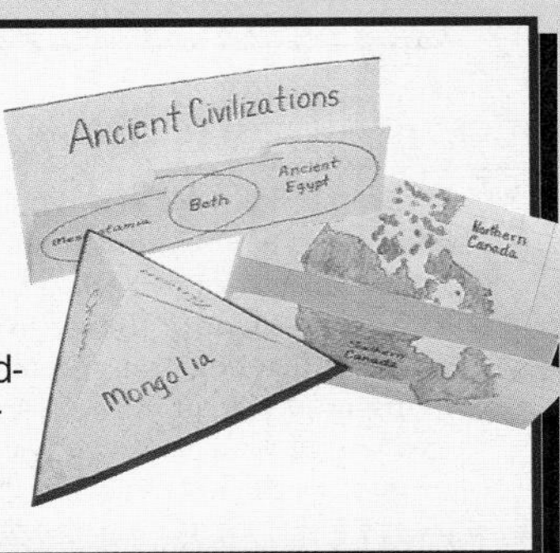

ENRICHMENT AND EXTENSION

Enrichment Activity 19

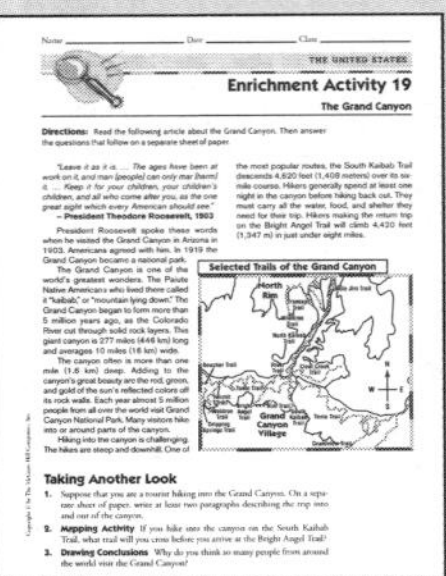

Cooperative Learning Activity 19

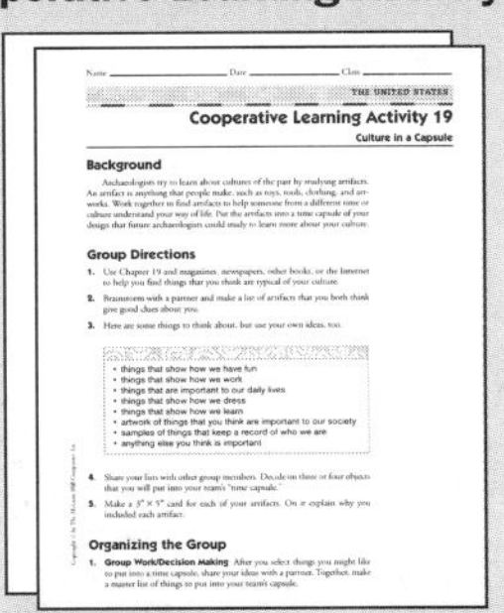

MAP AND GEOGRAPHY SKILLS

Chapter Map Activity 19

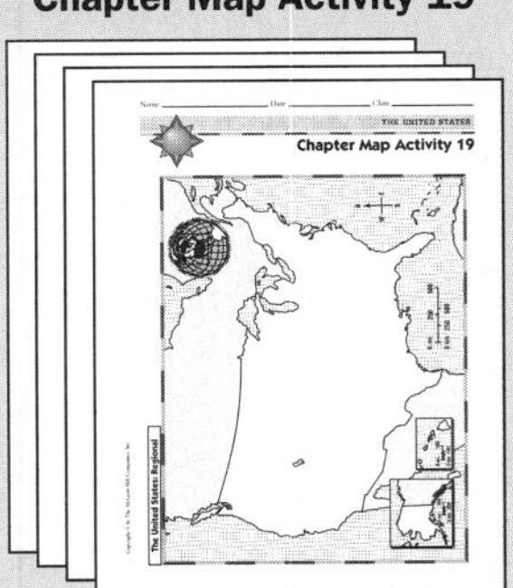

GeoLab Activity 19

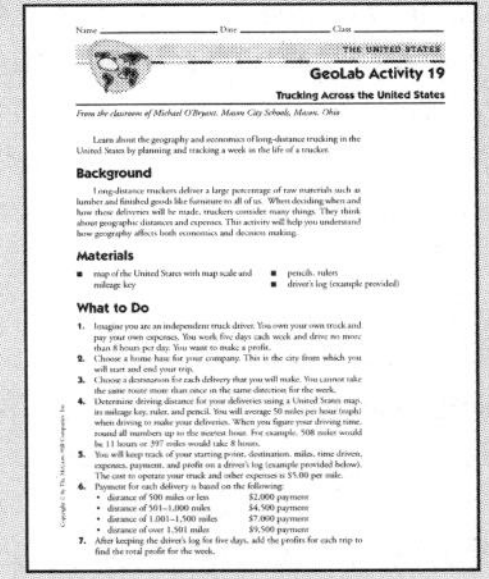

STANDARDIZED ASSESSMENT SKILLS

Critical Thinking Skills Activity 19

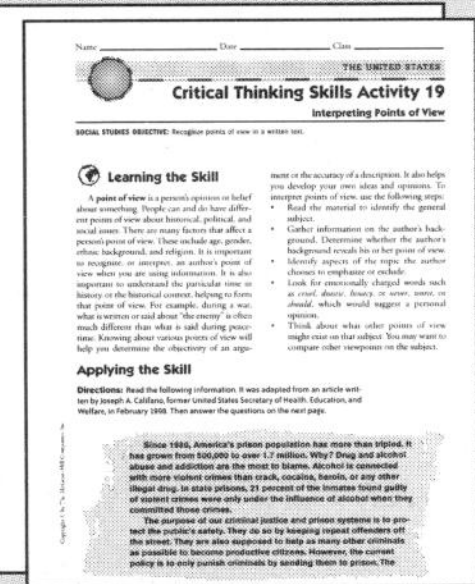

Map and Graph Skills Activity 19

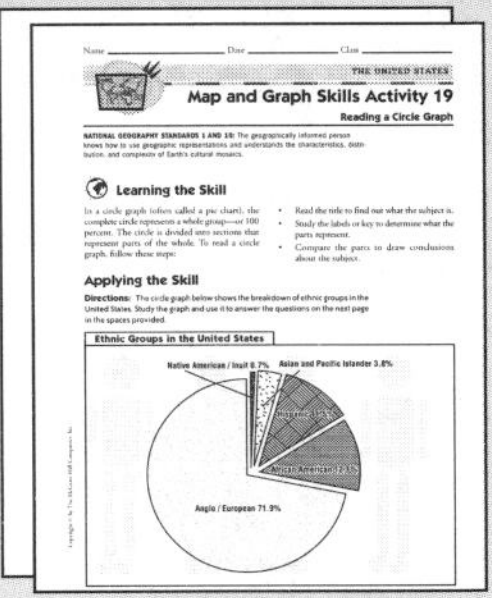

Reading and Writing Skills Activity 19

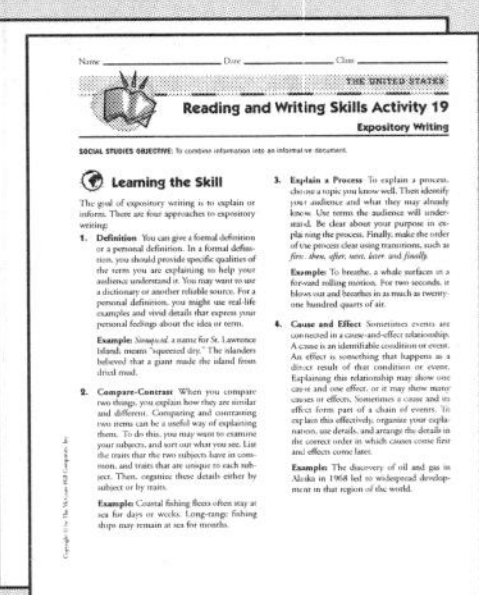

Standardized Test Practice Workbook Activity 19

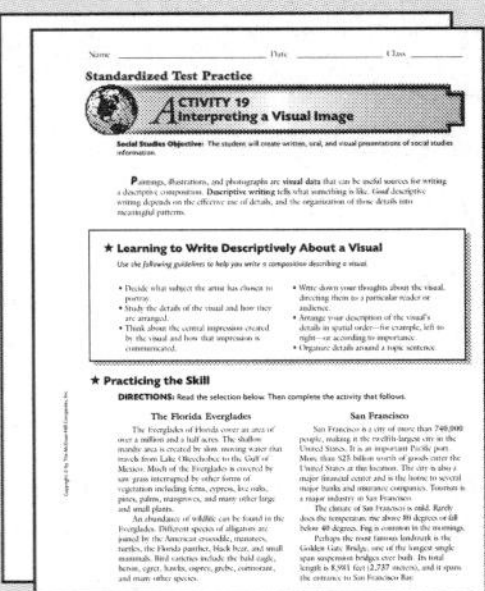

REVIEW AND REINFORCEMENT

Chapter Skills Activity 19

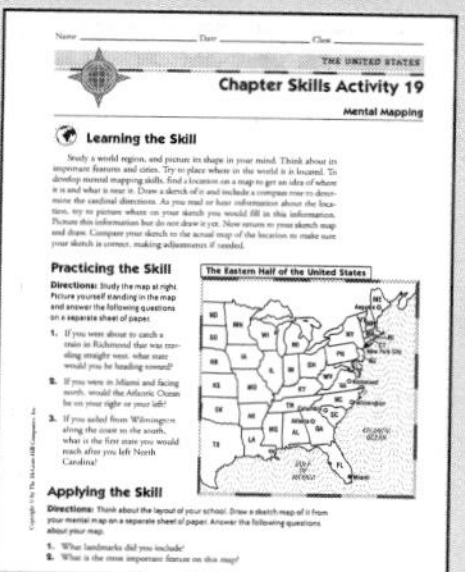

Take-Home Review Activity 19

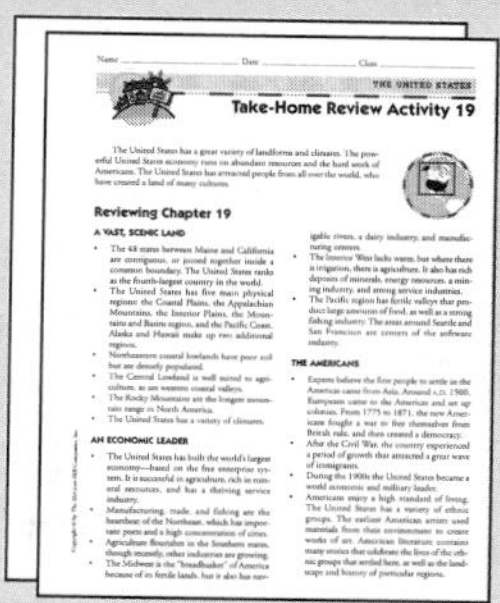

Reteaching Activity 19

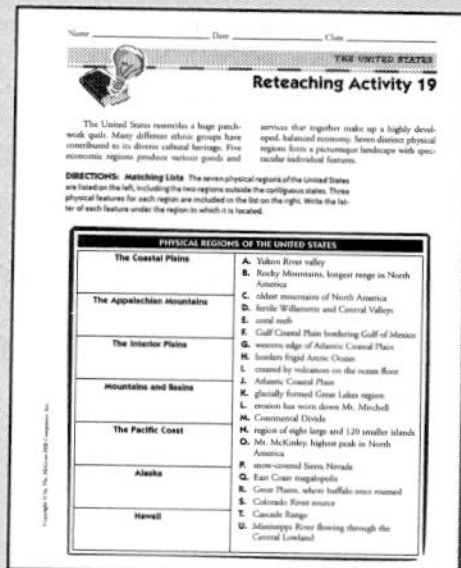

Vocabulary Activity 19

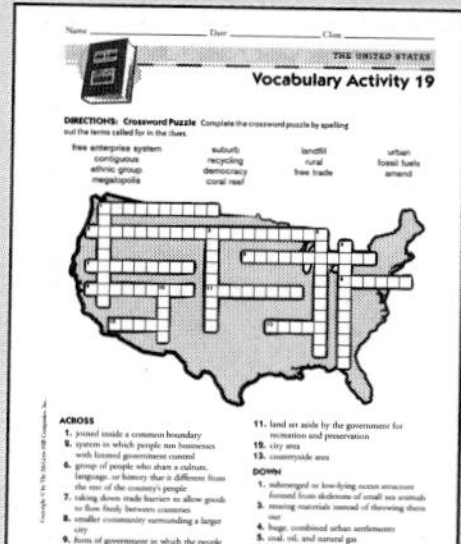

Workbook Activity 19

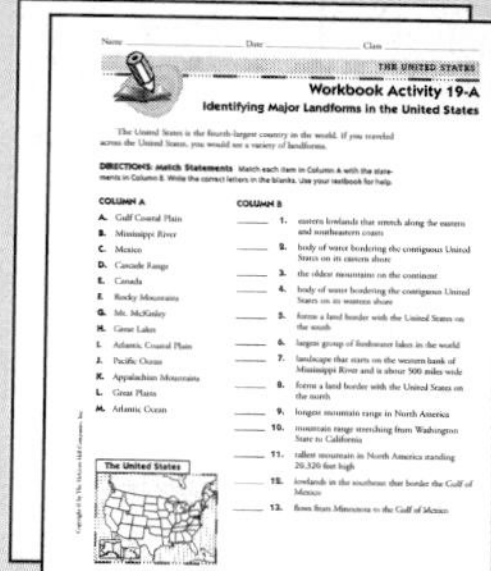

ASSESSMENT

GLENCOE'S ASSESSMENT ADVANTAGE

Chapter 19 Test, Form A

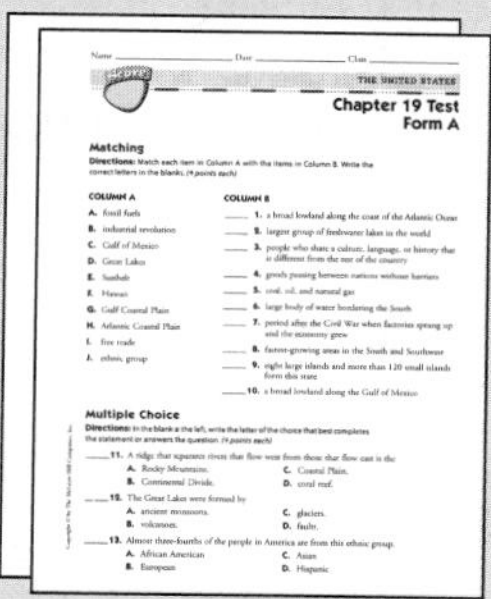

Chapter 19 Test, Form B

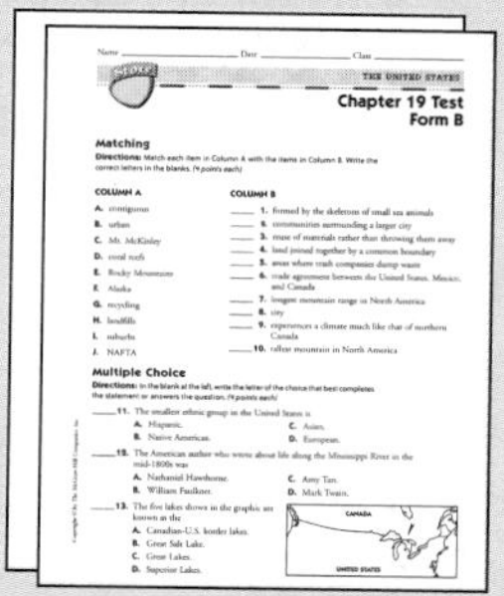

Performance Assessment Activity 19

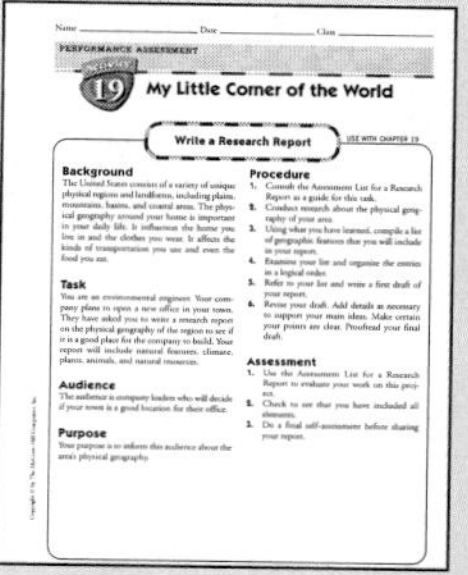

ExamView® Pro 3.0 Testmaker CD-ROM

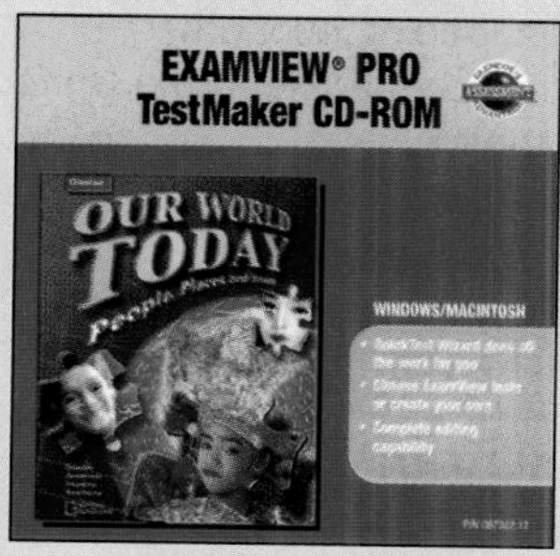

MULTIMEDIA

- National Geographic's The World and Its People
- MindJogger Videoquiz
- Vocabulary PuzzleMaker Software
- Interactive Tutor Self-Assessment CD-ROM
- ExamView® Pro 3.0 Testmaker CD-ROM
- Interactive Lesson Planner CD-ROM
- Interactive Teacher Edition CD-ROM
- Skillbuilder Interactive Workbook CD-ROM, Level 1
- Presentation Plus! CD-ROM
- Audio Program

SPANISH RESOURCES

The following Spanish language materials are available in the Spanish Resources binder:

- **Spanish Chapter Summaries**
- **Spanish Vocabulary Activities**
- **Spanish Guided Reading Activities**
- **Spanish Quizzes and Tests**
- **Spanish Take-Home Review Activities**
- **Spanish Reteaching Activities**

Meeting National Standards

Geography for Life

All of the 18 standards are demonstrated in Unit 7. The following ones are highlighted in Chapter 19:

Section 1 **EE1 The World in Spatial Terms: Standards 1, 3**
EE2 Places and Regions: Standards 4, 5

Section 2 **EE4 Human Systems: Standards 11, 12, 13**
EE5 Environment and Society: Standards 14, 16

Section 3 **EE4 Human Systems: Standards 11, 12, 13**
EE5 Environment and Society: Standards 14, 16

For a complete listing of National Geography Standards and entire text correlation, see pages T22–T29.

Local Objectives

Chapter 19 Planning Guide

SECTION RESOURCES

Daily Objectives	Reproducible Resources	Multimedia Resources
Section 1 **A Vast, Scenic Land** **Suggested Pacing = 1 day** **1.** Identify the landforms that are found in the United States. **2.** Contrast the climates of different areas of the United States.	Reproducible Lesson Plan 19-1 Daily Lecture and Discussion Notes 19-1 Guided Reading Activity 19-1 Reading Essentials and Study Guide 19-1 Section Quiz 19-1*	Daily Focus Skills Transparency 19-1 GeoQuiz Transparency 19-1 Vocabulary PuzzleMaker Software Interactive Tutor Self-Assessment CD-ROM ExamView® Pro 3.0 Testmaker CD-ROM Presentation Plus! CD-ROM
Section 2 **An Economic Leader** **Suggested Pacing = 1 day** **1.** Explain why the United States has the world's leading economy. **2.** Identify how people in the United States earn their livings. **3.** Describe the challenges facing the United States.	Reproducible Lesson Plan 19-2 Daily Lecture and Discussion Notes 19-2 Guided Reading Activity 19-2 Reading Essentials and Study Guide 19-2 Section Quiz 19-2*	Daily Focus Skills Transparency 19-2 GeoQuiz Transparency 19-2 Vocabulary PuzzleMaker Software Interactive Tutor Self-Assessment CD-ROM ExamView® Pro 3.0 Testmaker CD-ROM Presentation Plus! CD-ROM
Section 3 **The Americans** **Suggested Pacing = 1 day** **1.** Describe how the United States changed throughout its history. **2.** Explain what form of government the United States has. **3.** Identify what groups make up the American people. **4.** Discuss what has influenced American culture.	Reproducible Lesson Plan 19-3 Daily Lecture and Discussion Notes 19-3 Guided Reading Activity 19-3 Reading Essentials and Study Guide 19-3 Section Quiz 19-3*	Daily Focus Skills Transparency 19-3 Vocabulary PuzzleMaker Software Interactive Tutor Self-Assessment CD-ROM ExamView® Pro 3.0 Testmaker CD-ROM Presentation Plus! CD-ROM

00:00 **Out of Time?** Assign the **Reading Essentials and Study Guide** for this chapter.

*Also available in Spanish

KEY TO ABILITY LEVELS

Teaching strategies have been coded for varying learning styles and abilities.

- **L1** **BASIC** activities for all students
- **L2** **AVERAGE** activities for average to above-average students
- **L3** **CHALLENGING** activities for above-average students
- **ELL** **ENGLISH LANGUAGE LEARNER** activities

Blackline Master
Software
CD-ROM
Audiocassette
Transparency
Videocassette
Block Scheduling
DVD

Sister Cities

Connie Dunn
Mulberry High School
Mulberry, Arkansas

Have your students learn and compare information about their hometown to other towns in the United States with the same name. By using an atlas or the Internet, find "your" city in other states. Have students contact the chamber of commerce or, if possible, a geography class in each of these other cities. Ask students to find out information such as population data, date of settlement, and main economic activities. They may also want to compare fun information such as school colors and team names. The information can be compiled to create a "HOMETOWN, U.S.A." booklet.

OUR WORLD TODAY Online

Use our Web site for additional resources. All essential content is covered in the Student Edition.

You and your students can visit **owt.glencoe.com**, the Web site companion to *Our World Today*. This innovative integration of electronic and print media offers your students a wealth of opportunities. The student text directs students to the Web site for the following options:

- Chapter Overviews
- Student Web Activities
- Self-Check Quizzes
- Textbook Updates

Answers are provided for you in the Web Activity Lesson Plan. Additional Web resources and Interactive Tutor puzzles are also available.

NATIONAL GEOGRAPHIC TEACHER'S CORNER

Index to National Geographic Magazine:

The following articles may be used for research relating to this chapter:

- "The Way West," by John G. Mitchell, September 2000.
- "Big Sur," by Pico Iyer, August 2000.
- "Playing the Slots," by Scott Thybony, July 2000.
- "Cape Hatteras Lighthouse," by Angus Phillips, May 2000.
- "San Pedro River," by Barbara Kingsolver, April 2000.

National Geographic Society Products Available From Glencoe:

To order the following products for use with this chapter, contact your local Glencoe sales representative or call Glencoe at 1-800-334-7344:

- *GeoBee* (CD-ROM)
- *PictureShow: Earth's Endangered Environments* (CD-ROM)
- *PicturePack: Looking at Ecosystems* (Transparencies)
- *PicturePack: Geography of North America* (Transparencies)
- *PicturePack: Earth's Climate* (Transparencies)
- *PicturePack: Geography of North America* (Transparencies)
- *MapPack: Continents: North America* (Transparencies)

Additional National Geographic Society Products:

To order the following products for use with this chapter, call National Geographic Society at 1-800-368-2728:

- *Complete National Geographic: 111 years of National Geographic Magazine* (CD-ROM)
- *PictureShow: U.S. Regional Geography Library* (CD-ROM)
- *GeoKit: American Revolution* (Kit)
- *GeoKit: Pollution* (Kit)
- *PicturePack: U.S. Regional Geography Library* (Transparencies)
- *MapPack: U.S.A. Regions Series* (Transparencies)
- *United States Geography Series* (3 Videos)
- *A Swamp Ecosystem* (Video)
- *An Ecosystem: A Struggle for Survival* (Video)
- *The Living Ocean* (Video)
- *Investigating Global Warming* (Video)
- *PictureShow: Native Americans, Part I* (CD-ROM)
- *PictureShow: Native Americans, Part II* (CD-ROM)

NGS ONLINE

Access National Geographic's Web site for current events, activities, links, interactive features, and archives.
www.nationalgeographic.com

Introducing Chapter 19

Introduce students to chapter content and key terms by having them access Chapter Overview 19 at owt.glencoe.com

Chapter Objectives

1. Compare the physical features and climates of the United States.
2. Describe the economy of the United States.
3. Discuss the challenges the United States faces in the 21st century.
4. Examine cultural influences on the people of the United States.

GLENCOE TECHNOLOGY

NATIONAL GEOGRAPHIC

The World and Its People Video Program

Chapter 4 The United States
The following segments enhance the study of this chapter:

- **America the Beautiful**
- **The American Bison**
- **Land of Opportunity**

Available in DVD and VHS.

MindJogger Videoquiz
Use MindJogger to preview the Chapter 19 content.

Available in VHS.

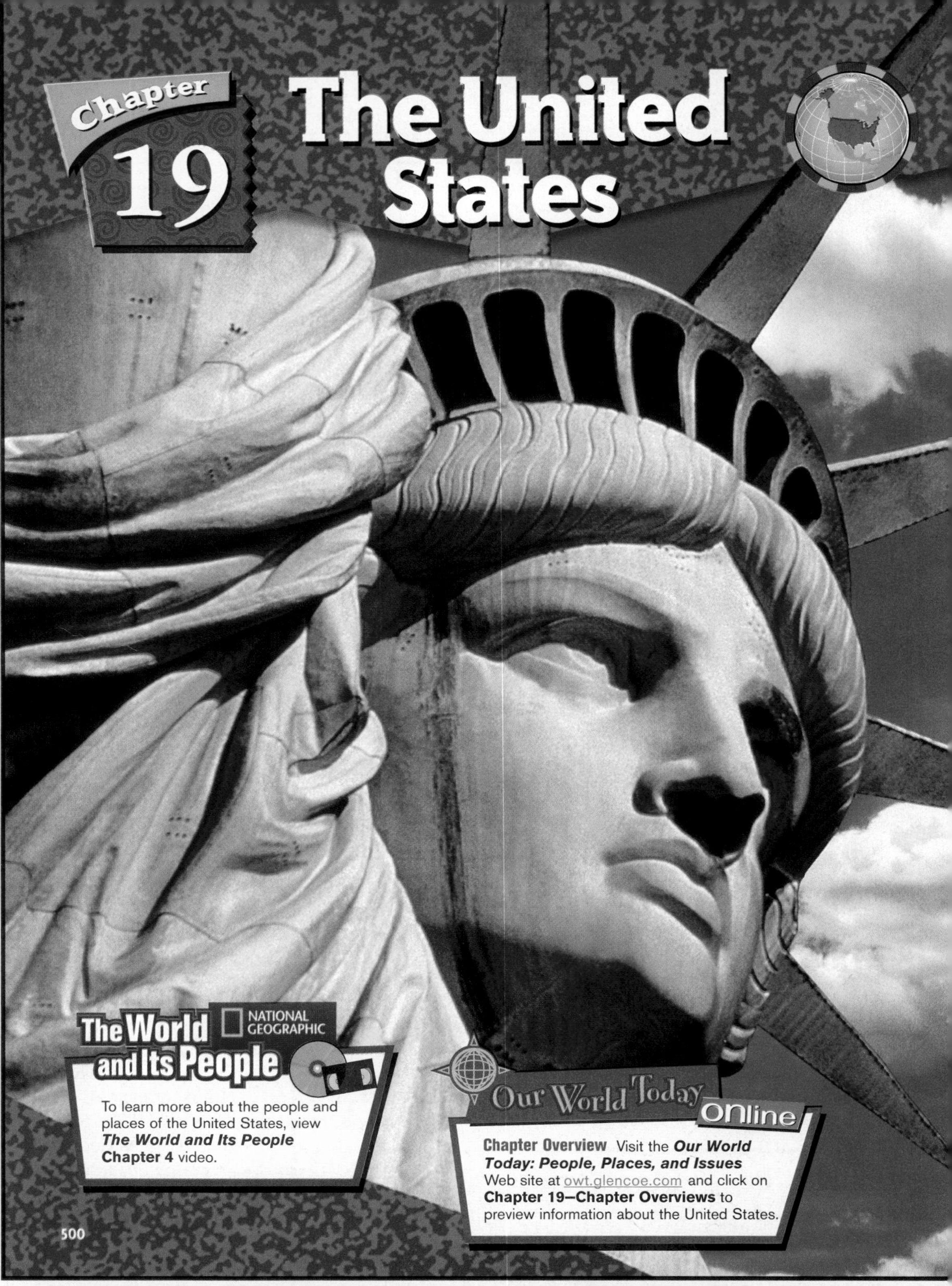

Chapter 19 The United States

The World and Its People NATIONAL GEOGRAPHIC

To learn more about the people and places of the United States, view ***The World and Its People* Chapter 4** video.

Our World Today Online

Chapter Overview Visit the ***Our World Today: People, Places, and Issues*** Web site at owt.glencoe.com and click on **Chapter 19—Chapter Overviews** to preview information about the United States.

500

Two-Minute Lesson Launcher

Have volunteers describe the different areas of the United States that they have lived in, visited, or seen on television or in movies. Write their responses. Try to group the responses under different headings, such as physical geography, economy, and culture. After writing down a few descriptions, ask students: **Based on these descriptions, how would you summarize the United States?** *(Possible answers include the following: varied; having many different landforms; prosperous economically; having free people; culturally diverse.)* **L1**

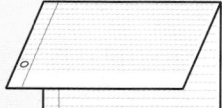

FOLDABLES™ Study Organizer

Identifying Main Ideas Study Foldable Asking yourself questions as you read helps you to focus on main ideas of the material and better understand it. Make this foldable and use it as a journal to record and answer your own questions about the United States.

Step 1 Fold a sheet of paper in half from top to bottom.

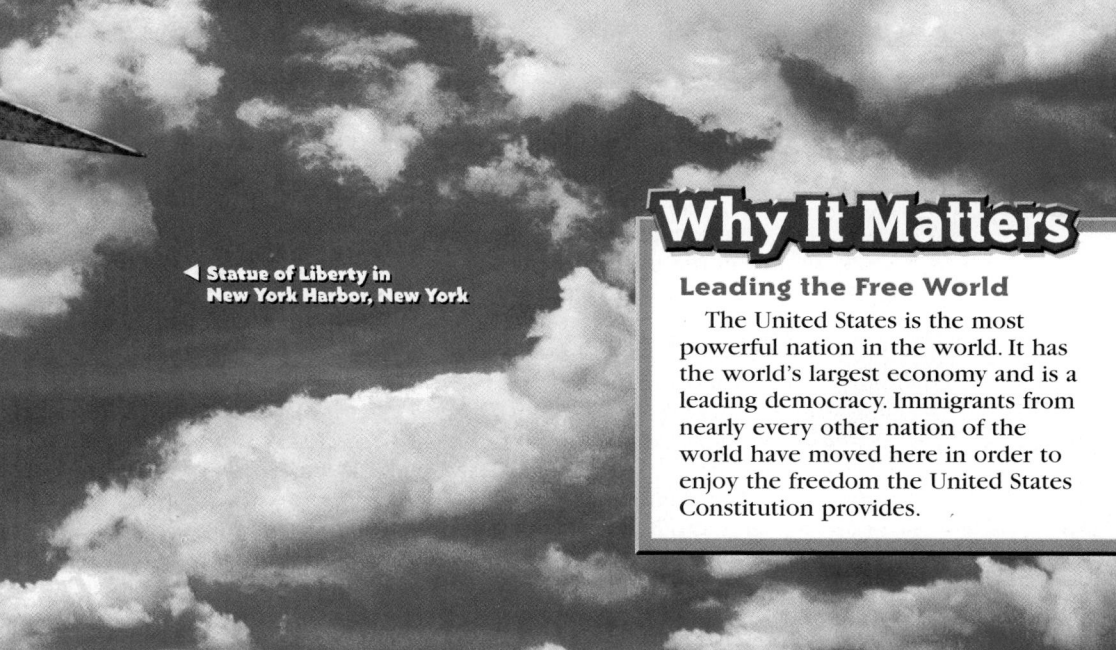

Step 2 Then fold the paper in half from side to side.

Step 3 Label the foldable as shown.

Reading and Writing Before you read the chapter, list questions you have about the land, people, and economy of the United States. Then, as you read the chapter, write down more questions that occur to you on the pages of your journal. Be sure to review your questions and fill in all the correct answers.

◀ Statue of Liberty in New York Harbor, New York

Why It Matters

Leading the Free World

The United States is the most powerful nation in the world. It has the world's largest economy and is a leading democracy. Immigrants from nearly every other nation of the world have moved here in order to enjoy the freedom the United States Constitution provides.

Introducing Chapter 19

FOLDABLES™ Study Organizer

Purpose When making this foldable, students are required to ask themselves questions about the land, people, and economy of the United States. This reading strategy requires students to ask questions of the chapter material as they read it, thereby helping them focus on main ideas and better understand the material.

Have students complete ***Reading and Study Skills Foldables*** Activity 19.

Why It Matters

Ask students to pretend they are from another country and have them write a letter to a relative explaining why they would like to move to the United States. Have them use outside sources to research geographic, economic, political, and social aspects of their "home" country and the United States. Tell them to include facts from their research in their letter when comparing the benefits of the United States to the negatives of their "home" country.

About the Photos

Located in New York Harbor, the Statue of Liberty was a gift of international friendship from the people of France to the people of the United States in recognition of the bond established between the two countries during the American Revolution. The monument was dedicated on October 28, 1886, and is one of the world's most universal symbols of political freedom and democracy. Visitors climb 354 steps to reach the crown. There are 25 windows in the crown that symbolize gemstones found on the earth and the heaven's rays shining over the world. The seven rays of the statue's crown represent the seven seas and continents of the world.

1 Focus

Section Objectives

1. Identify the landforms that are found in the United States.
2. Contrast the climates of different areas of the United States.

BELLRINGER Skillbuilder Activity

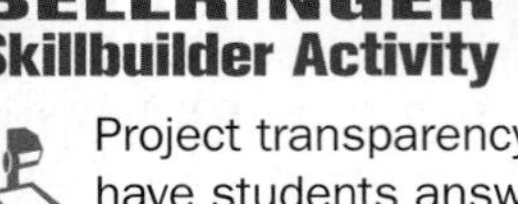

Project transparency and have students answer questions.

This activity is also available as a blackline master.

Daily Focus Skills Transparency 19-1

UNIT 7 DAILY FOCUS SKILLS Chapter 19 TRANSPARENCY 19-1

Interpreting Graphs

Highest Mountains in the United States

What is the highest point in the Appalachian Mountains?

A Mt. Elbert
B Mt. Ranier
C Mt. Michelson
D Mt. Mitchell

Mountain

Guide to Reading

■ **Accessing Prior Knowledge** Have students recite the words to "America, the Beautiful" and "This Land Is Your Land." Write key phrases (such as "amber waves of grain" or "New York highlands") on the board. **Ask: What do these phrases tell you about the United States?** *(It has a variety of different landforms.)*

Section 1: A Vast, Scenic Land

Guide to Reading

Main Idea

The United States has a great variety of landforms and climates.

Terms to Know

- contiguous
- megalopolis
- coral reef

Reading Strategy

Create a chart like the one below. Fill in details about each of the seven physical regions of the United States.

Region	Details

NATIONAL GEOGRAPHIC Exploring Our World

Who in the United States gets to see the sunrise first? The people in Maine are the first. As the earth rotates, the sun shines on an extremely varied land. It warms the valleys in the East, shimmers on the lakes in the North, and bakes the deserts in the Southwest. In the far Pacific, the sun greets Hawaii's tropical beaches. Finally, the sun sets beyond Alaska in the North.

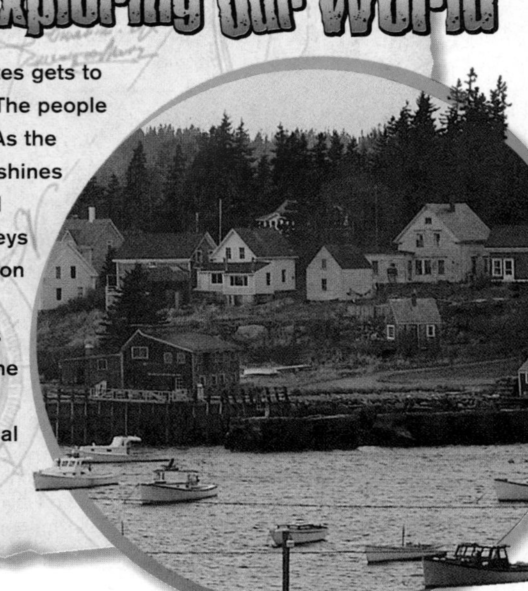

The United States stretches 2,807 miles (4,517 km) across the middle part of North America. The 48 states in this part of the country are **contiguous**, or joined together inside a common boundary. These states touch the Atlantic Ocean, the Gulf of Mexico, and the Pacific Ocean. Our neighbors are Canada to the north and Mexico to the south.

Two states lie apart from the other 48. Alaska—the largest state—lies in the northwestern portion of North America. Hawaii is in the Pacific Ocean about 2,400 miles (3,862 km) southwest of California.

From Sea to Shining Sea

The United States is ranked as the fourth-largest country in the world. Only Russia, Canada, and China are larger. Like a patchwork quilt, the United States has regional patterns of different landscapes. You can see swamps and deserts, tall mountains and flat plains.

The contiguous states have five main physical regions: the Coastal Plains, the Appalachian Mountains, the Interior Plains, the Mountains and Basins, and the Pacific Coast. Alaska and Hawaii each has its own set of physical landforms.

Section Resources

Reproducible Masters
- Reproducible Lesson Plan 19-1
- Daily Lecture and Discussion Notes 19-1
- Guided Reading Activity 19-1
- Reading Essentials and Study Guide 19-1
- Section Quiz 19-1

Transparencies
- Daily Focus Skills Transparency 19-1
- GeoQuiz Transparency 19-1

Multimedia
- Vocabulary PuzzleMaker Software
- Interactive Tutor Self-Assessment CD-ROM
- Presentation Plus! CD-ROM
- ExamView® Pro 3.0 Testmaker CD-ROM

The Coastal Plains A broad lowland runs along the eastern and southeastern coasts of the United States. The eastern lowlands are called the Atlantic Coastal Plain. The lowlands in the southeast border the Gulf of Mexico and are called the Gulf Coastal Plain. Find these coastal plains on the map below. Then look at the population map on page 522. What large cities lie in the Atlantic Coastal Plain?

Boston, New York City, Philadelphia, Baltimore, and Washington, D.C., all lie in the Atlantic Coastal Plain. These cities and their suburbs form an almost continuous line of settlement. Geographers call this kind of huge urban area a **megalopolis.**

The Gulf Coastal Plain is wider than the Atlantic plain. Soils in this region are better than those along the Atlantic coast. Texas and Louisiana both have rich deposits of oil and natural gas. The large cities

NATIONAL GEOGRAPHIC

The United States: Physical

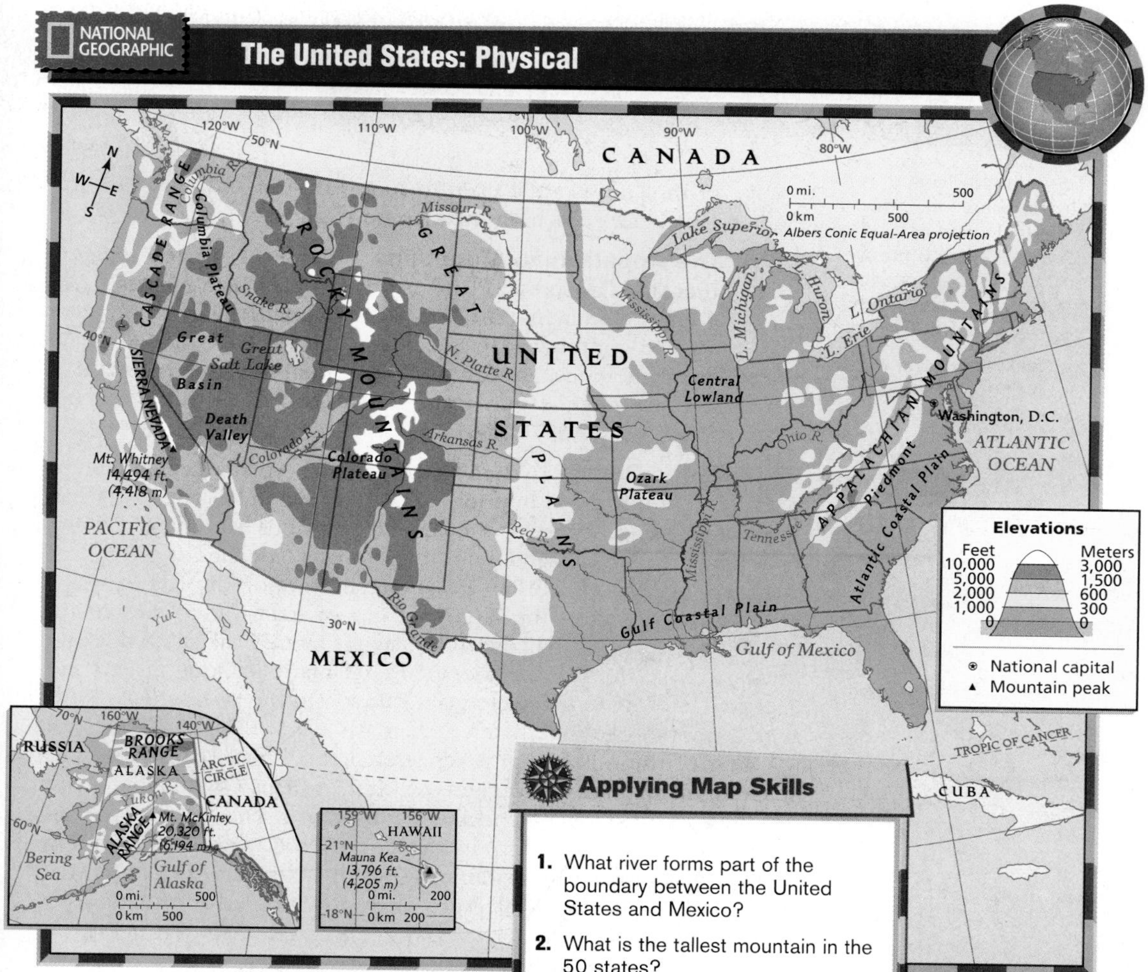

Elevations

Feet	Meters
10,000	3,000
5,000	1,500
2,000	600
1,000	300
0	0

⊛ National capital
▲ Mountain peak

Applying Map Skills

1. What river forms part of the boundary between the United States and Mexico?
2. What is the tallest mountain in the 50 states?

Find NGS online map resources @ www.nationalgeographic.com/maps

2 TEACH

Identifying Regions Have students identify the approximate location of their community on the map on this page. **Ask: In what physical region is your community located? What other physical regions are nearby? L1**

Daily Lecture Notes 19-1

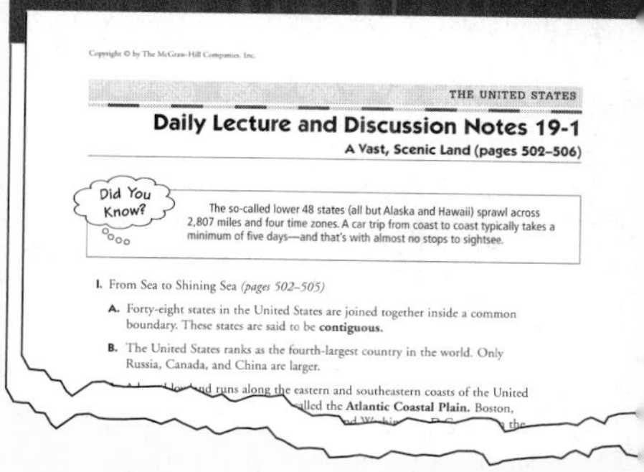

THE UNITED STATES

Daily Lecture and Discussion Notes 19-1
A Vast, Scenic Land (pages 502–506)

Did You Know? The so-called lower 48 states (all but Alaska and Hawaii) sprawl across 2,807 miles and four time zones. A car trip from coast to coast typically takes a minimum of five days—and that's with almost no stops to sightsee.

I. From Sea to Shining Sea (pages 502–505)

A. Forty-eight states in the United States are joined together inside a common boundary. These states are said to be **contiguous.**

B. The United States ranks as the fourth-largest country in the world. Only Russia, Canada, and China are larger.

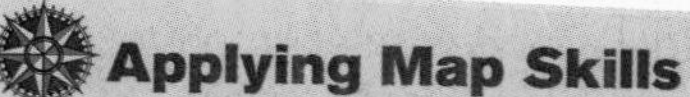

Applying Map Skills

Answers

1. the Rio Grande
2. Mt. McKinley, in Alaska

Skills Practice

Ask: How does the landscape of the United States change when moving from west to east? *(lowland on Pacific coast, then high mountains and plateaus, followed by high plains and lowlands in center, with mountains and lowlands in east)*

Meeting Special Needs

Naturalistic Organize students into seven groups and assign each group one of the physical regions of the United States. Instruct group members to locate photographs or make sketches of landscapes found in their assigned regions. Encourage groups to use their images to create a bulletin board display titled "America the Beautiful." Have groups arrange their illustrations around a large wall map of the United States. Remind students to be sure that each illustration has a caption and a leader line connecting it to its approximate location on the map. **L1**

Refer to *Inclusion for the Middle School Social Studies Classroom Strategies and Activities* in the TCR.

Measure student knowledge of physical features and political entities.

GeoQuiz Transparency 19-1

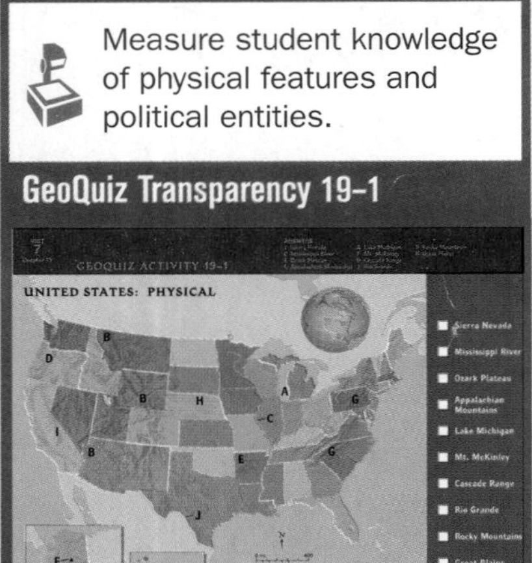

More About the Photos

Interior Plains Mineral resources in the Interior Plains helped build its industrial strength. Coal brought from nearby Appalachian foothills was used to power furnaces that make steel. To make that steel, workers used iron brought from the highlands near Lake Superior. The Mesabi Range in Minnesota was one of the richest sources of iron in the world. Cities such as Chicago, Detroit, Cleveland, and Pittsburgh became major industrial centers as a result of the availability of these resources.

Caption Answer the Mississippi River

NATIONAL GEOGRAPHIC **On Location**

City and Country

The Interior Plains of the United States include industrial cities of the North, such as Chicago (above), and the agricultural lands of the Great Plains, like this area in Texas (above right).

Region **What river divides much of the Interior Plains?**

of the Gulf Coastal Plain include Houston and New Orleans, which are shown on the map on page 522.

The Appalachian Mountains Along the western edge of the Atlantic Coastal Plain rise the Appalachian (A•puh•LAY•chuhn) Mountains. The Appalachians are the oldest mountains on the continent. How can you tell? Their rounded peaks show their age. Erosion has worn them down over time. The highest peak, Mount Mitchell in North Carolina, reaches 6,684 feet (2,037 m).

The Interior Plains When you cross the Appalachians heading west, you enter the vast Interior Plains. This region has two parts. East of the Mississippi River are the Central Lowlands. Here you will find grassy hills, rolling flatlands, and thick forests. The land is fertile, and farms are productive. This area also contains important waterways.

The Great Lakes—the largest group of freshwater lakes in the world—lie in the Central Lowlands. Glaciers formed Lake Superior, Lake Michigan, Lake Huron, Lake Erie, and Lake Ontario millions of years ago. The waters of these connected lakes flow into the St. Lawrence River, which empties into the Atlantic Ocean.

West of the Mississippi River stretch the Great Plains. The landscape in many places is blanketed with neat fields of grain and grassy pastures and takes on a checkerboard pattern. The Great Plains are about 500 miles (805 km) wide and stretch west to the Rocky Mountains, north into Canada, and south to the Mexican border. The rich grasslands of the Great Plains once provided food for millions of buffalo and the Native Americans who lived there. Today, farmers grow grains and ranchers raise cattle on the Great Plains.

Critical Thinking Activity

Drawing Conclusions Create a chart using the seven physical regions of the United States as horizontal column headings and "Population" and "Economic Activities" as vertical row headings. Call on volunteers to identify physical characteristics of each region. **Ask:** **How might these physical characteristics affect population in each region?** Note responses in the appropriate column and row. **How might physical features influence economic activities in the region?** Note these responses on the chart as well. Have students copy the chart into their notebooks. Encourage them to review and adjust chart entries as they study the chapter. **L2**

EE5 Environment and Society: Standard 15

Mountains and Plateaus The Rocky Mountains begin in Alaska and run all the way south to Mexico. Running along these mountains is a ridge called the Continental Divide. This ridge separates rivers that flow west—toward the Pacific Ocean—from those that flow east—toward the Mississippi River. Many important rivers begin in the high, snowy peaks of the Rockies. The Rio Grande, as well as the Missouri, Platte, Arkansas, and Red Rivers all flow east. The Colorado, Snake, and Columbia Rivers flow west.

Between the Rockies and the Pacific Coast are plateaus, canyons, and deserts. Plateaus are areas of flat land that rise above the land around them. A canyon is a deep valley with steep sides. The most famous of these is the Grand Canyon in Arizona.

The Pacific Coast Near the Pacific Coast rise two other mountain ranges, the Cascade Range and the Sierra Nevada. Find these ranges on the map on page 503. Even in a place as far south as California, the tops of these high mountains remain covered with snow year-round.

To the west of these Pacific ranges lie fertile valleys. The Willamette Valley in Oregon and the Central Valley in California both produce abundant crops. Many of the fruits and vegetables you eat may come from these valleys.

Alaska Mountain ranges form a semicircle over the northern, eastern, and southern parts of Alaska. Mount McKinley—the tallest mountain in North America—stands 20,320 feet (6,194 m) high in the Alaska Range. The northern part of the state borders on the frigid Arctic Ocean, and you can almost see Russia from Alaska's western shores. Most people in Alaska live along the southern coastal plain or in the central Yukon River valley.

Hawaii Eight large islands and more than 120 smaller islands make up Hawaii, our island state in the Pacific Ocean. Volcanoes on the ocean floor erupted and formed these islands. Some of the islands have coral reefs, formed by the skeletons of small sea animals. These structures lie just above or submerged just below the surface of the water.

Reading Check What is the Continental Divide?

NATIONAL GEOGRAPHIC On Location

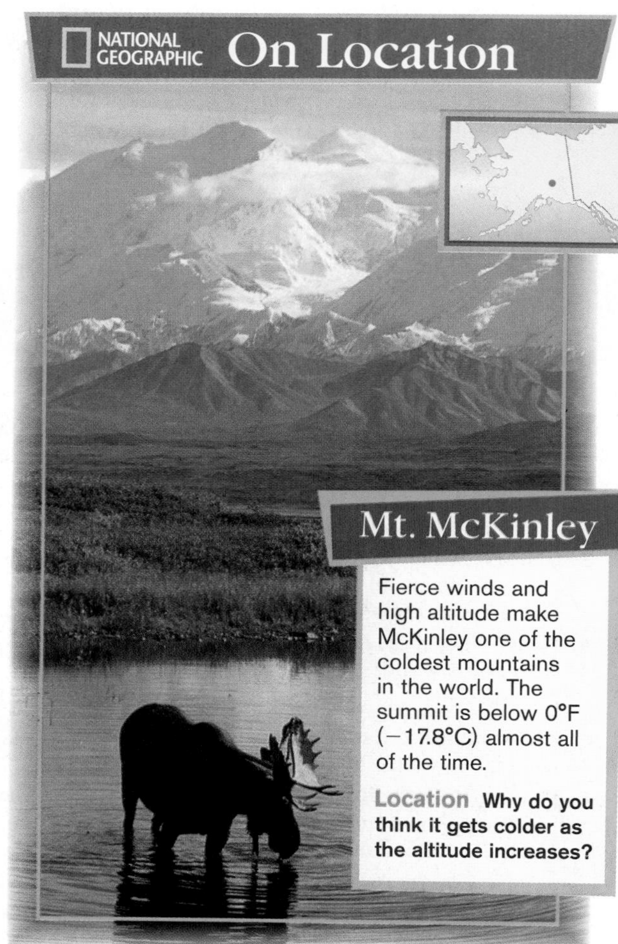

Mt. McKinley

Fierce winds and high altitude make McKinley one of the coldest mountains in the world. The summit is below 0°F (−17.8°C) almost all of the time.

Location Why do you think it gets colder as the altitude increases?

Critical Thinking Activity

Understanding Cause and Effect A plateau called the Piedmont lies at the eastern edge of the Appalachians. The eastern edge of the Piedmont rises sharply from the low-lying Atlantic Coastal Plain. Here fast-moving rivers drop from the plateau to the plains, forming many rapids and waterfalls. The line formed where this drop takes place is called the fall line. Early European settlers were unable to travel beyond the fall line by boat. The waterfalls and rapids, however, later provided waterpower for industries. Thus, many cities—including Macon, Georgia; Columbia, South Carolina; Raleigh, North Carolina; and Richmond, Virginia—developed along the fall line. Have students trace how rivers helped power early American industry. L3

EE6 The Uses of Geography: Standard 17

Chapter 19

Section 1, pages 502–506

More About the Photo

Mt. McKinley In 1917, Mount McKinley National Park was established as a wildlife refuge. In 1980, the park area was enlarged by 4 million acres and renamed Denali National Park. Denali, or "high one," is the name native people gave the massive peak.

Caption Answer At higher altitudes, the air is no longer warmed by the heat of the earth's surface.

Guided Reading Activity 19-1

Reading Check Answer

A ridge that runs along the Rocky Mountains separating rivers that flow west from those that flow east.

3 ASSESS

Assign Section 1 Assessment as homework or an in-class activity.

Have students use the Interactive Tutor Self-Assessment CD-ROM to review Section 19–1.

Chapter 19

Section 1, pages 502–506

Section Quiz 19-1

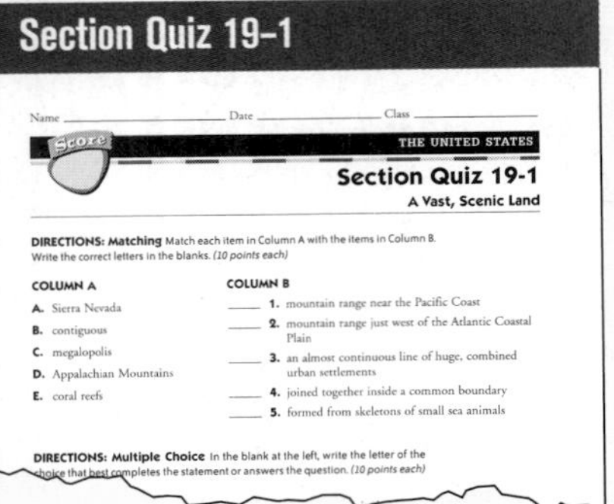
Name ____________ Date ____________ Class ____________

Score | THE UNITED STATES

Section Quiz 19-1
A Vast, Scenic Land

DIRECTIONS: Matching Match each item in Column A with the items in Column B. Write the correct letters in the blanks. (10 points each)

COLUMN A	COLUMN B
A. Sierra Nevada	___ 1. mountain range near the Pacific Coast
B. contiguous	___ 2. mountain range just west of the Atlantic Coastal Plain
C. megalopolis	___ 3. an almost continuous line of huge, combined urban settlements
D. Appalachian Mountains	___ 4. joined together inside a common boundary
E. coral reefs	___ 5. formed from skeletons of small sea animals

DIRECTIONS: Multiple Choice In the blank at the left, write the letter of the choice that best completes the statement or answers the question. (10 points each)

Reading Check Answer

mild, or temperate; Most places are not too hot or too cold.

Reteach
Have students work in small groups to outline Section 1. Assign one subsection to each group.

Reading Essentials and Study Guide 19-1

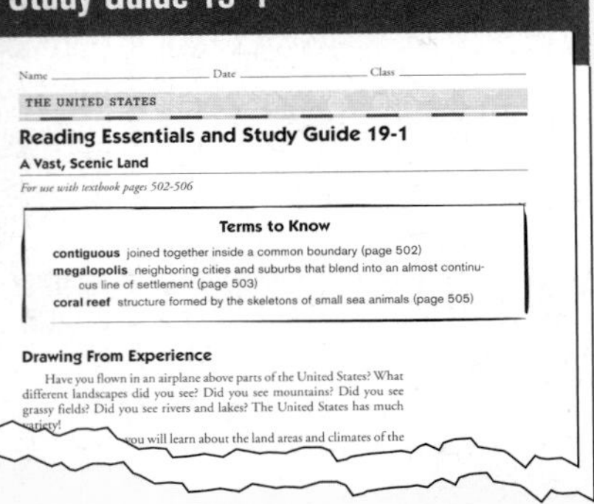
Name ____________ Date ____________ Class ____________

THE UNITED STATES

Reading Essentials and Study Guide 19-1
A Vast, Scenic Land
For use with textbook pages 502–506

Terms to Know
contiguous joined together inside a common boundary (page 502)
megalopolis neighboring cities and suburbs that blend into an almost continuous line of settlement (page 503)
coral reef structure formed by the skeletons of small sea animals (page 505)

Drawing From Experience
Have you flown in an airplane above parts of the United States? What different landscapes did you see? Did you see mountains? Did you see grassy fields? Did you see rivers and lakes? The United States has much variety! ... you will learn about the land areas and climates of the

Have students make a list of state nicknames and determine which are related to physical geography.

A Variety of Climates

Because the United States is such a large country, you probably expect it to have a variety of climates. You are right! Most of the country lies squarely in the middle latitude region—from 23°30′N to 66°30′N latitude. This means the region has the greatest variety of climates. With Alaska and Hawaii, our country also has high-latitude and tropical climates.

In spite of the great variety of climates in the United States, generally the climate is mild, or temperate. That means most places are not usually too hot or too cold. In general, the farther north you travel, the summers grow shorter and cooler and the winters become longer and colder. As you travel south, the summers become longer and hotter and the winters shorter and milder. Being located in the middle of North America gives the United States an average warmer climate than Canada, and an average cooler climate than Mexico.

It is important to remember that climate also changes with elevation. The higher the land, the cooler the temperatures. The highest mountain peaks are snow-covered year-round, while the low valleys and deserts stay much warmer year-round.

As you would expect, the climate in much of Alaska is similar to that of northern Canada. Hawaii and Florida have warm tropical climates with heavy rainfall much of the year.

Reading Check In general, what is the climate of the U.S.? What does this mean?

Assessment

Defining Terms

1. **Define** contiguous, megalopolis, coral reef.

Recalling Facts

2. **Place** How does the United States rank in size among all the countries of the world?
3. **History** Which region once supported millions of buffalo and the Native Americans who depended on them?
4. **Place** What is the largest group of freshwater lakes in the world?

Critical Thinking

5. **Understanding Cause and Effect** How were the Hawaiian Islands formed?
6. **Drawing Conclusions** What challenges do you think result from the distance between Alaska, Hawaii, and the other states?

Graphic Organizer

7. **Organizing Information** Create a diagram like this one to compare the Atlantic and Gulf Coastal Plains. In the separate outer parts of the ovals, write the qualities that make each region different. In the overlapping area, write the characteristics that the two areas share.

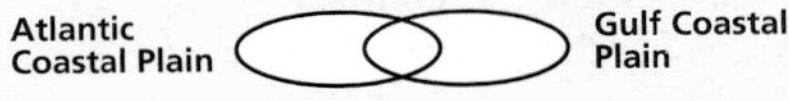

Applying Social Studies Skills

8. **Analyzing Maps** Look at the physical map on page 503 and the population map on page 522. At what elevations do the cities with more than 5 million people lie?

Section 1 Assessment

1. The terms are defined in the Glossary.
2. fourth-largest country in the world
3. Great Plains
4. the Great Lakes
5. volcanic eruptions on the ocean floor
6. *Possible answers:* problems communicating; extra time needed to ship goods
7. *Atlantic Coastal Plain:* continuous line of settlement; *Gulf Coastal Plain:* wider, good soil, has oil and natural gas; *Both:* have major cities, low-lying areas
8. 0–1,000 feet (0–300 m)

Section 2

An Economic Leader

Guide to Reading

Main Idea

The powerful United States economy runs on abundant resources and the hard work of Americans.

Terms to Know

- free enterprise system
- fossil fuel
- landfill
- recycling
- free trade

Reading Strategy

Create a chart like this one. List at least five challenges the United States faces in the twenty-first century.

Challenges

NATIONAL GEOGRAPHIC **Exploring Our World**

Have you ever seen an apartment building on wheels? You might in northern Alaska. Crews of oil companies there need a place to stay. They search constantly for new sources of oil in the area. Because they have to move often, the oil companies built homes on wheels. As a truck lumbers across the Alaskan ice, it tows a mobile apartment building.

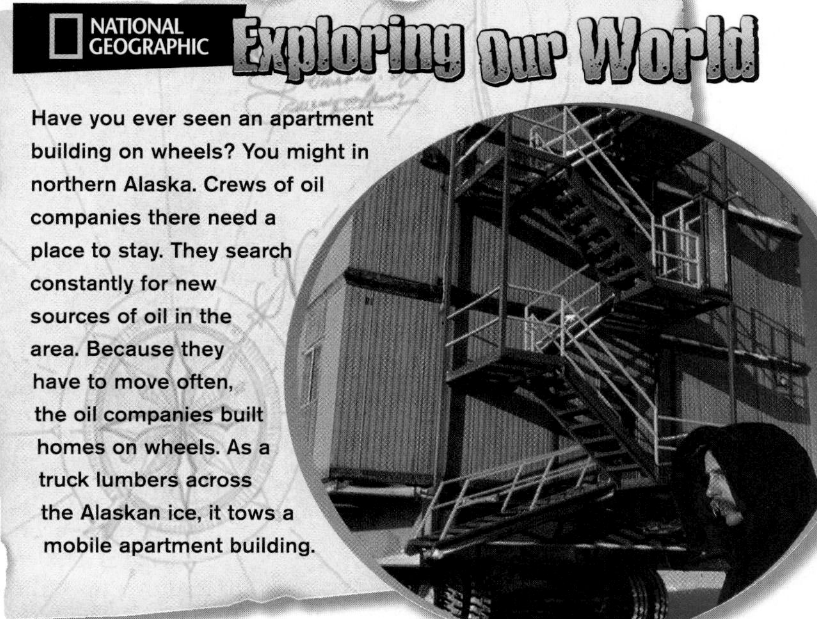

The United States has a large, energetic, and growing economy. Fueling all of this economic activity is freedom. The **free enterprise system** is built on the idea that individual people have the right to run businesses to make a profit with limited government interference and regulation. Americans are free to start their own businesses and to keep the profits they earn. They are free to work in whatever jobs they want—and for whatever employers they want. This has helped create great economic success.

The World's Economic Leader

The United States is rich in resources and has a hardworking labor force. As a result, the country has built the world's largest economy—in terms of how much money is made from the sale of its goods and services. In fact, the American economy is larger than the next two largest economies—China's and Japan's—combined.

Farms in the United States produce about one-half of the world's corn and about one-tenth of its wheat. American farmers raise about 20 percent of the world's beef, pork, and lamb. The country exports

507

1 FOCUS

Section Objectives

1. Explain why the United States has the world's leading economy.
2. Identify how people in the United States earn their livings.
3. Describe the challenges facing the United States.

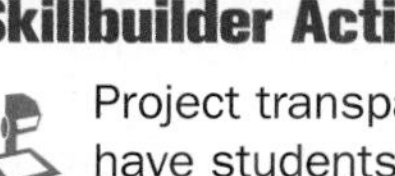

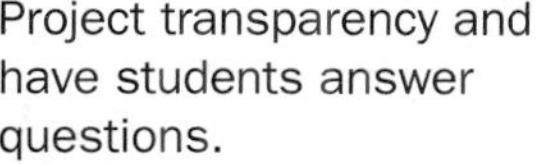

BELLRINGER Skillbuilder Activity

Project transparency and have students answer questions.

This activity is also available as a blackline master.

Daily Focus Skills Transparency 19-2

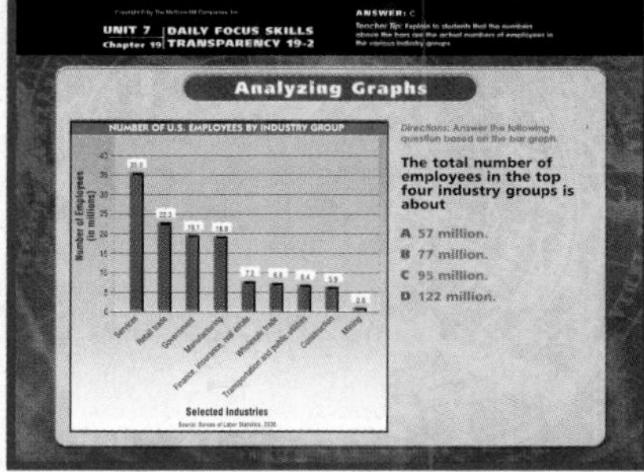

Guide to Reading

Accessing Prior Knowledge
Have students give examples of American industries. Choose one and have students suggest what jobs the industry might include.

Section Resources

Reproducible Masters
- Reproducible Lesson Plan 19-2
- Daily Lecture and Discussion Notes 19-2
- Guided Reading Activity 19-2
- Reading Essentials and Study Guide 19-2
- Section Quiz 19-2

Transparencies
- Daily Focus Skills Transparency 19-2
- GeoQuiz Transparency 19-2

Multimedia
- Vocabulary PuzzleMaker Software
- Interactive Tutor Self-Assessment CD-ROM
- Presentation Plus! CD-ROM
- ExamView® Pro 3.0 Testmaker CD-ROM

Analyzing the Graph

Answer
25 percent

Skills Practice
What is the second most important industry in the American economy? *(manufacturing)*

TEACH

Researching Jobs To reinforce the point that Americans are free to enter any career, bring in the want ads. Have each student find one job that interests him or her. Ask students to do research and create a fact sheet outlining what the job involves, what education or experience is needed, and how much it pays. L1

Daily Lecture Notes 19-2

THE UNITED STATES

Daily Lecture and Discussion Notes 19-2

An Economic Leader (pages 507–510)

Did You Know? The United States is the world's leading producer of electrical power from all sources. It also leads the world in production of natural gas, lead, aluminum, and several other minerals. It is among the leaders in the production of crude oil, coal, copper, iron ore, silver, and zinc. In total value of manufactured goods, the United States leads all other nations by a substantial margin.

I. The World's Economic Leader *(pages 507–508)*

A. In the United States, the **free enterprise system** allows individuals the right to run businesses and to make a profit with limited interference from the ... People are free to work in whatever job they wish.

Reading Check Answer

services

NATIONAL GEOGRAPHIC

The Economy of the United States

Analyzing the Graph

The economy of the United States is divided into the four main areas shown here.

Economics **What percentage of the U.S. economy is not made up of service/information industry?**

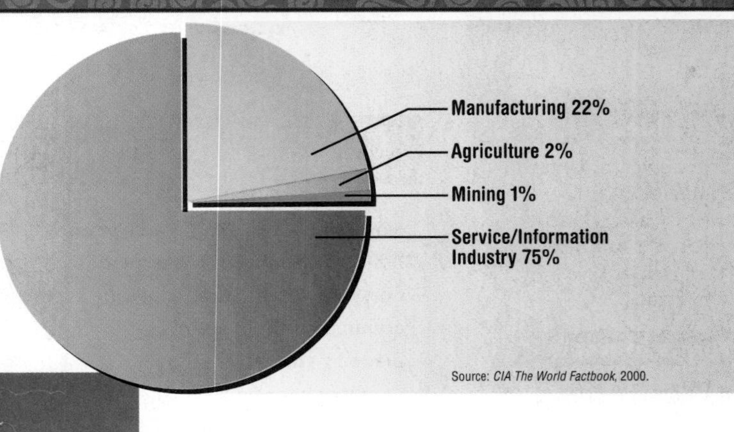

▲ **Filmmaking is a service industry.**

more food than any other nation. Yet agriculture is only a small part of the American economy. It makes up about 2 percent of the value of all goods produced in the country.

The United States has rich mineral resources. About one-fifth of the world's coal and copper and one-tenth of the world's petroleum come from the United States. The country also has large amounts of iron ore, zinc, lead, silver, gold, and many other minerals. Mining, though, makes up little more than 1 percent of the nation's economy.

American factory workers build cars and airplanes. They make computers and appliances. They process foods and make medicines. Manufacturing accounts for about one-fifth of the American economy.

By far, the largest part of the economy is services. A service industry is a business that provides services to people instead of producing goods. Banking and finance are services. So is entertainment—and people all over the world buy American movies and CDs. The United States is a leader in tourism, another service industry. Computer-based, online services have also emerged as an important American service industry.

Reading Check **What is the largest part of the United States economy?**

In the Twenty-First Century

The American economy, although strong, faces challenges in the twenty-first century. One of these challenges is how to clean up pollution and trash. Americans burn **fossil fuels**—coal, oil, and natural gas—to power their factories and run their cars. If not carefully controlled, burning these fuels pollutes the air. The pollution also mixes with water vapor in the air to make acid rain, or rain containing high amounts of

Critical Thinking Activity

Categorizing Information Have students refer back to the industry classification chart on page 32 of this text. Ask them to compare that to the graph on page 508 and classify each of the categories in the U.S. economy pie graph as either a primary, secondary, tertiary, or quaternary industry. **Ask:** **What percentage of the U.S. economy is based on primary industries?** *(3%)* Then have students make a four-column chart, with the headings "Primary," "Secondary," "Tertiary," and "Quaternary." As they read through this section, have them list the industries mentioned under the appropriate heading. L2

EE4 Human Systems: Standard 11

chemical pollutants. Acid rain damages trees and harms rivers and lakes. Acid rain that is produced in the United States and carried north by wind is a major environmental problem for Canada.

The fast-paced American way of life creates another problem. People generate huge amounts of trash. **Landfills,** the areas where trash companies dump the waste they collect, grow higher and higher each year. Many communities now promote **recycling,** or reusing materials instead of throwing them away. Recycling cuts down on the amount of trash.

Quality Schools The ability to develop new technology has been a major source of strength for the American economy. Researchers work constantly to find new products to make people's lives easier, healthier—and more fun. Quality schools that produce educated and creative people have helped the country become a world leader in satellites, computers, health care, and many other fields. Keeping our number one position will require just as much creative thinking and hard work. You will need to learn and use these new technologies to stay productive in your future jobs.

Health Care Some of the best health care in the world is available in the United States. New medical technologies are constantly being developed to improve the level of health care. These new technologies help to save lives, but they also raise medical costs overall.

The rising cost of medical care is a problem that affects the delivery of health care in the United States. Employers of temporary, contract,

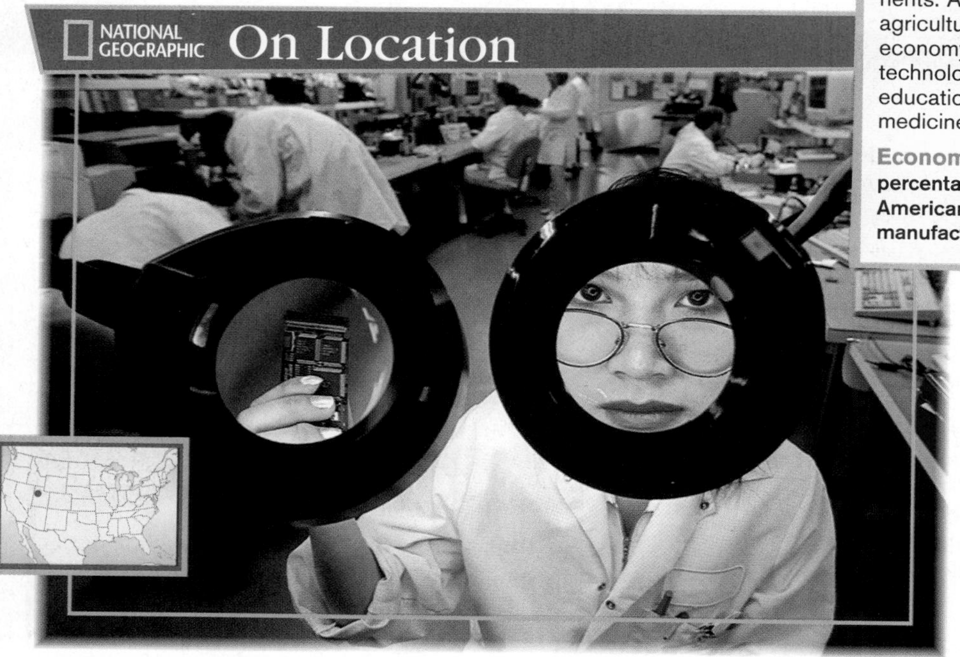

Factories

A worker inspects computer components. Along with agriculture, America's economy is strong in technology, science, education, and medicine.

Economics What percentage of the American economy is manufacturing?

Chapter 19

Section 2, pages 507–510

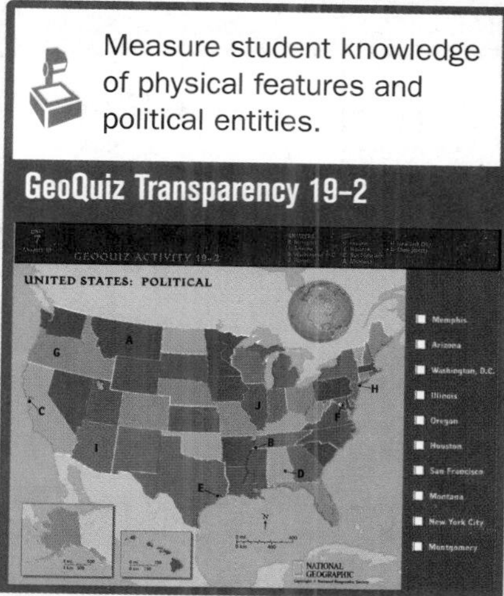

Measure student knowledge of physical features and political entities.

GeoQuiz Transparency 19-2

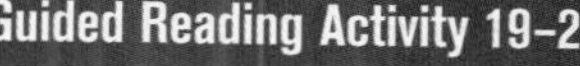

Guided Reading Activity 19-2

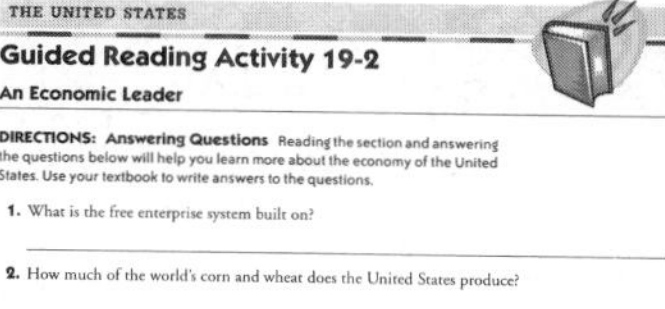

Name ______ Date ______ Class ______

THE UNITED STATES

Guided Reading Activity 19-2

An Economic Leader

DIRECTIONS: Answering Questions Reading the section and answering the questions below will help you learn more about the economy of the United States. Use your textbook to write answers to the questions.

1. What is the free enterprise system built on?

2. How much of the world's corn and wheat does the United States produce?

3. How important is agriculture to the nation's economy?

4. What makes up the largest part of the United States economy?

More About the Photos

Computer Technology An area near San Francisco called Silicon Valley is important for producing electronic equipment.

Caption Answer 22 percent

3 ASSESS

Assign Section 2 Assessment as homework or an in-class activity.

Team-Teaching Activity

Science Recycling, described on page 530, is an important way of contributing to a healthy environment. Many communities ask residents to recycle aluminum, glass, plastic, and paper. **Ask: Why is it important to recycle?** Work with the science teacher to outline for students the benefits of recycling, which include conserving resources and energy, reducing pollution, and saving landfill space. Ask the science teacher to discuss the different grades of plastic and explain why some can be recycled and others cannot. Finally, have students make a list of the things that they recycle—or could recycle—at home. Encourage them to carry out the practice. **L2**

EE5 Environment and Society: Standard 14

Chapter 19

Section 2, pages 507–510

Section Quiz 19-2

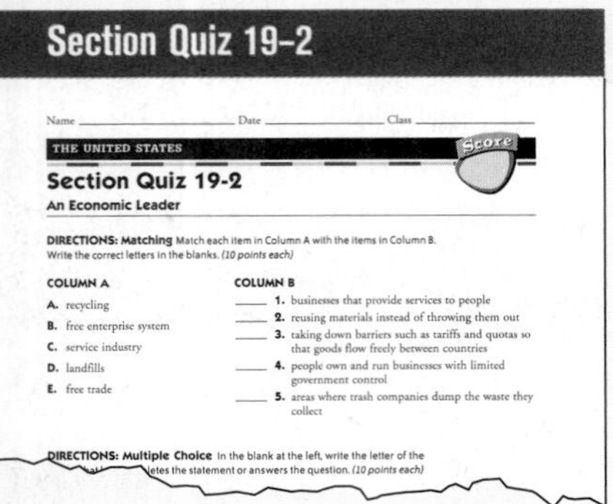

Name ______ Date ______ Class ______

THE UNITED STATES

Score

Section Quiz 19-2

An Economic Leader

DIRECTIONS: Matching Match each item in Column A with the items in Column B. Write the correct letters in the blanks. *(10 points each)*

COLUMN A	COLUMN B
A. recycling	____ **1.** businesses that provide services to people
B. free enterprise system	____ **2.** reusing materials instead of throwing them out
C. service industry	____ **3.** taking down barriers such as tariffs and quotas so that goods flow freely between countries
D. landfills	____ **4.** people own and run businesses with limited government control
E. free trade	____ **5.** areas where trash companies dump the waste they collect

DIRECTIONS: Multiple Choice In the blank at the left, write the letter of the ... letes the statement or answers the question. *(10 points each)*

Reading Check Answer

The fuels burned for factories and in cars pollute the air. The pollution also mixes with water vapor in the air to create acid rain.

Reading Essentials and Study Guide 19-2

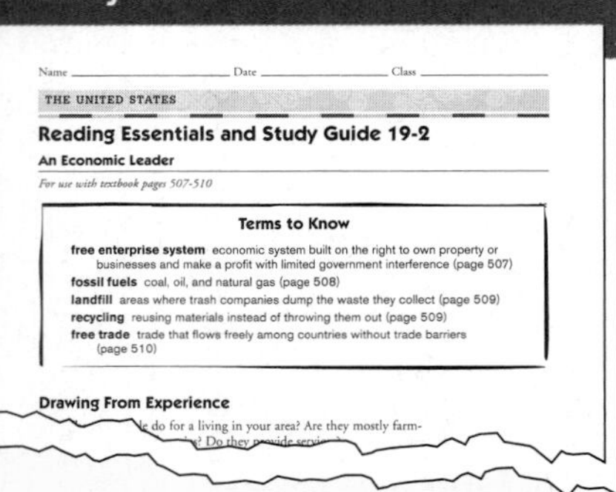

Name ______ Date ______ Class ______

THE UNITED STATES

Reading Essentials and Study Guide 19-2

An Economic Leader

For use with textbook pages 507-510

Terms to Know

free enterprise system economic system built on the right to own property or businesses and make a profit with limited government interference (page 507)
fossil fuels coal, oil, and natural gas (page 508)
landfill areas where trash companies dump the waste they collect (page 509)
recycling reusing materials instead of throwing them out (page 509)
free trade trade that flows freely among countries without trade barriers (page 510)

Drawing From Experience

...le do for a living in your area? Are they mostly farm-... Do they provide servi...

4 CLOSE

Have students work in pairs or small groups to identify recent changes in technology and how they have affected jobs. Encourage students to use photos and other media to present their findings.

and part-time workers do not usually offer health insurance as a benefit. Approximately one out of five people in the United States does not have medical insurance. The majority of these uninsured are children of lower income families. Because they do not have insurance, they might not be able to get some forms of medical care. For example, some emergency rooms will not treat people without medical insurance.

Some people think that the United States should have a national program of health insurance. In this type of program, the government provides some level of medical care at an affordable rate. Critics of nationalized health care point to countries such as Canada, where people may have lengthy waiting periods for operations and where there is little choice, if any, of doctors or hospitals.

World Trade The United States leads the world in the value of all its imports and exports. Millions of Americans depend on trade for their jobs. American leaders have worked hard to promote free trade. **Free trade** means taking down trade barriers such as tariffs or quotas so that goods flow freely between countries. In 1992 the United States, Mexico, and Canada entered into the North American Free Trade Agreement (NAFTA). This agreement, which took effect in 1994, promised to remove all barriers to trade among those three countries.

✓ Reading Check **How might burning fossil fuels harm the environment in the United States?**

Section 2 Assessment

Defining Terms

1. **Define** free enterprise system, fossil fuel, landfill, recycling, free trade.

Recalling Facts

2. **Economics** What is a major challenge of the American economy in the twenty-first century?
3. **Culture** What problem has been created by the fast-paced American way of life?
4. **Economics** What was the goal of the North American Free Trade Agreement (NAFTA)?

Critical Thinking

5. **Analyzing Information** Describe two characteristics of the United States that have helped it become a world leader.
6. **Understanding Cause and Effect** What reasons can you give for the fast-paced American way of life causing more trash?

Graphic Organizer

7. **Organizing Information** Create a diagram like this one. In the outer ovals, write one specific example under each heading.

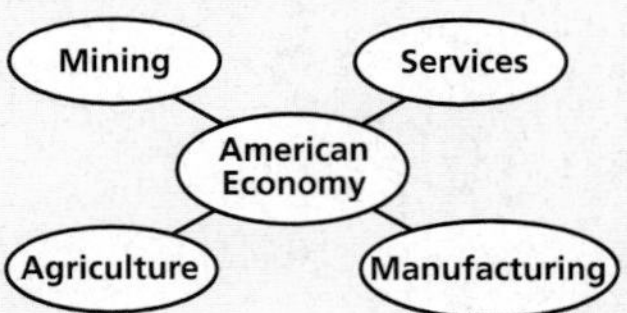

Applying Social Studies Skills

8. **Interpreting Graphs** Study the graph of the American economy on page 508. Then determine what part of the American economy is two times larger than mining.

510 CHAPTER 19

Section 2 Assessment

1. The terms are defined in the Glossary.
2. *Possible answers:* how to clean up pollution and trash; to develop new technology; affordable health care; world trade
3. trash
4. to remove all barriers to trade among the United States, Canada, and Mexico
5. The United States is rich in resources and has a hardworking labor force.
6. *Possible answers:* Fast-food consumption; inexpensive plastic and paper goods; products cost less to buy than repair; easier to throw things away than recycle
7. Answers will vary.
8. agriculture

TIME REPORTS

FOCUS ON WORLD ISSUES

A New Kind of War

Battling Terrorism in the Land of the Free

THOMAS E. FRANKLIN/RECORD/CORBIS SABA

Making Connections

Terrorism **Ask students:** **Do you remember where you were when the terrorist attacks on the World Trade Center and the Pentagon occurred on September 11, 2001?** After they have responded, **Ask:** **Did these attacks affect how safe you felt? Do you think they affected how safe the average U.S. citizen felt? What do you think were the goals of the terrorists? Do you think their attack achieved these goals? Why or why not?**

Focus on World Issues

Teacher Background

A long history of wars, displaced refugees, extreme poverty, and growing religious fundamentalism created the stew that boiled over into the horrific events of September 11, 2001. Many areas of Southwest Asia have long been ripe for extremist groups demanding retribution for perceived wrongs.

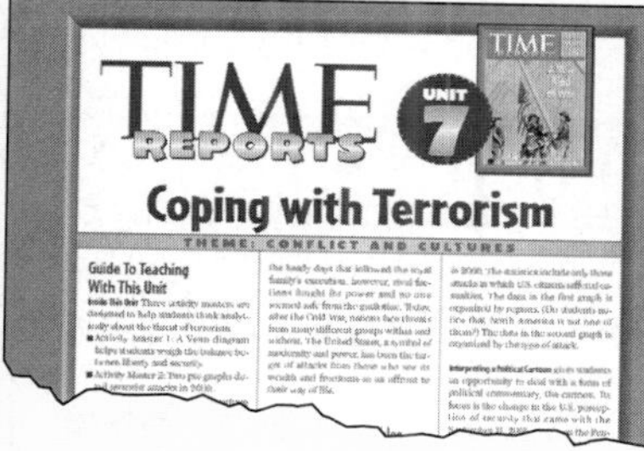
TIME REPORTS UNIT 7

Coping with Terrorism

THEME: CONFLICT AND CULTURES

Guide To Teaching With This Unit

Preparing the Student

Emphasize to students that although the terrorism of September 11 was linked to Muslim extremists, most Muslims are peace-loving. Terrorist acts have been done by many different people, from Basque separatists in Spain to Catholic and Protestant factions in Ireland to American Timothy McVeigh.

More About the Photo

Symbols Show students the famous photo of U.S. marines raising the American flag on Iwo Jima during World War II. Explain its background. **Ask:** **What are the similarities and differences between that photo and this one?**

1 Focus

Ask: **Did the word *terrorism* mean something different to you before the attacks of September 11, 2001, from what it meant to you afterward?** Encourage students to discuss how their thoughts and feelings changed. Then ask them to come up with a definition of the word *terrorism.* Ask students to think about how terrorism differs from traditional warfare. Write several definitions on the board and discuss them.

Did You Know?

On October 8, 2001, less than one month after the attacks on the World Trade Center and the Pentagon, President George W. Bush established the Office of Homeland Security.

EXPLORING THE ISSUES

ANSWERS

1. Answers will vary. Most people believe heroes are people who put their own lives and/or welfare at risk to help others, which the rescue workers certainly did.
2. Terrorism is by its nature unexpected and typically attacks civilians rather than soldiers.

1995
Terror strikes Oklahoma City.

LISA RUDY HOKE—BLACK STAR

1996
Terrorists in Saudi Arabia blow up housing for U.S. troops.

A Day for Heroes

September 11, 2001, was a day John Jonas will never forget. A New York City firefighter, Jonas was the captain of Ladder Company 6. That morning two **hijacked** airplanes were deliberately flown into the World Trade Center's twin towers.

Jonas and five other men in his company rushed to the scene. An hour later they were walking down the fire stairs of the south tower. An older woman they were rescuing told them she couldn't go on. They told her they wouldn't leave her. And just then the building collapsed around them in clouds of dust. "I'm thinking," Jonas said later, "'I can't believe this is how it ends for me.'"

But life didn't end either for Jonas or for the five firefighters with him. Nor did it end for Josephine Harris, the woman they saved. Above and below them and in the nearby north tower, more than 3,900 people died. But somehow the part of the stairway they were on didn't collapse. "It was a freak of timing," said Jonas. Another minute, either way, and the crumpling building would have crushed them like the others.

JAMES NACHTWEY—VII FOR TIME

▲ New York City firefighters battle the World Trade Center disaster on September 11, 2001.

More than 300 rescue workers lost their lives trying to save others that day. All of them were heroes.

No Ordinary Crime

Clearly, the horrible assault on the World Trade Center was no ordinary crime. It was an act of **terrorism**. Terrorism is the illegal use of violence against people or property to make a point. The point may involve a particular belief, such as religion or politics.

At the time, the U.S. government had named 27 foreign terrorist groups operating all over the world. Among them were groups in Asia, Europe, South America, and Africa. Many of the groups were foes of Israel, Southwest Asia's only democracy.

EXPLORING THE ISSUES

1. **Interpreting Points of View** Do you agree with the article's view of heroes? Why or why not?
2. **Making Inferences** How is the violence of terrorism different from the violence of war?

512

Meeting Special Needs

Interpersonal After the September 11, 2001, attacks on New York and Washington, D.C., many Americans said that they would not be defeated or frightened by the terrorists. Have students give an oral presentation, based on their personal experiences and what they have read and seen, that describes what they think is the essential American spirit. The presentation should discuss how and why Americans work as a group in times of crisis. Students should describe several instances they have personally witnessed, and what it is about our culture, society, and government that encourages this type of behavior. **L1**

Refer to *Inclusion for the Middle School Social Studies Classroom Strategies and Activities* in the TCR.

1998
Terrorists destroy the U.S. Embassy in Nairobi, Kenya.

2000
Terrorists in Yemen batter a U.S. warship, the USS Cole.

2001
Suicide pilots level the World Trade Center's twin towers.

TIME
REPORTS

Al-Qaeda

The most dangerous of the terrorist groups was al-Qaeda (al•KAY•dah). Its members hated the United States for supporting Israel. They hated freedom of speech and of religion. They wanted religious leaders to control the governments of all Muslim countries.

On September 11th, the terrorists attacked not only the World Trade Center, but also the Pentagon, the U.S. military headquarters outside Washington, D.C. These attacks horrified people around the world, including the nearly 7 million Muslims who live in the United States.

Al-Qaeda's leader, Osama bin Laden, told his followers that it was a Muslim's duty to kill Americans. No idea could be farther from Muslim teachings. The Quran, Islam's holiest book, tells soldiers to "show [civilians] kindness and deal with them justly." But the plane hijackers in September 2001 listened only to their terrorist leaders.

Closing in on America

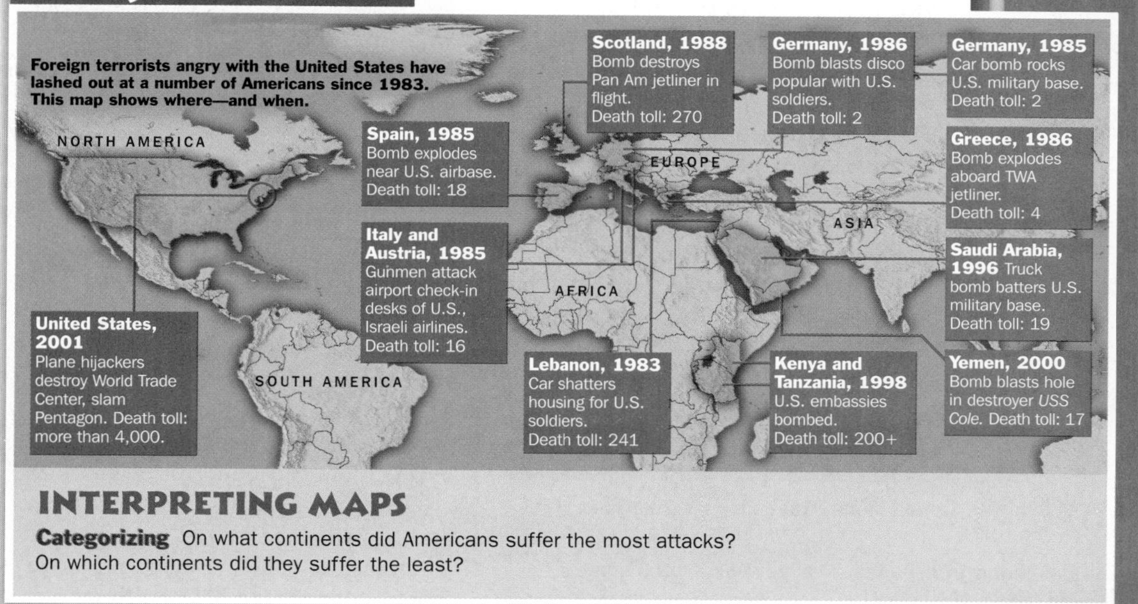
Foreign terrorists angry with the United States have lashed out at a number of Americans since 1983. This map shows where—and when.
NORTH AMERICA
EUROPE
ASIA
AFRICA
SOUTH AMERICA
Scotland, 1988 Bomb destroys Pan Am jetliner in flight. Death toll: 270
Germany, 1986 Bomb blasts disco popular with U.S. soldiers. Death toll: 2
Germany, 1985 Car bomb rocks U.S. military base. Death toll: 2
Spain, 1985 Bomb explodes near U.S. airbase. Death toll: 18
Greece, 1986 Bomb explodes aboard TWA jetliner. Death toll: 4
Italy and Austria, 1985 Gunmen attack airport check-in desks of U.S., Israeli airlines. Death toll: 16
Saudi Arabia, 1996 Truck bomb batters U.S. military base. Death toll: 19
United States, 2001 Plane hijackers destroy World Trade Center, slam Pentagon. Death toll: more than 4,000.
Lebanon, 1983 Car shatters housing for U.S. soldiers. Death toll: 241
Kenya and Tanzania, 1998 U.S. embassies bombed. Death toll: 200+
Yemen, 2000 Bomb blasts hole in destroyer USS Cole. Death toll: 17

INTERPRETING MAPS

Categorizing On what continents did Americans suffer the most attacks? On which continents did they suffer the least?

2 TEACH

Identifying Main Ideas As students read each subsection in the "A Day for Heroes" section, have them write one sentence that expresses the main idea of that subsection. Have the class share and discuss their sentences. Repeat this process for the sections titled "Behind the Hatred" and "War on All Fronts." **L1**

More About the Photos

Suicide Attackers The USS *Cole* and the World Trade Center attacks had something in common: both were committed by suicide attackers. **Ask:** **How does this fact make it difficult to prevent these attacks?**

Making Inferences The word *al-Qaeda* means "the base." Up until the emergence of al-Qaeda, large-scale terrorist networks had been funded by governments. Al-Qaeda was the first major terrorist network to be privately funded. **Ask:** **How has al-Qaeda affected the entire world? L2**

Closing in on America

ANSWER

The most attacks have occurred in Europe. No attacks have occurred in South America, Australia, and Antarctica.

Team-Teaching Activity

Sociology Invite a teacher to class who's knowledgeable about the role religion plays in some terrorist attacks. The teacher should also discuss how religion helps people in response to a crisis. A sociological perspective on the conditions under which religious fundamentalism thrives would be helpful to students. If the teacher has a specific knowledge of the role of religion in the lives of fundamentalist Muslims, encourage him or her to discuss this topic. With students' help, make a chart listing religious, political, and economic factors that might lead someone to commit a terrorist act. Find factors that may belong in more than one category or that have a cause-effect relationship with others. **L1**

EE6 The Uses of Geography: Standard 18

Recommended Internet Sites

www.un.org/terrorism
This United Nations Web site is titled "UN Action Against Terrorism." It contains UN statements and descriptions of current anti-terrorist actions.

usinfo.state.gov
This Web site is maintained by the U.S. Department of State and contains information on a broad range of issues, including terrorism, in addition to the U.S. government's response to terrorist activity.

www.pbs.org/americaresponds/educators.html
This site offers classroom resources and lesson plans in response to terrorist attacks.

EXPLORING THE ISSUES

ANSWERS

1. *Possible answers:* After World War II, many Americans felt the Jews deserved a homeland; Israel is the only democracy in the Middle East; Israel is an important ally in an unstable region.
2. *Possible answers:* Civilians typically do not expect to be attacked, so they are easy targets. Terrorism makes people fear that no one is safe.

TIME REPORTS

Behind the Hatred

What makes the United States the target of so much deadly anger? One answer is its support for Israel. Israel was founded in 1948. Soon afterwards, an Arab-Israeli war forced about 750,000 Palestinian Arabs from their homes.

Today many of those Palestinians live in refugee camps. So do their children and their grandchildren. Those 4 million Palestinians want a nation of their own. Israel has offered to exchange land for a promise of peace. But so far the Palestinians have rejected that offer. Many Muslims blame U.S. support for Israel for prolonging the Palestinians' suffering.

U.S. Troops in Saudi Arabia

Another source of anger is the presence of U.S. troops in Saudi Arabia. The Saudi government asked the United States to station troops there. But the holy cities of Makkah (Mecca) and Madinah (Medina) are in Saudi Arabia. To many Muslims, U.S. troops on Saudi soil are an insult to Islam.

To terrorist Osama bin Laden and his followers, the solution to these problems was violence. In 1996, he urged Muslims to kill U.S. troops in Saudi Arabia. In 1998, he called for attacks on American **civilians**. Civilians are people not in the armed forces or diplomatic services. By 2001, the death toll was more than 5,500 people.

The United States responded to September 11th with a determination and resolve bin Laden surely didn't expect. "Our war on terror begins with al-Qaeda," President George W. Bush said. "It will not end until every terrorist group of global reach has been found, stopped, and defeated."

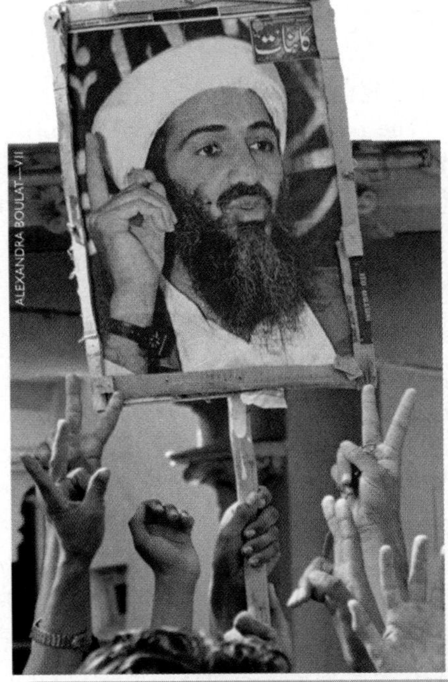

ALEXANDRA BOULAT—VII

▲ Fanatics hail terrorist Osama bin Laden in 2001.

EXPLORING THE ISSUES

1. **Drawing Conclusions** What are some reasons many Americans support Israel's presence in the Middle East?
2. **Making Inferences** Why are acts of terror against civilians often effective?

514

Critical Thinking Activity

Formulating an Opinion Tell students that Secretary-General Annan of the United Nations has stated, "To defeat terrorism, we need a sustained effort and broad strategy that unite all nations." **Ask:** **What do you think he means by this statement? Do you think that working through the United Nations is the best way to combat terrorism? Or, do you think it would be better for the countries that are actually attacked by terrorists to directly attack terrorism on their own?** Have students support their opinions with examples. After the class discussion, students should write a paragraph defending their position. **L2**

EE4 Human Systems: Standard 13

War on All Fronts

Americans were angry on September 11, 2001, as U.S. President George W. Bush spoke to the nation. "We will make no distinction," he said, "between those who committed these acts and those who harbor them."

He wasn't bluffing. The **Taliban** government of Afghanistan continued to protect Osama bin Laden. So in October the President ordered the U.S. military to attack Afghanistan and find him.

Aid for Children

The U.S. was not at war with the Afghani people, but with terrorists hiding in their country. During the attack, U.S. planes continually dropped shipments of food and medicine to the men, women, and children in the civilian population.

At the same time, the President held out an olive branch. The United States offered to stop its military action. But first the Afghanis had to turn bin Laden over to the United States.

Nations around the world backed America's actions. They promised to help the United States root out terrorism. Great Britain sent troops to Afghanistan to fight alongside U.S. forces.

Liberty and Security

At home, the United States opened still another front. Dozens of federal agencies stepped up their efforts to track down terrorists.

Do those agencies have enough power to fight terrorism? Some people don't think so. They want the U.S. Congress to make it easier to tap phones, intercept e-mail messages, and search homes.

Others think that's a bad idea. They fear that more powerful police forces would chip away at our **liberties**. Freedom of speech is one such liberty. The right to privacy is another.

The President urged Americans to protect those liberties. "We are in a fight for our principles," he said, "and our first responsibility is to live by them."

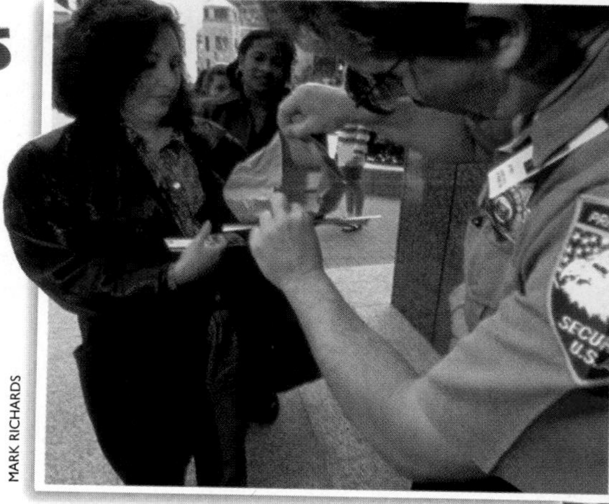

MARK RICHARDS

▲ **Safety checks help prevent terrorism. But the cost—less freedom—worries many Americans.**

EXPLORING THE ISSUE

1. **Analyzing Information** Shortly after September 11, 2001, President Bush said, "No one should be singled out for unfair treatment or unkind words because of their ethnic background or religious faith." What do you think he meant by that statement?
2. **Problem Solving** What liberties, if any, might you be willing to give up in order to feel safe?

Understanding Cause and Effect

Show several pictures of families, especially children, living in refugee camps. **Ask: Do you think these young people are more or less likely to grow up to become followers of terrorist leaders than young people in America? Why or why not?** If most student respond "yes," **Ask: Do you think the United States can do anything to prevent this from happening?** Encourage them to offer specific suggestions.

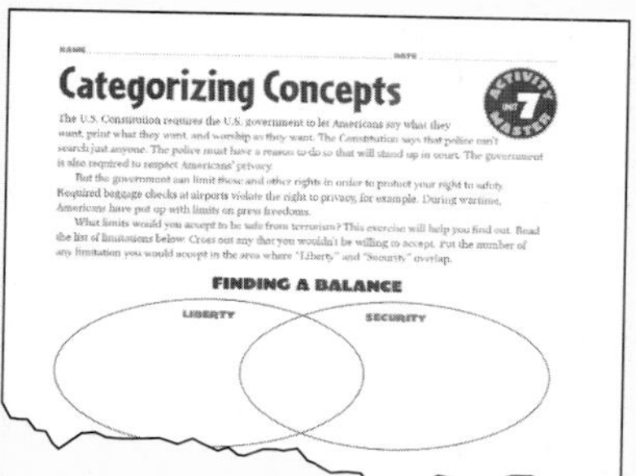

EXPLORING THE ISSUE

ANSWERS

1. Bush was concerned that Muslims and people of Middle Eastern descent might be targeted for abuse. He was telling the American people that such prejudice was wrong and the United States would not tolerate it.
2. Answers will vary, but might include freedom of speech, right to privacy, and freedom from illegal searches and seizures.

Interdisciplinary Activity

Art Have students create a work of art, such as a picture or sculpture, that embodies the qualities shown by American citizens after the September 11, 2001, terrorist attacks. Students may want to look at newspaper and magazine articles, television reports, or Web sites about that time to help them obtain ideas. Students can use any medium, such as watercolors, acrylic or oil paints, collage, and clay. Ask for volunteers to show their artwork to the class and explain why they chose that subject. The rest of the class should then be encouraged to describe their emotional response to the artwork. **L1**

EE4 Human Systems: Standard 10

Current Events Journal

Have students find first-person accounts of three or four heroic acts that occurred in response to a terrorist attack. The attacks do not have to be in the United States. The students should write a brief description of each act. They should also write a discussion of what they believe motivated the person, and how they might have acted under the same circumstances.

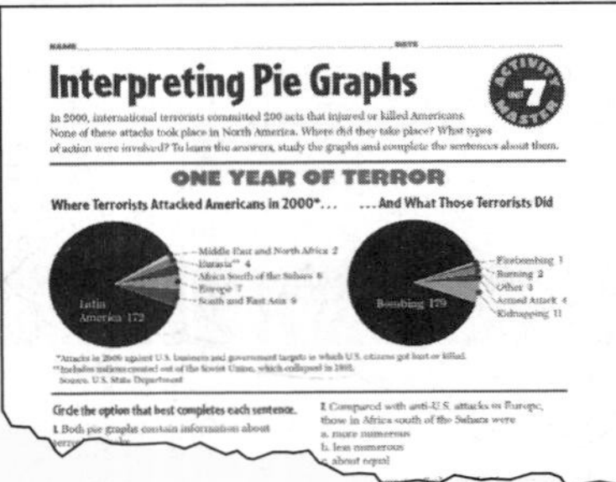

NAME ______ DATE ______

Interpreting Pie Graphs

ACTIVITY MASTER 7

In 2000, international terrorists committed 200 acts that injured or killed Americans. None of these attacks took place in North America. Where did they take place? What types of action were involved? To learn the answers, study the graphs and complete the sentences about them.

ONE YEAR OF TERROR

Where Terrorists Attacked Americans in 2000*...

Latin America 172
Middle East and North Africa 2
Eurasia** 4
Africa South of the Sahara 6
Europe 7
South and East Asia 9

...And What Those Terrorists Did

Bombing 179
Firebombing 1
Burning 2
Other 3
Armed Attack 4
Kidnapping 11

*Attacks in 2000 against U.S. business and government targets in which U.S. citizens got hurt or killed.
**Includes nations created out of the Soviet Union
Source: U.S. State Department

Circle the option that best completes each sentence.

1. Both pie graphs contain information about

2. Compared with anti-U.S. attacks in Europe, those in Africa south of the Sahara were
a. more numerous
b. less numerous
c. about equal

EXPLORING THE ISSUE

ANSWERS

1. Answers will vary. Talking with others can be helpful, especially talking with people who are determined not to let terrorists control their lives.
2. Answers will vary.

TIME REPORTS

Stopping Terrorism: What Can One Person Do?

The rescue workers who responded to the attacks on the World Trade Center and the Pentagon were true heroes. In the months that followed Americans honored them for their courage and sacrifice.

The response of Americans to tragedy showed the world the nation's hidden strengths—its people. Wherever they lived, Americans reacted. They gave blood. They held candlelight **vigils** to honor the victims. They flew flags to show their unity. They cut deeply into their budgets, contributing more than $200 million in the first week to help victims' families.

They all made it clear, as a girl from Ohio told TIME For Kids, that no terrorist can weaken the nation's spirit. "They bent steel," said Danielle, 12, of the World Trade Center murderers, "but they can't break the U.S."

Be a Local Hero

Wherever you live, you can help keep that spirit alive. And you can do it even years after the disasters of September 2001 took place.

Learn all you can about terrorism. Learn what it is, why it exists, and how people at all levels of government are fighting it.

Then join that fight any way you can. With posters and letters, report successful efforts to combat this evil. Raise money for groups that help out the victims of terrorism everywhere.

CHRIS USHER

▲ **Terrorist attacks in September 2001 trigger a burst of patriotism everywhere in America.**

Finally, refuse to give in to fear. Terrorists use fear as a weapon. If you can keep fear from changing your life, you will have taken a big bite out of terrorism.

One expert on fear, the novelist Stephen King, agreed. "If everybody continues working," he said, "they [the terrorists] don't win." ■

EXPLORING THE ISSUE

1. **Problem Solving** What might people do to stop the fear of terrorism from keeping them from doing what they want to do?
2. **Summarizing the Main Idea** Write a new title for this piece. Share it with your classmates. Explain why you think your title fits the story.

Your Government and You

After the September 11, 2001, terrorist attacks, the Office of Homeland Security was created to develop and implement a nationwide strategy to detect terrorist threats, prevent attacks from occurring, and execute the fastest possible recovery should an attack occur. The United States also has an Office of Counterterrorism (**www.state.gov/s/ct/**) that provides information and coordinates counterterrorist activities among U.S. governmental agencies and foreign governments. Print the Operation Enduring Freedom Overview for your students from that Web site (click "Coalition Against Terror" link, then "Fact Sheets" to get to the Overview link). Discuss the steps America has been taking in the "war on terrorism" and what the effects might be. **L2**

REVIEW AND ASSESS

UNDERSTANDING THE ISSUE

1. **Defining Key Terms** In your own words, define the following terms: *terrorism, hijacker, the Quran, the Pentagon, al-Qaeda, Taliban, liberty, security, principles, ideals,* and *vigil.*
2. **Writing to Inform** In a 300-word article, describe a terrorist act you heard or read about. Describe how you reacted when you heard about it.
3. **Writing to Persuade** What do you think Americans should know about terrorism? Put your answer in a 250-word letter to the editor of your local newspaper. Support your answer with facts. Use at least five of the terms listed above.

INTERNET RESEARCH ACTIVITY

4. Navigate to **www.libertyunite.org/kids.adp** to find out what kids are doing to help the victims of terrorism. Brainstorm ways you and your classmates can help, and send your ideas to **LibertyUnites@aol.com**.
5. Navigate to **www.terrorism.com/terrorism/links.shtml**. Scroll through the list of hyperlinks. Click on one or two that interest you. What do these sites teach you about terrorism? Put your answers in a list, under the title "What I Learned About Terrorism." Share your list with your classmates in a discussion about terrorism.

BEYOND THE CLASSROOM

6. **Study the map** on page 513. Research one of the terrorist attacks noted there. What does the attack tell you about the goals, thoughts, and methods terrorists have? Describe the attack and answer those questions in a brief oral report.

TERRY BARNER/SILVER IMAGE

▲ **Muslims mourn victims of the World Trade Center attack.**

7. **Visit your school or local library.** Research a country, such as Israel, Northern Ireland, or Bosnia where the people have suffered from terrorist attacks. Find out what programs have been started by groups or individuals to bring an end to the violence. Present your findings to the whole class.

FIGHTING TERRORISM: HOW FAR WOULD YOU GO?

What are Americans willing to do to fight terrorism? These pie graphs show what a TIME/CNN Poll found out.

To prevent terrorist attacks, would you favor or oppose the government doing each of the following?

	Favor	Oppose
1. Allow police to wire-tap phone conversations of suspected terrorists without a court's okay:	68%	29%
2. Let courts jail, for as long as they want, people suspected of links to terrorist groups:	59%	38%
3. Let police intercept e-mail messages sent by anyone in the United States and scan them for suspicious words or phrases:	55%	42%
4. Require everyone in the United States to carry an identification card issued by the Federal Government:	57%	41%
5. Let police stop people on the street and search them:	29%	69%

Source: TIME magazine, October 8, 2001; Gray slices indicate respondents who were not sure.

BUILDING GRAPH READING SKILLS

1. **Analyzing the Data** The U.S. Constitution bars the government from making "unreasonable searches and seizures" of citizens. Which of the graphs show how Americans think about this right? What's your thinking on this issue?
2. **Making Inferences** The U.S. Constitution bars the government from taking away a person's "life, liberty, or property" without a fair trial. What do most people who took part in this poll seem to think about this right? Why do you think they hold that view?

FOR UPDATES ON WORLD ISSUES GO TO www.timeclassroom.com/glencoe

517

TIME REPORTS

3 ASSESS

Have students take the Time Reports Quiz or do the Alternative Assessment project for this unit provided in the Teacher's Classroom Resources.

AIRPORT
WHERE DO YOU WISH TO TRAVEL TO?
SEPTEMBER 10th
Interpreting a

BUILDING GRAPH READING SKILLS

ANSWERS

1. graph #5; answers will vary
2. Most believe that when fighting terrorism the government should be able to violate our rights. Fifty-nine percent agreed that terrorist suspects should be jailed indefinitely. Many people are willing to give up liberties for greater security.

4 CLOSE

Ask students to write a paragraph starting with this topic sentence: *The best way that a democratic government can protect itself from terrorism is . . .*

Culminating Activity

To close this lesson, have students complete the Review and Assess section questions and activities above. Students should use classroom discussion, contextual clues, and their student dictionaries to write definitions for terms. Before assigning the Internet activities, it is recommended that you review your school district policy on student Internet use.

Focus on Debate

Mohandas Gandhi, who led the nonviolent fight for India's freedom, stated, "There is no way to peace. Peace is the way." Ask students what this statement means to them and how it relates to terrorism. Then have them debate the pros and cons of Gandhi's philosophy. **L2**

 **EE4 Human Systems: Standard 10**

Critical Thinking Skill

TEACH

Ask students to imagine that they have invited a new friend to visit them. Have them create a map of the route from the school to their home. Allow students a short time to make sketch maps. Then ask how many students made a mental picture of the route in order to create the map. Explain that the process of visualizing places and routes is called mental mapping. Direct students to read the skill and complete the practice questions. **L1**

Additional Skills Practice

1. **How would you create a map of the school?** *(Ask for volunteers to sketch their maps on the board.)*
2. **Why compare a map that you sketch to an actual map of the place?** *(to make any needed changes so it is accurate)*

Additional Skills Resources

 Chapter Skills Activity 19

 Building Geography Skills

GLENCOE TECHNOLOGY

 **Skillbuilder Interactive Workbook CD-ROM, Level 1**

This interactive CD-ROM reinforces student mastery of essential social studies skills.

Critical Thinking Skill

Mental Mapping

Think about how you get from place to place each day. In your mind you have a picture—or **mental map**—of your route. If necessary, you could probably create sketch maps like the one below of many familiar places.

Learning the Skill

To develop your mental mapping skills, follow these steps.

- When a country or city name is mentioned, find it on a map to get an idea of where it is and what is near it.
- Create a sketch map of it and include a compass rose to determine the cardinal directions.
- As you read or hear information about the place, try to picture where on your sketch you would fill in this information.
- Compare your sketch to an actual map of the place. Change your sketch if you need to, thus changing your mental map.

Practicing the Skill

Study the sketch map at the right. Picture yourself standing *in* the map, then answer the following questions.

1. If you were facing north, looking at the Chicago Cultural Center, what route would you take to reach the Chicago Harbor?
2. You are at the Sears Tower, one of the tallest buildings in the world. About how many miles would you have to walk to get to Medinah Temple?
3. If you met your friend at the cultural center, would it be too far to walk to the Art Institute? Should you take a taxi? Explain.

Applying the Skill

Think about your own neighborhood. Create a sketch map of it from your mental map. Which neighborhood streets or roads did you include? What are the three most important features on your map?

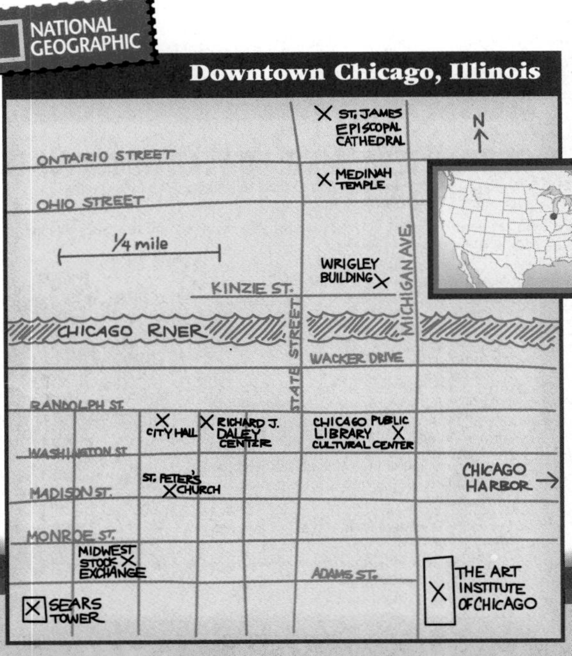

Practicing the Skill Answers

1. turn right and walk along Washington Street
2. about $1\frac{1}{4}$ miles
3. It would be easy to walk—the distance is only 3 blocks. There is no need to take a taxi.

Applying the Skill

Check students' mental maps for accuracy and to be sure they included at least three important features. Have students explain why they identified certain features as important.

Section 3

The Americans

Guide to Reading

Main Idea

The United States has attracted people from all over the world who have created a land of many cultures.

Terms to Know

- representative democracy
- federal republic
- amend
- ethnic group
- rural
- urban
- suburb

Reading Strategy

Create a diagram like this one. In each outer oval, write under the heading one fact about American society as it relates to the topic given.

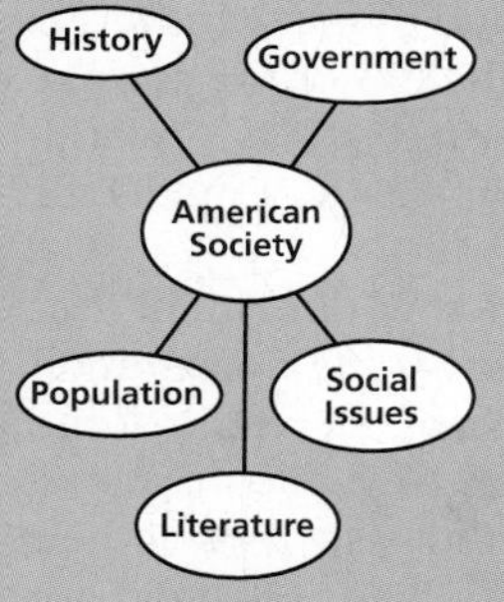

NATIONAL GEOGRAPHIC **Exploring Our World**

The United States has often been called a nation of immigrants. You might say that Elmhurst, New York, is the capital of this immigrant nation. (This area may have the greatest ethnic diversity in the country.) Elmhurst is a section of Queens, one of the boroughs of New York City. People from more than 120 different nations live in Elmhurst.

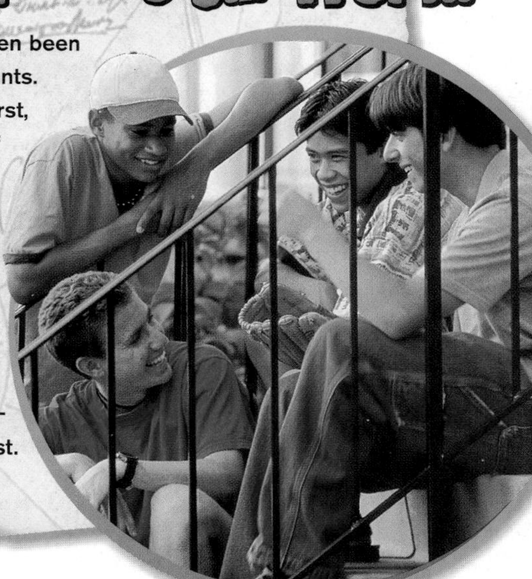

The United States is full of people from many different lands. What attracts people to the United States? One attraction is the freedom that Americans enjoy. Economic opportunity is another. The United States gives people in many other lands hope that they and their children can enjoy better lives.

A Rich History

The first Americans lived all over the continent. Over time, they developed different ways of life using local resources. Groups fished, planted corn and beans, or followed buffalo herds. Around A.D. 1500, Europeans began to explore the Americas. The raw materials they saw—forests, animal furs, and rich soils—soon led them to set up colonies, or overseas settlements that are tied to a parent country. The French built trading posts around the Great Lakes and interior river valleys. The Spanish built towns and missions in Florida and Georgia and fr

1 Focus

Section Objectives

1. Describe how the United States changed throughout its history.
2. Explain what form of government the United States has.
3. Identify what groups make up the American people.
4. Discuss what has influenced American culture.

BELLRINGER Skillbuilder Activity

Project transparency and have students answer questions.

This activity is also available as a blackline master.

Daily Focus Skills Transparency 19-3

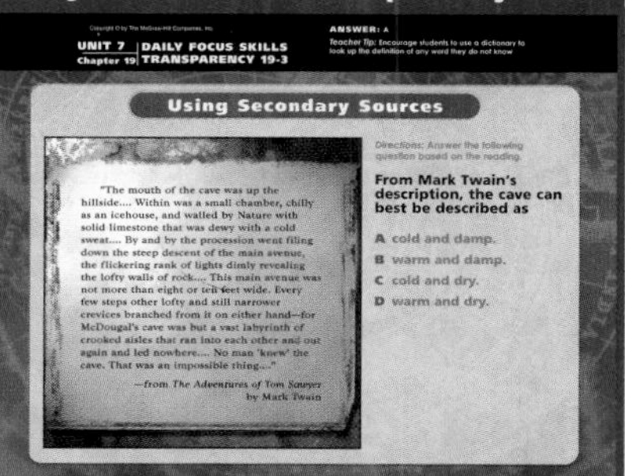

Copyright © by The McGraw-Hill Companies, Inc.

UNIT 7 Chapter 19 | DAILY FOCUS SKILLS TRANSPARENCY 19-3

ANSWER: A

Teacher Tip: Encourage students to use a dictionary to look up the definition of any word they do not know

Using Secondary Sources

"The mouth of the cave was up the hillside.... Within was a small chamber, chilly as an icehouse, and walled by Nature with solid limestone that was dewy with a cold sweat.... By and by the procession went filing down the steep descent of the main avenue, the flickering rank of lights dimly revealing the lofty walls of rock.... This main avenue was not more than eight or ten feet wide. Every few steps other lofty and still narrower crevices branched from it on either hand—for McDougal's cave was but a vast labyrinth of crooked aisles that ran into each other and out again and led nowhere.... No man 'knew' the cave. That was an impossible thing...."

—from *The Adventures of Tom Sawyer* by Mark Twain

Directions: Answer the following question based on the reading.

From Mark Twain's description, the cave can best be described as

A cold and damp.
B warm and damp.
C cold and dry.
D warm and dry.

Guide to Reading

Accessing Prior Knowledge Have students suggest the names of different ethnic restaurants. Then ask them why they think the United States has such a variety of foods.

Section Resources

Reproducible Masters

- Reproducible Lesson Plan 19-3
- Daily Lecture and Discussion Notes 19-3
- Guided Reading Activity 19-3
- Reading Essentials and Study Guide 19-3
- Section Quiz 19-3

Transparencies

- Daily Focus Skills Transparency 19-3

Multimedia

- Vocabulary PuzzleMaker Software
- Interactive Tutor Self-Assessment CD-ROM
- Presentation Plus! CD-ROM
- ExamView® Pro 3.0 Testmaker CD-ROM

Creating a Map Give students political maps of the United States. Have them write in the dates that each state entered the Union. Then have them color the states, grouping them by 1700s, 1800 to 1850, 1851 to 1900, and 1901 to today. Have them identify which period saw the most states enter the United States. *(1700s: 16; 1800–1850: 15; 1851–1900: 14: 1901–today: 5)* **L1**

Analyzing the Diagram

Answer
the legislative branch

Skills Practice
What are the two lawmaking bodies of the federal government? *(Senate and House of Representatives)*

Cultural Kaleidoscope

Spanish Settlements In 1565 the Spanish planted their first colony in what is today the United States, when Pedro Menéndez de Avilés founded a settlement at St. Augustine, Florida. In 1598, five years before the English settled in Jamestown, Virginia, the Spanish sent colonists to New Mexico. In 1610 they founded Santa Fe as the capital of this colony.

Branches of the United States Government

Analyzing the Diagram

The United States government has three main branches.

Government **Which branch makes the laws?**

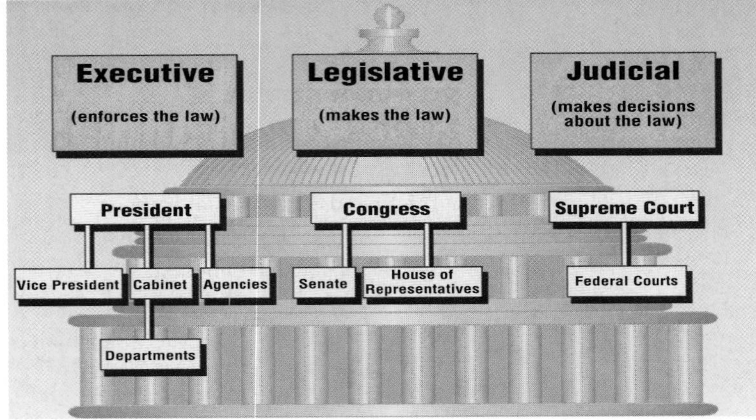

A Democratic Republic By the mid-1700s, the people living in the British colonies had started to see themselves as Americans. From 1775 to 1781, the new Americans fought a war that freed the colonies from British rule and formed a new country—the United States of America.

The United States is a **representative democracy,** in which voters choose leaders who make and enforce the laws for the benefit of the people they represent. The United States is also a **federal republic.** This means government is divided between national and state powers, with a president who leads the national government. As you can see from the chart above, the national government is divided into three branches.

A Living Document There are many different types of democracies, and you will be studying some of these in other units. One thing that most democracies have, however, is some kind of constitution, or document that identifies the rights and responsibilities of the people. The Constitution of the United States, written in 1787, is a world-famous document. It has been used by many countries as a model for their own constitutions.

There are many reasons for the success of this document, but experts believe that the most important reason is that the Constitution can be changed, when necessary, to meet the changing needs of the country's people. Through a process called **amending,** the people of the United States have a peaceful way to change the basic laws of their government. U.S. citizens can adapt their laws to situations that did not exist when the original Constitution was written. Americans can also correct injustices that arise from unequal treatment of people. Examples include the Thirteenth Amendment, which abolished slavery, and the Fifteenth Amendment, which gave the right to vote to all men regardless of color or race. (Sometimes, it took more than one

Meeting Special Needs

Visual/Spatial Students who learn best from visual aids may benefit from the following exercise. Have students tie the illustrations to text by finding sentences or paragraphs that relate to each picture, map, or diagram in the section. Then have them compare what they learn from the illustrations with what they learn from the text. **L1**

Refer to *Inclusion for the Middle School Social Studies Classroom Strategies and Activities* in the TCR.

amendment to correct the problem. The Nineteenth Amendment gave the right to vote to women also.) The Constitution is a remarkable document that grows with the needs of the country.

A Period of Growth From 1800 to 1900, the United States grew from the 13 states along the Atlantic coast to include 45 states that reached to the Pacific Ocean. The population boomed as millions of people settled here from other lands. They cleared forests, farmed, and often fought with Native Americans who were being pushed out of the way. Farmers grew corn in the Midwest and cotton in the South. Some people mined gold and silver in the Rocky Mountains and California.

In 1861, the nation experienced a crisis. Several Southern states seceded, or withdrew, from the national government over issues of slavery and states' rights. For four years, the North and the South fought a bitter civil war. In the end, the Southern states were brought back into the Union, and slavery was abolished. The Civil War did more than end slavery. It also launched the country into a period of great industrial and economic growth, the Industrial Revolution. Factories sprang up, especially in the Northeast and Midwest. Railroads reached out to bring faraway places into a national marketing system. This economic growth attracted another great wave of immigrants.

A World Leader During the early 1900s, the United States became one of the leading economies in the world. Automobiles rolled off assembly lines, electricity became common, and other technologies—the telephone and radio, for example—entered daily life.

The world plunged into two World Wars in the first half of the twentieth century. The United States took part in these wars. Our country's leaders urged the world's people to fight for freedom. American factories built tanks and airplanes, while American soldiers helped win the wars.

After World War II, the United States enjoyed great influence around the world. American companies shipped their products to all continents.

NATIONAL GEOGRAPHIC On Location

Ellis Island

In 1900, these immigrants waited to leave Ellis Island, New York, where they had been allowed to enter the United States.

Movement **What are some reasons people immigrate to the United States?**

Cooperative Learning Activity

Time Line Organize students into groups and assign each group a time period in American history: pre-Columbian, colonial, Revolution to early 1800s, nineteenth century, and twentieth century. Have students use several sheets of butcher paper to construct a time line running along one or more walls of the classroom. Direct groups to research their time period and select 10 important events from that period to enter on the time line. Have group representatives write their selections in the correct places on the line. Ask them to add annotations explaining their entries. **L1**

EE6 The Uses of Geography: Standard 17

2 TEACH

Analyzing Information

Have students define *culture region.* Write the following headings: "Cultures," "Homes," "Standard of Living," and "Recreation." Call on volunteers to identify characteristics of American people living in cities, suburbs, and rural areas under each heading. List the responses under the appropriate heading. Use this information to lead a discussion of why it is so difficult to describe a "typical American." **L1**

Daily Lecture Notes 19-3

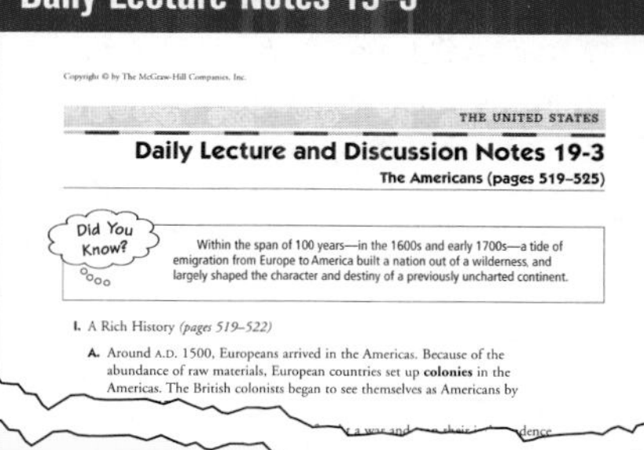

THE UNITED STATES

Daily Lecture and Discussion Notes 19-3

The Americans (pages 519–525)

Did You Know? Within the span of 100 years—in the 1600s and early 1700s—a tide of emigration from Europe to America built a nation out of a wilderness, and largely shaped the character and destiny of a previously uncharted continent.

I. A Rich History (pages 519–522)

A. Around A.D. 1500, Europeans arrived in the Americas. Because of the abundance of raw materials, European countries set up **colonies** in the Americas. The British colonists began to see themselves as Americans by

More About the Photo

Ellis Island From 1892 to 1954, over 12 million immigrants entered the United States through the portal of Ellis Island, a small island in New York Harbor. Ellis Island is located within the shadow of the Statue of Liberty.

Caption Answer freedom, economic opportunity, the hope of enjoying a better life

Chapter 19

Section 3, pages 519–525

Conducting Interviews

Have students interview an adult who immigrated to the United States. Encourage them to prepare a list of questions in advance. Examples of questions include the following: When did you or your ancestors come to the United States? Why did they come? From where did they come? What changes did they face in their new country? After they have completed their interviews, have students present their findings to the class. Students' results could be compiled in a class booklet called "Coming to America." **L2 ELL**

Reading Check Answer

After World War II, American companies shipped their products to all continents. American leaders worked to establish democracy and free enterprise in other countries.

Applying Map Skills

Answers

1. New York City, Chicago, Los Angeles, San Francisco, Boston, Philadelphia
2. Check answers for accuracy.

Skills Practice

In which region of the country do you find the highest population density? *(Northeast)*

American leaders worked to establish democracy and free enterprise in other countries. American culture spread around the globe.

At home, however, tensions existed among groups within American society. Many of the Americans who had fought in the two World Wars or had taken care of the home front were women, African Americans, Hispanic Americans, and Native Americans. After World War II, these groups became more active in seeking equal rights. Many people, including such leaders as Martin Luther King, Jr., developed methods that led to civil change. The poems on page 526 describe two views of Americans struggling to be accepted.

Reading Check **How did a strong economy in the U.S. help spread American culture?**

One Out of Many

About 285 million people live in the United States, making it the third most populous country in the world after China and India. Compared with people in most other countries, Americans enjoy a

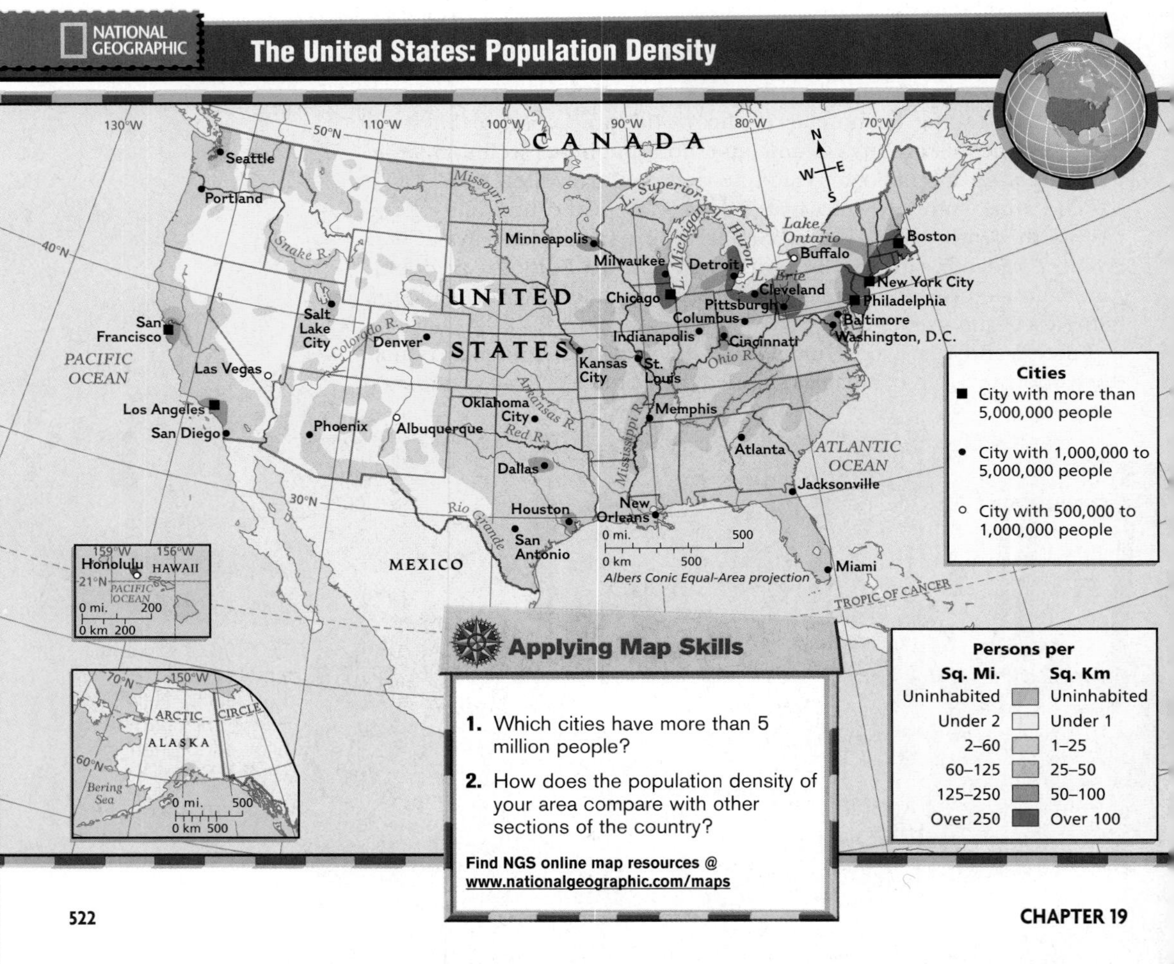

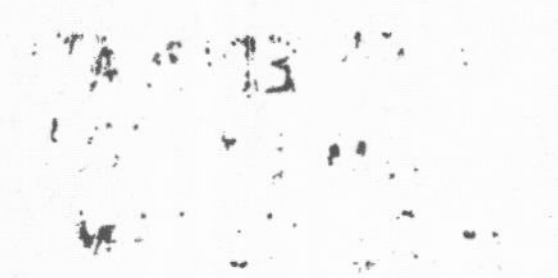

Content Background

Natural Disasters Severe weather in recent years has produced massive wildfires in the West, devastating hurricanes in the Southeast, mudslides along the Pacific, flooding on the Plains, and tornadoes in Florida. In addition, earthquakes have struck California, and a massive volcano erupted in Washington within the past two decades. These disasters have caused billions of dollars of damage—but cost very few lives. In an average year, fewer than 350 people die from natural disasters. In comparison, 42,000 Americans die each year from motor vehicle accidents, and more than 740,000 die from heart disease. **Ask: How do people adapt to environments prone to disasters such as an earthquake or hurricane?**

U.S. Population by Ethnic Groups

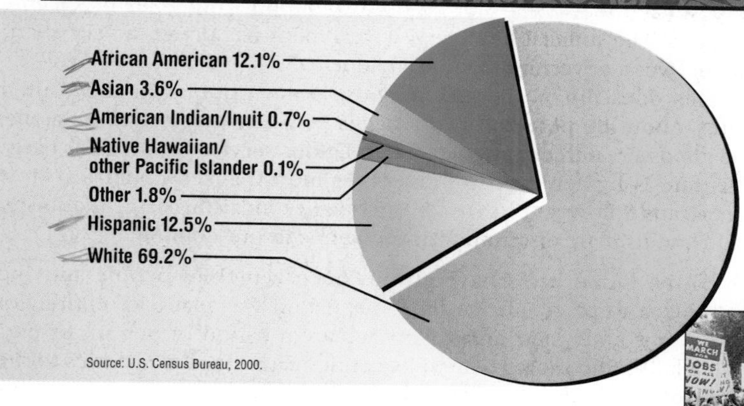

Analyzing the Graph

There are six main ethnic groups in the United States.

Culture **What percentage of the population is made up of Asians?**

▲ **The African American ethnic group has struggled to achieve equality with other Americans.**

very high standard of living. Americans, on the average, can expect to live about 76 years. Medical advances help people live longer than their grandparents could expect to live.

Almost three-fourths of the people in our country are descended from European ethnic groups. An **ethnic group** is a group of people who share a culture, language, or history. African American ethnic groups form about 12 percent of the population. Hispanics, who trace their heritages to the countries of Latin America and Spain, are the fastest-growing ethnic group. Today, many immigrants to the United States come from China, India, other Asian countries, and the Pacific Islands. The smallest ethnic groups have lived in the country the longest—Native Americans who live in Alaska.

Language The official language of the United States is English, but you can hear many different languages spoken on American streets. One of the concerns about language has centered around how to teach children who come to school not knowing English. Schools play an important role in developing good citizens. Learning a common language, sharing in national holidays, and being taught together with children from different countries help to create a feeling of patriotism and belonging. People who are against teaching immigrant children in their native languages believe that bilingual education discourages that sense of being an American. Other people think that it is just as important to preserve the culture and language of the immigrants, and that it is better for the students to learn in their own language, at least for some period of time. This debate has not been settled to most people's satisfaction one way or the other. It is likely that the debate will continue for years to come.

Religion Religion has always been an important influence on American life. One of the first laws passed by the new country stated that "Congress shall make no laws respecting an establishment of

Chapter 19

Section 3, pages 519–525

Analyzing the Graph

Answer
3.6 percent

Skills Practice
What is the smallest ethnic group in the United States? *(Native Hawaiian/Pacific Islanders)*

Guided Reading Activity 19-3

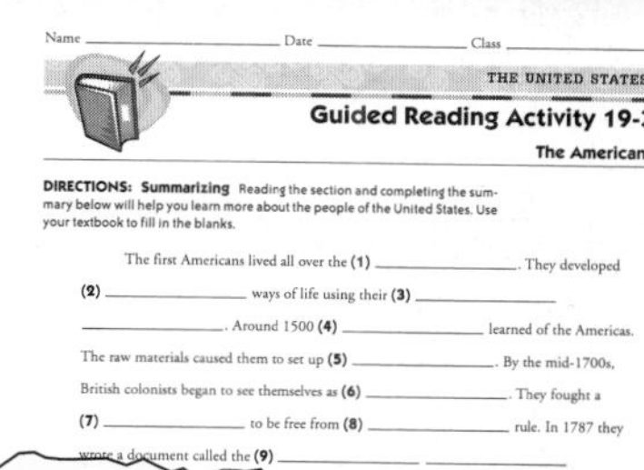
Name ______ Date ______ Class ______

THE UNITED STATES

Guided Reading Activity 19-3

The Americans

DIRECTIONS: Summarizing Reading the section and completing the summary below will help you learn more about the people of the United States. Use your textbook to fill in the blanks.

The first Americans lived all over the **(1)** ______. They developed **(2)** ______ ways of life using their **(3)** ______ ______. Around 1500 **(4)** ______ learned of the Americas. The raw materials caused them to set up **(5)** ______. By the mid-1700s, British colonists began to see themselves as **(6)** ______. They fought a **(7)** ______ to be free from **(8)** ______ rule. In 1787 they wrote a document called the **(9)** ______ ... that set up a type of

Interdisciplinary Connections

History The building of the transcontinental railroad in the 1860s opened up much of the West for settlement. The Union Pacific Railroad, which began in California, hired immigrant laborers, mostly from China, to lay track. Thousands of Chinese came to the United States to join this work.

Cooperative Learning Activity

Role Playing Assign student groups an ethnic group or minority that has had to fight for equal rights or been the victim of discrimination. Some possibilities are African Americans, Native Americans, Hispanics, Asians, Middle Eastern people, various religious groups, handicapped people, and women. Groups should research the history of their subject: examples of prejudice, significant events in the fight for equality or justice, important leaders. Each member of the group should write a short speech as if they were a member of the minority or one of its leaders, covering different aspects of their group's history. Have students make their speeches to the rest of the class. **L1**

EE4 Human Systems: Standard 13

Cultural Kaleidoscope

Los Angeles Los Angeles is one of the most racially and ethnically diverse cities in the United States. About 40 percent of the people in Los Angeles are from Spanish-speaking countries, 37 percent are white, 13 percent are African American, and 10 percent are Asian. There are more people of Mexican, Chinese, Taiwanese, Korean, and Philippine backgrounds in Los Angeles than in any other city in the United States.

Reading Check Answer

Hispanic ethnic groups

3 Assess

Assign Section 3 Assessment as homework or an in-class activity.

Have students use the Interactive Tutor Self-Assessment CD-ROM to review Section 19–3.

Section Quiz 19–3

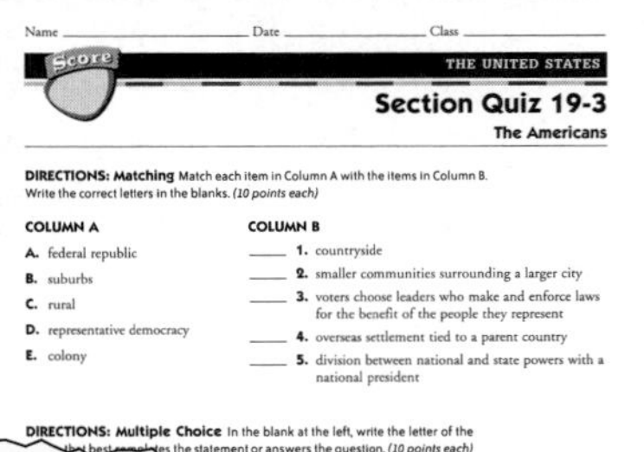

Name ______ Date ______ Class ______

Score | THE UNITED STATES

Section Quiz 19-3

The Americans

DIRECTIONS: Matching Match each item in Column A with the items in Column B. Write the correct letters in the blanks. *(10 points each)*

COLUMN A	COLUMN B
A. federal republic	____ **1.** countryside
B. suburbs	____ **2.** smaller communities surrounding a larger city
C. rural	____ **3.** voters choose leaders who make and enforce laws for the benefit of the people they represent
D. representative democracy	____ **4.** overseas settlement tied to a parent country
E. colony	____ **5.** division between national and state powers with a national president

DIRECTIONS: Multiple Choice In the blank at the left, write the letter of the ... es the statement or answers the question. *(10 points each)*

Rights and Responsibilities

The Constitution of the United States grants citizens certain rights. Many of those rights, such as freedom of religion and speech, are listed in the Bill of Rights. Along with our rights as citizens, however, we also have responsibilities. In the United States, everyone has a right to free public education. Attending school so that we will be informed and effective citizens is one of our responsibilities. Obeying school rules and local state laws is one of our most important responsibilities.

religion. . . ." In other words, this law said that the government could not say which religion people should follow. It also said that public or taxpayer money should not be used to support the goals of specific religions. The judicial branch of government has drawn a very sharp line between government and religion.

This does not mean that religion is not popular in the United States. About 80 percent of Americans consider themselves religious, and almost 50 percent attend some religious service on a regular basis. This rate is higher than in most other industrialized countries. Most Americans follow some form of Christianity. Judaism, Islam, Buddhism, and Hinduism are also important religions in our country.

Mobility Americans have always been a mobile people, moving from place to place. At one time, our nation was made up entirely of **rural,** or countryside, areas. Now we are a nation of **urban,** or city, dwellers. To find more room to live, Americans move from cities to the **suburbs,** or smaller communities surrounding a larger city. They also move from one region to another to seek a better climate or better jobs. Since the 1970s, the fastest-growing areas in the country have been in the South and Southwest—often called the Sunbelt.

Security Americans normally feel safe in their own country. After the terrorists attacks of September 11, 2001, this feeling of security was endangered. President Bush responded by creating the **Office of Homeland Security** on October 8, 2001. This office coordinates all government agencies fighting terrorism. In late October, Congress also passed a new anti-terrorism law to help police to track down terrorists.

Soon after the September 11 attacks, terrorists sent letters containing **anthrax**—a dangerous type of bacteria—to government offices and the news media. This kind of attack is called *bioterrorism.* Bioterrorism is the use of living organisms, such as bacteria or viruses, as weapons. The anthrax infected 17 people, including several postal workers. Five people died, and thousands more were given antibiotics as a safety measure. To deal with bioterrorism, the government created the **Office of Public Health Preparedness** and collected medicine in case of another attack.

Reading Check What ethnic groups are the fastest growing?

American Culture

American artists and writers have developed distinctly American styles. The earliest American artists used materials from their environments to create works of art. Native Americans carved wooden masks or made beautiful designs on pottery from clay found in their areas. Later artists were attracted to the beauty of the American land. Winslow Homer painted the stormy waters of the North Atlantic. Georgia O'Keeffe painted the colorful cliffs and deserts of the Southwest. Thomas Eakins painted scenes of city life.

Two themes are common to American literature. One theme focuses on the rich diversity of the people in the United States. The

Team-Teaching Activity

Language Arts Work with a foreign language teacher to help students learn a few common words in several different languages used in the United States. Words might include those for "hello," "goodbye," "dinner," and "friend." Languages could include Spanish, German, Italian, Chinese, Korean, Hindi, and Vietnamese, among others. If any students speak a language other than English at home, you might ask them to teach words from their language. **Ask: Why is it important to learn another language? L1 ELL**

EE4 Human Systems: Standard 10

poetry of Langston Hughes and the novels of Toni Morrison portray the triumphs and sorrows of African Americans. The novels of Amy Tan examine the lives of Chinese Americans. Oscar Hijuelos and Sandra Cisneros write about the country's Hispanics.

A second theme focuses on the landscape and history of particular regions. Mark Twain's books tell about life along the Mississippi River in the mid-1800s. Nathaniel Hawthorne wrote about the people of New England. Willa Cather and Laura Ingalls Wilder portrayed the struggles people faced in settling the Great Plains. William Faulkner examined life in the South.

Sports and Recreation Many Americans spend their leisure time at home, watching television, playing video games, or using a computer. Many also pursue active lives outdoors. They bike and hike, ski and skate, shoot baskets and kick soccer balls. Many enjoy spectator sports such as baseball and football. Stock-car races and rodeos also attract large crowds. Millions each year travel to national parks, or areas set aside to protect wilderness and wildlife and to offer recreation.

✓Reading Check **What are two common themes in American literature?**

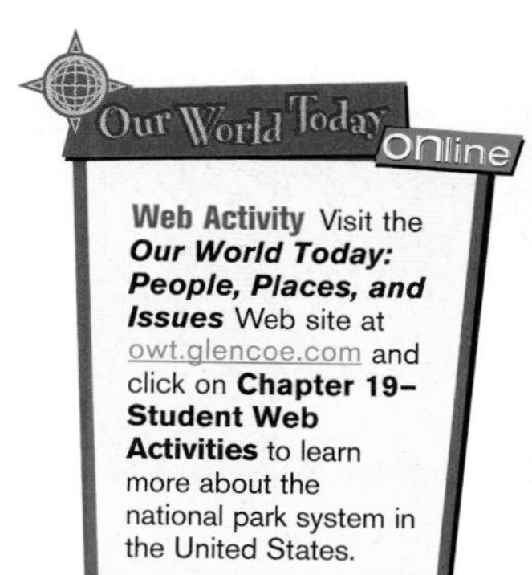

Web Activity Visit the ***Our World Today: People, Places, and Issues*** Web site at owt.glencoe.com and click on **Chapter 19–Student Web Activities** to learn more about the national park system in the United States.

Section 3 Assessment

Defining Terms

1. **Define** representative democracy, federal republic, amend, ethnic group, rural, urban, suburb.

Recalling Facts

2. **History** When was the war to free the colonies fought?
3. **History** Give two reasons people from other countries are attracted to the United States.
4. **Culture** What theme do the works of Langston Hughes and Toni Morrison share?

Critical Thinking

5. **Drawing Conclusions** Because the United States is a nation of immigrants, bilingual education is an issue. How would you resolve the issue of educating non-English-speaking students? Would you help these students preserve their native language and culture, or would you immerse these students in English-language education? Explain your reasoning.
6. **Drawing Conclusions** Why did the United States take part in two World Wars during the first half of the twentieth century?

Graphic Organizer

7. **Organizing Information** Create a diagram like the one below. At the tops of the three arrows, complete the diagram by listing three reasons that Americans today are moving more frequently than ever.

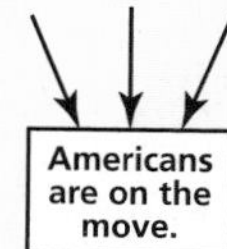

Applying Social Studies Skills

8. **Analyzing Maps** According to the population density map on page 522, what are the two largest cities in the northwest United States?

Section 3 Assessment

1. The terms are defined in the Glossary.
2. 1775–1781
3. *Possible answers:* freedom from persecution for beliefs or ethnicity, economic opportunity, the hope of enjoying a better life
4. the triumphs and sorrows of African Americans
5. Students' responses will vary. Ask them to support their opinions with historic and sociological facts.
6. Students' answers will vary but should be supported by historic facts.
7. to find more room to live, to seek a better climate, to find better jobs
8. Seattle and Portland

Objectives, goals, and answers to the Student Web Activity can be found in the Web Activity Lesson Plan at owt.glencoe.com

✓ Reading Check Answer

the rich diversity of the people; the landscape and history of regions

Reteach

Have students prepare an outline of the section.

Reading Essentials and Study Guide 19-3

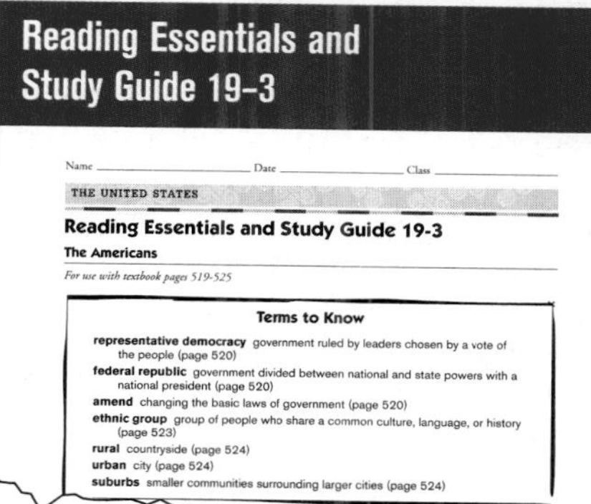

Name ______ Date ______ Class ______

THE UNITED STATES

Reading Essentials and Study Guide 19-3

The Americans

For use with textbook pages 519-525

Terms to Know

representative democracy government ruled by leaders chosen by a vote of the people (page 520)
federal republic government divided between national and state powers with a national president (page 520)
amend changing the basic laws of government (page 520)
ethnic group group of people who share a common culture, language, or history (page 523)
rural countryside (page 524)
urban city (page 524)
suburbs smaller communities surrounding larger cities (page 524)

Enrich

Have students create a poster that protests against intolerance.

4 CLOSE

Have students write a paragraph titled "What It Means to Be an American."

TEACH

Native American music and jazz, which influenced the work of Langston Hughes, both have strong rhythms. Play a selection of Native American music and a short jazz instrumental. **Ask:** **How do the two musical styles compare?** *(Possible answer: Native American music has simpler instrumentation.)* **L2**

More About the Poets

Simon Ortiz is an Acoma, one of the Pueblo peoples of the Southwest. His books include *A Good Journey* and *From Sand Creek.*

Langston Hughes first began writing poetry in high school. He became one of the leading figures of the Harlem Renaissance of the 1920s. He published many books, including collections of poems and short stories, plays, novels, essays, and two autobiographical works.

Interdisciplinary Connections

Literature Have students write their own poem about the experience of living in the United States. Encourage them to share their poems with the class.

Making Connections

CULTURE | GOVERNMENT | PEOPLE | TECHNOLOGY

Americans All

Native Americans and African Americans endured many years of injustice. Even so, the pride and determination of these Americans remained strong. Read the poems by Native American poet Simon J. Ortiz and African American poet Langston Hughes to see how they express these feelings.

▲ Picking cotton near Dallas, Texas, 1907

Survival This Way
by Simon J. Ortiz (1941–)

Survival, I know how this way.
This way, I know.
It rains.
Mountains and canyons and plants
grow.
We travelled this way,
gauged our distance by stories
and loved our children.
We taught them
to love their births.
We told ourselves over and over
again, "We shall survive
this way."

▲ Native Americans on the Great Plains, 1891

I, Too
by Langston Hughes (1902–1967)

I, too, sing America.

I am the darker brother.
They send me to eat in the kitchen
When company comes,
But I laugh,
And eat well,
And grow strong.

Tomorrow,
I'll be at the table
When company comes.
Nobody'll dare
Say to me,
"Eat in the kitchen,"
Then.

Besides,
They'll see how beautiful I am
And be ashamed—

I, too, am America.

Making the Connection

1. How does the poem "Survival This Way" tell how Native Americans feel about their children?
2. What does Langston Hughes mean by the phrase "I, too, sing America"?
3. **Making Comparisons** In what way do both poems convey a message of hope?

Making the Connection

1. *Possible answer:* With the lines "We taught them to love their births," Ortiz explains that they try to instill in their children a pride of their heritage to help them survive.
2. *Possible answer:* He is saying that even though the white majority often ignores African Americans, they also are beautiful Americans who have something to say about living in the United States.
3. *Possible answer:* The Ortiz poem affirms that Native Americans will survive and be proud of their heritage. The Hughes poem speaks of African Americans growing stronger, having a seat at the table, and being recognized.

Reading Review

Section 1 A Vast, Scenic Land

Terms to Know
- contiguous
- megalopolis
- coral reef

Main Idea

The United States has a great variety of landforms and climates.

✓ **Region** The United States has five main physical regions: the Coastal Plains, the Appalachian Mountains, the Interior Plains, the Mountains and Basins region, and the Pacific Coast. Alaska and Hawaii make up two additional regions.

✓ **History** Forty-eight of the United States are contiguous, joined together inside a common boundary between the Atlantic and Pacific Oceans.

✓ **Economics** The Central Lowlands area is well suited to agriculture, as are western coastal valleys.

✓ **Place** The high Rocky Mountains have a ridge called the Continental Divide, which separates rivers that flow east from rivers that flow west.

Section 2 An Economic Leader

Terms to Know
- free enterprise system
- fossil fuel
- landfill
- recycling
- free trade

Main Idea

The powerful United States economy runs on abundant resources and the hard work of Americans.

✓ **Economics** Because of many natural resources and a hardworking labor force, the United States has the world's most productive economy.

✓ **Economics** Service industries contribute the most to the American economy, followed by manufacturing, agriculture, and mining.

✓ **Economics** The economy of the United States faces many challenges in the twenty-first century. Some of those challenges include cleaning up pollution and trash.

✓ **Economics** Creativity and hard work are needed to continue to develop new technologies and help the American economy grow.

Section 3 The Americans

Terms to Know
- representative democracy
- federal republic
- amend
- ethnic group
- rural
- urban
- suburb

Main Idea

The United States has attracted people from all over the world who have created a land of many cultures.

✓ **Culture** The American people are immigrants or the descendants of immigrants who came from all over the world.

✓ **Government** The United States has a representative democratic government with power shared by the states and the national government.

✓ **Culture** Ethnic groups in America are descendants of five main peoples: Europeans, Africans, Hispanics, Asians and Pacific Islanders, and Native Americans.

✓ **Culture** American arts celebrate the country's ethnic and regional diversity.

Reading Review

Use the Chapter 19 Reading Review to preview, review, condense, or reteach the chapter.

Preview/Review

Use the Terms to Know lists to help students review and study.

Activity Have students create a quiz in which 10 terms from the chapter are to be matched to their definitions. Then have them exchange quizzes with another student and take the quiz their partners prepared.

Vocabulary PuzzleMaker Software reinforces the vocabulary terms used in Chapter 19.

The Interactive Tutor Self-Assessment CD-ROM allows students to review Chapter 19 content.

Condense

Have students read the Chapter 19 summary statements.

Chapter 19 Guided Reading Activities

Chapter 19 Audio Program

Reteach

Reteaching Activity 19

Chapter 19 Reading Essentials and Study Guide

Chapter Culminating Activity

Making Comparisons Ask students if they have friends or relatives living in another section of the country. Ask for volunteers to share descriptions of life in these areas. List their answers under the name of the location. Group the descriptions under specific characteristics: physical, people, cultural, etc. Then have the class compare these details to life in their own region. Afterwards, ask your students to find information about a part of the United States that they've never been to, but would like to visit. Have them write a paragraph describing what that area offers that is not available in their own location. **L1**

EE2 Places and Regions: Standard 6

Assessment and Activities

GLENCOE TECHNOLOGY

MindJogger Videoquiz
Use MindJogger to review the Chapter 19 content.

Available in VHS.

Using Key Terms

1.	c	6.	h
2.	g	7.	d
3.	e	8.	i
4.	a	9.	f
5.	b	10.	j

Reviewing the Main Ideas

11. The United States has an average cooler climate than Mexico and an average warmer climate than Canada.
12. the Coastal Plains, the Appalachian Mountains, the Interior Plains, the Mountains and Basins, and the Pacific Coast
13. Boston, New York City, Philadelphia, Baltimore, and Washington, D.C.
14. United States, Mexico, and Canada; North American Free Trade Agreement (NAFTA)
15. free enterprise
16. They are getting higher and higher because Americans are generating huge amounts of trash.
17. The Constitution can be changed, when necessary, to meet the changing needs of the country's people.
18. Hispanic
19. The South and the Southwest

Chapter 19 Assessment and Activities

Using Key Terms

Match the terms in Part A with their definitions in Part B.

A.

1. contiguous
2. megalopolis
3. free enterprise system
4. fossil fuel
5. suburb
6. amend
7. recycling
8. free trade
9. ethnic group
10. representative democracy

B.

a. oil, natural gas, and coal
b. smaller community surrounding a city
c. areas joined inside a common boundary
d. reusing materials
e. limited government control over the economy
f. group of people who share a common culture, language, and history
g. huge urban area
h. peaceful way to change laws
i. goods flow freely between countries
j. voters choose government leaders

Reviewing the Main Ideas

Section 1 A Vast, Scenic Land

11. **Region** How does the climate of the United States compare to those of Mexico and Canada?
12. **Region** What are the five main physical regions of the U.S.?
13. **Place** What cities make up the huge urban area along the East Coast of the United States?

Section 2 An Economic Leader

14. **History** What countries are part of the free trade agreement that took effect in 1994? What is the agreement called?
15. **Economics** What type of economic system does the United States have?
16. **Human/Environment Interaction** What is happening to America's landfills?

Section 3 The Americans

17. **Government** What is the most important reason for the success of the Constitution?
18. **Culture** Which ethnic groups are growing the fastest in the United States?
19. **Place** Which parts of the United States have the fastest-growing populations?

The United States

Place Location Activity

On a separate sheet of paper, match the letters on the map with the numbered places listed below.

1. Rocky Mountains
2. Mississippi River
3. Appalachian Mountains
4. Washington, D.C.
5. Chicago
6. Lake Superior
7. Ohio River
8. Gulf of Mexico
9. Texas
10. Los Angeles

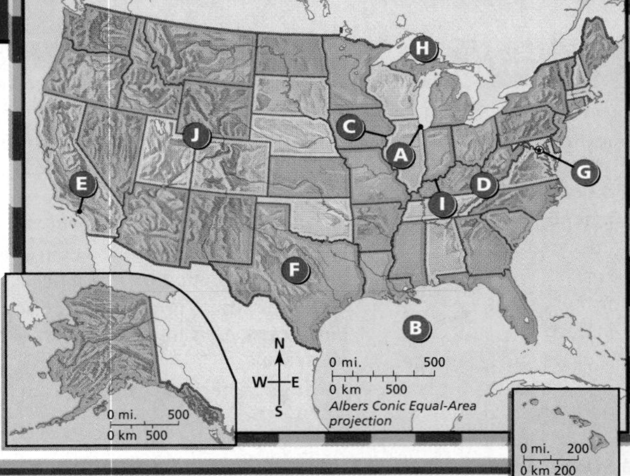

Place Location Activity

1.	J	6.	H
2.	C	7.	I
3.	D	8.	B
4.	G	9.	F
5.	A	10.	E

Critical Thinking

20. Flat land and fertile soil have made farming profitable. Its rivers are navigable, allowing Midwestern cities to become centers of trade. The Great Lakes also allow easy passage of shipping trade. Abundant mining resources have made many cities important manufacturing centers.
21. Answers will vary. Students should place facts from the textbook in the appropriate spaces.

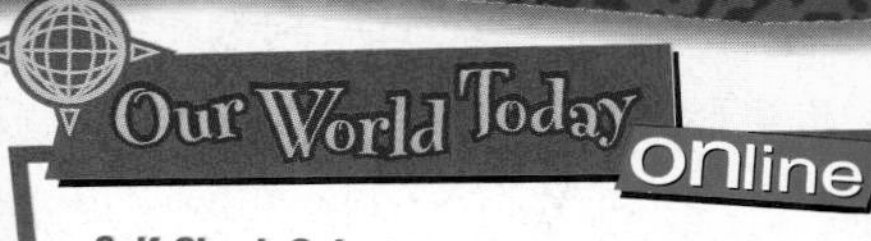

Self-Check Quiz Visit the ***Our World Today: People, Places, and Issues*** Web site at owt.glencoe.com and click on **Chapter 19–Self-Check Quizzes** to prepare for the Chapter Test.

Critical Thinking

20. **Understanding Cause and Effect** What physical features of the Interior Plains have affected the economy of that region?
21. **Categorizing Information** Create a diagram like the one below. In the outer ovals, write two facts about the United States under each heading.

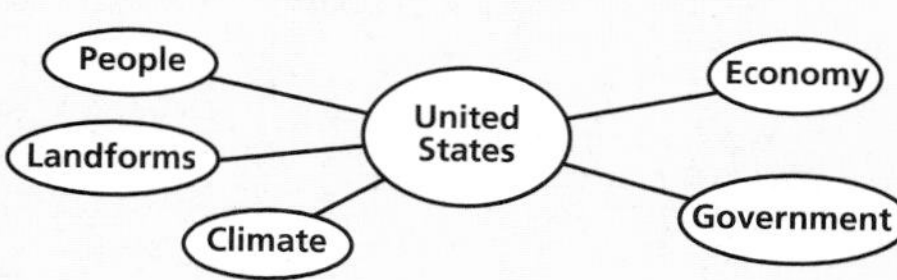

Current Events Journal

22. **Writing a Paragraph** Write a paragraph describing the recycling efforts of your school and community. Explain how you can help with these efforts.

Mental Mapping Activity

23. **Focusing on the Region** Create a simple outline map of the United States. Refer to the map on page 503, and then label the following:
    - Appalachian Mountains
    - Great Lakes
    - Alaska
    - Rocky Mountains
    - Hawaii
    - Mississippi River
    - Pacific Ocean
    - Atlantic Ocean
    - Gulf of Mexico
    - Great Plains

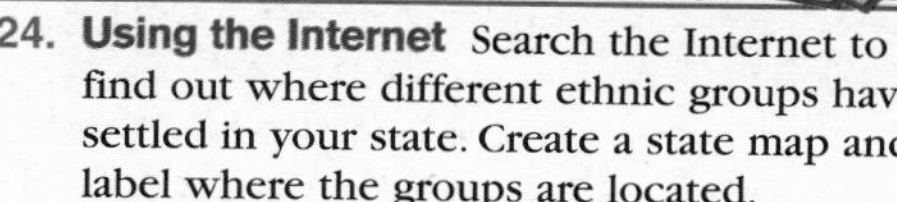

Technology Skills Activity

24. **Using the Internet** Search the Internet to find out where different ethnic groups have settled in your state. Create a state map and label where the groups are located.

The Princeton Review

Standardized Test Practice

Directions: Study the graph, and then answer the following questions.

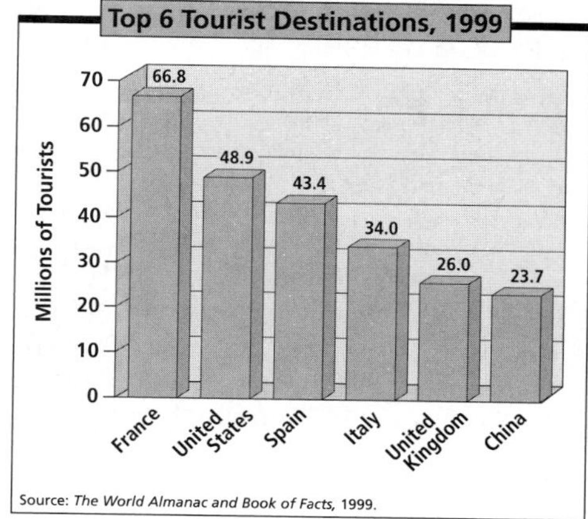

1. **According to the graph, about how many tourists visited the United States in 1999?**
   A 48.9
   B 66.8
   C 48,900
   D 48,900,000
2. **Which country on the graph had the least number of tourists?**
   F France
   G China
   H Spain
   J Italy

Test-Taking Tip: A common error when reading graphs is to overlook the information on the bottom and the side of the graph. Check these areas of the graph to see what the numbers mean.

529

Assessment and Activities

Standardized Test Practice

1. D
2. G

Tested Objectives:
Analyzing information, reading bar graphs

Chapter Test Bonus Question

This question may be used for extra credit on the chapter test.

What branch of the United States government enforces the laws? *(executive)*

Our World Today Online

Have students visit the Web site at **owt.glencoe.com** to review Chapter 19 and take the Self-Check Quiz.

Current Events Journal

22. Students' answers will vary but should be supported with facts.

Mental Mapping Activity

23. This exercise helps students visualize the countries and geographic features they have been studying and understand the relationships among various points. All attempts at freehand mapping should be accepted.

Technology Skills Activity

24. Students' maps should accurately present the data.

Focus

Mention that the United States generates more trash per person than any other country in the world. Then ask students what kinds of things they think Americans throw away. Note their responses on the board.

Teach

Graphing Information Next to the list of student responses generated above, write the following:

Paper products 37%
Yard waste 18%
Plastics 8%
Glass 7%
Aluminum 1%
Other metals 7%
Miscellaneous 22%

Have students present this information in a circle graph. Suggest that they highlight categories that are relatively easy to recycle—paper, yard waste, glass, and aluminum, for example—with shading or a different color. Encourage students to write a caption noting what percentage of American trash these recyclable materials represent. **L1**

Meeting National Standards

Geography for Life
The following standards are met in the Student Edition feature:

EE4 Human Systems: Standards 12, 13
EE5 Environment and Society: Standards 14, 15

EYE on the Environment

TOO MUCH Trash

Tons of Trash If you are an average American, you throw away about 4 pounds (2 kg) of trash each day. Not much, right? Think again. That is 1,460 pounds (663 kg) a year. By age 13, you have produced almost 10 tons (9 t) of trash!

Americans create more than one-third of the world's trash—200 million tons (181 million t) each year. That is enough to fill a line of garbage trucks that would circle the earth eight times!

State Recycling Rates
30% or greater
20–29%
10–19%
Less than 10%
Unavailable
Source: U.S. EPA Municipal Solid Waste Handbook—Internet Version.

What happens to trash?

- Most ends up in landfills.
- Some is burned in incinerators.
- Some is dumped into lakes, rivers, and oceans.

All of these disposal methods create pollution and harm living things. When landfills fill up, new ones must be created. However, sites for new landfills are getting hard to find. Would you want to live near one?

The Three R's Surprisingly, the solution to too much trash is simple. We need to produce less waste. How? By following the three R's—reduce, reuse, and recycle.

- REDUCE the amount of trash you throw away each day.
- REUSE products and containers.
- RECYCLE some of your trash. About 80 percent of household trash can be recycled.

If we reduce, reuse, and recycle, we can win the war against trash.

Trash piles up at a landfill in New Jersey.

More About the Issues

Hazardous Waste Point out to students that hazardous wastes are a particularly difficult problem. Hazardous wastes are materials, such as toxic chemicals, that present an exceptional threat to the environment. Disposal of these materials is closely regulated by the Environmental Protection Agency (EPA). In some places, however, businesses have dumped hazardous wastes without due care and attention. The EPA has identified more than 1,200 such hazardous waste sites throughout the country—an average of about 25 sites per state.

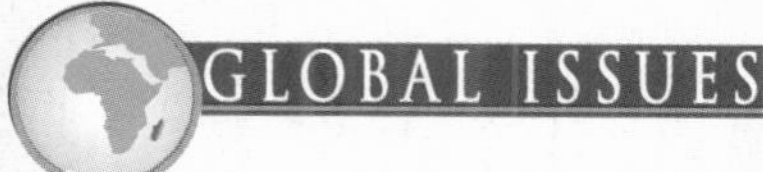

Pollution The most popular form of trash disposal worldwide is the open dump. Such dumps provide a breeding ground for rats and disease, foul the air with odors and smoke from burning garbage, and pollute nearby groundwater.

Have students write a paragraph summarizing why trash is a problem for the environment.

Discuss with students the What Can You Do? activities. Encourage students to research and report on trash disposal in their community. Consider inviting a representative of a local waste utility or an environmental group to give a brief presentation and answer students' questions.

For an additional regional case study, use the following:

Environmental Case Study 7

Making a Difference

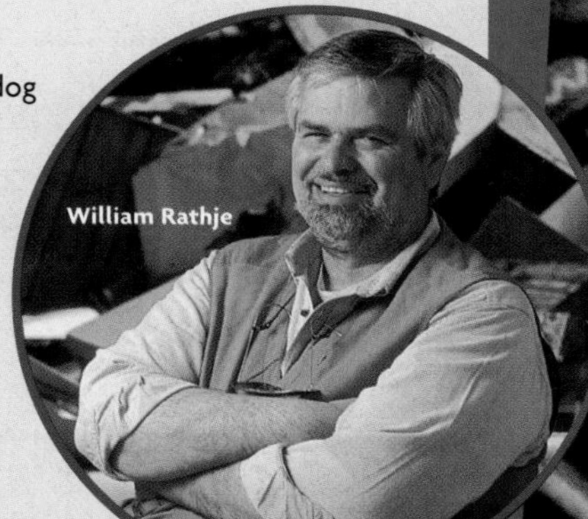

Dig It! You are at the ball game. You toss part of your hot dog into a trash can. Eventually, the hot dog goes to a landfill. How long will it take the hot dog to decay in a landfill?

In 1973 archaeologist William Rathje began the Garbage Project. He wanted to "dig up" facts about the trash Americans throw away. Rathje and his University of Arizona students spent years studying garbage from landfills across the United States. His research results are full of surprises. In some landfills, team members found foods such as steaks and hot dogs that were 15 to 20 years old! Lack of air, light, and moisture prevents wastes from breaking down. Another surprise: About a third of the trash in landfills is paper. Yard waste, food scraps, plastics, construction materials, and furniture are some of the other items we throw away.

William Rathje

Recycling to the Max Linda Munn and her husband, Frank Schiavo, are teachers in California. They have not set out a curbside garbage can in more than 20 years. That is because they recycle or compost almost everything they use. They produce only about two handfuls of trash a week—and that goes to a recycling center, too.

A student recycles aluminum cans.

What Can You Do?

Make Toys From Trash
Create toys from discarded clean paper, cardboard, or plastic. Have a class contest and award prizes to students who reuse trash in the most creative ways.

Campaign Against Waste
Investigate products used every day. Which ones have too much packaging—layers of plastic or paper thrown away once the product is used? Can you think of ways to eliminate the excess? Identify companies that make these products and send them a letter or an e-mail outlining your packaging changes.

Use the Internet
Click the Games option at *www.edf.org/Earth2Kids* to learn more about recycling. Also check out the Environmental Protection Agency's kids' page at *www.epa.gov/epaoswer/osw/kids.htm*

531

What Can You Do? Teacher Tips

Have students review the suggestions in What Can You Do? and then organize a recycling awareness campaign in their community. Have them brainstorm ways they can promote recycling. *(They might create posters promoting recycling or create and distribute brochures outlining the problem.)* Have the class discuss which idea—or ideas—they like best and then discuss what steps need to be taken to implement the idea or ideas. If students prefer more than one suggestion, you might break the class into groups, having each group develop an implementation plan for one of the ideas.

Chapter 20 Resources

Note: The following materials may be used when teaching Chapter 20.
Section level support materials are shown at point of use in the margins of the Teacher Wraparound Edition.

Timesaving Tools

TeacherWorks™ All-In-One Planner and Resource Center

- **Interactive Teacher Edition** See the **Interactive Teacher Edition** CD-ROM to electronically integrate your Teacher Wraparound Edition and blackline masters.
- **Interactive Lesson Planner** Organize your week, month, semester, or year with all the lesson helps you need. The **Interactive Lesson Planner** CD-ROM contains all Chapter 20 resources.

Use Glencoe's **Presentation Plus!** multimedia teacher tool to easily present dynamic lessons that visually excite your students. Using Microsoft PowerPoint® you can customize the presentations to create your own personalized lessons.

TEACHING TRANSPARENCIES

Graphic Organizer Transparency and Student Activity 20

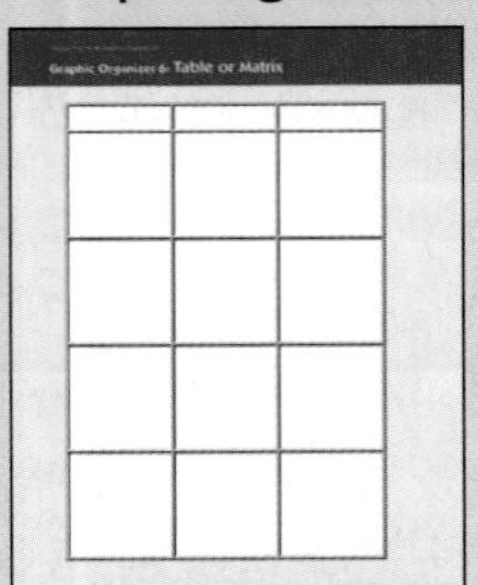

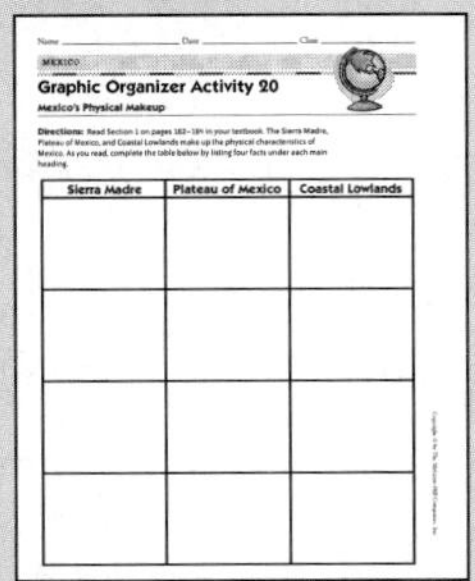

FOLDABLES™ Study Organizer

Foldables are three-dimensional, interactive graphic organizers that help students practice basic writing skills, review key vocabulary terms, and identify main ideas. Every chapter contains a Foldable activity, with additional chapter activities found in the ***Reading and Study Skills Foldables*** booklet.

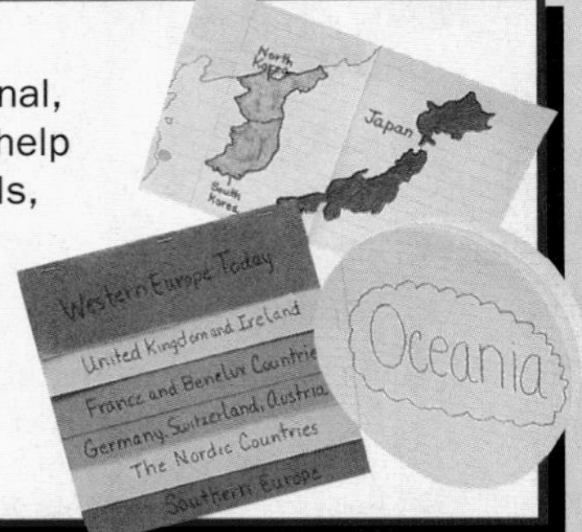

ENRICHMENT AND EXTENSION

Enrichment Activity 20

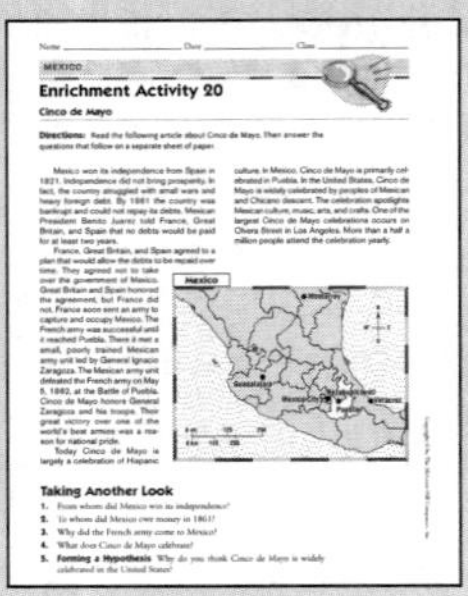

Cooperative Learning Activity 20

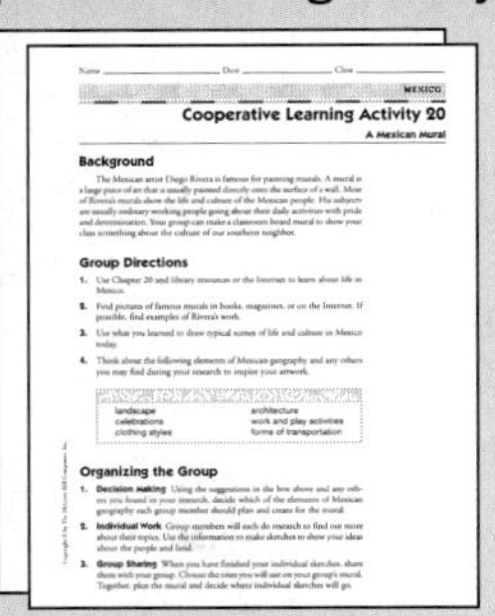

MAP AND GEOGRAPHY SKILLS

Chapter Map Activity 20

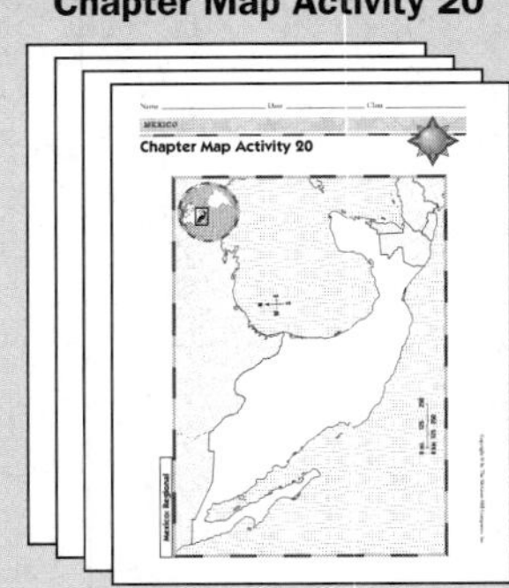

GeoLab Activity 20

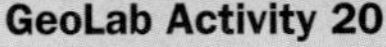

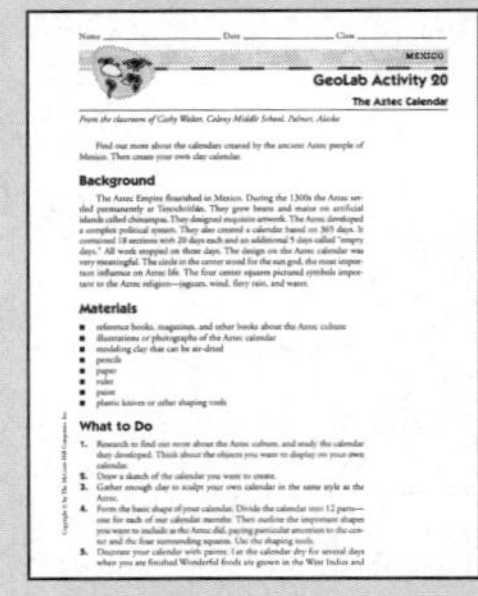

STANDARDIZED ASSESSMENT SKILLS

Critical Thinking Skills Activity 20

Map and Graph Skills Activity 20

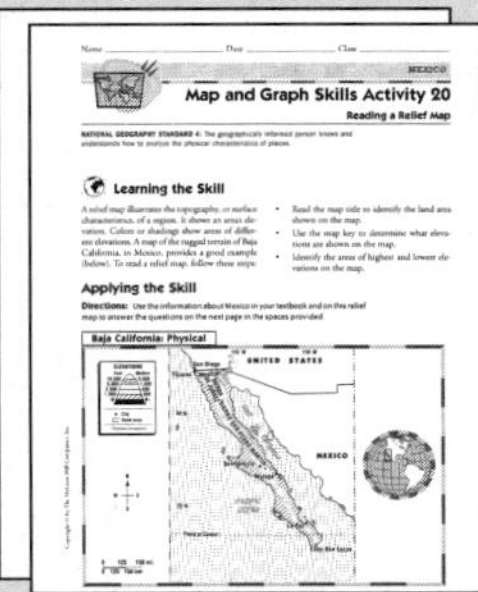

Reading and Writing Skills Activity 20

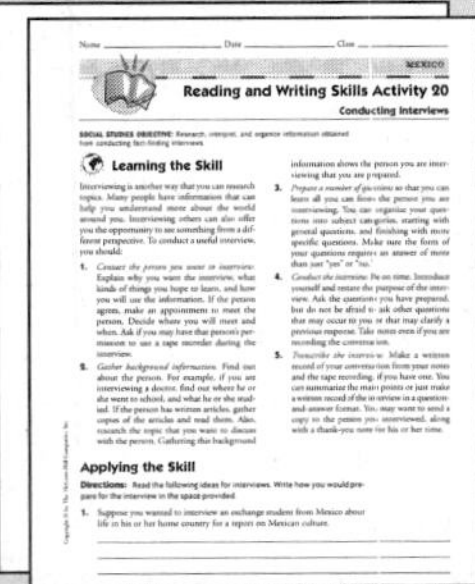

Standardized Test Practice Workbook Activity 20

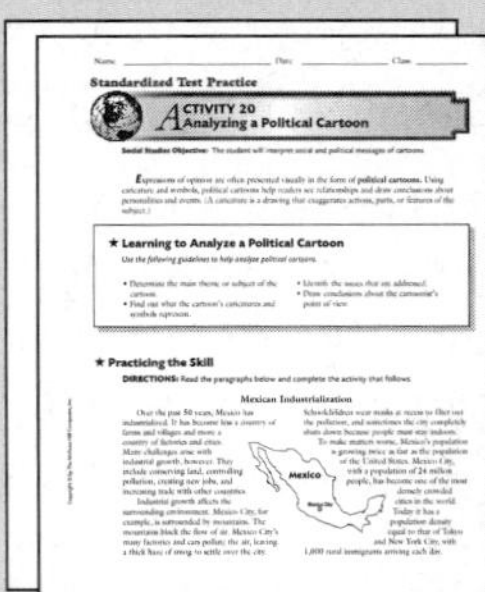

REVIEW AND REINFORCEMENT

Chapter Skills Activity 20

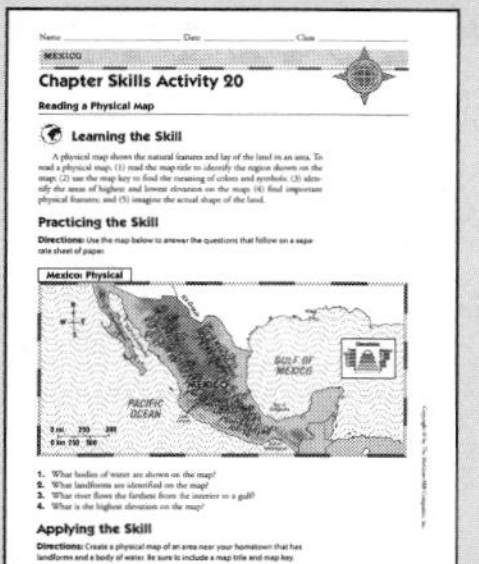

Take-Home Review Activity 20

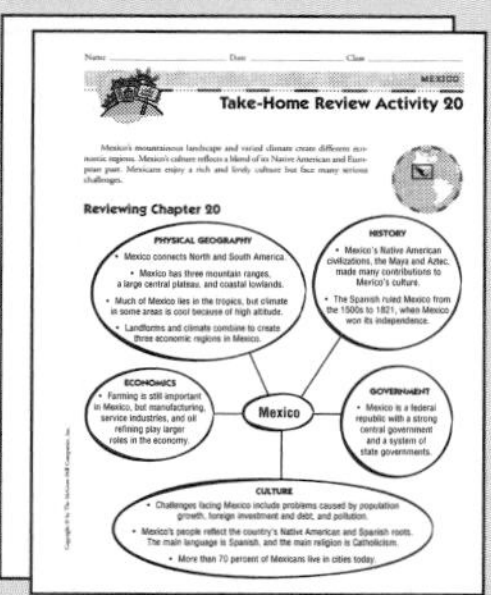

Reteaching Activity 20

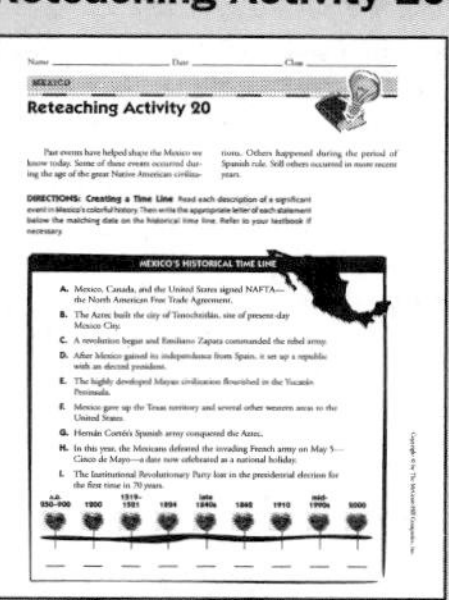

Vocabulary Activity 20

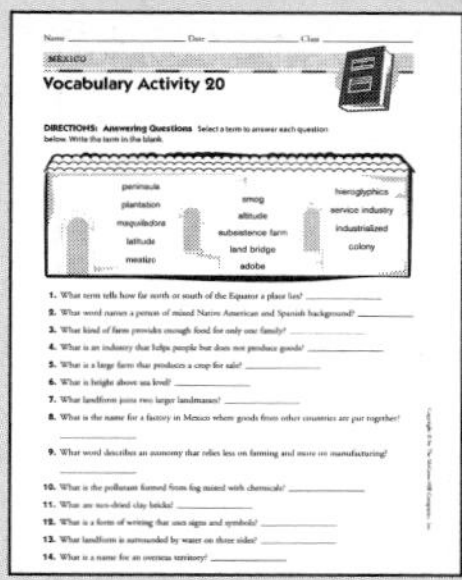

Workbook Activity 20

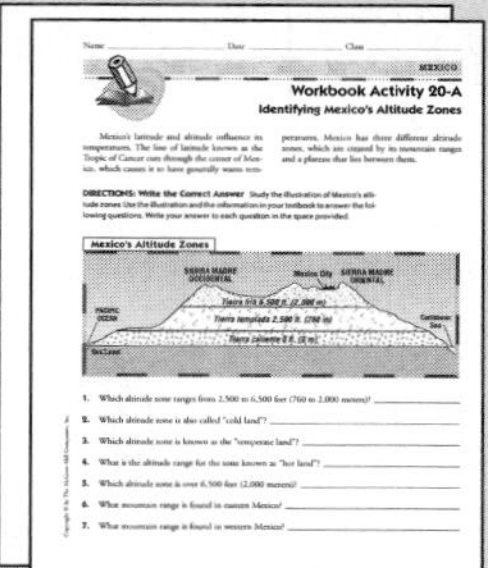

ASSESSMENT

GLENCOE'S ASSESSMENT ADVANTAGE

Chapter 20 Test, Form A

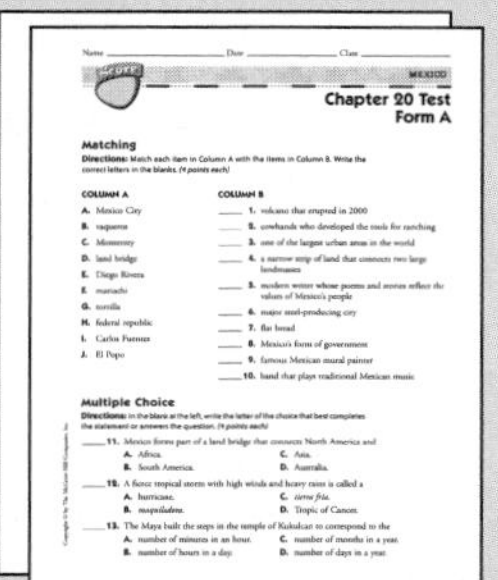

Chapter 20 Test, Form B

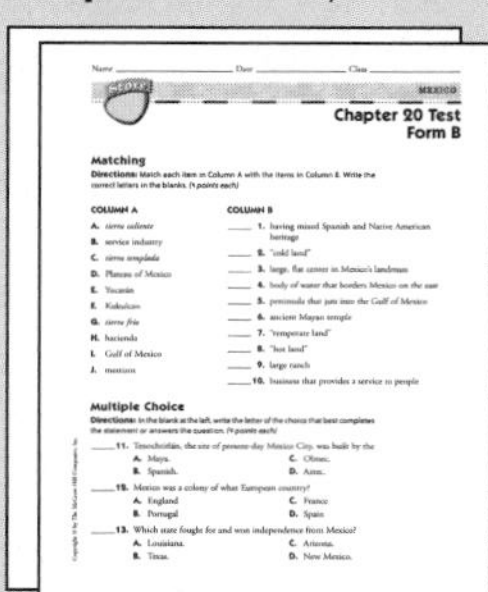

Performance Assessment Activity 20

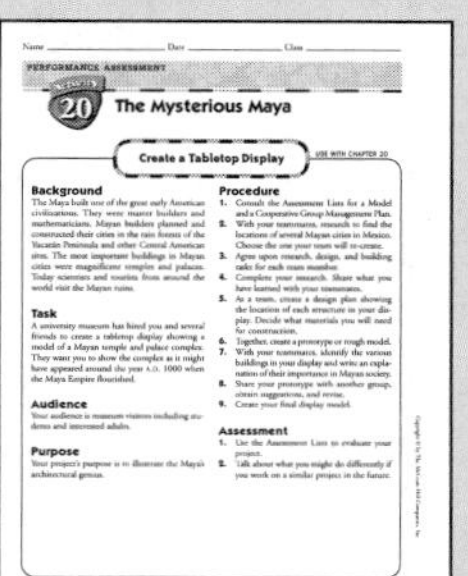

ExamView® Pro 3.0 Testmaker CD-ROM

MULTIMEDIA

- National Geographic's The World and Its People
- MindJogger Videoquiz
- Vocabulary PuzzleMaker Software
- Interactive Tutor Self-Assessment CD-ROM
- ExamView® Pro 3.0 Testmaker CD-ROM
- Interactive Lesson Planner CD-ROM
- Interactive Teacher Edition CD-ROM
- Skillbuilder Interactive Workbook CD-ROM, Level 1
- Presentation Plus! CD-ROM
- Audio Program

SPANISH RESOURCES

The following Spanish language materials are available in the Spanish Resources binder:

- Spanish Chapter Summaries
- Spanish Vocabulary Activities
- Spanish Guided Reading Activities
- Spanish Quizzes and Tests
- Spanish Take-Home Review Activities
- Spanish Reteaching Activities

Meeting National Standards

Geography for Life

All of the 18 standards are demonstrated in Unit 7. The following ones are highlighted in Chapter 20:

Section 1 EE2 Places and Regions: Standards 4, 5
EE3 Physical Systems: Standards 7, 8
EE5 Environment and Society: Standard 14

Section 2 EE4 Human Systems: Standards 9, 10, 12, 13

Section 3 EE4 Human Systems: Standards 9, 11, 12, 13
EE5 Environment and Society: Standard 14

For a complete listing of National Geography Standards and entire text correlation, see pages T22–T29.

Local Objectives

Chapter 20 Planning Guide

SECTION RESOURCES

Daily Objectives	Reproducible Resources	Multimedia Resources
Section 1 **Mexico's Land and Economy** **Suggested Pacing = 1 day** **1.** Describe the landforms found in Mexico. **2.** Describe how Mexico's climates vary with altitude. **3.** Compare the three economic zones of Mexico.	Reproducible Lesson Plan 20-1 Daily Lecture and Discussion Notes 20-1 Guided Reading Activity 20-1 Reading Essentials and Study Guide 20-1 Section Quiz 20-1*	Daily Focus Skills Transparency 20-1 GeoQuiz Transparency 20-1 Vocabulary PuzzleMaker Software Interactive Tutor Self-Assessment CD-ROM ExamView® Pro 3.0 Testmaker CD-ROM Presentation Plus! CD-ROM
Section 2 **Mexico's History** **Suggested Pacing = 1 day** **1.** Describe the groups that influenced Mexico's history. **2.** Discuss how Spaniards changed life in Mexico. **3.** Outline changes that took place in Mexico in the 1800s and 1900s.	Reproducible Lesson Plan 20-2 Daily Lecture and Discussion Notes 20-2 Guided Reading Activity 20-2 Reading Essentials and Study Guide 20-2 Section Quiz 20-2*	Daily Focus Skills Transparency 20-2 GeoQuiz Transparency 20-2 Vocabulary PuzzleMaker Software Interactive Tutor Self-Assessment CD-ROM ExamView® Pro 3.0 Testmaker CD-ROM Presentation Plus! CD-ROM
Section 3 **Mexico Today** **Suggested Pacing = 1 day** **1.** Describe life in the cities and villages of Mexico. **2.** Identify elements of Mexican culture. **3.** Discuss Mexico's government. **4.** Explain what challenges face Mexico.	Reproducible Lesson Plan 20-3 Daily Lecture and Discussion Notes 20-3 Guided Reading Activity 20-3 Reading Essentials and Study Guide 20-3 Section Quiz 20-3*	Daily Focus Skills Transparency 20-3 Vocabulary PuzzleMaker Software Interactive Tutor Self-Assessment CD-ROM ExamView® Pro 3.0 Testmaker CD-ROM Presentation Plus! CD-ROM

00:00 **Out of Time?** Assign the **Reading Essentials and Study Guide** for this chapter.

*Also available in Spanish

KEY TO ABILITY LEVELS

Teaching strategies have been coded for varying learning styles and abilities.

L1 BASIC activities for all students
L2 AVERAGE activities for average to above-average students
L3 CHALLENGING activities for above-average students
ELL ENGLISH LANGUAGE LEARNER activities

Blackline Master
Software
CD-ROM
Audiocassette
Transparency
Videocassette
Block Scheduling
DVD

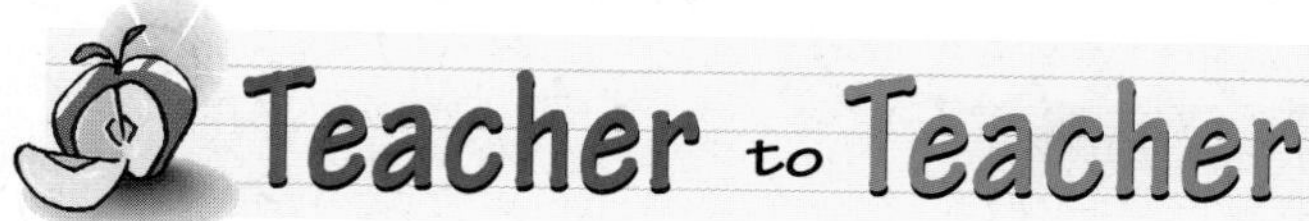

Catch the World!

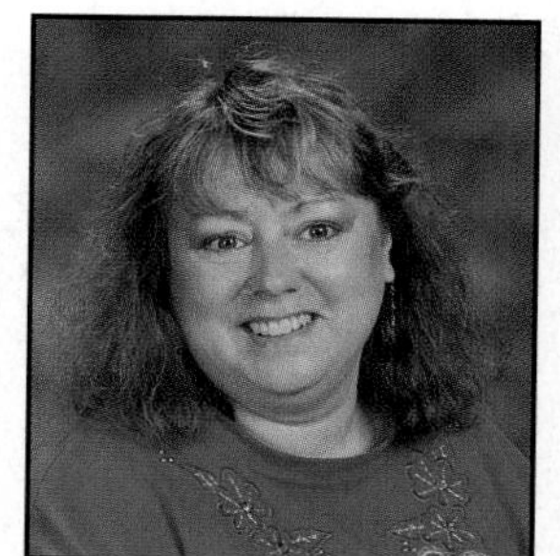

Donna Jett
Powell Middle School
Powell, Tennessee

You need an inflatable globe for this activity. Every so often, perhaps after each chapter or unit of study, have a student write two categories on the board: "Land" and "Water." Take out the inflatable globe and toss it to a student, who reports what is located at his or her right thumb. Write the country or body of water under its correct category on the board. Then have the student tell something about the place: its location in latitude and longitude or hemisphere, physical characteristics of the place, climate, capital, and so on. The student should toss the globe to another student, who repeats the process.

OUR WORLD Online

Use our Web site for additional resources. All essential content is covered in the Student Edition.

You and your students can visit **owt.glencoe.com**, the Web site companion to *Our World Today*. This innovative integration of electronic and print media offers your students a wealth of opportunities. The student text directs students to the Web site for the following options:

- Chapter Overviews
- Student Web Activities
- Self-Check Quizzes
- Textbook Updates

Answers are provided for you in the Web Activity Lesson Plan. Additional Web resources and Interactive Tutor puzzles are also available.

TEACHER'S CORNER

Index to National Geographic Magazine:

The following articles may be used for research relating to this chapter:

- "The Royal Crypts of Copán," by George E. Stuart, December 1997.
- *Mexico,* A National Geographic Special Edition, August 1996.
- "Tex-Mex Border," by Richard Conniff, February 1996.
- "The Timeless Vision of Teotihuacan," by George E. Stuart, December 1995.

National Geographic Society Products Available From Glencoe:

To order the following products for use with this chapter, contact your local Glencoe sales representative or call Glencoe at 1-800-334-7344:

- *PictureShow: Ancient Civilizations: Middle and South America* (CD-ROM)
- *PicturePack: Ancient Civilizations: Middle America* (Transparencies)
- *MapPack: Continents: North America* (Transparencies)
- *STV: North America* (Videodisc)

Additional National Geographic Society Products:

To order the following products for use with this chapter, call National Geographic Society at 1-800-368-2728:

- *Complete National Geographic: 111 years of National Geographic Magazine* (CD-ROM)
- *Spain in the Americas* (Video)
- *Mexico* (Video)
- *Lost City of the Maya* (Video)
- *The Maya Way of Death* (Video)
- *Population* (Map)
- *Cultures* (Map)
- *Central America Political* (Map)
- *National Geographic Desk Reference* (Book)
- *National Geographic Atlas of the World, Seventh Edition* (Book)
- *Voices: Poetry and Art From Around the World* (Book)

NGS ONLINE

Access National Geographic's Web site for current events, activities, links, interactive features, and archives.
www.nationalgeographic.com

Introducing Chapter 20

Introduce students to chapter content and key terms by having them access Chapter Overview 20 at owt.glencoe.com

Chapter Objectives

1. Identify the location of Mexico and describe its physical features and climate.
2. Describe the economy of Mexico.
3. Outline the history and government of Mexico.
4. Describe the Mexican people and the challenges they face today.

GLENCOE TECHNOLOGY

NATIONAL GEOGRAPHIC

The World and Its People Video Program

Chapter 6 Mexico
The following segments enhance the study of this chapter:

- **Mexico City**
- **Agua Azul**
- **Hills of Michoacán**

Available in DVD and VHS.

MindJogger Videoquiz
Use MindJogger to preview the Chapter 20 content.

Available in VHS.

Chapter 20 Mexico

The World and Its People NATIONAL GEOGRAPHIC

To learn more about the people and places of Mexico, view ***The World and Its People* Chapter 6** video.

Our World Today online

Chapter Overview Visit the ***Our World Today: People, Places, and Issues*** Web site at owt.glencoe.com and click on **Chapter 20—Chapter Overviews** to preview information about Mexico.

532

Two-Minute Lesson Launcher

Ask how many students enjoy eating corn in any of its forms (on the cob, cut, or as cornmeal). Point out that corn—or maize—was first cultivated in Mexico and that the oldest known examples of domesticated maize date from about 4,700 years ago. **Ask:** **How would you describe a corncob in terms of length and number of kernels?** *(as long as 1 foot (30.5 cm) with many rows and hundreds of kernels)* Inform them that ancient cobs of maize were much different. The first domesticated varieties were only about 1 inch (2.5 cm) long, with only eight rows, each of which had no more than nine kernels.

Categorizing Information Study Foldable

Categorizing Information Study Foldable When you group information into categories on a table, it is easier to study characteristics of items. Make this foldable to help you describe Mexico's land, economy, and government—past and present.

Step 1 Fold a sheet of paper into thirds from top to bottom.

This forms three sections.

Step 2 Open the paper and refold it into fourths from side to side.

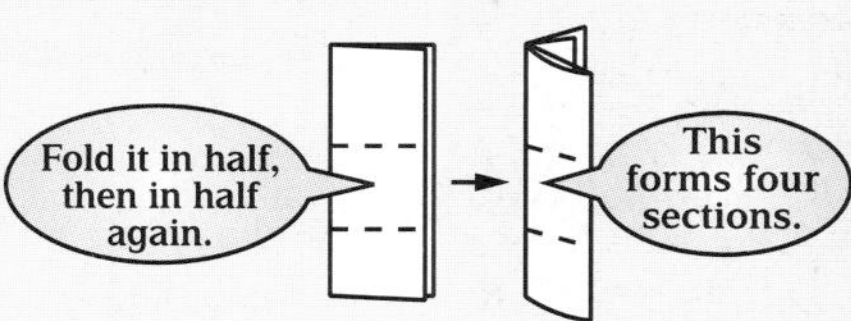

Fold it in half, then in half again.
This forms four sections.

Step 3 Unfold, turn the paper, and draw lines along the folds.

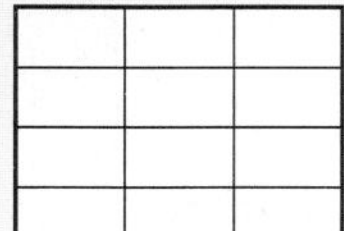

Step 4 Label your table as shown.

	Past	Present
Mexico's Land		
Mexico's Economy		
Mexico's Government		

Reading and Writing As you read the chapter, record key facts about Mexico's land, economy, and government in the appropriate places on your table foldable.

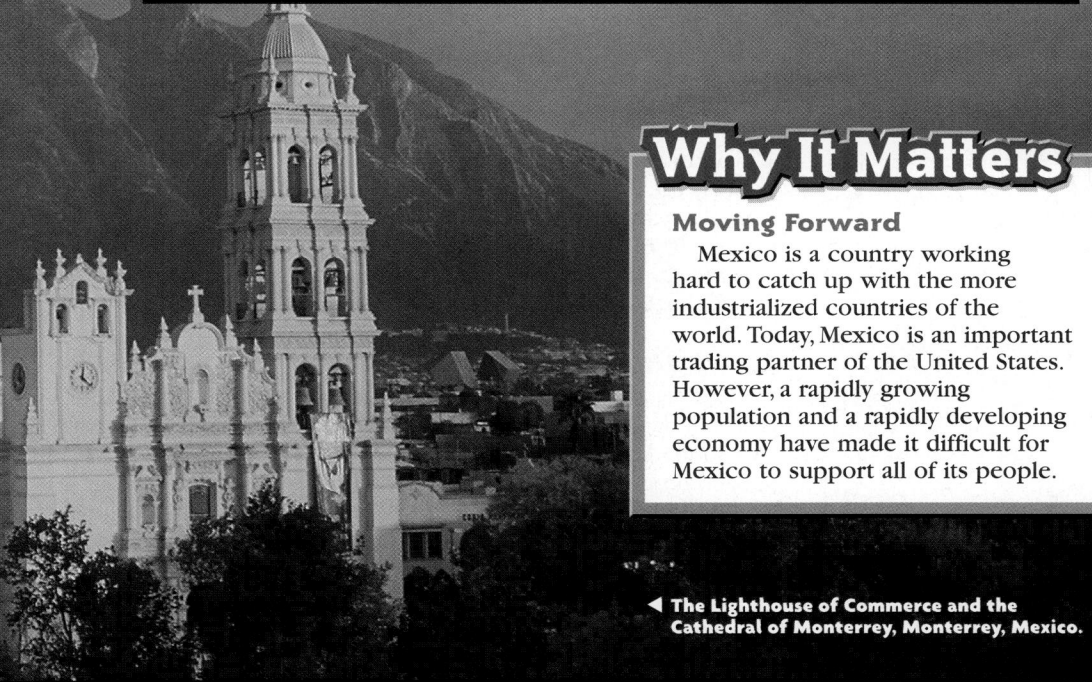

Why It Matters

Moving Forward

Mexico is a country working hard to catch up with the more industrialized countries of the world. Today, Mexico is an important trading partner of the United States. However, a rapidly growing population and a rapidly developing economy have made it difficult for Mexico to support all of its people.

◀ The Lighthouse of Commerce and the Cathedral of Monterrey, Monterrey, Mexico.

About the Photo

Monterrey is a blend of old and new. Its cathedral, which began construction in 1600, is a reminder of the city's beginnings as a Spanish colonial outpost. Today, modern skyscrapers reflect Monterrey's importance as a finance and industrial center. The city continues to prosper because of its proximity to the United States. Between 1995 and 1999, the number of maquiladoras—foreign-owned factories—in Monterrey's state of Nuevo León has grown from 5 to 124. More that 600 international firms have offices there. Workers, however, are very dependent on the American economy. When there is an economic slowdown in the United States, many workers lose their jobs. Since they work for low wages with no benefits, unemployment can lead to severe hardship.

Introducing Chapter 20

FOLDABLES™ Study Organizer

Purpose This activity requires students to create a table and organize information from the chapter on it. Students group information from the chapter into categories, in effect comparing Mexico's land, economy, and government of the past to the land, economy, and government of the present.

Have students complete ***Reading and Study Skills Foldables*** Activity 20.

Why It Matters

Have students pretend that they are editorial writers for a newspaper in Mexico. Using information in the chapter and from outside sources, have them write an editorial either supporting or criticizing Mexico's rapidly growing population and rapidly developing economy. Their editorials should include specific examples of how the growth in population and the expanding economy have affected daily life in Mexico.

Chapter 20

Section 1, pages 534–539

1 Focus

Section Objectives

1. Describe the landforms found in Mexico.
2. Describe how Mexico's climates vary with altitude.
3. Compare the three economic zones of Mexico.

BELLRINGER
Skillbuilder Activity

Project transparency and have students answer questions.

This activity is also available as a blackline master.

Daily Focus Skills Transparency 20-1

UNIT 7 Chapter 20 | DAILY FOCUS SKILLS TRANSPARENCY 20-1

ANSWER: A Teacher Tip: the average temperature for any day is found by adding the high temperature and the low temperature and dividing the sum by 2.

Interpreting Tables

Mexico City, Mexico	Latitude: 19°N					Elevation: 7,347 ft. (2,239 m)						
Month	Jan.	Feb.	Mar.	Apr.	May	June	July	Aug.	Sept.	Oct.	Nov.	Dec.
Average Temperature*	57°	59°	63°	66°	67°	67°	65°	65°	64°	63°	60°	58°
Highest Recorded Temperature*	86°	84°	88°	88°	91°	91°	86°	86°	86°	86°	91°	88°
Lowest Recorded Temperature*	26°	30°	28°	34°	36°	43°	37°	43°	36°	36°	33°	28°

Monterrey, Mexico	Latitude: 25°N					Elevation: 1,752 ft. (534 m)						
Month	Jan.	Feb.	Mar.	Apr.	May	June	July	Aug.	Sept.	Oct.	Nov.	Dec.
Average Temperature*	58°	62°	70°	76°	80°	84°	84°	85°	80°	74°	66°	60°
Highest Recorded Temperature*	95°	100°	108°	111°	109°	111°	109°	106°	102°	102°	99°	95°
Lowest Recorded Temperature*	32°	32°	34°	37°	36°	59°	59°	54°	54°	43°	34°	32°

*Temperatures in Fahrenheit

Directions: Answer the following question based on the table.

During which month are the average temperatures in these two Mexican cities most similar?

A January
B March
C July
D December

Guide to Reading

Accessing Prior Knowledge
Ask students what they know about Mexico. Write their responses. Have them write these ideas in their notebooks and refer to them after reading the chapter to see what they can add.

Section 1

Mexico's Land and Economy

Guide to Reading

Main Idea

Mexico's mountainous landscape and varied climate create different economic regions.

Terms to Know

- land bridge
- peninsula
- latitude
- altitude
- hurricane
- vaquero
- maquiladora
- subsistence farm
- plantation
- industrialize
- service industry
- NAFTA

Reading Strategy

Create a chart of Mexico's economic regions like this one. List the main economic activity of each region.

Region of Mexico	Economic Activity
Northern	
Central	
Southern	

NATIONAL GEOGRAPHIC **Exploring Our World**

Mexican farmer Dionisio Pulido was plowing his cornfield one day. Suddenly his son heard a rumble in the ground. Then white smoke began to spew into the air. When they awoke the next day, they saw a volcano 30 feet (9 m) high. Today, more than 50 years later, the volcano named Paricutín soars nearly 8,990 feet (2,740 m) high.

Paricutín and other volcanoes are scattered throughout Mexico because the country sits where three plates in the earth's crust collide. Sometimes the movement of these plates brings disastrous results. Hot magma, or melted rock, shoots through a volcano. The ground shifts violently in an earthquake. Do you see why Native Americans once called Mexico "the land of the shaking earth"?

Bridging Two Continents

Mexico forms part of a **land bridge,** or narrow strip of land that joins two larger landmasses. This land bridge connects North America and South America. Look at the map on page 535. You can see that Mexico borders the southern United States.

Physical geographers, people who study continents and landforms, think of Mexico as part of North America. It is also true, however, that cultural geographers think of Mexico as being part of Latin America.

Section Resources

Reproducible Masters
- Reproducible Lesson Plan 20-1
- Daily Lecture and Discussion Notes 20-1
- Guided Reading Activity 20-1
- Reading Essentials and Study Guide 20-1
- Section Quiz 20-1

Transparencies
- Daily Focus Skills Transparency 20-1
- GeoQuiz Transparency 20-1

Multimedia
- Vocabulary PuzzleMaker Software
- Interactive Tutor Self-Assessment CD-ROM
- Presentation Plus! CD-ROM
- ExamView® Pro 3.0 Testmaker CD-ROM

For cultural geographers, language, customs, religion, and history are important areas of study. Both groups are correct. Mexico is a Latin (Spanish-speaking) country on the continent of North America. Mexico's culture is closely tied to Central and South America. Its location in North America makes it an important trading partner to the United States and Canada. It is a country that bridges two continents.

The Pacific Ocean borders Mexico on the west. Extending south along this western coast is **Baja** (BAH•hah) **California.** It is a long, narrow **peninsula,** or piece of land with water on three sides. On Mexico's eastern side, the **Gulf of Mexico** and the **Caribbean Sea** border the coasts. Between the Gulf and the Caribbean Sea is another peninsula—the **Yucatán** (YOO•kah•TAHN) **Peninsula.**

Mexico is a rugged land. If you were to see it from space, you might think that the country looked like a crumpled piece of paper with deep folds. Towering mountain ranges and a huge, high plateau occupy the center of the country.

The Sierra Madre Three different mountain ranges in Mexico make up the **Sierra Madre** (SYEHR•rah MAH•thray), or "mother range." Because of

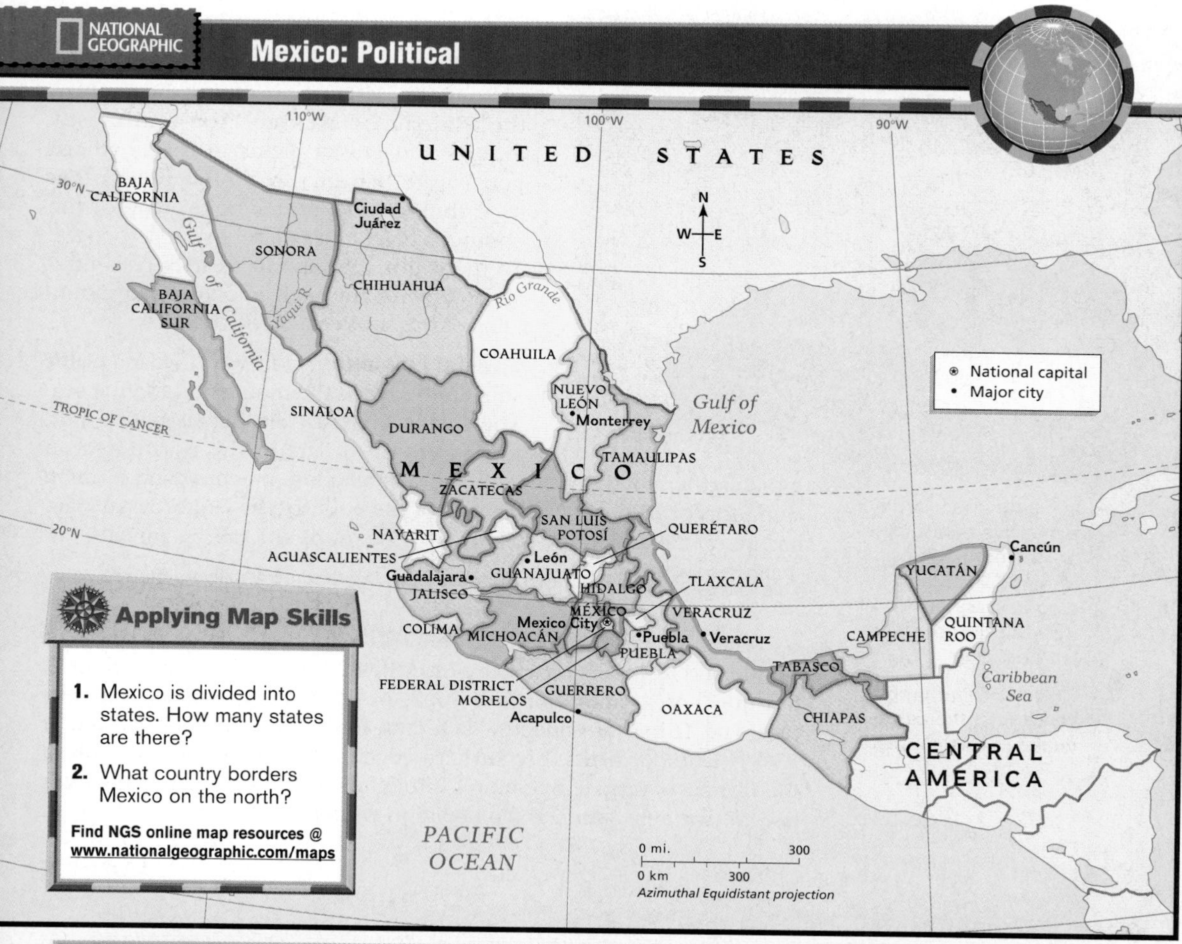

Applying Map Skills

1. Mexico is divided into states. How many states are there?
2. What country borders Mexico on the north?

Find NGS online map resources @ www.nationalgeographic.com/maps

Team-Teaching Activity

Language Arts Invite a Spanish teacher to the class to discuss words in English that are derived from Spanish. Have the teacher begin by focusing on those developed by Mexican vaqueros, which include the leather leggings called chaps (from *chaparreras*), the lariat (from *la reata*), and the wild horses called mustangs (from *mesteño*). Other possibilities include geographical terms such as *mesa*; food terms such as *taco* and *enchilada*; and musical forms such as *salsa* and *bolero*. **L1 ELL**

EE4 Human Systems: Standard 10

2 TEACH

Reading a Map Have students compare the physical map on page 476 to the physical map of the United States on page 474. Remind them that the United States and Canada share some physical features. Point out that Mexico, too, is part of North America. **Ask: What landforms in Mexico seem to be similar to landforms in the United States?** *(Mountains in Baja California extend from Sierra Nevada in California; the Sierra Madre Occidental extend from the Rocky Mountains; the Plateau of Mexico is part of the high plains east of the Rockies; the Gulf Coastal Plain is shared.)* **L1**

Daily Lecture Notes 20-1

MEXICO

Daily Lecture and Discussion Notes 20-1

Mexico's Land and Economy (pages 534–539)

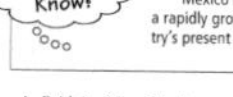

Did You Know? Mexico has a vast array of mineral resources, limited agricultural land, and a rapidly growing population. These factors are the basis for many of the country's present problems as well as opportunities for future development.

I. Bridging Two Continents *(pages 534–536)*

A. Mexico forms part of a **land bridge,** or narrow strip of land that joins two larger landmasses. This land bridge connects North America and South America.

B. Mexico is bordered by the Pacific Ocean on the west. Extending south along this western coast is Baja California, a **peninsula,** or piece of land with water ... On Mexico's eastern side, the Gulf of Mexico and the Caribbean

Applying Map Skills

Answers

1. 31 states and one Federal District
2. the United States

Skills Practice

What is the capital of Mexico? *(Mexico City)*

More About the Photo

Mexico City Mexico City is endangered by earthquakes. It lies on a fault, and much of the city rests on a former lake bed. As a result, the soil is soft, which means that buildings can move a great deal during a quake.

Caption Answer movement of the Pacific plate below the earth's crust

Interdisciplinary Connections

History In 1521 Spanish soldier Hernán Cortés conquered Mexico. When he returned to Spain, the Spanish king asked him to describe the land. Legend says that Cortés, to show the ruggedness of Mexico's land, crumpled a piece of paper and threw it on a table, saying "This, your Majesty, is the land of Mexico."

✓ Reading Check Answer

volcanoes and earthquakes

the rugged terrain, few people live in the Sierra Madre. The mountains are rich in resources, though. They hold copper, zinc, silver, and timber.

Many of Mexico's mountains are volcanoes. **Popocatepetl** (POH•puh•KAT•uh•PEHT•uhl), or "El Popo," as Mexicans call it, erupted violently centuries ago. In December 2000, El Popo erupted again, hurling molten rock into the sky. About 30,000 people from surrounding areas were forced to temporarily leave their homes. Tens of millions of people live 50 miles (80 km) or less from the mountain and could face even worse eruptions in the future.

Mexicans face another danger from the land. Earthquakes can destroy their cities and homes. A 1985 earthquake killed nearly 10,000 people in Mexico's capital, **Mexico City,** even though the earthquake's center was about 185 miles (298 km) away. You can understand why there are so many earthquakes here if you remember that Mexico is one of the countries that border the "Ring of Fire." This ring includes three-fourths of the world's active volcanoes. Earthquakes in the zone are common due to movement of the huge Pacific plate deep under the earth's crust.

NATIONAL GEOGRAPHIC On Location

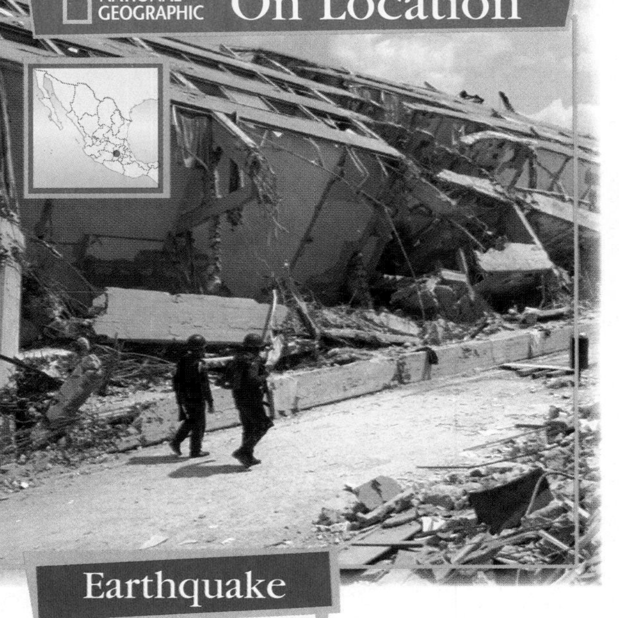

Earthquake

In September, 1985, a massive earthquake destroyed much of Mexico City. Many died and about 250,000 people were left homeless.

Region What probably caused the earthquake in Mexico City?

The Plateau of Mexico The Sierra Madre surround the large, flat center of the country, the **Plateau of Mexico.** You find mostly deserts and grassy plains in the northern part of the plateau. Broad, flat valleys that slice through the center hold many of the country's chief cities and most of its people. To the south, the plateau steadily rises until it meets with the high, snowcapped mountains of the southern Sierra Madre.

Coastal Lowlands Mexico's lowland plains squeeze between the mountains and the sea. The Pacific Coastal Plain begins with a hot, largely empty desert in the north. As you move farther south, better soil and rainfall allow ranching and farming along this plain. On the other side of the country, the Gulf Coastal Plain has more rain and fertile soil for growing crops and raising animals.

✓ Reading Check **What two dangers from the land do Mexicans face?**

Land of Many Climates

Mexico has many different climates. Why? As you read in Chapter 2, latitude—or location north or south of the Equator—affects temperature. The Tropic of Cancer, which cuts across the center of Mexico at 23½°N latitude, marks the northern edge of the Tropics. Areas south of this line have warm temperatures throughout the year. Areas north of this line are warm in summer and cooler in winter.

Meeting Special Needs

Visual/Spatial Have students construct a chart comparing Mexico's altitude zones. Bases of comparison might include location, temperature range, and vegetation. Have them use the completed chart to analyze the relationship between climate and altitude. L1

Refer to *Inclusion for the Middle School Social Studies Classroom Strategies and Activities* in the TCR.

Mexico's Altitude Zones

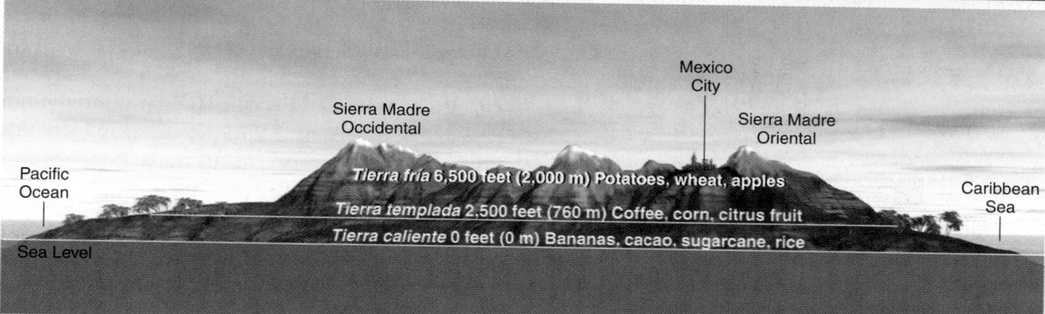

Altitude, or height above sea level, affects temperature in Mexico as well. The higher the altitude, the cooler the temperatures—even within the Tropics. The diagram above shows that Mexico's mountains and plateau create three altitude zones. You could travel through all of these zones in a day's trip across the Sierra Madre.

Because the coastal lowlands are near sea level, they have high temperatures. Mexicans call this altitude zone the *tierra caliente* (tee•AY•rah kah•lee•AYN•tay), or "hot land." Moving higher in altitude, you find the *tierra templada* (taym•PLAH•dah), or "temperate land." Here the climate becomes more moderate. In the highest zone, the climate becomes even cooler. Mexicans call this the *tierra fría* (FREE•ah), or "cold land."

Rainfall varies throughout Mexico. Baja California and northern Mexico receive very little precipitation. Other regions receive more, mostly in the summer and early fall. From June to October, Mexico can be hit by **hurricanes.** These fierce tropical storms with high winds and heavy rains form over the warm waters of the Atlantic or Pacific Oceans. They can strike Mexico with fury.

✓Reading Check **What is Mexico's warmest altitude zone?**

Analyzing the Diagram

Mexico has zones of different climates that result from different altitudes.

Location **In which altitude zone is Mexico City located?**

Mexico's Economic Regions

Mexico's physical geography and climate together give Mexico three distinct economic regions: the North, Central Mexico, and the South. Large stretches of northern Mexico are too dry and rocky to farm. By building canals to carry water to their fields, people without irrigation can grow cotton, fruits, grains, and vegetables.

Northern Mexico Did you know that the skills used by American cowhands originated in Mexico? Mexican cowhands, called **vaqueros** (vah•KEHR•ohs), developed the tools and techniques for herding, roping, and branding cattle. Vaqueros in northern Mexico carry on this work today.

Cooperative Learning Activity

Making Murals Point out to students that murals are popular vehicles for art in Mexico, dating back to the time of the Mayan civilization. In the twentieth century, artists such as Diego Rivera and José Clemente Orozco gained fame for their murals celebrating Mexico's past and present. Have students devise their own vehicle for celebrating the past of their community. Students should read about the history and development of the area, identifying famous individuals and significant events. They might also talk to older members of the community to gather stories about the past. Then have students work in groups to create a product—a mural, set of bulletin boards, or multimedia presentation—that describes the area's past. **L2 ELL**

EE6 The Uses of Geography: Standard 17

Analyzing the Diagram

Answer
tierra fría

Skills Practice
What products are grown in the *tierra templada*? *(coffee, corn, and citrus fruit)*

Guided Reading Activity 20-1

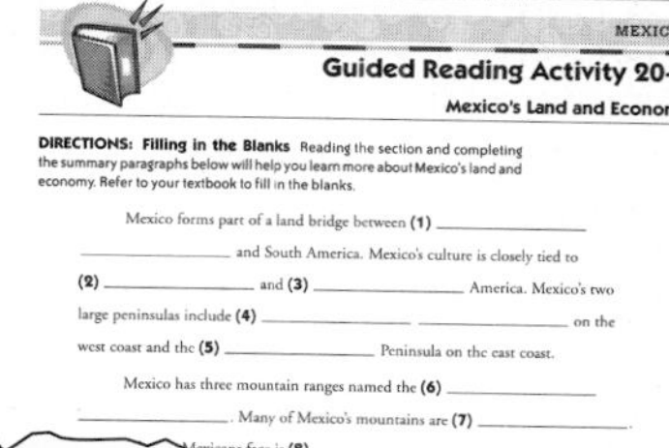

Name ______ Date ______ Class ______

MEXICO

Guided Reading Activity 20-1

Mexico's Land and Economy

DIRECTIONS: Filling in the Blanks Reading the section and completing the summary paragraphs below will help you learn more about Mexico's land and economy. Refer to your textbook to fill in the blanks.

Mexico forms part of a land bridge between **(1)** ______ ______ and South America. Mexico's culture is closely tied to **(2)** ______ and **(3)** ______ America. Mexico's two large peninsulas include **(4)** ______ ______ on the west coast and the **(5)** ______ Peninsula on the east coast.

Mexico has three mountain ranges named the **(6)** ______ ______. Many of Mexico's mountains are **(7)** ______.

(8) ______.

ASSESS

Assign Section 1 Assessment as homework or an in-class activity.

Have students use the Interactive Tutor Self-Assessment CD-ROM to review Section 20–1.

✓ Reading Check Answer

the tierra caliente ("hot land")

Chapter 20

Section 1, pages 534–539

Did You Know?

The clothing industry in Mexico experienced explosive growth after NAFTA was signed. Since then, Mexican clothing imports to Canada have quadrupled. The life of a maquiladora worker is not easy, however. Hours are long, wages are low, and conditions are sometimes very bad.

Reading Check Answer

Northern Mexico has seen a recent economic boom from growth in manufacturing; southern Mexico is based on farming and is poor.

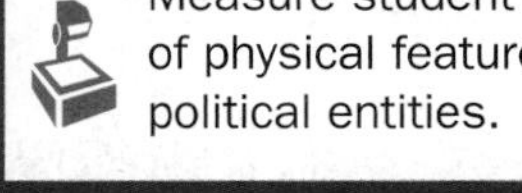

Measure student knowledge of physical features and political entities.

GeoQuiz Transparency 20-1

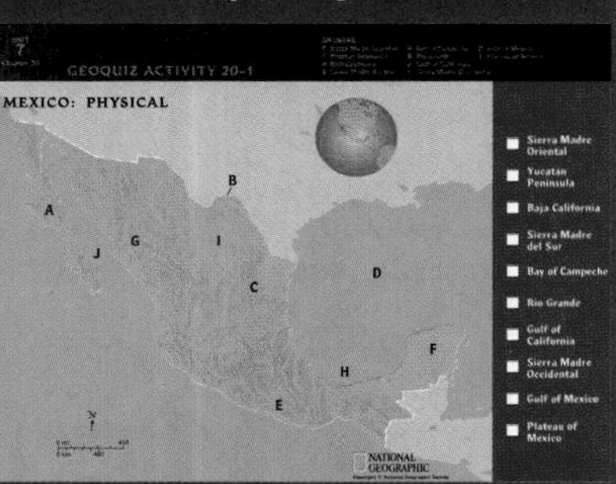

▲ A skilled seamstress makes clothing in a maquiladora in northern Mexico.

Northern Mexico has seen an economic boom. **Monterrey,** Mexico's main producer of steel and cement, has long been an important industrial city. In this and other cities, many companies from the United States and elsewhere have built **maquiladoras** (mah•KEEL•ah•DOHR•as), or factories that assemble parts made in other countries. As a result, thousands of Mexicans have flocked to cities such as **Tijuana** (tee•WAH•nah) and **Ciudad Juárez** (see•ooh•DAHD HWAH•rayz) along the border with the United States. The growth in these border cities has raised the standard of living in northern cities through factory work and increased trade. However, this quick growth has also brought concerns about damaging the environment, pollution, and dangers to the health and safety of workers.

Central Mexico More than half of Mexico's people live in the central region, the country's heartland. Why do they call this area home? The climate is one reason. Although central Mexico lies in the Tropics, its high elevation keeps it from being hot and humid. Temperatures are mild, and the climate is pleasant year-round. A second reason is the fertile soil created by volcanic eruptions over the centuries. This allows good production for farming and ranching.

Large industrial cities such as Mexico City and **Guadalajara** also prosper in central Mexico. More than 18 million people live in Mexico City and its suburbs, making it one of the largest cities in the world. Mexico City has been the largest city in the Americas since before the Spanish arrived in the early 1500s.

Southern Mexico The South is the poorest economic region of the country. The mountains towering in the center of this region have poor soil. **Subsistence farms,** or small plots where farmers grow only enough food to feed their families, are common here. In contrast, the coastal lowlands of this area have good soil and plentiful rain. Wealthy farmers grow sugarcane or bananas on **plantations,** large farms that raise a single crop for sale.

Both coasts also have beautiful beaches and a warm climate. Tourists from all over the world flock to such resort cities as **Acapulco** and **Puerto Vallarta** on the Pacific coast and **Cancún** on the Yucatán Peninsula.

Reading Check **How does the economic region of northern Mexico differ from that of southern Mexico?**

Mexico's Economy Today

With many resources and workers, Mexico has a growing economy. Did you know that Mexico's economy ranks among the top 12 in the world? As in the past, agriculture is important. Farmers raise food to feed people at home—and also to ship around the world. Corn, beans, wheat, and rice are the main crops grown for food. Exports include coffee, cotton, vegetables, fruit, livestock, and tobacco.

In recent years, Mexico has **industrialized,** or changed its economy to rely less on farming and more on manufacturing. Factories in

Critical Thinking Activity

Identifying Alternatives Although NAFTA has created many jobs in Mexican border towns, the area remains poor. Millions live in "colonias"—communities of ramshackle homes. Many of the colonias have no water, electricity, sewer systems, paved roads, or streetlights. Volunteers from both Mexico and the United States help residents by teaching proper health care, digging septic systems for waste disposal, and providing small loans of $100 to $200 to set up small businesses like dress-making or tire repair. Larger bank loans help the communities build garbage dumps and water purifying plants. **Ask: If you ran the bank, for what large and small needs would you lend people in colonias money?** Students should think about larger problems like electricity and safety, but also smaller needs like school supplies and child care. **L1**

Mexico now make cars, consumer goods, and steel. The labels on your clothing might even say "Made in Mexico."

Mexico has large deposits of petroleum and natural gas in the Gulf of Mexico and along the southern coast. As a result, Mexico is among the world's major oil-producing nations.

Mexico is also home to important service industries such as banking and tourism. **Service industries,** you recall, are businesses that provide services to people rather than producing goods.

NAFTA In 1994, Mexico, the United States, and Canada became partners in **NAFTA,** the North American Free Trade Agreement. Under this agreement, most goods traded between these countries would be free of tariffs, or special taxes. This means a homemaker in Canada would probably choose to buy a tablecloth made in Mexico rather than to pay more for a taxed tablecloth produced in Europe.

Some Americans have been afraid that belonging to NAFTA would mean American jobs would "go south." They feared that the lower rate of pay for labor in Mexico would encourage many manufacturers to move their businesses to Mexico rather than keep them in the United States. The debate about the overall affect of NAFTA is still going on. However, as one supporter of NAFTA stated, "As Americans, it is far better to have prosperous than struggling neighbors, and NAFTA contributes to this objective."

Reading Check **Why are some Americans afraid jobs will "go south"?**

Assessment

Defining Terms

1. **Define** land bridge, peninsula, latitude, altitude, hurricane, vaquero, maquiladora, subsistence farm, plantation, industrialize, service industry, NAFTA.

Recalling Facts

2. **History** How did the vaqueros of Mexico influence American ranching?
3. **Location** Why is Mexico a land bridge?
4. **Economics** Why have many Mexicans moved to the cities of the north?

Critical Thinking

5. **Understanding Cause and Effect** How has NAFTA affected the people in Canada and the people in Mexico? Do you think NAFTA has been good or bad for the people in border cities of the United States? Explain.
6. **Analyzing Information** Explain why Mexico is part of both North America and Latin America.

Graphic Organizer

7. **Organizing Information** Create a diagram like this one, and then list two facts that explain the large population of central Mexico.

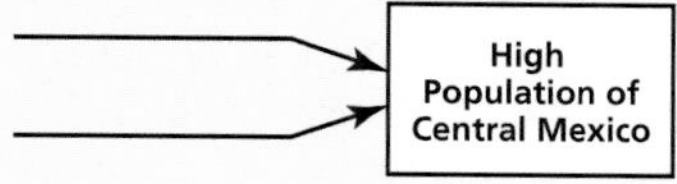

Applying Social Studies Skills

8. **Analyzing Diagrams** Study Mexico's altitude zones on page 537. At which elevation do you think most people live? Why do they live here?

Section 1 Assessment

1. The terms are defined in the Glossary.
2. American cowhands use tools and techniques for herding, roping, and cattle branding developed by vaqueros.
3. It joins two larger land masses, namely North America and South America.
4. to work in factories there
5. Answers will vary, but should be supported by facts.
6. Mexico is geographically part of North America and culturally part of Latin America.
7. pleasant climate and fertile soil for farming and ranching, and jobs in industrial cities like Mexico City and Guadalajara
8. 2,500 feet (760 m); moderate climate

Chapter 20

Section 1, pages 534–539

Section Quiz 20-1

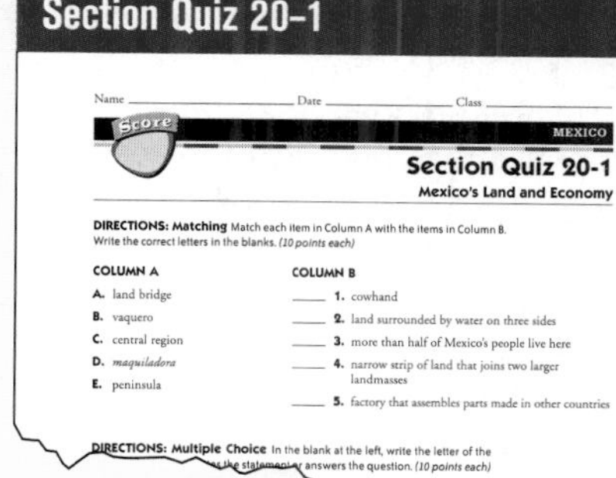
Name ____ Date ____ Class ____

MEXICO

Section Quiz 20-1

Mexico's Land and Economy

DIRECTIONS: Matching Match each item in Column A with the items in Column B. Write the correct letters in the blanks. (10 points each)

COLUMN A	COLUMN B
A. land bridge	____ 1. cowhand
B. vaquero	____ 2. land surrounded by water on three sides
C. central region	____ 3. more than half of Mexico's people live here
D. maquiladora	____ 4. narrow strip of land that joins two larger landmasses
E. peninsula	____ 5. factory that assembles parts made in other countries

DIRECTIONS: Multiple Choice In the blank at the left, write the letter of the ... answers the question. (10 points each)

Reteach

Write each term listed in the Guide to Reading on a slip of paper. Have students take turns drawing a slip and telling what they know about the term.

Reading Check Answer

They fear that Mexico's low wages will lure American businesses away from the United States.

Reading Essentials and Study Guide 20-1

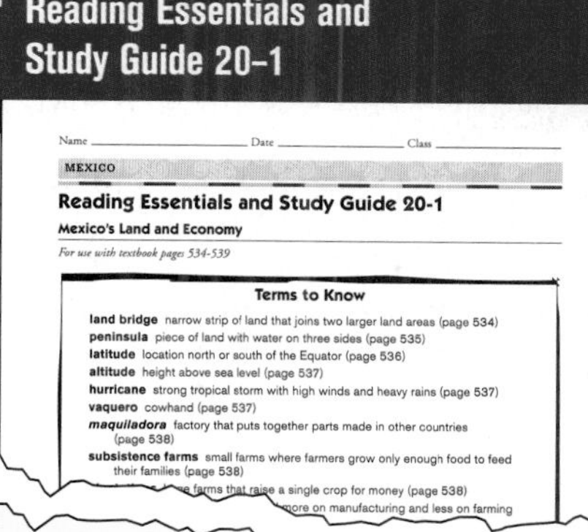
Name ____ Date ____ Class ____

MEXICO

Reading Essentials and Study Guide 20-1

Mexico's Land and Economy

For use with textbook pages 534–539

Terms to Know

land bridge narrow strip of land that joins two larger land areas (page 534)
peninsula piece of land with water on three sides (page 535)
latitude location north or south of the Equator (page 536)
altitude height above sea level (page 537)
hurricane strong tropical storm with high winds and heavy rains (page 537)
vaquero cowhand (page 537)
maquiladora factory that puts together parts made in other countries (page 538)
subsistence farms small farms where farmers grow only enough food to feed their families (page 538)
... farms that raise a single crop for money (page 538)
... more on manufacturing and less on farming

CLOSE

Have students make a concept web for Mexico's geography and climates.

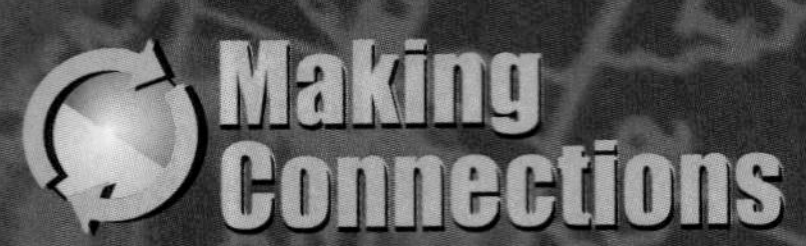

TEACH

Have students read Making Connections and the other passages that describe NAFTA in this text. Discuss some of the issues that are raised in these passages. Then have students write a letter to the editor explaining why they think NAFTA is good or bad for either the United States or for Mexico. (Students should choose only one country's perspective.) **L1**

More About NAFTA

The North American Free Trade Agreement (NAFTA), establishing a free-trade zone in North America, took effect on January 1, 1994. NAFTA immediately lifted tariffs on the majority of goods produced by Canada, Mexico, and the United States. After NAFTA was signed, maquiladoras, or assembly plants, flourished in Mexico. The maquiladoras are generally owned by non-Mexican corporations and produce such items as appliances, clothing, and automobiles. The maquiladoras have stimulated rapid population migration to the border region, particularly at its eastern and western extremities.

Making Connections

CULTURE | GOVERNMENT | PEOPLE | TECHNOLOGY

Good Neighbors

Every 60 seconds, goods worth more than $500,000 cross the U.S.-Mexican border. Goods worth nearly $750,000 cross the U.S.-Canadian border. Those numbers are double what they were in 1994. What made them grow, experts say, was the North American Free Trade Agreement, or NAFTA.

Map by Joe Lertola for TIME

Pros and Cons

NAFTA is an agreement that allows for the free movement of goods across the international borders of Canada, the United States, and Mexico. The free movement of goods means people are able to import goods from other countries without paying import taxes, called *tariffs.*

Since NAFTA took effect, millions of new jobs have been created in all three countries, especially Mexico. On the negative side, some U.S. and Canadian companies moved their factories to Mexico where wages are low. As a result, many U.S. and Canadian workers lost their jobs.

The United States and Mexico are interdependent. Mexicans depend on U.S. companies to create jobs in Mexico. The United States depends on the ability of Mexican workers to produce goods cheaply.

U.S. border communities depend on Mexico, too. From El Paso alone, Mexican factories buy $8 billion to $10 billion worth of goods and services every year. U.S. companies often try to make workers' lives easier by building safe and affordable housing.

Mexico's Future

Mexico's economy must get stronger. In 2001, one of every two people in Mexico was poor. One in five was desperately poor, scraping by on less than $2 per day. Farm workers earned only about $5 per day. That isn't nearly enough to support a family.

Jobs in border factories, or maquiladoras, that opened after NAFTA was signed pay on the average of $10 per day. This is still a small amount compared to U.S. jobs, but it is much better than before.

Mexico's president Vicente Fox is working closely with U.S. officials to ease such problems as immigration and trade restrictions. He would like to see the interdependence created by NAFTA continue to grow and benefit all its members.

Making the Connection

1. List the combined border cities on the map above in order of size, from largest to smallest.
2. **Drawing Conclusions** Which border cities would you expect to be connected by bridges? Why?

Making the Connection

1. San Diego/Tijuana; El Paso/Ciudad Juárez; McAllen/Reynosa; Brownsville/Matamoros; Calexico/Mexicali; Laredo/Nuevo Laredo
2. El Paso/Ciudad Juárez, Laredo/Nuevo Laredo, McAllen/Reynosa, and Brownsville/Matamoros; because the U.S./Mexican cities are separated by the Rio Grande

Section 2 Mexico's History

Guide to Reading

Main Idea

Mexico's culture reflects a blend of its Native American and Spanish past.

Terms to Know

- jade
- obsidian
- maize
- hieroglyphics
- mural
- colony
- hacienda

Reading Strategy

Create a chart like this one, then provide one example of how Native Americans and Europeans influenced Mexican culture.

Ethnic Groups	Influence on Mexican Culture
Native Americans	
Europeans	

NATIONAL GEOGRAPHIC Exploring Our World

Thousands of people visit an ancient temple in Mexico's Yucatán Peninsula on the spring and fall equinoxes. On those two days, the setting sun casts a shadow on the stairs of the temple's north face. The area that is not shadowed looks like the ancient Native American god called Kukulcan, or the Feathered Serpent, going down the temple stairs.

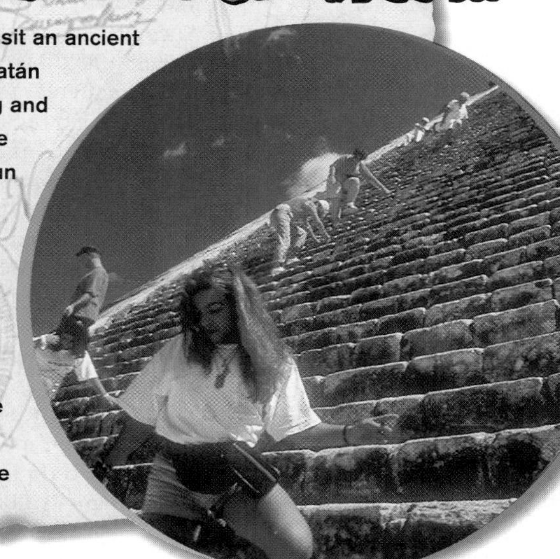

The first people to arrive in Mexico were the ancestors of today's Native Americans. Mexico's Native American heritage has shaped the country's culture. So has Mexico's European heritage, brought by the Spaniards who conquered the area in the 1500s.

Native American Civilizations

Native Americans came to Mexico thousands of years ago. From about 1200 B.C. to the A.D. 1500s, these people built a series of brilliant, highly advanced civilizations on Mexican soil. Of these, the Olmec, Mayan, and Aztec civilizations are the best-known. Look at the map on page 542 to see where the Olmec, Mayan, and Aztec civilizations thrived.

The Olmecs The **Olmecs** built the first civilization in the Americas around 1200 B.C. They decorated their cities with large carved stone statues, some standing about 10 feet (3 m) high and weighing over 20 tons (18 t). They also carved smaller and more personal objects like jewelry out of **jade,** a local shiny stone that comes in many shades of

1 Focus

Section Objectives

1. Describe the groups that influenced Mexico's history.
2. Discuss how Spaniards changed life in Mexico.
3. Outline changes that took place in Mexico in the 1800s and 1900s.

BELLRINGER Skillbuilder Activity

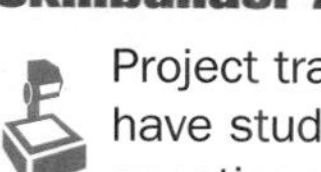

Project transparency and have students answer questions.

This activity is also available as a blackline master.

Daily Focus Skills Transparency 20-2

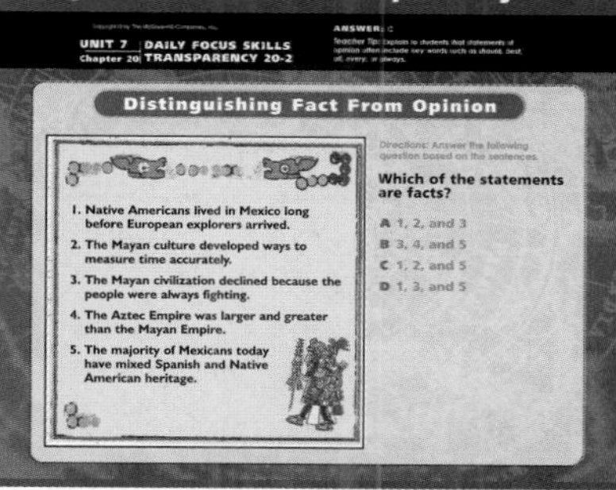

UNIT 7 Chapter 20 DAILY FOCUS SKILLS TRANSPARENCY 20-2

ANSWER: C

Teacher Tip: Explain to students that statements of opinion often include key words such as should, best, all, every, or always.

Distinguishing Fact From Opinion

1. Native Americans lived in Mexico long before European explorers arrived.
2. The Mayan culture developed ways to measure time accurately.
3. The Mayan civilization declined because the people were always fighting.
4. The Aztec Empire was larger and greater than the Mayan Empire.
5. The majority of Mexicans today have mixed Spanish and Native American heritage.

Directions: Answer the following question based on the sentences.

Which of the statements are facts?

A 1, 2, and 3
B 3, 4, and 5
C 1, 2, and 5
D 1, 3, and 5

Guide to Reading

■ **Accessing Prior Knowledge**
Ask: What European group colonized Mexico and the southwestern United States? Give clues by mentioning Spanish place names such as Los Angeles, Santa Fe, and San Antonio.

Section Resources

Reproducible Masters
- Reproducible Lesson Plan 20-2
- Daily Lecture and Discussion Notes 20-2
- Guided Reading Activity 20-2
- Reading Essentials and Study Guide 20-2
- Section Quiz 20-2

Transparencies
- Daily Focus Skills Transparency 20-2
- GeoQuiz Transparency 20-2

Multimedia
- Vocabulary PuzzleMaker Software
- Interactive Tutor Self-Assessment CD-ROM
- Presentation Plus! CD-ROM
- ExamView® Pro 3.0 Testmaker CD-ROM

Chapter 20

Section 2, pages 541–544

Teach

Identifying Main Ideas

Have students write each section subheading on a piece of paper. Under each subheading, have them identify the main idea of the subsection. L1

Daily Lecture Notes 20-2

MEXICO

Daily Lecture and Discussion Notes 20-2

Mexico's History (pages 541–544)

Did You Know? Texas was once part of Mexico. In 1836 General Antonio López de Santa Anna defeated a Texas force in the Battle of the Alamo at San Antonio. But later that year, Texas forces defeated his army at San Jacinto and captured him. Santa Anna signed a treaty recognizing the independence of Texas. In addition to what is now the state of Texas, the new republic of Texas included parts of present-day Colorado, Kansas, New Mexico, Oklahoma, and Wyoming.

I. Native American Civilizations (pages 541–543)

A. Native Americans came to Mexico thousands of years ago. These people built a series of brilliant, highly advanced civilizations on Mexican soil.

B. The people called the Maya lived on the Yucatán Peninsula. They built huge ... the shape of pyramids with steps. The Maya developed ... of writing that uses signs and symbols. Artists decorated ...

Applying Map Skills

Answers

1. the Maya
2. Tenochtitlán

Skills Practice

Which is the earliest Mexican civilization? *(the Olmec)*

Guided Reading Activity 20-2

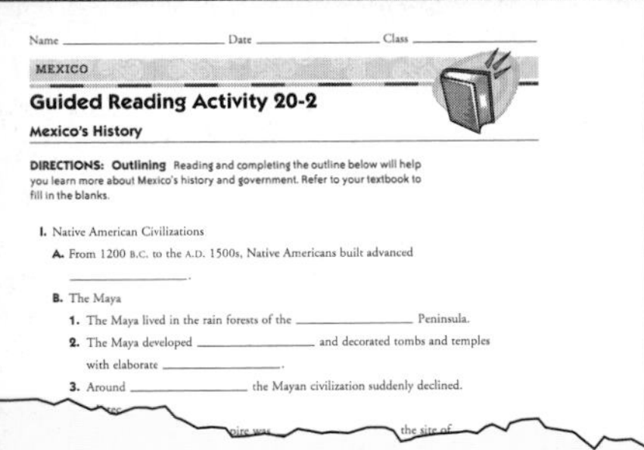
Name ______ Date ______ Class ______

MEXICO

Guided Reading Activity 20-2

Mexico's History

DIRECTIONS: Outlining Reading and completing the outline below will help you learn more about Mexico's history and government. Refer to your textbook to fill in the blanks.

I. Native American Civilizations

A. From 1200 B.C. to the A.D. 1500s, Native Americans built advanced ______

B. The Maya

1. The Maya lived in the rain forests of the ______ Peninsula.
2. The Maya developed ______ and decorated tombs and temples with elaborate ______.
3. Around ______ the Mayan civilization suddenly declined.

green as well as other colors. All these items were carved with **obsidian,** a hard, black glass created by the volcanoes in the area, because the Olmecs had no metals.

The Olmecs were the first to grow **maize,** or corn, to feed their many people. In addition to cities and ceremonial centers, they built large drainage systems to direct rainwater away from their fields and settlements. The Olmecs lasted longer than any other Native American civilization, finally disappearing in about 400 B.C.

The Maya The people called the **Maya** lived in the rain forests of the Yucatán Peninsula and surrounding areas from about A.D. 250 to 900. Religion held Mayan society together. Mayan priests needed to measure time accurately to hold religious ceremonies at the correct moment. They studied the heavens and developed a calendar of 365 days.

The Maya built huge stone temples in the shape of pyramids with steps. One of these structures, the temple of **Kukulcan,** showed careful planning. Each side of Kukulcan had 91 steps, totaling 364. The platform at the temple's top made one more step for a grand total of 365—just like the days in the year.

The Maya also developed **hieroglyphics,** a form of writing that uses signs and symbols. They had a complex number system. Artists decorated temples and tombs with elaborate **murals,** or wall paintings.

Around A.D. 900, Mayan civilization declined. Why? Historians do not know. Some suggest that the Maya overused the land and could not grow enough food. Others suggest that warfare or the spread of disease caused their decline. The Maya did not disappear, however. Their descendants still live in the same area and speak the Mayan language.

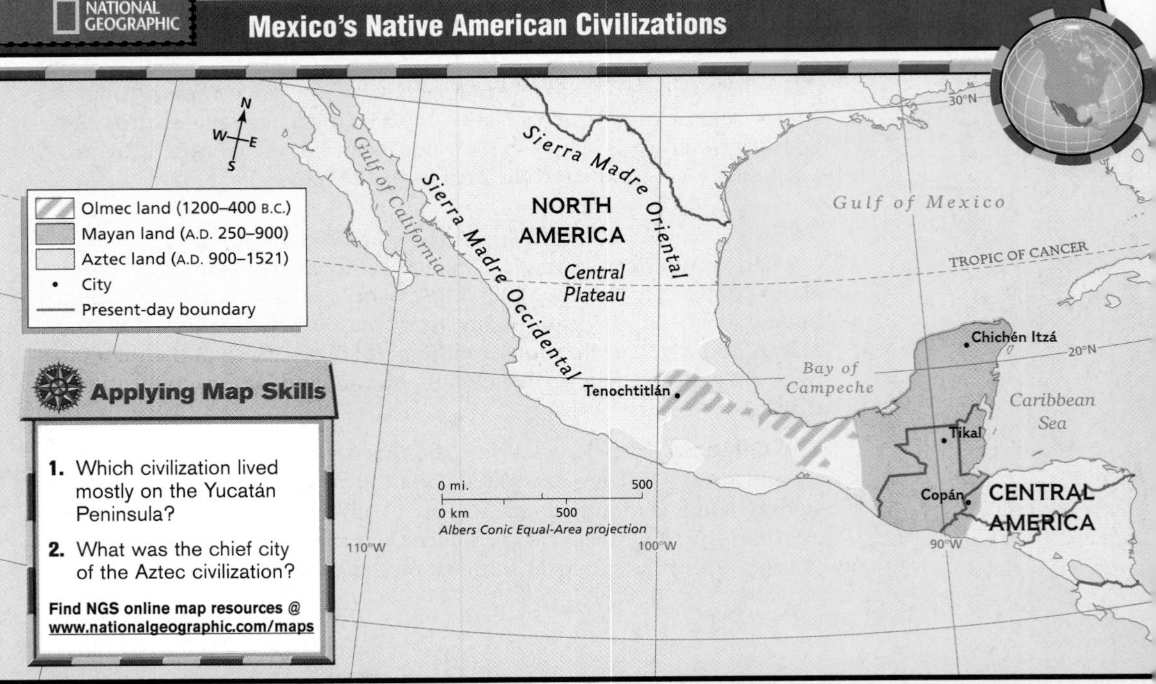

Cooperative Learning Activity

Making a Poster Organize students into three groups to research the cultural heritage of Mexico. Assign each group one of the following cultures: Maya, Aztec, or Spanish. Group members should research and report on the history of their assigned culture. Then they should find illustrations showing how that culture influences Mexico today. Have the groups use the illustrations to create a poster with captions, which they can present to the class. L2

EE6 The Uses of Geography: Standard 17

The Aztec Around A.D. 1200, a people called the Mexica moved into central Mexico from the north. The Spanish later called these people the Aztec. The **Aztec** conquered a large empire in central Mexico. Their capital, **Tenochtitlán** (tay•NAWCH• teet•LAHN) was magnificent. Today Mexico City—Mexico's capital—stands on this ancient site.

Tenochtitlán was originally built on two islands in the middle of Lake Texcoco. Long dikes connected it to land. The city had huge stepped pyramids. Merchants traded gold, silver, and pottery in busy marketplaces. Farmers grew their crops in structures called "floating gardens," or rafts filled with mud. The rafts eventually sank to the lake bottom and piled up, forming fertile islands.

The Aztec people and many of their traditions survive today in Mexico. The food, crafts, and language of Mexico have roots in Aztec culture. Even the name of the country comes from the word the Aztec called themselves—the *Mexica*. The flag of modern Mexico honors this ancient civilization. In the center of the flag is the Aztec symbol of an eagle with a snake in its beak.

✓ Reading Check **What Native American cultures flourished in Mexico?**

NATIONAL GEOGRAPHIC On Location

The Aztec

The Aztec capital of Tenochtitlán, shown here in ruins, flourished until the arrival of the Spaniards in 1519.

History **How was the small Spanish army able to defeat the Aztec?**

Spanish Mexico

In 1519 Mexico's history changed dramatically. A Spanish army led by **Hernán Cortés** landed on Mexico's Gulf coast. He and about 550 soldiers marched to Tenochtitlán, which they had heard was filled with gold.

But how did just 550 Spaniards conquer the heart of the Aztec Empire, which contained about 21 million people? There are several reasons for their success. First, the Spanish made treaties with the Indians who had been conquered by the Aztec. These treaties brought the Spanish thousands of warriors and many needed supplies. Second, Cortés's men had steel swords, muskets, and cannons, while the Aztec had only wooden weapons with jade and obsidian blades and points. Third, the Spanish had horses, which were unknown to the Indians until then. In fact, when Cortés was on his horse, the Aztec thought that he and his horse were one creature. They thought he was one of their most important gods, *Quetzlcoatl,* and that he had returned to punish them. So, of course, many were afraid of him.

Spain made Mexico a **colony,** or an overseas territory, because Mexico's rocky land held rich deposits of gold and silver. Many Spanish settlers came to live in Mexico. Some raised cattle on large ranches called **haciendas** (ah•see•AYN•dahs). Others started gold and silver mines. The Spaniards made Native Americans work on the ranches and

Chapter 20

Section 2, pages 541–544

More About the Photo

Tenochtitlán Tenochtitlán was founded around A.D. 1345. It was a flourishing city with an estimated population of between 200,000 and 300,000. The marshy island was connected to the mainland by three great causeways and had dams to protect against floods. People traveled by canals built throughout the city.

Caption Answer help from tribes conquered by the Aztec, superior weapons, and horses

✓ Reading Check Answer

the Olmecs, the Maya, and the Aztec

3 ASSESS

Assign Section 2 Assessment as homework or an in-class activity.

Have students use the Interactive Tutor Self-Assessment CD-ROM to review Section 20–2.

Section Quiz 20-2

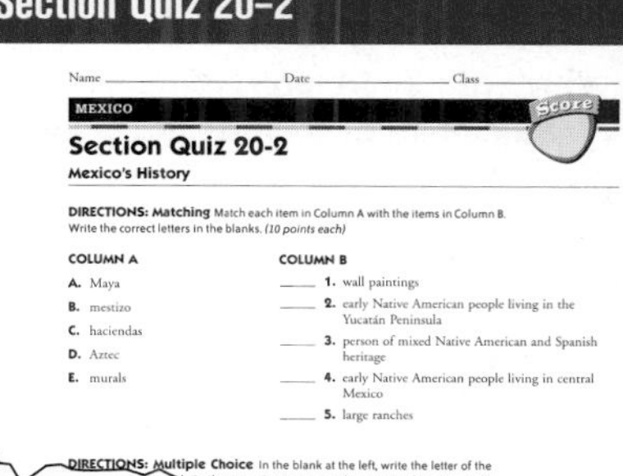

Name ______ Date ______ Class ______

MEXICO

Score

Section Quiz 20-2

Mexico's History

DIRECTIONS: Matching Match each item in Column A with the items in Column B. Write the correct letters in the blanks. *(10 points each)*

COLUMN A

A. Maya
B. mestizo
C. haciendas
D. Aztec
E. murals

COLUMN B

____ **1.** wall paintings
____ **2.** early Native American people living in the Yucatán Peninsula
____ **3.** person of mixed Native American and Spanish heritage
____ **4.** early Native American people living in central Mexico
____ **5.** large ranches

DIRECTIONS: Multiple Choice In the blank at the left, write the letter of the ... or answers the question. *(10 points each)*

Meeting Special Needs

Verbal/Linguistic Point out to students that some of the Terms to Know in this chapter are Spanish words. Remind them that the text often gives the pronunciations of these and other Spanish words. Have them follow the pronunciation guides and practice saying the Spanish words in this chapter aloud several times. **L1 ELL**

Refer to *Inclusion for the Middle School Social Studies Classroom Strategies and Activities* in the TCR.

Chapter 20

Section 2, pages 541–544

Reading Check Answer

because it held rich deposits of gold and silver

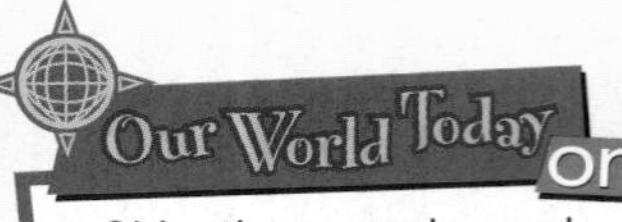

Objectives, goals, and answers to the Student Web Activity can be found in the Web Activity Lesson Plan at owt.glencoe.com

Reading Check Answer

Emiliano Zapata

Reading Essentials and Study Guide 20–2

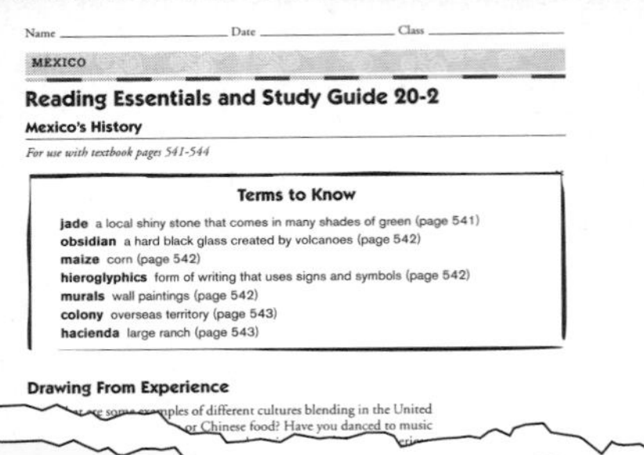

Name ____________ Date ____________ Class ____________

MEXICO

Reading Essentials and Study Guide 20-2

Mexico's History

For use with textbook pages 541-544

Terms to Know

jade a local shiny stone that comes in many shades of green (page 541)
obsidian a hard black glass created by volcanoes (page 542)
maize corn (page 542)
hieroglyphics form of writing that uses signs and symbols (page 542)
murals wall paintings (page 542)
colony overseas territory (page 543)
hacienda large ranch (page 543)

Drawing From Experience

...ples of different cultures blending in the United ... or Chinese food? Have you danced to music ...

Enrich

Have students learn more about Mayan culture, such as the calendar, the ritual ball game, or hieroglyphics.

4 Close

Have students create an annotated time line of Mexican history.

Web Activity Visit the ***Our World Today: People, Places, and Issues*** Web site at owt.glencoe.com and click on **Chapter 20–Student Web Activities** to learn more about Mexico's history.

in the mines. Thousands of Native Americans died from mistreatment. Many thousands more died of diseases such as the common cold and smallpox, which they caught from the Europeans. Spanish priests came to Mexico and in their own way tried to improve the lives of the Native Americans. Because of their work, many Native Americans accepted the priests' teachings. Today about 90 percent of Mexico's people follow the Roman Catholic religion.

Reading Check Why was Mexico a valuable colony for Spain?

Independence and Revolution

The people of Mexico eventually rebelled against Spanish rule and gained independence in 1821. In 1824 they set up a republic with an elected president. Soon after independence, Mexico lost some valuable territory to the United States. The territory included Texas and California.

For many decades, rich families, army officers, and Catholic Church leaders held most of the power and wealth in Mexico. In 1910 Mexican peasants revolted. **Emiliano Zapata,** who commanded a rebel army, stated the goals of this revolution. He wanted to give to the poor "the lands, woods, and water that the landlords or bosses have taken from us." Zapata's forces swooped down and seized many large haciendas. They divided the land among the poor. In the northwestern provinces along the U.S. border, **Francisco "Pancho" Villa** also tried to help the poor, mostly Indian peasants.

Reading Check Who led the 1910 revolution?

Section 2 Assessment

Defining Terms

1. **Define** jade, obsidian, maize, hieroglyphics, mural, colony, hacienda.

Recalling Facts

2. **History** Describe three achievements of the ancient Maya.
3. **History** Which European country conquered and colonized Mexico?
4. **History** What were Emiliano Zapata's goals?

Critical Thinking

5. **Sequencing Information** Put the following events in the correct chronological order: Cortés conquers the Aztec, Mexico wins independence from Spain, the Mexica move into central Mexico, Zapata leads a revolution.
6. **Understanding Cause and Effect** How did the arrival of Europeans affect the Native Americans in Mexico?

Graphic Organizer

7. **Organizing Information** Create a chart like this one. In each column list the major advancements of each civilization.

Olmec	Maya	Aztec

Applying Social Studies Skills

8. **Analyzing Maps** Refer to the map of Mexico's Native American civilizations on page 542. Which Native American group settled the farthest south?

Section 2 Assessment

1. The terms are defined in the Glossary.
2. a calendar of 365 days; pyramids; hieroglyphics; a number system; murals
3. Spain
4. to divide the lands of the rich among the poor
5. the Mexica move into central Mexico; Cortés conquers the Aztec; Mexico wins independence from Spain; Zapata leads a revolution
6. Many Native Americans worked on ranches and mines, died of mistreatment or disease, and accepted Catholicism.
7. Olmecs: built first civilization in Americas, carved statues and jewelry, grew maize, built drainage systems; Maya: developed 365-day calendar, built pyramids, developed hieroglyphics, painted wall murals; Aztec: built a magnificent city, conquered an empire
8. the Maya

Social Studies Skill

Reading a Physical Map

A map that shows the different heights of the land is called a physical map. Physical maps use colors and shading to also show relief—or how flat or rugged the land surface is. Colors are also used to show the land's elevation—or height above sea level. Green often shows the lowest elevations (closest to sea level). Yellows, oranges, browns, and reds usually mean higher elevations. Sometimes the highest areas, such as mountain peaks, are white.

Learning the Skill

To read a physical map, apply these steps:

- Read the map title to identify the region shown on the map.
- Use the map key to find the meaning of colors and symbols.
- Identify the areas of highest and lowest elevation on the map.
- Find important physical features, including mountains, rivers, and coastlines.
- Mentally map the actual shape of the land.

Practicing the Skill

Look at the map to answer the following:

1. What country is shown on the map?
2. What mountain ranges are labeled?
3. What is the elevation of the green areas on the map (in feet and meters)?
4. What color on the map means 2,000–5,000 feet (600–1,500 m)?
5. Briefly describe the physical landscape of the area shown on the map, moving from west to east.

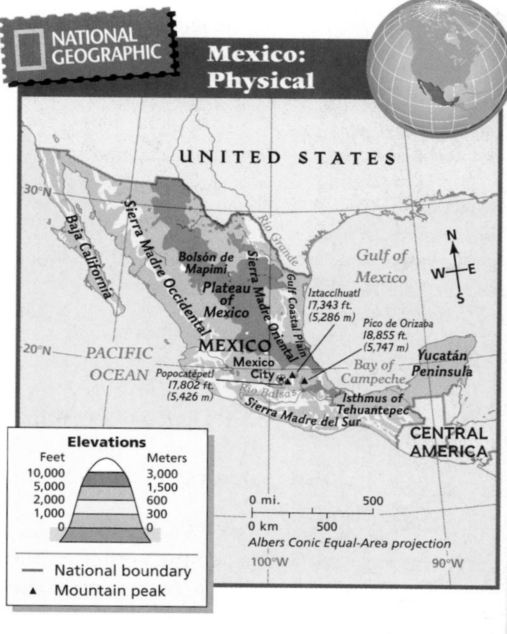

Applying the Skill

Look at the physical map of Canada on page 474. Describe the physical landscape of the country, moving from east to west.

GO TO Practice key skills with Glencoe **Skillbuilder Interactive Workbook, Level 1.**

TEACH

Display a photograph that shows mountains and lowlands. **Ask:** **How can geographers show the differences in the landforms?** If students are unable to answer, point to the physical map in the textbook on this page. Explain that the different colors indicate different elevations. Discuss the scale with the students so they can see how the color codes work. **L1**

Additional Skills Practice

1. **What elevation is represented by the color red?** *(5,000 to 10,000 feet or 1,500 to 3,000 meters)*
2. **What does it mean when the land around some of the rivers is colored yellow or green?** *(Rivers cut valleys in the mountains.)*
3. **How would you describe Mexico in terms of elevation?** *(Most of the country is 2,000 to 10,000 feet (600 to 3000 m) above sea level.)*

Additional Skills Resources

 Chapter Skills Activity 20

 Building Geography Skills for Life

GLENCOE TECHNOLOGY

 **Skillbuilder Interactive Workbook CD-ROM, Level 1**

This interactive CD-ROM reinforces student mastery of essential social studies skills.

Practicing the Skill Answers

1. Mexico
2. Sierra Madre Occidental, Sierra Madre Oriental, Sierra Madre del Sur
3. 0–1000 feet (0–300 m)
4. orange
5. lowlands on the west coast, increasing to higher elevations in the center of the country, then lowlands on the east coast and Yucatan Peninsula

Applying the Skill

Possible answer: Jagged coast rises to rolling hills; lowlands along the St. Lawrence River and near the Great Lakes; very low land dotted by lakes in the Canadian Shield; vast prairies in the Interior Plains; high Rocky Mountains; high plateaus; tall Coastal Mountains interspersed with river valleys

Chapter 20

Section 3, pages 546–550

1 Focus

Section Objectives

1. Describe life in the cities and villages of Mexico.
2. Identify elements of Mexican culture.
3. Discuss Mexico's government.
4. Explain what challenges face Mexico.

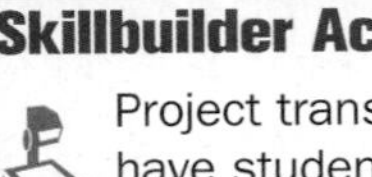

BELLRINGER
Skillbuilder Activity

Project transparency and have students answer questions.

This activity is also available as a blackline master.

Daily Focus Skills Transparency 20–3

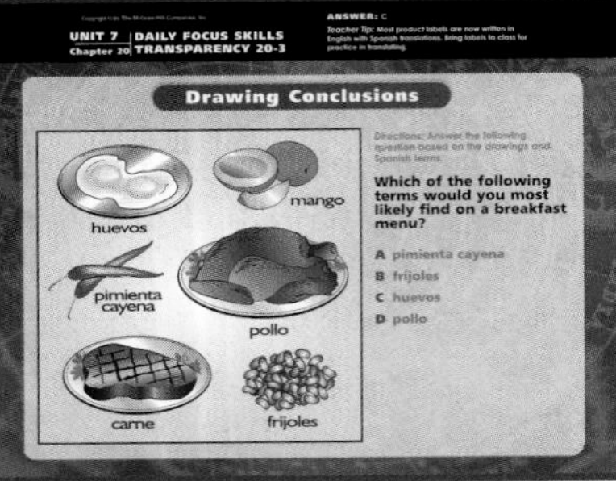

Reading Check Answer

plazas

Guide to Reading

■ **Accessing Prior Knowledge**
Have students predict what kinds of economic challenges they think Mexico might face based on what they know about Mexico's economy.

Section 3 Mexico Today

Guide to Reading

Main Idea

Mexicans enjoy a rich and lively culture but face many serious challenges.

Terms to Know

- plaza
- adobe
- federal republic
- migrant worker
- national debt
- smog

Reading Strategy

Create a diagram like this one. In each of the smaller ovals, write a feature of Mexican culture. Add as many smaller ovals as you need.

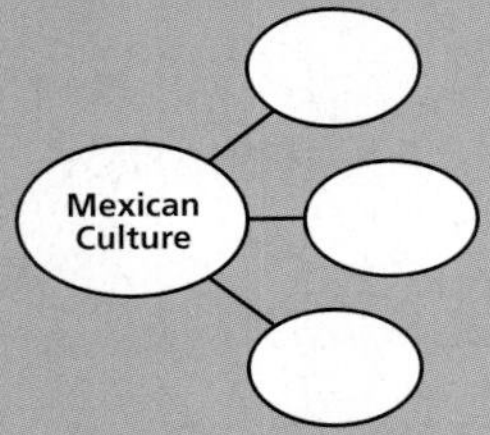

NATIONAL GEOGRAPHIC Exploring Our World

Mexican art reveals the pride that the people take in their rich heritage. The people of Taxco (TAHS•koh) call their city the "silver capital of the world." Though the nearby hills no longer hold any silver, the city remains a home to craftspeople who make silver jewelry, cups, and trays. Here, a designer and silversmith examine a new pitcher design.

Mexico—the third-largest country in area in Latin America, after Brazil and Argentina—has a large and dynamic population. About 75 percent of all Mexicans live in the country's bustling cities.

Mexico's Cities and Villages

In the center of Mexico's cities, you often find large **plazas,** or public squares. Around each city's plaza stand important buildings such as a church and a government center. When you look at the buildings, you can see the architectural style of Spanish colonial times. Newer sections of the cities have a mix of towering glass office buildings and modern houses. In the poorer sections of town, people build small homes out of whatever materials they can find. This may include boards, sheet metal, or even cardboard.

Rural villages also have central plazas. Streets lead from the plazas to residential areas. Many homes are made of **adobe** (uh•DOH•bee), or sun-dried clay bricks. The roofs might be made of straw or of colored tile, in the Spanish style.

✓Reading Check What do you find in the center of Mexico's cities and villages?

546 CHAPTER 20

Section Resources

Reproducible Masters

- Reproducible Lesson Plan 20-3
- Daily Lecture and Discussion Notes 20-3
- Guided Reading Activity 20-3
- Reading Essentials and Study Guide 20-3
- Section Quiz 20-3

Transparencies

- Daily Focus Skills Transparency 20-3

Multimedia

- Vocabulary PuzzleMaker Software
- Interactive Tutor Self-Assessment CD-ROM
- Presentation Plus! CD-ROM
- ExamView® Pro 3.0 Testmaker CD-ROM

Mexican Culture

Mexican artists and writers have created many national treasures. In the early 1900s, Mexican painters produced beautiful murals—just as Native American painters had done centuries before. Among the most famous of these mural painters were José Clemente Orozco, David Alfero Sequieros, and Diego Rivera. Rivera's wife, Frida Kahlo, became well-known for her paintings, which revealed her inner feelings. Modern writers such as Carlos Fuentes and Octavio Paz have written poems and stories that reflect the values of Mexico's people.

Food If you have tasted Mexican food, you know that it is a rich blend of flavors. Corn—first grown in Mexico—continues to be an important part of the Mexican diet. Chocolate, tomatoes, beans, squash, and chilies were all Native American foods as well. When the Spanish came, they brought beef, chicken, cheese, and olive oil, which Mexicans added to their cooking.

Today, Mexicans combine these different cooking traditions in popular foods such as tacos and enchiladas. Both dishes combine a flat bread called a tortilla with meat or beans, vegetables, cheese, and spicy chilies.

Celebrations Throughout the year, Mexicans enjoy several special celebrations called fiestas (fee•EHS•tuhs). These special days include parades, fireworks, music, and dancing. Mariachi (MAHR•ee•AH•chee) bands may play such traditional instruments as the violin, guitar, horn, and bass at fiestas. More likely, however, you will hear the fast-paced rhythms and singing of Latino bands, which have influenced the United States.

National holidays include **Independence Day** (September 16) and **Cinco de Mayo** (May 5). This holiday celebrates the day in 1862 that Mexicans defeated an invading French army in battle. November 2

Art

Mexican artist Diego Rivera is one of the most famous mural painters of the twentieth century. He believed that art belonged to the people. In Mexico City, Rivera's murals line the courtyard of the Ministry of Education building and cover the walls of the National Palace. With their characteristically vivid colors and distinctive style, Rivera's murals tell the story of the work, culture, and history of the Mexican people.

Looking Closer **How did Rivera's work support his belief that art belongs to the people?**

Mexico Through the Centuries ▶

Chapter 20

Section 3, pages 546–550

Making Comparisons Have students make a chart comparing Mexican culture to their culture. When they are done with their charts, have them discuss the similarities and differences. **L1 ELL**

Daily Lecture Notes 20-3

Copyright © by The McGraw-Hill Companies, Inc.

MEXICO

Daily Lecture and Discussion Notes 20-3

Mexico Today (pages 546–550)

Did You Know? The Treaty of Tlatelolco was the first treaty to ban nuclear weapons in a geographic region. Under the leadership of Mexico, the countries of Latin America signed the treaty in 1967.

I. Mexico's Cities and Villages *(page 546)*

A. In the center of Mexico's cities, large **plazas**—or public squares—are found. Around each city's plaza stand important buildings such as a church and a government center.

B. Many Mexican homes are made of **adobe**, or sun-dried clay bricks.

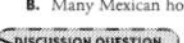

DISCUSSION QUESTION ...ffer between the newer sections and poorer

Answer His work tells the story of Mexico's people and culture and is displayed in public places.

Ask students: **If you were to create a mural celebrating Mexican culture, what would you include?** Discuss the significance of the people, events, and cultural elements that students suggest.

Team-Teaching Activity

Economics Have a teacher with a background in economics discuss the issue of international debt in the developing world. Have the teacher talk about growing calls by leaders of developing countries for debt relief and explain why lenders and international bodies like the World Bank and International Monetary Fund are reluctant to take that step without the countries involved taking additional actions. Then have students organize a debate on international lending. **L3**

EE4 Human Systems: Standard 11

More About the Photo

Fiestas Independence Day celebrates Mexico's independence from Spain. People decorate streets, houses, buildings and cars with Mexico's flag and national colors of green, white, and red. Lighted decorations are set up in every city, the most spectacular being those of the Zócalo, or main plaza, in Mexico City.

Caption Answer to celebrate special occasions in Mexico

Reading Check Answer

Independence Day, Cinco de Mayo, the Day of the Dead

Travel Guide

Mexico offers sport to deep-sea fishers. Marlin, swordfish, and tarpon are among the game fish caught off Mexico's coast. Many fishers enjoy the waters off Cape San Lucas at the southern tip of Baja California.

Guided Reading Activity 20-3

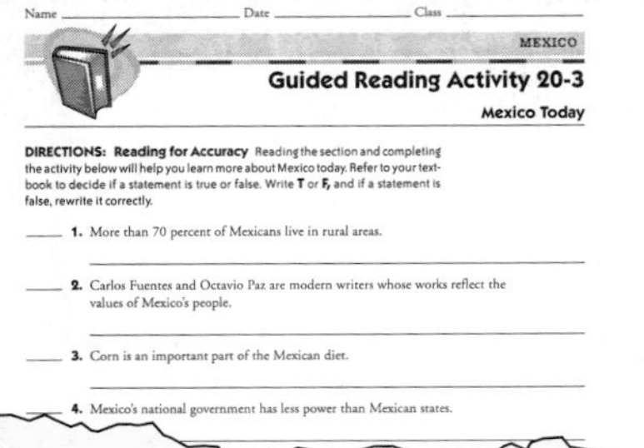

Name ______ Date ______ Class ______

MEXICO

Guided Reading Activity 20-3

Mexico Today

DIRECTIONS: Reading for Accuracy Reading the section and completing the activity below will help you learn more about Mexico today. Refer to your textbook to decide if a statement is true or false. Write **T** or **F**, and if a statement is false, rewrite it correctly.

____ **1.** More than 70 percent of Mexicans live in rural areas.

____ **2.** Carlos Fuentes and Octavio Paz are modern writers whose works reflect the values of Mexico's people.

____ **3.** Corn is an important part of the Mexican diet.

____ **4.** Mexico's national government has less power than Mexican states.

Reading Check Answer

federal republic

NATIONAL GEOGRAPHIC On Location

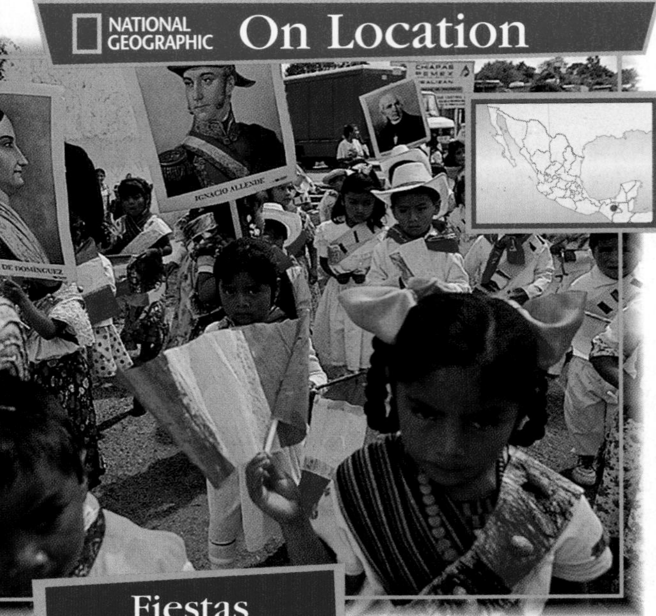

Fiestas

On September 16, parades celebrate the women and men who helped win Mexican independence.

Culture **What is the purpose of fiestas?**

is a special religious celebration called the **Day of the Dead.** On this day, families gather in cemeteries where they honor their departed loved ones by laying down food and flowers.

Reading Check **What are some important celebrations in Mexico?**

Mexico's Government

Mexico, like the United States, is a **federal republic,** where power is divided between national and state governments, and a strong president leads the national government. Mexico's national government differs in that it has much more power than the state governments. The president of Mexico is head of the executive branch of government. He or she can serve only one six-year term but has more power than the legislative and judicial branches.

For many decades, one political party, called the **Party of Institutional Revolution (PRI),** led Mexico. All the presidents and most other elected officials came from this party. In recent years, economic troubles and the people's lack of political power led to growing frustration. In the year 2000, the newly elected president of Mexico, **Vicente Fox,** came from a different political party—for the first time in 70 years.

Mexico's government faces many difficult challenges. People in Mexico are demanding more political freedom to make decisions that affect their everyday lives. Traffic in illegal drugs is protected by corrupt government officials. Nearly 40 percent of Mexico's 100 million people live below the poverty line. To fight the country's pressing problems, from poverty to drugs, a strong central government is needed. To increase democracy in Mexico, however, Fox must give power back to local and state agencies. Fox will have to help his country find the balance between these two levels of government.

Reading Check **What form of government does Mexico have?**

Mexico's Challenges

Mexico has tried to use its resources to improve the lives of its people. These actions have had strong effects on Mexican life—and created some challenges for the future.

Population Mexico's population has increased rapidly in recent decades. Because many people have moved to the cities to find jobs, the cities have grown quickly. Many people have been forced to take

Meeting Special Needs

Auditory/Musical Locate recordings of Mexican *mariachi* and *ranchero* (ranch hand) music. Play the music for students and ask them to characterize the differences between these folk styles and other forms of music. They might comment on the rhythms used or the instrumentation. Students who are familiar with other forms of music from Latin America might bring examples to class to provide additional contrasts. **L1 ELL**

Refer to *Inclusion for the Middle School Social Studies Classroom Strategies and Activities* in the TCR.

jobs that pay low wages. As a result, thousands of people crowd together in poor sections of the cities.

Those Mexicans who cannot find any work in their country may become **migrant workers.** These are people who travel from place to place when extra workers are needed to plant or harvest crops. They legally and sometimes illegally cross Mexico's long border to work in the United States. Though the pay is low, the migrant workers can earn more in the United States than in Mexico.

Another issue with people involves the descendents of the ancient Maya Indians. The present-day Mayans live in the southernmost state of Mexico called **Chiapas.** This state is one of the poorest states in Mexico. Over 75 percent of the people there live below the poverty level. Most of the wealth in Chiapas is concentrated in a very small number of ranching families who are of Spanish descent. Diseases and illness that result from the poverty and a lack of health care cause many thousands of deaths every year. Believing that the Mexican government would never help improve their situation, many Mayans rebelled. The Zapatista Army they formed is still fighting for independence from the central government.

Foreign Debt For decades, the Mexican government refused to let foreign companies build factories in Mexico. Leaders feared that the companies would take their profits to their own country, thus draining

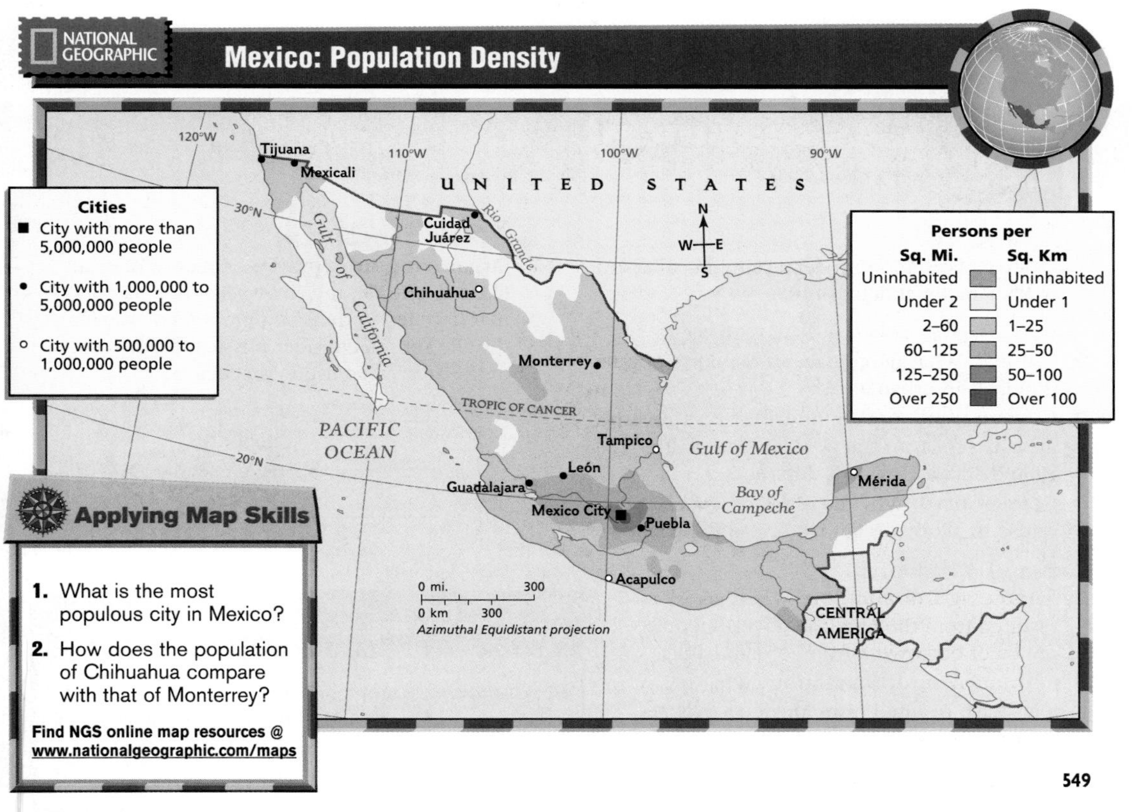

Applying Map Skills

1. What is the most populous city in Mexico?
2. How does the population of Chihuahua compare with that of Monterrey?

Find NGS online map resources @ www.nationalgeographic.com/maps

549

Chapter 20

Section 3, pages 546–550

3 ASSESS

Assign Section 3 Assessment as homework or an in-class activity.

Have students use the Interactive Tutor Self-Assessment CD-ROM to review Section 20–3.

Section Quiz 20-3

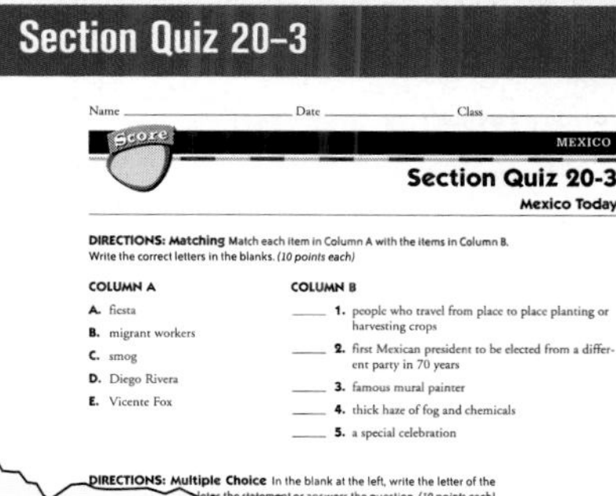

Name ______ Date ______ Class ______

MEXICO

Score

Section Quiz 20-3

Mexico Today

DIRECTIONS: Matching Match each item in Column A with the items in Column B. Write the correct letters in the blanks. *(10 points each)*

COLUMN A	COLUMN B
A. fiesta	____ 1. people who travel from place to place planting or harvesting crops
B. migrant workers	____ 2. first Mexican president to be elected from a different party in 70 years
C. smog	____ 3. famous mural painter
D. Diego Rivera	____ 4. thick haze of fog and chemicals
E. Vicente Fox	____ 5. a special celebration

DIRECTIONS: Multiple Choice In the blank at the left, write the letter of the ... the statement or answers the question. *(10 points each)*

Reteach

Have students work in pairs to quiz each other on the content of the text and map in this section.

Applying Map Skills

Answers

1. Mexico City
2. Chihuahua has 500,000 to 1 million people; Monterrey has 1 to 5 million

Skills Practice

Which part of Mexico has the lowest population density, the north or south? Why? *(north, because the climate and landscape are drier)*

Cooperative Learning Activity

Debating Organize the class into three groups and tell them that each group will debate solutions to one of the challenges facing Mexico. One group will discuss ways of solving Mexico's population problems, another will tackle the issue of foreign debt, and the third will explore pollution. Split each of the three groups into two parts, each of which is charged with developing a set of responses to their issue. Allow groups time to conduct their research and prepare their arguments before staging the three debates. **L2**

EE4 Human Systems: Standard 13

Chapter 20

Section 3, pages 546–550

Reading Check Answer

need to find jobs for growing population, diseases from poverty and lack of health care, repaying foreign debt, maintaining economic growth, pollution

Reading Essentials and Study Guide 20-3

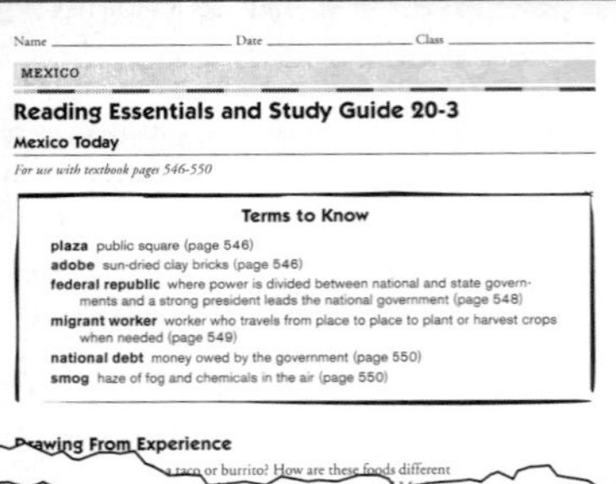

Enrich

Have students research one aspect of Mexican culture, such as the food, music, or celebrations, and prepare a multimedia presentation of their findings.

Have students write a letter to a friend describing Mexican culture.

money out of Mexico. In the 1990s, the government changed this policy. Mexican officials were still concerned that money would be lost, but hoped that the new factories would create more jobs for Mexicans.

To help its economy grow, Mexico borrowed money from foreign banks. The government then had to use any money it earned in taxes to pay back the loans. As a result, Mexico's leaders did not have enough funds to spend on the Mexican people when the economy began to struggle. Many Mexicans grew angry. Yet, if the government did not make the loan payments, banks would refuse to lend more money for future plans. Because there are still loans to be repaid, Mexicans will face this situation for many years. The problem of repaying a **national debt,** or money owed by the government, is one that is being faced by many countries in the world today.

Pollution As Mexico's population boomed, its cities grew very large. At the same time, the economy industrialized. Both of these changes contributed to rising pollution in Mexico.

The mountains that surround Mexico City trap the exhaust fumes from hundreds of thousands of cars. People wake each day to a thick haze of fog and chemicals called **smog.** Many people wear masks when they leave their homes to go to work or school. In northern Mexico, many factories release dangerous chemicals into the air or water. One environmental group says that the Rio Grande is now one of the most polluted rivers in North America.

Reading Check What challenges does Mexico face?

Assessment

Defining Terms

1. **Define** plaza, adobe, federal republic, migrant worker, national debt, smog.

Recalling Facts

2. **Culture** What percentage of Mexico's population lives in urban areas?
3. **Government** Explain how Mexico's government is similar to the government of the United States. How is it different?
4. **Government** Why did Mexico's government refuse to allow foreign factories in Mexico?

Critical Thinking

5. **Analyzing Information** What has resulted from the Mexican government's policy of borrowing from foreign banks?
6. **Summarizing Information** What problems have resulted from Mexico's expanding population?

Graphic Organizer

7. **Organizing Information** Create a diagram like this one. On the arrows list three factors that have led to the smog problem of Mexico City. Be sure to consider physical characteristics of the area when listing the factors.

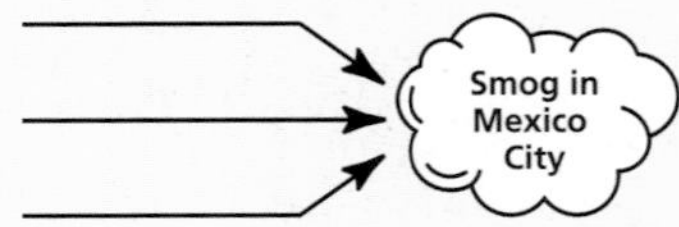

Applying Social Studies Skills

8. **Analyzing Maps** Look at the population density map on page 549. What is the population of Guadalajara? What is the population density of the area surrounding Mérida?

Section 3 Assessment

1. The terms are defined in the Glossary.
2. about 75 percent
3. similarity: federal republics, power divided between national and state governments, strong president; difference: Mexico's national government has much more power than the states.
4. Leaders feared companies would take their profits to their own countries.
5. Mexico must use tax money to repay loans and cannot spend money on its people.
6. increased poverty in the cities, low paying jobs, disease from poverty, conflict in Chiapas
7. growing population, industrialization, mountains trap smog
8. 1–5 million; 60–125 people per sq. mile (25–50 per sq. km)

Chapter 20 Reading Review

Section 1 Mexico's Land and Economy

Terms to Know
land bridge
peninsula
latitude
altitude
hurricane
vaquero
maquiladora
subsistence farm
plantation
industrialize
service industry
NAFTA

Main Idea
Mexico's mountainous landscape and varied climate create different economic regions.

✓**Location** Mexico is part of a land bridge that connects North and South America.

✓**Movement** Mexico's economy is growing; and many people are moving to the northern cities.

✓**Location** Much of Mexico lies in the Tropics, but the climate in some areas is cool because of high elevation.

✓**Economics** Landforms and climate combine to create three economic zones in Mexico.

Section 2 Mexico's History

Terms to Know
jade
obsidian
maize
hieroglyphics
mural
colony
hacienda

Main Idea
Mexico's culture reflects a blend of its Native American and Spanish past.

✓**History** Mexico's Native American civilizations—the Olmec, Maya, and Aztec—made many contributions to Mexico's culture.

✓**Culture** Mexico's people reflect the country's Native American and Spanish roots.

✓**History** The Spanish ruled Mexico from the 1500s to 1821, when Mexico won its independence.

✓**History** The poor people in Mexico revolted against the rich and powerful church and military leaders in 1910.

Section 3 Mexico Today

Terms to Know
plaza
adobe
federal republic
migrant worker
national debt
smog

Main Idea
Mexicans enjoy a rich and lively culture but face many serious challenges.

✓**Culture** About 75 percent of Mexicans live in cities today.

✓**Environment** Mexico is suffering from air pollution.

✓**Culture** Challenges facing Mexico include problems caused by population growth, foreign investment and debt, and pollution.

✓**Government** Mexico's government is a federal republic.

Reading Review

Use the Chapter 20 Reading Review to preview, review, condense, or reteach the chapter.

Preview/Review

Use the Terms to Know lists to help students review and study.

Activity Organize the class into teams and quiz students on the terms by offering the definition and asking them to supply the term.

Vocabulary PuzzleMaker Software reinforces the vocabulary terms used in Chapter 20.

The Interactive Tutor Self-Assessment CD-ROM allows students to review Chapter 20 content.

Condense

Have students read the Chapter 20 summary statements.

Chapter 20 Guided Reading Activities

Chapter 20 Audio Program

Reteach

Reteaching Activity 20

Chapter 20 Reading Essentials and Study Guide

Chapter Culminating Activity

Summarizing Information Have students complete the sentence "Mexico is a dynamic and diverse country because . . ." Explain that students can present their answers in many different ways—as a poster, a written report, an oral presentation, a multimedia presentation, or an annotated map. Whatever the vehicle, their answers should address such issues as the country's geography, climate, economy, people, and culture. *NOTE: This activity may be completed separately or you may wish students to incorporate it into their Current Events Journals.* **L1**

EE6 The Uses of Geography: Standard 18

Assessment and Activities

GLENCOE TECHNOLOGY

MindJogger Videoquiz

Use MindJogger to review the Chapter 20 content.

 Available in VHS.

Using Key Terms

1. e
2. h
3. b
4. a
5. j
6. c
7. i
8. f
9. d
10. g

Reviewing the Main Ideas

11. The Tropic of Cancer (the northern edge of the tropics) cuts across Mexico—areas south of the line have warm temperatures year-round, while areas north of the line are warm in summer and cooler in winter.
12. coffee, cotton, vegetables, fruit, livestock, tobacco, oil
13. They have caused an economic boom and attracted people looking for jobs. They have raised the standard of living in northern cities.
14. Tenochtitlán
15. Thousands died from mistreatment and diseases caught from Europeans; many were forced to work; many converted to Catholicism.
16. 1821
17. They are demanding more political freedom to make decisions that affect their everyday lives.
18. the day Mexico defeated an invading French army in 1862

Chapter 20 Assessment and Activities

Using Key Terms

Match the terms in Part A with their definitions in Part B.

A.

1. altitude
2. hurricane
3. vaquero
4. maquiladora
5. jade
6. adobe
7. plaza
8. smog
9. mural
10. subsistence farm

B.

a. factory that assembles parts from other countries
b. cowhand
c. sun-dried clay bricks
d. wall painting
e. height above sea level
f. fog mixed with smoke
g. produces only enough to support a family's needs
h. fierce tropical storm
i. public square
j. shiny stone that comes in many shades of green

Reviewing the Main Ideas

Section 1 Mexico's Land and Economy

11. **Location** How does Mexico's latitude affect its climate?
12. **Economics** What are Mexico's major exports?
13. **Movement** How have maquiladoras affected northern Mexico's cities?

Section 2 Mexico's History

14. **History** What was the capital city of the Aztec civilization?
15. **History** What effects did Spanish conquest have on Native Americans?
16. **History** When did Mexico win its independence from Spain?

Section 3 Mexico Today

17. **Government** What are people in Mexico demanding from the Mexican government?
18. **Culture** What does Cinco de Mayo celebrate?

Mexico

Place Location Activity

On a separate sheet of paper, match the letters on the map with the numbered places listed below.

1. Sierra Madre Occidental
2. Mexico City
3. Plateau of Mexico
4. Yucatán Peninsula
5. Baja California
6. Rio Grande
7. Gulf of Mexico
8. Guadalajara
9. Monterrey
10. Sierra Madre del Sur

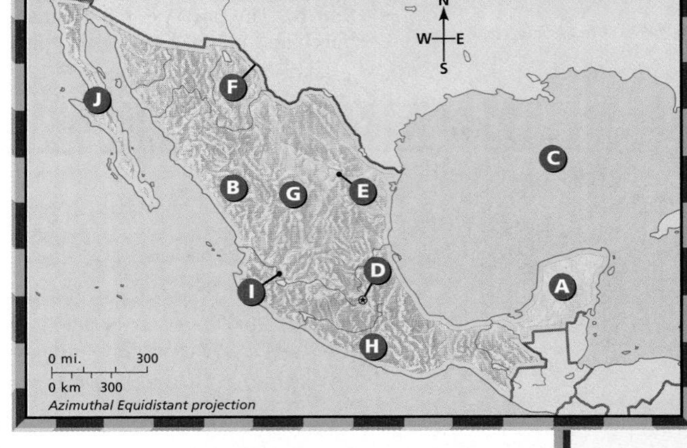

NATIONAL GEOGRAPHIC Place Location Activity

1. B
2. D
3. G
4. A
5. J
6. F
7. C
8. I
9. E
10. H

Critical Thinking

19. Leaders hope companies will open factories in Mexico, thus creating new jobs and economic growth.
20. Answers will vary, but should be well-reasoned and be supported by facts and examples.

Self-Check Quiz Visit the ***Our World Today: People, Places, and Issues*** Web site at owt.glencoe.com and click on **Chapter 20–Self-Check Quizzes** to prepare for the Chapter Test.

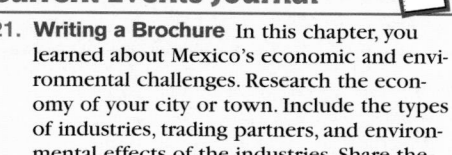

Critical Thinking

19. **Understanding Cause and Effect** Why have Mexico's leaders encouraged free trade agreements with other countries?
20. **Analyzing Information** If you were Mexico's president, what would you do to rid Mexico of the problems of illegal drugs and poverty?

Current Events Journal

21. **Writing a Brochure** In this chapter, you learned about Mexico's economic and environmental challenges. Research the economy of your city or town. Include the types of industries, trading partners, and environmental effects of the industries. Share the information you gather by making a brochure. Include a map of your area.

Mental Mapping Activity

22. **Focusing on the Region** Create a simple outline map of Mexico. Refer to the physical map on page 476 and then label the following:
    - Pacific Ocean
    - Gulf of Mexico
    - Yucatán Peninsula
    - Baja California
    - Mexico City
    - Rio Grande
    - Caribbean Sea

Technology Skills Activity

23. **Developing a Multimedia Presentation** Imagine that you work for Mexico's Economic Development Office. Create a multimedia presentation to present to a group of foreign investors. Use a software application such as PowerPoint® to showcase positive features like climate, resources, and labor supply. Your goal is to show investors that Mexico is a good place for them to invest their money.

The Princeton Review

Standardized Test Practice

Directions: Read the paragraph below, and then answer the question that follows.

The Aztec civilization was organized into classes. At the top was the emperor. His power came from his control of the army and the religious beliefs of the people. Next came the nobles, followed by commoners. Commoners included priests, merchants, and artists. Below commoners were the serfs, or workers who farmed the nobles' fields. Slaves, the lowest class, included criminals and people in debt, as well as female and child prisoners of war. Male prisoners of war were sacrificed to the Aztec gods. The Aztec believed that live human sacrifices were needed to keep the gods pleased and to prevent floods and other disasters.

1. Which of the following statements is an opinion about the information given above?

F The Aztec civilization was organized into classes.

G Male prisoners of war were sacrificed to the Aztec gods.

H Slaves included children.

J The Aztec should not have sacrificed people to the gods.

Test-Taking Tip: This question asks you to identify an opinion. An opinion is a person's belief. It is not a proven fact (such as answer F). Opinions often contain subjective words, such as *easier, best,* or *should.*

553

Assessment and Activities

Standardized Test Practice

1. J

Tested Objectives:
Distinguishing between fact and opinion, analyzing information

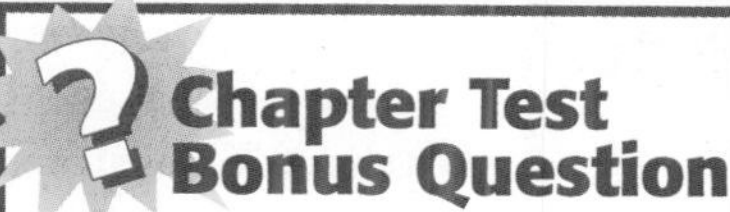

Chapter Test Bonus Question

This question may be used for extra credit on the chapter test.

What industry is growing in the southern areas of Mexico? Why? *(Tourism; because tourists are attracted to beautiful beaches and warm climate)*

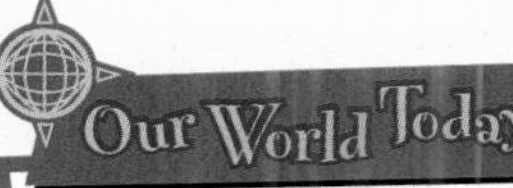

Have students visit the Web site at owt.glencoe.com to review Chapter 20 and take the Self-Check Quiz.

Current Events Journal

21. Students' brochures should include the requested information—types of industries, trading partners, and environmental effects of the industries—as well as the map.

Mental Mapping Activity

22. This exercise helps students visualize the countries and geographic features they have been studying and understand the relationships among various points. All attempts at freehand mapping should be accepted.

Technology Skills Activity

23. Students' multimedia presentations should include the requested information—climate, resources, and labor supply.

Chapter 21 Resources

Note: The following materials may be used when teaching Chapter 21. Section level support materials are shown at point of use in the margins of the Teacher Wraparound Edition.

Timesaving Tools

TeacherWorks™ All-In-One Planner and Resource Center

- **Interactive Teacher Edition** See the **Interactive Teacher Edition** CD-ROM to electronically integrate your Teacher Wraparound Edition and blackline masters.
- **Interactive Lesson Planner** Organize your week, month, semester, or year with all the lesson helps you need. The **Interactive Lesson Planner** CD-ROM contains all Chapter 21 resources.

Use Glencoe's **Presentation Plus!** multimedia teacher tool to easily present dynamic lessons that visually excite your students. Using Microsoft PowerPoint® you can customize the presentations to create your own personalized lessons.

TEACHING TRANSPARENCIES

Graphic Organizer Transparency and Student Activity 21

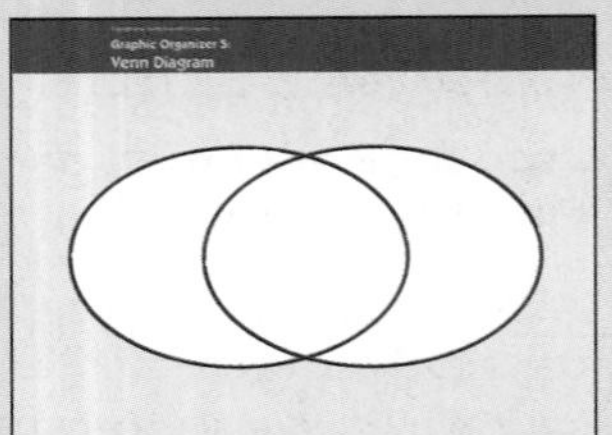

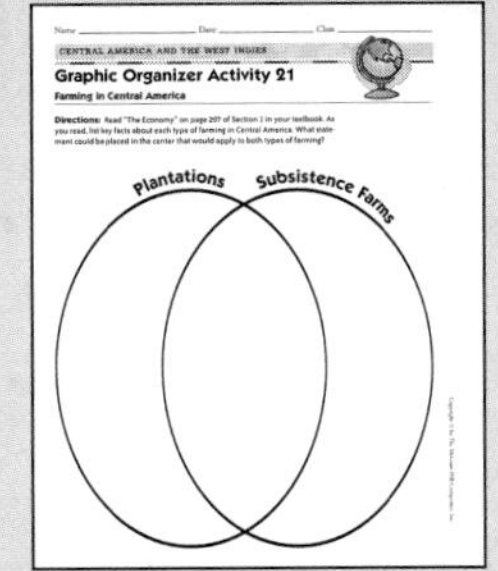

FOLDABLES™ Study Organizer

Foldables are three-dimensional, interactive graphic organizers that help students practice basic writing skills, review key vocabulary terms, and identify main ideas. Every chapter contains a Foldable activity, with additional chapter activities found in the ***Reading and Study Skills Foldables*** booklet.

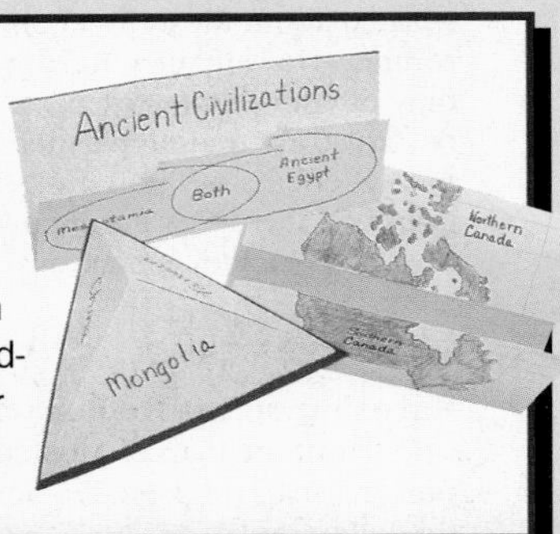

ENRICHMENT AND EXTENSION

Enrichment Activity 21

Cooperative Learning Activity 21

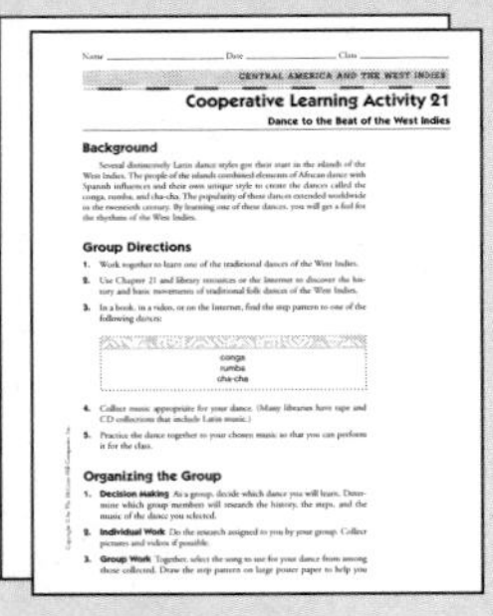

MAP AND GEOGRAPHY SKILLS

Chapter Map Activity 21

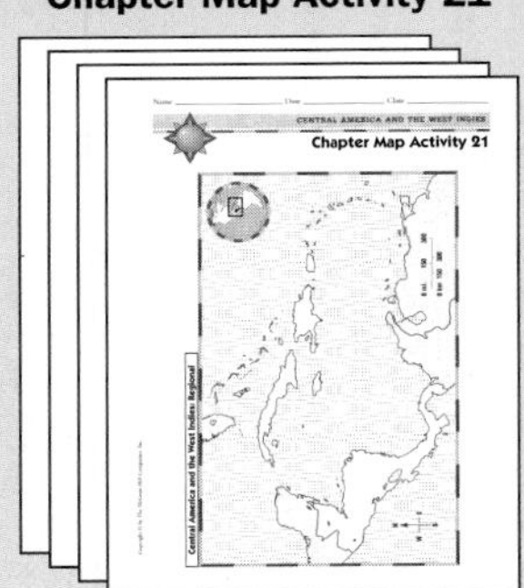

GeoLab Activity 21

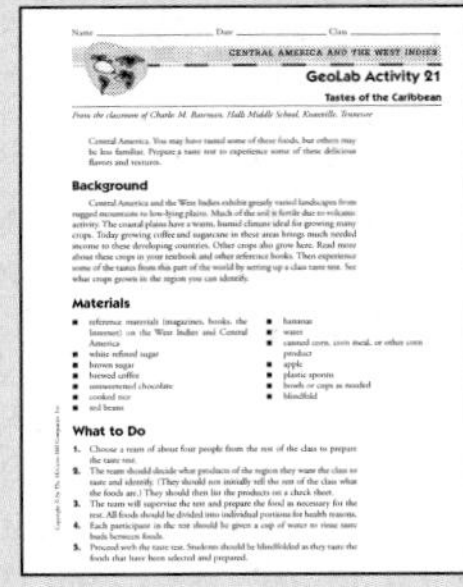

STANDARDIZED ASSESSMENT SKILLS

Glencoe's Assessment Advantage

Critical Thinking Skills Activity 21

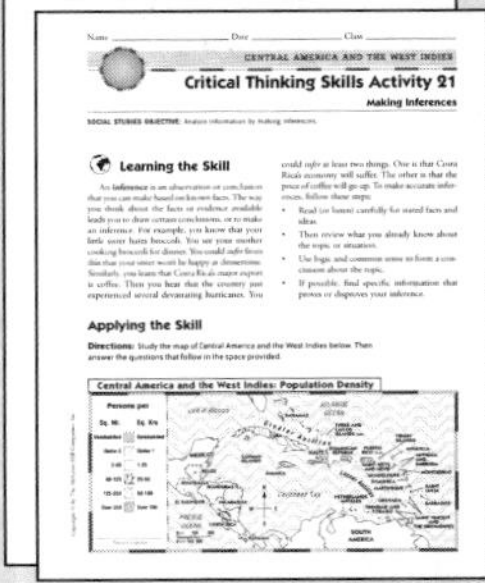

Map and Graph Skills Activity 21

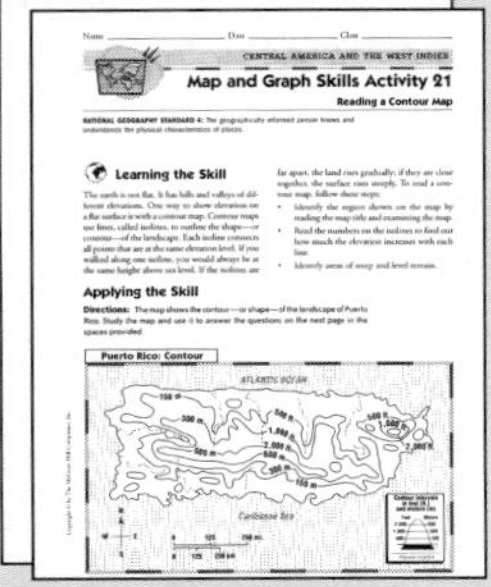

Reading and Writing Skills Activity 21

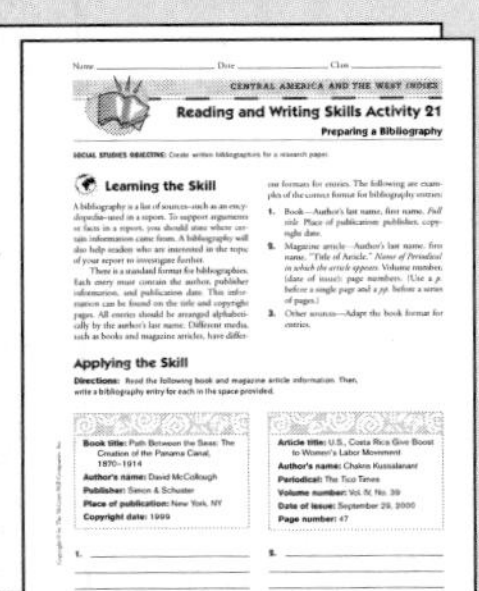

Standardized Test Practice Workbook Activity 21

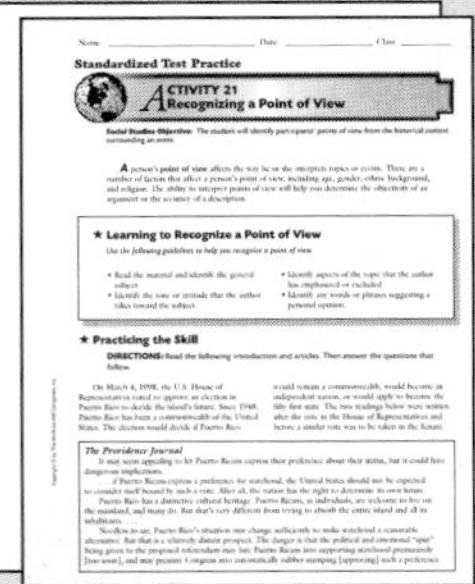

REVIEW AND REINFORCEMENT

Chapter Skills Activity 21

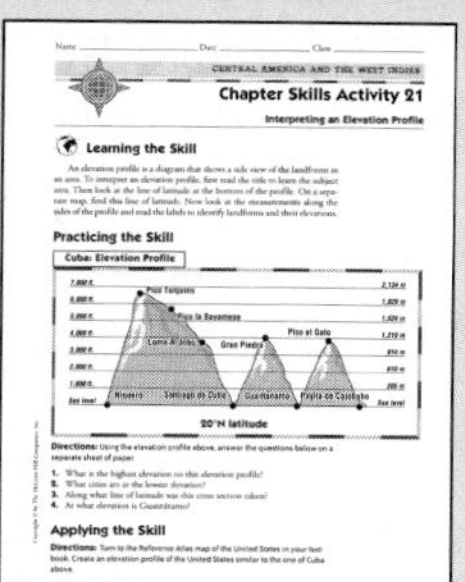

Take-Home Review Activity 21

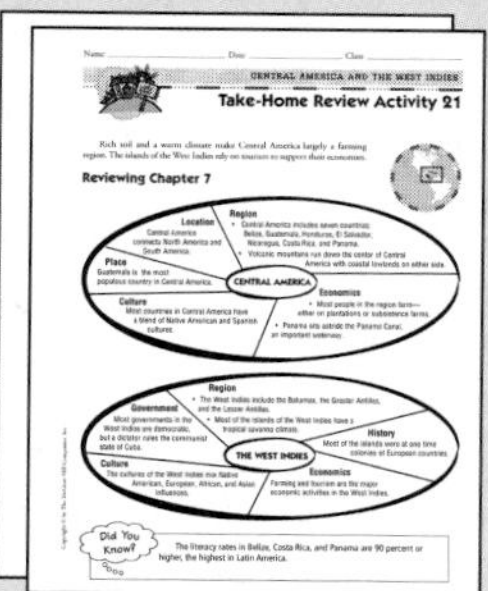

Reteaching Activity 21

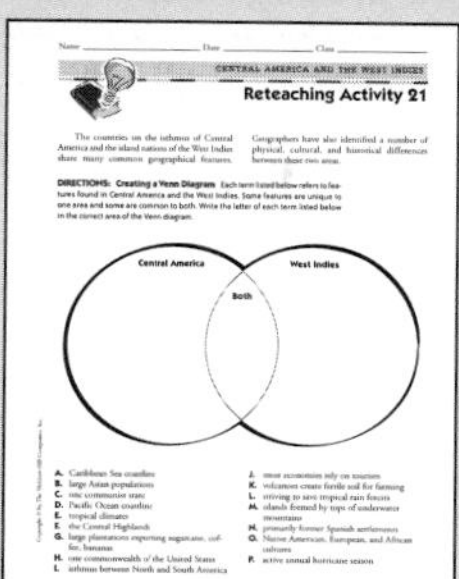

Vocabulary Activity 21

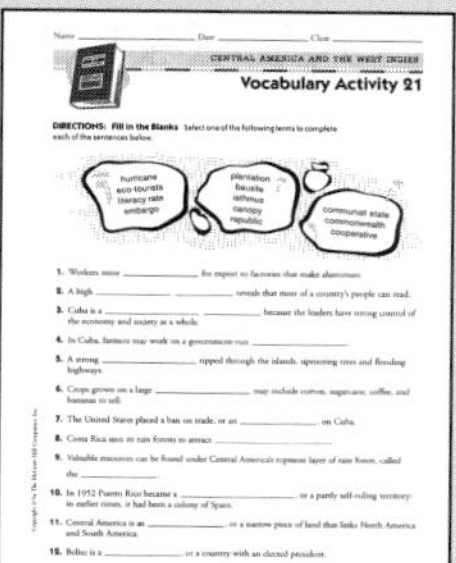

Workbook Activity 21

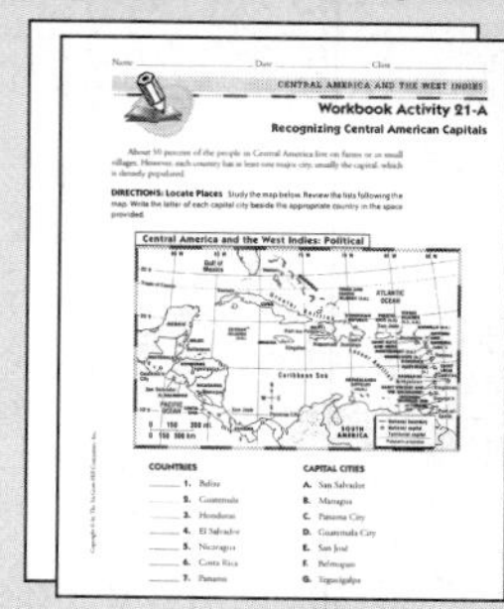

ASSESSMENT

GLENCOE'S ASSESSMENT ADVANTAGE

Chapter 21 Test, Form A

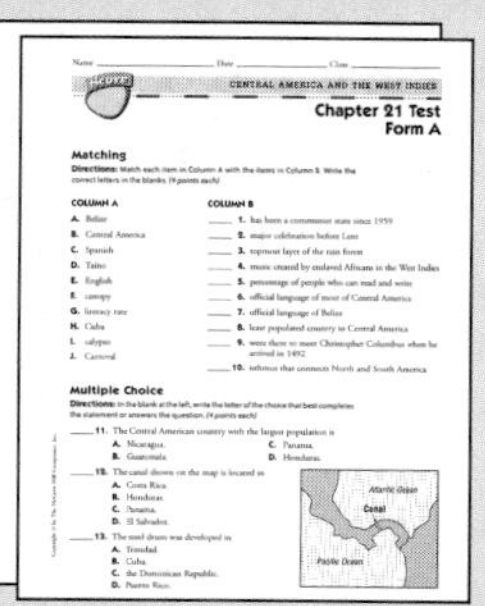

Chapter 21 Test, Form B

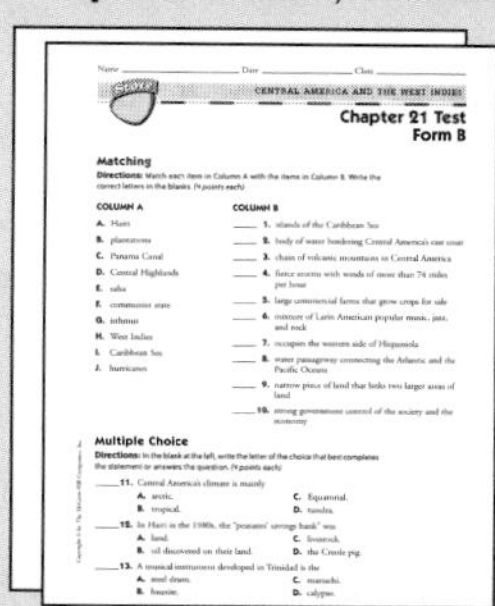

Performance Assessment Activity 21

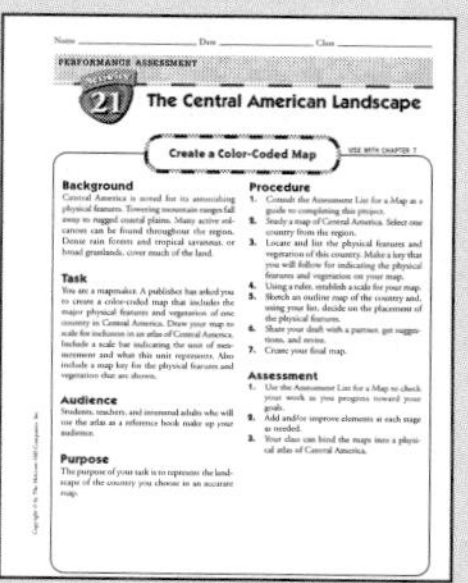

ExamView® Pro 3.0 Testmaker CD-ROM

MULTIMEDIA

- **National Geographic's The World and Its People**
- **MindJogger Videoquiz**
- **Vocabulary PuzzleMaker Software**
- **Interactive Tutor Self-Assessment CD-ROM**
- **ExamView® Pro 3.0 Testmaker CD-ROM**
- **Interactive Lesson Planner CD-ROM**
- **Interactive Teacher Edition CD-ROM**
- **Skillbuilder Interactive Workbook CD-ROM, Level 1**
- **Presentation Plus! CD-ROM**
- **Audio Program**

SPANISH RESOURCES

The following Spanish language materials are available in the Spanish Resources binder:

- **Spanish Chapter Summaries**
- **Spanish Vocabulary Activities**
- **Spanish Guided Reading Activities**
- **Spanish Quizzes and Tests**
- **Spanish Take-Home Review Activities**
- **Spanish Reteaching Activities**

Meeting National Standards

Geography for Life

All of the 18 standards are demonstrated in Unit 7. The following ones are highlighted in Chapter 21:

Section 1
- **EE2 Places and Regions: Standards 4, 5, 6**
- **EE3 Physical Systems: Standards 7, 8**
- **EE5 Environment and Society: Standards 14, 16**

Section 2
- **EE2 Places and Regions: Standards 4, 5, 6**
- **EE3 Physical Systems: Standards 7, 8**
- **EE5 Environment and Society: Standards 15, 16**

For a complete listing of National Geography Standards and entire text correlation, see pages T22–T29.

Local Objectives

___

Chapter 21 Planning Guide

SECTION RESOURCES

Daily Objectives	Reproducible Resources	Multimedia Resources
Section 1 **Central America** **Suggested Pacing = 1 day** **1.** Identify where Central America is and what nations make up this area. **2.** Describe the landforms and climate found in Central America. **3.** Explain the economy of Central America. **4.** Discuss the people and history of Central America's countries.	Reproducible Lesson Plan 21-1 Daily Lecture and Discussion Notes 21-1 Guided Reading Activity 21-1 Reading Essentials and Study Guide 21-1 Section Quiz 21-1*	Daily Focus Skills Transparency 21-1 GeoQuiz Transparency 21-1 Vocabulary PuzzleMaker Software Interactive Tutor Self-Assessment CD-ROM ExamView® Pro 3.0 Testmaker CD-ROM Presentation Plus! CD-ROM
Section 2 **The West Indies** **Suggested Pacing = 1 day** **1.** Identify and compare the islands of the West Indies. **2.** Describe the landforms and climates of the West Indies. **3.** Explain the economic activities of the islands. **4.** Compare the cultures and history of the islands.	Reproducible Lesson Plan 21-2 Daily Lecture and Discussion Notes 21-2 Guided Reading Activity 21-2 Reading Essentials and Study Guide 21-2 Section Quiz 21-2*	Daily Focus Skills Transparency 21-2 GeoQuiz Transparency 21-1 Vocabulary PuzzleMaker Software Interactive Tutor Self-Assessment CD-ROM ExamView® Pro 3.0 Testmaker CD-ROM Presentation Plus! CD-ROM

00:00 **Out of Time?** Assign the **Reading Essentials and Study Guide** for this chapter.

*Also available in Spanish

KEY TO ABILITY LEVELS

Teaching strategies have been coded for varying learning styles and abilities.

- **L1** **BASIC** activities for all students
- **L2** **AVERAGE** activities for average to above-average students
- **L3** **CHALLENGING** activities for above-average students
- **ELL** **ENGLISH LANGUAGE LEARNER** activities

Blackline Master
Software
CD-ROM
Audiocassette
Transparency
Videocassette
Block Scheduling
DVD

Teacher to Teacher

Show Me the Money

Mary Ann Polve
Mesa High School
Mesa, Arizona

Gale Olp Ekiss
Powell Junior High School
Mesa, Arizona

You need a variety of foreign currency and coins for this activity. Inform students that they will be looking at a variety of money to find clues about the countries from which the money comes. Organize students into small groups and give each group a sample of coins and bills that you have collected. Students will examine the money to locate symbols and images. Then have them chart the information on a worksheet with the headings "Country of Origin," "Monetary Unit," "Year," "Watermarks or Authenticators," "People Pictured," "Buildings," "Natural Features," "Animals," "Symbols," and "Other." Have groups share their findings with the class. Finally, ask students to design the front and back of a bill for any country in this chapter.

OUR WORLD TODAY Online

Use our Web site for additional resources. All essential content is covered in the Student Edition.

You and your students can visit **owt.glencoe.com**, the Web site companion to *Our World Today*. This innovative integration of electronic and print media offers your students a wealth of opportunities. The student text directs students to the Web site for the following options:

- Chapter Overviews
- Student Web Activities
- Self-Check Quizzes
- Textbook Updates

Answers are provided for you in the Web Activity Lesson Plan. Additional Web resources and Interactive Tutor puzzles are also available.

NATIONAL GEOGRAPHIC TEACHER'S CORNER

Index to National Geographic Magazine:

The following articles may be used for research relating to this chapter:

- "Cuba's Colonial Treasure," by A.R. Williams, October 1999.
- "Cuba," by John J. Putman, June 1999.
- "Feast of the Tarpon," by David Doubilet, January 1996.
- "El Salvador," by Mike Edwards, September 1995.
- "Treasure From the Silver Bank," by Tracy Bowden, July 1996.

National Geographic Society Products Available From Glencoe:

To order the following products for use with this chapter, contact your local Glencoe sales representative or call Glencoe at 1-800-334-7344:

- *PictureShow: Ancient Civilizations: Middle and South America* (CD-ROM)
- *PicturePack: Ancient Civilizations: Middle America* (Transparencies)
- *MapPack: Continents: North America* (Transparencies)
- *STV: Rain Forest* (Videodisc)

Additional National Geographic Society Products:

To order the following products for use with this chapter, call National Geographic Society at 1-800-368-2728:

- *Complete National Geographic: 111 years of National Geographic Magazine* (CD-ROM)
- *Spain in the Americas* (Video)
- *Lost City of the Maya* (Video)
- *The Maya Way of Death* (Video)
- *Population* (Map)
- *Cultures* (Map)
- *Central America Political* (Map)
- *National Geographic Desk Reference* (Book)
- *National Geographic Atlas of the World, Seventh Edition* (Book)
- *Voices: Poetry and Art From Around the World* (Book)

NGS ONLINE

Access National Geographic's Web site for current events, activities, links, interactive features, and archives.
www.nationalgeographic.com

Introducing
Chapter 21

Introduce students to chapter content and key terms by having them access Chapter Overview 21 at owt.glencoe.com

Chapter Objectives

1. Describe the physical and cultural geography of Central America.
2. Compare the major physical and cultural features of the West Indies islands.

GLENCOE TECHNOLOGY

NATIONAL GEOGRAPHIC

The World and Its People Video Program

Chapter 7 Central America and the West Indies

The following segments enhance the study of this chapter:

- **Ancient Maya**
- **A Deadly Game**
- **Modern Maya**

Available in DVD and VHS.

MindJogger Videoquiz

Use MindJogger to preview the Chapter 21 content.

Available in VHS.

Chapter 21

Central America and the West Indies

The World and Its People — NATIONAL GEOGRAPHIC

To learn more about the people and places of Central America and the West Indies, view ***The World and Its People* Chapter 7** video.

Our World Today online

Chapter Overview Visit the ***Our World Today: People, Places, and Issues*** Web site at owt.glencoe.com and click on **Chapter 21–Chapter Overviews** to preview information about Central America and the West Indies.

554

Two-Minute Lesson Launcher

Ask students what they think of when they hear the name West Indies. Responses might include words like *tropical, warm, beaches, salsa music, political turmoil, hurricanes,* and many others. Ask them how they developed these images of this part of the world. Responses might include movies, television programs, songs, news stories, and advertisements. **Ask: Do you think this is an accurate picture of the West Indies? What information might be missing?** *(inaccurate; missing facts such as how people live, how they get along, and so on)* Explain that in this chapter students will learn more about this nearby part of the world.

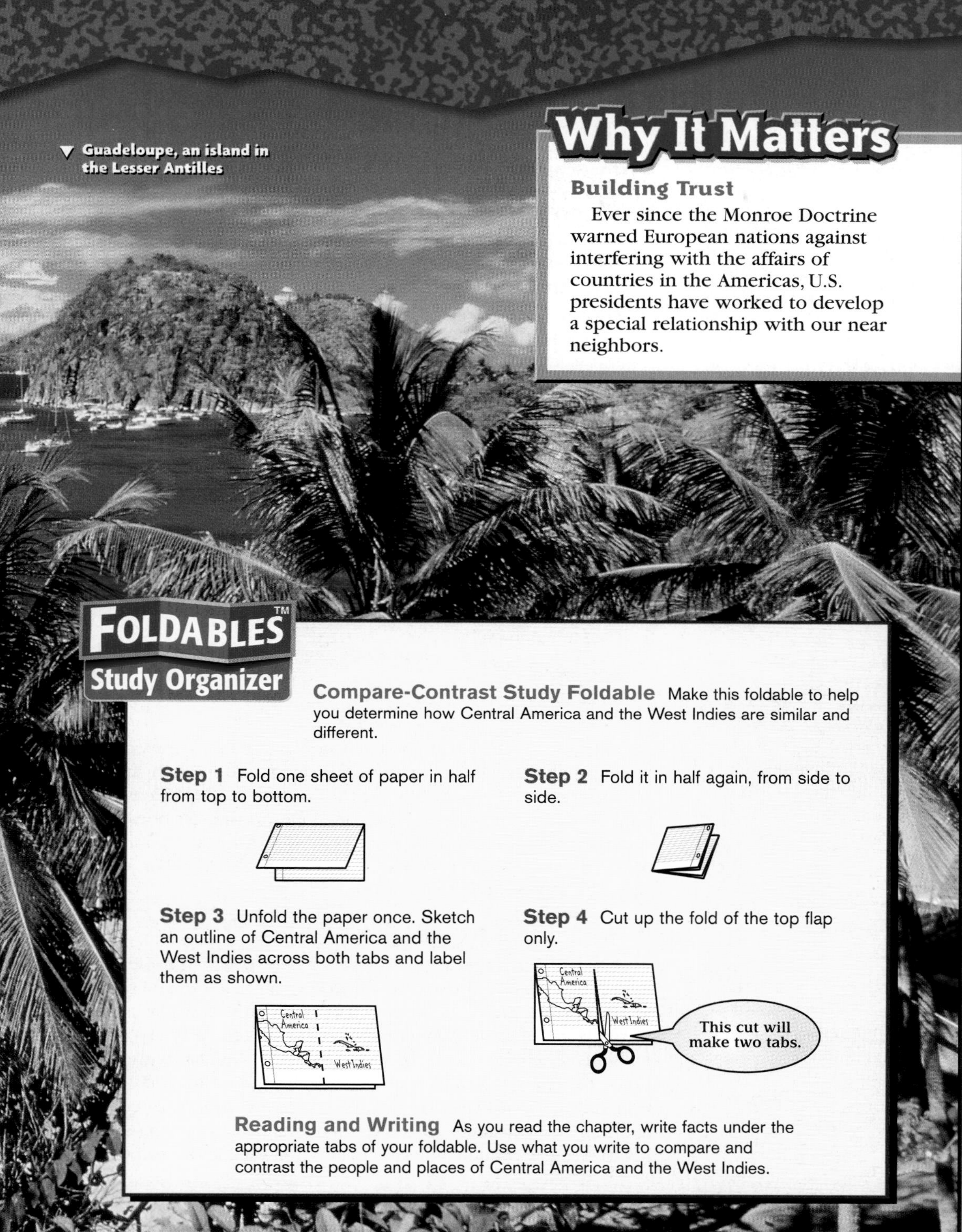

▼ Guadeloupe, an island in the Lesser Antilles

Why It Matters

Building Trust

Ever since the Monroe Doctrine warned European nations against interfering with the affairs of countries in the Americas, U.S. presidents have worked to develop a special relationship with our near neighbors.

FOLDABLES™ Study Organizer

Compare-Contrast Study Foldable Make this foldable to help you determine how Central America and the West Indies are similar and different.

Step 1 Fold one sheet of paper in half from top to bottom.

Step 2 Fold it in half again, from side to side.

Step 3 Unfold the paper once. Sketch an outline of Central America and the West Indies across both tabs and label them as shown.

Step 4 Cut up the fold of the top flap only.

Reading and Writing As you read the chapter, write facts under the appropriate tabs of your foldable. Use what you write to compare and contrast the people and places of Central America and the West Indies.

Introducing
Chapter 21

FOLDABLES™ Study Organizer

Purpose Students will make and use a compare-contrast foldable to help them organize the similarities and differences between Central America and the West Indies. As students read the chapter and fill in information on their foldable, they analyze how the people and places of Central America and the West Indies are similar and how they are different.

Have students complete ***Reading and Study Skills Foldables*** Activity 21.

Why It Matters

Have students use outside sources and the Internet to research ways in which United States presidents became involved in the affairs of Central America and the West Indies throughout history. Has the "special relationship" between the United States and its near neighbors always been a positive one? What is the relationship between the current United States president and our near neighbors?

About the Photo

The West Indies can be divided into three clusters of islands: the Bahamas to the north, the Greater Antilles in the middle, and the Lesser Antilles off the northern coast of South America. The Lesser Antilles, where Guadeloupe is located, extends from below Puerto Rico to Trinidad and Tobago. Unlike Central America, which was mostly colonized by Spain, the islands in this region were claimed by France, England, and the Netherlands. Today, some of the islands are independent, but many are still dependencies of their European colonizers. Although Guadeloupe has a popularly elected general council, the head of government is a commissioner appointed by France. Citizens can vote in French elections and they are represented in the French Parliament.

Chapter 21

Section 1, pages 556–561

Focus

Section Objectives

1. Identify where Central America is and what nations make up this area.
2. Describe the landforms and climate found in Central America.
3. Explain the economy of Central America.
4. Discuss the people and history of Central America's countries.

BELLRINGER
Skillbuilder Activity

Project transparency and have students answer questions.

This activity is also available as a blackline master.

Daily Focus Skills Transparency 21-1

UNIT 7 Chapter 21 DAILY FOCUS SKILLS TRANSPARENCY 21-1

Reading a Bar Graph

LITERACY RATES IN CENTRAL AMERICA

Which country has the highest literacy rate in Central America?

A Belize
B Costa Rica
C Honduras
D Panama

Guide to Reading

■ **Vocabulary Precheck**
Have students guess at the meaning of the word *eco-tourist* from its prefix and root. Have them identify other words that begin with *eco-* *(ecology, ecosphere, ecosystem).*

Guide to Reading

Main Idea

Central America is made up of seven nations that are home to a variety of peoples, exotic animals, and diverse landforms.

Terms to Know

- isthmus
- hurricane
- plantation
- subsistence farm
- canopy
- eco-tourist
- literacy rate
- republic
- parliamentary democracy

Reading Strategy

Create a chart like this one, listing each country in Central America and two key facts about each country.

Country	Key Facts

Unusual animals found nowhere else on the earth roam the floor and canopy of Central America's rain forests. The small frog here seems as if it would be a snack for other, larger animals. Do not be fooled by the enlargement of the photo, however. Many frogs like this one hold a deadly poison in their skin, which would quickly kill anything that tried to eat them.

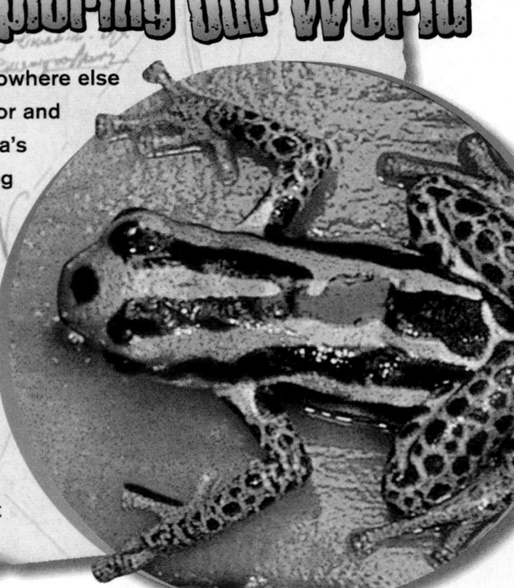

Central America, part of Middle America, is an **isthmus,** or a narrow piece of land that links two larger areas of land—North America and South America. Most of the countries on the isthmus have two coastlines—one on the Pacific Ocean and one on the Caribbean Sea. This narrow region is actually part of North America. Seven countries make up Central America: Belize, Guatemala, El Salvador, Honduras, Nicaragua, Costa Rica, and Panama.

A Rugged Land

Like Mexico, Central America sits where plates in the earth's crust meet. The collision of these plates produces volcanoes and earthquakes in the region. The Central Highlands, which curve like a backbone through inland Central America, are actually a chain of volcanic mountains. Because of their ruggedness, the Central Highlands are difficult to cross. This causes serious problems for transportation and communication and has also kept many of the region's people isolated from one another. The volcanoes of the Central Highlands do bring some benefits to farmers, though. Volcanic material has made the soil very fertile.

Section Resources

Reproducible Masters
- Reproducible Lesson Plan 21-1
- Daily Lecture and Discussion Notes 21-1
- Guided Reading Activity 21-1
- Reading Essentials and Study Guide 21-1
- Section Quiz 21-1

Transparencies
- Daily Focus Skills Transparency 21-1
- GeoQuiz Transparency 21-1

Multimedia
- Vocabulary PuzzleMaker Software
- Interactive Tutor Self-Assessment CD-ROM
- Presentation Plus! CD-ROM
- ExamView® Pro 3.0 Testmaker CD-ROM

Central America is mostly tropical, although the mountainous areas are cool year-round. The Caribbean Lowlands have a hot, tropical rain forest climate throughout the year. Here you can expect about 100 inches (254 cm) of rain each year. Breezes from the Caribbean Sea provide some cooling relief. These breezes can be replaced by deadly hurricanes during the summer and fall, though. **Hurricanes** are fierce storms with winds of more than 74 miles (119 km) per hour.

✓Reading Check **How have the volcanoes in Central America been helpful?**

The Economy

The economies of the Central American countries depend on farming and harvesting wood from their rain forests. Central America has two kinds of farms. Wealthy people and companies own **plantations**—commercial farms that grow crops for sale. Major crops include coffee, bananas, cotton, and sugarcane. Plantations export their harvest to the United States and other parts of the world. Farmers in Guatemala and Costa Rica also grow flowers and ornamental plants for export.

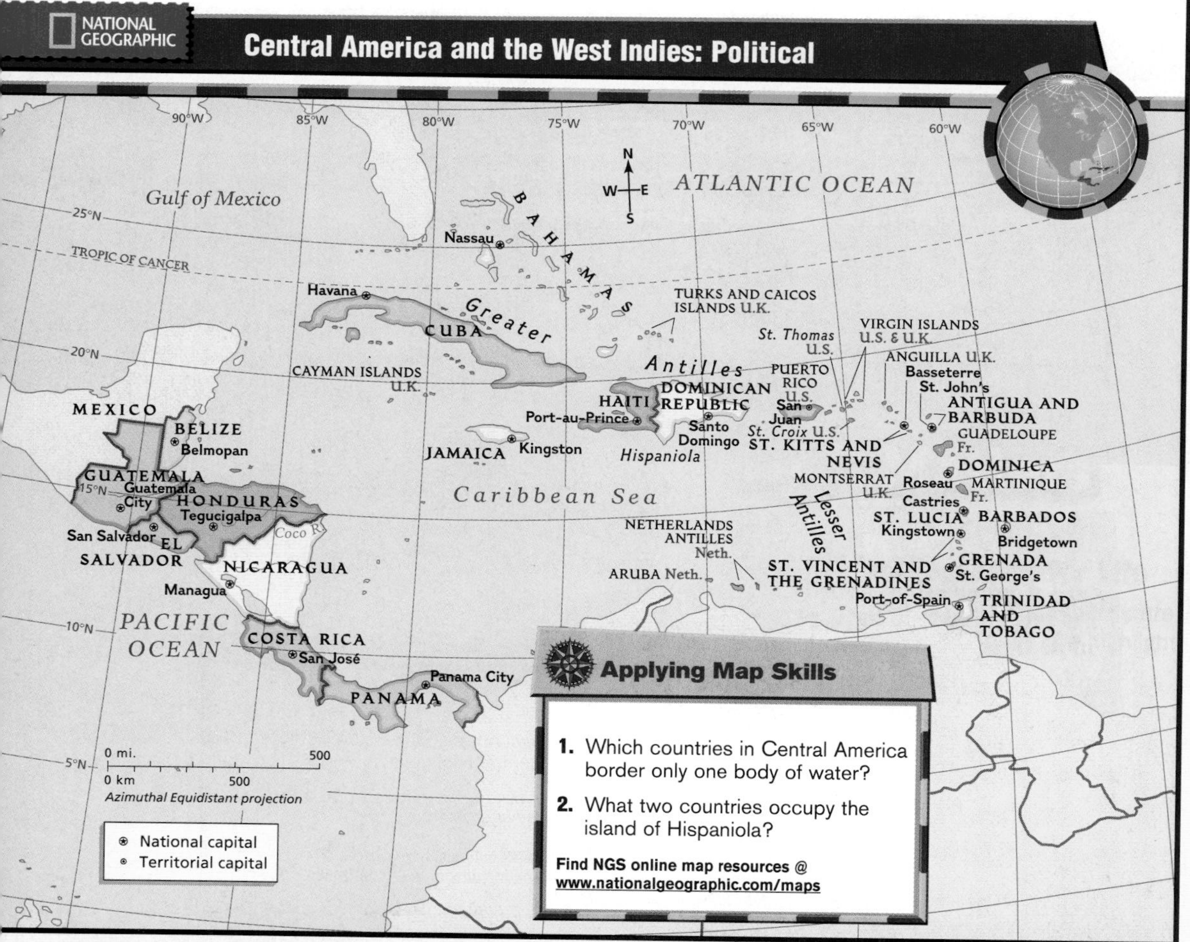

Applying Map Skills

1. Which countries in Central America border only one body of water?
2. What two countries occupy the island of Hispaniola?

Find NGS online map resources @ www.nationalgeographic.com/maps

Chapter 21

Section 1, pages 556–561

Evaluating Information
Have each student make up one riddle for each of the countries of Central America. Each riddle must be specific enough so that the country can be identified. Have students share and solve their riddles. **L1**

✓ Reading Check Answer
Volcanic material has broken down to create fertile soil.

Daily Lecture Notes 21–1

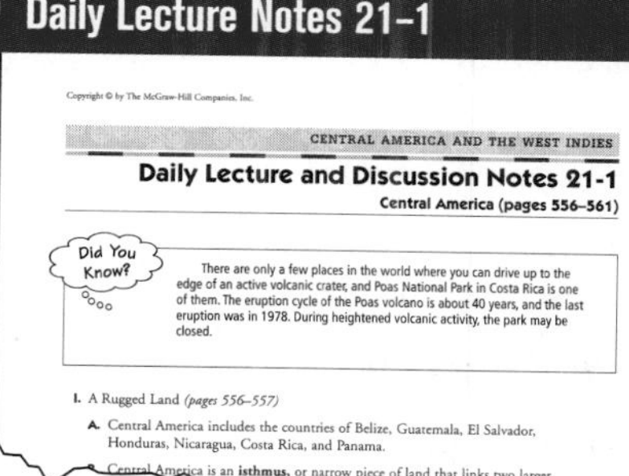
Copyright © by The McGraw-Hill Companies, Inc.

CENTRAL AMERICA AND THE WEST INDIES

Daily Lecture and Discussion Notes 21-1

Central America (pages 556–561)

Did You Know? There are only a few places in the world where you can drive up to the edge of an active volcanic crater, and Poas National Park in Costa Rica is one of them. The eruption cycle of the Poas volcano is about 40 years, and the last eruption was in 1978. During heightened volcanic activity, the park may be closed.

I. A Rugged Land (pages 556–557)

A. Central America includes the countries of Belize, Guatemala, El Salvador, Honduras, Nicaragua, Costa Rica, and Panama.

B. Central America is an **isthmus**, or narrow piece of land that links two larger ... South America.

Applying Map Skills

Answers
1. El Salvador, Belize
2. Haiti, Dominican Republic

Skills Practice
Using the map scale, find the shortest distance between Cuba and the southern tip of Florida. *(about 90 miles or 145 km)*

Team-Teaching Activity

Science Invite the science teacher to class to discuss the ecology of the rain forest. Ask the teacher to emphasize the biodiversity of rain forest flora and fauna, the fragility of this ecosystem and why it is important to humans. Afterwords, have students create diagrams that describe and explain the physical processes that produce the fertile soil and timber that grows in the rain forest. What happens if these processes are stopped due to deforestation? **L2**

EE3 Physical Systems: Standard 8

Chapter 21

Section 1, pages 556–561

Note-taking tip

Suggest that students write two questions and answers for each of the subheadings in the section. In writing them, they should aim to identify the main ideas of the subsections.

Guided Reading Activity 21-1

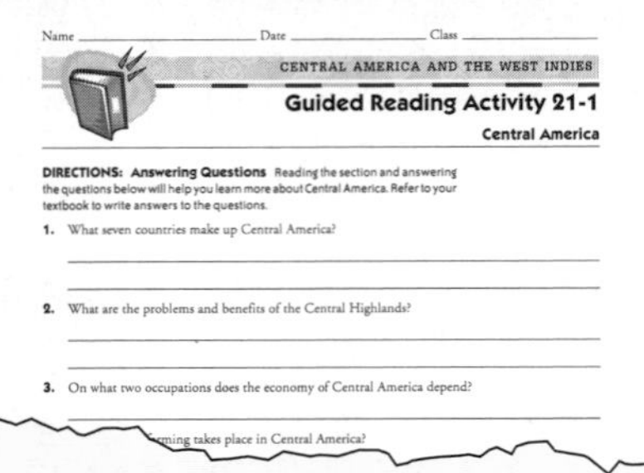
Name ______ Date ______ Class ______

CENTRAL AMERICA AND THE WEST INDIES

Guided Reading Activity 21-1

Central America

DIRECTIONS: Answering Questions Reading the section and answering the questions below will help you learn more about Central America. Refer to your textbook to write answers to the questions.

1. What seven countries make up Central America?
2. What are the problems and benefits of the Central Highlands?
3. On what two occupations does the economy of Central America depend?

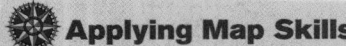

Applying Map Skills

Answers

1. Caribbean Lowlands, Pacific Lowlands
2. Puerto Rico

Skills Practice

Which is higher, the highest point in Central America or the highest point in the West Indies? By how much? *(Volcán Tajumulco, the highest point in Central America, is 3,428 feet, or 1,045 m, higher than Pico Duarte, on Hispaniola.)*

Many farms in Central America are not plantations but **subsistence farms,** or small plots of land where poor farmers grow only enough food to feed their families. Subsistence farmers typically raise livestock and grow corn, beans, and rice.

Rain Forests Under Central America's green **canopy,** or topmost layer of the rain forest, which shades the forest floor, valuable resources and ancient ruins of past empires can be found. The dense forests offer expensive woods—mahogany and rosewood, for example. Unusual animal and plant species also thrive here. Scientists research the plants to develop new medicines.

Both local and foreign-owned companies have set up large-scale operations in the rain forests. Lumber companies cut down and export the valuable trees. Other companies and local farmers also cut or burn the trees to clear land for farming. Without trees to hold the soil in place, heavy rains wash it and its nutrients away. As a result, the land becomes poor just a few years after being cleared. The businesses and farmers then move on, clearing trees from another piece of land.

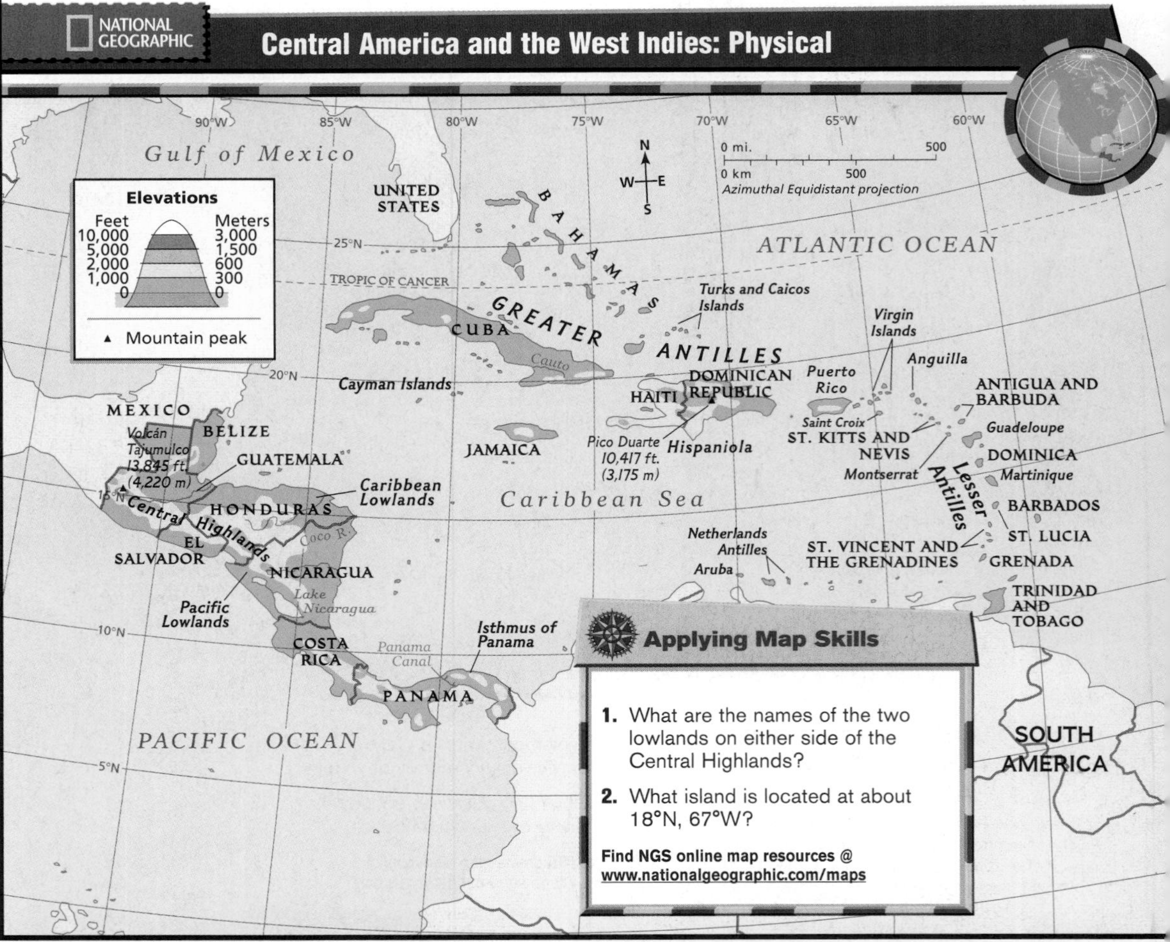

Applying Map Skills

1. What are the names of the two lowlands on either side of the Central Highlands?
2. What island is located at about 18°N, 67°W?

Find NGS online map resources @ www.nationalgeographic.com/maps

Meeting Special Needs

Visual/Spatial You can help visual learners keep track of the characteristics of the different countries of Central America by providing an outline map of the region. Have them write in the names and capitals of each country. Then suggest they annotate the map with information about the physical geography, climate, economy, and people, color coding their annotations by using a different color for each class of information (such as red for landforms, blue for climate, and so on). Students can use their completed maps as a study aid. **ELL L2**

Refer to *Inclusion for the Middle School Social Studies Classroom Strategies and Activities* in the TCR.

Many Central Americans worry about the rapid destruction of the rain forests. Some countries are responding to this crisis by helping workers replant cleared areas. Costa Rica has set aside one-fourth of its forests as national parks. It uses the rain forests to attract **eco-tourists**, or people who travel to other countries to enjoy natural wonders.

Industry Missing from the skylines of most major Central American cities are the smokestacks of industry. The few industries that exist generally focus on preparing foods. In Guatemala, Honduras, and Nicaragua, some factories produce clothing for export.

Guatemala, which has some oil reserves, exports crude oil. Costa Rica produces computer chips, other electronic goods, and medicines. With its varied economy, Costa Rica enjoys one of the highest standards of living in Latin America. It also has one of the highest **literacy rates**, or percentage of people who can read and write.

The Panama Canal The economy in Panama is based on farming—as the economy is throughout Central America—but Panama also earns money from its canal. The **Panama Canal** stretches across the narrow **Isthmus of Panama.** Ships pay a fee to use the canal to shorten travel time between the Atlantic and Pacific Oceans. Turn to page 562 to see how the canal works.

The United States built the canal and owned it for more than 80 years. In 2000 Panama was given final control of the canal. Panama hopes to use this important waterway to build its economy. Nearly half of Panama's 2.9 million people live and work in the canal area.

Reading Check What are the major crops grown on Central America's plantations?

NATIONAL GEOGRAPHIC **On Location**

Economic Highs and Lows

San José, Costa Rica's capital (top), has shopping malls and fast-food chains like many North American cities. In 1998 Hurricane Mitch caused massive mudslides that buried whole villages and destroyed crops in Honduras (bottom).

Issues **During what seasons do hurricanes strike Central America?**

The History and People of Central America

Native Americans settled Central America thousands of years ago. The Olmecs were the first civilization in the area, from about 1200 B.C. to 400 B.C. The Maya flourished in the rain forests of the north from about A.D. 250 to 900. Look at the Native American civilizations map on

More About the Photos

Hurricane Mitch The devastation wrought by Hurricane Mitch was extreme. The storm struck almost every country in the region (Costa Rica and Panama were spared) and left in its wake about 11,000 dead, about 2 million people without their homes, and about $10 billion in damages. Only the fierce "Great Hurricane" of 1780, which killed 22,000, was worse.

Caption Answer in the summer and fall

TRAVEL GUIDE

A blending of Native American, African American, and European—especially Spanish—cultures adds to the richness of Central American traditions. In each country, corn, beans, and rice are mixed with spices for a tasty variety of dishes. The music heard in these countries shares certain traits—rhythms, for instance—yet each country has its unique musical styles.

Reading Check Answer

coffee, bananas, cotton, sugarcane

3 ASSESS

Assign Section 1 Assessment as homework or an in-class activity.

Have students use the Interactive Tutor Self-Assessment CD-ROM to review Section 21–1.

Critical Thinking Activity

Making Comparisons Have students construct a classroom chart comparing the seven countries of Central America. Ask students to suggest topics for comparison. These might include physical geography, economic activities, history, government, or culture. Use the completed chart to prepare national profiles of the seven countries. L1

EE2 Places and Regions: Standard 4

Chapter 21

Section 1, pages 556–561

Measure student knowledge of physical features and political entities.

GeoQuiz Transparency 21-1

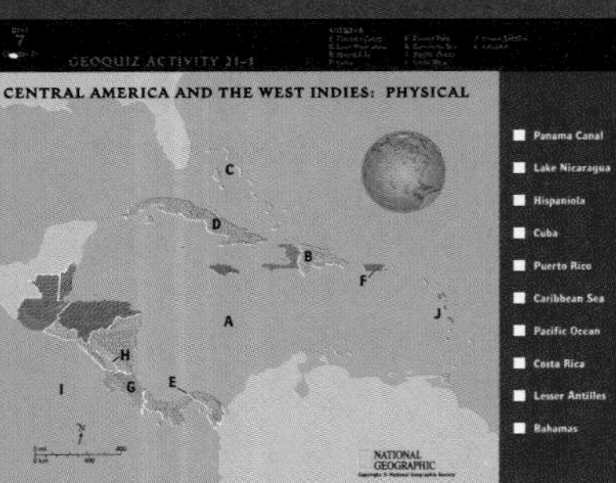

Building Skills

Research and Debate Have students research the Panama Canal treaties of 1977. Direct students to pay close attention to opinions, both for and against, of the transfer of control of the canal to Panama. Have volunteers debate the issue. Then poll the class to determine which viewpoint students favor.

Section Quiz 21-1

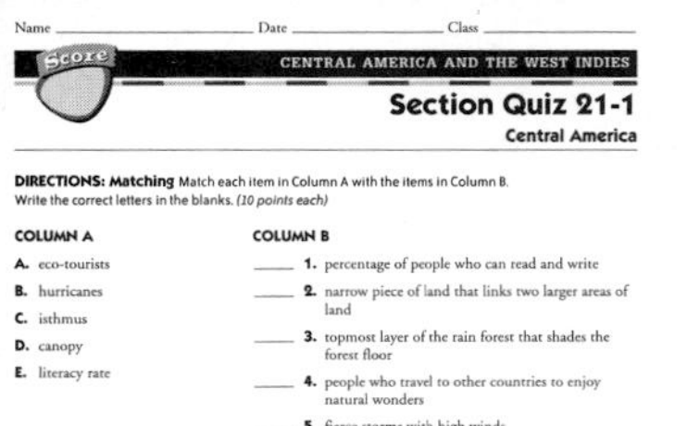

Name ______ Date ______ Class ______

CENTRAL AMERICA AND THE WEST INDIES

Section Quiz 21-1
Central America

DIRECTIONS: Matching Match each item in Column A with the items in Column B. Write the correct letters in the blanks. *(10 points each)*

COLUMN A	COLUMN B
A. eco-tourists	____ 1. percentage of people who can read and write
B. hurricanes	____ 2. narrow piece of land that links two larger areas of land
C. isthmus	____ 3. topmost layer of the rain forest that shades the forest floor
D. canopy	____ 4. people who travel to other countries to enjoy natural wonders
E. literacy rate	____ 5. fierce storms with high winds

Choice In the blank at the left, write the letter of the ... statement or answers the question. *(10 points each)*

What a Catch!

The deep blue waters of Lake Nicaragua are home to the world's only freshwater sharks and swordfish. Now the lake holds one less swordfish. Amadeo Robelo, who lives in Granada, Nicaragua, just spent three hours battling the powerful fish. Amadeo enjoys fishing with his father on weekends. His father wants Amadeo to become part of Nicaragua's middle class—something new in a region where you are either one of the few with wealth or one of the many who live in poverty.

page 542. In **Tikal** (tee•KAHL), Guatemala, and **Copán** (koh•PAHN), Honduras, the Maya created impressive temples and sculptures. Before Columbus arrived, Tikal was the site of the highest structure in the Americas, a 212-foot (64.6-m) temple rising from the floor of the rain forest. The Maya were a very highly developed civilization. Their religion focused on the careful study of time and the stars, astronomy, and mathematics. The Maya developed a calendar and kept records on stone slabs. Then the Maya mysteriously left their cities. Many of their descendants still live in the area today.

In the 1500s, Spaniards established settlements in Central America. For the next 300 years, Spanish landowners forced Native Americans to work on plantations. The two cultures gradually blended. Native Americans started to speak the Spanish language and follow the Roman Catholic faith. Native Americans taught the Spanish about local plants for medicines and how to trap animals for food and hides.

Most Central American countries gained independence from Spain by 1821. The two exceptions are Panama and Belize. Panama was part of the South American country of Colombia for decades. In 1903 the United States helped Panama win its independence in exchange for the right to build the Panama Canal. Belize, a British colony until 1981, was the last Central American country to gain independence.

After Independence Most Central American countries faced constant strife after they became independent. A small number of people in each country held most of the wealth and power. Rebel movements arose as poor farmers fought for changes that would give them land and better lives. Civil wars raged in Nicaragua, El Salvador, and Guatemala as recently as the 1980s and 1990s.

In Guatemala from 1960 to 1996, government military forces fought rebel groups living in the highlands. About 150,000 people died, and the civil war severely weakened Guatemala's economy. Tens of thousands of Guatemalans left the country to look for work in the United States.

In contrast, Costa Ricans have enjoyed peace. A stable democratic government rules, and the country has avoided conflict for most of its history. As a result of these peaceful relations, the country has no army—only a police force to maintain law and order.

Today each country in Central America has a democratic government, with voters choosing government officials. Six countries are also **republics,** with elected presidents as head of the government. Belize is a British-style **parliamentary democracy,** in which an elected legislature chooses a prime minister to head the government.

Daily Life Nearly 38 million people live in Central America. About one-third of this number live in Guatemala, the most heavily populated country in the region. Only about 300,000 people live in Belize, the region's least populous country. Spanish is the official language

Cooperative Learning Activity

Annotated Time Lines Organize students into seven groups and assign one of the countries of Central America to each group. Instruct groups to use the text and other references to find out their assigned country's political history. They should choose five or more important events to share with the class. Then have groups use these events to create annotated time lines. Call on groups to display and discuss their time lines. L2

EE6 The Uses of Geography: Standard 17

throughout the region, except for English-speaking Belize. Many Central Americans also speak Native American languages, such as Mayan. Guatemala's population, for instance, is largely Native American and has 21 different Native American languages. Most Central Americans follow the Roman Catholic religion.

About 50 percent of all Central Americans live on farms or in small villages. At least one major city, usually the capital, is densely populated in each country. Guatemala's capital, **Guatemala City,** ranks with **San José,** Costa Rica, as one of the most populous cities in Central America. People living in urban areas hold manufacturing or service industry jobs, or they work on farms outside the cities. Those living in coastal areas may harvest shrimp, lobster, and other seafood to sell in city markets or for export.

Whether rural or urban, most people enjoy a major celebration called **Carnival.** This festival comes before Lent, a solemn period of prayer and soul-searching before the Christian celebration of Easter. During Carnival—and at other times—bands play salsa, a mixture of Latin American popular music, jazz, and rock. Do you like baseball? It is a national sport in Nicaragua and very popular in Panama, too. Most people throughout the region also enjoy *fútbol,* or soccer.

✓ Reading Check **Why is the government of Belize different from that of other countries in Central America?**

Section 1 Assessment

Defining Terms

1. **Define** isthmus, hurricane, plantation, subsistence farm, canopy, eco-tourist, literacy rate, republic, parliamentary democracy.

Recalling Facts

2. **Economics** What is the difference between plantation and subsistence farming?
3. **Culture** What is the major religion and language of Central America?
4. **Place** Which country in Central America is the most heavily populated? The most sparsely populated?

Critical Thinking

5. **Making Comparisons** How have the differences in government stability affected the citizens of Guatemala and Costa Rica?
6. **Analyzing Cause and Effect** Explain why rain forest soil does not keep its nutrients long.

Graphic Organizer

7. **Organizing Information** Create a diagram like this one. On the lines list the major products and industries of Central America.

Major products and industries

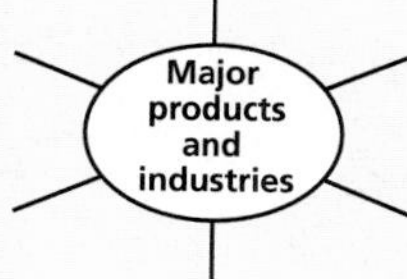

Applying Social Studies Skills

8. **Analyzing Maps** Refer to the political map on page 557. Which countries of Central America border Mexico? Which border the Pacific Ocean?

Section 1 Assessment

1. The terms are defined in the Glossary.
2. Plantations: owned by wealthy people and companies, grow crops for sale; subsistence farms: poor farmers grow only enough to feed their families.
3. Roman Catholicism, Spanish
4. Guatemala; Belize
5. Civil war in Guatemala has weakened the economy, causing many people to seek work in the United States. Stability in Costa Rica has provided peace for its people.
6. Trees hold soil in place. Without trees, rains wash away soil and its nutrients.
7. Coffee, bananas, cotton, sugarcane, flowers, ornamental plants, clothing, oil, computer chips, medicine
8. Guatemala, Belize; Guatemala, El Salvador, Honduras, Nicaragua, Costa Rica, Panama

Chapter 21

Section 1, pages 556–561

Reading Essentials and Study Guide 21–1

Name ______ Date ______ Class ______

CENTRAL AMERICA AND THE WEST INDIES

Reading Essentials and Study Guide 21-1

Central America

For use with textbook pages 556-561

Terms to Know

isthmus narrow piece of land that links two larger areas of land (page 556)
hurricanes strong storms with winds of more than 74 miles per hour (page 557)
plantations commercial farms that grow crops for sale (page 557)
subsistence farms small farms that grow just enough for farmers to feed their families (page 558)
canopy top layer of the rain forest that shades the forest floor (page 558)
eco-tourists people who travel to other countries to enjoy natural wonders (page 559)
literacy rate percentage of people who can read and write (page 559)
republic country with an elected president as head of the government (page 560)
democracy form of government in which an elected legislature ... the government (page 560)

Reteach

Have students work in pairs to review the content of the section. Partners should take turns asking and answering questions based on the section text and maps.

✓ Reading Check Answer

Because it was once a British colony, and not a Spanish one, Belize has a British-style government.

Enrich

Have students research ecotourism or plantation farming in Central America. Have them present their findings in a report.

CLOSE

Have students write a paragraph comparing daily life in Central America with that in the United States.

TEACH

Ask students what they know about canals. Use a map to show where the Panama Canal is and ask students to explain why this structure would be beneficial to shipping. **L1**

More About Panama Canal

Many people in the United States favored building the canal across Nicaragua, not Panama. Philippe Bunau-Varilla, a Panamanian who had invested in the French project, helped change their minds. Before the final vote, each senator received an envelope sent by Bunau-Varilla. The envelopes contained a Nicaraguan stamp that showed a volcano in Nicaragua in mid-eruption. The implication—that the volcano might destroy the canal—won the route for Panama.

Interdisciplinary Connections

Science Dr. Walter Reed had proved that mosquitoes carried yellow fever. Dr. William Gorgas was in charge of removing the threat of the mosquito-borne diseases in the canal. His work was so successful that yellow fever was completely wiped out of the isthmus of Panama in 1905.

Making Connections

CULTURE | GOVERNMENT | PEOPLE | TECHNOLOGY

The Panama Canal Locks

Before the Panama Canal was built, ships had to sail around the southern tip of South America to go from the Atlantic Ocean to the Pacific Ocean and vice versa. The canal provides a shortcut that reduces that trip by about 9,200 miles (14,802 km).

Digging the Canal

The first attempts to build a canal across Panama were begun in 1881 by a private French company. Huge expenses, poor planning, and the effects of diseases such as malaria and yellow fever stopped construction. In 1904 the United States government took over. Doctors had recently learned that bites from infected mosquitoes caused malaria and yellow fever. Workers drained swamps and cleared brush to remove the mosquitoes' breeding grounds. Then the digging began. The canal's course ran through hills of soft volcanic soil. Massive landslides regularly occurred before the 50-mile (80-km) canal was completed in 1914.

An Engineering Masterpiece

To move ships through the canal, engineers designed three sets of locks—the largest concrete structures on the earth. They allow ships to move from one water level to another by changing the amount of water in the locks. Together, the locks can raise or lower ships about 85 feet (26 m)—the height of a seven-story building. The diagram below shows you how these locks work.

Making the Connection

1. Why was a canal through Panama desirable?
2. What function do locks perform?
3. **Understanding Cause and Effect** How did medical advances affect the building of the Panama Canal?

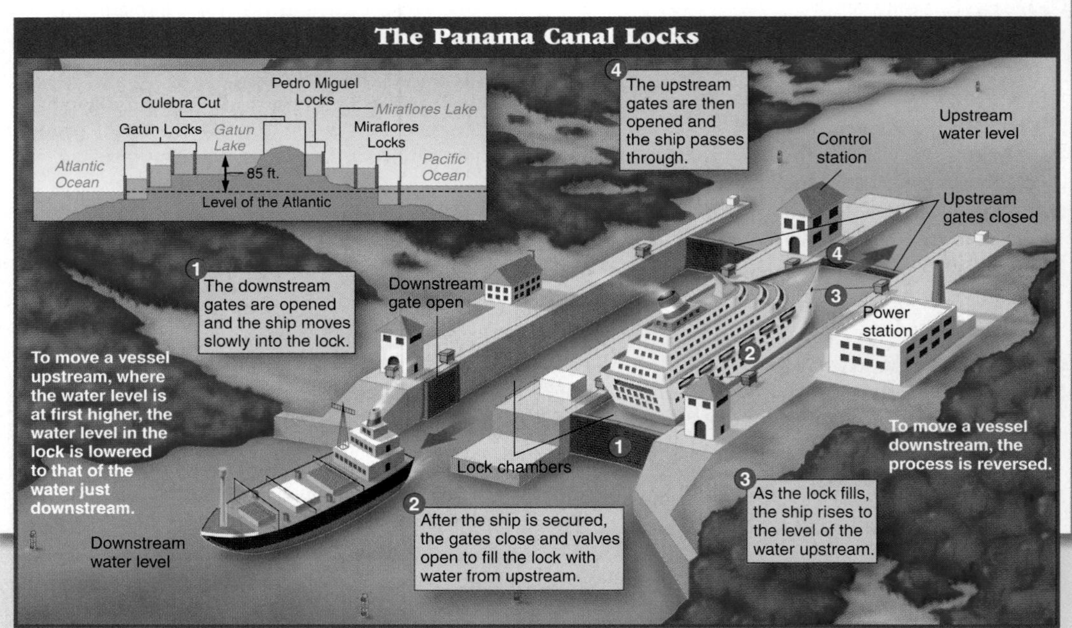

Making the Connection

1. to cut travel time between the Atlantic and Pacific Oceans
2. Locks allow ships to move from one water level to another by changing the amount of water in the locks, thereby raising or lowering the ships.
3. The impact of diseases such as malaria and yellow fever stopped construction, and the curing and prevention of these diseases spurred construction.

Section 2

The West Indies

Guide to Reading

Main Idea

The islands of the West Indies rely on tourism to support their economies.

Terms to Know

- commercial crop
- bauxite
- cooperative
- communist state
- embargo
- free trade zone
- commonwealth

Reading Strategy

Create a diagram like this one. In each oval, list a country in the West Indies and features that are specific to it. Where the ovals overlap, list features that are similar to both countries.

NATIONAL GEOGRAPHIC **Exploring Our World**

The warm waters of the Caribbean Sea lure millions of tourists to the West Indies every year. Some tourists go scuba diving so they can see the colorful fish, which swim in the islands' clear waters. Others shop at the local stores, buying handcrafted goods. This diver uses a metal detector to look for objects from a Spanish ship that sank in the 1600s.

A number of islands dot the Caribbean Sea. Some of these islands form groups that are known as the West Indies. Study the political map on page 557 to become familiar with the names of these island groups.

Mountaintop Islands

When you look at the islands of the West Indies, you are really looking at the tops of mountains. Many West Indian islands are part of an underwater chain of mountains formed by volcanoes. A typical volcanic island has central highlands ringed by coastal plains. The volcanic soil in the highlands is rich.

Other islands are limestone mountains pushed up from the ocean floor by pressures under the earth's crust. Limestone islands generally are flatter than volcanic islands. The sandy soil found on many limestone islands is not good for farming.

Climate The West Indies lie in the Tropics. Most islands have a fairly constant tropical climate. Sea and wind, more than elevation, affect the climate here. Northeast breezes sweep across the Caribbean Sea,

1 Focus

Section Objectives

1. Identify and compare the islands of the West Indies.
2. Describe the landforms and climates of the West Indies.
3. Explain the economic activities of the islands.
4. Compare the cultures and history of the islands.

BELLRINGER Skillbuilder Activity

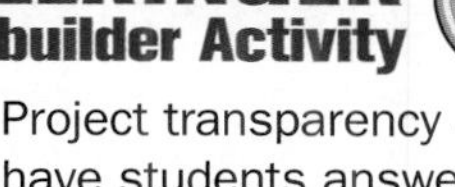

Project transparency and have students answer questions.

This activity is also available as a blackline master.

Daily Focus Skills Transparency 21-2

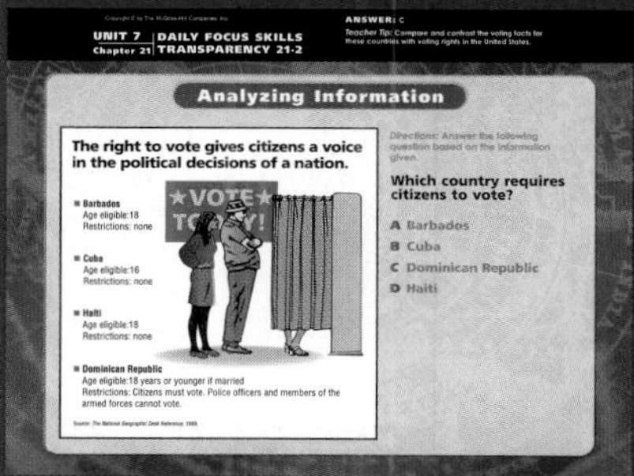

Guide to Reading

■ **Accessing Prior Knowledge**
Ask students to identify the citizenship of people born in Puerto Rico. *(They are citizens of the United States.)*

Section Resources

Reproducible Masters
- Reproducible Lesson Plan 21-2
- Daily Lecture and Discussion Notes 21-2
- Guided Reading Activity 21-2
- Reading Essentials and Study Guide 21-2
- Section Quiz 21-2

Transparencies
- Daily Focus Skills Transparency 21-2
- GeoQuiz Transparency 21-1

Multimedia
- Vocabulary PuzzleMaker Software
- Interactive Tutor Self-Assessment CD-ROM
- Presentation Plus! CD-ROM
- ExamView® Pro 3.0 Testmaker CD-ROM
- MindJogger Videoquiz

TEACH

Synthesizing Information After students have read the section, organize them into two teams to take a quiz. Offer the first team a clue that will help them identify a West Indian country. If the team cannot answer correctly, offer a second clue to the second team. If that team cannot answer correctly, give a third clue and invite either team to answer. **L1**

Reading Check Answer

The islands are actually mountains made by volcanoes or composed of limestone pushed up from the ocean floor.

Daily Lecture Notes 21-2

EARTH PATTERNS

Daily Lecture and Discussion Notes 2-1

Thinking Like a Geographer (pages 52–55)

Did You Know? Geography is the science of space and place on the earth's surface. We human beings are constantly interacting with the earth. The earth shapes our lives just as we shape the face of the earth. Studying geography enables us to better see and understand our own home and culture and our relationships to other cultures and environments. Clear vision and understanding form a basis for nearly any kind of communication and constructive action.

I. A Geographer's View of Place *(pages 53–54)*

A. Geographers study places. They ask: What features make a place similar to or different from other places?

B. **Landforms** are individual features of the land, like mountains, valleys, and water.

Reading Check Answer

tourism and farming

taking on the temperature of the cooler water beneath them. When the winds blow onshore, they keep temperatures pleasant.

For half the year, hurricanes threaten the West Indies. The word *hurricane* comes from the Taíno, an early Native American people who lived on the islands. They worshiped a god of storms named Hurakan. (Two other terms that we have borrowed from the Taíno include *canoe* and *hammock,* a bed made by stringing ropes or plant fibers between two trees.)

Reading Check **What formed the islands of the West Indies?**

The Economy of the West Indies

Farming and tourism are the main economic activities in the West Indies. Wealthy landowners grow crops such as sugarcane, bananas, coffee, and tobacco for export. Many laborers work on the plantations that grow these **commercial crops.** Commercial crops are grown to sell, not to be eaten by the grower. The Caribbean islands face an economic danger by depending on one commercial crop. If the crop fails, no income is earned. If too much of the crop is produced worldwide, overall prices fall and the economy is in serious trouble. Most of the islands do not have large amounts of minerals, although several islands have some resources. Jamaica, for example, mines **bauxite,** a mineral used to make aluminum. The country of Trinidad and Tobago exports oil products. In Puerto Rico, companies make chemicals and machinery. Haiti and the Dominican Republic have textile factories that make cloth.

Reading Check **What are the two major industries in the West Indies?**

History and Culture

When Christopher Columbus reached San Salvador in the Bahamas in 1492, who met him? As you probably guessed, it was a Native American group—the Taíno. The Taíno and other Native Americans lived on the islands long before the coming of Europeans.

The Spaniards established the first permanent European settlement in the Western Hemisphere in 1496. That settlement is now the city of Santo Domingo, capital of the Dominican Republic. During the next 200 years, the Spaniards, the English, the French, and the Dutch also founded colonies, or overseas settlements, on many of the islands. They found the soil and climate perfect for growing sugarcane.

By the mid-1600s, most Native Americans had died from European diseases and harsh treatment. The Europeans then brought enslaved Africans to work on sugar plantations. When the slave trade ended in the early 1800s, plantation owners still in need of workers brought them from Asia, particularly India. The Asians agreed to work a set number of years in return for free travel to the West Indies and low wages.

Independence During the 1800s and 1900s, many Caribbean islands won their freedom from European rule. The first to become independent were the larger island countries, such as Haiti, the Dominican Republic, and Cuba. Later, smaller islands such as Barbados

Meeting Special Needs

Inefficient Readers Students who do not read efficiently benefit from having a specific purpose for reading. Point out the Guide to Reading at the beginning of the section. Demonstrate how to use this study guide to preview the lesson and to find main ideas in the section. As you complete each section, have students identify the Terms to Know and fill in a diagram like the one in Reading Strategy. **L1**

Refer to *Inclusion for the Middle School Social Studies Classroom Strategies and Activities* in the TCR.

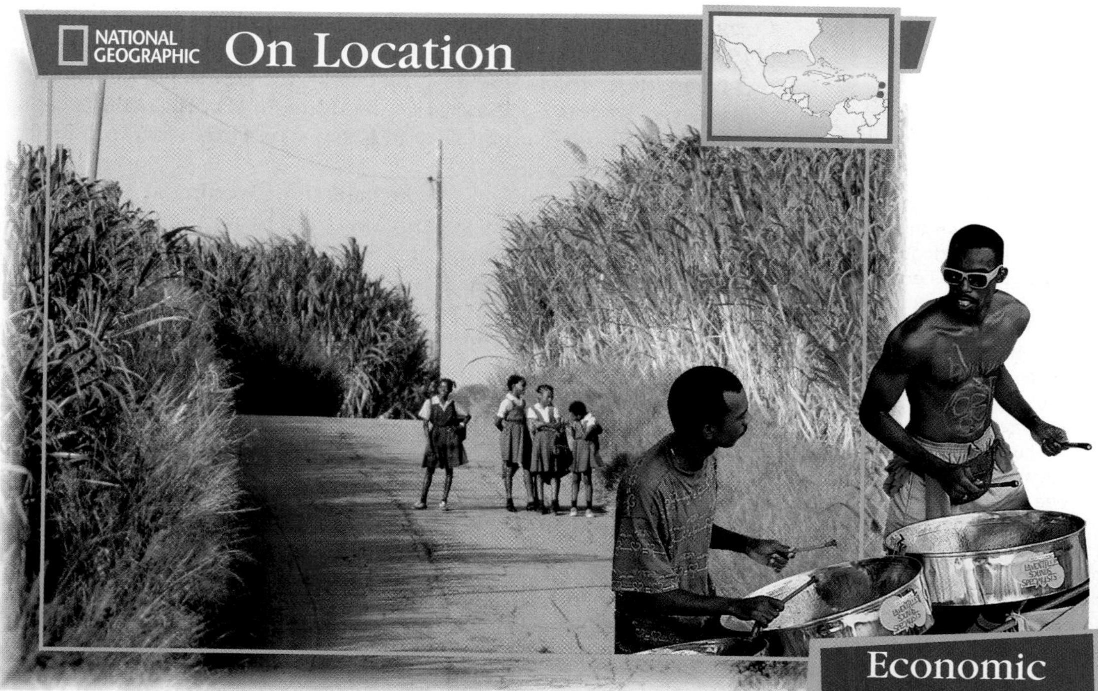

Economic Activities

Schoolgirls on Barbados walk past vast sugar plantations that European countries started in the colonial period (left). A steel-drum band entertains tourists in Trinidad (above).

Region **What attracts so many tourists to the islands of the West Indies?**

and Grenada became nations. Many countries—like Haiti and the Dominican Republic—are republics. Others—like Jamaica and the Bahamas—are British-style parliamentary democracies.

Daily Life About 60 percent of West Indians live in cities and villages. The other 40 percent live and work in the countryside. Many islanders have jobs in the hotels or restaurants that serve the tourist industry.

If you visit the Caribbean, you are likely to hear lively music. The bell-like tones of the steel drum, developed in Trinidad, are part of the rich musical heritage of the region. Enslaved Africans created a kind of music called calypso. Jamaica's reggae and calypso music combines African rhythms and American popular music. Cuban salsa blends African rhythms, Spanish styles, and jazz.

On several islands, you will hear a different sound—the crack of a baseball bat. People in Puerto Rico, the Dominican Republic, and Cuba have a passion for baseball. Soccer and cricket are other popular sports.

✓ Reading Check **Where was the first permanent European settlement in the West Indies?**

Island Profiles

The islands of the West Indies share many similarities, but they also have differences. Some of these differences can be seen in Cuba, Haiti, the Dominican Republic, and Puerto Rico.

Chapter 21

Section 2, pages 563–567

Guided Reading Activity 21-2

Name ______ Date ______ Class ______

CENTRAL AMERICA AND THE WEST INDIES

Guided Reading Activity 21-2

The West Indies

DIRECTIONS: Filling in the Blanks Reading the section and completing the activity summary paragraphs below will help you learn more about the West Indies. Refer to your textbook to fill in the blanks.

The West Indies is a group of islands in the (1) ______. Some islands of the West Indies are part of an underwater chain of mountains formed by (2) ______. Other islands are (3) ______ mountains. Most of the islands have a (4) ______ climate.

Many laborers work on plantations that grow (5) ______. ______ Commercial crops are grown to (6) ______. Most of the West Indies islands do not have large amounts of

More About the Photos

Steel Drums The idea of using steel drums as an instrument. started in Trinidad. Ordinary metal drums used for shipping liquid cargo are cut and hammered to take a concave shape, which can play different notes. Steel drum bands can include anywhere from 4 to 100 members.

Caption Answer warm, sunny climate and beautiful beaches

✓ Reading Check Answer

the Spanish settlement that is now Santo Domingo, the Dominican Republic

Assign Section 2 Assessment as homework or an in-class activity.

Have students use the Interactive Tutor Self-Assessment CD-ROM to review Section 21–2.

Critical Thinking Activity

Analyzing Information Pose the following question for students to consider: **Is tourism beneficial or harmful to the West Indies? Why?** Provide time for students to reflect on the question and discuss it among themselves. Then ask several volunteers to present opposing viewpoints. *(Some may feel that tourism is beneficial because it helps local economies. Others may argue that countries that rely on tourism fail to develop other industries.)* Ask the entire class what steps a nation could take to address the problems raised by tourism. **L2**

EE4 Human Systems: Standard 11

Chapter 21

Section 2, pages 563–567

Building Skills

Making Comparisons Have students create a six-column chart with the headings "Region," "Landforms," "Climate," "Economy," "People," and "History." Have them then write two row headings under the "Region" column—"Central America" and "West Indies." Have them complete the chart by filling in details about the five categories.

Travel Guide

In Santo Domingo, Dominican Republic, you will find the oldest street in the Americas: Calle Las Damas. On it you can see sixteenth-century homes and a grand Jesuit monastery. The Cathedral of Santa Mariá la Menor, the oldest church in the Americas, is a short distance away.

Section Quiz 21–2

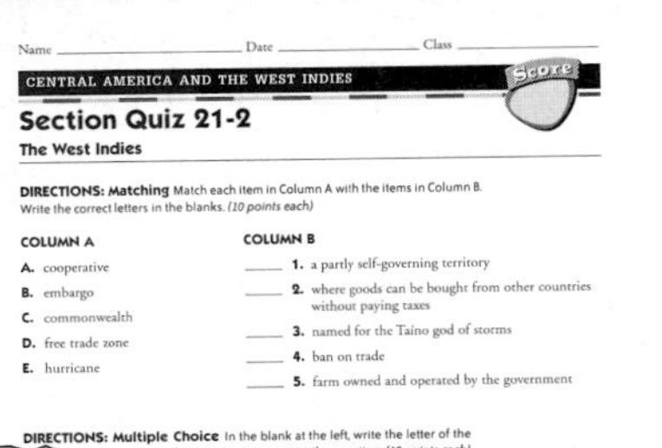

Name ______ Date ______ Class ______

CENTRAL AMERICA AND THE WEST INDIES

Score

Section Quiz 21-2

The West Indies

DIRECTIONS: Matching Match each item in Column A with the items in Column B. Write the correct letters in the blanks. *(10 points each)*

COLUMN A	COLUMN B
A. cooperative	____ **1.** a partly self-governing territory
B. embargo	____ **2.** where goods can be bought from other countries without paying taxes
C. commonwealth	____ **3.** named for the Taino god of storms
D. free trade zone	____ **4.** ban on trade
E. hurricane	____ **5.** farm owned and operated by the government

DIRECTIONS: Multiple Choice In the blank at the left, write the letter of the ... the statement or answers the question. *(10 points each)*

Believe It or Not!

Bee Hummingbird

How small is this bird? The bee hummingbird of Cuba measures only 2 inches (5.1 cm) from head to tail. That is small enough to make it the tiniest bird in the world. The bird's wings move so fast—80 beats per second—that the human eye cannot see them. At two grams, the bee hummingbird weighs less than a penny.

Cuba One of the world's top sugar producers, Cuba lies about 90 miles (145 km) south of Florida. Most farmers work on **cooperatives,** or farms owned and operated by the government. In addition to growing sugarcane, they grow coffee, tobacco, rice, and fruits. In **Havana,** Cuba's capital and the largest city in the West Indies, workers make food products, cigars, and household goods.

Cuba is a **communist state,** where the government has strong control over the economy and society. Cuba is the only communist state in the Western Hemisphere. A dictator, President Fidel Castro, leads the country. Cuba won its independence from Spain in 1898. The country had a democratic government, although military leaders sometimes seized power. In 1959 Castro led a revolution that took control of the government. He set up a communist state and turned to the Soviet Union for support. When he seized property belonging to American companies, the United States government responded. It put in place an **embargo,** or a ban on trade, against Cuba.

Before 1989, Cuba relied on aid from the Soviet Union. The Cuban people benefit from good education and healthcare, but the economy is struggling. The Cuban economy is struggling, and many Cubans live in poverty. With the end of the Cold War, some Americans favor ending the trade embargo with Cuba. Other Americans, especially relatives of Cubans who suffered under Castro and refugees who fled to the United States for safety, strongly oppose recognizing Castro's Cuban government.

Haiti On the western half of the island of Hispaniola, you will find the country of Haiti. Led by a former slave, Francois-Dominique Toussaint-Louverture, Haiti fought for and won its independence from France in 1804. It was the second independent republic in the Western Hemisphere (after the United States). It became the first nation in the history of the world to be founded by former slaves. About 95 percent of Haiti's 7 million people are of African ancestry.

Civil war has left Haiti's economy in ruins, and most Haitians are poor. In the 1980s, the staple of the people's diet was the Creole pig. Creole pigs were also important as a source of income. When it came time to send a child to school, a pig could be sold to pay for books, fees, and a uniform. When planting season came, selling a pig paid for seeds and tools. Having a pig around often meant the difference between life and death when health emergencies arose. Creole pigs were known as the "peasants' savings bank." In 1983 a swine flu outbreak forced the government to destroy the population of Creole pigs to prevent an epidemic in the Americas. A plan to substitute pigs from the United States failed. Unlike the Creole pigs, which had foraged for their own food, the U.S. breeds required expensive feed, which Haitian farmers could not afford. The imported pigs required housing with cement floors, while most Haitian peasants lived in homes with dirt floors. The U.S. pigs were not used to Haiti's tropical climate. Within a short time, most of the U.S. pigs had died. Today, the Haitian government, with U.S. help, has begun a program to help communities replace the destroyed Creole pig population and try to lessen the poverty of the families.

Cooperative Learning Activity

Helping a Relief Agency Central America and the West Indies sometimes suffer devastating damage from natural disasters, as can people in your area. Agencies like the Red Cross respond quickly to these situations by providing food, clothing, emergency shelter, blood, and medical supplies. Have students identify a relief agency and find out what help it needs. Students should consider the ways they can help this organization. They might collect food and clothing, organize fund-raising activities or blood drives, or create promotional posters. Once students have considered the advantages and disadvantages, they should choose the best solution and implement it. Afterwards, have the class write a report evaluating the effectiveness of their project. **L2**

EE6 The Uses of Geography: Standard 18

Dominican Republic The Dominican Republic shares the island of Hispaniola with Haiti, filling the eastern part. Though they share the same island, the two countries have different histories and little contact. Haiti was a French colony. The Dominican Republic was settled by Spaniards, who brought enslaved Africans to work on sugar plantations. Sugar is still an important crop to the Dominicans. Tourism is growing, too, and many Dominicans sell goods in the country's free trade zone. **Free trade zones** are areas where people can buy goods from other countries without paying taxes.

Puerto Rico To be or not to be a state in the United States, that is the question that Puerto Ricans ask themselves every few years. The last time they voted on the question, they said no. How did Puerto Rico become part of the United States? The island was a Spanish colony from 1508 to 1898. After the Spanish-American War in 1898, the United States won control of Puerto Rico. Since 1952 the island has been a **commonwealth**, or a partly self-governing territory, under American protection. By law, Puerto Ricans are citizens of the United States. They can come and go from the island to the United States as they wish. Today nearly 3 million Puerto Ricans live in the United States. The island itself holds about 3.9 million and boasts a high standard of living compared to most other Caribbean islands.

✓ **Reading Check** What is a commonwealth?

Our World Today online
Web Activity Visit the ***Our World Today: People, Places, and Issues*** Web site at owt.glencoe.com and click on **Chapter 21–Student Web Activities** to learn more about Puerto Rico.

Section 2 Assessment

Defining Terms

1. **Define** commercial crop, bauxite, cooperative, communist state, embargo, free trade zone, commonwealth.

Recalling Facts

2. **Economy** What are the two main economic activities in the West Indies?
3. **History** Name four groups who have influenced the culture of the Caribbean region.
4. **Government** How is Cuba different from every other country in the Western Hemisphere?

Critical Thinking

5. **Drawing Conclusions** Explain why you think Puerto Ricans might be satisfied remaining a commonwealth, rather than becoming a state.
6. **Making Predictions** What is the danger of a country's depending on only one crop?

Graphic Organizer

7. **Organizing Information** Complete a chart like the one below with facts about Haiti and the Dominican Republic.

Country	Haiti	Dominican Republic
Location		
Colonized by		
Economy		

Applying Social Studies Skills

8. **Cause and Effect** Create a cause and effect chart that explains why the U.S. pigs did not adapt to Haiti.

Section 2 Assessment

1. The terms are defined in the Glossary.
2. farming and tourism
3. Native Americans, Europeans, Africans, and Asians
4. It is a communist state.
5. People on the island are already U.S. citizens and are partly self-governing.
6. If the crop fails, no income is earned. Overproduction causes prices to fall, threatening the country's economy.
7. Haiti: western part of Hispaniola, France, civil war and poverty; Dominican Republic: eastern part of Hispaniola, Spain
8. U.S. pigs required expensive feed that Haitians could not afford, liked cement floors while most farmers had dirt floors, were not used to Haiti's climate

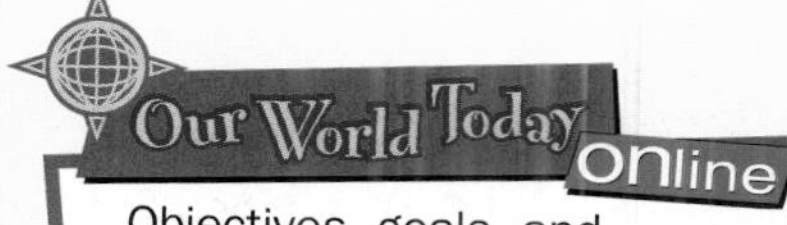

Objectives, goals, and answers to the Student Web Activity can be found in the Web Activity Lesson Plan at owt.glencoe.com

✓ Reading Check Answer

a partly self-governing territory

Reteach

Have students prepare an annotated map highlighting the cultural characteristics of the West Indies.

Reading Essentials and Study Guide 21–2

Name ____ Date ____ Class ____

CENTRAL AMERICA AND THE WEST INDIES

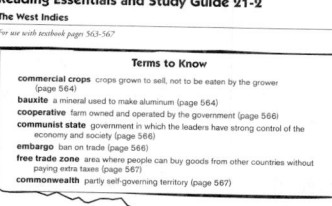

Reading Essentials and Study Guide 21-2

The West Indies

For use with textbook pages 563-567

Terms to Know

commercial crops crops grown to sell, not to be eaten by the grower (page 564)
bauxite a mineral used to make aluminum (page 564)
cooperative farm owned and operated by the government (page 566)
communist state government in which the leaders have strong control of the economy and society (page 566)
embargo ban on trade (page 566)
free trade zone area where people can buy goods from other countries without paying extra taxes (page 567)
commonwealth partly self-governing territory (page 567)

4 CLOSE

Have students write a brief essay that explains what the island nations of the West Indies have in common and how they differ.

Social Studies Skill

TEACH

Direct students to study the physical map of Central America and the West Indies on page 558. Point out that a physical map is similar to an elevation profile in that they both provide information about relief and landforms. Ask students to try to translate information on the map into an elevation profile. Suggest that they create a cross section from the Pacific coast of Guatemala through Honduras. Call on volunteers to use their profiles to locate and identify the highest and lowest points in this cross section. **L2**

Additional Skills Practice

1. **What sea surrounds Jamaica?** *(Caribbean Sea)*
2. **Is Kingston on the coast? How can you tell?** *(You cannot tell, because although it is shown between landforms, the profile does not show a north-south cross section.)*
3. **How high are the Blue Mountains?** *(about 7,200 feet, or 2,200 m)*

Additional Skills Resources

- Chapter Skills Activity 21
- Building Geography Skills for Life

Social Studies Skill

Interpreting an Elevation Profile

You have learned that differences in land elevation are often shown on physical or relief maps. Another way to show elevation is on **elevation profiles.** When you view a person's profile, you see a side view. An elevation profile is a diagram that shows a side view of the landforms in an area.

Learning the Skill

Suppose you could slice right through a country from top to bottom and could look at the inside, or *cross section.* The cross section, or elevation profile, below pictures the island of Jamaica. It shows how far Jamaica's landforms extend below or above sea level.

Follow these steps to understand an elevation profile:

- Read the title of the profile to find out what country you are viewing.
- Look at the line of latitude written along the bottom of the profile. On a separate map, find the country and where this line of latitude runs through it.
- Look at the measurements along the sides of the profile. Note where sea level is located and the height in feet or meters.
- Now read the labels on the profile to identify the heights of the different landforms shown along with their elevation.
- Compare the highest and lowest points.

Practicing the Skill

Use the elevation profile below to answer the following questions.

1. At what elevation is Kingston?
2. What are the highest mountains, and where are they located?
3. Where are the lowest regions?
4. Along what line of latitude was this cross section taken?

Applying the Skill

Turn to page 13 in the **Geography Handbook.** Use the elevation profile of Africa to answer questions 2–4 above about *that* continent.

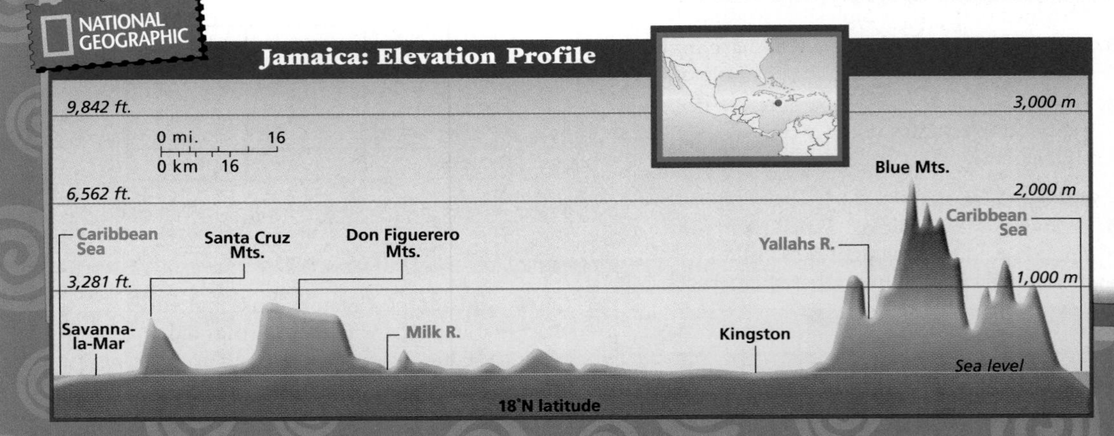

Practicing the Skill Answers

1. at about sea level
2. Blue Mountains, in the east
3. the Savanna-la-Mar in the west and the eastern valley where Kingston is located
4. 18°N

Applying the Skill

Highest mountain: Mt. Kenya in the east; Lowest region: Congo River valley; line of latitude is 0° (Equator)

Chapter 21

Reading Review

Section 1 Central America

Terms to Know
- isthmus
- hurricane
- plantation
- subsistence farm
- canopy
- eco-tourist
- literacy rate
- republic
- parliamentary democracy

Main Idea

Central America is made up of seven nations that are home to a variety of peoples, exotic animals, and diverse landforms.

✓ **Region** Central America includes seven countries: Belize, Guatemala, Honduras, El Salvador, Nicaragua, Costa Rica, and Panama.

✓ **Region** Volcanic mountains run down the center of Central America with coastal lowlands on either side.

✓ **Economics** Most people in the region farm—either on plantations or subsistence farms.

✓ **Culture** Most countries in Central America have a blend of Native American and Spanish cultures.

The Panama Canal ►

Section 2 The West Indies

Terms to Know
- commercial crop
- bauxite
- cooperative
- communist state
- embargo
- free trade zone
- commonwealth

Main Idea

The islands of the West Indies rely on tourism to support their economies.

✓ **History** Christopher Columbus landed in this region in 1492.

✓ **History** Most of the islands were at one time colonies of European countries.

✓ **Economics** Farming and tourism are the major economic activities in the West Indies.

✓ **Culture** The cultures of the West Indies mix Native American, European, African, and Asian influences.

✓ **Government** Most governments in the West Indies are democratic, but a dictator rules Communist Cuba.

Reading Review

Use the Chapter 21 Reading Review to preview, review, condense, or reteach the chapter.

Preview/Review

Use the Terms to Know lists to help students review and study.

Activity Have students write the terms and definitions on index cards and group themselves into pairs. Have the pairs quiz each other on the terms.

Vocabulary PuzzleMaker Software reinforces the vocabulary terms used in Chapter 21.

The Interactive Tutor Self-Assessment CD-ROM allows students to review Chapter 21 content.

Condense

Have students read the Chapter 21 summary statements.

Chapter 21 Guided Reading Activities

Chapter 21 Audio Program

Reteach

Reteaching Activity 21

Chapter 21 Reading Essentials and Study Guide

Chapter Culminating Activity

Writing a Letter Point out to students that life in the region has changed tremendously in the past 500 years or so since Christopher Columbus first landed in the region. Invite students to write a letter to Columbus describing these changes. Encourage them to include both positive and negative changes. They should use standard grammar, sentence structure, and punctuation. Call on volunteers to share their letters with the class. *NOTE: This activity may be completed separately or you may wish students to incorporate it into their Current Events Journals.* **L1**

EE6 The Uses of Geography: Standard 18

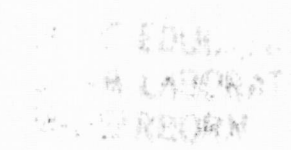

Assessment and Activities

GLENCOE TECHNOLOGY

MindJogger Videoquiz
Use MindJogger to review the Chapter 21 content.

Available in VHS.

Using Key Terms

1. d
2. h
3. a
4. f
5. j
6. b
7. i
8. c
9. e
10. g

Reviewing the Main Ideas

11. Guatemala, Belize, Honduras, El Salvador, Nicaragua, Costa Rica, and Panama
12. Lumber companies cut down and export valuable trees; other companies and local farmers cut or burn trees to clear land for farming. When the land loses its nutrients, the businesses and farmers clear trees from another piece of land.
13. Guatemala and Honduras
14. about 50 percent
15. farming and tourism
16. volcanoes
17. steel drums, calypso, reggae, African rhythms, American popular music, salsa, Spanish styles, jazz
18. Haiti
19. If the crop fails, no income is earned. Overproduction worldwide causes prices to fall, threatening the country's economy.

Chapter 21 Assessment and Activities

Using Key Terms

Match the terms in Part A with their definitions in Part B.

A.

1. isthmus
2. literacy rate
3. plantation
4. eco-tourist
5. commercial crop
6. bauxite
7. commonwealth
8. embargo
9. free trade zone
10. republic

B.

a. large commercial farm
b. mineral ore from which aluminum is made
c. ban on trade
d. narrow piece of land connecting two larger pieces of land
e. area where people can buy goods from other countries without paying taxes
f. person who travels to another country to enjoy its natural wonders
g. country with an elected president
h. percentage of adults who can read and write
i. partly self-governing territory
j. product grown to sell rather than to eat

Reviewing the Main Ideas

Section 1 Central America

11. **Region** What seven countries make up Central America?
12. **Economics** Why are the Central American rain forests being destroyed?
13. **History** In what Central American countries did the Maya live?
14. **Culture** What percentage of Central Americans live on farms or in small villages?

Section 2 The West Indies

15. **Economics** What two activities form the basis of the West Indian economies?
16. **Region** Many of the Caribbean islands were formed by what type of tectonic activity?
17. **Culture** What types of music can you find in the West Indies?
18. **History** What was the first nation in the world to be founded by formerly enslaved people?
19. **Economics** Why are commercial crops sometimes a risky business?

NATIONAL GEOGRAPHIC Central America and the West Indies

Place Location Activity

On a separate sheet of paper, match the letters on the map with the numbered places listed below.

1. Guatemala
2. Caribbean Sea
3. Cuba
4. Puerto Rico
5. Costa Rica
6. Panama
7. Bahamas
8. Haiti
9. Jamaica
10. Honduras

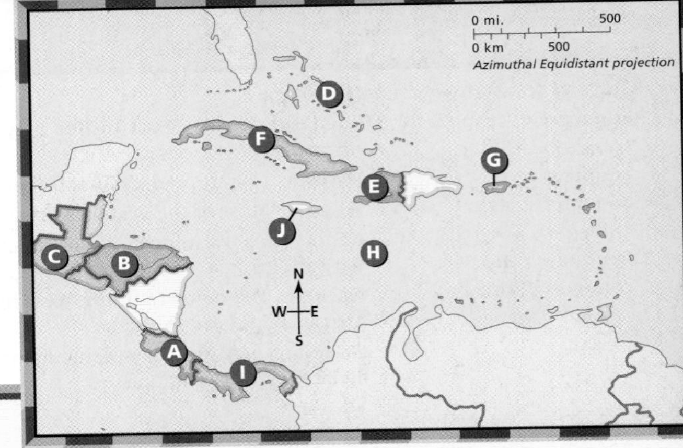

570

NATIONAL GEOGRAPHIC Place Location Activity

1. C
2. H
3. F
4. G
5. A
6. I
7. D
8. E
9. J
10. B

Critical Thinking

20. Because Cuba is only about 90 miles (145 km) from the United States, American officials keep a close watch on the island.

21. Answers will vary based on the country the student chooses. Check students' completed diagrams to be sure accurate facts are placed in appropriate places.

Self-Check Quiz Visit the ***Our World Today: People, Places, and Issues*** Web site at owt.glencoe.com and click on **Chapter 21–Self-Check Quizzes** to prepare for the Chapter Test.

Critical Thinking

20. **Analyzing Information** Explain why Cuba's location is an important factor in the United States's relationship with that nation.
21. **Categorizing Information** Create a diagram like this with details about the people, history, and economy of a country in Chapter 21.

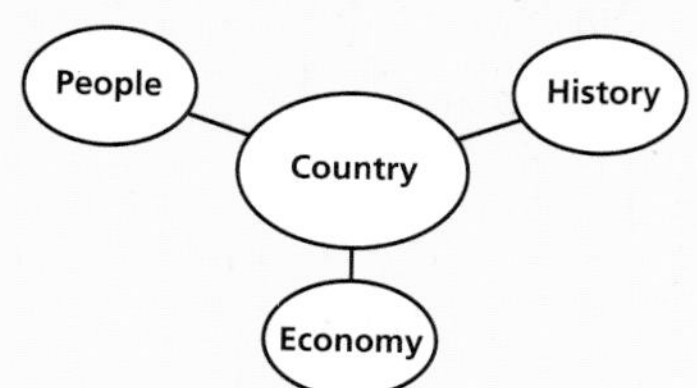

Current Events Journal

22. **Writing an Itinerary** Write an itinerary, or travel plan, for a cruise ship that makes five stops in the Caribbean. Include a map showing the route and descriptions of the sites and activities at each stop.

Mental Mapping Activity

23. **Focusing on the Region** Create an outline map of Central America and the West Indies, and then label the following:

- Pacific Ocean
- Cuba
- Caribbean Sea
- Puerto Rico
- Guatemala
- Jamaica
- Panama
- Bahamas

Technology Skills Activity

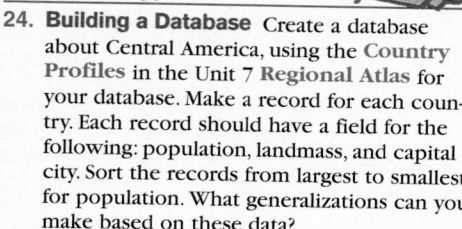

24. **Building a Database** Create a database about Central America, using the **Country Profiles** in the Unit 7 **Regional Atlas** for your database. Make a record for each country. Each record should have a field for the following: population, landmass, and capital city. Sort the records from largest to smallest for population. What generalizations can you make based on these data?

Standardized Test Practice

Directions: Study the map below, and then answer the question that follows.

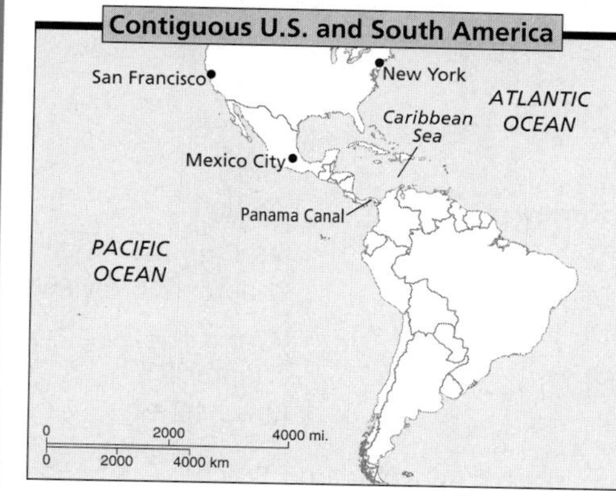

1. **Which of the following was true before the Panama Canal was completed?**
   - **A** A ship sailing from New York to California had to travel nearly 10,000 additional miles.
   - **B** A ship sailing from New York to California had to travel nearly 5,000 additional kilometers.
   - **C** The completion of the canal increased trade between Mexico City and San Francisco.
   - **D** Mexico City was extremely far away from New York City.

Test-Taking Tip: The scale shows you the actual distance between places on a map. Use your finger or a piece of paper to mark off the distance of the scale. Then, use your finger or piece of paper to gauge the distance between two places on the map.

Assessment and Activities

Standardized Test Practice

1. A

Tested Objectives:
Interpreting bar graphs, analyzing information

Chapter Test Bonus Question

This question may be used for extra credit on the chapter test.

Which country has taken steps to preserve its rain forests by declaring them national parks? *(Costa Rica)*

Our World Today online

Have students visit the Web site at **owt.glencoe.com** to review Chapter 21 and take the Self-Check Quiz.

Current Events Journal

22. Students' itineraries should include a map, descriptions of sites and activities at five stops, and a weather forecast. Students may want to do additional research to write about the tourist attractions of various places.

Mental Mapping Activity

23. This exercise helps students visualize the countries and geographic features they have been studying and understand the relationships among various points. All attempts at freehand mapping should be accepted.

Technology Skills Activity

24. Students' databases should include the needed information: population, landmass, and capital city. In addition, the data should be organized according to population, and students should include a generalization about the data.

Unit 8 Planning Guide

SUGGESTED PACING CHART

Unit 8 (1 day)	Chapter 22 (4 days)	Chapter 23 (5 days)	Unit 8 (2 days)
Day 1 Introduction	**Day 1** Chapter 22 Intro, Section 1	**Day 1** Chapter 23 Intro, Section 1	**Day 1** Wrap-Up/Projects
	Day 2 Section 2	**Day 2** Section 2	**Day 2** Unit 8 Assessment
	Day 3 Chapter 22 Review	**Day 3** Section 3	
	Day 4 Chapter 22 Assessment	**Day 4** Chapter 23 Review	
		Day 5 Chapter 23 Assessment	

For a complete course pacing guide and Teacher Classroom Resources, see:

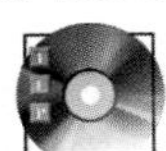

Interactive Lesson Planner

Use the following tools to easily assess student learning in a variety of ways:

- **Performance Assessment Activities and Rubrics**
- **Section Quizzes**
- **Chapter Tests and Unit Pretests and Posttests**
- **Interactive Tutor Self-Assessment CD-ROM**
- **ExamView® Pro 3.0 Testmaker CD-ROM**
- **MindJogger Videoquiz**
- **owt.glencoe.com**
- **Standardized Test Practice Workbook**

Note: The following materials may be used when teaching Unit 8.
Chapter level support materials can be found on the chapter resource pages.

TEACHING TRANSPARENCIES

Political Map Transparency 8

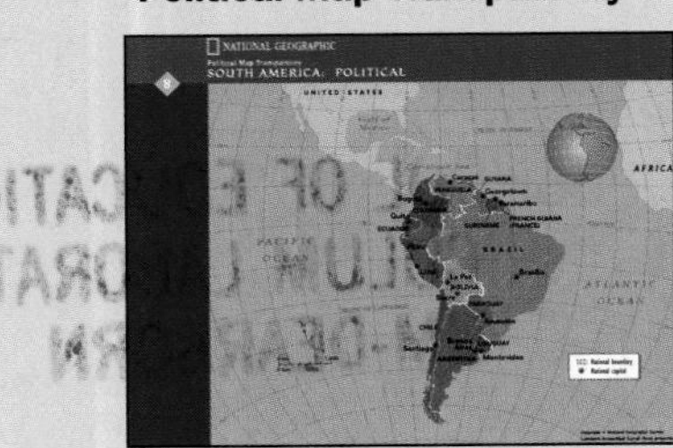

Unit 8 Map Overlay Transparencies

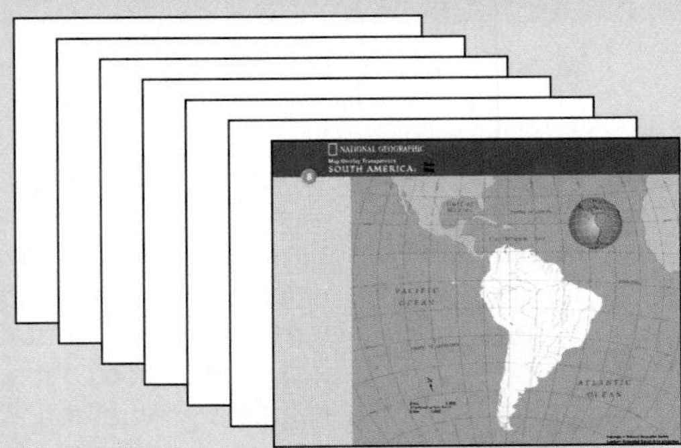

World Cultures Transparencies 13 and 14

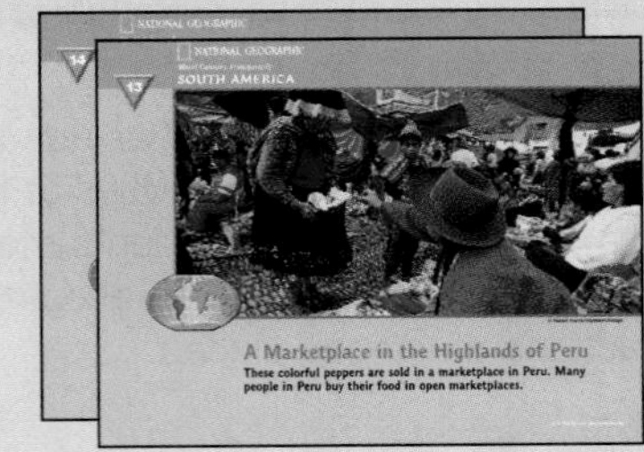

Unit 8 Resources

INTERDISCIPLINARY CONNECTIONS

World Literature Reading 8

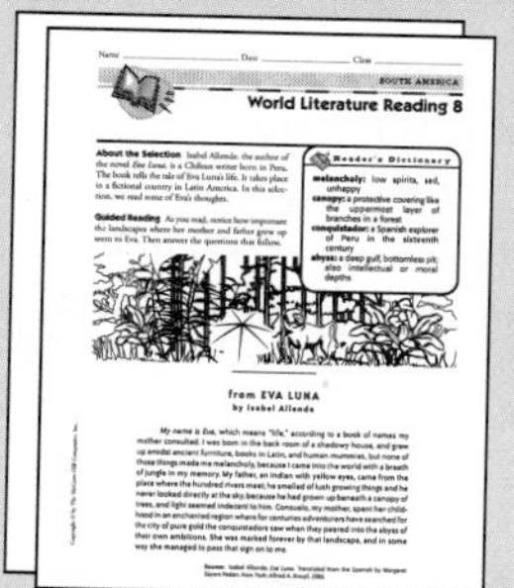

Economics and Geography Activity 8

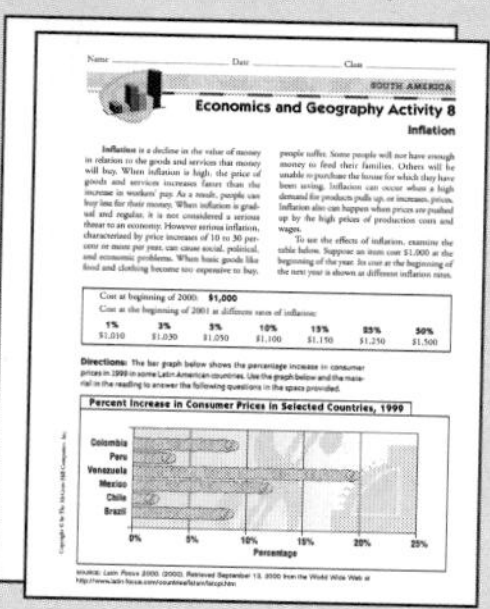

History and Geography Activity 8

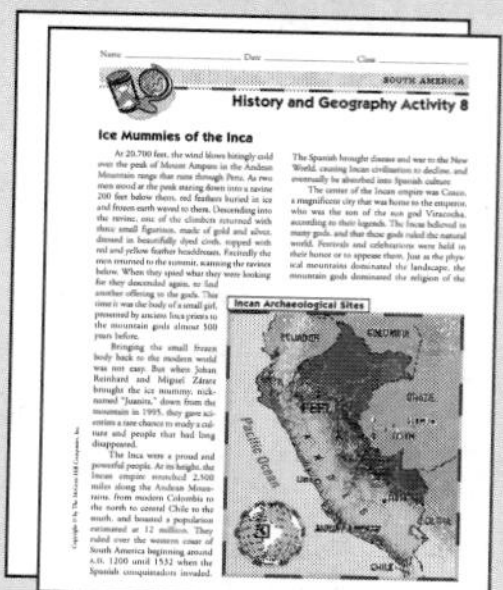

MAP AND GEOGRAPHY SKILLS

Building Geography Skills for Life

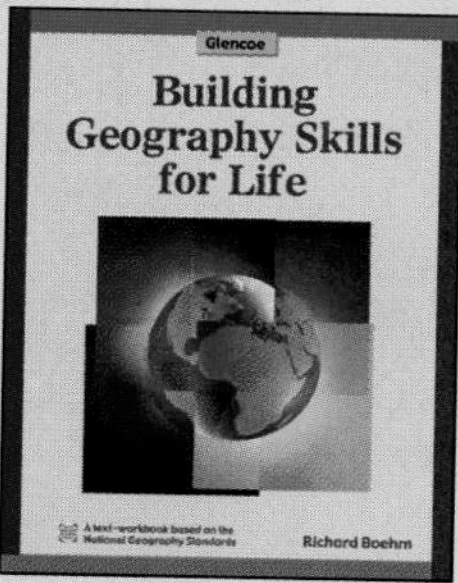

NGS Focus on Geography Literacy

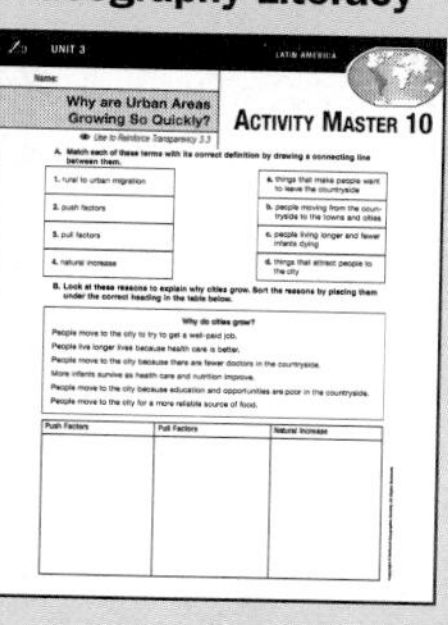

Regional Atlas Activity 8

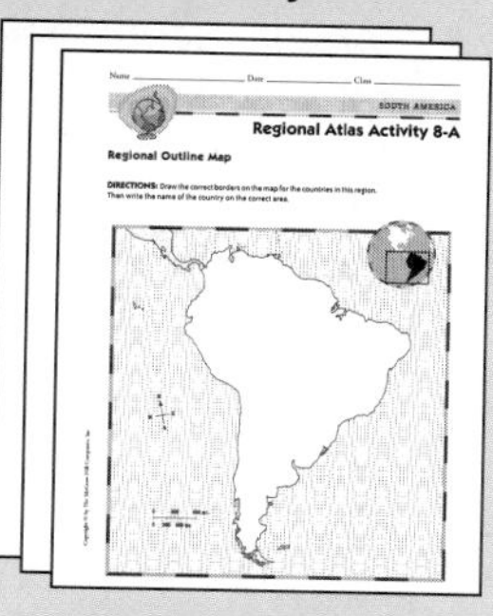

NATIONAL GEOGRAPHIC MapMachine

Find the latest coverage of geography in the news, atlas updates, cartographic activities with interactive maps, an online map store, and links at www.nationalgeographic.com/maps

APPLICATION AND HANDS-ON

Citizenship Activity 8

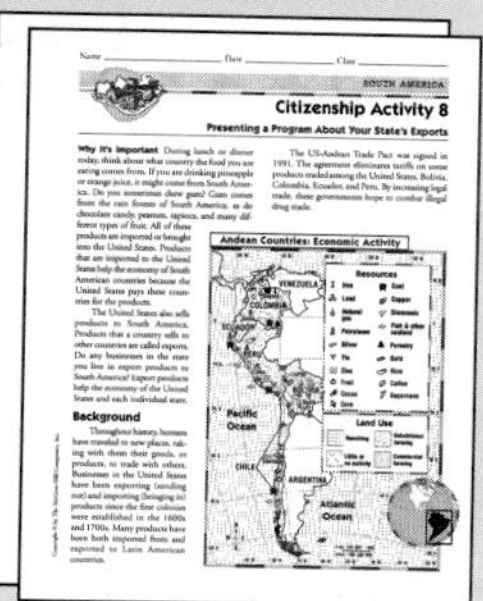

Foods Around the World 3

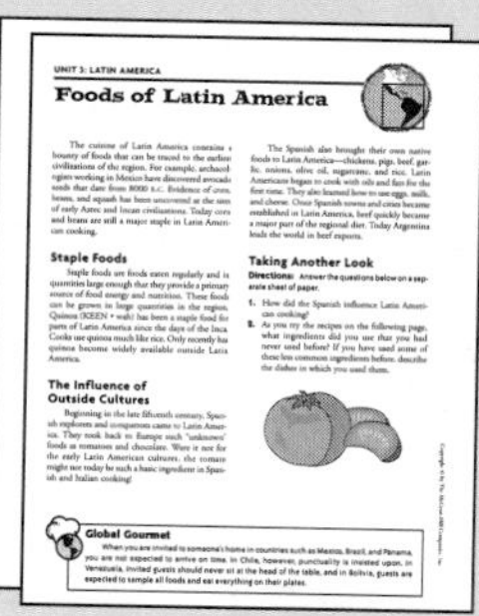

ENRICHMENT AND EXTENSION

Environmental Case Study 8

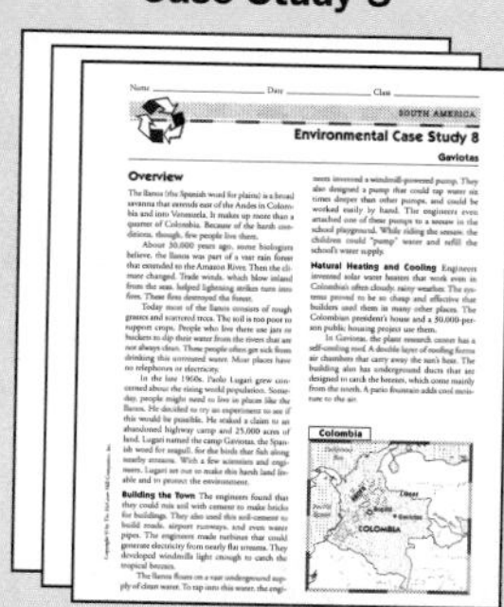

World Music: A Cultural Legacy

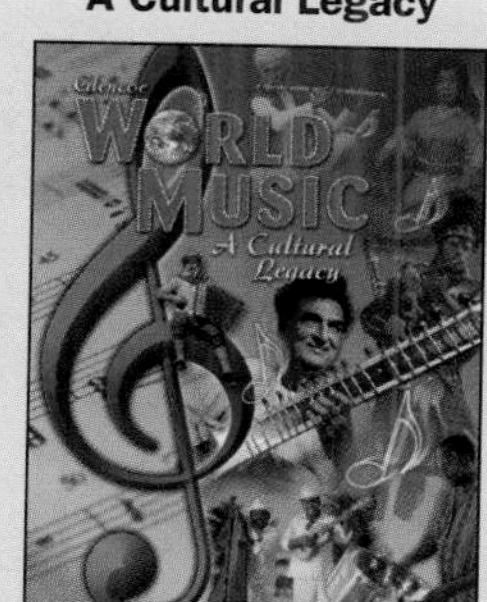

ASSESSMENT AND EVALUATION

GLENCOE'S ASSESSMENT ADVANTAGE

Unit 8 Pretests

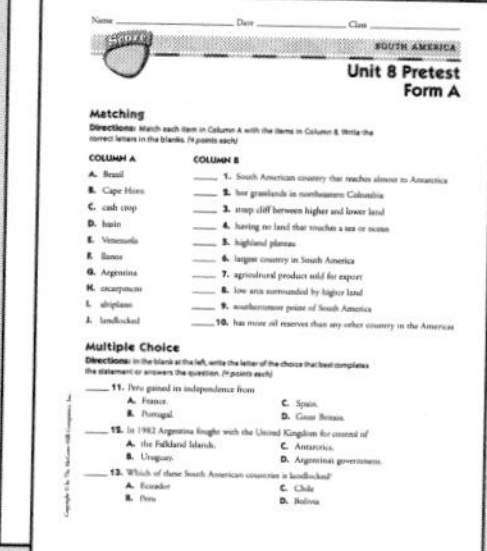

Unit 8 Posttests

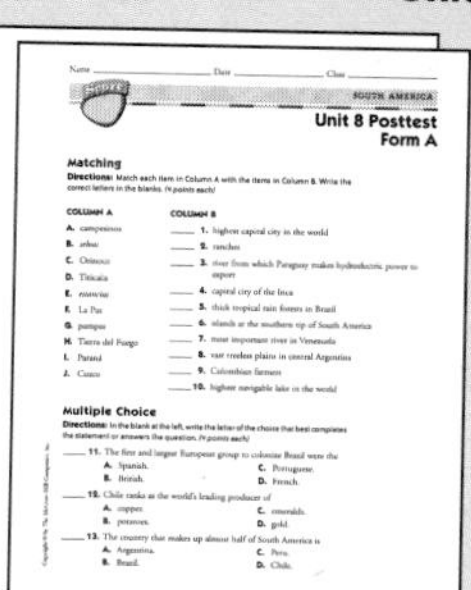

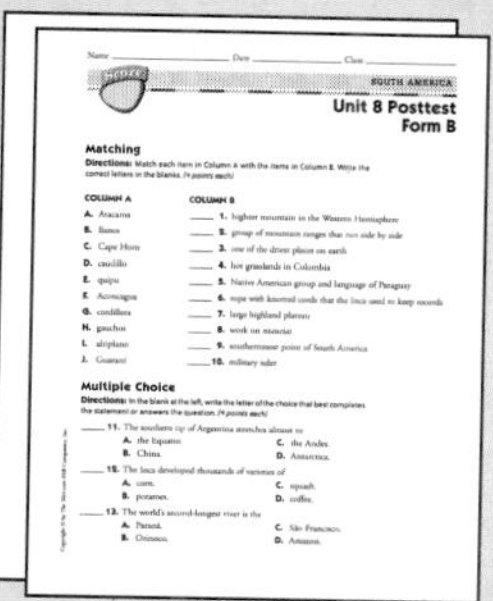

- owt.glencoe.com

  Our World Today: People, Places, and Issues
  Visit the Glencoe *Our World Today: People, Places, and Issues* Web site for overviews, activities, assessments, and updated charts and graphs.

- socialstudies.glencoe.com

  Glencoe Social Studies
  Visit the Glencoe Web site for social studies activities, updates, and links to other sites.

- www.teachingtoday.glencoe.com

  Glencoe Teaching Today
  This Web site features daily teaching tips, free PDF downloads, annotated Web resources, educational news, and more.

- www.nationalgeographic.com

  NGS ONLINE Visit the National Geographic Society Web site for the latest coverage of geography in the news, atlas updates, activities, links, interactive features, and archives.

- **Glencoe's Guide to Using the Internet**
  Provides an introduction to many of the current technologies on the Internet. Professional resources and teaching strategies included.

Our Web sites provide additional resources. All essential content is covered in the Student Edition.

Bibliography

Literature for the Student

- ***Jacques Cousteau's Amazon Journey,*** by Jacques Yves Cousteau and Mose Richards. New York: Abrams, 1984.
- ***Incas: Lords of Gold and Glory.*** Alexandria, VA: Time-Life, 1995.
- ***Prisoner Without a Name, Cell Without a Number,*** Jacobo Timerman. An Argentinean newspaper publisher struggles to tell the world about Argentina's repression under a dictator.

Readings for the Teacher

- ***The Cambridge Encyclopedia of Latin America and the Caribbean.*** New York: Cambridge University Press, 1992.
- ***Into the Amazon: The Struggle for the Rain Forest,*** by Augusta Dwyer. San Francisco, CA: Sierra Club Books, 1991.

Multimedia Links

- ***Around South America.*** International Film and Video. Available through Social Studies School Service (800) 421-4246. VHS.
- ***STV: Rain Forest.*** National Geographic Society, Washington, DC (800) 368-2728. Mac Laserdisc.
- ***Amazon Trail Third Edition: Rainforest Adventure.*** Novato, Calif.: Learning Company. Mac/Windows CD-ROM.

Refer to owt.glencoe.com for additional literature titles and study guides related to this region.

Additional Glencoe Teacher Support

- **Teaching Strategies for the Geography Classroom**
- **Reproducible Lesson Plans**
- **Outline Map Resource Book**
- **Reading in the Content Area**

The following videotape programs are available from Glencoe:

- **Evita: The Woman Behind the Myth** 0-7670-0029-3
- **Machu Picchu: City in the Sky** 0-7670-0143-5
- **Peru: Warriors and Treasure** 0-7670-1861-3

To order, call Glencoe at 1-800-334-7344. To find classroom resources to accompany many of these, check:

A&E Television: www.aetv.com

The History Channel: www.historychannel.com

Service Learning Project

Connecting Classroom With Community

Have students work in groups to review current children's books about South America in the local library. Students should research to find new books to purchase. Alternatively, students could set up a story hour in which they read several of the books to young children. Have students complete a project summary report that includes such information as: How did this project help my community? What did I learn while completing this project?

Content Background Notes

Use this additional information as lecture notes or discussion prompts throughout the study of Unit 8.

Chapter 22 Brazil and Its Neighbors (pp. 580–599)

One Step Forward . . . The effort to save Brazil's Amazon rain forest has moved in fits and starts in recent years. Brazil's government has made some moves to preserve the region:

- In 1998 the World Bank, the World Wide Fund for Nature, and the government announced a program in which the groups would provide funds to protect 61.8 million acres (25 million hectares) of rain forest. Brazil also passed a law setting harsh penalties for those who break environmental laws.
- In 1999 Brazil's government used army, navy, and air force personnel to prevent illegal logging in the rain forest. The government says that 80 percent of the logging there is illegal.
- In 2000 the government launched a new effort to improve monitoring of illegal logging by using satellites, radar, and airplanes.

However, in 2000 a special commission of Brazil's legislature recommended the easing of limits on rain forest logging. If approved, the move would allow landowners to clear up to 50 percent of their land instead of the current limit of 20 percent. This action alarmed environmentalists, especially in light of a 1999 study arguing that tree-cutting in the Amazon Basin is taking place two times faster than scientists had thought.

The Amazon South America's mighty Amazon River is one of the world's great rivers. It begins high in the Andes, less than 100 miles (161 km) from the Pacific Ocean. The river flows nearly 4,000 miles (6,437 km) and empties into the Atlantic Ocean. Its length is about equal to the distance from New York City to Rome, Italy. This immense river carries a huge amount of water. Some scientists estimate that the Amazon River alone funnels about 20 percent of all the freshwater that flows over the earth. The Amazon discharges so much freshwater at its mouth that water up to 100 miles (161 km) offshore in the Atlantic Ocean still does not taste salty.

Chapter 23 The Andean Countries (pp. 602–627)

The Revolution of Monte Verde Archaeologists have long believed that the first inhabitants of the Americas crossed the Bering land bridge to North America about 12,000 years ago. These first arrivals then spread throughout the Americas over a few thousand years. The oldest known settlement dated from about 11,500 years ago. Recent work at the site called Monte Verde, in central Chile, is turning these long-held theories upside down.

Scientists have used radiocarbon methods to date artifacts found at Monte Verde to about 12,500 years ago. If the Monte Verde dates are true, scientists are left to figure out how people crossed from Asia to the Americas. Did they use boats to move down the Pacific coast when glaciers covered the Bering land bridge? Or did they cross before glaciers formed? If so, the arrival of humans in the Americas is pushed back even further, because the last glacial age began 20,000 years ago.

A Traditional Language Quechua is the name for a family of peoples that share a common language. The Quechua tribes became the most powerful and advanced element of the Incan empire. Before the arrival of Europeans in South America during the 16th century, the Quechua contributed artistic achievements as well as scientific advances in such areas as engineering and architecture. Even after the Spanish conquest of Peru, Quechua remained the dominant language of the region and is still spoken by several million people today in Peru, Bolivia, Ecuador, Chile, and Argentina. While the Spanish used the Quechua language to teach Christianity in South America, the Quechua Indians themselves resisted European influences on their culture and retain close ties to their heritage to this day. There is a sharp division in Peru, even today, among the highlander Indians and the coastal people of mixed Spanish and Indian descent.

Introducing
Unit 8

00:00 OUT OF TIME?

If time does not permit teaching each chapter in this unit, you may use the **Reading Essentials and Study Guide** for each chapter.

Unit Overview

The two chapters that make up this unit introduce students to the geography and peoples of South America. The chapters detail the landforms, economy, history, government, and lifestyles found in these countries. Before beginning to study the unit, point out to students that—although the countries of South America are diverse—most have the following features in common:

- a strong Spanish or Portuguese influence on language and culture
- a blend of Native American and European heritages
- the world's largest zone of tropical rain forest

Peruvian Indian woman and child

Peaks of the Andes, Chile

Using the Illustration

Rio de Janeiro is instantly recognizable by the rock formation rising from its harbor. This peak is called Sugar Loaf, or Pão de Açúcar. Although Rio looks stunning from a distance, the city's beauty diminishes up close. Shantytowns cloak the city's hillsides, and during heavy rains, shacks and garbage will often wash down the slopes. Like Rio, South America has much potential for beauty and a wealth of riches, yet there is still a great deal of poverty. Have students form groups, with each choosing a particular country. Then have the groups research the people of the country, how they make a living, the average income, where the majority live, and how the people benefit or don't benefit from the country's resources. Each group should present their information to the class for discussion and a comparison of the countries. L2

NATIONAL GEOGRAPHIC

South America

South America is a continent in change. It contains 350 million people. Today, the larger countries of this region are diversifying their economies and attempting to meet the demands of rapidly growing populations. Many are becoming urban nations as people leave the countryside for the cities. Other countries are burdened by social stress and political turmoil.

NGS ONLINE
www.nationalgeographic.com/education

573

Unit Launch Activity

Why Study South America? Have students look at the photo above and the physical map on page 574. Ask them how they picture South America and its people. They will probably use the photo to say it has cities and mountains and Native Americans. **Ask:** **How do these elements fit together? Where do you think the Native Americans might traditionally live? Who lives in the cities? Are there parts of South America that look like nobody could live there?** Tell them to read the chapter with these questions in mind and see if they can find the answers. L1

NATIONAL GEOGRAPHIC

These materials are available from Glencoe.

Software

ZipZapMap! World

Transparencies

PicturePack Transparencies

CD-ROM

Picture Atlas of the World, Second Edition

Current Events Journal

Have students find an article about recent events in any South American country. They should paste the article in their journals and write the following information about it: the source and date of the article, the country that it is about, a brief summary of the article, an explanation of why this subject is important.

NGS ONLINE
www.nationalgeographic.com/education

This online resource provides lesson plans, atlas updates, cartographic activities with interactive maps, an online map store, and geography links.

Lesson Plan

Using the Regional Atlas
These features and activities may be used as an introduction to the unit or as teaching tools throughout the course of the unit.

Focus

Objectives

1. Describe the relative size and location of South America.
2. Name the major physical features of South America.
3. List the nations that make up South America.
4. Describe the population density of South America.

More About the Profile

In order to show a variety of physical features, this cross section begins at Lima, Peru, and ends at Salvador, Brazil, along 10°S latitude.

NATIONAL GEOGRAPHIC

Regional Atlas

South America

Physical

- ⦿ National capital
- Territorial capital
- ▲ Mountain peak

0 mi. 1,000
0 km 1,000
Lambert Azimuthal Equal-Area projection

Regional Atlas Activity

Class Challenge Organize students into small groups to write at least five questions about the physical map of South America. Tell students to include direction, key, scale, or physical map questions, such as: **In what direction would you travel from Tierra del Fuego to Venezuela** *(north)*; or **In the elevation profile, how do the Brazilian Highlands compare in elevation to the Andes?** *(The Andes, at about 15,000 feet, are about seven-and-one-half times higher than the Brazilian Highlands, at 2,000 feet.)* Allow time for groups to write questions and challenge one another. You may also want to repeat this activity at the end of the unit. **L1**

EE1 The World in Spatial Terms: Standard 1

UNIT 8

Political

90°W 80°W 70°W 60°W 50°W 40°W 30°W
10°N 0° 10°S 20°S 30°S 40°S 50°S
EQUATOR
TROPIC OF CAPRICORN
VENEZUELA
Caracas
COLOMBIA
Medellín
Bogotá
Cali
ECUADOR
Quito
Galápagos Is. Ecua.
GUYANA
Georgetown
SURINAME
Paramaribo
FRENCH GUIANA Fr.
Cayenne
PERU
Lima
BRAZIL
Manaus
Recife
Salvador
Brasília
Belo Horizonte
Rio de Janeiro
São Paulo
Curitiba
Porto Alegre
BOLIVIA
La Paz
Sucre
Lake Titicaca
PARAGUAY
Asunción
CHILE
Valparaíso
Santiago
ARGENTINA
Rosario
Buenos Aires
URUGUAY
Montevideo
Río de la Plata
Negro R.
Amazon R.
Madeira R.
Paraná R.
Paraguay R.
PACIFIC OCEAN
ATLANTIC OCEAN
Falkland Is. U.K.
South Georgia I. U.K.
N S E W
0 mi. 1,000
0 km 1,000
Lambert Azimuthal Equal-Area projection
⊛ National capital
◎ Territorial capital
• Major city

MAP STUDY

1. What huge lowland area lies in northern Brazil?
2. What is the capital of Chile?

Unit 8

2 TEACH

Making Comparisons Ask students to compare the population map on page 576 to the other maps in the Unit 8 Regional Atlas. **Ask:** **What are the physical locations like of the cities that are growing the fastest?** *(Possible answers: São Paulo, Lima, and other cities are located on the coast; Bogotá is by a river, Medellín is close to two oceans and Central America.)* **Why doesn't Bolivia have any large urban growth?** *(Its main cities are in the Andes.)* **L1**

Por puesto is a popular system of transportation in Venezuela. Taxi-like automobiles travel a regular route throughout a city, picking up and dropping off passengers at any point. The fare is more than a bus but less than a taxi.

MAP STUDY

Answers

1. Amazon Basin
2. Santiago

Skills Practice

What is the largest South American country? *(Brazil)*
What are the only two countries in South America that do not share a border with Brazil? *(Ecuador and Chile)*

Regional Atlas Activity

Categorizing Regions Tell students that South America can be divided into three areas: the Atlantic countries, the Andean countries, and the Caribbean countries. Each of these regions shares certain characteristics based on terrain, climate, and resources. Have students divide a sheet of paper into three columns labeled "Atlantic Countries," "Andean Countries," and "Caribbean Countries." Then have them use the maps to group the nations of South America under the correct heading. *(Atlantic—Brazil, Uruguay, Paraguay, Argentina; Andean—Chile, Bolivia, Peru, Ecuador, Colombia; Caribbean—Venezuela, Guyana, Suriname, French Guiana)* **L1**

EE2 Places and Regions: Standard 5

NATIONAL GEOGRAPHIC

REGIONAL ATLAS

TRAVEL GUIDE

Among the main food crops in Brazil are white rice, black beans, and manioc. These ingredients are combined with steak, chicken, or fish. Traditional Brazilian dishes include *moqueca,* a seafood stew flavored with dendê oil and coconut milk; *caruru,* which is okra and other vegetables mixed with shrimp, onions, and peppers; and *feijoada,* a bean and meat stew.

Interdisciplinary Connections

Math Inform students that the distance overland from western Peru to eastern Brazil is about 47 degrees of longitude. Tell students that each degree of longitude corresponds to about 69 miles (111 km). Have them calculate the width of South America at this point. *(about 3,243 miles [47 × 69] or about 5,217 km [47 × 111])* **L1**

MAP STUDY

Answers

1. by 14,706,000
2. 8,400,000

Skills Practice

Which city has grown faster between 1950 and 2001—Medellín or Belo Horizonte? *(Belo Horizonte)*

South America

Urban Population Growth

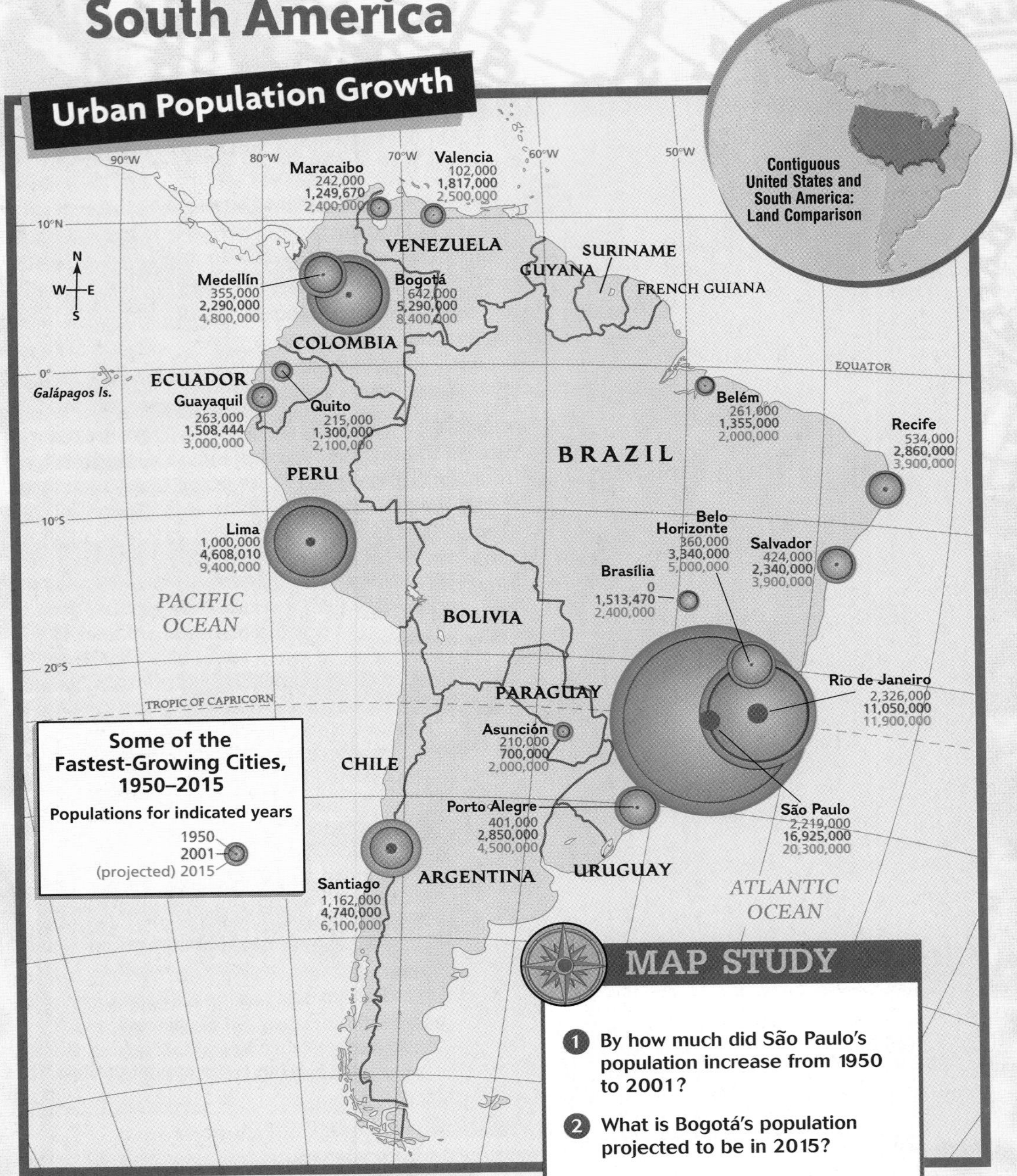

Maracaibo 242,000 1,249,670 2,400,000

Valencia 102,000 1,817,000 2,500,000

Medellín 355,000 2,290,000 4,800,000

Bogotá 642,000 5,290,000 8,400,000

Guayaquil 263,000 1,508,444 3,000,000

Quito 215,000 1,300,000 2,100,000

Lima 1,000,000 4,608,010 9,400,000

Belém 261,000 1,355,000 2,000,000

Recife 534,000 2,860,000 3,900,000

Belo Horizonte 360,000 3,340,000 5,000,000

Salvador 424,000 2,340,000 3,900,000

Brasília 0 1,513,470 2,400,000

Rio de Janeiro 2,326,000 11,050,000 11,900,000

Asunción 210,000 700,000 2,000,000

São Paulo 2,219,000 16,925,000 20,300,000

Porto Alegre 401,000 2,850,000 4,500,000

Santiago 1,162,000 4,740,000 6,100,000

VENEZUELA, GUYANA, SURINAME, FRENCH GUIANA, COLOMBIA, ECUADOR, Galápagos Is., PERU, BRAZIL, BOLIVIA, PARAGUAY, CHILE, ARGENTINA, URUGUAY, PACIFIC OCEAN, ATLANTIC OCEAN, EQUATOR, TROPIC OF CAPRICORN

90°W, 80°W, 70°W, 60°W, 50°W, 10°N, 0°, 10°S, 20°S

Some of the Fastest-Growing Cities, 1950–2015

Populations for indicated years

1950
2001
(projected) 2015

Contiguous United States and South America: Land Comparison

MAP STUDY

1. By how much did São Paulo's population increase from 1950 to 2001?
2. What is Bogotá's population projected to be in 2015?

576 UNIT 8

Regional Atlas Activity

Unit Project Point out that some of South America's cities are among the fastest-growing cities in the world. **Ask: Why have many South Americans been moving to cities in recent years?** Have students investigate the answer to this question by identifying and researching the largest cities in South America. They should look at the cities' growth over time and determine what push-and-pull factors have motivated people to move into these cities. Students should research this question throughout their study of Unit 8. They can present their answers in the form of annotated graphs or oral presentations. **L3**

EE4 Human Systems: Standard 9

Unit 8

Regional Atlas

Fast Facts

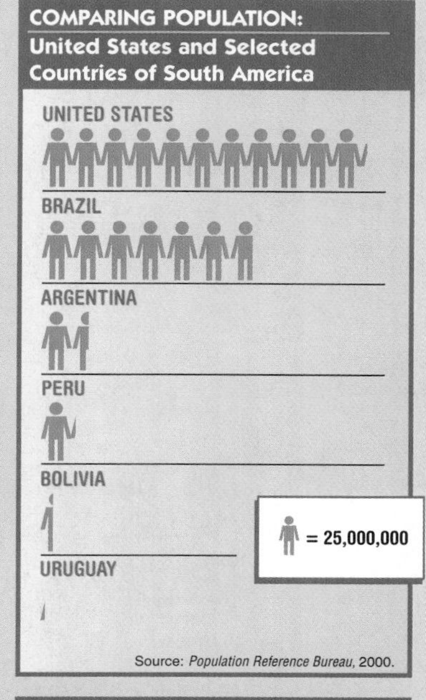

ETHNIC GROUPS: Selected Countries of South America

ARGENTINA	97%, 3%
BOLIVIA	55%, 30%, 15%
BRAZIL	55%, 38%, 6%, 1%
PERU	45%, 37%, 15%, 3%
URUGUAY	88%, 8%, 4%

Black · Indian · African/European · White · Mestizo · Other

Source: *Population Reference Bureau*, 2000.

Data Bits

Country	Automobiles per 1,000 people	Telephones per 1,000 people
Chile	71	180
Colombia	19	148
Ecuador	40	75
Suriname	59	130
Venezuela	68	116

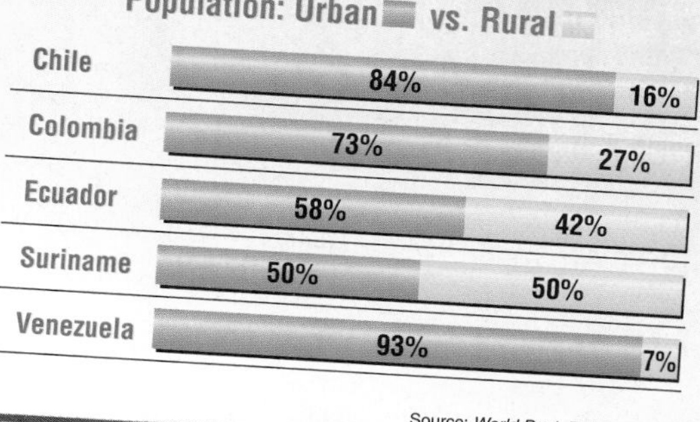

Source: *World Desk Reference*, 2000.

GRAPHIC STUDY

1. Which country has the fewest automobiles per 1,000 people, and which has the fewest telephones?
2. What country has a majority of Indians?

As an introduction to this region, you may want to engage students by studying an important contemporary issue in this region of the world. The **TIME REPORTS: FOCUS ON WORLD ISSUES** for this region is found on pages 609–615. The feature examines the causes and consequences of South America's drug wars.

Reading Graphics Have students use the graphic on this page to answer this question: **How does the population of Brazil compare to that of the United States?** *(Brazil has just under two-thirds of the people the United States has—about 175 million compared to about 280 million.)* **L1**

GRAPHIC STUDY

Answers

1. Colombia and Ecuador
2. Bolivia

Skills Practice

Which country has the lowest percentage of people living in rural areas? *(Venezuela)*

FUN FACTS

- **Brazil** On New Year's Eve, some Brazilians traditionally honor *lemanja,* the sea goddess. They dress in blue and white and place flowers and candles on the beach.
- **Peru** Iquitos, Peru, on the Amazon River is farther inland than any large port in the world.
- **Venezuela** When the Spanish explorer Alonso de Ojedo was sailing along Venezuela's coast in 1499, he saw Native American houses built on stilts over the water. He named the area "Little Venice," or Venezuela, because it reminded him of that famous Italian city.

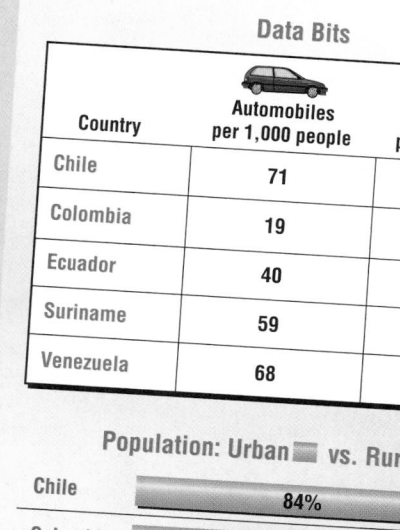

Regional Atlas

Using Maps and Charts Assign a South American country to each student. Have students make up riddles about their country based on its location—in relation to bodies of water and other countries—or its characteristics as described in the Country Profile. Have students take turns reading their riddles and calling on classmates to identify their country. **L1**

The Humanities Connection

World Music: A Cultural Legacy

World Art and Architecture Transparencies

3 Assess

Organize students into groups. Have groups use the maps and graphs from the Unit 8 Regional Atlas to quiz one another on the geography of South America.

Did You Know?

The Amazon River was named by Spanish explorer Francisco de Orellana for the Amazons, a band of female warriors in Greek mythology. Orellana supposedly chose the name after he was attacked by a group of female warriors.

Country Profiles

ARGENTINA
POPULATION: 37,500,000; 35 per sq. mi.; 14 per sq. km
LANGUAGE: Spanish
MAJOR EXPORT: Meat
MAJOR IMPORT: Machinery
CAPITAL: Buenos Aires
LANDMASS: 1,068,302 sq. mi.; 2,766,889 sq. km

BOLIVIA
POPULATION: 8,500,000; 20 per sq. mi.; 8 per sq. km
LANGUAGES: Spanish, Quechua, Aymara
MAJOR EXPORT: Metals
MAJOR IMPORT: Machinery
CAPITALS: La Paz, Sucre
LANDMASS: 424,164 sq. mi.; 1,098,581 sq. km

BRAZIL
POPULATION: 171,800,000; 52 per sq. mi.; 20 per sq. km
LANGUAGE: Portuguese
MAJOR EXPORT: Iron Ore
MAJOR IMPORT: Crude Oil
CAPITAL: Brasília
LANDMASS: 3,286,488 sq. mi.; 8,511,965 sq. km

CHILE
POPULATION: 15,400,000; 52 per sq. mi.; 20 per sq. km
LANGUAGE: Spanish
MAJOR EXPORT: Copper
MAJOR IMPORT: Machinery
CAPITAL: Santiago
LANDMASS: 292,135 sq. mi.; 756,626 sq. km

COLOMBIA
POPULATION: 43,100,000; 98 per sq. mi.; 38 per sq. km
LANGUAGE: Spanish
MAJOR EXPORT: Petroleum
MAJOR IMPORT: Machinery
CAPITAL: Bogotá
LANDMASS: 439,737 sq. mi.; 1,138,914 sq. km

ECUADOR
POPULATION: 12,900,000; 118 per sq. mi.; 45 per sq. km
LANGUAGES: Spanish, Quechua
MAJOR EXPORT: Petroleum
MAJOR IMPORT: Transport Equipment
CAPITAL: Quito
LANDMASS: 109,484 sq. mi.; 283,561 sq. km

FRENCH GUIANA*
POPULATION: 200,000; 6 per sq. mi.; 2 per sq. km
LANGUAGE: French
MAJOR EXPORT: Shrimp
MAJOR IMPORT: Foods
CAPITAL: Cayenne
LANDMASS: 34,749 sq. mi.; 89,999 sq. km

* Territory of France

GUYANA
POPULATION: 705,000; 8 per sq. mi.; 3 per sq. km
LANGUAGE: English
MAJOR EXPORT: Sugar
MAJOR IMPORT: Manufactured Goods
CAPITAL: Georgetown
LANDMASS: 83,000 sq. mi.; 214,969 sq. km

PARAGUAY
POPULATION: 5,700,000; 36 per sq. mi.; 14 per sq. km
LANGUAGES: Spanish, Guaraní
MAJOR EXPORT: Cotton
MAJOR IMPORT: Machinery
CAPITAL: Asunción
LANDMASS: 157,048 sq. mi.; 406,752 sq. km

PERU
POPULATION: 26,100,000; 53 per sq. mi.; 20 per sq. km
LANGUAGES: Spanish, Quechua, Aymara
MAJOR EXPORT: Copper
MAJOR IMPORT: Machinery
CAPITAL: Lima
LANDMASS: 496,225 sq. mi.; 1,285,217 sq. km

Countries and flags not drawn to scale

578 UNIT 8

Fun Facts

- **Chile** The *abrazo* is the most common greeting among relatives and friends in Chile. It consists of a handshake and a hug, sometimes followed by a kiss to the right cheek for women or family members.
- **Colombia** This country is the world's leading producer of emeralds. The value of the rich green gemstones depends on their color and lack of flaws. Perfect emeralds are more valuable than diamonds.
- **Peru** The Central Railway of Peru climbs from sea level to 15,800 feet (4,816 m). On its journey from Lima to Huancayo, the train crosses 59 bridges and goes through 66 tunnels.

For more information on countries in this region, refer to the Nations of the World Data Bank on pages 690–699.

BUILDING CITIZENSHIP

Public and Private Needs More than one-third of the area of Brazil is covered by a rain forest. This fragile ecosystem is home to millions of plant, animal, and insect species. Some of the plants are important sources of medicines. According to scientists, more than 50 percent of the world's species live in the rain forest.

The rain forest is also a major source of timber, minerals, fruits, and vegetables. Building roads and clearing land to reach these resources has led to major destruction of the rain forest habitat. The government of Brazil has tried to set aside large portions of the rain forest as preserves while allowing development of its natural resources, as income for its citizens.

Because of its affect on climate, the rain forest is important not just to Brazil but to the whole world. Who should have more say about how much of the rain forest is preserved—Brazil or the United Nations?

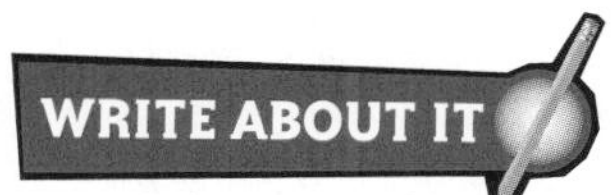

Imagine that a new golf course is being built in your city and the area where it is being built includes natural wetlands where birds and animals live. Write a letter to the city council outlining what steps you think the golf course developers should take to protect the wetlands.

Brazilian rain forest ▲

Country Profiles Activity

Classifying Exports Have students create a chart called "Chief Exports" with four columns headed "Food Product," "Mineral," "Petroleum," and "Manufactured Good." Have them look in the Country Profiles to find the chief export of each country in South America. Then have them write the name of each country in the appropriate column based on which category its chief export belongs. When they have completed their charts, have students analyze their results and make generalizations about the economies of South America. **L1**

EE2 Places and Regions: Standard 5

BUILDING CITIZENSHIP

Answer Students will have a hard time pitting the ownership rights of Brazil against what is for the greater common good. Some interesting opinions and debates should arise from discussion of this question.

Write About It! Students' papers should recognize the potential conflict between the property rights of the golf course developers and the need to protect the environmental resources and endangered species. They should also realize that compromise is possible by incorporating the wetlands into the design of the golf course or by donating other land to compensate for damage to the wetlands.

Cultural Kaleidoscope

Tierra del Fuego Have students find the Straits of Magellan and Tierra del Fuego on the physical map on page 574. Tell students that as he sailed past the island, Magellan named it *Tierra del Fuego,* or "Land of Fire," because he noticed large fires on the land.

Have students draw and label the countries of South America.

Chapter 22 Resources

Note: The following materials may be used when teaching Chapter 22. Section level support materials are shown at point of use in the margins of the Teacher Wraparound Edition.

Timesaving Tools

TeacherWorks™ All-In-One Planner and Resource Center

- **Interactive Teacher Edition** See the **Interactive Teacher Edition** CD-ROM to electronically integrate your Teacher Wraparound Edition and blackline masters.
- **Interactive Lesson Planner** Organize your week, month, semester, or year with all the lesson helps you need. The **Interactive Lesson Planner** CD-ROM contains all Chapter 22 resources.

Use Glencoe's **Presentation Plus!** multimedia teacher tool to easily present dynamic lessons that visually excite your students. Using Microsoft PowerPoint® you can customize the presentations to create your own personalized lessons.

TEACHING TRANSPARENCIES

Graphic Organizer Transparency and Student Activity 22

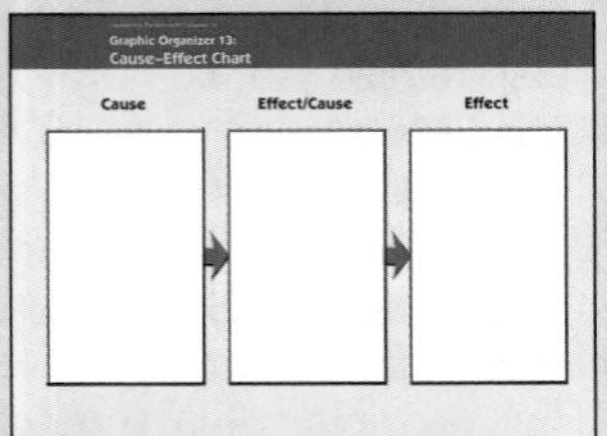
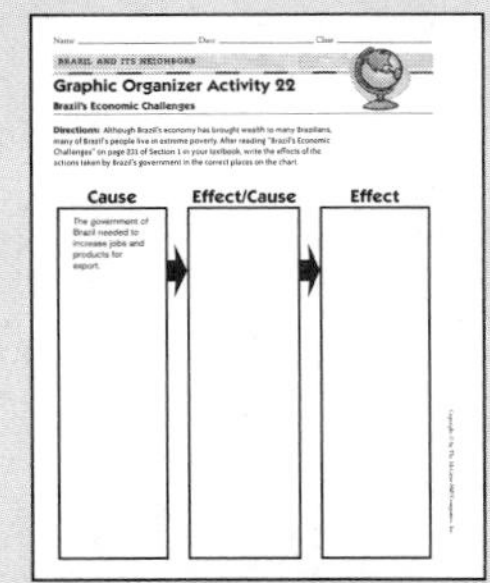

FOLDABLES™ Study Organizer

Foldables are three-dimensional, interactive graphic organizers that help students practice basic writing skills, review key vocabulary terms, and identify main ideas. Every chapter contains a Foldable activity, with additional chapter activities found in the ***Reading and Study Skills Foldables*** booklet.

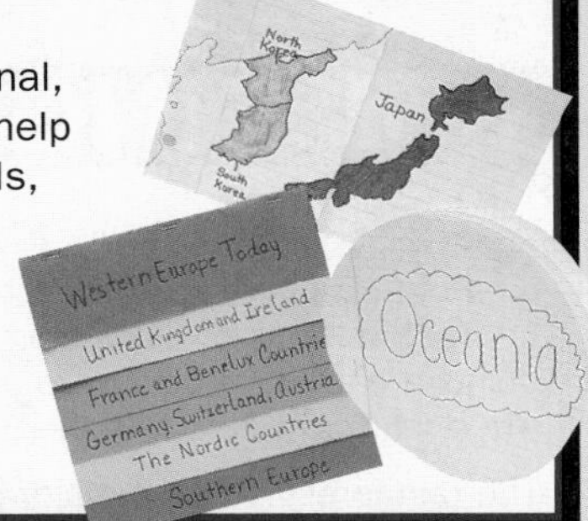

ENRICHMENT AND EXTENSION

Enrichment Activity 22

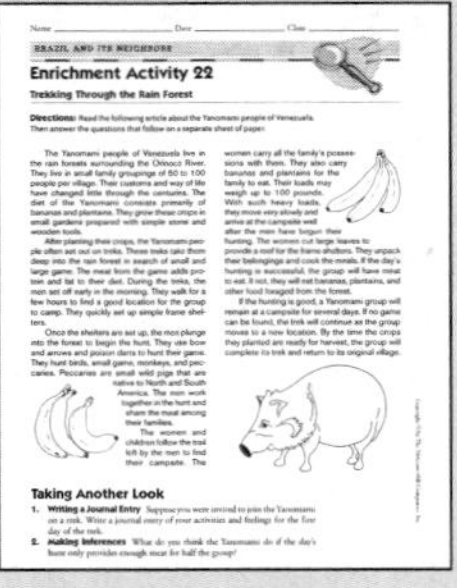

Cooperative Learning Activity 22

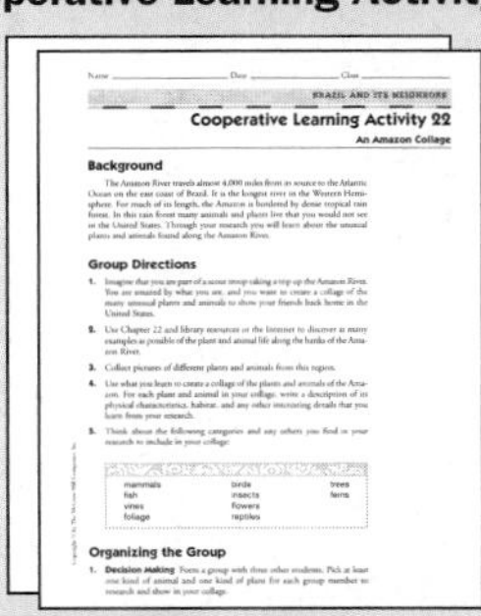

MAP AND GEOGRAPHY SKILLS

Chapter Map Activity 22

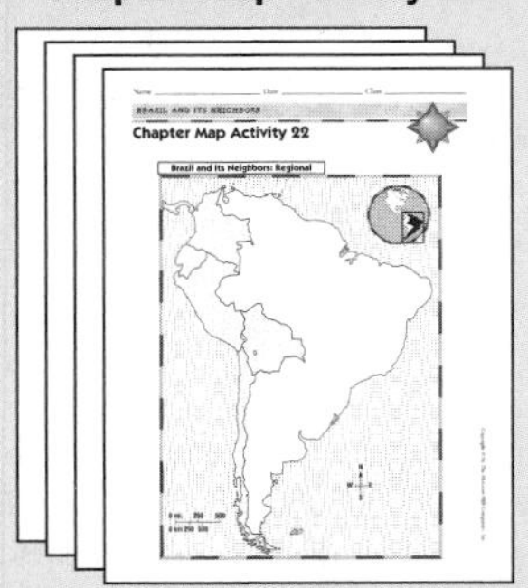

GeoLab Activity 22

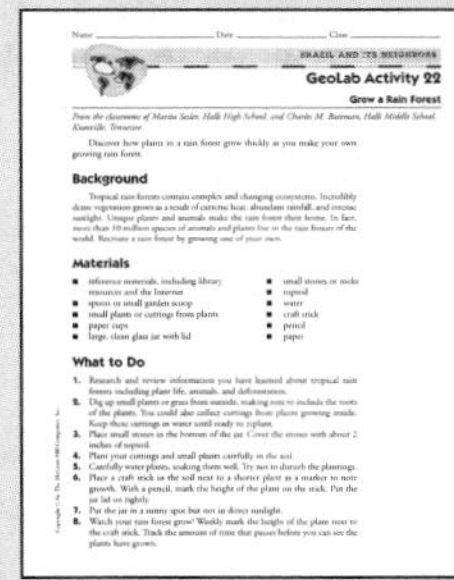

STANDARDIZED ASSESSMENT SKILLS

Glencoe's Assessment Advantage

Critical Thinking Skills Activity 22

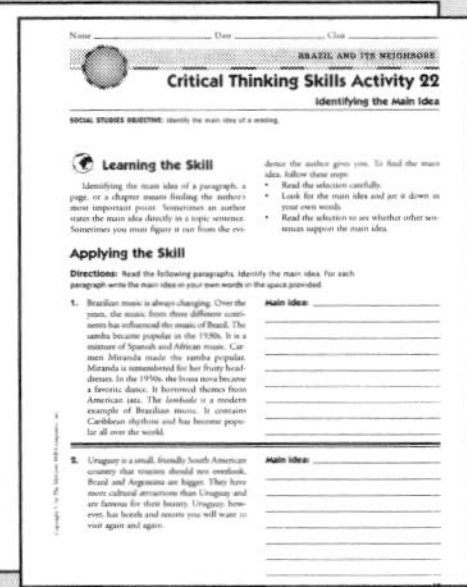

Map and Graph Skills Activity 22

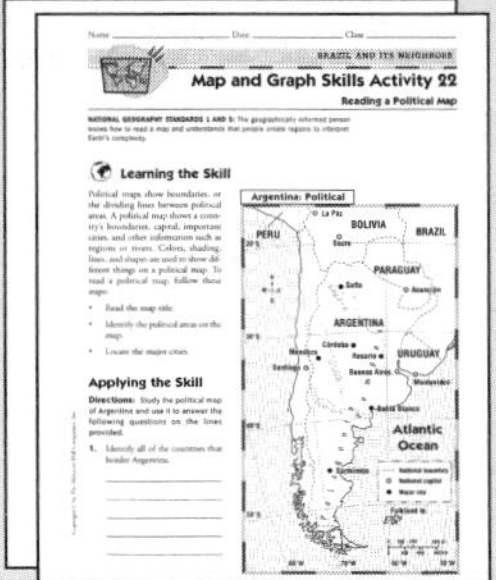

Reading and Writing Skills Activity 22

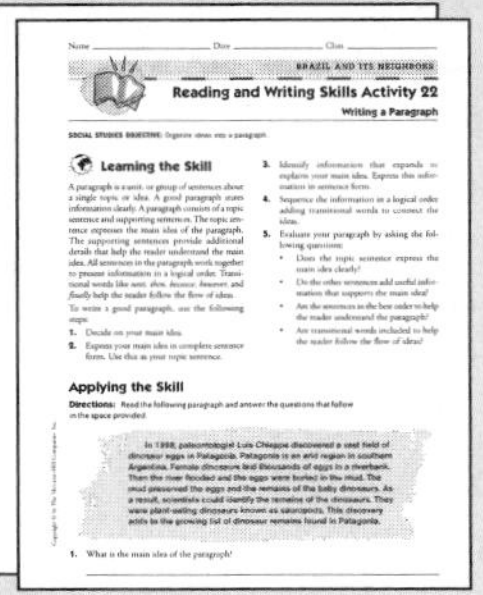

Standardized Test Practice Workbook Activity 22

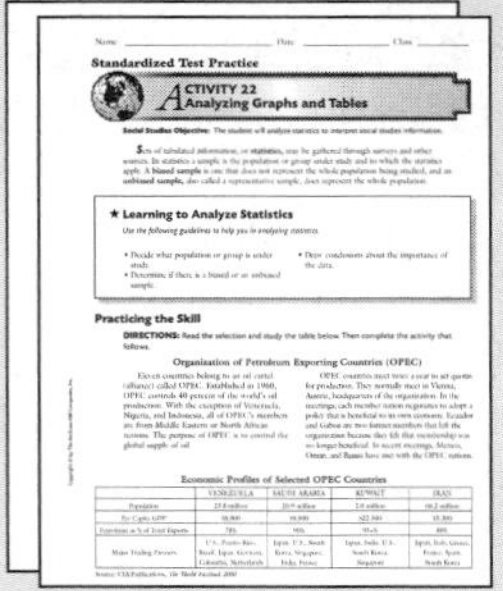

REVIEW AND REINFORCEMENT

Chapter Skills Activity 22

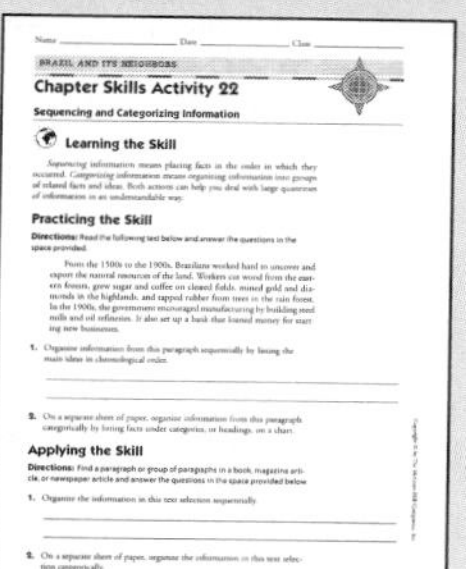

Take-Home Review Activity 22

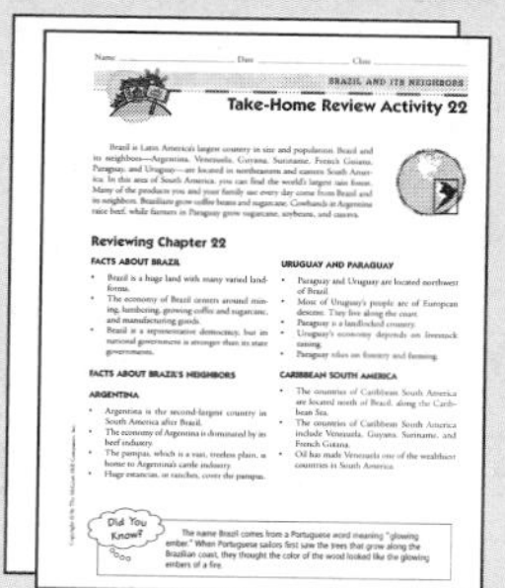

Reteaching Activity 22

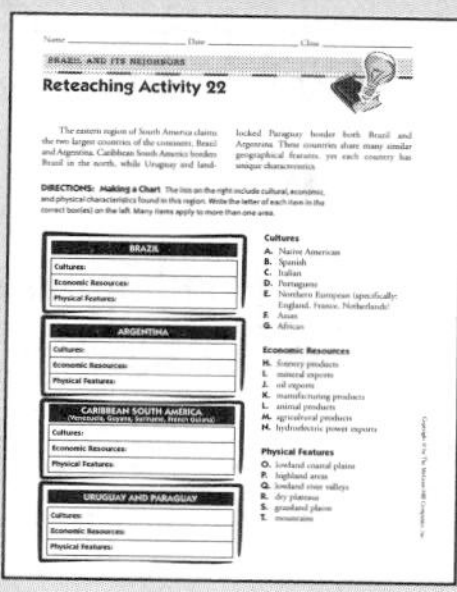

Vocabulary Activity 22

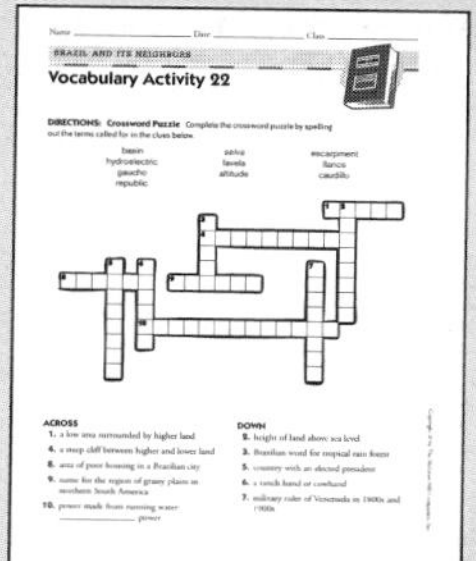

Workbook Activity 22

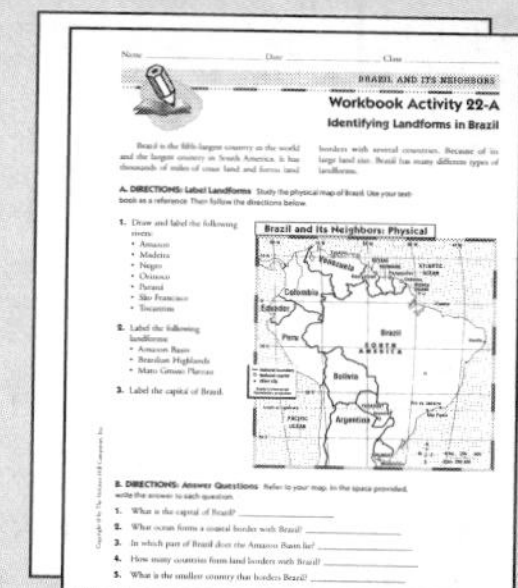

ASSESSMENT

GLENCOE'S ASSESSMENT ADVANTAGE

Chapter 22 Test, Form A

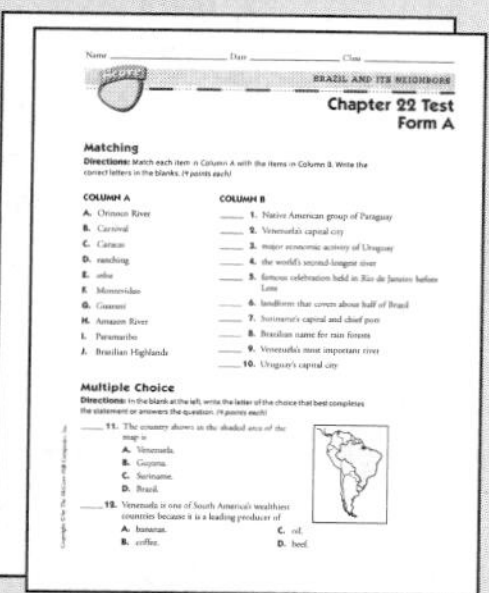

Chapter 22 Test, Form B

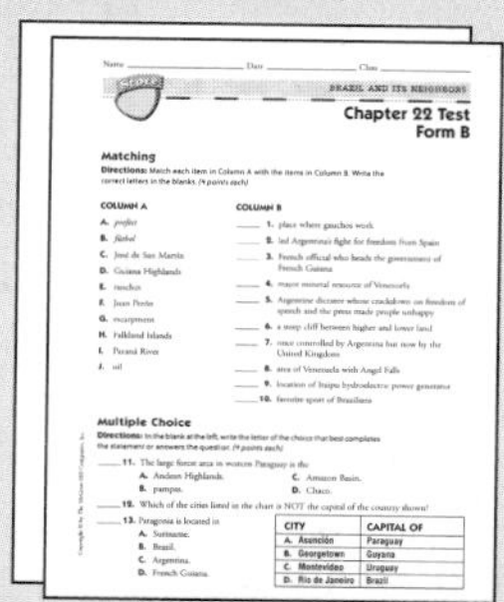

Performance Assessment Activity 22

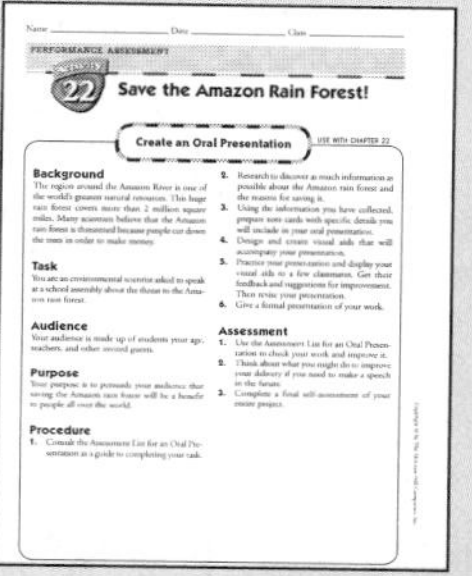

ExamView® Pro 3.0 Testmaker CD-ROM

MULTIMEDIA

- National Geographic's The World and Its People
- MindJogger Videoquiz
- Vocabulary PuzzleMaker Software
- Interactive Tutor Self-Assessment CD-ROM
- ExamView® Pro 3.0 Testmaker CD-ROM
- Interactive Lesson Planner CD-ROM
- Interactive Teacher Edition CD-ROM
- Skillbuilder Interactive Workbook CD-ROM, Level 1
- Presentation Plus! CD-ROM
- Audio Program

SPANISH RESOURCES

The following Spanish language materials are available in the Spanish Resources binder:

- Spanish Chapter Summaries
- Spanish Vocabulary Activities
- Spanish Guided Reading Activities
- Spanish Quizzes and Tests
- Spanish Take-Home Review Activities
- Spanish Reteaching Activities

Meeting National Standards

Geography for Life

All of the 18 standards are demonstrated in Unit 8. The following ones are highlighted in Chapter 22:

Section 1
- **EE2 Places and Regions: Standards 4, 6**
- **EE3 Physical Systems: Standards 7, 8**
- **EE4 Human Systems: Standard 13**

Section 2
- **EE1 The World in Spatial Terms: Standard 1**
- **EE2 Places and Regions: Standards 4, 5, 6**
- **EE4 Human Systems: Standards 9, 10**
- **EE5 Environment and Society: Standard 15**

For a complete listing of National Geography Standards and entire text correlation, see pages T22–T29.

Chapter 22 Planning Guide

SECTION RESOURCES

Daily Objectives	Reproducible Resources	Multimedia Resources
Section 1 **Brazil** **Suggested Pacing = 1 day** **1.** Describe Brazil's landforms and climates. **2.** Identify the natural resources Brazil's economy depends on. **3.** Discuss the people and culture of Brazil.	Reproducible Lesson Plan 22-1 Daily Lecture and Discussion Notes 22-1 Guided Reading Activity 22-1 Reading Essentials and Study Guide 22-1 Section Quiz 22-1*	Daily Focus Skills Transparency 22-1 GeoQuiz Transparency 22-1 Vocabulary PuzzleMaker Software Interactive Tutor Self-Assessment CD-ROM ExamView® Pro 3.0 Testmaker CD-ROM Presentation Plus! CD-ROM
Section 2 **Brazil's Neighbors** **Suggested Pacing = 1 day** **1.** Compare the landscapes and climates of Venezuela and Argentina. **2.** Describe the economies of Brazil's northern and southern neighbors. **3.** Discuss the histories of the Guianas and Argentina.	Reproducible Lesson Plan 22-2 Daily Lecture and Discussion Notes 22-2 Guided Reading Activity 22-2 Reading Essentials and Study Guide 22-2 Section Quiz 22-2*	Daily Focus Skills Transparency 22-2 GeoQuiz Transparency 22-1 Vocabulary PuzzleMaker Software Interactive Tutor Self-Assessment CD-ROM ExamView® Pro 3.0 Testmaker CD-ROM Presentation Plus! CD-ROM

00:00 **Out of Time?** Assign the **Reading Essentials and Study Guide** for this chapter.

*Also available in Spanish

KEY TO ABILITY LEVELS

Teaching strategies have been coded for varying learning styles and abilities.

L1 **BASIC** activities for all students
L2 **AVERAGE** activities for average to above-average students
L3 **CHALLENGING** activities for above-average students
ELL **ENGLISH LANGUAGE LEARNER** activities

Blackline Master
Software
CD-ROM
Audiocassette
Transparency
Videocassette
Block Scheduling
DVD

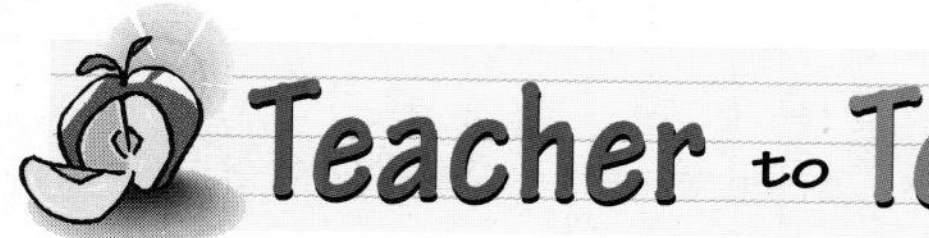

Travel Brochure

Lee Ann Burrow
Bob Courtway Middle School
Conway, Arkansas

Julie Hill
Bob Courtway Middle School
Conway, Arkansas

Have students create their own "South American Travel Brochure." Students can use the textbook, the Internet, travel agency brochures, or other sources to find information. Students' brochures should include information on climate, places to visit, interesting facts and information, currency, history, and landforms. Foods and recipes should also be added. Ask students to put their information on colored paper folded like a brochure, and to use pictures, drawings, and attractive fonts.

OUR WORLD TODAY Online

Use our Web site for additional resources. All essential content is covered in the Student Edition.

You and your students can visit owt.glencoe.com, the Web site companion to *Our World Today*. This innovative integration of electronic and print media offers your students a wealth of opportunities. The student text directs students to the Web site for the following options:

- Chapter Overviews
- Student Web Activities
- Self-Check Quizzes
- Textbook Updates

Answers are provided for you in the Web Activity Lesson Plan. Additional Web resources and Interactive Tutor puzzles are also available.

TEACHER'S CORNER

Index to National Geographic Magazine:

The following articles may be used for research relating to this chapter:

- "Feast of the Tarpon," by David Doubilet, January 1996.
- "Leafcutter Ants," by Mark W. Moffett, July 1995.
- "Poison-Dart Frogs," by Mark W. Moffett, May 1995.
- "The Amazon," by Jere Van Dyk, February 1995.
- "Remote World of the Harpy Eagle," by Neil Retting, February 1995.

National Geographic Society Products Available From Glencoe:

To order the following products for use with this chapter, contact your local Glencoe sales representative or call Glencoe at 1-800-334-7344:

- *PictureShow: Ancient Civilizations: Middle and South America* (CD-ROM)
- *PicturePack: South America* (Transparencies)
- *MapPack: Continents: South America* (Transparencies)
- *STV: Rain Forest* (Videodisc)
- *Eye on the Environment* (Posters)

Additional National Geographic Society Products:

To order the following products for use with this chapter, call National Geographic Society at 1-800-368-2728:

- *Complete National Geographic: 111 years of National Geographic Magazine* (CD-ROM)
- *MapPack: South America* (Transparencies)
- *South America* (Video)
- *Spain in the Americas* (Video)
- *Population* (Map)
- *Cultures* (Map)
- *South America Political* (Map)
- *National Geographic Desk Reference* (Book)
- *National Geographic Atlas of the World, Seventh Edition* (Book)
- *Discovering the Inca Ice Maiden* (Book)
- *Voices: Poetry and Art From Around the World* (Book)

NGS ONLINE

Access National Geographic's Web site for current events, activities, links, interactive features, and archives.
www.nationalgeographic.com

Introduce students to chapter content and key terms by having them access Chapter Overview 22 at owt.glencoe.com

Chapter Objectives

1. Describe the major physical, economic, and cultural features of Brazil.
2. Compare and contrast the physical, economic, and cultural characteristics of Brazil's neighbors.

GLENCOE TECHNOLOGY

NATIONAL GEOGRAPHIC

The World and Its People Video Program

Chapter 8 Brazil and Its Neighbors

The following segments enhance the study of this chapter:

- **Samba**
- **Amazon Basin**
- **Jungle Countdown**

Available in DVD and VHS.

MindJogger Videoquiz

Use MindJogger to preview the Chapter 22 content.

Available in VHS.

Chapter 22 Brazil and Its Neighbors

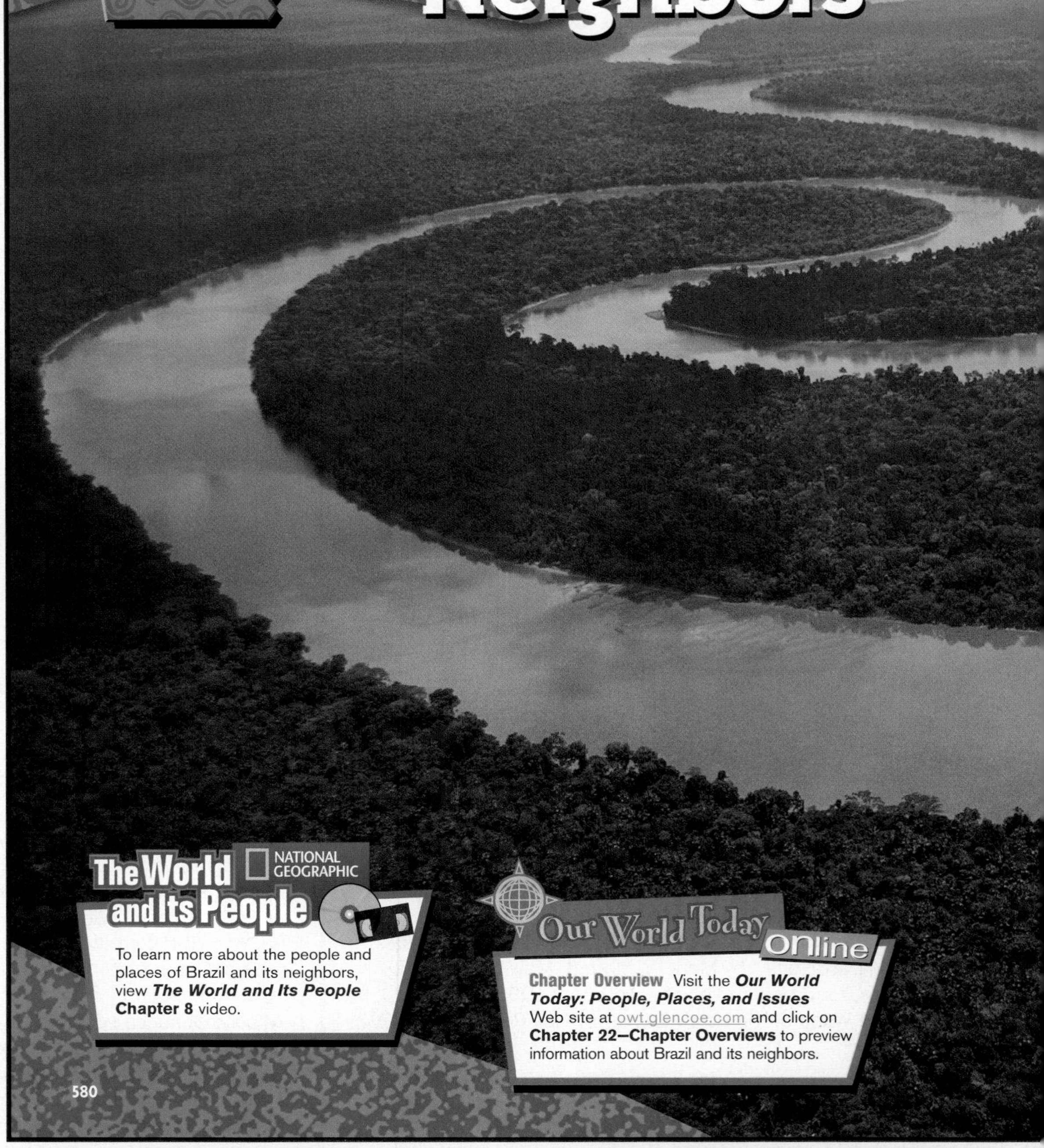

The World and Its People NATIONAL GEOGRAPHIC

To learn more about the people and places of Brazil and its neighbors, view ***The World and Its People* Chapter 8** video.

Our World Today online

Chapter Overview Visit the ***Our World Today: People, Places, and Issues*** Web site at owt.glencoe.com and click on **Chapter 22—Chapter Overviews** to preview information about Brazil and its neighbors.

580

Two-Minute Lesson Launcher

Ask students what they think of when they hear "Amazon River." They might mention rain forests, Native Americans, or diverse plant and animal life. Tell your class that although such descriptions are characteristic of the river, it is also an important transportation corridor. Commercial ships can travel as far as the port of Iquitos, Peru, located 2,300 miles (3,700 km) from the mouth. Using a physical map, have students trace the Amazon from its mouth on the Atlantic to Iquitos, and then to its source in the Andes. **Ask:** **Why might it be difficult to navigate the river beyond Iquitos?** *(It disappears into narrower headstreams and the elevation increases.)*

Summarizing Information Study Foldable Make this foldable and use it to organize note cards with information about the people and places of Brazil and its neighbors.

Step 1 Fold a 2-inch tab along the long edge of a sheet of paper.

Fold the left edge over 2 inches.

Step 2 Fold the paper in half so the tab is on the inside.

The tab can't be seen when the paper is folded.

Step 3 Open the paper pocket foldable, turn it, and glue the edges of the pockets together.

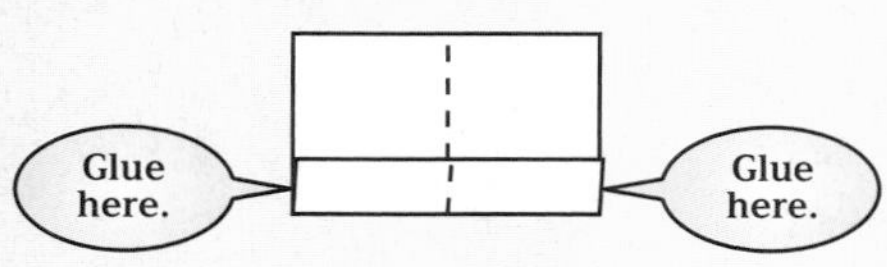

Step 4 Label the pockets as shown.

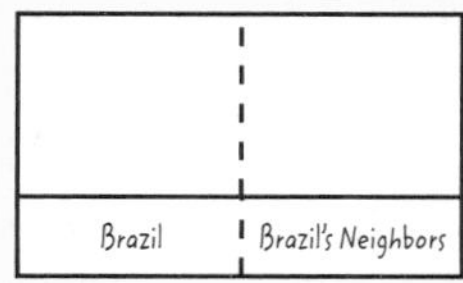

Reading and Writing As you read the chapter, summarize key facts about Brazil and its neighbors on note cards or on quarter sheets of notebook paper. Organize your notes by placing them in your pocket foldable inside the appropriate pockets. (Keep your pocket foldable to use with Chapter 23.)

Why It Matters

Preserving the Environment

The Amazon rain forest—sometimes called the "lungs of the planet" because of the huge amounts of oxygen given off by its trees—is home to up to 30 percent of the animal and plant life on Earth. Destroying these trees may cause the extinction of many wildlife species and damage to the earth's environment—on which we all depend for our own lives. This is just one of many issues facing the people and government of Brazil.

◀ **The Amazon River, Brazil**

About the Photos

Rivers are powerful forces which shape the earth's surface. Great civilizations sprung up along such rivers as the Tigris-Euphrates, the Nile, and the Indus. The Amazon is bordered by thick rain forest along much of its 4,000 mile (6,437 km) length. It is only 100 miles (120 km) shorter than the world's longest river, the Nile-Kagera in Africa, though the Amazon carries a much larger volume of water to the sea. The Amazon and the Congo carry the greatest volume of water of any of the world's rivers. Why so much water? Both rivers are located on the Equator, fed by tropical rains, and have many tributaries, or smaller streams feeding into them.

Introducing Chapter 22

FOLDABLES™ Study Organizer

Purpose This activity requires students to create note cards and a pocket foldable to organize information from the chapter. Students record key facts about the countries in the chapter and then group the information into categories, in effect, comparing the people and places of Brazil and its neighbors.

Have students complete ***Reading and Study Skills Foldables*** Activity 22.

Why It Matters

How Much Rain? Ask students if they have a rain gauge at their house. Discuss the concept of "annual rainfall," and what the average annual rainfall is where they live. Provide a supply of 1" by 1" construction paper squares, and a piece of butcher paper 12 feet long. (Some 1" by 10" strips will save time.) Create a chart with 11 foot columns for each location you choose to list. Ask volunteers to glue the correct number of squares in a straight line to represent inches of rainfall.

Annual Rainfall in Inches

Location	Inches
Your Town	??
Amazon Rain Forest	120
Mt. Waialeale, HA (world's highest)	460
Arica, Chile (world's lowest)	.03
Death Valley, CA (lowest in the U.S.)	1.66
Beaumont, TX (highest in Texas)	50
El Paso, TX (lowest in Texas)	8

1 FOCUS

Section Objectives

1. Describe Brazil's landforms and climates.
2. Identify the natural resources Brazil's economy depends on.
3. Discuss the people and culture of Brazil.

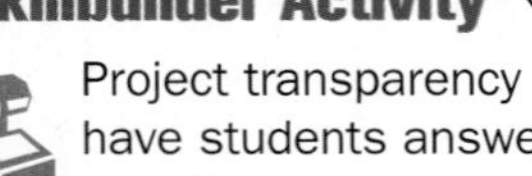

BELLRINGER Skillbuilder Activity

Project transparency and have students answer questions.

This activity is also available as a blackline master.

Daily Focus Skills Transparency 22-1

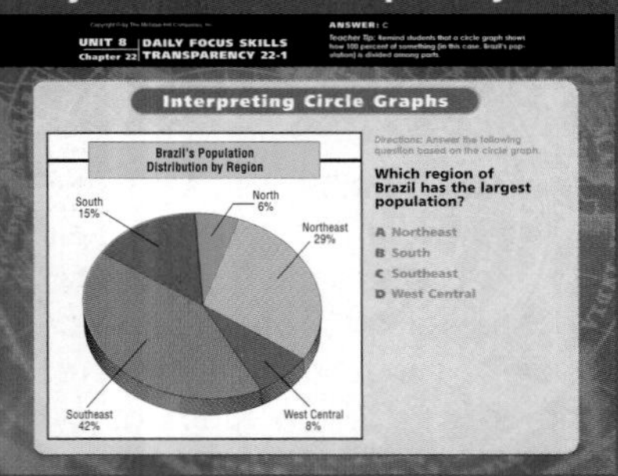

Guide to Reading

■ **Accessing Prior Knowledge**
Ask: What do you know about Brazil? List students' responses. As they read, have students determine if the items on the list are true.

■ **Vocabulary Precheck**
Have students find or create illustrations for each landform word on the Terms to Know list.

Section 1 Brazil

Guide to Reading

Main Idea

Brazil is a large country with many resources, a lively culture, and serious economic challenges.

Terms to Know

- basin
- *selva*
- escarpment
- favela
- deforestation
- republic

Reading Strategy

Create a chart like the one below and fill in at least one key fact about Brazil in each category.

Brazil	
Land	
Climate	
History	
Economy	
Government	
People	

NATIONAL GEOGRAPHIC Exploring Our World

Some of the world's largest freshwater fish swim in the mighty Amazon River in Brazil. Called pirarucu (pih•RAHR•uh •KEW), these fish can grow up to 15 feet (4.6 m) long. What a catch! The people who catch these huge fish often make the fish scales into souvenir key chains for tourists.

Like the pirarucu fish, Brazil is BIG. It is the fifth-largest country in the world and the largest in South America. In fact, Brazil makes up almost half of South America. It borders every South American country except Chile and Ecuador.

Brazil's Land

Because Brazil covers such a large area, it has many different types of landforms and climates. The map on page 583 shows you that Brazil has narrow coastal plains, highland areas, and lowland river valleys.

The **Amazon River** is the world's second-longest river, winding almost 4,000 miles (6,437 km) from the Andes mountain ranges to the Atlantic Ocean. On its journey to the Atlantic, the Amazon drains water from a wide, flat basin. A **basin** is a low area surrounded by higher land. In the **Amazon Basin,** rainfall can reach as much as 120 inches (305 cm) a year. These rains support the growth of thick tropical rain forests, which Brazilians call ***selvas.*** Turn to page 600 to learn more about this rain forest, which covers one-third of Brazil.

Section Resources

Reproducible Masters
- Reproducible Lesson Plan 22-1
- Daily Lecture and Discussion Notes 22-1
- Guided Reading Activity 22-1
- Reading Essentials and Study Guide 22-1
- Section Quiz 22-1

Transparencies
- Daily Focus Skills Transparency 22-1
- GeoQuiz Transparency 22-1

Multimedia
- Vocabulary PuzzleMaker Software
- Interactive Tutor Self-Assessment CD-ROM
- Presentation Plus! CD-ROM
- ExamView® Pro 3.0 Testmaker CD-ROM

Brazil has lowlands along the Paraná River and the São Francisco River. The Brazilian Highlands cover about half of the country, then drop sharply to the Atlantic Ocean. This drop is called the **Great Escarpment.** An escarpment is a steep cliff between higher and lower land.

Reading Check What is significant about the Amazon River?

Brazil's Economy

How do Brazilians earn a living? Agriculture, mining, and forestry have been important for centuries. The Amazon Basin has been a mysterious region whose secrets were guarded by the Native Americans

NATIONAL GEOGRAPHIC **Brazil and Its Neighbors: Physical**

Elevations

Feet	Meters
10,000	3,000
5,000	1,500
2,000	600
1,000	300
0	0

▲ Mountain peak

0 mi. 800 / 0 km 800

Azimuthal Equidistant projection

Applying Map Skills

1. Which area of Brazil—the north or the south—has the highest elevation?
2. Name two rivers that flow into the Amazon River.

Find NGS online map resources @ www.nationalgeographic.com/maps

Chapter 22

Section 1, pages 582–587

TEACH

Brainstorming Ask students what comes to their minds when they hear "rain forest." *(Answers might include insects, tall trees, steamy heat, and exotic plants and animals.)* Point out that about half of Brazil's area is covered by a tropical rain forest. Explain that this rain forest covers 2.3 million square miles (nearly 6 million sq. km), and receives between 60 and 120 inches (152 to 305 cm) of rain a year. **L1**

Reading Check Answer

It is the world's second longest river.

Daily Lecture Notes 22-1

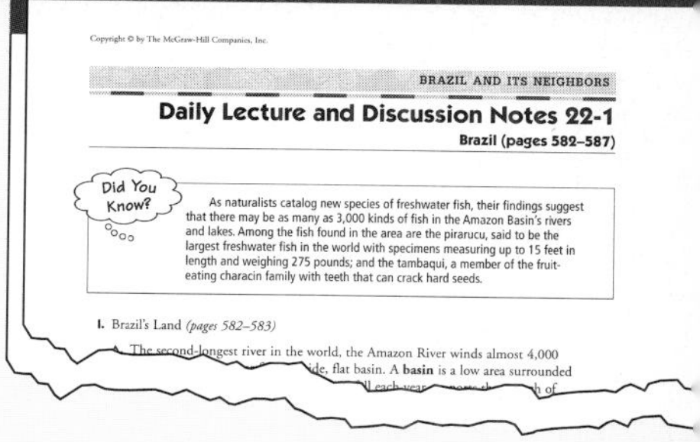

BRAZIL AND ITS NEIGHBORS

Daily Lecture and Discussion Notes 22-1

Brazil (pages 582–587)

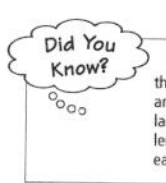

Did You Know?

As naturalists catalog new species of freshwater fish, their findings suggest that there may be as many as 3,000 kinds of fish in the Amazon Basin's rivers and lakes. Among the fish found in the area are the piraruci, said to be the largest freshwater fish in the world with specimens measuring up to 15 feet in length and weighing 275 pounds; and the tambaqui, a member of the fruit-eating characin family with teeth that can crack hard seeds.

I. Brazil's Land (pages 582–583)

A. The second-longest river in the world, the Amazon River winds almost 4,000 ...

Applying Map Skills

Answers

1. the south
2. Negro River, Madeira River, Xingu River, Tocantins River

Skills Practice

Where do you think most people in Brazil live? Why? *(along the coast; because inland areas are more difficult to reach)*

Meeting Special Needs

Visual/Spatial Have students work in small groups to create an annotated map of Brazil's regions. Their maps should include illustrations and captions that identify the region's natural features, climates, major economic activities, cities, and environmental issues. Groups can be subdivided, with each smaller group researching a particular region. Then the small groups can reassemble to prepare their annotated map. Have groups present their maps to the class. **L3 ELL**

Refer to *Inclusion for the Middle School Social Studies Classroom Strategies and Activities* in the TCR.

Guided Reading Activity 22-1

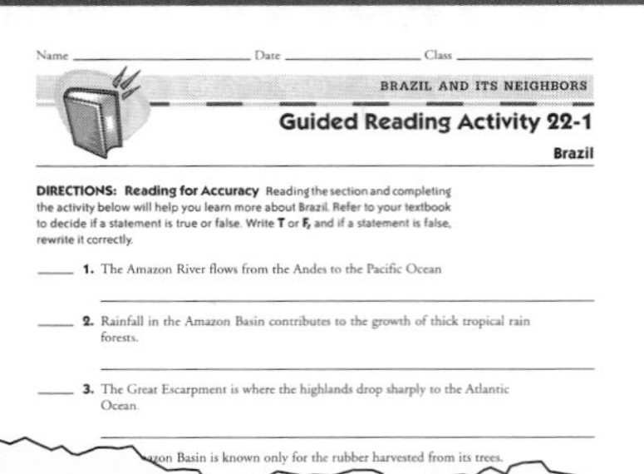
Name ______ Date ______ Class ______

BRAZIL AND ITS NEIGHBORS

Guided Reading Activity 22-1

Brazil

DIRECTIONS: Reading for Accuracy Reading the section and completing the activity below will help you learn more about Brazil. Refer to your textbook to decide if a statement is true or false. Write T or F, and if a statement is false, rewrite it correctly.

____ 1. The Amazon River flows from the Andes to the Pacific Ocean.

____ 2. Rainfall in the Amazon Basin contributes to the growth of thick tropical rain forests.

____ 3. The Great Escarpment is where the highlands drop sharply to the Atlantic Ocean.

...zon Basin is known only for the rubber harvested from its trees.

Interdisciplinary Connections

Science Brazilians are harnessing the power of their water resources to supply their energy needs. The Itaípu Dam on the Paraná River is a joint $20-billion project of Brazil and Paraguay. The dam is designed to supply one-fifth of Brazil's electricity.

Analyzing the Graph

Answer
Brazil and Colombia

Skills Practice
Which country is the leading coffee producer? *(Brazil)* **How much coffee does this country produce each year?** *(about 2 1/2 billion pounds per year)*

Leading Coffee-Producing Countries

Analyzing the Graph

Brazil's highlands have the right soil and climate to grow coffee.

Economics Which leading coffee-producing countries are in South America?

Visit owt.glencoe.com and click on **Chapter 22–Textbook Updates.**

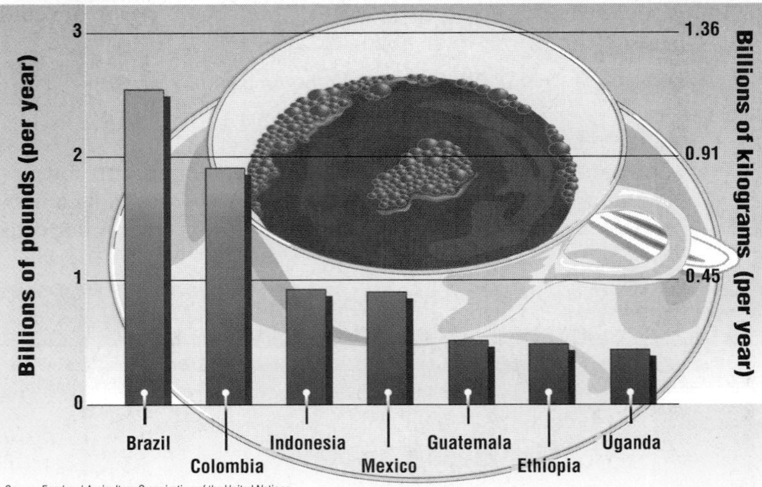

Source: Food and Agriculture Organization of the United Nations.

living there. This began to change in the mid-1800s. World demand skyrocketed for the rubber harvested from the basin's trees, and new settlers streamed to Brazil's interior. Today, mining companies dig for minerals such as bauxite, tin, and iron ore. Logging companies harvest mahogany and other woods from the rain forest. Farmers use the cleared land to grow soybeans and tobacco and to graze cattle.

Brazil's Economic Challenges Today Brazil's economy is diverse and productive, yet the country still faces serious economic challenges. Brazil's economy has brought wealth to many Brazilians and built a large and strong middle class. Yet as many as one-fifth of Brazil's people live in extreme poverty. Many Brazilian cities are surrounded by **favelas,** or slum areas. Thousands of poor people move to cities looking for work in the factories. They live in crude shacks with neither running water nor sewage systems. City governments have tried to clean up these areas, but people continue to settle here because they have no money to pay for housing. Many children as young as 10 years old go to work to help earn money for their families.

While Brazil has the largest area of remaining rain forest in the world, it also has the highest rate of **deforestation.** Deforestation is the cutting down or destroying of large areas of forest. To increase jobs and products for export, the government has encouraged mining, logging, and farming in the rain forest. The main causes of deforestation, however, are the building of roads and the clearing of land for farms. Roads allow both poor farmers and rich landowners to use parts of the rain forest that used to be out of reach. The forest is cut down on each side of the road to create long strips of land for farming.

Critical Thinking Activity

Identifying Cause and Effect Have students create a chart to illustrate the cause-and-effect relationships that have influenced life in Brazil. For example, the government built roads in the Amazon Basin, leading more people to settle there. Also, the cool climate and rich soil of Brazil's highlands make it appropriate for growing coffee. Have students add other examples from the section to their chart. When students have completed their charts, ask for volunteers to read an example to the class. Discuss how landforms, climate, settlement patterns, and history all influence the way people live in Brazil. **L2**

 **EE5 Environment and Society: Standard 14**

Deforestation is an issue because tropical forests are of great importance to the regulation of the earth's climate. The rain forests help move heat from the Equator to the more temperate regions. Scientists are still studying the role of the rain forest in global warming. Although the Amazon rain forest belongs to Brazil, the effects of deforestation are worldwide. An important issue, then, is how to balance the needs of a country to develop jobs and revenue for its people and the climate needs of the planet.

In addition, deforestation threatens the Native Americans who live in the rain forest. As more people settle in the Amazon Basin, Native Americans find it difficult to follow traditional ways of life. In the 1990s, the government announced plans to set aside 10 percent of the Amazon forest as parks. Another 10 percent will be set aside for native peoples.

✓Reading Check **What are the leading causes of deforestation in the Amazon Basin?**

Brazil's History and Culture

With about 172 million people, Brazil has the largest population of all South American nations. Brazil's culture is largely Portuguese. The Portuguese were the first and largest European group to colonize

Literature

BOTOQUE

Kayapo Indian Myth

In this myth of central Brazil, the hero brings fire to his people.

"Botoque and the animals safely returned to their village with Jaguar's possessions. Everyone was delighted to eat grilled meat. They loved being able to warm themselves by the fire when the nights became cool. And they liked having the village fires provide protection from wild animals.

As for Jaguar, when he returned home and found that he had been robbed of his special possessions, his heart flooded with fury. 'So this is how Botoque has repaid me for adopting him as my son and teaching him the secret of the bow and arrow!' he exclaimed. 'Why, he did not even leave me fire. Well, no matter. In memory of this theft, from this time forth and evermore, I will eat my catch raw! This will keep the memory of my adopted son before my eyes and hatred for him—and all who walk the earth as he does—alive in my heart!'"

Botoque, Bringer of Fire, p. 298–299, Folklore, Myths, and Legends, A World Perspective, edited by Donna Rosenberg, NTC Publishing, 1997.

Analyzing Literature

Do you think the Kayapo Indians feared jaguars? Why or why not?

Cooperative Learning Activity

Making Dioramas Have students work in groups to create a diorama of the Amazon rain forest. Individual students in each group can focus on specific topics for their diorama. For instance, one student can concentrate on trees; another on plants; and still others on birds, reptiles, mammals, or amphibians. Instruct members of each group to research their assigned topic. Then have them choose representative species to include in their group's diorama. Have students work in their groups to assemble the display. When it is complete, have students discuss the challenge of portraying the incredible variety of plant and animal life in this region. **L2 ELL**

EE3 Physical Systems: Standard 8

Cultural Kaleidoscope

Brazil The name *Brazil* comes from a Portuguese word meaning "glowing ember." When Portuguese sailors first saw the trees that grow along the Brazilian coast, they thought the color of the wood looked like the glowing embers of a fire.

Literature

Answer Yes, because they portray the jaguar as being angry at Botoque and his people and keeping his hatred for Botoque "alive in his heart."

Activity Read other South American Indian myths to your class. Discuss the concepts the myths explain, and how animals and humans are portrayed.

✓ Reading Check Answer

the building of roads and the clearing of land for farms

3 Assess

Assign Section 1 Assessment as homework or an in-class activity.

Have students use the Interactive Tutor Self-Assessment CD-ROM to review Section 22–1.

More About the Photos

Carnival Carnival is a four-day celebration that takes place before the Christian religious period called Lent. The famous Mardi Gras of New Orleans celebrates the same event.

Caption Answer people of European, African, Native American, Asian, or mixed ancestry

Measure student knowledge of physical features and political entities.

GeoQuiz Transparency 22-1

Section Quiz 22-1

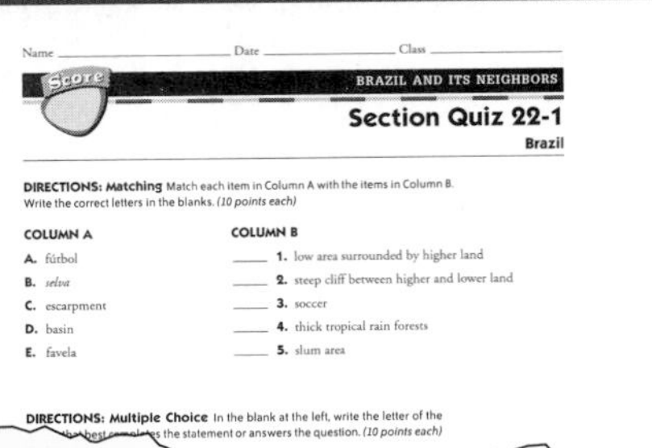

Name _______ Date _______ Class _______

BRAZIL AND ITS NEIGHBORS

Section Quiz 22-1

Brazil

DIRECTIONS: Matching Match each item in Column A with the items in Column B. Write the correct letters in the blanks. (10 points each)

COLUMN A	COLUMN B
A. fútbol	____ 1. low area surrounded by higher land
B. selva	____ 2. steep cliff between higher and lower land
C. escarpment	____ 3. soccer
D. basin	____ 4. thick tropical rain forests
E. favela	____ 5. slum area

DIRECTIONS: Multiple Choice In the blank at the left, write the letter of the ... the statement or answers the question. (10 points each)

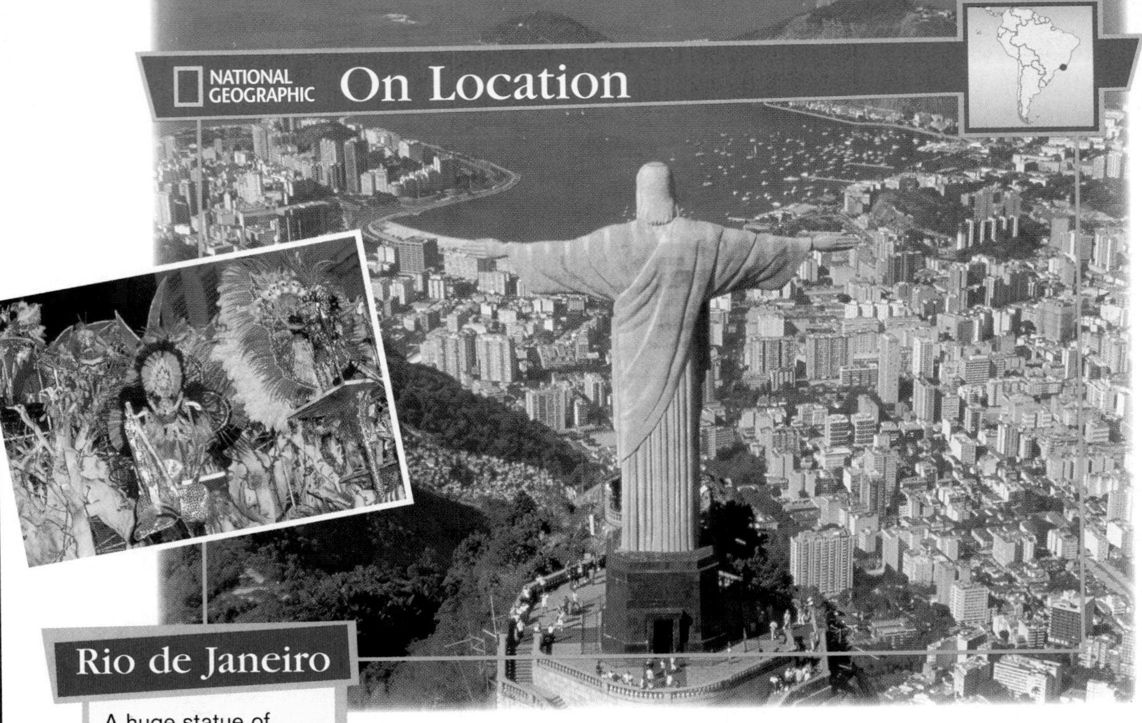

Rio de Janeiro

A huge statue of Christ overlooks Rio de Janeiro (right). Crowds of people in Rio de Janeiro celebrate Carnival wearing brightly colored costumes (above).

Culture What groups make up Brazil's population?

Brazil. Today Brazilians are of European, African, Native American, Asian, or mixed ancestry. Almost all of them speak a Brazilian form of Portuguese, which includes many words from Native American and African languages. Most of the population follow the Roman Catholic religion, but many Brazilians combine Catholicism with beliefs and practices from African and Native American religions.

Influence of History Native Americans were the first people to live in Brazil. In the 1500s, the Portuguese forced Native Americans to work on large plantations that grew tobacco and, later, sugarcane. Many Native Americans died from disease or overwork. To replace them, early Portuguese settlers brought people from Africa and enslaved them. Slavery finally was banned in 1888, but Africans remained in Brazil, most of them living in the northeastern part of the country. Over the years, African traditions have influenced Brazilian religion, music, dance, and food.

Moving to the Cities Much of Brazil is sparsely populated. Millions of people have moved from rural areas to coastal cities in hopes of finding better jobs. Now the government is encouraging people to move back to less populated inland areas. Highways now crisscross the country and reach many once remote regions. In 1960 Brazil moved its capital from coastal **Rio de Janeiro** 600 miles (966 km) inland to the newly built city of **Brasília.** With more than 1.5 million people, Brasília is a modern and rapidly growing city.

Content Background

Brazil's Economy For many centuries, Brazil swung between good and bad economic times because its economy was focused on producing only one or two commodities. When prices dropped or supplies were used up, the economy suffered. For most of that period, the economy centered on exploiting Brazil's resources. Lumber and sugar were the first main exports in the 1500s. By the 1700s, those seeking wealth mined Brazil's gold and diamonds. When easy-to-find supplies of these minerals were depleted, people built vast rubber plantations. Rubber was a major source of wealth in the late 1800s and early 1900s. Today Brazil's economy is more diverse. With its strong manufacturing and service industries, the country is somewhat better equipped to absorb price drops or falling demand for its minerals and export crops.

The Government Brazil declared independence from Portugal in 1822. At first the new nation was an empire, with emperors ruling from 1822 to 1889. Like some other countries in Middle and South America, Brazil was ruled by military dictators. Today Brazil is a democratic **republic,** where people elect a president and other leaders. In Brazil, though, citizens cannot choose whether to vote or not vote. People from ages 18 to 70 are required by law to vote. Brazil has more than a dozen political parties—not just two main ones, as in the United States.

The national government of Brazil is much stronger than its 26 state governments. Brazil's president has more power over the country than an American president does in the United States.

Leisure Time Brazilians live for soccer, which they call fútbol. Every village has a soccer field, and the larger cities have stadiums. Maracana Stadium in Rio de Janeiro seats 220,000 fans. Basketball is another important sport.

Brazil is also famous for **Carnival.** This festival is celebrated just before the beginning of Lent, the Christian holy season that comes before Easter. The most spectacular Carnival is held each year in Rio de Janeiro. The celebration includes Brazilian music and showy parades.

Brazil has one of the largest television networks in the world. This network produces prime-time soap operas called *telenovelas.* These programs are wildly popular in Brazil—and viewers in more than 60 other nations enjoy them too.

✓Reading Check **Why do most Brazilians speak a form of Portuguese?**

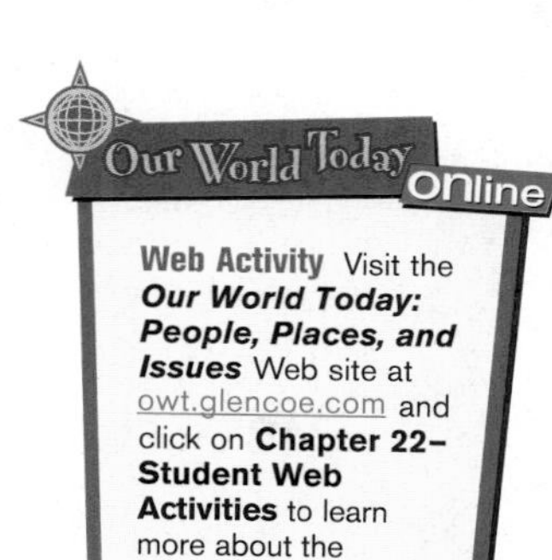

Web Activity Visit the ***Our World Today: People, Places, and Issues*** Web site at owt.glencoe.com and click on **Chapter 22–Student Web Activities** to learn more about the destruction of the rain forest.

Section 1 Assessment

Defining Terms

1. **Define** basin, *selva,* escarpment, favela, deforestation, republic.

Recalling Facts

2. **History** Who were the first and largest group of Europeans to colonize Brazil?
3. **Economics** What resources attract companies to the Amazon Basin?
4. **Culture** What is the major religion of Brazil?

Critical Thinking

5. **Drawing Conclusions** In what way is deforestation threatening the Native Americans who live in the rain forest?
6. **Summarizing Information** What economic challenges face Brazilians?

Graphic Organizer

7. **Organizing Information** Create a diagram like this one. Beside the left arrow, write the cause of the government action. On the right, list results of this action.

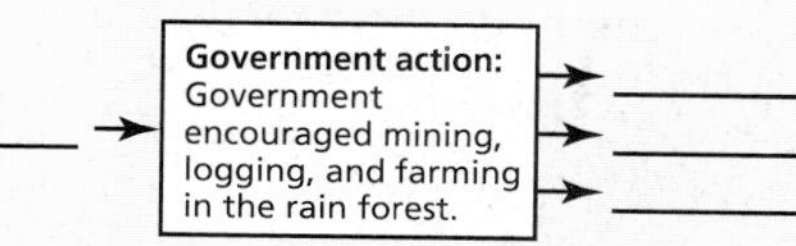

Applying Social Studies Skills

8. **Analyzing Maps** Look at the physical map on page 583. What large landform in Brazil surrounds the Amazon River?

Chapter 22

Section 1, pages 582–587

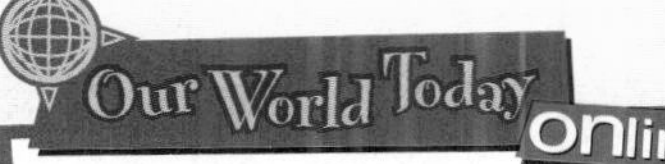

Objectives, goals, and answers to the Student Web Activity can be found in the Web Activity Lesson Plan at **owt.glencoe.com**

✓ Reading Check Answer

because Brazil was once a Portuguese colony

Reteach

Write false statements about Brazil. Ask for volunteers to correct the statements.

Reading Essentials and Study Guide 22-1

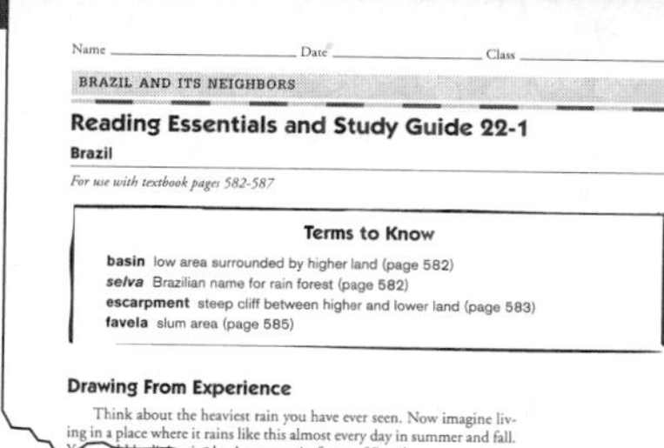
Name Date Class

BRAZIL AND ITS NEIGHBORS

Reading Essentials and Study Guide 22-1

Brazil

For use with textbook pages 582–587

Terms to Know

basin low area surrounded by higher land (page 582)
selva Brazilian name for rain forest (page 582)
escarpment steep cliff between higher and lower land (page 583)
favela slum area (page 585)

Drawing From Experience

Think about the heaviest rain you have ever seen. Now imagine living in a place where it rains like this almost every day in summer and fall.

Close

Have each student list five facts about Brazil from this lesson. Then have students work in groups to create a summary of the lesson based on their lists.

Section 1 Assessment

1. The terms are in the Glossary.
2. the Portuguese
3. rubber, minerals, wood
4. Roman Catholicism
5. Native Americans find it difficult to follow traditional ways of life.
6. poverty, destruction of rain forest and Native American lands
7. Cause: desire to increase jobs and products for export; Effect: land is damaged, deforestation, Native Americans threatened
8. the Amazon Basin

Critical Thinking Skill

TEACH

To demonstrate the importance of sequencing information correctly, write the following three steps: "Put the two pieces of bread together," "Spread peanut butter on one piece of bread," "Spread jelly on the other piece of bread." Ask for volunteers to explain the problem with this sequence. *(Putting the bread together should be done last.)* **L1**

Additional Skills Practice

1. **Why are words like *first*, *then*, and *finally* useful in determining sequence?** *(They show the order in which things happened.)*
2. Read the subsection Brazil's Economy, which begins on page 583. **What categories could you use to group the information that you read?** *(Possible answers: crops and industries; economic successes and challenges)*

Additional Skills Resources

 Chapter Skills Activity 22

 Building Geography Skills for Life

GLENCOE TECHNOLOGY

 **Skillbuilder Interactive Workbook CD-ROM, Level 1**

This interactive CD-ROM reinforces student mastery of essential social studies skills.

Critical Thinking Skill

Sequencing and Categorizing Information

Sequencing means placing facts in the order in which they occurred. *Categorizing* means organizing information into groups of related facts and ideas. Both actions help you deal with large quantities of information in an understandable way.

Learning the Skill

Follow these steps to learn sequencing and categorizing skills:

- Look for dates or clue words that provide you with a chronological order: *in 2004, the late 1990s, first, then, finally, after the Great Depression,* and so on.
- If the sequence of events is not important, you may want to categorize the information instead. Categories might include economic activities or cultural traits.
- List these characteristics, or categories, as the headings on a chart.
- As you read, fill in details under the proper category on the chart.

Brasília

Practicing the Skill

Read the paragraphs below, and then answer the questions that follow.

After Brazil's independence from Portugal in 1822, a bill was presented to build a new capital named Brasília. More than 100 years later, in 1955, a planning committee chose the site for the new capital. The first streets were paved in 1958. On April 20, 1960, the festivities to officially "open" the new capital started at 4:00 P.M.

Brasília has both positive and negative aspects. The positive include virtually no air pollution, no threat of natural disasters, many green areas, and a pleasant climate. The negative aspects of the capital include very high housing prices, inefficient public transportation, few parking spaces, and long distances between the various government buildings.

1. What information can be organized sequentially?
2. What categories can you use to organize the information? What facts could be placed under each category?

Applying the Skill

Find two newspaper or magazine articles about Brazil or another South American country. Sequence or categorize the information on note cards or in a chart.

GO TO Practice key skills with **Glencoe Skillbuilder Interactive Workbook, Level 1.**

CHAPTER 22

Practicing the Skill Answers

1. The facts about the development of Brasília; 1822—proposal to build a new capital; 1955—site chosen; 1958—first streets paved; 1960—new city officially opened
2. Positive and negative aspects of Brasília; Positive—low pollution, low threat of natural disasters, presence of open space, pleasant climate; Negative—high housing prices, poor transportation and parking, need to travel long distances

Applying the Skill

Students' cards or charts should show the information properly categorized or sequenced. You might wish to ask them to supply the original source along with their completed work.

Section 2

Brazil's Neighbors

Guide to Reading

Main Idea

Brazil's neighbors give South America a diverse array of landforms, climates, and cultures.

Terms to Know

- pampas
- *estancia*
- gaucho
- hydroelectric power
- llanos
- altitude
- caudillo

Reading Strategy

Create a diagram like this one. Fill in the names of Brazil's neighbors to the south and north, and then write at least one key fact about the people from each country.

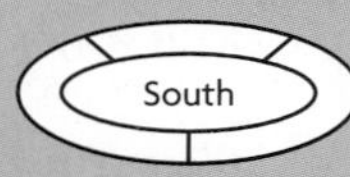

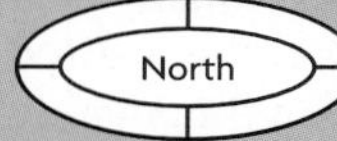

NATIONAL GEOGRAPHIC **Exploring Our World**

The traditional music of Paraguay seems to be out of place with the rest of its culture. The harp is the country's national instrument, and Paraguayans are famous for their slow, mournful guitar playing. In contrast, the traditional dances are much livelier. Here, a woman performs the bottle dance—a difficult feat even though the bottles are attached to one another.

South of Brazil lie **Argentina, Uruguay,** and **Paraguay.** To the north of Brazil are countries that border the Caribbean Sea—**Venezuela, Guyana, Suriname,** and **French Guiana.**

Argentina

Argentina is South America's second-largest country, after Brazil. Its southern tip reaches almost to the continent of Antarctica. Argentina is about the size of the United States east of the Mississippi River. Within this vast area, you can find mountains, deserts, plains, and forests.

The Andes tower over the western part of Argentina. Snowcapped peaks and clear blue lakes draw tourists for skiing and hiking. **Aconcagua** (AH•kohn•KAH•gwah) soars to a height of 22,834 feet (6,960 m), making it the highest mountain in the Western Hemisphere.

South and east of the Andes lies a dry, windswept plateau called **Patagonia.** Most of Patagonia gets little rain and has poor soil. As a result, sheep raising is the only major economic activity. Find Patagonia on the physical map on page 583.

Focus

1. Compare the landscapes and climates of Venezuela and Argentina.
2. Describe the economies of Brazil's northern and southern neighbors.
3. Discuss the histories of the Guianas and Argentina.

BELLRINGER Skillbuilder Activity

Project transparency and have students answer questions.

This activity is also available as a blackline master.

Daily Focus Skills Transparency 22-2

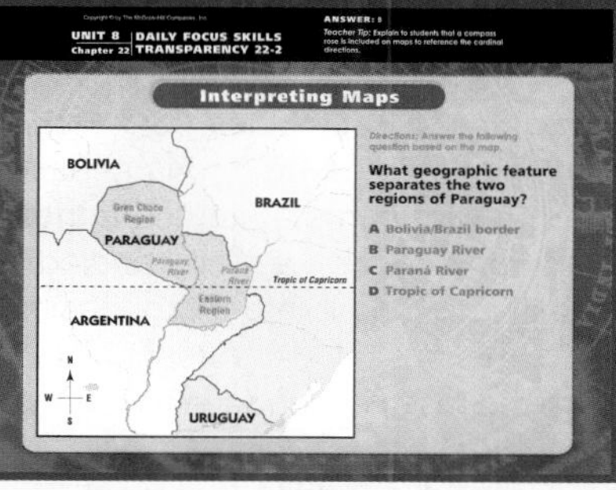

Guide to Reading

■ **Accessing Prior Knowledge** Ask students to describe the American West. *(large open spaces; ranches; cattle and sheep; grasslands)* Point out that these words apply to large parts of Argentina as well.

Section Resources

Reproducible Masters

- Reproducible Lesson Plan 22-2
- Daily Lecture and Discussion Notes 22-2
- Guided Reading Activity 22-2
- Reading Essentials and Study Guide 22-2
- Section Quiz 22-2

Transparencies

- Daily Focus Skills Transparency 22-2
- GeoQuiz Transparency 22-1

Multimedia

- Vocabulary PuzzleMaker Software
- Interactive Tutor Self-Assessment CD-ROM
- Presentation Plus! CD-ROM
- ExamView® Pro 3.0 Testmaker CD-ROM

TEACH

Outlining Have students create an outline for the section by writing down the headings and subheadings and then writing two facts under each subheading. **L1**

Daily Lecture Notes 22-2

BRAZIL AND ITS NEIGHBORS

Daily Lecture and Discussion Notes 22-2

Brazil's Neighbors (pages 589–595)

Did You Know? From 10,000 to 30,000 citizens "disappeared" in Argentina's Dirty War. From 1976 to 1983, a military government in Argentina conducted a reign of terror, destroying government opponents.

I. Argentina *(pages 589–591)*

A. Nearly reaching the continent of Antarctica, Argentina is approximately the size of the United States east of the Mississippi River.

B. The Andes tower over the western part of Argentina. South and east of the Andes is Patagonia, a dry and windswept plateau.

C. More than two-thirds of Argentina's population lives in the region known as the … area with fertile soil and mild climate similar to the Great Plains of

Determining Cause and Effect Many Argentines play *pato,* which combines polo and basketball. Players on horseback form two teams. Each team tries to keep control of a six-handled ball and toss it into the opposing team's basket. After describing the game, ask students: **What features of Argentina's physical geography and life provide a basis for this game?** *(gaucho culture of horseback riding)* **L1**

The center of Argentina has vast treeless plains known as the **pampas.** Similar to the Great Plains of the United States, the pampas are home to farmers who grow grains and ranchers who raise livestock. More than two-thirds of Argentina's people live in this region.

Argentina's Economy Argentina's economy depends heavily on farming and ranching. The country's major farm products include beef, sugarcane, wheat, soybeans, and corn. Huge ***estancias*** (ay•STAHN•see•ahs), or ranches, cover the pampas. **Gauchos** (GOW•chohs), or cowhands, take care of the livestock on the ranches. Gauchos are the national symbol of Argentina, admired for their independence and horse-riding skills. The livestock that the gauchos herd and tend are a vital part of the country's economy. Beef and food products are Argentina's chief exports. Turn to page 596 to read more about gauchos.

Argentina is one of the most industrialized countries in South America. Most of the country's factories are in or near **Buenos Aires,** Argentina's capital and largest city. The leading manufactured goods are food products, automobiles, chemicals, textiles, books, and magazines.

Petroleum is Argentina's most valuable mineral resource. The country's major oil fields are in Patagonia and the Andes. Other minerals—zinc, iron, copper, tin, and uranium—are mined in the Andes as well. Despite these resources, Argentina's economy has struggled during the early years of the twenty-first century.

Argentina's History In the late 1500s, the Spanish settled in Argentina. In 1816 a general named **José de San Martín** led Argentina in its fight for freedom from Spain. After independence, the country was torn apart by civil war. By the mid-1850s, a strong national government had emerged, and Argentina entered a time of prosperity. During the first half of the 1900s, Argentina's elected leaders governed poorly. The economy suffered, and the military took over. One of these military leaders, **Juan Perón,** became a dictator in the late 1940s. With his popular wife, Eva, at his side, Perón tried to improve the economy and give more help to workers. His crackdown on freedom of speech and the press made people unhappy, however. In 1955 a revolt drove Perón from power, and democracy returned.

Military officers again took control of Argentina in the 1970s. They ruled harshly, and political violence resulted in the deaths of many people. In 1982 Argentina suffered defeat in a war with the United Kingdom for control of the **Falkland Islands,** which lie in the Atlantic Ocean off the coast of Argentina. Argentina's loss forced the military to step down, and elected leaders regained control of the government.

Today Argentina is a democratic republic. As in the United States, the national government is much stronger than the provincial, or state, governments. A powerful elected president leads the nation for a four-year term. A legislature with two houses makes the laws.

Strong Presidency

In Argentina, the president is very strong. Checks and balances present in the American system to control the power of the president do not exist in Argentina. In the United States, the Supreme Court may declare acts or laws unconstitutional. Or, the legislature may pass laws to limit the power of U.S. federal agencies. In Argentina, it is harder to prevent a popular leader from forcing his programs through the legislature.

Argentina's People About 85 percent of Argentina's people are of European ancestry. During the late 1800s, immigrants in large numbers came to Argentina from Spain and Italy. They drove out or killed many

Critical Thinking Activity

Categorizing Information Have students work in pairs to organize this section's information in a chart. Have each student prepare a chart with the column headings "Landforms," "Climate," "Economy," "People," and "History." Then have both students in each pair write a list of 10 to 12 facts about Brazil's neighbors. Have students take turns reading their facts to each other. The partner then has the task of placing each fact in the correct category by writing it under the appropriate column heading. **L1**

EE2 Places and Regions: Standard 4

NATIONAL GEOGRAPHIC On Location

Itaipu Dam

About 40,000 workers labored to build Paraguay's Itaipu Dam. Brazil funded its construction. In return, Brazil pays low prices for the electricity it buys from Paraguay.

Human/Environment Interaction **How do both Paraguay and Brazil benefit from this arrangement?**

Native Americans who inhabited Argentina. Their arrival greatly influenced Argentina's society and culture. Many more immigrants arrived from Europe after World War II. European ways of life are stronger in Argentina today than in most other South American countries.

The official language of Argentina is Spanish, although the language includes many Italian words. Most people are Roman Catholic. About 80 percent of Argentina's people live in cities and towns. Buenos Aires and its suburbs hold more than 12 million people. Buenos Aires has wide streets and European-style buildings. Its citizens call themselves *porteños* (pohr•TAY•nyohs), which means "people of the port." Many have a passion for the national dance of Argentina, the tango.

✓ Reading Check **Why does Argentina have a strong European culture?**

Uruguay and Paraguay

Uruguay and Paraguay differ from each other in environment, population, and development. Uruguay, with its mild climate, low-rolling terrain, and rich grasslands, is a buffer zone between the two large and powerful nations of Brazil and Argentina. Originally settled by the Portuguese, then taken over by Spain, Uruguay revolted against both countries and eventually became independent in 1825.

Immigration from Spain and Italy and the introduction of sheep are keys to Uruguay's modern development. The country's 3.4 million people are mostly of European descent. Its economy is extremely dependent on sheep and cattle raising. In fact, sheep and cattle outnumber people by ten to one in Uruguay, and about 70 percent of the territory of the country is in pasture. These grasslands produce the wool, hides, and meat that Uruguay exports.

Chapter 22

Section 2, pages 589–595

More About the Photos

Itaipu Dam More than 99 percent of Paraguay's energy comes from hydroelectric projects like the Itaipu Dam. Only .7 percent comes from fossil fuels.

Caption Answer Brazil's financial help allowed Paraguay to build the dam, which it would not otherwise have been able to do. Brazil benefits by receiving inexpensive power.

✓ Reading Check Answer

because about 85 percent of Argentina's people are of European ancestry

Guided Reading Activity 22-2

Name Date Class

BRAZIL AND ITS NEIGHBORS

Guided Reading Activity 22-2

Brazil's Neighbors

DIRECTIONS: Answering Questions Reading the section and answering the questions below will help you learn more about Brazil's neighbors. Use your textbook to write answers to the questions.

1. Describe the plateaus and plains of Argentina.
2. What does Argentina's economy depend on?
3. What two groups greatly influenced Argentina's society and culture?

Meeting Special Needs

Verbal/Linguistic Have students organize into pairs and have each member of a pair write a set of fill-in-the-blank questions using information from this section. On a separate sheet of paper, have them prepare a list of answers for all the questions, but with the letters of the answer words scrambled. Have one student in each pair ask the other his or her questions, with the respondent student referring to the scrambled words to identify the answer. When the first student has asked all of his or her questions, have the students reverse roles. **L1**

Refer to *Inclusion for the Middle School Social Studies Classroom Strategies and Activities* in the TCR.

Paraguay's flag has a different design on each side. On one side is the country's coat of arms. On the other side is the seal of the national treasury.

3 ASSESS

Assign Section 2 Assessment as homework or an in-class activity.

Have students use the Interactive Tutor Self-Assessment CD-ROM to review Section 22–2.

Reading Check Answer

hydroelectric power

In Uruguay, the expected social pattern of a wealthy landowning elite and poverty-stricken working class did not evolve. The large haciendas were complemented by many medium-sized and small farms on which wheat, flax, wine, and vegetable production has doubled in recent years. Enlightened government policies have provided social welfare to the poor. The Uruguayans, half of whom live in the capital city of **Montevideo,** have the highest literacy rate, the lowest rate of natural increase, the best diet, and one of the highest standards of living of any South American country. Spanish is the official language, and the Roman Catholic faith is the major religion.

Paraguay In Paraguay, the society and economy followed a quite different course. The eastern third of Paraguay, with its rich soils and fertile grasslands, was settled by the Spanish. The western two-thirds of the country, the great forest area known as the **Chaco,** was brought into the Spanish territory by Roman Catholic missionaries.

In the 1800s and 1900s a series of wars severely hurt Paraguay, destroying the economy of the country. After the worst of these—the five-year War of the Triple Alliance against Brazil, Argentina, and Uruguay in the 1860s—Paraguay's population was cut in half. Experts estimate that only 28,000 adult males were left alive, and Paraguay had lost 55,000 square miles of territory. The country has yet to recover from this catastrophe.

Currently, the only area with success in agriculture in Paraguay is located near the capital city of **Asunción** (ah•SOON•see•OHN). Cotton, tobacco, soybeans, and cassava are among Paraguay's crops.

Paraguay also exports electricity. The country has the world's largest hydroelectric power generator at the **Itaipu** (ee•TY•poo) **Dam,** on the Paraná River. **Hydroelectric power** is electricity that is generated by flowing water. Paraguay sells nearly 90 percent of the electricity it produces to neighboring countries.

Paraguayans today are mostly of mixed Guaraní—a Native American group—and Spanish ancestry. Both Spanish and Guaraní are official languages, but more people speak Guaraní. Most people practice the Roman Catholic faith. About one-half of the people live in cities.

Paraguayan arts are influenced by Guaraní culture. Guaraní lace is Paraguay's most famous handicraft. Like people in Uruguay, the people of Paraguay enjoy meat dishes and sip yerba maté, a tealike drink.

Reading Check **What important export is generated at the Itaipu Dam?**

Believe It or Not!

Roping a Capybara

Capybaras are the world's largest rodents. They may grow to be 2 feet tall and 4 feet long, and weigh more than 100 pounds. Found in Central and South America, the capybara (ka•pih•BAR•uh) lives along rivers and lakes, and eats vegetation. Here, a gaucho ropes a dog-sized capybara in Venezuela. Some Venezuelans eat capybara during the Easter season.

Venezuela

Venezuela (VEH•nuh•ZWAY•luh) is the westernmost country of Caribbean South America. In the northwest lie the lowland coastal areas surrounding **Lake Maracaibo** (MAH•rah•KY•boh), the largest lake in South America. Swamps fill much of this area, and few people live here. The great number of towering oil wells, however, gives you a clue that rich oil fields lie under the lake and along its shores. Venezuela has more oil reserves than any other country in the Americas.

Team-Teaching Activity

Mathematics The Itaipu Dam is huge. In fact, it may be difficult for students to appreciate its size. Give students the following statistics: The dam has a reservoir capacity of 1.02 trillion cubic feet (28.9 billion cubic m). The waters of the Paraná River explode through a 400-yard-wide spillway at more than 90 miles per hour. The force of the water is transformed into 12,600 megawatts of electricity. One megawatt is equal to 1 million watts. Have students work with the math teacher to compare these figures to those of other structures, so they understand how large the dam is. **L1**

EE5 Environment and Society: Standard 14

The Andean highlands begin south of the lake and are part of the Andes mountain ranges. This area includes most of the nation's cities, including **Caracas** (kah•RAH•kahs), the capital and largest city.

East of the highlands, you see grassy plains known as the **llanos** (LAH•nohs). The llanos have many ranches, farms, and oil fields. Venezuela's most important river—the **Orinoco**—flows across the llanos. This river is a valuable source of hydroelectric power for Venezuela's cities.

South and east of the llanos rise the Guiana Highlands, deeply cut by rivers. **Angel Falls**—the world's highest waterfall—spills over a bluff in this region.

Because it is close to the Equator, Venezuela has a mostly tropical climate. In the Guiana Highlands to the south, you enter a steamy rain forest. As in Mexico, temperatures in Venezuela differ with **altitude,** or height above sea level. Higher altitudes have cooler climates.

Venezuela's Economy Venezuelans once depended on crops such as coffee and cacao to earn a living. Since the 1920s, petroleum has changed the country's economy. Venezuela is a world leader in oil production and one of the chief suppliers of oil to the United States. Because the government owns the oil industry, oil provides nearly half of the government's income. Iron ore, limestone, bauxite, gold, diamonds, and emeralds also are mined. Factories make steel, chemicals, and food products. About 10 percent of the people farm, growing sugarcane and bananas or raising cattle.

History and Government With its many rivers, the land in South America reminded early Spanish explorers of Venice, Italy, which is full of canals. They named the area *Venezuela,* which means "Little Venice."

In the early 1800s, rebellion swept across the Spanish colonial empire. **Simón Bolívar** (see•MOHN boh•LEE•VAHR), who was born in Venezuela, became one of the leaders of this revolt. He and his soldiers freed Venezuela and neighboring regions from Spanish rule. In 1830 Venezuela became independent.

During most of the 1800s and 1900s, the country was governed by military rulers called **caudillos** (kow•THEE•yohz). Their rule was often harsh. Since 1958, Venezuela has been a democracy led by a president and a two-house legislature.

NATIONAL GEOGRAPHIC On Location

Angel Falls

Angel Falls—the highest waterfall in the world at 3,212 feet (979 m)—roars over a cliff in Venezuela. It would take 11 football fields stacked end-to-end to reach the top.

Economics What is one of the rivers that provides Venezuela with hydroelectric power?

Cultural Kaleidoscope

Venezuela Most Venezuelan cities have a *Plaza Bolívar*—a public square honoring the South American liberator, Simón Bolívar. Venezuelans consider it rude to behave disrespectfully in one of these squares. They also take negative comments about Bolívar as an insult.

More About the Photo

Angel Falls The water at Angel Falls does not pour over the top of the mesa—which is named Auyán Tepui, or "Devil's Mountain." Rather, the river flows in underground streams beneath the mesa's surface and emerges 200 to 300 feet (61 to 91 m) below the top.

Caption Answer the Orinoco

Cooperative Learning Activity

Comparing Governments Organize students into four groups and assign one of the countries of Caribbean South America to each group. Direct groups to research the history and government of their assigned country. Have groups present their findings in an illustrated report. After all the reports have been presented, have students discuss the similarities and differences among the governments of these countries. A fifth group may prepare a presentation on the similarities and differences of these governments and that of the United States. **L2**

EE4 Human Systems: Standard 12

More About the Photo

Celebration Most Venezuelans follow the Roman Catholic faith, so many of the celebrations are associated with religious observances. While some celebrations involve dancing, music, costumes, and parades, many involve attending Mass, a type of worship service.

Caption Answer Roman Catholicism

Reading Check Answer

oil/petroleum

Section Quiz 22-2

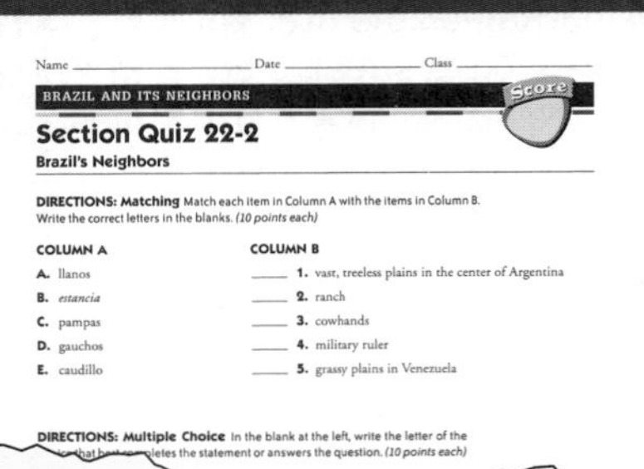

Name ______ Date ______ Class ______

BRAZIL AND ITS NEIGHBORS

Score

Section Quiz 22-2

Brazil's Neighbors

DIRECTIONS: Matching Match each item in Column A with the items in Column B. Write the correct letters in the blanks. *(10 points each)*

COLUMN A	COLUMN B
A. llanos	____ **1.** vast, treeless plains in the center of Argentina
B. *estancia*	____ **2.** ranch
C. pampas	____ **3.** cowhands
D. gauchos	____ **4.** military ruler
E. caudillo	____ **5.** grassy plains in Venezuela

DIRECTIONS: Multiple Choice In the blank at the left, write the letter of the ... letes the statement or answers the question. *(10 points each)*

Celebration

Venezuelan dancers in costumes and playing maracas take part in Corpus Christi, a local Roman Catholic celebration.

Religion What is the major religion in Venezuela?

Rising oil prices during the 1970s brought more money to the country. The middle class grew, and many people prospered. When oil prices fell in the 1990s, the country suffered. The government did not have the money to give the poor and unemployed the services they needed. In 1998 Venezuelans showed their impatience with the government. They elected a former military leader, **Hugo Chavez,** as president. Chavez proposed major changes to the country's constitution and economy. In December 1999, the Venezuelan people voted to accept the new constitution.

Venezuela's People Most of Venezuela's 24.6 million people have a mix of European, African, and Native American backgrounds. Spanish is the major language of the country, and the major religion is Roman Catholicism. More than 90 percent of Venezuelans live in cities. More than 4 million people live in Caracas, which holds towering skyscrapers surrounded by mountains.

Reading Check What product changed Venezuela's economy?

The Guianas

Caribbean South America also includes the countries of Guyana (gy•AH•nuh) and Suriname (SUR•uh•NAH•muh) and the territory of French Guiana (gee•A•nuh). Guyana was a British colony called British Guiana. Suriname, once a colony of the Netherlands, was called Dutch Guiana. As a result, these three lands are called "the Guianas."

The climate in the Guianas is hot and tropical. Most people live on the coastal plains because of the cooling ocean winds. Sugarcane grows in Guyana and French Guiana, while rice and bananas flourish in Suriname. Many people also earn their living mining gold and bauxite.

Guyana In the early 1600s, the Dutch were the first Europeans to settle in Guyana. They forced Native Americans and Africans to work on tobacco, coffee, and cotton farms and, later, on sugarcane plantations. The United Kingdom won possession of the Dutch colonies in the early 1800s and ended slavery. Still needing workers, the British paid Indians from Asia to move here. Today people from India make up most of Guyana's population. Another one-third are of African ancestry. Small numbers of Native Americans and Europeans also live here. Christianity and Hinduism are the chief religions. Most people speak English. **Georgetown,** the capital, is the major city.

Guyana won its independence from Britain in 1966. Guyana remains a very poor country, however, and depends on aid from the United Kingdom.

Meeting Special Needs

Interpersonal Have students research the ethnic, political, and religious differences among major components of the population in Guyana and Suriname. Have students think about what problems might arise because of these differences. **Ask: How might these differences divide society? How could they hold back economic development? What steps could a government take to try to overcome these differences?** Have students discuss their answers to these questions as a class. **L1**

Refer to *Inclusion for the Middle School Social Studies Classroom Strategies and Activities* in the TCR.

Suriname The British were the first Europeans to settle Suriname, but the Dutch gained control in 1667. As in Guyana, the Dutch brought enslaved Africans to work on large sugar plantations. Because of harsh treatment, many Africans fled into the isolated interior of the country. Their descendants still live there today. Later the Dutch hired workers from the Asian lands of India and Indonesia.

Asians form a large part of Suriname's population. About half of Suriname's people practice Christianity. The rest follow Hinduism or Islam. The main language is Dutch. **Paramaribo** (PAH•rah•MAH•ree•boh) is the capital and chief port. In 1975 Suriname won its independence from the Dutch. The country is poor, so it still relies on Dutch aid.

French Guiana French Guiana became a colony of France in the 1600s and remains one today. The country is headed by a French official called a *prefect,* who lives in the capital, **Cayenne** (ky•EHN). The French government provides jobs and aid to many of French Guiana's people.

Most people in French Guiana are of African or mixed African and European ancestry. They speak French and are Roman Catholic. In Cayenne, you see sidewalk cafés, police in French uniforms, and shoppers using francs, the French currency—just as you would in Paris, France. You also see local influences, such as Carnival, Native American woodcarving, and Caribbean music and dance.

✓Reading Check **What European countries influenced the development of Guyana, Suriname, and French Guiana?**

Section 2 Assessment

Defining Terms

1. **Define** pampas, *estancia,* gaucho, hydroelectric power, llanos, altitude, caudillo.

Recalling Facts

2. **Region** Describe two ways in which the pampas are similar to the Great Plains of the United States.
3. **Human/Environment Interaction** What is the significance of the Itaipu Dam?
4. **History** Who was Simón Bolívar?

Critical Thinking

5. **Analyzing Cause and Effect** Which of Juan Perón's policies led to his removal from office?
6. **Drawing Conclusions** Why is Hinduism one of the major religions of Guyana?

Graphic Organizer

7. **Organizing Information** Create a diagram like this one. In the top box, under the heading, list similarities about the Guianas. In the bottom boxes, under the headings, write facts about each country that show their differences.

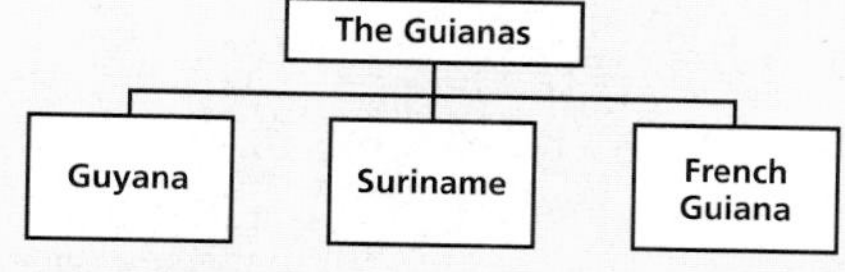

Applying Social Studies Skills

8. **Analyzing Maps** Look at the physical map on page 583. Which of Brazil's neighbors in this section have mountain elevations above 10,000 feet?

Section 2 Assessment

1. The terms are defined in the Glossary.
2. They have fertile soil and a mild climate; they are home to farmers who grow grains and ranchers who raise livestock.
3. It is the world's largest hydroelectric power generator.
4. leader of the revolt against Spanish rule that gained independence for Venezuela and neighboring regions
5. cracking down on freedom of speech and press
6. People from India make up most of Guyana's population.
7. Students should list differences as found in the textbook.
8. Argentina

Chapter 22

Section 2, pages 589–595

✓ Reading Check Answer

Guyana—Great Britain; Suriname—Netherlands; French Guiana—France

Reteach

Give students an outline map of the region and have them label Brazil's seven neighboring countries, their capitals, major landforms, and economic activities.

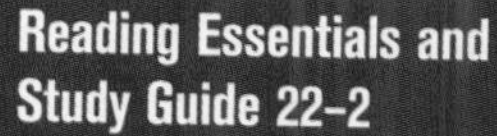

Reading Essentials and Study Guide 22-2

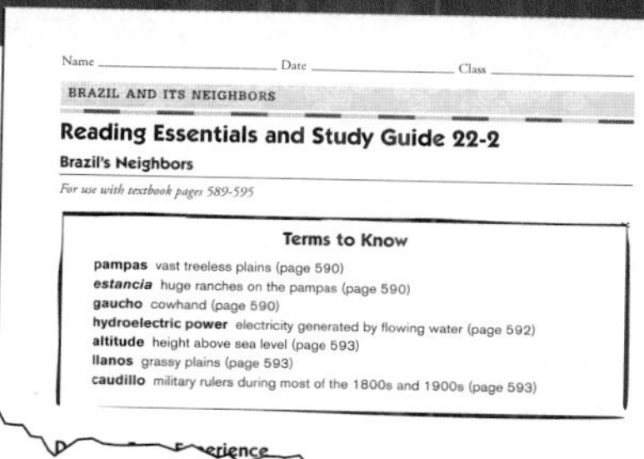

Name ______ Date ______ Class ______

BRAZIL AND ITS NEIGHBORS

Reading Essentials and Study Guide 22-2

Brazil's Neighbors

For use with textbook pages 589-595

Terms to Know

pampas vast treeless plains (page 590)
estancia huge ranches on the pampas (page 590)
gaucho cowhand (page 590)
hydroelectric power electricity generated by flowing water (page 592)
altitude height above sea level (page 593)
llanos grassy plains (page 593)
caudillo military rulers during most of the 1800s and 1900s (page 593)

Enrich

Have students research the history of one of the countries in this region and create an annotated time line, complete with illustrations and captions.

4 CLOSE

Have students write a paragraph contrasting life in the United States with life in one of the countries covered in this section.

TEACH

Ask students if they are familiar with songs, books, or movies about the life of American cowboys. Ask volunteers to identify what values these works often portray. *(Possible answers include self-reliance, hard work, toughness, affection for animals, and respect for others.)* Suggest that they look for similar values in this poem. **L1**

More About José Hernandez

Hernández was born in Buenos Aires, but he became acquainted with the life of the gaucho in his teens when he was sent to live in the countryside for his health. His poem aimed to celebrate the lost life of the gauchos to whom, Hernández felt, the people of Argentina owed much and who were threatened by modernization.

Interdisciplinary Connections

Literature *The Gaucho Martín Fierro* is now seen as the impassioned praise of a persecuted minority. Have students select a group that they feel is threatened by social changes and write a short poem celebrating that group's way of life. Ask for volunteers to read their poems to the class.

Making Connections

CULTURE | GOVERNMENT | PEOPLE | TECHNOLOGY

Poetry on the Pampas

As you learned in Section 2, gauchos herd cattle on the pampas. In 1872 José Hernández wrote the epic poem *El Gaucho Martín Fierro.* The poem tells the story of Martín Fierro, who recalls his life as a gaucho on the pampas. The following lines were translated from the poem.

El Gaucho Martín Fierro

by José Hernández (1834–1886)

A son am I of the rolling plain,
A gaucho born and bred;
For me the whole great world is small,
Believe me, my heart can hold it all;
The snake strikes not at my passing foot,
The sun burns not my head.

. . . .

Ah, my mind goes back and I see again
The gaucho I knew of old;
He picked his mount, and was ready aye,
To sing or fight, and for work or play,
And even the poorest one was rich
In the things not bought with gold.

The neediest gaucho in the land,
That had least of goods and gear,
Could show a troop of a single strain,
And rode with a silver-studded rein,
The plains were brown with the grazing herds,
And everywhere was cheer.

And when the time of the branding came,
It did one good to see
How the hand was quick and the eye
was true,
When the steers they threw with the
long lassoo [lasso],
And the merry band that the years have swept
Like leaves from the autumn tree.

Gauchos on Argentina's pampas ▲

Making the Connection

1. How does the poet describe the land on which the gaucho lives?
2. How can you tell from the poem that a gaucho is often on the move?
3. **Drawing Conclusions** What evidence does the poem give that the gaucho's way of life was a proud and happy one?

Making the Connection

1. Hernández describes the land as a rolling plain that has snakes and hot sun and is full of the vast herds of cattle.
2. The poem mentions that snakes cannot strike at the passing gaucho; a gaucho picked his horse and was ready to ride.
3. The lines printed here mention that even the poorest gaucho was rich and rode with a silver-studded rein, and everywhere there was cheer.

Chapter 22 Reading Review

Section 1 Brazil

Terms to Know
- basin
- *selva*
- escarpment
- favela
- deforestation
- republic

Main Idea

Brazil is a large country with many resources, a lively culture, and serious economic challenges.

✓ **History** Brazil declared independence in 1822 after centuries of colonial rule by Portugal.

✓ **Economics** Brazil is trying to reduce its number of poor people and balance the use of resources with the preservation of its rain forests.

✓ **Culture** Most Brazilians are of mixed Portuguese, African, Native American, and Asian ancestry.

Section 2 Brazil's Neighbors

Terms to Know
- pampas
- *estancia*
- gaucho
- hydroelectric power
- llanos
- altitude
- caudillo

Main Idea

Brazil's neighbors give South America a diverse array of landforms, climates, and cultures.

✓ **History** Simón Bolívar led a revolt that freed Venezuela from Spanish rule in 1830.

✓ **Culture** Argentina's capital, Buenos Aires, is a huge city with European style.

✓ **Economics** Uruguay and Paraguay have large areas of grass-covered plains that support ranching and industries that depend on raising livestock.

✓ **Culture** Most Venezuelans are of mixed European, African, and Native American ancestry. Most live in cities in the central highlands.

✓ **Culture** Guyana and Suriname have large numbers of people descended from workers who were brought from Africa and Asia.

Shepherd and sheep dogs on plateau of Patagonia in southern Argentina ▶

Reading Review

Use the Chapter 22 Reading Review to preview, review, condense, or reteach the chapter.

Preview/Review

Use the Terms to Know lists to help students review and study.

Activity Have students group the terms according to the category to which they belong—physical geography, economics, human geography. Read the terms aloud, one at a time, and ask for volunteers to categorize each.

Vocabulary PuzzleMaker Software reinforces the vocabulary terms used in Chapter 22.

The Interactive Tutor Self-Assessment CD-ROM allows students to review Chapter 22 content.

Condense

Have students read the Chapter 22 summary statements.

Chapter 22 Guided Reading Activities

Chapter 22 Audio Program

Reteach

Reteaching Activity 22

Chapter 22 Reading Essentials and Study Guide

Chapter Culminating Activity

Creating a Photo Album Have students choose one of the countries studied in this chapter and imagine that they have visited there. Ask them to create a photo album that shows what they saw in the country. They should look for photographs that show the landscape, cities, places of interest, and people of their chosen country. With each photograph, have them write a brief caption that identifies the subject of the photo and gives additional information about it. *NOTE: This activity may be completed separately or you may wish students to incorporate it into their Current Events Journals.* **L1**

EE2 Places and Regions: Standard 4

Assessment and Activities

GLENCOE TECHNOLOGY

MindJogger Videoquiz
Use MindJogger to review the Chapter 22 content.

 Available in VHS.

Using Key Terms

1. g
2. j
3. a
4. d
5. f
6. b
7. i
8. c
9. e
10. h

Reviewing the Main Ideas

11. Millions of inland-dwellers have moved to coastal cities to find better jobs.
12. People from 18 to 70 are required by law to vote.
13. 1960; to encourage people to move inland
14. 85 percent of Argentina's people are European immigrants or of European ancestry.
15. Spanish; Roman Catholicism
16. agriculture and hydroelectric power
17. oil
18. Most live on the coastal plains because the ocean keeps the climate temperate.
19. French Guiana

Chapter 22 Assessment and Activities

Using Key Terms

Match the terms in Part A with their definitions in Part B.

A.

1. basin
2. *estancia*
3. escarpment
4. caudillo
5. altitude
6. gaucho
7. *selva*
8. deforestation
9. llanos
10. pampas

B.

a. steep cliff separating two flat land surfaces, one higher than the other
b. cowhand
c. cutting down large areas of forest
d. military ruler
e. large, grassy plains region with many ranches, farms, and oil fields
f. height above sea level
g. broad, flat lowland surrounded by higher land
h. vast treeless plains
i. rain forest in Brazil
j. large ranch in Argentina

Reviewing the Main Ideas

Section 1 Brazil

11. **History** Why are Brazil's inland areas sparsely populated?
12. **Government** What are the voting requirements in Brazil?
13. **History** When and why did Brazil's government move the capital city to Brasília?

Section 2 Brazil's Neighbors

14. **Culture** Why is the European influence so strong in Argentina today?
15. **Culture** What are the major language and religion of Uruguay?
16. **Economics** What are the major economic activities of Paraguay?
17. **Economics** Which of Venezuela's resources is its main source of income?
18. **Culture** Where do most of the people of the Guianas live? Why do they live there?
19. **History** Which of Brazil's neighbors has been a colony of France since the 1600s?

NATIONAL GEOGRAPHIC Brazil and Its Neighbors

Place Location Activity

On a separate sheet of paper, match the letters on the map with the numbered places listed below.

1. Brazil
2. Amazon River
3. Argentina
4. Rio de Janeiro
5. Paraguay
6. Orinoco River
7. Río de la Plata
8. Venezuela
9. Brasília
10. Suriname

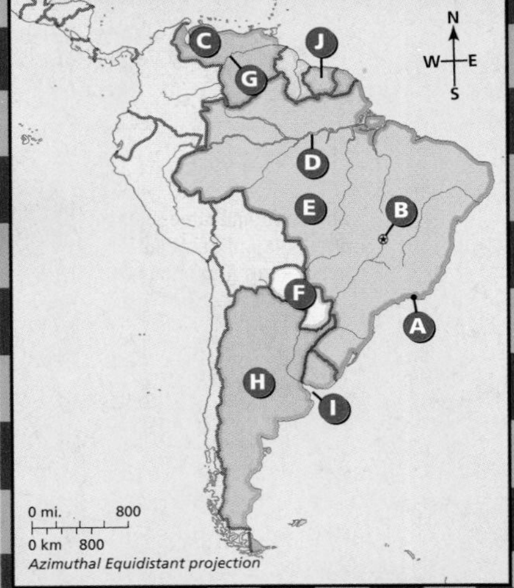

NATIONAL GEOGRAPHIC Place Location Activity

1. E
2. D
3. H
4. A
5. F
6. G
7. I
8. C
9. B
10. J

Critical Thinking

20. Argentina produces many manufactured goods, such as food products, automobiles, chemicals, textiles, books, and magazines.
21. Students' charts will vary. Possible answers: *For*—to help economy, provide jobs and products; *Against*—damages the land, mercury builds up in streams, Native Americans threatened

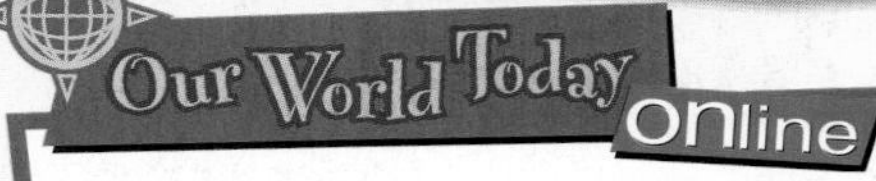

Self-Check Quiz Visit the ***Our World Today: People, Places, and Issues*** Web site at owt.glencoe.com and click on **Chapter 22–Self-Check Quizzes** to prepare for the Chapter Test.

Critical Thinking

20. **Analyzing Information** What facts support the statement "Argentina is one of the most industrialized countries in South America"?
21. **Identifying Points of View** In a chart like the one below, identify arguments for and against the cutting down of the rain forest.

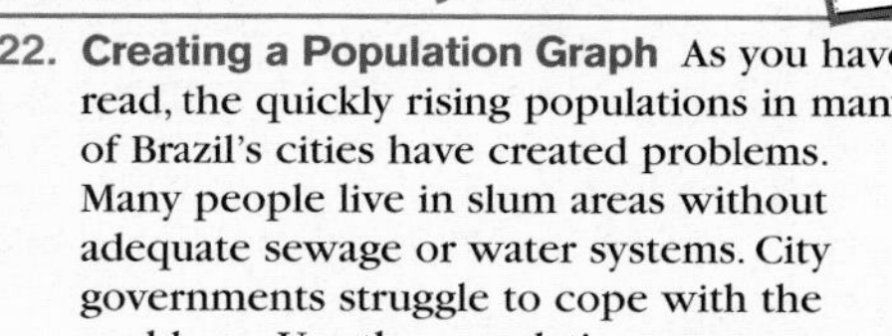

Cutting Down the Rain Forest	
For	Against

Current Events Journal

22. **Creating a Population Graph** As you have read, the quickly rising populations in many of Brazil's cities have created problems. Many people live in slum areas without adequate sewage or water systems. City governments struggle to cope with the problems. Use the population map on page 576 to create a bar graph of Brazil's five largest cities for the year 2001.

Mental Mapping Activity

23. **Focusing on the Region** Create an outline map of South America. Refer to the map on page 574; then label the following:

- Caribbean Sea
- Brazil
- Atlantic Ocean
- Argentina
- Pacific Ocean
- Brazilian Highlands
- Amazon River
- Río de la Plata
- Venezuela
- Guiana Highlands

Technology Skills Activity

24. **Using the Internet** Conduct a search for information about the Amazon rain forest and create an annotated bibliography of five useful Web sites. Your bibliography should contain the Web address, a brief summary of the information found on the site, and a statement of why you think the site is useful.

Standardized Test Practice

Directions: Read the passage below and answer the question that follows.

The Amazon Basin is a gigantic system of rivers and rain forests, covering half of Brazil and extending into neighboring countries. Much of the Amazon is still unexplored, and the rain forest holds many secrets. Some of the animals found here include the jaguar, tapir, spider monkey, sloth, river dolphin, and boa constrictor. Forest birds include toucans, parrots, hummingbirds, and hawks. More than 1,800 species of butterflies and 200 species of mosquitoes give you an idea about the insect population. In addition, the fish—such as piranha, pirarucu, and electric eel—are very unusual. Biologists cannot identify much of the catch found in markets.

1. On the basis of this passage, which of the following generalizations is most accurate?

F The Amazon rain forest covers about one-third of the South American continent.
G Native Americans living in the rain forest are losing their old way of life.
H The Amazon Basin is huge, and its rain forests hold thousands of animal species.
J The Amazon Basin is located only in Brazil.

Test-Taking Tip: This question asks you to make a generalization about the Amazon Basin. A *generalization* is a broad statement. Look for facts and the main idea *in the passage* to support your answer. Do not rely only on your memory. The main idea can help you eliminate answers that do not fit. Also, look for the statement that is true and that is covered in the paragraph.

Assessment and Activities

Standardized Test Practice

1. H

Tested Objectives:
Analyzing information, making generalizations

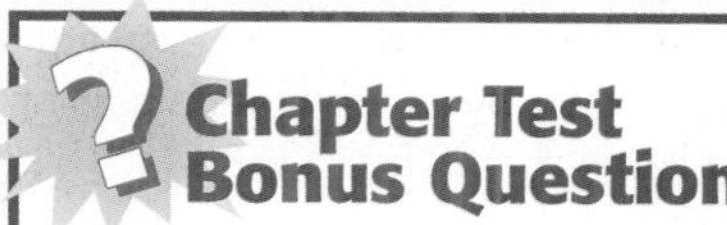

Chapter Test Bonus Question

This question may be used for extra credit on the chapter test.

This country is the only one in the region that was once a colony of Portugal. *(Brazil)*

Have students visit the Web site at **owt.glencoe.com** to review Chapter 22 and take the Self-Check Quiz.

Current Events Journal

22. Students' bar graphs should accurately present the following information for the year 2001:

São Paulo	16,925,000
Rio de Janeiro	11,050,000
Belo Horizonte	3,340,000
Recife	2,860,000
Porto Alegre	2,850,000

Mental Mapping Activity

23. This exercise helps students visualize the countries and geographic features they have been studying and to understand the relationship among various points. All attempts at freehand mapping should be accepted.

Technology Skills Activity

24. Students' bibliographies should include at least five sites, each of which is evaluated in terms of its usefulness.

Ask students to imagine the following situation: A lake near their town is about to be filled in to allow a shopping mall to be built. The lake is the only place where gilded grumpfish are known to live. Would students vote for the mall plan to proceed, or would they vote to stop the project to protect the grumpfish? Why? After discussion, tell students that governments controlling rain forest areas face similar problems.

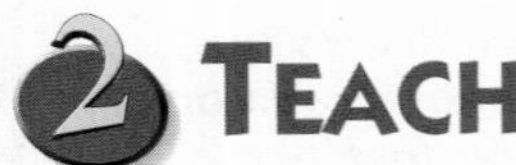

Designing Campaign Buttons Have students research animals that live in the rain forests of Brazil. Tell them to choose one animal and to use this animal as the basis of the slogan and design of a "Save the Rain Forest Wildlife" campaign button. Have students display their button designs. **L1 ELL**

Meeting National Standards

Geography for Life

The following standards are met in the Student Edition feature:

EE4 Human Systems: Standards 11, 12

EE5 Environment and Society: Standard 14, 15, 16

EE6 The Uses of Geography: Standard 18

EYE on the Environment

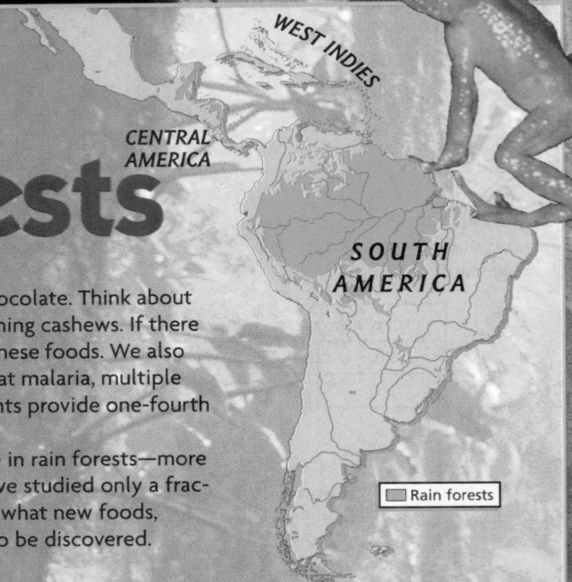

VANISHING Rain Forests

Rain Forest Riches Imagine never tasting chocolate. Think about never eating a banana, chewing gum, or munching cashews. If there were no rain forests, we would have none of these foods. We also would not have many of the drugs used to treat malaria, multiple sclerosis, and leukemia. In fact, rain forest plants provide one-fourth of the world's medicines.

Millions of kinds of plants and animals live in rain forests—more than half of all species on Earth. Scientists have studied only a fraction of these species. So no one really knows what new foods, medicines, or animals are there, just waiting to be discovered.

Rain Forest Destruction Yet we may never know. Why? Because a chunk of rain forest the size of two football fields vanishes every second! The forests are being destroyed for many reasons.

- Loggers cut trees and sell the lumber worldwide.
- Ranchers and farmers clear land for cattle and crops.
- Miners level acres of forest to get at valuable minerals.

People are trying to find ways to use rain forests without destroying them. Changing farming practices and developing different forest industries are possible solutions. However, time is running out. Can we afford to lose rain forests and all their treasures?

Settlers clear trees for a home in the rain forest.

Male golden toad

600 UNIT 3

More About the Issues

Environment and Society One of the many problems resulting from the development of the rain forests is the displacement of indigenous peoples. These native peoples, recognized by countries as an important resource, are as endangered as the plants and animals in the region. Throughout the Americas and beyond, local, national, and international organizations have begun to protest the displacement of these peoples and to work to secure their land and resource rights. See if students can come up with similar examples of cultural conflicts and cooperation in the United States. **L2**

Making a Difference

Discovering New Monkeys How would it feel to discover an animal that no one knew existed? Dutch scientist Marc van Roosmalen knows. He recently discovered a new species of monkey (photo, at right) in Brazil.

Van Roosmalen runs an orphanage for abandoned monkeys. One day, a man showed up with a tiny monkey van Roosmalen had never seen before. He spent about a year tracking down a wild population of the monkeys deep in the Amazon rain forest. Of some 250 kinds of monkeys known worldwide, about 80 live in Brazil. At least 7 new species have been discovered since 1990.

New species *Callithrix humilis*, a dwarf marmoset

Rain Forest Field Trip With help from the Children's Environmental Trust Foundation, students from Millbrook, New York, traveled to Peru's Yarapa River region, deep in the Amazon rain forest. Students studied the forest from platforms built in the canopy, and they soared among the tall trees using ropes. The students met rain forest creatures at night, went bird-watching at dawn, and swam in the Yarapa River—home to crocodiles called caimans.

Back in Millbrook, the students educate others about saving rain forests. They also raise money to help support a Peruvian zoo that protects rain forest animals.

Millbrook student traps insects for study.

What Can You Do?

Write a Note
Write to your government representatives and encourage them to support plans that help save rain forests.

Check Out Your Community
What environmental problems face your community? What can you do to help solve the problems? For example, does your community have problems with water pollution or water shortages? What steps does your community take to make sure you have clean water to drink?

Use the Internet
Learn more about efforts to save rain forests. Check out the Rainforest Action Network at *www.ran.org* or search National Geographic's Web site at *www.nationalgeographic.com*

601

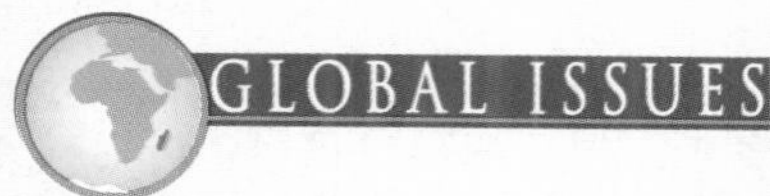

Interdependence Many scientists believe that the medicinal applications of rain forest plants and animals have been only partially explored. Further experimentation might also help to preserve the rain forest.

Have students work individually or in groups to complete the What Can You Do? activities.

Discuss with students the What Can You Do? activities. Encourage them to find out more about the groups that are working to save the rain forest. Students might want to start their own local organization to help in this work.

For an additional regional case study, use the following:

Environmental Case Study 8

What Can You Do? Teacher Tips

Write a Note: Remind students who write to a public official to include statistics and rational arguments supporting their position. Remind them also to carefully proofread their work. You might research in advance to locate the addresses of your state's senators and member of the House of Representatives.

Check Out Your Community: Have students brainstorm possible sources of information on local environmental issues. The telephone book and the Internet might provide some suggestions if they are having difficulty generating ideas.

Chapter 23 Resources

Note: The following materials may be used when teaching Chapter 23.
Section level support materials are shown at point of use in the margins of the Teacher Wraparound Edition.

Timesaving Tools

TeacherWorks™ All-In-One Planner and Resource Center

- **Interactive Teacher Edition** See the **Interactive Teacher Edition** CD-ROM to electronically integrate your Teacher Wraparound Edition and blackline masters.
- **Interactive Lesson Planner** Organize your week, month, semester, or year with all the lesson helps you need. The **Interactive Lesson Planner** CD-ROM contains all Chapter 23 resources.

Use Glencoe's **Presentation Plus!** multimedia teacher tool to easily present dynamic lessons that visually excite your students. Using Microsoft PowerPoint® you can customize the presentations to create your own personalized lessons.

TEACHING TRANSPARENCIES

Graphic Organizer Transparency and Student Activity 23

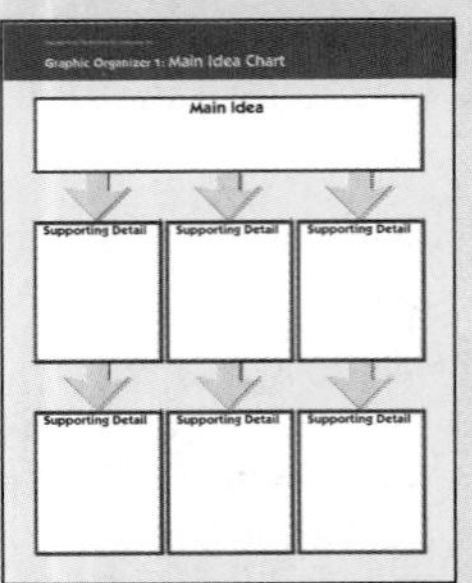

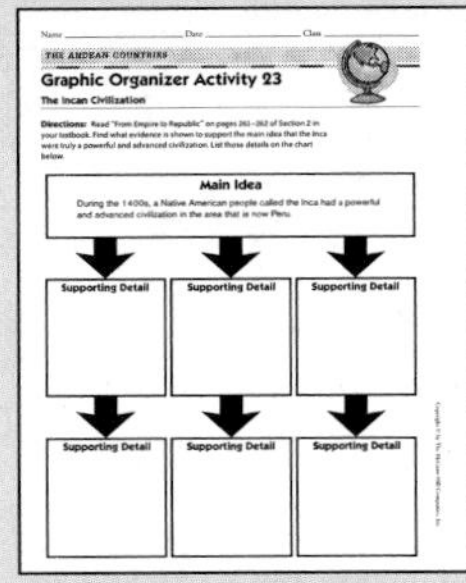

FOLDABLES™ Study Organizer

Foldables are three-dimensional, interactive graphic organizers that help students practice basic writing skills, review key vocabulary terms, and identify main ideas. Every chapter contains a Foldable activity, with additional chapter activities found in the ***Reading and Study Skills Foldables*** booklet.

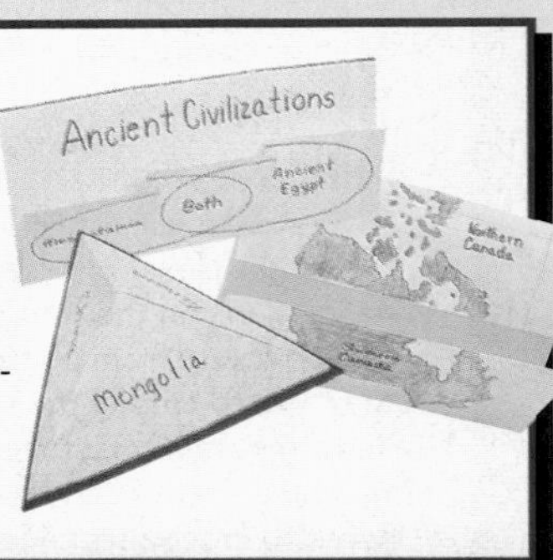

ENRICHMENT AND EXTENSION

Enrichment Activity 23

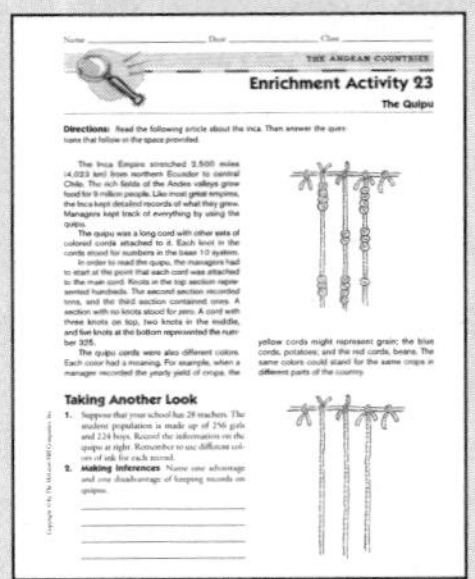

Cooperative Learning Activity 23

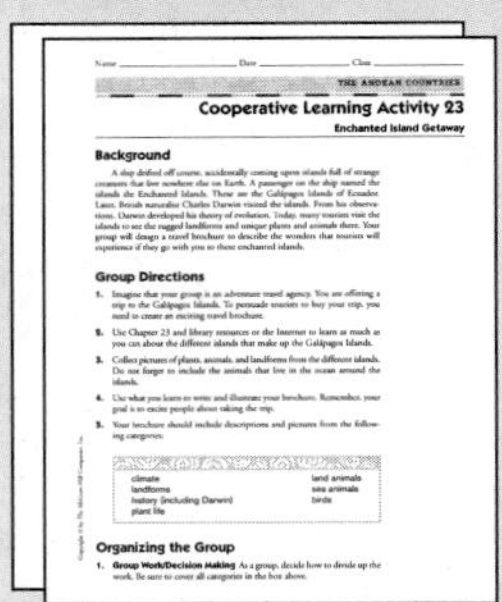

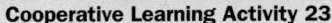

MAP AND GEOGRAPHY SKILLS

Chapter Map Activity 23

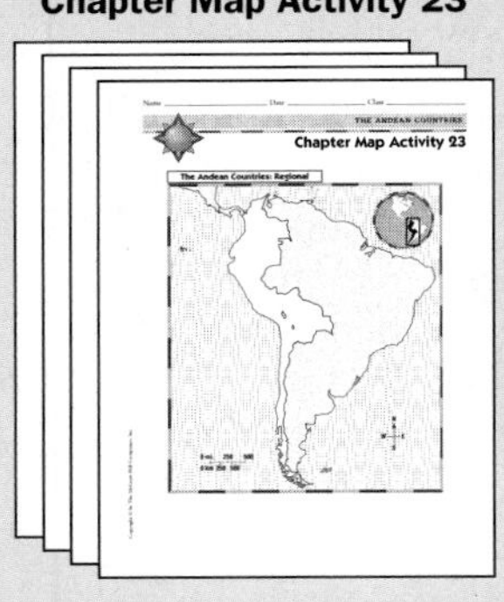

GeoLab Activity 23

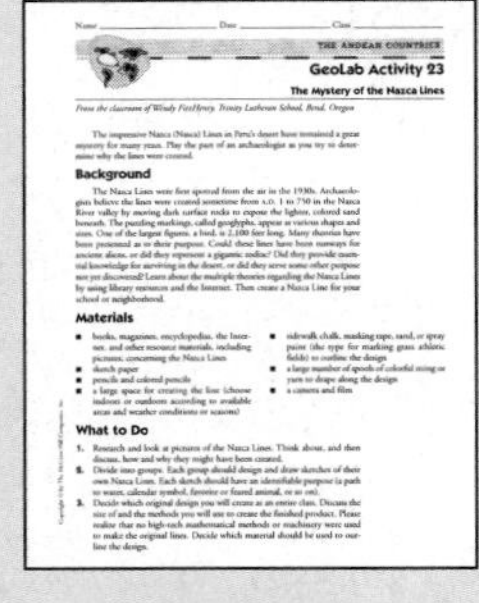

STANDARDIZED ASSESSMENT SKILLS

Glencoe's Assessment Advantage

Critical Thinking Skills Activity 23

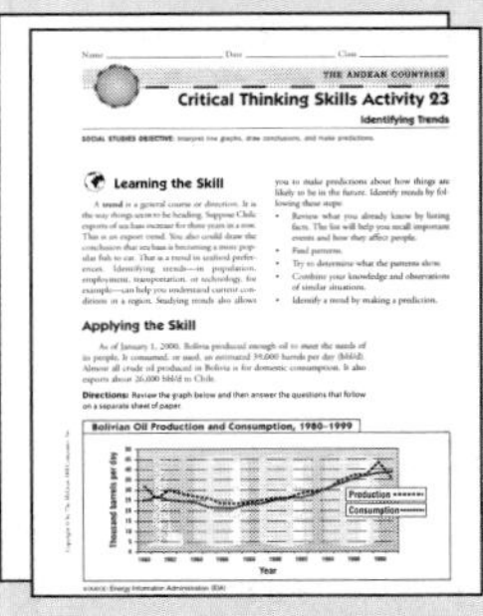

Map and Graph Skills Activity 23

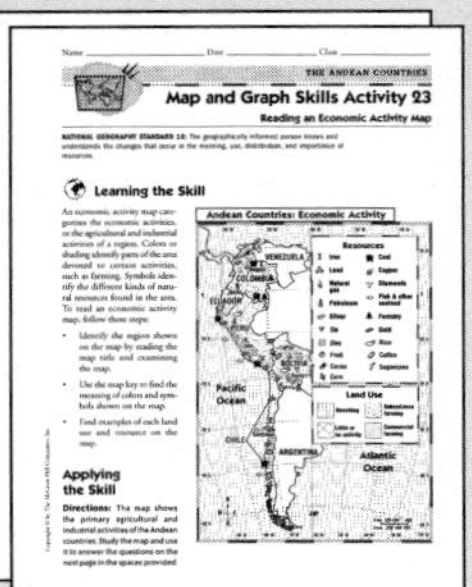

Reading and Writing Skills Activity 23

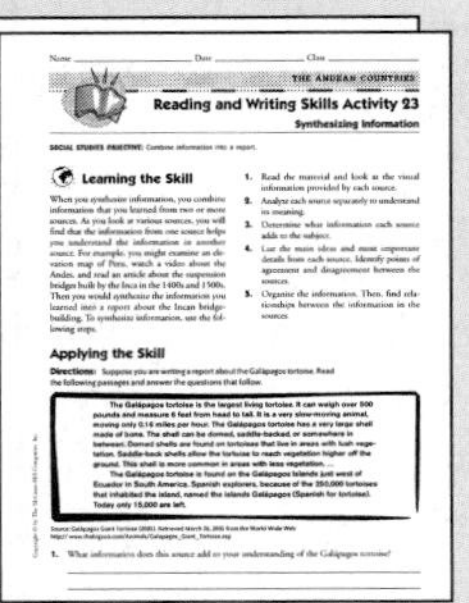

Standardized Test Practice Workbook Activity 23

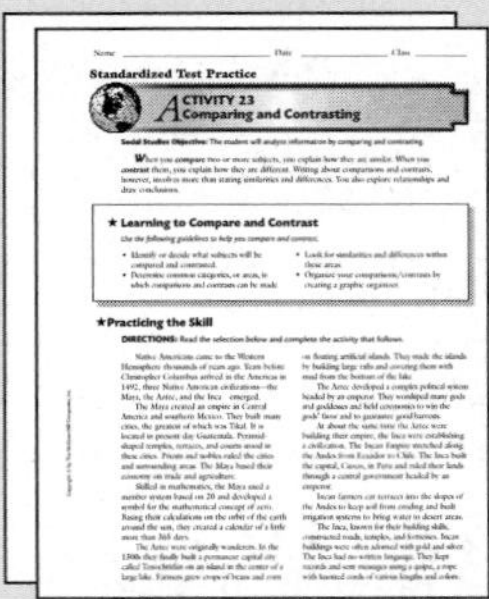

REVIEW AND REINFORCEMENT

Chapter Skills Activity 23

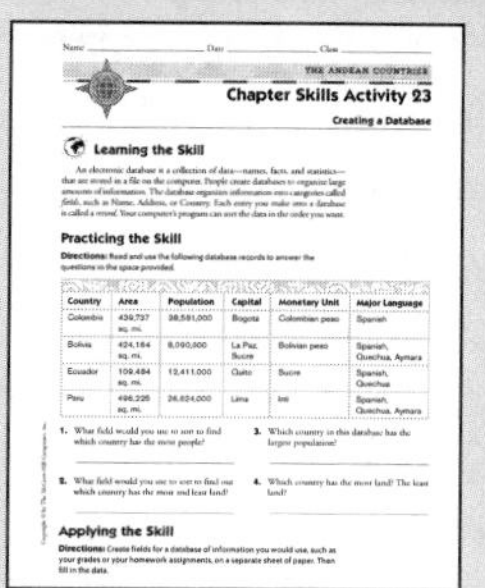

Take-Home Review Activity 23

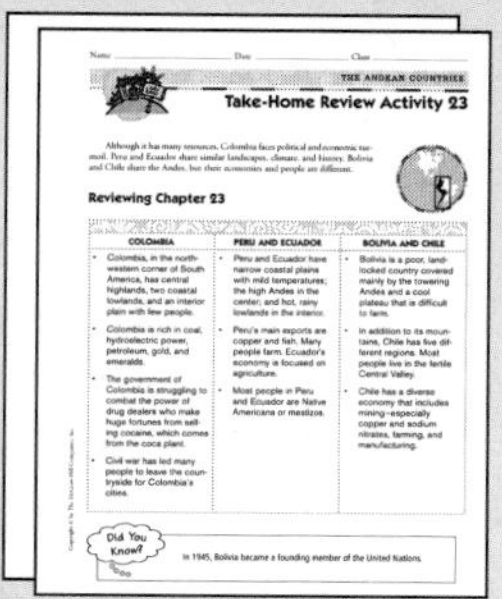

Reteaching Activity 23

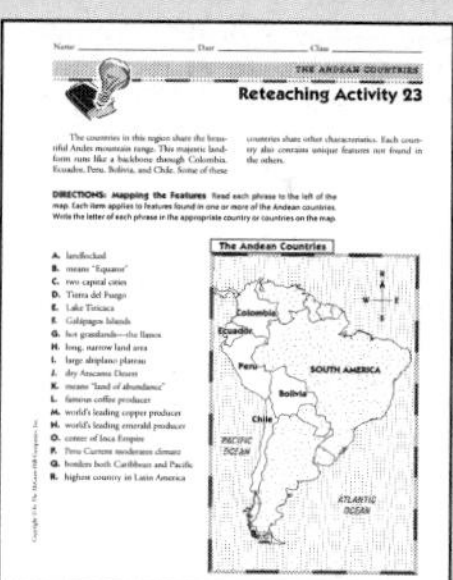

Vocabulary Activity 23

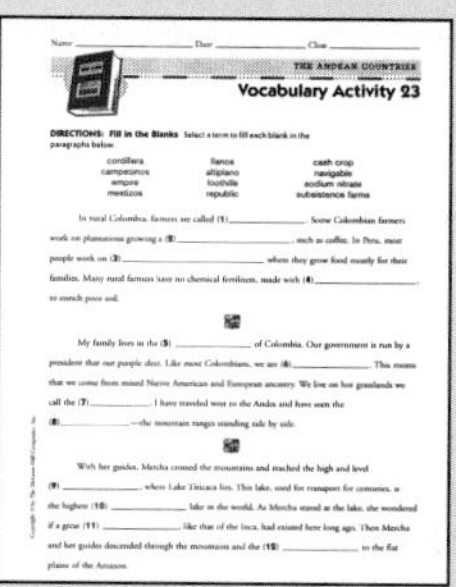

Workbook Activity 23

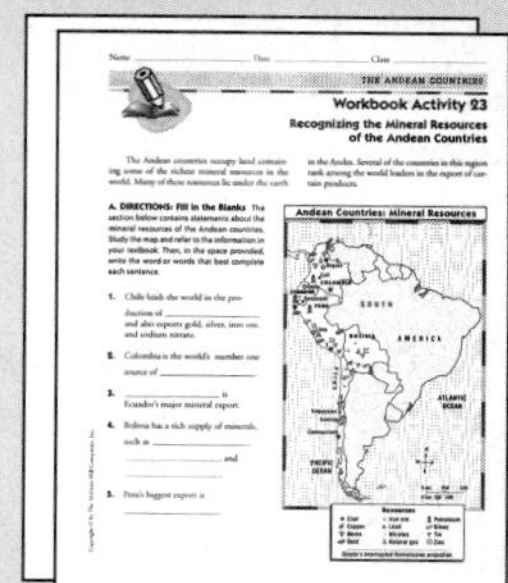

ASSESSMENT

GLENCOE'S ASSESSMENT ADVANTAGE

Chapter 23 Test, Form A

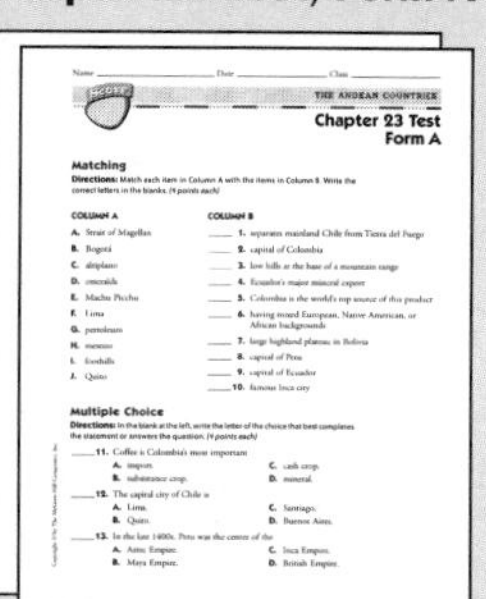

Chapter 23 Test, Form B

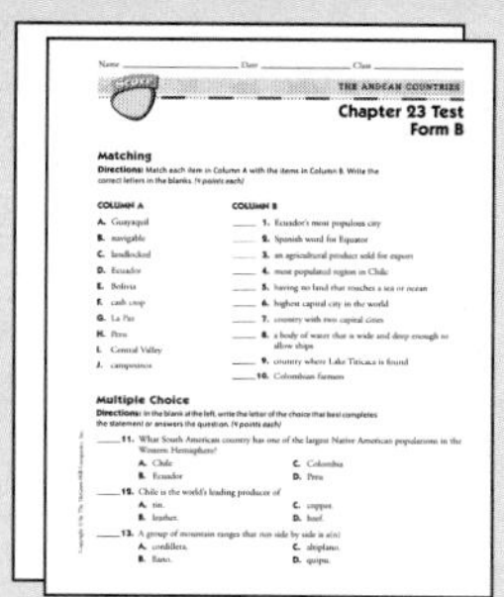

Performance Assessment Activity 23

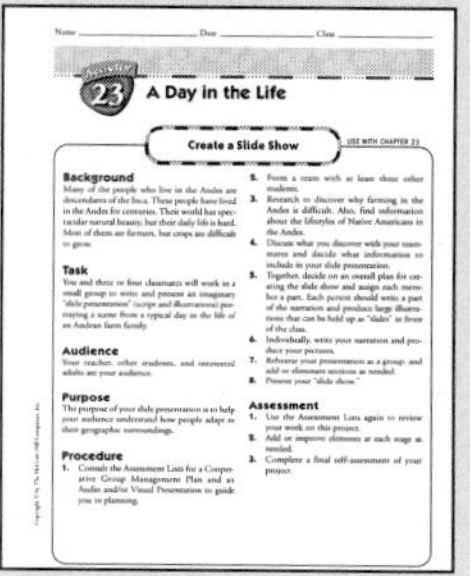

ExamView® Pro 3.0 Testmaker CD-ROM

MULTIMEDIA

- National Geographic's The World and Its People
- MindJogger Videoquiz
- Vocabulary PuzzleMaker Software
- Interactive Tutor Self-Assessment CD-ROM
- ExamView® Pro 3.0 Testmaker CD-ROM
- Interactive Lesson Planner CD-ROM
- Interactive Teacher Edition CD-ROM
- Skillbuilder Interactive Workbook CD-ROM, Level 1
- Presentation Plus! CD-ROM
- Audio Program

SPANISH RESOURCES

The following Spanish language materials are available in the Spanish Resources binder:

- Spanish Chapter Summaries
- Spanish Vocabulary Activities
- Spanish Guided Reading Activities
- Spanish Quizzes and Tests
- Spanish Take-Home Review Activities
- Spanish Reteaching Activities

Meeting National Standards

Geography for Life

All of the 18 standards are demonstrated in Unit 8. The following ones are highlighted in Chapter 23:

Section 1 **EE4 Human Systems: Standards 11, 12, 13**

Section 2 **EE4 Human Systems: Standards 9, 10**

EE5 Environment and Society: Standards 14, 15

Section 3 **EE4 Human Systems: Standards 9, 10, 11, 12, 13**

EE5 Environment and Society: Standards 14, 15, 16

For a complete listing of National Geography Standards and entire text correlation, see pages T22–T29.

Local Objectives

____

____

Chapter 23 Planning Guide

SECTION RESOURCES

Daily Objectives	Reproducible Resources	Multimedia Resources
Section 1 **Colombia** **Suggested Pacing = 1 day** **1.** Locate Colombia on a map or globe and describe its landforms. **2.** Discuss Colombia's economy and the challenges it faces. **3.** Describe Colombia's history and people.	Reproducible Lesson Plan 23-1 Daily Lecture and Discussion Notes 23-1 Guided Reading Activity 23-1 Reading Essentials and Study Guide 23-1 Section Quiz 23-1*	Daily Focus Skills Transparency 23-1 GeoQuiz Transparency 23-1 Vocabulary PuzzleMaker Software Interactive Tutor Self-Assessment CD-ROM ExamView® Pro 3.0 Testmaker CD-ROM Presentation Plus! CD-ROM
Section 2 **Peru and Ecuador** **Suggested Pacing = 1 day** **1.** Describe the landforms and climates of Peru and Ecuador. **2.** Compare how the people of Peru and Ecuador earn a living. **3.** Discuss what the people of Peru and Ecuador are like.	Reproducible Lesson Plan 23-2 Daily Lecture and Discussion Notes 23-2 Guided Reading Activity 23-2 Reading Essentials and Study Guide 23-2 Section Quiz 23-2*	Daily Focus Skills Transparency 23-2 GeoQuiz Transparency 23-1 Vocabulary PuzzleMaker Software Interactive Tutor Self-Assessment CD-ROM ExamView® Pro 3.0 Testmaker CD-ROM Presentation Plus! CD-ROM
Section 3 **Bolivia and Chile** **Suggested Pacing = 1 day** **1.** Identify where Bolivia and Chile are located. **2.** Describe the landforms and climates found in Bolivia and Chile. **3.** Compare the economies and people of Bolivia and Chile.	Reproducible Lesson Plan 23-3 Daily Lecture and Discussion Notes 23-3 Guided Reading Activity 23-3 Reading Essentials and Study Guide 23-3 Section Quiz 23-3*	Daily Focus Skills Transparency 23-3 GeoQuiz Transparency 23-1 Vocabulary PuzzleMaker Software Interactive Tutor Self-Assessment CD-ROM ExamView® Pro 3.0 Testmaker CD-ROM Presentation Plus! CD-ROM

00:00 **Out of Time?** Assign the **Reading Essentials and Study Guide** for this chapter.

*Also available in Spanish

KEY TO ABILITY LEVELS

Teaching strategies have been coded for varying learning styles and abilities.

L1 **BASIC** activities for all students
L2 **AVERAGE** activities for average to above-average students
L3 **CHALLENGING** activities for above-average students
ELL **ENGLISH LANGUAGE LEARNER** activities

Blackline Master
Software
CD-ROM
Audiocassette
Transparency
Videocassette
Block Scheduling
DVD

Teacher to Teacher

News Maps

Provide students with an outline map of the world with the seven culture regions separated by a thick border: North America; South America; Europe; Russia; Africa South of the Sahara; North Africa, Southwest Asia, and Central Asia; and Australia, Oceania, and Antarctica. Ask students to find one newspaper article for each culture region. They are to read the article and write a summary of its main points. Students then glue their summary to its proper place on the map. Then they must highlight the name of the country within the summary that shows it belongs in that particular culture region.

Nora Austin
Chestnut Community School
Belchertown, Massachusetts

Jean Serafino
Chestnut Community School
Belchertown, Massachusetts

*Adapted from John Daley's "Newsmap" at geobeast@massed.net

OUR WORLD TODAY Online

Use our Web site for additional resources. All essential content is covered in the Student Edition.

You and your students can visit owt.glencoe.com, the Web site companion to *Our World Today*. This innovative integration of electronic and print media offers your students a wealth of opportunities. The student text directs students to the Web site for the following options:

- Chapter Overviews
- Student Web Activities
- Self-Check Quizzes
- Textbook Updates

Answers are provided for you in the Web Activity Lesson Plan. Additional Web resources and Interactive Tutor puzzles are also available.

NATIONAL GEOGRAPHIC TEACHER'S CORNER

Index to National Geographic Magazine:

The following articles may be used for research relating to this chapter:

- "Lost Tombs of Peru," by Peter Lerche, September 2000.
- "Sierra Madre Pilgrimage," by Paul Salopek, June 2000.
- "Chiquibul Cave," by Thomas Miller, April 2000.
- "Madidi National Park," by Steve Kemper, March 2000.
- "Frozen in Time," by Johan Reinhard, November 1999.

National Geographic Society Products Available From Glencoe:

To order the following products for use with this chapter, contact your local Glencoe sales representative or call Glencoe at 1-800-334-7344:

- *GeoBee* (CD-ROM)
- *PicturePack: Geography of South America* (Transparencies)
- *MapPack: Continents: South America* (Transparencies)
- *STV: World Geography* (Videodisc)
- *STV: Rain Forest* (Videodisc)

Additional National Geographic Society Products:

To order the following products for use with this chapter, call National Geographic Society at 1-800-368-2728:

- *Complete National Geographic: 111 years of National Geographic Magazine* (CD-ROM)
- *MapPack: South America* (Transparencies)
- *South America* (Video)
- *Spain in the Americas* (Video)
- *South America Political* (Map)
- *National Geographic Desk Reference* (Book)
- *National Geographic Atlas of the World, Seventh Edition* (Book)
- *Discovering the Inca Ice Maiden* (Book)
- *Voices: Poetry and Art From Around the World* (Book)
- *PicturePack: Ancient Civilizations: South America* (Transparencies)
- *PictureShow: Ancient Civilizations: Middle and South America* (CD-ROM)

NGS ONLINE

Access National Geographic's Web site for current events, activities, links, interactive features, and archives.
www.nationalgeographic.com

Introducing
Chapter 23

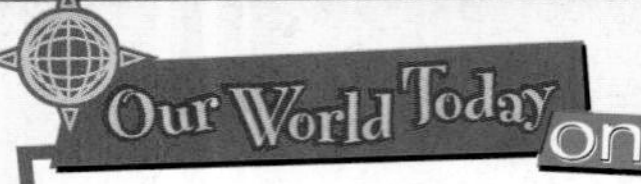

Introduce students to chapter content and key terms by having them access Chapter Overview 23 at owt.glencoe.com

Chapter Objectives

1. Describe the landforms and climates of the Andean countries.
2. Explain how the people of the Andean countries earn a living.
3. Discuss the culture of the Andean countries.

GLENCOE TECHNOLOGY

NATIONAL GEOGRAPHIC

The World and Its People Video Program

Chapter 9 The Andean Countries

The following segments enhance the study of this chapter:

- **Patagonia Puma**
- **Atacama Desert**

Available in DVD and VHS.

MindJogger Videoquiz

Use MindJogger to preview the Chapter 23 content.

Available in VHS.

Chapter 23 The Andean Countries

The World and Its People NATIONAL GEOGRAPHIC

To learn more about the people and places of the Andean countries, view ***The World and Its People*** **Chapter 9** video.

Our World Today online

Chapter Overview Visit the ***Our World Today: People, Places, and Issues*** Web site at owt.glencoe.com and click on **Chapter 23—Chapter Overviews** to preview information about the Andean countries.

602

Two-Minute Lesson Launcher

Point out to students that the photo on this page shows Quito, Ecuador, which is located over 9,000 ft (2,743 m) above sea level in the Andes mountains. Ask them to think about the effect this landscape would have on people's lives. **Ask:** **How will it affect where people live and what they do for a living? What impact would it have on how different groups communicate with one another?** Write their ideas on the board and suggest that students write them in their notebooks. They can check these notes as they read the chapter to see if they have any more ideas to add. **L1**

FOLDABLES™ Study Organizer

Summarizing Information Study Foldable Make this foldable and use it to organize note cards with information about the people and places of the Andean countries of South America.

Step 1 Fold a 2-inch tab along the long edge of a sheet of paper.

Fold the left edge over 2 inches.

Step 2 Fold the paper in half so the tab is on the inside.

The tab can't be seen when the paper is folded.

Step 3 Open the paper pocket foldable and glue the edges of the pockets together.

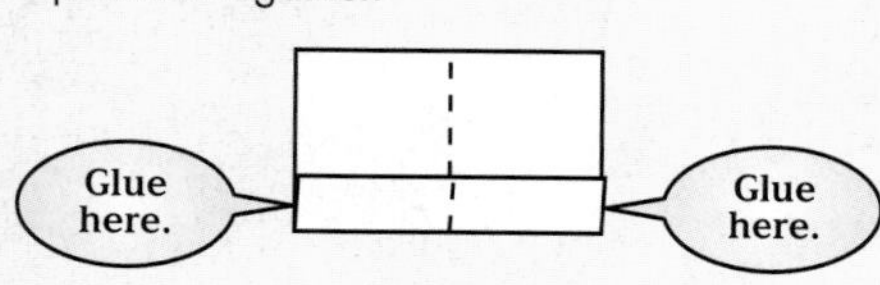

Step 4 Label the pockets as shown.

Reading and Writing As you read the chapter, summarize key facts about the Andean countries on note cards or on quarter sheets of notebook paper. Organize your notes by placing them in your pocket foldable inside the appropriate pockets. (Glue your foldable from Chapter 22 on the front cover of this foldable to form a four-pocket foldable on South America.)

Why It Matters

Wealth in the Andes

The Andes form the spine of South America and are the longest mountain chain on Earth. These high, rocky peaks are the source of some of the world's most highly desired substances, including oil, emeralds, gold and silver, coffee, and "Colombian Gold"—the illegal drug cocaine. Worldwide demand for these products has caused corruption and instability in the countries of this region.

◀ Monastery of San Francisco, Quito, Ecuador

About the Photos

Quito, Ecuador is the oldest capital city in South America. It was once settled by the Inca, but was captured by the Spanish in 1534. Like many colonial cities, it has narrow streets and a large central plaza that is dominated by a cathedral. Quito is located in the Andes on the slopes of the volcano Pichincha. Although the city lies near the Equator, it has a moderate climate because of its high altitude. Quito is the second largest city in Ecuador, where the chief economic center is Guayaquil.

Introducing

Chapter 23

FOLDABLES™ Study Organizer

Purpose This activity requires students to create note cards and a pocket foldable to organize information from the chapter. Students record key facts about the Andean countries of South America and then group the information into categories, in effect, comparing the people and places of the Andean countries. By combining the pocket foldables from Chapters 22 and 23, students can create a four-pocket foldable on South America.

Have students complete ***Reading and Study Skills Foldables*** Activity 23.

Why It Matters

Explain that the Andes have benefits as well as disadvantages for the people of South America. Create a **T** chart labeled "The Andes," with one side for "Advantages" and the other "Disadvantages." Ask students to think of ways these mountains help people *(providing building stone, mineral wealth, river sources, etc.)*, and ways they challenge people *(isolation, difficulty of transportation, poor farming, danger from earthquakes and volcanoes)*. Have volunteers fill in the chart with their ideas.

Chapter 23

Section 1, pages 604–607

Focus

Section Objectives

1. Locate Colombia on a map or globe and describe its landforms.
2. Discuss Colombia's economy and the challenges it faces.
3. Describe Columbia's history and people.

BELLRINGER Skillbuilder Activity

Project transparency and have students answer questions.

This activity is also available as a blackline master.

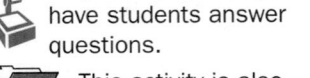

Daily Focus Skills Transparency 23-1

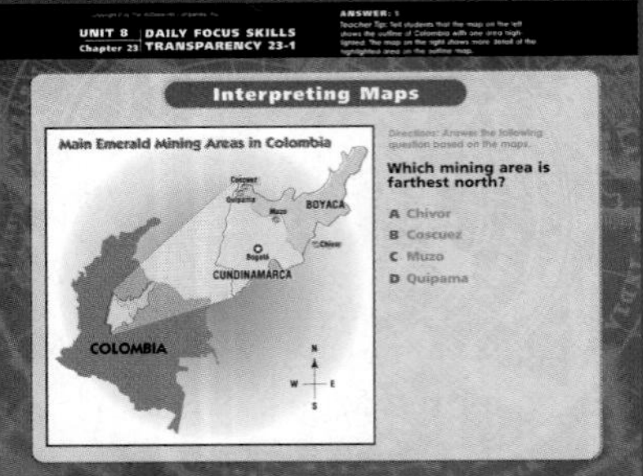

Guide to Reading

■ **Accessing Prior Knowledge**
Ask: What famous person do you think Colombia is named for? *(Christopher Columbus)* Why do you think the country was named for him? *(because he launched colonization of the Americas)*

Section 1 Colombia

Guide to Reading

Main Idea

Although it has many resources, Colombia faces political and economic turmoil.

Terms to Know

- cordillera
- llanos
- cash crop
- mestizo
- republic
- campesino

Reading Strategy

Create a chart like the one below and list advantages that Colombia enjoys in the left column. In the right column, list the challenges that it faces.

Colombia	
Advantages	Challenges

NATIONAL GEOGRAPHIC **Exploring Our World**

In a thin vein of black shale, a miner in Colombia spots a glistening green stone. He is not the first Colombian to mine the precious gemstones we call emeralds. The Colombian mine called Muzo has been producing top-quality emeralds for a thousand years. Early Native American rulers would offer these gems—more rare than diamonds—to their gods.

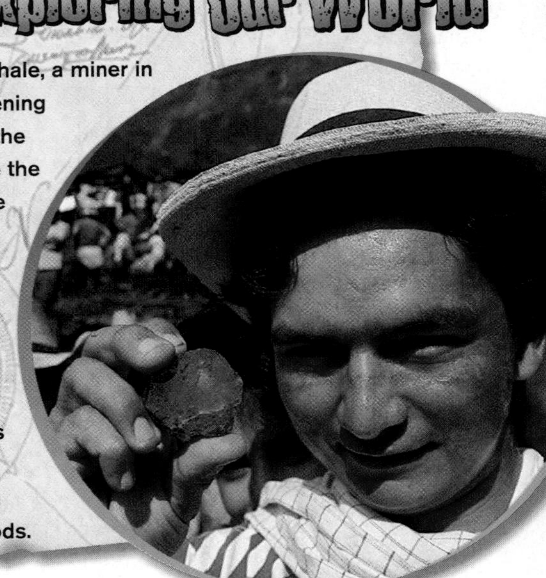

Colombia—named after Christopher Columbus—sits astride the lofty Andes mountain ranges at the northwestern edge of South America. These mountains continue south through five other countries—Ecuador, Peru, Bolivia, Chile, and Argentina.

Colombia's Land

Colombia—almost three times larger than Montana—has coasts on both the Caribbean Sea and the Pacific Ocean. The Andes sweep through the western part of Colombia. Here they become a **cordillera** (KAWR•duhl•YEHR•uh), or a group of mountain ranges that run side by side. Nearly 80 percent of Colombia's people live in the valleys and highland plateaus of the Andes. Thick forests spread over lowlands along the Pacific coast. Few people live there.

Only a few Native American groups live in the hot, steamy tropical rain forests of the southeast. In the northeast, ranchers drive cattle across the hot grasslands known as the **llanos.**

Colombia lies within the Tropics. Temperatures are very hot, and heavy rains fall along the coasts and in the interior plains. In the high

Section Resources

Reproducible Masters

- Reproducible Lesson Plan 23-1
- Daily Lecture and Discussion Notes 23-1
- Guided Reading Activity 23-1
- Reading Essentials and Study Guide 23-1
- Section Quiz 23-1

Transparencies

- Daily Focus Skills Transparency 23-1
- GeoQuiz Transparency 23-1

Multimedia

- Vocabulary PuzzleMaker Software
- Interactive Tutor Self-Assessment CD-ROM
- Presentation Plus! CD-ROM
- ExamView® Pro 3.0 Testmaker CD-ROM

elevations of the Andes, temperatures are very cool for a tropical area. **Bogotá,** Colombia's captial and largest city, lies on an Andean plateau at 8,355 feet (2,547 m) above sea level. Here high temperatures average only 67°F (19°C).

✓Reading Check **Where do most of Colombia's people live?**

Colombia's Economy

Colombia has many natural resources. The mountains hold valuable minerals and precious stones, and Colombia has more coal than any other country in South America. Second only to Brazil in its potential hydroelectric power, Colombia also has large petroleum reserves in the lowlands. In addition, the country is a major supplier of gold and

NATIONAL GEOGRAPHIC

The Andean Countries: Political

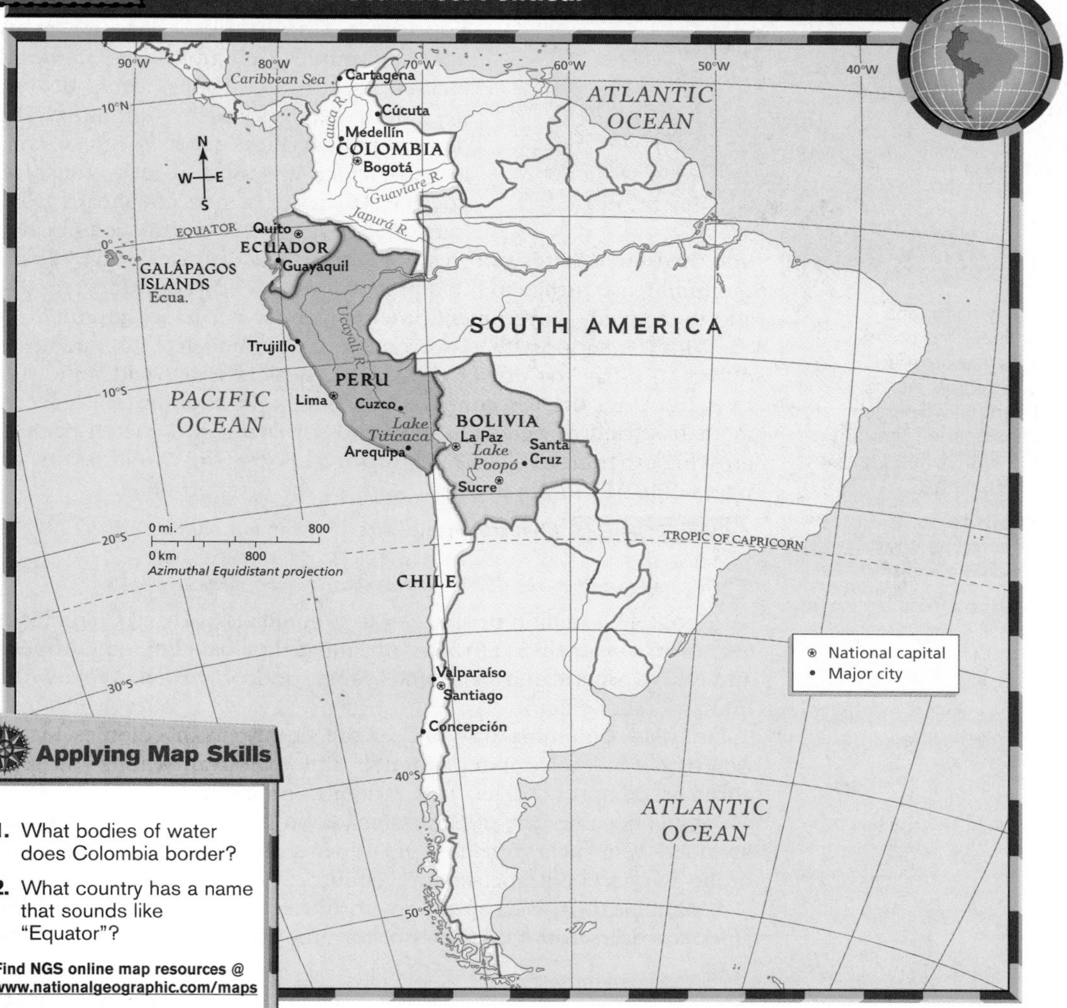

90°W
80°W
70°W
60°W
50°W
40°W
10°N
Caribbean Sea
Cartagena
Cúcuta
Medellín
COLOMBIA
Bogotá
Cauca R.
Guaviare R.
Japurá R.
ATLANTIC OCEAN
N
W
E
S
EQUATOR
0°
Quito
ECUADOR
Guayaquil
GALÁPAGOS ISLANDS
Ecua.
Ucayali R.
SOUTH AMERICA
Trujillo
PERU
10°S
PACIFIC OCEAN
Lima
Cuzco
Lake Titicaca
BOLIVIA
La Paz
Lake Poopó
Santa Cruz
Arequipa
Sucre
20°S
0 mi. 800
0 km 800
Azimuthal Equidistant projection
TROPIC OF CAPRICORN
CHILE
National capital
Major city
30°S
Valparaíso
Santiago
Concepción
40°S
ATLANTIC OCEAN
50°S

Applying Map Skills

1. What bodies of water does Colombia border?
2. What country has a name that sounds like "Equator"?

Find NGS online map resources @ www.nationalgeographic.com/maps

Chapter 23

Section 1, pages 604–607

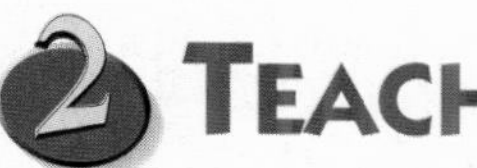

2 TEACH

Identifying Main Ideas As students read each subsection, have them write one sentence that expresses the main idea in that subsection. Have volunteers offer their sentences and discuss whether they do or do not capture the main idea of the subsection. **L1**

✓ Reading Check Answer

in the valleys and highland plateaus of the Andes

Daily Lecture Notes 23-1

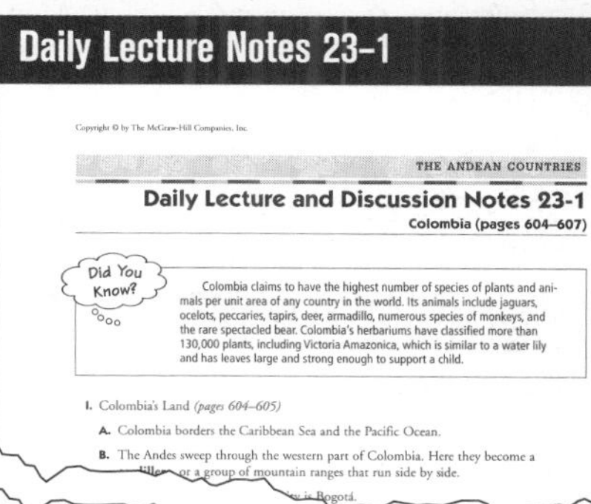

Copyright © by The McGraw-Hill Companies, Inc.

THE ANDEAN COUNTRIES

Daily Lecture and Discussion Notes 23-1

Colombia (pages 604–607)

Did You Know?

Colombia claims to have the highest number of species of plants and animals per unit area of any country in the world. Its animals include jaguars, ocelots, peccaries, tapirs, deer, armadillo, numerous species of monkeys, and the rare spectacled bear. Colombia's herbariums have classified more than 130,000 plants, including Victoria Amazonica, which is similar to a water lily and has leaves large and strong enough to support a child.

I. Colombia's Land *(pages 604–605)*

A. Colombia borders the Caribbean Sea and the Pacific Ocean.

B. The Andes sweep through the western part of Colombia. Here they become a ... or a group of mountain ranges that run side by side.

Applying Map Skills

Answers

1. Caribbean Sea, Pacific Ocean
2. Ecuador

Skills Practice

What is unusual about Bolivia's capital? *(There are two—La Paz and Sucre.)*

Team-Teaching Activity

Language Arts Literacy rates are low in some Andean countries. Difficulty with reading and writing—and learning problems in general—can also hold back children in our country. With the aid of the English teacher, students should use the decision-making process to 1) research and select a local group that provides assistance to children with learning problems, 2) identify ways they might help, 3) predict the consequences of their actions, and 4) follow through on their decision. Students should make a final presentation after their plan has been implemented. **L2**

EE4 Human Systems: Standard 10

More About the Photo

Coffee Coffee was first cultivated in either Arabia or Ethiopia. Coffee growing spread to the Americas in the 1700s. Colombia is the world's second-largest coffee producer.

Caption Answer bananas, cacao, sugarcane, rice, and cotton

Guided Reading Activity 23-1

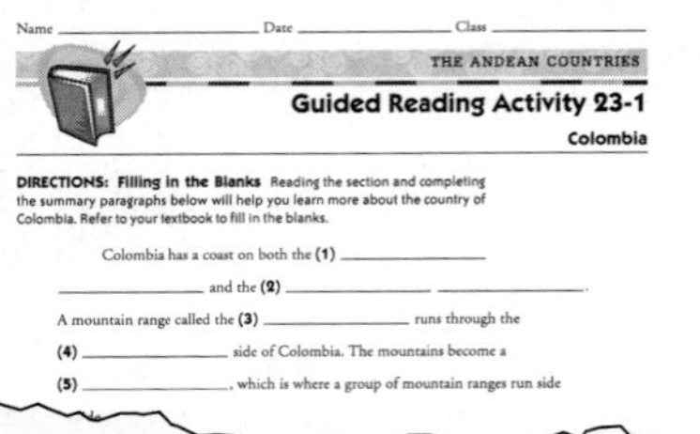
Name ______ Date ______ Class ______

THE ANDEAN COUNTRIES

Guided Reading Activity 23-1

Colombia

DIRECTIONS: Filling in the Blanks Reading the section and completing the summary paragraphs below will help you learn more about the country of Colombia. Refer to your textbook to fill in the blanks.

Colombia has a coast on both the **(1)** ______ ______ and the **(2)** ______ ______.
A mountain range called the **(3)** ______ runs through the **(4)** ______ side of Colombia. The mountains become a **(5)** ______, which is where a group of mountain ranges run side

Reading Check Answer

cocaine; powerful drug dealers protect the illegal trade through violence and corruption

Measure student knowledge of physical features and political entities.

GeoQuiz Transparency 23-1

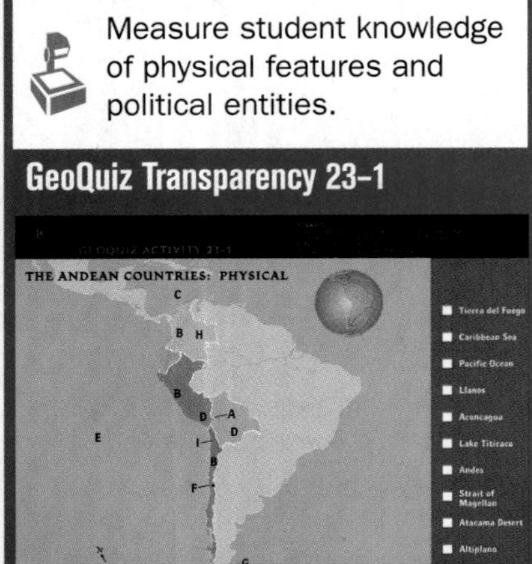

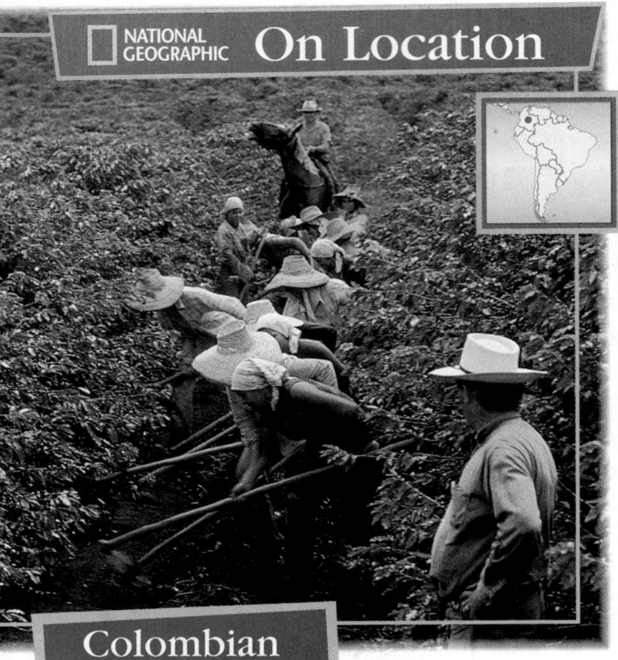

Colombian Coffee

Many historians believe that coffee was "discovered" in Ethiopia, Africa. Eventually Spanish missionaries brought the first coffee plants to Colombia.

Economics What other crops does Colombia export?

the world's number one source of emeralds. Manufacturing produces clothing, leather goods, food products, paper, chemicals, and iron and steel products.

Agriculture The coastal regions and the highlands have good soil for growing a variety of crops. Coffee is the country's major **cash crop**—a product sold for export. Colombian coffee is known all over the world for its rich flavor.

Colombia exports bananas as well as cacao, sugarcane, rice, and cotton. Huge herds of cattle roam large *estancias,* or ranches, in the llanos. The rain forests also supply a valuable resource—lumber.

Economic Challenges Despite many natural resources, Colombia faces economic challenges. In the 1980s, drug dealers became a major force in Colombia. The dealers paid farmers more to grow coca leaves—which are used to make the drug cocaine—than the farmers could earn growing coffee. Much of this cocaine is smuggled into the United States and western Europe. The drug dealers have used their immense profits to build private armies. They have threatened—and even killed—government officials who have tried to stop them.

With U.S. support, the government of Colombia has stepped up its efforts to break the power of the drug dealers. It has had some success, but drug dealers continue to flourish. In addition, the government has tried to persuade thousands of farmers to switch back to growing other crops. See **TIME Reports: Focus on World Issues** on pages 609–615 for an in-depth study of the drug problem.

Reading Check **What crop has been a problem in Colombia? Why?**

Colombia's History and People

About 43.1 million people live in Colombia. Nearly all Colombians are **mestizos** (meh•STEE•zohs), meaning they have mixed European and Native American backgrounds. Most speak Spanish and follow the Roman Catholic faith.

In 1810 Colombia was one of the first Spanish colonies in the Americas to declare independence. Simón Bolívar, whom you read about in Chapter 22, led this struggle for independence. In 1819 Colombia became part of New Granada, an independent country that included Venezuela, Ecuador, and Panama. Later, these other regions broke away and became separate countries.

Colombia today is a **republic** with an elected president. Political violence has scarred the country's history, though. During the late 1800s

Critical Thinking Activity

Expressing Problems Clearly Have students carefully review the information under the subheading Economic Challenges. After they have finished their reading, **Ask:** **What do you think is the most serious issue facing Colombia? Why?** Ask for volunteers to give their answers and explanations. After a few students have spoken, have the class discuss the different suggestions and the reasons given. **L1**

EE5 Environment and Society: Standard 16

alone, Colombia suffered through more than 50 revolts and 8 civil wars. Fighting broke out again in 1948. About 300,000 people died in this conflict, which ended in the late 1960s.

To prevent further turmoil, the two main political parties agreed to govern the country together. Efforts were made to improve the lives of poor farmers by giving them more land. Factories and industrial jobs opened up. Still, a wide gap between rich and poor remained, causing further troubles.

In the 1960s, groups of rebels in the countryside began fighting the government. This latest civil war has lasted more than 35 years and left more than 100,000 people dead. In late 1999, more than 13 million Colombians joined in a massive protest across the country, urging an end to the fighting.

A Diverse Culture Colombia has a rapidly growing urban population. Colombian farmers, or **campesinos,** and their families have journeyed to cities to look for work or to flee the fighting in the countryside.

You can see Colombia's Spanish, Native American, and African heritages reflected in its culture. Native American skills in weaving and pottery date back before the arrival of Columbus. Caribbean African rhythms blend with Spanish-influenced music.

Our World Today online

Web Activity Visit the ***Our World Today: People, Places, and Issues*** Web site at owt.glencoe.com and click on **Chapter 23–Student Web Activities** to learn more about Colombia.

✓Reading Check **What is a mestizo?**

Section 1 Assessment

Defining Terms

1. **Define** cordillera, llanos, cash crop, mestizo, republic, campesino.

Recalling Facts

2. **Economics** Colombia is the world's number one source of what resource?
3. **Culture** What language do most Colombians speak? What religion do they practice?
4. **History** Who led Colombia's struggle for independence from Spain?

Critical Thinking

5. **Analyzing Cause and Effect** Why does Bogotá, which is located in the Tropics, have an average temperature of only 67°F (19°C)?
6. **Drawing Conclusions** Why do you think it is so difficult for Colombian farmers to stop growing coca?

Graphic Organizer

7. **Organizing Information** Create a time line like this one; then put the following events and their dates in the correct order on it: Massive protest held by more than 13 million Colombians, groups of rebels fight the government, Colombia declares independence from Spain, Colombia suffers 50 revolts and 8 civil wars, Colombia becomes part of New Granada.

Applying Social Studies Skills

8. **Analyzing Maps** Study the political map on page 605. What rivers run through Colombia? What are Colombia's major cities?

Chapter 23

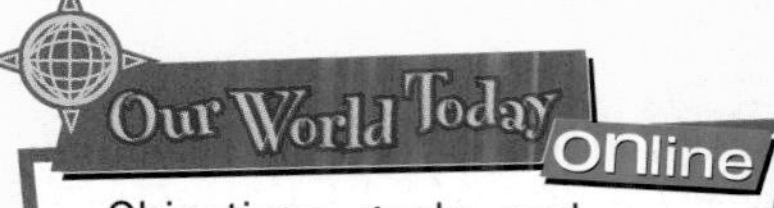
Section 1, pages 604–607

Our World Today online

Objectives, goals, and answers to the Student Web Activity can be found in the Web Activity Lesson Plan at **owt.glencoe.com**

3 Assess

Assign Section 1 Assessment as homework or an in-class activity.

Have students use the Interactive Tutor Self-Assessment CD-ROM to review Section 23–1.

✓ Reading Check Answer

a person of mixed European and Native American ancestry

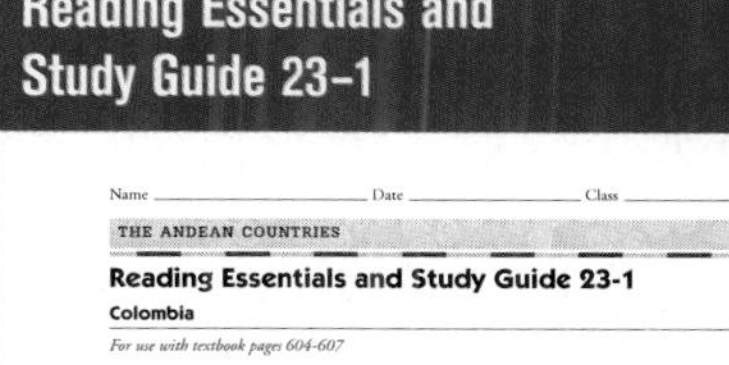
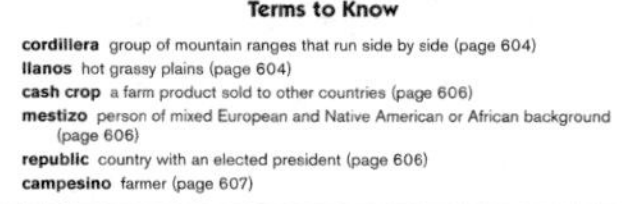
Reading Essentials and Study Guide 23–1

Name ________ Date ________ Class ________

THE ANDEAN COUNTRIES

Reading Essentials and Study Guide 23-1

Colombia

For use with textbook pages 604-607

Terms to Know

cordillera group of mountain ranges that run side by side (page 604)
llanos hot grassy plains (page 604)
cash crop a farm product sold to other countries (page 606)
mestizo person of mixed European and Native American or African background (page 606)
republic country with an elected president (page 606)
campesino farmer (page 607)

4 Close

Have students prepare a section quiz that tests mastery of the section content.

Section 1 Assessment

1. The terms are defined in the Glossary.
2. emeralds
3. Spanish, Roman Catholicism
4. Simón Bolívar
5. because of its high elevation
6. Farmers can earn more money growing coca, which has increased the amount grown.
7. Colombia declares independence from Spain (1810); Colombia becomes part of New Granada (1819); Colombia suffers 50 revolts and 8 civil wars (late 1800s); groups of rebels fight the government (1960s); massive protest by more than 13 million Colombians (1999)
8. Rivers: Cauca, Guaviare, Japurá; Cities: Cartagena, Cúcuta, Medellín, Bogotá

Technology Skill

TEACH

Begin discussion of this feature by surveying the class to find out if any students have done computer database searches (as in a library's electronic catalog). In discussing the construction of a database, refer to a phone directory. Give examples of *fields* (for example, name, phone number, and address); *records* (such as the specific names, phone numbers, and addresses of particular people); and *data files* (a collection of records). L1

Additional Skills Practice

1. **What is the difference between a field and a record?** *(A field is the category of information, whereas a record is a specific piece of information.)*
2. **What fields would you want in a database of a CD collection?** *(Possible answers: artist name, CD title, songs included, type of music)*
3. Look at the Country Profiles in the Unit 8 Regional Atlas on pages 578–579. **What fields are included for each country in this database?** *(country name, population, population density, languages, major exports, major imports, capital, landmass)*

Additional Skills Resources

 Chapter Skills Activity 23

Building Geography Skills for Life

Technology Skill

Using a Database

An electronic **database** is a collection of data—names, facts, and statistics—that is stored in a file on the computer. Databases are useful for organizing large amounts of information. The information in a database can be sorted and presented in different ways.

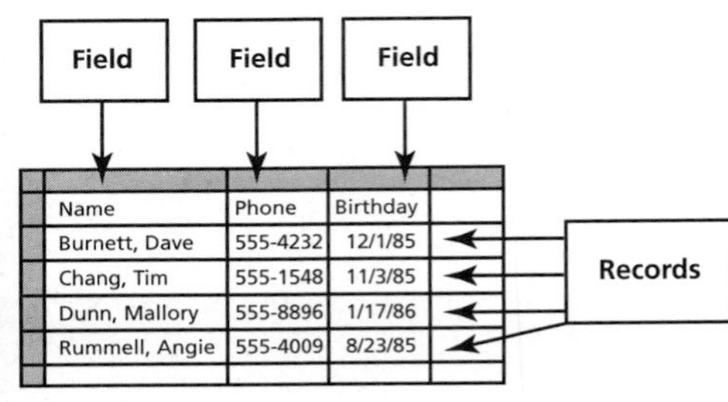

Field
Field
Field
Name | Phone | Birthday
Burnett, Dave | 555-4232 | 12/1/85
Chang, Tim | 555-1548 | 11/3/85
Dunn, Mallory | 555-8896 | 1/17/86
Rummell, Angie | 555-4009 | 8/23/85
Records

▲ **Using a database can help organize statistics, names and addresses, and even baseball card collections.**

Learning the Skill

The database organizes information in categories called *fields*. For example, a database of your friends might include the fields **Name, Address, Telephone Number,** and **Birthday.** Each person you enter into the database is called a *record*. After entering the records, you might create a list sorted by birthdays or use the records to create address labels. Together, all the records make up the database.

Scientists use databases for many purposes. They often have large amounts of data that they need to analyze. For example, a sociologist might want to compare and contrast certain information about the people of the Andean countries. A database would be a good place to sort and compare information about the languages, religions, and ethnic groups of these countries.

Practicing the Skill

Follow these steps to build a database about the Andean countries.

1. Determine what facts you want to include in your database and research to collect that information.
2. Follow the instructions in the database that you are using to set up fields. Then enter each item of data in its assigned field.
3. Determine how you want to organize the facts in the database—chronologically by the date, alphabetically, or by some other category.
4. Follow the instructions in your computer program to sort the information.
5. Check that all the information in your database is correct. If necessary, add, delete, or change information or fields.

Applying the Skill

Research and build a database that organizes information about an Andean country of your choice. Explain why the database is organized the way it is.

Practicing the Skill Answers

1. *Possible answers:* country name, landforms, resources
2. Monitor students' performance at this step.
3. Suggest that for this database, students organize their information by country.
4. Monitor students' performance at this step.
5. Have students present printed copies of the different records.

Applying the Skill

Students' completed databases should include different categories of information.

TIME REPORTS

FOCUS ON WORLD ISSUES

Waging War on Drugs

Small, hidden cocaine labs, like this one in Colombia, are difficult to eliminate.

CARLOS VILLALO/GETY/NEWSCOM

South America Fights a Global Problem

TIME REPORTS

Focus on World Issues

Teacher Background

Until the 1960s, illegal drug use was seen as primarily a lower-class activity. Recreational drug use grew in the 1960s, primarily as a social protest. In response to this surge in illegal drug use, the Bureau of Narcotics and Dangerous Drugs was founded in 1968, and the Drug Enforcement Administration (DEA) was founded in 1973. The current annual budget for drug enforcement is about $40 billion.

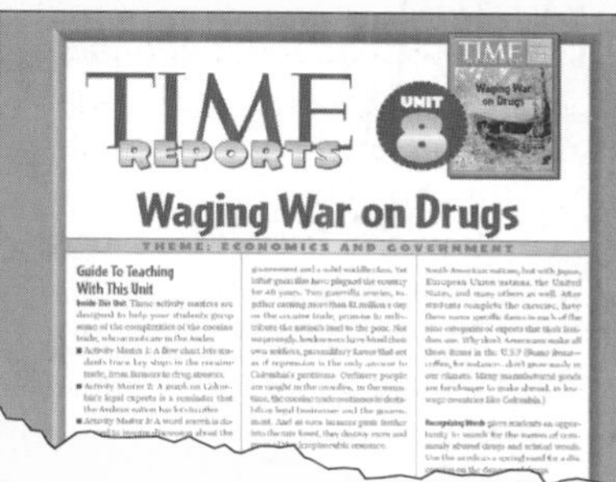
TIME REPORTS UNIT 8

Waging War on Drugs

THEME: ECONOMICS AND GOVERNMENT

Guide To Teaching With This Unit

Preparing the Student

The United States provides the world's largest market for those drugs that are commonly abused. A variety of government agencies and officials are involved in the "war on drugs," including the Drug Enforcement Administration (DEA), the FBI, and U.S. Customs.

Making Connections

Drug Abuse **Ask students:** How common do you think drug abuse is in our town? What kinds of drugs do you think are being abused? Write students' answers. **Ask:** How do young people get these drugs? Are the methods different for a legal drug (such as alcohol) than for an illegal drug (such as marijuana)? How does the use of illegal drugs affect your friends and our town? Tell students that this article will discuss some of the things being done to reduce drug abuse.

1 Focus

Ask students to write a paragraph suggesting ways to prevent drug abuse. They might include: interrupting drug routes and preventing cultivation, so people can't obtain drugs; and discouraging people from using drugs through education programs, imprisonment, or treatment programs. Students should support their ideas with facts or examples.

The Drug War in the Andes

ANSWERS

1. The U.S. has radar and facilities to fight drug trafficking in the Andes. It also spent large amounts of money in Bolivia and Peru, where coca cultivation has decreased. Cultivation increased in Colombia, where little money was spent.
2. The lines might go down in Colombia and increase in other countries, such as Ecuador.

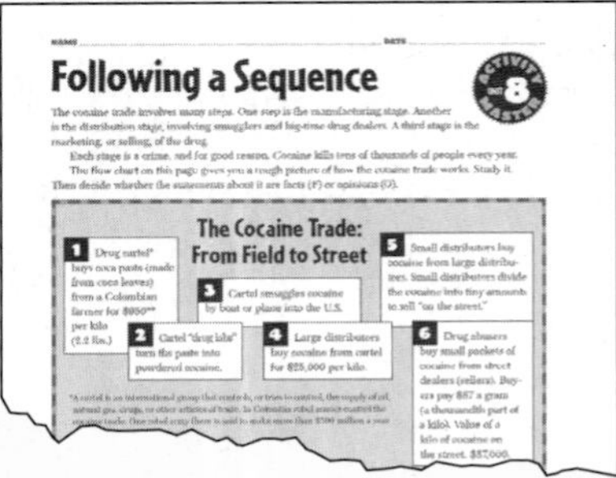

NAME ________ DATE ________

Following a Sequence

ACTIVITY MASTER 8

The cocaine trade involves many steps. One step is the manufacturing stage. Another is the distribution stage, involving smugglers and big-time drug dealers. A third stage is the marketing, or selling, of the drug.

Each stage is a crime, and for good reason. Cocaine kills tens of thousands of people every year.

The flow chart on this page gives you a rough picture of how the cocaine trade works. Study it. Then decide whether the statements about it are facts (F) or opinions (O).

The Cocaine Trade: From Field to Street

1. Drug cartel* buys coca paste (made from coca leaves) from a Colombian farmer for $950** per kilo (2.2 lbs.)
2. Cartel "drug labs" turn the paste into powdered cocaine.
3. Cartel smuggles cocaine by boat or plane into the U.S.
4. Large distributors buy cocaine from cartel for $25,000 per kilo.
5. Small distributors buy cocaine from large distributors. Small distributors divide the cocaine into tiny amounts to sell "on the street."
6. Drug abusers buy small packets of cocaine from street dealers (sellers). Buyers pay $87 a gram (a thousandth part of a kilo). Value of a kilo of cocaine on the street: $87,000.

*A cartel is an international group that controls, or tries to control, the supply of oil, natural gas, drugs, or other articles of trade. In Colombia rebel armies control the cocaine trade. One rebel army there is said to make more than $500 million a year [illegible]

A war on many fronts: U.S. Navy Seals on patrol in Brazil. Police in Peru seize cocaine.

LUKE FRAZZA/AFP

MARIANA BAZO/REUTERS

FOCUS ON WORLD ISSUES

The Drug Trade's Tragic Effect

In June 1986, Len Bias had everything to be happy about. The University of Maryland basketball star had just signed with the Boston Celtics, a pro team. The Celtics promised him $700,000 for his first season. A sneaker company agreed to pay him $325,000 to be their spokesman.

Len Bias (left) had a promising future.

MANNY MILAN

For this instant millionaire, it looked as if things could only get better. "That kid is going to be a superstar," a coach said. "What can't he do? He's got the whole package."

Bias also had a package of cocaine. **Cocaine** is a drug that can cause brain injuries even if taken only once. In 1986, scientists didn't know that for sure. Bias certainly didn't know it. Two days after he signed with the Celtics, he used cocaine and died.

A Deadly Import

The cocaine that killed Len Bias came from South America. And so did the 650 tons of cocaine smuggled into the United States in 2000. Everyday Americans died as a result of using this drug.

Cocaine is made from the coca plant, which is grown in only three countries. Colombia is by far the biggest producer followed by Peru and Bolivia.

In all three countries coca is grown high up in the Andes Mountains. Cocaine "factories" there turn coca leaves into a white powder. **Smugglers** use boats and airplanes to slip that powder, cocaine, into countries around the world.

The Drug War in the Andes

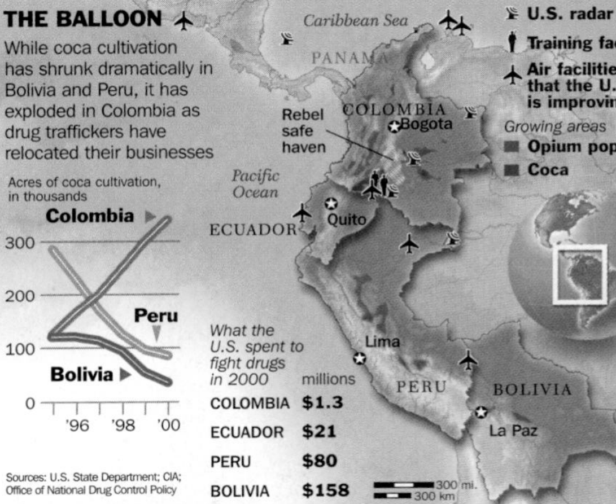

INTERPRETING MAPS AND CHARTS

1. **Interpreting Data** What does this map tell you about the U.S. role in South America's drug war?
2. **Making Inferences** Suppose the war against drugs succeeds in Colombia. How might the lines on the graph change?

610

Team-Teaching Activity

Government Invite a teacher to class who can discuss the impact government agencies have had on illegal drug trafficking and use. Ask the teacher to describe how these agencies' roles are different from one another, how the agencies work together to try to destroy illegal drug supply lines, and the relationship between federal and local officials. Have students find articles about either local or international drug enforcement activities. They should summarize the article and describe the role of the agencies involved and the results of their actions. Students should explain why this event was or wasn't an effective way of fighting drugs. **L2**

EE4 Human Systems: Standard 11

Len Bias became an instant millionaire. Then he made a choice that cost him his life.

LANE STEWART

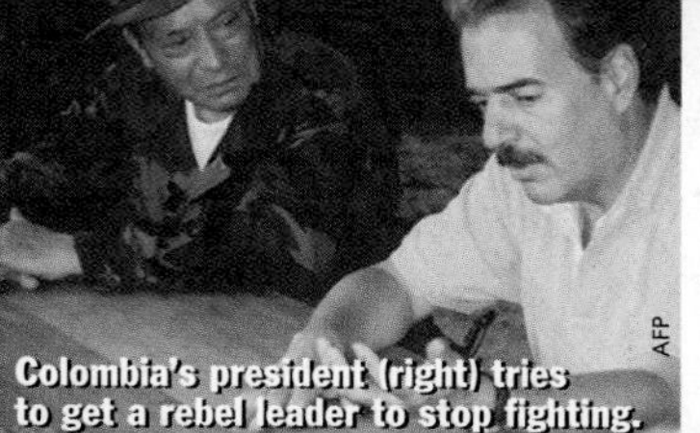
Colombia's president (right) tries to get a rebel leader to stop fighting.

AFP

The beautiful poppy is harvested for deadly heroin.

AFP/CORBIS

Heroin, another deadly drug, is made from the poppy plant. In South America, poppies are turned into heroin only in Colombia.

Rebels Businesses

Drugs have nearly brought Colombia to its knees. Colombia is a country about the size of Texas and California combined. Rebel armies based in Colombia's jungles have fought government troops for nearly 40 years. The rebels make and sell cocaine and heroin. Their dirty business brings them more than $1 million a day. They spend a lot of that money on weapons.

Paramilitaries add to Colombia's woes. These are armed men that landowners and businesses hire to protect their workers. In 2000, rebels and paramilitaries kidnapped eight innocent civilians every day and murdered 80 more. The chaos has forced more than 2 million Colombians to flee their homes.

U.S. money had helped Bolivia and Peru tackle drug problems during the 1990s. But many cocaine producers in those countries moved their operations to Colombia. Cocaine production in Colombia doubled between 1995 and 2000.

In 2000, the U.S. decided to help Colombia rid itself of the drug trade. It gave Colombia's government $1.3 billion to equip and train its army to fight drugs.

Fighters for Life

If no one bought drugs, no one would produce them. Len Bias's death in 1986 persuaded millions to avoid cocaine. But millions still use it, so the cocaine business remains strong.

Len Bias's mother, Louise, is happy that some good came out of her son's death. "Len Bias has done more in death," she said, "than he could have done in life. Life is what the fight against deadly drugs is all about."

EXPLORING THE ISSUE

1. **Explaining** What comment does this article's title make about the trade in illegal drugs?
2. **Cause and Effect** Describe how Len Bias's death could have persuaded millions of Americans to avoid cocaine.

2 TEACH

Identifying Main Ideas
Have students write down the headings for the four sections in this report. After each heading have them write the main idea of the section. Next have them write down the subheadings in each section, with the main idea and three supporting statements under each. **L1**

More About the Photo

Len Bias Ask: **Why do you suppose Len Bias took the cocaine that killed him?**

EXPLORING THE ISSUE

ANSWERS

1. It suggests that the drug trade is as much a threat to our nation as an attack, and the government will take action to fight it if necessary.
2. It was frightening because Bias had no history of cocaine use and yet died suddenly of brain injuries. Even occasional users are endangering their lives.

Did You Know

The international trade in illegal drugs is estimated to be a $400 billion dollar business. Its sheer size makes it difficult for law enforcement to control.

Meeting Special Needs

Logical/Mathematical According to the Office of National Drug Control Policy, in 1990 there were approximately 7,786,000 cocaine users in the United States, who used 271 metric tons of cocaine and spent a total of $61.3 billion. In 2000 there were 7,480,000 cocaine users who used 269 metric tons and spent a total of $36.1 billion. Have students put these figures into a chart and then compare the results. **Ask:** **How have the number of users, amount of cocaine, and total spent on cocaine changed in 10 years? How does this information relate to this report? Why is the change greater for the amount spent than the other two categories?** *(fewer users and greater availability of the drug might have reduced the cost)* **L2**

Refer to *Inclusion for the Middle School Social Studies Classroom Strategies and Activities*.

TIME REPORTS

Recommended Internet Sites

www.dea.gov/

The Web site of the Drug Enforcement Administration is a good source of information about drug use and drug deterrence programs.

http://www.pbs.org/wgbh/pages/frontline/shows/drugs/

This PBS's Frontline Web site covers 30 years of the war on drugs, including candid accounts from people directly involved, such as DEA and FBI agents. It also includes a CIA world map showing trafficking routes and crop areas, a time line, and a teacher's guide.

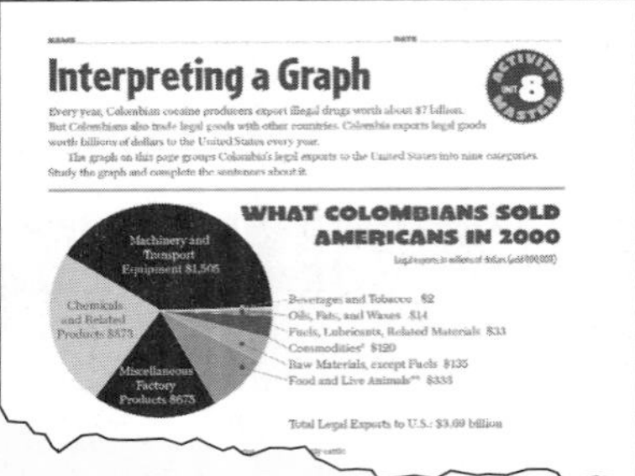

Interpreting a Graph

WHAT COLOMBIANS SOLD AMERICANS IN 2000

EXPLORING THE ISSUE

ANSWERS

1. As long as illegal drugs are being grown, suppliers will find ways to get them to those who will pay money for them.
2. Drug abuse is very difficult to prevent. However, Colombian farmers grow coca in order to support their families. If they can make the same amount of money in a different way, they are likely to switch.

TIME REPORTS

Targeting Drug Supplies

Pop works for the U.S. Customs Service in Hidalgo, Texas. He looks for illegal drugs in vehicles that cross into the United States from Mexico.

By any measure, Pop is good at his job. In 1998, he discovered 3,075 pounds of cocaine in a pineapple truck. In 1999, he found 50 pounds of marijuana hidden in an ice chest.

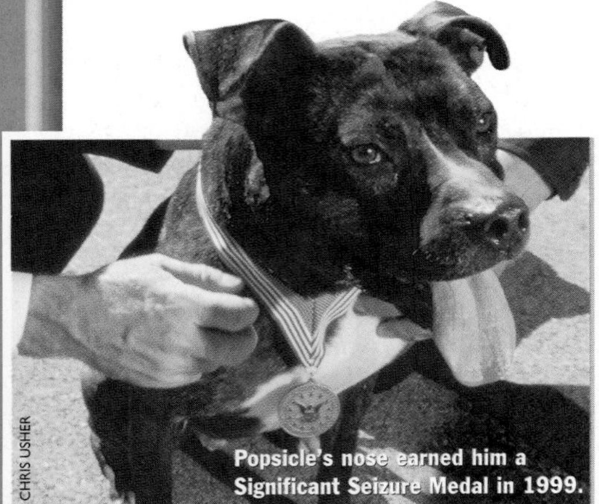

CHRIS USHER

Popsicle's nose earned him a Significant Seizure Medal in 1999.

What makes Pop so successful? His nose. Pop—short for Popsicle—is a pit bull. Like 500 other **customs dogs** in the U.S., he's been trained to sniff out drugs.

Popsicle plays a role in the worldwide effort to stop the flow of drugs. Many thousands of people are also part of that effort. Police officers, for example, arrest people who sell drugs on the street. Members of the U.S. Coast Guard head off smugglers at sea. Soldiers in Colombia destroy coca plants and cocaine factories.

U.S. Help

About 80 percent of the cocaine that reaches the United States comes from Colombia. That's why the U.S. has put more than $1.3 billion behind Colombia's fight against drugs. Colombia's armed forces use most of the money to train soldiers and buy equipment. Planes bought with U.S. dollars drop chemicals that kill growing coca plants. New helicopters rush soldiers to cocaine factories defended by heavily armed rebel troops.

Stopping cocaine at its source isn't just a military job. It's also an effort to change minds. Colombian officials are trying to persuade farmers to stop growing coca and poppies. They pay farmers to grow cocoa, coffee, palm hearts, and other crops instead.

Will those efforts work? Some experts think so. Others aren't so sure. "Those that profit from producing cocaine and heroin are not about to roll over and play dead," said one expert. "There is evidence that drug factories are moving into Brazil and Ecuador."

If she's right, Popsicle has a lot of work ahead of him.

EXPLORING THE ISSUE

1. **Explaining** Why is stopping cocaine at its source important to the war on drugs?
2. **Analyzing Information** Why might it be more effective to wipe out cocaine in Colombia than to stop it in the United States?

Critical Thinking Activity

Interpreting Points of View Tell students that in recent years there has been widespread public demand to get "hard on drugs," leading to a massive increase in the number of individuals incarcerated. The number of U.S. prisoners has doubled since 1994, with about 60% of federal prisoners being drug offenders. Ask students to explain why they think imprisonment is or isn't an appropriate solution to the drug problem. **Ask:** **Will jailing addicts help them get over their addiction in the long run? Why or why not? How does this treatment compare to that of people addicted to legal drugs like alcohol, cigarettes, or prescriptions? L2**

Dealing with Demand

It's tragic but accurate: Someone somewhere is always going to want to buy illegal drugs. And someone else will be willing to **supply** them. Worldwide, about 14 million people use cocaine today. About 5.3 million of them live in the United States. Nine million people in the world use heroin. More than 650,000 of them are Americans.

Suppose those numbers were cut in half. Heroin and cocaine production would plunge. And illegal drugs would cause far less misery than they do today.

Inside Drug Court

Is slashing the **demand** for drugs by 50 percent an impossible dream? Not in Baltimore, Maryland. Baltimore has a Drug Treatment Court. The court's goal is to help people arrested for carrying illegal drugs to stop abusing them. "If you ask for help," a Drug Court judge said in 2001, "you'll get it. If you don't ask, you'll go to jail."

Half the addicts placed in treatment by the Drug Court have stayed away from drugs. Copy that success rate throughout the nation, and the demand in the U.S. for illegal drugs would nose-dive.

Educating Americans

No war on drugs can be won without such a drop in usage, experts say. U.S. President George W. Bush shares their view. "The main reason drugs are shipped . . . to the United States," he said in 2001, "is because United States citizens use drugs. Our nation must do a better job of educating our citizenry about the dangers and evils of drug use."

Yes, someone somewhere is always going to want to buy illegal drugs. But proper education and treatment will surely reduce the demand for drugs everywhere.

PAUL F. GERO/SABA

▲ **Phoenix, Arizona, has a drug court like Baltimore's. Here a judge rewards a drug offender's good behavior with tickets to Phoenix's science museum.**

EXPLORING THE ISSUE

1. **Analyzing Information** Which is more important—reducing the demand for illegal drugs or stopping criminals from producing them? Why?
2. **Problem Solving** What could schools do to lower the demand for illegal drugs?

More About the Photo

Rewards Ask: **Do you think a reward such as the one given by this judge would affect whether a young person abuses drugs? Why or why not?**

Did You Know

Money is no good if you cannot spend it. Drug traffickers often receive large cash payments. They must then get the money into the mainstream without arousing suspicion. This process is referred to as "money laundering."

Synthesizing Information
Prescription drugs such as tranquilizers and amphetamines are also bought, sold, and used illegally. Have students research and write a report on the illegal use of prescription drugs, and how drug enforcement agencies handle this problem. L2

EXPLORING THE ISSUE

ANSWERS

1. Answers will vary. Many people believe it is most important to reduce demand, because as long as there is a market, dealers will provide the desired product.
2. *Possible answers:* teach students about the dangers of drugs; provide in-school treatment and counseling

Interdisciplinary Activity

Journalism Have students research anti-drug programs in your city, local area, or, if necessary, state. Then have them write a "pretend" newspaper article on these programs. If possible, they may want to talk to local enforcement agents. They might even include a question-and-answer style interview in their article. In addition, they should check out their state drug enforcement agency's Web site. They may want to pursue getting their article published in the school newspaper or elsewhere. L2

TIME REPORTS

Current Events Journal

Some people believe that part of the problem in reducing illegal drug use is that these drugs are sometimes glamorized in the press, movies, TV, and music. Have students ask 8 to 10 of their friends whether they think the media glamorizes drug use. If they say "yes," they should be asked for examples and whether they think this encourages young people to use drugs. Students should write a brief summary of each person's responses.

EXPLORING THE ISSUE

ANSWERS

1. Students should learn about the dangers of drugs before the sixth grade so that they are prepared with appropriate knowledge.
2. because he is famous in a sport (skateboarding) that is popular with teenagers and is sometimes associated with "outsiders," who may be more likely than the average student to abuse drugs

TIME REPORTS

Fighting Drug Abuse: What Can One Person Do?

Andy McDonald is a man with a mission—helping kids stay away from drugs. Andy is the national spokesperson for the Partnership for a Drug-Free America. His message: "Kids don't need drugs to succeed."

Andy should know. He's one of the few top-ranked skateboarders in the world. He's so good, he once jumped over three SUVs and one car—all at once. That feat landed him in *The Guinness Book of World Records*. "That right there," he says of skateboarding, "is my idea of getting high."

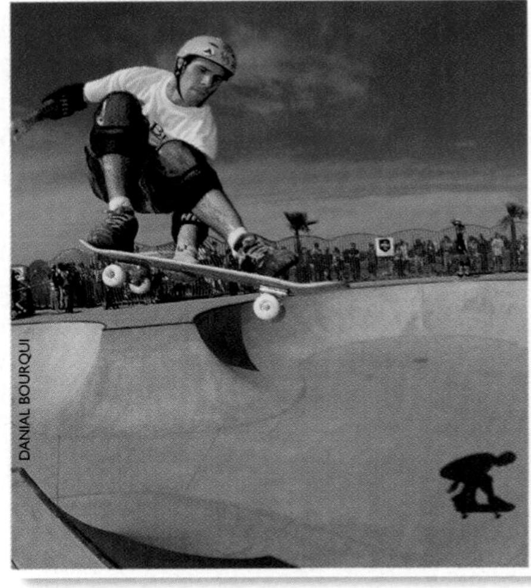
DANIAL BOURQUI

▲ **Andy McDonald: too active to do drugs**

Speaking Out

You don't have to be a champion athlete to fight drug abuse. Kaelin Weiler proved it. Between 1996 and 1998, heroin killed 11 teens in her hometown of Plano, Texas. The youngest victim was a seventh-grader.

Kaelin, 17, persuaded other kids to fight back. They tied white ribbons around traffic lights to remind people of the problem. They created a "memorial wall"—pictures of kids lost to drugs and the families they left behind. And they made videos about the dangers of drugs and showed them at assemblies.

You can work with school officials to start a similar program in your school and town. Learn as much as you can about the dangers of illegal drugs. Then design a program to teach what you learned to young students and their parents. Launch your program. Afterwards, describe the program and its results in a letter to your local newspaper's editor. E-mail a copy to the "In Your Own Words" website page of the Partnership for a Drug-Free America. (**...www.drugfreeamerica.org**).

EXPLORING THE ISSUE

1. **Making Inferences** Experts say that the risk for alcohol and other drug use skyrockets in the sixth grade. Assuming that's true, when—and why—should kids begin learning about the dangers of illegal drugs?
2. **Analyzing Information** What makes Andy McDonald an effective promoter of a drug-free life?

Your Government and You

There are a variety of government and government-funded anti-drug programs including D.A.R.E. (Drug Abuse Resistance Education) and the National Institute on Drug Abuse. In addition, there are many local programs sponsored by schools, law enforcement, and private agencies. Supply students with material from a variety of organizations. Much of this material can be found on the Internet. Have students make charts comparing the methods, budgets, results, and sponsors of at least three of these programs. Afterwards, students should compare charts and discuss which programs they believe would be the most effective and why. **L2**

REVIEW AND ASSESS

UNDERSTANDING THE ISSUE

1. **Defining Key Terms** Write definitions for the following terms: *drug abuse, cocaine, heroin, smuggler, paramilitary, customs dog, supply, demand.*
2. **Writing to Inform** In a 300-word article, explain why the drug trade needs both buyers and suppliers for its survival. Use at least five of the key terms listed above.
3. **Writing to Persuade** In your view, can the war against drugs ever be won? Support your answer to that question in a brief essay.

INTERNET RESEARCH ACTIVITY

4. Since 1998 the U.S. government has funded ads designed to combat drug abuse among young people. How good are the ads? You be the judge. Go to **www.mediacampaign.org.** Browse through the print ads aimed at parents and kids. Choose two you think are effective, and two you think are not effective. Print out all four. Attach a comment to each one explaining why it does or doesn't work well.
5. The No. 1 drug problem in America isn't cocaine or heroin. It's underage drinking. The Mothers Against Drunk Driving (MADD) website contains some startling facts on this issue. Navigate to **...http://www.madd.org/stats** Write down the five facts that you think best sum up the impact alcohol has on young people. Compare your choices with those of your classmates.

BEYOND THE CLASSROOM

6. **Research the way farmers live in Colombia, Bolivia, or Peru.** In a short article, explain why those farmers might see growing poppies or coca as a way to improve their lives.

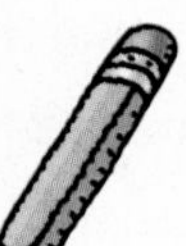

▲ **Venus and Serena Williams: At the top of their game—and far from drugs.**

7. **Research the geography and people of Afghanistan and Myanmar.** Most of the world's heroin is produced in those two countries. Make a list of conditions—poverty, climate, and location, for example—that each country shares with Colombia. In class, explain what your list suggests about places in which drug production thrives.

WHAT DRUG AND ALCOHOL ABUSE COST

Annual Cost of Alcohol Abuse in the U.S. $148 billion

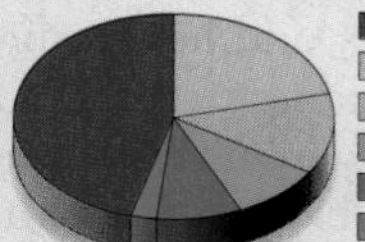

- Output[1] lost to alcohol-related illness: **$67.6 billion**
- Output lost to early deaths: **$31.4 billion**
- Healthcare: **$18.7 billion**
- Car-crash damage: **$13.6 billion**
- Alcohol-related crime: **$12.7 billion**
- Other costs: **$3.8 billion**

Annual Cost of Drug Abuse in the U.S. $98 billion

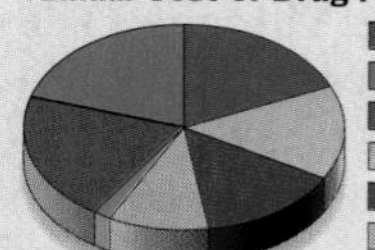

- Output[2] lost by crime victims: **$19.9 billion**
- Output lost to lives of crime: **$19.3 billion**
- Property damage, government expenses[3]: **$18 billion**
- Output lost to early deaths: **$14.6 billion**
- Output lost to drug-related illness: **$14.2 billion**
- Healthcare: **$9.9 billion**
- Other costs: **$1.8 billion**

[1]Output is the estimated amount of goods and services that workers would have produced if they had not died or gotten sick, injured, or jailed. [2]Includes output lost by victims of drug-related crimes and criminals jailed for those crimes. [3]Includes the cost of government anti-drug efforts, police, prisons, and other items.
Source: National Institutes of Health

BUILDING GRAPH READING SKILLS

1 **Explaining** A worker's "output" consists of the goods and services that he or she produces. The abuse of alcohol and other drugs costs the U.S. billions of dollars in lost output. How do these two graphs show that?

2 **Making Inferences** Suppose the U.S. Congress made cocaine and heroin as legal as alcohol. What might happen to the annual cost of drug abuse?

FOR UPDATES ON WORLD ISSUES GO TO www.timeclassroom.com/glencoe

615

3 ASSESS

Have students take the Time Reports Quiz or do the Alternative Assessment project for this unit provided in the Teacher's Classroom Resources.

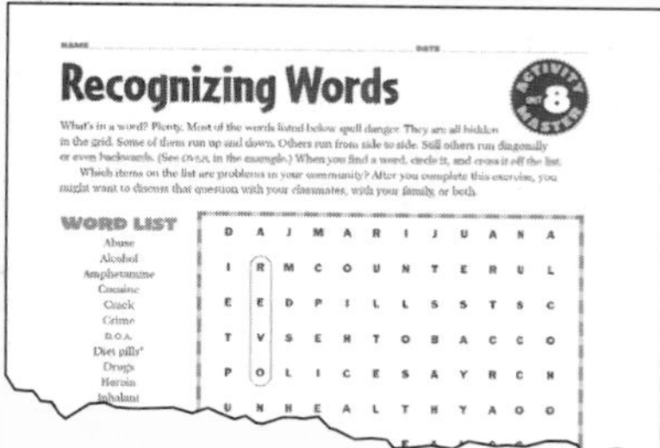

BUILDING GRAPH READING SKILLS

ANSWERS

1. Output lost to illness and early death from alcohol abuse costs $99 billion. Output lost by crime victims, lives of crime, illness, and early death due to drug abuse costs $68 billion.
2. *Possible answers:* The cost might drop because of lower drug prices and fewer related crimes. Also there would be fewer costs for sending people to jail. The cost might rise because of illnesses and accidents related to drug use.

4 CLOSE

Ask students to write a paragraph starting with this sentence: *The U.S. war on drugs would be more effective if . . .*

Culminating Activity

To close this lesson, have students complete the Review and Assess section questions and activities above. Students should use classroom discussion, contextual clues, and their student dictionaries to write definitions for terms. Before assigning the Internet activities, it is recommended that you review your school district policy on student Internet use.

Focus on Debate

As a final activity for further student understanding of the issue, have students debate the pro and con position of the following topic: **As long as there is a demand for illegal drugs, suppliers will find a way to obtain them. L2**

EE4 Human Systems: Standard 11

Focus

Section Objectives

1. Describe the landforms and climates of Peru and Ecuador.
2. Compare how the people of Peru and Ecuador earn a living.
3. Discuss what the people of Peru and Ecuador are like.

BELLRINGER
Skillbuilder Activity

Project transparency and have students answer questions.

This activity is also available as a blackline master.

Daily Focus Skills Transparency 23-2

Guide to Reading

■ **Accessing Prior Knowledge** Have students look at the photograph in Exploring Our World. Ask why they think this ancient site was not discovered until 1911.

Peru and Ecuador

Guide to Reading

Main Idea

Peru and Ecuador share similar landscapes, climates, and history.

Terms to Know

- navigable
- foothills
- subsistence farm
- empire

Reading Strategy

Create two ovals like these. Under each heading list facts about Peru and Ecuador in the outer parts of the ovals. Where the ovals overlap, write facts that apply to both countries.

NATIONAL GEOGRAPHIC Exploring Our World

They built thousands of miles of roads. They built a city on mountain peaks and were expert bridge builders. The Inca accomplished these feats in western South America during the 1400s and 1500s. The ruins of their ancient city of Machu Picchu (MAH•choo PEEK•choo), built nearly 8,000 feet (2,438 m) high in the Andes, were not even known to modern people until 1911.

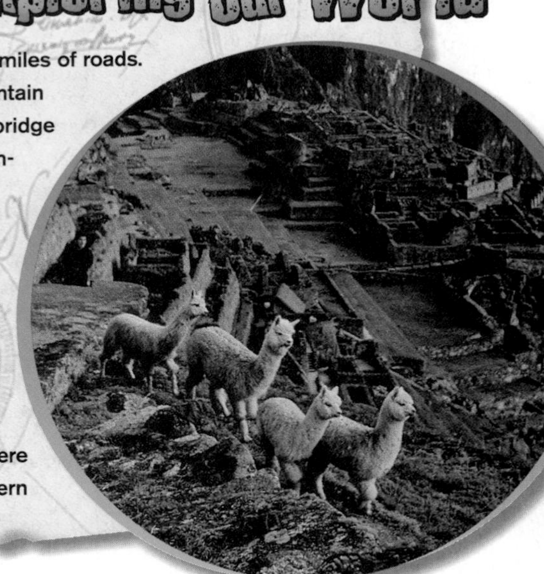

Peru and **Ecuador** lie along the Pacific coast of South America, west of Brazil and south of Colombia. The Andes form the spine of these countries. *Peru*—a Native American word that means "land of abundance"—is rich in mineral resources.

Peru

Dry deserts, snowcapped Andes mountain ranges, and hot, humid rain forests greet you in Peru. Most of Peru's farms and cities lie on a narrow coastal strip of plains and deserts. The cold Peru Current in the Pacific Ocean keeps temperatures here fairly mild even though the area is very near the Equator.

On the border with Bolivia, you can see **Lake Titicaca** (TEE•tee•KAH•kah), the highest navigable lake in the world. **Navigable** means that a body of water is wide and deep enough to allow ships to travel in it. East of the Andes you descend to the foothills and flat plains of the **Amazon Basin. Foothills** are the low hills at the base of a mountain range. Rainfall is plentiful here, and thick, hot rain forests cover almost all of the plains area.

Section Resources

Reproducible Masters

- Reproducible Lesson Plan 23-2
- Daily Lecture and Discussion Notes 23-2
- Guided Reading Activity 23-2
- Reading Essentials and Study Guide 23-2
- Section Quiz 23-2

Transparencies

- Daily Focus Skills Transparency 23-2
- GeoQuiz Transparency 23-1

Multimedia

- Vocabulary PuzzleMaker Software
- Interactive Tutor Self-Assessment CD-ROM
- Presentation Plus! CD-ROM
- ExamView® Pro 3.0 Testmaker CD-ROM

Peru's Economy Peru's economy relies on a variety of natural resources. The Andes contain many minerals, including copper, silver, gold, and iron ore. Peru's biggest export is copper. The second-largest export—fish—comes from the Peru Current, the cool Pacific Ocean current that parallels the coast.

About one-third of Peru's people farm the land. Some grow sugarcane, cotton, and coffee for export. Like Colombia, Peru grows coca leaves. Most people, however, work on **subsistence farms,** where they grow only enough food to meet their family's needs. The chief crops are rice, plantains (a kind of banana), and corn. Native Americans in the Andes were the first people ever to grow potatoes. Today, potatoes are Peru's main food crop, and farmers grow hundreds of varieties in different colors and shapes.

From Empire to Republic During the 1400s, a Native American people called the **Inca** had a powerful civilization in the area that is now Peru. Their **empire,** or group of lands under one ruler, stretched more than 2,500 miles (4,023 km) along the Andes.

The Incan emperor developed a complex system of tax collection, courts, military posts, trade inspections, and work rules. Work crews built irrigation systems, roads, and suspension bridges that linked the regions of the empire to **Cuzco,** the capital city of the Inca. You can still see the remains of magnificent fortresses and buildings erected centuries ago by skilled Incan builders. The photograph on page 616 shows the ruins of one of the Inca's most famous cities—**Machu Picchu.**

In the early 1500s, Spaniards arrived in Peru, craving the gold and silver found here. They defeated the Inca and made Peru a Spanish territory. Peru gained its freedom from Spain in the 1820s.

Peru is now a republic with an elected president. In recent years, the country's economy has grown very rapidly. Many of Peru's people, however, still live in poverty and cannot find steady jobs.

The Columbian Exchange Besides gold and silver, many other items were found in the Americas. The next time you eat a french fry, you might remember that the potato first grew wild in the mountains of Peru. By the 1400s, the Inca had developed thousands of varieties of potatoes. But no one in the Eastern Hemisphere had ever seen a potato. With Christopher Columbus's second trip, what became known as the "Columbian Exchange" began—an exchange of people, animals, plants, and even diseases between the two hemispheres.

From the Americas, explorers returned home with a wide variety of plants. Nutritious and easy to grow, the potato became one of Europe's most important foods. Corn from the Americas fed European cattle and pigs. Tobacco grown there became as valuable as gold.

The Europeans brought many new things to the Americas, including horses, sheep, cattle, and pigs. Crops that were introduced include oats, wheat, rye, barley, and sugarcane. Some parts of the exchange were disastrous, however. European diseases killed millions of Native Americans.

The Quipu

The Inca did not possess a written language. In order to record events and other aspects of their lives that they wished to remember, they used a system of knotted strings, called the quipu. Men in charge of the quipu recorded on the knots all the taxes brought each year to the Inca, noting details on everything. They recorded the number of men who went to the wars and how many were born and died every year. In short, they may be said to have recorded on their knots everything that could be counted.

Chapter 23

Section 2, pages 616–619

TEACH

Determining Cause and Effect Have students write down these key facts about Peru and Ecuador: "High altitude," "Peru Current nearby," "Ancient Native American culture," and "Once a colony of Spain." Tell them that each of these statements is a cause and that they are to identify the effects of these causes. Have volunteers read their suggestions to the class. L2

Daily Lecture Notes 23-2

THE ANDEAN COUNTRIES

Daily Lecture and Discussion Notes 23-2

Peru and Ecuador (pages 616–619)

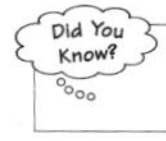

Ecuador is home to some of the world's most extraordinary national parks. In a matter of 200 miles, a traveler can visit parks in all of the country's defining regions—the coastal lowlands in the west, the volcanic central highlands, and the rain forests of the east.

I. Peru *(pages 616–618)*

A. Here you can see Lake Titicaca, the highest navigable lake in the world. **Navigable** means that a body of water is wide and deep enough to allow ships to travel in it.

B. East of the Andes you descend to the foothills and flat plains of the Amazon Basin. **Foothills** are the low hills at the base of a mountain range. Thick forests ... area.

Did You Know

In the Inca Empire, relay teams of messengers carried messages and packages along the Incan roads. One team had a special task—carrying fresh fish from the Pacific Ocean to the emperor's palace high in the Andes. They completed the journey in less than a day.

Meeting Special Needs

Interpersonal Organize students into three groups and assign one of the following topics to each group: landforms, economy, or people. Group members should work together to prepare a map of Peru and Ecuador depicting their assigned topic. Display the completed maps and have student groups discuss how economic activities in these two countries are related to the landforms, climates, and resources found there. L2

Refer to *Inclusion for the Middle School Social Studies Classroom Strategies and Activities* in the TCR.

Chapter 23

Section 2, pages 616–619

Answer a short stalk; The sound (pitch) is determined by the length of each stalk.

Take a Deep Breath
Because of the high altitudes, the lungs of many Andean people may be up to 30 percent larger than those of lowland inhabitants.

World Music: A Cultural Legacy

Use the accompanying Teacher Guide for more about the music of this region.

ASSESS

Assign Section 2 Assessment as homework or an in-class activity.

Have students use the Interactive Tutor Self-Assessment CD-ROM to review Section 23–2.

Reading Check Answer

the Inca

Section Quiz 23–2

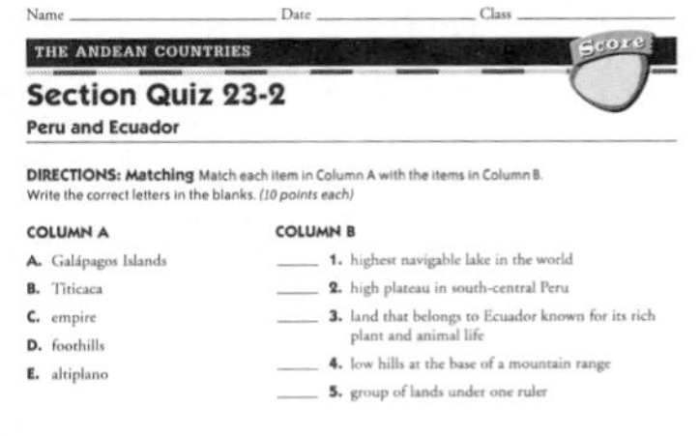

Name ____________ Date ____________ Class ____________

THE ANDEAN COUNTRIES

Score

Section Quiz 23-2

Peru and Ecuador

DIRECTIONS: Matching Match each item in Column A with the items in Column B. Write the correct letters in the blanks. *(10 points each)*

COLUMN A	COLUMN B
A. Galápagos Islands	____ **1.** highest navigable lake in the world
B. Titicaca	____ **2.** high plateau in south-central Peru
C. empire	____ **3.** land that belongs to Ecuador known for its rich plant and animal life
D. foothills	____ **4.** low hills at the base of a mountain range
E. altiplano	____ **5.** group of lands under one ruler

DIRECTIONS: Multiple Choice In the blank at the left, write the letter of the ... the statement or answers the question. *(10 points each)*

Music

Dating back thousands of years, the panpipe is one of the most common musical instruments from the Andes region. Panpipes are made of bamboo in various sizes. Individual bamboo stalks are carefully cut and lashed together with strips of bamboo and woolen string. The notes often alternate from one set of pipes to another. To play a complete melody, then, the two rows of pipes are often stacked one on top of the other.

Looking Closer **Which do you think produces a higher note–a short or long stalk? Explain.**

GO TO **World Music: A Cultural Legacy**
Hear music of this region on Disc 1, Track 10.

Peru's Culture Peru's 26.1 million people live mostly along the Pacific coast. Lima (LEE•mah), with more than 4 million people, is the capital and largest city. In recent years, many people from the countryside have moved to Lima in search of work. Because of this sudden rise in population, the city has become overcrowded, noisy, and polluted.

About half of Peru's people are Native American. In fact, Peru has one of the largest Native American populations in the Western Hemisphere. Most of them blend the Catholic faith, Peru's main religion, with traditional beliefs of their ancestors.

Peruvians also include many people of mixed or European ancestry. People of Asian heritage form a small but important part of the population. In the 1990s, **Alberto Fujimori** (FOO•jee•MAW•ree), a Peruvian of Japanese ancestry, was Peru's president for 10 years.

Spanish is Peru's official language, but about 70 Native American languages also are spoken. You can hear the sounds of **Quechua** (KEH•chuh•wuh), the ancient language of the Inca, in many Native American villages.

Reading Check **Who built a huge empire centered in Peru?**

Ecuador

Ecuador is one of the smallest countries in South America. Can you guess how it got its name? *Ecuador* is the Spanish word for "Equator," which runs right through Ecuador. West of Ecuador and also on the Equator are the **Galápagos Islands.** Owned by Ecuador since 1832, these scattered islands are known for their rich plant and animal life. Turn to page 620 to learn more about the unusual Galápagos Islands.

Critical Thinking Activity

Categorizing Information Read to students a series of statements, such as "Was once the center of an ancient Native American empire," "Sits on the Equator," and so on. Have students identify whether each statement refers to Peru or to Ecuador. **L1**

EE2 Places and Regions: Standard 4

Ecuador's Economy Agriculture is Ecuador's most important economic activity. Because of the mild climate, bananas, cacao, coffee, rice, sugarcane, and other export crops grow plentifully in the coastal lowlands. Farther inland, farms in the Andean highlands grow coffee, beans, corn, potatoes, and wheat. The eastern lowlands yield petroleum, Ecuador's major mineral export.

Ecuador's People About half of Ecuador's nearly 13 million people live along the coast. The important port of **Guayaquil** (GWY•ah•KEEL) is the most populous city. The other half of the population live in the valleys and plateaus of the Andes. **Quito** (KEE•toh), Ecuador's capital, lies more than 9,000 feet (2,743 m) above sea level. The city's historic center has Spanish colonial churches and old whitewashed houses with red-tiled roofs built around central courtyards. You will not find flashing neon signs here because the building of modern structures has been strictly controlled since 1978. In that year, the United Nations Educational, Scientific, and Cultural Organization (UNESCO) declared the "old town" section of Quito a protected world cultural heritage site. Quito does have a "new town" section, though, in the north. This area contains modern offices, embassies, and shopping centers.

✓ Reading Check **Why are Ecuador's eastern lowlands important economically?**

Assessment

Defining Terms

1. Define navigable, foothills, subsistence farm, empire.

Recalling Facts

2. History Who were the first people to grow potatoes?

3. Culture What has been the result of Lima's sudden population growth?

4. Economics What is Ecuador's major mineral export?

Critical Thinking

5. Analyzing Information Why is Peru's name, which means "land of abundance," appropriate? Why is it also inappropriate?

6. Analyzing Cause and Effect What effect does the Peru Current have on the coastal areas of Peru?

Graphic Organizer

7. Organizing Information Create two diagrams like this one, one for Peru and one for Ecuador. Under each heading list facts about the countries.

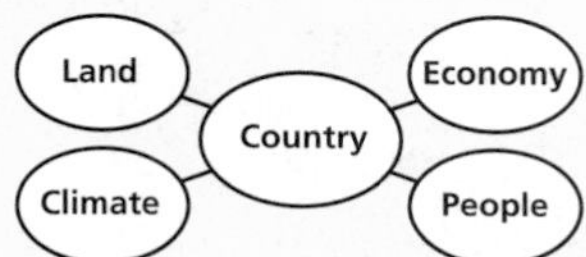

Applying Social Studies Skills

8. Analyzing Maps Turn to the political map on page 605. What Andean capital city lies closest to the Equator?

Section 2 Assessment

1. The terms are defined in the Glossary.
2. Native Americans in the Peruvian Andes
3. Lima has become overcrowded, noisy and polluted.
4. petroleum
5. It is appropriate because Peru is rich in a variety of natural resources, including copper, silver, gold, iron, and fish. It is inappropriate because most people work on subsistence farms.
6. The Peru Current, which is cool, keeps the climate mild, even though the area is very near the Equator.
7. Students' organizers will vary. Check facts for accuracy.
8. Quito, Ecuador

Chapter 23

Section 2, pages 616–619

✓ Reading Check Answer

They have petroleum, the major mineral export.

Reteach

Have students write five questions about Peru and Ecuador using the section text and chapter maps. Then put students in pairs and have them take turns asking and answering questions.

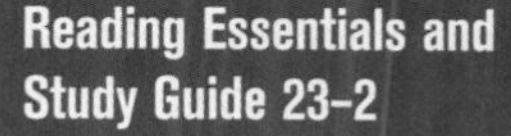

Reading Essentials and Study Guide 23-2

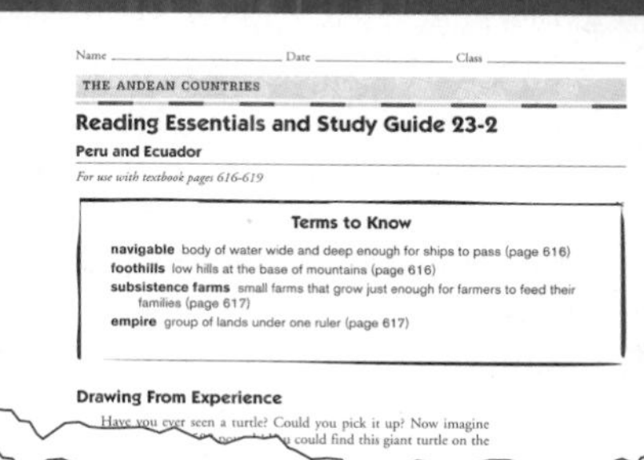
Name Date Class

THE ANDEAN COUNTRIES

Reading Essentials and Study Guide 23-2

Peru and Ecuador

For use with textbook pages 616–619

Terms to Know

navigable body of water wide and deep enough for ships to pass (page 616)
foothills low hills at the base of mountains (page 616)
subsistence farms small farms that grow just enough for farmers to feed their families (page 617)
empire group of lands under one ruler (page 617)

Drawing From Experience

Have you ever seen a turtle? Could you pick it up? Now imagine ... could find this giant turtle on the

Enrich

Have students research and report on the animals of the Galápagos Islands.

Close

Have students choose a destination in Peru or Ecuador that they would like to visit. Have them prepare a brochure about the place.

Teach

Point out to students that the Galápagos Islands were never connected to a larger body of land. **Ask:** **If that is true, how did plants and animals get there?** *(birds by flying; plants carried by the wind or in bird droppings; other animals by sea; plants and animals brought by humans)* **L1**

More About the Galápagos

Pirates used the islands as a base for attacking Spanish treasure ships. In the 1680s, the English pirate Ambrose Cowley first mapped the islands, giving them English names. Today most islands have Spanish names although one remains named for Cowley himself.

Interdisciplinary Connections

Science The Galápagos offer insight into the problems raised by introduced species—plants and animals that are not native to an area but brought there. Less than 20 years ago, Isabela Island had no wild goats. Today there are about 40,000 of these animals. Their efficient foraging of the island's vegetation threatens one species of tortoise and is causing deforestation.

Making Connections

CULTURE | GOVERNMENT | PEOPLE | TECHNOLOGY

The Galápagos Islands

The Galápagos Islands are located in the eastern Pacific Ocean about 600 miles (966 km) west of mainland Ecuador. Since 1959 about 95 percent of the islands has been maintained as a national park.

History of Exploration

From the first documented visit to the Galápagos Islands in 1535, people have commented on the islands' unusual wildlife. Sailors, including pirates and whalers, stopped on the islands to collect water and to trap the huge *galápagos*, or tortoises, found on the islands. Sailors valued the tortoises as a source of fresh meat because the giant tortoises could live on ships for months without food or water.

Charles Darwin

The most famous visitor to the Galápagos Islands was Charles Darwin, a scientist from England. He was studying animals all over the world. In 1835 Darwin spent five weeks visiting four of the biggest islands in the Galápagos. He carefully studied the volcanic landscape and the plant and animal life that he saw. He took notes on the differences between animals such as finches, mockingbirds, and iguanas from island to island. Darwin believed that these differences showed how populations of the same species change to fit their environment.

A Fragile Environment

Today the Galápagos Islands are still prized for their amazing variety of animal and plant life. Many of the species found here exist nowhere else on the earth. For instance, the Marine iguana that lives here is the only seagoing lizard in the world.

Unfortunately, years of contact between the islands and humans have had serious effects. Three of the 14 types of tortoises are extinct, and others are seriously threatened. Populations of goats, pigs, dogs, rats, and some types of plants, brought by visitors, have grown so large that they threaten the survival of native plants and animals. Demand for exotic marine life, including sharks and sea cucumbers, has led to overfishing. The government of Ecuador, along with environmentalists worldwide, is now working to protect the islands.

▲ Giant Galápagos tortoise

Making the Connection

1. Why did sailors long ago stop at the islands?
2. What did Darwin observe about the islands?
3. **Drawing Conclusions** Why are environmentalists and the government of Ecuador working to protect the Galápagos Islands?

Making the Connection

1. to collect water and to trap the large tortoises found there
2. He used them to help understand how populations change to fit their environments.
3. because many species found there exist nowhere else on the earth and because many species are threatened with extinction

Section 3

Bolivia and Chile

Guide to Reading

Main Idea

Bolivia and Chile share the Andes, but their economies and people are different.

Terms to Know

- landlocked
- altiplano
- sodium nitrate

Reading Strategy

Create a chart like the one below. In each row, write at least one fact about Bolivia and one about Chile.

	Bolivia	Chile
Land		
Climate		
Economy		
People		

NATIONAL GEOGRAPHIC **Exploring Our World**

The woman hides her face from the gusting wind as she follows her herd of sheep across the plains of Bolivia. She worries about her teenage children, who want to leave their home to find work in the city. The woman is part of a Native American group called the Chipaya, who raise sheep and farm in the dusty altiplano of Bolivia.

At first glance, Bolivia and Chile seem very different. Bolivia lacks a seacoast, while Chile has a long coastline on the Pacific Ocean. The Andes, however, affect the climate and cultures of both countries.

Bolivia

Bolivia lies near the center of South America. It is a **landlocked** country, having no sea or ocean touching its land. Fortunately, in 1993 Peru agreed to give Bolivia a free trade zone in the port city of **Ilo.** In this way Bolivia has had better access for the free flow of people, goods, and ideas. Bolivia also is the highest and most isolated country in South America. Why? The Andes dominate Bolivia's landscape. Look at the physical map on page 574. You see that in western Bolivia, the Andes surround a high plateau called the **altiplano.** Over one-third of Bolivia is a mile or more high. Unless you were born in this area, you would find that the cold, thin air makes it difficult to breathe. Few trees grow on the altiplano, and most of the land is too dry to farm. Still, the vast majority of Bolivians live on this high plateau. Those areas that have water have been farmed for many centuries.

621

Chapter 23

Section 3, pages 621–624

Focus

Section Objectives

1. Identify where Bolivia and Chile are located.
2. Describe the landforms and climates found in Bolivia and Chile.
3. Compare the economies and people of Bolivia and Chile.

BELLRINGER Skillbuilder Activity

Project transparency and have students answer questions.

This activity is also available as a blackline master.

Daily Focus Skills Transparency 23-3

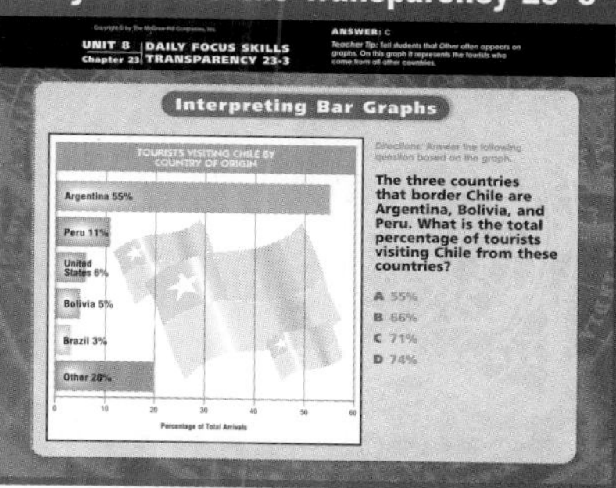

Guide to Reading

Accessing Prior Knowledge

Have students look at the Exploring Our World photograph and discuss what conclusions they can draw from it about life in Bolivia.

Section Resources

Reproducible Masters

- Reproducible Lesson Plan 23-3
- Daily Lecture and Discussion Notes 23-3
- Guided Reading Activity 23-3
- Reading Essentials and Study Guide 23-3
- Section Quiz 23-3

Transparencies

- Daily Focus Skills Transparency 23-3
- GeoQuiz Transparency 23-1

Multimedia

- Vocabulary PuzzleMaker Software
- Interactive Tutor Self-Assessment CD-ROM
- Presentation Plus! CD-ROM
- ExamView® Pro 3.0 Testmaker CD-ROM

TEACH

Drawing Conclusions Have students suggest what challenges Bolivia might face because of its high altitude, dry climate, and status as a landlocked country. **L1**

More About the Photos

Santiago Santiago was founded in 1541 by the Spanish. It became the capital of newly independent Chile in 1818. Today it is Chile's chief industrial city, main highway and railroad hub, and cultural center. Although the city is Chile's capital, the country's legislature meets in Valparaíso.

Caption Answer Tierra del Fuego

Daily Lecture Notes 23-3

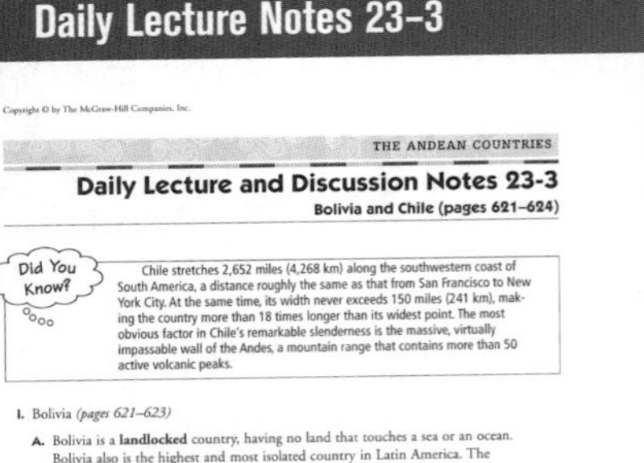

THE ANDEAN COUNTRIES

Daily Lecture and Discussion Notes 23-3

Bolivia and Chile (pages 621–624)

Did You Know? Chile stretches 2,652 miles (4,268 km) along the southwestern coast of South America, a distance roughly the same as that from San Francisco to New York City. At the same time, its width never exceeds 150 miles (241 km), making the country more than 18 times longer than its widest point. The most obvious factor in Chile's remarkable slenderness is the massive, virtually impassable wall of the Andes, a mountain range that contains more than 50 active volcanic peaks.

I. Bolivia *(pages 621–623)*

A. Bolivia is a **landlocked** country, having no land that touches a sea or an ocean. Bolivia also is the highest and most isolated country in Latin America. The Andes dominate Bolivia's landscape. In western Bolivia, the Andes surround a ... led the altiplano. Most Bolivians live on the altiplano.

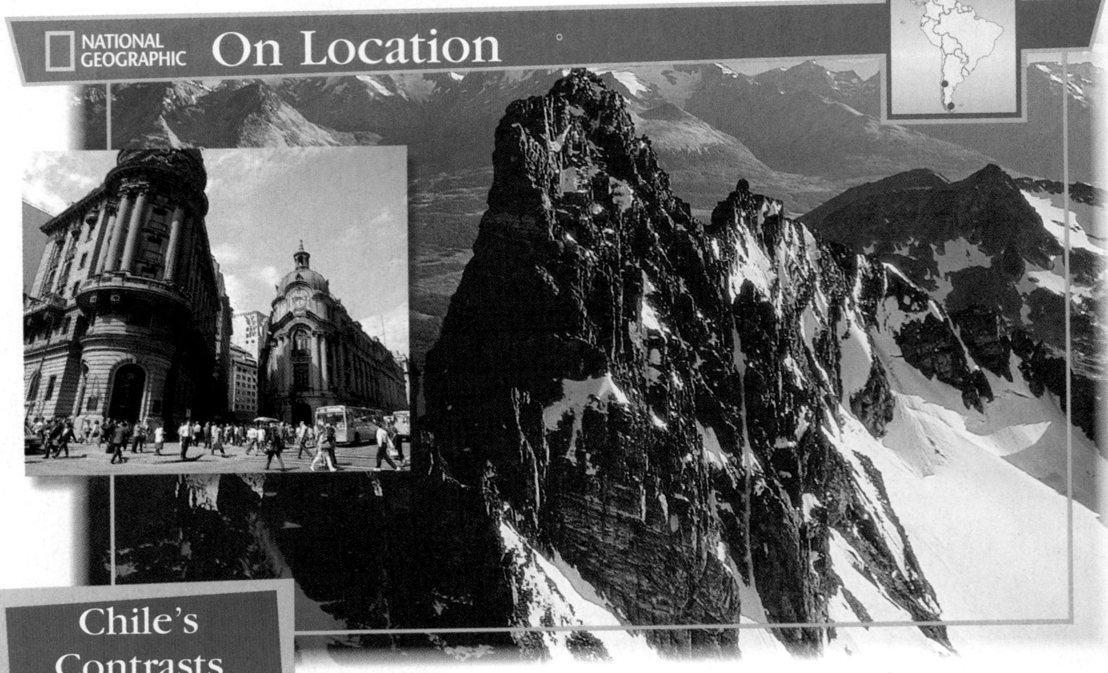

Chile's Contrasts

Chile has a wide variety of climates and landforms. The moderate capital city of Santiago in central Chile (above) contrasts sharply with the icy southern region (right).

Location **What group of islands lies at the southern tip of Chile?**

Bolivia also has lowland plains and tropical rain forests. Most of this area has a hot, humid climate. South-central Bolivia, however, has more fertile land, and many farms dot this region.

Bolivia's Economy Bolivia is rich in minerals such as tin, silver, and zinc. Miners remove these minerals from high in the Andes. Workers in the eastern lowlands draw out gold, petroleum, and natural gas.

Still, Bolivia is a poor country. About two-thirds of the people live in poverty. Throughout the highlands, many villagers practice subsistence farming. Subsistence farming is growing just enough food to feed yourself and your family. There is little, if any, left over to sell for cash. They struggle to grow wheat, potatoes, and barley. At higher elevations, herders raise animals such as alpacas and llamas for wool and for carrying goods. In the south, farmers plant soybeans, a growing export. Timber is another important export. Unfortunately, one crop that can be grown for sale is coca, which is made into coca paste from the leaves of the bush. The paste is then made into cocaine. The **Time Reports: Focus on World Issues** on pages 609–615 looks at the efforts to reduce the flow of drugs from South America.

Bolivia's People What is unusual about Bolivia's capital? There is not just one capital city, but two. The official capital is **Sucre** (SOO•kray). The administrative capital and largest city is **La Paz** (lah•PAHZ). Both capital cities are located in the altiplano. La Paz—at 12,000 feet (3,658 m)—is the highest capital city in the world.

Team-Teaching Activity

Science Point out to students that the altiplano of Bolivia and the mountains and deserts of Chile are very different environments. Remind them that a special community of plants and animals are suited to each of those environments. With the aid of the biology or other science teacher, have students research an environment found in Bolivia or Chile. Have them prepare dioramas that illustrate the plant and animal life found in those environments. Afterwards, have them compare the two countries using the dioramas. **L2**

EE3 Physical Systems: Standard 8

Most of Bolivia's 8.5 million people live in the Andean highlands. About half are of Native American ancestry, and another 40 percent are mestizos. In the cities, most people follow modern ways of living. In the country, you may hear traditional sounds—music played with flutelike instruments.

Reading Check What is the altiplano?

Chile

Chile is almost twice the size of California. Though its average width is only 110 miles (177 km), Chile stretches 2,652 miles (4,267 km) along the Pacific Ocean.

About 80 percent of Chile's land is mountainous. The high Andes run along Chile's border with Bolivia and Argentina. Except in the altiplano area of Chile's north, very few Chileans live in the Andes.

Also in the north is the **Atacama Desert.** It is one of the driest places on the earth. Why? This area is in the rain shadow of the Andes. Winds from the Atlantic Ocean bring precipitation to regions east of the Andes, but they carry no moisture past them. In addition, the cold Peru Current in the Pacific Ocean does not evaporate as much as a warm current does. As a result, only dry air hits the coast.

A moderate zone lies just north of **Santiago,** Chile's capital. Most of Chile's people live in a central region called the Central Valley. The fertile valleys here have the largest concentration of cities, industries, and farms.

The lake region, also known as "the south," supports thick forests. Chile's far south is a stormy, windswept region of snowcapped volcanoes, thick forests, and huge glaciers. The **Strait of Magellan** separates mainland Chile from a group of islands known as **Tierra del Fuego** (FWAY•goh)—or "Land of Fire." This region is shared by both Chile and Argentina. Cold ocean waters batter the rugged coast around **Cape Horn,** the southernmost point of South America.

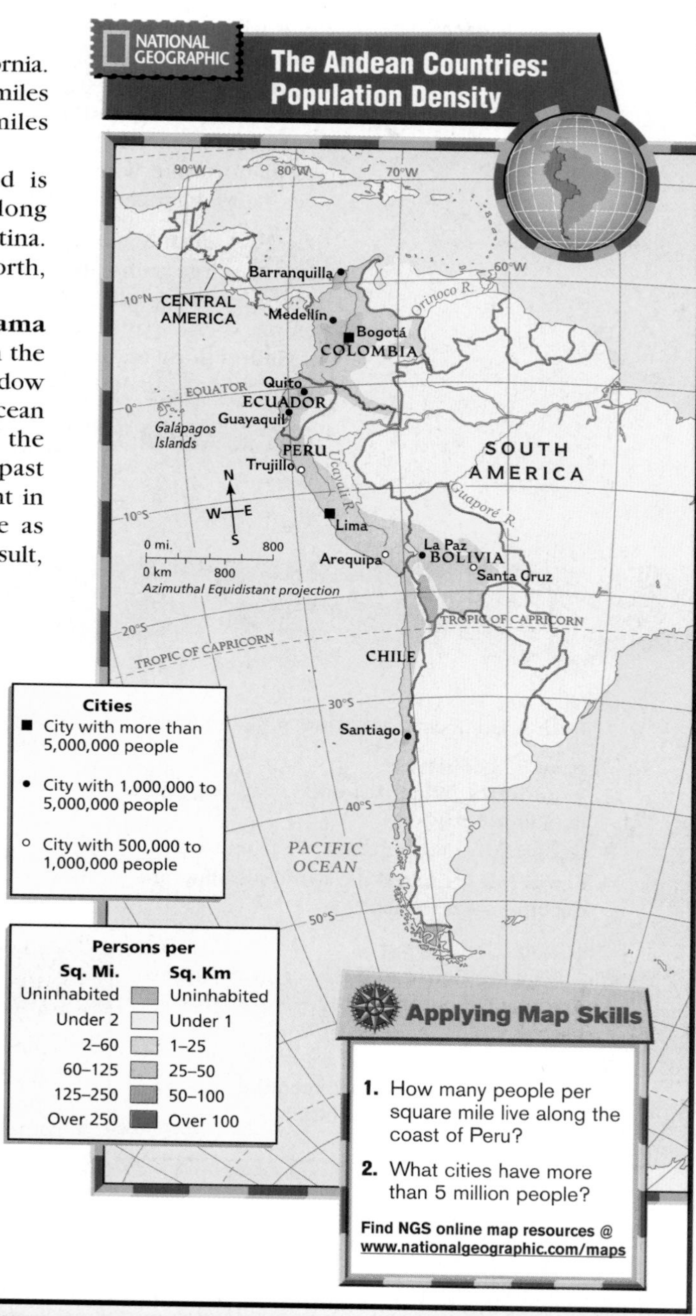

Applying Map Skills

1. How many people per square mile live along the coast of Peru?
2. What cities have more than 5 million people?

Find NGS online map resources @ www.nationalgeographic.com/maps

Chapter 23

Section 3, pages 621–624

Reading Check Answer

a high plateau

Guided Reading Activity 23-3

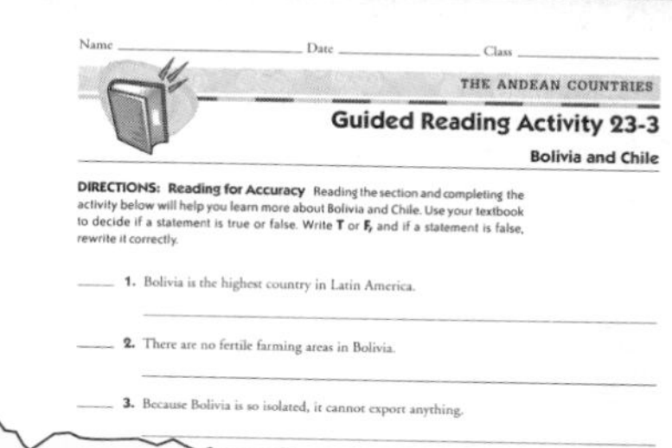
Name ______ Date ______ Class ______

THE ANDEAN COUNTRIES

Guided Reading Activity 23-3

Bolivia and Chile

DIRECTIONS: Reading for Accuracy Reading the section and completing the activity below will help you learn more about Bolivia and Chile. Use your textbook to decide if a statement is true or false. Write T or F, and if a statement is false, rewrite it correctly.

____ 1. Bolivia is the highest country in Latin America.

____ 2. There are no fertile farming areas in Bolivia.

____ 3. Because Bolivia is so isolated, it cannot export anything.

Assign Section 3 Assessment as homework or an in-class activity.

Have students use the Interactive Tutor Self-Assessment CD-ROM to review Section 23–3.

Applying Map Skills

Answers

1. about 2 to 60 per square mile (1 to 25 per sq. km)
2. Bogotá, Lima

Skills Practice

What are the largest cities in Ecuador? *(Quito, Guayaquil)* **in Bolivia?** *(La Paz, Santa Cruz)*

Cooperative Learning Activity

Creating a Dictionary Have students work in groups to create an illustrated dictionary of Latin American terms. They can begin with the term in this section—altiplano—but can add those from other sections (cordillera, llano, mestizo, and campesino from the section on Colombia, for example). Assign a specific task to each group member, such as finding terms, writing definitions, illustrating the words, and collating pages. Make sure that all group members receive a copy of the dictionary. **ELL L1**

EE2 Places and Regions: Standard 6

Chapter 23

Section 3, pages 621–624

Section Quiz 23-3

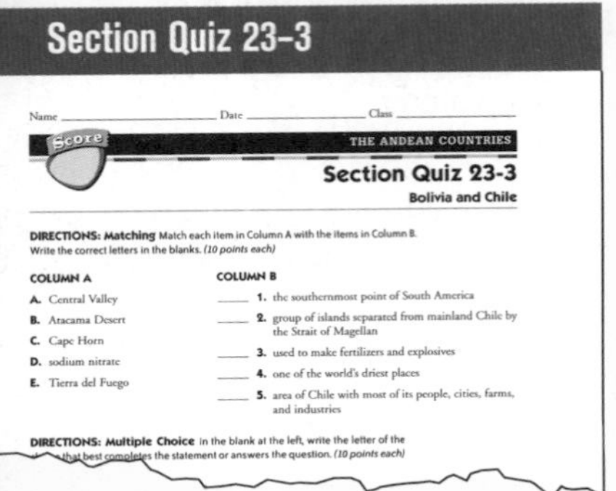

Name ______ Date ______ Class ______

Score — THE ANDEAN COUNTRIES

Section Quiz 23-3

Bolivia and Chile

DIRECTIONS: Matching Match each item in Column A with the items in Column B. Write the correct letters in the blanks. *(10 points each)*

COLUMN A

A. Central Valley
B. Atacama Desert
C. Cape Horn
D. sodium nitrate
E. Tierra del Fuego

COLUMN B

____ **1.** the southernmost point of South America
____ **2.** group of islands separated from mainland Chile by the Strait of Magellan
____ **3.** used to make fertilizers and explosives
____ **4.** one of the world's driest places
____ **5.** area of Chile with most of its people, cities, farms, and industries

DIRECTIONS: Multiple Choice In the blank at the left, write the letter of the ... that best completes the statement or answers the question. *(10 points each)*

✓ Reading Check Answer

mestizos, European descendants, Native Americans

Reteach

Name a physical feature, type of climate, resource, economic activity, or culture group. Have students identify whether the characteristic refers to Bolivia, Chile, or both countries.

Reading Essentials and Study Guide 23-3

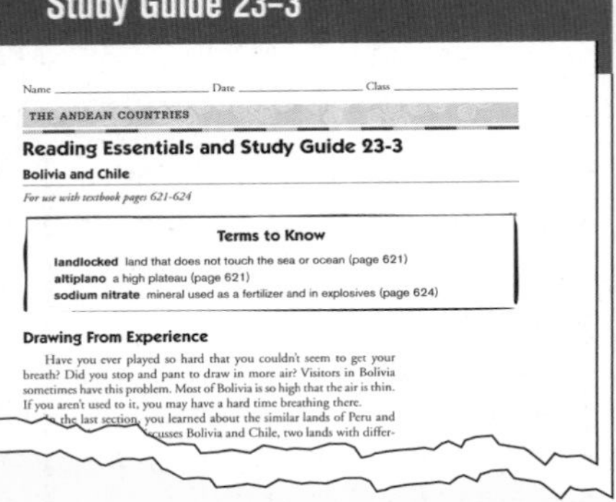

Name ______ Date ______ Class ______

THE ANDEAN COUNTRIES

Reading Essentials and Study Guide 23-3

Bolivia and Chile

For use with textbook pages 621-624

Terms to Know

landlocked land that does not touch the sea or ocean (page 621)
altiplano a high plateau (page 621)
sodium nitrate mineral used as a fertilizer and in explosives (page 624)

Drawing From Experience

Have you ever played so hard that you couldn't seem to get your breath? Did you stop and pant to draw in more air? Visitors in Bolivia sometimes have this problem. Most of Bolivia is so high that the air is thin. If you aren't used to it, you may have a hard time breathing there.

... the last section, you learned about the similar lands of Peru and ... cusses Bolivia and Chile, two lands with differ-

4 Close

Have students prepare an annotated map highlighting the key characteristics of Bolivia and Chile.

Chile's Economy In recent years, Chile has enjoyed high economic growth, and the number of people living below the poverty line has fallen by half. Mining forms the backbone of Chile's economy. The Atacama region is rich in minerals. Chile ranks as the world's leading copper producer. The country also mines and exports gold, silver, iron ore, and **sodium nitrate**—a mineral used as a fertilizer and in explosives.

Agriculture is also a major economic activity. Farmers produce wheat, corn, beans, sugar, and potatoes. The grapes and apples you eat in winter may come from Chile's summer harvest. Many people also raise cattle, sheep, and other livestock.

Chile has factories that process fish and other foods. Other workers manufacture wood products, iron, steel, vehicles, cement, and textiles. Service industries such as banking and tourism also thrive.

Chile's Culture Of the 15.4 million people in Chile, most are mestizos. A large minority are of European descent, and some Native American groups live in the altiplano and "the south." Nearly all the people speak Spanish, and most are Roman Catholic. Some 80 percent of Chile's population live in urban areas. Chile has been a democratic republic since the end of strict military rule in 1989.

✓ Reading Check **What three cultural backgrounds make up Chile's 15.4 million people?**

Section 3 Assessment

Defining Terms

1. **Define** landlocked, altiplano, sodium nitrate.

Recalling Facts

2. **Economics** What part of Bolivia's population lives in poverty?
3. **Geography** What makes La Paz unusual?
4. **Economics** Chile is the world's leading producer of what mineral?

Critical Thinking

5. **Analyzing Cause and Effect** Why is the Atacama Desert one of the world's driest places?
6. **Making Comparisons** What are differences and similarities between the economies of Bolivia and Chile?

Graphic Organizer

7. **Organizing Information** Create a diagram like this one. Under each arrow list supporting facts for the main idea given.

Main Idea: Bolivia is rich in minerals but is still a poor country.

↑ ↑ ↑ ↑

Applying Social Studies Skills

8. **Analyzing Maps** Study the physical map on page 574. The southernmost tip of South America is part of what country? What is the name of the group of islands at the southern tip of South America? What does its name mean?

Section 3 Assessment

1. The terms are defined in the Glossary.
2. about two-thirds of the people
3. It is the world's highest capital city.
4. copper
5. Moist winds from the Atlantic do not reach past the Andes. Also, winds from the Pacific are dry because the current is cold.
6. *Differences:* Bolivia is landlocked, Chile has a coast; Bolivia is mostly poor, Chile has more economic growth; Bolivians practice subsistence farming, Chilean farmers export products; Chile has factories and services. *Similarities:* Both have mineral resources and depend upon agriculture.
7. Farmers struggle to grow food; two-thirds live in poverty; needs to expand economy; hopes to increase trade.
8. Chile; Tierra del Fuego; "Land of Fire"

Reading Review

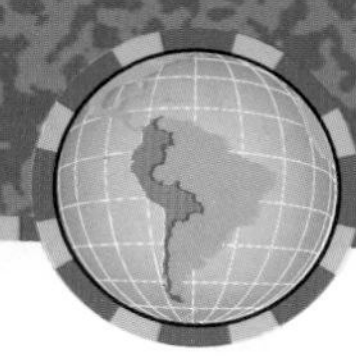

Section 1 Colombia

Terms to Know
- cordillera
- llanos
- cash crop
- mestizo
- republic
- campesino

Main Idea

Although it has many resources, Colombia faces political and economic turmoil.

✓Culture Most Colombians speak Spanish and follow the Roman Catholic faith.

✓Economics Colombia is rich in hydroelectric power, gold, and emeralds.

✓Government The government of Colombia is struggling to combat the power of drug dealers who make huge fortunes from selling cocaine, which comes from the coca plant.

✓History Civil war in Colombia has lasted for more than 35 years.

Section 2 Peru and Ecuador

Terms to Know
- navigable
- foothills
- subsistence farm
- empire

Main Idea

Peru and Ecuador share similar landscapes, climates, and history.

✓History The Inca had a powerful civilization in the area that is now Peru. They developed a complex system of record-keeping.

✓Economics Peru's main exports are copper and fish. Many people farm. Ecuador's economy is focused on agriculture.

✓Culture Most people in Peru and Ecuador live along the coast.

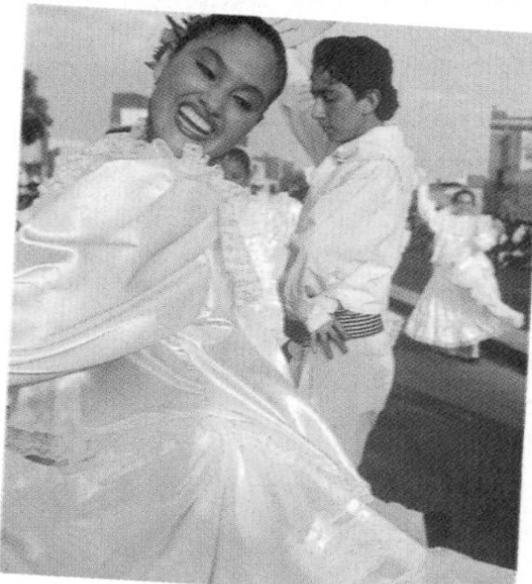

▲ Dancers in Peru

Section 3 Bolivia and Chile

Terms to Know
- landlocked
- altiplano
- sodium nitrate

Main Idea

Bolivia and Chile share the Andes, but their economies and people are different.

✓Human/Environment Interaction Bolivia is a poor country consisting mainly of the towering Andes and a high plateau that is difficult to farm.

✓Culture Most of Chile's people speak Spanish and follow the Roman Catholic faith.

✓Economics Chile has a diverse economy that includes mining—especially copper and sodium nitrate—farming, and manufacturing.

Reading Review

Use the Chapter 23 Reading Review to preview, review, condense, or reteach the chapter.

Preview/Review

Use the Terms to Know lists to help students review and study.

Activity Have students form into teams and play a game in which teams have to provide the correct definitions for the terms from the chapter.

Vocabulary PuzzleMaker Software reinforces the vocabulary terms used in Chapter 23.

The Interactive Tutor Self-Assessment CD-ROM allows students to review Chapter 23 content.

Condense

Have students read the Chapter 23 summary statements.

Chapter 23 Guided Reading Activities

Chapter 23 Audio Program

Reteach

Reteaching Activity 23

Chapter 23 Reading Essentials and Study Guide

Chapter Culminating Activity

Ask students: How do the Andes affect the lives of people in the countries from Colombia to Chile? Have them prepare a report that focuses on one area of life, such as earning a living, clothing, food, housing, and so on. Have them research life in each of the Andean countries in terms of this area and prepare an illustrated display that shows the impact of the Andes on at least three of the five countries. *NOTE: This activity may be completed separately or you may wish students to incorporate it into their Current Events Journals.*

EE5 Environment and Society: Standard 15

Assessment and Activities

GLENCOE TECHNOLOGY

MindJogger Videoquiz
Use MindJogger to review the Chapter 23 content.

 Available in VHS.

Using Key Terms

1. e
2. i
3. b
4. j
5. f
6. h
7. d
8. c
9. g
10. a

Reviewing the Main Ideas

11. *Any four:* petroleum, gold, emeralds, coal, hydroelectric power, timber
12. mestizo
13. political violence (revolts and civil wars)
14. Lake Titicaca
15. the Inca
16. Ecuador
17. They are poor subsistence farmers or herders, living on the altiplano.
18. democratic republic
19. mestizo

Chapter 23 Assessment and Activities

Using Key Terms

Match the terms in Part A with their definitions in Part B.

A.

1. cordillera
2. campesino
3. cash crop
4. llanos
5. navigable
6. foothills
7. empire
8. sodium nitrate
9. landlocked
10. mestizo

B.

a. person of mixed Native American and European ancestry
b. crop grown to be sold, often for export
c. mineral used in making fertilizer
d. group of lands under one ruler
e. group of mountain ranges that run side by side
f. when a body of water is wide and deep enough for ships to pass through
g. land that doesn't have a sea or ocean touching it
h. low hills at the base of a mountain range
i. farmer in Colombia
j. hot grasslands

Reviewing the Main Ideas

Section 1 Colombia

11. **Economics** List four of Colombia's natural resources.
12. **History** What is the heritage of most of Colombia's people?
13. **History** What type of activities have scarred Colombia's history?

Section 2 Peru and Ecuador

14. **Place** What is the highest navigable lake in the world?
15. **History** What ancient Native American civilization of the Andes lived in Peru?
16. **Government** Who owns the Galápagos Islands?

Section 3 Bolivia and Chile

17. **Culture** What is life like for about two-thirds of Bolivia's people?
18. **Government** What type of government does Chile have?
19. **Culture** What is the ethnic background of most Chileans?

The Andean Countries

Place Location Activity

On a separate sheet of paper, match the letters on the map with the numbered places listed below.

1. Colombia
2. Peru
3. Chile
4. Andes
5. Lake Titicaca
6. Quito
7. Bogotá
8. Strait of Magellan
9. Lima
10. Bolivia

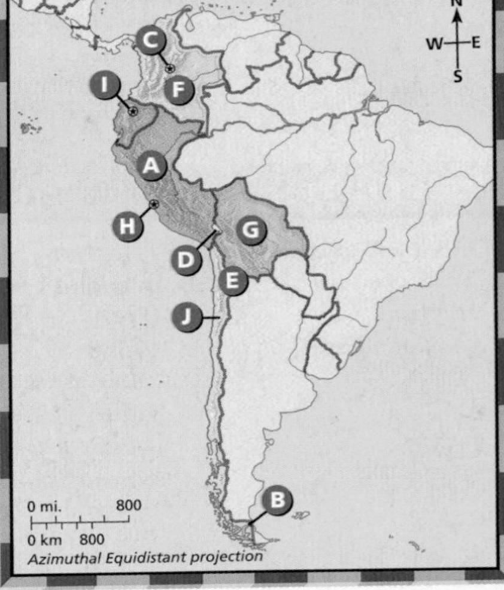

NATIONAL GEOGRAPHIC Place Location Activity

1. F
2. A
3. J
4. E
5. D
6. I
7. C
8. B
9. H
10. G

Critical Thinking

20. In isolated regions, these groups do not come into contact with more modern ways of doing things, so they are likely to follow traditional ways of life.
21. Factors should include drug wars, poverty (wide gap between rich and poor), and differences between major political parties.

Our World Today online

Self-Check Quiz Visit the ***Our World Today: People, Places, and Issues*** Web site at owt.glencoe.com and click on **Chapter 23–Self-Check Quizzes** to prepare for the Chapter Test.

Critical Thinking

20. **Making Inferences** Why are Native Americans who live in the Andean highlands more likely to follow a traditional way of life than those who live in the cities?
21. **Analyzing Cause and Effect** On a diagram like the one below, list factors that have led to political violence during Colombia's history.

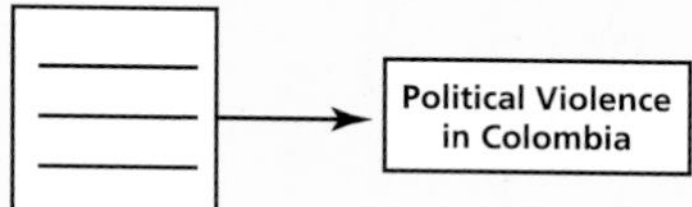

Current Events Journal

22. **Writing About Cities** Research one of the major cities of the Andean countries. Prepare a report that includes a map, a fact bank, pictures, and a T-shirt design that shows a famous landmark of the city.

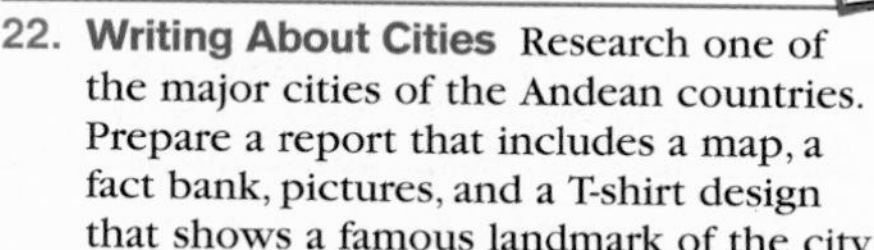

Mental Mapping Activity

23. **Focusing on the Region** Create a simple outline map of South America; then label the following:

- Pacific Ocean
- Peru
- Andes
- Colombia
- Atacama Desert
- Galápagos Islands
- Strait of Magellan
- Lake Titicaca
- Chile
- Ecuador

Technology Skills Activity

24. **Building a Database** Create a fact sheet about the Andean countries by building a database. Create fields for such categories as physical features, natural resources, capital cities, population, and type of government. When you have entered data for each field, print your fact sheet.

Standardized Test Practice

Directions: Read the paragraphs below, and then answer the question that follows.

Simón Bolívar, an aristocrat from Venezuela, led many of South America's lands to independence. He believed in equality and saw liberty as "the only object worth a man's life." Called "the Liberator," Bolívar devoted his life to freedom for Latin Americans.

Bolívar was the son of a rich family in New Granada, or what is today Colombia, Venezuela, Panama, and Ecuador. In 1805 he went to Europe. There he learned about the French Revolution and its ideas of democracy. He returned home, vowing to free his people from Spanish rule. In 1810 Bolívar started a revolt against the Spaniards in Venezuela. Spanish officials soon crushed the movement, but Bolívar escaped and trained an army. During the next 20 years, Bolívar and his forces won freedom for the present-day countries of Venezuela, Colombia, Panama, Bolivia, and Ecuador.

1. What is the main idea of the paragraphs above?

A Bolívar was the son of a rich family.
B Bolívar traveled to Europe and learned about democracy.
C Simón Bolívar was called "the Liberator."
D Bolívar devoted his life to freedom for Latin Americans.

Test-Taking Tip: This question asks you to find the main idea, or to make a generalization. Most of the answer choices provide specific details, not a general idea. Which of the answers is more of a general statement?

Assessment and Activities

Standardized Test Practice

1. D

Tested Objectives:
Making generalizations, identifying the main idea

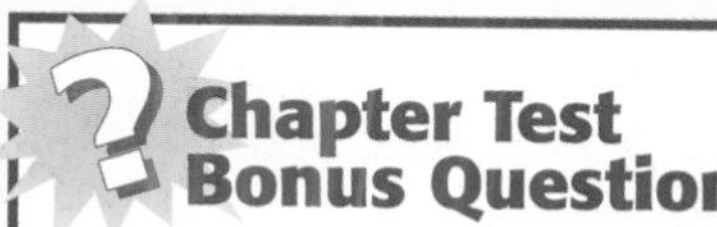

This question may be used for extra credit on the chapter test.

Is Ecuador in the Northern Hemisphere or the Southern Hemisphere? *(both)*

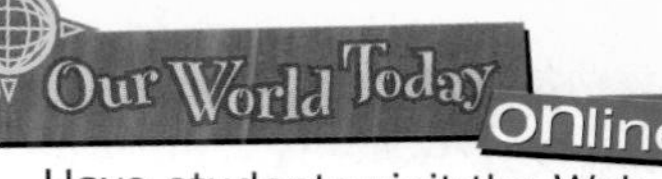

Have students visit the Web site at **owt.glencoe.com** to review Chapter 23 and take the Self-Check Quiz.

Current Events Journal

22. Students' reports should include all of the required elements: map, fact bank, pictures, and T-shirt design. Possible cities include Bogotá, Lima, Quito, La Paz, Sucre, and Santiago.

Mental Mapping Activity

23. This exercise helps students visualize the countries and geographic features they have been studying and to understand the relationships among various points. All attempts at freehand mapping should be accepted.

Technology Skills Activity

24. Students' fact sheets should include all the required information for each of the five countries covered in the chapter.

Unit 9 Planning Guide

SUGGESTED PACING CHART

Unit 9 (1 day)	Chapter 24 (4 days)	Chapter 25 (4 days)	Unit 9 (2 days)
Day 1 Introduction	**Day 1** Chapter 24 Intro, Section 1	**Day 1** Chapter 25 Intro, Section 1	**Day 1** Wrap-Up/Projects
	Day 2 Section 2	**Day 2** Section 2	**Day 2** Unit 9 Assessment
	Day 3 Chapter 24 Review	**Day 3** Chapter 25 Review	
	Day 4 Chapter 24 Assessment	**Day 4** Chapter 25 Assessment	

For a complete course pacing guide and Teacher Classroom Resources, see:

Interactive Lesson Planner

Use the following tools to easily assess student learning in a variety of ways:

- **Performance Assessment Activities and Rubrics**
- **Section Quizzes**
- **Chapter Tests and Unit Pretests and Posttests**
- **Interactive Tutor Self-Assessment CD-ROM**
- **ExamView® Pro 3.0 Testmaker CD-ROM**
- **MindJogger Videoquiz**
- **owt.glencoe.com**
- **Standardized Test Practice Workbook**

Note: The following materials may be used when teaching Unit 9.
Chapter level support materials can be found on the chapter resource pages.

TEACHING TRANSPARENCIES

Political Map Transparency 9

Unit 9 Map Overlay Transparencies

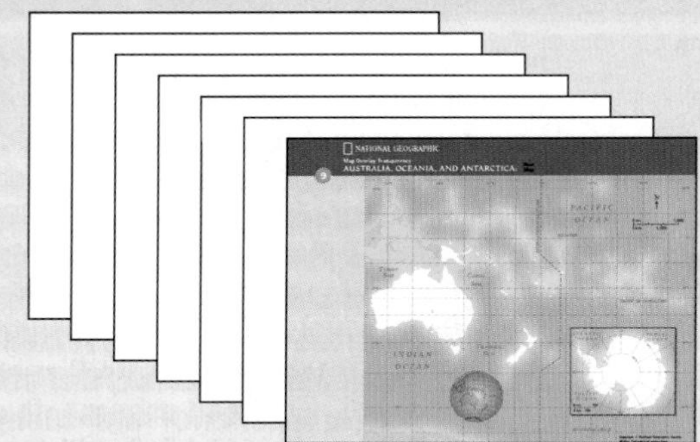

World Cultures Transparencies 15 and 16

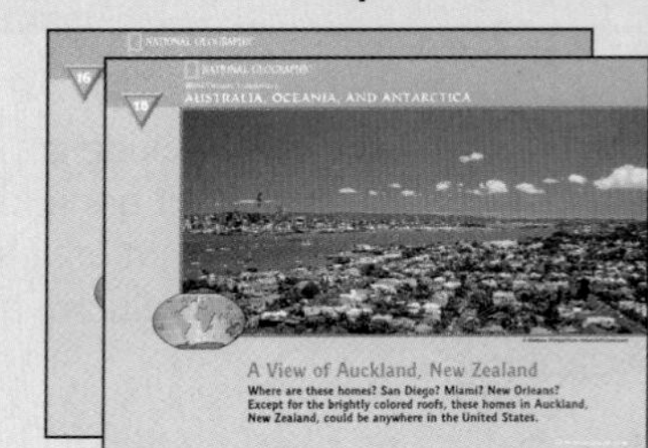

Unit 9 Resources

INTERDISCIPLINARY CONNECTIONS

World Literature Reading 9

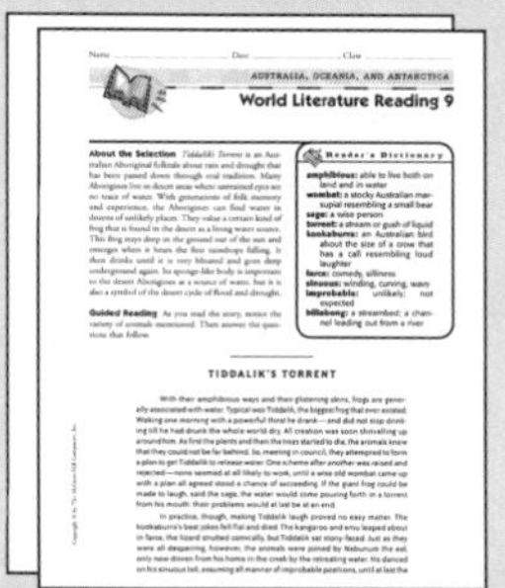

AUSTRALIA, OCEANIA, AND ANTARCTICA

World Literature Reading 9

TIDDALIK'S TORRENT

Economics and Geography Activity 9

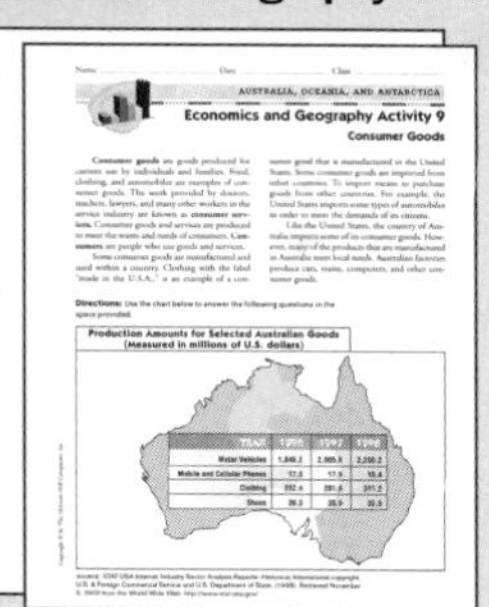

AUSTRALIA, OCEANIA, AND ANTARCTICA

Economics and Geography Activity 9

Consumer Goods

Production Amounts for Selected Australian Goods (measured in millions of U.S. dollars)

History and Geography Activity 9

AUSTRALIA, OCEANIA, AND ANTARCTICA

History and Geography Activity 9

New Zealand's Struggle for Women's Right to Vote

THE WOMAN SUFFRAGE MOVEMENT IN NEW ZEALAND

MAP AND GEOGRAPHY SKILLS

Building Geography Skills for Life

NGS Focus on Geography Literacy

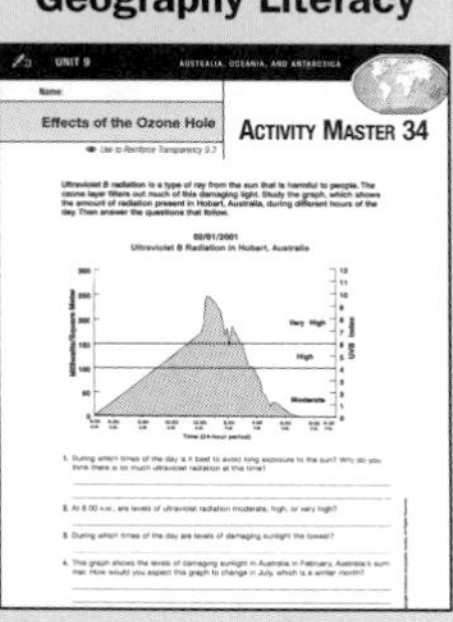

UNIT 9 AUSTRALIA, OCEANIA, AND ANTARCTICA

Effects of the Ozone Hole

ACTIVITY MASTER 34

Regional Atlas Activity 9

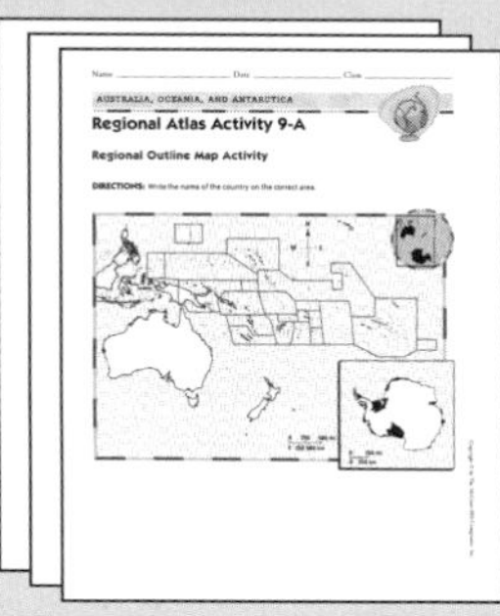

AUSTRALIA, OCEANIA, AND ANTARCTICA

Regional Atlas Activity 9-A

Regional Outline Map Activity

NATIONAL GEOGRAPHIC MapMachine

Find the latest coverage of geography in the news, atlas updates, cartographic activities with interactive maps, an online map store, and links at www.nationalgeographic.com/maps

APPLICATION AND HANDS-ON

Citizenship Activity 9

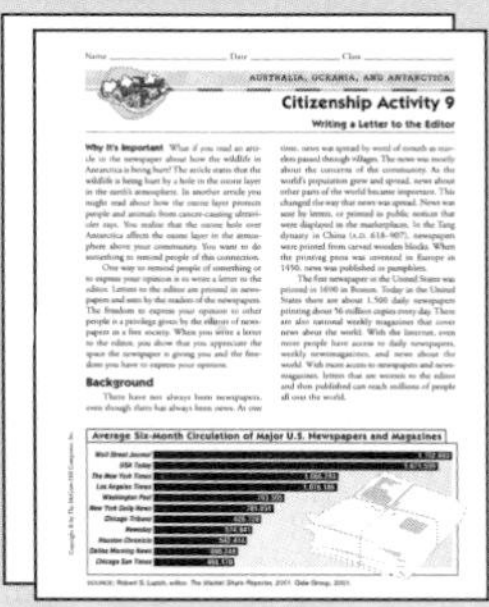

AUSTRALIA, OCEANIA, AND ANTARCTICA

Citizenship Activity 9

Writing a Letter to the Editor

Foods Around the World 9

UNIT 11: AUSTRALIA AND OCEANIA

Foods of Australia and New Zealand

ENRICHMENT AND EXTENSION

Environmental Case Study 9

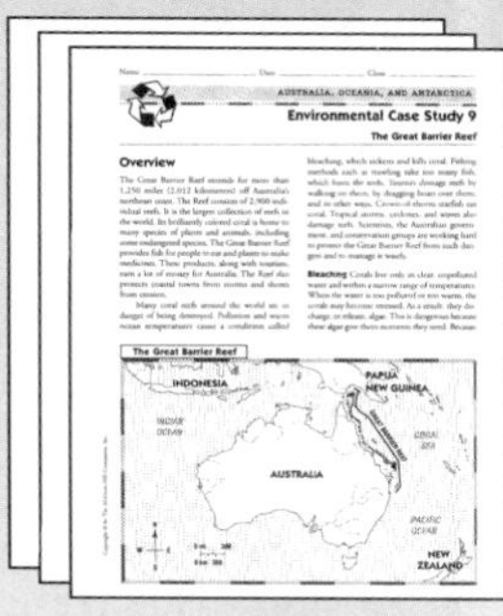

AUSTRALIA, OCEANIA, AND ANTARCTICA

Environmental Case Study 9

The Great Barrier Reef

World Music: A Cultural Legacy

ASSESSMENT AND EVALUATION

GLENCOE'S ASSESSMENT ADVANTAGE

Unit 9 Pretests

AUSTRALIA, OCEANIA, AND ANTARCTICA

Unit 9 Pretest Form A

Unit 9 Pretest Form B

Unit 9 Posttests

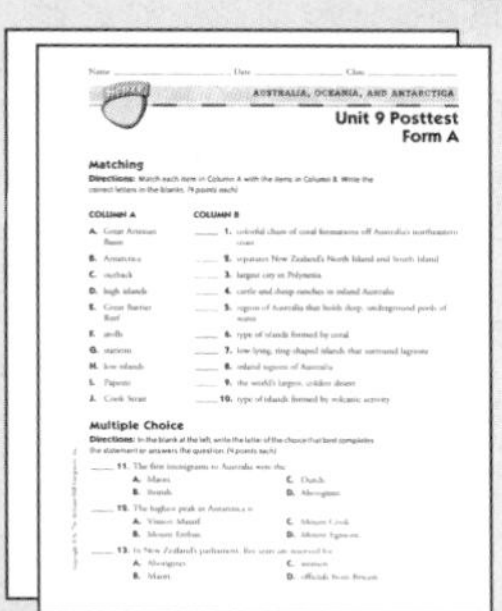

AUSTRALIA, OCEANIA, AND ANTARCTICA

Unit 9 Posttest Form A

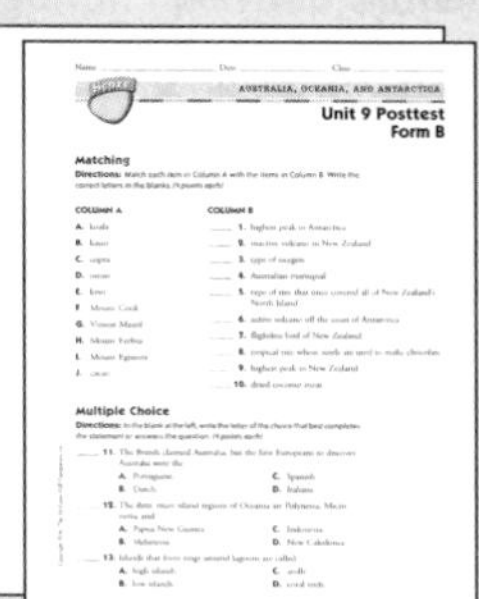

AUSTRALIA, OCEANIA, AND ANTARCTICA

Unit 9 Posttest Form B

Additional Unit 9 Resources

- owt.glencoe.com
  Our World Today: People, Places, and Issues
  Visit the Glencoe *Our World Today: People, Places, and Issues* Web site for overviews, activities, assessments, and updated charts and graphs.
- socialstudies.glencoe.com
  Glencoe Social Studies
  Visit the Glencoe Web site for social studies activities, updates, and links to other sites.
- www.teachingtoday.glencoe.com
  Glencoe Teaching Today
  This Web site features daily teaching tips, free PDF downloads, annotated Web resources, educational news, and more.
- www.nationalgeographic.com
  NGS ONLINE Visit the National Geographic Society Web site for the latest coverage of geography in the news, atlas updates, activities, links, interactive features, and archives.
- **Glencoe's Guide to Using the Internet**
  Provides an introduction to many of the current technologies on the Internet. Professional resources and teaching strategies included.

Our Web sites provide additional resources. All essential content is covered in the Student Edition.

The following videotape programs are available from Glencoe:

- **Admiral Richard Byrd** 1-56501-888-5

To order, call Glencoe at 1-800-334-7344. To find classroom resources to accompany many of these, check:

A&E Television: www.aetv.com

The History Channel: www.historychannel.com

Bibliography

Literature for the Student

- **Glencoe Middle School World Literature Library**
- ***The Great Barrier Reef,*** by Maura M. Gouck. Plymouth, Minn.: Child's World, 1993.
- ***New Zealand in Pictures.*** Minneapolis: Lerner, 1993.
- ***Antarctica,*** by Laurence Pringle. New York: Simon & Schuster, 1992.

Readings for the Teacher

- ***The Happy Isles of Oceania: Paddling the Pacific,*** by Paul Theroux. New York: G.P. Putnam's Sons, 1992.
- ***Ticket to Ride: A Rail Journey Around Australia,*** by Anthony Dennis. New York: Prentice-Hall, 1990.

Multimedia Links

- ***History and Culture of Australia.*** Fairfield, Conn.: Queue. CD-ROM, Win/Mac.
- ***The Pacific World.*** New York: Educational Design, VHS, 45 minutes.
- ***Touring New Zealand.*** Chicago: Questar, 1989. VHS, 60 minutes.
- ***WorldWalker: Destination Australia.*** Palo Alto, Calif.: Soleil Software. CD-ROM, Win/Mac.

Refer to owt.glencoe.com for additional literature titles and study guides related to this region.

Additional Glencoe Teacher Support

- **Teaching Strategies for the Geography Classroom**
- **Reproducible Lesson Plans**
- **Outline Map Resource Book**
- **Reading in the Content Area**

Service Learning Project

Connecting Classroom With Community

Many islands in Oceania promote tourism as a vital part of their economies. Have students help an agency that promotes tourism in their community. They could participate in clean-up campaigns, work in promotional activities, or work in many different capacities at a local tourist attraction. After they have completed their work, have students complete a project summary report that includes such information as: How did this project help my community? What did I learn while completing this project?

Content Background Notes

Use this additional information as lecture notes or discussion prompts throughout the study of Unit 9.

Chapter 24 Australia and New Zealand (pp. 636–657)

Preserving the Land Australia's fragile landscape has suffered at the hands of humans. Only in recent years has the extent of the damage become known. In fact, that damage may not yet be fully clear. A report on the issue recently stated that Australia has far less information on "the condition and productive capacity of its land" than other industrialized nations.

Some signs of damage are evident. Australia's wheat belt, in western Australia, is suffering from salinity. The cause was deforestation, which was carried out to clear the fields for planting. The loss of trees caused the water table to rise, bringing underground salt water to the surface. One study says that 10 percent of the wheat-producing area is now affected by this problem, but that the proportion may rise to 40 percent. The highly saline water also threatens the water supplies used by cities. The effects of deforestation have been harsh. About 40 percent of the country's forests have been cut down. That includes nearly three-fourths of the country's rain forests. In addition, an Australian government agency calls the country's record on animal extinctions "the worst for any country." Australians are taking steps to be kinder to the environment.

Splitting Families One reason for Australia's long history of poor relations between whites and Aborigines was the deliberate taking of children. From 1910 to the 1970s, nearly 100,000 Aborigine children were taken from their parents. Children who had light skins were adopted. Those who were darker were put in orphanages. The actions were part of the government's attempt to assimilate Aborigines into white culture. Recently, Australia's prime minister expressed his regret over the policy, calling it "a blemished chapter in our national history."

Saving the Whales All across the world, scientists are trying to understand why marine mammals occasionally beach themselves. Whatever the cause, the result is death—unless the creatures can be returned to the sea. A group in New Zealand has dedicated themselves to trying to do just that. Workers for Project Jonah roll the animals onto a mat that has inflatable pontoons attached. As the tide rises, the pontoons can be used to float the animal out to sea. In the 15 years it has used this system, the project has saved about 2,000 marine mammals.

The Kiwi The kiwi bird is the national symbol of New Zealand. Soon, however, it may be just a memory. The kiwi is a small flightless bird that has nostrils on its beak to sniff out worms—a unique feature among birds. The bird's numbers are falling sharply. There were an estimated 5 million kiwis in 1923, but now scientists think there are only about 70,000. A recent report said that an area rich in kiwis saw a population drop of 18 percent in one year alone. Stoats and possums eat the eggs, stoats and cats kill young birds, and dogs and ferrets attack adults. The result is an alarming decline in population—and a prediction that the bird will become extinct in the next 5 to 10 years unless the trend is reversed.

Chapter 25 Oceania and Antarctica (pp. 658–673)

Dangerous Place The city of Rabaul in Papua New Guinea has a dangerous distinction—it is the only community in the world built completely within the rim of a volcano. The crater formed by the volcano was created 6,000 years ago. Part of the volcano lies underwater. The crater filled with sea water—and formed a perfect harbor. That harbor attracted settlers and explains why Rabaul is located in such a dangerous place.

Open volcanic vents around the city prove that the volcano is still active. In 1994 one of those vents erupted, spreading a thick coat of volcanic ash over much of the city and forcing the evacuation of thousands of people. The warm, rainy climate of the South Pacific made the situation worse. Rain water mixed with the ash and then was baked into a hard, concrete-like substance by the hot sun.

The government wants to abandon the city. It has tried to persuade businesses and people to live elsewhere by refusing to repair or rebuild Rabaul. Some in Rabaul still hold out hope that their city can revive. Geologists say that the volcano will erupt again. It has erupted every 50 or 60 years in the past. In fact, natives to the area have a saying that reveals their own understanding of the volcano's regularity. "Once in your lifetime," the saying goes, "you will hear Rabalanakaia, the Fire God, speak."

Introducing Unit 9

00:00 Out of Time?

If time does not permit teaching each chapter in this unit, you may use the **Reading Essentials and Study Guide** for each chapter.

Unit Overview

The two chapters that make up this unit introduce students to the geography and peoples of Australia, New Zealand, Oceania, and Antarctica. The chapters describe the physical and human features of these unique areas, including cultural and social issues. Before beginning to study the unit, point out to students the following features of these regions:

- location in or near the Pacific Ocean, mostly south of the Equator
- unique animals and plants
- specialized economies
- indigenous peoples

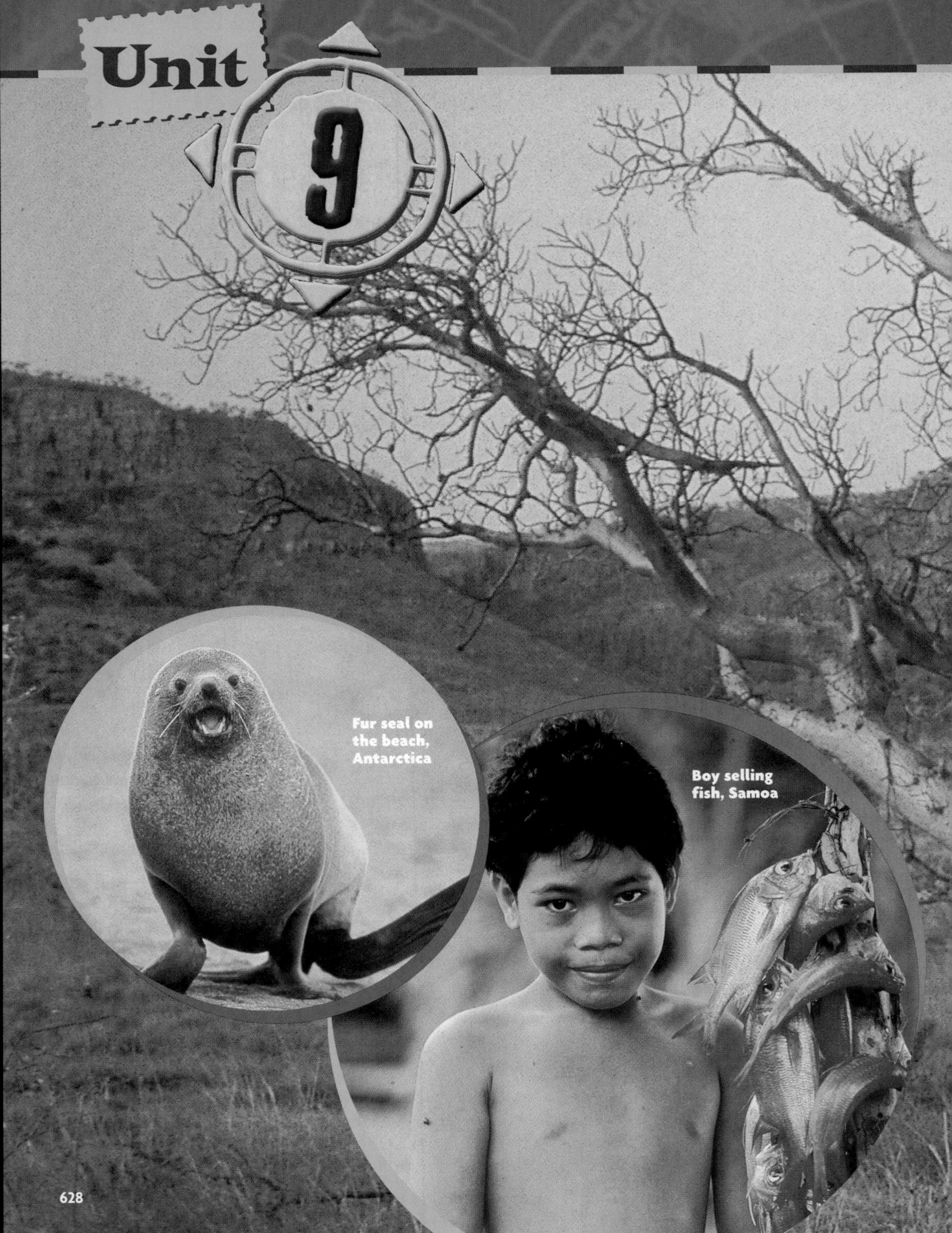

Fur seal on the beach, Antarctica

Boy selling fish, Samoa

Using the Illustration

The people who live in Australia's outback live isolated lives in remote areas. Getting supplies to them is difficult. Trucks called "road trains" solve the problem. These trucks carry supplies like food, gasoline, and even animals to towns across the outback. These vehicles are so named because of their size—the cabs haul three long trailers worth of supplies, making the vehicles so long that they need 62 wheels and so heavy that they weigh as much as 140 tons (127 t). **Ask:** **Can you think of places that are this remote in the United States? How do you think people get supplies in these places? What are some other ways that people in remote locations can stay in communication and receive information?**

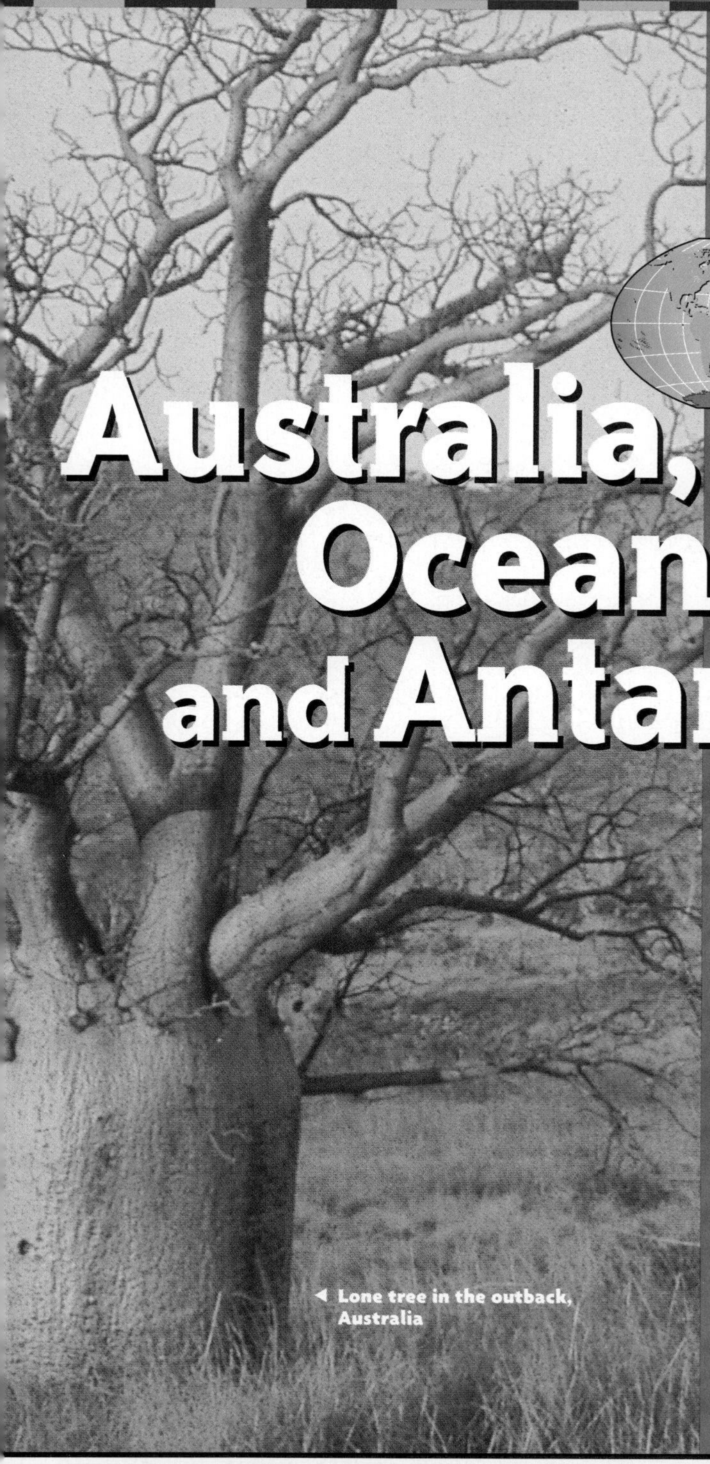

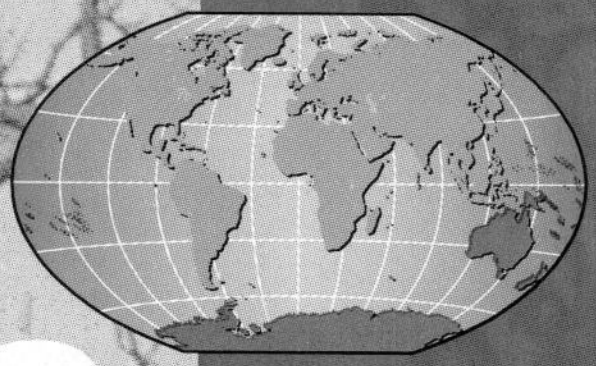

NATIONAL GEOGRAPHIC

Australia, Oceania, and Antarctica

Australia, Oceania, and Antarctica are grouped together more because of their nearness to one another than because of any similarities among their peoples. These lands lie mostly in the Southern Hemisphere. Australia is a dry continent that is home to unusual wildlife. Oceania's 25,000 tropical islands spread out across the Pacific Ocean. Frozen Antarctica covers the earth at the South Pole.

◂ Lone tree in the outback, Australia

NGS ONLINE
www.nationalgeographic.com/education

629

These materials are available from Glencoe.

Software
ZipZapMap! World

Transparencies
PicturePack Transparencies

CD-ROM
Picture Atlas of the World, Second Edition

Current Events Journal

Many unique and interesting animals live in Australia, Oceania, and Antarctica. As students read the unit, have them choose one of these animals as the subject of a children's book. Have them write the story in their journals, possibly illustrating them with drawings of the subject's adventures.

NGS ONLINE
www.nationalgeographic.com/education

This online resource provides lesson plans, atlas updates, cartographic activities with interactive maps, an online map store, and geography links.

Unit Launch Activity

Finding Similarities Australia, New Zealand, Oceania, and Antarctica are all very different places. The hot desert of Australia is unlike the frigid land of Antarctica. The cool highland meadows of New Zealand contrast with the warm tropical beaches of Oceania. Yet these very different lands have many things in common as well. One unfortunate similarity is that the indigenous cultures of this region are in danger of being absorbed into a global culture. As students study the unit, have them take notes on the people who inhabit this area, focusing on the aspects that link them. Then have them create a presentation that uses text and pictures to explain what they found. L2

EE4 Human Systems: Standard 10

NATIONAL GEOGRAPHIC

REGIONAL ATLAS

Australia, Oceania, and Antarctica

Physical

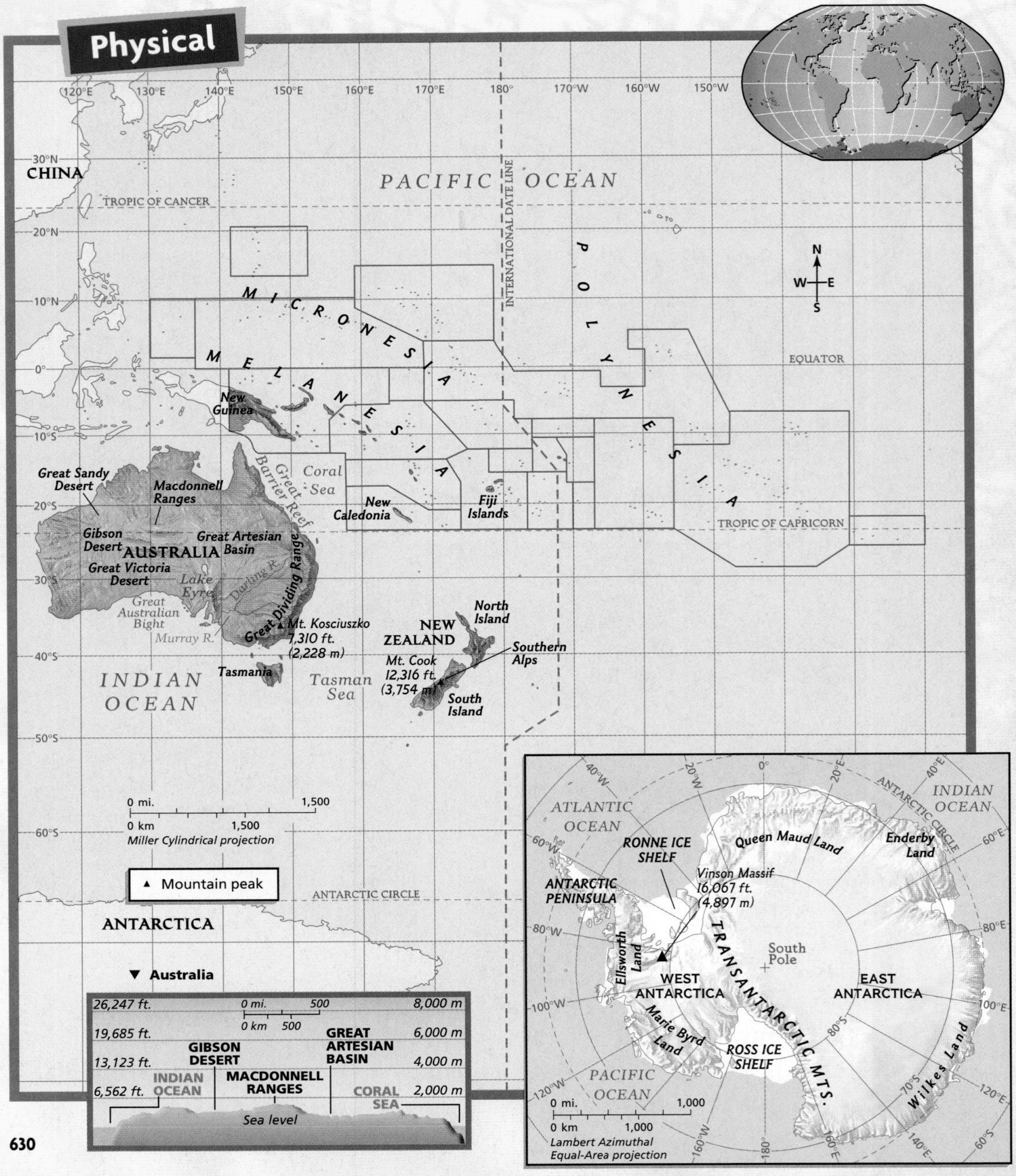

LESSON PLAN

Using the Regional Atlas
These features and activities may be used as an introduction to the unit or as teaching tools throughout the course of the unit.

FOCUS

Objectives

1. Locate the countries in this region and describe their landforms and endangered environments.
2. Describe the populations of the countries in this region.
3. Identify key facts about these countries.

5-Minute Precheck

Ask: **How does Antarctica's climate affect life forms there?** *(Species that live on Antarctica have to be able to cope with blizzards, darkness for months, and brutal cold. Because of the climate's severity, Antarctica has no permanent human inhabitants, although scientists do conduct research there.)*

More About the Profile

This cross section of Australia was taken along the Tropic of Capricorn at 23½°S latitude.

Regional Atlas Activity

Analyzing Maps Explain that Western Australia covers one-third of the country and has the largest area of Australia's six states. It also has the lowest population density. Have students look at the map above. **Ask:** **Why is Western Australia so sparsely populated?** *(The deserts there discourage settlement.)* Explain that about 80 percent of all Australians live in a crescent-shaped stretch of coast from the middle of the east coast to the southeast coast. **What factors explain why people settled there?** *(The low coastal plain and rivers made the area better for farming.)* **L1**

EE5 Environment and Society: Standard 15

Political

0 mi. 1,500
0 km 1,500
Miller Cylindrical projection

⊛ National capital

0 mi. 500
0 km 500
Lambert Azimuthal Equal-Area projection

MAP STUDY

1. What body of water separates Australia from Melanesia?
2. What is the capital of New Zealand?

Regional Atlas Activity

Practicing Map Skills Write the names of islands in Oceania on the board, and assign each island to a different student. Have each student use a globe or map to determine the absolute location of his or her island by finding its latitude and longitude. Then ask each student to express the island's relative location by figuring out its distance and direction from three or four other places. Direct students to list the absolute and relative locations on the board below the name of their islands. **L2**

EE1 The World in Spatial Terms: Standards 1, 3

TEACH

Drawing Conclusions Ask: Which country would you expect to have a cooler climate, Australia or New Zealand? Why? *(New Zealand, because Australia is nearer to the Equator)* **What would you expect to be an important part of the economy of Oceania?** *(fishing, sea products, and tourism)* **L1**

Interdisciplinary Connections

History The first European settlers in New Zealand were sealers and whalers. They set up stations on both islands to take advantage of the seals and whales in the nearby ocean.

History Ancestors of the Aborigines arrived in Australia during the Ice Age, before rising seas cut off the land passage between this continent and the rest of Asia.

MAP STUDY

Answers

1. Coral Sea
2. Wellington

Skills Practice

What is the highest point in all these lands? Where is it? *(Vinson Massif, in Antarctica)* **What is the capital of Australia?** *(Canberra)*

REGIONAL ATLAS

Australia, Oceania, and Antarctica

Interdisciplinary Connections

Science Some coral reefs were formed almost 600 million years ago and make up the earth's oldest ecosystems. Worldwide, there are more than 60,000 miles (96,560 km) of coral reefs lining the coastlines of some 109 nations. Many are threatened by human actions.

TRAVEL GUIDE

If you like scuba diving, you would love visiting the Great Barrier Reef of Australia. This reef—the largest structure built by living creatures anywhere in the world—is home to more than 1,500 species of fish, 400 types of coral, 4,000 species of mollusks, and 22 types of whales. The reef is so huge—about 135,000 square miles (350,000 sq. km)—that it is visible from space.

MAP STUDY

Answers

1. low to medium risk
2. an area protect by the Antarctic Treaty

Skills Practice

What is the status of the coral reefs surrounding the Philippines? *(high risk)*

Endangered Environments

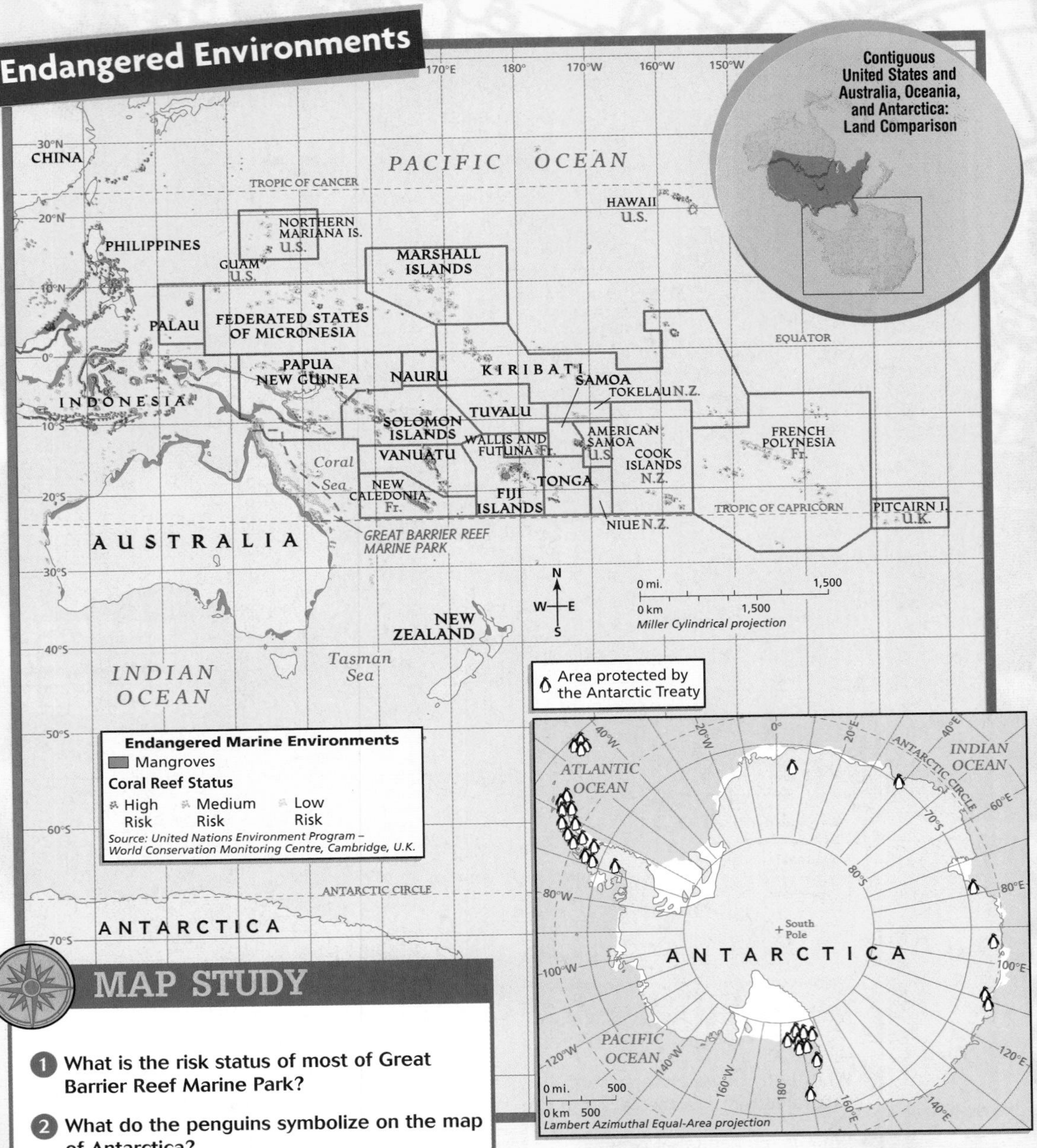

CHINA
PHILIPPINES
PACIFIC OCEAN
TROPIC OF CANCER
NORTHERN MARIANA IS. U.S.
GUAM U.S.
HAWAII U.S.
MARSHALL ISLANDS
PALAU
FEDERATED STATES OF MICRONESIA
EQUATOR
PAPUA NEW GUINEA
NAURU
KIRIBATI
SAMOA
TOKELAU N.Z.
INDONESIA
SOLOMON ISLANDS
TUVALU
WALLIS AND FUTUNA Fr.
AMERICAN SAMOA U.S.
FRENCH POLYNESIA Fr.
VANUATU
Coral Sea
COOK ISLANDS N.Z.
NEW CALEDONIA Fr.
FIJI ISLANDS
TONGA
TROPIC OF CAPRICORN
PITCAIRN I. U.K.
NIUE N.Z.
AUSTRALIA
GREAT BARRIER REEF MARINE PARK
NEW ZEALAND
Tasman Sea
INDIAN OCEAN
ANTARCTIC CIRCLE
ANTARCTICA
Miller Cylindrical projection

Contiguous United States and Australia, Oceania, and Antarctica: Land Comparison

Endangered Marine Environments
Mangroves
Coral Reef Status
High Risk — Medium Risk — Low Risk
Source: United Nations Environment Program – World Conservation Monitoring Centre, Cambridge, U.K.

Area protected by the Antarctic Treaty

ATLANTIC OCEAN
INDIAN OCEAN
PACIFIC OCEAN
ANTARCTICA
South Pole
Lambert Azimuthal Equal-Area projection

MAP STUDY

1. What is the risk status of most of Great Barrier Reef Marine Park?
2. What do the penguins symbolize on the map of Antarctica?

UNIT 9

Content Background

The Great Barrier Reef The Great Barrier Reef has been under construction for perhaps as long as 30 million years. Pollution, commercial fishing, and tourism have caused damage to the reef in just decades, however. The Australian government has taken a number of steps to stop this damage. In 1975, for example, the government declared the reef a national park. Laws restrict where tourists can dive, snorkel, or carry out other activities. Other laws require ships that carry hazardous cargo to have specially trained pilots guide them through the area. The park authority has developed a plan setting aside certain parts of the reef for specific uses, which has become a model for other countries trying to preserve their own coral reefs.

Unit 9

Fast Facts

COMPARING POPULATION: United States and Selected Countries of Australia, Oceania, and Antarctica

UNITED STATES

AUSTRALIA

PAPUA NEW GUINEA

NEW ZEALAND

= 15,000,000

Source: *Population Reference Bureau,* 2000.

POPULATION GROWTH: Australia, 1958–2008

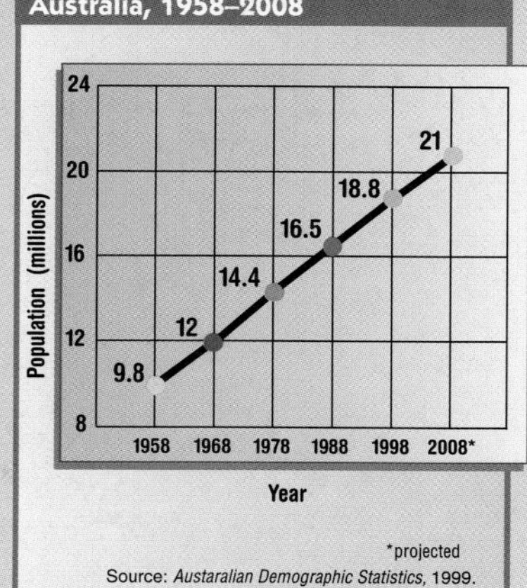

*projected

Source: *Austaralian Demographic Statistics,* 1999.

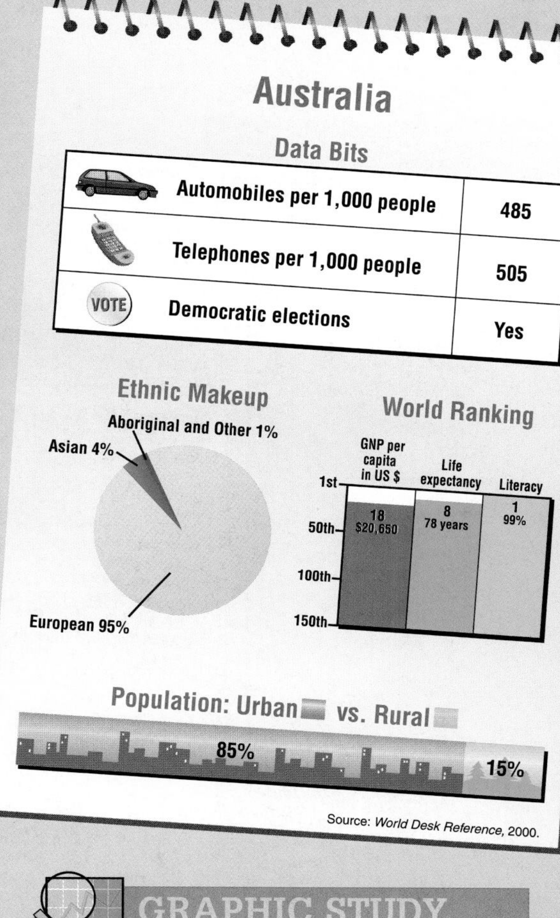

Australia

Data Bits

Automobiles per 1,000 people	485
Telephones per 1,000 people	505
Democratic elections	Yes

Source: *World Desk Reference,* 2000.

GRAPHIC STUDY

1. What is Australia's world ranking for life expectancy?
2. By how much is Australia's population expected to have grown between 1958 and 2008?

Unit 9 Regional Atlas

As an introduction to this region, you may want to engage students by studying an important contemporary issue in this region of the world. The **TIME REPORTS: FOCUS ON WORLD ISSUES** for this region is found on pages 647–653. The feature examines the struggle of indigenous peoples to maintain their cultural identity in an increasingly globalized world.

Cultural Kaleidoscope

New Zealand Most New Zealanders refer to themselves as *Kiwis,* after the symbol of their country. Maoris call white New Zealanders *Pakeha*—a Maori word meaning "fair skinned."

GRAPHIC STUDY

Answers

1. 8

2. by 11.2 million

Skills Practice

How does Australia compare to the United States in population? *(Australia has about 20 million people; the United States has about 285 million.)*

FUN FACTS

- **Antarctica** Antarctica is the world's highest continent, averaging 8,000 feet (2,438 m) in elevation.
- **Marshall Islands** The Marshall Islanders' greeting *lokwe* (YAH-quay) is similar to the Hawaiians' aloha. It can mean "hello," "good-bye," "love," or "like."
- **Kiribati** Mealtimes on the islands of Kiribati occur whenever fresh fish is available, although some islanders believe that fish for breakfast makes people lazy.
- **Fiji Islands** In January, village women play a game called "kick the orange" to welcome the New Year.

Did You Know?

The *woomera* was one of the many useful tools employed by Australia's Aborigines. This wooden rod with a hooked end was used to launch spears a great distance. The Australian government named its rocket and missile testing range *Woomera* after this device.

Making Comparisons Have students use the Country Profiles stamps in the Unit 9 Regional Atlas to create a chart showing the languages spoken in each country in the region. Then have students create another languages chart using the Country Profiles stamps from a different Regional Atlas in this text. Ask students to use the data in their two charts to write a brief summary comparing the number and types of languages spoken in these two world regions. L2

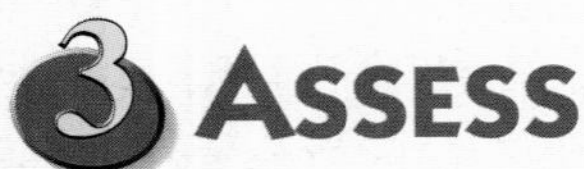

3 ASSESS

Organize students into groups. Have groups use the maps and graphs from the Unit 9 Regional Atlas to quiz one another on the physical and human geography of Australia, New Zealand, Oceania, and Antarctica.

NATIONAL GEOGRAPHIC

REGIONAL ATLAS

Country Profiles

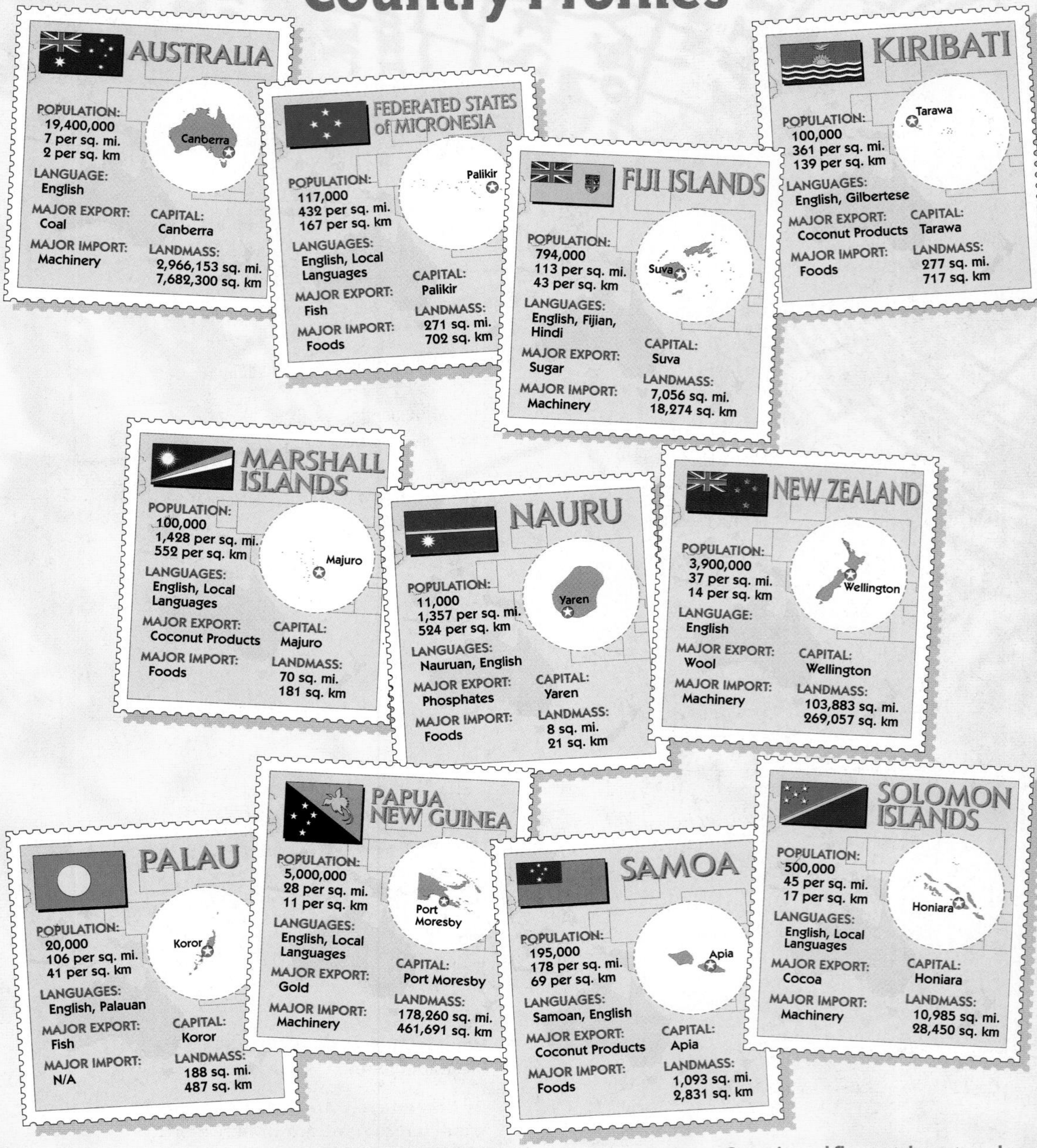

AUSTRALIA
POPULATION: 19,400,000 7 per sq. mi. 2 per sq. km
LANGUAGE: English
MAJOR EXPORT: Coal
MAJOR IMPORT: Machinery
CAPITAL: Canberra
LANDMASS: 2,966,153 sq. mi. 7,682,300 sq. km
Canberra
FEDERATED STATES of MICRONESIA
POPULATION: 117,000 432 per sq. mi. 167 per sq. km
LANGUAGES: English, Local Languages
MAJOR EXPORT: Fish
MAJOR IMPORT: Foods
CAPITAL: Palikir
LANDMASS: 271 sq. mi. 702 sq. km
Palikir
FIJI ISLANDS
POPULATION: 794,000 113 per sq. mi. 43 per sq. km
LANGUAGES: English, Fijian, Hindi
MAJOR EXPORT: Sugar
MAJOR IMPORT: Machinery
CAPITAL: Suva
LANDMASS: 7,056 sq. mi. 18,274 sq. km
Suva
KIRIBATI
POPULATION: 100,000 361 per sq. mi. 139 per sq. km
LANGUAGES: English, Gilbertese
MAJOR EXPORT: Coconut Products
MAJOR IMPORT: Foods
CAPITAL: Tarawa
LANDMASS: 277 sq. mi. 717 sq. km
Tarawa
MARSHALL ISLANDS
POPULATION: 100,000 1,428 per sq. mi. 552 per sq. km
LANGUAGES: English, Local Languages
MAJOR EXPORT: Coconut Products
MAJOR IMPORT: Foods
CAPITAL: Majuro
LANDMASS: 70 sq. mi. 181 sq. km
Majuro
NAURU
POPULATION: 11,000 1,357 per sq. mi. 524 per sq. km
LANGUAGES: Nauruan, English
MAJOR EXPORT: Phosphates
MAJOR IMPORT: Foods
CAPITAL: Yaren
LANDMASS: 8 sq. mi. 21 sq. km
Yaren
NEW ZEALAND
POPULATION: 3,900,000 37 per sq. mi. 14 per sq. km
LANGUAGE: English
MAJOR EXPORT: Wool
MAJOR IMPORT: Machinery
CAPITAL: Wellington
LANDMASS: 103,883 sq. mi. 269,057 sq. km
Wellington
PALAU
POPULATION: 20,000 106 per sq. mi. 41 per sq. km
LANGUAGES: English, Palauan
MAJOR EXPORT: Fish
MAJOR IMPORT: N/A
CAPITAL: Koror
LANDMASS: 188 sq. mi. 487 sq. km
Koror
PAPUA NEW GUINEA
POPULATION: 5,000,000 28 per sq. mi. 11 per sq. km
LANGUAGES: English, Local Languages
MAJOR EXPORT: Gold
MAJOR IMPORT: Machinery
CAPITAL: Port Moresby
LANDMASS: 178,260 sq. mi. 461,691 sq. km
Port Moresby
SAMOA
POPULATION: 195,000 178 per sq. mi. 69 per sq. km
LANGUAGES: Samoan, English
MAJOR EXPORT: Coconut Products
MAJOR IMPORT: Foods
CAPITAL: Apia
LANDMASS: 1,093 sq. mi. 2,831 sq. km
Apia
SOLOMON ISLANDS
POPULATION: 500,000 45 per sq. mi. 17 per sq. km
LANGUAGES: English, Local Languages
MAJOR EXPORT: Cocoa
MAJOR IMPORT: Machinery
CAPITAL: Honiara
LANDMASS: 10,985 sq. mi. 28,450 sq. km
Honiara

Countries and flags not drawn to scale

Country Profiles Activity

Ethnic Groups The countries in this region have people from many different groups. In Australia and New Zealand, native peoples (the Aborigines and Maoris) are minorities, and the descendants of European settlers are in the majority. The islands of Oceania are mostly populated with islanders, but there are many other groups as well. Assign each student one of these countries. Have students research relations among the different groups in that country and report on their findings. L2

EE4 Human Systems: Standard 10

Unit 9

Regional Atlas

For more information on countries in this region, refer to the Nations of the World Data Bank on pages 690–699.

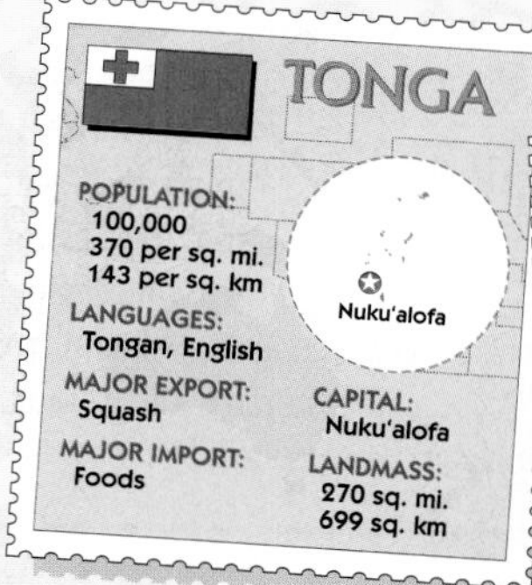

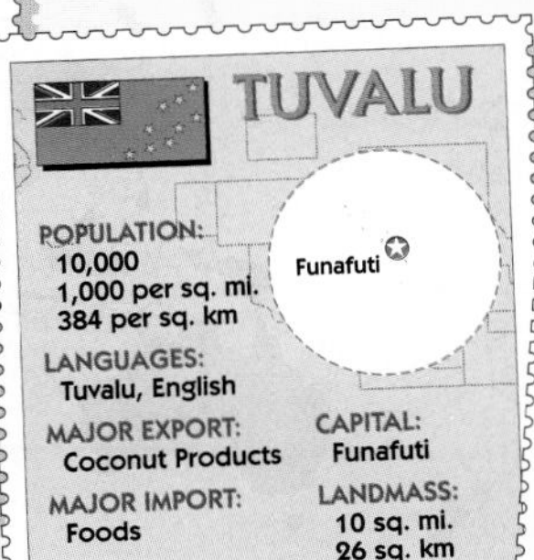

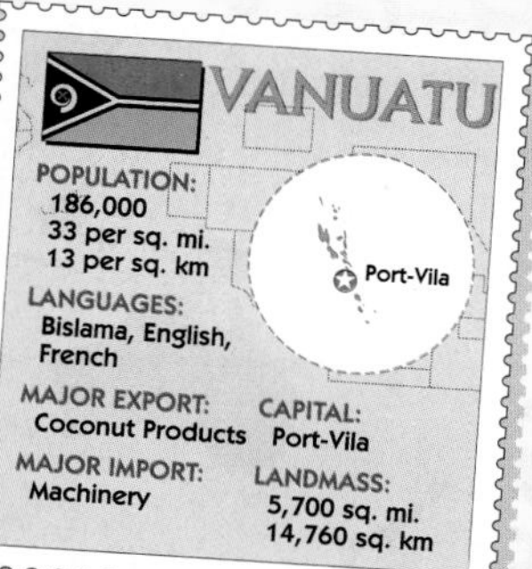

BUILDING CITIZENSHIP

Voting Nearly all eligible voters participate in elections in Australia. All citizens over 18 years old are required to vote in all local, state, and national elections. If they don't vote they can be fined up to 50 Australian dollars. To make it easier, elections are held on Saturdays and voting is done at schools, churches, and other convenient locations. In the United States, only about half of eligible people vote in the presidential elections.

Why do so many people in the United States not exercise their right to vote?

WRITE ABOUT IT

Voting and participating in political activities are important parts of belonging to a democratic society. Yet in the United States most people do not vote. Pretend you are the head of elections for your city and it is your responsibility to encourage people to vote in upcoming elections for mayor and the city council. Design a flyer that will be mailed to all households to encourage people to vote.

This woman is exercising her right to vote. ▼

FUN FACTS

- **Tonga** The people of Tonga have always considered obesity as a sign of good health, especially among their leaders. The *Guinness Book of World Records* listed their 462-pound (210-kg) King Tapou as the world's heaviest monarch. In recent years, however, the government launched a weight awareness campaign, and the king lost 182 pounds (83 kg).
- **Papua New Guinea** Traditional musicians play the *kundu*—an hourglass-shaped drum covered with lizard skin.
- **New Zealand** The people of this country eat a food, called vegemite, made from yeast extract. They spread it on their bread as Americans spread peanut butter.

Reteach

Give students an outline map of the region. Have them complete the map by writing in the names of the islands and major physical features.

BUILDING CITIZENSHIP

Answer Many students will respond that it is too much trouble to vote or that people don't feel their vote is important. Point out that not all people have always been allowed to vote. Women and African Americans won the right to vote through protests and political battles.

Write About It! Flyers should be imaginative and interesting to attract people's attention and have basic information on date, time, and place for voting. They should also include motivation for people to participate, pointing out the importance of the election and the civic responsibility to vote.

CLOSE

Have students prepare a chart that compares the populations of the different countries and territories in Oceania. They can find the population figures in the Country Profiles on pages 634–635.

Chapter 24 Resources

Note: The following materials may be used when teaching Chapter 24.
Section level support materials are shown at point of use in the margins of the Teacher Wraparound Edition.

Timesaving Tools

TeacherWorks™ All-In-One Planner and Resource Center

- **Interactive Teacher Edition** See the **Interactive Teacher Edition** CD-ROM to electronically integrate your Teacher Wraparound Edition and blackline masters.
- **Interactive Lesson Planner** Organize your week, month, semester, or year with all the lesson helps you need. The **Interactive Lesson Planner** CD-ROM contains all Chapter 24 resources.

Use Glencoe's **Presentation Plus!** multimedia teacher tool to easily present dynamic lessons that visually excite your students. Using Microsoft PowerPoint® you can customize the presentations to create your own personalized lessons.

TEACHING TRANSPARENCIES

Graphic Organizer Transparency and Student Activity 24

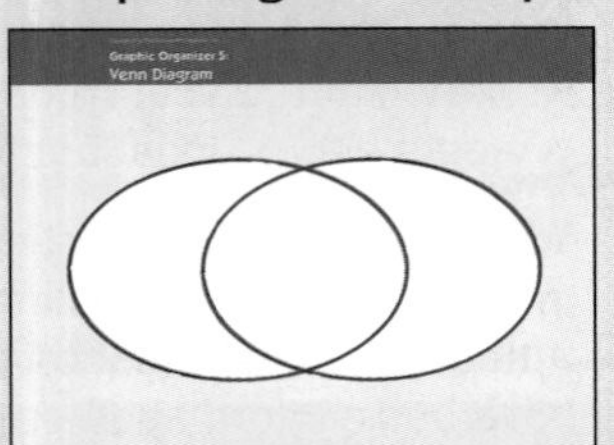

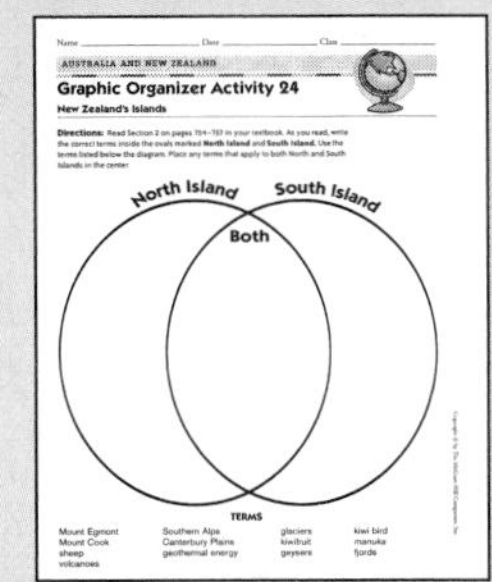

Graphic Organizer Activity 24
New Zealand's Islands

North Island | South Island | Both

FOLDABLES™ Study Organizer

Foldables are three-dimensional, interactive graphic organizers that help students practice basic writing skills, review key vocabulary terms, and identify main ideas. Every chapter contains a Foldable activity, with additional chapter activities found in the ***Reading and Study Skills Foldables*** booklet.

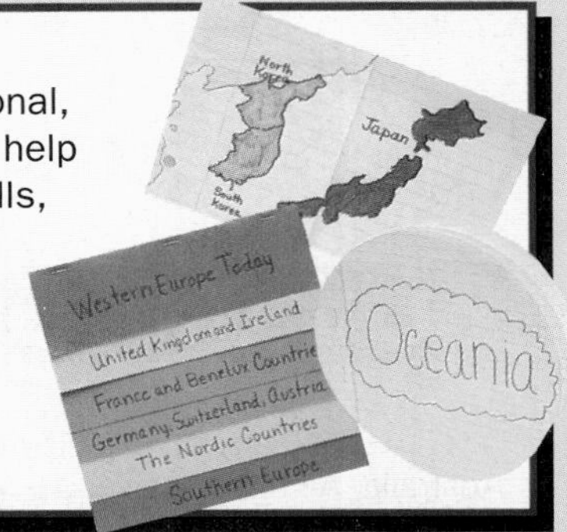

ENRICHMENT AND EXTENSION

Enrichment Activity 24

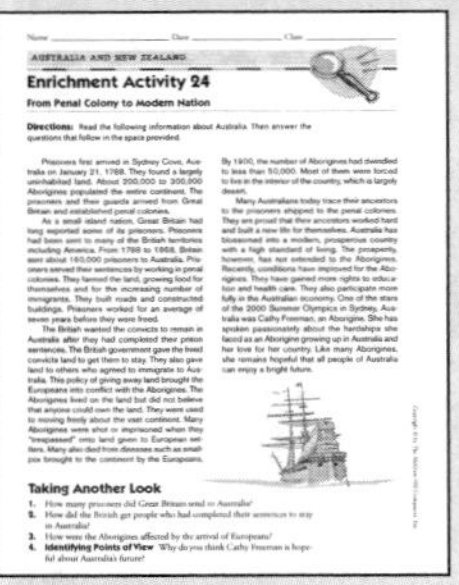

Enrichment Activity 24
From Penal Colony to Modern Nation

Cooperative Learning Activity 24

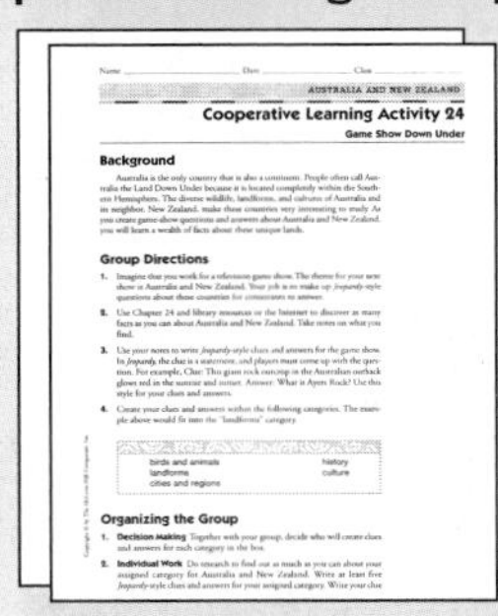

Cooperative Learning Activity 24
Game Show Down Under

MAP AND GEOGRAPHY SKILLS

Chapter Map Activity 24

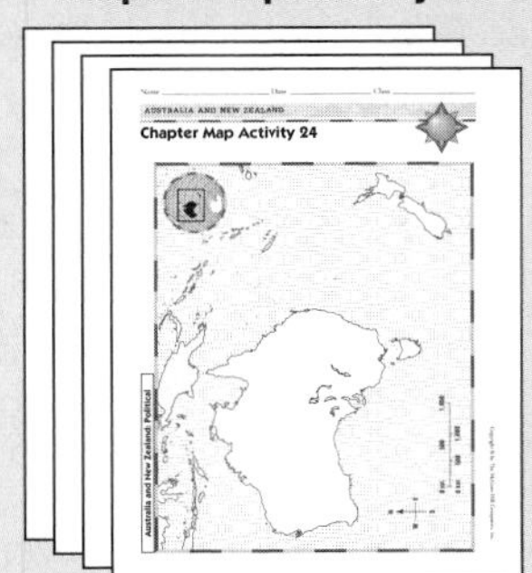

Chapter Map Activity 24

GeoLab Activity 24

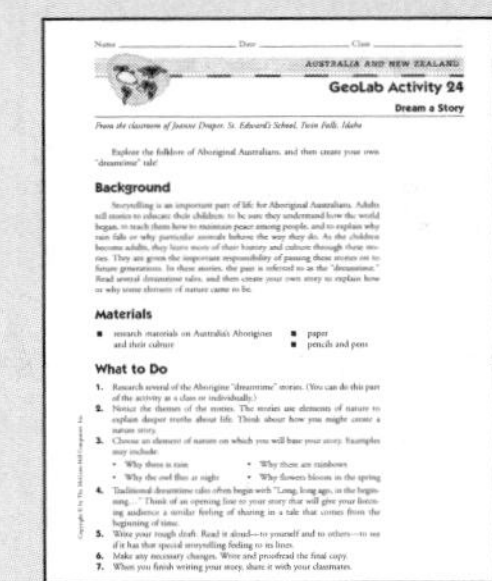

GeoLab Activity 24
Dream a Story

STANDARDIZED ASSESSMENT SKILLS

Glencoe's Assessment Advantage

Critical Thinking Skills Activity 24

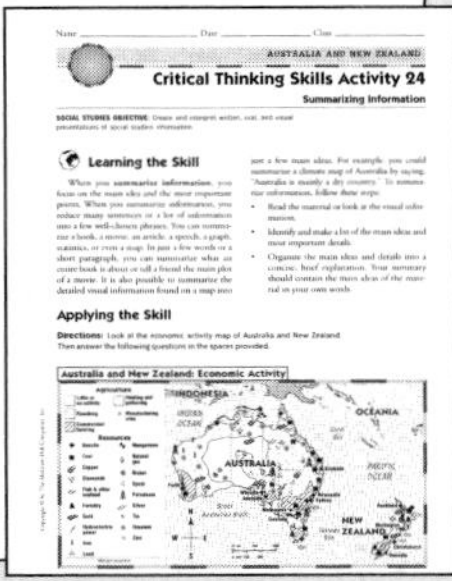

Critical Thinking Skills Activity 24
Summarizing Information

Map and Graph Skills Activity 24

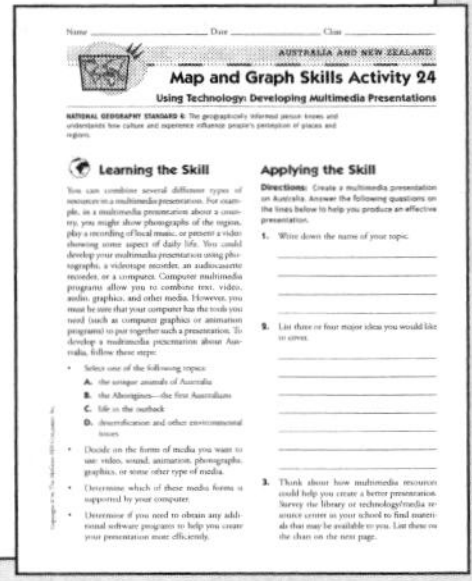

Map and Graph Skills Activity 24
Using Technology: Developing Multimedia Presentations

Reading and Writing Skills Activity 24

Reading and Writing Skills Activity 24
Using Word Resources

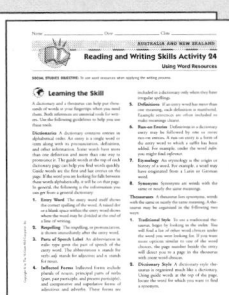

Standardized Test Practice Workbook Activity 24

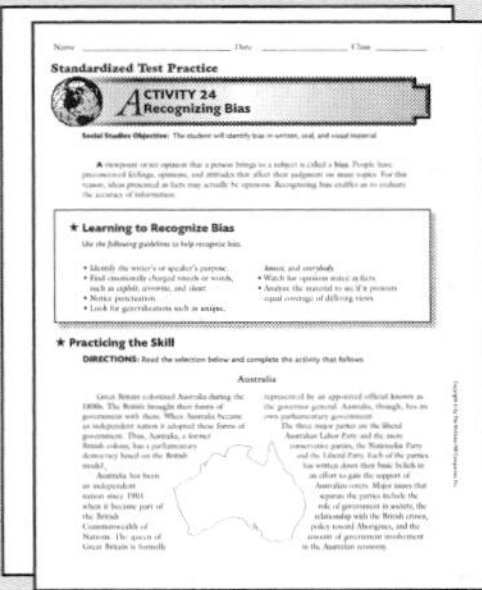

Standardized Test Practice
Activity 24
Recognizing Bias

REVIEW AND REINFORCEMENT

Chapter Skills Activity 24

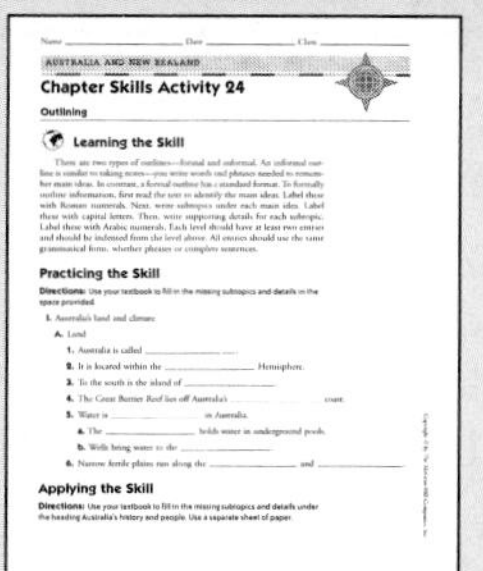

Take-Home Review Activity 24

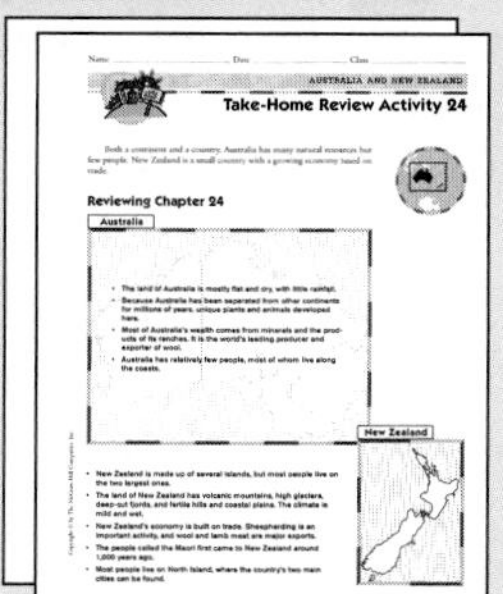

Reteaching Activity 24

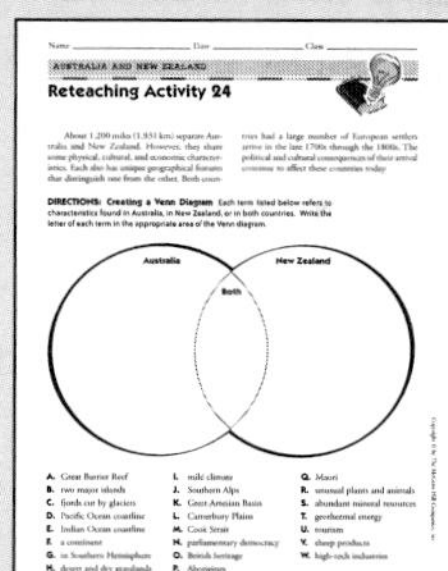

Vocabulary Activity 24

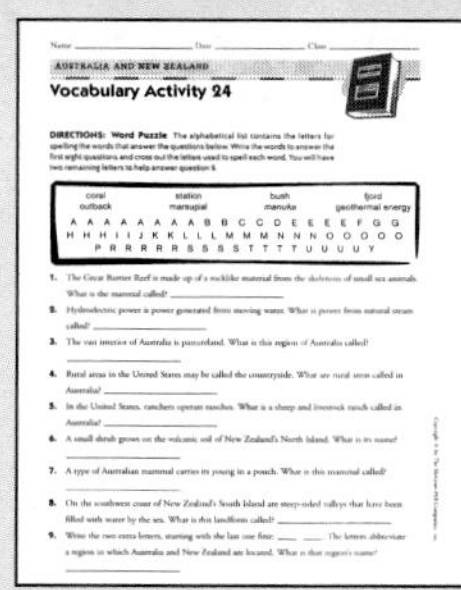

Workbook Activity 24

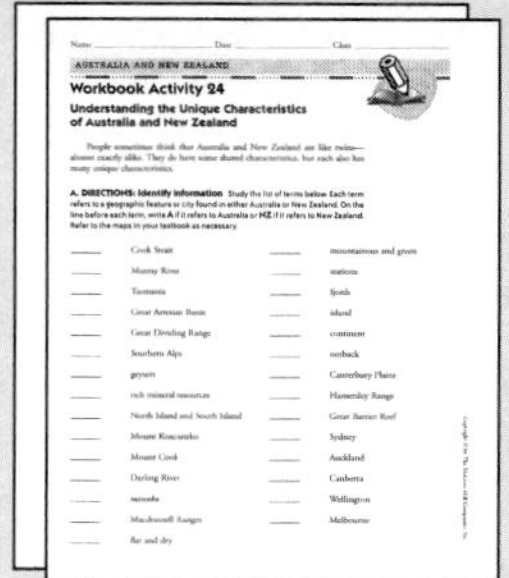

ASSESSMENT

Chapter 24 Test, Form A

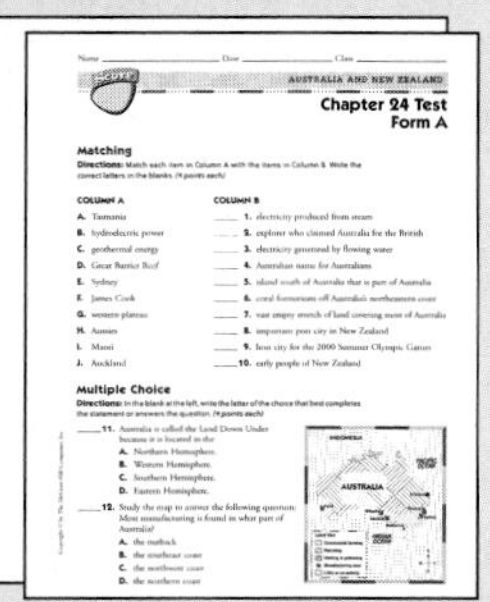

Chapter 24 Test, Form B

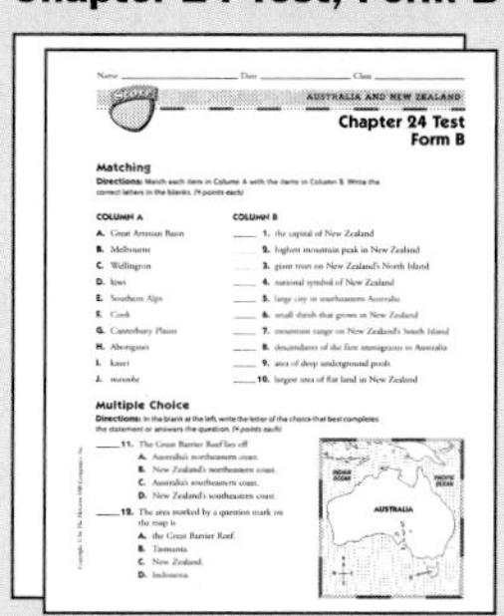

Performance Assessment Activity 24

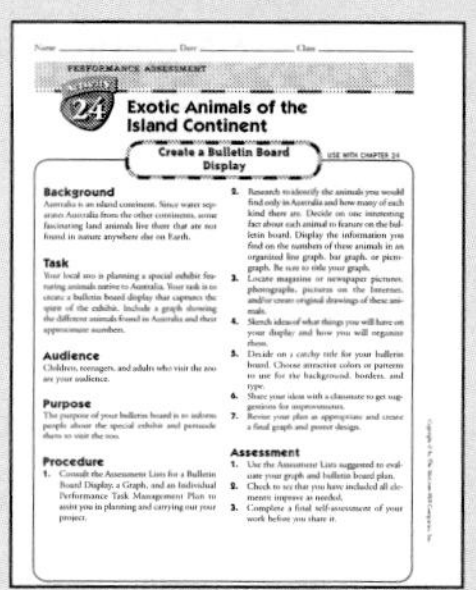

ExamView® Pro 3.0 Testmaker CD-ROM

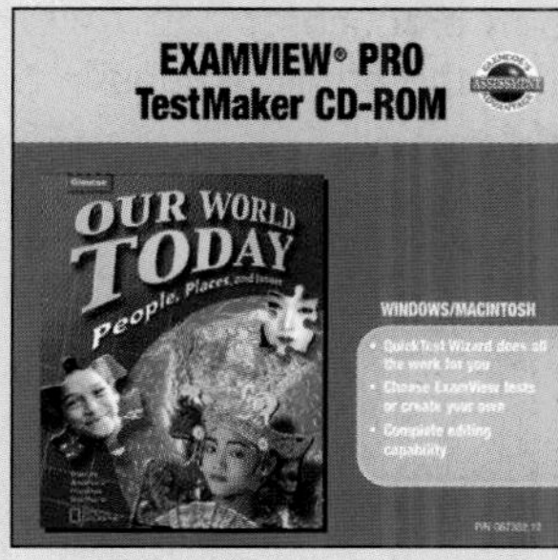

MULTIMEDIA

- **National Geographic's The World and Its People**
- **MindJogger Videoquiz**
- **Vocabulary PuzzleMaker Software**
- **Interactive Tutor Self-Assessment CD-ROM**
- **ExamView® Pro 3.0 Testmaker CD-ROM**
- **Interactive Lesson Planner CD-ROM**
- **Interactive Teacher Edition CD-ROM**
- **Skillbuilder Interactive Workbook CD-ROM, Level 1**
- **Presentation Plus! CD-ROM**
- **Audio Program**

SPANISH RESOURCES

The following Spanish language materials are available in the Spanish Resources binder:

- **Spanish Chapter Summaries**
- **Spanish Vocabulary Activities**
- **Spanish Guided Reading Activities**
- **Spanish Quizzes and Tests**
- **Spanish Take-Home Review Activities**
- **Spanish Reteaching Activities**

Meeting National Standards

Geography for Life

All of the 18 standards are demonstrated in Unit 9. The following ones are highlighted in Chapter 24:

Section 1 **EE2 Places and Regions: Standards 4, 5, 6**
EE4 Physical Systems: Standards 7, 8
EE4 Human Systems: Standards 9, 10, 13

Section 2 **EE4 Human Systems: Standards 9, 10, 11, 13**

For a complete listing of National Geography Standards and entire text correlation, see pages T22–T29.

Local Objectives

Chapter 24 Planning Guide

SECTION RESOURCES

Daily Objectives	Reproducible Resources	Multimedia Resources
Section 1 **Australia** **Suggested Pacing = 1 day** **1.** Discuss how the people of Australia earn a living. **2.** Explain how history has influenced the people of Australia.	Reproducible Lesson Plan 24-1 Daily Lecture and Discussion Notes 24-1 Guided Reading Activity 24-1 Reading Essentials and Study Guide 24-1 Section Quiz 24-1*	Daily Focus Skills Transparency 24-1 GeoQuiz Transparency 24-1 Vocabulary PuzzleMaker Software Interactive Tutor Self-Assessment CD-ROM ExamView® Pro 3.0 Testmaker CD-ROM Presentation Plus! CD-ROM
Section 2 **New Zealand** **Suggested Pacing = 1 day** **1.** Summarize what goods New Zealand's economy produces. **2.** Describe the ethnic groups in New Zealand.	Reproducible Lesson Plan 24-2 Daily Lecture and Discussion Notes 24-2 Guided Reading Activity 24-2 Reading Essentials and Study Guide 24-2 Section Quiz 24-2*	Daily Focus Skills Transparency 24-2 GeoQuiz Transparency 24-1 Vocabulary PuzzleMaker Software Interactive Tutor Self-Assessment CD-ROM ExamView® Pro 3.0 Testmaker CD-ROM Presentation Plus! CD-ROM

00:00 **Out of Time?** Assign the **Reading Essentials and Study Guide** for this chapter.

*Also available in Spanish

KEY TO ABILITY LEVELS

Teaching strategies have been coded for varying learning styles and abilities.

- L1 **BASIC** activities for all students
- L2 **AVERAGE** activities for average to above-average students
- L3 **CHALLENGING** activities for above-average students
- ELL **ENGLISH LANGUAGE LEARNER** activities

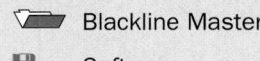

Blackline Master	Transparency
Software	Videocassette
CD-ROM	Block Scheduling
Audiocassette	DVD

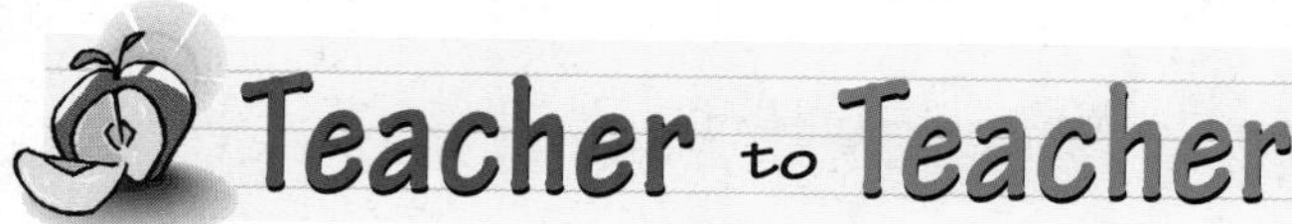

Lake Comparison

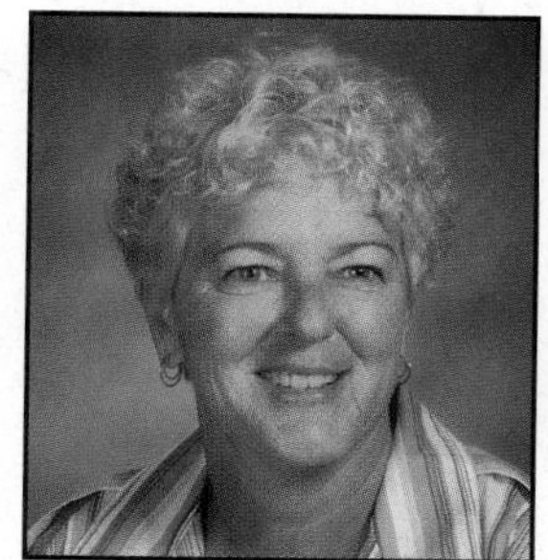

Sara Monschein
Oakridge Middle School
Naples, Florida

Have students gather information from the Internet regarding Lake Eyre in Australia, the Great Salt Lake in Utah, and the Dead Sea between Israel and Jordan. Ask them to make a chart or Venn diagram comparing the following information: (1) elevation at which the lakes lie; (2) the average annual temperature in the location; (3) the source of the salt content and the saline percentage in the lakes; (4) how the lake waters are used; (5) animal life near the lakes; and (6) other interesting information. When their research and charts are completed, have students write a paragraph summarizing the comparison.

OUR WORLD TODAY Online

Use our Web site for additional resources. All essential content is covered in the Student Edition.

You and your students can visit owt.glencoe.com, the Web site companion to *Our World Today*. This innovative integration of electronic and print media offers your students a wealth of opportunities. The student text directs students to the Web site for the following options:

- Chapter Overviews
- Student Web Activities
- Self-Check Quizzes
- Textbook Updates

Answers are provided for you in the Web Activity Lesson Plan. Additional Web resources and Interactive Tutor puzzles are also available.

NATIONAL GEOGRAPHIC TEACHER'S CORNER

Index to National Geographic Magazine:

The following articles may be used for research relating to this chapter:

- "Kingdom of Coral: Australia's Great Barrier Reef," by Douglas H. Chadwick, January 2001.
- "Fiordland: New Zealand's Southern Sanctuary," by Kennedy Warne, December 2000.
- "Sydney: On Top of the World Down Under," by Bill Bryson, August 2000.

National Geographic Society Products Available From Glencoe:

To order the following products for use with this chapter, contact your local Glencoe sales representative or call Glencoe at 1-800-334-7344:

- *STV: World Geography* (Videodisc)
- *Picture Atlas of the World* (CD-ROM)
- *PictureShow: Earth's Endangered Environments* (CD-ROM)
- *ZipZapMap! World* (Software)
- *GeoBee* (CD-ROM)
- *Images of the World* (Posters)
- *Eye on the Environment* (Posters)

Additional National Geographic Society Products:

To order the following products for use with this chapter, call National Geographic Society at 1-800-368-2728:

- *Complete National Geographic: 111 Years of National Geographic Magazine* (CD-ROM)
- *Voices: Poetry and Art From Around the World* (Book)
- *National Geographic Desk Reference* (Book)
- *National Geographic Atlas of the World, Seventh Edition* (Book)
- *Australia* (Video)
- *Healing the Earth* (Video)
- *Physical Earth* (Map)
- *Asia Political* (Map)
- *Cultures* (Map)
- *Population* (Map)
- *Technology's Price* (Video)

NGS ONLINE

Access National Geographic's Web site for current events, activities, links, interactive features, and archives.
www.nationalgeographic.com

Introducing
Chapter 24

Introduce students to chapter content and key terms by having them access Chapter Overview 24 at owt.glencoe.com

Chapter Objectives

1. Discuss the geography and economy of Australia.
2. Describe the people and culture of Australia.
3. Explain how the geography of New Zealand affects its people and its relations with other countries.

GLENCOE TECHNOLOGY

NATIONAL GEOGRAPHIC

The World and Its People Video Program

Chapter 27 Australia and New Zealand

The following segments enhance the study of this chapter:

- **Amazing Animals**
- **Hot and Steamy**
- **Snakes**

Available in DVD and VHS.

MindJogger Videoquiz

Use MindJogger to preview the Chapter 24 content.

Available in VHS.

Chapter 24 Australia and New Zealand

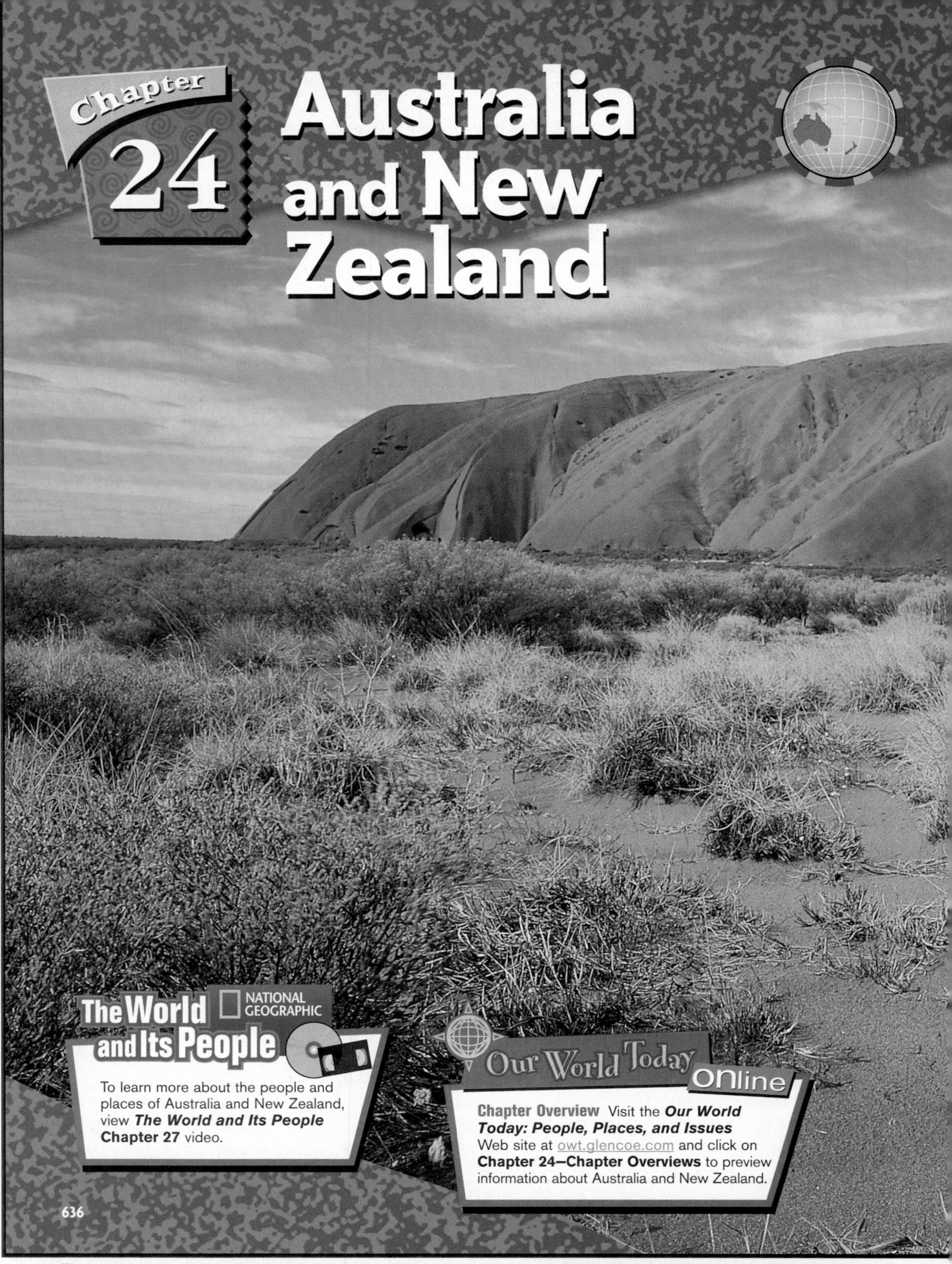

The World and Its People NATIONAL GEOGRAPHIC

To learn more about the people and places of Australia and New Zealand, view ***The World and Its People* Chapter 27** video.

Our World Today online

Chapter Overview Visit the ***Our World Today: People, Places, and Issues*** Web site at owt.glencoe.com and click on **Chapter 24—Chapter Overviews** to preview information about Australia and New Zealand.

636

Two-Minute Lesson Launcher

Ask students if they have heard the phrase "the Land Down Under." Ask what it means. *(Australia is below the Equator.)* Ask what effect Australia's location will have on its seasons. *(They will occur at opposite times of the year to the seasons in North America.)* Explain that although the seasons may take place in opposite months, Australia has many similarities to North America—and several distinctions that make it unique, too. Have students look at the physical and political maps of Australia and the United States in this text to compare the two countries. **L1**

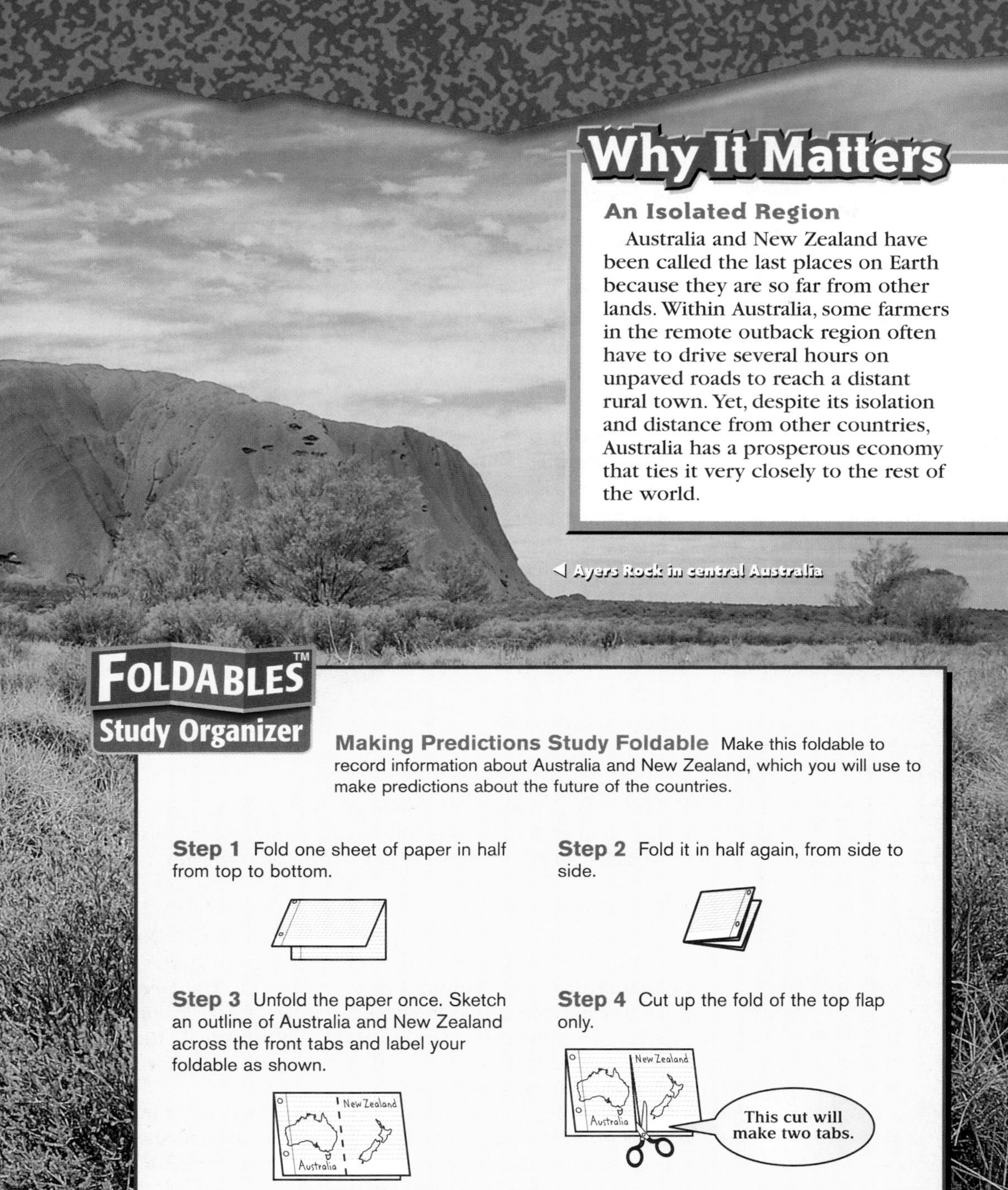

Why It Matters

An Isolated Region

Australia and New Zealand have been called the last places on Earth because they are so far from other lands. Within Australia, some farmers in the remote outback region often have to drive several hours on unpaved roads to reach a distant rural town. Yet, despite its isolation and distance from other countries, Australia has a prosperous economy that ties it very closely to the rest of the world.

◁ Ayers Rock in central Australia

FOLDABLES™ Study Organizer

Making Predictions Study Foldable Make this foldable to record information about Australia and New Zealand, which you will use to make predictions about the future of the countries.

Step 1 Fold one sheet of paper in half from top to bottom.

Step 2 Fold it in half again, from side to side.

Step 3 Unfold the paper once. Sketch an outline of Australia and New Zealand across the front tabs and label your foldable as shown.

Step 4 Cut up the fold of the top flap only.

Reading and Writing As you read the chapter, write what you learn about these countries under the appropriate tabs of your foldable. Then use that information to make predictions about the future economic growth and development of these countries.

FOLDABLES™ Study Organizer

Purpose Students will make and use a foldable to record information about Australia and New Zealand. As students read the chapter, they are required to write what they learn about these countries under the appropriate tabs on their foldables. They will then use this information to make predictions about the future economic growth and development of Australia and New Zealand.

Have students complete ***Reading and Study Skills Foldables*** Activity 24.

Why It Matters

Using the maps, graphs, charts, and photos in this unit, have students work in groups to write 10 questions they expect to be answered about Australia, Oceania, and Antarctica. When this task is completed, each group should write three of their questions on the board. Eliminate duplicate questions. Use the rest to create a poster that students will complete as the unit progresses.

About the Photos

Ayers Rock is the world's largest monolith, or stand-alone rock formation, in the world. It rises 1,143 feet (348 m) and is almost 6 miles (9 km) around the base. Under the desert's surface, it descends over 3.5 miles (5.6 km). Considered one of the great wonders of the modern world, Ayers Rock is located in the Kata Tjuta National Park, which is owned and run by the local Aborigines. The Aboriginal name for the rock is Mount Uluru, and the whole area is an important center of the Aborigines' spiritual beliefs. Depending on the time of day and the atmospheric conditions, the rock can dramatically change color—anywhere from blue to glowing red.

Focus

Section Objectives

1. Discuss how the people of Australia earn a living.
2. Explain how history has influenced the people of Australia.

BELLRINGER Skillbuilder Activity

Project transparency and have students answer questions.

This activity is also available as a blackline master.

Daily Focus Skills Transparency 24-1

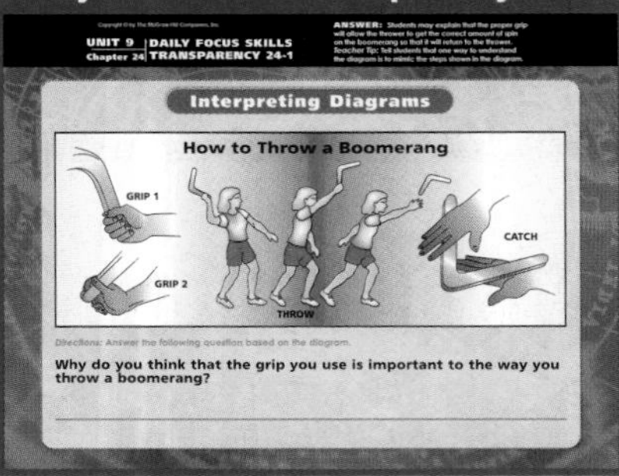

Guide to Reading

■ **Accessing Prior Knowledge** Write the words *kangaroo, koala,* and *platypus*. Ask students what they know about these animals. Explain that these three species—and several others—are unique to Australia. **Ask:** **What geographical feature explains why Australia has animals not found elsewhere in the world?** *(It is separated from other areas by water.)*

Section 1 Australia

Guide to Reading

Main Idea

Both a continent and a country, Australia has many natural resources but few people.

Terms to Know

- coral reef
- outback
- station
- marsupial
- immigrant
- boomerang
- bush

Reading Strategy

Create a chart like this one. Then fill in two facts about Australia for each category.

Land	History
Climate	Government
Economy	People

NATIONAL GEOGRAPHIC Exploring Our World

Signs along Australia's lonely outback warn drivers that they may meet camels, wombats, or kangaroos. This road stretches for 800 miles (1,287 km) between Western and South Australia. With only 11 rest stops along the way, perhaps meeting a kangaroo would be a good thing. It might make the drive seem less lonely.

Is Australia a country or a continent? It is both. Australia is the sixth-largest country in the world. Surrounded by water, Australia is too large to be called an island. So geographers call it a continent.

Australia's Land and Climate

Australia is sometimes referred to as the Land Down Under because it is located in the Southern Hemisphere. The island of **Tasmania,** to the south, is part of Australia. The **Great Barrier Reef** lies off Australia's northeastern coast. Coral formations have piled up for millions of years to create a colorful chain that stretches 1,250 miles (2,012 km). A **coral reef** is a structure formed by the skeletons of small sea animals.

The people of Australia use the name **outback** for the inland regions of their country. Mining camps and cattle and sheep ranches called **stations** dot this region. Some stations are huge. One cattle station is almost twice as large as Delaware.

Water is scarce in Australia. In the **Great Artesian Basin,** however, water lies in deep, underground pools. Ranchers drill wells and bring

Section Resources

Reproducible Masters

- Reproducible Lesson Plan 24-1
- Daily Lecture and Discussion Notes 24-1
- Guided Reading Activity 24-1
- Reading Essentials and Study Guide 24-1
- Section Quiz 24-1

Transparencies

- Daily Focus Skills Transparency 24-1
- GeoQuiz Transparency 24-1

Multimedia

- Vocabulary PuzzleMaker Software
- Interactive Tutor Self-Assessment CD-ROM
- Presentation Plus! CD-ROM
- ExamView® Pro 3.0 Testmaker CD-ROM

the underground water to the surface for their cattle. Australia's western plateau is even drier. Imagine a carpet of sand twice as large as Alaska, Texas, California, and New Mexico combined. Most people who cross this vast, dry plateau do so by plane. Narrow plains run along the south and southeast of Australia. These fertile flatlands hold Australia's best farmland and most of the country's people.

Unusual Animals About 200 million years ago, the tectonic plate upon which Australia sits separated from the other continents. As a result, Australia's native plants and animals are not found elsewhere in the world. Two famous Australian animals are kangaroos and koalas. Both are **marsupials**, or mammals that carry their young in a pouch. Turn to page 642 to read about some of Australia's animals.

Reading Check Where do most of Australia's people live?

Australia's Economy

Australia has a strong, prosperous economy. Australia is a treasure chest overflowing with mineral resources. These riches include iron ore, zinc, bauxite, gold, silver, opals, diamonds, and pearls. Australia also

Primary Source

GREAT MOTHER SNAKE

Aboriginal Legend

All cultures developed stories to help explain their beginnings. In this Aboriginal legend the Great Mother Snake is credited with creating Australia as well as all of its human and animal inhabitants. In this culture, the snake is a symbol of good rather than evil.

"... Then finally She awoke and brought from the womb on the Earth itself, man and woman. And they learned from the Mother Snake how to live in peace and harmony with all these creatures who were their spiritual cousins ...And man and woman were now the caretakers of this land. And the Great Snake then entered a large water hole where she guards the fish and other water creatures, so that when the Aboriginal people fish they know to take only as much as they can eat, because if someone should take more than they need through greed or kills for pleasure, they know that one dark night, the Great Mother Snake will come ... and punish the one who broke this tribal law."

Source: *Great Mother Snake* an Aboriginal legend.

Analyzing Primary Sources

1. What do you think the term "spiritual cousins" means?
2. Why would it be important for people in this culture to take from the earth only as much as they needed?

Meeting Special Needs

Visual/Spatial Give visual learners an outline map of Australia. As they study the section, they can take notes on the map. Suggest that they use different colors to indicate different kinds of information—green for physical and climate features, red for natural resources and economic activities, and blue for cities and cultural features, for example. This visual presentation will make it easier for visual learners to study the material. **L1** **ELL**

Refer to *Inclusion for the Middle School Social Studies Classroom Strategies and Activities* in the TCR.

TEACH

Cause and Effect Give students a fact about Australia. (*The interior of the country is very dry.*) Have them state an effect that results from the fact. (*The land is not good for farming.*) **L1**

Reading Check Answer

in the narrow plains along the south and southeast coasts

Daily Lecture Notes 24-1

AUSTRALIA AND NEW ZEALAND

Daily Lecture and Discussion Notes 24-1

Australia (pages 638–641)

Did You Know? When people moved to Australia from the United Kingdom, they took many British customs with them. For example, Australians drive on the left side of the road, as do British drivers. Tea is the favorite hot drink in Australia, as it is in the United Kingdom.

I. Australia's Land and Climate (*pages 638–639*)

A. Sometimes called the Land Down Under, Australia is a country and a continent.

B. The Great Barrier Reef lies off Australia's northeastern coast. Coral formations have piled up for millions of years to create a colorful chain that stretches 1,250 miles. A **coral reef** is a structure formed by the skeletons of small sea animals.

...h and southeast. These fertile flatlands hold ...the country's people.

Primary Source

Answers

1. creatures from the same spiritual source
2. for balance with nature and equality for everyone

Activity Ask students to think of another creation story that has a snake in it. The story of Adam and Eve will probably be mentioned. How is this story, or any others, the same or different from the Aboriginal legend?

Answer oboe, bassoon

The Art of Breathing The *digeridoo* is played by using circular breathing. This means blowing air out through the lips into the instrument, while simultaneously taking in air through the nostrils and storing it by puffing up the cheeks.

World Music: A Cultural Legacy

Use the accompanying Teacher Guide for background information and worksheets about the music of this region.

Reading Check Answer

raising livestock

Guided Reading Activity 24-1

Name ______ Date ______ Class ______

AUSTRALIA AND NEW ZEALAND

Guided Reading Activity 24-1

Australia

DIRECTIONS: Answering Questions Reading the section and answering the questions below will help you learn more about the country of Australia. Use your textbook to answer the questions.

1. Why is Australia not considered an island?
2. Why is Australia called the Land Down Under?
3. What type of land is found in the western part of Australia?

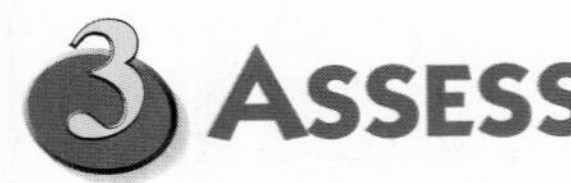

ASSESS

Assign Section 1 Assessment as homework or an in-class activity.

Music

The *digeridoo* is the most famous musical instrument from Australia. In its original form, it was made when a eucalyptus branch fell to the ground and was hollowed out by termites. Someone playing a *digeridoo* creates a variety of sounds by making a combination of lip, tongue, and mouth movements. Once you hear the eerie sounds, it is easy to understand why the Aborigines considered this instrument sacred and made it part of their ceremonies.

Looking Closer What other instruments are similar to the *digeridoo?*

GO TO

World Music: A Cultural Legacy
Hear music of this region on Disc 2, Track 28.

has energy resources, including coal, oil, and natural gas. Mineral and energy resources make up more than one-third of Australia's exports.

Australia's dry climate limits farming. With irrigation, however, farmers grow grains, sugarcane, cotton, fruits, and vegetables. The main agricultural activity is raising livestock, especially cattle and sheep. Australia is the world's top producer and exporter of wool. Ranchers also ship beef and cattle hides.

Manufacturing, which is growing in importance, includes processed foods, transportation equipment, metals, cloth, and chemicals. High-technology industries, service industries, and tourism also play a large role in the economy.

Reading Check **What is Australia's main agricultural activity?**

Australia's History and People

Despite its huge area, Australia has few people—only 19.4 million. Australia has long needed more skilled workers to develop its resources and build its economy. More than 5 million **immigrants,** or people who move from one country to live in another, have arrived in recent decades.

Aborigines (A•buh•RIHJ•neez) are a small part of Australia's population. They are the descendants of the first immigrants who came from Asia about 30,000 to 40,000 years ago. You may have heard of one of their weapons—the **boomerang.** This wooden tool is shaped like a bent bird's wing. Hunters throw their boomerangs to stun prey. If the boomerang misses, it curves and sails back to the hunter.

Australia was first discovered by the Dutch in the late 1600s. In 1770 **Captain James Cook** reached Australia and claimed it for Great

Team-Teaching Activity

Science Australia's government recently announced that it will test methods for extracting oil from deposits offshore. These deposits are potentially very large—they may hold more oil than all of North America. The problem is that the oil deposits are found in the waters near the Great Barrier Reef. Environmentalists worry that extracting the oil will damage this sensitive area. They also fear that tapping the oil will increase shipping in the area, heightening the danger of a damaging oil spill. Invite the science teacher to class to describe the situation. Then have students debate the scientific and economic issues involved. **L1**

EE5 Environment and Society: Standard 14

Britain. At first the British government used Australia as a place to send prisoners. Then other British people set up colonies, especially after gold was discovered in the outback in 1851. Land was taken from the Aborigines, and many of them died of European diseases.

Today about 300,000 Aborigines live in Australia. Growing numbers of them are moving to cities to find jobs. In 1967 the Australian government finally recognized the Aborigines as citizens.

The Government In 1901 the Australian British colonies united to form the independent Commonwealth of Australia. Today Australia has a British-style parliamentary democracy. A prime minister is the head of government.

Like the United States, Australia has a federal system of government. This means that political power is divided between a national government and state governments. The country has six states and two territories, the **Northern Territory** and the **Australian Capital Territory.**

City and Rural Life About 85 percent of Australia's people live in cities. **Sydney** and **Melbourne** are the largest cities. Sydney gained the world's attention as the host city for the 2000 Summer Olympic Games. About 15 percent of Australians live in rural areas known as the **bush.** Many rural people also live and work on the stations that dot the outback.

Australians speak English, but "Aussies," as they call themselves, have some different words. For example, Australians say "G'Day," as a form of hello and cook beef on a "barbie," or barbeque grill.

✓ Reading Check What kind of government does Australia have?

Our World Today Online

Web Activity Visit the ***Our World Today: People, Places, and Issues*** Web site at owt.glencoe.com and click on **Chapter 24–Student Web Activities** to learn more about the Great Barrier Reef.

Section 1 Assessment

Defining Terms

1. **Define** coral reef, outback, station, marsupial, immigrant, boomerang, bush.

Recalling Facts

2. **History** Why does Australia have animals not found on other continents?
3. **Economics** What are four mineral resources found in Australia?
4. **History** Who are the Aborigines?

Critical Thinking

5. **Understanding Cause and Effect** How does climate affect agriculture in Australia?
6. **Drawing Conclusions** How does life in Australia show that the country was once a colony of the United Kingdom?

Graphic Organizer

7. **Organizing Information** Create a time line like this one with at least four dates in Australia's history. Write the dates on one side of the line and the corresponding event on the opposite side.

Applying Social Studies Skills

8. **Analyzing Maps** Look at the physical map on page 644. What mountain peak represents the highest elevation in Australia? What mountain range is it part of?

Section 1 Assessment

1. The terms are defined in the Glossary.
2. because it is separated from other lands by oceans and seas
3. *Any four:* iron ore, zinc, bauxite, gold, silver, opals, diamonds
4. descendants of the first people to come to Australia—from Asia—about 30,000 to 40,000 years ago
5. The dry climate limits farming.
6. use of the English language and a British-style parliamentary democracy
7. 1770—James Cook claimed Australia for Great Britain; 1851—gold discovered in outback and land taken from Aborigines; 1901—Commonwealth of Australia formed; 1967—Aborigines recognized as citizens
8. Mt. Kosciuszko; Great Dividing Range

Chapter 24

Section 1, pages 638–641

Section Quiz 24-1

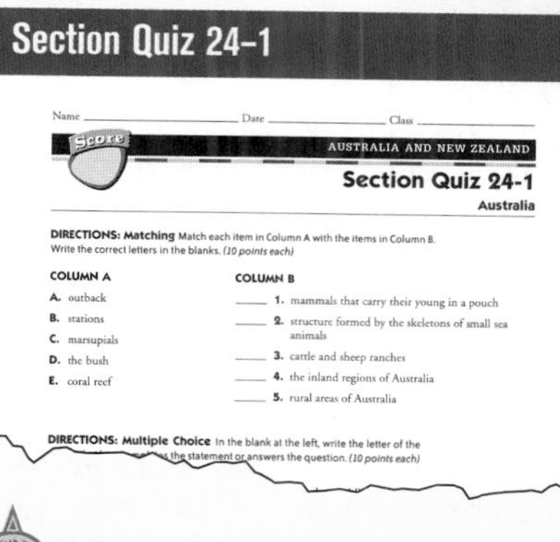

Name ______ Date ______ Class ______

AUSTRALIA AND NEW ZEALAND

Section Quiz 24-1

Australia

DIRECTIONS: Matching Match each item in Column A with the items in Column B. Write the correct letters in the blanks. *(10 points each)*

COLUMN A	COLUMN B
A. outback	____ 1. mammals that carry their young in a pouch
B. stations	____ 2. structure formed by the skeletons of small sea animals
C. marsupials	____ 3. cattle and sheep ranches
D. the bush	____ 4. the inland regions of Australia
E. coral reef	____ 5. rural areas of Australia

DIRECTIONS: Multiple Choice In the blank at the left, write the letter of the ... the statement or answers the question. *(10 points each)*

Our World Today Online

Objectives, goals, and answers to the Student Web Activity can be found in the Web Activity Lesson Plan at owt.glencoe.com

✓ Reading Check Answer

parliamentary democracy

Reading Essentials and Study Guide 24-1

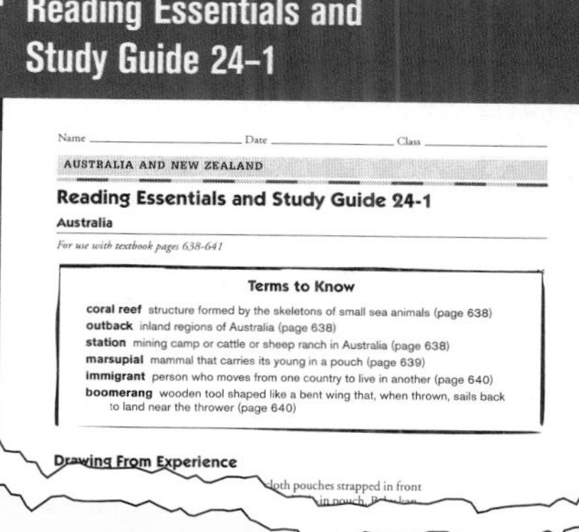

Name ______ Date ______ Class ______

AUSTRALIA AND NEW ZEALAND

Reading Essentials and Study Guide 24-1

Australia

For use with textbook pages 638-641

Terms to Know

coral reef structure formed by the skeletons of small sea animals (page 638)
outback inland regions of Australia (page 638)
station mining camp or cattle or sheep ranch in Australia (page 638)
marsupial mammal that carries its young in a pouch (page 639)
immigrant person who moves from one country to live in another (page 640)
boomerang wooden tool shaped like a bent wing that, when thrown, sails back to land near the thrower (page 640)

Drawing From Experience

Close

Have students write a paragraph comparing life in North America to life in Australia.

Teach

Ask students to identify the major characteristics of the kangaroo and the koala. Note their suggestions. Circle the word *pouch,* or add it if students do not identify this feature. Point out that the presence of the pouch puts both animals in the category of marsupials. Explain that the opossums of North America and the shrew opossums of South America are the only marsupials native to lands other than Australia. **L1**

More About Kangaroos

When they move slowly, kangaroos balance on their small front legs and their tails, shifting the larger hind legs forward. When they run, they hop. Kangaroos must move both hind legs together when on land—but in water, they can use them separately.

Interdisciplinary Connections

Science Koalas are almost the only animals to survive on eucalyptus leaves, which are very tough and have very few nutrients. They have developed adaptations that allow them to digest these leaves. One is a slow metabolism that permits a long period of time for digestion but requires little expenditure of energy. As a result, koalas may sleep 16 hours a day.

Making Connections

CULTURE | GOVERNMENT | PEOPLE | TECHNOLOGY

Australia's Amazing Animals

Australia is home to some fascinating and unusual animals. In fact, many of Australia's animal species are found nowhere else in the world.

Kangaroos

Ask people what comes to mind when they think of Australian animals, and they will probably say the kangaroo. Kangaroos are marsupials—mammals whose young mature inside a pouch on the mother's belly. The young kangaroo, called a joey, stays there for months, eating and growing. Australia is home to more than 50 species of kangaroo, ranging in size from the 6-foot (2-m) red kangaroo to the 9-inch (23-cm) musky rat-kangaroo. No matter what their size, all kangaroos have one thing in common—big hind feet. Kangaroos bound along at about 20 miles (32 km) per hour. In a single jump, a kangaroo can hop 10 feet (3 m) high and cover a distance of 45 feet (14 m).

Koalas

Because of their round face, big black nose, large fluffy ears, and soft fur, people sometimes call these animals koala bears. Yet they are not bears at all. The koala is a marsupial. The female's pouch opens at the bottom. Strong muscles keep the pouch shut and the young koalas, also called joeys, safe inside. The koala is a fussy eater who feeds only on leaves of eucalyptus trees. Although there are over 600 species of eucalyptus that grow in Australia, koalas eat only a few types. The leaves also provide the animals with all the moisture they need. Quiet, calm, and sleepy, koalas spend most of their time in the trees.

▲ Koala and joey

Platypus and Emu

The odd-looking platypus is one of the world's few egg-laying mammals. Sometimes called a duck-billed platypus, the animal has a soft, sensitive, skin-covered snout. The platypus is a good swimmer who lives in burrows along the streams and riverbanks of southern and eastern Australia. It uses its bill to stir the river bottom in search of food.

After the ostrich, the Australian emu is the world's second-largest bird. Although the emu cannot fly, its long legs enable it to run at speeds of up to 30 miles (48 km) per hour. Another interesting characteristic of the emu is its nesting behavior. Although the female lays the eggs, the male emu sits on them until they are ready to hatch.

◀ Kangaroo and joey

Emu ▼

Making the Connection

1. What are marsupials?
2. How far can a kangaroo hop in a single jump?
3. **Making Comparisons** Compare two different animals that live in Australia. Tell how they are alike. Tell how they are different.

Making the Connection

1. mammals whose young mature inside a pouch on the mother's belly
2. 10 feet (3 m) high and 45 feet (14 m) long
3. Comparisons will vary.

Section 2 New Zealand

Guide to Reading

Main Idea

New Zealand is a small country with a growing economy based on trade.

Terms to Know

- geyser
- *manuka*
- fjord
- geothermal energy
- hydroelectric power

Reading Strategy

Create a time line like this one with at least four dates in New Zealand's history. Write the dates on one side of the line and the corresponding event on the opposite side.

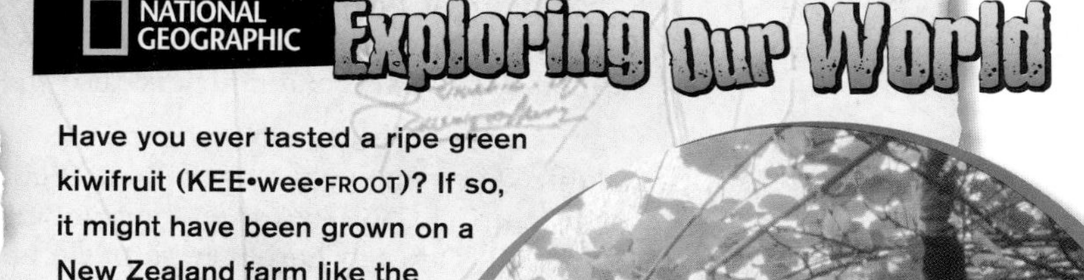

Have you ever tasted a ripe green kiwifruit (KEE•wee•FROOT)? If so, it might have been grown on a New Zealand farm like the one shown here. After all, New Zealand is one of the world's leading producers of this tasty fruit. The kiwifruit, once known as the Chinese gooseberry, is now named for the kiwi bird—New Zealand's national symbol.

New Zealand lies in the Pacific Ocean about 1,200 miles (1,931 km) southeast of its nearest neighbor, Australia. In contrast to Australia's flat, dry land, New Zealand is mountainous and very green. Its climate is mild and wet.

New Zealand's Land

New Zealand is about the size of Colorado. It includes two main islands—**North Island** and **South Island**—as well as many smaller islands. The **Cook Strait** separates North Island and South Island.

North Island A large plateau forms the center of North Island. Three active volcanoes and the inactive Mount Egmont are located here. You also find **geysers,** or hot springs that spout steam and water through a crack in the earth.

Small shrubs called ***manuka*** grow well in the plateau's fertile volcanic soil. Fertile lowlands, forested hills, and sandy beaches surround North Island's central plateau. On the plateau's slopes, sheep and cattle graze. Fruits and vegetables are grown on the coastal lowlands.

1 Focus

Section Objectives

1. Discuss New Zealand's land and how it affects its economy.
2. Describe the ethnic groups in New Zealand.

BELLRINGER Skillbuilder Activity

Project transparency and have students answer questions.

This activity is also available as a blackline master.

Daily Focus Skills Transparency 24-2

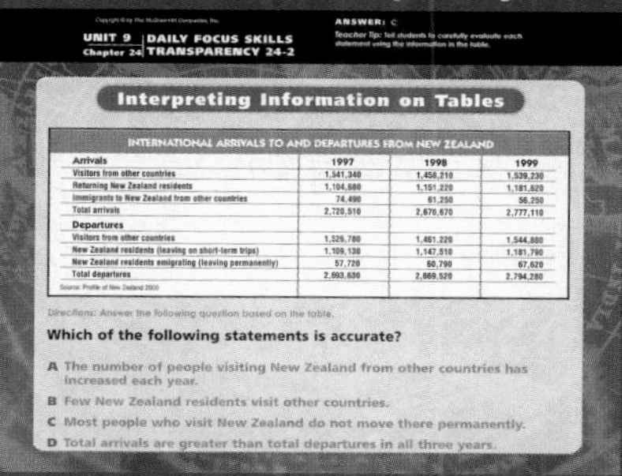

ANSWER: C

Teacher Tip: Tell students to carefully evaluate each statement using the information in the table.

UNIT 9 Chapter 24 DAILY FOCUS SKILLS TRANSPARENCY 24-2

Interpreting Information on Tables

INTERNATIONAL ARRIVALS TO AND DEPARTURES FROM NEW ZEALAND

Arrivals	1997	1998	1999
Visitors from other countries	1,541,340	1,458,210	1,539,230
Returning New Zealand residents	1,104,680	1,151,220	1,181,620
Immigrants to New Zealand from other countries	74,490	61,250	56,250
Total arrivals	2,720,510	2,670,670	2,777,110
Departures			
Visitors from other countries	1,526,780	1,461,220	1,544,880
New Zealand residents (leaving on short-term trips)	1,109,130	1,147,510	1,181,790
New Zealand residents emigrating (leaving permanently)	57,720	60,790	67,620
Total departures	2,693,630	2,669,520	2,794,280

Source: Profile of New Zealand 2000

Directions: Answer the following question based on the table.

Which of the following statements is accurate?

A The number of people visiting New Zealand from other countries has increased each year.
B Few New Zealand residents visit other countries.
C Most people who visit New Zealand do not move there permanently.
D Total arrivals are greater than total departures in all three years.

Guide to Reading

Accessing Prior Knowledge Ask students if they can identify "Old Faithful." After they name Yellowstone's landmark geyser, inform them that New Zealand has many geysers as well.

Vocabulary Precheck Explain that *geo-* comes from a Greek word meaning "earth" and that *thermal* comes from a Greek word for "heat." Then ask students what they think *geothermal energy* means.

Section Resources

Reproducible Masters

- Reproducible Lesson Plan 24-2
- Daily Lecture and Discussion Notes 24-2
- Guided Reading Activity 24-2
- Reading Essentials and Study Guide 24-2
- Section Quiz 24-2

Transparencies

- Daily Focus Skills Transparency 24-2
- GeoQuiz Transparency 24-1

Multimedia

- Vocabulary PuzzleMaker Software
- Interactive Tutor Self-Assessment CD-ROM
- Presentation Plus! CD-ROM
- ExamView® Pro 3.0 Testmaker CD-ROM

Chapter 24

Section 2, pages 643–646

TEACH

Making Comparisons Create a chart with the headings "Physical Features," "Agriculture," "Other Products." Have students copy the chart into their notebooks and then fill in details as they read the section. L1

✓ Reading Check Answer

South Island

Daily Lecture Notes 24-2

Copyright © by The McGraw-Hill Companies, Inc.

AUSTRALIA AND NEW ZEALAND

Daily Lecture and Discussion Notes 24-2

New Zealand (pages 643–646)

Did You Know? New Zealand offers students free elementary and secondary education up to age 19. The law requires children from 6 through 15 years of age to attend school, but most youngsters enter school at 5. Many children under 5 attend free kindergartens or play centers.

I. New Zealand's Land (pages 643–644)

A. In contrast to Australia's flat, dry land, New Zealand is mountainous and very green. Its climate is mild and wet.

B. New Zealand consists of two main islands—North Island and South Island—and many smaller islands.

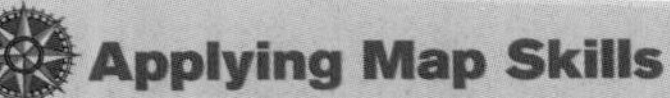

Applying Map Skills

Answers

1. Great Dividing Range
2. below sea level

Skills Practice

Where is the Great Barrier Reef? *(off Australia's northeast coast)*

South Island The **Southern Alps** run along South Island's western coast. Snowcapped **Mount Cook,** the highest peak in New Zealand, soars 12,316 feet (3,754 m) here. Glaciers lie on mountain slopes above green forests and sparkling blue lakes. These glaciers once cut deep **fjords** (fee•AWRDS), or steep-sided valleys, into the mountains. The sea has filled these fjords with crystal-blue waters.

To the east of the Southern Alps stretch the Canterbury Plains. They form New Zealand's largest area of flat or nearly flat land. Farmers grow grains and ranchers raise sheep here.

Plants and Animals New Zealanders take pride in their unique wildlife. Their national symbol is a flightless bird called the kiwi. Giant kauri (KOWR•ee) trees once dominated all of North Island. About 100 years ago, European settlers cut down many of these trees, using the wood to build homes and ships. Today the government protects kauri trees. One of them is more than 2,000 years old.

✓ Reading Check Which island of New Zealand has glaciers and fjords?

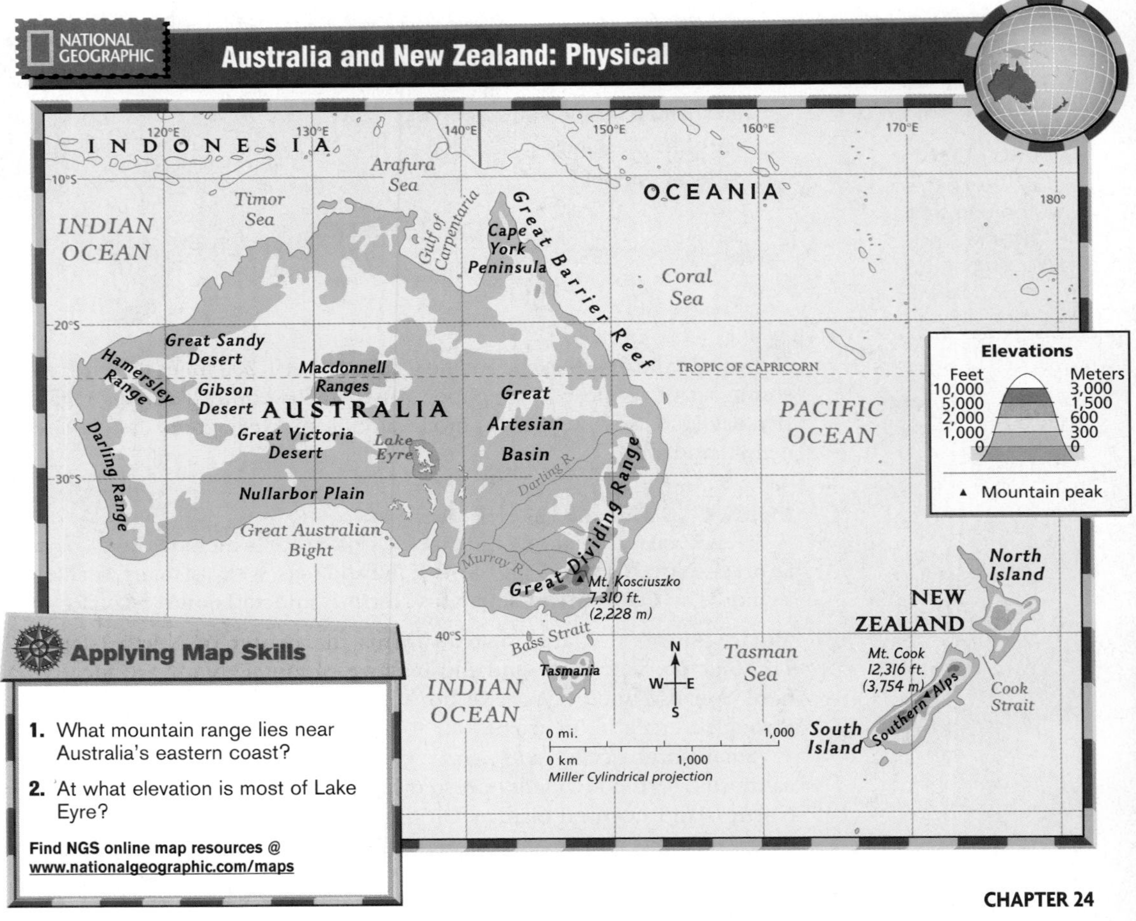

Applying Map Skills

1. What mountain range lies near Australia's eastern coast?
2. At what elevation is most of Lake Eyre?

Find NGS online map resources @ www.nationalgeographic.com/maps

Team-Teaching Activity

History Waitangi Day, February 6, is a national holiday in New Zealand. The holiday commemorates the 1840 treaty in which the Maoris agreed to accept British rule and the British, in turn, recognized the Maoris as the landowners of New Zealand. Hone Heke Pokai was the first Maori chief to sign the treaty. Four years later, he was one of the first chiefs to declare war on the British because they were not honoring their commitments in the treaty. The British defeated him and his followers in 1846. Since then, the Maori have used the treaty to reclaim land that was misappropriated by white settlers. Invite the history teacher to class to discuss relations between whites and the Maori and compare them to the situation with whites and Aborigines in Australia. L1

EE4 Human Systems: Standard 9

New Zealand's Economy

New Zealand has a thriving agricultural economy. Sheep are an important agricultural resource. New Zealand is the second-leading wool producer in the world. Lamb meat is another important export. Apples, barley, wheat, and corn are the main crops.

Trade with other countries is an important part of New Zealand's economy. Its main trading partners are Australia, Japan, the United States, and the United Kingdom. Depending on trade brings both benefits and dangers to New Zealand. If the economies of other countries are growing quickly, demand for goods from New Zealand will rise. If the other economies slow, however, they will buy fewer products. This can cause hardship on the islands. In recent years, trade has grown, and New Zealanders enjoy a high standard of living.

Mining and Manufacturing New Zealand sits on top of the molten rock that forms volcanoes. As a result, it is rich in **geothermal energy,** electricity produced from steam. The major source of energy, however, is **hydroelectric power**—electricity generated by flowing water. New Zealand also has coal, oil, iron ore, silver, and gold.

The country is rapidly industrializing. Service industries and tourism play large roles in the economy. The main manufactured items are wood products, fertilizers, wool products, and shoes.

✓ Reading Check **Why does trade with other countries offer both benefits and dangers to New Zealand?**

New Zealand's History and People

People called the **Maori** (MOWR•ee) are believed to have arrived in New Zealand between A.D. 950 and 1150. They probably crossed the Pacific Ocean in canoes from islands far to the northeast. Undisturbed for hundreds of years, the Maori developed skills in farming, weaving, fishing, bird hunting, and woodcarving.

The first European explorers came to the islands in the mid-1600s. Almost 200 years passed before settlers—most of them

NATIONAL GEOGRAPHIC On Location

Maori

In recent years the Maori culture has experienced a revival in New Zealand. Some Maori dress in traditional costumes for special celebrations.

History **How did the Maori arrive in New Zealand?**

Chapter 24

Section 2, pages 643–646

More About the Photo

Maori The Maori name for New Zealand before the arrival of the Europeans was *Aotearoa.* The Maori people call their language *te reo.*

Caption Answer The Maori came to New Zealand by canoe from islands far to the northeast.

Guided Reading Activity 24-2

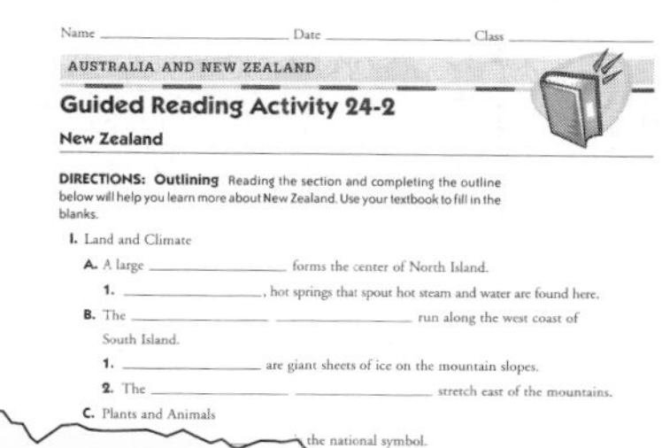

Name ______ Date ______ Class ______

AUSTRALIA AND NEW ZEALAND

Guided Reading Activity 24-2

New Zealand

DIRECTIONS: Outlining Reading the section and completing the outline below will help you learn more about New Zealand. Use your textbook to fill in the blanks.

I. Land and Climate

A. A large ______ forms the center of North Island.

1. ______, hot springs that spout hot steam and water are found here.

B. The ______ ______ run along the west coast of South Island.

1. ______ are giant sheets of ice on the mountain slopes.

2. The ______ ______ stretch east of the mountains.

C. Plants and Animals

3 ASSESS

Assign Section 2 Assessment as homework or an in-class activity.

✓ Reading Check Answer

High demand from those countries can lead to prosperity, but if demand slips, New Zealand's economy will suffer.

Meeting Special Needs

Naturalistic Explain to students the mechanics of geysers so they understand why these phenomena erupt. In a geyser, water is at rest in a column of space within rock. That column of water must be sitting near hot magma within the earth. The heated rock causes the water at the bottom to boil, pushing out some of the water above it. The remaining water becomes even hotter, turning to steam and shooting out into the air. Most geysers are found in only two countries besides New Zealand—Iceland and the United States. **Ask: Where are geysers found in New Zealand? What other landforms are found there?** **L1**

Refer to *Inclusion for the Middle School Social Studies Classroom Strategies and Activities* in the TCR.

Chapter 24

Section 2, pages 643–646

Section Quiz 24-2

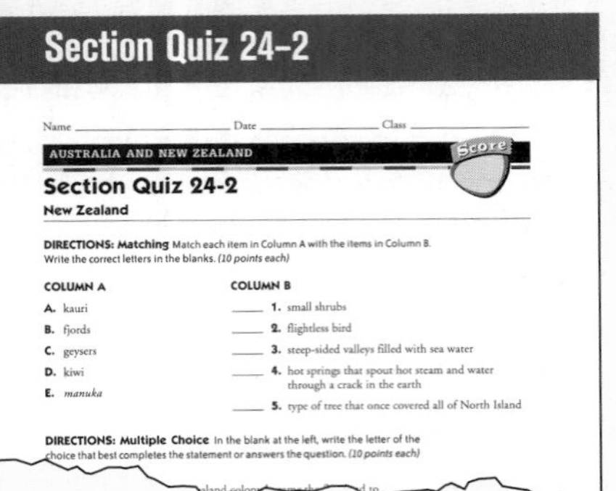
Name ________ Date ________ Class ________

AUSTRALIA AND NEW ZEALAND

Section Quiz 24-2

New Zealand

DIRECTIONS: Matching Match each item in Column A with the items in Column B. Write the correct letters in the blanks. *(10 points each)*

COLUMN A	COLUMN B
A. kauri	____ 1. small shrubs
B. fjords	____ 2. flightless bird
C. geysers	____ 3. steep-sided valleys filled with sea water
D. kiwi	____ 4. hot springs that spout hot steam and water through a crack in the earth
E. *manuka*	____ 5. type of tree that once covered all of North Island

DIRECTIONS: Multiple Choice In the blank at the left, write the letter of the choice that best completes the statement or answers the question. *(10 points each)*

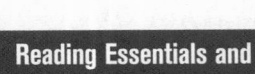

Reading Check Answer

the Maori

Reading Essentials and Study Guide 24-2

Name ________ Date ________ Class ________

AUSTRALIA AND NEW ZEALAND

Reading Essentials and Study Guide 24-2

New Zealand

For use with textbook pages 643–646

Terms to Know

geyser hot spring that spouts hot steam and water through a crack in the earth (page 643)
manuka small shrub that grows in New Zealand's volcanic soil (page 643)
fjord steep-sided valley filled with seawater (page 644)
geothermal energy electricity made from steam rising from deep inside the earth (page 645)
hydroelectric power electricity made from flowing water (page 645)

Drawing From Experience

Enrich

Have students research and report on traditional Maori crafts, either showing a variety of crafts or presenting in-depth information on one.

4 Close

Have students create a concept web for New Zealand that includes the geography, economy, history, and culture of the country.

British—arrived. In 1840 British officials signed a treaty with Maori leaders. In this treaty, the Maori agreed to accept British rule in return for the right to keep their land. More British settlers eventually moved onto Maori land. War broke out in the 1860s—a war that the Maori lost.

In 1893 the colony became the first land to give women the right to vote. New Zealand was also among the first places in which the government gave help to people who were old, sick, or out of work.

New Zealand became independent in 1907. The country is a parliamentary democracy in which elected representatives choose a prime minister to head the government. Five seats in the parliament can be held only by Maoris. Today about 10 percent of New Zealand's 3.9 million people are Maori. Most of the rest are descendants of British settlers. Asians and Pacific islanders, attracted by the growing economy, have increased the diversity of New Zealand's society.

About 85 percent of the people live in urban areas. The largest cities are **Auckland,** an important port, and **Wellington,** the capital. Both are on North Island, where about 75 percent of the people live.

New Zealanders take advantage of the country's mild climate and beautiful landscapes. They enjoy camping, hiking, hunting, boating, and mountain climbing in any season. They also play cricket and rugby, sports that originated in Great Britain.

Reading Check What group settled New Zealand about 1,000 years ago?

Section 2 Assessment

Defining Terms

1. **Define** geyser, *manuka,* fjord, geothermal energy, hydroelectric power.

Recalling Facts

2. **Region** How do New Zealand's land and climate compare to Australia's?
3. **Economics** What two animal products are important exports for New Zealand?
4. **History** Most of New Zealand's people are descendants of settlers from what European country?

Critical Thinking

5. **Analyzing Information** Why do you think New Zealand's government guarantees the Maori a certain number of seats in the parliament?
6. **Making Predictions** With so many different peoples settling in New Zealand, how do you think the country's culture might change?

Graphic Organizer

7. **Organizing Information** Imagine that you are moving to New Zealand. Write a question you would ask for each topic in the chart below.

Physical features	Economy	Recreation
Climate	Government	Culture

Applying Social Studies Skills

8. **Analyzing Maps** Look at the physical map on page 644. Which New Zealand island has higher mountains?

Section 2 Assessment

1. The terms are defined in the Glossary.
2. New Zealand is smaller, more mountainous, and wetter than Australia.
3. wool, lamb meat
4. United Kingdom
5. *Possible answer:* to protect their rights
6. *Possible answer:* The country will probably develop a more diverse culture.
7. Students' questions will vary.
8. South Island

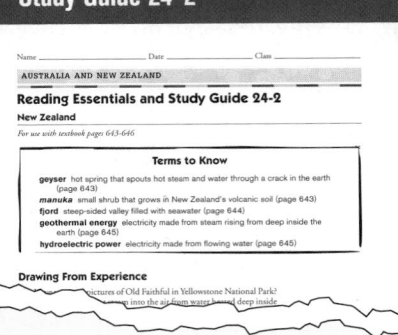

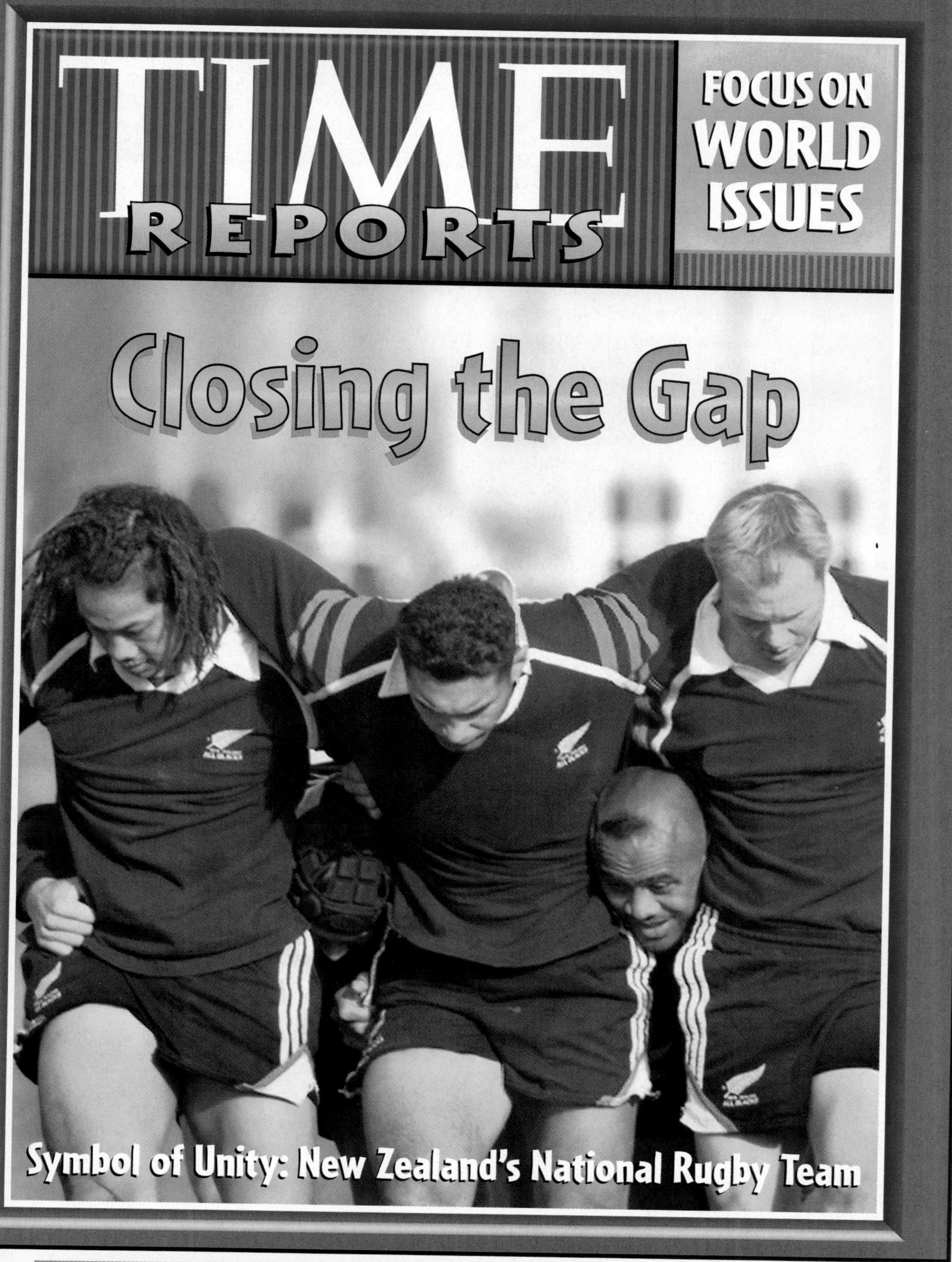

TIME REPORTS

FOCUS ON WORLD ISSUES

Closing the Gap

Symbol of Unity: New Zealand's National Rugby Team

AFP/CORBIS

TIME REPORTS

Focus on World Issues

Teacher Background

Indigenous people around the world have suffered when others have settled on their lands. The Maoris of New Zealand are one example. After the immigration of Europeans, they were discouraged from following their traditions, and many succumbed to illnesses. Amidst a feeling of hopelessness, some began abusing alcohol. By the late 19th century, there were only approximately 40,000 remaining Maoris.

Today the Maoris number over 500,000. New Zealanders are now trying to right many of the wrongs committed against the Maoris.

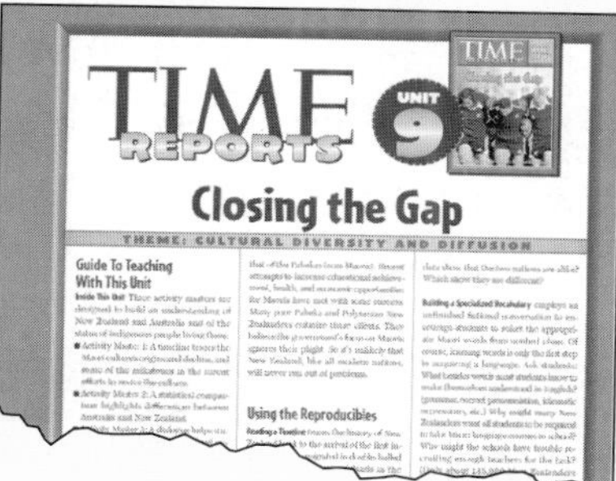
TIME REPORTS UNIT 9

Closing the Gap

THEME: CULTURAL DIVERSITY AND DIFFUSION

Guide To Teaching With This Unit

Using the Reproducibles

Preparing the Student

Students should be aware that the Maori people of New Zealand actually consist of a complex group of tribes and subtribes with a variety of customs and dialects.

Groups such as the Maoris, Aborigines, and Native Americans are commonly referred to as "indigenous peoples."

Making Connections

Tradition **Ask students:** **What kind of traditions does your family follow? What are some of the holidays your family celebrates?** Ask students to imagine that they could no longer celebrate these occasions. **Ask:** **How would that make you feel? Why do you think cultural traditions are important to people?** Then discuss the fact that when Europeans settled in various parts of the world, including New Zealand, Australia, and North America, they typically saw the cultures of those already living there as being inferior. They often discouraged the native people from practicing their religions, celebrating festivals, or speaking their language. While attitudes have changed in recent times, the actions of the Europeans greatly damaged these cultures.

TIME REPORTS

TIME REPORTS

FOCUS ON WORLD ISSUES

DAVE E. HOUSER/ CORBIS

In their ancestors' clothes, Maoris do a fierce dance. Land is sacred to Australia's Aborigines (right).

1 Focus

If there are any Native American students in your classroom, you may wish to ask them to share whether they feel they are sometimes treated differently from Caucasians. Otherwise, you may want to ask the class if they feel Native Americans are treated differently from Caucasians. Ask students to explain their responses. As students know, Native Americans are the indigenous people of North America. This article discusses the indigenous people of New Zealand and Australia.

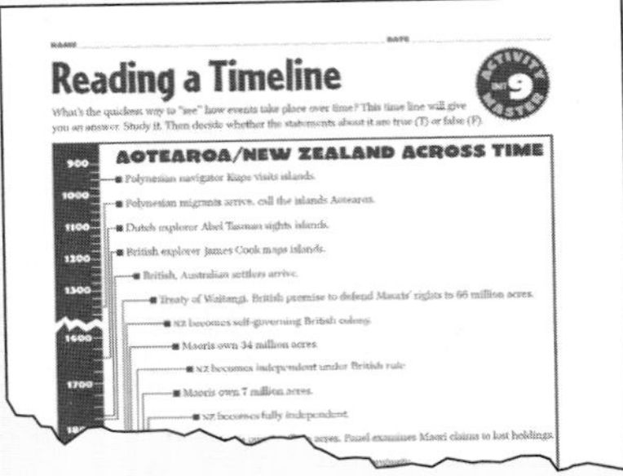

Maori Iwi Lands

ANSWER

It is approximately 500 miles. At least part of the journey would have to be over water, which could be treacherous; in addition, much of the land is mountainous, and you would have to pass through other tribes' lands.

The New World Down Under

When Ngataua Omahuru was five years old, he made a big mistake. Ngataua (en•gah•TOW•ah) was a **Maori**, a native New Zealander. He and his family lived in the forest beneath Mount Taranaki, a volcano on New Zealand's North Island.

One day in 1869, Ngataua made the mistake of wandering away from his parents. A band of British soldiers kidnapped him.

New Zealand was a British colony then. Europeans had been settling there in great numbers for more than 40 years. They had moved onto Maori land, paying nothing or very little for it. Maoris who tried to protect their land were often forced off it at gunpoint.

Ngataua ended up in the home of William Fox, the head of the colony's government. Fox and his wife changed Ngataua's name to William Fox. They sent him to English schools. They cut all his links to the Maori world.

A Rich Culture

Through their religion, the Maoris felt close to their ancestors and to nature. They expressed themselves through song, poetry, weaving, woodcarving, even tattooing. They were brave and clever warriors.

The British, called **Pakehas** (pa•KAY•haws) by the Maoris, did not value the Maori culture. The Pakehas were convinced that no way of life was better

Maori Iwi Lands

About 200 years ago, New Zealand was home to dozens of iwi, or tribes. This map shows where 10 of them were.

INTERPRETING MAPS

Making Inferences Suppose you were a Ngapuhi living 200 years ago. About how far would you have had to travel to reach the Ngai Tahu? What might have made this trip difficult and dangerous?

648

Team-Teaching Activity

Sociology Have a teacher who's knowledgeable about sociology talk to the class about the importance of preserving different cultures throughout the world. Ask the teacher specifically to discuss the importance of traditions such as celebrating harvests and religious events, as well as birth, death, and marriage rituals. The teacher should emphasize the differences and similarities among cultural observances. For example, many cultures have "coming-of-age" ceremonies for young people. Emphasis should be placed on the fact that celebrating these kinds of events creates common bonds within the community. Have students write a paragraph describing a ritual they've participated in and how it made them feel. **L1**

EE4 Human Systems: Standard 10

JOHN VAN HASSELT—CORBIS SYGMA

Maori children. Maoris and Pakehas often marry one another.

PAUL A. SOUDERS/CORBIS

Women in traditional dress perform Maori dances.

BETTINA A. STAMMEN

Aborigine Cathy Freeman lights the Olympic flame in 2000.

AL BELLO—ALLSPORT

TIME REPORTS

than their own. They believed the Maori would be better off leaving their ways behind.

That **ethnocentric** decision guided Pakeha thinking for a century. The Maoris were taught they had nothing in their culture to be proud of. Cut loose from their traditions but not fully accepted by whites, the Maoris fell on hard times.

They are still trying to recover. Compared with Pakehas, Maoris today learn less and earn less. They die more readily from cancer, diabetes, and heart disease.

New Zealanders are trying to close the gaps between the two groups. They are doing it both to be fair and to keep their nation strong. In 50 years the Maoris will make up almost a quarter of the country's population.

Australia's Ghosts

A similar issue haunts Australia, 1,400 miles (2,250 kilometers) west of New Zealand. Australia's native people, the **Aborigines**, make up 2 percent of the population. For tens of thousands of years, all of Australia was theirs. In 1788 British settlers arrived. They began almost immediately to separate the Aborigines from their culture. They drove them off land that was **sacred** to them. They killed many who resisted.

The Australian settlers repeated the New Zealand settlers' mistakes. They tried to make the first Australians more like them.

Some of their methods were especially harsh. The government decided that Aborigine children would be better off in the hands of white families. So from 1910 to 1971, as many as 100,000 Aborigine children were removed from their parents. White families adopted most of them. Few of the children ever saw their birth mothers again.

Ngataua Omahuru got to see his mother again. As a young lawyer, he returned to his homeland on business. His real family recognized him, and he saw how badly they had been treated. He devoted the rest of his life to helping the Maoris fight for their rights.

It would take the Maoris almost a century to get a fair hearing. By then, Maori foods, words, art, and songs had become part of New Zealand's culture. New Zealanders today realize just how much they would lose if the Maori way of life ever disappeared. ■

EXPLORING THE ISSUES

1. **Making Inferences** Why do you think British settlers believed their way of life was best?
2. **Problem Solving** If you could, what two things would you change to improve the Maori's lives?

2 TEACH

Identifying Main Ideas
Ask students to identify the main idea of the section titled "The New World Down Under." Write several suggestions and have students discuss them. Students should understand the concept of *ethnocentricity*. **Ask:** **How did ethnocentricity play an important role in the Pakehas's treatment of the Maori?** **L1**

More About the Photos

Olympics Ask: **Why do you think Cathy Freeman was chosen to light the flame at the 2000 Olympics?**

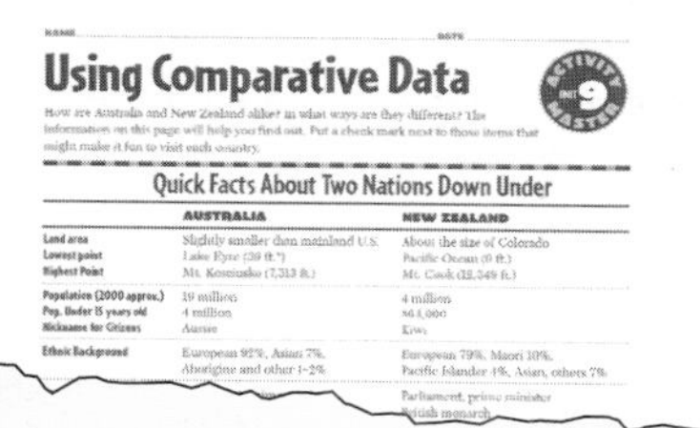

NAME ______ DATE ______

Using Comparative Data

ACTIVITY 9 MASTER

How are Australia and New Zealand alike? In what ways are they different? The information on this page will help you find out. Put a check mark next to those items that might make it fun to visit each country.

Quick Facts About Two Nations Down Under

	AUSTRALIA	NEW ZEALAND
Land area	Slightly smaller than mainland U.S.	About the size of Colorado
Lowest point	Lake Eyre (39 ft.*)	Pacific Ocean (0 ft.)
Highest Point	Mt. Kosciusko (7,313 ft.)	Mt. Cook (12,349 ft.)
Population (2000 approx.)	19 million	4 million
Pop. Under 15 years old	4 million	864,000
Nickname for Citizens	Aussie	Kiwi
Ethnic Background	European 92%, Asian 7%, Aborigine and other 1–2%	European 79%, Maori 10%, Pacific Islander 4%, Asian, others 7%
		Parliament, prime minister British monarch

EXPLORING THE ISSUES

ANSWERS

1. *Possible answers:* native cultures were less advanced in their use of technology; the natives' dress, customs, and manners might have seemed "improper" by British standards of the time
2. Answers might include better health care, education, and job training.

Critical Thinking Activity

Understanding Cause and Effect Tell students that for about a hundred years after their arrival, the Pakehas continually told young Maoris that the Maori way of life, including its language, religion, and traditions, was inferior to European culture. **Ask:** **How do you think this affected the way these young people felt about themselves? How do you think it might affect their success in society?** Have students research an indigenous group other than Maoris or Aborigines. They should then write a report about how these groups were treated by outsiders who came to their lands, how it affected their culture and people, and what steps have been taken to improve their situation. **L2**

EE4 Human Systems: Standards 10, 13

TIME REPORTS

Recommended Internet Sites

www.maori.culture.co.nz
Contains Maori history, examples of art and music, and a wide range of other information, along with links to related sites.

www.un.org/cyberschoolbus/
Enter "indigenous" in the Search box to find teaching units on indigenous people, including cultural information, a discussion of their rights and even a presentation on Maori schools.

www.aboriginalaustralia.com/
Contains examples of aboriginal art, discussions of culture, spirituality, sports, and other interesting information.

More About the Photos

Maoris Ask: **Do you think these children would prefer wearing traditional clothing or Western-style clothing? Why?**

EXPLORING THE ISSUES

ANSWERS

1. If the government chooses not to enforce a law (typically because the majority of people do not want it enforced), the law might as well not exist.
2. Many settlers did not agree with the treaty and routinely violated it. In order to enforce it, the government would have to go against British settlers.

TIME REPORTS

Broken Promises

Around noon on February 6, 1840, about 75 people stood under a tent in the coastal hamlet of Waitangi, New Zealand. The gathering included Maori chiefs, British settlers, missionaries, and military men.

BETTMANN/CORBIS

▲ Maori children in traditional dress.

They were there to sign a treaty. The treaty gave Britain the right to rule New Zealand. It gave the Maoris Britain's promise to protect them and their land.

The deal made sense to the Maoris. Shady businessmen had begun grabbing Maori land. The chiefs felt that Britain's military muscle was the only thing that could stop the thefts.

Founding Charter

The **Treaty of Waitangi** became New Zealand's founding document. It is as important to New Zealanders as the U.S. Constitution is to Americans. It granted British citizenship to the Maoris. It also described how Maoris and European settlers would share responsibility for New Zealand.

But an agreement is only as strong as the will to enforce it. Greedy settlers took control of New Zealand's government. They used small conflicts as excuses to take over huge pieces of Maori land.

The Maoris tried to embarrass the Pakehas into living up to the treaty. They plowed up the lawns of rich settlers who lived on stolen land. They met Pakeha troops with singing children who offered the soldiers bread.

But in the end nothing, not even the support of many white settlers, could keep the Maoris from losing more land. **Waitangi Day** is a national holiday in New Zealand. Many Maoris refuse to celebrate it, and few people wonder why. ■

EXPLORING THE ISSUES

1. **Explaining** What does the phrase "the will to enforce it" mean? How might the phrase apply to any law?
2. **Making Inferences** Why might it have been hard for Great Britain's government to live up to its side of the agreement?

650

Meeting Special Needs

Visual/Spatial The Maoris make extensive use of skin art, especially tattoos, which they call *kiri tuhi.* In many instances, both the application of the tattoo and its design have sacred meanings. Have students use reference books and the Internet to determine the types of symbols used, their meanings, etc. Two Web sites that contain useful information are **www.culture.co.nz/kirituhi** and **www.tamoko.org.nz**. Then have students draw examples of Maori tattoos on paper. They may want to combine several different symbols in their artwork. **L1**

Refer to *Inclusion for the Middle School Social Studies Classroom Strategies and Activities* in the TCR.

TIME REPORTS

Closing the Gap

How do you fix a problem that began 200 years ago? New Zealanders have three answers. They hope to keep the Maori culture alive. They want Maoris to have the skills they need to succeed. And they want to pay the **iwi** for land their ancestors lost.

Maoritanga, the Maori way of life, is in trouble. Few people speak the Maori language. To help more people learn it, schools have begun to teach it. They also teach Maori traditions, along with Maori arts and crafts, music, and dance. Maoris now have an "all-Maori" TV channel, too.

Prescription for Success

Equipping Maoris to succeed is another challenge. The government calls its solution "closing the gap"—in skills, wages, housing, and health care. Maoris are being encouraged to stay in school longer, so that they can find and keep good jobs.

The land issue is difficult. The government can't return land to the Maoris that it doesn't own without hurting the people who live on it now. The Maori will be paid for lost land and other lost "treasures," such as fishing rights.

By 2001, the Waitangi Tribunal had awarded several iwi a total of $300 million. The tribunal, or claims court, won't finish its work until around 2012.

"The process [of sorting through Maori claims] is about more than money," one panel member said. "It is about renewing a relationship that was intended to be based on trust."

That was the spirit of the Treaty of Waitangi. This time, New Zealanders are determined to make it work.

REUTERS NEW MEDIA INC/CORBIS

▲ New Zealand Prime Minister Helen Clark in 2001. New Zealand was the first nation to let all women vote.

EXPLORING THE ISSUE

1. **Summarizing** What does the title of this article mean? Where is the gap, and why do you think it exists?
2. **Making Inferences** Why might some Maoris be unhappy with the Waitangi Tribunal's decisions?

651

Identifying Main Ideas

Ask students to list the three solutions New Zealanders have for rectifying past mistreatment of the Maoris. Then have students discuss the methods New Zealanders are using to achieve these solutions.

Did You Know?

In 1995, Queen Elizabeth II formally apologized to the Maoris for the treatment they had received from the British.

Interpreting Points of View

Have students write a fictional account of a young Maori being taken from his or her family to be raised by Pakehas. The story should emphasize how this experience might affect the Maori's self-esteem and feelings toward his or her birth family.

EXPLORING THE ISSUE

ANSWERS

1. It refers to equalizing the treatment of the Maoris and Pakehas, with equal treatment under the law, equal wages, and equal education. In the past, the Maoris were treated as inferiors and their land and culture was taken from them.
2. The Tribunal is not returning land that was taken illegally, but is rather compensating iwi for the land.

Interdisciplinary Activity

Art Have students find a work of art by Maoris or Aborigines that transcends the boundaries of those cultures or societies and conveys a universal theme. Samples of artwork can be found in reference books and on the Internet. They should then write a brief report discussing the background of the work and what it means to them. The report should include illustrations and discuss what the artwork reveals about the Maori or Aborigine culture or religious beliefs. Students may work individually or in small groups. You may want to have the student examine music, literature, or poetry rather than works of visual art. L2

EE4 Human Systems: Standard 10

Current Events Journal

Tell students that indigenous people such as the Maoris and Aborigines are typically bi-cultural. They follow both their own culture and that of the dominant culture in their society.

Many people in America are multi-cultural, participating in traditions from various backgrounds. Have students write about two or three events or holidays from different cultures that they or people they know celebrate.

EXPLORING THE ISSUE

ANSWERS

1. *Possible answers:* Many people see the United States as a country where they can have religious or political freedom and be successful if they work hard and have the needed skills.
2. Answers will vary.

Did You Know

The Waitangi Tribunal is governed by the expression "Kia puta ki te whai ao ki te ao marama," meaning "From the world of darkness, moving into the world of light."

Bridging the Gaps at Home: What Can One Person Do?

Ngataua Omahuru, the Maori who was raised in the Pakeha world, did a lot to help his people. He was successful in part because he knew both worlds well.

Americans are fortunate to live in a country blessed with many cultures.

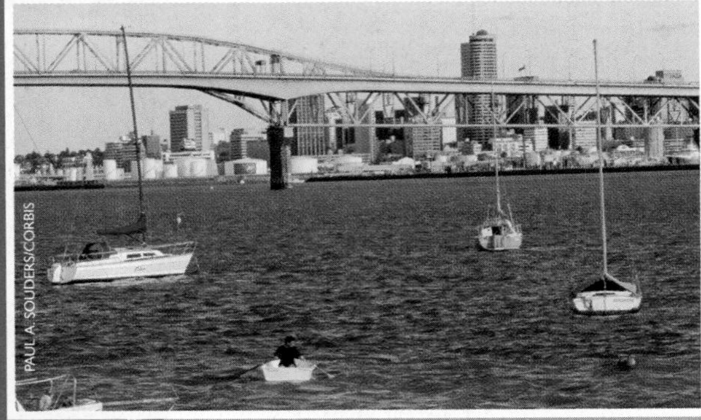

▲ Auckland, with 400,000 people, is New Zealand's largest city.

But how many of us take the time to really understand another culture? Do so, and you will help bridge the gaps that often keep Americans apart.

Here's one way to start. First, choose an immigrant group that you would like to learn more about. You'll have a lot of choices, because all Americans have immigrant roots. And that includes Native Americans, whose ancestors came from Asia thousands of years ago.

Detective Work

Second, get together with a couple of friends who share your interest in this group. As a team, find out all you can about it. When did members of the group come to the United States in large numbers? One of you could find out. Did a particular event prompt them to leave their homeland at that time? One of you could find an answer. How did Americans view the newcomers? How have those views changed? How do members of this group see themselves today—as members of an ethnic group, as Americans, or as both? How has this group changed the way Americans define themselves? By dividing up the work, you could find answers to all these questions fairly quickly.

Share your findings. Publish an article about them in a school newspaper or on a Web page. Illustrate your findings on a poster. Display the poster at school, at your local library, or with a church group. By doing so, you will help others appreciate the glittering mosaic of American life.

EXPLORING THE ISSUE

1. **Making Generalizations** In 2001, one of every 10 Americans had been born in another country. Why do you think the United States acts as a magnet for people from other countries?
2. **Cause and Effect** Write a new title for this *TIME Reports* feature. Share it with your classmates. Explain why you think your title fits the story.

Your Government and You

The United States Department of Interior Bureau of Indian Affairs (BIA) Web site (www.doi.gov/bureau-indianaffairs.html) contains information on the goals and programs of the BIA, including its adherence to the concept of self-determination for Native Americans. Have students examine this site to learn more about the Bureau's programs. It also contains links to other useful Native American sites. Have students discuss the information provided about the U.S./Tribal government-to-government relationship (click on the home page history link or go to www.doi.gov/bia/infoindex). Students should understand the mission of the BIA, its policy history, and recent measures taken by tribal governments. **Ask:** **What might be the advantages or disadvantages of the BIA's policy? L3**

 **EE4 Human Systems: Standard 13**

REVIEW AND ASSESS

UNDERSTANDING THE ISSUE

1. **Defining Key Terms** Write definitions for the following terms: *Maori, Aborigine, Pakeha, sacred, Treaty of Waitangi, culture, Maoritanga, iwi, traditions, rights.*
2. **Writing to Inform** Write a short article describing the history of the Treaty of Waitangi. Use at least five of the terms listed above.
3. **Writing to Persuade** Why is it important to respect other cultures? Write a short article to support your view, using the experiences of New Zealand and Australia as examples.

INTERNET RESEARCH ACTIVITY

4. Navigate to **www.tetaurawhiri.govt.nz**. Click on the English Gateway. Browse through the site. Read about the history of the Maori language. Read about Maori Language Commission, and what it does. How important is language to a culture's survival? Write a short essay answering that question, using facts picked up on this site.
5. Navigate to **www.culture.co.nz/recipes**. What can food tell you about people who eat it? The Maori recipes you find on this site will suggest answers. Browse through the traditional recipes. Then write a 250-word article explaining how those recipes provide clues to where the Maoris live, how they cook, and what foods their great-grandparents ate.

BEYOND THE CLASSROOM

6. **Compare the map** on the opening page with the physical map of New Zealand in the text on page 644. What does the physical map tell you about the land the iwi occupied? In a short essay, describe in general terms what one iwi's traditional land may have looked like.
7. **Visit your school or local library** to find books on the Maori or Aborigines. (A good but long one is Peter Walker's *The Fox Boy*, which tells Ngataua Omahuru's story.) Prepare an oral book report to deliver in class. Make sure to note the author's point of view.

BETTINA A. STAMMEN

▲ **A banana leaf serves as a plate for traditional Maori food.**

The Making of a Multicultural Society

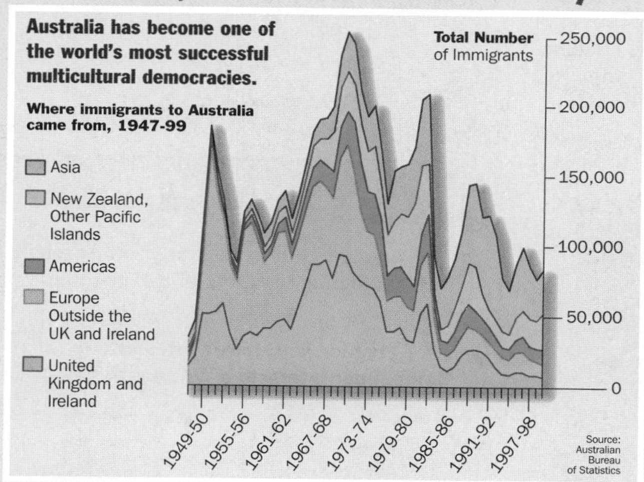

BUILDING GRAPH READING SKILLS

1. **Analyzing the Data** In 1999 there were about 80,000 immigrants. What were the two largest sources?
2. **Making Inferences** What might make people want to leave their homelands and settle in Australia?

FOR UPDATES ON WORLD ISSUES GO TO www.timeclassroom.com/glencoe

653

TIME REPORTS

3 ASSESS

Have students take the Time Reports Quiz or do the Alternative Assessment project for this unit provided in the Teacher's Classroom Resources.

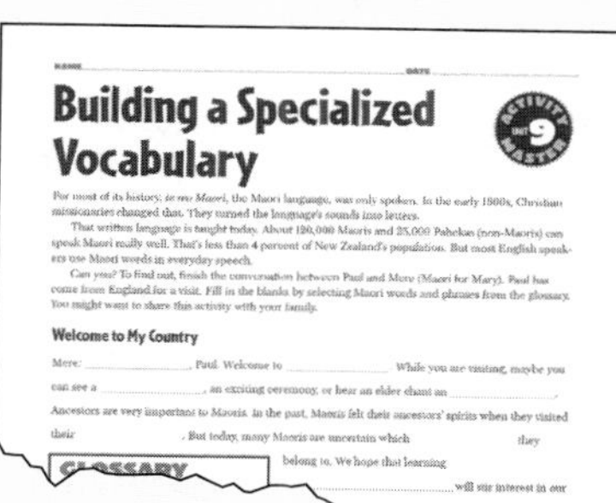

Building a Specialized Vocabulary

For most of its history, *te reo Maori*, the Maori language, was only spoken. In the early 1800s, Christian missionaries changed that. They turned the language's sounds into letters.

That written language is taught today. About 120,000 Maoris and 25,000 Pahekas (non-Maoris) can speak Maori really well. That's less than 4 percent of New Zealand's population. But most English speakers use Maori words in everyday speech.

Can you? To find out, finish the conversation between Paul and Mere (Maori for Mary). Paul has come from England for a visit. Fill in the blanks by selecting Maori words and phrases from the glossary. You might want to share this activity with your family.

Welcome to My Country

Mere: ________, Paul. Welcome to ________. While you are visiting, maybe you can see a ________, an exciting ceremony, or hear an elder chant an ________. Ancestors are very important to Maoris. In the past, Maoris felt their ancestors' spirits when they visited their ________. But today, many Maoris are uncertain which ________ they belong to. We hope that learning ________ will stir interest in our ...

GLOSSARY

BUILDING GRAPH READING SKILLS

ANSWERS

1. Asia and New Zealand and other Pacific islands
2. *Possible answers:* People (especially poor people) want to start a new life; there are many job opportunities; there's a lot of open land to settle

4 CLOSE

Ask students to write a paragraph starting with this topic sentence: *Preserving the culture of indigenous people, such as the Maoris and Aborigines, is important because . . .*

Culminating Activity

To close this lesson, have students complete the Review and Assess section questions and activities above. Students should use classroom discussion, contextual clues, and their student dictionaries to write definitions for terms. Before assigning the Internet activities, it is recommended that you review your school district policy on student Internet use.

Focus on Debate

For further student understanding of the issue, have students debate the pro and con positions of the following topic: **There should be a statute of limitations (time limit) on claims made by indigenous peoples against governments for loss of property. L2**

EE4 Human Systems: Standard 13

TEACH

Give students the following situation: Suppose you had seen a new movie that you enjoyed and wanted to tell your friends about it. How would you relate what happened in the movie? Would you tell them everything that happened or only the main events? Most students realize that they would describe only the main events. Explain that an outline is similar to this condensed version of the movie's plot—it contains the main points of a piece of writing. **L1**

Additional Skills Practice

1. **Why are different symbols—Roman numerals, capital letters, and Arabic numbers—used to show different entries?** *(to organize points that belong together; to show things that are of the same level of importance)*
2. **What is the purpose of indenting entries?** *(to show how one level is subordinate to the previous one)*

Additional Skills Resources

 Chapter Skills Activity 24

 Building Geography Skills for Life

Study and Writing Skill

Outlining

Outlining may be used as a starting point for writing. The writer begins with the rough shape of the material and gradually fills in the details in a logical manner. You may also use outlining as a method of note taking and organizing information as you read.

Learning the Skill

There are two types of outlines—formal and informal. An informal outline is similar to taking notes—you write words and phrases needed to remember main ideas. In contrast, a formal outline has a standard format. Follow these steps to formally outline information:

- Read the text to identify the main ideas. Label these with Roman numerals.
- Write subtopics under each main idea. Label these with capital letters.
- Write supporting details for each subtopic. Label these with Arabic numerals.
- Each level should have at least two entries and should be indented from the level above.
- All entries should use the same grammatical form, whether phrases or complete sentences.

▼ **A huge sheep herd pours down a ravine on New Zealand's North Island.**

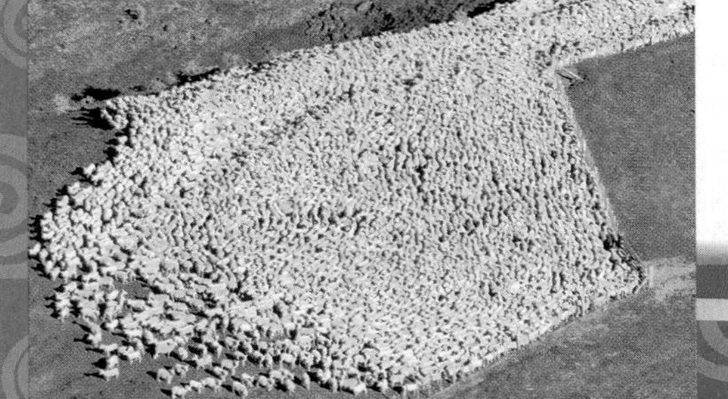

Practicing the Skill

On a separate sheet of paper, copy the following outline for Section 2 of this chapter. Then use your textbook to fill in the missing subtopics and details.

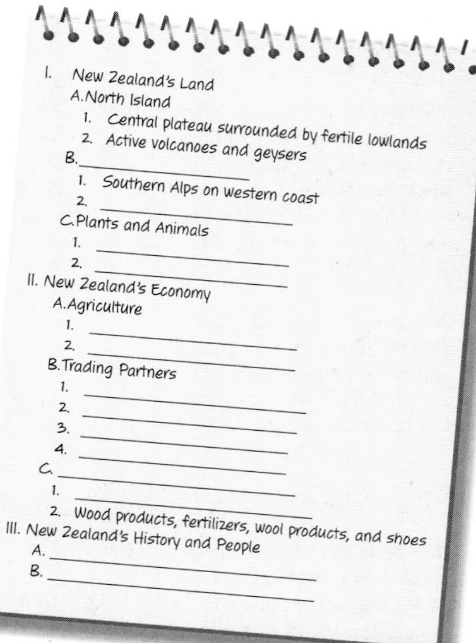
I. New Zealand's Land
  A. North Island
    1. Central plateau surrounded by fertile lowlands
    2. Active volcanoes and geysers
  B. ____
    1. Southern Alps on western coast
    2. ____
  C. Plants and Animals
    1. ____
    2. ____
II. New Zealand's Economy
  A. Agriculture
    1. ____
    2. ____
  B. Trading Partners
    1. ____
    2. ____
    3. ____
    4. ____
  C. ____
    1. ____
    2. Wood products, fertilizers, wool products, and shoes
III. New Zealand's History and People
  A. ____
  B. ____

Applying the Skill

Following the guidelines above, prepare an outline for Section 1 of this chapter.

GO TO Practice key skills with **Glencoe Skillbuilder Interactive Workbook, Level 1.**

Practicing the Skill Answers

I.B.—South Island
I.B.2.—Canterbury Plains in the east
I.C.1.—National symbol is kiwi
I.C.2.—Giant kauri trees
II.A.1.—Wool and lamb meat
II.A.2.—Apples, barley, wheat, and corn
II.B.1–4—Australia; Japan; United States; United Kingdom
II.C.—Mining and Manufacturing
II.C.1—Geothermal energy, hydroelectric power, coal, oil, iron ore, silver, gold
III.A.—Maori; came around 950 to 1150
III.B.—Europeans, mainly British, began arriving in the mid-1800s

Applying the Skill
Check outlines when completed.

Chapter 24 Reading Review

Section 1 Australia

Terms to Know
coral reef
outback
station
marsupial
immigrant
boomerang
bush

Main Idea

Both a continent and a country, Australia has many natural resources but few people.

✓Place The land of Australia is mostly flat and dry, with little rainfall.

✓History Because Australia has been separated from other continents for millions of years, unusual plants and animals developed here.

✓Economics Most of Australia's wealth comes from minerals and the products of its ranches. It is the world's leading producer and exporter of wool.

✓Culture Australia has relatively few people, most of whom live along the coasts.

Sydney Opera House in Sydney, Australia ▶

Section 2 New Zealand

Terms to Know
geyser
manuka
fjord
geothermal energy
hydroelectric power

Main Idea

New Zealand is a small country with a growing economy based on trade.

✓Place New Zealand has volcanic mountains, high glaciers, deep-cut fjords, fertile hills, and coastal plains. The climate is mild and wet.

✓Economics New Zealand's economy is built on trade. Sheepherding is an important activity, and wool and lamb meat are major exports.

✓History The people called the Maori first came to New Zealand about 1,000 years ago.

✓Culture Most people live on North Island, where the country's two main cities can be found.

✓History New Zealand was the first land to allow women to vote.

Reading Review

Use the Chapter 24 Reading Review to preview, review, condense, or reteach the chapter.

Preview/Review

Use the Terms to Know lists to help students review and study.

Activity Assign students a selection of terms from each section and have them write sentences using the assigned words. Have volunteers read their sentences aloud.

Vocabulary PuzzleMaker Software reinforces the vocabulary terms used in Chapter 24.

The Interactive Tutor Self-Assessment CD-ROM allows students to review Chapter 24 content.

Condense

Have students read the Chapter 24 summary statements.

Chapter 24 Guided Reading Activities

Chapter 24 Audio Program

Reteach

Reteaching Activity 24

Chapter 24 Reading Essentials and Study Guide

Did You Know?

Some cattle or sheep stations in Australia are so large that workers use airplanes or helicopters to watch the herds or flocks.

Chapter Culminating Activity

Creating Maps Have students create a salt-flour physical model of Australia and New Zealand. Their model should highlight the geographical features, with food coloring showing the different types of climates or vegetation and the landscape. Students should also show the resources and economic activities of the two countries. Finally, they should display historical and cultural sites in these countries.

EE2 Places and Regions: Standard 4

GLENCOE TECHNOLOGY

MindJogger Videoquiz
Use MindJogger to review the Chapter 24 content.

 Available in VHS.

Using Key Terms

1. b
2. e
3. h
4. a
5. g
6. j
7. c
8. i
9. b
10. d

Reviewing the Main Ideas

11. because it is in the Southern Hemisphere
12. mining camps and cattle and sheep ranches
13. wool
14. Great Britain
15. 85 percent
16. North Island
17. 1907
18. because it depends heavily on trade; if other countries' economies suffer, they will be less willing to buy goods from New Zealand
19. about 10 percent
20. camping, hiking, hunting, boating, and mountain climbing

Chapter 24 Assessment and Activities

Using Key Terms

Match the terms in Part A with their definitions in Part B.

A.

1. boomerang
2. bush
3. station
4. geothermal energy
5. outback
6. *manuka*
7. marsupial
8. hydroelectric power
9. coral reef
10. geyser

B.

a. electricity produced from steam
b. wooden weapon that returns to the thrower
c. mammal that carries its young in a pouch
d. hot spring that shoots hot water into the air
e. rural area in Australia
f. structure formed by the skeletons of small sea animals
g. name for entire inland region of Australia
h. cattle or sheep ranch in Australia
i. electricity generated by flowing water
j. small shrub found in New Zealand

Reviewing the Main Ideas

Section 1 Australia

11. **Location** Why is Australia called the Land Down Under?
12. **Place** For what is the outback used?
13. **Economics** What does Australia lead the world in producing and exporting?
14. **History** What country colonized Australia?
15. **Culture** What percentage of people live in Australia's cities?

Section 2 New Zealand

16. **Location** On which island do most New Zealanders live?
17. **History** When did New Zealand gain its independence from Britain?
18. **Economics** Why can New Zealand's economy suffer if other countries have economic problems?
19. **Culture** How many New Zealanders have Maori heritage?
20. **Human/Environment Interaction** What leisure activities do New Zealanders enjoy that are made possible by the country's climate?

NATIONAL GEOGRAPHIC Australia and New Zealand

Place Location Activity

On a separate sheet of paper, match the letters on the map with the numbered places listed below.

1. Auckland
2. Sydney
3. Tasmania
4. Great Barrier Reef
5. Great Dividing Range
6. Southern Alps
7. Darling River
8. Wellington
9. Canberra
10. Perth

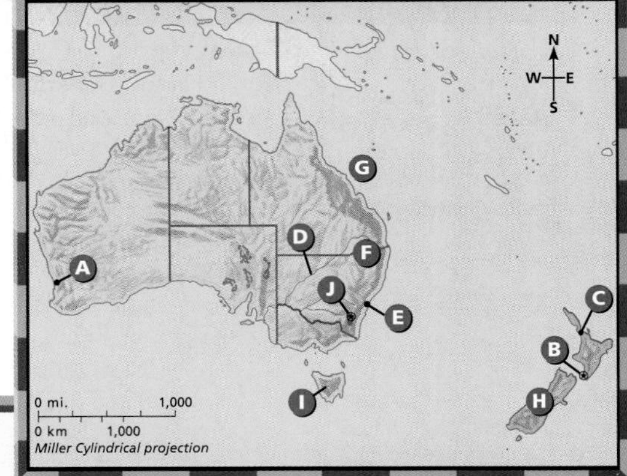

656

NATIONAL GEOGRAPHIC Place Location Activity

1. C
2. E
3. I
4. G
5. F
6. H
7. D
8. B
9. J
10. A

Critical Thinking

21. In Australia, the coastal areas are the most fertile. In New Zealand, the interiors are mountainous.
22. Diagrams will vary.

Current Events Journal

23. Suggest that students use the Internet or magazines to locate the photographs that they need.

Self-Check Quiz Visit the ***Our World Today: People, Places, and Issues*** Web site at owt.glencoe.com and click on **Chapter 24–Self-Check Quizzes** to prepare for the Chapter Test.

Critical Thinking

21. **Understanding Cause and Effect** Why do most Australians and New Zealanders live in coastal areas?
22. **Organizing Information** Create two ovals like these. In the outer ovals, write four facts about each country under its heading. Where the ovals overlap, write three facts that are true of both countries.

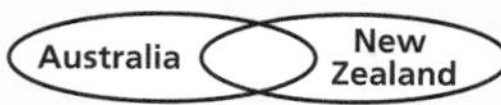

Current Events Journal

23. **Designing a Poster** Choose one of the unusual physical features found in Australia or New Zealand. You might choose the Great Barrier Reef, the Great Artesian Basin, or the geysers or glaciers of New Zealand. Research to learn more about this physical feature and how the people of the country relate to it today. Create an illustrated poster that includes a map, four photographs, and four facts about the feature.

Mental Mapping Activity

24. **Focusing on the Region** Create a simple outline map of Australia and New Zealand; then label the following:

- North Island
- South Island
- Sydney
- Auckland
- Tasmania
- Tasman Sea
- Coral Sea
- Darling River
- Great Artesian Basin
- Hamersley Range

Technology Skills Activity

25. **Using the Internet** Use the Internet to find out more about one of Australia's or New Zealand's cities. Prepare a travel brochure aimed at a tourist who might visit the city. Describe the city's main attractions.

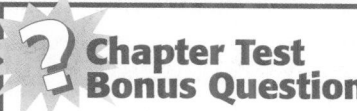

The Princeton Review

Standardized Test Practice

Directions: Study the graph below, and then answer the following question.

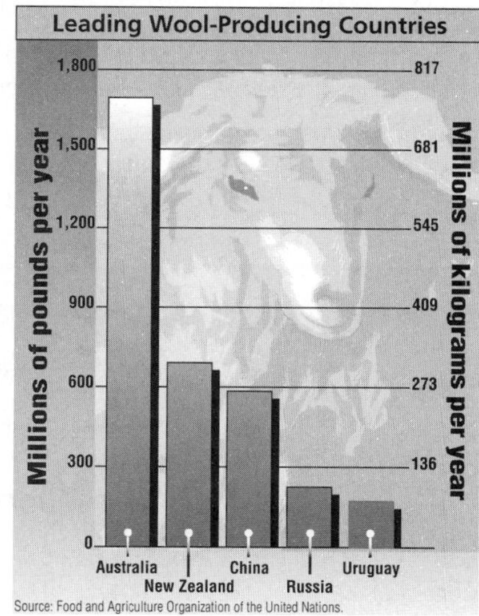

1. **How much wool does Australia produce per year?**
   - **A** 1,800 pounds
   - **B** 1,800,000 pounds
   - **C** about 1,700 pounds
   - **D** about 1,700,000,000 pounds

Test-Taking Tip: Remember to read the information along the sides of the graph to understand what the bars represent. In addition, eliminate answers that you know are wrong.

Assessment and Activities

Standardized Test Practice

1. D

Tested Objectives:
Reading a graph, analyzing information

Chapter Test Bonus Question

This question may be used for extra credit on the chapter test.

What area on New Zealand's South Island is good for farming? *(Canterbury Plains)*

Our World Today online

Have students visit the Web site at owt.glencoe.com to review Chapter 24 and take the Self-Check Quiz.

Mental Mapping Activity

24. This exercise helps students visualize the countries and geographic features they have been studying and understand the relationship among various points. Accept all attempts at freehand mapping that show places in the correct relationship to one another.

Technology Skills Activity

25. Students' brochures could be enhanced with photographs from the chosen country.

Chapter 25 Resources

Note: The following materials may be used when teaching Chapter 25.
Section level support materials are shown at point of use in the margins of the Teacher Wraparound Edition.

Timesaving Tools

TeacherWorks™ All-In-One Planner and Resource Center

- **Interactive Teacher Edition** See the **Interactive Teacher Edition** CD-ROM to electronically integrate your Teacher Wraparound Edition and blackline masters.
- **Interactive Lesson Planner** Organize your week, month, semester, or year with all the lesson helps you need. The **Interactive Lesson Planner** CD-ROM contains all Chapter 25 resources.

Use Glencoe's **Presentation Plus!** multimedia teacher tool to easily present dynamic lessons that visually excite your students. Using Microsoft PowerPoint® you can customize the presentations to create your own personalized lessons.

TEACHING TRANSPARENCIES

Graphic Organizer Transparency and Student Activity 25

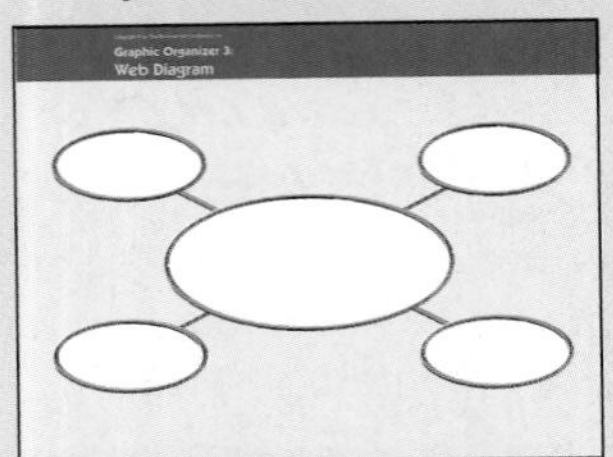
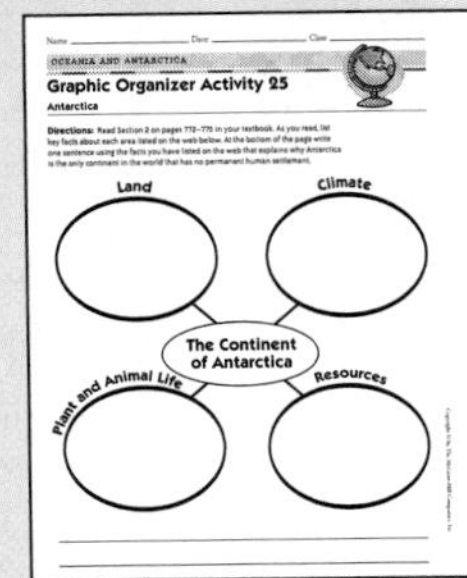

FOLDABLES™ Study Organizer

Foldables are three-dimensional, interactive graphic organizers that help students practice basic writing skills, review key vocabulary terms, and identify main ideas. Every chapter contains a Foldable activity, with additional chapter activities found in the ***Reading and Study Skills Foldables*** booklet.

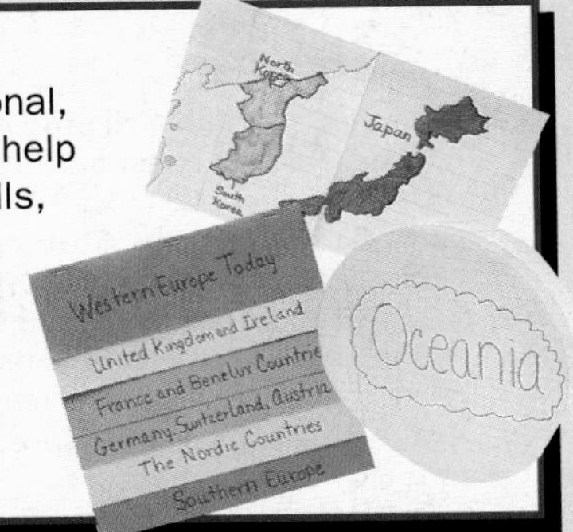

ENRICHMENT AND EXTENSION

Enrichment Activity 25

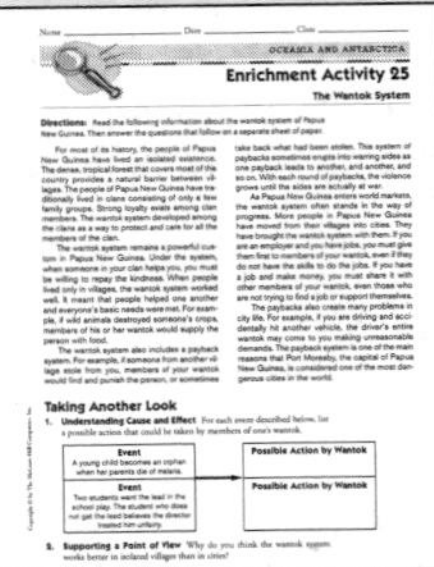

Cooperative Learning Activity 25

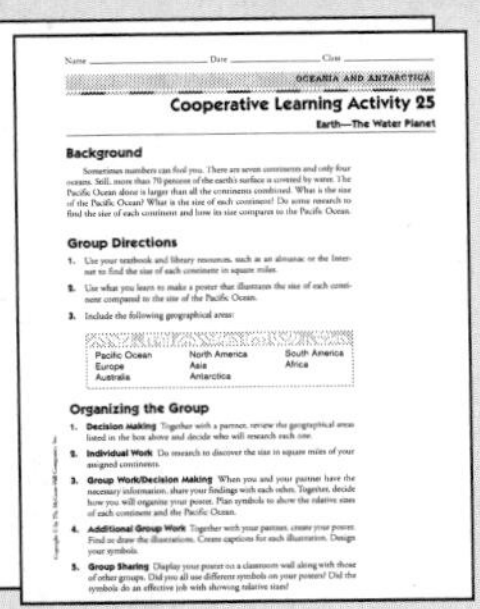

MAP AND GEOGRAPHY SKILLS

Chapter Map Activity 25

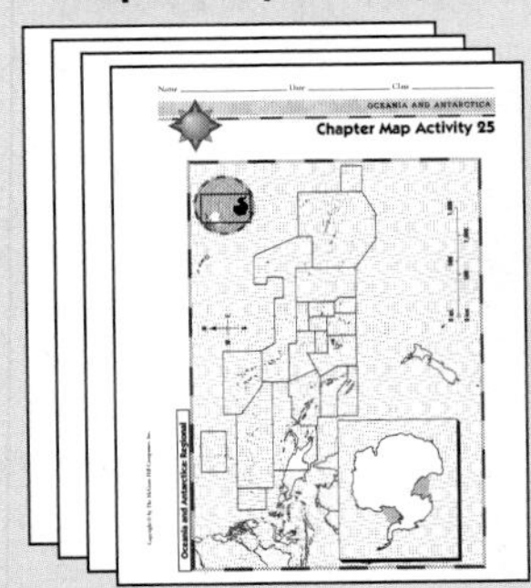

GeoLab Activity 25

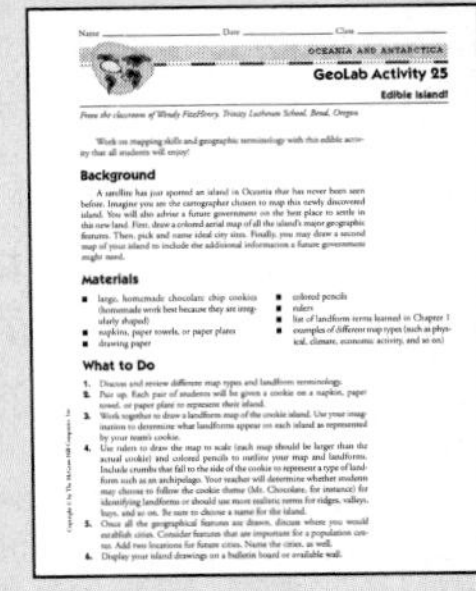

STANDARDIZED ASSESSMENT SKILLS

GLENCOE'S ASSESSMENT ADVANTAGE

Critical Thinking Skills Activity 25

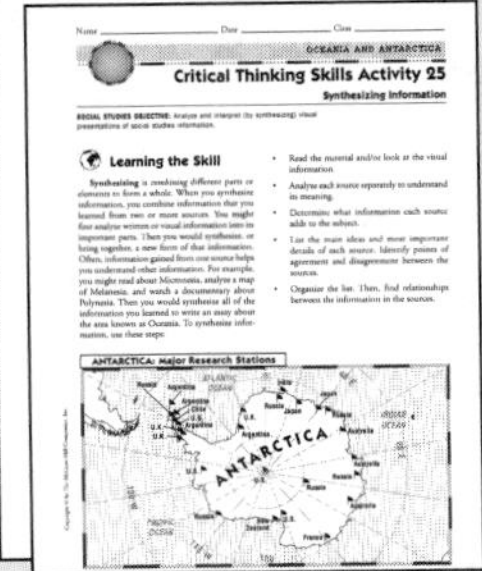

Map and Graph Skills Activity 25

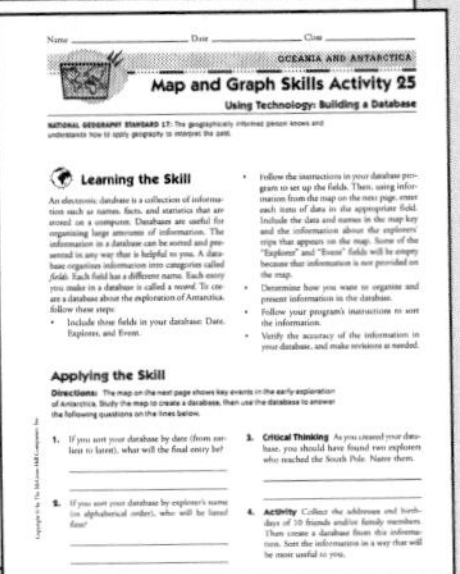

Reading and Writing Skills Activity 25

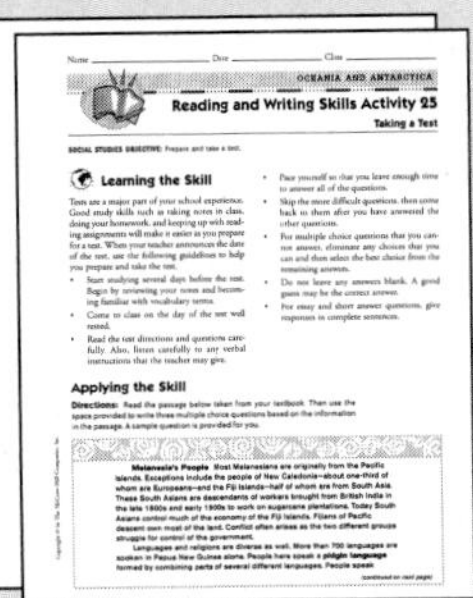

Standardized Test Practice Workbook Activity 25

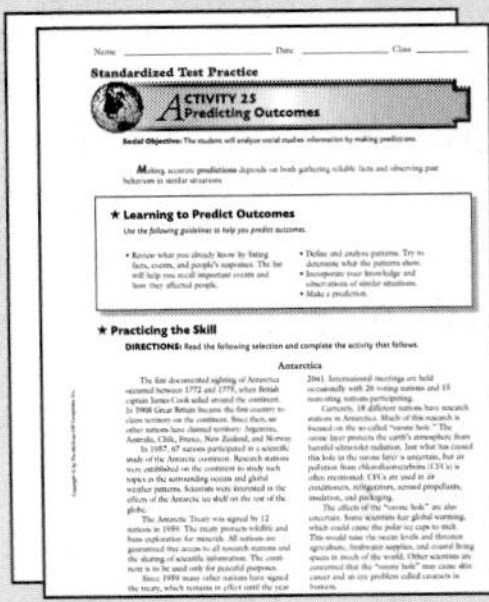

REVIEW AND REINFORCEMENT

Chapter Skills Activity 25

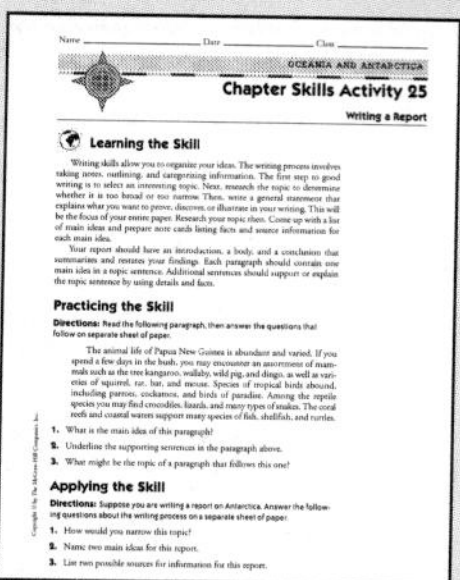

Take-Home Review Activity 25

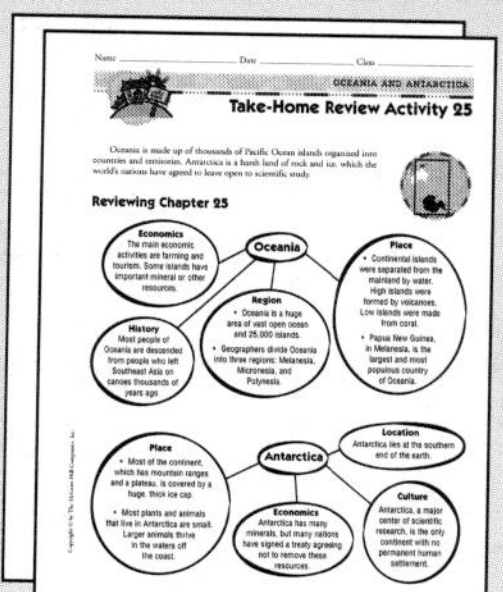

Reteaching Activity 25

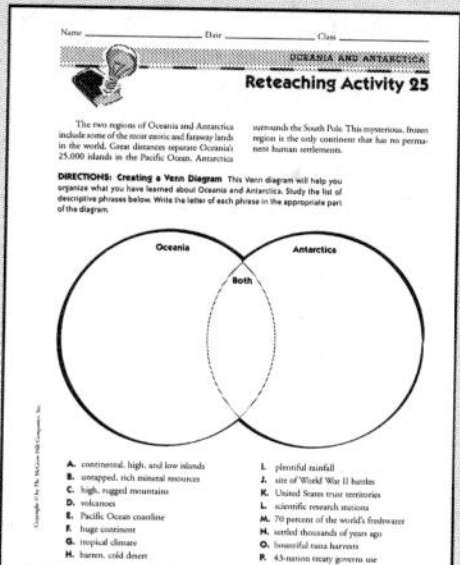

Vocabulary Activity 25

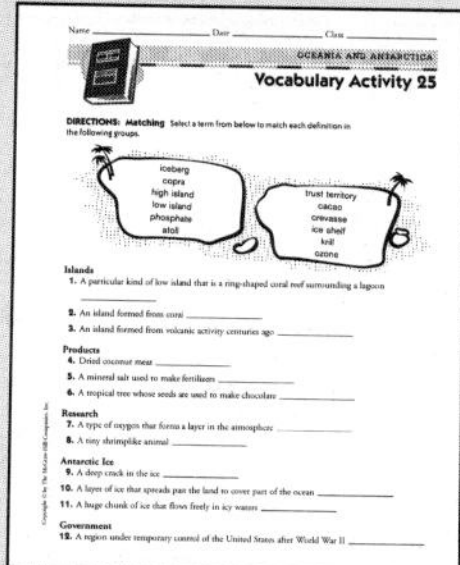

Workbook Activity 25

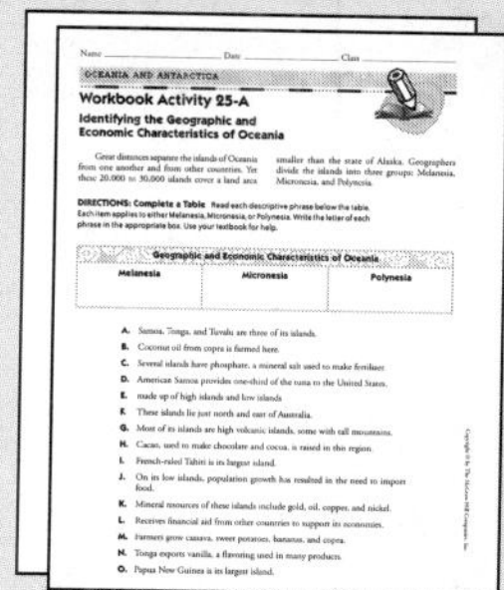

ASSESSMENT

GLENCOE'S ASSESSMENT ADVANTAGE

Chapter 25 Test, Form A

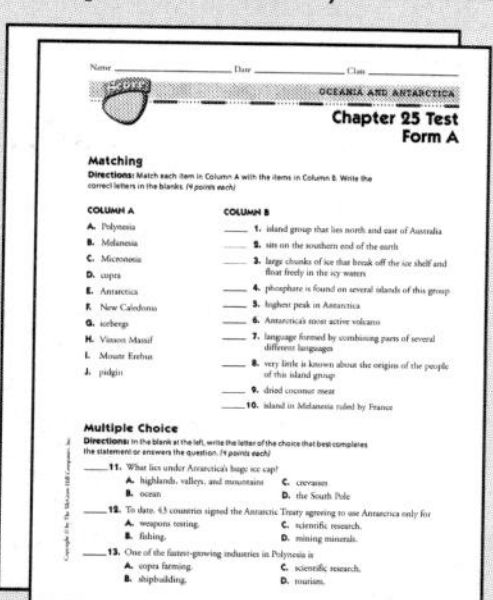

Chapter 25 Test, Form B

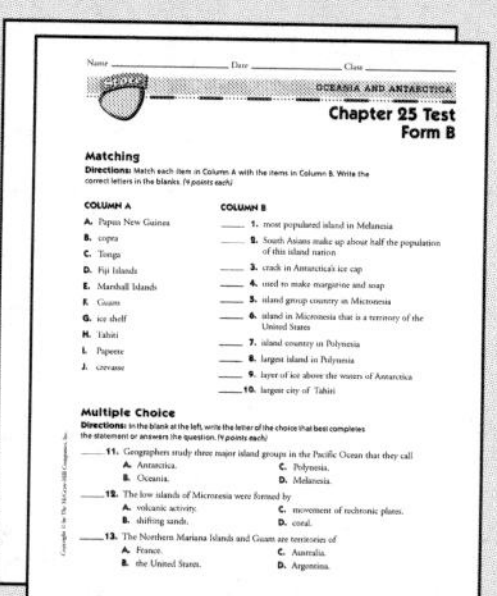

Performance Assessment Activity 25

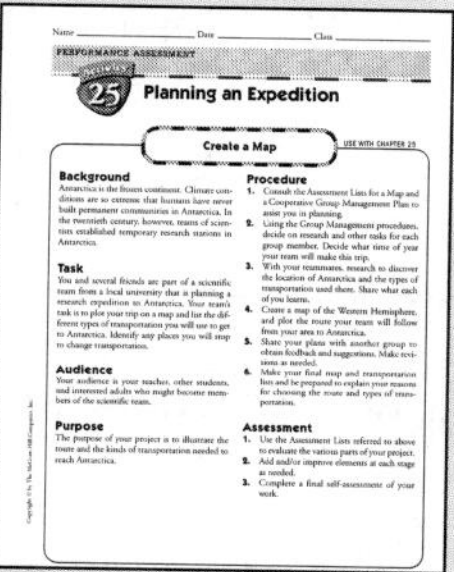

ExamView® Pro 3.0 Testmaker CD-ROM

MULTIMEDIA

- National Geographic's The World and Its People
- MindJogger Videoquiz
- Vocabulary PuzzleMaker Software
- Interactive Tutor Self-Assessment CD-ROM
- ExamView® Pro 3.0 Testmaker CD-ROM
- Interactive Lesson Planner CD-ROM
- Interactive Teacher Edition CD-ROM
- Skillbuilder Interactive Workbook CD-ROM, Level 1
- Presentation Plus! CD-ROM
- Audio Program

SPANISH RESOURCES

The following Spanish language materials are available in the Spanish Resources binder:

- Spanish Chapter Summaries
- Spanish Vocabulary Activities
- Spanish Guided Reading Activities
- Spanish Quizzes and Tests
- Spanish Take-Home Review Activities
- Spanish Reteaching Activities

Meeting National Standards

Geography for Life

All of the 18 standards are demonstrated in Unit 9. The following ones are highlighted in Chapter 25:

Section 1
- **EE1 The World in Spatial Terms: Standards 1, 3**
- **EE4 Human Systems: Standards 9, 10**
- **EE5 Environment and Society: Standard 14**

Section 2
- **EE3 Physical Systems: Standards 7, 8**
- **EE4 Human Systems: Standards 9, 10, 12, 13**
- **EE5 Environment and Society: Standard 15**
- **EE6 The Uses of Geography: Standard 17**

For a complete listing of National Geography Standards and entire text correlation, see pages T22–T29.

Chapter 25 Planning Guide

SECTION RESOURCES

Daily Objectives	Reproducible Resources	Multimedia Resources
Section 1 **Oceania** Suggested Pacing = 1 day **1.** Explain how the three regions of Oceania differ. **2.** Describe how the people of Oceania earn a living.	Reproducible Lesson Plan 25-1 Daily Lecture and Discussion Notes 25-1 Guided Reading Activity 25-1 Reading Essentials and Study Guide 25-1 Section Quiz 25-1*	Daily Focus Skills Transparency 25-1 GeoQuiz Transparency 25-1 Vocabulary PuzzleMaker Software Interactive Tutor Self-Assessment CD-ROM ExamView® Pro 3.0 Testmaker CD-ROM Presentation Plus! CD-ROM
Section 2 **Antarctica** Suggested Pacing = 1 day **1.** Describe what kinds of life are found in Antarctica. **2.** Explain why scientists study Antarctica.	Reproducible Lesson Plan 25-2 Daily Lecture and Discussion Notes 25-2 Guided Reading Activity 25-2 Reading Essentials and Study Guide 25-2 Section Quiz 25-2*	Daily Focus Skills Transparency 25-2 GeoQuiz Transparency 25-1 Vocabulary PuzzleMaker Software Interactive Tutor Self-Assessment CD-ROM ExamView® Pro 3.0 Testmaker CD-ROM Presentation Plus! CD-ROM

00:00 **Out of Time?** Assign the **Reading Essentials and Study Guide** for this chapter.

*Also available in Spanish

KEY TO ABILITY LEVELS

Teaching strategies have been coded for varying learning styles and abilities.

- **L1** **BASIC** activities for all students
- **L2** **AVERAGE** activities for average to above-average students
- **L3** **CHALLENGING** activities for above-average students
- **ELL** **ENGLISH LANGUAGE LEARNER** activities

Blackline Master
Software
CD-ROM
Audiocassette

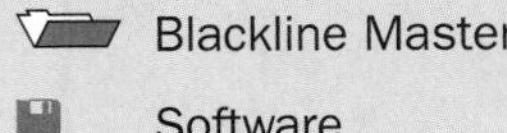

Transparency
Videocassette
Block Scheduling
DVD

Coloring Book

Have students make a coloring book about an island in Oceania. Have them research the island on the Internet or in encyclopedias to find such information as the island's landscape, climate, foods, clothing, economic activities, religions, festivals, types of money, and types of homes. Also have them research what teenagers on the island do for fun and learn in school. Then have students sketch simple drawings for each piece of information, with one sketch per page. At the bottom of the page, students should write a caption summarizing the sketch. Remind students to create a title page for the coloring book before binding the pages together. Donate the coloring books to an elementary school.

Joseph Turso
Wayne Hills High School
Wayne, New Jersey

OUR WORLD TODAY Online

Use our Web site for additional resources. All essential content is covered in the Student Edition.

You and your students can visit owt.glencoe.com, the Web site companion to *Our World Today*. This innovative integration of electronic and print media offers your students a wealth of opportunities. The student text directs students to the Web site for the following options:

- Chapter Overviews
- Student Web Activities
- Self-Check Quizzes
- Textbook Updates

Answers are provided for you in the Web Activity Lesson Plan. Additional Web resources and Interactive Tutor puzzles are also available.

NATIONAL GEOGRAPHIC TEACHER'S CORNER

Index to National Geographic Magazine:

The following articles may be used for research relating to this chapter:

- "Inside the Volcano," by Donovan Webster, November 2000.
- "Deep Sea Vents," by Richard A. Lutz, October 2000.
- "New Caledonia," by Thomas O-Neill, May 2000.
- "Under Antarctic Ice," by Norbert Wu, February 1999.
- "On the Edge of Antarctica: Queen Maud Land," by Jon Krakauer, February 1998.

National Geographic Society Products Available From Glencoe:

To order the following products for use with this chapter, contact your local Glencoe sales representative or call Glencoe at 1-800-334-7344:

- *STV: World Geography* (Videodisc)
- *PictureShow: Earth's Endangered Environments* (CD-ROM)
- *Physical Geography of the World* (Transparencies)
- *PicturePack: Oceania and Australia* (Transparencies)
- *ZipZapMap! World* (Software)
- *MapPack: Oceania and Antarctica* (Transparencies)

Additional National Geographic Society Products:

To order the following products for use with this chapter, call National Geographic Society at 1-800-368-2728:

- *Complete National Geographic: 111 Years of National Geographic Magazine* (CD-ROM)
- *Voices: Poetry and Art From Around the World* (Book)
- *National Geographic Desk Reference* (Book)
- *National Geographic Atlas of the World, Seventh Edition* (Book)
- *Antarctica* (Video)
- *Pollution: World at Risk* (Video)
- *Healing the Earth* (Video)
- *Technology's Price* (Map)

NGS ONLINE

Access National Geographic's Web site for current events, activities, links, interactive features, and archives.
www.nationalgeographic.com

Introducing Chapter 25

Introduce students to chapter content and key terms by having them access Chapter Overview 25 at owt.glencoe.com

Chapter Objectives

1. Identify the regions of Oceania.
2. Describe the economies and peoples of Oceania.
3. Discuss the scientific importance of Antarctica.

GLENCOE TECHNOLOGY

NATIONAL GEOGRAPHIC

The World and Its People Video Program

Chapter 28 Oceania and Antarctica

The following segments enhance the study of this chapter:

- **Antarctic Vacation**
- **Ice**
- **The Razor**

Available in DVD and VHS.

MindJogger Videoquiz

Use MindJogger to preview the Chapter 25 content.

Available in VHS.

Chapter 25 Oceania and Antarctica

The World and Its People — NATIONAL GEOGRAPHIC

To learn more about the people and places of Oceania and Antarctica, view ***The World and Its People* Chapter 28** video.

Our World Today Online

Chapter Overview Visit the ***Our World Today: People, Places, and Issues*** Web site at owt.glencoe.com and click on **Chapter 25—Chapter Overviews** to preview information about Oceania and Antarctica.

658

Two-Minute Lesson Launcher

Ask students what they think of when they hear the words *Polynesia* or *South Sea island*. They are likely to respond with such words as *warm, tropical, paradise, beautiful, beaches.* Then ask what they think of when they hear the name *Antarctica*. Answers are likely to be words like *cold, freezing, ice, snow, penguins.* Explain that in this section, they will learn how both of these places are similar in that they both have fragile environments that need to be protected.

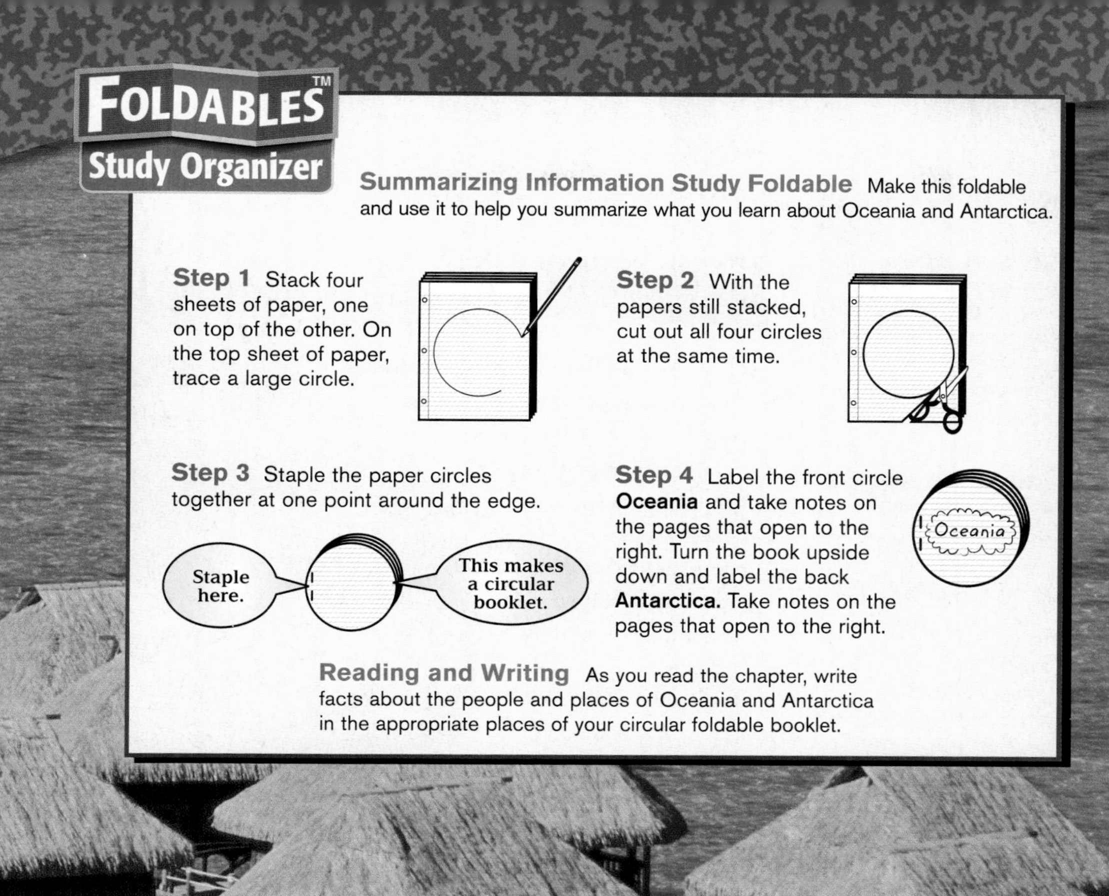

FOLDABLES™ Study Organizer

Summarizing Information Study Foldable Make this foldable and use it to help you summarize what you learn about Oceania and Antarctica.

Step 1 Stack four sheets of paper, one on top of the other. On the top sheet of paper, trace a large circle.

Step 2 With the papers still stacked, cut out all four circles at the same time.

Step 3 Staple the paper circles together at one point around the edge.

Staple here.
This makes a circular booklet.

Step 4 Label the front circle **Oceania** and take notes on the pages that open to the right. Turn the book upside down and label the back **Antarctica.** Take notes on the pages that open to the right.

Reading and Writing As you read the chapter, write facts about the people and places of Oceania and Antarctica in the appropriate places of your circular foldable booklet.

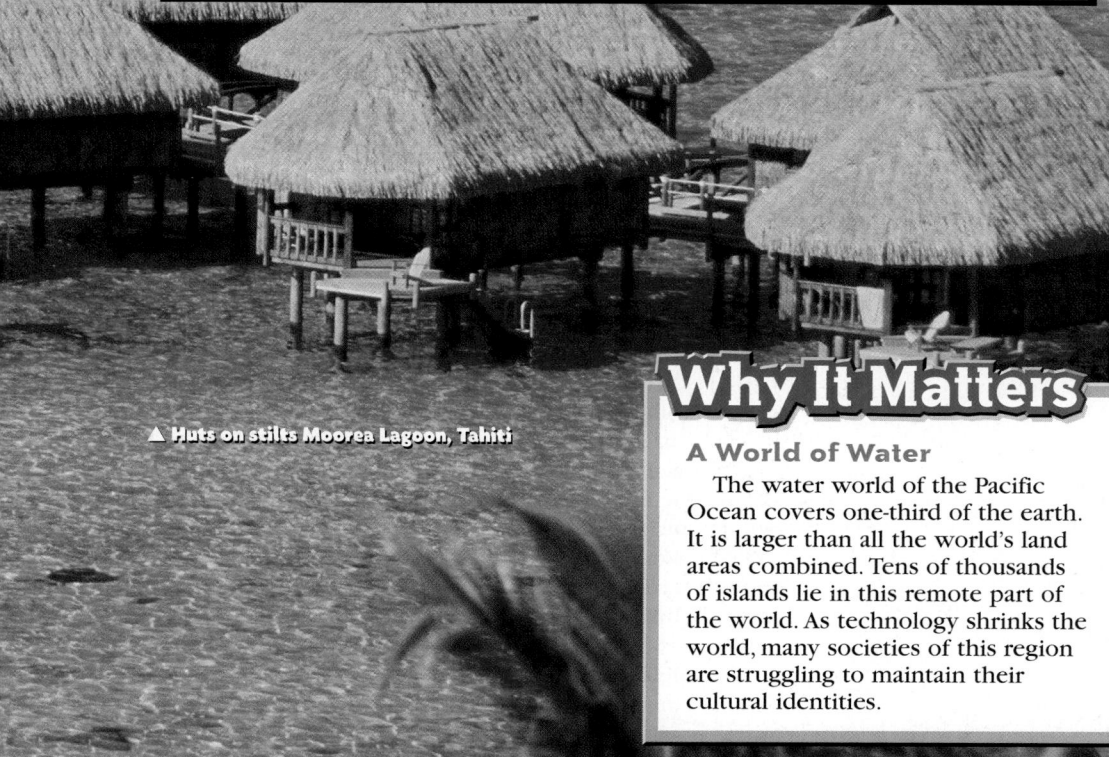

▲ Huts on stilts Moorea Lagoon, Tahiti

Why It Matters

A World of Water

The water world of the Pacific Ocean covers one-third of the earth. It is larger than all the world's land areas combined. Tens of thousands of islands lie in this remote part of the world. As technology shrinks the world, many societies of this region are struggling to maintain their cultural identities.

FOLDABLES™ Study Organizer

Purpose This activity requires students to create a booklet to organize information from the chapter. Students group information from the chapter into categories, in effect comparing the people and places of Oceania and Antarctica.

Have students complete ***Reading and Study Skills Foldables*** Activity 25.

Why It Matters

Global warming has a potentially devastating effect on Pacific Island nations. Some islands may disappear entirely. Have students write and perform a skit about an island village that is threatened by rising sea levels. Assign different roles to be portrayed—some that want to stay and preserve the village, some that are forced to move, and some that want the government to solve the problem for them.

About the Photos

Ask students to study the photograph and use it to discuss how humans interact with and are affected by their environment. Why do the Tahitians build houses on stilts? Explain that the houses are built high off the ground because of the ocean tides. Some people from Oceania have become very adept at using stilts themselves.

To avoid climbing ladders endlessly when visiting other houses, some islanders move among the houses on stilts of their own. In Tahiti, villages used to hold stilt races on festival days. Boys and girls of all ages would run like storks along the beaches.

Focus

Section Objectives

1. Explain how the three regions of Oceania differ.
2. Describe how the people of Oceania earn a living.

BELLRINGER Skillbuilder Activity

Project transparency and have students answer questions.

This activity is also available as a blackline master.

Daily Focus Skills Transparency 25-1

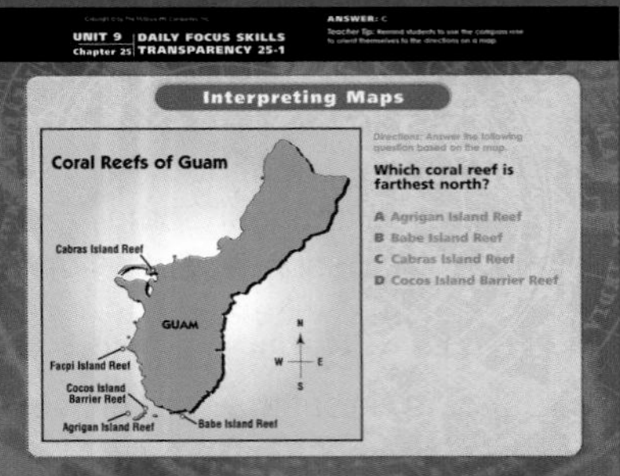

Guide to Reading

Accessing Prior Knowledge Ask students how many islands there are in Oceania. Then have them read the first paragraph of the section to see the answer.

Vocabulary Precheck Ask students what they think *pidgin language* means. Then have them look up the word in the section to verify their guesses.

Section 1 Oceania

Guide to Reading

Main Idea

Oceania is made up of thousands of Pacific Ocean islands organized into countries and territories.

Terms to Know

- cacao
- copra
- pidgin language
- high island
- low island
- atoll
- phosphate
- trust territory

Reading Strategy

Create a chart like this one. In the right column, write two facts about each region.

Region	Facts
Melanesia	
Micronesia	
Polynesia	

Plants and animals in coral reefs sometimes cooperate with one another. Here a sea anemone (uh•NEH•muh•nee) and an anemonefish live together peacefully. The anemonefish helps the anemone by eating debris on its tentacles and by driving predators away. In turn, the anemone offers the fish protection. Most anemonefish spend their lives inside an anemone.

Oceania is a culture region that includes about 25,000 islands in the Pacific Ocean. Geographers group Oceania into three main island regions—**Melanesia, Micronesia,** and **Polynesia.**

Melanesia

The islands of Melanesia lie just to the north and east of Australia. The largest country in size is **Papua New Guinea** (PA•pyu•wuh noo GIH•nee). Slightly larger than California, the country's 5 million people also make it Oceania's most populous island. Southeast of Papua New Guinea are three other independent island countries: the **Solomon Islands,** the **Fiji** (FEE•jee) **Islands,** and **Vanuatu** (VAN•WAH•TOO). Near these countries is **New Caledonia,** a group of islands ruled by France.

Rugged mountains and dense rain forests cover Melanesia's islands. Strips of fertile plains hug island coastlines. Most of Melanesia has a tropical climate with nearly constant temperatures between 70°F (21°C) and 80°F (27°C).

Most Melanesians work on subsistence farms. Coffee, palm oil, and cacao are important exports. **Cacao** is a tropical tree whose seeds are

Section Resources

Reproducible Masters
- Reproducible Lesson Plan 25-1
- Daily Lecture and Discussion Notes 25-1
- Guided Reading Activity 25-1
- Reading Essentials and Study Guide 25-1
- Section Quiz 25-1

Transparencies
- Daily Focus Skills Transparency 25-1
- GeoQuiz Transparency 25-1

Multimedia
- Vocabulary PuzzleMaker Software
- Interactive Tutor Self-Assessment CD-ROM
- Presentation Plus! CD-ROM
- ExamView® Pro 3.0 Testmaker CD-ROM

used to make chocolate. Sugarcane is exported as sugar and molasses. Coconut oil from **copra,** dried coconut meat, is used to make margarine, soap, and other products.

Some Melanesian islands hold rich mineral resources such as gold, oil, copper, and nickel. Several Melanesian islands export timber and fish. Melanesia is also becoming a popular tourist destination.

Melanesia's People Most Melanesians are originally from the Pacific islands. Exceptions include the people of New Caledonia—about one-third of whom are Europeans—and the Fiji Islands—half of whom are from South Asia. These South Asians are descendants of workers brought from British India in the late 1800s and early 1900s to work on sugarcane plantations. Today South Asians control much of the economy of the Fiji Islands. Fijians of Pacific descent own most of the land. Conflict often arises as the two different groups struggle for control of the government.

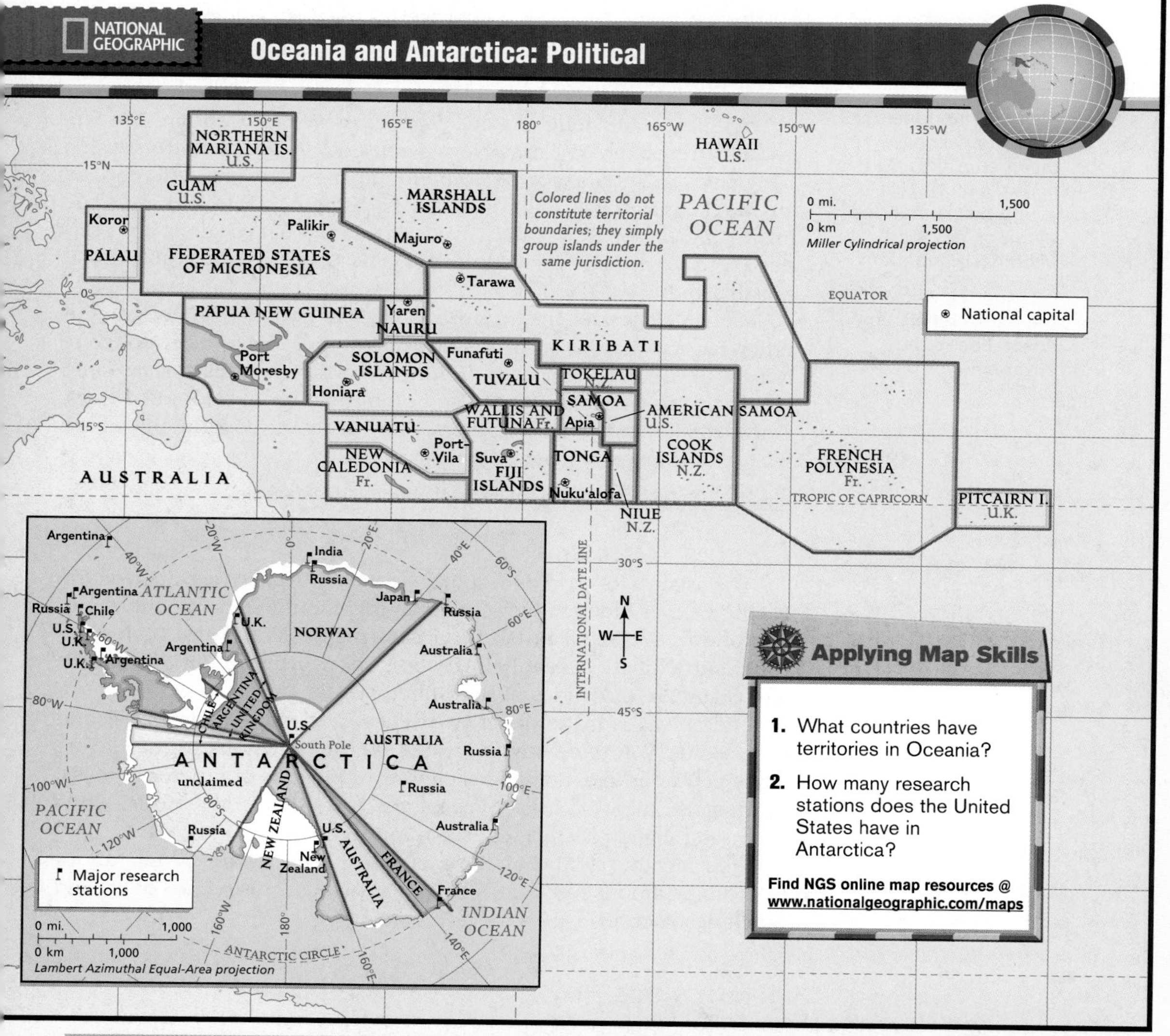

NATIONAL GEOGRAPHIC

Oceania and Antarctica: Political

Colored lines do not constitute territorial boundaries; they simply group islands under the same jurisdiction.

Miller Cylindrical projection

Lambert Azimuthal Equal-Area projection

Applying Map Skills

1. What countries have territories in Oceania?
2. How many research stations does the United States have in Antarctica?

Find NGS online map resources @ www.nationalgeographic.com/maps

Chapter 25

Section 1, pages 660–664

Making Comparisons

Have students use the Nations of the World Databank on pages 690–699 to identify the countries that rank in the bottom 10 (180th to 190th) for Gross National Product (GNP). **Ask:** **What world region dominates this list?** *(Oceania)* Have students pose and answer five questions comparing other data about the countries on their list. **L1**

Daily Lecture Notes 25-1

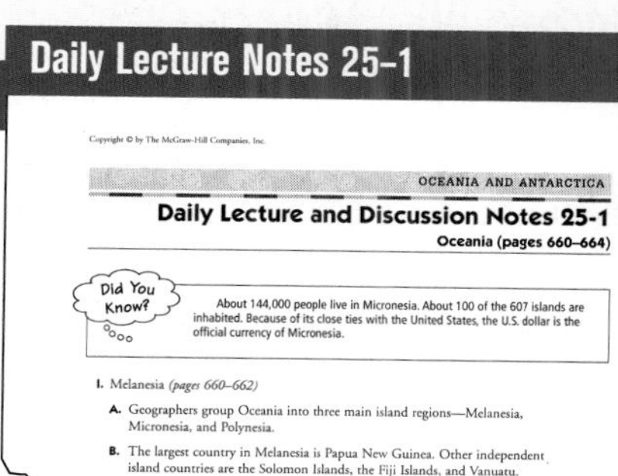

OCEANIA AND ANTARCTICA

Daily Lecture and Discussion Notes 25-1

Oceania (pages 660–664)

Did You Know? About 144,000 people live in Micronesia. About 100 of the 607 islands are inhabited. Because of its close ties with the United States, the U.S. dollar is the official currency of Micronesia.

I. Melanesia *(pages 660–662)*

A. Geographers group Oceania into three main island regions—Melanesia, Micronesia, and Polynesia.

B. The largest country in Melanesia is Papua New Guinea. Other independent island countries are the Solomon Islands, the Fiji Islands, and Vanuatu.

Applying Map Skills

Answers

1. France, United Kingdom, United States, and New Zealand
2. three

Skills Practice

What is the capital of the Fiji Islands? *(Suva)*

Team-Teaching Activity

Science Invite the science teacher to class to describe the particular dangers that global warming poses for the islands of the South Pacific. Many of these islands are low-lying atolls that emerge only a few feet above the sea. If sea levels rise, as scientists studying global warming suggest will occur, these islands are likely to suffer. French Polynesia, the Cook Islands, Samoa and American Samoa, Niue, Tonga, Nuvalu, Nauru, Kiribati, the Marshall Islands, and Palau are all thought to be at risk of being flooded by the end of the century. Have the science teacher discuss with the class the steps being considered to reduce global warming. **L1**

EE5 Environment and Society: Standard 14

Chapter 25

Section 1, pages 660–664

TRAVEL GUIDE 

Across the Pacific islands, coconut is a staple. The Kiribati people, for example, eat coconut with fish, grate it into tea, and use its milk to sweeten breadfruit soup. For many islanders, coconut sap provides a rich source of vitamin C. Twice a day, young boys on Kiribati cut *toddy,* meaning they gather coconut sap and boil it to make a thick, sweet molasses used to sweeten drinks or to make candy.

Reading Check Answer

Papua New Guinea

Guided Reading Activity 25-1

More About the Photos

Homes of Micronesia Some houses are built on stilts over water. When on land, the houses are much larger.

Caption Answer The houses in this photo reflect the use of natural materials. The shape allows for the escape of heat. Rain flows down the roof without causing damage.

NATIONAL GEOGRAPHIC **On Location**

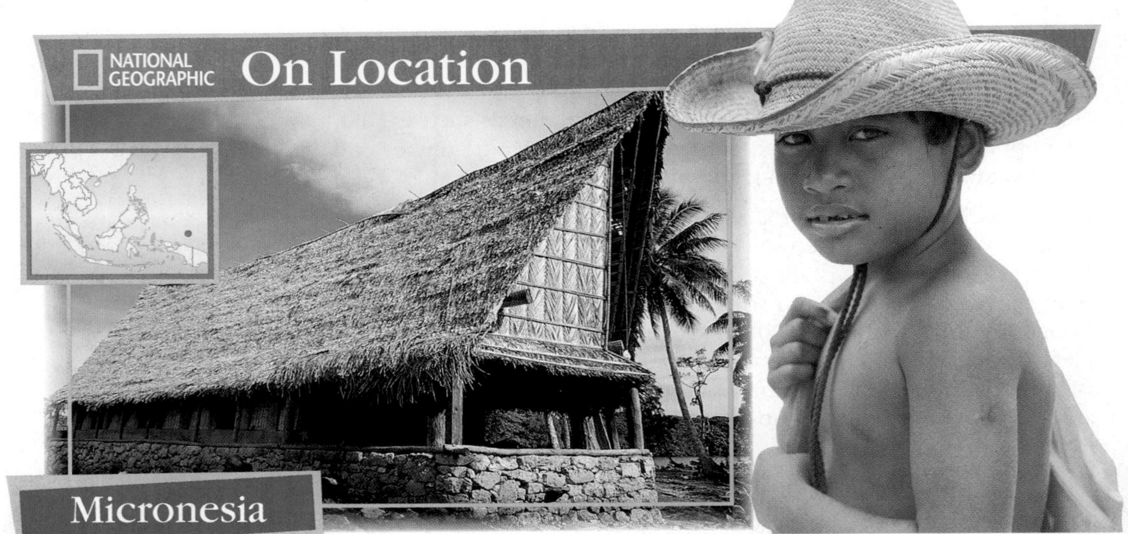

Micronesia

Many of the homes in Micronesia have thatched roofs and no walls (left). This young boy is from the island of Yap in Micronesia (right).

Culture **How does the house reflect an adaptation to the environment?**

Languages and religions are diverse as well. More than 700 languages are spoken in Papua New Guinea alone. People here speak a **pidgin language** formed by combining parts of several different languages. People speak English in the Fiji Islands, while French is the main language of New Caledonia. Local traditional religions are practiced, but Christianity is widespread. The South Asian population is mostly Hindu.

Many Melanesians live in small villages in houses made of grass or other natural materials. In recent years, people have built concrete houses to protect themselves from tropical storms. Melanesians keep strong ties to their local group and often hold on to traditional ways. Only a small number live in cities. Many of those living in cities have jobs in business and government.

Reading Check **What is the largest country in Melanesia?**

Micronesia

The islands of Micronesia are scattered over a vast area of the Pacific Ocean. Independent countries include the Federated States of Micronesia, the Marshall Islands, Palau (puh•LOW), Nauru (nah•OO•roo), and Kiribati (KIHR•uh•BAH•tee). The Northern Mariana Islands and Guam are territories of the United States.

Micronesia is made up of two types of islands—high islands and low islands. Volcanic activity formed the mountainous **high islands** many centuries ago. Coral, or skeletons of millions of tiny sea animals, formed the **low islands.** Most of the low islands are **atolls**—low-lying, ring-shaped islands that surround lagoons.

Like Melanesia, Micronesia has a tropical climate. From July to October, typhoons sometimes strike the islands, causing loss of life and much destruction.

Critical Thinking Activity

Determining Cause and Effect Remind students that Melanesians have many different cultures and languages, including hundreds on Papua New Guinea alone. Point out that isolation of groups of people often results in this kind of diversity. Have students look at a physical map of the region. **Ask:** **What geographical factor could cause this isolation on the small islands of Melanesia?** *(The islands are distant from one another.)* **What could cause this isolation on Papua New Guinea?** *(mountains).* **L1**

EE4 Human Systems: Standard 9

On Micronesia's high islands, soil is rich. Most people here engage in subsistence farming—growing cassava, sweet potatoes, bananas, and copra. Some high island farmers also raise livestock. People in the low islands obtain food from the sea. On some low islands, recent population growth has resulted in the need to import food.

Micronesia receives financial aid from the United States, the European Union, and Australia. With this money, the Micronesians have built roads, ports, airfields, and small factories. Clothing is made on the Northern Mariana Islands. Beautiful beaches draw many tourists here.

Several Micronesian islands have **phosphate,** a mineral salt used to make fertilizer. Phosphate supplies are now gone on Kiribati, and they have almost run out on Nauru. The Federated States of Micronesia and the Marshall Islands have phosphate but lack the money to mine this resource.

Micronesia's People Southeast Asians first settled Micronesia about 4,000 years ago. Explorers, traders, and missionaries from European countries came in the 1700s and early 1800s. By the early 1900s, many European countries, the United States, and Japan held colonies here.

During World War II, the United States and Japan fought a number of bloody battles on Micronesian islands. After World War II, most of Micronesia was turned over to the United States as **trust territories.** These territories were under temporary United States control. Some of these islands served as sites for hydrogen bomb testing. Since the 1970s, most have become independent.

Many of Micronesia's people are Pacific islanders. They speak local languages, although English is spoken on Nauru, the Marshall Islands, and throughout the rest of Micronesia. Christianity, brought by Western missionaries, is the most widely practiced religion. Micronesians generally live in villages headed by local chiefs. In recent years, many young people have left the villages to find jobs in towns.

✓Reading Check **In what two ways were Micronesia's islands formed?**

Polynesia

Very little is known about the origins of the Polynesians. Historians believe that their ancestors sailed from Asia hundreds of years before the birth of Christ. We know that the first people to settle the islands must have been extremely gifted navigators. Today, the influence of the early Polynesians in language, music, and dance can be seen throughout the South Seas.

When the Polynesian people traveled from island to island, they carried all the supplies they would need with them, including pigs, hens, and dogs. Young banana and breadfruit plants were put in the ground as soon as the Polynesians landed.

Today, Polynesia includes three independent countries—Samoa, Tonga, and Tuvalu. Other island groups are under French rule and are known as French Polynesia. Tahiti, Polynesia's largest island, is part of this French-ruled area. American Samoa, a United States territory, is

The Fate of Nauru

Micronesia's most famous phosphate island is Nauru, an 8-square-mile coral atoll. The name *Nauru* means "nowhere." Over the last 90 years, Nauru's citizens have chosen to "consume" their island by mining the coral as phosphate and selling it as fertilizer. The government of Nauru is now working to develop other industries such as fishing and tourism in preparation for the day when the phosphate is gone.

Chapter 25

Section 1, pages 660–664

Interdisciplinary Connections

Economics The small islands of Oceania have few resources, but some have made great use of those resources. Nauru has done so well selling phosphate that it has not taxed its citizens. Aware that the phosphate supply is running out, the island invested money in other businesses. Tuvalu makes beautiful stamps, raising revenue by selling them to stamp collectors.

Assign Section 1 Assessment as homework or an in-class activity.

✓ Reading Check Answer

by volcanic activity or by the formation of coral atolls

Measure student knowledge of physical features and political entities.

GeoQuiz Transparency 25-1

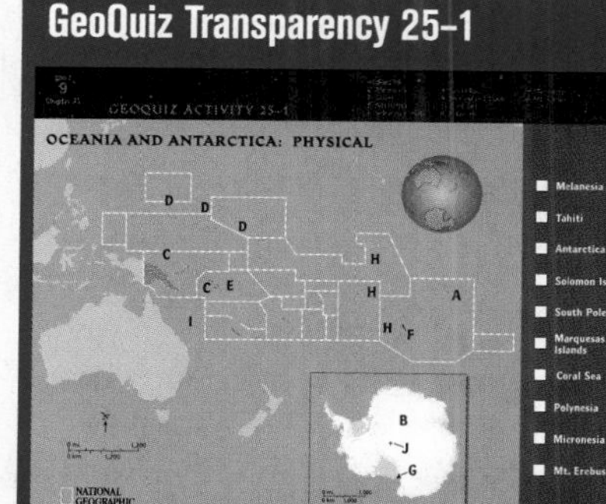

Team-Teaching Activity

History Invite the history teacher to class to discuss the story of the mutiny on H.M.S. *Bounty* and the adventurous aftermath. Have the teacher describe the mission of the ship—to bring breadfruit trees to the West Indies in hope of providing a nutritious food for enslaved plantation workers there—the mutiny itself, and the fates of the mutineers and of Captain William Bligh and those who stayed with him. Have students use a globe to trace the route of the *Bounty* from England to Tahiti and to modern Tuvalu, where the mutiny occurred. Then have them follow Bligh's journey on an open boat to East Timor and the mutineers' voyage back to Tahiti and on to Pitcairn Island. **L1**

EE1 The World in Spatial Terms: Standard 3

Chapter 25

Section 1, pages 660–664

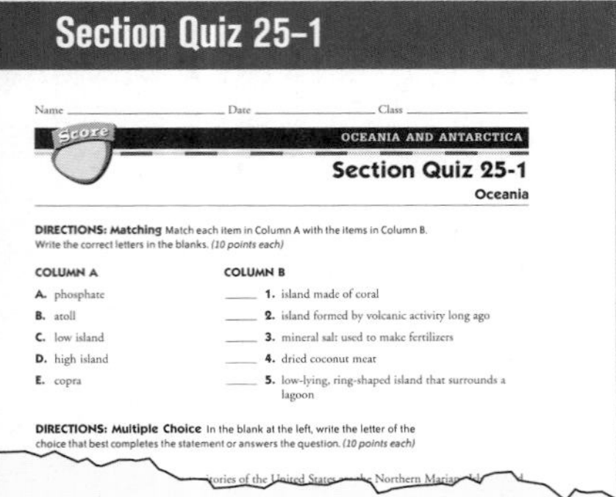

Section Quiz 25-1

Name ______ Date ______ Class ______

Score

OCEANIA AND ANTARCTICA

Section Quiz 25-1

Oceania

DIRECTIONS: Matching Match each item in Column A with the items in Column B. Write the correct letters in the blanks. *(10 points each)*

COLUMN A	COLUMN B
A. phosphate	____ **1.** island made of coral
B. atoll	____ **2.** island formed by volcanic activity long ago
C. low island	____ **3.** mineral salt used to make fertilizers
D. high island	____ **4.** dried coconut meat
E. copra	____ **5.** low-lying, ring-shaped island that surrounds a lagoon

DIRECTIONS: Multiple Choice In the blank at the left, write the letter of the choice that best completes the statement or answers the question. *(10 points each)*

Reteach

Ask volunteers, using their own words, to express each paragraph's main idea and supporting details.

Reading Check Answer

Tahiti

Reading Essentials and Study Guide 25-1

Name ______ Date ______ Class ______

OCEANIA AND ANTARCTICA

Reading Essentials and Study Guide 25-1

Oceania

For use with textbook pages 660-664

Terms to Know

cacao tropical tree whose seeds are used to make chocolate and cocoa (page 660)
copra dried coconut meat (page 661)
pidgin language language formed by combining parts of several different languages (page 662)
high island island formed by volcanoes (page 662)
low island island made of coral (page 662)
atoll low-lying, ring-shaped island that surrounds a lagoon (page 662)
phosphate mineral salt used to make fertilizer (page 663)
trust territory land put under temporary control of another country (page 663)

4 CLOSE

Have students imagine they have a chance to interview a teen who lives on one of these islands. Have them draft the questions they would ask.

also part of this region. Most Polynesian islands are high volcanic islands, some with tall, rugged mountains. Some of the islands are of the low atoll type. Because Polynesia lies in the Tropics, the climate is hot and humid.

Polynesians grow crops or fish for their food. Some farmers export coconuts and tropical fruits. The main manufacturing activity is food processing. The tuna you eat for lunch might have come from American Samoa. This island supplies about one-third of the tuna brought into the United States. Tonga exports squash and vanilla. Tourism is one of the fastest-growing industries of Polynesia. Tourists come by air or sea to the emerald green mountains and white palm-lined beaches.

Polynesia's People Settlers came to Polynesia later than they did to the other island regions. The first to arrive were probably Melanesians or Micronesians who crossed the Pacific Ocean from Asia in canoes.

During the late 1800s, several European nations divided Polynesia among themselves. They built military bases on the islands and later added airfields. The islands served as excellent refueling stops for long voyages across the Pacific. Beginning in the 1960s, several Polynesian territories chose independence, while others remained territories.

About 600,000 people live in Polynesia. Most Polynesians live in rural villages and practice traditional crafts. An increasing number live in towns and cities. **Papeete** (PAH•pay•AY•tay), located on Tahiti, is the capital of French Polynesia and the largest city in the region.

Reading Check What is the largest island in Polynesia?

Assessment

Defining Terms

1. Define cacao, copra, pidgin language, high island, low island, atoll, phosphate, trust territory.

Recalling Facts

2. Region What three regions make up Oceania?

3. Economics What two kinds of economic activities are most important in these regions?

4. History What groups first settled the lands of Micronesia?

Critical Thinking

5. Summarizing Information What is copra, and what is it used for?

6. Drawing Conclusions Why do many people in Melanesia speak a pidgin language?

Graphic Organizer

7. Organizing Information Create a chart like this one. List all the islands of Oceania under their specific region; then note whether they are independent countries or territories.

Melanesia	Micronesia	Polynesia	Country/Territory of ?

Applying Social Studies Skills

8. Analyzing Maps Look at the political map on page 661. Which two territories are colonies of France?

Section 1 Assessment

1. The terms are defined in the Glossary.
2. Melanesia, Micronesia, and Polynesia
3. tourism and farming
4. Southeast Asians
5. dried coconut meat; margarine, soap
6. to communicate better because so many different languages are spoken
7. *Melanesia*: Papua New Guinea, Solomon Islands, Fiji Islands, Vanuatu; territory is France's New Caledonia. *Micronesia*: Federated States of Micronesia, Marshall Islands, Palau, Nauru, Kiribati; territories are the U.S.'s Northern Mariana Islands and Guam. *Polynesia*: Samoa, Tonga, Tuvalu; territories are French Polynesia and American Samoa.
8. New Caledonia, French Polynesia, and Wallis and Futuna

Study and Writing Skill

Writing a Report

Writing skills allow you to organize your ideas in a logical manner. The writing process involves using skills you have already learned, such as taking notes, outlining, and sequencing information.

Learning the Skill

Use the following guidelines to help you apply the writing process:

- Select an interesting topic. Do preliminary research to determine whether your topic is too broad or too narrow.
- Write a general statement that explains what you want to prove, discover, or illustrate in your writing. This will be the focus of your entire paper.
- Research your topic by coming up with a list of main ideas. Prepare note cards listing facts and source information for each main idea.
- Your report should have an introduction, a body, and a conclusion summarizing and restating your findings.
- Each paragraph should express one main idea in a topic sentence. Additional sentences should support or explain the main idea by using details and facts.

An atoll in the Pacific Ocean ▼

Practicing the Skill

Read the following paragraph, and then answer the questions that follow.

> Most of Micronesia's low islands are atolls—low-lying, ring-shaped islands that surround lagoons. An atoll begins as a ring of coral that forms around the edge of a volcanic island. Over time, wind and water erode the volcano, wearing it down to sea level. Eventually only the atoll remains above the surface. The calm, shallow seawater inside the atoll is called a lagoon.

1. What is the main idea of this paragraph?
2. What are the supporting sentences?
3. What might be the topic of an additional paragraph that follows this one?

Applying the Skill

Suppose you are writing a report on Oceania. Answer the following questions about the writing process.

1. How could you narrow this topic?
2. What are three main ideas?
3. Name three possible sources of information.

Practicing the Skill Answers

1. Most of Micronesia's low islands are atolls.
2. the remaining sentences that define atolls
3. *Possible answers:* type of vegetation and wildlife found on atolls, description of Micronesia's high islands

Applying the Skill

1. by choosing to focus on one island or group of islands or by focusing on one aspect of life
2. Papua New Guinea is the largest and geographically most diverse country of Oceania; mountains on Papua New Guinea divide different groups from one another; or Papua New Guinea exports coffee, palm oil, and cacao.
3. encyclopedia; almanac; Web site about the country

TEACH

Give students the following situations: A student preparing a project about tourism in the South Pacific; a travel agent addressing colleagues at a convention about cost trends on cruises in Tahiti; an anthropologist describing traditional life on Samoa; a government leader on Nauru readying a speech about plans for the future of the country's economy. **Ask: What do all of these people have in common?** *(They are communicating information and ideas.)* **How can they most effectively carry out that task?** *(by writing down their ideas first)* **L1**

Additional Skills Practice

1. **What problem results when a topic is too broad?** *(There is too much material on which to report.)*
2. **How can outlining help you write a report?** *(It allows you to structure what you are going to say.)*

Additional Skills Resources

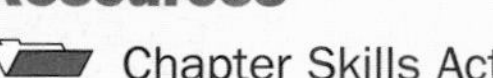

Chapter Skills Activity 25

Building Geography Skills for Life

GLENCOE TECHNOLOGY

Skillbuilder Interactive Workbook CD-ROM, Level 1

This interactive CD-ROM reinforces student mastery of essential social studies skills.

1 Focus

Section Objectives

1. Describe what kinds of life are found in Antarctica.
2. Explain why scientists study Antarctica.

BELLRINGER Skillbuilder Activity

Project transparency and have students answer questions.

This activity is also available as a blackline master.

Daily Focus Skills Transparency 25–2

UNIT 9 Chapter 25 | DAILY FOCUS SKILLS TRANSPARENCY 25-2

ANSWER: The chicks depart during the warmest months in Antarctica.

Teacher Tip: Explain to students that a generalization is a basic idea that can be formed from a set of facts.

Making Generalizations

Adelie and Emperor Penguins of Antarctica

	Adelie Penguins	Emperor Penguins
Size	29.5" (75 cm)	47" (120 cm)
Maximum weight	14 lbs. (6.5 kg)	99 lbs. (45 kg)
Egg laying	November	May
Hatching	December	July
Chicks depart	February	December/January
Main food	Krill	Squid and fish

Directions: Answer the following question based on the information about Adelie and Emperor penguins.

Why do you think both species of penguins have chicks departing the nest in December through February?

Guide to Reading

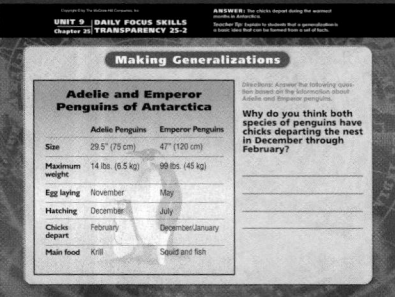

■ Accessing Prior Knowledge
Ask students what value they think Antarctica has. After they have offered their ideas, tell them that they will learn of its value to scientists when they read this section.

■ Vocabulary Precheck
Have students scan the section to find the terms listed in the Terms to Know. Have them use each one in a sentence.

Section 2 Antarctica

Guide to Reading

Main Idea

Antarctica is a harsh land of rock and ice, which the world's nations have agreed to leave open to scientific study.

Terms to Know

- crevasse
- ice shelf
- iceberg
- krill
- ozone

Reading Strategy

Create a chart like the one below. Under each heading, fill in at least one fact about Antarctica.

Antarctica	
Land	Climate
Resources	People

NATIONAL GEOGRAPHIC Exploring Our World

Whee! These Emperor penguins live on the harsh continent of Antarctica. Their shiny "tuxedos" and waddling walk fascinate people. Although they cannot fly, their feathers provide excellent insulation against the ice, snow, and freezing water. Emperor penguins often travel 30 miles (48 km) a day to bring food to their rookeries, or nests. Sometimes walking takes too long, so penguins simply slide on their bellies, which is called tobogganing.

Antarctica sits on the southern end of the earth. Icy ocean water surrounds it. Freezing ice covers it. Cold winds blow over it. The least explored of all the continents, this frigid mysterious land is larger than either Europe or Australia.

A Unique Continent

Picture Antarctica—a rich, green land covered by forests and lush plants. Does this description match your mental image of the continent? Fossils discovered here reveal that millions of years ago, Antarctica's landscape was inhabited by dinosaurs and small mammals.

Today, however, a huge ice cap buries nearly 98 percent of Antarctica's land area. In some spots, this ice cap is 2 miles (3.2 km) thick—about the height of 10 tall skyscrapers stacked upon one another. This massive "sea" of ice holds about 70 percent of all the freshwater in the world.

The Antarctic ice cap is heavy and strong, but it also moves. In some areas, the ice cap forms **crevasses,** or cracks, that plunge more than 100 feet (30 m). At the Antarctic coast, the ice cap spreads past

Section Resources

Reproducible Masters

- Reproducible Lesson Plan 25-2
- Daily Lecture and Discussion Notes 25-2
- Guided Reading Activity 25-2
- Reading Essentials and Study Guide 25-2
- Section Quiz 25-2

Transparencies

- Daily Focus Skills Transparency 25-2
- GeoQuiz Transparency 25-1

Multimedia

- Vocabulary PuzzleMaker Software
- Interactive Tutor Self-Assessment CD-ROM
- Presentation Plus! CD-ROM
- ExamView® Pro 3.0 Testmaker CD-ROM

the land into the ocean. This layer of ice above the water is called an ice shelf. Huge chunks of ice sometimes break off, forming icebergs, which float freely in the icy waters.

Highlands, Mountains, and Valleys Beneath the ice cap, Antarctica has highlands, valleys, and mountains—the same landforms you find on other continents. A long mountain range called the **Transantarctic Mountains** crosses the continent. The highest peak in Antarctica, the **Vinson Massif,** rises 16,067 feet (4,897 m). The Transantarctic Mountains sweep along the Antarctic Peninsula, which reaches within 600 miles (966 km) of South America's Cape Horn. East of the mountains is a high, flat plateau where you find the **South Pole,** the southernmost point of the earth. On an island off Antarctica's coast rises **Mount Erebus** (EHR•uh•buhs). It is Antarctica's most active volcano.

Climate Now that you have a mental picture of Antarctica's ice cap, think about this: Antarctica receives so little precipitation that it is the world's largest, coldest desert. Inland Antarctica receives no rain and hardly any new snow each year. Antarctica has a polar ice cap climate. Imagine summer in a place where temperatures may fall as low as −30°F (−35°C) and climb to only 32°F (0°C). Antarctic summers last from December through February. Winter temperatures along the coasts fall to −40°F (−40°C), and in inland areas to a low of −100°F (−73°C).

✓ Reading Check **What landforms are found under Antarctica's ice cap?**

NATIONAL GEOGRAPHIC On Location

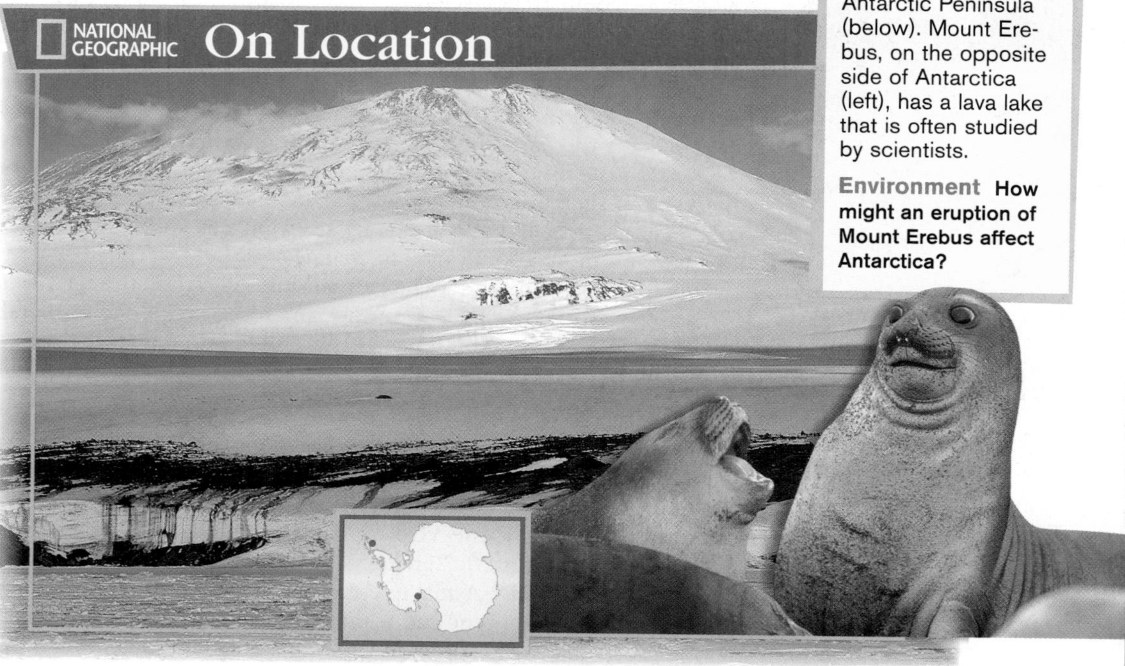

Antarctica

Elephant seals lounge on the coast of Elephant Island off the Antarctic Peninsula (below). Mount Erebus, on the opposite side of Antarctica (left), has a lava lake that is often studied by scientists.

Environment How might an eruption of Mount Erebus affect Antarctica?

Chapter 25

Section 2, pages 666–669

TEACH

Making Predictions Before students read the section, have them predict the kinds of animals, plants, and resources that might be found in Antarctica and make a list. As students study the section, have them check the accuracy of their predictions. **L1**

Daily Lecture Notes 25-2

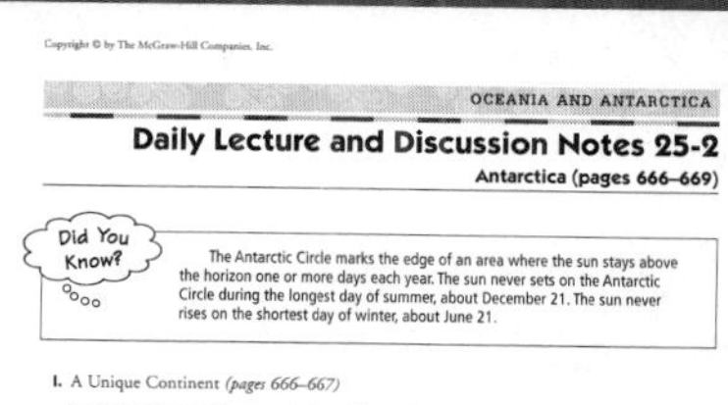

Copyright © by The McGraw-Hill Companies, Inc.

OCEANIA AND ANTARCTICA

Daily Lecture and Discussion Notes 25-2

Antarctica (pages 666–669)

Did You Know? The Antarctic Circle marks the edge of an area where the sun stays above the horizon one or more days each year. The sun never sets on the Antarctic Circle during the longest day of summer, about December 21. The sun never rises on the shortest day of winter, about June 21.

I. A Unique Continent *(pages 666–667)*

A. Fossils discovered here reveal that millions of years ago, Antarctica's landscape was inhabited by dinosaurs and small mammals. Today, however, a huge ice cap buries nearly 98 percent of Antarctica's land area.

B. In some areas, the ice cap forms **crevasses,** or cracks, that plunge more than 100 feet. At the Antarctic coast, the ice cap spreads past the land to cover part [illegible] above the water is called an **ice shelf.** Huge [illegible]

✓ Reading Check Answer

highlands, valleys, and mountains

More About the Photos

Antarctica Since 1972, Mount Erebus has had continuous activity in the lava lake and occasional explosions that eject lava bombs onto the crater rim. Since the lava pools in the cone are open, it does not build up great pressure.

Caption Answer Most eruptions of Mount Erebus are small, but can cause icequakes in nearby glaciers, and a violent eruption might even cause parts of the land to break away.

Team-Teaching Activity

Science Invite a science teacher to class to discuss the earth's magnetic properties. Have him or her explain to the students the difference between the geographical South Pole, the magnetic South Pole, and the geomagnetic South Pole. Ask the teacher to also explain why the latter two spots actually move over time. Give students an outline map of Antarctica and have them use latitude and longitude to plot the three Poles where they currently stand. **L1**

EE1 The World in Spatial Terms: Standard 1

Chapter 25

Section 2, pages 666–669

Guided Reading Activity 25-2

Name ______ Date ______ Class ______

OCEANIA AND ANTARCTICA

Guided Reading Activity 25-2

Antarctica

DIRECTIONS: Reading for Accuracy Reading the section and completing the activity below will help you learn more about Antarctica. Use your textbook to decide if a statement is true or false. Write **T** or **F**, and if a statement is false, rewrite it correctly.

____ **1.** Antarctica is covered with freezing ice and is the least explored continent.

____ **2.** There are not any landforms here; the continent is one huge sheet of ice.

____ **3.** Antarctica is the world's largest desert.

____ **4.** There is not any evidence of life here.

✓ Reading Check Answer

an international treaty to protect Antarctica

3 ASSESS

Assign Section 2 Assessment as homework or an in-class activity.

Have students use the Interactive Tutor Self-Assessment CD-ROM to review Section 25–2.

✓ Reading Check Answer

to learn more about possible climate changes

Section Quiz 25-2

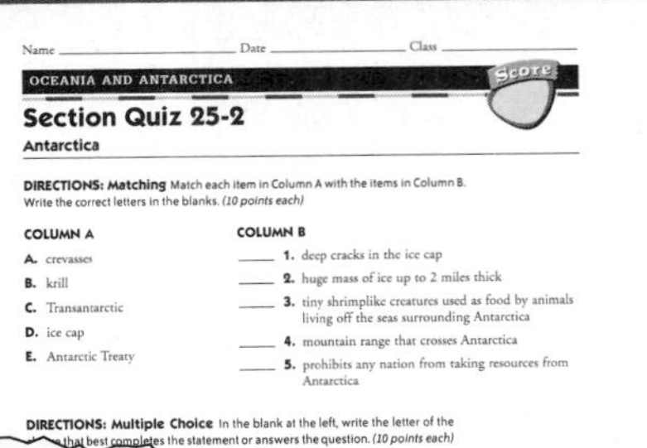

Name ______ Date ______ Class ______

OCEANIA AND ANTARCTICA

Section Quiz 25-2

Antarctica

DIRECTIONS: Matching Match each item in Column A with the items in Column B. Write the correct letters in the blanks. *(10 points each)*

COLUMN A	COLUMN B
A. crevasses	____ **1.** deep cracks in the ice cap
B. krill	____ **2.** huge mass of ice up to 2 miles thick
C. Transantarctic	____ **3.** tiny shrimplike creatures used as food by animals living off the seas surrounding Antarctica
D. ice cap	____ **4.** mountain range that crosses Antarctica
E. Antarctic Treaty	____ **5.** prohibits any nation from taking resources from Antarctica

DIRECTIONS: Multiple Choice In the blank at the left, write the letter of the choice that best completes the statement or answers the question. *(10 points each)*

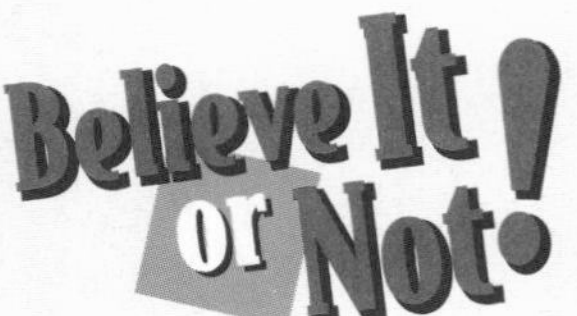

The *Endurance*

In January 1915, Ernest Shackleton and his crew in the *Endurance* became trapped in Antarctica's freezing seawater. In late October, ice crushed the wooden ship, forcing the explorers to abandon it (below). They spent five more months drifting on the ice until they reached open water and used lifeboats to get away.

Resources of Antarctica

Antarctica has a harsh environment, but it can still support life. Most of the plants and animals that live here are small, however. The largest inland animal is an insect that reaches only one-tenth of an inch in length. Penguins, fish, whales, and many kinds of flying birds live in or near the rich seas surrounding Antarctica. Many eat a tiny, shrimp-like creature called **krill.**

Scientists believe that the ice of Antarctica hides a treasure chest of minerals. They have found major deposits of coal and smaller amounts of copper, gold, iron ore, manganese, and zinc. Petroleum might lie offshore.

These mineral resources have not yet been tapped. To do so would be very difficult and costly. Also, some people feel that removing these resources would damage Antarctica's fragile environment. A third reason is that different nations would disagree over who has the right to these resources. Forty-three nations have signed the **Antarctic Treaty,** which prohibits any nation from taking resources from the continent. It also bans weapons testing in Antarctica.

✓ Reading Check **What is the Antarctic Treaty?**

A Vast Scientific Laboratory

The Antarctic Treaty does allow for scientific research in Antarctica. Many countries have scientific research stations here, but no single nation controls the vast continent. In January—summer in Antarctica—about 10,000 scientists come to study the land, plants, animals, and ice of this frozen land. Some 1,000 hardy scientists even stay during the harsh polar winter.

Much of the research focuses on ozone. **Ozone** is a type of oxygen that forms a layer in the atmosphere. The ozone layer protects all living things on the earth from certain harmful rays of the sun. In the 1980s, scientists discovered a weakening, or "hole," in this layer above Antarctica. If such weakening continues, some scientists say, climates around the world will get warmer. By studying this layer further, they hope to learn more about possible changes.

This frozen world attracts more than just scientists, though. Each year, a few thousand tourists come to Antarctica. With such a harsh environment, however, Antarctica is the only continent in the world that has no permanent population.

✓ Reading Check **Why are scientists studying the ozone layer?**

Living in Antarctica

Humans can adapt to life under the most difficult of conditions. One example of this is the Villa Las Estrellas, or Village of the Stars. Located in Chile's Antarctic Territory, the "town" has a school, hospital, supermarket, post office, bank, telephone, television, and Internet systems. There is even a gym and a sauna. Village residents are mostly members of Chile's Air Force and their families and scientists from

Meeting Special Needs

Inefficient Readers Students who do not read efficiently benefit from having a specific purpose for reading. Point out the Reading Strategy at the beginning of the section. Have students read the instructions and copy the grid into their notebooks. Then have them look for information to fill in the chart as they read. **L1**

Refer to *Inclusion for the Middle School Social Studies Classroom Strategies and Activities* in the TCR.

various countries. In all, a total of 88 people live in Villa Las Estrellas, including 24 children under the age of 12.

Like Penguins Daily dress here means wearing thermal underclothes, warm boots and dark sunglasses to protect against the sun's strong ultraviolet rays. Villagers must survive extreme temperatures—down to −13°F (−25°C) below zero with an even more bone-chilling wind factor—but they don't stay inside all day. Adults walk from house to house to visit their neighbors. The children seem to enjoy the experience more than anyone else. One resident describes outdoor playtime. "The children go crazy over the snow and enjoy sledding or just tobogganing downhill on their stomachs. They look like penguins!"

Global Village The countries of Russia, China, Korea, Brazil, Poland, Argentina, and Uruguay have military or scientific bases close to the village. In Antarctica, normal tensions between countries do not seem to matter. Every Wednesday afternoon the different bases send soccer teams to the Chilean gymnasium for a game of indoor soccer. Once a year a "winter Olympics" is held in volleyball and basketball. Visitors to the different bases mix freely with the people who live in the bases. Villa Las Estrellas may be as close to a real global village as the earth has ever seen.

✓ Reading Check **What is one way that humans have adapted to the harsh Antarctic environment?**

Web Activity Visit the ***Our World Today: People, Places, and Issues*** Web site at owt.glencoe.com and click on **Chapter 25–Student Web Activities** to learn more about Antarctica.

Section 2 Assessment

Defining Terms

1. **Define** crevasse, ice shelf, iceberg, krill, ozone.

Recalling Facts

2. **Place** What covers nearly 98 percent of Antarctica?
3. **Location** Where in Antarctica would you find the most living things?
4. **Human/Environment Interaction** Why do scientists come to Antarctica?

Critical Thinking

5. **Summarizing Information** Why have countries agreed not to use the resources of Antarctica?
6. **Writing Questions** Imagine that you are planning a trip to Antarctica. What questions would you ask scientists working there?

Graphic Organizer

7. **Organizing Information** Create a chart like the one below, and then look at the political map on page 661. In your chart, list the various national claims made in Antarctica by the world's countries. Then give the number of research stations for each country.

Countries With Claims in Antarctica	Number of Research Stations

Applying Social Studies Skills

8. **Analyzing Maps** Look at the physical map on page 630. What mountain range cuts across Antarctica?

Section 2 Assessment

1. The terms are defined in the Glossary.
2. an ice cap
3. along the coast
4. to study the ozone as well as plants, animals, ice, and resources of Antarctica
5. to protect its environment and avoid disputes over who owns them
6. Students' questions will vary.
7. Chile—1 station, Argentina—4 stations, U.K.—3 stations, Norway, Australia—3 stations, France—1 station, New Zealand—1 station, India has no claims but 1 station, Russia has no claims but 6 stations, U.S. has no claims but 4 stations, Japan has no claims but 1 station
8. the Transantarctic Mts.

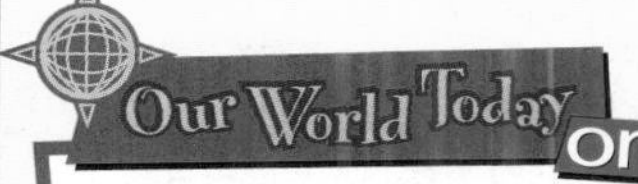

Objectives, goals, and answers to the Student Web Activity can be found in the Web Activity Lesson Plan at **owt.glencoe.com**

✓ Reading Check Answer

by wearing special warm clothing and dark sunglasses

Reading Essentials and Study Guide 25–2

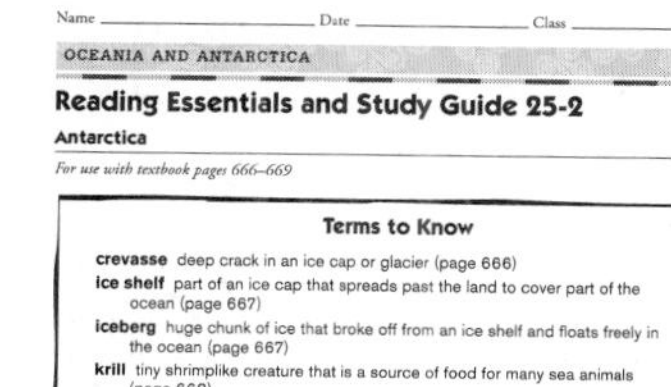

Name ______ Date ______ Class ______

OCEANIA AND ANTARCTICA

Reading Essentials and Study Guide 25-2

Antarctica

For use with textbook pages 666–669

Terms to Know

crevasse deep crack in an ice cap or glacier (page 666)
ice shelf part of an ice cap that spreads past the land to cover part of the ocean (page 667)
iceberg huge chunk of ice that broke off from an ice shelf and floats freely in the ocean (page 667)
krill tiny shrimplike creature that is a source of food for many sea animals (page 668)
ozone type of oxygen that forms a layer in the atmosphere (page 668)

Drawing From Experience

Enrich

Have students research and report on the current status of the ozone layer.

4 Close

Have students write a summary explaining why Antarctica's environment is fragile and why its resources have not been tapped.

TEACH

Have students describe the environment of outer space. Possible answers include cold, dark, and lifeless. **Ask: Where is the best place on the earth to test ways of surviving in such an environment?** *(Antarctica)* Then have them read the feature. L1

More About Antarctica

In 2000, scientists from the United Kingdom published the first map of the landforms found beneath Antarctica's ice cap. The map was created by combining the results of research gathered by scientists from 15 different countries over a 50-year period.

Interdisciplinary Connections

Science Some scientists hope to take samples from Lake Vostok, a large lake in Antarctica. They wish to see if the lake contains any life-forms. The purpose is not only to learn about life in Antarctica itself, but also to apply this knowledge to space. If there is life in harsh Antarctica, some scientists believe, similar forms may survive on the moons that circle other planets in the solar system.

Making Connections

CULTURE | GOVERNMENT | PEOPLE | TECHNOLOGY

Antarctica's Environmental Stations

For nearly 200 years, adventurers, explorers, geographers, and scientists have been drawn to the icy wilderness of Antarctica. Scientific research is the major human activity on this remarkable continent.

Polar Science

In the 1950s, countries began to talk of preserving Antarctica as an international laboratory for scientific research. Today a formal treaty guarantees free access and research rights for scientists of many countries. Antarctica now holds more than 40 research stations.

Types of Research

Geologists, biologists, climatologists, and astronomers are some of the many scientists who come to Antarctica to study. Understanding the earth's environment is a major focus. The Antarctic ice cap contains 90 percent of the world's ice and 70 percent of its freshwater. Changes here can affect the world's oceans and climates.

Scientists in Antarctica were the first to discover the holes in the ozone layer. Such holes can expose life on the earth to too much ultraviolet radiation.

Researchers in Antarctica also study the earth's history. Locked in the continent's ice crystals and air bubbles are clues to the earth's past. Fossils show how landmasses existed before the formation of today's continents.

The harsh living conditions of Antarctica provide another subject for study. The National Aeronautics and Space Administration (NASA) sends engineers and scientists to Antarctica to learn how to survive in extreme conditions, such as those humans might someday encounter on visits to other planets.

Research station at the South Pole ▶

Life at the Edge

Living and working in Antarctica's polar wilderness demands special equipment, well-trained people, and a sizable dose of caution. Freeze-dried food, layers of warm, quick-drying clothes, insulated boots, and specially designed pyramid tents keep researchers well-fed, warm, and dry. Researchers quickly learn the importance of staying inside during whiteout conditions, when snow and fog create a total lack of visibility.

The Antarctic environment is a fragile one, and researchers take care to protect it. All trash and wastes are removed from the continent. Mining of mineral resources is banned, and laws protect native plants and animals. Such care ensures that Antarctica will continue to hold exciting discoveries for years to come.

Making the Connection

1. What do researchers study in Antarctica?
2. What discovery did researchers make about the ozone layer?
3. **Summarizing Information** What items do researchers in Antarctica use to stay warm and dry?

Making the Connection

1. the earth's environment and atmosphere; the ice; fossils; living conditions in the cold
2. They found holes in the ozone layer, which can expose life on the earth to too much ultraviolet radiation.
3. warm, quick-drying clothes; insulated boots; and specially designed pyramid tents

Reading Review

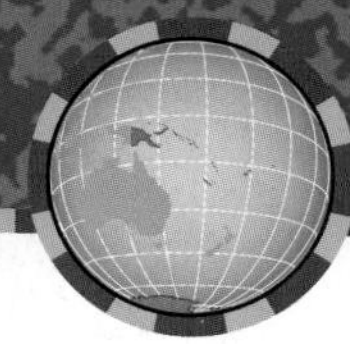

Section 1 Oceania

Terms to Know

cacao
copra
pidgin language
high island
low island
atoll
phosphate
trust territory

Main Idea

Oceania is made up of thousands of Pacific Ocean islands organized into countries and territories.

✓ Region Oceania is a huge area of vast open ocean and about 25,000 islands.

✓ Region Geographers divide Oceania into three regions: Melanesia, Micronesia, and Polynesia.

✓ Place High islands were formed by volcanoes. Low islands were made from coral.

✓ Place Papua New Guinea, in Melanesia, is the largest and most populous country of Oceania.

✓ Economics The main economic activities are farming and tourism. Some islands have important minerals or other resources.

✓ History Most people of Oceania are descendants of people who left Southeast Asia on canoes thousands of years ago.

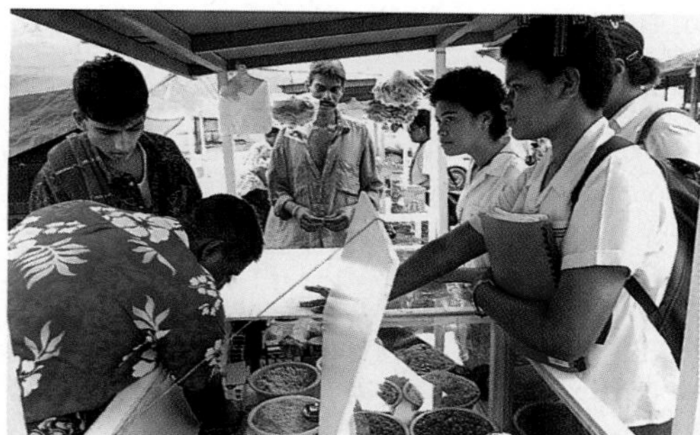

Fijian schoolgirls buy snacks from an Indian merchant in Suva. ▶

Section 2 Antarctica

Terms to Know

crevasse
ice shelf
iceberg
krill
ozone

Main Idea

Antarctica is a harsh land of rock and ice, which the world's nations have agreed to leave open to scientific study.

✓ Location Antarctica lies at the southern end of the earth.

✓ Place Most of the continent, which has mountain ranges and a plateau, is covered by a huge, thick ice cap.

✓ Place Most plants and animals that live in Antarctica are small. Larger animals thrive in the waters off the coast.

✓ Economics Antarctica has many minerals, but many nations have signed a treaty agreeing not to remove these resources.

✓ Culture Antarctica is a major center of scientific research, but is the only continent with no permanent human population.

Reading Review

Use the Chapter 25 Reading Review to preview, review, condense, or reteach the chapter.

Preview/Review

Use the Terms to Know lists to help students review and study.

Activity Have students create crossword puzzles for 10 of the terms from the chapter, exchange papers with another student, and try to complete their partner's puzzle.

Vocabulary PuzzleMaker Software reinforces the vocabulary terms used in Chapter 25.

The Interactive Tutor Self-Assessment CD-ROM allows students to review Chapter 25 content.

Condense

Have students read the Chapter 25 summary statements.

Chapter 25 Guided Reading Activities

Chapter 25 Audio Program

Reteach

Reteaching Activity 25

Chapter 25 Reading Essentials and Study Guide

Chapter Culminating Activity

Travel Brochure Have students create a four-page travel brochure that highlights the attractions for one of the countries in Oceania. Explain that the travel brochure should include both physical and cultural features that visitors would want to see. Remind students that one part of the brochure should have practical information such as clothing appropriate for the climate, language used in the country, and currency employed. Advise students that an effective brochure includes appealing visuals as well as brief, engaging text. *NOTE: This activity may be completed separately or you may wish students to incorporate it into their Current Events Journals.*

EE2 Places and Regions: Standard 2

GLENCOE TECHNOLOGY

MindJogger Videoquiz
Use MindJogger to review the Chapter 25 content.

 Available in VHS.

Using Key Terms

1. d
2. f
3. h
4. g
5. a
6. j
7. i
8. e
9. c
10. b

Reviewing the Main Ideas

11. They are descendants of workers brought by colonial powers.
12. high island; because it was formed by volcanic activity and has fertile soil
13. France
14. *Possible answers:* warm climate; beautiful beaches; attractive environment
15. Southeast Asia
16. It is Antarctica's most active volcano.
17. penguins
18. large amounts of coal and smaller quantities of copper, gold, iron ore, manganese, and zinc
19. Antarctic Treaty
20. to observe any possible changes in this layer, which protects all living things on the earth from dangerous rays of the sun

Chapter 25 Assessment and Activities

 Using Key Terms

Match the terms in Part A with their definitions in Part B.

A.

1. pidgin language
2. copra
3. trust territory
4. ice shelf
5. phosphate
6. ozone
7. low island
8. iceberg
9. high island
10. krill

B.

a. mineral salt used to make fertilizer
b. tiny, shrimp-like animal
c. Pacific island formed by volcanic activity
d. combines elements of several languages
e. chunk of a glacier that floats free
f. dried coconut meat
g. layer of ice above water in Antarctica
h. area temporarily placed under control of another nation
i. Pacific island formed of coral
j. layer in the atmosphere that blocks certain harmful rays of the sun

 Reviewing the Main Ideas

Section 1 Oceania

11. **History** Why are there South Asians on the Fiji Islands?
12. **Human/Environment Interaction** Which is likely to have better farmland—a high island or a low island? Why?
13. **Government** New Caledonia is ruled by what European country?
14. **Economics** What attracts tourists to Oceania?
15. **History** From where did the people who first settled Oceania originally come?

Section 2 Antarctica

16. **Place** What is significant about Mount Erebus?
17. **Location** What marine birds feed in the seas near Antarctica?
18. **Economics** What resources have been found in Antarctica?
19. **Government** What agreement bans the use of Antarctica's resources?
20. **Human/Environment Interaction** Why do scientists study the ozone layer in Antarctica?

Oceania and Antarctica

Place Location Activity

On a separate sheet of paper, match the letters on the map with the numbered places listed below.

1. Antarctic Peninsula
2. South Pole
3. Vinson Massif
4. Marshall Islands
5. Papua New Guinea
6. Fiji Islands
7. French Polynesia
8. Coral Sea
9. Solomon Islands

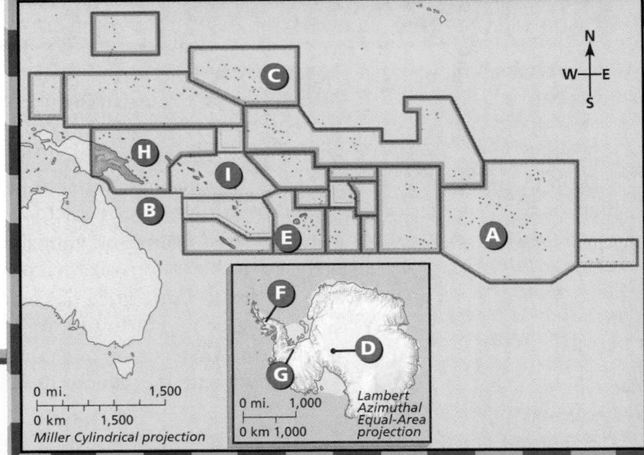

672

NATIONAL GEOGRAPHIC Place Location Activity

1. F
2. D
3. G
4. C
5. H
6. E
7. A
8. B
9. I

Critical Thinking

21. *Possible answer:* The warm, pleasant climate of Oceania makes life there easier in regards to clothing and shelter. Many crops grow in the fertile soil of the high islands, helped by the warm, tropical climate. The harsh climate of Antarctica has prevented permanent settlements, although technology allows a few scientists to stay there year-round.
22. Students' charts will vary.

Self-Check Quiz Visit the ***Our World Today: People, Places, and Issues*** Web site at owt.glencoe.com and click on **Chapter 25–Self-Check Quizzes** to prepare for the Chapter Test.

Critical Thinking

21. **Making Generalizations** You have read about two areas with very different climates. Write a generalization about how climate affects the way people live in each area.
22. **Organizing Information** Make a chart like this one. Under each heading, write a fact about each of the four regions you studied in this chapter: Melanesia, Micronesia, Polynesia, and Antarctica.

Region	Landforms	Climate	Economy or Resources	People

Current Events Journal

23. **Writing a Pamphlet** Choose one island country from Oceania. Research current topics such as the land, economy, daily life, or culture. After you have completed your research, create a pamphlet about your island, encouraging tourists to visit there.

Mental Mapping Activity

24. **Focusing on the Region** Create an outline map of Antarctica. Refer to the map on page 630, and then label the following:
    - Antarctic Circle
    - Vinson Massif
    - Antarctic Peninsula
    - Pacific Ocean
    - Atlantic Ocean
    - South Pole

Technology Skills Activity

25. **Building a Database** Research three animals of Oceania. Create a database of the information you find. Include separate fields for the following items: name of species, location, type of habitat, diet, natural predators, and population status. Then use the database information to create a map showing the location of each species.

The Princeton Review

Standardized Test Practice

Directions: Read the paragraph below, and then answer the following question.

Because of the clear Pacific waters, fresh fish is the primary traditional food of Oceania's people. This is especially true in the low coral islands, where there is little land suitable for farming. The rich volcanic soil of the high islands allows pineapples, coconuts, bananas, and sweet potatoes to grow. In Papua New Guinea, pork is a favorite food. Great feasts of pork, greens, and yams are social gatherings for whole villages. At these feasts, pigs are cooked for about eight hours over hot stones set in an "earth oven"—or large hole in the ground.

1. Which of the following statements best summarizes the paragraph above?

F People in the high islands are able to grow and eat pineapples, bananas, and sweet potatoes.

G In the low islands, the coral prevents much farming.

H The Pacific Ocean is the source of the fish that most people eat.

J Physical geography influences the traditional foods of Oceania's people.

Test-Taking Tip: When a question uses the word *best,* it means that more than one answer might be correct. Your job is to pick the *best* answer. This question also asks for a summary of the passage. Read through all of the answer choices before choosing the one that provides a more general restatement of the information.

673

Assessment and Activities

Standardized Test Practice

1. J

Tested Objectives: Summarizing information, making generalizations

Chapter Test Bonus Question

This question may be used for extra credit on the chapter test.

What mineral is used to make fertilizers? *(phosphate)*

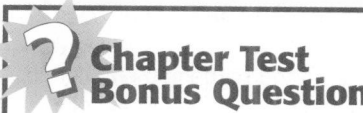

Our World Today Online

Have students visit the Web site at **owt.glencoe.com** to review Chapter 25 and take the Self-Check Quiz.

Current Events Journal

23. Suggest that students use Internet resources to find images that they can copy and paste into their pamphlets.

Mental Mapping Activity

24. This exercise helps students visualize the countries and geographic features they have been studying and understand the relationship among various points. Accept all attempts at freehand mapping that show places in the correct relationship to one another.

Technology Skills Activity

25. Have students hand in both the database and the map. They might also include photographs of the animals they selected.

Ask students what characteristics they think people would need to to be willing to brave the fierce conditions of Antarctica.

2 Teach

Developing a Point of View Have students discuss whether they would be willing to undergo the hardships entailed in exploring Antarctica. Have volunteers explain what aspects of such work appeal to them and what parts of it they find unattractive. Then ask students the same question about other areas of exploration, including deep in the oceans, in the deserts, and in space. **L1**

Meeting National Standards

Geography for Life

The following standards are met in the Student Edition feature:

EE2 Places and Regions: Standard 4

EE3 Physical Systems: Standards 7, 8

EE5 Environment and Society: Standard 15

Alone in a hut in 1934, Byrd fell ill from inhaling stove fumes.

"BYRD'S"-EYE VIEW: Exploring Antarctica

What sound does your breath make when it freezes? On his first expedition to Antarctica, United States Navy officer Richard E. Byrd found out. When the temperature dropped to –64°F (–53°C), Byrd heard what sounded like Chinese firecrackers as a slight breeze crackled across his frozen breath.

Beyond Imagination

Strange things happen in Antarctica. The sun lurks near the horizon for months and never sets. Then from mid-March to mid-September, the dark winter sets in, and the sun never rises. Antarctica is covered by thick ice and snow. Huge glaciers spill out between mountains that rim the coast, creating shelves of ice that extend out over the sea. Sometimes chunks of ice break off to form huge icebergs.

In the early 1900s, little was known about Antarctica. A few brave explorers had traveled on foot, skis, and sleds across the frozen land. Several made it to the South Pole. Much of the continent remained a mystery, however. Admiral Richard Byrd was determined to change that.

Mapping the Continent

With detailed planning, Byrd launched a major scientific expedition to Antarctica in 1928. He brought 650 tons (590 t) of supplies on his ship—everything from fur clothing and folding bathtubs to 80 sled dogs and a snowmobile! He also brought the latest technology, including radios, cameras, and three airplanes. His team of 53 professionals set up a complete village on the Ross Ice Shelf. They named it Little America.

From this base, Byrd and his crew explored the continent. On short flights from Little America, they used a mapping camera to gather data on vast areas never seen by humans. In 1929 Byrd and three companions were the first to fly over the South Pole. Such feats took great courage. Twice during flights, the engines failed. Once the pilot was able to restart them; once the plane crashed. Luckily, everyone survived. On a later expedition, huddled alone in a hut for months, Byrd almost died.

Byrd led five Antarctic expeditions and mapped nearly all of the continent. He supervised the completion of five Antarctic stations—Little America I through Little America V. His work paved the way for future researchers.

Today the United States and many other countries have scientific stations on Antarctica. From these stations, scientists record weather data, measure ozone levels, analyze ice and rock samples, and record animal behavior. Such research may answer important questions about future life on the earth.

QUESTIONS

1 What conditions did Byrd and his fellow explorers face in Antarctica?

2 Why is Byrd's work still important today?

Crunching through ice, the *U.S.S. Glacier* brings Admiral Byrd back to Antarctica in 1955. ▶

674

Answers to the Questions

1. freezing cold, long periods of darkness, danger from moving ice
2. Scientific stations in Antarctica are still carrying out important research, including the study of the ozone layer.

NATIONAL GEOGRAPHIC

Byrd's First Flight to the South Pole

Polar Plateau
South Pole
ANTARCTICA
Byrd's 1st Flight, November 1929
ROSS ICE SHELF
Little America
Bay of Whales
Ross Sea
ANTARCTICA
Ross Ice Shelf
Area enlarged
0 mi. 200
0 km 200
Lambert Azimuthal Equal-Area projection

Time Line

- **c. 650**: Maori legends tell of a canoe trip to a frozen ocean
- **1820**: Antarctica first sighted
- **1898–1899**: *Belgica* becomes first ship to spend winter in Antarctic waters
- **1901–1904**: Robert F. Scott leads *Discovery* expedition
- **1907–1909**: Ernest Shackleton leads *Nimrod* expedition
- **1911**: Roald Amundsen becomes first to reach South Pole
- **1912**: Scott reaches South Pole
- **1908–1942**: Seven nations claim parts of Antarctica
- **1929**: Richard Byrd leads his first exploratory expedition; flies over South Pole
- **1935**: Lincoln Ellsworth completes first crossing of Antarctica by air
- **1957**: Vivian Fuchs leads first expedition to cross Antarctica
- **1959**: Antarctic Treaty signed

ASSESS

Have students answer the questions on page 674.

CLOSE

Have students summarize the benefits gained from research in Antarctica.

Geography and History Activity

Researching Mapmaking Explain how scientists have used sonic depth recorders and satellite imaging to determine the landforms of Antarctica as well as the shape of the ocean floor. Have students create a dictionary of ocean topography that includes such terms as *abyssal plain, basin, continental shelf, continental slope, fracture zone, guyot, ridge, seamount, trench,* and *trough.* Suggest that students include a pronunciation along with the definition for each term. When students have completed their dictionaries, have them compare the landforms found in oceans to those found on land.

EE6 The Uses of Geography: Standard 18

Appendix

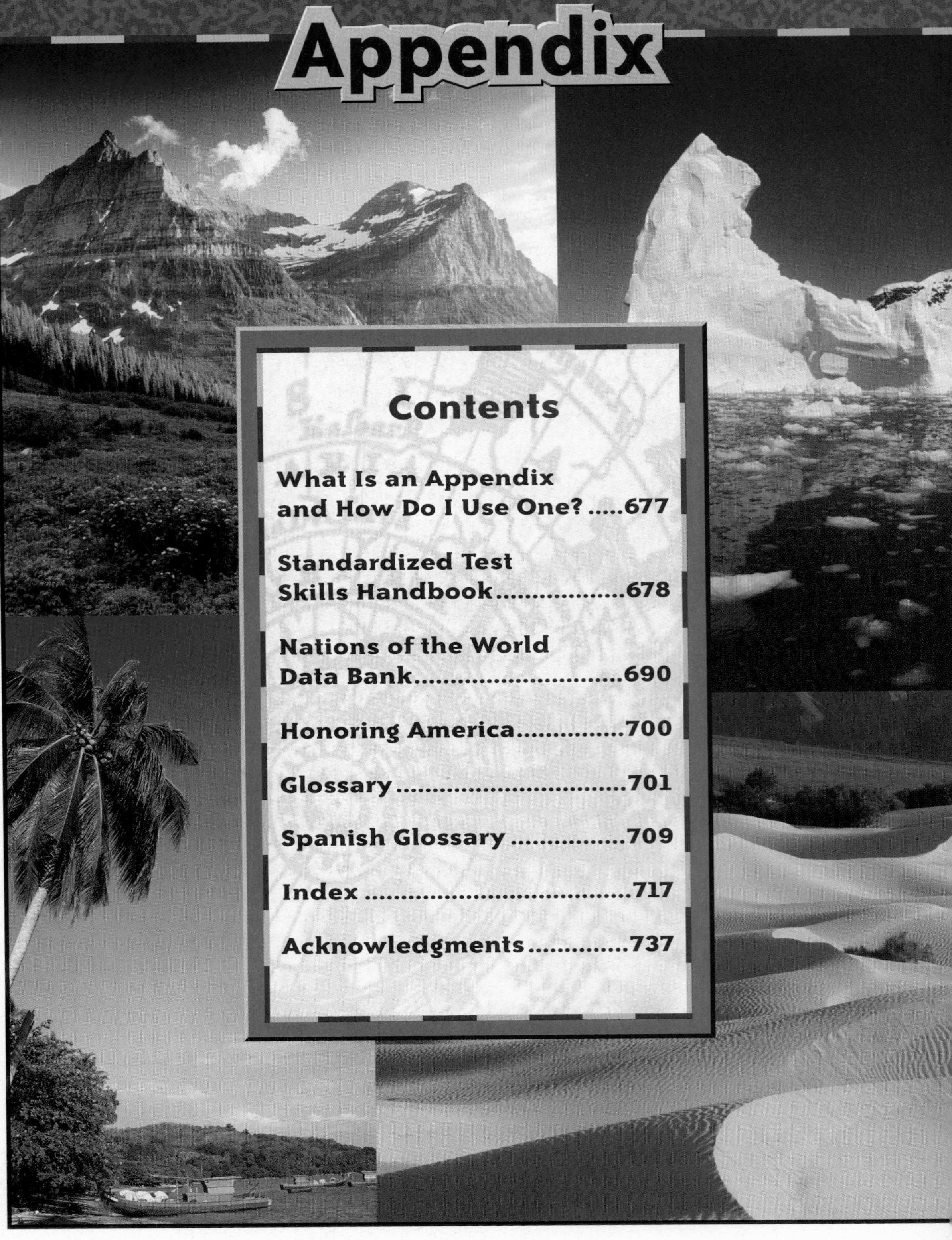

Contents

What Is an Appendix and How Do I Use One?

An appendix is the additional material you often find at the end of books. The information below will help you learn how to use the appendix in *Our World Today*.

SKILLS HANDBOOK

The **Standardized Test Skills Handbook** requires you to learn and apply many key skills that you will use throughout the study of geography as well as other subject areas.

NATIONS OF THE WORLD DATA BANK

The **Nations of the World Data Bank** that begins on page 690 lists all of the world's countries and various categories of information for each. For example, each country's type of government, form of currency, and literacy rate—among other topics—are listed in the data bank.

GLOSSARY AND SPANISH GLOSSARY

A **glossary** is a list of important or difficult terms found in a textbook. The glossary gives a definition of each term as it is used in the book. Since words sometimes have other meanings, you may wish to consult a dictionary to find other uses for the term. The glossary also includes page numbers telling you where in the textbook the term is used. The **Spanish glossary** is the English glossary translated into Spanish.

INDEX

An **index** is an alphabetical listing at the end of a book that includes the subjects of that book and the page numbers where those subjects can be found. The index in this book also lets you know that certain pages contain maps, graphs, photos, or paintings about the subject.

ACKNOWLEDGMENTS

This section lists photo credits and/or literary credits for the book. You can look at this section to find out where the publisher obtained the permission to use photographs or to use excerpts from other books.

Test Yourself!

Do you think you can use an appendix quickly and easily? Try it. Find the answers to these questions by using the appendix on the following pages.

1. What does *canopy* mean?
2. Where in the book is the word *canopy* used?
3. What is the Spanish word for *cassava?*
4. What kind of currency does Saudi Arabia use?
5. On what page can you find out about the climate of Iceland?
6. On what pages can you find information about Cuba?
7. What is the literacy rate in Nepal?

Appendix User Tip

When using an appendix, be sure to notice and use the guide words at the top of the page. These guide words indicate the alphabetically first and last entries on that page.

What is an Appendix and How Do I Use One?

By definition, an appendix is supplementary material attached to the end of a piece of writing. Students can use appendices to help them navigate through and understand the main material in their textbooks. Explain to them that they may use an appendix to find out what a word means, how to pronounce a word, or where else in the book they could find additional information about a particular word or topic.

Appendix User Tip

Be sure to review the beginning page of each section of an appendix. Often, the first page of a section contains a key that explains symbols or terms used in the entries of that section. For example, the abbreviation *ptg,* used in several Index entries, refers to specific paintings that appear in the book.

Other Useful Information Found in Books

Explain to students that useful material appears in the front of the book. Usually this information includes the following:

- The **title page** contains the book title, author's name, and the name of the publisher.
- The **copyright page** gives the publication date. Students should check this date to determine how current the book is.
- The **table of contents** lists the main topics covered in the book.

Test Yourself! Answers

1. Students can find the definition of *canopy* in the Glossary. It is the umbrella-like covering formed by the tops of trees in a rain forest.
2. Students can find this information in the Index or the Glossary.
3. Students can find the Spanish word for *cassava*, which is *yuca*, in the Spanish Glossary.
4. Students can find this answer by looking in the Index or in the Nations of the World Data Bank. Saudi Arabia's currency is the Saudi Riyal.
5. Students should look up Iceland in the Index to find that information.
6. Have students find Cuba in the Index.
7. By reviewing the Nations of the World Data Bank, students can find this information.

TEACH

Have students write down everything they associate with the word "test." Ask them to list helpful hints for taking tests. Lead a class discussion on successful test-taking strategies. For example suggest that when taking tests students look for clues in the question that support their answers, eliminate answers that don't make sense, and read the titles or keys of any graphics presented (graphs, charts, time lines, maps).

Standardized Test

Skills Handbook

Standardized tests are one way educators measure what you have learned. This handbook is designed to help you prepare for standardized tests in social studies. On the pages that follow, you will find a review of the major social studies critical thinking skills that you will need to master to be successful when taking tests.

Standardized Test Skills Practiced in This Handbook:

- Interpreting a Map
- Interpreting a Political Map
- Interpreting Charts
- Making Comparisons
- Interpreting Primary Sources
- Interpreting a Political Cartoon
- Interpreting a Circle Graph
- Drawing Inferences and Conclusions
- Comparing Data
- Categorizing and Analyzing Information
- Sequencing Events

Author
Tara Musslewhite
Humble I.S.D.
Humble, Texas

Reviewed by

Additional Glencoe TEST PRACTICE RESOURCES:

The following materials are available for further test practice:

- Glencoe Skillbuilder Interactive Workbook, Level 1
- ExamView® Pro Testmaker CD-ROM
- Reading Essentials and Study Guide
- Quizzes and Tests
-  Critical Thinking Skills Activities
- 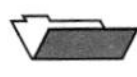 Standardized Test Practice Workbook (and TAE)
-   Daily Focus Skills Transparencies and Blackline Masters

Test Practice Lesson 1

Interpreting a Map

Before 1492 people living in Europe in the Eastern Hemisphere had no idea the continents of North America and South America in the Western Hemisphere existed. That was the year Christopher Columbus first reached the Americas. His voyage of exploration paved the way for other European voyages to the Western Hemisphere. The voyages of the early explorers brought together two worlds. Previously these parts of the globe had no contact with each other. Trade between the hemispheres changed life for people on both sides of the Atlantic Ocean. The trade between the peoples of the Eastern Hemisphere and the Western Hemisphere is referred to as the Columbian Exchange.

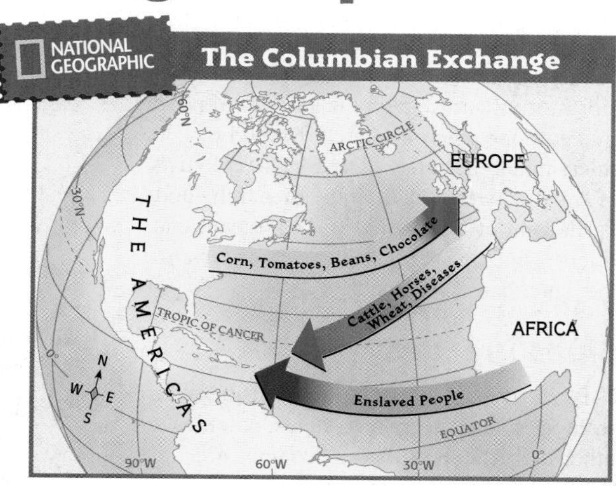

Skills Practice

Although globes are the best, most accurate way to show places on the round earth, people can more easily use maps to represent places. A map is made by taking data from a round globe and placing it on a flat surface. To read a map, first read the title to determine the subject of the map. Then read the map key or the labels on the map to find out what the colors and symbols on the map mean. Use the compass rose to identify the four cardinal directions of north, south, east, and west. Study the map of the Columbian Exchange and answer the questions that follow on a separate sheet of paper.

1. What is the subject of the map?
2. What do the arrows represent?
3. What continents are shown on the map?
4. What foods did Europeans acquire from the Americas?
5. What did the Americas acquire from Europe?
6. What people were brought from Africa to the Americas?
7. In what direction is Europe from the Americas?

Standardized Test Practice

DIRECTIONS: Use the map and your knowledge of social studies to answer the following question on a separate sheet of paper.

1. All of the following statements about the Columbian Exchange are true EXCEPT
   - **A** food products were traded between the continents.
   - **B** enslaved Africans were brought to the Americas.
   - **C** Europeans introduced diseases to Native Americans.
   - **D** Europeans acquired cattle from the Americas.

TEACH

Write the following on the overhead or board: "In fourteen hundred ninety-two, Columbus sailed the ocean blue." Ask students to analyze the verse. Ask: What is the significance of 1492? What century is represented by that date? Who was Columbus? To which ocean does the verse refer?

Review the steps of reading a map with students. (1. Read all the map labels; 2. Identify each symbol and color shown in the map key and locate these on the map; 3. Use this information to look for similarities and differences in the regions shown on the map.)

Skills Practice Answers:

1. the Columbian Exchange
2. trade routes between continents or hemispheres
3. North America, South America, Europe, Africa
4. corn, tomatoes, beans, chocolate
5. cattle, horses, wheat, diseases
6. enslaved people
7. east

Standardized Test Practice Answer:

1. D

Test-Taking Strategy: Explain to students that determining the meaning of the question will help them find the right answer. "EXCEPT" at the end of a question can be interpreted to mean, "Which answer is false?" Students should verify each answer choice against the map to find the one that is NOT true.

TEACH

Ask students: Why did people come to live in the British colonies in North America? Have students discuss the many reasons why someone might want to go on a dangerous voyage to a new land. *(Students should be able to explain that the various colonies were founded and populated for religious freedom, for profit, for trade, for political freedom, and to escape debt.)*

Remind students to use the various parts of the map to help them interpret the map. These map parts include the map key, labels, and compass rose.

Skills Practice Answers:

1. Massachusetts, Rhode Island, New Hampshire, Connecticut
2. New Jersey, Pennsylvania, New York, Delaware
3. New York
4. Georgia
5. Atlantic Ocean
6. in the Southern Colonies; in South Carolina

Test Practice Lesson 2

Interpreting a Political Map

By 1750, or the middle of the eighteenth century, there were 13 British colonies in North America. A colony is a group of people living in one place who are governed by rulers in another place. The British colonists in America were ruled by the monarchy and Parliament of Great Britain. That meant that rulers living 3,000 miles away made laws for the American colonists.

Skills Practice

Political maps illustrate divisions between territories such as nations, states, colonies, or other political units. These divisions are called boundaries. Lines represent the boundaries between political areas. To interpret a political map, read the map title to determine what geographic area and time period it covers. Identify the colonies or other political units on the map. Look at the map key for additional information. Study the map on this page and answer the questions that follow on a separate sheet of paper.

1. List the New England Colonies.
2. Which were the Middle Colonies?
3. Which Middle Colony bordered Pennsylvania to the north?
4. Which was the southernmost early British colony?
5. Name the body of water that formed the eastern border of the colonies.
6. Where was Charles Town located?

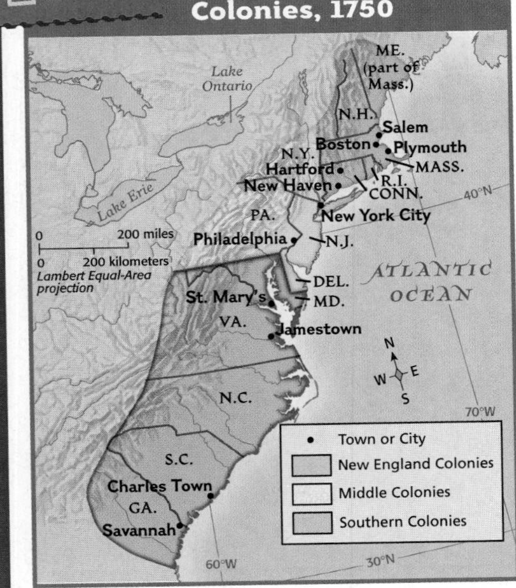

Standardized Test Practice

DIRECTIONS: Use the map and your knowledge of social studies to answer the following questions on a separate sheet of paper.

1. The New England Colony that covered the largest land area was
   A Virginia.
   B Pennsylvania.
   C Massachusetts.
   D New Hampshire.
2. The northernmost Middle Colony is the present-day state of
   F Maryland.
   G New York.
   H Massachusetts.
   J Pennsylvania.
3. The settlement of Plymouth was located
   A near Jamestown.
   B in Massachusetts.
   C in the Southern Colonies.
   D in Virginia.

The Princeton Review

Standardized Test Practice Answers:

1. C
Test-Taking Strategy: Be sure students identify the New England Colonies before they choose their answer.
2. G
Test-Taking Strategy: Tell students: First locate the Middle Colonies. Next determine which Middle Colony is farthest north.
3. B
Test-Taking Strategy: Have students answer the question before reviewing the answer choices to see which answer choice matches their answer.

Interpreting Charts

Government is a necessary part of every nation. It gives citizens stability and provides services that many of us take for granted. However, governments can sometimes have too much power.

The United States was founded on the principle of limited government. Limited governments require all people to follow the laws. Even the rulers must obey rules set for the society. A democracy is a form of limited government. Not all forms of government have limits. In unlimited governments, power belongs to the ruler. No laws exist to limit what the ruler may do. A dictatorship is an example of an unlimited government.

LIMITED GOVERNMENTS	
Representative Democracy	**Constitutional Monarchy**
People elect leaders to rule	King or queen's power is limited
Individual rights important	Individual rights important
More than one political party	More than one political party
People give consent to be governed	People elect governing body

UNLIMITED GOVERNMENTS	
Dictatorship	**Absolute Monarchy**
One person or small group rules	King or queen inherits power
Little personal freedoms	Usually some freedoms
Rule by force, often military	Officials are appointed by king or queen
Ruler does not have to obey rules	Monarch has complete authority

Skills Practice

Charts are visual graphics that categorize information. When reading a chart be sure to look at all the headings and labels. Study the charts on this page and answer the questions that follow on a separate sheet of paper.

1. What do the charts compare?
2. Which political systems are forms of limited government?
3. Which form of government often uses military rule?
4. In which political system does the king or queen have complete power?

The Princeton Review

Standardized Test Practice

DIRECTIONS: Use the charts and your knowledge of social studies to answer the following questions on a separate sheet of paper.

1. Information found in the charts shows that the most restrictive form of government is a
   - **A** dictatorship.
   - **B** representative democracy.
   - **C** absolute monarchy.
   - **D** constitutional monarchy.
2. Under which type of government do citizens have the most power?
   - **F** unlimited government
   - **G** limited government
   - **H** absolute monarchy
   - **J** dictatorship
3. An example of an unlimited government is
   - **A** the United States in the 1960s.
   - **B** Libya in the 1970s.
   - **C** the United Kingdom in the 1980s.
   - **D** Mexico in the 1990s.

TEACH

Ask how many students play a sport. How many have after-school jobs? What kinds of jobs? Then tell them that information like this could be explained in text form, but placing the information or statistics in a table or chart would present the information in a more concise and easily interpreted format. Have students practice analyzing a chart by reading the information and answering the questions that follow.

Skills Practice Answers:

1. types of government or limited versus unlimited governments
2. representative democracy, constitutional monarchy
3. dictatorship
4. absolute monarchy

Standardized Test Practice Answers:

1. A
Test-Taking Strategy: Make sure students have a clear understanding of the meaning of key words in the question. The most restrictive government is the one with the fewest freedoms.

2. G
Test-Taking Strategy: Tell students to be sure to read all the headings on the chart.

3. B
Test-Taking Strategy: Students can narrow the answer choices by eliminating choices they know are incorrect.

TEACH

Making comparisons is an important skill in all academic areas. Help students to realize that making comparisons is also a life skill that we use every day by having volunteers give examples of a situation in which they have had to make a comparison recently.

You may wish to create, as a class, a comparison chart of two professional sports teams, two entertainers, and so on.

Skills Practice Answers:

1. The chart compares the two houses of the United States Congress—the House of Representatives and the Senate. It compares the qualifications, numbers of representatives, and the terms of office for senators and representatives.
2. To become a member of the U.S. Congress (in either house), you must live in the state you represent.

Test Practice Lesson 4

Making Comparisons

The roots of representative democracy in the United States can be traced back to colonial times. In 1607 English settlers founded the colony of Jamestown in present-day Virginia. As the colony developed, problems arose. Later colonists formed the House of Burgesses to deal with these problems. Citizens of Virginia were chosen as representatives to the House of Burgesses. This became the first legislature, or lawmaking body, in America.

Today citizens of the United States elect representatives to Congress. The major function of Congress is to make laws for the nation. There are two houses, or chambers, of the U.S. Congress. Legislative bodies with two houses are said to be bicameral. The bicameral Congress of the United States includes the Senate and the House of Representatives. Article I of the U.S. Constitution describes how each house will be organized and how its members will be chosen.

THE U.S. CONGRESS

House of Representatives	Senate
Qualifications: • Must be 25 years old • Must be U.S. citizen for 7+ years • Must live in the state they represent	**Qualifications:** • Must be 30 years old • Must be U.S. citizen for 9+ years • Must live in the state they represent
Number of Representatives: • 435 total representatives; number of representatives per state is based on state population	**Number of Representatives:** • 100 total senators; two senators elected from each state regardless of state population
Terms of Office: • Two-year terms	**Terms of Office:** • Six-year terms

Skills Practice

When you make a comparison, you identify and examine two or more groups, situations, events, or documents. Then you identify any similarities and differences between the items. Study the information presented on the chart on this page and answer the questions that follow on a separate sheet of paper.

1. What two things does the chart compare?
2. How are the qualifications for each house of the U.S. Congress similar?

Standardized Test Practice

DIRECTIONS: Use the chart and your knowledge of social studies to answer the following questions on a separate sheet of paper.

1. Which of the following statements best reflects information shown in the chart?
   - **A** The Senate has more members than the House of Representatives.
   - **B** Representatives to the House are elected to two-year terms.
   - **C** House members must be residents of their states for at least 9 years.
   - **D** A state's population determines its number of senators.
2. One inference that can be made from information shown on the chart is that
   - **F** Texas elects more senators than Rhode Island.
   - **G** Texas elects more House members than Rhode Island.
   - **H** Texas elects fewer senators than Rhode Island.
   - **J** Texas elects fewer House members than Rhode Island.

The Princeton Review

Standardized Test Practice Answers:

1. B

Test-Taking Strategy: Tell students: Don't rely on your memory alone to answer the question. Check each answer choice with information presented in the chart.

2. G

Test-Taking Strategy: Ask: What do you know about the populations of Texas and Rhode Island? Which house uses population to determine the number of members?

Interpreting Primary Sources

When Thomas Jefferson wrote the Declaration of Independence, he used the term "unalienable rights." Jefferson was referring to the natural rights that belong to humans. He and the other Founders of our nation believed that government could not take away the rights of the people.

Skills Practice

Primary sources are records of events made by the people who witnessed them. A historical document such as the Declaration of Independence is an example of a primary source. Read the passage below and answer the questions that follow on a separate sheet of paper.

> "We hold these truths to be self-evident, that all men are created equal, that they are endowed by their Creator with certain unalienable Rights, that among these are Life, Liberty, and the pursuit of Happiness . . ."
>
> —Declaration of Independence, July 4, 1776

1. What does the document say about the equality of men?
2. List the three natural, or unalienable, rights to which the document refers.

After gaining independence, American leaders wrote the U.S. Constitution in 1787. The Bill of Rights includes the first 10 amendments, or additions, to the Constitution. The First Amendment protects five basic rights of all American citizens. Study the chart on this page and answer the questions that follow.

1. Which right allows Americans to express themselves without fear of punishment by the government?
2. Which right allows people to worship as they please?
3. Which right allows citizens to publish a pamphlet that is critical of the president?
4. What is the Bill of Rights?

Rights Protected by the First Amendment

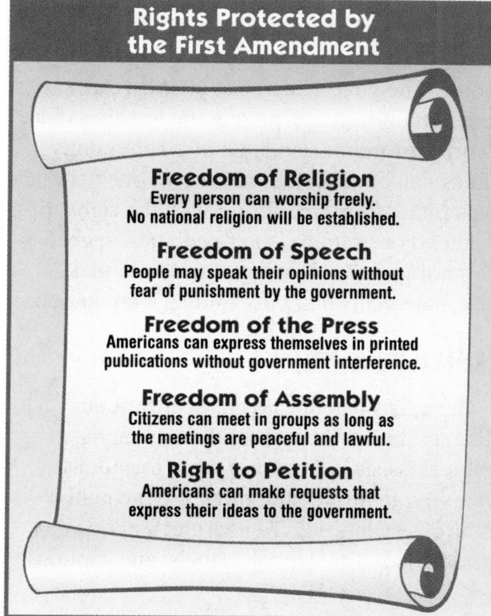

Freedom of Religion
Every person can worship freely.
No national religion will be established.
Freedom of Speech
People may speak their opinions without fear of punishment by the government.
Freedom of the Press
Americans can express themselves in printed publications without government interference.
Freedom of Assembly
Citizens can meet in groups as long as the meetings are peaceful and lawful.
Right to Petition
Americans can make requests that express their ideas to the government.

Standardized Test Practice

DIRECTIONS: Use the chart and your knowledge of social studies to answer the following question on a separate sheet of paper.

1. Which First Amendment right protects citizens who are staging a protest outside a government building?
   A freedom of speech
   B freedom of the press
   C freedom of assembly
   D freedom of religion

TEACH

Ask students to explain the phrase "Founders of our nation." What does it mean? Who were the Founders of the United States? What did they do? Have students speculate as to why the term *Founders* is capitalized.

Tell students that Thomas Jefferson was one of the most famous of the Founders of our nation because he wrote the Declaration of Independence. Ask students to recall the country from which Americans were declaring independence. Have students locate Great Britain on a map before they read these pages.

Skills Practice Answers:

1. All men are created equal.
2. life, liberty, and the pursuit of happiness

1. freedom of speech
2. freedom of religion
3. freedom of the press
4. The Bill of Rights includes the first 10 amendments to the United States Constitution. These amendments protect basic liberties and rights.

Standardized Test Practice Answer:

1. C

Test-Taking Strategy: Have students check each answer choice against the information presented in the chart. Words in the question may not exactly match information in the chart. Encourage students to look for synonyms, or words of similar meanings, to support their answers.

Standardized Test Skills Handbook

TEACH

Point out that the main purpose of political cartoons is to comment on a situation and, sometimes, to suggest a course of action. Help students understand that political cartoonists often use caricatures and symbols. (A caricature is an unrealistic drawing of a real person. A symbol is a real drawing of a concept.)

Skills Practice Answers:

1. a man sitting at a desk writing (about what freedoms to grant to Americans)
2. freedom, liberty, rights, but not too much/many
3. a Founder of our nation (the writer of the U.S. Constitution or Bill of Rights)
4. writing the Bill of Rights
5. They suggest that the nation's Founders had to create a balance between freedoms and rights and the limits to them.
6. Americans' rights are restricted so that one person cannot interfere in the rights of another person. These limits are necessary to keep order in a society of so many people.

Standardized Test Skills Handbook

Test Practice Lesson 6

Interpreting a Political Cartoon

Just as the government of the United States is limited in its powers, freedoms extended to Americans also have limits. The First Amendment was not intended to allow Americans to do whatever they please without regard to others. Limits on freedoms are necessary to keep order in a society of so many people. The government can establish laws to limit certain rights to protect the health, safety, security, or moral standards of a community. Rights can be restricted to prevent one person's rights from interfering with the rights of another. For example, the freedom of speech does not include allowing a person to make false statements that hurt another's reputation.

Skills Practice

The artists who create political cartoons often use humor to express their opinions on political issues. Sometimes these cartoonists are trying to inform and influence the public about a certain topic. To interpret a political cartoon, look for symbols, labels, and captions that provide clues about the message of the cartoonist. Analyze these elements and draw some conclusions. Study the political cartoon on this page and answer the questions that follow on a separate sheet of paper.

1. What is the subject of the cartoon?
2. What words provide clues as to the meaning of the cartoon?
3. Whom does the person in the cartoon represent?
4. What is the person doing?
5. What do the subject's thoughts suggest about the task faced by those involved in planning the new nation's government?
6. What limits are placed on First Amendment rights? Why are these rights limited?

The Princeton Review

Standardized Test Practice

DIRECTIONS: Use the political cartoon and your knowledge of social studies to answer the following questions on a separate sheet of paper.

1. The most appropriate title for the cartoon is
   - **A** Limits on Government.
   - **B** Parliament at Work.
   - **C** Limiting Rights.
   - **D** Unlimited Government.
2. The sources of our rights as citizens of the United States come from all of the following EXCEPT
   - **F** the will of the president.
   - **G** the Declaration of Independence and the U.S. Constitution.
   - **H** laws enacted by Congress.
   - **J** the interpretation of laws by the courts.

The Princeton Review

Standardized Test Practice Answers:

1. C
Test-Taking Strategy: Encourage students to look for clues. Words found in the cartoon show that the man is trying to grant limited rights.

2. F
Test-Taking Strategy: This question requires students to understand the sources of our rights. Since our government is a limited one, the president must also obey the laws.

Test Practice Lesson 7

Interpreting a Circle Graph

"E pluribus unum" is a Latin phrase found on United States coins. It means "Out of many, one." The United States is sometimes called a "nation of immigrants." Unless you are a Native American, your ancestors came to America within the last 500 years.

Groups of people who share a common culture, language, or history are referred to as ethnic groups. American neighborhoods include many different ethnic groups. The circle graph on this page shows the major ethnic groups in the United States.

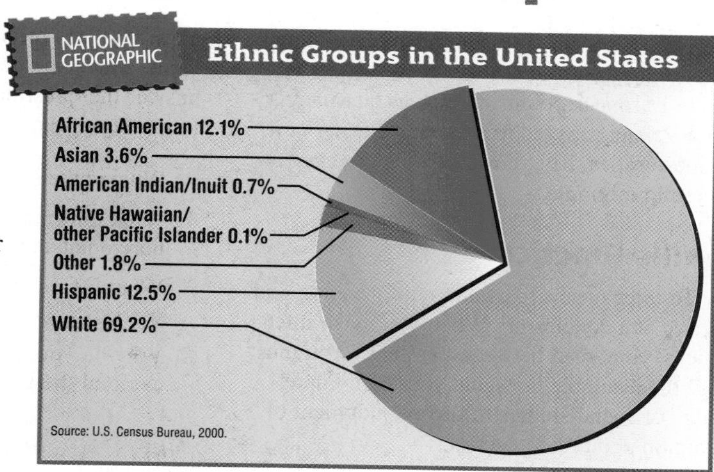

Skills Practice

A circle graph shows percentages of a total quantity. Each part, or slice, of the graph represents a part of the total quantity. To read a circle graph, first read the title. Then study the labels to find out what each part represents. Compare the sizes of the circle slices. Study the circle graph and answer the questions that follow on a separate sheet of paper.

1. What information does this circle graph present?
2. Which ethnic group includes the largest percentage of Americans?
3. Which groups represent less than 1 percent of the people in the United States?
4. What percentage of the United States population is represented by African Americans?
5. The smallest ethnic groups have lived in the United States the longest. What are these ethnic groups?

The Princeton Review

Standardized Test Practice

DIRECTIONS: Use the graph and your knowledge of social studies to answer the following questions on a separate sheet of paper.

1. Which group's population is about three times greater than the number of Asians and Native Hawaiians/Pacific Islanders?
   - **A** African American
   - **B** White
   - **C** American Indian/Inuit
   - **D** Hispanic
2. How does the Hispanic population compare to the African American population of the United States?
   - **F** It is greater than the African American population.
   - **G** It is the smallest segment of the United States population.
   - **H** It is less than half the size of the African American population.
   - **J** It is slightly less than the African American population.

TEACH

Ask students to name a custom practiced in the United States that originated in another country. Examples include celebrations, types of food, music, dance, or other cultural practices. Lead a discussion focusing on the diverse cultural heritages of Americans. Explain to students that the practice of adopting the cultural traits of another group is called cultural borrowing.

Explain to students that a circle graph is like a sliced pie; often it is even called a pie chart. Circle graphs show proportions rather than absolute amounts. They often are used when the information being compared totals 100 percent.

Skills Practice Answers:

1. ethnic groups in the United States
2. White
3. American Indian/Inuit and Native Hawaiian/other Pacific Islander
4. 12.1 percent
5. American Indian/Inuit and Native Hawaiian/other Pacific Islander

Standardized Test Practice Answers:

1. A

Test-Taking Strategy: Remind students to eliminate answers that don't make sense. Then students should multiply the percentage of Asians, Native Hawaiians, and Pacific Islanders by three to come up with the correct answer.

2. F

Test-Taking Strategy: To answer this question, students must compare two slices of the total circle.

TEACH

To help students become comfortable with making inferences and drawing conclusions, write the following sports page headline on the board: "Another Year of Futility—Hawks Fail to Make the Playoffs Again!" Ask students what information about the team they can draw from the headline. *(Most students will infer that it has been a long time since the Hawks had a successful season.)* Then have students suggest how the writer might feel about the situation. (*Students may suggest that the writer seems upset or frustrated.*) Then point out that students have just been drawing inferences and conclusions.

Skills Practice Answers:

1. immigration to the United States from 1820 to 1860
2. years (from 1820 to 1860)
3. number of immigrants
4. Students' answers will vary. Students may mention push and pull factors that push people out of their homelands to the U.S. and opportunities in the U.S. that pull people to this country.

Test Practice Lesson 8

Drawing Inferences and Conclusions

During the mid-nineteenth century, immigration to the United States increased. People from European countries such as Germany and Ireland traveled to America seeking new opportunities. Life, however, was not easy for these immigrants.

Skills Practice

To infer means to evaluate information and arrive at a conclusion. When you make inferences, you "read between the lines." You must use the available facts and your own knowledge of social studies to form a judgment or opinion about the material.

Line graphs are a way of showing numbers visually. They are often used to compare changes over time. Sometimes a graph has more than one line. The lines show different quantities of a related topic. To analyze a line graph read the title and the information on the horizontal and vertical axes. Use this information to draw conclusions. Study the graph on this page and answer the questions that follow on a separate sheet of paper.

1. What is the subject of the line graph?
2. What information is shown on the horizontal axis?
3. What information is shown on the vertical axis?
4. Why do you think these immigrants came to the United States?

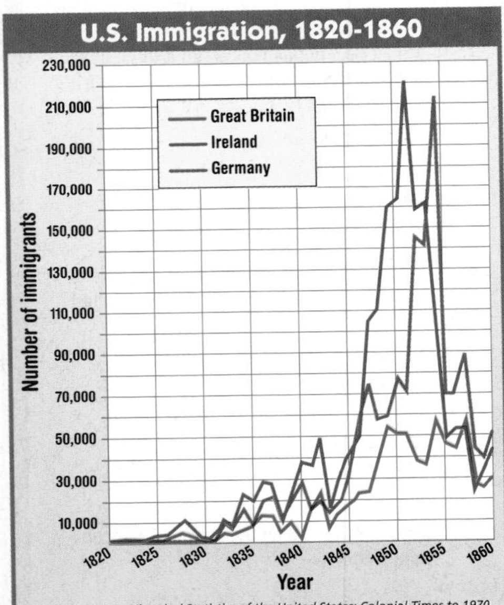

Source: *Historical Statistics of the United States: Colonial Times to 1970.*

Standardized Test Practice

DIRECTIONS: Use the line graph and your knowledge of social studies to answer the following questions on a separate sheet of paper.

1. The country that provided the most immigrants to the United States between the years 1820 and 1860 was
   A Great Britain.
   B Ireland.
   C Germany.
   D France.
2. In about what year did the number of German immigrants to the United States reach a peak?
   F 1845
   G 1852
   H 1855
   J 1860
3. Irish migration to the United States increased in the mid-1800s because of
   A a terrible potato famine in Ireland.
   B the failure of a German revolution in 1848.
   C the nativist movement.
   D the availability of low-paying factory jobs.

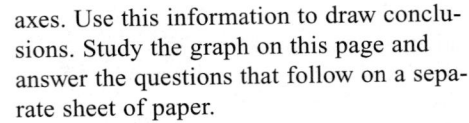

Standardized Test Practice Answers:

1. B
Test-Taking Strategy: Remind students to check each answer choice against the graph to eliminate wrong answers.
2. H
Test-Taking Strategy: Students must first find the line that represents Germany and estimate the year of the peak.
3. A
Test-Taking Strategy: Students must make an inference. Ask: What would force people from Ireland to leave their country?

Comparing Data

The world's earliest civilizations developed more than 6,000 years ago. The discovery of farming led to the rise of ancient cities in Mesopotamia and the Nile River valley. These early cities shared one important characteristic—they each arose near waterways. Since water was the easiest way to transport goods, the settlements became centers of trade.

Since then cities have grown all over the world. Every 10 years, the United States Census Bureau collects data to determine the population of the United States. (A census is an official count of people living in an area.) The first census was conducted in 1790. At that time, there were 3.9 million people in the 13 original states. The most recent census occurred in 2000. The results of that census showed that more than 280 million people reside in the 50 states that make up our nation.

POPULATION OF FIVE LARGEST U.S. CITIES, 1790

City	Number of People
New York City	33,131
Philadelphia	28,522
Boston	18,320
Charleston	16,359
Baltimore	13,503

POPULATION OF FIVE LARGEST U.S. CITIES, 2000*

City	Number of People
New York City	8,008,278
Los Angeles	3,694,820
Chicago	2,896,016
Houston	1,953,631
Philadelphia	1,517,550

*Numbers do not include metropolitan areas.

Skills Practice

The charts on this page show populations of the five most populous cities in the United States during different time periods. When comparing information on charts be sure to read the titles and headings to define the data being compared. Study the charts and answer the questions below on a separate sheet of paper.

1. Which U.S. city had the greatest population in 1790?
2. Which U.S. city had the greatest population in 2000?
3. What was the population of Philadelphia in 1790?
4. What was Philadelphia's population in 2000?
5. Which city had the third-largest population in 1790?
6. Which cities are on both lists?

Standardized Test Practice

DIRECTIONS: Use the charts and your knowledge of social studies to answer the following questions on a separate sheet of paper.

1. One inference that can be made from the charts is that the most populous cities in the United States
   - A have good weather.
   - B were founded early in our nation's history.
   - C are port cities.
   - D are in the eastern United States.
2. In 1790 the major cities of the United States were all
   - F larger than 20,000 people.
   - G located in the East.
   - H Northern cities.
   - J founded for religious reasons.

TEACH

Tell students the following: Determining populations is necessary for many reasons. For example, it is important to know the number of students in schools and school districts. The student population in each school helps officials decide how many teachers to hire. It also determines the amount of money districts receive. Find the total population of students in your school. What percentage of total students makes up each grade level? Create a circle graph that shows this information. *(Students should find the number of students in each grade and convert those numbers to percentages before drawing slices of the circle graph. Check graphs for accuracy.)*

Skills Practice Answers:

1. New York City
2. New York City
3. 28,522
4. 1,517,550
5. Boston
6. New York City, Philadelphia

Standardized Test Practice Answers:

1. C

Test-Taking Strategy: To answer this question students must make an inference, or "read between the lines." Encourage students to read each answer choice, eliminating ones that don't make sense.

2. G

Test-Taking Strategy: To answer this question students must examine the map carefully, and one by one, eliminate incorrect answer choices.

TEACH

Have students divide a piece of paper into two columns entitled "Wants" and "Needs." Ask students to list their wants and needs under the appropriate heading. Explain to students that balancing our wants and needs helps us to make decisions about our individual economic situations. Countries of the world use different methods to meet the economic needs of their people.

Tell students that categorizing information helps them deal with large quantities of information in an understandable way.

Skills Practice Answers:

1. command economic system
2. traditional economic system
3. Students should create a circle graph with the following slices: Manufacturing, 22 percent; Agriculture, 2 percent; Mining, 1 percent; Service and Information Industries, 75 percent. Industries related to farming make up 2 percent of the U.S. economy.

Test Practice Lesson 10

Categorizing and Analyzing Information

Economic systems describe the ways in which societies produce and distribute goods and services. Early societies, such as Mesopotamia, used bartering as their system of trade. In the seventeenth and eighteenth centuries, European countries practiced mercantilism in which colonies provided wealth to their parent countries. Great Britain used this idea to gain wealth from its North American colonies. The economy of the United States is based on the principle of free enterprise. Americans have the freedom to own businesses with limited interference from the government.

Because Americans are employed in a variety of industries, our economy is the largest and among the most diverse in the world. The U.S. economy includes the following parts:

- Manufacturing makes up 22 percent of the economy.
- Agriculture makes up 2 percent of the economy.
- Mining makes up 1 percent of the economy.
- Service and information industries make up 75 percent of the economy.

Skills Practice

Grouping information into categories is one way of making the information easier to understand. The economic systems of today's world can be classified into four basic groups. Study the chart on this page and answer the questions that follow on a separate sheet of paper.

1. Under which economic system does the government have the most control?
2. Under which system would people be most likely to have the same job as their parents?
3. Use the information about the U.S. economy on this page to create a circle graph. Then answer this question: Industries related to farming represent what percentage of the U.S. economy?

WORLD ECONOMIC SYSTEMS

Traditional	Command	Market	Mixed
Based on customs	Government controls production, prices, and wages	Individuals control production, prices, and wages	Individuals control some aspects of economy
Trades are passed down through generations	Communism; Government owns businesses	Free enterprise; Individuals own businesses	Government regulates selected industries and restricts others

Standardized Test Practice

DIRECTIONS: Use the chart and your knowledge of social studies to answer the following questions on a separate sheet of paper.

1. Which economic system provides individuals with the most economic freedom?
   - **A** traditional
   - **B** command
   - **C** market
   - **D** mixed
2. The United States has this type of economic system.
   - **F** traditional
   - **G** command
   - **H** market
   - **J** mixed

Standardized Test Practice Answers:

1. C
Test-Taking Strategy: Students should look for key words in the question. Encourage students to determine whether any of the key words are used on the chart. Under which category do they appear?

2. J
Test-Taking Strategy: Students should recall that the United States has a mixed economy. Although the economy is based on free enterprise, the government can step in when needed to regulate industry.

Sequencing Events

The free enterprise economic system of the United States has encouraged Americans to invent and produce new technology throughout the history of our nation. Using its rich natural and human resources, Americans are continually advancing the economy through technology. The tremendous economic growth of the United States at certain times in history, such as after the Civil War, resulted from foundations laid early in the nation's history and affects the growth of the United States economy today.

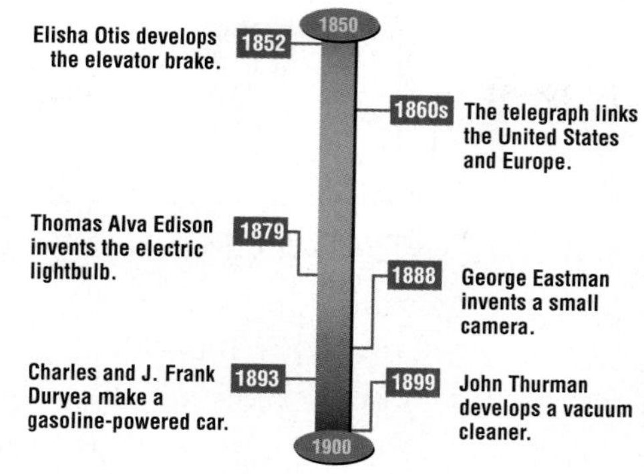
1850
1852 Elisha Otis develops the elevator brake.
1860s The telegraph links the United States and Europe.
1879 Thomas Alva Edison invents the electric lightbulb.
1888 George Eastman invents a small camera.
1893 Charles and J. Frank Duryea make a gasoline-powered car.
1899 John Thurman develops a vacuum cleaner.
1900

Skills Practice

Sequencing information involves placing facts in the order in which they occurred. Listed below are technological advances that occurred at different times in history, transforming the world economy. Find the date of each invention by studying the time line on page 23 of your textbook. On a separate sheet of paper take notes by writing the date beside a brief description of each invention. Then sequence the events by rewriting them in the correct order.

• Telephone	• Airplane
• Cellular phone	• Automobile
• Steamboat	• Steam locomotive
• Space shuttle	• Internet
• Radio	• Television

In the late 1800s, innovations in technology and new business combinations helped the United States grow into an industrial power. By the year 1900, the United States's industrial production was the greatest around the world.

Read the time line on this page. Determine the subject of the time line and summarize it in a few words. Then write a title for the time line on a separate sheet of paper.

The Princeton Review

Standardized Test Practice

DIRECTIONS: Use the events you have sequenced and your knowledge of social studies to answer the following questions on a separate sheet of paper.

1. Which of the following inventions occurred last?
   A steam locomotive
   B telephone
   C airplane
   D steamboat

2. During the late 1700s, 1800s, and early 1900s, new inventions and developments in the area of transportation, such as the steamboat, steam locomotive, and airplane, resulted in
   F increased poverty among urban Americans.
   G an end to westward migration.
   H the creation of new markets for trade.
   J rural growth.

3. In the early 1800s steamboats dramatically improved the transport of goods and passengers
   A along major roads.
   B along major inland rivers.
   C between the Americas and Africa.
   D in the West.

Standardized Test Skills Handbook

TEACH

Tell students it is easier to understand the order of events and their relationship to one another if the events are sequenced, or placed in order, on a time line.

Skills Practice Answers: Students' descriptions of each invention may vary. Check answers for accuracy.

1. 1787 — Steamboat
2. 1803 — Steam locomotive
3. 1876 — Telephone
4. 1885 — Automobile
5. 1903 — Airplane
6. 1920 — Radio
7. 1940 — Television
8. 1981 — Space shuttle
9. 1983 — Cellular phone
10. 1986 — Internet

Possible titles include: The Growth of Industry in the United States; The Growth of Technology in the United States, and Inventions and Developments in the U.S. (1860–1908).

Standardized Test Practice Answers:

1. C
Test-Taking Strategy: Students will have to have correctly sequenced the events to answer this question correctly.

2. H
Test-Taking Strategy: Students should eliminate answers they know are incorrect or that do not make sense.

3. B
Test-Taking Strategy: Students should recall when steamboats were invented and why they were important.

Nations of the World

DATABANK

Today we are learning to understand the global, connected world in which we live. Technological advances have made global communication and interaction much easier. We must interact with many different countries—more than at any other time in the world. Every country of the world has its own identity, culture, economy and government. This information about each country has been charted here for you. Using the chart will make it easier for you to compare and contrast the information.

	GOVERNMENT		ECONOMICS			SOCIAL & CULTURAL		
COUNTRY	Type of Government	Date Founded	*GNP Ranking	GNP Per Capita	Currency	Literacy	**Infant Mortality	Religion
Afghanistan	Religious Regime	1919	101st	$270	Afghani	32%	151	Muslim
Albania	Democracy	1912	131st	$760	Leke	85%	26	Muslim, Catholic
Algeria	Military Republic	1962	52nd	$1,500	Dinar	60%	32	Muslim
Andorra	Parliamentary Democracy	1278	155th	$15,600	Fr. Franc, Sp. Peseta	99%	4	Catholic
Angola	Multiparty Democracy	1975	126th	$260	Kwanzaa	45%	186	Indigenous, Catholic, Protestant
Antarctica	n/a	1961	n/a	n/a	n/a	100%	n/a	n/a
Antigua & Barbuda	Parliamentary Democracy	1981	166th	$7,380	E.C. Dollar	95%	17	Protestant, Catholic
Argentina	Republic	1816	17th	$8,950	Argentine Peso	96.5%	22	Catholic
Armenia	Republic	1991	137th	$560	Dram	99%	15	Orthodox
Australia	Democracy	1901	14th	$20,650	Australian Dollar	99%	5	Catholic, Anglican

*Gross National Product

**deaths/1,000 live births

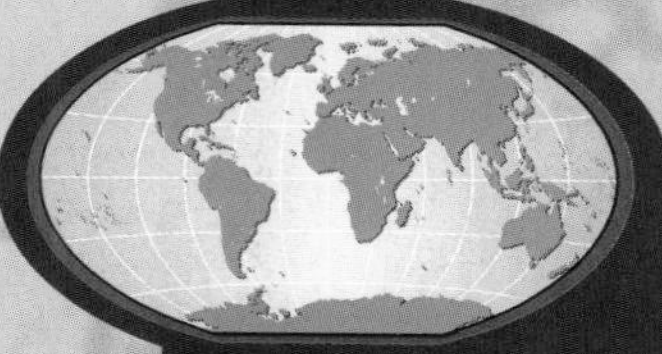

COUNTRY	 GOVERNMENT: Type of Government	Date Founded	 ECONOMICS: *GNP Ranking	GNP Per Capita	Currency	 SOCIAL & CULTURAL: Literacy	**Infant Mortality	Religion
Austria	Federal Republic	1918	22nd	$27,920	Austrian Schilling	99%	5	Catholic
Azerbaijan	Republic	1991	118th	$510	Manat	96%	20	Muslim
Bahamas	Commonwealth	1973	124th	$11,940	Bahamian Dollar	96%	19	Protestant, Catholic
Bahrain	Monarchy	1971	104th	$7,800	Bahrain Dinar	86%	9	Muslim
Bangladesh	Republic	1971	51st	$360	Taka	40%	14	Muslim, Hindu
Barbados	Parliamentary Democracy	1966	145th	$6,560	Barbados Dollar	98%	14	Protestant
Belarus	Republic	1991	61st	$2,150	Belarus Rouble	99%	12	Eastern Orthodox
Belgium	Parliamentary Democracy	1830	19th	$26,730	Belgian Franc	99%	6	Catholic, Protestant
Belize	Parliamentary Democracy	1981	162nd	$2,670	Belizean Dollar	75%	32	Catholic, Protestant
Benin	Republic	1960	133rd	$380	CFA Franc	34%	88	Indigenous, Christian, Muslim
Bhutan	Monarchy	1656	172nd	$430	Ngultrum	44%	63	Buddhist, Hindu
Bolivia	Republic	1825	91st	$970	Boliviano	84%	66	Catholic
Bosnia & Herzogovina	Democracy	1992	160th	$288	Maraka	93%	13	Muslim, Catholic, Orthodox
Botswana	Republic	1966	105th	$3,310	Pula	74%	58	Indigenous, Christian
Brazil	Federal Republic	1822	8th	$4,790	Real	84%	34	Catholic
Brunei	Constitutional Sultanate	1984	116th	$14,240	Brunei Dollar	90%	9	Muslim, Buddhist
Bulgaria	Republic	1908	82nd	$1,170	Lev	98%	9	Orthodox, Muslim
Burkina Faso	Parliamentary	1960	130th	$250	CFA Franc	21%	99	Traditional, Muslim
Burma	Military Regime	1948	41st	$1,500	Kyat	83.6%	79	Buddhist
Burundi	Republic	1962	157th	$140	Burundi Franc	45%	119	Indigenous, Catholic
Cambodia	Federal Democracy	1953	125th	$300	Riel	66%	105	Theravada Buddhism

*Gross National Product

**deaths/1,000 live births

GOVERNMENT | ECONOMICS | SOCIAL & CULTURAL

Nations of the World DATABANK

COUNTRY	Type of Government	Date Founded	*GNP Ranking	GNP Per Capita	Currency	Literacy	**Infant Mortality	Religion
Cameroon	Unitary Republic	1960	86th	$620	CFA Franc	72%	52	Indigenous, Christian, Muslim
Canada	Parliamentary Democracy	1867	9th	$19,640	Canadian Dollar	99%	6	Catholic, Protestant
Cape Verde	Republic	1975	169th	$1,090	C.V. Escudo	71%	56	Catholic, Protestant
Central African Republic	Republic	1960	152nd	$320	CFA Franc	42%	98	Indigenous, Catholic, Protestant, Muslim
Chad	Republic	1960	147th	$230	CFA Franc	50%	100	Muslim, Christian, Indigenous
Chile	Republic	1818	43rd	$4,820	Chilean Peso	95%	11	Catholic, Protestant
China	Communist State	1949	7th	$860	Yuan	84%	32	Officially Atheist, Buddhist, Taoist
Colombia	Republic	1819	39th	$2,180	Col. Peso	91%	24	Catholic
Comoros	Independent Republic	1975	181st	$400	Comoros Franc	55%	65	Catholic, Muslim
Congo, Democratic Republic	Dictatorship	1960	103rd	$110	Congolese Franc	77%	66	Indigenous, Catholic, Protestant
Congo, Republic	Republic	1960	144th	$670	CFA Franc	77%	90	Catholic, Protestant, Kimbanguist
Costa Rica	Democratic Republic	1838	85th	$2,680	Colones	95%	12	Catholic
Croatia	Parliamentary Democracy	1991	69th	$4,060	Kuna	98%	9	Catholic, Orthodox
Cuba	Communist State	1902	72nd	$1,650	Cuban Peso	96%	7	Catholic
Cyprus	Republic	1960	92nd	$9,400	Cyprus Pound	96%	8	Christian, Muslim
Czech Republic	Parliamentary Democracy	1993	48th	$5,240	Koruny	99%	6	Catholic, Atheist
Denmark	Constitutional Monarchy	1950	25th	$38,890	Kroner	99%	6	Lutheran
Djibouti	Republic	1977	167th	$750	Djib. Franc	49%	106	Muslim
Dominica	Parliamentary Democracy	1978	179th	$3,040	E. Car. Dollar	94%	16	Catholic, Protestant
Dominican Republic	Republic	1865	76th	$1,750	Dom. Rep. Peso	83%	40	Catholic
Ecuador	Republic	1830	71st	$1,570	Sucre	91%	33	Catholic

*Gross National Product

**deaths/1,000 live births

COUNTRY	GOVERNMENT: Type of Government	GOVERNMENT: Date Founded	ECONOMICS: *GNP Ranking	ECONOMICS: GNP Per Capita	ECONOMICS: Currency	SOCIAL & CULTURAL: Literacy	SOCIAL & CULTURAL: **Infant Mortality	SOCIAL & CULTURAL: Religion
Egypt	Republic	1936	42nd	$1,200	Egyp. Pound	53%	51	Muslim
El Salvador	Republic	1841	78th	$1,810	Colones	77%	32	Catholic, Protestant
Equatorial Guinea	New Democracy	1968	168th	$1,060	CFA Franc	80%	108	Catholic
Eritrea	New Democracy	1993	158th	$230	Nafka	80%	108	Christian, Muslim
Estonia	Parliamentary Democracy	1991	107th	$3,360	Kroon	99%	10	Protestant
Ethiopia	Federal Republic	1896	99th	$110	Birr	35%	107	Muslim, Orthodox, Animist
Fiji	Republic	1970	139th	$2,460	Fiji Dollar	92%	18	Hindu, Protestant
Finland	Republic	1917	31st	$24,790	Markka	99%	4	Evangelical Lutheran
France	Republic	1919	4th	$26,300	Franc	99%	5	Catholic
Gabon	Republic	1960	110th	$4,120	CFA Franc	66%	87	Christian
Gambia	Republic	1965	170th	$340	Dalasi	33%	78	Muslim
Georgia	Republic	1991	111th	$860	Lari	99%	17	Orthodox, Muslim
Germany	Federal Republic	1871	3rd	$28,280	Deutsche Mark	99%	5	Protestant, Catholic
Ghana	Democracy	1957	95th	$390	Cedis	66%	66	Christian, Muslim, Indigenous
Greece	Republic	1829	32nd	$11,640	Drachma	97%	7	Greek Orthodox
Grenada	Parliamentary Democracy	1974	174th	$3,140	E. Car. Dollar	96%	7	Catholic, Protestant, Anglican
Guatemala	Republic	1838	74th	$1,580	Quetzales	67%	42	Catholic, Protestant
Guinea	Republic	1958	119th	$550	Guinea Franc	38%	120	Muslim
Guinea-Bissau	Republic	1974	176th	$230	Guinea Peso	34%	130	Indigenous, Muslim
Guyana	Republic	1966	162nd	$800	Guy. Dollar	98%	58	Christian, Hindu
Haiti	Republic	1804	128th	$380	Gourdes	46%	58	Catholic, Protestant

*Gross National Product

**deaths/1,000 live births

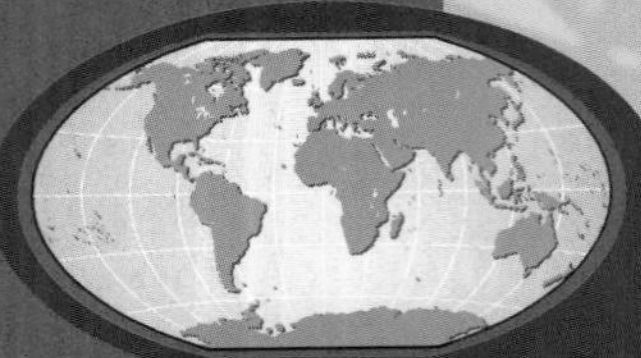

COUNTRY	GOVERNMENT: Type of Government	GOVERNMENT: Date Founded	ECONOMICS: *GNP Ranking	ECONOMICS: GNP Per Capita	ECONOMICS: Currency	SOCIAL & CULTURAL: Literacy	SOCIAL & CULTURAL: **Infant Mortality	SOCIAL & CULTURAL: Religion
Honduras	Republic	1838	113th	$740	Lempira	71%	36	Catholic
Hungary	Republic	1918	50th	$4,510	Forint	99%	10	Catholic, Protestant
Iceland	Constitutional Republic	1944	94th	$26,580	Ic. Krona	99%	6	Evangelical Lutheran
India	Federal Republic	1947	15th	$370	Ind. Rupee	54%	71	Hindu, Muslim
Indonesia	Republic	1949	23rd	$1,110	Rupiah	85%	47	Muslim
Iran	Religious Regime	1502	34th	$1,780	Ir. Rial	73%	32	Muslim
Iraq	Dictatorship	1932	65th	$950	Ir. Dinar	58%	112	Muslim
Ireland	Republic	1922	44th	$17,790	Punt	99%	5	Catholic
Israel	Republic	1948	37th	$16,180	Shekel	95%	7	Jewish, Muslim
Italy	Republic	1870	6th	$20,170	Lira	98%	5	Catholic
Ivory Coast	Republic	1960	81st	$710	CFA Franc	43%	87	Indigenous, Muslim, Christian
Jamaica	Parliamentary Democracy	1962	117th	$1,550	Jamaican Dollar	86%	12	Protestant
Japan	Constitutional Monarchy	1600	2nd	$38,160	Yen	99%	4	Shinto, Buddhist
Jordan	Constitutional Monarchy	1946	96th	$1,520	Jordanian Dinar	87%	29	Muslim
Kazakhstan	Republic	1991	62nd	$1,350	Tenge	99%	24	Muslim, Orthodox
Kenya	Republic	1963	83rd	$340	Kenya Shilling	79%	74	Protestant, Catholic, Indigenous
Kiribati	Republic	1979	188th	$910	Australian Dollar	98%	60	Catholic, Protestant
Korea, North	Communist State	1948	64th	$1,390	Won	95%	56	Buddhist, Confucian
Korea, South	Republic	1948	11th	$10,550	Won	97%	9	Buddhist, Protestant, Catholic
Kuwait	Constitutional Monarchy	1961	58th	$17,390	Kuwaiti Dollar	80%	12	Muslim
Kyrgyzstan	Republic	1991	134th	$480	Som	97%	26	Muslim, Orthodox

*Gross National Product

**deaths/1,000 live births

COUNTRY	Type of Government	Date Founded	*GNP Ranking	GNP Per Capita	Currency	Literacy	**Infant Mortality	Religion
Laos	Communist State	1953	142nd	$400	New Kip	59%	96	Buddhist, Animist
Latvia	Parliamentary Democracy	1991	100th	$2,430	Lati	99%	15	Lutheran, Catholic, Russian Orthodox
Lebanon	Republic	1944	77th	$3,350	Leb. Pound	84%	28	Muslim, Christian
Lesotho	Constitutional Monarchy	1966	150th	$680	Maloti	82%	93	Christian, Indigenous
Liberia	Republic	1847	154th	$330	Liberian Dollar	38%	116	Indigenous, Muslim, Christian
Libya	Dictatorship	1951	57th	$5,220	Libyan Dinar	77%	24	Muslim
Liechtenstein	Constitutional Monarchy	1719	151st	$40,000	Swiss Franc	99%	24	Catholic
Lithuania	Parliamentary Democracy	1991	88th	$2,260	Lita	99%	10	Catholic
Luxembourg	Constitutional Monarchy	1867	70th	$45,360	Lux. Franc	99%	5	Catholic
Macedonia	Democracy	1991	135th	$1,100	Mac. Denar	94%	16	Orthodox, Muslim
Madagascar	Republic	1960	120th	$250	Malagasy Franc	47%	94	Indigenous, Christian
Malawi	Democracy	1964	136th	$210	Kwacha	58%	135	Protestant, Catholic, Muslim
Malaysia	Constitutional Monarchy	1963	36th	$4,530	Ringgit	86%	11	Muslim, Buddhist, Chinese Faiths
Maldives	Republic	1965	173rd	$1,180	Rufiyaa	96%	32	Muslim
Mali	Republic	1960	129th	$260	CFA Franc	36%	118	Muslim
Malta	Parliamentary Democracy	1964	122nd	$9,330	Maltese Lira	91%	7	Catholic
Marshall Island	Constitutional Republic	1986	185th	$1,610	U.S. Dollar	91%	46	Protestant
Mauritania	Republic	1960	153rd	$440	Ouguiyas	38%	92	Muslim
Mauritius	Parliamentary Democracy	1968	112th	$3,870	Mauritian Rupee	83%	92	Hindu, Catholic, Muslim
Mexico	Federal Republic	1836	16th	$3,700	Mexican Peso	90%	31	Catholic
Micronesia	Constitutional Federation	1986	180th	$1,920	U.S. Dollar	89%	30	Catholic, Protestant

*Gross National Product

**deaths/1,000 live births

COUNTRY	GOVERNMENT: Type of Government	GOVERNMENT: Date Founded	ECONOMICS: *GNP Ranking	ECONOMICS: GNP Per Capita	ECONOMICS: Currency	SOCIAL & CULTURAL: Literacy	SOCIAL & CULTURAL: **Infant Mortality	SOCIAL & CULTURAL: Religion
Moldova	Republic	1991	140th	$460	Leu	98%	20	Orthodox
Monaco	Constitutional Monarchy	1861	106th	$11,000	French Franc	99%	7	Catholic
Mongolia	Republic	1924	156th	$390	Tughrik	84%	52	Buddhist
Morocco	Constitutional Monarchy	1956	54th	$1,260	Dirham	46%	51	Muslim
Mozambique	Republic	1975	132nd	$140	Metical	41%	135	Indigenous, Christian, Muslim
Namibia	Republic	1990	123rd	$2,110	Namibian Dollar	80%	65	Christian, Indigenous
Nauru	Republic	1968	187th	$7,270	Aus. Dollar	99%	41	Protestant, Catholic
Nepal	Parliamentary Democracy	1769	108th	$220	Nepalese Rupee	38%	83	Hindu
Netherlands	Constitutional Monarchy	1815	12th	$25,830	Guilder	99%	5	Catholic, Protestant
New Zealand	Parliamentary Democracy	1926	47th	$15,830	N. Z. Dollar	99%	7	Protestant, Catholic
Nicaragua	Republic	1838	143rd	$410	Cordobas Oro	83%	43	Catholic
Niger	Republic	1960	141st	$200	CFA Franc	14%	118	Muslim
Nigeria	New Republic	1960	55th	$280	Naira	60%	77	Muslim, Christian, Indigenous
Norway	Constitutional Monarchy	1905	27th	$36,100	Norwegian Krone	99%	4	Evangelical Lutheran
Oman	Monarchy	1951	79th	$4,820	Omani Rial	67%	18	Muslim, Hindu
Pakistan	Federal Republic	1947	45th	$500	Pakistani Repee	41%	95	Muslim
Palau	Constitutional Republic	1994	186th	$5,000	U.S. Dollar	92%	25	Christian, Indigenous
Panama	Constitutional Republic	1903	92nd	$2,670	Balboa	91%	21	Catholic, Protestant
Papua New Guinea	Parliamentary Democracy	1975	115th	$930	Kina	74%	61	Indigenous, Catholic, Protestant
Paraguay	Republic	1811	80th	$200	Guaranies	92%	29	Catholic, Protestant
Peru	Republic	1824	46th	$2,610	New Sol	89%	40	Catholic

*Gross National Product

**deaths/1,000 live births

COUNTRY	Type of Government	Date Founded	*GNP Ranking	GNP Per Capita	Currency	Literacy	**Infant Mortality	Religion
Philippines	Republic	1946	38th	$1,200	Ph. Peso	95%	35	Catholic
Poland	Democratic State	1918	29th	$3,590	Zloty	99%	10	Catholic
Portugal	Parliamentary Democracy	1640	33rd	$11,010	Escudo	91%	6	Catholic
Qatar	Monarchy	1971	93rd	$11,600	Qatar Rial	80%	32	Muslim
Romania	Republic	1878	56th	$1,410	Lei	98%	22	Romanian Orthodox
Russian Federation	Federation	1991	13th	$2,680	Rouble	99%	17	Russian Orthodox
Rwanda	Republic	1962	146th	$210	R. Franc	63%	124	Catholic, Protestant, Indigenous
St. Kitts & Nevis	Constitutional Monarchy	1983	177th	$6,260	E. Car. Dollar	90%	22	Protestant, Catholic
St. Lucia	Constitutional Monarchy	1979	163rd	$3,510	E. Car. Dollar	82%	16	Catholic, Protestant
St. Vincent & the Grenadines	Constitutional Monarchy	1979	175th	$2,420	E. Car. Dollar	82%	18	Protestant, Catholic
Samoa	Constitutional Monarchy	1962	182nd	$1,140	Tala	98%	22	Christian
San Marino	Republic	301	183rd	$7,830	Italian Lira	96%	6	Catholic
São Tome & Principé	Republic	1975	189th	$290	Dobra	75%	50	Catholic, Protestant
Saudi Arabia	Monarchy	1932	187th	$7,150	Saudi Riyal	73%	21	Muslim
Senegal	Republic	1960	109th	$540	CFA Franc	35%	70	Muslim
Seychelles	Republic	1976	165th	$6,910	S. Rupee	84%	15	Catholic
Sierra Leone	Democracy	1961	161st	$160	Leone	33%	170	Muslim, Indigenous, Christian
Singapore	Commonwealth	1965	35th	$32,810	Singapore Dollar	91%	4	Buddhist, Muslim
Slovakia	Parliamentary Democracy	1993	66th	$3,680	Koruna	99%	9	Catholic, Protestant
Slovenia	Parliamentary Democracy	1991	67th	$9,840	Tolar	99%	5	Catholic
Solomon Islands	Parliamentary Democracy	1978	171st	$870	Solomon Is.Dollar	62%	23	Catholic, Protestant

*Gross National Product

**deaths/1,000 live births

COUNTRY	GOVERNMENT: Type of Government	GOVERNMENT: Date Founded	ECONOMICS: *GNP Ranking	ECONOMICS: GNP Per Capita	ECONOMICS: Currency	SOCIAL & CULTURAL: Literacy	SOCIAL & CULTURAL: **Infant Mortality	SOCIAL & CULTURAL: Religion
Somalia	None	1960	159th	$100	Somali Shilling	24%	9	Muslim
South Africa	Republic	1934	30th	$3,210	Rand	84%	48	Christian, Indigenous
Spain	Constitutional Monarchy	1492	10th	$14,490	Spanish Peseta	97%	16	Catholic
Sri Lanka	Republic	1948	75th	$800	Sri Lanka Rupee	91%	14	Buddhist, Hindu
Sudan	New Republic	1956	90th	$290	Sudanese Dinar	53%	71	Muslim, Indigenous
Suriname	Republic	1975	164th	$1,320	S. Guilder	94%	29	Hindu, Muslim, Catholic, Protestant
Swaziland	Monarchy	1968	149th	$1,520	Lilangeni	78%	65	Christian, Indigenous
Sweden	Constitutional Monarchy	1809	21st	$26,210	Swedish Krona	99%	4	Evangelical Lutheran
Switzerland	Federal Republic	1291	18th	$26,210	Swiss Franc	99%	5	Catholic, Protestant
Syria	Military Republic	1046	73rd	$1,120	Syrian Pound	72%	31	Muslim, Christian
Taiwan	Democracy	1949	20th	$10,320	Taiwanese Dollar	94%	6	Buddhist, Confucian, Taoist
Tajikstan	Republic	1991	138th	$330	Taj. Rouble	99%	30	Muslim
Tanzania	Republic	1961	97th	$210	T. Shilling	72%	85	Muslim, Christian
Thailand	Constitutional Monarchy	1782	26th	$2,740	Baht	95%	33	Buddhist
Togo	New Democracy	1960	148th	$340	CFA Franc	53%	86	Indigenous, Muslim, Christian
Tonga	Constitutional Monarchy	1970	184th	$1,810	Pa'anga	99%	22	Protestant, Catholic
Trinidad & Tobago	Parliamentary Democracy	1962	102nd	$4,250	T&T Dollar	98%	12	Catholic, Protestant, Hindu
Tunisia	Republic	1956	68th	$2,110	T. Dinar	67%	30	Muslim
Turkey	Republic	1923	24th	$3,130	Turkish Lira	86%	40	Muslim
Turkmenistan	Republic	1991	127th	$640	Manat	98%	12	Muslim, Eastern Orthodox
Tuvalu	Constitutional Monarchy	1978	190th	$330	Australian Dollar	95%	40	Congregationalist

*Gross National Product

**deaths/1,000 live births

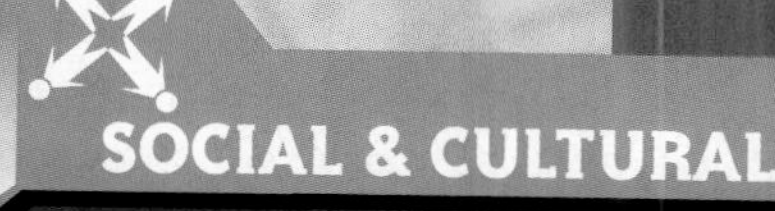

COUNTRY	Type of Government	Date Founded	*GNP Ranking	GNP Per Capita	Currency	Literacy	**Infant Mortality	Religion
Uganda	Republic	1962	98th	$330	New Uga. Shilling	64%	90	Catholic, Protestant, Muslim, Indigenous
Ukraine	Republic	1991	49th	$1,335	Hryvna	99%	14	Ukranian Orthodox
United Arab Emirates	Federation	1971	53rd	$17,400	UA.E. Dirham	75%	8	Muslim
United Kingdom	Constitutional Monarchy	1707	5th	$20,870	Pound Sterling	99%	6	Protestant, Catholic
United States	Federal Republic	1776	1st	$29,080	U.S. Dollar	99%	7	Protestant, Catholic
Uruguay	Republic	1828	63rd	$6,130	U. Peso	98%	16	Catholic
Uzbekistan	Republic	1991	59th	1,020	Som	99%	24	Muslim
Vanuatu	Republic	1980	178th	$1,340	Vatu	64%	37	Protestant, Catholic
Vatican City	Sacerdotal State	1929	n/a	n/a	Vat./Ita. Lira	n/a	n/a	Catholic
Venezuela	Republic	1821	40th	$3,480	Bolivar	92%	21	Catholic
Vietnam	Communist State	1954	60th	$310	Dong	92%	29	Buddhist
Yemen	Republic	1990	114th	$270	Rial, Dinar	43%	96	Muslim
Yugoslavia	Republic	1992	84th	$900	Dinar	93%	14	Eastern Orthodox, Muslim
Zambia	Republic	1964	121st	$370	Zambian Kwacha	75%	370	Christian, Muslim, Hindu
Zimbabwe	Parliamentary Democracy	1980	89th	$720	Zimbabwe Dollar	91%	69	Christian, Indigenous

*Gross National Product

**deaths/1,000 live births

Honoring America

For Americans, the flag has always had a special meaning. It is a symbol of our nation's freedom and democracy.

Flag Etiquette

Over the years, Americans have developed rules and customs concerning the use and display of the flag. One of the most important things every American should remember is to treat the flag with respect.

- The flag should be raised and lowered by hand and displayed only from sunrise to sunset. On special occasions, the flag may be displayed at night, but it should be illuminated.
- The flag may be displayed on all days, weather permitting, particularly on national and state holidays and on historic and special occasions.
- No flag may be flown above the American flag or to the right of it at the same height.
- The flag should never touch the ground or floor beneath it.
- The flag may be flown at half-staff by order of the president, usually to mourn the death of a public official.
- The flag may be flown upside down only to signal distress.
- When the flag becomes old and tattered, it should be destroyed by burning. According to an approved custom, the Union (stars on blue field) is first cut from the flag; then the two pieces, which no longer form a flag, are burned.

The Star-Spangled Banner

O! say can you see, by the dawn's early light,
What so proudly we hail'd at the twilight's last gleaming,
Whose broad stripes and bright stars through the perilous fight,
O'er the ramparts we watched, were so gallantly streaming?
And the Rockets' red glare, the Bombs bursting in air,
Gave proof through the night that our Flag was still there;
O! say, does that star-spangled banner yet wave
O'er the Land of the free and the home of the brave!

The Pledge of Allegiance

I pledge allegiance to the Flag of the United States of America and to the Republic for which it stands, one Nation under God, indivisible, with liberty and justice for all.

GLOSSARY

absolute monarchy form of government in which the king or queen governs with complete power (p. 31)
acid rain rain containing high amounts of chemical pollutants (pp. 65, 306)
adobe sun-dried clay bricks (p. 546)
airlift system of carrying supplies by aircraft (p. 263)
alliance political agreement between countries to support each other in disputes with other countries (p. 258)
alluvial plain area that is built up by rich fertile soil left by river floods (p. 122)
altiplano large highland plateau (p. 616)
altitude height above sea level (pp. 537, 593)
amend to change the basic laws of a government (p. 520)
apartheid system of laws that separated racial and ethnic groups and limited the rights of blacks in South Africa (p. 456)
apprentice young worker who learned a trade or skill from a master teacher (p. 244)
aquifer underground rock layer that stores large amounts of water (pp. 59, 101)
archipelago group of islands (p. 192)
atoll low-lying, ring-shaped island that surrounds a lagoon (p. 662)
autobahn German, Swiss, or Austrian superhighway (p. 289)
autonomy right of self-government (p. 494)
axis horizontal (bottom) or vertical (side) line of measurement on a graph (p. 10)

bar graph graph in which vertical or horizontal bars represent quantities (p. 10)
basin low area surrounded by higher land (p. 582)
bauxite mineral used to make aluminum (pp. 309, 444, 564)
Bedouin nomadic Arab of the deserts of Southwest Asia (p. 111)
bilingual having or expressed in two languages (p. 493)
bishop official of the Christian Church (p. 241)
blockade to forcibly prevent entry to an area (p. 263)
Boer South African of Dutch ancestry (p. 456)
bog low swampy land (p. 278)
boomerang Australian weapon shaped like a bent wing that either strikes a target or curves back toward the hunter (p. 640)
bush rural areas of Australia (p. 641)

cacao tropical tree whose seeds are used to make chocolate and cocoa (pp. 436, 660)
calligraphy art of beautiful writing (p. 172)
campesino Latin American farmer or farm laborer (p. 607)
canopy umbrella-like covering formed by the tops of trees in a rain forest (pp. 423, 558)
canyon deep, narrow valley with steep-sides, which a river has cut through a plateau (p. 59)
capitalism economic system that allows private ownership and open competition of businesses (p. 265)
cash crop crop grown to be sold for export (p. 606)
cassava plant with roots that can be ground to make porridge (p. 405)
caste social class based on a person's ancestry (p. 147)
caudillo military ruler (p. 593)
chart graphic way of presenting information clearly (p. 11)
charter written agreement guaranteeing privileges and freedoms (p. 244)
circle graph round or pie-shaped graph showing how a whole is divided (p. 11)
city-state city and its surrounding countryside (p. 83)
civilization culture that includes certain elements such as a system of writing, cities, and workers with specialized jobs (p. 82)
civil war fight between different groups within a country (pp. 213, 438)
clan family, or group of related people (pp. 195, 413)
classical relating to the ancient Greek and Roman world (p. 236)

climate usual, predictable pattern of weather in an area over a long period of time (p. 60)
climograph combination bar and line graph giving information about temperature and precipitation (p. 12)
coalition government government in which two or more political parties work together to run a country (p. 298)
Cold War conflict between the United States and the Soviet Union dating from the late 1940s to the late 1980s, when the two superpowers competed for world influence without declared military action at each other (pp. 261, 370)
colony overseas territory or settlement tied to a parent country (pp. 492, 543)
Columbian Exchange process in which people, diseases, ideas, and trade were distributed around the world from the Americas (p. 247)
commercial crop crop grown for the purpose of selling (p. 564)
common law unwritten set of laws based on local customs (p. 242)
commonwealth partly self-governing territory (p. 567)
communism economic, social, and political system based on the teachings of Karl Marx, which advocated the elimination of private property (pp. 258, 346)
communist state country whose government allows little or no private ownership of property and has strong control over the economy and society as a whole (pp. 165, 369, 566)
compound group of houses surrounded by walls (p. 437)
conservation careful use of resources so they are not wasted (p. 64)
constitution formal agreement that establishes the basis for a country's laws (p. 248)
constitutional monarchy government in which a king or queen is the official head of state, but elected officials run the government (pp. 31, 104, 196, 280)
consul elected chief official of the Roman Republic (p. 238)
consumer goods goods people buy to use for themselves, such as household products, clothing, and cars (pp. 165, 311, 344)
contiguous areas that are joined together inside a common boundary (p. 502)
continental divide mountainous area from which rivers flow in different directions (p. 290)
contour line line connecting all points at the same elevation on a contour map (p. 8)
convent place where nuns live, pray, and study (p. 242)
cooperative farm owned and operated by the government (p. 566)
copper belt large area of copper mines (p. 460)
copra dried coconut meat (p. 661)
coral reef structure formed by the skeletons of small sea animals (pp. 404, 505, 638)
cordillera group of mountain ranges that run side by side (p. 604)
cottage industry home- or village-based industry in which family members supply their own equipment to make goods (pp. 146, 257)
crevasse deep crack in the Antarctic ice cap (p. 666)
crop rotation varying what is planted in a field to avoid using up all the minerals in the soil (p. 65)
Crusades holy wars sponsored by the Catholic Church to capture Jerusalem from the Muslims (p. 91)
cultural borrowing when a group of people adopt another's cultural traits (p. 29)
cultural diffusion process of spreading new knowledge and skills to other cultures (p. 29)
culture way of life of a group of people who share similar beliefs and customs (p. 28)
cuneiform Sumerian form of writing using wooden triangular-shaped sticks in the form of hundreds of different wedge-shaped markings on moist clay tablets (p. 83)
custom practice handed down from the past (p. 24)
cyclone intense storm system with heavy rain and high winds (pp. 151, 467)
czar title of Russian emperor (p. 367)

deforestation widespread cutting of forests (pp. 65, 211, 426, 466, 585)
delta area formed from soil deposited by a river at its mouth (pp. 84, 100, 213)
democracy form of government in which citizens choose the nation's leaders by voting for them (pp. 31, 236)
desalinization process of removing salt to make seawater drinkable (p. 114)
desertification process by which grasslands change to desert (p. 441)
deterrence maintenance of military power for the purpose of discouraging an attack (p. 262)

GLOSSARY

diagram drawing that shows steps in a process or parts of an object (p. 13)
Diaspora collective name for scattered Jewish settlements around the world (p. 89)
dictator all-powerful government leader (p. 102)
dictatorship government under the control of one all-powerful leader (p. 31)
dike high bank of soil built along a body of water to control floods (p. 164)
disciple follower of a specific teacher (p. 90)
divine right of kings belief that royalty ruled by the will of God (p. 248)
dominion self-governing nation that accepts the British monarch as head of state (p. 492)
drought long period of extreme dryness and water shortages (pp. 412, 441)
dry farming method in which the land is left unplanted every few years so that it can store moisture (p. 296)
dynasty line of rulers from the same family (pp. 168, 200)
dzong Buddhist center of prayer and study (p. 154)

ecosystem place where the plants and animals are dependent upon one another and their surroundings for survival (p. 64)
eco-tourist person who travels to another country to view its natural wonders (pp. 408, 559)
elevation height of land above sea level (pp. 8, 358)
elevation profile cutaway diagram showing changes in elevation of land (p. 13)
embalm to treat a dead body to protect it from decay (p. 84)
embargo order that restricts or prohibits trade with another country (pp. 123, 566)
emperor absolute ruler of an empire (p. 238)
empire group of lands under one ruler (pp. 83, 182, 617)
enclave small territory entirely surrounded by a larger territory (p. 457)
endangered species plant or animal under the threat of completely dying out (p. 414)
environment natural surroundings (p. 54)
erosion process of moving water and wind across the earth's surface, leaving the land less fertile than before (p. 65)
escarpment steep cliff between higher and lower land (p. 583)
estancia huge ranch (p. 590)
ethnic cleansing forcing people from a different ethnic group to leave their homes (p. 313)
ethnic conflict dispute between two or more ethnic groups (p. 357)
ethnic group people who share a common culture, language, or history (pp. 24, 523)
ethnocentrism attitude that one's own ethnic group is superior (p. 29)
Eurasia region that lies on both the European and Asian continents (p. 342)
Euro common currency adopted by countries in the European Union (p. 268)
European Union trade alliance among many European countries, formerly called the Common Market (p. 268)
exclave small part of a country that is separated from the main part (p. 464)
exile unable to live in one's own country, usually because of political beliefs (p. 171)

famine extended, usually widespread, severe lack of food (p. 203)
fault crack in the earth's crust (pp. 57, 164)
favela slum area (p. 585)
federal republic form of government in which the national and state governments share powers (pp. 289, 375, 520, 548)
feudalism political and social system in which a lord gave land to a noble to work, govern, and defend, in return for the noble's loyalty (p. 242)
five pillars of faith basic religious obligations of Islam (p. 92)
fjord steep-sided valley cut into mountains by the action of glaciers (pp. 292, 643)
foothills hilly region at the base of a mountain range (p. 616)
fossil fuel fuel formed in the earth, such as coal, oil, or natural gas (p. 508)
free enterprise system economic system that operates on free competition, in which people start and own businesses with limited government intervention (pp. 165, 405, 507)
free market economy economy driven by forces including competition, supply, and demand (p. 373)
free port place where goods can be loaded, stored, and shipped again without import taxes (p. 218)

free trade trade without barriers like tariffs or quotas so that goods flow freely between countries (p. 509)
free trade zone area where people can buy goods from other countries without paying import taxes (p. 567)

gaucho cowhand (p. 590)
genocide mass murder of a people because of their race, religion, ethnicity, politics, or culture (pp. 259, 414)
geographic information systems (GIS) special software that helps geographers gather and use different kinds of information about a place (p. 54)
geography study of the earth in all its variety—land, water, plants, and animals (p. 52)
geothermal energy electricity produced by natural underground sources of steam (pp. 295, 643)
geyser spring that shoots hot water through a crack in the earth's crust (pp. 295, 643)
glacier giant, slow-moving sheet of ice (p. 487)
glasnost Russian policy of "openness," which permitted Soviet people to criticize the government without punishment (pp. 265, 371)
Global Positioning System (GPS) group of satellites that travels around the earth, which can be used to pinpoint an exact location on the earth (p. 54)
globalization development of a world culture and interdependent world economy (p. 38)
greenhouse effect buildup of certain gases in the atmosphere that, like a greenhouse, prevent the warm air from escaping into the atmosphere, resulting in increase of the earth's overall temperature (p. 61)
green revolution great increase in food grains production due to the use of improved seeds, pesticides, and efficient farming techniques (p. 145)
guild medieval workers' organization (p. 244)

habitat type of environment in which a particular animal species lives (p. 408)
hacienda large ranch (p. 543)
hajj religious journey to Makkah that Muslims are expected to make at least once during their lifetime if they are able to do so (p. 114)
harmattan dry, dusty wind that blows south from the Sahara (p. 434)
heavy industry industry that produces goods such as machinery, mining equipment, and steel (pp. 294, 347)
hemisphere one-half of the globe; the Equator divides the earth into Northern and Southern Hemispheres; the Prime Meridian divides it into Eastern and Western Hemispheres (p. 5)
hieroglyphics ancient form of writing that used signs and symbols (pp. 85, 542)
high island Pacific island formed by volcanic activity (p. 662)
high-technology industry industry that produces computers and other kinds of electronic equipment (p. 180)
Holocaust systematic murder by Adolf Hitler and his followers of more than 12 million people, including 6 million European Jews, during World War II (p. 259)
human resources supply of people who can produce goods (p. 256)
human rights basic freedoms and rights, such as freedom of speech and freedom of assembly, that all people should have (p. 171)
hurricane tropical storm with winds of more than 74 miles (119 km) per hour and heavy rains (pp. 537, 557)
hydroelectric power electricity generated by flowing water (pp. 423, 592, 643)

iceberg chunk of a glacier that has broken away and floats free in the ocean (p. 667)
ice shelf layer of ice above water in Antarctica (p. 666)
immigrant person who moves to a new country to make a permanent home (p. 640)
imperialism system of building foreign empires for military and trade advantages (p. 258)
indigenous native to or originating from a place (p. 486)
indulgences pardons for sins, given or sold by the Catholic Church (p. 246)
industrialize to change an economy to rely more on manufacturing and less on farming (pp. 368, 534)

industrialized country country in which a great deal of manufacturing occurs (p. 455)
intensive cultivation growing crops on every available piece of land (p. 194)
interdependence dependence of countries on one another for goods, raw materials to make goods, and markets in which to sell goods (p. 37)
invest to put money into a business (p. 165)
irrigation system planned series of ditches to control flooding and to better water land (p. 83)
Islamic republic government run by Muslim religious leaders (p. 124)
isthmus narrow piece of land that connects two larger pieces of land (p. 556)

jade shiny, usually green gemstone (p. 541)
jute plant fiber used for making rope, burlap bags, and carpet backing (p. 145)

kibbutz settlement or farm in Israel where the people share property and produce goods (p. 108)
krill tiny, shrimp-like animal that lives in the waters off Antarctica and is food for many other animals (p. 668)

land bridge narrow strip of land that joins two larger landmasses (p. 534)
landfill area where trash companies dump the waste they collect (p. 509)
landform individual feature of the land, such as a mountain or valley (p. 53)
landlocked not bordering a sea or an ocean (pp. 309, 621)
latitude location north or south of the Equator, measured by imaginary lines (parallels) numbered in degrees north or south (pp. 5, 536)
light industry industry that produces goods such as clothing, shoes, furniture, and household products (p. 347)
limited government type of government where, through law, some control is placed on leadership's powers (p. 31)
line graph graph in which one or more lines represent changing quantities over time (p. 10)
literacy rate percentage of people who can read and write (p. 559)
llanos grassy plains (pp. 593, 604)
longitude location east or west of the Prime Meridian, measured by imaginary lines (meridians) numbered in degrees east or west (p. 6)
low island Pacific island formed of coral and having little vegetation (p. 662)

maize Native American name for corn (p. 542)
majority culture dominant or main culture of a region (p. 350)
majority group group in society that controls most of the wealth and power, though not always the largest group in numbers (p. 24)
mangrove tropical tree with roots that extend both above and beneath the water (p. 434)
manor feudal estate made up of a manor house or castle and land (p. 243)
manuka small shrub of New Zealand (p. 643)
maquiladora factory that assembles parts made in other countries (p. 538)
marsupial mammal that carries its young in a pouch (p. 639)
megalopolis huge urban settlement made up of several large cities (pp. 196, 503)
messiah in Judaism and Christianity, a savior sent by God (p. 90)
mestizo person with mixed European and Native American ancestry (p. 606)
migrant worker person who travels from place to place when extra help is needed to plant or harvest crops (p. 549)
migrate to move from one place to another (p. 34)
minister to take care of or tend to another's needs (p. 91)
minority culture culture other than the majority culture in a region (p. 350)
minority group group of people who are different in some characteristic from the group with the most power and wealth in a region (p. 24)

GLOSSARY

missionary teacher of Christianity (p. 242)
monastery place where monks live, pray, and study (p. 242)
monotheism belief that there is only one God (p. 88)
monsoon seasonal wind that blows for months at a time, often affecting a region's climate (pp. 145, 201, 210)
moshav cooperative settlement of small individual farms in Israel where people share in farming, but also own some private property (p. 108)
mosque place of worship for followers of Islam (pp. 106, 314)
multilingual able to speak several languages (p. 286)
multinational company firm that does business in several countries (p. 286)
mural wall painting (p. 542)

NAFTA (North American Free Trade Agreement) free trade agreement among United States, Mexico, and Canada (p. 539)
national debt money owed by a nation's government (p. 549)
navigable describes a body of water wide and deep enough to allow the passage of ships (pp. 283, 616)
neutrality refusing to take sides in disagreements and wars between countries (p. 290)
nomad person who moves from place to place with herds of animals (pp. 182, 357)
nuclear energy power created by a controlled atomic reaction (p. 374)
nuclear weapon weapon whose destructive power comes from an uncontrolled nuclear reaction (p. 261)
Nunavut Canadian province created in 1999 from land that was part of the Northwest Territories (p. 486)

oasis green area in a desert fed by underground water (pp. 101, 358)
obsidian hard, black glass created by the cooled molten lava of a volcano (p. 542)
"one-country, two-systems" China's policy of blending capitalism and some Western freedoms with Chinese communism (p. 166)
outback inland regions of Australia (p. 638)
overfishing taking fish from the ocean so fast that it threatens their existence in that region (p. 488)
overgraze to allow animals to strip areas so bare that plants cannot grow back (p. 440)
ozone type of oxygen that forms a layer in the atmosphere and protects all living things on the earth from certain harmful rays of the sun (p. 668)

pagoda many-storied Buddhist temple (p. 172)
pampas vast treeless, grass-covered plains of South America (p. 590)
papyrus tall plant of the Nile valley, used in making a form of paper (p. 85)
Parliament supreme legislative body in the United Kingdom and other countries (p. 248)
parliamentary democracy system of democratic government where the executive power is held by a cabinet composed of members of the legislature; headed by a prime minister (pp. 279, 493, 560)
parliamentary republic parliamentary government that also has a president, who acts as head of state (p. 296)
peat wet ground with decaying plants that can be dried and used for fuel (p. 280)
peninsula piece of land with water on three sides (p. 535)
perestroika Soviet policy that loosened government controls and permitted its economy to move towards capitalism (p. 265)
pesticide powerful chemical that kills crop-destroying insects (pp. 64, 146)
pharaoh ruler of Ancient Egypt (p. 84)
philosophy term derived from Greek, meaning "love of wisdom" (p. 236)
phosphate mineral salt used in fertilizers (pp. 444, 663)
pictograph graph in which small symbols represent quantities (p. 12)
pidgin language language formed by combining elements of several different languages (p. 662)
plain low-lying stretch of flat or gently rolling land (p. 59)
plantation large farm that grows a single crop for sale (pp. 538, 557)
plate huge slab of rock that makes up the earth's crust (pp. 216, 412)

plateau flat land with higher elevation than a plain (p. 59)
plate tectonics theory that the earth's crust is not an unbroken shell but consists of plates, or huge slabs of rock, that move (p. 57)
plaza public square (p. 546)
poaching illegal hunting of protected animals (p. 404)
polder area of land reclaimed from the sea (p. 285)
polis Greek term for "city-state" (p. 236)
polytheistic believing in more than one god (p. 84)
pope head of the Roman Catholic Church (pp. 241, 308)
potash type of mineral salt that is often used in fertilizers (p. 319)
precious gems valuable gemstones, such as rubies, sapphires, and jade (p. 211)
prime minister official who heads the government in a parliamentary democracy (pp. 146, 493)
productivity measurement of the amount of work accomplished in a given time (p. 256)
Protestant person who "protested" Catholic practices; today, a member of a non-Catholic Christian church (p. 246)
province regional political division similar to a state (p. 486)
pyramid huge stone structure that served as an elaborate tomb or monument (p. 85)

recycling reusing materials instead of throwing them away (p. 509)
reform to improve by changing (p. 245)
refugee person who flees to another country to avoid persecution or disaster (pp. 35, 313, 414)
region area that shares common characteristics (p. 54)
reincarnation rebirth of a soul in a new body (p. 142)
relief differences in height in a landscape; how flat or rugged the surface is (p. 8)
representative democracy government where the people are represented by elected leaders (p. 520)
republic nation with a strong national government headed by elected leaders (pp. 236, 283, 560, 587, 606)
responsibilities duties owed by citizens to their government to make sure it can continue its functions (p. 37)
reunification bringing together the two parts of Germany under one government (p. 289)
revolution great and often violent change (p. 247)
rights benefits and protections that are guaranteed by law (p. 36)
rural relating to the countryside (pp. 344, 524)

samurai powerful land-owning warriors in Japan (p. 195)
satellite nation nation politically and economically dominated or controlled by another, more powerful country (p. 263)
sauna wooden room heated by water sizzling on hot stones (p. 294)
savanna broad grassland with few trees, found in the tropics (pp. 422, 434)
scale relationship between distance on a map and actual distance on the earth (p. 7)
scale bar on a map, a divided line showing the map scale, usually in miles or kilometers (p. 7)
scapegoat one who is wrongly blamed by others (p. 89)
scribe one who records information by writing (p. 85)
secular nonreligious (p. 103)
selva tropical rain forest in Brazil (p. 582)
Senate legislative body of government; the supreme council of the ancient Roman Republic (p. 238)
serf peasant laborer (pp. 243, 368)
service industry industry that provides services like banking, education, and tourism to people rather than producing goods (pp. 487, 539)
shah title given to kings who ruled Iran (p. 124)
shogun military leader in Japan (p. 195)
silt small particles of rich soil (p. 100)
sirocco hot, dry winds from North Africa that blow mainly across Italy (p. 298)
sisal plant fiber used to make rope and twine (p. 407)
slash-and-burn farming method of clearing land for planting by cutting and burning forest (p. 466)

GLOSSARY

Slav person from the ethnic group originating in northeast Europe whose native tongue is a Slavic language (p. 350)
smog thick haze of fog and chemicals (p. 559)
socialism economic system in which many businesses are owned and run by the government (p. 211)
social scientist scientist who studies the interaction of people and society (p. 27)
sodium nitrate chemical used in fertilizer and explosives (p. 623)
sorghum tall grass with seeds that are used as grain (p. 460)
spa resort that has hot mineral springs that people bathe in to regain their health (p. 309)
station cattle or sheep ranch in Australia (p. 638)
steppe partly dry, treeless grassland often found on the edges of a desert (pp. 182, 317, 346)
strait narrow body of water between two pieces of land (p. 218)
strike refusal to work, usually by a labor organization, until demands are met (p. 257)
subcontinent large landmass that is part of a continent but distinct from it (p. 144)
subsistence farm small plot where a farmer grows only enough food to feed his own family (pp. 435, 538, 558, 617)
suburb smaller community located in the area surrounding a city (pp. 344, 524)

taiga huge forests of evergreen trees that grow in subarctic regions (p. 345)
tenant farmer or other who pays rent to another for the use of land or property (p. 243)
terraced field strips of land cut out of a hillside like stair steps so the land can hold water and be used for farming (p. 219)
terrorism systematic use of violence or terror to achieve certain goals (p. 102)
textiles woven cloth (p. 257)
theocracy form of government in which one individual ruled as both religious leader and king (p. 83)
township South African neighborhood created for the housing of people of non-European descent (p. 457)
tropics low-latitude region between the Tropic of Cancer and the Tropic of Capricorn (p. 60)
trust territory area temporarily placed under control of another nation (p. 663)
tsetse fly type of fly found in Africa south of the Sahara, whose bite can transmit a parasite that carries a disease called sleeping sickness (p. 425)
tsunami huge sea wave caused by an earthquake on the ocean floor (p. 192)
tundra vast, rolling, treeless plain in high latitude climates in which only the top few inches of ground thaw in summer (pp. 344, 487)
typhoon hurricane that occurs in Asia (p. 165)

union labor organization that negotiates for improved worker conditions and pay (p. 257)
unlimited government government in which leaders rule without any restrictions (p. 31)
urban relating to the city (pp. 343, 524)
urbanization movement to cities (p. 34)

vaquero cowhand (p. 537)
vassal noble in medieval society who swore loyalty to a lord in return for land (p. 243)

wadi dry riverbed filled by rainwater from rare downpours (p. 113)
welfare state country that uses tax money to provide social services for sick, needy, jobless, or retired people (p. 294)

yurt large, circle-shaped tent made of animal skins that can be packed up and moved from place to place (p. 183)

absolute monarchy/monarquía absoluta forma de gobierno en la cual el rey o la reina gobierna con absoluto poder (pág. 31)

acid rain/lluvia ácida lluvia que contiene grandes cantidades de contaminantes químicos (págs. 65, 306)

adobe/adobe ladrillos secados al sol (pág. 546)

airlift/puente áereo sistema de transportar suministros por avión (pág. 263)

alliance/alianza acuerdo político entre dos países para apoyo mútuo en disputas contra otros países (pág. 258)

alluvial plain/llanura aluvial área creada por el suelo fértil que se acumula después de las inundaciones causadas por los ríos (pág. 122)

altiplano/altiplano meseta grande y muy elevada; también se llama altiplanicie (pág. 616)

altitude/altitud altura sobre el nivel del mar (págs. 537, 593)

amend/enmendar cambiar las leyes básicas de un gobierno (pág. 520)

apartheid/apartheid sistema de leyes que separaba los grupos raciales y étnicos y limitaba los derechos de la población negra (pág. 456)

apprentice/aprendiz jóven trabajador quien aprende un oficio o destreza bajo tutela de un maestro experto (pág. 244)

aquifer/manto acuífero capa de rocas subterránea en que el agua es tan abundante que corre entre las rocas (págs. 59, 101)

archipelago/archipiélago grupo de islas (pág. 192)

atoll/atolón isla de muy poca elevación que se forma alrededor de una laguna en la forma de anillo (pág. 662)

autobahn/autobahn autopista muy rápida (pág. 289)

autonomy/autonomía gobernarse por sí mismo (pág. 494)

axis/eje terrestre la línea vertical (del lado) u horizontal (de abajo) de una gráfica que se usa para medir (pág. 10)

bar graph/gráfica de barras gráfica en que franjas verticales u horizontales representan cantidades (pág. 10)

basin/cuenca área baja rodeada de tierras más elevadas (pág. 582)

bauxite/bauxita mineral que se usa para hacer aluminio (págs. 309, 444, 564)

Bedouin/beduino persona nomádica del desierto del sudoeste de Asia (pág. 111)

bilingual/bilingüe se refiere a un país que tiene dos idiomas oficiales (pág. 493)

bishop/obispo oficial de la Iglesia Cristiana (pág. 241)

blockade/bloquear impedir por la fuerza la entrada a un área (pág. 263)

Boer/bóer uno de los holandeses que fueron los primeros colonos en Sudáfrica (pág. 456)

bog/ciénaga tierra baja y pantanosa (pág. 278)

boomerang/bumerán arma australiana con forma de ala que se lanza para que golpee un objetivo o de la vuelta y caiga a los pies de la persona que la lanzó (pág. 640)

bush/campo áreas rurales de Australia (pág. 641)

cacao/cacao árbol tropical cuyas semillas se usan para hacer chocolate y cocoa (págs. 436, 660)

calligraphy/caligrafía el arte de escribir con letra muy bella (pág. 172)

campesino/campesino agricultor (pág. 607)

canopy/bóveda techo formado por las copas de los árboles en los bosques húmedos (págs. 423, 558)

canyon/cañón valle profundo y estrecho, con laderas escarpadas, formado por un río que corta una meseta (pág. 59)

capitalism/capitalismo sistema económico que permite propietarios privados y la competencia abierta de negocios (pág. 265)

cash crop/cultivo comercial producto que se cultiva para exportación (pág. 606)

cassava/yuca planta con raíces que se pueden convertir en harina para hacer pan o que se pueden cocinar de otras formas (pág. 405)

caste/casta clase social basada en la ascendencia de una persona (pág. 147)

caudillo/caudillo gobernante militar (pág. 593)

chart/cuadro manera gráfica de presentar información con claridad (pág. 11)

charter/cédula acuerdo escrito garantizando privilegios y libertades (pág. 244)

circle graph/gráfica de círculo gráfica redonda que muestra como un todo es dividido (pág. 11)

city-state/ciudad estado ciudad junto con las tierras que la rodean (pág. 83)

civilizations/civilizaciones culturas altamente desarrolladas (pág. 82)

civil war/guerra civil pelea entre distintos grupos dentro de un país (págs. 213, 438)

clan/clan grupo de personas que están emparentadas (págs. 195, 413)

classical/clásico relacionado a la antigua Roma y Grecia (pág. 236)
climate/clima el patrón que sigue el estado del tiempo en un área durante muchos años (pág. 60)
climograph/gráfica de clima gráfica que combina barras y líneas para dar información sobre la temperatura y la precipitación (pág. 12)
coalition government/gobierno por coalición gobierno en que dos o más partidos trabajan juntos para dirigir un país (pág. 298)
Cold War/Guerra Fría período entre los fines de los 1940 y los fines de los 1980 en que los Estados Unidos y la Unión Soviética compitieron por tener influencia mundial sin pelear uno contra el otro (págs. 261, 370)
colony/colonia territorio o poblado con lazos a un país extranjero (págs. 492, 543)
Columbian Exchange/Intercambio Colombiano proceso en el cual personas, enfermedades, ideas y comercio fueron distribuidos alrededor del mundo desde las Américas (pág. 247)
commercial crop/cosecha comercial cultivo agrícola para propósito de venta (pág. 564)
common law/derecho común grupo de leyes no escritas basadas en costumbres locales (pág. 242)
commonwealth/estado libre asociado territorio que en parte se gobierna por sí solo (pág. 567)
communism/comunismo sistema económico, social y político basado en las enseñanzas de Karl Marx, el cual abogaba por la eliminación de propiedades privadas (págs. 258, 346)
communist state/estado comunista país cuyo gobierno mantiene mucho control sobre la economía y la sociedad en su totalidad (págs. 165, 369, 566)
compound/complejo residencial grupo de viviendas rodeadas por una muralla (pág. 437)
conservation/conservación uso juicioso de los recursos para no malgastarlos (pág. 64)
constitution/constitución acuerdo formal que establece las bases para las leyes de un país (pág. 248)
constitutional monarchy/monarquía constitucional gobierno en que un rey o reina es el jefe de estado oficial pero los gobernantes son elegidos (págs. 31, 104, 196, 280)
consul/cónsul oficial en jefe electo en la república romana (pág. 238)
consumer goods/bienes de consumo productos para la casa, ropa y otras cosas que la gente compra para su uso personal (págs. 165, 311, 344)
contiguous/contiguas áreas adyacentes dentro de la misma frontera (pág. 502)
continental divide/línea divisoria continental área montañosa de la cual los ríos desciendan en diferentes direcciones (pág. 290)
contour line/curva de nivel línea que conecta todos los puntos a la misma elevación en un mapa de relieve (pág. 8)
convent/convento lugar donde viven, rezan y estudian monjas (pág. 242)
cooperative/cooperativa granja que es propiedad y es operada por el gobierno (pág. 566)
copper belt/cinturón de cobre área extensa de minas de cobre en el norte de Zambia (pág. 460)
copra/copra pulpa seca del coco que se usa para hacer margarina, jabón y otros productos (pág. 661)
coral reef/arrecife coralino estructura formada al nivel del mar o cerca de éste por los esqueletos de pequeños animales marinos (págs. 404, 505, 638)
cordillera/cordillera grupo de cadenas paralelas de montañas (pág. 604)
cottage industry/industria familiar industria basada en una casa o aldea en que los miembros de la familia usan sus propias herramientas para hacer productos (págs. 146, 257)
crevasse/grieta rajadura profunda en el casquete de hielo de la Antártida (pág. 666)
crop rotation/rotación de cultivos variar lo que se siembra en un terreno para no agotar todos los minerales que tiene el suelo (pág. 65)
Crusades/Cruzadas guerras religiosas patrocinadas por la Iglesia Católica para capturar Jerusalén de los musulmanes (pág. 91)
cultural borrowing/adopción cultural cuando un grupo de personas adoptan las características culturales de otro grupo (pág. 29)
cultural diffusion/difusión cultural el proceso de esparcir nuevos conocimientos y habilidades a otras culturas (pág. 29)
culture/cultura modo de vida de un grupo de personas que comparten creencias y costumbres similares (pág. 28)
cuneiform/cuneiforme forma de escritura sumeria que utiliza trozos triangulares de madera para hacer cientos de diferentes figuras en forma de cuña en tabletas de barro húmedo (pág. 83)
custom/costumbre práctica aceptada a través de los siglos (pág. 24)
cyclone/ciclón tormenta violenta con vientos muy fuertes y mucha lluvia (págs. 151, 467)
czar/zar título de los antiguos emperadores rusos (pág. 367)

deforestation/deforestación la extensa destrucción de los bosques (págs. 65, 211, 426, 466, 585)
delta/delta área formada por el suelo que deposita un río en su desembocadura (págs. 84, 100, 213)
democracy/democracia tipo de gobierno en que los ciudadanos seleccionan los líderes de la nación por medio del voto (págs. 31, 236)
desalinization/desalinización proceso de hacer el agua de mar potable (pág. 114)
desertification/desertización proceso por el cual los pastos se convierten en desiertos (pág. 441)
deterrence/disuasión el mantener el poder militar con el propósito de desalentar un ataque (pág. 262)
diagram/diagrama dibujo que muestra los pasos en un proceso o las partes de un objeto (pág. 13)
Diaspora/diáspora nombre dado a los poblados judíos alrededor del mundo (pág. 89)

SPANISH GLOSSARY

dictator/dictador individuo que toma control de un país y lo gobierna como quiere (pág. 102)
dictatorship/dictadura gobierno bajo el control de un líder que tiene todo el poder (pág. 31)
dike/dique muros de tierra muy altos construidos a lo largo de los ríos para controlar las inundaciones (pág. 164)
disciple/discípulo partidario de un maestro específico (pág. 90)
divine right of kings/derecho divino de los reyes la creencia de que los reyes gobernaban por la voluntad de Dios (pág. 248)
dominion/dominio naciones que se gobiernan por sí solas que aceptan al monarca británico como jefe de estado (pág. 492)
drought/sequía largos períodos de sequedad y de escasez de agua (págs. 412, 441)
dry farming/agricultura en seco método de cultivar en que la tierra se deja sin sembrar cada varios años para que almacene humedad (pág. 296)
dynasty/dinastía serie de gobernantes de la misma familia (págs. 168, 200)
dzong/ dzong centro budista en Bután para rezar y estudiar (pág. 154)

ecosystem/ecosistema lugar en el cual las plantas y animales dependen unos de otros y de sus alrededores para sobrevivir (pág. 64)
eco-tourist/ecoturista persona que viaja a otro país para ver sus bellezas naturales (págs. 408, 559)
elevation/elevación altura por encima del nivel del mar (págs. 8, 358)
elevation profile/perfil de elevaciones diagrama que muestra los cambios en la elevación de la tierra como si se hubiera hecho un corte vertical del área (pág. 13)
embalm/embalsamar tratar un cuerpo sin vida para protegerlo de la descomposición (pág. 84)
embargo/embargo orden que limita o prohibe el comercio con otro país (págs. 123, 566)
emperor/emperador gobernante absoluto de un imperio (pág. 238)
empire/imperio grupo de países bajo un gobernante (págs. 83, 182, 617)
enclave/enclave territorio pequeño totalmente rodeado por un territorio más grande (pág. 457)
endangered species/especie en vías de extinción planta o animal que está en peligro de desaparecer completamente (pág. 414)
environment/medio ambiente alrededores naturales (pág. 54)
erosion/erosión proceso de mover los materiales desgastados en la superficie de la tierra (pág. 65)
escarpment/escarpa acantilado empinado entre un área baja y una alta (pág. 583)
***estancia*/estancia** rancho (pág. 590)
ethnic cleansing/limpieza étnica forzar a personas de un grupo étnico distinto a abandonar el lugar donde viven (pág. 313)
ethnic conflict/conflicto étnico disputa entre dos o más grupos étnicos (pág. 357)
ethnic group/grupo étnico personas que comparten una cultura, idioma o historia en común (págs. 24, 523)
ethnocentrism/etnocentrismo la actitud que el grupo étnico de uno es superior a los demás (pág. 29)
Eurasia/Eurasia región que se ubica en los dos continentes de Europa y Asia (pág. 342)
Euro/eurodólar moneda común adoptada por los países de la Unión Europea (pág. 268)
European Union/Unión Europea alianza comercial entre muchos países europeos formalmente llamado el Mercado Común Europeo (pág. 268)
exclave/territorio externo parte pequeña de un país que está separada de la parte principal (pág. 464)
exile/exilio tener que vivir fuera de su país nativo por causa de sus creencias políticas (pág. 171)

famine/hambruna falta de alimentos (pág. 203)
fault/falla fractura en la corteza de la tierra (págs. 57, 164)
favela/favela barrio pobre y deteriorado (pág. 585)
federal republic/república federal nación en que el poder está dividido entre el gobierno nacional y el de los estados (págs. 289, 375, 520, 548)
feudalism/feudalismo sistema político y social en el cual un lord cedía tierra a un noble para que la trabajara, gobernara y defendiera, obligándose éste rendirle fidelidad (pág. 242)
five pillars of faith/cinco pilares de fé obligaciones religiosas básicas del Islam (pág. 92)
fjord/fiordo valle creado por el movimiento de glaciares en las montañas que deja laderas sumamente empinadas (págs. 292, 643)
foothill/estribaciones colinas bajas al pie de una cadena de montañas (pág. 616)
fossil fuel/combustibles fósiles carbón, petróleo o gas natural (pág. 508)
free enterprise system/sistema de libre empresa sistema económico en que la gente empieza y administra negocios con poca intervención del gobierno (págs. 165, 405, 507)
free market economy/economía del libre comercio economía llevada por fuerzas como la competencia, oferta y demanda (pág. 373)
free port/puerto libre lugar donde las mercancías se pueden cargar, almacenar y embarcar de nuevo sin tener que pagar derechos de importación (pág. 218)
free trade/libre comercio eliminar las barreras al comercio para que se puedan mover productos libremente entre países (pág. 509)
free trade zone/zona de cambio libre área donde la gente puede comprar bienes de otros países sin pagar impuestos adicionales (pág. 567)

gaucho/gaucho vaquero (pág. 590)

genocide/genocidio asesinato en masa de personas a causa de su raza, religión, etnicidad, política o cultura (págs. 259, 414)

geographic information systems (GIS)/ sistemas de información geográfica (SIG) programas de computadoras especiales que ayudan a los geógrafos a obtener y usar la información geográfica sobre un lugar (pág. 54)

geography/geografía el estudio de la tierra y de toda su variedad (pág. 52)

geothermal energy/energía geotérmica electricidad producida por fuentes de vapor subterráneas naturales (págs. 295, 643)

geyser/géiser manantial de agua calentado por rocas fundidas dentro de la tierra que, de vez en cuando, arroja agua caliente al aire (págs. 295, 643)

glacier/glaciar capa de hielo inmensa que se mueve muy lentamente (pág. 487)

glasnost/glasnost política rusa de "franqueza," la cual permitió que la gente soviética criticara al gobierno sin castigo (págs. 265, 371)

Global Positioning System (GPS)/Sistema de posición global (GPS) grupo de satélites alrededor de la tierra que se usan para localizar lugares exactos en la tierra (pág. 54)

globalization/globalización desarrollo de una cultura y economía interdependiente mundiales (pág. 38)

greenhouse effect/efecto invernadero la acumulación de ciertos gases en la atmósfera que mantienen más del calor del sol, como hace un invernadero (pág. 61)

green revolution/revolución verde gran aumento en la producción de granos debido al uso de semillas, pesticidas, y técnicas agrícolas perfeccionadas (pág. 145)

guild/gremio organización de trabajadores en la época medieval (pág. 244)

habitat/hábitat tipo de ambiente en que vive una especie animal en particular (pág. 408)

hacienda/hacienda un rancho grande (pág. 543)

hajj/*hajj* viaje religioso a La Meca que todo musulmán debe hacer por lo menos una vez en la vida si puede (pág. 114)

harmattan/harmattan viento seco y lleno de polvo que sopla hacia el sur desde el Sahara (pág. 434)

heavy industry/industria pesada manufactura de productos como maquinaria, equipo de minería y acero (págs. 294, 347)

hemisphere/hemisferio una mitad del globo terráqueo; el ecuador divide la tierra en los hemisferios norte y sur; el primer meridiano la divide en hemisferios este y oeste (pág. 5)

hieroglyphics/jeroglíficos forma de escribir que usa signos y símbolos (págs. 85, 542)

high island/isla oceánica isla del Pacífico formada por actividad volcánica (pág. 622)

high-technology industry/industria de alta tecnología industria que produce computadoras y otras clases de equipo electrónico (pág. 180)

Holocaust/Holocausto la matanza sistemática de más de 6 millones de judíos europeos por Adolfo Hitler y sus seguidores durante la Segunda Guerra Mundial (pág. 259)

human resources/recursos humanos suministro de personas quienes pueden producir bienes de consumo (pág. 256)

human rights/derechos humanos libertades y derechos básicos que todas las personas deben disfrutar (pág. 171)

hurricane/huracán tormenta tropical violenta con vientos y lluvias fuertes (págs. 537, 557)

hydroelectric power/energía hidroeléctrica electricidad generada por una corriente de agua (págs. 423, 592, 643)

iceberg/iceberg pedazo de un glaciar que se ha desprendido y flota libremente en los océanos (pág. 667)

ice shelf/plataforma de hielo capa de hielo sobre el mar en la Antártida (pág. 666)

immigrant/inmigrante persona que se muda permanentemente a un país nuevo (pág. 640)

imperialism/imperialismo el sistema de desarrollar imperios extranjeros para ventaja militar y comercial (pág. 258)

indigenous/indígeno nativo u originario de un lugar (pág. 486)

indulgences/indulgencias perdón por los pecados concedido o vendido por la Iglesia Católica (pág. 246)

industrialize/industrializar cambiar una economía de manera que dependa más de la manufactura que de la agricultura (pág. 368, 534)

industrialized country/país industrializado país en el cual ocurre mucha manufactura (pág. 455)

intensive cultivation/cultivo intensivo labrar toda la tierra posible (pág. 194)

interdependence/interdependencia países que dependen unos de otros para bienes, materia prima para producir bienes, y mercados en los cuales vendan sus productos (pág. 37)

invest/invertir poner dinero en un negocio (pág. 165)

irrigation system/sistema de irrigación sistema planeado de zanjas para prevenir inundaciones y mejorar el riego de tierra (pág. 83)

SPANISH GLOSSARY

Islamic republic/república islámica gobierno dirigido por líderes musulmanes (pág. 124)

isthmus/istmo extensión de tierra que conecta a dos masas de tierra más grandes (pág. 556)

jade/jade piedra preciosa reluciente, usualmente de color verde (pág. 541)

jute/yute fibras de una planta que se usan para hacer soga, sacos y el revés de alfombras (pág. 145)

kibbutz/kibutz poblado en Israel donde las personas comparten la propiedad y producen bienes (pág. 108)

krill/krill animales diminutos parecidos a los camarones que viven en las aguas alrededor de la Antártida y sirven de alimento para muchos otros animales (pág. 668)

land bridge/puente terrestre franja de tierra que une a dos masas de tierra mayores (pág. 534)

landfill/vertedero de basura lugar donde las compañías que recogen la basura botan los residuos que colectan (pág. 509)

landform/accidente geográfico característica particular de la tierra (pág. 53)

landlocked/rodeado de tierra país que no tiene tierras bordeadas por un mar u océano (págs. 309, 621)

latitude/latitud posición al norte o al sur del ecuador, medida por medio de líneas imaginarias (paralelos) numeradas con grados norte o sur (págs. 5, 536)

light industry/industria ligera fabricación de productos como muebles, ropa, zapatos y artículos para el hogar (pág. 347)

limited goverment/gobierno limitado tipo de gobierno donde, a través de la ley, hay algo de control sobre el poder del liderazgo (pág. 31)

line graph/gráfica lineal gráfica en que una o varias líneas representan cambios de cantidad a través del tiempo (pág. 10)

literacy rate/índice de alfabetización porcentaje de personas que saben leer y escribir (pág. 559)

llanos/llanos planicie cubierta de hierba (págs. 593, 604)

longitude/longitud posición al este o el oeste del primer meridiano, medida por medio de líneas imaginarias (meridianos) numeradas con grados este u oeste (pág. 6)

low island/isla coralina isla del Pacífico formada por coral que tiene poca vegetación (pág. 662)

maize/maíz nombre Nativo Americano del elote (pág. 542)

majority culture/cultura mayoritaria cultura dominante o principal de una región (pág. 24)

majority group/grupo mayoritario grupo en una sociedad que controla la mayoría de la riqueza y el poder, el cual no siempre es el grupo más numeroso (pág. 24)

mangrove/mangle árbol tropical con raíces que se extienden por encima y por debajo del agua (pág. 434)

manor/feudo estado feudal compuesto de una casa solariega o castillo y tierra (pág. 243)

manuka/ manuka pequeño arbusto de Nueva Zelanda (pág. 643)

maquiladora/maquiladora fábrica donde se ensamblan piezas hechas en otros países (pág. 538)

marsupial/marsupial mamífero que lleva a sus crías en una bolsa (pág. 639)

megalopolis/megalópolis área extensa de mucha urbanización (págs. 196, 503)

messiah/Mesías en judaísmo y cristianismo, el salvador enviado por Dios (pág. 90)

mestizo/mestizo persona cuya ascendencia incluye indios americanos o africanos y españoles (pág. 606)

migrant worker/trabajador itinerante persona que viaja a distintos lugares donde hacen falta trabajadores para sembrar y cosechar cultivos (pág. 549)

migrate/migrar mudarse de un lugar a otro (pág. 34)

minister/atender cuidar las necesidades de otro (pág. 91)

minority culture/cultura minoritaria cultura aparte de la cultura mayoritaria en una región (pág. 350)

minority group/grupo minoritario grupo de gente quien es diferente en alguna característica del grupo con mayor poder y riqueza en una región (pág. 24)

missionary/misionario maestro del cristianismo (pág. 242)

monastery/monasterio lugar donde viven, rezan y estudian monjes (pág. 242)

monotheism/monoteísmo creencia en un solo Dios (pág. 88)

monsoon/monzón vientos que soplan en un continente por varios meses seguidos en ciertas estaciones del año (págs. 145, 201, 210)

moshav/*moshav* poblados en Israel en que la gente comparte alguna propiedad pero también tiene propiedad privada (pág. 108)

mosque/mezquita edificio de devoción islámico (págs. 106, 314)

multilingual/multilingüe que puede hablar varios idiomas (pág. 286)

multinational company/compañía multinacional compañía que hace negocios en varios países (pág. 286)
mural/mural pintura hecha sobre una pared (pág. 542)

NAFTA (North American Free Trade Agreement)/TLC (Tratado de Libre Comercio) convenio de libre comercio entre Estados Unidos, México y Canadá (pág. 539)
national debt/deuda pública dinero debido por el gobierno de una nación (pág. 549)
navigable/navegable describe una masa de agua ancha y profunda suficiente para que los barcos puedan viajar por ella (págs. 283, 616)
neutrality/neutralidad negarse a ponerse a favor de uno de los adversarios en un desacuerdo o una guerra entre países (pág. 290)
nomad/nómada alguien que se muda de un lugar a otro con sus manadas o rebaños de animales (págs. 182, 357)
nuclear energy/energía nuclear energía producida por medio de una reacción atómica controlada (pág. 374)
nuclear weapon/arma nuclear arma cuya fuerza destructiva viene de una reacción nuclear no controlada (pág. 261)
Nunavut/Nunavut provincia canadiense creada en 1999 de terrenos que fueron parte de los Territorios del Noroeste (pág. 486)

oasis/oasis área verde en medio de un desierto adonde llegan aguas subterráneas (págs. 101, 358)
obsidian/obsidiana piedra vítrea de color negro formada por el enfriamiento de la lava líquida de un volcán (pág. 542)
"one country, two systems"/un país, dos sistemas política de China de combinar el capitalismo y algunas libertades occidentales con el comunismo chino (pág. 166)
outback/tierra adentro el interior de Australia (pág. 638)
overfishing/sobrepesca pesca excesiva que pone en riesgo la existencia de una especie marina en una región del océano (pág. 488)
overgraze/pastar excesivamente cuando el ganado despoja los pastos hasta tal punto que las plantas no pueden crecer de nuevo (pág. 440)
ozone/ozono tipo de oxígeno que forma una capa en la atmósfera que protege a todas las cosas vivas de ciertos rayos del sol que son peligrosos (pág. 668)

pagoda/pagoda templo budista de muchos pisos (pág. 172)
pampas/pampa llanura de gran extensión en América del Sur sin árboles y cubierta de hierba (pág. 590)
papyrus/papiro planta alta de la valle del Nilo, usada para hacer un tipo de papel (pág. 85)
Parliament/Parlamento cuerpo legislativo supremo en Inglaterra y otros países (pág. 248)
parliamentary democracy/democracia parlamentaria gobierno en que los votantes eligen a representantes a un cuerpo que hace las leyes y que selecciona a un primer ministro para que sea el jefe del gobierno (págs. 279,493, 560)
parliamentary republic/república parlamentaria *véase* parliamentary democracy/democracia parlamentaria (pág. 296)
peat/turba suelo mojado con plantas en descomposición que se puede secar y usar para combustible (pág. 280)
peninsula/península masa de tierra con agua alrededor de tres lados (pág. 535)
perestroika/perestroika política soviética que relajó los controles gubernamentales y permitió que la economía se moviera hacia el capitalismo (pág. 265)
pesticide/pesticida sustancia química poderosa que mata a los insectos que destruye los cultivos (págs. 64, 146)
pharaoh/faraón soberano del antiguo Egipto (pág. 84)
philosophy/filosofía término derivado del griego que significa "amor a la sabiduría" (pág. 236)
phosphate/fosfato sal mineral que se usa en los abonos (págs. 444, 663)
pictograph/pictograma gráfica en que pequeños símbolos representan cantidades (pág. 12)
pidgin language/lengua franca lenguaje formado al combinar elementos de varios idiomas distintos (pág. 662)
plain/llanura extensión de tierra plana u ondulante a elevaciones bajas (pág. 59)
plantation/plantación granja grande en que se siembra un solo cultivo para venderse (págs. 538, 557)
plate/placa plancha de roca inmensa que forma parte de la corteza de la tierra (págs. 216, 412)
plateau/meseta planicie a elevaciones más altas que las llanuras (pág. 59)
plate tectonics/tectónica de placas teoría que dice que la corteza de la tierra no es una envoltura enteriza, sino que está formada por placas, o planchas de roca inmensas, que se mueven (pág. 57)
plaza/plaza sitio donde se reúne el público (pág. 546)
poaching/caza furtiva cacería ilegal de animales protegidos (pág. 404)

SPANISH GLOSSARY

polder/pólder área de tierra ganada del mar (pág. 285)
polis/polis término griego para "ciudad estado" (pág. 236)
polytheistic/politeísta que cree en más de un dios (pág. 84)
pope/papa líder de la Iglesia Católica Apostólica Romana (págs. 241, 308)
potash/potasa tipo de sal mineral que a menudo se usa en los abonos (pág. 319)
precious gems/piedras preciosas valiosas piedras preciosas, como el rubí, el zafiro y el jade (pág. 211)
prime minister/primer ministro líder del gobierno en una democracia parlamentaria (págs. 146, 493)
productivity/productividad la medida de la cantidad de trabajo ejecutado en un tiempo dado (pág. 256)
Protestant/protestante persona que "protestaba" contra las prácticas católicas; hoy en día, miembro de la iglesia cristiana pero no católica (pág. 246)
province/provincia división política regional, parecida a un estado (pág. 486)
pyramid/pirámide estructura de piedra gigantesca que sirvió como tumba o monumento elaborado (pág. 85)

recycling/reciclaje usar materiales de nuevo en vez de botarlos (pág. 509)
reform/reforma mejorar cambiando (pág. 245)
refugee/refugiado persona que huye de un país a otro para evitar la persecución o un desastre (págs. 35, 313, 414)
region/región área destacada por ciertas características (pág. 54)
reincarnation/reencarnación renacimiento del alma en un cuerpo nuevo (pág. 142)
relief/relieve las diferencias en altitud de una zona; lo plana o accidentada que es una superficie (pág. 8)
representative democracy/democracia representativa gobierno donde las personas están representadas por dirigentes elegidos (pág. 520)
republic/república gobierno nacional fuerte encabezado por líderes elegidos (págs. 236, 283, 560, 587, 606)
responsabilities/responsabilidades deberes que la gente debe a su gobierno para asegurar que éste puede seguir funcionando (pág. 37)
reunification/reunificación juntar de nuevo las dos partes de Alemania bajo un solo gobierno (pág. 289)
revolution/revolución una órbita completa alrededor del sol (pág. 247)
rights/derechos beneficios y protecciones que están garantizados por ley (pág. 36)
rural/rural área en el campo (págs. 344, 524)

samurai/samurai propietarios y guerreros poderosos del Japón (pág. 195)
satellite nation/nación satélite nación dominada o controlada política y económicamente por otro país más poderoso (pág. 263)
sauna/sauna cuarto de madera calentado por agua que hierve sobre piedras calientes (pág. 294)
savanna/sabana pastos extensos en los trópicos con pocos árboles (págs. 422, 434)
scale/escala relación entre las distancias en un mapa y las distancias verdaderas en la tierra (pág. 7)
scale bar/regla de medida en un mapa, línea con divisiones que muestra la escala del mapa, generalmente en millas o kilómetros (pág. 7)
scapegoat/chivo expiatorio una persona que es acusada erróneamente por otras (pág. 89)
scribe/escribiente persona que registra información por medio de la escritura (pág. 85)
secular/secular no religioso (pág. 103)
***selva*/selva** bosque húmedo tropical, como el de Brasil (pág. 582)
Senate/Senado asamblea legislativa gubernamental; el consejo supremo de la antigua República Romana (pág. 238)
serf/siervo labrador que podía ser comprado y vendido con la tierra (págs. 243, 368)
service industry/industria de servicio negocio que proporciona servicios a la gente en vez de producir productos (págs. 487, 539)
shah/sha título de los reyes que gobernaban Irán (pág. 124)
shogun/shogún líder militar en Japón (pág. 195)
silt/cieno pequeñas partículas de suelo fértil (pág. 100)
sirocco/siroco vientos calurosos y secos que soplan a través de Italia desde el norte de África (pág. 298)
sisal/sisal fibra de una planta que se usa para hacer soga y cordel (pág. 407)
slash-and-burn farming/agricultura por tala y quema método de limpiar la tierra para el cultivo en que se cortan y se queman los bosques (pág. 466)
Slav/eslavo persona originaria del grupo étnico del noreste de Europa cuya lengua nativa es un idioma eslavo (pág. 350)
smog/smog neblina espesa compuesta de niebla y sustancias químicas (pág. 559)
socialism/socialismo sistema económico en que muchos negocios son propiedad y están dirigidos por el gobierno (pág. 211)
social scientist/sociólogo científico que estudia la interacción de la gente y la sociedad (pág. 27)
sodium nitrate/nitrato de sodio sustancia química usada en abonos y explosivos (pág. 623)
sorghum/sorgo cereal de tallo alto cuyas semillas sirven de alimento y del cual se hace un jarabe para endulzar (pág. 460)

spa/termas balneario con manantiales de agua mineral caliente en que la gente se baña para recobrar su salud (pág. 309)

station/estación rancho donde se crían ganado vacuno u ovejas en Australia (pág. 638)

steppe/estepa pastos parcialmente secos que a menudo se encuentran en los bordes de un desierto (págs. 182, 317, 346)

strait/estrecho masa de agua delgada entre dos masas de tierra (pág. 218)

strike/huelga una negativa a trabajar, usualmente por una organización de trabajo, hasta que las demandas sean solucionadas (pág. 257)

subcontinent/subcontinente masa de tierra grande que forma parte de un continente pero se puede diferenciar de él (pág. 144)

subsistence farm/granja de subsistencia terreno pequeño en el cual un granjero cultiva sólo lo suficiente para alimentar a su propia familia (págs. 435, 538, 558, 617)

suburb/suburbio comunidad pequeña en los alrededores de una ciudad (págs. 344, 524)

taiga/taiga bosques enormes de árboles de hoja perenne en regiones subárticas (pág. 345)

tenant/arrendatario agricultor u otra persona que paga renta a otra persona por el uso de una propiedad o terreno (pág. 243)

terraced field/terrazas franjas, parecidas a escalones, que se cortan en la ladera de una colina para que el suelo aguante el agua y se pueda usar para la agricultura (pág. 219)

terrorism/terrorismo uso sistemático de violencia o terror para lograr ciertas metas (pág. 102)

textiles/textiles tela tejida (pág. 257)

theocracy/teocracia forma de gobierno en la cual un individuo gobernaba como líder religioso tanto como rey (pág. 83)

townships/municipios barrios abarrotados de gente en las afueras de las ciudades de Sudáfrica donde viven la mayoría de las personas que no son blancas (pág. 457)

tropics/trópicos región entre el Trópico de Cáncer y el Trópico de Capricornio (pág. 60)

trust territory/territorio en fideicomiso área que está bajo el control temporario de otra nación (pág. 663)

tsetse fly/mosca tsetsé insecto cuya picada puede matar al ganado o a los seres humanos por medio de la enfermedad del sueño (pág. 425)

tsunami/tsunami ola inmensa causada por un terremoto en el fondo del mar (pág. 192)

tundra/tundra inmensas planicies ondulantes y sin árboles en latitudes altas con climas en que sólo varias pulgadas del suelo de la superficie se deshielan (págs. 344, 487)

typhoon/tifón nombre para un huracán en Asia (pág. 165)

union/sindicato organización laboral que negocia para mejorar las condiciones y pago de los trabajadores (pág. 257)

unlimited goverment/gobierno ilimitado gobierno en el cual los líderes gobiernan sin ninguna restricción (pág. 31)

urban/urbano parte de una ciudad (págs. 343, 524)

urbanization/urbanización movimiento hacia las ciudades (pág. 34)

vaquero/vaquero pastor de ganado vacuno (pág. 537)

vassal/vasallo noble en la sociedad medieval quien juraba lealtad a un lord en cambio de tierra (pág. 243)

wadi/uadi lecho de un río seco que llenan los aguaceros poco frecuentes (pág. 113)

welfare state/estado de bienestar social estado que usa el dinero recaudado por los impuestos para mantener a personas que están enfermas, pobres, sin trabajo o jubiladas (pág. 294)

yurt/*yurt* tienda de campaña grande y circular hecha de pieles de animales que se puede desmantelar y llevar de un lugar a otro (pág. 183)

SPANISH GLOSSARY

INDEX

c=chart	*m=map*
d=diagram	*p=photo*
g=graph	*ptg=painting*

INDEX

INDEX

C

INDEX

INDEX

INDEX

INDEX

INDEX

INDEX

INDEX

INDEX

N

O

INDEX

INDEX

INDEX

INDEX

INDEX

INDEX

ACKNOWLEDGMENTS

Text

37 From **Millennium Report, April 3, 2000** by Kofi Annan, secretary-general of the United Nations. United Nations Press Release SG/SM/7343 GA/9705, April 3, 2000. Copyright 2001 by United Nations; **194** From **Sadako and the Thousand Paper Cranes** by Eleanor Coerr. Copyright 1977. The Putnam Publishing Group; **199** From **Haiku, Volume II.** Copyright 1952 by R.H. Blyth. Reprinted by permission of Hokuseido Press; **248** From **The Scarlet Pimpernel** by Baroness Orzy. Copyright 1961 Doubleday and Company, Inc; **314** From **Zlata's Diary: A Child's Life in Sarajevo** translated with notes by Christina Pribichevich-Zoric. Translation copyright by Fixot et editions Robert Laffont, 1994 Viking, published by the Penguin Group, Penguin Books USA Inc. NY; **353** From **Nobel Lecture, 1972** by Alexander Isayevich Solzhenitsyn in *Bartlett's Familiar Quotations.* Copyright 1992 by Little, Brown and Company Inc, Boston; **355 The Grandfather and His Little Grandson** by Leo Tolstoy in *A Harvest of Russian Children's Literature,* edited by Miriam Morton. Copyright 1967 by Miriam Morton. University of California Press, Berkeley and Los Angeles, CA; **405** From **Where are those Songs** by Micere G. Mugo. Reprinted by permission of the author; **456** From **Long Walk to Freedom: The Autobiography of Nelson Mandela by Nelson Mandela.** Copyright 1994 by Nelson Rolihlahla Mandela. Little, Brown and Company; **493 A Declaration of First Nations.** Copyright 2001 by Assembly of First Nations National Indian Brotherhood. (http://www.afn.ca/About%AFN/a_declaration_of_first_nations.htm) **526 Survival This Way** by Simon J. Ortiz. Reprinted by permission of the author. **I, Too** in *Collected Poems* by Langston Hughes. Copyright 1994 by the Estate of Langston Hughes. Reprinted by permission of Alfred A. Knopf, a Division of Random House, Inc; **585** From **Botoque, Bringer of Fire** in Folklore, *Myths, and Legends, a World Perspective,* edited by Donna Rosenberg. Copyright 1977. NTC Publishing; **596** From **The Gaucho Martín Fierro** adapted from the Spanish and rendered into English verse by Walter Owen. Copyright 1936 by Farrar & Rinehart. Reprinted by permission of Henry Holt and Company, LLC; **639** From **Great Mother Snake** an Aboriginal legend.

Photographs

Cover (background)3D Spherical Jigsaw™ Puzzle World Globe made in USA by Buffalo Games, Inc., (l)PhotoDisc, (c)William Waterfall/Pacific Stock, (r)Jodi Cobb/National Geographic Image Collection; **iv–v** Ken Stimpson/Panoramic Images; **vi–vii** PhotoDisc; **viii** Art Wolfe; **ix** Jeff Schultz/Alaska Stock Images; **x** Owen Franken/CORBIS; **xi** (l)KS Studios, (r)Thomas E. Franklin/Record/Saba/CORBIS; **1** PhotoDisc; **2** (l)Todd Gipstein/CORBIS, (tr)Craig Aurness/CORBIS, (br)Craig Lovell/CORBIS; **3** (l)Peter Turnley/CORBIS, (tr)Robert Caputo/Aurora, (br)Roger Ressmeyer/CORBIS; **16** Aaron Haupt; **18** (l)Robert Landau/CORBIS, (r)Digital Stock; **18–19** S. Purdy Matthews/Stone; **20–21** Anthony Cassidy/Stone; **22** AP/Wide World Photos; **23** (t)Private Collection/The Bridgeman Art Library, London/New York, (cl)Hulton/Archive/Getty Images, (cr)Glencoe photo, (bl)NASA, (br)Glencoe photo; **24** Richard Hutchings/PhotoEdit; **26** Bettmann/CORBIS; **27** Kenneth Garrett/National Geographic Image Collection **28** (l)Black Star/National Geographic Image Collection, (r)Steven L. Raymer/National Geographic Image Collection **29** (l)Jeff Schultz/Alaska Stock Images, (tr)Will & Deni McIntyre/Stone, (br)Yellow Dog Productions/The Image Bank; **31** Hilarie Kavanagh/Stone; **34** Gerd Ludwig/National Geographic Image Collection; **35–37** AFP/CORBIS; **51** NASA/National Geographic Image Collection; **50–51** Norman Kent Productions/oi2.com; **53** (l)Richard T. Nowitz/National Geographic Image Collection, (r)Yann Arthus-Bertrand/CORBIS; **54** Doug Martin; **56** Courtesy Environmental Systems Research Institute, Inc.; **57** Natalie Fobes/National Geographic Image Collection; **59** (l)Michael K. Nichols/National Geographic Image Collection, (r)Wolfgang Kaehler/CORBIS; **60** Alberto Garcia/Saba; **63** Bryan & Cherry Alexander/National Geographic Society; **64** Robert Harding/CORBIS; **65** Jodi Cobb/National Geographic Image Collection; **67** George Grall/National Geographic Image Collection; **70** (background)Michael Nichols/National Geographic Society, (l)Gerry Ellis/ENP Images, (r)Jose Azel/Aurora/PictureQuest; **71** (bl)Art Wolfe/Stone, (others)Lisa Hoffner/Wildeye Photography; **72** (l)Hugh Sitton/Stone, (r)David Coulson; **72–73** X. Richer/Hoaqui/Photo Researchers; **79** AP/Wide World Photos; **80–81** Wolfgang Kaehler; **82** Kenneth Garrett/National Geographic Image Collection; **85** (l)Gianni Dagli Orti/CORBIS, (c)Wolfgang Kaehler, (r)Charles & Josette Lenars/CORBIS; **87** Steve Vidler/SuperStock; **88** ASAP Ltd./Index Stock; **90** (l)A. Ramey/Woodfin Camp & Associates, (c)Alan Oddie/PhotoEdit, (r)R & S Michaud/Woodfin Camp & Associates; **91** (t)CMCD/PhotoDisc, (c)C Squared Studios/PhotoDisc, (b)Robert Harding/CORBIS; **95** Kenneth Garrett/National Geographic Image Collection; **98–99** Wolfgang Kaehler/CORBIS; **100** George Steinmetz/National Geographic Image Collection; **105** Patrick Ward/CORBIS; **106** James L. Stanfield/National Geographic Image Collection; **107** Richard T. Nowitz/CORBIS; **109** Arthur Thevenart/CORBIS; **110** Dean Conger/National Geographic Image Collection; **111** Brian Haimer/PhotoEdit; **112** Annie Griffiths Belt/National Geographic Image Collection; **122** Charles & Josette Lenars/CORBIS; **123** AP/Wide World Photos; **124** (l)Alexandra Avakian/National Geographic Image Collection, (r)Jon Spaull/CORBIS; **126** National Geographic Society; **130** Ed Kashi; **130–131** James L. Stanfield; **131** (r)courtesy Sandra Postel, (others) Ed Kashi, ; **132** (l)Tim Davis/Stone, (r)David Sutherland/Stone; **132–133** Waranun Chutchawan-Tipakorn; **140** Steve Raymer/CORBIS; **141** Keren Su/Stone; **142–143** Tibor Bognar/CORBIS Stock Market; **144** George F. Mobley/National Geographic Image Collection; **145** Steve McCurry/National Geographic Image Collection; **146** (l)SuperStock, (c)Bettmann/CORBIS, (r)Hulton/Archive/Getty Images; **147** Rudi Von Briel/PhotoEdit; **148** Oriental Museum, Durham University, UK/The Bridgeman Art Library, London/New York; **149** Brian Vikander/CORBIS; **150** Steve McCurry/National Geographic Image Collection; **151** Brian Vikander/CORBIS; **153** Paul Chesley/Stone; **157** Robert Holmes/CORBIS; **160–161** Christopher Arnesen/Stone; **162** Keren Su/CORBIS; **165** (l)Michele Burgess/CORBIS Stock Market, (r)Kevin R. Morris/CORBIS; **167 168** AFP/CORBIS; **171** Joseph Sohm/ChromoSohm/CORBIS; **180** How-Man Wong/CORBIS; **181** Marc Garanger/CORBIS; **182** Nik Wheeler/CORBIS; **184** AFP/CORBIS; **188** Cary Wolinsky/Stock Boston; **189** Keren Su/CORBIS; **190–191** Dallas and John Heaton/CORBIS; **192** Reuters NewMedia/CORBIS; **194** Steve Cole/PhotoDisc; **195** Karen Kasmauski/Matrix; **196** Roger Ressmeyer/CORBIS; **199** Asian Art & Archaeology/CORBIS; **200** Carmen Redondo/CORBIS; **201** (l)Nathan Benn/CORBIS, (r)Wolfgang Kaehler/CORBIS; **202** Chris Lisle/CORBIS; **205** Neil Beer/CORBIS; **208–209** Bob Krist/Stone; **210 212** Paul Chesley/National Geographic Image Collection; **213** Kevin R. Morris/CORBIS; **216** Roger Ressmeyer/CORBIS; **218** Earl & Nazima Kowall/CORBIS; **220** David Hanson/Stone; **221** AP/Wide World Photos; **224** (l)IFA-Bilderteam-Travel/Bruce Coleman, Inc., (r)Robert Everts/Stone; **224–225** SuperStock; **233** Mary Kate Denny/PhotoEdit; **234–235** Christian Sarramon/CORBIS; **236** Ira Block/National Geographic Image Collection; **237** Vanni Archive/CORBIS; **238** Richard T. Nowitz/National Geographic Image Collection; **239** Museo della Civilta Romana, Rome/Art Resource; **241** Richard List/CORBIS; **242** SuperStock; **244** Archivo Iconografico, SA/CORBIS; **245** David Lees/CORBIS; **246** Sistine Chapel, Vatican, Rome/Fratelli Alinari/SuperStock; **247** The Art Archive; **248** Matt Meadows; **250** (l)Bettmann/CORBIS, (r)Gianni Dagli Orti/CORBIS; **254–255** Philippa Lewis/CORBIS; **256** Dagli Orti/Musee National d'Art Moderne, Paris/The Art Archive; **257** North Wind Picture Archives; **258** (l)CORBIS, (r)Craig Aurness/CORBIS; **259** Hulton-Deutsch Collection/CORBIS; **260** V. Yudin/Sovfoto/Eastfoto/PictureQuest; **261** Owen Franken/CORBIS; **264** (l)Culver Pictures/PictureQuest, (r)Bettmann/CORBIS; **267** James Stanfield/National Geographic Image Collection; **268** Shone/Sipa Press; **269** AFP/CORBIS; **274** (l)Robert Winslow, (r)Johan Elzenga/Stone; **274–275** Oliver Strewe/Stone; **275** (l)Martin Bond/Science Photo Library/Photo Researchers, (r)Mike Lewis, Northamptonshire Grammar School, UK; **276–277** Photowood/CORBIS Stock Market; **278** London Aerial Photo Library/CORBIS; **280** (l)Tim Thompson/CORBIS, (r)Stephen Beer/Stone; **282** Adam Woolfit/CORBIS; **283** James L. Stanfield/National Geographic Image Collection; **284** Mandalay/Rolph Konow/Kobal Collection; **285** Michael John Kielty/CORBIS; **287** SuperStock; **288** Ric Ergenbright/CORBIS; **289** Owen Franken/CORBIS; **290** Sisse Brimberg/National Geographic Image Collection; **291** AFP/CORBIS; **292** Tomasz Tomaszewski/National Geographic Image Collection; **293** (l)Buddy May/CORBIS, (r)Richard S. Durrance/National Geographic Image Collection; **294** Sisse Brimberg/National Geographic Image Collection; **296** David Cumming/Eye Ubiquitous/CORBIS; **297** Gerard Degeorge/CORBIS; **298** (t)Glen Allison/PhotoDisc, (b)Vittoriano Rastelli/CORBIS; **299** Louis O. Mazzatenta/National Geographic Image Collection; **300** Gail Mooney/CORBIS; **304–305** Foto World/The Image Bank; **306** Priit J. Vesilind/National Geographic Image Collection; **308** Steven L. Raymer/National

Geographic Image Collection; **309** Owen Franken/CORBIS; **311** Steve Raymer/CORBIS; **312** Peter Wilson/CORBIS; **313** Francoise de Mulder/CORBIS; **314** Aaron Haupt; **316** (l)Kelly-Mooney Photography/CORBIS, (r)Craig Aurness/CORBIS; **317** Gerd Ludwig/National Geographic Image Collection; **328** James Stanfield/National Geographic Image Collection; **329** Tomasz Tomaszewski/National Geographic Image Collection; **332** (l)Bruce Dale, (r)Alain Le Garsmeur/Stone; **332–333** Marc Moritsch/National Geographic Society; **338** Paul Harris/Stone; **339** KS Studios; **340–341** David & Peter Turnley/CORBIS; **342** Tom Brakefield/CORBIS; **343** (l)Marc Garanger/CORBIS, (r)David Turnley/CORBIS; **344** (l)Andre Gallant/The Image Bank, (c)Wolfgang Kaehler/CORBIS, (r)A. Solomonov/Sovfoto/Easfoto/PictureQuest; **349** Doug Martin; **350** Gerd Ludwig/National Geographic Image Collection; **352** Bob Krist/CORBIS; **353** Richard Howard/Black Star/PictureQuest; **354** David & Peter Turnley/CORBIS; **355** Roger-Viollet/Musee du Petit Palais, Paris/Bridgeman Art Library, London/New York; **356** Wolfgang Kaehler; **357** Gerd Ludwig/National Geographic Image Collection; **358** Ron Rovtar; **361** Gerd Ludwig/National Geographic Image Collection; **364–365** John Lamb/Stone; **366** Sisse Brimberg/National Geographic Image Collection; **367** Stock Montage; **369** Scala/Art Resource; **370** Kremlin Museums, Moscow, Russia/Bridgeman Art Library; **371** David & Peter Turnley/CORBIS; **373** Dean Conger/CORBIS; **374** Peter Turnley/CORBIS; **375** Reuters NewMedia/CORBIS; **384** Farrell Grehan/CORBIS; **385** Jay Dickman; **388** Giraudon/Art Resource; **389** Sovfoto/Eastfoto/PictureQuest; **390** (l)Hugh Sitton/Stone, (r)Jacques Jangoux/Stone; **390–391** Manoj Shah/Stone; **400** David & Peter Turnley/CORBIS; **401** Nicholas Parfitt/Stone; **402–403** W. Perry Conway/CORBIS; **404** Carol Beckwith & Angela Fisher/Robert Estall Photo Agency; **405** Courtesy of the author; **406** The Purcell Team/CORBIS; **408** Frank Lane Picture Agency/CORBIS; **409** Darrell Gulin/CORBIS; **410** Dave Bartruff/CORBIS; **412** AP/Wide World Photos; **413** Chinch Gryniewicz/Ecoscene/CORBIS; **422** AP/Wide World Photos; **425** Daniel Laine/CORBIS; **426** (l)Ann and Carl Purcell/Words & Pictures/PictureQuest, (r)James A. Sugar/Black Star/PictureQuest; **428** David Turnley/CORBIS; **432–433** Paul Almasy/CORBIS; **434 436–437** AP/Wide World Photos; **437** Robert W. Moore/National Geographic Image Collection; **439** (l)Bowers Museum of Cultural Art/CORBIS, (r)Davis Factor/CORBIS; **440** Steve McCurry/Magnum; **441** Carol Beckwith & Angela Fisher/Robert Estall Photo Agency; **443** Robert W. Moore/National Geographic Image Collection; **446** Nik Wheeler/CORBIS; **447** AP/Wide World Photos; **450** Michael A. Hampshire; **451** James L. Stanfield; **452–453** Pictor; **454** Wolfgang Kaehler; **456** Turnley Collection/CORBIS; **459** Walter Edwards/National Geographic Image Collection; **461** Jack Vartoogian; **463** (l)Chris Johns/National Geographic Image Collection, (r)Aaron Haupt; **464** Des & Jen Bartlett/National Geographic Image Collection; **466** AP/Wide World Photos; **467** Art Wolfe/Stone; **472** (l)Sisse Brimberg, (r)Michael Lewis; **472–473** David R. Stoecklein; **482** Aaron Haupt; **483** Kenneth Garrett/National Geographic Society; **484–485** SuperStock; **486** Raymond K. Gehman/National Geographic Image Collection; **488** David A. Harvey/National Geographic Image Collection; **491** Marie-Louise Brimberg/National Geographic Image Collection; **492** Michael Evan Sewell/Visual Pursuit; **493** Index Stock Imagery/PictureQuest; **494** Marie-Louise Brimberg/National Geographic Image Collection; **496** Reuters NewMedia/CORBIS; **497** Richard T. Nowitz/National Geographic Image Collection; **500–501** Mitchell Funk/The Image Bank; **502** David Hiser/National Geographic Image Collection; **504** (l)Steven L. Raymer/National Geographic Image Collection, (r)Vincent Musl/National Geographic Image Collection; **505** Roy Corral/Stone; **507** Karen Kasmauski/Matrix; **508** Joseph Sohm/ChromoSohm/CORBIS; **509** Joel Satore/National Geographic Image Collection; **519** Mug Shots/CORBIS Stock Market; **521** Bettmann/CORBIS; **523 526** CORBIS; **530** Ray Pfortner/Peter Arnold, Inc.; **531** (background)Michael Mathers/Peter Arnold Inc., (l)David Young-Wolff/Stone, (r)David Schmidt; **532–533** Randy Faris/CORBIS; **534** Bettmann/CORBIS; **536** Nik Wheeler/CORBIS; **538** Joel Satore/National Geographic Image Collection; **541** Tomasz Tomaszewski/National Geographic Image Collection; **543** Vladimir Pcholkin/FPG; **545** James L. Amos/National Geographic Image Collection; **546** David A. Harvey/National Geographic Image Collection; **547** Nik Wheeler/CORBIS; **548** Tomas Tomaszewski/National Geographic Image Collection; **554–555** Sylvain Grandadam/Stone; **556** Art Wolfe; **559** (l)Vincent Musl/National Geographic Image Collection, (r)Jan Butchofsky-Houser/CORBIS; **560** Michael S. Yamashita/CORBIS; **563** Jonathan Blair/National Geographic Image Collection; **565** (l)Tony Arruza/CORBIS, (r)Michael K. Nichols/National Geographic Image Collection; **566** Robert A. Tyrrell; **569** George Mobley/National Geographic Image Collection; **572** (l)David Levy/Stone, (r)William J. Herbert/Stone; **572–573** Ecoscene/CORBIS; **579** Michael K. Nichols/National Geographic Image Collection; **580** Layne Kennedy/CORBIS; **582** Alex Webb/Magnum; **585** Kennan Ward/CORBIS Stock Market; **586** (l)Jim Zuckerman/CORBIS, (r)Yann Arthus-Bertrand/CORBIS; **588** Jeremy Horner/CORBIS; **589** Louis O. Mazzatenta/National Geographic Image Collection; **591** (l)Jack Fields/CORBIS, (r)Louis O. Mazzatenta/National Geographic Image Collection; **592** Robert Caputo/Aurora & Quanta Productions; **593** Pablo Corral V/CORBIS; **594** Jacques Jangoux/Stone; **596** Kit Houghton Photography/CORBIS; **597** Robert van der Hilst/CORBIS; **600** (br)William Albert Allard, (others) Michael & Patricia Fogden; **601** (l)Michael Doolittle, (r)Marc Van Roosmalen Conservation International; **602–603** Paul Harris/Stone; **604** Fred Ward/Black Star; **606** Richard S. Durrance/National Geographic Image Collection; **616** Frank & Helen Schreider/National Geographic Image Collection; **618** Tiziana and Gianni Baldizzone/CORBIS; **620** Art Wolfe; **621** Maria Stenzel/National Geographic Image Collection; **622** (l)Richard T. Nowitz/National Geographic Image Collection, (r)James L. Stanfield/National Geographic Image Collection; **625** William A. Allard/National Geographic Image Collection; **628** (l)David Madison/Stone, (r)David Hiser/Stone; **628–629** Oliver Strewe/Stone; **635** Elaine Shay; **636–637** Larry Williams/CORBIS Stock Market; **638** R. Ian Productions P Lloyd/National Geographic Image Collection; **639 640** Penny Tweedie/CORBIS; **642** (t)Australian Picture Library/CORBIS, (bl)Charles Philip Cangialosi/CORBIS, (br)Earl & Nazima Kowall/CORBIS; **643** Kevin Fleming/CORBIS; **645** Neil Rabinowitz/CORBIS; **654** Kevin Fleming/CORBIS; **655** Australian Picture Library/CORBIS; **658–659** Dana Edmunds/FPG; **660** Hal Beral/CORBIS; **662** (l)Ben Simmons/CORBIS Stock Market, (r)SuperStock; **665** David Doublet/National Geographic Image Collection; **666** Wolfgang Kaehler/CORBIS, **667** (l)SuperStock, (r)David Madison/Stone; **668** Underwood & Underwood/CORBIS; **670** Galen Rowell/CORBIS; **671** AP/Wide World Photos; **674** Byrd Antarctic Expedition; **675** Andrew H. Brown; **676** PhotoDisc; **684** Sidney Harris.